WHO'S WHO
IN THE
COMMONWEALTH

WHO'S WHO IN THE COMMONWEALTH

Hon. General Editor:
ERNEST KAY, D.Litt

Managing Director:
R. Rayner

Sales Director:
Roger W. G. Curtis M.A. (Cantab)

Production Manager:
Nicholas Law

Editorial Manager:
Patricia McClatchie

Editorial Assistants:
Joan Doran
Jennifer Jordan

Researcher:
Sheila Ellwood

All communications to: Who's Who in the Commonwealth
International Biographical Centre
Cambridge CB2 3QP, England.

WHO'S WHO
IN THE
COMMONWEALTH

FIRST EDITION

Hon. General Editor
ERNEST KAY

INTERNATIONAL BIOGRAPHICAL CENTRE
Cambridge, England

ISBN 0 900332 63 8

Printed and bound in the UK by Clarke Constable Ltd., *Printers to the University of Edinburgh*, Tanfield, Edinburgh, Scotland.

FOREWORD BY THE HON. GENERAL EDITOR

It is with considerable pride and satisfaction that I present this First Edition of *Who's Who in the Commonwealth* for the approval of readers throughout the world. No less than twenty months has been taken from the time the first questionnaires were mailed to the date of publication, Commonwealth Day 1982, and work had begun on the Second Edition of this work long before this volume went to press.

As a matter of interest, it is three years since it was brought to my attention that no biographical reference book relating to the entire Commonwealth was in existence and it was then that we at the International Biographical Centre, here in Cambridge, England, decided to remedy this defect. The Commonwealth, of course, fully justifies a work of this kind for it is the most important grouping of nations in the world, being larger in both area and population than the United States of America, the Union of Soviet Socialist Republics, or the People's Republic of China.

The principal aims of *Who's Who in the Commonwealth* can be summarized as follows:-

To provide universal information about men and women of contemporary achievement throughout the Commonwealth;

To bring all these nations and peoples together in understanding and fellowship;

To promote the interests and aspirations of the people not only to the entire Commonwealth but also to the rest of the world.

The compilation and production of this pioneer work has been a monumental task indeed. Every one of the many thousands of completed biographical questionnaires returned to us has been carefully examined by one or more of our Editiors who have then compiled entries for those who qualified for inclusion. Typescripts of entries have been sent to all our biographees for correction before publication in order to eliminate errors. Many did not return the corrected typescripts in time (or at all) and we have assumed, in these cases, that the entries were correct in all details.

It is obvious that a First Edition of this kind cannot possibly be completely comprehensive and I am the first to admit that omissions will be discovered by our readers. You are cordially invited to write to me personally if you wish to suggest additions for future issues of *Who's Who in the Commonwealth* which is now planned as an annual publication.

It cannot be emphasized too strongly that it is not possible to "buy" inclusion into this work: there is no charge for entry nor is there any obligation to purchase the book.

Who's Who in the Commonwealth will be distributed to libraries, institutions, universities and individuals in most countries of the world and it is, I think, significant that there has been a considerable demand for copies in non-Commonwealth nations including, particularly, the United States and many countries in Europe.

Finally, I would like to record my personal appreciation as well as that of the IBC to all those universities, learned societies and professional institutions throughout the Commonwealth for their active co-operation in the publication of this work.

International Biographical Centre,
Cambridge, England CB2 3QP.
January 1982

THE INTERNATIONAL BIOGRAPHICAL CENTRE
RANGE OF REFERENCE TITLES

From one of the widest ranges of contemporary biographical reference works published under any one imprint, some IBC titles date back to the 1930's. Each edition is compiled from information supplied by those listed, who include leading personalities of particular countries or professions. Information offered usually includes date and place of birth; family details; qualifications; career histories; awards and honours received; books published or other creative works; other relevant information including postal address. Naturally there is no charge or fee for inclusion.

New editions are freshly compiled and contain on average 80-90% new information. New titles are regularly added to the IBC reference library.

Current titles include:

Dictionary of International Biography

Who's Who in the Commonwealth

Who's Who in Western Europe

Dictionary of Scandinavian Biography

Dictionary of Latin American and Caribbean Biography

International Who's Who in Art and Antiques

International Authors and Writers Who's Who

International Who's Who in Community Service

International Who's Who in Education

The World Who's Who of Women in Education

International Who's Who in Engineering

International Who's Who in Music and Musicians' Directory

International Who's Who in Poetry

Men and Women of Distinction (illustrated)

Men of Achievement (illustrated)

The World Who's Who of Women (illustrated)

International Youth in Achievement

Enquiries to:
International Biographical Centre
Cambridge CB2 3QP
England

A

AARONS, Barrie John, b. 26 Jan. 1934, Melbourne, Victoria, Australia. Surgeon. m. 30 Mar. 1958, 3 sons, 1 daughter, *Education:* Won Full Scholarship to Melbourne Church of England Grammar School, 1947; Scholarship to Trinity College, Melbourne University, 1951; Medicine, Melbourne University, 1952-57; MB; BS, Melbourne, 1957; Fellow of Royal Australasian College of Surgeons, 1963. *Appointments:* J.R.M.O. Alfred Hospital, Melbourne, 1958; R.M.O. Royal Childrens Hospital, Melbourne, 1959; Surgical Registrar, Royal Children's Hospital, Melbourne, 1960; Surgical Registrar, 1961-62, Surgical Supervisor, Repatriation General Hosp., Melbourne, 1963; Assistant Specialist to Thoracic Unit, Alfred Hospital, Melbourne, 1964-65; Surgeon Consultant, Hamilton Medical Group and Hamilton Base Hospital Hamilton Victoria Australia, 1966-. *Memberships:* Member of Victorian State Committee of Royal Australasian College of Surgeons 1974-; President, Hamilton ABC Subscriber's Committee 1974, President, Hamilton Gallery Concert Committee 1974, Rotary International 1968, President of Hamilton North Rotary Club 1980-81; District Governor's representative District 978 Rotary; Clarinet & Saxophone Society of Victoria. *Publications:* Associate Contributor; The Practice of Biliary Surgery -KUNE/S-ALI Blackwell Publications; A number of papers have been published in medical and veterinary journals on Hyatid Surgery and other diseases; Several surgical instruments have been designed and made and one is about to be produced commercially. *Honours:* Albert Jackson & William Newton Memorial Prize, 1947; Exhibitions Pure Maths, Applied Maths, General exhibitions (2), 1950-51; Honour in Surgery at Final MB, BS, 1957. *Hobbies:* Woodturning; Music, Amateur Clarinettist; Engineering and motor mechanics; Vintage Car restoration, Surgical Instrument design, manufacture and repair. *Address:* 13 Martin Street, Hamilton, Victoria 3300, Australia.

ABA, Andrew, Ame-Odindi, b. 29 May 1947, Otukpo, Benue State. Teaching/Educational Administration. m. Lucy Adoo Jir, 11 April 1977, 1 son, 1 daughter. *Education:* MEd, (Administration) State University of New York, Buffalo, USA, 1974-75; BA, (English) University of Ibadan, Nigeria, 1969-72. *Appointments:* Secondary School teacher, Government Secondary School, Kuru-Jos, 1972-; Lecturer, Advanced Teachers' College, 1972-74, Institute of Education, Zaria, Nigeria, 1975-76; Lecturer and Head of Division of Languages, Advanced T.C. KAla, Benue State of Nigeria, 1976-81-; Executive Admin. Secretary Advanced T C Oju, Benue State of Nigeria, 1981-. *Memberships:* Assistant Secretary, Nigeria Folklore Society. *Publications:* Mixed Dreams, work in final stage (novel); Contributed poems to Poems from A.B.U, 1976; Introducing Poetry, Enugu. *Honours:* John F Kennedy Scholar, (National 1st prize in John F Kennedy Memorial essay competition, 1968). *Hobbies:* Writing/Play Directing; Classical Music; Conversation. *Address:* 27 Lumumba Street, Otukpo, Benue State, Nigeria.

ABANGWU, (Chief) Charles Aniweta, b. 1923, Eha Alumona, Nsukka, Anambra State, Nigeria. Barrister-at-Law & Solicitor of the Federal Supreme Court of Nigeria, Politician, Educationist and Humanist. m. Christiana Nwuku, 15 Dec. 1948, 2 sons, 3 daughters. *Education:* First School Leaving Certificate, 1938; Cambridge Senior School Certificate Grade 1, 1942; Bachelor of Laws London, 1954; Council of Legal Education, 1954. *Appointments:* Practising Lawyer, 1954-80; Member House of Assembly Eastern Region, 1955-62; Commissioner, East Central State of Nigeria, 1970-75; Traditional Ruler of Eha Alumona, 1977-79; Chairman Institute of Management and Technology Enugu, 1980-. *Memberships:* Hon. Society of Lincoln's Inn, London, 1954; Recreation Club Enugu to date. *Publications:* Seven Books in Composition awaiting Publication. Autobiography, Vols. I & II; Mermaid of the Niger; Politics of the Nigerian Civil War, 1970; The Last Testament; City of Angels. *Honours:* Igwe of Isienu, 1962; Igwe of Eha Alumona, 1977. *Hobbies:* Reading; Farming; Meditation. *Address:* Igwe's Palace, Eha Alumona, Njukka, P.O.Box 12, Anambra State, Nigeria.

ABAYOMI (Chief) Kole, b. 20 Aug. 1940, Lagos, Nigeria. Lawyer. m. Elfrida Apinke Fajemisin, 5 Jan.

1965, 3 sons, 3 daughters. *Education:* LL.B.(Hons.), King's College, University of Durham, UK, 1962-65; Called to Bar, Nigerian Law School, Lagos, Nigeria, 1965-66; LL.B., PhD., Clare College, University of Cambridge, UK, 1966-70. *Appointments:* Senior Lecturer, Nigerian Law School, Lagos, Nigeria, 1970-78; Senior Partner, Abayomi & Co., Solicitors, 1970-; Director of: Phoenix Assurance of Nigeria Limited; Avon Cosmetics Nigeria Limited; Degremont Nigeria Limited; African Ivory Insurance Co. Limited; Garment Manufacturing Nigeria Limited; Eros Nigeria Limited. *Memberships:* Ikoyi Club. *Publications:* Parliamentary Democracy and Control of the Administration in Nigeria 1960-65, 1970. *Honours:* Commonwealth Scholar, 1966-69; Scholar of Clare College, Cambridge, UK, 1969-70; Created Chief the Otun Baba Sale of Lagos by His Royal Majesty the King of Lagos, 1979. *Hobbies:* Reading; Walking. *Address:* Kofoworola Villa, 11 Eric Moore Close, Surulere, Lagos, Nigeria.

ABBA, Abubakar Alkali, b. 22 Nov. 1946, Yola Town, Yola Local Government Area of Gongola State, Nigeria. Legal Practitioner. m. (1) Jamilatu, 30 Aug. 1967, (2) Mairamu, 14 Aug. 1981, 5 sons, 1 daughter. *Education:* Diploma in Law, 1968-69, Diploma in Islamic Law, 1970-71, LL.B.(Hons.), 1971-74, Ahmadu Bello University, Zaria, Nigeria. *Appointments:* State Counsel, Gongola State Government, 1969-79; Company Secretary/Legal Adviser, New Nigerian Newspapers Limited, Kaduna, Kaduna State, Nigeria. *Memberships:* Moslem Society; Ja'Amatul Nasrul Islam; Yola Club. *Hobby:* Athletics. *Address:* 54 Tafida Road, PO Box 1048, Jimeta Yola, Gongola State, Nigeria.

ABBA, Alhaji Abubakar, b. 25 Dec. 1932, Zaria, Kaduna State, Nigeria. Banker. m. 26 June, 1954, 9 sons, 16 daughters. *Education:* Middle School (now Government Secondary School, Zaria), Kaduna State, Nigeria, 1946-49; Barewa College, Zaria, 1949-52. *Appointments:* Sub-Accountant, 1957-60, Accountant, 1960-61, Branch Manager, 1961-75 (Retired), Barclays Bank D.C.O. (now Union Bank); Board Member of Kaduna Cooperative Bank Ltd, 1975-79. *Memberships:* Committee Member of Jamaatu Nasril Islam, Zaria; Zaria Social Club. *Honours:* First Northern Nigerian to Join Barclays Bank in 1953; First Northern Nigerian to be sent to UK on Banking Course, 1958; First Northerner to be Appointed Manager, 1961. *Hobbies:* Photography; Shooting. *Address:* No. 328 Kwarbai, Zaria City, Kaduna State, Nigeria.

ABBA, Hilda May, (The Reverend), b. 30 May 1916, Birmingham, England. Minister of Religion. m. Raymond Abba, 29 June 1940, 1 son, 1 daughter. *Education:* Teacher's Certificate, Distinction in History, Homerton College, Cambridge, UK, 1936-38; BA., Honours History Class II, Div.1, University of Sheffield, England, 1940-43; BD. (Melbourne), 1951; Certificate of Camden College, Sydney, and Ordination, 1951. *Appointments:* Secondary teacher, Birmingham, UK., 1938-40; Tutor, Camden College, Sydney, and Lecturer in Church History, United Faculty of Theology, University of Sydney, Australia, 1948-55; Minister, Balmain Congregational Church, Sydney, Australia, 1952-55; Head of Religious Education in Technical, Grammar and Comprehensive Schools, UK., 1955-76; Minister, Hampton Uniting Church Parish, Melbourne, Australia, 1977-80; Minister, St. John's Uniting Church, Essendon, Melbourne, Australia, 1981-. *Memberships:* Society for Old Testament Study, UK; Fellowship for Biblical Studies, Australia; Association for Religious Education, England & Wales; Australian Federation of University Women; Graduate Union, Melbourne. *Publications:* The Venture, 1948; The Congregationalist, 1951-55. *Honours:* First woman in Australia to be ordained as a theological lecturer, 1951. *Hobbies:* Reading; Tennis. *Address:* St. John's Manse, 853 Mt. Alexander Road, Essendon, Victoria 3040. Australia.

ABBA, (The Reverend. Dr.) Raymond, b. 11 Oct. 1910, Beverley, Yorkshire, England. Minister of Religion. m. Hilda May Blackham, 29 June, 1940, 1 son, 1 daughter. *Education:* Fitzwilliam & Cheshunt Colleges, University of Cambridge, England, 1935-40; MA, Cantab. & Sydney, Australia; BD, Melbourne, Australia. *Appointments:* Minister, Cemetery Road Congregational Church, Sheffield, UK, 1940-48; Principal & Professor of Theology, Camden College, Sydney, Australia, 1948-55; Schoolmaster, Willenhall, UK., 1955-57; Acting Professor of Old Testament Studies, University of Durham, 1958; Head of Department of Religious Studies, Swansea College of Education, University of Wales, 1958-76; Visiting Professor and Goldstein Memorial Lecturer, California State University, Fullerton, USA, 1973-74; Senior Minister, Hampton Uniting Church Parish, Melbourne, Australia, 1977-80; Senior Minister, St. John's Uniting Church, Essendon, Melbourne, 1981-. *Memberships:* Chairman, Association for Religious Education of England & Wales, 1974-77; President, Sheffield Free Church Council and Council of Churches, 1947-48; President, Swansea Council of Churches, 1969-71; Secretary, Faith & Order Commission, Australian Council of Churches, 1953-55; Chairman, United Faculty of Theology, Sydney, 1949; Chairman, Sheffield Theological Society, 1945-48; Chairman, Swansea University Teachers' Group, 1963-77; Society for Old Testament Study (UK) 1947-; Fellowship for Biblical Studies (Australia) 1952-; American Academy of Religion (USA), 1973-; Australian and New Zealand Society for Theological Studies (Australia), 1981. *Publications:* Things Which Abide, 1944; Principles of Christian Worship, 1957; The Nature and Authority of the Bible, 1958, revised and enlarged edition, 1982; Athens and Jerusalem, 1975; Editor: Bulletin of the Association for Religious Education, 1975-77; Training the Specialist Religious Education Teacher for Tomorrow, 1975; Religious Education Abroad, 1978; Contributor to The Interpreter's Dictionary of the Bible and many religious journals. *Honours:* Bronze Medal, Trinity College of Music, London, 1933; Astbury Exhibition, Cheshunt College, Cambridge, 1935; DD (honoris causa), Atlanta, 1973. *Hobbies:* Reading; Music; Walking; Swimming. *Address:* St. John's Manse, 853 Mt. Alexander Road, Essendon, Victoria. 3040, Australia.

ABDOOLCADER, Dato, Eusoffe, b. 18 Sept. 1924. Judge of the High Court, West Malaysia. m. Datin Haseenah binte Abdullah, 6 May 1968. *Education:* LL.B. (London) (1st Class Hons), 1949; Barrister at Law of Grays' Inn, 1950; Called, Malayan Bar, Notary Public, West Malaysia, 1951; Called to Singapore Bar, 1969; *Appointments:* Advocate, High Court in Malaya, 1951-74; Judge, High Court, West Malaysia, 1974. *Memberships:* State Goodwill Committee to 1974; Chairman, 1968 and 1969, member, 1970-, Penang Bar Committee; Bar Council 1963-74; Rules Committee of Malaysia 1963; External Examiner for LLB, University of Singapore, 1963-; Council and Court of University of Malaya, 1962-67; Advisory Editorial Board, Malaya Law Journal; Penang Club; Honary Member, Royal Perak Golf Club; Ipoh Club. *Honours:* Freeman, of the City of London, 1950; J.M.N. by H.M. the King of Malaysia, 1966; Dato, (Malaysian Knighthood), by HRH Sultan of Penang 1967; A.D.K by Governor of Sabah, 1969; D.P.C.M, (Malaysian Knighthood) by HRH Sultan of Perak, 1979 D.M.P.N. (Malaysian Knighthood), by Governor of Penang, 1981. *Hobbies:* Law; Electronics. *Address:* 23 Tiger Lane, Ipoh, Perak, Malaysia.

ABDUL KARIM BIN OTHMAN, b. 10 April, 1935, Muar, Johor, West Malaysia. Architect/Urban Planner. m. 1957, 3 sons, 2 daughters. *Education:* Diploma in Architecture, Singapore Polytechnic, Singapore, 1966; Master of Arts Degree in Urban Planning, University of Singapore, 1975. *Appointments:* Architectural Technician in the Jabatan Kerja Raya, Johor, Malaysia, 1957-63; Building Inspector in the Majlis Bandaran Johor Bahru, 1963-68; Assistant Architect in an Architectural Firm in Singapore, 1968-70; Architect in A. Karim Akitek (Own Practice), 1970-75; Architect/Planner in Kumpulan Karim-Lai (Partnership), 1975-. *Memberships:* Councillor in the Town Municipality Johor Bahru (Ahli Majlis MPJB); Committee Member, Malaysian Institute of Architects, Southern Chapter; Deputy Chairman, Rukun Tetangga Sektor Kebun Teh, Johor Bahru; Committee Member, UMNO Cwg. Bukit Chagar, Johor Bahru; Associate Member of Malaysian Institute of Architects (P.A.M.); Member of Singapore Institute of Architect; Member of British Institute of Management. *Honours:* Pingat Ibrahim Sultan, Johor (P.I.S.). *Hobbies:* Reading; Motoring; Touring; Self Study. *Address:* 43 Jalan Gelam, Majidee Park, Johor Bahru, W. Malaysia.

ABDUL KHALID BIN AWANG OSMAN, (Tan Sri Datuk Haji), b. 4 June 1925, Penang, Malaysia. Chairman and Managing Director. m. Puan Sri Laily bte. Hashim, 30 Apr. 1950, 4 sons, 2 daughters. *Education:* Diploma College of Agriculture, Malaya, 1949; *Ap-*

pointments: Rubber Instructor, 1950-51; Labour Officer, 1951-55; Elected Member of Federal Legislative Assembly, 1955-57; Elected Member of Parliament, 1957-69; Member of Railway Board, 1959; Member of Electricity Board, 1959; Malaysian Ambassador to: Netherlands, 1966, Federal Republic of Germany, 1966-70, Egypt, Lebanon and Sudan, 1970-74; Nepal, 1974-78; High Commissioner of Malaysia to India, 1974-78. *Memberships:* Malaysian Institute of Management; The Malaysian Royal Asiative Society; Malay Chamber of Trade & Industry, Kuala Lumpur; Royal Selangor Golf Club, Kuala Lumpur; Fellow, British Institute of Management 1980. *Publications:* Malaysia—An Anthology, 1978. *Honours:* Iron Cross, Second Class, 1967, Iron Cross, First Class, 1970, by President of the Federal Republic of Germany; P.S.M. with title of 'Tan Sri' by his Majesty the King of Malaysia, 1974; Order of the Arab Republic of Egypt Class One (Grand Cordon) by the President of Egypt, 1974; D.P.M.T. with title of 'Datuk' by H.R.H. the Sultan of Trengganu, Malaysia, 1975; D.P.M.K. with title of 'Dato' by H.R.H. the Sultan of Kedah, Malaysia, 1977. *Hobbies:* Reading; Golf. *Address:* KHALILI, Lot 35/37, Taman Tenaga, Batu 9, Jalan Puchong, Puchong, Selangor, Malaysia.

ABDULLAH, Fatma Shaaban, b. 2 Nov. 1939, Zanzibar,Tanzania. Artist and Teacher. m. (1) S. Abubakar, 10 Aug. 1964, (2) S Mohammed, 14 Nov. 1971. *Education:* Diploma in Fine Art, 1st Division, 1963, Diploma in Education, 2nd Division, 1964, Makerere University College, Uganda. *Appointments:* Vice Principal, Teacher Training College, Zanzibar, 1964; Head, Graphic Section, Television, Zanzibar, 1973; Art and Craft Promoter, 1975, Director, Culture, Art and Museums, Ministry of Culture and Sports, Zanzibar 1978-. *Memberships:* Vice Chairman, National Arts Council of Tanzania; Member of The Board of Directors, State Leather and Shoe Corporation, Zanzibar; Vice Chairman, Board of Directors, National Tourist Corporation, Zanzibar. *Creative Works:* Premantis a mural painting, 1964; May Day Procession, 1965; One-Woman exhibition, Nommo Gallery, Kampala, 1965; Study tour in East Germany, 1969; Worked with British designer in renewing the Tanzania Pavilion, Commonwealth Institute, London, 1975-76; Study tour, on Africa Crossroads Programme, USA, 1979. *Honours:* Margaret Trowell Prize, School of Fine Art, Makerere, award for the best 1st year student, 1959-60. *Hobbies:* Photography; Sewing. *Address:* PO Box 949, Zanzibar, Tanzania.

ABDULLAHI, Alhaji Halliru, b. 7 Sept. 1934, Katsina, Nigeria. Director. m. 2 wives, 10 Oct. 1952, 2 sons, 2 daughters. *Appointments:* Director, U T C. Nigeria Limited, Keno, Nigeria; Chairman: HALI Brothers Limited; A P I Limited, Keno, Nigeria; A C P., Kaduna, Nigeria; N E M Insurance, Lagos, Nigeria. *Memberships:* State Treasurer, W P W., Kaduna, Nigeria; Kano State Movement. *Hobbies:* Driving; Horse riding. *Address:* 683 Halliru Road, Gwagwarwa Kano, NIgeria.

ABECASIS, Isaac, b. 25 Aug. 1929, Gibraltar. Politician. m. Frances Pizzarello, 15 May 1959, 1 son, 1 daughter. *Education:* Diploma, Lycee Francais, Tangier, 1945. *Appointments:* Banking; Businessman; Elected to Legislature, 1969. *Memberships:* Member of the Gibraltar Labour Party and Association for the Advancement of Civil Rights; Minister for Tourism and Postal Services, Secretary, 1969-; Member of Gibraltar House of Assembly, 1969, Secretary, 1969; Minister for Tourism and Postal Services, 1972-75; Member of Gibralta House of Assembly, 1969; Minister for Housing and Postal Services, 1972-; Minister for Postal Services, 1972-75; Minister for Postal Services, 1972; Minister for Information, 1975-76; Regional Representative of the British Islands and Mediterranean Region of the Commonwealth Parliamentary Association, 1976-79. *Memberships:* Vice Chairman, Gibraltar Branch, Transport & General Workers Union, and Chairman, Gibraltar Trades Council, 1963-71. Attended UK and Mediterranean Regional Conferences, Isle of Man 1972 & 1979, Guernsey, 1974 & 1978, Westminster, 1977, Plenary Conference India, 1975, Canada, 1977, Jamaica, 1978, New Zealand, 1979, Parliamentary Seminar, Westminster, 1970, Commonwealth Parliamentary Visit, 1972, Meetings of Executive Committee of General Council Freetown, Sierra Leone, 1977, Penang, Malaysia, 1978, Perth, Australia, 1979. *Hobby: Languages. Address:* 2A, Castle Steps, Gibraltar.

ABEGG, Rudolf, b. 29 July 1943, Uster, (ZH), Switzerland. Physicist, Professor. m. Helene Jacot Abegg, 6 August, 1971, 1 son, 1 daughter. *Education:* BSc, College Minerva, Basle, Switzerland, 1962; MSc, 1970; PhD, 1974, University of Basle, Basle, Switzerland. *Appointments:* Research Associate, University of Wisconsin, Madison, Madison, USA, 1974-77; Professional Associate, Sessional Assistant Professor, 1978; University of Manitoba, Winnipeg, Canada, 1978; Research Assistant Professor, University of Manitoba, TRIUMF, Vancouver, BC, Canada, 1979-80; Research Scientist, TRIUMF and Research Assistant Professor, University of Alberta, Edmonton, Alberta, Canada, 1981. *Memberships:* Canadian Association of Physicists; American Physical Society; Swiss Physical Society. *Publications:* Numerous publications in scientific journals including: Nuclear Physics A, Physical Review C, Physics Letters, Nuclear Instruments and Methods; Numerous contributions to International Conferences on selected topics. *Hobbies:* Literature; Classical music; Swimming; Photography. *Address:* 8251 Luton Rd, Richmond, British Columbia, Canada, V6Y 2H1.

ABIDI, Saiyed Asif Husain, 4 Apr. 1940, Baragaon District., Jaunpur (U.P.) India. Scientist (Marine Biology and Fisheries). m. Sayeeda Tasneem, 30 Jan. 1967, 1 son, 2 daughters. *Education:* Doctor of Philosophy, 1981; Master of Philosphy, 1968; Master of Science, 1962; Bachelor of Science, 1960; UNESCO training in Oceanography and Marine Biology, 1966. *Appointments:* Senior Fisheries Inspector, Government of Uttar Pradesh, India, Directorate of Fisheries, 1962-65; Junior Scientist, National Institute of Oceanography, Cochin, New Delhi, Goa, 1965-70; Fisheries Officer, AG. Director of Fisheries, Fisheries Division, Ministry of Natural Resources and Tourism, Government of United Republic of Tanzania, 1970-76; Scientist, A, 1976-77, Scientist B, 1978, National Institute of Oceanography, Bombay Regional Centre, India; Director of Fisheries, Andaman and Nicobar Islands, Government of India, Port Blair, 1978-81; Scientist, C, 1980, Scientists-in-Carge, 1981, National Institute of Oceanography, Government of India, Bombay Regional Centre, India. *Memberships:* Marine Biological Association of United Kingdom; Limnology and Oceanography, USA; Marine Biological Association of India; Fishery Technologist Society of India; Also member of the Managing Committee and Editorial Board, Indian Fisheries Association; Society for Offshore Engineering and Underwater Technology of India, Honorary Treasurer. *Publications:* Twelve Scientific Research Publications; One Booklet on Fish Culture; 40 Scientific popular articles; Ten General articles; Ten Project Reports. *Honours:* Certificate of Honour, TAM PATRA, 1980. *Hobbies:* Photography; Writing. *Address:* Flat, 110-C, Janak Deep, Jai Prakash Road, Versova, Bombay, 400061, India.

ABIDI, Syed Ameer Haider, b. 28 Nov. 1940, Nowgianwan Sadat, India. Librarianship. m. 28 Aug. 1967, 2 sons, 1 daughter. *Education:* BA, 1958; MA, 1965; Certificate in Library Science, 1960; Post Grad. Diploma in Library Science, 1963; MLiB.Sc. 1967; ADEEB, 1956; ADEEB MAHIR, 1957; ADEEB KAMIL, 1958; Diplomas in Arabic, Persian, Hindi and German Languages. *Appointments:* Assistant Librarian, Indian Council for Cultural Relations, 1960-67; Lecturer in Library Science, Aligarh Muslim University, 1967-71; Senior Lecturer, later Acting Director, East African School of Librarianship, Makerere University 1971-73; Director of Libraries, Institute of History of Medicine and Medical Research, New Delhi, 1973-74; Director, East African School of Librarianship, Makerere University, Kampala, Uganda, 1975-. *Memberships:* include: Secretary, Council for Library Training in East Africa; Executive, Standing Conference of African Library Schools; Uganda Public Libraries Board; Chairman, Indian Association, Uganda; Life Member, Indian Association of Special Libraries and Information Centres; Indian Library Association; Makerere University Academic Staff Association; Uganda Library Association. *Publications:* Author of: Improving Library and information training facilities in Eastern Africa; The introduction of information science elements into library training schemes in Eastern Africa (with Professor Wersiq and Thomas Seeger); Librarianship as a career in East Africa (with Zaidir); Editor of: Ugandan Libraries, Six monthly journal of Uganda Library Associations and East African School of Librarianship; 18 papers and 14 conference papers and 4 proceedings of Seminars.

Honours: U.P. Govt. Scholarship, 1954-56; Rockefeller Foundation Aid Scholarship 1966-67; M.M.H. College Prize for standing first at MA, (Pol.Sc.) 1965; University of Delhi Gold Medal for standing first at Post. Grad. Dip. Lib. 1963. *Hobbies:* Urdu Poetry; Swimming; Driving. *Address:* Quary House, Makerere University PO Box 7062, Kampala, Uganda.

ABIDOGUN, Ayoade, b. 5 Oct. 1937, Ogbomosho, Oyo State, Nigeria. Agricultural Economist. m. Olatorera Oyesola, 2 sons, 3 daughters. *Education:* BSc., (Agric.), 1957-62, PhD. (Agric.Econs.), 1975, University of Ibadan, Nigeria; MSc., Wye College, University of London, UK, 1963-65. *Appointments:* Agricultural Officer, Ministry of Agriculture and Natural Resources, Western Region, Nigeria, 1963-68; Lecturer, Institute of Agricultural Research and Training, University of Ife, Nigeria, 1969-72; Chief Scientific Officer, former Agricultural Research Council of Nigeria, 1976; Assistant Director, National Cereals Research Institute, Ibadan, Nigeria, 1977-. *Memberships:* Society for International Development; Association for Advancement of Agricultural Sciences in Africa; Agricultural Economics Society of Great Britain; West African Association of Agricultural Economists; Nigerian Economic Society; Nigerian Association of Agricultural Economics. *Publications:* Published poems in literary journals including: Nigeria, a cultural periodical, Ibadan, a quarterly journal; Faces and Masks, a collection of poems in preparation. *Hobbies:* Gardening; Photography; Reading Music; Dancing. *Address:* Bodija Estate, Ibadan, Nigeria.

ABIOSE, Adenike Olatoke, b. 16 Oct. 1943, Eruwa, Nigeria. Doctor. m. Popoola Abiose, 2 Sept. 1967, 1 son, 3 daughters. *Education:* MB, BS, Ibadan. Distinctions in Pathology, Pharmacology, Paediatrics, Surgery, University of Ibadan, Nigeria, 1961-67; DO, RCS, RCP, London FRCS, ED, Institute of Ophthalmology, London, 1970-74. *Appointments:* House Officer, Obstetrics and Gynaecology, Surgery, Medicine, 1967-68, Senior House Officer, Ophthalmology, 1968-69, U.C.H. Ibadan, Senior House Officer, Ophthalmology, Sunderland Eye Infirmary, 1970; Registrar, Ophthalmology, U.C.H. Ibadan, 1971-72; Registrar, Opthalmology, Royal Victoria Infirmary, Newcastle, England, 1973; Registrar, Ophthalmology, Sussex Eye Hospital, Brighton, England, 1973-74; Senior Registrar, Lagos University Teaching Hospital, 1974-75; Senior Lecturer, University of Lagos, 1975; Senior Lecturer, Ahmadu Bello University, Zaria, 1978; Reader, Ophthalmology, Ahmadu Bello University, Zaria, 1979-. *Memberships:* Fellow West African College of Surgeons; International Society of Geographical Ophthalmology; Nigerian Ophthalmological Society; Medical Women's Association; Recreation Club. *Publications:* Numerous publications including: The Clinical Biochemical manifestations of Glucose-6-Phosphhate dehydrogenase deficiency DOKITA No. 9, April, 1967; Eye Injuries as seen in the Lagos University Teaching Hospital, Nigerian Medical Journal 5: 105, 1975; Retinal Diseases in Nigeria. A preliminary report, Nigeriah Medical Journal 6: 180, 1976; Pattern of Retinal Diseases in Lagos Annals of Ophthal. (Chicago) 11(7): 1967, 1979; Problems of Cataract Surgery in Lagos, Nigerian Medical Journal 9(2): 253-257, 1979. Submitted for Publication: Hypertensive Retinopathy in Nigerians, Abiose A and Mabadeje A.F.B; In preparation: Anterior Segment Diseases in Nigerian Children. *Honours:* Departmental Prize in Obstetrics & Gynaecology, 1965-66; Departmental Prize in Surgery, 1966-67; Faculty Prize in Medicine, 1966-67; Departmental Prize in Medicine, 1966-67; Sir Kofo Abayomi Prize and Gold Medal in Psychiatry, 1967; Blair-Aitken Prize in Clinical Surgery, 1967; Diploma in Ophthalmology (England), 1970; Passed Final Fellowship Examination of the Royal College of Surgeons of Edinburgh in Ophthalmology, 1974. *Hobbies:* Gardening; Reading. *Address:* 7 Yakubu Avenue, Kaduna, Nigeria.

ABIOYE, Ayinla Adewunmi, b. 13 Mar. 1929, Abeokuta, Nigeria. m. 25 Dec. 1954, 2 sons, 2 daughters. *Education:* LRCPI, LRCSI, LM, 1964; Certificate in Immunology, University of Ibadan, Nigeria, 1968; PhD, Pathology, 1971; FMC Pathology, (Nigeria) Nigerian Medical Council, 1977; MRC Pathology, London, England, 1979; FWACP, 1980. *Appointments:* House Surgeon/Physician, Bury General Hospital, England, 1964-65; Registrar in Medicine, University College Hospital, Ibadan, 1965-66; Registrar (pathology), 1966-68; Rockefeller Medical Research Training Fellow (pathology), 1968-71; Senior Registrar (pathology), 1971; Lecturer Non-Consultant (pathology), 1971-72; Lecturer/Consultant (pathology), 1972-74; Senior Lecturer/Consultant (pathology), 1974-77; Professor of Pathology, 1977-. *Memberships:* Nigerian Medical Association; British Medical Association; American Association for the Advancement of Science; Association of Pathologists of Nigeria; Nigerian Society for Immunology; Islamic Medical Association of Canada; Nigeria Muslim Mission Hospital Committee. *Honours:* Rockefeller Foundation Fellowship, 1968-71; WHO Research Fellowship, 1974-75; WHO Parasitic Diseases Programme Meeting in Geneva, Switzerland, 1980. *Hobbies:* Table Tennis; Reading; Writing. *Address:* 20 Paul Hendrickse Road, Bodija Housing Corporation, Ibadan, Nigeria.

ABLIZA, Togbe Kwasi, III, b. 1917, Somanya, Ghana. Paramount Chief of Volo Traditional Area of Ghana. *Education:* Certificates and Diploma in religion, at Elm advanced Bible Course College, Hampton, Ohio, USA, and Baptist Mission of Ghana. *Appointments:* Posts and Telegraphs Department, 1940-43; Paramount Chief, Abliza Paramount Stool, Menourfeme Royal Ruling House, Volo Traditional Area, 1943-. *Memberships:* Numerous memberships including: Chairman, Tongu Paramount Chiefs Council; Sogakofe; Tongu Local Management Committee; Volta Region Scholarships Selection Board. *Honours:* Knighthood diploma in the Order of the Sacred Cup, an ecumenical Christian men's organization of noted leaders around the world; Honorary degree of Doctor of Public Service from Bodkin Bible Institute with Headquarters in Brazil. *Address:* PO Box 1, Volo via Akuse, Tongu District, Volta Region Ghana West Africa.

ABODUNRIN, Yinka, b. 15 June 1947, Ibadan, Nigeria. Architect. m. 15 Mar. 1973, 1 daughter. *Education:* Bachelor of Architecture, 1976; Master of Urban Planning 1977. *Appointments:* Chicago Urban League, USA 1975-76; Solomon Cordwell and Buenz-Chicago, 1976-78; Allied Architects, Ibadan, 1978; Niger, 1978-81. *Memberships:* Nigerian Institute of Architects; Nigerian Institute of Town Planners; President, University of Illinois Student Senate, 1975-76. *Publications:* The Role of Architecture in the Prevention of Crime; The Challenge of Urban Renewal versus New Extension—The Nigerian Experience. *Honours:* Students Activity Honorary Award, University of Illinois, 1976. *Hobbies:* Swimming; Volley Ball. *Address:* 4B Otiti Crescent, Kongi Layout, Ibadan, Nigeria.

ABRAHAM, Abu, b. 11 June 1924, Tiruvalla, India. Political Cartoonist; Journalist. m. Sarojini, 29 Jan. 1962, 2 daughters. *Education:* BSc., Maths, English, French, Kerala University, India, 1945. *Appointments:* Bombay Chronicle, 1946-49; Shankar's Weekly, New Delhi, India, 1951-53; The Observer, London, England, 1956-66; The Guardian, London, England, 1966-69; Indian Express, New Delhi, India, 1969-81. *Memberships:* International Institute of Communications, London, UK. *Publications:* Editor, Verdicts on Vietnam; Abu on Bangladesh; Games of Emergency; Private View. *Hobby:* Tennis. *Address:* 153 Kakanagar, New Delhi 3, India.

ABRAHAM, (Sir), Edward Penley, b. 10 June 1913, Southampton, England. m. Asbjörg Harung, 1 Nov. 1939, 1 son. *Education:* MA., D.Phil., Queen's College, Oxford, UK, 1932-38. *Appointments:* Fellow, Lincoln College, Oxford, 1948, Senior Research Officer, 1948-60, Reader in Chemical Pathology, 1960-64, Professor of Chemical Pathology, 1964-80, Oxford, UK. *Memberships:* Royal Society; Athenaeum; Royal Society of Arts; Royal Society of Chemistry; Ed. board, Biochemical Society; Society for General Microbiology; American Society for Microbiology; British Society for Antimicrobiol Chemotherapy. *Publications:* Numerous publications in scientific journals on penicillins, cephalosporins and other substances with biological activity. *Honours:* FRS., 1958; CBE., 1974; Knighted, 1980; Hon. Fellow, Queen's College, Oxford, Linacre College, Oxford, Lady Margaret Hall, Oxford; Royal Medal, Royal Society, 1973; Mullard Award, Royal Society, 1980; Scheele Medal, Swedish Academy Pharmaceutical Sciences, 1975; Chemical Society Award in Medicinal Chemistry, 1975; Hon. DSc., University of Exeter, UK, 1980. *Hobbies:* Skiing; Gardening. *Address:* Badgers Wood, Bedwells Heath, Boars Hill, Oxford, England.

ABRAHAM, Kulangara Chacko, b. 16 Oct. 1942 Mekozhoor, Kerala State, India. Animal Husbandry Research Officer. m. Lissy Mathew, 8 May 1974, 1 son. *Education:* Bachelor of Veterinary Science, Kerala University, India, First Class, 1965; MSc, (Animal Science), Haryana Agricultural University, India, Animal Breeding, Major, 1973, First Class, Statistics Minor. *Appointments:* Veterinary Officer, Cattle Breeding Farm, Morvi India, 1965-66; Veterinary Officer, Veterinary Hospitals, Broach District, India, 1966-67; Veterinary Surgeon, Veterinary Hospitals and A I Centre, 1968-71; Veterinary Surgeon, i/c of Jersey Farm, Indo-Swiss Dairy Project, Kerala State, India, 1973-75; Assistant Professor, Department of Animal Brooding and Genetics, Faculty of Veterinary and Animal Science, Kerala Agricultural University, India, 1975-78; Foreign Assignment to Zambia, Animal Husbandry Research Officer, Ministry of Agriculture and Water Development Government of Zambia, 1978-. *Memberships:* Joint Secretary, 1977-78, Kerala Veterinary Teachers Association; Secretary, 1976-77, Kerala Agricultural University Faculty Club; Gideans International; Secretary, Animal Husbandry Research Committee, Zambia, 1979 and 1980; MSc Thesis Effects of Crossbreeding on grading Reproduction and Production Performances in Dairy Cattle, Haryana Agricultural University, 1973. *Publications:* Investigations on reproduction and production effeciency of different grades of Jersey and Red Sindhi with Local Cattle of Kerala, 1978; Evaluation of Brown Swissbulls by different Sire Indices 1978; Cattle Industry in Western Province, to appear shortly in Western Province Handbook; Also published popular articles in vernacular language and English in Dailies and Journals of Kerala, India, on different aspects of Goat breeding management and Dairy cattle management. *Honours:* Winner, M.O Thornakulty Gold Medal, Kerala University India, 1965; Winner, K.S. Mair Gold Medal, Kerala University India. *Hobbies:* Games; Reading; Gardening; Music. *Address:* Kulangara House, Mekozhoor, 689678, Kerala State, India.

ABRAHAMS, Ellis William, b. 7 May 1918. Warrnambool, Victoria, Australia. Physician. m. Mary Jean Hoy, 28 Apr. 1947, 3 sons, 1 daughter. *Education:* MB, BS, MD, University of Melbourne, 1946; MRCP, 1947, FRACP, 1972, FRCP, London, 1974. *Appointments:* Resident Medical Officer, Senior Resident Medical Officer and Assistant Medical Superintendent, Royal Melbourne Hospital, 1941-46; Post Graduate Study, London, England 1946-49; Medical Officer (Tuberculosis) Commonwealth Department of Health, Canberra, A.C.T. 1949; Director of Tuberculosis, Department of Health, Queensland, 1950-. *Memberships:* Australian National Tuberculosis Advisory Council; International Union Against Tuberculosis. *Publications:* Original contributions to medical literature include: Original Mycobacterial Sin, Tubercle (1970) 51, 316; Tuberculosis in Indiginous Australians, Medical Journal of Australia 1975. *Hobbies:* Orchids; Books; Travel. *Address:* 21 Stevens Street, Yeronga, 4104, Australia.

ABRAHAMS, Eric Wordsworth, b. 20 Feb. 1904, Kingston, Jamaica. Company Director; Financial Consultant. m. Lucille I, 16 June 1931, 2 sons, 2 daughters. *Education:* FAIA. *Appointments:* Managing Director (retired) Facey Commodity Co. Limited, Jamaica; Director, Gleaner Co. Limited, Jamaica; Vice-Chairman, Jamaica Citizens Bank Limited; Chairman: Palace Amusement Co. Group; Carib Pipe; Caribbean Health and General Insurance Co. *Memberships:* Vice President: Jamaica Chamber of Commerce, 1970; Jamaica Manufacturers Association, 1972. *Hobbies:* Golf; Magic; Music. *Address:* 8 West Armour Heights, Kingston 8, Box 32, Constant Spring PO., Jamaica, West Indies.

ABU KASSIM DATO', Bin Haji Mohammed, b. 31 Mar. 1921, Johore, Malaysia. Director of National Productivity Centre of Malaysia. m. Datin Mariam, 11 July 1957. *Appointments:* Public Health Inspector, Ministry of Health, Johore, Malaysia, 1940-50; State Commissioner for Labour, Regional Industrial Relations Officer, Southern Region, Ministry of Labour and Manpower, 1950-63; Assistant Controller of Trade, Ministry of Trade and Industry, July, 1963—Sept. 1963; Training & Investigating Officer, 1963-66, Director, 1966-, National Productivity Centre, Ministry of Trade and Industry; Served on numerous Government Committees including: National Productivity Council, 1966-; Industrial Court, Ministry of Labour and Manpower, 1973-; Cabinet Sub-Committee, Ministry of

Education on Manpower Development,1974-75; Advisory Panel, Tourist Development Corporation, Ministry of Trade & Industry, 1975; National Committee, Affairs of Bumiputra Small Businesses, 1977-. *Memberships:* Member of numerous associations including: Institute of Administrative Management, UK, 1964-; Governing Council, Malaysian Institute of Management, 1972-75; Founder member and Vice-President, Management Training Association of Malaysia, 1972; Founder member and National President, Malaysian Association of Productivity, 1970-; Founder member and Vice-President, Malaysian Institute of Personnel Management, 1975; British Institute of Management, 1975-. *Creative Works:* Attended numerous Seminars, Workshops including: Colonial Service Training Course, UK; Head of Malaysian Delegation to Regional Conference on Productivity and Emerging Economies, Singapore, 1968; Study Tour Fellowship in Federal Republic of West germany, 1973; Study Tour in Europe, UK., USA., and Japan, 1974; International Symposium on Entrepreneurship and Enterprise Development in Cincinnati, Ohio, USA., and Weekend Seminar on Entrepreneurship Development in Cleveland, USA, 1975; Study Tour in Ireland, Hotel Training Activities; Seminar, Transnational Corporation, National Public Administration Institute, Malaysia, 1979. *Hobbies:* Fishing; Reading; Stamp collecting. *Address:* 475 Section 17/13A, Petaling Jaya, Selangor, Malaysia.

ABUBAKAR, Iya, b. 14 Dec. 1934, Belel, Nigeria. Politician; University Professor. m. 1 Jan. 1963, 1 son, 2 daughters. *Education:* PhD., University of Cambridge, UK, 1962; BSc., (1st Class Hons.), University of Ibadan, Nigeria, 1958; DSc.(hons.), University of Ife, Nigeria, 1977; DSc.(hons.), Ahmadu Bello University, Nigeria, 1980. *Appointments:* Lecturer in Maths, 1962-64, Senior Lecturer in Maths., 1964-67, Professor and Head of Department of Maths. and Computer Science, 1967-75, Dean, Faculty of Science, 1968-69, 1972-75, Vice Chancellor, 1975-78, Ahmadu Bello University, Nigeria; Visiting Professor, University of Michigan, USA, 1965-66; Visiting Professor, New York, USA, 1971-72; Minister of Defence, Nigeria, 1979-81; Minister of Interior, Nigeria, 1981-. *Memberships:* Fellow, Nigerian Academy of Sciences; Fellow, Royal Astronomical Society, UK; Fellow, Institute of Maths and It's Applications, UK; New York Academy of Sciences, USA. *Publications:* Several research papers on Mathematics and geophysics in various international journals. *Honours:* Several in academic field. *Hobby:* Reading. *Address:* 11 Okotie Eboh Street, Lagos, Nigeria.

ACAMOVIC, Thomas, b. 17 Feb. 1952, Scotland. Chemist. *Education:* Licentiate of Royal Society of Chemistry, 1975; Graduate of Royal Society of Chemistry, 1979; MRSChem. 1981. *Appointments:* Higher Scientific Officer, Edinburgh School of Agriculture. *Publications:* 11 Scientific Publications including J. Chromatography, 206 (2) 416-420, 1981; J. Sci. Food Agric. 30 97-106, 1979; Leucaena Newsletter 1 38, 39, 40, 1980; *Honours:* Scottish Agricultural Industries Prize, 1979. *Hobbies:* Judo; Skiing; Chess; Karate; Philately. *Address:* 6 Dalhousie Drive, Bonnyrigg, Midlothian, EH19 2NA, Scotland.

ACHEBE, Chinua, b. 16 Nov. 1930, Ogidi, Nigeria. Writer & Teacher. m. C. Chinwe Okoli, 10 Sept. 1961, 2 sons, 2 daughters. *Education:* Government College, Umuahia (1944-47); University College, Ibadan (1948-53); BA, (London) 1953. *Appointments:* Producer- Controller- Director, Nigerian Broadcasting Corporation, 1954-66; Senior Research Fellow, Professor, University of Nigeria, Nsukka, 1967-; Professor of English, University of Massachusetts, Amherst USA, (1972-75); University Professor of English, University of Connecticut, Storrs, 1975-76. *Publications:* Things Fall Apart, No Longer at Ease, Arrow of God, A Man of the People (Novels); Girls at War (Short stories); Beware Soul Brother (Poems); Morning Yet on Creation Day (Essays); Chike and the River, How the Leopard Got his Claws, The Drum, The Flute (Juvenile); Editor: Don't Let Him Die (Poems), Okike (a literary journal). *Honours:* D.Litt (Dartmouth College, USA) 1972; (Southampton Univ, UK) 1975; LL.D Prince Edward Island 1976; DHL Massachusetts 1978; Honorary Fellow, Modern Language Association of America 1975; Neil Gunn Fellow, Scottish Arts Council 1975; Commonwealth Poetry Prize 1973; Nigerian National Merit Award 1979; Order of the Federal Republic 1979. *Hobbies:* Music. *Address:* University of Nigeria, Nsukka, Anambra State, Nigeria.

ACHESON, Jack, b. 20 Jan. 1925, Melbourne, Australia. Medical. m. Judith Maddern-Wellington, 21 Sept. 1965, 2 sons, 1 daughter. *Education:* Bachelor of Medicine, Bachelor of Surgery, Melbourne University, Australia, 1956; Fellow, Australian College of General Practitioners, 1974. *Appointments:* Resident Medical Officer, Prince Henry's Hospital, Melbourne, Australia, 1957; Geriatrics Resident Medical Officer, Cheltenham Home and Hospital for the Aged, Victoria, Australia, 1962; Paediatric ENT Registrar, Austin Hospital, Heidelberg, Victoria, Australia, 1963; Medical Superintendent, Mooroopna Base Hospital, Victoria, Australia, 1964-66; Medical Superintendent, Ballarat Base Hospital, Ballarat, Victoria 3350, Australia, 1970-; Service, Ex Prisoner of War; Ex RAAF, Flying Duties, World War II. *Memberships:* Australian Medical Association; Melbourne Cricket Club; Ballarat Regional Alcohol and Drug Dependance Association; Air Force Club; Air Force Association; Pacific Conference of Police Surgeons. *Hobbies:* Art; Writing; Golf; Drug education; Counselling drug addicts. *Address:* 1101 Norman Street, Wendouree 3355, Victoria, Australia.

ACKON, John Alexander, b. 14 Dec. 1937, Cape Coast, Ghana. Priest; Schoolmaster. m. Matilda Mercer-Ricketts, 10 May 1969, 2 sons, 2 daughters. *Education:* Dip.Th., Kelham Theological College, Newark, Notts, UK, 1963-68; B.Theol., University of Nottingham, UK, 1969-72; University of Lancaster's Post Graduate Certificate of Education, St. Martin's College, Lancaster, UK, 1973. *Appointments:* Curate, Holy Trinity Cathedral, Accra, Ghana, 1968-69; Chaplain, House-master, Head of Religious Studies Department, Adisadel College, Cape Coast, Ghana, 1973-77; Canon Precentor, Holy Trinity Cathedral, Accra, Head of Social Studies Department, Cathedral Secondary School, 1977-80; Archdeacon of Cape Coast, Priest in Charge, Christ Church Cape Coast, Rector of St. Nicholas Theological College, Cape Coast, 1980; Elected and Appointed Bishop of Cape Coast, 1981. *Memberships:* West African Association of Theological Institutions. *Publications:* Notable Problems Facing West African Students in London, 1966; Montamism as Compared to Spiritual Churches in Ghana, 1977, (unpublished). *Honours:* Made Deaon and Priested, 1968; Lord Coggan, former Archbishop of Canterbury, conferred the Lambeth S.T.H., 1979; Consecrated Bishop, 1981; Enthroned as First Bishop of Cape Coast, 1981. *Hobby:* Church music. *Address:* Christ Church House, PO Box 38, Cape Coast, Ghana.

ACORN, Glendyn Wallace, b. 18 Apr. 1928, Regina, Saskatchewan, Canada. Law. m. June Marie Carlson, 8 June 1957, 1 son, 1 daughter. *Education:* Bachelor of Laws, 1950, Bachelor of Arts, University of Saskatchewan, 1953. *Appointments:* Grant, Cavanagh and Rolf, 1954-55; Government of Alberta, 1955-79: Solicitor, Department of Lands and Forests, 1955-59; Solicitor, Department of Mines and Minerals, 1959-63; Assistant Legislative Counsel, 1963-71; Chief Legislative Counsel, 1971-78; Special Counsel-Legislation, 1978-79; Acorn Elliott, 1979-. *Memberships:* Law Society of Alberta; Cosmopolitan Music Society; Canadian Bar Association; Statute Law Society, UK. *Publications:* Constitutional Law Problems in Canadian Oil and Gas Legislation—The Background, 1964. *Honours:* Queen's Counsel, Alberta, 1974. *Hobby:* Music. *Address:* 39 Wolf Crescent, Edmonton, Alberta, T5T 1E1, Canada.

ADABA, John Osakenvem Renison, b. 29 Jan. 1942, Illah, Nigeria. Consultant Architect. m. Helen Gladys Abuah, 3 sons, 2 daughters. *Education:* Bachelor of Architecture (Honours), Ahmadu Bello University, Samaru, Zaria, Nigeria, 1973. *Appointments:* Project Architect, James Cubitt Fello Atkinson & Partners, Lagos, Nigeria, 1973-76; Partner, 1976-77, Senior Partner, 1977-, James Cubitt & Partners Nigeria. *Memberships:* Full member, Ikoyi Club, 1938, Ikoyi, Lagos Nigeria; Full member, Nigerian Institute of Architects, and member of the Institute's Education Board. *Publications:* None published. Work entitled SAHE-School of Architecture Africa, a dissertation on revolutionizing architectural education in Africa, in a Private Collection. *Honours:* Books prize for Academic Proficiency in 1971, after Intermediate Bachelor of Architecture Degree examinations in the University. *Hobbies:* Creative works; Painting; Drawing; Sculpture to a small degree due to insufficient time; Sports; Squash; Swimming; Listening to music. *Address:* Aquarian

House, Plots A2-A3, Razaq Gbadamosi Avenue, Aguda, Surulere, Lagos, Nigeria.

ADADEVOH, Babatunde Kwaku, b. 4 Oct. 1933, Lagos, Nigeria. Physician, Pathologist. m. Deborah Regina McIntosh, 21 July 1956, 1 son, 3 daughters. *Education:* Baptist Academy, Lagos, (1939-45); Igbobi College, Yaba, Nigeria (1946-51); University College, Ibadan (1952-56); University of Birmingham, UK (1956-59) Postgraduate Medical School & London School of Tropical Medicine (1960-61); Harvard Medical School, Boston, USA (1962-64). MD(Birmingham); FRCP (London); DTM&H (England); FRCPath (london); FWACP (West Africa); FMCP, FNIM; FSAN; FAS (Nigeria). *Appointments:* House Surgeon & Physician Birmingham Medal School, UK (1959-60); House Physician, Hammersmith Hospital, London, (1960-61); Research Fellow (Medicine & Biological Chemistry) Harvard Medical School & Massachusetts General Hospital, Boston, USA (1962-64); Lecturer/Senior Lecturer (Medicine) University of Lagos, Medical School (1964-67); Professor (Chemical Pathology), University of Ibadan (1968-78); Director of Medical Research, National Institute for Medical Research, Yaba, Nigeria (1977-); Vice-Chancellor, University of Lagos, Nigeria (1978-80); Professor (Chemical Pathology), University of Maiduguri, Nigeria (1981-). *Memberships:* Vice-President, Council for International Organisation of Medical Sciences (Cioms), 1979-; Vice-President, Nigerian Society of Endocrinology & Metabolism, 1978-; Member, International Society of Endocrinology; WHO expert Advisory Panel in Human - reproduction; WHO Africa Region Advisory Committee on Medical Research; International Association of Biological Standardization; Last twelve years served as Expert, Consultant, Adviser to Who, IAEA, IPPF etc. *Publications:* Over 150 publications in Medicine, Pathology, Endocrinology & Human Reproduction; including the book Sub-Fertility and Infertility in Africa 1974 pp 144, refs. 167. *Honours:* Cricket Colours (Igbobi College, 1950; University of Ibadan, 1955); Runner Up Lalcaca Medal & William Simpson Prize, London School of Tropical Medicine; Foundation Fellow, Science Association of Nigeria 1974; West African College of Physicians 1976; Nigeria Medical Council in Physics, 1970; Nigerian Academy of Science, 1977. *Hobbies:* Reading; Music; Tennis; Golf. *Address:* Plot 1195, 55 Bishop Oluwole Street, Victoria Island, Lagos State, Nigeria.

ADAMS, Ishmael Kwesi-Mensah, b. 8 Feb. 1920, Accra, Gold Coast, Ghana. Choral Conductor, Broadcaster, Music Teacher. m. Rebecca Ashiorkor Yebuah, 24 Dec. 1952, 7 sons, 6 daughters. *Education:* Government Junior Boys' School, James Town, Accra, 1925-28; Government Senior Boys' School, Kinbu, Accra, 1929-34; Extra Mural Music School, Accra, 1948-51; Curwen College of Music (Tonic Solfa College), Bayswater, London, 1952; Royal School of Church Music, Surrey, England, 1952. *Appointments:* Messenger, 1935-38; Stenographer/Secretary, 1938-51 City Press Ltd., Accra, Music Assistant, Ghana Broadcasting System, 1953-56; Senior Programme Assistant, 1956-59; Producer/Programme Organizer, 1960-65; Assistant Controller of Programmes, 1966-75 Ghana Broadcasting Corporation, Assistant Master of the Music, Holy Trinity Cathedral, Accra, 1965-68; Master of the Music, Holy Trinity Cathedral, Accra 1978-. *Memberships:* Founder, Leader & Musical Director, The Damas Choir, Accra; Singing Master, GA Choir, (Anglican), Accra; Secretary, Union of Anglican Church Choirs, Greater Accra Region; Member of Board of Governors, Holy Trinity Cathedral Church Secondary School, Accra. *Publications:* Compositions: Tatale-O (Choral); School Anthem - St. Anthony's Preparatory School, Accra; School Anthem - North Ridge Lyceum, Accra; 222nd Anniversary Outing Song, Anglican Church, Accra; Various arrangements of Ga Folk and Traditional songs. *Honours:* Bishop's Badge of Honour (Religious), 1960; Grand Medal (Civil Division) - Ghana National Honours Award 1975. *Hobbies:* Choral Adjudication; Walking; Drama; Table Tennis. *Address:* 3595/6, Abose Okai, Accra, Ghana.

ADAMS, John Michael Geoffrey Manningham, (Rt. Hon.) b. 24 Sept. 1931, Queen's Counsel, St Michael, Barbados. Barrister and Attorney at Law. m. Genevieve Turner, 2 June 1962, 2 sons. *Education:* MA(Oxon) Politics, Philosophy and Economics, Magdalen College, Oxford University; Called to the Bar, Gray's Inn, 1959; President, Oxford University, West Indian Association; Vice President, West Indian Students' Union, London. *Appointments:* BBC and TV Freelance Broadcaster and Producer 1957-62; General Secretary, Barbados Labour Party, 1965; Chairman and Political Leader, Barbados Labour Party 1971-; Member of Parliament for St. Thomas, 1966-; Leader of the Opposition, 1971; Prime Minister of Barbados, 1976, re-elected, 1981. *Memberships:* Clubs and Study Groups concerned with Stamp Collecting; Union Club, Bridgetown Barbados; Masonic Lodge. *Hobbies:* Gardening; Watching, Reading and Writing about Cricket; Philately. *Address:* 14 Walkers Terrace, St. George, Barbados.

ADAMSON, Jennifer Lilian, b 5 Dec. 1937, Adelaide, Australia. Legislator. m. Ian Kenneth Adamson, 10 Jan. 1959, 1 son, 2 daughters. *Education:* Leaving Honours, Walford House School, 1943-54. *Appointments:* Advertising copywriter 1955-59; Freelance promotion consultant and political research assistant 1971-77; Liberal candidate, Australian Senate election 1975; S.A. House of Assembly, Member for Coles, 1977; Minister of Health and Tourism, 1979. *Memberships:* Association of Women Journalists; Liberal Party; Walford CEGGS Council of Governors; Board of Botanic Garden; Parish Council, St. Matthews Church of England, Marryatville. *Hobbies:* Reading; Sewing; Music; Sailing. *Address:* 57 Kennaway Street, Tusmore, 5065, Australia.

ADAMSON, Vera, b. 8 Dec. 1909, Scarborough, England. University Lecturer. *Education:* King's College, London University, 1928-31; Institute of Education 1931-32; BA Hons. English, 1931; Diploma in Education, 1932; MA, Birmingham University. *Appointments:* Head, English Department, Twickenham County Grammar School, 1946; British Council Officer: Jerusalem, Palestine, 1946-48; Montevideo, Uruguay, 1948-50; London, Overseas, Student Centre, Director of Studies, 1950-58; Israel, British Council, English Language Officer, Hebrew University, 1959-61; Lecturer, English Department, and Advisor to Overseas Students, Birmingham University, 1962-76; Chairman, BBC's Midlands Regional Advisory Council, 1971-76; BBC's General Advisory Council, 1971-76. *Memberships:* Royal Institute of International Affairs; The Fabian Society; The British Council Retirement Association; Friends of Covent Garden Association, 1962-76; Philological Society; English Speaking Union. *Publications:* Oxford University Press—English Studies; Contributions to The Listener, Times Educational Supplement, Modern English Language Review. *Hobbies:* Reading; Walking; Travel. *Address:* 27 Lord's View, St John's Wood Road, London NW8 7HL, England.

ADAMU, Alhaji Hassan, b. 25 May 1940, Yola, Nigeria. Industrialist. m. 1 Jan. 1968, 2 daughters. *Education:* West Africa School Certificate, 1959; G.C.E. A Levels, 1961; National Diploma M. Eng. 1961-62; Diploma in Transport Studies 1963-65; Graduate Institute of Transport, 1963-65; Associate Member of Institute of Traffic Administration, 1963; Member of British Institute of Management, 1970. *Appointments:* Traffic and Commercial Officer, Nigerian Ports Authority, 1966-68; Deputy General Manager, Kadara Traction, N.N.D.C. (Subsidiary), 1969-71; General Manager, Nigerian Leather Works Company, 1971-74; Managing Director, Nigerian Industrial Complex, 1975-80; Chairman, Niger Bran Shipping Line, 1981. *Memberships:* Vice-Chairman, Kano Metropplitan Club, 1971-73; Director, Borin Porono (Largest Civil Engineering Co.,); Director, Yolo Polytechnic (Federal Government Instructor); Member of the Executive Council of Manufacturing Association of Nigeria; Member of Export Council of Nigeria. *Hobbies:* Reading, Horse riding and travelling. *Address:* 9 Sokoto Road, G.R.A. Nasarawa, Kano, N. Nigeria.

ADDAE, Stephen Kojo, b. 31 July 1936, Tsito, Ghana, West Africa. Doctor of Medicine - Physiologist. m. Felicia Addae, 20 Dec. 1959, 2 sons, 1 daughter. *Education:* MB., BS. (With Honours, London.), 1962; MSc., (Rochester), 1967; PhD., (Rochester), 1968; MD., (London), 1972. *Appointments:* Postdoctoral Fellow, University of Rochester, 1968-69; Lecturer, 1969-72, Senior Lecturer, 1972-74, Associate Professor, 1974-78, Professor 1978, University of Ghana Medical School. *Memberships:* West African Physiological Society; Nigerian Physiological Society; West African Society of Pharmacology; Ghana Medical Association;

Fellow, Ghana Academy of Arts & Science. *Publications:* Has published about 50 papers mainly on sickle cell disease; Has published a book The Kidney in Sickle Cell Disease. *Honours:* Best student awards in Physiology Biochemistry & Anatomy, 1960; Graduated with Honour MB. BS. OF London. 1962 with distinction in Surgery. *Hobbies:* History Reading (ancient); Tennis; Carpentery. *Address:* No 5 Church Crescent, North Lahore, Accra.

ADDENBROOKE, David Anthony, b. 3 Jan. 1944, Perth, Western Australia. Theatre Director; Academic; Film Executive; Author. m. Vivienne Katrinka Bailey (Deceased) 12 Apr. 1967. (2) Maureen Van Der Heyden, 10 Aug. 1979, 3 sons. *Education:* Hale School Western Australia, 1953-60; University of Western Australia, Bachelor of Arts, 1967; University of Warwick (UK), Master of Philosophy, 1972; Royal Academy of Dramatic Art, (London), 1971; University of Western Australia, Doctor of Philosophy (currently completing thesis). *Appointments:* Senior English Master, Wesley College, Perth, W. Australia, 1968; Freelance Theatre Director, Australia/London, 1969-72; Head of Theatre, Western Australian Institute of Technology, 1969-77; Head of Performing Arts, Darling Downs Institute of Advanced Education, Queensland Australia, 1977-80 (Theatre/Music/Film/TV); Founding Artistic Director, Western Australian Theatre Company, 1972-77; Founding Artistic Director, Performance Centre, Queensland, 1977-80; Royal Shakespeare Company UK. Work under secondment, 1971 Stratford Season; Royal Court Theatre, London, Assistant to Administrator under Arts Council of G.B. Trainee Administrator Scheme, 1972; Managing Director David Addenbrooke and Associates, Western Australian Artists Management, The Perth Stage Company, Asile Holdings, Gemini Press, 1981-; Executive Director, Film Corporation of Western Australia, 1981-. *Memberships:* Australian Society of Authors; Producers and Directors Guild of Australia; Australian College of Education; Actors and Announcers Equity of Australia; Liberal Party of Australia; Festival of Perth Drama Committe, 1972-77; Durling Downs Youth Theatre, Queensland, Executive Committe, 1977. *Publications:* The Royal Shakespeare Company, William Kimber Ltd., (London), 1974; Numerous articles for State and National Press in Australia on the Performing Arts. Regular talks and interviews for Radio/TV; Over 30 major Theatre and Opera productions for companies in Australia and London; Executive Editor, Performance Magazine, Perth, W. Australia, 1973-75. *Hobbies:* Breeding Siamese Cats, Antiques. *Address:* 82 Bagot Road, Subiaco 6008, Western Australia.

ADDICOTT, George Eric, b. 29 Apr. 1918, Plymouth, Devon, England. Journalist. m. Mollie Dorothy Phyllis Fereday, 24 Jan. 1942, 3 daughters. *Education:* Sutton High School, Plymouth, 1928-36; Oxford School Certificate with Honours, Distinction in French, Georgraphy and Mathematics and Exemption from London Matric, 1933; London Higher School Certificate with Exemption from Intermediate BA (London), 1935; and with Distinction in French (Written and oral), 1936; *Appointments:* Western Press Agency, Plymouth; 1936-38; Daily Mirror, London, 1938-39; Royal Corps. of Signals, 1939-43 (seconded to Indian Civil Service, 1941-43); Royal Indian Navy, 1943-46; Wartime employment including Army clerk; civilian journalist with GHQ (India) GS (MI8a); Counter-Propaganda Officer with civil Department of Information & Broadcasting, New Delhi; Public Relations Officer with Royal Indian Navy, specializing in cloak-and-dagger work with Fairmile motor launches on enemy-held Burma coast; Rhodesia Herald, Salisbury, 1946-52; Independent Public Relations Consultant (specializing in tobacco industry), 1952-65; Herald and Sunday Mail, Salisbury, 1966-. *Memberships:* President, Rhodesian Guild of Journalists, 1955-57; Elected Honorary Life Member, 1965; Vice-President, Old Suttonian Association since 1956; Chairman, The Press Club, Salisbury, 1960-62; Committee, The National Club, Salisbury, 1965; Member, Victory Services Club, London since 1980. *Publications:* Editor: RIN Log, 1944-45, Rhodesian Tobacco, 1953-59, The Rhodesian Tobacco Journal, 1965-66; Rhodesian Tobacco and World Markets, South African Journal of Economics, Vol. 26 No.1 March, 1958; Sundry publications for Tobacco Research Board of Rhodesia and Nyasaland, 1953-65. *Honours:* Ballard Open Scholarship to University College of the South-West, Exeter, Devon, 1936; Mention in Despatches (Burma Campaign - Arakan Coastal Forces) published

in New Year Honours List, 1946. *Hobbies:* Arboriculture, woodcarving, reading. *Address:* Lusty Glaze, 37 Harvey Brown Avenue, Milton Park, P.O. Belvedere, Salisbury, Zimbabwe.

ADDO-FENING, Robert Yaw, b. 7 Mar. 1935. University Teacher. m. Comfort Oduraa Asomaning, May 1956, 3 sons, 2 daughters. *Education:* BA(Hons) History, University of Ghana, 1963; MA, History Australian National University, Canberra, 1967; PhD (African History) University of Ghana, 1980. *Appointments:* History Tutor, Ofori Panin Secondary School, New Tafo, Ghana, 1963-65; Lecturer in History, University of Ghana, 1967-77; Visiting Assistant Professor, University of California, San Diego, 1977-78; Senior Lecturer, University of Ghana, 1977-. *Memberships:* Historical Society of Ghana; National Archives of Ghana; Ghana Academy of Arts & Sciences Committee, Documents, Oral Tradition and Cultural Heritage; Ghana Co-operating Committee, Encyclopaedia Africana Project; Editor, Transactions of the Historical Society of Ghana. *Publications:* Gandhi & Nkrumah: A study of non-violence & non-co-operation campaigns in India and Ghana as anti-colonial strategy, 1972; Some Aspects of the History of Asante & Maratha confedermies in the 18th and 19th C. 1972; The Pax Britanica and Akyem Abuakwa c 1874-1904, 1974; The Gold Mining Industry in Akyem Abuakwa c 1850-1910, 1976. *Honours:* Commonwealth Scholarship and Fellowship Plan: Australian Award, 1965-67; Visiting Senior Fulbright-Hays Scholar, UCLA, 1972; Fellow, Historical Society of Ghana, 1972; Linguist to the Royal Stool of Adadientam, 1973. *Hobbies:* Gardening; Table Tennis; Lawn Tennis. *Address:* No 3 Ayido Circle, Legon, Accra, Ghana.

ADDO, Nelson Otu, b. 4 Nov. 1933, Adukrom, Ghana. University Professor. m. Alice Dansoa Kwapong, 2 sons, 1 daughter. *Education:* BSc. (Soc.), University of Ghana, Legon, 1962; MSc. (Econ.), 1964, PhD, 1969, London School of Economics, University of London. *Appointments:* Agricultural Officer, Ghana Ministry of Agriculture, 1952-59; University Lecturer, Professor and Research Administrator, University of Ghana; Served as Consultant to UN ECA, UNESCO, World Bank etc. *Memberships:* International Union for the Scientific Study of Population (IUSSP), Association of African Statisticians; Ghana Sociological Association; Council Member, Population Association of Africa, (PASSAF). *Publications:* Population Growth & Socio Economics Change, Collaborating editor with J.C. Caldwell, Population Comment, 1975; Dynamics of Urban Growth in Ghana (Monograph); Siblings in Ghana, 1976 (with J.R. Goody); Editor and co-editor of 8 other monographs; Published 54 other articles and papers. *Honours:* Population Council, New York - Fellow: 1962-65; 1968-69; Visiting Scholar, Department of Sociology, University of North Carolina, USA, 1976; Commonwealth Visiting Professor, Smith Memorial Visiting Fellow, University of Cambridge, UK, 1977-78; Visiting Fellow, Clare Hall, Cambridge, UK, 1977-78. *Hobbies:* Football, Table Tennis, Farming. *Address:* No. 38, Lower Hill, University of Ghana, Legom, Ghana, West Africa.

ADEBISI, Ayoola, b. 25 Nov. 1936, Igboho, Oyo State, Nigeria. Tobacco Agronomist. m. Gbonjubola Afolabi, 13 Nov. 1965, 2 sons, 3 daughters. *Education:* BA-(Hons), University College Ibadan, 1959-62; MA, Dip Ed, McGill University, Montreal Canada, 1963-65. *Appointments:* Senior Geography Master, Olivet Baptist High School, Oyo, 1962-63 and 1965-66; Nigerian Tobacco Company Limited 1967-; Area Leaf Manager, 1967; District Leaf Manager, 1968-71; Divisional Leaf Manager, 1972-74; Leaf Operations Manager, 1975-79; Leaf Manager, Head Office, 1979-. *Memberships:* Nigerian Institute of Management; British Institute of Management; Ikoyi Club, Lagos; Igboho Premier Club. *Publications:* Unpublished MA Thesis: Dysfunctionalities of Nigerian Education in Relation to Post-Independence Aims of Social, Economic and Political Development MA Education, 1965. *Honours:* Commonwealth Scholarship, Canada, 1963-65. *Hobbies:* Hunting; Lawn Tennis. *Address:* 1, Alhaji Kanike Close, S.W. Ikoyi, Lagos, Nigeria.

ADEBIYI, Adekunle Augustine, b. 2 Jan. 1939, Lagos, Nigeria. Engineer. m. Sherifat Folashade Akanbi, 27 June 1970, 3 sons, 1 daughter. *Education:* West African School Certificate, Abeokuta Grammar School,

1955-58; Diploma, Engineering, College of Technology, 1960-65 & 1971-72. *Appointments:* Nigerian Army, 1968-74; Henry Stephes Engineering Co., 1974-76; Finlay Engineering Co., 1976-. *Memberships:* Chartered Member, Institution of Engineers of Ireland; Associate Member, Institution of Production Engineers; Affiliated Member, Nigerian Institute of Management. *Publications:* Weldability of Free Cutting Steels, 1972. *Honours:* High and Long Jump 1st, 1961; Long Jump 1st, 1962 & 1963; Long Jump 2nd, 1964. *Hobbies:* Table Tennis, Lawn Tennis; Squash. *Address:* 23 Eletu Odibo St, Abule Ijesha, Yaba, Lagos, Nigeria.

ADEBONOJO, Samuel Adetola, b. 7 July 1935, Lagos, Nigeria. Thoracic and Cardiovascular Surgeon. m. 6 July 1962, 2 sons, 1 daughter. *Education:* BSc. (Honour) Chemistry Howard University, USA, 1962; MD, University of Pennsylvania, USA, 1966; American Board of Surgery, 1972; American Board of Thoracic Surgery, 1976. *Appointments:* Associate Instructor Surgery, Bryn Mawr Medical Hospital, 1968-71; Instructor Thoracic Surgery, Hahnemann Medical College, 1971-73; Clinical Instructor, Cardiac Surgery, University of California, San Diego, 1973-75-; Lecturer, Consultant, Thoracic Surgery, University of Ibadan, Nigeria, 1975-76; Senior Lecturer- Consultant, Thoracic Surgery, University of Ibadan, Nigeria, 1976-. *Memberships:* Treasurer/Secretary, Nigerian Cardiac Society; Treasurer, Nigerian Surgical Research Society; Publicity Secretary, Nigerian Medical Association; Ass. Secretary General, Fellow, West African College of Surgeons; Fellow, International College of Surgeons, USA; Fellow, American College of Surgeons, USA; Society for Thoracic Surgeons, USA. *Publications:* Author of over 50 Publications on various aspects of Thoracic and Cardiovascular Surgery in Nigeria. *Honours:* Dean Honours Roll, Howard University, 1959-62; Phi Beta Kappa, 1962; Beta Kappa Chi Scientific Honours, 1962; International Who's Who, 1969; Marquis Who's Who in the World, 1978; American Medical Association Recognition Award. *Hobbies:* Squash; Tennis; Soccer; Swimming. *Address:* E9/881 Olabode Oloro St. off New Ife Road, Agodi, Ibadan, Nigeria.

ADEDEJI, Adebayo, b. 21 Dec. 1930, Ijebu-Ode, Nigeria. Economist. m. Aderinola Ogun, 11 Aug. 1957, 5 sons, 2 daughters. *Education:* Diploma in Local Goverment Administration, University College of Ibadan, Nigeria, 1953-54; BSc.Econ, University College, Leicester, University of London, England, 1955-58; Masters Degree in Public Administration, Harvard University, USA, 1960-61; PhD, University of London, England, 1967. *Appointments:* Senior Assistant Secretary (Revenue) Nigerian Civil Service, 1958-63; Deputy Director, Institute of Administration, University of Ife, 1963-67; Director, Institute of Administration, Unife, 1967-71; Professor of Public Administration, 1968; Federal Commissioner (Minister) for Economic Development and Reconstruction, 1971-75; United Nations Under Secretary-General and Executive Secretary of Economic Commission for Africa, 1975-. *Memberships:* Chairman, Western Nigerian Government Broadcasting Corporation, 1966-67; Nigerian National Manpower Board, 1968-71; President, Nigerian Economic Society, 1971-72; Board Member, Nigerian Institute of Management, 1968-75; Chairman, Directorate of the National Youth Service Corps of Nigeria, 1973-75; Ad Hoc Committee of Experts on the finances of the United Nations and its Specialized Agencies, 1965; Royal Commonwealth Society, 1970-; Vice President, African Association for Public Administration and Management (AAPAM), 1971-74; President, AAPAM, 1974-; Expert Committee on the Restructuring of the Economic and Social Sectors of the United Nations System, 1975; Chairman of the Senate of the United Nations Institute for Namibia, 1975-; Board of Trustees of the Department of Economics, University of Boston, Boston, Mass., USA, 1978-. *Publications:* Numerous Publications including: A Survey of the Highway Development in the Western Region of Nigeria, 1960; Nigerian Administration and Its Political Setting, 1968; Nigerian Local Government Finance: Development, Problems, and Prospects, 1972; Africa, the Third World and the Search for a New Economic Order, 1976. *Honours:* Fellow of the Nigerian Institute of Management (FNIM), 1974; Doctor of Letters (Honoris Causa), Ahmadu Bello University, 1976; Commander of the Order of Merit of the Islamic Republic of Mauritania, 1977. *Hobbies:* Photography; Walk-

ing; Lawn Tennis; Golf. *Address:* Adeola Lodge, 122 Apebi Street, Ijebu-Ode, Nigeria.

ADEDEJI, Joel Adeyinka, b. 4 Sept. 1932, Aboso, Ghana. Professor. m. Cecilia Folasade Adedeji, 6 Jan. 1962, 2 sons, 2 daughters. *Education:* Diloma in Drama, Rose Bruford College, Sidcup, Kent, UK, 1962; Master of Arts, New York University, New York, USA, 1964; Doctor of Philosophy, University of Ibadan, Ibadan, Nigeria, 1969. *Appointments:* Lecturer, University of Ibadan, Nigeria, 1964-71; Senior Lecturer, University of Ibadan, 1971-75; Professor, Theatre Arts and Head of Department, 1975-; Director, University Theatre Company, 1976-. *Memberships:* Executive Committee Member, International Theatre Institute, (UNESCO, Paris), 1977-; Executive Committee Member, International Federation for Theatre Research, 1979-; Society of Teachers of Speech and Drama, Great Britain. *Publications:* Many Articles and Monographs on the Drama and Theatre in Africa; Author of Three Books (in press). *Creative Works:* Director/Producer of Several Stage Plays. *Honours:* Certificate of the International Phonetic Association, 1962; Licentiate of the Royal Academy of Music, 1964; Fellow of the Royal Society of Arts, 1980. *Hobbies:* Squash; Golf; Theatre Visits; Walking. *Address:* 1 Kurunmi Road, University of Ibadan, Ibadan, Nigeria.

ADEDIRAN, Babaseinde Olufolahan, b. 3 Dec. 1940, Ado-Ekiti, Nigeria. Librarian. m. O. Atinuke Adediran, 21 Dec. 1968, 3 sons. *Education:* Bachelor of Arts, University of Ibadan, Ibadan, Nigeria, 1963-66; Postgraduate Diploma in Librarianship, University of Ibadan, Ibadan, Nigeria, 1966-67; Master of Library Science, School of Library & Information Science, University of Western Ontario, London, Ontario, Canada, 1971-72. *Appointments:* Assistant Librarian to Senior Sub-Librarian, Ibadan University Library, Ibadan, Nigeria, 1967-75; Head, Technical Services Division, Ibadan Polytechnic Library, Ibadan, Nigeria, 1975-79; Acting Chief Librarian, Ibadan Polytechnic Library, Ibadan, Nigeria, 1979-. *Memberships:* Music Circle, University of Ibadan; Ibadan Tennis Club, Ibadan. *Publications:* The role of the Association as regards research, in Proceedings of the Annual Conference of the Western State Division of the Nigerian Library Association, 1969; The design and operation of reference systems in libraries and information centres. Nigerian Libraries, vol. 9 Nos. 1 and 2 , 1973; Centralization of University Library Services: some compelling factors in Nigerian universities, 1974; Research projects in librarianship in Nigeria: financial provision, 1976; A Study of the acquisition pattern in Ibadan University Library over a five-year period: 1968/69-1972/73. *Honours:* Federal Government Scholarship for undergraduate studies at the University of Ibadan; Canadian International Development Agency Award to do Master's degree in Library Science at the University of Western Ontario, Canada. *Hobbies:* Music; Squash rackets; Football. *Address:* No.6, Block IV, Busari Akande Layout, Bodija, Ibadan, Nigeria.

ADEFOLAJU, Pamela Ibironke, b. 26 July 1950, Owo. Librarianship. m. 23 Aug. 1975, 1 son, 2 daughters. *Education:* BSc (Hons), Agricultural Biology, 1974; MLS, 1977. *Appointments:* Research Officer, 1975-76; Librarian, 1977-. *Memberships:* Nigerian Library Association; International Federation of Documentalists. *Publications:* A survey of the use of library materials in National cereals research Institute, Ibadan Nigeria—MLS, thesis; Abstracts of theses submitted to the library of National cereals research Institute, A memo. *Hobbies:* Sports; Gardening. *Address:* Odo-Ona Elewe, Challenge Area, Ibadan, Nigeria.

ADEGBITE, Josiah Adegoke, b. 12 Mar. 1938, Dorowa Babuje, Via B/Ladi, Nigeria. m. (1) Comfort Oluremi Jeje, 1966, (2) Grace Olufunmilayo Falase, 1979, 5 sons, 1 daughter. *Education:* Bachelor of Architecture, Ahmadu Bello University, Zaria, 1970. *Appointments:* Architect with Ikeja Area Planning Authority, Lagos, Nigeria, 1970-74; Architect, Lagos State Ministry of Works and Planning, 1974-76; Principal Partner and Chief Coordinator, Skyline Design Teamsters, 1976-; Partner, Housing Development Consortium, 1980-. *Memberships:* Associate Member, Nigerian Institute of Architects, 1975; Faboso Friendly Society. *Honours:* Federal Goverment of Nigeria Scholarship Award, 1964; Foundation Scholarship Awards, University of Nigeria, Nsukka, 1966; Staff Prize for best overall

Performance 3rd year, Ahmadu Bello University, Zaria, 1967-68; Atlas Prize for best overall Performance 4th year, Ahmadu Bello University, Zaria, 1968-69; Adeyemi Prize for Exceptional ability in developing some low-cost prototype building elements-Innovation, 1969-70. *Hobbies:* Running; Drawing; painting; Designing of Building Materials; Farming. *Address:* Plots 9 to 10 Sasegbon Estate, Tabon Tabon, Agege, PO Box 320, IKEJA, Lagos State, Nigeria.

ADEGBULE, Ezekiel Kayode, b. 18 Nov. 1942, Akure, Ondo State, Nigeria. Librarianship. m. Grace Modupe Mabadeje, 14 May 1977, 3 sons. *Education:* ALA, 1971, Liverpool Polytechnic, Liverpool, England, 1969-70; MA(Ed), MS in LS, Case Western Reserve University, Cleveland, Ohio, USA, 1977-78. *Appointments:* Library Assistant, Western Regional Library, Ibadan, Nigeria, 1962-65; Senior Library Assistant, College of Medicine, University of Lagos, Surulere, Lagos, Nigeria, 1965-67; Assistant Library Officer, Librarian Grade 1, Yaba College of Technology Library, Lagos, Nigeria, 1967-77; Assistant Librarian, Wigan Technical College Library, Wigan, England, 1970-71; Senior Librarian, Ondo State Library, P.M.B. 719, Akure, Ondo State, Nigeria, 1978-. *Memberships:* Nigerian Library Association; The Library Association, London; American Society of Information Science. *Publications:* Performance appraisal: criteria for self-actualization, In Public Servant, 1979; Views and Perspectives on supervision of instructions, In Modern Teacher, 1980. *Honours:* Ford Foundation Award, 1968. *Hobbies:* Photography; Table Tennis; Motoring. *Address:* 15, Esho Street, Akure, Ondo State, Nigeria.

ADEGUNLE, Olabisi, b. 28 Mar. 1938, Ondo, Ondo State, Nigeria. Legal Practitioner. m. 15 Jan. 1966, 1 son, 4 daughters. *Education:* LL.B., Hons., University of London, UK, 1967; Called to Bar, Middle Temple, UK, 1978; LL.M., University College, London, UK, 1979. *Appointments:* Private Legal Practitioner with Federal Republic of Nigeria, 1971-. *Memberships:* Executive member, Nigerian Bar Association; Student member, AMORC. *Hobby:* Hunting. *Address:* Olowo-Ade House, 61 Oshola Street, New Ifako, Ikeja Area, Lagos, Nigeria.

ADEJORO, Samuel Sunday, b. 13 Nov. 1938, Daja-Ajowa, Nigeria. Economist. m. Terressa Olayinka Epega, 28 Mar. 1967, 2 sons, 3 daughters. *Education:* Certificate in Coop Studies, Cooperative College, Ibadan, Nigeria; BSc. (Econ), London University, UK, 1963. *Appointments:* Government Cooperative Inspector, 1956-60; Lecturer, Yaba College of Technology, 1963-64; Officer, Nigerian Army, 1964-67; Comptroller, ITT, 1967; Nigerian Army, 1967-69; Nigerian Air Force, 1969-70; Director, S S Adejoro and Co. Ltd., 1970-. *Hobbies:* Billiards; Table Tennis. *Address:* 7 Oduduwa Way GRA, PO Box 598, Ikeja, Nigeria.

ADEKUNLE, Arthur Oludotun, b. 4 Apr. 1921, Igbogun, Abeokuta, Nigeria. Forester. m. Felicia Siju Taiwo, 6 Apr. 1950, 3 sons, 1 daughter. *Education:* BSc. (Forestry), Wales, UK, 1960; Forest Officers' Course in Forestry, Commonwealth Forestry Institute, Oxford, UK, 1965. *Appointments:* Nigerian Forest Service, 1941-54; State Forest Services, Nigeria, 1955-77. *Memberships:* Assistant Secretary, 1970-72, Secretary, 1972-76, President, 1977-78, 1978-79, Forestry Association of Nigeria. *Hobbies:* Reading; Driving; Lawn Tennis. *Address:* 1 B Ijeja Stadium Road, P.O.Box 1423, Ogun State, Abeokuta, Nigeria.

ADELANA, Bamidele Oladejo, b. 29 Jan. 1940, Owo, Ondo State, Nigeria. Agricultural Scientist. m. Florence Mojisola Osho, 22 Aug. 1971, 1 son, 3 daughters. *Education:* BSc., Hons., University of Ibadan, Nigeria, 1961-64; PhD., University of London, UK, 1967-70. *Appointments:* Agricultural Officer, Ministry of Agriculture, Western Nigeria, 1964-67; Research Fellow, 1972, Research Fellow I, 1974, Senior Research Fellow, 1976, Principal Research Fellow, Head, Vegetables Production Programme, 1979, Institute of Agricultural Research and Training, Ibadan, Nigeria; Served on advisory panels to Government Agricultural projects. *Memberships:* Science Association of Nigeria; Agricultural Society of Nigeria; Horticultural Society of Nigeria; Indian Horticultural Society; International Society for Horticultural Science. *Publications:* 22 publications in field of agronomy and crop physiology including: The Growth of two varieties of tomato at Ibadan, Western Nigeria, 1975; Effects of staking on the growth and yield of tomatoes, 1976; Relationship between leaf area and crop growth rate in maize, 1976; Effects of flower removal on the growth of tomato, 1978; Relationship between lodging, morphological characters and yield of tomato cultivators, 1980. *Honours:* awarded Government Scholarship, 1953-57; awarded Government Scholarship to University of Ibadan, Nigeria. *Hobbies:* Sports; Football; Travelling; International politics. *Address:* Plot 4, 10th Avenue, Oluyole Estate, Ibadan, Nigeria.

ADELEKAN, James Adeyi, b. 2 Oct. 1947, Ogbomosho, Oyo State, Nigeria. Librarian. m. Ruth Adeleye IE, 4 Apr. 1972, 2 sons, 1 daughter. *Education:* National Certificate, Medical Laboratory Technician, 1975; Diploma, Library Science, Ahmadu Bello University, Zaria, 1978. *Appointments:* Self Employed, 1961-70; WHO Malaria Research Project, Kano, 1970-73; WHO Anophele Control Unit, Kaduna, 1974-75; Micro-Biology Laboratory, 1975-76; Medical Library 1978, Ahmadu Bello University. *Memberships:* Baptist Choir Member, Leader. *Creative Works:* Christian Religious Music. *Hobbies:* Music; Lawn Tennis. *Address:* 16 Aliyu Road, T/Wada, Zaria, Nigeria.

ADELEYE, Ademola, b. 16 Nov. 1932, Ayede-Ekiti, Ondo State, Nigeria. Administrator. m. Agnes Olufunke Osekita, 3 May, 1962, 2 sons, 3 daughters. *Education:* BA. (MOD.), History, 1958, Higher Diploma in Education, 1959, Dublin University, Ireland, UK, MA. (Education) University of California, Los Angeles Campus, (California) USA, 1966. *Appointments:* Diocesan Lay Preacher, Ondo-Benin and Ekiti Dioceses, 1962-; Vice Principal, Ayede Grammar School, Ayede-Ekiti, Ondo State, Nigeria.; Acting Head of Department of History, Federal Advanced Teachers' College, Lagos; Deputy Delegate of Nigeria to UNESCO, Unesco Headquarters, Paris; Senior Assistant Registrar, Yaba College of Technology, Yaba-Lagos; Director of Administration, Managing Director, Ameniger Construction (Nigeria) Co. Ltd. *Memberships:* Nigeria Historical Association; Ikoyi Club (1938), Lagos, Nigeria. *Hobbies:* Reading; Gardening; Bird watching; Table Tennis; Music. *Address:* Plot 14, Bamisile Estate, Opebi Village, Onigbagbo, PO Box 3026, Ikeja, Lagos, Nigeria.

ADEMOSUN, Akinmolayemi Akinrinnibade, b. 28 Aug. 1935, Ile-Oluji, Ondo State, Nigeria. Agriculturalist; Animal Nutritionist; Animal Production Expert. m. Felicia Adenike Ademukolu, 14 Jan. 1962, 2 sons, 4 daughters. *Education:* University College, Ibadan, 1955-60; BSc, Agriculture, London; MSc, Animal Nutrition, McGill University, Montreal, Canada, 1962-64; PhD, Animal Nutrition, University of Wisconsin, Madison, USA, 1964-66. *Appointments:* Agricultural Officer, Western Region Nigeria, 1960-66; Research Assistant, Dairy Science Department, University of Wisconsin, USA, 1964-66; Lecturer, 1966-70, Senior Lecturer, 1970-73, Reader, 1973-74, Professor of Animal Science, 1974-; Dean, Faculty of Agriculture, 1974-77, Head, Department of Animal Science, 1977-, Ife Nigeria. *Memberships:* Fellow of the Royal Society of Chemistry, London; Chartered Chemist; Assistant Secretary, 1971-74, Secretary, 1974-77, Agricultural Society of Nigeria; President, 1977-78, Nigerian Society for Animal Production; Member of Council, 1975-, World's Poultry Science Association; Member of Council, 1967-71, Science Association of Nigeria; Member of Council, 1978-, Association for the Advancement of Agricultural Sciences in Africa. *Publications:* Over 60 articles, based on original research, in many learned Journals all over the world; Contribution to books eg. a chapter in Animal Production in Tropics, 1974. *Honours:* Government Scholar, 1950-55; College Scholar, University College Ibadan, 1957-60; Visiting Fellow, Department of Agricultural Biochemistry, University of Newcastle, England, 1970. *Hobbies:* Reading; Table Tennis. *Address:* Olayemi House, PO Box 182, Ile-Oluji, Ondo State, Nigeria.

ADEMUWAGUN, Zacchaeus Akingbade, b. 17 Feb. 1934, Ode-Aye, Ondo State, Nigeria. Public Health Education. m. Olujoke Popoola, 13 July 1962, 3 sons, 2 daughters. *Education:* BA (London), University College, Ibadan, 1962; MEd, 1963, EdD, 1965, Boston University, Boston, USA; MPH, School of Public Health, University of California, Berkeley, USA, 1969. *Appointments:* Lecturer in Education, 1965-69, Lecturer in Health Education, 1969-72, University of Lagos; Lecturer/Professor of Health Education, Department of Preventive and Social Medicine, College of Medicine, University of Ibadan, 1972-80; Special Adviser on Health, Education and Welfare matters to Ondo State Governor, Chairman, Ondo State Health Management Board, Akure, Nigeria, 1980-. *Memberships:* International Union of Health Education; American Public Health Association; Nigerian University Teachers Association; Nigerian Society of Health; Nigerian School Health Association, National President; Nigerian Union of Teachers; Phi Delta Kappa, USA; Nigerian Sociological and Anthropological Association; Commonwealth Universities Travelling Fellowship to India and Malaysia, 1979. *Publications:* Major Publications Include: Health Education: A Conceptual Approach, 1975; Certificate Health Science, 1976; The Ibadan Comfort Stations Geneva, WHO, 1975/76; Articles that have already appeared in Learned Journals Include: Problems and Prospect of Legitimatizing Aspects of Traditional Health Care Systems and Methods with Modern Medical Therapy: The Igbo-Ora Experience, Nigerian Medical Journal, 1975; Preparing the Physical and Health Education Teachers for Secondary Schools in Developing Countries, West African Journal of Education, 1975; Determinants of Pattern and Degree of Utilization of Health Services in Two Divisions of Western State, Nigeria, Israel Journal of Medical Sciences, 1977; General Publications: Education for Social Change, Ghana Journal of Education, 1971; Effective Reading and the Background Reading, Nigerian Libraries, 1970; African Therapeutic Systems, 1978. *Honours:* Western Region Scholarship, Undergraduate Programme, University College, Ibadam, 1958-62; State Department Fellowship, Postgraduate Programme, Boston University, USA, 1962-65; WHO Fellowship, MPH, Post Doctural Course, University of California, Berkeley, 1967-69; Pfizer Travelling Fellowship to Canada, 1978; Commonwealth University Travelling Fellowship to India and Malaysia, 1979. *Hobbies:* Music, Singing and Dancing; Swimming; Volley Ball; Reading Novels. *Address:* Massaba Road, Block 1, Flat 3, University of Ibadan, Ibadan, Nigeria.

ADENIJI, Adegoke Kolade, b. 23 Nov. 1941, Agege, Lagos State, Nigeria. Librarianship. m. Honoria Olayinka Irele, 28 June 1969, 2 sons, 3 daughters. *Education:* BA, Hons. English, 1966, Postgraduate Diploma in Librarianship, University of Ibadan, 1967; MLS, University of Pittsburgh, 1973. *Appointments:* Temporary Assistant, Librarian, University of Ife, Ile-Ife, 1967; Assistant Librarian, University of Lagos Library, 1967; Sub-Librarian Gandhi Memorial Research Collections, 1970; Circulation Librarian, 1971; Consultant Librarian, Bookmobile Services to Penal Institutions, DC Public Library, USA, 1973-74; Reference Librarian, University of Lagos, 1975-78; Education Librarian, 1979; Also includes: Sub-Librarian and Head of Circulation Department 1971, Reference Department 1971; Graduate Assistant, Hillman Library, University of Pittsburgh, 1972-73; Field Sales Supervisor, Grolier Publishing Company, 1973; Consultant Librarian, Bookmobile Services to Penal Institutions DC Public Library 1973-74. *Memberships:* American Library Association; Secretary, 1969-71, Nigeria Library Association, Lagos; President, University of Lagos Senior Staff Club; *Publications:* Times of Nigeria Index Lagos, 1978; List of subject headings for indexing Nigerian newspapers; The Place of Libraries in Educational Planning, 1974; Targets of research in librarianship, 1976; *Honours:* Ibadan Grammar School Leadership prizes 1972; Ibadan Grammar School English Prize for Senior classes 1960; Ibadan Grammar School Football and Cricket colours 1960. *Hobbies:* Lawn tennis; Billiards; Darts. *Address:* 6, Ozolua Road, University of Lagos, Akoka, Lagos.

ADENIKA, Frederick Boluwaji, b. 16 May 1940. Pharmacist. m. 27 July 1967, 2 sons, 1 daughter. *Education:* Nigerian College of Arts and Science 1959-60; Pharm D, University of California, San Francisco, 1966; MA, Business Management, San Francisco State University, 1968; PhD, Business Administration, Florida State University, Tallahassee, 1970; Post Doctoral Work in Industrial Pharmacy, University of London, Chelsea, United Kingdom. *Appointments:* Marketing Manager and Later Business Manager, Pfizer Products Limited, Ikeja-Nigeria, 1971-77; General Manager, 1978, Nigeria Limited, 1978; Managing Director, 1979, The Boots Company, Nigeria, *Memberships:* Pharmaceutical Society of Nigeria; American Pharmaceutical Association; Ikeja Country Club, Nigeria; Editor-in-Chief, West African Pharmaceutical Federation.

Publications: Various Publication: mostly in Pharmacy, Pharmacy Administration and Business Management. *Honours:* Aspau Scholarship for USA Education, 1961-1966; School of Pharmacy Essay Prize, University of California, 1964. *Hobbies:* Reading and Writing; Lawn Tennis; Gardening. *Address:* 12A Herbert Macaulay Crescent, G.R.A., Ikeja, Nigeria.

ADEOBA, Adetunji, b. 18 Oct. 1929, Oshogbo, Nigeria. Gynaecologist; Business Promoter and Investor. m. Stella Adeoba 18 Nov. 1961, 1 son, 3 daughters. *Education:* L.R.C.P.&S (Ireland); M.R.C.O.G. (England); F.M.C.O.G. (Nigeria); F.W.A.C.S. (West Africa); A.M.I.M.N (Institute of Management in Nigeria). *Appointments:* Visiting Registrar, Obstetrics and Gynaecology, University of Birmingham, 1966-67; Senior Gynaecologist, Lagos State of Nigeria; Chief Gynaecologist, Soar Hospital, Ikeja, Nigeria; Chairman: Lovell Stewart, Construction, Nigeria Limited; Health Care, Soar Hospital; Trading, Soar Enterprises; Paper Conversion, International Packaging Industry. *Memberships:* Institute of Management, Nigeria; American Geographical Society; Fellow, West African College of Surgeons; Fellow, Nigerian Medical Council in Obstetrics and Gynaecology; Fellow, Society of Gynaecologists and Obstetricians in Nigeria. *Publications:* Interpretation of Positive Serological Tests in Pregnancy in Nigeria; Nigerian Proud Heritage. *Hobbies:* Photography; Table Tennis; Reading. *Address:* 1, Adetunji Adeoba Street, G.R.A, PO Box 189, Ikeja, Nigeria.

ADEOYE, Adedeji David, b. 7 Dec. 1945, Daja-Ajowa, Akoko, Ondo State, Nigeria. Architecture. m. V B Adenola, 25 Nov. 1978, 1 son. *Education:* General Certificate of Examination, 1970; Bachelor of Environmental Studies, (B.E.S. Hons), Sec. Class. Lower Div. 1974; Master of Environmental Design, 1976. *Appointments:* National Youth Service Corps. Ministry of Works, Minna, Niger State, Nigeria, 1976-77; Deji Dyenuga and Partners, Architects and Planners, 1977-81; Echo-Mold Collaborative Partners, Architects and Development Consultants, 1981-. *Memberships:* Foursquare Gospel Church, Nigeria; Nigerian Institute of Architects, (M337). *Publications:* Traffic in Minna, 1977; The Impassable, Eric Moore Road Way out of the Present Congestion, 1980; Reducing Traffic Jam along Ikorodu Road, 1980. *Honours:* Deans Award, Faculty of Environmental Design University of Lagos, 1973; Science Society of Nigeria award, for being the best student in Elementary Mathematics, in the West African School Certificate Examination, conducted in December, 1968. *Hobbies:* Table Tennis. *Address:* 47 Omilade Street, Mafoluku, Oshodi, Lagos State, Nigeria.

ADEPOJU, Rasaki Adeyemi, b. 7 May 1951 Iseyin. Researching. *Education:* Diploma in Journalism, London School of Journalism, 1975; Diploma in Yoruba studies, Lagos University, 1979; Diploma Yoruba studies, Broadcasters, Yoruba and Publishers, Yoruba. *Appointments:* Primary School Teacher, 1972; Clerk, 1973-74; Field Assistant, 1974-77; Senior Field Assistant, 1977-80; Assistant Field Officer, 1980, Field Officer, 1980-, University of Lagos, Akoka - Yaba, Lagos. *Memberships:* Egbe Ijinte Yoruba; Nigerian Folklore Society; President, Pendite Club; General Secretary, Friendly Brothers Club. *Publications:* Contributed to some editions of Gboùngboùn, A Yoruba weekly newspaper; Example: Esù asoore se ìkà, 1978; Ìdí Abájo Awon Owe Yorùbá, 1979; Owó L'ègbón omo L'àbúro, 1979; Pípé Láyé Ni Erè Ayé?, 1979; Freelancing with Radio and Television as a Producer and Presenter of Yoruba programmes. *Hobbies:* Reading Novels; Watching Films; Indoor Games. *Address:* 1, Allen Road, Surulere, Lagos State, Nigeria.

ADESANY, Obafemi Adeyemi, b. 3 Feb. 1943. Architect. m. Bolajoko Olaremi Ogunbawo 22 Dec. 1973, 2 daughters. *Education:* Student of Architecture at Ahmadu Bello University, Zaria, Graduated with honours from the Faculty of Architecture, Passed the Nigerian Institute of Architects Professional Examination, 1965-70. *Memberships:* Chairman, Club Mermaid; Ibadan Tennis Club; Ibadan Recreation Club. *Creative Works:* Practice of Architecture. *Hobbies:* Swimming; Squash Racket; Hockey; Judo; Music, (Clarinet). *Address:* 186 Fagbemi Street, Iyaganku, Jericho Reservation, Ibadan Oyo State, Nigeria, W.A.

ADESINA, Ademola, b. 20 July 1940, Erin-Ile, Kwara State of Nigeria. Barrister and Solicitor. m. Moji Lawal,

21 Apr. 1967, 4 sons, 1 daughter. *Education:*
LLB(Hons), Ahmadu Bello University, 1967; Certificate
in Tax Administration, University of Ife, 1970; Barrister
at Law Certificate, Nigerian Law School, Lagos. *Ap-
pointments:* Inspector of Taxes, Kano State, 1967-76;
Company Secretary/Legal Adviser, 1976-80; Com-
pany Director and Legal Practitioner. *Memberships:*
Nigerian Bar Association. *Hobbies:* Farming; Hunting;
Fish farming; Travelling. *Address:* Demola House, Ile
Inurin, Erin-Ile, Kwara State, Nigeria.

ADESINA, Gabriel Olusanjo, b. 29 Dec. 1934, Abeokuta, Ogun State, Nigeria, Insurance. m. 29 Aug. 1964,
3 sons, 2 daughters. *Education:* Associate member,
Chartered Institute of Insurance, West London College
of Commerce, London, UK. *Appointments:* Hobbs Pad-
get Group, Lloyds Underwriters, London, UK, 1962-64;
Eagle Star Insurance Co., London, UK, 1964-67; Sun
Alliance and London Insurance Group, London, UK,
1968-72; NEM Insurance Co. Nigeria Limited, Lagos,
Nigeria, 1973-77; Nigeria Reinsurance Corporation,
Lagos, Nigeria, 1977-. *Memberships:* Ikoyi Club, Lagos,
Nigeria; Apostle and Prophet, Cherubim and Seraphim
Movement, Surulere, Lagos, Nigeria. *Hobbies:* Tennis;
Singing; Reading. *Address:* Plot 1202 or 41 Bishop
Oluwole Street, Victoria Island, Lagos, Nigeria.

ADESIYAKAN, Nathaniel Adelayi, b. 2 Oct. 1937, Ile-
Oluji Nigeria. Company Director. m. R.F A. Adesiyakan,
1967, M.F. Adesiyakan 1977, 4 sons, 2 daughters.
Education: Bachelor of Arts Econ. Studies of Durham
University 1966. *Appointments:* Assistant Manager,
Admin. and Packing, Nigerian Maritime Service, 1966-
69; Manager Coastal Services Nigeria Limited, 1969-
70; Shipping Manager Aircool Nig. Limited, 1970-72;
Managing Director Transaltic Nig. Limited, 1972-;
Managing Director Nats Food Industries Limited 1978-;
Director Caprihans Nigeria Limited; Director Glamour
Foundations Limited. Proprietor of Transaltic Nigeria
Limited which is Shipping Agency and Forwarding
Company; Proprietor of Nats Food Industries Nigeria
Limited; Proprietor of Glamour Foundations Nigeria
Limited. *Memberships:* Lagos Chamber of Commerce;
Manufacturers Association of Nigeria. *Honours:* Fa-
culty Price Winner, 1963/64 Academic Year of Fourah
Bay College Freetown Sierra Leone, 1964. *Hobbies:*
Watching Football; Swimming. *Address:* 34A Abata
Street, Orile, Iganmu, Nigeria.

ADEWUNMI, Clement Shodeinde, b. 13 Jan. 1935,
Lagos, Nigeria. Business. m. Theresa Clegg, 10 Oct.
1959, 3 sons, 1 daughter. *Education:* Diploma in Ma-
nagement Studies, 1962; Fellow of the Royal Econom-
ics Society 1962; Associate member of B.I.M 1963;
Associate member of Nigerian Institute of Manage-
ment, 1964. *Appointments:* Marketing Executive, BP,
West Africa, 1963-70; Company Manager, BP Super-
gas, Nigeria Limited, 1970-73; Managing Director,
Cotsgas Nigeria Limited, 1973-. *Memberships:*
President, Nigerian Association of Liquified Petroleum
Gas Marketers (NALPGAM); Chairman, L.P.G. Trade
Group; Lagos Chamber of Commerce and Industry;
Social Clubs inc: Metropolitan Club, Lagos; Lagos Din-
ing Club and Ikoyi Club. *Hobbies:* Golf; Reading. *Add-
ress:* 20 Jalupon Close, Surulere, Lagos State, PO Box
2159, Surulere, Nigeria.

ADEY, Philip Stanworth, b. 9 May 1939, Sevenoaks,
Kent, England. Educational Consultant. m. Jennifer
Margaret Preston, 28 Mar. 1964, 2 sons. *Education:*
BSc, Chemistry, Northern Polytechnic, London University, 1962; PGCE Academic Diploma, Institute of Education, 1967-68; PhD, Chelsea College, 1979. *Appointments:* Teacher, De Lodge School, Barbados, 1963-70;
Consultant, Caribbean Regional Science Project, 1970-
73; Research Fellow, Chelsea College, 1974-78; Education Officer, Re British Council, 1979-.
Memberships: Royal Society of Chemistry; Association
for Science Education. *Publications:* Science and People in the Caribbean, 1975; Editor, Boleswa Integrated
Science, 1978, 79; Towards a Science of Science
Teaching, (with Michael Shayer), 1981. *Hobbies:* Photography; Cycling. *Address:* 39 Oxford Road, London,
SW15 2LH.

ADEYEMI, Adesanya, b. 2 Aug. 1924, Isara, Ijebu
Remo, Nigeria. Chartered Architect. m. Agnes Dele
Diagi, 30 Mar. 1961, 1 son, 3 daughters. *Education:*
Certificate in Architecture, Leicester, England, 1961;
Associate of Royal Institute of British Architects, 1963;

Diploma in Housing, Rotterdam, 1970; Fellow of Nigerian Institute of Architects, 1978. *Appointments:* Architect, Federal Ministry of Works, Lagos; Architect then
Deputy Chief Architect, Lagos Executive Development
Board, Lagos; Associate then Partner, Watkins Gray
Woodgate, now Interstate Architects, Lagos. *Memberships:* Association of Nigerian Housing Corporations -
Secretary Technical Committee, 1968-73; St. John's
Church Parish Council, Lagos; Ikoyi Club, Lagos. *Publications:* Housing Policy for Nigeria. *Hobbies:* Photography, Golf. *Address:* 74 Adeniran Ogunsanya, St., Surulere, Lagos Nigeria.

ADEYEMI, Ekundayo Adeyinka (Professor), b. 27
Feb. 1937, Iyin-Ekiti, Ondo State, Nigeria. Architect. m.
14 Aug. 1965, 2 sons, 5 daughters. *Education:* Bachel-
or of Architecture, Ahmadu Bello University, Zaria,
Nigeria, 1963; Master of Science (Architecture), Columbia University, New York, USA. 1965; Master of
Urban Planning, New York University, New York, USA.
1973; Doctor of Philosophy, New York University, New
York, USA. 1974. *Appointments:* Resident/Senior Architect, Fed. Ministry of Works, Lagos, Nigeria, 1963-
68; Lecturer/Senior Lecturer, Faculty of Environmental Design, 1969-74, Professor & Head of Department
of Architecture, 1975-; Dean of Faculty of
Environmental Design, 1976-80, Ahmadu Bello University Zaria, Nigeria.) Nigeria. *Memberships:* Nigerian
Institute of Architects; American Instutue of Planners;
Architects Registration Council of Nigeria; Visitation
Panel, Commonwealth Board of Architectural Education. *Publications:* Institutional and Administrative
Framework for Urban Land Planning and Development:
Metropolitan Lagos and Kaduna Capital Territory;
Changing Traditional Culture and Modern Architec-
ture. *Honours:* African/American Institute Award,
1971; Certificate of Merit (USAID), 1965. *Hobbies:*
Reading (African Novels & writers, Biographies). *Add-
ress:* House 7, 7 Etsu Nupe Road, Main Campus,
Ahmadu Bello University, Zaria, Nigeria.

ADEYEMI, Larami-Dele, b. 27 July 1945, Lagos.
Architect. m. Mojirayo Emily Coker, 8 Dec. 1973, 3
sons, 1 daughter. *Education:* Diploma, Yaba College of
Technology, Yaba, 1966; Federal School of Science,
Lagos, 1967; B. Arch. First class Honours, Ahmadu
Bello University, Zaria, 1972. *Appointments:* Niger
Consultants Architects, Lagos, 1972-74; Huts Consult-
ing Architects, Lagos, 1974-79; Darchiworkgroup Ar-
chitects, Lagos, 1979-. *Memberships:* Nigerian Institue
of Architects Offices; Assistant General Secretary,
Editor Newsletter Nigerian Institute of Architects; Is-
land Club, Lagos. *Publications:* Design of Kaduna Dur-
bar Stand. *Honours:* NIA Prize for Best Theseis, 1972.
Hobbies: Swimming, Lawn Tennis, Reading, Writing.
Address: 12 Olaribiro Street, Opebi-Ikeja.

ADEYOJU, Samuel Kolade, b. 17 Sept. 1936, Ijan-
Ekiti,Nigeria. University Professor. m. 26 June 1965, 1
son, 1 daughter. *Education:* B.A. (Hons.) Exeter Univer-
sity, 1963; PhD, LSE, London University, 1966; Dip. for
St. John's Coll. Oxon. 1968. *Appointments:* University
of Ibadan, 1965-. FAO Consultant, 1975; Professor and
Head, Department of Forest Resources Management,
Universiyt of Ibadan, 1976-79; Project Manager, UN-
ECA/UNDP, 1979-81. *Memberships:* Life Member,
Commonwealth Forestry Association; Life Member,
Nigerian Forestry Association; International Union of
Forestry Research Organizations; Nigeria Economic
Society; Nigeria Agricultural Society. *Publications:* For-
estry and the Nigerian Economy, IUP, 308 PP, 1975; A
Study of Forestry Administration Problems in Six Se-
lected African Countries, FAO, 60 PP. 1976; Our For-
ests and Our Welfare, Inaugural Lecture, University of
Ibadan, 45 PP. 1978. *Honours:* Federal Nigerian Government. Scholarships (Undergraduate & Postgraduate), 1960-65; University of London Research Grant,
1964-65; Commonwealth Postgraduate Scholarship,
1965-66; FAO Fellowship, 1967-68. *Hobbies:* Rambling, Chess, Table Tennis & Photography. *Address:*
Dept. of Forest Resources Management, University of
Ibadan, Ibadan, Nigeria.

ADIO-MOSES, Afolabi Adenekan, b. 18 Sept. 1914,
Lagos, Nigeria. m. Adefunke Oyedele, 5 Oct. 1939, 7
sons, 3 daughters. *Education:* Ibadan, Grammar School
Nigeria, 1930-32- Preliminary Preceptors; St. Grego-
ry's College, Lagos, Nigeria, 1933-35; Snr. Cambridge;
Ruskin, College, Oxford, 1947-48. *Appointments:*
Branch Managerin-Training, United Africa Company,

Lagos, 1936-42; Secretary-General, Nigerian Trades Union Congress, 1942-50; Development Officer (Civil Service) Administration, 1952-53; Students Liaison Officer, Colonial Office then London, Welfare Administration, 1954-55; Labour Officer (Trade Unions), Employment Commissioner, Industrial Relations Commissioner, 1956-67; General Manager, Nigeria Shipping Federation, 1967-71; Territorial Personnel Manager, John Holt Group of Companies, Nigeria, 1971-76; Member, Industrial Arbitration Panel, 1976-. *Memberships:* Institute of Personnel Management, Nigeria; Institute of Management, Nigeria; Island Club, Lagos; National Parents Association of Nigeria. *Publications:* Regular Columnist, Nigerian Daily Times - late 1940's early 1950's The Trade Union World; Nigerian Trade Unions - unpublished manuscript; Flashes of ideas, (not yet published) on Nigerian Problems, morals etc; prose poem. *Honours:* Fellow of the Nigeria Institute of Personnel Management, 1975; Officer of the Order of the Federal Republic of Nigeria, 1980. *Hobbies:* Photography, Dancing, Writing, Religion - Lay Preacher, United African Methodist church. *Address:* 2nd Avenue, 23 Road, A Close, House, 5, P.O. Box 767, Festac Town, Badagry Road, Lagos, Nigeria.

ADISESHIAH, Malcolm Sathianathan, b. 18 Apr. 1910, Madras, India. Economist; Member of Parliament. m. 26 Dec. 1952, 1 son, 1 daughter. *Education:* MA., Madras University, India, 1930; PhD., London University, UK, 1938. *Appointments:* Lecturer, Economics, University of Calcutta, India, 1930-36; Head, Department of Economics, University of Madras, India, 1940-46; Deputy Director, Exchange of Persons Service, 1948-50, Director, Department of Technical Assistance, 1950-54, Assistant Director-General, 1955-63, Deputy Director-General, 1963-70, UNESCO; Director, Madras Institute of Development Studies, India, 1971-78; Vice Chancellor, Madras University, 1975-78; Member of Parliament, 1978. *Memberships:* Indian Adult Education Association, New Delhi; International Council for Adult Education, Canada; Indian Economic Association; International Economic Association; Chairman, International Institute for Educational Planning, Paris, 1981; World Social Science Development Committee; India International Centre. *Publications:* Let My Country Awake, 1970; Madras Development Seminar Series, 1971; It is time to Begin, 1972; Techniques of Perspective Planning, 1973; Plan Implementation: Problems and Prospects for the Fifth Plan, 1974; Science in the Battle Against Poverty, 1974; Towards a Functional Learning Society, 1976; Backdrop to Learning Society, 1978; A Mid Year Review of the Economy, 1979; Adult Education Faces Inequalities, 1981, Mid Year Review of the Economy, 1980, 1981. *Address:* Sadhana, 21 Cenotaph Road, Madras 600018, India.

ADJEI, Angelina Angeley, b. 18 Mar. 1936, Christiansborg. Nurse. m. 1 Son. *Education:* Elementary Education, Middle School Leaving Certificate, 1943-52; Secondary Education, G.C.E. Ordinary Level, 1978-79; State Registered Nuse, 1953-57; State Certified Midwife, 1959-60; Casualty O.P.D. Certificate, 1965-, Traumatic Surgery Certificate, 1966. *Appointments:* Staff Nuse, 1957-60; Staff Nurse-Midwife, 1960-61; Nursing Officer, 1961-72; Senior Nursing Officer, 1972-. *Memberships:* Current Chairman, Ghana Registered Nurses' Association, Greater Accra Region; Nurses and Midwife Council; Member Representative, Christian Council, Ghana Registered Nurses Association; Current Vice-Chairman, Labadi Presbyterian Old Girls Association; Past Choir Mistress, Choirister, Labadi Presbyterian Church; Choirister: Osu, Presbyterian Church and Ridge Church; Presbyterian Womens Fellowship. *Hobbies:* Singing, Sewing, Women's Voluntary Work, Net Ball, Tennis & Reading. *Address:* P.O. Box 0962, Osu-Accra, Ghana W.A.

ADOMAKOH, Albert, b. 8 Apr. 1924, Bomfa, Ashanti. Banker, Economist, Lawyer. m. Fitnat, 15 Oct. 1966, 5 sons, 1 daughter. *Education:* Downing Coll., Cambridge; Post-graduate, London School of Economics, 1961-62. *Appointments:* Barrister-at-Law; Secretary Bank of Ghana, 1957-62; Managing Director and Chairman National Investment Bank, 1962-65; Governor Bank of Ghana, 1965-68; Commissioner for Agriculture, 1968-69; Assistant Director General, FAO, 1969-70; Director Department of Investments, Africa and the Middle East, IFC, 1970-72; Development and Finance Consultant, 1972-; Chairman Ghana

Consolidated Diamonds Ltd., 1973-; Director C.F.A.O. (Ghana) Ltd., 1975-; Vice-Chairman Society International pour les Investissements et le Développement en Afrique S.A. 1978-. *Publications:* The History of Currency and Banking in West African Countries, 1962. *Address:* P.O. Box 4104, Accra, Ghana.

ADUHENE II, Nana Kwadwo, (John Samuel Brenya Tano), b. 1922, Sefwi, Wiawso, Ghana. Paramount Chief and Farmer. m. 1953, 2 sons, 2 daughters. *Education:*Elementary education at the former Sefwi Wiawso Government School, 1942; Agricultural Course at the Royal College of Cirencester, UK. for 4 months. *Appointments:* Field Assistant, Department of Agriculture, Swollen Shoot Unit, later resigned to become Building Contractor until he was enstooled as the Omanhene of the Sefwi Wiawso Traditional Area under the Stool name of Nana Kwadwo Aduhene II, 1953; Chief for period of 3 years. *Hobbies:* Tennis. *Address:* PO. Box. 42, Sefwi Wiawso, Ghana

AFERI, Nathan, Apeah, Major General (Retired), b. 21 Sept. 1922, Mampong (Akwapim), Ghana. Shoolmaster, Soldier, Diplomat, Politician. m. Georgina Lucy MacCarthy, 25 May 1946, 2 sons, 4 daughters. *Appointments:* Schoolmaster, 1942-44; Soldier, (British Army, RWAFF, Ghana Army, Major General, DSO Retired), 1944-66; Diplomat, Mexico, Jamaica, Trinidad, Tobago, Nigeria, 1967-72; Politician Minister of Foreign Affairs and Local Government, 1972-75; Member, Council of State, (Senate), 1980-. *Memberships:* Scout Master, Rotarian, Mason - Odd Fellow, Star of the East Lodge. *Publications:* Publication, Careers in the Army, 1964. *Honours:* Distinguished Service Order, 1965; Honour of Merit (Class One) by President of UAR, 1963; Gold Aztec Eagle (First Class) by the Mexican Government, 1970. *Hobbies:* Music, Poetry, Reading, Lawn Tennis, Driving and Farming. *Address:* Crown of the Magi, No. 6 Mankralo Close, East Contonments, Accra, Ghana

AFRAM (Mrs.) Adelaide Nyane, b. 28 July 1930, Suhum. m. Oheneba Kwaku, 30 June 1956, 1 son, 3 daughters. *Education:* State Registered Nurse, 1953; Registered Midwife 1955; Ward Administration Certificate, Royal College of Nursing, London, 1960; Senior Hospital Administrator's Course Certificate, Internationl Hospital Federation, Kingsford College, London, 1975. *Memberships:* Assistant Secretary, Zonta International Tema Branch, Ghana; Divisional Superintendent, St. John Ambulance Brigade; Grand United Oder of Odd Fellows; Young Womens Fellowship. *Hobbies:* Gardening, Sewing. *Address:* P.O. Box 959, Tema, Ghana.

AFRIK, Tai, b. 31 Mar. 1942, Freetown, Sierra Leone. Education Officer, Programme Assistant. m. Hawa Baio, 29 May 1973, 4 sons, 2 daughters. *Education:* Bachelor of Arts, Political Science and Sociology, Monash University, Australia, 1968; Advanced Diploma in Adult Education, Manchester University, UK, 1973; Diploma in Community Development and Adult Education, University of Haifa, Israel, 1970. *Appointments:*Teacher, Freetown Commercial College, 1962; Assistant Librarian, Sierra Leone Library Board, 1963-66; Teacher, Alliance Secondary School, Kenya, 1969; Social Development Officer, Ministry of Social Welfare, 1970-76; Education Officer, 1976-78, Senior Education Officer, Adult Education, 1978-81, Ministry of Education Programme Assistant, UNESCO, Adult Education and Rural Development, 1981-. *Memberships:* Chairman, National Literacy Committee; President, Sierra Leone Volunteers Association; Chairman, Interim Committee, Peoples Education Association; Secretary-General, Sierra Leone Adult Education Association; Chairman, National Orthography Committee; Secretary-General, Sierra Leone Cuban Friendship Society; Secretary-General, Sierra Leone Rural Development Agency. *Publications:* Adult Education for the Deprived and Apathetic. Numerous articles including: Adult Education and you; Historical perspective of Adult Education in Sierra Leone; Methodologies in Adult Education; Distance Teaching by Radio; Adult Literacy and National Development. *Hobbies:* Gardening; Creative Writing. *Address:* 5 Ogoo Lane, Brook Fields, Freetown, Sierra Leone.

AGAMAH, Daniel Attah, b. 12 Jan. 1950, Uewolawoldah, Nigeria. Architect. m. Ruth Ladi Ogu, 25 Mar. 1978, 1 son, 1 daughter. *Education:* Bachelor of

Science, 2nd Class Upper Honours Degree in Architecture, 1974, Master of Science Degree, Architecture, 1976, Ahmadu Bello University, Zaria, Nigeria. *Appointments:* National Service Architect with Ministry of Works and Housing, Owerri, Nigeria, 1976-77; Architect, Archcon Nigeria Architects, 1977-. *Memberships:* Architects' Registration Council of Nigeria; Nigerian Institute of Architects; Chairman, Sokoto State Chapter of the NIA, 1981. *Publications:* MSc. Architecture thesis on Nigerian Centre for Scientific Research and Development, 1976. *Honours:* Best Graduate Student Prize, Gindiri Secondary School, 1968; Excellence in Character Prize, Offa Grammer School, 1970; Ahmadu Bello University Scholarship award for MSc. Architecture course, 1974-75 & 1975-76; BSc. Architecture Prize for Best Working Drawings, Ahmadu Bello University, 1974. *Hobbies:* Table Tennis; International Current Affairs; Pleasure Driving. *Address:* No. 43, Runji Sambo Layout, Sokoto, Nigeria.

AGARWAL, Beni Prasad, b. 25 Sept. 1036, Allahabad (UP), India. Diplomat. m. Manjulika, 11 May 1961, 2 sons, 2 daughters. *Education:* MA., University of Allahabad, India, 1959; Certificate in Diplomacy, University of Oxford, UK, 1974. *Appointments:* Assistant Professor, University of Allahabad, India, 1959-60; Joined Indian Foreign Service, 1960; Third/Second Secretary, Embassy of India, Moscow, 1961-63; Second Secretary, Embassy of India, Prague, 1964; Under Secretary, Ministry of External Affairs, 1964-67; Consul of India, New York, USA, 1967-71; Deputy Secretary/Director, Ministry of External Affairs, 1971-75; Ambassador of India to Somalia, 1975-78; Minister, 1978-, Charge d'Affaires, Embassy of India, Bonn, 1980-. *Memberships:* Life member, Oxford Society. *Honours:* Award prize for best student, Allahabad University, India, 1955. *Hobbies:* Swimming; Music; Reading. *Address:* c/o Ministry of External Affairs, South Block, New Delhi 110011, India.

AGARWAL, Satish Chandra, b. 1 Sept. 1924, Bulandshahr, Uttar Pradesh, India. Law. m. Sheela Rani, 20 Feb. 1948. *Education:* BSc., 2nd class, 1944; LL.B., 1st class, 1946. *Appointments:* Advocate, 1947-63, Judge, 1963-, Chief Justice, 1978-, High Court, Allahabad, India. *Memberships:* Secretary, 1960, President, 1960 & 1969, Cosmopolitan Club, Allahabad, India. *Publications:* Judgements published in Law reports. *Hobby:* Gardening. *Address:* Chief Justices Residence, Elgin Road, Allahabad, Uttar Pradesh, India.

AGARWAL, Satish, b. 27 Sept. 1928, Rajasthan, India. Legal Advocate. m. Shanta, 16 Feb. 1953, 2 sons, 1 daughter. *Education:* Master of Commerce Degree, 1951; Bachelor of Laws, 1952. *Appointments:* Advocate with the Rajasthan High Court, 1952-; Municipal Council, Jaipur, 1956-58; Rajasthan Legislative Assembly, 1957-62; Detained under MISA during Emergency for 19 months in prison; Minister of State for Finance, Government of India, 1977-79; Elected Member of Parliament, 1977 and again in 1980. *Memberships:* Executive Committee, Commonwealth Parliamentary Association, Rajasthan Branch, 1967-72; Secretary-Rajasthan Legislative Assembly Members' Club, 1962-72; Vice-President and Secretary of Rajasthan State Council for Child Welfare; President, Agarwal College, Jaipur; Constitution Club, New Delhi, 1977-; Attended C.P.A. Conference in Malaysia, 1971; Leader of the Indian delegation to Colombo Plan Conference in Kathmandu, 1977, Washington, 1978; Attended Study Group of C.P.A., London, 1979. *Hobby:* Social Welfare Activities. *Address:* Dhuleshwar Gardens, Jaipur, India

AGBAROJI, Prince Chikwendu, b. 9 Jul. 1933, Amakama, Umuahia, Nigeria. Chartered Quantity Surveyor; Regional Planning Consultant. m. Gloria Onyedikachi Nwabuko, Apr. 1962, 2 sons, 1 daughter. *Education:* Diploma, Civil Engineering, Technical Institute, Yaba, Lagos, 1955-58; College of Estate Management, London, 1961-66 (ARICS, AIQS, 1968); LLB, 1969, University of London; MA, Regional Studies, University of Sussex, England, 1970; PhD, University of London, UK, 1978. *Appointments:* Technical Officer, Federal Ministry of Works, Lagos, 1955-61; Quantity Surveying Assistant, Harris & Porter, London, 1963-64; Assistant Quantity Surveyor, R. Gordon Fanshawe & Ptns, London, 1964-67; Quantity Surveyor, Widnell & Trollope, London, 1967-69; Main Grade Quantity Surveyor, Department of the Environment, London, 1969-72;

Principal, P.C. Agbaroji & Partners, 1972-. *Memberships:* Member of Council and Education Committee, Chairman of Registration Committee, Nigerian Institute of Quantity Surveyors, formerly 1st Vice President; Regional Studies Association, London; Sports Club, Enugu. *Publications:* Several articles for Journals and Seminars. *Honours:* Appointed Chief of Amakama Community in Ikwuano/Umuahia Local Government Area, 1980. *Hobbies:* Interested in Charitable Organizations; Reading; Golf. *Address:* No. 4 Unije Street, Independence Layout, Enugu.

AGBASI, Amanchuku John, b. 27 Sept. 1933, Nnewi, Nigeria. Chartered Accountant. m. Elizabeth Inenwa Egbuonu, 2 Jan. 1956, 4 sons, 3 daughters. *Education:* Member, 1965, Fellow, 1976, Institute of Cost and Management Accountants; Member, Chartered Accountant of Nigeria, 1974. *Appointments:* District Accountant, Chief Internal Auditor, Chief Accountant, Nigerian Railways. *Memberships:* Former Member, National and International Panel for Review of Principles of Account West African Examinations Council; Vice Chairman, Nnewi Youth League, Lagos; Auditor, Anaedo Social Club of Nigeria, Lagos; Treasurer, Railway Institute, Lagos; Life member, Nigeria/India Friendship Association. *Publications:* Editor: Nmwei Youth League Directory with Brief History of Social/Economic Life in Nnewi. *Hobbies:* Reading; Music; Gardening. *Address:* 45 Nnamdi Aziiciwe Drive, Railway Compound, Ebute Metta, Lagos, Nigeria.

AGBASI, Francis Christian Nnodu, b. 16 Nov. 1924, Uruagu Nnewi, Nigeria. m. Sussannah Ifeoma Obiegbu, 18 Mar. 1948, 4 sons, 4 daughters. *Education:* Diploma, Civil Engineering, P.W.D. Technical School, Lagos, 1944-48; BSc(Hons), Engineering, London University, UK, 1951-56; MSc, Iowa State University of Technology, USA, 1974. *Appointments:* Agricultural Assistant, 1943; Engineering Assistant, 1944-56; Executive Engineer P.W.D., 1956-60; Senior Lecturer, Head of Department, Yaba College of Technology, 1960-62; Chief Executive, Yaba College of Technology, 1962-65; Adviser on Technical Education to F.M.G., 1966; Senior Inspector, Technical Education, Republic of Biafra, 1967-69; Deputy Chief Inspector of Education,East Central State of Nigeria, 1970; Senior Lecturer, University of Nigeria, 1971-77; Principal Consultant in Design Construction Group, 1977-; Director and Chairman Board of Director, DCG & Associates Limited, 1977-; Vice President, Whiteley-Jacobson International/Design Construction Group, 1978-. *Memberships:* Fellow Nigerian Society of Engineers; Institution of Civil Engineers; American Society of Civil Engineers; National Board Technical Editor, 1977-79; Past Member Lagos Sports Council; Anaedo Social Club of Nigeria; Anglican Church. *Publications:* Establishment of Comprehensive Secondary Schools in Nigeria; Colleges of Technology in Developing Countries; Organisation and Administration of Two year Colleges in OWA State *Honours:* Proficiency Certificate in Geometry. 1941. *Hobbies:* Photography. *Address:* 68 Mbanefo St, New Haven, Enugu, Nigeria.

AGEDAH, Horatio Nelson Oyenke, b. 24 Jul. 1929, Odi, Rivers State, Nigeria. m. 19 Jan. 1961. *Education:* Bachelor of Laws(Hons), University of London, UK, 1970; Legal Practitioner's Certificate, Nigerian Law School, 1972. *Appointments:* Junior Clerk, Stenographer, Confidential Secretary, Nigeria Marine Department, 1948-55; Assistant Editor, Editor, Director of News and Current Affairs, 1956-62, Deputy Director-General and Alternate Director-General,1975-77, Nigerian Broadcasting Corporation; Chief Executive, News Agency of Nigeria, 1977-78; Federal Electoral Commissioner, 1978-79; Chairman, African Continental Bank Ltd, 1980-. *Memberships:* Past President, Nigerian Guild of Editors; Life Member, Nigerian Institute of International Affairs; Chairman, National Amamteur Wrestling Association; Boy Scouts Association of Nigeria; Bulletin Editor, Rotary Club of Lagos. *Publications:* Numerous articles in newspapers and journals; Professional papers at National and International Seminars and Conferences. *Honours:* Chevalier de la Medalle de la Reconnaissance Cetrafricaine, Central African Republic, 1972; Officier de l'Ordre National, Senegal, 1972. *Hobbies:* Reading; Writing; Sports Administration. *Address:* Aluku Lodge, 7 Falolu Road, Suru-Lere, Lagos, Nigeria.

AGER, Brian Cecil, b. 31 Aug. 1930, Calcutta, India. Architect. m. Yvonne Edwards, 22 Dec. 1963, 3 sons.

Education: Intermediate and Final Examinations, Royal Institute of British Architects, Hammersmith Polytechnic, London, UK. *Appointments:* Ministry of Works, London, UK, 1958-65; London Borough of Brent, UK, 1965-71; Ministry of Local Government, Kingston, Jamaica, 1972-. *Memberships:* Royal Institute of British Architects; Jamaican Institute of Architects. *Address:* 'Mountainside', Coopers Hill, St. Andrew, Jamaica.

AGHIMIEN, Jonah Obika, b. 15 Nov. 1941, Igbanke, Bendel State, Nigeria. Solicitor; Lawyer. m. Esther Ogbomo, 15 Nov. 1964, 3 sons, 1 daughter. *Education:* LLB, Honours, University of Lagos, Nigeria, 1969; Called to Nigerian Bar, Nigeria Law School, 1970. *Appointments:* State Counsel, 1970-71; Private Legal Practitioner, 1971-81; Member of Constitution drafting Committee for Bendel State, 1975; Nigerian Constituent Assembly, 1977-78; Legal Adviser to number of Companies and Corporations, e.g. N. TV. Benin. *Memberships:* Assistant Secretary, Literal Society of Government College Abraka; Editor-in-Chief, Law Society, University of Lagos; Legal Adviser, Igbanke Welfare Club; General Secretary, Federated Union of Midwest (BENDEL) Students. *Publications:* Editor of The Lawyer, a Law Journal. *Honours:* Won first Prize in Annual debating contest of the Literal Society of Government College Abraka. *Hobbies:* Sports; Music; Public Debates. *Address:* No. 1, Adesuwa Lane, New - Benin, Benin City, Bendel State, Nigeria.

AGRAWAL, Bhagwan Das, b. 23 Aug. 1932, Varanasi (U.P.), India. Teaching Profession. m. Kailash Agrawal, MA 23 May, 1959, 2 sons. *Education:* BSc., 1951, MSc., 1953, PhD(Maths)., 1960, Banaras Hindu University, India. *Appointments:* Lecturer, Mathematics, Faculty of Science, 1961, Reader, Mathematics, Faculty of Science, Banaras Hindu University, Varanasi 221005, India. *Memberships:* Life Member, Indian Mathematical Society, Progress of Mathematics; Indian Science Congress Association; Bhartiya Ganita Parishad; Calcutta Mathematical Society; Hon. Secretary, Sri Agrawal Samaj of Varanasi, 1978-79. *Publications:* 40 research papers in field of Mathematics. *Honours:* Numerous honours in field. *Hobbies:* Philately; Swimming; Gardening; Numesmatics; Book Collecting. *Address:* Ck. 52/11, Rajadarwaza, Varanasi-221001, India.

AGRAWAL, Naresh Chandra. b. 22 May, 1927, Gaya (Bihar) India. Teacher. m. Sarla Agrawal, 23 Nov. 1953, 2 sons, 1 daughter. *Education:* M. Com. 1949; PhD., 1957. *Appointments:* Lecturer in Commerce, Gaya College, Gaya, India, 1949-64; Lecturer and In-Charge, 1964-66, Reader and Head, University Department of Commerce, Magadh University, Bodh Gaya, India, 1966-79; University Professor of Business Finance and Head, Commerce Department, Bombay University, Bombay, India, 1979-; University Professor, Head and Dean, University Department of Commerce, Magadh University, 1980-. *Memberships:* Indian Commerce Association; Indian Management Association. *Publications:* Numerous publications including: The Food Problem of India, The Art and Technique of Budgeting. *Address:* West Jagjiwan Road, Civil Lines, Gaya (Bihar), India.

AGRAWAL, S.C, b. 8 Jul. 1943, Mathura, India. Teacher. m. Kusum Agarwal, 21 Apr. 1970, 2 sons, 1 daughter. *Education:* Bachelor's Degree, 1962, Master's Degree, 1964, Agra University, Agra, India; PhD, 1969, IIT, Kampur, India. *Appointments:* Lecturer, Agra College, Agra, India, 1964-65; Research Assistant, I.I.T. KAMPUR, India, 1966-69; Lecturer, Meerut University, Merrut, India, 1969-72; Guest Member of Staff, University of Newcastle-on-Tyne, UK, 1972-73; Lecturer, 1973-76, Reader, 1976-, Meerut University, India. *Memberships:* Board of Editors, Journal 'Acta Cinencia Indica'; Member of Council, Indian Science Congress Association; Indian Mathematical Society; Mathematical Association of India; Member of Board, Studies of Kumaun University, Nainital; Referee for a number of Journals. *Publications:* Numerous publications in field. *Honours:* Academic staff Fellowship (Commonwealth) for one year to visit UK in 1972-73; Selected to visit Hungarian Universties for 6 months; Gold Medal for 1st position in MA/MSc. in University; Chancellor's Silver medal for best student in postgraduate of all faculties in whole University; Scholarship of merit all through career. *Hobbies:* Badminton. *Address:*

C-5, University Campus, Merrat University, Meerat, Meerat-25005, V.P., India.

AGUSIOBO, Obiora Nnaemeka Abiodun, b. 26 Dec. 1926, Lagos, Nigeria, West Africa. Lecturer. m. Obiageli Onyejekwe 27 Jan. 1961, 2 sons, 1 daughter. *Education:* Cambridge School Certificate, St. Gregory's College Lagos 1947; BS degree in Technical Agriculture, Langston University Oklahoma USA 1957; MS degree in Agriculture Extesnion, 1958, PhD degree in Agriculture Education, 1966, University of Wisconsin, Madison, Wisconsin, USA. *Appointments: Appointments:* Instructor in Agricultural Science, Cuttington College, Suakoko, Liberia 1959-61; Rural Education Officer, Umudike, Umuahia 1961; Assistant Lecturer, 1961, Lecturer, 1962-72, Senior Lecturer, University of Nigeria, Nsukka 1973; Associate Professor in Vocational and Agricultural Education 1976-. *Memberships:* Alpha Phi Omega; Omega Psi Phi; American Country Life Association; National Education Association, USA; American Teachers of Vocational Agriculture; Agricultural Panel of National Research Council; Nigerian Society for Animal Production; Nigerian Association for Agricultural Education; Agriculture Education Association of England and Wales. *Publications:* Personal Factors Influencing the Occupational Choice of Selected Undergraduates at the University of Nigeria. Unpublished PhD Thesis, University of Wisconsin, Madison, Wisconsin, USA; Competencies Developed Through Occupation Experience for Agricultural and Home Economics Education Teachers, 1978; Implications of Vocational Education Programmes for the Nigerian School Systems, 1973; The Guidance Role of the Teacher of Agricultural Science in Nigerian Secondary Schools, 1974; Comparative Study of Four Methods of Teaching Agricultural Science, Agricultural Progress 1975; Patterns, Issues and Trends in Vocational Education, 1976; World of Work Assumptions, 1980; The Role of African Women in Rural Development, 1981; Vocational Education: The Nigerian Pattern: Proceedings of the 7th World Congress of the International Association for the Advancement of Educational Research, 1977; Vocational Education: 1976; Vegetable Gardening: Tropical Agricultural Handbook Series, 1977; School and Home Gardening, Book One, 1977; Swine Production in Tropical Climates, Book Two: 1977; Handbook of Teaching Practice, 1979; Introduction to Teaching Home Economics, 1979; Soil Science and Plant Growth, 1979; Agricultural Science Questions and Answers, 1981; Teaching Guide for Agricultural Science Teachers in Nigerian Secondary Schools and Colleges, 1979; Technical Competencies Needed by Higher Diploma (N.N.D.) Students in Schools and Colleges of Agriculture, 1979. *Honours:* Member, Board of Governors, Division of Agricultural Colleges, Ahmadu Bello University, Zaria, 1976-80-; First National Vice President, Nigerian Association for Agricultural Education 1975/76; 1976/77; Patron, Nigerian Vocational Association 1979; Patron, Vocational Education Students' Association; University of Nigeria Careers Board; Staff Adviser, St. Gregory's College Old Boys' Association University of Nigeria, Nsukka 1979-; Staff Adviser, National Union of Cameroon Students, U.N.N.; Executive Member, Nigerian Association for Agricultural Education; Collaborator: International Investigation on Articulation of Post-Secondary Education and the World of Labour; Pioneer Leader in Nigerian Vocational Education. *Hobbies:* Music; Tennis; Naturalist; Informal Education. *Address:* 13 Isagba Street, Onitsha Inland Town, Nigeria.

AGUTA, Rowland Nwanebu, b. 6 June 1944, Mbieri-Owerri, Nigeria. Civil Servant. m. 2 Feb. 1976 1 son, 2 daughters. *Education:* BSc(Hons.)1975; MA1977; PhD 1979. *Appointments:* Teacher 1962; Headmaster 1970; Tutor, Oma Grammar School, 1975; Principal Education Officer, Federal Ministry of Education Nigeria; Lecturer and Head of English Department, Federal Advanced Teachers' College, Katsina. *Memberships:* Auditor, General, Nwanne Dinamba Social Club of Nigeria; Nigeria English Studies Association; Educational Studies Association of Nigeria; Linguistic Association of Nigeria; Nigeria Folklore Association. *Hobbies:* Photographing; Gardening; Hunting; Swimming. *Address:* PO Box 1, Mbieri-Owerri, Nigeria.

AGYEI, Samuel Kwasi, b. 15 Mar. 1936. University Lecturer. m. Dorothy Amele Dagadu, 18 Apr. 1964, 1 son, 3 daughters. *Education:* MA., History, University of Ghana, 1970-76; Graduate Diploma, Archives Administration, University of New South Wales, Kensington, Australia, 1977. *Appointments:* Lecturer, Archives Administration, University of Ghana, Legon, 1978-. *Memberships:* Hon. Secretary, 1980-, Historical Society of Ghana; Australian Society of Archivists. *Publications:* Fionization of Records—With Particular Reference to Smaller Archival Institutions, 1979. *Hobbies:* Music; Gardening. *Address:* No. 3 Link Road, Achimota, Legon, Ghana.

AH KOY, Lavinia Beulah, b. 22 June 1940, Suva Fiji. Clerk to Fiji Parliement. m. James Michael Ah Koy, 2 sons, 2 daughters. *Education:* Suva Girls Grammar School 1945-55. *Appointments:* Fiji Civil Service, 1956-; Shorthand Writer Supreme Court of Fiji, 1958-60; Hansard Reporter, Legislative Council, 1960-68; Clerk to Legislative Council, 1968-70; Clerk to Fiji Parliament, 1970-. *Memberships:* Honorary Secretary/Treasurer, Fiji Branch Commonwealth Parliamentary Association; Pan Pacific South East Asia Women's Association; Seventh Day Adventist Church. *Honours:* OBE, 1975; Commissioned Justice of the Peace, 1976. *Hobbies:* Culinary Arts; Reading; Dressmaking; Interior decorating; Welfare work. *Address:* 22 Verrier Road, Tamavua Heights, Suva, Fiji.

AHEARNE, Millicencia, b. 25 Jan. 1945, Road Town, Tortola, Br. Virgin Island. Nursing. m. William B Ahearne, 12 Aug. 1972. *Education:* State Registered Nursing Certificate, 1966; State Certified Midwifery Certificate 1969; Neonatal Paediatric Nursing Certificate 1970; Nursing Administration Certificate 1978. *Appointments:* Junior Staff Nurse, University Hospital of the West Indies, Jamaica, 1966-67; Staff Nurse Operating Theatre, Peebles Hospital, Br. Virgin Island, 1967-68; Staff Nurse Labour Ward, Glasgow Royal Maternity Hospital, Scotland, 1970; Staff Nurse, 1970, Assistant Matron, 1970-77, Matron, 1978, Peebles Hospital, Br Virgin Island. *Memberships:* British Virgin Islands Nurses Association; The Friends of the Blind Society. *Hobbies:* Classical Music; Collecting Recipes and Coins; Cooking; Singing. *Address:* Havers, PO Box 252, Road Town, Tortola, British Virgin Islands.

AHLUWALIA, Isharsingh Ahluwalia, b. 13 Aug. 1924, Sialkot, West Punjab, Pakistan. Medical, (Dental). m. Inderjit Kaur, 6 June 1948, 3 sons. *Education:* BDs, 1948; MDs, 1962. *Appointments:* Dental Surgeon, 1949; Assistant Professor, 1956; Professor, 1962; Principal, 1979, Government Dental College and Hospital, Administrator, Punjab, India. *Memberships:* President, 1979, Indian Dental Association; Executive member, Dental Council of India; Founder member, Indian Prosthodontic Society; Rotary Club; Masonic Lodge. *Publications:* Eight publications done. *Hobbies:* Social activity. *Address:* 29 Taylor Road, Amritsar, Punjab, India.

AHMAD, Mohammad, b. 1 Jan. 1939, India. Librarian. m. Jamal Fatma, 3rd June 1970, 1 son, 1 daughter. *Education:* Certificate in Library Science, 1960; Bachelor of Arts, 1965; Bachelor of Library Science, 1967. *Education: Appointments:* Librarian Indian Council for Africa, New Delhi, 1961-66; Librarian, United Service Institution of India, 1967-68; Archivist/Librarian National, Archives of Zambia 1968-71; Senior Librarian, Botswana National Library Service 1971-79; Acting Director, Botswana National Library Service 1979-80; Senior Librarian, Botswana National Library Service 1981-. *Memberships:* British Institute of Management; Botswana Library Association; Social and Sports Clubs in Gaborone, Botswana. *Publications:* Compilor of Documentation List, Africa (monthly) 1961-66; Bibliographies for Africa Quarterly, 1961-66; Compilor Annual Bibliography, for school and college libraries in Africa, 1978-. *Hobbies:* Gardening; Sports. *Address:* PO Box 493, Gaborone, Botswana, Africa.

AHMAD, Qazi Jalaluddin, b. 1 Jan. 1930, District Rajshahi, Bangladesh. Civil Servant. m. Hashmat Hedayet, 17 July 1953, 1 son, 2 daughters. *Education:* BSc Honours in Chemistry, 1951; MSc Thesis Group, 1952. *Appointments:* Assistant Magistrate and Collector, Dacca; Sub-Divisional Officer, Sylhet; Under-Secretary, Deputy Secretary, Finance Department, Government of East Pakistan; Deputy Commissioner, District Pabna; Deputy Commissioner, District Chittagong; Director-General, Civil Defence and Joint Secretary, Home; Director-General, Commerce and Industries; Secretary, Ministry of Works, Ministry of Railways,

Waterways, Roads and Highways and Road Transport; Officer on Special Duty, Establishment Division, Government of Bangladesh; Secretary, Forest, Fisheries and Livestock, also Agriculture, Government of Bangladesh; Secretary, Election Commission and Returning Officer of Presidential Election of 1978; Conducted Bangladesh Parliamentary Election; Secretary, Bangladesh Parliament, 1979. *Memberships:* Chariman, Chittagong Press Club; Chairman, Chittagong Rifle Club. *Publications:* Thesis on Vapour Pressure of solid Amman bicarbonate as function of temperature; Salt production in East Pakistan; Flood Control in East Pakistan; Food Transport plan in East Pakistan; Administrative Leadership; Government Business Relations. *Honours:* Many Prizes for academic proficiency; Prizes for sports; Prizes for shooting; Honour: Tamgha-e-Qaide Azam. *Hobbies:* Hunting; Photography; Reading. *Address:* "Al-Kahaf", 155, Manipuri Para, Tejgaon, Dacca, Bangladesh.

AHMADU, Mansur Kurfi, b. 19 Dec. 1952, Nigeria. Architect. m. Hassana. *Education:* West African School Certificate, Div.I 1970; School of Basic Studies, Zaria, Nigeria, 1971-72; BSc (2nd class), 1975, MSc, 1977, Architecture, Ahmadu Bello University. *Appointments:* Rational Architects Ibadan, 1977-78; Fed. Cap. Dev. Authority, Lagos, 1978; Rational Architects Ibadan 1978-80; Benna Associates Zaria, 1980-. *Memberships:* Nigerian Institute of Architects; Zaria Club. *Publications:* Institute of Tropical Medicine, MSc. (thesis); Research on Design Problems and Solutions on a Medical Research Centre in the Tropics. *Honours:* Class Prizes at Government College, Kaduna, 1968-70. *Hobbies:* Art; Music; Current Affairs. *Address:* 5A Yakubu Ave, Kaduna, Nigeria.

AHMADULLAH, Abul Khayer, b. 1 Jan. 1927, Iswarganj, Mymensingh, Bangladesh. Teacher. m. (1) Gulenoor Begum (div.) 3 sons, 3 daughters, (2) Begum Jahan Ara, 11 Jan. 1977. *Education:* BCom. University of Calcutta, India, 1946; MCom. University of Dacca, Bangladesh, 1952; MSc (Economics), London School of Economics, United Kingdom, 1959; MSW, McGill University, Canada, 1964. *Appointments:* Professor, Jamalpur College, 1948-51, Ananda Mohan College, Mymensingh, 1953; Principal, Netrokona College, Mymensingh, 1953-55, H.G. College, Munshiganj 1956-59 and College of Social Welfare and Research Centre, University of Dacca, 1959-73; Professor and Director, Institute of Social Welfare and Research, University of Dacca 1973-. *Memberships:* Vice-President, Bangladesh Association for Mental Health; President, Bangladesh Balika Sadan; Chairman, Centre for Management and Socio-economic Research. *Publications:* Labour-Management Relations in Bangladesh—A Country Monograph prepared for ILO, 1977; A Study on Social Security in Bangladesh. *Hobbies:* Voluntary social service; Travelling; Reading. *Address:* 39H Dacca University Quarters, Dacca-2, Bangladesh.

AHMED, A.K.Shamsuddin, b. 2 Jan. 1930, Bangladesh. Teaching Professor of Chemistry. m. Nurunnahar Ahmed, 26 Nov. 1952, 4 sons, 1 daughter. *Education:* PhD, Chemistry, (Inorganic), University of Sheffield, United Kingdom, 1960; MSc, Chemistry, 1953; BSc, (Honours) Dacca University, Bangladesh 1952. *Appointments:* Lecturer in Chemistry, Government College, Chittagong, Bangladesh, 1954; Lecturer and Reader in Chemistry, Rajshahi University, Bangladesh, 1960-63; Professor of Chemistry, University of Chittagong, Bangladesh, 1971. *Memberships:* Bangladesh Academy of Sciences; Bangladesh Association for the Advancement of Science; Former Member, AAAS. *Publications:* About 50 research papers in the field of Coordination Chemistry in the National and International Journals; Executive Editor, Chittagong University Studies Part II (Science). *Hobbies:* Playing Tennis; Listening to music. *Address:* Village, Rampur, PO Shonaimuri, District, Noakhali, Bangladesh.

AHMED, Ekhlasuddin, b. 1 Oct. 1938, Dacca, Bangladesh. University Teaching. m. Hamida Banu, 28 Jan. 1962, 2 sons. *Education:* Matriculation, East Pakistan Secondary Education Board, 1955; Inter Science, Dacca University, 1957; BSc (Honours in Physics), University of Dacca, 1960; MSc (Physics), University of Dacca, 1961; D.I.C. (Imperial College,), London, 1963; PhD, University of London, 1967; Diploma in Russian, University of Dacca, 1969. *Appointments:* Assistant to the Professor of Physics, Dacca University, 1961-62;

Scientific Officer, Pakistan Atomic Energy Commission, 1962-67; Senior Scientific Officer, Pakistan Atomic Energy Commission, 1967-69; Associate Professor of Physics, University of Chittagong, 1969-75; Professor of Physics, University of Chittagong, 1975-. *Memberships:* Life Member of: The Asiatic Society of Bangladesh, The Bengali Academy, The Physical Society of Bangladesh; Member of: Bangladesh Association for the Advancement of Science, The Geophysical Society of Bangladesh; Foreign member of The Royal Meteorological Society, London. *Publications:* Classical Mechanics (Bengali); Research and Popular Science articles. *Honours:* Raja Kali Narayan Scholar, University of Dacca, 1960; The Royal Commission for the Exhibition of 1851 Scholar, 1962; Commonwealth Academic Staff Fellow, 1977. *Hobbies:* Popular Science writings and speeches, Literary activities. *Address:* Dattapara, P.O. Mannoonagar, Tangi, Dacca, Bangladesh

AHMED (Mrs.), Salima, b. 11 June 1926, Bangalore, South India. Pakistan Government Civil Servant. m. 23 Sept. 1954, 2 sons, 1 daughter. *Education:* Good Shepherd's Convent, Bangalore, O levels 1942; St. Joseph's College, Bangalore, A levels; Queen Mary's College, Madras, Graduate in Economics, 1946; Presidency College, Madras, M.A. Economics, 1948. *Appointments:* Programme Producer, Radio Pakistan, 1949; Assistant Accountant General Pakistan Revenue, 1949; Assistant Financial Adviser, Defence Finance, 1954; Director of Accounts & Financial Advisor, State Trading Food Department of Pakistan Government, 1960; Accountant General, Government of E. Pakistan, 1965; Director of Audit, Defence Services of Pakistan, 1971; Finance Director, State Trading Corporation of Pakistan, 1973; Finance Director, Pakistan Industrial Development Corporation, 1978-. *Memberships:* Founder-President , Pakistan Federation of Business & Professional Women's Clubs, 1974-80; Vice-President, International Federation of Business & Professional Women; President, All Pakistan Women's Association (E. Pakistan), 1960-70; Member of Honour, All Pakistan Women's Association 1970-. *Publications:* Various publications in newspapers and magazines on Women's Rights and Responsibilities; Status of Women in Islam; Finance and Accounting, Public Sector Corporations. *Honours:* President of Pakistan award for Meritorious services in Social Welfare; Sitaran Khidmat awarded in 1966. *Hobbies:* Music, dancing, working with women's organizations. *Address:* 49-I Khyabani Ghazi, Defence Housing Society, Karachi, Pakistan.

AHSAN, Syed Ali, b. 26 Mar. 1922, Jessore, Bangladesh. Professor of Literature and Fine Arts. m. Begum Quamar Mushtari, 7 July 1946, 2 sons, 2 daughters. *Education:* B.A. Honours, English, University of Dacca, 1943; M.A. in English, University of Dacca, 1944; *Appointments:* Chairman, Department of Bengali, University of Karachi, Pakistan, 1953-60; Director, Bengali Academy, Dacca, 1960-66; Dean of Faculty of Arts, University of Chittagong, 1967-70; Professor of Benfali, University of Chittagong, 1967-71; Vice-Chancellor, Jahangir Nagar University, Savar, 1972-75; Professor of Bengali, University of Chittagong, 1975; Vice-Chancellor, Rajshahi University, 1975-77; Honourable Member (Minister) in charge of Education, Government of Bangladesh, 1977-78; Professor, Jahangir Nagar University since 1978. *Memberships:* Member of: South East Asia Advisory Board, Obor International; Syndicate, University of Chittagong since 1972; International Board of Judges, The Literary Competition, Manila, 1964; Modern Languages Association, USA. Fellow of: International Poetry Society, Cambridge; Bangla Academy, Dacca. Secretary-General, Pakistan Committe for Cultural Freedom, 1956-65. President, International PEN. Bangladesh Centre since 1975. *Publications:* 35 published works including: poetry, literary criticism, Art Criticism, Literary History, Treatise on Poetry, Linguistic Study and Comparative Literature. Edited six books and anthologies; Edited six literary journals; At present editing a quarterly in English entitled Approach. *Honours:* Advisor to the UNESCO Secretariat, Tokyo, May, 1966; Awarded Bengali Academy Award for Poetry, 1968; Awarded Dawood Prize for original Research, 1969; Awarded Sufi Motahar Husain Award for Literary Criticism, 1975; The Nobel Committee of the Swedish Academy nomination candidate for the Nobel Prize for Literature for the years, 1976, 77, 78, 79, 80 & 1981. *Hobbies:* Walking,

Gardening. *Address:* 60/1 Bashiruddin Road, North Dhanmondi, Dacca 5, Bangladesh.

AICHROY, Bimal Ranjan, b. 25 July 1937, Baichatory, Bangladesh. General Surgeon. m. Ann Patricia Kane, 13 July 1968, 1 son, 1 daughter. *Education:* MBBS., 1960; FRCS.(Ed), 1971; FICS., 1978. *Appointments:* Senior House Surgeon, Professorial Unit, R G Kar Med-College, Calcutta, India, 1961-63; House Surgeon and Physician, War Memorial Hospital, Wrexham, North Wales, UK, 1964-65; Senior House Surgeon, Bradford 'A' HMC., Yorkshire, UK, 1966-68; Senior House Surgeon, Otley General Hospital, Yorkshire, UK, 1968-69; Surgical Registrar, Royal Cornwall Hospitals, UK, 1969-72; Visiting Consultant Surgeon to: Wagga Wagga Base Hospital, Calvary Hospital, Wagga Wagga, Tumut District Hospital, Batlow District Hospital, 1973-. *Memberships:* Australian Medical Association; Australian Association of Surgeons; Association of Surgeons of India; Provincial Surgeons Association of Australia; International Society for Burns; Australia and New Zealand Burns Association; Pan Pacific Surgical Association. *Hobbies:* Fishing; Skiing; Bushwalking; Travelling. *Address:* Churchill Avenue, Kooringal, Wagga Wagga, New South Wales 2650, Australia.

AIRD, Alastair, Sturgis, b. 14 Jan. 1931, Sial Kot, West Punjab, Pakistan. Comptroller to H.M. Queen Elizabeth, The Queen Mother. m. Fiona Kyddelton, 22 July 1963, 2 daughters. *Education:* Eton College, 1944-49; Royal Military Academy, Sandhurst, 1950;-51. *Appointments:* Commissioned 9th Lancers 1951; Adjutante, 1956; Equery to H.M. Queen Elizabeth, The Queen Mother, 1960; Retired from Army, 1963; Assistant Private Secretary to The Queen Mother, 1964; Comptroller of H.M. Household, 1974. *Appointments:* Army Ski. Association. *Honours:* K.V.O. 1969; C.V.O. 1977. *Hobbies:* Shooting, Fishing and Tennis. *Address:* 31 St. James's Palace, London, S.W.1.

AIREY, Ian Lintern, b. 11 Nov. 1947, Brisbane, Queensland, Australia. Medical Practitioner. m. Judeen Rose Daly, 6 Dec. 1975, 1 son. *Education:* Bachelor of Medicine, Bachelor of Surgery, 1973; Fellow of Faculty of Anaesthetists, Royal Australasian College of Surgeons, 1979. *Appointments:* Resident Medical Officer, 1973-75; Anaesthetic Registrar: 1976-77, Princess Alexandra Hospital, Brisbane; Anaesthetic Registrar 1978-79, Staff Anaethetist, 1979-81, Director Intensive Cars Unit, 1981-. Mater Misericordiae Hospital, Brisbane. *Memberships:* Australasian Society of Anaesthetists; Royal Automobile Club of Queensland. *Hobbies:* Photography. *Address:* P.O. Box 24, Coorparoo, Queensland 4151, Australia.

AITCHISON, Roderick Mailer, b. 16 Jan. 1921, Melbourne, Victoria, Australia. Psychiatrist. m. (1) Meredith Clark (Died 1961) (2) Joy Howard (Nee Kerr), 4 sons, 2 daughters. *Education:* Scotch College, Melbourne, 1935-39; 1st Year BA. (Honours), University of Melbourne, 1940; M.B.B.S. (Melbourne), 1950; D.P.M. (Melbourne), 1970. *Appointments:* Lieutenant, Armoured Corps, Australian Imperial Force, 1940-44; R.M.O. Mildura Base Hospital, Victoria, 1951; General Practitioner, Melbourne, 1952-61; R.M.O. Kew Mental Hospital, Victoria, 1961-67; R.M.O. Parkville Psychiatric Unit, Victoria, 1967-; R.M.O. Royal Park Psychiatric Hospital, Victoria, 1968-69; Psychiatrist, Willsmere Hospital, Kew, Victoria, 1970-74; Consultant Psychiatrist, Willsmere Hospital, Kew, Victoria, 1974-76; Psychiatrist Superintendent, Willsmere Hospital, Kew, Victoria 1976-81, Retired April, 1981, Planning to do Sessional & Private Psychiatry. *Memberships:* Captain, Reserve of Officers, R.A.A.M.C.; Rotary International; Australian Medical Association; Australian Association of Gerontology; National Trust, Australia; Graduate Union, University of Melbourne; Victorian Association for Mental Health; Life Governor, Royal Freemasons Home of Victoria. *Honours:* Shared exhibitions, Latin, Greek, School Leaving Honours Examination, Victoria, 1939; Hastie Exhibition, Philosophy, University of Melbourne, 1940. *Hobbies:* Reading, (Mainly non-fiction, History, Classics, Languages), Botany, Plant Propagation. *Address:* c/o 4 Bright Street, Kew, Victoria 3101, Australia.

AITKEN, Russell Faulkner, b. 15 Sept. 1913, Outram, Otago, New Zealand. m. Rhoda, Ruth, Bransome, 23 Dec. 1939, 1 daughter. *Education:* Secondary, Gore and Timaru, New Zealand; London University; R.A.F.

Staff College; N.A.T.O. Defence College and Joint Services Staff College. *Appointments:* Assisting Parents on New Zealand Sheep and Cattle Station, 1934-36; Royal Air Force, 1936-61; Director, National Safety Association of New Zealand, 1962-75; Accident Compensation Commission, Head Office, Wellington, New Zealand, 1975-78. *Memberships:* Rotary Club of Wellington; Wellington and District Justices of the Peace Association; The Institution of Industrial Safety Officers. *Publications:* Various articles on the Principles of Safety, mainly in Industry. *Honours:* Officer, Order of the British Empire, 1943; Commander, Order of the British Empire, 1958; Air Force Cross, 1941. *Hobbies:* Gardening and Music. *Address:* Rixlade, 64 Seaview Road, Paremata, New Zealand.

AJAYI, Ezra Oyegoke, b. 8 July 1937, Ara Via Ede. Librarian. m. Elizabeth, 2 Feb. 1955, 3 sons, 3 daughters. *Education:* Primary Ara Baptist Day School, 1943-48; College, Baptist Teachers College Benin City, 1953-54; College, Government Teacher Training College, Ibadon, 1959-60; G.C.E. Ordinary & Advanced Levels (Private Tuition) 1961-65; A.L.A. Associate of Library Association (London) 1971. *Appointments:* Library Assistant, 1965-68; Senior Library Assistant 1969-70; Assistant Librarian, 1971-72; Senior Assistant Librarian, 1973-77; Deputy Librarian, 1978; Librarian, 1979-. *Memberships:* Special Library Association. *Publications:* Newspaper article, The Need for Library Legislation in Nigeria, Punch, Oct.12, 1978. *Address:* 6 Adeniyi Adefioye Street, Ikate, Surulere, Lagos.

AJAYI, Olatunde Olabode, b. 30 Jan. 1944, Okeopin, Kwara State, Nigeria. Architect. m. Emily Mojisola Esechie, 9 Nov. 1974, 2 sons, 1 daughter. *Education:* Ahmadu Bello University, Zaria, Nigeria; Bachelor of Architecture, 1970; Member, Nigerian Institute of Architects, 1972. *Appointments:* Architect, Adedokun Adeyemi Associates, 1970-72; Architect, Marquis & Partners, 1973; Architect (Salaried Partner), Modulor Group, 1973-76; Architect (Partner), Team Architectural, Nigeria, 1976-. *Memberships:* Social and Publicity Secretary, October Klobb. *Publications:* Building for Development, 1967; Development and Economics of System Building, 1968; Resulting Responses, 1968; Ventilation for Human comfort, 1969; Fire Station for Ilorin (Thesis), 1970. *Hobbies:* Music, Photography, Travels & Chess. *Address:* 23 Rotimi Street, Surulere, Lagos, Nigeria.

AJAYI, Samuel Adebayo, b. 13 July 1940, Ile-Obaala, Oke-Illa, Orangum, Oyo State, Nigeria. Architect - Planner & Landscape Specialist. m. Florence Taiwo 27 July 1967, 4 sons. *Education:* Bachelor Architecture 1972, Masters Degree in Architecture, Howard University, Washington DC., 1974; Diploma in Landscape; Graduate School of the Department of Agriculture Washington, DC., 1975. *Appointments:* Draftsman, James Cuffs, Washington, DC., 1973; Messrs., Oluwole Olvoovylve & Associates, 1975-78; Established own firm, Messrs., Innovative Design Associates, Lagos, 1978-. *Memberships:* Nigeria Institute of Architecture; Oke-illa Orangun Progressive Union, Vice-President, Lagos Branch; Illa-Orangun Charity Club; Island Club, Lagos; Ikoyi Club, Lagos. *Publications:* The Federal Diagnostic Center, (the only one of its kind in Nigeria); University of Calabar, Teaching Hospital; Production of Rabies vaccine, Polio and Measles vaccine for the Federal Government of Nigeria. *Honours:* Best Academic Performance, James E Walker American Legion Award, Washington DC., 1967; Best performance in Science High School, Salvtarian Award, Washington DC., 1967. *Hobbies:* Lawn Tennis, Swimming, Photographing, Planting of shrubs and flowers for beautification purposes. *Address:* 17 Femi Adebule Street, Off, Fok Agoro Street, Abule-Ijesho, Yaba, Lagos, Nigeria.

AJEGBO, Michael Nnanye Ifeanyi, b. 23 Mar. 1949, Obosi, Anambra State, Nigeria. Legal Practitioner. m. Julie Kechi, 8 Nov. 1980, 1 daughter. *Education:* First School Leaving Certificate, Holy Trinity School, Onitsha; Grade 1, WASC, Christ the King College, Onitsha; L.LB (Honours), University of Ife, Ile-Ife; Barrister & Solicitor, Nigerian Law School. *Appointments:* Partner in Law Firm of Abuka, Ajegbo, Ilogu & Nwaogu. *Memberships:* Treasurer, All Nigerian United Nations Students Association, 1970-71; Secretary-General National Union of Nigerian Students, 1971-72; Member, Nigerian Bar Association; Associate Member American

Bar Association; Associate Member, New York Bar Association; Member, Ikoyi Club, 1938 of Nigeria. *Hobbies:* Lawn Tennis, Table Tennis, Hockey. *Address:* 7 Oshinkalu Close, Surulere, Lagos, Nigeria.

AJIBADE, Adeyemi (Yemi), b. 28 July 1929, Otta, Nigeria. Actor, Playwright, Director. m. Gwendoline Ebony Augusta, 25 May 1973, 2 daughters. *Education:* Abeokuta Grammar School, Nigeria; Kennington College of Law & Commerce, London, 1955-58; The Actors Workshop, London, 1960-62; London School of Film Technique, London, 1966-67; British Drama League, London, 1968; Diploma in Dramatic Arts; Diploma Film Technique, Associate of Drama Board. *Appointments:* Acted in Films, on Radio, Stage and Television from 1960 to date. In between acting engagements: Visiting Director, Actors Workshop, London, 1962; Artistic Director, Pan-African Players, London, 1965; Artistic Director, Keskidee Centre, London 1974; Tutor and Producer of Drama on the Panel of Inner London Education Authority, 1968; Artistic Advisor & Assistant to Lord Snowden on Mary Kingley, 1974; Artist-in Residence, Senior Arts Fellow, and Artist Director, Acting Company at the University of Ibadan, Nigeria, 1976-80; Variety of roles played. *Memberships:* Theatre Writers Association, Amateur Golfers Association, Union of African People Writers; British Kinematographic Society; President IlaOrangun Elements Society of Great Britain. *Publications:* Lagos, Yes Lagos; The Black Knives; Award; Parcel Post; Behind the Mountain; Mokai; The Girl from Bulaway, and Emma Mendero. *Honours:* Fellow of Royal Society of Arts. *Hobbies:* Golf, Travelling, Dancing, Jazz. *Address:* Flat 29, Seymour House, Churchway, London, N.W.1.

AJIBOYE, Anthony Babayemi, b. 16 Nov. 1943, Jogga-Ilaro, Ogun State, Nigeria. Medical Records Administrator. m. Funmilayo A, 5 Feb. 1965, 1 son, 1 daughter. *Education:* BSc., Medical Records, USA, 1975; Diploma in Medical Records, UK, 1969. *Appointments:* Medical Records Officer, Ministry of Defence, Armed Forces Medical Services; Staff Officer II, HQ. Infantry Division, Medical, Kaduna; Staff Officer II AHQ Name, Lagos, Nigeria. *Memberships:* Egbado Students Society. *Honours:* Conduct Award, 1976. *Hobby:* Football. *Address:* 44, Wosilatu Daldu St, c/o Mr. S.A.E.Oladeinde, PO Box 545, Lagos, Nigeria.

AJIT, Singh, b. 8 Nov. 1932, Amritsar, India. Medical Consultant; Teacher. m. Harbir Kaur, 29 Dec. 1963, 2 sons. *Education:* MBBS, Panjab University, India, 1955; MD Medicine, 1959; FCCP, USA, 1967; MAMS, Indian Academy, India, 1971. *Appointments:* Houseman in Medicine, 1956; Casualty Medical Officer, V.J. Hospital, Amritsar, 6 months, 1957; Research Scholar in Medicine, 8 months; Assistant Registrar, Medicine, 2 years; Registrar-cum-Senior Lecturer, Medicine, 1960-64; Assistant Professor Medicine, 1964-73; Professor of Medicine, 1973-. *Memberships:* College of Chest Physicians, USA; Indian Academy of Medical Sciences; Indian Medical Association; Indian Diseases of Chest; Indian Cardiology Society; Editorial Board of Punjab Medical Journal, Journal of Medicine and Surgery (Gujrat); current medical Practice (Bombay); Indian Adult Education Association. *Publications:* Numerous publications in field of Medicine including: Specialities of Cardiology. *Honours:* Numerous honours in academic field. *Hobbies:* Lawn Tennis; Urdu Ghazals and Poetry. *Address:* 4, Race Course Road, Amritsar 143001, India.

AJIWE, Onyenso, b. 8 July 1943, Umungasi, Aba, Nigeria. Chartered Secretary; Administrator. m. Ogbonyealu Ebere Onyeije, 20 June 1973, 2 sons, 2 daughters. *Education:* HND, Business Studies, Thurrock Technical College, Grays, Essex, UK, 1965-66; ACIS., Blackburn College of Technology, Blackburn, UK, 1966-69; MA., Accounting and Finance, University of Lancaster, Lancaster, UK, 1972-73; Membership, British Institute of Management, 1980. *Appointments:* Company Secretary, Silentnight Upholstery Limited, Barnoldswick, Lancashire, UK, 1970-72; Lecturer in Financial & Management Accounting, University of Dar-es-Salaam, Dar-es-Salaam, Tanzania, 1973-75; Lecturer in Management Accounting, University of Nigeria, Enugu Campus, 1975-76; Company Secretary, 1976-80, Director and Company Secretary, June 1980-Dec.1980, Company Secretary, 1981-, Golden Guinea Breweries Limited, Umuahia, Nigeria. *Memberships:* American Accounting Association, 1975;

Rotary Club International, Umuahia Branch; Executive member, Ngwa Social Club of Nigeria, Umuahia Branch. *Publications:* Accountant's contribution to profitability in the brewing industry, 1978; The Design of Cost Information System: Some Observations, 1978. *Hobbies:* TV .Viewing; Social Work; Thinking about work. *Address:* Plot 5A, Okpara Avenue, PO Box 686, Umuahia, Nigeria.

AJUWON, Bade, b. 25 Dec. 1940, Oyo, Nigeria. University Lecturer. m. 26 Dec. 1966, 1 son, 3 daughters. *Education:* BA(Hons.) English/History, 1969, Diploma in Law, 1972, University of Lagos, Nigeria; MA(Folklore), 1973, PhD(Folklore),1977, Indiana University, Bloomington, Indiana, USA. *Appointments:* Primary School Headmaster, Kosofe Baptist, Ikeja, 1958-60; Head, Department of English, Ajeromi Secondary Grammar School, Ipapa, 1970-71; Research Fellow, Institute of African Studies, Unife, 1974-75; Lecturer in African Languages and Literatures, Unife, 1976-. *Memberships:* Secretary/Treasurer, Yoruba Studies Association of Nigeria; International Folk Narrative Research; American Folklore Society; Nigerian Folklore Society. *Publications:* Funeral Dirges of Yoruba Hunters; Iremoje: Evé Ispa Ode. *Honours:* Indiana University African Studies Fellowship, 1972. *Hobbies:* Gardening. *Address:* Department of African Language and Literature, Unife, Nigeria.

AKANDA, Safar A, b. 2 Dec. 1934, Mohanganj, Mymensingh, Bangladesh,. University Professor. m. Gul Hasna, 17 Feb. 1971, 3 sons. *Education:* BA, Honours, History, 1951, MA, History, 1952, Dacca University, Bangladesh; MA, International Relations, 1965, PhD, International Studies, 1970, Denver University, Colorado, USA. *Appointments:* Lecturer, Department of History, Dacca University, 1954-55; Lecturer/Senior Lecturer/Assistant Professor, Department of History, Rajshahi University, 1955-71; Visiting Lecturer, Kalamazoo College, Michigan, USA, 1966-67; Visiting Fellow, University of Rajasthan, Jaipur, India, 1971; Associate Professor, Department of History, Rajshahi University, 1972-73; Associate Professor, Department of History, Jahangirnagar University, 1973-75; Professor of History & Joint Director IBS, 1975-77, Director, IBS, 1977-, Rajshahi University. *Memberships:* President, Pakistan Students Association of America, 1966-67; Asiatic Society of Bangladesh, Dacca; Bangla Academy, Dacca; Secretary, Rajshahi University Club, 1970-72; General Secretary. R.U.T.A, 1972-73. *Publications:* Numerous publications including: The Journal of the Institute of Bangladesh Studies, 1976-80; Editor, Studies in Modern Bengal, 1981; The Emergence of Bangladesh: Regionalism to Nationalism (in Press). *Honours:* Sir Jadunath Sarkar Post-Graduate Scholarship, Dacca University, 1951-52; University Prize for standing First in the First Class in MA Examination in History, 1952; Outstanding Pakistani student in USA, 1964-65; Social Science Foundaation Fellowship, Denver University, 1962-64; Hill Foundation Fellowship, 1964-65, Ford Foundation Fellowship, 1965-67, Denver University, USA; Commonwealth Academic Staff Fellowship at SOAS, 1976-77. *Hobbies:* Travelling. *Address:* Vill. Telikuri, PO. Mohanganj, Dt. Mymensingh, Bangladesh.

AKANDE, Adebowale Durojaiye, b. 9 June 1938, Ibadan, Oyo State of Nigeria. Lawyer and Member of the Nigerian National Assembly. m. Jadesola Olayinka, 31 Aug. 1963, 1 daughter. *Education:* LLB(Hons) London; Barrister-at-Law. *Appointments:* Self Employed. *Memberships:* Member, House of Representatives, National Assembly Nigeria, and Committees for Judiciary ad Public Petitions; Secretary General, African Bar Association, 1981-83; General Secretary, Nigerian Bar Association, 1977-79; International Bar Association, International Legal Aid Association, World Peace Through Law, Nigerian Council of Legal Education, Nigerian Bar Council, 1977-80; Island Club, Lagos Nigeria; Yoruba Tennis Club, Lagos Nigeria. *Publications:* Farewell to an upright Judge—A biographical tribute to Late Justice J.I.C. Taylor, Chief Justice of Lagos State, Nigeria. *Hobbies:* Reading; Travelling; Watching Football; Musical Films and Shows. *Address:* 7 Alawode Street, Ikate, Surulere, Nigeria.

AKANDE, Christopher Sunday Olutunde, b. 28 Dec. 1927, Arigidi, Akoko, Ondo State, Nigeria. Chartered/Registered Civil Engineer. m. Christiana Olufunke, Adefarati, 19 July 1957, 2 sons, 2 daughters. *Educa-*

tion: Inter BSc, University College Ibadan, 1948; BSc, Battersea Polytechic, London, 1950-53; Diploma, Royal College of Science and Technology, Glasgow, 1959-60; Summer School, Certificate, Stanford University, USA, 1969; Fellow, Institution of Civil Engineers, UK, 1968; Fellow, Nigerian Society of Civil Engineers, 1968. *Appointments:* Graduate Engineer, Ove Arup and Partners, London, 1953-55; Executive, Senior, Chief Engineer, Ministry of Works, W. Nigeria, 1955-67; Controller, (Director), Public Works, Services, W. Nigeria, 1967-74; Permanent Secretary, Ministries of Lands and Housing, Works and Transport 1974-75; Secretary, Military Government and Head of Service, Western State and Oyo State, 1975-76; Group Managing Director, Odu'a Investment Company Limited, 1976-79, Vice Chairman-Chief Executive, West African Portland Cement, Company Limited, 1979-; Chairman: National Bank of Nigeria Limited, 1976-80; Western Nigeria Housing Corporation, 1966-67; National Road Safety Committee, 1967-74, etc; Member, Senate of the University of Lagos, 1981-; Chairman, Tilbury Contracting Company Nigeria Limited, 1980-. *Memberships:* President: Nigerian Society of Engineers; Association of Professional Officers; Ibadan Government College Old Bosy Association; Ibadan Tennis Club; Member: Ibadan Dining Club; Metropolitan Club Lagos; Lagos Island Tennis Club; Lions Club. *Publications:* Papers/Lectures e.g.: The Engineer; Alternative Approaches to Decision Taking; Challenges to the Nigerian Engineer in 2000 AD; Infra-structural Requirements for Technological Development in Nigeria. *Hobbies:* Reading; Lawn and Table Tennis; Billiards; Swimming; Light game hunting. *Address:* Plot 1393 Tiamiyu Savage Road, Victoria Island, Lagos, Nigeria.

AKANNI, Adetunji Boladale, b. 27 Sept. 1937, Ibadan, Oyo State, Nigeria. Insurance. m. Bolatito Diekola Adeniyi, 12 Mar. 1964, 3 sons, 1 daughter. *Education:* Associate member of the Chartered Insurance Institute, London, 1967. *Appointments:* Underwriter, Holloway Insurance Brokers, London, 1964-66; Aviation Official, Aviation Department, English and American Insurance Company Limited, 1967-69; Manager/Secretary, Associate Insurance Brokers, Lagos, 1969-71; District Manger, The Nigerian General Insurance Company Limited, Lagos, 1971-. *Hobbies:* Reading; Travelling; Football. *Address:* Block 14, Plot 6 Modern Farmers Association, Moor Plantation, PO Box 12101, Ibadan, Nigeria.

AKANO, Joseph Jimoh, b. 15 Aug. 1941, Oshogbo, Oyo State of Nigeria. Accountant. m. Jokotade Brown, 31 May 1965, 2 sons, 2 daughters. *Education:* Associate of Institute of Chartered Accountants of Nigeria, 1973-75; Fellow, Institute of Cost and Management Accountants, 1981. *Appointments:* Chief Accountant, Daily Times of Nigeria Limited; Cost Accountant, 1972-75, Financial Accountant, 1975-77, Chief Accountant, Niger Pak Limited, 1977-80; Accountant, Mansa Construction Company Limited; Assistant Accountant, Wiggins Teape (W.A) Limited. *Memberships:* Assistant Secretary, Oshogbo Union, Lagos; Member, Lagos District Society of Accountants; Oshum Development Association; Oshogbo Sports Club; Lagos Country Club. *Publications:* Several Articles on Finance in the Nigerian Business Times. *Hobbies:* Music; Reading; Dancing; Table Tennis. *Address:* 5, Ishola Street, Surulere, Lagos State, Nigeria.

AKEL, Richard Livingston, b. 25 Oct. 1946, Whakatane, New Zealand. Lawyer. div. 2 sons, 1 daughter. *Education:* LLB, Honours, Auckland University, 1971; LLB(Cantab), Cambridge University, UK, 1972. *Appointments:* Meredith, Connell Gray & Co., Barristers & Solicitors (incorporating Crown Solicitor), Auckland, 1968-70; Senior Tutor, Faculty of Law, University of Western Australia, Perth, W.A., 1974; Buddle, Weir & Co, Barristers & Solicitors, Auckland, New Zealand, 1975-76; Office of Ombudsman, Auckland, New Zealand, 1976-77; Department of Labour, Auckland, New Zealand, 1977-78; New Zealand Forest Products Limited, 1979-. *Memberships:* Auckland Council for Civil Liberties; Amnesty International. *Hobbies:* Jogging. *Address:* 6 Thorp Street, St. Johns, Auckland 6, New Zealand.

AKERELE, Oluwalope Ezekiel Benjamin, b. 20 June 1943, Akure, Ondo State, Nigeria. Management Consultant. m. Florence Eugenia Tachie-Menson, 19 June 1971, 2 sons, 1 daughter. *Education:* MPhil, Leeds,

1970; Post-graduate Diploma in Textile Industries 1978; College Associateship Diploma, Blackburn College of Technology, 1967. *Appointments:* Quality Controller and Technologist, Customer Complaints Investigations, Qualitex Yarns Limited, Burnley 1967; Production Manager, Westexinco, Ado-Ekiti Textile Mills, 1970-72; Acting Technical Manager,, Westexinco, 1972-73; Management Consultant and Lecturer, Nigerian Institute of Management, 1973-80; Managing Director, Benol International Management Consultants Limited, 1980-. *Memberships:* Nigerian Institute of Management; Textile Institute of Nigeria; Institute of Management Consultants of Nigeria. *Publications:* Articles in Management in Nigeria, Magazine. *Hobbies:* Music; Reading Investment and Economic Reviews. *Address:* 3 Ayodele Ojo St, Ilupeju Estate, Lagos, Nigeria.

AKERHOLT, May-Brit, b. 19 Apr. 1943, Drammen, Norway. Tutor. m. Vidar Akerholt, 4 June 1965, 2 daughters. *Education:* Cand. mag.(BA) Oslo University, 1974; BA(Hons) Macquarie University, 1976; MA(Hons.) thesis to be handed in shortly. *Appointments:* Part-time tutor, University of New South Wales, 1977; Part-time tutor, Macquarie University, 1977-78, Tutor, 1979-. *Memberships:* Association for the Study of Australian Literature; Association for Commonwealth Literature and Language Studies. *Publications:* Structure and Themes in Patrick White's Four Plays, Patrick White: A Critical Symposium 1978; Henrik Ibsen in English Translation, The Languages of Theatre, 1980; Story Into Play: The Two Versions of Patrick White's A Cheery Soul, forthcoming in Southerly. *Address:* 38 Jopling Street, North Ryde, NSW, Australia 2113.

AKHTAR, Md. Shakil, b. 4 Apr. 1953, Bihar, India. Physician. *Education:* MBBS, 1978. Internship completion, 1979; JHP, Radiology, 1980; JHP, General Medicine, 1980; *Appointments:*JHP, Orthopaedics, 1981. Female Psychology, Radiology, General medicine, Orthopaedic, Cardiovascular surgery. *Address:* c/o Dr. Md. Sulaiman, Head of Urdu Department, L.S.College, Muzaffarpur, North Bihar, India.

AKIN DEKO, High Chief, Gabriel, b. 30 Oct. 1913, Lagos, Nigeria. Teaching; Engineering. m. Caroline Ebun Odeyemi, 15 Mar. 1946, 5 sons, 5 daughters. *Education:* Government College Ibadan, Nigeria, 1930-33; Yaba Diploma, Higher College Yaba, Lagos, Nigeria, 1934-37; HND, Brixton School of Building, London, 1947-50; DSc (Honorary), University of Benin. *Appointments:* School Master, Government College, Ibadan, Nigeria, 1937-47 and 1950-51; Managing Director, Akin Deko Kontrakts, 1951-55; Regional Minister, Minister of Agriculture and Natural Resources, 1956-61; UN-FAO Regional Representative for Africa, 1962-68; Chairman, Western Nigeria Development Corporation, 1968-71; Pro-Chancellor, University of Benin, 1976-80; Chairman, Modern Nigeria Kontrakts Limited, 1972-; Chairman Solel Boneh Nigeria Limited, 1978-. *Memberships:* GCIOBA; Ondo State National Party of Nigeria; Youths Christian Circle St James's Cathedral Ibadan; Royal Commonwealth Society, London; Fellow, Nigerian Institute of Building. *Honours:* Honorary LLD, University of Ibadan; High Chief Lasa of Idanre; The Basorun of Ile Oluji; The Salagwe of Owo; The Obanla of Idepe; The Arabanla of Apoiland; Pro-Chancellor, Chairman of Council, Federa University of Technology, Akure Ondo State. *Hobbies:* Music; Swimming. *Address:* SW8/801 Oke Ado, Ibadan, Nigeria.

AKINDELE, Labode Oladimeji (Chief), b. 2 June 1933, Ibadan, Nigeria. Company Director. m. Olabisi Ayeni, 2 sons, 4 daughters. *Education:* Grammar School, Abeokuta, 1945-50. *Appointments:* Western Nigeria Union of Importers & Exporters; Ibadan Traders Association Ltd; Ibadan Bus Service Ltd; Presently, Chairman Umarco Nig. Ltd; Standard Breweries Nig. Ltd; Damen Nig. Ltd; Contex Nig. Ltd; Coastal Services Nig. Ltd; Modandola Investments Ltd; Roro Terminal Co. Nig. Ltd; Nigerian Biscuit Manufacturing Co. Nig. Ltd; Riv Biscuit Nig. Ltd; Obelawo Farcha Fishing Co. Ltd. *Memberships:* Oluyole Club. *Honours:* The Parakoyi of Ibadan (Chieftaincy Title), 1981. *Hobbies:* Fishing; Lawn Tennis. *Address:* 6B Lander Close, Apapa, Lagos, Nigeria.

AKINKUGBE, Oladipo Olujimi, b. 17 July, 1933, Ondo, Nigeria. Physician. m. Folasade Dina, 8 May 1965, 2 sons. *Education:* University College, Ibadan,

1951-55; MB, BS, LRCP, MRCS, The London Hospital, London University, 1955-58; DTM & H, University of Liverpool, 1960; Balliol College, University of Oxford, 1962-64; MRCP, Edinburgh, 1961; DPhil, Oxon, 1964; MD, London, FRCP, Edinburgh, 1968; FWACP, 1976; FAS, 1980. *Appointments:* House Surgeon, The London Hospital, 1958; House Physician, Kings College Hospital, London, 1959; Med. Off. Special Grade, Western Nigeria, 1961; Lecturer in Medicine & Cons. Physician to the University College Hospital, 1964; Rockefeller fellow to six renal centres in the US, 1966; Professor of Medicine, University of Ibadan, 1968; Visiting Renal fellow, Department of Medicine, Universities of Manchester, Oxford, Cambridge & London, 1969; Vis. Professor of Medicine, Harvard University, 1974-75; Head of Medicine, 1972; Dean of Medicine University of Ibadan, 1970-74; Principal & Vice-Chancellor, University of Ilorin, 1975-78; Vice-Chancellor Ahmadu Bello University, Zaria, 1978-79; Visiting Fellow, Balliol College, Oxford, 1981-82. *Memberships:* Medical Research Society of Gt. Britain; International Society for Hypertension; International Society of Nephrology; Scientific Advisory Panel, Ciba Foundation; WHO Scientific Adviser, Panel on Professional Manpower Development. *Publications:* High Blood Pressure in the African, 1972; Priorities in National Health Planning, Edited Proceedings of an international symposium, 1974; Cardiovascular Disease in Africa, Edited Proceedings of the first All-Africa Cardiovascular Symposium, 1976; Various papers on Cardiovascular & Renal Diseases and medical education. *Honours:* Commander of the Noble Order of the Niger, 1979; Officer de l'Ordre National de la Republique de Cote d'Ivoire, 1981. *Hobbies:* Music; Gardening; Riding. *Address:* 17 Parry Road, University of Ibadan, Nigeria.

AKINMOLAYAN, Festus Oriola Oluwole, b. 16 Dec. 1935, Nigeria. Chartered Architect; Planning Consultant. m. Florence Olawoye, 15 Dec. 1962, 1 son, 3 daughters. *Education:* BSc, Honours Architecture, 1968, Diploma, Architecture, 1972, Northern Polytechnic, London, UK; Certificate in Building Technology, Yaba, Lagos, Nigeria, 1961. *Appointments:* Principal Partner, Oceanid Architects, Nigeria, a consulting firm of Architects, Engineers and Planners; Resident Partner, 'Oceanid International Consultants', a Co-partnership registered in Nigeria incorporating 'Oceanid Architects Nigeria,' the resident firm and 'Mayell Hart & Partners,' London, the Consultants. In association with Anderson and Anderson of Zambia and Botswana. *Memberships:* Royal Institute of British Architects; Incorporated Association of Architects and Surveyors; Nigeria Institute of Architects; Chartered Institute of Arbitrators; Architect Registration Council of Nigeria. *Creative Works:* Several Architectural & Planning Projects in Nigeria and Britain. *Hobbies:* Travelling; Reading; Writing. *Address:* PO Box 5695 Lagos, Nigeria.

AKINSANYA, Justus Akinbayo, b. 31 Dec. 1936, Lagos, Nigeria. Tutor. m. Cynthia Yolanda Marcelle, 6 May 1965, 3 sons, 1 daughter. *Education:* Crumpsall Hospital, Manchester, 1960-62; Treloar Hospital, Alton, Hants., 1963-64; Bristol Technical College, Bristol, 1966-68; Borough Polytechnic, London, 1969-71; Chelsea College, University of London, 1971-74, 1978-81; BSc; SRN; ONC; STD; BTA Cert; RNT; FRSH; FWACN. *Appointments:* Tutor, Mayday Hospital, Thornton Heath Surrey, England, 1971-74, King's College Teaching Hospital, London, 1974-75; Deputy Registrar (Education & Research), Nursing Council of Nigeria, 1975-78; Research Associate, Chelsea College, University of London, 1979-80; Lecturer, North East Surrey College of Technology, England, 1981. *Memberships:* Royal College of Nursing Research Society, London; Royal Society of Health, London; Foundation Fellow, West African College of Nursing. *Publications:* Human Biology for Nurses & Allied Professions, 1980; Microbiology, Health & Hygiene, 1980; Behavioural Sciences for Nurses (w. Prof. J C Hayward) forthcoming. *Honours:* Mary Girdlestone Memorial Prize, 1962; Lord Mayor Treloar Honours, 1964; Speaker of the Year, International Students Hostel, London, 1972; External Examiner, Nurses & Midwives Board, Sierra Leone, 1978-82. *Hobbies:* Debating; Writing; Travels; DIY; Tennis; Badminton. *Address:* 24 Croydon Road, Beddington, Croydon, Surrey, CRO 4PA, England.

AKINSEYE, Bamidele, b. 19 Mar. 1941, Ondo, Nigeria. University Administrator. m. Helen Aibinu Oyedepo,

17 Dec. 1967, 3 sons, 1 daughter. *Education:* Bachelor of Arts, Classics, University of Ibadan, Nigeria, 1966; Master of Public Administration, University of Ife, Nigeria, 1980. *Appointments:* Various Management positions including Acting General Manager, 1967-75; Assistant Registrar, 1975; Senior Assistant Registrar, 1976; Principal Assistant Registrar, 1978. *Memberships:* Finance Minister, Independence Hall, University of Ibadan, 1964; Secretary, Hoi Phrontistae, Classics Society, University of Ibadan, 1964; Editor, Student Christian Movement Magazine, University of Ibadan, 1964; Executive Secretary, University Booksellers Association of Nigeria, 1971-75; Dynamic Activities Club, Ikole-Ekiti, 1958-; British Instituto of Management, 1978; Nigerian Institute of Management, 1969. *Honours:* Western Nigeria Government Scholar, 1956-60; Various Secondary School Prizes, 1956-60; Various Higher School Prizes, Ibadan Grammar School, Ibadan, 1961-62; University of Ibadan Scholar, 1964-66; Various prizes , 1964, 65 and 66 including Sir James Robertson's Prize (Joint Winner) and Medal, 1966. *Hobbies:* Dancing; Photography. *Address:* 4 Pepple Road, University of Ibadan, Ibadan, Nigeria.

AKINSIKU, Fola, b. 14 Feb. 1948, Ondo, Nigeria. Pharmacist. m. Kehinde Keye Adetujoye, 4 Oct. 1980, 1 daughter. *Education:* General Diploma in Education, Federal City College, Washington DC, USA, 1972; BSc., cum laude in Pharmacy, Howard University, Washington, DC., USA., 1976. *Appointments:* Pharmacist, Pfizer Products (Nigeria) Limited, 1977; Branch Manager, Ikoyi, Juli Pharmacy and Stores Limited, Dresa, Lagos, Nigeria, 1978-81; Medical Representative, Boehringer Ingelheim, Lagos State, Nigeria, 1981-. *Memberships:* Rho Chi Pharmaceutical Honor Society, 1976; American Pharmaceutical Association, 1975; Treasurer, 1975, Vice-President, 1976, Nigerian Student Pharmaceutical Society; Pharmaceutical Society of Nigeria, 1977; Nigerian Association of General Practice Pharmacists, 1980. *Publications:* The Use of Antibiotics in Renal Disease, 1976; The Organization and Administration of Pfizer Pharmaceutical production plant in Oregun, Nigeria, 1977. *Hobbies:* Table tennis; Lawn tennis; Reading; Movies. *Address:* 41 Olufemi Peters Street, Ire-Akari Estate, Isolo, Lagos, Nigeria.

AKINWUNMI, Idowu, b. 10 Aug. 1943, Igede Ekiti. Accountancy. m. 6 June 1970, 3 daughters. *Education:* Diploma in Accountancy. *Appointments:* Accounts Officer, 1966, Assistant Accountant, 1972, Oxford Press; Accountant, 1975, Chief Accountant, 1981, Memco Steel Co. Limited, Nigeria. *Hobby:* Table tennis. *Address:* SW8/1884 Anfani Road, off Rind Road, Ibadan, Nigeria.

AKIRI, Chris William Amahwe, b. 3 Sept. 1947, Kokori-Inland, Bendel State, Nigeria. Management Consultant. m. Cecilia Erekahwevwe, 24 Dec. 1973, 1 son, 4 daughters. *Education:* BA.(Hons.), Ibadan, Nigeria, 1972; Certificate in Human Resources Project Appraisal, Bradford, UK, 1975; Certificate in Management Consultancy, Urwick Management Centre, Urwick, UK, 1977. *Appointments:* Teacher, St. Peter's Catholic School, Esa-Oke, 1964-67; Techer, Esa-Oke Community Grammar School, 1968-69; Lecturer, Planning and Development Division, Federal Ministry of Education, Lagos, June 1972—Dec. 1972; Lecturer, Federal Government College, Maiduguri, Borno State, 1973-74; Project Co-ordinator, IDA/IBRD Education Projects in Nigeria, 1974-77; Administrative Officer, Management Services Department, Federal Ministry of Establishments, Lagos, May 1977—Aug. 1977; Company Secretary, Western Textile Mills Limited, Lagos, Nigeria, 1977-. *Memberships:* British Institute of Management. *Publications:* Essays in African and European History, (unpublished); The British Imperial Factor and African Nationalist Development in South Africa: 1871-1931, (unpublished); Editor, 'Zikmag', an Ibadan University journal. *Hobby:* Reading. *Address:* 3 Ololade Odeyemi Close, Anthony Village, Lagos, Nigeria.

AKKERMANS, Charles Henry, b. 23 Jul. 1935, Munich, West Germany. Ophthalmologist. m. Maureen Joan Carroll, 6 Feb. 1960, 2 sons, 1 daughter. *Education:* Bachelor of Medicine and Bachelor of Surgery, University of Adelaide, Australia, 1959; Diploma in Ophthalmology, University of Sydney, Australia, 1963. *Appointments:* Private practice as an ophthalmologist, 1963-; Consultant Ophthalmologist to Royal Australian

Air Force, 1963-; Visiting Ophthalmologist to Royal Adelaide Hospital, Glenside Mental Hospital, Port Lincoln Hospital, 1963-70; Consultant Ophthalmologist, Adelaide Children's Hospital, 1963-; Chairman, Department of Ophthalmology, Adelaide Children's Hospital, 1981. *Memberships:* Australian College of Ophthalmologists, 1969; Fellow, Royal Australian College of Ophthalmologists, 1978; Aviation Medical Society of Australia and New Zealand; Sturt Football Club. *Publications:* Publication in British Journal of Ophthalmology, 1979. *Honours:* Adelaide University Football 'Blue', 1955; Shorney Medal, Adelaide University, 1958. *Hobbies:* Music; Sport; Reading; Short wave radio; Netherlands and early Australian history. *Address:* 9 Grenache Avenue, Wattle Park, South Australia 5066.

AKMEEMANA, A.D.D, b. 30 Sept. 1942, Sri Lanka. Accountant. m. Anoma Priyanwada , 31 Jan. 1971, 1 son, 1 daughter. *Education:* BA, Ceylon Peradeniya, 1965; Diploma, Management Process and Organisational Behaviou, 1974. *Appointments:* Accountant, Lanka Salu Sala, 1971-73; Finance Officer, Peoples Bank, 1973-75; Management Accountant, Bank of Ceylon, 1975-76; Research Associate, National Institute of Management, 1976-77; Visiting Lecturer, 1974-78, Lecturer, Head of Dept., University of Sri Lanka, 1977-78; Accountant, University of Zambia, 1978-79; Chief Internal Auditor, Zambia Electricity Supply Corporation, 1979-. *Memberships:* Institute of Cost and Management Accountants, 1975; Institute of Chartered Accountants of Sri Lanka, 1977; Chairman, Finance Committee of International Management Club. *Publications:* Contributed article Financial System in Sri Lanka to Bankers Handbook for Asia published in Hong Kong, 1976. *Honours:* Scholarship holder of the Institute of Chartered Accountants of Sri Lanka. *Hobbies:* Tennis; Photography. *Address:* Mahara, Kadawata, Sri Lanka.

AKO, Aaron Osuman, b. 22 Mar. 1941, Etteh, Nigeria. Economist; General Manager. m. Deborah, 31 May 1969, 2 sons, 1 daughter. *Education:* Diploma in Social Administration, London School of Economics, UK, 1965; BSc., Social Sciences, University of Southampton, UK, 1968; MA. (Econs.), Dalhousie University, Halifax, Canada, 1970; Diploma, Banking and Finance, Manchester Business School, UK, 1978. *Appointments:* Lecturer, Grade 1, Kaduna Polytechnic, Nigeria, 1971; Senior Marketing Officer, Nigerian Livestock and M. Authority, 1972; Senior Investment Executive, NNDC Limited, Kaduna, Nigeria, 1976; Coordinator, Benue Investment Co. Limited, Nigeria, 1980. *Memberships:* National Treasurer, Katsina-Ala Old Boys Association; Kaduna Club; Makurdi Club; Chairman, Benue State Volley Ball Association, 1981; Chairman, Makurdi Zonal Sports Committee, 1981. *Hobbies:* Football; Photography; Travelling; Stock Exchange Trends; Current Affairs; Radio and TV. Commentator & Critic; Crusader for Social Justice and Boundary Adjustment. *Address:* No. 1 Ogiri Oko Crescent, GRA Makurdi, Benue State, Nigeria.

AKPABIO, Monde Joseph, b. 3 May 1937, Efa Iman, Cross River State, Nigeria. Architect. m. 1 son, 6 daughters. *Education:* B. Arch., Ahmadu Bello University, Zaria, Nigeria, 1965; Diploma Housing Policy & Administration, Boucentrum, Rotterdam, Holland, 1969. *Appointments:* Architect, Federal Ministry of Works Lagos, 1965-74; Chief Architect, Ministry of Works, Calabar, 1975-. *Memberships:* Nigerian Institute of Architects; Architects Registration Council of Nigeria. *Publications:* Several newspaper articles on Housing and Social problems. *Honours:* Winner of British Council 'Writing for the Young' Competition, 1969,. The entry was a story entitled: 'The Trip to Atlantic'. *Hobbies:* Reading; Photography; Philosophy; Writing. *Address:* B6 Housing Estate, PO Box 752, Calabar, Nigeria.

AKPABOT, Samuel Ekpe, b. 3 Oct. 1932 Etinan, Cross River State, Nigeria. Musicologist/Composer/Educationist. m. Beatrice Dalmedida 10 Jan. 1962, 3 sons. *Education:* MA University of Chicago, 1967; PhD, Michigan State University, 1975; FTCL, Music Research, London, 1967; ARCM, 1957; LTCL 1959. *Appointments:* Senior Music Producer, Nigerian Broadcasting Corporation, 1959-62; Lecturer in Music, University of Nigeria, Nsukka, 1967-70; Senior Research Fellow, University of Ife, Nigeria 1970-73; Visiting Scholar and Artist in Residence, Michigan State University 1973-

75; Associate Professor and Chairman Division of Arts, College of Education Uyo, Nigeria 1975-79; Visiting Scholar and Professor of Music, University of Ibadan, 1980-. *Memberships:* Royal College of Organists, 1958; Fellow and Publicity Secretary, Society of Nigerian Broadcasters, 1980; Society for Ethnomusicology; Songwriters Guild; African Studies Association, USA; International Folk Music Council. *Publications:* Ibibio Music in Nigerian Culture, 1975; Foundations of Nigerian Traditional Music; Many articles in Learned Journals, example African Music; Bulletin of International African Institute; African Arts; Presence Africaine; Cantata: Verba Christi (Soloists, chorus, orchestra); Orchestral works: Overture for a Nigerian Ballet; Nigeria in Conflict Scenes from Nigeria; Cynthia's Lament; Three Nigerian Dances. *Honours:* Exhibitioner, Royal College of Music London, 1959; First Prize, Cannes Film Festival for Commercial Jingle for Barclay's Bank, 1956; First Prize (Composition) organized by UCLA for 41 African Countries, 1972; Participating Conductor, 4th International Choral Festival, Lincoln Centre, NY, 1974; Orchestral Music Commissioned by Symphony Orchestra American Wind, 1963, 1965, 1973; Sports Editor, Daily Times, Lagos, 1952; Orchestral and Choral works performed by: BBC Welsh Orchestra, Commonwealth Arts Festival, 1965; Chicago Chamber Orchestra, 1974; Church of the Holy Sepulchre, St. Louis Mississippi, 1975. *Hobbies:* Watching human behaviour; Athletics; Boxing; Sportswriting for Nigerian National Dailies. *Address:* "Music Villa", Press Road, Etinan, Cross River State, Nigeria.

AKWIWU, Emanuel Chikere, b. 23 July 1924 Port, Harcourt, Nigeria. Solicitor and Advocate. m. Joy Nkechinyere 5 June 1952, 4 sons, 3 daughters. *Education:* MA (Econs), LLB, Fitzwilliam College, Cambridge, 1945-50; Grays Inn, London 1950-51. *Appointments:* Legal Practice 1951-; Director, Nigerian Ports Authority 1954-59; Chairman, Golden Guinea Breweries Limited 1977-79; Director, Nigerian Services of Supply Company Limited 1962-; Vice-Chairman, Delattre Bezons Nigeria Limited 1978-; Director, Profield Nigeria Limited 1980-; Director, Agricultural Development Board 1970-75. Chairman and Managing Director, Akwiwu Motors Ltd., ECA Enterprises (Nig.) Ltd., ECA Kranzielder (Nig.) Ltd., Eman Akwiwu & Sons Ltd., *Memberships:* Patron Sports Clubs Imo St Anambra States; Recreation Club, ABA; Island Club, Lagos; Metropolitan Club, Lagos. *Creative Works:* Music; Organ; Piano. *Honours:* Deputy Speaker, Federal House of Representives 1960-64. *Hobbies:* Billiards; Golfing; Debating. *Address:* 1-2 Umuahim Avenue, GRA, PmB 7188, ABA, in Nkwerre Isu L.G.A., Imo State, Nigeria.

ALA, Alireza Parviz, b. 19 July 1932, Teheran, Iran. Consultant Physician. m. 15 Sept. 1966, 1 son. *Education:* Doctor of Medicine, University of Geneva, Medical School, Switzerland, 1958. *Appointments:* Associate Professor, Internal Medicine in Charge of The Cardiology Division, 1978; Consultant Physician, to the Western Health Board, Northern Ireland 1978-. *Memberships:* British Medical Association; Fellow, American College of Cardiology; International Society of Cardiology; Sloane Club, London; Founder and Master Lodge Saebe, Iran. *Publications:* Research into rheumatic Fever and rheumatic endoeanditis; Several articles published on the subject. *Honours:* Fellowship of the Central Treaty Organisation, 1962. *Hobbies:* Raading and writing. *Address:* 3 Hazelwood Omagh, Co. Tyrone, N. Ireland.

ALABA, Isaac Olugboyega, b. 19 May 1945 Igangan. Teaching. m. 9 Sept. 1976, 1 son, 2 daughters. *Education:* Teacher's Grade II Certificate 1968; GCE, DL, Six Subjects, 1969-70; GCE Three Subjects 1970-71; BA Hons, Yoruba Upper Second, Unilagos, 1974; MA, Linguistics, Unibadan, 1978. *Appointments:* Pupil Teacher, Methodist Mission Ibarapa, 1963; Class Teacher, Egba Local Schools Board Abeskuta, 1969-71; Form Master, House Master NYSC, Government Secondary School, Gusau, 1974-75; Graduate Assistant, Yoruba, Unilag, 1975-76; Assistant Lecturer, Yoruba, Unilag, 1976-78; Lecturer Grade II, Yoruba, Unilag, 1978-81; Lecturer Grade I Yoruba, Unilag, 1981-. *Memberships:* West African Linguistic Society; Yoruba Studies Association of Nigeria; Nigeria Folklore Society; Egbe Ijinle, Yoruba; Vice President, Igangan Development Association, Lagos; Nigerian Folk Dancing Club; Patron, Egbe Akeko Ijinle Yoruba. *Publications:* Amúmóra and Ilu Egàn Dà?; The Study of Individ-

ual African Oral Poets: The Example of Múrànà Alàbi; Virtue is Knowledge: Illustrations from Yoruba Life and Thought; Natural Versus Artificial Translation: A Case for Folk Etimology; Akojopo Orin Múrànà. *Honours:* National Award Covering University Tuition Boarding and book fees 1972-74 in honour of one of the best two results in the Faculty of Arts Degree Part I exams, 1972. *Hobbies:* Gardening; Reading for pleasure; Listening to music. *Address:* Alaagbaa Compound, Igitele, Igangan, Ibarapa Division, Qyo State, Nigeria.

ALADE, Isaac Fola, b. 24 Nov. 1933, Aramoko, Ekiti, Nigeria. Chartered Architect. m. (1) Yeeuni Alade (dec.) (2) Yinka Arogbonlo 30 Nov. 1980, 3 sons, 2 daughters. *Education:* Cambridge School Certificate, Nigerian College of Arts, Science and Technology, 1954-56, Preprofessional; Abmadu Bello University 1957-61; Diploma Architecture, Architect Association School of Tropical Studies, London, 1964-65; Post Graduate Certificate, 1964. *Appointments:* Architect, Western State government of Nigeria, Ibadan, 1961-67; City Architect to Lagos City Council, 1967-8; Principal Architect, 1968-72, Chief Project Architect, Federal Ministry of Works, Lagos, 1972-75; Director, Public Buildings, Federal Government, 1975-76; Permanent Secretary, Special Duties, 1976-79; Established, Fola Alade Group Practice, 1979-. *Memberships:* ARIBA; Nigerian Institute of Architects; Architects Registration Council of Nigeria; Commonwealth Association of Architects; Ikoyi Club of Lagos; Club Arcade of Nigeria; Royal Society of Health. *Creative Works:* The National Remèmbrance Arcades, Tajava Balawa Square, Lagos; Designed: Federal Special Court House, Vic. Island, Lagos; Federal Secretariat in State Capitals; Ministry of External Affairs, Marina, Lagos; National Institute of Policy and Strategic Studies; Nigerian Embassies in Cotonou, Alsijan, Bonn, Brazilia, Monoria, Dakar, Washington, Rome, Delhi, Islamabad etc.; Projects in respect of which publications were made by me. *Honours:* Atlas Award for Best student academic performance, 1958; Honoured as Man-of-the-Year 1978; National Honours: Officer of the Federal Republic of Nigeria, 1979; Chieftaincy title of Mayegum of Aramoko Ekiti, 1979; Chieftaincy title of Sobalojug Ido Faboro, 1980. *Hobbies:* Community Development Project in rural areas; Tennis; Swimming; Squash Racket; Golf; Cricket; etc.; Research into the Structures and history of Traditional Architecture; Gardening and Game-hunting. *Address:* 7081 Finbarr's College Road, Okoka, Yaba, Lagos, Nigeria.

ALAGOA, Ebiegberi Joe, b. 14 Apr. 1933 Nembe, Rivers State, Nigeria. Professor of History. 1 son. *Education:* Government College, Umuahia, 1948-54; BA, Honours History, University College, Ibadan, 1954-59; PhD History, University of Wisconsin, Madison, USA, 1962-65; Certificate in Archives Administration, American University, Washington DC, 1960. *Appointments:* ArchivistSenior Archivist, National Archives of Nigeria, 1959-62; Lecturer in History, University of Lagos, 1965-66; Senior Research Fellow, Institute of African Studies University of Ibadan, 1966-72; Professor of History, Director, Centre for Cultural Studies, University of Lagos, 1972-77; Professor of History, Dean, School of Humanties, University of Port Harcourt, 1977-80; Deputy Vice-Chancellor, University of Port Harcourt, 1980-. *Memberships:* President, Historical Society of Nigeria, 1981-; Council, Historical Society of Nigeria; International African Institute, London. *Publications:* A History of the Niger Delta, 1972; A Chronicle of Grand Bonny, 1972; The Small Brave City-State, 1964. *Honours:* College Scholar, University of London, 1956; History Prize, 1959; Carnegie Fellowship, University of Wisconsin, 1962-65. *Hobbies:* Swimming; Photography; Sound Recording. *Address:* Tombi, Nembe, Rivers State, Nigeria.

ALAKIJA, Tejumade, b. 17 May 1925, Ile-Ife, Nigeria. Chief Executive. 2 daughters. *Education:* BA.(Hons.) History, Westfield College, University of London, UK, 1946-50; Diploma in Education, Oxford University, UK, 1950-51. *Appointments:* Graduate teacher, 1951-53; Founder/Principal, Ijebu-Ode Girls Grammar School, 1953-56; Teacher, Abeokuta Grammar School, 1956-57; Served in different capacities in Civil Service, 1958-59; Permanent Secretary, Western State Civil Service and Oyo State Civil Service, 1975-79; Head of Service of Oyo State, Nigeria Civil Service, 1980-. *Memberships:* YWCA; University Woman Society; Historical Society of Nigeria. *Honours:* MFR., 1980. *Hob-*

bies: Reading; Gardening. *Address:* Quarter 1065, Humani Alaga Close, Onikoko Avenue, Agodi, Ibadan, Oyo State of Nigeria.

ALATISE, Alhaji Sikiru Olatunji, b. 4 Nov. 1937, Ojebu-Ode, Ogun State, Nigeria. Company Director. m. Oluyemisi Oyenuga, 15 May 1972, 2 sons, 3 daughters. *Education:* University education, Fourah Bay College, Sierra Leone, 1957-61; BA., Durham University, UK, 1961. *Appointments:* Sales Manager, Shell Company of Nigeria Limited, 1961-67; Sales Administration Manager, 1967-69, Direct Consumer Contact Manager, 1969-72, General Sales Manager, 1972-76, Sales Director, 1977-, Lever brothers Nigeria Limited. *Memberships.* Rotary Club of Lagos. *Hobbies:* Swimming; Table tennis. *Address:* 2B Badagry Road, Apapa, Lagos, Nigeria.

ALA-UD-DIN, Sahibzada, b. 18 Apr. 1933, Murshidabad, West Bengal, India. International Management Consultant. m. 12 Feb. 1971, 1 son, 1 daughter. *Education:* BComm, Dacca University, Bangladesh, 1952; MComm, 1954; Associate, Institute of Bankers, Pakistan, 1958; MSc, University of St. Andrews, Scotland, 1967-68; LLB, Blackstone School of Law, Chicago, USA, 1973-76; Doctor Juris, Thomas Jefferson College, California, 1980-81; As Associate, Faculty of Secretaries, England, 1977; Associate, British Association of Accountants & Auditors, 1976; Fellow, Institute of Management Accountants, Eire, 1977; Fellow, British Institute of Management, 1978; Associate, Irish Institute of Secretaries, 1980; Post-graduate Research Scholar, University of Oxford, 1968-69. *Appointments:* Lecturer in Economics, Sir Salimullah College, Dacca, 1954-55; Officer, State Bank of Pakistan, Dacca, 1955-60; Pakistan Government Scholar for Training in Banking in Westminster Bank, London, 1956-57; President, Pakistan Institute of International Affairs, UK, 1958-69; President, Afro-Asian Society Council of Immigrants' Welfare Service, 1969-; Founder, President, Travellers' Aid Centre, UK and National Charity; Director and General Secretary, Association of Business Managers and Administrators Limited by Guarantee; Founder leader of Political Party in Bangladesh; Bangladesh Patriotic Front. *Statuatory Positions:* Many held under HM Government, local Authorities and statuatory bodies: Local Valuation Court, Greater Manchester, 1976-82; Transport Users' Consultative Committee, North West, 1977-83; Passenger Transport Executive Advisory Committee, Greater Manchester, 1978-82; The University Court, University of Salford, 1980-85; Post Offices & Telecommunication Advisory Committee of the Electricity Consultative Council North West, 1981-83; Central Manchester Health Authority, 1981-83; The Central Community Health Council, Manchester, 1978-80; Supplementary Benefit Appeal Tribunal, Manchester, 1977-79. Fought unsuccessfully Central Constituency Manchester By- Election 1979, Independent Labour Parliamentary Candidate; Director, Secretary & Financial Advisor to numerous companies; Political Advisor, Manipur Minorities in Bangladesh; Ex-President, The Bangladesh Association, Oxford, 1970-76. Participated in liberation movement of Bangladesh. Numerous memberships of societies and charitable associations. *Hobbies:* Charitable and Social work; Travel; Football; Badminton; Rambling. *Address:* 23 Sunnybank Road, Longsight, Manchester, MI3O OXF, England.

ALA-UD-DIN, Tahmina, (Mrs.), b. 31 Dec. 1945, Pirojpur, Bangladesh. Sociologist; Housewife. m. 12 Feb. 1971, 1 son, 1 daughter. *Education:* BA(Hons), 1971, MA, Sociology, 1974, Dacca University; Member, Institute of Social Welfare, 1973; Diploma in Community Development, Manchester University, 1980-81. *Appointments:* Project Director, Training of Asian Women, 1978-79; Director, Asian Aid and Advisory Service, Manchester, and Asian Women and Children's Welfare Advisory Service, Manchester; General Secretary (Administration), Afro-Asian Society, Manchester, 1972-. *Memberships:* Social Services Government Committee, Manchester Council for Community Relations, 1978-79; Asian Battered Wives Unit, Manchester, 1978-79; Executive Committee, The Bangladesh Women's and Children's Project, 1978-81; Vice-Chairman, National Society for Prevention of Cruelty to Children, Longsight Branch, Manchester; Vice-Chairman, Travellers Aid Centre, (National charity); Active in the liberation movement of Bangladesh. *Publications:* The Bangladesh Women in Manchester, (in

Press). *Honours:* Hon. President, The Bangladesh Family Welfare Association (UK), 1976. *Hobbies:* Travel; Social Work; Reading. *Address:* 23 Sunnybank Road, Manchester MI3 OXF, England.

ALBINO-deCOTEAU, Merle, b. 29 June 1937, P.O.S. Trinidad. Teacher. 1 son. *Education:* Cambridge School Certificate, 1953-54; Trained Teachers' Diploma, 1963; Associate Teachers' Diploma, 1973; Licentate, Trinity College of Music, London, 1975. *Memberships:* Committee, Trinidad & Tobago Music Festival Association; Secretary, Trinidad & Tobago, Music Teachers' Association; Organist, St. Dominic Church Choir; Arranger, Musical Director, Talent Steel Orchestra. *Publications:* Own Musical Compositions: Summer '74; Happiness. *Hobbies:* Arranging Tunes for Steel Orchestras; Designing Ladies' Garments. *Address:* 206 Eastern Main Road, Laventille, Trinidad, West Indes.

ALBURY, Basil Hugh, b. 21 Jan. 1942, San Salvador, Bahamas. General Manager, Development & Europe. m. Cheryl AP Thompson, 31 Aug. 1968, 2 daughters. *Education:* Grade 1, Cambridge Certificate, St. FX University, Nova Scotia, Canada, 1959-61; BSc., Biology, St. Meinrad Seminary College, Indiana, USA, 1961-63; M.Ed., Administration, University of Toronto, Canada, 1968-70; Diploma, International Centre for Advanced Tourism Studies, Milan, Italy, 1972; MBA., University of Miami, USA, 1979-81. *Appointments:* Teacher, Government High School, Nassau, Bahamas, 1965-70; Assistant Secretary to the Cabinet, Bahamas Government, 1970-71; Assistant Director of Tourism, 1974-76, Deputy Director of Tourism, 1974-76, General Manager, Development, 1976-78, General Manager, Development and Europe, 1978-, Ministry of Tourism, Nassau, Bahamas. *Memberships:* American Society of Travel Agents; German-Bahamian Society; Chairman, Masquerade Committee, 1973-; Chairman, Advisory Development Council to St. Martin's Convent; Rotary Club; Executive Committee, Bahamas National Trust. *Hobbies:* Travel; Reading; Gardening; Swimming. *Address:* 'Sanctuary', Yamacraw Hill Road, PO Box 5860SS, Nassau, Bahamas.

ALDERTON, Robert Bozon, b. 19 Apr. 1919, Sydney, Australia. Surveyor. *Education:* Diploma, Civil Engineering, 1947. *Appointments:* Partner, 1947-81, Consultant, 1981-, PW Rygate & West, Surveyors, Sydney, Australia. *Memberships:* Past President, Institution of Surveyors, Australia Australian Institute of Cartographers; Director, 1975-77, Rotary Club of Sydney; The Sydney Club; Vice-President, 1979-80, Senior Vice President, 1980-81, West Lindfield Bowling Club. *Address:* 17/197 Pacific Highway, Lindfield, Australia 2070.

ALDINGTON, (Lord) Toby (Austin Richard William) Low, b. 25 May 1914 London. Banker/Industrialist. m. Araminta Machmichael 10 May 1947, 1 son, 2 daughters. *Education:* Winchester College; BA, New College, Oxford, 1936; Bar Middle Temple 1939. *Appointments:* Chairman Grindlays Bank, 1964-76; Chairman Port of London Authority, 1971-77; Chairman, Jt. Special Committee on Ports Industry, 1972; Chairman National Nuclear Corporation, 1973-80; Present Chairman Sun Alliance and London Insurance Limited; Westland Aircraft Limited; Dep. Chairman GEC Limited; Director Lloyds Bank Limited; Director Citicorp (USA). *Memberships:* Carlton Club; Chairman of Committee of Management, Institute of Neurology, 1962-80; Chairman BBC General Advisory Council, 1971-78. *Honours:* TD and Clasp 1950; PC 1954; KCMG 1957; CBE 1945; DSO 1941 Croix de guerre arec palmes, Commander of Legion of Merit (USA) D.L of Kent. *Hobby:* Golf. *Address:* Knoll Farm, Aldington, Ashford, Kent, England.

ALDISS, Brian Wilson, b. 18 Aug. 1925, East Dereham, Norfolk, UK. Writer & Critic. m. Margaret Manson, 11 Dec. 1965, 2 sons, 2 daughters. *Education:* West Buckland School, 1939-43. *Appointments:* Bookseller, 1948-56; Literary Editor, Oxford Mail, 1957-69. *Memberships:* Chairman, Society of Authors, 1977-78; Literary Panel, Arts Council, 1978-80; Past President, British Science Fiction Association; SF Writers of America; SF Research Association; World SF, Founder Member, British Trustee. *Publications:* Novels including: The Brightfount Diaries; Non-Stop; Male Response; The Primal Urge; Hothouse; Dark Light Years; Greybeard; Earthworks; The Eighty-Minute Hour; The Malacia Tapestry; Life in the West, 1980; Moreau's

Other Island, 1980; Helliconia, Spring 1982. Non-Fiction: Cities & Stones; The Shape of Further Things; Billion Year Spree; Science Fiction Art. *Honours:* Hugo Award, 1962; Nebula Award, 1965; Special BSFA Award, 1964; BSFA Award, 1972; DITMAR Award, 1970; Eurocon III Award, 1976; James Blish Award, 1977; Ferara Silver Comet, 1977; Prix Jules Verne, 1977; SFRA Pilgrim Award, 1978. *Hobby:* Travel. *Address:* 16 Moreton Road, Oxford, OX2 74X, England.

ALDOUS, Alice Mabel (Mrs), b. 13 Nov. 1902, Balcombe, Sussex. Public Service. m. Samuel Aldous, Jan. 1925, 2 sons, 1 daughter (dec). *Education:* Haywards Heath College for Pupil Teachers, 1914-19. *Appointments:* Public Service, 1917-20; Emigrated to Australia, 1920; Radio Singer; Hospital & Welfare Charity Work; War Office, interviewer in Man Power; Sunday Night Concerts at Air Force House, concert parties to various camps. *Honours:* MBE, 1971; Medal of St Kilda. *Address:* 6/88 Ailand Street, St Kilda, Victoria, Australia.

ALEXANDER, Kenneth John Wilson (Sir), b. 14 Mar. 1922. Economist. m. Angela May Lane, 24 Sept. 1949, 1 son, 4 daughters. *Education:* Diploma in Rublic Administration, School of Economics, Dundee; BSc, Economics, University of London. *Appointments:* Research Assistant, University of Leeds, 1949-51; Lecturer, University of Sheffield, 1951-57; Lecturer, University of Aberdeen, 1957-62; Professor of Economics, University of Strathclyde, 1962-76; Chairman, Highlands & Islands Development Board, 1976-81; Principal & Vice-Chancellor, University of Stirling, 1981-. *Memberships:* Fellow, Royal Society of Edinburgh; Executive Council, Scottish Council Development & Industry; President, Saltire Society; Council, Scottish Economic Society. *Publications:* The Economist in Business—Blackwells, 1967; Fairfields—A Study of Industrial Change—Allen Lane, 1970; The Political Economy of Change, 1975. *Honours:* Knight Bachelor, Hon LL.D CNAA, 1976; Hon.D University of Stirling, 1977; FBIM, 1977; CBIM, 1980. *Hobbies:* Sea Fishing; Scottish antiquarianism. *Address:* No 1 Airthrey Castle Yard, The University, Stirling, FK9 4LA, Scotland.

ALEXANDER-SINCLAIR, John Alexis Clifford Cerda. b. 22 Feb. 1906, Simla. India. Diplomatist, International Civil Servant. m. Maureen Wood Dover, 1965, 1 son, 2 daughters, (previous marriages). *Education:* Charterhouse, 1918-22; Göttingen and Munich Universities 1927-28; Foreign Service Examination 1928. *Appointments:* HM Foreign Service, Interpreter, Chinese, 1928. Served in 1929-43 as Vice-Consul, Consul, First Secretary of Embassy. Mentioned in Despatches (Admiralty) 1938; Founder and member of Chinese Industrial Co-operatives 1940-41; Liaison Free French in Far East 1941 (POW Shanghai 1942); British Embassy in Washington, 1st Sec. of Embassy, 1943; UNRRA, London and Paris 1944; CCG-Controller (Colonel) Economic Plans; UK delegation to UN NY 1946, 47, 48; Vice-Chairman UNICEF, UN/NY 1949-50; Director UN High Commissioner for Refugees Geneva, 1951-52; UN High Commissioner for Refugees, Rome (local Rank Minister). European Dir Int Rescue Cee. Seconded UN Technical Assistant. Thailand, Iran, Morocco (FAO). *Memberships:* Hansard Society for Parliamentary Reform 1944; Exec. Sec. Liberal International London 1963-64; Honorary Campaign Director UK Cee for Human Rights Year Founder and member of British Institute of Human Rights (Chairman and then Vice-Chairman 1939-73); Vice-Chairman Anti-Slavery Society 1971-; Secretary General British Group International League for Animal Rights; Royal Society of Miniature Painters Gravers and Scultors. *Creative Works:* Wood carvings, designed jewellery etc. *Honours:* Knight of Magistral Grace of the order of St John of Jerusalem Rhodes, Cyprus and Malta 1957; Distinguished Service Award International Rescue Cee NY 1959; Life Fellow R S. of Arts UK Cee of the Association Int.des Arts Plastiques Paris. *Hobbies:* $wood Carving, Designing Jewellery; Sports: Polo. *Address:* 5, Aysgarth Road, Dulwich Village, London, SE21. 7JR England.

ALI, Mohammad, b. 1 Dec. 1934, Chittagong, Bangladesh. University Teacher. m. Khaleda Hanum, 28 Apr. 1956, 1 son. *Education:* B.A. Honours in English, 1955; MA in English, University of Dacca, 1956; BA in English, 1961; MA in English University of Oxford, 1966. *Appointments:* Lecturer in English, 1958-62; Reader in

English, University of Rajshahi, Bangladesh, 1962-66; Associate Professor in English, 1966-72; Professor, University of Chittagong, Bangladesh, 1972-. *Publications:* Edited, a Critical edition of Thornton Wilder's play, The Skin of Our Teeth (in Bengali), 1978; Co-Editor, A Book of Modern English Essays, 1974; Co-Editor, A Selection of English Prose & Poetry for Higher Secondary Stage, 1968. *Honours:* Awarded & held Commonwealth Academic Staff Fellowship, University of Edinburgh, 1975-76. *Hobbies:* Music, Chess and Gardening. *Address:* 11 Rafiuddin Siddiqui Lane, Enayet Bazar, Chittagong.

ALI, Muhammad Ashraf, b. 1 Dec. 1930, Gabtali, Bogra District, Bangladesh. Teacher. m. Begum Faizun Nahar, 26 June 1952, 2 sons, 1 daughter. *Education:* Matriculation, Calcutta University, 1946-; Intermediate of Arts, 1948-; B.A. Honours in Statistics, 1951-; M.A. in Statistics, Dacca University, 1952-; PhD. in Statistics, Texas A & M University, 1966-. *Appointments:* Statistical Inspector, Bureau of Statistics, Government of East Pakistan, 1953-; Statistician, Pakistan Central Jute Committee, 1954-63; Associate Professor, 1966-72; Professor, Department of Agri. Statistics, Bangladesh Agri. University, 1973-. *Memberships:* Vice-President, Bangladesh Statistical Association; Former Member, American Statistical Association; Bangladesh Association for Advancement of Science; Bangladesh Agri. Economists Association. *Publications:* Three Text Books on Statistics for BSc. Honours and MSc Level courses; Ten Publications in different journals. *Hobby:* Football. *Address:* B/3 Agri. University, Campus, Mymensing, Bangladesh.

ALI, Muhammad Raushan, b. 18 May 1938, Jessore, Bangladesh. Teacher. m.Johora K, 21 Dec. 1957, 5 daughters. *Education:* Matriculation, Muslim Academy, Jessore, Bangladesh, 1954; I.A., Michael Madhusudan College, Jessore, 1956; B.A. University of Rajshahi, Bangladesh, 1958; M.A. (Psychology), University of Rajshahi, 1960; M.A. (Social Work), University of Dacca, 1963; PhD. (Psychology), University of London, 1967; Diploma in Arabic, University of Dacca, 1978.. *Appointments:* Headmaster, Hat Barobazar High School, Jessore, 1960-61; Senior Lecture, Psychology, University of Dacca, 1967-72; Associate Professor & Chairman, Psychology Department, 1972-78; Professor, Psychology, University of Dacca, 1978-; Lecturing in Industrial Psychology, University of Zambia on temporary assignment. *Memberships:* Fellow, British Psychological Society; Fellow, British Institute of Management; General Secretary, Bangladesh Psychological Association, 1972-78. *Publications:* Approximately 25 papers published in National & International journals; 4 books on Psychology. *Honours:* Director of Public Instructions Scholarship, 1956; The Government of East Pakistan Scholarship of higher studies abroad, 1963. *Hobbies:* Reading and gardening. *Address:* Department of Psychology, The University of Zambia, P.O. Box 32379, Lusaka, Zambia.

ALI, Wahid, b. 28 June 1928, Trinidad, West Indies. Medical Practitioner; President, Senate of the Republic of Trinidad & Tobago. m. Mariam Ibrahim 8 Aug. 1951, (Deceased Feb, 1972), 6 sons, 2 daughters. *Education:* Medical Board of Trinidad & Tobago; License of Pharmacist, 1950; University College of the West Indies (University of London) MB., BS., 1963. *Appointments:* Pharmacist (Private practice), 1951-56; Medical Officer, Hospital Practice, Government of Trinidad & Tobago, 1963-68; Private Medical Practice (Full-time 1968-70), (Part-time 1970); Senator on Government Benches, 1970; Senator and President of Senate, 1971and 1976. *Memberships:* Vice-President, Central Muslim Youth Organisation of Trinidad & Tobago; Former Chairman, National Youth Conference of Trinidad & Tobago; International Executive, World Assembly of Youth, 1954-58; Senior Vice-President, World Assembly of Youth, 1964-67; Former President, Guild of Undergraduates, University of West Indies, 1959-60; Former President, Regional Union of West Indian Students, 1961-62; Chairman, International Student Conference, (Switzerland), 1960; Chairman, International Student Conference (Canada), 1962; Observer from Guild of Undergraduates of University of the West Indies to World Youth Forum, Moscow, 1962; Pharmacy Board of Trinidad & Tobago 1968-70; Medical Board of Trinidad & Tobago; Queen's Park Cricket Club; Executive Committee, Secretary and Vice-President of Anjuman Sunnat-ul-Jammat Assocation Incorporated of

Trinidad & Tobago; President of Inter-religious Organisation of Trinidad & Tobago, 1971-74; People's National Movement. *Publications:* Founder and Editor of Trinidad Muslim Annual, 1950-55. *Honours:* First Recipient of Sir Thomas Taylor Award, by the Taylor Hall Society, University College of West Indies, 1959; Awarded Silver Medal for Surgery (Clinical Prize in final Examination), 1963; Awarded Trinity Cross, for distinguished service to Trinidad & Tobago in the sphere of Public Service, 1977; Awarded Gold Medal by VISHVA Hindu Parishad for Public Service, 1979. *Hobbies:* Cricket and Comparative Religion. *Address:* 15 Sweet Briar Road, St. Clair, Port of Spain

ALI KAWI, b. 12 June 1934, Kuching, Sarawak. Advocate. m. Fatimah Jamel, 8 Jan. 1956, 2 sons, 1 daughter. *Education:* Police Course, Hendon, England, 1961-, Police Course, Australian Police College, Sydney, 1967-, Barrister-at-Law, 1971-. *Appointments:* Assistant Commandant; Police Training School, Sarawak; Divisional Superintendent, Limbang; Superintendent, Finance, Sarawak; Head Crime Branch, Sarawak; Head Special Branch, Sarawak; Deputy Commissioner, Sarawak; Deputy Director, Management, I.G.P. Headquarters, Kuala Lumpur. *Memberships:* President, Parti Rakyat Jati, Sarawak, 1978-79. *Publications:* Police Handbook; Selected Ordinances (Sarawak) in Malay. *Honours:* Pegawai Bintang Sarawak; Pingkat Perhidmatan Cemerlang. *Hobbies:* Reading; Golf. *Address:* 22-A, Bampfylde Road, Kuching, Sarawak.

ALIMI, Shittu Olarewaju, b. 28 Feb. 1938, Ife-Olukotun (Oyi Lga), Kwara State of Nigeria. Librarian. m. Alimotu Bola Balogun, 15 Dec. 1967, 5 daughters. *Education:* B.A. Honours, Makerere University, Uganda, 1966; P.G. Diploma, Lib. University of Ibadan, Nigeria, 1967; Certificate of Attendance, British Council Course, 730, 1977; Library Planning Design, London and Birmingham. *Appointments:* First Graduate Librarian, North Regional Library, Kaduna, Nigeria, 1966-68; First State Librarian, Kano State Library, Kano, Nigeria, 1968-; First Librarian, Nigerian Civil Aviation Training Centre, Zaria, Nigeria, 1968-70; First Librarian, Kwara State College of Technology, Ilorin, Nigeria, 1972-77; College Librarian, Kwara State College of Technology, Ilorin, 1977-80; Chief Librarian, Kwara State College of Technology, Ilorin, 1980-. *Memberships:* Nigerian Library Association, Council Member, 1968-74, 1977-; Secretary-Treasurer, 1969-72, Editor, Special Libraries Association (NLA), Northern Nigeria Library Notes, 1969-70, Editorial Board, 1970-71, NLA Standing Committee on Salaries, Wages & Conditions of Service, 1970-71, NLA Committee on Legal Recognition, 1970-73, Unesco National Sub-Committee on University & College Library Statistics, 1973-, Chairman, Kwara State Branch, 1977-; Nigerian Book Development Council, 1978-; Steering Committee, International Board on Books for Young People; Current Affairs Society, Kwara State of Nigeria; General Secretary United Nations Students Association (Makerere Branch), 1964-65; Publicity Secretary, World University Service (Makerere Branch), 1964-65; Jama'Atu Nasril Islam Society of Nigeria; Muslim Council of Nigeria, Kwara State Branch; Red Cross Society of Nigeria; Nigerian Boy Scout Movement. *Publications:* Journalism in Nigeria with an Introductory Survey & Bibliography, 1967; Brief Survey & Bibliography of Nuclear Physics, 1967; Library Development & Bibliograpic Control in Eastern Africa, Contribution to Ogunsheye, F.A. Sources for African Studies, 1967; Conference: An Impression, South-East Yagba Past & Present, a brief Historial, Social & Economic Survey, Nigerian Herald, 1975. *Honours:* Usaid Scholar, 1963-66; College Exhibition Award, for All-round-undergraduate student, Makerere University, 1964-65. *Hobbies:* Mountaineering; Political Analyses and Current Affairs; Debating; Gardening; Museum Pieces Collection. *Address:* 10 New Market Road, Ife-Olukotunn Oyi LGA, Kwara State of Nigeria.

ALIMI, Shittu Olarewaju, b. 28 Feb. 1938, Ife-Olukotun (Oyi Lga), Kwara State of Nigeria. Librarian. m. Alimotu Bola Balogun, 15 Dec. 1967, 5 daughters. *Education:* B.A. Honours, Makerere University, Uganda, 1966; P.G. Diploma, Lib. University of Ibadan, Nigeria, 1967; Certificate of Attendance, British Council Course, 730, 1977; Library Planning Design, London and Birmingham. *Appointments:* First Graduate Librarian, North Regional Library, Kaduna, Nigeria, 1966-68; First State Librarian, Kano State Library, Kano, Nigeria, 1968-; First Librarian, Nigerian Civil Aviation Training Centre, Zaria, Nigeria, 1968-70; First Librarian, Kwara State College of Technology, Ilorin, Nigeria, 1972-77; College Librarian, Kwara State College of Technology, Ilorin, 1977-80; Chief Librarian, Kwara State College of . Technology, Ilorin, 1980-. *Memberships:* Nigerian Library Association, Council Member, 1968-74, 1977-, Secretary-Treasurer, 1969-72, Editor, 1969-70, Editorial Board, 1970-71, NLA Standing Committe on Salaries, Wages & Conditions of Service, 1970-71, NLA Committee on Legal Recognition, 1970-73, Unesco National Sub-Committee on University & College Library Statistics, 1973-, Chairman, Kwara State Branch, 1977-; Nigerian Book Development Council, 1978-; Steering Committee, International Board on Books for Young People; Current Affairs Society, Kwara State of Nigeria; General Secretary United Nations Students Association (Makerere Branch), 1964-65; Publicity Secretary, World University Service (Makerere Branch), 1964-65; Jama'Atu Nasril Islam Society of Nigeria; Muslim Council of Nigeria, Kwara State Branch; Red Cross Society of Nigeria; Nigerian Boy Scout Movement. *Publications:* Journalism in Nigeria with an Introductory Survey & Bibliography, 1967; Brief Survey & Bibliography of Nuclear Physics, 1967; Library Development & Bibliograpic Control in Eastern Africa, Contribution to Ogunsheye, F.A. Sources for African Studies, 1967; Conference Edition, Nigerian Library Association, 1970; South-East Yagba Past & Present, a brief Historial, Social & Economic Survey, Nigerian Herald, 1975. *Honours:* Usaid Scholar, 1963-66; College Exhibition Award, for All-round-undergraduate student, Makerere University, 1964-65. *Hobbies:* Mountaineering; Political Analyses and Current Affairs; Debating; Gardening; Museum Pieces Collection. *Address:* 10 New Market Road, Ife-Olukotunn Oyi Lga, Kwara State of Nigeria.

ALJEFFRI, Syed Amin, b. 10 Nov. 1947, Malaysia. Chartered Accountant. m. 14 Apr. 1979, 1 daughter. *Education:* Bachelor of Economic (Honours), Malaysia; Chartered Accountant, Canada. *Appointments:* Touche Ross & Co., Vancouver, B.C. Canada, Chartered Accountants, 1973-76; Hanafiah Raslan & Mohamad, Kuala Lumpur, Malaysia, Chartered Accountants, 1977-; Esso Malaysia Ltd., Kuala Lumpur, Malaysia, 1977-79; Esso Eastern Inc., Houston, TX., USA., 1979-80; Aljeffri, Siva, Heng & Company, Kuala Lumpur, Malaysia, Chartered Accountants, 1981-. *Address:* 67 Jalan Setiakaseh, Damansara Heights, Kuala Lumpur, Malaysia.

ALLAN, Colin Hamilton, b. 23 Oct. 1921, Wellington, New Zealand. H.M.O.C.S. (Retired). m. Betty Dorothy Evans, 29 Oct. 1955, 3 sons. *Education:* MA, New Zealand, 1945; Diploma of Anthropology (Cantab), 1950. *Appointments:* Various Appointments, Colonial Administrative Service, British Solomons, 1945-58; Assistant, 1959; BRC, New Hebrides, 1966; Governor & Commander in Chief Seychelles & Commissioner BIOT, 1973-76; Governor, Solomon Islands & HC for the Western Pacific, 1976-78. *Memberships:* Fellow, RAI; Royal Commonwealth Society. *Publications:* Various papers on Colonial Administration. *Honours:* OBE, 1959; Commandeur, l'Ordre Nationale du Mérite, France, 1966; CMG, 1968; KCMG, 1977. *Hobbies:* Reading the Financial Times & The Times. *Address:* Glen Rowan, 17 Sale Street, Howick, Auckland, New Zealand.

ALLBROOK, Edward Kenneth, (Deceased), b. 26 Nov. 1913, London, England. Parliamentary Counsel, Tasmania. m. Jean, 22 Mar. 1944, 1 son, 1 daughter. *Education:* Caterham Shool (for the sons of clergymen); BSc, Imperial College of Science, 1935; LLB, London School of Economics, 1939; Barrister, Grays Inn, 1946. *Appointments:* Legal Assistant, London County Council, 1934-57; Royal Air Force Voluntary Reserve, 1940-46; Solicitor, 1952; Second Assistant Parliamentary Draftsman, Tasmania, 1957; Parliamentary Counsel, 1973. *Memberships:* Tasmanian Secretary to Amnesty International. *Publications:* Instrumental in the writing of The Law of Town and Country Planning, J. R. Howard Roberts, 1948. *Hobbies:* Woodcarving, Bushwalking. *Address:* 512A Nelson Road, Mt. Nelson, Hobart, Tasmania, 7007 Australia.

ALLEN, Garry Kellar, b. 18 Mar. 1934, Sydney, Australia. Merchant Banker. m. Janet Caroline, 4 Nov. 1959, 2 daughters. *Education:* Balgowlah High School; Tamworth High School. *Appointments:* Bank of New South Wales, 1950-68; Partnership Pacific Limited, 1968-69; General Manager, Continental Development Corporation Ltd. (now Barclays Australia Ltd.), 1969-71; Managing Director, Transia Corporation Ltd., 1972-. *Memberships:* Australian Institute of Management; Securities Institute of Australia; Institute of Directors; Society of Senior Directors. *Honours:* Justice of the Peace; Senator; Junior Chamber International. *Hobbies:* Flying; Scuba Diving; Jet Skiing; Golf; Squash; Engineering. *Address:* 8/4 Mitchell Road, Darling Point, New South Wales.

ALLEN, Rudolph Theodore, b. 4 Oct. 1929, Georgetown, Guyana, South America. Teacher. m. Eulalie Undine, 12 Dec. 1956. *Education:* B.A. London, 1962; Diploma in Education, University of West Indies, 1966; Diploma of Geography, London, 1968; Diplôme D'Etudes Francaises, The Centre International d'Etudes, Francaises, Universite de Bordeaux, 1968; M.A. in Counsellor Education, Loma Linda University, California, 1981; Ontario Teacher's Certificate, Canada. *Appointments:* First teaching post at Wray High School, Georgetown, Guyana, 1948-53; Barbados S.D.A. Secondary School, 1953-57; Caribbean Union College, Trinidad, 1957-60; Graduate Master, St. Benedict's College, La Romaine, Trinidad, 1962-64; Hillview College, Tunapuna, Trinidad, 1964-65; Hillview College, 1966-69; Jarvis Collegiate, Toronto, Canada, 1970-71; New Liskeard Secondary School, Ontario, Canada, 1971-75, 1976-78; Cobalt Haileybury High School, 1978-80. *Memberships:* Scottish Association of Geography Teachers; Geographical Association, Sheffield, England. *Honours:* Diploma in Education Scholarship Mona Campus, Jamaica, 1965-66; Bourse du Centre International d'Etudes Francaises, 1968. *Hobby:* Travel. *Address:* 2737 Kipling Avenue «611, Rexdale, Ontario, Canada, M9V 4C3.

ALLEN, Thelma Olive (Mrs) (nee Stone), b. 5 June 1919, Melbourne, Victoria, Australia. Company Director. m. Christopher John Allen, 29 May 1937, 2 sons, 2 daughters. *Appointments:* 35 Years Design Development & Manufacture of Industrial & Leisure Protective Garments, Alsafe Industries Pty Ltd & Alston Safety Equipment Pty Ltd. *Memberships:* Former Vice-President, Beaumaris Childrens Hospital Committee; Former President, Moorabbin Lions Club Ladies Aux; Former President, Ladies Auxiliary of the Jan Juc Surf Lifesaving Club. *Hobbies:* Pottery; Porcelain Artistry. *Address:* 46 Wells Road, Beaumaris 3193, Victoria, Australia.

ALLENDER, Peter John, b. 15 Sept. 1927, Somerset, England. Materials Engineer. m. Marjorie Edith Tomkins, 6 Nov. 1955. *Education:* Birmingham Central Technical College, London Ext. BSc, Chemistry, 1948; London, PhD., 1954; Reading M.A. 1960. *Appointments:* Senior Metallurgist, BSA Group Research, 1948-54; Senior Research Metallurgist, James Booth Ltd., 1954-56; Research Manager, Homa Foundry Ltd., 1956-57; Materials Engineer, Metro-Cammell Ltd., 1958-. *Memberships:* Royal Geographical Society, Royal Society of Chemistry; Society of Company and Commercial Accountants; Institution of Metallurgists; Plastics and Rubber Institute; Club Royal Overseas. *Publications:* Various papers and articles on Materials Engineering and Technical Management Subjects; Editor, Railway Industry Association Firenotes. *Honours:* Brassworkers Bursary, 1943; Alfred Rosling Bennett Award, Institute Mechanical Engineers, 1980. *Hobbies:* Writing, Motoring, History. *Address:* 9 Jeremy Grove, Solihull, West Midlands, B92 8JH.

ALLES, Joseph Mohan, b. 17 Mar. 1949, Sri Lanka. Chartered Accountant. m. Chandi Panambalana, 22 Jan. 1977, 1 daughter. *Education:* St. Joseph's College, Colombo 10, Sri Lanka. *Appointments:* Ford, Rhodes, Thornton & Co., Sri Lanka, 1971-77; Coopers & Lybrand, Kitwe, Zambia, 1977-79; Press Group of Companies, Blantyre, Malawi, 1979-. *Memberships:* Treasurer, Institute of Cost and Management Accounts, Malawi Centre. *Hobbies:* Badminton & Squash. *Address:* c/o Press (Holdings) Ltd., Internal Audit Department, P.O. Box 682, Lilongwe, Malawi.

ALLEYNE, George Allanmoore Ogarren, b. 7 Oct. 1932, Barbados, West Indies. Physician. m. Sylvan l

Chen, 20 Dec. 1958, 2 sons, 1 daughter. *Education:* Harrison College, Barbados, 1944-51; MB BS, University College of West Indies, 1951-57; MRCP, London, 1962; FRCP, 1972; MD, London, 1965; FACP (Hon), 1975. *Appointments:* Senior Registrar, University of the West Indies, 1962-63; Research Fellow & Senior Research Fellow, Medical Research Council, Tropical Metabolism Research Unit, 1963-72; Professor of Medicine, University of West Indies, 1972-81; Chief, Research Promotion & Coordination, Pan American Health Organization, 1981-. *Memberships:* Royal Commonwealth Society; International Society of Nephrology; American Society of Nephrology; Past Chairman and President, University Guild of Graduate. *Publications:* Over 100 publications in scientific journals related to research in the fields of nutrition, rural medicine, renal biochemistry. *Honours:* Barbados Scholar (classics), 1950; University Silver & Gold Medals, 1957; Pelican Award of University of the West Indies, Guild of Graduate; Sir Arthur Sims Commonwealth Travelling Professor. *Hobby:* Reading. *Address:* 6308 Landon Lane, Bethesda, MD. 20817, USA.

ALLINSON, Leonard (Walter) Sir, b. 1 May 1926. HM Diplomatic Service. m. Margaret Patricia Watts, 1951, 3 daughters. *Education:* MA, Merton College, Oxford, 1947. Assistant Principal, Ministry of Fuel & Power, 1947-48; Principal, Ministry of Education, 1948-58; Assistant Private Secretary to Minister, 1953-54; Transferred CRO, 1958; First Secretary in Lahore and Karachi, 1960-62, Madras and New Delhi, 1963-66; Counsellor and Head of Political Affairs Department, 1968; Deputy Head later Head, of Permanent Under Secretary's Department, FCO, 1968-70; Counsellor and Head of Chancery, subsequently Deputy High Commissioner, Nairobi, 1970-73; RCDS, 1974; Diplomatic Service Inspectorate, 1975; Deputy High Commissioner and Minister, New Delhi, 1975-77; High Commissioner, Lusaka, 1978-80; Assistant Under Secretary of State (Africa), Foreign & Commonwealth Office, 1980-. *Memberships:* Travellers' Club; Nairobi Club; Ndola Club. *Honours:* MVO, 1961; CMG, 1976; KCVO, 1979. *Address:* c/o Foreign and Commonwealth Office, King Charles Street, London SW1, England.

ALLMAN, John Stuart, b. 27 Sept. 1929, Sydney, Australia. Academic. m. Betty Joy Watt, 3 sons, 3 daughters. *Education:* BSurv, 1962, PhD, 1968, University of New South Wales. *Appointments:* Royal Australian Survey Corps, 1950-54; The University of New South Wales, 1955-. *Memberships:* The Australian Institute of Cartographers; The Canadian Institute of Surveyors. *Publications:* Many publications in the fields of Geodesy and Surveying. *Hobbies:* Sailing; Beach Fishing. *Address:* 35 Bluegum Crescent, Frenchs Forest, Sydney 2086, Australia.

ALLSTON, Desmond Kenneth, b. 27 July 1922, Guernsey, Channel Islands. Company Director; Management Consultant. m. Irene Marjorie, 10 July 1948, 1 son, 1 daughter. *Education:* Southampton University, 1939-43; FlMechE; FlMarE; Professional Canadian Engineer (Retired); Fellow, British Institute of Management; Member, Institution of Management Consultants; Associate Member Institute of Brewing. *Appointments:* Marine Engineer Apprentice, JI Thornycroft & Co. Ltd., 1939-43; Merchant Navy Officer, Furness Withy Co. Ltd., 1943-50; Engineer, British Electricity Authority, 1950-52; Director & General Manager, Diesel Injection Ltd., 1952-58; Senior Management Consultant, Associated Industrial Consultants Ltd., 1958-65; Head of Managenment Services to Canadian Operations, Booker Brothers, McConnell Ltd., 1965-67; Independent Consultant, 1967-68; Executive Director, Commonwealth Industrial Gases Ltd., 1968-76; Managing Director, Barrett Burston (Aust) Ltd., 1976-80; Deputy Managing Director, Henry Jones (IXL) Ltd., 1980-81; Appointed one of three Commissioners by the Hamer Government to take over the responsibilities of the previous Melbourne City Council, 1981-. *Memberships:* The Australian Club. *Hobbies:* Poll Hereford Stud Breeding; Boating; Antique collecting. *Address:* Waterford Farm, Launching Place, Victoria 3139, Australia.

ALLY, Ariff I, b. 19 Sept. 1951, Georgetown, British Guiana. Medical Research Scientist. m. Verna Rae Bartlett, 8 Jan. 1981. *Education:* BSc., University Western Ontario, London, Ontario, Canada, 1973; MSc,

Queens University, Kingston, Ontario, Canada, 1976; PhD, McGill University, Montreal, Quebec, Canada, 1979. *Appointments:* Queens University, (Pharmacology), Canada, 1974-76; Clinical Research Institute'of Montreal, Canada, 1976-79; Henderson Cancer Clinic, McMaster University, Canada, Jan-Mar, 1980; National Institutes of Environmental Health Sciences, Research Triangle Park, North Carolina, USA, 1980-; National Research Council, Ottawa, Canada, 1981. *Memberships:* American Association for the Advancement of Science; Canadian Pharmacological Society; New York Academy of Science. *Publications:* Author of 32 papers including: Adenosine as a natural prostaglandin antagonist in vascular smooth muscle, 1977; Quinacrine is a prostaglandin antagonist, 1977; The roles of prostaglandins and calcium in muscular dystrophy, 1977; Effect of prostacyclin on heart rate and perfusion pressure in the isolated rat heart, 1977; Dantrolene blocks intracellular calcium release in smooth muscle: Competitive antagonism of thromboxane A2, 1978; Prostaglandins as second messengers of prolactin action, 1978; Ultraviolet radiation and inhibition of thromboxane synthesis have similar actions on vascular reactivity. Histidine blocks their effects, 1978; Thromboxane A2 in blood vessel walls and its physiological significance: Relevance to thrombosis and hypertension, 1980 Papers Contributed to: Bulletin de Physiopathologie Respiratoire, 1981; Pulmonary Toxicology, 1982; Prosaglandins and Arachidonate Metabolites, 1981. *Honours:* Eldon Boyd Fellowship in Pharmacology, 1975-76; RHODA Scholarship, 1975; Predoctoral Fellowship, IRCM, 1976-79; NIH Visiting Fellowship, 1980-; NRC Associateship, 1981. *Hobbies:* Reading; Science fiction; Photography; Travel. *Address:* 244 Glebemount Avenue, Toronto, M4C 3T6, Ontario, Canada

ALMEDA, Alexis Jesus George, b. 4 Aug. 1936, Gibraltar. Environmental Health Officer. m. Irene Fava, 4 May, 1962, 2 daughters. *Education:* Diploma, Public Health (Hons.), Royal Technical College, Salford, UK., 1958-60; Diploma, Public Health Inspection, Diploma, Food Hygiene, Royal Society of Health, London, UK.; Diploma, General Hygiene, Royal Institute of Public Health and Hygiene, London, UK. *Appointments:* Public Health Inspector, City Council of Gibraltar, 1960-71; Senior Public Health Inspector, 1971-74, Chief Environmental Health Officer and Superintendent of Markets, 1974-, Government of Gibraltar. *Memberships:* Vice Chairman, Gibraltar Rabies Committee; Member of the Board of Management, Medical and Health Department; Royal Society of Health; Institution of Environmental Health Officers; His Lordship the Roman Catholic Bishop's Diocesan Pastoral Council; The Gibraltar Horticultural Society; Calpe Rowing Club. *Honours:* Fellowship in Epidemiology and Surveillance of Communicable Diseases, World Health Organization, 1979. *Hobbies:* Gardening; Viticulture. *Address:* 37 Irish Town, Gibraltar.

ALUFANDIKA, Donny Ronald Damiton, b. 12 Feb. 1952, Lulwe, South West Nsanje District, Malawi. Lawyer. m. Stella D. Kaitano, 13 Dec. 1977, 1 son. *Education:* LLB, University of Malawi, 1977. *Appointments:* Acting Co-Secretary, Lilley, Wills & Co., Solicitors, 1977-81; Assistant Company Secretary, Capital City Development Corporation, 1981-. *Memberships:* Malawi Law Society; Geographical Society, University of Malawi. *Publications:* Substitute Love, 1974; Pangs of Love, 1976; A Promise is for Ever, 1979. *Creative Works:* Radio Plays: Wedding Sacrifice, 1977; On the Brink of Disintegration, 1977; A Step to Immortality, 1977; Beyond the Misty Horizon. 1981. *Hobbies:* Writing Plays; Reading Classics; Rhetoric; Football; Films. *Address:* Capital City Development Corporation, PO Box 30139, Capital City, Lilmgwe 3, Malawi.

ALUKO, Samuel Adepoju, b. 18 Aug. 1929, Ode Ekiti, Ondo State, Nigeria. Economist. m. Joyce Anomoghan Ofuya, 1954, 4 sons, 2 daughters. *Education:* BSc, Economics, 1954, MSc, Economics, 1957, PhD, Economics, 1959, London, UK. *Appointments:* Lecturer, Nigerian College of Arts, Science and Technology, 1959-62; Lecturer, University of Ife, Nigeria, 1962-64; Senior Lecturer/Associate Professor, University of Nigeria, NSukka, 1964-66; Professor of Economics, University of Ife, Nigeria, 1967-79; Economic Adviser, Ondo State Government, Akure, Nigeria, 1979-. *Memberships:* Nigerian Economic Society; International Institute of Public Finance; World Council of

Churches, Geneva; Unity Party of Nigeria. *Publications:* Planning and Growth in Nigeria, 1959; Economic Growth and World Perspective, 1966; Christianity and Communism: An Economic Analysis, 1964 and 1978; Several articles in Economic Journals. *Honours:* London University Scholar, London School of Economics, 1957-59. *Hobbies:* Lawn Tennis; Table Tennis. *Address:* Plot 17, Owo St, PO Box 1594, Akure, Ondo State, Nigeria.

ALUSI, Moses Kenechuku, b. 15 June 1930, Awka, Nigeria. Architect. m. (1) Yetunde, Aug. 1962, (2) Oby, 8 Apr. 1979, 4 sons, 2 daughters. *Education:* Diploma, Architecture, Birmingham School of Architecture, UK, 1956-58; Diploma, Town Planning, University of Manchester, Manchester, UK, 1959-61; Nigerian College of Arts Science and Technology, 1952-55; Municipal College, Southen-on-Sea, UK, 1955-56. *Appointments:* Federal Ministry of Works and Housing, Lagos, 1961-75; Self Employed, Inter Group Architects, 1975-81. *Memberships:* Chairman, Inter Group International Ltd, 1978-; NUCCON GROUP,consultants to the National Universities Commission; Nigerian Institute of Town Planners; and Architects; AWKA Improvement Union; Patron, Womens Cultural Dance Group, Lagos; Nigerian Ports Authority Sports Club; NISER ad hoc Committee on Solid Waste Disposal; American Institute of Planners, 1975. *Creative Works:* Development of War time emergency Airfields and landing strips; Specialist Hospital for Aba; Master Plans for Nnewi and participated in preparing the Master Plan for Oritsha; Participated as a principal in drawing up of the physical Planning standards Guides and the implementation guides for Universities in Nigera, 1977-79; Several domestic buildings. *Address:* 127 Bode Thomas Street, PO Box 469, Surulere, Nigeria.

AMADI, Edward Sotonye, b. 12 July 1940, Amadi Town-Ogoloma/Okrika. Business Executive. m. Viola Opuine Amadi, 26 Oct. 1963, 2 sons, 2 daughters. *Education:* Teachers Grade II Certificate, St. John's College, Port Harcourt, Nigeria, 1961-63. *Appointments:* Headmaster of Anglican School, 1964-66; HM Customs and Excise, 1967-70; Self Employed, Shipping, Transportation (Haulage), Kennedy Transport (Nig.) Ltd, 1970-. *Memberships:* International Entrepreneurs Association (IEA); Institute of Managing Directors of Nigeria; Economic Society of New York; The Embassie Club of (UCI) Nigeria; Masonic Scotish Lodge of Nigeria; Nigerian Union of Rivers State Students. *Publications:* On the Shipping Industry in Nigeria; On Purchasing Economics; On Approach and Ethics in Business Studies, thesis. *Honours:* Honorary Doctorate Degree for Business Studies, London School for Business Studies, 1975. *Hobbies:* Football; Cricket; Novelling; Golf; Fishing; Farming. *Address:* No. 3 Chf. Nduka, Lane 'D' Line. G.R.A. Port Harcourt, Nigeria.

AMADI, Godfrey Nnanta (Dr), b. 18 Sept. 1947, Rumuchiolu Village, Rumueme, Port Harcourt. Engineer; Manager. m. Elizabeth, 11 Feb. 1970, 1 son, 3 daughters. *Education:* Institute for Foreign Students of Lower Saxony Hannover, 1971-72; West-Germany Institutes Final Certificate; BSc, MSc, University of Hildesheim West-Germany, 1972-75; PhD, University of Wales, United Kingdom, 1975-78. *Appointments:* Resident Engineer, Site Manager, Rivers State Ministry of Works & Transport, Port Harcourt, Nigeria, 1978-81. *Memberships:* German Society of Engineers; British Institute of Management; Nigerian Institute of Management; Nigerian Society of Engineers. *Publications:* Thesis: Forecasting in Nigerian Agriculture; Seminar paper: The Use of System Dynamics in Forecasting. *Honours:* PhD, Management Science. *Hobbies:* Dancing; Music; Table Tennis; Lawn Tennis; Photography. *Address:* PO Box 1479, Port Harcourt, Nigeria, West Africa.

AMAKIRI, Sotonye Fiberesima, b. 2 June 1942, Okrika, Rivers State, Nigeria. Veterinary Surgeon; University Lecturer. m. 3 Apr. 1971, 2 sons, 5 daughters. *Education:* BSc, Anatomy, University of Ibadan, Nigeria, 1964-68; DVM, Ahmadu Bello University, Zaria, Nigeria, 1968-70; PhD, Anatomy, University of Ibadan, Nigeria, 1970-74; Rockefeller Fellow, University of California, Davis, California, USA, 1974-75. *Appointments:* Lecturer, Acting Head of Department of Veterinary Anatomy, University of Ibadan, Nigeria, 1970-. *Memberships:* World Association of Veterinary Anatomists; International Society of Biometeorology; Nigerian Veterinary Medical Association; Nigerian Society of Animal Production; Nigerian Institute of Management. *Publications:* 40 Scientific publications in various International and National Journals in areas of Anatomy, Veterinary Medicine and Skin Diseases; Chapters in Books. *Honours:* German Academic Exchange Scholar, 1967-70; Postdoctoral Fellow, Rockefeller Foundation, New York, USA, 1974-75. *Hobbies:* Reading; Swimming. *Address:* 4 Amina Way, University of Ibadan, Ibadan, Nigeria.

AMANCHUKWU, Nnamdi Peter, b. Abagana. Engineer. m. Rose Ngozi Onuah, 29 July 1978, 1 son, 1 daughter. *Education:* Post-Graduate Diploma, Production Engineering, Polytechnic of the South Bank, London, 1970; MSc, University of Aston-in-Birmingham, 1973. *Appointments:* Assistant Tech. Officer, Electricity Corporation of Nigeria; Mechanical Engineer, Michelin Tyre Company, Staffordshire; Works Manager, Gas Producers Ltd., Port Harcourt, Nigeria. *Memberships:* Institution of Mechanical Engineers; Institution of Production Engineers. *Hobbies:* Reading; Football; Lawn Tennis. *Address:* No. 2 Asinobi Street, Port Harcourt, Nigeria.

AMAZU, Lawrence Chukwunenye, b. 4 Apr. 1932, Nigeria. Managing Director. m. 5 sons, 3 daughters. *Education:* Taking tuition course leading to Law Degree. *Appointments:* Managing Director, Chi Di Ebere Transport Limited and Amazu Motors Limited. *Publications:* Portrait of a Nigerian Businessman, 1974. *Hobbies:* Physical Exercise. *Address:* No. 2, Azikiwe Road, Umuahia, Imo State, Nigeria.

AMBOGA, George Mark, b. 20 July 1923, Maragoli, Kakamega, Kenya. Librarian. m. Rachel Indasi, 3 May 1950, 4 sons, 2 daughters. *Education:* Makarere College, Kampala, Uganda, 1943. *Appointments:* Clerk, East African Railways and Harbours, 1944-46; Warden, Community Welfare Centre, East African Groundnut Scheme, Tanganyika, 1947-52; Library Assistant, Makerere University, 1953-61; Chief Librarian, East African Community, Industrial Research, Nairobi, Kenya, 1962-77; Chief Librarian, Ministry of Commerce and Industry, Nairobi, Kenya, 1978-80; retired 1980. *Memberships:* Library Association, London, UK, 1957; Kenya Library Association. *Hobbies:* Music; Golf. *Address:* PO Box 185, Maragoli, Kenya.

AMEH, John Ameh, b. 12 June 1944. Architect. m. Aladi Echono, 19 Mar. 1976, 1 son. *Education:* B. Arch., Ahmadu Bello University, Zaria, Nigeria, 1971. *Appointments:* Architect, Public Service of Defunct Benue Plateau State of Nigeria, 1971-76; Public Service of Benue State of Nigeria, February-June, 1976; Self Employed, John Ameh and Associates, 1976-. *Memberships:* Nigerian Institute of Architects, 1974. *Hobbies:* Hockey; Cricket; Tennis; Current Affairs. *Address:* 8 Nunku Road, Jos, Plateau State, Nigeria.

AMERASEKERA, Errol Clement Anthony, b. 22 Nov. 1943, Colombo, Sri Lanka. Chartered Engineer. m. Shirlene Mary Mendis, 27 June 1967, 2 sons. *Education:* Advanced Diploma in Engineering, 1971; Master of Science in Technological Economics, 1972. *Appointments:* Post-graduate Research, GR Stein Refrectories Ltd., Scotland, 1972-73; Contracts Manager, Oxy Metal Finishing (GB) Ltd., Surrey, UK, 1973-74; Executive Officer, British Post Office, London, UK, 1974-75; Planning Officer, Australian Postal Commission, Melbourne, 1975-77; Senior Planning Officer, Australian Telecommunications Commission, Melbourne, 1977-. *Memberships:* Institution of Mechanical Engineers, London, 1973; British Institute of Management, London, 1975; Institution of Engineers, Australia, 1977. *Publications:* Production Information Systems using Linear Programming and Matrix Generation, 1972; MSc Degree Thesis. *Hobbies:* Athletics; Travel; Youth work; Philately. *Address:* 1 Evelyn Street, Glen Waverley, Victoria, 3150, Australia.

AMERY, Rt. Hon. Julian, b. 27 Mar. 1919, m. Catherine, 1950, 1 son, 3 daughters. *Education:* Summerfields; Eton; Balliol College, Oxford War Correspondent in Spanish Civil War, 1938-39; Attaché HM Legation, Belgrade, and on special missions in Bulgaria, Turkey, Roumania and Middle East, 1939-40; Sergeant in RAF, 1940-41; commissioned and transferred to army, 1941; on active service, Egypt, Palestine and Adriatic, 1941-42; liaison officer to Albanian resistance move-

ment, 1944; served on staff of General Carton de Wiart, VC, Mr. Churchill's personal representative with Generalissimo Chiang Kai-Shek, 1945. Contested Preston in Conservative interest, July 1945; MP (C) Preston North, 1950-66; Delegate to Consultative Assembly of Council of Europe, 1950-53 and 1956. Member Round Table Conference on Malta, 1955. Parliamentary Under-Secretary of State and Financial Secretary, War Office, 1957-58; Parliamentary Under-Secretary of State, Colonial Office, 1958-60; PC, 1960; Secretary of State for Air, October 1960-July 1962; Minister of Aviation, 1962-64; MP (C), Brighton Pavilion, 1969-; Minister of Public Building and Works, June-October, 1970; Minister for Housing and Construction, DoE, 1970-72; Minister of State, FCO, 1972-74. *Publications:* Sons of the Eagle, 1948; The Life of Joseph Chamberlain: vol. IV, 1901-3; At the Height of his Power, 1951; vols V and VI, 1901-14; Joseph Chamberlain and the Tariff Reform Campaign, 1969; Approach March (Autobiography), 1973; articles in National Review, Nineteenth Century and Daily Telegraph. *Hobbies:* Ski-ing; Mountaineering; Travel. *Address:* 112 Eaton Square, London, SW1.

AMIN, Mansurul, b. 1 July 1942, Noakhali, Bangladesh. Teacher. *Education:* BSc., 1965, MSc., 1968, Bangladesh Agricultural University, Mymensingh, Bangladesh; Master of Veterinary Science, 1974, PhD, 1977, University of Liverpool, UK. *Appointments:* Thana Livestock Officer, Director of Livestock Services, Bangladesh, 1966; Assistant Research Officer, 1969-72, Lecturer, 1972, Assistant Professor, 1975-, Bangladesh Agricultural University, Mymensingh. *Publications:* Numerous publications in Veterinary Journals including: Isolation and Identification of Salmonella from wild birds, rodents and insects, 1969; Comparative serological studies of the selected isolates of Newcastle disease Virus of Bangladesh with GB, 1977; A comparative study of some cultural methods in the isolation of avian mycoplasma from field material, 1978; Infection of chicken with a virulent or avirulent strain of Mycoplasma gallisepticima alone and together with Newcastle disease virus or E. Coli or both, 1979; A preliminary investigation on Mycoplasma tesuie inhibitors in chicken bing, 1980. Presentations: Published as abstracts in the proceedings, Association of Veterinary Teachers and Research Workers, England: The isolation of mycoplasma with particular reference to avian species, 1976; Mycoplasma in avian species other than poultry, 1978. *Memberships:* Managing Editor, Bangladesh Veterinary Journal; Vice President, Students Union, Bangladesh Agricultural University; President, Literary Societics, Teacher-Students Centre, Bangladesh Agricultural University; Bangladesh Society of Microbiologist; Bangladesh Krishibid Samity; Bangladesh Agricultural University Old Boys Association. *Honours:* Awarded prizes on debates and Literary activities and general proficiencies. *Hobbies:* Lawn Tennis; Badminton; Volley Ball; Literary and Cultural activities; Photography. *Address:* Lakshmipur, Noakhali, Bangladesh.

AMINUL HAQUE, Abul Kalam Muhammad, b. 1 July 1929, Mymensingh, Bangladesh. University Teacher. m. Sitara Begum, 4 July 1963, 3 sons, 1 daughter. *Education:* Bachelor of Science, Dacca University, Bangladesh, 1950; Master of Science, Panjab University, Pakistan, 1952; Doctor of Philosophy, Nottingham University, UK, 1957; Postdoctoral Fellowship, Tokyo University, Japan, 1970-71. *Appointments:* Lectureship in Zoology, Dacca University, Bangladesh, 1952-54; State Scholarship in UK., Goverment of Pakistan, 1954-57; Senior Lectureship in Zoology, Dacca University, Bangladesh, 1957-62; Reader in Zoology and Head of Departments of Zoology and Fisheries, 1962-67, Professor of Fisheries and Head of Department, 1967-80, Dean of Faculty of Fisheries, 1969-80, Vice-Chancellor, 1980-, Bangladesh Agricultural University, Mymensingh, Bangladesh. *Memberships:* Founder President, Council Member, Fellow, Zoological Society of Bangladesh; Founder Member, Bangladesh Association for the Advancement of Science; Founder - President, Fisheries Society of Bangladesh; Asiatic Society of Bangladesh; Bangladesh Geographical Society; Bangladesh Marine Biological Association; Fisheries Research Society of the Philippines; Life Member, Marine Biological Association of India; Inland Fisheries Society of India; Indian Science Congress; Honorary Member, Industrial Fisheries Association, Cochin, India; Editor, Bangladesh, Journal of Fisheries. *Publica-*

tions: 6 books; 26 research papers in international journals published from India, Italy, Japan, Pakistan, UK., and Bangladesh; 24 abstracts of research articles in proceedings of science conferences in Pakistan and Bangladesh; Many Seminar papers; innumerable articles on popular science. *Honours:* UNESCO Prize on book under UNESCO's Reading Materials Project, 1961-62; National Bank of Pakistan Prize awarded by Pakistan Writer's Guild for best science book in Bengali, 1964; UNESCO Prize on a book of commoner birds of Bangladesh, 1963-64. *Hobbies:* Wildlife Conservation; Bird Watching; Travelling. *Address:* Vice-Chancellors House, PO Agricultural University, Mymensingh, Bangladesh.

AMOFAH, Agnes, Gifty, b. 8 December, 1936, Kumasi, Librarianship. m. Joel Kwasi Amofah, 6 August 1960, 1 son, 3 daughters. *Education:* Associate of Library Association 1970; Fellow of the Library Association 1978. *Appointments:* Ashanti Regional Library 1959-1960; University of Science and Technology, U.S.T. Kumasi, 1960-1976; Animal Research Institute, 1976-. *Memberships:* Past Noble Adviser, Ladies of Marshall; National Secretary Holy Child Past Students Association; Past National Treasurer, Research Staff Association; Secretary Ashanti Cultural Ladies; Asante Kotoko Society, Accra Branch; Tesano Club, Accra; Past Vice-President, Christ the King Marshallan Association. *Publications:* An evaluative study of the University Library systems in Ghana, Thesis for Fellowship of the Library Associations 1977; Finding Knowledge on the shelf, 1980; Animal Research Staff Publications, 1981. *Honours:* Fellow of the British Library Association, 1st June, 1978. *Hobbies:* Reading; Marriage and Family Councelling; Youth Activities. *Address:* North Kaneshie, House No. 563A, Accra, Ghana.

AMONI, Samuel S, b. 7 Apr. 1940, Uneme, Bendel State, Nigeria. Ophthalmologist. m. Memmeh Femora Williams, 15 June 1968, 1 son 3 daughters. *Education:* AB, Harvard University, Cambridge, Mass, USA, 1964; MD, Boston University Medical School, USA, 1968; National Board of Medical Examiners, USA, 1969; American Board Certificates in Ophthalmology, 1974; FACS, 1979; Fellow, American Academy of Ophthalmology, USA, 1979; FMCS, Nigeria, 1976. *Appointments:* Internship, Genesee Hospital, Rochester, New York, USA, 1968-69; Resident Surgeon in Ophthalmology, Wills Eye Hospital and Research Institute, Philadelphia, USA, 1969-72; Staff Ophthalmologist, Kaiser Foundation Hospital, Fontana, California, USA, 1972-74; Lecturer with Consultant status in Ophthalmology, 1974-77, Senior Lecturer, 1977-, Ahmadu Bello University Hospital, Kaduna, Nigeria. *Memberships:* Nigerian Medical Association; Executive Council Member, Nigerian Ophthalmological Society; Kaduna Club. *Publications:* Articles in professional journals. *Honours:* Prize for most useful student in a secondary school, Edo College, Benin City 1957; School Head Prefect, 1958; School Science Prize, 1958; School Library Prefect, Goverment College, Ibadan, 1960. *Hobbies:* Music; Tennis. *Address:* 15 Queen Amina Road, (Near Ungwar-Rimi), Kaduna, Nigeria.

AMONOO, Edwin, b. 18 Oct. 1937, Accra, Ghana. Economist. m. Grace Yvonne Koryoe Mate-Kole, 27 July 1974, 1 son, 2 daughters. *Education:* Candidaats Economics, 1966, Doctoraal Theoretical Economics, 1969, PhD. Economics, 1978, Free University, Amsterdam, The Netherlands; Postgraduate Diploma, Economic Planning, Institute of Social Studies, The Hague, The Netherlands, 1969. *Appointments:* Posts and Telecommunications Officer, Ghana, 1957-60; Weighing Supervisor, Ghana Cocoa Marketing Board, 1960-61; Research Fellow (Special Assignment) Social Studies Project, August-December, 1969; Research Fellow and Acting Director, Centre for Development Studies, 1977, University of Cape-Coast, Cape-Coast, Ghana. *Memberships:* West African Economic Association; Regional Loans Board, Central Region, Ghana; Board of Governors, Ghana Education Service, Cape-Coast Technical Institute, Cape-Coast, Ghana; Vocation Training and Rehabilitation Extension Programme, Biriwa, Central Region, Ghana Executive and Senate Committees, Research and Conferences Committee, University of Cape-Coast, Ghana, 1977-; Central Regional Food Distribution Board, 1971-72; Ghana Food Distribution Corporation, Accra, Ghana, 1972-73; Ghana Food Production Corporation, Accra, Ghana, 1972-73; Ghana Liaison Committee, Institute of Social Studies, The Hague, The Netherlands, 1973-76. *Publications:* Numerous publications including: The Flow of Marketing of Cassava in the Central Region with Special Reference to Cape-Coast, Centre for Development Studies, University of Cape-Coast, 1972; The Flow and Marketing of General Agricultural Produce in the Central Region with Special Reference to Cape-Coast, 1974; The Concept of Savings in the National Accounts of Ghana, 1969; Agricultural Production and Income Distribution in Ghana. A Case Study of Incomes of Farm Households in Two Rural Areas, 1967-73, 1978; Agricultural Resource Allocation and Income Distribution in Ghana, 1980. *Honours:* Netherlands Goverment Scholarship, 1963-69; Netherlands Universities Foundation for International Co-operation Award, 1970-71; British Council Award (Seminar on International Commodities, Institute of Development Studies, University of Sussex, May-June 1977. *Hobbies:* Gardening; Reading. *Address:* Bungalow 192 Northern Section, Campus, University of Cape-Coast, Ghana.

AMOORE, Dorothy Mary (Mrs), b. 9 Feb. 1920, East End Finchley, London, UK. Theatre Director, Actress, Theatre Tutor. m. Geoffrey Wighs Amoore (dec.), 20 June 1945, 1 son, 3 daughters. *Education:* Queen's College, London, 1928-34; St Stephen's College, Kent, 1934-38; Diploma, Bagot Stack School, London, 1938-40. *Appointments:* Wartime Nursing Services, 1939-45; Co-Director, Central Theatre, Auckland & Director of the Central Theatre Child Drama Department, 1961-71; Drama Tutor for Emotionally Handicapped Children, Mt. Wellington, Auckland, 1964-65; Co-Director for the Preliminary Drama School run by the Auckland Theatre Trust, 1966; Artistic Director, Central Theatre, 1971-76; Ensemble Theatre Sydney Box Office Administration; Tutor/Play Director; Tutor Joan Halliday Ballet School & Australian Theatre for Young People; TV Actress, 1976-78; Actress/Play Director, Mercury Theatre, Auckland, 1978-79; Artistic Director, Auckland Youth Theatre Inc., 1978-. *Memberships:* Actress/Producer, Henderson Little Theatre, 1955-61; Actress/Producer, Auckland Repertory Theatre, 1959-61; British Drama League, Chairman Auckland Branch, 1958. *Publications:* Wrote Book & Lyrics of On Our Way for Central Theatre, 1970. *Honours:* Awards for British Drama League Festivals, Acting & Producing, 1955-62; Queen Elizabeth II Arts Council Fellowship, 1966; Neboa Merit Award for long service and devotion to theatre, 1974. *Hobbies:* Reading; Letter writing; Travel. *Address:* 65 Onslow Avenue, Epsom, Auckland, 3, New Zealand.

AMORY, Derick Heathcoat, KG, b. 26 Dec. 1899. Member of Parliament. m. M Margaret Isabella Dorothy Evelyn, Doyle, 2 sons, 2 daughters. *Education:* MA, Christ Church. Oxford, UK. *Appointments:* War Service 1939-45; Governor, Hudson's Bay Company, 1965-70; Director, Lloyds Bank, 1948-51 abd 1964-70; Oresudebtm John Heathcoat and Company 1973, Chairman, 1966-72; Director, ICI, 1964-70; Member Devon CC, 1932-51; Member of Parliament, Tiverton Devon, 1945-60; Minister of Pensions, 1951-53; Minister of State, Board of Trade, 1953-54; Minister of Agriculture and Fisheries, 1954; Minister of Agriculture and Fisheries and Minister of Food, 1954-55; Chancellor of the Exchequer 1958-60; High Commissioner for the United Kingdom in Canada, 1961-63; Jt. Pro-Chancellor, University of Exeter, 1966-72; Chairman Medical Research Council, 1960-61 and 1965-69; Voluntary Service Overseas, 1964-75; *Memberships:* President, Association of County Councils; County Councils Association; London Federation of Boys' Clubs; Exeter Cathedral Appeal; Prime Warden, Goldsmiths' Company; High Steward Borough of South Molton; *Honours:* KG, 1968; PC, 1953; GCMG, 1961; TD; DL; Bt cr 1874; Lieutenant-Colonel (hon. rank); RA (TA) retired; Chancellor of Exeter University; Honary FRCS 1974; Hon LLD; Exeter University 1959; Heir, (to baronetcy only). *Address:* 150 Marsham Court, The Wooden House, Chevithorne, Tiverton Devon

AMOS, Francis John Clarke, b. 10 Sept. 1924, London, England. University Fellow. m. Geraldine Mercy Sutton, 15 Aug. 1956, 1 son, 1 daughter. *Education:* Diploma in Architecture, Polytechnic, London, 1951; Diploma in Planning, School of Planning, London, 1953; BSc (Sociology), University of London, 1956. *Appointments:* Assistant Architect, Harlow Development Corporation, 1951; Planning Officer, London County Council, 1953-58, Ministry of Housing & Local

Government, 1958-63; Seconded as Adviser to Ethiopian Government, 1959-62; Divisional Planning Officer, 1962-66, City Planning Officer, 1966-73, Liverpool City Council; Chief Executive, Birmingham City Council,1973-77; Senior Fellow, Institute of Local Government, University of Birmingham, 1977-. *Memberships:* Royal Institute British Architects; President, 1971-72, Hon. Secretary, 1979-, Royal Town Planning Institute; International Society of City & Regional Planners, 1973; Royal Society of Arts, 1978; Professor of Planning Practice & Management, University of Nottingham, 1979. *Publications:* Education for Planning & Urban Governance, 1972; City Centre Redevelopment (Part), 1973; Planning & The Future; Inner Cities & Social Policies, 1977; Social Malaise in Liverpool, 1972. *Honours:* Commander of British Empire, 1972. *Hobby:* Community Welfare work. *Address:* 20 Westfield Road, Edgbaston, Birmingham B15 3QG, England.

AMPONSAH, Kinabema, b. 23 Aug. 1945, Msoajre, Ghana. Teacher/Publisher. m. Mar. 1968, 3 sons, 2 daughters. *Education:* BA Honours, Study of Religions, University of Ghana Legon, 1968-71; Post Graduate Certificate in Education, University of Cape Coast, 1974-75; MA African Studies (part one), University of Ghana, 1976-77. *Appointments:* English and Bible Knowledge Master, ODA Secondary School, Akim, ODA, Ghana, 1971-72; Senior Bible Knowledge Master, Adisadel College Cape Coast Ghana, 1972-74; Teaching Assistant, Curriculum Department, University of Cape Coast, 1975-76; Senior Religious Studies Master, Presbyterian Boys' Secondary School and Sixth Form Science College, 1976-78. *Memberships:* Ghana Publishers' Association. *Publications:* Topics on West African Traditional Religions Volumes I and II; Studies in Acts of the Apostles "O" Level Commentary; Studies in the Gospels, Mark, Luke and Matthew. *Hobbies:* Writing; Farming. *Address:* Adwinsa House, A/M&N/942, Madina, Accra.

AMULI, Beda Jonathan, b. 27 May, 1938 Masasi, Tanzania. Architect. m. Luchia, Violet 23 Sept. 1965, 1 son, 2 daughters. *Education:* St Andrews College Minaki, 1956-57; 1st year Architecture, University of Nairobi, 1958-59; 2nd year-5th year (Technion), Israel Institute of Technology, 1960-64; B.Arch. Degree, 1964. *Appointments:* Junior Partner in Tanzania Practice with "ZEVET", Tanzania Architects and Engineers, 1964-69; Principal of B. J. Amuli Architects, 1969-. *Memberships:* Registered Architect, Board of Registration of Architects in Tanzania, Kenya, Uganda and Zambia; Architectural Association of Tanzania; Uganda Society of Architects; Zambian Institute of Architects; Commonwealth Association of Architects, Africa Region. *Publications:* Author and executive Architect for Kariakoo Produce Market of Dar Es Salaam Tanzania. *Hobbies:* Swimming, Squash. *Address:* PO Box 20861 Dar Es Salaam, Tanzania.

ANAKWENZE, (Chief) Francis Nwoye, b. 4 May 1926 Anambra State, Nigeria. Civil Servant. m. Rebecca Nwakego Ikeme 1 Nov. 1951, 1 son, 2 daughters. *Education:* Cambridge School Leaving Certificate, Christ the King College Onitsha, 1940-44; Forest Assistant Certificate, Forest School, Ibadan, 1977; Scottish Highers, Dundee Technical College, Scotland, 1954; BSc, Forestry, Aberdeen University, 1958; Forest Management Certificate, Oxford University, England, 1964-65. *Appointments:* Forest Assistant, 1946-58; Assistant Conservator of Forests, 1958-63; Conservator of Forests 1964-70; Chief Conservator of Forests, Anambra State of Nigeria, 1970-. *Memberships:* National Forest Development Committee of Nigeria; President, 1977-78, Forest Association of Nigeria; Commonwealth Forestry Association; Wildlife Conservation of Nigeria; Vice-President General, Abagana, Anambra State of Nigeria; Cabinet of the Warrat Chief, Abagana, Ananbra State of Nigeria. *Publications:* History of Natural Regeneration in Nigeria, 1964; Nursery Techniques in Nigeria 1965; Timber Trends Study in West Africa 1965; Socio-Economic Role of Forestry in Eastern Nigeria 1966; Nigerian Civil War and Forestry Practice 1970; The Role of Forestry in National Development 1977; The Role of Forestry in Food Production in Nigeria 1974. *Honours:* First Prize in Survey, Forest School Ibadan, Nigeria 1947, Oke-Ofia of Abagana, 1977; Knight of St John, 1978; Anambra State Governor's Merit Award 1980; Merit Scholarship Award, to study for MSc Forestry 1958. *Hobbies:* Gardening;

Farming; Billiards. *Address:* No. 6 Bent Lane, Government Residential Area, Enugu, Nigeria.

ANAND, Narendra Nath, b. 7 Dec. 1935, New Delhi, India. Defence Services, Indian Navy. m. Vijaya N 22 Oct. 1962, 2 sons. *Education:* Joined National Defence Academy, 1952, Graduated, 1955; Completed Naval Training, 1956; Specialised in Naval Communications, HMS Mercury, UK, 1961; *Appointments:* Head of Wireless Departments, Indian Navy Signal School, 1962; Squadron Communication Officer, 11 Destroyer Squadron, 1962-63; Signal Communication Officer, INS Mysore, 1963-64; Head of Technical Department & Chief Instructor, Indian Navy Signal School, 1964-66; Staff Officer, Naval Headquarters, 1966-68; On Secondment to Government of Nigeria, for services with Nigerian Navy, 1968-70; Second in Command, INS, Trishul, 1970-71; Commanding Officer, INS Cauvery, 1972-74; HQ Eastern Naval Command, 1974-76; Commanding Officer, INS Himgiri, 1976-77; Attachment with Ministry of Defence, 1978-81; National Defence College, India, 1981. *Memberships:* Institute of Electronic & Telecommunication Engineers, India, 1977, Fellow, 1979; Institute of Public Administration; United Services Club, Bombay; Defence Service Officers Institute, New Delhi. *Publications:* Secure Communications, Indian Navy; Communications Organisation & Training of Nigerian Navy. *Honours:* Best All Round Cadet, Naval Training, 1955; First in Advanced Communication Course, 1963; National Security Management, 1968; Gallantry Award, Nao Sena Medal, 1971; Awarded AVSM, 1981. *Hobbies:* Music; Photography. *Address:* 8 Rafiya Manzil, Wode House Road, Colaba, Bombay, 400039, India.

ANATOLITOU, Vanna, b. 16 Oct. 1929, Limassol, Cyprus. Director. m. Takis Anatolitis 26 Dec. 1948, 3 sons, 1 daughter. *Education:* American Academy Larnaca 1946-48; International Union of Official Travel Organisation, Diploma on Tourism Studies 1964; Cyprus Government Licenced Guide 1964. *Appointments:* Private Secretary, 1955-60, Tours Manager 1960-67, Francoudi and Stephanou Limited, Assistant General Manager Esperia Tower Hotel, Famagusta, 1967-69; Assistant General Manager 1969-70, Director and General Manager, 1970-, Exchange Travel Cyprus. *Memberships:* Committee, Famagosta Chambers of Commerce and Industry; Famagusta Lioness Club. *Hobbies:* Reading; Swimming; Making fancy cakes. *Address:* 16 Alassia Street, Limassol, Cyprus.

ANAVHE, Paul Momodu Charles, b. 3 Mar. 1934, Fugar, Bendel State of Nigeria. Business. m. 3 Mar. 1964, 4 sons, 4 daughters. *Education:* Holds General Certificate of Education, attended several courses & seminars in various field of higher learning, nationally & internationally. *Appointments:* Surveys Dept., Richard Costain (WA), 1956; Wireless Dept., Post & Telecomms, 1958; Cashier, United Africa Company Ltd., 1959; Accounts Dept., Leventis Co. Ltd., 1964; Transport Officer, USAID, 1965; AREWA Textiles Ltd., 1967; Secretary/Accounts, KLM, 1968. *Memberships:* Chairman/Managing Director, Panav International Limited, Building & Civil Engineers. *Honours:* A Knight of the Catholic Church in Nigeria. *Hobbies:* Running; Lawn Tennis; Singing. *Address:* KK6 Abidjan Road, Ungwa Rimi Village, Kaduna, Nigeria.

ANDERSEN, Neville Arthur, b. 14 July 1922, Albury, New South Wales, Australia. Medicine: General Practice; Community Health. m. Marie Patricia Vines 20 Dec. 1947, 1 son, 2 daughters. *Education:* MB, BS, Sydeny University, 1945; DTM and H, 1948; MRACGP, 1967; FRACGP 1970; FRCGP, 1972. *Appointments:* R. M.O. Marrickville District Hospital 1945-46; Cloncurry Base Hospital 1946-47; Medical Officer in Charge, London Missionary Society Hospital, Kapuna, Papua, 1948-53; General Practice, Fairfield New South Wales, 1953-73; Acting Co-ordinator, Community Medicine, 5th year programme, University of New South Wales, 1975; Hon. Associate, School of Community Medicine, University of New South Wales, 1977-; Director of Community Medicine, St. Vincent's Hospital, Sydney, 1973-; Director, Primary Care, Westmead Centre, Westmead, New South Wales. *Memberships:* Numerous Societies, Clubs etc. including: Royal Australian College of General Practitioners; National Health and Medical Research Council; World Organisation of National Colleges and Academies of General Practice-/Family Medicine; Australian and New Zealand Society for Epidemiology and Research in Community Health; Australian Medical Association. *Publications:* Numerous publications including: Obstetric Experience in the Purari Delta, Papua 1954; Assessment of the Structure of General Practice in New South Wales Report of a survey, 1968; Postgraduate Medical Education for General Practitioners, 1973; Joint Authorships: Articles, Reports and Conference Papers: General Practice and its Future in Australia, 1972; The Health Status and Needs of the Urban Aged, 1979; A Comparison between Hospital Patients with Drinking Problems and Court Referred Drinking Drivers, 1980. *Creative Works:* Community Attitudes to General Practice 1971; Community Health in Australia, 1979. *Honours:* Tasmanian Prize Essay (2nd prize) 1967; Nuffield Travelling Fellowship in General Practice 1970; Departments of General Practice: Their Role in Teaching and Research; Report to the Nuffield Foundation, 1972. *Address:* 11 Barker Road, Strathfield 2135, Australia.

ANDERSON, Diana, b. 11 Dec. 1940, South Wales, United Kingdom. Scientist, m. Dr John Julian Anderson 22 Dec. 1967, 2 daughters. *Education:* BSc Faculty Science, University of Wales, 1963; DipEd, Faculty of Education, University of New South Wales, 1965; MSC, 1971, PhD 1973, Faculty of Medicine University of Manchester. *Appointments:* Biology teaching, Doonside High School, Comprehensive, Sydney, New South Wales, Australia, 1964-65; Tutor/demonstrator, School of Biological Sciences, Sydney University, New South Wales, Australia, 1965-68; Research Assistant, Department of Cancer Research, Leeds University, United Kingdom, 1968-69; Lecturer in Biology, Didsbury Teacher Training College, Manchester, 1969-70; Research worker, Paterson Laboratories, Christie Hospital, University of Manchester, 1970-74; Head of Mutagenesis Work Group, Central Toxicology Laboratory, Imperial Chemical Industries Limited, Alderley Park, United Kingdom, 1974-81; Head of Genetic Toxicology, British Industrial Biological Research Association, Carshalton, United Kingdom, 1981-. *Memberships:* Institute of Biology; Secretary, United Kingdom Environmental Mutagenesis Society; Governor Stockport College of Technology; Stockport College Science Advisory Board; Validation and Examination Board, Institute of Biology. *Publications:* Contributed book chapters to: Genetic Damage in Man caused by Environmental Agents, 1979; Mutagenesis in Sub-Mammalian Systems, 1979; Chemical Mutagenesis, Human Population Monitoring and Genetic Risk Assessment, 1981. *Hobbies:* Interior Design; Antique Collecting; Music. *Address:* Oakdene, Leicester Road, Hale Cheshire.

ANDERSON, Donald, b. 17 June 1939, Swansea. MP and Barrister. m. Dorothy Mary Trotman, 28 Sept. 1963, 3 sons. *Education:* BA (1st) University College, Swansea, 1957-60; Called to bar Inner Temple, 1969. *Appointments:* Foreign Office, 1960-64; Lecturer University College, Swansea, 1964-66; MP Monmouth (Labour), 1966-70; Barrister 1969-; MP Swansea East, 1974-. *Memberships:* Minister of Defense, 1969-70; Councillor, Kensington and Chelsea, 1971-75; Attorney General 1974-79; Chairman Environment Group 1974-79; President, Gower Society 1977-79; Chairman Welsh Labour Group 1978-79. *Hobbies:* Church; Walking. *Address:* House of Commons, London SW1.

ANDERSON, Eric St. George, b. 18 June 1914 Free Hill, St Mary, Jamaica West Indies. Physician and Surgeon. m. Aneta Wright, 31 July, 1940. *Education:* Teachers Diploma, Mico College, Teachers Training College, 1931-33; BSc, New York University, 1946-47; LRCP, LRCS, LM, Royal College of Physicians and Surgeons, Dublin, Ireland, 1947-52; Yale University USA, 1955-56, MD, Toronto University, 1969-70. *Appointments:* Medical Officer, Harlem Hospital, New York, 1953-54; Medical Officer, Kingston Public Hospital 1954; St Anns Bay Hospital 1954-1955; M.O.H. Clarendon 1955-62; Private Practice, 1962-. *Memberships:* Justice of the Peace; Right Worshipful Master, Masonic Lodge Clarendon Kilwinning. S.C; Chairman of the Police Services Commission of Jamaica; Commander of the Order of Distinction. *Publications:* First Steps in Public Health Administration in Jamaica, 1956. *Honours:* Government WHO Fellowship to Yale 1956; M.P.H Honours Student; Masters Degree in Public Health; Commander of the Order of Distinction, 1979. *Hobbies:* Motoring; Cricket; Football;

Music; Reading. *Address:* "Vermont", PO Box 2, Chapelton, JA OV1.

ANDERSON, Graham Roland, b. 13 July 1922, Brisbane. Orthopaedic Surgeon. m. Joan Blandford Earnshaw, 4 Dec. 1948, 4 daughters. *Education:* MBBS (Qld), 1945; FRCS (England) 1950; FRACS 1961. *Appointments:* Orthopaedic Surgeon, 1956-, Orthopaedic Supervisor, 1951-56, Royal Brisbane Hospital. *Memberships:* President, 1980, Australian Orthopaedic Association; President, 1969-71, Executive, 1959-, Federal Secretary, 1969-73, Royal Flying Doctor Service (Queensland Section); Federal Secretary; Court of Examiners RACS; *Publications:* A few medical publications, journals. *Honours:* Hallett Prize 1949. *Hobbies:* Golf; Tennis; Fishing; Painting; Photography. *Address:* 25 Bennison Street, Ascot, Brisbane, 4007, Australia.

ANDERSON, (Sir) John Muir, b. 14 Sept. 1914, Windsor, Victoria, Australia. Company Director. m. Audrey Drayton Jamieson 26 Aug. 1949, 1 son, 1 daughter. *Education:* Brighton Grammar School; Melbourne University. *Appointments:* Managing Director, John M. Anderson Company Pty. Limited; Managing Director, King Oscar Fine Foods Pty. Limited; Commissioner of State Bank of Victoria; Commissioner, Port of Melbourne Authority; Director Victoria Insurance Limited 1965-69; Director, New Zealand Insurance Company Limited, Australia 1969; Service 1939-42, 2/6th Commando Company 1st Australian Paratroop Battalian. *Memberships:* Melbourne Club; Victoria Racing Club. *Honours:* C.M.G. 1957; Knight Batchelor 1969; Coronation Medal; Jubilee Medal. *Hobbies:* Swimming; Gardening. *Address:* 25 Cosham Street, Brighton Victoria 3186, Australia.

ANDERSON, Kenneth Paxton, b. 7 Mar. 1915, Pittenweem, Fife, Scotland. Veterinary Surgeon. m. Bets Welch Westwater, 17 Sept. 1928, 3 sons, 1 daughter. *Education:* Waid Academy, Anstruther, 1926-31; Edinburgh University, 1931-36; Royal Dick Veterinary College, 1931-35. *Appointments:* House, Surgeon, Royal Dick Vet. College, 1936-37; Assistant to SJ Motton, Penzance, 1937-38; Assistant to R Turnbull, Eastbourne, 1938-40; Own Practice, Stirling, 1940-77. *Memberships:* British Veterinary Association 1941-; Royal College of Veterinary Surgeons, 1974-; Society Practising Veterinary Surgeons, 1974-; President, Scottish Branch BVA, 1960; President, Scottish Metropolitan Division, BVA, 1958. *Publications:* Several papers for British Veterinary Association Congresses subsequently published in veterinary journals. *Honours:* OBE, 1979. *Hobbies:* Wild Life; Photography & Film making; Gardening; Golf. *Address:* Balcormo, 16 Ladysneuk Road, Cambuskenneth, Stirling, FK9 5NF, Scotland.

ANDERSON, Robert David, b. 20 August 1927, Shillong, Assam, India. Musician and Egyptologist. *Education:* Gonville and Caius College, Cambridge, 1948-1954; First class honours in Classical Tripos part 1, 1950; First Class honours in Oriental Languages Tripos part 2, 1952; B.A. 1950; M.A. 1957. *Appointments:* Assistant Editor, Record News 1954-1956; Director of Music, Gordonstoun School 1958-1962; Conductor, Moral Choral Union 1958-1962; Extra-Mural Lecturer in Egyptology, University of London 1966-1977; Associate Editor, The Musical Times, 1967-; Conductor, St. Bartholomew's Hospital Choral Society, 1965-; Administrative Director, Egypt Exploration Society Excavations at Qasr Ibrim, 1977-. *Memberships:* Honorary Secretary, Egypt Exploration Society, 1971-; Member of Council, The British Institute in Eastern Africa, 1977-; Liveryman, Worshipful Company of Musicians, 1977-; Royal Musical Association. *Publications:* Catalogue of Egyptian Antiquities in the British Museum, III: Musical Instruments (1976); Wagner (1980). *Hobbies:* Music; Egyptology. *Address:* 54 Hornton Street, London W8 4NT, England.

ANDERSON, Roderick Allan McBeth, b. 6 Sept. 1947 Palmerston North, New Zealand. Medical Laboratory Technologist. m. 15 Feb. 1969, 1 son, 2 daughters. *Education:* University Entrance, 1965; Certificate of Proficiency (Haematology and Blood Bank Serology II) (Immunohaematology II), Medical Laboratory Technology, 1970; Certificate in Radiochemistry, Elementory Stage III, 1981. *Appointments:* Trainee Technologist, National Women's Hospital Laboratory, 1966-69; Trainee Technologist, Blood Transfusion Centre, Auckland, New Zealand, 1969-70; Staff Technologist, Groote Schuul, Medical School, Tissue Typing Laboratory, Cape Town, South Africa, 1971; Charge Technologist, Reference Laboratories, Blood Transfusion Centre, Auckland New Zealand, 1972-81. *Memberships:* Associate of the New Zealand Institute of Medical Laboratory Technology. *Publications:* New Zealand Journal Medical Laboratory Technology, 1975, 1979, 1981, 1981. *Honours:* Outward Bound Award, 1966; First Prize in Immunohaematology, 1971; First Prize for Best Scientific paper presented at National Conference, 1980. *Address:* F3/335 Mt. Eden Road, Mt. Eden, Auckland, New Zealand.

ANDERSON, Spencer Roy, b. 12 Jan. 1927, Brisbane, Queensland, Australia. Manufacturers' Agent & Importer. m. Jill Rodgers, 6 June 1951 (div. 30 Nov. 1976), 3 sons, 1 daughter. *Education:* Brisbane Boys' College, 1940-43; Senior Pass Matriculation, 1943. *Appointments:* War Service RANR, 1944-46; Clerk, HM Russell & Co. Pty. Ltd., 1946-51; Len Anderson & Son Pty. Ltd., 1951-81, Managing Director, 1970-. *Memberships:* Royal Queensland Yacht Squadron; Southport Yacht Club; Indooroophilly Golf Club; Tattersall's Club. *Honours:* Reserve Decoration, 1963; Clasp to Reserve Decoration, 1973. *Hobbies:* Yachting; Golf. *Address:* 24/128 Oxlade Drive, New Farm, Brisbane, 4005, Australia.

ANDERSON, William Alexander Beaumont, b. 7 May 1915, Montreal, Canada. Military, Civil Service. m. Caroline Jane Waddell, 4 Nov. 1939, 2 sons. *Education:* Diploma, Royal Military College of Canada, 1932-36; BA, Queen's University, Kingston, Canada, 1936-37; DMil.Sc., 1977; Graduate, US Army & Navy Staff College, 1945, Canadian National Defence College, 1950, Imperial Defence College, 1956. *Appointments:* Commissioned Royal Canadian Artillery, 1936; Second World War, North-West Europe, 1939-45; Director of Military Intelligence, Ottawa, 1946-49; Commander First Infantry Brigade, Germany, 1953-55; Commandant, Royal Military College, 1960-61; Adjutant General, Canadian Army, 1962-64; Commander, Mobile Command, Canadian Forces, 1966-69; Retired, Lieutenant General, 1969. Deputy Minister, Ontario Civil Service; Chairman, Civil Service Commission, 1969-74; Secretary, Management Board of Cabinet, 1974-79; Deputy Provincial Secretary, Resources Development, 1979; Seconded as Special Adviser to Government of Canada, 1980-81. *Memberships:* Royal Artillery Association; Royal Canadian Artillery Association; Canadian Institute of International Affairs, Niagara Institute, Canada, Royal Canadian Military Institute, Toronto, Canada. *Honours:* Gold Medallist, Rothesay Collegiate School, 1931; Sword of Honour, Royal Military College of Canada, 1936; OBE, 1945; Canadian Forces Decoration; Officer, Belgian Order of Leopold, 1945; Officer, Belgian Order of the Crown, 1946. *Hobbies:* Golf; Skiing. *Address:* 1 The Mews, Ottawa, Canada, K1M 2G3.

ANDERSON, William Eric Kinloch, b. 27 May 1936, Edinburgh, Scotland. Headmaster. m. Poppy Mason, 20 Apr. 1960, 1 son, 1 daughter. *Education:* MA, University of St Andrews, 1953-57; B.Litt, Balliol College, Oxford, 1957-59. *Appointments:* Assistant Master, Fettes College, Edinburgh, 1960-64, 1966-70, Gordonstoun, 1964-66; Headmaster, Abingdon School, 1970-75, Shrewsbury School, 1975-80, Eton College, 1980-. *Memberships:* President, Edinburgh Sir Walter Scott Club, 1981. *Publications:* The Written Word, 1964; Editor The Journal of Sir Walter Scott, 1972; Essays and articles. *Honours:* Hon. D.Litt University of St Andrews, 1981. *Hobbies:* Golf; Fishing. *Address:* Eton College, Windsor, Berkshire.

ANDERSON, William Joseph (The Honourable), b. 20 Apr. 1918 Oakville, Manitoba, Canada. Judge: High Court of Justice for Ontario. m. Alison Rosamond Morgan 2 July 1951, 2 sons. *Education:* BA(Hons) University of Manitoba 1942; Barrister-at-Law, Osgoods Hall Law School, 1948. *Appointments:* Practised law with Gardiner Roberts or predecessor firms, 1948-77; Appointment to the Bench, 1977-. *Memberships:* Advocates Society, Ontario; Foundation for Legal Research; Phi Delta Phi; York Co. Law Association; Anglican. *Hobbies:* Reading; Fishing; Liturgical music. *Address:* 43 Roxborough Street E, Toronto, Canada, M4W 1U5.

ANDOH, Dominic Kodwo, b. 4 May 1929, Shama, Ghana. Catholic Bishop of Accra. *Education:* Philoso-

phy and Theology, St Teresa's Minor Seminary, Amisano Elmina, 1950-56; Doctorate in Canon Law, Pontifical Urban University, Rome, 1961-64; *Appointments:* General Manager of Catholic Schools, 1957-60; Director of Catechetical Centre, Asamankese, 1964-67; Holy Spirit Cathedral Administrator, 1967-69; Vicar General, Diocese of Accra, 1969-70; Rector of St Peter's Regional Seminary, Pedu Cape Coast 1970-71. *Memberships:* Judicial Council of Ghana; Board of Directors, International Institute of the Heart of Jesus, inc; President, Ghana Bishops' Conference. *Creative Works:* Catechetical Education in Ghana. *Hobbies:* Gardening; Music. *Address:* Biship's House, PO Box 247, Accra.

ANDREW, Donald, James, Clifford, b. 26 May 1920, Barnstaple, N. Devon, England. Professional Oboist. m. Oct. 1959, 1 daughter. *Education:* Choristers' School, Exeter Cathedral, 1929-36; Royal Military School of Music 1938-39; Royal Academy of Music, London, 1947-48; ARCM 1942. *Appointments:* Cor Anglais and Sub Principal Oboe, Sadlers Wells Opera Orchestra, 1947-48; Principal Oboe, The Royal Liverpool Philharmonic Orchestra 1948-49; Principal Oboe, The BBC Review Orchestra 1950-54; Principal Oboe, The Leighton Lucas Chamber Orchestras 1955-57; Principal Oboe, The Ballet Rambert 1958-59; Member, The Wind Band, The Royal Shakespear Theatre, Stratford-upon-Avon 1959-60; Principal Oboe, Sadlers Wells Opera Orchestra 1960-63; Woodwind Instructor, Edinburgh Education Authority 1968-77. *Memberships:* London Musical Club; Edinburgh Society of Musicians. *Creative Works:* BBC Soloist, 1945-; Recitals: Wigmore Hall, 1962; (RFH) 1972, 77, 80; Broadcast, Haydn Oboe Concerto; Has played with Leading London Orchestras; Liverpool Philharmonic Orchestra. *Honours:* IBC Diplomas: International Who's Who in Music, 1976 and 1980; Companion of Western Europe Diploma 1980; FIBA, 1978. *Address:* Broxburn, Broxburn Junction, West Lothian, Scotland.

ANDREW, James Harvey, b. 23 Feb. 1921 Dunfermline Scotland. Medical Practitioner. m. Alison Mary Andrew 12 Sept. 1953, 3 sons, 1 daughter. *Education:* Edinburgh Academy 1928-39; MB, ChB, Edinburgh University 1946-51; Member 1961, Fellow 1975, Royal College of Obstesricians and Gynaecologists. *Appointments:* Consultant Obstetrician and Gynaecologist, HM Forces, 1965-72; Assistant Director Medical Services, 1972-76; Medical Officer, Department Health and Social Security 1977-; Her Majesty's Inspector of Anatomy 1980-. *Memberships:* British Medical Association; Anatomical Society of Great Britain; Federation of British Artists; Foxhills Golf and Country Club. *Hobbies:* Golf; Gardening; Collecting water colour paintings. *Address:* Birchwood, Springfield Road, Camberley, Surrey, GU15 1AB UK.

ANDREW, Warwick John, b. 29 Mar. 1941, Sydney, Australia. Judge. *Education:* Sydney University, 1951-58; Admitted to Practice as Barrister, 1970. *Appointments:* Barrister, 1970-76; Public Solicitor of Papua New Guinea, 1973; Judge of Supreme Court of Papua New Guinea, 1978-. *Publications:* Criminal Law & Practice of Papua New Guinea. *Hobbies:* Flying; Farming; Horse breeding. *Address:* Port Moresby, Papua New Guinea.

ANDREWS, John Thomas, b. 20 Mar. 1927, Brighton. Nuclear Medicine Physician. m. Iris Mary Groves, 17 May 1957, 4 sons. *Education:* St. John the Baptist and Xaverian College, Brighton, Sussex 1941; HMS Cadet Ship, Conway, 1942-43; Queen Mary College and London Hospital, University of London, 1949-55. LRCP(London) MRCS(England) 1955; MB, BS(London) 1955; DObst. RCOG 1958; MRACP 1960; MRACR 1963; FRACP 1970; Certificate American Board Nuclear Medicine 1973; FRACR 1977; MD(Melbourne) 1979. *Appointments:* Cadet to 2nd Officer Merchant Navy, 1943-48; House Surgeon London Hospital 1955-56; House Physician Dover Hospital 1956-57; Resident Accoucheur, Assistant in Morbid Anatomy and Junior Medical Registrar London Hospital, 1957-59; Medical Registrar Launceston General Hospital and General Practice Launceston Tasmania, 1959-61; Trainee Radiotherapist and Radiotherapist Peter MacCallum Clinic, Melbourne, 1961-66; Director of Nuclear Medicine, The Royal Melbourne Hospital, 1966-; Senior Associate in Medicine, Lecturer and former Clinical Instructor, University of Melbourne; Physician Assisting Thyroid and Special Breast Clinics, Royal Melbourne Hospital. *Memberships:* Australian and New Zealand Society of Nuclear Medicine; Special Advisory Committee on Nuclear Medicine, Royal Australasian College of Physicians; Australian and New Zealand Association of Physicians in Nuclear Medicine; Advisory Committee and former Lecturer Department of Applied Physics, Royal Melbourne Institute of Technology; British and Australian Medical Associations; American College of Nuclear Medicine; Life Member Gardenvale Squash Club. *Publications:* Nuclear Medicine. Clinical and Technological Bases, (with M. J. Milne) 1977; Publications on Clinical Medicine, Radiotherapy and Nuclear Medicine. *Honours:* Frederick Treves Prize London Hospital 1955, Baker Travelling Fellow Royal Australasian College of Radiologists 1969. *Hobbies:* Squash; Music; Skiing; Art. *Address:* 400 New Street, Elsternwick, Victoria 3185, Australia.

ANDREWS, John William, b. 8 May 1891, Masterton, New Zealand. Joinery Merchant and Company Director. m. Margaret Latham 11 Mar. 1921 (dec.), 1 son, 1 daughter. *Education:* Masterton District High School. *Memberships:* President, Municipal Association of New Zealand, 1945-47; Local Government Commission 1947-54; Town Planning Board; Board of Health; Rabbit Board; Soil Conservation Council; Decentralisation of Industry Committee; Mayor of City of Lower Hull, 1933-47; Chairman Hult Valley Power Board; Founder Chairman Hult Valley Milk Board; Wellington Harbour Board; Wellington Hospital Board; City and Suburban Highways Board; Founder President Hull Valley Red Cross; Charter President Rotary Club of Hull; Active Service: First World War; Captain, New Zealand Rifle Brigade. *Honours:* OBE; Counsellor of Honour, Red Cross Society; Gold Star, New Zealand Returned Services Association; Life Member Amateur Athletic Club; Wellington Builders Association. *Hobby:* Gardening. *Address:* 36 Hinau Street, Lower Hutt, New Zealand.

ANDREWS, Stuart Alexander, b. 21 Mar. 1920 London, England. Chartered Engineer. m. 23 July 1946. *Education:* Engineering Apprenticeship, with De Havilland Aircraft Company, 1941; Aeronautical and Mechanical Engineering, City University, 1938-41 and 1945; HNC, Aeronautical; HND Mechanical. *Appointments:* Assistant Chief Engineer, Rolls Royce Small Engines Division, 1960-68; Chief Technical Engineer, Birmingham Small Arms, 1968-73; Manager, Electrical Engineering, British Leyland, 1973-79; Executive Engineer, Design Analysis, British Leyland, 1979-. *Memberships:* Chartered Engineering Institutions; Fellow, Institution of Mechanical Engineers; Fellow, Royal Aeronautical Society; British Institute of Management; Group 'A' Registration with European Federation of National Engineering Associations. *Publications:* Structural Design and Diesel Engine Noise, 1979; Analysistechniques in Gearbox and Axle Noise Investigation; Analysis and Mechanism of Petrol Engine Crank Rumble. Automobile Division Conference at Cranfield, 1979; The Noise and Source Identification of Automobile Gearboxes and Final Drives.—Proceedings of the Institute of Acoustics. Interests Are: Vibration, Noise and Stress Engineering; Instrumentation Electronics. *Hobbies:* Gardening; Motoring; Photography; Wine Making. *Address:* 4 Elmbank Road, Kenilworth, Warwickshire, CV8 1AL UK.

ANDREWS, Timothy Douglas, b. 9 Mar. 1938, Birmingham, England. Microfilm Consultant. m. Margaret Hazel Edmonds 31 Aug. 1963, 2 daughters. *Education:* Foundation Scholar, King Edwards School, Birmingam 1949-56; MA, DPhil. Merton College, Oxford, 1958-64. *Appointments:* University of California, 1964-65; MHD, Inc. California, 1965-66; Douglas Aircraft Company, Astro Power Laboratory, 1966-67; ICI Limited 1967-75; Xidex (UK) limited 1975-81; Independent Consultant 1981-. *Memberships:* Fellow, Royal Society of Chemistry; Fellow, British Interplanetary Society; Royal Photographic Society; Society of Photographic Scientists and Engineers. *Publications:* British Patents: 1,310,812; 1,335,962; 1,354,322; 1,360,521; 1,391,423; 1,395,713; 1,410,519; 1,422,631; 1,427,932; United States Patents: 3,697,528; Technical Papers: J Gas Chromatography, 1963; Chemical Communications, 1965; J American Chemical Society, 1965; 1968; Contributor to: Inorganic Syntheses, 1967; Non-Silver Photographic Processes, 1975; Abstractor for Chemical Abstracts. *Hobbies:* Photography; Sailing; Shooting; Skiing; Scuba; Diving; Sky-diving;

Horse-riding. *Address:* Clapper Farm House, East Bergholt, Colchester, Essex, England CO7 6UN.

ANG, Sum, b. 9 May 1946, Tumpat, Malaysia. Orthodontist. m. Yoon-Wan Koo, 28 Apr. 1973. *Education:* BDS, University of Singapore, 1972; Dip. Orth. Royal College of Surgeons, England, 1977; MSc, University of London, 1978. *Appointments:* General Hospital in Singapore, demonstrator at the Operative Dept., University of Singapore, 1972; General Practice in Ilford, London, 1972-75; House Officer/Post Graduate Student, Royal Dental Hospital, London, 1975-78; Specialist Orthodontic Practice, Sydney, NSW, Australia, 1979-; *Memberships:* Australian Dental Associaton; Australian Society of Orthodontists; Australian Begg Study Group; British Society for the Study of Orthodontics. *Publications:* Contributor to Dental Journal; MSc Dissertation, University of London, 1978. *Honours:* Various Book Prizes in Primary Schools, and Secondary Schools; Government Scholarship, Malaysia, 1965-72; Kelantan School Boys Champion in Badminton, Singapore, 1964; Singapore University Badminton Champion for five years, 1965-72. *Hobbies:* Keeping physically fit; Listening to Jazz Music; Interested in energy conservation and being self-sufficient. *Address:* 5/47 Milson Road, Cremorne Point, NSW, 2090, Australia.

ANGELO, Homer G, b. 8 June 1916, Alameda, California, USA. Professor of Law; Company Director. m. Ann Berryhill, 12 Nov. 1943, 1 son, 2 daughters. *Education:* AB, JD, University of California, Berkeley; LL.M, Columbia Law School. *Appointments:* US Department of State, 1949-50; Adviser, US Representative to the United Nations, 1951; Acting Professor Law, Stanford Law School, 1954-57; Founder Governor, International Council of Environment Law, 1968-; Visiting Professor, School of Law, University of California, Berkeley, 1967; Professor, Institut d'Etudes Europeennes, Free University of Brussels, 1968-; Professor of Law, University of California, Davis, 1968-. *Memberships:* Chairman: Section of International and Comparative Law, American Bar Association; Executive Council, American Society of International Law; Executive Committee, American Branch of International Law Association, 1957-59; Vice-Chairman, Commission on Legislation, International Union for the Conservation of Nature, 1966-74; Club De La Fondation Universitaire (Brussels). *Publications:* Multinational Corporate Enterprises—Hague Academy of International Law, 1968. *Address:* Sagehouse Drive, Genoa, Nevada, 89411, USA.

ANGOVE, Thomas William Carlyon, b. 8 Aug. 1917, Adelaide, South Australia. Vigneron & Distiller. m. (1) Jean Primrose Sawers, 10 Feb. 1942 2 sons, 1 daughter, (2) Beverley Robertson DuRieu, 7 Aug. 1958, 2 daughters. *Education:* R.D.Oen (Hons), Roseworthy Agricultural College. *Appointments:* Managing Director, Angove's Pty. Ltd., Renmark, SA; St Agnes Wines Pty. Ltd., Tea Tree Gully, SA; Lyrup Wine Co. Pty. Ltd., Lyrup, SA; Cole & Woodham Pty. Ltd. Renmark, SA; Chairman, Sth. Aust., Local Board, GRE Insurance Ltd; Angove Investments Pty. Ltd., Renmark, SA; Angove Nominees Pty. Ltd., Renmark, SA. *Memberships:* Royal Agricultural & Horticultural Society of South Australia; Association of Agricultural Technologists of Australasia; Chairman, Australian Wine Research Institute; Management & Executive, Australian Wine & Brandy Producers Association; Wine & Brandy Producers Association of South Australia. *Honours:* Star, 1939-45; Pacific Star; War Medal, 1939-45; Australian Service Medal, 1939-45; Silver Jubilee Medal, 1977; Justice of the Peace, South Australia, 1948. *Hobbies:* Flying; Yachting & Power Boating; Hunting; Shooting; Fishing. *Address:* Evans Road, PO Box 12, Renmark, South Australia, 5341.

ANGUS, Barbara, b. 15 Jan. 1924 Woodville, New Zealand. Diplomat. *Education:* MA(Hons) Otago University, New Zealand. *Appointments:* Second Secretary, Singapore, 1962-64; First Secretary, Sydney, 1964-68; Deputy High Commissioner, Kuala Lumpur, 1972-75; Minister, Washington, 1976-78; Ambassador, Manila, 1978-. *Hobbies:* Swimming; Walking; Reading; Bridge. *Address:* 12 Banaba Street, Forbes Park, Metro Manila.

ANGUS, John Colin, b. 8 Dec. 1907 Wangaratt, Victoria, Australia. Artist. m. Lilian Christina Roberts 20 May 1939, 1 son, 2 daughters. *Education:* Wangaratta and Dandenong High Schools. *Appointments:*

Own Business 1929-68; Part-time Painting 1940-68; Full-time painting 1968-. *Memberships:* Executive and Honary Life Member North-Eastern Historical Society; Delegate North-Eastern Historical Association; Royal Historical Society of Victoria; Vice-president North-Eastern Branch National Trust of Australia; Victorian Artists' Society; Australian Guild Realist Artists, Melbourne; Ferntree Gully Art Society; Life Member Benalla Art Gallery; Bega Art Society; President, Anvil Art Society; Executive El Dorado Museum Trust; Executive Centennial Park Trust. *Publications:* Author, Wangaratta Shire Centenary 1967; Mining at El Dorado 1966; Co-Author (with Harley Forster) The Ovens Valley; co-author (with Hilde Knorr) J. Colin Angus Landscapes 1955-1978 (1978 and 1981); Contributed articles to The Artist, London; The Riverlander; The Antique Collector; Albury Border Morning Mail; Wangaratta Chronicle; one time editor N.E.H.S. Newsletter. *Honours:* Painting awards: Albury, N.S.W. 1955, 1961, 1968, 1970; Sherbrooke (Vic) Shire Award, 1970; Harriëtville, Victoria, 1962; Warrnambool, Victoria, 1964; Rutherglen, Victoria, 1970; Bega, N.S.W., 1976; Wodonga, Victoria, 1968, 1969; Galerie 34 Grand Prix award, Paris, 1979; One main exhibitions in all Australian States, London, Paris, Cologne and Singapore. *Hobbies:* Historical Research; Gardening. *Address:* "Wandana", El Dorado, Victoria, 3746, Australia.

ANGWENYI, Charles Peter, b. 1 Jan. 1939 Kisii, Kenya. Banker; Economist. m. Susan Njeri 20 Mar. 1971, 2 sons, 1 daughter. *Education:* 1st Division Cambridge School Certificate; BA Economics, Colby College USA; MA Economics, University of Massachusettes USA; Completed requirements for PhD Degree except dissertation. *Appointments:* Planning Officer, Ministry of Finance and Economics Planning 1968; Lecturer in Economics, University of Nairobi 1968 and 1969; Appointed Visiting Lecturer Chapman College, USA, (World Campus Afloat Programme, 1970); Management Trainee, Standard Bank Limited, 1970; 10 years in various capacities and positions including Marketing and Business Departments, Senior Manager of Standard Bank; Chairman, National Bank of Kenya Limited. *Memberships:* United Kenya Club; Kenya Institute of Management—Director Kiambu Club; Free Mason, Lodge Unity; Diners Club; Kenya Economic Association; Public Relations Society of Kenya. *Publications:* Two Tone—Shakespeare's Othello; African Economic Problems; Population and Economic Growth; Inflation in Kenya; Devaluation in Kenya; Access to Credit—Commercial Bank Lending in Kenya. *Honours:* Blue Hill Foundation Scholarship Award, Colby College, USA, 1963; Institute of International Education Fellowship 1966/68; Who's Who in Dictionary of International Biography; Who's Who in the World 1979. *Hobbies:* Swimming; Golf; Reading; Writing; Travelling. *Address:* PO Box 67899, Nairobi, Kenya.

ANIELO, Alexis Iloegbunam, b. 13 July 1936, Enugu, Nigeria. Engineer; Industrial Consultant. m. Irene Ogochi Madubico 22 Apr. 1972, 3 daughters. *Education:* Technical University Hannover; Engineering University Düsseldorf, 1963-69; BSc, Engineering; Diploma Industrial Economics; Diploma Comp. Sciences. *Appointments:* Study Engineering, Westinghouse, Hannover, West Germany, 1965; Project Engineer, Siemens AS, Düsseldorf, 1969; Project Engineer, Kessler University, Luch, 1970; Project Engineer, International Harverster Company Neuss, 1970-71; Industrial Engineer, Nigerian Industrial Development Bank, Lagos, Nigeria, 1971-74; Chairman/Managing Director, Maurice Project Centre Limited, 1974-. *Memberships:* Geman Society of Engineers; American Management Association; Presidents Association of American; Institute of Management Consultants, Nigeria; Nigerian Institute of Management; Lagos Chamber of Commerce, Nigera. *Publications:* Labour Problems of Developing Countries; Industrial Application of Differential Equalities; The Challenge of Industrial Take off. *Honours:* Silver Medal Award High Jump, Wollwich Poly, London, 1959. *Hobbies:* Piano and Organ; Table Tennis. *Address:* Plot 94 Animashaun Close, off Aledlaton Street, Surulere, Lagos, Nigeria.

ANI, Godwin Njokuji, b. 20 Mar. 1945, Ohofia Oduma, Awgu Local Government Area. Company Secretary; Administration Manager. m. A Chukwu, 31 Mar. 1973, 1 son, 1 daughter. *Education:* ACIS Finals, 1967; ACCA (Section 1 Finals), 1973. *Appointments:* Cooperative Officer, 1966-73; Government Auditor, 1973-77; Company Secretary, Administration Manager, 1977-81. *Memberships:* President, Oduma Improvement Union; ACIS, London & Wales; Nigerian Chartered Institute of Secretaries; Nigerian Institute of Public Relations; Nigerian Institute of Personnel Management. *Publications:* Contributed to various journals. *Honours:* Eastern Nigeria Government Scholarship, 1960-65. *Hobby:* Reading, Law & Literature. *Address:* Ohofia Oduma, Awgu Local Government Area, Anambra State, Nigeria.

ANIGBORO, Pius Jeremiah Orieoghenebrulu, b. 16 Mar. 1942, Emevor, Bendel State of Nigeria. Legal Profession. m. 5 Aug. 1974, 1 daughter. *Education:* LL.B.(Hons), Ife, 1971; Called to the Nigerian Bar, 1972. *Appointments:* Private legal practice. *Memberships:* First Assistant General Secretary, Nigerian Bar Association, 1980-81, 1981-82. *Publications:* An Outline of Emevor History and Organisation; Contributor to Professional Journals. *Honours:* Notary Public for Nigeria, 1980-. *Hobbies:* Reading; Writing. *Address:* 34 Upper Ereguwa Road, PO Box 128, Warri, Bendel State of Nigeria.

ANIYOM (Chief), Dien Akankpo, b. 1 Apr. 1926, Umon Town, Cross River State, Nigeria. Land Surveyor. m. Arit Etim Duke, 19 Dec. 1953, 2 sons, 4 daughters. *Education:* Associate, Royal Institution of Chartered Surveyors, 1963; Licensed Surveyor (Nigeria), 1964. *Appointments:* Survey Assistant, Survey Department, Nigeria, 1949-56; Student Nigerian College of Technology 1956-60; Technical Officer, Federal Survey Department, 1960-63; Staff Surveyor, Federal Survey Department, 1963-65; Chief Surveyor, Electricity Corporation of Nigeria, 1966-67; Licensed Surveyor in private practice, 1970-81; Managing Director. Aniyom Surveys Ltd., 1978-; Director, Cross River State Water Board. *Memberships:* President, Nigerian Instituion of Surveyors, 1978-79; Chairman, Commission 7 of the International Federation of Surveyors, 1976-78; Fellow Royal Institution Chartered Surveyors Britain; Chairman, Rotary Club, 1979-80. *Publications:* Papers on, The Principal Land Tenure Systems of Nigeria and The Prospects of Nigeria Having a National Cadastre; Editor, Rot Aba, Jour Rotary Club, Aba, 1977-79. *Honours:* Chief of Umon, Nigeria, 27 Dec. 1980; Elder of the Presbyterian Church of Nigeria, 15 Oct. 1972; Certificate of Appreciation, International Federation Surveyors, 1978. *Hobbies:* Singing in choirs, Listening to Classical music; Church Activities; Swimming; Dancing; Rotary. *Address:* 3 St. Michael's Road, P.M.B. 7223, Aba, Nigeria

ANKOMAH, Kofi, b. 20 May 1942, Nkronso-Akim, Eastern Region, Ghana. Senior Lecturer. m. Elsie Honny, 25 Oct. 1980. *Education:* AB, Parsons College, Fairfield, Iowa, USA, 1960-63; MPA, 1963-66, PhD, 1966-74, New York University. *Appointments:* New York City Central Baour Council AFL-CIO; Assistant Research Officer, 1967, Lecturer, 1967-74, Senior Lecturer, 1974-, Co-ordinator, International Relations Course, 1975-76, Co-ordinator, Ghana Police Course, 1977-79, Ghana Institute of Management and Public Administration; Part-time Library Assistant, Parson's College, 1961-63; Swaziland Institute of Management & Public Administration. *Memberships:* American Society for Public Administration; Royal African Society; African Association of Public Administration & Management. *Publications:* Numerous articles and book reviews in professional journals including: Spear and Scepter—Army, Police and Politics in Tropical Africa, 1972; The Administration of Nigeria, 1972; African Perspectives—Papers in The History, Politics and Economics of Africa, 1973. *Honours:* Phelps Stokes Fund, 1963-64; Paulstudenski Award, 1964-65; Ford Foundation, 1970. *Hobbies:* Tennis; Travelling & Camping; Book reviewing and writing Radio Commentaries on National Affairs. *Address:* c/o Swaziland Institute of Management & Public Administration, PO Box 495, Mbabane, Swaziland.

ANNAN, Joseph Samuel, b. 1 Jan. 1914, Sekondi, Ghana. Electrical Engineer and Retired International Civil Servant. m. Elizabeth Aba , 30 Dec. 1944, 1 son, 3 daughters. *Education:* BSc (London), Achimota University College (External London), 1935-40; Associate, Heriot-Watt College, Edinburgh, 1941-42. *Appointments:* Probationer Electrical Engineer, Gold Coast Railway, 1940-41; Assistant Electrical Engineer, 1943-45; Labour Officer, Senior Labour Officer, 1945-

54; Senior Assistant Secretary, Permanent Secretary, Government of Ghana, 1955-60; Liaison Officer for Africa, F.A.O. Rome, 1960-62; Assistant to the Executive Director UN/FAO, World Food Programme, 1962-77; Director,. Retired from International Civil Service, 1977. *Memberships:* International Biographical Association. *Hobbies:* Church music, Gardening, Rural Development. *Address:* P.O. Box A408, Labadi, Accra, Ghana, West Africa.

ANNAN, MacDonald Ako, b. 2 Jan. 1933, Labadi. Bookseller. m. Comfort Wellington, 3 Aug. 1962, 2 sons, 1 daughter. *Education:* Stenographer Grade I Certificate, Government Secretarial School, 1957; Proficiency Certificate, Booksellers' Middle Management, Training Course, 1976. *Appointments:* Stenographer, Grade II, Electricity Corporation of Ghana, 1957-; Stenographer, Grade I, Ghana Broadcasting Corporation, 1959-; Clerk, Grade I, 1962-, Senior Clerk, 1967-, Assistant Bookshop Manager, 1975, Senior Assistant Bookshop Manager, 1981- University of Ghana Bookshop. *Memberships:* Ghana Bookseller's Association; Accra Horse Owners Association; La Salem Old Students Association (Secretary); La Town Development Committee. *Hobbies:* Horse Racing; Card Playing, Reading, Swimming. *Address:* N11. Adjei.Odai. WE, Onidin's Lodge, Emmaus, Labadi-Accra, Ghana, West Africa.

ANSETT, Reginald Myles (Sir), b. 13 Feb. 1909, Inglewood, Victoria. Company Director. m. Joan McAuliffe Adams, 17 June 1944, 3 daughters. *Education:* State School & Swinburne Technical College. *Appointments:* Chairman & Managing Director, Ansett Transport Industries Ltd., 1936-80. *Memberships:* VRC; VATC; MVRC. *Honours:* Knight Commander of the British Empire, 1969. *Hobbies:* Horse Racing; Game Shooting. *Address:* Gunyong Valley, Mount Eliza, Victoria. Australia.

ANSETT, Robert Graham, b. 8 Aug. 1933. Managing Director. m. Josie 1 Jan. 1975, 2 sons, 1 daughter. *Education:* High School, Vista California USA, 1951. *Appointments:* Salesman Carnation Company Los Angeles California; Salesman Oroweat Company San Diego California; General Manager, Managing Director Budget Rent A Car Melbourne Australia. *Memberships:* President, Melbourne Chamber of Commerce, 1981; President North Melbourne Football Club; Vice-Chairman Moomba Festival; Australian Tourist Advisory Council. *Honours:* Charles McGrath Award, Marketing, 1979. *Hobbies:* Skiing-Water/Snow; Tennis. *Address:* 53 Wilson Street, Princess Hill, Victoria, Australia.

ANSFORD, Anthony Joseph, Pathologist. *Education:* Entered Otago University after three years training as a Medical Laboratory Technologist, 1960; MB.,Ch.B., 1965; Diploma Clinical Pathology, Otago, 1972; Fellow, The Royal College of Pathologists of Australasia, 1975; Fellowship, The Royal Australasian College of Physicians, 1975. *Appointments:* Resident House Officer, Timaru Hospital, 1966-67; Resident Medical Officer, Middlemarch Special Area (General Practice at direction of NS Health Department, bonded bursar), 1968 Cardiological, Renal & General Medical Registrar & Assistant Lecturer in Medicine, 1969, Registrar & Assistant Lecturer in Pathology, 1970-72, Dunedin Hospital and Otago University; Registrar in Histopathology, Fairfax Institute of Pathology, Royal Prince Alfred Hospital, Camperdown, New South Wales, 1972-74; Part-time Government Medical Officer, Division of Forensic Medicine, Glebe, NSW, 1974; Pathologist, 1974-, Pathologist in Charge, Cytogenetics Section, 1974-, Haematology Section, 1974-, Deputy Director, 1980-, Laboratory of Microbiology and Pathology and Institute of Forensic Pathology, Brisbane; Tutor (Part-time) in Pathology, 1975-, in Child Health, 1976-, Visiting Lecturer in Forensic Pathology, 1976-, University of Queensland; Visiting Pathologist, Wolston Park Hospital, Wacol, 1977-. *Memberships:* Executive Otago University Medical Students Association, 1963-64; Royal Australasain College of Physicians, 1970; Medical Faculty, Otago University; Vice-Patron of Otago University Medical Students Association; Chairman and elected representative of Dunedin Hospital Pathology Registrars, 1970-71; New Zealand Society of Pathologists, 1971; Australasian Division, International Academy of Pathology, 1973; Committee on Anaesthetic Deaths, Queensland Health Department, representing College

of Pathologists of Australasia; Queensland Perinatal Mortality Committee. *Publications:* Numerous papers and Case Reports; Contributor to medical journals including: Malignant Brenner Tumour (w. H McKenna), 1976; Fatal Oleander Poisoning, 1981. *Honours:* Scott Memorial Prize and Sistinction in Human Anatomy, 1962; William Ledingham Christie Prize in Surgical Anatomy, 1964; Fowler Scholarship in Medicine, 1965; James Boyd Prize in Clinical Medicine, Wellington Hospital, 1965; Smith Kline and French Prize with Distinction in Clinical Psychiatry, 1965; International Cancer Conference, Sydney, 1972; Visited Melbourne as sponsored Fellow of the New Zealand Cancer Society, 1972. *Address:* 15 Montanus Drive, Bellbowrie Queensland, 4070, Australia.

ANSTEE, Dorothy Rae, b. 15 Aug. 1932, Melbourne, Victoria, Australia. Nursing. *Education:* General Nurse Training, Royal Children's Hospital, Melbourne, Australia, 1957-61; Ward Sister's Diploma, College of Nursing, Australia, 1965-; Midwifery Certificate, Box Hill & District Hospital, Melbourne, Australia, 1969-70; Infant Welfare Certificate, Presbyterian Babies Home, Melbourne, Australia, 1972-72; Diploma of Nursing Administration, College of Nursing, Australia, 1973-. *Appointments:* Royal Children's Hospital, Melbourne, Australia - Staff Nurse & Sister, 1961-63, Charge Nurse, 1963-65, Supervisory Sister, 1965-69, Assistant Director of Nursing, 1970-77; Director of Nursing, Austin Hospital, Melbourne, 1977-. *Memberships:* League of Former Trainees, Royal Children's Hospital, 1961-; Honorary Secretary, Paediatrics Special Interest Group, R.A.N.F., 1975-78; Surveyor for the Australian Council on Hospital Standards, 1976-; Chairman, Nursing Services Standing Committee, R.A.N.F. (Victoria), 1976-78; Chairman, Child Health Co-ordinating Interim Committee R.A.N.F., 1977-79; Austin Hospital Graduate Nurses' Association, 1978-; President, Royal Australian Nursing Federation (Victoria Branch), 1978-80; Association of Directors of Nursing and Principal Nurse Teachers, 1979-; Victorian Nursing Council Committee, 1980-; Monash University Research Project, 1980-; Chairman, The Methicillin Resistant Committee, 1980-; Representative, The Association of Directors of Nursing on the Political Action Group of the R.A.N.F., 1980-. *Hobbies:* Child and Family Health Care, World Affairs, Music and People. *Address:* Unit 3, 6 Carlyle Street, Hawthorn, 3122, Victoria, Australia.

ANSTEY (Lilly), Marjorie Daphne, b. 6 Oct. 1915, Sherbrooke, Quebec, Canada. Documentary Film Maker. m. Edgar Anstey OBE, 2 Apr. 1949, 1 son, 1 daughter. *Education:* Alberta, British Columbia; One year specialized course, University of Western Ontario. *Appointments:* Calgary & Ottawa branches, Bank of Montreal, 1936-41; National Film Board of Canada, 1941-47; Worked on theatrical series World in Action and Canada Carries On; Free-lance film editor in New York with Standard Oil and World Today, 1947-49; Subsequent occasional consultation and representational work including Editor on experimental programmes for young people at London's National Film Theatre and return visit to NFB, Montreal, in International Women's Year, 1975, to take part in retrospective on women's role in documentary films; Participated with Edgar Anstey in film conferences/festivals worldwide. *Memberships:* General Purposes and United Nations Committees (former Chairman of each); Associated Country Women of the World; Executive committees Commonwealth Human Ecology Council and Institute of Rural Life at Home and Overseas; Women's Advisory Council United Nations Association. *Publications:* Arctic Jungle, National Film Board of Canada documentary, 1946. *Hobbies:* Visiting old cathedral towns; Commonwealth and international communication; Reading; Travel. *Address:* 6 Hurst Close, Hampstead Garden Suburb, London, N.W.11, 7BE, England.

ANSTEY, Thomas Herbert, b. 27 Dec. 1917, Victoria B.C. Canada. Agrologist. m. Laura Winifred Ferguson 6 July 1945, 1 son, 2 daughters. *Education:* BSA, 1941, MSA, 1943, University of British Columbia, PhD, University of Minnesota, 1949. *Appointments:* Research Scientist, Experimental Farm, Agassiz BC 1946-52; Superintendent, Experimental Farm, Summerland BC 1952-58; Superintendent, Experimental Farm, Kentville NS 1958-59; Director, Research Station, Lethbridge Alta 1959-69; Director General (West) Research Branch, Agriculture Canada 1969-79; Senior Advisor

Internation R&D, Research Br. Agr. Cam 1979-. *Memberships:* National President, Agriculture Institute of Canada; Ontario Institute of Agrologists; Canadian Society for Horticluture Science; Canadian Society of Genetics and Cytology. *Publications:* 20 Scientific papers on Plant Breeding. *Honours:* Conway Memorial Research Fellowship 1959; Nuffield Travelling Fellowship 1969; Fellow, Agriculture Institute of Canada 1980. *Hobbies:* Downhill Skiing; Sailing; Gardening. *Address:* 12 Warbonnet Drive, Nepeam, Ontario, Canada, K2E 5M2.

ANTESON, Reginald Kwaku, b. 28 Nov. 1936, Accra, Ghana. University Lecturer (Scientist). m. Grace Akuoko Abbey-Mensah, 24 June 1961, 2 sons, 2 daughters. *Education:* BSc (General), 1960, BSc (Special), University College, Ghana; MSc, Medical Parasitology, McGill, Canada, 1964; PhD, Parasitology, University, Conn. USA, 1968; Diploma, Microbial Diseases, Osaka University, Japan, 1978; Diploma, Parasitological Techniques, Fakushome, Japan, 1981. *Appointments:* Assistant Research Officer in Parasitology, Ghana Academy of Sciences, 1961-63; Assistant Professor, Lecturer, University of Rhode Island Kingston, Rhode Island, USA, 1968; Teacher, Department of Microbiology, University of Ghana Medical School, 1968-. *Memberships:* American Society of Parasitologists; American Society of Tropical Medicine and Hygiene; Sigma Xi. *Publications:* Published scientific papers in the field of Filarial Diseases, Schiestosomiasis and Toxoplasmosis. *Honours:* Afgrad Fellowship, 1967; Canadian Government Fellowship, 1962-64; WHO Fellowship, Denmark, 1972; WHO Postdoctoral Fellowship, USA 1973-74; Japan Government Fellowship, 1977, 1981. *Hobbies:* Listening to Jazz, Blues and Country Music; Poultry Farming; Gardening; Playing Table Tennis. *Address:* 12 Nicodemus Road, Lartebiokorshie. Accra, Ghana.

ANTHONIO, Quirino Bandele Olatunji, b. 16 May 1932. Professor, Agricultural Economics. m. Henrietta Olaitan Sholade, 26 Dec. 1957, 5 sons. *Education:* BSc., (agriculture), London; University College, Ibadan, 1958-; Diploma Agricultural Economics, St. Catherine's College, Oxford, England, 1959-; MSc University of California, Berkeley, USA., 1966-; PhD. University of London, England, 1968-. *Appointments:* Agricultural Officer, Ministry of Agriculture, Ibadan, Nigeria, 1958-; Agricultural Economist, Ministry of Economics, Planning, Ibadan, Nigeria, 1969-; Lecturer, Agricultural Economics, University of Ibadan, Nigeria, 1968-; Professor of Agricultural Economics, 1975-; Director, ECA/FAO Agriculture Division, Addis Ababa, Ethiopia, 1976-. *Memberships:* General Secretary, Agricultural Society of Nigeria, 1960-63; Agricultural Economics Society, U.K.; Nigerian Economic Society, Nigeria; Editor-in-Chief, Nigerian Journal of Agriculture, 1970-75; Country Representative, International Association of Agricultural Economists. *Publications:* Economic Problems of Peasant Storage, Ministry of Economics Planning, Ibadan, 1962-; Upton & Anthonio, Farming as a Business, Oxford University Press, 1964-; Q.B.O. Anthonio, General Agriculture for West Africa, 1980-. *Honours:* Scholarship, University College of Ibadan, 1953-58; Rockefeller Fellowship, Oxford University, 1958-60; Rockefeller Fellowship, University of California, 1963-66. *Hobbies:* Photography, Cinema, Tennis and Music. *Address:* 3/4 Benin Road, Sogunle, Lagos State, Nigeria.

ANTHONY, John, Douglas, b. 1929. Australian Politician and Farmer. m. Margot McD. Budd, 1957, 2 sons, 1 daughter. *Education:* Murwillumbah, Kings School; Parramatta, New South Wales; Queensland Diploma of Agriculture. *Appointments:* Minister for the Interior 1964-1967; Minister for Primary Industry 1967-1971; Leader, Australian Country Party since 1971 (called National Country Party of Australia since 1975); appointed a Privy Councillor 1971; Deputy Prime Minister, Minister for Trade and Industry 1971-1972; Deputy Prime Minister, Minister for Natural Resources and Minister for Overseas Trade 1975-1977; Deputy Prime Minister and Minister for Trade and Resources since 1977. *Hobbies:* Sunnymeadows, Murwillumbah, N.S.W. 2484, Australia.

ANTIA, Dara Pirojshaw, b. 31 May 1914, Bulsar, Surat District, Gujarat State, India. Industrial and Management Consultant. m. Jeroo H Wania, 17 Sept. 1950, 1 son, 2 daughters. *Education:* BSc, Metallurgy,

Banaras University, 1938; ScD, Physical Metallurgical and Mineral Economics, Massachusetts Institute of Technology, Cambridge, Massachusetts, USA, 1943; Diploma, Advanced Management, Harvard Business School, Cambridge, Massachusetts, 1959; Founder, Indian Institute of Metals, 1946. *Appointments:* Director of Metals, Government of India, 1946-50; Director and Deputy Managing Director, Union Carbide India Ltd., 1955-72; Chairman and Director of Numerous Companies including: Machine Tools (India) Ltd.; Tega India Ltd.; Techno Electric and Engineering Company Ltd.; Kayshree Chemical Ltd.; Willard India Ltd.; Cominco Binani Zinc Ltd.; Bhartia Electric Steel Company Ltd.; Uni Abex Alloy Products Ltd.; Metal Distributors Ltd.; Tata-Yodogawa Ltd.; Nilhat Shipping Company Ltd.; Jessop and Company Ltd.; 1973-79; Incheck Tyres Ltd., 1973-75; Bharat Aluminium Company Ltd., 1969-73. *Memberships:* Fellow, Indian National Science Academy; Institution of Metallurgists, UK; American Society for Metals; Numerous other Indian and Foreign Societies. *Publications:* 34 publications including: Quantitive Determination of Retained Austenite by X-Ray, 1943; Tempering of High Carbon Steels, 1945; Some Aspects of Industrial Management and Productivity, 1946; Anant Pandya Memorial Lecture, 1972; Technology, Organisation and Management, 1973; Tego Endowment Lecture, 1979; Reduction of Wear in Mineral Handling and Processing Industries; First Syed Husain Zaheer Medal Lecture, 1980; Materials Science and Engineering—an Overview. *Honours:* Honorary Member, Metals Society, UK; Indian Institute of Metals; Henry Marion Howe Medal of the American Society for Metals, 1946; Indian Institute of Metals Platinum Medal, 1947; S H Zaheer Medal, Indian National Science Academy, 1980. *Hobbies:* Golf; Bridge; Reading. *Address:* 10 Judges Court Road, Flat No 7, Calcutta 700 027, India.

ANTIPPA, Adel Fadel, b. 17 Mar. 1942, Beirut, Lebanon. Professor of Physics. m. Monique Vaillancourt, 28 Dec. 1969, 1 son, 1 daughter. *Education:* Baccalauréat II (Mathématiques) International College, Beirut, 1960; BSc, Physics, American University of Beirut, 1964; PhD, Physics, Tufts University, Boston, USA, 1970. *Appointments:* Assistant Professor, 1970-73, Associate Professor, 1973-81, Professor, 1981-, Department of Physics, Université du Québec à Trois-Rivères, Québec, Canada. *Memberships:* American Physical Society, 1969; L'Association canadienne-fraîse pour l'avancement des sciences, 1970; American Association of Physics Teachers, 1973; Canadian Association of Physicists, 1974; Canadian Applied Mathematical Society, 1979. *Publications:* Various Major Scientific Contribution in The Physical Review, Journal of Mathematical Physics, Discrete Mathematics, CAnadian Journal of Physics, Il Nuovo Cimento, Chemical Physics Letters, Journal of Theoretical Biology and American Journal of Physics. Contributions on Graph Theory, Calculus of Finite Differences, Polynomial Potentials, High Energy Physics, Theory of Relativity, Photosynthesis, Kinetics of Germination. *Honours:* Penrose Award, American University of Beirut, 1964. *Hobbies:* Listening to music; Playing the piano; Swimming; Cycling. *Address:* 235 rue Ringuet, Trois-Rivieres, Quebec, Canada, G9A 3C6, Canada.

ANUKPE, Walter Jemeje, b. 9 Apr. 1927, Warri, Nigeria. Civil Servant, Banker. m. Rebecca Oritsematosan Nanna, 22 Mar. 1951, 4 daughters. *Education:* BSc. Honours Economics, University of Southampton, UK., 1953-56; Postgraduate inservice course in Public Administration, University of Ibadan, Nigeria, 1958-59; MA, Williams College, Williamstown, Massachusetts, USA., 1962-63. *Appointments:* Administrative Officer, Class IV, 1956-60, Class III, 1960-63, Western Nigerian Government; Administrative Officer, Class II, 1963-65, Staff Grade, 1965-70, Midwestern Nigerian Government, Chairman/Managing Director, New Nigeria Bank, 1970-80. *Memberships:* Past President Rotary Club of Benin City, Nigeria; Past President, Gideons International, Benin Club. *Hobbies:* Photography, Swimming, Table Tennis. *Address:* 22 Ovie-Whiskey Avenue, Off Aghu Street, Off Ekenwan Road, Benin City, Nigeria.

ANYA, Anya Oko, b. 3 Jan. 1937, Umuahia-Ibeku, Nr. Abiriba, Nigeria. Research Biologist/University Teacher. m. Inyang Oji Iboko, 7 Aug. 1965, 3 sons. *Education:* Hope Waddell Training Institution, Calabar, Nigeria, 1950-56, BSc. (Special Honours, London 1961), University College, Ibadan, 1958-61; PhD, St. Johns College, University of Cambridge, England, 1965-. *Appointments:* Fisheries Research Officer, Nigeria, 1961-63; Agricultural Research Officer, Nigeria, 1963-65; Lecturer in Zoology, University of Nigeria, 1965-70; Senior Lecturer, 1970-73; Professor of Zoology, 1973-; Dean of Faculty of Biological & Pharmaceutical Sciences, 1976-78; Head Department of Zoology, 1978-79; Director, School of Postgraduate Studies, University of Nigeria, 1979-. *Memberships:* Ecological Society of Nigeria, 1973-79; Editor-in-Chief and Council Nigeria Society for Parasitology, 1974-79; Science Association of Nigeria; Cambridge Philosophical Society; British Society for Parasitology, Institute of Biology, UK.; New York Academy of Science; Nigerian Academy of Science; Chairman, Imo State Library Board, Nigeria, 1976-79; Chairman Federal Government of Nigeria Committee on Academic Freedom, 1978-79; Governing Board, Lake Chad Research Institute, 1980; Secretary, Council for Public and International Relations and Academis Secretary Biological Sciences, 1980-. *Publications:* Biological professional papers in Nature; Parasitology; International Journal of Parasitology; Comparative Physiology and Biochemistry; Advances in Parasitology. Forth-coming book, An African Perception: Science, Man and Development, 1980-; Nigerian Institute of International Affairs, Lagos, Science Policy and the development of Nigeria's geopolitical potential, 1977-. *Honours:* Fellow, Institute of Biology, 1976-; Fellow, Nigerian Academy of Science, 1979-. *Hobbies:* Reading, Tennis, Music (listening), Conversation. *Address:* 307 Marquerite Cartwright Avenue, University of Nigeria, Nsukka.

ANYA, Udegbunem Nwokolo, b. 23 Apr. 1936 Ezeagu Nigeria. Legal Practitioner. m. Marie Shirley Fraser, 18 Feb. 1962, 3 sons, 2 daughters. *Education:* North-Western Polytechnic, London, 1959-60; LLB. Hons, Hull University, England 1963; D.Ilsm., B.L. Hon. Society of Middle Temple, London and Nigerian Law School 1964. *Appointments:* Solicitor and Advocate of the Supreme Court of Nigeria, 1964-. *Memberships:* Chairman, Nigeria Bar Association, Emugu, Nigeria; Anambra State of Nigeria Law Reporting Committee. *Publications:* Author of fictions: She died in the Bloom of Youth; Bitter Days; Matter of Life and Death; Wretched Orphan. *Hobbies:* Gaming; Hunting. *Address:* 4 Mgbemena Street, Ogbete, Box 744, Emugu, Nigeria.

ANYANWU, Enoch Agulanna, b. 15 Oct. 1933, Umuariam, Nigeria. Professor and Secretary, Imo State Government. m. Beatrice Ngozi Ikeazota, 27 July 1962, 1 son, 1 daughter. *Education:* BA(Hons) Econs. Durham University, England, 1958; MA(Econs) Yale University, USA, 1963; DPhil.(Econs) Oxford University, Oxford, 1967. *Appointments:* School teacher and Master, 1943-50; Clerical Officer, Regional Treasury Department Enugu, 1951-53; Senior Assistant Secretary, Ministry of Finance and Economic Development, Enugu production and compilatio, Development Plan, 1962-68; Research Officer, Institute of Economics and Statistics, Oxford University, 1967-68; Research Officer, National Institute for Economic and Social Research, Smith Square, London, 1968; Economic Adviser, Economic Services Div. Department of Trade and Industries, London, 1969-71; Industrial Econ. Development Experts, International Bank for Reconstruction and Development, Washington DC, 1972-77; World Bank Industrial Economic Dev. Expert and Adviser for Ethiopia, Liberia and Nepal, 1973-76; Associate Professor of Economics and Head of Economics, African Studies and Research Programme, Howard University, 1972-75; Professor of Economics, University of Nigeria, 1977; Head, Department of Economics, University of Nigeria, Nsukka, 1976-79; Secretary, Imo State Government, Nigeria, 1979-. *Memberships:* American Economic Association; International Studies Association, USA; Nigerian Economic Society; Royal Economic Society UK; Association of University Teachers of Great Britain and Northern Ireland; ECOWAS. *Publications:* 15 Books, Monographs and Articles including: Regional Index of Industrial Consuption in Great Britain, 1970; Evaluation of Some Export Projections for Developing Countries, 1973; Problems of Industrialization in Least-Developed Countries, 1974; Small Scale, Cottage and Handicraft Industries Development in Ethiopia, 1977. *Honours:* Eastern Nigerian Regional Government Scholarship, 1955-58; Oxford University post graduate scholarship, distinction in academic work; Outstanding

Student, Department of Economics, Durham University 1958. *Hobbies:* Lawn and Table Tennis; Golf. *Address:* Umuariam Obowo, Etiti Local Government Area, Imo State, Nigeria.

ANYAOKU, Eleazar Chukwuemeka, b. 18 Jan. 1933, Obosi, Nigeria. Diplomat; Deputy Secretary-General of the Commonwealth. m. Ebunola Olubunmi Solanke, Oct. 1962, 3 sons, 1 daughter. *Education:* BA(Hons) London, University College of Ibadan, 1954-59; Special courses, Cambridge University, Royal Institute of Public Administration, London, and Cavillam Institute, Vichy, France. *Appointments:* Executive Assistant, Colonial Development Corporation, Regional Office, Lagos, 1961; Ministry of External Affairs, Lagos, 1962-63; Permanent Mission of Nigeria, UN, New York, 1963-66; Assistant Director, International Affairs Division, Commonwealth Secretariat, London, 1966-71; Director, International Affairs Division, 1971-75; Assistant Secretary General 1975-77; Deputy Secretary General 1978-. *Memberships:* Chairman, Africa Centre, London; Vice President, Royal Commonwealth Society, London; Governing Board of English Speaking Union and Save the Children Fund; Overseas Development Institute, London. *Publications:* The Racial Factor in International Politics, published by the Nigerian Institute of International Affairs, Lagos; Other papers and Lectures. *Hobbies:* Reading; Tennis; Swimming. *Address:* 1 Halkin Place, Belgravia, London, SW1, England.

APTE, Nilkantha, b. 26 July 1923, Baroda, India. Ear, Nose and Throat Surgeon. m. 30 Nov. 1949, 3 daughters. *Education:* MBBS, 1946; MS, 1949; FCPS, General Surgery, 1948; DLO, 1951; MS, in Otorhinolaryngology with Distinction, Bombay, 1953; FACS, USA, 1976. *Appointments:* Professor and Head of the Department of Ear Nose and Throat, Grant Medical College, Bombay, India; Hon. Surgeon, J.J. Government Hospital, Bombay Hospital. *Memberships:* Otolaryngologists of India; Rotary Club of Bombay. *Publications:* Scientific articles in the field of Ear Nose and Throat; Published in Journal of Laryngology and Otology, London, and other Journals in India. *Honours:* MS (E.N.T.) Passed with Distinction, 1953; FACS, 1976; Regional Conference Guest Lecture Awards, A.O.O.I., West Bengal (Br) 1974, Hyderabad (Br) 1975, Jodhpur (Br) 1980. *Hobbies:* Painting; Dramas; Movies. *Address:* 3 D, Ananta, B. Desai Road, Bombay 400026, India.

AQUINAS (Monahan), Sister Mary, b. 30 Aug. 1919, Cappatagle, Galway, Ireland. Medicine. *Education:* MB, BCh, B.A.O., N.U.I. (Dublin) 1947; LM (Coombe) 1947; TDD (Wales) 1953; FRCP (Edin.) (Hon.) 1977. *Appointments:* Medical Superintendent, Ruttonjee Sanatorium, Hong Kong, 1949; Hon. Clinical Lecturer, Department of Medicine, University of Hong Kong, 1958. *Memberships:* BMA, Hong Kong; Hong Kong Medical Association; Federation of Medical Societies of Hong Kong; The Society for the Aid and Rehabilitation of Drug Abusers; Soroptimist International of Hong Kong. *Publications:* Participating with British Medical Research Council in co-operative Clinical Chemotherapeutic Trials for Tuberculosis for over 15 years. *Honours:* Sir Robert Philip Gold Medal 1965; Honorary, Doctor of Social Sciences, University of Hong Kong, 1978; OBE 1980. *Hobby:* Music. *Address:* Ruttonjee Sanatorium, 266, Queen's Road, East Hong Kong.

ARABA, Adekunle Babatunde, b. 27 September, 1936 Lagos Nigeria. Medical Practitioner, University Lecturer. 1 son, 3 daughters. *Education:* Ogbobi College Yaba, Lagos Nigeria 1951-1955; B.Sc.(Hon) King's College London; A.K.C. London 1958-1961; Westminster Medical School, London, S.W.1 1961-1964; Rikshospitalet, Klinisk Nervofysiolog, Oslo 1970-1971, Diploma in Clinical Neurophysiology. *Appointments:* Queen Mary's Hospital, Roehampton, London, England, 1964; Hackney Hospital, London, E.9, 1965; Lagos University Teaching Hospital, Lagos, Nigeria, 1965; Lecturer (Consultant in Physiology) College of Medicine, University of Lagos, Nigeria; Senior Lecturer in Physiology, CM.VL 1974-1978; Consultant in Clinical Neurophysiology, Lagos University Teaching Hospital, 1975-1978; Medical Director, Alaka Essate Clinic, 1978-. *Memberships:* Secretary, Nigerian Society of Neurological Sciences; Secretary, Physiological Society of Nigeria; British Medical Association; Nigerian Medical Association. *Publications:* Several Contributions to Medical Journals. *Honours:* King's College Scholarship for Physiology, 1960; Entrance Scholarship to Westminster Medical School, 1961; Federal Government of Nigeria Scholarship for Clinical Studies. *Hobbies:* Table Tennis; Swimming; Photography; Hunting. *Address:* 10, Kernel Street, P.O. Box 1112, Surulere, Lagos, Nigeria.

ARBI, Ezrin, b. 24 Oct. 1936, Bukittinggi, Sumatra. Architect-Planner. m. Nursasi Tubangi 10 Mar. 1966, 1 son, 2 daughters. *Education:* Bachelor of Architecture, University of Melbourne, Australia, 1961; Certificate in Project Analysis, United Nations' Asian Institute for Economic Development and Planning, Bangkok, 1968; Post Graduate Diploma in Town and Regional Planning, University of Melbourne, Australia, 1973. *Appointments:* Tutor, International House, University of Melbourne, 1960-61; C.M. Morgan and Associates, Architects, Melbourne 1961-62; Ministry of Industry, Jakarta, 1962-69; Lecturer, Architecture and Planning, MARA Institute of Technology, Senior Lecturer, 1974-; Principle Lecturer, 1981; Head, Department of Architecture, 1970-74; Head, School of Architecture, Planning and Surveying 1974-75; Project Manager, Master Plan Unit, City Hall, Kuala Lumpur, 1980-. *Memberships:* Royal Australian Institute of Architects; Incorporated Association of Architects and Surveyors, United Kingdom; Malaysian Institute of Architects; Royal Australian Planning Institute; Malaysian Institute of Planners; International Association for Housing Science, USA. *Publications:* Numerous Publications and Papers including: 'Architectural Course at ITM' in 'Majallah Akitek', 1972; The Building Industry: Past, Present and Future in the Development of Malaysia, 1977; A Report for Jabatan Perumahan Negara, 1978; Berita Perancang, 1978; *Honours:* Colombo Plan Scholarship, Australian Government, 1955-60; United Nations, Fellowship, Bangkok, 1968; Colómbo Plan Special Visiting Award, Australian Government, 1974. *Hobbies:* Painting; Stamp Collecting. *Address:* 20 Jalan SS 22 A/3, Petaling Jaya, Selangor, Malaysia.

ARCH, Richard Edward, b. 2 Oct. 1938, George Town, Grand Cayman, B.W.I. Company Director. m. Beryl Margaret Bodden, 24 June 1962, 1 son, 1 daughter. *Education:* Leaving Diploma, Cayman High School, 1956. *Appointments:* Seaman, Merchant Marine, 1956-60; British West Indian Airways, 1960-71; Owner: English Shoppe Limited and Margaret's Boutique, 1971-; Represents, Air Jamaica, Cayman Islands, 1971-. *Memberships:* Commonwealth Parliamentary Association; National Council of Social Service; Cayman Islands Corporation, Airport Authority; Planning Appeal Tribunal; Museum Committee; Chairman, Adoption Board. *Honours:* MBE 1981. *Hobbies:* Social Service; Travel; Music; Fishing. *Address:* Hospital Road, George Town, PO Box 165, Grand Cayman, British West India.

ARCHER, Brian Roper, b. 21 Aug. 1929, Calder, Tasmania, Australia. Senator. m. Dorothy Margaret Bird, 15 Oct. 1955, 1 son, 3 daughters. *Education:* Fellow, Australian Institute of Valuers; Fellow, Real Estate Institute of Australia; Fellow, Australian Institute of Management. *Appointments:* C.J. Weedon and Company Real Estate/Share Broker, 1947-54; Brian R Archer and Company 1955-75; Australian Senate, 1975-. *Memberships:* Commonwealth Parliamentary Association; Inter Parliamentary Union; Australian Limousin Breeders Society. *Hobby:* Philately. *Address:* Bass Highway, Boat Harbour, Tasmania 7321, Australia.

ARCHER, Geoffrey Thynne Valentine, b. 25 Apr. 1919, London, England. President/Owner, Archer Group of Companies. m. The Hon. Sonia Gina Ogilvie Birdwood, 21 July 1957, 1 son, 1 daughter. *Education:* Epsom College, Oxford and Cambridge School Certificate, Law Society Preliminary and Intermediate Examinations. *Appointments:* Law Student; British Army, Cavalry Officer, 1st Cavalry Division, Palestine, 8th Army Western Desert, European Campaign, 1940-46; Oil Executive, British Petroleum, Australia, Persia, Aden, Portugal, Canada, 1946-65; Executive Director, Hong Kong Chamber of Commerce, 1965-67; Chairman, Archer Group of Companies, 1968-. *Memberships:* Cavalry Club, London; Hong Kong Club; Hong Kong Country Club; Harlequin Football Club; Ski Club of Hong Kong; Hong Kong General Chamber of Commerse; American Chamber of Commerce in Hong Kong. *Hobbies:* Hunting; Steeplechasing; Show Jump-

ing; Skiing; Music. *Address:* 63 Repulse Bay Road, Hong Kong.

ARCHER, Hal D, b. 23 Sept. 1936, USA. Exporter. m. Penny Yong Archer, 8 Dec. 1973. *Education:* Bachelor of Arts, University of Kansas, USA. *Appointments:* Joint Managing Director, The Exco Group of Companies Limited, International Export Corporation, Hong Kong; Chairman, Projection Television Limited, Manufacturer of Large Screen Televisions, Hong Kong. *Hobbies:* News and Sports Announcer, Rediffusion Television Limited; Programme Presenter, Radio Television Hongkong; Television Commercial Voiceovers. *Address:* Block 40/15th floor, Baguio Villas, 550 Victoria Road, Hong Kong.

ARCHER, Jeffrey Howard, b. 15 Apr. 1940, London. Author. m. Mary Weeden 14 June 1966, 2 sons. *Education:* Wellington School Somerset; Brase Nose College Oxford. *Appointments:* Member of G.L.C. 1966-69; Member of Parliament 1969-74. *Memberships:* President Somerset AAA; Chairman Cambridge RFU; MCC; Louth Working Mens Club. *Publications:* Not A Penny More, Not A Penny Less, 1976; Shall We Tell The President, 1978; Kane and Abel, 1980; A Quiver full of Arrows, 1981. *Hobby:* Watching Somerset Play Cricket. *Address:* The Old Vicarage, Grantchester, Cambridge.

ARCHER, Patricia Dawn, b. 18 Aug. 1935, Melbourne, Australia. Cytotechnologist. *Education:* BSc Melbourne, 1972; Associate of the Australian Institute of Medical Laboratory Scientists, 1974; Certified Technologist of the International Academy of Cytology, 1973; Cytotechnologist member of International Academy of Cytology, 1974, Fellow, 1979. *Appointments:* Laboratory Assistent, CSIRO Division of Food Preservation and Transport, 1956; Medical Technologist in Cytology Department, Royal Womens' Hospital, Melbourne, 1959-60; Medical Technologist, Cytology Department, Westminster Hospital, London, England, 1960-61; Senior Cytotechnologist, Prince Henry's Hospital Melbourne, 1961-81; Educational Co-ordinator, Prince Henry's Hospital School of Cytotechnology. *Memberships:* Committee on Constitution and By-Laws of the International Academy of Cytology; President, Victorian Branch of the Australian Society of Cytology; Cytotechnologist Fellow of International Academy of Cytology; Australian Institute of Medical Laboratory Scientists; Hospital Scientists Association in Victoria; The Graduate Union, University of Melbourne; The Australian Elizabethan Theatre Trust. *Publications:* Nasal Colmnar Cell Exfoliation in the Asthmatic; The Effects of Infection and Allergy, 1961; The Training of Cytotechnologists in Melbourne, Australia—Cytotechnologists Forum, 1979. *Honours:* Rona Martelli Murray Memorial Prize for Proxime Accesit, 1953; Matriculation, 1953; Commonwealth Scholarship and Free Place at University, 1953; John F Funder Travel Award, 1979. *Hobbies:* Music; Watercolour Painting; Tapestry; Sewing; Philately; Travelling; Siamese Cats; Photography. *Address:* 4 Highland Avenue, Balwyn 3103, Victoria, Australia.

ARCHER, Peter Kingsley, b. 20 Nov. 1926, Wednesbury, England. Politician. m. 6 Aug. 1954, 1 son. *Education:* LLB, External, London, 1946; LLM, London School of Economics, 1950; BA, Philosophy, University College, London, 1952. *Appointments:* Barrister, 1953-; Member of Parliament, 1966-; Queen's Counsel, 1971-; Solicitor General, 1974-79; Opposition Front Bench Spokesman on Legal Affairs. *Memberships:* Amnesty International; Fabian Society; Society of Labour Lawyers; Gray's Inn. *Publications:* The Queen's Courts; Communism and the Law; Human Rights; The Role of the Law Officers; Freedom at Stake; Social Welfare and the Citizen. *Honours:* Bacon Scholar of Grays Inn, 1952; Bencher of Grays Inn, 1974-; Fellow of University College, London, 1977-; Privy Councillor, 1977-. *Hobbies:* Music; Writing; Talking. *Address:* 5 Penn Close, Chorleywood, Herts., England.

ARCHER, Richard Kendray, b. 13 Apr. 1921, London. Haematologist. m. Mary Tavy Morton, 2 Oct. 1948, 1 son (dec.). *Education:* BA(Hons, Trinity Hall, Cambridge, 1939-42; MRCUS, Royal Veterinary College, 1942-45; PhD, Cambridge University, 1954-56; ScD, 1956-. *Appointments:* Veterinary Practice, Eastbourne, 1945-52; Equine Research Station, Newmarket, Fellowship, 1953-56; Haematologist, 1956-66; Director 1966-78;

Medical Research Council, Laboratory Animals Centre, 1978-. *Memberships:* British Society for Haematology; International Society Haematology; Royal Society of Medicine; Zoological Society London; British Veterinary Association; British Equine Veterinary Association; British Laboratory Animals Veterinary Association. *Publications:* Many papers on comparative Haematology and two monographs and a text book (jointly). *Hobbies:* Boating; Bird Watching; Wood Turnery. *Address:* 23 Stagbury Avenue, Chipstead, Surrey CR3 3PD.

ARCHONTIDES, Ioannis C, b. 19 Nov. 1942, Limassol, Cyprus. Economist Company Director. m. Popi Archontides, Sept. 1962, 1 son, 1 daughter. *Education:* BSc(Economics) London University, United Kingdom; Financial Analysis and Policy Diploma, I.M.F. Institute, USA. *Appointments:* Economist, Central Bank of Cyprus, Economic Research Department, 1966-68; Personal Assistant to the Chairman of Lanitis Group of Companies, 1968-70; Director/General Manager of Amathus Navigation Company Limited, Hotels Department, 1970-80. *Memberships:* Vice Chairman, Cyprus Hotel Association; Cyprus Employers Federation; Vice Chairman of Limassol Sporting Club; Rotary Club, Limassol. *Publications:* Various articles on the Hotel and Tourist Industry in Cyprus and their significance to the National Economy. *Hobbies:* Tennis. *Address:* 14 Evagora, Papachristoforou Street, Limassol, Cyprus.

ARCULUS, (Sir), Ronald, b. 11 Feb. 1923, Birmingham. Diplomat. m. Sheila Mary Faux, 7 Nov. 1953, 1 son, 1 daughter. *Education:* BA, Exeter College, Oxford, 1942 and 1946-47. *Appointments:* Captain, 4th Queen's Own Hussars, 1943-45; Diplomatic Service, 1946-; San Francisco, 1948; La Paz, 1950; Aukara, 1953; Washington, 1961; New York, 1965; Imperial Defence College, 1969; Paris, 1973; Ambassador to Law of the Sea Conference, UN, 1977; Ambassador, Rome, 1979. *Memberships:* Army and Navy Club. *Honours:* CMG, 1968; KCMG, 1979; KCVO, 1980; Grand Cross Italian Order of Merit, 1980. *Hobbies:* Travel; Fine Arts. *Address:* British Embassy, Rome, Italy.

ARDAGH, James Warne, b. 5 Dec. 1920 Christchurch New Zealand. Surgeon. m. Margaret Christine Meehan, 6 Jan. 1951, 4 sons, 3 daughters. *Education:* MB, ChB, Otago University 1939-44; Fellow Royal College Surgeons, England, 1948; Fellow Royal Australasian College Surgeons, 1949. *Appointments:* House Surgeon, Ch.Ch. Hospital 1945, Queen Mary's Hospital, 1946; Barnet General Hospital 1947; Surgical Registrar, Barnet General Hospital 1948; Surgical Registrar, Ch. Ch. Hospital 1949-51; Visiting Surgeon, Plastic Surgical Unit, 1954-55; Visiting General Surgeon, Ch. Ch. Hospital 1955-79; Chairman Surgical Services, Head of Department General Surgery, Ch. Ch. Hospital, 1979-. *Memberships:* Chairman, Ch. Ch. Hospital's Post-graduate Society, 1970-72; Chairman, Ch. Ch. Hospital's Medical Staff Association, 1973-74; President, Canty, Div. N. Z. Medical Association, 1975. *Honours:* OBE, 1967; OSt.J. 1979; CBE, 1981. *Hobbies:* Member Tree Crops Association; Part-time farmer. Gardening; Philately. *Address:* Bong Son, Ivey's Road, 1 Rural Delivery, Christchurch, New Zealand.

ARDEN, Donald Seymour, b. 12 Apr. 1916, Boscombe, Hants. Bishop. m. Jane Grace Riddle, 29 Sept. 1962, 2 sons. *Education:* St Peter's College, Adelaide, S. Australia, 1926-33; BA (1st class Gen. Hons) Leeds University, 1934-37; College of the Resurrection, Mirfield, 1937-39. *Appointments:* Assistant Priest: St. Catherine's, New Cross, Southwark Diocese, 1939-40, Nettleden with Potten End, St. Alban's Diocese, 1941-43, Pretoria African Mission, Pretoria Diocese, 1944-51; Director, Usuthu Mission, Swaziland, 1951-61; Bishop of Nyasaland, renamed Malawi 1964, 1961-71; Bishop of Southern Malawi, 1971-81; Archbishop of Central Africa, 1971-80; Priest-in-charge, St. Margaret's, Uxbridge, Diocese of London, 1981-. *Publications:* Youth's Job in the Parish, 1938; Out of Africa something new? 1976. *Honours:* Canon of the Diocese of Zululand, 1959; CBE, 1981. *Hobby:* Photography. *Address:* 72 Harefield Road, Uxbridge, UB8 1PL, England.

AREJE, Raphael Adekunle, Chief, b. 24 Mar. 1925, Ora Ekiti, Ondo State, Nigeria. Librarian. m. Abigail Moradeun, 18 Nov. 1948, 3 sons, 2 daughters. *Education:* A.L.A. and 2 Parts F.L.A. Post Secondary Education, 1954-57; Loughborough University and Lough-borough College. *Appointments:* Library Assistant, 1950-54; Librarian Grade II 1958-64; Librarian Grade I, 1965-69; Senior Librarian, 1970-73; Principal Librarian, 1973-75; State Librarian, 1975-81. *Memberships:* President, Ora Ekiti Progressive Union, 1960-66; Treasurer, Ibadan Red Cross Society, 1965-75; Egbe Ijinle Yoruba; National Library Board, 1975-78. *Publications:* The Place of Libraries in a Nation's Life, Daily Times, 1960-; Library Service in Modern State, Daily Times, 1960-; Public Libraries, Development and Legislation W.N. Libraries, 1964-; Western State (Nigeria), Library Service, Teachers Forum, 1974-. *Honours:* Chieftaincy (Traditional), The Olora of Ora Ekiti, 1979-. *Hobbies:* Gardening, Reading, Photography. *Address:* 1 Ogboriefon Street, Bodija, Ibadan, Oyo State, Nigeria.

ARENE, Eugene Onyekwelu, b. 17 May 1937, Eziowelle. University Teacher. m. Dr. Violet Nwakaego Ezeanata, 1 Oct. 1966, 1 son, 2 daughters. *Education:* BSc (Honours, London), University College Ibadan, 1956-60; PhD. (London), University of Ibadan and Oxford University, 1960-63. *Appointments:* Post-Doctorate Lecturer, University of Ibadan, 1964-66; Lecturer, University of Nigeria, Nsukka, 1966-70; University of Lagos, Nigeria, 1970-; Associate Professor, Arizona State University, USA., Research Association Cancer Research Institure, 1975-76. *Memberships:* Fellow, Chemical Society of London; American Chemical Society; Chairman, Chemical Society of Nigeria (Lagos Chapter); President, University of Lagos Staff Club, 1974-75; President, University of Lagos Film Society. *Publications:* Various research papers in Natural Products, Chemistry; Co-author of a Text Book, An Introduction to the Chemistry of Carbon Compounds. *Honours:* College Scholar, 1957-63, Faculty of Science and Chemistry Department Prize-Winner, 1969, University College, Ibadan, Nigeria, 1969-. *Hobbies:* Lawn Tennis, Table Tennis, Billiards. *Address:* Flat 4, Block 4, Ozolua Road, University of Lagos, Yaba, Nigeria.

ARGENT, Edward, b. 21 Aug. 1931, London, England. Director: School of Drama. m. Christine Walma Tuck, 19 Apr. 1952, 1 son, 2 daughters. *Education:* Diploma, Royal Academy of Dramatic Art, UK, 1952-54. *Appointments:* As actor/stage manager/director, 1954-70; In repertory, on tour, and with Royal Court Theatre, Royal Shakespeare Company, Mermaid Theatre, etc. As teacher of acting, 1962-70; Guildhall School of Music and Drama, Webber-Douglas Academy, British Theatre Association, Morley College. Head of School of Theatre, Manchester Polytechnic, UK, 1970-74; Director, School of Drama, The Royal Scottish Academy of Music and Drama, 1974-. *Memberships:* Executive committee, Conference of Drama Schools; Chairman, 1977-80, Committee of Heads of Drama Departments in Scotland; Board of Directors, Citizens Theatre; Management Committee, Glasgow Theatre Club; National Council for Drama Training. *Creative Works:* Directed productions of: Miss Julie, Caucasian Chalk Circle, Troilus and Cressida, War and Peace, Antigone, Black Comedy, Heartbreak House, The Matchgirls, The White Devil, Midsummer Night's Dream, Winter's Tale, Titus Andronicus, Comedy of Errors, Oedipus, Camino Real, Fanny's First Play, Live Like Pigs, Dangerous Corner, etc.; Adapted for the Stage and directed: Great Expectations; Designed: Summer Visitors. *Honours:* Fellowship of the Guildhall School of Music and Drama, 1969. *Hobbies:* Mask making; Unskilled interior decorating. *Address:* 2 Glenbank Road, Lenzie, Scotland.

ARIF, Bin Kamal, b. 12 Jan. 1951, Gopeng, Perak, Malaysia. Architect. m. 4 Oct. 1976, 2 daughters. *Education:* Diploma in Architecture, Institiut Teknologi Kebangsaan, Kuala Lumpur, Malaysia, 1968-72; AA Diploma, Architectural Association School of Architecture, London, 1973-75. *Appointments:* Lecturer, School of Architecture, Institute Technology, Mara, Shah Alam, Malaysia, 1975-; Architect, Jabatan Kerja Ray (Public Works Department), Ipoh, Perak, Malaysia, 1976-77; Architect, (private practice), with Akitek Fawizah, Kuala Lumpur and was also Senior Partner, 1978-79; Own Practice, A.B. Kamal Akitek Incorporated, 1980-. *Memberships:* Royal Institute of British Architects; Pertubuhan Akitek, Malaysia; Registed Architect in Malaysia. *Hobbies:* Painting. *Address:* 3 Club Road, Batu Gajah, Perak, Malaysia.

ARIFF, Abdul Wahab (Datuk Dr.), b. 24 Dec. 1919, Penang, Malaysia. Medical Practitioner. m. Intan binti Haji Mustapha, 24 Sept. 1952, 2 sons, 2 daughters.

Education: Penang Free School, King Edward VII College of Medicine, Singapore, University of Malaya, Singapore Institute of Child Health, University of London, Royal Instititute of Public Health & Hygiene, London. Rotunda Hospital Dublin, Republic of Ireland, and School of Tropical Medicine, Calcutta. *Appointments:* C.M. & H.O. Trengganu, State M.O. Brunei, Maternal & Child Health Officer, Ministry of Health, C.M. & H.O. Kelantan, Pahang Penang and Johore. Health Officer for District Town Councils of Kota Bahru, Pasir Mas, Tumpat, Tanah Merah/Machang, Kuala Krai, Besut and Pasir Puteh of Kelantan State 1966-; Director of Health Services, Ministry of Health, Malaysia, 1970-71, Director of Planning & Development, Ministry of Health 1971-74; Acting Director-General of Health, Malaysia, Ministry of Health, Malaysia, K.L. on five occasions. *Memberships:* President, Malaysian Medical Council; Deputy Chairman, University Council, University of Malaya; Registrar of Medical Practioners, Malaysia; Chairman of Dental Board, Malaysia; Chairman of Pharmacy Board, Malaysia; Chairman Nursing Board, Malaysia; Chairman Midwives Board, Malaysia; Chairman, Board of Examiners for Certificate of Royal Society of Health, London; First President Federation of Malaya Students Union, 1948-49; National Association for Mental Health, London, 1958-; Royal Society of Health, London, 1958-77; Malaysian Medical Association and Chairman, National Committee for The Man and The Biosphere Programme, 1971-74; Represented Brunei Government at Western Pacific Regional Session of Who in Manila and Wellington, 1960, 61. *Honours:* Datuk, States of Brunei, Kelantan and Penang; Penang Free School Centenary Gold Medal, 1938-; Penang Kapitan Kling Mosque Scholarship, King Edward VII College of Medicine Singapore, 1939-; Malayan Government Queen's Fellow, 1955-; Fellowship of World Health Organisation in Public Health Administration, 1967-; Singapore Defence Medal, 1946-; Pingat Peringatan Malaysia, 1966-; Brunei Government Coronation Gold Medal, 1969-; Certificate of the Royal Life Saving Society of London; Athletic Captain of Medical College Union, Singapore, 1946-. *Address:* 543-B Tanjong Bungah, Penang, Malaysia.

ARIFFIN BIN NGAH MARZUKI (Datuk), b. 3 Sept. 1925, Perak, Malaysia. Consultant Obstetrician and Gynaecologist. m. Margaret Mariam, 26 June 1962 1 son, 2 daughters. *Education:* M.B.B.S., University of Malays, 1954-; London Membership, Royal College of Obstetrician and Gynaecologist, 1960-; London Fellowship, Royal College of Obstetrician and Gynaecologist, 1969-. *Appointments:* Registrar of Obstetrician and Gynaecologist, Carlisle Maternity Hospital, UK., 1958-60; Consultant Obstetrician and Gynaecologist, General Hospital, Ipoh, Malaysia, 1960-65; Senior Consultant Obstetrician and Gynaecologist, Ministry of Health, Malaysia, 1965-71; Vice-Chancellor National University of Malaysia, 1971-74. *Memberships:* Past President, Rotary Club of Gombak, Malaysia; Malaysian Zoological Society; Past President, Amateur Swimming Association, Malaysia. *Publications:* Various publications in local Medical Journals. *Honours:* 2nd. Calss Order of the Crown of Trengganu, Malaysia, 1970-; 2nd. Calss Order of the Crown of Kelantan, Malaysia, 1970-; 1st. Class Order of the Royal Household, Malaysia, 1974-. *Hobbies:* Golf, Swimming, Photography. *Address:* 53 Jalan Damai, Off Jalan Aman, Kuala Lumpur.

ARIGBABU (Dr.), Surajudeen Oladele, b. 2 Feb. 1945, Ijebu-Ode, Nigeria. Neuro Surgeon. m. Esther Abosede 9 Sept. 1971, 1 son, 2 daughters. *Education:* M.B.B.S., Lagos, 1971-; F.R.C.S., Edinburgh, 1976-. *Appointments:* Lecturer and Consultant Neuro Surgeon, College of Medicine, University of Lagos, Nigeria. *Memberships:* Nigerian Medical Association; Fellow of Royal College of Surgeons of Edinburgh; Society of British Neurological Surgeons; British Society of Sports and Medicine. *Honours:* Commonwealth Schlarship Award, 1975-79. *Hobbies:* Reading, Walking, Squash. *Address:* Neurosurgical Unit, Department of Surgery, L.U.T.H. P.M.B. 12003, Lagos, Nigeria.

ARINZE, Francis Anizoba, b. 1 Nov. 1932, Eziowelle, Anambra State, Nigeria. Clergyman. *Education:*Secondary School, All Hallows Seminary, Onitsha, 1947-51; Philosophy, Bigard Memorial Seminary, Enugu, 1953-55; Theology, Urban University, Rome, 1955-60, (Doctor of Divinity, 1960); Postgraduate Certificate in Education, London University, 1963-64. *Appointments:* Lecturer in Logic and Liturgy in Bigard Memorial Seminary, 1961-62; Regional Education Secretary, 1962-65; Auxiliary Bishop of Onitsha, 1965-67; Archbishop of Onitsha, 1967-. *Memberships:* President, National Episcopal Conference of Nigeria; Vatican Sacred Congregation for the Doctrine of the Faith; Vatican Sacred Congregation for the Causes of Saints. *Publications:* Sacrifice in Ibo Religion, 1970-; More Justice for the Poor; The Church and Nigerian Culture; The Rights of the Child; The Christian and the Family. *Hobbies:* Lawn Tennis, Walking. *Address:* Archbishop's House, Onitsha, Nigeria.

ARINZE, Michael Okoye, b. 15 Mar. 1932, Awka-Etiti, Nigeria. Business man. m. Bernice Uche Emeli, 20 Nov. 1961, 3 sons, 3 daughters. *Appointments:* Director of: GMO & Co. Limited, 1957, United African Drug Co. Limited, 1964, GMO Rubber Products, 1976, GODM Shoes Limited, 1978, Petrogas (Nigeria) Limited, 1979. *Memberships:* Executive member, Peoples Club of Nigeria; Executive member, Awka-Etiti Social Club; Patron, St. Joseph's Christian Workers' Society. *Honours:* Ozo Title-Ezissi Akubeze. *Hobbies:* Social Welfare activities; Club activities. *Address:* 8 Otigba Crescent, GRA, Onitsha, Nigeria.

ARIPPOL, Marc, b. 18 Feb. 1924, Alexandria, Egypt. Chartered Textile Technologist. m. Irene Oudiz, 9 June 1946, 2 daughters. *Education:* London University Matriculation, 1942; Diploma in Textile Designing, Weaving, Finishing, Diploma in Organisation and Management, 1946. *Appointments:* Planning Department, Usines Textiles Al Kahira, Cairo, Egypt, 1943; Technical Manager, Societe Industrielle Spahi Des Files et Textiles, Cairo, Egypt, 1945; Technical Manager, Tissage Castro Freres, Cairo, Egypt, 1946; Owner Manager, Tissage El Sahel, Cairo, Egypt, 1948-56; Mill Manager, Etablissements LecLerc Dupire, Saint Python, Nord, France, 1956-58; Technical Director and General Manager, Classweave Industries P/L, Melbourne, Victoria, Australia, 1958-. *Memberships:* Poast Management Committee Member, Textile Institute Southern Australia Section; Associate member, The Textile Institute. *Creative Works:* Patented Lineal Jacquard Card Cutting Machine, 1946. *Honours:* Awarded 1st prize Pure Wool Apparel Rachel Knitted Fabric by the Australian Wool Corporation. *Hobbies:* Research and Development; Mechanical Engineering; Woodwork. *Address:* 17 Nowra Street, Moorabbin, Victoria 3189, Australia.

ARKFELD, Leo, b. 4 Feb. 1912, Butte, Nebraska, USA. Archbishop, Missionary. *Education:* 3 years, Philosophy, 4 years, Theology at Divine Word Siminary, Illinois, USA. B.A. Doctor of Divinity, Honorary. *Honours:* Order of British Empire, England, 1976-; Commander of the British Empire. *Hobbies:* Pilot, Films and Photography. *Address:* Box 750, Madang, Papua, New Guinea.

ARKU, Emmanuel Edmeston Deodat, b. 24 July 1940, Volo, Volta Region, Ghana. Textile Technician. m. Beatrice Awusi Nyamedi & Grace Enyonam Lodo, 4 sons, 1 daughter. *Education:* Secondary School, 1964-; Quality Control Course, 1972, Supervisory Course, 1974, Management Development and Productivity Institute, Accra, Ghana. *Appointments:* Care-taker, Government Rest House, Volo, Volta Region; Headteacher, Vome-Battor Middle School, Tongu District; Headteacher, Volo L.A. Middle B School, Tongu District; Akosombo Textiles Ltd., Akosombo, Ghana. *Memberships:* Ghana Boy Scouts, Volo Branch, Secretary; Auditor, Aka Branch of Volo Youth Association; Advisory Board, Tongu Youth Association, Akosombo Branch; Ghana Red Cross Society. *Hobbies:* Painting, Designing, Music, Football, Domestic Poultry Farming, Stamp Collecting, Photography, Travelling and Technical Work. *Address:* Royal House, c/o P.O. Box 1, Volo, Via Akuse, Tongu District, Volta Region, Ghana, West Africa.

ARMITAGE, (Sir) Arthur Llewellyn, b. 1 Aug. 1916, Marsden, Yorkshire, England. Chairman, Social Security Advisory Committee. m. Joan Kenyon Marcroft, 1940, 2 daughters. *Education:* BA., 1936, LL.B., 1937, MA., 1940, Queen's College, Cambridge, UK; Yale University Commonwealth Fund Fellow, 1937-39. *Appointments:* Military Service, 1940-45; Fellow, 1945-58, President, 1958-70, Queen's College, Cambridge, UK; Vice-Chancellor, University of Cambridge, UK,

1965-67; Vice-Chancellor, University of Manchester and Professor of Common Law, 1970-80; Chairman, Social Security Advisory Committee, 1980-. *Memberships:* President, 1967-68, Society of Public Teachers of Law; Athenaeum Club. *Publications:* Case Book on Criminal Law (with JWC Turner), 1952, 1958, 1964; Jt. Editor Clerk and Lindsell on Torts, 1954, 1961, 1969, 1975. *Honours:* Kt., 1975; Hon. Fellow, Queen's College, Cambridge, 1970; Hon. LL.D., Manchester, 1970; Hon. LL.D., Queen's University of Belfast, 1980; Hon. LL.D., Liverpool, Birmingham, 1981. *Address:* Rowley Lodge, Forty Acre Lane, Kermincham, near Holmes Chapel, Cheshire CW4 8DX, England.

ARMSTRONG, Alexander Ewan, b. 16 June 1916, Sydney, New South Wales, Australia. Company Director. m. (1) Marjorie A Goodhew, 1945, 2 daughters; Josephine Ann MacMahon, 1978-. *Education:* Matriculation, Scots College, Sydney. *Appointments:* Personally managed family pastoral properties until 1955, since then engaged in commercial and real estate development in Sydney and Surfers Paradise; Engaged in large scale real estate development in the Albert Shire, and surfers Paradise, estates being Highland Park, Nerang and Wide Horizons, Mudgeeraba. *Memberships:* New South Wales Legislative Council, 1952-69; Commonwealth (Canberra); Huntington Country and Yacht (Southport, Gold Coast). *Hobbies:* Tennis, Swimming, Water-skiing, Photography, Travel. *Address:* Allawah, The Esplanade, Surfers Paradise, Q. 4217, Queensland, Australia.

ARMSTRONG, William Edward Iredale, b. 6 June 1920, Birkenhead. England. Arbitrator; Construction Claims Advisers. m. Louise Parker Blackley, 6 Dec. 1956, 2 daughters. *Education:* BEng with First Class Honours, Liverpool University, 1938-41; MEng, Liverpool University, 1943-. *Appointments:* Assistant Engineer, Sir Alexander Gibb & Partners, 1941-42; Officer REME finishing as Second in Command to Commander, REME Gibraltar, 1942-46; Assistant Lecturer, Faculty of Engineering, University of Liverpool, 1949-; Senior Scientific Officer, Road ResearOh Laboratory, 1948-53; Agent and Engineering Manager, Mears Construction Ltd., 1953-65; Director, Mears Construction Ltd., 1965-74; Partner, Ashcroft & Armstrong, 1974-. *Memberships:* Fellow of the: Insitituion of Civil Engineers, Institution of Mechanical Engineers, Chartered Institute of Building, Chartered Institute of Arbitrators, Institute of Directors; Past President of: The University of Liverpool Engineering Society, The Lancashire & Cheshire Federation of Scottish Societies, The Chester Caledonian Association. *Publications:* Bond in Prestressed Concrete, 1948-49; Renovations to deteriorated reinforced concrete structures, 1954-; Concrete versus flexible method of road construction, 1957-; Various other papers and articles on civil engineering and building subjects; Contractural Claims under the ICE Conditions of Contract, 1977-. *Honours:* Hely-Shaw Prize, Liverpool University, 1940-; Rathbone Medal, Liverpool University, 1941-; Officer of the Most Excellent Order of the British Empire (Military Division), 1961-; Territorial Decoration, 1953-, and two Bars; Deputy Lieutenant of Lancashire 1970-74 and of Merseyside 1974-. *Hobbies:* Mountain walking, Swimming, Highland Games, Scottish Country Dancing, Burns, The Armstrong Clan, Travel. *Address:* Harwood House, Overdale Road, Willaston, South Wirral, L64 1SX.

ARMSTRONG, William Louther Hunter, b. 27 Oct. 1924, Melbourne, Australia. General Surgeon. m. Susanna Heath, 6 Mar. 1962, 1 son, 1 daughter. *Education:* Geelong Grammar School, 1936-42; Royal Australian Air Force, 1943-46; (Flight Lieutenant, 77 Aquadron); Melbourne University, Trinity College, 1946-51; M.B.B.S. 1951-; F.R.C.S., 1958-; F.R.A.C.S., 1960-. *Appointments:* R.M.O. Royal Melbourne Hospital, 1952-53; Austin Hospital, Heidelberg, 1954-; Assistant Surgeon, Consultant Surgeon, Geelong & District Hospital. *Memberships:* Naval & Military Club, Melbourne; Barwon Heads Golf Club. *Hobbies:* Cricket, Golf, Agriculture. *Address:* Oak Grove, Whites Road, Mount Duneed, Victoria, 3216, Australia.

ARNOLD, Thomas Richard, b. 25 Jan. 1947, London. Member of Parliament. *Education:* Bedales, Hampshire, 1954-57; Le Rosey, Geneva, 1957-64; Pembroke, Oxford, 1964-67, (M.A.). *Appointments:* British Malawi, Theatre Producer; Member of Parliament; Parliamentary Private Secretary to the Secretary of State for Northern Ireland since 1979; Palimentary Private Secretary to the Word Privy Seal since September 1981. *Memberships:* Vice-Chairman, Theatre Producer and Publisher, Anglo-Malawi Parliamentary Group; Carlton, R.A.C. *Address:* House of Commons, London, S.W.1.

ARORA, Ramesh Chandra, b. 1 Aug. 1944, DI Khan, (formerly India). Physician: Cardiologist. m. Sunita, 11 Oct. 1972, 2 daughters. *Education:* BSc., 1961; MBBS., 1966; MD., 1969; Educational Council of Foreign Medical Graduates, 1966. *Appointments:* House Physician, Jan.1967—Dec.1967; Demonstrator, Medicine, 1968-69; Rosident Physician, Jan.1970—Dec.1970; Lecturer in Medicine, 1971-73; Reader in Medicine, 1973-; Head of Department of Medicine and allied Specialities, 1981-. *Memberships:* Association of Physicians of India; Indian Medical Association; Diabetic Association of India; North India Chapter of American College of Chester Physicians; Rotary International, Jhansi; Masonic Lodge of India. *Publications:* 30 Scientific Publications; Contradicted the Use of Garlic Oil, as a hypocholestraric and fibrinolytic drug, which was being marketed in India. The contradictions had received wide international and national aclaims; Is engaged in assessing various new drugs, indigenous herb's fractions to lower cholesterol and enhance fibrinolysis with the aims to prevent Ischemic Heart Disease; Establishing Cholesterol/Fat Tolerence Test, to predict hyperlipidemia at early stages. *Honours:*Received 6 honours including: Certificate of Honour with Silver Medal of Merit in Physiology; Certificate of Honour with Silver Medal of Merit in Medical Jurisprudence and Toxicology; Certificate of Honour in Ophthalmology; Certificate of Honour in Pharmacology; 35 Prizes including: Chancellors Medal for best student; Buckley Bharecha Silver Medal for top in Final MBBS., Examinations; Mrs Vazir Saran Silver Medal for Obstetrics and Gynaecology; Silver Medal for General Proficiency in Final MBBS (Part 1) Examination; Devi Dayal Khanna Shield for Best Medical Student, 1967; numerous Book prizes. *Hobbies:* Reading; Writing.*Address:* PR-13, MLB Medical College Campus, Jhansi 284001, India.

AROSANYIN, Olatunji, b. 3 Sept. 1938, Egbe, Kwara State, Nigeria. Legal Practitioner. m. Janet Omolara, 11 Apr. 1967, 2 sons, 2 daughters. *Education:* Judicial Course Certificate, Institute of Administration, Zaria, 1960-; LL.B. (Honours) Second Class, Ahmadu Bello University, Zaria, 1970-; BL., Law School, Lagos, 1971-. *Appointments:* Court Registrar to Kabba Divisional Criminal Court, 1960-64; Grade B Court Judge, Bacita Arca Court, 1965-; Plateau Upper Area Court Registrar, 1968-; Chairman, Kwara State Rent Tribunal, 1973-79; Assistant National Legal Adviser to the National Party of Nigeria, 1978-. *Memberships:* President, Ahmadu Bello University Law Association, 1969-70;State Secretary to Nigerian Bar Association, Kwara State Branch, 1973-78; Chairman, Kwara State Football Association, 1975-; Nigerian Football Association, 1975-. *Hobbies:* Football, Lawn Tennis, Farming. *Address:* No. 7 Unity Road, Ilorin, Kwara State, Nigeria.

ARTHINGTON-DAVY, Humphrey, Augustine, b. 1920. British Diplomat. *Education:* Eastbourne College; Trinity College, Cambridge. *Appointments:* Indian Army 1941-1946; Indian Political Service 1946-1947; Civil Service of Pakistan 1947-1956; H.M. Diplomatic Service 1957-; British Representative in the Maldives 1959-65; Deputy High Commissioner, Botswana 1966-1968; Mauritius 1968-1970, Tonga and Samoa 1970-1973; British High Commissioner Tonga since 1973, and Western Samoa(non-res.) 1973-1977. *Memberships:* Naval and Military Club, London, S.W.1 *Address:* c/o Foreign & Commonwealth Office, London, S.W.1, England.

ARTHUR, Geoffrey George, b. 19 Mar. 1920, Burton-on-Trent, England. Diplomatic Service (retired). m. Margaret Woodcock, 31 July 1946. *Education:* Christ Church, Oxford, UK, 1938-40, 1946-47. *Appointments:* Served in Army, 1940-45; Entered HM Foreign (later Diplomatic) Service, 1947; Served in Baghdad, Ankara, Foreign Office, Bonn; Counsellor, HM Embassy, Cairo, Egypt, 1959-63; Head of Department, Foreign Office, 1963-66; HM Abassador, Kuwait, 1967-68; Assistant Under-Secretary, 1968-70, Deputy Under-Secretary, 1973-75, Foreign and Commonwealth Office; Political Resident in the Persian Gulf, 1970-72; Master of Pembroke College, Oxford, UK, 1975-; Adviser to the British Bank of the Middle East. *Memberships:* United Oxford and Cambridge University Club; Beefsteak Club. *Honours:* CMG., 1963; KCMG., 1971. *Address:* Pembroke College, Oxford, OX1 1DQ, England.

ARTHUR, James Stanley, b. 3 Feb. 1923, Aberdeen, Scotland. H.M. Diplomatic Service. m. Marion North, 26 Aug. 1950, 2 sons, 2 daughters. *Education:* Trinity Academy, Edinburgh; BSc., Liverpool University, 1944-. *Appointments:* Scientific Civil Service, 1944-46; Assistant Principal Scottish Education Department, 1946-; Ministry of Education, Department of Education & Science, 1947-66; Private Secretary to Parliamentary Secretary, 1948-50; Principal Private Secretary to Minister, 1960-62; Counsellor Foreign & Commonwealth Office, 1966-; Nairobi, 1967-70; DHC Malta, 1970-73; High Commissioner, Suva, 1974-78; 1st High Commissioner (non-Resident), Nauru, 1977-78; High Commissioner, Bridgetown, since 1978-; High Commissioner, Dominica (Non-Resident) since 1978-; St. Lucia since, 1979-; Grenade, 1980-; Concurrently British Government Representative, West Indies Associated States of Antigua and St. Kitts/Nevis/Anguilla. St. Vincent and the Grenadines, since 1979-. *Memberships:* Royal Commonwealth Society and Travellers Club. *Honours:* C.M.G., 1977-. *Hobbies:* Music, Golf. *Address:* c/o Foreign & Commonwealth Office, London S.W.1.

ARTHUR, William Seymour, b. 26 March, 1909, St. Philip Parish, Barbados, School Teacher. m. Enid Odle, 10 December, 1936 (deceased), 3 sons, 4 daughters. *Education:* Board of Education Teachers' Examinations, 1925-1929; Rawle Training College (Codrington) 1929-1931; Teachers' Observation Course, United Kingdom, 1961. *Appointments:* Buxton Primary School, 1927-1932; Montgomery Primary School, Assistant Teacher, 1932-1937; Buxton Primary School, Head Teacher 1938-1969; Industry High School, Administrator, 1969-. *Memberships:* Cubmaster, Montgomery Pack; Chairman, Sharon Moravian Church 1964-1967; Barbados Museum; Barbados Teachers' Union; Founder, President, World-Wide Friendship Club, Pen Pal Associates. *Publications:* Short Stories and Poems published in local magazines, including BIM and Mary were broadcast on the BBC Programme: Caribbean Voices; Poetry publications:-Whispers of the Dawn 1941; Morning Glory 1944; No Idle Winds 1955; Editor of Cosmos. *Honours:* Justice of Peace 1976; Silver Medals for Poetry Italy) 1976, 1977, 1978. *Hobbies:* Literary; Philately. *Address:* Arthur Seat, St. Thomas, Barbados, West Indies.

ARULANANDOM, Frederick Christian, b. 4 Jan. 1920, Kuala Lumpur, Malaysia. Barrister-at-Law; Judge, High Court, Malaya. m. Lucy Yong, 16 Dec. 1967, 2 daughters. *Education:* Diploma in Arts, Diploma in Education, Raffles College, 1941; Diploma in Social Science and Administration, London University, UK, 1948; Barrister-at-Law, Middle Temple, London, UK, 1949. *Appointments:* Teacher, 1945-46; Social Welfare Officer, 1950-52; Advocate and Solicitor, 1953-74; Judge, High Court, Malaya, 1974-. *Memberships:* Vice President, Law Association for West Asia and the Pacific, 1968-71; President, Malayan Youth Council, 1950-54; President, Bar Association of Perak, 1963-74; Bar Council, States of Malaya, 1955-73. *Publications:* Through My Tainted Glasses. *Honours:* DMPN., 1978. *Hobbies:* Reading; Writing. *Address:* No. 1 Sepoy Lines Road, Penang, Malaysia.

ARYEMO, Mary Ursula, b. 12 Apr. 1957, Gulu, Uganda. Physiotherapist. *Education:* O Level Certificate, 1973-; A Level Certificate, 1975-; Diploma in Physiotherapy, 1980. *Appointments:* Physiotherapist. *Memberships:* Uganda Associaton of Physiotherapy. *Hobbies:* Hockey, Music. *Address:* Department of Physiotherapy, Mulugo Hospital, Box 7051, Kla, Uganda.

ASARI, S. Velayudhan, b. 9 Aug. 1936, Trivandrum. Teacher. m. Rajalakshmi, 2 Sept. 1960, 1 son, 1 daughter *Education:* BSc, 1956, MA, 1958, Kerala University, Trivandrum; M.A., University of Bhagalpur, Bihar, 1963-; Diploma in Linguistics, University of Kerala, 1964-; Diploma in Linguistics, University of Poona, 1966-; Diploma in Applied Linguistics, University of Reading, UK., 1969-; A.M., University of Missouri,

Columbia, USA., 1970-; PhD., University of Kerala, 1971-. *Appointments:* Research Associate, 1958-64; Lecturer in Linguistics, 1964-70, University of Kerala; Lecturer in English, University of Calicut, 1970-74; English Studies Officer, British Council, Bombay, 1974-77; Reader in English & Head of the Department, 1977-80; Professor & Head of the Department of English, 1981, University of Calicut. 1981-. *Memberships:* Linguistic Society of India, Poona; Dravidian Linguistics Society, Trivandrum. *Publications:* Contemporary English Prose, Oxford University, 1977-; Golden Cadence, Oxford University, 1978-; The Phonetics and Structure of English, 1978-; Thinking and Doing, Oxford University, 1980-; An Essay of Dramatic Poetry, 1980-; A Slection of Keats's Letters, 1981. *Honours:* Dr. Godavarma Memorial Medal, 1958-; British Council Scholarship, 1968-. *Hobby:* Translating from Malayalam to English and vice-versa. *Address:* Lakshmi, Calicut University, P.O. 673 365, Kerala, India.

ASEKUN, Daniel Oluremilekun, b. 16 Oct. 1925, Ijebu-Ode, Nigeria. Obstetrician and Gynaecologist. m. 11 Oct. 1955, 2 sons, 2 daughters. *Education:* C.M.S. Grammar School, Lagos, 1938-44; King's College Medical School, University of Durham, M.B.B.S., 1948-55, M.R.C.O.G., 1967-, F.R.C.O.G., 1980-, F.M.C.O.G., 1968-. *Appointments:* House Surgeon & Physician, 1955-56; Medical Officer, 1956-67; Medical Officer Special Grade, 1967-; Consultant, 1968-; Senior Consultant, 1971-; Chief Consultant, 1978-; Lagos Island Maternity Hospital, Lagos. *Memberships:* Federation International Natacion Amateur, 1976-80, 1980-84; Vice-President African Swimming Confederation, 1974-78. *Hobbies:* Swimming; Photography. *Address:* 16 Ilaka Street, P.o. Box 2482, Lagos, Nigeria.

ASEMOTA, Solomon Adun, b. 8 Dec. 1938, Benin City, Bendel State, Nigeria. Barrister-at-Law: Solicitor. m. Irene Osayuwame Ighodaro, 8 May 1965, 2 daughters. *Education:* Diploma, Police College, Wakefield, UK, 1962; Diploma, Scottish Police College, UK, 1959; LL.B.(Hons.), University of Lagos, Nigeria, 1964-69; BL., Nigerian Law School, Nigeria, 1969-70. *Appointments:* Teacher, 1958-59; Police Officer, Superintendent of Police, 1959-70; Private Legal Practice, 1970-. *Memberships:* Benin Club; Metropolitan Club, Lagos; Chairman, Bendel Football Association, 1970-75, Nigeria Football Association; Match Inspector, African Football Confederation, 1973-75; Secretary Benin Branch, 1973-77, National Treasurer, 1978-80, Nigerian Bar Association; International Bar Association. *Publications:* Article in press in IBA Journal. *Honours:* Independence Medal; ONUC Medal; Republican Medal. *Hobbies:* Soccer; Golf. *Address:* 15 Ogbenede Street, Benin City, Bendel State, Nigeria.

ASH, Stuart, Bradley, b. 10 July 1942, Hamilton, Ontario. Principal, Gottschalk & Ash International, Design Consultants. Graphic Design. *Education:* Western Technical School, Graphic Design; Ontario College of Art (Graphic Design) graduate, 1962-; Instructor, Ontario College of Art, Advanced Typography, 1978-. *Appointments:* Principal, Gottschalk & Ash International, Toronto, Montreal, New York, Zurich. *Publications:* Design work exhibited and given awards internationally. *Hobbies:* Sailing, Skiing. *Address:* 167 Madison Avenue, Toronto, M5R256, Ontario, Canada.

ASHCROFT, William David, b. 28 Apr. 1946, Sydney, Australia. Lecturer. m. Judy Lee Souter, 3 Mar. 1972, 2 sons. *Education:* Bachelor of Arts, Sydney University, 1968-; Master of Arts (Honours), Sydney University, 1974-; Doctor of Philosophy Australian National University, 1980-. *Appointments:* Teaching Fellow, University of Sydney, 1970-73; Lecturer, Guild Teacher's College, Sydney, 1974-75; Tutor, Australian National University, 1975-79; Lecturer, MacAuley Teacher's College, Brisbane, 1979-. *Memberships:* Executive Council, Association for the Study of Australian Literature; South Pacific Association for Commonwealth Literature and Language Studies. *Publications:* Poetry in various journals; Various articles on Australian and Commonwealth Literature and theory Literary; Editor of New Literature Review, a journal concerned with the study of New Literatures in English migrant writing, and literary theory. *Honours:* Commonwealth Post-graduate Scholarship, 1964-; Colin Roderick Prize for Australian Literature, 1974-; Nominated for Crawford Prize for Post-graduate study, 1979-. *Hobby:*

Sports. *Address:* 2 Hefferan Street, Fairfield, Queensland, 4103.

ASHE, (Sir) Derick Rosslyn, b. 20 Jan. 1919, Guildford, Surrey, England. HM Diplomatic Service (retired). m. Rissa Parker, 5 June 1957, 1 son, 1 daughter. *Education:* MA., Trinity College, Oxford, UK, 1937-39. *Appointments:* HM Forces, 1940-46; 2nd Secretary, Control Commission for Germany, 1947-49; Private Secretary to Permanent Under-Secretary of State for German Affairs, 1950-53, 1st Secretary, La Paz, 1953-55, 1 Secretary Information, Madrid, 1957-61, Foreign Office, 1961-62; Counsellor and Head of Chancery: Addis Ababa, 1962-64, Havana, 1964-66; Head of Security Department, Foreign and Commonwealth Office, 1966-69; Minister, Tokyo, 1969-71; Ambassador to: Romania, 1972-75, Argentina, 1975-77; Alternate Leader of: UK Delegation to Disarmament Conference, Geneva, 1977-79, UK Delegation to United Nations Special Session on Disarmament, New York, 1977-78. *Memberships:* White's Club, London; Travellers' Club, London; Beefsteak Club, London. *Honours:* Mentioned in Despatches, 1945; Knight of Order of Orange-Nassau (with swords), 1945; CMG., 1966; KCMG., 1978. *Address:* Dalton House, Hurstbourne Tarrant, Andover, Hampshire SP11 OAX, England.

ASHENDEN, Edward Scott, b. 5 Oct. 1939, Gumeracha, South Australia. Member of Parliament. m. Wendy Loraine Mickan, 30 Dec. 1961, 2 sons, 1 daughter. *Education:* BA., Dip.Ed., University of Adelaide, Australia. *Appointments:*Assistant, Murray Bridge High School; Senior Master, Price Alfred College; Regional Manager, Shell Co. (Australia) Limited; Senior Executive, Chrysler, Australia. *Memberships:* Board member, Lions International; Tea Tree Gully Golf Club. *Hobbies:* Golf; Photography. *Address:* 12 Dernancourt Drive, Dernancourt 5075, Australia.

ASHMORE, Edward Beckwith, b. 11 Dec. 1919, Queenstown. Naval Officer; Company Director. m. 11 Dec. 1942, 1 son, 2 daughters. *Education:* Royal Naval College, Dartmouth, 1933-37; Cambridge University, 1946; Naval Staff Course, 1949. *Appointments:* War Service, 1939-45; Staff of Naval Attache, Moscow, 1946-47; Commander, 1949-50; Radio Equipment Department, 1951-53; Captain, 1955; 6 Frigate Squadron, 1958-60; Plans Division, Ministry of Defence, 1960-63; Commander British Forces, Caribbean Area, Commodore and Senior Naval Officer, West Indies, 1963-64; Rear Admiral, ACDS (Sigs). FO and i/c Far East Fleet, 1965-68; Vice Admiral, 1969-70; VCNS Admiral, C in C Fleet, C in C Eastern Atlantic Area; Allied C in C; First Sea Lord and Chief of Naval Staff UK, 1970-77; Chief of Defence Staff UK; Admiral of the Fleet, 1977; Inactive duty, 1977; Director, Racal Electronics Limited, 1978-. *Memberships:* Naval and Military Clubs, London; Honorary Life Member, Royal Signals Institution; US Naval Institute; Naval President, The Officers Association, UK; Freeman of City of London and Liveryman of Shipwrights Company; Governor, Sutton's Hospital in Charterhouse. *Honours:* Jackson Everett Prize, 1943; DSc, 1942; Mentioned in Despatches, 1946; CB, 1966; KCB, 1971; GCB, 1974. *Hobbies:* Travel; Swimming; Gardening. *Address:* South Cottage, Headley Down, Hampshire, England.

ASHU, Dawuda Philip, b. 12 Dec. 1935, Takum in Takum, Nigeria. Educationist. m. Helen Matangona Angve, 12 July 1952, 3 sons, 3 daughters. *Education:* Teachers Certificate, 1950-55; General Cettificate of Education, 1963; National Certificate in Education, 1966. *Appointments:* Teaching in Primary School, 1951-53; Headmaster of Senior Primary School, 1958-63; Supervisor of Primary Schools, 1965-66; Vice Principal of Wukari Combined Secondary School, 1967; Civil Commissioner in forme Benu-Plateau State of Nigeria, Commissioner for Trade and Industry, Local Government, Internal Affairs and Information, and Works and Housing, 1968-73; Personnel Manager, Nasreddin Group International Jos, in Riceco, Bry-Tex and Northern Nigeria, Fibre Products Limited, Jos-Nigeria, 1974-. *Memberships:* Historical Society of Nigeria; Secretary, Registered Trustees of the Christian Reformed Church of Nigeria; Benue-Plateau Water Board; Gongola State Scholarship Board, 1976-79; Chairman, Bible Society of Nigeria Benu-Plateau Area. *Publications:* My Visit to America, 1961; Translated a book into Hausa; Article published in a booklet. *Hobbies:* Gardening; Music; Reading; Writing; Table Ten-

nis; Volleyball; Driving. *Address:* No 2 Wase Close, PO Box 1028, Jos-Plateau State, Nigeria.

ASHWIN, Charles Robin, b. 27 Sept. 1930 Adelaide, South Australia. Diplomat. m. Okche Chon 16 May 1959, 1 son, 1 daughter. *Education:* BA(Hons) University of Adelaide, 1952; BA(Hons) University of Oxford, 1954; MA 1956; South Australian Rhodes Scolar, 1952. *Appointments:* Department of Foreign Affairs, Canberra, Australia 1955; Deputy Permanent Representative of Australia, United Nations, New York 1971-73; Australian Ambassador Egypt and Sudan 1975-78; First Assistant Secretary, Western Division, Foreign Affairs, 1978-80. First Assistant Secretary, International Organisations, Africa and Middle East Division, 1980-. *Hobbies:* Mountains; Reading. *Address:* 39 Kidston Cr. Curtin, Canberra, Australia.

ASIBEY, Emmanuel Osei Agyeman, b. 21 Nov. 1935 Kwaso. Civil Servant. m. Joyce Lucy Konama Kyei, 18 Dec. 1971, 2 daughters. *Education:* Cambridge Higher School Certificate, Prempeh College, Kumasi, 1955; BSc(for). 1960; PhD(Zoo). 1974; Aberdeen University, Scotland; Certificate in Development Studies, Wolfson College, Cambridge, United Kingdom, 1975. *Appointments:* Assistant Conservater of Forests 1960-; Assistant Game Warden; Game Warden; Chief Game and Wildlife Officer; Chief Administrator, Forestry Commission 1980-. *Memberships:* Numerous Memberships including: British Ecological Society; British Mammal Society; Ghana Forestry Association; Ghana Science Association; International Union for the Conservation of Nature and Natural Resources Council—Africa Regional councillor, etc. *Publications:* Numerous publications including: Reproduction in the Grasscutter in Ghana, 1974; Black-fly and the Environment. Environmental Conservation, 1975; Wildlife and Sport 1963; Proceedings of the Ghana Working Group on the Environment 1972; Tick-borne Diseases and their Vectors, 1978; Proceedings of the 7th Congress of the International Primatological Society. *Honours:* Asanteman Council Scholar 1950-55; Ghana Government Scholar 1957-62, 1970-75; Grand Medal, Ghana National award for wildlife work done at home and abroad, 1978; Knight, of the Order of the Golden Ark, 1979. *Hobbies:* Photography; Writting; Gardening. *Address:* PO Box 58, Mampong, Ashanti, Ghana.

ASIBEY, Joyce Lucy Konama, b. 31 Jan. 1931 Agogo, Ghana. Headmistress. m. Emmanuel Osei Agyeman Asibey 18 Dec. 1971, 2 daughters. *Education:* BA-(Hons); Dip. ED. *Appointments:* Geography Teacher 1957-67; Assistant Headmistress 1967-71; Headmistress 1971-. *Memberships:* Secretary, Ghana Geographical Association 1967-70; Conference of Heads of Assisted Secondary Schools. *Honours:* Given a citation and a painting by the Old Girls' Association of the School for long and meritorious service, 1978. *Hobbies:* Reading; Gardening. *Address:* PO Box 104, Kumasi, Ghana.

ASIRWATHAM, Rajanayagam Nalliah, b. 26 Aug. 1942, Negiombo, Sri Lanka. Chartered Accountant. m. 7 Jan. 1972 3 daughters. *Education:* Final Examination, Institute of Chartered Accountants, Sri Lanka, 1967; G.C.E. Advanced level, English Literature, British Constitution, Economics, London, 1961. *Appointments:* Qualified Assistant, 1967-72, Partner, Ford Rhodes Thornton and Company, 1972-. *Memberships:* British Institute of Management; Executive Committee of Old Boys' Association of St Thomas College Mount Lavinia, Sri Lanka. *Publications:* History and Nature of Free Trade Zones- Thesis submitted to Bandaranaike Centre for International Studies. *Honours:* Diploma in International Relations by Bandaranaike Centre for International Studies. *Hobbies:* Reading; Squash. *Address:* 265/1 R.A.De Mel Mawatha, Colombo 3, Sri Lanka.

ASIWAJU, Anthony Ijaola, b. 27 Apr. 1939 Imeko, Ogun State, Nigeria. Teacher. m. Victoria Fatuyi 10 May 1970, 1 son, 3 daughters. *Education:* BA(Hons.) History 1966, PhD 1971 Ibadan; Teachers' Grade II Certificate, Western Nigeria, 1960. *Appointments:* Primary School Teacher, Roman Catholic Mission Schools, Ado-Odo and Abeokuta, Ogun State of Nigeria, 1960-62; Secondary School Teacher R.C.M. Schools and Colleges, Iperu-Remo and Ijebu Ode 1962-63; 1966; Lecturer in History, University of Lagos, 1969-; Professor of History, 1978; Head of Department,

University of Lagos, 1979-82. *Memberships:* Secretary, University of Lagos Staff Union, 1972-73; Hon. Secretary, The Historical Society of Nigeria; *Publications:* Western Yorubaland Under European Rule, 1889-1945; Editor of Tarikh, Journal of African History, 1975; A Comparative Analysis of French and British Colonialism, 1976; Plus chapters in books and articles in a variety of learned journals of international reputation. *Honours:* Fulbright Scholar, The Hoover Institution for War, Peace and Revolutions, Stanford, California, USA 1979. *Hobby:* Travels. *Address:* Department of History, University of Lagos, Lagos, Nigeria.

ASORO, Michael Dee, b. 15 Oct. 1942, Jesse, Bendel State, Nigeria. Artist. m. Elizabeth U Asoro, 13 Dec. 1964, 5 sons 2 daughters. *Education:* BA, Ahmadu Bello University, 1971. *Appointments:* Assistant Chief Inspector of Education; Chief Co-ordinator of Art and Cultural Education, Bendel State Schools. *Memberships:* Society of Nigerian Artists; Financial Secretary, Bendel State Branch. *Publications:* A Guide to School Certificate and GCE Art (Design), A Guide to School Certificate and GCE Art (Still-Life and Nature). *Creative Works:* Numerous Paintings and Sculptors. *Hobbies:* Table Tennis; Tennis; Hunting. *Address:* No 3 Igiozee Street, 33 KV Line, Upper Sakpoba Road, Benin City, Nigeria.

ASPER, Israel, Harold, b. 11 August 1932, Minnedosa, Manitoba, Canada. Chairman & Chief Executive Officer CanWest Capital Corporation. m. Ruth Miriam Bernstein, 27 May 1956, 2 sons, 1 daughter. *Education:* Bachelor of Arts, University of Manitoba, 1943; Bachelor of Law University of Manitoba, 1957; Master of Law 1964; created Q.C. 31 December, 1975. *Appointments:* Called to the Bar of Manitoba, July 1957; Member of Law firm Drache, Meltzer, Esses, Gold & Asper, Winnipeg, 1957-1959; Senior Partner, Asper & Company, 1959-1970; Senior Partner, Buchwald, Asper, Henteleff, 1970-1977; Chairman and Chief Executive Officer, CanWest Capital Corporation; Vice-Chairman, Chairman and Director of several other companies; Chairman, Policies for Development Committee, Manitoba Government Commission on Targets for Economic Development; Leader of the liberal Party in Manitoba and Member of the Legislative Assembly, 1970-1975. *Memberships:* Canadian Bar Association; Canadian Tax Foundation; Manitoba Law Society and Manitoba Bar Association; National Vice President Canadian Council on International Law(Manitoba); Honourary Council, Winnipeg Chamber of Commerce. *Publications:* The Benson Iceberg: A Critical Analysis of the White Paper on Tax Reform in Canada, 1970; Newspaper columnist on the subject of taxation, nationally syndicated with the Toronto Globe & Mail Tax Column, 1966-1967. *Honours:* University of Manitoba Alumni Award-Outstanding 25th year graduate - 1979. *Hobbies:* Music; Tennis. *Address:* 1063 Wellington Crescent, Winnipeg, Manitoba, Canada.

ASPIN, Norman, b. 9 Nov. 1922, Darwen, Lancashire. Business Adviser. m. Elizabeth Irving, 18 Sept. 1948, 3 sons. *Education:* BA, 1947, MA, 1948, Durham University; Imperial Defence College, 1970. *Appointments:* Royal Navy, 1942-45; Commonwealth Relations Office, 1948-68; Foreign and Commonwealth Office, 1969-80; Adviser and Secretary, East African Association, 1980-. *Memberships:* The Naval Club; The Institute of Directors. *Honours:* CMG, 1968. *Hobbies:* Sailing; Tennis; Gardening. *Address:* 4 Mayfield Lodge, 28 Brackley Road, Beckenham, Kent, England.

ASQUITH, Leonard Keith, b. 19 Apr. 1920, Sydney, New South Wales, Australia. Company Secretary and Director. m. Betty Munro, 24 July 1943, 1 son, 1 daughter. *Education:* Certificate of Accountancy, 1937. *Appointments:* Laboratory Assistant, 1938; War Service, 1940-46; Senior Clerk, 1946, Company Accountant, 1953, Company Secretary, 1955, Executive Director, 1956-59, Lindemans Wines; Group Secretary, Group Executive Director, Lindeman (Holdings) Limited, and Seven Subsidiary Companies. *Memberships:* Treasurer, Rotary Club. *Honours:* Paul Harris Fellow Award; Philip Morris, The Silver Ring Award. *Hobbies:* Rotary Club Projects; Gardening. *Address:* 29 Bodem Avenue, Strathfield, New South Wales, Australia.

ASTON, Harold George, b. 13 Mar. 1923 Sydney Australia. Company Director. m. Joyce Thelma Smith 25 Mar. 1948, 1 son, 1 daughter. *Appointments:* Past Deputy Chairman Presently Chairman, Bonds Coats Patons Limited Camperdown, New South Wales, 2050 Australia. *Memberships:* Royal Sydney Yacht Squadron; Concord Golf Club. *Honours:* CBE, Services to Industry, 1976. *Hobbies:* Gardening; Bowling. *Address:* 44 Greenway Drive, Pymble, New South Wales, Australia 2073.

ASTOR, Hugh Waldorf, b. 20 Nov. 1920, m. Emily Lucy Kinloch, 1950, 2 sons, 3 daughters. *Education:* Eton, New College, Oxford. *Appointments:* Intelligence Corps, Europe and SE Asia, Lieutenant Colonel, 1939-45; Assistant, Middle East Correspondent, The Times, 1947; Elected to Board, 1956, Deputy Chairman, 1959-67; Justice of the Peace, Berkshire, 1953; High Sheriff of Berkshire, 1963. *Memberships:* Chairman: The Times Book Company Limited, 1960; Times Trust; Council of Trusthouse Forte Ltd. Director: Hambros Bank Ltd, Phoenix Assurance Company Limited, Winterbottom Trust Limited; Sotra Property Company Ltd; Universal Shipyards (Solent) Ltd. Governor: Peabody Trust, Deputy Chairman 1979, Chairman, 1981, Bradfield College; King Edward's Hospital Fund for London; Deputy Chairman, Council of Governing body of the Middlesex Hospital, 1956-74; Royal National Life-Boat Institution; Royal Yachting Association; Hon. Treasurer Air League; Franco-British Society; Marine Biological Association, United Kingdom; Director: Hutchinson Limited, 1959-78; Vice-President: Aircraft Owners and Pilots Association; Prime Warden, Fishmongers' Company, 1976-77. *Hobbies:* Flying; Sailing; Farming; Underwater Fishing; Photography. *Address:* 14 Culross Street, London W1, England.

ASTOR of HEVER, Gavin, b. 1 June 1918 Taplow, Bucks. m. 4 Oct. 1945 2 sons, 3 daughters. *Education:* Eton and New College, Oxford. *Appointments:* Chairman, The Times Publishing Company Limited 1959-66; President, Times Newspapers Limited 1967-; Chairman, Commonwealth Press Union 1959-71, President, 1971-81; Chairman, Royal Commonwealth Society 1972-75; Lord Lieutenant of Kent 1972-; Chairman, Royal Commonwealth Society, 1972-75; Chairman 1968-77, President 1977-, Pilgrims' Society of Great Britain. *Hobbies:* Golf; Painting; Shooting. *Address:* Hever Castle, Edenbridge, Kent.

ATEKHA, Jude Irobun, b. 25 Jan. 1952 Benin City. Economist. m. 2 sons. *Education:* Immaculate Conception College, Benin City 1965-70; MA Comb. III. BS Geology, 1976, MA Comb. III. MA Economics, Western Illinois University, 1981. *Appointments:* Manager, Concrete Poles Industries Limited, 1977-78, General Manager 1978-80, Chairman-Managing Director 1980-. *Memberships:* Omicron Delta Epsilon (Honorary Economics Society); Lotus Club of Nigeria. *Hobbies:* Swimming; Reading; Tennis. *Address:* 1 Atekha Street, Benin City, Nigeria.

ATKINS, Geoffrey Gilbert, b. 14 Oct. 1930, Reading, England. Actor, Director Producer, Broadcaster. *Appointments:* Various Theatrical Companies, UK, 1954-59; Donovan Maule Theatre, Nairobi, Kenya, 1959-61; Rhodesia Television, Salisbury, Rhodesia, 1961-65; Free-Lancing, 1966-74; Artistic Director, Seven Arts Theatres, Salisbury, Zimbabwe, 1974-81. *Memberships:* British Film Institute; Vegetarian Society of the UK. *Honours:* Top Television Personality, 1961-81. *Hobbies:* Reading; Films; Theatre; Gardening; Yoga. *Address:* Box HG 233, Highlands, Salisbury, Zimbabwe.

ATKINS, George Stuart, b. 1 July 1917, Maplewood, New Jersey, USA. Agrologist/Agricultural Broadcaster. m. Janet Babion Blackwood, 27 Dec. 1941, 4 daughters. *Education:* Bachelor of Science in Agriculture, University of Toronto, Toronto, Ontario, Canada, 1939; Graduate School Certificates, Agricultural Studies, University of Wisconsin, Madison, Wisconsin, USA, 1940; Graduate School Certificate, Agricultural Extension/Communications, Colorado State University, Fort Collins, Colorado, USA, 1954. *Appointments:* Manager, 1940-58-; President and General Manager, Woodlands Orchards Limited, Bronte, Ontario, 1958-; Instructor, Ontario Agricultural College and Ontario Department of Agriculture 1942-46; Farm Director, Niagara TV Limited, Hamilton, Ontario, 1954-55; Farm Commentator 1955-59, Regional Producer, 1959-60; Regional Supervisor, 1960-61; Senior Agricultural Commentator, Canadian Broadcasting Corporation,

Toronto, 1962-80; Agricultural Broadcast Workshop Leader, University of Zambia, on secondment by Commonwealth Broadcasting Association, 1975; Sp. Project Consultant, Climate/Food Project, Massey-Ferguson Limited, Toronto, 1977-79; Director, Developing Countries Farm Radio Network, Toronto, 1979-; Agricultural Radio Communications Consultant, US Agency for International Development, Washington, DC, USA, 1980. *Memberships:* President, Canadian Farm Writers' Federation, Eastern Canadian Farm Writers Association; Vice-President and Parliamentarian, National Association of Farm Broadcasters; Executive Director, Ontario Federation of Agriculture; Junior Farmers' Association of Ontario; Councillor, Ontario Institute of Agrologists, Ontario Forestry Association and Ontario Welfare Council; Halton Region Conservation Authority; Ontario Federal of Home and Schools Associations; Diocese of Niagara Laymen's Council, University of Guelph Alumni Association. *Publications:* Originated, planned, developed and produced numerous agricultural radio and TV program series in both public and private broadcasting; *Honours:* Awards of Merit, Canada Farm Writers' Federation 1958-74 CBC Cowhide Trophy, 1962; 50th Year Gold Medal, 1972; OAC Centenniel Medal, 1974; Elected Fellow of the Agricultural Institute of Canada, 1980. *Hobbies:* Research and recording of local history; Living History; Natural History; Archaeology; Audio tape recording and editing; Collecting and restoring antique farm equipment and automobiles. *Address:* "The Woodlands", R. R. #2, Oakville, Ontario, L6J 4Z3, Canada.

ATKINS, Humphrey Edward Gregory, b. 12 Aug. 1922 Chalfont St. Peter, Bucks, England. Member of Parliament. m. Adela Margaret Spencer-Nairn, 21 Jan. 1944, 1 son, 3 daughters. *Education:* Wellington College Crowthorne Berks, 1935-40. *Appointments:* Royal Navy 1940-48, Lieutenant 1943; Manager, Michael Nairn and Company Limited 1948-60; Director, Foster Turner and Benson Limited 1960-65; Member of Parliament, Merton and Morden Surrey 1955-70, Spelthorne, Surrey, 1970-; Assistant Conservative Whip 1967-70; Treasurer of the Royal Household, 1970-73; Parliamentary Secretary to the Treasury, 1973-74; Opposition Chief Whip 1974-79; Secretary of State for Northern Ireland, 1979-; Lord Privy Seal, 1981-. *Memberships:* Brooks's Club London, Royal London Yacht Club, Cowes, Isle of Wight. *Honours:* Privy Counsellor 1973. *Hobbies:* Sailing; Golf. *Address:* House of Commons, London S W 1.

ATKINS, Robert James, b. 5 Feb. 1946, Hampstead, England. Member of Parliament. m. 1 Oct. 1969 1 son, 1 daughter. *Education:* Highgate School. *Appointments:* Marine Insurance Broker, 1962-70; Salesman, IBM(UK) Limited 1970-76; Sales Executive, Rank Xerox United Kingdom Limited 1976-79. *Memberships:* Honary Secretary, Conservative Parliementory Defence and Aviation Committees; National Vice-President, Conservative Trades Unionists. *Hobbies:* Old Churches; Wine; Cricket. *Address:* 29 Haringey Park, Hornsey, London, N8 9JB.

ATKINSON, (Sir) Leonard Henry, b. 4 Dec. 1910, Hale, Cheshire, England. Regular Army Officer, retired; Chartered Engineer. m. Jean Eileen Atchley, 6 May 1939, 1 son, 3 daughters. *Education:* University College, London, 1929-32; BSc, 1932; Fellow, University College, London, 1977. *Appointments:* Satchwell Controls, GEC, 1932-36; British Army, REME, retired as Major General, 1936-66; Directorships include: Harland Engineering; Weir Engineering Industries; C & W Walker; EMRAY; Harland Simon; Technology Transfer Associates. *Memberships:* FIMechE; FIEE; FIGasE; FIERE, President, 1968/9; Chairman, Council of Engineering Institutions, 1974. *Honours:* KBE, 1966; OBE, 1945. *Hobby:* Photography. *Address:* Pound Cottage, Silchester, Reading, England.

ATKINSON, Norman, b. 25 Mar. 1925, Manchester, England. Design Engineer; Member of Parliament. m. Irene Parry, 15 May 1948. *Appointments:* Apprentice Toolmaker, Draughtsman, Metropolitan Vickers Limited, Manchester; Engineering Designer in Machine Tools, Chief Designer, Manchester University Engineering Department; Member of Parliament, Tottenham, London, 1964-; National Treasurer, British Labour Party, 1976-81. *Publications:* Political Pamphleteer. *Creative Works:* Oil Paintings. *Hobbies:* Sport;

Oil Painting; Walking. *Address:* House of Commons, London, England.

ATKINSON-O'DONNELL, Diana Margaret Mary, b. 10 Dec. Subiaco, Western Australia. Geologist. m. Peter Robert Atkinson (div. 1978), 11 Oct. 1966, 1 son, 3 daughters. *Education:* Bachelor of Science with majors in Geology, Anthropology and Archaeology, University of Western Australia. *Appointments:* Alcoa of Australia, Kwinana, Western Australia; Bureau of Mineral Resources, Canberra A.Ct. C.R.A Exploration (nickel exploration); One of the first women Geologists in Australia to work in the field for a Mining Company C.R.A Exploration, Geologist, P.D.C Constructions Mining Company; Employed on diamond exploration, C.R.A.E, Western Australia. *Memberships:* Australasian Institute of Mining and Metallurgy; Geological Society of Australia; Royal Society of Western Australia; Anthropological Society of Western Australia; Gemmological Society of Australia; Australian Marine Sciences Association of Australia; Women's Auxiliary of the Australasian Institute of Mining and Metallurgy; Newman Society, University of Western Australia; Women's Auxiliary, Royal Guide Dogs for the Blind; National Trust of Australia; Royal Western Australian Historical Society; Art Gallery Society of Western Australia; Convocation, University of Western Australia; Royal Kings' Park Tennis Club; Nedlands Tennis Club. *Hobbies:* Family Life; Music; Oil painting; Archaeology; Gemmology; Squash Tennis; Skin-Diving; Gold Prospecting and Jewellery Making; Designer of a Registered wine-label. *Address:* 74 Watkins Road, Dalkeith 6009, Western Australia.

ATOKI, Christopher Adesanmi, b. 16 Nov. 1934, Ikere-Ekiti, Ondo State, Nigeria. Legal Practitioner; Director and Secretary. m. Grace Oyeyemi Oyedele, 16 July 1960, 3 sons, 1 daughter. *Education:* Council of Legal Education, Middle Temple Inn of Court, London, 1959-62; BSc University of Lagos, Nigeria, 1966-71. *Appointments:* Private Legal Practice, Nigeria, 1962-64; Assistant Company Secretary, 1964-67, Company Secretary, 1967-, Executive Director/Head of Legal and Secretarial Department, 1977-, Nigerian Tobacco Company Limited. *Memberships:* Nigerian Bar Association; International Bar Association; Vice President, Association of Arbitrators of Nigeria. *Publications:* Rights of Shareholders. *Honours:* FCIS; FCIArb. *Hobbies:* Reading; Swimming. *Address:* 52 Upper Drive, Palmgrove Estate, Off Ikorodu Road, Yaba, Lagos, Nigeria.

ATTALIDES, Michael, b. 15 Nov. 1941 Leonarisso, Cyprus. Head, International Relations Service, House of Representatives, Cyprus. *Education:* BSc(Econ.), London School of Economics and Political Science, 1963; MA 1965, PhD 1974, Princeton University. *Appointments:* Lecturer in Sociology, University of Leicester, United Kingdom; Sociologist, Department of Town Planning and Housing, Cyprus; Project Director, Social Research Centre Cyprus; House of Representatives, Cyprus. *Publications:* Cyprus: Nationalism and International Politics 1980; Social Change and Urbanization in Cyprus: A Study of Nicosia 1981. *Hobbies:* Swimming; Photography. *Address:* River Court, 11, Demou Herodotou Street, Apartment 33, Nicosia, Cyprus.

ATTIS, Joel, b. 16 Feb. 1952, Moncton, New Brunswick, Canada. Lawyer. *Education:* BComm, Dalhousie University, Halifax, Canada, 1973; University of Auckland, New Zealand, 1974; LLB, University of New Brunswick, Canada, 1977; Admitted to Barrister's Society of New Brunswick, 1977. *Appointments:* Senior Partner, Attis and Attis, 1977-79; Senior Partner, Johnson Attis, 1979-. *Memberships:* Moncton Barristers Society; Chamber of Commerce; Past President, Management of Independent Living Experiences; Director and Solicitor, Moncton Central Business Development Corporation; Member and Consumer Arbitrator, Better Business Bureau; Independent Chairperson, Dorchester Penitentiary. *Honours:* Numerous Service Awards. *Hobbies:* Squash; Backgammon; Reading. *Address:* 219 Gaspe Street, Dieppe, New Brunswick, Canada.

AUBREY, Irene Elizabeth, b. 7 Jan. 1928 Ottawa, Canada. Professional Librarian. *Education:* BA, University of Ottawa, 1949; Diploma, Lafortune Business College Ottawa, 1950; B.L.S. University of Toronto 1951. *Appointments:* Children's Librarian; Branch Librarian, West Branch, Ottawa Public Library, 1951-60; Stagiaire, Hachette Publishing Company, Paris, France, 1960-61; Branch Librarian, St. Laurent Branch, Ottawa Public Library, 1962-66; Coordinator of Children's Services, West-Island Regional Library Service, Pointe Claire, Quebec, 1966-68; Children's Librarian, Westmount Public Library, Quebec, 1968-75; Chief, Children's Literature Service, National Library of Canada, 1975. *Memberships:* Chairperson, Notable Canadian Children's Book Committee and the Comité pour la sélection des meilleurs livres canadiens pour les jeunes (National Library of Canada); IFLA Round Table of Librarians Representing Documentation Centres Serving Research in Children's Literature; Liaison Officer, Executive Board, Canadian Section of IBBY (International Board on Books for Young People); Editorial Advisory Panel of In Review; Advisory Board for All About Us/Nous Autres. *Publications:* La biche miraculeuse 1973, Original version: The Miraculous Hind; Storytellers' Rendezvous: Canadian Stories to Tell to Children, 1979; Considered for inclusion: Notable Canadian Children's Books and Un choix de livres canadiens pour la jeunesse and Pictures to Share/Images pour tous. *Hobbies:* Music; Book collecting. *Address:* 195 Clearview Avenue, Apt. 714, Ottawa, Ontario, Canada, K1Z 6S1.

AUCHMUTY, James⊙Johnston, b. 29 Nov. 1909, Portadown, N. Ireland. Emeritus Professor of History, and Retired Vice-Chancellor. m. Margaret Walters Vassar, 20 Oct. 1934, 1 son, 1 daughter. *Education:* Armagh Royal School and Trinity College Dublin, Scholar of the House 1929; First Class Moderatorship and Gold Medal, BA 1931; MA 1934; PhD 1935; Hon. LL.D 1974. *Appointments:* Lecturer School of Education University of Dublin 1936-46; Head, Department of Modern History, Farouk University, Alexandria Egypt, 1946-52; Professor of History, New South Wales, Newcastle, 1955-74, Emeritus; Warden Newcastle University College 1960-64; Vice Chancellor University of Newcastle, NSW 1965-74; Hon. Visiting Fellow Humanities Research Centre ANU, 1975-76; First Visiting Professor of Modern Commonwealth History, University of Leeds 1976-77. *Memberships:* F R Hist. S. 1938; MRIA 1941; Foundation Fellow of the Australian Academy of the Humanities 1971; Patron, Australian University Sports Association, since 1975; Athenaeum, London; Pioneers, Sydney; Commonwealth Canberra. *Publications:* US Govt. and Latin American Independence 1810-1830, 1937; Irish Education 1937; Sir Thomas Wyse, 1969; The Teaching of History, 1940; Lecky, 1946; The Voyage of Governor Phillip to Botany Bay, 1970; Contributor to the Australian Dictionary of Biography; The Australian Encyl. *Honours:* CBE 1971; Silver Jubilee Medal 1977; Hon D.Litt Sydney 1974; Hon D Litt Newcastle NSW 1974; Symons award for Services to Commonwealth Universities 1974; First Chairman of Irish Committee of Historical Sciences 1938-44; Plus Chairman of various Committees, and National Commissions. *Hobbies:* Golf; Swimming. *Address:* 9 Glynn Street, Hughes A.C.T. 2605, Australia.

AUGUSTINE, Fennis, Lincoln, b. 22 April 1932. High Commissioner for Grenada in London, 1979nh. m. Oforiwa Augustine, 1 son, 1 daughter. *Education:* LL.B London University; Labour Studies, Ruskin College, Oxford, Called to the Bar Gray's Inn, 1972. *Hobbies:* Cricket; Music. *Address:* 18 Langham Road, London, N15 England.

AULD (Hon), James Alexander Charles, b. 22 July 1921, Toronto, Ontario, Canada. Minister of the Crown. m. Nancy Eleanor Gilmour, 3 May 1946, 1 son, 1 daughter. *Education:* St. Andrew's College, Aurora, Canada; University of Toronto Schools, Toronto, Canada. *Appointments:* Alderman, Corporation of Brockville, Ontario, Canada, 1952-54; Elected to Ontario Legislature, 1954; Minister of Transport, 1962-63; Minister of Tourism and Information, 1963-71; Minister of Public Works, 1971-72; Minister of the Environment, 1972-74; Minister of Colleges and Universities, 1974-75; Chairman, Management Board of Cabinet, 1975-78; Minister of Natural Resources and Minister of Energy, 1978-79; Minister of Natural Resources, 1979-; Minister of Natural Resources, 1979-81; Chairman, St. Lawrence Parks Commission, 1981. *Memberships:* Canadian Legion; Royal Canadian Military Institute; Monarchist League of Canada; Sussex Lodge, Royal Arch Masons; Anglican Foundation of Canada; Heral-

dry Society of Canada; Albany Club of Toronto; Kiwanis Club of Brockville; Brockville Country Club. *Honours:* Doctor of Laws (honoris causa), University of Dundee, Scotland, 1974. *Hobbies:* Boating; Woodworking; Cross-country skiing. *Address:* 173 Hartley Street, Brockville, Ontario, Canada K6V 3N4.

AULD, Robin Ernest, b. 19 July 1937, England. Queen's Counsel; Recorder of the Crown Court. m. Catherine Eleanor Mary Pritchard, 8 June 1963, 1 son, 1 daughter. *Education:* LL.B., 1955-58, PhD., 1959-62, King's College, University of London, UK; Called to the Bar by Gray's Inn, London, UK, 1959. *Appointments:* Practised at English Bar, 1959-; Member of Commission of Inquiry into Casino Gambling in the Bahamas, 1967; Prosecuting Counsel to Department of Trade, 1969-75; Called to Northern Ireland Bar, 1973; Appointed Queen's Counsel, 1975; Chairman of Public Inquiry into William Tyndale Schools, 1975-76; Department of Trade Inspector, Ashbourne Investments Limited, 1975-79; Appointed Recorder of the Crown Court, 1977. *Memberships:* Worshipful Company of Woolmen; City Livery Club; Moor Park Golf Club. *Publications:* Various Reports of Public Inquiries. *Honours:* Macaskie Scholarship, Lord Justice Holker Senior Scholarship, 1959. *Address:* Lamb Building, Temple, London EC4, England.

AUSTIN, Michael, b. 5 November 1935, Portsmouth, England. Chartered Accountant. m. Joan Wendy Sunley, 19 March, 1966, 2 sons. *Education:* Eltham College, Kent, England; Qualified as Chartered Accountant 1964; Fellow of the Institute of Chartered Accountants; in England and Wales; Associate of the Institute of Taxation. *Appointments:* Peat, Marwick, Mitchell & Co. Jamaica 1966-1968; Peat, Marwick, Mitchell & Co, Cayman Islands 1968nh; Managing Partner 1969-. *Memberships:* Past President, Cayman Islands Society of Professional Accountants; Grand Cayman Yacht Club(Former Commodore); Cayman Islands Chamber of Commerce; Cayman Drama Society. *Hobbies:* Sailing; Theatre; Gourmet Foods-International Cuisine; Music; Reading; Travel. *Address:* 6 Lime Tree Bay, P.O. Box 493, Grand Cayman, Cayman Islands, British West Indies.

AUSTIN, Reginald, b. 16 Oct. 1936 Gulgons New South Wales. Salesman-Superannuation. m. Jane 28 Feb. 1981, 2 sons. *Education:* Dip. A.I.T.; A.A.I.M. *Memberships:* Life Member, New South Wales Professional Athletic Association. *Hobbies:* Rugby League Football; Current World Veteran Sprint Champion. *Address:* 80 Rathowen Pde, Killarney Heights 2087, New South Wales, Australia.

AVALON, Phillip Anthony Holbrow, b. 24 Feb. 1945 Newcastle. Film Producer. m. 6 Mar. 1977, 1 son. *Education:* St Josephs College Newcastle NSW, 1950-56; Marist Brothers College Newcastle NSW, 1956-60; Physical Education Course and Crew Commanders Course, Caribou and Hercules Aircraft, Australian Army 1962-68; Independant Theatre Drama School, 1970. *Appointments:* Australian Army Air Supply 1962-68; Physical Education Teacher YMCA 1968-70; Professional Model-Actor 1970-76; Produced and Wrote, The Backstreet General, Play, 1972, and 1978; Double Dealer, Film, 1975; Summer Boy, Film, 1976; Little Boy Lost, 1978. *Memberships:* Film and Television Producers Association of Australia; Autralian Writers Guild; Actors and Announcers Equity; Film Makers Co-operative; The Wave-Ski Surfers Association; Rostrum Club. *Publications:* Co-author novels: Summer City, 1978; The Backstreet General, 1980; Screenplays: Zodiac Fairground; Waterfront; Double Dealer; Summer City. *Honours:* Australian Army, Marksman Owen Machine Gun, 1962; Highest Point Score, Surf Ski, NSW 1978; Highest Point Score Overall Surf Ski NSW 1979. *Hobbies:* Films; Reading; Surf Skiing; Public Speaking. *Address:* 16 Lindley Avenue, Narrabeen 2101 New South Wales, Australia.

AVOINE (De), Jean-Claude, b. 14 Mar. 1935 Mauritius. Writer, Journalist. *Appointments:* Co-founder and editor, in Belgium, of "L'Etoile et la clef", international French poetry magazine: First issue: September 1975. *Publications:* La cité fondamentale, poems; Le testament de noirault-le-Blond, novel, to be published. *Honours:* A Laureate of Hachette-Larousse Prize, Great Britain, 1965. *Hobbies:* Music composition, (piano);

Painting. *Address:* 38, d'Epinay Street, Rose Hill, Mauritius.

AVON, Nicholas Eden, 2nd Earl of Avon, b. 3 Oct. 1930 London. Politician. *Education:* Eton 1944-49. *Appointments:* Served with KRRC, 1949-51; ADC to Governor General of Canada, 1952-53; TA 1953-75, Major 1959, Lt.Col 1965, Colonel 1972; Hon Col. NE Sector, Army Cadet Force, 1970; Vice Chairman, Greater London TA & VRA, 1976-81; Opposition Whip, 1978-79. *Memberships:* Master, Salters' Company, 1979-80; Party delegate to N Atlantic Assembly, 1979-80; Lord-in-waiting (Government Whip), 1980-. *Honours:* OBE 1970; TD 1965; ADC 1978-; DL 1973-. *Creative Works:* All England Lawn Tennis Club. *Address:* House of Lords, London SW1 A0PW.

AVRAM, His Grace, The Duke of, John Charlton Rudge, b. 12 Mar. 1944, Kalgoorlie, Western Australia. Admiral; Professor; Banker; Company Director. m. Maureen Agnes Markham, 1 son, 2 daughters. *Education:* D.Litterarum, R.C.D., 1977; DSc, R.A.I.C. 1978; MBA, R.C.D. 1978; D.Phil. 1979; D.B.A. 1981; Honorary Degrees, D.S.T. 1978; D.C.L 1978; D.Eng. 1980. *Appointments:* Managing Director: Aaron Pty. Limited 1969-; Mary-Ellen Mines Pty. Limited 1969-; Aabec Investments Pty. Limited 1971-; Governor, The Royal Bank of Avram, 1979-; Admiral, Australian Navy, 1979; The Royal Australian Exchange. 1979; Professor of Business Administration, R.C.D. 1980-; Professor of Science, R.A.I.C. 1980-; Life Administrator, R.C.D. 1977-; Registrar, R.A.I.C. 1978-. *Memberships:* FRCD; FRAIC; AMAus.IMM; ARACI; The Royal Society of Tasmania, 1978-; Masons various 1964-; Apex, acclaimed 1st. peer president, 1976-77; Chartered Scientist, Chemist, Engineer; Member and past officer of numerous clubs and associations. *Publications:* Editor, The Cyclopedia of Tasmania; Author of Selected Speeches and Scientific Papers in Fields. *Honours:* Knight of the Sword, 1971; Royal Knight, 1975; Knight of Honour, 1976; Chevalier of Honour, 1979; Knight of Bountiful Endeavours, 1976; Grand Knight Cross of the Order of Leonard, 1979; Chevalier, 1981; Cr. the Rt. Hon. The Earl of Enoch, 1976; Cr. His Grace, The most Noble, Admiral, The Duke of Avram, 1979; Cr. the Most Hon. The Marquis of Mathra 1980; Cr. The Rt. Hon. Viscount ULOM, 1981; Cr. The Rt. Hon. Lord Rama, 1981. *Hobbies:* Reading about life and the law; Play most sports. *Address:* Tamar Avenue, George Town, Tasmania, Australia, 7253.

AWA, Eme Onuoha, b. 15 Dec. 1921, Nigeria. Political Scientist. m. Pauline Seromi Kempi, 12 Dec. 1957, 2 sons, 1 daughter. *Education:* B.A. (Honours), Lincoln University, Philadelphia, 1951-; PhD., New York University, 1952 & 1955-. *Appointments:* Assistant Secretary, Federal Ministry of Economic Development, 1956-57; University Teaching, Universities of Ibadan, Lagos, Nigeria (Nsukka). *Memberships:* Nigerian Political Science Association; African Political Science Association; African Association for Public Administration; Nigerian Association for Public Administration. *Publications:* Books on, Federal Government in Nigeria, Issues in Federalism and The Transformation of Rural Society. *Honours:* Grant by the I.D.R.C., Canada, for the study of Rural Development in Nigeria, 1973-. *Hobby:* Farming. *Address:* 302 Cartwright Avenue, Nsukka, Nigeria.

AWACHIE, James Brinsley Egbunike, b. 2 Feb. 1934, Umunnachi, Nigeria. Professor. m. Carol Ifeyinwa Nwangwu, 26 Dec. 1965 3 sons, 3 daughters. *Education:* BSc., University of London, 1958-; PhD., University of Liverpool, England, 1963-. *Appointments:* Lecturer, in Zoology, Nigerian College of Technology, Zaria, 1959-61; Ahmadu Bello University, Zaria, 1961-63; University of Lagos, 1964-65; Faculty, University of Nigeria, Nsukka, 1965-; Professor of Zoology, 1973-; Head of Department, 1975-; Visiting Professor, University of Waterloo, Canada, 1980-81. *Memberships:* Nigerian & British Societies, Parasitology, Feshwater Biology Association; Institute of Biology, UK.; Insititute of Fisheries M.G.M.T; Nsukka Philosophy Society; Government Council, University of Ife; Government Board, Lake Chad Research Institute, Chairman Research & Publications; Chairman National Advisory Commission, Fisheries Research; Council Science Association, Nigeria; Expert Consultation Group on River Fisheries Management. *Publications:* Author of over 60 papers in National & International

Journals in the areas of Parasitology, Hydrobiology & Fishery Science. Consultant in Aquaculture & Floodplain Fisheries Management. *Honours:* Fellow, Nigerian Academy of Sciences; Linnean Society; Commonwealth Scholar, 1961-63; Norad Fellow, 1973-; Research Grantee several National & Internation Organisations. *Hobbies:* Photography, Gardening, Table Tennis, Folk Singing, Dancing. *Address:* Egbunamnike House, Ezimili, c/o Postal Agency, Umunnachi, Idemili, Anambra State, Nigeria.

AWERE, Daniel, b. 16 July 1928, Accra, Ghana. Journalist and Public Relations Practitioner. m. Joana Iagoe, 1963, 4 sons, 5 daughters. *Education:* Achimota School; Cambridge School Certificate, 1946 ; Diploma, Thompson Foundation TV College, Glasgow, 1970-. *Appointments:* Civil Service, Ghana, 1947-56; Ghana Broadcasting Corporation, 1956-75; Head of News & Current Affairs, 1973-75; Public Relations Officer, Ghana Publishing Corporation, 1975-; Chief Press Secretary to Head of State, 1978-79; Public Relations Manager, Ghan Publishing Corporation, 1979-. *Address:* No. 21 Ist Labone Street, Osu, Accra, Ghana.

AWOKOYA, Stephen Hezekiah Oluwole Oluremilekun, b. 9 July 1913, Awa, Ijebuode, Nigeria. Educationalist. m. (1) 5 Jan. 1941, (2) 2 Jan. 1950, 3 sons, 6 daughters. *Education:* Science Diploma, Higher College, Yaba; BSc., (Special), University College, London. *Appointments:* Science Tutor, St Andrew's College, Oyo, Nigeria, 1937-40; Principal, Molusi College, Ijebu-Igbo, Nigeria, 1949-51; Minister of Education, Western Region, Nigeria, 1952-56; Head, Federal Emergency Science School, Lagos, 1958-61; Permanent Secretary and Chief Federal Adviser on Education, 1961-67; Unesco Director, Department of Scientific and technological Research and Higher Education, 1967-73; Professor of Educational Planning, University of Ife, Nigeria, 1973-. *Memberships:* President, Nigeria Chemical Society; Science Teachers Association of Nigeria; Island Club, Lagos. *Publications:* England as I Saw Her; The Science of Things Above Us; The Crisis Child of Our Time. *Honours:* DSc, Lagos, 1973-; C.B.E. *Hobbies:* Music, Sketching. *Address:* Gimh Terrace, 78 Obanta Avenue, Awa, Ijebuode, Nigeria.

AWONIYI, Sunday Bolorunduro, b. 30 Apr. 1932, Mopa, Kwara State, Nigeria. Public Administrator; Management Consultant. m. (1) Florence Ebun Oyewole, 1959; (2) Benedicta Omowunmi Omopariola, 1973, 7 sons, 4 daughters. *Education:* BA., University College, Ibadan, Nigeria, 1956-59; Imperial Defence College (now Royal College of Defence Studies), London, UK, 1970-71. *Appointments:* Administrative Officer Class IV, Northern Nigeria Civil Service, 1959; Divisional Officer, Bauchi, 1959-60; Assistant Secretary, Federal Ministry of Mines and Power, 1961-62; Secretary, Northern Nigeria Government Executive Council, Kaduna, 1963; Provincial Secretary in Charge, Niger and Plateau Provinces, 1964-65; Under Secretary, Military Governor's Office, Kaduna, 1966-68; Permanent Secretary, Ministry of Finance, Kwara State, Ilorin, 1968-70; Permanent Secretary, Federal Ministry of Internal Affairs, Lagos, 1971-75; Permanent Secretary, Ministry of Petroleum Resources, 1975-77; Elected member, Nigerian Constituent Assembly, 1977; Board of Governors, National Institute for Policy and Strategic Studies, Kuru, 1979-; Board of Governors, Institute of Administration, Ahmadu Bello University, Zaria, Nigeria. *Memberships:* Mopa Welfare Society. *Honours:* Commander of the Order of the Niger; CON., 1977. *Hobbies:* Reading; Badminton. *Address:* 6 Rumsey Road, Ikoyi, PO Box 15664, Lagos, Nigeria.

AWWAL, Mohammad Abdul, b. 25 May 1932, Comilla, Bangladesh. Teacher. m. Saleha, 16 June 1960, 1 son, 1 daughter. *Education:* B.A. Honours, 1957-; M.A. (in Bengali language & literature), Dacca University, 1958-; PhD. in Bengali literature, London University, 1967-; M.A. course attended in Linguistics, London University, 1963-. *Appointments:* Lecturer in Bengali in different colleges, 1958-68; Senior Lecturer & Reader, Chittagong University, Bangladesh, 1968-77; Professor of Bengali, Rajshahi University, 1977-. *Memberships:* Bengali Academy, Dacca, Bangladesh; Royal Asiatic Society, Great Britain; Asiatic Society of Bangladesh, Dacca. *Publications:* Books in Bengali: Samudre Sisire, Chaya O Chanda, Godhulir Akas, Piccadilli Circus; Namita Boser Dairy (All fictions);

Bngla Bhasar Itihas, Mir Masaf Hosen, Mir Masarrafer Gadya Racana (All Critical Essays); Edited Books: Ucit Sraban, Ratnabati, Basantakumar, Sindhu Hillol, Mrigbati; Book in English, The Prose works of Mir Masarraf Hosen. *Hobbies:* Painting, Photography. *Address:* 17/6 KM. Das Lane, Dacca 3, Bangladesh.

AYAZ, Iftikhar, Ahmad, b. 18 Jan. 1934, Tanga, Tanzania. Teacher. m. Amtul Basit Maulana Abul Ata, 6 Dec. 1959, 1 son, 4 daughters. *Education:* Teachers Certificate, Nairobi, Kenya, 1957-; B.Ed., with Honours in Education, University of Newcastle-upon-Tyne UK., 1975-; Diploma in TEFL, University of London, 1976-; M.A. Language and Literature in Education, 1977-. *Appointments:* Ministry of National Education, Tanzania, 1957-77; Insitutue of Education, 1978-. *Memberships:* Secretary General, Tanzania Commonwealth Society; Training Commissioner Boy Scouts; Royal Commonwealth Society; International Association of Teachers of English as a Foreign Language; Language Association of Tanzania; Secretary, Tanzania Literary Lights Club; Red Cross Society; T.S.P.C.A. and other official advisory Committees on education in Tanzania. *Publications:* Patterns of Development, Africa, Commonwealth Institute, 1978-; Tanzania in the Commonwealth; Several professional papers and feature articles on topics related to understanding of the Commonwealth. *Honours:* British Council Scholarship for Educational visits, 1966-; Commonwealth Fellowship Award, 1973-76; British Council Bursary Award for participation in IATEFL Conference, 1979-; Queen Scouts Certificate, Badge, 1953-. *Hobbies:* Reading, Writing and Public Service. *Address:* P.O. Box 376, Daressalaam, Tanzania.

AYER, Sir, Alfred Jules, b. 29 Oct. 1910. m. (1) Grace Isabel Renée Lees, 1932, (2) Alberta Constance Wells, 1960, 2 sons, 1 daughter. *Education:* Scholar, Hon. Student, Christ Church, Oxford, 1979; 1st class Lit. Hum., 1932; MA., 1936; Lecturer in Philosphy at Christ Church, Oxford, UK, 1932-35; Research Student, 1935-44; Fellow of Wadham College, Oxford, UK, 1944-46; Hon. Fellow, 1957. *Appointments:* Dean, 1945-46; Grote Professor of the Philosophy of Mid and Logic in the University of London, UK, 1946-59; Hon. Fellow, UCL., 1979; Wykeham Professor of Logic, University of Oxford and Fellow of New College, Oxford, UK, 1957-78; Fellow of Wolfson College, Oxford, UK, 1978-; Visiting Professor at: NY University, USA, 1948-49, City College, New York, USA, 1961-62; Surrey University, UK, 1978-. *Memberships:* Central Advisory Council for Education, 1963-66; President, Humanist Association, 1965-70; Modern Languages Association, 1966-67; Chairman, Booker Prize Committee, 1978; Hon. member, American Academy of Arts and Sciences, 1963; Foreign member, Royal Danish Academy of Sciences and Letters, 1976; Chevalier de la Legion d'Honneur, 1977; Order of Cyril and Methodius, 1st Cl. (Bulgaria), 1977. *Publications:* Language, Truth and Logic, 1936 (revised edition 1946); The Foundation of Empirical Knowledge, 1940; Thinking and Meaning, 1947; British Empirical Philosophers (ed.with Raymond Winch), 1952; Philosophical Essays, 1954; The Problem of Knowledge, 1956; Editor, Logical Positivism, 1959; Privacy, 1960; Philosophy and Language, 1960; The Concept of a Person and Other Essays, 1963; Man as a Subject for Science, 1964; The Origins of Pragmatism, 1968; Editor, The Humanist Outlook, 1968; Metaphysics and Common Sense, 1969; Russell and Moore: the analytical heritage, 1971; Probability and Evidence, 1972; Russell, 1972; Bertrand Russell as a Philosopher, 1973; The Central Questions of Philosophy, 1974; Part of my Life, 1977; Perception and Identity, 1979; Hume, 1980; articles in philosophical and literary journals. *Creative Works:* Lectures: William James, Harvard, 1970; John Dewwey, Columbia, 1970; Gifford, St. Andrews, 1972-73. *Address:* 51 York Street, London W1, England.

AYIDA, Allison Akene, b. 16 June 1930, Nigeria. Economist and Administrator. m. Remi Victoria, 3 sons, 2 daughters. *Education:* King's College, Lagos; Queen's College, Oxford; London School of Economics & Political Science; M.A. Oxon. *Appointments:* Permanent Secretary, Federal Ministry of Economic Development and Reconstruction and Secretary, National Economic Council, 1963-71; Chairman UN Economic Commission for Africa, 1967-68; Permanent Secretary, Federal Ministry of Finance, Lagos, 1971-75; Secretary to the Federal Military Government & Head of the Federal

Civil Service, 1975-77; Financial Consultant and Company Director, 1977-. *Memberships:* President, Nigerian Economic Society, 1971-; Nigerian Institute of Management. *Publications:* Common Markets and Industrialisation; contractor Finance and Supplier Credit in Economic Growth; Development Objectives for Nigeria in the Seventies; Nigerian Revolution, 1966-70; Federal Civil Service and Nation Building. *Hobbies:* Lawn Tennis and Swimming. *Address:* 6 Idowu Martins Street, Victoria Island, Lagos, Nigeria.

AYIM, Emmanuel Nuwokpor, b. 15 July 1933. Anaesthetist and Educator. m. Elsie Seyena Hosu-Porbley, 15 May 1976, 2 sons. *Education:* Achimota School, Ghana, 1948-53; University of Hamburg; University of Goettingen; University of Hamburg, 1955-60; German State Examination Certificate, 1960-; M.D. 1963-; D.T., M & H., 1961-. *Appointments:* Intern, Allgemeines Krankenhaus (A.K.), Hamburg, Altona and A.K. St. George, Hamburg; Resident, A.K. St. George, Hamburg, Albertinen Krankenhaus, Hamburg; Universitaetskliniken, Zurich; Research Fellow, Anaesthesia, University of Zurich; Senior Lecturer & Head of Anaesthesia, University of Dares Salaam, 1969-71; University of Nairobi, Senior lecturer, 1971-74; Associate Professor, 1975-79; Professor and Head of Anaesthesia, 1979-; Visiting Professor of Anaesthesia, University of Khartoum, 1976-. *Memberships:* Society of Anaesthesiologists of East Africa; Founder, Chairman for 3 terms, Executive Committee World Federation of Societies of Anaesthesiologists; International College of Surgeons; Neurological Society of Kenya; Nairobi Hospital Clinincal Club; Associaton of Physicians of East Africa; Kenya Medical Association. *Publications:* Author of over 30 articles on Anaesthesia, Intensive Care and related fields in professional journals. Author of 3 chapters in a textbook of Surgery; One chapter in Modern Textbook of Surgery in preparation. *Honours:* Foreign corresponding member to Anaesthesia, Association of Anaesthetists of Great Britain and Irelands, 1977-; Foreign corresponding member to Anaesthesist, Organ des Osterreichschen Gesselschaft fur Anaestheriologie & Internsive Care, der Deutschen Gesselschaft fur Anaesthesitogie & Intensiventisen und des Schwerzerischen Gesselschaft fur Anaesthesiologie; Special Consultant Anaethetist to Aga Khan Hospital, Nairobi, 1980-; Honorary Consultant, Kenyattan National Hospital, 1972-. *Hobby:* Horse riding. *Address:* Karuna Close, Westland, Nairobi, Kenya.

AYLESFORD, 11th Earl of, Charles Ian Finch-Knightley, b. 2 Nov. 1918, Melbourne, Australia. Landowner. m. Margaret Rosemary Tyer, 21 Mar. 1946, 1 son, 2 daughters. *Education:* Oundle School. *Appointments:* Sun Fire Insurance Company, 1937-39; London Scottish Regiment, 1937-40; Royal Scots Fusiliers, 1940-42; The Black Watch, 1942-46; Secretary to Packington Estate, 1946-58; Landowner, Packington Estate, 1958-. *Memberships:* County Commissioner, Boy Scouts, 1947-74; President, Royal Scoeity of St. George, Warwickshire, 1960-71; President, Warwickshire Magistrates Association, 1964-; President, Warwickshire County Cricket Club, 1979-; Lord Warden of the Woodmen of Arden, 1958-. *Honours:* Knight of the Order of St. John, 1974-; The Queen's Silver Jubilee Medal, 1977-. *Hobbies:* Archery, Fishing, Shooting, Nature Conservation. *Address:* Packington Old Hall, Meriden, Nr. Coventry, CV7 7HG.

AYLETT, Allen James, b. 24 Apr. 1934, Melbourne, Australia. Dental Surgeon. m. Marjorie Anne Wappet, 7 Feb. 1958, 3 sons, 1 daughter. *Education:* University High School; Bachelor of Dental Science, Melbourne University; Licensed Dental Surgeon. *Memberships:* President of: North Melbourne Football Club, 1971-76; Victorian Football League, 1977-, National Football League, 1978-; Chairman of: Australian Football Championship, 1978-, Young Presidents Organisation, 1981-. Director, Rothmans National Sports Foundation, World of Sport Foundation, Sir Robert Menzies Memorial Trust; Clubs include: Carbine (Melbourne), V.R.C., M.V.R.C., V.A.T.C., M.C.C., Eildon Boat (Victoria), Ski Club, (Victoria). *Honours:* O.B.E., 1979-. *Hobbies:* Cricket, Football, Tennis. *Address:* 65 Park Street, Moonee Ponds 3039, Melbourne, Australia.

AYUB, Arshad, b. 15 Nov. 1928, Johor, Malaysia. Administrative Officer of the Administrative & Diplomatic Service of the Government of Malaysia. m. Zaleha Mohd., 29 Dec. 1960, 5 sons, 2 daughters. *Education:* Malay School, Parit Keruma, Government Preparatory English School, Government English School, (Muar); College of Agriculture Malays (Diploma Agriculture, 1954-); BSc., Honours, University College of Wales, Aberystwyth, 1958-; Management Development Institute, Lausanne, Switzerland (Postgraduate Diploma in Business Administration), 1964-. *Appointments:* Secretary-General, Ministry of Agriculture, Ministry of Primary Industries; Deputy Director General, Economic Planning Unit; Deputy Governor, Central Bank of Malaysia; Director, MARA Institute of Technology; Principal Assistant Secretary (Finance), The Treasury; Deputy Controller, Industrial Development Division, Ministry of Trade & Industry; Economic Officer Penang, Ministry of Trade & Industry; Assistant Economist, Rural & Industrial Development Authority. *Memberships:* Institute of Statisticians; British Institute of Management; Malay Officers' Cooperative & Credit Investment Society, Malaysia; National Archery Association of Malaysia; President, Parents Teachers Association. *Honours.* J.M.N. 1971-, D.P.M.P. 1974 , P.G.D.K. 1976-, D.P.M.J. 1979-, P.S.M. 1980-. *Hobbies:* Gardening, Travelling. *Address:* 25 Jalan 16/6, Petaling Jaya, Selangor, Malaysia.

AZIM, Mohammad Anwarul, b. 31 Jan. 1940, Noakhali, Bangladesh. Teacher. m. Fazila, 14 Dec. 1970, 1 son, 1 daughter. *Education:* BSc., (Mech.) Engineering Dacca, 1961-; Diploma-Ing., Aachen, West Germany, 1965-; Dr.-Ing., Braunschweig, West Germany, 1975-. *Appointments:* Lecturer, Bangladesh University of Engineering. & Technology 1961-66; Assistant Professor, 1966-71, Associate Professor, 1971-76, Professor of Mech. Engineering since Jan. 1976-. *Memberships:* Institution of Engineers, Bangladesh; Fellow, Bangladesh Computer Society; Institute of Welding, Bangladesh. *Publications:* Numerous and varied works in field in journals and publications. *Hobbies:* Tennis, Swimming. *Address:* Faculty of Engineering University Quarters, Dacca-2, Bangladesh.

AZIZ, Hamza, b. 28 Feb. 1930, Dar-es-Salaam, Tanzania. Civil Servant; Chief of Police; Diplomat; Businessman. m. Naimi A Shangali, 5 Sept. 1959, 2 sons, 4 daughters. *Education:* Diploma, East African Staff College; Diploma, International Police Academy, USA; Diploma, Diplomacy, USA; Masters Degree, Politics, Johns Hopkins University, USA. *Appointments:* Civil Servant; Chief of Police; Diplomat; Business Consultancy. *Memberships:* Rotary Club; Red Cross; British Council. *Publications:* Poetry. *Honours:* Cross of the Nile. *Hobbies:* Swimming; Football; Squash. *Address:* 109 B Msasani, Old Bagamoyo Street, Dar-Es-Salaam, Tanzania.

AZIZ, Ungku A, b. 28 Jan. 1922, London. Economist. m. Shari Fah Azah, 5 May, 1946, 1 daughter. *Education:* Diploma in Arts (Class II), Raffles College, Singapore, 1940-41 and 1947-; Bachelor of Arts (Honours) Class I in Economics, University of Malaya, Singapore, 1951-; Doctor of Economics (Hakase), Waseda University, Tokyo, 1964-; Honorary Doctor of Humane Letters, University of Pittsburgh, 1971-; Honorary Doctor of Education, Chulalongkorn University Bangkok, 1977-.

Appointments: Johore State Civil Service; Lecture in Economics University of Malay, Singapore, 1952-; Head Department of Economics Faculty of Arts, University of Malaya Kuala Lumpur, 1961-; Dean Faculty of Economics and Administration, University of Malaya, Kuala Lumpur, 1965-; Vice-Chancellor University of Malay, 1968-; Vice-Chancellor, University of Malaya, Kuala Lumpur & Royal Professor of Economics. *Memberships:* Committee for Development Planning United Nations, 1978-80; International Advisory Council, University College at Buckingham, England, 1976-; Scientific Commission of International Council of Research in Co-operative Development; International Association of Agricultural Economics; Joint Advisory Committee FAO/UNESCO/ILO; Advisory Group Research Register of Studies on Co-operatives in Developing Countries & Selected Biography; Editorial Advisory Board of Asia Pacific Community (The Asian Club), 1978-; UNU Council, 1980-86; Chairman Malaysian Examinations Council, 1980-; National Farmers' Organisation, Malaysia; Malaysian National Council of ASAIHL; Malaysian Rubber Research and Development Board; National Co-operative Movement of Malaysia; Board of Directors, Malaysian Co-operative Bank; Commission Joint UNESCO-IAU Research Programme in Higher Education Kuala Lumpur; Economic Association of Malaysia; Chairman Board of Trustees, National Art Gallery. *Publications:* Numerous and varied papers and publications in field. *Honours:* Order Des Arts et Des Lettres, Government of France, 1965-; Fellow, World Academy of Arts and Science, 1965-; Malaysian Award of the Tun Abdul Razak Foundation Awards, 1978-; Royal Professor of Economis, 1978-. *Hobbies:* Reading, Photography, Jogging. *Address:* Vice-Chancellor's House, University of Malay, Kuala Lumpur 22-11, Malaysia.

AZNAM, Raja Tan Sri bin Raja Haji Ahmad, b. 21 Jan 1928, Taiping, Malaya. Malaysian High Commissioner in London, 1979nh. m. Tengku Puan Sri Zailah Btd T. Zakaria, 1954, 1 son, 2 daughters. *Education:* King Edward VII College, Taiping; Malay College, Kuala Kangsar; University of Malaya, Singapore. *Appointments:* Malayan Civil Service 1953, Foreign Service 1956; Second Secretary, Bangkok, 1957; First Secretary, Cairo, 1960-1962; Principal Assistant Secretary, Minister of Foreign Affairs, 1962-1965; Deputy Permanent Representative to UN, 1965-1968; High Commissioner in India, 1968-1971; Ambassador to Japan, 1971-1974, Ambassador to USSR, Bulgaria, Hungary, Mongolia, Poland and Romania, 1974-1977, to France, Morocco, Portugal and Spain, 1977-1979. *Hobbies:* Reading; Golf. *Address:* Malaysian High Commission, 45 Belgrave Square, London, SW1X 8QT England.

AZOPARDI, Dick Joseph, b. 19 Aug. 1956, Gibraltar. Barrister-at-Law. m. Marilyn Josephine, 16 Aug. 1978. *Education:* Second Calss Honours Degree in Law, The Polytechnic of North London, 1975-78; Second Class Award in Part II Bar Examinations, 1978-79. *Appointments:* Barrister-at-Law with J. A. Hassan & Partner since called to the Bar of Gibraltar in 1979-. *Memberships:* Gibraltar Bar Association. *Hobbies:* Football, Squash, Golf, Writing and all types of Music. *Address:* 5 Chicardo's Passage, Gibraltar.

B

BABAJIDE, Solomon Babatunde, b. 29 Jan. 1950, Fajoye, Ibadam East, Oyo State, Nigeria. Shipping. m. Patricia Ojorumi Emina, 29 Mar. 1975, 1 son, 3 daughters. *Education:* GCE A/Level, University of London, 1972-73; Shipping Course, Home Studies, 1968-69. *Appointments:* Panalpina World Transport Limited, Nigeria, 1969-74; Life Flour Shipping Agency, 1974-. *Memberships:* Nigerian Institute of Management; British Institute of Management; Institute of Transport Administration; Board of Directors, Life Flour Mill Limited, 1980; Board of Directors, West African Shrimps Limited. *Hobby:* Reading. *Address:* Life Flour Mill Qtr., Omoraka Estates, Nr. Eternit, Sapele/Warri Road, Sapele, Bendel State, Nigeria.

BABIIHA, KABWIMUKYA, John, b. 17 Apr. 1913, Toro, Uganda. Veterinarian. m. Elizabeth Kabahuma, 10 June 1940, 4 sons, 7 daughters. *Education:* Diploma Veterinary Science, Makerere University College, 1934-39; BA, Social Anthropology, Pretoria University External Division, 1950-53. *Appointments:* Assistant Veterinary Officer, Uganda Government, 1939-45; Department Treasurer, Toro Kingdom Government, Uganda, 1946-53; Uganda Leg. Council Member, 1954-60; Minister of Animal Resources and Vice-President of the Republic of Uganda, 1961-71; Presidential Advisor on Animal Resources, 1973-80; National Chairman of Uganda Peoples Congress and Pensionable ex Vice President. *Memberships:* Hon. Fellow, Louanium University, Kinshasha, Zaire; American Veterinary Medical Association of USA and Canada; Lions Clubs International; Fellow of International Biographical Association. *Publications:* Bayaga Clan in Western Uganda, 1957, new editions, 1975 and 1978. *Honours:* Knight of the Grand Cross of the Order of Pius XI, 1969; Knight Commander of the Grand Order of the Stars of Honour, 1963; Chevalier of the Grand Cordon of the Order of The Leopard, Zaire, 1966; International Order of the Lion, 1970; Medalha Pro-Mundi Benefilio, 1975. *Hobbies:* Walking; Anthropological pursuits. *Address:* PO Box 7168, Kampala, Uganda.

BACHAN, Nirmal Kant, b. 12 Apr. 1940, Dhamtari, M.P., India. Medical Doctor. m. Lydia Solomon Rao, 5 Feb. 1965, 2 sons, 2 daughters. *Education:* M.B.B.S. (Bachelor in Medicine and Bachelor in Surgery), Jabalpur University, 1963-; D.P.H. (Post Graduate Diploma in Public Health), Calcutta University, 1980-. *Appointments:* Staff Doctor, Dhamtari Christian Hospital, Dhamtari, 1964-65; General Duty Medical Officer, Ministry of Health, India, 1965-72; Medical Superintendent and Director Community Health, Harriet Benson Memorial Hospital, India, 1973-. *Memberships:* Christian Medical Association of India; Indian Medical Association. *Publications:* Alternative approaches to Health Care a paper published 1976 at the National Symposium, Hyderabad. *Hobbies:* Photography, Hunting. *Address:* Staff Bungalow, Harriet Benson Memorial Hospital, P.O. Lalitpur, U.P. 284403, India.

BACHELARD, Eric Peter, b. 1 Mar. 1931, Melbourne, Australia. Professor of Forestry. m. Sally Beatrice Lodge, 6 Jan. 1966, 2 sons, 1 daughter. *Education:* A. Diploma For. (Creswick), 1952-; BSc. (For.), Melbourne, 1958-; M.F. Yale, 1959-; PhD., Yale, 1962-. *Appointments:* Assistant Forest Officer, Forests Commission, Victoria, 1953-63; Instructor in Biology, Harvard University, 1963-64; Research Officer, 1964-65, Chief Silvicultural Research Officer, 1965-, Forests Commission, Victoria, Lecturer, Forestry, Australian National University, 1965-69; Senior Lecturer in Forestry, 1969-78; Professor of Forestry, 1978-; Dean Faculty of Science, ANU., 1980-. *Memberships:* Institute of Foresters of Australia; Australian Society of Plant Physiologists; Ecological Society of Australia. *Publications:* Editor, Australian Forestry, 1974-79. *Honours:* Exhibition, Agricultural Chemistry, Melbourne, 1956-; Exhibition, Forestry, Melbourne, 1957-; Fellowships from Yale, 1958-61. *Hobbies:* Tennis, Squash, Golf, Reading, Gardening. *Address:* 29 Mackellar Crescent, Cook, A.C.T. 2614, Australia.

BADA, Mudashiru Atanda, b. 18 Nov. 1948, Nguru, Borno State of Nigeria. Accountant. m. Lolade Ayinke Adeleke, 12 Dec. 1971, 4 daughters *Education:* St.

Pauls, Nguru, 1956-63; St. Pauls, Zaria, 1973-. *Appointments:* Senior Accounts Clerk United Nigeria Insurance Co., Ltd., 1967-71; Senior Accounts Clerk, Accountant, Chief Accountant, Executive Director, Femi Johnson & Company, Insurance Brokers. *Hobbies:* Football; Movies. *Address:* N4.337 Igesam Lane, Oje-Area, Ibadan, Nigeria.

BADGER, Edwin, b. 19 Aug. 1909, Worcester, England. Priest, Church of England. m. (1) Letitia Nancy Edwards, (dec.) 2 daughters, (2) Norah Constance Parsons, 4 Sept. 1943, 2 daughters. *Education:* St Boniface College, Warminster, Wiltshire, 1928 and 1932-34; BA, University of Bristol, 1929-32; BD, University of London, 1957. *Appointments:* Deacon 1934; Curate St John the Baptist, Kidderminster, England, 1934-36; Priest 1935: SPG Missionary, Nippon Seikokwai, Japan 1936-40; Vicar, Mordialloc, Victoria, Australia 1941-42; Japanese Language Officer, Australian Imperial Forces 1942-46; First Vicar, St Linus, Merlynston, Victoria, Australia 1946-51; Rector Nathalia, Victoria 1951-57; Avoca, Vic. 1957-59; Euroa, Vic. 1959-61; Warden, St Columb's Theological Hall, Wangaratta and Rector Milawa, Vic. 1961-64; First Rector, Moyhu, Vic. 1965-76. *Memberships:* Chaplain to Lay Readers Association, Diocese of Wangaratta 1972-76; Examining Chaplain to Bishop of Wangaratta 1971-76; Board of St John's Retirement Village, Wangaratta 1971-76; Council of Diocese of Wangaratta. *Publications:* History of Anglican Church in Euroa 1885-1960, 1960; Tapestries: Triptych (The Fall, Crucifixion, Resurrection); St John's Vision; The day Thou gavest; Come unto Me; etc. *Honours:* Honorary Canon, Holy Trinity Cathedral, Wangaratta 1969; Canon Emeritus 1976. *Hobbies:* Walking; Tapestry. *Address:* 6 Malcolm Street, Bacchus Marsh, Victoria 3340, Australia.

BADIANI (Dr.) Shashikant Vithaldas, b. 8 July 1947, Kisumu, Kenya. Doctor. m. Jyotsana, 27 Jan. 1973, 1 son, 1 daughter. *Education:* M.B.Ch.B. Makerere University, Uganda, 1972-; D.C.H. University of London, 1975-. *Appointments:* Medical Officer, Kenya Government, 1972-75; Private Medical Practice, 1975-. *Memberships:* Secretary, Kenya Medical Association, 1978-; Nairobi Club; Professional Society of Kenya; Kenya Hospital Association; Social Service League. *Hobbies:* Fine Art, Squash, Social Work. *Address:* PO Box 42455, Nairobi, Kenya.

BADIOZAMAN, Raja Mohar, b. 23 Mar. 1922, Kuala Kangsar, Malaysia. Civil Servant. m. Norella Talib, 17 Apr. 1954, 1 son, 3 daughters. *Education:* Diploma, Raffles College, Singapore, 1947-; Bachelor of Arts, Cambridge, 1951-; Diploma Agricultral Economics, Oxford, 1953-. *Appointments:* Economic Research Officer, Rural Industrial Development Authority; Controller of Trade; Secretary for Commerce and Industry; Secretary General, Ministry of Finance; Special Economic Adviser to Prime Minister; Chairman Malaysian Airline System. *Memberships:* President, Malaysian Institute of Management; President, Malaysian Economic Society; Royal Selangor Golf Club. *Honours:* Johan Mangku Negara, 1961-; Panglima Setia Mahkota, 1967-; Panglima Mangku Negara, 1977-; The Grand Cross first class of the Order of Merit, Federal Republic of Germany, 1976-; Honorary Doctor of Law, University of Science, 1977-. *Hobbies:* Photography, Stamps. *Address:* No. 3, Lorong Damai Sepuloh, Jalan Damai, Kuala Lumpur, Malaysia.

BAGGALEY, Norman Reginald, b. 23 Jan. 1937, Stoke-on-Trent, Staffordshire, England. College Dean. m. Jean Frost 26 Jan. 1956, 1 daughter. *Education:* School of Art, Newcastle under Lyme, 1953-55; National Diploma in Design, Painting (major) Ceramics (add), Stoke on Trent College of Art, 1955-57; Art Teachers Diploma University of Liverpool, 1957-58; Master of Science in Education, Southern Illinois University 1974-75. *Appointments:* Art Teacher, London, 1960-65; Art Teacher Sydney, Australia 1965-68; Head, Division of Creative and Fine Arts, Salisbury College of Advanced Education, South Australia 1969-78; Head, School of the Arts, Ballarat College of Advanced Education, Victoria, Australia 1978-80; Dean, School of Art and Design, Prahran College of Advanced Education Prahran, Melbourne, Australia, 1980-; *Memberships:* Australian Association for Tertiary Art and Design Education; Phi Kappa Phi. Chairman of several accreditation committees to asses new degree, diploma and post graduate awards in Australia; Member, Humanities Core Committee of the Teriary Education Authority of South Australia. *Creative Works:* Ten One-man Exhibitions of Painting in Australia and the USA; Several group shows in London, Sydney, Adelaide and Melbourne. *Hobbies:* Squash. *Address:* 300 Malvern Road, Prahran 3181, Melbourne, Australia.

BAHL, Rajnish, b. 22 Sept. 1927, Ferozepur, N. India. Ex Naval Officer; Engineer; Industrialist; Poultry/Dairy Farmer; Firlm Producer/Director/Script Writer. m. Nutan Samarth 11 Oct. 1959, 1 son. *Education:* Bishop Cotton School, Simla 1937-41; Aicheson Chief's College, Lahore 1941-45; Royal Naval College, Dartmouth 1945-52; Royal Naval Engineering College, Plymouth 1945-52; FIMechE, FIElecE, FIMarE. *Appointments:* Chief Engineer of various Naval Ships, India; Director Personnel and Training India; Industrial Manager Naval Dockyards, India 1952-65; Film Director, (film, Soorat aur Seerat, India) 1962; Poultry/Dairy Farming; Producer/Director/Script Writer 1965-. *Memberships:* Fellow, Institute of Marine Engineers, London; Aeronautical Society, London; Indian Motion Picture Producers' Association; Indian Film Directors' Association; Royal Western India Turf Club; Shikar Clubs throughout India. *Creative Works:* Invented Synchro Mesh Dog Clutch and Servo Operated Super-charger change-over for carburettors (cars) and for any other internal cubstion engine 1950; *Honours:* Acclaimed as artistic Film Director (Script and Direction) with film Soorat aur Seerat, 1962; Competence Certificate Deep Sea Diving 1949; Prizes Mill Miglia Monte Carlo car racing 1950; Gold medalist Army Rifle Association 1954 and 1956; Awards and recognition for hunting Maneating Tigers and Panthers 1952-. *Hobbies:* Big Game Hunting; Shikar, Rifle Marksmanship; Car Racing; Movie and Still Photography; Architecture designing and decoration; Collection of Antiques; Indian Miniature Paintings; Stones, Bronzes. *Address:* ''Numohraj'', Parsik Hill, PO Kalwa, Dist: Thane-400 605, India.

BAIANU, Ion, b. 18 Aug. 1947, TG. Logresti, Romania. Research Scientist. m. Kimiko Baianu 1979, 1 son. *Education:* Diploma in Physics, Faculty of Physics, Bucharest, Romania, 1968; First Honours degree and MSc(Biophysics); PhD, Queen Elizabeth College, University of London, 1974. *Appointments:* Assistant Professor of Electricity, Magnetism and Biophysics, 1968-71, Associate Professor of Biophysics and Biochemistry, Bucharest University, Faculty of Physics, Romania, 1974-76; SRC Research Fellow, Department, Physical Chemistry, University of Leeds, United Kingdom, 1976-77; Research Associate, The Cavendish Laboratory, University of Cambridge, United Kingdom, 1977-80; Senior Scientist, Biophysics Department, The Lord Rank Centre of Research, United Kingdom, 1980-; Visiting Research Associate, NSF Midwest Facility for High-Field Nuclear Magnetic Resonance and Department of Physical Chemistry, University of Illinois, USA, 1981-. *Memberships:* Institute of Physics, London; European Physical Society, Geneva; British Biophysical Society, London; Society for Mathematical Biology, Inc. Chicago, USA. *Publications:* Over 50 published and communicated scientific papers in the fields of: Magnetic Resonance (nuclear and electron spin resonance); Solid State Physics; X-Ray Diffraction; of disordered systems; Biophysics; Mathematical Biology; Photosynthesis; Protein Biochemistry; Plasma Physics. *Honours:* Romanian Ministry of Education Grant Award in Biophysics for Membrane Structure Investigations. *Hobbies:* English History and Literature; French Literature; Chess; Travel; Lawn Tennis; Swimming; Painting; Mathematics. *Address:* 611 W California Urbana, Ill. 61801, USA.

BAIGENT, Aubrey Gordon Amos, b. 24 Aug. 1910, Ashburton, New Zealand. Secondary School Teacher and Principal. m. M Joyce Limbrick 24 Aug. 1940, 1 son, 1 daughter. *Education:* BA, MA, (1st Class Honours); Canterbury University, 1928-33; MA Diploma of Honours, Latin 1933; Diploma in Education 1936; BComm. degree 1948; *Appointments:* Palmerston North Boys' High School 1934-41; Feilding High School 1941-47, including 3 years' New Zealand Defence Forces: Te Awamutu College 1944-55; Principal, Kaitaia College 1955-58; Headmaster, Hamilton Boys' High School 1958-70; Adult Education Lecturer, Palmerston North and Feilding 1938-46, Hamilton 1978. *Memberships:* Justice of the Peace, 1970; National Executive and President New Zealand Post-primary

Teachers' Assosiation; National Council Maori Education; National Teacher-Training Council; Rotarian; Waikoto Founders Society Foundation; Hamilton Cricket Association; Bryant Trust Board. *Honours:* University Entrance Scholarship, 1928; New Zealand University Senior Scholarship in English 1931; Carnegie Travelling Fellowship in Education, Great Britain. *Hobbies:* Cricket Administration; Dramatic work (Producer and Adjudicator); Gardening; Reading; Bowls. *Address:* 24 Kakanui Avenue, Hillcrest, Hamilton, New Zealand.

BAILEY, Jeffrey Gordon, b. 2 July 1942, Gilgandra, N.S.W. Australia. Associate Dean, (Academic). m. Robyn Dixon 22 Aug. 1969, 2 sons, 2 daughters. *Education:* Teachers Certificate, Alexander Mackie College, Sydney 1961; Bachelor of Arts 1970, Bachelor of Letters 1972, Master of Educational Administration 1976, University of New England, Armidale NSW Australia; Doctor of Education, University of Cincinnati, Ohio, USA 1979. *Appointments:* Teacher, 1961-69, Principal 1970-72, Special Education Consultant, NSW Department of Education, 1973-74, Darling Downs Institute of Advanced Education, Toowoomba Australia 1974-; Senior Lecturer in Special Education, Associate Dean, School of Education, 1980-. *Memberships:* Editor: Australian Journal of Special Education; The Official Publication of the Australian Association of Special Education; International Association of Applied Psychology; Australian College of Education; President, Toowoomba Branch, SPELD. *Publications:* Unpublished Dissertations: Xavier Herbert: Satirist; Morale in Special Education: A Regional Survey; The Development and Evaluation of a Simulation Course in Mainstreaming; Numerous articles in professional journals. *Honours:* Foundation Senior Lecturer in Special Education, DDIAE 1974; First Special Education Consultant, Country Regions, NSW Department of Education 1973; Nominated for publication in the US publication National Register of Outstanding College Graduates 1979. *Hobbies:* Family; Travel; Reading; Restoring old homes. *Address:* 88 Mary Street, Toowoomba 4350, Queensland, Australia.

BAILEY, Norman Stanley, b. 23 Mar. 1933, Birmingham, England. Operatic and Con*Education:* Bachelor of Music, Rhodes University, South Africa; Performer's and Teacher's Licentiate Singing; Diplomas in Opera, Lieder, and Oratorio, Vienna State Academy of Music Austria. *Appointments:* Linzer Landestheater, Austria, 1960-63; Wuppertaler Buhnen, Wuppertal, West Germany, 1963-64; Deutsche Oper am Rhein, Dusseldorf, West Germany, 1964-67; Sadlers Wells opera, london, 1967-71; Freelance, 1971-; Appeared as guest artist at major Opera Houses in the world including: La Scala, Milan; Bayreuth Wagner Festival; Royal Opera House, Covent Garden; Hamburg State Opera; Munich State Opera; New York Metropolitan; Chicago Lyric Opera; Vienna State Opera, Austria; CAPAB, Nico Malan Theatre, South Africa. *Creative Works:* Decca: Meistersinger/Holländer (complete operas), warlock recital and Ballads & Sacred Songs; EMI: Wotan's Farewell (w. O Klemperer), Ring in English, (w. R Goodall); SAGA: Songs of Love & Death; Songs of Hugo Wolf (two Lieder recitals); Deutsche Gramophon: Beethoven's Ninth Symphony. *Honours:* Prize International Song Competition, Vienna, 1960; CBE, 1977; The Worshipful Company of Musicians, Sir Charles Santley Memorial Gift, 1977. *Hobbies:* Chess; Notaphily; Golf; Swimming; D.I.Y. *Address:* Quarry Hangers, White Hill, Bletchingley, Surrey, RH1 4QZ, England.

BAINTON, Richard Leslie, b. 4 Mar. 1923 Bryn Mawr, Wales. Managing Director. m. 28 June 1954, 1 son, 3 daughters. *Education:* Fellow, Institute of Directors; Fellow, Chartered Institute of Secretaries; Fellow, Company Accountants; Fellow, British Institute of Management. *Appointments:* Law Clerk, W.G. Bradley and Sons, 1940-43; Managing Clerk, Hayes and Sons, 1944-48; Assistant Secretary, The Iveagh Trust, 1949-55; Assistant Company Secretary, Holloway Engineering Works Limited, 1956-60; Group Secretary, Portland Group of Companies, 1961-63; Company Secretary, IDM Electronics Limited, 1964-68; Executive Director, 1969-77; Managing Director, 1977-; IDM Engineering and Tooling Limited. *Memberships:* Reading and District Engineering Group Limited, Henley Badgemore Park Golf Club. *Honours:* Queen's Award for Export 1980. *Hobbies:* Youth Work; Music; Golf. *Address:* Apna-Gar, 139 Wilderness Road, Earley, Berkshire, England.

BAIRD, Nora, b. 13 Mar. N. Ireland. *Education:* LRAM, Piano 1922; LTCL Piano 1924; LTCL, Organ Performer. *Appointments:* Chief Music Teacher St Margaret's Girls College, 1928-74; Organist, Uniting Church Valley, Brisbane, 1942-; Lecturer in Piano, Queensland Conservatorium, 1957-75. *Memberships:* Executive Honorary Life Member, Australian Broadcasting Commission; Honorary Secretary, Royal Schools Music Club; Royal Schools Church Music; Royal College of Organists London; Australian Society Music Education Committee; Organ Society Queensland; Music Teacher's Queensland; Australian-American Association; Vice President, Australian Keyboard Music; Fellow, FIBA. *Creative Works:* Writing Archives Accompanist Memoirs etc. *Honours:* MBE, 1980; Presented to Her Majesty, Queen Elizabeth, The Queen Mother, 1967; ABC Conferred Hon. Life Membership, 1980; Queensland Music Teacher, St Margarets Girls College, Honorary Life Member, 50 years; Royal Schools Music, Honorary Life Member, 40 years. *Hobbies:* Travel; Correspondence; Stamp Collecting; Organising Charity Concerts etc. *Address:* 352 Newmarket Road, Newmarket, Brisbane, Australia 4051.

BAIYEWU, Darlington Olutade, b. 22 June 1941, Abeokuta. Company Director. m. Margaret A Baiyewu, 14 Apr. 1970, 3 sons, 2 daughters. *Education:* Small Scale Business Courses, Nigerian Institute of Management 1975-77; Seminars, Conferences and Business Management Courses, in Europe, and America. *Appointments:* Chairman/Managing Director, Landmark Industrial Supplies Limited. *Memberships:* Royal Commonwealth Society; Lagos Country Club, Ikeja; The Blue Elephant Club; World Federation of Democratic Youths; Nigerian Voluntary Service Association. *Hobbies:* Swimming; Table Tennis; Lawn Tennis; Golf. *Address:* 4 Baiyewu Close, Ijaiye Aguda, Agege, Lagos State, Nigeria.

BAKARI, Abubakar Bafetel, b. 27 Sept. 1942, Jos. Plateau State Nigeria. Economist and Businessman. m. Sakinatu 15 Feb. 1968, 3 sons, 2 daughters. *Education:* WAEC School Cert II, Barewa College Zaria 1956-60; Advance Level GCE, Reading Technical College 1961-62; London Russell College 1962-63; BA Economics, University of Strathclyde Glasgow 1963-66. *Appointments:* Commercial Officer, Ministry of Trade and Industry Kadona Northern Nigeria Government, 1967-68; Company Secretary Director, Achaji Bakari and Sons Limited, Yola, 1968-; Chairman/Managing Director, Gauni (Nig) Limited P.M.B. 2106 Yola Nigeria; Part Time Director: National Properties Limited, Lagos; Gongola Tomato Industries Yola; Committee member of the State National Youth Service. *Memberships:* Lake Chad Club; Yola Club; Kaduna Club; Le Circle Kano. *Hobbies:* Travelling; Farming; House Gardening. *Address:* Old Government Residential Area, Yola, Nigeria.

BAKER, Bruce Earle, b. 1 Aug. 1917 Stanbridge East, P.Que. Canada. Chemist. 4 sons, 1 daughter. *Education:* BSc Bishops University 1940; DSc Laval University 1945. *Appointments:* Research Chemist, Mallinckrudt Chemicals 1944-45, Munsanto Canada 1945-46; Lecturer Department Agriculture Chemistry, Faculty of Agriculture, McGill University 1946-48; Assistant Professor, 1948-57; Associate Professor 1957-64; Professor and Chairman of Department 1972-. *Memberships:* American Chemicl Society; American Dairy Science Association; Canadian Instutute of Chemistry; Canadian Institute of Food Science and Technology; Society of the Sigmaxi; Life Member, Missisquoi Historical Society. *Publications:* Numerous publications and patents on synthesis of sulfa drugs; Dairy Chemistry; Proteins from Leguminous seeds; Pollution of water and soils; Milks of wild animals; Protein Hydrolysates. *Honours:* Fessenden Scholarship for Mathematics. 1939. *Hobbies:* Farming; Reading; Travel. *Address:* PO Box 208, MacDonald Campus, McGill University, Ste Anne De Bellevue, P Que Canada.

BAKER, John Hamilton, b. 10 Apr. 1944, Sheffield, England. Barrister at Law; University Lecturer. m. Veronica Margaret Lloyd, 20 Apr. 1968, 2 daughters. *Education:* LLB (1st class hons.), 1962-65; PhD 1968, University College, London; MA, University of Cambridge, 1971; Barrister at Law, Inner Temple, 1966 and Gray's Inn, 1978. *Appointments:* Assistant Lecturer in Laws, 1965-67, Lecturer, University College London, 1967-71; Librarian of Squire Law Library, Cambridge,

1971-73; University Lecturer in Law, Cambridge, 1973-; Fellow, 1971-, Dean, 1977-79, Archivist 1979-, St Catharine's College, 1971-; Junior Proctor, University of Cambridge 1980-81; Lecturer in Legal History, Inns of Court School of Law, 1973-78. *Memberships:* Selden Society; Royal Historical Society; Society of Public Teachers of Law. *Publications:* An Introduction to English Legal History, 1979; English Legal Manuscripts, 1978; The Reports of Sir John Spelman 1977-78; Manual of Law French 1979; Over 40 articles and notes in periodicals. *Honours:* Andrews Silver Medal and Prize 1965; Yorke Prize, Cambridge 1975. *Hobbies:* Collecting portraits; visiting churches. *Address:* 75 Hurst Park Avenue, Cambridge, England.

BAKER, Joseph Thomas, b. 19 June 1932, Warwick, Queensland, Australia. Research Director. m. Valerie Joy Wormald, 5 Feb. 1955, 2 sons, 2 daughters. *Education:* BSc, 1956, BSc 1st Class Honours, Chemistry, 1958, MSc, 1960, PhD, 1966, University of Queensland. *Appointments:* Lab. Attendant, CSIRO, 1950-54; Teaching Fellow, 1955-57, Demonstrator, 1958, Senior Demonstrator, 1959-60, University of Queensland; Lecturer, Chemistry, 1961-62, Senior Lecturer, University College of Townsville, 1962-69; Associate Professor, Chemistry, James Cook University of North Queensland, 1970-74; Director of Research, RRIMP, 1974-81; Director of Research, Roche, Australia, 1976-81; Director, Centre for Tropical Marine Studies, James Cook University of North Queensland, 1981; Board of Directors, Roche Maag. 1978-. *Memberships:* President of the Trust, The Australian Museum; Vice-President, Australian National Commission for UNESCO; Great Barrier Reef Marine Park Authority; Autralian Marine Sciences and Technologies Advisory Committee; Vice President, Australian Marine Sciences Association; Chairman, Lizard Island Research Station Committee of Trustees; Heron Island Research Station Advisory Committee; Visiting Committees in Chemistry, University of New South Wales and University of Sydney; World Wildlife Fund, Australia. *Publications:* 26 Scientific Papers in Recognized Journals; Two books on Marine Chemistry. A third volume in Press. *Honours:* Carnegie Fellowship, 1967-68; Fellow, Royal Australian Chemical Institute; President, Pharmaceutical Sciences Section of ANZAAS, New Zealand, 1979; Honorary Life Member of three Rugby League Clubs in Queensland. *Hobbies:* Tennis; Squash; Surfing; Scuba Diving; Beach Fishing. *Address:* 28 Bilkurra Avenue, Bilgola Plateau 2107, New South Wales, Australia.

BAKER, June Rosalie, b. 27 June 1937 Murwillumbah NSW Australia. WRANS Officer. *Education:* Murwillumbah High School 1949-53; Sydney Teachers College 1955-57. *Appointments:* Primary School Teacher 1957-67; WRANS 1967-; General Administrative Appointments 1967-76; First WRANS Officer, RN Staff College Greenwich 1976-77; Exchange Posting with WRNS HMS Dauntless 1977-78, Ministry of Defence London 1978; Director, WRANS 1979-. *Memberships:* Australian Naval Institute, Canberra; Woden Squash Club; Coaching Director, Australian Capital Territory; Womens Hockey Association. *Hobbies:* Reading; Squash; Gardening; Umpiring Hockey; Golf. *Address:* Unit 10, Bourne Gardens, Bourne Street, Cook ACT Australia.

BAKER, Kenneth Wilfred, b. 3 Nov. 1934. Member of Parliament; Mir ster of State, Department of Industry. m. Mary Elizabeth Gray-Muir, 1963, 1 son 2 daughters. *Education:* St Paul's School; Magdalen College, Oxford; National Service, *Appointments:* 1953-55; Lieutenant in Gunners, N Africa; Artillery Instructor to Libyan Army; Oxford 1955-58 (Sec. of Union). Served Twickenham Borough Council 1960-62. Contested (C): Poplar, 1964; Acton, 1966; MP(C) Acton, 1968-70; Public Accounts Committee, 1969-70; PPS to Minister of State, Department of Employment 1970-72; Parliamentary Secretary, CSD, 1972-74; PPS to Leader of Opposition, 1974-75; Member Executive 1922 Committee, Chairman, Hansard Soc., 1978-. Chairman Computer Agency Council, 1973-74. *Hobbies:* Collecting books. *Address:* House of Commons, SW1A 0AA, England.

BAKER, Michael Warren, b. 10 July 1946. Management Consultant. m. Robyn 6 June 1976, 2 sons. *Education:* Melbourne High School. *Appointments:* Media Clerk, USP-Benson Advertising, 1965; Account

Director, Ogilvy and Mather Advertising, 1971; Managing Director, The Baker Consulting Group, 1976. *Hobbies:* Snow Skiing; Rugby Union. *Address:* c/o 150 Queen Street, Melbourne, Victoria, Australia, 3000.

BAKER, Norman Keith, b. 2 Sept. 1920, Melbourne, Australia. Chartered Accountant. m. Diane Ethel Weir, 7 July 1949, 2 sons, 2 daughters. *Education:* Fellow, Institute of Chartered Accountants in Australia, 1952. *Appointments:* Edwin V Nixon and Partners, Chartered Accountants, now Arthur Young and Company, Melbourne, 1937-81; Partner, 1952-81; Senior Partner, 1974-81; Director: Melbourne Branch Board, Australian Mutual Provident Society, 1970-77; Australian Consolidated Industries Limited, 1971-; Equity Trustees Executors and Agency Company Limited, 1971-. *Memberships:* Newcastle Club; Royal Automobile Club of Victoria; Institute of Chartered Accountants in Australia; Australian Branch, RAF Escaping Society; Australian Club, Melbourne; Melbourne Club; The Naval and Military Club, Melbourne. *Publications:* The Essential Simplicity of Accounting for Money Value Changes, 1966. *Honours:* Croix de Guerre avec Etoile de Vermeil, France; Mentioned in a Despatch for Distinguished Service, 1944-45. *Hobbies:* Squash; Fly Fishing; Golf. *Address:* 25 Stawell Street, Kew, Melbourne, Victoria, 3101, Australia.

BAKER, Peter Maxwell, b. 26 Mar. 1930, Sheffield, England. Queens Counsel; Recorder of the Crown Court. m. Jacqueline Mary Marshall, 15 May 1954, 3 daughters. *Education:* MA (oxon) 1952; Barrister-at-law, Gray's Inn 1956. *Appointments:* Barrister-at-Law 1956; Recorder of the Crown Court 1972; Queen's Counsel 1974. *Memberships:* Gray's Inn; North Easter Circuit, Junior 1960; President, South Yorkshire Medico-Legal Society 1980-81; Sheffield Club. *Honours:* Richard's Prize Exhibitioner, Exeter College Oxford 1948; Lord Justice Holker Senior Exhibtioner, Gray's Inn 1956. *Hobbies:* Music; Sailing; Travel. *Address:* 28 Snaithins Lane, Sheffield 10, England.

BAKER, Richard St. Barbe, b. 9 Oct. 1889, Southampton. Silviculturist; Forestry Advisor; Author. m. (1) Doreen Whitworth 23 Jan. 1946 1 son, 1 daughter, (div.) 1953, (2) Catriona Burnett 1959. *Education:* Dean Close School, Cheltenham; Emmanuel College, University of Saskatchewan; Ridley Hall and Caius College, Cambridge, School of Forestry; New College, Oxford, Commonwealth School of Forestry. *Appointments:* Assistant Conservator of Forests, Kenya, 1920-23; Forestry Sections, Kenya, Nigeria and Gold Coast Commonwealth Exhibition, Wembley 1924; Assitant Conservator of Forests, Nigeria 1924-29. *Memberships:* Overseas League; English Speaking Union; Royal Commonwealth Society; Diamond Jubilee, Men of the Trees 1982; Ecoworld Foundation. *Publications:* 30 published works on Trees and Forestry including: I Planted Trees and My Life-My Trees; Forthcoming My Horse—My Kingdom; My Health—My Wealth; Tall Timber, about the Great ones who have helped us. *Honours:* FIAL for Gruene Herrlichkeit 1958; Freshel Award for Book of the Year making The Greatest Contribution to Humanitarianism 1967; Friends of Nature Conservation Award 1962; Hon. Doctor of Law's University Saskatchewan Canada, 1971; OBE 1978; 1st President International Tree Crops Inst. *Hobbies:* Conservation Silvicultural and Ecological Consultant; Correspondence; Travelling; Riding; Tree Photography; Produced Tree Lovers' Calendar for 46 years. *Address:* Mt. Cook Street, Box 3, Lake Tekapo, New Zealand.

BAKER, Thomas Wilfred, b. 9 June 1923 Southport. *Education:* Stockport College for Further Education 1940-42 and 1944-45; Royal Technical College Salford 1945-46; Intermediate BSc, University of London 1946; Honours School of Physics, University of Manchester 1946-49; BSc(Honours Physics), 1949. *Appointments:* Laboratory Assistant, The British Cotton Industry Research Association, Didsbury, Manchester, 1940-42 and 1944-46; Royal Air Force 1942-44; Research Assistant, Jodrell Bank Radio Astronomy Station 1950; Section Leader, X-ray Diffraction, Atomic Energy Research Establishment, Harwell, 1950-77; Chief Experimental Officer, 1969, Principal Scientific Officer, 1971; Scientific Consultant and Director, Tirrold Scientific and Technical Services Limited 1977-. *Memberships:* Institute of Physics; The Committee of the Crystallography Group, Institute of Physics, 1977-

78; Scientific Committee of the Maharishi European Research University, Mentmore, 1979. *Publications:* Several contributions in scientific literature including: An X-ray Study of the Factors Causing Variation in the Heats of Solution of Magnesuim Oxide, 1959; Interatomic Distances in the Intermetallic Compound $MgBe_{13}$ and $CaBe_{13}$ 1961; High-Temperature Phase Transformation in Beryllia 1962; Very High Precision X-ray Diffraction, 1966; Fully Automated High Precision X-ray Diffraction, 1968; X-ray Diffraction, 1974; The APEX Goniometer System for X-ray Diffraction, 1975. *Hobbies:* Skin diving; Rugby. *Address:* Berry Croft, Spring Lane, Aston Upthorpe, Didcot, Oxfordshire, OX11 9EH England.

BAKER, (The Hon.), Walter David, b. 22 Aug. 1930, Ottawa, Ontario. Member of Parliament. m. Lois Patricia Welch, 2 June 1956, 2 sons, 1 daughter. *Education:* Graduated, Albert College, Belleville, Ontario, 1949; BA, Carleton University, Ottawa, Ontario, 1953; Called to the Bar, 1957; Queen's Counsel 1969. *Appointments: Appointments:* Partner Bell, Baker, Thompson, Oyen and Webber, 1957-79; Associate Counsel Bell, 1980; Member of Parliament, 1972; Deputy Opposition House Leader, 1973; Opposition House Leader, 1976; President, Queen's Privy Council and Minister of National Revenue, 1979; Opposition House Leader, 1980-. *Memberships:* Member of numerous Societies and Clubs including: Canadian Bar Association; Baltic Federation in Canada; Richmond Curling, Honorary Member; Prescott Fish and Game. *Publications:* Interest in Canada's Parliament and its ability to respond to Canadian needs, the morale and efficient operation of the Public Service as well as freedom of information and regulatory process of government. *Honours:* Queen's Counsel, 1969. *Hobbies:* Golf; Fishing; Cross-country skiing; Reading. *Address:* 8 Commanche Drive, Nepean, Ontario, K2E 6E9, Canada.

BAKEWELL, Robert David, b. 22 Sept. 1927, Wickham Skieth. Ombudsman for South Australia. m. Winifred Joan Millhouse 20 Dec. 1954, 2 sons, 1 daughter. *Education:* BSc Economics. *Appointments:* Director, Research Customs and Excise, Australia; Director and Chief Inspector, Petroleum Products, Australia; Commissioner, South Australian Public Servce Board; Permanent Head, Premier's Department, South Australia; Permanent Head, Economic Development, South Australia; Ombudsman for South Australia, 1980. *Memberships:* Australian Institute of Public Administration; Australian Institute of Management; Australian Institute of International Affairs; Stock Exchange Club of Adelaide; Commonwealth Club of South Australia; Army Navy and Military Club of Adelaide. *Publications:* Articles, Australian Journal of Public Administration; Articles, Australian Outlook; Numerous papers to national and international bodies. *Hobbies:* Golf; Tennis. *Address:* 29 Third Avenue, St. Peters, 5069, South Australia.

BALAAM, Leslie Norman, b. 11 Apr. 1925, Bundaberg, Australia. Academic. m. Winifred Ellen Mann 24 Mar. 1945, 2 sons, 1 daughter. *Education:* St Laurence's College, Brisbane 1937-42; BSc, University of Queensland 1947-49; MSc, University of Sydney 1960. *Appointments:* Biometrician, Department Agriculture and Stock 1950-59; Lecturer, Senior Lecturer in Biometry, University of Sydney 1959-67; Director of Biometric Services, University of Sydney 1968-; Dean, Faculty of Agrigulture, 1972-. *Memberships:* International Statistics Institute; International Biometrics Society; NSW Branch, Australian Statistical Society; Australian Institute of Agricultural Science. *Publications:* Fundamentals of Biometry; Fondamenti di Biometria. *Hobbies:* Wine collecting; Gardening; Painting. *Address:* 562 Warringah Road, Forestville, NSW 2087, Australia.

BALAKUMAR, Velupillai, b. 22 Apr. 1946 Colombo Sri Lanka. m. 20 Mar. 1974, 3 daughters. *Education:* Final Examination, Institute of Chartered Accountants, Sri Lank. *Appointments:* Finance Manager, Ceylon Paper Sacks Limited Sri Lanka, 1971-73; Chief Accountant, Indeco Limited Zambia 1973-76; Director of Studies, Institute of Chartered Accountants 1977; Director Finance, Mikechris Group, Sri Lanka, 1978-; Consistant voluntary involvement in the last 10 years as Lecturer and Examiner in Management Sciences both in Sri Lanka and Zambia. *Memberships:* Fellow, Institute of Chartered Accountants, Sri Lanka; Fellow, British Institute of Management; Rotarian President elect. *Hobbies:* Angling; Snorkeling; Chess. *Address:* C De Fonseka Place, Colombo 5, Sri Lanka.

BALASOORIYA, Indraratne, b. 12 Jan. 1934, Mapote, Sri Lanka. University Professor and Dean. m. Chintamani Singhabahu, 18 Aug. 1964, 1 son, 2 daughters. *Education:* BSc, Ceylon, 1957; PhD, Liverpool, 1964. *Appointments:* Temporary Assistant Lecturer, 1957-59, Assistant Lecturer, 1959-64, Lecturer, University of Ceylon, 1964-68; Professor of Botany, Vidyalankara University, 1968-; Dean, Faculty of Science, Vidyalankara Campus, University of Sri Lanka, 1977-78; Dean, Faculty of Science, University of Kelaniya, Sri Lanka, 1979-. *Memberships:* Ceylon Association for the Advancement of Science; Ceylon Association for the Advancement of Science; Ceylon National History Society. *Publications:* A study of the rate of respiration of coleoptile segments of Triticum sativum NP 165, 1956; An investigation on the suitabilty of tendril segments of Cissus quadrangulatis for auxin assay, 1959; A few species of fungi new to Ceylon, 1959; Nature and activity of fungi in a pine wood soil, 1964; Studies on fungi in a pine wood soil, 1967; Succession of microfungi on root surface of Oryza sativa, 1969; An investigation of microfungi in a grassland soil, 1969; The Living Soil, 1973; Preliminary Observations of a fungus which is pathogenic to Salvinia molesta, 1975; The Mangroves, 1978. *Honours:* Best student of the year, Ananda College, Colombo, 1952; University Exhibition, 1954; Commonwealth Academic Scholarship, 1961; Commonwealth Academic Fellowship, 1974; Fellow, Sri Lanka Academy of Science, 1977; National Coordinator, Research Project, Management of Water Hyacinth, Commonwealth Science Council, London. *Address:* 410/115 Bauddhaloka Mawatha, Colombo 7, Sri Lanka.

BALASUBRAMANI, S, b. 28 Dec. 1957, Salem, India. Business. m. B Umarani, 25 May 1981. *Education:* SSLC 1973; PUC 1975; BA, 1978; BCom. 1979; MBA 1981; Type writting 1976; National Language Hindi, High Grade 1977. *Appointments:* Export Business and Dyeing. *Memberships:* YMCA; Thiasophical Society. *Creative Works:* Painting; Scooter; Motor Cycle Rally. *Honours:* Scooter Prize one cup. *Hobbies:* Table Tennis; TV; Pop Music; Swimming; Picnic; Pen Friends; Photography etc. *Address:* 139 Ambalavana Samy Koil St., Gugai, Salem 636006, Tamil Ndu, India.

BALASUBRAMANIAN, S, b. 13 June 1938, Bhavani, Coimbatore Dt. S India. Professor of Physics. m. Rukmini, 9 Feb. 1970, 1 son, 1 daughter. *Education:* BSc(Hons.) Physics 1959; MSC Nuclear Physics 1963; MS Physics 1967; PhD Physics 1971. *Appointments:* Lecturer in Physics, Madura College, Madurai India, 1959-62; Research Associate, TIFR, Bombay, India 1963-64; Teaching/Research Assistant, Purdue University, USA 1964-67; CSIR Pool Officer, Madurai University, Madurai India 1967-68; P G. Lecturer in Physics, Madura College, Madurai, India, 1968-69; Lecturer, 1967-71, Reader, 1971-76, Professor, Madurai University, 1976-. *Publications:* About 35 research papers in International and National Journals; A book on problems in quantum mechanics is nearing completion. *Honours:* Swami Jnanananda 1963. *Hobby:* Chess. *Address:* 58 Dr. Janakinarayan Road, S.S. Colony, Madurai, 625016, India.

BALBAN, Mario, b. 10 July 1942, La Linea, Spain. Barrister-at-Law. m. Lucila Garcia 29 Sept. 1965, 1 son, 1 daughter. *Education:* Bar Exam. 1972. *Appointments:* Private Practice, Gibraltar 1972-74; Treasury Solicitor's Department, London, 1974-79; Registrar Supreme Court, Gibraltar 1979-. *Memberships:* The Hon. Society of the Middle Temple. *Hobby:* Pottery. *Address:* 19 Naval Hospital Hill, Gibraltar.

BALD, Rose Marion, b. 15 June 1913, Strathalbyn, Australia. Registered Semi-trained Nurse. m. Gordon Stanley Bald, 30 May 1942, 1 son. *Education:* AEC., Mt. Gambier Art Classes, 1960-64; Art and Craft Certificate, Distinction, Painting II, SE Community College, Semester, Mt. Gambier, Australia, 1979. *Appointments:* Private Nursing, Apr.1943—Aug.1943; Preparation for one-man painting Exhibitions, Original oil and watercolour, 1964-; Preparation for Exhibition, RSASA Art Gallery, Adelaide, South Australia, 1981-. *Memberships:* Associate member, RSASA, Adelaide, South Australia; Vice-President (1 term), Foundation Committee member, SE Art Society; Past (exhibiting) member, Victorian Artists Society, Melbourne, Victoria, Australia, 1960-68. *Creative Works:* 1st Exhibition, 53 paintings, Jen's Hotel, Mt. Gambier, South Australia, Apr. 1960; 2nd Exhibition, 36 works, City of Hamilton Gallery, Victoria, Australia, Apr. 1963; 3rd Exhibition, 28 works, Murray Bridge Gallery, South Australia, Mar. 1969; 4th Exhibition, Honour to be invited back to City of Hamilton Art Gallery showing 48 paintings, 1974. *Honours:* 1st Prize, (Oils), SE Land Art Festival Competition, Mt. Gambier, South Australia, 1972, 1975; 2nd Prize, (Oil and Watercolour sections), SE Land Art Festival, Mt. Gambier, 1976; 3rd Prize, (Egg-Tempera), SE Land Art Festival Mt. Gambier, 1980; Highly Commended: Watercolour, O'Donnell Art Award, Mt. Gambier, 1959, (Oil), Portland Art Competition, Victoria, 1966; Commended: (Oils), Portland Art Competitions, Victoria, 1969, 1971, (Oil), RSASA Associates and Lay members Exhibition, 1976. *Hobbies:* Small nature writings; Sewing; Crochet; Home cooking; Collecting, small museum attached to gallery. *Address:* 'Rosemead' 37 Canavan Rd., Mt. Gambier, South Australia 5290.

BALFOUR, Richard Creighton, b. 3 Feb. 1916, Vancouver, BC, Canada. Official of Bank of England, (retired); Company Director. m. Adela Rosemary Welch, 1943, 2 sons. *Education:* St Edward's School, Oxford, 1930-34. 03 The Agent, Bank of England, Leeds, 1961-65, Deputy Chief Cashier, 1965-70, Chief Accountant, 1970-75; Director, Datasaab Limited, 1976-. *Memberships:* Fellow, Institute of Bankers; Freeman, City of London; Liveryman, Worshipful Company of Gardeners; Numerous other Garden Societies. *Publications:* Author of many articles on Roses & photographs of them in various publications. *Honours:* MBE, (During Naval Service), 1945; Dean Hole Medal, highest award of Royal National Rose Society, 1974. *Hobbies:* Gardening, (especially Roses); Cine & Slide photography; Dancing; Travel; Collecting hatpins and rocks; Gem polishing; Wine; Sea floating; Writing; Compiling puzzles; International Rose Judge. *Address:* Albion House, Little Waltham, Chelmsford, Essex, CM3 3LA, England.

BALME, Charles Nicholas, b. 21 Dec. 1940, Cambridge, England. Barrister. m. Eithne Hanly, 4 Apr. 1962, 2 sons, 2 daughters. *Education:* Sir George Williams University, Montreal, Canada, 1963-67; LL.B., Queens University, Kingston, Ontario, Canada, 1973-76; Barrister CDP, Osgoode Hall, Toronto, Ontario, Canada, 1978; Institute for Certification of Computer Professionals, 1981. *Appointments:* CP Rail, Montreal, Quebec, Canada, 1962-69; Private Legal Practice, including Computer law, 1978-. *Memberships:* Law Society of Upper Canada; Canadian Bar Association; Frontenac Law Association; Canadian Information Processing Society. *Publications:* Papers and articles concerning Computer Systems and the Law. *Hobbies:* Music; Boating. *Address:* 528 Victoria Street, Kingston, Ontario, Canada.

BALOGH, Thomas, b. 2 Nov. 1905, Budapest. (Baron, 1968 (Life Peer), of Hampstead). m. Penelope, 1945 (marriage dissolved 1970), 2 sons 1 daughter; 1 step-daughter; m. Catherine Storr, 1970, 3 step-daughters. *Education:* The Gymnasium of Budapest University; Universities of Budapest, Berlin, Harvard; Fellow of Hungarian College., Berlin, 1927-; Rockefeller Fellow, 1928-30; National Insitutue of Economic Research, 1938-42; Oxford University, Institute of Statistics, 1940-55; Leverhulme Fellow, Oxford, 1973-76. *Appointments:* League of Nations, 1931; Economist in the City, 1931-39; Special Lecturer, 1955-60; Minister of State, Department of Energy, 1974-75; Visiting Professor, Minnesota and Wisconsin, 1951-; Delhi and Calcutta, 1955-; Member and acting Chairman Minerals Committee, Ministry of Fuel and Power, 1964-68; Consultant: Reserve Bank of Australia, 1942-64; UNRRA Mission to Hungary, 1946-; Government of Malta, 1955-57, of Jamaica, 1956-, 1961-62; UN Economic Committee for Latin America, 1960-; Government of India Statistical Institute, 1960, 1971-; Greece, 1962-; Mauritius, 1962-63; UN Special Fund, 1964, 1970, 1971-; OECD, 1964-; Turkey, Peru, 1964-; Member, Economic and Financial Committee of the Labour Party, 1943-64, 1971-; Economic Adviser to Cabinet, 1964-67; Consultant to Prime Minister, 1968-. Chairman., Fabian Society, 1979-. Deputy Chairman, British National Oil, 1976-77; Adviser

1978-79. *Publications:* Hungarian Reconstruction and the Reparation Question, 1946-; Studies in Financial Organisation, 1946-; Dollar Crisis, 1949-; Planning through the Price Mechanism, 1950-; The Economic Future of Malta, 1955-; Planning and Monetary Organisation .in Jamaica, 1956-; The Economic Problem of Iraq, 1957-; The Economic Development of the Mediterranean, 1957-; Economic Policy and Price Mechanism, 1961-; Development Plans in Africa, 1961-; Sugar Industry in Mauritius; Unequal Partners, 2 vos, 1963-; Planning for Progress, 1963-; Economics of Poverty, 1966-; Labour and Inflation, 1970-; Fact and Fancy, 1973-; Economics of Full Employment, 1945-; War Economics, 1947-; Foreign Economic Policy for the US; Fabian International and Colonial Essays; The Establishment, 1960-; Crisis in the Civil Service, 1968-; Keynes College Essays, 1976-; papers in Economic Journal, Bulletin of Oxford Institute of Statistics. *Honours:* Honorary Doctor of Law, York University, Toronto. *Address:* The Cottage, Christmas Common, Watlington, Oxon, England.

BALOGUN (Chief), Olayiwola Osuolale, b. 22 Sept. 1940, Lagos. Chartered Architect. m. Folake Olufunke Adebayo 26 Dec. 1970, 4 sons, 3 daughters. *Education:* Yaba Technical Instutute, Yaba College of Technology, Lagos 1955-59; Nigerian College of Arts, Science and Technology, Zaria, Kaduna State 1961; Ahmadu Bello University Zaria, 1962-66; Corporate member RIBA, Nigerian Institute of Architects. *Appointments:* Costain (W.A) Limited 1959-61; Equator Group, -lagos, 1966-67; Modulor Group, 1967-. *Memberships:* Secretary, Ikeja Lions Club; Ikoyi Club, Lagos; Lagos Country Club, Ikeia; Treasurer, Nigerian Institute of Architects, 1973-75, Secretary, 1975-79; President, Yaba College of Technology Alumni Association; President, Parents Association of Private Primary Schools, Lagos; Corona Schools Trust Council; Parent Teacher Association, Corona School,; Hon. Life Member, Nigerian Red Cross Society. *Creative Works:* Eko Court, Victoria Island Lagos; Residence and Block of Flats for RAO Investment Ikoyi; House for Late Chief Henry Fajemirokun, Ile-Oluji, Ondo State; Office Building (Elephant House) at Broad St., Lagos; Federal Palace Suites Hotel, Lagos. Abuja. *Hobbies:* Reading; Meditation; Table Tennis; Lawn Tennis. *Address:* 26 Oluwole Street, off St. Finbarr's College Road, Akoka, Nigeria.

BAMALLI, Yu Su Fu Muhammadu, b. 29 Aug. 1939 Zaria. Accountant. m. 1 Oct. 1960, Twelve Children. *Education:* Diploma in Public Accountancy, Abu Zaria 1969; Certificate Advanced Accountancy and Audit London, 1974. *Appointments:* Financial Controller, Sub-Treasury, Kaduna; Deputy Accountant General Kaduna State, Nigeria; Director, Kaduna Cooperative Bank. *Hobbies:* Reading of Islam Books; Lectures in Islam. *Address:* V27 Saminaka Road, New Extention T/Wada, Kaduna, Nigeria.

BAMBERG, Harold Rolf, b. 17 Nov. 1923, England. Chairman. m. June Winifred Clarke, 1957, 2 sons, 3 daughters. *Appointments:* Chairman of Bamberg Group Limited and other Companies including Eagle Aircraft Services Limited. *Memberships:* Chairman, Gamta, London. *Publications:* FRSA. *Honours:* CBE., 1968. *Hobbies:* Polo; Shooting; Bloodstock breeding. *Address:* Harewood Park, Sunninghill, Ascot, Berkshire, England.

BAMISAIYE, Joshua Adepitan, b. 29 Sept. 1937, Ilobgo-Ekiti, Ondo State, Nigeria. Chairman & Managing Director. m. 1 Aug. 1969, 1 son, 1 daughter. *Education:* B.A. Toronto, Canada, 1964-; M.A. Stockholm, Sweden, 1966-; PhD., Sweden, 1968-. *Appointments:* Lecturer, University of Ibadan, 1969-73; Research Fellow, Nigerian Institute of International Affairs, Lagos, 1973-75; Managing Director & Chairman, Nigerian Charter Associates Ltd., 1975-; Managing Director & Chairman, Concorde Furniture Manufacturing Co., Ltd., Lagos,; Director, Destination Africa Ltd., 1978-. *Memberships:* Law Society of Nigeria; Chairman, Wood & Furniture Manufacturing Association of Nigeria; Skoyi Club 1938; Lagos Lawn Tennis Club; Lagos Motor Club; Lagos Country Club. *Honours:* Honours Award, York College, University of Toronto, Canada, 1963-; First Class Blues winner for Tennis, University of Toronto, 1962-. *Hobbies:* Photography, Tennis, Squash, Table Tennis and Boating. *Address:* 101 Isaac John Street, G.R.A., Ikeja, Lagos, Nigeria.

BAMJI, Khurshid Soli, b. 10 Sept. 1925, Bombay, India. Government Official. m. 18 Jan. 1949, 1 son. *Education:* B.A. French (Honours), University of Bombay. *Appointments:* Assistant Director, Government of India Tourist Office, Bombay, 1950-54; Director, Tourist Office, Madras, 1955-; Director, Tourist Office, Bombay, 1956-60; Director, Tourist Office, Toronto, Canada, 1960-64; Director, Tourist Office, Calcutta, 1964-67; Director, Tourist Office, Paris, France, 1967-74; Deputy Director General, Department of Tourism, New Delhi, 1974-78; Regional Director, Tourist Office, Sydney, Australia, 1978-. *Memberships:* Zonta International (Executive Club for Women); Women's Club; Pacific Area Travel Association; Australian Federation of Travel Agents; Association of National Tourist Office Representatives. *Honours:* Several Prizes and Scholarships both in School and University. *Hobbies:* Travel; Reading; Music. *Address:* 228 Edinburgh Road, Castlecrag, Sydney 2068, Australia.

BANANA, Cde Cannan, b. 5 Mar. 1936, Esiphezine, Essexvale District. Teacher, Methodist Minister and Politician, Poet and Author, Journalist. m. Janet Mbuyazwe, 2 sons, 1 daughter. *Education:* Epworth Theological College, Salisbury; Wesley Theological Seminary, Washington DC, USA; Kansai Industrial Centre, Japan; University of South Africa. *Appointments:* Methodist Schools Manager, Wankie and Plumtree areas, 1963-66; Chaplain, Tegwani High School, 1965-75; Chairman, Bulawayo Council of Churches, 1969-71; Principal, Matjinge Boarding School, 1965-; Chaplain, American University, 1973-75. *Memberships:* First Deputy President, ANC., 1971-72; Chairman of the Southern Africa Content Group on Urban/Industrial Mission of the All Africa Conference of Churches, 1970-73; Publicity Secretary People's Movement Internal Co-ordinating Committee of ZANU (P.F.), 1976-77; Advisory Committee of W.C.C. Churches, 1970-80. *Publications:* Zimbabwe Exodus; Rhodesian Provincialisation Deepening Apartheid; The Gospel According to The Ghetto; The Woman of My Imagination; Several articles to several magazines. *Hobbies:* Travelling. *Address:* c/o President's Office, Government House, P.O. Box 368, Salisbury, Rhodesia.

BANATVALA, Jehangir, b. 7 Jan. 1934, London. Doctor of Medicine, Professor of Clinical Virology. m. Roshan Mugaseth, 15 Aug. 1959, 3 sons, 1 daughter. *Education:* B.A.; MB.B.Chir, M.A., M.D., Caius College, Cambridge, 1952-55; London Hospital Medical College, 1955-58. *Appointments:* House Physician & Surgeon, The London Hospital, 1959-60; Paediatrician, General Hospital, Kettering, 1960-61; Research Fellow, Department of Pathology, University Cambridge, 1961-64; American Thoracic Society, Post-Doctoral Research Fellow, University of Yale, 1964-65; Senior Lecturer, 1965-71; Reader, 1971-75; Professor, Clinical Virology, St. Thomas' Hospital Medical School, London. *Memberships:* President, European Association Against Virus Diseases, 1981-; M.C.C., Leander. *Publications:* Current Problems in Clinical Virology, 1970-; Recent Advances in clinical virology, Rubella vaccines, 1977-; Clinics in Gastroenterology, Viral Diarrhoed Diseases, 1979-; Various papers on clinical virology in various Medical Journals. *Honours:* Lionel Whitby Medal, University of Cambridge, 1964-. *Hobbies:* Tennis; Watching Cricket; Dogs. *Address:* Church End, Herham, Nr. Bishops Stortford, Herts, England.

BANCROFT, Harold Edward, b. 12 Mar. 1910, York, Western Australia. m. Muriel Jean Truscott, 2 June 1934, 1 son. *Education:* Northam High School, Western Australia. *Appointments:* Secretary to Royal Commission, for City of Perth Building By-Laws, 1937-; Managing Secretary of Zoological Gardens Board, 1956-68; Managing Secretary National Parks Board of Western Australia, 1956-71; Equipment Officer R.A.F. Second World War, 1939-45. *Memberships:* The Federal Institute of Accountants; The Australian Society of Accountants; The Chartered Institute of Secretaries. *Honours:* First Place, Final Examination, Federal Institute of Accountants, 1936-; Pacific Star. *Hobbies:* Golf; Gardening. *Address:* 16 Norland Street, Cheltenham, Victoria, 3192, Australia.

BANCROFT, Ian Powell, b. 23 Dec. 1922. Civil Servant. m. Jean Swaine, 1950. *Education:* MA., Balliol College, Oxford, UK. *Appointments:* Entered Treasury, 1947; Private Secretary to: Sir Henry Wilson Smith,

1948-50, Chancellor of the Exchequer, 1953-55, Lord Privy Seal, 1955-57, Cabinet Office, 1957-59; Principal Private Secretary to Sucessive Chancellors of the Exchequer, 1964-66; Under Secretary to: HM Treasury, 1966-68, Civil Service Department, 1968-70; Deputy Secretary Director General of Organisation and Establishments, DOE, 1970-72; Deputy Chairman of Board, Comissioner of Customs and Excise, 1972-73; Second Permanent Secretary, 1973-75, Head of the Home Civil Service and Permanent Secretary, 1978-, Civil Service Department; Permanent Secretary, DOE, 1975-77. *Memberships:* Visiting Fellow, Nuffield College, Oxford, 1973-; United Oxford and Cambridge University Club. *Honours:* CB., 1971; KCB., 1975; GCB., 1979. *Address:* 4 Melrose Road, West Hill, London SW18, England.

BANDA Hastings Kamuzu, (Life President of the Republic of Malawi). b. 14 May, 1906, Kasungu District, Nyasaland. *Education:* Graduate, Wilberforce Institute, Xenia, Ohio, USA. 1928-; Student, University Indiana, USA. 1928-; PhB., Chicago University, USA. 1931-; MD., Meharry Medical College, Nashville, USA., 1937-; Universities of Glasgow and Edinburgh, UK. BSc, MB, ChB., LRCSE and several Honorary Degrees. *Appointments:* Practised Medicine, Liverpool & Tyneside, 1939-45; Willesden, London, 1945-53; Practised Medicine, Gold Coast, 1953-58; Leader of the Nyasaland African Congress Party, 1958-; Minister of Natural Resources and Local Government, 1961-63; Prime Minister of Local Government, 1963-64; Prime Minister of Malawi, 1964-66; President of the Republic of Malawi, 1966-; Elected Life President, 1971-; Also Minister of External Affairs, Agriculture and Justice; Chancellor of the University of Malawi. *Address:* State House, Zomba, Republic of Malawi.

BANDE, Benedicto Panadza, b. 6 Aug. 1943. Personnel Manager. m. Virginia Stimah, 27 Sept. 1969, 2 sons, 4 daughters. *Education:* Professional Management, Practice of Management and Effective Presentation, Polytechnic University of Malawi, 1972-; Office Management, 1974, and General Management, 1979, School of Careers; Personnel, Recruitment and Selection, University of Malawi, 1978-. *Appointments:* Printer; Assistant Works Manager; Personnel Manager. *Memberships:* Christian Families, Cordinator; 1st Vice-Chairman, Preschool Playgroups Association in Malawi; Board of Trustees, Montfort College; Advisory Board, Orphan's Home. *Hobbies:* Reading; Football; Music. *Address:* c/O Montfort Press, P.O. Box 5592, Limbe, Malawi.

BANDYOPADHYAY, Shyama Prasad, b. 1 Feb. 1930, Calcutta. Reader in Pure Mathematics. m. 1953, 1 son. *Education:* B.A. Calcutta University, 1949-; M.A. in pure mathematics, Calcutta University, 1952-; D.Phil., Calcutta University, 1964-; PhD., Department of H.Alg, Moscow State University, 1968-; A research scholar, Calcutta University, Government of India, Government of USSR. *Appointments:* Formerly Professor Mathematics, the Karimgamj College, Assam; Lecturer in Mathematics at different colleges of the Government of West Bengal; Assistant Professor of Mathematics, Indian Institute of Technology, Kharagpur; Reader in Pure Mathematics, Calcutta University. *Memberships:* Indian Mathematical Society; Calcutta Mathematical Society; Indian Science Congress Association; Bangiya Bijnan Parishad; Editorial Board of the Bull. Cal. Mathematical Society. Director of Three U.G.C. and Two CSIR Projects. *Publications:* The lattice of subgroups of finite groups, 1956-; The lattice of normal subfields; Valuations in groups and rings; Valuations in groups and rings in Russian, 1969-, in Czechoslovak Mathematical Journal, 1969-; U-Semigroups, 1970-; Ring with valuation, 1970-; Valuation in universal algebras, 1976-; Valuation and archimedean classes in U-algebras, 1979-. Four PhD's in Algebra. *Hobbies:* Tourism. *Address:* Ground Floor, Flat A, Ripon Mansion, 107 Ripon Street, Calcutta - 700 016, India.

BANFIELD, Audray Margaret, b. 21 Dec. 1931, Melbourne. Art Gallery Director. m. Trevor, 13 Feb. 1953 (Divorced 1976), 1 son 2 daughters. *Education:* Fine Art, University of Melbourne, 1973-; Bendingo I.A.E., 1976-79; Riverina College, 1981-. Studied painting and drawing under Constance Coleman. *Appointments:* Director, Benalla Art Gallery, 1969-80; Director, Albury Regional Art Centre, 1980-. *Memberships:* Australian Gallery Directors' Council, 1975-76, 1980-

81; Regional Galleries Association of Victoria, 1978-80; Regional Gallery Directors' Conference, 1976-; Art Museums Association of Australia; Benalla Drama Club. *Publications:* Catalogue for M.J. MacNally Retrospective, 1974-; Catalogue for Spirit of Place, 1977-. *Hobbies:* Theatre; wine and food; Collecting inexpensive but beautiful objects. *Address:*7 333 Smith Street, Albury, Melbourne, Australia.

BANJOKO, Abayomi Olugbemiga, b. 10 Oct. 1937, Gwadabawa, Sokoto State, Nigeria. Architect. m. (1) Abigail Modupe, 21 May 1960, (1) Bosede Adesola, 2 May 1978, 3 sons, 2 daughters. *Education:* Molusi College, Ijebu-Igbo, 1951-60; Leeds School of Architecture, 1962-64; Huddersfield Polytechnic, 1964-71; Associateship in Architecture, (A. Arch.) (R.I.B.A.). *Appointments:* West Riding County Council, County Architects Department, 1962-64; Sheffield City Architects Department, 1970-72; Own Practice in Lagos, 1975-79; Partner, Banjoko Kukoyi & Flack, 1978-81. *Memberships:* Royal Institute of British Architects; Chartered Institute of Arbitrators; Nigerian Institute of Architects; I-Jay Klub, 1969-; Klub I5 Ago-Iwoye; Nigerian National Society for the Disabled. *Publications:* Masterplan for the new University of Maiduguri, in association with Messrs. Caudill Rowletts & Scott (Architects) Houston, Texas, USA. *Hobbies:* Driving, Gardening, Table Tennis. *Address:* 72 Osun Road, Atikori, Ijebu-Igbo, Ogun State, Nigeria.

BANJO, Ladipo Ayodeji, b. 2 May 1934, Nigeria. University Teacher. m. Alice Mbamali, 8 June 1963, 2 sons, 2 daughters. *Education:* MA., University of Glasgow, UK, 1955-59; Graduate Certificate in Education, 1959-60, Postgraduate Diploma in English Studies, 1964-65, University of Leeds, UK; MA., University of California, Los Angeles, USA, 1965-66; PhD., University of Ibadan, Nigeria, 1966-69. *Appointments:* Education Officer, 1960-64, Senior Education Officer, Apr-Oct. 1966, Western Nigeria; Lecturer in English, 1966-71, Senior Lecturer in English, 1971-73, Reader in English Language, 1973-75, Professor of English Language, 1975-, University of Ibadan, Nigeria. *Memberships:* Vice President, West African Modern Language Association, 1976-; President, Nigeria English Studies Association, 1968-78; Vice-President, Yoruba Studies Association, 1978-; West African Linguistic Society, 1966-. *Publications:* Oral English (with P Connell), 1971; Letter Writing, 1973; Effective Use of English,(with SO Unoh), 1976. *Hobbies:* Music; Reading; Cricket. *Address:* 15 Sankore Avenue, University of Ibadan, Ibadan, Nigeria.

BANKA, Niranjan Hanuman Prasad, b. 21 Aug. 1948, Malsisar, Rajasthan, India. Medicine, Consultant Gastroenterologist. m. Lata Sah, 14 June 1974, 1 son, 1 daughter. *Education:* M.B., B.S. University of Bombay, India, 1970-; F.C.P.S. (Medicine), The College of Physicians and Surgeons, Bombay, India, 1974-; M.D. (Medicine), University of Bombay, India, 1974-. *Appointments:* Clinical Assistant, Gastroenterology, Western General Hospital, Edinburgh, Scotland, 1975-76; Consultant Gastroenterologist at Bhartiya Arogyanidhi Hospital and Smt B.C.J. General Hospital, Bombay, 1976-; Medical Adviser to Inga Pharmaceuticals. *Memberships:* Indian Medical Association; Association of Physicians of India; Indian Society of Gastroenterology; Gastrointestinal Endoscopy Society of India; Consultants Association, Bombay. *Publications:* Original articles Drug trials and case reports published and read at various conferences and Journals. *Honours:* Gold Medal of Sir Hoshang Dhunjishaw Dastur Prize for standing first in the F.C.P.S. Examination, 1974-. *Hobbies:* Sports, Paintings, Reading, Writing. *Address:* B/7 Paradise Appartments, Behind Oscar Cinema, 137 S.V. Road, Andheri, Bombay, 400 058, India.

BANKOLE, Olawale Alabi, b. 3 Aug. 1942, Igan-Alade, Nigeria. Business Executive. m. Ayoade Abidemi Ladipo, 24 Dec. 1965, 2 sons, 3 daughters. *Education:* BSc.,(Hons.), University of Lagos, Nigeria, 1971. *Appointments:* Teacher, various schools, 1955-68; Merchandise Manager, Kingsway Stores Division of VAC. of Nigeria Limited, Lagos, Nigeria, 1971-75; Marketing Manager, Longman Nigeria Limited, Ikeja, Nigeria, 1975-78; Minister of Education, Ogun State of Nigeria, 1978-79; Marketing Manager, University Press Limited, Oxford House, Ibadan, Nigeria, 1979-. *Memberships:* British Institute of Marketing; Nigerian Marketing Association; Nigerian Institute of Management; Ibadan Tennis Club. *Publications:* Several articles on Management and Marketing in Journals and newspapers. *Honours:* University Scholar, University of Lagos, Nigeria, 1970; Faculty Prize Winner (overall), 1971; Appointment as Balogun of Igan Alade, Traditional Chieftaincy title, 1978. *Hobbies:* Photography; Farming. *Address:* Balogun Bankole House, Igan Alade, Via Ilaro, Nigeria.

BANKS, (Lord), Desmond Anderson Harvie, b. 13 Oct. 1918, Ascot, Berkshire, England. Insurance Broker. m. Barbara Wells, 12 June 1948, 2 sons. *Education:* University College School, Hampstead, 1932-36; Alpha Preparatory School, Harrow, 1928-32. *Appointments:* Canada Life Assurance Company, 1951-55; Life Association of Scotland, 1955-58; Life & Pensions Manager, Jago Tweddle Co., Ltd., 1960-62; Life & Pensions Director, D. G. Jago & Co., Ltd., 1962-65; Life & Pensions Manager, K. C. Hopkins Ltd., 1970;73; Life & Pensions Director, Tweddle French Ltd., 1973-. *Memberships:* President, Liberal Party, 1968-69; Chairman, Liberal Party Executive, 1961-63 & 1969-70; Deputy Liberal Whip, House of Lords, 1977-; Liberal Spokesman on the Social Services, 1977-; Vice-Chairman, Liberal Party Foreign Affairs Panel, 1972-; President, Liberal European Action Group, 1972-. *Publications:* Clyde Steamers, Albyn Press, Einburgh, 1947-; Numerous political pamphlets. *Honours:* Commander, O.B.E., 1972-. *Hobbies:* Enjoying Gilbert & Sullivan Opera, Pursuing interest in Clyde Steamers. *Address:* Lincoln House, The Lincolns, Little Kingshill, Great Missenden, Bucks HP16 0BH, England.

BANKS, Edgar Roger, b. 10 July 1930, Melbourne, Victoria, Australia. Engineer. m. Molly May Carmichael, 10 Nov. 1956, 1 son, 1 daughter. *Education:* Bachelor of Electrical Engineering, 1st Class Honours, Melbourne University. *Appointments:* Appointed to Postmaster-General's Department, 1948-; Assistant Director-General, Switching & Facilities Planning, H.Q. Chairman C.C.I.T.T. Working Party on National Networks, Vice-Chairman Special S.G.B. (World-wide Telephone) C.C.I.T.T., 1961-70; Director (Business Planning), Plessey Telecommunications Ltd., U.K. 1972-74; A/g A.D.G. Telephone Equipment Branch, H.Q. Appointed A.D.G. Fundamental Planning, 1974-; General Manager (Customer Services) H.Q., 1975-, Director Business Development 1980. *Memberships:* Institute of Engineers (Australia), Australian Insitutue of Management; Athenaeum West Brighton and R.A.C.V. *Honours:* Dixon Scholarship, Melbourne University, 1952-; Monash, Newbigin and Oral Presentation Prizes of I.E. (Australia), (Melbourne Division), 1953-; Federation of British Industries Overseas Fellowship, 1955-56. *Hobbies:* Swimming, Sailing, Church and School Administration, Wife's Music and Gardening. *Address:* 31 Cheviot Road, Mount Waverley, Melbourne, Victoria, 3000, Australia.

BANKS, Robert George, b. 18 Jan. 1937, Kent, England. Member of Parliament. m. Diana Margaret Payne Crawford, 3 June 1965, 4 sons, 1 daughter. *Education:* Haileybury. *Appointments:* Lieutenant Commander, Royal Naval Reserve; Joint Founder/Director, Antocks Lairn Limited, 1963-67; Member, Paddington Borough Council, London, UK, 1959-65; Member of Parliament for Harrogate, Yorkshire, UK, 1974-; Joint Secretary, Conservative Parliamentary Defence Committee, 1976-79; Secretary, 1976-77, Vice-Chairman, 1978, Conservative Parliamentary Horticulture Sub-Committee; Secretary, 1973-79, Vice-Chairman, 1979, All Party Tourism Group; Secretary, Anglo-Sudan Group, 1978; Parliamentary Private Secretary to Mr. Peter Blaker, Minister of State at Foreign Office, and to Mr Richard Luce, Under Secretary of State at the Foreign Office, 1979-. *Memberships:* Substitute member to the Council of Europe Assembly, Apr. 1977-; Western European Union, Apr. 1977-. *Publications:* Britain's Home Defence Gamble. *Honours:* TD; MBE. *Hobbies:* Farming; Shooting; Architecture. *Address:* House of Commons, London, SW1, England.

BANNENBERG, Roger James Nicholas, b. 2 Oct. 1939, Sydney, Australia. Librarian. m. Glenys Margaret Bolen, 30 Apr. 1966, 2 daughters. *Education:* Albury Grammar School, 1948-51; Rockhampton Grammar School, 1952-55; Brisbane Grammar School, 1956-57; Associate Library Association of Australia, 1966-; Bachelor of Laws, University of Queensland, 1972-. *Appointments:* Library Assistant, 1960-66; Library Of-

ficer, 1966-68; Queensland Parlimentary Library; Senior Assistant Librarian, 1968-72; Parliamentary Librarian, 1973-. *Publications:* Several articles on Librarianship; Edited Proceedings, Fourth Conference of Australian Parliamentary Librarians; Queensland Parliamentary Handbook. *Hobbies:* Veteran's Athletics, Music, Chess. *Address:* 46 Yallambee Road, Jindalee, Brisbane, Australia, 4074.

BANNER, Frederick Thomas, b. 12 Mar. 1930, Swaffham, Norfolk, UK. Professor of Oceanography. m. Aisha Osman, 14 Nov. 1975. *Education:* BSc Honours Geology, University College, London, 1951-; PhD. Micropalaeontology, University College, London, 1953-; DSc Marine Geology, University of London, 1980-. *Appointments:* Senior Micropalaeontologist, Australasian Petroleum Co. Ltd., Papua, New Guinea, 1953-56; Micropalaeontologist and Stratigrapher, BP Exploration Co. Ltd., 1956-66; Senior Lecturer, then Reader, Department of Geology and Oceanography, University College of Swansea, 1967-76; Professor of Oceanography and head of Department of Oceanography, University College of Swansea, 1976-; Visiting Professor, University Sierra Leone, 1979, 1980; University West Indies, 1978; University Legon, Ghana, 1980-. *Memberships:* Royal Society of Arts; The Geological Association; British Micropalaeontological Society; The Society for Underwater Technology; Sometime Council of the Palaeontologists Association; Committee of the Marine Studies Group of the Geological Society of London. *Publications:* Co-editor of: Fundamentals of mid-Tertiary Strategraphical Correlation, 1962-; The North West European Shelf Seas, Geology and Sedimentology, 1979-; The North West European Shelf Seas, Physical Oceanography, 1980-; Problems of industrialised embayments, 1980-; Approximately 50 papers in scientific journals. *Honours:* Honorary Research Fellow, University College, London, 1974-. *Hobbies:* Travel, Music. *Address:* 23 Windsor Street, Uplands, Swansea, West Glamorgan, SA20LN, England.

BANNISTER, Sir, Roger Gilbert, b. 23 Mar. 1929, Harrow, England. Consultant Neurologist. m. Moyra Elver Jacobsson, 11 June 1955, 2 sons, 2 daughters. *Education:* Oxford, Exeter and Merton Colleges, UK; St. Mary's Hospital Medical School, UK; MA., MSc., (Oxon.); DM., (Oxford). *Appointments:* Chairman, British Sports Council, 1971-74; Consultant Neurologist, St. Mary's Hospital, London, UK and The National Hospital for Nervous Diseases, London, UK. *Memberships:* Athenaeum Club. *Publications:* First Four Minutes, 1955; Editor, Brain's Clinical Neurology. *Honours:* CBE., 1955; Knight, 1975. *Address:* 16 Edwardes Square, London, W8, England.

BANSAL, Sundar Lal, b. 13 Apr. 1929, Machhrauli. Engineer. m. Gayatri , 14 Feb. 1951, 2 sons. *Education:* BSc Engineering (honours), Banaras Hindu University, 1950-; Diploma, Guided Weapons, College of Aeronautics, Cranfield, UK. 1959-; Graduate, National Defence College, New Delhi, 1969-; Senior Defence Management Course, Secunderabad, 1971-. *Appointments:* Defence Research & Development Organisation, Ministry of Defence, Goverment of India, 1951-; Group Leader Radar and Electronics Group, Defence Science Laboratory, New Delhi; Deputy Director, Defence Research & Development Laboratory, Hyderabad, 1963-73; Project Officer, 1971-73; Director, Rockets & Missiles, Ministry of Defence, New Delhi, 1973-80; Co-ordinator, Missile Development Panel, 1980-; Director, Defence Research & Development Laboratory, Hyderabad, 1980-; Director, Bharat Dynamics Limited, Hyderabad; Director, Hyderabad Batteries Ltd., Secunderabad. *Memberships:* Institute of Electronics and Telecommunication Engineers; Ex. Committee Hyderabad Centre, 1980-81. *Publications:* Technical Reports. *Honours:* Prince of Wales Gold Medal, Banaras Hindu University, 1950-; Distinguished Alumnus Award, Banaras Hindu University, 1980-. *Hobby:* Photography. *Address:* DRDL House, Kanchan Bagh Post, Hyderabad, 500 258, India.

BAPPU, Manali Kallat Vainu, b. 10 Aug. 1927, Madras, India. Scientist. m. Yemuna Sukumaran, 14 Nov. 1956. *Education:* MSc., University of Madras, 1949-; A.M. Harvard University, 1950-; PhD., Harvard University, 1952-. *Appointments:* Director, Uttar Pradesh State Observatory, Naini Tal, India, 1954-60; Director, Indian Institute of Astrophysics, Bangalore,

1960-. *Memberships:* President, International Astronomical Union, 1979-82; Vice-President, Indian Academy of Sciences, 1980-82; Foreign Associate, Royal Astronomical Society of London; Indian National Science Academy; Corresponding Member, Royal Society of Sciences, Liege. *Publications:* Research publications in several fields of astronomy. *Honours:* Donohoe Comet Medal, of the Astronomical Society of the Pacific, 1949-; Shanti Swarup Bhatnagar Prize of the CSIR, in Physical Sciences, 1970-; Padma Bhushan, 1981-. *Hobbies:* Painting, Photography. *Address:* Kadambari, 527, 16th Main Road, Koramangala, Bangalore, 560034.

BARAGWANATH, Owen Thomas, b. 12 Oct. 1913, Auckland, New Zealand. Minister of Religion. m. Eileen Georgia Richards, 20 Oct. 1939, 2 sons, 2 daughters. *Education:* BA., Auckland University, New Zealand, 1936; Theological College, Dunedin, New Zealand and University of Edinburgh, UK. *Appointments:* Assistant Minister, St. Giles Cathedral, Edinburgh, UK, 1938-39; Minister, Balclutha, New Zealand, 1939-41; Chaplain, NZ Military Forces, 1941-44; Associate Minster, Knox, Dunedin, New Zealand, 1945-47; Minister, Anderson's Bay, Dunedin, New Zealand, 1947-53; Minister, 1953-77, Associate, 1977-78, St. David's, Auckland, New Zealand. *Memberships:* Honorary member, Auckland Rotary Club; Whangaparaoa Golf Club; various other sporting, musical societies. *Honours:* OBE (Civil), 1970; Mention in despatches, 1944; Efficiency Decoration, 1953. *Hobbies:* Gardening; Music; Golf. *Address:* 15 Tyndalls Bay Road, Whangaparaoa, Auckland, New Zealand.

BARBACK, Ronald Henry, b. 31 Oct. 1919, London, England. Economist. m. Sylvia Chambers, 21 Oct. 1950, 1 son, 1 daughter. *Education:* University College, Nottingham, UK; BSc., (Econ.), London, UK; M. Litt., Queen's and Nuffield Colleges, Oxford, UK. *Appointments:* Assistant Lecturer in Economics, University of Nottingham, UK, 1946-48; Lecturer in Economics, Senior Lecturer, Canberra University College, Australia, 1949-56; Professor of Economics and Social Studies and Director, Nigerian Institute of Social and Economic Research, 1956-63; Professor of Economics, Trinity College, Dublin, Ireland, 1964-65; Professor of Economics, University of Hull, UK, 1965-76; Deputy Economic Director, Head, Economic Research, Confederation of British Industry, UK, 1977-. *Memberships:* Athenaeum Club; Royal Commonwealth Society; Royal Economic Society. *Publications:* The Pricing of Manufactures, 1964; The Conflict of Expansion and Stability, (with Prof. Sir D Copland), 1957; Australia, in The Commonwealth in the Modern World, 1956; Contribution on Nigerian Industry and Trade in The Commonwealth and Europe, 1960; Insurance in the English-Speaking Countries of West Africa, 1964; Articles on Commonwealth, economics, and fisheries topics in various journals; various official reports. *Hobbies:* Travel; Music. *Address:* 'Oakhurst', Beaconfields, Sevenoaks, Kent, England.

BARBOUR, Thomas Vevers-Redman, b. 22 Apr. 1919, Little Clandeboye, Co. Down, N. Ireland. Civil Servant. *Education:* Belfast College of Technology, 1938-39; H.M. Forces, 1939-. *Appointments:* H.M. Forces, 1939-46; British Control Commission, 1946-50; A.D.C. to the Governor of Northern Rhodesia, 1950-54; P.A. to successive High Commissioners in the U.K. of the Federation of Rhodesia and Nyasaland, 1954-64; P.A. to the High Commissioner of Rhodesia, in the U.K. 1964-; Assistant Chief of Protocol, Goverment of Rhodesia, 1965-; Comptroller to the Officer Administering the Government of Rhodesia, 1965-69; Comptroller to the H.E. The Life President of Malawi, 1969-. *Memberships:* Royal Commonwealth Society; Victory Club; Railway Club; Stephenson Locomotive Society; Railway Correspondence & Travel Society; Gymkhana Club and Turf Club, Zomba Malawi. *Honours:* M.B.E. (Civil), 1957-. *Hobbies:* Interior Decoration, Reading, Bridge, Study of the Pre-Grouping Railways of Great Britain, 1900-23. *Address:* PO Box 40, Zomba, Malawi.

BARING, (The Hon.), John Francis Harcourt, b. 2 Nov. 1928, London, England. Merchant Banker. m. The Hon. Susan Mary Renwick, 25 Nov. 1955, 2 sons, 2 daughters. *Education:* Eton College; Trinity College, Oxford; B.A. 1950-; M.A. 1950-. *Appointments:* Joined Barings 1950-; Seconded to associates in U.S.A. and

Canada, 1953-54; Appointed to Managing Director, 1955-; Appointed Chairman, 1974-. *Memberships:* President Overseas Bankers Club, 1977-78; Fellow Institute of Bankers. *Honours:* C.V.O., 1980-. *Address:* Lake House, Northington, Alresford, Hants., SO24 9TG, England.

BARKER, (Sir), Alwyn (Bowman), C.M.G., b. 5 Aug. 1900, Adelaide, South Australia. Chartered Engineer. m. Isabel Barron Lucas, 1 son (Deceased), 1 daughter. *Education:* St. Peters College, Adelaide, 1910-14; Geelong, C.E.G.S., 1915-18; University of Adelaide, 1919-22, 1930-31. *Appointments:* Tester, British Thompson Houston, Co., Rugby, England, 1923-24; Draughtsman, Hudson Motor Car Co., Detroit, USA., 1924-25; Production Manager, Holdens Motor Body Builders, Adelaide, 1925-30; Works Manager, Kelvinator Australia Limited, 1931-40; General Manager, Chrysler Australia Ltd., 1940-52; Managing Director, Kelvinator Australia Limited, 1952-67, Chairman, 1967-80. *Memberships:* Chairman, Adelaide Electrolysis Investigating Committee; Chairman, Board of Municipal Tramways Trust, 1953-68; President, Australian Insitute of Management, 1952-54; Federal President, Australian Institute of Management, 1952-53, 1959-61; President, Institution of Production Engineers, 1970-72; Faculty of Engineering, University of Adelaide, 1937-66; Lecturer, Industrial Engineering, University of Adelaide, 1929-53; Chairman, Industrial Development Advisory Council, 1968-70; Manufacturing Industries Advisory Council, 1958-72; Research and Development Advisory Committee, 1967-72; Director, 10 Public Companies, Chairman 2 Public Companies. *Publications:* Three Presidential Addresses, 1954-; William Queale Memorial Lecture, 1965-; *Honours:* John Storey Memorial Medal, 1965-; Jack Finlay National Award, 1964-. *Hobbies:* Pastoral. *Address:* 51 Hackney Road, Hackney, South Australia, 5069.

BARKER, James Rollins, b. 17 Apr. 1921 Kingston, Canada. Diplomat. m. Barbara Jane Bermingham 5 May 1951, 2 sons. *Education:* BA(Hons) Queens University, Kingston, 1948; Equtualances, and work on PhD, Instud de Hautes Etudes Internationales, Geneva, 1948-1950; National Defence College of Canada, 1966-67. *Appointments:* Canadian Armed Forces, 1941-46; Canadian Foreign Service, Ottawa and Abroad, 1950, Moscow, 1953-55, London, 1959-63; Highcommissioner, Tanzania with Concurrent Accreditation in Zambia and Mauritius, 1971-; Ambassador to Somalia, 1974; Chief of Protocol, Ottawa, 1975-78; Ambassador to Greece, 1978-. *Honours:* CD, Canadian Forces Decoration, 1951. *Hobbies:* Early New Brunswick History. *Address:* Canadian Embassy, 4 Ghennadiou Street, Athens, 140, Greece.

BARKER, Paul, b. 24 Aug. 1935, Halifax, West Yorkshire, England. Magazine Editor. m. Sally Huddleston, 15 Apr. 1960, 3 sons, 1 daughter. *Education:* BA(Oxon), 1958; MA, 1970. *Appointments:* Staff of The Times, 1959-64; Staff, New Society, 1964; Staff, The Economist, 1964-65; Assistant Editor, New Society, 1965-68; Editor, New Society, 1968-. *Memberships:* Council, Pennine Heritage Limited. *Publications:* A Sociological Portrait, 1972; One for Sorrow, Two For Joy, 1972; The Social Sciences Today, 1975; Arts in Society, 1977. *Address:* 26 Patshull Road, London, NW5, England.

BARKER, Sylvia, b. 13 Mar. 1944, Sydney, Australia. Medical Illustrator. *Education:* Tolworth County Secondary Girls School, 1955-60; National Diploma of Art and Design, Member of Medical Arts Association, Kingston Polytechnic, 1960-63. *Appointments:* Assistant Medical Artist, Department of Medical Illustration, Royal Postgraduate Medical School, Hammersmith Hospital, Du Cane Road, London, 1964-67; Medical Artist, Department of Medical Illustration, St Bartholomew's Hospital, London, 1967-70; Head, Graphic Section, Department of Medical Illustration, John Radcliffe Hospital, Headington, Oxford OX3 9DU, 1971-. *Memberships:* Medical Artists Association, Institute of Medical and Biological Illustration; Fellow of the Royal Society of Arts. *Publications:* Illustrations produced for various medical and scientific publication e.g. Butterworth's Text Book of Operative Surgery; Design and illustration of series of undergraduate/patient information and children's health education tape/slide programmes and videotapes. *Hobbies:* Photography, Travelling; Ethnic Music. *Address:* 55 Percy Street, Oxford, England.

BARKER, Wilfrid John, b. 1 Aug. 1928. General Manager. m. Alison, 1 Feb. 1962, 1 son, 1 daughter. *Education:* Matriculation, University of Tasmania. *Appointments:* Victorian Sales Manager, GTV 9 Melbourne, 1966; Sales Manager 1967, General Sales Manager, TCN 9 Sydney, 1968; GTV-TCN Network Sales Director, 1971; General Sales Manager ATV 10 Melbourne, 1972; Director of Sales and Marketing, 1976; General Manager, 1979; General Manager, Television Development, News Corporation, 1980; Director, United Telecasters Limited, Ten 10 Sydney; Director, Broadcast FM Pty Limited, 3 Fox-FM Melbourne. *Memberships:* Chairman, Federation of Australian Commercial Television Stations; Deputy Chairman, The Media Council of Australia; International Advertising Association Electronic Media Committee. *Hobbies:* Fishing; Boating. *Address:* 22 Belcote Road, Longueville, NSW 2066, Australia.

BARLTROP, Robert Arthur Horace, b. 6 Nov. 1922, Walthamstow, London E. Author. m. Mary Gleeson 18 July 1947, 3 sons. *Education:* Teacher's Certificate, Forest Training College 1949-50. *Appointments:* Worked in Manual Jobs and was a Professional Boxer; Schoolteacher, 1948-61; Strip-Cartoonist and Painter, 1948-; Full-time Writer, 1974. *Memberships:* Society of Authors; National Union of Journalists; East London Family History Society. *Publications:* The Monument, 1975; Jack London the Man, The Writer, The Rebel 1977; Editor, Revolution, Stories and Essays by Jack London 1979; The Bar Tree 1979; The Muvver Tongue 1980; The Word, to be published 1981; Contributor to many journals and newspapers; Radio and TV broadcaster; Lecturer to various societies. *Honours:* Arts Council Award 1981. *Hobbies:* Drawing and Painting; Genealogy; Reading and collecting Books; Sports. *Address:* 34 St Martin's Avenue, London E6 3DX, England.

BARLTROP, Roger Arnold Rowlandson, b. 19 Jan. 1930 Leeds, Yrkshire. HM Diplomatic Service. m. Penelope Pierrepont Dalton 1 Mar. 1962, 2 sons, 2 daughters. *Education:* BA(Hons.) Exeter College, Oxfoard, 1950-54. *Appointments:* Royal Navy, 1949-50; Commonwealth Relations Office, 1954-56; 2nd Scertary, New Delhi, 1956-57; Private Secretary to Parliamentary Under Secretary of State, then to Ministor of State, CRO, 1957-60; 1st Secretary, Inugu and Ibadan, Nigeria, 1960-62; Salisbury, Rhodesia, 1962-65; FO/FCO Commonwealth Office, 1965-69; 1st Secretary, Head of Chancery, Ankara, 1969-70; Dep. British Government Rep., West Indies Associated States, 1971-73; Counsellor, Head of Chancery, Addis Ababa, 1973-77; Head, Commonwealth Coordination Depatment, FCO, 1978-. *Memberships:* Royal Commonwealth Society; Royal Yachting Association; Sailing Division, Sussex Motor Yacht Club. *Hobbies:* Sailing; Genealogy; Music, especially opera. *Address:* Avalon, 1 Glendale Road, Burgess Hill, West Sussex RH15 0EJ.

BARNARD, Martin James Edwards, b. 5 July 1939, Trinidad West Indies. Agriculturist. m. Mary Ann Doransky, 27 Apr. 1962, 1 son, 3 daughters. *Education:* BSc Agriculture, MacDonald College of McGill University, Canada. *Appointments:* Managing Director, Orange Hill Estates Limited; Assistant Managing Director, Mustique Company; Director: St. Vincent Banana Growers Association, Marketing Board, Bonlers, St. Vincent, Limited, St. Vincent Development Corporation. *Memberships:* Chairman Vivcentian Publishing Company; Policy Adviser to Barclays Bank International; Director: Wayfarer Book Store, St Vincent Employers Federation; Chairman, Agricultural Committee Partners of the Americas. *Hobbies:* Tennis; Golf; Squash; Cricket; Sailing; Flying; Amature Radio. *Address:* Orange Hill Estates, St. Vincent, West Indies.

BARNES, Sir John, b. 22 June 1917, London. HM Diplomatic Service (retired); Company Director. m. Cynthia Stewart, 1 May 1948, 2 sons, 3 daughters. *Education:* Dragon School, Oxford 1928-30; Scholar, Winchester College 1930-36; MA, Trinity College Cambridge, 1936; Fellow, Center for International Affairs, Harvard University, 1961-62. *Appointments:* Lieutenant-Colonel, Royal Artillery, 1939-46; HM Diplomatic Service, 1946-77; Ambassador to Israel, 1969-72; Ambassador, The Netherlands, 1972-77; Director, Alliance Investment, Limited, 1977-; Director, Whiteaway Laidlaw Limited, 1979-. *Memberships:* Athenaeum, Beefsteak, Brooks's and MCC clubs (London). *Publications:* Ahead of His Age, 1979. *Honours:* Porson Scholarship, Cambridge, 1939; MBE (military) 1945; US Bronze Star, 1945; KCMG, 1974. *Address:* Hampton Lodge, Hurstpier Point, Sussex, BN6 9QN, England.

BARNES, Richard Marsden, b. 4 Aug. 1933, Sydney, Australia. Marketing Consultant. 2 daughters. *Education:* B. Economics, University of New South Wales; Management Certificate, Queensland Technical College. *Appointments:* Market Research Manager, E. R. Squibb & Sons Pty. Ltd.; Marketing Adviser-South East Asia, Lilly Industries Pty Ltd; Market Research Manager, Merck Sharp & Dohme Pty Ltd.; Richard Barnes & Associates. *Memberships:* Regional Vice-President, International Marketing Federation; Federal Chairman, N.S.W. Chairman, Market Research Society of Australia; Chairman, Australasian Pharmaceutical Market Research Group; Associate, Australian Institute of Management. *Publications:* Introduction to International Pharmaceutical; Market Research, U.S.A. 1966; Educating the Educators, New Zealand, 1980. *Hobby:* Genealogy. *Address:* 9/27-29 Church Street, Chatswood N.S.W. 2067, Australia.

BARNETSON, The R. Hon. Lord William Denholm, b. 21 Mar. 1917, Edinburgh, Scotland. Newspaper Publisher/Company Director. m. Joan Fairley Davidson, 6 July 1940, 1 son, 3 daughters. *Education:* MA, Edinburgh University. *Appointments:* Control Commission in British Zone of Germany: re-organisation of newspaper and book publishing 1944-47; Leader Writer, Editor and General Manager, Edinburgh Evening News, 1948-61; Director, United Newspapers, 1962, Chairman & Managing Director, 1966-; Chairman, Reuters Ltd. 1968-79; Chairman, The Observer Ltd. 1976-80; Chairman, Thames Television Ltd. 1979-; Director, British Electric Traction Co. Ltd. 1972, Deputy Chairman 1976-; Director, Hill Samuel Group 1977-; Bank of Scotland (London Board), 1979-; Trusthouse Forte Ltd. 1980-. *Memberships:* House of Lord, UK; Companion, Insitute of Management; Honourable Life Member, Commonwealth Press Union; Master of the Guild of St. Bride; Vice-President, Royal Commonwealth Society; Member Presidential Council, Canada-UK Chamber of Commerce; Member UK Committee, International Press Institute; Patron, Newsvendors' Benevolent Institution; Fellow, Institute of Directors. *Honours:* Knight Bachelor 1972, Life Peer 1975 (Great Britain); Officer of the Order of St. John 1972; Knight Grand Cross Italian Order of Merit 1973. *Hobbies:* Books; Gardening. *Address:* Broom, Chillies Lane, Crowborough, Sussex, England.

BAROOAH, Debo Prasad, 1 Oct. 1930, Gauhati. Professor of Political Science. m. Renu Debi, 10 May 1957, 1 son, 1 daughter. *Education:* Bachelor of Arts, 1954, Master of Arts, 1956, Bachelor of Laws, 1958, Doctor of Philosophy, 1969, Gauhati University. *Appointments:* Lecturer in History, 1957, Part time Lecturer, Political Science, 1964-65, Reader, Political Science, 1971, Head, Department of Political Science, 1973, also i/c Head, Department of Journalism, Professor & Head, Department of Political Science, 1978, i/c Head, Department of Journalism, Gauhati University. *Memberships:* Life Member, Indian Political Science Association; Indian Council of World Affairs; Asian Mass Communication Research and Information Centre; Amnesty International, Indian Section; President, Gauhati University Teachers' Association for six years through 1975; President, various empolyees' Unions. *Publications:* World History, 1963, Indo-British Relations 1950-60, World Wars I & II and Other Essays, 1978; Phulmoni (a social novel in Assamese), 1977; Prison Diary: Birnari (in Assamese), 1980; a number of academic papers. *Honours:* BA, Distinction First; MA, First Class First; LL.B. First Class. *Hobbies:* Reading. *Address:* Kharghuli, Gauhati-781 004, Assam, India.

BARR, John Wilmer Browning, b. 7 Dec. 1916, Lanark, Ontario, Canada. Physician (Health Administration). m. Marion Sarah Crawford, 10 May 1945. *Education:* MD, CM, Queen's University, Canada, 1940; PSC, Canadian Army Staff College, 1947; Senior Officers' Course, Royal Army Medical College, London, 1953; University of Toronto, Canada, Diploma in Hospital Administration, 1959; National Defence College, Canada, 1965. *Appointments:* Medical Officer, Canadian Army, in various units in Canada, United Kingdom, North West Europe and Canada, (Lt. to Maj.), 1940-49; Commander, Royal Canadian Army Medical Corps School (LCol.), 1950-52; Senior Medical Officer, Canadian Army Europe, 1953-54; Assistant Director of Medical Services, Canadian Army, 1954-57; Commander, Canadian Forces Hospital, Kingston (Col.), 1958-61; Director of Medical Training Canadian Forces, 1961-64; Deputy Surgeon General (Operations), Canadian Forces (BGen.), 1966-70; Surgeon General Canadian Forces (MGen.), 1970-73; Registrar, Medical Council of Canada, 1973-81; Colonel Commandant, Medical Branch, Canadian Forces (MGen Ret'd), 1976-. *Memberships:* Chief Medical Officer, Order of St. John, Priory of Canada; Honorary Vice-President, Defence Medical Association of Canada; Honorary Member, Army (Ottawa) Officers' Mess; College of Physicians and Surgeons of Ontario; Canadian Medical Association, Ontario Division; Institute of Association Executives. *Publications:* Author of 10 articles in the Journal of the Canadian Medical Association, About the Medical Council of Canada, 1974; Contributor to, 70 years of Service—The History of the Royal Canadian Army Medical Corps, 1975; Contributor to, The History of the Medical Council of Canada, 1979. *Honours:* Robert Wood Johnson Award in Hospital Administration, 1959; Officer Brother, 1967, Commander Brother, 1971, Order of St. John of Jerusalem; Commander, Order of Military Merit of Canada, 1973; Knight of Grace, Order of St. John of Jerusalem; Queen's Honorary Physician, 1967-73, 1977-. *Hobbies:* Scottish Country Dancing; Gardening; Philately. *Address:* 429 Huron Avenue South, Ottawa, Canada KIY OX3.

BARR SMITH, Tom Elder, b. 17 Feb. 1941, Adelaide, South Australia. Pastoralist. m. Jennifer Waterman, 24 Jan. 1964, 2 sons, 1 daughter. *Education:* Royal Agricultural College, Cirencester. *Memberships:* Adelaide Club, Committee; Melbourne Club. *Address:* 9 Edwintce, Gilberton, South Australia.

BARRETT, Alan Henry Bernard, b. 18 Aug. 1934, Manangatang, Victoria, Australia. Historian. *Education:* BA, 1959, MA, 1970, PhD, 1979, University of Melbourne. *Appointments:* Lecturer in Social and Political Studies, Swinburne Institute, Australia, 1963-77; State Historian, Government of Victoria, Australia, 1978-. *Publications:* The Inner Suburbs: the Evolution of an Industrial Area, 1971; The Civic Frontier: the Origin of Local Communities and Local Government in Victoria, 1979. *Honours:* Australia and New Zealand Bank prize, 1979. *Address:* 14 Buley Street, East Hawthorn, Victoria 3123, Australia.

BARRETT, Lewis, b. 18 July 1920, Adelaide, South Australia. Chartered Accountant. m. Hazel Jean Phelps, 5 May 1945, 1 son, 1 daughter. *Education:* University of Adelaide; A.C.I.S. 1947; F.C.A. 1950; F.A.S.A. 1953; F.T.C.L. 1956; F.A.I.M. 1974. *Appointments:* include Adelaide Children's Hospital Board of Management,1963-, Appointed Honorary Treasurer, 1977; Payroll Tax Tribunal of South Australia, 1971;80; Trustee of Savings Bank of South Australia, 1970-73, Appointed Chairman of the Board, 1980; Institute of Medical & Veterinary Science, Adelaide, Member of Council 1979-; Director of Santos Limited, 1978-80; Poseidon Limited, 1978-; Argo Investments Limited, 1980-; M.S. McLeod Limited, 1978-; Organist and Choirmaster, Tynte Street Baptist Church, North Adelaide, 1940-1972, Appointed Organist-Emeritus, 1972, Royal Adelaide Hospital Board of Management, 1979, Chairman 1980. *Memberships:* Organ Music Society of Adelaide, President, 1953-55; Adelaide Club, Committee of Management, 1976-78, Chairman Finance Committee, 1978-; Rotary Club of Adelaide; Commonwealth Club of Adelaide, Member of Committee of Management, 1979-; Member of Cpouncil, South Australian Institute of Technology, 1979. *Publications:* Minor organ and church music (unpublished). *Honours:* OBE. 1981; Institute of Chartered Accountants in Australia F.G. Wilson Prize, 1945; Justice of the Peace, 1947. *Hobbies:* Music; Walking; Gardening. *Address:* 8 View Road, Walkerville, South Australia 5081, Australia.

BARRETT, Stephen Jeremy, b. 4 Dec. 1931, Twickenham, England. Diplomat. m. Alison Mary Irvine, 9 Apr. 1958, 3 sons. *Education:* BA, MA, Christ Church, Oxford, 1950-53. *Appointments:* Foreign Office, 1955-57; Political Office with the Middle East Forces, 1957-59; Deputy Political Adviser, British Military Government, Berlin, 1959-62; Foreign Office, 1962-65; British Embassy, Helsinki, 1965-68; Foreign and Commonwealth Office, 1968-71; Councillor, British Em-

bassy, Prague, 1972-74; Head, South West European Dept FCO, 1974-75; Principal Private Secretary to Secretary of State, 1975; Head, Sciences and Technology Dept. FCO, 1976-77; Fellow, Center for International Affairs, Harvard University, 1977-78; Councillor, British Embassy, Ankara, 1978-81; Councillor, Tehran, 1981; Director of Communications and Technical Services, 1981-. *Hobbies:* Reading; Climbing. *Address:* 9 Beaufort Gardens, London, England.

BARROW, Errol Walton, b. 21 Jan. 1920, Barbados, west Indies. Barrister-at-Law. m. Carolyn Plaskett, 18 Nov. 1945, 1 son, 1 daughter. *Education:* University of London, LSE; BSc, 1950; Lincoln's Inn, Barrister, 1949; Queens Counsel. *Appointments:* Private Law Practice, 1950-61; Premier, Barbados, 196166; Prime Minister, 1966-76; Leader of Opposition, 1978-. *Memberships:* Democratic Labour Party, 1956-; Royal Economic Society. *Publications:* Democracy and Development, 1979; What Canada can do for the West Indies Institute of International Affairs, Canada, 1964. *Honours:* LL.D. McGill University, Canada, 1967; LL.D. Sussex University, England, 1970; Privy Counsellor, England, 1969; Fellow, London School of Economics, 1974. *Hobbies:* Flying; Sailing. *Address:* P O Box 125, Bridgetown, Barbardos, West Indies.

BARRY, Grahame Maxwell, b. 23 Oct. 1930, Sydney, Australia. Physician. m. Brenda Anita Major, 5 Sept. 1965, 3 daughters. *Education:* BA, 1950, MB, BS, 1955, Sydney University; DCH, Royal College of Physicians & Surgeons, 1963. *Appointments:* Royal North Shore Hospital of Sydney, 1956; Townsville General Hospital, 1957; DC General Hospital, Washington, DC, 1958; Princess Margaret Hospital, Nassau, Bahamas, 1959-63; Private Practice (Bahamas), 1964-79; Retired. *Memberships:* Secretary, 1964-69, President, 1970-74, Bahamas Lawn Tennis Association; Vice President, 1971-74, Commonwealth Carribbean Lawn Tennis Association; International Oceanographic Foundation; Consultant and Medical Adviser, Dive-Med. International; I.B.A.; Undersea Medical Society. *Publications:* Occasional articles in medical, diving and sporting publications. *Honours:* Blue in athletics, Sydney University, 1955; Community Service Award. *Hobbies:* Squash; Golf; Tennis; Scuba Diving; Photography; Philately. *Address:* 4 Tryon Ave, Wollstonecraft, NSW 2065, Australia.

BARWICK, Garfield Edward John, b. 22 June 1903, Stanmore, NSW, Australia. Law. m. Norma Mountier Symons, 23 Mar. 1929, 1 son, 1 daughter. *Education:* BA, 1923, LL.B, 1926, LL.D, 1972 (Hon.), University of Sydney. *Appointments:* Admitted to NSW Bar, 1927; KC, 1941; Victorian Bar, 1945; KC, 1945; Queensland Bar, 1958; QC, 1958; MHR for Parramatta, NSW, 1958-64; Commonwealth Attorney-General, 1958-64; Minister for External Affairs, 1961-64; Chief Justice of Australia, 1964-81; Chancellor, Macquarie University, NSW, 1967-78; Judge Ad Hoc, International Court of Justice, 1973 and 1974. *Memberships:* President, Australian Institute of International Affairs, 1972-; President, NSW Institute for Deaf and Blind Children, 1976-, Vice-President, 1966-76; President, Australian Conservation Foundation, 1965-71, Vice-President, 1971-73. *Publications:* Contributions to Commonwealth Law Reports. *Honours:* University Medal and Dalley Prize, 1926; Kt, 1953; PC, 1964; GCMG, 1965; AK, 1981. *Hobbies:* Gardening; Yachting. *Address:* 133 George Street, Careel Bay, NSW 2107, Australia.

BASHFORD, Victor Gwynne, b. 24 July 1918, Swansea, South Wales. Polytechnic Lecturer. m. Gladys May Taylor, 17 Aug. 1946, 2 sons, 1 daughter. *Education:* BSc, 1st Class Hons. Chemistry, 1939, MSc, 1941, PhD, 1947, Birmingham University. *Appointments:* ICI (Explosives) Limited, 1940-43; British Schering Limited, 1943-45; Ontario Research Foundation, 1947-49; Monsanto Chemicals Limited, 1949-54; Hardman & Holden Company Limited, 1954-60; Turner Brothers Asbestos Company Limited, 1960-66; John Dalton College of Technology, 1966-70; Manchester Polytechnic, 1970-. *Memberships:* Chairman of Pennine Training Area of N. Golden Retreiver Association; Porthmadog Yachting Club; Retriever S.C.I; Plastics & Rubber Institute. *Publications:* Papers in: J. Society Chemical Ind, J.C.S., Nature, J. Applied Polymers; Six Patents. *Honours:* University Research Scholarship, Birmingham University, 1939. *Hobbies:* Gun-Dog

Training; Gun-Dog Breeding; Sailing; Antiques. *Address:* 12 Whalley Ave, Sale, Manchester, England.

BASKIVILLE-ROBINSON, Victor Graham, b. 11 Nov. 1918, Auckland, New Zealand. Company Director. m. Joyce Elsie Sime, 4 Sept. 1943, 2 sons. *Education:* Seddon Memorial Technical Night School, Auckland. *Appointments:* Farmers Trading Company, Auckland, 1935-36; Abbott, Armstrong and Howie, Auckland, 1936-39; RNZAF, 1939; Officer commanding Movements Unit, Auckland, 1946-48; Senior Equipment Officer, Hobsonville, 1948-51; Exchange Duty RAAF 1951-53; Staff Officer, Air Depot, 1953-56; Chief Equipment Officer Te Rapa, 1956-57; Commanding Officer, Weedons, 1957-59; Qualified RNZAF Staff College, 1959; Senior Equipment Officer, Wigram, 1959-61; Commanding Officer, Te Rapa, 1961-63; Senior Equipment Officer, NZDS, Washington DC, 1964-69; Managing Director, Pacific Logistics Limited, 1969-. *Memberships:* Secretary, St. Albans Cricket Club, 1960-61; Northern Districts Cricket Association Exec. 1962-63; Paraparaumu & Waikanae Golf Clubs. *Honours:* MBE, 1947; Wing Commander RNZAF. (Retired, 1969). *Hobbies:* Golf; Gardening. *Address:* 15 Tui Crescent, Waikanae, New Zealand.

BASS, Harry Godfrey Mitchell, b. 26 Aug. 1914, Rainford, Lancashire. Diplomat (retired). m. Monica Mary Burroughs, 22 April 1948, 2 sons, 1 daughter. *Education:* Gonville and Caius College, Cambridge; BA, 1937, Marlborough College, MA 1940, St. Johns College, Oxford. *Appointments:* British Museum, Department of Egyptian and Assyian Antiquities, 1939-40; Admiralty, 1940-46; Dominions Office, Commonwealth Relations Office, Commonwealth Office, Foreign and Commonwealth Office, 1946-73; Assistant Secretary, Canberra, 1948-50; Counsellor, Calcutta, 1954-57; DHC, Salisbury, 1959-61; DHC, later Minister, South Africa, 1961-62; DHC, Ibidan, 1965-67; High Commissioner, Lesotho, 1970-73; Retired, 1973; Chapter Clerk, St. Georges Chapel, Windsor Castle, 1974-77. *Memberships:* Royal Commonwealth Society; British Ornithologists' Union. *Honours:* CMG, 1972; Jubilee Medal, 1977. *Hobbies:* Birdwatching; Gardening. *Address:* Tyler's Mead, Deneham Road, Deerham, Norfolk, England.

BASSETT, George William, b. 26 Mar. 1910, Orange, New South Wales, Australia. University Professor. m. Phyllis Adriana Breakwell, 29 Dec. 1934, 2 daughters. *Education:* BA, 1929, Dip.Ed, 1930, MA, 1932, Sydney University; PhD, 1940, London University. *Appointments:* Teacher, New South Wales, Department of Education, 1930-42; Lecturer, Sydney Teachers College, 1943-47; Principal, Armidale Teachers College, 1948-60; Professor, Education University of Queensland, 1961-80. *Memberships:* Australian College of Education, National President, 1967-68; Queensland, Australian, and Commonwealth Council for Educational Administration; Queensland Institute for Educational Research, President, 1962-63. *Publications:* Headmasters for Better Schools, 1963; Each One is Different, 1965; Teaching in the Primary School, 1967; Planning in Australian Education, 1970; Innovation in Primary Education, 1971; Primary Education in Australia, 1974; Individual Differences, 1978. *Honours:* Canadian Commonwealth Fellow, 1965; Fellow of the Royal College of Arts, 1970; Fellow of the Queensland Institute of Educational Admin, 1978; Honorary Fellow, Australian College of Education, 1978; Order of Australia, 1979; Mackie Medal, 1980. *Hobby:* Gardening. *Address:* 23 River Crescent, Cypress Gardens, Queensland, Australia.

BASSETT, , John Walter, b. 6 June 1925, Birmingham, England. Chartered Engineer. m. Ivy Ethel Mason 23 Aug. 1947, 1 son. *Education:* Part-time, Aston and Handsworth Technical Colleges, 1940-50; Studied, Higher National Certificate, CGLI Certificates etc. for Corporate membership of Professional Engineering Institutions. *Appointments:* Engineering Apprenticeship with Birlec Limited, Furnace Manufacturers, 1940-46; Furnace Design Draughtsman, Birlec Limited, 1946-48; Furnace Design Engineer, Metals Division, ICI Limited, 1948-59; Design Engineer, AWRE, Aldermaston, 1959-61; Senior Engineer, Metals/Imperial Metal Industries, ICI, 1961-71; Consultant Engineer, Tom Martin Metal Group, 1971-73; Present Divisional Mechanical Engineer, Delta Group, 1973-. *Memberships:* Fellow, Institution of Mechanical

Engineers; Institute of Energy; Institution of Nuclear Engineers; Institution of Refractories Engineers; Fellow of Royal Society of Arts; Black Country Energy Managers Group Committee. *Publications:* An Introduction to Furnace Design, 1950; Some Heat Treatment Problems of Non-Ferrous Metals, 1965; A Users Approach To A New Furnace Installation 1967; Part-time Lecturer at Technical College, 1947-56 and 1964-66. *Honours:* Awarded Institution of Mechanical Engineers Graduates Prize for Paper, 1950. *Hobbies:* Target Pistol Shooting; Gardening. *Address:* 72 Grange Road Erdington, Birmingham B24 0DF, England.

BASSETT, Michael Edward Rainton, b. 28 Aug. 1938, Auckland, New Zealand. University Teacher; Member of Parliament. m. Judith Ola Petrie, 17 Oct. 1964, 1 son, 1 daughter. *Education:* MA(Hons) University of Auckland, 1961; PhD Duke University 1963. *Appointments:* Lecturer, 1964-72, Senior Lecturer, University of Auckland, 1976-78; Member of Parliament, 1972-75 and 1978-. *Memberships:* Organisation of American Historians; Commonwealth Parliamentary Association. *Publications:* Confrontation '51, 1972; The Third Labour Government, 1976; Getting Together Again, 1979; Plus, Two school Text Books. *Honours:* James B Duke Fellowship 1961-63; American Council of Learned Societies, Scholar, 1967. *Hobbies:* Fishing; Gardening. *Address:* 17 Stilwell Road Auckland 3, New Zealand.

BASSETT, Michael Lindsey, b. 2 Feb. 1949, Erdington, Birmingham, United Kingdom. Doctor of Chiropractic. m. Rita Helen, 2 May 1981. 1 son, previous marriage. *Education:* DC awarded by Anglo European College of Chiropractic. *Appointments:* Private Practice; Outside Lecturer, Anglo European College of Chiropractic. *Memberships:* British Chiropractic Association; European Chiropractic Union; American Chiropractic Association; West Herts Golf Club. *Publications:* Doctoral Thesis: Cervical Spondylosis. *Hobbies:* Photography; Horticulture; Golf. *Address:* 19 Beaconsfield Road, St Albans, Herts, England.

BASTARACHE, J E Michel, b. 10 June 1947, Quebec, Canada. Dean of Law. m. Yolande Martin, 17 Aug. 1968, 1 son, 1 daughter. *Education:* BA, University of Moncton, 1967; LL.L., University of montreal, 1970; DES, University of Nice, 1972; LL.B., University of Ottawa, 1978. *Appointments:* Legal translator, Department of Justice, Province of New Brunswick; Vice-President, Marketing, Assumption Mutual Life Company, Moncton, N.B., Canada; Professor of Law, Dean of Law, University of Moncton, N.B., Canada. *Memberships:* Barristers' Society of New Brunswick; Canadian Bar Association; International Bar; Canadian Council on International Law; Canadian Institute of International Affairs; Canadian Law Teachers Association; Quebec Law Teachers Association; Canadian Law Deans; Corporation of Translators and Interpretors of New Brunswick. *Publications:* Founder of a political review entitled, Egalité; Many articles on constitutional law, public international law and Canadian politics; A legal vocabulary of the law of property (in co-operation); Two major studies on language rights in New Brunswick. *Honours:* Membre, Ordre des Francophones d'Amérique. *Hobbies:* Photography; Tennis; Squash. *Address:* 206 Bromley Avenue, Moncton, New Brunswick, E1 C5 V6, Canada.

BASU, Prahlad Kumar, b. 16 Dec. 1931, Bankura, India. Director General; Permanent Secretary. m. Aparna Mehta, 10 May 1959, 2 daughters. *Education:* BA Economics(Hons) (First Class) Presidency College, Calcutta University, 1951; BA(Cantab) Economics Tripos, King's College, University of Cambridge, UK, 1954; MA(Cantab) University of Cambridge, 1957. *Appointments:* Under Secretary/Special Officer for Aircraft Production, Ministry of Defence, Department of Defence Production, Government of India, 1962-64; Secretary, Bokaro Steel Corporation, 1964-67; Director, Bureau of Public Enterprises, 1967-72; Executive Director and full-time member, Board of Directors, Shipping Corporation of India, 1972-75; Joint Secretary, Department of Expenditure, Ministry of Finance, 1975-76; UN International Civil Service Staff and Development Economist-cum-Administration Expert, Asian and Pacific Development Administration Centre, Kuala Lumpur, 1976-79; Director General, Bureau of Public Enterprises and concurrently Additional Permanent Secretary, Ministry of Finance, Government of India,

1979-. *Memberships:* Visiting Professor of Economics and PhD Examiner, University of Minnesota, USA, 1971; Visiting Faculty Member, Harvard University-/DAS International Workshop on Public Enterprises 1973; Visiting Faculty, Institut International D'Administration Publique, Paris 1977; Member of High Table, King's College, Cambridge 1978; Board of Governors, Indian Institute of Management at Calcutta and Ahmedabad 1967-73 and 1979-; Council of Management, All India Management Association 1979-; Governing Body, Indian Statistical Institute 1974-75; Executive Board, Standing Conference of Public Enterprises 1979-; Governing Council, International Centre for Public Enterprises, Ljubljana, Yugoslavia, 1979-; Governing Body, Himalayan Mountaineering Institute, Darjeeling, India; Governing Body, National Productivity Council of India; Governing Body, Institute of Public Enterprise, Hyderabad, India. *Publications:* Public Enterprise Policy on Investment, Pricing and Returns, 1979; Approaches to Public Enterprise Policy in Asia on Investment, Prices and Returns Criteria, 1976; Towards a New Managerial Order in Asia, 1977. *Honours:* Awarded Overbrook Fellow, Yale Graduate School of Economics, USA 1954; Political Economy Club, Cambridge, 1953-54 *Hobbies:* European and Indian Classical Music; Golf. *Address:* 4, Lodhi Gardens, New Delhi-110003, India.

BATES, David Robert, b. 18 Nov. 1916, Omagh, Co. Tyrone, Northern Ireland. University Professor. m. Barbara Bailey Morris, 20 Mar. 1956, 1 son, 1 daughter. *Education:* MSc, Queen's University, Belfast, 1938; DSc, University College, London, 1950. *Appointments:* Admiralty Research Laboratory, Teddington, 1939-41; Mine Design Department of HMS Vernon, 1941-45; Lecturer in Mathematics, University College London, 1945-50; Consultant, US Naval Ordnance Test Station, Inyokern, California, 1950; Professor, Department of Applied Mathematics and Theoretical Physics, 1951-; Regent's Fellow, Smithsonian Astrophysics Observatory, Cambridge, Mass., 1982. *Memberships:* FRS; MRIA; Hon. Foreign Member Americaan Academy Arts, Science; Associate Royal Academy of Belgium. *Publications:* Scientific Papers. *Honours:* Hughes Medal, Royal Society, 1970; Chree Medal, Institute Physics, 1973; Gold Medal Royal Astronomical Society, 1977; Knighted, 1978. *Hobbies:* Reading; Listening to Radio. *Address:* Newforge Close, Belfast BT9 5JT Northern Ireland.

BATES, Lionel Henry, b. 14 Oct. 1933, Perth, West Australia. Architect. m. Eileen Emily Newcombe, 10 Mar. 1956, 2 sons. *Education:* Perth Technical College, 1955. *Appointments:* Cadet Architect, 1951-55, Senior Architect, 1958-63, Supervising Architect, 1964-72, Chief Architect (Defence), 1973-77, Department of Construction; Director General, Tasmanian Government, Department of Housing and Construction, 1977-. *Memberships:* Fellow, Royal Australian Institute of Architects; Associate Fellow, Australian Institute of Management. *Publications:* Various Government/Departmental projects, reports, texts, lectures. *Honours:* RAIA, Student Award, 1956. *Hobbies:* Building; Gardening; Lawn Bowls; Public Speaking; Reading. *Address:* 19 Karingal Court, Taroona, Tasmania, Australia.

BATES, Richard Heaton Tunstall, b. 8 July 1929, Sheffield, England. Engineering Scientist. m. Philippa Harding, 10 July 1954, 3 sons, 1 daughter. *Education:* Wellington College, Berkshire, England 1943-47; University College, University of London, 1949-52; BSc Engineering, 1952; DSc Engineering, 1972. *Appointments:* Research/Development Engineer, Vickers Armstrongs, Decca Radar, Canadian Westinghouse, United Kingdom and Canada, 1952-59; Systems Engineer, National Corporation, Mitre Corporation, Sperry-Rand Rsearch Center, USA 1960-66; Senior Lecturer, Engineering School, University of Canterbury, Christchurch, 1967, Reader 1969, Professor with Personal Chair 1975. *Memberships:* New Zealand Mathematics Society; New Zealand Institution of Engineers; Australasian College of Physical Scientists in Medicine; Optical Society of America; Fellow: Institution of Electrical Engineers, London; Institute of Electrical and Electronics Engineers, New York; Royal Society of New Zealand. *Publications:* Over 150 major reports, contributions to Conference proceedings and papers in internatonal learned journals. *Honours:* FRSNZ 1976; Fellow IEEE 1980; Cooper Memorial Award of Royal Society NZ 1980; UK Science Research

Council Senior Visiting Fellowship, Imperial College 1973/4; Erskine Travelling Fellowship, University of Canterbury 1977; Humanities and Social Sciences Research Council of Canada Visiting Foreign Lectureship 1979; Thomas Alvin Boyd Lecturer of Ohio State University 1979; Distinguished Visiting Scholar, University of Adelaide 1980. *Hobbies:* Dry-fly fishing; Tramping; Concert/Theatre. *Address:* Electrical Engineering Department, University of Canterbury, Christchurch, New Zealand.

BATLEY, Robert Anthony Leighton, b. 15 Sept. 1923, Taihape, New Zealand. Farmer; Company Director. m. Margaret Winifred Green, 11 Oct. 1947, 2 sons, 1 daughter. *Education:* Wanganui Collegiate School, 1938-40. *Appointments:* Managing Director, Batleys Limited. *Memberships:* Council Member, Polynesian Society Inc., since 1955; Representative, Royal Society of New Zealand on New Zealand Historic Places Trust, 1961-68; President, New Zealand Archaeological Association, 1967-69; Kaimanawa-Kaweka State Forest Park Advisory Committee, 1973-; Inland Patea Regional Filekeeper, New Zealand Archaeological Association Site Recording Scheme. *Publications:* Author, Moawhango Valley and School—A Short History of the Inland Patea, 1958; Papers on Archaeology, Maori Traditions and Natural History. *Hobbies:* Maori History, Archaeology and Ecology in the Central North Island, New Zealand; Established Motumatai Private Scenic Reserve in 1974 for protection of native flora and fauna; Preservation and Ecology of New Zealand Feral Horses. *Address:* The Homestead, Moawhango, Taihape, New Zealand.

BATSA, Kofi, b. 8 Jan. 1931, Odumase Krobo, Ghana. Publisher; Journalist; Politician. m. Georgina Aya, 2 sons, 3 daughters. *Education:* Read Journalism, Economics, Politics, 1945-52. *Appointments:* Newspapers: Takoradi Times, Ashanti Times, Ashanti Pioneer, 1953-59; Editor, The Spark, 1960; Editor-in-Chief, Voice of Africa 1966; Secretary General, All-African Union of Journalists 1964-67; Secretary General, Co-ordinating Secretariat of Inter-African Unions, in the field of Mass Communication. *Memberships:* Central Committee of People's National Party; Council of Elders; Chairman, Publicity Committee, PNP; Adviser on Political Matters to the President of Ghana, Ruling Party; Chairman, Ghana Industrial Holding Corporation; National Development Commission; Ghana Press Commission. *Publications:* Some Essential Features in the Teachings of Kwane Mkrumal. *Honours:* World Prize for Journalism by International Union of Journalists 1965. *Hobbies:* Football. *Address:* PO Box 346, Accra, Ghana.

BATT, John Michael, b. 22 Sept. 1935, Melbourne, Victoria, Australia. Barrister. m. Margaret Elizabeth Hodgkinson, 31 Aug. 1968, 1 son, 1 daughter. *Education:* University of Melbourne, 1954-59; Trinity College 1954-57; BA(Hons.) 1958; Wyselaskie Scholarship in Classical and Comparative Philology and Logic, 1957; LLB(Hons) 1960; Co-Editor, Melbourne University Law Review, 1958-59. *Appointments:* Barrister and Solicitor, Victoria, 1961; Articled clerk, Oswald Burt and Company, Solicitors, Melbourne, 1960-61; Victorian Bar, 1961-; Barrister, New South Wales, 1964; Barrister, Tasmania, 1966; Queen's Counsel, Victoria, 1977-, New South Wales and Tasmania, 1978-. *Memberships:* Director, Barristers' Chambers Limited; Management, The Mission of St. James and St. John, 1976-; 1971-80; Melbourne Club; RACV; Melbourne Cricket Club. *Hobbies:* Languages. *Address:* 16 Mayfield Avenue, Malvern, Victoria, Australia.

BATTEN, Jean Gardner, b. 15 Sept. 1909, Rotorua New Zealand. Airwoman, Long-distance air pioneer. *Education:* Cleveland House College, Auckland NZ; Gained Private Pilots Licence, London Aeroplane Club, 1930; Commercial Pilots Licence 1932. *Memberships:* Liveryman of Guild of Air Pilots and Air Navigators London, 1978; Jean Batten Archive, established at Royal Air Force Museum, Hendon, London, 1972. *Publications:* Solo Flight, 1934; My Life, 1938; republished 1979 with new title, Alone in the Sky. *Honours:* Officer of Order of Southern Cross, Brazil, 1935; Chevalier, Legion of Honour, France, 1936; Commander of Order of British Empire, 1936; First woman to receive medal of Federation Aeronautique International 1938; Britannia Trophy 1935 and 1936; Harmon International Trophy, USA 1935, 1936, 1937; Segrave Trophy; Great Britain awarded for greatest demonstration of possibilities of transport on land, water or in the air, 1936; City of Paris medal 1972; Received Freedom of the City of London, 1978; Opened National Bank in Jean Batten Place, Auckland, 1979; Brittania Airways named one of its Boeing 737 Airliners Jean Batten, 1980. *Hobbies:* Travel; Music; Swimming and walking. *Address:* c/o Barclays Bank Limited, 25 Charing Cross Road, London, WC2H OHZ, England.

BATTERSBY, Jean Agnes, b. 12 Mar. 1928 Drouin, Victoria, Australia. Arts Administrator. m. 11 Feb. 1950, 1 daughter. *Education:* BA, University of Melbourne, 1947; MA 1949; PhD 1954. *Appointments:* Lecturer, Canberra University College and Melbourne University, 1950; Freelance writer, broadcaster, television compere and contributor, 1958-; Project Officer, HRH The Duke of Edinburgh's Third Commonwealth Study Conference, 1966-68; Executive Officer, Australia Council for the Arts, 1968-72; Executive Officer and Chief Executive Officer, Australia Council, 1972; Vice-Chairman, Commonwealth Arts Organisation. *Memberships.* The Commonwealth Club, Canberra. *Publications:* The Arts Council Phenomenon; Cultural Policy in Australia; Teenagers in 10 Years of Television. *Honours:* Research Scholar, University of Melbourne, 1951-54; Travelling Fellowship from French Government, Centre Universitaire Internationale, Paris, 1956; L'ordre des Palmes Academiques, 1973. *Hobbies:* Sport. *Address:* 91 Cutler Road, Clontarf, New South Wales 2093, Australia.

BATUMA. Seduraka John. b. 1 Feb. 1929. Bubare. Kigezi, Uganda. Businessman. m. Beatrice Mary Keirungi, 17 Jan. 1953, 4 sons, 4 daughters.*Education:* Bubare Primary School, 1938-41; Kigezi High School, 1942-49; Veterinary Training Institute, Entebbe, Uganda, 1950-53; Poultry husbandry in Israel, 1963-. *Appointments:* Assistant & Senior Veterinary Assistant, 1953-67; Managing Director, Kigezi African Wholesale Company Ltd., 1967-. *Memberships:* Ex-Director, National Trading Corporation; Ex-Director, Uganda Dairy Corporation; National Transport Licencing Board; Director, National Tobacco Corporation; Chairman, District Chamber of Commerce, Kabale; Chairman, Dairy Co-operative Society, Kabale. *Honours:* Winner of Farmers Competition, 1970-71; Awarded Independence Medal. *Hobbies:* Music recording, swimming, Football, (watching & organising).*Address:* P.O. Box 95, Kebale, Uganda.

BAUME, Michael Ehrenfried, b. 6 July 1930, Sydney, New South Wales. Member of Parliament. m. Brigid Tancred, 22 Feb. 1963, 3 sons. *Education:* B.A. Sydney University, 1951-. *Appointments:* Financial Editor of: Australian Financial Review, 1963-66, "The Bulletin" Magazina, 1966-69; TV Panellist, ABC's "Would You Believe", 1970-74; ABC Radio Commentator on business, 1968-72; Member of Parliament for Federal Seat of Macarthur, 1975-. *Memberships:* Australian Society of Security Analysis; Australian Journalists Association; Councillor, Musiva Viva Australia, 1974-76. *Publications:* The Sydney Opera House Affair, 1967-. *Hobbies:* Tennis, cricket, skiing. *Address:* No 4 The Courtyard Houses, Charles Avenue, Minnamurra, N S W. 2532, Australia.

BAVAKUTTY, M b. 15 July 1946, Ponani, Kerala. Librarian and Teacher of Library Science. m. Zeenath, E. K, 25 May 1975, 1 son, 1 daughter. *Education:* BSc, 1967, BLibSc, 1969, University of Kerala; MLibSc, University of Delhi, 1970. *Appointments:* Librarian, MES Ponnani College, Ponani, 1969-70, Farook College, Calicut, 1970-72; Lecturer in Library Science, University of Kerala, Trivandrum, 1972-77; University Librarian & Head of the Department of Library Science, University of Calicut, Kerala, 1977-. *Memberships:* Kerala Library Association; Indian Library Association; Indian Association of Special Libraries and Information Centres. *Publications:* Published 30 Professional Articles and a Book on Library Classification. *Hobbies:* Reading; Gardening. *Address:* Lal Bhavan, Kohinoor, PO Thenhippalam, Malappuram District, Kerala, S India

BAWDEN, Thomas Arthur, b. 7 Feb. 1941, Douglas, Isle of Man. Legislative Officer. m. Rose Mary Marler, 21 Dec. 1968, 1 son, 1 daughter. *Education:* Douglas High School for Boys, 1952-59. *Appointments:* Isle of Man Civil Service, 1959-; Clerk to H.M. Second Deemster, 1963-66; Clark to H.M. First Deemster and

Clerk of the Rolls, 1966-76; Clerk of the Legislative Council, Clerk Assistant of Tynwald and Deputy Secretary of the House of Keys, 1977-; Secretary Isle of Man Law Revision Commission, 1966-76; Secretary Isle of Man Income Tax Commissioners, 1966-76. *Memberships:* Deputy Secretary, Commonwealth Parliamentary Association (Isle of Man Branch); Society of Clerks-at-the-Table in Commonwealth Parliaments; Secretary (Field section) Isle of Man Natural History and Antiquarian Society, 1969-71; Attended Commonwealth Parliamentary Association Regional Conferences, Guernsey, 1978-, Isle of Man, 1979-. *Publications:* Co-Author, The Industrial Archaeology of the Isle of Man, 1979-; Editor, The Statutes of the Isle of Man, 1960-65; Compiler, The Tynwald Companion, 1980-81; Contributions to various journals etc. *Address:* 56 Glenfaba Road, Peel, Isle of Man.

BAWLA, Ahmed, b. 11 June 1938, Bombay. Businessman. m. Qamar Jehan, 9 Aug. 1964, 2 sons, 1 daughter. *Education:* Bachelor of Technology, Electrical Engineering with Honours, 1962-; Post-Graduate Certificate, Statistical Quality Control, 1963-. *Appointments:* Production Engineer and Chief Engineer, Electric Fan Manufacturing Industry, Pakistan, 1962-67; Chief Electric Motor Production, Siemens Engineering Company Limited, Karachi, Pakistan, 1967-73; Own business in Partnerships with brothers in Pakistan and Dubai and established M/S Saya Hong Limited, in Hong Kong, 1973-, and Managing Director, 1975-. *Memberships:* Karachi Club and Karachi Gymkhano. *Publications:* Modification and design of Electric Fan. Developed and produced higher Horse Power Motors in Pakistan. *Honours:* Honours degree from Indian Institute of Technology, Bombay, 1962-. *Hobbies:* Sports, Music and large scale business. *Address:* 1-11 Tak Shing Street Hong Yuen Court, Block A A4, 2nd Floor, Kowloon, Hong Kong.

BAXTER, Authur Charles, b. 15 Feb. 1921, Australia. Hospital Administrator. m. Joyce Mabel Nicholls, 12 Apr. 1947. 3 daughters. *Education:* F.A.I.M.; L.M.R.S.H. *Appointments:* Canowindra Soldiers Memorial Hospital, 1961-67; The Governor, Phillip Special Hospital, Penreth, 1967-. *Memberships:* President, Australian Association of Gerontology, NSW Division; State Branch Counsellor, Australia Hospitals Association; Honorary Secretary, Mobile Meals Committee; Penrith City Council, Aged Persons Housing Committee; Community Advisory Committee, Penrith Legal Services. *Honours:* Overseas Study Leave Scholarship, U.K. & Europe, 1975-; 10th World Congress on Gerontology; Awarded Scholarship, 1978-, Present Paper 11th World Congress on Gerontology, Tokyo, Japan. *Hobbies:* Fishing, Gardening. *Address:* 30 Sheba Crescent, Penrith, New South Wales, Australia.

BAXTER, Denis Charles Trevor, b. 1 Mar. 1936, Southsea, Hampshire. English Language Tutor. *Education:* Dorset Farm Institute, 1954-55; Stockwell College of Education, 1965-68. *Appointments:* Assistant, Rubber and Tea Plantation, 1959-62; Manager, Kerala, South India, 1962-64; Teacher of English to Foreign Students, 1968-. *Memberships:* Royal Society of Arts; Printmakers Council; Society of United Artists; Turner Society; Chelsea Art Club; Thomas Hardy Society. *Hobbies:* Reading, Walking, Music, Rural preservation, Steam Train Societies. *Address:* 20 Church Road, Southbourne, Bournemouth, Dorset, BH6 4AT, England.

BAXTER, Laurence Henry, b. 26 Mar. 1923, Grantham, Lincolnshire. Technical College, Head of Department. m. June Louisa Gowland, 21 July 1951, 1 son, 2 daughters. *Education:* BSc (Engineering Metallurgy), University of London, 1949-; Member of Institution of Metallurgists, 1949-; Chartered Engineer, 1978-; Fellow of Institute of Ceramics, 1977-. *Appointments:* Metallurgical Apprentice, Ruston & Hornsby Limited, Grantham, 1939-45; Metallurgist, 1945-46; Head Metallurgist, 1946-50; Lecturer in Metallurgy, Nottingham & District Technical College, 1950-52; Senior Lecturer, Cumberland Technical College, 1952-68; Head of Department of Metallurgy, Science & Mathematics, Rotherham College of Arts & Technology, 1968-. *Memberships:* Founder Secretary, Cumbria Metallurgical Society, 1960-68; Chairman of County Advisory Committee for Metallurgy, Yorkshire & Humberside, Council for Further Education, 1978-; Institute of Ceramics Education Committee, 1977-; Institute of Ceramics Membership Committe, 1977-. *Hobbies:*

Photography, Angling. *Address:* The Willows, 2 Toad Lane, Brampton-en-le-Morthen, Rotheram, South Yorkshire, S66 9BG, England.

BAYLOR, Hilda Gracia, b. 8 Oct. 1929, Brisbane, Queensland. Member of Parliament. m. Richard Patrick, 23 Mar. 1959, 3 sons, 1 daughter. *Education:* Diploma Fine Arts, 1948-. *Appointments:* Secondary School Teacher, 1949-58; Voluntary Community worker, 1960-79. *Memberships:* Liberal Party, Victorian Division; Victorian Local Government Women's Association; Commonwealth Parliamentary Association. *Hobbies:* Reading, gardening and gourmet cooking. *Address:* 110 Badger Creek Road, Healesville, 3777, Victoria, Australia.

BAYLY, Kenneth Leslie, b. 14 Jan. 1936, Melbourne, Australia. Principal. *Education:* T.Mus.A, Melbourne Conservatorium of Music, 1968; TPTC, Melbourne State College, 1954. *Appointments:* Victorian Education Department, 1955-. *Memberships:* National Commissioner for Leader Training, Scout Association of Australia, 1976-; Asia Pacific Training Committee, Scout Association. *Publications:* Published 80 songs for Youth Groups. *Honours:* Award for Especially Distinguished Service, Scout Association, 1977. *Hobbies:* Production Director of the "Melbourne Gang Show" Piano and Organ; Music Composition. *Address:* 2 Wood Street, Strathmore, Melbourne, Australia.

BAYMAN, Irene. b. Wigan, Lancashire, England. Specialist Teacher of Art and Crafts. *Education:* Private School, Wigan; Teacher Training, Manchester; Art & Craft Training, School of Art & Craft, Technical College, Wigan. *Appointments:* Junior Schools, Wigan; Head of Department, Co-Educational Grammar School, Eccles, Manchester; Head of Department, Secondary Modern, Manchester Road, Leigh, Lancashire. *Memberships:* Lancashire Rural Studies Association; National Society for Art Education; International Arts Guild (Monaco); International Biographical Association (Cambridge). *Publications:* Exhibition of pictures in Preston, London and Monte Carlo; Colour Slide Exhibitions with talks on Sardinia, Iceland, Malta, Yugoslavia etc. Short Talks for Radio Merseyside. *Honours:* General Art Work & Fabric Printing, 1942-44; Diploma of Honour, International Arts Guild, Monaco, 1976-. *Hobbies:* Gardening, Reading, Music, Travel, Antiques, Outer Space Research. *Address:* 7 Elmfield Road, Wigan, WN1 2RG, England.

BBALE-MUGERA, Vincent Rick, b. 21 July 1944, Masaka, Uganda. Accountant/Economist. m. Princess Ann Sarah Kagere, 9 Nov. 1974, 1 son, 3 daughters. *Education:* Bachelor of Ecnomics and Accountancy (Honours), University of East Africa, Makerere College, 1970-; *Appointments:* Principal Accountant, E.A. Posts & Telcoms Corporation, 1974-; Chief Accountant, Uganda P & T. Corporation, 1978-. *Memberships:* Uganda Institute of Management; The Lions Club, International. *Honours:* Certificate of Merit, in English Language. *Hobbies:* Table Tennis; Travelling. *Address:* P.O. Box 85, Kampala, Uganda, East Africa.

BEADLE, Stanley Leslie, b. 21 Oct. 1913, London. Retired. m. Elsie Florence Woodard-Knight, 1 Mar. 1936, 3 daughters. *Education:* Bolt Court School of Graphic Arts, London, 1928-33; Camberwell School of Art, London, 1928-33. *Appointments:* Lithographic Artist, apprentice, 1928-33; after apprenticeship, Johnson, Riddle & Company, London, 1933-37; Reproduction Artist, Henry Hildesley, London, 1937-40; War Service, Air Force, 1940-45; Lithographic Reproduction Manager, Photoplate Limited, 1945-53; Emigrated to South Australia, 1953-; Adelaide Art Engravers, 1953-55; Reproduction Manager, Vardon Price, 1955-63; Manager, Lithoplate Makers, 1963-76. *Memberships:* Royal South Australian Society of Arts Incorporated; Mr. Lofty Ranges Art Society; Adelaide Art Society; Masonic Society; *Publications:* Editor of Kalori, official Journals of the Royal Society of Arts; Watercolours and Pastels in private collections in England, Canada & Australia. *Honours:* Royal Society of Arts, Watercolour Prize, 1979-. *Address:* 34 Eden Avenue, Bellevue Heights, South Australia, 5050.

BEALE (Honourable), Jack Gordon, b. 17 July 1917, Sydney, Australia. m. Stephania Toth-Dobrzanski, 9 Sept. 1958, 2 sons. *Education:* Diploma in Mechanical Engineering, with Honours, Sydney Technical College, 1939-; Associate Sydney Technical College, 1939-; Master of Engineering Degree, School of Civil Engineering, University of New South Wales, 1964-; Post Graduate, Engineering and Research Studies, Sydney Technical College, University of California and University of New South Wales, 1940-60. *Appointments:* International Consultant in Environmental Planning, Conservation, Resources Development, Engineering, Management, Environmental Legislation, 1974-; Consulting Chartered Engineer, Australia, 1942-; Minister for Environment Control, Government of New South Wales, 1971-73; Minister for Conservation, Government of New South Wales, 1965-71; Legislative Assembly of New South Wales, 1942-73; Company Director, several private and public companies, 38 years. *Memberships:* Fellow, Institution of Engineers, Australia; American Society of Civil Engineers, Agricultural Engineers and Mechanical Engineers; The Company Directors Association of Australia.. *Publications:* Cyclical Environmental Management System, 1975-; Protection and Management of the Environment, 1975-; The Manager and The Environment, Theory and Practice of Environmental Management, 1980-. *Address:* 95 Elizabeth Bay Road, Elizabeth Bay, New South Wales, 2011, Australia.

BEAMISH, Arthur Philippe, b. 21 Jan. 1924, Australia. Executive Director. m. Enid Jean Gibson, 9 Mar. 1946, 1 son, 1 daughter. *Education:* Diploma in Commerce, University of Melbourne, 1949. *Appointments:* State Savings Bank of Victoria, 1939-57; Royal Australasian College of Surgeons, 1957-61; Victorian Road Transport Association, 1961-. *Memberships:* Australian Chairman, Chartered Institute of Transport; Australian Institute of Management; Society of Association Executives. *Publications:* Returned Services League History; Several transport papers. *Hobbies:* Gardening; Golf. *Address:* 10 Goldthorns Avenue, Kew East 3102, Victoria, Australia.

BEARD, Evelyn Ruth, b. 24 Feb. 1908, Tipton, Staffordshire, England. Insurance Broker. m. Frederick Brentnall, 15 Aug. 1936, 1 son. *Education:* Miss Withers' Private High School for Girls, West Bromwich, Staffordshire. *Appointments:* Phoenix Assurance Company Limited, 1926-36; Founder Member & Executive Director of Brentnall Beard & Company Limited, 1936-; Founder Member, first Secretary and Executive Director of Brentnall Beard (Holdings) Limited, 1969-; Retirement in 1974-; 18 years Voluntary Service on Panel, Appeals Tribunal, DHSS. *Memberships:* Associate of the Chartered Insurance Institute; Fellow of the Corporation of Insurance Brokers; Founder Member & President of the Chinchilla Breeders' Association; Chairman of local Conservative Pary; Lady Captain, Shrewsbury Golf Club; Hawkestone Park and Aberdovey Golf Clubs; Guild of Craft Enamellers, Treasurer, 1979-81; *Honours:* Co-author, with London Zoo and others on book on Care of Chinchillas. *Hobbies:* Piano, Golf, Gardening, Travel, Sewing, Photography, Skiing, Enamelling, Care of small animals, Lecturing. *Address:* Green Lane, Lyth Bank, Nr. Shrewsbury, England, SY3 0BQ.

BEASLEY, Donald Maurice Geddes, b. 10 Apr. 1920, Auckland, New Zealand. Medical Practitioner, Consultant Paediatrician. m. Caroline Lucy Graham, 3 Aug. 1947, 4 sons. *Education:* M.B. Ch.B, Otago, 1946-; Royal Australasian College of Physicians, Member, 1950, Fellow, 1965-; D.C.H. London, 1953-. *Appointments:* House Physician, 1947-49, Registrar, 1950, Auckland Hospital; Lecturer, Child Health, Department of Child Health, Sheffield, England, 1952-53; Junior Specialist, Auckland, 1954-; Consultant Paediatrician, Department Health, Whangarei, 1955-61; Consultant Paediatrician, Northland Hospital Board, Whangarei, 1961-. *Memberships:* Council member, 1966-74, President, International League of Societies for the Mentally Handicapped, Brussels, 1974-78; President, New Zealand Society for the Intellectually Handicapped, 1964-79; Director, Trustee, New Zealand, Institute of Mental Retardation and New Zealand Trust for Intellectually Handicapped Persons; Member Northland Hospital Board, Whangarei, 1971-, Deputy Chairman, 1980-. Fellow, Royal Society of Medicine, London. *Publications:* Numerous papers, publications National & International on Mental Retardation. *Honours:* O.B.E., 1977-. *Hobbies:* Fly fishing, Watching Cricket, 17th Century English History, Music.

Address: 1 Bedlington Street, Whangarei, New Zealand.

BEASLEY, Michael Charles, b. 20 July 1924, Hereford, England. County Treasurer. m. Jean Anita Mary Webber, 18 Nov. 1955, 1 son. *Education:* BSc., Economics Honours, London University, 1948-; IPFA Honours, 1950-; FCA, 1956-; FCCA, 1981-. *Appointments:* East Suffolk County Council; Staffordshire County Council; Glamorgan County Council; Nottinghamshire County Council; Royal County of Berkshire, County Council. *Memberships:* Society of County Treasurers, President, 1981-82, Vice-President, 1980-81, Honorary Secretary, 1971-80. *Publications:* Numerous contributions to journals etc., on local Government Finance & Computers. *Hobbies:* Pottering and Pondering. *Address:* Greenacre, Hyde End Road, Spencers Wood, Berkshire.

BEATH, Terence, b. 27 Oct. 1946, Belmont, New South Wales, Australia. Forester. m. Christine Fay Hicken, 29 May 1976, 3 sons. *Education:* BSc Foreign, Australian National University, Canberra, 1969-; MSc, Australian National University, 1976-. *Appointments:* Forester at Dungog, Bermagui, Bega, Eden & Bombala, Forestry Commission of New South Wales, 1965-80; Wood Production Superintendent, Australian Newsprint Mills Limited, Albury, 1980-. *Memberships:* Institute of Foresters of Australia Incorporated. *Publications:* The Effect of Road Gradient & Load on the Speed of log trucks, MSc Thesis; Co-author with EA Nicholson, Woodchipping at Eden, a catalyst for better Forest Management, 1977. *Hobbies:* Sport, Mens Hockey & Cricket, Coaching & playing both, Gardening. *Address:* 10 Snubba Crescent, Tumuf, New South Wales, 1720, Australia.

BEATTIE (Sir) David Stuart, b. 29 Feb. 1924, Sydney, Australia. Governor General Designate of New Zealand. m. Norma Margaret Sarah MacDonald, 1 Mar. 1950, 3 sons, 4 daughters. *Education:* LL.B. 1948-; Q.C., 1965-. *Appointments:* Barrister; Queens's Council; Judge of Supreme Court. *Memberships:* Chairman, Sir Winston Churchill Special Trust Board. Chairman, Royal Commission on the Courts; Chairman, Admiralty Reform Committee. *Honours:* G.C.M.G., 1980-; Kt. of St. John, 1980-; Q.C. 1965-. *Hobbies:* Golf, Tennis, Fishing, Music. *Address:* 53B Chatsworth Road, Silverstream, Wellington, New Zealand

BEATTIE, John Maxwell, b. 4 Oct. 1932, Melbourne, Victoria. Member of Tasmanian State Parliament. m. Barbara Alison Little, 25 Feb. 1956, 1 son, 3 daughters. *Education:* Friends School Hobart; Diploma Australian Insurance Institute. *Appointments:* Accountant, R. R. Emmett, 1949-52; Commonwealth Bank, 1952-60; AMP Society, 1960-; Member for Franklin, 1972-, Re-elected, 1976, 1979. Represented Tasmanian Parliament, Commonwealth Parliamentary Association Conference, Lusaka, Zambia, 1980. *Memberships:* Past President, Rotary Club, Bellerive; Royal Yacht Club of Tasmania; Motor Yacht Club of Tasmania; *Honours:* Queens Silver Jubilee Medal. *Hobbies:* Boating, Woodwork. *Address:* 52 Esplanade, Lindisfarne, 7015, Tasmania, Australia.

BEAUDOIN, Gérald A, b. 15 Apr. 1929, Montréal, Canada. Professor of Constitutional law; Lawyer. m. Renée Desmarais, 11 Sept. 1954, 4 daughters. *Education:* BA., summa cum laude, 1950, LL.L., Magna cum laude, 1953, MA., 1954, University of Montreal, Canada; DES., Cum laude, University of Ottawa, Canada, 1958. *Appointments:* Practiced law with Paul Gérin-Lajoie, QC of Montreal, Canada, 1955-56; Advisory Counsel, Department of Justice, Ottawa, Canada, 1956-65; Assistant Parliamentary Counsel of the House of Commons of Canada, 1965-69; Civil Law DEAN, University of Ottawa, 1969-79; Professor of Constitutional and parliamentary law; President of Constitutional Section of Canadian Bar Association, 1971-73; Member of Task Force on Canadian Unity (Pépin-Robarts Commission), 1977-79; Member, Goldenberg Committee on the Constitution, 1967. *Memberships:* Quebec Bar; Canadian Bar Association; Royal Society of Canada, 1977; Institut international de droit d'expression française; Cercle universitaire in Ottawa; National Gallery. *Publications:* Essais sur la Constitution, 1979; Le partage des pouvoirs, 1980; 50 articles in Constitutional Law in Canadian and Foreign reviews. *Honours:* Officer of the Order of Canada, 1980;

Queen's Counsel, 1969. *Hobbies:* Travelling; Reading. *Address:* 4 St. Thomas Street, Hull, Quebec, Canada.

BEAUGRAND, Kenneth Louis, b. 19 Oct. 1938, New York, U.S.A. Lawyer and Business Executive. m. Augusta Newell Wood Barnard, 22 Nov. 1969, 2 sons, 1 daughter. *Education:* B.A. Brown University, Providence, Rhode Island, U.S.A. 1960-; LL.B. Columbia Law School, New York, U.S.A. 1963-; LL.M. University of London, England, 1964-. *Appointments:* Willkie, Farr & Gallagher, Solicitors, New York, 1964-68; I.O.S. Limited, Financial Services, Geneva, Switzerland, 1968-72; Solicitor, 1968-69; Secretary, 1969-71; Vice-President, General Counsel and Director, 1971-72; Value Capital Services, Financial Services, Amsterdam, Holland, Vice-President, General Counsel and Director, 1971-72; Aird, Zimmerman & Berlis, Solicitor, 1973-77; Eaton Bay Fanancial Services Limited, Financial Services, Totronto, Ontario, Canada. Vice-President, Secretary and General Counsel, 1977-79 Senior Vice-President and General Counsel, 1979-. *Memberships:* Granite Club, Toronto Lawn Tennis Club; Whiff of Grape. *Hobbies:* Tennis, Squash, Skiing, Sailing, Coaching children's hockey. *Address:* 427 Russell Hill Road, Toronto, Ontario, Canada.

BECK, Gustav Theodor, b. 8 Apr. 1910, Albstadt-Ebingen, West Germany. Managing Director. m. Mary Elizabeth Arundell, 15 Jan. 1941, 1 son, 2 daughters. *Education:* Commercial College, 1923-27. *Appointments:* Apprenticeship and Commerce Employment, Germany, 1927-32; Manager, Tool Factory, Germany, 1932-34; Assistant Manager, Importing Company, Australia; Founded Beck & Coram, Importers and Distributors, November 1935, Sole Owner, 1936, Managing Director and Chairman of Directors, 1956-. *Memberships:* Danish Club Dannebrog, Middle Park, Melbourne; Tivoli Club, Richmond, Melbourne. *Publications:* Various articles in Trade Journals. *Honours:* 2 Prizes in Commercial College, 1926 & 1927. *Hobbies:* Reading; Classical Music; Photography; Swimming; Gardening; Collecting Oil and Water Colour Paintings; Languages; Ceramics; Ivory and Wood Carvings; Antique Furniture. *Address:* PO Box 194, North Melbourne, Victoria, 3051, Australia.

BEDBROOK, (Sir), George Montario, b. 8 Nov. 1921, Melbourne, Victoria, Australia. Orthopaedic Surgeon. m. Jessie Violet Page, 23 Feb. 1946, 2 sons, 3 daughters. *Education:* Medical School, University of Melbourne, Australia; JP Ryan Scholarship in Surgery, 1944; MB BS., 1944, MS., 1950, FRACS., 1950, Melbourne; FRCS., 1950, England; DPRM., 1970, Sydney, Australia. *Appointments:* Resident, Medical Officer, Royal Melbourne Hospital, Victoria, Australia, 1944-45; Lecturer in Anatomy, University of Melbourne, Australia, 1946-50; Resident Medical Officer, National Orthopaedic Hospital, England, 1951; Registrar, Orthopaedic Deoartment, Croydon Group Hospitals, England, 1951-53; Private Practice, Perth, Western Australia, Consultant, Orthopaedic Department, 1953, Head, Department of Paraplegia, 1954-72, Senior Surgeon, 1972, Head, Department of Orthopaedics, 1965-75, Chairman, Department of Orthopaedics, 1975-79, Senior Surgeon, Department of Orthopaedics, 1979, Senior Surgeon, Spinal Injuries Unit, 1981-, Royal Perth Hospital/Royal Perth Rehabilitation Hospital, Australia. *Memberships:* ex-Vice President, Australian Council for Rehabilitation of the Disabled; Vice Chairman, National Advisory Council for the Handicapped; State Chairman, Committee for 1981 International Year of Disabled Persons; President, International Medical Society of Paraplegia; Chairman, Organising Committee for the 1982 Congress of the Western Pacific Orthopaedic Association; Past President, Australian Orthopaedic Association; Court of Examiners (Orthopaedic Surgery) Royal Australian College of Surgeons; Rehabilitation International; Scoliosis Research Society. *Publications:* 61 publications, 55 Medical and scientific publications including: The Care and Management of Spinal Cord Injuries. *Honours:* numerous honours including: OBE., 1963; O.St.J., 1973; Hon. MD., West Australia University, 1973; Kt. Bachelor, 1978; Hon. FRCS., Edinburgh, Scotland, 1981. *Hobbies:* Reading; Farming; Sporting activities for the disabled. *Address:* 29 Ulster Road, Floreat Park 6014, Western Australia.

BEDLOE, Norman Christopher, b. 25 Aug. 1937, East Horsley, Surrey, England. Director, Canberra Theatre Centre. m. Janet Elizabeth Aplin, 19 Feb. 1966, 1 son, 2

daughters. *Education:* Nautical College, Pangbourne, UK, 1950-55. *Appointments:* Assistant Purser, P. & O.S.N Co., 1958-62; Stage Management, Repertory Theatre, Guildford and Mermaid Theatre, London, UK, 1962-63; Production Management and Direction, BBC TV., UK, 1963-80; Director, Canberra Theatre Centre for Canberra Theatre Trust, Australia, June 1980. *Publications:* Musical Version of A Christmas Carol, (Co-adaptation with J Wood and M Shapcott), 1967. *Hobbies:* Swimming; Music; Opera; Woodwork. *Address:* 2 Niblo Place, Chapman, ACT 2611, Australia.

BEEBY, Clarence Edward, b. 16 June 1902, Leeds, England. International Educational Consultant and Writer. m. Beatrice Eleanor Newnham, 3 June 1926. 1 son 1 daughter. *Education:* M.A. Philosphy, University of New Zealand, 1923; PhD. Psychology, University of Manchester, 1927-. *Appointments:* Lecturer, Canterbury University College, New Zealand, 1923-34; Director, New Zealand Council for Educational Research, 1934-38; Director of Education, New Zealand, 1940-60; Assistant Director General of UNESCO, 1948-49; New Zealand Ambassador to France and Permanent Delegate to UNESCO, 1960-63; Research Associate Harvard University, 1963-67; Commonwealth Visiting Professor University of London 1967-68; Educational consultant to Australian Government in Papua New Guinea; 1969-; Ford Foundation Consultant in Indonesia, 1970-75; UNDP Consultant, Malaysia, 1966-; Consultant to New Zealand Council for Educational Research, 1969-80. *Memberships:* New Zealand Association for Research in Education; New Zealand Book Council (President); New Zealand PEN; New Zealand Council for Civil Liberties. *Publications:* The Intermediate Schools of New Zealand, 1938-; Entrance to the University, 1939-; Report on Education in Western Samoa, 1954-; The Quality of Education in Developing Countries, 1966-; Planning and the Educational Administrator, 1967-; Qualitative Aspects of Educational Planning 1969-; Report of the Advisory Committee on Education in Papua and New Guinea 1969-; Assessment of Indonesian Education; *Honours:* C.M.G. 1956; Order of St. Gregory, 1964-; Hon. LL.D., Otago, 1969-; Hon. Lit. D. Wellington, 1970-; Mackie Medal, ANZAAS, 1971-; Hon. Fellow New Zealand Educational Institute, 1974-. *Hobbies:* Words and wood. *Address:* 73 Barnard Street, Wellington, 1, New Zealand.

BEETZ, Jean, b. 27 Mar. 1927, Montreal, Quebec, Canada. Puisné Judge, The Supreme Court of Canada. *Education:* College Notre-Dame, Montreal, Canada; College de Saint-Laurent, Montreal, Canada; University of Montreal, Montreal, Canada; Oxford University, Pembroke College; BA, LL.L University of Montreal; MA Oxford University. *Appointments:* Practiced law in Montreal, 1950-51; Assistant Professor, Civil Law, Faculty of Law, University of Montreal, 1953-59; Associate Professor, Constitutional Law, Faculty of Law, 1959-66; Assistant Secretary to the Cabinet, Ottawa, 1966-68; Dean of Law, University of Montreal, 1968-70; Special Counsel, to the Prime Minister of Canada on constitutional matters, 1968-71; Professor, Faculty of Law, 1966-73; Appointed Puisné Judge, Quebec Court of Appeal, 1973-; Puisné Judge, The Supreme Court of Canada, 1974-. *Memberships:* Fellow of the Royal Society of Canada; Le Cercle Universitaire d'Ottawa. *Publications:* Attribution et changement de nom patronymique, 1956; Le contrôle juridictionnel du pouvoir législatif et les droits de l'homme dans la constitution du Canada, 1958; Avant-projet de constitution fédérale pour la République du Congo, 1962; Les attitutdes changeantes du Québec à l'endroit de la Constitution de 1867, 1965; Uniformité de la procédure administrative, 1965; Rapport sur l'évolution du Gouvernement dans les Territoires du Nord-Ouest, 1966; Réflections on Continuity and Change in Law Reform, 1972. *Honours:* Rhodes Scholarship, 1951; Honary LL.D, University of Ottawa, 1975; Honary Fellow of Pembroke College, Oxford, 1976; Honary LL.D, University of Montreal, 1977; Honary DCL, University of Windsor, 1978. *Address:* 2405-400 Stewart, Ottawa, Ontario, Canada K1N 6L2.

BEEVOR, John Grosvenor, b. 1 Mar. 1905, Newark on Trent, Nottinghamshire, England. Solicitor; Development Banking. m. (1) Carinthia Jane Waterfield, 1933, (divorced, 1956), 3 sons, (2) Mary C. Grepe, 1957. *Education:* 1st class honours in Mods and Greats, New College, Oxford, UK, 1924. *Appointments:* Solicitor of

Supreme Court, 1931-53; Slaughter and May, London, Director, Legal and General Assurance, 1947-56; Managing Director, Commonwealth Development Finance Co. London, UK, 1954-56; Director, Industrial Credit and Investment Corporation of India, 1955-56; Vice President, International Finance Corporation (World Bank group, Washington, USA), 1956-64; Director, Industrial Development Finance Comapnies in Malaysia, Nigeria, Pakistan and other non-Commonwealth countries, 1963-65; Director and Chairman, various Banking and Industrial Companies in UK and France, 1965-80. *Memberships:* Member of Council, Overseas Development Institute, London. *Publications:* The Effective Board—A Chairman's View, 1975; SOE -Recollections and Reflections, 1981. *Honours:* OBE., (Military), 1945; Officer of Order of Leopold, Belgium, 1979. *Address:* 51 Eaton Square, London, SW1W 9BE, England.

BEG, M K A, b. 1 Jan. 1945, Gorakhpur-273001, India. Government Service. m. Durdana, 18 June 1972, 2 daughters. *Education:* MA(English), 1968; MA(Linguistics), 1971; BA, 1966; PhD(Linguistics), 1976. *Appointments:* Lecturer in Linguistics, Aligarh Muslim University, Aligarh-202001, 1973-77; Principal, Urdu Teaching and Research Centre, Solan-173211, 1977-. *Memberships:* Linguistic Society of India, India; Dravidian Linguistics Association, India. *Publications:* 30 articles and 5 books on language and linguistics with special reference to the Urdu language. *Hobbies:* Reading. *Address:* 105, Nizampur, Gorakhpur-273001, India.

BEGG, John Elly, b. 24 July, 1929, Sydney, Australia. Agricultural Scientist. m. 24 Aug. 1962, 3 sons. *Education:* BSc, Agricultural Honours, Sydney University, Australia; PhD, Cornell University, New York, USA. *Appointments:* CSIRO, 1951-58, 1962-68, 1969-78, 1979-; Cornell University, New York, 1958-62; Connecticut Agricultural Experimental Station, 1968-69; USDA, 1978-79. *Memberships:* Australian Institute Agricultural Science; Australian Society Plant Physiology; ANZAAS. *Publications:* Numerous scientific papers, Review articles and chapters in books. *Hobbies:* Sailing; Squash; Golf. *Address:* 19 Colvin St, Hughes ACT 2605 Australia.

BEGG, Varyl Cargill, b. 1 Oct. 1908, London, England. Naval Officer. m. Rosemary Cowan, 7 Aug. 1943, 2 sons. *Education:* Special entry, Royal Navy, 1926; Staff College, 1946; Imperial Defence College, 1954. *Appointments:* Qualified Gunnery Officer, 1933; 2nd World War in Atlantic, Mediterranean, Far East, 1939-45; Commander, 1943, Captain, 1947, Commanded HM Gunnery School, Chatham, 8th Destroyer Flotilla, HMS Cossack, HMS Excellent, HMS Triumph; Rear Admiral, 1957; Chief of Staff to CinC, Portsmouth, 1957-58; Flag Officer i/c 5th Cruiser Squadron, 1958-60; Vice Admiral, Vice Chief of Naval Staff, 1960; Admiral, CinC, British Forces, Far East, 1963; CinC, Portsmouth and Channel (Nato), 1965; First Sea Lord, 1966; Governor and CinC, Gibraltar, 1969-73. *Memberships:* United Service Club; Army-Navy Club. *Honours:* DSC., 1941; DSO., 1952; CB., 1959; KCB., 1962; GCB., 1965; PMN., 1966; K.St.J., 1969. *Hobbies:* Shooting; Fishing; Gardening. *Address:* Copyhold Cottage, Chilbolton, Stockbridge, Hampshire, England.

BEHRENS, Robert, b. 19 Jan. 1952, Manchester, England. Polytechnic Lecturer. *Education:* BA.(Hons.), University of Nottingham, UK, 1973; MA, Politics, University of Exeter, UK, 1976. *Appointments:* Lecturer in Public Administration, 1975-81, Senior Lecturer in Public Administration, 1981-, Lanchester Polytechnic, Coventry, UK. *Memberships:* Founder member, Social Democratic Party; Political Studies Association. *Publications:* The Conservative Party from Heath to Thatcher: Policies and Politics, 1974-1979, 1980. *Hobby:* Football supporter. *Address:* 'Meyerson', 19 Henry Street, Kenilworth, Warwickshire, England.

BELINO, Eleuterio D, b. 10 Oct. 1930, Philippines. Veterinarian. m. Paz G. Dia, 25 June 1960, 2 sons, 2 daughters. *Education:* Doctor of Veterinary Medicine, University of the Philippines, 1957; Post Graduate, Diploma in Veterinary Public Health, University of Toronto, Canada, 1967; MSc, University of Guelph, Canada, 1968; Master of Public Administration, University of the Philippines, 1970. *Appointments:* Veterinary Officer, Bureau of Animal Industry, Albay, Philippines, 1957-60; Research Veterinarian, Bureau of Animal Industry, Manila, Philippines, 1961-64; Supervising Veterinarian, Veterinary Inspection Board, Manila, 1964-72; Animal Health Officer (Veterinary Public Health and Meat Inspection), Food and Agricultural Organization of the United Nations, Nigeria, 1972-78; Reader and Head, Department of Veterinary Public Health and Preventive Medicine, Ahmadu Bello University, Zaria, Kaduna State, Nigeria, 1978-. *Memberships:* Philippine Veterinary Medical Association; Radioisotope Society of the Philippines; Philippine Society for the Advancement of Science; Association of Public Health Veterinarians. *Publications:* Education and Training in Meat Inspection and Veterinary Public Health in Nigeria. Technical Report, AG. DP/NIR/71/OO9, United Nations Development Programme - Food and Agricultural Organization of the United Nations, Rome 1979; Integrated studies on the Processing and Utilization of Animal and Plant Wartes with Livestock Feed in Nigeria. *Honours:* Most outstanding Goverment Employee of the year, Awarded by Philippine Government Employee Association in 1970 for outstanding works in veterinary public health and meat hygiene. *Hobbies:* Stamp, Coin, and Spoon collection; Book collection on meat hygiene. *Address:* C-25 Harry Darling Road, Area C, Samaru, Zaria, Kaduna State, Nigeria.

BELISLE, Louis Alexandre, b. 7 Mar. 1902, Trois-Pistoles, Quebec, Canada. Lexicographer; Publisher; Translator. m. Gabrielle Deschênes, 1 Sept. 1929, 3 sons, 1 daughter. *Education:* ACBA, Kingston (Queens) University, Canada, 1922-23. *Appointments:* Banque Nationale, 1920-23; Power Lumber Co, Paymaster, 1924-27; Financial Editor, 'Le Soleil', leading daily of Québec City, Canada, 1927-36; Publisher and Editor, 'La Semaine Commerciale', Financial Weekly, Québec, Canada, 1936-74. *Memberships:* President of La Société Canadienne de Technologie, 1942-; l'Association des Editeurs Canadiens, 1960-61; President du Salon International du Livre de Québec; invited speaker with all social and business Clubs around the Province of Québéc, main Radio and Television stations (French) in Canada; l'Association des Ecrivains Québécois, of l'Association des Employeurs de l'Imprimierie; Comité de Québec, 1941-64. *Publications:* Le Dictionnaire Général de la Langue française su Canada the first author having written a complete dictionary of one of the two Official Languages of Canada, 1932-57, reprinted four times and of which more than 360 000 copies were sold; Le Petit Dictionnaire Canadien de la Langue française, 125,000 copies; Le Dictionnaire Nord-Américain de la Langue française, 1979; Le Dictionnaire Général de la Langue française au Canada, 1958; Le Dictionnaire Nord-Americain de la Langue Francaise, 1980. Numerous Manuals and translations. *Honours:* His Dictionnair Général was honoured by L'Académie française by the Médaille de la Langue française 1958; La Vie Française en Amérique awarded him its gold medal, 1971, for the whole of his contributions to the French-Canadian culture in North America; was proposed for the first Médaille du Mérite to be awarded by The Québec Department of Cultural Affairs next year. *Hobbies:* Hockey; Wrestling; Boxing; Skiing; Baseball; Tennis; Walking; Gardening. *Address:* 1404 Avenue des Pins, Sillery, Québec, Canada G1S 4J5.

BELISLE, Rheal, b. 3 July 1919, Blezard Valley, Ontario, Canada. Senator. m. Edna Rainville, 21 Aug, 1941, 4 sons, 4 daughters. *Education:* LLD (Honoris Causa), University Laurentian, Sudbury, Canada, 1971; Theology Graduate, St. Paul University of Ottawa, Canada, 1977. *Appointments:* Councillor of Rayside, 1944; Mayor from 1945-52; Clerk Treasurer for two years; President and Director of Sudbury and District Municipal Association; Director of Sudbury and District Home for the Aged; President and Director of Sudbury and District Chamber of Commerce, 1950-55 and Chelmsford and Valley Chamber of Commerce, 1952; Director of Fielding Lumber Co. Ltd; Director of Whitefish Pallet Co. Ltd; Director of Montfort Hospital; Director of the Banque Canadienne Nationale; Director of l'Union du Canada. *Memberships:* Honourary President of the Wellington Club of Ottawa; Charter member of the National Advisory Council of the Canadian Cystic Fibrosis Foundation; Chairman of the Financial Committee 1975; Director of the Canadian Wildlife Federation; Trustee of the Canadian Wildlife Foundation; Member of the Board of Governors of the Sudbury University, 1963; Chairman of the Board, 1964-74; Lifetime Ho-

nourary President of the University of Sudbury. Godfather of five universities. *Honours:* Named lifetime Honourary President of l'Association d'éducation d'Ontario, 1965; Named lifetime member of l'Ordre de mérite de la culture française au Canada by the Honourable Gérard Pelletier, Secretary of State, 1969. Summoned to the Senate on 4 Feb. 1963; Senate Representative to numerous conferences including: NATO Conference, Paris, 1963; United Nations for the visit of Pope Paul VI , 1965; Commonwealth Parliamentary Association Conference in Trinidad and Tobago, 1969; European Common Market in Brussels and Strasbourg on a fact-finding tour, 1973; 20th Commonwealth Parliamentary Conference at Sri Lanka, Ceylon, 1974; South African Government, 1977; Canadian Section, International Association of French Parliamentarians Meeting in Brussels, 1978; 66th Inter-parliamentary Conference in Caracas, Venezuela, 1979. *Address:* 403 Simpson Road, Ottawa, Ontario, K1H 5A8, Canada.

BELL, Geoffrey, b. 5 May 1928, Melbourne, Australia. Consulting Geologist. m. Jill Griffin, 29 Dec. 1951, 2 sons, 2 daughters. *Education:* BSc., Geology and Metallurgy, Melbourne, University Australia, 1951. *Appointments:* Mount Isa Mines Limited, 1952; Victorian Geological Survey, 1952; E A Webb & Associates Pty. Limited, 1968; Self Employed, 1973. *Memberships:* Australasian Institute Mining and Metallurgy; Geological Society of Australia. *Publications:* Geological Survey publications. *Hobby:* Photography. *Address:* 62 Russell Street, Surrey Hills, Victoria, Australia 3127.

BELL, Geoffrey Sydney, b. 11 June, 1942, Sydney, New South Wales, Australia. Company Director and Investment Manager, Public Trusts. m. Salley Lynne Cousens, 20 Aug. 1977, 1 son, 2 daughters. *Education:* The Scots College, Sudney, 1949-59; University of New England, USA, 1960-63. *Appointments:* Teacher of Agriculture, Economics and Commerce; Grazier; Property Development and Project Management; Theatrical Entrepreneur and Agent; Founding Shareholder and Director, Macquarie Counsellors, Management Unit Trust, Trustee Management and Superannuation Funds. *Memberships:* Royal Sydney Golf Club; Australian Jockey Club; Elanora Country Club; The Armidale Club. *Hobbies:* Surfing; Horse riding; Golf; Skiing; Opera and Theatre. *Address:* Tanglewood, Bogangar, 2413, New South Wales, Australia.

BELL, Glen Wesley, b. 22 Aug. 1945, Toronto, Canada. Lawyer. *Education:* BA., 1967, LL.B., 1970, Queen's University, Kingston, Ontario, Canada. *Appointments:* Canadian Civil Liberties Association, Toronto, Canada, 1972-74; Indian Brotherhood of the Northwest Territories, Yellowknife, Canada, 1974-76; Regina Community Legal Services, Regina, Canada, 1976-78; Parkdale Community Legal Services, Toronto, Canada, 1978-81; B.C. Ombudsman, Vancouver, Canada, 1981-. *Memberships:* Law Societies of: Upper Canada, Northwest Territories, Saskatchewan, British Columbia; Canadian Bar Association; Canadian Civil Liberties Association; Board member, Oxfam, Canada. *Address:* 202-1275 W. 6th Avenue, Vancouver, British Columbia, Canada, V6H 1A6.

BELL, Gordon John, b. 27 Nov. 1923, Hinckley, Leicestershire, England. Civil Servant/Scientist. m. Kaia Ranghild Ringnes, 22 Feb. 1954, 2 sons, 1 daughter. *Education:* MA, St. Johns College, Cambridge University, England, 1942-43, 1946-49. *Appointments:* Scientific Officer, 1949, Deputy Director, 1963, Director, 1965-81, Royal Observatory, Hong Kong; Science Adviser to the Hong Kong Government, 1981-. *Memberships:* FRMetS; Commonwealth Club, London; Oriental Club, London. *Publications:* Numerous papers and articles in the meteorological literature especially on tropical cyclones. *Honours:* OBE, 1975; AE-Air Efficiency Award, 1958; First clasp, 1965; Hon. FHKIE-Hon. Fellow, Hong Kong Institution of Engineers; Hon. Research Fellow, Hong Kong University, 1968-77; Hon. Air Commodore, Royal Hong Kong Auxiliary Air Force, 1977. *Hobbies:* Walking in hills and mountains; Squash; Sailing; Music. *Address:* Tylers Meadow, Castle Walk, Wadhurst, East Sussex, England, TN5 6DB.

BELL, Kathleen Hazel, b. 11 Jan. 1920, Masterton, New Zealand. Headmistress. *Education:* Otago University, New Zealand; Dunedin Teachers' College, New Zealand; LRSM,; LRAM,; Royal Academy of Music, London. *Appointments:* Assistant Mistress, Raetihi,

New Zealand, 1942-44; Assistant Mistress, Woodford House, Havelock North, New Zealand, 1944-48; Assistant Mistress, S.Peter's Square, London, England, 1949; Choir Mistress, 1950-63, House Mistress, 1956-63, Wycombe Abbey, Bucks, England; Head Mistress, Woodford House, Havelock North, New Zealand, 1964-75. *Memberships:* Royal Commonwealth Society; Former Member, Association of Heads of Independant Schools, New Zealand and United Kingdom; Royal School of Church Music, Zonta. *Hobbies:* English Literature; Music; Travel. *Address:* 10 Sharon Place, Palmerston North, New Zealand.

BELL, Robert J, b 22 July, 1950, Tripoli, Lebanon. Vice President, International Services Extendicare Ltd., Toronto, Canada. m. Patricia L Neate, 8 Sept. 1973, 2 daughters. *Education:* Bachelor of Applied Science (Industrial Engineering), University of Toronto, Canada, 1973; Post-graduate Studies in Economics, York University, Canada, 1974-76; Master of Public Administration, Queen's University, 1980. *Appointments:* Systems Engineer, Hospital for Sick Children, Toronto, 1972-74; Executive Officer, Ministry of Health, Ontario, 1974-75; Treasury Board Officer, Management Board of Cabinet, Ontario, 1975-76; Executive Director, District Health Council, Peterborough, Ontario, 1976-79; Executive Coordinator, Metropolitan Toronto District Health Council, 1979-80; Vice President, Development and Management, Extendicare Ltd., Toronto, 1980-. *Memberships:* Association of Professional Engineers of Ontario; Canadian College of Health Service Executives; Oriental Rug Society. *Hobbies:* Collector of Oriental Rugs and Carpets; Islamic Art; Collector of Miniature Military Models. *Address:* 94 Woodsford Square, London W14 England.

BELL, Ronald McMillan, b. 14 Apr. 1914, Cardiff. Queen's Counsel; Member of Parliament. m. Elizabeth Audrey Gossell, 15 Apr. 1954, 2 sons, 2 daughters. *Education:* Magdalen College, Oxford, 1933-37; BA, Medieval and Modern Languages, 1936; BA, Jurisprudence, 1937; MA, 1941. *Appointments:* Called to Bar, Gray's Inn, 1938; Queen's Counsel 1966; Contested Caerphilly Parliamentary by-election, 1939; Royal Naval Volunteer Reserve, 1938-46; Member of Parliament for Newport, Mon., 1945, and for South Bucks. and Beaconsfield, 1950-. *Memberships:* Oxford Union Society; Oxford University Conservative Association; Court of Reading University. *Publications:* Tory Oxford, 1936; Crown Proceedings, 1948; Many press articles. *Honours:* Heath Harrison Travelling Scholar, University of Oxford, 1935; Knight Bachelor, 1980. *Hobbies:* Work; Gardening. *Address:* West Witheridge, Beaconsfield, Bucks. England.

BELLEH, Godfrey Sanfiye, b. 14 Dec. 1940, Angiama, Bendel State, Nigeria. Librarian. m. Mary E Ighobunor, 24 Nov. 1967, 2 sons, 3 daughters. *Education:* Diploma in Librarianship, University of Ibadan, Nigeria, 1964; ALA, Library Association, UK, 1972; Intermediate Exam. in Laws, University of London, UK, 1974; MSLS, Case Western Reserve University, Cleveland, Ohio, USA, 1975. *Appointments:* Assistant Librarian, 1965-70, Librarian Grade II, 1970, Librarian Grade I, 1972, Senior Librarian, 1976-77, Principal Librarian, 1977-1979, Medical Librarian, 1980-, Library, College of Medicine of the University of Lagos. *Memberships:* Nigerian Library Association; Health Sciences Libraries and Information Services Group of the Nigerian Library Association; International Cooperation Committee of the American Medical Library Association; Eagle Tennis Club, Lagos, Nigeria. *Publications:* Belleh, G S Medical Librarianship in Nigeria - a review of the literature and comments on some problems and prospects, 1975; Hospital Libraries in Nigeria, Mar. 1977; Towards a national biomedical information network for Nigeria, 1978; Libraries and nursing objectives, 1977. *Honours:* Won Cunningham International Fellowship for Medical Librarianship in 1975, awarded by the Medical Library Association of the US. *Hobbies:* Lawn Tennis; Swimming; Reading. *Address:* 94 Adeniran Ogunsanya Street, Surulere, Lagos, Nigeria.

BELLO, Mohammed, b. 1930, Katsina, Nigeria. Lawyer. m. (1) Zainab Abubakar, (2) Daula Selem. *Education:* Kaduna College, Nigeria, 1951-52; University College, Ibadan, Nigeria, 1950-52; At the Inns of Court, London, UK and called to the Bar in Lincoln's Inn, London, 1955; Harvard Law School, Massachussetts, USA, 1962-63. *Appointments:* Crown Counsel, North-

ern Nigeria Government, 1956-61; Chief Magistrate, Northern Nigeria, 1961; Director of Public Prosecutions, Northern Nigeria, 1964; Judge of the High Court, Northern Nigeria, 1966; Senior Puisne Judge in the former North-Central and Kwara States, 1968; Chief Justice of the Northern States, 1969-75; Appointed a Justice of the Supreme Court, 1975; Legal Secretary to the Cameroons under the British Mandate, 1961; Deputy Commissioner for Native Courts, Northern Nigeria, 1965; Chairman of the Commission of Inquiry: Affairs of Electricity Corporation of Nigeria, 1966; Chairman of the Visitations to the Universites of Ibadan and Lagos, 1971; Chairman of the Nigerian Institute of Advanced Legal Studies, 1980. *Memberships:* National Commissioner of the Sheriff Guard of Nigeria; Chairman of St. John Council of Nigeria; Commonwealth Magistrates Association; Harvard Law School Association; Nigerian Institute of International Affairs; Chairman of Rehabilitation Commission, North-Central State of Nigeria, 1968-71; Chairman, Body of Benchers, 1981-82. *Honours:* Commander of the Order of the Niger (CON), 1965; Fellow of the Nigerian Institute of Advanced Legal Studies, 1981. *Address:* 12 Second Avenue, Ikoyi, Lagos, Nigeria.

BELLWOOD, Peter Stafford, b. 10 Aug. 1943, Leicester, England. Archaeologist. 1 son. *Education:* BA, 1966, MA, 1970, PhD, 1980, Cambridge University, England. *Appointments:* Lecturer in Prehistory, University of Auckland, New Zealand, 1967-72; Lecturer, 1973-76, Senior Lecturer, 1976-, in Prehistory, Australian National University. *Publications:* Man's conquest of the Pacific, 1978; The Polynesians, 1978; The peopling of the Pacific, 1980. *Hobbies:* Cycling; Observing other cultures. *Address:* 6 Hale Crescent, Turner, Act 2601, Australia.

BEL-MOLOKWU, Josef Chukwumah, b. 6 Apr. 1947, Onitsha, Nigeria. Journalism. m. Chinwe Umunna, 26 Aug. 1978, 1 son. *Education:* BA, University of Nigeria, Nsukka, 1970-73. *Appointments:* Acting Editor/Night Editor, New Age—ABA, 1967-68; Assistant Production Editor, Biafra Ministry of Information, 1968-70; Diamond Food Co., Enugu, 1970; Reporter, Daily Times, Lagos, 1971-72; Ministry of Agriculture, Kano, 1973-74; Star Printing & Publishing Co., Ltd., Enugu, Editor Daily Star, 1975-80, Editorial Adviser, 1980; Managing Editor, Ivory Trumpet Publishing Co., Ltd., Enugu, 1980-. *Memberships:* Nigerian Institute of Management, 1975; Nigerian Institute of Public Relations, 1977; Fellow, Institute of Intercontinental Communication, 1980. *Publications:* Numerous publications in newspapers and magazines worldwide; Currently working on two books—This is PR and Who's Who in Onitsha, due to be completed 1981 and 1982 respectively. *Honours:* Department of Journalism Prize, 1973, Faculty of Arts Prize, 1973, Daily Times Award, 1973, University of Nigeria. *Hobbies:* Photography; Watching sports; Reading. *Address:* 9 Western Close, Ekulu Layout, Enugu, Nigeria.

BELMONTE, Peter George Colaco, b. 29 Apr. 1942, Georgetown, Guyana. Insurance Unit Manager. m. Loleita Alli-Shaw, 4 May 1963, 1 son, 1 daughter. *Education:* Convent of the Good Shepherd; St Stanislaus College; Central High School. *Appointments:* Customs Clerk, Bookers Stores Ltd., 1959; Joined Guyana & Trinidad Mutual Fire & Life Insurance Co., 1960, Unit Manager, 1974-; Established timber business in Essequibo, 1965; Manager, Golden Lotus Night Club and Farm Fresh Inn Restaurant, 1967; Managing Director, Andlosim & Co. Ltd; Director, Alli-Shaw & Co., Ltd; Director, Jesus Rescue Mission of Guyana. Member, Insurance Institute of Guyana; Life Underwriters Association of Guyana; Caribbean Association of Life Underwriters. *Honours:* GTM Premium Club Certificate of Excellence, 1974-78; Caribbean Quality Award by the Caribbean Association of Life Underwriters, 1977-81; International Quality Award by the Life Insurance Marketing & Research Association, 1975-81. *Hobbies:* Swimming; Walking; Music. *Address:* 78 Ixora Avenue, Bel Air Park, Georgetown, Guyana.

BELO, Olatunji Kolade, b. 15 Dec. 1942, Lagos, Nigeria. Banking. m. Adebola Titilola Omitola, 6 June 1979, 1 daughter. *Education:* MBA, University of Western Ontario, 1971; BSc, ACGI, Imperial College of Science and Technology, London, 1966. *Appointments:* Associate Research Engineer (SST Program), The Boeing Company, Seattle, Washington, USA, 1967-69; Lecturer,

Business Administration, University of the West Indies, Mona, Jamaica, 1971-73; Investment Officer, World Bank Group, Washington DC, 1973-77. *Memberships:* Victoria Island Lions Club. *Honours:* Federal Government of Nigeria University Scholarship, 1963-66. *Hobbies:* Squash; Table Tennis; Reading; Travelling. *Address:* 9 Musa YarAdua Street, Victoria Island, PO Box 9707, Lagos, Nigeria.

BELOFF, Max (Lord), b. 2 July 1913. *Education:* Corpus Christi College, Oxford; Gibbs Scholar in Modern History, 1934, First Class Hons, School of Modern History, 1935; Senior Demy, Magdalen College, Oxford, 1935; Junior Research Fellow, Corpus Christi College, 1937. *Appointments:* War of 1939-46, Royal Corps of Signals, 1940-41; Assistant Lecturer in History, Manchester University, 1939-46; Nuffield Reader in Comparative Study of Institutions, Oxford University, 1946-56; Fellow of Nuffield College, 1947-57; Gladstone Professor of Government and Public Administration, Oxford University, 1957-74, now Professor Emeritus, and Fellow, All Souls College, 1957-74, Emeritus Fellow, 1980-; Principal, University College, Buckingham, 1974-79, Retired, 1979; Supernumerary Fellow, St. Antony's College, Oxford, 1975-82. *Publications:* Public Order and Popular Disturbances, 1660-1714, 1938; The Foreign Policy of Soviet Russia, Vol. 1, 1947, Vol. 2, 1949; Thomas Jefferson and American Democracy, 1948; Soviet Policy in the Far East, 1944-51, 1953; The Age of Absolutism, 1660-1815, 1954; Foreign Policy and the Democratic Process, 1955; Europe and the Europeans, 1957; The Great Powers, 1959; The American Federal Government, 1959; New Dimensions in Foreign Policy; The United States and the Unity of Europe, 1963; The Balance of Power, 1967; The Future of British Foreign Policy; Imperial Sunset, Vol. 1, 1969; The Intellectual in Politics; The Government of the United Kingdom, (w G R Peele), 1980; Edited: The Federalist, 1948; Mankind and his Story, 1948; The Debate on the American Revolution, 1949; On the Track of Tyranny, 1959; L'Europe du XIXe et XXe siècle, 1960-67; American Political Institutions in the 1970's, 1975 (w. V Vale); Articles in English, French, Italian and American Journals. *Honours:* Hon. LLD, Pittsburgh, USA, 1962; Hon. DCL, Bishop's University, Canada, 1976; Hon. DLitt Bowdoin Coll., USA, 1976; Hon. Dr.Univ. Aix-Marseille III, 1978; Kt., 1980; Life Peer, 1981. *Hobby:* Watching Cricket. *Address:* House of Lords, London SW1, England.

BELO-OSAGIE, Tiramiyu, b. 1 Oct. 1926 Benin City, Nigeria. Professor. m. Maria Bazuaye 3 Apr. 1954, 3 sons, 1 daughter. *Education:* Faculty of Medicine, McGill University, Montreal, Canada; BSc(First Class Honours) 1949; MD 1953; LMCC 1954; MRCOG 1963; FMCOG 1971; FRCOG 1977 *Appointments:* House Physician, Southampton General Hospital, 1953; House Surgeon, Royal South Hants Hospital, Southampton 1953; Paediatric House Physician, St. Charles Hospital, London 1954; Medical Officer, Obstetrics and Gynaecology, Massey Street Maternity Hospital and General Hospital, Lagos, 1958; Clinical Assistant in Gynaecology, 1959; Obstetric House Surgeon, Hammersmith Hospital, London 1959; Senior House Officer, Maternity Hospital, Leeds, 1950; Registrar, Professorial Unit, Maternity Hospital and Hospital for Women, Leeds 1960-61; Assistant Lecturer, Department of Obstetrics and Gynaecology, Leeds University 1972; Registrar in Obstetrics and Gynaecology, North Middlesex Hospital London 1963; Specialist Obstetrician and Gynaecologist, Lagos Island Maternity and General Hospital, Lagos 1963-68; Chief Consultant, 1971-72, Consultant, Obstetrician and Gynaecologist, Teaching Hospital, 1965-72, Associate Lecturer Department of Obstetrics and Gynaecology, University of Lagos, 1965-72; Professor and Head of Department of Obstetrics and Gynaecology 1972-75, Dean, Faculty of Medicine and Pharmacy, 1972-74, Provost, College of Medical Sciences, University of Benin 1974-75; Teaching and Tutorial Posts at: Leeds University 1960-62, North Middlesex Hospital, London 1962-63, Gynaecologist, Lagos University Teaching Hospital 1963-66, 1972-. *Memberships:* Examining Board in Obstetrics and Gynaecology, Nigeria Medical Council; Treasurer, Society of Gynaecology and Obstetrics of Nigeria; Board of Management, Lagos University Teaching Hospital; Court of Governors, College of Medicine, University of Lagos; Action and Planning Committee, Maiduguri Teaching Hospital. *Publications:* Papers at. 4th World Congress in Buenos Aires 1964, in

the field of Gynaecology and Obstetrics; Articles on Ruptured Uterus, Postpartum Haemorrhage in manual used by students studying Obstetrics. *Address:* 30 Catholic Mission Street, Lagos, Nigeria.

BENADY, Samuel, b. 21 May 1905, Gibraltar. Barrister-at-Law. m. Pat 17 Jan. 1968, 1 son, 2 daughters. *Education:* MA, Jesus College, Cambridge University; Barrister, Inner Temple London, 1926; Queen's Counsel 1954. *Appointments:* Private Practice. *Memberships:* Gibraltar Garrison Library; Royal Gibraltar Yacht Club. *Honours:* Officer of the British Empire; Leader of the Gibraltar Bar. *Hobbies:* Bridge. *Address:* 124 Main Street, Gibraltar.

BENCSIK, Albert Frank, b. 15 Oct. 1931, Sydney Australia. Orthopaedic Surgeon. m. Diana Margaret Meurer 14 Nov. 1964, 2 sons, 2 daughters. *Education:* The University of Sydney, 1950-56; MBBS, 1956; Royal College of Surgeons, Edinburgh University, 1960; Fellowship Royal College of Surgeons Edinburgh 1964; Fellowship Royal Australasian College Surgeons 1968; Fellow Australian College Rehabilitation Medicine 1980. *Appointments:* Mater Misericordiae Hospital North Sydney 1957-59; Royal Portsmouth Hospital United Kingdom 1962-63; Royal Infirmary Edinburgh 1963; St George Hospital Sydney 1964-66; St Vincents Hospital Sydney 1967; Prince of Wales Hospital Sydney 1968; Sydney Hospital and Royal Alexandra Hospital for Children 1969; Private Practice, Consultant Orthopaedic Surgeon, Sydney, 1970-. *Memberships:* Australian Orthopaedic Association; Australian Medical Association; Fellow Royal Colleges of Surgeons of Edinburgh and Australasia. *Hobbies:* Gardening; Travel; Photography. *Address:* "Ysabel" 6 Ernest Street Hunters Hill 2110 NSW Australia.

BENERJEE (Dr.) Santosh Kumar, b. 1 Mar. 1932, Calcutta, India. Ceramic Technologist. m. Shefali Banerjee, 12 June 1959, 1 son, 1 daughter. *Education:* BSc., (Honours), 1951-; MSc., 1954-; PhD., Calcutta University, 1968-; *Appointments:* Research Chemist, Bengal Ceramic Institute, 1954-; Assistant Director of Industries, 1958-; Project Engineer, Ceramic Department Gibbons Brothers, UK., 1961-; Director, G. Atherton Engineering, 1969-; Managing Director, West Bengal Ceramic Development Corporation, 1976-; Assistant Director, Central Glass & Ceramic Research Institute, Calcutta, 1980-. *Memberships:* Institute of Engineers, 1979-; Indian Institute of Ceramics, 1980-; Institute of Clay Technology, London; Institute of Energy, London; Council of Engineering Institution, UK. *Publications:* Approximately 50 research papers, articles, review papers, study etc., on Glass and Ceramics, Raw-materials, turn Key projects, project engineering, ceramic Tunnel Kilns, Instruments etc., Papers on Scientific planning, Research Management, productivity in Scientific Research. Booklets on Technology Transfer. *Honours:* Nilkanta-Sarda Gold Medal, 1946-; Dr. M.N. Goswami Medal, 1953-; Participation in All India Radio Programme, 1969 — 1973-; Television programme, 1980-. *Hobbies:* Reading; Seminars; Touring; Study of Human Beings. *Address:* Sirsa, Flat 3D, 59 Lake Road, Calcutta 700 029, West Bengal, India.

BENFIELD, Kenneth Michael, b. 7 Oct. 1940, Coventry England. Managing Director. m. Ann Cheswick 4 Apr. 1962, 2 sons. *Education:* Civil Engineering, Loughborough College; Diploma in Management Studies, Lanchester Polytechnic. *Appointments:* Construction Surveyor, Site Agent, Works Manager, Marketing Manager, General Manager, J Poulton, Ascot Limited; Managing Director, Classic Homes; Chairman and Joint Managing Director, Jones Benfield Construction Limited; Principle, Surveyors and Consultants, Edward Savage and Associates; Managing Director, International Trading Company, Export Guarantee. *Memberships:* Senator; Junior Chambers International; Commonwealth Human Ecology Council; Ecology Party; Institute of Marketing; Faculty of Building; Fellow, British Institute of Management; Guild of Surveyors; Faculty of Architects and Surveyors; Association of Cost and Executive Accountants; Construction Surveyors Institute. *Publications:* Contributor to newspapers and periodicals on Ecological, Political and Future Studies orientated topics. *Honours:* 1st Prize, National Management Scholarship, Management Centre Europe, 1975; 1st Prize, World Trade Management Exercise, Keyser Ulman Limited, 1980; Knight Commander of the Sovereign Order of St Johns of Jerusalem; Knights of Malta, 1972. *Hobbies:* Photography; Travel; Writing; Public Speaking; Swimming; Sailing; Flying-/Gliding; Committee Work. *Address:* Tudor Lodge, Hob Lane, Burton Green, Nr. Kenilworth, Warwickshire, England.

BENJAMIN, Victor Ariyaratnam, b. 19 Feb. 1928, Jaffna, Sri Lanka. Medical Practitioner, General Surgeon. m. Saraswathy Louise Rasiah, 31 Dec. 1957, 1 son, 2 daughters. *Education:* Medical Studies, University of Ceylon, Colombo, 1946-52; MBBS, Ceylon, 1952; FRCS, England, 1959; Fellow of International College of Surgeons, 1962; MS, Ceylon, 1965; LMSSA, London, 1980. *Appointments:* Medical Officer, Department of Health, Sri Lanka, 1952-78; Demonstrator in Pathology, University of Ceylon, 1953-55; Consultant Surgeon, Trincomalee, Batticoloa, Jaffna, Kandy and Colombo, 1959-; Visiting Consultant Teacher in Surgery, and Examiner in Surgery, University of Sri Lanka, 1972-78; Visiting Lecturer in Anatomy, New Faculty of Medicine, 1978-79, Professor of Surgery, University of Jaffna, 1981. *Memberships:* President, Jaffna Medical Association, 1970; Ceylon Medical Association; Government Medical Officers' Association; College Old Boys' Association, Jaffna, Sri Lanka, 1980. *Honours:* Exhibitioner, University of Ceylon, 1946-47; Jeejeebhoy Medical Scholar, University of Ceylon, 1947-52. *Hobbies:* Amateur Photography; Short Wave Radio Listening; Music. *Address:* 15 Campbell Place, Dehiwala, Sri Lanka.

BENN, Edward Glanvill, b. 31 Dec. 1905, London. Publisher. m. Catherine Newbald, MBE, 4 June 1931, 1 son, 1 daughter. *Education:* Clare College, Cambridge, 1926-27. *Appointments:* New York Times, 1925; Benn Brothers Limited, 1927-80, Chairman, 1945-75, Life President, 1976; Exchange Telegraph Co., Ltd., 1956-73, Chairman, 1969-72. *Memberships:* Council Advertising Association, 1951-67, Hon. Treasurer, 1960-65; Council Commonwealth Press Union, 1956-, Hon. Treasurer, 1967-77, Hon. Life Member, 1975-; Chairman, Independent Television Authority Advertising Advisory Committee, 1959-64; President Periodical Publishers Association, 1976-78; Master, Stationers Company, 1977; Life Vice-President Newspaper Press Fund, 1965-; Trustee, 1951-80, President, 1961-62, National Advertising Benevolent Society. *Honours:* Mentioned in Despatches, Italy, 1944; Mackintosh Medal, 1967. *Address:* Crescent Cottage, Aldeburgh, Suffolk, IP15 5HW, England.

BENNESS, Edwin Charles, b. 18 Aug. 1915, Coolgardie, Western Australia. Company Director. m. 17 Apr. 1944, 2 sons, 1 daughter. *Education:* Perth Technical College, 1932-37; Fellow: Australian Society of Accountants; Institute of Chartered Secretaries; Australian Institute of Management. *Appointments:* Company Secretary, 1951-65, Finance Director, 1965-70, Managing Director, 1970-78, Boans Ltd; Commissioner, Australia Post, 1978-; Director, Swan Brewery, 1974-. *Memberships:* President, Perth Chamber of Commerce; Councillor, Australian Chamber of Commerce; State Chairman, Chartered Institute of Secretaries; Institute of Directors in Australia; State President, Retail Traders Association of Western Australia. *Honours:* Citizen of the Year, Western Australia, 1978; Order of Australia, 1979. *Hobbies:* Tennis; Music; Gardening. *Address:* 16 Linden Street, Dianella, Western Australia, 6062.

BENNETT, David Louis, b. 29 Oct. 1944, Brisbane, Australia. Physician in Adolescent Medicine. m. Anne Lipski 17 Dec. 1968, 2 sons, 2 daughters. *Education:* MB, BS, University of Queensland 1968; Member, Royal Australasian College of Physicians, 1973; Fellow, Royal Australasian College of Physicians 1977; Teaching Certificate in Adolescent Medicine, The University of Alabama School of Medicine, 1976. *Appointments:* Resident Medical Officer and Registrar in Internal Medicine, Princess Alexandra Hospital, Brisbane, Australia, 1969-73; Associate Director, The Adolescent Unit, University of Alabama School of Medicine, Birmingham, Alabama, USA, 1974-76; Head, Adolescent Medical Unit, Royal Alexandra Hospital for Children, Sydney, Australia, 1977-. *Memberships:* Australian College of Paediatrics; Short Term Consultant, World Health Organization (Chairman, Western Pacific Region Expert Working Group on, Health Needs of Adolescents, Manila, Philippines; International Pedi-

atric Association; Royal Australasian College of Physicians; Society for Adolescent Medicine; Australian Association for Adolescent Health; International Study Group on Diabetes in Children and Adolescents. *Publications:* Publications on varied aspects of adolescent medicine (including hypertension, diabetes, nutrition, anabolic steroids, sexuality and abnormal illness behaviour) and health care delivery (general approach, inpatient care, health needs of adolescents in Australia, world wide problems). *Hobbies:* Classical pianist. *Address:* 72 Provincial Road, Lindfield, NSW, 2070, Australia.

BENNETT, Eleanor Marion (Mrs John Bennett), b. 4 Feb. 1942 Subiaco, Western Australia. Botanist. m. John Bennett, 6 Jan. 1968, 1 son, 1 daughter. *Education:* BSc(Hons), 1964; Teachers Certificate, 1964; Diploma Ed, 1965; MSc, 1971. Studing PhD. *Appointments:* Botanist, W A Herbanum, South Perth, 1965-70, Part-time, 1971-72; Part-time Demonstrator Botany, University of West Australia, 1973; Part-time with Emeritus Professor B J Grieve, How to know Western Australian Wildflowers, 1974-76; Part time Lecturer in Horticultural Botany, Bentley Technical College, Western Australia, 1978; Lecturer Technical Education Course, Ravensthorpe, 1979. *Memberships:* International Association of Plant Taxonomists; Royal Society of Western Australia; Australian Systematic Botany Society; Naturalist Club of Western Australia; Australian Society for Growing Ferns; Los Angeles Fern Club; Fitzgerald River National Park Association. *Publications:* A revision of the Australian species of Hybanthus Jacquin, 1972; New taxa and new combinations in Western Australian Pittosporaceae, 1972; New taxa and new combinations in Australian Pittosporaceae, 1976; Wildflowers of the Geraldton District, 1969. *Honours:* Grant from the Australian Biological Resources Study Interim Council 1974-75. *Hobbies:* Philately; Spinning. *Address:* 21 Currawong Drive, Gooseberry Hill, 6076, Western Australia.

BENNETT, Frederick Douglas, b. 16 Sept. 1925, Spencerville, Ontario, Canada. Director (Entomologist). m. Elizabeth Margaret Rapsey, 24 Jan. 1953, 2 sons, 1 daughter. *Education:* Diploma Agriculture, Kemptville Agricultural School, 1947; BSc Agric. University of Toronto, 1950; PhD, University of California, 1962. *Appointments:* Entomologist, Department of Agriculture, Bermuda, 1950-52; Entomologist, 1952-58, Entomologist in Charge, 1958-76, Director, 1976-, Commonwealth Institute of Bio Control, Trinidad. *Memberships:* Treasurer, International Organization for Biological Control, 1980; President, Western Hemisphere Regional Section/International Organization for Biological Control, 1972-73; American, Florida, Canadian, Colombian, Georgia, Peruvian and Brazilian Entomological Societies. *Publications:* Over 70 scientific papers including Review articles and original research and chapters in several books on biological control. *Hobby:* Woodworking. *Address:* Laurie Drive, Santa Margarita Circular Road, Curepe, Trinidad.

BENNETT, Frederic Mackarness, b. 2 Dec. 1918, United Kingdom. Member of Parliament, Barrister. m. Marion Patricia Burnham, 16 Feb. 1945. *Education:* Westminster School. *Appointments:* Called to Bar: Lincoln's Inn, 1946; Called to Southern Rhodesia Bar, 1947; Diplomatic Correspondent, Birmingham Post, 1950-51; Elected to Parliament, Reading N., 1951-55, Torbay, 1955-; Director, Various Financial, Banking, Insurance Institutions. *Memberships:* Leader Parliamentary Delegation to Council of Europe Assembly and Western European Union Assembly; President, Anglo Turkish Society; Chairman, Anglo Jordania Society; Chairman, Foreign Affairs Research Institute. *Honours:* Knighted, 1964; Order of Phoenix, Greece, 1963; (Sithari) Star of Pakistan, 1st Class, 1964; Commander of Polonia Restituta (Poland), 1977; The Order of AL-IS-TIQLAL-1st Class-(Jordan), 1980. *Hobbies:* Shooting; Tennis; Skiing; Sailing. *Address:* No. 2 Stone Buildings, Lincoln's Inn, London WC2, England.

BENNETT, Ian Cecil, b. 2 Aug. 1931, Bebington, Cheshire, England. Dentist. m. Loreen Alberta Bayer, 20 Aug. 1960, 1 son, 1 daughter. *Education:* Bachelor of Dental Surgery, Liverpool University, UK, 1956; Doctor of Dental Surgery, University of Toronto, Ontario, Canada, 1959; Master of Science in Dentistry, University of Washington, Seattle, USA, 1964. *Appointments:* Associate Professor and Head of the Division of Pedodontics, Dalhousie University, Halifax, Nova Scotia, 1963-65; Head of Dental Department, The Children's Hospital, Halifax, Nova Scotia, 1963-65; Assistant Professor of Pedodontics, 1965, Associate Professor of Pedodontics, University of Kentucky, Lexington, Kentucky, 1968; Assistant Coordinator of Medical Center Television, 1966-67; Assistant Coordinator of the Division of Medical Center Communications and Services, 1967; Director of Medical Center Communication and Services, University of Kentucky, Lexington, 1967-68; Associate Dean, College of Dentistry, Associate Professor of Pedodontics, 1968-69, Dean, College of Dentistry, Professor of Pedodontics, 1969-70, New Jersey College of Medicine and Dentistry, Jersey City, New Jersey. Dean and Professor of Pedodontics, 1970-76, New Jersey Dental School, College of Medicine and Dentistry, Newark, USA; Consultant, East Orange Veteran's Administration Hospital, East Orange, New Jersey, USA, 1969-76; Dean of the Faculty of Dentistry, Professor of Pedodontics, Dalhousie University, Halifax, Nova Scotia, Canada, 1976-; Active Consultant, The Izaak Walton Killam Hospital for Children, Halifax, Nova Scotia, Canada, 1976-. *Memberships:* Member of numerous Associations including: American Academy of Pedodontics; American College of Dentists; American Society of Dentistry for Children; Canadian Association for Dental Research; Federation Dentaire Internationale; International College of Dentists. *Publications:* Numerous publications including: Non-Antibiotic Properties of Tetracycline, 1964; Measurement of Tetracycline Incorporated in Enamel and Dentin, 1966; Technique for Producing Powdered Human or Canine Teeth, 1967; Why a Division of Communication in a Medical Center, 1967; Why a Division of Communication in a Medical Center?, 1968; How Should the Dental Association 'Adapt' to prepare for the 'New Student', 1972; New Jersey Dental School: History and Progress, 1974. *Honours:* Scholarship to Birkenhead, School, Birkenhead, Cheshire, England, 1943,50; County Major University Scholarship Tuition to Attend Liverpool University School of Dentistry, 1950-56; American Academy of Pedodontics Research Award for paper 'Incorporation of Tetracycline in the Developing Enamel and Dentin in Dogs' presented at the 19th Annual Meeting in Toronto, Ontario, 1966. *Address:* 1703-6369 Coburg Road, Halifax, Nova Scotia, B3H 4J7,Canada.

BENNETT, Jack Hubert, b. 15 Nov. 1930, Beira, Mocambique. Legal Practitioner. m. Elva Edith Patricia Leslie, 26 Apr. 1958, 1 son, 1 daughter. *Education:* BA, Rhodes University, Grahamstown, South Africa, 1952; Attorneys Admission Certificate, 1956; Associate of Chartered Institute of Secretaries, 1968. *Appointments:* Articled Clerk, 1953-55, Professional Assistant, 1956-62, Partner, 1963-, Firm of Legal Practitioners, Salisbury, Zimbabwe. *Memberships:* President, Law Society of Zimbabwe; Past President, Salisbury Association of Attorneys; Councillor, Zimbabwe Institute of Patents and Trade Mark Agents; Board Member, National Gallery of Zimbabwe; The Salisbury Club. *Hobbies:* Art. *Address:* 11 Quorn Avenue, Mount Pleasant, Salisbury, Zimbabwe.

BENNETT, John Christopher, b. 20 Mar. 1943, Krugersdorp, Transvaal, South Africa. Market Researcher. m. Carolynne Renee Berry, 17 Oct. 1970, 1 son, 1 daughter. *Education:* Bachelor of Commerce, University of NSW, 1967. *Memberships:* Market Research Society. *Hobbies:* Skiing; Sailing; Windsurfing. *Address:* 75 Belmont Road, Mosman, NSW, Australia.

BENNETT, Reginald, (Sir), b. 22 July 1911. m. Henrietta, 28 Nov. 1947, 1 son, 3 daughters. *Education:* Winchester College, 1924-30; New College, Oxford, 1930-34; St George's Hospital, 1934-37; Institute of Psychiatry, 1946-49; MA, BM, B.Ch., (Oxon), 1942; LMSSA, 1937;DPM, 1948. *Appointments:* Medical, Navy, 1934-46; Member of Parliament, Gosport and Fareham, 1950-79. *Memberships:* Council, International Institute of Human Nutrition, 1970; Chairman of many Committees, Societies & Companies. *Publications:* Articles and broadcasts on Medicine, Politics, Yachting, Aviation, Wine and Navy paintings. *Honours:* RNVR Officer Decoration (VRD), 1944; Grand Officer, Italian Order of Merit, 1977; Knight Bachelor, 1979. *Hobbies:* Yacht racing; Painting. *Address:* 37 Cottesmote Court, London, W.8, England.

BENNETT, Tressa Carnine, b. 17 Aug. 1901, Moultrie County, Illinois, USA. Teacher and Librarian. m. John

Arthur Bennett, deceased, July, 1933, 1 stepson. *Education:* AB, Illinois Wesleyan University, USA, 1923; Easter Illinois State University, summers, 1925-28-30; University, Wisconsin, 1926; University of Minnesota, 1932; Eastern Illinois University-Masters in education, 1959. *Appointments:* Social service and church work, Hillsboro, Illinois, USA, 1924; Teacher, History, Mt. Pulaski, Illinois, 1926-27; Teacher, English, history, journalism, Clinton, Illinois, 1928-33; Homemaker, Kansas, Illinois, 1933-45; Teacher, English and Latin, and librarian, 1945-66; Librarian, Sullivan, Illinois High School, 1966-70; Librarian, Medical Training Centre, Nairobi, Peace Corps Volunteer, Kenya-U.S., 1972-79. *Memberships:* Womens Club; Business and Professional Clubs; Illinois Education and National Education Association; Kenya Library Association; American Association of Women; Kenya Association of University Women; Museum Society; Wild Life Society; Theatre and Music Society, USA; National English Teachers Association; Illinois Librarians. *Publications:* Since 1929, newspaper publicity for church organizations and schools; Sponsored newspapers and yearbooks for schools for 34 years Edited and wrote for organization papers and magazines. *Honours:* The Eastern Illinois University Distinguished Alumnus Award, 1980. *Hobbies:* Reading; Writing; Travel; Photography. *Address:*209 Grist Mill Road, RRI, Glenn Mills, PA 19342, USA.

BENNETT-ENGLAND, Rodney Charles, b. 16 Dec. 1936, Romford, Essex, England. Journalist, Writer. *Education:* Royal Liberty School, 1948-53. *Appointments:* Various Local Weekly Newspapers in Metropolitan Essex, 1953-61; Reporter and Columnist, Sunday Express, 1961-67; The Journal Editor, 1965-67; Fashion Editor, Penthouse, 1967-70; Leisure Editor, Men Only, 1970-73; Freelance Writer, Broadcaster and Lecturer, 1973-; Chairman and Managing Director, RBE Associates Ltd, 1968-; European Editor, Business and Energy International, Houston, Texas, 1977-79; Consultant Editor, Various Publications, Principal Editorial Training Services, 1980-. *Memberships:* Member of numerous societies including: Chairman, 1968-69 and 1977-79, National Council for Training of Journalists; Fellow, Institute of Journalists; Fellow, Royal Society of Arts; Fellow, Institute of Directors; Member, Institute of Public Relations. *Publications:* Numerous publications including: Faith in Fleet Street; As young as you Look; First Eat Your Starter; Contributor to over 300 publications Worldwide. *Honours:* Freeman, City of London, 1967; First Fashion Writer of the Year, 1968; Scripps Lecturer in Journalism, University of Nevada, Reno, 1978; Hon Member, Society of Collegiate Journalists, USA, 1980. *Hobbies:* Food; Wine; Travel; Antiques. *Address:* 3 Oakley Street, Chelsea, London, SW3 5NW, England.

BENNIGSEN (Baron Von) Sergei, b. 4 July 1940, Dvinsk, Latvia. Financial Consultant. m. 19 June 1971, 2 sons, 1 daughter. *Education:* Bachelier En, Lycee Russe, Paris, France, 1959; Bachelier en Philosphie, Faculte de Droit Et Des Sciences; Economiques Paris, Ecole Superieeure de Publicite de Paris.*Appointments:* Bank Manager, 1962-65; Public Relations and Political Consultant, 1965-79; Co Founder, Officer National Tourism of Argentine, Paris, 1966; Co Founder, Inforel Films-Renova Films, Sescor-Commodities, 1968-69; Political & Press Adviser to Mr Raymond Triboulet, Former Minister, Member of Institut de France, 1966-70; Special Adviser to Archbishop Makarios of Cyprus, 1973-77; Director, Esni France, Esni Bankok, 1978; Director, Signtest Ltd, Coreter, Liberia, 1979; Chairman, Internava Services UK Ltd, Chairman, Sersei Von Bennigsen and Associates Ltd, 1980; President, Provident, Investment and Finance-Hong Kong Ltd. Provident, Investment and Finance, Panama Corporation. *Memberships:* Rotary Club International; Sublime Society of Beefsteak 1730; Most Sacred Order of the Orthodox Hospitallers Grand Commander. *Publications:* Articles in Argentinian and French Press; Contributor to Genealogical and Heraldic Works. *Honours:* Star and Cross of American International Academy; Chevalier de la Courtoisie Française; Grand Bailliff Order of Orthodox Hospitallers. *Hobbies:* Gipsy Singing. *Address:* 36 Warwick Avenue, London, 9 2 PT, England.

BENNISON, John, b. 3 July 1924, Mandalay, Burma. Chief Executive. m. Joyce Norma Brearley, 16 Dec. 1946, 1 son, 3 daughters. *Education:* New England

Pilot, RAAF, 1943-46; Joined Westralian Farmers Co-operative, 1954; Manager, Wesfarmers Kleenheat Gas, 1958-66; Wesfarmers Industrial Divisional Manager, 1967-69; Wesfarmers Assistant General Manager, 1970-73; General Manager, 1974; Member Australian Wool Corporation, 1975-77; Director CSBP and Farmers, 1979-. *Memberships:* Weld Club, Perth; Lake Karrinyup Golf Club; Cottesloe Golf Club. *Hobbies:* Golf; Fishing; Reading. *Address:* 3 Hill Terrace, Mosman Park, Western Australia, 6012.

BENNY, Henry Robert Clifford, b. 8 Aug. 1922, Balclutha, New Zealand. Obstetrician and Gynaecologist. m. Marion Margaret Scott, 23 Feb. 1946, 3 sons, 2 daughters. *Education:* MBCLB, 1946; MRCOG, 1955; FRCOG, 1971. *Appointments:* Resident, Waikato Hospital, 1947-48; General Practice, 1949-51; Post-graduate Training in Obstetrics and Gynaecology in UK, 1952-55; Consultant, Obstetrics and Gynaecology, Timaru, 1955; Consultant, Timaru Hospital, 1960-; Superintendent in Chief to South Canterbury Hospital Board and Senior Gynaecologist, 1981-. *Memberships:* Timaru Rotary Club, 1960-77. *Publications:* An Aid in Mini-Laparotomy Tubal Ligation, 1977. *Hobbies:* Golf; Bridge; Gardening; Fishing. *Address:* 24 Selwyn Street, Timaru, New Zealand.

BENOIT, Gaetan Michel, b. 15 Apr. 1942, Mauritius. Librarian. m. Marie Said, 20 June 1974, 2 daughters. *Education:* Higher School Certificate, Cambridge, UK, 1959; Associateship of Library Association, UK, 1973; Fellowship of Library Association, UK, 1977. *Appointments:* City Librarian, City Hall, Port-Louis, Mauritius, 1974-. *Memberships:* Vice Chairman, 1974, Secretary, 1975, Mauritius Library Association. *Publications:* City Library of Port-Louis: A brief history (1851-1968), 1977; Mauritius Newspaper Index, 1979; Eugene Morel: His life and work, 1980; various articles in foreign and local press. *Hobbies:* Journalism; Antiques; Bibliography. *Address:* 5 Bis Anderson Street, Curepipe, Mauritius.

BENOIT, Germain Edmour, b. 19 June 1919, Montreal, P. Quebec, Canada. Vice-President, Atlantic Region, Canadian Pacific Limited. m. Edith Diana Beasley, 4 Nov. 1951. *Education:* BA, Loyola College, 1940. *Appointments:* Trainman, Laurentian Division, 1942, Safety Agent, Conductor, 1947, Supervisor, Safety Loss and Damage, 1950, Quebec District, CP Rail, Montreal; Assistant Superintendent, Quebec Central Railway, Sherbrooke, 1951; Assistant Superintendent, St. Luc Terminal, CP Rail, Montreal, 1957; Assistant Superintendent, Montreal Terminals Division, CP Rail, Montreal, 1958; Manager, Quebec Central Railway, Sherbrooke, 1961; Assistant General Manager, 1963, General Manager, 1964, Vice-President, 1965-, Atlantic Region, CP Rail, Montreal, Canada. *Memberships:* Member of Numerous Associations including: President of the Arrostook River Railroad Company, Brunterm Limited; International Railway Company of Maine, Newport and Richford Railroad Company; Director of the Fredericton Railway Company; La Chambre de Commerce du District de Montréal; Montreal Board of Trade; Commission d'initiative et de développement économiques de Montréal (CIDEM). *Hobbies:* Golf; Curling. *Address:* 4583 Earsncliffe Avenue, PO Box 521, Snowdon Branch, Montreal, Quebec, Canada H3X 3T7.

BENSON, Babatunde Olusola, b. 4 July 1932, Ikorodu, Lagos State, Nigeria. Legal Profession. m. Olabisi Adunola Obafemi, 11 July 1959, 3 sons, 6 daughters. *Education:* Inns of Court, Lincoln's Inn, London; Called to the English Bar 1959; Enrolled in Nigeria 1959. *Appointments:* T.O. Shobowale Benson & Company (Solicitors), 1959-; General Secretary, Nigerian Bar Association, 1968-71; Chairman, African Bar Association, 1971, 1974-78; President, Nigerian Bar Association, 1978-80; Chief Host of the Sixth Commonwealth Law Conference in Lagos, 1980. *Memberships:* Metropolitan Club; Island Club; Lagos Lawn Tennis Club; Yoruba Tennis Club; Chairman, The Exclusives. *Hobbies:* Tennis; Swimming. *Address:* 50 Ogunlana Drive, Surulere, Lagos, Nigeria.

BENSTED, John, b. 12 Mar. 1942, Erith, Kent. Chartered Chemist. m. Josephine Marian Hobday, 6 July 1976. *Education:* BSc, 1964, PhD, 1968, DSc, 1981, London University; FRSC, 1977; FICeram, 1979. *Appointments:* Research Chemist, Associated Portland

Cement Manufacturers Limited (now Blue Circle Industries Limited), 1967; Principal Scientist, Head of Materials Section, Blue Circle Industries Limited, 1978. *Memberships:* Programme Secretary, Road and Building Materials Group, Society of Chemical Industry; Concrete Society; Inter-Varsity Club. *Publications:* Research Papers in Technical Journals; Research Presentations at International Cement Congresses. *Hobbies:* Walking; Foreign Languages; Vintage Transport; The Countryside. *Address:* Blue Circle Industries Limited, Research and Development Division, London Road, Greenhithe, Kent, England.

BENTLEY, David Bernard, b. 7 May 1925, Cushendall, Co. Antrim, Northern Ireland. Chemical Engineer. m. Barbara Anne Skinner, 10 Oct. 1952, 3 sons, 2 daughters. *Education:* BSc (Hons.), Queen University, Belfast, 1944-48; University New South Wales, 1953-54. *Appointments:* Chief Chemist, Courtaulds, Australia, 1956; Superintendent, Research & Development, Bapco, Bahrain, 1961; Production Manager, Monsanto, Coleraine, 1969; Technical Manager, ICI, (Richardsons), Belfast, 1974; Manufacturing Director, Belfast Rope Works, 1976; Managing Director, Bagco, Lagos, Nigeria. *Memberships:* Keyhaven Yacht Club; Apapa Boat Club, Sailing Secretary; Eb Golf Club. *Honours:* BOT, Yachtmasters Certificate, 1974; Institute Advanced Drivers, 1973. *Hobbies:* Sailing; Golf; Motoring. *Address:* 76 Marine Road, Apapa, Lagos, Nigeria.

BENTLEY, William, b. 15 Feb. 1927, Bury, Lancashire, England. Diplomat. m. Karen Bentley, 2 sons, 3 daughters. *Education:* Manchester University; Wadham College, Oxford, (1st class Modern History); College of Europe, Bruges. *Appointments:* HM Diplomatic Service: Tokyo, 1952-57, Foreign Office, 1957-60, 1963-65, 1973-76, UK Mission to UN, New York, 1960-63, Kuala Lumpur, 1965-69, Osaka, 1969-70, Belgrade, 1970-73; Ambassador to the Philippines, 1976-81; High Commissioner to Malaysia, 1981. *Memberships:* Brook's, London; Roehampton, Surrey. *Honours:* CMG, 1977. *Hobbies:* Golf; Fishing; Shooting; Skiing. *Address:* Carcosa, Kuala Lumpur.

BERGER, Peter Egerton Capel, b. 11 Feb. 1925, Hatfield, Herts. Royal Navy (ret.); College Bursar. m. June Kathleen Pigou, 1 dec. 1956, 3 daughters. *Education:* Harrow School, 1938-43. *Appointments:* Cadet Royal Navy, 1943; Normandy & South of France landings, HMS Ajax, 1944; Sub-Lieutenant, 1945, Lieutenant, 1946; Yangste incident, HMS Amethyst, 1949; Leiuteneant-Commander, 1949; Commander, Fleet Navigating Officer, Home Fleet, 1956; Navigating Officer, HM Yacht Britannia, 1956-58; Commanded HMS Torquay, 1962-64; Captain, Defence, Military Attaché The Hague, 1964; Commanded HMS Phoebe, 1964-66; Commodore Clyde, 1971-73; Rear-Admiral, Assistant Chief of Naval Staff, 1973; Vice-Admiral, 1975; Chiefof Staff to Commander-in-Chief, Fleet, 1976-78; Flag Officer Plymouth, NATO Commander Central Atlantic, 1979-81; Retired Royal Navy, 1981; Appointed Bursar of Selwyn College, Cambridge, 1981-. *Honours:* DSC, 1949; MVO, 1960; KCB, 1979; cbim, 1979. *Hobbies:* Shooting; Fishing; Reading; Walking. *Address:* Pincotts, Meadow Way, West Horsley, Surrey, KT24 6LL, England.

BERGERON, Viateur, b. 23 Aug. 1932, Ville-Marie, Province de Québec, Canada. Lawyer and Professor of Law. m. Claudette Roy, 27 Dec. 1958, 2 daughters. *Education:* BA, 1956, LL.L, 1959, DESD, (equivalent to a Master of Laws), 1960, LL.D, 1980, University of Ottawa, Canada. *Appointments:* Lecturer, 1960, Assistant Professor, 1962, Associate professor, 1966, Professor, 1971, Faculty of Law, Civil Law Section, University of Ottawa, Canada, 1971; General Practice in Law, 1961-; Barrister and Counsel, Bergeron, Gaudreau, 1974-. *Memberships:* Canadian Bar Association, President Québec Branch, 1981-82, Vice-President, 1980-81; Bar of the Province of Québec, Canada, President (batonnier), 1977-78; Vice-President, 1967-77, Vice-President, 1976-77, Bar of Hull; Acting Dean, Civil law Section, University of Ottawa, 1976-77; Associated with numerous other legal societies and committees. *Publications:* L'attribution d'une protection Légale aux malades mentaux, 1981; Jurivoc - Words, Computers and Communication in Law/Lexicographie, 1976, second edition, 1977. *Honours:* Queen's Counsel, 1976; Bilinguisme Juridique et Ordinateur, Scholarships, 1956, 57, 58, 59; Research Grants, 1969, 70; Research contracts, 1972-75; Research Grant, University of Ottawa to complete and publish book on Jurivoc, 1975-76. *Address:* 17 Lavallée Street, Hull, Québec, Canada, J8Z 1N9

BERGLUND, Cedric Ross, b. 20 July 1935, Young, New South Wales, Australia. Managing Director. m. Joan Beverley Antcliff, 11 Jan. 1958, 3 daughters. *Education:* ASTC Diploma (Credit) in Chemical Engineering, Newcastle College, 1958, BSc (Hons), 1961, University of New South Wales; Australian Administrative Staff College 1C4, 1964. *Appointments:* Trainee through to Assistant Production Director, John Lysaght (Australia) Ltd., 1952-64; Executive Assistant-Chairman, Guest Keen & Nettlefolds Aust. Ltd., 1964-69; New South Wales; Manager, Australian Packaging Inductries Ltd., now Van Leer Australia, 1969-74; Commercial Manager, Gillespie Bros. Holdings Ltd., 1974-78; Managing Director, Steetley Industries Limited, 1978-. *Memberships:* Australian Club, Sydney; Executive Committee of the Committee for Economic Development of Australia; Royal Australian Chemical Institute. *Hobbies:* Music; Opera; Ballet; Literature; Art; Botany; Squash. *Address:* 65 Minimbah Road, Northbridge, 2063 New South Wales, Australia.

BERKELEY, Hartog Carel, b. 14 Aug. 1928, London, England. Barrister. m. Margaret Diana Bingham, 24 Mar. 1954, 1 son, 1 daughter. *Education:* Eltham College, Kent, 1941-47. *Appointments:* Rouseabout, 1949-54; Public Servant, 1955-58; Barrister, 1959-; Queens Counsel (Victoria), 1972; Queens Counsel in NSW, Tasmania, Western Australia, Australian Capital Terriority. *Memberships:* Chairman, 1979, Victorian Bar Council; President, 1980, Australian Bar Association; Chairman, Essoign Club, 1981. *Hobbies:* Jogging; Farming. *Address:* 21 Selbourne Road, Toorak, Victoria, Australia.

BERKELEY, Kenneth Gordon Charles, b. 30 July 1929, Watford, Hertfordshire, England. Metallurgical Engineer. m. Elizabeth Anne Bocock, 13 Oct. 1956, 1 son. *Education:* Battersea College of Technology, 1949-53; ACT (Batt).; CEng; FIM; FICorrT. *Appointments:* Metal & Pipeline Endurance Limited, UK, 1953-56; Electrorust Proofing Inc., USA, 1956-57; Wallace & Tiernan, UK, 1957-59; Sturtevant Engineering Company, UK, 1959-62; Morgan, Berkeley & Company, UK, 1962-68; P.I. Corrision Engineering Limited, UK, 1968-. *Publications:* Corrosion Control on Buried Pipelines, (Department of Industry—Guide to practice); 15 papers on aspects of Cathodic Protection. *Honours:* IMM Travelling Scholarship, 1952. *Hobbies:* Vintage Cars; Wine; Philately; Theatre. *Address:* Coachmans Cottage, Rotherwick, Basingstoke, Hants, England.

BERKELEY, Lennox Randal, b. 12 May 1903, Boars Hill, Oxford. Composer. m. 14 Dec. 1946, 3 sons. *Education:* BA, Merton College, Oxford. *Appointments:* Member of BBC Music Division, 1942-45; Professor, Royal Academy of Music, 1947-68. *Publications:* Compositions: Chamber Music; Orchestral Music; Piano and Vocal Music of all Kinds; Three One-act Operas; One full length Opera. *Honours:* CBE, Knighthood, 1974. *Address:* 8 Warwick Avenue, London W2, England.

BERNABE, Juan Carrasco, b. 27 May 1932, Tipas, Tagig, Rizal, Philippines. Professional Electrical, Mechanical Engineer. m. Corazon C. Fermin, 28 Jan. 1956, 3 sons, 2 daughters. *Education:* Bachelor of Science in Electrical Engineering, 1952, Bachelor of Science in Mechanical Engineering, 1956, Mapua Institute of Technology. *Appointments:* Draftsman, Bureau of Telecommunication, Philippines, 1950-52; Electrician, Master Electrician, Acting Assistant Dredge Engineer V, Electrical Engineer, Bureau of Public Works, Philippines, 1958-65; Senior Engineer-/Consultant, Progressive Development Corporation, Araneta Enterprises, Philippines, 1966-68; General Manager/Chief Engineer, Secretary/Member, Tonga Electric Power Board, Tonga, 1968-. *Memberships:* Member of numerous Societies including: Philippine Professional Regulation Commission; National Standing Committee on Energy, Tonga; Nuku'alofa Club; Tonga Club. *Publications:* Planned, Designed and Implemented the Electricity Development Programme of the Kingdom of Tonga; Prospect of Mini-Hydro Power Development in the Kingdom of Tonga, seven pages, 1979. *Honours:* Third place, Board examination, Asso-

ciate Electrical Engineer, Philippine Board of Electrical Engineering Examiners, 1960; Certificate of Attendance, Seminar/Workshop on Mini-Hydro Power Generation, Katmandu, Nepal, 1979; Certificate of Attendance, Symposium on Master Plans for Electricity Supply, Kuching, Malaysia, 1981. *Hobbies:* Movies; Reading. *Address:* Fasi-moe-afi, Nuku'alofa, Tonga, SW Pacific.

BERNADT, Ian Nolan, b. 2 June 1941, Cape Town, South Africa. Ear Nose Throat Surgeon. m. Susan Queen, 15 April 1973, 1 son, 1 daughter. *Education:* MB, ChB, 1964; FRCS (ENG), 1970; FRACS, 1974. *Appointments:* Pravate Practice Perth & Fremantle, Western Australia; Consultant , Ear Nose Throat Surgeon, Fremantle Hospital. *Memberships:* Australian Medical Association; Secretary, Otolaryngological Society of Western Australia; Fremantle Sailing Club. *Publications:* Publications on Otorhinolargngological Topics. *Honours:* Two Silver Medals, 1966, 1967, Two Bronze Medals, 1971, 1972, Comrades Marathon, South Africa. *Hobbies:* Long Distance Running; Jazz; Australian Art. *Address:* 1 Sayer Street, Swanbourne, Western Australia.

BERNARD, Claude Charles Andre, b. 4 Mar. 1944, Paris, France. Scientist. m. Ora Zev Degani, 7 Mar. 1969, 1 son, 1 daughter. *Education:* Conservatoire des Arts et Metiers, Paris, 1963-65; Centre Departmental de transfusion sanguine, Paris, 1964-65; Diplome d'Etudes Superieures en Sciences Naturelles, Faculty of Sciences, Paris, 1965-68; Master of Sciences in Microbiology and Immunology, Faculty of Medicine, Montreal, Canada, 1969-70; Doctorate in Microbiology and Immunology, Faculty of Graduate Studies, University of Montreal, Canada, 1970-73; Doctorat es Sciences d'Etat, Universite Louis Pasteur, Strasbourg, France, 1978. *Appointments:* Biologiste adjoint at Experimental Immuno-Pathology Laboratory, Centre National de la Recherche Scientifique, Hopital St. Antoine, Paris, 1964-69; Demonstrator in Immunology, Faculty of Medicine, University of Montreal, Canada, 1970-72; Lecturer in Immunology, Microbiology and Biology, University of Quebec-Montreal, Canada, 1970-73; Visiting Research Fellow, Walter and Eliza Hall Institute, Melbourne, Victoria, 1973-77; Member of the Basel Institute for Immunology, Basel, Switzerland, 1977-79; Research Fellow, 1979-81, Senior Research Fellow, 1981, La Trobe University, Bundoora, Victoria. *Memberships:* Executive member and Honorary Treasurer, Brain-Behaviour Research Institute, 1981; Senior Associate Member, Clinical Research Unit, Walter and Eliza Hall Institute of Medical Research, 1979; Australian Society of Medical Research, 1979; Australian Society of Immunology, 1976; French Society of Immunology, 1977; Canadian Society of Immunology, 1973. *Publications:* Numerous scientific papers on immunity, Multiple Sclerosis, and autoimmunity. *Honours:* National Health and Medical Research Council of Australia, Senior Research Fellowship, 1981-86; La Trobe University, Research Fellowship, 1979-81; Multiple Sclerosis Society of Canada, Postdoctoral Fellowship, 1970-73, 1973-76; NS Award, Ministry of Foreign Affairs, France, 1969; NS Award, Quebec Ministry of Cultural Affairs, Canada, 1970. *Hobbies:* Skiing; Sailing; Classical Music; Tennis; Culinary Arts. *Address:* 18 Trentwood Avenue, North Balwyn 3104, Victoria, Australia.

BERRY, The Hon. Anthony George, b. 12 Feb. 1925, Farnham Royal, England. Member of Parliament. m. Hon. Mary Roche, 1954 (Div., 1965), 1 son, 3 daughters; m. Sarah Clifford-Turner, 5 April 1966, 1 son, 1 daughter. *Education:* Eton College, 1938-43; MA, Christ Church, Oxford, 1947-50. *Appointments:* Assistant Editor, Sunday Times, 1952-54; Editor, Sunday Chronicle, 1954-55; Director, Kemsley Newspapers, 1955-59; Member of Parliament for Southgate, 1964-; Opposition Whip, 1975-79; Government Whip and Vice-Chamberlain of the Household, 1979-81; Comptroller of the Household, 1981. *Memberships:* Whites; Portland. *Honours:* Commander, Order of St. John, 1962; Fellow, Royal Society of Arts, 1969; Justice of the Peace, Cardiff, 1960; High Sheriff of Glamorgan, 1961. *Address:* 1 Graham Terrace, London SW1, England.

BERRY, Duncan Elmslie, b. 9 Feb. 1936, Derby, England. Barrister; Chief Parliamentary Counsel for Tasmania. 2 sons, 2 daughters. *Education:* LLB(Hons),

Nottingham, England, 1957; LLM (Hons), Victoria University of Wellington, New Zealand, 1963; Barrister-at-Law, Grays Inn, 1961; Barrister & Solicitor of the High Court of New Zealand; Barrister of the Supreme Court of New Zealand; Barrister of the Supreme Court of New South Wales, 1975; Barrister of the Supreme Court of Tasmania, 1978. *Appointments:* Examiner of Titles, Wellington District Land Registry, 1961-63; Assistant Land Registrar, South Auckland Land District, 1964; Assistant Parliamentary Counsel, New Zealand, 1965-71; Crown Counsel, Hong Kong, 1971-75; Senior Legislative Draftsman, NSW Parliamentary Counsel's Office, 1975-78; Chief Parliamentary Counsel for Tasmania, 1978-. *Memberships:* President, Amnesty International, Tasmania. *Publications:* Thesis: A Strata Titles Act for New Zealand? *Hobbies:* Cricket; Squash; Bushwalking; Table Tennis; Music; Cinema. *Address:* 15 Nile Avenue, Sandy Bay, Tasmania 7005,

BERRYMAN, Douglas Barrie, b. 30 Dec. 1926, Christchurch, New Zealand. Consulting Orthopaedic Surgeon. 4 sons. *Education:* Selwyn College, University of Otago (Medical School), 1946-50; Auckland (University) Hospital, 1951-53; Demonstrator Physiology Department, University of Otago, 1957; FRCS, Finals Course, Guy's Hospital, London, 1958; FRCS Ed, 1958; FRACS, 1961. *Appointments:* Senior Registrar, Orthopaedic Surgery, Royal Children's Hospital, 1959, Austin Hospital, Heidelberg, Melbourne, 1960; Assistant Orthopaedic Surgeon, St. Vincent's Hospital, Melbourne, 1962-69, Austin Hospital, Heidelberg, 1963-73; Consultant Orthopaedic Surgeon, Williamstown & District Hospital, 1970-73, Albury Base Hospital, 1973-75, Mercy Hospital, 1973-75; Private Practice as Consulting Orthopaedic Surgeon, 1975-. *Memberships:* Pan Pacific Surgical Association; Australian Orthopaedic Association; Syllabus Organiser, Archaeological & Anthropological Society of Victoria. *Publications:* Coauthor: Evaluation of Raised Serum Amylase Levels in Non-Pancreatic Disease; Management of Flexion Rotation Injuries of the Cervical Spine; Wilson's Osteotomy of the 1st Metatarsal in the Adolescence and the Young Adult. *Hobbies:* Collecting Asian and Pacific flutes, oboes and trumpets; Archaeology. *Address:* Iris Court, The Bluff, Cannon's Creek 3930, Victoria, Australia.

BESSBOROUGH, Frederick Edward (Earl of), b. 29 Mar. 1913. Parliamentarian. m. 1948, Mary, 1 daughter. *Education:* Eton; MA, Trinity College, Cambridge. *Appointments:* Secretary, League of Nations High Commission for Refugees, 1936-39; War Service, 1939-45; Second and subsequently First Secretary, British Embassy, Paris, 1944-49; Director, Associated Broadcasting Development Company Ltd, ATV, Glyndebourne Arts Trust; English Stage Company Ltd, etc, 1950-63; Member of UK Parliamentary Delegation to USSR, 1960; Parliamentary Secretary for Science, 1963; Jt Parliamentary Secretary Under-Secretary of State for Education and Science, 1964; Conservative front bench spokesman, 1964-70; Minister of State, Ministry of Technology, 1970; Chairman, Committee of Inquiry into the Res. Assocs, 1972-73; Lectures throughout the world on British Science & Industry Member, European Parliament, 1972-79; Deputy Leader, European Conservative Group, 1972-77; Member, EP Committees on Budgets, Energy, Research and Technology; House of Lords Select Committees on European Communities and Science and Technology, 1979-. *Memberships:* President, SE Association of Building Societies; Men of Trees; Chichester Conservative Association; Chairman of Governors, Dulwich College, 1972-73, International Atlantic Committee, 1952-55; European Atlantic Group, 1954-61; British Society for International Understanding, 1939-71. *Publications:* Nebuchadnezzar, 1939; The Four Men, 1951; Like Stars Appearing, 1953; The Noon is Night, 1954; Darker the Sky, 1955; Triptych, 1957; A Place in the Forest, 1958; Return to the Forest, 1962; Articles and reviews. *Honours:* Order of St John of Jerusalem; Chevalier Legion of Honour; MRI; FRGS. *Address:* 4 Westminister Gardens, London SW1, England.

BESSELL, Michael John, b. 22 Oct. 1946, Launceston, Tasmania. Legal Practitioner. m. Suzanne Tyson, 29 Mar. 1969, 2 sons, 2 daughters. *Education:* Matriculation, St Patrick's College, Launceston, 1955-64; LLB, University of Tasmania, 1965-69. *Appointments:* Dobson Mitchell and Allport, Hobart Tasmania, 1968-69; B S Sproule and Company, Burnie, Tasmania 1970-72; Crisp, Hudson and Mann, Burnie, Tasmania, 1972-. *Memberships:* Council, Law Society of Tasmania; President, North-West Law Society; Tasmanian Legal Assistance Committee; North-West Legal Aid Committee; Fellow, Taxation Institute of Australia; Board of Management Stella Maris School; Burnie Club; Seabrook Golf Club; Cooee Football Club; Burnie Cricket Club. *Hobbies:* Golf; Bridge; Cricket. *Address:* 26 Seaview Avenue, Burnie, Tasmania, Australia.

BEST, James Calbert, b. 12 July 1926, New Glasgow, Nova Scotia, Canada. Public Service Executive. m. Barbara Doreen Phills, 19 Oct. 1957, 3 sons, 1 daughter. *Education:* BA, Dalhousie University, 1948; Diploma Journalism, 1948; MA, Political Science—1 year. *Appointments:* National President, Civil Service Association, Canada, 1957-65; Director, Personnel & Administration, Office of Comptroller of Treasury, Canada, 1965-69; Director General Administration, Department of Supply & Services, Canada, 1969-70; Assistant Deputy Minister, Department of Manpower & Immigration, 1970-74; Assistant Deputy Minister Administration, 1974-75; Director, Applied Studies in Government Commonwealth Secretariat, London, 1975-77; Executive Director, Immigration & Demographic Policy Department of Employment & Immigration, 1978-. *Memberships:* Institute of Public Administration of Canada; World Commonwealth Society; Federal Institute of Management. *Publications:* Various articles. *Honours:* Centennial Medal, Canada, 1967. *Hobbies:* Reading; Music; Photography. *Address:* 2067 Delmar Drive, Ottawa, K1H 5P6, Canada.

BEST, Keith, b. 10 June 1949, Brighton, England. Member of Parliament and Barrister. *Education:* Brighton College; BA(Hons) Jurisprudence, Keble College, Oxford University, 1967-70. *Appointments:* Called to the Bar by the Inner Temple, 1971. *Memberships:* Captain, Territorial Army, Royal Artillery. *Publications:* Write Your Own Will, 1978; The Right Way to Prove a Will, 1981. *Hobbies:* Walking; Photography. *Address:* 7, Alderley Terrace, Holyhead, Anglesey.

BESWICK, (The Rt. Hon. The Lord), b. 21 Aug. 1911, Hucknall, Notts, England. m. Dora, 1935, 1 son, 1 daughter. *Appointments:* Pilot, Royal Air Force, 1940-45; Pilot British Overseas Airways, 1945-46; Member of Parliament, 1945-59; PPS, Secretary of State, ATV, 1946-49; Under Secretary of State, Civil Aviation, 1950-51; Parliamentary Secretary Commonwealth Office 1965-67; Chief Whip House of Lords, 1967-70; Captain, Queens Bodyguard 1967-70; Special Advisor, Chairman British Aircraft Corporation, 1971-74; Minister of State, Industry, 1974-76; Chairman, British Aerospace, 1977-80. *Publications:* Plan for the Aircraft Industry 1955. *Honours:* Life Peerage, Baron, 1964; Member Privy Council 1968; Deputy Leader House of Lords 1974-76; Companion Royal Aeronautical Society 1977; Fellow Royal Society of Arts 1978. *Address:* House of Lords, London SW1.

BETHAM, Valerie Joan (Mrs), b. 4 July 1933, Harrow. Medical Practitioner. m. Dr Geoffrey Furnival Howden, 28 July 1962, 1 son, 1 daughter. *Education:* MB, BS, FFARCS, 1971, Westminster Hospital Medical School, 1962. *Appointments:* SRA, St Thomas's Hospital, London; Registrar, Bristol Royal Infirmary; Rotating Senior Registrar, National Hospital for Nervous Diseases, London, Brompton Hospital and Royal Free Hospital; Consultant Anaesthetist, Royal Gwent Hospital; SMO, Port Moresby Hospital; Senior Lecturer, University PNG. *Memberships:* Association of Anaesthetists UK; South Western Association of Anaesthetists. *Hobbies:* Reading; Travel. *Address:* 66 Linden Road, Bristol 6, England.

BETHEL, Harcourt Rodney, b. 29 May 1913, Cherokee Sound, Abaco, Bahamas. Advertising Manager. m. Kathleen Agatha Bethel, 31 Mar. 1944, 1 son, 1 daughter. *Appointments:* Royal Bank of Canada, 1927-36; Ships Wireless Operator, 1936-38; General Manager ZNE Radio Station, Nassau, 1938-70; Advertising Manager, The Tribune, 1970-. *Honours:* Chamber of Commerce Award, 1971. *Hobbies:* Boxing; Reading; Travelling. *Address:* Camperdown Heights, Eastern Road, Nassau, Bahamas.

BEVEGE, David Ian, b. 29 Mar. 1939, Brisbane, Queensland, Australia. Forest Scientist. m. Valerie Mae Edmonds, 1972, 2 sons, 1 daughter. *Education:* Matriculation, University of Queensland, Undergraduate, 1957-58; Australian Forestry School Canberra 1960-61; Diploma of Forestry, (Distinction), AFS 1962; BSc, Forestry, University Queensland, 1962; BSc, Forestry (First Class Honours), 1965; PhD, University New England, 1972. *Appointments:* Management Surveys, Native Forests, 1962, Silvicultural Research, Conifer Plantations, Queensland State Department Forestry, 1962-67; Junior Research Fellow in Botany, Ecophysiology and Native Conifers, University of New England, Armidale, NSW, 1967-70; Visiting Scientist, Ecophysiology of conifers and crop plants, CSIRO Division of Soils, Adelaide, South Australia, 1971-72; Officer-in-Charge, Forest Soils and Nutrition and Biology Laboratory, Queensland State Department Forestry, 1972 81-; Numerous Consultancies in the field of Forest nutrition, soils and microbiology. *Memberships:* Institute of Foresters of Australia; Forest Soils and Nutrition Working Group, Australian Forestry Council; Australian New Zealand Association for the Advancement of Science; Ecological Society of Australia*Publications:* Over 50 papers 1963-81 covering the fields of plantation silviculture, nursery nutrition, fertilization and nutrition of plantation conifers, eucalypts, physiology of mycorrhizas, nitrogen fixation, biomass and mineral cycling, reforestation following surface mining. *Honours:* State Fellowship in Forestry, University of Queensland, 1957-61; Schlich Memorial Gold Medal, Australian Forestry School, 1961; Hedges Prize, Institute of Foresters of Australia, 1965; Junior Research Fellowship, Rural Credits Development Fund, Reserve Bank of Australia, 1967-70; Nuffield Foundation Research Grant, 1971; Rural Credits Development Fund Research Grant, Reserve Bank of Australia, 1978-81; International Union Forestry Research Organisations, Scientific Achievement Award, 1981. *Hobbies:* Reading; Gardening; Photography; Music. *Address:* 22 Goolman Street, Chapel Hill, Q4069, Australia.

BHANDARI, Sunder Singh, b. 12 Apr. 1921, Udaipur, India. Advocate. *Education:* BA, 1939, MA, 1941, SD College, Kanpur; LLB, 1942, DAV College, Kanpur. *Appointments:* Advocate, Mewar High Court, Udaipur, 1942-43; Headmaster, Shiksha Bhawan, Udaipur, 1943-46; Divisional Organiser RSS Jodhpur, 1946-50; General Secretary, Bharatiya Jama Sangh, Rajasthan, 1951-60; Secretary, All India Bharatiya Jana Sangh, 1960-67; General Secretary BJS, 1967-77; Member, National Executive Janta Party, 1977-80; Treasurer, Bharatiya Janata Party, 1980-; Deputy Leader, Janata Parliamentary Party, 1977-80; Deputy Leader, Bharatiya Janata Parliamentary Party, 1980-. *Memberships:* Rashtriya Swayamsewak Sangh, 1939-; Bharatiya Jana Sough; 1951-77; B.J.P. 1980-; Council of Scientific and Industrial Research Enquiry Committee, 1968-71; Agricultural Prices Commission, 1977-79; Central Posts and Telegraphs Advisory Council, 1978-; Parliament Committee on Office of Profits, 1968-72; Parliament Committee on Public Undertakings, 1980-; Member, Rajya Sabha (Council of States) 1966-72, and since 1976. *Hobbies:* Social and Cultural Activities; Reading. *Address:* 11 Ashoka Road, New Delhi, 1, India.

BHARGAVA, Rai, Narender, Kumar, b. 7 June 1944, Hyderabad, India. Doctor, General Surgeon. *Education:* MBBS, Marathwada University, Aurangabad, 1967; MS, General Surgergy, Osmania University, Hyderabad, 1971; FICS, General Surgery, USA, 1979. *Appointments:* Assistant Professor of Surgery, Osmania Medical College, 1975-80; Surgeon, Government General Hospital King Kothi. *Memberships:* Indian Medical Association; Association of Surgeons of India; Gastroenterology Society of India; Past President, Civil Assistant Surgeons Association, Osmania Medical College and Osnamia Hospital; Member Nizam Club; Fateh Maidan Club; Boat Club; Hyderabad Race Club. *Publications:* Metabolism of Drugs and Carcinogens in Man: Antipyrine Elimination as an Indicator, 1979; Study of Incidence of Liver Disease in Grape Wine Sprayers around Hyderabad, 1978. Treatment of Trigeminal Neuralgia by Injection of Alcohol in Gaserion Ganglion, 1979. *Hobbies:* Cricket; Table Tennis; Lawn Tennis; Social Service. *Address:* 5-4-7, Jawaharlal Nehru Road, Hyderabad, 500001, A.P. India.

BHAT, Panemangalore Appraya, b. 21 Oct. 1920, Panemangalore, Karnatak, India. Business. m. Jahnavi Bai, 16 June 1948, 2 sons, 3 daughters. *Education:* Business Management. *Appointments:* Director, Morvi Vegetable Products Limited, 1944-59; Chief Executive,

PolyChemn Limited 1961-63; Committee Executive, Hindustan Times Limited 1959-60; Managing Director, Asian Electronics Limited 1963-78; President, Bhat and Pikale Electronics Consultancy 1978-; Dir. Goa Resistors P Ltd., Goa Teletubes P Ltd., Goa Ceramics P Ltd., Collem Electrolytics P Ltd. *Memberships:* Honorary Secretary, South Kanara District Congress Committee; Honorary Secretary, Morvi District Congress Committee, 1945-48; Rotary Club of Morvi; Morvi Chamber of Commerce and Industry; Sir Lukhdirji Endowment Trust, Orphanage; Electronics Components Industries Association; All India Instrument Manufacturers' Organisation; President, Santa Cruz Electronics Manufacturers Exporters Association; National Advisory Committee on Electronics and several government bodies. *Publications:* Regular contributor of articles and letters to the press, magazines and organising seminars, symposia. *Honours:* President of India-Padmashri Award, 1973; Acting President of India: Award of Self Made Business man and Industrialist of India, 1975; Invited to serveral International Delegations sponsored by Government of India. *Hobbies:* Yachting; Stamp-collection; Collection of Liberation movement archives. *Address:* Firdosh Manzil, 41, Byramji Jijibhoy Road, Band Stand, Bandra, Bombay 400050, India.

BHATHAL, Ragbir Singh, b. Malaysia. Director, Singapore Science Centre. *Education:* BSc(Hons) 1965; PhD(Physics) 1968. *Appointments:* University Professor 1969-75; Director 1976-. *Memberships:* Singapore National Academy of Science; Singapore Association for the Advancement of Science. *Publications:* Over 50 publications in international and regional journals; 25 Paintings; Co-Editor, Singapore in the Year 2000; University and Government Research in Singapore. *Honours:* Commonwealth Scholar. *Hobbies:* Abstract Art. *Address:* Singapore Science Centre, Science Centre Road, Jurong, Singapore 2260.

BHAUMIK, Rabi Nanda, b. 12 Dec. 1944, Deora, East Bengal, Bangla Desh. Teaching. m. Alo Sarkar 8 Feb. 1975, 1 son. *Education:* Higher Secondary, 1961; Bachelor of Science, 1964; Master of Science, 1967; Doctor of Philosophy, (Topology), 1972. *Appointments:* Assistant Professor, Saugor University, M.P., India, 1970-71; Assistant Professor, M.B.B. College, Tripura, India, 1971-80; Lecturer in Mathematics, Calcutta University, P. G. Centre, Agartala, Tripura, India, 1980-. *Memberships:* American Mathematical Society; Indian Mathematical Society; Tripra Mathematical Society; Allahabad Mathematicla Society. *Publications:* Six Research articles on Topology published and few others are sent for publications; Seven Popular articles on Mathematics; Editor of Bulletin/Journal of Tripura Mathematical Society. *Honours:* Member of Management Committee, Central School, Agartala, 1980-83; General Secaretary, Tripura Mathematical Society, 1981. *Hobbies:* Reading Books; Forming a personal Library. *Address:* 32, Dhaleswar, PO Agartala College, Triphra, India, 799004.

BHIM, Tamesar, b. 10 Jan. 1925, Navua, Fiji. Auditor-General of Fiji. m. Mankuár, 13 Mar. 1944, 2 sons, 2 daughters. *Education:* Fellow, New Zealand Society of Accountants; Fellow, Institute of Chartered Secretaries and Administrators; Fiji Institute of Accountants. *Appointments:* After some years service in Fiji Government, appointed, Auditor, 1955; Senior Auditor, 1964; Deputy Director of Audit, 1969; Auditor-General, 1970-; Member, Fiji Institute of Accountants. *Publications:* Papers for various conferences. *Honours:* CBE, 1978; Justice of Peace, Fiji, 1980. *Hobbies:* Gardening; Reading; Sport. *Address:* 287 Princes Road, Tamavua, Suva, Fiji, South Pacific.

BHOGA, Mehnga Singh, b. 1 Jan. 1924. Accountant (Incorporated). m. 26 Nov. 1943, 4 sons, 3 daughters. *Education:* Master of Commerce degree, 1952; PhD (Com) 1956. *Appointments:* Managing Director, Bhogal General Mills and Rural Industries, (Regd) Kamam (144513) District Jullunduz, Punjab, India; Managing Partner, Bhogal Globe Travel Corporation. *Memberships:* Senate and Syndicate, Commercial University, New Delhi; Fellow: Institute of Commerce, Birmingham, United Kingdom; Society of Incorporated Accountants and Auditors of India; Society of Incorporated Secretaries of India. *Publications:* Agricultural Commercial Products in India. *Honours:* Golden Medal in Master of Commerce (Degree) Examination. *Hob-*

bies: Music. *Address:* Kamam (144513) Distt Jullundur, Punjab, India.

BIALOGUSKI, Michael, b. 19 Mar. 1917, Kiev, Ukraine. Conductor. m. Nonnie Peifer 16 Jan. 1957, 1 son, 2 daughters. *Education:* Violin, Vilna Conservatorium, Poland; MB, BS, University of Sydney. *Appointments:* Leader, Operetta Theatre, Vilna, Poland, 1939-41; Solo Violinist, Sydney, Australia, 1941-64; Member of Sydney Symphony Orchestra, 1950-51; Free-lance Conductor, London, 1965-; Principal Conductor, Commonwealth Philharmonic Orchestra, 1974-. *Memberships:* Incorporated Society of Musicians, London; Lions Club; Royal Automobile Club; St. James Bridge Club. *Publications:* The Petrou Story, 1955. *Hobbies:* Golf; Bridge; Medicine. *Address:* 'Poynings', Waterhouse Lane, Kingswood, Surrey, KT20 6HU, England.

BICKERTON, Arthur William, b. 27 Aug. 1919, Ringwood, Victoria, Australia. Member of Parliament, retired. m. Marjorie Jean Campbell, 1944, 1 son 1 daughter. *Education:* Several Victorian Schools. *Appointments:* Captain, Australian Infantry Forces, 1939-45; Coal mining and Tin mining Industry, New South Wales and Western Australia, 1946-58; Western Australian Parliament, 1958-74. *Memberships:* Commonwealth Parliamentary Association; Press Club; Royal Commonwealth Society. *Honours:* Queen's Silver Jubilee Medal. *Hobbies:* Painting; Writing; Poetry. *Address:* 4 Mandurah Road, Mandurah. 6210, West Australia.

BIDE, Austin Ernest, b. 11 Sept. 1915, London, England. Chemist. m. Irene Ward, 16 June 1941, 3 daughters. *Education:* BSc, University of London, 1933-39; Fellow of the Royal Society of Chemistry. *Appointments:* Research Chemist Glaxo, 1940-44, responsible for Chemical Development and Industrial Property, 1944-54; Deputy Company Secretary, 1954-59, Company Secretary, 1959-65, Director, 1963-71, Deputy Chairman, 1971-73, Chairman and Chief Executive, 1973-80, Chairman, 1980-, Glaxo Holdings Ltd; Non-executive Director, 1977, Non-Executive Deputy Chairman, 1980, British Leyland Limited; Non-Executive Director, J Lyons & Co. Ltd., 1977-78. *Memberships:* Companies Committee, 1974-80, Council, 1974-, Chairman, Research & Technology Committee, 1977-, Confederation of British Industry; Council of British Institute of Management and Companions Committee, 1976-; Chairman, BIM Finance Committee and Director, BIM Foundation, 1977-79; Member of the Council of the Imperial Society of Knights Bachelor. *Honours:* Knight Bachelor, 1980. *Hobbies:* Fishing; Handicrafts. *Address:* Clarges House, 6-12 Clarges Street, London, W.1., England.

BIELESKI, Roderick Leon, b. 3 Aug. 1931, Auckland, New Zealand. Research Scientist. m. Valerie Mary Harvey, 17 Aug. 1957, 2 daughters. *Education:* BSc., Junior and Senior Lancaster Prizes, 1950-52, MSc. (1st Hons) (Kauri Research Scholarship), 1953-55, Auckland University College, University of New Zealand; PhD (CSIRO Research Studentship), University of Sydney, Australia, 1955-58. *Appointments:* Fruit Research Division(DSIR), 1958-60; On Leave; University of California, Los Angeles, USA, 1960-61; Fruit Research Division (DSIR), 1961-69; On Leave; UCLA, 1969-70; Plant Diseases Division (DSIR), 1970-79; On Leave; UC Davis, 1979-80; Director, Division of Horticulture and Processing (DSIR), 1980-. *Memberships:* Royal Society of New Zealand; National Committee of Biological Sciences; Auckland Institute and Musuem; American Society of Plant Physiologists; Australian Society of Plant Physiologists; New Zealand Society of Plant Physiologists; American Orchid Society; New Zealand Biochemical Society; Royal New Zealand Society of Horticulture; New Zealand Association of Scientists. *Publications:* 50 Scientific Publications on Sugar Transport; Phosphate Metabolism and Nutrition; Phloem Physiology; Methods of Plant Analysis; Polyol Metabolism. *Honours:* Research Medal, New Zealand Association of Scientists, 1966; Senior Fulbright Fellow, 1960; FRS, NZ, 1973. *Hobbies:* Gardening; Tramping; Fabric Dyeing. *Address:* 176 Redoubt Road, Manukau City, New Zealand.

BIESHAAR, Theodorus, b. 30 June 1927, Amsterdam, Holland. Company Secretary. m. Wiebrigge Anna Bosma, 21 Mar. 1953, 3 sons, 2 daughters. *Education:*

Diploma, Hotel School, Holland, 1946; Degree, Accountancy, Australia, 1958; Degree, Cost Accountancy, Australia, 1961; Degree Secretarial, Australia, 1963; Diploma, Computer Technology, 1966. *Appointments:* Chief Accountant, 1952-59, Company Secretary, 1959-61, Chief Cost Accountant Controller, 1961-69, Company Secretary, Finance Manager Controller, 1969-, various subsidiaries of Ansett Transport Industries Ltd. *Memberships:* Associate and Senior Associate, Australia Society of Accountants; Associate, Chartered Institute of Secretaries; Australian Computer Society; Associate Fellow, Australian Institute of Management. *Hobbies:* Woodworking; Reading; Outdoor sports. *Address:* 22 Haroldstreet, Glenroy, Victoria, Australia, 3046.

BIGGS-DAVISON, John Alec (Sir), b. 7 June 1918, Boscombe, Bournemouth, England. Member of Parliament. m. 27 Nov. 1948, 2 sons, 4 daughters. *Education:* Scholar, Clifton College; Exhibitioner, MA, Magdalen College, Oxford, England. *Appointments:* Commissioned in Royal Marines, 1939; Indian Civil Service(last British Officer appointed to Punjab Commission), 1942; Forward Liaison Officer Cox's Bazar, 1943-44; Political Assistant and Commandant Border Military Police and later Deputy Commissioner Dera Ghazi Khan, 1946-48; Conservative Research Department, 1950-55; Secretary, British Conservative Delegation to Council of Europe, 1952 and 1953; Conservative MP for Chigwell, 1955-74; Conservative MP for Epping Forest, 1974-. *Memberships:* European Movement; European League for Economic Co-operation; Pan-Europe Club; Deputy Parliamentary Chairman, Conservative Commonwealth and Overseas Council; Royal Stuart Society; Founder, Pakistan Society; Trustee and Member of Board of Management, Aid to the Church in Need; Carlton Club; Special Forces Club. *Publications:* George Wyndham, A Study in Toryism, 1951; Tory Lives, 1952; The Uncertain Ally 1917-1957, 1957; The Walls of Europe, 1962; Portugues Guinea, Nailing a Lie, 1970; Africa, Hope Deferred, 1972; The Hand is Red, 1974; Rock Firm for the Union, 1979; Broadcasts, many pamphlets and articles on political and historical subjects. *Honours:* Gold Medal, London to Brighton Pacesetters' Walk, 1963; Knight Bachelor, 1981. *Hobbies:* Reading; Riding; Tennis; Walking; Jogging. *Address:* House of Commons, London, SW1A OAA, England.

BIGGS, Frederick William, b. 8 Apr. 1927, Adelaide, South Australia. Chairman, Woodham Biggs Group of Companies (Real Estate). m. Roslyn Claire, 1 son, 2 daughters. *Education:* Prince Alfred's College, Adelaide, South Australia; Licensed Valuer, Auctioneer, Registered Manager (Real Estate). *Appointments:* Chairman and Managing Director of several companies, all related to Real Estate - real estate agency, development company, finance company, investment company, valuation company; Owner of these companies. *Memberships:* Stock Exchange; Naval & Military Club. *Hobbies:* Hunting; Fishing; Sailing; Gulf. *Address:* Ceywood, 7 Sturt Valley Road, Stirling, 5152, South Australia.

BIKANGAGA, John, b. 1 July 1921, Kabale, Uganda. Teacher. m. 22 Dec. 1945, 4 sons, 3 daughters. *Education:* Diploma in Education, Makerere College, 1938-40; BSc, University of Wales, UK, 1949-53. *Appointments:* Headmaster, Kigezi High School, 1941-49; Headmaster, Makerere College School, 1956-62; Backbench Member, Legislative Council, 1958-60; Deputy Chairman, Uganda Public Service Commission, 1962-63; Chairman, Public Service Commission, 1979; Chairman, National Housing Corporation, 1967-74; Chairman, Makerere University Council, 1974-; Chairman, Boys Brigade of Uganda, 1968-; Chairman, Uganda YMCA, 1961-68; Constitutional Head of Kigezi District. *Memberships:* Boys Brigade; YMCA; Lions President, Lions Club; Trustee, Church of Uganda; Trustee, International Year of Child, Uganda. *Publications:* Church of Uganda: Report-Survey on Administration; Uganda Government: Report-Public Service Salaries Commission; Grading Committee on Parasatal Bodies and Companies. *Honours:* Canon of St. Paul's Cathedral (Namirembe). *Hobbies:* Classical Music; Walking; Football; Tennis; Cricket. *Address:* PO Box 3265, Kampala, Uganda.

BILISH, Anthony George, b. 26 May 1941, Tekopuru, New Zealand. Machinery Company Executive. m. 10 Sept. 1966, 1 son, 2 daughters. *Appointments:* Clerk,

New Zealand Post Office, Auckland, 1957-60; Sales Manager, International Harvester Co., 1960-75; Sales Representative, Industrial Steel and Plant, 1975; Managing Director, Machinery Equipment Ltd, Earthmoving and Construction Machinery, Auckland, New Zealand, 1975-. *Memberships:* Auckland Trotting Club. *Hobbies:* Athletics; Swimming. *Address:* 14 Wayne Place, Mt. Roskill, Auckland, New Zealand.

BILLINGTON, Harry George Read, b. 7 Mar. 1930, Sydney, New South Wales, Australia. Inspector of Schools. m. Elaine Audrey Muir, 6 Feb. 1952, 2 sons, 2 daughters. *Education:* Dip. T. Mus, New South Wales State Conservatorium of Music; BA(Hons), Sydney University, Australia; Member, Australian College Education. *Appointments:* Teacher, Sydney Boys' High School; Assistant Supervisor of Music, Department of Education; Inspector of Schools, Department of Education. *Memberships:* International Society for Music Education; Foundation Secretary, NSW Chapter, ASME; Association Music Education Lecturers; Board of Governors, NSW State Conservatorium of Music. *Publications:* Creative Music Making; Sounds and Western Music; Your World of Sounds. *Hobbies:* Travel; Book collecting. *Address:* 6 O'Brien's Road, Hurstville, NSW 2220, Australia.

BIMPONG-BUTA, Seth Yeboa, b. 4 June 1940, Accra. Lawyer. m. 23 Aug. 1979, 1 son, 3 daughters. *Education:* University of Ghana, Legon, 1963-67; Kings College, University of London, UK, 1977-78; LLB (Hons) (Ghana), 1966; LLM (London), 1978; Summer Advanced International Law Course at Hague Academy of International, Netherlands, 1979. *Appointments:* Private Legal Practitioner, 1967-72; Law Reporting - Council for Law reporting, Accra, 1972-; Promoted Assistant Editor, Ghana Law Reports, 1975; Appointed Assistant Editor Review of Ghana Law, 1976; Acting Editor, Ghana Law Reports, 1979; Editor, Review of Ghana Law, 1980; part-time Senior Lecturer in Law, Ghana School of Law, 1979-. *Publications:* Articles published in Review of Ghana Law include: Caveats in application for grant of Probate or Letters of Administration, 1972; Customary Mores and Sale of Photographs of a married woman, 1973; When may an alien be deported, 1974; Certiorari and inferior courts, 1976; Joinder of insurers in actions for damages against their insured, 1977; Detention in the interest of national security, 1979. *Honours:* Commonwealth Fund Award for attachment course in Law Reporting with Butterworths, London, 1972; Advanced International Law Course award per Hague Academy of International Law, 1979. *Hobbies:* Backyard farming including rearing of rabbits. *Address:* Bungalow No. 2, Nima Avenue, Accra.

BINGHAM, Warren Davis, b. 20 Feb. 1940, USA. Executive/Publisher. m. Janet A Ward, 18 Oct. 1957, 1 son, 4 daughters. *Education:* BA, 1960, MS, 1961, Massachusetts Institute of Technology, USA; PhD, Harvard University, USA, 1966; ADM Diploma, Wharton School of Business, USA. *Appointments:* Managing Director, Richard de Boo Ltd., Toronto, Canada; Director, Oyez (Canada) Ltd., Toronto, Canada; President, MWM/Dexter, Inc., New York, USA; President Harbour Press, Boston, USA; Research Associate, Harvard University, Cambridge, Massachusettes, USA. *Memberships:* AMA-Presidents Association; Alpine Club of Canada; Audubon Society. *Publications:* Various scientific papers. *Honours:* Presidents Award CFC, 1976-78. *Hobbies:* Alpinism; Photography; Skiing. *Address:* 133 Shanley Terrace, Oakville, Ontario, Canada.

BINNIE-DAWSON, John Lewis Mervyn, b. 7 Feb. 1930, Sydney, Australia. Professor of Psychology. m. Judith Ridgley, 22 Mar. 1966, 1 son, 1 daughter. *Education:* BA, University of California, USA, 1951; Dip. Anthropology, 1960, DPhil, 1963, MA, 1969, University of Oxford, UK. *Appointments:* Post Graduate Research Scholar, University of Oxford, UK, 1960-61; Research Lecturer, University of Edinburgh, Scotland, 1961-65; Senior Lecturer, University of Sydney, Australia, 1965-67; Foundation Professor, 1967-, Dean, Faculty of Social Sciences, 1968-, University of Hong Kong; Visiting Fellow, Wolfson College, University of Oxford, UK, 1969-70; Visiting Professor, Latro University, Bristol University and E.T.S., 1976-. *Memberships:* Founder President, IACCP, 1978-80; Founder Chairman, H. K. Psychological Society, 1968-72; Fellow, New York Academy of Science; Fellow FRAI;

Fellow, B. Psy. Society; Fellow, H.K. Psychology Society; Fellow, Australian Psychology Society. *Publications:* Numerous papers in Journals, review articles; 12 Books; 15 Chapters in books; 29 Conference papers. *Honours:* Reserve Decoration, R.D. Royal Navy, 1971; Retired List with rank of Lieutenant Commander, 1980. *Hobbies:* Yachting; Painting. *Address:* 6 Felix Villas, 61 Mt. Davis Rd, Hong Kong.

BIRCH, William Francis, b. 9 Apr. 1934, Hastings, New Zealand. Consulting Surveyor; Member of Parliament. Minister of Energy, Minister of Regional Development, Minister of National Development. m. Rosa Mitchell, 28 Nov. 1953, 3 sons, 1 daughter. *Education:* Hamilton Technical College; Professional Surveying (MNZIS). *Appointments:* Consulting Surveyor, Pukekohe, New Zealand, 1957-72. *Memberships:* Member, Pukekohe Borough Council, 1965-74; Deputy Mayor Pukekohe Borough Council, 1968-74; President, Pukekohe Jaycees Inc., 1962. *Honours:* Life Member J C International. *Hobbies:* Gardening; Tramping; Fishing. *Address:* 188 Kitchener Rd, Pukekohe, New Zealand.

BIRCHALL, James, b. 29 June 1945, Solihull, England. Physicist. *Education:* BSc, Hons. Physics, 1966, PhD, Nuclear Physics, 1969, University of Birmingham. *Appointments:* Université Laval, Québec, 1969-72; Lawrence Berkeley Laboratory, University of California, Berkeley, 1972-74; Institut für Physik, University of Basel, Switzerland, 1974-76; Physics, Department, University of Manitoba, Winnipeg, 1976-. *Memberships:* Canadian Association of Physicists; Institute of Physics, UK. *Publications:* Approximately 62 Scientific Publications of which 25 are in referred Scientific Journals, most of remainder appear in the Proceedings of International Conferences. *Honours:* Natural Sciences and Engineering Research Council of Canada, National Research Associate, 1979-. *Hobbies:* Music; Languages. *Address:* 801-2295 Pembina, Winnipeg, Manitoba, Canada.

BIRCHAM, Deric Neale, b. 16 Dec. 1934, Wellington, New Zealand. Visual Communicator & Administrative Executive. m. Patricia Frances Simkin, 18 Apr. 1960, 2 daughters. *Education:* St. Patricks College, Silverstream; Honorary Degrees, Victoria University. *Appointments:* Senior Photographer, Ministry of Works & Development, Chief Photographer, Tourist & Publicity, New Zealand Public Service, 1954-78; Head of Photography, 1979, Head of Art & Medical Illustration, 1981, University of Otago & Dunedin Hospitals. *Memberships:* Fellow of the New Zealand Professional Photographers Association, Chairman, Qualifications Board, 1974-76; National Chairman Scientific and Technical 1967-71, National Executive Councillor, 1967-71, 1974-76; Chairman Wellington District Council, 1974-76; Royal Photographic Society of Great Britain; Royal Society of Arts; Institute of Incorporated British Photographers; International Institute of Community Service; International Institute of Professional Photography; Federation de Industrie Photographique. *Publications:* Seeing New Zealand, 1st edition 1971, 4th edition 1975; Waitomo Tourist Caves, 1975; New Zealanders of Destiny, 1978; Old St. Paul's Cathedral, 1981; Towards a More Just World, (co-author)1973; Table Tennis (co-author) 1976; 12 book reviews. *Honours:* Numerous International Awards and Honours including The Bank of New Zealand purchasing the Bircham Collection for Auckland City Art Gallery, the first collection on canvas of its type to be preserved in Australasia; Commissions: 4 Royal, 3 Vice-Regals, 4 Prime Ministers, VIP's. *Hobbies:* Classical piano. *Address:* 130 Easther Crescent, Dunedin, New Zealand.

BIRD, Eric Charles Frederick, b. 2 Sept. 1930, Tunbridge Wells, England. Environmental Scientist. m. Juliet Frances Wain, 30 June 1962, 3 daughters. *Education:* BSc, 1953, MSc, 1955, King's College, London, 1950-55; PhD, 1960, Australian National University, 1957-59. *Appointments:* Assistant Lecturer, King's College, London, 1960; Lecturer, University College, London, 1960-63; Senior Lecturer, Australian National University, 1963-66; Reader, University of Melbourne, 1966-; Project co-ordinator United Nations University, 1978-; Managing Director, Geostudies, 1978-. *Memberships:* Chairman, International Geographical Union Commission on the Coastal Environment; Fellow, Royal Geographical Society, London; Coastal Society, USA; Royal Society of Victoria, Australia. *Publications:* Coastal Landforms, 1964; Coasts 1968,

2nd edition, 1976; The Gippsland Lakes, 1978; 150 scientific papers. *Honours:* Cuthbert Peek Prize, 1969. *Hobbies:* Walking; Photography; Cricket; Natural History. *Address:* 343 Beach Road, Black Rock, Victoria, 3193, Australia.

BIRD, John Frederick, b. 12 June 1914, Gosforth, Northumberland, England. Chartered Engineer. m. Joan Clark Taylor, 6 June 1947, 1 son, 3 daughters. *Education:* BSc, Durham University, 1933-36; Staff College (Haifa), 1942. *Appointments:* A Reyrolle and Co., 1932, Engineer in charge Testing and certification, 1947-54; Managing Director, Reyrolle (Rhodesia) Ltd., 1955-60; Overseas Manager, 1961-69, Director, 1965, A Reyrolle & Co; Managing Director, Reyrolle Parsons International Ltd., 1969-76; Chairman, Parolle Ltd., 1970-76. *Memberships:* Fellow, Institution of Electrical Engineers, Council, 1951-54. *Honours:* Military Cross, 1941; Territorial Decoration, 1949; CBE, 1970. *Hobbies:* Golf; Gardening; Fishing; Painting. *Address:* 17 Radcliffe Road, Bamburgh, Northumberland, England.

BIRIBONWOHA, Aloysius Rwamwema, b. 15 June 1939, Bugoma, Hoima District, Uganda. Fisheries Biologist. m. 6 July 1968, 3 sons, 3 daughters. *Education:* Bachelor of Science (London), 1963; Master of Science (Mass), 1966. *Appointments:* Fisheries Officer, 1963-67; Principal (Fisheries Tl, Uganda), 1967-71; AG. Chief Fisheries Officer, 1971-78; Commissioner for Fisheries, 1978-. *Memberships:* American Fisheries Society; Uganda Ecological Committee of National Research Council; Scientific Advisory Committee—Uganda National Parks; President, UMASS African Students Association. *Publications:* Age and Growth of Yellow Perch in Quabbin Reserviour; Training Aspects for a Trawling Fishery; Fish Processing & Marketing in Uganda. *Hobbies:* Reading; Music; Walking. *Address:* c/o Fisheries Training Institute, PO Box 124, Entebbe, Uganda.

BIRT, Lindsay Michael, b. 18 Jan. 1932, Melbourne, Victoria, Australia. Vice-Chancellor. m. Avis Jennypher Tapfield, 25 July 1959, 2 sons. *Education:* B.Agr.Sc. and BSc, 1949-54, PhD (Biochemistry), 1955-57, University of Melbourne; D.Phil (Biochemistry), University of Oxford, 1957-59. *Appointments:* Lecturer in Biochemistry, 1960-63, Senior Lecturer in Biochemistry, 1964, University of Melbourne; Senior Lecturer in Biochemistry, University of Sheffield, 1964-67; Foundation Professor and Head Department of Biochemistry, Australian National University, 1967-73; Vice-Chancellor designate, Wollongong University College, 1973-75; Foundation Vice-Chancellor, The University of Wollongong, 1975-81; Vice-Chancellor, University of New South Wales, 1981-. *Memberships:* The Biochemical Society; Fellow, Australian Institute of Management, 1981. *Publications:* Biochemistry of the Tissues: Textbook with W. Bartley & P. Banks, 1968, editions in German, Japanese, Italian and Malaysian. *Honours:* Scholarship from the Royal Commission for the Exhibition of 1851, 1958; Emeritus Professor, The Australian National University, 1974; Commander of the British Empire, 1980; Honorary DLitt, Wollongong, 1981. *Hobbies:* Music; Reading. *Address:* 76 Wentworth Street, Randwick, NSW 2031, Australia.

BIRTLES, Eric Arthur, b. 3 May 1924, Melbourne, Australia. Valuer. m. Margaret Hood, 8 August 1956. *Education:* Diploma in Land Valuation, Fellow of Australian Institute of Valuers. *Appointments:* Land Valuer. *Memberships:* State Rivers & Water Supply Commission of Victoria; State Savings Bank of Victoria; Camberwell City Council; Government of Tasmania; President of Tasmanian Section of Royal Flying Doctor Service of Australia; Treasurer of Tasmanian Aero Club. *Hobbies:* Flying, Golf. *Address:* 109 Cormiston Road, Riverside, 7250, Australasia.

BISHOP, George Sidney, b. 15 October 1913, Wigan, Lancashire, UK. Company Executive. m. Una Padel, 1961. *Education:* Ashton-in-Makerfield Grammar School; London School of Economics (B. Sc. Econ.). *Appointments:* Director of: Booker MacConnell Limited,1961-, Barclays Bank International, 1972-, Barclays Bank Limited, 1974-, Ranks Hovis MacDougall, 1976-, Agricultural Mortgage Corporation, 1973-79, Industry Council for Development. Chairman of: Overseas Development Institute, Booker MacConnell Limited, 1972-79, Vice Chairman Booker MacConnell Limited, 1970-71. President West India Committee. Ministry of Agriculture, Fisheries and Food 1940-61, (1959-61, Deputy Secretary). *Memberships:* Reform Club, MCC, Club Alpin Francais. Fellow: Royal Geographical Society. President: Britain-Nepal Society. *Honours:* OBE, 1947, CB, 1958, Knighted 1975. *Hobbies:* Mountaineering and photography. *Address:* Brenva, Eghams Wood Road, Beaconsfield, Bucks, England.

BISHOP, James William, b. 19 June 1918, Wimbledon, UK. Ophthalmic Surgeon. m. Doctor Mary Fitzclarke, 19 August 1942, 1 son, 1 daughter. *Education:* School of Medicine, University of Leeds, 1935-42; MRCS English, LRCP (London) 1942; MB, Ch B (Leeds) 1943; DOMS 1943; FRACO. *Appointments:* House Surgeon: Leeds General Infirmary, 1941-42; Royal Westminster Ophthalmic Hospital, 1942; RAMC Ophth. Spec. (Major) 1942-46; Ophth. Surgeon Coventry & Warwickshire Hospital, 1946-55, The Geelong Hospital, 1955-. *Memberships:* British and Australian Medical Association, (Chairman of Geelong Subdivision 1963). Royal Australian College of Ophthalmology (Member of Council 1971-73, President Victoria Section 1972) Faculty of Ophthalmologists, Rotary Club of Geelong West President 1962-63, Barwon Heads and Geelong Golf Clubs, Australian Simmental Breeders Association. *Publications:* Caterpillar Hair Kerato Conjunctivitis, American Journal Ophth. 1967; Cataract Surgery in the Dog; The Dispensing Optician 1956. *Hobbies:* Simmental Cattle Breeding; Golf. *Address:* 27 Park Street, East Geelong, Victoria, 3220 Australia.

BISHOP, Kenneth Ernest, b. 9 May 1925, Croydon, England. Chartered Engineer. m. Mary Margaret Hempson, 30 June 1951, 2 sons. *Education:* Croydon Polytechnic, 1943-46; Diploma in Mechanical/Electrical Engineering; C.Eng; MIMech.E; MBIM. *Appointments:* Commission in Royal Engineers, 1946-48; Babcock & Wilcox Ltd., UK, 1948-60; Stewarts & Lloyds of India Ltd., Calcutta, India, 1961-75; Dorman Long & Amalgamated Engineering Ltd., Lagos, Nigeria, 1975-. *Address:* 22 Stokes House, Sutherland Avenue, Bexhill-on-Sea, East Sussex, TN39 3QT, England.

BISHOP, Maurice. Grenadian Politician. *Appointments:* Leader New Jewel Movement (Joint Endeavour for Welfare, education and Liberation), 1972-; Prime Minister of Grenada and Minister for Foreign and Home Affairs, Information and Culture, National Security and Carriacou Affairs, 1979-; Minister for Petit Martinique Affairs. *Address:* Office of the Prime Minister, St George's, Grenada.

BISHOP, Norah Jane (Mrs), b. 3 June 1932, Toronto, Ontario, Canada. Co-Owner of Importer Firm for Musical Instruments. m. 15 Apr. 1954, 2 sons, 1 daughter. *Education:* Physical Occupational Therapy, University of Toronto, 1953. *Appointments:* Physiotherapist for crippled children, 1953-54; Physiotherapist at convalescent Hospital, 1970-72; Commercial Traveller, 1972-79; Co-Owner of Import Business, 1977-. *Memberships:* Toronto Symphony WomenOs Association; Chairman & Administrator, 1966-69, Prologue to the Performing Arts; Alpha Gamma Delta Fraternity President, 1952-53. *Publications:* Board, commissioning new plays, operas & musical work to be perfomed for school age children in Ontario. *Hobbies:* Opera; Symphony; Hockey; Theatre; Golf; Cross country skiing; Painting. *Address:* 15 Urbandale Avenue, Willowdale, Ontario, Canada, M2M 2G9.

BISHOP, Thomas Augustus, b. 15 June 1895, Auckland, New Zealand. Farmer (Retired). m. Lilian Constance Lusty, 20 July 1920, 2 sons, 1 daughter. *Education:* Auckland University Gollege, 1914-19; BA, 1919. *Memberships:* Auckland Harbour Board, Chairman 1951-53, Sinking Fund Commissioner, 1954, Represented Harbour Board on the Committee of Auckland Chamber of Commerce, 1944-54; Veteran Member, Auckland Officers' Club, 1943; New Zealand Returned Services Association, 1919; New Zealand Founders Society, 1954; Clan Mac Leod Society of New Zealand, 1953; Trustee, Titirangi Soldiers' Memorial Church, 1924; Life Member, Auckland Institute & Museum. *Honours:* OBE, 1963; MM, 1918; JP, 1922. *Hobbies:* Reading; Gardening. *Address:* 75 Waima Road, Titirange, Auckland 7, New Zealand.

BISSEMBER, Neville James, b. 12 Mar. 1928. Barrister-at-Law. m. Mary Noel Durham, 1 Aug. 1954, 2 sons,

1 daughter. *Appointments:* School Teacher, 1943-46; Civil Servant, 1946-47; Degree of the Letters Bar at the Honourable Society of the Middle Temple, London, 1951; Crown Prosecutor, 1958-60; Deputy Prime Minister and Leader of House, 1964-69; Member of Parliament 1961-73. *Memberships:* Senior Vice Chairman of the Peoples National Congress. *Hobbies:* Boxing; Cricket. *Address:* 149 Church Street, Albertown, Georgetown, Guyana.

BISSON, André, b. 7 Oct. 1929, Trois-Rivières, Québec, Canada. Banker. m. Reine Lévesque, 13 June 1953, 2 daughters. *Education:* BA, 1950, MCom, 1953, Laval University; MBA, Harvard Business School, 1955. *Appointments:* Associate Professor of Business Administration, Laval University, 1955-73; Director of Education, The Canadian Bankers' Association, 1966-71; General Manager, 1971-77, Vice-President & General Manager, 1977-, Province of Québec, The Bank of Nova Scotia. *Memberships:* Chairman, Board of Directors: Hôpital Notre-Dame, Gestion, Revue Internationale de Gestion; Vice-President, French Chamber of Commerce in Canada; Member, Board of Directors: Centraide, United Way, Canada, European Institute of Business Administration, Fontainebleau, France, Montréal Symphony Orchestra, Fondation de l'Université du Québec à Montréal, Université de Montréal, Davie Shipbuilding Limited, Logistec Corporation, Miron Inc., Rougier Inc., L'Union Canadienne, Cie d'Assurances; Member, Board of Governors, Conseil du Patronat. *Honours:* Man of the Month, Revue Commerce, 1979. *Address:* 2 Poplar Place, Baie d'Urfé (Québec), Canada.

BISWAS, Ahsan Ali, b. 10 Jan. 1936, Pabna, Bangladesh. Director. m. Lutfun Nessa 23 Dec. 1963, 1 son, 1 daughter. *Education:* BSc, Rajshahi University, 1954; MSc (Chemistry), Dacca University, 1956; Trained, Documentation and Information, Australia 1959, Japan, 1964, USSR 1970, Poland 1976, Canada 1978, UK 1981; Attended many international seminars. *Appointments:* Junior Documentation Officer 1956; Documentation Officer PANSDOC, Karachi, Pakistan 1962; Officer-in-Charge, 1963; Director, BANSDOC, Dacca, Bangladesh 1972. *Memberships:* President, Bangladesh National Committee for Cooperation with Internaltional Federation for Documentation; Library Association of Bangladesh; Library Association of Australia; Japan Documentation Society; Abstractor: Chemical Abstracts, American Chemical Society. *Publications:* Editors: A Directory of Scientists and Technologists of Bangladesh; Current Scientific and Technological Research Projects in the Universities and Research Institutions of Bangladesh; National Catalogue of Scientific and Technical Periodicals of Bangladesh; Bangladesh Science and Technology Index; Authors of six papers in different international periodicals in the field of Documentation and Information. *Hobbies:* Study of Philosophy and Astronomy. *Address:* B-30, Science Laboratories, Staff Quarters, Dhanmondi, Dacca-5, Bangladesh.

BJELKE-PETERSEN, Johannes, b. 13 Jan. 1911, Dannevirke. Premier of Queensland. m. 31 May 1952, 1 son, 3 daughters. *Education:* Correspondence Courses and Private Studies, Taabinga Valley State School. *Appointments:* Nanango 1947-50; National Party Member for Barambah, 1950-; Minister for Works and Housing 1963-68; Premier of Queensland 1968-. *Hobbies:* Flying; Physical Culture; Reading. *Address:* "Bethany", Kingaroy, Queensland, Australia.

BLACK, Edith Ruth (Dr.), b. 2 June 1925, Austria. Medical Practitioner. m. Harry 30 Aug. 1954 (deceased), 2 sons. *Education:* BA, 1947, MB, Ch.B, 1952, University of New Zealand; Dip.F.P., 1952. *Appointments:* Resident Medical Officer, Auckland Hospital Board, 1952-54; Clinic Doctor, Auckland FPA, 1954-76; General Practice, 1954-57; Medical Officer, Health Department, 1957, Student Health Service, 1959-; Medical Director, Auckland Family Planning Clinics, 1954-73; Visiting Medical Officer, Carrington Hospital, 1976-. *Memberships:* Chairman, Medical Advisory Committee, New Zealand Family Planning Association, 1963-74; Council of International Planned Parenthood Federation for SE Asia and Oceania and of Medical and Education Sub-Committees, 1964; Delegate/Participant to a number of W.H.O and I.P.P.F. Meetings; NZMA, Medical Womens Association, 1955-; Board & Executive, Metal Health Foundation of NZ; Chairman of Education & Information Committee; Member, Board,

New Zealand Broadcasting Corporation and Television, 1973-77. *Publications:* Articles in popular press mainly concerned with population and family planning problems, also some papers in medical journals. *Honours:* New Zealand Council Richmond Fellowship, 1979. *Hobbies:* Music; Walking; Family activities; Reading; Interest in broadcasting & current affairs. *Address:* 25 William Fraser Crescent, Kohimarama, Auckland, 5, New Zealand.

BLACKBURN, Charles Archie D'Arcy, b. 8 May 1899, Hamilton, New Zealand. Retired Chartered Accountant. m. Eileen Mary Bindon, 23 Nov. 1923, 4 sons, 1 daughter. *Education:* Gisbourne, Central School, New Zealand, 1905-11; Gisborne High School, 1912-16; Royal Military College, Australia, 1917-20. *Appointments:* Lieutenant New Zealand Staff Corps, 1921-22; Chartered Accountant, 1923-39, 1945-58; Served in New Zealand Territorial Force, 1924-39 (attaining rank of Major); Commanded 19th Battalion through campaigns in Greece & Crete, 1941-; Commanded 1st Army Tank Battalion, 1942-43. *Memberships:* Ornithological Society of New Zealand, 1961-67; Fauna Protection Advisory Council, 1962-68; Gisborne Conservation Society; 2 Masonic Orders with past Grand Rank in Grand Lodge of New Zealand; Past-president Gisborne United Officers Institute. *Publications:* Numerous papers in field of ornithology contributed to Notornis, the Journal of the Ornithological Society of New Zealand. *Honours:* E.D. 1942-; Mentioned in Despatches, Crete, 1941-. *Hobbies:* Field Ornithology, Trout fishing. *Address:* 10 Score Road, Gisborne, New Zealand.

BLACKBURN, Edward Kenyon, b. 12 Jan. 1918, Morley, Yorkshire, England. Medical-Haematologist. m. Fanny Elizabeth Norris 30 Nov. 1943, 2 sons, 1 daughter. *Education:* MB, ChB(Honours) Leeds, 1942; DRCOG (London) 1944; MD, Leeds 1945; FRFPS (qua Physician), Glasgow 1947; FRCP, Glasgow 1964; FCPath 1963; FINucE 1970; FRCP, London 1974. *Appointments:* House Physician and House Surgeon, Leeds Hospitals 1940-42; House Surgeon and R.S.O., Royal Infirmary, Doncaster, 1942-43, Resident Medical Officer, 1943; General Practitioner, Stainforth Area, 1943-44; Medical Officer, Fighter Command, RAF Station, Orby, Lincs, and Physician, Skegness and District General Hospital and Skegness Isolation Hospital 1944-45; Clinical Assistant and First Assistant in Clinical Pathology, Royal Infirmary, Sheffield, 1945-47; Postgraduate Fellowship, Departments in Oxford, London, Edinburgh and Glasgow, 1947-48; Haematologist, Royal Infirmary, Sheffield, 1948-80; Consultant Haematologist, United Sheffield Hospitals and subsequently Sheffield Area Health Authority 1951-; Professor Associate, University of Sheffield 1970-. *Memberships:* President, British Society for Haematology, 1965; President, Association of Clinical Pathologists, 1973-74; Haemophilia Centre Directors of the United Kingdom, 1968-80; Royal College of Pathologists, 1974-77; Panel of Examiners, Haematology, Royal College of Pathologists, 1970-80; British Journal of Haematology, 1969-79. *Publications:* Approximately 140 papers, chapters in various books between 1948 and 1981. *Honours:* West Riding of Yorkshire County Major Scholar, 1936-42; Lord Kitchener's National Memorial Scholar 1936-42; *Hobbies:* Music; Golf; Gardening. *Address:* 20 King Ecgbert Road, Totley Rise, Sheffield S17 3QQ, South Yorkshire, England.

BLACKHALL, William John, b. 26 Feb. 1934, Cronulla, New South Wales, Australia. Company Director. m. Roma Audrey, 30 Oct. 1954, 2 sons, 1 daughter. *Education:* Certificate in Marketing, Institute of Administration, University of New South Wales, 1971-; *Appointments:* Australiasian Director, Syntex Agribusiness Incorporated, Chairman of Directors, Syntex Laboratories New Zealand Limited, Director, Syntex Australia Limited, 1979-; Marketing Director, Smith Kline Animal Health, Australia, 1977-79; Managing Director, Marupi, Merck Sharp & Dohme K.K. Osaka, Japan, Marketing Manager, Veterinary Division, Merck Sharp & Dohme, Australia, Limited, Australian Sales Manager & other positions, Vet. Division MS&D Australia, 1961-77. *Memberships:* Agricultural & Veterinary Chemicals Association of Australia, Chairman, New South Wales Division, Former Federal Vice President, Former member Board of Directors; World Poultry Science Association, Former Vice President New South Wales Division; Royal Agricultural Society of New South Wales. *Honours:* Fellow, Australian Marketing

Institute, 1980-; Associated Fellow, Australian Institute of Management, 1977-. *Hobbies:* Golf, Tennis, Squash, Numismatics. *Address:* 49 Renway Avenue, Lugarno, New South Wales, Australia, 2210.

BLACKMAN, Francis Woodbine, b. 21 Sept. 1922, Barbados. Campus Secretary. m. 18 Dec. 1943, 2 sons, 1 daughter. *Education:* South East Essex Technical College, 1948; BSc., London, 1953. *Appointments:* Assistant Master (Science), Foundation School, Barbados, 1940-43; Temporary Science Teacher, Department of Agriculture, Barbados, 1943-45; Assistant Master (Science), St Vincent Grammar School, 1945-49; Assistant Master, 1949-53, Headmaster, St Kitts Nevis Grammar School, 1957-59; Principal, Secondary School, Montserrat, 1953-57; Chemist & later Agronomist, St Kitts Sugar Association, St Kitts, 1960-66; Campus Secretary, University of the West Indies, Barbados, 1966-. *Memberships:* Junior Chamber International Senator. *Honours:* Justice of the Peace, Barbados, 1973. *Address:* Cherwood, 22 Rowans, Rowans, St George, Barbados, West Indies.

BLACKMORE, Keith Wilbur, b. 4 Apr. 1911, Dunedin, Otago, New Zealand. Local Body Administrator, Director. m. Agnes Anderson Hill, 19 Oct. 1938, 1 son, 4 daughters. *Education:* Anderson's Bay Primary School, 1916-24; King Edward Technical College, 1925-30. *Appointments:* Carpenter, 1930-38; Foreman, 1938-44; Master Builder, 1944-72. *Memberships:* Mayor of Alexandra, 1959-80; Chairman, Central Otago Local Bodies Association, 1959-80; Chairman of Alexandra Blossom Festival Executive, 1959-80; Trustee, Flood Relief Committee, 1978-; Executive, New Zealand Municipalities Association, 1964-80; Soil Conservation and Rivers Control Council of New Zealand, 1968-80; New Zealand Milk Board, 1971-80; Director Municipal Cooperative Insurance Company of New Zealand, 1978-; Upper Clutha Development Committee; Gold Parks Advisory Committee; Numerous local committees and patron of many local organisations. *Honours:* M.B.E. 1973-; Queen's Jubilee Medal, 1977-; J.P. 1979-. *Hobbies:* Gardening, Golf and Bowls. *Address:* 25 Old Bridge Road, Alexandra, Central Otago, New Zealand.

BLACKWELL, Basil Davenport, b. 8 Feb. 1922, Whitkirk, Yorkshire, England. Engineer & Company Director. m. Betty Meggs, 4 Sept. 1948, 1 daughter. *Education:* MA, St John's College, Cambridge; BSc, London University. *Appointments:* Rolls-Royce, 1945; Engineering Division of Bristol Aeroplane Co. Ltd., 1949; Deputy Chief Engineer, 1959, Sales Director, 1963, Managing Director, 'Amall Eng. Division, 1965, Bristol Siddeley Director Westland Aircraft Ltd., 1970; Managing Director, 1972, Chairman, 1976, Westland Helicopters Ltd; Vice-Chairman & Chief Executive Westland Group of Companies, 1974; British Hovercraft Corporation Limited, 1979; Normalair-Garrett Ltd., 1979. *Memberships:* Council CBI; NDIC; SBAC (President 1979-80, 1980-81); CBIM; F.Eng; FIMech.E; FRAES; United Oxford & Cambridge University Club. *Publications:* Contributions to Professional Journals. *Honours:* Hughes' Prize, St John's College, Cambridge. *Hobby:* Gardens and Gardening. *Address:* High Newland, Newland Garden, Sherborne, Dorset DT9 3AF, England.

BLACKWELL, Richard John Neal, b. 14 May 1909, Melbourne, Australia. Retired Banker. m. Edna Agnes Dawson, 5 Dec. 1939, 1 son. *Education:* Haselor, Winnington and Scotch Colleges; FASA. *Appointments:* Joined Bank of NSW, in Melbourne, 1924; Various positions London England Branch of the Bank, 1936-46; Assistant Manager, 1946-50, Chief Manager, 1950-54, International Division, Head Office, Sydney; State Manager, Returning Division, 1954-57, City Division, 1957-60; Chief Manager for Victoria, 1960-63, for NSW, 1963-64; Assistant General Manager, 1964-71, General Manager, 1971-74. *Memberships: Hobbies:* Yachting; Water colour painting. *Address:* 6 High Street, Beaumaris, Victoria, Australia.

BLACKWOOD (Dame) Margaret, b. 26 Apr. 1909, Melbourne, Australia. University Lecturer. *Education:* Melbourne Church of England Girls Grammar School, 1916-27; University of Melbourne, BSc, MSc, 1930-38; PhD., Cambridge University, 1948-50. *Appointments:* Lecturer Senior Lecturer, Reader in Botany & Genetics, University of Melbourne, 1946-74; Dean of Women, Mildura Branch University, 1946-48; Rese-

arch Assistant, University of Wisconsin, U.S.A. 1958-; Senior Associate, Cytogencticist, University of Melbourne, 1974-; Council of the University of Melbourne, 1976-; Deputy Chancellor, 1980, 1981-. *Memberships:* One-time Secretary, International Federation of University Women; British Lichen Society; Lyceum Club, Melbourne; Royal Society of Victoria Australian Genetics Society; Beta Sigma Phi, A.N.Z.A.A.S; Organising Secretary, Melbourne Congress, 1977-; Soroptimist International, National, State & Club President; Honorary Member, Soroptimist International of the South West Pacific Federation. *Publications:* Various scientific articles in journals. *Honours:* Carnegie Travel Fellow, 1959-; Honorary Research Fellow, Birmingham University, 1959-; Founder Fellow, Janet Clarke Hall, University of Melbourne, 1961-; Fellow, Trinity College, University of Melbourne, 1980-; Fellow, Australian & New Zealand Association for the Advancement of Science, 1979-; Chapman Medal, Institute of Engineers, 1975-; War Service, Wing Officer, Womens Australian Air Force, 1941-46; Dame Commander of the Most Excellent Order of the British Empire, 1981-. *Hobbies:* Music, Photography, Lichenology. *Address:* 63 Morrah Street, Parkville, Victoria, Australia, 3052.

BLADEN, Anthony William, b. 18 Jan. 1924, Worcester, England. Musician and Free-lance Journalist. m. Eileen Ruth MacDermott, 18 Jan. 1951. *Education:* Birmingham School of Music, 1939-47, subsequently violin studies with Albert Sammons, C.B.E; Associate of Birmingham School of Music, 1947-; Associate of the Royal College of Music, 1948-. *Appointments:* Principal Viola, BBC West of England Players, 1962-65; Principal Viola, BBC Scottish Radio Orchestra, 1965-66; Assistant Master, King's College, Taunton, 1971-73; Since 1973, Arts Critic, Somerset County Gazette, and Private Music Teacher. *Memberships:* Incorporated Society of Musicians; Past Committee Bristol Branch; Past Vice-Chairman, Bristol Branch and Member of South West District Council, Musicians Union. *Honours:* Bentley Scholarship, 1942 and 1943; Dowler Scholarship, 1944-. *Hobbies:* Reading, Travelling. *Address:* 31 Abbey Close, Curry Rivel, Langport, Somerset, TA10 OEL, England.

BLAGROVE, Robert John, b. 17 Jan. 1944, Adelaide, South Australia. Research Scientist. m. Lynette Engel, 25 Feb. 1967, 2 sons, 1 daughter. *Education:* BSc., 1964-, BSc Honours, 1965-, PhD., 1979-, Department of Physical and Inorganic Chemistry, University of Adelaide. *Appointments:* CSIRO Post-Doctoral Fellowship, Nuffield Department Clinical Biochemistry, Oxford, 1969-70; Research Scientist, Principal Research Scientist, CSIRO Division of Protein Chemistry, 1970-. *Memberships:* Australian Biochemical Society; Cereal Chemistry Division, Royal Australian Chemical Institute; Australian Society Plant Physiologists; Phytochemical Club, Melbourne, Member and Foundation Secretary, 1979-80. *Publications:* Author and Co-author of 40 scientific papers dealing with aspects of physical biochemistry, plant protein biochemistry and wool dyeing technology. *Honours:* J.L. Young Scholarship for Research, University of Adelaide, 1963-; CSR Chemicals Prize, University of Adelaide, 1964-; CSIRO Junior Postgraduate Scholarship, 1964-; CSIRO Senior Postgraduate Scholarship, 1965-69; CSIRO Postdoctoral Fellowship, 1969-. *Hobbies:* Gardening, Tennis. *Address:* 14 Terrara Court, Montmorency 3094, Victoria, Australia

BLAIR, Ian Scott, b. 18 May 1933, Stretford, England. Metallugist. m. Telika-Shane Pickard, 19 July 1958, 3 sons. *Education:* B.Sc Hons, Metallurgy, Manchester University, 1951-54. *Appointments:* National Service, Commissioned in Royal Corps of Signals, 1954-56; Roan Consolidated Mines Limited, Zambia, 1956-; Various posts to Asst. Smelter Supt., Luanshya Division, 1956-67; Refinery Superintendent, Ndola Copper Refinery, 1967-70; Refinery Superintendent, 1970-72, Assistant Manager, 1972-73, Manager, 1973-75, General Manager, 1975-, Mufulira Division. *Memberships:* Fellow, Institute of Metals; Chartered Engineer; Fellow, Institution of Mining and Metallurgy; Fellow, Engineering Institute of Zambia; Canadian Institution of Metallurgists. *Publications:* Co-Author of paper 'Recent Developments in the design and operation of Copper Tankhouses', AIME Congress, United States of America, 1970; Co-Author of paper 'The Introduction of Electric Furnace Smelting Technology to Mufulira, Zambia' contained in 'The Extractive Metallurgy of Copper', 1976. *Hobbies:* Golf; Tennis; Swimming; Church Music. *Address:* P.O. Box 1039, Newlands House, Mufulira, Zambia.

BLAKE, Anne, b: Cambridge, England. Editor. *Appointments:* Researcher, Field Publications, 1969-71; Sub-Editor, (Diary Column), 1971-76, Editor, 1976-, Anglian Magazine. *Publications:* All magazines published by Field publications (articles); Many contributions to Hare and Hounds, Country Times, Daily Telegraph. *Hobby:* Walking. *Address:* 17 Cambridge Road, Ely, Cambridge, CB7 4HJ, UK.

BLAKE, Byron Wycliffe, b. 15 Apr. 1945, Dalton, St. Elizabeth, Jamaica. Economist. m. Clare Patricia, 1 Jan. 1972, 3 sons. *Education:* Trained Teachers Certificate, 1966-; Bachelor of Sciences Economics, 1970-; Master of Sciences, Economics, 1978-. *Appointments:* Teacher, Ministry of Education, 1966-77; Caribbean Community Secretariat, 1970-; Public Service, Government of Jamaica, 1977-79. Numerous and varied publications including: The Caribbean Community & Five Years On: An Assessment, Paper, 1979-; MSc Thesis, Anti-Polarisation and Distribution Mechanisms, 1978-; Pamphlet, The Multi-national Corporation and Caribbean Economic Integration, 1973-; The Multi-national Corporation and the Under-developed Countries, 1972-. *Honours:* Willie Henry, Prize for Hisitory, Mico Teachers College, 1966-; Chalres Kennedy, Prize for Economics, 1970-. *Address:* 121 Akawini & Stone, Avenue, Section K, Campbellville, Greater Georgetown, Guyana.

BLAKE, Douglas Harold, b. 6 Nov. 1921, Worcester, England. Medical. m. Olive May Lister, 21 June 1950, 2 sons. *Education:* Birmingham University Medical School, 1939-44; M.B. Ch.B. Birmingham, 1944-; M.R.C.S. England; L.R.C.P. London, 1944-; Postgraduate course in Internal Medicine, Edinburgh University, 1956 & 1957; M.R.C.P. Edinburgh, 1960-; Post-graduate course in Geriatric Medicine, Glasgow, 1962-; Fellow of the Royal Australian College of Medical Administrators, 1969-; F.R.C.P. Edinburgh, 1974-. *Appointments:* Assistant Chest Physician, Markfield Hospital & the County of Leicester, 1952-62; Chest Physician, Northern Territory of Australia, 1963-64; Senior Medical Officer, Perth Chest Clinic, Western Australia, 1964-67; Medical Superintendent & Specialist Geriatrician, Bendigo Home & Hospital for the Aged, Victoria, Australia, 1967-70; Regional Specialist Geriatrician, Loddon & Mallee Region, Victoria, Australia, 1970-72; Specialist Geriatrician-in-charge, Geriatrics Division, Caulfield Hospital & Consultant Geriatrician to the Alfred Hospital, Melbourne, Australia, 1972-76; Regional Specialist Geriatrician, Warrnambool Base Hospital, the Corangamite Region of Victoria, Australia, 1976-. *Memberships:* British Medical Association; Australian Medical Association; Australian Association of Gerontology; Australian Geriatrics Society; British Geriatrics Society; British Thoracic Society. *Publications:* Numerous publications in field including: The Treatment of Chronic Cavitating Pulmonary Tuberculosis by Long-term Chemotherapy, Tubercle, London, 1961-; The Northern Territory of Australia, 1964-; A Day Hospital for Geriatric Patients, 1968-. *Honours:* Carter-Downs Medical Prize, Worcester Royal Grammar School, 1939-; Bertram-Windle Anatomy Prize, Birmingham University, 1941-. *Hobbies:* Music, Photography, Travel, Caravaning & boating, Cycling, Stamp collecting, Carpentry. *Address:* 14 Riverview Terrace, Warrnambool, Victoria, 3290, Australia.

BLAKE, Leslie Bamford James, b. 5 Mar. 1913, Bendigo, Victoria, Australia. Author and Historian. m. Shirley Jean Woodfine, 16 Apr. 1938, 1 son, 2 daughters. *Education:* B.A. University of Melbourne, 1952: B.Ed., University of Melbourne, 1956-; Master of Education, 1974-. *Appointments:* Teacher, Victorian Education Department, 1931-41; 2nd World War Service, 1942-46 Lecturer Geelong Teachers College, 1953-58, University of Melbourne, 1965-; Inspector of schools, 1958-72; Official historian Victorian Education Department, 1966-74; State Historian of Victoria, 1975-76; Retired 1976 to work as free-lance writer. Government positions held, Chairman State Education History Committee, 1966-73; Education Department Centenary Celebrations, 1972-73; *Memberships:* President, Royal Historical Society of Victoria, 1966-71; President

Western Victorian Association of Historical Societies, 1963-64; Vice-president, PEN, Melbourne, 1971-72; Victorian Working Party, Australian Dictionary of Biography project, Australian National University, 1972-80; Historic Schools Society of Victoria; Historical societies at Nhill, Horsham, Geelong and Dandenong. *Publications:* Varied and numerous publications including: Tales From Old Geelong, 1979-; Peter Lalor, the man from Eureka, 1979-; Covered Wagons in Australia, 1979-; Schools of The Tattyara, 1981-. *Honours:* Officer of the Most Excellent Order of the British Empire, 1974-; Fellow, Australian College of Education, 1980-; Fellow of Royal Historical Society of Victoria, 1970-; F.I.B.A., Cambridge, 1978-; Official historian for Shires of Lowan, Wimmera and Kaniva. *Hobbies:* Writing, Historical research, book collecting. *Address:* 4 Anton Court, Karingal, 3199, Victoria, Australia.

BLAKE, Michael Jon, b. 18 June 1946, Geelong, Victoria, Australia. Teacher. *Education:* BA, Bachelor of Education, Melbourne University. *Appointments:* Teacher, 1968-74, Senior Teacher, Melton High School, 1975-77; Reservoir High School, 1978-. *Memberships:* Australian College of Education; Victorian Secondary Teachers Association; Graduate Union, Melbourne University. *Publications:* Co-editor & writer for Catch; Articles concerning school theatre; Bibliography: MJ Blake; History of Reservoir High School; Revue theatre, various submissions to Government authorities; Design in Theatrical productions, Fiddler on the Roof, The Music Man, Oliver, The King & I, Camelot; Directed 31 productions, designing 23; worked in various other capacities on a further 29 productions. *Hobby:* Theatre and its promotion in the community; The development of amateur theatre, including the foundation & development of Catchment Players. *Address:* Unit 5, 58 Mount Street, Heidelberg, Victoria, 3084, Australia.

BLAKENEY, Allan Emrys, b. 7 Sept. 1925, Bridgewater, Nova Scotia. Canadian Politician. m. (1) Mary Schwartz, 1950 (Deceased 1957), 1 son 1 daughter, (2) Anne Gorham, 1959, 1 son, 1 daughter. *Education:* BA, LLB, Dalhousie University; BA, MA, Oxford University. *Appointments:* Secretary and Legal Advisor to Crown Corporations, 1950-55, Minister of Education, 1960-61, Government of Saskatchewan; Chairman, Saskatchewan Securities Commission, 1955-58; Partner, law firm of Davidson, Davidson & Blakeney, 1958-60; Provincial Treasurer, 1961-62; Minister of Health, 1962-64; Partner, Griffin, Blakeney, Beke, 1964-70; Leader of the Opposition, 1970-71; Premier of Saskatchewan, 1971-. *Memberships:* University of Saskatchewan Senate, 1960-62; Chairman, Wascana Centre Authority, 1962-64; President, New Democratic Party of Canada, 1969-71; United Nations Association. *Publications:* Articles on Saskatchewan Crown Corporations in Proc. of the Institute of Public Administration of Canada and The Public Corporation; Press Coverage of Saskatchewan Medicare Dispute, 1963. *Honours:* University Medal, Dalhousie University; Nova Scotia Rhodes Scholarship, 1947; Honorary Doctorate, Mount Allison University, 1980. *Hobbies:* Reading; Swimming; Walking. *Address:* 837 King Street, Regina, Saskatchewan, Canada.

BLAKENEY, Eugene Algernon, b. 3 Dec. 1932, Hamilton, Bermuda. Politician & Trade Union Official. m. Shirley Gwendoline Pearman, 2 July 1959, 2 sons, 2 daughters. *Education:* Berkeley Institute; Bermuda College; University of West Indies; American Institute for Free Labour Development. *Appointments:* Member of Parliament, Warwick West Constituency, Elected 1980, Legislative Council, 1976-80, Opposition Spokesman; General Secretary, Bermuda Public Services Association, formerly Secretary General, Bermuda Industrial Union. *Memberships:* President, BIU Credit Union; Labour Advisory Council; Government Economic Forum. *Honours:* Award presentation from Bus Operators, 1968; Award presentation from Bermuda Industrial Union, 1979. *Hobbies:* Fishing; Reading. *Address:* Sweeds, Warwick Park Estate, Warwick West 7-26, Bermuda.

BLAKER, Peter Allan Renshaw, b. 4 Oct. 1922, Hong Kong. Member of Parliament. m. Jennifer, 14 Oct. 1953, 1 son, 2 daughters. *Education:* BA, Toronto University; MA, New College, Oxford. *Appointments:* Served with the Canadian Infantry, 1942-46; Admitted as Solicitor, 1948; Called to the Bar, Lincoln's Inn, 1952; Foreign Service, 1953-64; Joint Secretary Conservative Parl. Foreign Affairs Committee, 1965-66; Opposition Whip, 1966-67; Joint Secretary Conservative Parl. Trade Committee, 1967-70; Parliamentary Under-Secretary of State for Defence (Army), 1972-74, for Foreign & Commonwealth Office, 1974; Vice-Chairman, Conservative Parl. Foreign Affairs Committee, 1974-79; Minister of State, Foreign and Commonwealth Office, 1979-81; Minister for the Armed Forces, Ministry of Defence, 1981. *Hobbies:* Shooting; Tennis; Swimming; Opera. *Address:* House of Commons, London SW1A OAA, England.

BLAKEY, Frank Alexander, b. 13 Sept. 1923, Melbourne, Australia. Rsearch Engineer. m. Barbara Brent, 4 Sept. 1946, 1 son, 2 daughters. *Education:* Bachelor of Engineering, 1st Class Honours, University of Western Australia, 1945-; Doctor of Philosophy, University of Cambridge, 1949-. *Appointments:* Assistant Lecturer in Civil Engineering, University of Tasmania, 1944-47; Research Student, University of Cambridge, 1947-49; Head of Concrete Structures Research Division of Building Research, CSIRO, 1949-68; Assistant Chief, Division of Building Research, CSIRO 1968-79; Chief, Division of Building Research, CSIRO, 1979-; Seconded to Department of Housing & Construction as First Assistant Secretary, Technology, 1974-76. *Memberships:* Instituion of Engineers, Australia; Fellow, Australian Institute of Building. *Publications:* 150 publications in technical journals. *Honours:* Hackett Travelling Studentship, 1946-; Rex Moir Studentship, 1948-. *Hobbies:* Work. *Address:* 11 Fuge Street, Highett, Victoria, Australia 3190

BLANCH (Archbishop of York), Stuart Yarworth, b. 2 Feb. 1918, Blakeney, Gloucester, England. British Ecclesiastic. m. Brenda Gertrude Coyte, 10 July 1943, 1 son, 4 daughters. *Education:* Alleyns School, Dulwich; B.A. (1st cl.Th.), M.A. St. Catherine's College and Wycliffe Hall, Oxford. *Appointments:* Law Fire Insurance Society Limited, 1936-40; Royal Air Force Navigator, 1940-46; Curate, All Saints, Highfield, Oxford, 1949-52; Vicar of Eynsham, Oxford, 1952-57; Vice-Principal, Wycliffe Hall, 1957-60; Oriel Canon of Rochester and Warden of Rochester Theological College, 1960-66; Bishop of Liverpool, 1966-75; Archbishop of York 1975-; Primate of England and Metropolitan. *Memberships:* Royal Commonwealth Society; House of Lords, 1972-. *Publications:* The World our Orphanage, 1972-; For All Mankind, 1976-; The Christian Militant, 1978-; The Burning Bush, 1978-; The Trumpet in the Morning, 1979-; The Ten Commandments, 1981. *Honours:* Honorary, LLD Liverpool University, 1975-; Honorary DD Hull University, 1977-; Honorary Doctorate York University, 1979-; Honorary DD Wycliffe College, Toronto, 1979-. *Hobbies:* Squash, Walking, Music. *Address:* Bishopthorpe, York YO2 1QE, England.

BLANCKENSEE, Alan Eric, b. 3 July 1926, Perth, Western Australia. Solicitor and Company Director. m. Anne Elizabeth Alexander, 14 Sept. 1949, 1 son, 2 daughters. *Education:* Wesley College South Perth, Western Australia, 1937-43; The University of Western Australia, LL.B., 1944-47; 03 Admitted Barrister & Solicitor Supreme Court of Western Australia, 1949-; Partner Stone James & Company, Solicitors, Perth, Western Australia, 1949-. *Memberships:* President Law Society of Western Australia, 1977-79, (Vice-President, 1973-77); Chairman, Planning Committee 17th Australian Legal Convention, Perth, 1973-; Treasurer of Law Council of Australia, 1980-81; Law Council of Australia Representative on the Council of the International Bar Association 1980-81. *Hobbies:* Gardening, Golf, Music. *Address:* 102 Matheson Road, Applecross, Western Australia, 6153.

BLANDFORD, Douglas Charles, b. 25 Mar. 1941, Macksville, New South Wales. Consulting Environmental Geologist. m. Edwina Lilley, 16 Dec. 1965, 1 son, 1 daughter. *Education:* H.D.A. Hawkesbury Agricultural College, Richmond, New South Wales; B.A. Geology, Macquarie University, Sydney, New South Wales; Litt. B. The University of New England, Armidale, New South Wales. *Appointments:* Soil Conservationist, Soil Conservation Service of New South Wales, 1966-73; Officer, in charge, Australian National Antarctic Research Expedition, Davis Station, Antarctica, 1973-75; Research Fellow, University of New England,

Armidale, 1975-76; Research Officer, Division of Land Utilization, Queensland, 1976-78; Officer in Charge, Soil Conservation Section, Territory Parks & Wildlife Commission, Darwin, 1978-79; Consulting Environmental Geologist, Dames & Moore, Perth, Western Australia, 1979-. *Memberships:* Geological Society of Australia; Institute of Australian Geographers; Royal Agricultural Society of New South Wales; Australian National Antarctic Research Expedition Club. *Publications:* Various publications including: Paper, Rangelands and Soil Erosion Research—A Question of scale, 1980-; Ord River Catchment (N.T.) Regeneration and Research, 1979-; The Geology and Soils of the Bombala District Soil Conservation Service of New South Wales, 1975-. *Honours:* Land Prize for practical agruculture, 1964-, Yates Prize for proficiency in practical economic botany, 1965-, Hawkesbury Agricultural College; Travel Scholarship, Royal Agricultural Society of New South Wales, 1967-. *Hobbies:* Reading, Tennis, Rifle Shooting, Photography. *Address:* 38 Ronneby Road, Lesmurdie, Western Australia, 6076.

BLATT, Jack b. 18 Jan. 1909, Warsaw, Poland. m. Devida Williams, 4 Sept. 1941, 1 son, 4 daughters. *Appointments:* Chairman of the Board, Electricite Standard Inc; President of: Standard Holdings Ltd; Standard Enterprises Inc; Blaman Investments Inc; Henja Investments Corp; Madabar Ltd; Building Enterprises Inc; Bonaventure of Florida; Prime Corporation (Florida). *Memberships:* British Society of Commerce; Institute of Commerce. *Honours:* Canadian Man of the Year, State of Israel Bonds, Received the Eleanor Roosevelt Humanities Award and 12 Tribes of Israel Torah Breast Plate; Man of Honour Award, Les Associations De L'Industrie Electrique; The Israel Prime Minister's Medal; Chevalier Du Tastevin, 1978 (The Knight of Tastevin). *Address:* 4300 Blvd De Maisonneuve, P.H.9, Montreal, Quebec, Canada.

BLAXALL, Peter Norris George, b. 12 Jan. 1929, Wellington, New Zealand. Exporter, Manufacturer, Importer. m. Helen Marguerite, 19 Dec. 1958, 1 son, 1 daughter. *Education:* Christ's College, 1943-46; Canterbury University, 1947-52. *Appointments:* Accountancy Office, 1947-52; Founder Blaxall & Steven Limited, 1954-; Founder Blaxall Science Company Limited, 1978-. *Memberships:* Executive, Canterbury Aged Peoples Welfare Council, 1967-80; Chairman of Executive Aged Peoples Committee, 1972-76; City Councillor, Christchurch, 1968-71, 1974-80; Chairman Community Service City Council, 1974-77; New Zealand Social Development Council, 1976-; Chairman Parks & Recreation City Council, 1977-80; Patron Canterbury Repertory Society, 1976-. *Honours:* Queen's Service Order for work with aged, 1977-. *Hobbies:* Theatre, Music, Cooking, Jogging, Golf. *Address:* 165F Rockinghorse Road, Southshore, Christchurch, New Zealand.

BLAZEY, Cecil Albert, b. 21 July 1909, Hastings New Zealand. Retired. m. Mavis Emily Peek, 13 Feb. 1935 (Died, 1978-), 1 daughter. *Education:* Christchurch Boys High School, 1922-26; University of Canterbury, Associate Australian Insurance Institute; Fellow, Insurance Institute of New Zealand. *Appointments:* Australian Mutual Provident Society, 1927-70 (Finally, Senior Assistant Manager for New Zealand). President, Council of Insurance Institute of New Zealand, 1959-60; Chairman, Insurance Tutorial School, 1945-78; Lt. Colonel, Retired, R.N.Z.A.S.C. Director, Realty Development Corporation Limited; Twice Chairman Dividends Appeal Committee; Chairman, Programme Advisory Committee of New Zealand Broadcasting Corporation for 3 years. *Memberships:* Wellington Club; United Services Officers Club; East India, Devonshire, Sports & Public Schools Club, London; International Rugby Football Board; Chairman, Council of New Zealand Rugby Football Union; Chairman New Zealand Amateur Athletic Association; Patron Wellington Centre. *Honours:* O.B.E. Military, 1945-; Efficiency Decoration, with 2 clasps, 1945-. *Hobbies:* Gardening. *Address:* 318 Karori Road, Wellington 5, New Zealand.

BLEAKLEY, David Wylie, b. 11 Jan. 1925, Belfast, Northern Ireland. Chief Executive; Educationist and Politician. m. Winifred Wason, 5 Aug. 1949, 3 sons. *Education:* Diploma Econ. Political Science (Distinction), Ruskin College, Oxford, 1946-48; BA(Hons), MA, Queen's University, Belfast, 1948-51. *Appointments:* Principal, Belfast Further Education College, 1951;

Member of Parliament Northern Ireland, 1958-; Industrial Relations Lecturer, Adult Education College, Dar es Salaam, 1967; Minister of Community Relations, Government of Northern Ireland, 1971; Member, Northern Ireland Assembly, 1975; Head of Department, Economics, Methodist College, Belfast, 1978; Chief Executive and General Secretary, Irish Council of Churches, 1981. *Memberships:* Anglican Consultative Council; Fellowship of Reconciliation; Standing Committee CMS; Fabian Society; Amnesty International; Christian Understanding Everywhere. *Publications:* Young Ulster and Religion in the Sixties; Peace in Ulster; Faulkner—a biography; Saidie Patterson—Irish Peacemaker; In Place of Work—the Sufficient Society. *Honours:* Privy Councellor, 1971; Honorary Degree, Open University, 1975. *Address:* 8 Thornhill, Bangor, Co. Down, Northern Ireland.

BLEASEL, Kevin Fabian, b. 13 April 1924, Sydney. Neurosurgeon. m. Marianne Connelley, 21 May 1955, 4 sons, 1 daughter. *Education:* Marist Brothers High School, Darlinghurst; University of Sydney MB, BS, 1946; Fellow College of Surgeons, London, 1951, Australia, 1956. *Appointments:* Resident Medical Officer, 1946, Medical Superintendent, 1948-50, Neurosurgeon, 1960, Saint Vincent's Hospital, Sydney, Australia; Neurosurgical Registrar, National Hospital for Nervous Diseases, London 1952. *Memberships:* President, Neurosurgical Society of Australasia, 1980; Past President, Association of Neurological Surgeons of New South Wales; Foundation President, Association Medicale Francophone D'Australia; American Association of Neurological Surgeons; Societe De Neurochirugie De Langue Francaise; Australian Club; Royal Sydney Golf Club; Tattersalls Club. *Publications:* Nerve Root Radiography — British Journal of Radiograph, 1961, New Approach to Stereotactic Surgery — Medical Journal of Australia, 1964; Cryo Hypophysectomy: A Technique for the Therapeutic Induction of Hypopituitarism — Medical HJournal of Australia, 1965. *Hobbies:* Photography; French Language; Golf. *Address:* 13 Etham Ave., Darling Point 2027, Sydney, Australia.

BLICQ, Anthony Norman, b. 15 Nov. 1926, Guernsey, Channel Islands. Publishers. m. Laura P Engelbach, 9 Oct. 1958. *Appointments:* Manitoba Civil Service, Canada; Freelance Writer; Oxford University Press, Oxford UK; Executive Director, University of British Columbia Press, Vancouver, Canada; Established the Press, 1970. *Publications:* Novel, The Rise and Fall of Married Charlie, Andre Deutch, London, 1970; Short stories published under pseudonym, published in 10 countries, 1960. *Address:* 305 — 1990 W. 41st Avenue, Vancouver, B.C. V6N 1Y4, Canada.

BLUMHARDT, Doreen Vera, b. 7 Mar. 1914, Whangarei, New Zealand. Art Lecturer (Retired); Potter. *Education:* Christchurch Teachers College, University and Art School, 1934-39. *Appointments:* Appointed to pioneer art and craft education in primary schools throughout New Zealand, 1942-48; Studied art education in Britain and UNESCO in Paris, 1949-50; Head, Art Department, Wellington Teachers College, 1951-72; Pottery Exhibitions, 1955-; Co-founder N.Z. Potter, 1958; President, New Zealand Society of Potters, 1969-70; Advisory Panel for Expo '70, Osaka, Japan. *Memberships:* Advisory Panel, QEII Arts Council of New Zealand, 1973; International Academy of Ceramics; New Zealand Society of Potters; Wellington Potters Society; Craft Council of New Zealand; New Zealand Academy of Fine Arts. *Publications:* New Zealand Potters: Their Work and Words, 1976; Craft New Zealand, 1980-81; Editorial Committee New Zealand Potter; Contributions in many art and craft magazines. *Honours:* CBE, 1981, QEII Arts Council of New Zealand, travel awards to study oriental ceramics in Philippines, Japan, Korea, Taiwan, USA, UK, Greece, Turkey, and Middle East. *Hobbies:* Gardening; Music. *Address:* 35 Harbour View Road, Wellington 5, New Zealand.

BLUNDELL, (Sir) Michael, b. 1907. Director; Farmer. m. Geraldine Lotte Robarts 1946, 1 daughter. *Education:* Wellington College. *Appointments:* Second Lieutenant R.E., 1940; Major, 1940; Lieutenant Colonel, 1941; Colonel, 1944; Commissioner for European Settlement, 1946-47; Member, Legislative Council, 1948: Legislative Council of Kenya, Rift Valley constituency, 1948-63. *Memberships:* Chairman, Pyrethrum Board of Kenya, 1949-54; Leader, New Kenya Group, 1959-63; Leader, European Members 1952: Minister on

Emergency War Council, 1954; Minister of Agriculture, 1955-59 and 1961-62; Chairman, E.A. Breweries Limited, 1964-77; Egerton Agricultural College, 1962-72; Director, Barclays Bank Kenya Limited, 1968; Chairman, Kenya Society for the Blind, 1978; President's Award Scheme, Kenya, 1978. *Publications:* So Rough a Wind, 1964. *Honours:* MBE(Mil), 1942; KBE, 1963; Freeman, Goldsmiths Company, 1953; Honorary Colonel 3rd King's African Rifles, 1955-61; Judge, Guernsey Cattle RASE Show, 1977. *Address:* Box 30181, Nairobi, Kenya.

BLUNN, Oswald Maurice, b. 1 Nov. 1926, Wolverhampton, England. Economist. m. Barbara Mary Saddington, 2 Dec. 1957, 1 son, 2 daughters. *Education:* S.C., H.S.C., George Dixon Grammar School, Birmingham, 1938-44; Bachelor of Commerce, Faculty of Commerce and Social Science, University of Birmingham, 1948-51. *Appointments:* British Railways, Rating and Charging, Curzon Street, Birmingham, 1952. Bank Officer: Chartered Bank of India; Australia; China; Singapore, 1952-55. Cost Investigator and Translator for The General Electric Company Limited, Witton, 1955-59; Translator, B S A Group Research Centre, Birmingham, 1959-60. Portering, Queen Elizabeth Medical Centre, Birmingham, 1974-79; Author/Writer, Contributor to Technical Publications. *Memberships:* Centre for Russian and East European Studies, University of Birmingham, UK. Confirmed Methodist. M.I.B.A. *Publications:* Electric Technology U.S.S.R. by arrangement with Pergamon Institute, Oxford, from London Conference on U.N.E.S.C.O. Editorials and other publications translating from French, FGerman And Russian. *Honours:* William Morton Memorial Prize, The University of Birmingham, 1949. *Hobbies:* Gardening; Music. *Address:* 28 Greville Drive, Sir Harry's Road, Edgbaston, Birmingham, B15 2UU, England.

BOARDMAN, Alexander James, b. 27 Sept. 1938, Brisbane, Australia. Dental Surgeon. m. Susan Maynard Crabbe, 4 Apr. 1964, 2 sons, 1 daughter. *Education:* Commerce, 1957, Bachelor of Dental Science, University of Queensland, 1958-62. *Appointments:* Commonwealth Oil Refineries, 1957; Dentist in Charge, Roma District Hospital, 1963-64; Dental Practice, London, 1964-66; Part time Private Practice, Brisbane, 1966-67; Part-time Civilian Employee, Army, Brisbane, 1966-67; Private Practice, Brisbane, 1968-. *Memberships:* President, Queensland Yachting Association, 1979-; Commonwealth Games Foundation, 1982; President, Appollonian Dental Society, 1977-78; Queensland Rugby Union Club; Australian Yachting Federation; Australian Dental Association; Royal Yachting Association; United States Yacht Racing Union; Queensland Cricketers Club. *Hobbies:* Yachting; Cricket; Tennis; Rugby Union; Music. *Address:* 54 Oriel Road, Yeronga West, Brisbane, 4104, Queensland, Australia.

BOARDMAN, The Rt. Hon. The Lord Thomas Gray, b. 12 Jan. 1919, Staverton Hall, Northamptonshire, England. Company Chairman. m. Norah Mary Deirdre, 14 July 1948, 2 sons, 1 daughter. *Education:* Bromsgrove School. *Appointments:* Solicitor, 1947; Chairman, The Steetley Company Limited; Director, National Westminster Bank Limited; Chairman, Eastern Regional Board of National Westminster Bank; Director, MEPC Limited. *Memberships:* Cavalry & Guards Club. *Honours:* Military Cross, 1944; Territorial Decoration; Deputy Lieutenant (Northamptonshire); High Sheriff of Northamptonshire, 1979-80; President of the Association of British Chambers of Commerce, 1978-80. *Hobbies:* Riding; Hunting. *Address:* The Manor House, Welford, Northants, England.

BODDEN, Truman Murray, b. 22 Apr. 1945, George Town, Grand Cayman. Attorney-at-Law, Barrister. m. 21 Jan. 1975. *Education:* LLB(Hons), London, 1972; Barrister-at-Law, 1969; Associate of Institute of Bankers, London, 1966; Fellow, Institute of Administrative Accounting, 1975; Fellow, Institute of Commerce, 1970; Fellow, British Institute of Commerce, 1970; Fellow, British Institute of Management 1976; Fellow, British Society of Commerce, 1975; Fellow, Institute of Credit Management, 1976; Fellow, Chartered Institute of Arbitrators, 1980. *Appointments:* Banker, 1960-66; Her Majesty's Coroner, 1971; Legal Assistant to Attorney General, 1969-72; Acting Attorney General, 1970, 71 and 72; Senior Partner, Truman Bodden and Company; Attorneys-at-Law; Director of Several Banks. *Memberships:* Executive Council of the Cayman Islands; Legislature for George Town Constituency; Law Society of the Cayman Islands; Honourable Society of Inner Temple, London. *Hobbies:* Sailing; Weight Training. *Address:* North Church Street, Grand Cayman, British West Indies.

BODDINGTON, Thomas James, b. 20 Feb. 1910,. Great Britain. Consulting Engineer. m. Janet Mary Dallison, 1 Apr. 1939, 1 daughter. *Education:* BSc (Eng.), 1931, University of Wales, Cardiff, 1928-31. *Appointments:* Assistant, 1931-34; J.D. & D.M. Watson, Westminster, 1934-43; War Office, British Government, 1943-45; Sir Alexander Gibb & Partners, 1945-58; Rofe & Raffety (Senior Partner, 1968) Rofe Kennard & Lapworth, Senior Partner, 1958-75; Consultant, Sir Frederick Snow & Partners, 1975-. *Memberships:* Fellow, Institution Civil Engineer; Fellow, Institute Water Engineers & Scientists; Institute Water Pollution Control; Life Fellow, Royal Society of Arts; Life Fellow, Royal Commonwealth Society; Life Fellow, Zoological Society; St. Stephens Club; Cardiff & County Club. *Publications:* Papers; Water for Peace, for World Conference, Washington, USA. *Honours:* Decorated Order Homayoun (3rd) H.I.M. Shah-in-Shah, Iran; Trevithick Premium Institution of Civil Engineers, President's Premium, Institute's Premium, Institute Water Engineers & Scientists. *Hobbies:* Sport: Vice President of Rugby Club, Member National Sporting Club. *Address:* 6 Clarendon Court, Kew Gardens Road, Richmond, Surrey, England.

BODLEY, Philip Francis Arthur, b. 26 May 1945, Sydney, Australia. Fine Art Publisher. *Education:* Leaving Certificate, Vaucluse Boys High School. *Appointments:* Foundation member and Manager of House of Bodleigh. Specialises in Fine Art publishing featuring reproductions of works by well known artists. *Hobbies:* Classical Music; Historical Literature; English Literature; Theatre; Football; Cricket; Squash; Tennis. *Address:* 45 Russell Street, Vaucluse, New South Wales 2030, Australia.

BODYCOMB, John Francis, b. 12 Aug. 1931, Melbourne, Victoria, Australia. Minister; Dean. m. Mavis Marjorie Forward, 15 Dec. 1956, 1 son, 3 daughters. *Education:* LTh, 1954, Dip. R.E., Melbourne College of Divinity, 1956; S.T.M. Boston University School of Theology, 1970. *Appointments:* Parish Minister, Geelong, Victoria, 1957-61; Director, Christian Education, Congregational Union of South Australia, 1961-67; Parish Minister, Kensington, New Hampshire, USA, Post-graduate studies, Boston University, 1967-70; Parish Minister, Elizabeth S.A, 1970-74; Church Research and Planning Consultant, South Australia, 1975-76; Dean, Uniting Church Theological Hall, Melbourne, 1977-. *Memberships:* Religious Research Association, USA; Society for the Scientific Study of Religion, USA; Sociological Association of Australia and New Zealand; Australian Association for the Study of Religions; Australia and New Zealand Society for Theological Studies; World Future Society; etc. *Publications:* Southern California Baptist Study; The Kensington Study; HELP! Needs and Welfare of Youth; A Way with Youth; The Naked Churchman; What Price Partnership? plus sundry booklets, journal articles etc. *Hobbies:* Music; Sport (cricket); Camping and other outdoor interests. *Address:* #2 Residence, Ormond College Grounds, Parkville Victoria 3052, Australia.

BODY, Denis Roger, b. 18 Sept. 1937, Wellington, New Zealand. Lipid Chemist (Scientist). m. Jennifer Alison Tindill, 27 Jan. 1968, 2 sons. *Education:* BSc, 1959, MSc (1st class Hons), 1960, Victoria, University of Wellington. *Appointments:* Lister Institute of Preventive Medicine, London, 1964-67; Fats Research Laboratory, 1960-64, Food Chemistry Division, 1968-69, Applied Biochemistry Division, 1970-, Department of Scientific and Industrial Research. *Memberships:* New Zealand Institute of Chemistry; New Zealand Biochemistry Society; Presbyterian Church Elder (Session Clerk); Avalon Rugby Union Football Club, (Secretary); Acting Officer, Boys' Brigade. *Publications:* Approximately 20 publications of scientific papers in International Journals; Chapter on Branched-chain fatty acids, in CRC Handbook on Chromatography of Lipids. *Honours:* National Research Fellowship, 1961. *Hobbies:* Gardening. *Address:* 63 Wikiriwhi Crescent, Palmerston North, New Zealand.

BODY, Richard Bernard Frank Stewart, b. 18 May 1927, Windsor, England. Member of Parliament. m. Doris Marion Graham, 31 Mar. 1959, 1 son, 1 daughter. *Education:* Reading School; Inns of Court, School of Law, (called to the Bar by Middle Temple, 1949). *Appointments:* Barrister, 1949-70; Member of Parliament, 1955-59, 1966-; Underwriting Member of Lloyds, 1979-. *Memberships:* Chairman of the Open Seas Forum, 1970-; Joint Chairman of the Council of 'Get Britain Out', in the Referendum on EEC, 1975; Vice President of Free Trade League, Selsdon Group; Carlton Club; Reform Club. *Publications:* Architect and the Law, 1954; Destiny or Delusion (co-author), 1971; Freedom and Stability in the World Economy (co-author), 1976. *Address:* Jewell's Farm, Stanford Dingley, Reading, Berkshire, England.

BOERNER, Wolfgang-Martin, b. 26 July 1937, Finschhafen, Papua New Guinea. University Professor; Researcher. m. Eileen-Annette Hassebrock, 23 Dec. 1967, 2 sons, 1 daughter. *Education:* St. Peter's College Intermed. Indooroopilly, Queensland, Australia, 1947-48; Neuedettelsau, Federal Republic of Germany, 1949; Arbitur, A von Platen Gymnasium, Ansbach, 1950-58; Dipl. Ing. El. Eng., Technical University, Munich, 1959-63; PhD, Moore School EE, University of Pennsylvania, 1963-67. *Appointments:* Research Student, HF-Institute TV, Munich, 1960-63; Research Fellow, MSEE, University of Pennsylvania, 1963-67; Research Assistant, Elect. and Compt. Eng., Radiation Laboratory, University of Michigan, 1967-68; Research & Teaching PDF, Electrical Engineering, University of Manitoba, 1968-69; Assistant, 1969-71, Associate, 1971-75, Professor, Electrical Engineering, University of Manitoba; Professor Elect. and Info Engineer, 1978; Dir. Communications Laboratory, University of Illinois at Chicago Circle. *Memberships:* Sigma Xi; IEEE (APPT, MTT AES, GES) CAP; SEG; SPIE; NTG VDE; MBESC; SES; Fulbright Alumni Association; Association of Professional Engineers of the Province of Manitoba American Association for the Advancement of Science; Society of Exploration Geophysicists; Electromagnetic Society; Society of Engineering Sciences; Optical Society of America. *Publications:* Approximately 100 papers in international journals, three monographs; Guest Editor, Special Journal Issue on Inverse Methods in Electromagnetic Imaging, 1981. *Honours:* Markgraf Georg der Fromme Scholarship, Ansbach, Federal Republic of Germany, 1956-58; Bad Honeff Scholarship, 1958-64; TV University Munich/University of Pennsylvania Fulbright exchange scholar, 1963-67; IEASTE Exchange scholar, Netherlands, 1961 62; Alex von Humboldt Fellow, 1974-76; Distinguished Humboldt Visiting Scientist, 1980; Distinguished DFVLR Visiting Professorship, 1980. *Hobbies:* Hiking; Travelling. *Address:* 1021 Cedar Lane, Northbrook, IL 60062, USA.

BOFFA, Joseph, b. 6 Feb. 1944, Malta. Librarian. m. 1 daughter. *Education:* Teacher Training Course, 1968-70; Polytechnic of North London, 1973-75. *Appointments:* Teacher, 1970-73; Officer, Public & School Libraries, 1976-. *Memberships:* Honorary Vice-Chairman, Library Association; Public Libraries Advisory Committee; National Commission for UNESCO; Maltese Publications Subsidies Committee. *Publications:* Thesis: An intergrated public and schools library system for Malta (covers 1980-89). *Honours:* ALA, 1976; FLA, 1981. *Hobbies:* Reading; Driving; Photography. *Address:* 35A/4 Mannarino Road, B'Kara, Malta.

BOGLO, Ambrose, b. 7 Dec. 1942, Badagry, Lagos State. General Manager. m. Elizabeth, 24 Nov. 1970, 3 sons, 2 daughters. *Education:* Business and Industry, Lagos University, 1971; Sales Management, 1975; Financial Management, 1978. *Appointments:* Manager, Industrial Machinery Department, 1972, Western Area Manager, 1974, Mid-West Area Manager, M&E Division of UAC, 1975; Divisional Manager, 1976, General Manager, BTD, UYB(Nig) Limited, 1981. *Memberships:* Ikoyi Club; Apapa Club. *Hobbies:* Football; Swimming. *Address:* 3, Chief Bereola Street, c/o PO Box 1000, Surulere, Lagos, Nigeria.

BOJUWOYE, Funso Michael, b. 12 Jan. 1935, Oro, Kwara State, Nigeria. Medicine. m. Susan Ebun Bojuwoye, 2 Oct. 1960, 2 sons, 1 daughter. *Education:* MB, BS, University College, Ibadan, 1965; Certificate in Senior Health Services Management of the Kings Fund Centre & Kings Fund College, London, 1977; Fellow,

Nigeria Post Graduate Medical College, 1981. *Appointments:* Teacher, 1955-57; Trained as Doctor, 1957-65; House Officer in Surgery & Obstetrics and Gynaecology, 1965-66; SHO/Registrar in Surgery, 1966-67; Registrar in Surgery, 1967-68; Staff Medical Officer, 1967-75; Senior Staff Medical Officer, & Head of Staff Health Services, 1975-76; Principal Staff Medical Officer I. *Memberships:* Boy Scouts of Nigeria; International Hospital Federation; Nigerian Medical Association; Deputy Chairman, Catholic Archidiocesan Social Welfare Commission, Lagos; Founding Member, Society of Occupational Health Medicine, Nigeria; President, Oro Development Association; Board Management, Prestigious Sacred Heart Hospital, Abeokuta, Nigeria; Board of Governors, St. Josephs Teacher Training College, Surulere, Lagos. *Publications:* Catholic Position Papers, Co-editor (Nigerian Chapter). *Hobbies:* Fishing; Swimming; Reading; Tourism. *Address:* 5 Anifowose Close, Surulere, Lagos, Nigeria.

BOLAND, Clifford Anthony, b. 8 Nov. 1937, Malta. Medical Practitioner. m. Moira Bencini, 24 Feb. 1963, 2 daughters. *Education:* MD, Royal University of Malta, 1961; DPM (RCP & S Eng.), Royal College of Physicians & Surgeons, England, 1969. *Appointments:* Residential Medical Officer, St. Luke's Hospital, Malta, 1961-63; Captain, 1963-68, Major, 1968-70, Royal Army Medical Corps; Psychiatrist, Royal Derwent Hospital, New Norfolk, Tasmania, 1970-73; Regional Psychiatrist, Hobart & Southern Suburbs, Tasmania, 1973-78; Superintendent, John Edis Hospital, Newtown, Tasmania, 1978-81; Stase Director, Alcohol & Drug Dependency Services; Governor, Council Appointment as Chairman, Medical Commissioner, Mental Health Services Commission, Tasmania; Senior Specialist, Repatriation Department, Hobart, 1973-81; Clinical Supervisor, University of Tasmania, Psychiatry Department, Tasmania, 1971-81; Consultant Psychiatrist (private practice), 1981-. *Memberships:* British Medical Association; Royal Australian & New Zealand College of Psychiatry, Treasurer, 1972-79; Psychotropic Drug Committee for Australia; Army & Navy Club; Medico Legal Society; Australian & New Zealand College of Psychiatry; Royal College of Psychiatry, United Kingdom; Fellow of the Royal Australian & New Zealand College of Psychiatry. *Honours:* Honorary Psychiatrist, Royal Hobart Hospital, Tasmania, 1971-81; Vice-Chairman, Alcohol & Drug Dependency Board, Tasmania, 1978-81. *Hobbies:* Tennis; Billiards; Swimming. *Address:* 22 Mawhera Avenue, Sandy Bay, Tasmania 7005, Australia.

BOLAND, John Cowan, b. 24 July 1927, Muirkirk, Ayrshire, Scotland. Construction. m. 7 Nov. 1953, 4 sons, 2 daughters. *Education:* Fellow, Chartered Institute of Building. *Appointments:* Various positions in construction, 1941-49; Construction Site Manager, Area Manager, J Dickie and Sons, 1949-54; Section Manager, A A Stuart Limited, 1954-57; Construction Superintendent, 1957-58; Construction Manager, Regional Manager, 1958-71; Regional Manager, Crudens Limited, 1971-73; Director, Chief Executive for Scotland, 1973, Henry Boot Construction Limited. *Memberships:* Glasgow College Building; Board of Management, Scottish Building Contractors Association; Senior Vice President, 1981, President, 1982, Scottish Building Employers Federation; Serra International; The Joint Standing Committee of Architects, Surveyors and Building Contractors, Scotland; Scottish Regional Committee, National Joint Council for the Building Industry; National Federation of Building Trades Employers; Royal Troon Golf, Pollock Golf; Royal Scottish Automobile. *Hobbies:* Golf. *Address:* "Kirkhouse", Humbie Road, Newton Mearns, Glasgow G77 5DF, Scotland.

BOLARINWA, Ayodeji Olusola, b. 29 June 1939, Ilesa, Oyo State, Nigeria. Architect and Planner. m. Adeyombo Folasade Sokunbi, 9 Dec. 1972, 1 son, 2 daughters. *Education:* B.ARC, Ahmadu Bello University, 1958-63; MSc(Trop.Arch), Pratt Institute, New York, 1964-66; Post Graduate Research, 1966-68. *Appointments:* Architect, Federal Ministry of Works, Lagos, 1963-64; Architect, Smith Haines Lundberg and Weahler, New York, 1966-; Architect, Ministry of Works, Barbados, West Indies, 1968-70; Architect, Private Practice, Principal Partner, Enplar Nigeria, Ibadan, Nigeria, 1970-. *Memberships:* Royal Institute British Architects; Nigerian Institute of Architects.

Hobbies: Billiards; Travels. *Address:* No 1, Mofolasade Bolarinwa Drive, Kongi, PO Box 2513 Ibadan, Nigeria.

BOLARINWA, Janet Egbinola, b. 18 Aug. 1922, Ibadan City, Oyo State, Nigeria. Educationist. m. 3 Feb. 1945, 2 sons, 4 daughters. *Education:* Nigerian Teacher Education 1941; University of London 1953-55. *Appointments:* Teacher, Primary School Shagamu 1941; Oyo, Teacher Training College, 1941-44; Princess School, Lagos 1945-46; Nursery School, Nigeria Lagos 1946; Alafia Nursery/Primary School, Mokola, Ibadan, 1947-. *Memberships:* National Council of Women, Road Safety, experiment in International wing; Oluyole Cooperative Society Ibadan Face Lift. *Publications:* Radio and Television programmes on Education; Writing in local papers and presentation of papers in International Conferences. *Honours:* MON, 1963; A Chief, Ibadan, 1977. *Hobbies:* Travelling; Reading; Talking; Organising Parties; Planner, Community, State and Federal. *Address:* Alafia Nursery/Primary School, PO Box 5483, Ibadan Oyo State Nigeria.

BOLKIAH MU'IZUDDIN WADDAULAH, H H Sultan Hassanal, b. 15 July 1946. Sultan of Brunei. *Education:* Privately and Victoria Institute, Kuala Lumpur, Malaysia; Royal Military Academy, Sandhurst. DK; PSPNS; PSNB; PSLJ; spmb; PANB. *Appointments:* Appointed Crown Prince and Heir Apparent, 1961; Ruler of State of Brunei, 1967-. *Honours:* Honorary Captain, Coldstream Guards, 1968; Sovereign and Chief of Royal Orders instituted by Sultans of Brunei. *Address:* Istana Darul Hana, Brunei.

BONAR, James Charles, b. 27 Sept. 1906, Montreal, Quebec, Canada. Archivist. m. Andrée Beaubien, de Gaspé, 3 June 1944, 3 sons, 2 daughters. *Education:* Faculty of Letters, University of Montréal; Doctor of Social, Economic and Political Sciences (Hons), University of Montréal; Fellow, The Chartered Institute of Secretaries of Joint Stock Companies and other Public Bodies. *Appointments:* Canadian Pacific Railway Company, Traffic Department; Advertising Supervisor, Secretary, Educational Committee, Chief of Office of Chairman and President, C.P.R. Company; Officer, Assistant Secretary, 1946, Archivist, 1965-70; Chairman and President, The Business Archives Council of Canada, 1968-73. *Memberships:* St James's Club, Montreal; Royal and Ancient Golf Club of St Andrews, Scotland; The Newcomen Society in North America; Canadian Historical Association; Hudson's Bay Record Society; Canadian Authors' Association; The Canadian Club of Montreal; Governor: The Montreal General Hospital, Montreal; St Justine's Hospital for Children; Antiquarian and Numismatic Society, Montreal; Past President, Better Business Bureau of Montreal Inc.; Canadian Railway Club; Past Official, Canadian Conferences on Social Work; Canadian Association for Adult Education. *Publications:* (co-author) The Dominion of Canada; Montreal and the Inauguration of Trans-Canada Transportation; British Columbia and the Highway to the Far East; The Centenary of Sir William Van Horne; Canada Greets Kittery; Canada Upon the Seas; (co-author) Survey of Canadian Political Parties; (co-author) Survey of Civil Service in Canada; (co-author) Canadian Pacific Railway Company; Contributions to Early development and continued progress of Canada. *Honours:* Certificate of Merit, Canadian Legion, British Empire Service League, 1947; Distinguished Professional Service Award, The Institute of Chartered Secretaries and Administrators, 1960; *Hobbies:* Walking; Swimming. *Address:* 599 Lansdowne Avenue, Westmount, Quebec, H3Y 2V7, Canada.

BOND, Anthony Derek, b. 18 Dec. 1944, Bristol, United Kingdom. Gallery Director. m. Jan Bond, 11 July 1970, 1 son, 1 daughter. *Education:* Isleworth Polytechnic Art Department 1962-64; Ruskin School of Drawing, Oxford, 1965; BEd Hons. London 1974. *Appointments:* Assistant, Phillip Bentram Sculptor, 1964; Various exhibitions, 1965-69; Teaching, Ceramics, Kingston on Thames, 1974; Teaching Art, NSW, 1975-77; Director Wollongong City Gallery, Chairman of Regional Galleries Association, NSW, 1978-; Member of the Visual Arts Board of the Australia Council, 1980; Writing, Weekly Column, Illawarra Mercury, NSW, 1976-; Assistant Director, Curatorial, Western Australia Art Gallery. *Memberships:* Regional Galleries Association NSW; Wollongong Gallery Society. *Publications:* Weekly articles for Illawarra Mercury; Several Catalogues of exhibitions; Painting; Sculpture; Printmaking. *Honours:* Award, Best Painting, Ruskin, 1965. *Hobbies:* Bush walking; Wine collecting and Drinking; Reading; Photography. *Address:* Wollongong City Gallery, Wollongong 2500, NSW Australia.

BONDI, (Sir) Hermann, b. 1 Nov. 1919, Vienna, Austria. Mathematician; Chairman. m. Christine M Stockmann, 2 sons, 3 daughters. *Education:* Trinity College, Cambridge, 1937-40; BA(Cantab), 1940; MA(Cantab), 1944; DSc(Hons), University of Bath, 1974; DSc, University of Sussex, 1974; DSc, University of Surrey, 1974; University of York, 1981. *Appointments:* Fellow, Trinity College Cambridge, 1943-49 and 1952-54; Assistant Lecturer, Mathematics, Cambridge, 1945-48; University Lecturer, 1948-54; Professor of Mathematics, Kings College, London, 1954-; Director-General European Space Research Organisation 1967-71; Chief Scientific Adviser, Ministry of Defence 1971-77; Chief Scientist, Department of Energy 1977-80; Chairman, Natural Environment Research Council 1980-. *Memberships:* FRS; FRAS; FIP; Fellow and Past President, Institute of Mathematics and its Applications; Rationalist Press Association Limited; British Humanist Association; Science Policy Foundation; Advisory Centre for Education. *Publications:* Cosmology 1952, 1960; The Universe at Large 1961; Relativity and Common Sense, 1964; Assumption and Myth in Physical Theory 1967. *Honours:* KCB, 1973; FRS, 1959; Hon FIEE 1979. Hobby: Travelling. *Address:* East House, Buckland Corner, Reigate Heath, Surrey, England.

BONE, Thomas Renfrew, b. 2 Jan. 1935, Port Glasgow, Scotland. College Principal. m. Elizabeth Stewart 31 July 1959, 1 son, 1 daughter. *Education:* MA 1st Class Honours, English Language and Literature, Glasgow University 1952-56; Teaching Qualification, Jordanhill College 1956-57; MEd 1st Class Honours, 1958-62; PhD 1963-66, Glasgow University. *Appointments:* Teacher of English, Paisley Grammar School, 1957-61; Lecturer, Glasgow University, 1963-67; Lecturer, 1961-63, Principal Lecturer, 1967-71, Principal, 1972, Jordanhill College. *Memberships:* Chairman, Scottish Council for Educational Technology, Vice Chairman, Standing Conference, Studies in Education; Vice Chairman, Scottish Certificate of Education Examination Board; General Teaching Council for Scotland; Commonwealth Council for Educational Administration; Educational Research Board, Social Science Research Council; Education Committee, Council for National Academic Awards; Educational Advisory Council, Independent Broadcasting Authority. *Publications:* Studies in the History of Scottish Education, 1967; School Inspection in Scotland, 1968; Chapters in: Whither Scotland, 1971; Educational Administration in Australia and Abroad, 1975; Administering Education, International Challenge, 1975; European Perspectives in Teacher Education, 1976; World Yearbook of Education, 1980. *Hobbies:* Golf. *Address:* 16 Thornly Park Avenue, Paisley, Scotland, PA2 7SD.

BONER, J Russell, b. 25 July 1930 Boulder, Colorado, USA. Editor. m. Darryl Anne Alkire 22 Dec. 1954, 1 son, 2 daughters. *Education:* High School Diploma, American School, Tokyo, Japan, 1948; BA Economics, History and Political Science, Yale University, New Haven, Connecticut, USA, 1952. *Appointments:* Bureau Manager, Reporter, International News Service, Atlanta, Georgia, Hartford, Connecticut, USA, 1956-58; Reporter, United Press International, Hartford, Connecticut, Buffalo, NY, USA, 1958-59; Staff Reporter, The Wall Street Journal, Chicago, Illinois, Pittsburgh, Pennsylvania, USA, London, 1959-70; Editor-in-chief, International Management, 1970-; Publisher, Maidenhead, Berks, 1977-79. *Address:* 61 Cadogan Place, London SW1X 9RS, England.

BONINGTON, Christian John Storey, b. 6 Aug. 1934, London. Mountaineer; Writer and Lecturer. m. Wendy Marchant, 25 May 1962, 2 sons. *Education:* University College School, 1944-51; Royal Military Academy, Sandhurst, 1953-55. *Appointments:* Officer, Royal Tank Regiment, 1956-58; Army Outward Bound School, 1958-60; Management Trainee, Unilever, 1961-62; Freelance Mountaineer, Writer, Lecturer 1962-. *Memberships:* Alpine Climbing Group; Alpine Club; British Mountaineering Council; Army Mountaineering Association; Youth Hostels Association; Climbers Club; Carlisle Mountaineering Club; Army and Navy Club; FRGS. *Publications:* I Chose to Climb, 1966; Annapurna South Face, 1971; Next Horizon, 1972;

Everest South West Face, 1972; Everest the Hard Way, 1976; Quest for Adventure, 1981. *Honours:* Honorary MA, Salford University, 1973; Founders Medal, RGS, 1974; CBE, 1976; Doctor of Science, Sheffield University; Fellow, UMIST. *Hobbies:* Climbing; Squash; War Games. *Address:* Badger Hill, Hesket Newmarket, Wigton, Cumbria, England.

BOOTH, Charles Leonard, b. 7 Mar. 1925, Littleborough, Lancs. Diplomatic Service. m. Mary Gillian Emms, 1 Aug. 1958, 2 sons, 2 daughters. *Education:* Pembroke College, Oxford 1942-43 and 1947-50; MA(Hons), Modern History. *Appointments:* Captain, Royal Artillery, 1943-47; HM Foreign Service, 1950-80; HM Ambassador in Rangoon. *Memberships:* Travellers' Club, London. *Honours:* CMG, 1979; MVO, 1961. *Hobbies:* Gardening; Walking; Italian Opera. *Address:* British Embassy, Rangoon, Burma.

BOOTH, David Robert, b. 27 Aug. 1937, Southport, England. Oral Surgeon. m. Judith Urania Savage, 15 July 1961, 3 sons, 1 daughter. *Education:* BDSc, University of Western Australia, 1959; MDSc, 1970; Fellow, Royal Australasian College of Dental Surgeons, 1972; Member, Australian College of Education, 1976. *Appointments:* Dentist, England and Western Australia, 1959-60; Private Practice, 1961-66; Surgical Registrar, Perth Dental Hospital, 1966-70; Senior Lecturer in Oral Pathology, University of Western Australia, 1970-; Visiting Oral Surgeon, Royal Perth Hospital, 1972. *Memberships:* Chairman, W.A. Committee, Royal Australasian College of Dental Surgeons, 1975-80; Chairman, Federation of Independent Schools Parents Associations, 1980-81; Secretary, The New Church in Australia, 1964-73. *Publications:* Journal Articles on Oral Surgery and Oral Pethology. *Honours:* Certificate of Merit, American Society of Dentistry for Children, 1960; Professor KJ Sutherland Prize (Inaugural award), Dental Study Group of Western Australia. *Hobbies:* Walking; Classical Guitar. *Address:* 17 Leonora Street, Como, 6152, Western Australia.

BOOTH, John Moss, b. 23 Mar. 1933 Glossop, Derbyshire. Endodontist. m. 12 Sept. 1964, 3 sons. *Education:* BDS, Manchester University 1957; DDS, Toronto University 1962. *Appointments:* Dental General Practitioner, Oxford 1962-74; Specialist Dentist, Adelaide 1975-. *Hobbies:* Golf; Gardening; Squash. *Address:* 11 Peroomba Avenue, Kensington Gardens, South Australia.

BOOTHROYD, Rockley Garrick, b. 5 Oct. 1937, Cossipore, Calcutta, India. Chartered Mechanical Engineer/Academic. m. Margaret Mary Faith Boyle, 4 Feb. 1961, 1 son, 2 daughters. *Education:* BA(Cantab) 1960; MA 1964 Magdalene College, Cambridge; MSc, Nuclear Reactor Physics and Technology, 1961, PhD, Mechanical Engineering, 1967, Birmingham University. *Appointments:* Lecturer, Nuclear Engineering, Department of Mechanical Engineering, University of Birmingham 1961-71; Senior Rsearch Scientist, CSIRO Division of Environmental Mechanics, Canberra, Australia 1971-73; Foundation Head of Department of Mechanical Engineering, Capricornia Institute of Advanced Education, Rockhampton, Queensland Australia 1973-. *Memberships:* Fellow, Institution of Mechanical Engineers, London; Fellow, Institution of Engineers, Australia. *Publications:* Flowing Gas-Solids Suspensions, Chapman and Hall, London 1971; Over 40 Technical/Research papers also newspaper/journal articles. *Honours:* Jeanne Liquier-Millward Prize, Birmingham University, 1961. *Hobbies:* Reading; Music; Travel. *Address:* Alton Downs, Nr. Rockhampton, Queensland 4702, Australia.

BORCHARDT, Dietrich Hans, b. 14 Apr. 1916, Hanover, Germany. Librarian. m. Janet Duff Sinclair, 1 son, 2 daughters. *Education:* MA, (NZ) 1947; Dip. NZ Lib.Sch. 1947; FLAA 1963. *Appointments:* Acquisition Librarian, University of Otago, Dunedin, New Zealand, 1948-50; Deputy Librarian, 1950-53, Librarian, 1953-65, University of Tasmania, Hobart, Tasmania; Chief Librarian, La Trobe University, Bundoora, Victoria, 1965-81; UNESCO Library Expert, Ankara, Turkey, 1964-65; Visiting Professor, Geo. Peabody College School of Library Science, Nashville Tennessee, USA, 1968 and 1973. Memberships include: Australian Advisory Council on Bibliographical Services, 1960-; Consultant, National Library of Australia; Advisor to Indonesian University's on Library Services. *Publica-*

tions: Australian Bibliography, 1979; Australian Official Publication, 1979; Librarianship in Australia, New Zealand and Oceanica, 1975; Editor: Australian Academic and research libraries, 1970. *Honours:* H.C.L. Andersen Award of the Library Association of Australia, 1979. *Hobbies:* Bibliography; Gardening. *Address:* 57 Aylmer Street, North Balwyn, Victoria, Australia, 3104.

BORNEMISSZA, George Francis, b. 11 Feb. 1924, Baja, Hungary. Ecologist m. Helen Patricia Insley, 9 May, 1972, 1 son. *Education:* Undergraduate Studies, Eotvos Lorand University, Budapest, 1943-48; PhD, University of Innsbruck, Austria, 1949-50; Research Fellow of A. von Humboldt Foundation, Munchen, Germany, 1960-61. *Appointments:* Graduate Assistant (Demonstrator in Entomology) at Zoology Department, University of Western Australia, 1951-54; Senior Principal Research Scientist, Division of Entomology, Commonwealth Scientific and Industrial Research Organization, Australia, 1954-. *Memberships:* Entomological Society of Australia; Ecological Society of Australia; Entomological Society of Southern Africa. *Publications:* Seventeen Scientific Publications. *Creative Works:* The Burning Bush, (Reinvasion of burnt areas by insects). Won numerous Australian and international prizes, including Third prize at International Film Competition in Sydney, 1963. *Honours:* Gold Medal by Britannica Australia Awards, 1973 and citation For His Application of Ecology for Human Benefit; Honourable mention in a scroll from Rolex Awards for Enterprise, 1981. *Hobbies:* Morphological collection of beetles; Thematic collection of stamps (Insects, Environment); Photography; Hiking. *Address:* 78 Nelson Road, Hobart, Tas. 7005, Australia.

BOROWITZKA, Michael Armin, b. 1 Oct. 1948, Vienna, Austria. Phycologist. m. Lesley Joyce Antill, 23 Oct. 1971, 1 daughter. *Education:* BSc.(Hons.), 1970, PhD, 1975, University of Sydney, Australia. *Appointments:* Post-Doctoral Fellow at the Scripps Institution of Oceanography, La Jolla, USA, 1975-76; Queens Fellow in Marine Science at the Australian Institute of Marine Science, Townsville, Australia, 1977-78; Section Leader in Marine Biology, 1979-81, Senior Project Scientist, 1981-, Roche Research Institute of Marine Pharmacology, Dee Why, Australia. *Memberships:* Committee Member, Great Barrier Reef Committee; Council Member and Newsletter Editor, Australasian Society for Phycology and Aquatic Botany; Treasurer, Australian Marine Sciences Association, N S W Branch; International Phycological Society; Phycological Society of America. *Publications:* Various publications in the scientific literature. *Hobbies:* Music; Sailing; Stamp collecting. *Address:* 115 Prince Alfred Pde., Newport, N S W 2106, Australia.

BOSAH, Chuba Benedict, b. 28 Nov. 1932, Onitsha, Anambra State, Nigeria. Ceramist. m. Bessie Nwando, 16 Feb. 1964, 3 sons, 1 daughter. *Education:* Dipl.Ing, Ceramics, West Germany, 1968-69; Associate Nigerian Institute of Management, 1980; Fellow, British Institute of Ceramics, 1981. *Appointments:* Assistant Works Manager, Winterling Ceramics, 1968-70; Assistant Works Manager, Hutsche Nreuther, 1970-71; Assistant Works Manager, Electro Ceramics Industry Neuerer, 1971; Production Manager/Head of Production Department, Modern Ceramics Industries Limited, Umuahia, Nigeria, 1972-. *Memberships:* West Germany Ceramics Society; Chemical Society of Nigeria, 1979. *Creative Works:* Successfully conducted a research work on the possibility of using 100% local Nigerian raw materials for the production of Ceramics Wares. Composed a Ceramics Body for the manufacture of Sanitary wares and Dinner wares using 100% local Nigerian raw materials (except chemicals), 1975. Since 1975 Modern Ceramics Industries, Umuahia still use the Body Composition and glaze. *Hobbies:* Football; Music. *Address:* 44 School Road, Umuahia, Imo State, Nigeria.

BOSE, Tapan Kumar, b. 12 Oct. 1938, Calcutta, India. Professor of physics. m. Gouri Paul-Chaudhuri, 10 July 1966, 1 son, 1 daughter. *Education:* BSc. (Hons), 1957, MSc. (Physics), 1959, University of Calcutta, India; DSc. (Physics), University of Louvain, 1965. *Appointments:* Post doctoral Fellow, Kammerlingh Onnes Laboratorium, Leiden, Holland, 1965-67; Research Associate, Brown University, Providence, R I. USA,

1967-69; Assistant professor of physics, 1969-71, Associate professor of physics, 1971-75, Full professor of physics, 1975-, Director, Department of Physics, 1972-75, Université du Québec, Trois-Rivières, Québec, Canada; Visiting professor, University of Nancy I, Nancy, France, 1976-77; Director, Graduate studies, Department of Physics, Université du Québec, Trois-Rivières, Québec, Canada, 1979-. *Memberships:* American Physical Society; Canadian Association of Physicists; Institute of Electrical and Electronics Engineers; Canadian Association of Chemists. *Publications:* Author of twenty five publications in the field of dielectrics with particular emphasis on molecular interactions, time domain spectroscopy and critical phenomena. *Hobbies:* Stamp collection; Reading; Travel; Tennis; Badminton; Table tennis. *Address:* 3965 De Châteaufort, Trois-Rivières, Québec G8Y 2A8, Canada.

BOSSOM (Hon Sir) Clive, b. 4 Feb. 1918, New York, USA. Past Member of Parliament; Company Director. m. The Lady Barbara North, 28 Sept. 1928, 3 sons, 1 daughter. *Education:* Eton. *Appointments:* Regular Soldier, The Buffs, 1937-48; Kent County Council, 1949-52; Conservative MP., Leominster Division (N Hereford), 1959-74, (PPS. Mrs Margaret Thatcher MP. 1961 at Ministry of Pensions and National Insurance); Chairman, Europ Assistance Ltd; Director, Vosper Ltd. *Memberships:* Chairman, R A C., 1975-78; Chairman, British Motor Sports Council, 1975-; Vice President, Federation International de L'Automobile 1975-81; Chairman, Ex-Service War Disabled Help; Committee, St. John and Red Cross; President, Anglo-Netherlands Society; Vice President, Anglo-Belgian Union; Past Master, Worshipful Company of Grocers, 1979-80; Past Council Member, Royal Geographical Society, 1971-78; Past Council Member, Royal Society of Arts, 1969-72; President, Industrial Fire Protection Association, 1969-; Council Fire Protection Association. *Honours:* Knight of Justice, Order of St.John; Fellow of the Royal Society of Arts; Commander, Order of Leopold II (Belgium); Order of Homayoun (Iran); Commander of Order of The Crown (Belgium); Knight Commander of Orange Nassau (Netherlands). *Hobbies:* Travel. *Address:* 3 Eaton Mansions, London, SW1.

BOTA, Watson S C, b. 15 Apr. 1927, Chama District, Zambia. Controller, Educational Broadcasting Services. m. Emmie Kumwenda, 12 June 1950, 5 sons, 2 daughters. *Education:* Diploma in Educational Administration, 1965; Diploma in Educational Broadcasting, 1971. *Appointments:* Headmaster; Education Officer; Inspector of School; Lecturer Grade I/Producer; Head of Educational Radio; Controller of Educational Broadcasting and Television Services. *Memberships:* Session Clerk of Presbyterian Church in Zambia. *Publications:* School Broadcasts 1973 Social Studies Teachers' Handbook. *Hobbies:* Church activities. *Address:* 2 Nyati Road, off Addis Ababa Drive, Lusaka, Zambia.

BOTHWELL, John Charles, b. 29 June 1926, Toronto, Ontario, Canada. Clergyman. m. Joan Cowan, 29 Dec. 1951, 3 sons, 2 daughters. *Education:* BA, 1948, LTh, 1951, BD, 1952, DD, 1972, Trinity College, Toronto. *Appointments:* Curate, St James' Cathedral, Toronto, 1951; Curate, Christ Church, Vancouver, BC, 1953; Rector, St Aidan's Church, Oakville, 1956; Rector, St James' Church, Dundas, 1960; Canon Missioner of Niagara, 1965; Executive Director of Program for thw Anglican Church of Canada, 1969; Elected First Coadjutor Bishop of Niagara, 1971; Succeeded to the See of Niagara, 1973-. *Memberships:* Executive Member Hamilton Social Planning and Research Council, President, 1976-78; Board Member, Hamilton United Way and Ontario Welfare Council; Official Visitor Ridley College, St. Catharines, St John's Boys School and St. Margaret's Girls School, Elora, Ontario and Canadian Chapter of the Sisters of the Church; Member of General Synod and Ontario Provincial Synod of Anglican Church of Canada; Member of various ecumenical and inter-church committees and boards. *Address:* 838 Glenwood Avenue, Burlington, Ontario, Canada.

BOTTOMLEY, Arthur George, b. 7 Feb. 1907, London. Member of Parliament. m. 25 July 1936. *Education:* Gamuel Road Council School; Extension Classes at Toynbee Hall. *Appointments:* Under Secretary of State for the Dominions; Secretary for Overseas Trade; Secretary of State for Commonwealth Relations; Minister of Overseas Development; House of Commons Commissioner. *Memberships:* Ex-Vice Chairman of the UK Branch of Commonwealth Parliamentary Association; Ex-Treasuer of Commonwealth Parliamentary Association; Chairman of British India Forum, President of the Britain Burma Society. *Publications:* The Use and Abuse of Trades Unions; Why Britain Should Enter the European Common Market. *Honours:* OBE, 1941; Privy Councillor, 1951. *Hobbies:* Walking; Theatre-going. *Address:* 19 Lichfield Road, Woodford Green, Essex.

BOTTOMLEY, James Reginald Alfred, b. 12 Jan. 1920, London, England. British Diplomat (Retired); Company Director. m. Barbara Evelyn Vardon, 23 Aug. 1941, 3 sons, 2 daughters. *Education:* MA, Trinity College, Cambridge, 1938-40. *Appointments:* British Army, 1940-46; Dominions Office, 1946-47; Commonwealth Relations Office, 1947-67; Foreign and Commonwealth Office, 1968; Deputy Under-secretary of State, 1967; Ambassador to South Africa, 1973; Permanent Representative at Geneva, 1976; Retired, 1978; Director, Johnson, Matthey and Company Limited, 1979. *Honours:* KCMG, 1973. *Hobbies:* Golf; Gardening; Reading. *Address:* Chiltern Rise, Aldbury, Tring, Herts, England.

BOULT, Reynald, b. 20 Nov. 1916, Hull, Canada. Lawyer. m. Lyone Migneron, 5 Oct. 1940, 1 son, 2 daughters. *Education:* BA, B.Ph, 1938, L.LL, 1958, University of Ottawa, Canada. *Appointments:* Inspecting Officer, Inspection Board of UK and Canada, 1941; Administrator, UNRRA Sponsored relief campaigns, 1945; Translator, House of Commons Debates, 1947; Solicitor, Department of Secretary of State, 1961; Librarian, Supreme Court of Canada, 1962. *Memberships:* Cercle Universitaire, Ottawa. *Publications:* A Bibliography of Canadian Law, 1977; Articles in Legal journals. *Honours:* Paris Bar Gold Medal at Quebec Bar Admission examinations, 1959; Appointed Queen's Counsel, 1976. *Address:* 330 Metcalfe, Ottawa, Canada, K2P 1S4.

BOURCHIER, Murray Goulburn Madden, b. 28 Mar. 1925, Melbourne, Australia. Australian Diplomatic Service. m. Ray Francis, 8 Dec. 1951, 3 sons, 2 daughters. *Education:* Gordon Technical College, 1942; LLB, Melbourne University, Australia, 1947-50. *Appointments:* Department of External Affairs, 1951; 3rd Secretary, Australian High Commission, London, 1954-57; 2nd Secretary, Australian High Commission, Colombo, 1959-62; Head, South East Asia Section, Department of External Affairs, 1962-65; Counsellor, Australian Embassy, Moscow, 1965-68; Ambassador, Republic of Korea, 1971-75; Head, Legal and Treaties Division, ·Department of Foreign Affairs, Canberra, 1975-77; Ambassador Moscow, 1977-. *Hobbies:* Literature; Fishing. *Address:* Australian Embassy, Moscow.

BOURCHIER, Ursula, b. 15 Nov. 1921, Hamburg, W Germany. Secretary. m. James William Bourchier, 24 Dec. 1948. *Education:* Commercial Assistant Diploma, given by Chamber of Commerce, Hamburg, W Germany, Sept. 1941. *Appointments:* Insurance Brokers, Hamburg, W Germany, 1938-46; 94th British Military Hospital, Hamburg, W Germany, 1946-48; Overseas Buying and Confirming House., London, 1953-55 and 1957-58; Machine Tool Importers, London, UK, 1955; Sign Manufacturers, London, UK, 1956; Lloyd's Underwriter, London, UK, 1958-. *Memberships:* MIBA; ex Woolwich, Bexley and District Canine Association; ex Dartford and District Canine Society. *Publications:* In letter form only, Birds Illustrated, 1961; Our Dogs, 1960, 1965, 1967. *Honours:* Between 1960 and 1977 collected about 400 prizes at home and abroad. 1951 at HQ Hamburg Garrison, BAOR., Highly Commended in both embroidery and knitting. *Hobbies:* Dog Breeding; Showing; Keeping of Foreign Birds; Crochet; Embroidery; Knitting; Mosaic; Writing. *Address:* 149 Northumberland Ave, Welling, Kent, DA16 2QE England.

BOURGEAU, Pierre G, b. 21 Jan. 1939 Ottawa, Ontario Canada. Barrister and Solicitor. m. Nicole de Terwangne 1973, 1 son. *Education:* BA, Political Science, University Ottawa, 1961; LLB, 1965; Postgraduate Studies, Doctorate Course, Civil Law, 1965-66; Osgood Hall Bar Admission Course, 1967-68. *Appointments:* Called to Ontario Bar, 1968; Canada Diplomatic Corporations Department External Affairs, 1968-70; Legal Advisor, UN Session, 1969, Department of Secretary of State for Federal Department

Justice, 1970-72; Legal Advisor, Canadair Limited, Montreal, 1972-74; Vice President, General Counsel and Sec., Churchill Falls, Labrador, Corporation Limited, 1974-79; General Counsel and Secretary Celanese Canada Incorporated; President, Clean Properties Limited; Vice-President, Secretary and Director, Celanese Canada (Millhaven) Inc., Vice President and Director, Lethbridge Rehabilitation Centre. Memberships include: Law Society Upper Canada; Bar Quebec; Canadian Bar Association; Canadian Council on International Law; The International Law Association; Lethbridge Rehabilitation Centre; Institute Chartered Secretaries and Administrators of Canada; St James Club; St Denis Club. *Hobbies:* Travel; Reading. *Address:* 615 Lazard Avenue, Mt. Royal, Quebec, Canada H3R 1P6.

BOURNE, Naomi Margaret, b. 16 July 1950, Gosport, Hampshire, England. Theatre Manager. *Education:* Teachers Diploma, Claremont Teachers College, Western Australia, 1968-69. *Appointments:* Music Mistress, Narrogin Agricultural Senior High School, Western Australia, 1970; Music Mistress, Cannington Senior High School, Western Australia, 1971; Music Mistress, Marylebone C of E Girls School, London, UK, 1973; Administrative Assistant, XI ISME Conference, Western Australia, 1974; Production Co-Ordinator, 1974, Manager, 1980, Perth Concert Hall, Australia. *Hobbies:* Piano; Guitar; Dancing. *Address:* 9/25 Eric Street, Como, Western Australia.

BOURN, John Bryant, b. 21 Feb. 1934, London, England. Economist. m. Ardita Ann Fleming, 21 Mar. 1959, 1 son, 1 daughter. *Education:* London School of Economics, 1951-56; BSc, 1954, PhD, 1958. *Appointments:* Air Ministry, 1956-63; HM Treasury, 1963-64; Private Secretary to Permanent Under Secretary of State, 1964-69, Assistant Secretary, 1972-74, Assistant Under Secretary of State, 1977-, Ministry of Defence; Director of Programmer, Civil Service College, 1969-72; Under Secretary, Northern Ireland Office, 1974-77. *Memberships:* Political Studies Association. *Publications:* Management in Central and Local Government, 1979; Memorandum to Report of Committee on the Civil Service, 1968; Contributions to degree courses. *Honours:* Postgraduate Studentship in Economics, 1954 and 1955. *Hobbies:* Swimming; Squash Rackets. *Address:* 11 Cresswell Way, London, England.

BOURRE, John Mountfort, b. 12 May 1916, Sydney, Australia. Chairman, Housing Commission of New South Wales. *Education:* B Econ., 1948, Diploma of Town and Country Planning, 1950, University of Sydney, Australia. *Appointments:* NSW Department of Local Government, 1935-37; Secretary, Relief Works Regulation Committee, 1937-40; RAAF., 1940-45; Housing Commission of NSW, Australia, 1945-50; Secretary, 1950-70; Chairman, 1970-; Member of Macarthur Development Board, Campbelltown, NSW, Member, Public Servants Housing Authority, NSW, Australia. *Memberships:* Life Fellow, Royal Australian Planning Institute; Life Fellow and Chairman of NSW Division, Australian Society of Senior Executives; Fellow, Australian Institute of Administration; Councillor, Australian Institute of Urban Studies; Civic Design Society. *Honours:* Imperial Service Order. *Address:* 34 Palace Street, Petersham, New South Wales, Australia.

BOUSFIELD, Edward Lloyd, b. 19 June 1926, Penticton, B C., Canada. Museum biologist. m. Barbara Joyce Schwartz, 20 June 1953, 1 son, 3 daughters. *Education:* BA, 1948, MA, 1949, University of Toronto, Canada; PhD, Harvard University, USA, 1954. *Appointments:* Invertebrate Zoologist, 1950-64, Chief Zoologist, 1964-74, Senior Scientist, 1974-, National Museum of Natural Sciences, National Museums of Canada, Ottawa, Canada. *Memberships:* President, 1979-80, Archivist, 1971-, Canadian Society of Zoologists; President, Ottawa Field-Naturalists' Club, 1959-61; Fellow, Royal Society of Canada, 1978-; Biological Council of Canada, 1974-80; Director Youth Science Foundation, 1977-80; Canadian Committee on Oceanography, 1970·; American Society of Limnology and Oceanography (ALSO); Ecological Society of America; Sigma Xi; Arctic Institute of N America; Society of Systematic Zoology; Canadian Museums Association. *Publications:* Author of more than 70 scientific and popular publications on aquatic invertebrate animals, mainly crustaceans and mollusks including: Ecological Control of the Occurrence of Barnacles in the Miramichi Estuary, 1955; Freshwater Amphipods of Glaciated North America, 1958; Canadian Atlantic Seashells, 1960; Shallow-water Gammaridean Amphipoda of New England, 1973; A Revised Classification and Phylogeny of Amphipod Crustaceans, 1979. *Hobbies:* Curling; Lawn Bowling; Golf; Music: SPEBSQSA; Trumpet; Guitar. *Address:* 48 Farlane Blvd., Ottawa, Ontario, Canada, K2E 5H5.

BOUTIN, Maurice, b. 10 June 1938, St.-Camille, PQ, Canada. Professor of Fundamental Theology. *Education:* BA, 1959, BA(Theol.), 1963, University of Montreal, Canada; ThD, University of Munich, German Federal Republic, 1973. *Appointments:* Assistant Professor, 1973-78, Associate Professor, 1978-, Fundamental Theology, University of Montreal, PQ, Canada. *Memberships:* Vice-president, Canadian Corporation for Studies in Religion, 1979; Member of Executive, Canadian Society for the Study of Religion, 1978, President, 1981; International Colloquiums on Hermeneutics, Rome, Italy, 1975; Christians Associated for Relationships with Eastern Europe, (New York, USA) 1979. *Publications:* Contributions to various professional journals and publications in German, English and French including: Relationalität als Verstehensprinzip bei Rudolf Bultmann, 1974; L'homme en mouvement: Le sport, le jeu, la fête, 1976; Christianisme - Marxisme: positions et questions: Prêtre et Pasteur, 1980. *Hobbies:* Skiing; Swimming; Canoeing. *Address:* 2835 Goyer, Montreal, PQ, H3S 1H2, Canada.

BOWEN, Glynn Demsey, b. 14 Sept. 1930, Brisbane, Australia. Scientist. m. 24 Sept. 1955, (Div., 1981), 2 sons, 1 daughter. *Education:* BSc., 1948-53, BSc. (Hons.) 1st Class, 1955, MSc., 1961, DSc., 1980, University of Queensland, Australia. *Appointments:* Queensland Department, Primary Industries, 1948-58; Assistant Chief (Adelaide) and Chief Research Scientist, Division Soils, CSIRO, Glen Osmond, South Australia, 1959-. *Memberships:* Australian Society Plant Physiologists; Australian Society Soil Science; Australian Institute Foresters; Scientific consultant to International Foundation of Science, Stockholm. *Publications:* Several scientific papers and chapters for books dealing with effects of soil micro-organisms on plant productivity and on root physiology. *Honours:* Nuffield Foundation Award, 1969. *Hobbies:* Sculpture; Ceramics; Music; Squash. *Address:* CSIRO Division of Soils, Private Bag No. 2, Glen Osmond, S A 5064, Australia.

BOWEN, James Vincent Seaton, b. 22 Feb. 1923, Adelaide, Australia. Company Director. m. Natalie Anne, 3 daughters. *Education:* Queen's College and St. Peter's College, Adelaide, Australia; S A School of Mines and University of Adelaide, Australia. *Appointments:* Chairman of Chesser Cellars and Associates; Director of Sabco Limited; Lord Mayor of Adelaide, 1979-81. *Memberships:* Adelaide County Council since 1966; Royal S A Yacht Squadron; Royal Adelaide Golf Club; Naval, Military and Air Force Club, Adelaide, Australia. *Hobby:* Gardening. *Address:* 195 Stanley Street, North Adelaide 5006, Australia.

BOWEN, Nigel Hubert, b. 26 May 1911, Summerland, British Columbia. Chief Judge, Federal Court of Australia. m. Eileen Cecily Mullens, 21 Feb. 1947, 3 daughters. *Education:* BA, LLB, St Paul's College, Sydney University. *Appointments:* Admitted New South Wales Bar, 1936; Victorian Bar, 1954; QC, 1953; Liberal MP for Parramatta, New South Wales, 1964-73; Commonwealth Attorney-General, 1966-69, 1971; Minister for Education, 1969-71; Minister for Foreign Affairs, 1971-72; Head Australian Delegation to United Nations General Assembly, 1971 and 1972; Judge New South Wales Court of Appeal and Supreme Court, 1973-76; Chief Judge in Equity, 1974-76; Chief Judge, Federal Court of Australia, 1976-. *Publications:* Reports: Conflict between Public Duty and Private Interest, 1979; Legal Education in New South Wales, 1979. *Honours:* QC, 1953; KBE, 1976. *Hobbies:* Swimming; Music. *Address:* 43 Grosvenor Street, Wahroonga, New South Wales, Australia.

BOWETT, Druie, b. 3 Jan. 1924, Ripon, Yorks, England. Artist. m. 28 Aug. 1943, 3 sons. *Education:* Harrogate School of Art; Pupil of Jean-Georges Simon. *Appointments:* Vice Chairman, Loughborough College of Art and Design. *Memberships:* AIAP; IAA, Paris. *Creative Works:* Numerous One Man Shows including: Midland Group, Gallery, Nottingham, 1957,1961; Aus-

ten Hayes Gallery, York, 1961; Wakefield City Art Gallery, 1964; Sheffield University, 1965; Vaccarino Arte Contemporanea, Florence, Italy, 1970; 359 Gallery, Nottingham, 1975; Rotherham (recent work), 1980; Group Shows: Midland Group; Nottingham University; Festival of Church and Art; Exhibitions include: Paris Salon; Royal Academy; Scottish Royal Academy; Artists' International Association; Women's International Association; Work reproduced includes: BBC Television 'Artist at work in the Studio', 1963; BBC Woman's Hour-Guest of the Week, 1965. *Hobby:* Racing. *Address:* Wilton Lodge, Blyth, Nr. Worksop, Notts, England.

BOWLES, John Ferdinand, b. 22 June 1909, Birmingham, England. Clvll Servant, Diplomat (Retired). m. Kathleen Beryl Truscott, 4 Dec. 1937, 2 sons. *Education:* BA, 1932, MA, 1947, Oriel College, Oxford, UK. *Appointments:* District Administration, 1934-51, Chief Information Officer, 1951-54, Native Affairs Department, S Rhodesia; Ministry of External Affairs, Federation of Rhodesia and Nyasaland, 1954-63; Commission for Federation in East Africa, 1956-58; Counsellor (Political), Federal High Commission, London, UK, 1958-60; High Commissioner for Rhodesia and Nyasaland in Nigeria, 1960-62; Counsellor (Political), Rhodesia and Nyasaland Affairs Office, British Embassy, Washington, 1962-63; Rhodesian Ministry of External Affairs, Salisbury, Under-Secretary, 1964-65. *Memberships:* Rhodesia Constitutional Association; Secretary, Settlement Council, Rhodesia; Rhodesian National Affairs Association; Royal Commonwealth Society; Salisbury Club. *Publications:* Editor, Rhodesia Constitutional Association Newsletter, 1967-68. *Hobbies:* African Politics and constitutional affairs. *Address:* 20 Hawick Road, PO Borrowdale, Zimbabwe.

BOWYER, Philip Desmond, b. 27 Dec. 1917, Llantarnam, Monmouthshire, Wales. Anthropologist; Superintendent (Community Welfare). m. Audrey Barrett, 3 Feb. 1940, 1 son, 2 daughters. *Education:* Abersychan Technical School, Abersychan, Wales, 1929-32; Newport Technical College, Newport, Wales, 1947-50; Guildford Technical College, Guildford, Surrey, England 1956; BA, Anthropology, University of Western Australia, Perth, Western Australia, 1967-75. *Appointments:* Apprentice then journeyman bricklayer, England 1933-41; Able Seaman, Royal Navy, 1941-46; various surveying and teaching/building positions: Ministry of Labour, Cardiff, Min. of Works, London, Inland Revenue, Liskeard, St. Loyes College, Exeter, 1946-53; Vocational Training Specialist (Building), Middle East, under International Labour Office, Geneva, 1953-55; Building Instructor, Park House School, Godalming, Surrey, England 1955-56; Vocational Training Specialist, ILO., Geneva, Malaya and India, 1956-57; Group Worker, Aftercare Officer, Senior G Worker, Assistant Superintendent, Superintendent, Department for Community Welfare, Western Australia in Government Training Centres, 1960-. *Memberships:* Royal Society of Western Australia; Australian Archaeological Association; Anthropological Society of Western Australia; Western Australian Archaeology Group; Convocation, University of Western Australia. *Publications:* Thesis: The Bearing of Ethnographic Evidence on Prehistory. *Hobbies:* Classical music; Study of the Arabic language; Reading prehistory; Writing poetry; Chess; Cricket. *Address:* Benbow, Newman Road, Yanchep, Western Australia.

BOYD, John Charles, b. 3 Dec. 1921, Murwillumbah, Australia. Member of the New South Wales Parliament. m. Nancye Winifred McIlvride, 16 Oct. 1943, 1 son 1 daughter. *Education:* Murwillumbah High School, Passed 21/A Course for Lt./Col. 1956. *Appointments:* Elected 1973, Re-elected, 1973, New South Wales Parliament; Appointed to Parliamentary Select Committee Fishing Industry, 1975; Re-elected New South Wales Parliament, 1976; Member of House Committee, 1976; Re-Elected New South Wales Parliament, 1978; Member Public Accounts Committee, 1978; Shadow Minister for Housing and Co-operative Societies, 1980. *Hobbies:* Golf; Bowls; Fishing; Bush Walking; Gardening. *Address:* Dulguigan, Via Murwillumbah, 2484, New South Wales, Australia.

BOYD, Philip Irving, b. 13 Dec. 1912, Dominica, West Indies. Medical Doctor. m. Margaret Joan Hemstock, 4 June 1938, 2 sons, 2 daughters. *Education:* MRCS, LRCP, 1935. MBBS, 1935, MD, 1937, University of

London, 1929-35; MPH, 1944, Johns Hopkins University. *Appointments:* Resident Hospital Posts in the United Kingdom, 1935-38; Certain Posts in the Public Service of Caribbean Territories, 1938-63; Employment with PAHO/WHO, 1963-76; Chief of the Health Section, Caribbean Community Secretariat, 1971-. *Memberships:* Formerly President, Leeward Islands Branch of British Medical Association; Formerly President of Caribbean Federation for Mental Health; Vice-President of the American Public Health Association. *Publications:* Various papers on the health situation and services in the Commonwealth Caribbean. *Honours:* Fellows Silver Medal, 1932; Gold Medal, London, 1937; DSc, Honorary, University of the West Indies, 1975; Award of Honour, Dominica, 1978. *Hobby:* Swimming. *Address:* A70 Issano Place West, Bel Air Park, Greater Georgetown, Guyana.

BOYD-CARPENTER, John Archibald (The Right Honourable Lord), b. 2 June 1908, Harrogate, England. Barrister at Law; Administrator, Company Chairman. m. Margaret Mary Hall, 25 June 1937, 1 son, 2 daughters. *Education:* Stowe; BA(Hons.) History, 1930, Diploma in Economics, 1931, Balliol College, Oxford. *Appointments:* Barrister at Law, 1934-39; Officer, Scots Guards, 1940-45; MP for Kingston-upon-Thames, 1945-72; Financial Secretary, Treasury, 1951-54; Minister, Transport and Civil Aviation, 1954-55; Minister, Pensions and National Insurance, 1955-62; Chief Secretary, Treasury and Paymaster-General, 1962-64; Chairman, Public Accounts Committee, 1964-70; Chairman, Orion Insurance Co., 1968-72; Chairman, Civil Aviation Authority, 1972-77; Chairman, Rugby Portland Cement Co., 1976-. *Memberships:* President, Oxford Union, 1930; Chairman Carlton Club, 1979-; Deputy Chairman, Association of Independent Unionist Peers, Chairman, 1979-. *Publications:* Way of Life, 1979. *Honours:* Privy Councillor, 1954; Life Baron, 1972; High Steward of Kingston-upon-Thames, 1973; Deputy Lieutenant for Greater London, 1973-. *Hobbies:* Tennis; Swimming; Walking; Gardening. *Address:* 12 Eaton Terrace, London, SW1 England.

BOYLE, Lawrence, b. 31 Jan. 1920, Balerno, Midlothian, Scotland. Accountant. m. Mary McWilliam, 12 Aug. 1952, 1 son, 3 daughters. *Education:* BCom, 1952, PhD, 1963, Edinburgh University; Member of the Chartered Institute of Public Finance and Accountancy, 1954. *Appointments:* Accountant, Deputy County Treasurer, Midlothian County Council; Deputy City Chamberlain, City Chamberlain, Glasgow, 1970-74; Chief Executive, Strathclyde Regional Council, 1974-80; Partner, Sir Lawrence Boyle Associates, 1980-; Director: Short Loan and Mortgage Company Limited, Pension Fund Property Unit Trust; Scottish Mutual Assurance Society. *Memberships:* Chairman, Scottish National Orchestra Society Limited, 1980-; Member of Court and Finance Committee, Business School Steering Board, Visiting Professor, Strathclyde University; British Institute of Management Advisory Board for Scotland; Royal Commonwealth Society; Chartered Institute of Public Finance and Accountancy; Companion, British Institute of Management. *Publications:* Equalisation and the Future of Local Finance, 1966; Articles on Finance Accountancy and Management in Professional Journals. *Honours:* Justice of Peace, 1970-; Knight Bachelor, 1979. *Hobby:* Music. *Address:* 24 Broomburn Drive, Newton Mearns, Glasgow, Scotland.

BOYSON, Rhodes, b. 5 Nov. 1925, Haslingden, Lancashire, United Kingdom. Government Minister. m. (1) Violet Burletson, (2) Florette MacFarlane, 2 daughters. *Education:* University College, Cardiff, 1943-44; BA, MA, Manchester University 1946-50; PhD, London School of Economics; Corpus Christi College, Cambridge. *Appointments:* Teacher, Ramsbottom Secondary Modern School, Lancashire, 1950-55; Headmaster, Lea Bank Secondary School, 1955-61; Headmaster, Robert Montefiore Secondary School, 1961-66; Headmaster, Highbury Grammar School, 1966-67; Headmaster, Highbury Grove School, 1967-74; Member of Parliament, Brent North 1974-; Parliamentary under Secretary, Department of Educational Science, 1979-. *Memberships:* St. Stephens; Carlton. *Publications:* Crisis in Education; Centre Forward; The Ashworth Cotton Enterprise; The Story of Highbury Grove; Co-editor, Black Papers on Education; Centre Forward: A Radical Conservative Programme,

1978. *Hobbies:* Gardening; Reading; Writing. *Address:* 71 Paines Lane, Pinner, Middlesex, England.

BRADDON, Russell Reading, b. 21 Jan. 1921, Sydney, Australia. Author; Broadcaster; Lecturer. *Education:* Sydney Church of England Grammar School, 1933-38; BA Sydney University 1941; Held in Various Japanese Prisoner of War Camps and gaols; Abandoned Law in Final Year, 1948; Writing 1949. *Publications:* The Piddingtons; The Naked Island; Those in Peril; Cheshire V.C; Out of the Storm; Nancy Wake; Gabriel Comes to 24; End of a Hate; Proud American Boy; Joan Sutherland; Year of the Angry Rabbit; Roy Thomson; Committal Chamber; When the Enemy is Tired; The Inseparables; Will You Walk A Little Faster; The Siege; Suez; The Hundred Days of Darien; The Progress of Private Lilyworth; Prelude and Fugue for Lovers; End Play; All the Queen's Men; The Finalists; The Predator; A Clock Striking, 1982. *Address:* c/o John Farqharson Limited, Bell House, 8 Bellyard, London, WC2 England.

BRADLEY, John Martin, b. 6 Mar. 1925, Sydney, NSW, Australia. Medical Practitioner. m. Veronica Brennan, 27 Feb. 1960, 1 son, 3 daughters. *Education:* MB, BS, 1947; MD, 1957; DTR 1948, University of Melbourne; MRACP 1956; MRACR 1959; FRCR 1966; FRACR 1969; FRACP 1970. *Appointments:* Resident Medical Officer, Prince Henry's Hospital, 1947-48; Resident Medical Officer, St. Vincents Hospital 1949; General Practise, 1950; Resident Medical Officer, Repatriation General Hospital 1951; Regular Army, 1952-55; Clinical Supervisor, University of Melbourne, 1956; Radiotherapist, 1956-65, Consultant Radiotherapist, 1966-73, Peter MacCallum Clinic. Assistant Radiotherapist, 1956-66, Honorary Radiotherapist 1966, Royal Melbourne Hospital, 1966-. *Memberships:* Australian Medical Association; Naval and Military Club; Australian Hereford Society. *Publications:* Radiation of Central Nervous System Tumours 1963; Tolerance of Central Nervous Tissue to Megavoltage Radiation, 1964; Radiotherapy of Pituitary Tumours, 1965. *Honours:* David Grant Scholarship, 1957; Thomas Baker Memorial Fellowship 1959. *Hobbies:* Cattle Breeding; History; Current Affairs. *Address:* 274 Alma Road, North Caulfield, Victoria 3161, Australia.

BRADMAN, Donald George, b. 27 Aug. 1908, Cootamundra, NSW Australia. Company Director; Stock and Share Broker. m. Jessie Martha Menzies, 30 Apr. 1932, 1 son, 1 daughter. *Education:* Bowral Intermediate High School. *Publications:* Don Bradman's Book, 1930; How to Play Cricket, 1935; Farewell to Cricket 1950; The Art of Cricket, 1958. *Honours:* Knight Bachelor 1949; Companion of the Order of Australia, 1979. *Hobbies:* Golf; Squash; Billiards; Music. *Address:* 2 Holden Street, Kensington Park 5068, South Australia.

BRADSHAW, Neville, b 19 Mar. 1937 Colne, Lancs, England. Geologist. m. Jil Towers, 2 sons, 1 daughter. *Education:* BSc, Hons. Geology Class I, 1958, PhD, 1962, Manchester University. *Appointments:* Geological Survey of Tanzania, 1962-64; Mineral Resources Division, Overseas Geological Surveys, London, 1964-65; Institute of Geological Sciences, London, 1965-70; UN/OTC Mineral Exploration Project, Ecuador, 1970-72; UNESCO Postgraduate Training in Mineral Exploration, Burma, 1972-76; IAEA, Consultant, Uranium Exploration Project, Chile, 1977-79; Exploration Unit, Atomic Energy Organisation of Iran, 1977-79; UN/DTCD, Consultant, Kerala Mineral Exploration and Development Project, India, 1979-80; UNFRNRE, Gold and Precious Metals Exploration Project, Liberia, 1980-81. *Memberships:* Mineralogical Society, United Kingdom; Mineralogical Society of America; Mineralogical Association of Canada. *Hobbies:* Reading; Gardening; Golf. *Address:* Keepers Cottage, High Head, Ivegill, Carlisle CA4 0PJ, Cumbria England.

BRAIN, Gary Clifford Dennis, b. 12 Aug. 1943, Palmerston North, New Zealand. Symphonic Musician. m. June Brain, 14 Aug. 1969, 1 son, 1 daughter. *Education:* Bursary given for study and Scholarship to, Staatliche Hochschule für music, Berlin Germany, University of Indiana, USA. *Appointments:* Trainee New Zealand Symphony Orchestra; BBC Training Orchestra, Bristol; Ulster Orchestra, Belfast; BBC, Welsh Orchestra, Cardiff; Principal Timpanist and Percussionist, New Zealand Symphony Orchestra, 18 Years. *Member-*

ships: Percussive Arts Society, USA; Society for Music Education, New Zealand; Tutor Victoria University, New Zealand; Director, New Zealand Percussion Ensemble; Director Music Players; Manager TV Programmes and Commercial Recordings. *Creative Works:* Quartet Violin and Percussion; Vere Et Violin, for Solo Violin; Three Movements for String Orchestra; History of Percussion 1977; Music Players 70 LP Record; New Zealand Symphony Orchestra LP's and Radio Documentaries. *Honours:* Solo Recital 1979; Hong Kong Arts Festival; Solo Television Programme, RJVHK, Hong Kong; National Tour for Musica Viva Australia; Eight Tours for New Zealand, Music Federation; Solo Television Programme TVNZ. *Hobbies:* Art; Fishing; Philosophy; Own Children; School's Concerts. *Address:* New Zealand Symphony Orchestra, BC New Zealand, Box 11-440, Wellington 1, New Zealand.

BRAINE, Bernard Richard, (Sir), b. 24 June 1914, Ealing, Middlesex, England. Member of Parliament. m. 21 Dec. 1935, 3 sons. *Education:* Hendon County Grammar School. *Appointments:* Essex South East, 1955-; Civil Servant 1931-39; Army 1940-46; Member of Parliament 1950-; MP for Billericay, 1950-55; Essex South East, 1955-; Parliamentary Secretary Ministry of Pensions and National Insurance 1960-61; Under Secretary of State and Commonwealth Relations 1961-62; Parliamentary Secretary Ministry of Health 1962-64; Deputy Chairman, Commonwealth Parlimentary Association 1964, 1970-74 and Treasurer, 1964-70 and 1974-78; Leader of British Parliamentary missions, India 1963, West Germany 1973 and Greece 1980; Governor of the Commonwealth Institute, 1965-; Opposition Front Bench Spokesman on Foreign and Commonwealth Affairs, Overseas 1967-70; Chairman Parliamentary Select Committees on Overseas Aid, 1970-74 Chariman: British German Parliamentary Group, British Greek Parliamentary Group, Isle of Man Parliamentary Group. Chairman, UK Chapt of Society for International Development; National Council on Alcoholism; Campaign for Justice for the Banabans; Society for the Defence of the Unjustly Prosecuted British Solidarity with Poland Campaign. *Honours:* Knight Bachelor 1972; Commander of the Order of St John of Jerusalem; Grand Cross of the German Order of Merit, 1974; Deputy Lieutenant for Essex, 1978; European Peace Cross, 1979; Fellow of the Royal Society of Arts; Associate of the Institute of Development Studies, Sussex University. *Address:* Kings Wood, Rayleigh, Essex, England.

BRAITHWAITE, Peter, b. 15 Sept. 1913, London, England. m. Maura Lynch, 26 Nov. 1971. *Education:* Matric, North Sydney Boys High School, 1930; MB, BS, Sydney University, 1936; FRACS 1948; FCCP 1958. *Appointments:* Military Service, 1933-36; RMO Sydney Hospital 1937; RMO Royal Hobart Hospital 1938-39; AAMC, AIF 1939-45; Surgeon Superintendant R.H.H 1945-48; Clinical Assistant Royal Melbourne and Heidelberg Hospitals 1949; Thoracic Surgeon, Royal Hobart and Repatriation Hospitals, 1950-78. *Memberships:* Royal Australasian College of Surgeons; Australian Red Cross Society; Lannec Society; Thoracic Society Australia; Caridiac Society Australia and New Zealand; Sustralian Resuscitation Council; National Heart Foundation; Naval Military Tasmania Racing Clubs; Royal Yacht Club of Tasmania. *Publications:* Articles in Journals. *Honours:* AO 1979; CBE 1968; ED 1953. *Hobbies:* Cruising; Fishing; Racing. *Address:* 8 Quamby Avenue, Sandy Bay 7005, Tasmania, Australia.

BRAMALL, Edwin Noel Westby (Gen. Sir), b. 18 Dec. 1923, Westby England. Chief of the General Staff. m. Dorothy Avril Wentworth Vernon, 1949, 1 son, 1 daughter. *Education:* Eton College. *Appointments:* Commissioned, KRRC, 1943; Served in NW Europe, 1944-45; Occupation of Japan, 1944-45; Instructor School of Infantry, 1949-51; PSC 1952; Middle East 1953-58; Instructor Army Staff College, 1958-61; Staff of Lord Mountbatten with Special responsibility for reorganisation of MOD 1963-64; CO, 2 Green Jackets, KRRC, Malaysia during Indonesian confrontation, 1965-66; Commander, 5th Airportable Bde, 1967-69; idc 1970; GOC 1st Div. BAOR, 1972-73; Lt-General. 1973; Commander. British Forces, Hong Kong, 1973-76; General., 1976; C-in-C, UK Land Forces, 1976-78. *Memberships:* Traveller's; Pratt's; MCC; I Zingari; Free Foresters; Butterflies. *Honours:* Fellow of Royal Society of Art. *Hobbies:* Cricket; Painting; Tennis; Travel. *Add-*

ress: MOD Main Building, Whitehall, London SW1A 2HB, England.

BRANCKER, John Eustace Theodore, b. 9 Feb. 1909, Barbados. Queens Counsel. m. Eshe Gwendolyn Walcott, 18 Dec. 1967. *Education:* Harrison College, Barbados; Council of Legal Education, England; Course in Colonial Administration, London School of Economics; Graduate of Institute of Political Secretaries, Mayfair, London. *Appointments:* Barrister-at-Law, Private practice; Member of House of Assembly (MP), 1937-71; Queen's Counsel, 1961; Deputy Speaker; Leader of Opposition, 1956-61; Speaker, 1961-66, 1966-71; President of Senate, 1971-76. *Memberships:* Life Fellow, Royal Commonwealth Society; Honorary Corresponding Secretary, Royal Overseas League; Fellow, Royal Society of Arts; Commonwealth Parliamentary Association; Honorary Legal Adviser of RSPCA. *Honours:* Queen's Counsel, 1961; Knight Bachelor, 1969; Queen's Coronation Medal; Queen's Silver Jubilee Medal; Honorary LL.B., University of Soochow. *Hobbies:* Chess; Music; Drama. *Address:* Valencia, Holetown, St James, Barbados, West Indies.

BRANDFORD, Gilbert Baldwin, b. 16 June 1914, Barbados, West Indies. Auditor General (Retired); Chairman. m. Phyllis Elaine White, 29 Nov. 1969, 1 son, 1 daughter. *Education:* Private School; Correspondence Course in Accountancy. *Appointments:* Clerk, Magistrates Courts, 1936-53; Currency Officer, Currency Board, 1953-56; Auditor, Audit Department, 1956-57; Assistant Auditor General, 1959-66; Auditor General, 1966-75; Chairman, Public Utilities Board, 1976-. *Honours:* OBE, 1972. *Address:* Bewdley, Navy Gardens, Christ Church, Barbados, West Indies.

BRANDON, Brian Joseph (Rev. Brother), b. 5 Apr. 1938, West Wyalong, NSW, Australia. School Teacher. *Education:* Parade College, East Melbourne; Christian Brothers' Teachers' College, Melbourne, 1957; BSc, University of Melbourne, 1963. *Appointments:* St. Bernard's College, Moonee Ponds, Australia, 1959-62; St Leo's College, Box Hill, Australia, 1964-65; Rostrevor College, Adelaide, Australia, 1966-68; Deputy Headmaster, 1969-72, Headmaster, 1973-77, St. Patrick's College, Prospect Vale, Australia; Headmaster, St Kevin's College, Toorak 3142 Australia, 1978-. *Memberships:* Congregation of Christian Brothers; Religious Superior of C.B. Community, Prospect Vale and Toorak; Australian College of Education; Schools Board of Tasmania. *Hobbies:* Running; Squash; Reading; Music. *Address:* St. Kevin's College, Moonga Road, Toorak, Victoria, 3142, Australia.

BRANGMAN, E.M. Lovette, b. 18 Jan. 1936, Bermuda. Teacher/Administrator. m. Walter S Brangman, 7 Aug. 1958, 3 sons. *Education:* General Teaching Course, 1955, Primary Specialist Course, 1956, Ontario, Canada; Institute of Supervisory Management, England, 1975; Master of Business Administration Degree, Nova University, Florida, USA, 1980. *Appointments:* Kindergarten Teacher; Nursery School Teacher/Administrator. *Memberships:* Secretary-General, Progressive Labour Party; Church Treasurer, Bright Temple AME Church; Past Secretary, Bermuda Workers Cooperative Society. *Publications:* Poem Writing, Playlets. *Hobbies:* Travel; Creative Writing. *Address:* Welms-B, Hermitage Road, PO Box 20, Smith's 3-16, Bermuda.

BRANGMAN, Walter Sinclair, b. 11 July 1930, Bermuda. Architect; Member of Parliament. m. E.M. Lovette Brown, 7 Aug. 1958, 3 sons. *Education:* Ryerson School of Architecture, Toronto, Canada, 1952-55. *Appointments:* Principle Architect, Walter S.S. Brangman, 1958-; Member of Parliament. *Memberships:* The Institute of Bermuda Architects; Director, Bermuda Provident Bank Limited; Salvation Army Advisory Board; Conference Trustee of AME Churches. *Honours:* Florida International University, 1974; Bermuda Football Association, 1978. *Hobbies:* Carpentry; Music; Gardening; Bee-Keeping; Photography; Art. *Address:* Welms-B, Hermitage Road, PO Box 20, Smith's 3-16, Bermuda.

BRANN, Conrad Max Benedict, b. 20 July 1925, Rostock. Socio-linguist. *Education:* St.John's College, Oxford, University, UK, 1946-50; Hamburg University, Germany, 1952-57; College of Europe, Bruges, 1957-58. *Appointments:* Lecturer in English, Hamburg University, Germany, 1952-57; Programme Specialist, Unesco, Paris, France, 1958-65; Senior Lecturer, Language Education, University of Ibadan, Nigeria, 1966-77; Professor of Applied Linguistics, University of Maiduguri, Nigeria, 1978-. *Memberships:* Editor, 1975-, West African Modern Languages Association; Research Committee, Socio-Linguistics, International Sociological Association; Association Internationale de Linguistique Appliquée; Associate Res.Fellow, Institute of African Studies, University of Ibadan, Nigeria; National Language Centre, Lagos, Nigeria. *Publications:* Monographs and articles in field of Language Education and Language Planning.*Hobbies:* Bibliophagy and bibliography; African Art and Literatures. *Address:* University of Maiduguri, Borno State, Nigeria.

BRASH, Alan Anderson, b. 5 June 1913, Lower Hutt, New Zealand. Minister. m. Eljean Ivory Hill, 23 Nov. 1938, 1 son, 1 daughter. *Education:* MA, Hons. Otago University; BD, cum laude, Edinburgh University. *Appointments:* Parish Minister, 1938-46, 1952-56; General Secretary, National Council of Churches, 1947-52, 1956-64; East Asia Christian Conference, Singapore, 1957-68; Christian Aid Director, London, 1968-70; World Council of Churches, 1970-78; National Council of Churches, 1979-. *Honours:* DD, Knox College, Canada, 1971; OBE, 1972. *Address:* 13 Knightsbridge Drive, Auckland 10, New Zealand.

BRASH, Barbara, b. Melbourne, Australia. Artist. *Education:* National Gallery of Victoria Art School, 1948; Studied with George Bell, & printmaking at RMIT, 1950. *Appointments:* Art Therapist, Mental Health Department, 1953-56; Lecturer, Free Drawing and Design, School of Architecture, Royal Melbourne Institute of Technology, 1956-70; Lecturer, Free Drawing and Design, Building Industries Division, Royal Melbourne Institute of Technology, 1970-80. *Memberships:* Treasurer, Committee Member, Print Council of Australia; Art Advisory Committee, Lyceum Club; Art Advisor, Caulfield Council, 1978; World Print Council; Women's Art Forum; Victorian Artist Society. *Creative Works:* Represented in State Galleries of Victoria, New South Wales, South Australia, West Australia, Queensland; Regional Galleries of Newcastle, Latrobe Valley, Warnambool, Gold Coast Collection, Stanthorpe—also in National Collection, Canberra; In collections of Australian National University, Canberra; Universities of Adelaide, Melbourne, Monash & Flinders; collections of World Record Club, B.H.P. Collection; I.C.I. House, Marland House, A.M.P. Building; Comalco & Premier's Department Adelaide; Department of Foreign Affairs; Queensland Arts Council, C.B.A. ahd Commonwealth Art Bank; Teacher's training colleges and private collections in Australia & other countries, Australian Embassy, Belgrade, Yogoslavia. *Honours:* Numerous National & International honours including: Print Council of Australia members Print, 1972; Tenth International Biennial Exhibition of Prints in Tokyo, Japan, 1976; Contemporary Australian Prints, Perth-Fiji, 1977; Pratt Benefir International Exhibition, New York, 1971.*Address:* 735 Toorak Road, Malvern, Victoria 3144, Australia.

BRAY, John Jefferson, b. 16 Sept. 1912, Adelaide, South Australia. Law. *Education:* St Peter's College, Adelaide, University of Adelaide; LL.B (Ordinary, 1932, (Honours), 1933, LL.D, 1937. *Appointments:* Admitted to Bar, 1933; Act. Lecturer in Jurisprudence, University of Adelaide, 1941, 1943, 1945, 1951, and in Legal History, 1957-58; QC, 1957; Lecturer in Roman Law, 1959-66; Lieutenant-Governor's Deputy, 1968; Chief Justice of South Australia, 1967-78 (retired); Chancellor, University of Adelaide, 1968-. *Memberships:* State Libraries Board of South Australia. *Publications:* Poems, 1962, 1961-71, 1972-79. *Honours:* AC, 1979.*Hobby:* Reading. *Address:* 39 Hurtle Square, Adelaide, South Australia, 5001.

BRAYSICH, Joseph Micheil, b. 28 Sept. 1935, Boulder, Western Australia. Sociologist/Author/Management Consultant. m. Robin Haselhurst, 2 sons, 1 daughter. *Education:* Teachers Certificate, 1954; Teachers Higher Certificate, 1961; Associateship in Soc. Sc., 1967; Diploma in Educ. Administration, 1969; Master of Science (Wisconsin), 1970; Doctor of Philosophy, 1971. *Appointments:* Grade School Teacher, 1955-67; Deputy Headmaster, 1968-69; Lecturer Teachers College, 1969-70; Head of Social Science, Claremont C.A.E., 1971-78; Management Consultant-

/Speaker Internationally, 1979-. *Memberships:* Fellow Australian Institute Management; Fellow & Past President, Institute Educational Administration. *Publications:* Body Language—The Art of Seeing What Others are Thinking; Keys to Dynamic Marketing, Video Training Programme; Audio Cassette Series on Sales & Management. *Honours:* Wisconsin Alumni Research Foundation Fellowship Award, 1970. *Hobbies:* Researching; Making Video Programmes. *Address:* 13 Weldon Way, City Beach, Western Australia.

BREARLEY, Maurice Norman, b. 21 Jan. 1920. Professor of Mathematics. m. (1) Patricia Mary Gluyas 20 May 1948 (marriage dissolved 1977) (2) Patricia Ann Norman 4 Nov. 1977 1 son, 2 daughters. *Education:* Hale School, Perth, Western Australia. 1928-36; Bachelor of Engineering, University of Western Australia, 1942; Bachelor of Science, University of Sydney, 1952; Master of Arts, University of Cambridge, 1958; Doctor of Philosphy, University of Adelaide, 1958; Master of Science, University of Melbourne, 1967. *Appointments:* Engineer, de Havilland Aircraft Company Sydney, 1942, Hatfield, England, 1946-47; Pilot, Royal Australian Air Force, 1943-45; Lecturer in Mathematics, University of Sydney, 1948-52, University of Adelaide, 1955-65; Professor of Mathematics, University of Melbourne and RAAF Academy, Point Cook, Victoria, 1966-. *Memberships:* Australian Mathematical Society; International Society for Prosthetics and Orthotics; Society for Medical and Biological Engineering (Victoria); Technical Aid to the Disabled (Victoria). *Publications:* Book: Born to Fly, a biography of Wayne Blackmore, (in preparation). Articles: Numerous learned Journals of Mathematics and Engineering. *Honours:* University Medal for Mathematics, Barker Prize for Mathematics, University of Sydney, 1951; Rayleigh Prize, ibid., University of Cambridge, 1956. *Hobbies:* Music (piano, composition); Application of mathematics to sport. *Address:* 29/8 The Strand, Williamstown, Victoria 3016, Australia.

BREED, Ian Douglas, b. 1 July 1948, Raetehi, New Zealand. Medical Laboratory Technologist. m. 6 Dec. 1969, (seperated 1980), 2 sons. *Education:* University Entrance (Science Subjects) 1965; Qualified Medical Technologist, 1970; Higher Technology Examination (Chemical Pathology) 1971; Management Course, Auckland Technical Institute, 1973. *Appointments:* Trainee, Pathology Department, Greenlane Hospital, Auckland, 1966-70, Technologist and Graded Officer, 1971-77. Self employed, 1977-79; Travenol Laboratories, 1979-. *Memberships:* Mount Albert Presbyterian Church Elder; Eden, Epsom Lions Club New Zealand Institute of Medical Laborartory Technology; Associate, Auckland Branch 1974-75; St. John Ambulance Brigade, 1957-79, Outward Bound Old Boys Association (secretary, Vice President). *Publications:* An Assessment of the Radiometer ABL 1 — N Z Journal of Medical Laboratory Technology, 1976; Quality Control in Blood Gas Measurement — N Z Journal of Medical Laboratory Technology, 1976. *Honours:*Colombo Plan aid Project to Thailand November 1975,76. *Hobby:*Music. *Address:* 18 Adam St., Greenlane, Auckland, New Zealand.

BREEN, Kerry John, b. 29 Aug. 1941, Bright, Victoria, Australia. Physician. m. Maria Vice, 24 Feb. 1969, 2 sons, 1 daughter. *Education:* MB., BS., 1964, MD., 1975, University of Melbourne, Australia; FRACP., 1972. *Appointments:* Resident Medical Officer, 1965-68, Staff Gastroenterologist, 1975-78, Director, Gastroenterology Unit, 1978-, St. Vincent's Hospital, Melbourne, Australia; Medical Registrar, Royal Prince Alfred Hospital, Sydney, Australia, 1969-70; Fellow in Gastroenterology, Vanderbilt University Medical School, Nashville, Tennessee, USA, 1970-72; Senior Lecturer in Medicine, University of Melbourne, Australia, 1972-74. *Memberships:* Royal Australasian College of Physicians; Councillor, 1977-, Gastroenterological Society of Australia; Australian Medical Association, Nutrition Society of Australia; American Association for Study of Liver Diseases. *Publications:* 40 publications in the Medical literature in the fields of gastroenterology and nutrition. *Hobbies:* Tennis; Basketball; Carpentry. *Address:* 7 Derwent Square, Bulleen 3105, Australia.

BREINBURG, Petronella Alexandrina, b. 16 Apr. 1928, Paramaribo, Surinam, South America. Lecturer; Writer; Researcher. m. Emile Charles Breinburg, 12

Dec. 1945, 2 sons. *Education:* Diploma, English, City of London College, England, 1965; Diploma of Education, University of London, 1972; BA Honours Education, C.N.A. 1977; Doctor of Philosophy, Keele University, 1981. *Appointments:* Teaching, 1951-74; Lecturing including Germany, Holland and Scotland, 1974-; Researcher, 1978-; Writer, 1969-. Numerous books including US Boys of Westcroft, 1975; One/Another day; Brinsley's Dream. 1980; Numerous short stories in Anthologies and Magazines. *Honours:* Honororary Mention — Legend of Surinam, 1972; Children's Book of the Year Award, 1976, 77, 80. *Hobbies:* Painting; Playing Badminton. *Address:* 7 Tuam Road, Plumstead, London SE18, England.

BRENNAN, Francis Gerard, b. 22 May, 1928, Rockhampton, Queensland, Australia. Justice of the High Court of Australia. m. Patricia O'Hara, 26 May 1953, 3 sons, 4 daughters. *Education:* Christian Brothers College,ʹRockhampton, Qld. 1935-40; Sacred Heart College, Downlands, Toowoomba, Qld. 1941-45; University of Queensland, Brisbane, Qld. 1945-51; B.A. 1948; Ll.B. 1951. *Appointments:* Barrister, 1951-76 (Q.C. 1965-76); Judge, Australian Industrial Court, Australian Capital Territory Supreme Court, 1976-81; Federal Court of Australia, 1977-81; President, Adminstrative Appeals Tribunal and Adminstrative Review Council, 1976-79; Justice of the High Court of Australia, 1981. *Memberships:* President, National Union of Australian University Students, 1949-50; President, Bar Association of Queensland, 1974-76; Executive Member, Law Council of Australia, 1974-76; President, Australian Bar Association, 1975-76; part-time member, Australian Law Reform Commission, 1975-78; Commonwealth Club, Canberra; Canberra Club, Canberra. *Honours:* Knight Commander in the civil division of the Order of the British Empire, 1981. *Hobbies:* Tennis; Gardening. *Address:* 10 Kurundi Place, Hawker. A.C.T. 2614,. Australia.

BREWER, Roy, b. 29 Sept. 1918, Helensburgh, New South Wales, Australia. Soil Scientist. m. Mary Agnes Cox, 24 July 1943, 2 sons. *Education:* Christian Brothers College, Waverley, N.S.W. 1931-35; University of Sydney, 1936-41, BSc (Hons I) 1941, Doctorate of Science, 1963. *Appointments:* Commonwealth Scientific and Industrial Research Organization, Chief Research Scientist, Honorary Research Scientist -1979-. *Memberships:* International Society of Soil Science: Senior Vice President, 1960-64; Secretary, 1964-68; Working Group in Soil Micromorphology, 1969-73. Australian Society of Soil Science, Branch President, 1959-60; Geological Society of Australia 1979; Royal Canberra Golf Club. *Publications:* Fabric and Mineral Analysis of Soils, 1964; Co-author, A Handbook of Australian Soils, 1968; over 50 Scientific papers in International Journals. *Honours:* Leverhulme Trust -Fellowship, 1964-65; Commonwealth Research Fellowship, 1971-72; Prescott Medal, 1980; Editorial Board, Geoderma, 1967-79; Invited Lecturer, International Society of Soil Science, 1960. *Hobbies:* Golf; Gardening; House Maintenance. *Address:* 13 Miller St., O'Connor, A.C.T. 2601, Australia.

BRIDGE, Gerald Hastings, b. 22 Nov. 1911, Christchurch, New Zealand. Company Director, Formly Bank Executive. m. Gwenda Ethelwynne Kenderine, 29 Mar. 1937, 1 son, 1 daughter. *Education:* Auckland New Zealand, Primary School, 1917-25, Grammar School, 1926; Christchurch, (NZ) Boys High School, 1927-28. *Appointments:* Bank of Australasia, Christchurch, Taumarunui, Marton, Wellington (NZ), 1928-50; Senior Appointments Australia and New Zealand Banking Group, Melbourne, 1950-58, Wellington, 1958-71; Director Bata Company (NZ) Ltd., since 1972. *Memberships:* Honorary Treasurer New Zealand Red Cross Society, 1968-76; Christchurch N.Z. Club; Wellington N.Z. Club. President Royal Commonwealth Society, Wellington Branch, 1974-79; Member London Central Council, 1972-; National President New Zealand Founders Society, 1979-. *Honours:* Queen's Silver Jubilee Medal, 1977; Justice of the Peace for New Zealand since 1966; Counsellor of Honour New Zealand Red Cross Society, 1976; Service Medal New Zealand Founders Society, 1978. *Hobbies:* Golf; Fishing; Gardening. *Address:* 5 Cooper Street, Karori, Wellington 5, New Zealand.

BRIDGES (Sir) Phillip Rodney, b. 9 July 1922, Bedford, England. Judge. m. 8 Nov. 1962, 2 sons, 1 daughter. *Education:* Bedford School. *Appointments:* Private Practice, London as a Solicitor, 1951-54; Legal and Judicial service in The Gambia, 1954-; Attorney General, 1964-68; Chief Justice, 1968-. *Memberships:* Law Society; Travellers Club. *Honours:* Knight Bachelor, 1973; CMG, 1967; QC (Gambia), 1964. *Hobby:* Reading. *Address:* c/o Chief Justice's Chambers, Banjul, The Gambia.

BRIDGEWATER, Peter, b. 31 Dec. 1945, Bristol, England. Botanist; Ecologist. m. Gillian Mary Hunter Edwards, 1 Dec. 1973, 1 daughter. *Education:* BSc.(Hons), 1964-67, PhD, 1967-70, University of Durham, England. *Appointments:* Lecturer, Monash University, Victoria, Australia, 1970-75; Senior Lecturer, Murdoch University, Western Australia, 1976-81. *Memberships:* British Ecological Society; Secretary, Royal Society of Western Australia; Royal Society of Victoria; Councillor, Ecological Society of Australia. *Publications:* 30 papers concerning the vegetation of Australia and Britain. *Hobbies:* Gardening; Broadcasting. *Address:* 17 Third St, Bicton 6157, Western Australia, Australia.

BRIDGLAND, Lionel Cedric, b. 28 Nov. 1910, Adelaide, South Australia. Company Director. m. Joy Cranswick, 14 Sept. 1940, 4 sons. *Education:* Associate Diploma in Commerce, Adelaide University, Australia, 1928-32; Associate Member, Institute of Cost Accountants, Dacomb College, Australia, 1937-38; *Appointments:* Elder, Smith & Co. Ltd., Pastoral, Stock and Wool Brokers, 1928-38; Imperial Chemical Industries of Australia and New Zealand Ltd, 1938-70, Executive Director - Commercial and Finance, 1967-70; Sundry Public Corporations/Private Company Directorships, 1971-. *Memberships:* Vice President, Financial Executives Institute of Australia; Vice President of Council (and Hon. Treasuer) of Royal Melbourne Institute of Technology, Victoria, Australia; Trustee, Committee for Economic Development of Australia; Australian Committee, Pacific Basin Economic Council; Fellow, Australian Society of Accountants; The Athenaeum Club, Melbourne, Australia. *Publications:* Monograph: Some Aspects of Tariff Policy and Procedures, 1967; Memoirs: The Bridgland Papers, 1981. *Hobbies:* Pastoralist - Hereford Cattle Breeding. *Address:* 4 Kyora Parade, North Balwyn, 3104, Victoria, Australia.

BRIGHT, Charles Hart, b. 25 Nov. 1912, Adelaide, Australia. Law. m. Dr. Elizabeth Holden Flaxman, 31 Aug. 1940, 2 sons, 1 daughter. *Education:* B.A. Ll.B. Adelaide University, 1936-; *Appointments:* Private Law Practice, 1935-63; Judge, Supreme Court of South Australia, 1963-78. *Memberships:* President, Law Society of South Australia, 1960-; Vice-President, Law Council of Australia, 1960-. *Publications:* Various contributions to learned books and journals, various reports of Royal Commissions and Government enquiries. *Honours:* Q.C., 1960-; K.B.E., 1980-. *Address:* IA/97 Mackinnon Parade, North Adelaide, Australia, 5006.

BRIGHT, Michael Robert, b. 7 Sept. 1946, Plymouth, England. Producer. m. Susanna Koschland, 9 Oct. 1976. *Education:* BSc., (London); MI Biol. *Appointments:* Rentokil Limited, 1970; BBC Radio and Television, 1971-. *Memberships:* Fellow, Royal Entomological Society; Marine Biological Association; British Association of British Science Writers. *Publications:* Various Radio features and documentaries, 1971-; Answers from Dial-a-Scientist, 1976; Living with your Allergy, 1982; Music for Catch me a Butterfly and TO Fly Where the Sun Never Sets, 1981. *Hobbies:* Photography; Music; Fishing; Natural history. *Address:* 62 Somerset Street, Kingsdown, Bristol, England.

BRINCKEN (Von), Alexander Christoph, b. 30 Mar. 1943, Freiburg, West Germany. Banker. m. Janina Irena, 17 July 1971, 2 sons. *Education:* High School Matrriculation, 1954-63; Army, 1963-65; Studied Law, University at Munich, 1965-68; Banking apprenticeship, 1969-70. *Appointments:* Bayerische Vereinsbank, Loan Officer, domestic, 1971-73, internal banking officer, 1974-; Holder of procuration, 1977-; Regional Representative in Hong Kong, 1979-. *Memberships:* Royal Hong Kong Yacht Club; Overseas Bankers Club, Hong Kong. *Hobbies:* History, Antiques, Books, Sailing. *Address:* 22 Coombe Road, A1 Carolina Gardens, The Peak, Hong Kong.

BRITTAN, Samuel, b. 29 Dec. 1933, London. Journalist. *Education:* Kilburn Grammar School, Jesus College, Cambridge, 1955-; MA Cantab. *Appointments:* Various posts in Financial Times, 1955-61; Economics Editor, Observer, 1961-64; Adviser, DEA, 1965-; Fellow, Nuffield College, Oxford, 1973-74; Visiting Fellow, 1974-; Visiting Professor of Economics, Chicago Law School, 1978-. *Publications:* The Treasury under the Tories, 1964, revised edition, Steering the Economy, 1969, 1971; Left or Right: The Bogus Dilemma, 1968-; The Price of Economic Freedom, 1970-; Capitalism and the Permissive Society, 1973-; Is There an Economic Consensus?, 1973-; Seocond Thoughts on Full Employment Policy, 1975-; The Delusion of Incomes Policy, 1977-; The Economic Consequences of Democracy, 1977; How to end the Monetarist Controversy, 1981; articles in various journals. *Honours:* Financial Journalist of the Year Award, 1971; George Orwell Memorial Prize, 1981. *Address:* Flat 10, The Lodge, Kensington Park Gardens, W11.

BROADBENT, John Edward, b. 21 Mar. 1936, Oshawa, Ontario, Canada. Member of Parliament. m. Lucille Allen, 29 Oct. 1971, 1 son, 1 daughter. *Education:* BA., Hons.Philsophy, 1959, MA., Philosophy of Law, Doctorate, Political Science, University of Toronto and London School of Economics, UK. *Appointments:* Professor of Political Science, York University, Toronto, Ontario, Canada; Member of Parliament, 1968-. *Memberships:* RCAF Wing Association; Vice-President, Socialist International; Royal Canadian Legion, Branch 43. *Publications:* The Liberal Rip-Off, 1970. *Honours:* Recipient of two University of Toronto Open Fellowships and two Canada Council Scholarships for post-graduate study in Canada and England. *Hobbies:* Cross-Country Skiing; Reading; Classical Music. *Address:* 450 Laurier Avenue E, Ottawa, Ontario, Canada, K1N 6R3.

BROCK, Jeffry Vanstone, b. 29 Aug. 1913, Vancouver, British Columbia, Canada. Retired Naval Officer. m. Patricia Elizabeth Folkes, 11 March 1950, 2 sons, 1 daughter. *Education:* St. Johns College School; University of Manitoba. *Appointments:* Western Manager, Great West Life Assurance Company , Cockfield Brown and Company; 1st Lieutenant, Winnipeg Division, R.C.N.V.R. 1934; In Command Vancouver Division, 1936; Staff Signals Officer to Flag Officer, Pacific Coast, 1939; On loan service with Royal Navy, 1940; Served afloat in North Atlantic, West Africa, North Africa, Italy, East Mediterranean, in Command of HMS Kirkella, HMS Rununculus, HMS Stonecrop, HMS Bazely, and as spare Escort Commander W. approaches, 1940-44; D.S.C. promoted Commander, 1944-45; Senior Officer, 6th Canadian Escort Group, 1945-47; Senior Officer, Western Naval Reserve Divisions; In Command HMCS Ontario; R.C.A.F., Staff Coll. Dir of Naval Plans, Ottawa, 1948-50; Appointed Captain, West Coast Canadian Destroyer Flotilla, 1950; Departed for Far East and Korean War as Commander, Canadian Destroyers Far East; Mentioned in Despatches; D.S.O. U.S. Legion of Merit Officer; Returned to Canada, July 1951 on appointment as Naval member of Directing Staff, National Defence College of Canada; Naval member Canadian Joint Staff, London England, and Naval advisor to the High Commissioner for Canada, 1953-55; Appointed Senior Naval Officer afloat 'Atlantic'; Assistant Chief of the Naval Staff (Air and Warfare) and member of the Naval Board, 1958; Promoted Rear Admiral and Vice Chief of Naval Staff, 1961; Member of Canada U.S. permanent Joint Board on Defence; Appointed Flag Officer, Atlantic Coast and Maritime Commander Atlantic, 1963; Retired 1965; Parliamentary Conservative Candidate for Nanaimo Cowichan and The Islands, 1968. *Publications:* 'With Many Voices', an autobiography in two volumes, Volume 1 subtitled 'The Dark Broad Seas', 1981. *Honours:* Distinguished Service Order; Distinguished Service Cross; U.S. Legion of Merit (Degree of Officer); Thrice mentioned in Dispatches. *Hobbies:* Sailing; Fishing; Travel. *Address:* P.O. Box 314, Westport, Ontario, Canada KOG 1XO.

BROCK, Peter Geoffrey, b. 26 Feb. 1945, Hurstbridge, Victoria. Motor Racing Driver, Company Director. *Education:* Eltham High School. *Appointments:* Comapny Director, Partner, 1967-69; Motoring Consultant with G.M.H. 1969-; Professional Racing Driver, 1969-; Road Safety Campaigner with Road Safety and Traffic Authority, 1975-; Managing Director P.G.B. Pty., Ltd.

Memberships: Victorian Game Fishing and Sport Club; Collingwood Football Club; Light Car Club of Australia. *Publications:* Peter Brock on Class Driving, 1976, reprint, 1978-; Hardie Ferodo 500, Films, 1972,73,75-80; Road Safety Film on Class Driving, 1976-. *Honours:* Order of Australia, 1980-; 5 Times winner Australias' most prestigious motor race at Bathurst, Hardie Ferodo 1000. *Hobbies:* Fishing, Cricket, Football. *Address:* 146 Chetwynd Street, North Melbourne, 3051 Victoria, Australia.

BROCKEAY, Baron Archibald Fenner, b. 1888, Calcutta. m. Lilla, 1914, 4 daughters. m. Edith Violet, 1946, 1 son. *Education:* School for the Sons of Missionaries (now Eltham College). *Appointments:* Joined Staff Examiner, 1907-; Sub-Editor, Christian Commonwealth, 1909-; Lbour Leader, 1911-; Editor, 1912-17-; Secretary No Conscription Fellowship, 1917-. Joint Secretary British Committee of Indian National Congress and Editor, India, 1919-; Joint Secretary Prison System Enquiry Committee, 1920-; Organising Secretary ILP, 1922-; General Secretary ILP, 1928 and 1933-39; Editor of New Leader, 1926-29 and 1931-46; Labour candidate Lancaster, 1922-; Chairman No More War Movement and War Resister's International, 1923-28; Labour candidate Westminster, 1924-; Executive Labour and Socialist International, 1926-31; Fraternal Delegate Indian Trade Union Congress and Indian National Congress, 1927-; M.P. Labour East Leyton, 1929-31; Chairman ILP, 1931-33; Political Secretary ILP, 1939-46; German British Centre for Colonial Freedom, 1942-47; ILP candidate, Upton Division of West Ham, 1934, Norwich, 1935-, Lancaster, 1941-, and Cardiff East, 1942-; ILP Fraternal Delegate Hamburg Trade Union May Day Demonstrations and German Social Democratic Party Conference, Hanover, 1946-. Resigned from ILP 1946-, and rejoined Labour Party; MP Labour Eton and Slough, 1959-64; Member International Committee of Socialist Movement for United Europe, 1947-52; first Chairman of Congress of Peoples against Imperialism, 1948-; Fraternal Delegate, Tunisian Trade Union Conference, 1951-; Chairman, Liberation (formerly Movement for Colonial Freedom,), 1954-57, President, 1967-; British Asian and Overseas Socialist Fellowship, 1959-66; Peace in Nigeria Committee, 1967-70; Peace Mission to Biafra and Nigeria, 1968-; British Council for Peace in Vietnam, 1965-69; President British Campaign for Peace in Vietnam, 1970-; Co-Chairman, World Disarmament Campaign, 1979-. *Publications:* Numerous and varied contributions including: The Next Step to Peace, 1970-; The Colonial Revolution, 1973-; Autobiography, Towards Towmorrow, 1977-; Britain's First Socialists, 1980-; Numerous ILP and Movement for Colonial Freedom pamphlets. *Address:* 67 Southway, London, N20 8DE.

BRODERICK, Golda Avril, b. 24 Apr. 1919, Walcs. Music Teacher. m. 29 Oct. 1941, 2 sons, 1 daughter. *Education:* Associate of London College of Music, 1946-; Associate Imperial Society Teachers of Dancing, 1945-. *Appointments:* Music Teacher, (Guitar, piano, piano accordion, violin), Film Work. *Memberships:* Incorporated Society of Musicians; Musicians Union; Music Teachers Association; Film Artists Association. *Hobbies:* Singing, Dancing. *Address:* 2 Whittlesea Path, Harrow Weald, Harrow Middlesex, HA3 6LP.

BRODIE, Graeme Neill, b. 10 Feb. 1939, Sydney, Australia. Medical Practitioner. m. Sally Rosemary Gorer, 15 Aug. 1964, 1 son, 1 daughter. *Education:* MB., BS.(Hons.), 1963, BSc.(Med.), 1961, Sydney University Medical School, Australia; MRACP., 1967; FRACP., 1973; FRCPA., 1975. *Appointments:* Junior Resident Medical Officer, 1963, Senior Resident Medical Officer, 1964, Pathology Registrar, 1965, Medical Registrar, 1966-67, Sydney Hospital, Australia; Research Fellow, Clinical Research Unit, 1968-69, Staff Specialist in Haematology, 1970, Royal Prince Alfred Hospital, Sydney, Australia; Instructor in Medicine, Division of Haematology, Washington University School of Medicine, St. Louis, Missouri, USA, 1970-72; Senior Lecturer in Medicine, Monash University School of Medicine, Assistant Physician, Alfred Hospital, Melbourne, Australia, 1972-77; Director of Medical Oncology, Senior Lecturer in Medicine, Monash University School of Medicine, Prince Henry's Hospital, Melbourne, Australia, 1977-. *Memberships:* Member of numerous associations including: Chairman, Medical Oncology Group of Clinical Oncological Society of

Australia; Executive Secretary, Specialist Advisory Committee in Medical Oncology; Royal Australasian College of Physicians; Councillor, Clinical Oncological Society of Australia. *Publications:* numerous publications including: The Effect of Thrombin on a membrane protein and odenylate cyclase activity in Human platelets, 1971; The Binding of Lectins to Human Platelets, 1972; Adenocarcinoma of Unknown Primary Site: Investigation, Prognosis and Management, 1980. *Honours:* G S Caird Award for General Proficiency, Sydney University, Australia. *Hobbies:* Classical Music; Photography; Stamp collecting. *Address:* 161 Finch Street, Glen Iris, Victoria 3146, Australia.

BRODIE, Wilfred John, b. 4 July 1906, Euroa, Victoria, Australia. Accountant. m. Thyra Ross Campbell, 27 Mar. 1936, 2 daughters. *Education:* Associate Australian Society of Accountants; Associate Chartered Institute of Secretaries. *Appointments:* Inspector of Co-operative Housing Societies, 1945-49; Registry of Co-operative Housing Societies and Co-operative Societies, Chief Clerk, 1950-62, Deputy Registrar, 1962-64, Registrar, 1964-69; Chairman of Home Finance Trust, 1964-69. *Memberships:* Melbourne Cricket Club; Royal Automobile Club of Victoria; Brighton Bowls Club. *Hobbies:* Bowls, Cricket, Music. *Address:* 4 Harrow Court, 211 Church Street, Middle Brighton, 3186, Victoria, Australia.

BROGAN, Bernard Alwyn, b. 29 July 1911, Melbourne, Australia. Architect. m. Dorothy Eileen Withers, 28 Feb. 1942, 2 daughters. *Education:*ASTC., (Arch.), Sydney Technical College, Australia, 1932; Registered Architect, New South Wales, Australia, 1936. *Appointments:* Cadet Architect, Architect, New South Wales Public Works Department, Australia, 1927-37; Architect, Commonwealth Department of Interior, Canberra, Australia, 1937-39; Supervising Architect, 1945, Executive Architect, 1946-57, Commonwealth Department of Works, Melbourne, Australia; Assistant Director of Works: Adelaide, Australia, 1958-59, Sydney, Australia, 1960-65; Director of Works, Sydney, Australia, 1965-73; Director of Construction, Department of Construction, Sydney, Australia, 1973-76. *Memberships:* Retired Fellow, Royal Australian Institute of Architects; Associate, Royal Institute of British Architects; New South Wales Building Industry Advisory Council; Visiting Committee, School of Building, University of New South Wales; Architectural Course, Advisory Committee, New South Wales Institute of Technology; New South Wales Divisional Committee, Building Science Forum. *Hobbies:* Golf; Swimming. *Address:* 33 Yarrara Road, Pymble, New South Wales 2073, Australia.

BROMFIELD, Donald Hamilton, b. 23 Mar. 1922, Perth, Western Australia. Medical Practitioner. m. Sylvia Nolan, 12 Dec. 1946, 2 sons, 1 daughter. *Education:* Hale School, Perth; M.B.B.S., University of Adelaide, 1946-. *Appointments:* Resident Medical Officer, 1947-48; Clinical Assistant Ophthalmologist, Royal Perth Hospital, 1948-53; Resident Medical Officer, Ear, Nose & Throat, Victorian Eye & Ear Hospital, 1954-; Registrar, 1955-; Out-Patients Medical Officer, 1956-;Assistant Surgeon, Oto-Rhino-Laryngologist, Princess Margaret Hospital, 1957-58; Clinical Assistant O.R.L. Royal Perth Hospital, 1956-62; Assistant Surgeon, O.R.L., 1962-63; Honorary Senior O.R.L., Fremantle Hospital, 1966-. *Memberships:* Honorary Secretary Oto-Laryngological Society of Australia, Western Australia State Section, 1956-65, Chairman, 1965-66, 1979-80-81, Organising Secretary, 1972-. Chairman State Committee and Council Member Australian Association of Surgeons, 1977-; Federal Executive 1979-, Treasurer, 1979-. Royal Perth Yacht Club; Western Australia Turf Club; Perth Gun Club; Fremantle Lacrosse Club. *Publications:* The Use of Fibro Fat in Myrincoplasty; A Modern Version of an Operation Performed by Daggert. *Hobbies:* Orchardist, Boating, Fishing, Shooting. *Address:* 65 The Avenue, Nedlands 6009, Western Australia.

BRONSVELD, Paulus Maria, b. 15 July 1936, Ryswyk, The Netherlands. Physicist. m. Yessonda Vandenberg, 16 May 1964, 1 son, 1 daughter. *Education:* Engineering Degree, 1962; MSc, Toronto, 1966; PhD., Toronto, 1971. *Appointments:* Department of Applied Physics, University of Groningen, The Netherlands. *Memberships:* Dutch Association of Physicists; European Physical Society; Canadian Association of Phy-

sicists. *Publications:* Co-author of about 20 articles in physics. *Honours:* Province of Ontario Scholarships, Reginald Blyth Scholarships, 1965-70. *Hobby:* French Language. *Address:* Van Dam laan 8, G831 PE-Aduard, The Netherlands.

BROOK, John Howard, b. 25 Jan. 1931, Melbourne, Australia. Public Servant. *Education:* Dandenong High School & Scotch College, Melbourne; LL.B. Honours, University of Melbourne, 1949-52. *Appointments:* Department of External (later Foreign) Affairs, 1953-; Ambassador to Vietnam, 1976-78, Algeria, 1979-80. *Address:* 8 Richardson Street, Garran, A.C.T. Australia.

BROOKE, Peter Leonard, b. 3 Mar. 1934, London, England. Member of Parliament. m. 6 Apr. 1964, 3 sons. *Education:* MA., Balliol College, Oxford, UK, 1953-57; MBA., Harvard Business School, Boston, Massachusetts, USA, 1957-59. *Appointments:* Research Associate, IMEDE, Lausanna and Swiss Correspondent, Financial Times, 1960-61; Director, 1965-79, Chairman, 1974-79, Spencer Stuart Management Consultants, 1961-79; Member of Parliament for the City of London and Westminster South, UK, 1977-; Assistant Government Whip, UK, 1979-. *Memberships:* President, 1964-65, Harvard Business School Club of London. *Honours:* Harkness Fellow, Commonwealth Fund, 1957-59. *Hobbies:* Cricket; Churches; Conservation; Planting things. *Address:* 110A Ashley Gardens, London SW1, England.

BROOKS, Barry Hewitt, b. 27 Dec. 1932, Wellington, New Zealand. Diplomat. m. Joan Aroha Kermode, 3 Nov. 1961, 1 son, 2 daughters. *Education:* MA., Victoria University, Wellington, New Zealand. *Appointments:* Clerk, Department of Foreign Affairs, 1952-54; Dunlop New Zealand Limited, 1954-57; Ministry of Foreign Affairs, Wellington, New Zealand, 1957-58; Administrative and Consular Attache, Kuala Lumpur, 1959-60; Attache, Jakarta, 1960-61; Registrar, MFA, Wellington, New Zealand, 1962-63; Second and First Secretary, Washington DC, USA., 1963-67; Acting Head and Deputy Head, 1974-75, Economic Division, MFA, Wellington, New Zealand, 1968-69, 1974-75; First Secretary, Economic Affairs, Paris, France, 1969-73; Deputy High Commissioner: Suva, 1975-77, Ottawa, Canada, 1977-81; High Commissioner, New Delhi, India; concurrently Ambassador to Nepal and High Commissioner to Bagladesh, 1981-. *Honours:* Gold Medal, Men's Vocal Championship, Wellington Competitions, 1958; Gold Medal, Society of Australian Teachers of Ballroom Dancing, 1958. *Hobbies:* Music; Philately; Cricket; Tennis. *Address:* New Zealand High Commission, 39 Golf Links, New Delhi, India, 110003, India.

BROOKS, Hector George, b. 21 Sept. 1905, New South Wales, Australia. Grazier. m. Edna Joan Kelly, 14 June 1930, 2 sons, 1 daughter. *Education:* Queen's School, Adelaide; St. Peter's College, Adelaide, 1924-. *Appointments:* Managing Director of: Dandarage Pastoral Company, Munarra Pastoral Company, Two Wells Pastoral Company, Western Australia; Ilya Pty. Limited South Australia; Director of Nilpinna Pty. Limited: G. & E.A. Brooks Limited, & Brooks Estates, South Australia, 1938-73. *Memberships:* Vice-President Associate Delegate National Farmers' Union, South Australian Branch, 1967-69; Vice-President and President, Stockowners' Association, South Australia, 1961-74; Representative of Australian Woolgrower's & Graziers Council, 1967-75, Australian Wool Industry Conference, 1966-74, Australian Wool Industry Policy Committee, 1972-75, Wool Study Tour - France and Italy, 1974-; Vice-President and President, Australian American Association; President, Mens Branch, Walkerville Liberal Party, 1971-73; Executive, English Speaking Union of South Australia, 1954, Deputy President, 1976, Council of St. Mark's College, Adelaide, 1959-, St. Ann's College, ibid., 1957-, Synod Church of England, South Australia; Justice of the Peace, South Australia; Adelaide Club; Stock Exchange; Adelaide Oval Bowling Club *Honours:* OAM, 1981. *Hobbies:* Shooting, Fishing, Boating, Bowling. *Address:* 14 Burlington Street, Walkerville, 5081, South Australia.

BROOKS, Malcolm Edmund, b. 6 Apr. 1909, South Australia. Pastoralist and Company Director. m. Margaret Alison James, 14 Dec. 1938, 3 sons. *Education:* St. Peters College, Adelaide, 1924-27. *Appointments:* Pastoralist; Company Director, G & E.A. Brooks Partnerships Limited, Nilpinna Partnerships Limited; Two

Wells, Dandaraga, and Munarra Pastoral Company. *Memberships:* Federal President, 1978-79; State Council, 1956-80; State President, Royal Flying Doctor Service, 1967-69, 1973-74; Council of Royal Automobile Association of South Australia, 1959-; Vice-President, Royal Automobile Association of South Australia, 1981-. *Honours:* Commissioned Pilot, Royal Australian Air Force, 1941-45; Mention in Despatch, 1944-; O.B.E. 1980-; Justice of the Peace, State of South Australia. *Hobbies:* Boating, Fishing, Swimming, Golf. *Address:* 8 Wilsden Street, Walkerville, South Australia, 5081.

BROOKS, Patricia Ann Lorraine, b. 30 Jan. 1933, Adelaide, South Australia. Sculptor. m Colin, 20 Feb. 1960, 3 daughters. *Education:* Diploma Fine Art (Sc.), South Australia Shool of Art, 1969-; Masters Diploma Sculpture, National Gallery School of Victoria, 1972-. *Appointments:* Department of Further Education. *Memberships:* Associate, Royal South Australian Society of Arts Contemporary Art Society. *Creative Works:* Various R.S.A.S.A. Exhibitions; Mildura City Council Commission, 1959-; S.A. Government Commission; Mildura Triennial Exhibition, 1960-; Cobar Centenary Stele, 1969-; Various Group Exhibitions; St. Peters Collegiate School Wall Sculpture, 1980-. *Honours:* Harry Gill Memorial Medal, 1949-; Clarkson Memorial Prize, 1950-; R.S.A.S.A. Portrait Prize, 1959-. *Hobbies:* Girl Guides Association; Needlework. *Address:* 45 High Street, Burnside, South Australia, 5066.

BROOKS, Peter Wright, b. 8 Jan. 1920, Teddington, Middlesex, England. Executive in Aerospace Industry. m. Patricia Graham Thomson, 18 Aug. 1951, 1 son, 1 daughter. *Education:* BSc.,(Eng.), Imperial College, London University, UK, 1937-41; Associate of City and Guilds of London Institute; Chartered Engineer. *Appointments:* Editorial Staff of The Aeroplane, Air Correspondent, Manchester Evening News, 1940-41; Officer and Pilot, Fleet Air Arm, Royal Navy, 1941-46; Technical Officer, Ministry of Civil Aviation, 1947-50; Technical Assistant to Chief Executive, Assistant to Chairman, Fleet Planning Manager, British European Airways, UK, 1950-61; Deputy Managing Director, Joint Managing Director, Beagle Aircraft Limited, UK, 1961-68; Manager, International Collaboration, British Aircraft Corporation Limited, UK, 1968-79; Regional Executive, British Aerospace, UK, 1979-. *Memberships:* Fellow, Royal Aeronautical Society; Institute of Directors; Fellow, Institute of Transport; Council, Royal Aero Club. *Publications:* The World's Sailplanes, 1958; Contributor, History of Technology, Vols.V & VII., 1958-78; The Modern Airliner: Its History and Development, 1961; The World's Airliners, 1962; Flight Through the Ages, (with CH Gibbs Smith), 1974; Historic Airships, 1975. *Hobbies:* Writing; Private flying; Gardening. *Address:* The Pightle, Ford, Nr. Aylesbury, Bucks, England.

BROOKS, Robert Richard, b. 9 Apr. 1926, Bristol, England. University Teacher and Scientist. m. Mary Yvonne Myatt, 25 Aug. 1950, 1 son, 3 daughters. *Education:* BSc., Honours, Bristol University, 1948-52; PhD., Geochemistry, University of Cape Town, 1957-60; BA., German & Russian, Massey University, 1971-77; DSc, Massey University, 1976-. *Appointments:* ES & A Robinson, Bristol, 1952-56; University of Cape Town, 1957-60; Massey University, New Zealand, 1960-. *Memberships:* Fellow of the New Zealand Institute of Chemistry. *Publications:* Two books, Geobotany & Biogeochemistry in Mineral Exploration, 1972-; Trace Element Analysis of Geological Materials, 1979-; 170 Scientific Papers. *Hobbies:* Philately; Hiking. *Address:* 4 Seaton Court, Palmerston North, New Zealand.

BROUN, Catherine Jane, b. 5 Jan. 1949, London, England. Medical Practitioner. m. Peter Scott Ramsay, 9 July 1977, 1 daughter. *Education:* Liverpool University Medical School, 1967-72; L.R.C.P., M.R.C.S., London, 1972-; M.B. C.H.B., Liverpool, 1972-. *Appointments:* David Lewis Northern Hospital, Liverpool, England, Medical House Officer, 1972-73; Surgical House Officer, 1973-; Senior House Officer, Gynaecology, The Womens Hospital, Liverpool, 1973-74; Resident Medical Officer, The Mersey General Hospital, Devonport and Latrobe, Tasmania, 1975-76; Medical Officer-in-charge, Outpatients, Devonport, Tasmania, 1978-. *Memberships:* The Horsehead Water Ski Club, Australia, 1975-; The East Devonport Squash

Club and Theogenes Squash Club, Launceston, Tasmania. *Honours:* Nuffield Scholarship, 1970-. *Hobbies:* Squash, Tennis, Waterskiing, Sno-skiing, gardening, swimming, reading and knitting. *Address:* Orchard Hill, Spreyton, Tasmania, 7310, Australia.

BROWN, Barrington, Edmunsom Obryan, b. 31 July 1942, Lucea, Hanover, Jamaica. Teacher/Handicraft Consultant. m. 17 Dec. 1972, 1 daughter. *Education:* Various Courses in Craft Work Metal, Industrial Arts and Vocational Education Teacher Training, Senior Management Devlopment, Handicraft and Historical Development, Marketing of Handicraft and small scale industries, 1960-79. *Appointments:* Handicraft and small scale industries research, Development and implementation; Appropriate Industrial Technology Transfer; Junior Master, Knockalva Rural Secondary Technical Hish School Jamaica, 1960; Assistant Woodwork Instructor, Montego Bay Boys School, Jamaica, 1961-; Assistant Industrial Arts Instructor, Kingston College, Jamaica, 1962; Head, Industrial Arts Department, Cornwall College Jamaica, 1963; Tutor, Industrial Arts and Vocational subjects in Winnipeg, Department of Education, Manitoba, Canada, 1964; Factory and Operation Manager, Whitecraft Jamaica Limited, 1969-71; PlusAssociate Consultant, Third World Consultants, Yale Station, Yale University, OAS Handicraft Adviser, Grenada Government Tech. Mission to Mexico, 1981. *Memberships:* Adviser and Consultant to numerous Committee's Conference's and Clubs including: re Design and Production of Handicraft; J.M.A. Furniture and Woodworking Industries Development Seminar. *Address:* 23c Oakridge, Kingston 8, Jamaica, West Indies.

BROWN, Bernard, b. 10 Feb. 1933, Deal, Kent, England. Actor. m. Joyce Mary Finch, 2 daughters. *Education:* Haileybury College, 1947-50; Diploma, Royal Academy of Dramatic Art, London, 1953-54. *Appointments:* Starred as Hamlet, Baalbeck Festival, The Lebanon, 1956; Bristol Old Vic Co. Theatre Royal Bristol, 1957; A Stranger in the Tea, Arts Theatre, London, 1957; Dear Augustine, Royal Ct. Theatre, London, 1958; Robert and Elizabeth, Lyric Theatre, London, 1965; Fallen Angels, Vaudeville Theatre, London, 1966; Dir. Macbeth, Capetown, 1972; Member, Royal Shakespeare Co., London and Stratford-upon-Avon, 1975-79; Played Ghost, 1st Player and Osric in Hamlet, Old Vic Co., London, Athens, Elsinore, Denmark, Japan, China and Australia, 1979; Guest Dir., Lectr. Brigham Young University 1980; Robert Brand in Nancy Astor, BBC TV, 1982; Freelance actor, London; Royal Navy, 1951-53. *Memberships:* British Actors' Equity Association; Royal Naval Sailing Association. *Hobbies:* Sailing; Gardening; Listening to Music; Opera. *Address:* "Nauvoo", 79 Victoria Road, Emsworth, Hants, PO10 7NJ, England.

BROWN, Bruce Macdonald, b. 24 Jan. 1930, Wellington, New Zealand. Civil Servant and Diplomat. m. Edith Irene Raynor, 3 Jan. 1953, 2 sons, 1 daughter. *Education:* MA(Hons), Victoria University, Wellington. *Appointments:* Private Secretary to Leader of the Opposition, 1955-57 and Prime Minister, 1957-59; Ministry of Foreign Affairs, 1959-; Director, New Zealand Institute of International Affairs 1969-71; Deputy High Commissioner, Canberra, 1972-75; Ambassador to Iran, 1975-78 and Pakistan 1976-78; Assistant Secretary, Ministry of Foreign Affairs 1978-81; Deputy High Commissioner, London, 1981-. *Memberships:* International Institute of Strategic Studies, London; New Zealand Institute of International Affairs. *Publications:* The Rise of New Zealand Labour, 1962; The United Nations 1966; Asia and the Pacific in the 1970's, 1971. *Hobbies:* Reading; Golf. *Address:* New Zealand High Commission, Haymarket, London, England.

BROWN, Geoffrey Bruce, b. 24 Oct. 1926, Adelaide, Australia. Artist. Lecturer. m. Jennifer Anne Barratt, 3 Feb. 1958, 1 son. *Education:* South Australian School of Art, 1946-48; Academie de la Grande Chaumiere, Paris, 1952-; Diploma in Etching, Central School of Art, London, 1960-. *Appointments:* Teacher in Art, St. Peters College, Adelaide, South Australia, 1961-62; Lecturer at South Australia School of Art, 1963-. *Memberships:* Fellow of the Royal South Australian Society of Arts, 1961-67; Vice-President Contemporary Society of Art of Australia Incorporated, 1966-68; President of Contemporary Art Society of Australia,

1971-76; Experimental Art Foundation, 1976-; Interstate Vice-President of Print Council of Australia, 1977-80; World Print Council, San Francisco, U.S.A. 1979-. *Creative Works:* Numerous one-man and group exhibitions including: Contemporary Art Society Gallery, 1980, Australia and Overseas including: Contemporary Australian Printmakers II, Print Council of Australia Touring Exhibitions; Represented in various Galleries including: South Australia, New South Wales, Western Australia, Queensland, Victoria; National Gallery Canberra; Private Collections in Australia, U.S.A. and U.K. *Honours:* Maude Vizard-Wholohan Prize for a Print, 1966-. *Hobbies:* Travel, Tennis, Theatre and Music. *Address:*232 Cross Road, Unley Park, South, South Australia, 6045.

BROWN, Jacob A, b. 12 July 1926, Swift Current, Sask., Canada. Economist and Farmer. m. Elizabeth Hildebrandt, 17 Aug. 1952, 2 sons, 2 daughters. *Education:* B.S.A., University of Sask., Canada, 1951-; M.S. University of North Dakota, U.S.A., 1953-; PhD., University of Minnesota, U.S.A., 1964-. *Appointments:* Director Sask Farm Management Programme, 1957-; Department of Agriculture, Director of Research and Planning, Director Economics Branch, Government of Sask., 1960-61; Professor, Agricultural Economics, University of Sask., Canada, 1967-; Professor and Dean of Agruclutre, 1974-; Sask., Land Bank Commission, 1971-; Chairman, Sask., Farm Ownership Board, 1974-. *Memberships:* Past-President, Canadian Agricultural Economic Society; American Agricultural Economic Association; International Agricultural Economics Association International Right of Way Association Agricultural Institute of Canada; Sask., Institute of Agrologists. *Publications:* Research and Scholarly work in agricultural policy. *Honours:* Two Agricultural College Scholarships, 1962, 1963; Phi Kappa Phi honorary academic award, 1952-; Gamma Sigma Delta academic award, 1963-; Fellow, Agricultural Institute of Canada, 1980-; Economic Council of Canada, 1974-80-. *Hobbies:* Photography, Farming. *Address:* Box 338 Sub. P.O. 6. Saskatoon, Sask., Canada, S7N0W0.

BROWN, John Gilbert Newton (Sir), b. 7 July 1916, London. Publisher & Bookseller. m. Helen Virginia Violet, 25 May 1946, 1 son, 2 daughters. *Education:* Lancing College, 1930-34; M.A. Zoology, Hertford College, Oxford, 1934-37. *Appointments:* Oxford University Press, 1937-80; B. H. Blackwell Ltd., 1980-; Royal Artillery, 1940-45. *Memberships:* President, Publishers Association, 1963-65. *Honours:* Kt., 1974-; C.B.E. 1966-. *Address:* Milton Lodge, Great Milton, Oxford, OX9 7NJ England.

BROWN, Mervyn, b. 1923. British Deiplomat. m. Elizabeth Gittings, 1949. 02 MA, St John's College, Oxford. *Appointments:* Third Secretary, Buenos Aires, 1950-53; Second Secretary, New York, 1953-56; First Secretary, Foreign Office, 1956-59; Singapore, 1959-60; Vientiane, 1960-63; Foreign Office, 1963-67; H M Ambassador, Tananarive, 1967-70; Inspector, Diplomatic Service, 1970-72; Head of Communication Department, Foreign and Commonwealth Office, 1973-74; Assistant UnderSecretary (Director of Communications), 1974; British High Commissioner, Dar es Salaam and concurrently H M Ambassador to Tananarive, 1975-78; Deputy Permanent Representative at UN., New York, 1978; British High Commissioner, Lagos, 1979-. *Memberships:* Royal Commonwealth Society. *Publications:* Madagascar Rediscovered. *Honours:* Companion of the Order of St Michael & St George, 1975; Officer of the Order of the British Empire, 1963. *Address:* c/o Foreign and Commonwealth Office, London, SW1, England

BROWN, Mervyn, (Sir), b. 24 Sept. 1923, Durham, England. Diplomat. m. Elizabeth Gittings, 12 Nov. 1949. *Education:* Ryhope Grammar School, 1935-41; St. John's College, Oxford, 1941-42, 1946-68, (M.A. History). *Appointments:* Foreign Office, 1949-; Buenos Aires, 1950-; New York, 1953-; Foreign Office, 1956-; Singapore, 1959-; Vientiane, 1960-; Foreign Office, 1963-; Ambassador Madagascar, 1967-; Diplomatic Service Inspector, 1970-; Director of Communications, 1973-; High Commissioner, Tanzania, 1975-; Deputy Permanent Representative New York, 1978-; High Commissioner, Nigeria, 1979-. *Memberships:* Royal Commonwealth Society; Corresponding member, Academie Malgache. *Publications:* Madagascar Redis-

covered (A History), 1978-. *Honours:* O.B.E., 1963-; C.M.G., 1975-: K.C.M.G., 1981-. *Hobbies:* Music, Tennis, History. *Address:* 3 Queen's Drive, Ikoyi, Lagos, Nigeria.

BROWN, Michael Russell, b. 3 July 1951. Member of Parliament. *Education:* Degree in Economics & Politics, University of York, 1969-72; *Appointments:* Graduate Trainee Barclays Bank, 1972-74; Lecturer & Tutor, Swinton Conservative College, 1974-76; Personal Assistant to Nicholas Winterton M.P. 1976-79; Elected M.P. for Brigg & Scunthorpe, 1979-. *Memberships:* British Atlantic Committee. *Hobbies:* Cricket, Walking. *Address:* House of Commons, London, S.W.1.

BROWN, Neil Anthony, b. 22 Feb. 1940, Melbourne, Victoria, Australia. Member of the Parliament *Education:* Bachelor of Laws, University of Melbourne, 1963-. *Appointments:* Barrister, 1964-69; Member of Parliament, 1969-72; Barrister, 1972-75; Member of Parliament, 1975-. *Honours:* Parliamentary Adviser to Australian Delegation to U.N. General Assembly, 1976-; Leader of Australian National Observer Group to Southern Rhodesian Elections, 1980-. *Address:* Parliament House, Canberra, A.C.T., Australia, 2600.

BROWN, Raymond Frederick, b. 19 July 1920, London. Chairman; Director; Consultant. m. (1) Evelyn Jennings, 1942, 1 daughter, (2) Carol Jacquelin Elizabeth, 1953, 2 sons, 1 daughter. *Education:* South East London Technical College; Morley College; DSc(Hons), Bath University, 1980. *Appointments:* Apprentice Engineer, Redifon 1934; Sales Manager Communications Division, Plessey Limited 1949-50; Chairman, Managing Director, President, Racal Electronics Limited 1950-66; Head, Defence Sales, Ministry of Defence, 1966-69; Consultant Adviser, Commercial Policy and Exports, Department of Health and Social Security 1969-72; Chairman, Racecourse Technical Services Limited, 1970-. *Memberships:* British Overseas Trade Board Working Party, Innovation and Exports 1972-74; President, Electronic Engineering Association; National Economic Development Office; Director, National Westminster Bank Limited; President, Egham and Thorpe Royal Agricultural and Horticultural Association; Governor, South East London College; Liveryman, Scriveners Company, London; Society of Pilgrims; City Livery; Travellers'. *Honours:* OBE 1966; Knighted 1969. *Hobbies:* Polo; Farming; Shooting; Golf. *Address:* Westcroft Park, Windlesham Road, Chobham, Surrey GU24 8SN, England.

BROWN, Robert James, b. 2 Dec. 1933, Pelaw Main, NSW, Australia. Member of Parliament. m. Elizabeth Joy Hirschausen, 27 Aug. 1960, 1 son, 1 daughter. *Education:* Bachelor of Economics, 1954; Diploma in Education, 1955. *Appointments:* High School Deputy Principal; Legislative Assembly, NSW Parliament; House of Representatives, Australian Parliament. *Memberships:* Australian Labour Party; Amnesty International; Lions International; Inter Parliamentary Union; Commonwealth Parliamentary Association; Council for Civil Liberties;. Australian Consumers Association. *Publications:* Student Economics, Parts I and II; Economics Workbook, Parts I and II. *Hobbies:* Philately; Numismatics. *Address:* 31 Rawson Street, Kurri Kurri, New South Wales, Australia.

BROWN, Theo Watts, b. 11 Oct. 1934, Melbourne, Victoria, Australia. Marine Biologist. *Education:* University Matriculation, Perth Technical College, 1956-; Affiliated with University of Sydney, 1969-72. *Appointments:* Director, Marine Research Division, Australian Deep Sea Diving & Salvage Service, 1957-; Research Associate, Institute of Medical Research of French Polynesia Papeete, Tahiti, 1967-; Research Associate, World Life Research Institute, Colton, California, 1968-; Consultant, South Pacific Commission, 1970-74; Director, Australian Division, World Life Research Institute, 1978-; Research Associate, Academy of Applied Science, Boston, 1978-. *Memberships:* Manly Life Saving Club, N.S.W. Australia; Australian Society of Authors. *Publications:* Crown of Thorns, The Death of the Great Barrier Reef?, 1972-; Sharks, The Search for a Repellent, 1973-; Sharks, The Silent Savages, 1975-; The Boy and the Shark, 1979-; Numerous science papers. *Honours:* Silver Medal for Bravery, Royal Humane Society, NS.W. Australia, 1960-. *Hobby:* Egyptology. *Address:* 68 Seaview Avenue, Newport Beach, New South Wales, 2106, Australia.

BROWN, Thomas Christopher Kenneth, b. 9 Dec. 1935, Kenya. Anaesthetist. m. Janet Patricia Penfold, 8 July 1961, 3 sons, 2 daughters. *Education:* MB.ChB., St. Andrews University, Scotland 1960-; Licentiate, Medical Council of Canada, 1961-; Fellowship, Faculty of Anaesthetists, Royal Australasian College of Surgeons, 1967-; MD., Melbourne University, 1980-. *Appointments:* Intern, Victoria Hospital, London, Ontario, 1960-61; G.P. Yellowknife, Canada, 1961-62; Anaesthesia Resident, Vancouver General Hospital, Research Fellow, Department of Medicine, University of British Columbia 1963-65; Anaesthesia Resident, Hospital for Sick Children, Toronto, 1965-; Anaesthetic Registrar, Royal Melbourne Hospital, Australia, 1966-; Royal childrens Hospital, Melbourne, Fellow in ICH., 1967-69, Anaesthetist, 1970-74, Director of Anaesthesies, 1974-. *Memberships:* Faculty of Anaesthetists, Royal Australisian College of Surgeons; Chairman, Education Officer, Victorian Regional Committee; Examiner, Primary FFA. R.A.C.S. Australian Society of Anaesthetists, Convenor Scientific Programme Committee; Editorial Board, Anaesthesia and Intensive Care; Australian College of Paediatrics. *Publications:* Textbook, Anaesthesia for Children, 1979-; M.D. Thesis, Tricyclic antidepressant overdosage in Children; 32 scientific papers. *Honours:* Gilbert Brown Medal, Faculty of Anaesthetists R.A.C.S., 1977-. *Hobbies:* Painting; Photography. *Address:* 13 Alfred Street, Kew, Victoria, 3101, Australia.

BROWNBILL, David Scott Barrington, b. 15 Nov. 1938, Melbourne, Australia. Neurosurgeon. m. Susan Victoria Symonds, 13 Aug. 1970. *Education:* Caulfield Grammar School; MB. BS., Melbourne University, 1962-; Fellow Royal Australasian College of Surgeons, 1968-. *Appointments:* Australian Surgical Team, South Vietnam, 1966-; Nuffield Department of Neurosurgery, Oxford, 1970-; Department of Neurosurgery, Queen Square, London, 1971-; Senior Clinical Assistant, Neuro/Ophthalmology, Moorefield's Eye Hospital, 1971-; Locum Consultant Neurologist, Royal Devon and Exeter Hospital, 1972-; Senior Neurosurgeon, Royal Melbourne Hospital, 1975-; Consultant Neurosurgeon, Royal Women's Hospital, 1975-; Senior Associate Department of Surgery, Melbourne University, Royal Melbourne Hospital, 1975-. *Memberships:* Melbourne Club; Royal Melbourne Tennis Club; Fellow Royal Australasian College of Surgeons; Neurosurgical Society of Australasia; Australian Medical Association; South Pacific Underwater Medicine Society. *Honours:* Royal Australasian College of Surgeons, Edward Lumley, Surgical Research Travelling Fellowship, 1970-. *Hobby:* Underwater photography. *Address:* 21 Grant Street, North Fitzroy, Victoria, Australia

BROWNE, Stanley George, b. 8 Dec. 1907, London England. Consultant Leprologist. m. Ethel Marion Williamson, 15 Nov. 1940, 3 sons. *Education:* King's College, London, 1927-30, Hospital, 1930-35; Institut de Medécine Tropicale, Antwerp, 1935-36; MD, London; FRCP; FRCS; DTM; FKC; Fellow, King's College Hospital Medical School. *Appointments:* Baptist Medical Missionary, Belgian Congo 1936-58; Director, Leprosy Research Unit, East Nigeria 1959-65; Director, Leprosy Study Centre, London, 1966-80; Consultant Adviser in Leprosy, DHSS 1966-79; Honorary Consultant, University College Hospital, 1966-79; Medical Consultant, Leprosy Mission, 1966-78; Medical Consultant, Hospital and Homes of St Giles 1966-80. *Memberships:* Secretary, International Leprosy Association; Fellow and Past President, Royal Society of Tropical Medicine and Hygiene; Christian Medical Fellowship. *Publications:* Over 450 papers in Scientific journals on medical subjects, especially Leprosy, Tropical Dermatology, Onchocerciasis; Congo—as the Doctor Sees It; Leprosy—new hope and continuing challenge; etc. *Honours:* Murchison Scholarship, Royal College of Physicians, 1934; Africa Medal, Royal African Society, 1970; Stewart Prize, British Medical Association 1975; Ambuj Nath Bose Prize, Royal College of Physicians, Edinburgh, 1977; Chaudury Gold Medal, Calcutta, 1978; Chevalier, Ordre Royal du Lion, 1948; Officier, Ordre de Léopold II, 1958; Commandeur, Ordre de Léopold, 1980; OBE, 1965; CMG, 1976; Commandeur, Ordre de Malte, 1973. *Hobbies:* Reading; Writing; Photography. *Address:* 16 Bridgefield Road, Sutton, Surrey, SM1 2DG, England.

BROWNE, Stevenson Alfred, b. 1 Jan. 1934, St. John's, Antigua, West Indies. Barrister-at-Law. m. Daphne, 30 Jan. 1957, 4 sons. *Education:* Antigua Grammar School, 1946-52; Sheffield University, 1959-63; LL.B. Degree 2nd Class Honours, 1962-; Called to the Bar by Honourable Society of Gray's Inn, 1964-; LL.M. Degree, Sheffield University, 1964-. *Appointments:* Private Practice, Antigua, 1964-; Legal Assistant and Additional Magistrate, St. Lucia, 1965-67; Magistrate, St. Vincent, 1967-69; Acting Attorney General, St. Vincent, 1968-; Crown Counsel, St. Vincent, 1970-71; Private Practice, Antigua, 1971-. *Memberships:* Lions Club; Angigua Cricket Association. *Hobbies:* Bridge, Tennis, Reading. *Address:* Bendals Village, Antigua.

BROWNING, Stella Daniel. b. 22 June 1917, New Rcmney, Kent. Poet, Author, Publisher, Editor, Teacher (Retired). m. J.J. Duffey (Divorced), m. Kenneth Martin, 1978, 2 sons. *Education:* Southlands Grammar School, London University with M.A. Honours, English and Psychology and extension courses at different Universities. Convent, Loire Valley, Finishing School, 1922-40; French and Music Diplomas and additional in Domestic Sciences-cordon-bleu. *Appointments:* Pianist, Schools, Gold Medallist Reader to Schools. Infant Teacher; Poetry Promotions, Scotland & England; S.E. Secretary & Treasurer; B.B.C. Reader to Schools; Journalist; Writer Educational Verses for Children; Promotion of Poetry S.E. Kent with Cinque Parts Poets International; Anthology Collator & Editor Horizon Magazine; Publisher of Educational Material for Schools, Kent Education Committee, 1980, Hertfordshire, 1977; South-South East Television Programme for the Arts, 1981. *Memberships:* Runnymede Association of the Arts; National Poetry Society, London; Founder, Editor, Cinque Parts Poets, own Society; Society of Authors; P.E.N. International; Poetry Secretariat, London; World Brotherhood of Peace; Acadamy of Poets, Cambridge; Accademia Italia Delle Arti Del Lavoro, Roma. *Publications:* Pilgrimage & Other Poems, 1972; Horizon Magazine; Children's Educational Verses; Butter-in-the-Buttercups, Parts I, 2 & 3 (A private collection) of Oil & Watercolour Paintings. Notail at Wesley; Adventures of Hoodie the Crow; Pilgrimage & other Poems (Adult); On Wings of Sound, 12 Year autobiography in Poetry, 1981. *Honours:* Poetry & Prose, 1926 & 1928-; Southlands Grammar School, Dr. F.W. Cox Reading Prize (Snr), 1933-, Rev. F.H. Manser Reading prize, Snr. with Gold Medal & the Reading of Prayers Daily, 1934-35; Schools Pianist, Diploma; London Literary Award for Poetry, 1971-; Listed Best Poems Choice Years consecutive, 1972-77; Alice Gregory Memorial Runner-up, 1977-; Jubilee Highland Arts Award, 1977-; 3 Poem Book Awards. *Hobbies:* Schools Writing and Reading for Children, Gardening, Motoring, Fellowship with own Society. *Address:* 2 Highfield, Sussex Road, New Romney, Kent, England.

BROWNLIE, Alistair Rutherford, b. 5 Apr. 1924, Edinburgh. Solicitor Supreme Courts. m. 20 June 1970. *Education:* George Watson's College, Edinburgh; M.A. 1948-; LL.B. 1950-; Diploma Administrative Law, Edinburgh University, 1951-. *Appointments:* Cochrane & Blair Paterson, S.S.C., Edinburgh; External Examiner in Forensic Medicine, Dundee University. *Memberships:* Secretary, Society of Solicitors in the Supreme Courts of Scotland; Past President and founder member, Forensic Science Society; Former Member, of Council Law Society of Scotland; Legal Aid Central Committee, Scotland. *Publications:* Co-author of Drink Drugs & Driving, 1970-; Contributor to Criminal Law Review; Book Reviews Editor, Journal of Forensic Science Society. *Honours:* John Hastie Scholarship, 1950-; James Brierley, Firth Memorial Lecturer, 1977-. *Hobbies:* Writing, Gardening, Travel. *Address:* 8 Braid Mount, Edinburgh Scotland.

BRUCE, Peter Thomas, b. 26 Feb. 1931, Vienna, Austria. Urological Surgeon. m. Carlin Connan, 27 Nov. 1976, 1 son, 3 daughters. *Education:* Geelong Grammar School, 1943-49; M.B., B.S., Melbourne University, 1950-55; Post-Graduate Ch,M. Liverpool University, England. Post-Graduate, Vienna University. *Appointments:* Senior Urologist to Queen Victoria Medical Centre, Monash University; Senior Urologist to Sandringham & District Memorial Hospital. Fellow Royal College of Surgeons of England; Fellow Royal Australisian College of Surgeons; International Society of Urological Surgeons; *Memberships:* British Association of Urological Surgeons; Urological Society of Australasia; The Savage Club, Melbourne; The Lawn Tennis Association of Victoria. *Publications:* Ch,M., Thesis, Lymphography, Liverpool University, Liverpool, England. Surgery, Urology, Medicine, in International Journals. *Honours:* Commonwealth Scholarship to Melbourne University, 1949-; British Council Scholarship to Vienna University, 1958-; Biennial Essay Prize, Urology Society of Australisia, 1964-. *Hobbies:* Music, Harness Horse Driving. *Address:* Yarrimbah, Wandong, Victoria, Australia, 3656.

BRYAN, Arthur (Sir), b. 4 Mar. 1923, Stoke-on-Trent, England. Company Chairman. m. Betty Ratford 1947, 1 son, 1 daughter. *Education:* Longton High School. *Appointments:* Joined Wedgwood, 1947; Assistant London Manager, 1950-53; London Manager General Manager, Wedgwood Rooms, 1953-59; General Sales Manager, 1959; President, Board of Josiah Wedgwood and Sons Inc. of America, 1960-62; Managing Director, Chief Executive, and Chairman, 1968-. *Memberships:* Director, Phoenix Assurance Company; Court of the University of Keele, Staffordshire; Companion, British Institute of Management; Companion, Institute of Ceramics; Fellow, Institute of Marketing; Fellow, Royal Society of Arts. RSA. *Honours:* Honorary Degree, Master of the University, 1977; Knight of the Order of St. John; Knighted, 1976; Her Majesty's Lord Lieutenant for Staffordshire, 1968. *Hobbies:* Walking; Tennis; Reading. *Address:* Parkfields Cottage, Tittensor, Stoke-on-Trent, Staffordshire, England.

BRYAN, Garlan Henry, b. 27 July 1927, Launceston, Tasmania, Australia. Magistrate. m. Shirley Eileen Kingsley, 18 Oct. 1952, 4 daughters. *Education:* Bachelor at Laws, University of Tasmania, 1963. *Appointments:* Legal Officer, Tasmania Police Department, 1965-71; Senior Assistant, Parliamentary Counsel, Tasmania, 1971-77; Magistrate, Hobart, Tasmania, 1977-; Captain, Legal Officer, Citizen Military Forces, 1969-75. *Memberships:* Civic Club, Hobart, Tasmania. *Hobbies:* Music; Walking. *Address:* 39 Centenary Crescent, Claremont, Tasmania 7011, Australia.

BRYCE, Wyatt Errington, J.P., b. 24 Nov. 1915, Black River, Jamaica. association Executive. m. Vivia Ellene Simpson, 6 May 1955, 2 sons, 1 daughter. *Education:* Grad. High School. *Appointments:* Sub-editor, Jamaica Standard, 1938-39; Co-publisher, editor, Evening Post, 1940-41; Chief Reporter, Daily Express, 1942-43; News Editor, 1943; News Editor Daily News, 1945; Pub. Reference Book Jamaica, 1946; Pocket Reference Book Jamaica, 1947; Assistant, Government Publicity Services: Jamaics Agricultural Society, Kingston, 1947-51, Assistant Secretary, Information and Publicity, 1951-66, Secretary/Treasurer, 1966-77; Personal Assistant to Managing Director, Jamaica Livestock Association, 1978-; Hon. Secretary/Treasurer, National. Farmers Union Jamaica, 1973-75. *Memberships:* Jamaica Press Association, Founder 1943, Hon. Secretary, 1945-46, Treasurer, 1968-73; Jamaica Press Club. *Honours:* Officer of Order of Distinction (Jamaica), 1979. *Address:* 4 Hope Plaza, Hope Pastures, Kingston 6, Jamaica.

BRYDEN-BROWN, John Trevor, b. 23 Oct. 1929, Sydney, Australia. Advertising & Marketing Consultant. m. 1 son, 3 daughters. *Education:* Fellow, Advertising Institute. *Appointments:* Accountant, Qantas Airways, 1945-47; Director, Maxwell Advertising, 1947-53; Editor, Modern Motor, 1953-54; Advertising Manager, Email Limited, 1954-56; Director, Fortune Advertising, 1956-58; Managing Director, Bryden-Brown & Associates Partners Limited, 1958-81. *Memberships:* American Club; American Chamber of Commerce in Australia; Journalists Club; Advertising Club; Life Education (Wayside Chapel); Advertising Institute of Australia. *Publications:* Advertising-The First 10,000 Years; Marketing-The First 10,000 Years; The Ads. That Made Australia. *Honours:* Advertising Age - International Award; Two F.A.C.T.S., TV Awards; Fellow, Institute Advertising. *Hobbies:* Vintage Cars; President Australian Auburn Cord Duesenberg Club. *Address:* 81 Ben Boyd Road, Neutral Bay 2089, Australia.

BRYDON, Adam Howie, b. 14 Apr. 1921, Armidale, NSW, Australia. Newspaper Executive. m. (1) Lois Stevens, 16 July 1954 (Div.) 1 daughter, (2) Jocelyn Peters, 23 May 1975. *Education:* The Armidale School, Armidale, Australia, 1931-38; Royal Australian Air Force College, 1939. *Appointments:* Squadron Leader, RAAF, 1939-44; Lieutenant, RANVR.(Fleet Air Arm),

1944-45; Brydon Motors, 1947-54; Diners Club Limited, 1954-60; News Limited, 1960-70; Herald & Weekly Times Limited, 1970-77; General Manager, New York Post, 1977-. *Memberships:* Naval & Military Club (Melbourne); Royal Brighton Yacht Club (Melbourne); Cruising Yacht Club of Australia. *Honours:* Distinguished Flying Cross (1944) & Bar (1944). *Hobbies:* Automobile Racing; Yacht Racing. *Address:* 180 East End Avenue, New York, NY 10028, USA.

BUCABUSHAKA, Nicolas, b. 21st Dec. 1946, Nkoronko, Karusi, Burundi. Professor at University of Burundi. m. 15 Sept. 1969, 1 son, 4 daughters. *Education:* Certificate in humanities, 1966; 1st and 2nd. candidatures in philosophy and letters, Romance Philology, Official University of Bujumbura, 1966-67, 1967-68; 1st and 2nd. Licenciates in Romance Philology (with distinction), Free University of Brussels, Belgium, 1968-69, 1969-70; UNESCO scholarship, work on doctoral thesis, distinction, University of Lille III, France, 1972-75. *Appointments:* Lecturer, Department of Letters, 1970-72, Professor, 1975-78, Teacher Training College, Burundi; Professor, 1975-78, Head of Department of Letters, Faculty of Letters and Humane Sciences, 1975-78, University of Burundi; Director, Technical Service in EACROTANAL, Zanzibar, Tanzania, 1979-81. *Memberships:* Association of Partly and Wholly French-speaking Universities. *Publications:* Le problème des masses et des élites vu à travers Ernest Renan et Jean Guehenno, 1970; Tradition et modernité dans les conceptions du héros intellectuel à travers les romans négro-africains d'expression française, 1975; Contributor of articles to: Liaison, Revue de l'Ecole Normale Supérieure. Revue de l'Université du Burundi. *Hobbies:* Reading; Cinema; Organisation of Drama productions at University of Burundi. *Address:* Université du Burundi. BP 1550 Bujumbura. Republic of Burundi.

BUCIL, Milan Bohumil, b. 4 Apr. 1936, Prague. Musician; Teacher; Composer. m. Leticia Maria Cornejo, 4 Feb. 1978, 1 son, 1 daughter. *Education:* Prague Conservatory of Music, 1959; Studies in Misucology, Charles University, Prague, 1962-67; Mus. Bac, 1969, B Ed, 1975, University of Toronto, Canada. *Appointments:* Professional Musician, 1958; Teacher and Lecturer, 1961; Freelance Writer and Journalist, 1962; Band Leader and Conductor, 1969; Composer and Arranger: Theatre and Chamber Music, Songs, Popular and Jazz Music. *Memberships:* Toronto Musicians Association; Composers, Authors and Publishers Association of Canada; American Musicological Society; Toronto Secondary Schools Teachers Association. *Publications:* The Guitar-How to Play and Enjoy Music, 1981; Contributions to various newspapers; Scenic and Stage Music. *Creative Works:* Performances and Engagements in Europe and North America. *Hobbies:* Fina Arts; Literature; Outdoor Living; Travel. *Address:* 344 Military Trail, West Hill, Ontario, M1E 4E6, Canada.

BUCKNER, Garth Samuel Harold, b. 4 Apr. 1934, Melbourne, Victoria, Australia. Barrister; Cattle Grazier. m. Sarah Alicia Latham, 19 Dec. 1963, 2 daughters. *Education:* Bachelor of Laws (Hons.), 1957, University of Melbourne, Australia, 1953-56. *Appointments:* Admitted to Victorian Bar, 1960; Admitted to New South Wales Bar, 1969; Admitted to Bars of Australian Capital Territory and Tasmania, 1975; Appointed Queen's Counsel in the State of Victoria, Australia, 1977; Cattle Grazier, 1971-. *Memberships:* British Film Institute; National Film Theatre of Australia; Collingwood Football Club, V.F.L. Park; Royal Automobile Club of Victoria; Vintage Club. *Publications:* Notes on American Film Comedies of the Thirties, 1958, Stanley Kubrick: Film Director, 1960, The Development of the Comédie Noire, 1958. *Hobbies:* Jazz Dance; Squash; Jogging; Reading; Cinema; Theatre; Book Collecting. *Address:* 10 mackennel Street, East Ivanhoe 3079, Melbourne, Victoria, Australia.

BUCKWOLD, Sidney Labe, (Hon), b. 3 Nov. 1916, Winnipeg, Manitoba, Canada. Vice President & General Manager of Buckwold's Ltd. m. Clarice Rabinovitch, 17 Sept. 1939, 1 son, 2 daughters. *Education:* Nutana Collegiate, Saskatoon; University of Saskatchewan, Alaska; B Comm., McGill University, Canada. *Appointments:* Salesman, 1936; Manager, 1946; General Manager, Buckwold's Ltd., Saskatoon, 1952; Mayor, Saskatoon, Saskatchewan, 1958-63, 1967-71; Director and

Member of Executive Committee, Bank of Montreal; Director, SED Systems Ltd., Consolidated Pipeline Company, Mutual Life Assurance Co. of Canada. *Memberships:* Member of numerous Associations including: President, Canadian Federation of Mayors and Municipalities; The Canadian National Committee for Habitat: The United Nations Conference on Human Settlements; Co-Chairman Joint Senate/H. of C. Comm. on Employer-Employee Relations; Chairman Palimentary Committee on International Hockey; Government Whip in Senate, 1973-74; National Council of Duke of Edinburgh's Awards in Canada; Vice-Chairman of the National Liberal Caucus, 1979-80. *Honours:* Salesman of the Year, 1971; Saskatoon Citizen of the Year, 1971. *Hobby:* Golf. *Address:* 824 Saskatchewan Cresc. E. Saskatoon, Saskatchewan, S7N OL3, Canada.

BUDD, Alfred Hamilton Dale, b. 4 Apr. 1944, Sydney, New South Wales, Australia. Management Consultant. m. Dianna Suzette Banks, 21 Dec. 1970, 2 sons, 1 daughter. *Education:* Graduated Bachelor of Engineering in Mechanical Engineering (Hons III), Sydney University, Australia, 1961-64. *Appointments:* Engineering and management positions, Containers Limited, 1965-70; Private Secretary to Minister for Defence 1970-71; Private Secretary to Minister for Education and Science, 1971; Private Secretary to Minister for Defence, 1971-72; Defence Department, Logistics Division, several positions, 1973-74; Consultant, PA Consulting Services, Sydney, Australia, 1974-75; Principal Private Secretary to Leader of the Opposition, 1975; Principal Private Secretary to the Prime Minister, 1975-78; Partner in own consultancy, Dale Budd & Associates, 1978- *Memberships:* N.S.W. Rail Transport Museum, 1962-70, 1974-75. *Publications:* Flyer, 1970; West by Steam, 1972. *Honours:* Officer of the Order of the British Empire, 1978. *Hobbies:* Reading; Photography. *Address:* 19 Hooker Street, Yarralumla, A C T 2600, Australia.

BUDD, Stanley Alec, b. 22 May 1931, Edinburgh, Scotland. Scottish Representative, Commission of the European Communities. m. Wilma McQueen Cuthbert, 5 Nov. 1955, 3 sons, 1 daughter. *Education:* George Heriot's School, Edinburgh, Scotland. *Appointments:* Newspaper reporter and sub-editor, 1947-57; Research writer, Foreign Office, 1957-60; Second Secretary, British Embassy, Beirut, 1960-63; First Secretary, British High Commission, Malaysia, 1963-69; Foreign Office, 1970-71; Deputy Director of Information, Scottish Office, 1972; Press Secretary, Chancellor of Duchy of Lancaster, 1973; Chief Information Officer, Cabinet Office, 1974-75. *Hobbies:* Oriental antiques; Bridge; Music; Painting. *Address:* 2 Bellevue Crescent, Edinburgh, Scotland.

BUDDEE, Paul Edgar, b. 12 Mar. 1913, Perth, Western Australia. Author; Educationalist; Musician. m. Elizabeth Vere Bremner, 12 Jan. 1944, 1 son, 1 daughter. *Education:* Western Australia College of Advanced Education; Elected to Australian College of Education, 1963. *Appointments:* Journalist, 1930-33; Teacher, Principal Lecturer, 1933-76; Australian Imperial Forces, 9th Division-Service in Tobruk and North Australia, 1940-47. *Memberships:* President of Fellowship of Writers, 1947-49; President Rockingham Sub-branch Returned Soldiers League, 1953-54; Vice-president, Western Australia Teachers Union, 1956-57; President, Thornlie Rotary Club, 1973-74; South Perth City Council, 1963-71; Australian Society of Authors; Life Member Rats of Tobruk Association. *Publications:* Stand to and Other War Poems, 1944; Author of over 30 childrens books published in Australia, England and translated into Polish and Danish; Has written music for public performance since 1935. *Honours:* Special Purpose Grant by Literary Board of Australia Council; State Citizenship award for 40 years of service to the State in Art Culture and Entertainment, 1977; General Purpose Grant by Literary Board of Australia Council, 1978; Elected Paul Harris Fellow in Rotary International, 1980; Made Life Member of Fellowship of Writers (WA) for Service to the Fellowship and to Literature, 1981. *Hobbies:* Travel; Photography. *Address:* 11 The Parapet, Burrendah, Western Australia 6155.

BUGEMBE-KIGONGO, Samuel Muye, b. 12 July 1942, Bukto,Kampala, Uganda. Broadcaster. m. Margaret N Kawuma, Feb. 1974, 2 sons, 1 daughter. *Education:* Cambridge School Certificate and Oral English Certificate, 1962;Training by Unesco and BBC, Feb.

1963: Certificate in Journalism and Broadcasting Techniques, 1972. *Appointments:* Social Researcher, Marco Surveys Ltd, Uganda; Parcels Department, Uganda Bookshop, 1963; Radio Uganda, Aug,1963-, First as Programme Assistant, secondly as Cont/Announcing, thirdly, Commentaries, mainly in Sports; Newcaster on Radio and Television; Producing Commercials; Programme Organiser of Presentation Unit of External Service of Radio Uganda, 1975; Currently in Charge of Music and Light Entertainment, External Service of Radio Uganada. *Memberships:* Uganda Sports Writers' Association; The Express Football Club; Ministry of Information and Broadcasting Co-operative Society; Commonwealth Jounralists' Association. Uganda YMCA. *Creative Works:* Two Paintings: Cating Grasshoppers; Fighting it Out. *Honours:* Certificate for reaching Finals in the Uganda Junior Boxing Championship, 1957; Awarded Book for Best Artist Award at Kokolo Senior Secondary School, 1962. *Hobbies:* Listening to other Radio Stations; Music; Football; Gardening. *Address:* c/o Dr. D N Kiremerua, P O Box 16096, Kandegeya,Kampala, Uganda.

BUGOTU, Francis, b. 27 June 1937, Tasimboko, Guadalcanal, Solomon Islands. Diplomat. m. Ella Vehe 28 May, 1962, 1 son, 1 daughter. *Education:* Educated in New Zealand, Australia, Scotland and England besides Solomon Islands. *Appointments:* Teacher and Inspector of Mission Schools for the Church of Melanesia (Anglican), 1959-60; Lecturer at Solomon Island Teachers College, 1964-68; Chief Education Officer and Permanent Secretary, Ministry of Education, 1968-75; Chairman of Review Committee on Education, 1974-75; Permanent Secretary to Chief Minister and Council of Ministers, also titular Head of Solomon Islands Civil Service, 1976-78; Secretary for Foreign Affairs and Roving Ambassador/High Commissioner, 1978-; accredited as Ambassador to USA, West Germany, Sweden, United Nations and European Economic Community, High Commissioner to UK, Australia, New Zealand and Canada. *Memberships:* Member of Solomon Islands 1st Legislative Council, 1960-62; Chief Commissioner of Scouts for Solomon Islands, 1970-71; Founder member and Chief Adviser of Kakamora Youth Club, 1968-75; Lay-Canon, Church of Melanesia, 1970-; First Chairman of Solomon Islands Tourist Authority, 1970-73; Chairman of Solomon Islands Scholarship Committee. *Publications:* The Impact of Western Culture on Solomon Island Society-A Melanesian reaction, 1969; Politics, economics and Social aspects in the developing Solomons, 1970; Recolonising and Decolonising: the case of the Solomons, 1975; Solomon Islands Pidgin - a comparative study, 1974. Play entitled: This Man, later became an award winning film. *Honours:* CBE, 1979. *Hobby:* Travel. *Address:* Foreign Affairs Department, Homiara, Solomon Islands.

BUJANG, Abdul Ghani, b. 2 July 1945, Kuala Belait, Brunei. Senior Education Officer. m. Hasnah Wahab, 3 July 1969, 3 sons. *Education:* Cert. ED, 1969; B.Ed, 1975. *Appointments:* Teacher, 1969-73; Lecturer, 1975-78; Deputy Principal, 1976-78; Principal, 1978-81. *Memberships:* Founder member, Persatuan Pendidik National Brunei; National Association of Educators, Brunei; Vice-President, Brunei Artists Association. *Publications:* Pengajaran: Prinsip dan Amalan. *Hobbies:* Painting; Reading; Travel; Writing. *Address:* PO Box 2918, Bandar Seri Begawan, Brunei.

BULLEN, Leslie Raymond, b. 30 Oct. 1918, Sydney, Australia. Managing Director. m. Joan Margaret, 4 Feb. 1950, 2 daughters. *Appointments:* National Cash Register Company, Australia, 1946-59; General Manager and Director of Victoria and Tasmania, 1959-64, Sales & Marketing Director of Australia and New Zealand, 1964-68, Australian Board of Directors, 1963-68, Lewis Berger & Sons (Australia) Pty. Limited; Self Employed Management Consultant, 1968-69; Managing Director, Eutectic (Aust(Pty. Limited, Area Director, South East Asia & Pacific Zones, Eutectic Corporation of New York, 1969-71; Managing Director, Fire Fighting Enterprises Limited, 1971-; Consultant to Australian Institute of Management, 1962-63. *Memberships:* Member of numerous associations including: Fellow, Institute of Chartered Secretaries and Administrators; Fellow, Institute of Sales & Marketing Executives, President NSW Division, 1967-68; Chairman of Steering Committee for formation of Australia-Philippines Business Co-operation Committee, Inaugural

President, 1975-77; Chairman, Tourism and Cultural Exchange Sub-Committees, Joint Meetings, 1979-80; Vice Chairman and Sponsor, Filipino Community Centre, Marrickville, Sydney; Hon. Life Governor, Royal Children's Hospital, Melbourne, 1960-; Australia-New Zealand Marketing Association; Australian Fire Protection Association; Australian Institute International Affairs. *Honours:* Special award from Confederation of Filipino Clubs, June 1979, in recognition of assistance given to Philippine Community. *Address:* 6 Pearl Bay Avenue, Beauty Point, 2088 New South Wales, Australia.

BULTEAU, Volney Gordon, b. 17 Dec. 1915, Sydney, NSW, Australia. Surgeon m. Ann Holme, 28 Dec. 1945, 3 daughters. *Education:* MBBS, 1938, DLO, 1949, FRACS, 1959, University of Sydney, Australia. *Appointments:* Ear, Nose and Throat Surgeon. *Memberships:* Vice President, Australian Post Graduate Medical Federation; Hon. Treasurer, Post Graduate Medical Committee, University of Sydney; Councillor, New South Wales Medical Defence Union; Consulting Otologist, National Accoustic Laboratories, Northcott Neurological Centre, Department of Veterans Affairs; Representative, Honorary Colonel, Royal Australian Army Medical Corps. *Publications:* Articles in various medical publications.*Honours:* Commander-in-Chief's Award, El Alamein, 1942; Efficiency Decoration, 1975. *Hobbies:* Books; Tennis; Swimming. *Address:* 4/2 Highview Avenue, Neutral Bay, New South Wales 2089, Australia.

BULUBA, Arnold Mont., b. 15 July 1949, Bariadi District, Shinyanga Region, Tanzania. Social Planner. m. 30 Oct. 1979, 1 son. *Education:* Bachelor of Arts in Social Work and Social Administration, Makerere University, 1975; Masters of Science, Economics, Social Planning in Developing Countries, London School of Economics, 1977. *Appointments:* Assistant Secretary, Ministry of Lands, Housing and Urban Development, Tanzania; Social Town Planner, World Bank Finaces, Sites and Services Project, Tanzania; Projects Manager, Community Development Trust Fund of Tanzania. *Memberships:* Msasani Beach Club; Tanzania Rural and Agriculture Society; The Tanzania Commonwealth Society. *Publications:* Housing Policy for Urban Door in Tanzania. *Hobbies:* Football; Swimming; Church Singing. *Address:* Bhesco Flats 6A, Ursino Estate, Bagamoyo Road, D'Salaam, Tanzania.

BUNCE, Ian Hugh, b 20 Dec. 1942, Brisbane, Australia. Medical Practitioner; Consultant Haematologist. m. Margaret Elizabeth Allan, 14 Sept. 1968, 1 son, 1 daughter. *Education:* MB BS (QLD), 1967; Fellow Royal Australasian College of Physicians, 1977; Fellow Royal College of Patholgoists of Australasia, 1977. *Appointments:* Haematologist, Department of Pathology, North Brisbane Hospitals Board; Clinical Haematologist, Royal Brisbane Hospital, Australia. *Memberships:* United Service Club; Haematology Society of Australia; Australasian Society of Blood Transfusion; International Society of Haematology. *Publications:* Publications on Disseminated Intravascular Coagulation and Lymphoproliferative Disease. *Honours:* Efficiency Decoration, Military Division, 1976; Australian Kidney Foundation Research Scholar, 1971; Royal Australasian College of Physicians, Travelling Scholarship, 1977. *Address:* 51 Charlton Street, Ascot, Brisbane, Australia, 4007.

BUNTING, (Edward) John, b. 13 Aug. 1918, Ballarat, Australia. Civil Servant, Retired. m. Pauline Peggy MacGruer, 4 Apr. 1942, 3 sons. *Education:* BA(Hons), Diploma Public Administration, Trinity College, University of Melbourne. *Appointments:* Assistant Secretary, 1945-53, Deputy Secretary, 1955-58, Secretary, 1959-68, Prime Minister's Dept., Canberra; Official Secretary, Australia House, London, 1953-55; Secretary, Dept. of Cabinet Officer, Canberra, 1968-71; Secretary, Dept. of Prime Minister & Cabinet, Canberra, 1971-75; Secretary to the Australian Cabinet, 1959-75; High Commissioner for Australia, London, 1975-77; Australia Council, 1978-; Chairman of Directors, 1978-. *Memberships:* Commonwealth Club, Canberra. *Honours:* Knight Bachelor, 1964; KBE, 1977. *Hobbies:* Reading; Music; Golf. *Address:* 8 Arnhem Place, Red Hill, Canberra, 2603, Australia.

BUNWAREE, Goorpersad, b. 12 May 1919, Mauritius. Central Banker. m. Ambicka Ghoorun, 2 sons, 1 daughter. *Education:* Royal College, Mauritius; Diploma in Public and Social Administration, Wadham College, Oxford, England; Economic Development Institute, Washington D.C, USA. *Appointments:* Assistant Secretary, Central Administration, 1956-57; Principal Assistant Secretary, Chief Secretary's Office, 1957-60; Principal Assistant Secretary, Ministry of Industry, Commerce and External Communications, 1960-63; Deputy Financial Secretary, 1963-66; Permanent Secretary, Ministry of Works and Internal Communications, 1966-67; Financial Secretary, 1967-69; Managing Director, Bank of Mauritius, 1970-72; Governor, Bank of Mauritius, 1973-. *Address:* 67 Sir Virgile Naz Avenue, Quatre Bornes, Mauritius.

BURBURY, Donald Leslie, b. 26 Dec. 1907, Oatlands, Tasmania, Australia. Pastoralist. m. Jessie Wade Gatehouse, 23 June 1937, 1 son. *Education:* Hutchins School, Hobart, Australia, 1921-25. *Memberships:* Hon. Life Councillor, Royal Agricultural Society of Tasmania; Hon. Life Member, Australian Hereford Society Ltd; Hon. Life Member, Tasmanian Working Sheepdog Association; Trustee, Tasmanian Farmers and Stockowners Association; Tasmanian Club; Royal Automobile Club of Tasmania; Past Member, Oatlands Municipal Council 33 years and held Office of Warden 8 years; Past Member, Municipal Association of Tasmania; Past President of Royal Agricultural Society of Tasmania; Past President Tasmanian Working Sheepdog Association; Past President Tasmanian Farmers and Stockowners. *Honours:* Appointed Justice of the Peace, 1955; Queen's Jubilee Medal, 1977. *Hobbies:* Land Valueling; Bowls. *Address:* Wyndham, York Plains 7206, Tasmania, Australia.

BURGESS, Anthony Langbien, b. 1 Oct. 1953, Sydney, Australia. Photogrammetrist. *Education:* Certificate in Cartography; Associate Diploma in Cartography, Sydney; Diploma in Photogrammetry, Holland. *Appointments:* Consulting Photogrammetrist, 1978-. *Memberships:* Australian Institute of Cartographers; Australian Photogrammetric Society. *Publications:* Bogangar Beach, Sawtell Beach, New South Wales, Photogrammetric Analysis. *Hobbies:* Early Australian Art; Sport; Skiing; Scuba Diving. *Address:* 58 Cromwell Street, Leichhardt 2040, Australia.

BURGESS, Ellis Howard, b. 8 Oct. 1916, Adelaide, South Australia. Chartered Accountant. m. Marjorie Carlisle Stevens, 2 Mar. 1943, 1 son, 1 daughter. *Education:* Diploma in Commerce, University of Adelaide, South Australia, 1935-39. *Appointments:* Chartered Accountant in Pulic Practice; Senior Adelaide Partner, Arthur Young & Company, retired 1977; Director of Following Public Companies: Bennett & Fisher Ltd Group since 1968, Chairman since 1974; Bradford Insulation (SA) Holdings Ltd Group since 1969, Chairman since 1978; G & R Wills Holdings Ltd, since 1971, Chairman since 1976; Advertiser Newspapers Ltd, since 1974; Executor Trustee & Agency Co. of S.A. Ltd Group since 1976; Bennett Farmers Ltd, since 1978; Australia and New Zealand Banking Group Ltd, since 1980. *Memberships:* Institute of Chartered Accountants in Australia, Australian President 1972-74; South Australian Chairman 1970-72; Australian Society of Accountants; Institute of Chartered Secretaries and Administrators; Finance Committee, University of Adelaide; Faculty of Economics, 1953-80; Board of Governors, Adelaide Festival of Arts, 1970-, Deputy Chairman, 1972-78, Chairman, 1978-80; Hon. Australian Commissioner TOCH, 1957-62. *Publications:* Technical Papers Presented at Australia and International Congresses of Accountants. *Honours:* Mentioned in Despatches 1945; OBE, 1980. *Address:* 74 Kingston Terrace, North Adelaide, S.A. 5006.

BURGESS, Michael Webster, b. 24 June 1938, Nairobi, Kenya. Agriculturalist. m. June Ann Fitzgerald, 12 Aug. 1961, 2 daughters. *Education:* University of London, 1958-61; BSc Agric, NDA, Leeds; Cambridge University, 1962; DTA, University of West Indies, 1963. *Appointments:* Agricultural Officer, Tobacco Officer, Tobacco Training Officer for Zambia, Zambian Govertment, 1963-69; Cotton Advisory Officer, Zimbabwe Government, 1969-74; Cotton Productivity Advisor, Commercial Cotton Growers Association, 1974-80; Director Cotton Training Centre, Gatooma Zimbabwe, 1980-. *Memberships:* Crop Science Society; Caravan Association, Chairman, 1978-80. *Publications:* 20 Publications in various professional Journals. *Hobbies:*

Golf; Squash; Reading. *Address:* PO Box 530, Gatooma, Zimbabwe.

BURGOYNE, John Henry, b. 4 Aug. 1913, Luton, Bedfordshire, England. Consulting Scientist, Engineer. m. 8 Mar. 1944, 1 son. *Education:* ARCS, BSc, Royal College of Science, 1931-33; DIC, PhD, DSc, City and Guilds College, 1934-40. *Appointments:* Department of Scientific and Industrial Research, 1940-42; Ministry of Home Security, 1942-46; Imperial College London, 1946-64; Independent Consultant, Dr J.H. Burgoyne and Partners, 1964-. *Memberships:* Fellow, The Royal Society of Chemistry; Fellow, The Institution of Chemical Engineers; Senior Fellow, The Institute of Energy; The Combustion Institute; Fellow, Institute of Petroleum, Institution of Fire Engineers. *Publications:* Many Scientific and Technical Publications in the field of Combustion, Explosion and Fire Technology; Report of the Committee of Inquiry into Offshore Safety, 1980. *Honours:* CBE, 1980. *Address:* 1 Redlynch Court, 70 Addison Road, London, England.

BURKE, Joseph Terence Anthony, b. 14 July 1913, England. Emeritus Professor. m. Agnes Middleton, 1940, 1 son. *Education:* King's College, University of London; Courtauld Institute of Art; Yale University. *Appointments:* Victoria and Albert Museum, 1938; Private Secretary to successive Lord Presidents of the Council, 1942-45; Private Secretary, to the Prime Minister, 1945-46; Herald Professor of Fine Arts, University of Melbourne, 1947. *Memberships:* Australian UNESCO Committee for Visual Arts; Fellow, President, 1971-73, Australian Academy of the Humanities. *Publications:* Hogarth and Reynolds: A Contrast in English Art Theory, 1943; William Hogarth's Analysis of Beauty and Autobiographical Notes, 1955; Hogarth: The Complete Engravings, (with Colin Caldwell), 1968; Oxford History of English Art 1714-1800, 1976; Contributor to Magazines, Journals. *Honours:* OBE, 1946; FAHA, The Herald Professor of Fine Arts, University of Melbourne, 1947; CBE, 1973; MA; Hon. D.Litt. Monash, 1977; KBE, 1980. *Hobbies:* Golf; Swimming. *Address:* Dormers, Falls Road, Kalorama 3766, Australia.

BURKE, Samuel Martin, b. 3 July 1906, Pakistan. Judge; Ambassador; Professor (retired). m. Queenie Louise Neville, 4 daughters. *Education:* BA(Hons); MA, Government Central School, Lahore; Government College, Lahore; School of Oriental Studies, London. *Appointments:* Indian Civil Service, 1931-47; District Officer, District and Sessions Judge; President, Election Petitions Commission, Punjab, 1946; Pakistani Foreign Office, 1948-49; Counsellor, Pakistani High Commission in London, 1949-52; Minister, Embassy of Pakistan, Washington, 1952-53; Special Missions to Mexico and Dominican Republic, Charge d'affairs, Rio de Janeiro, 1953; Deputy High Commissioner for Pakistan in UK., 1953; Minister to Sweden, Norway, Denmark, Finland, 1953-56; Ambassador to Thailand, Minister to Cambodia and Laos, 1956-59; Member Pakistani Delegation to SEATO Council Meetings, 1957-59; High Commissioner to Canada, 1959-61; Leader Special Mission to Argentina, 1960; Professor cons. South Asian studies, department international relations, University Minnesota, 1961-75. *Memberships:* United Nations Committee on Contributions, 1953-55; Fellow, Royal Society of Arts. *Publications:* Zafrulla Khan: The Man and His Career; Pakistan's Foreign Policy, An Historical Analysis; Mainsprings of Indian and Pakistani Foreign Policies. *Honours:* Founder, Burke Library, South Asia Collection, Hamline University, Minnesota, USA; Awarded Star of Pakistan, 1962. *Hobbies:* Cricket; Tennis; Riding. *Address:* 44 Roehampton Close, London SW15 5LV, England.

BURNHAM, Linden Forbes Sampson, b. 1923. Guyanese politician; Prime Minister of Guyana. m. (1) Sheila Bernice Lataste, 1951, 3 daughters, (2) Viola Victorine Harper, 1967, 2 daughters. *Education:* British Guiana; BA, London University; Bachelor of Laws, Gray's Inn. *Appointments:* President, West Indian Student's Union, London, 1947-48; Delegate, International Union Students' Congress, 1947-48; Co-founder, Chairman, People's Progressive Party, 1949; Elected Georgetown Town Council, 1952-56; President, Guyana Labour Union, 1963-65; Minister, Education PPP Government, 1953; Founder, Leader People's National Congress, 1957; Leader Party Opposition, 1957-64; Mayor of Georgetown, 1959 and 1964; Premier, British Guiana, 1964; Prime Minister of Guyana, 1966-; Re-elected Prime Minister, 1968, 1973. *Memberships:* The bar Association of Guyana (President, 1959); *Publications:* A Destiny to Mould. *Honours:* British Guiana Scholarship, 1942; Best Speaker's Cup, London University, 1947; Queen's Counsel, 1960; Senior Counsel, 1966; Order of Excellence of Guyana, 1973. *Address:* The Residence, Vlissengen Road, Gorgetown, Guyana.

BURNS, Douglas Roland Bonser, b. 20 Apr. 1937, Streatham, London England. Adminstration. m. Wendy Erica Steward-Anderson, 29 Mar. 1962, 2 daughters. *Education:* Reading School, Reading, Berks; Writtle Agricultural College, Chelmsford; National Diploma in Agriculture, College Diploma in Agriculture, Diploma in Local Government (Town Clerks), Diploma in Local Government (Treasurers). *Appointments:* Farms Manager, Suffolk, 1960-64; Farm Management & Economics Lecturer, Chadacre Agricultural College, Bury St. Edmunds, 1964-66; Farm Management Consultant, Perenjori, 1966-70; Shire Clerk, Laverton, 1970-75; Shire Clerk, Wongan Hills, 1975-78; Executive Director, Western Australia Division Red Cross Society, 1978-. *Memberships:* Fellow of the Australian Institute of Management; Associate of the Australian Institute of Municipal Adminstration; Member of the Institute of Emergency Services; Member of Perth Rotary Club. *Honours:* Justice of the Peace; Commissioner for Declarations. *Hobbies:* Woodwork; Gardening; Rugger. *Address:* 10 Brian Avenue, Mt. Pleasant, Western Australia 6153.

BURNS, Eedson Louis Millard, Lieutenant General (Retired), b. 17 June 1897, Montreal, Canda. Soldier; Civil Servant. m. 3 Dec. 1927, 1 daughter. *Education:* LLD, Universities of British Columbia and Alberta, New Brunswick, Windsor, Carleton, Canada; Royal Military College, Kingston. *Appointments:* Commissioned, Royal Canadian Engineers, June 1915, Served in World War I, signals and staff; Officer i/c Geographical Secretary. G.S., 1931-37; At outbreak World War II, GSO. 1, Canadian Military HQ., London; ADC.GS, NDHQ Ottawa, 1940; Comdr. 4th Canadian Armoured Bde, 1942; Comdr. 2nd Canadian Division, 1943; Comdr, 1st Canadian Corps, ITALY, 1944; Director General, Rehabilitation Department, Veterans' affairs, 1946; Deputy Minister, DVA, 1950; Comdr., United Nations Emergency Force, (Suez), 1956; Adviser to Canadian Government on disarmament, 1960; Canadian Representative at Disarmament conferences, Geneva, 1960-68. *Memberships:* Rideau Club, Ottawa; President, Canadian Institute of Surveying, 1936-37; President, United Nations Association of Canada, 1936. *Publications:* Between Arab and Israeli, 1962; Megamurder, 1966; General Mud, 1970; A Seat at the Table, 1972; Defence in the Nuclear Age, 1976. *Honours:* MC, 1916; OBE, 1935; DSO, 1944; CC, 1967. *Hobbies:* Gardening; *Address:* R R I., Box 132, Manotick, Ontario, KOA 2NO, Canada.

BURNS, Elton Owen, b. 1 July 1917, Brisbane, Queensland, Australia. Agricultural Economist. m. Mary Margaret Sheehan, 24 Dec. 1941, 2 daughters. *Education:* B. Com. University of Queensland. *Appointments:* Queensland Department of Primary Industries , Director of Economic Services, 1962-73, Deputy Director, Marketing Division, 1973-74, Chief Advisory Officer (Adminstration), 1974-76, 1976-78, Deputy Director General, Director General and Under-Secretary, 1978-80. *Memberships:* Australian Institute of Agricultural Science (M.A.I.A.S.). Australian Farm Management Society; Fellow, Royal Institute of Public Adminstration; Fellow, Australian Society of Accountants (F.A.S.A.) Australian Agricultural Economics Society (President 1972, Queensland President, 1965. Chairman, Queensland Fish Board, 1971-75; Marketing Advisor, Queensland Trade Mission to Middle East and Asia,1975, Australian Delegate to F.A.O. Conference, Rome, 1979 Council Member, Queensland Agricultural College 1970-. *Hobbies:* Chess; Golf; Music. *Address:* 71 Graham Road, Carseldine, Qld. 4034, Australia.

BURNS, Jeffrey Howard, b. 21 Dec. 1946, Toronto. Barrister & Solicitor. m. Audrey Loeb, 12 Aug. 1969. 02 BA, Waterloo University College, 1968; LL.B., Osgoode Hall Law School, 1970; MBA., York University, 1971; LLM., London School of Economics, 1972; Law Society of Upper Canada Bar AD Course, 1973; Barrister-at-Law. *Appointments:* Partner in Law Firm of McDonald & Hayden, Toronto and Calgary; Member of Panel of

Experts assigned to the United Nations Centre on Transnational Companies. *Memberships:* Canadian Bar Associaton; Canadian Tax Foundation; London School of Economics Society. *Publications:* Co-author, Foreign Investment in Canada - a Guide to the Law; Regulation of Foreign Investment in Canada; Author of numerous articles in learned journals. *Honours:* American City Managers' Association Studentship. *Hobby:* Politics. *Address:* 2 Dunloe Road, Toronto, Ontario, Canada.

BURNS, Thomas James, b. 27 Oct. 1931, Maryborough. Member of Parliament. m. Angela MacDonald, 29 Nov. 1968, 1 daughter. *Education:* Brisbane Grammar School, Queensland. *Appointments:* State Organizer Queensland Branch Australian Labour Party, 1960-65; State Secretary, ibid., 1965-72; Member of Legislative Assembly Queensland Parliament, 1972; National President Australian Labour Party, 1970-73; Leader of Her Majesty's Opposition, Queensland Parliament, 1974-78; Shadow Minister for Transport & Main Roads, 1979. *Publications:* Booklets, Journals and Articles on Australian Politics. *Hobbies:* Bowls; Fishing. *Address:* 20 Aster Street, Cannon Hill 4170, Australia.

BURNS, William Gregory, b. 29 Apr. 1924, Queenstown, Tasmania. Senior Trade Commissioner. m. Joan Hagger, 13 Feb. 1948, 2 sons. *Education:* Xavier College, Kew, 1934-40; R.M.I.T. 1940-45; Fellowship Diploma of Civil Engineering, 1946; Commercial Pilot Licence 1952/72. *Appointments:* Airport Engineer, 1945; Civil Air Attaché, London, 1956; Business Manager, Department of Civil Aviation, 1960; Regional Director, Vic.-Dept. of Trade And Resources, 1966; Assistant Secretary, Trade Relations, 1968; Senior Trade Commissioner Minister (Commercial), Kuala Lumpur, 1973, Tehran, 1976, Peking, 1979-. *Memberships:* Institution of Engineers, Australia; Federal Golf Club, Canberra. *Publications:* Numerous technical papers; Trade relations articles. *Hobbies:* Tennis; Golf; Cars; Music. *Address:* Australian Embassy, Peking, China

BURRELL, Anthony Richard, b. 22 May 1946, Sydney, Australia. m. Ruth Gibson, 24 July 1971, 1 son, 1 daughter. *Education:* MB, BS, University of Sydney, 1964-71; Fellow, Faculty of Anaesthetists, Royal Australasian College of Surgeons, 1976. *Appointments:* Resident Medical Officer, Royal Newcastle Hospital, 1971-72; Registrar in Anaesthesia, 1973-75, Senior Registrar, 1976, Royal North Shore Hospital; Anaesthetist, Orange Base Hospital, 1977-; Director of Intensive Care, Orange Base Hospital, 1979-; Consultant Anaesthetist to Forbes, Parkes and Molong District Hospitals. *Memberships:* Australian: Medical Association; Society of Anaesthetists; Australian & New Zealand Intensive Care Society; Western Pacific Association of Critical Care Medicine. *Hobbies:* Music: Whisky; MG Cars; Farming. *Address:* "Ngumby", Cargo Road, Lidster 2800, Australia.

BURRELL, George Albert, b. 20 May 1924, Newcastle, New South Wales, Australia. Metallurgy. m. 5 Apr. 1952, 1 son, 1 daughter. *Education:* ASTC (Hons), Diploma of Metallurgy, 1946; BSc, 1956; Diploma of Management, 1952. *Appointments:* Metallurgist, 1941-48; Production Manager, 1949-72; Personnel Manager, 1973-76; General Manager, 1977-. *Memberships:* Chairman, Heavy Engineering Manufacturers Association; Councillor, Australian Industries Development Association; Heavy Industry Advisory Council; Australian Institute of Management; Australian Institute of Metals; Metals Society; Newcastle Club. *Publications:* Australian Engineer: Tool Steels, 1946; Heavy Forgings, 1952. *Honours:* Institute of Metals Award, 1946. *Hobbies:* Music; Woodworking; Painting. *Address:* 33 Mountainview Parade, New Lambton Heights, New South Wales, Australia.

BURRELL, Michael Philip, b. 12 May 1937, Harrow, England. Actor/Director. *Education:* John Lyon School, Harrow, 1949-56; Peterhouse, Cambridge, 1958-61, M.A. 1965. *Appointments:* Associate Director, Royal Lyceum Theatre, Edinburgh, 1966-68; Director, Marklew & Hunt Ltd., 1972-75; Associate Director, Derby Playhouse, 1975-77. *Publications:* Hess, 1980. *Honours:* OBIE Award for performance in HESS, New York, 1980. *Hobbies:* Reading; Music; D-I-Y; Gardening;

Travel. *Address:* Pump Lodge, 406 Cherry Hinton Road, Cambridge, CB1 4BA. England.

BURRENCHOBAY, Dayendranath, (Sir), K.B.E., C.M.G., C.V.O. b. 24 Mar. 1919,m. . Governor-General of Mauritius. m. 1 son, 2 daughters. *Education:* Royal College, Curepipe; Graduated in electrical engineering at the Imperial College, London University- Imperial College Scholarship, 1946-48; Postgraduate Certificate in Education, 1951; B.Sc. (Eng.) Hons. (London); A.C.G.I.; P.G.C.E. *Appointments:* Education Officer, 1951; successively Senior Education Officer, Chief Education Officer, Permanent Secretary, Ministry of External Affairs, Tourism & Emigration, and also Permanent Secretary, Primo Minister's Office, 1968-76; Secretary to the Cabinet, Head of the Civil Service & 1976; Part-time Chairman, Central Electricity Board, 1968-79; Attended various conferences and seminars as a representative of the Government. *Honours:* CVO, 1972; Chevalier de la Légion d'Honneur, 1975; CMG, 1977; Knight Commander, KBE, 1978; Grand Croix 1ere Classe de l'ordre du mérite de la République Fédérale d'A llemagne, 1978. *Hobbies:* Mathematics; History; Philosophy; Politics. *Address:* Government House, Le Réduit, Mauritius.

BURRUMARRA, Bukulatjpi, b. 1918, Wodanga'Yu, Elcho Island, N.T. Australia. Traditional Leader. m. Lawuk, 1943, 4 sons, 3 daughters. *Education:* Milingimbi School, Milingimbi; Teachers' College, Darwin; Strong Traditional Education (Totems, Whale, Octopus). *Appointments:* Chairman of Mala (Tribal); Leaders' Council, 1956-80. *Memberships:* Institute of Aboriginal Studies; Aboriginal Material Culture Organisation; Australian Cancer Society. *Publications:* Totem Ceremonies; Mirror to the Man, 1978; Land Rights Paper, 1980; Life and Opinions of Burrumarra (unpublished manuscript). *Honours:* MBE, 1978. *Hobbies:* Conversationalist; Traditional Narrator. *Address:* Galiwin'Ku, Elcho Island, N.T.5791, Australia.

BURTON, Barry Lawson, b. 30 Dec. 1942, Ulverston, Cumbria, England. Librarian. m. Wendy Fay Monks, 4 Dec. 1970, 2 sons, 1 daughter. *Education:* BA, 1965; ALAA, 1968; MBIM, 1974. *Appointments:* Reference Officer, Flinders University of South Australia, 1966-67; Chief Librarian, Salisbury College for Advanced Education, 1968-71; Deputy Librarian, Makerere University, Uganda, 1972; Polytechnic Librarian, Hong Kong Polytechnic, 1973-. *Memberships:* Chairman, Hong Kong Library Association, 1975; FID Representative for Hong Kong, 1979-; Board of Governors, Foreign Correspondents' Club, 1979. *Publications:* Many journal articles. *Honours:* President, International Federation for Documentation/Commission for Asia and Oceania FID/CAO, 1981-; Member, Australian Open Bridge Team. *Hobbies:* Bridge; Horse Racing; Wine Tasting. *Address:* D13, Pak Sui Yuen, Science Museum Road, Tsim Sha Tsui East, Hong Kong.

BURTON, Thomas Leonard, b. 1 Sept. 1941, March, Cambridgeshire, England. University Professor. m. Lynne Marion Dale, 14 Apr. 1972. *Education:* B. Sc. (Economics), University College, London, 1963; PhD, (Land Economics), Wye College, London, 1967; MCIP (Member, Canadian Institute of Planners), 1977. *Appointments:* Assistant Lecturer, Wye College, London, 1963-67; Lecturer, University of Birmingham, 1967-69; Assistant Professor, Michigan State University, USA, 1969-70; Associate Professor, University of Waterloo, Canada, 1970-73; Policy and Research Coordinator, Government of Canada, 1973-76; Professor, University of Alberta, Canada, -, Chairman, since 1979-. *Memberships:* Commonwealth Human Ecology Council, (London, England); Canadian Parks/Recreation Association; Alberta Recreation and Parks Association; Ontario Research Council on Leisure; Chairman Canadian Association for Leisure Studies. *Publications:* Recreation Research and Planning, 1970; Social Research Techniques For Planners, 1970; Experiments in Recreation Research, 1971; Natural Resource Policy in Canada, 1972; Making Man's Environment & Leisure, 1976; Guidelines for Urban Open Space Planning, 1977. *Honours:* Numerous research grants and awards from Governments of Canada, Alberta, Ontario and United Nations Economic Commission for Europe. *Hobbies:* Cross Country and Downhill Skiing; Photography; Music; Drama; Cookery. *Address:* 8912-140 Street, Edmonton, Alberta, Canada, T5R OJ3

BURTON-BRADLEY, Burton Gyrth, b. 18 Nov. 1914, Sydney, Australia. Transcultural Psychiatrist, Author. m. Ingeborg, Roeser, 7 Oct. 1950 (deceased, 1972). *Education:* DPM, University of Melbourne, 1956; DTM & H, 1963, Dip. Anth. 1964, University of Sydney; FRACMA, Royal Australian College of Medical Administrators, 1967; MD, University New South Wales, 1969; FRANZCP, Royal Australian and NZ College of Psychiatrists, 1970; FRCPsych. Royal College of Psychiatrists England, 1972. *Appointments:* Medical Officer, Psychiatric Services, Queensland, 1951-57; Lecturer in Psychological Medicine, University of Malaya, 1957-59; Chief Mental Health PNG. 1959-75; Chairman Permanent Committee on Mental Health and Cultural Development, 1961-75; Associate Professor of Psychiatry, University of Papua New Guinea, 1972-75; Clinical Associate Professor of Psychiatry, University of Hawaii , 1976-; Professor of Psychiatry (Hon) University of Papua, New Guinea, 1978-. *Memberships:* Abraham Flexner Lecturer, Vanderbilt University, USA, 1973; Advisory Panel on Mental Health of World Health Organisation, 1977-; Counsellor World Association for Social Psychiatry, 1977-; Vice-President, International College of Psychosomatic Medicine, 1977-79; Regional Cousellor World Association for Social Psychiatry since 1977; 32 other professional associations in Medicine. *Publications:* South Pacific Ethnopsychiatry, 1967-; Mixed-Race Society in Port Moresby, 1968-; Psychiatry and the Law in the Developing Country, 1970-; Longlong, 1973-; Stone Age Crisis, 1975-; Plus 120 Scientific Papers in Professional Learned Journals. *Honours:* Wenner Gren Research Award, 1970-; Benjamin Rush Bronze Medal, 1974-; Yale-Based Foundations Fund for Research in Psychiatry Award, 1975-; Independence Medal, Papua New Guinea, 1978-; Organon Psychiatric Research Award, 1980. *Hobbies:* Historical Research in Medicine and Psychiatry; Patrolling in Papua, New Guinea. *Address:* Mental Health Services, P.O. Box 1239, Boroko, Papua, New Guinea.

BURTT, Thomas Browning, Tom, b. 22 Jan. 1915, Christchurch, New Zealand. Company Manager. m. 31 Oct. 1942, 3 sons, 2 daughters. *Memberships:* Christchurch Savage Club; St. Albans Cricket Club; Selwyn Hockey Club; Chamber of Commerce; Ellesmer Golf Club; Waitikiri Golf Club. *Honours:* Represented New Zealand in Hockey, 1937, 1938, and Cricket, 1949, 1950. *Hobbies:* Fishing; Golf. *Address:* 6 Weka Street, Christchurch, New Zealand.

BURVILL, Peter Walter, b. 27 Apr. 1933, Perth, Western Australia. Psychiatrist. m. Marilyn Ann Hogan, 5 June 1961, 6 sons, 1 daughter. *Education:* M.B.B.S., Adelaide, 1957-; M.D., West Australia, 1970-; D.P.M. , Edinburgh University, 1963-; M.R.C.P.E., 1964-; M.R.A.N.Z.C.P., 1966-; F.R.A.N.Z.C.P., 1977-; M.R.C., Psychiatry, 1971-; M.F.C.M., 1972-. *Appointments:* Senior Lecturer Psychiatry, 1965-73; Associate Professor of Psychiatry, University of Western Australia, 1973-; Head, Department of Psychiatry, Royal Perth Hospital, 1973-; Head, University Department of Psychiatry & Behavioural Science, University of Western Australia, 1980-. *Memberships:* Chairman, Western Australia Schizophrenia Research Foundation; Chairman, Board of Censors; Chairman, Surveys, Questionnaire Committee, Royal Australian & New Zealand College of Psychiatrists. *Publications:* Various publications in psychiatric epidemiology, psychogeriatrics, suicide, migrants, general practice, psychiatric service delivery. *Address:* 35 Gardner Street, Como, Western Australia, 6152.

BURWELL, Richard Geoffrey, b. 1 July 1928, Leeds. University Professor. m. Helen Mary Petty, 19 Jan. 1963, 1 son, 1 daughter. *Education:* University of Leeds, 1945-52; BSc., 1st Class Honours, 1949-; M.B., Ch.B., 2nd Class Honours, 1952-; M.D. Distinction, Leeds, 1955-; F.R.C.S., England, 1955-. *Appointments:* House Officer, Senior House Officer, Registrar, General Infirmary Leeds, 1952-58; Lecturer Anatomy and Surgery, University of Leeds, 1958-65; Registrar, Senior Registrar, Robert Jones and Agnes Hunt Orthopaedic Hospital, Oswestry, England, 1965-68; Professor of Orthopaedics, Institute of Orthopaedics, University of London, Honorary Consultant Surgeon, Royal National Orthopaedic Hospital, London, 1968-72; Professor of Human Morphology and Experimental Orthopaedics, University of Nottingham, Honorary Consultant in Orthopaedics, Nottinghamshire Area Health Authority, 1974-. *Memberships:* Honorary Secretary, British Orthopaedic Research Society Association 1974-77; British Orthopaedic Research Society Association; British Association of Clinical Anatomists Council; British Scoliosis Society; International Society of Orthopaedic Surgery and Traumatology; Society for Human Biology; Anatomical Society; *Publications:* Numerous publications on: Congenital Anomalies, The Kidney, Lymphoid Tissue, transplantation (Skin & Bone), Osteoarticular allografting, Scoliosis, Perthes' Disease, Burns, Acrylic Bone Cement in Orthopaedic Surgery and General Orthopaedics. *Honours:* Chairman, Committee on Acrylic Cement in Orthopaedic Surgery, Department of Health and Social Security, 1971-73; Chair endowed by Action Research for the Crippled Child, 1974-; MacMurray Lecturer, University of Liverpool, 1976-. Gold Medal Lecturer, Oswestry, 1977-. *Hobbies:* Family, Local History, Church Architecture, Economics. *Address:* 63 Rodney Road, West Bridgford, Nottingham NG2 6JH.

BUSHARA, John Bunyan, b. 11 Sept. 1937, Mbarara, Ankole, Uganda. Teacher and Conservationist. m. Ruth Zerida Kabajumba, 17 July 1965, 4 sons, 2 daughters. *Education:* School Certificate 1st Class, Nyakasura School, 1955-; BSc., Honours, London University, (Obtained at Makerere University College), 1961-; Diploma in Education, 2nd Grade, Makerere University College, 1962-; Certificate in Tourism Studies, Tel Aviv, Israel, 1964-. *Appointments:* Biology Master & Head of Biology Department, Ntare School, 1962-64; Assistant Secretary, Ministry of Tourism, 1964-66; Tourism Attache Uganda High Commission in London, 1966-; Assistant Secretary, Ministry of Tourism, 1966-69; Senior Game Warden Ministry of Animal Industry, 1969-73; Deputy Director, Uganda National Parks, 1973-75; Chief Game Warden, 1975-79 to Date; Acting Permanent Secretary Ministry of Lands and Natural Resources, 1979-. *Memberships:* Former Chief Commissioner of Scouts, Uganda, 1973-75; Vice-Chairman Wildlife Clubs of Uganda, 1978-; Survival Service Commission of International Union for Conservation of Nature; Consultant on Commission of National Parks and Protected areas of IUCN-; Trustee of Uganda National Parks Board; National Museum and Historical Monuments Committee; East African Wildlife Society (Ex-officio). *Hobbies:* Reading, Scouting, Squash, Swimming, Gardening, Farming. *Address:* P.O. Box 4, Entebbe, Uganda.

BUSHELL, John Christopher Wyndowe, b. 27 Sept. 1919, Harrow, UK. Diplomat. m. Theodora Senior, 1 son, 1 stepson, 1 stepdaughter. *Education:* Winchester College; Clare College, Cambridge. *Appointments:* War Service RAF, 1939-45; HM Diplomatic Service, 1945, Served in Moscow, Rome, Baghdad, Ankara, Berlin; HM Ambassador, Saigon, 1974-75; HM Ambassador, Islamabad, 1976-79. *Memberships:* Travellers Club, London. *Honours:* CMG, 1970. *Hobbies:* Various. *Address:* 19 Bradbourne Street, London SW6, England.

BUTLER, Adam Courtauld, b. 11 Oct. 1931, London. Member of Parliament, Government Minister. m. Felicity Molesworth-St. Aubyn, 21 Oct. 1955, 2 sons, 1 daughter. *Education:* Eton College, 1944-49; B.A. History Economics, Pembroke College, Cambridge, 1951-54. *Appointments:* Courtaulds Limited, 1955-73; Member of Parliament, 1970-; Minister of State, Department of Industry, 1979-; Minister of State for Northern Ireland, 1981. *Memberships:* National Farmers Union. *Publications:* Principal Editor, One Nation at Work. *Address:* House of Commons, London, England.

BUTLER, Esmond Unwin, b. 13 July 1922, Wawanesa. Secretary to the Governor General. m. 19 Mar. 1960, 1 son, 1 daughter. *Education:* Weston Collegiate; University of Toronto; University of Geneva; Institute of International Studies, Geneva, Switzerland, with B.A., License ès sciences politiques. *Appointments:* Journalist, United Press, Geneva, Switzerland, 1950-51; Assistant Secretary General, International Union of Official Travel Organisations, Geneva, 1951-52; Information Officer, Department Trade & Commerce, Ottawa, 1953-Information Officer, Department Health & Welfare, 1954-; Assistant to the Secretary to the Governor General, Government House, Ottawa, 1955-58; Assistant Press Secretary to The Queen, London, England, 1958-59; Acting Press Secretary to The Queen, Royal Tour of Canada, 1959-; Secretary to the Governor General, Ottawa, 1959-; Secretary General of the Order of Canada, 1967-; Secretary General Order of Military Merit, 1972-. *Memberships:* Zeta Psi Fraternity; Advisory Board of The Salvation Army. *Honours:* Commander of the Royal Victorian Order; Commander Brother, Order of St. John of Jerusalem. *Hobbies:* Fishing, Shooting, Collecting Canadiana, Skiing. *Address:* Rideau Cottage, Government House, Ottawa, Ontario, K1A 0A1.

BUTLER, Frederick Edward Robin, b. 3 Jan. 1938, Poole, England. Treasury Official. m. Gillian Lois Galley, 15 Aug. 1962, 1 son, 2 daughters. *Education:* Orley Farm School, Harrow, 1946-51; Harrow School, 1951-56; B.A. Literae Humaniores, University College Oxford, 1957-61. *Appointments:* H.M. Treasury, 1961-; Private Secretary to Financial Secretary, 1964-65; Secretary to Budget Committee, 1965-69; Seconded to Bank of England, 1969-; Seconded to Cabinet Office, Member of Central Policy Review Staff, 1971-72; Private Secretary to Prime Minister, 1972-75-; Under Secretary, General Expenditure Policy Group, Treasury, 1977-80; Principal Establishment Officer, H.M. Treasury, 1980-. *Memberships:* Vincents Club, Oxford; Anglo-Belgian Club. *Hobbies:* Sports; Opera; Ballet. *Address:* 28 Half Moon Lane, London, SE24 9HU.

BUTLER, Michael Dacres, b. 27 Feb. 1927, Nairobi, Kenya. Diplomat. m. Margaret Ann Clyde, 3 Feb. 1951, 2 sons, 2 daughters. *Education:* Exhibitioner, Winchester College, UK, 1940-45; Honours degree in Politics, Philosophy, Economics, Trinity College, Oxford, UK, 1948-50. *Appointments:* Foreign Office: Western Department, 1950-52, South East Asia Department, 1958-61; UK Mission to the UN., New York, USA, 1952-56; Embassies in: Baghdad, 1956-58, Paris, France, 1961-65, Washington, USA, 1971-72; Foreign and Commonwealth Office, 1965-68; UK Mission, Geneva, 1968-70; Fellow, Center for International Affairs, Harvard University, USA, 1970-71; Head of European Integration Department, Foreign and Commonwealth Office, 1972-74; Assistant Under-Secretary, 1974-76, Deputy Under-Secretary, Economic Affairs, 1976-79, Permanent Representative, 1979-, EEC, Brussels. *Memberships:* Council, 1977-80, Oriental Ceramic Society. *Honours:* CMG., 1975; KCMG., 1980. *Hobbies:* Collecting Chinese porcelain; Skiing; Tennis. *Address:* Avenue Henri Pirenne 21, 1180 Brussels, Belgium.

BUTLER, Richard Edmund, b. 25 Mar. 1926, Melbourne, Victoria, Australia. Deputy Secretary-General of International Telecommunication Union. m. Patricia Carmel Kelly, 18 Aug. 1951, 3 sons, 2 daughters. *Education:* Diploma Public Administration Qualified Public Account. *Appointments:* From 1941 to 1968 various posts in the Australian Post Office, including Chief Industrial Officer, 1955-60; Executive Officer-Deputy Assistant Director-General, 1960-68; in absentia Secretary, and later Director Corporate Planning Directorate, Australian Telecommunications Commission; current post Deputy Secretary-General of International Telecommunication Union, elected 1968-, re-elected 1973-. *Memberships:* A.A.S.A., R.I.P.A. C.T.A., Melbourne; Royal Commonwealth Society; Royal Overseas League, London. *Hobbies:* Reading, Golf. *Address:* 222B route d'Hermance, 1246 Corsier (GE), Switzerland.

BUTLER, Stuart Thomas, b. 4 July 1926, Naracoorte, South Australia. Scientist. m. Miriam Stella Silver, 11 Dec. 1948, 2 sons, 1 daughter. *Education:* University of Adelaide, BSc., 1945-, BSc 1st Class Honours, 1946-, MSc., 1947-; PhD., Birmingham University, England, 1951-; DSc., Australian National University, 1961-. *Appointments:* Research Associate, Cornell University, USA., 1951-53; Senior Research Fellow, Australian National University, 1953-54; Reader in Physics, University of Sydney, 1954-59; Professor of Physics, (Theoretical), University of Sydney, 1959-77; Director, Australian Atomic Energy Commission Research Establishment, Lucas Heights, New South Wales, Australia, 1977-. *Memberships:* Fellow Australian Academy of Science; Fellow, Australian Institute of Physics; Fellow of Senate University of Sydney. *Publications:* 62 Scientific Publication in International Journals; 8 Scientific Books; 20 Science Books for High School Students. *Honours:* Thomas Ranken Lyle Medal, 1966-; Tom W Bonner Prize, 1977-. *Hobby:* Sport. *Address:* 6 The Grove, Mosman, New South Wales, 2088, Australia.

BUTLER, William Henry (Harry), b. 25 Mar. 1930, Subiaco, Western Australia. Conservation Consultant; Naturalist. m. Margaret Alice Elliott, 10 Sept. 1969, 2 sons, 1 daughter. *Education:* Teachers Certificate, Claremont Teachers College, Western Australia, 1953; Courtesy Doctorate, Western Washington State College, USA, 1966; Hon. Fellow, Environmental Science, Griffith University, Queensland, Australia, 1980. *Appointments:* Fitter and Turner, SECWA, 1946-51; Education Department, Western Australia, 1954-62; Self employed as a Conservation Consultant, 1963-. *Memberships:* member of numerous associations including: Honorary Wildlife Officer, Department of Fisheries and Wildlife, W.A., 1957-; Advisory Board State Pollution Control Commission, NSW., Moomba/Sydney Pipeline, 1973; Uranium Advisory Council, 1978-; Adviser to WA Offshore Operators Committee, 1978-79; Honorary Life member, Busselton Wildlife and Nature Society, 1979-; Council member, Energy Advisory Council, WA, 1980-. *Publications:* numerous publications including: Articles: Growth of the Blackboy, 1947; Living off the Land, 1950; First Record of Spurwing Plover for Western Australia, 1957; A Record of an Invertebrate preying on a Vertebrate, 1970; Breeding Behaviour in the Atherine Fish Craterocephalus, 1979; Books: Australian Outback Cooking, 1971; Barrow Island, 1975; Food, in Help Yourselves: an anthology of contemporary writing on food, 1979; Looking at the Wild, 1980. *Creative Works:* Numerous films including: Outback, 1968; Looking at the Wild, 1979; Harry Butler's Tasmania, 1980; Things aren't what they seem to be and Isolated Island, 1980. *Honours:* Numerous honours including: MBE., 1970; Gold Sammy Australian Television and Film Awards for Best Male TV Personality, 1977; Penguin Award, In the Wild—The Killers, Series, Best Documentary Programme, 1977; Australian of the Year, 1979; Citizen of the Year, The Professions Category, 1980; CBE., 1980. *Hobbies:* Gardening; Photography; Woodworking; Skin diving; Bird watching. *Address:* Wildflower Nursery, Wanneroo Road, Wanneroo, Western Australia 6065.

BUTTERFIELD, Cyril Sinclair, b. 23 June, 1916, Pembroke, Bermuda. Clergyman. m. Helen Louise, 9 Apr. 1942, 3 sons. *Education:* B.Th., College and Seminary, 1947-51; Hon.DD., Payne Seminary, Wilberforce, Ohio, USA, 1972. *Appointments:* Ministry, Bermuda, 1951-; Presiding Elder of Bermuda Conference, African Methodist Episcopal Church, 1969-; Justice of the Peace, 1981. *Memberships:* Past President, Secretary, Treasurer, Bermuda Ministerial Association; Charter member, YMCA and Kiwanis Club; Chairman, LCCA; Served on Several Government Boards. *Honours:* Queen's Certificate and Badge of Honour, 1972; several Church Awards. *Hobbies:* Crossword Puzzles; Working with the Youth; Social and Welfare Organizations. *Address:* PO Box 133, Lighthouse Road, St. David's, Bermuda.

BUTTERFIELD, William, b. 10 Apr. 1934, Sunderland, England. Company Director. m. 6 July 1957, 2 sons. *Education:* HNC., Mech., Sunderland Technical College, UK, 1957; Assoc. MIGasE., Newcastle Rutherford Technical College, UK, 1959. *Appointments:* Junior Clerk, 1949-51; Technical Assistant, 1951-59; Project Engineer, 1959-60; Project Manager, 1960-62; ARGA Agent, 1962-66; Gas Conversion Manager, 1966-69; Construction Manager, Australia, 1969-73; Operations Manager, 1973-78; Director, 1978-81; Managing Director, 1981-. *Memberships:* Chartered Engineer, 1968; Chartered Fuel Technician, 1974; Institute Energy, UK, 1974; Fellow, Australian Institute Energy, 1975; Institute Engineers, Australia, 1979. *Publications:* Some Trade Papers Conference Presentations. *Hobbies:* Rotary; Golf; Tennis; Music. *Address:* 232 Warrimoo Avenue, St Ives, New South Wales 2075, Australia.

BUTTERFIELD, William John, (Sir), b. 28 Mar. 1920, Birmingham, England. Physician; Educationalist. m. Isabel Ann Foster Kennedy, 16 Mar. 1950, 3 sons, 1 daughter. *Education:* Exeter College, Oxford, UK, 1939-45; Rockefeller Scholar, Johns Hopkins, Baltimore, USA, 1942-44. *Appointments:* External Staff, Medical Research Council; Professor of Experimental Medicine, Professor of Medicine, Goys Hospital, London, UK; Vice-Chancellor, University of Nottingham, UK; Regius Professor of Physic, University of Cambridge, UK. *Memberships:* Fellow, Royal College of Physicians; Fellow, Royal Society of Arts; Association of Physicians of GB; Overseas Fellow, American College of Physicians; Hon. Fellow, New York Academy of Sciences; Athenaeum,UK; Vincents, Oxford; Pitt, Cambridge. *Publications:* Over 100 articles, books, reviews in the biomedical and educational literature. *Honours:* OBE., 1953; Rock Carling Fellowship, 1968; Knight Bachelor, 1978. *Hobbies:* Cricket; Real tennis; Talking. *Address:* Mastors Lodge, Downing College, Cambridge, England.

BUTTIGIEG, Anton, b. 1912. President of the Republic of Malta. m. (1) Carmen Bezzina, 1944, (2) Connie Scicluna, 1953, (3) Margery Patterson, 1975, 2 sons, 1 daughter. *Education:* St Aloysius College, Malta; BA, LL.D., University of Malta. *Appointments:* Notary Public, 1939-41; Advocate, 1941-71; Police Inspector, 1942-44; Law Reporter and Leader Writer for Times of Malta, 1944-48; Acting Magistrate, 1955; Editor, Voice of Malta, 1959-70; Member of Parliament, 1955-76; President, Malta Labour Party, 1959-61; Deputy Leader, 1962-76; Delegate to Malta Constitutional Conferences, London, 1958, 1964; Representative to Consultative Assembly, Council of Europe, 1967-71, Vice-President, 1967-68; Deputy Prime Minister, 1971-76; Minister of Justice and Parly. Affairs, 1971-76; President, Republic of Malta, 1976-. *Memberships:* Academy of the Maltese Language. *Publications:* Lyric Poetry: Mill-Gallarija ta' Zghoziti, 1945; Fanali bil-Leil, 1949; Qasba mar-Rih, 1968; Fl-Arena, 1970; Ballati Maltin, 1973; Il-Ghania tas-Sittin, 1975; Collected Poems, 1978; and various selections translated into other languages; Autobiography, Toni tal-Bahri, 1978; L-ghazla tat-triq, 1980; Fil-morsa tal-gwerra, 1981. *Honours:* First Prize for Poetry, Government of Malta, 1971; Guze' Muscat Azzopardi Prize for Poetry, 1972; Silver Plaque for Poetry, Circolo Culturale Rhegium Julii of Reggio Calabria, 1975; International Prize of Mediterranean Culture for Poetry, Centro di Cultura Mediterranea, Palermo, 1977; First Prize and Special Diploma for Poetry, 1979; First Prize of the Malta Literary Award, 1979. *Address:* Villa Mnara, 65 Annibale Preca Street, Lija, Malta.

BUTTROSE, Ita Clare, b. 17 Jan. 1942, Sydney, Australia. Company Director & Editor-in-Chief. m. Alasdair MacDonald, 20 Dec. 1963 (Divorced 1977-) 1 s, 1 d. *Education:* Dover Heights High School, Sydney, Australia. *Appointments:* Women's Editor Daily Telegraph & Sunday Telegraph, 1970-; Founding Editor, Cleo Magazine, 1972-; Board, Australian Consolidated Press Ltd., 1974-; Editor, The Australian Women's Weekly, 1975-; Editor-in-Chief, The Australian Women's Weekly & Cleo, 1976-; Publisher, ACP Women's Magazines, 1977-; Board, Murray Leisure Group Ltd., 1978-; Resigned from Australian Consolidated Press Ltd., 1980-; Joined News Limited, Editor-in-Chief, The Daily Telegraph & The Sunday Telegraph. Appointed to Board, News Limited, 1981-. *Memberships:* The Australian Japan Foundation; The Executive Committee of the New South Wales Bicentennial Council; The Board of the James MacGrath Foundation; The Advisory Board of the Girl Guides Association of Australia; The New South Wales Chapter of the Company Directors Association of Australia; The National Trust of Australia; The Australian Opera Co., Ltd.; Friends of Vaucluse House; The American Club; White City Tennis Club; Fellow of The Institute of Directors in Australia; Fellow of The Australian Institute of Management, New South Wales Division; Fellow of Society of Senior Executives; Councillor of The Royal Blind Society of New South Wales. *Honours:* O.B.E., 1979-. *Hobbies:* Tennis, Opera, Ballet, Reading. *Address:* 2 Holt Street, Sydney, New South Wales, 2000, Australia.

BUTTROSE, Stroma, b. 20 Oct. 1929, Adelaide, South Australia. Commissioner Legal. *Education:* Bachelor of Arts 1955; Bachelor of Arts (Honours in Geography) University of Adelaide 1956; Master of Town Planning 1972. *Appointments:* Common Law Clerk, Thomson, Buttrose, Ross and Lewis, Barristers and Solicitors 1949; Secretary, Department of Architecture, School, of Mines 1952-54; Geography Teacher St. Peters Collegiate School, North Adelaide, 1954-56; Tutor, Geography, University of Adelaide 1955-56; Geography Teacher, The Wilderness School, Medindie 1956; Planning Officer State Planning Office 1957-73; Tutor in Town Planning, South Australia Institute of Technology 1966-69; Commissioner, Planning Appeal Board since 1973. *Memberships:* Eight Educational Councils, Federations and Associations; Five Planning; Four

Geography; Five Conservation; Eight Writing; Three Books; Ten Musical; Five Art & Craft; Five Animals & Plants; etc. *Publications:* Various poems in numerous publications and public poetry readings of own poems 1952-; The Future of the Adelaide Hills, 1972; City Planning in Australia 1975. *Honours:* Rhodes Prize, 1947; Club Letters, university sport, 1950 and 1951; First Prize for Poetry, 1953. *Hobbies:* Dance; Music; Writing; Local History; Animals; Plants. *Address:* PO Box 2465, Adelaide, South Australia 5001, Australia.

BUZZARD, Anthony John, b. 9 May, 1941, Australia. Surgeon. m. Gaye Lorraine Dunlop, 7 Aug. 1971, 1 son. *Education:* Melbourne Grammar School; M.B.,B.S. Melbourne University, 1960-65; F.R.A.C.S., 1971-; F.R.C.S., 1972-. *Appointments:* Honorary Lecturer, Monash University Department of Surgery, Melbourne; Visiting Lecturer Melbourne University Department of Anatomy. *Memberships:* Corresponding Fellow, British Society Clinical Anatomist; Visiting Examiner, Melbourne University Department of Anatomy; Board of Examiners Royal Australisian College of Surgery; Council, Trinity College University of Melbourne; Fellow of International College of Surgeons. *Publications:* Various contributions to Surgical Journals. *Hobby:* Snow Skiing. *Address:* 16 Dixon St. Malvern, Victoria, Australia.

BWATWA, Yosiah Dag Magembe, (Dr.), b. 20 Dec. 1939, Musoma, Tanzania. University Professor. m. 1 son. *Education:* Diploma in Education, 1967-; B.A., 1972-; M.A., 1973-; Ed.D., 1975-. *Appointments:* Secondary School Teacher, 1965-75; University Teaching, 1975-. *Memberships:* Tanzania Adult Education Association; African Adult Education Association; Unified Teaching Service; Tanzania Society; International Council of Adult Education. *Publications:* Publications in Illiteracy, Concepts of Adult Education, Planning & Administration of Adult Education and in Psychology and Methods in Adult Education. *Honours:* Captain, Regional Soccer Team in Tanzania, 1965-69; Captain, Goshen College Soccer Team, 1971-; All American Soccer Team, 1970-; Most Valuable Soccer Conference Team, 1971-; All State Soccer Team, Indiana, U.S.A., 1971-. *Hobbies:* Sports, Soccer, Volleyball, Music, Gardening. *Address:* University of Dar-es-Salaam, P.O. Box 35048, Dar-es-Salaam, Tanzania.

BYATT, Hugh Campbell, b. 27 Aug. 1927, Edinburgh, Scotland. HM Diplomatic Service. m. Fiona Mary McKenzie, 19 June 1954, 2 sons, 1 daughter. *Education:* MA., New College, Oxford, UK, 1945, 1948-51. *Appointments:* HMOCS., Nigeria, 1952-57; Commonwealth Relations Office, 1957-60; Subsequently served India; Cabinet Office, Portugal; London; Consul General, Mozambique; Diplomatic Service Inspectorate; Royal College of Defence Studies, 1976; Deputy High Commissioner, Kenya; First British Ambassador, People's Republic of Angola, 1978-; British Ambassador to Portugal, 1981. *Memberships:* Travellers Club; Royal Ocean Racing Club; Leander, Henley-on-Thames Club. *Honours:* CMG. *Hobbies:* Sailing; Fishing; Gardening. *Address:* c/o The Foreign and Commonwealth Office, Downing Street, London, SW1, England.

BYATT, Ronald Archer Campbell, b. 14 Nov. 1930, England. Diplomatic Service. m. Ann Brereton Sharpe, 1954, 1 son, 1 daughter. *Education:* Gordonstoun; New College, Oxford; King's College, Cambridge. *Appointments:* RNVR, 1949-50; Colonial Admin. Service, Nyasaland 1955-58; HM Foreign Service 1959; Foreign Office 1959; Havana 1961; FO 1963; UK Mission to UN, NY 1966; Kampala 1970; Head of Rhodesia Department, FCO 1972-75; Visiting Fellow, Glasgow University 1975-76; Counsellor and Head of Chancery, UK Mission to UN, NY 1977-79; Assistant Under Secretary, FCO 1979-80; High Commissioner in Salisbury 1980-. *Memberships:* United Oxford and Cambridge University; Leander, Henley on Thames. *Honours:* CMG 1980. *Hobbies:* Sailing; Boating; Bird-watching; Gardening. *Address:* c/o Foreign and Commonwealth Office, London, SW1, England.

BYER, David, b. 5 Sept. 1946, Montreal, Quebec, Canada. Barrister and Solicitor. m. Barbara Joan, 23 July 1971, 2 sons. *Education:* BSc., Sir George Williams University, Canada, 1969; BA., (cum laude), University of Montreal, Canada, 1970; BCL., 1973, LL.B.,

1974, McGill University, Canada; MA., (in progress), Carleton University. *Appointments:* Private Practice; Legal Counsel, Campeau Corporation; Executive Officer, Surety Management Group; Secretary and Legal Counsel, Digital Equipment of Canada Limited. *Memberships:* Law Society of Upper Canada; Licensed Mortgage Broker; Ontario, 1979; Board of Directors, United Way of Ottawa; Board of Directors, Catholic Family Service; Board of Directors, Centre. *Hobbies:* Skiing; Tennis; Golf; Photography. *Address:* 992 Plante Drive, Ottawa, Ontario, Canada, K1V 9E6.

BYNOE, Jacob Galton, b. 8 May 1933, Berbice, Guyana. University Teacher. m. Janet Brenezes Grant, 2 Aug. 1975, 2 sons. *Education:* B A London, External First Division, 1957-; Diploma Education, University of the West Indies, 1959-; M.A. Education, 1964-; Ed.D., University of British Columbia, 1972-. *Appointments:* Teacher, Tutorial High School, Georgetown, Guyana, 1951-58; Guyana Teachers Training College, 1959-64; Lecturer, University of the West Indies, 1964-65, 1967-68; Senior Lecturer, University of Guyana, 1970-; Principal, College of the Bahamas, 1979-81. *Publications:* Articles on Education, including: Education for Political Socialisation; A Guyana Case Study, Equality and High School Opportunity, 1972-; Problems Strategies and Objectives, Towards a Programme of Politcal Education, 1977-. *Honours:* British Council Fellowship, 1973-; University of British Columbia Fellowship, 1968, 1969-; Commonwealth Scholarship, Canadian Award, 1963-; U.W.I. Fellowship, 1963-; Government of Guyana Teachers Scholarship, 1959-. *Hobbies:* Dancing, Draughts, Reading Political Literature. *Address:* University of Guyana, Box 841, Georgetown, Guyana.

BYRNE, David Edward, b. 20 Ja. 1951, Sydney, N.S.W. Australia. Lecturer. *Education:* Associate Diploma (Speech and Drama),1972-; Philosophy Certificate, Augustinian College, 1972-; L.A.C.M., (Speech and Drama), 1979-; F.A.C.M., (Public Speaking), 1979-, Australian College of Music, B.A. University of Queensland, 1975-. *Appointments:* English Master, Villanova College, Brisbane, Australia, 1971-72; History Master, San Sisto College, Brisbane, Australia, 1974-; Member of Parliament, Queensland Legislative Assembly, Australia, 1974-77; Lecturer in Communications, Queensland Policy Academy, 1978-80; Director, Australian College of Human Studies, 1980-. *Memberships:* Commonwealth Parliamentary Association; Chairman, Queensland Council of Youth Associations; Patron, Carina Galleries, Queensland; Secretary-Treasurer, Australian Breeders Association, 1973-74; Honorary member, Lions International. *Publications:* Harmony in Becoming (Philosopy), Australia under Challenge, (Political Manifesto), Imitations (Book of Poetry). *Hobbies:* Reading, Writing, Debating, Horse-riding, surfing, Athletics, Travel. *Address:* 11 Glindemann Drive, Holland Park, 4121, Queensland, Australia.

C

CABRAAL, Nivard Ajith Leslie, b. 14 Dec. 1954, Tangalle, Sri Lanka. Chartered Accountant. m. Roshini Sunethra, 5 Feb. 1981. *Education:* G.C.E. Advanced Level, Distinctions in Physics, Applied & Pure Mathematics & Credit in Chemistry, University of London, 1970-; First Examination in Laws, University of Sri Lanka, 1978-; Completed Examinations of the Institute of Cost & Management Accountants, England, 1976-. *Appointments:* Finance Manager, Secretary, The Cargo Boat Despatch Co., Ltd., 1977-79; Director, Sri Lanka State Trading (Textile) Corporation, Salu-Sala, 1979-; Director, Cargo Boat Development Co., Ltd., 1981-; Financial Consultant, The Cargo Boat Despatch Group of Companies, 1979-; General Manager, Renuka Hotels Ltd., 1979-. *Memberships:* President, Chartered Accountants Students Society, 1975-; Institute of Chartered Accountants, Sri Lanka, 1976. *Honours:* Institute of Chartered Accountants, Final Examination, Partnership ·& Company Law Prize, Mercantile Law Prize, 1976-; Institute of Cost & Management Accountants Part III Examination, 3rd in Accountancy 2, 1974-. *Hobbies:* Philately, Music. *Address:* 146/5, Havelock Road, Colombo, 5, Sri Lanka.

CABUTEY-ADODOADJI, Edmund, b. 18 July 1945, Akuse, Ghana. Bookshop Manager, Librarian. m. Victoria Kofilotie, 20 Dec. 1977, 3 sons. *Education:* B.L.S., (A. Bello Nigeria), 1975-; P.G.C.E. (Cape Coast), 1977-; Certificate in Bookshop Management, London, 1978-. *Appointments:* Library Assistant with Ghana Library Board, British Council, University of Cape Coast, 1963-72; Assistant Librarian, University of Cape Coast, 1975-; Bookshop Manager, University of Cape Coast, 1977-. *Memberships:* Ghana Library Association; Ghana University Booksellers Group; West African University Booksellers Association; University Tennis Club. *Hobbies:* Gardening, Tennis, Music. *Address:* 144 Farm Road, Univesity Campus, U.C.C. Cape Coast.

CACCIA, Harold Anthony, b. 21 Dec. 1905, India. Chairman, ITT (UK) Ltd., m. Anne Catherine Barstow, 1932, 1 son, 2 daughters. *Education:* Eton; Trinity College, Oxford. Laming Travelling Fellowship; Queen's College, Oxford, 1928-, Honorary Fellow, Trinity College, 1963-; Honorary Fellow Queen's College, 1974-; M.A. *Appointments:* Diplomatic Service: from 1929-65; British High Commissioner in Austria, 1959-54; British Ambassador, Austria, 1951-54; British Ambassador, Washington, 1956-61; Permanent Under-Secretary of State Foreign Office, 1962-65; Head of H.M. Diplomatic Service, 1964-65, retired; Chairman, Standard Telephones & Cables, 1968-79; Chairman, ITT(UK) Ltd., 1979-; Director, Prudential Assurance Co., F & C Eurotrust; Orion Bank (Chairman, 1973 74); Provist of Eton 1965-77; *Memberships:* President MCC, 1973-74; Lord Prior of the Order of St. John of Jerusalem, 1969-80; President, Anglo-Austrian Society; Chairman The David Davies Institute of International Studies; MCC Committee; Athenaeum Club; All England Lawn Tennis and Croquet Club; Metropolitan Club New York; Grillions; Pitt Club. *Honours:* C.M.G., 1945-; K.C.M.G., 1950-; K.C.V.O., 1957-; G.C.M.G., 1959-; G.C.V.O., 1961-; Cr. Baron of Abernant, 1965-, Life Peer; G.C.St.J. *Address:* 1 Chester Place, Regent's Park, London NW1 4NB.

CADMAN, Alan Glyndwr, b. 26 July 1937, Sydney, N.S.W. Australia. Member of House of Representatives, Australian Parliament. m. Judith Pattinson, 1 Apr. 1961, 3 sons. *Education:* Certificate of Agriculture, University of N.S.W., Australia, 1958-. *Appointments:* Jackaroo, 1955-; Overseer, 1959-; Manager, Company Director, 1967-; Entered House of Representatives, 1974-; Re-elected to House of Representatives, 1975-,1977,1980; Parlimentary Secretary to the Prime Minister, 1981. *Memberships:* Chairman of House of Representatives Select Committee on Specific Learning Difficulties; Parliamentary Committee on Public Accounts, 1978-81; Chairman Chairmen's Committee, 1978-81; Chairman Parties' Committee on Housing, Construction and Transport, 1979-81; Industry and Commerce Committee, 1978; Government Parties' Parliamentary Reform Committee; Advisory Council for Intergovernmental Relations, 1981. *Honours:* Japan Foundation Guest, 1966-; Leader, Australian Delegation to Greece, 1976-; Guest of British

Government 1979-, Emissary to Caribbean for Commonwealth Heads of Government Conference 1981. *Hobbies:* Sailing, Painting, Tennis. *Address:* 11 Mansfield Road, Galston, N.S.W. 2159, Australia.

CAINES, John, b. 13 Jan. 1933, Sherborne, Dorset, England. Civil Servant. m. 28 Sept. 1963, 1 son, 2 daughters. *Education:* Sherborne Preparatory School, 1940-45; Westminster School, 1945-50; Christ Church, Oxford, 1951-55; B.A. 1st Class Honours Modern Language, 1955-; M.A. 1958-. *Appointments:* Assistant Principal Ministry of Supply, 1957-60; Assistant Private Secretary to Minister of Aviation, 1960-61; Principal, Ministry of Aviation, 1961-64; Civil Air Attache in Middle East, 1964-66; Manchester Business School, 1967-; Secretary, Commission on Third London Airport, 1968-71; Assistant Secretary, Department of Trade & Industry, 1971-72; Principal Private Secretary to Secretary of State for Trade & Industry, 1972-74; Under-Secretary, Department of Trade, 1974-77; Secretary of National Enterprise Board, 1977-79; Member & Deputy Chief Executive N.E.B., 1979-80; Deputy Secretary, Department of Trade and Chief Executive British Overseas Trade Board, 1980-. *Address:* 19 College Road, London, SE21 7BG.

CAIRNS, Richard Blakely, b. 9 Apr. 1934, Los Angeles, California, USA. President Hallmark Cards of Canada. m. Hazel Anna Campbell, 15 Nov. 1956, 1 son, 1 daughter. *Education:* Queen's University, Chartered Accountant, 1961-. *Appointments:* Arthur Anderson & Co., Senior Manager, Chartered Accountants, 1960-71; Chief Financial Officer, 1971-75; President, Hallmark Cards, 1976-. *Memberships:* Chairman, Greeting Card Association of Canada; Past-President Canadian Water Ski Association; Granite Club; Board of Trade. *Honours:* Ontario Water Ski Champion, 1970,71,72 & 73-; Ontario Discus Champion, 1953-. *Hobbies:* Golf, Skiing, Water Skiing, Squash, Reading, Travelling. *Address:* R.R.#1, Uxbridge, Ontario, Canada, LOC1KO.

CAIRNS, William James, b. 13 Mar. 1936, Cawdor, Nairn, Scotland. Environmental Planner. m. Barbara Mary Russell, 3 Oct. 1962, 1 son, 1 daughter. *Education:* Diploma LD University of Durham; MC P., Massachusetts Institute of Technology. *Appointments:* Lanark County Council Department of Town and Country Planning, 1960-62; Glasgow Corporation Department of City Planning, 1962-; Assistant Professor, University of Georgia Athens, Georgia, 1962-64; Whitney Fellow, Massachusetts Institute of Technology, ; New City Planning and Design Team Head, Craigavon Development Commission, Northern Ireland, 1966-68; Senior Associate, Land Use Consultants, London, 1968-72; W J Cairns and Partners, Planners, Architects and Landscape Architects, Edinburgh, Scotland, 1972-. *Memberships:* Fellow, Landscape Institute London; International Association of Environmental Coordinators; Institute of Petroleum; International Society of City and Regional Planners; Bruntsfield Golfing Society, Einburgh; Scottish Arts Club. *Publications:* Numerous professional and technical articles and papers in journals. *Honours:* Jonathon Whitney Fellowship for MIT, 1964-66; Research Associate Joint Center Urban Studies, Harvard University and MIT, 1965-66. *Hobbies:* Hill walking, Skiing, Golf, Tennis, Fishing, Gardening, Foreign travel. *Address:* 32 Garscube Terrace, Edinburgh EH12 6BH Scotland.

CAKOBAU, George Kadavulevu, b. 6 Nov. 1911, Fiji. Governor-General, Fiji. m. Lealea Seruwaia Balekiwai, 3 sons, 1 daughter. *Education:* Newington College, Australia; Wanganui Technical College, New Zealand. *Appointments:* Captain Fiji Military Forces, 1939-45; Member of Council of Chiefs, Fiji, 1938-72; Legislative Council, Fiji, 1951-70; Minister for Fijian Affairs & Local Government, 1970-71; Minister Without Portfolio, 1971-72; Governor-General, Fiji, 1973-. *Honours:* OBE, 1953; K.St.J, 1973; GCMG, 1973; GCVD, 1977. *Hobbies:* Rugby; Cricket; Fishing. *Address:* Government House, Suva, Fiji.

CALDER, Donald Malcolm, b. 6 July 1933, Christchurch, New Zealand. Botanist. m. Jane Julia Palmer, 20 Dec. 1958, 1 son, 2 daughters. *Education:* BSc., New Zealand, 1956-; MSc., Canterbury, 1958-; PhD., Wales, 1963-; M.I. Biology, 1963-. *Appointments:* Assistant Lecturer in Botany, Massey University, New Zealand, 1958-60; Research Assistant, Welsh Plant Breeding Station, Aberystwyth, Wales, 1960-63; Senior Scientific Officer, Welsh Plant Breeding Station, 1963-66; Senior Lecture in Botany, University of Melbourne, Australia, 1966-77; Reader in Botany, Melbourne University, 1978-; Chairman of Botany School, University of Melbourne, 1975-79. *Memberships:* Various Professional societies in Britain & Australia; Chairman of the National Parks Advisory Council of Victoria; Victorian National Parks Association (President, 1971-73, 1975-76); Environment Studies Association of Victoria, (President, 1978-79); Melbourne Beefsteak Club. *Publications:* Scientific and semi-popular articles in botany and conservation. *Hobbies:* Enjoyment of the open air, Travel, Creative crafts. *Address:* 146 Waiora Road, Rosanna, Victoria, 3084, Australia.

CALDER (A Canadian Indian Chief of the Nishga Tribe), Frank Arthur, b. 3 Aug. 1915, Nass Harbour, British Columbia, Canada. Consultant, Politician. m. Tamaki, 26 Feb. 1975. *Education:* Graduated, Chilliwack High School, Canada, 1937-; Graduated, Anglican Theological College, University of British Columbia, Canada, 1946-; Degree, Licentiate in Theology. *Appointments:* Commercial Fisherman, B.C. Packers Ltd.; Canadian Indian Association Organiser; Politician, Member Legislative Assembly for 26 Years; Consultant, Domain Consultants. *Memberships:* Founder of the Nishga Tribal Council, 1955-, President 1955-74; Research Director, since 1974-. A Leading Advocate for Government Recognition of Aboriginal Rights in the New Canadian Constitution, 1980-81. *Honours:* First Canadian Indian ever elected to any Canadian Parliament, 1949-; First Canadian Indian ever appointed to a Cabinet Post in any Canadian Parliament, 1972-; Known for famous Calder Case, a Landmark decision of the Supreme Court of Canada on the Nishga Land Claims, 1973-; Or achievement and leadership on behalf of the Indians of British Columbia and Canada honoured with the Indian Hereditary name of Chief Lissims, by the Nishga Nation, 1955-. *Hobby:* Photography. *Address:* 906 Parklands Drive, Victoria, British Columbia, V9A 4L7, Canada.

CALDER, Michael William, b. 27 May 1941, Christchurch, New Zealand. Economist. m. Hilary Joan Grieve, 6 Apr. 1968, 2 sons. *Education:* Christs College, Christchurch, N.Z. 1954-58; Graduated M.Agr.Sc., Lincoln College, University of Canterbury, New Zealand, 1959-66. *Appointments:* Research Officer, N.Z. Meat and Wool Boards Economic Serivvice, Wellington, 1966-70; Research Officer, N.Z. Meat Producers Board, Wellington, 1970-72; Economist, N.Z. Meat Producers Board, London, 1972-75, 1975-80; Assistant General Manager, 1980-. *Memberships:* New Zealand Institute of Agricultural Science. *Hobbies:* Squash, Amateur Photography. *Address:* 61 Wilton Road, Wellington, 5,, New Zealand.

CALLA, Om Prakash Narayan, b. 6 Dec. 1935, Jodhpur, Rajasthan State, India. Engineer. m. Tara, 23 May 1959, 2 sons. *Education:* BSc, Jaswant College, Jodhpur, 1956; BD, 1960, ME, 1961, Birla Engineering College, Pilani, Rajasthan State. *Appointments:* Radar and high power transmitter development Systems, Atomic Engery Establishment, 1962; Development of Rocket borne C-band Radar Tranponder, Incospar, 1964; Member of team to conduct joint study by Incospar and Hughes Aircraft Co., USA, on Indian Domestic Satellite Systems for Television & Telephony; Associated in the preparation of total budget for Site experiment and Augmentation of ESCES for SITE; Microwave Antenna Systems Engineering Group (Maseg), 1970; ISRO as Secretary of MASEG Board and Head of the Electronics Division of MASEG which later became Microwave Division, 1972; Appointed Principal investigator for propagation experiment with Ministry of Communications, Department of Electronics, Wireless Planning Commission and ISRO; Appointed as Principal Scientist for Satellite Microwave Radiometer (SAMIR), 1979; Project Director, for Satellite Telecommunications Experiments Project (STEP), 1977-79; At present, Chairman, Communications Area and Chairman of Apple Payload Coordination Committee at SAC. *Memberships:* Fellow, Institution of Electronics & Telecommunication Engineers, New Delhi; Chairman, local centre of IETE, Ahmedabad; Astronomical Society of India, Hyderabad; Founder President, Biomedical Engineering Society of Gujarat, Ahmedabad. *Publications:* More than 100 contributions. *Honours:* Hari Om Ashram Prerit Vikram Sarabhai Award, 1978. *Hobby:* Music. *Address:* 1 Ahmedabad District, Co-operative

Bank Employees' Society, Dr. Vikram Sarabhai Marg, Abmedabad - 380 015, India.

CALLAGHAN, Allan Robert, b. 24 Nov. 1903, Perthville, New South Wales. Agricultural Consultant. m. (1) Zillah May Sampson 25 Oct. 1928 (Deceased), (2) Doreen Winifred Draper, 12 Nov. 1965, 3 sons, 1 daughter. *Education:* BSc, St Pauls College, University of Sydney, 1921-24; BSC., D.Phil., St Johns College, University of Oxford. *Appointments:* Plant Breeder, NSW, Department of Agriculture, 1928-32; Principal, Roseworthy Agricultural College, S. Australia, 1932-49; Director of Agriculture, Permanent Head, South Australian Department of Agriculture, 1949-59; Commercial Counsellor, Australian Embassy, Washington, DC, 1959-65; Chairman, Australian Wheat Board, 1965-71; Agricultural Consultant, 1972-. *Memberships:* Past President, Australian Institute of Agricultural Service. *Publications:* Co-author, The Wheat Industry in Australia; Two Brochures: Sheep Husbandry & Crop Culture for Post War Training; Numerous publications on agriculture, agronomy and animal husbandry. *Honours:* NSW, Rhodes Scholar, 1925; CMG, 1945; Farrer Medal, 1954; Fellow, AIAS, 1956; Carnegie Travelling Scholarship, 1956; Knight Bachelor, 1972. *Hobby:* Gardening. *Address:* 22 Murray Street, Clapham, South Australia, 5062.

CALLAGHAN, Joseph Clair, b. 21 Feb. 1933, St. Louis, Prince Edward Island, Canada. Engineer. m. 2 sons, 1 daughter. *Education:* Bachelor of Arts (cum laude), St. Dunstan's University, 1953; Engineering Diploma, St. Francis Xavier, 1954; Bachelor of Electrical Engineering (with honours), Nova Scotia Technical College, Halifax, 1956; Master of Science, Massachusetts Institute of Technology, Cambridge, Massachusetts, USA, 1963. *Appointments:* Professor, Engineering, St. Dunstan's University, 1956-58; Teaching and Research Assistant, Massachusetts Institute of Technology, 1958-60; Assistant Professor Electrical Engineering, Nova Scotia Technical College, 1960-66; Consultant Warnock Hersey, Moisture Measurement by Electrical Techniques, 1964; Consultant Computing Devices of Canada, Power Plant Studies for Aircraft, 1965; Visiting Professor, Northern Electrical Research and Development Labratory, Ottawa, Phase Equalization in RAI, 1965; Technical Director Research and Development Programme for Helicopter Hauldown System, Fairey Canada Limited, 1966; Senior Consultant Fairey Canada Limited, Nova Scotia, 1966; Associate Professor Engineering, 1966-69, Chairman, Department of Electrical Engineering, 1968-70, Sir George Williams University; Consultant Du Pont of Canada Limited on Process Control of a Batch Polymerization Process, 1968; Full Professor and Dean of Engineering, 1969-77; Consultant Chemcell on failure of Brown Boveri, 1972; Air Compressor, 1973; Consultant Canadian International Development Agency, French Equatorial Africa, Dahomey, Ivory Coast, Zaire, Niger, 1975; President, Technical University of Nova Scotia, 1977-. *Memberships:* Numerous Societies including: Association of Professional Engineers of Nova Scotia; Order of Engineers of Quebec; American Society of Electrical Engineers; Engineering Institute of Canada; · Institute of Electrical and Electronic Engineers; Chairman, Nova Scotia Educational Computer Network Board; Chairman, Council of University Presidents of Nova Scotia; Province of Nova Scotia Task Force on Research & Technology; Director, NS Tidal Power Corporation. *Publications:* Contributor to various scientific journals and conferences. *Honours:* Fellow, Engineering Institute of Canada, 1980. *Address:* 1334 Barrington Street, Halifax, Nova Scotia.

CALLAGHAN, Leonard James, b. 27 Mar. 1912, Portsmouth, England. Member of Parliament. m. Audrey Elizabeth Moulton, July, 1938, 1 son, 2 daughters. *Appointments:* Tax Officer, Inland Revenue Department, 1929; Assistant Secretary, Inland Revenue Staff Federation, 1936-47; Lieutenant, Royal Navy Volunteer Reserve, 1942; Member of Parliament for Cardiff South East, 1945-; Parliamentary Secretary, Ministry of Transport, 1947-50; Parliamentary and Financial Secretary to the Admiralty, 1950; Opposition, Transport Spokesman, 1951-53; Opposition, Fule & Power Spokesman, 1953-55; Opposition, Colonial Affairs Spokesman, 1956-61; Shadow Chancellor, 1961-64; Chancellor of the Exchequer, 1964; Home Secretary, 1967-70; Shadow Home Secretary, 1970; Opposition Spokesman for Employment, 1971-72; Shadow Foreign Secretary, 1972-74; Secretary of State for Foreign and Commonwealth Affairs, 1974-76; Prime Minister and First Lord of the Treasury & Leader of the Labour Party, 1976; Resigned as Leader of Labour Party, 1980. *Memberships:* President, Advisory Committee on Oil Pollution of the Sea, 1963-; Consultant and Adviser to the Police Federation of England and Wales and to the Scottish Police Federation, 1954-64; President, United Kingdom Pilots Association, 1963-76; Honorary President, International Maritime Pilots Association, 1971-76. *Publications:* A House Divided, 1973. *Honours:* Honorary Freeman of the City of Cardiff, 1974; Honorary Life Fellow, Nuffield College, 1967; Honorary Freeman, City of Sheffield; Honorary Degrees- University of Wales, Sardar Patel University, Gujarat, India; Honorary Bencher of the Inner Temple; Hubert Humphrey Award, 1978; Grand Cross First Class of the Order of Merit of the Federal Republic of Germany, 1979; Honorary LID, University of Birmingham. 1981; Honorary Fellow, Portsmouth Polytechnic, 1981. *Address:* House of Commons, London, SW1A OAA.

CALLANDER, John, b. 30 Jan. 1925, Liverpool, England. Chief Education Officer. m. 18 Apr. 1949, 1 son, 2 daughters. *Education:* London University Institute of Education, T.Certificate, Academic Dip. Ed. MA. *Appointments:* Teacher, Liverpool, 1949-51; HMOCS, Education Officer, Kenya, 1951-63; Chief Education Officer, City of Nairobi, 1963-67; Commonwealth Institute, London, 1968-; Chief Education Officer. *Memberships:* Royal Commonwealth Society, Member of Public Affairs Committee; Chairman, 1975-, The League for the Exchange of Commonwealth Teachers. *Hobbies:* Commonwealth Teacher Exchange; African Affairs; Wine. *Address:* 29 Beauchamp Road, E. Molesey, Surrey, England.

CALLENDER, Bradley Walter, b. 19 Jan. 1944, Nassau, NP, Bahamas. Counsel & Attorney-at-Law. m. Addie E Moree, 7 Nov. 1969, 2 sons, 1 daughter. *Education:* St Francis Xavier College, Nassau, Bahamas, 1951-55; Seaford College, Sussex, England, 1956-60; Davies College, London, England, 1960-62. *Appointments:* Admitted as a Member of the Bahamas Bar Association, 1969; Active Practice at the Bahamas 1969-. *Hobbies:* Boating; Hunting; Fishing. *Address:* PO Box N7117, Nassau, NP, Bahamas.

CALLIL, Alexander Stephen, b. 2 Feb. 1902, Melbourne, Australia. Company Chairman. m. Henriette Marie Haddad, 4 Jan. 1940, 4 daughters. *Education:* Melbourne University. *Appointments:* Entered Family Firm, Latoof & Callil Pty. Ltd. (Founded by Father, 1884), 1924; Managing Director; Chairman; RAAF, World War II. *Memberships:* Victoria Racing Club; Victorian Amateur Turf Club; Moonee Valley Racing Club; Melbourne Cricket Club; Melbourne Football Club; Surrey County Cricket Club. *Hobbies:* Cricket; Horse Racing; World Travel; Reading. *Address:* 59 St. Georges Road, Toorak, Melbourne, Australia.

CALVERT, Barbara Adamson, b. 30 Apr. 1926, Leeds, Yorkshire, England. Barrister at Law. m. 3 Apr. 1948, 1 son, 1 daughter. *Education:* Bsc (Econ.), London University, 1943-45; Member Honourable Society Middle Temple, 1957; Called to Bar, 1959. *Appointments:* Administrative Officer, City & Guilds London Institute, 1961-62; Barrister, 1962-; Part-time Chairman, Industrial Tribunals, 1974-; Appointed Queens Counsel, 1975; Admitted Senior Northern Ireland Bar, 1978; Appointed Recorder of The Crown Court, 1980. *Memberships:* Trustee International Students Trust. *Hobbies:* Gardening; Swimming; Poetry. *Address:* 158 Ashley Gardens, London, SW1P 1HW

CALVERT, Philip James, b. 16 Sept. 1949, Hitchin, Herts, England. Librarian. m. Sylvia Powell, 12 Feb. 1978, 1 son, 1 daughter. *Education:* BA(Hons), History, University of Warwick, 1971; Associate Library Association, 1973. *Appointments:* Luton Public Library, 1971-74; Bedfordshire County Library, 1974-75; Fiji Institute of Technology, Librarian, 1976-78; C.F.T.C. Operational Expert, P.N.G; University of Technology, 1979; Librarian, Goroka Teachers College, University of Papua New Guinea, 1980-. *Memberships:* Library Association; PNG Library Association. *Hobbies:* Travel; Golf. *Address:* Goroka Teachers College, Box 1078 Goroka, Papua, New Guinea.

CAMARA, Assan Musa, b. 1923, Mansajang. Gambian Politician. *Appointments:* Teacher in Government

and Mission schools, 1948-60; Independent member, House of Assembly, 1960-; Ministerial posts held: without Portfolio, 1960; Health and Labour, 1960-62; Education and Social Welfare, 1962-65, 1966-68; Works and Communications, 1965-66; External Affairs, 1968-74; Local government and Lands, 1974-77; Education, Youth and Sports, 1977; Finance and Trade, 1977-79; Vice President of the Gambia, 1973-77, 1978-. *Honours:* Order of the Cedar of Lebanon; Commander, National Order of Senegal, Grand Band; Order of Star of Africa; Grand Cross, Brilliant Star of China. *Address:* Office of the Vice-President, Banjul, The Gambia.

CAMERON, Fiona Jacqueline, b. 27 May 1952, Epsom, Surrey, England. Dental Surgeon. *Education:* Bachelor of Dental Surgery, 1975, University of Newcastle upon Tyne, 1970-75. *Appointments:* General Practice, Cambridge, 1975-77; Senior House Officer, Dental Hospital, Newcastle upon Tyne, 1977-78; General Practice, London, 1978-80; General Practice, Barbados, West Indies, 1980-. *Memberships:* British Dental Association; Barbados Dental Association. *Hobbies:* Squash; Sailing; Swimming; Reading. *Address:* Springham, Sheringham Gardens, Maxwell Christchurch. Barbados, West Indies.

CAMERON, Grant Robert, b. 25 Aug. 1947, Sydney, Australia. Medical Practitioner. m. Treena Del Crompton, 19 Jan. 1974, 2 sons. *Education:* MB, BS, Queensland, 1972; Graduate Diploma in Management (CAIE), 1979. *Appointments:* Resident Medical Officer, Royal Brisbane Hospital, 1972; Medical Officer, HMAS Supply, 1973; Medical Superintendent, General Hospital, Manus Island, Papua, New Guinea, 1974-76; Assistant Medical Superintendent, The Prince Charles Hospital, 1976 *Memberships:* Executive Secretary, Queensland State Government Co-ordinating Committee on Child Abuse; Executive Secretary, Queensland Health Department, Medical & Surgical Equipment Committees; British Institute of Management; Fellow, Australian Institute of Management; Executive, Private Hospitals Association, Queensland. *Hobbies:* Piper in the City of Brisbane Pipe Band; Squash; Tennis; Gardening. *Address:* 311 Kitchener Road, Stafford 4053, Brisbane, Queensland, Australia.

CAMERON, Ian George Dewar, b. 4 June 1929, Brisbane, Australia. Consulting Engineer. m. June Prentice Meek, 17 Feb. 1955, 1 son, 3 daughters. *Education:* Bachelor of Engineering (lst class honours), Queensland University, 1951. *Appointments:* Queensland Main Roads Department, 1951-60; Partner, Cameron McNamara & Ptns, 1960-72; Director, Cameron McNamara Pty. Limited, 1972-; Director, Carricks Limited (Dep. Chairman), 1970-; Director, Evans Deakin Industries Limited, 1971-; Director, Austral Group Limited, 1980-. *Memberships.* Fellow, The Institution of Engineers, Australia; Fellow, The Institute of Arbitrators, Australia; Fellow, The Institution of Civil Engineers; Member The American Society of Civil Engineers. *Honours:* The Institution of Engineers, Australia, Chapman Medal, 1959. *Hobbies:* Gardening; Bush Walking. *Address:* 460 Herron Road, Pullenvale, Brisbane 4069, Australia.

CAMERON, James, b. 17 June 1911, London, England. Journalist; Author. m. Moneesha Srkar, 25 Jan 1971, (Two Stepchildren). Honorary LLD, Lancaster University, UK, 1970; LLD, Bradford University, UK, 1977; LLD, Dundee University, Scotland, UK, 1980; Hon. D. Univ., Essex University, UK, 1978. *Appointments:* Many newspapers and publications, mostly as Foreign Correspondent. Documentary and drama films for BBC and ITV. *Memberships:* National Union of Journalists; Society of Authors; Savile Club. *Publications:* Touch of the Sun, 1950; 1914, 1959; The African Revolution, 1961; Point of Departure, 1967; What a Way to Run a Tribe, 1968; The Making of Israel, 1967; An Indian Summer, 1974; Witness in Vietnam, 1969. *Creative Works:* Two Plays: The Pump; Sound of the Guns; Many Documentary Features for BBC radio and TV. *Honours:* Prix Italia for The Pump; Three times Journalist of the Year Granada award. *Hobby:* Working. *Address:* 3 Eton College Road, London NW3, England.

CAMM, Harold, b. 7 Sept. 1903, Geraldton, Western Australia. Surveyor. m. Dorothea Laura Hill Parker, 12 July 1932, 1 son. *Education:* Bachelor of Laws, University of Western Australia, 1937-40. *Appointments:*

Staff Surveyor, Department of Lands and Surveys; Inspector of Plans and Surveys; Deputy Surveyor General; Surveyor General of Western Australia. *Memberships:* Former President, Institution of Surveyors, Western Australia; Fellow, Institution of Surveyors, Australia; Former President, Western Australia Golf Association; Former President, Life Member, Royal Fremantle Golf Club; Chidley Point Golf Club. *Publications:* Various articles dealing with Astronomy and mathematics. *Hobbies:* Golf; Gardening; Mathematical Problems. *Address:* 1 Saunders Street, Mosman Park, Western Australia, 6012.

CAMMACK, Peter, b. 15 Oct. 1932, Boston, Lincolnshire, England. Deputy Chief Coal Preparation Engineer. m. Valerie Caldwell, 30 Mar. 1959, 4 sons. *Education:* BSc.(Hons.)Mining, MSc.(Coal Preparation), Diploma Fuel Tech, C. Eng, University of Durham, Kings College, England, 1949-56. *Appointments:* Project Engineer, Senior Project Engineer, Head of Processes Group, Central Engineering Establishment, National Coal Board; Head of Development Branch, Deputy Chief Coal Preparation Engineer, Mining R & D Establishment, National Coal Board. *Memberships:* M. Institute Energy; M. Minerals Engineering Society. *Publications:* Author of numerous papers on all aspects of Coal Preparation Engineering, especially to the International Coal Preparation Congresses held at 4 yearly intervals in the various Capital Cities of Countries involved with Coal Mining. *Honours:* British Ropes Prize, 1953; Mather Scholarship, 1954, State Scholarship, 1954, University of Durham, England; Filtration Prize, Institute of Mechanical Engineering, 1974. *Hobbies:* Reading; Walking; Foreign Travel; Cricket; Gardening. *Address:* 10 Vicarage Close, Winshill, Burton on Trent, Staffordshire, England.

CAMPBELL, Alan Hugh, b. 1 July 1919, Worthing, Sussex. Retired Diplomat. m. Margaret Jean Taylor, 27 Sept. 1947, 3 daughters. *Education:* First class Honours, Modern & Medieval Languages, BA, Caius College, Cambridge, 1937-39. *Appointments:* Devonshire Regiment, 1940-45; H.M. Diplomatic Service, 1946-79; Ambassador to Italy, 1976-79; Foreign Affairs adviser to Rolls Royce Ltd., 1980-; Director, National Westminster Bank, 1980-. *Honours:* GCMG, 1979. *Address:* 45 Carlisle Mansions, Carlisle Place, London, S.W.1, England.

CAMPBELL, Alan Johnston, b. 31 July 1895, Dubbo, New South Wales, Australia. Retired Grazier. m. Barbar Jane, 19 Aug. 1965. *Education:* Private tuition, 1905-08; Toowoomba Grammar School, 1908-10. *Appointments:* Chairman, Directors of Charles Campbell & Manager, Merino Douns & Cooinda near Roma; Manager/Owner, Wallen Station near Cunnamulla; Mt Alfred station near Wyandra; Spring Creek station near Eulo; Dalamlly near Roma, 1920-50. *Memberships:* Life Fellow, Royal Geographical Society of Austrasasia and of London; The United Graziers Association of Queensland; The Maranoa Graziers Association, 1952; State President Queensland Country Party, 1943-51. *Publications:* Memoirs of the Country Party, Queensland, 1920-1974, 1975; History of the Charles Campbell Clan, 1781-1974, 1975. *Honours:* Companion of St George & St Michael, 1973; Chairman, Gallipoli Fountain of Honour Committee, 1975-80. *Hobbies:* Photography; Politics; World Travel; Livestock. *Address:* 24 Dusk Street, Kenmore, Queensland, 4069, Australia.

CAMPBELL, Alexander Colin, b. 16 Apr. 1932, Cheltenham, England. Civil Servant. m. Judith Meriel Strachan, 2 Dec, 1961, 2 sons, 1 daughter. *Education:* BA, Sindebele (Distinction) & Social Anthropology, Rhodes University, Grahamstown, South Africa, 1959-61. *Appointments:* British South Africa Police, Southern Rhodesia, 1951-54; Department of Tsetse and Trypanosomiasis, LAF, 1954-58; District Officer, Bechuanaland Protectorate, 1962-66; Senior Game Warden, Botswana Government, 1966-71; Director of Wildlife and National Parks, Botswana, 1971-74; Director of National Museum and Art Gallery, Botswana, 1974-80; Principal Administrative Officer, National Museum and Art Gallery, Botswana, 1980-. *Memberships:* Place Names Commission, Botswana; Chairman, Editorial Board, Botswana Society. *Publications:* The Guide to Botswana, 1978 revised 1980; About 40 papers in Scientific and semi-scientific journals. *Honours:* MBE,

1966. *Hobbies:* Photography; Painting. *Address:* Crocodile Pools Farm, Ngotwane, Nr Gaborone, Botswana.

CAMPBELL, Andrew Hugh, b. 19 Jan. 1946, Sydney, NSW, Australia. Surveying. m. Brenda Joan Coy, 17 May 1969, 2 sons, 1 daughter. *Education:* Bachelor of Surveying, 1968, Master of Surveying Science, 1972, University of New South Wales; Certificate of Competency, Board of Surveyors, NSW, 1968. *Appointments:* Bannister & Hunter, Surveyors, Gosford, NSW; Rygate & West, Surveyors, Sydney, NSW; University of New South Wales; King & Campbell Pty, Ltd., Consulting Surveyors & Engineers, Port Macquarie, NSW. *Memberships:* The Institution of Surveyors Australia; Australian Institute of Cartographers; Australian Photogrammetric Society; American Photogrammetric Society; Urban Development Institute of Australia. *Publications:* Two Unisurv Reports (University of NSW); Congress Paper and Several Reports in Surveying Journals in Australia and South Africa; Contributed several reports in Surveying Journals. *Hobbies:* Sailing; Squash. *Address:* 162 Oxley Highway, Port Macquarie, New South Wales, 2444, Australia.

CAMPBELL, Bruce Alpin, b. 4 Sept. 1931, Longreach, Queensland, Australia. Company Director and General Manager. m. 28 Oct. 1961, 1 son, 1 daughter. *Education:* Advanced Course, Administrative Staff College, Mt. Eliza, Victoria, Australia. *Appointments:* Wool Valuer, Branch Manager, Branch Superintendent, Assistant General Manager, General Manager, The Queensland Primary Producers Co-operative Association Ltd, 1949-74; General Manager, Primaries Mactaggarts Association Ltd, 1975-77; Director and Group General Manager, Primac Holdings Limited, 1977-; Director, Australian Farmers Pty. Limited, 1977-. *Memberships:* Australian President, The National Council of Wool Selling Brokers of Australia; Queensland Chairman, Australian Society of Senior Executives; Queensland President, The Royal Life Saving Society Fellow of The Australian Institute of Management; Fellow of The Institute of Directors; The Queensland Club; The Brisbane Club; Royal Queensland Golf Club. *Honours:* Recipient of: Queen's Silver Jubilee Medal; Serving Brother of the Order of St. John of Jerusalem; Meritorious Medal and Distinguished Service Cross of the Royal Life Saving Society. *Hobbies:* Swimming; Golf; Farming; Reading. *Address:* 6 Armagh Street, Clayfield. 4011, Queensland, Australia.

CAMPBELL, Henry Cummings, b. 22 Apr. 1919, Vancouver, British Columbia, Canada. Librarian; Adult Educator. m. Sylvia Frances Woodsworth, 10 Sept. 1943, 1 son, 2 daughters. *Education:* BA, University of British Columbia, Canada, 1937-40; BLS, University of Toronto, Canada, 1940-41; MA, Columbia University, New York, USA, 1946-47. *Appointments:* National Film Board of Canada, Ottawa, Canada, 1941-46; United Nations, Lake Success, New York, USA, 1946-48; Libraries Division, UNESCO, Paris, France, 1948-56; Chief Librarian, Toronto Public Library, Toronto, Canada, 1956-78; General Manager, Espial Productions, Toronto, Canada, 1978-81. *Memberships:* First Vice-President, International Federation of Library Association, 1973-79; President, Canadian Library Association, 1974-75; President, Ontario Association for Continuing Education, 1972-73. *Publications:* Manual on Public Library Systems & Services, 1981; Canadian Art-Auction Prices, 1980; Early Days on the Great Lakes, 1976; How to Find out about Canada, 1967. *Honours:* Honorary Fellow, IFLA, 1979. *Hobby:* Preparation of Machine Readable Data Bases. *Address:* 373 Glengrove Avenue, Toronto, Canada.

CAMPBELL, Ivan Gustavivs, b. 6 Sept. 1920, New Works, Westmoreland, Jamaica. Educator. m. 3 Aug. 1950, 1 son, 3 daughters. *Education:* Teachers Certificate, 1942-44; High School Certificate, 1955; BSc, (London), 1961. *Appointments:* Pre-Train Teacher, 1938-41; School Principal, 1945-47; Lecturer, Bethlehem Teachers College, 1947-57; Education Officer, Civil Servant, 1963-73; Registrar of Independent Schools, 1973-75; Senior Education Officer, Secondary Supervision, 1975-79; Lecturer, Teachers College, 1979-80. *Memberships:* Civil Service Association; Jamaica Teachers Association; Jamaica Association of Teacher Educators. *Publications:* Hymns & Their Message, contributed to Journal. *Honours:* Justice of the Peace, St Elizabeth. *Hobbies:* Farming;

Bridge playing; Reading; Research in Hymnology. *Address:* Malvern PO, St Elizabeth, Jamaica, West Indies.

CAMPBELL, Kate Isabel, b. 22 Apr. 1899, Melbourne, Victoria, Australia. Paediatrician. *Education:* Methodist Ladies' College, Melbourne, 1916; Melbourne University, 1917-22; MB,BS, 1922; MD, 1924; FRCOG (Hon.), 1961; LL.D (Hon.), 1966; Fellow, Royal Australian College Ophthalmologists (Hon.), 1968. *Appointments:* RMO Melbourne, Children's and Women's Hospitals; Hon. Paediatrician, Queen Victoria Hospital; Medical Officer, Victorian Baby Health Centres; General Medical Practice; Specialist Paediatrician; Lecturer, Neonatal Paediatrics, Melbourne University; Paediatrician, Women's Hospital; Consultant Paediatrician to Dept. of Maternal & Child Welfare, Victoria; Associate Paediatric Dept., Monash University. *Memberships:* Australian Medical Association; President, Victorian Medical Women's Society; President, Australian Paediatric Association. *Publications:* Guide to the Care of the Young Child (with collatborators); Section on the Newborn in Townsend's Obstetrics for Students, First Editition; Papaers on Retrolental Fibroplasia in Premature Infants; Various other medical papers. *Honours:* CBE, 1954; DBE, 1971; Brittanica Encyclopaedia Award in Medicine (Shared with Sir Norman Gregg), 1964. *Hobby:* Literature. *Address:* 1293 Burke Road, Kew, Victoria, Australia, 3101.

CAMPBELL(Mensah), Keith Bernard, b. Pine Ridge, Grand Bahama, The Bahamas. Doctor of Veterinary Medicine. 1 son. *Education:* BSc. Animal Science, 1974, DVM, 1976, Tuskeyere Institute, Alambama, USA. *Appointments:* Veterinary Officer, Ministry of Agriculture, Fisheries, Local Government, Crown Lands and Cooperatives, 1976-. *Memberships:* Phi Zeta Veterinary Honor Society; President, Veterinary Medical Association, Bahamas, 1981. *Honours:* Emminent Scholar, Tuskeyere Institute, 1972; Dean's List and Honour Roll throughout University Years. *Hobbies:* Sailing; Swimming; Snorkelling; Chess; Cycling; Reading; Music. *Address:* PO Box 5826 ES, New Providence Island, Commonwealth of the Bahamas, West Indies.

CAMPBELL, Meldrum James Arthur, b. 10 July 1922, Melbourne, Victoria, Australia. Senior Lecturer. m. 11 Dec. 1954, 1 son, 1 daughter. *Education:* BSc, 1952, MDSc, 1956, DDSc, 1969, University of Melbourne. FRACDS, 1965. *Appointments:* Clerk, Kanematsu Pty Ltd., 1939-40, Bank of Australasia, 1940-42; Member, Fourth Flash Spotting Battery, AIF, 1942-44; Senior Lecturer, Faculty of Dental Science, University of Melbourne, 1952-; Associate Dean, Faculty of Dental Science, University of Melbourne, 1977-. *Memberships:* Diabetes Foundation, Victoria, 1956-, Deputy Chairman, 1960-64. *Publications:* Numerous contributions to Dental Journals, including· Preventive dentistry in general practice, 1972; The effect of age and the duration of diabetes mellitus on the width of the basement membrane of amall vessels, 1974; An activity survey of dentists, 1971. *Hobbies:*Painting; Gardening; Reading. *Address:* 2/19 Kalang Road, Camberwell, 3124, Victoria, Australia.

CAMPBELL, Peter Ellis, b. 17 Oct. 1930, Geelong, Australia. Paediatric Pathologist. m. Helen Elizabeth Emonson, 9 Feb. 1957, 3 sons, 2 daughters. *Education:* MB,BS, University of Melbourne, 1948-53; Fellow, Royal College of Pathologists of Australia, MDI, Melbourne, 1959. *Appointments:* Resident Medical Officer, Geelong Hospital, 1954-56; Trainee in Pathology, Victoria, 1956-61; Histopathologist, 1961-70, Director of Anatomical Pathology, 1970-, Royal Childrens Hospital, Melbourne. *Memberships:* Graduate Union, Melbourne University, 1971-; President, Royal Childrens Hospital Ski Club, 1968-74. *Publications:* Tumours of Infancy and childhood, (w. E P G Jones), 1976; Articles on a variety of pathological topics. *Honours:* Exhibition chemistry, MBBS, Part One, 1948; Uncle Bobs Travelling Fellow, 1965-66; UICC Committee on Epidemiology childhood Cancer, 1970-73; Mollison Prize in Pathology, Melbourne, 1980. *Hobbies:* Skiing; Woodwork; Wine appreciation. *Address:* 6 Adeney Avenue, Kew 3101, Australia.

CAMPBELL, Peter Leonard, b. 29 Jan. 1932, London, England. Consulting Structural, Civil & Marine Engineer. m. Pamela, 19 Dec. 1953, 1 son, 2 daughters. *Education:* C. ENG., DIC., FISTRUCT.E., ACI.ARB., Imperial College of Science, London, 1953-54. *Ap-*pointments: Ove Arup & Partners; Campbell Reith & Partners; Managing Director, Downland Technical Services Limited; Trustee, Dunottar School Foundation Limited. *Memberships:* Council Member, The Institution of Structural Engineers; The Association of Consulting Engineers; The British Consultants Bureau; The Concrete Society; The Architectural Association; The Institute of Directors; The French Society of Civil Engineers; The American Society of Civil Engineers; Founder, First Museum of Concrete. *Publications:* Numerous articles, papers and book reviews. *Honours:* Justice of the Peace, 1976; Civic Trust Commendation, 1979; Civi Trust Award, 1980; Civi Trust Commendation, 1980. *Hobbies:* The History of Engineering; Painting; Power Boats; Horsemanship. *Address:* Earlymist, The Bridle Path, Leazes Avenue, Chaldon, Surrey, CR3 5AG, England.

CAMPBELL, Walter Benjamin, b. 4 Mar. 1921, New South Wales. Judge, Supreme Court of Queensland. m. Georgina Margaret Pearce, 18 June 1942, 1 son, 1 daughter. *Education:* MA, 1947, LLB (1st Class Hons), 1948, LLD (Hons), 1980, University of Queensland. *Appointments:* Barrister, 1948; Queen's Counsel, 1960; Judge, Supreme Court of Queensland, 1967-; Chairman, Law Reform Commission of Queensland, 1969-73; Chairman, Australian Remuneration Tribunal (Commonwealth), 1974-; Academic Salaries Tribunal (Commonwealth), 1974-78. *Memberships:* Chancellor, University of Queensland, 1977-; Chairman, Board of Governors, Utah Foundation, 1977-; President, Queensland Bar Association, 1965-67; President, Australian Bar Association, 1966-67; Executive of Law Council of Australia, 1966-67; Director, Winston Churchill Memorial Trust, 1969-80. *Honours:* Knight Bachelor, 1979. *Hobbies:* Golf; Fishing. *Address:* 71 Enderley Road, Clayfield, Brisbane, Queensland, Australia 4011.

CAMPBELL OF CROY, Gordon Thomas Calthrop, b. 8 June 1921, Quetta. Member of Parliament. m. Nicola Elizabeth Gina Madan, 21 July 1949, 2 sons, 1 daughter. *Education:* Wellington College, 1934-39. *Appointments:* Regular Army, 1939-46(Wounded and disabled 1945); Diplomatic Service, 1946-57; Member of House of Commons for Moray and Nairn, 1959-74; Member of the Cabinet and Secretary of State for Scotland, 1970-74; Member of House of Lords, 1974-; Estate Owner and farmer; Consultant Oil Industry; Member Building Society and on several Company Boards. *Honours:* Military Cross, 1944, Bar 1945; Privy Councillor, 1970; Peerage, 1974. *Hobbies:* Music; Birds. *Address:* Holme Rose, Cawdor, Nairn, Scotland.

CANTO, Victor M, b. 28 Dec. 1917, San Pedro De Macoris, Dominican Republic. Ranch Owner. m. Olga Del Giudice de Canto, 19 Dec. 1942, 1 son, 3 daughters. *Education:* High School, 1935. *Appointments:* Advisor to: Consejo Estatal Del Azucar, Junta Monetaria, Instituto Azucarero; Director of the Agricultural Bank, 1963; British Vice-Consul, 1970-. *Memberships:* Consular Corps; Rotary International; several Cultural Societies. *Honours:* Condecorated by the British Government as a Member of the Highest Excellent Order of the British Government, 1981. *Hobbies:* Baseball; Paso Fino Show Horses. *Address:* Jose Carbuccia 41, San Pedro De Macoris, Dominican Republic.

CAPON, Edmund George, b. 11 June 1940, Kent, England. Art Museum Director. m. Joanna Susan Hirsch, 8 July 1978, 1 son, 1 daughter, from previous marriage. *Education:* PhD, Chinese and Chinese Archaeology, School of Oriental and African Studies, University of London, UK, 1966-68. *Appointments:* Richard Ellis & Son, Chartered Surveyors; Assistant Keeper, Far Eastern Section, Victoria and Albert Museum, London; Director, Art Gallery of New South Wales, Sydney, Australia, 1978-. *Memberships:* Royal Society for Asian Affairs; Oriental Ceramic Society, London; Oriental Ceramic Society of Hong Kong; Director, Australian Gallery Directors Council; Director, International Cultural Corporation of Australia; Oriental Club, London; Australian Club, Sydney. *Publications:* Princes of Jade, 1973; Art & Archaeology of China, 1977; Chinese Painting, 1980; numerous articles including: Chinese Buddhist Sculpture, 1974; Theory and Practice in Chinese Museums, 1975; K'ossu and its relationship with painting, 1975; Ancient Chinese Ceramic Sculpture, 1978. *Hobbies:* Sailing;

Writing. *Address:* 3 Mansion Road, Bellevue Hill, Sydney, New South Wales 2023, Australia.

CARDEN, Anthony Basil George, b. 27 Feb. 1933, Melbourne, Australia. Surgeon. m. Janet Ramsay Webb, 30 Aug. 1958, 1 son, 3 daughters. *Education:* Medical School, Melbourne University, 1952-57; Residency, Royal Melbourne Hospital, 1958-62. *Appointments:* Residency in Surgery, Queen Elizabeth Hospital, Birmingham, England, 1962, St Mark's Hospital, London, 1962-63, St George's Hospital, London, 1963; Fellow in Surgery, Cleveland Clinic, 1964; Assistant Surgeon, Royal Melbourne Hospital, 1964-69; Surgeon, Queen Victoria Medical Centre, 1964-; Currently Chairman Division of Surgery. *Publications:* Papers in field of Surgery. *Hobbies:* Surfing; Sailing; Golf; Skiing; Photography. *Address:* 26 KooYong Koot Road, Hawthorn, Victoria 3122, Australia.

CAREY, Samuel Warren, b. 1 Nov. 1911, Campbelltown, New South Wales, Australia. Geologist. m. 15 June 1940, 2 sons, 2 daughters. *Education:* BSc, 1931, BSc, 1st Class Honours, 1932, MSc, 1933, DSc, 1939, University of Sydney, Australia. *Appointments:* Geologist, Oil Search Ltd., New Guinea, 1934-38; Senior Geologist, Australasian Petroleum Company, Papua, 1938-42; Chief Geologist, Tasmanian Government, 1944-46; Professor of Geology, University of Tasmania, 1946-76; Consultant, Tasmanian Hydro-electric Commission, 1946-60; Consultant, mining and engineering geology, many companies and instrumentalities, 1946-81; Visiting Professor, Yale, 1959-60; Western Ontario, 1967-68; UN Technical Adviser, Israel, 1963. *Memberships:* President, Australian & New Zealand Association for Advancement of Science, 1970; President, Geological Society of Australia, 1977-78; Chairman of Trustees, Taasmanian Museum & Art Gallery, 1951-52; Chairman of Professorial Board, 1954-55, Dean of Faculty of Science, 1950,51, 1970, President, Staff Association, 1947-48, 1952-53, 1964-65, University of Tasmania, Australia; President, Tasmanian Paratroopers Association, 1962-81; Founder & President, Tasmanian Caverneering Club, 1945-50; Founder & President, Sydney University Students Geological Society, 1931-33; Honorary Life Fellow: Indian National Academy of Science, 1977, Geological Society of America, 1977; Honorary Life Member: Geological Society of London, 1970, Royal Society of New South Wales, 1976; Honorary Doctor of Science, University of Papua and New Guinea, 1970. *Publications:* The Expanding Earth, 1976; Editor of Symposiums on: Continental Drift, 1956; Dolerite, 1958; Syntaphral Tectonics, 1963; Earth Expansion, 1981; 53 scientific research papers in technical journals. *Honours:* Officer of the Order of Australia, 1977; Gondwanaland Gold Medal, 1963; Clarke Medal, 1969; Johnston Medal, 1976. *Hobbies:* Beekeeping; Hydroponics; Parachuting; Caverneering. *Address:* 24 Richardson Avenue, Dynnyrne, Taasmania, 7005, Australia.

CARLISLE, John Russell, b. 28 Aug. 1942, Henlow, Bedfordshire, UK. Member of Parliament. m. 4 July 1964, 2 daughters. *Education:* St Lawrence College, 1954-61; London University, 1961-64. *Appointments:* Director of Grain Trading Company. *Memberships:* Farmers Clubs. *Hobbies:* Sport. *Address:* 18b Leagrave Road, Luton, England.

CARLYON, Norman Dean, b. 4 Sept. 1903, Ballarat. Chairman of Directors. m. Enid Murdoch, 25 May 1935, 1 son, 1 daughter. *Education:* Geelong Church of England Grammar School, Corio, Victoria, Australia. *Appointments:* Chairman of Directors, Carlyon Holdings Pty Ltd; Managing Director, Hotel Australia, Melbourne, Australia; Chairman, Housing and Catering Committee, responsible for Olympic Village, Melbourne Olympics, 1956; Chairman, Corps of Commissionaires Victoria, 1947-81. *Memberships:* Victorian Racing Club; Metropolitan Golf Club; Victorian Amateur Turf Club; Moonee Vaalley Racing Club. *Publications:* I Remember Blamey, 1980. *Honours:* OBE, Military Mention in Despatches; CBE, Civil. *Hobbies:* Golf; Horse Racing(Owner). *Address:* Apartment 11, 'Clarendon', 58 Clarendon Street, East Melbourne 3002, Australia.

CARMICHAEL, Alexander John, b. 21 July 1919, Sydney, Australia. Engineer; President, Hunter District Water Board. m. 29 Mar. 1941, Frances Ezart, 1 son, 2 daughters. *Education:* Diploma: Electrical Engineering,

1940, Mechanical Engineering, 1948, Sydney Technical College; Hons. Degree, Mechanical Engineering, 1952, Doctorate in Engineering, 1962, University of New South Wales, Australia; Degree in Civil Engineering, University of Illinois, USA, 1958. *Appointments:* Senior Planning Engineer, Standard Telephones & Cables Pty. Ltd, 1943-47; Research Officer, CSIRO, Applied Mechanics, 1947-49; Lecturer in Civil Engineering, 1949-56, Senior Lecturuer in Civil Engineering, 1957-61, Associate Lecturer in Civil Engineering, 1962-74, University of New South Wales, Australia; Professor Mechanical Engineering and Dean of Faculty, University of Newcastle, Australia, 1967-74; President and Chairman, The Hunter District Water Board, 1974-. *Memberships:* Fellow, Royal Society of Arts; Fellow, American Society of Civil Engineers; Fellow, Institution of Mechanical Engineers, London; Fellow, Institution of Engineers, Australia; Newcastle Club; Newcastle Rotary Club; Newcastle Tattersalls Club. *Publications:* 80 technical papers, monographs and significant reports. *Honours:* James Clayton Fellowship to United Kingdom, 1961-62; Fulbright Scholarship to USA, 1965 and 1970; Award of Professor Emeritus, University of Newcastle, 1974; CBE, 1980. *Hobbies:* Swimming; Photography; Antiques. *Address:* 31 Madison Drive, Adamstown Heights, New South Wales, 2289, Australia.

CARNE, Ian Hamilton, b. 10 Aug. 1915, Murray Bridge, South Australia. Metallurgical Engineer. m. Mary Steel Scott, 8 May 1943, 2 sons, 1 daughter. *Education:* Bachelor of Engineering, Diploma of Applied Science, Adelaide University; Fellowship Diploma of South Australian School of Mines. *Appointments:* Technical Officer, 1939-51, American Representative, 1951-55, Executive Assistant, Chief General Manager, 1955-59, Manager Overseas Division, 1959-61, Executive Officer Operations & Distribution, 1961-64, General Manager, Western Australian Operations, 1964-72, General Manager, Minerals Western Australia, 1972-77, General Manager, Western Australia, 1977-79, Broken Hill Proprietary Company Limited. *Memberships:* Advisory Council, State Energy Commission of Western Australia; Advisory Committee, Solar Energy Research Institute of Western Australia; Australasian Institute of Mining & Metallurgy; Deputy, Conservation & Environment Council; Chairman, The Structural Engineering Company of Western Australia, 1970-78; Deputy Chairman, Orbital Engine Company Pty. Ltd., 1972-79, Texada Mines Pty. Ltd., 1976-78; Director, WA Mining Engineering Services Pty. Ltd., 1973-79, Widgiemooltha Pastoral Company Pty. Ltd., 1978-79. *Honours:* Awarded Her Majesty's Silver Jubilee Medal, 1977. *Hobbies:* Lawn Bowls; Gardening; Electronics; Music. *Address:* 108 Burke Drive, Attadale 6156, Australia.

CARRICK, John Leslie, b. 4 Sept. 1918, Sydney, Australia. Senator and Cabinet Minister. m. Diana Margaret Hunter, 2 June 1951, 3 daughters. *Education:* Bachelor of Economics, University of Sydney, Australia. *Appointments:* Research Officer, 1946-48, General Secretary, 1948-71, Liberal Party of Australia, New South Wales Division; Senator, Commonwealth Parliament of Australia, 1971-; Minister for Education, 1975-79; Minister for National Development and Energy, 1979-; Leader of the Government in the Senate, 1978-; Vice-President of the Executive Council, 1978-. *Hobbies:* Swimming; Reading. *Address:* 8 Montah Avenue, Killara, New South Wales 2071, Australia.

CARRINGTON, (6th Baron) Peter Alexander Rupert, b. 6 June 1919, London. British Politician. m. Iona McClean, 1 son, 2 daughters. *Education:* Eton College; Royal Military College, Sandhurst. *Appointments:* Grenadier Guards, 1939, served N.W. Europe; Parliamentary Secretary, Ministry of Agriculture, 1951-54; Ministry of Defence, 1954-56; High Commissioner in Australia, 1956-59; First Lord of the Admiralty, 1959-63; Minister without Portfolio (Foreign Office), Leader, House of Lords, 1963-64; Leader of the Opposition, House of Lords, 1964-70; Secretary of State for Defence, 1970-74; Minister of Aviation Supply, 1971-74; Secretary of State for Energy, 1974; Foreign and Commonwealth Affairs, 1979; Minister of Overseas Development, 1979; Leader of the Opposition, House of Lords, 1974-79. *Memberships:* Chairman, Conservative Party, 1972-74; Chairman, Australia and New Zealand Bank Limited, 1969-70; Director, Amalgamated Metal Corporation Limited, 1965-70; Cadbury

Schweppes Limited, 1968-70, 1974-79; Barclays Bank Limited, 1967-70, 1974-79; Hambros Bank Limited, 1967-70; Rio Tinto Zinc Corporation Limited, 1974-79. *Honours:* Hon. LLD (Cambridge) 1981; PC; KCMG; MC. *Address:*Manor House, Bledlow, nr. Aylesbury, Buckinghamshire, England.

CARROL, Charles Gordon, b. 21 Mar. 1935, Edinburgh, Scotland. Director, Commonwealth Institute, Scotland. m. Frances Anne Sinclair, 5 Sept. 1970, 3 sons. *Education:* MA, Edinburgh University, Scotland, 1957; Dip. Ed. Moray House College, Scotland, 1958. *Appointments:* Education Officer, Government of Northern Nigeria, 1959-65; Education Officer, Commonwealth Institute, Scotland, 1965-71; Director, Commonwealth Institute, Scotland, 1971-. *Memberships:* Lay member of Press Council, 1978. *Hobbies:* Hill Walking; Reading; Cooking. *Address:* 11 Dukehaugh, Peebles, EH45 9 DN, Scotland.

CARROLL, Ernest Michael, b. 2 Feb. 1925, Mareeba, Queensland, Australia. Air Vice Marshal, Royal Australian Air Force. m. Shirley Ray Agnew, 30 July 1947, 1 son, 2 daughters. *Education:* Diploma of Commerce, University of Queensland, Australia, 1947-51; RAAF Staff College, Canberra, Australia, 1962. *Appointments:* Navigator RAAF, Commissioned 1944, 1943-46; Banking, Commonwealth Bank of Australia, 1946-51; RAAF ACtive Reserve, Navigator, 1949-51; Apoointed Equipment Officer, Permanent Air Force, 1952; Unit, Depot, and Command Duties, 1953-57; Aircraft Procurement Support, USA, 1957-61; SESO RAAF Edinburgh, 1963-64; SESO RAAF, Paris, 1965-67; Director Equip Policy & Administration, 1968-70; CO No 2 Stores Depot, 1970-73; SESO Hqs Operational Command, 1973-74; Director General Movements and Transport, 1975-77; SESO HQs Support Command, 1978-79; Chief of Supply, Department of Defence, 1980-. *Memberships:* Naval and Military Club, Melbourne; Royal Canberra Golf Club, Canberra. *Honours:* Fellow: Chartered Institute of Transport, 1975, Australian Institute of Management, 1980. *Hobbies:* Golf; Philately; Gardening. *Address:* 17 Galway Place, Deakin, ACT, 2600, Australia.

CARROLL, Henry Thomas, b. 6 July 1911, Sydney, Australia. Veterinary Surgeon, Animal Production Specialist and International Civil Servant. m. Gwendoline Rose Conn, 13 Aug, 1966, 2 sons, 1 daughter. *Education:* Hawkesbury Dip. of Agric. (HDA), 1930; Bachelor of Vet. Science, Sydney University, Australia, 1938. *Appointments:* Veterinary Adviser, Golds, Mort & Co. Ltd, Western Australia, 1945-53; Staff member, FAO of UN, 1953; Veterinary Parasitol., Sheep Diseases and Production Expert in Brazil, 1953,-54, Uruguay, 1954, Chile 1955, Peru and Ecuador 1956, Yugoslavia 1957-58, Ethiopia 1958-59, Kenya 1960-63; FAO Regional Animal Production and Health Officer for Africa E/S Zone (permanent staff) i/c Ethiopia, Kenya, Uganda, Tanzania, Ruanda, Burundi, Zambia, Malawi, Rhodesia, Botswana, Mauritius, 1964-66; Director, UN/SD Project, Sheep Husbandry Research in Argentina, Patagonia, 1966-71; Official advisory visit to Poland, 1970. Staff member, FAO Hq. Rome, Italy, 1971; Member, UNDP Mission to Yemen and World Food Programme Mission to NE Turkey, 1971-72; Officer i/c Sheep Production Research, NE Brazil, 1972-74; Retired 1974; Consultant to FAO of UN Rome, UN Development Programme, New York and Dalgety Farm Management Pty. Ltd. (Aust.), 1975. *Memberships:* Australian Veterinary Association, New South Wales and Western Australia. *Publications:* Diseases of Sheep in Western Australia and South Australia, 1949, 1953; Enfermedades de los Ovinos, 1957; Official FAO Reports on each country of assignment. *Honours:* Justice of the Peace of New South Wales, 1939; Foundation Member Australian College of Veterinary Scientists, 1971; Second recipient, Kesteven Medal, 1980. *Hobbies:* Literature; Music; International Affairs; Golf. *Address:* 2 'Miramar' 7 Aston Gardens, Bellevue Hill 2023 Australia.

CARRUTHERS, John, b. 12 Mar. 1937, Edinburgh, Scotland. Insurance Broker; Pension Consultant. m. Wilfrida Nayiga Musoke, 2 sons, 3 daughters. *Education:* Scottish Higher Certificate, 1955; Associate Chartered Insurance Institute, 1961. *Appointments:* Royal Air Force, 1955-57; Scottish Widows Fund, 1957-61; Hogg Robinson Kenya, 1962-63; Director, Hogg Robinson, Uganda, Uganda Life & Pensions Consultants,

1963-73; Director, Nigerian Life & Pensions Consultants, 1973-; Nigerian Universities Pensions Management Company, 1973-; Director, Hogg Robinson, Nigeria, 1975; Director, Hogg Robinson Overseas ltd., 1977. *Memberships:* Institute of Directors; Nigerian Institute of Management; Chartered Insurance Institute, Commonwealth Society; Lions International. *Hobbies:* Swimming; Golf; African History. *Address:* PO Box 1156, Lagos, Nigeria.

CARSON, William Hunter, b. 16 Nov. 1942, Riverside, Stirling, Scotland. Jockey. m. Carole Jane Sutton, 1963, (div.), 3 sons. *Appointments:* Apprenticed to Captain G Armstrong, 1957; Transferred to Fred Armstrong, 1963-66; First Jockey to Lord Derby, 1967; First classic win, High Top, 1972; Champion Jockey, 1972, 1973 and 1978; became First Jockey to WR Hern, 1977; also appointed Royal Jockey, riding Dunfermline to the Jubilee Oaks and St Leger wins in the colours of HM the Queen; won the 200th Derby on Troy, trained by WR Hern, 1979; the same combination won the 1980 Derby, with Henbit, and the 1980 Oaks, with Bireme; also won King George VI and Queen Elizabeth Stakes on Ela-Mana-Mou, 1980. *Hobby:* Hunting. *Address:* West Ilsley, Nr. Newbury, Berks., England.

CARTER, Bruce Northleigh, b. 21 July 1939, Sydney, New South Wales, Australia. Headmaster. m. Jann Williamson, 2 May 1975, 2 sons. *Education:* BA, University of Sydney, Australia, 1963; Ed.M, Harvard University, USA, 1964; Ed.D, University of Toronto, Canada, 1967. *Appointments:* Assistant Master, Knox Grammar School, Wahroonga, New South Wales, Australia, 1958-63; Don, Knox College, University of Toronto, Canada, 1965-67; Research Fellow, University of Toronto, Canada, 1965-66; Assistant Master, Newington College, New South Wales, Australia, 1967-68; Senior English Master, The King's School, New South Wales, Australia, 1969; Deputy Headmaster and Boarding Housemaster, Knox Grammar School, Wahroonga, New South Wales, Australia, 1970-77; Principal, Scotch College, Launceston, Tasmania, Australia, 1978; Principal, Scotch Oakburn College, Launceston, Tasmania, Australia, 1979-. *Memberships:* Chairman, Association of Heads of Independent Schools in Tasmania, 1979-80; Australian College of Education; Phi Delta Kappa, USA Harvard Chapter. *Honours:* Walker-Beale Scholar to Harvard University, 1963-64. *Hobbies:* Cricket; Tennis; Squash; Literature; Theatre. *Address:* Scotch Oakburn College, 85 Penquite Road, Launceston, Tasmania, Australia 7250.

CARTER, Charles Frederick (Sir), b. 15 Aug. 1919, Rugby, Warwickshire. Economist. m. Janet Shea, 1 Jan. 1944, 1 son, 2 daughters. *Education:* MA, St John's College, Cambridge. *Appointments:* Lecturer in Statistics, University of Cambridge, 1945-51; Fellow of Emmanuel College, 1947-51; Professor of Applied Economics, The Queen's University, Belfast, 1952-59; Stanley Jevons Professor of Political Economy & Cobden Lecturer, University of Manchester, 1959-63; Vice-Chancellor, University of Lancaster, 1963-79; Chairman, Research Committee, Policy Studies Institute, 1978-. Author or Co-author: Industry & Technical Progress, 1957; Investment in Innovation, 1958; Science in Industry, 1959; The Northern Ireland Problem, 1962; The Science of Wealth, 1960; Wealth, 1968; British Economic Statistics, 1954; Higher Education for the Future, 1980. *Honours:* Fellow, British Academy; Hon. Fellow Emmanuel College, Cambridge, 1965; Hon. Doctor of Science, University of Lancaster, 1979; Hon. Doctor of Science, New University of Ulster, Coleraine, 1979; Hon. LLD, University of Dublin, 1980; Hon. Doctor of Economic Science, University of Belfast, 1980 & National University of Ireland, 1968. *Hobby:* Gardening. *Address:* Bank Head, The Banks, Seascale, Cumbria CA20 1QN, England.

CARTER, Michael Percy, b. 22 Sept. 1929, Hove, Sussex, England. Professor of Sociology. m. Diana Brown, 5 Sept. 1953, 1 son, 2 daughters. *Education:* BA, University of Nottingham, UK, 1952; PhD, University of Edinburgh,UK, 1969. *Appointments:* Research Assistant, University of Nottingham, UK, 1952-54; RAF Education Officer, 1954-57; Research Associate, University of Birmingham, 1957-58; Senior Research Worker, University of Sheffield, UK, 1958-63; Lecturer in Social Anthropology, University of Edinburgh, Scotland, 1963-70; Professor of Sociology, Fourah Bay College, University of Sierra Leone, 1968-70; Professor and subsequently Head of Department of Sociology, University of Aberdeen, Scotland, 1970-76; Professor and Head of Department of Sociology, University of Newcastle, New South Wales, Australia, 1976-; Dean of Arts, 1977-78, Deputy Chairman of Senate, 1979-, Member, New South Wales Institute of Psychiatry, 1980-. *Memberships:* Association of Social Anthropologists; British Socilogical Association; Sociological Association of Australia and New Zealand. *Publications:* The Social Background of Delinquency(with Pearl Jephcott), 1954; Home, School and Work, 1963; Education, Employment and Leisure, 1964; Into Work, 1966; Co-author, Sociology and Social Research, 1981; Various Articles. *Hobbies:* Reading; Cooking. *Address:* 33 Lloyd Street, Newcastle, New South Wales, Australia. 2291.

CARTER, Rosemary Margaret, b. 24 Nov. 1920, Adelaide, Australia. m. Walter Aileyne Carter, 25 Nov. 1953. *Education:* Certificates, South Australia School of Art. *Appointments:* Wireless Telegraphist, Womens Royal Australian Navy, 1942-45; Began business in flower arrangements, 1946-60. *Memberships:* Womens Australian National Services; Various Offices held in the Red Cross, 1940-65; Member of National Flower Day Committee, Chairman of various sub committees within this South Australia Government Committee, 1950-74. *Creative Works:* Exhibited paintings in Royal Society of Arts Exhibitions, also exhibited and sold paintings in other exhibitions, 1967-70; Designer of Floral Carpet for National Flower Day, 1970. *Honours:* Presented at Buckingham Palace, 1951; Associate Member, Royal Society of Arts. *Hobbies:* Golf; Gardening. *Address:* 7 Buckingham Close, 11 Walkerville Terrace, Gilberton, South Australia. .

CARTER, Wilfred, (Air Vice-Marshal), b. 5 Nov 1912, Ratcliffe, England. International Disaster Preparedness Consultant. m. Margaret Enid Bray, 15 Apr. 1950, 1 son, 1 daughter. *Education:* Middle East Centre for Arab Studies, 1946-47; Royal Airforce Staff College, 1949; Joint Services Staff College, 1953. *Appointments:* Apprentice, Pilot, World War Two, Bomber Command, World War 2, Director of Studies RAF Staff College, Head Plans & Operations CENTO, Air Officer Administrative, Royal Air Force, 1929-67; Director Australian Counter Disaster College, 1969-78; International Disaster Preparedness Consultant, 1978-. *Memberships:* Patron, Australian Institute of Emergency Services; Fellow, Australian Institute of Management; Upper Freeman, Guild of Air Pilots & Navigators; International Institute for Strategic Studies. *Honours:* DFC, 1943; Officer of Order of Cedars of Lebanon, 1954; CB, 1963; Winner of Gordon Shephard Memorial Prize for Strategic Studies, 1955, 1956, 1957, 1961, 1965, 1967; Companion of Order of Bath (CB), 1963. *Hobbies:* Walking; Swimming. *Address:* Blue Range, Macedon, Victoria 3440, Australia.

CARTLAND, (Sir) George Barrington, b. 22 Sept. 1912, Manchester, England. British Colonial Service (Ret.); University Vice Chancellor (Ret.) m. Dorothy Rayton, 24 July 1937, 2 sons. *Education:* Manchester University; Hertford College, Oxford. *Appointments:* Entered Colonial Service, Gold Coast, 1935; Colonial Office, 1944-49, Head of African Studies Br. and Ed. Jl of Afr. Adminis., 1945-49; Sec. London Afr. Conference, 1948; Admin. Secretary, Uganda, 1949; Secretary for Social Services and Local Government, Uganda, 1952; Minister for Social Services, Uganda, 1955; Minister of Education and Labour, Uganda, 1958; Chief Secretary Uganda, 1960; Deputy Gov. of Uganda, 1961-62, (Acting Gov., various occasions, 1952-62); Registrar of University of Birmingham, 1963-67. *Memberships:* Chairman, Australian National Accreditations Authority for Translators and Interpreters, 1977-; Deputy Chairman Australian Vice-Chancellors' Committee, 1975 and 1977; Chairman, Adv. Committee on National Park in South West Tasmania, 1976-78; Tasmanian Council of Australian Trade Union Trng Authority, 1979; Appointed to review: Library and Archives Legislation of Tasmania, 1978; Tasmanian Govt Adm, 1979. Australian National Committee of Hoover Awards for Marketing, 1968-; Chm., St John Council, Uganda; President St John Council, Tasmania; Member Council: University of East Africa; Royal Technical College, Nairobi; University College of Rhodesia; University of the South Pacific. *Honours:* Belgian Medal, 1960; CMG, 1956; Kt, 1963; Fellow, Australian College of Education, 1970; KStJ, 1972; Honorary LLD, Univer-

sity of Tasmania, 1978. *Hobbies:* Mountaineering; Fishing. *Address:* 5 Aotea Road, Sandy Bay, Hobart, Tasmania, Australia.

CARTWRIGHT, John Cameron, b. 29 Nov. 1933, Lincoln, England. Member of Parliament. m. Iris June Tant, 23 Feb. 1959, 1 son, 1 daughter. *Appointments:* Executive Class, Civil Service, 1952-55; Labour Party Organiser, 1955-67; Co-operative Society, Political Organiser, 1967-72; Co-opertive Society, full time Director, 1972-74; Member of Parliament, 1974-. *Memberships:* London Borough of Greenwich Council, 1971-74; PPS to Rt. Hon. Shirley Williams, 1976 78; Chairman, Labour Party Defence Group, 1979-. *Hobby:* Do-It-yourself Home Maintenance. *Address:* 17, Commonwealth Way, London, SE2 OJZ, England.

CARUNAKARAN, Arunachalam, b. 24 Jan. 1937, Klang, Malaysia. Chartered Accountant. m. Nagaletchumie Velupillai, 15 Nov. 1964, 1 son, 1 daughter. *Education:* Associate Member of Institute of Chartered Accountants, Sri Lanka, 1971. *Appointments:* Lecturer/Registrar, Brighton Institute, Sri-Lanka; Accountant, Ministry of Finance, Republic of Zambia; Area Accountant, Zambia Electricity Supply Corporation; Expert, Lecturer in Accountancy, Commonwealth Fund for Technical Co-Operation based in Jamaica. *Hobbies:* Photography, Badminton, Yoga. *Address:* P.O. Box 49, Mona, Kingston, Jamaica.

CARVER Richard Michael Power, (Field Marshal Lord), b. 24 Apr. 1915, Bletchingley, Surrey, England. Army Officer. m. Edith Lowry-Corry, 22 Nov. 1947, 2 sons, 2 daughters. *Education:* Winchester College, 1928-33; Royal Military College, Sandhurst, Kings Gold Medal, 1933-34. *Appointments:* 2nd Lieut. Royal Tank Corps, 1935; Lt-Col. GSO1 7th Armd Div. 1942; OC 1st Royal Tanks, 1943-44; Comd. 4th Armd BDE, 1944-47; Chief of Staff, East Africa, 1955-56; Director Army Plans, 1958-59; Comd. 6th Infantry, BDE, 1960-62; Comd. 3rd Division, 1962-64; Director Army Staff Duties, 1964-66; Comd Far East Land Forces, 1966-67; Commander-in-charge, Far East, 1967-69; Commander-in-charge, Southern Comd, 1969-71; Chief General Staff, 1971-73; Chief Defence Staff, 1973-76. *Memberships:* Fellow Royal Society of Arts. *Publications:* Second To None, 1952; El Alamein, 1962; Tobruk, 1964; The War Lords, 1976; Harding of Petherton, 1978; The Apostles of Mobility, 1979; War Since 1945, 1980. *Honours:* GCB, 1971; CBE, 1945; DSO, 1943, Bar 1944; MC, 1942. *Hobbies:* Gardening; Sailing; Tennis. *Address:* Wood End House, Wickham, Fareham, Hants, PO17 6JZ, England.

CASEY, Brian Hal, b. 23 Nov. 1936, Sydney, Australia. Orthopaedic Surgeon. *Education:* Waverley College, Sydney Maximum Pass, Leaving Certificate, 1953; Sydney University, M.B.,B.S., Honours, 1960; Royal College of Surgeons, Edinburgh, Fellow, 1965; Royal Australian College of Surgeons, Fellow, 1978. *Appointments:* Resident Medical Officer, Royal Prince Alfred Hospital, 1960-61; Anatomy Demonstrator, Sydney University, 1962; Surgical Registrar, Prince Henry-/Prince of Wales Hospital, 1963; Teaching Fellow Physiology, University of New South Wales, 1964-65; Surgical Fellow, Heidelberg University, Germany, 1966; Surgical Research Fellow, Harvard University U.S.A. 1966-67; Senior Orthopaidic Registrar, Luton & Dunstable Hospital, U.K. 1967-68; Senior Orthopaedic Registrar, Royal Perth Hospital, 1969-70; Clinical Fellow, Hospital For Sick Children, Toronto, Canada, 1970-71; Fellow Arthritis Service, Rancho Los Amigos Hospital, Los Angeles, California, 1971; Honorary Orthopaedic Surgeon, Royal South Sydney Hospital, Sydney, 1972; Honorary Orthopaedic Surgeon, War Memorial Hospital, Waverley, N.S.W. 1977-. *Memberships:* Australian Orthopaedic Association; American Orthopaedic Society for Sports Medicine; Australian Knee Club; Australian Medical Association; Australian Hand Club; N.S.W. Hand Surgery Association. *Publications:* Contributed to various professional journals. *Honours:* Robin May Memorial Prize, Graduation, Sydney University, 1960; Elected Fellow, Royal Australian College of Surgeons, 1978. *Hobbies:* Sailing, Body Surfing, Water Skiing, Scuba Diving. *Address:* 8/4 Dundas Street, Coogee, 2034, N.S.W. Australia.

CASEY, Edmund Denis, b. 2 Jan. 1933, Mackay, Australia. Politician. m. Laurette Norma Reeves, 20

Feb. 1955, 5 sons, 1 daughter. *Education:* Matriculation. *Appointments:* Bank Clerk; Managing Director, Family Contracting Business; Legislative Assembly, 1969-. *Memberships:* Vice-Patron, Queensland Council of Social Service; Vice-President, Queensland Social Service League. *Honours:* Deputy Mayor of Mackay City Council, 1967-69. *Hobbies:* Rugby League; Swimming; Tennis. *Address:* 1 Henderson Street, Mackay, Queensland, 4740, Australia.

CASH, Earl Douglas, b. 15 July 1919, Gladstone, Manitoba, Canada. Law Librarian. m. Margaret Joan Moore, 11 May 1946, 2 daughters. *Education:* BA, University of Western Australia, 1966; Graduate Diploma in Librarianship, Western Australia Institute of Technology, 1975. *Appointments:* MHR (Lib) for Stirling WA, 1958, 1961, for Mirrabooka WA, 1968-71; Research Officer, Liberal Party of Australia, WA Division, 1971-74; Special Collections Librarian, Darwin Community College, 1976-78; Law Librarian Northern Tertitoty Department of Law, 1978-. *Memberships:* Associate, Library Association of Australia; Chairman, Council Royal Commonwealth Society WA, 1963-64; Council Joint Council of Commonwealth Societies, 1963-64. *Honours:* Justice of the Peace. *Hobbies:* Writing; Travel; Bowls; Fishing; Photography. *Address:* 42/114 Smith Street, Darwin, N7, Australia, 5790.

CASH, Sir Gerald (Christopher), b. 28 May 1917, Nassau, Bahamas. Governor-General, Commonwealth of the Bahamas. m. Dorothy Eileen Long, 2 sons, 1 daughter. *Education:* Called to the Bar, Middle Temple, 1948. *Appointments:* Counsel and Attorney, Supreme Court of Bahamas, 1940; Member: House of Assembly, Bahamas, 1949-62; Executive Council, 1958-62; Vice President, 1970-72. President, 1972-73, Senate, 1969-73; Chairman, Labour Board, 1950-52; Board of Education, 1950-62; Police Service Commission, 1964-69; Immigration Committee, 1958-62; Road Traffic Committee, 1958-62; Represented Bahamas, Independence Celebrations of Jamaica, Trinidad and Tobago, 1962; Acting Governor-General, 1976-79, Governor-General, Commonwealth of the Bahamas, 1979-. *Memberships:* Chairman, Visiting Committee, Boys Industrial School, 1952-62; Board of Governors, Government High School, 1949-63, 1965-76; Bahamas National Committee, United World Colleges, 1977-; Formerly: Hon. Vice-Consul for Republic of Haiti; Vice-Chancellor, Anglican Dio.; Administrative Adviser, Rotary Clubs in Bahamas to President of Rotary International; Treasurer and Director, YMCA; Treasurer, Bahamas Cricket Association; Chairman, Boy Scouts Executive Council; Member of Board of: Directors of Central Bank of Bahamas; Bahamas Association for Mentally Retarded. *Honours:* JP, Bahamas, 1940; Coronation Medal, 1953; Silver Jubilee Medal, 1977; GCMG., 1980; KCVO., 1977; OBE., 1964. *Hobbies:* Golf; Tennis; Table tennis; Swimming. *Address:* Government House, PO Box N 8301, Nassau, Bahamas.

CASSAB, Judy, (Mrs), b. 15 Aug. 1920, Wien, Austria. Artist. m. John Kampfner, 31 Apr. 1939, 2 sons. *Education:* Studies in Budapest & Prague. *Appointments:* One-man-shows: 1953,55,61; Macquarie Galleries Sydney, 1959-61; Crane Kalman Gallery London, 1959; Newcastle City Art Gallery, 1962; Argus Gallery, Melbourne, 1963/67/72/75/79; Rudy Komon Gallery Sydney, 1964; Georges Gallery Melbourne, 1964/70/75/79; Von Bertouch Gallery, Newcastle, 1967/69/73; Skinner Gallery, Perth, 1969; Studio White Gallery, Adelaide, 1973; Reid Gallgery, Brisbane, 1976; South Yarra Gallery, Melbourne, 1978; New Art Centre, London, 1979; Gallery One, Sydney, 1980; Masterpieces Fine Art Gallery, Hobart, 1980; Town Gallery, Brisbane, 1980; Australian Embassy, Paris, 1981; New Art Centre, London, 1981. *Memberships:* Council for the Order of Australia, 1975-79; Trustee for the Art Gallery of NSW, Sydney, 1980. *Publications:* Recent Australian Painting, 1957; Australian Painting & Sculpture, 1962; Contemporary Drawing 1963; Australian Painters, 1963; Modern Australian Painting 1963; Present Day Art in Australia, 1969; Modern Australian Painging 1960-70, 1970; Encyclopedia of Australian Art, 1970; Australian Painting, 1788-1970, 1971; Modern Australian Paintings, 1970-75, 1975; The Ephemeral Vision, 1975; Australian Landscape, 1976; ABC TV One hour Documentary Judy Cassab, Woman in Focus, 1979; Artists and Galleries of Australia and New Zealand, 1980; Master-

pieces of Australian Painting, 1969; Modern Australian Painting, 1975-80, 1980; Art International, Lugano: Review in Lettres De Paris. *Honours:* Perth Prize, Woman's Weekly Prize, 1955; W.W. Prize, 1956; Archibald Prize, 1960; Helena Rubinstein Prize, 1964-65; Sir Charles Lloyd Jones Prize, 1965/71/72/73; Archibald Prize, 1968; CBE, 1969. Represented: Art Gallery NSW; Western Australia Art Gallery; Rugby Museum, England; Nuffield Foundation, Oxford, England; Newcastle City Art Gallery; Tasmanian Art Gallery; Australian National Gallery, Canberra; Art Gallery South Australia; Bendigo City Art Gallery; National Gallery, Budapest; National Portrait Gallery, London; Museum Pecs, Hungary; Queensland Art Gallery; Rockhampton City Art Gallery. *Hobbies:* Writing; Music. *Address:* 16 C Ocean Avenue, Double Bay, Sydney 2028, Australia.

CASSAR-PULLICINO, Joseph, b. 21 Sept. 1921, Birkirkara, Malta. Civil Servant. m. Céline Bonett, 31 Jan. 1954, 2 sons, 1 daughter. *Education:* Martriculated, University of Malta, 1938; Academical Course of Literature, 1939-40; British Council Scholarship in Librarianship, Leeds & London, 1950-51; Associate of the Library Association, 1952. *Appointments:* Librarian, University of Malta, 1953-58; Assistant Director of Information, 1959-65; Assistant Secretary, Ministry of Trade, 1965-68; Senior Assistant Secretary, Ministry of Health, 1969-70; Director of Industry, 1971-79; Librarian, Faculty of Theology, Archbishop's Seminary, Rabat, Malta, 1980-. *Memberships:* Society of Maltese Writers, Servedas Council, 1942-45; Folklore Society, London, 1946; The Library Association, London, 1950; Malta Historical Society, Secretary, 1952; Accademia di Studi Superiori, Phoenix, Bari, 1956-58; Casino Maltese, 1971. *Publications:* 11 Books and Longer Studies, 'Folklore', from An Introduction to Maltese Folklore, 1947 to Background Material for the Study of Folk Arts and Crafts in Malta, 1972; 18 Other Studies from, Kifighajtu 1-bejjiegha, a collection of Maltese street-cries, 1943 to The Mediterranean Islands as Places of Synthesis of the Arab and European Cultures, 1979; Numerous Books on Language, Literature and History, from 1947-72; Many Communications at Congresses, etc., Editorial Activities, 1944-61. *Honours:* Malta Government Prize for book, Aquilina ul-Malti, 1975; Malta Literary Award, Studies in Maltese Folklore, 1979. *Address:* 'Lares' Dr. Zammit Str, Balzan, Malta.

CASSELL, David John Allenby, b. 30 June 1943, Dumfires, Scotland. Headmaster. m. 2 Apr. 1963, 2 sons, 1 daughter. *Education:* Birkbeck College London, History, French, English degree course; I.A.P.S. awarded 1972. *Appointments:* Parkside School, East Horsley Surrey, 1960-62; New Beacon School, Sevenoaks, Kent, 1962-70; Smallwood Manor School, Uttoxeter, 1970-72; Headmaster, St. Michael's, Tavistock Court, Barnstaple, 1972. *Memberships:* S.A.T.I.P.S ; I.S.I.S.; Monday Club. *Honours:* Surrey County Hockey colours, 1969; Captain of Staffordshire Hockey colours, 1971; Scotland Hockey, 1968. *Hobbies:* Sports; Gardening; Do-it-yourself; Reading. *Address:* St. Michael's, Tawstock Court, Barnstaple, Devon.

CASSON, Hugh Maxwell, b. 23 May 1910, London. Architect. m. Margaret Macdonald Troup, 19 Nov. 1938, 3 daughters. *Education:* St John's College, Cambridge; Craven Scholar, British School at Athens, 1933. *Appointments:* Private practice, 1937; Camouflage Office, Air Ministry, 1940-44; Technical Officer, Ministry of Town & Country Planning, 1944-46; Private practice, Senior Partner, Casson Conder & Partners, 1946-; Director of Architecture, Festival of Britain, 1948-51; Professor, Environmental Design, Royal College of Art, 1953-75; President the Royal Academy of Arts, 1976-. *Memberships:* Trustee, British Museum (Natural History) and National Portrait Gallery; Royal Fine Art Commission; Royal Mint Advisory Committee; Board British Council; National Trust Executive Council; GLC Historic Buildings Board. *Publications:* New Sights of London, 1937; Bombed Churches, 1946; Homes by the Million, 1947; Houses—Permanence and Prefabrication, 1947; Victorian Architecture, 1948; Inscape the Design of Interio, 1978; Nanny Says, 1972 (w. Joyce Grenfell), 1972; Spirit of the Age (w. others); Wines with Long Noses (w. G Bijur), 1978; Set designs for Covent Garden—Troilus and Cressida late 1950's; Glyndebourne, 1953/4/8 Alceste, 1962/3/4; Poppea, 1979; La Fedelta and three musicals in the West End including the sets for The World of Paul

Slickey, 1959; Regular exhibitor at Royal Academy—watercolours. *Honours:* Knight; Royal Designer for Industry, 1952; Royal Danish Academy, 1954; Hon. Associate American Institute of Architects, 1968; Hon. Doctorate Royal College of Art, 1975; Hon. Doctorate Southampton University, 1977; Hon. LLD Birmingham University, 1977; KCVO, 1978; Italian Order Al Merito della Repubblica Italiana; Hon. Doctorate, Glasgow University; Hon. Doctorate, Loughborough University of Technology, 1980. *Hobbies:* Watercolour painting; Drawing. *Address:* 60 Elgin Crescent, London, W11 2JJ, England.

CASTLE, (Rt. Hon.) Barbara Anne, (Mrs), b. 6 Oct. 1910. Member of European Parliament. m. 26 July, 1944. *Education:* BA, St Hugh's College, Oxford. *Appointments:* Member of Parliament, 1945-79; Minister of Overseas Development, 1964-65, of Transport, 1965-68; Secretary of State for Employment & Productivity, 1968-70, for Social Services, 1974-76; Member of European Parliament, 1979-. *Publications:* The Castle Diaries, 1974-76. *Honours:* Hon. Fellow, St Hugh's College, Oxford, 1968-; Hon. Doctor of Technology, Loughborough University, 1968-. *Address:* 2 Queen Anne's Gate, London, SW1, England.

CATCHESIDE, David Guthrie, b. 31 May 1907, London, England. Biologist. m. Kathleen Mary Whiteman, 19 Dec. 1931, 1 son, 1 daughter. *Education:* King's College London, BSc, MSc, DSc, 1925-36; MA, Cambridge, 1937. *Appointments:* Assistant to Professor of Botany, Glasgow University, 1928-30; Assistant Lecturer, Lecturer, Kings College, London, 1931-36; Rockefeller Fellow, 1936-37; University of Cambridge, Lecturer, 1937-50; Reader in Cytogenetics, 1950-51; Trinity College, Cambridge, Lecturer and Fellow, 1944-51; University of Adelaide, Professor of Genetics, 1952-55; University of Birmingham, Professor of Microbiology, 1956-64; Australian National University, Professor of Genetics, 1964-72; Director of Research School of Biological Sciences, 1967-72. 1964-72. *Memberships:* Fellow, Royal Society, 1951; Fellow, Australian Academy of Science, 1954; Foreign Associate, American Academy of Science, 1974. *Publications:* Genetics of Micro-organisms, 1951; Genetics of Recombination, 1977; Mosses of South Australia, 1980. *Hobbies:* Natural History, Archaeology. *Address:* 16, Rodger Avenue, Leabrook, South Australia, 5068.

CATHERWOOD, Fred, b. 30 Jan. 1925, Castledawson, Co. Londonderry N. Ireland. Chartered Accountant. m. Elizabeth Lloyd-Jones, 27 Feb. 1954, 2 sons, 1 daughter. *Education:* Cambridge University, MA; Fellow Institute of Chartered Accounts. *Appointments:* Price Waterhouse & Co., Chartered Accountants, 1946-52; Secretary Laws Stores, Gateshead, 1952-54; Secretary and Controller, 1954-55, Chief Executive, 1955-60, Richard Costain Ltd.; Assistant Managing Director, 1960-62, Managing Director, 1962-64, The British Aluminium Co, Ltd., Chief Industrial Adviser Department of Economic Affairs, 1964-66; Director General, Nation Economics Development Council, 1966-71; John Laing & Son Ltd., Managing Director, 1971-74. Mallinson Denny Ltd., Director, 1974-81; Goodyear Tyre, Director, 1974; British Institute of Management, Chairman, 1974-76; British Overseas Trades Board, Chairman, 1975-79; Member, European Parliament for Cambridgeshire and Wellingborough, 1979; Chairman, European Parliament's Committee on External Economics Relations. *Publications:* The Christian in Industrial Society, 1964, 2nd Edition, 1980; The Christian Citizen, 1969; A Better Way, 1975; First Things First, 1979. *Honours:* University of Aston, Hon DSc, 1972; Queens University Belfast, Hon DSc, 1973; University of Surrey, Hons D, 1979. *Address:* 7 Rose Crescent, Cambridge, CB2 3LL, England.

CATO, Rt. Hon. Robert Milton, b. 3 June 1915. Leader of Saint Vincent Labour Party. *Appointments:* Premier of Saint Vincent, 1967-72, 1974-79; Prime Minister of Saint Vincent and the Grenadines, 1979-. *Address:* Office of the Prime Minister, Kingstown, Saint Vincent and the Grenadines.

CATT, Shirley Pearson Clifford, b. 31 Oct. 1916, Leabrook, South Australia. Musician and Artist. m. Sydney Philip Coombe, 18 Dec. 1961. *Education:* Elder Conservatorium, University of Adelaide, 1934; Kendall Taylor for piano, London, 1950-54; Harold Darke, or-

gan; Eric Thiman, composition; South Australian School of Art, 1966-72. *Appointments:* Private Teaching; Teacher, Woodlands Church of England Girls Grammar School, Girton School, Musical Director and Organist of various churches; Burnside Painting Group, Tutor; Workers Education Association, Lecturer; Organ Recitals: Australian Broadcasting Commission; Elder Conservatorium; Adelaide Town Hall, Lunch Hour; Organ Music Society. *Memberships:* Organ Music Society, Adelaide; London Society of Organists; Adelaide Art Society; Royal South Australia Society of Arts; Music Teachers Association. *Publications:* Oil Paintings including 'The Dreaming Land'; Series of 10 paintings; Landscapes in oils and water colours. Sketching, Church Music; One Man Art Exhibitions; Several exhibitions with other artists. *Honours:* Diplomas: AMUA, L Mus A, ARCO; Bach Prize for Organ Australian Society for encouragement of music and art, 1948; Kiwanis award of Merit, 1977-80; Highly commended West Lakes exhibition, 1977; Salvation Army Centenary Exhibition, Merit Award, 1980; Highly commended, Tea Tree Gully, 1981. *Hobbies:* Gardening; Chess. *Address:* 7, Treloar Avenue, Kensington Park, South Australia 5068.

CATTERMOLE, Edward Francis, b. 12 May 1946, Bury-St-Edmunds, Suffolk, England. Director of Charity; Minister of United Reformed Church. m. Helen Jennifer Bisset, 15 July 1972, 2 sons, 1 daughter. *Education:* St. Nicholas GS, Northwood, Middlesex, 1957-64; Bristol University, (B.Sc. in Psychology) 1964-67; Westminister College, Cambridge (Certificate in Theology) 1967-70; Westhill College, Birmingham (Certificate in Youth Work) 1970-71. *Appointments:* Assistant Minister St Andrew's Presbyterian Church, Eastbourne, 1970-72; Minister St Andrew's Reformed Church, Kenton, Newcastle-Upon-Tyne, 1972-77; Youth Leadership Training Officer, United Reformed Church, Southern & Wessex Provinces, 1977-80; Director National Council For Voluntary Youth Services, 1980-. *Memberships:* Department of Education & Science Review Group of the Youth Service. *Hobbies:* Rugby Football Refereeing; Choral Singing; Humankind. *Address:* 39 Springfield Road, Leicester, LE2 3BB, England.

CAUCHI, George William, b. 1 Mar. 1925, Port Said, Egypt, Nationality, Maltese. Senior Medical Technologist — Manager. m. Edith Joyce, 21 Feb. 1964, 3 sons. *Education:* British School, Port Said, Egypt. *Appointments:* Active Service, RAF Air Sea Rescue, World War II; Royal Children's Hospital, Melbourne, 1954-; Adminstrator, Animal Research Laboratory, 1963-; Animal Research Laboratory, Parkville, Victoria, Australia. *Publications:* Has been involved in numerous projects, including: The Venturi Bronchoscopic Attachment — Paediatric Considerations; The Effect of Parathyroid Extract On Renin Release In The Dog: Comparison of the Cardiovascular Toxity of Three Tricyclic Antidepressent Drugs, Imipramine, Amitriptyline, and Doxepin; Assisting S.K. Sutherland in the Local Inactivation of Funnel-Web Spider Venom by First-Aid Measures. *Hobbies:* Gold Fossicking; Gardening; Fishing; Walking; Cycling. *Address:* 228 Melrose Drive, Tullamarine, Victoria, Australia.

CAUSE, Noel Francis, b. 7 Apr. 1927, Ipswich, Queensland, Australia. Dental Surgeon. m. Carmel Catherine Weedman, 4 sons, 3 daughters. *Education:* BDSc, Queensland University, 1950. *Appointments:* Private Practice; Staff Dentist, Senior Dentist in Orthodontia, Deputy Superintendent, Brisbane Dental Hospital; Assistant, Superintendent, South Brisbane Dental Hospital; Dentist-in-charge, Wynnum Dental Clinic; Superintendent, Brisbane Childrens Dental Hospital. First Superintendent of the Brisbane Childrens Dental Hospital, the first Paediatric Dental Hospital in Australia; Initiated the early orthodontic correction of babies born with cleft palates from the time of birth and organised the formation of the cleft palate clinic of review involving both University and North Brisbane Hospitals Board Staff. *Memberships:* Member, The Creative Glass Guild. *Hobbies:* Gemmology; Gem cutting and faceting; Silver Jewellery; Bee keeping; Fibreglass construction; Metal work; Woodwork; House renovations. *Address:* 36 Annie Street, Woody Point, Queensland 4019, Australia.

CAVDARSKI, Vanco, b. 3 Mar. 1930, Vladimirovo. Orchestral Conductor. m. Elisabeth Lythgoe, 28 Apr.

1961, 2 sons. *Education:* Diploma, Teachers' College, Skopje, Yugoslavia, 1948; Degree, Music Academy of Belgrade, 1957; Staatliche Hochschule für Musik Hamburg, Germany, 1959; Ford Foundation Scholarship, USA, 1964. *Appointments:* Conductor, Musical Director, Macedonian Philharmonic, Skopje, Yugoslavia, 1960-70; Conductor Australian Opera Sydney, Australia, 1970-72; Musical Director Christchurch Symphony Orchestra, New Zealand, 1972-74; Chief Conductor Tasmanian Symphony Orchestra, 1974-78; Chief Conductor Queensland Symphony Orchestra, 1978-; Chief Conductor, Symphony Orchestra, Radio, Television, Belgrade, Yugoslavia, 1982. *Honours:* Second Prize at the Liverpool International Conductors Competition, 1962; Macedonian Arts Award, 1962; Australian Music Critics Award, 1976. *Address:* 307 Cavendish Road, Coorparoo 4151, Brisbane, Queensland, Australia.

CEDERHOLM-WILLIAMS, Stewart Anthony, b. 8 Mar. 1947, Northampton, England. Research Biochemist. m. Gunnel Marianne, 3 Aug. 1968, 2 daughters. *Education:* BSc(Hon),CNAA, 1972; DPhil. -)-Oxon), 1977; MA, 1980; MIBiol. 1977; MRSC, 1980; CChem, 1980; MRCPath (ptl), 1980. *Appointments:* Biochemist, United Oxford Hospitals, 1972-78; Senior Biochemist, Oxford Area Health Authority, 1978-; Royal Society Travelling Fellowship, 1979; Senior Biochemist, Oxford Area Health Authority, 1979-. *Memberships:* Association of Clinical Biochemist; Complement-Haemostasis Discussion Group (Co-ordinator); British Society for Haemostasis and Thrombosis; Oxford Area Health Authority Staff Council; St. Clements, Parish Church, Oxford. Current Responsibilities for research into the mechanism of thrombosis, Supervisor for post graduate students and MRC, CRC, BHF grant holder. *Address:* Department of Haematology, John Radcliffe Hospital, Oxford, OX3 9DU, UK.

CELERMAJER, John Marian, b. 13 May 1935, Lwow, Poland. Physician. m. 8 Jan. 1961, 1 son, 1 daughter. *Education:* Lycée Charlemagne, Paris, France, 1949-50; Randwick High School, Sydney, Australia, 1950-53; Sydney University, 1953-56; MB, BS, Sydney University, (hons), FRACP, 1959. *Appointments:* Resident Medical Officer, Royal Prince Alfred Hospital, Sydney, 1960; RMO, Medical Registrar, 1961-65, Fellow, Paediatric Cardiology, 1965-67, Royal Alexandra Hospital for Children, Sydney, Senior Fellow, Paediatric Cardiology, The Johns Hopkins Hospital, Baltimore, USA, 1967-68; Staff Cardiologist, 1968-, Director, Institute of Cardiology, 1970-, Consultant Physician, 1965-, Royal Alexandra Hospital for Children, Sydney; Consultant Paediatric Cardiologist, The Women's Hospital, Sydney, 1980-; Consultant Paediatric Cardiologist, The Westmead Centre, Sydney, 1981-. *Memberships:* International Society and Federation of Cardiology (Member of Scientific Council on Paediatric Cardiology); Cardiac Society of Australia and New Zealand; Australian College of Paediatrics; Australian Medical Association; Australian Golf Club, Sydney, Australia. *Publications:* Scientific articles in Medical journals including: Circulation, American Heart Journal, British Heart Journal, The Lancet, American Journal of Diseases of Children, Journal of Paediatrics, Paediatric Radiology, Medical Journal of Australia, Australian and New Zealand Journal of Medicine, Australian Paediatric Journal, Journal Thoracic and Cardiovascular Surgery etc. *Hobbies:* Collecting modern Australian Art; Antique Silver; Golf. *Address:* 7 Hopetoun Avenue, Vaucluse, Sydney, N.S.W., 2030, Australia.

CHABRIA, Narain. L, b.27 May 1934, Shikarpur, India. Physician. m. Shilu, 30 Dec. 1962, 1 son, 1 daughter. *Education:* MBBS, Bombay, 1959; MD, Bombay, 1964; ECFMG, United States, 1961. *Appointments:* Research Fellow, G. S. Medical College, Bombay, 1961-62; Junior Lecturer in Pharmacology, Grant Medical College, Bombay, 1962-65; Assistant Professor of Pharmacology & Matera Medica, T.N. Medical College, Bombay, 1965-68; Senior Medical Adviser, Hoechst Pharmaceuricals, 1968-77; Vice President-Medical Services, Warner-Hindustan Ltd., Bombay, 1977-. *Memberships:* Indian Pharmacological Society; Diabetic Association of India; Association of Physicians of India; Indian Association for Chest Diseases; Indian Society of Gastroenterology; Cardiological Society of India; Association of Medical Advisers to the Pharmaceutical Industry (India). *Publications:* Author and co-author, Nine research papers in National and International Journals and Publications. *Honours:* Bombay University Exam for 2nd MBBS, 1967-68. *Hobbies:* Swimming; Literature; Reading. *Address:* Flat No. 10, Bhole Apartments, Jn. of 17th & 13th Roads, Khar, Bombay 400 052, India.

CHADWICK, Clarence Earl, b. 29 May 1909, Billinudgel, N.S.W. Australia. Entomologist. *Education:* University of Sydney, B.Sc., 1932. *Appointments:* Teacher, N.S.W. Department of Education, 1933-46; Lecturer Broken Hill, Technical College, 1941-42, 1944; Systematic Entomologist and Curator of Collection, N.S.W. Department of Agriculture, 1947-74. *Memberships:* Entomological Society of Australia (N.S.W.), Founder 1953, President, 1953-60, 1963-78, Vice President 1961, Council, 1962, Hon. Editor, 1964-77; Royal Zoology Society N.S.W., Entomology Section Chairman, 1979-; Barrier Field Naturalists' Club, President, 1942-44; Sturt Centenary Celebrations, Broken Hill, 1944, President, Illawarra Natural History Society, Founder, 1946, President, 1946, 1948, Vice President, 1947, 1949; Honorary Secretary, 1951-56; Honorary Treasurer, 1951-52, Council, 1957-58; Naturalists' Society, N.S.W. Vice President, 1947-48; Wild Life Preservation Society Council, 1949-52. *Publications:* 58 mostly on entomology; others in press and in preparation. *Honours:* Illawarra Natural History Society, Honorary Life Member, 1959; Entomological Society of Australia (N.S.W.), Honorary Life Member, 1975; Australian Museum (Honorary) Research Associate, 1976-. *Hobbies:* Photography; Motoring. *Address:* 1/155 Herring Road, North Ryde, N.S.W. Australia, 2113.

CHAKAIPA, Patrick Fani, b. 25 June 1932, Mhondoro, Zimbabwe. Roman Catholic Priest. *Education:* St Michael's Mission, Mhondoro; Minor and Major Seminaries, Chishawasha; Kutama Teacher Training College. *Appointments:* Ordained Priest, 1965; Auxiliary Bishop of Salisbury, 1973; Archbishop of Salisbury, 1976. *Publications:* Karikoga Gumiremiseve; Pfumo Reropa; Rudo Ibofu; Garandichauya; Dzasukwa Kwana Asina Hembe (Shona Novels). *Address:* Archbishop's House, 66 Fifth Street, Salisbury, Zimbabwe.

CHAKKO, Puthenpurayil Thommy, b. 3 Feb. 1927, Ranny, Kerala, India. Medical Doctor, Ophthalmologist. m. Aley Poothicot, 14 Feb. 1954, 1 son, 1 daughter. *Education:* Intermediate Science with distinction in Chemistry, 1945; LMP, 1949; LCPS, 1950; MBBS, with distinction in Pathology, 1959; DO (Diploma in Ophthalmology, London), 1962; MS (Master of Surgery, Ophthalmology), 1964. *Appointments:* General Practitioner, Bahrain, Arabian Gulf, 1953-57, 1959-61; Lecturer in Ophthalmology, Christian Medical College, Vellore, India, 1964-67; Department Head, Ophthalmology, Lisie Hospital, Kerala, India, 1967-73; Director, Chief Consultant, Lumas Eye Hospital, Kerala, India, 1973-76; Consultant in Ophthalmology Ahmedu Belle University teaching Hospital, Kaduna, Nigeria, 1976-80, promoted to Senior Consultant, 1980-; Reader and Head of Department of Ophthamology, School of Medicine, University of Calabar, Nigeria, 1981. *Memberships:* Indian Medical Association; All, India Ophthalmological Society; Madras State Ophthalmological Association; Founder Secretary and later Vice-President and President Elect, Kerala State Ophthalmological Society; Founder Secretary, National Society for the prevention of Blindness, Kerala State Branch; Ophthalmological Society of Nigeria; Pan-African Ophthalmological Society; International Filariasis Association, London; International Agency for the Prevention of Blindness; The Society of Eye Surgeons of International Eye Foundation; Secretary, Vice-President and President-elect, Rotary Club of Cochin; Director International Service TRotary Club of Kadune, Nigeria. *Publications:* A number of new concepts and techniques in Surgery including: A new technique of trabeculectomy in difficult glaucoma, a new concept in corneal graft for rather hopeless cases, skin graft technique, Scleral inlay technique for correction of entropion and trichiasis. New instruments including: New lid clamps for whole lid surgery, new speculum cum, holder for beta-ray applicator; Many ongoing research projects. *Hobbies:* Philately; Photography. *Address:* Department of Opthalmology, University of Calabar Teaching Hospital, Calabar, Cross River State, Nigeria.

CHAKRABARTI, Radharaman, b. 9 Dec. 1939, Hooghly, West Bengal, India. University Professor. m.

Krishna (Roy Choudhury), 13 August 1963, 1 son, 1 daughter. *Education:* BA, Hons. Economics & Political Science, Presidency College, Calcutta University, 1960; MA, Political Science, Calcutta University, 1962; PhD, International Relations, University of London, 1969. *Appointments:* Assistant Professor, Political Science, Presidency College, Calcutta, 1963-71; Reader in Political Science, University of Burdwan, 1971; Professor Political Science, Chairman of the Subject, 1972-; Dean Faculty of Arts, 1977, University of Burdwan. *Memberships:* Vice-President, Council Political Studies, Calcutta, 1972-; Executive Committee, Indian Political Science Association, 1975-76; Editor-Secretary, Journal of Humanities, Burdwan University, 1972; Board of Editors, Socialist Perspective, Calcutta. *Publications:* Intervention & the Problem of its Control in the 20th Century; In preparation: The Political Economy of India's Foreign Policy; Understanding International Politics. *Honours:* Proficiency Prize in History, 1956; Duff Scholarship in Languages, Calcutta University, 1958; Surendranath Banerjee Prize in International Relations and Gold Medal, Calcutta University, 1962; LSE Scholarship in International Law 1967. *Hobbies:* Drama. *Address:* C-5 Tarabag, PO Burdwan, W. Bengal, India 713104.

CHALLIS, Louis Aron, b. 20 July 1936, Sydney, New South Wales, Australia, Consulting Acoustical Engineer. m. Anna Mariana Wollner, 28 Jan. 1962, 2 sons. *Education:* Bachelor Electrical Engineering, 1961, Master Science Archtiecture, 1979, Sydney University. *Appointments:* Royal Australian Navy Experimental Laboratory, 1961-62; Overseas Telecommunications Commission, Australia, 1962-66; Founder & Senior Partner of Louis A. Challis & Associates Pty. Limited, 1966-. *Memberships:* Member, Founder, Divisional Committee Member, Australian Acoustical Society; Fellow, Institution of Engineers of Australia; Association of Consulting Engineers, Australia; Standards Association of Australia Acoustics Committee; Australia Delegate, IEC TC29 and ISO SC43, 1973-, 1975, 1977, 1979, 1980. *Publications:* Consultant and Senior Review writer, Electronics Today International; Author of numerous papers at National & International Acoustical Conferences; Three patents on Acoustical Products. *Honours:* Australia Engineering Merit Awards, Association of Consulting Engineers, Australia, 1976 and 1981. *Hobbies:* Sailing, Photography; Music; The Arts. *Address:* 3 Macleay Street, Dover Heights, New South Wales 2030, Australia.

CHALLIS, Reuben Lionel Grover, b. 12 Mar. 1916, New Zealand. Foreign Correspondent & Lecturer. *Appointments:* Commissioned RNZNVR and seconded to RN Squadron Radar Officer, to British Eastern Fleet, 1941-45; Executive Officer, United Nations in China and deputy political liaison officer to Chinese National Government in Nanking, 1946-47; Attached to New Zealand Legation Washington as New Zealand official to Far Eastern Commission for Japan, 1947; Head of New Zealand Government Reparations and Trade Mission in Occupied Japan, 1947-51; Head of New Zealand Diplomatic Mission in Occupied Japan, 1951-52; Charge d'affaires e.p. of New Zealand Legation in Japan, 1952-56; Charge d'affaires of New Zealand Embassy in Thailand Acting New Zealand member of SEATO Council Representative in Bangkok, 1956-58; High Commissioner for New Zealand in India, 1958-60; Consul General for New Zealand for the Western USA, 1960-63; Commissioner for New Zealand in Singapore and Borneo Territories, 1963-64; Head of New Zealand Legation in Indonesia, 1965; Commissioner for New Zealand in Hong Kong and concurrently Minister of New Zealand to the Philippines, 1965-68; Ambassador of New Zealand to Indonesia, 1968-72; Foreign Correspondent and Lecturer, 1972-. *Hobbies:* Tennis; Golf; Fishing; Boating; Skiing. *Address:* Box 74, Wakatipu Post Office, Otago, New Zealand.

CHAMBERS, Jim Bernard, b. 18 Feb. 1919, Napier, New Zealand. Minister of Religion (Congregational). m. Marcelle Jeanne Connor, 10 Dec. 1945, 3 sons, 1 daughter. *Education:* Auckland University, 1940-43; Otago University, 1944-46; Trinity Methodist Theological College, Auckland, 1940-42; BA, 1945; MA, 1947. *Appointments:* Assistant Minister, Congregational Churches, New Lynn, Auckland, 1940-42, Beresford Street, Auckland, 1944; Ordained 1945; Minister, Ravensbourne & Port Chalmers, 1944-50, Timaru, 1950-54, Karori, Wellington, 1954-59, Maungaturoto, 1959-

63, Cambridge Terrace, Wellington, 1963-. *Memberships:* Chairman, Congregational Union of New Zealand, 1952-53, 1966-68, 1969-79; Council for World Mission, 1966-; Executive, 1977, Secretary for Australia, New Zealand, Pacific Islands, Hong Kong, India, 1979-, International Congregational Fellowship; The Order of St Luke the Physician in New Zealand, Senior Chaplain, 1965-69, Warden 1972-75, Missioner at Large, 1978-; New Zealand Marching Association, 1954-59, 1963-79, New Sealand President, 1967-77; Patron Wellington Centre, 1976-, Wellington Association, 1977; Grand Master, Grand Orange Lodge of New Zealand, 1970-74. *Publications:* The Karori Congregational Church 1842-1956, 1956; Hands Can Heal, 1968; Is Any Sick Among You, 1962 (11th printing 1980); To God Be The Glory, 1965; The Cambridge Terrace Congregational Church, 1877-1967, 1967; Editor New Zealand Marching Association, Bulletin, 1965-77, Quick Step, 1977-79. *Honours:* Ordinary Officer of the Civil Division of the Most Excellent Order of the British Empire (OBE), 1978. *Hobbies:* Lodges; Druids; Masons. *Address:* 29 Alexander Road, Raumati, New Zealand.

CHAMBERS, John Harrison, b. 13 Sept. 1939, Ipswich, Queensland, Australia. Philosopher of Education. *Education:* B.A., University of Queensland, 1964-; M.A., University of London, 1971-; M.Ed. Administration, University of New England, 1980-; University of Tasmania. *Appointments:* Queensland Education Department; New Zealand Education Department; Inner London Education Authority; Hereford College of Education; Maria Grey College, University of London; Tasmanian College of Advanced Education. *Memberships:* Secretary, London & Middlesex Archaeological Society Schools' Section, 1965-69; Chairman, Royal Society of St. George, Ipswich Branch, 1961, 1962-; Royal Institute of Philosophy, 1969-; Philosophy of Education Society of Australasia, 1974-. *Publications:* Examining Key Concepts in Education, 1981-; The Achievement of Education (Accepted, forthcoming), 1982; Knowledge Authority & Tertiary Educational Administration, (Accepted, forthcoming), 1981-; 50 articles in educational/literary journals. *Hobbies:* Cricket, Jogging, The Arts, History. *Address:* 6 Matthew Place, Launceston, Tasmania.

CHAMPION, Geoffrey David, b. 16 Mar. 1937, Parramatta, N.S.W., Australia. Medical Practitioner (Consultant Physician). m. Caroline Mayhew Thompson, 3 May 1962, 1 son, 2 daughters. *Education:* M.B., B.S., University of Sydney, 1962-; Royal Australasian College of Physicians, Membership, 1966-, Fellowship, 1972-. *Appointments:* Junior R.M.O. The Royal North Shore Hospital of Sydney, (R.N.S.H.), 1962-63; Srnior R.M.O., R.N.S.H., 1963-64; Medical Resident, Repatriation General Hospital, Concord, N.S.W., 1964-67; Spurway Fellow in the Rheumatic Diseases, 1967-69, Clinical Superintendent, 1969, R.N.S.H., 1969-; Research Fellow, Medical Research Council Rheumatism Unit, Canadian Red Cross Memorial Hospital, Taplow. U.K., 1969-70; Research Fellow, Division of Rheumatology, Department of Medicine, University of California, U.S.A., 1970-71; Clinical Fellow, Medical Professorial Unit, St. Vincent's Hospital, Darlinghurst, N.S.W., 1972-73; Honorary Rheumatologist, Ryde District Soldiers Memorial Hospital, N.S.W., 1972-74; Visiting Physician, Repatriation General Hospital, Concord, N.S.W., 1972-77; Honorary, Visiting Physician in Rheumatologyk St. Vincent's Hospital, Darlinghurst, N.S.W., 1973-; Honorary, Visiting Consultant Physician in Rheumatology (Paediatric), Prince Henry and Prince of Wales Hospitals, later Prince of Wales Children's Hospital, N.S.W., 1974-; *Memberships:* Australian Medical Association; Royal Australasian College of Physicians; Australian Rheumatism Association; Australian Arthritis & Rheumatism Foundation; Arthritis & Rheumatism Council; National Health & Medical Research Council; Commonwealth Department of Health; Heberden Society, London; Australasian Society of Clinical and Experimental Pharmacologists; International Association for the Study of Pain; University of N.S.W. *Publications:* Author and co-author of numerous and varied articles in professional journals, 1968-; Papers presented to learned societites, 1969-. *Honours:* Commonwealth Travelling Fellowship by The Australian Arthritis and Rheumatism Foundation, in conjunction with a Geigy Grant of the Arthritis & Rheumatism Council of Great Britain, 1969-; Abbott Fellowship of the Royal Australasian

College of Physicians, 1971-; Research Award, Southern California Rheumatism Society, 1971-; Part-time Research Grant, Royal Australasian College of Physicians, 1972-; Part-time Research Grant, Tweddle Fellowship, Royal Australasian College of Physicians, 1975-. *Hobbies:* Tennis, Books, Music. *Address:* 69 Northwood Road, Northwood, 2066 Australia

CHAN, Cecil Shu On, b. 24 Oct. 1938, Hong Kong. Chartered, Professional Engineer. m. Rita H.Y. 23 Dec. 1965, 1 daughter. *Education:* Diploma E.E./Grad. IEE (U.K.), 1963-; Chartered Engineer, (U.K.), 1968-; Registered Professional Engineer, Toronto, Canada, 1972-; Senior Member, IEEE (U.S.A.), 1974-; Fellow, Royal Society for Health, (U.K.), 1974-; Fellow IEE (U.K.), 1975-. *Appointments:* Head, Electrical Design, Taikoo Dockyard and Engineering. Co., Ltd., Hong Kong, 1963-69; Technical Director, Federation of Hong Kong Industries, 1969-72; Executive Director, Federation of Hong Kong Industries, 1972-; Director, Hong Kong Standards & Testing Centre, 1969-; Director, Hong Kong Industrial Design Council, 1976-; Director, Hong Kong Packaging Council, 1976-; Director, Asian Packaging Information Centre, 1976-. *Memberships:* Chairman, Hong Kong Section, Institute of Electrical & Electronics Engineers; Governor, Hong Kong Baptist College, Hong Kong; Director, Chinese Y.M.C.A. Hong Kong; President, Asian Baptist Youth Fellowship; Chairman, Electronic Engineering Advisory Committee, Hong Kong Polytechnic. *Publications:* Guide to Design of Marine Electrical Systems; Selection of H.R.C. Fuses. *Honours:* Governor Appointed Adjudicator in Immigration Tribunal, 1980-; Governor Appointed Lay Assessor in Magistracies, 1978-; Institution of Electrical Engineers Prize, 1962-. *Hobbies:* Photography, Swimming, Soccer. *Address:* Blk. 4 Balwin Court, A-11, 154-164 Argyle Street, Kowloon, Hong Kong.

CHAN, Heun Yin, b. 22 July 1942, Kuala Lumpur, Malaysia. Principal Soil Scientist. m. Katherine Tung Hoh Yun, 18 Jan. 1969, 1 son, 1 daughter. *Education:* B. Agric. Sc., University of Malaya, Kuala Lumpur, Malaysia, 1965-; M.S., Cornell University, Ithaca, USA., 1974-. *Appointments:* Principal Soil Scientist, Rubber Research Institute of Malaysia, 1965-; Consultant in World Bank/FAO Feasibility Study Team on rubber projects in Tanzania, Africa. *Memberships:* Associate Malaysian Scientific Association; Agricultural Institute of Malaysia; Honorary Sercetary, Malaysian Society of Soil Science, 1976-78; International Society of Soil Science. *Publications:* Author 19 papers and co-author of 17 papers in Technical publications on soil surveys, pedology and land use; Nine local and One International, Technical consultancy/feasibility study reports. *Honours:* Gold Medalist for best all-round student, University of Malaya, 1964-; Invited to present specialist papers in International Confernces in India, Rome and Philippines; Congress Award Recipient, International Society of Soil Science XIth Congress, Edmonton, Canada, 1978-. *Hobbies:* Golf, Cricket, Badminton, Swimming. *Address:* 25D Hillside Estate, Ampang Jaya, Kuala Lumpur, Malaysia.

CHAN, Jimmy, Wing-Cheung, b. 10 Dec. 1934, Hong Kong. Education. m. 31 Mar. 1962, 2 sons, 1 daughter. *Education:* BSc., Dip. Ed., MA. (Ed.), University of Hong Kong; BSc., Sp. Honours Ac.Dip. Ed., M.Phil., PhD. University of London. *Appointments:* Senior Education Officer, Educational Research Establishment, Education Department, Hong Kong; Honorary Lecturer, Psychology Department, Part-time Lecturer, Department of Extra-Mural Studies, University of Hong Kong; Part-time Lecturer, School of Education, Part-time Lecturer, Department of Extramural Studies, The Chinese University of Hong Kong. *Memberships:* Vice-President, Hong Kong Teachers' Association; Chief Editor, New Horizons, Journal of Education, Hong Kong; Chairman, Hong Kong Research Council in Biological Education; Deputy Chairman, Convocation, University of Hong Kong; Executive Committeee, International Association for Cross-Cultural Psychology; World Congress Committee and International Development Committee, International Reading Association; Treasurer, Hong Kong Reading Association. *Publications:* Over 30 articles in various Hong Kong and overseas learned journals, more than ten papers presented at international educational and psychological conferences; Four books on different school teaching subjects. *Honours:* Sino-British Scholarship, 1966,67,69,73,77-; British

Council Visitorship, 1969,73,77-; Commonwealth Scholarship, 1970-72; International Fellow, Melbourne University, 1975-; Fellow of College of Preceptors, London, 1977-; Consultant Western Kentucky University, 1979-; Consultant South-West Texas State University, 1981-; Visiting Scholar, University of California, Berkeley, 1981-. *Hobbies:* Stamp collecting, Photography. *Address:* Palm Court, B10, 55, Robinson Road, Hong Kong.

CHAN, Julius (The Rt. Hon. Sir), b. 29 Aug. 1939, Tanga Island, New Ireland Province, Papua New Guinea. Politician. m. Lady Stella, 27 Aug. 1966, 3 sons, 1 daughter. *Education:* Agricultural Science, University of Queensland, Australia, 1959. *Appointments:* Co-operative Officer, Papua New Guinea Administration, Australian Government, 1960-62; Private business in coastal shipping and merchandise, 1963-70; Elected Member of Papua New Guinea House of Assembly, Deputy Speaker of the House of Assembly, Vice-Chairman of Public Accounts Committee, 1968-72; Elected Parliamentary Leader of the People's Progress Party, 1970-; Re-elected Member of the House of assembly and Minister for Finance, Governor Asian Development Bank, 1972-77; Nominated Vice-Chairman of the Asian development Bank (Governor for PNG); Governor, World Bank/IMF; Re-elected Member of Parliament, Deputy Prime Minister and Minister for Primary Industry, 1977; Withdrew from Government coalition to take People's Progress Party into Opposition; Elected Prime Minister, 1980. *Memberships:* Elected Fellowship Member of International Banker Association Incorporation (FIBA), USA, 1976; Member of several Delegations and Commissions; Attended numerous Conferences; Several State Visits, as Prime Minister, to Australia, Indonesia, United Kingdom, France, Belgium, Italy and New Zealand. *Honours:* CBE, 1975; Honorary DEc., Dankook University, Seoul, Republic of Korea, 1978; Granted the title Honourable, by Her Majesty the Queen, 1979; KBE, 1980; Privy Councillor, 1981. *Hobbies:* Speedboat; Fishing. *Address:* P O Box 423, Rabaul, ENBP, Papua New Guinea.

CHAN, Michael Chew Koon, b. 6 Mar. 1940, Singapore. Senior Lecturer in Tropical Paediatrics, Honorary Consultant Paediatrician. m. Irene Chee, 13 Nov. 1965, 1 son, 1 daughter. *Education:* M.B., B.S. London, M.R.C.S., England, L.R.C.P., London, Guy's Hospital Medical School, University of London, 1958-64; M.D., University of Singapore, 1969-; M.R.A.C.P. Paediatrics, 1971-; F.R.A.C.P. 1975 Royal Australasian College of Physicians. *Appointments:* House Surgeon, Hackney General Hospital, London; House Physician Brook General Hospital, London; Medical Officer, Kandang Kerbau Hospital for Women, Singapore; Research Fellow in Neonatology, Department of Paediatrics, Lecturer, Department of Paediatrics, University of Singapore; Heinz Fellow, Department of Haematology, Institite of Child Health, University of London; Senior Lecturer and Consultant Paediatrician, Department of Paediatrics, University of Singapore and Singapore General Hospital; Senior Lecturer in Tropical Paediatrics, School of Tropical Medicines, University of Liverpool; Honorary Consultant Paediatrician, Mersey Regional Health Authority. *Memberships:* British Paediatric Association, Convenor Overseas Committee, 1980-, Convenor, British Tropical Child Health Group, 1980-; British Medical Association; Christian Medical Fellowship; Liverpool Medical Institution; Royal College of Physicians, London; Royal Society of Tropical Medicine and Hygiene; Singapore Medical Association; Singapore Paediatric Society, Honorary Treasurer, 1968-69; Merseyside Chinese Community Serviives, Honorary Medical Consultant since, 1977-. *Publications:* Thesis, Bleeding Disorders in Infants; Chapters on Neonatal Jaundice, Childhood Anaemias & Dengue Haemorrhagic Fever, 1981-; Chapter on Tropical Child Health and Paediatrics, 1982-; More than 30 papers on haematology, neonatology and tropical paediatrics in medical journals. *Honours:* Heinz Fellowship, British Paediatric Association, 1974-75; Post-graduate Research Fellowship, University of Singapore, 1966-68. *Hobbies:* Colour photography, Badminton, Student welfare work, Chinese cooking. *Address:* 1 Rathmore Drive, Oxton, Birkenhead, Wirral, Merseyside L43 2HD, England.

CHAN, Roland Man Sang, b. 28 Jan. 1949, Hong Kong. Managing Director. m. Jannie Ng Sui Shan, 19 Aug. 1976, 1 son. *Education:* Tak Sun Anglo-Chinese

School, 1956-61; Diocesan Boys' School, 1961-63; Greenmore College, England, 1963-64; Quantock School, England, 1964-68; BSc, Woodbury University, Los Angles, U.S.A. 1968-73. *Appointments:* Kowloon Rattanware Co., Ltd., 1973-. *Memberships:* Architectural Association, London; Heraldry Society, London; Fellow Royal Numismatic Society, London; British Numismatic Society, London; American Numismatic Society; American Society of Interior Designers; Hong Kong Designers Association. *Hobbies:* Swimming, Reading, Tennis, Fishing, Music. *Address:* Kowloon Rattanware Co. Ltd., 24 Ashley Road, 1st Floor A, Astoria Building, Kowloon, Hong Kong.

CHAN, Wing On, b. 16 Feb. 1922, Kwangtung, China. Architect. m. Leung Siu Ying, 21 Apr. 1952, 2 daughters. *Education:* Mapua Institute of Technology, Philippines, 1938-46; BSc., Architecture, Diploma 1942. *Appointments:* Assistant Architect Hong Kong Engineering & Construction Co., Ltd., 1947-59; Authorized Architect in Private Practice, 1960-. *Memberships:* The Hong Kong Institute of Architects; Airline Passengers Association Incorporated. *Hobbies:* Reading, Painting Travelling. *Address:* Pearl City Mansion, 7th Floor, Flat A2, 22-36 Paterson Street, Hong Kong.

CHANA, Tara Singh, b. 28 Oct. 1948, Nairobi, Kenya. Architect, Planner. m. 2 Sept. 1973, 2 daughters. *Education:* B.A. (Arch. St.), 1971-; M. Arch., 1973-, University of Nairobi, 1969-73; M.A.A.S., 1974-; Master of City Planning, Massachusetts Institute of Technology, M.I.T., 1971-75. *Appointments:* Teaching Assistant, Massachusetts Institute of Technology, U.S.A., 1974-; Consultant & Research Assistant, Internation Bank for Reconstruction & Development, World Bank, U.S.A., 1975-; Project Architect Planner & Acting Assistant Director, Housing Development Department, Nairobi City Council, Kenya, 1976-; Director, Housing Research & Development Unit, 1978-; Senior Lecturer, 1978, University of Nairobi, Kenya. Director, Human Settlement Consultants, 1978-. *Memberships:* Director, Vice-Chairman, Executive Committee, Environment Liaison Centre; Director, Chairman, Mazingira Institute; Architectural Association of Kenya, Town Planning Chapter; American Institute of Architects. *Publications:* Post Habitat Evaluation of Human Settlements in Kenya & Tanzania, 1978-; Nairobi's Informal Economic Sector, Ekistics, 1975-; Land Crisis, Ekistics, 1974-; Village 4B, Documentary Film, 1973-; 20 Published & unpublished papers; 15 Research Reports. *Honours:* American Institute of Architects Foundation Scholastic Award, 1973-. *Hobbies:* Swimming, Golf, Travel. *Address:* P.O. Box 41591, Nairobi, Kenya.

CHANDARIA, Nemu, b. 12 Sept. 1939, Ravalsar, India. Managing Director. m. Meena, 16 Apr. 1964, 2 sons, 1 daughter. *Education:* Duke of Gloucester High School, Nairobi, Kenya. *Appointments:* General Manager, Ethiopian Aluminium Co., Asmara, Ethiopia, 1963-73; Chairman, Steel Co., of Ethiopia, Asmara, Ethiopia, 1965-73; Managing Director, Petroplastics & Chemicals Ltd., U.K., 1974-; Director, Nigerian Synthetic Chemical Industry Ltd., *Memberships:* Institute of Directors; Rotary Club, London. *Hobbies:* Devotional Music, Badminton, Table Tennis. *Address:* 6 Hall Farm Close, Stanmore, Middlesex, HA7 4JT, England.

CHAND, Khub, b. 16 Dec. 1911, Khurd, Dist. Jhelum, India. Diplomat; Consultant. m. Nirmal Singh, 18 Jan. 1948. *Education:* BA(Hons), University of Delhi and Oriel College, Oxford. *Appointments:* Civil Service, Joint Magistrate, Shajahanpur and Moradabad, Additional District Magistrate, Cawnpore, Assistant Commissioner, Lucknow, 1935-39; Under Secretary, Department of Defence, Assistant Financial Adviser, Military Finance, 1939-43; District Magistrate, Azamgarh, 1943-45; Regional Food Controller, United Provinces 1945-47; Head, Indian Military Mission, Allied Control Council for Germany, Major-General, Indian Army, 1948-50; Diplomatic Service numerous appointments including: Acting High Commissioner, India in Pakistan, 1950-52; Ambassador of India to Italy, 1957-60 and Federal Republic of Germany, 1967-70; Consultant for International Development and Business Relations, 1972-. *Memberships:* Director, Kiwanis Club of New Delhi; President, Federation of Indo-German Societies in India. *Publications:* Several books and journals, in the field of Political and Economic affairs; Co-author, Im Urteil des Auslands—Dreissig Jahre Bundesrepublik, 1979. *Honours:* Grand Cross of the Order of Merit, Federal Republic of Germany, 1978; President, Oxford-Cambridge Society, Delhi, 1979. *Hobbies:* Bridge; Travel. *Address:* 1/8A Shanti Niketan, New Delhi 110021, India.

CHANDLER, Geoffrey, b. 15 Nov. 1922, London. Manager. m. Lucy Bertha Buxton, 12 Aug. 1955, 4 daughters. *Education:* Sherborne School, 1936-41; M.A., Trinity College, Cambridge, 1947-49; Commonwealth Fund Fellow, Columbia University, New York, 1953-54. *Appointments:* War Service, 1942-46; B.B.C. Foreign News Service, 1949-51; Financial Times, 1951-56; Shell International Petroleum, 1956-64; Shell Trinidad, Chairman & Managing Director, 1964-69; Coordinator, Shell International Public Affairs, 1969-78; Director, Shell International Shell Petroleum Ltd., Shell Petroleum, N.Y. Director General, National Economic Development Office, 1978-. *Memberships:* President, Institute of Petroleum, 1972-74; Athenaeum; Hawks, Cambridge. *Publications:* Books on Greece, Trinidad and Tobago; Numerous articles on Oil, Energy and Economic subjects. *Honours:* C.B.E., 1976-. *Hobbies:* Oboe Playing, Gardening. *Address:* 57 Blackheath Park, London, SE3 9SQ.

CHANDLER, Peter Charles, b. 7 Mar. 1941, Melbourne, Australia. Marketing Academic. *Education:* Bachelor of Commerce, University of Melbourne, 1966-; Master of Arts (Marketing), University of Lancaster, 1977-. *Appointments:* Marketing Executive, Bunge (Aust.,) Pty., Ltd., (Melbourne), 1960-66, McCall Corporation (New York), 1967-; Assistant to Marketing Director, Walpamur Paints, Melbourne, 1968-; Executive Assistant to General Manager, Australian Tourism Commission, Melbourne, 1969-72; Present Head of Marketing Department David Syme Business School, Caulfield Institute of Technology, Melbourne, 1971-; Consultant, 1971-; Director, Australian Apple and Pear Corporation, 1973-; Marketing Consultant, Australian Administrative Staff College, 1979-; Chairman, City Wide Industrial Work Garment Services; 1979-; Chairman, Marketing Strategy Services Pty. Ltd., 1980-. *Memberships:* Australian Institute of Export; Market Research Society; Australian Institute of Management; Royal Tennis Club. *Publications:* Agricultural Marketing Education in the U.S.A., 1973-. *Honours:* Honorary Life Membership, A.I.E.S.E.C., Australia, 1966-. *Hobbies:* Farming. *Address:* Timbarra, Flinders Road, Red Hill, Victoria 3937, Australia.

CHANDRA, Lokesh, b. 11 April 1927, Ambala, India. Member of Parliament. m. 1952, 2 sons. *Education:* M.A., D.Litt. *Appointments:* Director, International Academy of Indian Culture, New Delhi 16. *Publications:* 300 publications on Sanskrit, Tibetan, Mongolian, Chinese, Japanese, Manchu, Indonesian Art, Literature and History. *Honours:* Jauahaulah Nehru Fellowship, 1973. *Hobbies:* Social work; Iconography. *Address:* J22 Hauz Khas Enclave, New Delhi 110016.

CHANDRATREYA, Gopal Lakshman, b. 18 Nov. 1911, Nasik, India. m. 13 June 1937, 1 son, 1 daughter. *Education:* B.A. 1st Class, Mathematics, 1930-; BSc., 1st Class Distinction, Physics, 1932-; M.A., 1st Class, Mathematics, 1933-, Bombay University. B.A., 1st Class Mathematics, Wrangler, 1935-; M.A. Mathematics, Cambridge University, 1945-. *Appointments:* Professor of Mathematics, Fergusson College, Poona & University of Bombay & Poona, 1936-54; Professor & Principal, Willingdon College, Sangli University of Poona, 1954-59; Professor, Principal and Dean, University of Delhi, Delhi, 1959-75; Honorary Professor, 1975-81. *Memberships:* Treasurer, Indian Science Congress; Treasurer Indian Mathematic Society, 1939-55; Treasurer Delhi Mathematical Society, 1959-75; President, Society for Unification of Science and Culture, 1975-81; Chairman, Dean of Board, Studies Senates Executive Committee, Academic Councils of Bombay, Poona, Delhi, Mysore, Baroda, Banaras & other Universities. *Publications:* Calculus, Geometry, Higher Mechanics, Advanced Text books in Mathematics and Physics (Books); Published papers, in journals of India and foreign Countries (12). *Honours:* Fitzwilliam Prize, Cambridge University, 1935-; Approximately 30 scholarships and 50 prizes. Dinanath Manker, Gold Medal; Dinshaw Petit Science Scholarship; Publication grants for Monographs; Visiting Professor to U.S.A., 1957-58. *Hobbies:* Interpreting Ancient literature scientifically; Written articles and monographs in Veda

Upanishads Cosmology and Cosmogony of Ancient literature. *Address:* Seetaram, 1233-B, Apte Road, Pune 411004, India.

CHANEN, William, b. 6 May 1927, Melbourne, Australia. Gynaecologic Surgeon. m. Ann Mordech, 8 June 1960, 2 sons, 1 daughter. *Education:* Melbourne Church of England Grammar School, 1938-44; M.B.B.S., University Melbourne, 1951-; D.G.O., Melbourne, 1955-; M.R.C.O.G., London, 1956-; F.R.C.S., Edinburgh, 1957-; F.R.A.C.S., 1964-; F.R.C.O.G., 1971-; F.R.A.C.O.G., 1979-. *Appointments:* Resident Medical Officer, Royal Melbourne Hospital, 1952-; R.M.O., Registrar, Royal Women's Hospital, Melbourne, 1953-54; 2nd Assistant to Professor Obstetrics & Gynaecology, University Melbourne, 1955-; Registrar, Royal Salop Infirmary, Shrewsbury U.K. 1957-58; Honorary Associate, Obst., & Gynaec., Royal Women's Hospital, 1959-66; Honorary Obst., & Gynaec., Footscray & District Hospital, 1961-66; Honorary Surgeon, Gynaec., Outpatients Royal Women's Hospital, 1965-70; Senior Gynaecologist, Royal Women's Hospital, 1971-; Senior Associate, Department Obst., & Gynaec., University Melbourne, 1971-. *Memberships:* Honorary Secretary, Australian Society of Colposcopy & Cervical Pathology; The Naval & Military Club; Victorian Amateur Turf Club. *Publications:* Numerous scientific articles on cancer and pre-cancerous lesions of the female Genital tract to Australian, British and American Journals; Contributing author, Gynaecologic Oncology, 1981-. *Hobbies:* Modern Australian Art. *Address:* 2 St. James Place, Toorak, 3142, Melbourne, Australia.

CHANG, Allan Mang Zing, b. 28 Mar. 1940, Shanghai, China. Medical Practitioner. m. 4 Mar. 1967, 2 sons. *Education:* MB, BS, Sydney University, 1964; MRCOG, London, 1970; PhD, Monash University 1976; MRACOG, Brisbane, 1980. *Appointments:* Jessops Hospital for Women, Sheffield, United Kingdom, 1971-76; Tutor, Monash University, 1973-76; Lecturer, 1976-78, Senior Lecturer, Queensland University 1970-. *Publications:* Thesis, Effects of some drugs on fetal acid base status, 1977; Perinatology: Nuchal encirclement of the umbilical cord, 1971; Intrapartum drugs and fetal blood pH and gaseous state, 1973; A decrease in fetal pH during the second stage of labour when conducted in the dorsal position, 1974; The effects of intravenous Ritodrine on the acid base status of the fetus during the second stage, 1975; The effects of narcotics and their antagonists on fetal acid base balance, 1976; Clinical trials, Control trial of fetal intensive care, 1976; Clinical case reports, Acute traumatic tetraplegia during pregnancy, 1978; Epidemiology and measurements, The reduction of the intrapartum stillbirth rate at the Queen Victoria Memorial Hospital, 1977; A comparison of maternal serum levels of alpha-fetoprotein in normal and pre-eclamptic pregnancies, 1978; Perinatal death: Audit and classification, 1979; A comparison of obstetric morbidity and management between clinic and private patients, 1979, etc. *Honours:* University Blue, Judo, 1964. Hobby: Computer programming. *Address:* 6 Sirius Street, Coorparoo, Queensland 4151, Australia.

CHANG, Brian, b. 4 Apr. 1943, South Africa. Chairman, Managing Director. m. Yap Foi Fong, Sept. 1975, 1 son, 2 daughters. *Education:* Christ's Hospital, U.K., 1961-62; Honours Graduate in Electrical Engineering, London University, U.K., 1962-65. *Appointments:* Sales Executive, Mobil Oil Refinery, 1965-66; Marketing Executive, Jardine Waugh, 1966-67; Assistant Marketing Manager, Vosper Thornycroft, 1967-68; Sales, Contracts Manager, Far East Shipbuilding, 1968-69; Area Manager, M J Batty, South East Asia, 1969-70; Marketing Director, Transworld Marine Ltd., 1970-71; Chairman, Managing Director, Promet Private Limited, 1971-. *Memberships:* Young Presidents' Organisation; Singapore Association of Shipbuilders & Repairers; American Club; Petroleum Club. *Honours:* Christ's Hospital, Scholarship, 1961-. *Hobby:* Fishing. *Address:* 25 Gallop Park, Singapore, 1025.

CHANG, Min Phang, Paul, b. 6 Apr. 1918, Malaysia. Education Consultant. m. 8 Nov. 1943, 5 sons, 2 daughters. *Education:* Diploma in Arts, 1st Class, Raffles College, Singapore, 1938-; B.A. Honours, 2nd Class Upper, University of Malaya, Singapore, 1951-; Diploma in Education, University of Malaya, Singapore, 1952-; Academic Diploma in Education, University of London, 1967-; Master of Arts, Education, University of London, 1968-. *Appointments:* Teacher, 1938-42; Petitioner Writer-Self employed, 1942-45; Teacher, 1945-52; Head Master, Secondary Schools, 1953-57; Federal Inspector of Schools, 1957-60; Education Adviser to the Malaysian High Commission, London, 1961-63; Chief Inspector of Schools, Malaysia, 1964-70; Co-ordinator, Centre for Educational Studies and Unit for Off-Campus Academic Studies, University Science, Malaysia, Penang, Malaysia, 1970-75; Associate Professor of Education, 1975-78; Visiting Professor of Education, Unit for Commonwealth and Overseas Studies in Educational Development, Department of Administrative and Social Studies in Education, school of Education, University of Birmingham, United Kingdom, 1978-; Education Consultant, 1980-. *Memberships:* Commonwealth Council for Educational Administration; Fellow The Royal Geographical Society; Malaysian Institute of Management; Chairman, English Language Teaching Association, Malaysia; Adviser, Art Choir, Penang; Committee of Management, Arts Council, Penang; Trustee, Association for Retarded Children, Selangor, Malaysia. *Publications:* Contributed articles to the following journals: International Review of Education, UNESCO, Institute of Education, W. Germany, Teacher Education for Developing Countires, London, Bulletin of the UNESCO Regional Office for Education in Asia, Thailand. Malaysian Journal of Education, Singapore, Journal of Education, Malaysia, Education and the Educators Journal of the School of Educational Studies, Penang, Malaysia.Readings in Malaysian Education; Geography for Primary Schools. *Honours:* Open Raffles Scholarship, 1935-38; Ministry of Education Fellowship, 1951-53; UNESCO Fellowship, 1967-68; Johan Setia Makhota an award by the Paramount King of Malaysia, 1966-; Fellow of the Commonwealth Council for Educational Administration, 1980-. *Hobbies:* Performing arts, Reading, Badminton, Music and Art Appreciation. *Address:* 26 Jalan 21/9, South East Asia Park, Petaling Jaya, Selangor, Malaysia.

CHANG, Min Tat, b. 2 Apr. 1916, Ipoh, Perak, Malaysia. Judge, Federal Court, Malaysia. m. Grace Tan, 21 June 1941, 1 son, 1 daughter. *Education:* Diploma Arts & Diploma Education, Raffles College, Singapore, 1936-40; M.A. (Oxon), Exeter College, Oxford, 1950-52; Inner Temple London, Barrister-at-law. *Appointments:* Called to the English Bar, 1953-; Advocate & Solicitor, 1954-; Judge, High Court, Ipoh, 1966-71; Judge, High Court, Penang, 1972-74; Judge, High Court, Kuala Lumpur, 1975-77; Judge, Federal Court, Malaysia, 1977-. *Memberships:* Vice-President, Oxford-Cambridge Society of Malaysia; President, Selangor Cheshire Home, 1980-; Chairman, Board of Governors, St. John's Institutuion, 1979-80; Penang Club; Penang Turf Club, Golf Section; Perak Turf Club, Sports Club; Royal Salangor Golf Club; Malayan Golf Association. *Honours:* D.M.P.N, Penang, 1972; P.S.M, Malaysia, 1978. *Hobbies:* Reading Golf, Orchids. *Address:* 7 Jalan Gallagher, Kuala Lumpur, Malaysia.

CHANG, Shu-Ting, b. 30 Sept. 1930. Shansi, China. Professor of Biology. m. five children. *Education:* BSc, National Taiwan University, 1949-53; MSc, 1956-58, PhD, 1958-60, University of Wisconsin; Postdoctoral Fellow, Harvard University, 1966-67; Visiting Fellow,, University of Tokyo, Japan, 1969; Visiting Fellow, Jointly, Australian National University and Commonwealth Scientific and Industrial Research Organization, 1972-73. *Appointments:* Assistant Lecturer in Biology, The Chinese University of Hong Kong, 1960-61; Lecturer in Biology, 1961-70; Senior Lecturer in Biology; 1970-74; Reader in Biology, 1974-78; Professor of Biology, 1978-. *Memberships:* American Association for the Advancement of Science; American Institute of Biological Sciences; Scandinavian Society for Plant Physiology; The Botanical Society of America; The Botanical Society of Japan; The Genetics Society of America; The Mycological Society of America; Vice Chairman, Hong Kong Reserach Council in Biological Education; President, The International Mushroom Society for the Tropics. *Publications:* The Chinese Mushroom, 1972; The Biology and Cultivation of Edible Mushrooms, (w. W A Hayes) 1978; Tropical Mushrooms, (w. T H Quimio) in press; Editor in Chief, The Mushroom Newsletter for the Tropics; 50 papers in scientific journals. *Honours:* Appointed, Head, Hong Kong delegation to the 12th Pacific Science Congress, Canberra, Australia, 1971 and 13th Parific Science

Congress, Vancouver, BC, Canada 1975; Appointed by the Council, International Cell Research Organixation, Alternate Member, UNEP UNESCO ICRO Panel on Microbiology; Representative, National point-of-contact, Hong Kong, UNESCO Regional Network of Microbiology, Southeast Asia. *Address:* Flat 6B, University Residence No. 1, The Chinese University of Hong Kong, Shatin, N.T., Hong Kong.

CHAPMAN, George Alan, b. 13 Apr. 1927, Trentham, Wellington, New Zealand. Chartered Accountant. m. Jacqueline Sidney Irvine 9 Sept. 1950, 2 sons, 5 daughters. *Education:* Victoria University College, Wellington; Fellow New Zealand Society of Accountants; Fellow Chartered Institute of Secretaries. *Appointments:* Chartered Accountant, Upper Hutt, New Zealand, 1948; Senior Partner, Chapman Ross and Company, Chartered Accountants, Upper Hutt; Chairman, BNZ Finance Company Limited; Deputy Chairman, Bank of New Zealand, Property Securities Limited; Director, Maui Developments Limited, Offshore Mining Company Limited; Director, Liquigas Limited. *Memberships:* President New Zealand National Party, 1973, Vice President, 1966-73; Upper Hutt Chamber of Commerce, President, 1956-57; Councillor Upper Hutt Borough Council, 1952-53; Deputy Mayor of Upper Hutt, 1953-55; Hutt Valley Drainage Board; Heretaunga College Board of Governors, 1953-55. *Publications:* The Years of Lightning, 1980. *Hobbies:* Tennis; Golf; Reading; Politics. *Address:* 53 Barton Avenue, Heretaunga, Wellington, New Zealand.

CHAPMAN, John Clifford, b. 21 Feb. 1923, London, England. Civil Engineer. m. Roberta Blanche Gingell, 1 son, 1 daughter. *Education:* BSc 1942; PhD 1950. *Appointments:* Royal Engineers 1942-46; Various appointments to Reader in Structural Engineering, Imperial College, 1946-71; Director, Constructional Steel Research and Development Organisation, 1971-73; Director, George Wimpey Limited 1973-81; Consulting Engineer 1981-. *Memberships:* Fellow, Fellowship of Engineering; Fellow, Institution of Civil Engineers; Fellow, Royal Institution of Naval Architects; Fellow, Institution of Naval Architects; The Athenaeum. *Publications:* 40 papers on engineering in journals in the field of Engineering. *Honours:* Two awards from ICE, three from International Structural Engineers, one from RINA, one from American Society for Metals. *Hobbies:* Tennis; Squash; Skiing; Mountain Walking; Cycling. *Address:* 41 Oathall Road, Haywards Heath, Sussex.

CHAPMAN, Keith Samuel Roy, b. 2 Nov. 1945 Adelaide. Biochemist. m. Gillian Woolhouse 4 Nov. 1972. *Education:* BA Agriculture, Adelaide, 1968; BA (Hons), 1969; PhD, Adelaide 1973. *Appointments:* Research Associate, MSU/DOE Plant Research Laboratory, Michigan State University, Michigan, USA 1973; Research Fellow, Department of Botany, University of Edinburgh, Edinburgh, Scotland, 1974-76; Research Scientist, CSIRO, Division of Plant Industry, Canberra, Australia, 1976-. *Memberships:* Australian Biochemical Society; Australian Society of Plant Physiologists; New Zealand Alpine Club; Australian Conservation Foundation. *Hobbies:* Mountaineering; Photography; Skiing. *Address:* 5 Rich Street, Higgins, Act 2615, Australia.

CHARLES, Robert, b. 11 July 1933, Essex, England. Institution Administrator. m. Molly Evelyn Branch, Mar. 1970, 1 daughter. *Education:* BSc(Eng), CEng., CMPN. SCP., FIMechE, FRAES; Harrow Weald County Grammar School, HSC and State Scholarship London University, Bachelor of Science (Internal); Wulfruna College of Advanced Technology, British Institute of Management Certificate, Honours. *Appointments:* Engineer Officer, Royal Air Force; Development Engineer, Rolls Royce, Rotol; Stress Analysis Consultant, Auster Aircraft, Boulton Paul Aircraft, Saunders Roe, Fairey Aviation; Chief Stressman, Heslop and Company; Chairman, Mathematics Limited, Turner Charles Group of Companies; General Secretary, The Society of Certified Professionals. *Memberships:* Companion, The Society of Certified Professionals; Fellow, The Institution of Mechanical Engineers; Fellow, The Royal Aeronautical Society; British Computer Society. *Publications:* Vibration Analysis of Curved Cantilevers; Manufacture of Ultralight Artificial Arms; Business Terms for Self-Employed Engineers; Limited Companies for Contract Professionals; Various papers on new

law related to professional employment and associated taxations. *Hobbies:* Small firm enterprise and finance; Contract Law for Entrepreneurs; Lawn Tennis. *Address:* Newton House, Newmarket Road, Cambridge CB5 8HA ,England.

CHARLES, Robert James, b. 14 Mar. 1936, Carterton, New Zealand. Golf Professional. m. Verity Joan Aldridge, 19 Dec. 1962, 1 son, 1 daughter. *Education:* Wairarapa College, Masterton, NZ, 1949-53. *Appointments:* National Bank of New Zealand, 1953-60; Golf Professional 1960-. *Memberships:* President, Professional Golfers Association, NZ; PGA, Great Britain; PGA, America. *Publications:* Left Handed Golf. *Honours:* OBE, 1972. *Hobbies:* Tennis; Cricket; Farming. *Address:* Lytham, Burnt Hill Road, Oxford, New Zealand.

CHARLTON, Graham, b. 15 Oct. 1928, Newbiggin-by-the-Sea, Northumberland, United Kingdom. Dental Surgeon/University Professor. m. Stella Dobson 14 July 1956, 2 sons, 1 daughter. *Education:* Cert.ED, St. John's College, York, 1946-48; BDS, University of Durham, 1952-58; MDS, University of Bristol, 1970; FDS, RCS, Royal College of Surgeons, Edinburgh, 1978. *Appointments:* Teacher, Northumberland, 1948-52; General Practice, Torquay, Devon, 1958-64; Lecturer, University of Bristol, 1964-72; Consultant Senior Lecturer, Bristol, 1972-78; Dental Clinical Dean, Bristol, 1975-78; Dean of Dental Studies, University of Edinburgh,, Professor of Conservative Dentistry, 1978. *Publications:* Papers in dental journals. *Address:* Carnethy, Bog Road, Penicuik, Edinburgh, EH26 9BT, Scotland.

CHARNLEY, (Sir) John, b. 4 Sept. 1922, Liverpool. Government Service/Aeronautical Engineer. m. Mary, 2 June 1945, 1 son, 1 daughter. *Education:* BEng. (1st class Hons), Civil Engineering, Liverpool University, 1942; MEng, 1945; AFRAeS, 1949; Imperial Defence College, 1962; Fellow Royal Institute of Navigation, 1963; FRAeS, 1966. *Appointments:* Aerodynamics Department, RAE, Farnborough, 1943-55; Superintendent, Blind Landing Experimental Unit, 1955-61; Imperial Defence College, 1962; Head, Instruments and Electrical Engineering Department, RAE, 1963-65; Head, Weapons Department, 1965-68; Head, Research Planning, Min. Tech. 1968; Deputy Controller Guided Weapons, 1969-72; Controller Guided Wpns. and Electronics, MOD(PE), 1972-75; Chief Scientist, (RAF) and Deputy Controller, R&D Establishments and Research, 1975-77; Controller, R&D Establishments and Research, 1977-. *Memberships:* RAF Club, Piccadilly. *Publications:* Papers on subjects in aerodynamics; Aircraft all weather operation;. Aircraft navigation. *Honours:* Bronze Medal of Institute of Navigation, 1959; Guild Air Pilots and Navigators, Cumberbatch Trophy, 1964; Silver Medal Royal Aeronautical Society, 1973; CB, 1973; gold Medal Royal Aeronautical Society, 1980; Knighted, 1981. *Hobbies:* Gardening; Walking; Foreign travel. *Address:* 'Kirkstones', Brackendale Close, Camberley, Surrey, England.

CHARPENTIER, Fulgence, b. 29 June 1897, Ontario Canada. Diplomat, Journalist. m. Louise Dionne, 1934. *Education:* Classical College, Joliette, P.Q.; BA, Laval University 1917; Osgoode Hall, Toronto, 1919. *Appointments:* Department of External Affairs, 1947; Adviser, UNO Conference, Paris, 1948; Candain Delegete, UNESCO Fourth Session, Paris, 1949; Information Officer, Canadian Embassy, Paris, 1948-53; Adviser, UNO Conference, Paris, 1951; Delegate, 8th UNESCO Conference, Montevideo, 1954; Chargé d'Affaires, Canadian Embassy, Uruguay, 1953-56, Brazil, 1956-57 and Haiti, 1957-60; Ambassador, Cameroun, Gabon, Chad, Congo and Central African Republic 1962-65; Assistant, Candian World Exhibition, Montreal 1967; Assistant, Editor-in-Chief, Le Droit, 1968; President, L'Alliance Française; Parliamentary Correspondent, 1926-30. *Memberships:* Private Secretary, Hon. Fernand Rinfret, 1926-30; Chief French Journals, 1936-47. *Publications:* Author, Le Mirage Américain, 1934; Les Patriotes, drama, 1938; Editorialist, Le Droit, Ottawa; Bailli national Confrérie Chaîne des Rôtisseurs. *Honours:* Confederation Medal; several foreign orders; King's Coronation Medal; MBE 1944; CM 1978. *Address:* 42 Southern Drive, Ottawa, Ontario, K1S 0P6, Canada.

CHARPENTIER, Reinhold, b. 1 Aug. 1936, Lund, Sweden. Research Leader. m. Birte von Cappelen 14

Nov. 1975, 3 daughters. *Education:* BA, Lund, 1959; PhD, Montpellier, France, 1968; Academical docent, Lund, 1973; University studies on Zoology, Botany, Chemistry, Genetics, Sweden, 1955-65; Intervebrate Pathology and Parasitology, France, 1967-68. *Appointments:* Assistant Professor, Zoological Institute, Lund University, 1958-68; Scientist, 1969-79; Research Leader, Experimental Division of Plant Resistance, Swedish University of Agricultural Sciences, 1980-. *Memberships:* Society for Invertebrate Pathology; The New York Academy of Sciences; Japanese Society of Applied Entomology and Zoology; Swedish Entomological Societies, Stockholm and Lund. *Publications:* About 50 publications on Insect Taxonomy, Insect Pathology and Microbiological Control, Insect Tissue Culture; Insect Rearing Methods; etc. Hobby: Old Entomological Books. *Address:* Holländarehusvägen 7, S 23700-Bjarred, Sweden.

CHASE, Ashton Alton, b. 18 July 1926, Guyana. Attorney-at-Law. m. Deborrah Ann Ross 27 Sept. 1977, 1 son, 2 daughters. *Education:* Ruskin College, Oxford 1948-49; Barrister-at-Law, Gray's Inn, London 1954-57; LLB(Hons.), London University, 1953-57. *Appointments:* Trade Union Secretary 1950-54; Minister of Labour, Trade and Industry 1953; Member, Public Service Commission, 1970-74; Private Practice, Barrister-at-Law 1957-. *Memberships:* Honorary President, National Association of Agricultural Commercial and Industrial Employees; President, Guyana Bar Association; Vice-Chairman, Guyana Leprosy Relief Association; Treasurer, Guyana Legal Aid Company Limited. *Publications:* 133 Days Towards Freedom in Guyana; The Law of Workmen's Compensation; A History of Trade Unionism in Guyana 1900-61; Industrial Law; Trade-Union Law in the Caribbean; Industrial Relations. *Address:* 30 b Eping Avenue, Bel Air Park, Georgetown, Guyana.

CHASE, Roger Trevor, b. 8 Apr. 1953, London, England. Musician, (Violist). m. Helene Barriere, 24 Sept. 1977, 1 daughter. *Education:* Studied Viola with Bernard Shore, Royal College of Music; Studied with Steven Staryk, in Toronto Canada. *Appointments:* Solo Viola with The Ballet Rambert; Chamber Music and Solo Recitals; Professor of Viola and Chamber music with, The Académie Internationale De Musique, De Chambre, The International School, Directed by Yehudi Menuhin; Principal Viola, London Sinfonietta; Solo Viola, The Nash Ensemble. *Memberships:* President, Students Association, Royal College of Music, 1973-74. *Honours:* Sir Arthur Bliss Prize for Services to RCM, 1974. *Hobbies:* Sailing; Spelaeology; Photography; Carpentry. *Address:* Canal Cottage, 5 The Pry, Purton, Swindon, Wiltshire, Wiltshire.

CHATAWAY, (Rt. Hon.) Christopher John, b. 31 Jan. 1931 England. Vice Chairman, Orion Bank Limited 1980-. *Education:* Magdalen College, Oxford. *Appointments:* Junior Executive, Arthur Guinness Son and Company, 1953-55; Staff Reporter Independent Television News 1955-56; Current Affairs Commentator for BBC Television 1956-59; North Lewisham, LCC 1958-61; Lewisham North 1959-66; Chichester, 1969-74; PPS, Minister of Power 1961-62; Joint Parliamentary Under-Secretary of State, Department of Education and Science 1962-64; Alderman GLC 1967-70; Leader Education Committee ILEA 1967-69; Minister of Posts and Telecommunications 1970-72; Minister for Industrial Development 1972-74; Director, British Electric Traction Company 1974-; Chairman, Honeywell UK Advisory Board 1978-; Chairman, British Telecommunications Systems Limited 1979-; Chairman, United Medical Enterprises Limited 1980-; Director, International General Electric Company of New York Limited; Treasurer, National Committee for Electoral Reform 1976; Treasure, Action in Distress 1976. *Honours:* Represented Great Britain Olympic Games 1952 and 1956; Held world 5,000 metres and 3 miles records. *Address:* 40 Addison Road, London W14.

CHATILLON, Claude, b. 29 Dec. 1917, Ottawa, Canada. Diplomat. m. Simone Boutin, 24 Jan. 1948, 1 son, 2 daughters. *Education:* BA., BPH., University of Ottawa, Canada, 1940; LPH., 1941. *Appointments:* Vice-Consul, New York, USA,1946; 2nd Secretary, Canadian Embassy, New Delhi, 1948; 2nd Secretary, Paris, France, 1953, 1955; National Defence College, Kingston, Ontario, Canada, 1956; Assistant Director of Information, Department of External Affairs, Ottawa, 1957; Consul, Seattle, USA, 1959, Boston, USA, 1962; Counsellor, Canadian Embassy, Madrid and Rabat, 1965; Director of Consular Affairs, 1970, Director of Consular Policy, 1972, Ottawa, Canada; Ambassador to Cameroons, Gabon, ECA and Chad, 1975-; Ministry representative on Refugee Staus Advisory Committee, 1978-; Volunteer Private, Canadian Forces, 1942; Service in UK., North Africa, Sicily, Italy; Demob. as Liet., 1945. *Memberships:* Association of Old Students of University of Ottawa; Association of Royal 22nd Regiment. *Hobbies:* Painting; Tennis; Swimming; Fishing; Golf. *Address:* Department of External Affairs, Ottawa, Ontario, Canada.

CHATSIKA, Lewis Alexander, b. 18 Nov. 1934, Blantyre Malawi. Lawyer. m. Phyllis Enna Mituka 5 Sept. 1959, 2 sons, 3 daughters. *Education:* Higher Cambridge School Certificate 1956; Barrister at Law, Lincoln's Inn 1965. *Appointments:* State Counsel 1965; Legal Aid Counsel 1966; Traditional Courts Commissioner 1967; Director of Public Prosecutions, 1968; Judge of the High Court and Supreme Court, 1970-. *Hobbies:* Football; Reading. *Address:* 1 Kabula Hill, PO Box 1763, Blantyre, Malawi.

CHATTERJEA, Santi Kumar, b. 5 Nov. 1930, Howrah, West Bengal, India. Reader in Pure Mathematics, Calcutta University. m. Momota Banerjea 3 Mar. 1957, 1 son, 3 daughters. *Education:* MSc (1st class third), Pure Mathematics. Calcutta University, 1953; PhD (Special Functions), Jadapur University, 1964; DSc, (Lie theory and Special Functions), Calcutta University 1976. *Appointments:* Lecturer in Mathematics, 1954-65, Senior Lecturer, Bangabasi College and Bangabasi Morning College, Calcutta, 1965-71; Lecturer, 1971-79 and Reader, 1979-, in Pure Mathematics, Calcutta University. *Memberships:* Reviewer, American Maths Society; Zentralblatt für Mathematik; Board of Editors, Calcutta Maths Society; Referee, Jadapur Maths Society; Indian Maths Society; Academia Sinica, Republic of China. *Publications:* Numerous publications in special functions and lie theory; Seven publications on Fixed Point Theory; One-parameter group and differential equations, Semigroups, complex analysis, mathematical economics and Biomathematics; Book: Matematic Analysis. *Honours:* Invited, NSF-CBMS Regional Research Conference 1979; Attended and delivered lectures in the Intensive Summer Seminar, S.N. Bose Institute, Calcutta, 1980; Second Mathematics. Conference Dacca, Bangladesh, 1980. *Hobbies:* Palmistry; Astrology. *Address:* 28/1B Serpentine Lane, Calcutta 700014, W.B., India.

CHATURVEDI, Arun, b. 12 May 1947, Varanasi, India. Teaching. m. Anubhuti Chaturvedi, 6 June 1978, 1 son. *Education:* Bachelor of Music, Violin, 1965; Master of Arts, Hindi, 1966; Master of Arts, Linguistics, 1968; Doctor of Philosophy, Linguistics, 1979. *Appointments:* Research Assistant, 1968-70, Jr. Research Fellow, 1975-79, Lecturer, 1979-, Central Institute of Hindi, Agra; Language Teacher, American Peace Corps, 1970-71; Lecturer, Banasthali Vidyapith (Rajasthan), 1971-74; Sr. Research Fellow, Keral University, Trivandrum, 1974-75. *Memberships:* Linguistic Society of India. *Publications:* Ten books; Poems; Three Articles. *Honours:* Prizes, Music Competitions, 1956-66, games and sports, 1975-79; Gold Medal, 1966; Gold Medal, Agra University, 1979. *Hobbies:* Indian Classical Music; Philately; Sports & Games; Teaching. *Address:* Central Institute of Hindi, Shitla Road, Agra 282005, India.

CHAUDHARY, Binod Kumar, b. 13 Nov. 1938, Patna, India. Dentist. m. Jayanti Kumari, 11 July 1962, 2 sons, 2 daughters. *Education:* Bachelor of Dental Surgery, Lucknow University, 1961; Doctor of Philosophy, Bihar University, 1967; Fellow of International College of Dentists. *Appointments:* Tutor, Lecturer, Government Dental College & Hospital, Patna, Bihar, India; Professor of Dentistry & Head of Oral Pathology & Oral Medicines Deptt. Patna Dental College; Head, Dental Department, Patna Medical College. *Memberships:* President Elect, Indian Dental Association; Member Executive Committee, Bihard State Health Services; Dental Council of India; Treasurer, Biahrd State Dental Council. *Publications:* 11 Research Papers and Articles in Professional Journals. *Honours:* Fellowship, Murry Lunnie Dental Clinic Guggenheim, USA. *Hobbies:*

Sports; Reading. *Address:* Road No. 1 C, Rajendra Nagar, Patna-800016, Bihar, India.

CHAUDHURI, Asok Kumar, b. 1 Apr. 1924, West Bengal, India. m. Gita Chaudhuri, 9 Mar. 1955, 2 sons. *Education:* Matriculation, 1941, Calcutta University; Intermediate in science, 1943; BSc, 1945; BCom, 1948; MCom, 1959. *Appointments:* General Assistant, A B Cement Company Limited, Calcutta, 1946-51; Assistant Secretary, Board of Secondary Education, West Bengal, Calcutta, 1951-62; Audit & Accounts Officer, 1962-63, Finance Officer, 1963-78, Registrar, 1978-, Burdwan University, West Bengal, India. *Publications:* Several papers on financial and educational matters. *Address:* Rajbali, PO Burdwan, Dt. Burdwan, West Bengal, India.

CHAUDHURY, Abdul Matin, b. 1 May 1921, Dacca, Bangladesh. Bose Professor of Physics. m. Razia Matin Chaudhvry, 18 Nov. 1943, 3 sons, 1 daughter. *Education:* BSc, 1942, MSc, 1943, PhD, 1962, Dacca University; PhD, 1949, Chicargo University. *Appointments:* Reader in Physics, 1950, Professor of Physics, 1962, Vice-Chancellor, 1973, Dacca University; Member, 1967, Chairman, 1969, Atomic Energy Commission; Defence Advisor, Ministry of Defence, Pakistan, 1970. *Memberships:* Bangladesh Association for the Advancement of Science; Bangladesh Physicans Society. *Publications:* Works on Structure Analysis by X-ray Diffraction Method. *Honours:* Recommending Member for the award of Nobel Prize in Physics, 1976; Jury for the Award of Neheru Award for International Understanding. *Hobbies:* Reading; Painting. *Address:* Dacca University, Dacca, Bangladesh.

CHAUHAN, A.R., b. 23 May 1939, Kotkhai, Simla, India. Administration. m. Kamla Chauhan, 1 July 1963, 2 sons, 1 daughter. *Education:* Matriculation, 1949-55, FA (Intermediate), 1955-57, BC, 1957-60, Punjab University; MA (Econ), University of Delhi, 1960-62. *Appointments:* Senior Lecturer in Economics, 1963-73; Company Secretary, 1973-76; General Manager, Secretary, 1976-81; Registrar, Himachal Pradesh University, India, 1981-. *Memberships:* Fellow, Society of Incorporated Accountants & Auditors of India; Fellow, Society of Incorporated Secretaries of India; Affiliate fellow, International Creative Centre, Switzerland; Secretary General, H.P. United National Association, Simla, India; Secretary, National Executive Council of Indian Federation of United Nationals Association of India; Bellavista Association of Administrative Staff College of India, Hyderabad; H.P. Productivity Council; H.P. Chamber of Commerce; Alumini Association of Indian Institute of Management, Bangalore; H.P. State Fertilizers Advisory Committee. *Publications:* Contributor of articles to professional journals and conferences. *Hobbies:* Gardening. *Address:* V.P.O. Tharola, Kot Khai, Dist. Simla (H.P.), India.

CHEATLEY, Alice Mary-Elizabeth, b. 26 Oct. 1918, Fisher Branch, Manitoba, Canada. Educator. m. J. Bruce Cheatley, 10 July 1948. *Education:* BA, MED, Enrolled in Phd Programm, University of Manitoba; EDD, University of North Dakota. *Appointments:* Teacher, various schools; School Administrator, Winnipeg. *Memberships:* Elected Vice President, Executive and Administrative Board, Delta Kappa Gamma International; Honorary Life Member, Manitoba Teachers' Society; Manitoba Education Association; Winnipeg Teachers' Association; President, University Women's Club, Manitoba; Board of Teacher Education & Certification (Provincial); Board of Continuing Education, Manitoba; Board of Nursing Education (Provincial); Board of Assocation, Manitoba, North Dakota, St. John's College; Canadian College of Teachers; Manitoba Association of Principals Manitoba Council of Women; Diocesan Board, The Diocese of Ruperts Land, Anglian Church of Canada. *Publications:* Master's Thesis and other papers. *Honours:* Distinguished Service Award, Manitoba, 1979; Nominated Woman of the Year, 1980; Honorary Life Membership, Manitoba Teachers' Society, 1981; Nominated Carter Woman of the Year, 1981. *Hobbies:* Travel; Ballet; Theatre. *Address:* 290 Montgomery Avenue, Winnipeg, Manitoba, Canada.

CHEETHAM, Francis William, b. 5 Feb. 1928. Director of Museums. m. Monica Fairhurst, 19 Apr. 1954, 3 sons, 1 daughter. *Education:* BA, University of Sheffield, 1945-48 and 1950-51. *Appointments:* Deputy Art Director and Curator, City of Nottingham, 1960-63; Director, City of Norwich Museums, 1963-74; Director Norfolk Museums Service, 1974-. *Memberships:* Norfolk and Norwich Triennial Festival Committee; Crafts Advisory Committee; National Heritage; Norfolk Contemporary Crafts Society; Museums Association. *Creative Works:* Medieval English Alabaster Carvings in the Castle Museum, Nottingham. *Honours:* Associate of the Museums Association 1959; Fellow, Museums Association, 1966; Winston Churchill Fellow, 1967; OBE, 1979. *Hobby:* Hill walking. *Address:* 25 St. Andrews Avenue, Thorpe, Norwich, Norfolk, England.

CHEETHAM, John Stewart, b. 5 Nov. 1948, Melbourne, Australia. Education Consultant and Author. m. Roberta Christine Spence, 23 Aug. 1980. *Education:* BA, Monash University, 1973; BEd, 1975; Primary Teachers Certificate, 1971. *Appointments:* Secondary Teaching, 1968-77; Head, Yarra Valley Special Education Community Centre, 1975-77; Education Officer, Victorian Foundation on Alcoholism and Drug Dependence, 1977-81; Acting Executive Director, 1980; Education Consultant in Private Practice, 1981-. *Memberships:* President, Victorian Council for Handicapped Readers; Fellow, Society of Senior Executives; Australian College of Education; American Personnel Guidance Association; Board of Directors Victorian Foundation on Alcoholism and Drug Dependence. *Publications:* Co-author, Parent Power; O.K. Lets' Go; Your Child Can Succeed; Co-editor, Readings in Illicit Drug Use, in Press. *Honours:* Outstanding Young Australian Award, 1980. *Hobbies:* Yachting; Squash; Skiing. *Address:* 45 Albert Street, Port Melbourne 3207, Victoria, Australia.

CHELLAH, Mwimanji Ndota, b. 14 Nov. 1944, Nakakola Village, Isoka, Zambia. Museum Administrator, Artist. m. Suzyo Ndhlovu, 9 Sept. 1967, 3 sons, 1 daughter. *Education:* Certificate in Fine Art, 1967, Diploma in Fine Art, 1969, University of East Africa; Canadian Museums Association Certificate, 1980. *Appointments:* Graphic Artist, Rural Development, Government of Zambia; Technical Officer, Chief Technical Officer, Deputy Director, Acting Director, Director, Livingstone Museum. *Memberships:* International Council of Museums; Commonwealth Association of Museum; Zambia National Commission for UNESCO; Zambia National Commission for the Preservation of Natural and Historical Monuments and Relics; Zambia National Crafts Committee. *Creative Works:* Exhibitions of Paintings. *Hobbies:* Music; Stage Acting. *Address:* 45 Kanyanta Road, Livingstone, Zambia.

CHELLAPPAH, Sinnathamby Thambiah, b. 26 Mar. 1909, Jaffna, Sri Lanka, Ceylon. Professional & Practising Accountant. m. V Rasammah, 24 Aug. 1930, 1 son (dec.), 8 daughters. *Education:* Senior Cambridge Grade I London; Certified Accountant, Royal Charter, London; Institute of Chartered Secretaries, UK; British Institute of Management. *Appointments:* First Collector of Income Tax, Malaysian Inland Revenue Department, 1947-52; Practicing Professional Accountant, & Professional Secretary, 1954-; Tax Adviser, Property Valuer, Consultant, Business Management Accountants & Auditors. *Memberships:* Pure Life Society; Devine Life Society; Blind Deaf & Retarded Assocations; Patron of Certified Public Accountants & Students Association, Malaysia; President, Chairman, Ceylonese Malayan Death Provident Fund; Honorary Treasurer of Central Welfare & Social Council. *Honours:* Honoured by Sultan of Selangar, Malaysia; Honored by Agong Beusar (King), Malaysia. *Hobbies:* Reading; Walking; Farming. *Address:* No. 11 Lorong, Travers, Kuala Lumpur, Malaysia.

CHEN, Fong-ching, b. 15 Dec. 1939, Chungking, China. University Administration. m Ngar-sheung Lam, 6 Sept. 1964, 2 sons. *Education:* BA, Physics, magna cum laude, Harvard, 1962; MA, 1964, PhD, 1967, Physics, Brandeis. *Appointments:* Lecturer in Physics, 1966-76, Senior Lecturer in Physics, 1977-80, Secretary of University, 1980-, The Chinese University of Hong Kong. *Memberships:* American Physical Society; Hong Kong Physical Society. *Publications:* 20 Articles published in International Journals, mainly in the area of polymer physics and occasional journalistic pieces. *Honours:* Phi Beta Kappa Society, 1962. *Hobbies:* Reading; Music; Hiking. *Address:* Flat 5B, Residence No. 4, The Chinese University of Hong Kong, Shatin, New Territories, Hong Kong.

CHEONG, Mervyn, b. 20 Oct. 1933, Darwin, Northern Territory, Australia. Medicine. m. Frances Woon Kwai Lau Gooey, 6 Jan. 1962, 3 sons, 2 daughters. *Education:* MB. BS, University of Queensland, 1951-56; MRCP (Edin), 1968. *Appointments:* Resident Medical Officer, Royal Brisbane Hospital, 1957; Resident Medical Officer, 1958, Medical Registrar, 1959-62, Director of Geriatrics, Marjory Warren Geriatric Unit, 1968-76, Princess Alexandra Hospital; Medical Officer, Division of Geriatrics, 1963-68, Director, Division of Geriatrics, 1968-76, Director, Division of Community Medicine, 1976-, Queensland Department of Health. *Memberships:* Numerous Societies including: Gerontology (Standing) Committee, National Health and Medical Research Council; Australian Geriatrics Society, (Vice-President); Chairman, Hospital Services Committee, Australian Red Cross Society; Chairman, Physiotherapy Board of Queensland; Australian National Council of and for the Blind. *Honours:* Public Health Travelling Fellowship, National Health And Medical Research Council, 1971; Churchill Fellowship, 1971; Red Cross Service Award, 1975. *Address:* 228 Station Road, Sunnybank, Brisbane, Queensland, Australia.

CHERIAN, Maliakal Eapen, b. 6 July 1926, Kerala, India. Teaching-College President. m. Premila Ohal, 7 June 1950, 2 sons, 1 daughter.*Education:* BLA, Spicer Memorial College, Poona, India, 1949; MA(Philosophy), Andrews university, Michigan, USA, 1956; MA (History), University of Maryland, USA, 1957; PhD (Political Science), University of Poona, India, 1965. *Appointments:* Teacher,1949, Librarian 1951, Registrar 1957, Head, History Department 1958, Head, Philosophy Department, 1960, Dean, Academic 1962, President (Principal) 1963-, Spicer Memorial College, Poona, India. *Memberships:* Member of numerous associations including: President, Rotary Club of Poona North; Executive Board, All India Association for Christian Higher Education; President, The Bhasker P Hivale Education Society, Bombay; Senate member, University of Poona; Executive Magistrate, Government of Maharashtra; Board member, Symbosis School of Management. *Honours:* Honorary Doctor of Laws, 1980; Alumni of Distinction, Andrews University, Michigan, USA; Cited by the Michigan State Government, USA, as a distinguished educator, who graduated from a Michigan centre of higher learning, cited during Michigan International week, October 1975. *Address:* Dr M E Cherin, Spicer Memorial College, Poona 7, India.

CHESHIRE, (Geoffrey) Leonard, b. 7 Sept. 1917, Chester, England. RAF.retired. m. Susan Ryder, 5 Apr. 1959, 1 son, 1 daughter. *Education:* 2nd Class Hons., School Jurisprudence, Merton College, Oxford, 1939. *Appointments:* OU Air Squadron, 1936; RAFVR, 1937; Permanent Commission, RAF, 1939; Served i Bomber Command, 1940-45 including: 617 Squadron(Dambusters) 1943; Attached HQ Eastern Air Command, South East Asia, 1944; Official British observer at dropping of Atomic Bomb on Nagasaki, 1945; Retired December, 1945; Founder, Cheshire Foundation Homes (200 Homes for the disabled in 38 countries). *Memberships:* Royal Air Force Club; Queen's; All England Lawn Tennis Club; Pathfinder Association; Air Crew Association. *Publications:* Bomber Pilot, 1943; Pilgrimage to the Shroud, 1956; The Face of Victory, 1961; A Hidden World, 1981. *Honours:* War of 1939-45: Victoria Cross; Distinguished Service Order (and 2 bars); Distinguished Flying Cross; Civilian Order of Merit, 1981; Variety Club Humanitarian Award (jointly with wife), 1975; Hon. LLD Liverpool University,1973; Hon. LLD, Manchester Polytechnic, 1978; LLD, Nottingham University, 1981. *Hobbies:* Tennis; Photography. *Address:* Cavendish, Suffolk.

CHESTER, Sir (Daniel) Norman, b. 27 Oct. 1907, Manchester, England. Academic. m. Eva Jeavons, (deceased), 14 May 1936. *Education:* BA., 1927-30, MA., 1933, Manchester University, UK; MA., Oxon., 1946. *Appointments:* Research Assistant, Economics Research Section, Manchester University, UK, 1933-34; Rockefeller Fellow, USA., 1935-36; Lecturer in Public Administration, 1936-40; Economic Section, War Cabinet Secretariat, 1940-45; Fellow, 1945-54, Warden, 1954-78, Honorary Fellow, 1978-, Nuffield College, Oxford, UK. *Memberships:* President, 1961-64, International Political Science Association; Vice President, Royal Institute of Public Administration; Vice President, UK Political Studies Association; Chairman, Oxford Centre for Management Studies, 1965-75; Chairman,

Football Grounds Imporovement Trust, 1975-80; Deputy Chairman, Football Trust English Administrative System 1780-1870, 1981. *Publications:* Central and Local Relations, 1951; British Central Government, 1914-1956, (with F.M.G. Willson), 1957; Questions in Parliament, (with N. Bowring), 1962; Nationalisation of British Industry, 1975. *Honours:* CBE., 1951; Knight Bachelor, 1974; Chevalier de la Legion d'Honneur, 1976; Corresp. member, Academie des Sciences Morales et Politiques. *Hobbies:* Association football. *Address:* 136 Woodstock Road, Oxford OX2 7NG., England.

CHESTERMAN, Ronald George Arthur, b. Chester, Cheshire, England. Archivist. m. Marion Clarke, 18 June, 1971, 1 son, 2 daughters. *Education:* BA (Hons.) History (London), North Western Polytechnic, Kentish Town, London, as London University full-time external student, 1965-68; Postgraduate Diploma in Archives Administration, University College, London, UK, 1971-73. *Appointments:* Archives Assistant, India Office Library and Records, Foreign and Commonwealth Office, London, UK, 1971-73; Senior Assistant Archivist (Modern Records), East Sussex County Record Office, Lewes, Sussex, UK, 1973-75; Records Administration Officer, Cheshire County Record Office, Chester, UK, 1975-79; Government Archivist, Solomon Islands National Archives, Honiara, Guadalcanal, Solomon Islands, 1979-. *Memberships:* Society of Archivists (UK); British Records Association; International Records Management Federation; International Records Management Federation; Society for Army Historical Research; Society for Maritime Reearch; Richard III Society; English Folk Dance and Song Society. *Publications:* Proceedings of an International Seminar on Automatic Data Processing in Archives, 1975; Laughter in the House: Local Taxation and the Motor Vehicle in Cheshire, 1887-1977, 1977; Cheshire at War, 1914-18, 1978. *Creative Works:* Sound recordings: Bass Player, Strawbs, 1968; Dragonfly, 1969; Sandy Denny and the Strawbs, 1973; More Folk in Worship, 1974; A Kiss in the Morning Early, 1977; Broadcasting: Producer and Presenter, Sunday Morning Jazz Session, 1979. *Hobbies:* Music; Military and Naval History; Wargaming; Chess; Golf; Swimming; Sailing; Fishing; Gardening; Home brewing and wine making. *Address:* c/o PO Box 781, Honiara, Guadalcanal, Solomon Islands.

CHESWORTH, John Coventry, b. 22 June, 1930, Manchester, England. Artistic Director; Choreographer. m. Valerie Jane Marsh, 26 Feb. 1960, 2 daughters. *Education:* Rambert Schooll of Ballet, 1950-52. *Appointments:* Dancer, rising to Principal, 1952, Assistant to Artistic Director, 1966, Appointed Associate Director 1973, Appointed Co-Artistic Director, 1974, Appointed Artistic Director 1974, Ballet Rambert. *Memberships:* Ballet Sub-Committe, Arts Council of Great Britain, 1969-74; Gulbenkian Foundation Dance Panel, 1975; Council of National Academic Awards Dance Committee, 1978; Fellow of Royal Society of Arts, 1978; External examiner BA (Hons) Degree in Dance at Laban Centre, 1979; Honorary Dance Adviser on the Education Arts Committee to County of Leicester, 1979; Committee member, National Youth Dance Festival, 1979; Director, Creative Dance Artists, 1979; Director, Board of Extemporary Dance Comapny, 1980; Vice Chairman, Accreditation Committee of Council for Dance Education and Training. *Creative Works:* Ballets: Timecase, 1966; Tic-Tack, 1967; H and Pawn to King Five, 1968; Four According, 1970; Games for Five Players, 1971; Ad-Hoc, Pattern for an Escalator, 1972; Project 6354/9116 Mark 2, 1974; Selected Scenes, 1979; Television Ballets: Work for Granada Television 1970; Work for BBC Television Produced and Co-Directed, 1972; Films, Imprints, 1973; Dancers 1978. *Honours:* Documentary Sound Award,Cracow Film Festival, 1979; Gold Plaque Award, Chicago Film Festival, 1979. *Hobbies:* Theatre; Cinema; 20th Century Art. *Address:* 194 Lower Ham Road, Kingston-upon-Thames, Surrey, KT2 5BD, England.

CHIA, Chin Shin, b. 4 Nov. 1922, Miri, Sarawak, Malaysia. Member of State Legislative Council. m. Jong Tze Min, 25 June 1943, 4 sons, 3 daughters. *Education:* St. Joseph's School, Kuching, Sarawak, Malaysia, 1937-41. *Appointments:* Life Member of Commonwealth Parliamentary Association, Sarawak Branch, 1954-; Councillor, Miri District Council, 1951-63; Sarawak Development Board, Sarawak, 1957-63; Sarawak Legislative Council, Sarawak, 1954-63; Sarawak Executive Council, Sarawak, 1961-63; Member of

Parliament, Malaysia, 1964-69; Sarawak Legislative Council, Sarawak, 1970-; Chairman, Syarikat Thye Seng Hardware Sdn. Bhd., Miri, Sarawak, Malaysia; Managing Director, Thai Poo Rubber Estate Co. Snd. Bhd., Miri, Sarawak, Malaysia; Managing Director, Miri Daily Sdn. Bhd., Miri, Sarawak, Malaysia; Managing Director, Kenderaan Piasau Sdn. Bhd., Miri, Sarawak, Malaysia. *Memberships:* Vice Chairman, Sarawak United Peoples Party; Chairman, Miri Branch, Sarawak Peoples Party; Chairman, Chinese Chamber of Commerce, Miri, Sarawak; Chairman, Thai Poo Community Association; Chartered President, Lions Club of Miri. *Honours:* Ahli Bintang Sarawak, 1964; Panglima Negeri Bintang Sarawak, 1972. *Hobbies:* Stamp and Souvenir Collecting. *Address:* 4 Ricemill Road, PO Box No. 1, Miri, Sarawak, Malaysia.

CHIA, Peter Joe, b. 26 Apr. 1935, Singapore. Educational Administrator. m. 3 Apr. 1961, 2 daughters. *Education:* Teachers' Training College, Singapore, 1955-57. *Appointments:* Teacher, 1955-71, Senior Education Officer, 1971-78, Senior Assistant, 1979, Anglo-Chinese School, Singapore; Vice-Principal, Anglo-Chinese Junior School, Singapore, 1980-. *Memberships:* Member of numerous associations including: Executive Council, The Methodist Church Singapore; Chairman, Regional Guidance Committee Group 1, Ministry of Education; Appeals Committee, Singapore Children's Society; Assistant General Secretary, Singapore Youth Council; Board of Directors, Metropolitan YMCA; Central Committee, World Association for Christian Communication; Executive Committee, Singapore Children's Society; District Vice President: Singapore Scout Association, Singapore Girl Guide Association; Honorary Assistant Secretary, Citizens Consultative Committee. *Publications:* Editor, Methodist Message, 1972-; Editor, Our Neighbours. *Honours:* Gold Award, 1971, Pewter Award, 1975, Champion Donor Award 1980, Singapore Blood Transfusion Service; Long Service Award 1968, Meritorious Service Award 1970, Superior Service Award 1973, Singapore Scout Association. *Hobbies:* Swimming; Community Service. *Address:* M256 Lagoon View, Singapore 1544.

CHIANG, Hai Ding, b. 27 Apr. 1938, Malaysia. Ambassador. m. Patricia NG, 12 Aug. 1961, 4 sons. *Education:* BA (Hons.) History, University of Singapore, 1959; PhD. (Pacific History), Australian National University, Canberra, ACT, 1964. *Appointments:* Lecturer in History, University of Singapore, 1963-71; Singapore High Commissioner to Malaysia, 1971-73; Officer, Citibank, NA in Singapore, 1973-78; Singapore Ambassador to the Federal Republic of Germany, 1978-; Elected Member of Parliament in 1970, re-elected in 1972, 1976 and 1980. *Publications:* A History of Straits Settlements Foreign Trade 1870-1915, 1978; Indochina: Der Permanente Konflict?, 1981. *Address:* PO Box 1000, Tanglin Post Office, Singapore 10.

CHIANG, On Khiong, b. 10 Apr. 1944, Sandakan, Sabah, Malaysia. Director, Computer Service Unit, State Government of Sabah. m. Fung Hiong Mee, 4 Feb. 1971, 1 son, 2 daughters. Bachelor of Surveying (Hons.), 1970, Diploma in Computer Science, 1971, University of Queensland, Australia. *Appointments:* Computer Grade I, Lands Dept., Queensland, Australia, 1972; Systems Analyst, Lands and Surveys Department, Sabah, 1973-75; Director, Computer Service Unit, Sabah, 1975-. *Memberships:* Voting member of ACM; Malaysian Computer Society. *Publications:* Problems and Issues Facing Government Computer Installations, 1980. *Honours:* Cohen Memorial Prize for 1964 awarded in 1965 for topping Sabah in COSC examination. *Hobbies:* Television; Stamps; Swimming; Badminton. *Address:* Lot 49, Fook Tin Villa, Reservoir Road, Kota Kinabalu Malaysia.

CHIBESAKUNDA, Lombe Phyllis, b. 5 May, 1944. Barrister-at-Law; Zambian Lawyer and diplomatist. *Education:* National Institute of Public Administration, Lusaka, Zambia; Gray's Inn, London, UK. *Appointments:* State Advocate, Ministry of Legal Affairs, 1969-72; private legal practice, Jacques and Partners, 1972-73; Member of Parliament, Matero, 1973-; Ambassador to Japan, 1975-77; High Commissioner in the UK, concurrently Ambassador to the Netherlands and the Holy See, 1977-81; Chief Zambian delegate, UN Law of the Sea Conference, 1975. *Memberships:* Founder, Social Action charity, Lusaka, Zambia; Life

member, Commonwealth Parliamentary Association. *Address:* c/o Ministry of Foreign Affairs, Lusaka, Zambia.

CHICHESTER-CLARK, (Sir) Robert, b. 10 Jan. 1928. m. (1) Jane Helen Goddard, 1953, 1 son, 2 daughters, (2) Caroline Bull, 1974, 2 sons. *Education:* Royal Naval College; BA.(Hons.), Magdalene College, Cambridge, UK. *Appointments:* Journalist, 1950; Public Relations Officer, Glyndebourne Opera, 1952; Assistant to Sales Manager, Oxford University Press, UK, 1953-55; Member of Parliament,(UU), Londonderry City and Co., 1955-1974; PPS to Financial Secretary to the Treasury, 1958; Assistant Government Whip (unpaid), 1958-60; a Lord Comr. of the Treasury, 1960-61; Comptrollor of HM Household, 1961-64; Chief Opposition Spokesman on N Ireland, 1964-70, on Public Building and Works, 1965-70; Minister of State, Department of Employment, 1972-74; Director: The Welbeck Group, Alfred Booth and Co.; Management Consultant. *Honours:* Hon. FIWM., 1972; Kt., 1974. *Hobbies:* Reading; Fishing. *Address:* The Welbeck Group, 25 The Haymarket, London SW1, England.

CHIDUME, Eusebius Nwankwo, b. 24 Dec, 1933, Nimo, Njikoka LGA, Anambra State, Nigeria. Doctor of Medicine. m. Patricia Nwamaka Omeili, 26 Dec. 1960, 2 sons, 4 daughters. *Education:* University College, Dublin, Ireland, 1953-54; Royal College of Surgeons, Ireland, 1954-55; BSc. Hons. in Anatomy, 1958, MB, B.Ch, BAO, 1961, Queen's University of Belfast, 1955-61; FRCS, Edinburgh University, Scotland, 1964. *Appointments:* Surgical Registrar, Belfast, Ireland, 1963-64; Medical Officer Special Grade 1964, Consultant Surgeon 1970, Senior Consultant Surgeon 1976, Nigeria; Now owns and runs 104-bedded Private Hospital as Chief Specialist Surgeon/Medical Director. *Memberships:* Nigerian Medical Association; Peoples Club of Nigeria; Ozo Society. *Publications:* Thesis: Cartilage Crafts and Transplants, presented to Queen's University, Belfast, Ireland. *Honours:* Queen's University Scholarship Award for BSc.(Hons) degree course. *Hobbies:* Music; Gardening; Art collection. *Address:* Mater Infirmorum Hospital Ltd, PO Box 95, Nimo, Anambra State, Nigeria.

CHIDYAUSIKU, Godfrey Guwa, b. 27 Mar. 1947, Goromonzi, Zimbabwe. Advocate. m. Mary Machekera, 1973, 3 sons. *Education:* LLB.(Lon.) 1970, LLB, University of Rhodesia, 1968-71. *Appointments:* Practising Advocate, January 1972; Elected to Parliament, 1974-77, re-elected February 1980 and appointed Deputy Minister of Local Government and Housing, March 1980. *Memberships:* Chairman, Legal Committee of the People's Movement; Chairman, Legal Committee of the ZANU (PF) Election Directorate; Secretary African Bar Association. *Honours:* Independence Medal, 1980. *Hobby:* Soccer. *Address:* Stand No. 7553, Mangwonde Drive West, Old Highfield, Salisbury, Zimbabwe.

CHIEPE, Gaositwe Keagakwa Tibe, b. Serowe Botswana. *Education:* BSc, Fort Hare, 1946, Education Diploma, SA University, 1947; MA, 1958, LLD (Hon.), Bristol University, United Kingdom, 1958. *Appointments:* Assistant Education Officer, 1948; Education Officer 1953; Senior Education Officer 1962; Deputy Director of Education 1965; Director of Education 1968; High Commissioner/Ambassador to UK, Federal Republic of Germany, France, Sweden, Norway, Nigeria, Denmark concurrently 1970 and Belgium, EEC 1973-74; Minister for Commerce and Industry 1974-77; Minister for Mineral Resources and Water Affairs, 1977-. *Memberships:* Girl Guides Association; Fellow of the Royal Society of Arts; Vice-Chairman, Notwane Club; Vice President, Botswana Branch of the Commonwealth Parliamentary Association, 1978-. *Publications:* Political Education pamphlets. *Honours:* MBE; Presidential Honour for Meritorious Service. *Hobbies:* Gardening; Walking; Reading; Swimming. *Address:* 2454 Tshekedi Road, Gaborone, Botswana.

CHIFUNYISE, Tisa Mwape, b. 31 May 1948, Chiundaponde, Mpika, Zambia. Teacher/Editor. m. Stephen Joel Chifunyise, 5 Oct. 1974, 1 son, 2 daughters. *Education:* BA, University of Zambia, 1972; MED (Comprehensive Curriculum), University of California, Los Angeles, 1977. *Appointments:* Teacher, Chipembi Girls Secondary School, 1972; Language Instructor, Sida Training Centre, Vasterås, Sweden, 1973; Lecturer, English Department, Curriculum Development Centre, Lusaka, Zambia, 1974; Editor, Orbit Magazine, Lusaka, Zambia, 1977. *Memberships:* Founder Secretary, Zambia National Theatre Arts Association; Historical Association of Zambia; International Theatre Institute Zambia Associate Centre; Lioness Club of Kapila. *Hobbies:* Reading; Gardening; Theatre; Tennis. *Address:* 4 Juniper Avenue, Chelston, Lusaka.

CHIKELUBA, George Godwin Ekejekwu, b. 18 June 1933, Awka-Etiti, Nigeria. Businessman. m. Mercy Olikeze, 15 June 1958, 5 sons, 3 daughters. *Education:* St Michael's School Aba, 1939-46; St Joseph's College Awka-Etiti, 1951. *Appointments:* Managing Director, GMO and Company Limited, 1957; Director, United African Drug Company Limited, 1964; Chairman, GMO Group of Companies, 1976; Chairman, GODM Shoes Limited, 1978; Director, Ciana Agencies Limited, 1979. *Memberships:* People's Club of Nigeria; Awka-Etiti Social Club; Ikembe Age Group; British Institute of Management, Awka-Etiti. *Honours:* Ezissi Ezenyimba Title 1978. *Hobbies:* Swimming; Table Tennis. *Address:* 18 Obanikoro Road, Ikorodu Road, Vie Yaber, Nigeria.

CHIKWENDU, Arthur Aniemeka Obi, b. 6 Mar. 1943, Kano, Nigeria. Chemical Engineer; Management. m. 2 July 1977, 2 daughters. *Education:* Diploma, Chemical Engineering, UK, 1970; Graduate, British Institution of Chemical Engineers, 1972. *Appointments:* Technical Manager, British Steel Corporation, Middlesborough, UK, 1970-75; Engineer, 1975-77, Chief Engineer/Production Manager, 1977-79, General Manager, 1979-, Nigergas Limited, Enugu, Nigeria. *Memberships:* Council of Registered Engineers of Nigeria; Associate member, Nigerian Institute of Management; British Institute of Management; Chairman, Programme Committee, Rotary Club of Enugu; Enugu Sports Club; Nigerisn Society of Chemical Engineers. *Publications:* Several articles and speeches. *Hobbies:* Car mechanic; Beer and wine brewing; Reading Science fiction; Coin collecting; Home Decorating and improving. *Address:* 3 Igboeze Street, Independence Layout, Enugu, Nigeria.

CHILD, Graham Foster Tamplin, b. 6 June 1936, Bulawayo Zimbabwe. Wildlife Ecologist. m. Diana 7 May 1960, 1 son, 2 daughters. *Education:* BSc 1957; BSc(Hons) 1958; PhD 1965. *Appointments:* Junior Lecturer, Zoology, University of Cape Town, 1959; Wildlife Ecologist, Department of National Parks and Wildlife Management, Zimbabwe, 1959-61; Keeper of Ventebrates, National Museum, Bulawayo, 1961-65; F.A.O UN Wildlife Ecologist, Advising Botswana Government, 1965-71; Director National Parks and Wildlife Management, Zimbabwe, 1971-. *Memberships:* Trustee National Museums and Art Gallery, Botswana; Scientific Council of Zimbabwe; Elephant Group S.S.C of IUCN; IUCN National Parks Commission; Plumtree School Board. *Publications:* 50 Scientific Papers; Two Books. *Honours:* Officer of the Legeon of Merit. *Address:* 7a Old Catton Road, Mt. Pleasant, Salisbury, Zimbabwe.

CHILOPE, Seriano Morris, b. 1 Apr. 1934 Malawi. Land Surveyor and Civil Engineer. 3 sons, 5 daughters. *Education:* Oversea's Cambridge School Certificate, 1957; GCE Certificates, 1963-65; Society of Engineers Graduateship Examinations, Part I, 1972-75, Part II 1978; Technical Certificate Practical Test, 1979; Eligible to sit for Direct Membership Examination 1979. *Appointments:* Senior Engineering Surveyor, City Engineers Department, City of Blantyre, 1965-74; Land Surveyor, Malawi Housing Corporation, Blantyre, 1974-77; Senior Land Surveyor, M.H.C., Blantyre, 1977-. *Memberships:* Society of Surveying Technicians; Surveyors Institute of Malawi; Associate Member of the Society of Engineers. *Creative Works:* LONG LIVE KAMUZU, with two National flags below them, were designed by S M Chilope, 1966. *Hobbies:* Teaching Music; Reading; Football. *Address:* Malawi Housing Corporation, PO Box 414, Blantyre, Malawi.

CHIN, Fung Kee, b. 27 Feb. 1920, Penang, Malaysia. Civil Engineer. m. Wong Swee Yong, 3 sons, 1 daughter. *Education:* Diploma in Arts, Raffles College, Singapore, 1946; BSc(First Class Honours), Civil Engineering, Belfast, 1952; MSc, Engineering, Belfast 1953. *Appointments:* Assistant Master, Education Department, Malaya; Assistant Lecturer, Queen's University, Belfast; Engineer, Ferguson amd Millveen, Belfast; Engineer, Drainage and Irrigation Department, Malaya; Lecturer/Senior Lecturer/Professor of Engineering,

University of Malaya; Deputy Vice Chancellor/Dean of Engineering, University of Malaya; Acting Vice Chancellor; Consulting Engineer. *Memberships:* Fellow: Institution of Civil Engineers, UK; Institution of Structural Engineers, UK; Institution of Engineers of Ireland, Malaysia and Singapore; World Academy of Art and Science; President, Institution of Engineers, Malaysia; President, Southeast Asia Society of Soil Engineering; Vice President, International Society of Soil Mechanics and Foundation Engineering; Chairman, Governing Council, Standards and Industrial Researach, Malaysia; Vice Chairman, Science Council, Malaysia; Three Royal Commissions. *Publications:* More than 50 papers in International Engineering Journals. *Honours:* Foundation Scholarship, Queens University, Belfast, 1949; Belfast Association of Engineers Prize 1951; Raffle College Scholarship 1939; Queen Victoria Scholarship 1946; Johan Mangku Negara 1967; Panglima Setia Mahkota Knighthood, 1980; Honorary Fellow, Institution of Civil Engineers, UK 1977; Honorary Doctor of Science, University of Singapore, 1975; Professor Emeritus, University of Malaya. *Address:* 14 Road 12/19, Petaling Jaya, Selangor, Malaysia.

CHIN, Hoong Fong, b. 21 Feb. 1935, Kuala Lumpur Malaysia. Professor. m. Annie Sim Hooi Guat 27 Feb. 1965, 3 sons. *Education:* BSc Agriculture, Melbourne University 1960; MSc Agriculture 1970; PhD 1973. *Appointments:* Agronomist, Department of Agriculture 1961; Senior Lecturer, 1962, Lecturer, 1972, Associate Professor, 1975, Professor 1981, University of Agriculture, Malaysia. *Memberships:* Agricultural Institute of Malaysia; Australian Institute of Agricultural Science; Australian Society of Plant Physiologist; Malaysian Nature Society; Institute of Biology London. *Publications:* Malaysian Flowers in Colour; Malaysian Fruits in Colour; Recalcitrant Crop Seeds. *Hobbies:* Photography; Fishing. *Address:* 15, Jalan 1/9c, Bandar Barn Bangi, Bangi, Selangor, Malaysia.

CHING, Julia Chia-Yi, b. 15 Oct. 1934 Shanghai, China. Academic. *Education:* BA, College of New Rochelle 1958; MA Catholic University of America 1960; PhD Australian National University 1971. *Appointments:* Lecturer, Australian National University 1969-74; Associate Professor, Columbia University 1974-75; Associate Professor, Yale University 1975-78; Associate Professor, University of Toronto, 1978-81; Professor, University of Toronto, Canada, 1981-. *Memberships:* Association of Asian Studies; American Society for the Study of Religion; American Catholic Philosophical Society. *Publications:* Confucianism and Christanity 1977; To Acquire Wisdom: the Way of Wang Yang-ming 1976; The Philosophical Letters of Wang Yang-ming 1971. *Honours:* Phi Tau Phi Scholastic Honours Society, 1974-. *Hobbies:* Photography; Languages. *Address:* 66 Helena Avenue, Toronto, Canada.

CHINOY, Phiroze Behramji, b 7 Sept. 1924 Bombay. Chief Executive. m. Homsi 14 Mar. 1954, 1 son, 1 daughter. *Education:* BSc(Hon.) 1945, BSc(Tech.) 1947, MSc(Tech.) 1949, Fellow, Institute of Engineers, India. *Appointments:* Superintendent, Production Manager, National Rayons, Bombay 1948; Works Manager, Chief Executive, Baroda Rayons, Udhna, 1960-81. *Memberships:* Past President, Rotary Club Udhna; Rotary Foundation Committee; Surat Gymkhana Club; Surat Management Association. *Creative Works:* Responsible for the commercial development of Finer denier yarns in Rayon viz. in 25,30 and 40 Deniers for the first time in India. This greatly helped in saving foreign exchange to the country by replacing the imported Cuprammoniam Yarn. *Honours:* Singhanee Scholar in 1947 and 1948. *Hobbies:* Reading-Technical; Travel; Classical Music. *Address:* A-2, B.R.C. Colony, PO Baroda Rayon 394 220, (Udhna) Dist. Surat, Gujarat, India.

CHIOKE, Nwanne Obiajulu, b. 7 Oct. 1952 Ogidi. Veterinary Surgeon. m. 19 Dec. 1979 1 daughter. *Education:* WASC 1971; (DMGS Onitsha); Doctor of Veterinary Medicine U.N.N. 1979. *Appointments:* Teaching; Veterinary Officer. *Memberships:* Society for Animal Production, Nigeria; Society of Theriogeniologists, Nigeria; Beta Sigma Fraternity, Nigeria; Nigerian Veterinary Medical Association. *Honours:* Governor Beta Sigma Fraternity 1978; Certificate Award, as the National President, Nigerian Association of Veterinary Medical Students, 1979. *Hobbies:* Collecting stamps and old Currencies; Morning Runs; Listening to Jazz Music. *Address:* PO Box 32, Afor-Igwe PO, Ogidi, Anambra State, Nigeria.

CHIPASULA, James Cuthbert, b. 16 Apr. 1941, Yofu Village, Likoma Island, Nkhata Bay. Manager. m. Esther Kamana 8 Sept. 1973, 2 sons, 2 daughters. *Education:* Cambridge School Certificate 1959-61; Cambridge Higher School Certificate 1962-64; Certificate in French Language 1965-66; BSc Political Science 1966-69; PhD Political Science 1969-72. *Appointments:* Research and Administrative Assistant, University of Aix-Marseille 1970-72; Lecturer in Public Administration, University of Malawi, 1973-76; Training Manager, Hogg Robinson, Malawi Limited 1978-79; Group Training Manager, Import and Export Company of Malawi Limited 1979-. *Publications:* PhD thesis (unpublished) on East African Socialism, 1972, Awarded with distinction. *Hobbies:* Fishing; Swimming; Football; Reading. *Address:* Yofu Village, PO Likoma, Malawi.

CHIPP, Donald Leslie, b. 21 Aug. 1925, Melbourne, Victoria, Australia. Senator. m. (1) 2 sons, 2 daughters, (2) Idun Guda Welz, 25 Nov. 1979. *Education:* University of Melbourne, Commerce Degree, 1946. *Appointments:* RAAF, Air Crew, 1943-45; Registrar, Commonwealth Institute of Accountants and the Australian Society of Accountants, 1950-55; Member of the Council of the City of Kew, 1955-62; Minister for the Navy and first Minister for Tourism, 1966; Minister for Customs and Excise, 1969-72; Leader of the House of Representatives in the Australian Parliament, 1972; Founder of the Australian Democrats, 1977-. *Memberships:* Chief Executive Oficer of the Olympic Civic Committee, 1954; Member of the Council of the City of Kew. *Publications:* Numerous papers and articles; The Third Man. *Hobbies:* Cricket; Football; Tennis; Rafting. *Address:* Commonwealth Parliament Offices, 400 Flinders Street, Melbourne, Victoria, 3000, Australia.

CHIRAMBO, Mzondi Haviland, b. 27. Apr. 1956, Rumphi District, Malawi. Lawyer. m. Margaret Miriam Chirambo, 8 Nov. 1978, 1 son, 1 daughter. *Education:* Law Degree, credit, 1973-78. *Appointments:* Assistant Registrar General; Deputy Registrar of Patents, Marks and Designs; Attended the Austria WIPO Training Course in Patent Documentation, Vienna, 1979; Various WIPO Conferences, Industrial Property Geneva, Switzerland. *Memberships:* Member of the Malawi Law Society. *Publications:* Article on the Sale of Goods Act of Malawi for the Students Law Journal. *Hobbies:* Music; Dancing; Reading; Soccer. *Address:* SE/17, Soche East, Blantyre, Malawi.

CHISAKA, Kingstone Mumba, b. 20 Jan. 1944, Luanshya Mine, Zambia. City Librarian. m. 1970, 4 sons, 1 daughter. *Education:* Certificate in Library Studies, Evelyn Hone College of Further Education, Lusaka, 1969-70; Diploma in Library Studies, University of Zambia, Lusaka, 1972-74. *Appointments:* Senior Clerk, Bank of Zambia, Lusaka, 1966-71; Senior Library Assistant, 1971-72; Professional Training, University of Zambia, 1972-74; Assistant Librarian, 1974-75; Senior Assistant Librarian, 1975 76; City Librarian, 1976-, Ndola Public Libraries Ndola City. *Memberships:* Council Member, Zambia Library Association; Treasurer, Copperbelt Branch, Zambia Library Association; Team Manager, City of Ndola Football Club. *Hobbies:* Playing, Coaching and watching Soccer; Films. *Address:* 105 Broadway, Ndola, Zambia.

CHISANGA, Matthews Machlen, b. 1st Aug. 1938, Kitwe Zambia. Registrar. m. Theresa Mwamba, 6 Apr. 1972, 3 sons, 1 daughter. *Education:* St. Francis, Xavier College, Kutama Southern Rhodesia; Royal Institute of Public Administration. *Appointments:* Clerical Officer, Accountant, Manager, Bangweulu Water Transport, 1958-65; Zambian Diplomatic Service, 1965-71; Principal Training Officer, Ministry of Information and Broadcasting Services, 1972-77. *Memberships:* Chairman, Lusaka Central Sports Club, 1976-78. *Hobbies:* Tennis; Reading; Golf. *Address:* House No. 4, Chikuni Road, Northmead, Lusaka.

CHISMAN, Dennis Geoffrey, b. 21 Oct. 1927, Leeds, England. Education Consultant. m. Sheila Dorothy Lister, 29 July 1950, 1 son. *Education:* B.Sc. Kings College London, 1948; Dip. Ed. London Institute of Education, 1949. *Appointments:* Senior Science Master, Shene School, 1949-57; Education Officer Royal Institute of Chemistry, 1957-66; Director of Schools Dept, British Council, 1966-81; Education Consultant, 1981-. *Memberships:* Royal Society of Chemistry; Royal Commenwealth Society. *Publications:* University Chemical Education, Butterworths, 1970; British Science Curriculum Development, Ohio University, 1973; Integrated Science Education Worldwide, 1978. *Honours:* Honorary Member, Association for Science Education, 1980. *Hobbies:* Philately; Music. *Address:* 114 The Avenue, Sunbury-on-Thames, Middlesex, TW16 5EA, England.

CHISWELL, Peter, b. 18 Feb. 1934, Oatley, New South Wales, Australia. Bishop of Anglican Diocese of Armidale, Australia. m. Betty Marie Craik, 8 Jan. 1960, 2 sons, 1 daughter. *Education:* Bach. of Engineering, 1955; BD., 1961; Scholar in Theology, 1965. *Appointments:* Engineer, New South Wales Department of Main road, Australia, 1955-56; Vicar of Bingara, New South Wales, 1961-68; Vicar of Cummedeh, New South Wales, Australia, 1968-76; Bishop of Armidale, New South Wales, Australia, 1976-. *Address:* Bishopscourt, Armidale, New South Wales, Australia.

CHITTY, Joseph Charles Oliver, b. 28 Oct. 1917, Sleaford, Lincs, England. Director of Companies. m. Liv Helga Bakke, 26 Sept. 1942, 2 daughters. *Education:* Royal Naval College, Dartmouth, Devon, England. *Appointments:* Various Appointments in Royal Navy, 1935-47; Deputy Chairman (Managing Director 1947-81), Bakke Industries Ltd., Various Directorships, including: Central African Building Society; Zimbabwe Banking Corporation Ltd.; Syfrets Merchant Bank Ltd.; Quality Boxes Ltd., Lancashire Steel Ltd; Salwire Ltd. *Memberships:* Chairman, Commercial & Industrial Medical Aid Society; President, Salisbury Chamber of Industries, 1962-63; President, Association of Rhodesian Industries, 1975-76; Chairman, Lumber Millers & Timber Processors Association, 1957 and numerous subsequent years, Fellow, Institute of Directors. *Publications:* Several entomological papers. *Hobby:* Entomology. *Address:* Torrie Lodge, St. Michael's Lane, Borrowdale, Salisbury, Zimbabwe.

CHIUME, Murray William Kanyama, b. 22 Nov. 1929, Usisya, Nkata Bay, Malawi. Journalist, Author; Educationist. m. (1) Edas Ngoza, 31 July 1955; (2) Natalia, 13 Oct. 1966, 4 sons, 3 daughters. *Education:* Diploma in Education, Makerere University College, 1949-53. *Appointments:* Teacher, Assistant Education Officer, Dodoma, Tanzania, 1954; Publicity Secretary, Nyasaland African Congress, 1955-64; Feature Writer, Tanu Party Papers, 1965-75; Editor, Drum and Trust, 1975-76; Managing Director, Pan-African Publishing Co. Ltd., 1977-. *Memberships:* President, Makerere College Education Society, 1952; President, Makerere College Political Society, 1953; Selander Bridge Club, Daressalaam; Leader, The Congress for the Second Republic of Malawi, 1975-. *Publications:* Caro Ncinonono; Mwana wa Ngoza; Dunia Ngumu; Mbutolwe Mwana wa Umma; Hadithi Za Kwetu; The African Deluge; Several Tranlations, including: Ndugu Nkruma; Kwacha (Autobiography). *Honours:* Student of the Year, Daresalaam, 1946; Student of the Year, Tabora, 1948; Swimming, Makerere, 1949. *Hobbies:* Swimming; Hunting; Writing. *Address:* P.O. Box 4212, Daressalaam, Tanzania.

CHIU, Frank Tjie-Sien, b. 5 Dec. 1932. Medical Practitioner. m. 26 Jan. 1964, 2 sons, 1 daughter. *Education:* MB., BS., Medical School, University of Queensland, Australia, 1960; MRACP., 1970; FRACP., 1975; Royal Australasian College of Physicians. *Appointments:* Resident Medical Officer, Royal Brisbane Hospital, Australia, 1961-62; Medical Registrar, 1963-65; Teaching Medical Registrar, Medical Professorial Department, University of Queensland, Australia, 1966-67; Cardiothoracic Registrar, Chermside Hospital, Brisbane, Australia, 1968; Chest Registrar, Repatriation General Hospital, Heidelberg, Melbourne, Australia, 1970; Registrar to Pulmonary Function Unit, Chest Physician, 1971-74; Visiting Chest Specialist, Austin Hospital, Heidelberg, Melbourne, Australia, 1973-74; Chest Physician, Royal Adelaide Hospital, Australia, 1975-; Senior Visiting Chest Specialist, Repatriation General Hospital, Daw Park, Australia, 1975-. *Memberships:* Fellow, Royal Australasian College of Physicians; Thoracic Society of Australia; Australian

Medical Association; Chairman, 1975-78, President, 1978-80, Chinese Association of South Australia, Inc.; Australian Asian Family Association; IndoChinese Refugee Association. *Publications:* Publications include: Cavitation in Lung Cancer, 1975; Bronchogenic Carcinoma causing Non-Terminal Saccular Bronchiectasis , 1973; Effects of Disodium Cromoglycate and Beclomethasone Dipropionate on Methacholine Provocation, 1977; Unusual Biochemical Abnormalities in a Case of Pulmonary Tuberculosis, 1978; Hypercalcaemia Associated with Tuberculosis, 1980; Ritampicin Associated Renal Dysfunction during Antituberculous Therapy, 1980. *Hobbies:* Chinese martial arts; Tennis; Table tennis; Swimming; Photography; Piano; Violin; Chess. *Address:* 11 Sleeps Hill Drive, Panorama, South Australia 5041, Australia

CHOA, Gerald Hugh, b. 21 March 1921, Hong Kong. Physician. m. Peggy Leung, 18 Dec. 1954. *Education:* M.B. B.S. Hong Kong, 1946; D.T.M. & H., Liverpool, 1948; M.R.C.P., London, 1952-53; M.D., Hong Kong, 1960; F.R.C.P., London, 1968; F.R.C.P., Edinburgh, 1972; F.F.C.M., 1974. *Appointments:* Lecturer in Medicine, Hong Kong University, 1949-56; Medical Specialist, Medical and Health Department, 1956-67; Deputy Director, Medical and Health Department, 1967-70; Director of Medical & Health Services, Hong Kong, 1970-76; Dean, Faculty of Medicine, Chinese University of Hong Kong, 1977-. *Memberships:* President, Hong Kong Mental Health Association; Vice-President, Hong Kong Anti-Tuberculosis and Thoracic Diseases Association; British Medical Association; British Medical Association, Hong Kong; Medical Association, Hong Kong. *Publications:* The Life and Times of Sir Kai Ho Kai; The History of Medicine in Hong Kong; The Phenomenon of Drug Addiction in Hong Kong; Medical Education in Hong Kong. *Honours:* C.B.E., 1972. *Hobbies:* Reading; Writing; Music. *Address:* Faculty of Medicine, Chinese University of Hong Kong, Shatin, New Territories, Hong Kong.

CHOE, Jimmy C.Y. b. Taiping, Perak, Malaysia, 5 Jan. 1941, Companies Director, Planter. *Education:* St. George's Institution, Taiping, Perak, Malaysia; Perth Technical College, Western Australia. *Appointments:* Managing Director, Yoong Heng Hardware Sdn. Bhd., Hup Heng Pembekal Ladang Sdn. Bhd., Kimiajaya Sdn. Bhd., Hi-Top Pub Sdn. Bhd., Executive Director of Choe Mock Heng Holdings Sdn. Bhd., Director of Hup Heng Motor Sdn. Bhd., Epak Services Enterprise Sdn. Bhd., *Memberships:* Protem Chairman, Old Georgians' Association Ipoh, 1974; Founder Member and President, Hon. Secretary, 1974-80; -incorporated Society of Planters, Central Perak Branch, 1966-77; Vice-Chairman, 1978-79; Chairman, 1980. *Hobbies:* Photography; Flying; Motoring; Acting; Football; Travelling. *Address:* 32, Jalan Sultan Yussuf, Belfield Street, P.O. Box 154, Ipoh, Perak, Malaysia.

CHOI, Cheung-Kok, b. 20 Oct. 1912, China. Industrialist. m. 2 Aug. 1947, 4 sons, 3 daughters. *Education:* Ho Dung College, Kwantung, China. *Appointments:* Managing Director, Ting Tai Metal Ware Factory Limited; Chairman, Tingtai Wahchong Metal Manufacturing Co. Limited; Managing Director, The Excelsior Metallurgical Works Co. Limited. *Memberships:* Past Chairman, Honorary Chairman, The Chinese Manufacturers' Association of Hong Kong; Past Chairman, life-time Honorary Chairman, Hong Kong Chiu Chow Chamber of Commerce Ltd.; Vice Chairman, Chiu Chow Association Building (Property Holding) Ltd.; Life-time Chairman, Gee Tuck World Association Limited; Past President, Rotary Club of Kowloon West; The Royal Hong Kong Golf Club; The Hong Kong Association (Hong Kong Branch). *Creative Works:* Rings Brand Aluminiumware. *Honours:* JP, 1968. *Hobbies:* Reading. *Address:* 2A Green Lane, Happy Valley, Hong Kong.

CHONG, Wilson, b. 5 July 1922, Santiago, Cuba. Architect Planner. m. Inez Holung, 27 Apr. 1952, 4 sons, 2 daughters. *Education:* University of Notre Dame, Indiana, USA, 1942-45; BS., Architect, University of Illinois, USA, 1952. *Appointments:* William Zook, Chicago, USA, 1952-53; Private Practice, Jamaica, 1953-. *Memberships:* President, 1963-65 and 1966-67, Jamaican Society of Architects; Honorary Member, Mexican Society of Architects; Institute of Patentees and Inventors; American Society of Cost Engineers; Construction Specification Institute; Chairman, 1972-76, Town and County Planning Authority; Chairman,

1972-, Advisory Planning Committee. *Creative Works:* Marly Grandstand, Arch Record, 1952; National Stadium, Arch Record, 1962; Arch Forum, 1963; Holder of: British German and US Patents for hand pile borer; British patent for a rat trap; British patent for Seat for non-ambulatory patients. *Publications:* Various papers and forums. *Honours:* Commander of the Order of Distinction, 1978; Silver Musgrave medal, 1976; Governor General award in Architecture, 1962. *Hobby:* Research. *Address:* 3 Allerdyce Drive, Allerdyce Court, Apartment 4, Kingston 8, Jamaica.

CHONGO, Julius Anderson, b. 6 Sept. 1943, Chipata, Eastern Province, Zambia. Magistrate. m. Averess Mwanza, 25 May 1966, 3 sons, 2 daughters. *Education:* BBC. course in Broadcasting, 1964; Journalism course, Evelyne Home College, Lusaka, Zambia, 1965; Diploma, Journalism, International Press Institute, University College, Nairobi, Kenya, 1968; Diploma, Mass communication, Indian Institute of Mass Communication, Delhi, India, 1970; Magistracy, 1974. *Appointments:* Broadcaster; Journalist; Magistrate. *Memberships:* Past Vice Treasurer, Press Club; Writers Association of Zambia; Founder Chairman, Zambezi Drama Club. *Publications:* Fumbi Khobod; Pondo, (under print); TV and Radio plays; Short Story contributor to Zambia magazine; Writer and narrator of Poceza Madzulo, radio stories. *Hobbies:* Short story writing; Poetry writing; Writing and producing plays. *Address:* PO Box 30, Zambezi, Zambia.

CHOO, Samuel Kam Chee, b. 16 Mar. 1916, Chemor, Perak, Malaysia. Clergyman. m. Dorothy King Cheung Man, 4 Feb. 1950, 1 daughter. *Education:* BSc., Lingnan University, Canton, China, 1941; MRE. Golden Gate Baptist Theological Seminar, Berkeley, California, USA, 1958; post graduate, University of California, Berkeley, California, USA, 1958-60; Sign Language, Red River Community College, Winnipeg, Manitoba, Canada, 1975. *Appointments:* Teacher, Lingnan Middle School, Hong Kong, 1945-55; Church worker and interpreter, Chinese Baptist Mission, Berkeley, California, USA, 1955; Chinese language teacher and evangelist, Ottawa Chinese Mission, Canada, 1955-60; Ordained, The United Church of Canada, 1962; Founder and Minister, Chinese United Church, Ottawa, Ontario, Canada, 1962-68; Minister, Chinese United Church, Winnipeg, Manitoba, Canada, 1968-77; President, Chinese United Church Conference of Canada, 1963-67. *Memberships:* Adult Training Union, Kowloon City Baptist Church Hong Kong; Manitoba Chinese Fellowship; Chinese United Church, Building Committee, Winnipeg, Canada; Senior Citizen's Housing Building Committee, Winnipeg, Canada. *Creative Works:* Built the Winnipeg Chinese United Church, $65000.00 new sanctuary, 1970; Built the $2 mil. 13 storey 88 units Sek On Toi Chinese Senior Citizen's Home, Winnipeg, Canada, 1978. *Hobbies:* Reading; Badminton; Table-tennis; Sports. *Address:* 415 Beverley Street, Winnipeg, Manitoba, Canada R3G 1T9.

CHOPPING, Steven Charles, b. 7 July 1948, Hobart, Tasmania, Australia. Barrister; Solicitor. m. Robyn Dell Shipp, 23 Dec. 1972, 2 sons. *Education:* Bachelor of Laws degree, 1971. *Appointments:* Barrister and Solicitor admitted 1972; Employed by Simmons Wolfhagen, 1971-74, Partner in firm, Ogilvie McKenna, 1974-. *Memberships:* Law Council (Tasmania); National Council of Confederation of Australian Motor Sport; State Chairman, Confederation of Australian Motor Sport; President, Hobart Sporting Car Club; President, Tasmania Auto Sport Incorporated; Athenaeum Club; Royal Hobart Golf Club; Light Car Club of Australia; Australian Institute of Advanced Motorists. *Publications:* Tasmanian Editor, Racing Car News Magazine; Columnist, Saturday Evening Mercury Newspaper; Broadcasting: Motor Racing Contributor Radio 7HT; Australian Broadcasting Commission. *Honours:* Tasmanian Sportsman of Year (Motor Racing), 1980; Butterworths Prize (Mercantile Law), 1969. *Hobbies:* Motor Racing; Golf; Sailing; Photography; Scouting. *Address:* 21 Darling Parade, Mt. Stuart, Hobart, Tasmania, Australia.

CHOUDHARY, Lakshman 'Lalit', b. 1 Nov. 1945, Mishratola, Darbhomge, Bihar, India. University Lecturer. m. 9 June 1969, Sudha, 2 sons, 1 daughter. *Education:* Pre-Arts, 2nd Div., 1963, Part-one Arts, 2nd Div., 1964, BA(Hons.) 1966, MA(Maithili) 1968, Bihar University, India; PhD, Mithila University, India, 1974. *Appointments:* Lecturer in Maithili, CM College, Darbhange, Bihar, India; Lecturer in Maithili, JN College, Madhubani, Bihar, India; Lecturer in Post-Graduate Dept. of Maithili Language and Literature, Mithila University, India. *Memberships:* Maithili Sahitya Parishad, Darbhanga; Linguistic Society of India. *Publications:* Research work: Maithili Sahitya Par Pauranic Prabhav; numerous research articles in journals of Bihar and Bengal. *Honours:* Gold medal at both the Hons. and Post-graduate level examinations; National merit Scholarships at the Post-Graduate studies. *Hobbies:* Travel. *Address:* Mishratola, PO and District, Darbhanga 846004, Bihar, India.

CHOUDHRI, Saif-Ur-Rahman. b. 5 Apr. 1934, Khamachun, British India. Dean, Faculty of Management Sciences. m. Zakia Sultana, 16 Sept. 1965, 1 son, 2 daughters. *Education:* BA, Punjab University, Lahore, Pakistan, 1955; National Diploma, Manchester College of Science and Technology, Manchester, England, 1961; MSc.Tech., University of Manchester, England, 1963; Post Graduate Diploma, S.M. Law College, Karachi University, Pakistan, 1964; MSc., University of Salford, England, 1968; PhD Candidate, University of Lancaster, England, 1971-78. *Appointments:* Management Counsellor in Labour-Management Relations at Pakistan Institute of Management, Karachi, 1964-66; Visiting Lecturer in Management Studies Salford Technical College, Salford, England, 1966-69; Lecturer in Industrial Relation, Sunderland Polytechnic, Sunderland, England, 1969-71; Senior Lecturer in Personnel Management/Industrial Relations, Salford College of Technology, Salford, England, 1971-78; Principal Lecturer/Acting Head of Department of Business Administration, College of Science and Technology, Port Harcourt, Nigeria, 1978-80; Dean, Faculty of Management Sciences, River State University of Science and Technology, Port Harcourt, Nigeria. *Memberships:* British Institute of Management, London; Institute of Personnel Management, London; Society of Industrial Tutors, London; Associate Member, Nigerian Institute of Management, Lagos. *Publications:* Numerous articles in British Management Journals including: A Worm's Eye View, 1968; Personality, Shop Stewards and Managerial Behaviour, 1970; Management through Shop Steward's Eyes, 1970; Brotherly Spirit, 1970; Employing Pakistanis, A Sense of Responsibility, 1973; Numerous Broadcasts made on NTV Channel 10 Port Harcourt in field; Papers read at Conferences in field;Prepared the first student handbook of the School of Business Studies, 1979. *Hobbies:* Reading Ancient History; Classical Eastern and Western Music. *Address:* Bungalow 3, Road C, University Campus, PMB. 5080, Port Harcourt, Nigeria.

CHOUDHURY, Abdur Razzaque, b. 1 Mar. 1923, Habiganj, Sylhet, Bangladesh. Teacher. m. 28 June 1951. *Education:* ISC 1941, BSc 1943, Calcutta University, India; MSc, Botany, Dacca University, Bangladesh, 1950; MSc, Botany, Manchester University, England 1963; PhD, Texas A & M University, USA, 1970. *Appointments:* Teacher, High School, Sylhet, Bangladesh, 1943-48; Research Assistant, Daaca University, Bangladesh, 1950-51; Lecturer, Veterinary College, 1951-59; Assistant Professor 1964-72, Associate Professor 1972-77, Professor 1977-, Agricultural University. *Memberships:* Indian Association of Genetics & Plant Breeding; Society for Advancement of Breeding Research in Asia and Oceania; Bangladesh Association for Advancement of Science. *Publications:* 28 publications in International Scientific journals. *Honours:* Numerous Scholarships, Academic Career. *Hobbies:* Flower and Vegetable gardening. *Address:* D9/2 Professor's Colony, University Campus, Mymensingh, Bangladesh.

CHOUDHURY, Amalendu, b. 29 June 1930, Tangail, Bengal, India. Research and Teaching. m. Molina, 27 Jan. 1966, 1 daughter. *Education:* MSc., 1952; PhD., 1959; Diploma for Specialised Training in France, 1965; Visited various Research laboratories in England, Germany, France and many European Countries. *Appointments:* Lecturer in Physics, 1960, Reader in Physics, 1965, Professor of Physics, 1976, Head of Department of Physics, 1977-80, Jadavpur University, Calcutta, India; French Government Fellowship, 1963. *Memberships:* Indian Physical Society; Mineralogical Society of France; Past Vice President and Treasurer, Indian Physics Association, Calcutta Chapter; Cryogenic Society of India; Indian Science Congress Association. *Publications:* Pioneer in developing a method for Study of Electron channelling in ionic crystals by using

color centres; 40 original research publications in International Journals. *Creative Works:* Developed a School of Physicists in the domain of solid state physics, Jadavpur University, India. *Address:* 108 Maniktala Main Road, Flat 14, Block 2, Calcutta 54, India.

CHOW, Timothy Albert, b. 23 Oct. 1923, Shanghai, China. Librarian. m. 30 Dec. 1948, 2 sons, 1 daughter. *Education:* Licencie-ès-lettres, Aurora, 1946; Diploma in Librarianship, New South Wales, Australia, 1967; Associateship, Library Association of Australia, 1967. *Appointments:* Assistant Librarian, Aurora University, Shanghai, China, 1946-57; Assistant Librarian, 1962-68, Chief Librarian, 1969-, Urban Council Public Libraries, Hong Kong. *Memberships:* Hong Kong Library Association; Australian Library Association. *Publications:* Numerous papers submitted to Government in field; Created first library course at Hong Kong University Extra Mural Department, 1980. *Hobbies:* Reading; Classical Music; Travel. *Address:* 6c/19 Broadcast Drive, Kowloon, Hong Kong.

CHOWDHRY, Surendra Vir Singh, b. 2 May 1933, Kanpur, India. Army Officer. m. Shashi Dagur, 25 June 1963, 4 daughters. *Education:* BSc. Physics 1953, MSc. Physics 1954, Lucknow University, India; Graduate, Telecommunication Engineering, Military College of Telecommunication Engineering, Mhow, India, 1969; National Security Management Course, National Defence University, Washington, USA, 1978. *Appointments:* Commissioned in Army, 1957-; Specialised in EDP, 1972; Faculty member in Computer Technology Wing of MCTE, Mhow,1973-74; Promoted to Lt. Col., 1974; Officer in Charge of Section responsible for EDP activity at Army Headquarters, New Delhi, 1974-76; Commanded Static Signal unit, 1976-78; Member of Study team connected with introduction of field computers in the Army 1978-79; Associated with design and development of field computer systems, 1979-80; Promoted to Colonel, 1980; Deputy Chief Signal Officer at a Corps Headquarters, 1980-. *Memberships:* Chartered Engineer (India); Fellow, Institution of Engineers (India); Fellow, Institution of Electronics and Telemcommunication Engineers; Computer Society of India. *Creative Works:* Associated with analysis, design and development of several computerised information systems to cater for training as well as other peacetime Army requirements. *Honours:* Awarded Chief of Army Staff's Commendation Card for contribution in the planning of communication support during Indo-Pak Conflict, 1971. *Hobbies:* Golf. *Address:* A-7 Terrace Apartments, Navrangpura, Ahmedabad (Gujarat), India.

CHOWDHURY, Abu Sayeed, b. 31 Jan. 1921. Former President of Bangladesh. m. Khurshid 1948, 2 sons, 1 daughter. *Education:* MA., Bachelor Laws, Calcultta University, India; Called to the Bar, Lincoln's Inn, London, 1947. *Appointments:* Member, Pakistan Delegation to General Assemby of the UN, 1959; Advocate-General, E Pakistan, 1960; Member, Constitution Commission, 1960-61; Judge, Dacca High Court, 1961-72; Chairman, Central Board for Development of Bengali, 1963-68; Leader, Pakistan Delegation to World Assembly of Judges and 4th World Conference on World Peace through Law, 1969; Vice-Chancellow, Dacca University, 1969-72, in addition to duties of Judge of Dacca High Court; Member, UN Commission on Human Rights, 1971; Ambassador-at-large for Government of Bangladesh, designated by Bangladesh Government as High Commissioner for UK and N Ireland, 1971, and Head of the Bangladesh Missions at London and New York, April 1971-Jan. 1972; President of Bangladesh, 1972-73; Chancellor, all Bangladesh Universities, 1972-73; Special Representative of Bangladesh, 1973-75; Leader, Bangladesh Delegations: Conference on Humanitarian Law, Geneva, 1974, 1975 (Chairman, Drafting Committee); World Health Assemblies, Geneva, 1974, 1975; International Labour Conferences, Geneva, 1974, 1975 (Chairman, Human Resources Committee); Conferences on Law of the Sea, Caracas, 1974, Geneva, 1975; General Conference International Atomic Energy Agency, Vienna, 1974; Non-aligned Foreign Ministers' Conference, Lima, 1975; UN Special Session, Sept. 1975, NY; 30th Session of General Assembly, UN, 1975; Islamic Foreign Ministers' Conference, Jeddah, 1975; led goodwill missions to Saudi Arabia, Egypt, Syria, Lebanon and Algeria, 1974; Turkey, 1975 Foreign Minister 1975. *Honours:* Hon. Fellow, Open University, 1977; Hon.

Deshikottama Viywabharati (Shantiniketan), India, 1972; Hon. LLD Calcutta, 1972. *Memberships:* Athenaeum Club; Royal Over-Seas League; Royal Commonwealth Society. *Hobbies:* Reading; Gardening. *Address:* 2 Paper Buildings, Temple, London, EC4, England.

CHOWDHURY, Fazlul Halim, b. 1 Aug. 1930, Comilla, Bangladesh. University Teacher. m. Shamsun Nahar, 17 July 1960, 1 son, 3 daughters. *Education:* BSc.(Hons.) 1950, MSc 1951, Dacca University, Bangladesh; PhD, Manchester University, England, 1956. *Appointments:* Lecturer, Chemistry, Dacca University, Bangladesh, 1952-56; Reader in Chemistry, 1956-58, Professor of Chemistry, 1963-67, Provost, Nawab Abdul Latif Hall, 1967-70, Professor and Chairman, Department of Applied Chemistry, 1967-74, Dean of the Faculty of Science, 1972, Rajshahi University, Bangladesh; Member, Bangladesh University Grants Commission, Aug. 1974-Feb. 1976; Vice Chancellor, University of Dacca, Bangladesh, 1976-. *Memberships:* Fellow of Bangladesh Academy of Sciences; Bangladesh Association for Advancement of Science; Bangladesh Chemical Society. *Publications:* Published large number of Scientific papers in National and International Journals. *Honours:* Overseas scholar of the Royal Commission for Exhibition of 1851 at the University of Manchester, UK, 1953-55; Patuch Prize, Manchester College of Science and Technology, 1956; Fellowship awarded by the Nuffield Foundation, University of Cambridge, UK, 1960-62; Commonwealth Academic Staff Fellowship at the University of Cambridge - attached to Sydney Sussex College 1972-73. *Hobbies:* Music; Travel. *Address:* Vice-Chancellor's House, University of Dacca, Dacca, Bangladesh.

CHOWDHURY, Jugal Kishore, b. 1 Mar. 1918, Assam, India. Chartered Architect & Chartered Town Planner. *Education:* Associateship Examination, Royal Institute of British Architects, London, 1948; Diploma in Town Planning and Civic Architecture, University of London, 1948; University of Tennessee, USA, 1948-49. *Appointments:* Chief Architect & Town Planner Gandhidham Township, 1949-50; Consulting Architect, Govt Punjab, Chandigarh, 1950-57; Consultancy Practice, Architect and Town Planner, Delhi, 1957-; Proprietor, Chowdhury & Gulzar Singh, New Delhi, 1957-. *Memberships:* Fellow: Royal Institute of British Architects, London; Royal Town Planning Institute, London, Indian Institute of Architects; Fellow, Vice President, President, Institute of Town Planners, India; Executive Council, Eastern Regional Organization Planning and Housing. *Honours:* Padma Shree award, 1977. *Address:* 145-A Jorbagh, New Delhi-110003, India.

CHOWDHURY, Kabir, b. 9 Feb. 1923, Brahmanbaria, Bangladesh. Educationist;University Professor. m. Meher Timur, 29 June 1945, 3 daughters. *Education:* Matriculation, 1938; Intermediate Arts, 1940; BA Hons. English, 1st Class, Dacca University, 1943; MA, English, 1st Class, Dacca University, 1944; Studied American Literature, University of Minnesota, 1959-58; Master Degree, Public Administration, University of Southern California, 1964. *Appointments:* Subdivisional and District Controller, Civil Supplies, 1945-55; Professor and Principal of Colleges, 1955-69; Director, Bengali Academy, 1969-72; Member-Secretary, National Education Commission, Bangladesh, 1972-73; Secretary, Government of Bangladesh, Ministry of Education, Cultural Affairs, Sports, 1973-74; Professor, Department of English, University of Dacca, 1974-. *Memberships:* Chairman, United Nations Association of Bangladesh, 1975-; Chairman of the Presidium, Afro-Asian Writers Union of Bangladesh, 1975-; President, Federation of Film Societies of Bangladesh, 1978-; Chairman, School of Drama, Dacca, 1977-; Fellow, Bengali Academy, Dacca, 1978-. *Publications:* Bengali translation, works of Eugene O'Neill, Jack London, Chekov, J B Priestly and others, and English translation, works of Kazi Nazrul islam, Shamour Rahman and many others *Honours:* Bengali Academy Prize for Translation, 1974; Samakala Literary Award tor significant contribution to arts and letters, 1979. *Hobbies:* Reading; Music. *Address:* 35F,, Fuller Road, Dacca University Quarters, Dacca — 2, Bangladesh.

CHOWDHURY, Mafizul Islam, b. 1 Dec. 1920, Dacca, Bangladesh. University Teacher. m. Feroza Begum, 4 July 1944, 2 sons, 4 daughters. *Education:* BA, (Hons.), 1943, MA, 1944, MSc, 1959. *Appointments:* Professor,

Afghan Education Service, Kabul, Afghanistan, 1944-46; Lecturer, Islamia College, Calcutta, Bengal Jr. Education Service, 1946-47; E.P. Education Service, 1950-73; Jahangirnagar University, 1973-. *Memberships:* President, Bangladesh Society of Natural Sciences; President, National Geographical Association; President, National Committee of Geographers; President, Monsoon Region Environment Society; President, SCOPE, Bangladesh. *Publications:* Articles in Newspapers; Papers in Scientific Journals, and proceedings of Symposium, Seminars, & Conferences. *Honours:* Honourary Life Member, Bangladesh Geographical Society, Dacca. *Address:* Rd. 1, Block 1, No. 61 Banani, Dacca, Bangladesh.

CHRISTENSEN, Eric Herbert, b. 29 Oct. 1923, Banjul, The Gambia, West Africa. Company Director. m. Diana Dixon-Baker, 16 June 1951, 4 sons, 3 daughters. *Education:* St. Augustine's Primary School, 1928-36; St. Augustine's Secondary School, 1937-40; Cambridge University School Certificate, 1940. *Appointments:* Teacher, St. Augustine's Secondary School, 1941-43; Military Service, 1944-45; Vice Consul for France, Banjul, 1947-60; Counsellor Senegalese Consulate General, 1961-65; Secretary External Affairs, Banjul, 1965-66; Principal Assistant Secretary Prime Minister's Office, 1966-67; Permanent Secretary, PMO & External Affairs, Secretary to the Cabinet, Secretary General President's Office, Head of the Civil Service, 1970-78; Chairman, Atlantic Hotel Ltd., 1980; Director, Seagull Coldstores, Ltd., 1980. *Memberships:* President, Gambia Cricket Association, 1958-68; Honorary Secretary British Legion (Gambia B4anch), 1965-; President Alliance Francaise de Gambie, 1968-78. *Honours:* Knight Commander, Order of Merit, GFederal German Republic, 1968; Companion of the Most Distinguished Order of St. Michael & St. George (CMG), 1968; Grand Officer of the National Order of the Gambia (GORG), 1970; Chevalier de la Legion d'Honneur (France), 1975. *Hobbies:* Reading; Philately; Photography; Chess; Golf. *Address:* Pipeline Road, Latrikunda, The Gambia.

CHRISTIAN, Millicent Lilian, b. 5 Mar. 1905, Johannesburg, South Africa. Teacher. m. 11 Feb. 1929, 3 daughters. *Education:* Bachelor of Arts, Sudney University, 1926; Diploma of Education, Sydney University, 1927. *Appointments:* Teacher. *Memberships:* President, United Associations of Women; President, Nth. Sydney Club, Business & Professional Women; Former President, Kuringai Historical Society (NSW); Former President & Secretary various other local Committees. *Publications:* Various short articles and letters for newspapers and magazines. *Honours:* Distinguished Citizens Award from Kuringai Municipality for Historical Work and community service on the occasion of Kuringai's Jubilee celebrations in 1978. *Hobbies:* Reading; Music; Politics; Sport; Family Relations (eight grandchildren). *Address:* Warrel, 48 Warrimoo Avenue, St. Ives, N S W 2075, Australia.

CHRISTODOULOU, Aris John, b. 16 Jan. 1939, Nicosia, Cyprus. Horticulturist. m. Stella Pittas, 14 June 1970, 1 son, 1 daughter. *Education:* N.C.A.Houghall School of Agriculture, Durham, 1959; B.Sc. Agriculture, Durham University, 1963; M.Sc. Horticulture, U.C. California, 1966. *Appointments:* Lanitis Farm Limited, 1964-. *Memberships:* Limassol International Rotary, Board of the Limassol Chamber of Commerce & Industry, Attended The Royal Society of the Commonwealth Conference in Canada — Jamaica, 1977; Newcastle University Agricultural Society, American Society of Enology. *Publications:* Papers Published: California Agriculture,(Vol.20, Number 11), 1966; Vitis 6, Seite 303-308, 1967; Proceedings International Symposium on Sub-tropical & Tropical Horticulture, 1967; American Society for Horticulture Science, Vol. 92, 1968. *Hobbies:* Game Shooting; Tennis; Wine making; Horticulute. *Address:* 4 Herodotou Street, Limassol, Cyprus.

CHRISTOFIDES, Andreas N, b. 20 Aug. 1937, Nicosia, Cyprus. Director-General of the Cyprus Broadcasting Corporation. m. Theofile Papadopoulou, 28 July 1957, 1 son, 1 daughter. *Education:* Pancyprian Gymnasium, 1948-54; Philosophic School of the University of Athens, 1954-58; Columbia University, N.Y. (M.A.Columbia), 1963-64. *Appointments:* Teacher, Pancyprian Gymnasium, 1958-63; Director of Radio Programmes, 1964-67; Director-General, 1967 Cyprus

Broadcasting Corporation. *Memberships:* Secretary General, Secondary School Teacher's Association; Administrative Council of the E B U, 1972-76, 1980-; International Broadcast Institute; UNESCO, WIPO and other conferences. Chairman of Select Committee of experts on the Electronic Media Council of Europe, 1979; Chairman, State Theatre of Cyprus; Founder member, Editorial Board of the monthly literary magazine, Cultural Cyprus. *Publications:* Love Poems from Cyprus, 1962; Letters from New York, 1966; Introduction to Propaganda, 1966; Points of View, 1966; Strange Illustrations, 1969; Analytical Propositions, 1971; Anthology of Verse of Cyprus, 1972,74; Conversation of the Night, 1979, and other Poems and Essays. *Honours:* State Prize for Literature, Points of View, volume I and II, 1970, 1974. *Hobbies:* Reading; Music. *Address:* Romanos Street, No. 18A, Nicosia, Cyprus

CHUA,Song Lim, b. 31 Oct. 1920, Muar, Johore, Malaysia. Company Chairman; Land Developer. m. Koh Sai Eng, 5 Feb. 1943, 3 sons, 4 daughters. *Education:* St. Andrew's School, Muar; English High School, Muar. *Appointments:* Elected Johore State Assembly, Alliance Party, 1954,59,64,69,74; Johore Executive Council, Public Works, 1956-78; Chairman Johore Malaysian Chinese Association until 974; Senator Johore State Assembly, 1978-. *Memberships:* President of: Teochew Association Muar, The Chua Clan Association Muar, The Moral Uplifting Association Muar, Kwang Tong Association Muar, Old People Homes Muar, The Lion Club Muar, and others; Malaysian Chinese Association, Johore, Honorary Secretary, 1951, State Chairman & National Vice-President, 1963-73. *Honours:* J.P. (Justice of Peace), 1957; J.M.N., 1958; P.I.S., 1961; D.P.M.J. (Title of DATO), 1962; S.P.M.J. (Highest rank Datoship), 1972; S.S.I-.J.(Another Title of Dato), 1976; B.S.I., 1977. *Hobbies:* Art Collector; Photoghy; Chinese Paintings and Antiques. *Address:* 18, Jalan Parit Hj. Baki, Muar, Johore, Malaysia.

CHUKE, Paul Okwudili, b. 15 July 1936, Enugu, Nigeria. Neurologist; Professor. m. Mary Lily Oranika, 15 Nov. 1969, 2 sons, 1 daughter. *Education:* University College, Ibadan, 1956-61; M.B., B.S.(London); Johns Hopkins Hospital Baltimore, USA; F.R.C.P.(Canada) 1967; Diploma American Board of Neurology, 1968; F.M.C.P.(Nigeria) F.A.W.C.P. *Appointments:* Consultant Physician, Lusaka Central Hospital, Zambia, 1969-71; Senior Lecturer, (Medicine) University of Zambia, Lusaka, 1971-74; Director of Medical Services, Zambia Ministry of Health, 1974-77; Reader in Medicine, University of Nigeria, 1977-78; Professor of Medicine, University of Nigeria, Enugu Campus, 1978-. *Memberships:* -Nigerian Medical Association; Canadian Neurological Association; Pan-African Association of Neurological Sciences; President, Association of Physicians of East Africa, 1974; Treasurer, Enugu Golf Club, 1978-80. *Publications:* Pernicious Amaemia in Africans; Cerebrospinal fluid protein in Africans; Neurological Complications by high iron diet; Peripheral Neuropathy. *Honours:* Executive Board, World Health Organisation, 1975-77; Advisory Committee on Medical Research Who, African Region; Physician, State House, Lusaka, Zambia, 1969-77. *Hobbies:* Golf; Photography. *Address:* 4 Charles Lemeh Street, University of Nigeria Campus Enugu, Anambra State, Nigeria.

CHUKS-ADOPHY, (Chief) Victor, b. 12 Mar. 1920. Publisher. m. 14 Oct. 1961, 1 son, 2 daughters. *Education:* Government College, Umuahia; Kings College, Lagos; London School of Journalism & Regent Institute; University of London, Faculty of Laws; London School of Economics. *Appointments:* Presidential Press Secretary, State House, Nigeria, 1963-66; Press Secretary, (Asika's Administration) Government, Eastern Nigeria, 1967-69; Foreign Service. *Memberships:* National Press Club, Lagos; Ikoyi Club. Lagos. *Publications:* Marriage an International Problem; Japan's Daylight; Diplomatic Significance of Holy See in International Relations. F.R.S.A; F.R.G.S, 1948; F.R.A.I. (Great Britain & Ireland), 1949; F.R.Econ.S, 1955; Member Institute of Journalists London, 1956; Life Member, International Institute of Arts & Letters, 1962. *Address:* P.O. Box 123, Yaba, Lagos State, Nigeria.

CHUKWU, Ethelbert Nwakuche, b. 22 Nov. 1940, Mbano Imo, Nigeria. Mathematician, University Administrator. m. Rega Chifo Chukwunyere, 26 Dec. 1966, 1 son, 2 daughters. *Education:* BSc., Applied Mathematics, University, Providence, Rhode Island, 1965-; MSc., University of Nigeria, Nsukka, 1973-; PhD., Case Western Reserve University, Cleveland, Ohio, 1972-. *Appointments:* Chairman, Department of Maths, Holy Ghost College, Owerri, 1966-; Teaching Assistant, University of Nigeria, Enugu Campus, 1966-68; Acting Chairman, Mathematics, University of Nigeria, Enugu Campus, 1966-67; Assistant Lecturer, University of Nigeria, Nsukka, Spring, 1970-; Lecturer in Mathematics, The Cleveland State University, 1972-; Assistant Professor of Mathematics, 1972-76, Associate Professor of Mathematics, 1976, The Cleveland State University, Reader, 1978-; Professor, 1978-; Head, Department of Mathematics, 1979-; Dean of Postgraduate Studies, 1977-. University of Jos, Nigeria. *Memberships:* Representative of Basic Sciences, National Universities Commission; N.U.C. University Expansion Committee; National Vice-President, Nigerian Mathematical Society and Mathematical Association of Nigeria; Science Association of Nigeria; University of Jos Council. *Publications:* Symmetries and Identifications of Non-Autonomous Control Systems; Differential Games and Control Theory, 1975-; A Connection Between Optimal Control Pro and Disconjugacy, 1974-; On the Null Controllability of a Control Process Satisfying a Nonlinear Fifth Order Differential Equation, 1976-. *Honours:* Nigerian State Scholar, 1954-60; African Scholarship Program for American Universities, 1962-65; University Fellow, Case Western Reserve University, 1970-72; Research Initiatiion Award, The Cleveland State University, 1974-; Senior Research Initiation Award, 1977-; N.A.S.A. Research Grant NSG, 1445, 1977-79; University of Jos Research Grant, 1977-80. *Hobbies:* Music, Cycling, Reading. *Address:* Umuaro, Nsu PA, Umuahia, Imo State, Nigeria.

CHUKWU, Nnamdi Chimere Ifeoma, b. 15 Nov. Amakohia Ihitte, Etiti, Nigeria. Education; Company Director. m. Sussy, 3 Mar. 1979. *Education:* WASC/HSC., Government College, Afikpo, 1971; H/Diploma in Education, 1977; ACP., London, 1977; LCP., 1978. *Appointments:* Lecturer i/c Science, Chemistry and Physics: Government College, Takum, Gongola State, Nigeria; Combine Secondary School, Takum, Nigeria; Chairman/Chief Executive, Chukwu (WA) Organisation; Chairman, C.N. Chukwu Int. Agency; Executive Director, Henry Hudson (WA) Limited. *Memberships:* Publicity Secretary, College of Preceptors Association of Nigeria; President, Club of Friends. *Honours:* Holds an 'Ozo' title, of Honour and Achievement, awarded by His Royal Highness, the Chief of the Land. *Hobbies:* Football; Table tennis; Swimming. *Address:* 26 Nwodo Street, Ekulu, GRA. Enugu, Nigeria.

CHUKWU-IKE, Muo, b. 26 Nov. 1946, Mgbowo, Agwu Local Goverment, Nigeria. Geologist. m. 25 Jan. 1975, 3 sons, 2 daughters. *Education:* BSc.(Hons.), University of Nigeria, NSUKKA, Nigeria, 1971; MSc., Imperial College of Science and Technology, London, UK, 1974; DIC., Royal School of Mines; PhD., London, UK. *Appointments:* Exploration Geologist, Nigerian Steel Development Authority, 1971-73; Imperial College, London, UK, 1974-77; Planning Manager, Nigerian Coal Corporation, Enugu, Nigeria, 1977-. *Memberships:* Nigerian Institute of Mining and Geosciences; Institute of Mining and Metallurgy, London, UK. *Publications:* Over 10 publications including: Mineralised crustal failures shown in Satellite images of Nigeria, 1977; Crustal suture and lineament in North Africa, 1977; Astrons—the Earth's oldest scars, 1977. *Honours:* Merit award in Geology, University of Nigeria; Distinguished lectureship award, Nigerian National Institute for Policy and Strategic Studies. *Hobbies:* Tennis; Photography; Travelling. *Address:* 7 Colliery Avenue, Enugu, Nigeria.

CHUKWUMAH, Patrick Azuka Lionel, b. 19 June 1926, Asaba, Nigeria. Senior Professional Official of International Labour Organisation. m. Bernadette Nkem Ikediashi, 19 Mar. 1963, 1 son. *Education:* H.A. Honours, Sociology, Diploma Social Studies, Leeds University, 1954-58; Certificate in French, University Besancon, 1961-62. *Appointments:* Postal clerk and telegraphist, 1943-49; Senior Official Federal Ministry of Labour, Nigeria, 1949-61; Director Inter-African Labour Institute, Brazzaville, Africa, 1962-65; Counsellor Labour Nigerian Permanent Mission, Geneva, 1966-67; Social Affairs Officer, UNECA Addis Ababa,

1968-; Senior Professional Officer ILO Regional Office, Addis Ababa, 1968-72; Director ILO Area Office for East Africa, Dar es Salaam, 1972-79; Senior ILO Official in charge Co-ordination of Technical Co-operation Unit, Labour Administration Branch, Geneva, 1979-. *Memberships:* F.B.I.M. (U.K.); International Tennis Club, Geneva. *Honours:* Knight of Congolese Order of Merit, 1965-. *Hobbies:* Lawn Tennis, Amateur Photography, recreational music and electronics. *Address:* 31 Rue de La Prulay, 1217 Meyrin, Geneva, Switzerland.

CHUNG, Arthur, b. 1918. President of the Republic of Guyana. m. Doreen Pamela Ng-See-Quan, 1954, 1 son, 1 daughter. *Appointments:* Land Surveyor, 1940; Assistant Legal Examiner, UK Inland Revenue Department, 1947; Magistrate, 1954, Senior Magistrate, 1960; Registrar of Deeds of the Supreme Court, Guyana, 1961; Judge of the Supreme Court, Guyana, 1962-70; First President, Republic of Guyana, 1970, re-elected 1976. *Address:* Guyana House, 95 Carmichael Street, Georgetown, Guyana.

CHUNG, Manuel Konveng, b. 20 Dec. 1945, Canton, China. Musician. m. Eliza Chui-King Lam, 15 July 1975, 1 son. *Education:* Diploma, Accordion, Centro Venzolano Para El Estudio del Acordeon, 1961-65; Graduate Diploma, Comosition, Double bass and Piano, Escuela Superior de la Musica, 1963-74; Titulo de Professor, Ministerio de Educacion, Venezuela, 1974; Studied Conducting, Instituto Nacional de la Cultura, 1970-73; ARCM., 1976, LRAM, 1976, FTCL., 1976, Royal Northern College of Music, 1975-77. *Appointments:* Piano Tutor, Academia de Musica Fischer, 1967-70; Bass Player, Orquesta Sinfonica Venezuela, 1970-74; Bass Player, Hong Kong Philharmonic Orchestra, 1977-80; Instructuro, Hong Kong Youth Orchestra, 1978; Tutor, Hong Kong Conservatory of Music, 1979; Master Classes and Recital, University of the Philippines, 1979; Founder and Conductor, Hong Kong Victoria Children's Choir, 1979; Conductor, Hong Kong Lutheran Youth Band, 1979; Resident Conductor, Hong Kong City Symphony Orchestra, 1980; Artistic Director, Hong Kong Victoria Music Centre, 1980. *Memberships:* Chairman, Hong Kong Chung Wah Symphonic Society; Chairman, Players' Committee, Hong Kong Philharmonic; Members Committee, Hong Kong City Symphony Orchesstra. *Creative Works:* 4 Sonatas for the Piano; Suite for Orchestra; Fuga en Re menor para Orquesta, 1970; String Quartets. *Honours:* Post-graduate Scholarship for Double bass and Conducting, Instituto Nacional de la Cultura y Bellas Artes Venezuela. *Hobby:* Swimming. *Address:* 16H Nam Shan Mansion, Taikoo Shing, Hong Kong.

CHURCHILL, Winston Spencer, (MP), b. 10 Oct. 1940. Member of Parliament. m. Mary Caroline d'Erlanger, 1964, 2 sons, 2 daughters. *Education:* Eton; MA., Christ Church, Oxford. *Appointments:* Correspondent in: Yemen, Congo and Angola, 1964-; Borneo and Vietnam, 1966-; Middle East, 1967-; Czechoslovakia, 1968-; Nigeria, Biafra and Middle East, 1969-. Correspondent of The Times, 1969-70. Lecture tours of the US and Canada, 1965,69,71,73,75,78,80-. Contested Gorton Division of Manchester in By-election, 1967-. PPS to Minister of Housing and Construction, 1970-72, to Minister of State, FCO, 1972-73; Secretary Conservative Foreign and Commonwealth Affairs Committee, 1973-76; Conservative Party front-bench spokesman on Defence, 1976-78; Vice-Chairman, Conservative Defence Committee, 1979-. Elected to Executive of Conservative 1922 Committee, 1979-. Chairman & Managing Director of Gatwick Air Taxis Limited. Sponsored Motor Vehicles (Passenger Insurance) Act, 1972-. *Memberships:* President, Trafford Park Industrial Council, 1971-; Trustee of: Winston Churchill Memorial Trust, 1968-, National Benevolent Fund for the Aged, 1973-; Governor, English-Speaking Union, 1975-80; Vice-President, British Technion Society, 1976-; White's Club; Buck's Club; Press Club. *Publications:* First Journey, 1967-; Six Day War, 1967-; Defending the West. *Honours:* Honorary Fellow, Churchill College, Cambridge, 1969,; Honorary LLD., Westminster College, Fulton, Mo, USA. *Hobbies:* Tennis, Sailing, Skiing. *Address:* House of Commons, London, SW1A OAA, England.

CHYE, Andrew Miang San, b. 2 May 1941, Kuala Lumpur. Principal, Director. m. Margaret Yoong Lin

Yong, 2 sons, 1 daughter. *Education:* St. John's Institution, Kuala Lumpur; Royal Academy of Music, London; Degrees: LRAM & ARCM. *Appointments:* BBC Scottish Symphony Orchestra; Deputy Director, The Malaysia Conservatorium of Music; Director, The Malaysia Conservatorium of Music. *Memberships:* Petaling Jaya Rotary Club. *Honours:* Associated Board of the Royal Schools of Music Scholarship, 1959-; Alfred Waley Prize for Violin; MacEwen Prize for Chamber Music; Dominions Fellowship Trust Award; Gordon Bryan Award; Bach & Beethoven Scholarship. *Address:* 58 Jalan Selangor, Petaling Jaya, Selangor, Malaysia.

CIAPPARA, Joseph M, b. 18 Mar. 1933, Valletta, Malta. Advocate. m. Ina Azzopardi, 24 Apr. 1960, 1 daughter. *Education:* University of Malta: B.A., 1955-; LL.D., 1958-. *Appointments:* Practising Lawyer; Magistrate in the Courts of Malta; Legal Adviser to the Broadcasting Authority, Malta and to the Association of Insurance Companies, Malta; Electoral Commissioner, 1980-. *Memberships:* Member & President, Students' Representative Council, Malta, 1952-56; Malta Delegate , International Student Conference, Birmingham, U.K., 1955-, and at Peradeniya, Ceylon 1956-; Membe & Chairman of various Government sponsored and private Commissions and Committees. *Hobbies:* Philately. *Address:* Amaryllis, 2nd New Street, Parallel to Sliema Road, Kappara, Malta.

CIROMA, Adamu Liman, b. 30 Sept. 1930, Potiskum, Borno Staste, Nigeria. Retired Public Officer. m. Madiya Ciroma, Aug. 1959, 4 sons, 1 daughter. *Education:* Institute of Archaeology, University of London, 1953-54; BA, Birmingham University, 1956-59. *Appointments:* Technical Assistant, Nigeran Museum, 1949-53; Government Archaeologist, Curator, 1959-61; Administrative Officer, Northern Nigeria Public Service, 1961; Permanent Secretary, Northern Nigeria Public Service, 1965-68; Permanent Secretary, North Eastern State Public Service, 1968-70; Permanent Secretary, Federal Ministry of Industries, 1971-75; Permanent Secretary, Ministry of Education, 1975-77; Secretary to the Federal Military Government and Head of Service, 1977-79. *Memberships:* Foundation member and Councillor of the Zoological Society of Jos. *Honours:* Commander of the Order of the Federal Republic, 1979. *Hobbies:* Walking; Gardening. *Address:* 4 Kabala Close, PO Box 755, Kaduna, Nigeria.

CLAFFEY, Thomas Joseph, b. 10 Jan. 1925, Sydney, Australia. Orthopaedic Surgeon. m. Esther Patricia O'Neill, 26 May 1951, 1 son, 1 daughter. *Education:* M.B.,B.S. Class II Honours, Sydney University, 1948-; F.R.C.S., London, 1955-; F.R.A.C.S., Orthopaedics, 1959-. *Appointments:* Jnr. & Snr. Medical Officer, 1948-50; Student Supervisor & Surgical Associate, 1951-; Surgical Resistrar, 1952 St. Vincent's Hospital; Nuffield Orthopaedic Centre & Radcliffe, Accident Service, Oxford, 1955-57; Visiting Orthopaedic Surgeon, Director, Accident & Emergency Centre, St. Vincent's Hospital, Sydney; Consultant Surgeon, N.S.W. Society for Crippled Children; Consultant Orthopaedic Surgeon, Canterbury Hospital, Sydney; Tutor, Orthopaedic Surgery, University of New South Wales. *Memberships:* British Orthopaedic Association; Australian Orthopaedic Association, Honorary Secretary, 1968-72, Censor-in-Chief, 1973-77; Board of Orthopaedics Surgery of the Royal Australasian College of Surgeons, 1969-77. *Publications:* Acute Infections of the Fingers and Hand, 1953-; Avascular Necrosis of the Femoral Head, 1960-; Compound Fractures of the Tibia, 1961-; Gastrostomy in the Treatment of Advanced Sepsis; Major Arterial Injury in Road Accidents, (Co-author), 1969-; Common Fractures of the Lower Limb, 1980-. *Hobbies:* Golf & Swimming. *Address:* 26 Gordon Avenue, Coogee, New South Wales, 2034.

CLAMPETT, Robert Wyndham, b. 27 June 1920, Adelaide, Australia. Merchant. m. Juliet Mary O'Dea. *Education:* St. Peters College. *Appointments:* Wine & Spirit Merchant & Company Director. Chairman of Directors: R.W. Clampett — Co., Pty., Ltd., Clampett Beverages Pty., Ltd., Clampett Properties Pty. Ltd., South Australian Wine & Spirit Co., Pty., Ltd. Director, R.E.I. Imperaial Building Society. *Memberships:* South Australian Totalizator Agency Board; Board of Governors, St Andrews Hospital; Returned Soldiers League, Legacy Club, Naval & Military; Royal Adelaide Golf Club; South Australian Cricket Association; Peninsula Golf Club; Chairman, South Australian Jockey Club

Incorporated. *Honours:* Order of Australia, A.M. 1977-; Justice of the Peace, 1966-; Honorary Consul for Mexico, South Australia, 1977-. *Hobbies:* Golf, Horse racing. *Address:* Blakiston, Littlhampton, South Australia, 5250.

CLARK (Hon.), Alan Kenneth MacKenzie, b. 13 Apr. 1928, London. Member of Parliament. m. 31 July 1958, 2 sons. *Education:* Eton, 1942-45; Christ Church, Oxford, 1946-49. *Appointments:* Member of Parliament for Plymouth, 1974-. *Address:* Saltwood Castle, Hythe, Kent.

CLARK, Alastair Trevor, b. 10 June 1923, Glasgow. Retired overseas Civil Servant, elected local government member. m. Hilary Agnes Mackenzie Anderson, 1 May 1965. *Education:* Glasgow Academy, 1929-35; Edinburgh Academy, 1935-41; BA., MA., Magdalen College, Oxford, 1941-42, 1947-48; Middle Temple, Inns of Court, called to English Bar, 1963-. *Appointments:* Queen's Own Cameron Highlanders & Royal West African Frontier Force, 1942-46; District Officer, Secretary to Executive Council, Senior District Officer, Northern Nigeria, 1949-59; Clerk of Councils, Director of Social Welfare, Principal Assistant Colonial Secretary, Resettlement and Urban Services Departments, Hong Kong, 1960-72; Deputy Chief Secretary, Chief Secretary Western Pacific High Commission & Deputy Governor Solomons, 1974-77 Elected Member City of Edinburgh Council, 1980-; Chairman, Edinburgh International Festival Council, Council for Museums & Galleries in Scotland, 1981; Edinburgh Film Council; Lothian Health Board, 1981-; Director Edinburgh Academy. *Memberships:* New Club, Edinburgh; Royal Overseas League; Scottish National Trust; Cockburn Association; Old Town Association; Sir Walter Scott Club. *Publications:* Contribution to Journal of Commonwealth & Comparative Politics, 1980-. *Honours:* Leverhulme Trust Grant, 1979-81; Country Leader Fellowship to United States, 1972-; CBE., 1976-; MVO., (4th Class), 1974-. *Hobbies:* Music, Reading, Theatre, Collecting Netsuke and Cartophily. *Address:* 11 Ramsay Garden, Edinburgh EH1 2NA, Scotland.

CLARK, C David, b. 22 Feb. 1939, Hamilton, Ontario, Canada. President & Chief Operating Officer. m. Mary Edna Kelly 25 Aug. 1965, 3 daughters. *Education:* MBA, University of Western Ontario, 1966-; BA., MacMaster University, 1963-. *Appointments:* Colgate Plamolive; 7 Up (Canada) Ltd.; Thomas J. Lipton, Limited. *Memberships:* Young Presidents Organisation; Grocery Products Manufacturers of Canada; Metro Toronto Y.M.C.A. Tea & Coffee Association. *Honours:* Deans Honour List, University of Western Ontario, 1966-. *Hobbies:* Jogging, Sailing, Squash, Skiing. *Address:* 25 Farmington Crescent, Agincourt, Ontario, Canada, M1S 1E9.

CLARK, David George, b. 19 Oct. 1939, Castle Douglas. Member of Parliament. m. 24 Mar. 1970, 1 daughter. *Education:* BA., Economics, 1963; MSc., 1965; Manchester University, PhD., Sheffield University, 1978. *Appointments:* Forestor, 1956-; Mill Worker, 1957-79; Teacher (Unqualified), 1959-60; Student, 1960-63; Lecturer, 1963-65; University Lecturer, 1965-70; MP., Colne Valley, 1970-74; Polytechnic Lecturer, 1974-79; MP., South Shields, 1979-. *Publications:* Two Books: Industrial Manager, 1966-; Colne Valley, Radicalism to Socialism, 1981-. *Address:* House of Commons, London S.W.1, England.

CLARK, Graeme Milbourne, b. 16 Aug. 1935, Camden, N.S.W., Australia. Professor of Otolaryngology. m. 27 Dec. 1961, 2 sons, 4 daughters. *Education:* The Scots College, Sydney, 1948-51; MB., BS., Honours, The University of Sydney, 1952-57; F.R.C.S., Edinburgh, 1961-; F.R.C.S., England, 1962-; F.R.A.C.S., 1966-; M.S. Sydney, 1968-; PhD., Sydney, 1969-. *Appointments:* Senior Ear, Nose & Throat Surgeon, Royal Victorian Eye & Ear Hospital; Consultant Otolaryngologist to the Royal Melbourne Hospital; Alfred Hospital, Royal Women's Hospital and Repatriation General Hospitals; William Gibson Professor of Otolaryngology University of Melbourne, 1970-. *Memberships:* Chairman, Regional Committee, Postgraduate Training in Otolaryngology; Chairman, Steering Committee for Deafness Foundation of Victoria and Deafness Council; Foundation Member, Executive, Deafness Foundation of Victoria; Vice-Chairman, Advisory Council for Children with Impaired Hearing; Chairman, Otolaryngological Society of Australia; Chairman, Consultative Council on Maternal and Child Health. *Publications:* 100 contributions to International Professional and Scientific Journals; Science and God, 1979-. *Honours:* Prosector in Anatomy, University of Sydney, 1953-; First Place in Final Year Medicine, 1957-; Bertha Sudolz Prize in Otolaryngology, 1970-. *Hobbies:* Music, Reading, Swimming and Theology. *Address:* 13 Banoon Road, Eltham, 3095, Victoria, Australia.

CLARK, Howard Hewlett, (Rev.), b. 23 Apr. 1903, Fort Macleod, Alberta, Canada. Archbishop, Anglican Clergyman. m. Anna Evelyn Wilson, 3 June 1935, 1 son, 4 daughters. *Education:* BA., University of Toronto, 1932-; Divinity Testamor, University of Trinity College, 1930-; Ordained Deacon, 1930-; Ordained Priest, 1932-. *Appointments:* Assistant Curate, St. John's Norway, Toronto, 1930-32; Christ Church Cathedral, Ottawa: Assistant Curate, 1932-38, Priest-in-Charge, 1938-, Rector, 1939-, Canon, 1941-, Dean, 1945-54; Bishop of Edmonton, 1954-; Archbishop of Edmonton, 1959-61; Primate of the Anglican Church of Canada, 1959-70; Archbishop of Rupert's Land, 1961-69; Chancellor, University of Trinity College, Toronto, 1971-; Tutor, Trinity College, 1971-. *Publications:* The Christian Life According to the Prayer Book, 1957-. *Honours:* Companion Order of Canada, 1970-; D.D., University of Trinity College, Toronto; D.D. & Other Honorary D.D.s, from Canadian & American Colleges, also St. Pauls University, Tokyo, Japan; D.C.L. St. John's College, Winnipeg, & Bishops University, Lennoxville; LL.D., University of Manitoba, Winnipeg. *Address:* 252 Glenrose Avenue, Toronto, Ontario, Canada.

CLARK, I, b. 28 Aug. 1922, Lancaster, England. Political Writer. m. Mary Heathers, 16 Apr. 1945, 2 sons, 1 daughter. *Education:* BA, University of Lancaster, 1948; Honorary Degree in Political Science, London University, 1972. *Appointments:* Army (Intelligence Corps), to Rank of Major, 1944-56; Librarian, City Bank, 1957-59; Chief Researcher, Government Departments, 1959-63; Freelance writer on political and recent historical affairs, particularly in Middle East, 1963-. *Memberships:* National Trust; British Historical Society; Army and Navy; British Universities Club. *Publications:* Books: The Princes of the Middle East, 1964; The Cradle of Modern History, 1965; Article, The Sands of Time Run Out, 1979. *Honours:* Honorary Fellow, Islamic Research Institute. *Hobbies:* Reading; Writing; Travelling. *Address:* 11 Madingley Road, Cambridge, UK.

CLARK, Ian Hall, b. 27 Apr. 1935, Hay, New South Wales, Australia. Finance Director. m. 11 Feb. 1961, 3 daughters. *Education:* B. of Commerce, Melbourne, 1958; FASA, 1959. *Memberships:* Australian Society of Accountants; Financial Executives Institute; International Treasury Club. *Hobbies:* Running; Reading; Gardening. *Address:* 23 Bay Street, Brighton, Victoria, Australia.

CLARK Joe, (Right Honourable), b. 5 June 1939, High River, Alberta. Member of Parliament. Alberta. m. Maureen Anne McTeer, 30 June, 1973, 1 daughter. *Education:* High River High School; B.A. History, University of Alberta, 1960-; M.A. Political Science, 1973-. *Appointments:* Lecturer, Political Science, University of Alberta, Journalist CBC Radio & TV, Calgary Herald, Edmonton Journal, 1965-67; Private Secretary, Alberta PC Leader, 1959-; National President, PC Student Federation, 1962-64; Director of provincial organisation for Alberta PC Leader, 1966-67; Special Assistant to Hon. Davie Fulton, Ottawa, 1967-; Executive Assistant to National PC Leader, 1967-70; PC Candidate in Alberta Provincial General Election, 1967-; Elected to House of Commons for Rocky Mountain, Alberta, 1972-; Re-elected for Rocky Mountain, 1974-; Chairman, PC caucus Committee on Youth, 1972-74; Chairman, PC Caucus Committee on the Environment, 1974-76; Elected National Leader of the Progressive Conservative Party of Canada, 1976-; Elected Prime Minister of Canada, 1979-; Won personal election in Yellowhead riding in general election which saw the defeat of the Progressive Conservative Government, 1980-; Resigned as Prime Minister, becoming leader of the Opposition, 1980-. *Memberships:* Hillcrest Miners' Literary and Athletic Association; Ottawa Athletic Club; Honorary Member, Cercle Universitaire. *Honours:* Honorary Doctor of Laws, University of New Brunswick,

1976-. *Address:* House of Commons, Ottawa, Ontario, K1A 0A6, Canada.

CLARK, John Richard James, b. 30 Oct. 1932, Hobart, Tasmania. Director, The National Institute of Dramatic Art. m. Henrietta Mary Hartley, 28 Jan. 1958, 1 son, 2 daughters. *Education:* Clemes College, Hobart, 1937-41; Caulfield Grammer School, Melbourne, 1942-45; The Hutchins School, Hobart, 1946-50; B.A. Honours, 1954, M.A., 1956, The University of Tasmania, M.A., The University of California at Los Agneles, 1966-. *Appointments:* School Teacher, London & Hobart, 1958-59; Lecturer in Theatre History, The National Institute of Dramatic Art, Sydney, Australia, 1960-68; Director, NIDA., 1968-; Artistic Advisor, inaugural season of the Sydney Theatre Company, 1979-; Chairman, Advisory Council on Cultural Grants, Premier's Department, Government of New South Wales, 1976-80. *Memberships:* Vice-President, Producers & Directors Guild of Australia, 1964-65. *Publications:* Plays directed for the Old Tote Theatre Company including: The Fire Raisers and The Bald Prima Donna, Entertaining Mr. Sloane, The Homecoming, The Alchemist; Play directed for the Sydney Theatre Company: The Caucasian Chalk Circle; Plays directed for the National Institute of Dramatic Art including: The Crucible, Blood Wedding, A Midsummer Night's Dream, King Edward, The Dybbuk, Twelfth Night; Play directed for The National School of Drama, India: The Skin of Our Teeth. *Honours:* Harkness Fellowship of the Commonwealth Fund, New York, 1965-66; A.M. Member in the General Division of the Order of Australia, 1981-. *Hobbies:* Boating. *Address:* 41 Regent Street, Paddington, New South Wales, 2021, Australia

CLARK, Leroy Maxwell, b. 27 Feb. 1926, Boston, USA. Police Commissioner (Ret). m. Clarine Marie Jones, 13 Nov. 1951, 1 daughter. *Education:* National Police College, England. *Appointments:* Royal Canadian Navy, 1941-45; Bermuda Police, 1949-81, Commissioner, 1972-81. *Honours:* General Service Medals, World War II; Colonial Police Medal for Meritorious Service, 1967; Colonial Police Long Service and Good Conduct Medal, 1972; Queen's Police Medal, 1975; Member of Royal Victorian Order, 4th Class, 1975; Order of British Empire, 1978. *Hobbies:* Fishing; Reading; Woodworking. *Address:* Littorina, Gables Road, Devonshire, Bermuda.

CLARK, Marvin Ramsay, b. 17 July 1936, Kensington, Prince Edward Island, Canada. Medical Doctor. m. Marla MacKenzie Clark, 20 Jan. 1960, 3 sons. *Education:* Mount Allison University, Sackville, New Brunswick, 1953-56; MD, Dalhousie University, Halifax, Nova Scotia, 1956-61; MA, Michigan State University, USA, 1971-72. *Appointments:* Family Physician and Health Officer, Kensington, PEI, 1961-69; Coroner, Prince County, Prince Edward Island, 1964-69; Assistant Director, 1969-72, Demonstrator, 1969-77, Assistant Lecturer, 1970-77, Assistant, Dean of Medicine, 1972-77, Associate Professor, 1973-77, Director, 1972-77, Assistant Professor, 1977, Dalhousie University, Halifax, Nova Scotia; Deputy Health Minister, Department of Health and Social Services, Province of Prince Edward Island, 1977-; Chief Health Officer, Province of Prince Edward Island, 1977-. *Memberships:* including: Prince Edward Island Medical Society; Medical Society of Nova Scotia; Canadian Medical Association; Chairman, Committee on Examinations, College of Family Physicians of Canada; American Educational Research Association; President, Canadian Association for Continuing Medical Education; Canadian Public Health Association; Institute of Public Administration of Canada; College of Family Physicians of Canada. *Publications:* Contributed to various medical journals. *Honours:* Licentiate of the Medical Council of Canada, 1961; Certificate of the College of Family Physicians of Canada, 1971. *Hobbies:* Swimming; Skiing; Reading; Music; Photography. *Address:* Bonshaw R. R. #3, Prince Edward Island, Canada.

CLARK, Robin Hamley, b. 10 June 1921, Otahuhu, New Zealand. Professor of Geology. m. Maureen Lyndley O'Donnell, 8 May 1948, 1 son, 1 daughter. *Education:* BSc, 1947, MSc, 1949, University of New Zealand; PhD, University of Edinburgh, 1952. *Appointments:* Lecturer in Geology, University of Edinburgh, 1951-54; Professor of Geology, and Head of Department, Victoria University of Wellington, 1954-; Convener, Antarctic Research Committee, 1958-. *Memberships:* Fellow of Geological Society; Fellow of Explorers' Club of New York; New Zealand Geological Society. *Publications:* Numerous Scientific Papers. *Honours:* Sir Julius Von Haast Prize, 1949; Carnegie Fellow, 1961; Japan Society for Promotion of Science Fellowship, 1976. *Hobbies:* Sailing; Restoring old houses. *Address:* 14 Highbury Crescent, Wellington, New Zealand.

CLARK, William Donaldson, b. 28 July 1916, Haltwhistle, England. International Civil Servant. *Education:* Modern History, (1st class hons), Oriel College, Oxford, 1938. *Appointments:* Assistant Professor and Commonwealth Fellow, University of Chicago, 1938-39; Press Attaché, British Embassy, Washington, 1944-47; Observer Newspaper, Diplomatic Correspondent, 1948-55; Asia Correspondent, 1957-59; Public Relations Adviser to Prime Minister, 1955-56; Director, Overseas Development Institute, 1960-68; Vice President, World Bank, Washington DC, 1968-80; President, International Institute for Environment and Development, 1980-. *Publications:* Less than Kin, 1957; What is the Commonwealth?, 1963; Number 10, 1965, (also play and TV film); Special Relationship, 1968. *Honours:* Finalist in Empire Quiz Contest, 1949. *Address:* The Mill, Cuxham, Oxford, England.

CLARKE, Alfred MacDonald, b. 13 Aug. 1912, Port-of-Spain, Trinidad, West Indies. Barrister-at-Law. m. Stella Martin, 27 May 1944, 1 son, 1 daughter. *Education:* Trained Teacher's Diploma, Government Training College, 1935-; B.A. Honours in History, London University, 1950-; Called to the Bar, Middle Temple, Barrister-at-Law, 1962-. *Appointments:* Elementary School Teacher, 1930-; Graduate Master & Lecturer of St. James Government Secondary School, 1963-; Vice-Principal, St. James Government Secondary School, 1966-; Legal Adviser, Ministry of Education, 1968-70; Private Practice, Barrister-at-Law, 1973-. *Memberships:* The Writers Union, Trinidad. *Publications:* Co-author, Short Stories, 1939-; Co-author, Ma Mamba & Other Stories, 1940-; Edited, Best Poems of Trinidad, 1941-; Co-author, Burnt Bush, a collection of poems, 1947-; Published a Verse Play, Green Magic, subsequently staged, 1962-; Wheels within Wheels, a collection of verse, 1975-; Revolution at Grass Roots, a collection of short stories, 1976-; Caribbean* Coup, a Novel, 1980-; Lord Constantine and Sir Hugh Wooding, a biography, 1981-. *Honours:* National 1st Prize, Essay Writing, 1935-; Winner Playwright award Cellar Club, 1st Prize, Verse Play, Road to Glory, 1953-. *Hobbies:* Spectator at all kinds of Sports, Listening to Steelband music. *Address:* 16 Ward Lane, Belmont, Port-of-Spain, Trinidad, West Indies.

CLARKE, Arthur C, b. 16 Dec. 1917, Minehead, England. Writer. *Education:* BSc, Kings College, London, 1948. *Appointments:* War Service, (originated proposal for use of satellites for communications, 1945) 1941-46; Assistant Editor, Science Abstracts, 1949-50; Underwater Exploration on Great Barrier Reef of Australia and coast of Sir Lanka, 1954; Full-time Writer, 1950-. *Memberships:* Patron, Sri Lanka Astronomical Association; Past Chairman, British Interplanetary Society; International Academy of Astronautics; World Academy of Art and Science; Science Fiction Writers of America; Royal Astronomical Society; Association of British Science Writers; International Science Writers Association; British Astronomical Association; American Association for the Advancement of Science; Council Member; Society of Authors; Fellow, American Astronautical Association. *Publications:* Author of 46 Non-Fiction and Fiction books including: Interplanetary Flight; Going into Space; The Promise of Space; The First Five Fathoms; The View from Serendip; Islands in the Sky; The Other Side of the Sky; Dolphin Island; The Lion of Comarre; The Wind from the Sun; Imperial Earth; The Fountains of Paradise; Childhood's End; Co-author of six other books including: 2001: A Space Odyssey with Stanley Kubrick. Editor: The Coming of the Space Age; Time Probe; Three for Tomorrow; Numerous Anthologies. *Honours:* Numerous awards including: International Fantasy Award, 1952; UNESCO Kalinga Prize, 1961; Robert Ball Award of Aviation Space-Writers' Association, 1965; Fellow, Franklin Institute, 1971; AIAA Aerospace Communications Award, 1974; Bradford Washburn Award, Boston Museum of Science, 1977; Fellow of King's College, London, 1977; Hon. DSc, University of Moratuwa, 1979. *Address:* 25 Barnes Place, Colombo 7, Sri Lanka.

CLARKE, Ellis (Sir) (Emmanuel Innocent), b. 1917. President of the Republic of Trinidad and Tobago. m. Eyrmyntrude Hagley, 1952, 1 son, 1 daughter. *Education:* LL.B., London University, UK, 1940; Gray's Inn, London, UK. 03 Private Practice at Bar of Trinidad and Tobago, 1941-54; SolicitorGeneral, 1954; Deputy Colonial Secretary, 1956; acted as Colonial Secretary and as Governor's Deputy; Attorney-General, 1957-62; Acting Governor of Trinidad and Tobago, 1960; Chief Justice (designate), 1961; Constitutional Adviser to the Cabinet, 1961; Trinidad and Tobago Permanent Representative to UN, 1962-66; Ambassador to USA, 1962-73, Mexico, 1966-73; Ambassador, Representative on Council of OAS, 1967-73; Chairman of Board, British West Indian Airways, 1968-72; Governor-General and C-In-C of Trinidad and Tobago, 1973-76. *Honours:* TC., 1969; CMG., 1960; GCMG., 1972; Kt., 963; K St. J., 1973. *Address:* President's House, Port of Spain, Trinidad.

CLARKE, Kenneth Charles, b. 5 Feb. 1916, Kent Town, Australia. Chairman. m. Jean L Miles, 14 Dec. 1944, 1 son, 2 daughters. *Appointments:* Deputy General Manager, Standard Motor Products, 1948-54; General Manager, Hilton Corporation, Limited, 1954-58; Director, Australian Motor Industries Limited, 1958-62; Director, Japan, 1962-67; Regional Director, Asia, 1967-63; Managing Director, International Wool Secretariat London, 1973-76; Director, Dalgety Japan, 1976-; Chairman, Domino Industries Group, 1977-. *Honours:* OBE, 1971; Order of The Rising Sun, Japan, 1972; MC; FISM; psc. *Hobbies:* Sailing; Tennis. *Address:* 77 Caroline Street, South Yarra, Victoria, Australia.

CLARKE, Kenneth Henry, b. 17 May 1923, London, England. Medical Physicist. m. Vivienne Edith Williams, 29 Jan. 1959, 1 son, 2 daughters. *Education:* Associate Royal College of Science, Physics & Mathematics, London, 1943-; BSc., Physics & Mathematics, London University, 1944-; MSc., University of Melbourne, 1953-. *Appointments:* Radar Officer, Royal Navy, Burma & Pacific theatres of war, 1943-47; Physicist, The Middlesex Hospital, London, 1947-49; Physicist, Commonwealth X-Ray & Radium Laboratory, Australia, 1950-54; Deputy Physicist-in-Charge, Cancer Institute, Melboure, 1954-60; Head, Department of Physical Sciences, Cancer Institute, Melbourne, 1960-; Honorary Consultant Physicist to Alfred, Prince Henry's & Royal Women's Hospitals, Victoria, Australia. *Memberships:* Foundation President & Fellow, Australasian College of Physical Scientists in Medicine; Fellow, Institute of Physics, London, England; Foundation Fellow, Australian Institute of Physics, Federal Secretary for two years; Hospital Physicists' Association, U.K.; Australia and New Zealand Society for Nuclear Medicine; Institution of Biomedical Engineering, Australia; National Committee for Biophysics, Australian Academy of Science, 1968-79; Governing Council, Chairman, Advisory Council, Swinbourne Institute of Technology, Melbourne; Consultative Council in Radiation Safety, Victoria; National Committee, Biomedical Engineering. Institution of Engineers, Australia. *Publications:* 20 Scientific Publications. *Hobbies:* Classical Music, Theatre, Art, History & Gardening; Editor, Publisher, Journal Australasian Physical & Engineering Sciences in Medicine. *Address:* 19 Marlborough Avenue, Camberwell, Victoria, 3124, Australia.

CLARKE, Randall Emile, b. 24 Sept. 1918, Scaford Town, Westmoreland, Jamaica, West Indies. Land Surveyor. m. Bertha Elizabeth Heusner, 2 Jan. 1953, 1 son. *Education:* Cambridge School Certificate, 1935-; R.I.C.S., Student, 1939-; City & Guilds Certificate, Surveying; Commissioned Land Surveyor, Jamaica, 1942-; Corporate member, American Congress on Surveying and Mapping, 1963-; Fellow, 1972; Fellow, corporate Land Surveyor, Incorporated Assocaition of Architects and Surveyors, 1980-. *Appointments:* Private Practice, 1943-51; Government of Jamaica, 1951-53; Government of Liberia, 1953-55; Private Practice, 1956-62; Government of Liberia, 1963-66; United Geophysical Canada, 1966-68; Government of Jamaica, Central, 1969-77; Local, Government 1977-. *Memberships:* Land Surveyors Association of Jamaica; Permanent Committee, International Federation of Surveyors, 1963-65; Kingston Cricket Club, Jamaica; Caledonian Society; Masonic Lodge. *Hobbies:* Reading, Photography. *Address:* 5 Carvalho Drive, Kingston, 10, Jamaica, West Indies.

CLARKE, William Malpas, b. 5 June 1922, Ashton-under-Lyne, England. Writer; Economist; Bank Director. m. (1) Margaret Braithwaite, 2 daughters, (2) Faith Elizabeth Dawson, 3 May 1973. *Education:* BA, Manchester University, 1941-42 and 1946-48; Shuttleworth Research Scholarship, 1948. *Appointments:* Assistant Financial Editor, Manchester Guardian, 1948-56; Deputy City Editor, The Times, 1956-66, City Editor, 1957-63, Financial and Industrial Editor, 1963-66; Director of Studies into enquiry into Britain's invisible earnings, 1966; Joined Boards of: United Kingdom Provident Institution, Cincinnati Milacron Limited, Trade Indemnity Company Limited, Euromoney Publications, Romney Trust Limited, 1966-68; Director-General and Deputy Chairman, Committee on Invisible Exports, 1976-; Deputy Chairman: City Communications Centre; Director, Grindlays Bank, Grindlay Brandts Limited, Swiss Reinsurance, UK, Raeburn Investment Trust Limited. *Publications:* The City in the World Economy, 1965 and 1967; Private Enterprise in Developing Countries, 1966; Britain's Invisible Earnings, 1967; The City's Invisible Earnings, 1968; Money Markets of the World, 1971; The World's Money, 1970, US edition, 1972; Inside the City, 1979. *Honours:* CBE, 1976. *Hobby:* Opera. *Address:* 37 Park Vista, Greenwich, London, England.

CLARKO, James George, b. 21 July 1932, Cottesloe, Western Australia. Member of Parliament. m. Edith Laurel Loudon, 25 Aug. 1958, 3 daughters. *Education:* Bachelor of Arts, University of Western Australia; Diploma of Education, University of Western Australia; Teachers Higher Certificate, Education Department of Western Australia. *Appointments:* Oil Company Representative, 1950-57; University Student, 1958-61; Secondary Teacher and Senior Master, 1961-68; Lecturer Nedlands Advanced College of Education, 1969-74; Elected Western Australian Legislative Assembly, Member for Karrinyup, 1974-; Appointed Government Whip, 1975-; Elected Chairman, Parliamentary Public Accounts Committee, 1975-; Elected Deputy Speaker & Chairman of Committees, 1977-; Re-elected Deputy Speaker & Chairman of Committees, 1980-. *Memberships:* Australian College of Education; Past Member, Board of the Nedlands College of Advanced Education; Executive, Liberal Party of Australia (W.A. Division), 1970-74; President, North Beach & Districts Sportsmens Club, 1973-74; President, Claremont Teachers College Student Council, 1961-; Flight Lieutenant, Number 25 Squadron City of Perth Citizen Air Force, 1959-71. *Honours:* Air Efficiency Award, 1970-; Justice of the Peace, 1972-. *Hobbies:* Cricket, Rugby Union & Rugby League Football, Australian Rules Football, Crustacean Fishing, Golf. *Address:* 14 Lynn Street, Trigg, 6020, Western Australia.

CLAY, Trevor, b. 10 May 1936, Nuneaton, Warwickshire, England. Registered Nurse. *Education:* MPhil., Brunel, 1977. *Appointments:* Assistant Regional Nursing Officer, North West Metropolitan Regional Hospital Board, 1967-69; Director of Nursing, Whittington Hospital, London, 1969-70; Chief Nursing Officer, North London Group Hospital Management Committee, 1970-73; Area Nursing Officer, Camden and Islington AHA, 1973-79; Deputy General Secretary, Royal College of Nursing, 1979-81. *Memberships:* Royal Commonwealth Society. *Publications:* Thesis. *Hobbies:* Friends; Music. *Address:* Royal College of Nursing of the United Kingdom, 1a Henrietta Place, London, England.

CLEARY, Jon Stephen, b. 22 Nov. 1917, Sydney, Australia. Author. m. Constantina Lucas, 6 Sept. 1946, 2 daughters. *Education:* Marist School, Randwick, New South Wales, 1924-32. *Appointments:* Various jobs including: Laundry worker, Textile worker, Animated cartoonist, Commercial Artist, 1932-40; Served with the Australian Imperial Forces, Middle East & New Guinea, 1940-45; Journalist, Australian News & Information Bureau, London & New York, 1948-51. *Memberships:* Australian Society of Authors; Australian Writers Guild. *Publications:* Novels including: You Can't See Round Corners, The Sundowners, A Flight of Chariots, The Climate of Courage, The High Commissioner, Peter's Pence; Also Two Books of Short Stories, plus Screen plays and Television Plays. *Honours:* Co-winner ABC National Radio Play Competition, 1945-; 2nd Prize Winner Sydney Morning Herald Novel Competition, 1946-; Winner Crouch Medal, Best Australian Novel, 1950-; Regional Winner New York

Herald Tribune World Story Competition, 1951-; Winner Edgar Allen Poe Award, Best Crime Novel, 1974-. *Hobbies:* Cricket, Tennis, Reading. *Address:* 1 Upper Pitt Street, Kirribilli, New South Wales, 2061, Australia.

CLEASBY, John Michael, b. 4 Nov. 1953, Ndola, Zambia. Cartographer. m. Bronwyn Lenore Hancox, 2 Dec. 1978. *Education:* Cartography Certificate, 1977; Drafting Certificate, Land and Engineering Survey, 1977; Drafting Cerificate, Post Land and Engineering Survey, 1978; Art Certificate. *Appointments:* Universal Business Directories, Pty. Ltd. Australia, 1973-77; Macquarie University 1977-. *Memberships:* Australian Institute of Cartographers. *Creative Works:* Exhibited paintings: Macquarie University Art Shows; Southern Cross Art Shows. *Honours:* Queen Scout Award, 1972; Geospectrum Award, 1977. *Hobbies:* Watercolour painting; Drawing; Sport. *Address:* 7/12 Early Street, Parramatta 2150, NSW, Australia.

CLEAVER, Maxwell George, b. 21 Mar. 1914, Launceston. Company Director. m. Elizabeth Wauburton-Gray, 17 Jan. 1940, 1 daughter. *Education:* Launceston Grammar School. P.SC., Australian Military Staff College, 1942-; Fellow Australian Institute of Management, 1964-. *Appointments:* Australian Military Forces, 1938-49; Chairman & Managing Director, The Cleavers Ltd., Launceston, Tasmania, 1951-. *Memberships:* Launceston Club; Peninsular Golf Club; Tasmanian Naval & Military Club; Launceston Golf Club; Alderman, Launceston City Council, 1969-; General Committee, Launceston Bank for Savings, 1960-; Board, Northern District Ambulance Service, 1971-; Commissioner, Tasmanian Ambulance Committion, 1971-77; President, Northern Tasmanian Branch, Australian American Association, 1979-81; Chairman, Ainslee Home for the Aged, 1977-; President, Launceston Chamber of Commerce, 1967-68; Tasmanian Federated Chambers of Commerce, 1969-70, Launceston Rotary Club, 1962-63; Governor, Rotary District 282, 1966-67; Mayor of City of Launceston, 1977-78. *Honours:* O.B.E., 1967-; United States of America Bronze Star Medal, 1944-; Efficiency Decoration, (Army), 1950-. *Hobbies:* Golf, Fishing, Gardening. *Address:* 15 York Street, Launceston, Tasmania.

CLEMENT, Hope Elizabeth Anna, b. 29 Dec. 1930, North Sydney, Nova Scotia, Canada. Associate National Librarian. *Education:* BA, English 1948-51; MA, French, Dalhousie University 1951-53; BLS, Library Science, University of Toronto, 1954-55. *Appointments:* Chief, National Bibliography Division, National Library, 1966-70; Assistant Director, Research and Planning, 1970-73; Director, Research and Planning Branch, National Library, 1973-77; Associate National Librarian, 1977. *Memberships:* Canadian Library Association; Canadian Association for Information Science. *Publications:* Developments toward a National Bibliographic Data Base, 1974; The Canadian Union Catalogues: plans and developments, 1973; The Automated Authority File, 1980; Editor, Canadiana, 1966-69. *Honours:* Governor General's Medal, High School, 1946; Governor General's Medal, University 1951. *Address:* 252 Daniel Street, Ottawa, Ontario, Canada K1Y 0C8.

CLEMENTS, Christopher John, b. 21 Jan. 1946, Ledsham, Cheshire, England. Medical Practitioner. m. Vivienne Mary Driscoll, 11 Dec. 1976, 2 sons. *Education:* Merchant Taylors School, Crosby, Liverpool, 1956-65; London Hospital Medical College, London University, 1965-69 University of Manchester, 1978-80; M.B.,B.S., London, 1969-; L.R.C.P., M.R.C.S., Royal College, 1969-; Diploma of Obstetrics, University of Auckland, 1972-; Diploma of Child Health, Royal College, 1973-; M.Sc., Community Medicine, Manchester University, 1980-; M.F.C.M., Royal College of Physicians, U.K., 1980-; M.C.C.M., New Zealand, 1980-. *Appointments:* House Surgeon, The London Hospital, 1969-; Resident in Paediatrics, University of Western Ontario, 1970-; Registrar in Obstetrics, Waikato Hospital, New Zealand, 1971-; Senior House Officer in Paediatrics, Alder Hey Childresn Hospital, Liverpool, 1972-; Medical Director, Hospital del Valle Apurimac, Peru, 1973-; Registrar in Paediatrics, Royal Lancaster Informary, 1975-; Chief Medical Officer, Bangladesh Project for Save the Children Fund, 1977-; Chief Medical Officer, Afghanistan Project for Save The Children Fund, 1978-; Locum Medical Assistant in Paediatrics, Royal Lancaster Informary, 1978-; Registrar in Community Medicine, North West Regional Health Authority, 1978-80; Specialist in Community Medicine, Wellington Health District, Department of Health, New Zealand, 1980-. *Memberships:* British Medical Association; New Zealand Medical Association; Faculty of Community Medicine, U.K.; College of Community Medicine, New Zealand; Paediatric Society of New Zealand;Australia and New Zealand Society for Epidemiology and Research in Community Health; Editorial Committee of New Zealand Health Review, 1981. *Publications:* Co-author, third edition, Diseases of Children in the Tropics and Subtropics; Various articles in Medical Journals on: Infant Feeding, Health Education, Community Medicine, Travel and Medical Practice in the Third World; Consultant Editor, Annals of Tropical Paediatrics, 1980. *Hobbies:* Photography, Natural History, Travel. *Address:* 19 Gurkha Crescent, Khandallah, Wellington, New Zealand.

CLERIDES, John Zacharias, b. 10 Jan. 1918 Rizokarpasso, Famagasta Distric, Cyprus. Travel Agent. m. Salomi Constantinou 9 Sept. 1938, 1 son, 1 daughter. *Education:* Commercial Lyceum of Famagusta; Bennett College Sheffield, Accountancy, English Literature, Business Administration and Auditing 1937-38. *Appointments:* Secretary, Co-operatives, Rizokarpasso 1937; Chief Accountant, Secretary, Shipping Agency 1938-74; Correspondent, Greek Newspaper, Eleftheria 1940-74; Correspondent, Econreuter, 1963-; Travel Agent 1977-; Managing Director: Intercontinents Limited, Intercontinental Holidays Selefkia Maritime Limited, Evolusion Shipping Limited. *Memberships:* Lions International; Famagusta Red Cross; Association for the Blind; Hellenic Club; Famagusta Chamber of Commerce; Famagusta Refugees Association; Institute of Directors. *Honours:* Gold Medal from Lions International President 1973. *Hobbies:* Reading; Fishing. *Address:* 10 Damaskinou, PO Box 5072, Nicosia Cyprus.

CLERIDES, Lefkos, b. 15 Aug. 1923, Cyprus. Advocate. m. Popie Syrimis 30 Dec. 1947, 3 children. *Education:* English School, Nicosia; Barrister-at-Law, Gray's Inn; Called to L Bar 1946. *Appointments:* Senior Partner, Lefkos Clerides & Sons. *Memberships:* Chairman, Bar Council Cyprus; Ex-Minister of Justice Cyprus; Editor-in-Chief, Cyprus Law Tribune. *Publications:* Many articles on legal topics and contributions in literary magazines on art poetry etc. *Hobbies:* Literature; Poetry; Folk-lore. *Address:* 30 Stassinos, Avenue, Nicosia, Cyprus.

CLINCH, Peter Gladstone, b. 26 June 1930 Geraldton, Western Australia. Senior Lecyurer in Music. m. Joy Iolanthe Richmond 5 Nov. 1953 1 son, 1 daughter. *Education:* Licentiate in Music 1962; Bachelor of Music 1972; Master of Music 1974; Doctor of Philosophy 1981. *Appointments:* Australian Opera Orchestra; HSV7 TV Studio Orchestra; Western Australia Symphony Orchestra; Melbourne State College. *Memberships:* President, Founder, Clarinet and Saxophone Society of Victoria. *Creative Works:* Various music compositions and arrangements; Clarinet Tutor; Edited Concerto for Clarinet and Orchestra by Franz Tausch; Various commercial solo recordings including works dedicated to me. *Honours:* A grant from, Western Australian Government, Australian Arts Council, to assist studies and to perform in Europe, UK, Canada and USA, 1972-73; Grant from, Australian Music Board to perform Australian Music in France, 1976. *Hobbies:* Weight lifting; Running. *Address:* 57 Woodhouse Road, East Doncaster 3109, Victoria, Australia.

CLOUSTON, John Gannon, b. 15 Mar. 1923 Sydney, New South Wales Australia. Scientist. m. Dorothy Downing 27 Feb. 1954, 2 sons, 1 daughter. *Education:* BSc(Hon) Sydney University 1949; MSc 1950; PhD London 1958; DIC Imperial College, 1958. *Appointments:* Scientific Officer, Rocket propulsion Department, Westcott UK 1950-53; Weapons Research Laboratory, Adelaide South Australia 1953-56; Assistant Lecturer, Physics, Imperial College London 1956-58; Scientific Officer Australian Atomic Energy Commission, Harwell, UK 1958-60; Section Head, Lucas Heights, Australia 1963-74; Deputy Chief 1974-77; Chief, Isotope Division, AAEC, Research Establishment 1977-. *Memberships:* Fellow, Australian Institute of Physics; Royal Society of New South Wales; Australian and New Zealand Society for Nuclear Medicine; Australian and New Zealand Society for the Advancement of Science; Saint Vincent de Paul Society; Australian Golf Club; St. George Motor Boat Club. *Publications:* Contributed Research Papers to Science publications, 1950-. *Hobbies:* Golf; Skiing; Fishing. *Address:* 24 Bunyala Street, Carss Park Sydney, New South Wales, 2221 Australia.

CLUNIE, Fergus G A U, b. 10 Dec. 1948 Suva, Fiji. Museum Director, Fiji Museum. m. Susan Frances Airlie 9 Feb. 1976, 1 son, 1 daughter. *Education:* Bachelor Science, Victoria University of Wellington, 1978. *Appointments:* Fiji Museum 1969-81. *Memberships:* Fiji Society for Science and Industry; National Trust for Fiji. *Publications:* Fijian Weapons and Warfare, Bulletin of Fiji Museum, 1977, numerous ornithological papers in Notornis; ethnological papers in Fiji Heritage; Miscellaneous Museum booklets. *Address:* 32 Des Voeux Road, Suva, Fiji.

COALES, John Flavell, b. 14 Sept. 1907, Harborne Birmingham, United Kingdom. Chartered Engineer. m Mary Dorothea Violet Alison, 1936, 2 sons, 2 daughters. *Education:* MA, Sidney Sussex College, Cambridge. *Appointments:* Department of Science Research, Admiralty, 1929-46; Research Director, Elliott Brothers, (London) Limited 1946-52; Assistant Director of Research, Engineering Department, University of Cambridge, 1953; Lecturer, 1956; Reader, 1958; Professor 1965; Chairman: United Kingdom Automation Council 1963-66; President, International Federation of Automatic Control (IFAC), 1963-66; President, Institution of Electrical Engineers, 1971-72; Chairman, Council of Engineering Institutions, 1975; Commonwealth Board for Engineering Education and Training 1975-79; Executive Committee National Physical Laboratory, 1958-64; Governing Body Royal Military College of Science, 1963-73; Governing Body National Institute of Agric. engineering 1970-75; RAF Training and Education Advisory Committee 1976-79; British Library Advisory Council 1975-80; Foreign Member, Serbian Academy of Sciences, 1981-. *Memberships:* Fellow Royal Society; Fellowship of Engineering; Honorary Fellow, Institute of Measurement and Control; Fellow, Clare Hall, Cambridge, 1964-; Fellow, Institute of Electrical & Electronic Engineers; Mackay Visiting Professor, University of California, Berkeley, USA, 1963; Eastern Electricity Board, 1967-73; Director, Delta Mats. Research Limited, 1974-77. *Publications:* Author, many original papers on communications, radar, magnetic amplifiers, computers, control and systems engrng., engrng. education and training. *Honours:* Hon. Fellow Hatfield Polytechnic; OBE, 1946; CBE, 1975; Harold Hartley Medal, 1971; Hon. DEng, Sheffield, 1978; Hon. ScD, City, 1970; Hon. DTech, Loughborough, 1977; Giorgio Quazza Medal of IFAC, 1981. *Hobbies:* Mountaineering; Gardening; Music; Reading. *Address:* 4 Latham Road, Cambridge, CB2 2EQ, England.

COATES, Peter Cunliff, b. 11 June 1928, Norton-on-Tees, England. Mechanical Engineer; Director. m. Margaret Hamilton McMullan, 7 Mar. 1979, 3 daughters. *Education:* Constantine Technical College; Kings College, Durham University; CEng, AMIMechE, AMInstE, FAIE. *Appointments:* Project Manager, Power Gas Corporation, United Kingdom, 1957-62, General Manager, Power Gas, Bombay, 1962-66; Managing Director, Davy McKee Pacific Pty Limited, Melbourne, 1967-81. *Memberships:* The Asutralia British Trade Association; Process Engineers and Constructors Association; The Australian Club, Melbourne; The Sciences Club, Melbourne; Royal Commonwealth Society; Australia Britain Society; Green Acres Golf Club. *Honours:* CBE, 1977. *Hobbies:* Golf; Tennis. *Address:* 1 Laurel Grove, Blackburn, Victoria 3130, Australia.

COBBETT, Stuart Hanson, b. 3 June 1948, Montreal, Canada. Lawyer. m. Jill Rankin, 7 Sept. 1973, 2 sons, 1 daughter. *Education:* BA, McGill University, 1969; BCL, 1972. *Appointments:* Heenan, Blaikie, Jolin, Potvin, Trépanier, Cobbett, Lawyer and Partner, 1972-; Part-time Lecturer, McGill University, 1976-. *Memberships:* Barreau du Québec; Canadian Bar Association; Mount Bruno Country Club; University Club of Montreal; Montreal Racket Club. *Honours:* University Honours. *Hobbies:* Golf; Squash; Theatre. *Address:* 422 Roslyn Avenue, Westmount, Montreal, Quebec, H3Y 2T5, Canada.

COBBOLD, Allen Edward, b. 9 Aug. 1943 Cambridge. Designer and Design Administrator. m. Hazel Wendy

Clay 22 Aug. 1964, 2 daughters. *Education:* Lincoln School of Art; Studied Painting Lithography and Stained Glass, Hornsey College of Art; Certificate, Further Education, teaching qualification, London University; National Diploma in Design. *Appointments:* Central Display Limited; Lep Exhibition Contractors; The Electricity Council; The Central Office of Information; The Medway College of Design; The Commonwealth Institute; Lecturer II and Head of Interior & Exhibition Design Department, Medway College of Design; UNESCO Consultant, Museum Interiors. *Memberships:* Fellow, Society of Industrial Artists and Designers. *Publications:* Design Magazine, India's Design Dilema, 1979. *Honours:* Ralph Yablon Award 1969. *Hobbies:* Early English Music; Fine Art and Applied Art and Design from all Cultures; Drawing. *Address:* 7 Saltcoats Road, Chiswik, London W4 1AR, England.

COBBOLD, Cameron Fromanteel, (Lord), b. 14 Sept. 1904 London England. Central Banker and Palace Official. m. Lady Hermione Bulwer Lytton 3 Apr. 1930 2 sons, 2 daughters. *Education:* Eton 1917-23; Scholar, Kings College Cambridge 1923-24. *Appointments:* Advisor, Bank of England 1933, Executive Director, 1938, Deputy Governor 1945, Governor 1949-61; Lord Chamberlain of HM Household 1963-71- Chairman Malaysian Commission 1962; Chairman Middlesex Hospital Board of Governors Medical School Council 1963-74; President British Heart Foundation 1963-74. *Address:* Lake House, Knebworth, Herts.

COCHRANE, Gordon Ross, b. 12 Mar. 1930, Ngaruawahia, New Zealand. University Professor; Director. m. Moyreen Glynn Chamberlin, 1957, 1 son, 4 daughters. *Education:* Auckland Teachers College; BA, Auckland University 1952; MA(Hons), 1954; BSc Otago University 1957; PhD, 1977. *Appointments:* Secondary School Teacher, Avondale College, 1953-54; Lecturer, Otago University 1955-56, Adelaide University 1957-60; Research Fellow, Australian National University Canberra, 1960; Senior Lecturer, Melbourne University 1961-65; Auckland University 1965-68; Visiting Research Professor, Kan. University 1968; Associate Professor, Auckland University 1969; Visiting Research Professor University California Santa Barbara, 1976,78; Director Remote Sensing Research Unit, University Auckland 1980. *Memberships:* President and Chairman, Auckland Br., NZ Geographical Society (various times); Institute of Australian Geographers; New Zealand Ecological Society; British Interplanetary Society; American Society of Photogrammetry. *Publications:* Vegetation Map of Australia and Vegetation Regions of Australia, 1967; Flowers and Plants of Australia, 1968, 1973; numerous papers on biogeography and remote sensing. *Honours:* Fowld's Member Certificate, Auckland University, most disting. student, Fac. Arts, 1954; Fellow, Netherlands Min. Science and Education 1968; numerous awards from NASA for research into satellite mapping. *Hobbies:* Yachting; Swimming; Ice Figure Skating. *Address:* (Koa Kohanga', 35 Kohimarama Road, Kohimarama, Auckland 5, New Zealand.

COCKCROFT, John Hoyle, b. 6 July 1934. Economist. m. Tessa Fay Shepley, 1971, 3 daughters. *Education:* BA Hons, History and Economics, St. John's College, Cambridge, 1958. *Appointments:* Royal Artillery, 1953-55; Feature Writer and Investment Analyst, Financial Times, 1959-61; Economist, GKN, 1962-67; seconded to Treasury, 1965-66; Econ. Leader-writer, Daily Telegraph, 1967-74; Member of Parliament, Conservative, Nantwich, 1974-79; Duff Stoop & Company (stockbrokers), 1978-. *Memberships:* Member, Council, European Movement, 1973-74; Member, Select Committee on Nationalised Industries, 1975-79. *Publications:* Why England Sleeps, 1971; A History of Guest Keen and Nettlefolds, (co-author. *Hobbies:* Walking; Reading; Swimming; Entertaining. *Address:* Mitchell's Farmhouse, Stapleford Tawney, Essex.

COCKERELL, Christopher, (Sir), b. 4 June 1910, Cambridge, England. Engineer. m. 4 June 1910, 2 daughters. *Education:* Peterhouse, Cambridge University. *Appointments:* W.H. Allen & Sons, Bedford, 1931-33; Radio Research, Cambridge, 1933-35; Airborne and Navigational Equipment, Research and development, Marconi Company Limited, 1935-50; Chairman, Ripplecraft Company Limited, 1950-79; Consultant (Hovercrasft) Ministry of Supply, 1957-58; Consultant of Hovercrasft Development Limited, 1958-70, Director, 1959-66; Member, Ministry of Technology's Advisory Committee for Hovercrasft, 1968-70; Consultant British Hovercraft Corporation, 1973-79; Chairman, Wavepower Limited, 1974-. *Memberships:* Fellow of the Royal Society; Fellow, Royal Society of Arts; Honorary Fellow, Swedish Society of Aeronautics; Honorary Fellow, Society of Engineers; Honorary Fellow, Manchester Institute of Science and Technology; Honorary Member Southampton Chamber of Commerce; President, Int. Air Cushion Engineering Society; President, UK Hovercraft Society. *Creative Works:* Patents: Electronics 36; Hovercraft 56; Wavepower 3. *Honours:* Numerous honours including: CBE; FRS; Viva Shield, Worshipful Co. of Carmen, 1961; Thulin Medal, Swedisch Society of Aeronautics, 1963; Howard N Potts Medal of Franklin Institute, 1965; Churchill Medal of Society of Engineers, 1966; Honorary DSc, Leicester University, 1967; Honorary Dr of Arts, Royal College of Art, 1968; Columbus Prize of Genoa, 1968; John Scott Award of Philadelphia, 1968; Elmer A Sperry Award, 1968; Gold Medal of Ewing Medal of Institute of Civil Engineers, 1977; Honorary Fellow of Downing College, Cambridge, 1969; Honorary Freeman, Borough of Ramsgate, 1971; Honorary DSc, Heriot - Watt University, 1971; Honorary Fellow of Peterhouse, Cambridge, 1974; Honorary DSc, London University, 1975. *Hobbies:* Antiquities; Gardening; Fishing. *Address:* 16 Prospect Place, Hythe, Southampton, England.

COCKRAM, Walter William, b. 9 Oct. 1909, Melbourne, Australia. Chairman of Directors. m. Kathleen Rose Canty, 30 June 1934, 2 sons. *Education:* Northcote State School, Collingwood Technical College. *Appointments:* W.H. Cockram and Sons, Pty Ltd, 1948-; Chairman, Arundel Farm Pty Ltd, 1958-; *Memberships:* Vice Chairman, Victoria Amateur Turf Club; Blood Horse Breeders Association; Fibrous Plaster Manufacturers Association, Australia and New Zealand; CSIRO Plater Research Liason Committee; Atheneum; Victoria Racing Club, Moonee Valley, R.C. *Hobbies:* Racing; Golf. *Address:* Arundel Farm, Arundel Road, Keilor, Victoria 3036, Australia.

COGGAN, (Baron) Frederick Donald, b. 9 Oct. 1909, London. Archbishop of Canterbury, (Retired). m. 17 Oct. 1935, 2 daughters. *Education:* Merchant Taylors School, London, 1923-28; St John's College, Cambridge, 1928-31; Wycliffe Hall, Oxford, 1934. *Appointments:* Assistant Lecturer, Semitic Languages and Literature, University of Manchester, 1931-34; Curate of St Mary Islington, 1934-37; Professor of New Testament, Wycliffe College, Toronto, 1937-44; Principal, London College of Divinity, 1944-56; Bishop of Bradford, 1956-61; Archbishop of York, 1961-74; Archbishop of Canterbury, 1974-80. *Memberships:* Chairman, Liturgical Commission; President, Society for Old Testament Studies; Pro-Chancellor, York University, Hull University; Prelate, Order of St John of Jerusalem. *Publications:* A People's Heritage, 1944; The Ministry of the Word, 1945; The Glory of God, 1950; Stewards of Grace, 1958; Five Makers of the New Testament, 1962; Christian Priorities, 1963; The Prayers of the New Testament 1967; Sinews of Faith, 1969; Word and World, 1971; Convictions, 1975; On Preaching, 1978; The Heart of the Christian Faith, 1978; Sure Foundation, 1981; contributions to Theology, etc. *Honours:* BD 1941; DD(hc) 1944; DD, Lambeth 1957; Hon.DD, Cambridge 1962; Leeds, 1958; Aberdeen, 1963; Tokyo, 1963; Saskatoon, 1963; Huron 1963; Hull, 1963; Manchester, 1972; Moravian Theol. Seminary, 1976; Virginia Theol Seminary, 1979; Hon. LLD Liverpool, 1972; HHD Westminster Choir College, Princeton 1966; Hon. DLitt Lancaster, 1967; STD(hc) Gen. Theol Seminary, NY, 1967; Hon. DCL Kent, 1975; DUniv. York, 1975; FKC 1975; Royal Victorial Chain, 1980. *Hobbies:* Gardening; Motoring; Music. *Address:* Kingshead House, Sissinghurst, Kent, England.

COGSWELL, Frederic Neil, b. 28 Dec. 1938, Surbiton, England. Research Scientist. m. Valerie Wigg, 7 July 1967, 2 daughters. *Appointments:* Research Associate, ICI Limited, 1958-. *Memberships:* British Society of Rheology; Plastics and Rubber Institute; Society of Rheology; *Publications:* Polymer Melt Rheology: A Guide for Industrial Practice. *Honours:* Honorary College Fellow, University College of Wales, 1977; Plastics Institute, Silver Medal, 1972. *Hobbies:* 18th Century Military History. *Address:* 67 Daniells, Welwyn Garden City, Herts, England.

COHEN, Douglas Harry, b. 10 Feb. 1920, Sydney, Australia. Paediatric Surgeon. m. Lysbeth Rose Sloman, 15 Feb. 1943, 1 son, 1 daughter. *Education:* MB, BS, 1942, Master of Surgery, 1950, University of Sydney; Fellow, Royal Australasian College of Surgeons, 1950. *Appointments:* War Service, 1944-46; Resident Medical Officer, Royal Prince Alfred Hospital, 1943; Private practice, 1946-52; Post-graduate training, Hospital for Sick Children, Great Ormond Street, London, 1954-55; Consulting practice in Paediatric Surgery, 1956-70; Honorary Surgeon, 1950-70, Head, Department of Surgery, 1971-, Royal Alexandra Hospital for Children; Consulting Paediatric Surgeon: The Women's Hospital, The Royal Newcastle Hospital, The Westmead Centre, Marrickville District Hospital. *Memberships:* British Association of Paediatric Surgeons; Foundation Member, Pacific Association of Paediatric Surgeons, President, 1979-80; Member, New South Wales State Committee, Royal Australasian College of Surgeons, Chairman, 1975-76; Australian College of Paediatrics, Member of Council, 1979-. *Publications:* Numerous publications on paediatric surgery and child safety. *Honours:* Order of Australia, 1980; Pfizer Guest Lecturer to Paediatric Society of New Zealand, 1961; Visiting Professor, Royal College of Physicians and Surgeons of Canada and Canadian Association of Paediatric Surgeons, 1980. *Hobbies:* Sailing; Tennis; Music. *Address:* 8/84 Milray Avenue, Wollstonecraft, New South Wales, Australia.

COHEN, (Sir), Rex Arthur Louis, b. 27 Nov. 1906, Liverpool. Company Chairman, (Retired). m. Nina Alice Castello, 7 July 1932, 1 daughter. *Education:* Rugby School; BA, Trinity College, Cambridge. *Appointments:* Chairman: Lewis's Investment Trust Croup, 1958-65; NAAFI, 1961-63; Higgs and Hill Limited, 1966-71; Meat and Livestock Commission, 1966-70; Director: Barclays Bank, London Local Board, 1979; Director, Tribune Investment Trust. *Memberships:* Jockey Club; Whites. *Honours:* KBE, 1964; OBE, 1944. *Hobbies:* Racing; Horse-Breeding; Shooting. *Address:* Rucknans Farm, Oakwood Hill, Nr. Dorking, Surrey, England.

COKER, Judith Corsen, b. 24 Oct. 1941, New York, USA. Librarian; Library Sales Manager. m. Akinola Coker, 23 July 1968, 1 son, 1 daughter. *Education:* MSLS., Drexel Institute of Technology, Philadelphia, Pennsylvania, USA, 1967; BA., Wilson College, Chambersburg, Pennsylvania, USA, 1963. *Appointments:* United Nations Development Programme, Lagos, Nigeria, 1968-70; New York Public Library, USA, 1968, 1970-74; The British Council, Lagos, Nigeria, 1975-77; Nigerian Book Suppliers, 1979-. *Memberships:* Assistant Treasurer, Nigerwives, 1981; President, 1980-81, Contact International. *Honours:* Graduated Cum Laude, Wilson College, USA, 1963. *Hobbies:* Travel; Crossword puzzles; Reading; Baking. *Address:* 45 Mercy Eneli Street, Surulere, Lagos, Nigeria.

COKER, R Oluwole, b. 11 Nov. 1923, Lagos, Nigeria. Surveyor. m. J Coker, 5 sons, 6 daughters. *Education:* BSc, (Special) Hons. Mathematics, University College, London, 1948-52; Postgraduate Diploma in Surveying. *Appointments:* Surveyor, Nigeria Government, 1946; Senior Surveyor, Western Nigeria Government, 1955-61; Assistant Surveyor General Western Nigeria Government, 1961-63; Director of Federal Surveys Nigeria, 1963-78; Chairman, Kenting Africa Resource Services Limited, 1978-. *Memberships:* President, Nigerian Association of Geodesy; President, Nigerian Institution of Surveyors; American Congress on Surveying & Mapping; American Society on Photogrammetry; Nigerian Society of Photogrammetry; Canadian Institute of Surveying; President, Commission for Geodesy in Africa of the International Assocation of Geodesy; Chairman, Inter-African Committee on Surveys and Maps of Scientific Technical & Research Commission of the O.A.U. *Publications:* Author of numerous papers in field. *Hobbies:* Music; Photography. *Address:* 18 Odaliki Street, Ebute-Meta, Lagos, Nigeria.

COLCHESTER, Thomas Charles, b. 18 Apr. 1909, London, United Kingdom. Administrator. m. Nancy Russell, 17 Feb. 1937, 1 daughter. *Education:* MA(Cantab), First Class Honours, History, Corpus Christi College, Cambridge, 1930. *Appointments:* HMOCS, 1931-61; District Officer, Kenya; Various Posts in Local Government Housing, Works, Cabinet Secretary, 1953-56; Permanent Secretary, Commonwealth Association of Architects, 1963-74; Commonwealth Legal

Education Association 1975-. *Memberships:* Royal Institute of British Architects; Royal Commonwealth Society. *Creative Works:* Active in Suffolk Conservation and Aldeburgh Music Festival. *Honours:* CMG. *Hobbies:* Fishing; Gardening; Music; Architecture; Conservation. *Address:* Warren Hill Lane, Aldeburgh, Suffolk, England.

COLE, Bernadette Philomena, b. 19 July 1945, Freetown, Sierra Leone. Journalist. m. Tunde Cole, 5 Apr. 1975, 1 son, 1 daughter. *Education:* Bachelor of Arts, Durham, 1969; Diploma in Journalism, Cardiff University, 1972; Post Graduate Diploma in Journalism, Indiana, 1973; Diploma in Communication for Social Development, Chicago, 1976. *Appointments:* Teacher, St. Edwards Secondary School, 1969-70; Information Officer, Ministry of Information, 1970-76; Senior Information Officer, 1976-80; Editor, 1973-, Assistant Controller, 1980, Sierra Leone Trade Journal, AG Controller and Head of Publications Division in the Ministry, Correspondent for a number of overseas magazines; Communications Consultant, AHEA Project, Sierra Leone. *Memberships:* Sierra Leone YWCA; Publicity Commissiner, Sierra Leone Girl Guides Association; Treasurer, Sierra Leone Association of Journalists, 1978-80. *Hobbies:* Reading; Gardening; Writing. *Address:* Government Rest House, Flat 14 Brookfields, Freetown, Sierra Leone.

COLE, Frederick Georgius Adekunle, b. 19 June 1938, Port Harcourt, Nigeria. House Governor/Director. m. Dora Emedo Okposuogu, 1 Dec. 1962, 2 sons, 2 daughters. *Education:* BSc Economics; CHA. *Appointments:* Executive Officer, West African Council for Medical Research; Establishments Officer, University College Hospital; Director/Chief Executive, University of Benin Teaching Hospital, Benin; House Governor, Director/Chief Executive, University College Hospital, Ibadan. *Memberships:* State Chairman, Nigerian Institute of Management; Chairman, Committee of Teaching Hospitals Chief Executives; Argonauts Society of Nigeria *Honours:* Justice of the Peace. *Hobbies:* Golf; Current Affairs; Reading; Tennis. *Address:* Directors Lodge, University College Hospital, PMB 5116, Ibadan, Nigeria.

COLE, Oswald Elliott, b. 28 Nov. 1933, Kingsbridge, England. Electrical Engineer; Chartered Engineer. m. Marjorie Ann Phillips, 31 Dec. 1960, 2 sons, 1 daughter. *Education:* BSc Eng., Plymouth Technical College, Devon, 1952-56. *Appointments:* College Apprentice, AEI Limited, Manchester, 1956-58; National Service Commission, REME, 1958-60; Design Engineer, AEI-GRS, London, 1960-61; Westinghouse Brake & Signal Company Limited, Chippenham, 1962-65; Section Engineer, NCCM Limited, Zambia Chingola Division, 1966-69; Project Engineer, NCCM Limited, Kitwe, Zambia, 1969-72; General Manager, Instelec Limited, Kitwe, Zambia, 1972-74; General Manager, Cutler Hammer Zambia Limited, 1974-. *Memberships:* Past President, Secretary, Treasurer, Lions Club; I.E.E.; Engineering Institute of Zambia; Chairman 1980-81, 1981-82, Kitwe and District Chamber of Commerce. *Hobbies:* Private Flying. *Address:* PO Box 28068, Kitwe, Zambia.

COLEMAN, William Peter, b. 15 Dec. 1928, Melbourne, Victoria, Australia. Member of Parliament. m. Verna Susannah Scott, 5 Apr. 1952, 1 son, 2 daughters. *Education:* Bachelor of Arts, University of Sydney, 1946-49; Master of Science, Economics, London School of Economics; Barrister-at-law, 1965. *Appointments:* Associate Editor, The Observer, 1958-61; Editor, The Bulletin, 1964-67; Editor Quadrant, 1968-77, 81-; Member of Parliament, Legislative Assembly of New South Wales, 1968-78; Administrator of Norfolk Island, 1979-81; Member of Parliament, House of Representatives, 1981-. *Memberships:* Union Club, Sydney. *Publications:* Australian Civilisation; Obscenity, Blasphemy and Sedition. Censorship in Australia; Cartoons of Australian History; The Heart of James McAuley. *Address:* 196 Queen Street, Woolahra, New South Wales 2025, Australia.

COLES, Kenneth George, b. 30 June 1926, Melbourne, Australia. Company Chairman. m. Thalia Helen, 1950 (Div), 1 son, 2 daughters. *Education:* BE., 1948, MIE(Aust), FIMechE., 1969, FAIM., 1959, Sydney University, Australia. *Appointments:* Gained engineering experience in appliance manufacturing

and automotive industries Nuffield Aust. Pty. Limited, General Motors, Holden Pty. Limited and Frigidaire, before commencing own business manufacturing conveyors, 1955; Chairman and Managing Director, 1955-76, Chairman, 1976-, K.G. Coles & Co. Pty. Limited; Chairman and Managing Director, K.G.C. Magnetic Tape Pty. Limited, 1973-80; Director: Australian Oil & Gas Corporation Limited, 1969-, AO G Minerals Limited, 1969-, G.J. Coles & Co. Limited, 1976-, Electrical Equipment Limited, 1976-, Permanent Trustee Co. Limited, 1978-, *Memberships:* General Councillor, NSW Branch, Metal Trades Industries Association of Australia, 1976-; International Solar Energy Society, 1957-; Councillor and Member, Board of Governors, Ascham School, 1972-; Employers' Representative, NSW Secondary Schools Board, 1979-. *Hobbies:* Tennis; Skiing; Bridge; *Address:* 24 Rosemont Avenue, Woollahra, New South Wales 2025, Australia.

COLLAKIDES, Stanley, b. 20 June 1944, Sydney, New South Wales, Australia. Insurance Broker. m. Prudence Anne Cooper, 19 Jan. 1975, 2 sons. *Education:* PALUA., 1969; AAIM., 1971. *Appointments:* Founding Director, Kollington Weber and Carroce Pty. Limited, Insurance Brokers, 1972-. *Memberships:* Chairman, Sydney, National Heart Foundation of Australia; Vice Commodore, Botany Bay Yacht Club; Cruising Yacht Club of Australia. *Honours:* NSW State Title Holder Enveavour 26 Yachting Association, 1973; Australian Title Holder, Endeavour 26 Yachting Association, 1974; Australian Quarter Ton Champion. *Hobbies:* Ocean Racing Yachting; Tennis; Fly fishing. *Address:* 54 Gordon Street, Clontarf, New South Wales 2093, Australia.

COLLARD, Stanley James, b. 25 Mar. 1936, Maleny, Queensland, Australia. Senator. m. Gloria Pearl Auld, 3 May 1958, 1 son, 2 daughters. *Appointments:* Locomotive engineman, Queensland Railways, Australia; Elected to Senate, 1975. *Memberships:* Former Secretary, Kennedy Divisional Council of NPA; Former Representative, North Queensland NPA to Queensland Management Committee; Campaign Director each election 1966-74 for Hon. Bob Katter, MP. *Address:* 6 Suthers Avenue, North Rockhampton, Australia.

COLLETT, Jill, b. 4 Oct. 1932, Kasauli, India. Historical Gardener. m. Gerald David Martin Collett, 9 Dec. 1953, 1 son, 1 daughter. *Appointments:* Secretary, Solicitors, Cheltenham; Secretary, Department of Agriculture, Nyasala, Central Africa; Secretary, Manager, Cheltenham Racecourse. *Memberships:* Bermuda National Trust; Garden History Society. *Creative Works:* Exhibition, Guildhall School of Music and Drama, 1948. *Hobbies:* Gardening; Sailing; Music; Needlework. *Address:* The Coach House, Mangrove Bay, Bermuda.

COLLIER, Helen Louisa, b. 17 Nov. 1929, Taihape, New Zealand. Musician. m. Ronald Claris Gordon, 17 Nov. 1962, 3 sons. *Education:* Diploma, New South Wales Conservatorium of Music, 1952; Diploma, Konservatorium Der Stadt Wien, 1960. *Appointments:* Samuel Marsden Collegiate School, Wellington, New Zealand, 1953-57; New South Wales Conservatorium of Music, Sydney, 1961; Radio New Zealand, Australian Broadcasting Commission, 1961-80. *Memberships:* Composers Association of New Zealand; Registered Music Teachers Society, New Zealand; President, 1963-80, Taihape Music Group. *Publications:* Numerous Concert Performances as Solo Pianist and Concerto Soloist. *Honours:* New Zealand Government Bursary, 1951. *Hobbies:* Arts; Cooking. *Address:* Rongoiti, R.D.I. Taihape, New Zealand.

COLLINGS, Richard Varwell, b. 30 Jan. 1927 Churston Ferrers, South Devon United Kingdom. Company Director; Industrial Company Manager. m. Audrey Elizabeth Brown 26 Dec. 1950, 2 sons, 1 daughter. *Education:* MA (Cantab) 1949; Associate 1953; FCIS 1962. *Appointments:* Salisburg Board of Executors 1953-64; Industrial Development Corporation of Zimbabwe 1964-80; Berkshire International Zimbabwe 1980-. *Memberships:* Salisbury Club; Bulawayo Club; Rotary. *Hobbies:* Gardening. *Address:* 26 Chipping Way, Burnside, Bulawayo, Zimbabwe.

COLLINS, James Slade, b. 15 May 1916 Bexley, New South Wales, Australia. Designer, Draftsman, Artist. m. Mabel Noeleen Waite 5 Feb. 1949, 2 sons. *Educa-*

tion: High School and Technical College, Sydney and Lithgow, NSW, 1928-34; Darlinghurst Art College, NSW 1946-48. *Appointments:* Oil Industry 1936-50; War Service 1941-45; Local Government 1953-59; Private Practice, Design and Drafting, 1951-52 and 1960-74. *Memberships:* Honorary Life Member, Billiards and Snooker Association of New South Wales and also of the Australian Billiards and Snooker Council; Sydney Club; Cronulla Golf Club; Sutherland Leagues Club; Cronulla and Caringbah R.S.L Clubs. *Publications:* Compiled collection of Pencil Portraits of Fellow Prisoner-of-war. The collection has since been donated to the Australian War Memorial; Wrote a Mathematical Work, Reduction Check; Designed instrument for solution of Spherical Triangles, intended as a navigational aid to escapees. *Honours:* Five Service Awards: 1939/45 Star, Pacific Star, Defence Medal, War Medal 1939/45, Australia Service Medal; Awarded Queen's Silver Jubilee Medal 1977; Awarded A.M.(Member of the Order of Australia) 1980, for services to the sport of Billiards and Snooker. *Hobbies:* Lapidary; Silvercraft; Art; Chess; Billiards; Snooker; Golf; Tennis. *Address:* 30 Oleander Pde, Caringbah 2229, New South Wales, Australia.

COLLINS, John James, b. 3 May 1926, Sydney, Australia. Orthopaedic Surgeon. m. Maureen Byrne, 31 Aug. 1957, 4 sons, 1 daughter. *Education:* MBBS., 1951, FRACS., 1960, University of Sydney, Australia. *Appointments:* Visiting Orthopaedic Surgeon, 1963-, Lewisham Hospital, Sydney, Australia; Plastic and Jaw Unit, Rooks Down House, Basingstoke, Hants, UK, 1956; Robert Jones and Agnes Hunt Orthopaedic Hospital, Oswestry, Salop, UK, 1957; Life Consulting Medical Officer, Orthopaedic Surgery, Canterbury Hospital, Sydney, Australia, 1977. *Memberships:* Royal Australasian College of Surgeons; Australian Orthopaedic Association; Australian Medical Association; Chairman-elect, Medical Board, Lewisham Hospital, Sydney, 1981. *Publications:* Retrosternal Dislocation of the Clavicle, (with M C Mehta and A Sachdev), 1973. *Honours:* University Exhibition, 1943, 1944. *Hobbies:* Golf; Reading. *Address:* 6 Belcote Road, Longueville, New South Wales 2066, Australia.

COLLINS, Lewis John, b. 23 Mar. 1905, Hawkhurst, Kent, England. Minister of Religion. m. Diana Clavering Elliot, 21 Oct. 1939, 4 sons. *Education:* 1st class Theology Tripos, Part II, Sidney Sussex College and Westcott House, Cambridge, UK, 1924-28. *Appointments:* Curate at Whitstable, Kent, UK, 1928-29; Chaplain, Sidney Sussex College, Cambridge, UK, 1929-31; Minor Canon, St. Paul's Cathedral, London, UK, 1931-34; Deputy Priest-in-Ordinary, 1931-32, Priest-in-Ordinary, 1932-35, HM The King; Vice-Principal, Westcott House, Cambridge, UK, 1934-37; Chaplain, RAFVR., 1940-45; Dean, 1938-48, Fellow, Lecturer, Lecturer and Chaplain, 1937-48, Oriel College, Oxford, UK; Canon of St. Paul's Cathedral, London, UK, 1948-81; Chairman, Campaign for Nuclear Disarmament, 1958-64; Martin Luther King Foundation, 1969-73; President, 1959-, Chairman, 1946-73, Christian Action; International Defence and Aid Fund, 1964. *Memberships:* Studiorum Novi Testamenti Societas. *Publications:* The New Testament Problem, 1937; A Theology of Christian Action, 1949; Faith under Fire, 1966; Contributor to Journal of Theological Studies, Hibbert Journal, Three Views of Christianity. *Honours:* Order of Hrand Companion of Freedom (Third Div), Zambia, 1970; Commander, Order of the Northern Star, Sweden, 1976; Awarded Gold Medal of the Special Committee of UN against Apartheid, 1978 *Hobbies:* Gardening; Walking. *Address:* Mill House Chappel, Mount Bures, Suffolk, England.

COLLINS, Michael Brendan, b. 9 Sept. 1932 Exmouth Devon. HM Diplomatic Service Officer. m. Elena Lozar 2 Apr. 1959. *Education:* St Illtyd's College Cardiff 1942-51; BSc(Econ.) University College London 1951-53. *Appointments:* HM Forces 1953-55; HM Diplomatic Service: Foreign Office 1956-59; Santiago Chile 1959-61; Santiago Cuba 1962-64; F.C.O 1964-67; HM Consul, Prague 1967-69; Deputy High Commissioner, The Gambia 1969-72; Head of Chancery, Algiers 1972-75; FCO 1975-78; Consul, Commercial, Montreal 1978-80; Consul Halifax 1980-. *Memberships:* Army and Navy Halifax Clug. *Honours:* MBE 1969. *Hobbies:* Reading; Golf; Fishing; Shooting. *Address:* 5961 Balmoral Road, Halifax, Nova Scotia Canada.

COLLINSON, Kenneth Edward, b. 8 Mar. 1945 Kingston-on-Thames, Surrey, England. Proprietor, Advertising Business. m. Heather Isabel Wise 17 June 1967 2 sons. *Education:* Huntingdon, UK 1950-59; Unley High School, South Australia 1959-60; Scholarship Student, South Australian School of Art 1960-61. *Appointments:* Advertising Layout/Copywriter, Myer Emporium South Australia, 1961-65; Assistant Advertising Manager, Woolworths, South Australia, 1965-67; Account Manager, Berwen Paine Advertising, South Australia, 1967-70; Proprietor, Collinson Advertising, 1970-75; General Manager and Associate Director, Ogilvy and Mather, South Australia 1975-76; Manager Retail Division, Ogilvy and Mather, Victoria, Australia 1976-77; Proprietor, Collinson, Murray Evans Advertising, 1977-81. *Memberships:* Advertising Federation of Australia; Australian Bureau of Circulations; Young Mens Christian Association; Angora Mohair Association of Australia; Commercial Travellers Association of Australia; Onkaparinga Racing Club Incorporated. *Hobbies:* Snow Skiing; Game Fishing; Farming; Building. *Address:* PO Box 91, Oakbank, South Australia 5243.

COLLINS-WILLIAMS, Cecil, b. 31 Dec. 1918 Toronto, Canada. Physician. m. Jean Hamilton 30 June 1944, 1 son, 1 daughter. *Education:* BA, University of Toronto, 1941; MD 1944; Postgraduate work in Toronto, Boston, New York City; FRCP(C) in Paediatrics, 1950. *Appointments:* Staff, Hospital for Sick Children, 1950-; Senior Physician; Staff, Medical School, University of Toronto, 1950-; Professor of Paediatrics; Head, Allergy Division, Hospital for Sick Children, Toronto 1952-; Consultant, Ontario Crippled Children's Centre, 1967-. *Memberships:* Canadian Society of Allergy and Clinical Immunology; American Academy of Pediatrics; American Academy of Allergy; American College of Allergists; Canadian Paediatric Society; Canadian Society for Immunology; Asthma Care Association of America; Association for the Care of Asthma; Asthma Society of Canada; Academy of Medicine, Toronto; American Thoracic Society; Canadian Thoracic Society; British Society for Allergy and Clinical Immunology; Affiliate member, Royal Society of Medicine. *Publications:* One hundred and nine published papers in the field of Paediatric Allergy and Clinical Immunology; Editorial Board, Annals of Allergy; Editorial Board, Journal of Asthma Associate Editor, Allergia. *Hobbies:* Photography; Cross-country skiing. *Address:* 39 Bennington Heights Dr. Toronto, Ontario, Canada, M4G 1A8.

COLMAN, Fraser MacDonald, b. 23 Feb. 1925 Wellington, New Zealand. Member of Parliament. m. 13 Dec. 1958 3 daughters. *Appointments:* Engineering 1939-55; Assistent General Secretary, NZ Labour Party 1955-67; Minister of Immigration, Mines, 1972-75; Postmaster General 1974-75; Shadow Transport Minister. *Memberships:* Lions International *Address:* 103 Hine Road, Wainuiomata, New Zealand.

COLOCASSIDES, Michael George, b. 9 Sept. 1933, Nicosia, Cyprus. Economist. m. Nedy Tryfonos 11 Jan. 1959, 2 sons, 1 daughter. *Education:* BSc(Econ) London School of Economics 1952-55. *Appointments:* Director, 1963-70, Chairman Cyprus Development Bank, 1968-70; Chairman, Cyprus Tourism Organization 1970-72; Minister of Commerce and Industry 1972-76; Governor, Bank of Cyprus 1976-79; Chairman, Town and Country Planning Council 1979-; Chairman, Cyprus Industrialists and Employers Federation, 1981-. *Memberships:* President, Friends of LSE in Cyprus. *Publications:* Various articles and lectures on issues relevant to the Cyprus economic and political scene in local and foreign journals. *Hobbies:* Tennis; Music; Photography; Stamp Collecting; Map Collecting. *Address:* 4, Aetolon Street, Nicosia, Cyprus.

COLTMAN, Owen McKay, b. 12 May 1929, Ballarat Victoria Australia. Obstetrician and Gynaecologist. m. Barbara Alixe Dalton 27 May 1955, 2 sons, 1 daughter. *Education:* Ormond College, Melbourne University; MBBS 1953; MRCOG 1961;FRCOG 1976; Foundation Fellow RACOG 1979. *Appointments:* J.R.M.O. Alfred Hospital, Melbourne; S.R.M.O. Ballarat Base Hospital; S.R.M.O. (Gyn. Royal Melbourne Hospital); Registrar Obs. Footscray Hospital; J.R.M.O. Royal Berkshire Hospital; J.R.M.O. Hammersmith Hospital; Registrar ? & G. Paddington General Hospital; ? & G. Geelong Hospital 1962-; Clinical Tutor O & G. 1971-; Clinical Dean Geelong Hospital Clinical School Monash University

1974-77. *Memberships:* AMA; Medical Advisory Council; Honorary Life Member VFPA 1977. *Publications:* With Crosby, Jones and Mestitz, Auditing at Geelong Hospital, Australian Clinical Review, 1981. *Hobbies:* Skiing; Sailing; Flying; Outback Travelling; Bird Watching; Australian Wines. *Address:* 11 Stephen Street, Newtown 3220, Australia.

COLVIN, Alfred Cephus, b. 21 May 1937 Grafton New South Wales. Public Servant. m. Frances Vere Pierce, 3 sons, 1 daughter. *Education:* Dip.P.E Sydney Teachers College, 1957; BA(Hons) 1966; MEd(Hons 1972; Sydney University; PhD Alberta University 1975. *Appointments:* Teaching in various Government schools, 1958-66; State Advisor in Health Education 1966-70; Assistant Director, Sport and Recreation Service of NSW, 1970-73; Teaching and Study, University of Alberta 1973-75; Chief Curriculum Officer NSW Department of Education 1975-. *Memberships:* Numerous memberships in Scientific, Professional and Other Societies including: Mental Health Association; Church of England Youth Council; Sports Medicine Federation; Australian College of Education; Director of Physical Education Publications. *Publications:* Numerous publications and Conference Reports including: An Analysis of the Health Interests of Secondary School Students from Non-Departmental Schools in the Sydney Metropolitan and Parramatta Areas, 1968; Sex Education in Secondary Schools, 1972; Recreational Potential of Land in Industrial Areas, 1976; Health Interests in Secondary Schools, Australian Physical Education Conference Report, 1966; Drama in Education—National Drama in Education Conference 1979. *Hobbies:* Ocean Racing; Skiing; Swimming; Golf. *Address:* 151 Awaba Street, Mosman, New South Wales, 2008, Australia.

COLVIN, Gordon Stirling, b. 16 Sept. 1912, Chatsworth, New South Wales, Australia. Orthopaedic Surgeon. m. Joan Allen, 7 May, 1943, 1 son, 1 daughter. *Education:* MBBS., Sydney University Australia, 1936; Fellow, University of Liverpool, UK, 1973. *Appointments:* Orthopaedic Surgeon at: Hon. Consultant, 1973-, RAHC; Consultant, 1977-, Ryde Hospital, 1940-76; Royal South Sydney Hospital, Australia, 1949-61. *Memberships:* Killara Golf Club; Killara Tennis Club; AMA; AOA; Life member, APA. *Publications:* Various medical publications. *Honours:* OBE., 1967. *Hobbies:* Golf; Tennis. *Address:* 3/2 Mount Street, Hunters Hill, New South Wales 2110, Australia.

COLVIN, Michael Keith Beale, b. 27 Sept. 1932, London, England. Member of Parliament; Farmer; Landowner. m. Nichola Cayzer, 12 Sept. 1956, 1 son, 2 daughters. *Education:* Eton; Royal Military Academy, Sandhurst; Royal Agricultural College, Cirencester. *Appointments:* Grenadier Guard, retired T/Captain, 1950-57; J Walter Thompson & Co. Limited, 1957-62; Farmer, Landowner and Company Director, 1962-. *Memberships:* Andover and Trust Valley District Councillor, 1964-76; Vice Chairman, Conservative Aviation Committee; Secretary, Conservative Smaller Businesses Committee; Member Parlimentary Select Commitee on Employment; Governor of the Village Settlement Association; Country Landowners Association; National Farmers Union; National Union of Licenced Victuallers; Association of Scientific Secretarial and Managerial Staffs; Turf Club. *Publications:* Blueprint for Bristol, 1978; An Open Tech-training for skills, 1980. *Hobbies:* Painting; Designing. *Address:* Tangley House, Andover, Hampshire, England.

COMANS, Charles Kennedy, b. 21 Oct. 1914, Melbourne, Australia. Lawyer. m. Nancy Louisa Button, 14 Aug. 1944, 3 sons, 1 daughter. *Education:* LL.M., University of Melbourne, Australia. *Education:* Various Legal Positions, Commonwealth Attorney-General's Department, 1938-48; Assistant Parliamentary Draftsman, 1948; Second Parliamentary Counsel, 1970; First Parliamentary Counsel, 1972-77; Consultant to Commonwealth Attorney-General, 1977-. *Honours:* QC, 1974; CBE, 1977. *Hobby:* Golf. *Address:* 21 Tasmania Circle, Forrest.ACT.2603, Australia.

COMBEN, Graeme Maxwell, b. 6 Jan. 1933, Melbourne, Australia. Chartered Accountant; Manager. m. Shirley Lorraine Martin, 24 Mar. 1956, 1 son, 1 daughter. *Education:* Associate, Chartered Institute of Accountants, 1960; Associate, Chartered Institute Secretaries and Managers, 1960; Associate, Chartered

Institute of Transport, 1981. *Appointments:* Watson Niven & Co., Chartered Accountants, 1950-61; Self-Employed, 1961-66; West Gate Bridge Authority, 1966-. *Memberships:* President, Apex Club of Portland; President, Rotary Club of Werribee; Werribee Park Golf Club. *Hobbies:* Golf; Travel; Swimming; Gardening. *Address:* 'Marlo', 93 Princess Highway, Werribee Victoria. 3030, Australia.

COMBER, Kenneth Mark, b. 20 Jan. 1939, New Plymouth, New Zealand. Member of Parliament. m. Diane Holyoake, 8 July 1966, 1 son, 2 daughters. *Education:* Victoria University of Wellington, New Zealand, 1958-64; U.E.(Accredited); A.C.A.(Chartered Accountant). *Appointments:* McCulloch, Butler and Spence, Chartered Accountants, 1958-60; N.Z. Counties' Association, 1961-69; National Electric, 1969-72; John H Walker & Co. Limited, 1972-73; Member of Parliament, 1972-. *Memberships:* Lions Club of Wellington; Congregation of St. Vincent de Paul Parish, Northland; Patron, Wellington Multiple Sclerosis Society. *Hobbies:* Swimming; Water-Skiing; Reading Politics; Tennis; Squash. *Address:* 54 Harbour,View Road, Northland, Wellington, New Zealand.

COMIS, Spyridon Dimitri, b. 26 May 1941, Alexandria, Egypt. Physiologist; Lecturer. m. Diane Margaret Rimmer, 27 Apr. 1968, 2 sons. *Education:* BSc., University College, London, UK, 1963; PhD., University of Birmingham, UK. *Appointments:* Research Fellow, 1966-73, Lecturer, 1973-, University of Birmingham, UK. *Memberships:* Physiological Society; Institute of Biology. *Publications:* Contributions to numerous scientific journals. *Hobbies:* Music; Phtography; Gardening. *Address:* 20 Greenside, Harborne, Birmingham, B17 OBT, England.

COMMON, Frank Breadon, Jr., b. 16 Apr. 1920, Montreal, Quebec, Canada. Lawyer. m. Katharine Ruth Laws, 7 Sept. 1946. *Education:* Royal Military College of Canada, Kingston, Ontario, Diploma in Engineering, 1938-40; Graduated as Bachelor of Civil Law, McGill University, Montreal, Canada, 1948; Admitted to Bar of Province of Quebec, Canada, June 1948; *Appointments:* Active service with Royal Engineers of Canada, 1940-45; Member of Law Firm of Montgomery, McMichael, Common, Howard, Forsyth & Ker and Soccessor Firms (now Senior Partner of Ogilvy, Renault), 1948-; Created Queen's Counsel, April, 1959. *Memberships:* Candian Bar Association, 1948-; Canadian Tax Foundation, 1948-; also member of numerous committees and associations. *Address:* apartment B-101, 'Gleneagles', 3940 Cote des Neiges Road, Montreal, Quebec, Canada H3H 1W2.

COMPTON, Everald Ernest, b. 5 Oct. 1931, Toowoomba, Australia. Fund Raising Consultant. m. Helen Eva Wyllie, 11 Oct. 1958, 1 son, 3 daughters. *Education:* Associate of Acountancy, University of Queensland, Australia, 1957; Associate, Australian Society of Accountants, 1960; Associate, Australian Marketing Institute, 1962; Associate, Public Relations Institute of Australia, 1976; Fellow, Institute of Directors, 1971; Associate, Australasian Institute of Fund Raising; Fellow, Australian Institute of Management. *Appointments:* Secretary, St. Andrews Hospital, Brisbane, Australia, 1956-60; Director, Cosway Public Relations Pty. Limited, Brisbane, Australia, 1961-63; Managing Director, Compton Associates Pty. Limited, Fund Raising Consultants, Brisbane, Australia, 1964-; also Compton Associates (NZ) Limited, Wellington, New Zealnd; Compton Associates Limited, London ,UK; Compton Associates Consulting Limited, Vancouver, Canada. *Memberships:* Deputy Chairman, Later Years; Secretary, Queensland Foundation for Family Life; Chairman, Everald Compton Charitable Trust, Australia; Chermside Rotary Club; Brisbane Club, Australia; Sloane Club, London, UK; Elder, Uniting Church of Australia. *Publications:* Ten Steps to Successful Fund Raising; Where Have the Christian Stewards Gone?. *Hobbies:* Writing Feature Articles. *Address:* 31 Glengellan Street, Aspley Q4054, Australia.

COMPTON-HALL, Patrick Richard, b. 12 July 1929, Reigate, Surrey, England. Museum Director; Author. m. Eve Margery Cameron, 27 Dec. 1961, 4 sons, 2 daughters. *Education:* Graduated Royal Naval College, Dartmouth, UK, 1947; Naval Staff College, UK, 1961; Joint Services Staff College, UK, 1967. *Appointments:* Cadet to Commander, Royal Navy, 1943-68; Director of

Services, John Lewis Partnership, UK, 1969-71; Author, Scriptwriter, BBC., UK, 1971-75; Director, RN Submarine Museum, Gosport, Hants, UK, 1975-. *Memberships:* Royal United Services Institute; Writers Guild; Translators Association; Museums Association. *Publications:* Various radio comedy series, BBC., NZBC., BFBS; BBC & ITV Documentaries on Submarines; the Second Underwater War, (in press); Submarines, (in press). *Honours:* MBE., 1964. *Hobbies:* Translation technical and literary; Restoring old houses; Reading for PhD. *Address:* Upper Ffynnon Fair, Rhayader, Powys, Wales LD6 5LA.

CONDELL, Aurelio Figuriedo, b. 18 May 1937, Manchester, Jamaica, West Indies. Dental Surgeon; Anesthesiologist. *Education:* BA., St. Johns University, New York, USA, 1961; BSc., Benedict College, Columbia, South Carolina, USA, 1965; MSc., Purdue University, USA, 1967; DDS., Meharry Medical College, Nashville, Tennessee, USA, 1971; Diploma in Oral Surgery, 1973, Diploma, Anesthesiology, 1975, Columbia University, Harlem Hospital, USA; Diploma, Journalism, Trans World College, 1979. *Appointments:* Resident Oral Surgery Department, Resident, Department of Anesthesiology, Harlem Hospital, USA; Clinical Dental Surgeon, Government of Jamaica; Private Practice, General Dentistry, Oral Surgeon, Anesthesiologist. *Memberships:* English Freemason Constitution; Freemason Scottish Constitution; American Society of Chemists; Liguance Club, Kingston, Jamaica; Jamaican Dental Association. *Publications:* Book of Poetry (unpublished). *Creative Works:* Sculpture. *Honours:* Award for Bedside manner, Harlem Hospital, 1973. *Hobbies:* Song writing; Learning to play different musical instruments; Writing poetry and short stories; Farming; Public Speaking; Sculpture; Painting. *Address:* 23B Oakridge, Kingston 8, Jamaica, West Indies.

CONDON, Michael John, b. 4 July 1937, Oldbury, Worcestershire, England. Dental Surgeon. *Education:* Bachelor of Dental Surgery, University of St. Andrews, Scotland, 1963. *Appointments:* Associate in Private Practice, Slough, Berkshire, UK, 1963; Junior Partner in Private Practice, Redditch, Worcestershire, UK, 1963-67; Government Dental Surgeon, Lilongwe and subsequently, Blantyre, Malawi, 1967-70; Principal Dental Officer, Ministry of Health, Gaborone, Botswana, 1971-. *Memberships:* Medical and Dental Association of Botswana; Lions Club of Gaborone. *Publications:* Preliminary Report of a Survey of Dental Disease conducted in two selected Villages of Botswana, 1978; A system for drug administration, 1978. *Hobbies:* Riding; Reading. *Address:* 2654 Kgori Close, Gaborone, Botswana.

CONIBEER, George William Neame, b. 21 May 1925, Plymouth, Devon, England. Chartered Mechanical and Electrical Engineer. m. 26 Dec. 1953, 1 son, 2 daughters. *Education:* HM. Dockyard Technical College, 1940-43; Graduateship, Institution of Mechanical Engineers, 1943-46; Corporate Membership Examination of Institution of Mechanical Engineer, 1947; Qualifications giving Graduateship of Institution of Electrical Engineers, 1950; Chartered Mechanical Engineer, 1953; Chartered Electrical Engineer, 1973. *Appointments:* Site Mechanical Engineer, Ewbank & Partners Limited, 1952-55; Head of Mechanical Engineering Office, British Nuclear Design and Construction Limited, 1955-65; Chief Engineer, Yarrow-Admiralty Research Department Limited, 1965-73; Chief Design Engineer, Berkeley Nuclear Laboratories, 1973-. *Memberships:* Chartered Engineer; Fellow, Institution of Mechanical Engineers; Member, Institution of Electrical Engineers. *Publications:* Numerous Classified Papers on Nuclear Submarine Developments and the Design and Safety of Nuclear Power Stations and Test Rigs. *Honours:* Institution of Marine Engineers Prize for Thermodynamics, 1944. *Hobbies:* Christian Theological Studies. *Address:* 17 Holywell Road, Norman Hill, Dursley, Gloucestershire GL11 5RS, England.

CONNELL, Henry Barry, b. 7 June 1928, Melbourne, Australia. International Lawyer. m. Carmel Therese Slaweski, 5 May, 1962 (div.), 1 daughter. *Education:* BA(Hons.) 1950, LL.B. 1959, Diploma of Education 1959, Melbourne University, Australia. *Appointments:* History Master, Geelong Grammar School, Corio, Victoria, Australia, 1951-57; Resident Tutor, Trinity College, University of Melbourne, Australia, 1958-60; Practice Law, The Victorian Bar, 1961-; Senior Legal

Adviser, Advisings Division, Attorney-General's Department, Commonwealth of Australia, 1963-65; Senior Lecturer in Law, 1965-70, Associate Professor, 1973-, Monash University; Legal Adviser, Foreign Affairs, Kingdom of Lesotho, 1969-70; Chief Secretary, 1971-73, Civil Aviation Adviser, 1973-, Republic of Nauru; Chairman, Victorian Committee on Discrimination in Employment and Occupation, 1978; Chairman, Victorian Dissemination Committee, Australian Red Cross, 1981; Member, Nauru Phosphate Royalties Trust, 1981. *Memberships:* The Victorian Bar; International Law Association; Australian Institute of International Affairs; Australian Institute of Political Science; Law Asia; Melbourne Cricket Club; Lawn Tennis Association of Victoria; Metropolitan Golf Club; Moonee Balley Racing Club; Royal Automobile Club of Victoria. *Publications:* Editor: Australian Yearbook of International Law, 1970-71. *Hobbies:* Golf; Tennis; Squash; Herb Gardening. *Address:* 'Buckhurst', 42 O'Connors Road, The Patch, Victoria 3972, Australia.

CONNELL, James Peter, b. 23 Sept. 1926, Halifax, Nova Scotia, Canada, Federal Public Servant. m. Ella Catherine Macleod, 5 sons, 3 daughters. *Education:* Acadia University. *Appointments:* Industrial Relations Manager, Union Carbide Canada Limited, 1955-60; Director, Employee Relations, Allied Chemical Canada Limited, 1961-66; Director, Personnel Administration, Department of National Revenue, Customs and Excise, 1966-67; Director General, Personnel, Department of Transport, 1967-68; Deputy Secretary for Personnel Policy, Treasury Board Secretariat, 1969-75; Deputy Minister of National Revenue, Customs and Excise, 1975-. *Honours:* Chairman of the Customs Co-operation Council, 1980, 1981; Vice-Chairman of the Customs Co-operation Council, 1979; Employer Vice-Chairman of the International Joint Committee on the Public Service, 1971. *Hobbies:* Farming; Fishing. *Address:* Oxford Station, Ontario KOG 1TO, Canada.

CONNELL, John Leonard, b. 26 Sept. 1922, Wangaratta, Victoria, Australia. Surgeon. m. Betty, 28 Jan. 1950, 2 sons, 3 daughters. *Education:* M.B. B.S. University of Melbourne, 1947; M.S. Melbourne, 1950; F.R.A.C.S. 1951; F.R.C.S. 1952; F.A.C.S. 1978. *Appointments:* Resident Medical Officer, St. Vincents Hospital, Melbourne, 1947-50; Surgical Registrar, West Middlesex Hospital, London, 1950-53; Surgeon to Outpatients, St. Vincents Hospital, Melbourne, 1954-80; Senior Vascular Surgeon, St. Vincents Hospital, Melbourne, 1980-. *Memberships:* Royal College of Surgeons, London; Royal Australian College of Surgeons; American College of Surgeons; Commonwealth Golf Club; Melbourne Cricket Club. *Publications:* Surgery for Nurses, 1980; Numerous Surgical Articles ; Surgery Journal; Australian Medical Journal. *Honours:* Divine Prize in English, 1939; Gordon Taylor Prize in Surgery, 1950. *Hobbies:* Chess; Tennis; Golf; Farming. *Address:* 7, Tregarron Avenue, Kew 3101, Victoria, Australia.

CONNELL, Philip Henry, b. 6 July 1921, Leeds, Yorkshire, Medical Practitioner. m. (1) Marjorie Helen Gilham, 31 March 1948, 2 sons, (2) Cecily Mary Harper, 1st Sept. 1973. *Education:* University of London, St. Bartholomews Hospital, London, 1945-51; The Maudsley Hospital and Institute of Psychiatry, 1953-57; M.R.C.S. L.R.C.P., 1951; M.B. B.S. 1951; D.P.M. 1956; M.D. 1957; M.R.C.P. 1969; F.R.c. Psychiatry, 1971; F.R.C.P. 1974. *Appointments:* St. Stephens Hospital, Fulham Road, London, 1951-53; The Bethlem Royal Hospital and The Maudsley Hospital, London, 1953-57; Consultant Psychiatrist, Newcastle General Hospital and Royal Victoria Infirmary; Physician in charge Child Psychiatry Unit, Newcastle General Hospital, 1957-63; Physician, The Bethlem Royal Hospital and The Maudsley Hospital, 1963-; Consultant Advisor, Department of Health and Social Security, 1967-71, 1981-. *Memberships:* Secretary, Child and Adolescent Psychiatry section of Royal Medico Psychological Association, 1961-64; Chairman, Child and Adolescent Psychiatry Specialist Section of the Royal College of Psychiatrists, 1971-75; Vice-President, Royal College of Psychiatrist, 1979-81; Appointed Member of General Medical Council, 1979-. Chairman, Institute for the Study of Drug Dependence, 1975-; The Athenaeum Club. *Publications:* Amphetamine Psychosis, Maudsley Monograph No.5, 1958; Cannabis and Man, (jointly) 1975; Contributions to the Scientific Literature on Drug Dependence, Maladjusted and Psychiatrically Disturbed Children and Adolescents. *Honours:* President, Society For The Study of Addiction, 1973-77; Chairman, Scientific and Professional Advisory Board of International Council on Alcohol and Addictions, 1972-79; Member, Council of British Association of Psychopharmacology, 1974-76; Elected Corresponding Fellow of American Psychiatric Association, 1970. *Hobbies:* Theatre; Bridge; Tennis. *Address:* 25 Oxford Road, Putney, London SW15 2LG.

CONNELL, William Fraser, b. 28 June 1916, Lockhart, N.S.W. Australia, Emeritus Professor of Education. m. Margaret Lloyd Peck, 20 Dec. 1939, 1 son, 2 daughters. *Education:* M.A., M.Ed. Melbourne, 1944; M.A. Illinois, 1949; Ph.D. London, 1948. *Appointments:* Lieutenant, RANVR, 1942-45; Lecturer in Education, University of Melbourne, 1946-50; Senior Lecturer, University of Sydney, 1951-53; Reader, 1953-55; Professor, 1955-76; Emeritus Professor, 1977-. Fellow of Faculty of Education, Monash University, 1978-; Visiting Professor for several Universities. *Memberships:* President, Australian and New Zealand History of Education Society, 1971; Chairman, Australian Unesco Education Committee, 1965-75; Chairman, Australian National Committee on Social Science Teaching, 1970-78; Fellow, Academy of the Social Sciences in Australia; President, Australian Association for Research in Education, 1973; Member, Phi Delta Kappa; Comparative Education Society. *Publications:* The Educational Thought and Influence of Matthew Arnold, 1950; Growing up in an Australian City, 1957; Foundations of Secondary Education, 1961; A History of Education in the Twentieth Century World, 1980; The Australian Council for Educational Research 1930-80, 1980; Co-author of several books including: The Foundations of Education, 1962; 1975; China at School, 1975;. *Honours:* Mackie Medal in Education awarded by the Australian and New Zealand Association for the Advancement of Science, 1977; Honorary Member, Australian Association for Research in Education, 1979; O.B.E., 1977. *Hobbies:* Tennis; Swimming; Gardening; Woodwork. *Address:* 34, Tanti Avenue, Mornington, Victoria, 3931, Australia.

CONNELLY, Eric, F.C.A, b. 2 June 1910, Amble, Northumberland, England. Chartered Accountant. m. Barbara Toole, 31 March 1948, 1 son. *Education:* University of Alberta, 1933; Fellow, Institute of Chartered Accountants of Alberta, 1957; Institute of Chartered Accountants of Alberta, 1975; Registered Industrial Accountants Society, 1942. *Appointments:* Student, Harvey Morrison, 1928-33; Staff, Harvey Morrison, 1933-35; Staff, Touche, Ross & company, Toronto, 1935-36; Vice President, Director, Northern Wood Preservers, Port. Arthur, 1936-37; Hospital, 1938-41; Vice President, Director, Barber Industries Ltd., 1941-47; Vice President, Mannix Cos., President Pembina Pipe Line Ltd., 1947-70; Chairman, Canex Trading Ltd., 1970; Ashland Oil Canada Ltd. 1965-80; Chairman, Barber Engineering Controls Ltd., Director, Eau Claire Estates Ltd., Merland Explorations Ltd. (Grosvenor), L.K. Resources Ltd., Turbo Resources Ltd., Bankend Mines Ltd., Queenston Gold Mines Ltd. *Memberships:* President, Alberta Tuberculosis Society, 1947; President, Institute of Chartered Accountants of Alberta, 1954; President, Calgary Chamber of Commerce, 1964; President, Ranchmens Club, 1977-78; Registered Industrial Accountants Society; Honorary Treasurer, Calgary Exhibition Stampede; Rotary Club, - Calgary; Calgary Golf and Country Club; Glencoe Club; Mill Reef Club (Antigua); Wailea Golf Club (Hawaii). *Honours:* Medal, Institute of Chartered Accountants, 1931; Lecturer, Banff School of Advanced Managment, 1954-58; Austrian School of Advanced Management, 1970; Papers, Canadian Tax Foundation; University of Alberta, Commerce Faculty. Golf. *Address:* Appt 4 S. 222 Eagle Ridge, W1. S.W. Calgary, Alberta, Canada, T2V2V7.

CONNELLY, Michael Aynsley, b. 21 Feb. 1916, Wellington, New Zealand. Member of Parliament. m. Margaret Joyce Kennedy, 29 Nov. 1941, 4 sons, 2 daughters. *Education:* Bachelor of Commerce, William Emery Scholarship for Commerce, University of Otago, Dunedin, New Zealand; Fellow Chartered Accountant. *Appointments:* Served in New Zealand and overseas, RNZAF, World War II; Elected Labour member of parliament for Riccarton, 1956-69; Represented Wigram, 1969-78, Yaldhurst, 1978-; In Third Labour Government,held following portfolios: Minister of

Works and Development, 1975; Minister of Police, 1972-75; Minister of Customs, 1972-74; Minister of Statistics, 1974-75; Minister in Charge of Erthquake and War Damage Commission, 1975; Associate Minister of Finance, 1972-74; Chairman, National Roads Board, 1975; Chairman, National Water and Soil Conservation Authority, 1975; Former Opposition spokesman on Social Welfare, Foreign Affairs, and Defence; currently Spokesman for Works and Development and for Police; Representative on Labour Party's Policy Council; Led New Zealand delegation to 30 session of ECAFE Conference, Colombo, Sri Lanka, 1974; member of various Parliamentary delegations to many countries. *Memberships:* Patron of numerous Associations including: New Zealand Greyhound Racing Association; New Zealand Antique Arms Association; Canterbury Area, Scout Association of New Zealand; New Zealand Riding for the Disabled Association, Christchurch Group; President, Adult Cerebral Palsy Society; Trustee, Christchurch Racecourse Reserve; Former Chairman, Executive Committee, Canterbury Provincial Buildings Board; Former President and Patron, Ferrymead Museum of Science and Industry. *Address:* Cnr. Yaldhurst and Pound Roads, Christchurch R D 5, New Zealand.

CONOLLY, Richard, b. 22 Dec. 1920, Uralla, N.S.W., Australia. Director and Chairman. m. Norma Marie Humphries, 18 May, 1944, 2 daughters. *Education:* Town Clerks' qualification, 1949; F.T.C.S. Fellow, Town Clerks' Society; F.I.M.A. Fellow, Institute of Municipal Administration; Fellow, Australian Institute of Public Administration; Institute of Administration, University of New South Wales; Management Course, 1962. *Appointments:* Deputy Town Clerk, Municipality of Yass, New South Wales, Australian, 1946-49; Town Clerk, Municipality of Yass, New South Wales, Australian, 1949-58; County Clerk, Burrinjuck County Council H.Q., Yass, New South Wales, Australia, 1954-58; County Clerk, South West Slopes County Council, H.Q. Young, New South Wales, Australia, 1959-65; Town Clerk, Willoughby Municipal Council, Sydney, Australia, 1965-71; Director and Chairman of the New South Wales Metropolitan Waste Disposal Authority, 1971-. *Memberships:* Chairman, Chatswood District Community Hospital; President and Member, Rotary Club of Chatswood, New South Wales; Director, Mercy Family Life Centre, Wahroonga, New South Wales; Vice-President, Gordon District Cricket Club, Chatswood, Australia; Member, Sydney Cricket Ground; Member, Roseville Golf Club, Sydney; Member, Gordon Rugby Club, Australia; Member, Chatswood Bowling Club, Australia. *Publications:* Numerous papers for National and International Conferences on Waste Management including: International Conferences 'Enviroment 1973', 'Enviroment 1975' and 'Enviroment 1978'; Institution of Engineers, Australia, National Conference, 1973, 1975, 1979; Internation Symposium on 'The Ultimate Disposal of Hazardous Wastes', Honolulu, Hawaii, U.S.A., 1979. *Hobbies:* Golf; Tennis; Reading. *Address:* 145 Deepwater Road, Castle Cove, New South Wales, 2069, Australia.

CONSITT, Frederick John Patrick, b. 14 Nov. 1911, Perth, Ontario, Canada, Physicist. m. Mary Holland, 24 Aug. 1943, 5 sons, 4 daughters. *Education:* Senior Matriculation, Perth Collegiate Institute, 1929; B.A., Physics and Geology, University of Toronto, 1933; M.A., Physics, University of Toronto, 1935. *Appointments:* Geophysicist, Hans Lundberg Limited, Toronto, 1936-41; Physicist, Research Enterprises Limited, Toronto, 1941-46; Optical Physicist, Canadian Arsenals Limited, Toronto, 1946-64; Staff Physicist, Ernst Leitz Canada Limited, Midland, 1964-76. *Memberships:* Charter Member, Canadian Association of Physicists; Optical Society of America. *Publications:* Proposed Standard for Measuring and Reporting Physical Properties of Optical Materials, 1965; OTF Techniques in the Routine Testing of Production Lenses, 1971. *Honours:* Teefy Gold Medal, 1933. *Hobbies:* Genealogy Research; Space Developments. *Address:* 333 Scott Street, Midland, Ontario, Canada, L4R 2M9.

CONTI, Mario Joseph, b. 20 March, 1934, Elgin, Scotland. R.C. Bishop of Aberdeen. *Education:* Ph. L. 1955, S.T.L. Gregorian University, Rome, 1959. *Appointments:* Curate, St. Mary's Cathedral, Aberdeen, 1959-62; Parish Priest, St. Joachim's, Wick, and St. Anne's, Thurso, Caithness, 1962-77; Bishop of the Roman Catholic Diocese of Aberdeen, 1977-.

Memberships: President-Treasurer of Scottish Catholic International Aid Fund; Vice-President and Chairman of National Commission for Migrant Workers and Tourists, Scotland; Vice-President and Chairman of Scottish Catholic Heritage Commission; Member, Episcopal Board of Internat Commission for English in the Liturgy; Member, Scottish Religious Advisory Committee (B.B.C.). *Hobbies:* Music; Art; Travel; Book Brousing. *Address:* Bishop's House, 156 King's Gate, Aberdeen AB2 6BR Scotland.

COOGAN, Allan Gordon, b. 23 Nov. 1922, Deniliquin, New South Wales, Australia. Company Chairman and Chief Executive Officer. m. Mary Milne Stephen, 28 Feb. 1956, 2 sons, 1 daughter. *Education:* Bachelor of Engineering, 1945, School of Engineering, St. Paul's College, University of Sydney, Australia, 1943-45. *Appointments:* Deputy General Manager, 1963-65, John Lysaght (Australia) Limited, 1946-65; General Manager, Engineering Division, Mauri Bros. & Thomson Limited, 1965-69; Chairman, Chief Executive Officer, Nabalco Pty. Limited, 1969-; Director of: Perpetual Trustee Co., Sydney, Australia; Swiss Aluminium Australia Limited. *Memberships:* Executive Committee, Australian Mining Industry Council; Australian Manufacturing Council; Science and Industry Forum, Australian Academy of Science; Commonwealth Committee of Inquiry into Technological Change in Australia. *Hobbies:* Golf; Fishing; Skiing. *Address:* 82 Victoria Road, Bellevue Hill, New South Wlaes 2023, Australia.

COOK, Brian Francis, b. 13 Feb. 1933, Bradford, Yorkshire, Museum Keeper. m. Veronica Mary Teresa Dewhirst, 18 Aug. 1962. *Education:* BA., University of Manchester, 1951-54; B.A. 1956, M.A. 1960, Downing College, Cambridge; St. Edmund's House, Cambridge; British School, Athens, 1960. *Appointments:* Curatorial Assistant, 1960-61; Assistant Curator, 1961-65, Associate Curator, 1965-69, Department of Greek Roman Art, The Metropolitan Museum of Art, New York, Assistant Keeper, 1969-76; Keeper of Greek and Roman Antiquities, British Museum, London, 1976-. *Memberships:* Fellow, Society of Antiquaries of London, 1971; Life Member, Society for the Promotion of Hellenic Studies, 1970-73, 1978-81; Challoner Club, London. *Publications:* Inscribed Hadra Vases in The Metropolitan Museum of Art; Greek and Roman Art in The British Museum, 1976; Articles, on Greek, Etruscan and Roman Antiquities in British and Foreign Periodicals. *Honours:* Rogers Scholar, University of Manchester, 1951-54; Dorrington, Kyd, Classical, Conway Prizes, University of Manchester, 1952-54. *Hobbies:* Reading; Gardening. *Address:* 4, Belmont Avenue, Barnet, Herts, England.

COOK, Gordon Charles, b. 17 Feb. 1932, London, England. Academic Medicine (clinical). m. Elizabeth Jane Agg-Large, 8 June 1963, 1 son, 3 daughters. *Education:* Royal Free Hospital School of Medicine, University of London, UK; MB., BS., 1957; MRCS., LRCP., 1957; MRCP., 1960; MD., 1965; DSc., 1976; FRCP., 1972; FRACP., 1978. *Appointments:* Junior Hospital appointments, Royal Free, Brompton, Royal Northern Hospitals, UK, 1958-60; Medical Specialist, Royal Nigerian Army, 1960-62; Lecturer in Medicine, Royal Free Hospital School of Medicine, UK, 1963-65, 1967-69; Lecturer in Medicine, Makerere University, Uganda, 1965-67; Professor of Medicine, University of Zambia, 1969-74; Professor of Medicine, Riyadh University, Saudi Arabia, 1974-76; Senior Lecturer in Clinical Tropical Medicine, London School of Hygiene and Tropical Medicine, UK, 1976-82; Professor of Medicine and Chairman of Clinical Sciences, University of Papua New Guinea, 1978-81. *Memberships:* Royal Society of Medicine; Association of Physicians of Great Britain and Ireland; Royal Society of Tropical Medicine and Hygiene; British Society of Gastroenterology; Medical Research Society; Physiological Society; Nutrition Society; Medical Society of London; Society of Apothecaries of London. *Publications:* Tropical Gastroenterology, 1980; some 120 medical and scientific papers on: gastroenterology; nutrition; tropical medicine and medical education in developing countries. *Honours:* Undergraduate and postgraduate prizes, Royal Free Hospital School of Medicine, 1952-69; Frederick Murgatroyd Memorial prize, Royal College of Physicians of London, 1973. *Hobbies:* Cricket; Walking; Medical history; African and Pacific artefacts. *Address:* 39 Alma Road, St. Albans, Herts. AL1 3AT, England.

COOK, Richard Lawson, b. 5 July 1951, London, England, Doctor of Chiropractic. m. Catherine Mary Jackson, 11 Dec. 1976, 2 sons. *Education:* Doctor of Chiropractic Degree, Anglo; European College of Chiropractic, 1976. *Appointments:* Self Employed Chiropractor, 1976-. *Memberships:* Member, British Chiropractors' Association; Member, American Chiropractors' Association; Editor, Association Magazine 'Contact', 1978-81; Executive Member, Chiropractic Advancement Association, 1977-80; Member, British Rheumatism and Athritis Association 1980-81; Harrow Round Table; Committee Member, Greenford Young Conservatives. *Publications:* Research Project, Spinal Problems in School Children; Thesis, Biomechanics of the Lumbar Intervertebral Disc, 1976. *Hobbies:* Astronomy; Boxing; Cricket; Football; Paleontology; Photography; Tennis; Sports Medicine. *Address:* 82, Lowlands Road, Harrow-on-The-Hill, Middlesex, England.

COOK, Robert Malcolm, b. 12 Nov. 1928, Bluff, New Zealand. Dental, Oral Surgeon. m. Gillian M Ferguson, 15 Mar. 1961, 3 sons, 1 daughter. *Education:* BDSc, 1952; MDSc, 1958; FDSRCS, 1956; FRACDS, 1965; FICD, 1972. *Appointments:* Resident Dental Officer, The Royal Melbourne Hospital, 1953-55; Dental Registrar, North Lancashire England 1956; Hon. Dental Surgeon, Prince Henrys Hospital, Melbourne, 1958-65; Hon. Dental Surgeon, Western General Hospital, Melbourne, 1961-71; Hon. Dental Surgeon, The Royal Melbourne Hospital, 1957-; Private Practice as Specialist Oral Surgeon, 1957-; Consultant Oral Surgeon, The Royal Australian Navy, 1962-; Senior Dental Surgeon, and Oral Surgeon, The Royal Melbourne Hospital, 1971-. *Memberships:* State President, Victoria, 1964, Fed. Council, 1966-70, Australian Dental Association; Secretary, 1964-67, President, 1978-81, Australian and New Zealand Society Oral Surgeons; Naval and Military Club; Metropolitan Golf Club. *Publications:* 21 Scientific Publications. *Honours:* John Iliffe Scholarship, 1952, Francis Gray Prize, 1952, Melbourne University. *Hobbies:* Tennis; Golf; Sking; Sailing; Farming, Simmental Beef Cattle. *Address:* 18 Robinson Road, Hawthorn, Victoria 3122, Australia.

COOK, William Richard Joseph, b. 10 Apr. 1905, Trowbridge, England. Consultant. m. G Allen 10 June 1939, 1 son, 2 daughters. *Education:* Trowbridge High School, 1922; BSc, Bristol University 1922-26. *Appointments:* Ballistics Research and Rocket Development, 1928-47; Director of Physical Research, Admiralty, 1947-50; Chief of Royal Naval Scientific Service, 1950-54; Deputy Director Atomic Weapons Research Establishment, 1954-58; Member for Reactors, Atomic Energy Authority, 1958-64; Deputy Chief Scientific Adviser, Ministry of Defence, 1964-67; Chief Adviser, Projects and Research, 1967-70; Director Rolls-Royce Limited, 1970-75; Director, GEC-Marconi Electronics, 1971-76; Director, Buck and Hickman Limited, 1970-. *Memberships:* Fellow, Royal Society; Fellow, Institute Physics; Athanaeum Club. *Honours:* CB, 1951; Kt, 1958; KCB, 1970; Hon.DSc, Strathclyde, 1967; Hon.DSc, Bath, 1975. *Address:* Adbury Springs, Newbury, Berkshire, RG15 8EX, England.

COOKE, Robin Brunskill, b. 9 May 1926, Wellington, New Zealand. Judge of Court of Appeal. m. Annette Miller, 1952, 3 sons. *Education:* LLM, Victoria University College; MA, PhD, Cambridge University. *Appointments:* Fellow, Gonville and Caius College, Cambridge; Barrister, New Zealand, QC, 1964; Judge of Supreme Court, 1972. *Honours:* Member of Privy Council, 1977; Knight Bachelor, 1977. *Address:* 4 Homewood Crescent, Wellington, New Zealand.

COOMBES, Anthony Henry George Richard, b. 11 June 1940, Curepipe, Mauritius. Professional Engineer. m. Marie Laurence De Foiard Brown, 20 Apr. 1967, 3 sons. *Education:* Imperial College of Sciences and Technology; ACGI, BSc Eng. Hons, CEng, MRINA, University of London. *Appointments:* Mechanical Engineer, Hall Geneve Langlois and Company Limited, 1964-66; Technical Manager, 1966-68, Managing Director, 1968-81, Director and Chief Executive, 1981, Taylor Smith and Company Limited. *Memberships:* Grand Bay Yacht Club; Grand Sable Club; Dodo Club; Club Hippique De Maurice. *Hobbies:* Chess; Reading; Water Skiing; Squash; Wind Surfing. *Address:* Avenue John Kennedy, Floreal, Mauritius.

COOPER, Ian Allan, b. 26 Sept. 1930, Sydney, New South Wales, Australia. Medical Practitioner. m. Mary Louise Rother, 1 son, 1 daughter. *Education:* MB, BS.1957; MRACP, 1962; FRACP, 1972; FRCPA, 1973. *Appointments:* Royal Prince Alfred Hospital, Sydney-J.R.M.O. 1957, S.R.M.O. 1958, Registrar, 1959-62; Clinical Superintendent, Research Fellow-Clinical Research Unit, Post-Graduate Committee in Medicine, University of Sydney, 1962-64; Fellow in Dept. of Medicine, Washington University, School of Medicine, St. Louis, Missouri, USA. 1964-66; Johnson & Johnson, Research Fellow, Clinical Research Unit, Royal Prince Alfred Hospital, Sydney, 1967; Clinical & Consultant Haematologist. Head Haemotology Research Unit, Cancer Institute, Melbourne, 1968. *Memberships:* Haematology Society of Australia — President, 1979-81, Councillor, 1980. International Society of Haematology; Australian Society of Medical Research; Victorian Society of Pathology and Experimental Medicine; Australian Society of Blood Transfusion; Royal Agricultural Society. *Publications:* 31 published Abstracts of Presentations to Major Scientific Meetings, including: Management of Myeloma, 1977; The Classification of Acute Leukaemia, 1979; Effects of Colchicine and Vincristin on Polymorphonuclear Leucocyte Function in Vitro. Contributor to 31 Medical papers including: Non-Hodgkin's lymphoma — current concepts, 1979; A Comparison of the use of Teniposide and Vincristine in Combination Chemotherapy for Non-Hodgkin's Lymphoma. *Hobbies:* Music; Choral Singing; Gardening. *Address:* 11 Widford Street, East Hawthorn, 3123 Australia.

COOPER, John Henry, b. 20 Sept. 1926, Rolleston, Nr. Burton-on Trent, Staffs. Chartered Engineer. m. 9 Feb. 1952, 1 son. *Education:* College of Technology, Burton Upon Trent; ONC, HNC, Mechanical Engineering with endorsements; Chartered Engineer. *Appointments:* Royal Navy, 1943-47; Joined The Clayton Equipment Company Limited as Trainee Draughtsman, 1951; Appointed Assistant General Manager, 1956; Appointed Director and General Manager, 1960; Part-time lecturer, Burton-on-Trent Technical College, 1957-60; Member, Engineering Advisory Committee, Burton-on-Trent, Technical College, 1964-65; Manager, Associated Electrical Industries, 1965-68; Founder, J H Cooper (Copying) Company Limited, 1968; Managing Director, David Whitehead Limited, 1971; Director, Hawker Siddeley Group, 1973; Director, General Manager, Walkers Rotary (Holdings) Limited, 1975; Founder, Cooper Electro Mechanical Limited, 1976; Chairman, Managing Director, Electrical Power Engineering Co. Ltd., J H Cooper Co. Ltd., David Whitehead Ltd., Cooper Electro Mech. Ltd., Richard Ashton & Co. Ltd., 1979-. *Honours:* Chartered Engineer; F.I. Mech. E.; F.I. Prod. E.; F. I I. M. (Industrial Managers). *Hobbies:* Tennis; Badminton; Swimming; Golf. *Address:* 15 Raad Ny Gabbil, Ballalough, Castletown, Isle of Man.

COOPER, Nigel Cookson, b. 7 May 1929, Leeds, England. Educational Administrator. m. June Elizabeth Smith, 18 Dec. 1972,2 sons, 1 daughter. *Education:* Teachers Certificate, Leeds Training College, 1946-48; Dip. Carnegie College of Physical Education, 1953-54; MA, in Education, State University of Iowa, USA, 1957-58; Bachelor of Law Degree (Hons), Leeds University, 1968-70. *Appointments:* Primary School Teacher, 1950-53; Head of Dept. Secondary Modern School, 1954-59; Lecturer in Education at Trent Training College, London, 1959-61; Lecturer in Education at Loughborough Training College, 1961-64; Supervisor, Schools for Nova Scotia, Canada, 1964-65; County Organiser of Schools for Norfolk, 1965-68; Assistant Education Officer for Oldham, 1970-72; Assistant Director, Education for British Families Education Service in Europe, 1972-78; Registrar, Kelvin Grove College Advanced Education, 1978-. *Memberships:* British Institute of Management; National Vice-President, Australian Institute of Educational Adminstrators; President, Taylor Range Squash Club, Brisbane; Secretary/Treasurer, Australian Flying Arts School. *Publications:* 18 articles in educational journals in Britain, Canada and Australia. *Honours:* Fulbright Travel Scholarship to USA. *Hobbies:* Trumpet Playing; Squash; Music. *Address:* 8 Barrabooka Drive, The Gap, Brisbane 4061, Queensland, Australia.

COOPER, Paul Kendall, b. 29 April 1948, Melbourne, Australia. Lawyer. *Education:* Melbourne Grammar School; Bachelor of Law, Trinity College, University of Melbourne, 1974; Barrister, Solicitor, Supreme Court of Victoria and the High Court of Australia, 1975. *Appointments:* Solicitor in private practice, 1975-; Director of Continuing Legal Education, Leo Cussen Institute of Continuing Legal Education, 1980-. *Memberships:* Melbourne Cricket Club; Royal Automobile Club of Victoria. *Hobbies:* Dillentantism; Gardening. *Address:* Little Broomfield, 93 & 95A Simpson Street, East Melbourne, 3002 Victoria, Australia.

COOPER, Roy Charles, b. 7 May 1915, Bexley, New South Wales. Company Director. m. Elizabeth Mary Dalrymple Hay, 19 July 1947, 2 sons, 1 daughter. *Education:* Leaving Certificate, Fort St Boys High School, New South Wales, 1931. *Appointments:* Commonwealth Bank of Australia, 1931-60; Reserve Bank of Australia 1960-79; Manager for Queensland, (Retired), 1979; Director, Metropolitan Permanent Building Society, Queensland 1979-. *Memberships:* Senate University of Queensland; Arts Council of Queensland; Arts Council of Australia; Lyric Opera of Queensland; Queensland Art Gallery Foundation; Migrant Settlement Council for Queensland; Queensland Club; United Service Club; Legacy Club of Brisbane. *Honours:* Fellow, Australian Institute of Management 1977; Commander, Order of British Empire, 1979. *Hobbies:* Bowls; Reading; Theatre. *Address:* 109 Hawken Drive, St Lucia, Queensland 4067, Australia.

COOPER, Whina,b. 9 Dec. 1895, Panguru, Hokianga, New Zealand. Domestic. m. William Cooper (deceased), 21 Feb. 1941, 2 sons, 2 daughters. *Education:* Secondary Education (Proficiency Certificate). *Appointments:* School Teacher, 1915-17; General Shopkeeper, 18 years (late 20's). *Memberships:* Played active part in Maori Land Development in the North Hokianga District, 1938; 1st Woman President in Southern Hemisphere of a Rugby Football Union, 1947; 1st Domonion President of the Maori Womens Welfare League, 1952; 1st Woman President of Panguru Federated Farmers, 1940; Established Te Unga Waka Marae Auckland, 1966. *Publications:* Maori Arts & Crafts; Tukutuku Weaving, (for Te Unga Waka Marae); Maori Cloak Making — Korowai (Modern) and Maori Kit Making. *Honours:* MBE, 1953; CBE, 1974; JP, 1953; DBE, 1981. *Hobbies:* Hockey; Basketball; Table Tennis. *Address:* 4 McCulloch Road, Panmure, Auckland, New Zealand.

COPEMAN, Herbert Arthur, b. 24 Sept. 1923, Brisbane, Queensland, Australia. Medicine; Medical Education. m. Margaret Jean Hill, 29 Nov. 1947, 3 sons, 1 daughter. *Education:* Toowoomba Grammar School, Queensland, 1937-41; Service with RAF, 1942-45; University of Queensland, 1946-51; MB, BS, 1951; Royal Australasian College of Physicians, Member 1957, Fellow 1969. *Appointments:* Royal Brisbane Hospital, 1952-54; University of Queensland, 1955-56; Physician, Part-time Lecturer, Research Fellow, University of Queensland, Royal Brisbane Hospital, 1957-74; Coordinator Postgraduate Studies, University of Western Australia, Royal Perth Hospital; Consultant Physician, University Department of Medicine, Royal Perth Hospital, 1975-. *Memberships:* President, Queensland Marriage Guidance Council, 1966-71; Vice-President, National Marriage Guidance Council of Australia, 1969-71; Deputy Chairman of the Postgraduate Medical Education Committee of the University of Queensland, 1970-74; Vice-President of the Australian Postgraduate Federation in Medicine, 1979-; Chairman of the Western Australian State Committee of the Royal Australasian College of Physicians, 1978-80; Member Queensland Club; Royal Society of Medicine; Endocrine Society of Australia; Australian Diabetes Association. *Publications:* Nine original papers including: The Role of Coordinator of Postgraduate Studies, 1976; Private Practice 1977: A Myth or A Must, 1977. Six Abstracts including: Was Henry Leighton Jones Australia's First Transplant Surgeon?, 1976; Toxaemia of Pregnancy as an Aetiological Factor in Obesity, a Prospective Study, 1978; Hormonal Influences in the Prevention and Regression of Atheroma, 1981, invitation to address the XIth Triennial Congress of the World Association of Societies of Pathologies, Jerusalem, 1981, paper to be published as chapter in a book, Healing and Scarring of Atheroma, 1982. *Hobbies:* Bush Walking; Fishing; Sailing; Gardening. *Address:* 46 Irvine Street, Peppermint Grove, Western Australia 6011.

COPLAND, Bruce McKenzie, b. 7 Oct. 1950, Kilwinning, Scotland. Hotel Manager. m. Frances Ann Scott,

16 Oct. 1971. *Education:* BA, Hotel and Catering Management, Strathclyde University 1971; Hotel Catering and Institutional Management Association, 1973. *Appointments:* Treasurer Princess Hotels Bermuda, 1971-74; General Manager, Royal Palms Hotel, 1974-76; Vice President, Cayman Isles Limited, 1977-. *Memberships:* Rotary Club of Grand Cayman; President, Cayman Islands Hotel Association, 1981-82; Cayman Islands Divers; Diving Officer, 1981; Professional Association of Diving Instructors; National Association of Underwater Instructors; British Sub Aqua Club; Royal Yachting Association. *Hobbies:* Diving; Sailing. *Address:* Tradewinds, West Bay, Grand Cayman, British West Indies.

CORBAN Alexander Annis, b. 17 Mar. 1925, Auckland, New Zealand. Oenologist. m. Muriel Gwen Jerram, 2 sons, 2 daughters. *Education:* Henderson Primary School; Mt. Albert Grammar School; Auckland, University College, B.Sc., 1949; Roseworthy, Agricultural College (Sth. Australia), R.D. Oen 1948. *Appointments:* Employed Corbans Wines Ltd., Winemaker, 1949-76; Winery Manager, 1950-76; Production Manager, 1952-76; Research & Product Development Manager, 1976-79; Commercial Relations Manager, 1979-. *Memberships:* Trustee, Western Districts Foundation; Patron, Henderson Squash Rackets Association; Founder member & Past President Wine & Food Society of Auckland; American Society of Enologists; Life Member, Auckland University Field Club. *Publications:* Wine Industry Study and Development Plan (1978) for the Wine Institute of New Zealand; Contributor to International Publications on Winemaking (Australian) and Viticulture (Italian). *Honours:* O.B.E. 1978; Memorial Medal for International Co-operation (German Agricultural Society), 1981. *Hobbies:* Photography; Travel; The Arts; Reading. *Address:* 21 Lincoln Road, Henderson, Auckland 8, New Zealand.

CORDINGLEY, John Edward, b. 1 Sept. 1916 Blandford, Dorset, England. Regular Army Officer. m. (1) Ruth Pamela Boddam Whetham, 2 sons, 2 daughters, (2) Audrey Helen Anne Beaumont-Nesbitt. *Education:* Sherborne School 1930-34; Royal Military Academy Woolwich 1935-36. 2nd Lieutenant Royal Artillery 1936; War, Europe and India 1939-45; Brigade Commander, 1961-62; Imperial Defence College, 1963; Director of Work Study, Ministry of Defence, Army 1964-66; Deputy Director, RA 1967-68; Major-General, RA, BAOR, 1968-71, retired; Colonel Commandant, RA 1973-; Bursar, Sherborne School, 1971-74; Controller, RA Institution, 1975-; Chairman, Board of Management, Royal Artillery Charitable Fund, 1977-. *Memberships:* Fellow, Institute of Work Study Practitioner, 1965; British Institute of Management; Army and Navy Club; Senior Golfers Society. *Honours:* OBE 1959. *Hobbies:* Golf; Gardening. *Address:* Church Farm House, Rotherwick, Nr. Basingstoke, Hants.

CORDNER, John Pruen, b. 20 Mar. 1929 Melbourne Australia. Company Director. m. Gwendolyn Aldyta Reed 23 June 1952, 2 sons, 2 daughters. *Education:* BSc Melbourne 1950; MSc, 1952; Fulbright Scholar 1956; FSSP Mit USA. *Appointments:* Research Chemist Docker Brothers UK 1952-54, Taubmens, Australia 1954-55; Work Study Officer, 1955-58; Production Superintendant, 1958-61; Works Manager, 1961-63; Product Manager, 1963-66; Division Manager, ICI, 1966-69; Marketing Manager, Australian Fertilizers Ltd., 1970-72; Managing Director Laporte 1972-80; Chairman, 1980-. *Memberships:* Australian Chemical Industrial Council; Royal Australian Chemical Institute; Killara Golf Club; Royal Sydney Yacht Squadron, Melbourne Cricket Club. *Publications:* Papers in journal Chemical society; Journal American Chemical Society. *Hobbies:* Cricket; Reading; Tennis; Golf. *Address:* 18 Nicholson Avenue, St Ives 2075, New South Wales, Australia.

CORMACK, Patrick Thomas, b. 18 May 1939, Grimsby, United Kingdom. Member of Parliament. m. Mary McDonald, 18 Aug. 1967, 2 sons. *Education:* Havelock School, Grimsby, 1951-57; BA(Hons), University of Hull, 1958-61. *Appointments:* Schoolmaster, 1961-70; Member of Parliament, 1970-. *Memberships:* Fellow of Society of Antiquaries; Historic Buildings Council; Liveryman of Worshipful Company of Glaziers; Athenaeum; Brooks's; Member, Royal Commission on Historical Manuscripts. *Publications:* Heritage in Danger, 1976; Right Turn, 1978; Westminster: Palace and Parliament, 1981. *Hobbies:* Fighting Philistines; Visiting Old Churches. *Address:* House of Commons, London SW1, England.

CORNER, Frank Henry, b. 17 May 1920 Napier, New Zealand. Civil Servant and Diplomat. m. Lynette Robinson 27 Nov. 1943, 2 daughters. *Education:* MA(First, History), Victoria University of Wellington. *Appointments:* Ministry of Foreign Affairs and War Cabinet Secretariat 1943; First Secretary, NZ Embassy, Washington 1948-51; Senior Counsellor, NZ High Commission, London 1952-58; Deputy Secretary of Foreign Affairs, Wellington 1958-62; Permanent Rep (Ambassador) to UN 1962-67; Ambassador to US 1967-72; Permanent Head, Prime Ministers Department 1973-75; Secretary of Foreign Affairs 1973-80; Administrator of Tokelan 1976-. *Honours:* CMG 1980. *Hobbies:* Gardening; Walking; Music and the Arts; Wine. *Address:* 26 Burnell Avenue, Wellington 1, New Zealand.

CORNISH, Augustus Morris, b. 21 Sept. 1928 Launceston, Tasmania, Australia. Public Servant. m. Margaret Patricia Furness 15 Aug. 1953, 1 son 1 daughter. *Education:* Launceston Technical College; FASA; FCIS; MAIES. *Appointments:* Social Service Department Tasmania 1943; Audit Department 1950; Public Service Inspector 1967; Secretary Acctt. Metro. Water Board. 1969; Deputy Under Secretary, Premier's Department 1973; Commsnr. Public Service Board 1977-; Chairman Public Service Board of Tasmania 1980-. *Address:* 25 Berega Street, Howrah, Tasmania, 7018 Australia.

CORNISH, Hugh (Hubert) Kestell, b. 6 Feb. 1934, Killarney, Queensland. Chemist. m. Joyce Mears, 25 Sept. 1958, 2 sons, 2 daughters. *Education:* Studied Dip. of Industrial Chemistry, 1952-54; AMusA, 1951; ATCL (Speech), 1953. *Appointments:* Industrial Chemist, Colonial Sugar Refining Company, 1952-54; Radio Announcer 41P Ipswich, 1954; Radio Announcer, 4BH Brisbane, 1955-59; Television Announcer, QTQ Channel 9, Brisbane, 1959; Programme Manager, QTQ9, 1967; Assistant General Manager, 1970; General Manager, 1981. *Memberships:* Royal Commonwealth Society, Queensland; Deputy Chairman, Council of the Conservatorium of Queensaland. *Creative Works:* Three long-playing record albums: A Twentieth Anniversary Collection; Piano Portraits (Gold Record); Keyboard Cocktails, to be released. *Hobby:* Playing Piano. *Address:* 25 Comus Avenue, Albion Heights, Brisbane 4010, Australia.

CORRIE, John Alexander, b. 29 July 1935, Kirkcudbright, Scotland. Member of Parliament; Farmer. m. Jean Sandra Hardie, 25 Aug. 1965, 1 son, 2 daughters. *Education:* George Watson's College, Scotland; Lincoln Agricultural College, New Zealand. *Appointments:* Lecturer, Agricultural Training Board, 1970-74; Lecturer, British Wool Marketing Board, 1970-74; Elected Member of Parliament, 1974; Served in European Parliament, 1975-76, 1977-79; Scottish Whip, 1976-77; PPS., Secretary of State for Scotland, 1979-81; Chairman, Back Bench Conservative Members, 1981; Elected Member, Scottish Committee on Select Affairs, 1981. *Memberships:* Vice President, Apprentice Committee, 1972, 1973, National Farmers Union; Rotary District Convener, Community Service, 1973-74. *Publications:* Towards a Community Rural Policy; Towards a Community Fisheries Policy; Forestry in Europe; Fish Farming in Europe; The Importance of Forestry in the Next Century; Island Problems—Some Answers. *Honours:* Nuffield Scholar in Agriculture, 1972-73. *Hobbies:* Shooting; Tennis; Water skiing; Hanggliding; Motor racing; Curling; Fly fishing; Riding. *Address:* Carlung Farm, West Kilbride, Ayrshire, Scotland.

CORRIGAN, M. Dorothy, (Mrs), b. 26 July 1913, Charlottetown, Prince Edward Island, Canada. Registered Nurse. m. 21 June 1944, 1 son, 1 daughter. *Education:* School of Nursing. *Appointments:* Registered Nurse; Alderman, Elected to City Council; Deputy Mayor, Mayor, City of Charlottetown, Prince Edward Island. *Memberships:* President, Chamber of Commerce (Board of Trade); Zonta International Women's Service Club. *Honours:* Hon. Degree DDL University of Prince Edward Island; Order of Canada. *Hobbies:* Swimming; Skating; Tennis; Knitting. *Address:* 228 Grafton Street, Charlottetown, Prince Edward Island, Canada.

CORRIN, John William, b. 6 Jan. 1932, Isle of Man. HM Second Deemster. m. Dorothy Patricia Lace, 30 Sept. 1961, 1 daughter. *Education:* King William's College, Isle of Man. *Appointments:* Admitted Manx Bar, 1954; Partner, Dickinson, Cruickshank & Co; Advocates, Isle of Man, 1959-74; HM Attorney General, Isle of Man, 1974-80; HM Second Deemster, Isle of Man, 1980-. *Memberships:* Criminal Injuries Compensation Tribunal; Licensing Appeal Court; Prevention of Fraud Tribunal; Wireless Telegraphy Appeal Board; Manx Blind Welfare Society. *Honours:* George Johnson Law Prize. *Hobbies:* Music; Gardening; Bridge. *Address:* Carla Beck, 28 Devonshire Road, Douglas, Isle of Man.

CORTAZZI, Henry Arthur Hugh, (Sir), b. 2 May 1924, Sedbergh, Yorkshire, England. Diplomat. m. Elizabeth Esther Montagu, 3 Apr. 1956, 1 son, 2 daughters. *Education:* MA, St. Andrews University 1944; BA, London University, 1949. *Appointments:* Diplomatic Service, Foreign Office, 1949; Third Secretary Singapore, 1950; Third later Second Secretary Tokyo, 1951; Foreign Office, 1954; First Secretary Bonn, 1958; Tokyo, 1961, (Head of Chancery, 1963); First Secretary, Notional Counsellor, Foreign Office, 1965; Counsellor (Commercial) Tokyo, 1966; Royal College of Defence Studies 1971; Minister (Commercial) Washington 1972; Deputy Under-Secretary of State FCO 1975; British Ambassador to Japan 1980-. *Memberships:* Army & Navy Club. *Publications:* Translation of Japanese Short stories, 1972. *Honours:* C.M.G., 1969; K.C.M.G., 1980. *Address:* British Embassy, Tokyo, Japan.

COSIER, Gary John, b. 25 Apr. 1953 Richmond Victoria. Sales Executive. m. 19 May 1978. *Education:* Leaving Standard, University High School, Melbourne. *Appointments:* SPEEDO, Australian Knitting Mills, 1971-76; 5AA, South Australia Radio Station 1976-77; 4IP, Queensland Radio Station 1977-79; TNT, Thomas Nation Wide Transport Melbourne 1979-. *Publications:* Poetry, Music; Guitar. *Honours:* Junior Cricketer of Year 1969; Junior Australia Cricket Captain 1970; Captained Queensland and South Australia Sheffield Shield Teams; Represented Australia in 19 tests; Test Debut Century Vice Captain Australia 1978-79; One of 3 players to represent more than 2 states in Sheffield Shield Competition. *Hobbies:* Cricket; Tennis; Golf; Squash; Music; Fishing; Horse Riding. *Address:* 136 Mullum Mullum Road, Ringwood, Melbourne, Victoria, Australia.

COSTER, Douglas John, b. 23 Apr. 1946, Melbourne, Australia. Ophthalmic Surgeon. m. Marion MacLennan Roberts, 8 Dec. 1973, 2 sons. *Education:* M.B.B.S., Melbourne, 1969; F.R.A.C.S., 1975; F.R.C.S., 1978; F.R.A.C.O., 1980. *Appointments:* Registrar (Ophthalmology), Royal Melbourne Hospital, 1969-72, Royal Victorian Eye and Ear Hospital, 1973, Moorfields Eye Hospital, London, 1974-78; Consultant Ophthalmologist, Moorfields Eye Hospital, London, 1979; Lions Professor of Ophthalmology, Flinders University of South Australia, 1980. *Memberships:* Fellow, Royal Australasian College of Surgeons, Royal College of Surgeons of England, Royal Australian College of Ophthalmology. *Publications:* Various scientific publications. *Honours:* Hunterian Professor, Royal College of Surgeons, 1980. *Address:* 2 Dalaston Avenue, Glenunga, South Australia.

COSTER, Hans Gerard Leonard, b. 11 Mar. 1939, Djakarta, Indonesia. University Professor. m. Marjorie Tillie Eakin, 4 Jan. 1964, 1 son, 1 daughter. *Education:* University of Sydney, Major in Physics and Mathematics B.Sc, 1962, Biophysics, M.Sc., 1964, Ph.D., 1966. *Appointments:* Experimental Officer, Commonwealth Scientific & Industrial Research Organisation, Division of Applied Physics, 1962-63; Experimental Officer, C.S.I.R.O. Plant Physiology Unit, 1963-64; Senior Tutor School of Physics, University of N.S.W., 1965-67; Lecturer, School of Physics, University of N.S.W., 1967-70; Senior Lecturer, School of Physics, University of N.S.W., 1970-74; Visiting Professor, Institute of Physical Chemistry, Nuclear Research Center, Julich, West Germany, 1974-75; Associate Professor Physics, University of N.S.W., 1976-. *Memberships:* Bioelectrochemical Society; Institute of Physics, London; Australian Institute of Physics; Australian Society for Biophysics, Secretary, 1975-78, President Elect. 1981; Biophysics Group A.I.P., Chairman, 1973; Aus-

tralian Society of Plant Physiologists. *Publications:* Thermodynamics of Life Processes, 1981; 80 Research Publications in International Scientific Journals; Two Patents in Biomedical field. *Honours:* Editorial Board, Bioelectrochemistry and Bioenergetics, Elsevier-Sequoia, Switzerland. *Hobbies:* Microcomputers; Electronics. *Address:* 34 Cook Street, Randwick, N.S.W., 2031, Australia.

COTTER, Arthur John Sandford, b. 28 Mar. 1908, Sydney, N.S.W., Australia. Chartered Accountant. m. Katherine Jordan Wells, 27 Aug. 1942, 1 daughter. *Education:* F.C.A., Institute of Chartered Accountant, Australia, 1937. *Appointments:* Chartered Accountant and partner, Messrs. Priestley & Morris, 1946-63; Own Practice as Accountant and Company Director. *Memberships:* Union Club, Sydney; Melbourne Club; White's, London; Imperial Service Club, Sydney; The Royal Sydney Golf Club; The Australian Jockey Club; United Service Institution of N.S.W: M.C.C. *Honours:* P.S.C., 1944; Effieiency Decoration, 1951; O.B.E., 1968. *Hobbies:* Cricket; Swimming; Racing. *Address:* 19 Bathurst Street, Woollabra, N.S.W. Australia, 2035.

COTTERILL, Benedict Gordon Ross, b. 26 Mar. 1918, Wareham, Dorset, England. m Violet Lorraine Clark, 12 Jan. 1946, 2 sons. Assistant Export Manager, Page-Hersey Tubes Ltd., 1938-43; Assistant Export Manager, 1945-46; Export Manager and Secretary, Sino-Canadian Development Co., 1946; Officer, Sinocan Forwarders Ltd., Manager and Secretary - Treasurer, Roy Peers Co. Ltd., 1946-52; Salesman, St. Regis Paper Co. (Canada) Ltd., 1952; Western Sales Manager, 1953, Ontario District Sales Manager, 1957, General Sales Manager, 1962, Director of Marketing, 1967, Vice President and General Manager, 1968, Consolidated Bathurst Packaging Ltd., Bag Division. *Memberships:* Mississaugua Golf & Country Club, Ontario; Capilano Golf & Country Club, British Columbia; Royal Montreal Golf Club, Montreal; Lambton Golf & Country Club, Toronto; Saint James's Club, Montreal; Empire Club of Toronto, Ontario. *Hobbies:* Golf; Fishing; Gardening; Travel. *Address:* 140 Wilder Drive, Oakville, Ontario, L6L 5G3, England.

COTTON, Richard Graham Hay, b. 10 Nov. 1940, Wangaratta, Victoria, Australia. Research Scientist. m. Elizabeth Smibert, 2 sons, 1 daughter. *Education:* B.Agr.Sci., 1959-62, PhD., 1963-66, University of Melbourne. *Appointments:* Research Fellow, John Curtin School of Medical Research, Australian National University, Canberra, 1967; Senior Research Fellow, Genetics Department, University of Melbourne, 1968-70, 1973-75, Genetics Research Unit, Royal Children's Hospital Research Foundation, 1968-70, 1973-81; Post Doctoral Fellow, Scripps Clinic, La Jolla, California, 1971, MRC Laboratory of Molecular Biology, Cambridge, UK, 1971-73; Foundation Deputy Director, Birth Defects Research Institute, Royal Children's Hospital Research Foundation, 1981-. *Memberships:* Australian Club; Australian Biochemical Society; Australian Paediatric Research Society; Human Genetics Society of Australia. *Publications:* Numerous publications in bacterial and human biochemical genetics particularly in the area of inborn errors of metabolism in man. Immediate practical and theoretical foundation for the monoclonal antibody technique while in Cambridge. *Honours:* Fulbright Travelling Fellowship, 1971; EMBO Award, 1972-73; Queen Elizabeth Fellowship, 1974-75. *Hobbies:* Classical Music; Travel; Horology; Wine; Current Affairs. *Address:* 25 Avenue Athol, Canterbury, 3126, Victoria, Australia.

COTTON-STAPLETON, Larry Henry Charles, b. 24 June, 1915, Napier, New Zealand. Property Valuer and Agent. m. Constance Alison Reid, 4 Oct. 1942, 1 son. *Education:* Foreign-Going Masters Certificate, 1942; Qualified Valuer, 1961. *Appointments:* Merchant Service, 1933-48; Own business as Land Agent and Valuer, 1948-; Foundation Director, Dandenong Westernport PB Society, 1970-. *Memberships:* Melbourne Club; President, Dandenong Club. *Honours:* Justice of Peace, 1962. *Hobby:* Chess. *Address:* Sevenoaks, Pakenham 3810, Victoria, Australia.

COTTRELL, Alan Hoard, (Sir), b. 17 July 1919, Birmingham, England. Scientist and Master of Jesus College, Cambridge. m. Jean Elizabeth Harber, 1944, 1 son. *Education:* BSc. 1939, PhD, 1942, University of Birmingham, UK; ScD., University of Cambridge, UK,

1976. *Appointments:* Lecturer in Metallurgy, 1943-49, Professor of Physical Metallurgy, 1949-55, University of Birmingham, UK; Deputy Head of Metallurgy Division, Atomic Energy Research Establishment, Harwelll, Berkshire, UK, 1955-58; Goldsmiths' Professor of Metallurgy, Cambridge University, UK, 1958-65; Deputy Chief Scientific Adviser (Studies), 1965-67, Chief Adviser, 1967, Ministry of Defence; Deputy Chief Scientific Adviser, 1968-71, Chief Scientific Adviser, 1971-74, HM. Government; Part-time Member, UKAEA, 1962-65; Member Advisory Council on Scientific Policy, 1963-64; Central Advisory Council for Science and Technology, 1967-; Executive Committee, British Council, 1974-; Advisory Council, Science Policy Foundation, 1976-; Security Commission, 1981. *Memberships:* Member of numerous Associations including: Fellow Royal Swedish Academy of Sciences; Hon. Fellow, Christ's College, Cambridge, 1970; Hon. Member., American Society for Metals 1972; Hon. Member, The Metals Society 1977; Fellow of The Fellowship of Engineering 1979. *Publications:* Theoretical Structural Metallurgy, 1948, 2nd ed. 1955; Dislocations and Plastic Flow in Crystals, 1953; The Mechanical Properties of Matter, 1964; Theory of Crystal Dislocations, 1964; AN Introduction to Metallurgy, 1967; Portrait of Nature, 1975; Environmental Economics, 1978; How Safe is Nuclear Energy?, 1981. Scientific papers to various learned journals. *Honours:* Knighted 1971; FRS, 1955; numerous other awards including: Hughes Medallist, Royal Society, 1961; James Alfred Ewing Medal, ICE, 1967; Albert Sauveur Achievement Award, American Society for Metals, 1969; The Rumford Medal of the Royal Society, 1974. *Hobbies:* Music. *Address:* The Master's Lodge, Jesus College, Cambridge, England.

COTTRELL, Peter John Waraker, b. 25 May 1928, Warwick, Queensland, Australia. Company Director. m. Barbara Jean Wheeler, 9 Aug. 1952, 2 sons, 2 daughters. *Education:* Bachelor of Mechanical & Electrical Engineering, 1951, Master of Engineering, 1956, University of Sydney; Post Graduate Diploma in Management, University of Birmingham, 1953. *Appointments:* Engineer to Assistant Manager, 1951-59, First Director Management Services, 1959, Department of Supply; Manufacturing Manager, 1960, Manager, 1962, General Manager, 1967, Group General Manager, 1971, Managing Director, 1974-, Email Limited. *Memberships:* Australian President, Institution of Production Engineers, 1979 & 1980; Australian Trade Development Council, 1974-80; NSW, Chairman, Export Now Campaign, 1979-81; Development Corporation of NSW, 1975-81; Chairman, First Regional College of Advanced Education to be established in NSW, 1967-70. *Publications:* Articles in various technical and management journals. *Honours:* Charles Kolling Graduation Prize, First Class Honours and University Medal, 1951; Silver Jubilee Medal, 1977; OBE, 1978. *Hobbies:* Golf; Family interests. *Address:* 35 Saiala Road, Killara, NSW, 2071, Australia.

COULSON, (Sir) John Eltringham, b. 13 Sept. 1909, Gosforth, England. Diplomat. m. 15 Apr. 1944, 2 sons. *Education:* MA, Corpus Christi College, Cambridge, 1928-31. *Appointments:* Joined Diplomatic Service, 1932; Various Posts at home and abroad including: Minister in UK Delegation to United Nations, New York, 1950-52; Minister, British Embassy, Washington, 1955-57; Ambassador to Sweden, 1960-63; Secretary General of European Free Trade Association, 1965-72. *Honours:* KCMG, 1957. *Address:* The Old Mill, Selborne, Alton, Hampshire, England.

COUPER-SMARTT, John David, b. 24 Dec. 1944, Northallerton, Yorkshire, England. Child and Family Psychiatrist. m. Islay Joy Kennedy, 22 Dec. 1979, 1 son, 2 daughters. *Education:* MB.Ch.B, 1969, DPM, 1972, University of Liverpool, MRC.Psych, 1974; MRANZCP, 1980. *Appointments:* House Physician, Sefton General Hospital, Liverpool, 1969; House Surgeon, Maelor General Hospital, North Wales, 1970; Registrar, North Wales Hospital for Nervous & Mental Disorders, 1970; Registrar in Psychiatry, Liverpool Psychiatric Day Hospital and Sefton General Hospital, Liverpool, 1972; Senior Registrar, Child & Family Psychiatry Clinic, Cambridge, 1973; Lecturer & Consultant Psychiatrist, University of Otago, Dunedin, New Zealand, 1974; Senior Psychiatrist, Mitchell House Clinic, Adelaide, South Australia, 1978; Current Positions: Consultant Psychiatrist in Private Practice; Visiting Psychiatrist,

Modbury Hospital, South Australia; Clinical Lecturer, University of Adelaide, South Australia. *Memberships:* Chairman, Northern Suburbs Family Services Board, Adelaide, South Australia; Secretary, Gawler and Districts Medical Practitioners Association; Committee Member, Family Therapy Association of South Australia. *Publications:* Publications in Scientific Journals on the subjects of obesity, psychiatric medication, pregnancy and psychological problems of childhood. *Hobbies:* Sailing; Reading. *Address:* 15 Blanche Street, Gawler East, South Australia.

COURT, Charles Walter Michael, (Hon. Sir), b. 29 Sept. 1911, Crawley, Sussex, England. Premier of Western Australia. m. 3 June 1936, Rita Maud Steffanoni, 5 sons. *Education:* LLD. Hons. University of Western Australia, 1969. *Appointments:* Commenced practice as Chartered Accountant, 1933; Partner, Hendry, Rae & Court, Chartered Accountants, 1938-70; AIF(Private to Lt. Colonel), 1940-46; Elected Member of Legislative Assembly, Parliament of Western Australia (Liberal Member for Nedlands), 1953; Minister for Industrial Development and North West, 1959-71; Minister for Railways, 1959-67; Minister for Transport, 1965; Deputy Leader of Opposition, 1957-59, 1971-72; Leader of Opposition, 1972-74; Premier of Western Australia, also Treasuerer and Minister Co-ordinating Economic and Regional Development, 1974. *Memberships:* State Registrar, Institute of Chartered Accountants in Australia, Western Australian Branch, 1946-52; State Councillor, The Institute of Chartered Accountants in Australia, Western Australian Branch, 1952-55; President, Western Australian Band Association, 1954-59; Honorary Colonel, University Regiment, University of Western Australia, 1969-75; Honorary Colonel, Special Air Services Regiment, 1976-80; FCA; FCIS; FASA; Senator, Jaycees International; Rotary Club; Lions Club. *Publications:* Has provided major contributions to international and Australian forums, especially on resources development. *Honours:* OBE.(Mil. Div.), World War II, 1946; Australian Manufactuers' Council Award for Personal Contribution to Exports, 1969; Kirby Award, Institute of Engineers. 1971; Created Knight Bachelor, 1972; Industrial Design Council of Australia Award, 1978; KCMG, 1979; Life Member, Australian Society of Accountants, 1979; Hon. FAIM, 1980. *Hobbies:* Music; Yachting; Reading. *Address:* 46 Waratah Avenue, Nedlands, 6009, Western Australia, Australia.

COURT, Robin Howell, b. 27 Mar. 1937, Lincoln, England. University Professor of Economics. m. Sandra Thelma Gillett, 17 Jan. 1966, 4 sons. *Education:* BSc, Victoria University of Wellington, 1958, BA, 1961 MA, 1964 University of Auckland, New Zealand; PhD, University of New South Wales, Australia, 1969. *Appointments:* Meteorologist, New Zealand Government, 1958-59; Research Economist, University of Canterbury, New Zealand, 1962-66; Lecturer in Economics, University of New South Wales, Australia, 1967-69; Senior Lecturer, Victoria University of Wellington, New Zealand, 1970; Senior Lecturer, University of Essex, 1971-72; Associate Professor, 1973-76, Professor of Economics, 1977-, University of Auckland, New Zealand; Visiting Professor, Simon Fraser University, British Columbia, 1981; Hallsworth Fellow, University of Manchester. *Memberships:* Economic Society of Australia and New Zealand; Ornithological Society of New Zealand; Environmental Defence Society. *Publications:* Various academic articles on Economics in scholarly journals. *Hobbies:* Farming; Fishing; Environmental activities; Reading; Photography; Water sports; Raquet Sports; Maori carving. *Address:* Bushvalley, R. D. 2, Albany, New Zealand.

COURTOIS, Edmond Jacques, b. 4 July 1920, Montreal, Quebec, Canada. Lawyer. m. Joan Miller, 23 Oct. 1943, 2 sons, 1 daughter. *Education:* BA., Collège de Montréal, 1940; LLB., Université de Montréal, 1943; Admitted to Quebec Bar, 1946; Created Queen's Counsel, 1963. *Appointments:* Partner in firm of Courtois, Clarkson, Parsons and Tétrault, 1953-; Vice-President and Director, The Bank of Nova Scotia; Chairman of the Board and Director, Gaz Métropolitain, inc; President and Director, CIIT Inc.; La Compagnie Foncière du Manitoba (1967), Limitée; President and Supervisory Director, Eastbourne N.V.; Director of numerous companies including: Brinco Limited; Canada Life Assurance Company; McGraw Hill Ryerson Limited; Norcen Energy Resources Limited; Ritz-Carlton Hotel Company of Montreal, Limited; UCL Securities, Inc. *Memberships:* Canadian Bar Association; Bar of Montreal; Bar of the Province of Quebec; Forest and Stream; St. Denis, York (Toronto); Saint James's, Mount Royal and Mount Bruno Country. *Hobbies:* Riding; Fishing. *Address:* 9 Chelsea Place, Montreal, Quebec, Canada, H3G 2J9.

COWAN, Henry Jacob, b. 21 Aug. 1919, Glogow, Poland. Professor of Architectural Science. m. Renate Proskaver, 23 June, 1952, 2 daughters. *Education:* BSc.(1st. class hons.), 1939, MSc, 1940, University of Manchester, PhD, 1952, D.Eng, 1963, University of Sheffield, *Appointments:* War Service, Royal Engineers, 1940-45; Lecturer, University College, Cardiff, Wales, 1946-48; Lecturer, University of Sheffield, 1948-53; Professor and Head of Department of Architectural Science, 1953-, Dean of Faculty of Architecture, 1966-67, University of Sydney, Australia; Visiting Professor, Cornell University, USA, 1962, Kumasi University (Ghana), 1973, Trabzon University, Turkey, 1976; Editor, Architectural Science Review, 1958-; Editor, Vestes Magazine of Federation of Australian University Staff Associations, 1965-78. *Memberships:* Fellow, Institution of Engineers, Australia; Fellow, Institution of Structural Engineers; Fellow, American Society of Civil Engineers; Fellow, Royal Society of Arts (Honorary Corresponding Member of Council); President, Building Science Forum of Australia, 1966-67; President, Architecture Section, Australia and New Zealand Association for Advancement of Science, 1963; Chairman, Australian Group International Association for Bridge and Structural Engineering, 1959-. *Publications:* Over 200 papers in various journals and 14 books, including: Design of Reinforced Concrete, 1963,68, 76, 77, 81; Architectural Structures, 1971, 75, 76, 79; Dictionary of Architectural Science, 1973, 78; The Master Builders, 1977; Science and Building, 1978. *Honours:* Chapman Medal, Institution of Engineers, Australia, 1956; Honorary Life Member, Australia and New Zealand Architectural Science Association, 1977; Honorary Fellow, Royal Australian Institute of Architects, 1979. *Hobbies:* Collecting Books, Stamps and Wines. *Address:* 93 Kings Road, Vaucluse NSW 2030, Australia.

COWEN, Zelman (His Excellency, The Right Honourable Sir), b. 7 Oct. 1919, St Kilda, Melbourne, Australia. Governor General. m. Anna Wittner, 7 June 1945, 3 sons, 1 daughter. *Education:* BA, 1939, LLB, 1941, LLM, 1942, University of Melbourne, Australia; BCL, MA, 1947, DCL, 1968, Oxford University, UK. *Appointments:* Dean of Faculty of Law and Professor of Public Law, University of Melbourne, Australia, 1951-66; Vice-Chancellor, University of New England, 1967-70; Vice-Chancellor, University of Queensland, 1970-77; Governor-General of Australia, 1977-. *Memberships:* Fellowships of: the Royal Society of Arts, 1971; the Academy of Social Sciences in Australia, 1971; the Australian College of Education, 1972. Queen's Counsel of the Queensland Bar; Member of the Victorian Bar; Privy Counsellor, 1981. *Publications:* Specialist Editor, Dicey: Conflict of Laws, 1949; American-Australian Private International Law, 1957; The British Commonwealth of Nations in a Changing World, 1964; Introduction to 2nd edition Evatt: The King and His Dominion Governors, 1967; Individual Liberty and the Law (Tagore Law Lectures, 1975); Chapters in books, articles and essays in journals in Australia, UK, USA, Canada and Europe, on legal, political, social and university matters. *Honours:* Honorary Fellow of: Oriel College, Oxford, UK, 1977; the Academy of Social Sciences in Australia, 1978; the Australian College of Education, 1978; New College, Oxford, 1978; the Australian National University, 1978; University House of the Australian National University, 1978; the Royal Australian Institute of Architects, 1978; the Australian Academy of Technological Sciences, 1979; the Australian College of Physicians, 1979; the Australian Academy of Humanities, 1980; the Australian Society of Accountants, 1980; the Royal Australian College of Medical Administrators, 1981; the Royal Australian College of Obstetricians and Gynaecologists, 1981. Honorary Master of the Bench of Gray's Inn; Honorary Life Member of the New South Wales Bar Association. Decorations: Chancellor and Principal Knight, Order of Australia, 1977; Knight Grand Cross, Order of St Michael and St George, 1977; Knight Grand Cross, Royal Victorian Order, 1980; Associate Knight of Justice of Order of St John of Jerusalem, 1977; Knight Bachelor,

1978; Companion Order of St Michael and St George, 1968. Honorary Degrees: LLD, University of Hong Kong, 1967; University of Queensland, 1972; University of Melbourne, 1973; University of Western Australia, 1981; University of Turin, 1981; DLitt, University of New England, 1979; University of Sydney, 1980; DHL, of Hebrew Union College-Jewish Institute of Religion, Cincinnati, 1980; D.University of Newcastle, Australia, 1980; Griffith University, Australia, 1981. Rhodes Scholar for Victoria, 1940; Supreme Court Prizeman, Melbourne, 1941; Vinerian Scholar, Oxford, UK, 1947; Emeritus Professor, University of Melbourne, 1967. *Hobbies:* Swimming; Tennis; Music; Performing and visual arts. *Address:* Government House, Canberra, ACT 2600, Australia.

COWLEY, Kenneth Edward, b. 17 Nov. 1934, Sydney, Australia. Publishing Executive. m. Maureen Manahan, 6 Oct. 1958, 1 son, 2 daughters. *Education:* Bankstown High School, Sydney. *Appointments:* Managing Director, News Limited; Director, Nationwide News Pty., Limited, 1974-; Director, Mirror Newspaper Limited, 1974-; Chairman, Cumberland Newspapers Pty., Limited, 1976-; Director, Austn. Stockman's Hall of Fame and Heritage Centre, 1976-; Deputy Chairman, F. S. Falkner and Sons Pty. Limited, 1978-; Director, Deputy Manager, Director, News Limited, 1978-; Chairman, Progress Press Pty. Limited, 1979-; Director, United Telecasters Sydney Limited, 1979-; Director, The News Corporation Limited, 1979-. *Memberships:* Councillor, Royal Agricultural Society of New South Wales; Director, Australian Stockman's Hall of Fame and Heritage Centre; Councillor, University of New South Wales. *Address:* 5 Burrawong Avenue, Clifton Gardens, New South Wales 2088, Australia.

COWLISHAW, Edith Fabian (Mrs), b. Adelaide, South Australia. Printmaker. m. John Abbott, 31 May 1947, 3 sons, 1 daughter. *Education:* HLC, Waverly, Adelaide; PLC, Pymble, Sydney; BSc, Sydney University; Painting, Drawing, Printmaking, Workshop Arts Centre. *Appointments:* Industrial Chemist. *Memberships:* Vice-President, 1979-80; Sydney Printmakers, 1971-80; Print Circle, 1972-80; 9 Printmakers, 1973-80; 8 Graphic Artists, 1975-80; Society of Wildlife Artists of Australia, 1978-80. *Creative Works:* Paint & Print, mainly Etching; Since 1970 have concentrated on the Flora of the Sydney Bush, The Trees, Bushfire, mainly the intricacies of the Wild Flowers. *Honours:* First Prize in Graphics Section in Country Exhibitions, Narrabri, Boggabri, Wellington, 1975-80; One man shows: Workshop Arts Centre, 1971; Kabuki Gallery, 1976; Barry Stern, Sydney, 1978-79; Bris & Print Makers Gallery, 1979; Cooks Hill Galleries, Newcastle, 1980; Print Circle in Cologne, Germany, 1980. *Hobbies:* Skiing; Tennis; Growing Australian native plants from seed; Wildflower Garden. *Address:* 139 Middle Harbour Road, East Lindfield 2070, New South Wales, Australia.

COWPER, Norman Lethbridge, b. 15 Sept. 1896, Chatswood, Sydney, Australia. Solicitor. m. Dorothea Huntly McCrae, 17 June 1925, 3 daughters. *Education:* BA, 1917, LLB, 1923, University of Sydney. *Appointments:* Partner, 1924, Senior Partner, 1955-70, Allen, Allen & Hemsley, 1919-70. *Memberships:* Chairman, 1934-38, Director, Australian Institute of Political Science; Chairman, 1937, Director, Australian Institute of International Affairs; Chairman, 1954-74, Trustees of the Sydney Grammar School. *Honours:* CBE, 1958; Knight, 1967. *Hobbies:* Reading; Gardening. *Address:* 9 Millewa Avenue, Wahroonga, New South Wales 2076, Australia.

COX, Patrick Brian, b. 19 Apr, 1914, London, England. Author; Public Relations Consultant; Welfare Officer. m. Patricia Elizabeth Jackson, 1 son, 1 daughter. *Education:* BA., Honours, University of Melbourne, Australia, 1949; Diploma in Journalism, ibid., 1968; Postgraduate Diploma in French Studies, ibid., 1977; Diploma in Public Relations, Royal Melbourne Institute of Technology, Australia, 1967; Diplôme de Langue Française, 1970, Diplôme Supérieur d'Etudes Françaises Modernes, 1971, Paris, France. *Appointments:* Reporter, Reviewer, The Argus and The Australasian Post, 1947-49; Contributing Editor, New International Illustrated Encyclopaedia, 1954; Concurrently Ballet Editor, Architecture and Arts; Executive Director, Cosmos P R Enterprises; Terra Australis Literary Circle; Editor, Kaleidoscope, 1959-62, suspended. *Memberships:* Melbourne Shakespeare Society; Grand Druid, International Guild of Contemporary Bards; Vice-Chancellor, International Academy of Poets; Regent for Oceania, World Poetry Society Intercontinental. *Publications:* Hooded Falcon/Faucon chaperonné, 1957; Singing Forest, 1958; Roses Aflame, 1964; Linéaments, 1968; Testament to Love, 1969; The Roseate Flame, 1971; Suite for Renaissance, 1976; La Déesse et la Licorne, 1978; Worldwide contributor to newspapers, magazines, reviews and anthologies in French, Spanish, German, etc., as well as English. *Honours:* Numerous honours including: Knight Grand Cross, Order of Justinian; Apostolic Delegate, Ancient and Mystical Order of Antioch; Many medals from Accademie Leonardo da Vinci; DD. (Université Philotecnique, Mysore) 1960; Two citations from World Poetry Society Intercontinental; Arts-Sciences-Lettres, Paris: Silver Medal, 1971, Silvergilt Medal, 1978; Jessie Litchfield Prize, Australia, 1976; The Trollope-Cagle Prize cited him as 'Greatest living Love poet'. *Address:* GPO Box 2108-S, Australia 3001.

CRABB, Fredrick Hugh Wright, b. 24 Apr. 1915, Honiton, Devon, England. Minister of Religion. m. A Margery Coombs, 26 Sept. 1946, 2 sons, 2 daughters. *Education:* Bachelor of Divinity (1st Class), London University, 1935-39; ALCD (1st Class), London College of Divinity. *Appointments:* Assistant Priest, St. James, West Feignmouth, Devon, 1939-41, St. Andrews, Plymouth, Devon, 1941-42; District Missionary, AKOT, S Sudan, 1942-45; Principal Bishop, Gwynne College, Mundri S Sudan, 1945-51; Vice-Principal, London College of Divinity, 1951-57; Principal, College of Emmanuel & St Chad, Saskatoon, Sask. Canada, 1957-67; Associate Priest, Christ Church, Calgary, Alberta, 1967-69; Rector, St Stephen's Church, Calgary, 1969-75; Bishop of Athabasco, Alberta, 1975-, Metropolitan of Rupertsland, 1978-. *Memberships:* Rotary Club. *Publications:* Articles in Theological Journals. *Honours:* Honorary DD, Wycliffe College, Toronto, 1958, St Andrew's College, Saskatoon, 1962, College of Emmanuel & St Chad, Saskatoon, 1979. *Hobbies:* Gardening; Mountain Trail Hiking. *Address:* Box 279 Peace River, Alberta, Canada, TOH 2XO.

CRABBE, Vincent Cyril Richard Arthur Charles, b. 29 Oct, 1923, Accra, Gold Coast, Ghana. Lawyer. m. 6 Jan. 1956, 3 sons, 3 daughters. *Education:* Accra Academy, 1939-43; City of London College, UK, 1950-52; Honourable Society of Inner Temple, August, 1952; Passed Bar Final, 1954; Called to the Bar, 1955. *Appointments:* Numerous appointments including: Lecturer in Law, Department of Extra-Mural Studies, University College of Ghana, 1959-63; First Parliamentary Counsel and Constitutional Adviser to Uganda Government, 1963-66; Leader, Ghana Delegation to Conference of Government Exports on Conventional Weapons, Lucerne, Switzerland, Sept-Oct. 1974; Observer, 1970 British General Election, at invitation of British Government; Principal State Attorney in charge of Drafting of Government Legislation both substantive and subsidiary, 1961-63; Justice of the High Court, 1966-70; Member, Central Council of the Ghana Red Cross Society, 1972-77; Chairman of the Drafting Committee of the Constituent Assembly Drafted the 1979 Ghana Constitution; Chairman, Constituent Assembly for the drafting of a new Constitution for Ghana, 1978-79. *Memberships:* Statute Law Society, London; American Judicature Society; London Institute of World Affairs; Fellow, Royal Commonwealth Society. *Honours:* Companion of the Order of the Volta. *Hobbies:* Gardening; Cooking; Baking. *Address:* 2 off Sixth Circular Road, East Cantonments, Accra, Ghana.

CRAFTER, Gregory John, b. 16 Sept. 1944, Mount Barker, South Australia. Barrister; Solicitor; Member of Parliament. m. Kathleen Rae Hurley, 14 Apr. 1973, 1 son, 1 daughter. *Education:* Bachelor of Laws (LlB), University of Adelaide. *Appointments:* South Australia Public Service, 1962-65, 1971-79; Professional Youth Leader, Young Christian Workers Movement, 1965-70; Elected Member for Norwood, South Australian House of Assembly, 1979; Re-elected, Seat of Norwood, 1980-. *Address:* 86 Edward Street, Norwood, South Australia 5067.

CRAIG Albert, James (Macqueen), (Sir), b. 13 July 1924, Liverpool, England. Diplomat. m. 5 July 1952, 3 sons, 1 daughter. *Education:* MA, Class I Honour Moderations, Class I Oriental Studies, Queen's College and Magdalen College, Oxford. *Appointments:* Lecturer in Arabic, Durham University, 1948-55; Principal Instructor Middle East Centre for Arab Studies, 1958; Foreign Office, 1958-61; H.M. Political Agent, Trucial States, 1961-64; British Embassy, Beirut, 1964-67; British Embassy, Jedda, 1967-70; Fellow of St. Antony's College, Oxford, 1970-71; Head of Near East and North Africa Department, F.C.O., 1971-75; Deputy High Commissioner, British High Commission, Kuala Lumpur, 1975-76; H.M. Ambassador, Damascus, 1976-79; H.M. Ambassador, Jedda, 1979-. *Memberships:* Travellers Club. *Honours:* C.M.G., 1975; KCMG, 1981. *Address:* c/o F.C.O. London, S.W.1, England.

CRAIG, Hugh Leslie, b. 24 Sept. 1912, Sydney, Australia. Public Servant. m. Ethel Kelley, 27 Jan. 1939, 1 son, 1 daughter. *Education:* Sydney Teachers' College, 1933; Sydney University, 1932-37; BA, 1938. *Appointments:* Teacher, Department of Education, New South Wales, 1935-37; Psychologist, Vocational Guidance Bureau, 1937-39; Officer, Public Service Board, 1939-56; Member, 1940-67, Chairman, 1961-67, Public Service Board Examinations Committee; Member, New South Wales Film Council, 1940-67; Adminstral Assistant, Department of Education, 1956-67; Executive Member, New South Wales Unversities Board, 1967-69; Secretary & Permanent Head, Ministry of Education, 1969-76; Member, Board of Governors, New South Wales State Conservatorium of Music, 1975-. *Memberships:* Fellow, Royal Institute of Public Administration, 1945-79, Australian Institute of Public Administration, 1980-. *Honours:* Companion of the Imperial Service Order, 1976. *Hobbies:* Gardening; Industrial Arts. *Address:* 16 Burmah Road, Denistone, NSW 2114, Australia.

CRAIK, Donald William, b. 26 Aug. 1931, Baldur, Manitoba, Canada. Professional Engineer. m. Shirley Yvonne Hill, 19 Sept. 1953, 3 daughters. *Education:* B.Sc., University of Manitoba, Canada, 1956; M.Sc. University of Minnesota, U.S.A., 1961. *Appointments:* Canadian Westinghouse Company, 1956-58; Engineering Professor, University of Manitoba, 1958-64; Executive Director of Manitoba Research Council, 1964-66; Minister of Mines & Natural Resources, Manitoba Government, 1967-68; Minister of Education, Manitoba Government, 1968-69; Private Consulting in Engineering and Environmental Projects, 1970-77; Minister of Finance, Minister of Energy and Mines, Deputy Premier , Chairman-Cabinet Committee on Economic Development, Minister responsible for Manitoba Hydro, Minister responsible for Manitoba Forestry Resources Ltd., 1977-. *Memberships:* Association of Professional Engineers of Manitoba. *Publications:* Thesis: Solar Energy; Heat Transfer. *Hobbies:* Fishing; Golfing; Jogging. *Address:* 3 River Lane, Winnipeg, Manitoba, Canada, R2M 3Y8.

CRAIK, Duncan Robert Steele, b. 17 Feb. 1916, Auckland, New Zealand. m. Audrey Mavis lon, 17 Feb. 1943, 4 daughters. *Education:* Bach. of Econs., University of Sydney, 1940. *Appointments:* Commonwealth Bank, 1933-40; Taxation Branch Treasury, 1940-60; Assistant Secretary, Treasury, 1960-66; First Assistant Secretary, Treasury, 1966-69; Deputy Secretary, Treasury, 1969-73; Auditor-General for Australia, 1973-; Part-time Member, Administrative Appeals Tribunal, 1981. *Memberships:* National President, Australian Institute of Public Administration, A.C.T. Divisional Council of Australian Society of Accountants; Fellow, Australian Institute of Management. *Publications:* Contributor to Economic Record. *Honours:* O.B.E., 1971; C.B., 1979. *Hobbies:* Bowls; Gardening. *Address:* 15 Meehan Gardens, Griffith A.C.T. 2603, Australia

CRANE, Brian Anthony, b. 19 Mar. 1930. Lawyer. m. Ann Kelly, 3 sons, 1 daughter. *Education:* BA Hons., Pol. Sci, University of British Columbia, 1950; AM Public Law, 1952; LLB, University of British Columbia 1960; Called to the Bar of Ontario (Osgoode Hall) 1962; QC 1977. *Appointments:* Canadian Member, UN Interne Programme, UN Secretariate, New York, 1951; Pickering College, Ontario 1951; Foreign Service Officer, Department of External Affairs 1952-57; Lecturer, History, University of British Columbia, 1959; Lawyer, Gowling and Henderson, Ottawa, 1962-67; Partner, 1967; Adviser to the Law Reform Commission of Canada on Administrative Law, 1976-; Editor, Recent Judgments of the Supreme Court of Canada, Canadian

Law Information Council 1975-81. *Memberships:* Canadian Bar Association; Commission on the Federal Court of Canada,; Canadian Institute of International Affairs; Chairman, National Executive Committee, 1970-74; Conseil d'Administration, Centre Québecois de Relations Internationales; Vice President, International Commission of Jurists, Canadian Section; Chairman, National Associations Active in Criminal Justice; National Scientific Planning Council; Canadian Mental Health Association. *Publications:* Arms Control: A New Approach to Disarmament, Behind The Headlines, 1962; Editor, Problems of Canadian Defence, 1963; An Introduction to Canada Defence Policy, 1964; Law Clerks for Canadian Judges, 1966; The Jurisdiction of the Supreme Court of Canada, 1967; Some Aspects of Constitutional Procedure, Constitutional Law in a Modern Perspective, 1970; Freedom of the Press and National Security, 1974; The Citizen and the State: Current Problems of Public Law, 1978. *Hobbies:* Canoeing. *Address:* 387 Mariposa Avenue, Rockcliffe, Ottawa, Ontario, Canada.

CRASWELL, Peter William, b. 14 June 1940 Brisbane, Queensland, Australia. Medical Practitioner (Nephrologist). m. Gail Annette Frances Cowell 9 Nov. 1966, 1 son, 1 daughter. *Education:* MB BS, University of Queensland, 1964; Member, 1970, Fellow Royal Australasian College of Physicians, 1975. *Appointments:* Resident Medical Officer, Princess Alexandra Hospital, 1965-66; Medical Registrar, Royal Brisbane Hospital, 1967-69; Teaching Registrar, University of Queensland, 1970; Research Fellow, Department of Nephrology and Transplantation, Royal Free Hospital, London, U.K. 1971-72; Research Fellow, Renal Unit, Victoria Hospital, London Ontario Canada, 1972-73; Clinical Warden, University of Queensland, Royal Brisbane Hospital and Visiting Nephrology, North Brisbane Hospitals' Board, 1973-75; Nephrologist, 1975; Physician-in-Charge, Department of Nephrology, Royal Brisbane Hospital, 1978. *Memberships:* Australasian Society of Nephrology; International Society of Nephrology; High Blood Pressure Research Council of Australia. *Hobbies:* Reading; Gennis. *Address:* 40 Ascog Terrace, Toowong, Queensland 4066, Australia.

CRAVEN, Anna, b. 7 Apr. 1941 Leicester U.K. Museum Curator. m. Joses T Tuhanuku 9 Nov. 1979, 1 son, 1 daughter. *Education:* Bedales School, Hampshire, U.K, 1953-59; MA(Honours Cantab.), Social Anthropology, New Hall, Cambridge, U.K, 1960-63. *Appointments:* Research Assistant, West African Research Unit, Cambridge, and Ghana, 1964; Keeper of Ethnography, Livingstone Museum, Zambia 1965; Researcher, British Institute for History and Archaeology, East Africa, project on Ssese Islands, Uganda, 1965-66; Assistant, Part-time, International African Institute Library 1966; Researcher, Survey of Race Relations London 1966-67; Researcher, (freelance: documentary films), Derrick Knight and Partners London 1967-68; Ethnographer, Federal Department of Antiquities, Nigeria 1968-73; Curator (Training), National Museum, Solomon Islands, ODA, United Kingdom Government 1973-79. *Memberships:* International Council of Museums; Museums Association United Kingdom; Cambridge Society; Fauna Preservation Society; Cultural Association of the Solomon Islands. *Publications:* West Africans in London, Institute of Race Relations, 1968; Editor of various publications for National Museum and Cultural Association of the Solomon Islands; Institute of Pacific Studies, University of the South Pacific, Fiji; Credits on documentary films: Reaching Out (Christian Aid); Witnesses (International Defence and Aid); The Tribal Eye; Man Blong Custom (BBC TV). *Address:* PO Box 271, Honiara, Solomon Islands.

CRAWFORD, Eusebius John, (Most Rev.), b. 4 Dec. 1917 Warrenpoint, Ireland. Catholic Bishop. *Education:* Theology, St Mary's Tallaght, Dublin; Priest 1941. *Appointments:* Professor, Dominican College, Newbridge, Co-Kildare, 1942-45; Professor of Philosophy and Theology, St Dominic's, Melbourne, Australia 1947-; Prior Dominican Community Sydney 1957-; Melbourne 1959-; Bishop Gizo 1960. *Honours:* CMG 1977. *Hobbies:* Music. *Address:* Bishop's House, PO Box 22, Gizo, Solomon Islands.

CRAWSHAW, Alwyn, b. 20 Sept. 1934 Mirfield, Yorkshire. Artist. m. June Eileen, Bridgman 16 Mar. 1957, 1 son, 2 daughters. *Education:* Hastings Grammer

School for Boys 1945-49; Hastings School of Art 1949-51. *Appointments:* Founder Partner, Director, Russell Artists Merchandising Limited, Commercial Art, Graphic Design, Kingston Upon Thames, 1958-80; Now Devoting all my time to Fine Art Painting in Acrylic, Watercolour and Oil; Lecturer and Demonstrator for George Rowney and Company Limited, Manufacturers of Artist Materials, Bracknell, Berkshire. *Memberships:* Fellow, Royal Society of Arts. *Publications:* Painting with Acrylic Colours, 1974; Learn to Paint with Acrylic Colours, 1979; Learn to Paint with Watercolours 1979; Learn to Paint Landscapes 1981; Learn to Paint Boats and Harbours 1982; Editorial Articles for The Artist and Leisure Painter; Paintings sold throughout the world. *Honours:* Fine Art Print, Wet and Windy, in top ten prints 1975. *Hobbies:* Fishing. *Address:* "Metcombe Vale House", Metcombe, Ottery St. Mary, Devon EX11 1RS.

CRAWSHAW (Edward) Daniel (Weston) Sir QC, b. 10 Sept. 1903, Yorkshire, England. Barrister-at-Law. m. Rosemary Treffry, 24 Jan. 1924, 2 sons (1 dec.), 2 daughters. *Education:* Selwyn College, Cambridge, 1923-26; Solicitor, Supreme Court of Judicature, England, 1929; Barrister-at-Law, Gray's Inn, 1946. *Appointments:* Solicitor, Northern Rhodesis, 1930-32, England, 1932-33; Colonial Legal Service, Tanganyika, 1933-39, Zanzibar, 1939-47; Attorney General, Aden, 1947-52; Puisne Judge, Tanganika, 1952-60; Justice of Appeal, Court of Appeal for Eastern Africa, 1960-65; Commissioner, Foreign Compensation Commission, London, 1965-76. *Memberships:* Royal Overseas League, London. *Honours:* Brilliant Star of Zanzibar, 1947; Coronation Medal, 1953. *Hobby:* Golf. *Address:* 1 Fort Road, Guildford, Surrey, GU1 3TB, England.

CREAN, John Gale, b. 4 Nov. 1910, Toronto, Canada. Executive. m. Margaret Elizabeth Dobbie, 2 Dec. 1939, 1 son, 3 daughters. *Education:* Upper Canada College; Bachelor of Commerce, University of Toronto. *Appointments:* President: Robert Crean & Company Limited; Adam Hats, Canada Limited; Canadian Chamber of Commerce. Chairman of Board, Ontario Science Centre; President: Canadian Business & Industry Advisory Committee; Canadian Council, Int. Chamber of Commerce; International Chamber of Commerce. Vice-Chairman, Canadian Business & Industry International Advisory Committee. *Memberships:* St. James's Club; University Club; Queen's Club. *Publications:* Several articles in various journals. *Honours:* Her Majesty the Queen Jubilee Medal. *Hobbies:* Tennis; Sailing. *Address:* 161 Forest Hill Road, Toronto, Ontario, M5P 2N3, Canada.

CREASEY Timothy May (General, Sir), b. 21 Sept. 1923, Bexley, Kent, England. Army Officer. m. Ruth Annette Friend, 11 Aug. 1951, 2 sons (1 dec), 1 daughter. *Education:* Clifton College. *Appointments:* Commissioned Indian Army, 1942, War service, Far East, Italy & Greece; Transferred to Royal Norfolk Regiment, 1946; Chief Instructor, School of Infantry, 1951-53; Brigade Major, 39 Brigade, Kenya & Northern Ireland, 1955-56; Instructor, Army Staff College, 1959-61, Royal Military Academy, Sandhurst, 1963-64; Commanded, 1st Royal Anglian Aden & BAOR, 1969-70; Commanded Sultan of Oman's Armed Forces, 1972-75; Director of Infantry, 1975-77; General Officer Commanding Northern Ireland, 1977-80; Commander in Chief, United Kingdom Land Forces, 1980-81; Chief of Defence Staff, Sultan of Oman's Armed Forces, 1981. *Memberships:* Army & Navy MCC. *Honours:* OBE, 1966; CB, 1975; KCB, 1977; Jordanian Order of Independence, 1974; Order of Oman, 1975. *Hobbies:* Golf; Shooting; Fishing. *Address:* c/o Williams & Glyn's Bank Limited, Holt's Whitehall Branch, Kirkland House, London SW1, England.

CREET, Peter John Ralli, b. 24 Sept. 1937 Ripley, Surrey England. Artist, Gallery Director and Teacher. m. Heather Hodgson 12 June 1964, 3 children. *Education:* Julian Ashton Art School Sydney, New South Wales, 1958-61; Academia de Belli Arti, Rome. Diploma of Fine Art 1961-63; London Central School of Arts. (stained glass). *Appointments:* Seaman; Professor; Artist; Teacher; Vitulturalist; Merchant; Gallery Director. *Memberships:* Contemporary Art Society, New South Wales; Craft Council of Tasmanian; Print Council of Australia; Australian Democrats. *Creative Works:* One-Man Exhibitions: Il Bilico, Rome 1963; Barry Stern, 1967; Gallery 100 1968; Helen Macquine 1969; Art

Centre Gallery 1980; Exhibitions: British Society of Artists CAS, Sydney; Sulman Prize, Sydney, etc. *Honours:* Silver Medal, IV Students International 1963. *Hobbies:* Bush Walking; Sailing; Chess. *Address:* 263 Nelson Road, Mt. Nelson 7007, Tasmania.

CREGIER, Don M(esick), b. 28 Mar. 1930 Schenectady, New York, USA. University Professor. m. Sharon Kathleen Ellis 29 June 1965. *Education:* BA Union College, New York 1951; MA University of Michigan 1952; Post-graduate studies Clark University (Mass.), Yale University, London School of Economics. *Appointments:* Instructor to Associate Professor of History, University of Tennessee, Baker University (Kansas), Keuka College (NY), St. John's University (Minnesota), St. Dunstan's University (Canada), and University of Prince Edward Island, Canada, 1956-; Editor, Quest for Education, 1966-67; Consultant, American Bibliographical Centre/Clio Press 1978-. *Memberships:* Phi Beta Kappa; Phi Kappa Phi; Pi Gamma Mu; Phi Sigma Kappa; American Historical Association; American Political Science Association; North American Conference on British Studies; Association of Contemporary Historians; Anglo-American Associates; Canadian Association of University Teachers, Mark Twain Society. *Publications:* Novel Exposures: Victorian Studies Featuring Contemporary Novels 1980; Bounder from Wales: Lloyd George's Career before the First World War, 1976; 18 articles in Academic American Encyclopedia 1980; contributions to American Historical Review, Canadian Journal of History, Victorian Studies, and other professional journals. *Honours:* Canada Council Fellow, 1972-73; Mark Hopkins Fellow, 1965-66. *Hobbies:* Writing and Editing; Humane work. *Address:* Valleyfield, Prince Edward Island, Canada.

CREMONA, John Joseph, b. 6 Jan. 1918, Gozo, Malta. Law. m. Marchioness Beatrice Barbaro of St. George, 25 Sept. 1949, 1 son, 2 daughters. *Education:* BA, Malta, 1936; D Litt, Rome, 1939; LL D, cum laude, Malta, 1942; BA, 1st class Hons, London, 1946; Ph D in Laws, London, 1951; Dr. Jur. Trieste, 1972. *Appointments:* Crown Counsel, 1947; Lecturer in Constitutional Law, 1947-65; Professor of Criminal Law, University of Malta, 1959-65; Drafted Malta Independence Constitution, 1963; Judge, European Court of Human Rights, Strasbourg, 1965; Vice-President, Constitutional Court and Court of Appeal, 1965-; Chief Justice and President of the Constitutional Court, Court of Appeal, Court of Criminal Appeal, Malta, 1971- Acting President of the Republic of Malta. *Memberships:* Editorial Advisory Board, Revue des Droits de l'Homme, Paris; Europäische Grundruhte Zeitschrift, Strasbourg; Checklist of Human Rights Documents, New York; Human Rights Law Journal, Arlington, USA; World Chairman of Human Rights Section of the World Association of Lawyers, Washington; Vice-President, International Institute of Studies, Documentation and Information for the Protection of the Environment; Committee of Experts on Human Rights; Committee of Experts on State Immunity Council of Europe; Hon. -Fellow of the London School of Economics, University of London; Fellow of The Royal Historical Society (England); International Academy of Legal and Social Medicine; Delegate and Rapporteur at several International Congresses, and numerous other memberships, Numerous publications. *Address:* Villa Barbaro, 45 Main Street, Attard, Malta.

CREQUE, James Robert Longden, b. 29 July 1942, Roadtown, Tortola, Virgin Islands. Permanent Secretary (BUI Government). *Education:* College of Virgin Islands, 1965-67; University of West Indies (DPA), 1972; Attended several Regional & International Conferences, Seminars & Workshops on MNational Parks & Environmental Management. *Appointments:* Permanent Secretary: Ministry of Natural Resources & Environment; Ministry of Natural Resources & Public Health; Ministry of Communications, Works & Industry. Comptroller of Inland Revenue; Labour Commissioner, Senior Labour Officer, Executive Officer, Ministry of Communications. *Memberships:* Secretary/Treasurer, Caribbean Conservation Association; Deputy Chairman, Caribbean Award Scheme Council; Chairman, Duke of Edinburgh Award Scheme; Past Chairman, The Scouts Council; Chairman, BUI's Conservation Society. *Hobbies:* Accomplished Pianist; Drama. *Address:* Road Town, Tortola, British Virgin Islands.

CRICHTON-BROWNE, Noel Ashley, b. 2 Feb. 1944. Parliamentarian; Senator. m. Esther Grace Stevens, 27

Dec. 1969, 2 sons, 1 daughter. *Education:* Scotch College, Perth, Australia. *Appointments:* Liberal Party of Australia, Western Australian Division: State Vice President, 1971-75, State President, 1975-79. *Hobbies:* Riding; Tennis; Golf. *Address:* 29 Pawlett Way, Karrinyup, Western Australia.

CRIPPS, Jerrold Sydney, b. 22 Apr. 1933, Blackheath, New South Wales, Australia. Justice of Land and Environment Court. m. Ann L Stephen, 28 June 1961, 3 sons, 1 daughter. *Education:* University of Sydney, Australia, 1950-55; St. Pauls College, Australia, 1950-55; LL.B., 1956, LL.M., 1973, Sydney University, Australia. *Appointments:* Appointed Queen's Counsel, 1974; Appointed District Court Judge, 1977; Judge of New South Wales Land and Environment Court, 1980. *Memberships:* President, New South Wales Anti-Discrimination Board, 1979; Chairman, New South Wales Legal Services Commission, 1981; New South Wales Bar Council, 1971-77. *Hobbies:* Tennis; Swimming; Theatre. *Address:* 21 Beach Road, Collaroy, New South Wales, Australia.

CRISPIN, Sheila Margaret, b. 21 Jan. 1944, Liverpool, England. Veterinary Surgeon. *Education:* BSc, Honours Degree in Zoology including Applied Zoology, University College of North Wales, 1964-67; University of Cambridge, 1967-72; Medical Science Tripos; Degree in Veterinary Medicine, with Distinction; Diploma in Veterinary Anaesthesia; Member of the Royal College of Veterinary Surgeons. *Appointments:* Mixed General Practice, Lake District; Clinical Research in Comparative Ophthalmology, Cambridge; House Surgeon to the Veterinary Hospital, University of Cambridge; Lecturer in Veterinary Surgery, Lecturer in Veterinary Anatomy, University of Edinburgh. *Memberships:* British Small Animal Veterinary Association; BSAVA Ophthalmology Special Study Group; Panel of Experts for Ophthalmology; Association of Veterinary Anaethetists of Great Britain and Ireland; Cambridge University Medical Society; Cambridge University Veterinary Graduates Society; Pinnacle Club. *Publications:* Numerous Scientific publications. *Honours:* Agricultural Research Council Veterinary Training Grant, 1967-72; College Prizes, Graduate Scholar, Bye-Fellow, Girton College, Cambridge, 1967-72; Peoples Dispensary for Sick Animals Scholar, 1972-74; Keeler Prize for Ophthalmology, 1979. *Hobbies:* Classical Music; Reading; Painting; Mountaineering; Sailing. *Address:* Garden Cottage, Otterston, by Aberdour, Fife, Scotland.

CRISP, Hon. Sir (Malcolm) Peter, b. 21 Mar. 1912, Devonport, Tasmania, Australia. Law. m. Edna Eunice Taylor, 27 Sept. 1935, 2 daughters. *Education:* LL.B., University of Tasmania, Australia, 1933. *Appointments:* Admitted legal practitioner, Tasmania, Australia, 1933; Solicitor Supreme Court and Sheriff's Department, 1935; Deputy Registrar, 1935; Solicitor, Solicitor General's Department, 1936; Crown Prosecutor, 1940; Crown Solicitor, 1947-51; Solicitor General, 1951; K.C., 1951; Lands Titles Commissioner, 1947-52; Lecturer, Law of Property, Tasmania University, Australia, 1947-52; Justice Supreme, Court of Tasmania, 1952-71. *Memberships:* Royal Commissioner, Fluoridation of Public Water Supplies, 1967-68; Chairman, Tasmania Soot Superannan Fund Board, 1947-52; Chairman, State Library Board, 1956-77; Chairman, 1971, Council, National Library of Australia; Chairman, Australian Advisory Council on Bibliographical Services, 1973-; President, Library Association of Australia, 1963-67; Trustee, Tasmanian Museum and Art Gallery, 1972-. *Honours:* Redmond Barry Award, Library Association of Angling; Cruising. *Address:* 10 Anglesea Street, Hobart, Tasmania, Australia.

CRITCHLEY, Julian Michael Gordon, b. 8 Dec. 1930, Chelsea, England. Member of Parliament, Author and Journalist. m. (1) Paula Baron, 1955, (2) Heather Goodrick, 1965, 1 son, 3 daughters. *Education:* MA, Oxford University. *Appointments:* Advertising Executive; Journalist; Author; Politician. *Memberships:* Chairman, Conservative Party MEDIA Committee, 1976-81; Chairman of the Bow Group, 1966-67. *Publications:* Warning and Response, 1978; Nato in the 1980s, 1982; Collective Security (with O Pick), 1974. *Hobbies:* Watching Boxing; the Country; Military and 19th century French history. *Address:* 18 Bridge Square, Farnham, Surrey, England.

CRITCHLEY, Thomas Kingston, b. 27 Jan. 1916, Melbourne, Australia. m. Susan Cappel, 1962, 4 daughters. *Education:* B.Ec., University of Sydney, Australia. *Appointments:* Research Officer, Premier's Department, Sydney, Australia, 1938-41; RAAF., 1941; Assistant Economic Adviser, Department of War Organization of Industry, 1943-44; Head, Research Section, Far Eastern Bureau, New Delhi, British Ministry of Information, 1944-46; Head, Economic Relations Section, 1946-47, Head, Pacific and Americas Branch, 1954-55, Department of External Affairs; Australian Representative, UN Good Offices Committee on Indonesian Question, 1948-49, UN Commission for Indonesia, 1949-50; Acting Australian Commissioner, 1951-52, Australian Commissioner, 1955-57, High Commissioner, 1957-65, Fed. of Malaya; Australian Representative, UN Commission for Unification and Rehabilitation of Korea, 1952-54; Senior External Affairs Representative, London, UK, 1966-69; Ambassador to Thailand, 1969-74; High Commissioner, 1974-75, Australian High Commissioner, 1975-78, Papua New Guinea; Ambassador to Indonesia, 1978-. *Publications:* Australia Foots the Bill, (co-author), 1941; Australia and New Zealand, 1947. *Honours:* PMN (Malaysia), 1965; CBE., 1964; AO., 1976. *Hobbies:* Golf; Tennis; Flying. *Address:* Australian Embassy, Jakarta, Indonesia.

CROCKER, Walter Russell, (Sir), b. 25 Mar. 1902. Diplomat. m. Claire Ward, 1951 (div. 1968), 2 sons. *Education:* University of Adelaide; Balliol College, Oxford; Stanford University, USA. *Appointments:* Entered Colonial-Administrative Service, Nigeria, 1930; League of Nations, 1934; ILO, Assistant to Director-General; War Service, 1940-45; Farmer, 1946; UN Secretariat, Chief of Africa Section, 1946-49; Prof. of International Relations, Australian National University, 1949-52; Acting Vice-Chancellor, 1951; High Commissioner for Australia to India, 1952-55; Ambassador of Australia to Indonesia, 1955-57; High Comr to Canada, 1957-58; High Comr for Australia to India and Ambassador to Nepal, 1958-62; Ambassador of Australia to the Netherlands and Belgium, 1962-65; Ambassador to Ethiopia and High Commissioner for Kenya and Uganda, 1965-67; Ambassador to Italy, 1967-70. *Memberships:* United Oxford and Cambridge University, Reform; Adelaide. *Publications:* The Japanese Population Problem, 1931; Nigeria, 1936; On Governing Colonies, 1946; Self-Government for the Colonies, 1949; Can the United Nations Succeed?, 1951; The Race Question as a factor in International Relations, 1955; Nehru, 1965; Australian Ambassador, 1971; Travelling Back: Memoirs, 1981. *Honours:* Croix de Guerre avec palme; L'Ordre royal du Lion, Belgium, 1945; CBE, 1955; Cavaliere di Gr. Croce dell'Ordine al Merito, Italy, 1970; Order of Malta, 1975; Honorary Colonel, Royal South Australia Regiment, 1977; KBE, 1978. *Hobbies:* Gardening; Walking; Music. *Address:* Government House, Adelaide, South Australia.

CROHAM, Douglas Albert Vivian, (Lord), b. 15 Dec. 1917, Wallington, Surrey, England. Company Director. m. Sybil Eileen Allegro, 16 Aug. 1941, 2 sons, 1 daughter. *Education:* BSc, London School of Economics, London University, 1935-39. *Appointments:* Civil Service, Board of Trade, 1939; Permanent Secretary, Department of Economic Affairs, 1966-68; Permanent Secretary, HM Treasury, 1968-74; Permanent Secretary, Civil Service Department and Head of Home Civil Service, 1974-77; Retired from Civil Service, 1977; Adviser, Governor, Bank of England, 1978-; Deputy Chairman, British National Oil Corporation, 1978; Director, Pilkington Brothers Limited, 1978-. *Memberships:* President, Institute of Fiscal Studies; Deputy Chairman, Anglo Anglo German Foundation; Fellow, Royal Statistical Society; Companion British Institute of Management; Fellow, Royal Society of Arts; Governor, London School of Economics; Governor, National Institute for Economic & Social Research; Member of Council, Manchester Business School. *Honours:* Farr Medal in Statistics, 1938; CB, 1963; KCB, 1967; GCB, 1973; Life Peerage, 1978. *Hobbies:* Woodwork; Tennis. *Address:* 9 Manor Way, South Croydon, Surrey, England.

CROLL, David Arnold, b. 12 Mar. 1900, Moscow, Russia. Lawyer, Parliamentarian. m. Sarah Levin, 1925, 3 daughters. *Education:* Osgoode Hall Law School, 1925. *Appointments:* Mayor of the City of Windsor, 1930; Elected to Provincial Legislature, 1934;

War Service, 1939-45; Liberal Member of House of Commons, 1945, re-elected in 1949 and 1953; Appointed to the Senate, 1955. *Memberships:* Chairman of the Senate Committee on Aging; Co-Chairman of the Joint Committee on Consumer Credit; Chairman of the Senate Committee on Poverty; Chairman of the Special Senate Committee on Retirement Age Policies; Senate Committees: Banking, Commerce, External Affairs, Health and Welfare, Legal and Constitutional Affairs and Finance. *Publications:* Handbook on dispatch riding; numerous reports. *Honours:* Delegate to United Nations, 1956-57; B'Nai B'Rith Humanitarian Award, 1956; United States National Community Service Award, 1961; Honoured by the Council of Reform Congregations for public service, Montreal, 1962. *Address:* 1603 Bathurst Street, Toronto, Ontario, Canada.

CROMER, D'Arcy Ananda Neil, b. 14 Mar. 1910, London, England. Consultant Forester. m. Edna May Featherstone, 27 Dec. 1935, 1 son, 1 daughter. *Education:* BSc, 1932, MSc, 1935, University of Adelaide; Diploma of Forestry, 1932, Australian Forestry School; DScFor, 1958, University of Queensland. *Appointments:* Forestry Commission of New South Wales, 1934-41; War Service, 1942-45; O/C Research Divisions, Forestry & Timber Bureau, 1946-63; Director, Forest Research Institute, Canberra, 1963-70; Director General, Forestry & Timber Bureau, Canberra, 1970-75. *Memberships:* International Union of Forestry Research Organisations, Executive Board/Permanent Committee, 1967-76; Institute of Foresters of Australia, President, 1949-53; Past Chairman, New South Wales Division, ACT Division; Commonwealth Forestry Association, Oxford, Governing Council; Explorers Club, New York, Fellow, 1978; Canberra Alpine Club. *Publications:* New Approaches in Forest Mensuration, 1961; Several Bulletins & Leaflets in Forestry and Timber Bureau series; Numerous papers in scientific journals. *Honours:* Ernest Ayers Scholarship, University of Adelaide, 1933; NW Jolly Memorial Medal, Institute of Foresters of Australia, 1964; Fellow, Institute of Foresters of Australia, 1969; Companion of the Imperial Service Order, 1976. *Hobbies:* Woodworking and Turning; Trout Fishing; Golf. *Address:* 11 Guilfoyle Street, Yarralumla, ACT 2600, Australia.

CROMPTON, Michael Robin, b. 19 Mar. 1938, Manchester, England. Diplomat. *Education:* Jesus College, 1956, MA, 1962, Cambridge University; Heidelberg University, 1959-63; Diplomatic Service Lower Standard examination in Swahili, 1980. *Appointments:* Lektor in English language and area studies, Heidelberg University, Interpreters' Institute, 1964-71; HM Diplomatic Service, 1971-, Nigeria, 1973-76, Kenya, 1978. *Memberships:* Royal Commonwealth Society; Diplomatic Service Association; Wexas International Limited; Jesus College Cambridge Society; East African Wildlife Society. *Publications:* Translations from German: The History of Heidelberg University, 1965; Johann Wolfgang von Goethe: Visits to Heidelberg; European Places of Culture, 1966; Theodor Fontane: Wanderings through Berlin, 1968; Gt Britain's Relations with SW Germany, 1965. *Honours:* Procter German Composition Prize, 1956, Procter French Reading Prize, 1956, Manchester Grammar School; Jesus College of Cambridge German Prize, 1957; Trinity College of Music, Intermediate Level, 1953. *Hobbies:* Motoring; Music; Walking; Golf; Tennis. *Address:* PO Box 30465 Nairobi, Kenya.

CROOKS, Barbara Gwendolen Anne, b. 4 July 1904, London, England. Retired Teacher, Artist in Oils. m. James Eric Crooks, 22 Dec. 1930, 2 daughters. *Appointments:* Teacher, 1948-62. *Memberships:* National Society of Painters, Sculptors & Printmakers. *Creative Works:* Painting in Paris Salon, 1973; 2 Ds in Royal Academy; Exhibitions ROI, NS, SWA, Debeu Art Gallery; International Amateur Art Gallery. *Honours:* Prize Royal Drawing Society, 1922; Bronze, Silver, Gold medals, London Academy Music & Drama. *Hobbies:* Patchwork; Knitting; Drama; Reading. *Address:* 85 Glynde Way, Thorpe Bay, Essex, England.

CROOME, Helen Angela, b. 22 Feb. 1925, Peking, China. Writer; Journalist. *Education:* WRNS technical course and service with recommendations, 1943-45; Open Scholar, 1945, BA. Hons, 1948, MA (Oxon), 1962, Somerville College, Oxford, UK; Alumnus, Salzburg Seminar in American Studies, 1951. *Appointments:* BBC, 1949-50; Special Correspondent, Discovery magazine, 1956-65; Science Staff, Daily Telegraph, 1961-; Editor, Spectrum, 1972-74; Reviews Editor, International Journal of Nautical Archaeology, 1971-. *Memberships:* Committee member, 1965-66, 1972-73, Association of British Science Writers; Founder member, Council for Nautical Archaeology; Hon. Secretary 1970-74, UK Hovercraft Society. *Publications:* PEP booklet - Decimalisation, 1957; Hover Craft, 1960, 64, 71, 73; Into the Air (children) 1964; Wrecks (Know about), 1964; Air, Earth and Sea (Research into), 1975; Transport entries in Readers Digest: Inventions that Changed the World, 1982; articles etc seriatim in Discovery, New Scientist, Daily Telegraph, Nature, 1956. *Honours:* US State Department travel award, 1970; Science Writer of the Year, 1972. *Hobbies:* Travel; Convivial conversation; Drawing and painting; Music. *Address:* 14 The Paragon, Blackheath, London SE3 OPA.

CROSBIE, Eric John, b. 28 Jan. 1907, London, England. Managing Director (retired). m. Doris Ivy Bessie Ward, 21 July 1932, 1 daughter. *Education:* Oxford Locals, St. Ignatius Jesuit College. *Appointments:* Professional Stage, 1917-23; West Indian Merchants, 1923-26; Manganese Steel Cartel, 1926-28; Timber Technology, 1928-32; Family Departmental Stores, 1932-39, 1945-74; Judge of Crown Court, 1977-79. *Memberships:* Chairman, Board of Pentonville Prison; Chairman, Income Tax Commissioners; Chairman, Supplementary Benefits Appeals; Chairman, Groups of Hospitals; Past President, English Bowling Association; Secretary, English Bowls Council; Chairman, Help the Aged, Haringey; Chairman, EBA Publications Limited; Chairman, Hospital Academic Centre; Chairman, Family Practitioner Committee. *Publications:* Various contributions on Bowls at all levels; Analysis of Value Added Tax for sporting aspects; Guidance on works of Benevolent Institutions. *Honours:* MBE., 1977. *Hobbies:* Antiques; Gardening; Scouting; Bowling; Administration at national levels. *Address:* 150 Wellington Road, Enfield, Middlesex, UK, EN1 2RH, England.

CROSBIE, John Shaver, b. 1 May 1920, Montreal, Canada. Author; Business Executive. m. Catherine Patricia James, 19 Nov. 1971, 4 sons, 1 daughter. *Education:* Universities of New Brunswick and Toronto, Canada. *Appointments:* Canadian Broadcasting Corporation, 1944; Managing Director, Purdy Productions, 1944-46; Assistant General Manager, Dancer Fitzgerald Sample (Canada) Limited; General Manager, Canadian Advertising Agency Limited, 1949; Vice-President in Chicago, San Francisco, J Walter Thompson Co.; President, The Magazine Association of Canada, 1967-. *Memberships:* Chairman, International Save the Pun Foundation; Past Chairman, Canadian Advertising Foundation; Past Vice-Chairman, The United Appeal, Toronto; Former President-Elect, The Canadian Club, Chicago; Director, The Canadian Club, New York; Founding Director, The Canadian-American Society of Northern California. *Publications:* The Incredible Mrs. Chadwick; Crosbie's Dictionary of Puns; Crosbie's Book of Punned Haiku; Crosbie's Dictionary of Riddles, etc; Publisher: The Canada Report, The Pundit (newsletters). *Address:* 107 Ridge Drive, Toronto, Ontario M4T 1B8, Canada.

CROSBIE, Joseph Stanislaus, b. 16 Feb. 1923, Surrey Hills, Victoria, Australia. Medical Practitioner. m. Joan Margaret, 12 Jan. 1949, 4 sons, 3 daughters. *Education:* MBBS, University of Melbourne, Australia, 1951; FRACGP, Royal College of General Practice, Australia, 1968. *Appointments:* Resident Medical Officer, St. Vincent's Hospital Melbourne, Australia, 1951; Hon. Obstetrician and Gynaecologist, 1954-64, Medical Superintendent (and Private Practice in Obstetrics), 1965-, Gippsland Base Hospital, Sale, Victoria, Australia. *Memberships:* Returned Soldiers League of Australia; Divisional Surgeon, St. Johns Ambulance Brigade. *Honours:* Full Blue Boxing, Melbourne University, Australia, 1947; Serving brother, Order of the Hospital of St. John of Jerusalem. *Hobbies:* Fishing; Camping; Gardening. *Address:* 225 York Street, Sale 3850, Victoria, Australia.

CROSS, David Stewart, b. 4 Apr. 1928, Hutton, near Preston, Lancashire, England. Clerk in Holy Orders. m. Mary Margaret Workman Colquhoun, 31 Aug. 1954, 1 son, 2 daughters. *Education:* Trinity College, Dublin, Ireland, 1948-52; BA, 1952, MA, 1956, Westcott House Theological College, Cambridge, UK, 1952-54.

Appointments: Assistant Curate, Hexham Abbey, 1954-57; Assistant curate, later Precentor, St Albans Abbey, 1957-63; Assistant Chaplain, University of Manchester, 1963-67; Religious Broadcasting Assistant, BBC North, 1968-71; Religious Broadcasting Organiser, BBC Manchester Network Production Centre, 1971-76; Bishop of Doncaster, 1976-; Chairman, Churches' Advisory Committee on Local Broadcasting, 1980; Chairman, BBC, Sheffield Local Radio Council, 1980; Chairman, British Churches' Committee for Channel Four, 1981. *Publications:* Hymn Father. Lord of All Creation (published in several hymn books). *Hobbies:* Music; Photography. *Address:* 5 Park Lane, Sheffield, S10 2DU Yorkshire.

CROSS, Kathleen, b. 1 Nov. 1943, Blackburn, Lancashire, England. Teacher. *Education:* 1st class Hons. Degree, Mathematics, Durham University, UK, 1962-65; Post Graduate Certificate in Education, Leicester University, UK, 1965-66. *Appointments:* Blackburn Girls' Grammar School, UK, 1966-68; Accrington High School for Girls, UK, 1968-75; Head of Mathematics and Science, Accrington and Rossendale College, UK, 1975-; Member of Cockcroft Committee, Inquiry into Mathematics Teaching, 1978-81. *Memberships:* Treasurer, 1981, Association of Teachers of Mathematics; Mathematics Association; Elder, United Reformed Church. *Hobbies:* Choral singing; Fell walking; Concert and Theatre going. *Address:* 46 Westcliffe, Great Harwood, Blackburn, Lancashire, BB6 7PW, England.

CROSSAN, Bruce Marshall, b. 21 Sept. 1934, Inglewood, Taranaki, New Zealand. Television Executive. m. Catherine Heather Walker, 4 Jan. 1958, 1 son, 2 daughters. *Education:* Stratford Technical High School, New Zealand. *Appointments:* Journalist Cadet, Taranaki Herald, New Plymouth, New Zealand, 1952-53; Journalist, Evening Post, Wellington, New Zealand, 1953-62; Chief Reporter, 1962-65, District Editor, 1965-70, Chief Reporter, Northern Region, 1970-75, New Zealand Broadcasting Corporation, Wellington, New Zealand; Editor, News and Current Affairs, South Pacific Television, Auckland, New Zealand, 1975-80; Controller, News, Current Affairs and Sport, Television New Zealand, Auckland, New Zealand, 1980-. *Memberships:* Remuera Golf Club. *Honours:* New Zealand Journalists' Association Prize for Investigative Journalism, 1965; Jefferson Fellow, East-West Centre, University of Hawaii, 1974. *Hobbies:* Gardening; Golf. *Address:* 28 Houghton Street, Meadowbank, Auckland 5, New Zealand.

CROSSLAND, Christopher John, b. 16 June 1944, Auckland, New Zealand. Marine Scientist. 2 daughters. *Education:* BSc., 1967, MSc.(Class II,Hons),1968, Auckland University, New Zealand; PhD, James Cook University of North Queensland, Australia, 1973; Diploma, Australian School Nuclear Technology, 1973. *Appointments:* Tutor, 1968-72, Lecturer, 1973-74, James Cook University of North Queensland, Australia; Research Scientist, Australian Institute of Marine Science, Australia, 1975-79; Senior Research Scientist, CSIRO, Division of Fisheries and Oceanography, 1979-. *Memberships:* Australian Society of Plant Physiologists; Australian Biochemical Society; Australian Marine Science Association; Royal Society of Queensland; Whitford Rotary Club. *Publications:* 23 Scientific publications in International Journals; 2 Industry Reports. *Honours:* Rotary International Foundation; Group Study Exchangee, 1979. *Hobbies:* Wine; Australian Marine Exploration; Rugby Union. *Address:* 76 High Street, Sorrento, Western Australia, Australia 6020.

CROSSLEY, Desmond Ivan, b. 10 Oct. 1910, Lloydminster, Saskatchewan, Canada. Forester. m. Isobel Willis Boyd, 9 Oct, 1937, 1 son, 1 daughter. *Education:* BSc., Forestry, University of Toronto, Canada, 1935; MSc., University of Minnesota, USA, 1940. *Appointments:* Tree Planting Supervisor, Dominion Department of Agriculture, 1935-40; Navigator, Discharged with rank of Squadron Leader, RCAF., 1941-45; Senior Forest Research Officer, Canadian Forestry Service, 1945-55; Chief Forester, North Western Pulp and Power, 1955-75; Forest Management Consultant, 1975-. *Memberships:* President, Canadian Institute of Forestry; Society of American Foresters; President, Forester Club, University of Toronto; President, Hinton Kiwanis Club. *Publications:* Some 50 publications including: Silvicultural research, Forest Management

Studies, Environment reviews, published by the Research Division, Canadian Forestry Service; Pulp and Paper, Invited paper, World Forestry Congress, Spain, 1966. *Honours:* Canadian Forestry Achievement Award, Canadian Institute of Forestry, 1970; Achievement Award, Alberta Government, 1975; Fellow, Canadian Institute of Forestry, 1979; Best Paper, Woodlands Section, Canadian Pulp and Paper Association, 1975; Member, Sigma Xi scientific fraternity; Guest Lecturer, Forestry Faculties, Universities of Toronto, Alberta and British Columbia; H.R. MacMillan Lecture, University of British Columbia, 1976; Honorary Testimonial, Royal Canadian Humane Association, 1946; Member, University of Alberta Senate, 1966-71; Panel Member, Environment Council of Alberta, 1978-79; Member, Arctic Land Use Research Committee, 1973-78. *Hobbies:* Breeding and training of Arabian horses; Growing miniature (bonsai) trees. *Address:* Box 247, Hinton, Alberta, Canada, TOE 1BO.

CROWDEN, Ronald Keith, b. 21 Oct. 1931, Scottsdale, Tasmania, Australia. University Lecturer. m. Stella Irene McDonald, 14 Nov. 1957, 3 sons, 1 daughter. *Education:* BSc.(Ist.Class Hons), University of Tasmania, Australia, 1954; PhD, University of New South Wales, Australia, 1960. *Appointments:* Technical Officer, 1955-56, Teaching Fellow, 1956-68, Lecturer in Biochemistry, 1958-60, Department of Biological Sciences, New South Wales University of Technology, Australia; Lecturer in Botany, 1960, Senior Lecturer in Botany, 1966, Reader in Botany, 1973, University of Tasmania, Australia. *Memberships:* Committee representative for Tasmania, Australian Society of Plant Physiologists; Australian Systematic Botany Society; Past Vice-President and President, Tasmanian Transport Museum Society; Tasmanian Division Secretary, Australian Railway Historical Society; Society for Growing Australian Plants. *Publications:* Approximately 40 scientific papers and publications. *Hobbies:* Transport History in Australia; Gardening,native plants and exotic bulbs. *Address:* PO Box 267 Kettering, Tasmania 7155, Australia.

CRYNGE, Frederick Xavier, b. 18 Sept. 1935, Enkeldoorn, Zimbabwe. Consultant Sybarite. m. Margot Butterworth Brown, 23 Feb. 1967, 1 son. *Education:* MA.(Oxon),Anthropology, 1956; D.Phil.(Ariz.), 1962. *Appointments:* Research Assistant, British National History Museum, London, UK, 1957; Assistant Professor, Arizona Lutheran College, Faculty of Antiquities, Phoenix, Arizona, USA, 1958-63; Professor, Department of Anthropology, Liberian School of Prehistory studies, University of Monrovia, 1964-72; Self employed consultant, Andorra, 1973-80; Adviser to Ministry of Education and Culture, Zimbabwe, 1980-. *Memberships:* FBMS, Anthropology; Council member, Council for Inter-African Cultural Exchange. *Publications:* Numerous publications in anthropological journals with a sybaritic theme. *Honours:* Julius Nyerere award for contributions to African self-awareness, 1971. *Hobbies:* Indigenous African poetry; West African musical instruments. *Address:* c/o Ministry of Education and Culture, PO Box 8022, Causeway, Zimbabwe.

CSORGO, Miklós, b. 12 Mar.1932, Hungary. Professor Mathematics. m. Anna Eszter Tóth, 10 Aug. 1957, 2 daughters. *Education:* BA., Budapest, Hungary, 1955; MA, 1961, PhD, 1963, McGill University, Canada. *Appointments:* Department of Mathematics, Princeton University, USA, 1963-65; Department of Mathematics, McGill University, Canada, 1965-71; Department of Mathematics and Statistics, Carleton University Canada, 1971-. *Memberships:* American Mathematical Society; Bernoulli Society for Mathematical Statistics and Probability; Member of Council, Canadian Mathematical Society; Fellow, Institute of Mathematical Statistics; International Statistical Institute; Statistical Society of Canada. *Publications:* Strong Approximations in Probability and Statistics, (with Pál Révész), 1981; approximately 60 publications in various journals of Mathematics and Statistics. *Honours:* Canada Council Leave Fellowship, 1969-70, 1976-77; Canada Council Killam Senior Research Fellowship, 1978-79, 1979-80. *Hobbies:* Reading; Canadian Hockey. *Address:* 18 Plaza Court, Ottawa, Ontario, Canada K2H 7W1.

CULATTO, Lionel William Gerard John, b. 11 June 1952, Gibraltar. Barrister-at-Law. *Education:* Stoney-

hurst College, Lancs., UK; College of Law, Chancery Lane, London, UK, 1972-76; Called to the Bar, Middle Temple, July 1976. *Appointments:* Barrister-at-Law. *Memberships:* Royal Gibraltar Yacht Club; Honourable Society of the Middle Temple; The Victorian Society; The Fortress Study Group; Chairman, Gibraltar Conservation Society; Stonyhurst Association. *Hobbies:* Painting; Sailing. *Address:* c/o PO Box 111, Gibraltar.

CULLEN, David Joseph, b. 6 Jan. 1929, London, England. Scientist. m. Pamela Mary Coker, 19 Sept. 1953. *Education:* B.Sc. Hons., Chelsea Colleg, University of London;, 1949-53; Ph.D., University of London, 1965. *Appointments:* Geologist, Bechuanaland Protectorate, 1953-59; Scientist, New Zealand Oceanographic Institute, DSIR, Wellington, 1960-. *Publications:* Numerous Scientific works on various aspects of the Marine Geology of the Southwest Pacific, and several on Southern African Precambrian Geology. *Honours:* Royal Society, Nuffield Foundation Commonwealth Bursary, University of Wales, Swansea, 1970-71. *Hobbies:* Music; Art; Literature; History; Archaeology; Walking; Swimming. *Address:* 277 Muritai Road, Eastbourne, Wellington, New Zealand.

CULLINGFORD, Ada Sophia, b. 14 March 1908, Berechurch, Essex, England. Mental Nurse, R.M.P.A. m. Arthur Albert Cullingford, 4 March 1937, 1 son, 1 daughter. *Education:* The Royal Medico Psychological Association Certificate, St. Audrys Hospital, Melton, Suffolk, 1930; Diploma in Gas Warfare, Woodbridge, 1936. *Appointments:* Student Nurse, 1926-30, Sister in Charge, 1930-37, St. Audrey's Hospital, Melton, Suffolk; Freelance Writer for British Naturalists Association, 1973-76; Bedsitter and B.A.P.A. *Memberships:* Winchester Amateur Orchestra, 1960-74; Hampshire Rural Music School, 1952-70; B.A.P.A. Adjudicator; Penman Literary Society, Southern Arts, 1971. *Publications:* Collection of Poems, 1969-71, 72, 74, 76, 79, 81; Poetry Workouts for Colour Television films, 1971, 1973, 1981; Several articles on Radio Solent, 1979. *Honours:* Plaques and certificates of merit for Poetry; Prize for poem, 1978; Poetry Judge, Winchester Festival of the Arts, 1980. *Hobbies:* Art Galleries; Exhibitions; Entomology; Music; Gardening. *Address:* Warden's Flat, The Beeches, Oxford Road, Sutton Scotney, Nr. Winchester, Hants SO21 3JW, England.

CULLING, George Charles, b. 13 Aug. 1925, London, England. Educational Advisor; British Council. m. Maureen Cleave, 29 July 1950, 3 sons. *Education:* ALCM., 1950; AMus., Trinity College, London, UK, 1960; LCP., 1965; Diploma in Child Development, London, UK, 1966; BSc., Economics, 1966; MA., Education, 1969. *Appointments:* Various teaching posts, 1950-60; Headmaster, Monson Primary School, UK, 1961; Principal Lecturer, Education, North East London Polytechnic, UK, 1967; Director, Schools and Teacher Training Department, 1972, Director, Courses Department, 1980, The British Council; Service, British Council in India, 1976. *Memberships:* Fellow, Royal Geographical Society. *Publications:* Teaching in the Middle School; Projects in the Middle School. *Hobbies:* Piano playing; Gardening. *Address:* 21 Claremont Gardens, Upminster, Essex, England.

CULLITON, (Hon.) Edward Milton, b. 9 Apr. 1906, Grand Forks, Minnesota, USA. m. Katherine M Hector, 9 Sept. 1939. *Education:* BA., 1926, LL.B., 1928, DCL.(Hons.), 1962, University of Saskatchewan, Canada. *Appointments:* Admitted to Bar of Saskatchewan, Canada, 1930; practised law at Gravelbourg, Saskatchewan, Canada, 1930-31; elected Member, 1935, re-elected 1938, Legislature of Saskatchewan, Canada; Provincial Secretary and Minister in charge of Tax Commission, Saskatchewan Government, Canada, 1938-41; Served in Canadian Army, Canada and Overseas, 1941-46; Defeated in Provincial election, 1944, re-elected in 1948; Appointed to Saskatchewan Court of Appeal, Canada, 1951-; Chief Justice, 1962-81. *Memberships:* Canadian Bar Association; Royal Canadian Legion; Royal Regina United Services Institute; Assiniboia Club; Wascana Country Club. *Honours:* Companion of Order of Canada; Knight Commander of St. Gregory. *Hobbies:* Curling; Golf; Travelling. *Address:* 1303-1830 College Avenue, Regina, Saskatchewan, Canada, S4P 1C2.

CULLITY, Thomas Brendan, b. 10 Sept. 1925, Adelaide, South Australia. Physician, Vigneron. m. Veronica Margaret Albrecht, 28 April 1956, 4 daughters. *Education:* MB BS., Adelaide, 1947; F.R.A.C.P., 1971; F.R.C.P., London, 1975. *Appointments:* Resident Medical Officer, Registrar, Royal Adelaide Hospital, 1947-48; Royal Perth Hospital, 1948; Princess Margaret Hospital, 1949; Clinical Research Unit, Alfred Hospital, Melbourne, 1950; National Heart Hospital, London, 1951-52; Consulting Physician, Departments of Cardiology, Freemantle Hospital, 1963; Royal Perth Ospital, 1979-. *Publications:* Planted and developed Vasse Felix vineyard and winery, the first such in South West Australia, 1967. *Hobbies:* French; Wine; Golf. *Address:* 33 View Street, Peppermint Grove, Western Australia 6011.

CULLIVER, Francis Edward, b. 11 Oct. 1920, Melbourne, Australia. Surveyor. m. Audrey Bell Dempster, 10 June 1943, 3 sons, 3 daughters. *Education:* Surveyors Board of Victoria, 1947; Registered Surveyor, Victoria, New South Wales and Northern Territory. *Appointments:* Royal Australian Survey Corps, 1940-46; Partner, Culliver and Sim, Consulting Surveyors, Melbourn, 1948-81. *Memberships:* President, Institution of Surveyors, Victoria, 1956; President, Institution of Surveyors, Australia, 1977; Surveyors Board of Victoria; Victorian Artists Society. *Hobbies:* Antique Furniture Restoration; Drawing. *Address:* 36 Cochrane Street, Brighton, Victoria, 3186, Australia.

CUMES, James William Crawford, b. 23 Aug. 1922, Rosewood, Queensland, Australia. Economist, Diplomat. *Education:* B.A., Queensland, 1945; Graduate, School of Diplomatic Studies, Canberra, 1945; Ph.D., London, 1951. *Appointments:* include: Australian Army, 1942-44; Assistant Secretary, Foreign Affairs, Canberra, 1958-61; Chage D'Affaires, Brussels, 1961-65; High Commissioner, Nigeria, 1965-67; Ambassador to Belgium, Luxembourg and European Communities, 1975-77; Ambassador to Austria and Hungry, 1977-80; Governor on IAEA Board of Governors, 1978-80; Ambassador to the Netherlands, 1980-. *Publications:* The Indigent Rich, 1971; Inflation, A Study in Stability, 1974; Their Chastity was not too Rigid, 1979. *Hobbies:* Writing; Tennis; Golf. *Address:* Tobias Asserlaan 6, 2517KC The Hague, Netherlands.

CUMINE, Eric Byron, b. 16 June 1905, Shanghai, China. Architect. m. (2) Yvonne Ho 25 June 1952, 1 son. *Education:* AAdip., RIBA., AIAA., School of Architecture, Bedford Square, London. *Appointments:* Private Professional Practice, Eric Cumine Associates, HongKong, 1929-. *Memberships:* Royal Institute of British Architects; Hong Kong Institute of Architects; Rainstorm Disaster Enquire; Examiner for Hong Kong Finals in Architecture, 1962-78; Steward, Royal Hong Kong Jockey Club; Member, Lotteries Board; Member, Town Planning Board, 1965-76. *Creative Works:* Architect to more than 500 projects in HongKong, Taiwan and Singapore; *Publications:*Cartoons on Internment Camp Life in Shanghai; Hong Kong Ways & Byways, 1981; Editor of: Hexagon a technical journal in Shanghai; Inuno. *Honours:* Tite Prize, 1927; RSA Measured Drawing Prize, 1927; OBE, 1977; Justice of the Peace, 1970. *Address:* 5B Rose Court, 119 Wongneichong Road, Hong Kong.

CUMMING, Douglas Graham, b. 21 Aug. 1938, Viking, Alberta, Canada. Senior Vice-President. m. Margaret Ann Roddick, 27 Aug. 1966, 1 son. *Education:* Harvard Advanced Management Program, 1980-81; Sales and Management Courses. *Appointments:* Vice President, Acklands Limited, 1981-. *Memberships:* Edmonton Petroleum Club; Edmonton Chamber of Commerce; Alberta Northwest Chamber of Mines. *Hobbies:* Golfing; Farming; Curling. *Address:* 7727-155 Street, Edmonton, Alberta, Canada T5R 1V9.

CUMMING, Ian, b. 28 Jan 1912, Kirkcaldy, Scotland. Associate Professor of Education (retired). m. Beth Hexter, 10 April 1939, 2 sons, 1 daughter. *Education:* BA., 1939, Dip.Ed., 1942, BEd, 1944, MEd, 1946, University of Melbourne; PhD, University of London, 1953. *Appointments:* Teacher, Victorian Education Department, Australia, 1930-46; Lecturer, 1947-64, Associate Professor of Education, 1964-77, University of Auckland; Unesco Expert, 1965-66; Project Manager and Chief Technical Adviser, 1966-68, U.N.E.S.C.O. *Memberships:* Elder, Presbyterian Church of New Zealand; Royal Historical Society; Australia and New Zealand History of Education Society; President, Auckland Institute for Educational Research; President, Auckland Federation of Parent-Teacher Associations, Representative of the Council of the University of Auckland on the Board of Governors of Mt Roskill Grammer School, Roskill; Board of Experts in Institute of Comparative Education, University of Barcelona; Various Antient, Free and Accepted Masons' Lodges, Mark Master Masons' Lodges, Chapters of Holy Royal Arch Freemasons. *Publications:* Helvetius: His Life and Place in the History of Educational Thought, 1955; Glorious Enterprise: The History of the Auckland Education Board 1857-1957, 1959; History of State Education in New Zealand 1840-1975, in conjuction with Professor Alan Cumming, 1978; Several articles and bulletins completing a study of the life and educational thought of James Mill; Numerous articles on the History of Education and Comparative Education in journals. *Honours:* Imperial Relations Trust Fellow for New Zealand, University of London Institute of Education, 1951-52; Fellow, Royal Historical Society, 1959. *Hobbies:* Reading; Writing. *Address:* 672A South Titirangi Road, Titirangi, Auckland 7, New Zealand.

CUMMING, John James, b. 14 Nov. 1921, Melbourne, Australia. Chairman, Director. m. 27 Feb. 1946, 1 son, 2 daughters. *Education:* Scots College, Melbourne, Australia. *Appointments:* Chairman, Nichols-Cumming Advertising Agency, 1946. *Memberships:* Australian Advertising Council. *Creative Works:* One man show of oil paintings, 1979; Number of important sculpture commissions. *Hobbies:* Sailing-Ocean Racing; Fishing. *Address:* 44 Union Street, Armadale, 3143, Australia.

CUMMINGS, Constance, b. Seattle, USA. Actress. m. Benn W Levy, July 1933, 1 son, 1 daughter. *Appointments:* Appeared in many plays including: Madam Bovary; Goodbye Mr Chips; Taming of the Shrew; The Good Natured Man; played Juliet and St. Joan at the Old Vic; The Petrified Forest; The Barretts of Wimpole Street; Skylark; Clutterbuck; Return to Tyassi; Country Girl; Lysistrata; The Rape of the Belt; J.B; Huis Clos; The Genius and the Goddess; Who's Afraid of Virginia Woolf; Fallen Angels; played Voluminia in Coriolanus; Leda in Amphitryon; Mary Tyrone in Long Day's Journey into Night; The Bacchae; Children; The Circle; Mrs Warren's Profession; All Over; Wings, in America and England; has made many films including: Blithe Spirit; The Battle of the Sexes. *Memberships:* Royal Society of Arts. *Honours:* CBE., 1974; Best Actress Wings; Antionette Perry Award, 1979. *Address:* 68 Old Church Street, London, SW3, England.

CUMMINS, James Thomas, b. 15 Nov. 1934, Warrnambool, Victoria, Australia. Neurosurgeon. m. 10 Oct. 1959, 1 son, 3 daughters. *Education:* MB, BS, Melbourne University, 1958; FRCS, London, 1967; FRACS, Australia. *Appointments:* Resident Medical Officer, Neurosurgical Registrar, 1964, Neurosurgeon, 1971-81, St Vincents Hospital, Melbourne, Victoria; Medical Officer, Royal Australian Air Force, 1960-63; Surgical Registrar Repatriation Hospital, Heidelberg, Victoria, 1965-67; Neurosurgical Registrar, Newcastle Upon Tyne, UK, 1968-69; Senior Neurosurgical Registrar, London Hospital, 1969-70. *Memberships:* Neurosurgical Society Australasia; Society of British Neurological Surgeons; Society for Research into Hydrocephalus & Spina Bifida. *Hobbies:* Malacology; Skiing. *Address:* 168 Doncaster Road, North Balwyn, Victoria, 3104, Australia.

CUMMINS, John Daniel, b. 9 Sept. 1934, Sydney, Australia. Barrister. m. 11 Dcc. 1964, 1 son, 3 daughters. *Education:* LLB., Sydney University, 1956; Queens Counsel Member, 1980. *Appointments:* Barrister, New South Wales Bar, 1961-. Appointed Queens Counsil, 1980-; Bar Association of New South Wales, 1979-80. *Memberships:* Australian Jockey Club. *Honours:* Queens Counsel, 1980-. *Hobbies:* Tennis; Horse Breeding; Swimming; Music. *Address:* 77 Alexandra Street, Hunters Hill, Australia.

CUNEO, Terence Tenison, b. 1 Nov. 1907, London. Artist. m. 27 Sept. 1934, 1 daughter. *Education:* Sutton Valence School; Chelsea and Slade. *Appointments:* Served War of 1939-45: RE, and as War Artist; Special propaganda paintings for Ministry of Information, Political Intelligence Department of FO, and War Artists Advisory Committee; Respresentative of Illustrated London News, France, 1940; Royal Glasgow Institute of Fine Arts; Exhibitor, RA, RP, ROI, Paris Salon (Hon. Mention, 1957); Has painted extensively in North Africa, South Africa, Rhodesia, Canada, USA, Ethiopia and Far East; One-man exhibition, Underground Activities in Occupied Europe, 1941; RWS Galleries, London, 1954 and 1958; Sladmore Gallery, 1971, 1972, 1974. *Creative Works:* Best known works include: Memorial Paintings of El Alamein and The Royal Engineers, King George VI at The Royal Artillery Mess, Woolwich; King George VI and Queen Elizabeth at The Middle Temple Banquet, 1950; Memorial Painting of The Rifle Brigade, 1951; Visit to Lloyd's of Queen Elizabeth II with the Duke of Edinburgh to lay Foundation Stone of Lloyd's New Building, 1952; Queen's Coronation Luncheon, Guildhall, The Duke of Edinburgh at Cambridge, 1953; Portraits of Viscount Allendale, KG, as Canopy Bearer to Her Majesty, 1954; Coronation of Queen Elizabeth II in Westminster Abbey (presented to the Queen by HM's Lieuts of Counties), 1955; Queen's State Visit to Denmark, Engineering Mural in Science Museum, 1957; Queen Elizabeth II at RCOG, 1960; Queen Elizabeth II at Guildhall Banquet after Indian Tour, 1961; Equestrian Portrait of HM the Queen as Col-in-Chief, Grenadier Guards, 1963; Garter Ceremony, 1964; first official portraits of Rt Hon Edward Heath, 1971, of Field Marshall Viscount Montgomery of Alamein, 1972; HM the Queen as Patron of Kennel Club, 1975; State Portrait of King Hussein of Jordan, 1980. *Publications:* The Mouse and his Mater, (autobiography), 1977; Articles in various journals. *Hobbies:* Writing; Sketching; Travel; Riding. *Address:* Freshfields, 201 Ember Lane, E Molesey, Surrey, England.

CUNNINGHAM, George, b. 10 June 1931, Dunfermline, Scotland. Member of Parliament. m. Mavis Walton, 1957, 1 son, 1 daughter. *Education:* BA., University of Manchester; BSc. Economics, University of London. *Appointments:* 2nd Lieutenant, Royal artillery, 1954-56; Commonwealth Relations Office, 1956-63; 2nd Secretary, British High Commission, Ottawa, 1958-60; Commonwealth Officer of Labour Party, 1963-66; Minister of Overseas Development, 1966-69; Member of Parliament of European Community, 1978-79. *Publications:* (Fabian pamphlet) Rhodesia the Last Chance, 1966; Britain and the World in the Seventies, 1970; The Management of Aid Agencies, 1974. *Address:* 28 Manor Gardens, Hampton, Middlesex, England.

CURRIE, Alexander Shand, b. 9 June 1939, Huntly, New Zealand. Minister of Religion, Theological Educator. m. Beverley Una Salmond, 21 Dec. 1961, 4 sons. *Education:* Normal Graduate, Longburn College, N.Z., 1957-58; BA., Theology, Avondale College, Australia, 1959-61; MA., Theology, 1974-75, Doctor of Education, 1975-77, Andrews University, Mich., USA. *Appointments:* Pastor-evangelist, North Queensland, Australia, 1962-65; Director Theological Education, Jones Missionary College, Kambubu, Papua New Guinea, 1966-67; Director Theological Education, Sonoma College, New Britain, Papua New Guinea, 1968-72; Director Theological Education, 1973-74, Deputy Principal and Director, 1977, Principal, 1978-79, Fulton College, Fiji Islands; Dean of Student Affairs, Avondale College, Australia, 1980-81. *Memberships:* American Society of Missiology; Asia Theological Association; Association of Adventist Educators; Commonwealth Council of Educational Administrators; Australian and New Zealand Student Services Association. *Publications:* Strategies for Seventh-Day Adventist Theological Education in the South Pacific Islands, 1977; Directed the theological education of more than 250 Seventh-day Adventist ministers in Papua New Guinea and Fiji , 1966-79. *Hobbies:* Stamp collecting; Reading; Coin Collecting; Sports, Squash and Tennis; Travel; Study of South Pacific Cultures. *Address:* 24 Meyers Crescent, Cooranbong, N.S.Wales, 2265.

CURRO, John Ronald, b. 6 Dec. 1932, Cairns, Queensland, Australia. Lecturer. m. Carmel Cusack, 1 son. 2 daughters. *Education:* Violin with Oscar Rosen, London, 1955; Private Study with Professor W Schweyda Klangenfurt (Conservatorium)., Austria, 1956-57; Private Study with Professor Remy Principe, Santa Cecilia (Conservatorium) Rome, Italy, 1957-58; Violin & Viola, Queensland Conservatorium with Jan Sedivka, 1962-65; Viola with Robert Pikler, Sydney, 1965-68; Conducting with Ezra Rachlin, Brisbane, 1968-72, London, 1976. *Appointments:* Specialists Tutor, Violin, Viola & Chamber Music, University of Queensland, 1968-74. Lecturer in Violin, Viola & Chamber Music, Queensland Conservatorium of Music, 1974-; Director of Music, Queensland Youth Orchestra 1966-; Conductor, Youth Orchestras Australia; Musical Director, Conducted several Australian professional Opera Companies & ABC Orchestras; Radio recitalist & Concerto Soloist ABC; Violist, Lazaroff String Quartet, 1964-72; Duo (viola) w. Ladislav Jasek, 1968-69; Leader Mayne String Quartet, University of Queensland, 1974-77; Principle Viola, University of Queensland Sinfonietta, 1973-; Senior Lecturer, Queensland Conservatorium. *Memberships:* Numerous professional organisations including: Australian Council, 1974, 75, 76; Advisory Committee, Australian Broadcasting Commission; Board Member, Queensland Theatre Orchestra, 1976-; Australian String Teachers Association; Australian Music Camp Association. *Publications:* Queen Elizabeth II Silver Jubilee Medal, 1977; M.B.E.M 1981. *Address:* 19 Moray Street, New Farm, Brisbane, Queensland, Australia.

CURTAIN, Ruth Frances, b. 16 July 1941, Melbourne, Australia. Professor of Mathematics. *Appointments:* Senior Tutor, Mathematics, 1964-75, Assistant Lecturer, 1966, University of Melbourne, Australia; Research Associate, Applied Mathematics, Brown University, R.I., USA., 1967-69; Assistant Professor, School of Engineering Sciences, Purdue University, Indiana, USA, 1969-71; Research Fellow, Control Theory, 1971-73, Lecturer, 1973-77, University of Warwick, Coventry, UK; Professor of Mathematics, Mathematics Institute, University of Groningen, Netherlands, 1977-. *Memberships:* American Mathematical Society; Society for Industrial and Applied Mathematics; I.E.E.E; Systeemgroep Nederland; Wiskundig Genootschap. *Publications:* Functional Analysis in Modern Applied Mathematics (with A J Pritchard), 1977; Infinite dimensional linear systems theory (with A J Pritchard), 1978; Several articles in mathematical journals and contributions to books. *Hobbies:* Squash; Cycling; Jogging; Travel. *Address:* Isebrandtsheerd 200, 9737LR Groningen, Netherlands.

CUSH, Neville McLeod, b. 3 June 1918, Sydney, NSW, Australia. Managing Director. m. Valerie Lorraine Sheel, 19 Aug. 1944, 2 sons, 3 daughters. *Education:* Commonwealth Institute of Accountants, Accountancy Degree, 1945. *Appointments:* Clerk, Accountant, Manager, Director, H.H. Cush & Co. Pty. Ltd., 1936-49; Managing Director, Neville Cush & Co. Pty. Ltd., 1949-81; Managing Director, Forest Timbers of Australia Pty Ltd. 1954-77; Neville Cush (Material Handling) Pty Ltd., 1981; Allury Sawmilling Pty Ltd. 1981. *Memberships:* Vice President, St George District Cricket Club; President, Honorary Sercretary, Congregational Men's Association, of New South Wales. *Honours:* First Prize, Economics, Geography, Sydney Grammar School; First NSW Honours, Banking Finance & Exchange; NSW Honours Company Law, Commonwealth Society of Accountants. *Hobbies:* Reading; Cricket; Squash; Baseball. *Address:* 123 Stuart Street, Blakehurst, Sydney, NSW, 2221, Australia.

CUSHEN, Arthur Thomas, b. 24 Jan. 1920, Bluff, New Zealand. Radio Journalist & Broadcaster. m. Ralda Maud Macdonald, 12 Mar. 1946. *Education:* Secondary education. *Appointments:* Appointed representative of BBC in New Zealand, 1942; Similar appointment with Radio Canada, 1945; Commenced features in New Zealand Listener and Electronics Australia, 1950; Appointed Voice of America Representative, 1972. *Memberships:* National President New Zealand Radio DX League; National Vice-President New Zealand Association of the Blind, 1968-78. *Publications:* Author & Publisher, The World in my Ears, 1979. *Honours:* MBE, 1970. *Hobbies:* Listening to Radio; Philately. *Address:* 212 Earn Street, Invercargill, New Zealand.

D

DADA, Gabriel Akintunde, b. 4 Dec. 1926, Lagos, Nigeria. Architecture. m. Marian Adebisi Olumide, 22 Apr. 1954, 2 sons, 3 daughters. *Education:* Technical Institute, Yaba, 1949-52; BA, Hons. Arch., Sheffield University, 1954-60. *Appointments:* Chief Architect, Federal Ministry of Works, Lagos, 1948-76, Consultant Architect, 1977-. *Memberships:* Nigerian Institute of Architects; Royal Institute of British Architects, 1965; Island Club, Lagos, 1970; Ancient Order of Foresters, 1963, Secretary, 1969-80. *Hobbies:* Table Tennis; Lawn Tennis; Gardening; Dancing. *Address:* 5 Oseni Close, Surulere, Lagos, Nigeria.

DADA, Titus Olufemi, b. 16 Aug. 1928, Lagos, Nigeria. Consultant Physician and Neurologist. m. Mollie Read, 20 Dec. 1958, 2 sons, 3 daughters. *Education:* MB, Chb, 1958, MD, 1968, University of Bristol; DT, M & H, University of Liverpool, 1961; Royal Postgraduate Medical School, London, and Institute of Neurology, London, 1962-64; MRCP, 1963, FRCP, 1970, Glasgow; MRCP, 1964, FRCP, 1970, Edinburgh; FMCP, 1970; FWACP, 1973; Johns Hopkins University, Baltimore, USA, 1970. *Appointments:* Clinical Assistant in Neurology, The London Hospital, 1964; Senior Registrar in Neurology, University College Hospital, Ibadan, 1964-65; Lecturer, 1965-68, Senior Lecturer, 1968-73, Associate Professor, 1973-75, in medicine and Consultant Neurologist, College of Medicine, University of Lagos; Director, Medical Consultant Service and Maryland Medical Centre, Ikeja, 1975-. *Memberships:* President, Nigerian Society of Neurological Sciences, 1966-70; President, Pan-African Association of Neurological Sciences, 1977-79; African Delegate, Council of World Fed. of Neurology, 1967-; World Health Organisation, Expert Panel on Neurosiences, 1974-; Research Group on Neuro-Epidemiology of World Federation of Neurology, 1979-; President, Rotary Club of Lagos, 1972-73. *Publications:* Epilepsy in Nigeria, 1968; Methods in Neurological Examination, 1975; Several Publications on Neurology, especially Epidemiology of Epilepsy, Strokes. *Honours:* Augustine-Pritchard Prize in Surgical Anatomy, United Bristol Hospitals, 1958; UK Commonwealth Scholar in Neurology, 1962-64; WHO Fellow, Johns Hopkins University, USA, 1970. *Hobbies:* Music; Dancing; Swimming. *Address:* Tomori House, Maryland, Ikeja, Lagos, Nigeria.

DAGENAIS, Camille A, b. 1920, Montréal. Chairman & Chief Executive Officer. m. Pauline Falardeau, 3 sons. *Education:* BASc, l'Ecole Polytechnique de Montréal, 1946. *Education:* CIL; Project Engineer, 1953, partner, 1959, Chairman of the Board & General Manager, 1965, Surveyer, Nenniger & Chênevert; President, Surveyor, Nenniger & Chênevert Inc., 1966, President of SNC Enterprises Ltd., 1967, Chairman of the Board and Chief Executive Officer, 1975. *Memberships:* National Research Council of Canada; Past Vice-President, Zone America of the International Commission on Large Dams; President of the Canadian Nuclear Association; Council of the Conference Board of Canada; Director, The Royal Bank of Canada, Canadian Liquid Air, Société d'Investissement Desjardins, Spar Aerospace Limited; Board of Governors of Le Conseil du Patronat, 1979-80. *Honours:* Officer of the Order of Canada; Fellow, Engineering Institute of Canada; Hon. LL.D, University of Toronto; Hon. DSc, Royal Military College of Canada; Hon. DASc, University of Sherbrooke; HON. DSc, Laval University; LL.D, Concordia University; l'Association des Diplômés de l'Ecole Polytechnique of Montréal, for services rendered to society as an Engineer, 1979; Medal of Merit, l'Association des Diplomes de l'Université de Montréal, 1980; Advisor of the International Management Centre of l'Ecole des hautes Etudes Commerciales of Montréal. *Address:* c/o Surveyor, Nenniger & Chênevert Incorporated, Montréal, Quebec, Canada.

DAHLSEN, John Christian, b. 3 Feb. 1935, Bairnsdale, Australia. Solicitor. m. Gillian Hamilton York Syme, 21 Sept. 1962, 1 son, 2 daughters. *Education:* Trinity College, University of Melbourne. *Appointments:* Corr & Corr, Solicitors, 1959, Partner, 1963-; Director, The Herald and Weekly Times Limited; Director, Queensland Press Limited; The Myen Emporium Ltd. *Memberships:* Advisory Board of Melbourne University School of Business Administration; Australian Club; Melbourne Club. *Hobbies:* Tennis; Sailing; Fishing. *Address:* 51 Albany Road, Toorak, 3142, Australia.

DAKE, Mawuse Kwaku, b. 12 Feb. 1936, Ziavi, Volta Region, Ghana. Water Resources Engineer. m. Edith Awo Acolatse, 26 Apr. 1962, 5 sons, 3 daughters. *Education:* MSc, 1963, University of Manchester Institute of Science and Technology; ScD, 1966, Massachussets Institute of Technology, 1963-66; BSc. University of Science and Technology, Kumasi, 1956-61. *Appointments:* Assistant Engineer, Ghana Waster Supplies Division, 1961; Assistant Lecturer, Lecturer, Senior Lecturer, University of Science and Technology, Kumasi, Ghana, 1962-70; Senior Lecturer, Professor of Civil Engineering, 1970-79, Dean, School of Engineering, 1973-78, University of Zambia; Project Coordinator, UNESCO, African Network of Scientific and Technological Institutions, 1980-. *Memberships:* Deputy Leader, Social Democratic Front, Ghana; Chairman, Committee on Engineering Education in Middle Africa; American Geophysical Union; Engineering Institute of Zambia. *Publications:* Essentials of Engineering Hydraulics, 1972; Approximately 12 scientific papers. *Honours:* Member of Constituent Assembly for drawing up the 1979 Constitution of Ghana. *Hobbies:* Sports; Writing. *Address:* UNESCO Regional Office for Science and Tech., PO Box 30592, Nairobi, Kenya.

DALAI, Upendra Prasad, b. 20 July 1941. Lecturer. m. Saila Bala Dalai, 5 June 1967, 2 sons, 1 daughters. *Education:* BA (Hons), 1964; MA (Origa), 1969; First Year Diploma in Linguistics, 1975. *Appointments:* Assistant Teacher, Ganailo High School, 1964-67; Lecturer, Nayagarh College, Nayagarh, 1970-. *Memberships:* Linguistic Society of India; Dravidian Linguistics Association. *Publications:* Thesis; Essays published in several Journals. *Hobbies:* Reading Ancient Indian Culture and Religion. *Address:* Village-Kanimul, PO Narijang, Via Tirtol, Dist. Cuttack, Orissa, India.

DALAL, Harshul, b. 8 Oct. 1947, Bombay, India. Business Executive. m. Nina Harshul, 20 Dec. 1970, 2 daughters. *Education:* BSc (hons), Chemistry. *Appointments:* Managing Director, Camphor & Allied Products Limited, 1970-; Director, Pine Chemicals Limited, Jammu; Director, Terpene Industries Limited, Nangal (HP). *Memberships:* Willingdon Sports Club, Bombay; The Chambers of Hotel Taj Mahal Hotel; Cricket Club of India, Bombay; Indo American Society, Bombay. *Honours:* Appointed as a Special Executive Magistrate by the Government of Maharashtra, 1975-80. *Hobbies:* Photography; Electronics. *Address:* 12 Belvedere Court, 148 Maharshi Karve Road, Bombay 400 020, India.

DALE, David Kenneth Hay, b. 27 Jan. 1927. Governor. m. Hanna Szydlowska, 1956, 1 son. *Education:* Dorchester Grammar School. *Appointments:* Queen's Royal Regiment 1944; 2/Lieutenant 8th Punjab Regiment 1945; Lieutenant 4 Bn(PWO), 1946; Lieutenant, Royal Artillery 1948; Captain 1955; Kenya and Malaya (despatches); District Officer, Kenya 1960; District Commissioner 1962; Admin Officer Cl.B, subseq. Cl.A, Anglo-French Condominium, New Hebrides, W Pacific, 1965-73; Permanent Secretary, Ministry of Aviation, Communications and Works, Seychelles, 1973-75; Dep. Governor, Seychelles 1975; Secretary to Cabinet, Republic of Seychelles 1976; FCO 1977-80; Governor, Montserrat, West Indies 1980-. *Memberships:* East India; Devonshire; Sports and Public Schools. *Honours:* CBE 1976. *Hobbies:* Birdwatching, Walking. *Address:* Government House, Montserrat, West Indies.

DALGLEISH, Angus Cheyne, b. 1 Jan. 1919, Woking, Surrey, England. Chartered Civil Engineer. m. Lorna Mary Waldron, 26 Jan. 1952, 1 son, 3 daughters. *Education:* Royal Military Academy, 1937-38; Trinity College, Cambridge, 1938-39; MA (Cantab), 1961. *Appointments:* Royal Engineers, Retired as Major, 1938-60; Civil and Transport Engineering; Fellow, Institution of Highway Engineers, 1965; Chairman, Railway Conversion League, 1975. *Memberships:* Fellow, Royal Commonwealth Society; Europe House Club. *Publications:* A Solution to our Transport Problems, 1979; Technical Publications on Transport Economics and Route Utilization. *Hobbies:* Scottish Country Dancing; Squash. *Address:* Shouson Hill, Ruxbury Road, Chertsey KT16 9NH, Surrey, England.

DALHAT, Macido, b. 31 Mar. 1935, Zaria City, Kaduna State of Nigeria. Administrator. m. 18 Nov. 1968, 3 sons, 5 daughters. *Education:* Administrative Service Training, Institute of Administration, Zaria, 1959-60; Commonwealth Services Course, Queens College, Oxford, 1963-64. *Appointments:* Assistant Publicity Officer, Ministry of Information, Northern Nigeria, 1955-60; Administrative Officer, District Officer, 1960-64; Assistant Secretary, Senior Assistant Secretary, Principal Assistant Secretary, 1964-68; Permanent Secretary, Ministry of Finance, North-Central (Kaduna) State of Nigeria, 1968-69; Permanent Secretary, Ministry of Education, 1967-73; Permanenet Secretary, Ministry of Agriculture, 1973-75; Secretary to the Government and Head of Civil Service, Kaduna, State of Nigeria, 1975-79. *Memberships:* Kaduna State Lawn Tennis Association, Vice Chairman, 1973-; Kaduna Lawn Tennis Club, Foundation Member and Member of Management Committee; Nigerian Lawn Tennis Association, 1981. *Honours:* Shooting Colours, Zaria, 1954. *Hobbies:* Horticulture; Lawn Tennis; Study in Arabic and Islamic Culture. *Address:* No. 8 Jabbi Road, GRA, Kaduna, Nigeria.

DALLAT, Cahal A, b. 12 Nov. 1921, Ballycastle, County Antrim, Ireland. m. (1) Mary C. Gilligan, 3 sons, 4 daughters, (2) Moira F Mullan, 14 Aug. 1967. *Education:* BA (QuB), 1943; DIP. Handicraft, 1959; DIP. RE, 1964; DIP. AD. Studies, Ed, 1974; Master of Philosophy, 1978. *Appointments:* Head of Craft Department, 1957-63, Headmaster, 1963-78, Star of the Sea; Project Officer, Schools Cultural Studies Project, 1974-76; Deputy Head, Cross & Passion College, Ballycastle, 1978-. *Memberships:* Vice-Chairman, Northern Health & Social Services Board; Vice-Chairman, Ulster Countryside Commission; Central Services Agency for Health and Social Services Norther Ireland; Chairman, Association of Teachers of Cultural and Social Studies; Federation for Ulster Local Studies; Chairman, Glens of Antrim Historical Society; President, County Antrim Council; Pioneer TA Association; President, N. Antrim Area Council, St. Vincent De Paul Society. *Publications:* Place names in the Glens of Antrim; A Study of the Teaching of Local History in Northern Ireland; Oh Maybe it was Yesterday, The Glens of Antrim in Early Photographys, (co-author). *Honours:* Justice of the Peace, 1965; Fellow, Society of Antiquaries of Scotland, 1975; Fellow, Royal Society of Antiquaries of Ireland, 1976. *Hobbies:* Genealogy; Folklore. *Address:* Drimargy, Atlantic Avenue, Ballycastle, County Antrim BT54 6A, Ireland.

DAN, Malcolm John, b. 27 May 1935, Babinda, North Queensland, Australia. Diplomat. m. Rosemary Lillian Kirton, 4 Jan. 1964, 2 daughters. *Education:* Bachelor of Economics, 1959, Bachelor of Arts, 1960, University of Sydney. *Appointments:* Ind. Rel. Department, Ford Motor Company, Sydney, 1958-60; Research Officer, Unilever Australia, 1960; Department of External Affairs, 1961; Buenos Aires, Australian Embassy, 1962-65; New Delhi, 1967-70; Counsellor OECD Paris, 1972-74; Minister and Deputy Head of Mission, Jakarta, 1974-76; Assistant Secretary, International Organisations Branch, Department of Foreign Affairs, Canberra, 1976-79; Australian Ambassador to Argentina, Uruguay, Paraguay, 1980-. *Memberships:* A.N.U. Staff Centre, Australian National University, Canberra. *Hobbies:* Chinese Porcelain; Fishing. *Address:* Zabala 1900, Belgrano, Buenos Aires, Argentina.

DANESI, Mustapha Abudu, b. 21 Aug. 1948, South Ibie, Bendel State, Nigeria. Medical. *Education:* MB, BS, 1972, University of Ibadan, 1967-72; Edinburgh Post-Graduate Internal Medicine Course, 1975; MRCP Diploma, Royal College of Physicians of Ireland, 1977. *Appointments:* Senior House Officer, UBTH Benin, 1973-75; Senior House Officer, Astley Ainslie Hospital, Edinburgh, 1976-77; Medical Registrar, Burnley Group of Hospitals, Burnley, England, 1977-78; Senior Registrar, 1978-79, Consultant Physician, 1979-, Luth, Idiavaba, Lagos. *Memberships:* Etsako Club, 1981. *Publications:* Research work in Epilepsy and Cerebrovascular disease; Some of the publications include Social problems of adolescent and adult Nigerian Epileptics—Risk factors associated with Cerebrovascular disease in Nigerians. *Hobbies:* Music; Reading. *Address:* 32 Sam Shonibare Street, Suru-Lere, Lagos.

DANGANA, Alhaji Abdurrahim, b. 20 Jan. 1942 Bida, Niger State, Minna, Nigeria. Public Servant. m. Safiya-

tu Haruna Aug. 1965 (Div.). 3 sons. *Education:* BA Ahmadu Bellow University, Zaria 1967; MSc(Econ.) University of Ghana, 1969. *Appointments:* Assistant Library Superintendant, Regional Library, Kaduna, 1964; External Affairs Officer, Ministry of External Affairs, Lagos, 1967; Assistant Lecturer Rural Economy Research Unit, Ahmadu Bello University Zaria, 1969; Principal Investment Executive, New Nigeria Development Company Kaduna, 1969-73; Director Investment Supervision, Nigerian Bank for Commerce and Industry, 1973; Commissioner for Social Development N/W State Sokoto, 1975-76; Commissioner for Agriculture, 1976, Commissioner for Health, Niger State, Minna, 1976-77. *Memberships:* Institute of International Affairs, Lagos; Nigerian Economic Society; American Economic Association. *Publications:* Railroads and Economic Development in Nigeria—The Case of Borno Railroad Extension, 1962-1968; MSc Thesis University of Ghana, 1969. *Honours:* Professor Edith Whetham Prize for Best First Year Economics Student, 1965; Nation-Wide Essay Contest Prize, three months' visit to USA, 1963. *Hobbies:* Reading; Travelling; Squash; Tennis; Swimming; Snooker. *Address:* Plot 1262, Adeola Odeku Street, Victoria Island, Lagos.

DANIELS, Eric Charles, b. 15 Mar. 1924, Sydney, Australia. Architect. m. Joan 12 Jan. 1946, 2 sons. *Education:* Diploma in Architecture (Honours) 1949; Master of Architecture, New South Wales, 1964. *Appointments:* Architecture Assistant, Government Architect, NSW, 1946-49; Architect, London, 1949-51; Lecturer, Architecture, Sydney Technical College, 1951-61; Senior Lecturer, UNSW, 1961-68; Visiting Fellow, School of Massachusetts Institute of Technology, USA; Design Tutor, Penn. University; Visiting Critic, Columbia University, NY; Visiting Lecturer, Bristol University, England; Associate Professor of Architecture; Professor of Architecture, 1974; Head, School of Architecture UNSW. *Memberships:* Life Fellow, Royal Australian Institute of Architecture; Honorary Member Illuminating Engineering Society; Bouble Bay Sailing Club; Lane Cove Cave Country Club. *Creative Works:* Several Residences in Sydney. *Honours:* President, RAIA (NSW Chapter), 1976-78; Chairman, HSC Art Examination Committee, 1972; Chairman, HSC Art Syllabus Committee, 1972-79; Member of Council, Alexander Mackey College of Advanced Education, 1978; RAIA Travelling Scholarship, 1949. *Hobbies:* Sailing; Squash; Golf. *Address:* 11 The Albany, 1 Selwyn Street, Woolstonecraft, NSW, Australia.

DANIELS, Frank James, b. 25 Nov. 1899, Chatham, Kent. Civil servant/Teacher. m. 6 Sept. 1932. *Education:* BSc(Econ), London, 1927. *Appointments:* Civil Servant, Admiralty, London, 1915; Army service, 1918-19; British Embassy, Tokyo, 1928-32; Teacher, English, Otaru Commercial College, Japan, 1933-36; Work on Japanese/Basic-English dictionary, 1936-39; Shizuoka Higher School, Japan, 1939-41; Teacher, Japanese, School of Oriental & African Studies; Senior Lecturer, 1941, Reader, 1947, Professor, 1961, London University. *Memberships:* Philological Society; Asiatic Society of Japan; Association of Teachers of Japanese; British Association of Orientalists; Japan Society of London; International Association of Teachers of English as a Foreign Language; Folklore Society. *Publications:* General Editor & contributor, Selections from Japanese Literature (12th-19th centuries), 1958, 1975; Compiler, Basic English: Japanese-English Wordbook, 1969; Translater into Basic English, Stories from Okinawa, 1981. *Honours:* Professor Emeritus, University of London, 1969; Hon. Fellow, School of Oriental & African Studies, 1967; Japan Foundation Award, 1978; British Association for Japanese Studies, 1979; European Association for Japanese Studies, 1979; Consultant, The Basic English Foundation, 1981. *Address:* 31A Abbey Road, St John's Wood, London NW8 9AU, England.

DANIELS, John Richard Sinclair, b. 2 May 1939, Wellington, New Zealand. Director. m. Jenifer Anne Christie, 9 Dec. 1962, 3 sons. *Education:* Scots College, Wellington, 1950-55; Master of Arts (Hons), Victoria University of Wellington, 1956-61. *Appointments:* Library Assistant, General Assembly Library, Wellington, 1960-62; Senior Research Officer, 1968-69, Department of Internal Affairs, Wellington, 1962-69; Research Officer, Municipal Association of New Zealand, 1969-71; Director, New Zealand Historic Places Trust, Wellington, 1971-. *Memberships:* NZ Archaeological

Association, Central Filekeeper, 1961-76, Committees of other historical and archaeological organisations. *Publications:* New Zealand Archaeology—A site recording handbook, First edition, 1970, second edition, 1979; Various articles and reports on New Zealands history and archaeology. *Hobbies:* Music; Reading; Gardening. *Address:* 49 Ganges Road, Khandallah, Wellington, 4, New Zealand.

DANYLIU, Paul George, b. 21 Feb. 1945, Reifnitz, Austria. Barrister. m. Dana Renix, 12 Jan. 1979, 1 son, 1 daughter. *Education:* Bachelor of Arts, 1967; Bachelor of Law, 1970. *Appointments:* Lundeen, Clancy & Mitchel, Dawson Creek, British Columbia, 1971-73; Thomas & Co., Fort St John, 1973-75; Danyliu, Kenny & Co., Vernon, 1975-. *Memberships:* Canadian Civil Liberties Association. *Hobbies:* Karate; Horses; Dogs; Racquetball; Theatre. *Address:* 3009-28th Street, Vernon, British Columbia, V1T 4Z7, Canada.

DARBY, Peter Howard, b. 8 July 1924, Birmingham, England. HM·Chief Inspector, Fire Services. m. Ellen Josephine Glynn, 1948, 1 son, 1 daughter. *Education:* City of Birmingham Advanced Technology. *Appointments:* Deputy Chief Officer, Suffolk & Ipswich Fire Brigade, 1963; Chief Officer, Nottingham, 1966, Lancashire, 1967, Greater Manchester, 1967, London, 1976; HM Chief Inspector of Fire Services, 1981. *Memberships:* Regional Fire Commander, (No 10) NW Region, 1974-76, (No 5) Greater London Region, 1977-80; President, Chief & Assistant Chief Fire Officers Association, 1975; Fire Adviser, Association of Metropolitan Authorities, 1975; Fire Service College Board, 1977; Central Fire Brigades Advisory Council, 1977; Advisor, National Joint Council for Local Authority Fire Brigades, 1977. *Honours:* Freeman of City of London; CBE, 1973; QFSM, 1970. *Hobbies:* Fell-walking; Golf; Fishing; Sailing. *Address:* c/o Fire Service Inspectorate, Home Office, Queen Anne's Gate, London SW1H 9ATA, England.

DARLING, James Ralph, b. 18 June 1899, Tonbridge, Kent, England. Schoolmaster. m. Margaret Dunlop Campbell, 21 Aug. 1935, 1 son, 3 daughters. *Education:* MA, Oriel College, Oxford, 1920-21; Honorary degrees, MA, LLD, Melbourne, DCL, Oxford. *Appointments:* Second Lieutenant, RFA, France & Germany, 1918-19; Assistant Master, Merchant Taylors School, Crosby, Liverpool, 1921-24, Charterhouse School, Gadalming, 1924-29; Headmaster, Geelong Church of England Grammar School, Corio, Victoria, Australia, 1930-61; Chairman, Australian Broadcasting Commission, 1961-67. *Memberships:* Honorary Secretary, 1931-45, Chairman, 1946-48, Headmasters Confernce of Australia; University of Melbourne Council, 1933-71; Commonwealth Universities Commission, 1942-51; Australian Immigration Advisory Council, 1955-61; Australian Broadcasting Control Board, 1955-61; President, Australian College of Education, 1959-63 (Honorary Fellow, 1970); Chairman, Australian Road Safety Council, 1961-70; Australian Immigration Publicity Council, 1962-71; Chairman, Victorian Branch, United World Colleges. *Publications:* The Education of a Civilized Man, 1962; Timbertop (w. E.H. Montgomery), 1967; Richly Rewarding, 1978; Contributions to Melbourne Studies of Education, The Independent School. *Honours:* OBE, 1953; CMG, 1958; Kt Bachelor, 1968. *Hobbies:* Reading; Writing; Bowls. *Address:* 3 Myamyn Street, Armadah, Victoria, 3143, Australia.

DA ROZA, Gustavo Uriel, b. 24 Feb. 1933, Hong Kong. Architect; Professor. m Gloria Go 17 June 1961, 2 sons, 3 daughters. *Education:* Bachelor of Architecture (First Class Honours) University of Hong Kong, 1955. *Appointments:* University of Hong Kong, 1956-58; University of California, Berkeley, California, USA, 1958-60; Professor in Architecture, University of Manitoba, Winnipeg, Canada, 1960-; Private practice, principal of Da Roza Architects, Winnipeg, Canada, 1961-. *Memberships:* Fellow, Royal Architectural Institute of Canada; Academician, Royal Canadian Academy of Arts; Canadian Housing Design Council; Architectural Advisory Board, Wascana Centre, Regina; Honorary Consul of Portugal in Winnipeg; Winnipeg Horsemen's Club; Board of Directors, Winnipeg Art Gallery. *Creative Works:* Architect: Man and His Home, Pavilion, Expo 67, Montreal, Quebec, 1966; Winnipeg Art Gallery, Winnipeg, Manitoba, 1971; Owens Art Gallery, Sackville, New Brunswick, 1972; Gull Harbour

Resort Hotel, Hecla Provincial Park, Manitoba, 1977; Church of the Immaculate Conception, Winnipeg, Manitoba, 1980; Over 50 private residences and numerous residential projects across Canada. *Honours:* Architectural Competitions: Finalist, design of New National Gallery of Canada, 1977; Honourable Mention for entries to Low Energy Building Design Award, 1979; First Prize, Design of Winnipeg Art Gallery, 1967; First Prize and 2 Hon. Mentions for house design by CLA, 1965; Finalist, design of 1968 Winter Olympic Games project in Alberta, 1963; Numerous awards and recognitions for residential projects. *Hobbies:* Art; Horses; Skiing; Travel. *Address:* 515 Shaftesbury Blvd. Winnipeg, Manitoba, Canada R3P 0M3.

DART, Rowland Stanley James, b. 20 Dec. 1906, Sydney, Australia. Education. m. Clarice Williams 27 Dec. 1929, 2 sons. *Education:* Sydney Teachers' College, 1926-27; Bachelor of Arts, Evening Student, 1941-43. *Appointments:* Teacher-in-charge, Public School, Merungle Hill, Leeton, 1927-36; Deputy Headmaster, Auburn North, 1937; Newtown, 1941; Granville Secondary, 1943; Principal Bourke Intermediate High School, 1948; Inspector of Schools (NSW) Temora, 1950; Lithgow/Bathurst, 1954; Kogarah (Sydney), 1957; Maroubra, 1963; Chatswood/Gordon, 1967-71. Retired Dec. 1971. *Memberships:* Australian College of Education; Scout Association of Australia; Warranted Scoutmaster, 1925-; Commissioner, 1942-; National, Australian Commissioner for Training, 1966-71; NSW HQ Commissioner for Training, 1942-66; Honorary Commissioner, 1975-; Rotary; President St. Ives Rotary Club; NSW National Fitness Council member, 1957-71; President, NSW Institute of Inspectors of Schools; Australasian Association of Institutes of Inspectors of Schools, 1963. *Honours:* Medal of Order of Australia, 1980; Paul Harris Fellow (Rotary), 1978; Scouting Awards: Medal of Merit, 1942; Silver Acorn, 1962; Silver Kangaroo, 1970; Leader, Australian Scout Delegation to World Scout Conference, Lisbon, 1961. *Hobbies:* Scouting; Caravanning; Travel. *Address:* 4 Tobruk Avenue, St. Ives, Sydney, Australia.

DAS, Anadi Kumar, b. 2 Nov. 1931, West Bengal, India. Dentist. m. Ila 18 May 1968, 1 son 1 daughter. *Education:* BSc, 1954; BDS, Calcutta University, 1958; MDS, Bombay University, 1961. *Appointments:* Lecturer in Dentistry, 1962; Assistant Professor Dentistry, 1964; Professor Dentistry, 1971; Principal, Dentistry, 1973. *Memberships:* Dental Council of India; Indian Dental Association; Indian Prosthodontic Society; Lions International; Beugate Association. *Publications:* Standardisation of Dental Materials; Philosophy of Partial Denture Service; Radio talk on oral Cancer; Transplantation of Teeth. *Honours:* Fellowship under Colombe Plan for training in Maxillo-Facial Surgery and Prosthesis, Royal Melbourne Hospital, Victoria, Australia, 1969-70. *Hobbies:* Reading; Sports and Games. *Address:* 4 Manoramagary, Agra Bombay Road, Indore, MP India 452001.

DAS GUPTA, Jyoti Bhusan, b. 1 Nov. 1926, Calcutta. University Professor. m. Namita Sen Gupta 10 May 1965, 2 sons. *Education:* BA, 1945, MA, Political Science, Calcutta University, 1954; Master of Social Sciences, Institute of Social Studies, The Hague, 1957; DSc, Political and Social Sciences, Amsterdam University, 1958. *Appointments:* Research Scholar, Indian Council of World Affairs, New Delhi, 1959-60; Lecturer, Political Science, Gauhati University, Assam, 1960-61; Reader in International Relations, 1961-71; Professor of International Relations, 1971-; Head of Department of International Relations, Jadaupur University, Calcutta, 1974-77. *Memberships:* Indian Council of World Affairs, New Delhi. *Publications:* Indo-Pakistan Relations, 1947-1955, 1958; Jammu and Kashmir, 1968. *Honours:* Gold Medal and Sir S N Banerjee Prizes, Calcutta University, 1954; Nuffic fellowship, The Hague, 1955-57; Ford Foundation fellowship, 1957; Senior Fulbright fellowship tenable at USA, 1967. *Hobbies:* Reading; Travelling. *Address:* CF 24 Salt Lake City, Calcutta 700064 India.

DAS Gupta, Shantimoy, b. 1 Feb. 1928, Rangoon, Burma. Medical Educator. m. Bela Das Gupta, May 1952, 2 daughters. *Education:* MBBS Calcutta University, India, 1955; MD (Pathology), Delhi University, India, 1964. *Appointments:* Lecturer and Head, Department of Forensic Medicine, Government Medical College, Jabalpur (UP), India, 1964-67; Reader and Head,

Department of Forensic Medicine, Institute of Medical Sciences, Banaras Hindu University, Varanasi, (UP) India, 1967-73; Professor and Head, Department of Forensic Medicine, Institute of Medical Sciences, Banaras Hindu University, India 1973-. *Memberships:* Indian Academy of Forensic Sciences; Indian Association of Forensic Medicine; Indian Academy of Forensic Medicine; Indian Association for Advancement of Medical Education; Indian Medical Association; Forensic Science Society, England. *Publications:* 14 Outstanding Achievements in the field of Forensic Pathology, Psychiatry, Anthropology, Immunology, Thanatology, Clinical Forensic Medicine; 15 Outstanding Achievements in Research and Academic; 22 Outstanding Achivements Academic Honours; Papers presented-/accepted at International and National Seminars and Conferences: 8 International; 68 National; 61 Publications; Five Books and Souveniers. *Honours:* Fellowship of Indian Academy of Forensic Sciences, 1974; Dr. B C Roy National Award and Gold Medical of 1979; Convenor, Speciality Board of Forensic Medicine, National Board of Examinations, India; Member, International Board of Editors, International Journal of Medicine and Law; National Correspondent, Board of National Correspondents for India for INFORM; Member of National Geographic Society of USA. *Hobbies:* Gardening; Outdoor Games; Music; General Knowledge; History and Geography. *Address:* A-4 New Medical Enclave, Banaras Hindu University, Varanasi 221005 (U.P.) India.

DAS GUPTA, Suhasini Jhunoo, b. Jalpaiguri, Bengal. Retired Gazetted, First Class Officer of Government of India. *Education:* Graduate, Calcutta University, History and Mathematics, 1937; Studied, MA, Ancient Indian History and Culture; Work Study Appreciation Course for Senior Officers, Defence Services Work Study Institute, Landour Mussorie, 1968; Studied Law Non Collegiate Women Student, New Delhi University Women's Educational Programme, 1954-56. *Appointments:* Women's Auxiliary Corps, India, 1942-46; Indian National Airways, New Delhi, 1946; Representative of Industrial firm of Bombay, 1948-49; Directorate of National Cadet Corps, Ministry of Defence Lady Staff Officer, Division Units of the National Cadet Corps all over Indian schools and Colleges, 1969-74. *Memberships:* Pensioners Associations in India; Red Cross and Hospital Welfare Committee; All India Women's Conference; Federation of Kennel Clubs of India; National Kennel Club, India; Wild Life Fund; Officers Club; Social Welfare Board; Girl Guides. *Honours:* Star, 1939-43; Burma Star; War Medal, 1942-46; NCC, National Award, 1971. *Hobbies:* Dog Breeding and Training; Needlework and Needle Craft; Sewing; Reading and Writing; Painting; Music; Animal and Social Welfare; Gardening; Cooking. *Address:* Ashirbad, Solan (H.P), Pin Code 173212, India.

DAS MUNSI PRIYA RANJAN, Priya, b. 13 Nov. 1943, Chirirbandar, Dinajpur, East Bangladesh. Advocate; Freelance Journalist. *Appointments:* School Teacher, Higher Secondary School, 1966-67; Accounts Assistant, Commercial Firm, 1967-70; Member, Lok Sajha, Parliament of India, 1971-77. *Memberships:* Vice President, All India Football Federation; Inter Parliamentary Union; Governing Body, Chittaranjan Cancer Research Institute, Calcutta. *Publications:* Take Over; Anek Rakta Anek Nam, 1967 and 1972; Composed and published stories, poetry in teaching journals. *Honours:* NCC; Physical Efficiency Star Holder; MA, Calcutta University; LLB; Vice Chancellor, Medal Winner, 1963. *Hobbies:* Singing; Playing Chess; Reading. *Address:* Ga Rani Bhawani Road, Calcutta 26, West Bengal, India.

DATTA, Anaida Kumar, b. 1 May 1916, Kushtia, Bangladesh. Electrical and Electronic Engineer. m. Nilima, 9 May 1949, 2 sons, 1 daughter. *Education:* BSc.(Physics), 1938, MSc.(Applied Physics), 1941, Calcutta University, India; Section A of Institution of Electrical Engineers (London), 1947; Advanced Electrical Technology & Power Distribution, 1947, Structural Engineering, Inter grade, 1947, Radio Service Work, Inter grade, 1947, City and Guilds of London Institute, London, UK. *Appointments:* Lecturer in Physics, Bangabasi College, Calcutta, India, 1943-44; Professor and Principal, Indian Engineering Institute, New Delhi, 1944-48; Technical Assistant, later Deputy Engineer in Charge, High Power Transmitters, All India Radio, Delhi, 1948-76; In charge, Electronic and Electrical workshop, Mother's International School, New Delhi,

1977-79; Consulting Engineer, 1976-. *Memberships:* India Society of Engineers, India; Institution of Engineers, India; Referee and Member Executive Committee, Gauhati Centre, 1968-70; Institution of Electrical Engineers, London, UK; Fellow, Institution of Electronic and Telecom Engineers, India. *Creative Works:* Design and Installation of emergency broadcasting station at Kohima, Nagaland, India; Installation of Recording vans at Calcutta, Cuttack, Vijayawada, Recording Studio at Imphal (Manipur), Receiving centre at Calcutta, Read over room, Diesel generator, Air conditioner, half-minute and second impulse clocks, Loud speaker network in Calcutta, Transmitters at Patna in All India Radio. *Honours:* Holder of Technological certificate of City and Guilds of London Institute; Commendation for installation work of broadcasting equipment at Cuttack and Nagaland in shortest time of one month each. Hobby: Study of languages. *Address:* B-192, Chittaranjan Park, New Delhi-110019, India.

DATTA, Bimal Kumar, b. 11 Mar. 1920, Mazilpur. University Librarian and Teacher-in-Charge. m. Seuli, 27 Jan. 1947, 1 son, 1 daughter. *Education:* BA, 1942; MA, 1949; Diploma in Lib. Sc., 1948; PhD., 1963. *Appointments:* Excavation Assistant, Archaeological Survey of India, 1946; Assistant Editor, Pratyaha, 1946; Assistant Librarian, Visva-Bharati University, 1947; University Librarian, Visva-Bharati, Santiniketan, W.B., 1949; Head of the Department of Library Science, 1952. *Memberships:* BLA; ALA; ILA; IASLIC; President, Bandhab Library, WB, 1980; President(R), Banga Sahitya Semml, 1981; Academic Council & Court, V B University. *Publications:* Introduction to Indian Art; Bengal Temples; A Practical Guide to Library Procedure; Libraries and Librarianship of Anc. & Med. India; Book in Bengali and Hindia; 150 articles in Indian and Foreign journals on Library Science and Indian Art. *Honours:* Senior Fellow, South East Asia Library Seminar, Australia, 1951; Fulbright & Smith Mundt Scholar, USA, 1952; Gold Medal, BLA, 1959. *Hobbies:* Collector of Art objects and books on Art. *Address:* 'Surendra Niketan', PO Jaynagar Mazilpur, 24 Paraganas, West Bengal, India.

DAUTH, John Cecil, b. 9 Apr. 1947, Brisbane, Australia. Diplomat. *Education:* BA(Hons.), Sydney University, Australia, 1968. *Appointments:* Department Foreign Affairs, Canberra, Australia, 1969; 2nd Secretary, Australia High Commission, Lagos, Nigeria, 1970-72; Department Foreign Affairs, Canberra, Australia, 1973-74; Concurrently Tutor, History, Burgmann College, ANV. Canberra, Australia, 1973-74; 1st Secretary, Australian Embassy, Islamadad, 1975-76; Assistant Press Secretary to HM Queen, Buckingham Palace, London, UK, 1977-80; Department of Foreign Affairs, Head, Commonwealth and Multilateral Organizations Section, 1980-. *Memberships:* National Press Club, Canberra, Australia. *Honours:* MVO.(iV), 1980. *Hobbies:* Music; Cricket; Squash. *Address:* 4 Hubba Street, Torrens ACT 2607, Australia.

DAVE, Trambaklal Nandakeshwar, b. 5 Jan. 1897, Muli, Dist. Surendranagar, Gujarat State, India. Retired Government Officer. m. Shrimati Sarasvati Umashankar, 10 May 1916, 1 son, 3 daughters. *Education:* BA, 1919, MA, 1928, BT, 1925, Bombay University; PhD, London University, 1931. *Appointments:* Professor of Sanskrit, Gujarat University, Ahmedabad, 1931-45; Vice-Principal, College for Princes, Rajkot, 1943-45; Principal, Dharmensasinhji Arts & Science College, Gujarat State, 1945-48; Lecturer in Sanskrit & Gujarate, London University, 1947-56; Director, Oriental Research Institute, Dwarka Gujarat, 1956-66. *Memberships:* Fellow, Royal Asiatic Society, London; Fellow, Gujarat Research Society, Bombay. *Publications:* Historical Grammar of Old Gujarati (15th Century); Languages of Aboriginal Tribes in the Border Lands of Gujarat; Language of Gujarati; Contributions to the Indo-Aryan Dictionary (w. Prof Dr R.L. Turner). *Honours:* North-Cote Gold Medal, Bombay University, 1921; PhD., Distinction Prize, London University, 1931; Royal Asiatic Society, London Prize, for best work in Gujarati Linguistics, 1935; Gold Medal from the Prime Minister of India, 1977. *Hobby:* Vedantic Studies. *Address:* Bhava-bhuti, Surendsa Mangaldas Road, Opp Govt. H Colony, Ahmedabad, 15, India.

DAVEY, Thomas Ronald Albert, b. 27 Mar. 1925, Melbourne, Victoria, Australia. Consulting Metallurgist. m. Kathleen Ann Bonython, 24 July 1954, 1 son, 2

daughters. *Education:* BSc, 1947, B.Met.E, 1948, M.Met.E, 1954, Doctor of Applied Science, 1967, University of Melbourne, Australia. *Appointments:* Research Officer, 1947-54, Chief Research Officer, Broken Hill Associated Smelters, 1959-60, Port Pirie, South Australia; Betriebsinginieur, Norddeutsche Affinerie, Hamburg, Germany, 1954-57; Research Officer, 1957-58, Consultant, 1958-59, Consultant, 1960-63, Imperial Smelting Corporation, Avonmouth, UK; Senior Principal Research Scientist, Chemical Engineering Division, Commonwealth Scientific & Industrial Research Organisation, Melbourne, Australia, 1963-69; Professor of Metallurgical Engineering, Colorado School of Mines, Golden, Colorado, USA, 1969-72; Research Planner, Minerals Research Laboratories, CSIRO, Melbourne, Australia, 1973-78; Visiting Professor of Metallurgy, University of Melbourne, Australia, 1979-80; Consultant, Metacon Consulting Services, Melbourne, Australia. 1981-. *Memberships:* Fellow, Institution of Mining and Metallurgy, London; Australasian Institute of Mining and Metallurgy; AIME; Founder member of Wilhelm Hofmann Memorial Prize International Consortium, 1968-81. *Publications:* over 60 publications in professional journals, or chapters in technical books. *Creative Works:* 22 Patents in many countries; Co-organizer of Symposia on Extractive Metallurgy, Melbourne, 1967 and 1974; Convenor of Australia-Japan Symposium on Extractive Metallurgy, Sydney, Australia, 1980. *Honours:* Australian IMM Student's Essay Prize, 1943 and 1944; Exhibition for Final Hons. in Metallurgy, Melbourne University, Australia, 1948; Gold Medal of AIME Extractive Metallurgy Division, 1955; Keynote Lecturer at International Tin Symposium, La Paz, Bolivia, 1977; Keynote Lecturer at International Symposium, Advances in Chemical Metallurgy, Bombay, India, 1979; Keynote Lecturer at International Symposium on Lead, Zinc, Tin, Las Vegas, USA, 1980. *Hobbies:* Music; Literature; Gardening. *Address:* 5 Rhodes Drive, Glen Waverley, Victoria 3150, Australia.

DAVID, Jean Marc, b. 22 Sept. 1925, Port Louis, Mauritius. Barrister-at-Law. m. Mary Doreen Mahoney, 4 Feb. 1948, 3 sons, 3 daughters. *Education:* Royal College, Port Louis, Mauritius, 1938-41; Laureate (of English Scholarship), Royal College, Curepipe, Mauritius, 1942-45; Middle Temple, London, England, 1946-49; Called to the Bar, Michaelmas, 1949; LLB(Hons.), London School of Economics and Political Science, England, 1946-50. *Appointments:* Started Practising at Mauritius Bar, 1950 and returned to practice, 1964; District Magistrate, Mauritius Judicial Department, 1955-59; Crown Law Officer, Mauritius Legal Department, 1959-64; Member, Electoral Supervisory and Boundaries Commissions, 1968-, and Chairman since, 1973-; Chairman of various Commissions of Enquiry and Arbitration Tribunals (relating to Industrial Disputes and Valuation on compulsory acquisition); Visitor, University of Mauritius, 1980. *Memberships:* Chairman, Mauritius Bar Association, 1968, 1979; Founder member, Lions Club of Port Louis; Mauritius Society for the Prevention of Cruelty to Animals; Mauritius Turf Club; Racing Club of Mauritius; Port Louis City Club; Action Civique; Stella Clavisque Club. *Honours:* Queen's Counsel, 1969. *Hobbies:* Reading; Horse Racing. *Address:* 'Hillview', Jenner Lane, Farquhar Avenue, Quatre Bornes, Mauritius.

DAVIDSON, James Alfred, b. 1922 England. British Diplomat. m. Daphne S, 1955, 2 stepsons, 2 daughters. *Education:* Christ's Hospital; Royal Naval College, Dartmouth; Barrister-at-Law, Middle Temple; Master Mariner's Certificate of Service. *Appointments:* Royal Navy, 1939-60; Commander, HM Ships Calder and Welfare, 1955; Called to the bar, 1960; Commonwealth Office, 1960; Port of Spain, Phnom Penh, 1970 and 71; Dacca, Chargé d'Affaires, and Dep. High Commissioner, 1972-73; Visiting Scholar, University of Kent, 1973-74; High Commissioner in Brunei, 1974-78; Governor, British Virgin Islands, 1978. *Memberships:* Army and Navy Club. *Honours:* Officer, Order of the British Empire, 1971. *Address:* c/o Foreign & Commonwealth Office, London, SW1, England.

DAVIDSON, Lindsay Alexander Gordon, b. 18 June 1926, Edinburgh. Professor. m. (1) Joyce Mary Mitcalfe 15 Sept. 1954, 1 son, 2 daughters, (2) Gillian Grubb, 21 Jan. 1977. *Education:* George Watsons College, Edinburgh, 1931-43; MB, ChB, Edinburgh University, 1943-48; MD, University of Birmingham, 1962; FRCP,

Edinburgh, 1962; FRCP, London, 1970; FRACP, 1977; FRACMA, 1980; MFCM, 1980. *Appointments:* Luccock Research Fellow, University of Durham, 1954-55; Lecturer, Research Fellow, University of Birmingham, 1956-62; John Polachek Fellow, Columbia University, New York, (Public Health Fellowship), 1959-60; Professor of Medicine, 1962-70, Dean of Medicine, 1967-69, University of Rhodesia; Senior Research Fellow, University of Glasgow, 1969-70; Consultant Physician, University Hospital of Wales, 1970-77; Principal and Director, School of Public Health and Tropical Medicine, Commonwealth Department of Health, 1977-80; Director, Commonwealth Institute of Health in the University of Sydney, 1980-; Professor, University of Sydney, 1977. *Memberships:* Royal Society of Medicine; Royal Medical Society; Thoracic Society; Thoracic Society of Australia; British Cardiac Society; Australian and New Zealand Society for Epidemiology and Research in Community Health/Australian Public Health Association Incorporated; Association of Physicians of Great Britain and Ireland; International Society of Epidemiology. *Publications:* Published papers on Cardiopulmonary Physiology, Medical Education, Health Promotion, Health Services Research, etc. *Address:* 6 Avon Close, Pymble, NSW, Australia, 2073.

DAVIDSON, William, b. 16 May 1924, Ardoe, Kincardineshire, Scotland. Professor of Applied Mathematics. m. Irene B Cook, 18 Dec. 1954, 1 son, 1 daughter. *Education:* BSc.(Hon.) Mathematics, 1950, MSc, PhD., DSc., Queen Mary College, University of London, UK. *Appointments:* Lecturer, Senior Lecturer, Reader in Applied Mathematics, Battersea College of Technology (later the University of Surrey, Guildford), 1950-66; Professor of Applied Mathematics, University of Otago, Dunedin, New Zealand, 1966-. *Memberships:* Fellow, Royal Society of New Zealand; Fellow, Institute of Mathematics and its Applications; Fellow, Royal Astronomical Society; International Astronomical Union and of its Commission 47 (Cosmology) and 48 (High Energy Astrophysics); New Zealand Mathematical Society; President, Local Branch (Otago) Royal Society of New Zealand, 1973. *Publications:* Astrophysics (W A Benjamin); numerous papers and encyclopedic articles in Cosmology and Relativity. *Honours:* Visiting Professor, Queen Elizabeth College, University of London, UK, 1971; Visiting Professor, University of Sussex Astronomy Centre, UK, 1978. *Hobbies:* Walking; Gardening. *Address:* 54 Tomahawk Road, Dunedin, New Zealand.

DAVID-WEST, Kelsey Benibo, b. 9 May 1938, Buguma, Rivers State, Nigeria. Veterinary Surgeon. m. Merlene Adela Johnson, 1 Dec. 1965, 2 sons, 2 daughters. *Education:* Doctor of Veterinary Medicine, Toronto, Canada, 1964. *Appointments:* Federal Department of Veterinary Research, Vum Nigeria, 1964-66; Eastern Nigeria Veterinary Services, 1966-70; Rivers State of Nigeria Veterinary Services, 1970-72; Deputy Chief Veterinary Officer, 1972-74, Chief Livestock Planning Officer, 1974-75, Deputy Director, 1975-79, Director, 1979-, Federal Livestock Department, Nigeria. *Memberships:* Nigerian Veterinary Medical Association; Royal College of Veterinary Surgeons; Animal Production Society of Nigeria. *Publications:* Newcastle Disease in Nigeria-Retrospection and Anticipation; Animal Health Problems and Livestock Development in Nigeria. *Honours:* Federal Government Scholar, 1959-64. *Hobbies:* Swimming; Table tennis; Badminton. *Address:* House 4, Closea 21st Road, 2nd Avenue, Festac Town, Lagos, Nigeria.

DAVIES, Arthur Llewellyn, b. 18 Aug. 1903, Brantford, Ontario, Canada. Newspaper and Broadcasting executive. m. (1) Dorothy Eleanor Porter, 5 May, 1934, 2 sons; (2) Jean Campbell Rowe, 8 July 1969. *Education:* Collegiate Institute, Renfrew, Ontario, Canada; Central Technical School, Toronto, Ontario, Canada. *Appointments:* General Manager, Kingston Whig-Standard, 1939-62; President, Peterborough Examiner, 1946-67; President, Kingston Whig-Standard, 1967-76; Director, 1942-77, President, 1967-77, Frontenac Broadcasting Co. and Kawartha Broadcasting Co; President, Alda Llyn Limited, 1968-. *Memberships:* Royal Edward Lodge AF & AM., Kingston; Past President, Ontario Provincial Daily Newspaper Association; Past-President, Canadian Daily Newspaper Association; President, Board of Governors, Kingston General Hospital, 1950-53; Board of Trustees, Queen's University, 1959-74; National Club, Toronto, Canada; Cataraque Golf and Country Club,

Canada; Kingston Yacht Club, Canada. *Publications:* Sketches, Scholars and Scandals of a Quiet College Town; Death Plays a Duet. *Honours:* Honorary Doctor of Laws, Queen's University, Canada, 1979; Officer Brother, Order of St. John, 1958; Confederation Medal of Canada, 1967; City of Kingston Award for Achievement, 1980; Honorary President, Kingston & District United Fund; Honorary President, St. John Ambulance association, Kingston; Patron, Welsh Society of Kingston. *Hobbies:* Yachting; Travelling. *Address:* 245 Alwington Place, Kingston, Ontario, Canada, K7L 4P9.

DAVIES, Bruce Richard, b. 8 Jan. 1925, Sydney, New South Wales, Australia. Under Secretary and Permanent Head, Department of Lands and Registrar General of the State of New South Wales. m. Gwenyth Joy Eldridge, 11 Oct. 1947, 2 sons. *Education:* Bachelor of Law, Sydney University, Australia; Admitted as Barrister, 1949; Admitted as Solicitor, 1954. *Appointments:* New South Wales Public Service, Registrar General's Office, 1942; Senior Deputy Registrar General, 1961; Deputy Under Secretary, Premier's Department, 1965; Under Secretary and Permanent Head, New South Wales Premier's Department and Secretary, New South Wales Cabinet, 1973; Under Secretary and Permanent Head, Department of Lands and Registrar General of the State of New South Wales, 1977; Royal Australian Naval Rsserve, 1943-46; Deputy Chairman, New South Wales Archives Authority, 1965-80. *Memberships:* Vice-President, 1979, President, 1978, International Nippon Australia New Zealand Club; Royal Automobile Club; Royal Commonwealth Society; Chairman, Lord Howe Island Board, 1981; Member, Zoological Parks Board of New South Wales, 1981. *Hobbies:* Golf; Tennis; Sailing; Japanese Language and culture. *Address:* A70 Carrington Road, Wahroonga, 2076, New South Wales, Australia.

DAVIES, Edward William, b. 28 April 1937, Neath, South Wales, Chartered Chemical Engineer. m. Lynne Maureen Hadley, 30 Sept. 1965, 2 daughters. *Education:* Neath Technical College, 1955-58. *Appointments:* British Petroleum, 1955-62; Wales Gas Board, Cardiff, 1962-65; East Midlands Gas Board, Leicester, 1965-68; Conoco Limited, Killingholme, 1968-72; Gulf Oil Raffinaderij B.V., Rotterdam, 1972-79; Gulf Oil Company International, London, 1979-. *Memberships:* Member, The Institution of Chemical Engineers; Fellow, Institution of Gas Engineers; Fellow, Institute of Petroleum. *Honours:* 4 Caps, Welsh Secondary Schools Rugby Union, 1955; British Army Rugby Cap, Dorset and Wiltshire, 1960-61; Neath R.F.C., Bridgend R.F.C. *Hobbies:* Philately; Golf. *Address:* 'Seven Ways', 15 St. Huberts Close, Gerrards Cross, Bucks, England.

DAVIES, Frank Thomas, b. 12 Aug. 1904, Merthyr Tydfil, Glamorgan, Wales, Polar Explorer, Research Scientist. m. Ada Eleanor Bennett, 29 July, 1931, 2 daughters. *Education:* B.Sc. University College, Aberystwyth, 1925; M.Sc. McGill University, 1928; D.Sc. McGill University, 1978; D.Sc. York University, 1977. *Appointments:* Lecturer in Maths and Demonstrator in Physics, University of Saskatchewan, 1925-26; Demonstrator in Physics, McGill University, 1926-28; Physicist, First Byrd Antarctic Expedition, 1928-30; Physicist, Carnegie Institute, Washington, 1930-32, 1934-39; Leader, Canadian 2nd Polar Expedition, 1932-34; Director, Carnegie Geophysical Observatory, Huancayo, Peru, 1936-39; Scientist, Defence Research Board, successively Superintendent Radio Physics Laboratory., Director Physical Research, Assistant Chief Scientist, Director General, Telecommunications 1949-69. *Memberships:* Fellow, The Royal Society of Canada; Governor and Fellow, Artic Institute of North America; Canadian Association of Physicists. *Publications:* Author of numerous papers in Scientific Journals. *Honours:* Fellow, Royal Society of Canada; ONT. D.Sc. York University, 1977; D.Sc. McGill University, 1978; U.S. Congressional Medal, 1930; Fellow, Arctic Institute of North America. Numerous other awards. *Hobbies:* Welsh Society of Ottawa; Arctic Circle Club. *Address:* 22, Clegg Street, Ottawa, KISOH8, Canada.

DAVIES, Jeffrey William, b. 25 June 1942, Leicester, England. Virologist and Molecular Biologist. m. Jean Hajek, 6 July 1977. *Education:* BSc Nottingham University, 1963; PhD. Nottingham University, 1966. *Appointments:* Lecturer in Molecular Biology, University of Edinburgh, 1966-70; Senior Virologist, Regional Virus Laboratory, Birmingham, 1970-72; Visiting Fel-

lowships in Leiden and Madison; Assistant Scientist, Biophysics Laboratory, University of Wisconsin, United States of America, 1972-76; Senior Research Fellow, University of Wageningen, The Netherlands, 1976-79; Head of Virus Research, John Innes Institute, Norwich, 1979-. *Memberships:* Member, Society for General Microbiology; Member, Institute of Biology; Member, American Society for Microbiology; Member, Biochemical Society; Member, New York Academy of Sciences. *Publications:* Nucleric Acids in Plants, Vols I and II; Various Scientific papers in several journals, in the fields of Virology, Biochemistry and Molecularbiology. *Honours:* Fellow, Linnean Society of London, 1975. *Hobbies:* Theatre; Music; Stage Director of Opera and Plays; Acting; Singing; Teacher of voice production and singing; Various sports and languages. *Address:* 7 Meadow Road, Costessey, Norwich NR5 ONF, England

DAVIES, Michael Bruce, b. 8 Aug. 1939, Berwyn, Alberta, Canada, Investment Banker. m. Susan Kirchheimer, 6 Dec. 1970, 1 son, 1 daughter. *Education:* Bachelor of Commerce, 1961, Bachelor of Law, University of British Columbia, 1964. *Appointments:* Lawyer, Davis and Company, 1965; First National City Bank, New York , and The Mercantile Bank of Canada, 1965-70; Vice-President and Director McLeod, Young Weir, Toronto, 1970-76; Vice President Finance, The Polar and Gas Project, Toronto, 1976-80; Vice-President, Morgan Stanley and Company 1980-. *Memberships:* Law Society of British Columbia, 1965; Canadian Bar Association; National Club; Royal Canadian Yacht Club; The Dellcrest Childrens Centre. *Hobbies:* Tennis; Jogging; Skiing. *Address:* 1148, 5th Avenue, New York, USA.

DAVIES, Peter Griffith, b. 8 Oct. 1946, Bloemfontein, South Africa, Pathologist. m. Beverley Howman, 23 Feb. 1974, 2 daughters. *Education:* M.B.C.H.B. Cape Town, 1971; F.F.Path, South Africa, 1978; M.M.E.D. Path, South Africa, 1978. *Appointments:* Housemanship year at Groote Schuur Hospital, Cape Town, 1972; Registrar, Mpilo Hospital, Bulawayd, Zimbabwe, 1973; Registrar in Pathology, Harare Hospital, Salisbury and Cape Town, 1974-78; Consultant Pathologist, Director, Hospital Laboratories, Salisbury, Zimbabwe, 1979-. *Memberships:* Various Medical Associations; Member, Old Georgians Sports Club. *Hobbies:* Tennis; Squash; Skiing; Swimming. *Address:* 11, Burnham Road, Highlands, Salisbury, Zimbabwe.

DAVIES, Richard, b. 14 Sept. 1924, Leeds, Yorkshire, Chartered Engineer. m. (1) Elsa Schneller, 12 Dec. 1953, 2 sons, 2 daughters. *Education:* M.A. Cambridge University, 1950-53. *Appointments:* Sutcliffe Speakman and Co. Ltd., Leigh, Lancashire, 1939-46; Ministry of Supply, Department Atomic Energy, Risley, 1946-50; United Kingdom Atomic Energy Authority, Risley, 1953-70; National Nuclear Corporation Limited, Risley, 1970-. *Memberships:* Member, Fitzwilliam Society; Fellow, Institution of Mechanical Engineers; Fellow, British Institute of Management; Fellow, Institute of Industrial Managers; Member, Institution of Production Engineers; Cambridge University Engineers Association. *Honours:* Technical State Scholarship, 1949. *Hobbies:* Reading; Photography; Philately; D.I.Y; Swimming. *Address:* Bry-Lyn, Cross Lane, Croft, Warrington, Cheshire, WA3 7AR, England.

DAVIS, Brian Newton, b. 28 Oct. 1934, Stratford, New Zealand. m. Marie Lynette Waters, 21 Jan. 1960, 4 daughters. *Education:* Teachers Training College, Ardmore, 1952-53; Auckland University, 1952-53; Victoria University of Wellington, 1955-58; BA, 1957, MA (1st class hons), Christchurch Theological College, 1959; Licentiate of Theology, 1965. *Appointments:* Teacher, Stratford Primary School, 1954; Lab. Assistant, Victoria University of Wellington, 1958; Ordained Deacon, 1960; Priest, 1961; Assistant Curate, St. Marks, Wellington, 1960-62; Assistant Curate, Parish of Karori and Makara, 1962-64; Vicar of Makara and Karori West, 1964-67; Vicar of Dannevirke, 1967-73; Vicar of Cathedral Parish of St. John The Evangelist and Dean of Waiapu, 1973-80; Vicar General of Waiapu, 1979-80; Bishop of Waikato, 1980-. *Memberships:* Lions International. *Publications:* Regular Columnist for Church Scene, Australian Anglican Newspaper; Contributor to Encyclopaedia of New Zealand, 1966. *Hobbies:* Wood Carving; Water Colour Painting; Squash Racquets. *Address:* P.O. Box 21, Hamilton, New Zealand

DAVIS, John Derek, b. 22 July, 1923, Bridlington, Yorkshire, England, Chartered Mechanical Engineer. m. Peggy Jean Hardiment, 5 June 1945, 1 son, 1 daughter. *Education:* Derby Technical College, 1940-41; Sidney Sussex College, Cambridge University, 1941-43; M.A. Mechanical Sciencestripos. *Appointments:* Apprentice, Rolls Royce Limited, Derby, 1940; Air Engineer Officer, Royal Navy, 1943-46; Research Engineer, Shell Research Limited, 1946-53; Head, Product and Marketing Development, Shell International Petroleum Company Limited; Chairman, Shell Composites Limited, 1971-74; Non-Executive Director, Jobling Purser Limited, 1976-81; Private Consultant, 1974-81; Adviser to Ministry of Defence, 1975-81. *Memberships:* Fellow, Institution of Mechanical Engineers; Fellow, Institute of Petroleum. *Publications:* 'Energy-to use or abuse.'; 'Technology for a changing world'. *Honours:* Crompton-Lanchester Medal, 1952; Eastlake Medal, 1976. *Hobbies:* Sailing; Writing. *Address:* 10, Grenfell Road, Beaconsfield, Buckinghamshire, England.

DAVIS, John Raymond, b. 5 May 1932, Sydney, NSW, Australia. Consultant Paediatrician. m. Marilyn Esther Saulwick, 5 Dec. 1956, 2 daughters. *Education:* MB, BS, Sydney University, 1956, FRACP. *Appointments:* Prince Alfred Hospital, Sydney; Parramatta Hospital, Sydney; Royal Hospital for Women; Currently, Physician, Royal Alexandra Hospital for Children; Head Department, Paediatrics, Royal North Shore Hospital, Mona Vale District Hospital. *Memberships:* Chief Medical Advisor, Variety Club of Australia. *Hobbies:* Tennis; Stamps; Horses. *Address:* 6 Heights Crescent, Middle Cove, NSW, 2068, Australia.

DAVIS, Phoebe Irene (Mrs), b. 27 Oct. 1898, Sydney, Australia. Accountant. m. (1) Leslie Sulman (dec.), 20 Apr. 1921, 1 son, 1 daughter, (2) Maurice Davis, 1950. *Education:* Sydney Technical High School until 1912; Sydney Metropolitan Business College until 1914. *Appointments:* Book-keeper, Typist, Director, Secretary, General Business Administration, 1952-75; Honorary Secretary to "Help-in-Need Society" since 1940; Secretary to Western Suburbs Synagogue, 1952-69; Honorary Treasurer to AJHS, since 1976. *Memberships:* Various Communal Organisations in Sydney. *Publications:* Contributor to Great Synagogue Journal. *Hobbies:* Drama & Concert Going; Reading; Exotic Cooking. *Address:* 4/282 New South Head Road, Double Bay, New South Wales, 2028, Australia.

DAVIS, Roy Cecil, b. 6 May 1932, Nassau, Bahamas. Sales Manager, Eastern Airlines. *Education:* Graduated Government High School, 1949. *Appointments:* BOAC, Nassau, 1950-59; Bahamas Airways, 1959-69; Office Manager, Law Chambers, 1969-72; Manager-Passenger & Cargo Sales, Eastern Airlines, 1972-. *Memberships:* Councillor, Executive Council, Chairman, Tourism Division, Deputy Chairman, Education Committee, Deputy Chairman, Bay Street Committee, Chamber of Commerce. *Honours:* Bahamas Chamber of Commerce Distinguished Citizen in Civics, 1981; Spirit of Service Award, Kiwanis International, 1976; Kiwanian of the Year, 1966, 77, 78; Life Member of Kiwanis International, 1981; Bahamas National Tourism Achieement Award, 1981. *Hobbies:* Old passenger liners—Member, Steamship Historical Society; Titanic memorabilia—Member, Titanic Historical Society. *Address:* Stevenson Subdivision, PO Box N 4786, Nassau, Bahamas.

DAVIS, Terence Newman, b. 25 Nov. 1930, Solihull, Warwickshire, England, University Dean. m. 1 Aug. 1960, 1 son, 1 daughter. *Education:* M.A. (Hons). University of Edinburgh, 1964; MEd. 1965, PhD, University of Birmingham, 1970. *Appointments:* Senior Lecturer, Homerton College, Cambridge, 1964-67; Lecturer, University of Bristol, 1967-70 Senior Lecturer, University of Stirling, Scotland, 1970-76; Dean, University of London Institute of Education, 1977-. *Memberships:* Fellow, Royal Statistical Society; Fellow, Royal Society Arts; Associate British Psychological Society. *Honours:* Gold Medal Psychology, 1963. *Hobbies:* Bridge; Theatre; Swimming. *Address:* Silverhurst, Fulmer Way, Gerrards Cross, Bucks., England.

DAVIS-PIERRE, Marie Lucilla(rs), b. 3 Dec. 1918, Roseau, Commonwealth of Dominica. Speaker of the House of Assembly. m. 23 Apr. 1957 (divorced). *Education:* Sat Senior Sheffield School Certificate passed in English Language, English Literature, Mathematics & Geography, 1937; Passed in Commercial subjects, Typing & Shorthand, 1938; Certificate of Merit, Record Management Studies, Canada, 1970; Certificate, Clerks of Parliamentary Assemblies, Westminister, 1971. *Appointments:* Ran a Private School, 1939-44; Entered Civil Service, 1944; Acting Deputy Registrar, 1965-67; Clerk of the House of Assembly, 1967-78; Speaker of the House of Assembly, 1980-. *Memberships:* Secretary, Commonwealth Parliamentary Association, Dominica Branch, 1967-78, President, 1980. *Publications:* Author: Procedure and Working Methods of the House of Assembly, Dominica, 1975. *Honours:* Her Majesty's Silver Jubilee Medal, 1977; 1st Prize, National Day Essay Competition; Attended Annual Regional CPA Conferences in the Caribbean, Plenary CPA Conference in Malawi, 1971, Residing Officers & Clerks Conference in Dominica, 1970, Grand Cayman, 1974. *Hobbies:* Singing; Drama. *Address:* 25 Cork Street, Roseau, Commonwealth of Dominica, West Indies.

DAWE, Colin Stuart, b. 1 Oct. 1930, London, England, Economist. m. Claire Esney Hastings, 26 Jan 1963, 3 sons, 1 daughter. *Education:* London University, England.; B.A. University of Wellington, New Zealand, 1963. *Appointments:* London Metropolitan Borough Lambeth, 1947-55; Research Officer, New Zealand Public Service, 1956-68; Economist, Chief Economist, Bank of New South Wales, 1969. *Memberships:* President, New Zealand Business Planning Society, 1980; Councillor, Economic Society of New Zealand; University Club of Wellington. *Publications:* Economic Outlook for New Zealand in the 1980's, 1980; Government and Business in New Zealand, 1970. Hobby: Mountaineering. *Address:* 57, Matai Road, Hataitai, Wellington, New Zealand.

DAWES, Edward Naasson, b. 30 Aug. 1914, Newtown, Sydney, Australia. Lawyer. m. Margaret Villiers Cathie, 27 Dec. 1941, 1 son, 2 daughters. *Education:* Bachelor of Laws, University of Sydney, 1934-37. *Appointments:* Barrister-at-Law, New South Wales and Commonwealth Bar, 1939-58; Master in Equity and Master in Lunacy, Protective Division, Supreme Court of New South Wales, 1958; Retired, 1976. *Memberships:* New South Wales Bar Association, Council, 1949; Returned Services League of Australia; Tattersall's Club; Royal Motor Yacht Club; Royal Automobile Club of Australia; North Sydney Anzac Memorial Club. *Publications:* Dawes' Australian Proprietary and Private Companies (Law and Management), 1955; Consulting Editor: Dawes' Australian Proprietary and Private Companies (Law and Management) 2nd Edition, 1964; Purvis, Proprietary Companies, 1973. *Honours:* War Medal, 1939-45; Australian Service Medal. *Hobbies:* Boating; Swimming; Fishing; Music. *Address:* 108 Prince Alfred Parade, Newport, New South Wales, 2106, Australia.

DAWKINS, Roger Letts, b. 25 June 1941, Perth, Western Australia. Clinical Immunologist. *Education:* BMed. Sci, 1965; MBBS, 1966; MRCP, 1970; MD, 1974; FRACP, 1974; FRCPA, 1974. *Appointments:* Head Departments of Clinical Immunology, Royal Perth Hospital and Queen Elizabeth II Medical Centre, Perth, Western Australia; Associate Professor Immunopathology, University of Western Australia. *Memberships:* President, Australian Society of Medical Research; President, Australian Tissue Typing Association; Treasurer, Australian Society of Immunology. *Publications:* Approximately 100 papers, chapters in medical journals. Hobby: Simmental Cattle breeding. *Address:* Melaleuka, Nicholson Road, Canning Vale, Western Australia 6155.

DAWSON, Daryl Michael, b. 12 Dec. 1933, Melbourne, Victoria, Australia. Solicitor-General for Victoria. m. Mary Louise Thomas, 12 Feb. 1971. *Education:* LLB (Hons), University of Melbourne, 1954; LLM, Yale University, 1956. *Appointments:* Barrister, 1959-74; Queens Counsel, 1971; Solicitor General for Victoria, 1974-. *Memberships:* University of Melbourne Council, 1975-; Australian Motor Sport Appeal Court, 1970-; Savage Club; Melbourne Club. *Honours:* Companion of the Order of the Bath, 1980; Fulbright Scholar, 1955; Sterling Fellow, Yale University, 1955-56. Hobby: Squash. *Address:* 221 Queen Street, Melbourne, Victoria 3000, Australia.

DAYSH, Zena, b. New Plymouth, New Zealand. Secretary General and Executive Vice Chairman. *Appointments:* Executive Officer and Secretary-General of te Commonwealth Human Ecology Council; Committee on Nutrition in the Commonwealth. *Creative Works:* Pioneer and Catalyst force in Human Ecology movement in the Commonwealth now widening to International. *Address:* 63 Cromwell Road, London, SW7 5BL, England.

DE, Subhas Kumar, b. 19 Jan. 1921, Calcutta, India, Medicine. m. Bina Basu, 13 Mar. 1950, 1 son. *Education:* MBBS (Calcutta), 1945; Tuberculosis Disease Diploma, 1954; MD, India, 1965. *Appointments:* Medical Officer, Medical College Hospitals, West Bengal, 1945-54; Physician, Willingdon Hospital, New Delhi, India, 1954-70; Physician, Consultasnt Physician, Mulago Hospital, Kampala, Uganda, 1973; Senior Consultant Physician and Officer in charge of Uganda TB. Control, Kampala, Uganda; Co-ordinator in Uganda of MRC, TB. Research, UK; Lecturer in Medicine and Examiner in MB ChB exam, Makerese University, Kampala, Uganda. *Memberships:* Indian Medical Association; Uganda Medical Association; East Africa, Association of Physicians; American College of Chest Physicians; Life member, Indian Association of Chest Physicians; International Union Against Tuberculosis. *Publications:* Numerous Publications on Tuberculosis and Respiratory diseases in journals; Conducting MRC, Short course Tuberculosis Chemotherapy in Uganda, East Africa, Research, 1975-. *Honours:* First Class Honours in Preventive Medicine, 1945. Hobby: Photography. *Address:* Box 7051, Kampala, Uganda, East Africa.

DEAKINS, Eric Petro, b. 7 Oct. 1932, London, England. Member of Parliament. *Education:* BA, (Hons), History, London School of Economics, 1950-53. *Appointments:* Executive, 1956-69, General Manager, 1969-70, Pigs Division, FMC Limited; MP Walthamstow West, 1970-74; MP Walthamstow, 1974-; Parliamentary under Secretary of State for Trade, 1974-76; Parliamentary under Secretary of State for Health and Social Security, 1976-79. *Publications:* A Faith to Fight for, 1964; Two Pamphlets, one as joint author. *Hobbies:* Cinema; Football; Squash; Writing. *Address:* House of Commons, London SW1, England.

DEAN, Beryl (Mrs Wilfred M Phillips), b. 2 Aug. 1911, Bromley, Kent. Embroiderer; Lecturer; Designer; Author. m. Wilfred M Phillips, 22 June 1974, 2 stepsons. *Education:* Diploma, Royal School of Needlework, 1929-32; Diplomas, Industrial Design, Bromley College of Art, 1934; Associate, Royal College of Art, 1934-37. *Appointments:* Part-time teacher various schools and Colleges of Art, 1938-; Eastbourne School of Art, 1939-45; Lecturership, University of Durham, 1941; Free Lance Dress design, 1943-48; Ecclesiastical Embroidery, for St. Paul's, Chelmsford, Guildford, Canterbury, St. George's Chapel, Windsor Castle, etc. *Memberships:* Embroiderers' Guild; Past member Executive Committee; Fellowship, Society of Designer Craftsmen. *Publications:* Ecclesiastical Embroidery; Church Needlework; Ideas for Church Embroidery; Creative Applique; Embroidery in Religion and Ceremonial. *Honours:* M.B.E. 1975; Runner-up, City of London Midsummer Prize, 1977; Awarded Royal Exhibition, 1934. Hobby: Gardening. *Address:* 59 Thornhill Square, London N1 1BE, England.

DEAN, Geoffrey, b. 18 Sept. 1940, Newcastle-upon-Tyne, England. Book Publisher. m. Philma Marina Patterson, 10 Aug. 1963, 1 son, 1 daughter. *Education:* BA, University of Toronto, 1961. *Appointments:* College Representative, Editor, McGraw-Hill Company of Canada, Ltd., 1961-66; General Sales Manager, Methven Publications, 1966-69; Marketing Manager, Van Nostrand Reinhold Ltd., 1970-76, Vice-President Marketing, 1972-76; President, John Wiley & Sons, Canada Ltd., 1976-. *Memberships:* Granite Club; Officer, Canadian Book Publishers' Council. *Hobbies:* Music; Travel. *Address:* John Wiley & Sons of Canada Limited, 22 Worcester Road, Rexdale, Ontario, M9W 1L1, Canada.

DEAN, Patrick Henry (Sir), b. 16 Mar. 1909, Berlin. Company Director; Formerly HM Diplomatic Service. m. Patricia Wallace Jackson, 26 July 1947, 2 sons. *Education:* Gonville & Caius College, Cambridge; 1st Class Hons, Classics & Law, 1928-32; Fellow, Clare College, Cambridge, 1932-35; Barstow Law Scholar, Inns of Court, 1934. *Appointments:* Called to the Bar, 1934 by Lincoln's Inn and practised Law to 1939; Assistant Legal Adviser, Foreign Office, 1939-45; Head of German Political Department, Foreign Office, 1946-50; Minister, British Embassy, Rome, 1950-51; Assistant & Deputy Under-Secretary, Foreign Office, 1953-60; Permanent Representative of the UK to the United Nations, 1960-64; British Ambassador to US, 1965-69; Director, Taylor Woodrow, 1969-; International Adviser, American Express, 1969-; Chairman of Governing Body, Rugby School, 1972-; Chairman, English-Speaking Union, 1974-. *Memberships:* Hon. Bencher Lincoln's Inn, 1965; Hon. Fellowship Clare College & Gonville & Caius College, Cambridge, 1965; Brook's Club; The Brook (New York). *Honours:* GCMG, 1963. *Hobbies:* Shooting; Fishing; Walking. *Address:* 5 Bentinck Mansions, Bentinck Street, London W1M 5RJ, England.

DEAN, Paul, b. 14 Sept. 1924, Cheshire, United Kingdom. Member of Parliament; Director. m. Margaret Frances Parker, 7 Apr. 1980, 2 Stepsons. *Education:* Ellesmere College, Shropshire; Exeter College, Oxford, MA, BLitt. *Appointments:* War Service, 1943-46; Farmer, 1951-57; Conservative HQ., 1957-64; M.P. for North Somerset, 1964-; Opposition Spokesman on Social Services, 1968-70; Pensions Minister, 1970-74; Member Chairmen's Panel (House of Commons), 1979-; Chairman Conservative Health & Social Services Committee, 1979-. *Memberships:* Executive Committee UK Branch Commonwealth Parliamentary Association, 1975-; UK Representative on CPA Executive Committee, 1975; Attended Annual Conferences of the CPA, India, 1975, Canada, 1977, Jamaica 1978, New Zealand, 1979; CPA events in Papua New Guinea, Australia, Cyprus & Jersey; Member, Governing Body of Commonwealth Institute, 1981. *Hobbies:* Walking; Gardening. *Address:* House of Commons, London SW1, England.

DEAR, John Stanley Bruce, b. 18 July 1925, St. Lucia, West Indies. Barrister and Attorney-at-Law. m. Jeanne Dylis Rawlins, 24 Sept. 1949, 2 sons, 1 daughter. *Education:* BA, 1947, MA, Pembroke College, Cambridge, England; Middle Temple, Inns of Court, London, England. *Appointments:* Barrister and Attorney-at-Law. *Memberships:* President, Organisation of Commonwealth Caribbean Bar Association, 1968-70; President, Barbados Bar Association, 1973-76; Member of the Executive Committee of the International Planned Parenthood Federation; President, Barbados Museum and Historical Society; Member of the Council of the Barbados National Trust; Chairman, Barbados Board of Tourism. *Honours:* Queen's Counsel, 1963. *Hobbies:* Swimming; Reading; Bridge. *Address:* Deal House, Maxwell Coast Road, Christ Church, Barbados, West Indies.

deBRUYN, Mary Jean Hicks, b. 24 Jan. 1933, Craigmyle, Alberta, Canada. Teacher. m. Hendrik deBruyn, 12 May 1971, 1 son. *Education:* B.Ed., University of Alberta, Edmonton, Alberta, Canada, 1956; M.A., Columbia University, New York, USA, 1960; Post-graduate studics, University of Minnesota, Minneapolis, Minnesota, USA, 1965-66, Summer 1969. *Appointments:* Elementary School Teacher, Calgary, Alberta, 1950-59; Visiting Teacher, Special Educational Services, Calgary Board of Education, 1960-65; Teaching Assistant, University of Minnesota, USA, 1965-66; Sessional Instructor, University of Calgary, Alberta, 1968-69, 1971; Instructor, Inservice Courses for Classroom Teachers, 1966-76; Supervisor and Reading Clinician, Learning Assistance Centre, Calgary Board of Education, Calgary, Alberta, 1966-76; Reading Specialist, School for Unwed Mothers, Board of Education, Clagary, Alberta, 1976-; Visiting Professor, University of Victoria, Victoria, Canada, 1977; Private Consultant in Learning Disabilities, 1966-. *Memberships:* International Reading Association; Calgary Association for Children with Learning Disabilities; President, International Reading Association, 1967-68; Coordinator for Alberta, International Reading Association, 1971; Secretary, Disabled Reader Special Interest Group, 1976-77; Learning Disabilities Fund Registry, Alberta, 1975-; University Women's Club; Christian Women's Club; Church of the Nazarene. *Publications:* Many articles including publication in: Journal for Children with Learning Disabilities International Reading Association, Calgary and District Council Newsletter; Reader's Digest. *Honours:* Special acknowledgments were made as various terms of office expired. *Hobbies:* Reading; Travelling; Collecting recipes and cookbooks; Cooking. *Address:* 231 Varsity Estates Link NW, Calgary, Alberta, Canada, T3B 4E1

DE BUNSEN, (Sir) Bernard, b. 24 July 1907, Cambridge, England. Education. m. Joan Allington Harmston, 25 Oct. 1975. *Education:* BA, MA, Balliol College, Oxford, 1926-30; Teachers Certificate, London Day Training College, 1930-31. *Appointments:* Schoolmaster, Liverpool Elementary Schools, 1931-34; Assistant Director of Education, Wiltshire, 1934-38; HM Inspector of Schools, 1938-46; Director of Education, Palestine, 1946-48; Professor of Education, 1948-50, Principal, 1950-52, Makerere University College, East Africa; Vice-Chancellor, The University of East Africa, 1962-64; Principal, Chester College of Education, 1965-71. *Memberships:* Chairman, The Noel Buxton Trust, 1976-; Chairman, The Africa Bureau, 1971-77; Chairman, Africa Education Trust, 1966-; Chairman, Council for Aid to African Students, 1975-; Vice President, The Royal African Society; Vice President, The Anti-Slavery Society. *Honours:* CMG, 1957; Knight Bachelor, 1962. *Address:* 3 Prince Arthur Road, London, England.

DE CASTRO, Barbara Elaine, b. 11 Dec. 1931, New York, USA. Social Worker. m. 15 June 1957, 2 sons. *Education:* BA, State University of NY, Plattsburgh, 1952; London School of Economics, 1955-56; Master in Social Work, Smith College, School of Social Work, Northampton, Mass., 1962. *Appointments:* New York City, Department of Social Welfare, Bureau of Child Welfare, 1952; Probation Officer, Juvenile Term Court; Housing Consultant, New York City, Housing Authority; Instructor, Hunter College Educational; Extra Mural Representative, University of the West Indies, Department of Extra mural Studies, 1975-80. *Memberships:* Caribbean Federation of Mental Health, New York Chapter, Life Honorary Member; Smith College Alumni Association; State of New York, Department of Education, Certified Social Worker; BVI, Mental Health Association; BVI, Ladies Association. *Publications:* Family Background And Occupational Aspirations; Clinical Training—A New Role in Teacher Education (with Janet Lieberman). *Honours:* James G Stevens Award, 1950; Jessie S Noyes Award, 1950, 1951; Mental Health Fellowship, 1961-62. *Hobbies:* Reading; Swimming; Travelling. *Address:* Box 271, Road Town, Tortola, British Virgin Islands.

DE CHASTEIGNER DU MEE, Paul Rene, b. 18 Aug. 1925, Mauritius. Chartered Accountant. m. Myriam Koenig, 9 Feb. 1954, 2 sons, 2 daughters. *Education:* BCom, University of Cape Town, 1947; Chartered Accountant, SA, 1951; Institute of Chartered Accountants, England and Wales. *Appointments:* Partner, De Chazal Du Mee and Company, Chartered Accountants, and Coopers and Ly Brand, 1962-81; Chairman and Managing Director, Mauritius Oil Refineries Limited, 1969-. *Memberships:* President, Association of Accountants of Mauritius, 1961-81; Treasurer, Mauritius Institute of Management. *Hobbies:* Golf; Horse-racing. *Address:* 29 Hitchcock Avenue, Quatre Bornes, Mauritius.

DEELEY, Richard Kenneth, b. 6 Sept. 1946, Winnipeg, Manitoba, Canada. Barrister and Solicitor. m. Joylynn Deeley, 22 July 1972, 1 son, 1 daughter. *Education:* BA, 1967, LLB, 1970, University of Manitoba, Canada. *Appointments:* Richardson and Company, Barristers and Solicitors, 1970-79; Special Lecturer, Faculty of Law, University of Manitoba, 1973-; Deeley, Fabbri, Sellen, Barristers and Solicitors, 1979-. *Memberships:* Executive Member, Canadian Club of Winnipeg; Canadian Bar Association; Manitoba Bar Association; Fort Garry United Church; Association of Trial Lawyers of America. *Hobbies:* Athletics; Theatre. *Address:* 14 Portsmouth Blvd, Winnipeg, Manitoba, Canada.

DEEN, Matthew Emen, b. 28 Nov. 1921, Sydney, Australia. Dental Surgeon. m. Jean Dorey 14 Apr. 1961, 1 son, 1 daughter. *Education:* Bachelor Dental Surgery, Sydney University 1955. *Appointments:* Lieutenant 104 Australian Tank Attack Regiment, 2nd AIR, 4 years; Self Employed. *Memberships:* British Dental Society; Middle Harbour Yacht Club, Sydney; Tattersalls Club, Sydney. *Hobbies:* Sailing; Squash;

Tennis. *Address:* 34 The Grove, Mosman 2088, Sydney, Australia.

DEER, (Sir Arthur), Frederick, b. 15 June 1910, Nebraska, USA. Company Director. m. Elizabeth Christine Whitney, 10 Oct. 1936, 1 son, 3 daughters. *Education:* BA, 1930; LLB, 1934; BEc, 1936, University of Sydney. *Appointments:* The Mutual Life and Citizens' Associate Company Limited, 1930, General Manager, 1955-74 (retired); Director, 1956-; Director, Glass Containers Limited, 1975-; Director, Bowater-Scott Corporation of Australia Limited, 1975-; Director, Dow Chemical Limited, 1976-; Director, Miller Street Investments Pty. Limited 1978-; Chairman Expo Oil N.L. 1980-. *Memberships:* Numerous Societies including; Fellow, Senate of University of Sydney; Salvation Army, Sydney; Australia-Britain Society; Cargo Movement Co-ordination Committee, Port of Sydney; Administrative Review Council; Rotary Club, Sydney; etc. *Honours:* Knight cr. 1979; CMG 1973; Order Distinguished Auxiliary Service, Salvation Army 1976. *Hobbies:* Golf; Tennis. *Address:* 1179 Pacific Highway, Turramurra, NSW, 2074, Australia.

DE FREITAS, (Rt Hon. Sir) Geoffrey, b. 1913. Member of Parliament. m. 1938, 4 children. *Education:* Honorary Fellow, Haileybury and Clare College, Cambridge; Mellor Fellow, Yale University; Cholmeley Scholar, Barrister-at-Law, Lincoln's Inn. *Appointments:* RAF 1940-45; Member of Parliament (elected 10 times, Labour); Parliamentary Private Secretary to Prime Minister, 1945-46; Under Secretary of State, Air Ministry 1946-50; Home Office, 1950-51; Delegate to United Nations, 1949 and 1965; British High Commissioner, Ghana, 1961-63, Kenya, 1963-64, President: Council of Europe's Assembly, 1966-69, Vice-President, European Parliament, 1975-79. *Memberships:* High Commissioner, East African Federation; North Atlantic Assembly, 1976-78; Ten times, Committee of Commonwealth Parliamentry Assembly; Director, Iopate Industries, 1968-78; President: Inland Waterways Association 1978-; International Social Service 1978-; Chairman, European Consultants Limited, 1979-; Guild of Air Pilots and Company of Builders. *Honours:* KCMG 1961; Privy Council 1967. *Address:* 34 Tufton Court, Tufton Street, London SW1P 3QH, England.

DEGARIS, (Hon.) Renfrey Curgenven, b. 12 Oct. 1921, Millicent, South Australia. Farmer; Glazier; Legislator. m. Norma Florence Willson, 14 Feb. 1948, 2 sons, 2 daughters. *Education:* Millicent HKH, Prime Alfred College, Matriculation Standard. *Appointments:* Elected Legislative Council 1962; Opposition Leader 1967; Chief Secretary Ministry Mines and Health 1968-70; Opposition Leader 1970-79. *Memberships:* Land Settlement Committee; Party Delegate to Commonwealth Constitution Convention. *Address:* 3 Avenuest, Millswood 50304, South Australia.

de GIORGIO, Roger, b. 29 Dec. 1922, Milan, Italy. Architect. m. 30 Apr. 1947, 4 sons, 1 daughter. *Education:* 'cum laude' Bachelor of Engineering & Architecture, Royal University of Malta, 1946. *Appointments:* Partner in architectural and civil engineering practice, Mortimer and de Giorgio, 1948-68; Senior Partner, Roger de Giorgio and Partners, 1968; Senior Partner, Malta Consult, 1976-79. *Memberships:* Associate of Royal Institute of British Architects, 1960; Elected Fellow of RIBA, 1962; Rotary Club of Malta, 1974. *Honours:* Knight of Magistral Grace of the Sovereign and Military Order of Malta. *Hobbies:* Fishing; Historical Research. *Address:* 'Ca'de Yoris', Madliena Hill, Madliena, Malta.

DEI, Richard Ellis, b. 15 Mar. 1936. m. Apr. 1958, 4 sons, 3 daughters. *Education:* Principles of Medical Records amd statistics, Lagos University Teaching Hospital, Nigeria, 1966-67; Vital and Health Statistics-WHO Fellowship, London School of Hygiene and Tropical Medicine, UK, 1971; Ghana Institute of Management and Public Administration, 1979. *Appointments:* General Administration, 1955-64, Medical Statistics Division, 1964-81, Federal Ministry of Health, Lagos, Nigeria. *Memberships:* Secretary, Nigerian Guild of Medical Records Officers; Nigerian Health Records Association. *Honours:* OPCS(London), 1971; Mgt. P.A-(Accra), 1979; West African Secretariat Award. *Hobbies:* Photography. *Address:* 36 Osholake Street (East), Ebufe-Metta, Lagos, Nigeria.

DEKORT, Joseph Augustine, b. 17 May 1942, Wal-laceburg, Ontario, Canada. President; Management Consultant. m. Mary Jane Gunn, 25 June 1966, 2 sons, 1 daughter. *Education:* BA, Honors Mathematics, Ap-plied Phsyics, University of Western Ontario, Canada, 1961-65; Basic Computer training, 1965; Cobol, RPG, DOS and OS, 1966; Project Management, Manage-ment by Objective, Computer Audit Fundamentals, 1967-72; Appraisal I, Economics I, Ryerson Polytechni-cal Institute, 1973-74. *Appointments:* IBM Canada Limited, 1965-68; Woods, Gordon & Company, 1970-72; Senior Vice President Administration, Vice Presi-dent Corporate Systems, The Metropolitan Trust Com-pany, 1972-79; Alderman, Borough of Scarborough, 1974-82; J A Dekort & Associates Limited, President, 1979-. *Memberships:* Board of Governors, Scarboro General Hospital; Recreation and Parks Committee; Curriculum Committee, Trust Companies Institute; Director, Scarboro East Federal Liberal Association. *Publications:* EFT Planning: Cooperation and Commu-nication are Critical, 1979; Formation of a Financial Institution, 1980; Financial Community Study, 1981. *Honours:* Plaque, Past Services Recreation and Park, Borough of Scarboro, 1980; Certificate, Trust Compan-ies Institute MTCI, 1976; Letter Thank you, office of Attorney General's Office, USA, 1963; Letter Thank-You Prime Minister Trudeau, 1976. *Hobbies:* Philately; Collecting Antique Books. *Address:* 64 Blueberry Drive, Agincourt, Ontario, Canada, M1S 3G3.

DEKU, Anthony Kwashie (Amega), b. 1923, Yapei, Northern Region of Ghana. Business Executive; Ma-naging Director. m. Docia Margaret Doe, 2 Mar. 1942 (div), 4 sons, 2 daughters. *Education:* Threetown, Denu, 1929-39. *Appointments:* Ghana Police Force, 1940-69; Managing Director and Proprietor, Securicor Limit-ed, Ghana, 1970-; Executive Committee, International Criminal Police Organization, 1964-67. *Memberships:* Noble Order of Knights of Marshall; Association of Retired Superior Police Officers; Accra Lawn Tennis Club; Achimota Golf Club. *Honours:* Colonial Police Medal, 1955; Distinguished Service Order, 1967; Member of the Order of the Volta, 1969. *Hobbies:* Lawn Tennis; Golf; Reading; Goat/Sheep rearing. *Address:* 35 Switchback Road, Residential Area, Accra, Ghana.

DELACOMBE, Rohan, b. 25 Oct. 1906, Malta. Army Officer; Governor; (Retired). m. 15 Feb. 1941, 1 son, 1 daughter. *Education:* Harrow School; Royal Military College, Sandhurst; Staff College Camberley. *Appoint-ments:* The Royal Scots, Egypt, North China, India and Palestine, 1926; Palestine 1937-39; France 1939-40; Norway 1940; Normandy 1944; Italy 1944-45; India and South East Asia 1945; Commander, BAOR, Colon-el, The Royal Scots, 1956-64; GOC, 51 Lowland Divi-sion; GOC Berlin, 1959-62; Governor of Victoria, 1963-74; Administer of Commonwealth of Australia. *Memberships:* Queens Body Guard of Scotland, Royal Company of Archers; Army and Navy Club, Pall Mall. *Honours:* LLD(Hon Causa) Melbourne and Monash; KCMG; ; CB; KCVO; DSO; KBE; Freeman of Melbourne. *Address:* Shrewton Manor, Nr. Salisbury, Wilts, SP3 4DB, England.

DELL, Miriam Patricia, b. 14 June 1924, Hamilton, New Zealand. Teacher. m. Richard Kenneth Dell, 3 Aug. 1946, 4 daughters. *Education:* Auckland University, New Zealand, 1940-43; BA. Teachers B. Certificate, Auckland Teachers Training College(Secondary Teach-ing), New Zealand, 1944. *Appointments:* Teaching full and/or part-time, 1945-47 and 1957-58, 1961-71. *Memberships:* Member of numerous associations in-cluding: Vice-Convenor Standing Committee on Physi-cal Environment 1973-76, Vice President 1976-79, President 1979-, International Council of Women; Inter Church Council of Public Affairs, 1974-; Convenor Council Tutor 1964-70, Convenor Tutor Training 1971, Hutt Valley Marriage Guidance; Council for Equal Pay and Opportunity, 1966-67; Urban Development Asso-ciation; National Council of Women *Publications:* Role of Women in National Development, 1970; Numerous magazine and newspaper articles. *Honours:* CBE, 1975; Adele Ristori Prize, 1976; Queen's Jubilee Med-al, 1978; DBE, 1980. *Hobbies:* Gardening; Reading; Handicrafts; Beachcombing. *Address:* 98 Waerenga Road, Otaki, New Zealand.

DELORME, Jean Claude, b. 22 May 1934, Montreal, Quebec, Canada. President and Chief Executive Offi-cer, Teleglobe, Canada. m. Paule Tardif, 2 daughters. *Education:* BA, Collège Sainte-Marie, Montreal, Cana-da; Licentiate in Law, Université de Montréal, Canada, 1959. *Appointments:* Admitted to Quebec Bar, 1960, joined law firm of Martineau, Walker, Allison, Beauli-eu, Tetley and Phelan; Appointed Secretary and Gener-al Counsel, Canadian Corporation for the 1967 World Exhibition, 1963; General Counsel and Assistant to Chairman and Chief Executive Officer, Standard Brands Limited, 1967; Vice-President Administration, Secretary and General Counsel, Telesat, Canada, 1969; President and Chief Executive Officer, Teleglobe, Canada, head office, Montreal, Canada, 1971; Cana-da's representative on the Commonwealth Telecom-munications Council, the Operating body of the Com-monwealth Telecommunications Organization and served as Chairman of the Council, 1973-80. *Member-ships:* Member of Board of Directors, Interprovincial Pipe Line Limited, The Canadian German Chamber of Industry and Commerce, May 1980; Chairman of the Comité consultatif du transport de la Commission d'initiative et de développement économiques de Mon-tréal (CIDEM); Member of Board of the Association montréalaise d'action récréative et culturelle (AMARC); President of the Régie de la Place des Arts and President of the Opéra de Montreal; Member of Board of Directors of International Institute of Music; Arthritis Society of Montreal; National Ballet of Cana-da; Montreal Board of Trade; Association internation-ale des étudiants en sciences économiques et Com-merciales (AIESEC.) McGill Board of Advisors; Quebec Bar Association; Saint-Denis Club; Cercle Universitaire d'Ottawa; Saint James's Club; Mount Royal Club. *Hon-ours:* Officer of Order of Canada; Centennial Medal of Canada; Gold Medal of the Czechoslovakian Society for International Relations. *Hobbies:* Skiing; Sailing. *Add-ress:* 3 Glendale Avenue, Beaconsfield, Quebec, Cana-da, H9W 5P6.

DELPH, Richard Michael Forbes, b. 20 Sept. 1927, Georgetown, British Guyana. Lawyer. m. Esther Früh, 17 Dec. 1955, 1 son, 2 daughters. *Education:* Bachelor of Laws, University College, London University, UK, 1946-49; Barrister at Law, Middle Temple, Inn of Court, London, UK, 1949-51; Bar Admission Course, 1977-78, Law Society of Upper Canada, Barrister and Solici-tor, Ontario, Canada. *Appointments:* Crown Counsel, British Guyana, 1956-60; Legal Adviser to Police, British Guyana, 1960; acting Solicitor General, British Guyana, 1961-1962; Legal Adviser at British Guyana Independence Conference, 1962; Parliamentary Coun-sel, Jamaica, 1963-65; Chief Parliamentary Counsel, Guyana, 1965-69; Draftsman of Caribbean Free Trade Agreement, Member of Guyana Delegation to United Nations Seminar on Human Rights, Jamaica, 1967; Senior Parliamentary Counsel, Jamaica, 1969-76; Le-gislative Counsel, Government of Canada, 1978-. *Memberships:* Law Society of Upper Canada; Bar Asso-ciation of Jamaica; Jackson Bay Gun Club, Jamaica; Ottawa Valley Trap and Skeet Club; Ottawa Civil Ser-vice Recreational Association; Swiss Club Ottawa Val-ley. *Hobbies:* Reading; Hunting; Shooting; Chess. *Add-ress:* 555 Brittany Drive, Apt. 909, Ottawa, Ontario, K1K 4C5, Canada.

DENBOROUGH, Michael Antony, b. 11 July 1929, Salisbury, Rhodesia. Research Physician. m. Erica Elizabeth Griffith Brown, 12 Dec. 1959, 2 sons, 3 daughters. *Education:* Cape Town University, 1947-52; Oxford University, 1953-56; MB, ChB, 1952; MD (Mel-bourne), 1969; DPhil.(Oxon) 1956; DSc, Melbourne, 1977. *Appointments:* House Physician, Salisbury Gen-eral Hospital, Rhodesia, 1953; House Surgeon, Rad-cliffe Infirmary, Oxford, 1953-54; Assistant, Nuffield Clinical Medicine Department, 1954-57; Resident Medical Officer, National Heart Hospital, London, 1958; Senior Lecturer, Reader in Medicine, University of Melbourne, Department of Medicine, The Royal Melbourne Hospital, 1960-74; Professorial Fellow, Department of Clinical Science, John Curtin School of Medical Research, Australian National University, 1974-. *Memberships:* Fellow, Royal College of Physi-cians; Fellow, Royal Australasian College of Physi-cians; Editorial Board, Pharmacology and Therapeutics. *Publications:* Numerous scientific papers on metabolic and genetic diseases in man. *Honours:* Rhodes Scho-larship (Rhodesia and Exeter), 1953; First Selwyn-Smith Prize for Medical Research, University of Mel-bourne, 1970; Eric Susman Prize for Medical Research, Royal Australasian College of Physicians. *Hobbies:* Music; Golf. *Address:* 38 Sheehan Street, Pearce, ACT 2607, Australia.

DENHAM, Lindsay William, b. 5 Dec. 1916, Somerville, Victoria, Australia. Automotive Engineer. m. Athalie O'Connell, 21 Oct. 1944, 1 son, 1 daughter. *Education:* Automotive Engineering Certificate, Victoria, Australia, 1937; Teaching Certificate, Department of Further Education, South Australia, 1968. *Appointments:* Automotive Engineer, 1934-40, 1945-64; Royal Australian Air Force, 1940-45; Lecturer, School of Automotive Engineering, 1964-76; Justice of the Peace, 1976; Justice of the Quorum, 1978. *Memberships:* Society of Automotive Engineers, Australasia, South Australian Division; Catalina Club (Ex Serviceman's Club). Hobby: Stamp Collecting. *Address:* 22 Mary Street, Pennington. 5013, South Australia.

DENISON (known as Dulcie Gray), Dulcia Winifred Catherine, b. 20 Nov. 1920, Kuala Lumpur. Actress; Writer. m. Michael Denison, 29 Apr. 1939. *Appointments:* First professional job as actress-Hay Fever, Aberdeen, Scotland, 1939; Has starred in West End of London on 38 occasions; Most recent appearance for the National Theatre at the Prince of Wales Theatre, London, UK; Most recent tour, Singapore, Hong Kong, Kuala Lumpur, Dubai, Bahrain, Abu Dabi, Muscat, appearing in Relatively Speaking, 1981. *Memberships:* Crime Writers Association; Mystery Writers of America; British Actors Equity; British Butterfly Conservation Society; The Society of Authors; The Lansdowne Club, London. *Publications:* 20 Crime novels including: Stage Door Fright, book of Short Horror Stories; Death in Denims, 1977; Butterflies on my Mind, on the Conservation of British Butterflies; numerous short stories in anthologies including: The Bedside Book of Great Detective Stories; The Midnight Ghost Book; The 3rd Bumper Book of Ghost Stories; I've seen a Ghost. *Honours:* Queen's Silver Jubilee Medal, 1977; The Times Education Supplement Senior Information Book Award, for Butterflies on My Mind, 1978. *Hobbies:* Swimming; Butterflies. *Address:* Shardeloes, Amersham, Buckinghamshire, England.

DENIZ, Clare Frances, b. 7 Apr. 1945, Highgate, London, England. Musician. *Education:* Won Junior Exhibition to Royal Academy of Music, London, UK, 1956; LRAM. Diploma, 1966; Private Lessons with Christopher Bunting, 1969-73; Personal invitation to attend private lessons with Paul Tortelier in 1976; Masterclasses with Karoly Boevay, Snape Maltings, 1978; Private Lessons with Jacqueline Dupre and Masterclasses, 1977-79; 6 months intensive study, 1979 with Antonia Butler. *Appointments:* Principle Cellist with Royal Ballet, 1969-71; Sub-principle Cellist, English National Opera, 1973-77; Cello Tutor at Stowe, Wycombe Abbey Schools, Bulmershe College of Further Education; Cellist in residence at South Mill Park Arts Centre, Bracknell, Berkshire, UK, 1979. *Memberships:* Incorporated Society of Musicians. *Creative Works:* Recitals given at: English Music Festival, 1979, 80, 81; City of London Festival, UK, 1978, 80; Appearances at European Festivals at Bath, 1978, Dorchester Abbey, Ware, UK, and Oxford, UK; Broadcasts in Ireland. *Honours:* LRAM Diploma. *Hobbies:* Walking; Badminton. *Address:* 31 Friday Street, Henley-On-Thames, Oxon RG9 1AN, England.

DENNISON, Victor Douglas, b. 14 July 1919, London, England. Lecturer. m. Betty Dickens (deceased), 23 Mar. 1942, 2 sons, 1 daughter. *Education:* BSc(Econ.),1947, London School of Economics, London, UK, 1938-40, 1946-47; Post Graduate Certificate in Education, 1948, Institute of Education, London University, UK, 1947-48; Certificate in Science (Geology), Bristol University, UK, 1974-76. *Appointments:* Senior Geography Master, Carre's Grammar School, Sleaford, Lincolnshire, UK, 1948-54; Lecturer in Geography, College of Commerce, Bristol, UK, 1954-65; Senior Geography Master, Queen Elizabeth's Hospital, Bristol, UK, 1966-69; Lecturer in Geography, Filton Technical College, Bristol, UK, 1969-. *Memberships:* Fellow, Royal Geographical Society; Chairman of Further Education Section, President, 1980-81, Geographical Association; Geological Association; President, Geological Section, 1978-80, Bristol Naturalists Society; Institute of British Geographers; Editor of Newsletter, Mendip Society; Churchill Parish Council. *Publications:* Notes on course of River Slea, 1957; Presidential Address, Geographical Association, 1981. *Hobbies:* Gardening; Conservation; Photography. *Address:* Heathercrest, The Batch, Churchill, Bristol, BS19 5PP, England.

DENNISS, Gordon Kenneth, b. 29 Apr. 1915 London, England. Chartered Surveyor; Farmer and Land Owner. m. Violet Lilia 19 Aug. 1939 1 son, 2 daughters. *Education:* Dulwich Prep. to Dulwich College, Dulwich 1925-32; College of Estate Management, Lincolns Inn 1932-35. *Appointments:* Pupil to Uncle Hugh F Thoburn, Chartered Surveyor Beckenham Kent 1932-35; Assistant Surveyor, 1935-37; Assistant Surveyor, H W Denniss, London, 1937-40; Partner, 1940-45; Principal Eastman and Denniss, Chartered Surveyors, London, 1945-72; Crown Estate Commissioner, 1965-71; Senior Partner, Eastman and Denniss, 1972-; Farmer, 1953-. *Memberships:* Fellow, Royal Institution of Chartered Surveyors; Royal Society of Health; Savile Club; Farmers Club; Marylebone Cricket Club; Surrey County Cricket Club. *Honours:* CBE 1979. *Hobbies:* Farming; Cricket; Politics; History. *Address:* 6 Belgrave Place, London, SW1, England.

DENSON, John Boyd, b. 13 Aug. 1926, Sunderland, England. Diplomat. m. Joyce Myra Symondson, 16 Nov. 1957. *Education:* Perse School, Cambridge, 1939-44; MA, St Johns College, Cambridge, 1947-51. *Appointments:* Royal Artillery and Intelligence Corps, 1944-47; Foreign Office, Hong Kong, Tokyo, Peking, London, Helsinki, Washington, Vientiane, 1951; Assistant Head, Far Eastern Department 1963-68; Chargé d'Affairs, Peking, 1969-71; Royal College of Defence Studies 1973; Counsellor, Consul General Affairs, 1973-77; Ambassador, Katmandu, 1977-. *Memberships:* United Oxford and Cambridge University Club; Achilles Club. *Honours:* OBE, 1965; CMG, 1972; Gurkha Dakshina Bahu 1st Class, 1980. *Hobbies:* Pictures; Wine; Theatre. *Address:* British Embassy, Katmandu, Nepal.

DENTON, Richard Norman Hamilton, b. 10 Oct. 1928, Sydney, Australia. Chartered Accountant. m. Patricia, 22 Jan. 1954, 2 sons, 2 daughters. *Education:* Canterbury Boys' High School. *Appointments:* Irish and Michelmore; Irish Young and Outhwaite; Deloitte Haskins and Sells. *Memberships:* Fellow, The Institute of Chartered Accountants in Australia; The Institute of Chartered Secretaries and Administrators; Club mmberships, Australian Club; Sydney Club; Royal Prince Alfred Yacht Squadron. *Honours:* Officer of the Order of Australia, 1980. *Hobbies:* Tennis; Squash; Boating; Piano. *Address:* 79 Lynbara Avenue, St. Ives 2075, Australia.

DENT-YOUNG, David Michael, b. 25 Mar. 1927, Bath, United Kingdom. Mining Engineer. m. Patricia McKeon, 12 July 1951, 3 daughters. *Education:* St Aidan's College, Grahamstown, SA, 1940-45; ACSM, Camborne School of Mines, Cornwall, 1947-51. *Appointments:* Mining Engineer, Nigerian Alluvials Limited, 1951-53; Mining Engineer, A O Nigeria Limited, 1953-57; Area Engineer, 1957-64; District Superintendent, 1964-67; Senior Superintendent, 1967-71; Managing Director, Amalgamated Tin Mines of Nigeria Limited, 1971-. *Memberships:* Fellow, Institute of Mining and Metallurgy; Nigerian Army Engineers; Nigerian Chamber of Mines; Nigerian Employers Consultative Association; Nigerian Mining Employers Association; Plateau (N) Horticultural Society; Rayfield (N) Sailing Club; Board of Governors, Jos School of Mines; Consultative Committee on Reclamation and Restoration; Plateau Turf Club; Board of Management Kduna Polytechnic. *Honours:* CBE 1977. *Hobbies:* Gardening; Painting; Swimming; Sailing; Tennis. *Address:* The Cloisters Cottage, Perrymead, Bath BA2 5AY, England.

DEORAS (Dr), Purushottam Jaikrishna, b. 20 July 1907, Bilaspur, India. Medical Biologist. m. Vatsala Ghate, 27 May 1936, 2 sons, 4 daughters. *Education:* BSc., 1931, MSc., 1933, LLB, 1935, Nagpur University; PhD. University of Durham, 1940. *Appointments:* Entomological Assistant, Agricultural College, 1936-38; Assistant to Imperial Entomologist, 1940-42; Professor of Zoology, 1943-46; Entomological Adviser, 1946-48; Professor of Entomology, 1948-50; Assistant Director & Head of Entomology Department, 1951-69; Officiating Director, Haffkine Institute, Bombay, 1968; Scientist Emeritusm 1969-75; Visiting Professor, 1976-81; Consultant Pesticides, Environment Post-Graduate Guide Bombay University, 1981-. *Memberships:* Life Fellow, Entomological Society, India; Life Fellow, Zoological Society, India; Life Fellow, Maharashta Academy of Sciences; Life Fellow, Ecological Society, India; International Society Toxinology; New York Academy of Sciences; Vice-President, Society for Clean Environment; Friends of Trees. *Publications:* Snakes of India, 1965; Pollution; Chapter, Handling Snakes, Scorpions, 1963; Chapter, Story of Indian Poisonous Snakes, 1971; 110 Scientific Papers; 210 General articles. *Honours:* Hindu Education Fund Scholar, 1938-40; Rockfeller Fund Scholar, 1959; Presidium, First International Congress, Ophiology, Caracas, 1976; Dr Bhansali Lecture Award, Bombay Medical Union, 1977; First Zoological Congress Gold Medal Award, Zoological Society of India, 1980. *Hobbies:* Writing, Travelogue & Science; Horticulture; Supervising Laboratory Animal Houses Pest Control. *Address:* Anandvan, Sahitya-Sahawas, Bandra-East, Bombay 400051, India.

DE PAIVA RAPOZO, Anthony Richard, b. 17 June 1946, London. Company Executive. *Education:* Sandroyd School, Wiltshire, United Kingdom, 1955-59; Lycee Jaccard, Lausanne, Switzerland, 1959-62; Brummana High School, Brummana, Lebanon, 1962-66. *Appointments:* Wilkinson Sword Limited, 1967-70; Ladbroke Group Limited, 1971-72; Lonrho Exports Limited, 1973-78; General Manager, WF Clarke, Nigeria Limited, 1978-. *Memberships:* Institute of Directors; British Institute of Management; National Geographic Society. *Hobbies:* Travelling; Deep Sea Fishing; Reading. *Address:* 14 Sussex Square, Kemptown, Brighton, Sussex, England.

DER, Benedict Godwin, b. 6 June 1939, Nandom, Ghana. Senior Lecturer in History. m. Josephine Catherine Mensah, 20 Oct. 1979. *Education:* BA Hons. 1965; MA, University of Ottawa, Canada, 1967; Doctoral Candidate, PhD, University of Ghana, Legon. *Appointments:* Teaching Modern European and British History; Russian History and American History; Specialising, West African History in Doctoral Work. *Memberships:* Historical Society of Ghana; fhsg; Council of the Historical Society of Ghana. *Publications:* Edmund Burke and Africa, 1772-1792, 1970; Church-State Relations in Northern Ghana, 1906-1940, 1974; Colonial Land Policy in the Northern Territories of the Gold Coast, 1975; Methodist-Presbyterian Relations in Northern Ghana, 1900-1960; God and Sacrifice in the Traditional Religions of the Kasena and Dagaba of Northern Ghana, in press; Tax Collection in Northern Ghana, 1898-1950: An Aspect of Administrative History, Part 1 and II; Na Gbewa, Dictionary of African Biography, 1977. *Honours:* Commonwealth Travel Grant, 1978. *Hobbies:* Travel; Gardening. *Address:* Bungalow 204, Arku Korsah Road, University of Cape Coast, Ghana, West Africa.

DERERA, Nicholas Frederick, b. 5 Jan. 1919, Budapest, Hungary. Plant Breeder. m. Roza Eva Gyarfas, 12 Jan. 1946, 1 son. *Education:* Diploma Agr. Sc. Budapest, 1942; Diploma P.B. Hungary, 1943. *Appointments:* Plant Breeder with private seed companies, 1942-48; Principal Research Officer, Ministry of Agriculture, 1949-56; Process Worker, 1957-58; Laboratory Assistant, Ryde School of Horticulture, Australia, 1958; Plant Breeder (cotton), N.S.W. Department of Agriculture, 1958-61; Plant Breeder, Senior Plant Breeder, Officer-in-Charge, 1961-81; Director of Wheat Breeding, The University of Sydney, Plant Breeding Institute, 1973-; Agricultural Science (Plant Breeding) Consultant, 1981-. *Memberships:* Australian Institute of Agricultural Science; Wheat Breeding Society of Australia; Crop Science Society of America; The Australian Society of Plant Physiologists; Society for the Advancement of Breeding Researches in Asia & Oceania; Rotary Club. Fellow, Australian Institute of Agricultural Science, 1977. *Publications:* Author and co-author of 39 scientific, 25 major conference papers and 17 semi-popular articles; Breeder and co-breeder of two grass, one bean, two tomato, one capsicum cultivars and the Australian prime hard wheat varieties Gamut, Mendos, Timgalen, Gatcher, Songlen, Timson, Shortim, SUN 39A, SUN 41A, SUN 43A and SUN 44E. *Honours:* Certificate of Appreciation, Returned Services League, N.S.W. Branch, 1979; Farrer Memorial Medal, 1981. *Hobbies:* Tropical fish breeding; Rock Gardens; Wine collection. *Address:* 5 Lister Street, Winston Hills, 2153, NSW, Australia.

DERHAM (Sir), Peter John, b. 21 Aug. 1925, Melbourne, Victoria, Australia. Company Director. m. Averil Cleveland Wigan, 8 June 1950, 2 sons, 1 daughter. *Education:* Bachelor Science, Ormond College, University of Melbourne 1958; Advanced Management Programme, Harvard University. *Appointments:* War Service, R.A.A.F., 1944, transferred to RAN in 1945, Served in South West Pacific and Japan. Joined Moulded Products (Australasia) Ltd., 1943, Appointed to Board, 1953, and Sales Director, 1960. Appointed General Manager, 1967 and Managing Director, 1972-. Director of Nine Companies (chairman of 2), Chairman: CSIRO Advisory Council, Australian Tourist Commission, Australia New Zealand Foundation, Australian Canned Fruits Corporation; Board member, Victorian Economic Development Corporation; Councillor of various Institutes and Councils. *Memberships:* Federal President, Institute of Directors in Australia and memver various boards, councils and committees; Australian Club; Melbourne Club; Commonwealth Club, Ca cerra; Royal Melbourne Golf Club; Frankston Golf Club; Flinders Golf Club; Davey's Bay Yacht Club; Royal South Yarra Lawn Tennis Club; Melbourne Cricket Club. *Honours:* Knight Bachelor, 1980. *Hobbies:* Golf; Sailing; Garden; Tennis. *Address:* 12 Glenbervie Road, Toorak, Victoria, 3142, Australia.

DeROBURT, Hammer, b. 25 Sept. 1923, Nauru. Politician and Administrator. *Education:* Nauru Secondary School, Geelong Technical College, Victoria, Australia. *Appointments:* Teacher, 1940-42, 1951-57; Educational Liaison Officer, Department of Nauruan Affairs, 1947-51. *Memberships:* Nauru Local Government Council, 1955-68; Chairman and Head Chief of Nauru, 1965-68; Chairman, Transitional Council of State, 1968; President of Nauru, 1968-76 and 1978-; Minister for Internal Affairs, External Affairs, Island Development Industry, Civil Aviation and Public Service; Leader of the Opposition, 1976-78. *Address:* Office of the President, Nauru, Central Pacific.

DESAI, Bachubhai Karimbhai, b. 15 Apr. 1932, Dhandhuka, Gujarat State, India. m. Zubedi Munshi, 14 Apr. 1961, 2 sons. *Education:* M.B.B.S., 1956; M.D., 1960. *Appointments:* Registrar, Medicine, 1958-60; Residency in Internal Medicine, Episcopal Hospital, Philadelphia, USA., 1963-64; Fellowship, Gastroenterology, Temple University Hospital, Philadelphia, USA., 1964-65; Honorary Physician, Giulabbai General Hospital, Ahmedabad, 1966-. *Memberships:* Honorary Visiting Physician, E.S.I.S., 1970-. *Publications:* Alkaptonuric Ochronosis, 1979; Peritoneal Dialysis—a clinical experience, 1970; Medical Management of Peptic Ulcer, 1980. *Hobbies:* Photography; Reading. *Address:* V J Hospital, Panchkuva, Ahmedabad 2, Gujarat, India.

DESAI, Dilip Chimanlal, b. 31 July 1934, Hansot, District Bharuch, Gujarat, India. Medical Physician, Gastroenterlogist. m. Mrunalini, 7 Dec. 1972, 2 daughters. *Education:* M.B.B.S. of the M.S. University of Baroda, 1957; M.D. General Medicine, 1962. *Appointments:* Shree Sayaji General Hospital and Medical College, Baroda, India, House Physician, Internal Medicine, 1958, Skin & Veneral Diseases, 1959, Registrar, Skin and V.D., 1958-59; Casualty Medical Officer, 1959-60; Junior Lecturer, Part-time, Pharmaceology, 1962-63; Registrar Internal Medicine, 1960-62; Resident, Internal Medicine, Freedman's Hospital & Howard University School of Medicine, 1963-64; Resident, Fellow in Gastroenterlogy, Cook County Hospital, 1964-65; Lecturer for Dietitian course students, Cook County Hospital, 1965-68; Pool Officer, appointed by C.S.I.R., working in capacity of Assistant Professor of Medicine, Department of Medicine, s.s.g. Hospital and Medical College, Baroda, India, 1968-70; Since then Treasurer, Association of Physicians of Gujarat, 1978. Executive Committee, Association of Physicians of Gujarat, 1979,80,81; Vice-President, Chairman and Representative of various Societies including Indian Society of Gastrointestinal Endoscopy and Indian Society of Gastroenterology. *Publications:* Contributions to various professional journals including: Treatment of Post-operative Esophageal Stricture by Dilitation with Metal Olive Bougies, 1969, Diagnosis and Treatment of Diffuse Esophageal Spasm, 1969, Role of Endoscopy in G.I. Diseases, 1980; Numerous papers at conferences including: Gastric Signs of Distal Duodenal Ulcer, 1975, Ulcerative Colitis, Differentiating Signs, 1976, Medical Management of Pyloric obstruction, 1979, Peritoneoscopy in Children, 1979; Contributed to various exhibitions and lectures in field. *Honours:* Thomas G Hullgold Medal Award, American Medical Association, 1967; City & County of San Francisco State Award, Certificate of Honour, 1968. *Hobbies:* Philately;

Amateur Flute, Indian Classical & Light Music; Nail Art Drawings. *Address:* at Amdavadi Pole Entrance, Vadodara 390 001, Gujarat, India.

DESAI, Ramesh Amratlal, b. 17 May 1939, India. Physician. m. 1964 (wife deceased), 2 sons, 1 daughter. *Education:* M.B.B.S., Grant Medical College, University of Bombay, 1963; M.D. Internal Medicine, Grant Medical College, University of Bombay, 1967. *Appointments:* Resident Medical Officer, six months at J.J. Group of Hospitals, Bombay; Resident in Neurology, six months; Registrar in Internal Medicine, two years; Registrar in Neurology, three months; Private Consultant Practice, Mombasa, 1967-. *Memberships:* Secretary, Treasurer, Vice-Chairman and Chairman, Coast Division, Kenya Medical Association; Executive Council of the National Association; Three times organising Secretary, Kenya Medical Associations Annual Conference; Representative, Commonwealth Medical Association, Jamaica, 1974; Lions Club. *Honours:* Arnott Scholarship, Grant Medical College; Twice winners, Bombay University Inter-collegiate Hockey Championships, Grant Medical Hockey Team; Grant Medical College Chess Team; Editor Grant Medical College Magazine & Wall Paper, 1963. *Hobbies:* Serious Amateur Photographer; Interest in Music; Sports, Tennis. *Address:* Vihiga Avenue, off Rasini Road, Tudor, Mombasa, Kenya.

DESCHAMP, Bryan Desmond, b. 3 June 1943, Townsville, Queensland, Australia. Dean, Trinity College, University of Melbourne, Public Servant. *Education:* S.T.L., Gregorian University, Rome, 1970; Diplôme d'Etudes Médiévales, Louvain, 1971; Ph.B., Louvain, 1972; S.T.D., Louvain, 1973. *Appointments:* Ordained R.C. Priest, 1967; Dean of Studies, Carmelite Theological College, Donvale, and Lecturer in Theology and History at the Yarra Theological Union, Melbourne, 1973-75; Tutor in History, Trinity College, Melbourne, 1976-79; State Director, Good Neighbour Council, Victoria, 1977-79; Chairman, Migrant Resource Centre, Melbourne, 1979-81; Dean and Sub-Warden, Trinity College, University of Melbourne, 1979-; Member of the Security Appeals Tribunal, 1980-81; Member of the Victorian Ethnic Affairs Advisory Council, 1980-81; Assistant Director, Victorian Regional Office, Commonwealth Department of Immigration and Ethnic Affairs, 1981-. *Memberships:* Australia Day Council, Victoria, 1980. Hobby: Medieval History. *Address:* Trinity College, Parkville, Victoria 3052, Australia.

DESCHENES, Bernard M.-, b. 8 April 1926, Sayabec, Province of Quebec, Canada. Advocate, Barrister and Solicitor. m. Lise Caron, 10 May 1952, 3 sons, 3 daughters. *Education:* Diploma in Science, Mont St-Louis College, Montreal, 1941-44; Bachelor of Arts, University of Montreal, 1944-46; Bachelor of Civil Law, McGill University, Montreal, 1946-49. *Appointments:* Lawyer, Private Practice, 1949-; Senior partner of de Grandpré, Colas, Deschênes, Godin, Paquette, Lasnier & Alary, 1965-; Senior Crown Prosecutor, Montreal, 1960-65; Member, Board of Directors of Canadair Limited, 1976-; Member, Aircraft Accident Review Board of Canada, 1978-; Chairman, Disciplinary Committee of Professional Corporation of Medical Doctors of Quebec, 1976-80. *Memberships:* National Vice-President, Liberal Party of Canada, 1968-78; Chairman, Legal Ethics Committee, Bar of the Province of Quebec, 1975-; Member, Canadian Bar Association; Richelieu Valley Golf and Country Club. *Honours:* Queen's Counsel, 1965-. *Hobbies:* Reading; Skiing; Golfing; Lapidary. *Address:* 6887-20th Avenue, Rosemont, Montreal, Quebec, HIX 2J6.

DESHPANDE, Balkrishna Ganesh, b. 29 Nov. 1911, Pune, Maharashtra, India. Geologist and Teacher in Earth Sciences. m. Shashi Debadghao. *Education:* BSc. University of Bombay, India, 1933; MSc. University of Bombay, India, 1936; Post Graduate, University of Melbourne, Australia, 1946-47; Ph.D. University of Poona, India, 1953. *Appointments:* Superintending Geologist, Geological Survey of India, 1936-51; Deputy Director, Indian Bureau of Mines, India, 1951-56; Chief of Geological Services, Oil and Natural Gas Commission, India, 1956-59; Professor of Geology and Head of Department, University of Poona, Pune, India, 1970-76; Professor of Geology, University of Dar es Salaam, Tanzania, 1977-. *Memberships:* Member, Association of Geoscientists for Internation Development, Caracus, Venezuela; Member, Mining, Metallurgical and Geological Institute of India; Member, Indian Association of Geohydrologists, Calcutta, India; Fellow, Indian National Science Academy, India; Fellow, Maharashtra Academy of Sciences, Bombay, India; Member, Indian Science Congress Association, Calcutta,. *Publications:* Numerous Scientific publications, published in Indian and Foreign Scientific Journals. *Honours:* Merit Award, 'Ideal Teacher', University, Government of Maharashtra, Bombay, India, 1977; Fellow, Indian National Science Academy, New Delhi, India, 1966; Founder Fellow, Maharashtra Academy of Sciences, India, 1975. *Hobbies:* Photography. *Address:* B 204 Ashit Apartments, Modi Baug, Pune 411016, India.

De SOMOGYI, Aileen Ada, b. 26 Nov. 1921, London, England. Librarian. *Education:* BA. MA. Royal Holloway College, University of London, 1939-43; Associate, Library Association, 1946; MLS. University of Western Ontario, London, Ontario, Canada, 1967-70; Certificate of Proficiency in Archive Management, Carleton University, Ottawa, 1969; Diploma in Computer Programming, Career Learning Centre, Toronto, 1979-80. *Appointments:* Librarian, Special and Public Libraries, Enfield, Shrewsbury and Reading, 1943-66; Senior Instructor, National Coal Board, 1956-57; Librarian, Lawson Memorial Library, University of West Ontario, 1966-71; Cataloguer, Co-operative Book Centre of Canada, 1971; Staff Member, East York P.I., Toronto, 1971-74; Librarian, Management and Information Services Library, Ontario Ministry of Government Services, 1975-78; Librarian, Sperry Univac Computor Services, Toronto, 1980. *Memberships:* American Library Association; Ontario Humane Society; International Fund for Animal Welfare; Royal Holloway College Association; Canadian Wildlife Federation; East York Historical Society. *Publications:* Contributor to Canadian Library Journal, School Library Journal; Studies in Islam, American Libraries. *Hobbies:* Reading; Animals. *Address:* 9 Bonnie Brae Boulevard, Toronto, Ontario, Canada, M4J 4N3.

De SOUZA, Terence Charles, b. 28 March 1927, Karachi. Insurance Company Director. m. Othelia Pereira, 7 June 1953, 2 sons, 2 daughters. *Education:* BA. University of Bombay, 1947; MA. Catholic University of America, 1949; Associate of the Chartered Insurance Institute, London, 1960. *Appointments:* Research Officer, Ministry of Economic Affairs, Goverment of Pakistan; Member, Pakistan Delegation to United Nations Economic Commission, Asia and The Far East, 1949-52; General Manager, Alpha Insurance Company Limited, Karachi, 1952-68; Managing Director, Industrial and Commercial Insurance Company Limited, Karachi; Technical Advisor, Eastern Federal Union Insurance Company Limited, Karachi, 1968-69; Director and General Manager, Walton Insurance Company Limited, Sydney, Australia, 1969-. *Memberships:* National Social Science Honor Society, Pi Gamma, United States of America; Chartered Insurance Institute, London; Australian Insurance Institute, Melbourne, Australia; Rotary Club, Turramurra, Australia; Mandarin Club, Sydney, Australia. *Publications:* 'The External Value of the Rupee', 1931-47. *Hobbies:* Philately; Historical Research. *Address:* 12 Alice Street, Turramurra, New South Wales, 2074, Australia.

DESPRÉS, Robert, b. 27 Sept. 1924, Quebec, Canada. Chairman of the Board of Atomic Energy of Canada Limited. m. Marguerite Cantin, 10 Sept. 1949, 2 sons, 2 daughters. *Education:* Commercial Course, Le College de Lévis, 1936-41; Senior Matriculation, L'Académie de Québec, 1941-44; BC, MD, L'Université Laval, 1944-47; Postgraduate, Western University, Ontario, 1961. *Appointments:* Comptroller, Quebec Power Company, 1947-63; Regional Manager, Administration and Trust Company, 1963-65; Deputy Minister, Quebec Department of Revenue, 1965-69; President and General Manager, Quebec Health Insurance Board, 1969-73; President, Université du Québec, 1973-78; President and Chief Executive Officer, National Cablevision Limited, 1978-80; President and Chief Exective Officer, Netcom Incorporated, 1978-; Chairman of the Board, Atomic Energy of Canada Limited, 1980-. *Memberships:* Member of the Board of Directors of several companies including: Campeau Corporation, Canada Malting Company Limited; International Centre for Research and Studies in Management; Member, Canadian Tax Foundation; French Chamber of Commerce; Presidents Association of America. *Publications:* Author of many publications in the management field. *Honours:* Officer of the Order of Canada, 1978; Fellow, Society of Management Accountants of Canada, 1979; Member, Fellow, Certified General Accountants' Association, 1948. *Hobbies:* Golf; Tennis; Reading. *Address:* 890 Dessane, Quebec, GLS 4J8, Canada.

DEVESI, Sir Baddeley, b. 16 Oct. 1941, Mostyn Tagabasoe, Norua and Laisa Otu. Governor-General. m. June Marie Barley, 1969, 3 sons, 2 daughters. *Education:* St Stephen's School Auckland, New Zealand; Ardmore Teachers' College, Auckland, New Zealand. *Appointments:* MLC and Member, Executive Council, 1967-69; Headmaster, St Nicholas School, Honiara, 1968; Education Officer and Lecturer, 1970-72; District Officer, 1973; District Commissioner and Clerk, Malaita Council, 1974; Permanent Secretary, 1976. *Memberships:* Deputy Chairman, Solomon Islands Broadcasting Corporation, 1976; Alternate Director Air Pacific Board of Directors; Member of UK Delegation on South Pacific Air Transport Council; Member of the Consultative Committee on Civil Aviation fo the South Pacific Bureau for Economic Co-operation; Captain Solomon Islands team, 2nd Pacific Games, 1969; Commissioner, Boy Scouts Association, 1968; Chancellor, University of South Pacific, 1980. *Honours:* GCMG, 1980; *Hobbies:* Reading; Swimming; Lawn Tennis; Cricket; Snooker. *Address:* Government House, Honiara, Solomon Islands.

DEVGUN, Manjit Singh, b. 17 Oct. 1952, Kenya. Clinical Biochemistry. *Education:* BSc. University of London, 1973-76; PhD. University of Dundee, 1976-79; MIBiol. Institute of Biology, 1980. *Appointments:* Post Graduate Assistant. University of Dundee, 1976-79; Post Doctoral Assistant, University of Dundee, 1979-80; Honorary Assistant, University of Dundee, 1981-; Biochemist, Tayside Health Board, 1980-. *Memberships:* Licenciate, Institute of Biology, 1976-79; Member, Institute of Biology, 1980; Member, Association of Clinical Biochemists, 1981. *Publications:* Several publications in Journals including: Ph.D. Thesis, University of Dundee, 1979; British Journal of Nutrition, 1981. *Honours:* Camilla-Samuel Fund Award, 1977-80. *Hobbies:* Squash; Hockey. *Address:* 36 Lochinver Crescent, Gowrie Park, Dundee DD2 4UA, Scotland.

DEVITT, Anthony Colin, b. 7 Nov. 1944. Senior Viticulturist and Oenologist. *Education:* BSc.(Hons.) Agriculture, University of Western Australia, 1968; R.D.Oen.(Hons), Roseworthy Agricultural College, South Australia, 1975. *Appointments:* Research Officer, Plant Research Division, Department of Agriculture, 1967-73; Viticulture Adviser, Division of Horticulture, Department of Agriculture, 1973-79; Senior Viticulturist and Oenologist, Department of Agriculture, 1979-; Chairman, WA Grapegrowers & Wine Producers Association; Chairman, Regional Certification of Wines Committee. *Memberships:* Member, Roseworthy Agricultural College; Member, Australian Institute of Agricultural Science; Secretary, Horticultural Industries Committee; Secretary, Table Grape Advisory Committee; Member of several Cricket Clubs. *Publications:* Numerous publications on pasture research, Viticulture and Oenology. *Honours:* Swan Brewery Prize, Faculty of Agriculture, 1967; Leo Buring Gold Medal, 1975; Rudi Buring Scholarship, Post Graduate, 1980. *Hobbies:* Sport; Reading; Farming. *Address:* 17 The Strand, Applecross, Western Australia.

DEWAN, Manik Lal Dewan, b. 5 Jan. 1935, Rangamati. University Teacher. m. Deepika, 31 Jan. 1954, 2 sons, 2 daughters. *Education:* B.Sc. East Park College, 1957; M.S., A & M Texas University, Texas, 1964; Ph.D. Moscow Academy, U.S.S.R., 1971; Post Doctoral Training, Royal School of Veterinary Medicine, Edinburgh, 1978. *Appointments:* Animal Husbandry Officer, Comilla, 1957-59; Assistant Lecturer, East Park Veterinary College, 1959-61; Assistant Professor, Bangladesh Agricultural University, 1964-73; Associate Professor, Bangladesh Agriculture University, 1973-79. *Memberships:* Member, Bangladesh Society for Advancement of Science; Member, Bangladesh Veterinary Association; Associate Editor, Bangladesh Veterinary Journal. *Publications:* Numerous Scientific publications in the field of Vetinary Pathology. *Hobbies:* Photography; Indoor Games. *Address:* Quarter No D-17/1, BAU Campus, Mymensingh, Bangladesh.

DEWAR-BEAUCLERK, Peter de Vere, b. 19 Feb. 1943, Tenterden, Kent, England. Accountant; Registered Genealogist. m. Sarah Ann Sweet Verge Rudder, 4 Feb. 1967, 1 son, 2 daughters. *Education:* Fellow, Institute of Administrative Accounting and Data Processing; British Institute of Management; Fellow, Society of Antiquaries of Scotland; International Institute of Genealogy and Heraldry. *Appointments:* Accountant, Hays Akers and Hays, London, UK, 1961-64; Account Executive, Masius Wynne Williams Limited, London, UK, 1964-66; Head of Organisation Department, National Farmers Union, Employers Association, London, UK, 1967-73; Regional Manager for Scotland, Tyndall Group, Fund Managers, Edinburgh, UK, 1973-75; Accountant, Dewar East & Co., London, UK, 1975-80; Chief Accountant, Hospital of St John & St. Elizabeth, London, UK, 1981-; Lieutenant Commander, 1977, Royal Naval Reserve, 1965-. *Memberships:* Founder member, 1968, Hon. Director and Treasurer, 1971-73, Council member, 1979-, Association of Genealogists and Record Agents; Hon. Treasurer, 1979-, Institute of Heraldic and Genealogical Studies; Liveryman, 1968, Worshipful Company of Haberdashers; Sub-Committee, 1968-73, Society of Genealogists. *Publications:* numerous publications including: The House of Nell Gwyn, 1670-1974, (with D Adamson), 1974; Contributor to A Handbook of British family History, 1979; Consultant Editor and Contributor to Burke's Scottish Family Records, unpublished; Contributor to The Armorial Who's Who. *Honours:* Knight of Malta, 1971; Knight of Order of Constantine St George, 1981; Falkland Pursuivant Extraordinary, 1975; Royal Naval Reserve Decoration (RD), 1980; Silver Stick Usher at HM Silver Jubilee Thanksgiving Service, 1977. *Address:* 45 Airedale Avenue, Chiswick, London W4 2NW, England.

DEWHURST, William George, b. 21 Nov. 1926, Frosterley, England. Physician, Psychiatrist, Teacher. m. Margaret Dransfield, 17 Sept. 1960, 1 son, 1 daughter. *Education:* Oxford University; London University; London Hospital Medical College; Insitute of Psychiatry; B.A. 1947; M.A. 1962; B.M., B.Ch., 1950; Internal Medicine, Royal College of Physicians, London, 1955; Academic Postgraduate Diploma in Psychological Medicine, London University, 1961; Certified Specialist, Alberta, 1970; Royal College of Psychiatry, 1971; F.R.C.P., 1978; F.A.C.P., 1980; F.A.P.A., 1980. *Appointments:* Senior Lecturer and Honorary Consultant Physician, Bethlem, Royal and Maudsley Hospitals, 1965-69; Professor and Associate Professor, Department of Psychiatry, 1969-75; Professor and Chairman, Department of Psychiatry, University of Alberta, 1975-; Consultant Psychiatrist, Royal Alexandra Hospital, 1976-; Co-Director, Neurochemical Research Unit, Department of Psychiatry, 1979-; Honorary Professor of Pharmacy and Pharmaceutical Sciences, 1979-. *Memberships:* Founding Vice-President, Canadian College of Neuropsychopharmacology; Past-President, Alberta Psychiatric Association; Fellow, American College of Psychiatrists, American Psychiatric Association and Royal Society of Medicine; Member of numerous other Scientific organizations including, American Association for the Advancement of Science; New York Academy of Sciences; Canadian Psychiatric Association and Medical Association. *Publications:* Author and co-author of over sixty publications in the Scientific Literature concerning the Biochemistry of Mental Illness. *Honours:* Open Scholarship to Kings College; Open Exhibition in Natural Science, University College, Oxford; Senior County Scholarship, Somerset; Distinction in Academic Diploma in Psychological Medicine, London University; Foundation member, Royal College of Psychiatrists, Royal College of Physicians, Canada, American College of Psychiatrists and American Psychiatric Association. *Hobbies:* Music; Books; Chess; Hockey; Football. *Address:* 92 Fairway Drive, Edmonton, Alberta, Canada, T6J 2C5.

DEXTER, Barrie Graham, b. 15 July 1921, Kilsyth, Australia. Diplomat. m. Judith MacWalter Craig, 30 May 1950, 1 son, 2 daughters. *Education:* MA; Dip; Ed; University of Melbourne, 1940-47. *Appointments:* School Teacher, Brighton Grammar School, Melbourne, 1940; Australian Army, 1941-43; Australian Navy, 1944-47; Head Federal Governments News Agency and Executive member of the Council for Aboriginal Affairs, 1967-77; School Teacher, Wesley College, Melbourne, 1947; Department of External Affairs, 1948-68; Australian High Commissioner in Ghana,

1963-64; Australian Ambassador to Laos, 1964-68; Australian Ambassador to Yugoslavia, Romania, Bulgaria, 1977-80; Australian High Commissioner in Canada, 1980-. *Memberships:* Associate Member, Australian Institute for Aboriginal Studies; Member, University House, Australian National University, Canberra; Member, Commonwealth Club, Canberra; Member, Naval and Military Club, Melbourne; Member, Victorian Commando Association; Associate Member, The Gallipoli Association, England. *Honours:* CBE. *Hobbies:* Music; Gardening; Skiing. *Address:* 407 Wilbrod Street, Ottawa KIN 6M6, Canada.

DEY, Subhas Chandra, b. 31 Dec. 1942, Gauhati, Assam, India. University Professor. m. Chhabi Das, 13 Mar. 1969, 1 son, 1 daughter. *Education:* Intermediate Science, First Division, Gauhati University, 1958; Bachelor of Science, First Class, Honours in Zoology, Gauhati, 1960; Master of Science in Zoology & Comp. Anatomy, First Class, Calcutta, 1962; Doctor of Science, Calcutta, 1976. *Appointments:* Head, BioScience Division, Rungta HS Institute, Calcutta, 1962-63; Assistant Professor (Lecturer) in Zoology & Head, Fish Division, Gauhati University, India, 1963-76; Associate Professor (Reader) in Zoology and Head, Fish Division, Gauhati University, 1976-. *Memberships:* Executive, Indian Society of Ichthyologist, Madras; Assam Science Society, Gauhati; Zoological Society of India; Indian National Science Academy, Delhi; Indian Science Congress Association, Calcutta; Council of Scientific & Industrial Research, Delhi; Zoological Society of Calcutta. *Publications:* Co-author of Four Text Books on General Science, (School level) and Zoology, (Under-Graduate level); 28 Research Papers on Hydrobiology, Experimental Ichthyology and Fish & Fishery Biology in reputed journals. *Honours:* All India Merit Scholarship, 1960-62; Fellow, Zoological Society of Calcutta, 1979. *Hobbies:* Excursions; Cricket and Book Reading. *Address:* 129 University Campus, Gauhati, Assam, 781014, India.

DEY, Victoria Aku (Mrs John Kwadzo Day), b. 16 Aug. 1933. Nursing. m. John Kwadzo, 12 July 1958, 3 sons, 3 daughters. *Education:* State Registered Nurse, 1954; Central Midwives Board, 1957; Diploma Nursing Administration, 1974; Family Planning, 1973; Community Health Nursing, 1979. *Appointments:* Principal Nursing Officer, General Nursing. *Memberships:* Christian Mothers Association; Our Lady of Perpetual Help; Church Choir. *Hobbies:* Gardening; Sewing; Reading. *Address:* No. 6 1st Circular Road, Cantonments, Accra, Ghana.

DHALLA, Om Parkash, b. 8 Aug. 1928, Bahawal Pur State, Pakistan. Surgeon, Dentist. m. Shobha, 31 Jan. 1952, 2 sons. *Education:* L.D.Sc., 1946; H.M.D.S., 1950. *Appointments:* Honorary Registrar, Delhi Dental Council, 1973-; Delhi Dental Council, 1973-; Dental Council of India, 1979-. *Memberships:* President, Dentists Association, Delhi Branch, 1977-78; Dentists Association, India, 1979,80,81; Divisional Warden, Civil Defence Delhi Administration; President National Tairak Sangh; General Secretary, Consumers Council of India; Executive, Rajput Association of India. Organiser Dental Camps, slums areas; Organiser T.B. Care & after Care Committee. *Honours:* State Award, Civil Defence; National Award, Civil Defence; Gold Medal, Organising Dental Camps. *Hobbies:* Social work. *Address:* Dhalla Niwas, Delhi Gate, New Delhi 2.

DHAMDHERE, Madhukar Narayanrao, b. 18 Oct. 1936, Vada, District, Thana, Maharashtra, India. Chartered Accountant. m. Asha Bhonsle, 16 Dec. 1961, 1 son, 1 daughter. *Education:* Bachelor of Commerce, 1956; Chartered Accountant, 1959; Bachelor of Laws, 1963. *Appointments:* Kodak Limited, Bombay, 1959-60; AF Ferguson and Company, Chartered Accountants, India, 1960-62; Indian Detonators Limited, India, 1962-65; Consultant, 1965-68; IDL Chemicals Limited, India, 1968-73; Vegatable and Fruit Processing Limited, 1973-78; Sona Breweries Limited, Azad Group, Nigeria, 1978-. *Memberships:* Fellow, Institute of Chartered Accountants, India. *Honours:* M.G. Desai Gold Medal, Final Examination, Institute of Chartered Accountants, India, 1959. *Hobbies:* Badminton; Bridge. *Address:* 10, Taslim Alias Close, Victoria Island, Lagos, Nigeria.

DHARMARAJU, Kalyanapu, b. 15 July 1953, Puttakonda. L.I.C. Agent; Treasurer, S.F.A. Manager,

U.L.T.C. Institute. *Education:* B.Com. Andhra University, 1975-78; Manual of Village Accounts, Certificate, 1975; Transport Section, Conductors Licence, 1975; Village Sanitation Test Certificate, 1976; Telephone Operator's Training Certificate, 1978; Wireless Telegraphy, Commercial University, 1978; National Cadet Corps, two years training Certificate; National Service Scheme two years Training Certificate; Social Service, five years. *Appointments:* L.I.C., India Agent; President & Manager V.L.T.C. Institute; Small Farmers Association. *Memberships:* New Delhi University; All India C.A., New Delhi. *Hobbies:* Kabbadi; Cricket; Khoko. *Address:* Puttakonda, Kakinada Taluk, East Godavari District, A.P. India.

DHILLON, Gurdial Singh, b. 6 Aug. 1915, Panjwar, Amritsar, India. High Commissioner for India in Canada. m. Ranbir K, Jan. 1953. *Education:* Graduated, Government College, Lahore, 1935; Law Degree with Distinction, University Law College, Lahore, 1937. *Appointments:* Practiced Law, 1937-47; Journalist for many years; Editor, Punjabi Daily Vartmen, 1948-52; Chief Editor, Urdu Daily Sher-e-Bharat, 1948-52; Managing Director, National Sikhs Newspapers Ltd., Punjab Legislative Assembly, 1952-57, Deputy Speaker, 1952-54, Speaker 1954-62; Secretary General & Chief Whip, Punjab Congress Legislature Party, 1964-67; Minister, Transport, Rural Electrification, Elections & Civil Aviation for Punjab, 1965-66; Parliament of India, 1967-77; Chairman, Parliamentary Committee on Public Undertakings, 1968-69, Speaker, 1969-75; Union Minister of Transport & Shipping, 1975-77; President, Commonwealth Speakers' Conference 70, Chairman, Standing Committee of Commonwealth Speakers' Conference 1971-74; Vice-President, Executive Committee of Commonwealth Parl. Association, 1969-74; President of C.P.A. 1973-74; Executive Committee of IPU 1969-73; President, Inter-Parl. Council of IPU 1973-76; Executive, Punjab University Senate and Syndicate, 1956-; Senate & Syndicate of G.N. University, Amritsar, Punjabi University, Patiala. *Memberships:* President of: Dr.Zakir Hussain Educational & Cultrual Foundation, Institute of Const. & Parl. Studies, Weight Lifting Association, Rifle Shooting Association of India, International Punjabi Society; Rotary Clubs of Delhi, Chandigarh and Amritsar; Trustee and Chairman of Managing Committee of Jalleanwala Bagh Memorial Trust. *Honours:* Dr.Pol.Sc. Punjab University, Chandigarh; Dr.Pol.Sc. Punjabi University; D.Litt. GN University, Amritsar; LL.D. Kurukshetra University; Dr.Pol.Sc. Humboldt Uni Berlan; Dr.Pol.Sc. Sub Kwan University; Awarded honours and medallions by various Parliaments; Medallion of Parliament of Canada, 1969. *Hobbies:* Promoting High Education; Social Service; Farming and rural sports. *Address:* 585 Acacia Avenue, Rockcliffe, Ottawa, Canada.

DHOKALIA, Ramaa Prasad, b. 17 Oct. 1925, Kota, India. Academic Lawyer Educator. m. Shyam Kumari Beohar, 18 May 1949, 2 sons, 3 daughters. *Education:* Allahabad University, India, B.A., 1946, M.A., 1948, LL.B., 1949; PhD., Manchester University, UK., International Law, 1964. *Appointments:* Allahabad University, Lecturer in Pol. Sc., 1948-55, Assistant Professor, Pol. Sc., 1955-62; Research Fellow in Law, Manchester University UK., 1962-64; Reader in Pol. Sc., Allababad University, 1964-66; Banaras Hindu University, Reader in Law, 1966-72; Professor of Law, 1972, Dean Law School, 1976-80; Visiting Professor of Law, University of Calabar, 1980-. *Memberships:* Indian Academy of Social Sciences, President, 1979-80, Regional President, 1977-79; President, Indian Law Teachers Association, 1979-80; Director, Clinical Legal Education Programme, 1974-80; Commonwealth Law Association; Commonwealth Legal Education Association, London; International Law Association; Indian & American Societies of International Law. *Publications:* Codification of Public International Law 1970; Democracy in India—Challenges and Perspectives, 1975; Human Rights in India, 1972. *Honours:* Research Grant in Law, University of Manchester, 1962-64; Hague Academy of International Law, 1968, International Law Association, 1974. *Hobbies:* Painting; Photography; Gardening. *Address:* Visiting Professor of Law, Unical, Calabar, Nigeria, West Africa.

DHONIRAM SAIKIA, Dhoronidhara Kamaleswara, b. 19 May 1943, Chakardhoragaon, Assam, India. Astrologist, Indian Medicine, Commerce. *Education:* Jyotisharnav, 1976; B.Com. Hons, 1978. *Appointments:* Astrology; Ayurvedic Medicine; Commerce.

Memberships: Indian Commercial Association; Indian Institute of Astrology. *Publications:* Articles on Astrology. *Hobbies:* To earn knowledge and realize with research; Humanity. *Address:* Chakardhoragaon, P.O. Borpothorua, Golaghat 785621, Assam, India.

DHU, Jenifer Elain, (Mrs Keith T E Dhu), b. 4 Nov. 1934, Adelaide, South Australia. Artist. m. Keith T Ellis Dhu (second marriage) 23 Dec. 1980, 3 sons, 1 daughter (by previous marriage). *Education:* Leaving Certificate, including Art, Adelaide Public Examinations Board; S.A. School of Arts. *Memberships:* Royal South Australian Society of Arts. *Creative Works:* Howqua Valley, 1977; Numerous paintings including: Progress, 1978, Tanunda Vineyards, 1979, Surf, 1978, Razorback, 1979, South-East Forests, 1979, Howqua II, 1980. *Honours:* Kernewek-Lowender Art Prize, (Shared), 1979. *Hobbies:* Tennis; Snow Skiing. *Address:* 3/168 Sydney Road, Fairlight, N.S.W. 2094, Australia.

DIANZUMBA, Sinda Balunga, b. 28 Aug. 1942, Ndembo, Masangi, Lower Zaire. Cardiologist. *Education:* B.S., Oregon State University, 1967; M.D., Northwestern University Medical School, 1971; *Appointments:* Internship, Passavant Memorial Hospital, 1971-72; Residency in Internal Medicine, Northwestern University, MacGaw Medical Center, 1972-74; Clinical Fellowship in Cardiology, Northwestern University, 1974-76; Research Fellowship in Cardiology (Echocardiography), Allegheny General Hospital, 1976-78; Faculty of Medicine, University of the West Indies and the University Hospital, West Indies, Consultant Cardiologist, Chief Cardiologist, Lecturer in Medicine, 1978-; Honorary Consultant, National Chest Hospital, Kingston, Jamaica, 1978-. *Memberships:* Board of Directors, The Heat Foundation of Jamaica; Jamaica Heart Health Club; Jamaica Cancer Society; American Heart Association; American Medical Association; Medical Association of Jamaica; Association des Médicines Francophones de la Jamaique; Association des Médinces de Longue Francaise du Canada. *Publications:* Poetry in French; 23 articles in Medical journals on heart diseases, 1976, 1981-; Landscape paintings. *Honours:* American Government Scholarship, 1963-67; American Medical Association Recognition award, 1975. *Hobbies:* Photography; Hiking; Swimming; Classical music collection; Stamp collection; Jogging; Leisure reading, science fiction. *Address:* Olympia Hotel, 33-34 University Crescent, Mona, Kingston 6, Jamaica, West Indies.

DIAS, Anthony Lancelot, b. 13 Mar. 1910, Poona, India. Chairman, National Book Trust, India. m. Joan Dias 7 Oct. 1939, 4 daughters. *Education:* BA(Econ.) (Hons. 1st Class), University of Bombay; BSc(Econ) London School of Economics, 1930-33; Magdalene College, Cambridge, 1933-34. *Appointments:* Civil Service, 1933; Secretary, Education Department, 1952-55; Agricultural Department, 1955-57; Home Department, 1957-60; Chairman, Bombay Port Trust, 1960-64; Secretary, Department of Food, Ministry of Food and Agriculture, 1964-70; Lt. Governor of Tripura, 1970-71; Governor of West Bengal, 1971-77; Chairman, Indian Institute of Management, Calcutta, 1976-; National Book Trust, 1978-; Member, Board of Governors, Int. Department Research Centre, Ottawa, 1970-74. *Publications:* Feeding India's Millions. *Honours:* London Cobden Club Gold Medal for Economics and the Hugh Lewis Prize of the London School of Economics 1932; Padma Vibhushan, Government of India, 1970. *Hobbies:* Golf; Photography. *Address:* No. 2, Kushak Road, New Delhi 110011, India.

DIAS, Lal Jayasri, b. 10 Nov. 1950, Galle, Sri Lanka. Chartered Accountant. m. Dushiyanthi M I Pimanda, 30 Oct. 1976, 1 son. *Education:* Articled Clerk with Chartered Accountants, Colombo, Sir Lanka, 1968-72; Final Examination of the Institute of Chartered Accountants of Sri Lanka, 1974; Associate Member of Institute of Chartered Accountants of Sri Lanka, 1975. *Appointments:* Accountant, Sri Lanka Sugar Corporation, 1973-75; Accountant, Brooke Bond, Ceylon, Ltd., 1975-76; Financial Controller, Ceylon Match Co., Ltd., 1976-78; Assistant Group Controller, 1978-; *Memberships:* National Geographical Society, Washington D.C. Tennis Club of Nyon, Switzerland; Touring Club of Switzerland; 80 Club of Colomboa, Sir Lanka. *Hobbies:* Home Movies; Tennis; Swimming; Skiing; Music (Country & Western); International Affairs. *Address:* La Levratte 16, 1260 Nyon, Switzerland.

DICK, Gavin Colquhoun, b. 6 Sept. 1928, Hamilton, Scotland. Civil Servant. m. Elizabeth Frances Hutchinson, 20 Dec. 1952, 2 daughters. *Education:* Hamilton Academy, 1933-45; MA, Glasgow University, 1945-49; MA, Baliol College, Oxford, 1949-52. *Appointments:* Royal Tank Regiment, 1952-54; Board of Trade, 1954; UK Trade Commissioner, Wellington, NZ, 1961-64; Under Secretary, 1975; Head of Regional Policy and Development Grants Division, Department of Industry, 1981. *Memberships:* United Oxford and Cambridge University Club. *Hobbies:* Words. *Address:* Fell Cottage, Bayley's Hill, Sevenoaks, Kent, England

DICK, John Young William, b. 15 Feb. 1916, Auckland, New Zealand. Education. m. Lilian Dalton, 23 Sept. 1939, 2 sons, 1 daughter. *Education:* Mount Albert Grammar School; Seddon Memorial Technical College; British Institute of Engineering Technology. *Appointments:* Royal Navy, 1939-45; Merchant Navy, 1945-49; New Zealand, Education Department, Technical Correspondence School, Tutor, 1949-53; Head, Technical Department, Hawera Technical High School, 1953-59; Head, Industrial Department, Wanganui Technical College, 1959-65; Director, Nelson Polytechnic, 1965-69; Foundation Principal, Manukau Technical Institute, New Zealand, 1969-. *Memberships:* National Executive, Technical Institutes Association; Rotary; Nelson Chamber of Commerce; Several Apprenticeship Committees; President, Royal Overseas League, Auckland Branch; Associate, Institute Marine Engineers, London; Associate, New Zealand Institute Motor Industry; Associate, Society Automotive Engineers, Australia. *Publications:* Mechanics of the Motor Vehicle. *Honours:* Apprentice of the Year, Gold Medal, 1937; Sir Woolf Fiaher Travel Award, 1970. *Hobbies:* Travel; Sailing. *Address:* 167 Beach Road, Castor Bay, Auckland, New Zealand.

DICKENS, David Robert Vernon, b. 24 Oct. 1938, Melbourne, Australia. Orthopaedic Surgeon. m. Susan Jean Roxburgh, 2 Feb. 1966, 3 sons. *Education:* MBBS, University of Melbourne, 1962; FRACS, Royal Australian College of Surgeons, 1967. *Appointments:* Orthopaedic Surgeon, Royal Childrens Hospital. *Memberships:* Australian Orthopaedic Association; Fellow, Royal Australian College of Surgeons; Royal Brighton Yacht Club. *Address:* 6 Kensington Road, South Yarra, Australia, 3141.

DICKENSON, Norris, Nathaniel, b. 17 May 1911, St. Kitts. Minister of Religion. m. (1) Mildred L Trott, 18 Dec. 1941, 2 daughters, (2) Miriam Ada Bascome, 30 Dec. 1971. *Education:* Study, Bennet College, Machine Shop Practice and General Education; American International College; Moody Bible Institute; Cerullo School of Ministry, San Diego, California, USA. *Appointments:* Machinist Apprentice, HMS Dockyard, Bermuda, 1927; Machinist, USA Air Base Kindley Field, Bermuda, 1941; Diesel Mechanic, Precision Engineering, 1942-66; District President, Christian Ministry, 1966-; Bishop of United Holy Church of America Inc; Bishop, Church to be consecrated outside of USA; First Bishop, Bermuda District; *Memberships:* The Annual Convocation; President, Pentecostal Ministerial Fellowship; The Bermuda Ministerial Association; Broadcasting Commissioner. *Publications:* The 50 Jubilee Historical Journal of the Bermuda District of the United Holy Church of America, 1971. Foreword, to several Church journals. *Honours:* Several awards and a certificate for outstanding performance as a Machinist, USA Air Base, Bermuda, 1963. *Hobbies:* Reading; Carpentry. *Address:* PO Box 32, Old Road, Shelly Bay, Bermuda, 2-12.

DICKINSON, Harley Rivers, b. 20 Oct. 1938, Melbourne, Australia. Registrar, Diocese of Melbourne. m. Nicola Charlotte Nina, 24 Nov. 1964, 3 sons, 1 daughter. *Education:* Geelong College, Geelong, Australia; Graduate, Australian School of Pacific Administration; Associate Australian Institute of Management. *Appointments:* District Officer PNG, 1958-70; Resident Magistrate, Coroner, Visiting Justice PNG, 1970-76; Chief Executive & Registrar, Anglican Diocese of Melbourne; Secretary VFGA, Bannockburn. *Memberships:* UK Magistrates Association; Point Leo Surf Life Saving Club; Toastmasters International; RACV Melbourne; Vice-President Liberal Speakers Group. *Publications:* Prepared 1971 Edition Field Officers Manual, Department Adminstrator PNG Synod Papers Diocese of Melbourne, 1980. *Honours:* Olympic Torch Bearer,

Melbourne, 1956; Oarsman, Geelong College Head of River Crew, 1957; Athletics GPS, Relay, 1957. *Hobbies:* Farming; Oil Painting; Antiques; Politics; Tennis. *Address:* Mt. Pleasant, Bannockburn 3331, Victoria, Australia.

DICKINSON, John Lawrence, (Bob), b. 16 Nov. 1913. Company Chairman. m. Bettine Mary Jenkins, 1937, 2 daughters. *Education:* Chartered Accountant, Taunton School, 1937. *Appointments:* Chief Accountant, Lucas Industries, 1937-44; Finance Director, Secretary, SKF (UK) Ltd., 1944-62; Sales Director, 1962-66; Managing Director, 1967-75; Retired Chairman, British Rail (Eastern) Board, 1970-. *Memberships:* National Enterprise Board, 1975-79; Chairman NEDO Industrial Engines Sector Working Party, 1976-79; Member, CBI Council, Finance, General Purposes Committee, until 1977; Chairman Cranfield Institute, High Sherrif, Bedfordshire, 1972-73; Deputy Chairman, Cranfield Institute, Deputy Lieutenant, Bedfordshire. *Honours:* Gold Medal, Royal Patriots Society, Sweden, 1975. *Hobbies:* Gardening; National Hunt Racing. *Address:* Arkle House, Upton End, Shillington, Hitchen, Herts, England.

DICKS, Paul David, b. 13 Apr. 1950, St John's, Newfoundland. Lawyer. m. Maureen Dunn, 12 Oct. 1974, 1 daughter. *Education:* College Rochelle, 1967-68; BA-(Hons.), BEd, Memorial University of Newfoundland, 1970-73; LLB, Dalhousie Law School. *Appointments:* Dicks, Dicks and Watton, Partner, 1977-81. *Memberships:* Liberal Party; Rotary. *Publications:* Novel, Presently being prepared for publication. *Honours:* Sir Allister Fraser Memorial Fellowship, 1974; Sir James Dunn Scholarship, 1973; Gold Medal in Physiology, 1973; NTA Medal, 1973; Centenary Scholarships, 1971; Deans List Iona College 1967; Grade Eleven, 1967. *Hobbies:* Writing; Painting; Photography; Stamp and Coin Collecting. *Address:* Steady Brook, Newfoundland, Canada.

DICKSON, Brian, b. 25 May 1916, Yorkton, Saskatchewan. Lawyer. m. Barbara Melville, 18 June 1943, 3 sons, 1 daughter. *Education:* LLB, 1938, Manitoba Law School; DCnL, 1965, Saint John's College; LLD, 1973, University of Manitoba; LLD, 1978, University of Saskatchewan; LLD, 1979, University of Ottawa; LLD, 1980, Queen's University. *Appointments:* Called to the Bar of Manitoba, 1940; Royal Canadian Artillery, 1940-45; Lawyer, Aikins, MacAulay and Company, 1945-63; Lecturer, Manitoba Law School, 1948-54; QC, 1953; Court of Queen's Bench of Manitoba, 1963; Court of Appeal for Manitoba, 1967; Supreme Court of Canada, 1973. *Memberships:* Law Society of Manitoba; Board of Trustees, The Sellers Foundation; Rideau; Maganassippi Fish and Game. *Hobbies:* Riding. *Address:* Marchmont, Dunrobin, Ontario, K0A 1T0, Canada.

DIGBY, Darcy Octavius, b. 14 Nov. 1911, Ashburton, New Zealand. Master Builder. m. Margaret Ella Ross, 28 Dec. 1961, 1 son. *Appointments:* Master Builder, 1947; Farmer, 1968-81; Director, Canterbury Sugar Development Society Limited, 1975-81. *Memberships:* Mayor of Ashburton, 1971-77; District Roads Board, 1965-77; South Island Local Bodies Association, 1975-77; Past President and Life Member Master Builders' Associated; Member and Past President, Ashburton Lions Club; Ashburton College Board, 1971-73; Member and Past President, Ashburton Chamber of Commerce; Member and Past President, Ashburton Senior Citizens Club; Save the Children Fund; Ashburton Hearing Association Incorporated; Vice-President, The Venerable Order of St. John, Ashburton. *Honours:* Justice of the Peace, 1971-81; Queen's Silver Jubilee Medal. *Hobbies:* Farming; Bowling; Fishing. *Address:* Pole Road, Winchmore, No 6 RD, Ashburton, New Zealand.

DIGGLE, John Lynton, b. 13 Oct. 1936, Paeroa, New Zealand. Film maker. m. Edith Grace Norgrove, 5 Sept. 1959, 1 son, 1 daughter. *Address:* 3 Ngaio Road, Titirangi, Auckland, New Zealand.

DIKSHIT, Hanuman Prasad, b. 27 Dec. 1941, Kanpur, India. Teaching and Research. m. Sujata Dikshit, 14 June 1974, 1 daughter. *Education:* MSc (Mathematics), 1961, DPhil, 1964, University of Allahabad; DSc, 1969, University of Jabalpur. *Appointments:* Lecturer, University of Allahabad, 1963-69; Reader, 1969-72;

Head of Mathematics Department, 1972-78, Professor, University of Jabalpur; Professor and Head, School of Mathematics, Jiwaji University, Gwalior, 1978-79. *Memberships:* Indian Mathematical Society; Indian Science Congress Association. *Publications:* 40 papers in Journals of mathematical research. *Honours:* A National Associate of the University Grants Commission of India, 1977-82. *Hobbies:* Music. *Address:* B 2 University Campus, PO Saraswati Vihar, Jabalpur 48200 1, India.

DILL, Nicholas Bayard, b. 28 Dec. 1905, Devonshire, Bermuda. Barrister-at-Law. m. Lucy Clare Watlington, 3 July 1930, 2 sons. *Appointments:* Trinity Hall, Cambridge, England; Middle Temple, London, England. *Appointments:* Partner, Conyers, Dill and Pearman, Hamilton, Bermuda, 1928-. *Memberships:* Royal Bermuda Yacht Club; Royal Thames Yacht Club; Royal Hamilton Dinghy Club, Bermuda; India House, New York, USA; Canadian Club of New York; Mid-Ocean Club, Bermuda. *Publications:* Reminiscences of an Islander. *Honours:* Commander of the British Empire, 1951; Knight Bachelor, 1955; Chancellor, Anglican Church of Bermuda 1950-; Captain, Bermuda Volunteer Engineers, 1933-44; Chairman, Five Government Boards. *Hobbies:* Sailing; Golf; Tennis. *Address:* "Newbold Place", Devonshire, Bermuda.

DILWORTH, Robert James, b. 13 July 1950, Kitchener, Ontario, Canada. Organist and Choirmaster. *Education:* BA, Wilfrid Laurier University, 1974; MA, University of Waterloo, 1975; ARCT, Royal Conservatory of Music, University of Toronto, 1971. *Appointments:* Assistant Teacher, University of Waterloo, 1974-77; Organist, St Timothy's United Church, 1975-78; Organist, Calvin Presbyterian Church, 1978-. *Honours:* Alumni Gold Medal for French and German, 1974; Ontario Graduate Scholarship, 1974-75 and 1975-76; Canada Council Doctoral Fellowship, 1976-77 and 1977-78. *Hobbies:* Stamp Collecting; Reading. *Address:* 75 Village Road, Kitchener, Ontario, Canada, N2M 4K9.

DINGLE, D Terence, b. 22 May 1935, Winnipeg, Manitoba, Canada. Lawyer and Businessman. m. Judith E Hingston, 16 Feb. 1963, 1 son, 2 daughters. *Education:* BA, Loyola College, 1957; BCL, McGill University, 1960. *Appointments:* Lawyer, Partner, Courtois, Clarkson, Parsons & Tétrault; President and Chief Executive Officer, Shawinigan Group Incorporated. *Memberships:* University Club of Toronto; Toronto Golf Club; Mount Bruno Golf and Country Club; Saint James's Club of Montreal; Hillside Tennis Club; Montreal Indoor Tennis Club; Montreal Badminton & Squash Club. *Hobbies:* Skiing; Tennis; Sailing; Squash. *Address:* 168 Inglewood Drive, Toronto, Ontario, Canada.

DINSDALE, Walter Gilbert, b. 3 Apr. 1916, Brandon, Manitoba, Canada. Member of Parliament; Privy Council; Professor. m. Lenore Gusdal, 17 Sept. 1947, Five children. *Education:* Public Schools Brandon, 1922-33; BA, Inchmaster University, 1937; MA, University of Toronto, 1951; Pre-doctoral Studies, University of Chicago. *Appointments:* Canadian Pacific Railway, 1935-39; Social Worker, Salvation Army, 1935-39; Royal Canadian Air Force, Night Fighter Pilot, 1942-45; Professor, Social Sciences, Brandon College, 1945-51; Member of Parliament, 1951-80; Cabinet Minister, Northern Affairs and Resources, 1960-63; Parliamentary Secretary, 1957-60. *Memberships:* Royal Canadian Legion; Royal Canadian Air Force Association; Kiwanis Club and Rotary Club; Salvation Army Divisional Bandmaster. *Publications:* MA Thesis, University of Toronto; The Prophet and the Sectarian Cycle; Numerous speeches and legislative initiations. *Honours:* Brandon College Honour Society, 1937; DFC Royal Canadian Air Force, 1945; Canadian Privy Council, 1960; Honorary LLD, Brandon University, and Richmond College, Toronto, 1977; Meritorious Service Medal Royal Canadian Legion, 1979. *Hobbies:* Music; Home Movies; Photography; Swimming; Tennis; Water Skiing; Travel. *Address:* 3205 Rosser Avenue, Brandon, Manitoba, Canada, R7B 0H1.

DIONNE, Jean-Guy, b. 14 June 1923, Stratford, Province of Quebec Canada. Industrialist. m. Clemence C Maheux 2 June 1947, 2 sons, 1 daughter. *Education:* Textile Engineering, Diploma, New Bedford Textile Institute 1945. *Appointments:* Professor, Institut Des

Textiles Du Quebec, 1948; Sales, Canadian Industries Limited 1956; President, Textiles Dionne Incorporated 1963. *Memberships:* Canadian Textile Institute; Textile Technical Federation of Canada; Textile Society of Canada; Texscope Foundation of Canada; Knight of Columbus; Rotary Club of St Georges. *Hobbies:* Tennis; Golf; Cross-country; Skiing. *Address:* 10945, 5th Avenue, St Georges De Beauce, Quebec, Canada, G1V 4N3.

DIPEOLU, Olusegun Oladipupo, b. 19 Oct. 1941, Ibadan, Nigeria. Veterinary Surgeon. m. Mofolasayo Mobolaji, 26 July 1960, 2 sons, 1 daughter. *Education:* Cambridge Overseas Higher School Certificate, Christ School, Ado-Ekiti, 1961; Diplom Tierarzt (Equivalent of BVMS/MRCVS) Justus Liebig University, Giessen, West Germany, 1969; PhD (Parasitology) University of Edinburgh, Edinburgh, Scotland. *Appointments:* Lecturer Grade II, 1972; Lecturer Grade I 1974; Senior Lecturer 1975; Professor of Parasitology, University of Ibadan, 1977; Head of Department of Veterinary Microbiology and Parasitology, 1979. *Memberships:* Nigerian Society for Parasitology; Fellow, Royal Entomological Society; Science Association of Nigeria; Entomological Society of Nigeria; Nigerian Veterinary Medical Association; Nigerian Society for Animal Production; Fellow, African Association of Insect Scientists. *Publications:* Thesis: The development of trypanosomes in tsetse flies; Chapters in Books and Monographs; Publications on Trypanosomiasis; Culicoides; On Ticks and Tick-Borne Diseases; On Insects of Veterinary Importance; On Veterinary Public Health; On General Parasitological Topics. *Honours:* Royal Society Commonwealth Award, 1976. *Hobbies:* Sports; Photography. *Address:* 21 Amina Way, University of Ibadan, Ibadan, Nigeria.

DIRI, Gladday Anson, b. 4 Apr. 1941, Kalaibiama, Opobo, Rivers State, Nigeria. Journalist. m. Nettie Jaja, 2 Sept. 1972, 3 sons, 2 daughters. *Education:* BA(Hon), 1976-79. *Appointments:* Journalist, Daily Times of Nigeria Limited; Sub-Editor, 1970-73; Chief Sub Editor Headlines, 1973-74; Ag. Editor Headlines, 1974; Editor Headlines, 1974-76; Service Training, 1976-79; Production Editor. *Memberships:* Secretary, Opobo Action Council; National Students' Union; Nigerian Union of Journalists; Nigerian Guild of Editors. *Hobbies:* Political Debates; Classical Music; Dancing; Cultural Plays; Photography; Swimming; Political Literature. *Address:* 9 Ojerinde Street, Idiaraba, Surulere, Lagos.

DITTERICH, Eric Keith, b. 8 Feb. 1913, East Melbourne, Victoria, Australia. Minister of Religion. m. Nancy Moyle Russell, 6 Aug. 1940, 1 son, 3 daughters. *Education:* BA, BD, Dip. Ed., University of Melbourne, 1936, 40, 47. *Appointments:* Ordained Methodist Ministry, 1940; Chaplain, RAAF, 1940-46; Citizen Air Force, 1948-70; Minister, East Malvern, 1946-50, Benalla, 1950-55, Horsham (Chairman of District), 1955-58; Managing Treasurer Methodist Supernumerary Fund, 1958-77, Uniting Church Beneficiary Fund, 1977-80; Chairman of Board, 1980; Director Methodist Publishing House, 1954-77; President, Methodist Conference, Victoria and Tasmania, 1969. *Memberships:* Royal Philatelic Society of Victoria; Royal Automobile Club of Victoria; Rotary President; President Queen's College, University of Melbourne, 1965-68; President, Wesley College Council, 1966-. *Publications:* Fourteen publications from 1945-80; Listed in Australian Books in Print and Who's Who in Australia. *Honours:* MBE 1979. *Hobbies:* Philately; Gardening. *Address:* 1574 High Street, Glen Iris, 3146, Australia.

DIXON, Lascelles Alphonso, b. 27 June 1940, Linstead, Jamaica. Architect. m. Sandra Elizabeth Wright, 26 Jan. 1980, 1 daughter. *Education:* Diploma, Construction Engineering, College of Arts, Science and Technology, Jamaica, 1964; Bachelor of Environmental Studies, 1972; Bachelor of Architecture, University of Manitoba, Canada, 1973. *Appointments:* Junior Engineer, Caribbean Construction Company; Assistant Lecturer, College of Arts, Science and Technology; Architect, Ministry of Works; Resident Architect, University of the West Indies; Project Manager, USAID/U-WI Project; Manager, Project Development Resource Team, Project Analysis and Monitoring Company Limited, Agency, Ministry of Finance; Appropriate Chairman, Projects Development Committee, Scientific Research Council. *Memberships:* Jamaican Institute of Architects; Association of Scientists and Technologists; President, Professional Societies Association of Jamaica; Board of Directors, Scientific Research Council; Managing Director, Architrend Jamaica Limited; Ikebana Chapter of Jamaica. *Publications:* Introduction to Contracts, Jamaican Contract Documents and Tendering Procedures; Selection and Use of Consultants; Programme Planning (as related to health planning); Low income Housing an Experiment. *Honours:* Scholarship, Jamaican Government, Architecture 1979. *Hobby:* Photography. *Address:* 1a Waterloo Avenue, Kingston 10, Jamaica WI.

DJENTUH, Anthony Kofi Mensah, b. 26 Sept. 1941, Kpando, Volta Region of Ghana. Administrator. m. Maria Enyonam O'Sullivan, Jan. 1974, 2 sons, 1 daughter. *Education:* BA, Economics, Sociology and Political Science, 1969; Diploma in Public Administration, 1971. *Appointments:* Administrative Officer, Ghana Civil Service, 1969: Regional Organisation, Ashanti, Kumasi; Regional Organisation, Eastern Region Koforidua; Chieftaincy Secretariat, Accra; Chief Executive, District Office, Odumase-Krobo and Akim-Oda; Ministry of Agriculture and Ministry of Information and Tourism, Accra. *Memberships:* President, Kpando Youth Association; Board of Directors of Ghana Film Industry Corporation. *Publications:* Tribalism and Nation Building in Ghana; Strategies of Economic Development in the Volta Region of Ghana. *Hobbies:* Coin Collection; Films; Music. *Address:* PO Box 28, Kpando, Volta Region of Ghana.

DLAMINI, Prince Mabandla N.F, Swazi Politician; Prime Minister November 1979. *Address:* Office of the Prime Minister, PO Box 395, Mbabane, Swaziland.

DLAMINI, Naphtal Leonard, b. 11 Nov. 1916. Parliamentary Clerk. m. Constance, 23 June 1954, 1 son, 3 daughters. *Education:* Higher Primary Course, Matriculation, 1947. *Appointments:* Teacher, 1948-67; Assistant Inspector of Schools, 1967; Parliamentary Clerk, 1970; Secretary of Minerals Committee. *Memberships:* Land Control Board; Secretary, Commonwealth Parliamentary Association. *Hobbies:* Gardening; Reading. *Address:* Box 39, Jawalusoni, Swaziland.

DOBBIE, David, b. 25 Feb. 1923, Hawthorn, Victoria, Australia. Banker. m. Evelyn Thompson, 28 Sept. 1946, 1 son, 1 daughter. *Education:* Fellow, Australian Society of Accountants; Associate, Royal Melbourne Institute of Technology. *Appointments:* Commercial Bank of Australia Limited, 1939: Deputy Chief Accountant, 1956-64; Chief Accountant, 1965-69; Chief Manager, Planning Division, 1969-71; Chief London Manager, 1971-74; Assistant General Manager, Branch Banking Division, 1974-76; Director and General Manager, Banking, 1976-78; Managing Director, 1978-. *Memberships:* Marylebone Cricket Club, London; Clubs in Melbourne: Australian (Melbourne), Athenaeum, RACV; Brighton Bowling. Hobby: Lawn Bowls. *Address:* C.B.A. House, 114 William Street, Melbourne, Victoria, 3000, Australia.

DOBSON, Esme Clarice, b. 24 Aug. 1914, Parkside, South Australia. Secretary, Typist/Clerk. m. William Thomas Ernest Dobson, 13 May 1939, 2 sons, 3 daughters. *Education:* University of Adelaide, 1929; Chartres Business College, Typing, Shorthand and Bookkeeping. *Appointments:* Cashier/Clerk/Bookkeeper, Retail Store, Adelaide 5 years; Bookkeeper, Finance Company 5 years; Receptionist, Bookkeeper and Typist, Professional Club, Adelaide, 1956-69; Hon. Secretary, Calisthenic Association, South Australia, 1937-81. *Memberships:* Calisthenic Association of South Australia Inc.; West Mitcham Calisthenic Club. *Honours:* Medal of Order of Australia, 1978. *Hobby:* Ten Pin Bowling. *Address:* 52 Price Avenue, Lower Mitcham, 5062, South Australia.

DOBSON, William Henry, b. 1 Nov. 1907, Toronto. Real Estate Broker. m. Rita M Cronin, 15 June 1931, 1 son. *Appointments:* Practice, Real Estate, 1928; Director, 1948, President, Toronto Real Estate Board, 1955; Degree FRI, 1956; Fellow of Institute of Realtors. *Memberships:* Toronto Board of Trade; Lambton Golf Club; Toronto Cricket Club; Vice President, Orangeville Investment Club. *Hobbies:* Golf; Curling; Photography. *Address:* R.R. 1 Orangeville, Ontario, Canada.

DOCTOR, Chandrakant C, b. 25 Oct. 1925, Rangoon, Burma. Government Service. m. Vidula 25 Jan. 1953, 2 sons, 1 daughter. *Education:* BA; MA, LLB; IAS. *Ap-*

pointments: Collector and District Magistrate, 1962-68; Director of Census 1969-73; Director of Education 1973-74; Municipal Commissioner, Ahmedabad, 1974; Administrator, Ahmedabad and Rajkot Municipal Corporations, 1975-; Development Commissioner, Gujarat State, 1976; Managing Director, Gujarat State Financial Corporation, 1976-80; Secretary Health, Government of Gujarat, 1980-. *Memberships:* Ellisbridge Gymkhana. *Publications:* 60 books dealing with Census of India 1971. *Honours:* Medal from President of India for meritorious work in census operations. *Hobbies:* Travelling; Swimming; Reading. *Address:* 23 Patel Society, Ellis-Bridge, Ahmedabad, 380 006, India.

DOCTOR, Hirjibhai Rustomji, b. 13 Apr. 1894, Vadodara (Gujarat). Musician, (Classical Indian). m. Avanbai Jamshedji Morenas, 31 Dec. 1931, 4 daughters. *Education:* BA, English, Physics, 1917; BSc, Chemistry and Botany, Bombay University, 1919. *Appointments:* Principal, College of Indian Music; Director of Amusements, Baroda State, 1928-; Principal New College of Indian Music, Dance and Dramatics, MS University of Baroda, 1951-. *Memberships:* Founder member, Indian Musicological Society; Swar Sadhana Samiti of Bombay. *Publications:* Prepared manuscript containing 420 musical compositions in 210 Ragas, for personal use; A Short History of North Indian Music. *Honours:* Honours by the Swar Vilas Samiti of Baroda; Swan Sadhana Samiti of Bombay; Shriram Bharatiya Kala Kendra of Delhi and the Bruhad Gujarat Sangeet Samiti organised by the Gandharve Mahavidyalaya at its triennial Sangeet Sammetan, 1977; Silver Trophy with Citation by the Samiti; Fellowship Award Fine Arts in India, 1977; Sangeet Neutya Natya Akadeny of the Guyarat State, 1981. *Hobbies:* Music; Sports; Scientific Study of the Theory and Practice of Classical Indian Music. *Address:* Shastri's Lane, Raopura, Kothi, Vadodara, (Gujarat), India.

DODD, Thomas, b. 19 June 1932, Liverpool, England. Director of Studies. m. Joyce E Clark, 31 Aug. 1955, 1 son, 2 daughters. *Education:* Teachers Certificate 1954; Academic Diploma 1972; Master of Arts (with Dist) 1974. *Appointments:* Assistant Teacher, Secondary School, Birkenhead, 1954; Head of Department, Ruffwood Comprehensive School, Kirkby, Lancs, 1965-69; Principal Lecturer, College of Education, Chorley, Lancs, 1965-69; Inspector and Staff Inspector, Inner London Education Authority, 1969-80; Director of Studies, Brunel University 1980-. *Memberships:* Dean of College of Craft Education; Association of Advisers in Design and Technical Studies; Chairman, Schools Technology Forum. *Publications:* Design and Technology in the School Curriculum, 1978; The Curriculum in Action, 1980; Many articles etc. in journals. *Honours:* Honorary Fellow Society of Engineers; Honorary Fellow, College of Craft Education; Fellow Royal Society of Arts. *Hobbies:* Cricket; Hockey; Golf. *Address:* Cedarwood, Grove Lane, Chalfont St Peter, Bucks SL9 9LN, England.

DODDS, Robert, b. 11 Mar. 1893, Hamilton Beach, Ontario, Canada. *Appointments:* Lieutenant, 1915; Captain, 1918; Major, 1922; Founder and first President and Instr., Hamilton Aero Club, 1928; Inspector, Airways and Airports, Civil Aviation, Deptartment of National Defence, 1930; Constr. and survey of Trans-Canada Airway, trans. to Department of Transport, 1936; Founder of Trans-Canada Airlines; Chief Inspector of Airways, 1940; Superintendent of Airways and Airports, 1941-50; Controller of Civil Aviation, Ottawa, 1950-56; Director, 1956-58; Retired, 1958. *Memberships:* Canadian Owerns and Pilots Assn.; British Commonwealth Alliance; Hamilton Aero; Hamilton Gun. *Honours:* OBE, 1955; MC, 1918. Hobby: Trap-shooting. *Address:* PO Box 102, Stoney Creek, Ontario, Canada.

DOELLE, Horst Werner, b. 1 Sept. 1932, Muehlhausen, Germany. Reader in Microbiology. m. Gabriele Dorothea Doelle, 15 Mar. 1958, 2 daughters. *Education:* Diplom-Biologe, University of Jena, Germany, 1954; Dr.rer.nat, University of Gottingen, Germany, 1957; PhD, 1966, DSc, 1975, University of Queensland. *Appointments:* Microbiologist, Scientif Inst. Brewery, Munich, 1959; Experimental Officer, Irrigation Res. Laboratory, CSIRO, Griffith, Australia, 1960-63; Senior Lecturer, 1964-73, Reader, 1974-, Department of Microbiology, University of Queensland, Australia. *Memberships:* Intern. Org. for Biotechnology and Bioengineering, Executive 1980-; Intern. Cell Res.

Organization; World Federation of Culture Collections; American Society Microbiology; British Society General Microbiology; Australian Society Microbiology, Chairman of Education Group, 1974-77; Australian Biochem. Society; British Biochem. Society. *Publications:* Bacterial Metabolism, 1969, 1975; Microbial Metabolism, 1973; Approximately 50 res. publications; Contributor to Handbook. *Honours:* Recipient of numerous honours including: Alexander v. Humboldt fellow, 1970, 1976; Intern. Organizer and Lecturer UNEP/Unesco/ICRO/IOBB, Lagos, 1978; Invited Speaker and Section Organizer, VIth International Fermentation Symposium, Canada, 1980. *Hobbies:* Reading; Gardening. *Address:* 21 Belsize Street, Kenmore, Queensland 4069, Australia.

DOHA, Aminur Rahman S, b. 1929. Bangladeshi Soldier; Journalist; Politician; Diplomat. *Education:* BSc(Hons); BA; various military degrees. *Appointments:* Commissioned Artillery, 2nd Lieutenant, 1952; Regimental Officer, Artillery Regiments, 1952-61; Command, General Staff College, Quetta 1962; General Staff Infantry Brigade HQ, 1963; Royal Military College of Science and Technology, Shrivenham, Berks, 1964-65; School of Artillery and Guided Missiles, Oklahoma, USA, 1957-58; Senior Instructor, Gunnery, 1965; General Staff, GHQ, 1965; Retired from Army, 1966; Editor and Publisher, Interwing, Rawalpindi, 1968-71; General Secretary, Awami League, Rawalpindi, 1969-71; Ambassador, Yugoslavia and Romania 1972-74; Iran and Turkey, 1974-77; United Kingdom, 1977-. *Memberships:* Central Executive Committee of ruling Bangladesh Nationalist Party. *Publications:* Arab-Israeli War, 1967; Aryans on the Indus. *Honours:* Commander-in-Chief's Commendation, 1964; several military awards and decorations; Yugoslav Order of the Lance and Flag, class 1. *Hobby:* Sports. *Address:* High Commission for the People's Republic of Bangladesh, 28 Queen's Gate, London, SW7 5JA, England.

DOMARADZKI, Theodore Felix, b. 27 Oct. 1910, Warsaw, Poland. University Professor, Writer and Editor. m. Maria Dobija-Domaradzki, 20 Apr. 1954. *Education:* Political Sciences Diploma, Warsaw, Poland, 1936; MA, History and Philosophy, University of Warsaw, Poland, 1939; Litt. Doctor in Slavic Philology, University of Rome, Italy, 1941. *Appointments:* Assistant, Academy of Political Sciences, Warsaw, 1936-39; Lecturer, University of Rome, 1941-47; Associate Professor, Pontificio Istituto Orientale, Rome, 1943-47; Representative in Italy of Polish Ministry of Education, 1942-45; Director and Professor, Department of Slavic Studies and Centre of Polish and Slavic Research, University of Montreal, 1948-76; Head, Polish Studies Program and Visiting Professor, Fordham University, USA, 1948-50; Director and Professor, Department of Slavic Studies, Ottawa University, 1949-53; Director and Professor, Institute of Comparative Civilizations of Montreal, 1976-; Professor and Director, Graduate Research Centre, Northland Open University, 1979-. *Memberships:* Canadian Association of Slavists, Honorary Life Member, 1976; Canadian International Academy of Humanities and Social Sciences, Vice-President, 1975; Canadian Society for Comparative Study of Civilizations, Honorary Life Member, 1976; Canadian Inter-American Research Institute, Vice-President, 1964-; Société des Ecrivains Canadiens; Quebec Ethnic Press Association, Vice-President, 1980-; Polish Institute of Arts & Sciences, Canada and America. *Publications:* numerous publications including Le symbolisme et l'universalisme de 1974; Le culte de la Vierge Marie et le Catholicisme de 1961. *Honours:* Research Scholarships holder of the Governments: Poland, Italy, Canada, France, 1938-68; Polish Golden Cross of Merit, 1958; Knight Commander, Papal Order of St. Gregory the Great, 1962; Knight, French Underground Forces Order, 1964; Golden Medal of Polish Educational Merits, 1970. *Address:* 5601 Av. des. Cèdres, Montréal, H1T 2V4, Canada.

DOMINGO, Rashid, b. 24 June 1937, Cape Town, South Africa. Biochemist, Managing Director. m. Maureen Virginia Scheffers, 3 Aug. 1962, 1 son, 1 daughter. *Education:* BSc, 1959. *Appointments:* Serav-ac Laboratories, Epping Industria, Cape Town, 1959-67; Miles-Seravac Laboratories, Holyport, Maidenhead, UK, 1967-71; Biozyme Laboratories Limited, Blaenavon, Gwent, UK, 1971-. *Memberships:* Fellow of Biochemical Society; Royal Society of Chemistry.

Publications: Two Piano Compositions. *Honours:* Class Medal for Chemistry, University Cape Town, 1957; Presented to Her Majesty Queen Elizabeth II, representing Biozyme Laboratories on winning Queens Award for Export Achievement, 1979. *Hobbies:* Music; Sea Angling; Ballroom Dancing. *Address:* The Beeches, 54 Pen-y-Pound, Abergavenny, Gwent, Wales.

DONALD, Kenneth John, b. 9 Aug. 1936, Ipswich, Queensland, Australia. Pathologist. m. Elizabeth Ann Cleeve, 4 Feb. 1961, 3 daughters. *Education:* MB.BS, 1962, PhD, 1973, University of Queensland; Post Doctoral Research, Department of Pathology, Erasmus University, Rotterdam, Holland and University of Edinburgh, Scotland. *Appointments:* Resident Medical Officer, 1963, Senior Resident Medical Officer, 1964, Registrar in Pathology, 1965-68, Royal Brisbane Hospital; Lecturer, 1969, Senior Lecturer, 1972, Reader, 1975-77, Department of Pathology, University of Queensland; Director, Department of Pathology, North Brisbane Hospitals Board, 1977-; Deputy Director-General, Health and Medical Services, Queensland, 1981. *Memberships:* Fellow Royal College of Pathologists of Australia; Royal College of Pathologists, UK; Australian Medical Association; Member of Board of Examiners, Royal Australasian College of Surgeons; Queensland Anti Cancer Council; Member of Board, Queensland Radium Institute; Chairman, Drug Testing Committee, Commonwealth Games, 1982; Red Cross Blood Transfusion Advisory Committee, Queensland Club; Tattersalls Club. *Publications:* A wide range of published medical and scientific papers and contributions to medical text books. *Honours:* Research Training Fellowship IARC, 1972-73. *Hobbies:* Gardening; Rugby Football. *Address:* 50 Woodville Street, Hendra Q 4011, Brisbane, Australia.

DONALD, Russell Hughes Oxby, b. 1 Jan. 1902, Lindfield, New South Wales, Australia. Medical Practitioner. m. Gwen Joynt Hargrave, 28 Jan. 1940, 2 sons. *Education:* P.HC, 1923, Sydney University; MB, BS, 1935, Dip. LO, 1946, Melbourne University; Royal College of Surgeons of Edinburgh, 1940. *Appointments:* ROMO, Prince Henry's Hospital, Melbourne, 1934-35; Senior RMO, St George District Hospital, Sydney, 1945-46; Medical Superintendent, Zeehan District Hospital, Tasmania, 1936-38; Medical Officer, RAAF, 1940-45; Assistant Surgeon, Vic. Eye and Ear Hospital, 1946-52; Clin. Assistant, Allergy, Alfred Hospital, Melbourne, 1946-49; Hon. Allergist and in Charge of Allergy Clinic, 1949-62; Hon. Consultant Allergist, 1962-, Royal Melbourne Hospital. *Memberships:* British Medical Association; Australian Medical Association; Fellow, Australian College of Allergists; Foundation Member, Collegium Internationale Allergologicum; British Association of Allergists. *Publications:* Contributor of reviews, monographs, articles to professional journals and conferences. *Hobbies:* Photography; Sailing. *Address:* 12 Beach Road, Hampton, Victoria, Australia.

DONALDSON, Edgar John, b. 13 Nov. 1920, Toowoomba, Queensland, Australia. Ophthalmic Surgeon. m. Marjorie Rosalind Bryant, 23 Oct. 1948, 1 son, 3 daughters. *Education:* MB, BS, University of Sydney, 1943, DO 1948; Fellow of Royal Australian College of Surgeons, 1968; Fellow of Royal Australian College of Ophtholomogists, 1971. *Appointments:* Junior Resident Medical Officer, Sydney Hospital, 1943-44; Ophthalmic Registrar, 1944-49, Honorary Assistant Ophthalmic Surgeon, 1950-63, Honorary Ophthalmic Surgeon, 1963-, Chairman Ophth. Staff, 1979, Sydney Eye Hospital; Director, Ophthalmic Studies & Eye Health, University of Sydney, 1970-77. *Memberships:* President, Royal Australian College of Opthalmologists, 1978-79; Chairman, Court of Examiners RACO, 1971-78; President, New South Wales Ophthol. Society, 1961-63; Secretary, Opthalmic Research Institute of Australia. *Publications:* Numerous papers in medical journals. *Honours:* Telfer Prize, Sydney Hospital, 1976. *Hobbies:* Photography. *Address:* 8 Braeside Street, Wahroonga, Sydney, Australia.

DONALDSON, John Francis, b. 6 Oct. 1920, London, England. Lord Justice of Appeal. m. Dorothy Mary Warwick, 6 Oct. 1945, 1 son, 2 daughters. *Education:* MA, Cambridge University, 1946. *Appointments:* Junior Barrister, 1946-61; QC, 1961-66; High Court Judge, 1966-79; Lord Justice, 1979-. *Memberships:* President, Chartered Institute of Arbitrators; President,

British Maritime Law Association; President, British Insurance Law Association. *Honours:* Knight Bachelor, 1966; Privy Councillor, 1979. *Hobby:* Sailing. *Address:* Royal Courts of Justice, Strand, London, England.

DONALDSON, Timothy Patrick, b. 29 Sept. 1947, Portstewart. Physicist. m. Elizabeth Margaret Feilden, 17 Aug. 1974. *Education:* BSc, 1969, PhD, 1973. *Appointments:* Research Fellow, Ukaea Culham Laboratory, 1974-76; Head of Plasma Physics Group, University of Berne, Switzerland, 1976-78; Technical Manager, Gas Tubes Division, English Electric Valve Company Limited, 1979-. *Memberships:* Institute of Physics; Institution of Electrical Engineers. *Publications:* Contributed to various professional journals. *Hobbies:* Gardening; Vegetable Growing. *Address:* 16 Eaton Way, Great Totham, Essex, England.

DONELAN, Stephen Sydney, b. 20 Mar. 1900, Melbourne, Australia. Pastoralist; Sheep Breeder; Director. m. 16 Jan. 1929. *Education:* Xavier College, Kew, Victoria. *Appointments:* Merino Stud sheep breeder, 1921-48; Shorthorn beef cattle breeder; Commercial fat stock grazier; Director, Property Trusts; Executive of various government committees dealing with finance, wool and farm products. *Memberships:* Australian Primary Producers Union, Federal President, 1952-62; Shepparton Agricultural Society, Council Member, 1948-68; The International Association of Agricultural Economists; Victorian Farmers' Union; Graziers Association; Royal Agricultural Society, Melbourne; Deniliquin Club, Foundation member, 1921; Riverina Picnic Race Club, Foundation member, 1922. *Publications:* Annual Federal Report, the Australian Primary Producers Union, Canberra, 1952-62. *Honours:* OBE, 1961, Coronation Medal, 1953; 79 show prizes for Stud Live Stock. *Hobbies:* Cricket; Tennis; Billiards; Motoring. *Address:* 33 Bruce Street, Toorak, Victoria 3142, Australia.

DONOVAN, Brian Harrie Kevin, b. 24 June, 1943, Middleton-on-Sea, Sussex, England. Barrister-at-Law. m. Noelene Lynette Bell, 18 Aug. 1974, 2 daughters. *Education:* BA, 1964, LL.B., 1967, LL.M., 1980, University of Sydney, Australia; Resident member of St. John's College, University of Sydney, Australia, 1961-66. *Appointments:* Solicitor, 1967-74; Barrister at Law, 1974-. *Memberships:* Member of Council of New South Wales Bar Association; Fellow of St. John's College, University of Sydney, Australia; Member of Council of St. John's College, University of Sydney, Australia; Secretary of Criminal Law Committee of Sydney University Law Graduates Association; Lector of St. Mary's Cathedral, Sydney, Australia; Member of Board of Directors, Australian Opera; Director of Young Opera; President, Sydney University Dramatic Society; President, Student's Club, St John's College, University of Sydney, Australia. *Publications:* The Law of Bail, 1981. *Honours:* Dalley Prize for Third Year Law, St. John's College, 1966. *Hobbies:* Theatre; Music; Cycling; Astronomy. *Address:* 4 Barina Road, Lane Cove, New South Wales 2066, Australia.

DONOVAN, John Kenmore, b. 23 May 1929, Melbourne, Australia. Medical Practitioner. m. Jennifer Hornsey, 6 Feb. 1981, 3 sons. *Education:* MBBS, 1952; DMRT, 1958; MRACR, 1961. *Appointments:* Resident Medical Officer, Royal North Shore Hospital, Sydney, 1952; Casualty Officer, Queen Marys for the East End, Stratford, London, 1954; Surgical Registrar, South Middlesex Hospital, 1955; Senior RMO in Radiotherapy, Royal Northern Hospital, London; 1956; Radiotherapy Registrar, Royal Marsden Hospital, London, 1957-59; Specialist Radiotherapist, Royal Prince Alfred Hospital, Sydney, Australia, 1959-; Visiting Specialist Radiotherapist, Royal Newcastle Hospital, and Parramatta Hospital, 1959-. *Memberships:* Royal Australasian College of Radiologists. *Publications:* Various Medical Publications in numerous medical journals. *Hobby:* Music. *Address:* 35/10 Mount Street, Hunters Hill, New South Wales 2110, Australia.

DOODY, Cyril William, b. 26 Feb. 1931, St. John's, Newfoundland, Canada. Politician. m. Doreen Elaine Jessop, 30 July 1960, 2 sons, 1 daughter. *Appointments:* Elected HR Main District, 1971; Minister of Mines and Resources, 1972; Minister of Industrial Development, 1973; Minister of Finance, 1975-78; Minister of Transport and Communications and Minister for Intergovt. Affairs, 1978-; Minister of Public

Works and Services, 1978; Appointed to the Senate of Canada, 1979. *Address:* 32 Bennett St., Ottawa, Ontario, Canada.

DOOLEY, Brian Stanislaus, b. 17 July 1927, Melbourne, Australia. Dental Surgeon. *Education:* BDSc., University of Melbourne, 1949; DDS., Northwestern University, USA, 1952; Fellow, Royal Australian College of Dental surgeons, 1968. *Appointments:* Senior Clinical Demonstrator, Dental Faculty, University of Melbourne, Australia, 1964-71; Private Practice, 1953-. *Memberships:* President, 1973, Australian Dental Association; Graduate Committee, University of Melbourne, Australia; Kelvin Club. *Publications:* 3 articles in Australian Dental journal; Lectures at Dental Congresses. *Hobbies:* Tennis; Gardening. *Address:* 10 Torresdale Road, Toorak, 3142 Australia.

DORAN, Isaac Gregg, b. 18 Jan. 1923, Belfast, Ireland. Consulting Engineer. m. Ainslie Elizabeth Graham, 1 son, 2 daughters. *Education:* BSc.(1st class hons.), 1944; MSc, 1945; PhD, 1948. *Appointments:* Queens University, Belfast, Ireland; Northern Ireland Materials Testing Station; Self-employed. *Memberships:* FICE; FISE; FIEI; FIHE; FGS. *Honours:* OBE. *Hobbies:* Fishing. *Address:* 47 Derryvolgie Avenue, Belfast BT9 6FN, Ireland.

DORION, Henri, b. 4 May 1935, Québec, Canada. Geographer. m. Renée Hudon, 28 July 1980, 4 daughters (from previous marriage). *Education:* Law Licence, 1957; Member of Québec Bar, 1958; MA (Geography), 1962. *Appointments:* Professor (geography, political science), Laval University, Québec, Canada, 1964-78; President, Québec Territory Commission (Dorion Commission), 1966-72, President, Toponymy Commission, 1978-80, Québec Government, Canada; Delegate General of the Québec Government in México, 1980. *Memberships:* Royal Society of Canada, 1971; Académie des Sciences Morales et Politiques (Montréal), 1970. *Publications:* 205 articles, books, reports on: Law, Political Geography, Place Names. *Honours:* Premier Prix du Concours symphonique, Québec, 1955; Prix de la Société de géographie de Québec, 1961; Prix de l'Association Canadienna des géographes, 1962; Prix du Concours littéraire et scientifique de la Province de Québec, 1964; Prix Bonaparte-Wyse de la Société de géographie de Paris, 1964; Prix de l'Agence de presse Novosti, Moskva, 1966; Election a la Société royale du Canada, 1970; Election a l'Académie des sciences morales et politiques, 1971; Médaille de bronze de la Société de géographie de Québec, 1977. *Hobbies:* Music; Travel. *Address:* 1354, Montpellier, Québec, PQ, Canada.

DORMAN, (Sir), Maurice Henry, b. 7 Aug. 1912, Stafford, England. Lord Prior, Order of St. John; Governor General (retired). m. Florence Monica Churchward Smith, 1937, 1 son, 3 daughters. *Education:* Magdalene College, Cambridge, UK. *Appointments:* Administrative Officer, 1935, Clerk of Councils, 1940-45, Tanganyika Territory; Assistant to Lt-Governor, Malta, 1945; Principal Assistant Secretary, Palestine, 1947; Seconded to Colonial Office as Assistant Secretary, Social Services Department, 1948; Director of Social Welfare and Community Development, Gold Coast, 1950; Colonial Secretary, Trinidad and Tobago, 1952-56; Acting Governor of Trinidad, 1954, 1955; Governor, Commander-in-Chief and Vice-Admiral, Sierra Leone, 1956-61, after independence, Governor-General, 1961-62; Governor and Commander-in-Chief, Malta, 1962-64, after independence, Governor-General, 1964-71; Deputy Chairman, Pearce Commission on Rhodesian Opinion, 1971-72; Leader, British Observers Zimbabwe Independence Elections, 1980. *Memberships:* Almoner, Venerable Order of St John, 1972-75; Chief Commander, St. John Ambulance, 1975-80; Chairman, Swindon HMC, 1972-74; Chairman, Wiltshire Area Health Authority, 1974-; Chairman, Swindon DHA; Chairman, Board of Governors, Badminton School, UK, 1975-; Trustee, Imperial War Museum, UK, 1972-; Director, Ramsbury Building Society, 1972-. *Honours:* CMG, 1955; KCMG, 1957; GCMG, 1961; GCVO, 1961; MA; DL Wilts, 1978; Hon. DCL, Durham, 1962; Hon. LLD, Royal University, Malta, 1964; GCStJ, 1978; KStJ, 1957; Gran Croce Al Merito Melitense (Society Ordine Militaire di Malta), 1966. *Hobby:* Golf. *Address:* The Old Manor, Overton, Marlborough, Wiltshire, England.

DORWARD, William, b. 25 Sept. 1929, Dundee, Scotland. Civil Servant. m. Rosemary Ann Smith, 26 Nov. 1960, 1 son. *Education:* Morgan Academy, Dundee, Scotland. *Appointments:* Colonial Office, 1951-53; Various posts, Hong Kong Government, Hong Kong, 1954-; Counsellor (Hong Kong Affairs), UK Mission, Geneva, 1974-76; Director of Trade Industry and Customs, Hong Kong. *Memberships:* Carlton Club, London, UK; Hong Kong Club; President, Studio One, Film Society of Hong Kong; Hon. Vice President, Hong Kong Economics Society. *Honours:* OBE, 1977. *Address:* A3101 Tregunter Mansions, Hong Kong.

DOUGLAS, Athol Mardon, b. 19 Oct. 1915, Albany, Western Australia. Museum Biologist. m. Marion Joan Schubring, 6 Aug. 1971, 2 sons, 3 daughters (by previous marriage). *Education:* Diplomas in the following: Assaying and Mineralogy; Applied Chemistry; Comparative Anatomy; Entomology; Microbiology and Morbid Pathology; Pathology and Laboratory Techniques; Technical and Applied Art; 1936-48. *Appointments:* Assistant to Director, Entomologist, Acting Director, Senior Experimental Officer, Western Australian Museum, Australia, 1935-76. *Memberships:* Legacy Club of Western Australia; Australian Forensic Society, Western Australian Branch. *Publications:* Our Dying Fauna, A Personal Perspective on a changing environment, 1980; 985 scientific papers in field. *Hobbies:* Photography; Restoration and Preservation of Antiques; Lecturing on the Changing Environment and Ecosystems. *Address:* 120 Third Avenue, Mt. Lawley, Western Australia, 6050.

DOUGLAS, Colin Roy, b. 22 May 1920, Brisbane, Queensland, Australia. Public Servant. m. 23 Aug. 1947, 1 son, 1 daughter. *Education:* Fellow, Australian Society of Accountants, 1946. *Appointments:* Audit Inspector, 1946-54, Senior Audit Inspector, 1954-64, Auditor General's Department, Secretary to Cabinet, 1964-67, Queensland Government, Australia; Commissionor of Land Tax, 1967-71; General Manager, State Government Insurance Office, Queensland, Australia, 1971-80; Chairman, Public Service Board, 1980-. *Memberships:* Fellow, Australian Society of Accountants; Fellow, Australian Institute of Management; Royal Australian Institute of Public Administration. *Address:* 10 Stardust Street, Kenmore, Brisbane, Queensland, Australia.

DOUGLAS, Neil, b. 17 Aug. 1911, New Zealand. Artist. m. 3 sons. *Education:* National Gallery Art School, Melbourne, Australia. *Appointments:* Self employed. *Memberships:* Royal Society; Bend of Islands Conservation Association; Honorary Member, Round the Bend Conservation Co-operative. *Creative Works:* Paintings; Pottery. *Honours:* MBE, 1975. *Address:* The Bend of Islands, Henley Road, Kangaroo Ground, Victoria, Australia 3097.

DOUGLAS, Robert Ramsay, b. 25 Nov. 1944, Brisbane, Queensland, Australia. Barrister-at-Law. m. Jennifer Farmar Horton, 1 Apr. 1970, 2 sons, 1 daughter. *Education:* LL.B., University of Queensland, Australia, 1963-68. *Appointments:* Associate to the Honourable Mr. Justice J A Douglas, 1965-67, Associate to the Honourable Mr. Justice Sheehy, 1968-69, Supreme Court of Queensland, Australia; Barrister in private practice, 1969-. *Memberships:* Honorary Secretary 1975-76, Australian Bar Association; Honorary Secretary 1972-77, Bar Association of Queensland; Committee member 1980-, The Brisbane Club; Committee Member, Queensland Art Gallery Foundation, 1980; United Service Club, Brisbane; Queensland Rugby Union Club; Queensland Turf Club; Brisbane Amateur Turf Club; Wine and Food Society of Queensland. *Hobbies:* Reading; Horse Racing; Wine and Food. *Address:* 18 Towers Street, Ascot, Brisbane, Queensland 4007, Australia.

DOUGLAS, Roderick Gavin Sholto, b. 24 June 1944, Maidenhead, Berkshire. Librarian/Archivist. *Education:* BA(Lond), University College of Rhodesia and Nyasaland, 1966; Dip.Lib.(Lond) School of Library, Archive and Information Studies, University College London, 1976. *Appointments:* National Archives of Rhodesia: Archivist, 1969-; Acting, Research Officer, 1973-; Librarian, 1974-78; Principal Archivist Editor, National Archives of Zimbabwe, 1978 . *Memberships.* Editor, Rhodesia/Zimbabwe Library Association, 1978-79; Associate of the Library Association United

Kingdom. *Publications:* Contributions (reviews, papers) to various professional journals; editorial comment in publications; General Editor, Zimbabwe Epic, a Pictorial History in Progress. *Hobbies:* Reading; Book-collecting; Study of History and Fine Arts; Landscape Gardening. *Address:* Giwonde, Pvt Bag 7540, Umvukwes, Zimbabwe.

DOUST, Leonard Thomas, b. 5 Feb. 1941, Geraldton, Ontario Canada. Barrister and Solicitor. m. Louise Sandra, 9 Sept. 1961, 3 sons, 1 daughter. *Education:* LLB, (Expertise-Criminal Law), University of British Columbia, 1966. *Appointments:* Clark, Wilson and Company, 1966-68; Crane Smith and Doust, 1968-70; Clark Wilson and Company, 1970-77; Doust and Smith, 1977-. *Memberships:* Canadian Bar Association; Law Society of British Columbia; Criminal Law Sub Section, BC Branch of Canadian Bar Association. *Hobby:* Fly Fishing. *Address:* 1380 Crestwell Road, West Vancouver, British Columbia, Canada V7S 2P2.

DOUST, Robin William, b. 27 Dec. 1941, Tunbridge Wells, Kent, United Kingdom. Librarian. *Education:* Brighton College of Technology 1962; Associate of the Library Association. *Appointments:* Deputy Branch Librarian, Kensington Public Library 1964-65; Children's Librarian, Penge Public Library 1965-68; School Librarian, Beaufoy Comprehensive School, I.L.E.A 1968-75; Librarian, Bulawayo Technical College, Rhodesia 1975-77; Librarian, Bulawayo Public Library 1977-. *Memberships:* Zimbabwe Library Association; Chairman, Bulawayo Railway Circle. *Publications:* Editor, The Zimbabwe Librarian; Author of several periodical articles on library development in Zimbabwe. *Hobbies:* Photography; Steam Railways; Collecting Railway Relics; Swimming; Cycling; Reading. *Address:* 18 Tenby Avenue, Bradfield, Bulawayo, Zimbabwe.

DOVENER, John Montague, b. 7 Dec. 1923, Liverpool, England. Queen's Counsel. m. Shirley Donn, 17 Apr. 1973. *Education:* Shrewsbury. *Appointments:* Called to Bar, Middle Temple, 1953; Queen's Counsel, 1972. *Publications:* Author Pseudonym 'Montague Jon' The Wallington Case, 1981; A Question of Law, 1981. *Address:* 2 Pump Court, Temple, London, England.

DOVLO, Florence Efua, b. Keta, Ghana. Home Scientist (Research). m. Moses Dovlo, 26 Dec. 1962. *Education:* Teachers' Certificate 'A' 1947; BSc (Home Science) 1959; Post Graduate Certificates: Food Science and Applied Nutrition, 1963; Food Consumption Studies, 1967. *Appointments:* Teaching, Volta Region of Ghana, 1948-55; Regional Nutrition Officer, Northern and Upper Regions of Ghana, 1961-63; Senior Research Officer, Head of Economics, Food Utilization Division, Food Research Institute, Accra; FAO Consultant on Foods and Food Habits, 1975-78, East, West and Southern Africa, 1980, Household Food Processing and Storage Somalia. *Memberships:* Ghana Home Science Association; Zonta International Club of Accra; Diocesan Council of Catholic Women; Study Group on the Environment; President, Ghan Home Science Association; President, Accra Diocesan Council of Catholic Women; Council member, International Federation of Home Economics; ECA Task Force Volunteer for Research and Training African Women, Project Advisory Committee of the National Council on Women and Development. *Publications:* Numerous publications including: Infant Feeding Practices in Accra, Ghana, 1968; Food Consumption patterns among the well-to-do in Ghana, 1966; Communal Catering and Contamination, 1974; Maize in the Ghanaian Diet; Chemical Composition of some Ghanaian Soups and Stews; Cassava as food in Ghana; Traditional Food Processing and Preservation in Ghana; Cowpeas: Home Preparation and Use in West Africa; Consumers Opinion on Malnutrition in Africa; Founder and Editor of The Home Scientist, 1973-; Conferences and Seminars Attended in Washington, USA, Sierra Leone, Hamburg West Germany Instanbul, Turkey, Helsinki, Finland, Mauduguri, Nigeria, Dakar, Senegal, Ottawa Canada, Tucson Arizona, Mysore, India, Manila Philippines. *Honours:* Honorary Doctorate Degree, St. Mary's College, Notre Dame, Indiana, USA, 1979; Associate Fellow of Volta Hall University of Ghana. *Hobbies:* Civic Education Activities; Sewing; Reading and Writing. *Address:* PO Box 6278, Accra, Ghana.

DOW, Marguerite Ruth, b. 13 June 1926, Ottawa, Ontario, Canada. Professor, English and Drama. *Education:* University of Toronto: BA English, 1949; BEd, 1971; MA English, 1970; Certificate in Drama, Queen's University, 1955; Senior Certificate in Drama, University of Alberta, 1956. *Appointments:* Laboratory Assistant, Division of Applied Biology, National Research Council, 1944-46; Librarian, Aeronautical Library, 1947-48; Librarian, Joint Intelligence Bureau, Defence Research Board, 1949-50; Teacher of English, Ontario High Schools, 1950-65, Head, English Department, Laurentian High School, Ottawa, 1959-65; Associate Professor, Department of English, Faculty of Education, University of Western Ontario, 1965-72; Professor 1972-; Acting Co-ordinator, 1977; Member, Creative Arts Committee, Ontario Institute for Studies in Education, 1966-68; Member, Theatre Arts, Comm., 1966-69. *Memberships:* United Empire Loyalists Association of Canada; Monarchist League of Canada; Canadian Heritage Writing Competition; Fellow, Intercontinental Biographical Association; Fellow, International Institute of Community Service; Fellow, American Biographical Institute; Fellow, World Academy, New Zealand. *Publications:* Editor, Light from other Windows, 1964; Author, The Magic Mask, 1966; co-author, Courses of Study in the Theatre Arts, 1969; Editor, My Canada, 1977; Heritage, 1977, 1978; Ecrits Heritage Writing, 1979, 80 and 81; author, numerous articles in scholarly journals. *Honours:* Founder-Fellow Silver Medal, International Institute of Community Service, 1975; Silver Medal, distinguished service to the community, 1976; Award, Contemporary Achievement, Dictionary of International Biog., 1976; Notable Americans Award, 1977; Appointment, 7 Ontario Ministry of Education Committees, 1958-64; Grant of Armorial Bearings, including the personal motto Nothing but well and fair, College of Arms, England 1974. *Hobbies:* Travel; Drama; Early Canadian History; Chinese Culture and Art. *Address:* 1231 Richmond Street, Apt. 909, London, Ontario N6A 3L9, Canada.

DOWN, (Sir) Alastair Frederick, b. 23 July 1914, Kirkcaldy, Fife, Scotland. Company Chairman. m. Bunny Mellon, 4 Oct. 1947, 2 sons, 2 daughters. *Education:* Edinburgh Academy, 1923-27; Marlborough College, 1927-32. *Appointments:* British Petroleum Company, 1938; Chief Representative of BP Canada, 1954-57; President, BP Group in Canada, 1957-61; Managing Director, London, 1962-74; Deputy Chairman and Managing, London, 1969-74; Chief Executive, The Burmah Oil Company, 1975-80; Chairman, The Burmah Oil Company Limited, 1975-. *Memberships:* Bath (London); Mount Royal (Montreal); York (Toronto); Ranchmen's (Calgary). *Honours:* MC, 1940; OBE, 1944; Kt. Comdr. Order of Orange Nassau with swords, 1946; Knighthood, 1978. *Hobbies:* Shooting; Golf; Fishing. *Address:* Stockleigh House, Stockleigh Pomeroy, Crediton, Devon, EX17 4AU, England.

DOWNER, (The Hon. Sir KBE), Alexander Russell, b. 7 Apr. 1910, Adelaide, South Australia. Barrister; Member of Parliament; Diplomat; Grazier. m. Mary Isobel Gosse, 23 Apr. 1947, 1 son, 3 daughters. *Education:* MA, Dip. Economics and Political Science, Brasenose College, Oxford; Called to Bar, Inner Temple, London, 1934; Hon. LLD, Birmingham, 1973. *Appointments:* Australian Imperial Force, 1940-45; Prisoner of War, Changi Singapore, 1942-45; Member Board, Electricity Trust, South Australia, 1946-49; Member Board, Art Gallery of South Australia, 1946-64; Member of Parliament, Angas, Australia, 1949-64; Parliamentary Delegation to Coronation 1953; Australian Minister for Immigration, 1958-63; High Commissioner for Australia to United Kingdom 1964-72. *Memberships:* Brooks's Lond; Hon. Cavalry; Adelaide Union, Sydney. *Publications:* Various Lectures. *Honours:* KBE, 1965; Freeman City of London, 1965; Liveryman Tallow Chandlers, 1965; Honorary Freeman, Butchers Company, 1965; Honorary Freeman, Woolmens Company, 1973; Fellow, Royal Society of Arts, 1968; Member, Parliamentary Foreign Affairs Committee, 1952-58; Constitutional Committee, 1956-59; Minister Assisting Prime Minister, 1959-62. *Hobbies:* Collecting Antiques; Reading; Travel; Walking. *Address:* Martinsell, Williamstown, South Australia.

DOWNER, Donovan Francis, b. 21 Nov. 1943, Indian Islands, Newfoundland, Canada. Teacher; Biologist. m. Winnifred Anne Shea, 25 June 1969, 2 sons, 1 daughter. *Education:* BSc, BEd, 1967; MSc. *Appointments:* Teacher, 1963-64, 1973-80; Biologist, 1967-69; Principal Teacher, 1969-71, 1972-73; Curriculum Supervisor, 1980-. *Memberships:* NTA, Special Interest Council, Science, Member and Vice President; Prov. Department of Education Science Curr. Comm; APICS; PTA, President; Layreader, Anglican Church of Canada. *Publications:* Masters Thesis, 1972; Article in professional journal. *Hobbies:* Writing; Gardening; Canoeing; Amateur Geology. *Address:* 99 East Valley Road, Corner Brook, Newfoundland, Canada.

DOWNES, Clive Stanley, b. 7 July 1920, Roseville, Sydney, Australia. Chartered Accountant; Company Director. m. 24 Apr, 1948, 1 son, 1 daughter. *Education:* Fellow, Institute of Chartered Accountants in Australia; Fellow, Australian Society of Accountants; Fellow, Institute of Directors in Australia. *Appointments:* Senior Partner, Downes, Barrington, Chartered Accountants; Director of: Fielder Gillespie Limited, J.B. Young Limited, Schlegel Property Limited; Chairman of Directors, Downes Stores Holdings Property Limited and subsidaries. *Memberships:* Commonwealth Club. *Hobby:* Golf. *Address:* 23A Linden Close, Pymble, Sydney, Australia.

DOWNES, Michael Geoffrey, b. 26 Feb. 1942, Adelaide, South Australia. Financial Director. m. Margaret Irene Allen, 5 Mar. 1966, 1 son, 1 daughter. *Education:* Diploma in Advertising, Royal Melbourne Institute of Technology, 1959-61. *Appointments:* W John Haysom, Advertising Melbourne, Victoria, 1959; Fortune (Aust), Melbourne, Victoria, 1960; McCann Erickson, Melbourne, Victoria, 1963; Dorland Advertising Group, London, United Kingdom, 1964; Benton and Bowles, London, 1966; McCannerickson Melbourne 1967; Managing Director, Stannard Patten Samuelson, Australia, 1969; Financial Director, Baker Medical Research Institute, 1978. *Memberships:* Fellow, Advertising Institute of Australia; Institute of Directors in Australia; Australian Institute of Management; Australasian Institute of Fundraising. *Publications:* Various Fundraising Papers; Design of Australian Fundraising Training Course; Various Scouting Publications. *Honours:* Australian Direct Mail Award, for Fundraising Mailing, 1979; Medal of Merit, Scout Association of Australia, 1980. *Hobbies:* Branch Commissioner for Scouts in Victoria. *Address:* 33 Butlers Road, Plenty Victoria 3090, Australia.

DOWNEY, Hugh Robert Hamilton, b. 28 Oct. 1930, Melbourne, Victoria, Australia. Director. m. Alison Mary Robinson, 5 Oct. 1974. *Education:* Royal Military College, Duntroon. *Appointments:* Australian Regular Army, 1952-59 (Retired: Captain); Manager Training and Salaried Personnel, Ford Motor Company of Australia, 1959-66; Corporate Personnel Manager, Australian Consolidated Industries, 1966-76; Director, State Government, Victorian Ministry of Immigration and Ethnic Affairs, 1977-. *Memberships:* Rotary Club of Melbourne; Australian Institute of International Affairs. *Hobbies:* Farming; Viticulture; Building in Rock. *Address:* 232 Victoria Parade, East Melbourne, 3002, Australia.

DOWNIE, Charles Francis Alphonsos, b. 2 Aug. 1927, Lanarkshire, Scotland. Dental Surgeon. m. Helen Heggarty, 10 Aug. 1955, 3 sons, 4 daughters. *Education:* LDS, RFPS, Glasgow Dental Hospital and School, Scotland, 1950. *Appointments:* Assistant, 1950-51, Principal, 1951-74, General Dental Practice; Chief Administrative Dental Officer, Lanarkshire Health Board, Scotland, 1974-; Honorary Visiting Dental Surgeon to Conservation Department, Glasgow dental Hospital, Scotland; Honorary Consultant to International Dental Federation. *Memberships:* Chairman of Special Purposes Committee, Member of Disciplinary Executive, General Dental Council; British Dental Association Rep. Board; British Dental Association Council; British Dental Association Ancilliary Committee; British Dental Association Joint Committee with Dental Surgery Assistant; Examining Board for Dental Surgery Assistants; Board of Management, New Cross School of Dental Therapists; Chairman, Coltbridge YMCA; Scottish Royal Automobile Club; Royal Commonwealth Society; British Hypnosis Society. *Publications:* Trends in Dental Practice, 1970; The NNS. Reorganisation, 1973; Emergency Dental Service, 1974; The Dental Surgery Assistant, 1980; Audio-Visual Tapes: Preventative Dentistry, 1978; Non-Accidental Injuries to Children, 1976. *Honours:* Glasgow Dental Hospital Golf Champion, 1947, 48, 49. *Hobbies:* Golf; Cricket; Swimming; Public Speaking; Hypnotherapy. *Address:* Belmont, Clark Street, Airdrie, Lanarkshire, Scotland.

DOWSLEY, Gordon Kenneth, b. 6 Oct. 1943, Kingston, Ontario, Canada. Financial Planning Officer. m. Marilyn Jean Elliott, 8 July 1972, 3 daughters. *Education:* BA.(Hon.), Queen's University, Kingston, Canada, 1966; MGA, Wharton School, University of Pennsylvania, Philadelphia, USA, 1969; New York University, USA; Rutger's University, USA. *Appointments:* Ontario Department of Health; Crown Life Insurance Company. *Memberships:* Registered Agent for Ontario, 1977-, Treasurer, 1976-78, Liberal Party of Canada; Multiple Sclerosis Society; Metro Toronto Director, University of Pennsylvania, USA; Canadian Alumni Fund Director; Queen's University Class Agent. *Publications:* Papers, articles and reviews on Economics and Finance. *Honours:* Member of the Canada Council, 1979. *Hobbies:* Public Affairs; Gardening; Crafts. *Address:* 9 Fairchild Avenue, Willowdale, Ontario, Canada, M2M 1T5.

DOYLE, Leslie Graeme, b. 21 Mar. 1947, Melbourne, Australia. Artist. *Education:* Diploma of Art, Swinburne Technical College, Australia, 1965; Art Course, Prahran Technical College, 1966; Studied Painting under Erica McGilchrist, 1972-75; Studied Print Making under Nola Hjorth, 1975; Studied Singing, Guitar, Piano and Musical Composition and Musical Theory. *Appointments:* 4 months in Public Service as a Clerk. *Memberships:* Poets Union of Australia. *Publications:* Poem published in Arts Magazine; Composed approximately 210 songs, and performed some of them in folk clubs. *Creative Works:* 7,000 Sketches and Drawings; 100 Prints; Sculptures; 1st One Man Exhibition of Drawings, Paintings and Prints, 1977 at Open Leaves Gallery; 2nd One Man Exhibition at Bookshelf Gallery, 1978. *Honours:* Matriculation Poetry Prize, 1964. *Address:* 89 Grange Road, Aphington Victoria 3078, Australia.

DRAFFIN, Rodney Fox, b. 26 Feb. 1925, Auckland, New Zealand. Architect. m. Evelyn Jean Gracey, 22 Jan. 1954, 3 daughters. *Education:* Diploma in Architecture, University of Auckland, 1943-47; Associate, 1947, Fellow, 1964, New Zealand Institute of Architects; Member, Royal Institute of British Architects, 1948. *Appointments:* Principal, Architectural Private Practise, 1949-. *Memberships:* Past President, Royal Commonwealth Society, Auckland Branch; President, New Zealand Conservation Society; Auckland Institute and Museum. *Creative Works:* Building Designs. *Hobbies:* Yachting; Skiing; Climbing; Conservation. *Address:* 8 Ridings Road, Remuera, Auckland 5, New Zealand.

DRAKE, (Sir) Eric, b. 29 Nov. 1910, Rochester, Kent, England. Oil Company Chairman (ret.) m. Margaret Elizabeth Wilson, 14 Sept. 1950, 2 sons, 2 daughters. *Education:* BA, 1931, MA, 1946, Honorary Fellow, 1976, Pembroke College, Cambridge. *Appointments:* Managing Director, 1958-75, Deputy Chairman, 1962-69, Chairman, 1969-75, Deputy Chairman, P and O Company, 1975-81; Director, Kleinvorth Benson and Lonsdale Limited, 1975-, Hudson Bay Company, 1975-81, Toronto Dominion Bank, 1975-81. *Memberships:* Honorable Elder Brothers of Trinity House, 1976-; Hon. Member the Honourable Company of Master Mariners, 1975-; One of Her Majesty's Lieutenants for the City of London; Hon. Petroleum Advisor to the British Army. *Honours:* William Quilter PriE, 1934; Cadman Memorial Medal, 1976; Hon. Doctor of Science, Cranfield; Hon. Fellow, University of Manchester Institute of Science and Technology; CBE; Knight Grand Cross of the Order of Merit, Italy; Officer of the Legion of Honour, France. *Hobbies:* Sailing; Shooting. *Address:* The Old Rectory, Cheriton, Alresford, Hampshire, England.

DRAKE (The Hon. Sir), Frederick Maurice, b. 15 Feb. 1923, London, England. High Court Judge. m. Alison May Waterfall, 21 Aug. 1954, 2 sons, 3 daughters. *Education:* MA(Hons.), Exeter College, Oxford, UK, 1946-48; Jurisprudence, Cholmonely Scholar, 1948, Lincoln's Inn, London, UK, 1945-49; Called to Bar, 1950. *Appointments:* Barrister, 1950-78, QC, 1968; Deputy Chairman, Bedfordshire Quarter Sessions, 1966-71; Recorder of Grimsby, UK, 1971; Recorder of the Crown Court, 1972-78; Standing Senior Counsel to Royal College of Physicians, 1972-78; Deputy Leader, Midland and Oxford Circuit, 1976-78; Judge of the High Court of Justice, Queen's Bench Division, 1978-;

Presiding Judge of the Midland and Oxford Circuit, 1979-. *Honours:* DFC, Royal Air Force, Italy, 1944. *Hobbies:* Music; Opera; Gardening; Forestry; Country-side. *Address:* 31 West Common Way, Harpenden, Herts., England.

DRAKE, Malcolm Ernest, b. 27 Mar. 1933, Erode, South India. Architect. m. Gillian Dudley Ward, 20 Nov. 1971. *Education:* Bachelor of Architecture, Sir J J School of Art, Bombay, 1953-58; Transportation and Town Planning, University College, London, UK, 1972. *Appointments:* Gregson Batley & King, Bombay, 1956; Junior Architect, Prynne Abbott & Davis, Madras, India, 1957-58; Job Architect, Messrs. Eric Marrett, Bombay, India, 1958-61; Senior Architect, Messrs. Mehta & Contractor, Bombay, India, 1961-62; Partner, Fernando, Madras, India, 1962-67; Principal Executive Architect (Road), London Transport Executive, London, UK, 1967-. *Memberships:* Associate of Royal Institute of British Architects, 1970; Associate of Institute of Arbitrators, 1964; Associate of Incorporated Association of Architects, 1963; Indian Institute of Architects, 1958-72; Royal Society of Health, 1971-. *Publications:* Several papers in field including: A J Journal, 1969; Papers for University of Washington, US; The Fifth Dimension in Architecture; Basic Freedom. *Creative Works:* Pilot Cinerama, Madras; Theosophical Society HQ Library, Adyar; Polytechnic at Manaparia; G J Block at Montfort School, Yercaud; Tata Steinmetz Garment Factory, Madras; Multi-storey flats at Nandanam; Several houses, factories and hospitals. *Honours:* Best Student Prize, Bombay, 1954; Professor Robert W Cable Prize in Architecture, 1954; Indian Government Scholar, 1954. *Hobbies:* Photography; Model making; Landscape architecture. *Address:* 91 South Farm Road, Worthing, West Sussex, BN14 7AN, England.

DRAPEAU, Jean, b. 18 Feb, 1916, Montréal, Canada. Lawyer. m. Marie-Claire Boucher, June, 1945, 3 sons. *Education:* Diploma, Social Economic and Political Sciences, 1937, Arts Degree, 1938, Faculty of Law, 1938-41, University of Montréal, Canada. *Appointments:* Practice of Law in the Criminal and Civil Courts while specialising in Commercial and Corporation Law, 1943-54; Mayor of Montréal, 1954-57, 1960-. *Memberships:* Member of many international and national organizations including: American Bar Association. *Publications:* Place des Arts; Le Métro; The 1967 Universal and International Exhibition; The 1976 Summer Olympic Games; Les Floralies Internationales de Montréal, 1980. *Honours:* Numerous honours including: Honorary Degree, University of Moncton, 1956; Honorary Degree, the University McGill, 1965; Honorary Degree, Sir George Williams University, 1967; Queen's Counsel, 1961; Gold Medal of the Royal Architectural Institute of Canada for 1967; Created Companion of the Order of Canada, the nation's highest decoration, 1967. *Address:* 5700 Avenue des Plaines, Montréal, Québec, Canada, H1T 2X1.

DREGO, Pearl Angela, b. 7 July 1946, Bombay, India. Psychotherapist. *Education:* BA, 1966, MA, 1968, University of Bombay; Clinical Member, 1978, Teaching Member, 1981, International Transectional Analysis Association. *Appointments:* Lecturer in Philosophy, Sophia College, Bombay; Lecturer in Philosophy, St Xavier's College, Bombay; Manager, Grail Mobile Units; Director, TA Centre for Education and Training. *Memberships:* Vice President, TA Society of India; Chairperson, Board of Trustees, Grail Mobile Education and Development Training Unit. *Publications:* Pathways to Liberation, 1974; The Illusioned Child, 1979; Ego State Models, 1981; Inculturation, 1981. *Honours:* 4 Prizes, University of Bombay, 1968. *Hobbies:* Music; Stamps. *Address:* 25 Dr Ambedkar Road, Bendra, Bombay, India.

DREHER, Goeffrey Hamilton, b. 30 June 1939, Bundaberg, Queensland, Australia. Medical Practitioner. m. Margaret Elizabeth Evans, 16 Sept. 1965, 1 son, 3 daughters. *Education:* Bachelor of Medicine, Bachelor of Surgery, Melbourne University, Australia, 1962; Master of Administration, Monash University, Australia, 1974; Associate of the Australian College of Health Service Administrators, 1976. *Appointments:* Junior Resident Medical Officer, 1963-64, Senior Resident Medical Officer, 1964-65, Footscray & District Hospital, Victoria, Australia; Medical Registrar, Prince Henry's Hospital, Melbourne, Victoria, Australia, 1965-66; Junior Resident Medical Officer, 1966-67, Medical

Registrar, 1967-69, Chief Resident Medical Officer, 1969-70, Acting Deputy Medical Director, June-Oct. 1969, Deputy Medical Director, 1970-76, Royal Children's Hospital, Parkville, Victoria, Australia; Medical Director, Dandenong & District Hospital, Dandenong, Victoria, Australia, 1976-78; Director of Medical Services, The Royal Melbourne Hospital, Parkville, Victoria, Australia, 1978-. *Memberships:* Member of numerous associations including: Board member, Resident Medical Officers Wages Board, Victoria; Board member, Course Advisory Committee for Diploma of Nursing, Caulfield Institute of Technology; Member of Committee of Management of Lincoln Community Health Centre, Abbotsford, Victoria; Member of Board of Studies, Mayfield Centre for Health Services Staff Training and Development; Surveyor, Australian Council on Hospital Standards; Board member, Hospital Ancillary Services Wages Board, Victoria. *Publications:* Numerous publications including: Cor Pulmonale following Primary Subclavian Vein Thrombosis (with A M King), 1966; Cushing's Syndrome in a three month old girl (co-author), 1969; Casualty and Outpatients at the Royal Children's Hospital, 1972; Improving the Productivity of a Casualty Department, 1974; Computerisation and Consequent Problems for Administrators, 1977. *Honours:* Hospitals and Charities Commission of Victoria - Scholarship to complete Master of Administration Course, Monash University, Victoria, Australia, 1971-73. *Address:* 126 Beverley Road, Heidelberg, Victoria 3084, Australia.

DRIDAN, David Clyde, b. 15 Dec. 1932, Adelaide, Australia. Artist; Winemaker. m. Sarah Gosse, 29 Apr. 1963, 1 son, 2 daughters. *Education:* St. Peters College, Adelaide, Australia, 1945-49. *Appointments:* Professional Assistant 1959-62, Keeper of Paintings 1962-64, National Gallery of South Australia; Senior Art Master, St. Peters College, Adelaide, Australia, 1965-68; Full time artist and Private Teaching, 1969; Director, Adelaide Art Leasing, Australia, 1972; Started Dridan Skottowe Winery, 1975. *Memberships:* Fellow, Royal Society of Arts, London; Adelaide Club; Clarendon Bowling Club; McLaren Vale Bacchus Club; Art Gallery Board, Adelaide, South Australia, 1980-. *Publications:* The Art of Sir Hans Heysen, 1966; Russell Drysdale co-author), 1980; David Dridan by Sir Arthur Rymill, 1972. *Honours:* British Council Grant, 1961. *Hobbies:* Silversmithing; Photography; Travel. *Address:* Gosse Road, PO Box 33, Clarendon South Australia, 5157.

DRINKALL, John, b. 1 Jan. 1922, Maymo, Burma. Diplomat. m. 1961, 2 sons, 2 daughters. *Education:* Brasenose College, Oxford University, UK. *Appointments:* Diplomatic appointments in Nanking, Taiwan, Cairo, Brasilia, Cyprus, Brussels; Canadian National Defence College, 1971-72; Ambassador to Afghanistan, 1972-76; High Commissioner, Jamaica Ambassador (non-resident) to Haiti, 1976-. *Memberships:* All England Lawn Tennis Club; Royal Automobile Club. *Honours:* CMG, 1973. *Hobbies:* Sports; Exploring. *Address:* Bolham House, Tiverton, Devon, EX16 7RA, England.

DRISCOLL, Kevin James, b. 10 July 1927, Townsville, Australia. Company Director. m. Thelma Thiess, 29 Sept. 1959, 2 sons, 2 daughters. *Appointments:* Managing Director of National Homes Property Limited Group of Companies, 1959-; Driscoll Pastoral Company; Driscoll Hotels Group; Director, Queensland Tourist and Travel Corporation, 1980. *Memberships:* Australian Institute of Directors; Past President, Housing Industry Association. *Honours:* Order of the British Empire, 1980. *Hobbies:* Boating; Golf. *Address:* 840 Beams Road, Bridgeman Downs, Australia.

DRISCOLL, Robert Mitchell, b. 9 July 1922, Haberfield, New South Wales, Australia. Taxation Consultant; Company Director; Secretary. m. Audrey Ellis Driscoll, 9 Nov. 1971. *Education:* Fellow, Taxation Institute Australia; Graduate Institute of Quarrying. *Appointments:* Director, JD Industrial Equipment Holdings; Secretary SD Investments; Ransome Equipment; JD Industrial Equipment; Secretary Span Developments; Span Corporation; Justice of the Peace; Registered Tax Agent. *Hobbies:* Music; Choir/Orchestra Conducting; Stamp Collecting. *Address:* 2 Markers Road, West Pennant Hills, New South Wales, Australia.

DRIVON, Roland, b. 29 June 1947, Lyon, France. Director of Alliance Française de Singapour. *Education:* Licence de Lettres Modernes, 1969, Maitrise de Lettres Modernes, 1970, Capes de Lettres Modernes, 1971, Université Paul-Valéry, Montpellier, France. *Appointments:* Lecturer, University of the West Indies, Kingston, Jamaica, 1972-74; Director of Alliance Francaise de la Jamaique, Kingston, Jamaica, 1974-78; Director, Alliance Francaise de Singapour, Singapore, 1978-. *Publications:* Editor of Lien-magazine, French monthly in Singapore; Numerous contributions in arts, travel reports. *Hobbies:* Cycling; Football; Squash; Reading. *Address:* 21 F, Balmoral Park, Singapore 1025.

DROVER, Donald Prosper, b. 7 May 1927, Narrandera, New South Wales, Australia. Professor of Chemistry. m. Christine Mary Hudson, 22 Nov. 1969, 1 son, 2 daughters. *Education:* BSc.(Hons.), University of Sydney, Australia, 1949; PhD, University of Western Australia, 1954. *Appointments:* Lecturer in Soil Science, 1949, Senior Lecturer in Soil Science, 1957, University of Western Australia; Professor and Head of Department of Agriculture, Biochemistry and Soil Science, University of Khartoum, 1960; Senior Research Scientist, CSIRO, Division of Land Research, Canberra, Australia, 1965; Foundation Professor of Chemistry, University of Papua, New Guinea, 1966; Chief Scientist, Department of Primary Production, 1981. *Memberships:* Fellow, Royal Society of Arts, London; Australian Institute of Agricultural Science; Australian Soil Science Society; Associate, Royal Australian Chemical Institute; Darwin Rotary Club. *Publications:* 40 research papers in scientific journals. *Honours:* Papua New Guinea Independence Medal, 1975. *Hobbies:* Philately; Food and wine; Home brewing. *Address:* 7 Nelson Street, Stuart Park, Northern Territory, Australia 5790.

DRUMALBYN, (Lord) Niall Malcolm Stewart Macpherson, b. 3 Aug. 1908, Gaya, India. Business and Politics. m. 27 July 1937, 3 daughters. *Education:* 1st class Hons, Classical Moderations, 1929, 1st class Hons., Litterae Humaniores, 1931, Trinity College, Oxford, UK, 1927-31. *Appointments:* Reckitt and Colman Limited, 1931-39; Major, Queen's Own Cameron Highlanders, Army, 1939-45; Elected National Liberal Member of Parliament for Dumfries, Scotland, 1945; Served as: Scottish Whip, National Liberal Unionist Group, 1950-55; Joint Under-Secretary of State for Scotland, 1955-60; Parliamentary Secretary, Board of Trade, 1960-62; Minister of Pensions and National Insurance, 1962-63; Minister of State, Department of Trade and Industry, 1963-64; Minister Without Portfolio, 1970-74. *Memberships:* Chairman, Advertising Standards Authority Limited, 1965-70, 1974-77; Fellow, Institute of Directors; Deputy-President, Association of British Chamber of Commerce, 1970; Chairman, Independent Unionist Peers Association, 1975-80; Chairman, British Commonwealth Producers Organisation, 1952-55; President, 1967-70; General Advisory Council of BBC, 1950-55; President, Highland Society of London, 1972-76. *Honours:* Created a Peer, Privy Counsellor, 1962, 1963; KBE., 1974. *Hobby:* Music. *Address:* Claytons Beeches Hill, Bishops Waltham, by Southampton, SO3 1FU, England.

D'SILVA, Roby James Francis, b. 12 Feb. 1932, Bombay. Educationist, Designer. *Education:* G.D. Bombay, 1954; N.D.D., United Kingdom, 1958; C.C.A.D.D., United Kingdom, 1959; Advertising Course, City of London College, London, 1958-59. *Appointments:* include: Art Director, Studio Boggeri, Milan, 1959-61; Expert Member, Board of Studies, University of Boroda, 1979-., Member of Selection, Advisory Committees of several Government and Educational Institutions, India. *Memberships:* Member, International Centre for Typographical Association, America, 1970; Fellow, J.J. School of Arts and Crafts, Bombay, 1955-56; Fellow, Society of Industrial Artists and Designers, London, England; Expert Member, Board of Studies, Maharaja Sayajirho University, Baroda; Chairman, Membership Expansion Committee, Rotary Club, Bombay, 1970. *Publications:* Exhibitions in Advertising, Art, Design, in various countries; Various publications including: 'Graphis', 'Designers in Britain', 'Penrose Annual',. *Honours:* First Prize, Government of India Art Exhibition, Bombay, 1953; First Prize, All India Child Welfare Society's Poster Design competition, 1954; First Prize, 2500th Buddha Jayanti, All India Postage Stamp Design Competition, 1955; First Prize, Diploma and Seal Design, Royal Society for Prevention of Accidents, United Kingdom, 1957. *Hobbies:* Photography; Reading;. *Address:* Desilva House, Papdy Church, Bassein, Dist-Thana, Maharashtra, India.

D'SOUZA, William Antony, b. 22 Dec. 1958, Puttur, South Kanara, Karnataka State, India. Industrialist and Technical Consultant. *Education:* Bachelor of Commerce; Diploma in Industrial Training; Diploma in Business Accounts; Master of Commerce. *Appointments:* include: Managing Director, Mangala Papers, Puttur; Managing Partner Souza Industrial Corporation, Supreme Blocks, Sweeta Bottling; Chief Executive, Great India Finance Corporation; Partner, Great India Sales Corporation. *Memberships:* Treasurer and Honorary Member, Catholic Student's Union; Member, Karnataka Catholic Education Society; Member, All India Commerce Association; Member, Industrial Development Bank; Member, Catholic Sabha, Managlore. *Publications:* Numerous Project reports on Small Scale Industries. *Honours:* Several Certificates for various competitions, including: Toy's Show, Cricket matches. *Hobbies:* Stamp Collection; Driving; Motor Bikes; Swimming; Reading; (interested in setting up small scale industries abroad or to become the technical advisor). *Address:* Souza Building, Puttur S.K. 574 201, Karnataka, India.

DUBUC (Colonel), Hector Philippe Jean-Claude, b. 10 Jan. 1924, Montreal, Canada. Insurance Executive. m. Louise MCGovern, 28 June 1958, 2 sons, 2 daughters. *Education:* Science, University of Montreal, Canada, 1943; Commerce, University of London, UK, 1945; Bach. of Commerce, McGill University, Canada, 1946-49; Chartered Life Underwriter, University of Toronto, 1955-58; Fellow, Royal Society of Arts, 1958. *Appointments:* Employee, Benfit Plans Consultant, 1949-52; Chartered Life Underwriter and Manager, 1952-68; President, J.C. Dubuc & Associates Limited, 1968-; Vice-President, Johnson & Higgins Willis Faber Limited, 1971-; Executive Vice-President, Dupuis, Parizeau, Tremblay, Inc., 1977-; Vice-President and Director, J. & H.W.F. Ltée, 1980; Vice-President and Director, Les Conseillers D.P.T. Inc., 1980. *Memberships:* Life member, Million Dollar Round Table; Past President, Club St.Denis, Montreal, Canada; Royal Canadian Military Institute; Past President, Royal Canadian Legion, Jean Brillant VC Branch; Chancellor, Order of St. John, Priory of Canada; Governor, Marie-Enfant Hospital and Institute of Cardiology, Montreal, Canada; McGill Graduate Society; Director, Knowlton Golf Club; Director, Montreal Military and Maritime Museum. *Honours:* Canadian Forces Decoration and bar, Order of Poland, Military Cross (Poland); Order of Merit S.R. (France); Silver Medal, Paris, France, Bronze Medal, Versailles, France, 1974; Past President, Life Underwriters Association of Canada, 1966; Knight of Justice, Order of St. John; Knight of Malta; Knight Commander of St. Lazarus; Armigerous, College of Arms, London, 1976. *Hobbies:* Fishing; Skiing; Tennis. *Address:* 2265 Kildare Road, Town of Mount Royal, Montreal, Quebec, H3R 3J6, Canada.

du CANN, Edward Dillon Lott, b. 28 May 1924, Beckenham, England. Member of Parliament. m. Sallie Innes Murchie, 1 son, 2 daughters. *Education:* MA Law, St. John's College, Oxford. *Appointments:* Privy Councillor, 1964; Conservative Member of Parliament for Taunton Division, Somerset, 1956-. *Memberships:* Commodore, Admiral, House of Commons Yacht Club, 1962, 1974; Chairman, Burke Club, 1968. *Publications:* Investing Simplified, 1959; Several articles on Financial and Internation Affairs including: The Case for a Bill of Rights; The Control of Public Expenditure. *Honours:* Privy Councillor, 1964; Elected Freeman of Taunton Deane Borough, 1977. *Hobbies:* Travel; Gardening; Sailing. *Address:* Cothay Barton, Greenham, Wellington, Somerset, England.

DUCK-CHONG, Robert Neil, b. 27 Sept. 1932, Sydney, Australia. Life Underwriter. m. Coral Gwenda Chamberlain, 6 Feb. 1960, 1 son, 1 daughter. *Education:* Leaving Certificate, 1959; Diploma, Australian Institute, 1969. *Appointments:* Life and Disability Insurance Broker, Life Management Pty. Ltd.; Superannuation and Pension Consultant, Supermaster, New South Wales, Ltd; Member, Life Insurance Consultative Committee; Grand Councillor (NSW) Rosicrucian Order, AMORC. *Memberships:* National President, Life Underwriters Association of Australia; Vice President,

Life Underwriters Association of Australia, New South Wales; Qualifying and Life Member, Million Dollar Round Table; Life Member, Rosicrucian Order, AMORC. *Honours:* International Quality Award, 1970-81. *Hobbies:* Music; Theatre; Teaching; Acting. *Address:* 92 Barons Crescent, Hunters Hill, New South Wales 2110, Australia.

DUCKER, John Patrick, b. 29 March 1932, Hull, Yorkshire, England. Public Service Administrator. m. Valerie Smith, 23 Sept. 1963, 2 sons. *Appointments:* Member of Legislative Council of New South Wales, 1972; Secretary, Labour Council of New South Wales, 1975; Vice President, Australian Council of Trade Unions, 1977; Member, Public Service Board of New South Wales, 1979. *Memberships:* Automobile Club; Sydney Rotary; Tattersalls Club. *Honours:* Order of Australia, 1979. *Hobbies:* Gardening; Sailing; Reading; Photography. *Address:* 2 Briony Place, Mona Vale, New South Wales 2103, Australia.

DUCKHAM, Alec Narraway, b. 23 Aug. 1903, Blackheath, London, UK. Professor of Agriculture. m. Audrey Mary Polgreen, 23 Dec. 1931, 1 son, 2 daughters. *Education:* Natural Science, Cambridge University. *Appointments:* Cambridge University, 1926-29; Rowett Research Institute, Aberdeen, 1929-32; Ministries of Agriculture and Food; British Embassy, Washington, United States of America, 1932-35; Department of Agriculture, Reading University, England, 1955-68. *Memberships:* Royal Agriculture Society of England; British Grassland Society; Agricultural Economics Society. *Publications:* Numerous books including: Livestock in British Commonwealth; American Agriculture; Fabric of Farming; Farming Seasons; Several Paintings. *Honours:* Silver Research Medal, 1926; Order of British Empire, 1945; C.B.E. 1950. *Hobbies:* Painting; Sketching. *Address:* 5 Woolacombe Drive, Reading, England. RG6 2UA.

DUCROS, (Hon. Mr. Justice), Jacques, b. 18 May, 1934, Toulon, France. Judge of the Superior Court, Province of Quebec. m. Patricia Marilynn McCoshen, 10 Sept. 1960, 5 daughters. *Education:* BA., Stanislas College, Putremont, Quebec, Canada, 1952; BCL., Law, McGill University, Canada, 1956. *Appointments:* Monette, Fillion & Labelle, 1957-60; Ducros, Tellier & Demers, 1960-62; Crown Attorney, 1962-64, Associate Deputy Minister of Justice, 1964-67, Province of Quebec, Canada; Geoffrion & Prud'Homme, 1967-71; Quebec Superior Court, 1971-; Supreme Court, NW Territories, 1975-; Law Reform Commission of Canada, 1979-. Professor Criminal Law: University of Montreal, Canada, 1964, Montreal Police Department, Canada, 1965-68; Chairman, Criminal Justice Section; Canadian Bar Association, 1969-71. *Hobbies:* Golf; Bridge. *Address:* 4458 de Maisonneuve Blvd., Westmount, Quebec, H3Z 1L7, Canada.

DUFFIELD, Peter R, b. 23 March 1938, Montreal, Quebec. Vice-President. m. Martha Richardson, 11 May 1963, 2 sons. *Education:* Senior Matriculation, (awarded Hooper Scholarship), Bishops College, Lennoxville, P.Q., 1952-55; Bachelor of Chemical Engineering, MacGill University, 1955-59; Ecole du Louvre, University of Paris, 1959-60; German Language, Goethe Institut, Munich, Germany, 1959; Spanish Language, Universidad de Menendez Pelayo Santander, Spain, 1959. *Appointments:* Shawinigan Engineering Company, 1955-56; Various positions in Export Division, including: Cellulose Film Sales Supervisor and Export Technical Supervisor; Several Managerial Positions including: Liquid Packaging, 1968; Woven Polyolefins, 1976-77; Special Advisor to Secretary of State, Government of Canada, 1977-78; Vice-President, Fibres Group, Du Pont Canada, 1978-. *Memberships:* Chemical Institute of Canada; Canadian Society for Chemical Engineers; Life Governor of Montreal General Hospital; University Club, Montreal. *Honours:* Student Executive Council Silver Award, 1958; MacGill Debating Union Executive Award, 1959. *Hobbies:* Squash; Skiing. *Address:* 132 Clandeboye, Westmont, Quebec H3Z 1Z1, Canada.

DUFFUS, Herbert George Holwell, b. 30 Aug. 1908, St. Ann's Bay, Jamaica, West Indies. Barrister-at-Law; Chief Justice of Jamaica (retired). m. Elsie Mary Hollinsed, 10 June 1939. *Education:* Articled to a Solicitor, 1925-30; Admitted to practice, 1930; Called to the Bar,

Lincoln's Inn, London, UK, 1956. *Appointments:* Private practice as a Solicitor, 1930-43; Acting Resident Magistrate, 1943-47, Resident Magistrate and member of Her Majesty's Overseas Judiciary, 1947-56, Jamaica; Puisne Judge of Supreme Court of Jamaica, 1958-62; Judge, 1962, President of Court of Appeal, 1964-68, Chief Justice Jamaica, 1968-73; Acted as Governor General, Jamaica, 1973. *Publications:* Editor of Jamaica Law Reports, 1958-60; Joint Editor, West Indian Law Reports, 1959-61; Commissioner in several Commissions of Enquiry in Jamaica, Grenada and Barbados, 1954-78. *Honours:* Knighthood, 1966. *Hobbies:* Gardening; Fishing. *Address:* 6 Braywick Road, PO Box 243, Kingston 6, Jamaica, West Indies.

DUFFY, Graeme Pat, b. 12 Dec. 1932, Wellington, New Zealand. Neurological Surgeon. m. Karen Jean Richmond, 20 Nov. 1973, 2 sons, 2 daughters. *Education:* M.B., ChB., University of New Zealand, 1955; F.R.C.S., Royal College of Surgeons of England, 1962; F.R.C.P., Royal College of Physicians, Edinburgh, 1975; F.R.A.C.S., Royal Australasian College of Surgeons, 1974. *Appointments:* Consultant Neurosurgeon, Birmingham Regional Hospital Board, Birmingham, England, 1967-73; Head of Department of Neurosurgery, Royal Hobart Hospital, 1973; Visiting Neurosurgeon, Tasmanian State Hospitals Supervisor, Neurosurgery, Medical School, University of Tasmania. *Memberships:* Member, Society of British Neurosurgeons; Fellow, Royal Society of Medicine; Member, Society of Hydrocephalus; Foundation Member, Brain Research Association; Member, Pan American Medical Association; Member, Neurosurgical Society of Australasia; Member, Royal Society of Tasmania. *Publications:* Various Medical Journals in the Medical Field including: Lumbar Puncture in Raised Intracranial Pressure, 1969; Anterior Interbody Fusion for Cervical Disc Desease, 1981; Surgical Treatment of Spontaneous Intrapontine Haemorrhage, 1981. *Hobbies:* Boating; Gardening. *Address:* 34 Wandella Place, Taroona, Tasmania 7006, Australia.

DUFRESNE, F Gerard, b. 22 July 1918, East Angus, Quebec, Canada. Chartered Insurance Broker; Professional Technician. m. Madeleine Cyr, 4 June 1949, 1 son, 2 daughters. *Education:* Graduated from Shawinigan Technical Institute, 1939. *Appointments:* Active Force, Canadian Army, 1939-46; Insurance Broker and Industrial, 1946-; Director, Canadian Universal Insurance; President, Gerard Dufresne Inc.; President, Moreco Electric; Vice-President, Trois Rivieres Chevrolet Inc. *Memberships:* Past President, Professional and Industrial Club; Past President: Local Branch of Junior Chamber of Commerce; Local Branch of Chamber of Commerce; Board of Directors, St. Thérése Hospital; Governor, Canadian Corporation of Commissionnaires; Director Cdn. Council St John's Ambulance; Past Mayor of Shawinigan; Past Vice-President, Royal Cnd. Artillery Association; Past Vice-President, Provincial Insurance Brokers Association. *Honours:* Member of Order of Canada; Efficiency Decoration; Canadian Decoration. *Hobbies:* Fishing; Hunting. *Address:* 1363 Des Eerables, Shawinigan, Quebec, Canada.

DUFTY, Norman Francis, b. 6 Apr. 1919, Sheffield, England. Educator. m. Dorothy Isobel Bowen, 1 June 1940, 3 sons. *Education:* A.Met., Sheffield University, UK, 1938; BA., 1956, PhD., 1962, M.Ed., 1966, University of Western Australia; MA., University of Illinois, USA, 1958. *Appointments:* Chemist, Vickers Limited, Sheffield, UK., 1934-35; Management Cadet, United Steel Cos., Sheffield, UK, 1935-38; Foreman, Samuel Fox, Stocksbridge, UK, 1938-39; Foreman, Brymbo Steel Co., Wrexham, UK, 1939-43; Commissioned Service, RAF., 1943-46; Manager, K and L Steelfounders, Letchworth, UK, 1946-48; Manager, BHP., Port Kimbla, Australia, 1948-50; Management Consultant, W D Scott, Sydney, Australia, 1950-52; Senior Lecturer, 1953-57, Department Head, 1957-62, Assistant Principal, 1964-66, Perth Technical College, Australia; International Labour Officer, Geneva, Switzerland, 1962-63; UN Spec. Fund, Republic of China, 1963-64; Professor, University of Wisconsin, USA, 1966-67; Dean of Social Sciences, 1967-80, Chairman, Division of Arts, Education and Social Sciences, 1981-, Western Australian Institute of Technology, Australia. *Memberships:* Fellow, Institution of Metallurgists; Fellow, Australian College of Education; Fellow, Australian Institute of Management; Chartered Engineer. *Publications:* Industrial Relations in India, 1964;

Managerial Economics, 1966; Editor, Essays on Apprenticeship, 1967; Editor, Sociology of the Blue Collar Worker, 1970; Industrial Relations in the Australian Metal Industry, 1972; Changes in Labour/Management Relations in the Enterprise, 1975; Industrial Relations in the Public Sector, 1979. *Honours:* Lancasterian Scholarship, 1st Class, 1934; Armorer's and Brasiers' Prizes, Sheffield University, 1938; Employers' Federation Prize, Perth Technical College, 1952; Fulbright Fellow, 1957; Rosenstamm Prize in Economics, University of Western Australia, 1953. *Hobbies:* Gardening; Swimming. *Address:* Walnut Road, Bickley 6076, Australia.

DUGGAL, Krisham Lal, b. 21 Dec. 1929, India. Mathematician. m. Asha Duggal, 22 Jan 1956, 2 sons, 1 daughter. *Education:* B.A., Panjab University India, 1951; M.A. Agra University, India, 1954; M.Sc., University of Windsor, Canada, 1967; Ph.D., University of Windsor, Canada, 1969; *Appointments:* Lecturer, Panjab University, India, 1954-66; Teaching Assistant, University of Windsor, Canada, 1966-69; Assistant Professor, Associate Professor, Professor, University of Windsor, Canada, 1969-; Visiting Professor, University of Waterloo, Canada and Mathematical Institute, Oxford, England, 1979-80. *Memberships:* Member of several Socities including: American Mathematical Society; London Mathematical Society; General Relativity and Gravitation Society; Life Member, Academy of Progress of Mathematics, India; Life Fellow, International Institute of Community Services; Life Fellow, International Biographical Association, London. *Publications:* Several publications in Internation Journals of Mathematics and Science on Global Differential Geometry, and General Relativity. *Honours:* National Research Council Fellowship, 1967-69; Bursary awarded by French Government under Scientific and Technical Exchange programme, 1970. *Hobbies:* Gardening; Chess; Cards; Reading; Travelling. *Address:* 335 Beneteau Drive, R.R. 4 Amherstburg, Ontario, Canada N9V 2Y9.

DUKURS, Verners Jakobs, b. 6 Nov. 1914, Riga, Latvija. Sculptor; Civil Engineer. *Education:* Diploma, Degree of Arts, Riga, Latvia, 1944; Diploma, Architecture, 1956, Diploma, Civil Engineering, 1962, International Correspondence Schools, Adelaide, Australia. College Lecturer, Riga, Latvia, 1939-43; Lecturer, Faculty of Architecture, Munich University, UNRRA, Germany, 1945-48; Survey Draughtsman, Chief Draughtsman, Assistant Engineer, Municipal Tramways Trust and State Transport Authority, Adelaide, Australia, 1950-79. *Memberships:* Fellow, Royal South Australian Society of Arts; Associate, Institution of Engineers, England, 1966-79; Australian Institute of Engineers Associates, 1978. *Creative Works:* Sculptors Exhibitions at: Riga, Latvia, 1943, 1944; Eslingen, Germany, Jan. & Nov. 1946; Memmingen, Germany, 1947; Adelaide, Australia, 1948, 1949 and 1981. *Hobby:* Opal and Gemstone cutting, polishing and grading. *Address:* 45 Curzon Street, Camden Park, S A 5038, Australia.

DUNCAN, James Francis, b. 25 July 1921, Liverpool, England. Chemist. *Education:* MA., 1943; BSc., 1943; D.Phil., 1944; DSc., Oxford, 1966; MSc., Melbourne, Australia, 1968. *Appointments:* Principal Scientific Officer, Atomic Energy Research Establishment, Harwell, UK; Reader in Radiochemistry, University of Melbourne, Australia; Professor of Inorganic and Theoretical Chemistry, Victoria University of Wellington, New Zealand. *Memberships:* National Treasurer, Royal Society of New Zealand; Wellington Branch Chairman, NZ Institute of Chemistry; President, NZ Association of Scientists; President, Association of University Teachers; IDA; UNESCO Commission; National Development Council; Trustee, National Library, New Zealand; Chairman, Commission for the Future. *Publications:* 150 papers on Professional Chemistry; Numerous papers on future studies in New Zealand. *Honours:* OBE., 1975. *Address:* 'Thorpe End', Akatarawa Road, Reikorangi, Waikanae RD1, New Zealand.

DUNCAN, John Soenser Ritchie, b. 1921, United Kingdom. British Diplomat. m. Sheila Conacher, 1950. *Education:* George Watson's Boys College; Glasgow Academy; Dundee High School; Edinburgh University. *Appointments:* Sudan Political Service, 1941; HM Forces, 1941-43; Head, Personnel Department, Diplomatic Service, 1966-68; Minister, Canberra, 1969-71; High Commissioner to Zambia, 1971-74; Ambassador to Morocco, 1975-78; High Commissioner, Bahamas 1978-. *Publications:* The Sudan: A Record of Achievement, 1952; The Sudan's Path to Independence, 1957. *Honours:* CMG; MBE. *Address:* c/o Foreign & Commonwealth Office, London, SW1, England.

DUNCAN, John Stuart, b. 21 June 1922, Timaru, New Zealand. Geographer. m. Betty Dallas Macdonald, 6 Aug. 1949, 3 daughters. *Education:* BA., 1943, MA., 1948, Canterbury University College, University of New Zealand; PhD., London School of Economics, England, 1949-51. *Appointments:* Assistant Lecturer, 1951-54, Lecturer, 1954-63, Department of Geography, University of Manchester, UK; Senior Lecturer, Geography, Monash University, Australia, 1963-. *Memberships:* Institute of Australian Geographers; Institute of British Geographers; New Zealand Geographical Society. *Publications:* Editor, Atlas of Victoria (in press); articles in geographical journals. *Honours:* Star, 1939-45, Italy Star, War Medal, 1939-45, New Zealand Service Medal, Service with New Zealand Army, 1941-46, including service with 2 New Zealand Division in Italy, 1944-45. *Hobby:* Chess. *Address:* 45 Yongala Street, Balwyn, Victoria 3103, Australia.

DUNCAN, Philip Pius, b. 5 Jan. 1943, Aishalton, Rupununi, Guyana. Motor Vehicle Mechanic. m. Edith Xavier, 11 Apr. 1966,.1 son, 5 daughters. *Appointments:* Pupil Teacher, 1959-62; Motor Vehicle Mechanic, 1964-66; Elected member of Parliament, 1964, 1968, 1973-80; Parliamentary Secretary for Amerindian Affairs, 1966-73; Minister of State-Regional, 1973-80; Commissioner of Oaths to Affidavits, 1968-; Member of Guyanese Delegation to United Nations, 1969; Vice-Chairman, Constituent Assembly, 1980. *Memberships:* Peoples National Congress; Secretary, People's National Congress Youth Organisation; National History and Art Council; Board of Directors, Guyana School of Agriculture; Rehabilitation Committee for Rupununi, 1969; Regional Minister and Regional Chairman, PNC., in Rupuni and North West Regions, 1973-80; Chairman, Hinterland Emergency Action Programme Committee, 1978-79. *Hobbies:* Travelling; Hunting; Photography; Camping. *Address:* 3153-4 Aubrey Barker Street and Congress Drive, South Ruimveldt Park, Georgetown, Guyana.

DUNCAN-SANDYS, Duncan Edwin, b. 24 Jan. 1908, Dorset, England. Former British Government Official. m. (1) Diana Churchill, 1935, 1 son, 2 daughters, (2) Marie-Claire Schmitt, 1962, 1 daughter. *Appointments:* Diplomatic Service, Foreign Office and British Embassy, Berlin, 1930-33; MP for Norwood div. of Lambeth, 1935-45; Streatham, 1950-74; Finance Secretary, War Office, 1941-43; Parliamentary Secretary, Ministry of Supply, 1943-44; Privy Councillor, 1944; Minister of Works, 1944-45; Member, General Advisory Council, BBC, 1947-51; Minister of Supply, 1951-54; Minister, Housing and Local Government, 1954-57; Minister of Defence, 1957-59; Minister of Aviation, 1959-60, Sec. of State for Commonwealth relations, 1960-64, also Sec. of State for the Colonies, 1962-64. Founder European Movement, 1947, Chmn. Internat. Exec., 1950; Member, Consultative Assembly Council of Europe, 1950-51, 65-; Founder-Pres. Civic Trust, 1956-; Pres. Europa Nostra 1969-; Chmn. Lonrho Limited, 1972-; Chmn. Internat. Organizing Com. European Archtl. Heritage Year, 1975. Joined royal arty. Territorial Army 1937, advanced through grades to Lt. col., 1941; Expeditionary Force, Norway, 1940; disabled, 1941. *Honours:* Life Peer, 1974; Companion of Honor (Eng.); Grand Cross Order of Merit, Italy; Medal City of Paris; Grand Cross Order of the Crown, Belgium; Comdr. Legion of Honor, France; Grand Cross of the Order of Merit of the Federal Republic of Germany; Fellow, Royal Institute British Architects (hon.); Member, Royal Town Planning Institute (hon.). *Address:* 86 Vincent Square, London, SW1 P 2PG England.

DUNCAN-SHORROCK, Sarah Esther Janina, b. 6 Aug. 1953. Wilpshire, Blackburn, England. Musician, Performer and Teacher. *Education:* Northern School of Music, Manchester; Manchester School of Music; London College of Music; Flute Diploma, Conservatory of Music, Berne. *Appointments:* Several Vocal Recitals; Flute and Recorder Recitals; Music Teacher for several schools including: Queen Elizabeth's Grammar School, Blackburn. *Memberships:* Incorporated Society of Musicians; London College of Music Society. *Hobbies:*

Music; Ballet; Theatre; Driving; Reading; Travel. *Address:* 'Isola Bella', 22 Alice Street, Oswaldtwistle, Lancashire BB5 3BL, England.

DUNDEE, John Wharry, b. 8 Nov. 1921, Larne, Northern Ireland. Professor Anaesthetics. m. Sarah Irwin Houston, 6 Sept. 1949, 1 son, 3 daughters. *Education:* MB, BCH, BAO, 1946; MD, 1951, The Queen's University of Belfast; PhD, University of Liverpool, 1953; DA (Ire) 1949; DA (Eng), 1951; FFARCS (Eng) 1953; FFARCS (Ire) 1959; MRCP (UK), 1975. *Appointments:* Senior Lecturer in Anaesthetics, University of Liverpool, 1953; Consultant Anaesthetist, Belfast Teaching Hospitals, 1958-; Professor of Anaesthetics, The Queen's University of Belfast, 1958-. *Memberships:* Dean, Faculty of Anaesthetists, Royal College of Surgeons, Ireland, 1970-73, Board Member, 1960-79; President, Section of Anaesthetics, Royal Society of Medicine, 1979-80; British Medical Association; British Pharmacological Society; Anaesthetic Research Society; American Society of Anaesthetics. *Publications:* 400-500 papers published in journals on the subject of clinical pharmacology and anaesthesia. *Hobbies:* Gardening. *Address:* 24 Old Coach Road, Belfast 9, Northern Ireland.

DUNN, Adrian Arthur, b. 8 Jan. 1929, Sydney, N.S.W., Australia. Dentist. m. Fay Noble Norris, 9 Jan. 1954, 1 son, 1 daughter. *Education:* Bachelor Dental Surgery, Sydney University, 1953; Master Dental Surgery, Sydney University, 1964; Fellow Royal Australian College Dental Surgeons, 1965. *Appointments:* Private Practice, 1954-; Lecturer in field at numerous Universities and Dental Associations. *Memberships:* Committee, Eastern Suburbs Dental Group, 1953; Foundation Member, Australian Endodontic Society; Foundation Member, Australian Prosthodontic Society, 1960; American Equilibration Society, 1964; Royal Australian College of Dental Surgeons, 1965; Foundation Member, International Academy of Gnathology, Australian Section, 1977; President, International Academy of Gnathology, Australian Section, 1981; Committee, Royal Motor Yacht Club. *Publications:* Thesis—Physical Properties of Dental Ceramics, Sydney University, 1964. *Hobbies:* Yachting. *Address:* 27 Parsley Road, Vaucluse, N.S.W., Australia.

DUNN, Hector Lockhart, b. 13 Jan. 1918, Warwick, Queensland. Presbyterian Minister. m. Joan Lolita Slatyer, 26 Nov. 1941, 1 son, 1 daughter. *Education:* BA., University of Queensland, 1941; University of Sydney. *Appointments:* Minister of St. Andrew's, Grenfell, N.S.W., 1945-48; The Scots Church, Hobart, Tasmania, 1948-63; Associate Minister, St. Columba's Church of Scotland, London, 1963-65; Senior Minister, St. John's Collegiate Church, Victoria, 1965-80. *Memberships:* Charter President, Rotary Club of Grenfell; Rotary Club of Hobart, 1949-60; Rotary Club of WWarrnambool, 1965-; Scottish Church Society. *Publications:* Regular broadcasts on Australian Broadcasting Commission national network on religious, social and historial clubjects. *Honours:* Rotary Vocational Service Award, 1976; M.B.E., 1981. *Hobbies:* Photography; Horticulture. *Address:* Pandora Court, 31 Queen Street, Bribie Island, Queensland, Australia.

DUNNET, George Mackenzie, b. 19 Apr. 1928, Caithness, Scotland, UK. Biologist. m. Margaret Henderson Thomson, 5 Jan. 1953, 1 son, 2 daughters. *Education:* Peterhead Academy; Aberdeen University, BSc., 1st Class Hons. Zoology, 1949, PhD., 1952. *Appointments:* Research Officer, Wildlife Survey Section, C.S.I.R.O., Australia, 1953-58; Lecturer, Senior Lecturer, Professor of Zoology, University of Aberdeen, 1958-74; Senior Research Fellow, D.S.I.R., New Zealand, 1968-69; Regius Professor of Natural History, University of Aberdeen, 1974-. *Memberships:* British Ecological Society, Vice-President, 1973-74, President, 1980-81; British Ornithologists Union; Fellow, Royal Society of Edinburgh, 1970, Institute of Biology, 1974, Royal Society of Arts, 1981. *Publications:* Numerous scientific papers in professional journals; Monograph of Australian Fleas. *Hobbies:* Photography; Walking. *Address:* Culterty House, Newburgh, Ellon, Aberdeen, Scotland, UK.

DUNNETT, Ludovic James, b. 12 Feb. 1914, Lahore, Pakistan. Civil Servant (retired). m. Olga Adair, 4 Sept. 1944. *Education:* Edinburgh Academy 1920-32; BA, University College, Oxford, 1932-36. *Appointments:*

Air Ministry, 1931-44; Ministry of Civil Avaition,1944-50; Ministry of Supply, 1950-59; Ministry of Transport, 1959-62; Ministry of Labour, 1962-66; Ministry of Defence, 1966-74. *Memberships:* President, Institute of Nature Studies, 1976-80; Chairman, Duke of Edinburgh Study Conference, 1974; Reform Club. *Publications:* Varous articles of Public Administration. *Honours:* CMG, 1949; GCH, 1969. *Hobbies:* Reading; Golf. *Address:* 2 Warwick Square, London SW1, England.

DUNROSSIL, 2nd Viscount, John William Morrison, b. 22 May 1926. HM Diplomatic Service. m. (1) Mavis Spencer-Payne, 3 sons, 1 daughter, (2) Diana Mary Cunliffe, 1969, 2 daughters. *Education:* Fettes; Oxford. *Appointments:* Royal Air Force, 1945-48; Flight Lieutenant, Pilot; Commonwealth Relations Office, 1951; Assistant Private Secretary, Secretary of State, 1952-54; Second Secretary, Canberra, 1954-56; CRO, 1956-58; First Secretary and Acting Deputy High Commissioner, Dacca, East Pakistan, 1958-60; First Secretary, Pretoria/Capetown, 1961-64; FO, 1964-68. *Memberships:* Intergovernmental Maritime Consultative Organisation, 1968-70; Counsellor and Head of Chancery, Ottawa, 1970-74; Counsellor, Brussels, 1975-78; Royal Air Force, Royal Commonwealth Society; Cercle Royal Gaulois, Brussels. *Address:* c/o Commonwealth Office, London SW1, England.

DUNSTAN, Allan Albert, b. 8 Apr. 1924, Donald, Victoria, Australia. Business & Farming. m. Lesley Hands, 1 Mar. 1947, 3 sons. *Education:* Leaving Certificate. *Appointments:* Newspaper; Farming; Commerce. *Memberships:* President, Victorian Country Football League; Lions Club; Donald District Cricket Association; Holder 20 year badge, Municipal Association of Victoria; S.P.A.S.M.S., Club, Donald; Returned Soldiers League. *Honours:* Justice of Peace, 1963; O.B.E., awarded for Municipal & Community Service, 1980. *Hobbies:* Football; Cricket. *Address:* 1 Cosack Street, Donald, 3480, Australia.

DUNWOODY, Gwyneth Patricia, b. 12 Dec. 1930. Member of Parliament. m. 1954, (divorced 1975), 2 sons, 1 daughter. *Education:* Notre Dame Convent; Fulham Secondary. *Appointments:* Member of Parliament, Labour, Exeter, 1966-70; Party Secretary to BoT, 1967-70; Member, European Parliament, 1975-79; Director, Film Production Association of Great Britain, 1970-74; Member of Parliament Labour Crewe, 1974; Opposition Front Bench Spokesman on Foreign and Commonwealth Affairs, 1979. *Address:* 113 Cromwell Tower, Beech Street, London EC2, England.

DUODO, Yeboa Alex, b. 1 Jan. 1937, Agona Nsaba, Ghana. Entomologist. m. Florence Banson, 3 sons, 1 daughter. *Education:* BA., Agriculture, University of Ghana, 1962; MA., Entomology, Utah State University, USA., 1968; Doctor of Philosophy, Entomology, Utah State University, 1972. *Appointments:* Research Assistant, Entomology, Crops Research Institute, Kumasi, Ghana; Teaching Assistant, Biology & Entomology, Utah State University, USA; Research Officer, Entomology, Crops Research Institute, Ghana, 1972-77, Senior Research Officer, 1977-; Officer-in-Charge, West African Substation of Commonwealth Institute of Biological Control, 1977-; Part-time Lecturer, Entomology & Biology, University of Science & Technology, Kumasi, Ghana, 1976-. *Memberships:* Entomological Society of America; Association of African Insect Scientists; Ghana Science Association; Ashanti Representative, Accra Great Olympics Football Club. *Publications:* Contributed articles to various professional journals. *Honours:* Prize for being School Organist and Singing Prefect, Presbyterian Secondary School, Odumase-Krobo, Ghana, 1955. *Hobbies:* Classical Music; International Affairs; Rabbit Rearing; Sports, especially Football and Boxing. *Address:* P.O. Box 16, Agona Nsaba, Ghana

DURACK, Elizabeth (Mrs F A Clancy), b. 6 July 1916, Perth, Western Australia. Artist & Writer. m. Francis A Clancy, 19 Aug. 1939, (Deceased), 1 son, 1 daughter. *Education:* Studied, Diploma Fine Arts, Chelsea Polytechnic, London, Antiquities, Rome, Naples, Sicily, 1936; Special Studies, National Gallery, London, Louvre, Paris, Prado, Madrid, 1966-68;. *Appointments:* Commissioned for Murals for University of Western Australia, Charles Gardiner Hospital, West Australian Tourist Bureau; Paintings and drawings for the Australian Wool Board, Broken Hill Proprietory Ltd., The Australian Institute of Aboriginal Stufies, Conzinc Rio Tinto, Australia, Hammersley Iron, Northern Cattle Company. *Memberships:* W.A. Art Gallery Society; Australian Society of Authors; PEN International; Australian Institute of International Affairs; Australia-Japan Society; Australian American Association; Royal Commonwealth Society. *Creative Works:* Author illustrator, Love Magic, 1956; Seeing Through New York, 1967; Face Value—Women of Papua New Guinea, 1968; Philippines, 1970; Seeing Through Nigeria, 1972; Seeing Through Indonesia, 1977; Co-productions (with sister, Dame Mary Durack), Allabout, Chunuma, Son of Djaro, Picanninies, Nungaree and Jungaree, The Magic Trumpet, The Way of the Whirlwind, The Courteous Savage, Kookanoo; Several articles in Newspapers and Magazines and illustrations for European, African and Asian travel; 46 solo exhibitions in capital cities of Australia; Innumerable group exhibitions, including Australian Exhibition, Whitechapel Gallery, 1961; Represented in State Galleries of Australia and private collections in Australia, Europe and the United States Collections in University of Western Australia, Murdock University, W.A. Institute of Technology, Australian National University Canberra, University of Texas. *Honours:* O.B.E., 1966. *Hobbies:* Swimming. *Address:* 47 Browne Avenue, Dalkeith, Western Australia, 6009.

DURACK, Mary, b. 20 Feb. 1913, Adelaide, South Australia. Writer. m. Captain H.C. Miller, 2 Dec. 1938, (Dec.), 2 sons, 4 daughters. *Education:* Loreto Convent, Adelaide Terrace, Perth, Western Australia. *Appointments:* Journalistic Staff, West Australian Newspapers Limited, 1937-38; Self-Employed. *Memberships:* Fellowship of Australian Writers; International PEN, Australia; Australian Society of Authors; National Trust; Royal Western Australian Historical Society; Kuljak Playwrights Incorporated; Aboriginal Cultural Foundation; Director, Australian Stockman's Hall of Fame and Outback Heritage Centre. *Publications:* All-about 1935; Chunuma, 1936; Son of Djaro, 1938; The Way of the Whirlwind, 1941; Piccaninnies 1943; The Magic Trumpet, 1944; Child Artists of the Australian Bush, (w. Florence Rutter) 1952; Keep Him My Country, 1955; Kings in Grass Castles, 1959; To Ride a Fine Horse, 1963; The Courteous Savage, 1964; Kookanoo and Kangaroo, 1963; An Australian Settler, 1964; The Rock and the Sand, 1969; The End of Dreaming, (w. Ingrid Ysdale) 1974; To Be Heirs Forever, 1976; Tjakamarra—Boy Between Two Worlds, 1977; Plays: The Ship of Dreams, 1968; Swan River Saga, 1972; Numerous scripts for ABC drama department, Young World, etc. *Honours:* Commonwealth Literary Grant, 1973 and 77; Dame Commander Order of the British Empire, 1978; Honorary, Doctor of Letters; Australian Research Grant, 1980. *Address:* 12 Bellevue Avenue, Nedlands, Western Australia 6009

DUREAU, Michael Bruce, b. 11 Feb. 1941, Brisbane, Queensland, Australia. Managing Director. m. Pamela Grace Partridge, 17 Aug. 1970, 1 son, 2 daughters. *Education:* BE(Chemical), Sydney University 1966; Master of Applied Science in Environmental Pollution Control, University of New South Wales, 1973. *Appointments:* Chemical Design Engineer and Project Engineer, Laport Industries Limited, 1966-70; Senior Project Engineer, Manager, Water and Wastewater Systems, Envirotech (Aust.) Pty. Ltd, 1970-76; Manager Victorian Division, 1976-77 and Managing Director, Kent Instruments, Australia, Pty. Limited, 1978-. *Memberships:* Institution of Chemical Engineers; Institution of Engineers Australia; Australian Water and Wastewater Association; Institute of Instrumentation and Control Australia; Industrial Instrument Industry Association of Australia; Melbourne Cricket Club; Northbridge Golf Club. *Publications:* Author of 12 technical papers on Water Pollution Control Techniques and advanced wastewater treatment. *Hobbies:* Golf; Sailing; Philately. *Address:* 3 Bourmac Avenue, Northbridge, NSW 2063, Australia.

DURIE, David John Bruce, b. 12 Feb. 1954, Kirkcaldy, Fife, Scotland. Science Writer/Broadcaster/Film-maker. *Education:* BSc., Honours Summa Cum Laude, Edinburgh University, 1976. *Appointments:* Research Student, Biochemistry Department, University of Edinburgh, 1976-79; Anaesthetics Specialist, Janssen Pharmaceuticals, 1979-80; Medical Editor, Pulse, 1980-81; Freelance medical writer, broadcaster and film maker 1976-; Director, Scott-Wenn Associates,

1980-; Editor, Arab Medical World, 1981. *Memberships:* Royal Zoological Society of Scotland; British Association of Psycho Pharmacology; National Union of Journalists; Medical Journalists Association; Jaguar Drivers Club. *Publications:* Many articles in the medical press, popular magazines, newspapers; Numerous radio programmes for BBC world service, Capital Radio. *Honours:* First in Class & Summa Cum Laude, 1976; IBRO-UNESCO Scholar, Leipzig, 1977. *Hobbies:* Writing, music and carousing; Restoring antique furniture and jaguar cars; Avoiding deadlines; Herbalism; Genealogy. *Address:* The Lodge, Jigs Lane, Warfield, Berkshire, England.

DURNFORD, Andrew Montague Isaacson Alexander William, b. 21 Aug. 1904, Sarnia, Ontario, Canada. Professor of Physics. m. Mary Isabelle Chestnut, 7 July 1933, 3 sons, 1 daughter. *Education:* BA, 1925, MA, 1926, University of Western Ontario; PhD, University of Toronto, 1931. *Appointments:* Technical Assistant, University of Toronto, 1929-30; Instructor, 1930-34, Assistant Professor, 1934-44, Associate Professor, 1944-66, Professor, 1966-70, Professor Emeritus, 1970-, University of Western Ontario. *Memberships:* Charter Member, Canadian Association of Physicists; American Physical Society. *Publications:* Contributed to various professional journals. *Honours:* Gold Medal for Physics, University of Western Ontario, 1925; Fellow, University of Toronto, 1928-29. *Address:* 283 Steele Street, London, Ontario, Canada.

DUROJAIYE, Harry Titi, b. 11 Feb. 1946 Awe, Oyo State, Nigeria. Insurance; Lawyer. m. 5 May 1972, 1 son, 1 daughter. *Education:* ACII; LLB (Hons); BLAI Arb; MBIM. *Appointments:* Management Trainee, 1967-70; Manager, 1970-72; District Manager, 1972-77; Acting Managing Director, 1977-78; Managing Director, 1978-. *Memberships:* Island Club; Ikoyi Club. *Publications:* Lectures; Symposia; Articles in Legal and Insurance Subjects. *Hobbies:* Reading; Table Tennis; Music; Dancing. *Address:* 40 Norman William Street, SW Ikoyi, Lagos.

DUTHIE, Robert, b. 5 Aug. 1917, Lerwick, Shetland Isles. Librarian. m. Roberta Fotheringhame Irvine, 20 July 1941, 2 sons. *Education:* BA, 1940; Diploma New Zealand Library School (Diploma NZLS), 1946. *Appointments:* War Service (Navy), 1941-45; Reference Librarian S Auckland Public Library, 1947-49; Librarian I/C Lending Services, 1949-51; Assistant Chief Librarian, 1951-52; Acting Chief Librarian, 1952-53; City Librarian, 1953-. Vice-President, New Zealand Library Association, 1972; Rotary Club of Auckland. *Publications:* Articles in Professional Journals. *Honours:* Fellow, New Zealand Library Association (FNZLA), 1966; OBE, 1979. *Hobbies:* Boating; Photography; Gardening; Reading. *Address:* 163 Hinemoa Street, Birkenhead, Auckland, New Zealand.

DUTT-MAJUMDAR, Nirmalendu, b. 29 Dec. 1911, Austagram, India. Barrister. *Education:* Advocates Examination of the High Court, Calcutta, 1941; Barrister-at-Law, Middle Temple, London, UK, 1956. *Appointments:* Director, General Industries Ltd., Calcutta, 1934-36; Managing Editor, Oriental Review, Bombay, 1937-38; Practising in the High Court, Bombay, 1941-44; Managing Director, Modern Farms Ltd., Calcutta, 1946-51; Practising in the High Court, Calcutta, 1951-. *Memberships:* Bar Council of W Bengal: elected three terms, 1962-75, Honorary Secretary, 1962-63; Executive Committee, 1964-72, Chairman, Disciplinary Committee 1972-75); Automobile Association of Eastern India, 1951-73; Life Member, Himalayan Association; Calcutta Bar Library Club; Indian Law Institute. *Publications:* Advocates Act & Professional Ethics; Conduct of Advocates & Legal Profession; Urban Land Ceiling Law. *Honours:* Honorarium of Rs 5000/- awarded by the Bar Council of West Bengal in 1963. *Hobbies:* Mountaineering; Trekking in the Himalayas. *Address:* 101-A Ballygunge Place, Calcutta-700 019, India.

DWYER, Anthony Paul, b. 14 Sept. 1940, Melbourne, Australia. Orthopaedic Surgeon. m. Judith Ann, 1 son, 1 daughter. *Education:* MB BS, Melbourne University Medical School, 1966; FRCS, Royal College of Surgeons, Edinburgh, 1971; FRCS, Royal College of Surgeons, England, 1971; FRACS, Royal Australian College of Surgeons, 1974. *Appointments:* Registrar, Australian Surgical Team, Bien Hoa, South Vietnam, 1969-70; Registrar, Orthopaedic Hospital, Oswestry,

UK, 1972-73; Lecturer, Duchess of Kent, Children's Orthopaedic Hospital, Sandy & Queen Mary's Hospital, University of Hong Kong, 1973-75; Research Fellow, Children's Hospital Medical Center, Harvard Medical School, Boston, USA, 1975-76; Senior Lecturer & Orthopaedic Surgeon, Department of Orthopaedics, University of Western Australia, 1976-81; Associate Professor, Department of Orthopaedics, University of Arkansas for Medical Sciences, 1981-; Chief of Orthopaedics, Veteran's Administration Medical Center, 1981-. *Memberships:* Scoliosis Research Society; International Society for the Study of the Lumbar Spine; Orthopaedic Research Society; Australian Orthopaedic Association; British Orthopaedic Association; Western Pacific Orthopaedic Association; Facet Club. *Publications:* National & International Presentations & Papers on Spinal Deformity, Spinal Degeneration & Spinal Cord Injury; Local & International Publications on Spinal Surgery, including Clinical Basic Research on Spinal Deformity, Degeneration & Injury. *Hobbies:* Family; Music; Films; Tennis; Antique Maps. *Address:* 31 Inverness Circle, Little Rock, Arkansas 72212, USA.

DWYER, Bernard Joseph, b. 25 Apr. 1926, Sydney, NSW, Australia. Public Servant. m. Marie Therese Kerwick, 8 Jan. 1955, 3 sons, 2 daughters. *Education:* BSc, University of Sydney, NSW, Australia. *Appointments:* Commonwealth Treasury, 1942-72, (War Service, 1944-46); Commonwealth Department of Repatriation and Compensation, 1974-75; Commonwealth Commissioner for Employees' Compensation, 1975-. *Memberships:* Canberra: Services Club, Southern Cross Club, Bowling Club; Hellenic Club of Canberra; Phillip Community Club Phillip ACT. *Hobbies:* Reading; Snooker. *Address:* 22 Hampton Circuit, Yarralumla, ACT 2600, Australia.

DWYER, James Gerard, b. 19 Feb. 1931, Perth, Western Australia. Educator; Librarian. m. Shirley May Riley, 3 sons, 1 daughter. *Education:* Teaching Certificate, Sydney, 1949; BA, University of Western Australia, 1959; Diploma, National Library of Australia Training School, 1962; Associate, Library Association of Australia, 1962. *Appointments:* Teacher, 1949-59; Cataloguing librarian, National Library, Canberra, 1960-61; Referemce Officer, Deputy Librarian, Canberra Public Library Service, 1962-64; Superintendant School Libraries, South Australian Education Department, 1964-. *Memberships:* Fellow, Australian College of Education; National President (1981), Library Association of Australia; Australian Advisory Council on Bibliographical Services; South Australian Institute

of Teachers; Knights of the Southern Cross; Sportsmans Association of Australia. *Publications:* Co-operation or Compromise, 1978; Consolidation, Compromise or Conquest, 1978; Co-Author: Changes and Exchanges, 1980; School Librarianship, 1981. *Honours:* Fulbright/Hayes Scholarship, 1971; Librarian-in-Residence, Kuring-gai College of Advanced Education, 1978. *Hobbies:* Classical Music; Wine Collecting; Tennis. *Address:* 9 Muller Road, Manningham 5086, South Australia.

DWYER, John Parkhurst, b. 19 Mar. 1901, Sydney, NSW, Australia. Civil Engineer and Town Planner. m. Emily M Lawson, 13 July 1929, 1 son. *Education:* Sydney Technical College, New South Wales; FIMunE; FIEAust. LFAPI. *Appointments:* Shire Engineer, Baulkham Hills, Shire Council 1927-29; Municipal Engineer, Petersham Municipal Council 1929-45; Chief Technical Officer, Housing Commission NSW 1945-65; Co-ordinating Engineer, NSW Defence Works, 1942-45; Royal Australian Engineers, 1940-42. *Memberships:* Institution of Engineers Australia; Institution of Municipal Engineers; The Royal Australian Planning Institute; Royal Automobile Club, Australia; Manly Civic Club; Manly Bowling Club. *Honours:* G.A. Taylor Memorial Medal 1931; Life Fellow, Royal Australian Planning Institute, 1980. *Hobbies:* Lawn Bowling; Philately; Photography. *Address:* 12 Marlborough Gardens, 140 Addison Road, Manly 2095, NSW, Australia.

DZANG, Chemogoh Kevin, (Rear Admiral), b. 27 July 1941, Nandom, Ghana. Naval/Diplomat. m. Emelia Kpinbo, 12 Feb. 1970, 2 sons, 1 daughter. *Education:* Ghana Military Academy, 1960-61; Britannia Royal Naval College, 1961-64; Graduate, Defence Service Staff College, Wellington, India, 1972; Graduate, Naval War College, Newport, USA, 1974-75; Graduate, Australian National University, Canberra, 1979-81; Graduate Diploma International Law. *Appointments:* 1st Lieutenant GNS AFADZATO, 1964-65, Commanding Officer, 1965-66; Commanding Officer, GNS EJURA, 1967-68; Director, Personnel & Administration, Navy Headquarters, 1968-70; Commanding Officer GNS KETA & Senior Officer Afloat, 1970-71; Chief of Naval Staff & Commander Ghana Navy, 1973-77; Member of Supreme Military Council, 1975-77; Appointed High Commissioner to Australia, 1978. *Memberships:* Accra Lawn Tennis Club; Royal Canberra Golf Club; Life Patron Nandom Youth Development Association. *Honours:* Member of the Star of Ghana MSG, 1979; Ordre National Republique de Guinee, 1976. *Hobbies:* Photography; Tennis; Golf. *Address:* 42 Endeavour Street, Red Hill, ACT, Australia.

E

EADE, John Christopher, b. 27 Oct. 1939. Research Fellow. *Education:* MA., St. Andrews, 1963; MA., Adelaide, 1966; Phd., Australian National University, 1973. *Appointments:* Tutor in English, Australian National University; Research Fellow, Humanities Research Centre, Australian National University. *Memberships:* Secretary/Editor, Australasian & Pacific Society for Eighteenth-Century Studies; Editor, Australian and New Zealand Association for Medieval & Renaissance Studies, 1970-; Executive Secretary, Australian and New Zealand Early Imprints Project. *Publications:* Bibliographical Essay on Studies in Eighteenth-Century European Culture since 1958, Sydney, 1970; Eighteenth-Century Studies in Australia since 1958, Sydney, 1979. *Honours:* J.G. Crawford, Prize, Australian National University, 1973. *Hobbies:* Sailing. *Address:* 49 Foveaux Street, Ainslie, ACT 2602, Australia.

EADIE, Edward Norman, b. 1 Nov. 1935, Melbourne, Australia. Scientist, Economist, Lawyer. *Education:* Geelong College; Trinity College; Melbourne University and Balliol College, Oxford; *Degrees:* B.Sc. Melbourne, 1959; M.Sc. Melbourne, 1971; B.Sc. (Econ.), London, 1972; D.Phil. Oxon, 1974; LL.B., London, 1977. *Appointments:* Geophysicist and Party Leader, Bureau of Mineral Resources, Department of National Development, Melbourne, Australia, 1959-65; Mining Investment Analyst, Davies and Dalziel, Stockbrokers, Melbourne, Australia, 1965-66; Senior Geophysicist and Chief Geophysicist, McPhar Geophysics Pty. Ltd., Adelaide, Australia, 1966-68; Research, Oxford University, 1968-72; Visiting Lecturer, Leicester University, England, 1970-72; Research and Business, Adelaide, Australia, 1973-74; Managing Director, Probex Pty., Ltd., Adelaide, Australia, 1975-. *Memberships:* Australasian Institute of Mining and Metallurgy; Australian Mining and Petroleum Law Association; Fellow, Royal Geographical Society; Fellow, London House; Senior Common Room, St. Mark's College, Adelaide University. *Publications:* Magnetic Survey of the Savage River and Long Plains Iron Deposits, Northwest Tasmania; Mineral Exploration—The role of geology, geophysics and geochemistry in an integrated approach to mineral exploration; Induced Polarization in Mineral Exploration. *Hobbies:* Collecting railway tickets and passes of all countries. *Address:* 46 Pennington Terrace, North Adelaide, South Australia, 5006.

EADIE, Hugh Angus, b. 23 June 1939, Hopetoun, Victoria, Australia. Minister of Religion, Educator, YMCA Executive. m. Wendy Tulloh, 14 Dec. 1965, 1 son, 1 daughter. *Education:* BA., University of Western Australia; Bachelor of Divinity Honours, Melbourne College of Divinity, 1962; Diploma of Education, University of Melbourne, 1963; Doctor of Philosophy, University of Edinburgh, 1970. *Appointments:* Assistant Minister, Prahran Presbyterian Church, Victoria, 1963; Chaplain & Senior History Master, Ballarat College, Victoria, 1964-65; Deputy Director, The Cairnmillar Institute, Melbourne, Victoria, 1966-67; Assistant Chaplain to Overseas Students, Edinburgh University, 1968-70; Director, Human Relations Training, The Cairnmillar Institute, Melbourne, Victoria, 1970-74; Director, YMCA College, Victoria, 1975-79; National Executive Officer, National Council of YMCA's of Australia, 1979-. *Memberships:* Australian College of Education; International Society of Community Educators; Rotary Club of Melbourne South; Huntingdale Golf Club. *Publications:* The Health of Scottish Clergymen, 1972; Stress and the Clergyman, 1973; Making Sense of Sex, 1974; The Helping Personality, 1975; Educating for the Future, 1975; Editor, Juvenile Justice and Youth Advocacy, 1978; The YMCA and Social Issues—The Fire to Come, 1979. *Honours:* Commonwealth Scholarship, 1957; George Hunter Doake Prize (Outstanding Student) and Connibere Prizes in Theology, Old and New Testament studies, Ormond College, Melbourne, 1962; Australia-Japan Foundation Study Award, 1978. *Hobbies:* Gardening; Painting; Conchology; Golf. *Address:* 2 Octavia Court, Burwood, Victoria, 3125, Australia.

EAMES, Robert Henry Alexander, b. 27 Apr. 1937, Belfast. Bishop of The Church of Ireland. m. Ann Christine Daly, 25 June 1966, 2 sons. *Education:* Belfast Royal Academy; Methodist College, Belfast; Queen's University, Belfast; Trinity College, Dublin; Divinity Testimonium (2nd Class), LL.B., (Hons. 1960; PhD., (Ecclesiastical Law and History), 1963. *Appointments:* Curate of Bangor, County Down, 1963-66; Incumbent of Gilnahirk, 1966-74, Dundela, 1974-75; Bishop of Derry and Raphoe, 1975-80; Bishop of Down and Dromore, 1980-. *Memberships:* University and Kildare Street Club, Dublin. *Publications:* Author of: A Form of Worship for Teenage Groups, 1965, The Quiet Revolution—The Disestablishment of the Church of Ireland, 1970, Through Suffering—The Church's response to a suffering community, 1973, Thinking through Lent, 1978; Contributor to: Irish Legal Quarterly, Northern Ireland Legal Quarterly, Criminal Law Review, New Divinity, University Review. *Honours:* Austin Memorial (Jurisprudence), 1958-59; Downes (Orat.), Composition, Sermon; Moncrieff Cox and King Prize; Pastoral Theological Prize; Liturgy Prize; Ecclesiastical History Prize; Research Scholar and Tutor, Queen's University, Belfast, 1960-63. *Address:* The See House, 32 Knockdene Park South, Belfast, BT5 7AB, Ireland.

EAST, Paul Clayton, b. 4 Aug. 1946, Optiki, New Zealand. Barrister and Solicitor; Member of Parliament. m. Marilyn Therese East, 25 Sept. 1972, 2 daughters. *Education:* Auckland University; University of Virginia School of Law. *Appointments:* President, Northern Industrial Legal Employees Union, 1970-71; Assistant to Vice President and General Council of Canada Dry Corporation, New York, 1971; Barrister and Solicitor and Partner, East, Brewster Parker and Company, 1972-; Deputy Mayor and City Councillor, City of Rotorua, 1974-; Member of Parliament, 1978-. *Memberships:* Chairman, Rotorua Airport Committee; Member of Executive of Airport Authorities of New Zealand; Committee Member, Rotorua Conservation Society; Regional Councillor in the Environmental Defence Society; Patron, Paraplegic and Physically Disabled Persons Association. *Publications:* Various legal articles in academic and professional journals. *Hobbies:* Skiing; Fishing. *Address:* 26 Sumner Street, Rotorua, New Zealand.

EASTICK, Bruce Charles, b. 25 Oct. 1927, Reade Park, South Australia. Veterinary Surgeon/Member of Parliament. m. Mary Dawn Marsh, 8 Dec. 1951, 3 sons, 1 daughter. *Education:* R.D.A. (1st Class Honours), Roseworthy Agricultural College, 1943-47; B.V.Sc. (2nd Class Honours, Sydney University, 1947-51. *Appointments:* Self-employed Veterinary Practice, 1951-70; Member of Parliament, 1970-; Leader of Opposition, 1972-75; Speaker, House of Assembly, 1979-. *Memberships:* Australian Veterinary Association, State President, 1961-62, Federal President, 1966-67; Australian College of Veterinary Scientists, President, 1972-73; Commonwealth Parliamentary Association, Vice-President, 1972-75; Rotary Club of Gawler, President, 1960-61; Former Mayor and Councillor of Gawler Corporation. *Publications:* Scientific papers on Veterinary subjects. *Honours:* Charter Fellow, Australian College of Veterinary Scientists, 1971; Fellow, Australian Veterinary Association, 1972; Queen's Silver Jubilee Medal, 1977. *Hobbies:* Lawn Bowls; Gardening; Travel. *Address:* 5 Bright Street, Willaston, South Australia, 5118.

EASTMAN, Creswell John, b. 30 Mar. 1940, Narrandera, N.S.W., Australia. Consultant Physician. m. Annette Mary Delaney, 15 Dec. 1964, 2 sons, 2 daughters. *Education:* M.B., B.S., Sydney, 1964; M.R.A.C.P., 1969; F.R.A.C.P., 1974; M.D., Sydney, 1978. *Appointments:* Resident Medical Officer & Medical Registrar, St. Vincent's Hospital, Sydney, 1965-71; Research Fellow, Middlesex Hospital Medical School, London, 1971-72; Assistant Director, Garvan Institute Medical Research, Sydney, 1973-74; Director Endocrinology, Canberra & Woden Valley Hospitals, Canberra, 1975-79; Director Endocrinology, Westmead Centre, Westmead, 1979-. *Memberships:* Chairman R.A.C.P., ACT Branch, 1978-79; Endocrine Society, Australia, Vice-President, 1978-80, President, 1980-82; Secretary, Treasurer, Asia Oceania Thyroid Association, 1975-80. *Publications:* Many original contributions to Medical and Scientific Journals in the fields of Endocrinology and Internal Medicine. *Honours:* Searle Travel Grant, Endocrinology, 1970; Overseas Travelling Fellow of Royal Australasian College of Physicians, 1971. *Hobbies:* Tennis; Skiing; Reading. *Address:* 64 Greenhaven Drive, Pennant Hills, N.S.W., Australia

EATON, Gordon Campbell, b. 1 June 1920, St. John's, Newfoundland, Canada. Director. m. M. Ruth Fraser, 26 June 1946, 3 sons, 3 daughters. *Education:* St. Bonaventures College, St. John's, Newfoundland, Canada. *Appointments:* Served Royal Artillery, 166th (Newfoundland) Field Regiment R.A., Great Britain, North Africa, Italy, 1940-45; Retired as Captain, Commanding Officer, Newfoundland Field Regiment R.C.A. 1949-52; Building Estimator, Concrete Products (Newfoundland) Ltd., St. John's, 1946-50; Secretary, Newfoundland Fish Trades Association, 1950-51; Director, Fishery Products Ltd., 1951-56; Sales Manager, Newfoundland Tractor & Equipment Co. Ltd., 1956-62; General Manager, 1962-68; Managing Director, 1968-; Director, Royal Bank of Canada; Chairman Seabase Ltd. *Memberships:* Past Chairman, General Hospital Corporation, 1969-7; Canadian Association of Equipment Distributors; St. John's Housing Authority, 1958-68; Newfoundland Division, Canadian Red Cross; Newfoundland Hospital Association; St. John's Hospital Council; Advisory Committee, Arctic Vessel and Marine Research of National Research Council; Vice-President, Associated Equipment Distributors of US; Director, Royal Canadian Corps Commissionaires; St. John's Heritage Foundation; Newfoundland Institute Management Advancement and Training; Canadian Chamber of Commerce; School of Business Advisory Board, Memorial University of Newfoundland; Rotary Club; Bally Haly. *Honours:* Military Cross, 1944; Canadian Decoration; St. John's Citizen of the Year, 1973; Honorary Lieutenant Colonel, Royal Newfoundland Regiment, 1972-76; Honorary Colonel, Royal Newfoundland Regiment, 1976; Officer of the Order of Canada, 1978; Honorary Doctor of Laws, 1978. *Hobbies:* Sports; Fishing. *Address:* 15 Dublin Road, St. John's, Newfoundland, Canada, A1B 2E7.

EBIE, John Chukunyelu, b. 5 May 1936, Agbor, Nigeria. Psychiatrist & University Teacher. m. 16 Apr. 1966, 1 son, 1 daughter. *Education:* University of Ibadan, Ibadan, Nigeria, 1958-64; University of Edinburgh, Scotland, 1966-69; Degrees & Diplomas: M.B., B.S., London, 1964; D.P.M., Edinburgh, 1968; M.Sc., Edinburgh, 1969; M.R.C., Psych., 1972; F.M.C., Psych., F.W.A.C.P. *Appointments:* House Physician & Surgeon, University College Hospital, Ibadan, 1964-65; Senior House Officer & later Registrar in Psychiatry, U.C.H. Ibadan, 1965-66; Clinical Assistant, Royal Edinburgh Hospital, 1966-68; Medical Research Council Unit for Epidermological Studies in Psychiatry, Edinburgh, 1968-69; Senior Registrar in Psychiatry, U.C.H., Ibadan, 1970; Lecturer in Psychiatry, University of Ibadan, 1970-71; Senior Lecturer in Psychiatry, University of Benin, 1972-74; Associate Professor, Professor of Mental Health, University of Benin, 1974-76; Consultant Psychiatrist, 1970-; Head, Department of Mental Health, University of Benin, 1976-80; Dean, School of Medicine, University of Benin, 1979-; Commissioner for Health, Bendel State, Nigeria, 1972-74; *Memberships:* Chairman, Management Board for Psychiatric Hospitals, 1977-; Rotary Club of Benin. *Publications:* Many publications in scientific & professional journals on mental health topics. *Honours:* Rockefeller Foundation Fellowship, 1966-69; Provisional Council, University of Calabar, 1976-80; Chairman, Ika Development Council, 1975; Editor-in-Chief, African Journal of Psychiatry. *Hobbies:* Reading; Hockey. *Address:* House B.20, University of Benin, Teaching Hospital, Benin City, Nigeria.

EBOKA, Michael Chukwunwike, b. 29 Sept. 1939, Forcados, Nigeria. Librarian. m. Caroline Nnabuife, 13 July 1965, 1 son, 3 daughters. *Education:* BA., (Hons.), University College, Dublin, Ireland, 1964; Diploma in Library Training, School of Librarianship, University College, Dublin, 1965; A.C.A., School of Librarianship, Liverpool Polytechnic, 1966. *Appointments:* Librarian, Ministry of Education, Benin City, Nigeria, 1967-69; Assistant Librarian, later sub-librarian, University of Ibadan, Ibadan, 1969-72; Senior Librarian, later Principal Librarian, Bendel State Library, Benin City, 1972-78; Senior Librarian, later Deputy University Librarian, Ahmadu Bello University, Samaru, Zaria, Nigeria, 1978-. *Memberships:* Library Association of the UK; Nigerian Library Association; Historical Association of Nigeria. *Publications:* Management of a University Library; Librarianship in developing countries—a collection of Essays (in publication); Bibliography of African Costumes (in publication). *Hobbies:* Cine-photography; Classical Music; Video-Photography. *Address:* No.

4. Nkwekagbor Street, Umuonaje, Asaba, Bendel State, Nigeria.

EBOO, (Sir) Pirbhai, b. 25 July 1905, Bombay, India. Representative of HH The Aga Khan; Director of Companies. m. Kulsumbhai Eboo, 1925, 2 sons, 3 daughters. *Appointments:* President, Aga Khan Supreme Council for Europe, Canada, USA and Africa; Member, Nairobi City Council, 1938-43; Kenya Legislative Council, 1952-60; Past President, Central Muslim Association; Member, various other official bodies. *Memberships:* Royal Commonwealth Society. *Honours:* OBE, 1946; Knight, 1952; Count, 1954; Order Brilliant Star of Zanibar; Order Crescent Cross Comores. *Hobbies:* Social Work; Travel. *Address:* PO Box 40898, Nairobi, Kenya.

EDEMA, Agbajegorite Adebanjo Omolade, b, 13 Apr. 1948. Vegetable Breeder and Geneticist. m. Nancy Adedoja Adepeju Grillo, 17 May, 1981. *Education:* BSc., 1976, M.Phil., 1981, University of Ife, Ile-Ife, Nigeria. *Appointments:* Nigeria Agricultural Officer, Ministry of Agriculture and Natural Resources, Abakaliki, Nigeria, 1976-77; Genetic Resources Officer, 1977-, Research Officer II, 1977-79, Research Officer I, 1979-, National Horticultural Research Institute, Ibadan, Nigeria. *Memberships:* International Society of Horticultural Science; Association for Advancement of Agricultural Science in Africa; Science Association of Nigeria; Horticultural Society of Nigeria; Genetic Society of Nigeria; Secretary-General, Social Justice Movement of Nigeria. *Publications:* Breeding for resistance to root knot nematodes in tomato, 1976; Natural variability in horticultural crops in Nigeria, 1978; Genetic variability studies in Amaranthus species (unpublished), 1981; Genetic variability of seedling emergence and its correlation with other traits of Amaranthus species, 1981. *Hobbies:* Gardening; Photography; Woodwork. *Address:* NH18, Nihort Quarters, Eleiyele, Ibadan, Nigeria.

EDGERTON, Richard Ernest Malcolm, b. 11 Aug. 1950, Cornwall, Ontario, Canada. Land Surveyor. m. 30 July 1978. *Education:* Diploma in Forestry, Sir Sandford Fleming College, 1972; Bachelor of Technology, Geodetic Sciences, Byerson Polytechnical Institute, 1976. *Appointments:* L.P. Stidwill & Associates; Energy Mines & Resources, Geodetic Survey, Government of Canada; Energy Mines & Resources, Legal Surveys, Government of Canada. *Memberships:* Association of Ontario Land Surveyors; Canadian Institute of Surveying; Bermuda Surveyors Association. *Hobbies:* Skiing; Golf; Scuba Diving; Sailing. *Address:* 326 Third Street East, Cornwall, Ontario, Canada.

EDINBOROUGH, Arnold, b. 2 Aug. 1922, Donington, England. Journalist; Consultant. m. Letitia Mary Woolley, 14 Jan. 1946, 1 son, 2 daughters. *Education:* St. Catharine's College, Cambridge, 1940-42, 1945-47; BA(Hons) English 1947; MA, 1949. *Appointments:* Assistant Professor of English, Queen's University, Kingston, Ontario, 1949-54; Editor, Kingston Whig-Standard, 1954-58; Editor, Saturday Night magazine, 1958-62, Publisher, 1962-70; President, Edina Productions Ltd., 1970; President & CEO, Council for Business and the Arts in Canada, 1974-. *Memberships:* President, Marlowe Society, Cambridge, 1946-47; President, Magazine Advertising Bureau, 1964; Albany Club; Arts & Letters Club; Stonecrop Trout Club. *Publications:* One Church, Two Nations, 1967; Some Camel, Some Needle, 1974; The Enduring Word, 1979; The Festivals of Canada, 1980. *Honours:* LLD, University of Guelph, 1968; Honorary Fellow, St. John's College, Winnipeg, 1976; Litt S.D, Wycliffe College, University of Toronto, 1980. *Hobbies:* Fishing; Reading. *Address:* 10 Ancroft Place, Toronto, Canada.

EDJE, Oghenetsaubuko Todo, b.4 Dec. 1940, Aladja, Warri, Nigeria. Professor; Vice-Principal. m. Louise Jordan, 1 son, 3 daughters. *Education:* Diploma, Agriculture, Nigeria, 1959; BS, MS, Michigan State University, USA, 1965, 66; PhD, Iowa State University, USA, 1970; Post-doctoral, Physiology, 1970. *Appointments:* Agricultural Superintendent, 1959-61; Lecturer, Crop Physiology, Bunda College, 1970-73, Senior Lecturer, 1973-78; Professor & Vice-Principal, Bunda College of Agriculture, 1978-. *Memberships:* Chairman, Association for the Advancement of Science of Malawi; National Research Council of Malawi; American Society of Agronomy; Crop Science Society of America;

Alpha Zeta; Sigma Xi. *Publications:* Several publications in International & National Journals. *Hobbies:* Football; Photography. *Address:* Bunda College of Agriculture, PO Box 219, Lilongwe, Malawi.

EDMOND, Robert, b. 20 Mar. 1927, Blair Drummond, Perthshire, Scotland. Medical Practitioner. m. Jean Radcliffe Dorsett, 6 Apr. 1979, 1 daughter, 1 stepdaughter. *Education:* Edinburgh University, 1945-50; MB, ChB, Edinburgh, 1950; DObst. RCOG, London, 1956; FRACGP, Sydney, 1977; RACOG, Melbourne, 1980. *Appointments:* House Surgeon, Bangour General Hospital, Broxburn, W Lothian, 1950-51; General Practice, Coxhoe, County Durham, 1951-57; Obstetric House Surgeon, Cresswell Maternity Hospital, Dumfries, 1955; Medical Officer-in-Charge, Segama Estate Hospital, Lahad Datu, North Borneo, 1957-62; SHO in Gynaecology, Dumfries & Galloway Royal Infirmary, Dumfries, 1962; Private Practice, Workington, Cumberland, 1962-64; Registrar in Anaesthetics, Dumfries & Galloway Royal Infirmary, 1964; Chief Medical Officer, Oil Industry Medical Society, Tripoli, 1964-72; Private Practice, Port Augusta, South Australia, 1972-74; General Superintendent, Launceston General Hospital, Tasmania, 1974-77; Private Practice, Launceston, Tasmania, 1977-. *Memberships:* Fellow, Royal Medical Society, 1949-; Australian Medical Association: Tasmanian Branch Council, 1978-; Chairman, Northern Tasmanian Division, 1979; President-elect, Tasmanian Branch, 1980; Chairman, Tasmanian Health Services Review Committee, 1979-; Board of Management, Launceston General Hospital, 1978-; Board, Tasmanian Faculty, RACGP, 1979-; President, Northern Tasmanian Medico-Legal Society, 1979; Associate Royal Society of Medicine, 1980. *Hobbies:* Music; Books; Photography; Gardening; Fishing; Motoring. *Address:* 52 Reatta Road, Launceston, Tasmania 7250, Australia.

EDMONDS, Harry Morton, b. 14 Apr. 1891, Merthyr Tydfil, Wales. Marine Engineer (retired); Author. m. 11 Nov. 1923, (wife dec. 1966), 2 sons, 1 daughter (dec.). *Education:* Merthyr County Grammar School, 1903-05; Alleyn's School, Dulwich, 1905-6; *Appointments:* Apprenticed to Sea in Barque 'Dunearn' and Schooner-rigged ship 'Port Kingston', 1906-08; Marine Engineer, Thornycroft's Yard, Chiswick, 1908-11; Manager, Machine Tool Exhibition, Australia & New Zealand, Selson Engineering Company, 1912-14; Professional soldier, 1914 rising to the rank of (acting) lieut-Colonel, 1918; Liaison Officer with Dr. Hugo Eckener & German Zeppelin Transport Company, 1936-38. *Memberships:* Life Member (Flying) The Kent Gliding Club; The East India Club, St. James Square, London. ; Founder, Vice-President for Life, The Wagner Society; Secretary, London Committee of Australian Red Cross, 1939-41; Founder, Secretary, Constitutional Research Association, 1941-55. *Publications:* Author of 15 Novels including: The North Sea Mystery, 1930; The Riddle of the Straits, 1931; Red Invader, 1933; Across the Frontiers, 1936; The Secret Voyage, 1946; The Clockmaker of Heidelburg, 1949; The Rockets, 1941; The Orphans of Brandenburg, 1953; Essay: A British Five Year Plan, 1932. Poetry, Homage to Southey, 1943. *Honours:* Diploma as Companion of Western Europe; MIBA, 1980; Received congratulatory letters from many famous men. *Hobbies:* Flying; Classical Music; Rugby Football; Sailing. *Address:* 1 Brockhill Road, Hythe, Kent, England.

EDODO, Oritsegbiten Popo, b. 8 June 1925, Sapele, Bendel State, Nigeria. Law. m. Diana Eyewumi Eyide, 20 Dec. 1951, 4 sons, 5 daughters. *Education:* St. Gregory's College, Lagos, 1942-46; Holborn College London, 1959-62; Lincoln's Inn, London, 1959-62; LLB BL. *Appointments:* Private Legal Practice; Appointed Commissioner in Bendel State's Executive Council, 1967, and held various Ministries (Local Government & Chieftaincy, Trade & Industry, Finance Works, etc), 1967-75. *Appointments:* Various. *Hobbies:* Swimming; Driving. *Address:* 1 Bungalow Road, Gra Warri, Bendel State, Nigeria.

EDOZIEN, John Dikenwiwe, b. 20 Apr. 1943, Enugu, Nigeria. Civil Servant. m. Victoria Amah Asumah, 24 Jan. 1976, 3 daughters. *Education:* BSc(Hons) Econs. University of Ibadan, 1964-67; MA (Econs.) University of Wisconsin, USA, 1970-72; Fellowship, Economic Development Institute, 1975; Fellowship, IMEDE, Lansanne, Switzerland, 1981. *Appointments:* National Planning Office of the Federal Ministry of National Planning: Planning Officer, 1967-72; Senior Planning Officer, 1972-74; Prinicipal Planning Officer, 1974-75; Chief Planning Officer, 1975-76; Assistant Director, 1976-80; Director of Planning (Social Service Department), 1980-. *Memberships:* Nigerian Economic Society; West African Economic Society; Lagos Lawn Tennis Club; Falcon Club of Asaba; Sigma Club, University of Ibadan; Public Sector Participation in Economic Activities; Social Services Sector; Management and Optimum Utilization of Resources; and various other papers. *Hobbies:* Lawn Tennis; Reading. *Address:* 5 Adeyemi Lawson Road, Ikoyi, Lagos, Nigeria.

EDWARDS, John Coates, b. 25 Nov. 1934, Tunbridge Wells, Kent, England. Government Service. m. 25 June 1959, 1 son, 1 daughter. *Education:* MA(Hons), History, Brasenose College, Oxford, 1955-58. *Appointments:* Lieutenant, Royal Artillery, 1953-55; Assistant Principal, Ministry of Supply, 1958; Assistant Principal, Colonial Office, 1960; Private Secretary to the Parliamentary Under Secretary of State for the Colonies, 1961-62; Principal, The Nature Conservancy, 1962-65; Principal, Ministry of Overseas Development, 1965-68; First Secretary, Development, British Embassy, Bangkok, Thailand, 1968-71; Assistant Secretary, Ministry of Overseas Development, 1971; Head of E Africa Development Division, Nairobi, Kenya, 1972-76; Assistant Secretary, Ministry of Overseas Development, 1976-78; Head of British Development Division in the Caribbean, Barbados, 1978-81; Head of West Indian and Atlantic Department, Foreign and Commonwealth Office, 1981. *Memberships:* Bridgetown Club, Barbados; Royal Commonwealth Society. *Address:* Fairways, Ightham, Sevenoaks, Kent, England.

EDWARDS, Keith William, b. 16 Sept. 1908, York, Western Australia. Business Manager (retired); Farmer; Director. m. 21 Sept. 1936, 2 sons, 1 daughter. *Education:* Primary Education, Western Australian State Schools. *Appointments:* Chief Executive, Westralian Farmers Cooperative Limited, 1958-73; Director of Public and other Companies; Member of Government Consultative Bodies. *Appointments:* Associate, Australian Society of Accountants; Chartered Institute of Shipbrokers, London. *Honours:* Companion St Michael & St George, 1979; Companion Order of the British Empire. *Hobbies:* Golf; Fishing; Reading. *Address:* 191 Wellington Street, Mosman Park, Western Australia 6012.

EDWARDS, Meredith Ann (Mrs), b. 10 May 1941, Sydney, Australia. Senior Lecturer in Economics—Economist. m. Clive Thomas Edwards, 19 Jan. 1963, 1 son, 1 daughter. *Education:* University of Melbourne, 1958-62; Bachelor of Commerce (Hons 1st Class), 1963. *Appointments:* Assistant Lecturer, University of Malaya, 1963-64; Senior Tutor (Economics), Australian National University, 1964-68; Lecturer in Economics, Canberra College of Advanced Education, 1972-79; Part-time Economic Consultant, Social Welfare Commission, 1974; Senior Lecturer in Economics, CCAE, 1980-. *Memberships:* Institute of Fiscal Studies; Australian Institute of Political Science; Women's Electoral Lobby. *Publications:* Report to the Australian National Women's Advisory Council on 'Financial Arrangements within Families'. *Honours:* Francis J Wright Exhibition in Economics, 1960; Chamber of Commerce Exhibition in Statistical Method, 1960; Katherine Woodruff Memorial Exhibition in Economic History, 1961; Scholarship in Political Economy, 1961. *Hobbies:* Jogging; Swimming; Bushwalking; Reading. *Address:* 1 Lomandra Street, O'Connor Act 2601, Australia.

EDWARDS, Nigel Rousseau, b. 11 May 1952, Rinteln, Germany. Journalist, Freelance Broadcaster. *Education:* BA, 1973, MA, 1977, Oxford University. *Appointments:* Assistant Master, Lime House School, Dalston, Cumbria, 1973-74; Head of English, Slindon College, Sussex, 1975; Director of Music, Hillstone School, Malvern, Worcestershire, 1976-80; Editorial Staff, Malvern Gazette, Ledbury Reporter, Worcester Evening News, 1980. *Memberships:* Conductor, Malvern Male Voice Choir; Aldwyn Consort of Voices; Board of 'management, Malvern Museum Society Limited; International Biographical Association; Institute of Journalists; Incorporated Society of Musicians; Music Masters' Association; Langland Consort of Recorders. *Publications:* On the music scene, weekly personal column; Reports on music festivals; a number of choral compositions and arrangements; LP Recording, Music from Malvern College Chapel, 1980. *Honours:* Centenary Scholarship, Brighton College, 1965; Richard Taylor Exhibition, Keble College, Oxford, 1970; Hungarian Radio and Television Kodaly Trophy w. Aldwyn Consort of Voices, 1980. *Hobbies:* Music; Singing; Organ; Piano; Recorders; Photography; Genealogy; Local History; Hymnology; Theology; Home Computing. *Address:* Flat 2 St. Helier's, 42 Abbey Road, Malvern, Worcestershire, England.

EDWARDS, Vivian Edward, b. 28 Feb. 1938, Brisbane, Australia. Neurophysician. m. Jennifer Jane Horton Tait, 27 Apr. 1962, 2 sons, 3 daughters. *Education:* Queensland University, MBBS, 1961, MRACP, 1968, FRACP, 1971. *Appointments:* Resident Medical Officer, 1962-64, Medical Registrar, 1965-66, Neurology Registrar, 1968, Visiting Consultant Neurologist, 1969-, Royal Brisbane Hospital; Teaching Medical Registrar, University of Queensland, 1967; Visiting Consultant Neurologist, Prince Charles Hospital, 1973; Visiting Consultant Physician, Gladstone Hospital, 1969-70; Honorary Medical Officer, Royal National Association, Queensland, 1970-. *Memberships:* Fellow, Royal Australian College of Physicians; Australian Association of Neurologists; Australian Medical Association; Chairman of Department of Neurology and Neurosurgery, Chairman, Neurology Unit, Royal Brisbane Hospital; President of Queensland Branch of Australian Pony Stud Book Society; Tattersalls' Club; Queensland Turf Club. *Publications:* Contributed to various professional journals. *Hobbies:* Breeder of Shetland and Australian Stud Ponies. *Address:* Moongalba, Two Tree Hill Road, Tallegalla, Queensland, Australia.

EDWARDS, William Philip Neville, b. 5 Aug. 1904, Littlehampton, Sussex, England. Industrialialist. m. (1) Sheila Cary, 2 sons, (2) Joan Mullins, 22 Dec. 1976. *Education:* BA, 1927, MA, 1932, Corpus Christi College, Cambridge; Princeton University, USA, Davison Scholar, 1925-26. *Appointments:* Underground Electric Group of Companies, 1927-33; London Transport, 1933-41; Ministry of Supply, Ministry of Production, Board of Trade, 1941-46; Head of British Information Services in USA, 1946-49; Director, Confederation of British Industry, 1949-66; Managing Director, 1959-66, Chairman, 1966-68, British Overseas Fairs Limited. *Memberships:* Carlton Club; The Pilgrims of Great Britain and USA; Walton Heath & West Sussex Golf Clubs. *Honours:* CBE, 1949; Chevalier (1st class) order of Dannebrog (Denmark), 1955; Commander of Order of Vasa (Sweden), 1962. *Hobbies:* Golf; Gardening. *Address:* Four Winds, Kithurst Lane, Storrington, Sussex, England.

EFEIZOMOR, Emmanuel Onyeike, b. 10 Mar. 1938, Owa-Bendel State, Nigeria. Traditional Ruler. m. Grace Ebomah, May 1962, 2 sons, 1 daughter. *Appointments:* Ibadan University, 1960; University of Sussex, England, 1972; University of Pittsburgh, USA, 1975. *Appointments:* Western House Of Chiefs, 1962-64; Chairman, IKA Divisional Education Board, 1972-75; Chairman, Bendel State Advisory Council on Education; Federal Government, 1977-79; Director, Nigerian Cocoa Board, 1977-80. *Honours:* Justice of Peace, 1967. *Hobbies:* Reading; Table Tennis. *Address:* The Royal Palace, Owa-Oyibu, Lowa Ika Local Government, Area-Bendel State, Nigeria.

EFI, The Hon. Taisi Tupuola Tufuga, b. 1938. Western Samoa. Politician. *Education:* Victoria University, Wellington, New Zealand. *Appointments:* Elected to Western Samoan Parliament, 1965; Minister of Works, Civil Aviation, Marine and Transport, 1970-73; Prime Minister, March 1976-; Minister of Foreign Affairs, Local and District Affairs and Police. *Address:* c/o Office of the Prime Minister, Apia, Western Samoa.

EGBE, Ogar Steve, b. 22 Apr. 1943, Cross River State, Nigeria. Medical Records and Statistics. m. Susana J Ibanga, 30 Sept. 1978, 3 sons, 1 daughter. *Education:* Diploma in Medical Records, 1972. *Appointments:* Medical Records Officer, 1974; Higher Medical Records Officer, 1976; Senior Medical Records Officer, 1978; Principal Medical Records Officer, 1980. *Memberships:* AMORC; Aetherius Society. *Publications:* Medical Records As a Profession; Lost Legion of the Health Service; Towards a Better Health Service in Cross River State; Statistics in the Management of Health Care Resources; Role of Medical Statistics in Tuberculosis Control; Hospital Bed Utilization Review in Cross River State of Nigeria. *Address:* 19B Chamley Street, Calabar, Cross River State, Nigeria.

EGBE, Patrick Chuks, b. 17 Mar. 1946, Onicha-Ugbo, Nigeria. Psychopharmacologist/Pharmacist. m. Kikelomo Yesufu, 17 July 1974, 2 sons, 1 daughter. *Education:* B.Pharm., Hons., IFE., 1971; U.W.I., Kingston, Jamaica, M.Sc., Neuropharmacology, 1975, PhD., Psychopharmacology, 1978. *Appointments:* Hospital Pharmacist, 1971-72; Research Assistant, 1975-78; Research Fellow, 1978-79; Lecturer, Grade I 1979-. *Memberships:* Pharmaceutical Society of Nigeria and Jamaica; Science Association of Nigeria; Nigerian Neurological Society. *Honours:* Commonwealth Post-Graduate Scholar, 1973-78; Sir Frank Worrell Memorial Scholar, 1978-79. *Hobbies:* Cricket; Listening to Music; Darts and Reading. *Address:* Adebayo's House, No. 220 Fajuyi Road, Ile-Ife, Nigeria.

EGBE, Webber George, b. 23 May 1923, Warri, Bendel State of Nigeria. Barrister-at-Law. m. Gladys Kalappa, 1949, 5 sons, 6 daughters. *Education:* King's College Lagos, Nigeria, 1936-42; Inter LLB (London), Port Harcourt; LLB (London), University College Hall, 1948-51; Called to the Bar, Middle Temple, 1952. *Appointments:* Enrolled in the Supreme Court of Nigeria, 1953; Junior, Law Firm of Thomas, Williams, Kayode, 1953; Legal Practice, Warri, 1953; Commissioner of Justice, 1962; Attorney General & Minister of Justice, Western Region Nigeria until 1963; Queen's Counsel of Nigeria, 1963; First Attorney General & Minister of Justice of the New Region, Bendel State, 1964-66; Private Legal Practice, Warri, 1966-. *Memberships:* American Society of International Law; International Bar Association; Life Member, Nigerian Body of Benchers, Nigerian Bar. *Hobbies:* Swimming; Hunting. *Address:* 12 Dore Street, PO Box 39, Warri Bandel State of Nigeria.

EGEGBARA, Aloysius Onwuegbuchulam, b. 31 Aug. 1944, Owerri, Nigeria. Architect. m. Daisy Ebere Okoroma, 3 Nov. 1979, 1 son. *Education:* Ahmadu Bello University, Zaria, Nigeria, 1964-66, Bachelor of Architecture, 1971-72; Certificate in Project Management for Practising Architects, York University, York, UK., 1974. *Appointments:* Architect, James Cubitt Pellow Aitkinson & Ptrs., 1971; Architect, Adedokun Adeyemi Associates, Lagos, 1972-74; Principal Partner, Designfold Consultants, Architects, Lagos, 1975-. *Memberships:* Nigerian Institute of Architects. *Publications:* Federal Government Girls College, Anambra, Nigeria; Master Plan Customs & Excise Headquarters, Olodi, Apapa, Lagos; Marian Hotel, Calabar. *Hobbies:* Cricket; Painting; Music. *Address:* B1 Terrace House, Alhaji Masha Street, Surulere, Lagos, Nigeria.

EGGAR, Timothy John Crommelin, b. 19 Dec. 1951, Burton, Staffs., UK. Member of Parliament & Merchant Banker. m. 2 Sept. 1977, 1 daughter. *Education:* Winchester College; BA., MA., Magdalene College, Cambridge, 1973. *Appointments:* Hambros Bank, 1974-75; European Banking Company Ltd., 1975-. *Publications:* British Gas—A Prospectus, 1980. *Hobbies:* Skiing; Simple Gardening; Village Cricket. *Address:* House of Commons, London SW1A OAA, England.

EGGLESTON, Richard Moulton, b. 8 Aug. 1909, Hampton, Victoria, Australia. Consultant in Law & Chancellor, Monash University. m. Isabel Marjorie Thom, 10 Jan. 1934, 1 son, 3 daughters. *Education:* Wesley College, Melbourne; LL.B., Queen's College, Melbourne University, 1930. *Appointments:* Barrister, 1932-41 & 1945-60; Staff of Defence Department, 1942-45; Independent Lecturer in Equity, Melbourne University, 1940-49; K.C., 1950; Honorary Treasurer Victoria Bar Council, 1953-56, Chairman, 1956-58; Board of Australian Elizabethan Theatre Trust, 1961-67; Fellow Queen's College Melbourne University, 1964-; Chairman Company Law Advisory Committee, 1967-73; President, Trade Practices Tribunal, 1966-74; Judge Commonwealth Industrial Court & Supreme Court, Australian Capital Territory, 1960-74; Supreme Court Norfolk Island, 1960-69; Director, Barclays Australia, 1974-80; Honorary Fellow, Institute of Arbitrators, Australia, 1977-; Fellow, Academy of Social Sciences in Australia, 1981. *Memberships:* Australian Club, Melbourne; Commonwealth Club, Canberra; Metropolitan Golf Club, Melbourne; Royal Automobile Club of Victoria. *Publications:* Industrial Relations, (2nd edition), 1961; Relevance and Admissibility, 1970; The

Assessment of Credibility, 1972; Subjective Probability and the Law, 1979; Evidence, Proof and Probability, 1978; Constitutional Seminar (with Edward St. John, Q.C. and others), 1977. *Honours:* Knight Bachelor, 1971; Hon. LL.D. Melbourne University, 1973. *Hobbies:* Painting; Golf; Billiards. *Address:* 3 Willow Street, Malvern, Victoria 3144, Australia.

EGIRI, Ogbu Peter, b. 4 Dec. 1940, Uga Adoka, Benue, Nigeria. Medical Records. m. Fatu, 29 May 1961, 5 sons, 3 daughters. *Education:* Medical Records Science Certificate, 1976; Seminar Workshop in Medical Records Science, 1979. *Appointments:* Church Leader; Local Teacher; Railway Worker; Medical Records Personnel. *Memberships:* Auditor, Treasurer, Secretary, Chairman, Adoka District Union; Secretary Medical & Health Department, Worker's Union of Nigeria; Chairman, Northern Idoma Divisional Union; President, Idoma Catholic Youth Association. *Publications:* Local publications on Medical & Health Records on Statistical Data, 1976, 77, 78, 79, 80; Development of Medical & Health Records in Benue State Health Establishments, 1976-81. *Honours:* Membership Certificate, Nigerian Health Records Association, 1980. *Hobbies:* Social Activities; State Affairs; World Affairs; Farming. *Address:* Uga Adoka, LGEA School, Via Otukpo, Benue State of Nigeria.

EGOLE, Eze, Cosmas Chukwumaeze, b. 29 Oct. 1929, Umuhu-Okabia, Nigeria. Commissioner for Finance, Imo State, Nigeria. *Education:* NRN., Nursing School, Ibadan, Nigeria; SRN., Whittington Hospital, London and General Hospital, Kingston-upon-Thames, UK; External student, Law, London University, UK; Bar examinations, Council of Legal Education, London, UK; Called to the Bar, Lincoln's Inn, UK, 1964. *Appointments:* Nigeria Police Force, 1949-53; Private business, CFOA and UAC., Yaba and Obalende, Lagos, Nigeria; Shell Co., Owerri, Nigeria; Practised Law until appointment; Solicitor, Co-operative Bank of Eastern Nigeria Limited, Nkwerre; Former Licensed Buying Agent; Commissioner for Finance, Imo State, Nigeria, 1979-. *Memberships:* Divisional School Management Board, Mgbidi, Nigeria; Orlu LGA Member Divisional Council, Orlu, Nigeria. *Hobbies:* Walking; Reading. *Address:* Ministry of Finance, Owerri, Imo State, Nigeria.

EGONU, Uzo, b. 25 Dec. 1931, Onitsha, Nigeria. Painter, Graphic Artist & Designer. m. Hiltrud Streicher, 20 Aug. 1971. *Education:* Diploma in Fine Art, Camberwell School of Arts & Crafts, London, 1949-52. *Memberships:* Fellow, The Royal Society of Arts, Great Britain; Printmakers Council, Great Britain. *Creative Works:* One man and mixed exhibitions of paintings, graphics, gouaches and drawings in various parts of England, Scotland, Ireland, Lagos, Nigeria, Nairobi, Kenya, Dakar, Senegal, Berlin, Cologne, Düsseldorf West Germany, Leipzig, East Germany, Brussels Belgium, Naples Italy, Holstebro Denmark, Michigan and Berkeley, California, USA., Nimes and Rheims, France. Exhibited in major International Graphic and drawing biennales. *Honours:* First Prize (oil painting), BBC Morning Show, 1970; Bronze Medal (graphics), Les Arts en Europe, 1971; Cup of the City of Caserta (oil painting), International Art Exhibition, Naples, Italy, 1972; Second Prize (oil painting), International Art competition, Los Angeles, 1972; UNESCO Prize (poster), Paris, France, 1976; Honorarium, International Association of Art, Paris, 1976; Purchase Prize (Screenprint) 13th International Biennial of Graphic Art, Ljubljana, Yugoslavia, 1979; Honorable Mention (Screenprints), Third World Biennale of Graphic Art, London & Baghdad, 1980. *Hobbies:* Reading. *Address:* 32 Coniston Gardens, South Kenton, Wembley, Middlesex, HA9 8SD, England.

EGUZORO, Luke Ngozi, b. 24 Sept. 1947, Abu Amumara, Mbaise, Imo State, Nigeria. Civil Servant. m. Rosemary Eguzoro, 19 Nov. 1970, 1 son, 1 daughter. *Education:* Stages I, II & III in Typing, Shorthand & Commerce, Pitmans Examination, London, Udumeze Institute of Commerce Aba; Certificate in Personnel Management, ICS, London. *Appointments:* Tutor, Modern Commercial Bureau for two years; Presently, Accountant, Manila Construction Company Limited. *Memberships:* Secretary, Ekwueme Social Club of Nigeria; Amumara Peoples Club; Secretary, Udo-Umara Social Club of Amumara; Mbaise United Social Club of Nigeria. *Hobbies:* Singing (Choirmaster); Travelling;

Wrestling. *Address:* Abu Amumara, Amamara Ezinihitte PA, Via Aba, Nigeria.

EHANIRE, John Agbonkonkon, b. 2 Apr. 1933, Benin City, Bendel State, Nigeria. Medical Practitioner. m. Jill Patricia Botham, 27 Aug. 1966, 3 sons. *Education:* Cambridge School Certificate Grade I, Edo College, Benin City, 1947-51; MB, BS, (London), University College, Ibadan, 1952-60; DTPH (London), London School of Hygiene & Tropical Medicine, 1975-76. *Appointments:* House Surgeon, Adeoyo Hospital, Ibadan, 1961; House Physician, 1961-62, House Surgeon, 1962, Royal South Hants Hospital; Senior House Officer, Radcliffe Infirmary, Oxford, 1963; SHO/Registrar in Surgery, several Hospitals in UK, 1963-70; General Practitioner, Stratford/Plaistow, London, 1970-72; Head of GOPD, University of Benin Teaching Hospital, 1973-, Chief Medical Officer, since 1979-. *Memberships:* British Medical Association, 1961-72; Nigerian Medical Association, 1972-; Fellow, Nigerian College of General Practitioners, 1981-; Benin Club, 1976-; Oak Club of Benin, 1980-. *Hobbies:* Lawn Tennis; Squash; Gardening. *Address:* B13 UBTH Staff Quarter, PMB IIII, Benin City, Nigeria.

EIDLITZ, Frank, b. 5 June 1933, Budapest, Hungary. Designer; Artist; Consultant. *Education:* Diploma of Royal Academy of Art, Budapest, 1955; First Artist to recieve the Winston Churchill Fellowship, 1967; Studied with Professor G Kepes, Massachusetts Institute of Technology, Boston, USA. *Appointments:* Art Director, Atlas Publications, 1955-57, USP-Benson Oil, 1957-66; Own Design Office, Melbourne, 1968-72; Design Studio, Sydney, 1970-; Design Consultant Women's Day Magazine, 1969. *Memberships:* Fellow, Industrial Design Institute of Australia; Fellow, ACIAA; Art Director's Club, Australia; Fellow, Winston Churchill Trust. *Publications:* Articles in various International Newspapers & Magazines. *Creative Works:* Exhibited in Galleries in Melbourne, Sydney, New York, Czechoslavakia, Poland, Berlin, Hungary, West Germany. *Address:* 27 Carr Street, Waverton, New South Wales 2060, Australia.

EINFELD, Marcus Richard, b. 22 Sept. 1938, Sydney, Australia. Queen's Counsel. m. Divorced, 1 son, 1 daughter. *Education:* BA; LLD. *Appointments:* Barrister 1962-72; Director African and Asian Affairs World Jewish Congress, 1972-75; Official Representative UNESCO, UNO, United Nations High Commission for Human Rights, 1972-75; Director, Marks-Spencer Limited, London, 1975-76; Queen's Counsel, 1977-. *Memberships:* New Bar Association; Council for Civic Liberties; University Club. *Hobbies:* Music; Sport; Farming. *Address:* 17/40 Penkiuk Street, Bondi, NSW 2026, Australia.

EINFELD, Sydney David, (The Honourable, b. 17 June 1909, Sydney, NSW, Australia. Politician. m. Billie Appelboom, 2 June 1934, 1 son, 1 daughter. *Education:* Bourke Street Public School, Paddington Public School; Fort Street Boys High School. *Appointments:* Chairman, 24 Welfare Co-operative Building Societies 1956-76; Chairman, Australian Council for Overseas Aid 1965-71; Deputy Chairman, Australian National Committee World Refugees Year, Geneva, 1960; National Vice President, Australian Committee for International Refugee Campaign, 1963; Vice President, International Council of Voluntary Agencies, 1968-71; President, Executive Council of Australian Jewry, 1953-66; Parliamentary Career: President, Bondi Branch, ALP 11 years; President, Phillip State Electoral Council, 14 years, Wentworth Federal Council, 9 years; Various Ministeries until 1976; Deputy Leader Opposition Leg. Assn., 1968-73; Shadow Minister, Consumer Affairs; Minister for Consumer Affairs and Minister for Co-Op. Societies since 1976; Minister for Housing since 1978; Deputy President, ECAJ, 1967-68; President, Federal Australian Jewish Welfare and Relief Societies; President, Australia Committee for O.R.T. *Memberships:* Dover Heights Bowling; City Tattersall's; Randwick Labor; Sydney Cricket Ground; Eastern Suburbs Rugby; Bowling Club, New South Wales; NSW Leagues; Member for Phillip National House of Representatives, 1961-63; Member for Bondi, 1965-71, Waverley since 1971, NSW Legislative Assembly; Member of NSW Parliamentary Executive of ALP since 1966; Life Member, Executive Council Australia Jewry, 1969; Member, Board of Management Benevolent Society, NSW. *Honours:* Australian

Jew of the Year, 1968. *Hobbies:* Treasury; Education; Prices; Inflation; Consumerism; Bowls; Reading; Relaxing with family. *Address:* 162 Military Road, Dover Heights 2030, Australia.

EJIGA, (Major General), Obiaje Ede, b. 15 Feb. 1940, Adoka, Benue State, Nigeria. Soldiering (Military). Military Serviceman. m. Obonu, 30 Mar, 1968, 2 sons, 3 daughters. *Education:* Cadet Training, Military Academy; various Military courses; Staff College. *Appointments:* Military Service: Command of: Platoon; Battalion; Brigade; Staff College, Division; Adjutant General of the Army. *Honours:* Awarded: Forces Service Star; Officer of Federal Republic. *Hobbies:* Hunting; Golf; Tennis. *Address:* 2 Babajimeta Road, Jos, Plateau State, Nigeria.

EJIKO, Emmanuel Oritsetseyi, b. 1 Nov. 1949, Koko, Bendel State, Nigeria. Librarianship. m. Esther Onajite, 1 Sept. 1964, 5 daughters. *Education:* BLS., 1972; MLS., 1978. *Appointments:* Librarian Ministry of Education, Benin City, Bendel State, Nigeria, 1972-73; Assistant Librarian, Senior Librarian, 1973-80, Principal Librarian, 1980, Kashim Ibrahim Library, Ahmadu Bello University, Zaria, Nigeria. *Memberships:* Hon. Secretary, 1978-80, Nigerian Library Association; Ahmadu Bello University Staff Club. *Publications:* Who's Who in the Nigerian Library World, (co-author), 1978. *Hobbies:* Table tennis; Swimming. *Address:* 10 Ogodo Road, Sapele, Bendel State, Nigeria.

EJIMKONYE, Christopher, Nwanana, b. 1 Jan. 1944, Awo-Omamma, Imo State, Nigeria. Librarianship. m. Maria Chinyere, 24 Dec. 1972, 4 daughters. *Education:* Diplôme d'Étude Françaises Université de Dakar, Senegal 1967; BA(Hons) Languages, French and German, University of Nigeria 1971; MA, Library Science, Rosary College, Graduate School of Library Science, River Forest, Illinois, USA, 1976. *Appointments:* Teacher, French Language, Girls Secondary School, Ogidi, Nigeria, 1971-75; Principal Librarian i/c Acquisitions Alvan Ikoka College of Education Library, Owerri, Nigeria 1977-. *Memberships:* Nigerian Library Association; Awo-Omamma Graduates Association. *Hobbies:* Reading; Gardening. *Address:* Alvan Ikoku College of Education, PMB 1033, Owerli, Imo State, Nigeria.

EKANAYAKE, Sariyan Elanga, b. 25 Apr. 1951, Colombo, Sri-Lanka. Chartered Accountant. m. Kusandra Carmell Fernando, 17 Jan. 1980, 1 son. *Education:* Associate Member, The Institute of Chartered Accountants, Sri-Lanka, 1977. *Appointments:* Audit Assistant M/S Thorntan Panditheratne and Company, Kandy, Sri-Lanka, 1972-76; Chief Finance Manager, The Central Finance Company Limited, Kandy, Sri-Lanka, 1976-80; Financial Advisor, (Large Projects), Department of Commerce, The Independant State of Papua New Guinea, 1980-. *Memberships:* The P.N.G. Association of Accountants. *Honours:* Awarded, Institute Prize for 'Partnership and Company Law', Final examination of The Institute of Chartered Accountants of Sri-Lanka. *Hobbies:* Motor Mechanism; Carpentry and Wood work. *Address:* PO Box 1779, Boroko, Papua New Guinea.

EKECHI, Aloysius Oguzie, b. 17 Nov. 1935, Owerri, Imo State, Nigeria. Sales Executive. m. 22 Sept. 1968, 4 daughters. *Appointments:* Traffic Department, Nigerian Railway; Depot Superitendent, Shell Co. of Nigeria Limited, 1959-70; Self Employed-Distribution General Goods, 1970-72; Company Director, E Osborne (Nigeria) Limited; Representing UK Manufacturers in Nigeria; Import Consultant. *Hobby:* Gardening. *Address:* 30 Ogbete Crescent, Abakpa-Nike H/E, Enugu, Nigeria.

EKE, Frank Adele, b. 23 July 1939, Woji Town. Physician. m. Beatrice C Eke, Aug. 1958, 3 sons, 3 daughters. *Education:* MB, BS(London), University College of Ibadan, Nigeria, 1964; MPH, Harvard University, Boston, Massachusetts, USA 1972. *Appointments:* Senior Medical Officer, General Hospital, Port Harcourt, Nigeria, 1970; Consultant Epidemiologist, 1972; Principal Health Officer, Ministry of Health Port Harcourt, 1974; Director, Health Service, College of Science and Technology, Port Harcourt, 1976; Chairman, Governing Council, Rivers State College of Education, 1975-79; Deputy Governor of the Rivers State of Nigeria, 1979-; Member, Board of Governors, African Institute of Development and Education, Washington, 1980;

Chairman, Nigeria Institute of Development and Education, 1981. *Memberships:* People's Club of Nigeria. *Publications:* Numerous publications including environmental polution in Port Harcourt; Organisation of Family Planning in Rivers State of Nigeria. *Honours:* Football Colours 1952; Cricket Colours 1953 and 56. *Hobbies:* Boating; Swimming; Diving; Lawn Tennis; Travelling. *Address:* Deputy Governor's Office, Government House, Port Harcourt, Nigeria.

EKEH, Peter Palmer, b. 8 Aug. 1937, Okpara Inland, Bendel State, Nigeria. University Teacher. m. 1 May 1965, 4 sons, 1 daughter. *Education:* BSc., University of Ibadan, 1961-64; MA, Stanford University, California, USA, 1965-66; PhD, University of California, Berkeley, USA, 1966-70. *Appointments:* Assistant Professor of Sociology, University of California, Riverside, USA, 1970-73; Research Fellow, Centre for Social and Economic Research, Ahmadu Bello University, Zaria, Nigeria, 1973-74; Lecturer, 1974-75, Senior Lecturer, 1975-78, Professor and Head of Department, 1978-, Department of Political Science, University of Ibadan, Nigeria. *Memberships:* International Sociological Association; Nigerian Political Science Association; Nigeria Anthropological and Sociological Association. *Publications:* Social Exchange Theory: The Two Traditions, 1974; Colonialism and Social Structure, 1982. *Honours:* Rockefeller Foundation Scholarship, 1965-70; Cadbury Visiting Fellowship, Birmingham University, 1978. *Hobbies:* Farming; Fishing. *Address:* 8 Crowther Lane, University of Ibadan, Nigeria.

EKELE, Michael Musa, b. 2 Oct. 1944, Ogugu, Ankpa, LGA. Benue State, Nigeria. Librarian. m. Agnes A Negeau, 18 July 1970, 2 sons, 3 daughters. *Education:* BSc.Zoology, 1966-70, MLS, 1976-78, Ahmadu Bello University, Zaria, Nigeria. *Appointments:* Assistant Librarian, July 1970, Sub-Librarian, October 1973, Medical Library, Ahmadu Bello University Teaching Hospital, Zaria, Nigeria; Visited 31 libraries in United Kingdom to study the administration and organization of British Medical libraries, 1974; Ag. Medical Librarian and Head of Department, July 1976; Chief Librarian, School of Basic Studies, Ugbokolo, Nigeria, 1977. *Memberships:* Nigerian Library Association, Benue State Division; Igala Students Association; Rainbow Club, Ahmadu Bello University, Zaria, Nigeria; Community of Ogugu Students. *Hobbies:* Reading; Cricket; Table-tennis. *Address:* c/o District Head, Ogugu, Ankpa PO, Benue State, Nigeria.

EKPENYONG, Efiong Esang, b. 29 Oct. 1941, Ikot Nkim, Uyo Local Government Area, Cross River State, Nigeria. Civil Servant. m. Ukeme Silas Udofia, 25 Mar. 1972, 3 sons. *Education:* A Level General Certificate of Education, University of London, UK, 1962; BSc. Hons.(Econ.), University of Ibadan, Nigeria, 1965. *Appointments:* Graduate Research Assistant, University of Ibadan, Nigeria, 1965-66; Administrative Officer/Loans Administrator serving Federal Goverment, 1966-67, Eastern Nigeria Government, 1967-68; Administrative Officer/Senior Divisional Officer, South Eastern State Government, 1968-72; Deputy Secretary, South Eastern State Executive Council, 1972-75; Permanent Secretary, Cross River State Government, 1975-. *Memberships:* Fellow, Nigerian Institute of Administrative Management. *Hobbies:* Photography; Reading; Driving. *Address:* No. B2/14, GRA, Ikot Ansa, Calabar, Nigeria.

EKPOTT, Ita Daniel, b. 1 Dec. 1938, Ibiaku Ikot Obong Itam, Cross River State, Nigeria. Management. m. Inyang Eyibio Effiong, 15 Dec. 1968, 2 sons, 3 daughters. *Education:* BSc.(Hons.), Business, University of Lagos, Nigeria; Several Management courses in Nigeria and Overseas. *Appointments:* Pamol Nigeria Limited, Calabar, 1958-61; AT & P Nigeria Limited, Sapele, 1961-63; General Management Trainee, 1966-69, Operations Planning Manager, 1969-73, Corporate Development Manager, 1973-75, Nigerian Breweries Limited, Lagos; General Manager, Cross River Breweries Limited, Uyo, Cross River State, Nigeria, 1975-. *Memberships:* Public Relations Officer, University of Lagos Students Union; Branch Secretary, Itam Development Union; Itam Leaders of Thought Committee; Vice President, Presbyterian Church Committee, Uyo; Fellow, The Great Alpha Fraternity; Patron, Itu Students Union; Patron, Cross River State Students Union; Vice-President, Unilag Alumni Association; Project Leader, Ibiaku Ikot Obong Itam Community Rubber

Estate; Chairman, Board of Governors, State Commercial Academy, North Itam; Vice President, Ukpaubong Development Association. *Publications:* Target Management: The Dynamics of Profitability Planning, 1979. *Honours:* Notable, Bier Convent International, 1978. *Hobbies:* Lawn tennis; Writing books and articles for management education. *Address:* 39 Udo Qtung Ubo Street, PO Box 358, Uyo, Cross River State, Nigeria.

EKWEGH, Chukwunonyere Charles, b. 22 Feb. 1946, Eziama Osuh, Imo State, Nigeria. m. Nnalu Juliet Okoroji, 20 June 1979, 1 son, 1 daughter. *Education:* Diploma Business Management, IMT., Enugu, Nigeria, 1972; ACCA, 1977, MBIM, 1979, ACA, 1980, South West London College, London, UK. *Appointments:* African Continental Bank Limited, Head Office, Lagos, Nigeria, 1972-74; Group Head Office, John Holt Limited, Lagos, Nigeria, 1978; Nigerian Ropes Limited, Lagos, Nigeria, 1978-. *Memberships:* Association of Certified Accountants; Institute of Chartered Accountants of Nigeria; British Institute of Management; Ikoyi Club. *Hobbies:* Swimming; Golf. *Address:* 23 Adisa Bashua Street, PO Box 4615, Surulere, Lagos, Nigeria.

EKWEGH, Samuel Chukuemeka, b. 18 Jan, 1944, Port Harcourt, Nigeria. m. 27 Dec. 1975, 1 son, 2 daughters. *Education:* Ordinary Diploma, Mechanical Engineering, 1964-67; Ordinary Diploma, Electrical Engineering, 1964-67; Higher Diploma, Environmental Engineering, 1967-70. *Appointments:* Design/Contracts Engineer, Young, Austen and Young, England, 1970-71; Design Engineer, W C Pearce and Partners, England, 1971-73; Technical Director, Eksons(Nig)Limited, Owerri, Nigeria, 1973-; Principal Consultant, Sase and Partners, Engineering Services Consultants, Owerri, Nigeria, 1980-. *Memberships:* Associate member, Illuminating Engineering Society, England; Institute of Refrigeration, England; Associate, Chartered Institute of Building Services, England; American Society of Heating, Refrigeration and Air Conditioning Engineers. *Hobbies:* Travel; Football. *Address:* Plot 741, Amakohia Layout, PO Box 486, Owerri, Nigeria.

EKWENSI, Walter Arthur Menkiti, b. 22 Oct. 1940, Nkwelle Ezunaka, Anambara Local Government Area, Anambra State, Nigeria. m. Joyce Akuabata Agunwah, 10 July 1965, 2 sons, 2 daughters. *Education:* AIB., ATII., South-West London College, UK, 1967; ACCA., London School of Accountancy, UK, 1973; ACA., 1979. *Appointments:* Accountant, Williams and Glyns Bank, London, UK, 1971-76; Financial Controller, Central Investment Co. Limited, Enugu, Nigeria, 1977-81; Financial Accountant, Anambra Motor Manufacturing Co. Limited, Enugu, Nigeria, 1981-. *Memberships:* Enugu District Society of the Chartered Accountants of Nigeria; Inner Circle Club, Enugu. *Honours:* Victor Ludorum, Merchants of Light School, Oba, Nigeria, 1953; Prize winner, South-West London College, UK, 1966, 1967. *Hobbies:* Photography; Gardening; Setting up Financial Reporting systems for new Companies. *Address:* Plot S-22, Ben Ene Lane, off Chief Edward Nnaji Street, New Haven Upper Extension, Enugu, Nigeria.

EKWERE, John Dickson, b. 26 Oct. 1933, Etinan, Cross River State, Nigeria. Broadcaster; Theatre Arts Practitioner; Speech writer. m. Ufok Regina Thompson Eboh, 5 June 1965, 2 sons, 2 daughters. *Education:* BA.(Hon.) English (London), University College, Ibadan, Nigeria, 1954-59; Post Graduate Certificate in Speech and Drama, Bruford College of Speech and Drama, Sidcup, Kent, UK, 1960; Associate of British Drama Board, 1960; Advanced Management Couse in Broadcasting, Unesco Fellowship, Netherlands, 1966. *Appointments:* Senior Producer, 1960-65, Deputy Director of Programmes, 1965-66, Director of Programmes, 1966-70, Eastern Nigeria Broadcasting Corporation, Nigeria; Director of Information, South Eastern State of Nigeria, 1970-74; Permanent Secretary, Cross River State, Nigeria, 1975; Chairman, Etinan Local Government, Nigeria, 1977-79; Publisher, Popsi Enterprises, 1980-. *Memberships:* Founder & Executive Secretary, Mbari-Enugu Artists and Writers Club, 1962-70; International Theatre Institute; Nigerian Arts Council, 1962-75; Nigerian Antiquities Commission, 1970-75.*Publications:* Short stories and poems for Radio(including BBC) and Sunday papers; Film commentaries; numerous creative works in theatre productions and acting, 1960-77. *Creative Works:* Author of the Modern over

1,000 capacity Theatre nearing completion in Calabar, Nigeria. *Honours:* Numerous honours including: Member of Federal Republic of Nigeria for outstanding contributions to the cultural artistic scene, 1965; Honorary Chieftancy titles. *Hobbies:* Photography; Lawn tennis. *Address:* Offiong Street, PO Box 80, Etinan, Cross River State, Nigeria.

EKWUEME, Alex Ifeanyichukwu, b. 21 Oct. 1932, Oko, Nigeria. Architect; Politician. *Education:* University of Washington, Seattle, USA; University of Strathclyde, Glasgow, UK; PhD. *Appointments:* Founded Ekwueme Associates, Architects, Nigeria, 1960; Vice-President of Nigeria, Oct. 1979-; National Party of Nigeria. *Memberships:* Former President, Architectural Registration Council of Nigeria. *Address:* Office of the Vice-President, Lagos, Nigeria.

ELDEN, John Charles, b. 2 Nov. 1917, Melbourne, Australia. Director. m. Betty Euphemia Lane, 6 June 1950, 1 daughter. *Education:* Royal Melbourne Institute of Technology; Fellow, Society of Senior Executives, 1965; Certified Facility Executive, International Association of Public Facility Managers, Chicago, USA, 1979. *Appointments:* Citizen Force, 1940-46, Permanent Force, 1950-60, Royal Australian Air Force; Assistant State Secretary, Air Force Association, 1947-50; Director, The Exhibition Trustees, 1961-; Secretary-General, Royal Exhibition Building Centenary Celebrations, Melbourne, Australia, 1980-81. *Memberships:* Naval and Military Club, Melbourne; Air Force Club, Melbourne; Royal Commonwealth Society, Melbourne; President School Council, Councillor, 1969-, Melbourne High School, Former President, Melbourne High School Old Boys' Association; Life member, Royal Historical Society of Victoria; Life member, United Services Institution of Victoria. *Publications:* Editor of: The Old Unicornian, 1973-; The School Register and Directory of Old Boys 1905-1927. *Hobbies:* Writing; Music; Wine. *Address:* The Residency, Royal Exhibition Building, Melbourne, At Carlton, Victoria, Australia 3053.

ELDERKIN, Caroline Sarah, b. 6 Feb. 1948, Salisbury, Wiltshire, England. Journalist. m. 28 Oct. 1966, Edward Derek, 3 daughters. *Appointments:* Editorial Assistant, Joe Magazine, 1973, Production Assistant, Sports Magazine, Business World, weekly television programmes, 1974, Editorial Assistant, The Weekly Review, 1975-79, Editor, Picture Post, 1976-77, Assistant Editor, The Weekly Review, 1980-, Editor, colour magazine, Assistant editor/Features editor, The Nairobi Times, 1977-, Director, 1976-, Stellascope Limited, publishers, Kenya. *Memberships:* Board of Directors, Press Trust of Kenya. *Hobbies:* Tennis. *Address:* Muthangari Drive, Nairobi, Kenya.

ELKINGTON, Christopher Richard, b. 9 Dec. 1933, Malvern, Worcestershire, England. Geologist. m. Jane Bale, 9 June 1967, 2 sons. *Education:* BSc.Hons., University of Western Australia, 1957; DIC., MSc., Imperial College of Science and Technology, London, 1965. *Appointments:* Western Mining Corporation, Western Australia, 1957-60, 1965-69; Falconbridge Nickel Mines Limited, Canada, 1961-64; Mineral Exploration Consultant, Principal, Ekomin Pty. Limited, South Perth, Western Australia, 1970-. *Memberships:* Geoloical Society of Australia; International Association of Cosmochemistry and Geochemistry; Royal Society of Western Australia; Australasian Institute of Mining and Metallurgy; Herbert Lapworth Club. *Publications:* Bronzite, Peridotite and Associated Metamorphic Rocks at Nunyle, Western Australia, 1963. *Hobby:* Gardening. *Address:* 25 Dyson Street, South Perth, Western Australia,6151.

ELKINS, Cyrus, b. 22 Mar. 1922, Haileybury, Ontario, Canada. Hotelier. m. Bridgette Mary, 19 Dec. 1980. *Education:* Haileybury School of Mines, Ontario, Canada. *Appointments:* Worked in mining field in Timmins, Ontario, Canada, 1938-40; Lieutenant, Canadian Army, 1940-46; Operated Guest House, Jamaica, 1946; General Manager of: Shaw Park Hotel, Jamaica, 1948-50, Seaway Hotel Corporation, 1958-59, Gold Head Hotel, Oracabessa, Jamaica, 1959-61, Elbow Beach Surf Club, Bermuda, 1961-71, The Princess Hotel, Pembroke, Bermuda, 1971-73, Southampton Princess Hotel, Bermuda, 1973-74; Part owner and Managing Director, Jamaica Inn, Jamaica, 1950-58; Promoted, built and Managing Director, Plantation Inn,

Ocho Rios, Jamaica, 1956-61; Regional Vice President, Princess Hotels, Bermuda, 1974-76; Vice President and General Manager, The Princess, Pembroke, Bermuda, 1976-. *Memberships:* President, Jamaica Hotel Association; President, Ocho Rios Chamber of Commerce; Chairman, Beach Control Authority; Jamaica Tourist Board; Palisadoes Development Committee; Justice of the Peace for Parish of St. Ann; Chairman, Civic Police Committee; Public Welfare Foundation; Bermuda Government Tourist Board; President, Bermuda Hotel Association; Vice-Chairman, Hotel Advisory Board; Bermuda College Board of Governors; Board of Governors, Bermuda Employers' Council; American Hotel and Motel Association Resort Committee; SKAL; Associate member, ASTA. *Honours:* Certified Hotel Administrator awarded by the Educational Institute of the American Hotel and Motel Association, 1980; Hon. member, Hotel Association of Greater Montreal, 1981. *Address:* 'Tamarisk Cottage', PO Box 837, Hamilton 5, Bermuda.

ELLICOTT, Dorothy, b. 30 June 1901, Portsmouth, England. Author; Housewife. m. John Teague Ellicott (Deceased), 24 Feb. 1926. *Appointments:* Journalist, Gibraltar Chronicle, 1920-24. *Memberships:* First woman ever elected member, Gibraltar City Council, 1947-56; First woman elected, Legislative Council, 1959-64; Chairman, Gibraltar Museum Committee, 1968-; Chairman, Gibraltar Branch, RSPCA, 1957-72; People's Warden, Cathedral of the Holy Trinity, 1952-78; Gibraltar Society for the Prevention of Blindness, Secretary, 1953-74, Vice-Chairman, 1976-. *Publications:* An Ornament to the Almeida, 1950; From Rooke to Nelson, 101 eventful years in Gibraltar, 1956; Bastion against Aggression, 1966; Our Gibraltar, 1975; Gibraltar's Royal Governor, 1981. *Honours:* MBE, 1957; OBE, 1972; First woman, Justice of the Peace in Gibraltar, 1970; Serving Sister, 1948, Sister, 1955, Order St. John of Jerusalem. *Hobbies:* Swimming. *Address:* 1 Town Range, Gibraltar.

ELLIOTT, John Patrick, b. 28 Apr. 1931, Tweed Heads, New South Wales, Australia. Judge. *Appointments:* Journalist, 1949-65; Barrister-at-Law, 1965; Solicitor of Supreme Court of Queensland, Australia, 1969; Apoointed Judge, Dec. 1979-. *Address:* c/- Family Court, GPO Box 9991, Brisbane 4000, Australia.

ELLIOTT, Katherine M, b. 28 May 1919, Lincoln, United Kingdom. Medical Practitioner. m. Alan Manton Elliott, 8 Sept. 1945 (Divorced 1969), 1 son, 2 daughters. *Education:* University of London (London School of Medicine for Women and The Royal Free Hospital); Member, Royal College of Surgeons of England 1943; Licentiate, Royal College of Physicians of London, 1943; Member, Faculty of Community Medicine, Royal Colleges of Physicians of the United Kingdom, 1979. *Appointments:* Resident Posts in General Medicine, Paediatrics, Obstetrics and Gynaecology, Addenbrooke's Hospital, Cambridge, United Kingdom; Captain, Indian Medical Service, Staff Surgeon, Ahmednagar Military Families' Hospital; Infant Welfare Medical Officer, London County Council; Assistant Director, Ciba Foundation, 1966-81; Founder and Honorary Director, Appropriate Health Resources and Technologies Action Group, 1977, Chairman, 1980-. *Memberships:* Royal Society of Medicine; Royal Society of Tropical Medicine; International Hospital Federation; Intermediate Technology Development Group; Society for International Developmemt; Commonwealth Human Ecology Council. *Publications:* Organizer and joint editor of 32 Ciba Foundation biomedical symposia; Author of numerous articles on aspects of primary health care in developing countries, and the training and use of health care auxiliaries; Editor of three annotated bibliographies; also Health Auxiliaries and the Health Team, 1977; More Technologies for Rural Health 1980. *Address:* 24 St George's Court, Gloucester Road, London, SW7 4OZ.

ELLIOTT, Lyla Daphne, b. 2 July 1934, Geraldton, Western Australia. Member of Parliament. m. Edwin John White, 22 May 1976. *Appointments:* Elected to Western Australia Legislative Council for North East Metropolitan Province, 1971-; Secretary to F.E. Chamberlain, 1956-65, 1967-71; Secretary to Overseas Department; Secretary to British Labour Party, 1966-67; Obersver, Socialist International Congress, Stockholm, Sweden, 1966; Member, British Labour Party Study delegation, Israel, 1966. *Hobbies:* Reading;

Swimming; Squash; Gardening. *Address:* Parliament House, Perth, Western Australia 6000.

ELLIOTT, Norman Randall, b. 19 July 1903, London, England. Engineer; Barrister. m. 16 Jan. 1960. *Education:* Cambridge University, UK, 1926-28. *Appointments:* Engineer and Manager, London and Home Counties Joint Electricity Authority; Chairman, South Eastern Electricity Board; Chairman, South of Scotland Electricity Board; North of Scotland Board; Chairman, Electricity Council; Chairman, Howden Group Limited. *Memberships:* Fellow, Institution of Civil Engineers; Fellow, Institution of Electrical Engineers; Middle Temple; Athenaeum Club. *Publications:* Electricity Statutes. *Honours:* Knighthood; CBE. *Hobbies:* Golf; Theatre. *Address:* 3 Herbrand Walk, Cooden, Sussex TN39 4TX, England.

ELLIS, Arthur, b. 10 Feb. 1932, Morecambe, England. Librarian. m. Margaret Mary Van Oriel, 22 Aug. 1956, 2 sons, 1 daughter. *Education:* Newcastle School of Librarianship, UK; BA., University of Western Australia, 1966; BA., FLA., ALAA. *Appointments:* Librarian, State Library of Western Australia; Principal Librarian, Assistant Director-General, National Library of Australia; University Librarian, University of Western Australia. *Hobbies:* Reading; Gardening. *Address:* 12 Vauduse Street, Claremont, Western Australia.

ELLIS, Eva Lillian Johnson, b. 4 June 1920, Seattle, Washington, USA. Artist. m. Professor Everett L Ellis, 1 May 1943, 4 daughters. *Education:* BA, University of Washington 1941; MA, University of Idaho 1950; Studied in United Kingdom, Greece, Italy, France, Scandinavia, Spain. *Appointments:* Art Director, Seattle University, Best and Company; Free lance Artist, New York City; NBC TV, New York City; York City; Lecturer, University of Idaho; Professional Seminars University of Michigan; Chairman, Armerican Art Week Idaho; Director Chirldren's Art, Oregon Lecturer in Art, New Zealand. *Memberships:* President, Susquekanna Arts Council NY; Michigan Academy of Art and Science; President National League of American PEN Women; Alpha Omicron Pi Society; Lambda Rho; Gamma Alpha Chi; President University Faculty Wives, New Zealand. *Creative Works:* Paintings on permanent display at Berkeley Campus, Universities of California, Washington, Oregon State, Christchurch, NZ Library; Many paintings in collections throughout world; Listed at Hirshorn Museum Washington DC, Swedish National Museum, Stockholm, Seattle Art Museum, Seattle Washington. *Honours:* Diploma with Gold Medal, Italian Academy of Art 1980. *Hobbies:* Cooking; Travel; Cancer Society; Girl Guides. *Address:* 71 Clifton Terrace, Christchurch, New Zealand.

ELLIS, George Ernest, b. 20 Aug. 1932, Cleethorpes, Lincolnshire. Chairman and Managing Director. m. Avril Violet Smith, 7 May 1954, 1 son, 1 daughter. *Education:* School Certificate, Wintringham Grammar School. *Appointments:* Remington Rand Limited, United Kingdom 1956-62; CFAO, Lagos, Nigeria 1963-66; NCR Lagos, Nigeria 1966-69; NCR Accra, Ghana, 1970-72; NCR (Nigeria) Limited, Lagos, Nigeria 1972-. *Memberships:* Ikoyi Club Lagos; Ikoyi Golf Club Lagos; Fellow Institute of Directors, United Kingdom; Fellow British Institute of Management; Nigerian Institute of Management, Lagos; Metropolitan Club, Lagos; Lagos Motor Boat Club; Race Horse Owners Association, United Kingdom. *Hobbies:* Golf; Horse Racing; Travel. *Address:* 6A Club Road, Ikoyi, Lagos, Nigeria.

ELLIS, Madeleine Blanche, b. 10 Mar. 1915, Vancouver, British Columbia, Canada. Writer; Scholar; University Professor. *Education:* BA., 1936, MA., 1937, University of British Columbia, Canada; French Fellow, Bryn Mawr College, Penn, USA, 1937-38; French Fellow, 1938-40, PhD, 1944, University of Toronto, Canada. *Appointments:* Summer School Lecturer, 1945, Lecturer in French, 1944-46, University of Toronto, Canada; Professor of French, Fine Arts and Humanities, 1946-80, Chairman of Department of Modern Languages, 1964-72, Marianopolis College, Montréal, Canada; Summer school 'chargée de cours', Laval University, Québec, Canada, 1949; Lecturer, University of Orange Free State, Bloemfontein, South Africa, Summer, 1964; Lecturer, McGill University International Jean-Jacques Rousseau Congress, Canada, Autumn, 1978; Reader for University Presses. *Memberships:* Life member, Société J.-J. Rousseau,

Geneva; Life member, Comité du Montlouis, Montmorency, France; Société française d'etude du XVIIIe siècle; American Society of Eighteenth Century Studies; Société canadienna d'étude du XVIIIe siècle. *Publications:* Robert Charbonneau et la creation romanesque, 1948; St-Denys-Garneau: art et réalisme, 1949; Julie or La Nouvelle Heloise: A Synthesis of Rousseau's Thought, 1949; Rousseau's Venetian Story: An Essay ypon Art and Truth in the Confessions, 1966; Rousseau's Socratic Aemilian Myths: A Literary Collation of Emile and the Social Contract, 1977; Collaborated on Dictionnaire international de Littérature comparée, 1970-; also articles in reviews. *Honours:* Bursaries awarded by University of British Columbia, 1934, 35, 36; Carnegie Foundation Scholarship, 1937-38; Grant in aid of publication from Humanities Research Council of Canada, 1949. *Hobbies:* Music and Art appreciation; Pianotforte performer. *Address:* 2045 Closse Street, Apt. % A-8, Montreal, Québec., H3H 1Z7,Canada.

ELLIS, Margaret Mary, b. 12 Jan. 1952 Sydney, Australia. Occupational Therapist. *Education:* Diploma Occupational Therapy, New South Wales, College of Occupational Therapy, 1970-72; Degree in Applied Science (Occupational Therapy) Conversion Course, Cumberland College of Health Sciences, Sydney, 1978-80. *Appointments:* Staff Therapist, 1973-77, Occupational Therapy Student Supervisor 1977-79, North Ryde Psychiatric Centre, Sydney; Staff Therapist, Queen Elizabeth II Rehabilitation Centre, Sydney 1979-. *Memberships:* Federal Observer, NSW Association of Occupational Therapists; Past Secretary, Occupational Therapy Vocational Branch of the Public Service Association. *Publications:* Writing Fiction. *Honours:*Runner-up in the American Study Tour of Occupational Therapy 1977, 1981. *Hobbies:* Writing Fiction; Tennis; Stamp/Coin Collecting. *Address:* 25 Twyford Avenue, Earlwood, Sydney 2206, Australia.

ELLIS, William Frank, b. 4 Apr. 1928, Hobart, Tasmania, Australia. Art Museum Director. m. (1) Vivienne Rae, (2) Margaret Anne Ferrall, 26 Oct. 1979, 1 son, 1 daughter. *Education:* University of Tasmania, Australia. *Appointments:* Cadet and Demonstrator, University of Tasmania, Australia, 1946-51; Curator of Anthropology and Archaeology, 1951-53, Assistant Director, 1953-55, Director, 1955-78, Queen Victoria Museum, Launceston, Tasmania, Australia; Director, Art Gallery of Western Australia, 1978-. *Memberships:* Hon. Secretary, Northern Branch, Royal Society of Tasmania, 1953-78; Hon. Life member, Royal Society of Tasmania; Chairman, Australian Society for Education through the Arts; Chairman, Australian Gallery Directors' Council. *Publications:* Penal Settlements of Van Diemens Land; Diaries of John Helder Wedge; various articles in journals. *Honours:* Churchill Fellowship, 1968; OBE., 1970. *Hobbies:* Photography; Reading; Sailing; Bushwalking. *Address:* 3 Trinnick Place, Booragoon, Western Australia 6154.

ELLISON, Gerald Alexander, b. 19 Aug. 1910. Minister of Religion. m. Jane Elizabeth Gibbon 1947, 1 son, 2 daughters. *Education:* St George's Windsor; Westminster School; New College Oxford (Hon. Fellow, 1974); Westcott House, Cambridge. *Appointments:* Curate, Sherborne Abbey, 1935-37; Domestic Chaplain to Bishop of Winchester, 1937-39; Chaplain RNVR, 1939-43 (despatches); Domestic Chaplain to Archbishop of York, 1943-46; Vicar, St Mark's Portsea, 1946-50; Hon. Chaplain to Archbishop of York, 1946-50; Canon of Portsmouth, 1950; Exam. Chaplain to Bishop of Portsmouth, 1949-50; Bishop of Willesden, 1950-53; Bishop of Chester, 1955-73; Bishop of London, 1973-81; Dean of the Chapels Royal, 1973-81; Prelate, Order of the British Empire, 1973-81; Episcopal Canon of Jerusalem, 1973-81. Chaplain: Master Mariners' Company, 1946-73; Glass Sellers' Company, 1951-73; Chaplain and Sub-Prelate, Order of St John 1973-. Hon. Chaplain, RNR. Member, Wolfenden Committee on Sport, 1960; Chairman: Board of Governors, Westfield College, University of London, 1953-67; Council of King's College London, 1973-80 (FKC 1968. Vice-Chm. newly constituted Council, 1980-); Archbishop's Commn on Women and Holy Orders, 1963-66; Mem., Archbishop's Commn on Church and State, 1967; President: Actors' Church Union, 1973-81; Pedestrians Assoc. for Road Safety, 1964-77. Hon. Bencher Middle Temple, 1976. Freeman, Drapers' Co.; Hon. Liveryman: Merchant Taylors' Co., Glass Sellers' Co., Painter Stainers' Co.; *Memberships:* Mariners' Co.

Chm., Oxford Society; Steward of Henley Regatta. *Publications:* The Churchman's Duty, 1957; The Anglican Communion, 1960. *Hobbies:* Oarsmanship; Walking. *Address:* Billeys House, 16 Long Street, Cerne Abbas, Dorset.

ELLMERS, Judith Corrighliee, b. 26 Apr. 1925, Gisborne, New Zealand. Farmer; Writer. m. K C Ellmers, 3 Sept. 1948, 1 son, 2 daughters. *Education:* Bachelor of Arts 1968; Certificate, Liaison Officer, (Advisor) NZ Playcentres Federation 1966; Member NZ Women Writers Society Inc. 1967; Judges Certificate Floral Art Society NZ Inc. 1972; Secondary Teachers Certificate 1975. *Appointments:* Teacher, Country School 1946-48; Farmers wife and Farmer, 1948-74; Director Farming Company Te Rawhiti Farms Limited; Country Librarian Station Branch 1956-62. *Memberships:* The Victoria League for Commonwealth Friendship, NZ; The Royal Society for Commonwealth Friendship London; The Maori Womens Welfare League, NZ; Women's Electoral Lobby 1979; Friend of St Martins; New Zealand Women Writers Incorporation; Federated Farmers, NZ; Country Womens Institute NZ; Town and Country Club Gisborne NZ; Royal Forest and Bird Protection Society Incorporation NZ. *Publications:* Articles NZ Weekly News, NZ Farmer, NZ Womens Weekly, Eve, magazine; Co-Founder of Playcentre Movement NZ 1964. *Honours:* NZ Wool Board Gold Medal Woolcraft 1965; Merit Certificate Hawkes Boy Education Board, Outdoor Camp Children 1972; Associated Countrywomen of 'World Essay (International) 1969; Rep. NZ as Freelance Writer London 1978; *Hobbies:* Gardening; Floral Art. *Address:* 171 Clifford Street, Gisborne, New Zealand.

ELLYARD, Peter Wake, b. 13 Apr. 1937, Wagga Wagga, NSW, Australia. Environmental Administrator. m. Heather Shain Ellyard, 2 daughters. *Education:* BSc Agriculture (Hons) University of Sydney 1959; MS Cornell University 1962; PhD 1966. *Appointments:* Academic and Administrative Positions in USA, Australia and United Kingdom; Senior Executive Officer, Office of Environment, Canberra; Senior Advisor Minister for Environment, Australia 1972-75; Director of Environment and Conservation, Papua New Guinea 1976-79; Director-General Department for the Environment South Australia 1979-. *Publications:* A number of publications in Environmental Field, (Approximately 12); Co-Editor of two books. *Honours:* William Farrer Memorial Scholar 1961-62. *Hobbies:* Yoga; Music; Reading. *Address:* 26 East Pallant Street, North Adelaide SA, 5006 Australia.

ELMSLY, John Anthony, b. 1 July 1952, Auckland, New Zealand. Composer. *Education:* BSc(Hons), 1972; BMus Victoria University of Wellington, 1974; First Prize in Composition, Royal Conservatory of Brussels, 1977; Special Certificates, Royal Conservatory of Liège, 1978; LTCL, 1970. *Appointments:* Belgian Government Scholar, Studying Composition in Brussels, Liege, 1975-78; Resident, London, Freelance Composer and Teacher, 1979-80; Mozart Fellow, University of Otago, New Zealand, 1981. *Memberships:* Australasian Performing Rights Association; Composers Association of New Zealand. *Creative Works:* Sinfonia, for Orchestra 1980; Exchanges for Chamber ensemble, 1980; Neither nor Towards, for String Orchestra, 1980; Dream Fragments, for soprano and 3 clarinets, 1980. *Honours:* Wellington City Council Music Prize, 1975. *Address:* c/o Department of Music, University of Otago, PO Box 56, Dunedin, New Zealand.

ELSWORTH, David Lindsay, b. 27 Mar. 1927, Melbourne, Victoria, Australia. Company Director. m. Margaret Elaine Stubbings, 5 July 1952, 1 son, 3 daughters. *Education:* Leaving Honours, Wesley College, Melbourne, 1943-44; Bachelor of Commerce, Melbourne University, 1945-48. *Appointments:* Rocla Industries Limited, Melbourne, 1949-50; P.A. Management Consultants, UK and Australia 1951-59; Managing Director, Lend Lease Corporation 1959-65; Managing Director, Power Corporation Australia Limited 1966-68; Self Employed, Company Director, Consultant to Company Boards and Entrepreneur, 1969-. *Memberships:* Director, Benevolent Society of New South Wales; American Club Sydney; Australian Institute of Management. *Honours:* Practical Music Exhibition, Victoria 1944; General Exhibition 1944; Senior Government Scholarship 1944. *Hobbies:* Classical

Music; Sailing. *Address:* 16 Burran Avenue, Mosman 2088, NSW, Australia.

ELTON, Rodney, b. 2 Mar. 1930, Oxford, England. Farmer; Teacher. m. (1) Anne Frances Tilney, 1 son, 3 daughters, (2) Richenda Gurney, 1979. *Education:* Eton College 1943-49; New College, Oxford 1950-53. *Appointments:* Farming, 1955-70; Teaching History, Loughborough Grammar School, Liecestershire 1962-67, Fairman Comprehensive School Nottingham, 1967-69, Bishop Lonsdale College, Derby, 1969-72; Eductional Publishing, 1973; Deputy Secretary, Committee on International Affairs, Church of England, 1974-76; Director, International Building Exhibition Limited, Overseas Exhibition Services Limited, 1976 79; Director and Deputy Chairman, Audry Montgomery Limited 1978-79; Parliamentary Under Secretary of State, Northern Ireland Office, 1979-81; Parliamentary Under Secretary of State, Department of Health and Social Services, 1981-. *Memberships:* National Service (Commissioned) BAOR 1949-50; Territorial Army Service 1950-70; Athaenum; Beefsteak and Cavalry and Guards Clubs. *Honours:* MA 1953; TD 1960. *Address:* The House of Lords, Westminister, London, England.

ELTRINGHAM, Donald Herbert, b. 22 Mar. 1924, Ballarat, Victoria, Australia. Head of Commonwealth Department of Productivity. m. Mary Bette Davies, 28 Apr. 1945, 2 daughters. *Education:* Diploma of Electrical Engineering and Mechanical Engineering, Ballarat School of Mines and Industries, 1942; Diploma of Radio Engineering, Royal Melbourne Institute of Technology. *Appointments:* including: Engineering Engineer, Department of Civil Aviation, 1947-62; Deputy Secretary, Department of Defence, 1965; Secretary, Department of Productivity, 1980. *Memberships:* Fellow, The Institution of Engineers, Australia. *Hobby:* Golf. *Address:* 12 Marawa Place, Aranda. A.C.T. Australia.

ELUFOWOPE, Amos Ademola, b. 31 Jan. 1941, Ile-Ife, Oyo State, Nigeria. Chartered Accountant and Administrator. m. Theresa Elufowope, 22 May 1969, 2 sons, 2 daughters. *Education:* Associate member, Institute of Costs and Management Accountants, 1970; Associate member, Institute of Chartered Secretaries and Administrators; Associate member, Institute of Chartered Accountants of Nigeria, 1974. *Appointments:* Secretary/Accountant, Zambia Pork Products Limited, Zambia, 1971-74; Management Accountant, Beecham Limited, 1974-75; IBRU Organization, Assistant, Group Financial Control, 1975-76; Chief Accountant/Company Secretary, Union Beverages Limited, 1976-79; Financial Controller/Company Secretary, New Nigeria Construction Company Limited. *Memberships:* Kaduna Club. *Hobbies:* Football; Debating; Squash. *Address:* 86A Dawaki Road, Gra, Kaduna State, Nigeria.

ELUOGU, Jonathan Chukwunwike, b. 9 June 1940, Ogbunike, Nigeria. Veterinary Surgeon. m. Henrietta N Uzodinma, 5 Feb. 1972, 1 son, 3 daughters. *Education:* B.V.M.S., Glasgow, 1966; M.R.C.V.S., London, 1966. *Appointments:* Various Vetinary positions from 1966-77; Deputy Chief Vetinary Officer, 1977; Associate Lecturer, University of Nigeria, Nsukka, 1970-77; Assistant Secretary, Ogbunike Progress Union, Ogbunike. *Memberships:* Member, Board of Governers, St. Monicas Teacher Training College, Ogbunika; Assistant Secretary, Ogbunike Progress Union, Ogbunika; Vice-President, Azu Village Union, Ogbunike; Chairman, Finance Committee, Ogbunike Rangers Internation F.C., Nigeria; Several Sports Associations. *Honours:* Imperial Chemical Industry Prize for Chemistry, 1961; Pharmacology Prize, University of Glasgow, 1964; Parasitology Prize, University of Glasgow, 1965; Sports Champion Award in Table Tennis, 1979. *Hobbies:* Various sporting activities including: Table Tennis; Football. *Address:* 50 Obioma Street, Achara Layout, Enuga, Nigeria.

ELUWA, Gabriel Ihie Chinenye, b. 10 Dec. 1928, Amapu Ntigha, Imo State, Nigeria. Educationist. m. 15 Dec. 1961, 2 sons, 4 daughters. *Education:* M.A., University of St. Andrews, Scotland, 1958; Dip.Ed., University of Edinburgh, Scotland, 1959; Ph.D., Michigan State University, United States of America., 1967. *Appointments:* Education Officer, Ministry of Education, 1959-62; University Lecturer, University of Nigeria, 1962-76; College of Education Lecturer, Alvan Ikoku

College of Education, 1976-. *Memberships:* Member of several Education Societies, including: Historical Society of Nigeria; University of St. Andrews Alumni Association; Michigan State University. *Publications:* Contributed to several learned articles including: Background to the Emergence of the National Congress of British West Africa; Edward Wilmot-Blyden; The Man and his Social and Political Ideas. *Honours:* Easter Nigerian Government Scholarship, 1953-59; Ford Foundation Fellowship, 1966-67; Certificate of Merit, University of St. Andrews. *Hobbies:* Walking; Table Tennis; Sight-Seeing. *Address:* Amapu Ntigha, Isiala Ngwa, Imo State, Nigeria.

ELVISH, Charles Edgar, b. 1 March 1907, Castlemaine, Victoria, Australia. Stipendiary Magistrate (Retired). m. Breta Lynda Lillington, 23 Oct. 1947, 2 sons. *Education:* Crown Law Departmental Examination, 1927. *Appointments:* Courts Branch of the Crown Law Department, Victoria, 1924; Clerk of Courts, Benalla, 1934-41; Relieving Clerk of Courts, 1941-46; Clerk of Courts, Richmond, 1946-49, and Ballarat 1949-51; Police Magistrate, 1951, and Deputy-Chief Stipendiary Magistrate, 1969-72; Chairman, Commonwealth Public Service Appeals Board, 1972-76. *Memberships:* Stipendary Magistrates' Association of Victoria; The Royal Automobile Club of Victoria; Caulfield Bowls Club. *Publications:* Collaborated in writing book of 'Instructions to Clerks of Courts', 1939. *Honours:* Her Majesty's Coronation Medal, 1953. *Hobbies:* Photography. *Address:* 1912 Malvern Road, East Malvern, 3145, Victoria, Australia.

ELWOOD, Brian George Conway, b. 5 April, 1933. Barrister, Solicitor. m. Dawn Ward, Dec. 1956, 1 son, 2 daughters. *Education:* L.L.B.; A.T.C.L. *Appointments:* Mayor of Palmerston North, 1971; President, Municipal Association, New Zealand, 1976-79; Chairman of Directors, Municipal Co-operative Insurance Co. Limited, 1979-81; Director, Monarch Life Insurance Co. Limited, 1980-. *Address:* 19 Cremorne Avenue, Palmerston North, New Zealand.

ELWORTHY, Jonathan Herbert, b. 1 July 1936, Timaru, New Zealand. Member of Parliament. m. 6 July 1963, 2 sons, 1 daughter. *Education:* Christs College; Lincoln College. *Appointments:* Farm Manager, Director, Craigmor and Farming Company, 1962-75; Member of Parliament, Waitak, 1975-. *Memberships:* School Farm Organisations; Political Party Organisation; Sundry Sports Club. *Hobbies:* Squash; Climbing; Jogging; Tennis. *Address:* 49 Wharfe Street, Oamaru, New Zealand.

ELWORTHY, Samuel Charles, b. 23 March 1911, Timaru, New Zealand. Company Director. m. Audrey Hutchinson, 5 June 1936, 3 sons, 1 daughter. *Education:* Marlborough College, 1924-29; Trinity College, Cambridge, 1929-33; Called to Bar (Lincoln's Inn), 1935. *Appointments:* Bomber Command, 1939-45; Constable and Governor, Windsor Castle, 1971-78; Lord Leiutenant of Greater London, 1973-78. *Memberships:* Hon. Bencher, Lincoln's Inn, 1970; Hon. Freeman, Skinners Company, 1968; Christchurch Club, New Zealand. *Honours:* D.S.O., A.F.C., 1941; D.F.C., 1941; C.B.E., 1946; M.V.D., 1953; G.C.B., 1962; Life Peerage, 1972; K.Sr.J., 1976; K.G., 1977. *Hobbies:* Fishing; Shooting. *Address:* Gordons Valley, R.D.2., Timaru, New Zealand.

ELWYN-JONES, Frederick, b. 24 Oct. 1909, Llanelli, Wales. Lord of Appeal. m. Pearl Binder, 27 Aug. 1937, 1 son, 2 daughters. *Education:* Llanelli Intermediate School, Aberystwyth University College Wales; MA-(Cantab), Gonville and Caius College, Cambridge, (President, Cambridge Union). *Appointments:* Barrister 1935-; Queen's Counsel 1953; Attorney General 1964-70; Lord Chancellor 1974-79; Member of Parliament for West Ham, 1945-74; Recorder of Merthyr Tydfil, Swansea and Cardiff; Major RA (TA), Member, British War Crimes Executive, 1945-46. *Publications:* Author, The A Hack From Within, 1939; Hitler's Drive to the East, 1937; The Battle for Peace, 1938. *Honours:* Freeman of Llanelli and London; Hon.LLD University of Wales, Ottawa, Warsaw, Philippines, Columbia University; Fellow of Gonville and Cauis College, Cambridge and Kings College, London. *Address:* 17 Lewes Crescent, Brighton BN2 1GB, England.

EL-ZEFTAWI, Bassam Mohamed, b. 7 March 1935, Alexandria Egypt. m. Mona Ahmed Abed-El-Khalek, 5

July 1962, 1 daughter. *Education:* B.Agricultural Science, Alexandria, 1956; Diploma Modern Chinese, Peking, 1957; M.Agricultural Science, Canton, 1960. *Appointments:* includes: Division of Horticulture, Cairo, Egypt, 1956-65; Research Scientist, 1965-81; Research Scientist, H.R.I., Knoxfield, 1981-. *Memberships:* Several Horticultural and Agricultural Societies including: Australian Institute of Agricultural Science; International Plant Growth regulators working group; Charter Secretary, Mildura Working Man's Club. *Publications:* Contributed to various Horticultural and Scientific research Journals; Numerous papers for International and Australian Conferences. *Honours:* The Peoples Republic of China Scholarship, 1956-60. *Hobbies:* Reading; History; Politics; Cheese and Wine Making. *Address:* 26 Bambara Street, Wantirna, Victoria, Australia.

EMA, Asuquo Ndon, b. 9 Oct. 1936, Ikot Ekpene. Veterinary Surgeon. m. 15 Dec. 1962, 2 sons, 2 daughters. *Education:* Hope Waddell Training Institution, 1955-57; B.Vet. Med., M.R.C.V.S., Royal Vetinary College, London University, 1967; M.Sc., Missouri University, 1973; PH.D., Ahmadu Bello University, 1976. *Appointments:* includes: Veterinary Surgeon, P.D.S.A., Clinic, Harrow, England, 1968-69; Senior Lecturer, Zaria, 1969-77; Reader and Head of Department, Veterinary Anatomy, Zaria, 1978-80; Professor of Veterinary Anatomy, 1980-; Dean of the Faculty of Veterinary Medicine, 1981. *Memberships:* Science Association of Nigeria; Association for Advancement of Agricultural Sciences in Africa; Several Veterinary Associations. *Publications:* 'The Mechanism of Emesis in the Dog'; 'The Vasculature of the Stomach during Emesis'; 'Vagotomy and Emesis in the Dog'. *Honours:* KSU/ABU Study Fellowship, 1971-73. *Hobbies:* Tennis; Dancing; Reading. *Address:* B.6. Main Campus, A.B.U., Zaria.

EMANI, Sankara Sastry, b. 23 Sept. 1922, Draksharama, Andhra Pradesh, India. Music. m Narasa Mamba, 1945, (Widower), 2 sons, 4 daughters. *Education:* BA, Andhra University, India, 1945. *Appointments:* Music Director, Gemini Studios (Films), 1945-58; Producer Music, 1959-61, Chief Producer, 1961-, All India Radio, Madras; Conductor, Composer, Director, National Orchestra, New Delhi, 1961-. *Memberships:* University Grants Committee, 1973-74; Chairman, Committee selection of candidates for scholarships of the Education Ministry, 1974-77; Expert Committee, Music Academy, Madras, 1975-; International Music Fund, Paris; Select Film Awards (National), 1974; Central Sangeet Natak Academy, 1975. *Creative Works:* Composed about 100 orchestral compositions; Composer of classical, folk melodies & light songs; Research on Gramakas—Graces or nuances of music. *Honours:* Asia Rostrum First Prize, 1973; Honorary doctorate, Delhi University; Doctorate degree from Andhra University, 1979; Central Sangeet Natak Academy Award, 1973; Republic Day honour, Padmasu award, 1973; Permanent State Musician of Andhra Pradesh, India; Permanent Musician, Tirupathi (Temple in South India). *Hobby:* Playing cards, favourite, Bridge. *Address:* 7 Market Road, Giole Market Area, New Delhi 110001, India.

EMEJUAIWE, Stephen O, b. 15 Sept. 1935, Nkpa, Bende LGA, Imo State, Nigeria. Microbiologist. m. Ihuoma Iroegbu, 5 April 1969, 2 sons, 3 daughters. *Education:* B.Sc. Howard University, 1962; M.Sc., Howard University, 1963; Ph.D., Immunology, Ibadan, 1971; Diploma in Radioisotope Technique, Oake Ridge National Institute for Nuclear Studies, United States of America, 1964-65; Certificate in Cellular Immunology, Lausanne, Switzerland, 1972. *Appointments:* Research Fellow, Department of Chemical Pathology, University College Hospital, Ibadan, 1965-66; Lecturer, Senior Lecturer, Reader, University of Nigeria, Nsukka, 1966-77; Professor of Microbiology, Faculty of Medicine, Science, Ahmadu Bello University, Zaria, 1976-. *Memberships:* includes: Member, International Union of Immunological Societies; Vice-President, Nigerian Society for Immunology; Editor, Nigerian Journal of Microbiology. *Honours:* include: Fellow, International Union of Immunological Societies; Norad Fellow, 1977; Fellow, International Union of Immunological Societies, 1979. *Hobbies:* Swimming; Table Tennis; Lawn Tennis. *Address:* NKPA, Bende LGA, Imo State, Nigeria.

EMENANJO Nwanolue Emmanuel, b. 21 Apr. 1943, Dandawa, Saria, Kaduna State, Nigeria. Teaching. m.

Nwamaka Florence Nwulia, 18 Dec. 1970, 1 son, 4 daughters. *Education:* BA, University of Ibadan, Nigeria, 1966, Post-Graduate Diploma, 1970, MA, 1975, PhD, 1981. *Appointments:* Education Officer, Federal Government College, Warri, 1966-69; Junior Research Fellow, Department of Linguistics & Nigerian Languages, University of Ibadan, 1969-72; Editor, Oxford University Press, Ibadan, 1972-75; Lecturer, Senior Lecturer, Principal Lecturer, Department of Igbo, Alvan Ikoku College of Education, Owerri, Nigeria, 1975-79; Reader in Igbo Linguistics, 1979-; Dean, School of Arts, 1980-. *Memberships: Memberships:* West African Linguistics Society; Linguistic Association of Nigeria; Literary Society of Nigeria; Folklore Society of Nigeria; Society for Promoting Igbo Language & Culture; Secretary, Igbo Standardization Committee; Co-ordinating Committee on Igbo Studies; Standard Igbo Dictionary Project. *Publications:* Elements of Modern Igbo Grammar, 1978; Utara Nti, 1980; Ukabuilu ndi Igbo, 1981; Igbo Language and Culture (Co-edited w. F.C. Ogbalu). *Honours:* Ford Foundation Research Fellow, University of Ibadan, 1969-72. *Hobbies:* Reading; Writing; Travelling; Music. *Address:* Idumuogbu-Umuodafe, Box 51, Ibusa, Bendel State, Nigeria.

EMENIKE, Emmanuel Ndubisi, b. 10 Sept. 1933, Nanka in Aguata, Anambra, Nigeria. Surveyor. m. Cecilia Amuche, 23 Dec. 1961, 4 sons, 2 daughters. *Education:* BSc.Hon.(London), University College, Ibadan, Nigeria, 1954-59; Diploma in Surveying, School of Military Survey, England, 1960-61; MSc.(Surveying Engineering), University of New Brunswick, Canada, 1963-65. *Appointments:* Staff Surveyor, 1961-63, Provincial Surveyor, 1965, Eastern Nigeria; Lecturer in Surveying, 1965-71, Senior Lecturer in Surveying, 1971-76, Reader in Surveying, 1976-, University of Nigeria. *Memberships:* Executive Member, Nigerian Association of Phtogrammetists; Nigerian Geodetic Association; Nigerian Institution of Surveyors. *Publications:* Several publications including: The Principles of Electronic Surveying, 1981; Aid to Large Scale Mapping - The Map Maker, 1976; High Density Survey - Control system for Nigeria, 1978. *Honours:* External Examiner in a Surveying subject, University of Science and Technology, Ghana, 1973-76; External Examiner in Surveying, Auchi Polytechnics, 1979-80. *Hobbies:* Farming; Poultry keeping. *Address:* 1 Rotinsi William, Enugu Campus, University of Nigeria, Enugu, Nigeria.

EMERUOM, Anthony Ugwunwune. b. 25 Dec. 1935, Mpam, Ekwerazu, Ahiazu, LGA, Mbaise. m. Selinah Nwanediuto Iwuoha, 3 Oct. 1964, 6 sons, 3 daughters. *Appointments:* Office messenger, 1955; Office Clerk, 1958-61; Company Secretary, 1964; Sales Director. *Memberships:* Ome-Okachie Social Club of Nigeria; Nueji, Social Club of Nigeria. *Hobbies:* Football; Music; Dancing. *Address:* No. 5, Orlu Street, Owerri, Imo State, Nigeria.

EMESSIRI, Solomon Anthony Johnnie, b. 21 Apr. 1930, Port Harcourt, Rivers State, Nigeria. Legal Practitioner. m. 1 Aug. 1962, 4 sons, 2 daughters. *Education:* LL.B., Holborn College of Law, London, UK, 1960-63; BL., Inner Temple, London, UK, 1963. *Appointments:* Legal practice. *Memberships:* 3rd National Vice President, 1979-80, 2nd National Vice President, 1980-81, Nigerian Bar Association; Chairman, Warri branch, 1979-81, Nigerian Bar Association. *Hobby:* Reading. *Address:* Daji Close, Effurun, Warri, Nigeria.

EMOKPAE, Ogieva Erhabor, b. 10 May 1934, Benin City, Nigeria. Artist. m. Oghogho Iroguehi Bazuaye, 9 May 1957, 4 sons, 12 daughters. *Appointments:* Commercial Artist at Eastern Nigeria Information Services, Enugu, Nigeria, 1954-59; Creative Advertising Visualiser, West Africa Publicity, later known as Lintas, West Africa, 1959-63; Senior Creative Visualiser, 1963-70, Group Head, Creative Department, 1970-74, Executive Creative Director, 1974-76, Lintas Nigeria Limited; Hon. National Secretary, Nigerian Arts Council, 1966-76; Secretary, Society of Nigerian Artists, 1966-69; Art Consultant, 1976-. *Memberships:* Aghama Youth Club of Fine Arts, 1950-53; British Council, 1953-59; Nigerian Society for Arts and Humanities, 1960; Publicity Secretary, 1964-65, Society of Nigerian Artists; Nigerian Arts Council, National Secretary, 1966-76; Island Club, Lagos; Ikoyi Club, Lagos. *Creative Works:* Numerous Murals and Paintings including: Murals: International Understanding Through Peace, 1965; Growth; Paintings: Cosmic Rendezvous; Journey; Dialogue;

Sculptures: Bankers; People; Form; Dialogue; Antelope; Mask; Several one-man Exhibitions at British Council, Enugu, Nigeria; Numerous Joint Exhibitions Internationally including: Bethoven Halle, 1962; London, 1963; Canada, 1965,66; Moscow and Leningrad, 1968; Sofia, Bulgaria, 1980; International Symposia, Sofia, Bulgaria, 1978, 79, 80. *Honours:* Four First Prizes in Painting, Drawing and Sculpture, Nigeria Festival of the Arts, 1953; Nigeria National Honours Award, Officer of The Order of the Niger, 1981. *Hobbies:* Reading; Golf; Swimming. *Address:* No. 7, Joseph Shynglo Street, Surulere, Lagos, Nigeria.

ENELI, Timothy Chukuemeka Maduegbuna, b. 6 April, 1922, Benin City, Nigeria. Educationist; Archivist; Administrator. m. Edna Nkiruka Nkemena, 1 Dec. 1956, 2 sons, 3 daughters. *Education:* BA.(Hons)History, Birmingham University, UK, 1949-52; Post-graduate Certificate in Education, Institute of Education, London University, UK, 1952-53; Diploma in Administrative Management, Washington, USA, 1960. *Appointments:* School Master/Tutor, Dennis Memorial Grammar School, Onitsha, 1942-54; First Nigerian Archivist, Federal Government National Archives of Nigeria, Ibadan, Nigeria, 1955-58; Administrative Officer in the Civil Service of Nigeria, 1959-71; Chairman, Nigerian Construction and Furniture Co. Limited, 1978-79; Director, UTC (Nigeria) Limited, 1977-; Director of numerous Government industrial projects and businesses including: Flour Mills of Nigeria Limited; Nigersteel Company Limited, 1966-70; Universal Insurance Company Limited, 1966-70; Elected Chairman of United Nations (UNCTAD) Committee on Commodities, 1964-65; Visited several Countries including: USA, World Bank Annual Conferences, 1962-65; India to study the industrial development programme with special emphasis on the Iron and Steel Industry; France - on Comparative Education Course,1952, and to make Trade Agreement, 1974-75; Indonesia and Singapore on Industrial Trade Mission, Dec. 1978. *Memberships:* Society of Archivists; Historical Association of Nigeria; Sports Club, Enugu. *Publications:* Essay: Oba Overanmon of Benin. *Hobbies:* Gardening; Music and Dancing; Lawn tennis; Sports. *Address:* 4b Nike Avenue, PO Box 282, Enugu, Anambra State, Nigeria.

ENGEL, Charles Edward, b. 16 Apr. 1921, Dortmund, Germany. Professor of Medical Education. m. Morag Beaufoy, 28 Mar. 1952, 1 son. *Education:* Birkbeck College, University of London, UK. *Appointments:* The Queen's Own Royal West Kent Regiment, Italy and Austria, 1941-46; Head, Department of Medical Photography, Guy's Hospital Medical School, London, UK, 1947-65; Reader, Department of Audio-Visual Aids, University of Melbourne, Australia, 1966-67; Director, British Life Assurance Trust for Health Education, London, UK, 1967-75; Director, BLAT Centre for Health and Medical Education, British Medical Association, London, UK, 1967-75; Head, Discipline of Medical Education, Faculty of Medicine, University of Newcastle, New South Wales, Australia, 1976-. *Memberships:* Fellow of the Royal Photographic Society; Fellow of the Biological Photographic Association; Foreign Corresponding Member, Deutsche Gesellschaft für Photografie; Association for the Study of Medical Education, UK; Australasian and New Zealand Association for Medical Education; Society for Research into Higher Education; Editorial Board, Encyclopaedia Cinematographica; Expert Advisory Panel, Health Manpower Development, World Health Organisation; Associate, WHO Regional Teacher Training Centre, University of New South Wales, Australia; The Athenaeum, London. *Publications:* Former Editor, Medical and Biological Illustration, BMA Quarterly; Photography for the Scientist; Author of over 100 text book chapters and scientific papers. *Honours:* Serving Brother of the Most Venerable Order of the Hospital of St. John of Jerusalem. *Address:* 40 Stuart Street, Kotara Heights, New South Wales 2288, Australia.

ENGLAND, Edgar Roy, b. 4 Jan. 1928, London, England. Consulting Civil Engineer; Town Planner; Arbitrator. m. Claire May Shortt, 25 Nov. 1950, 2 daughters. *Education:* BSc.(Eng)1948, MSc.(Eng), 1949, Westminster College, University of London, UK, 1945-49; Diploma, Town and Country Planning, 1958. *Appointments:* Lecturer, University of London, UK, 1948-49; Engineer, The Hydro-Electric Commission, Tasmania, Australia, 1949-51; Engineer, The Electrolytic Zinc Co. of Australasia Limited, Tasmania, Australia, 1951-55;

Engineer, J. Fowler consultant, 1955-58; Partner, Fowler and England, 1958-60; Partner, Fowler England & Newton, 1960-80; Director, England Newton Spratt & Murphy, 1980-; part-time Lecturer, University of Tasmania and Hobart Technical College, Australia, 1950-62. *Memberships:* Fellow, Institution of Engineers, Australia; Fellow, Institution of Civil Engineers, UK; Foundation Fellow, Institute of Arbitrators, Australia; Member Royal Australian Planning Institute; President, Tasmania Branch, Australian Water and Wastewater Association; Athenaeum Club, Hobart. *Publications:* The Effect on mild steel of cold working in forsion (thesis); The planning of airport environs (thesis); The design of subdivisions and courts. *Honours:* Hobart City Council prize in Town Planning, 1956; Institute of Australian Planning prize in Town Planning, 1957. *Hobbies:* Philately; Woodworking; Building. *Address:* 462 Churchill Avenue, Sandy Bay, Tasmania, Australia.

ENGLAND, Frederick John, b. 5 Mar. 1939, London, England. Painter; Lecturer; Gallery Owner. m. Sheelagh JANE, Apr. 1971. *Education:* National Diploma in Design, Brighton College of Art,UK,1959; Art Teachers Certificate, London University, UK, 1960; Norwegian Scholarship, Hardanger Folkschule, Norway, 1960. *Appointments:* Leek School of Arts and Crafts, UK, 1961-; Director, Englands Gallery, Stoke-on-Trent, UK, 1968-76; Director, Englands Gallery, Leek, UK, 1976-. *Memberships:* International Arts Guild; President, Secretary, Society of Staffordshire Artists; Society of Free Painters and Sculptors; Fine Art Organiser, Leek Arts Festival. *Creative Works:* Work in Permanent Collections at: Nicholson Institute,Leek; City of Stoke-on-Trent Museum and Art Gallery; Goritz Collection, London; Fenning Collection, Geneva; Keele University. *Honours:* Diploma D'Honneur, Monte Carlo,1971; Medaille D'Argent, 1972, Medaille D'Or, 1975, Paris Salon, Society des Artists Francais; Diploma of Art, Cannes, 1976; European Prize for Painting, Rome, 1977; Prix de Deauville, Deauville, 1975; Diploma for Services to Art and Antiques, 1980; European Master Framer, Belgium, 1977. *Hobbies:* Travel. *Address:* England's Gallery, 56/58 St. Edward Street, Leek, Staffordshire ST13 5DL, England.

ENGLAND, Glyn, b. 19 Apr. 1921, Llantrisant, Wales. Chartered Engineer. m. Tania Reichenbach, 28 Sept. 1942, 2 daughters. *Education:* BSc.(Eng),Queen Mary College, London University, UK; London School of Economics. *Appointments:* Department of Scientific and Industrial Research, 1939; War service, 1942-47; Chief Operations Engineer,1966-71, Director-General, South Western Region, 1971-73, Chairman,South Western Electricity Board, 1973-77, Chairman,Central Electricity Generating Board, 1977-, Electricity Supply Industry, 1947-. *Memberships:* Companion, British Institute of Management; Fellow, Institution of Electrical Engineers; Fellow, Institution of Mechanical Engineers. *Publications:* Papers on: Clean Air; Conservation of Water Resources; Economic Growth and the Electricity Supply Industry; Security of Electricity Supplies; Planning for Uncertainty. *Honours:* Hon. DSc Bath, 1981. *Hobbies:* Enjoying the Countryside. *Address:* Woodbridge Farm, Ubley, Bristol BS18 6PX, England.

ENUKE, Christopher Onyeji, b. 3 Nov. 1929, Arondizuogu, Imo State, Nigeria. Personnel Management. m. 23 Apr. 1955, 2 sons, 5 daughters. *Education:* BSc (London) Mathematics and Geography, University College, Ibadan, Nigeria, 1948-53; Post Graduate Studies: US Department of Agriculture Graduate School, Washington DC, USA, US Bureau of the Census, IBM School, Washington DC, USA, Jan-Nov.1962; Diploma in Data Processing. *Appointments:* Teacher, National High School, Arondizuogu, Education Officer and Senior Mathematics Master, Government College, Umuahia, Nigeria, 1953-61; Data Processor: Federal Census Office, Cabinet Office, Lagos, Nigeria, 1962-65; Labour/Staff Manager, 1965-66, Factory Personnel Manager, Aba Factory, 1966-71, Management Administrative Manager, 1971-73, General Personnel Manager, 1973-78, Personnel Director, 1978-, Lever Brothers Nigeria Limited. *Memberships:* Chairman, NJIC of the Chemical Industries Trade Group; Coordinating Committee of NECA; Institute of Personnel Management of Nigeria; Assessor in the Industrial Arbitration Panel; Apapa Club, Lagos; Chairman, Lagos Chapter of Arondizuogu Social Club of Nigeria. *Publica-*

tions: Preparing publication on: Industrial Relations in Nigeria. *Hobbies:* Reading. *Address:* c/o Lever Brothers Nigeria Limited, 15 Dockyard Road, PO Box 15, Apapa, Lagos, Nigeria.

ENWEZOR, Walter Okwundu, b. 3 July 1936, Awkuzu, Nigeria. Soil Scientist; Agriculturist. m. Ime Inyang, 2 Apr. 1966. *Education:* BSc.Agric., MSc., University College, Ibadan, Nigeria, 1955-62; PhD., DIC., Imperial College, London, UK, 1962-64. *Appointments:* Lecturer in Soil Science, University of Ibadan, Nigeria, 1965-66; Lecturer in Soil Science, 1966-76, Reader in Soil Science, 1976-78, Professor of Soil Science, 1978-, University of Nigeria, Nsukka, Nigeria. *Memberships:* Secretary, Soil Science Society of Nigeria,1971-; International Society of Soil Science; Agricultural Society of Nigeria; Science Association of Nigeria; Association for the Advancement of Agricultural Science in Africa. *Publications:* Contributor to Professional Journals in Soil Science, including: Soil Science; Plant and Soil; Geoderma; Nigerian Agricultural Journal. *Honours:* Commonwealth Academic Fellowship to Aberdeen University, Scotland, 1975-76; Departmental Prize in BSc. Degree Examination, 1960; State Scholarship to University College, Ibadan, Nigeria, 1955. *Hobbies:* Ballroom dancing; Photography; Cinematography; Farming; Gardening. *Address:* 911 Murtala Muhammed Road, University of Nigeria, Nsukka, Nigeria.

ENWONWU, Cyril Obiora, b. 12 Oct. 1935, Onitsha, Nigeria. University Professor and Research Director. m. 28 Dec. 1963, 2 sons, 2 daughters. *Education:* BDS, 1962, MDS, 1966, PhD, 1976, University of Bristol, England; ScD, 1968, Massachusetts Institute of Technology, Massachusetts, USA. *Appointments:* Assistant Professor, 1968-72, Associate Professor, 1972-73, Research Professor, 1973-74, University Washington, Washington, USA; Professor of Medical Biochemistry, 1974-, Head, Enugu Campus, 1975-79, University of Nigeria; Director, National Inst. Medical Research, Nigeria, 1979-. *Memberships:* American Institute of Nutrition; International Association Dental Research; World Health Organization Expert Working Group on Oral Health; President, Nutrition Society of Nigeria; Biochemical Society, Nigeria; International Relations Committee; Federation Dentaire Internationale; Consultant, Scientific Committee of FDI. *Publications:* Author and co-author of approximately 80 manuscripts in International Journals; Contributed several chapters in scientific professional textbooks. *Honours:* Fellow, Academy of Science of Nigeria, 1977; Honorary Fellow, Nigerian Institute of Food Science and Technology, 1978; British Dental Association Prize, 1959; Claudius Ash Prize, 1961. *Hobbies:* Reading; Music. *Address:* No. 4 Enwonwu Street, Onitsha, Nigeria.

ENYI, Wilson Obeya, b. 17 May 1939, Otukpo, Benue State, Nigeria. Architect. m. Victoria Otobo, 1 Sept. 1951, 1 son, 3 daughters. *Education:* Ahmadu Bello University, Zaria, 1962-67; MNIA, 1972, RIBA 1976. *Appointments:* Architect, Northern Nigeria Government, Kaduna, 1967; Chief Architect, Benue-Plateau State Government, Jos, 1975; Chief Architect, Benue State Government, Makurdi, 1976; Consultant Architect, 1976-. *Memberships:* President, Society of Architectural Students, 1966-67; Student Representative Assembly, 1965-66; Chairman, Plateau Dynamous Football Club, 1973-76; Chairman, Table Tennis Association, 1973-74; Chairman, Basketball Association, 1974-76. *Hobbies:* Football; Table Tennis; Music; Dancing; Filming. *Address:* 13 Railway By-Pass, Makurdi, Benue State, Nigeria.

EPELU-OPIO, Justin, b. 20 Oct. 1944, Soroti, Uganda. Veterinary. m. Gladys Epelu-Opio, 30 Dec. 1972, 1 son, 3 daughters. *Education:* BVSc, MSc, University of Nairobi, Kenya, 1967-72; PhD, Makerere University, Uganda, 1973-76. *Appointments:* Temporary Technician, 1971, Part-time Demonstrator, 1971-72, University of Nairobi, Kenya; Lecturer, Department of Veterinary Anatomy, Makerere University, Uganda, 1973-76; Senior Professional Officer, 1977-79, Principal Professional Officer, 1979, Scientific Officer, 1980-, National Council for Scientific Research, Animal Productivity Research Unit, Zambia. *Memberships:* Executive Member, Veterinary Association of Zambia; Uganda Veterinary Association; East African Academy; Lions Club; Wild Life Conservation Society of Zambia; Agricola Club; Chilanga Recreation Club. *Publications:* Author of 15 Reports and Papers in field of animal research.

Honours: DAAD Scholarship, 1971-72; DAAD Fellowship, 1975. *Hobbies:* Gardening; Sports; Films. *Address:* PO Box 605, Soroti, Uganda.

ERBY, Jonathan George Wycombe, b. 19 May 1938, Sydney, Australia. Architect. m. Christine Ann Creal, 21 May 1966, 2 sons. *Education:* B.Arch. Sydney University, 1957-61. *Appointments:* Devine, Erby & Mazlin Pty. Ltd., 1962-. *Memberships:* President, The Primary Club of Australia; Vice-President, Sydney University Cricket Club; The Australian Club; Pymble Golf Club; Cricketers Club of New South Wales. *Hobbies:* Cricket; Golf; Philately. *Address:* 191 Deepwater Road, Castle Cove, NSW, 2069, Australia.

EREKOSIMA, Isaac Dagogo, b. 11 Apr. 1912, Buguma City, Degema, Nigeria. Retired Educationist, Business Administrator. m. Victoria Kingba Charles Amachree, 14 Jan. 1939, 2 sons, 3 daughters. *Education:* Pupil Teacher, 1925-29; Government College, 1930-31; Government Class Six Certificate; Higher College, 1932-35; Teachers' Diploma; Associateship Course, University of London Institute of Education, 1960-61; Overseas Course B, London School of Economics, 1960-61; Certificate for Development Planning & Administration, UNESCO Regional Institute for Educational Planning, Dakar, 1965. *Appointments:* Education Officer, 1950-56; Principal, Government Secondary School, Owerri, 1957-59; Principal Government Teacher Training College, Uyo, 1960-61; First African Principal, Government College, Imuahia, 1962-65; In charge of Planning, Research and Statistics, Eastern Nigeria Ministry of Education, 1966-68; Chairman, Board of Director, Cooperative Bank of Eastern Nigeria, 1958-60 and of Port Harcourt Flour Mills, 1975-79. *Memberships:* Chairman, Eastern Nigeria Amateur Athletic Association; Chairman, Association of Education Officers of Eastern Nigeria. *Publications:* The Church in Nigeria, 1939; Chieftancy in Kalabari, 1975; Proposals for the Educational System of the Rivers State, 1968; Regular contributor to Magazines in Eastern Nigeria. *Honours:* Queen's Coronation Medal, 1953; Former Nigerian Mile Champion, 1933; Head of War Canoe House at Buguma, 1955; Halls of Residence named after him at Government Secondary School, Owerri, 1961, and at Government College, Umuahia, 1966; Meritorious Award by the Old Boys of Government College, Umuahia, 1980. *Hobbies:* Lawn Tennis; Chess; Reading; Choral Singing. *Address:* Seaview House, Buguma, Nigeria.

EREMIE, Deinma Ayo, b. 25 Mar. 1947, Okrika. Legal Practitioner. m. Furo Adoki, 8 Apr. 1976, 2 sons, 3 daughters. *Education:* LL.B., University of Ife, 1973; Called to the Bar as Barrister and Solicitor of the Supreme Court of Nigeria, 1975. *Appointments:* Legal Officer, Federal Ministry of Labour, Maiduguri, 1973-74, Pan African Bank Ltd., Port Harcourt, 1974-75; Company Secretary, 1975-78, Head of Administration, 1978-80, Pan African Bank Ltd., Port Harcourt; Private Commercial Law Consultancy and Practice. *Memberships:* International Bar Association. *Publications:* Regular contributions to the media. *Honours:* Okrika Progressive Educational Award, 1961; Shell BP Essay Prize, 1965; Students Leadership Award, University of Ife, 1973. *Hobbies:* Swimming; Travelling; Writing. *Address:* 10 Ngumezi Street, D/Line, Port Harcourt, Nigeria.

ERESI, Remissio Joseph, b. 22 June 1935, Nila, Shortlands. General Nursing Midwives, Medical Laboratory Assistant. m. Adella Dolores, 18 July 1964, 4 sons, 5 daughters. *Education:* General Nursing & Midwifery Certificate, Nursing School, Honiara, 1955; Medical Laboratory Assistant, Fiji School of Medicine, 1960; Six months course Radiographical School in Swoa, Fiji, 1960. *Appointments:* General Nursing & Midwife, 1952-55; Laboratory Assistant and Radiographer, Central Hospital, Homiara, 1961-65; Assistant Geochemist, Geological Survey Department, 1965-67. *Memberships:* Vice-President, 1968, President, 1969-70, Shortland Council; Governing Council; Secretary Famoa Council of Chiefs; Chairman, Parliamentary Business Committee. Several local songs in modern times. *Hobbies:* Pop singing; Gardening; Fishing; Soccer, Rugby; Philately; Playing guitar and ukalele; Dancing. *Address:* c/o Postal Agency, Nila, Shortlands, Solomon Islands.

ERICSON, John Frederick, b. 24 Aug. 1926, Ngapara, New Zealand. Automotive Engineer. m. June Morita

Day, 8 Oct. 1949, 1 son, 2 daughters. *Appointments:* Assistant Garage Supervisor, New Zealand Railway Road Services, New Zealand, 1960-64; Part time Lecturer, Automotive Engineering, Otahahu College, Auckland, New Zealand, 1962-64; Garage Supervisor, New Zealand Railways Road Services, Kaitaia, New Zealand, 1964-67; Garage Supervisor, NZ Railway Road Services, Wellington, New Zealand, 1967-75; Part time Lecturer, Automotive Engineering, Wellington Polytechnic, 1969-74; Assistant Director, New Zealand Railways Road Services, Wellington, New Zealand, 1975-. *Memberships:* Society of Automotive Engineer; New Zealand Institute of Motor Industry; Engineering Associates Registration Boards; Registered Engineers Associate; Life Member Society of Automotive Engineers; Naenae College Board of Governors. *Hobbies:* Golf; Fishing. *Address:* 28 Pilcher Crescent, Lower Hutt, New Zealand.

ERLWANGER, Stanley Herbert, b. 17 July 1934, Bulawayo, Zimbabwe. Mathematics Educator. m. Gladys Ruth Elizabeth Jeffery, 30 Apr. 1960, 2 sons, 1 daughter. *Education:* BSc, University of Cape Town, South Africa, 1955; MA, Eastern Michigan University, USA, 1969; PhD, University of Illinois, 1974. *Appointments:* Principal, Chizongwe Secondary School, Zambia, 1964-66; Inspector of Schools, 1967-69, Senior Inspector of Schools, 1970-71, Ministry of Education, Zambia; Visiting Professor, Florida State University, USA, 1974-75; Research Associate, Institute for Advanced Study, USA, 1974-76; Dean, Faculty of Education, University College of Botswana, Botswana, 1977-79; Visiting Professor, 1980, Associate Professor, 1981-, Maths. Department, Concorida University, Montreal, Canada; External Examiner, National University of Lesotho, Lesotho, 1979-. *Memberships:* The National Council of Teachers of Mathematics; The Mathematical Association of America; The National Education Association; The National Society for the Study of Education; American Educational Research Association. *Publications:* Several Working Papers and Publications. *Hobbies:* Reading; Fishing. *Address:* 4350 Mayfair Avenue, Montreal, Quebec, Canada.

EROJU, Bandele Olusegun, b. 28 Jan. 1940, Lagos Nigeria. Engineering. m. Theresa Ibidun Dossou, 1964, 2 sons, 1 daughter. *Education:* BSc, University of Surrey, Guildford, 1968. *Appointments:* Stress Engineer, Westland Helicopters, Hayes & Western Super Mare; Design Engineer, Balfour Kilpatrick Int., London; Divisional Manager, Mechnical, JKN Construction, Nigeria. *Memberships:* Institution of Chartered Engineers, UK; Institution of Mechanical Engineers, UK; American Society of Heating Refrigeration and Air Conditioning Engineers; Royal Aeronautical Society, UK. *Hobby:* Table tennis. *Address:* 7 Awoyemi Close, Surulere, Lagos, Nigeria.

ERRINGTON, William, b. 9 Aug. 1927, San Francisco, California, USA. Barrister & Solicitor. m. Elizabeth 3 June 1950. *Education:* B.Com, McGill University, Montreal, Quebec, 1950; Osgoode Hall Law School, 1954. *Appointments:* Partner, Stive Vale, Barristers & Solicitors. *Memberships:* Canada Bar Association; Fellow, Canadian Law Foundation. *Honours:* Queen's Counsel, 1964. *Address:* 175 Beechwood Crescent, Newmarket, Ontario, Canada.

ERUBU, Hamidu Gambari, b. 29 May 1931, Ilorin, Nigeria. Chairman, Kwara State Civil Service Commission. m. Sidikatu Bolajoko Maliki, 3 sons, 5 daughters. *Education:* Yale University, 1961; Hull University, 1963; BSc, University of Wisconsin, 1972. *Appointments:* Assistant Education Officer, 1957-60; Education Officer, 1960-62; Senior Education Officer, 1962-65, Princiapl Education Officer, 1965-66, Deputy Chief Education Officer, 1966-68, Ministry of Education, Northern Nigeria; Chief Education Officer, 1968-72, Deputy Chief Inspector of Education, 1972-74, Ministry of Education, North Western State; Deputy Chief Extension Coordinator, 1974-76; Director, Centre for Adult Education, 1976-77, Ahmadu Bello University, Zaria; Permanent Member, 1977-80, Chairman, 1980-, Kwara State Civil Service Commission. *Memberships:* Science Association of Nigeria; Executive Member, Nigerian National Council for Adult Education; African Adult Education Association. *Publications:* Editor, Adult Education in Nigeria; Elementary Science Texts. *Hobbies:* Badmington; Table Tennis. *Address:* 14 Umar Audi Road, GRA, Ilorin, Kwara State, Nigeria.

ESIMAI, Nelson Ifeanyichuku, b. 12 Nov. 1933, Ohita, Anambra State, Nigeria. Medical Practitioner. m. Esther Agwajinma Ajoku, 20 Jan. 1962, 2 sons, 3 daughters. *Education:* MB,BS., (London), University College Hospital, Ibadan, 1953-60; Diploma in Child Health (England), 1963; Fellow, Royal College of Physicians and Surgeons, Glasgow, 1978. *Appointments:* Junior hospital appointments in Surgery, Medicine and Paediatrics in Bath, Birmingham, West Bromwich andd Wolverhampton, 1961-65; Medical Officer, Special Grade, Onitsha, 1965-70; Consultant Physician, 1970; Senior Consultant Physician, 1974; Chief Consultant Physician, Anambra State, 1977; Medical Director, St Luke's Hospital, Onitsha, 1980-. *Memberships:* Royal College of Physicians and Surgeons, Glasgow, 1965. *Publications:* The Health of the Nation - Address to the Niger Diocesan Synod, 1979. *Honours:* Commissioner for Health, Anambra State, Nigeria, 1976-79. *Hobbies:* Music; Reading; Architecture. *Address:* 15 Old Nkissi Road, Onitsha, Anambra State, Nigeria.

ESPLIN, Air Vice-Marshal Ian George, b. 26 Feb. 1914. m. Patricia Kaleen Barlow, 1944, 1 son, 1 daughter. *Education:* Sydney University; BEc, 1936, MA, 1939, Oxford University. *Appointments:* Pilot, RAF, 1939-45; Comd. RASF Desford, 1947; Deputy Senior Personnel Staff Officer, HQ Reserve Comd, 1948; Directing Staff, RAF Staff College, 1950-51; Cmd first Jet All Weather Wing, Germany, 1952-54; Flying College Course, 1954; Dep. Director of Operational Requirements, Air Ministry, 1955-58; Cmdr, RAF Wartling, 1958-60; Director of Operational Reqts, 1960-62; Cmdr, RAF Staff and Air Attache, Washington, USA, 1963-65; Dean, Air Attache Corps, 1964-65; Managing Director, Computer Sciences, Australia, 1970-72. *Memberships:* Vincents; Leander; Elanora CC, Sydney. *Honours:* CB, 1963; OBE, 1946; DFC, 1943. *Hobbies:* Golf; Tennis; Swimming. *Address:* 47 Headland Road, Castlecove, New South Wales, Australia.

ESPLIN, Thomas, b. 26 Nov. 1915, Motherwell, Scotland. Artist and Teacher of Art. m. Edith Christina Leslie Mees, 22 June 1940, 2 sons, 2 daughters. *Education:* Diploma of Art, Edinburgh College of Art, 1939; Specialist Teacher of Art Diploma, 1940; Diploma of the College of Handicraft, 1953; Member of the New Zealand Society of Industrial Designers, 1970. *Appointments:* Associate Professor of Design and Fine Art, University of Otago, Dunedin, New Zealand, 1954-81. *Memberships:* Past President of the Dunedin Public Art Gallery; Past President of the Otago Art Society; Artist Member of the New Zealand Academy of Fine Art, Wellington. *Creative Works:* Represented in Public Art Galleries and Private Art Collections in New Zealand and Australia, Americas and Europe, many group and one man shows. *Honours:* Andrew Grant Commonwealth Open Scholar, 1934; Imperial Relations Trust Scholar, 1934; Fellow of the College of Handicraft, 1952. *Hobbies:* Trasvel. *Address:* 3 Prospect Row, Sawyers Bay, Otago, New Zealand.

ESSANG, Ita Okon, b. Aug. 1934, Adadia, Uyo Local Govt. Soldier. m. Akon Inyang Nuwak, 30 Dec. 1966, 1 son, 3 daughters. *Education:* Cambridge Overseas School Leaving Certificate, 1954; Diploma, School of Forestry, 1957; Mechanical Transport School, Bourden, England, 1961-62. *Appointments:* Forestry Assistant, 1956-58; Commissioned Officer, 1958-71; Active service with United Nations in the Congo, 1960-63; Chief Instructor, Nigerian Military Training College, 1964-66; Transport Control Supervisor, Shell-BP, 1972-77; Civil Commissioner, Commissioner for Education, 1978; Civil Commissioner, Commissioner for Lands, Surveys and Urban Development, 1979; Chairman, Cross River State Transport Corporation, 1976-79. *Memberships:* Sports Club; African Club; Pamol Club, Calabar. *Creative Works:* Paintings. *Hobbies:* Painting; Game Hunting. *Address:* No. 18 Eyamba Street, PO Box 58, Oron, Cross River State, Nigeria.

ESSIEN, Emmanuel Archibong, b. 6 May 1935, Atai Otoro, Cross River State, Nigeria. Teaching. m. Lucy Henry Ekpo, 27 Dec. 1956, 2 sons, 3 daughters. *Education:* BA, University of Nigeria, 1964. *Appointments:* Native Administration School, 1951; Holy Family College, Oku-Abak, 1952-54; Ibibio State College, Ikot Ekpene, 1954-61, 1964-68; Commissioner (Minister) of Works and Transport, 1968-71, Commissioner (Minister) of Education, 1973-75, South Eastern State; Government TTC, Ikot Osurua, Ikot Ekpene, 1975-.

Memberships: Memberships: President, Otoro Youth Association; President, Literary Society; Chairman, Calabar Sports Club; Secretary, Football Association, Secretary, Recreation Club. *Publications:* The Growth of the English Language; A Collection of Poems. *Honours:* Book Prizes for Poetry, 1964; Honorary Member of Nigerian Parliament, 1965-66; Visited United Kingdom as Guest of British Council, 1973. *Hobbies:* Lawn Tennis; Billiards; Farming; Music; Photography; Dog Raising. *Address:* Atai Otoro, PO Box 3, Abak CRS, Nigeria.

ETTE, Akpanoluo Ikpong, b. 23 Sept. 1930 Ibeno, Nigeria. University Teacher. m. Edak Ekpenyong Nsa 22 Apr. 1961, 3 Sons, 2 daughters. *Education:* University College, Ibadan 1949-54; BSc London 1954; PhD London 1966. *Appointments:* Physics Master, Hope Waddell Training Institution 1954-59; Lecturer in Physics, University College, Ibadan 1959-66; Senior Lecturer, Physics, University of Ibadan 1966-72; Professor, Physics 1972-; Dean, Postgraduate School, University of Ibadan 1976-78. *Memberships:* Nigerian Union of Planetary and Radio Science; Ad-hoc Working Group, International Commission on Atmospheric Electricity, on Long-range localization of lightning activity; Nigerian Institute of Physics; Science Association of Nigeria; Nigerian Academy of Science. *Publications:* 24 publications including: Anomalous electrical behaviour oa a tree looking in between metal electrodes, 1966; On starting voltages in a two-point discharger, 1966; On the ion space charge resitance in point-to-plane corona gaps, 1971; Education and Training of the Scientists: Deflects in our System of Training, 1975; The characteristics of rain electricity in Nigeria I—Magnitudes and variations, 1980. *Honours:* Fellow, Science Association of Nigeria 1975; Foundation Fellow, Nigerian Academy of Science 1977. *Hobbies:* Reading; Swimming; Dancing; Table tennis. *Address:* 12 Saunders Road, University of Ibadan, Nigeria.

ETTEH, Esoetok Ikpong Ikpong, b. 1 Sept. 1946 Upenekang, Ibeno, Cross River State, Nigeria. Architect. m. 29 July 1977 1 son, 1 daughter. *Education:* West African School Certificate 1965; GCE (A Level) 1968; BSc(Arch.) 1972; MSc(Arch.) 1974. *Appointments:* National Youth Service Corp. 1974-75; Niger Consultants, (Architects/Planners) 1975-. *Memberships:* Nigerian Institute of Architects; The Portharcourt Club; Patron, University of Science and Technology Association of Quantity Surveying Students. *Creative Works:* Architectural Design on Housing, Schools, Hospitals, Hotels Sports Stadia, Offices, and Industry. *Hobbies:* Football; Lawn/Table Tennis; Squash; Dancing. *Address:* 48c Nkpogu Road, Transamadi Layout, Portharcourt, Rivers State, Nigeria.

ETUK, Ekong Samson, b. 14 June 1942, Etinan, Cross River State, Nigeria. Architect-Urban Designer. m. Pamela Francine Etuk, 26 Dec. 1970, 1 son, 1 daughter. *Education:* McGill University, Montreal Canada 1963-67; Bachelor of Architecture, University of Manitoba Winnipeg, Canada 1970; Master of Architecture in Urban Design, Cornell University, Itacha, NY 1974. *Appointments:* Architects and Planners, Gardiner Thornton Davidson Garrett and Masson, Vancouver, BC, Canada 1970; Architects, Colebrooke Associates Nassau, Bahamas 1971; Architects, Engineers, Planners, Madison Madison International, Cleveland, Ohio, USA 1971-72; Planners, Urban Designers, EcoDesign Inc. Cambridge, Massachusetts, USA 1973; The Architects Collaborative Inc., Cambridge, Massachusetts, USA 1973-74; Architects, Femi Majekodunmi Associates, Lagos Nigeria 1975-76; Foundeed Intellect Associates, Architects, Engineers, Planners, 1976; President and Chief Executive of Intellect Associates, 1976-; Teaching: Part-time Lecturer University of Lagos, Faculty of Environmental Design. *Memberships:* Umuahia Government College Old Boys Association; Nigerian Institute of Architects; Royal Institute of British Architects; Director African Ivory Insurance Company Limited; Alternate Director, BFN Limited; Director Beaman Management Consultants; Director of Prodel Inc, Houston USA. *Publications:* Beyond Calabar 2000, 1974; Low Cost Housing in Developing Countries, 1973; Staging of a New Town Development, 1969; Systems Application to African Village Planning 1969; Paper on National Housing Policy—Housing as a Process and Accessibility 1980; Designed: Uyo Main Market (Phae I - 15 million); Federal Capital Development Authority Field Base, Abuja; Nigerian National Petro-

leum Corporation Petroleum Research Center, Port-Harcourt; Ajaokuta Steel Company Corporate Headquarters, Ajaokuta; Block of Flats at Plot 181 Victoria Island, Lagos. *Honours:* Class nomination Pilkington Travel Scholarship, 1970; Manitoba Association of Architects Book Prize 1970; Government College Umuahia, Colours in Cricket, Athletics, Hockey; Tuition Scholarship Cornell University 1973; McGill University colours in Athletics; Eastern Nigeria and Nigerian National Hockey team, 1962. *Hobbies:* Tennis; Music; Reading; Travelling. *Address:* 2 MaCarthy Street, Ilupeju, Lagos, Nigeria.

EUNSON, Richard Keith, b. 10 Apr. 1929 Invercargill, New Zealand. Journalist. m. Elizabeth Margaret Smith 7 July 1956, 3 daughters. *Education:* Southland Boys High School. *Appointments:* Southland Daily News 1946-49; Otago Daily Times, London correspondent NZ Associated Press 1954-56; Otago Daily Times, Parliamentary Press Gallery correspondent, Otago Daily Time, Editor, 1976-. *Memberships:* CPU; New Zealand Press Council; Otago regional executive National Children's Health Foundation; Dunedin Rotary Club; Otago Racing Club. *Publications:* Election 1969; In The Balance; The Wreck of the General Grant; Hunting With Harker; Harker Hunts the Coast. *Honours:* Queen's Silver Jubilee Medal; Cowan Memorial Prize (twice). *Hobbies:* Thoroughbred Racing; Otago goldfields history; 19th Centry sailing ships. *Address:* 37 Lundie Street, Dunedin, New Zealand.

EVANS, Arthur Mostyn (Moss), b. 13 July 1925 Methyr Tydfil. Trade Union Official. m. Laura Bigglestone 1947 3 sons, 3 daughters. *Education:* Cefn Coed Primary School, South Wales; Church Road Secondary Modern School, Birmingham. *Appointments:* District Officer, TGWU, Birmingha, Chemical and Engineering Industries, 1956; Regional Officer, Midlands, 1960; National Officer, Engineering Trade Group, 1966; National Secretary, Chemical Rubber and Oil Industries, 1969; National Secretary, Autmotive Section 1969-73; National Organiser 1973-78; General Secretary TGWU 1978. *Memberships:* Royal Instiute of International Affairs; Vice-President, Industrial Society Schrewsbury School, 1978. *Hobbies:* Music. *Address:* 6 Highland Drive, Leverstock Green, Hemel Hempstead, Herts HP3 8PT, England.

EVANS, Cyril Percival Victorious, b. 27 Apr. 1921 Sydney Australia. Medical Practitioner. m. Beryl 20 Dec. 1949 1 son, 3 daughters. *Education:* Sydney University; Postgraduate Medical Studies in England and USA; MBBS, Sydney; DTM, Sydney; FRACP London; DExp, FRACMA. *Appointments:* General and Senior Resident Medical Officer posts at Royal Prince Alfred Hospital Sydney, 1943-45; Captain, Australian Army Medical Corps. 1945-46; Medical Supertent, Aymes Memorial Hospital Solomon Islands 1946-49; Resident and Registrar, Royal Postgraduate Medical School, Lond, and Assistant Chest Physician, Cornwall and North Wales, 1950-54; Chest Physician, North Carolina Sanatorium USA 1954-55; Deputy Director of Tuberculosis, Department of Health, Queensland Australia, 1956-68; Seconded, WHO, Medical Officer Tuberculosis Chemotherapy Centre, Madras, India, 1963-65; Director Tuberculosis Services, Department Public Health, Adelaide, South Australia, 1969-73; First Assistant Director-General, Australian Department of Health, Canberra, 1974; Deputy Director-General, Department of Health, Canberra 1974. *Publications:* Tuberculous Menigitis—a Preventible Disease, 1956; The Histoplasmin Skim Test: A Brief Report, 1960; Varicella Pneumonia: A Possible Cause of Subsequent Pulmonary Calcification, 1964; A 2-year Follow-up of Patients with Quiescnt Pulmonary Tuberculosis following a Year of Chemotherapy, 1966; An Attempt at Group Therapy as a Cure for the Smoking Habit, 1967; The Assessment of Cavitation from Chest Radiographs, 1968; A Clinical Trial of Ethambutol plus Capreomycin in the Treatment of Atypical Tuberculosis, 1969; The Australian Rifampicin Trial 1972. *Address:* 57 Ambalindum Street, Hawker, ACT, Australia.

EVANS, Daniel Simon, b. 29 May 1921, Llanfynydd, Dyfed. University Professor. m. Annie Frances Richards, 29 Mar. 1949, 1 son. *Education:* Swansea University College; United Theological College, Aberystwyth; Jesus Collogo, Oxford; BA, (Wales), 1944, BD (Wales), 1947, MA (Wales), 1948; B.Litt (Oxon), 1952; D.Litt (Wales), 1979. *Appointments:* Assistant Lecturer in Welsh, 1948, Lecturer, 1951, Swansea University College; Professor of Welsh, University College, Dublin, 1956; Lecturer in Welsh, 1962, Professor of Welsh, 1974, St David's College, Lampeter; Head of Department of Celtic Studies, University of Liverpool, 1966. *Memberships:* London Philological Society; International Arthurian Society; The Honourable Society of Cymmrodorion; Secretary, Language & Literature Committee of the Board of Celtic Studies, University of Wales. *Publications:* Gramadeg Cymraeg Canol, 1951, 1960, 1977; Buched Dewi, 1959, 1965; A Grammar of Middle Welsh, 1964, 1970, 1976; Lives of the Welsh Saints, 1971; Historia Gruffud Vab Kenan, 1977. *Honours:* Vernam Hull Memorial Prize, University of Wales, 1978. *Address:* Hoddnant, New Street, Lampeter, Dyfed, Wales.

EVANS, David Denton Edward, b. 3 Jan. 1936, Adelaide, South Australia. Pathologist. m. Eleanor Elizabeth Johnson, 9 Jan. 1960, 1 son, 2 daughters. *Education:* Bachelor of Medicine & Surgery, University of Adelaide, 1960; $diploma of Tropical Medicine, University of Sydney, 1962; Diploma of Clinical Pathology, University of London, 1966; Fellowship, Royal Australasian College of Pathologists, 1978. *Appointments:* Resident Medical Officer, 1960,61; Pathology Registrar, 1962-66; Medical Officer, Research & Teaching, 1966,67; Histopathologist, Canberra Community Hospital, 1968-69; Pathologist-in-Charge, Commonwealth Pathology Laboratory, Hobart, 1969-81. *Memberships:* Australian Medical Association, Secretary, Hobart Division, 1978-79, Secretary 6th Australian Medical Congress 1981; Fellow, Royal Society of Tropical Medicine; Society of Friends. *Publications:* Contributions in journals on Sexually Transmitted Diseases, Australia Antigen, & Case Reports. *Honours:* WHO Fellow, 1965-66. *Hobbies:* Japanese game of Go; Royal Tennis; Choral Music. *Address:* 1 Swanston Street, New Town, Tasmania, Australia, 7008.

EVANS, David Mylor, b. 20 June 1934, Richmond, Victoria, Australia. Member Legislative Council, Victorian Parliament. m. 4 Aug. 1961, 1 son, 2 daughters. *Education:* Matriculation, 1951. *Appointments:* Farmer Redcamp Moyhu, Victoria, 1952-76; Member of Parliament, 1976-. *Hobbies:* Farming; Community Involvement; Sport. *Address:* Redcamp, Moyhu 3732, Victoria, Australia.

EVANS, Edward Howard Michael, b. 9 Oct. 1947, Tonbridge, Kent, England. Systems Programmer. *Education:* Imperial College, London, 1966-69, BS.c., 1969, A.R.C.S., 1969; University College, Cardiff and A.E.R.E., Harwell, 1970-73, Ph.D., 1980. *Appointments:* Systems Programmer, International Computers Limited, Putney, London, 1974-76; Post-Doctoral Assistant, Physics Department, University College, Cardiff, 1976-78; Post-Doctoral Fellow, Chemistry Department, University College, Cardiff, 1979; Systems Programmer, Computing Centre, University College, Cardiff, 1979-. *Memberships:* Institute of Physics; Institution of Electrical Engineers. *Publications:* Various contributions to scientific journals including: Phase Transitions in Triamantane, 1978; Diffracted Beam Monochromator in Single Crystal Diffractometry, 1980. *Hobbies:* Golf; Tennis; Snooker; Gardening; stamp collecting. *Address:* 3 Waverley Close, Llandough, Penarth, South Glamorgan, CF6 1PQ, Wales.

EVANS, Gareth John, b. 5 Sept. 1944, Melbourne, Australia. Senator, Australian Parliament. m. Merran Gael Anderson, 15 Jan. 1969, 1 son, 1 daughter. *Education:* BA., LL.B., Honours, Melbourne; MA., Oxon. *Appointments:* Lecturer, 1971-74; Senior Lecturer, Constitutional Law, University of Melbourne, 1974-76; Practising Barrister, 1977-78; Senator for Victoria, 1978-; Shadow Attorney-General, 1980-. *Memberships:* Foundation President, Australian Society of Labor Lawyers; Vice-President, Victorian Council for Civil Liberties; Director, Australian Institute of Political Science. *Publications:* Editor or Co-editor of: Labor and the Constitution, 1972-75; The Whitlam Years in Australian Government, 1977; Law Politics & the Labor Movement, 1980; Labor Essays, 1980,81; Author or Co-author of pamphlets, The Politics of Justice, 1981; Labor's Socialist Objective, 1981 and numerous published chapters & articles. *Hobbies:* Travel; Literature; Tennis. *Address:* 24 Maltravers Road, E. Ivanhoe, Victoria, 3079, Australia.

EVANS, Gregory Thomas, b. 13 June 1913, McAdam, New Brunswick, Canada. Chief Justice of the High Court, Supreme Court of Ontario. m. Zita Callon, 1 Oct. 1941, 5 sons, 4 daughters. *Education:* B.A., St. Josephs University; LL.D., St. Thomas University; Ph.D., University of Moncton. *Appointments:* includes: Call to Ontario Bar, 1939; Queen's Counsel, 1953; High Court, 1963, Court of Appeal, 1965, Supreme Court of Ontario; Chief Justice of the High Court, 1976-; Knight Commander of the Order of St. Gregory the Great, 1980; Vice-Chairman, Canadian Judicial Council. *Memberships:* Member, University Club, Toronto. *Address:* Osgoode Hall, 130 Queen Street West, Toronto M5H 2N5, Canada.

EVANS, Harold, b. 29 Apr. 1911. Journalist; Civil Servant; Adviser on Public Relations; Author. m. Elizabeth Jaffray, 8 Sept. 1945, 1 son, (Deceased), 1 daughter. *Education:* King Edward VI School, Stourbridge. *Appointments:* Journalist in Worcestershire and Sheffield, 1932-40; British Legation, Helsinki, 1940-41; Ministry of Information representative in West Africa (Staff of Resident Minister), 1942-46; Colonial Office, 1946-57 (Chief Information Officer from 1953); Adviser on Public Relations to Prime Minister, 1957-64; Head of Information and Research, Independent Television Authority, 1964-66; Adviser on Public Relations to Board of Vickers Limited, 1966-76; Chairman of Health Education Council, 1973-76. *Publications:* Men in the Tropics (Anthology); Vickers—Against the Odds; Downing Street Diary; Various articles and lectures. *Honours:* Baronet, 1963; CMG, 1957; OBE, 1945. *Hobbies:* Reading; Walking; Gardening; Travel; Photography. *Address:* 3 Challoners Close, Rottingdean, Brighton, England.

EVANS, Hywel David, b. 20 Dec. 1924, Wales. Member of Legislative Assembly. m. Betty June Rice, 5 Jan. 1952, 1 son, 2 daughters. *Education:* B.A. University of Western Australia. *Appointments:* Teacher; Deputy Principal; Senior English Master; Member Legislative Assembly, 1968; Minister for Lands, Forests and Agriculture, 1971-74; Deputy Leader of the Opposition, 1981-. *Memberships:* Commonwealth Parliamentary Association; Manjimup Country Club; President Manjimup Historical Society. *Hobbies:* Gardening; Fishing; Golf. *Address:* 26 Finch Street, Manjimup, Western Australia. 6258.

EVANS, John, b. 19 Oct. 1930, Aylesham, Kent. Member of Parliament. m. Joan Slater, 6 June 1959, 2 sons, 1 daughter. *Appointments:* Marine Fitter, 1946-74; Member of Parliament, 1974-. *Memberships:* Vice President, National Union of Labour and Socialist Clubs. *Hobbies:* Gardening; Reading; Rugby League; Football. *Address:* 6 Kirkby Road, Culcheth, Warrington, England.

EVANS, Rodney Michael, b. 26 Jan. 1938, Birmingham, England. Chartered Accountant. m. 11 Feb. 1961, 1 son, 2 daughters. *Education:* Associate, 1961, Fellow, 1969, Institute of Chartered Accountants; Associate, 1966 Chartered Institute of Secretaries. *Appointments:* Qualified with Peat Marwick Mitchell & Co.; Two years with O L Haines & Co.; Joined Melsom, Wilson & Partners, 1964, senior partner, 1967, *Publications:* Numerous technical papers. *Hobbies:* Sailing; Swimming. *Address:* c/o Melsom, Wilson & Partners, 37 St George's Terrace, Perth, Western Australia 6000.

EVERINGHAM, Douglas Nixon, b. 25 June 1923, Wauchope, Australia. Member of Parliament. m. Beverly May Withers, 10 Sep. 1948, 2 sons, 2 daughters. *Education:* M.B., B.S., Sydney, Australia, 1946. *Appointments:* include: R.M.O., General and Mental Hospitals, 1946-53; Private General Medical Practice, Sydney and Rockhampton, Australia, 1953-67; Australian House of Representatives, 1967-75, and since 1977; Minister for Health, 1972-75; Registrar in Psychiatry, Isle of Wight, 1977. *Memberships:* Amnesty Parliamentary Group, International Institute of Social Psychiatry; Humanist Society, World Association of World Federalists; Benevolent Home, Queensland; Trustee, Bliss Institute, Spelling Action Society and Benevolent Home, Rockhampton, Queensland; Australian Labour Party. *Publications:* Three Monographs. *Honours:* Assembly Vice-President, WHO, 1975; Leonard Ball Ovation, Australian Foundation on Alcoholism and Drug Dependance, 1978; WHO 1975. *Hobbies:*

Pasigraphy; Spelling reform; Interlinquistics. *Address:* 50 Corberry Street, Rockhampton 4700 Queensland, Australia.

EWEKA, Adeyemi Osasinmwidba, b. 1 Jan 1930, Benin City Nigeria. Chartered Accountant. m. Joannah Kofo Pinheiro, 21 Oct. 1956, 4 sons, 7 daughters. *Education:* Fellow, Institute of Chartered Accountants, England and Wales; Institute of Chartered Accountants, Nigeria. *Appointments:* include: Founder, Partner, Anjous, Uku, 1964-69; Director and Chairman to various Boards including: Lombard Insurance Company Limited, Lagos, Nigeria, 1970-.; Sellsoman Limited, 1974-.; Spasco Vehicle and Plant Hire Limited, 1974-. *Memberships:* Island Club, Nigeria's Premier Club, 1964-. *Hobbies:* Reading; Classics; History; Religion; Philosphy; Lawn Tennis; Golf. *Address:* Ovbi Udu Court, Oghosa Crescent, G.R.A. Benin City, Nigeria.

EYNAUD, Augustin Samuel Paul, b. 29 Oct. 1931, Mauritius. Director. m. Evelyne Carosin, 26 Apr. 1960, 2 sons, 1 daughter. *Education:* Barrister-at-Law 1956-59; Called to the Bar, at Middle Temple, 1956. *Appointments:* Assistant Secretary to Mauritius Chamber of Agriculture, 1959-60, Assistant to London Representative, 1960-67; Director, PRO Sugar Industry, 1968-70; Director Mauritius Sugar Syndicate, 1970-. *Memberships:* Lions International, Stella Clavisque. *Hobbies:* Amateur dramatics; Tennis; Squash. *Address:* Arbre Sec, Eau Coulée, Mauritius.

EYRE, Ivan, b. 15 April 1935, Saskatchewan, Canada. Painter. m. Brenda Yvonne Fenske, 14 June 1957, 2 sons. *Education:* Drawing and Painting, University of Saskatchewan, Saskatoon, 1952; University of Manitoba, School of Art, Winnipeg, 1953-57; Masters Programme, University of North Dakota, Grand Forks, North Dakota, 1958. *Appointments:* Drawing Instructor, University of North Dakota, 1958-59; Professor, University of Manitoba, 1959-81. *Memberships:* Member, R.C.A. *Creative Works:* Thirty-Two One-Man Exhibitions and Forty-Eight Group Exhibitions. *Honours:* include: Montreal Museum of Fine Arts Silver Commemorative, 1978; Queen's Silver Jubilee Medal, 1977; Elected to Royal Academy of Arts, 1974; Canada Council Art Bank Purchase, 1980. *Address:* 1098 rue des Trappistes, Winnipeg, Manitoba, Canada R3V 1B8.

EZEAKO, Onwuha Cletus, b. 20 Sept. 1928, Umuabi, Nigeria. Chartered Town Planner. m. Benedicta Iheoma Okonkwo, 28 Dec. 1963, 3 sons, 3 daughters. *Education:* Senior Cambridge Certificate, King's College, Lagos, 1942-47; Diploma in Town Planning, Nottingham College of Art, England, 1957-62; Post Graduate, Technical University of Szczecin, Poland, 1966; Certificate in Dev. Planning, University College, London, 1974. *Appointments:* Clerk, Survey Department, Lagos, 1947-48; Senior Town Planning Officer, Ministry of Lands, S. & T.P., Enugu, 1966-67; Chief Town Planning Officer, Ministry of Lands, Enugu, 1977-. *Memberships:* Fellow, Nigerian Institute of Town Planners; Elected Member, Royal Town Planning Institute of Great Britain, 1964; Director, Gion, Nigeria; Member, Rotary Internation, Enugu Branch; Council Member, Nigerian Institute of Town Planners; Patron of Several Cultural Organisations, Udi Local Government Area. *Publications:* Diploma Thesis, 1962; Planning

Administration in Eastern Nigeria, 1963; Planning problems of Eastern Nigeria, 1966; Post-war Planning Programme for East Central State, 1970. *Honours:* College of Art Board of Governors Prize for best student for the years, 1957-61; Thomas Earp Major Travel Scholarship, 1962. *Address:* 76 Akpabio Street, G.R.A., Enugu, Anambra State, Nigeria.

EZIKEOJIAKU, Paulinus Ajapurumba, b. 12 Nov. 1943, Umuezike Amaokpara Ihitenansa, Orlunig. Teacher. m. Angela Ezikeojiaku, 27 Dec. 1964, 5 sons, 2 daughters. *Education:* B.A. Hons. Linquistics, University of Ibadan, 1976; Ed.M. Suny, Buffalo, New York, 1981. *Appointments:* Primary School Teacher, 1962-73; Education Officer, 1976-77; Lecturer, AICE Owerri, 1977-81; Lecturer, Imo State University 1981-. *Memberships:* include: Member, West African Languages Congress; Member, Board of Governers, Ihitenansa Orlunig; Member, Traditional Council of Ichie, Ihitenansa, Nigeria. *Publications:* Agharata; Stailistiks Igbo; Fonoloji Na Utoasusu Igbo; Abu Nd! Pra! Mar!; Novel Nd Praimar; Ukabuilu Igbo; Ibegwam. *Honours:* Traditional Member of the Chiefs' Council; Certificate of Merit, spilc; Certificate of Honour, BHS. *Hobbies:* Football; Dancing; Touring. *Address:* Amaokpara, Ihitenansa, P.O. Box 565, Orlu, Imo State, Nigeria.

EZRA, Derek, b. 23 Feb. 1919, Tasmania. Industrialist. m. Julia Elizabeth Wilkins. *Education:* Hon. Fellow M.A., Magdalene College, Cambridge. *Appointments:* Marketing Department, National Coal Board, 1947; Member UK Delegation to European Coal and Steel Community, 1952-56; Regional Sales Manager, 1956-60; Director,-General, 'Marketing; 1960-65; Board Member, 1965-67; Deputy Chairman, 1967-71; Chairman, 1971-. *Publications:* 'Coal and Energy', First Edition, 1978, Second Edition, 1980. *Honours:* MBE, 1945; Knight Bachelor, 1974; Order of Merit of the Italian Republic, 1977; Commander of Oreder of Merit Luxembourg, 1981; Officer of the Legion of Honour of France, 1981. *Address:* Hobart House, Grosvenor Place, London SW1X 7AE, England.

EZUEH, Micah Ikechuku, b. 8 May 1938, Ogbunka Aguata LGA, Anambra State, Nigeria. Agricultural Scientist (Entomologist). m. Cecilia Chidi, 25 Aug. 1964, 1 son, 3 daughters. *Education:* BSc, University of Ibadan, 1963; MSc, Michigan State University, USA, 1966; PhD, University of Ibadan, 1979. *Appointments:* Research Officer, Nigerian Institute for Trypanosomiasis Research, Nigeria, 1964-66; Institute of Agricultural Research, Umuahia, Nigeria, 1966-71; Research Associate, Legume entomology, International Institute of Tropical Agriculture, Ibadan, 1971-73; Assistant Chief Research Officer, 1974-81, Leader of the Legume Research Programme, 1975-80, Head of Station, National Cereals Research Institute, Amakama, Umuahia, Nigeria. *Memberships:* Entomological Society of Nigeria; Nigerian Association of Soybean Scientists; Sigma Xi Association of America, 1966; Association of African insect scientists. *Publications:* An Introductory Economic Entomology for Nigeria; About 14 scientific papers in various learned journals in field of grain legume entomology, especially host plant resistance to major pests. *Hobbies:* Table tennis; Listening to music; Photography; Gardening; Excursions. *Address:* No 7 Macauly Street, Umuahia, Imo State, Nigeria.

F

FABB, Wesley Earl, b. 19 Mar. 1930, Ultima, Victoria, Australia. Medical practitioner. m. Margaret Rose Padersen, 15 Jan. 1957, 2 sons, 1 daughter. *Education:* MB, BS., University of Melbourne, Australia, 1948-55; Membership by Examination, Royal Australian College of General Practitioners, 1967. *Appointments:* Junior Resident Medical Officer, Royal Melbourne Hospital, Australia, 1956; Senior Resident Medical Officer, Mooroopna & District Base Hospital, Australia, 1957; General practice: Shepparton, Victoria, Australia, 1959-60, Yarra Junction, Victoria, Australia, 1960-71; Editor of Australian Family Physician, Director of CHECK programme of self-assessment,1971-74, Chief Examiner, 1968-77, Royal Australian College of General Practitioners; Director of Education, 1973-, Director, 1978-, Family Medicine Programme, Director of Examination Research and Development, 1978-, RACGP; Assistant Physician, Casualty Department, Alfred Hospital, Melbourne, Australia, 1972-; Honorary Senior Lecturer, Department of Community Practice, Monash University, Australia, 1976-. *Memberships:* Fellow of Royal Australian College of General Practitioners; Victoria Faculty Board; Chairman of the Practice Management Committee of Council,1966-67; RACGP College Council 1967-71; RACGP Censor 1972-73; Member of Council, Honorary Secretary 1973-75, Victorian Bush Nursing Association. *Publications:* Focus on Learning in Family Practice(with Heffernan, Phillips and Stone), 1976; Editor of Examination Handbook, 1976; Training in family medicine., A Study based on a Canadian Commonwealth Fellowship, 1979; Principles of Practice Management in Patient Care(co-editor). *Honours:* Fellowship, Royal Australian College of General Practitioners, 1971; Honorary Fellowship, College of General Practitioners Singapore, 1974; Honorary Fellowship, Faculty of General Practice, College of Medicine of South Africa, 1975; Honorary member, College of Family Physicians of Canada, 1979. *Hobbies:* Reading; Travel; Photography; Sailing. *Address:* 12 Westminster Avenue, Bulleen, Victoria 3105, Australia.

FABIYI, Joshua Olatuyi, b. 31 Oct. 1946, Iesha, Oyo State, Nigeria. Marketing Executive. m. Elizabeth Olalonpe Balogun, 31 Aug. 1974, 2 sons. *Education:* BSc.(Hons.) Pharmacology, 1972. *Appointments:* Trainee Medical Laboratory Technician, Wesley Guild Hospital, Ilesha, Oyo State, Nigeria, 1967-68; Medical Representative, Smith Kline & French, Nigeria, 1973-78; Medical Representative, 1976-77, Product Manager, 1978-80, Ciba-Geigy, Nigeria; Marketing Manager, Janssen Pharmaceutical Division, Johnson & Johnson (Nigeria) Limited, 1980-. *Memberships:* Associate member, Nigerian Institute of Management; British Institute of Management; American Institute of Management; Institute of Marketing M. Inst.M. *Hobbies:* Reading; Sports; Travel. *Address:* No. 30 Irepo Avenue, off Adeshina Street, Ijeshatedo, Surulere, Lagos, Nigeria.

FABUNMI, Lawrence Apalara, b. 12 Dec. 1925, Ilawi-Ekiti, Ondo State, Nigeria. International Relations. m. 16 July 1960, 1 son, 2 daughters. *Education:* BA, Hope College, Holland, Michigan, 1952; PhD, (London), Faculty of Economics, London School of Economics and Political Science, 1957. *Appointments:* Education Headquarters (Administration), Lagos, 1945-48; Research Assistant, London School of Economics & Political Science, 1958; Assistant Secretary, (External Affairs), Federal Government of Nigeria, 1958-61; Part-time Lecturer, International Affairs, University College of Ibadan, 1958-61; Acting Senior Assistant Secretary, 1961; First Political Affairs Officer, 1961-63; Director-General, Institute of International Affairs, Lagos, 1963-71; Head, Policy Planning Unit, Director, IOD and Director America Department, 1972-73; Nigerian High Commissioner to Zambia , 1973-76; Director, Consular and Legal Affairs Department, 1976-79; Ambassador of Nigeria to Poland (with concurrent accreditation to Czekoslovakia and Hungary), 1979-81. *Memberships:* Philosophy Club; Arcadian Fraternity; International Relations Club; Secretary-General, Nigerian Union of Great Britain and Ireland; President, African Society, London School of Economics and Political Science; Royal Institute of International Affairs, London, 1953; Senior Civil Service Association of Nigeria; Comteporary Society of Nigeria; President, Nigeria Society, 1966;

Executive, United Nations Association of Nigeria, 1966-; President, Nigeria Chapter of Society for International Development; Secretary, National Reconciliation Committee, Federal Republic of Nigeria, 1967; Directing Committee of the African-American Dialogues; Nigerian delegation to the Session of Commission for Technical Co-operation in Africa, 1959, Conference on Future Law in Africa, 1960; The CCTA Conference in Tananarive, 1960; United Nations General Assembly, New York, 1960-61; United Nations Economic Commission for Africa, 1961; Nigerial Delegation to Turkey, 1968; UN General Assembly, 1972. *Publications:* Thesis - The Sudan in Anglo-Egyptian Relations—A Case Study in Power Politics 1800-1956, 1960; Numerous articles in professional journals. *Address:* 28 Catholic Mission Street, Lagos, Nigeria.

FADAHUNSI, Samuel Olatunde, b. 17 Mar. 1920, Ilesha, Nigeria. Civil Engineer. m. 17 Mar. 1959, 2 sons, 3 daughters. *Education:* BSC, London University, 1948-51; Associateship of Battersea Polytechnic, 1952. *Appointments:* Engineer Grade IV, PWD, Lagos, 1947-48; Executive Engineer, Ministry of Works, Ibadan, 1954-59, Chief Water Engineer, 1960-63; Chief Executive Officer, LEDB, Lagos, 1963-72; Principal Partner, Comprehensive Engineer Consultants, Lagos, 1972-. *Memberships:* Fellow of: Institution of Civil Engineers and Nigerian Society of Engineers; Institution of Water Engineers; Past Chairman, Industrial Research Council, Nigeria; Past Chairman, Federal Housing Authority; President, Council of Registered Engineers of Nigeria. *Publications:* Contributor of several papers Hydro-Electrical Development, Housing and Urban Engineering. *Honours:* Honorary Fellowship of the Nigerian Institute of Chartered Surveyors and Valuers, 1979; Life Membership of the Association of Housing Corporation of Nigeria, 1980. *Hobbies:* Music; Tennis; Boating. *Address:* 2 Senbanjo Close, Apapa, Lagos, Nigeria.

FÁDÉLÉ, Adéyeyè Oláyemí, b. 23 May 1948, Okè-Ilá, Oràngún. Theatre Business Manager. m. 28 Dec. 1980, 2 sons. *Education:* BA, Lagos, 1979; Diploma in Mass Communication, Lagos, 1980. *Appointments:* Theatre Business Manager, Centre for Cultural Studies, University of Lagos, Akoka, Lagos, Nigeria, 1980. *Memberships:* Nigerian Institute of Public Relations, Lagos Chapter; Publicity Secretary, Senior Staff Club, University of Lagos, 1980-81. *Honours:* First Prize, Yoruba, Government College, Ibadan, 1967, Inter-University Radio Debate, 1973 and Nigerian Universities Games Association Debate 1974. *Hobbies:* Drama; Hockey;Cricket; Ayò Game. *Address:* Plot 635, Afolabi Brown Street, Akokà, Lagos, Nigeria.

FAGAN, Warren Christopher, b. 5 Feb. 1937, Melbourne, Victoria, Australia. Barrister. m. Beverley MAIE Stiffe, 27 Jan. 1964, 2 sons, 4 daughters. *Education:* Melbourne University, Australia, 1961. *Appointments:* Barrister at Law, Victoria, Australia, 1962-; Acting Chairman, Town Planning Appeals Tribunal, 1975-76; Local Government Arbitrator, Victoria, Australia, 1977-78; Acting Judge and Chairman, Liquor Control Commission, Victoria, Australia, 1980; Member, New South Wales Bar, Australia, 1978-. *Memberships:* Victoria Golf Club; Royal Automobile Club of Victoria; Royal Melbourne Tennis Club. *Publications:* Various reports of Bar sub-committees including: Delays in Hearing of Criminal Trials, 1980; various Book Reviews. *Honours:* LL.B., 1961; Queen's Counsel, 1978. *Hobbies:* Golf; Tennis. *Address:* 87 Bowen Street, Camberwell, Melbourne 3124, Australia.

FAGBAMIGBE, Mercy Ebun, b. 2 Jan. 1934, Akure. m. 2 sons, 5 daughters. *Education:* Teachers Grade III Certificate, Divisional Teachers Training College, Ondo; Teachers Grade II Certificate, Provincial Grade II College, Osogbo; National Certificate of Education, Institute of Education, University of London, UK. *Appointments:* L A School, Iju, Akure, 1957-59; St. Francis Modern School, Akure, 1962-63; St. Theresa Practising School, Akure, 1964-72; United Missionary College, Ibadan, 1975-77; St. Peter's Teacher Training College, Akure, 1978-79; Olaiya Fagbanugbe, Publishers, 1980-. *Memberships:* Honorary Secretary,Ondo State, Ondo State Chairman, Fund Raising Committee, Treasurer-Akure Branch, Red Cross Society; General Secretary, Akure Dynamic Women Association; General Secretary, National Council of Women Societies; Executive member of Akure Branch, Queen of Apostles; Treasurer and Vice Chairman, Fund Raising Committee of the International Year of the Disabled Persons Ondo State Executive Committee. *Publications:* Release on Current Affairs; One of the Artists of the NTV Akure and OSBC Akure. *Honours:* Medals for singing in 1954 at the Cathedral in Ondo. *Hobbies:* Photography. *Address:* 11 Methodist Church Road, PO Box 14, Akure, Nigeria.

FAICHNEY, Norman, b. 29 July 1910, Midland Junction, Western Australia. Minister of Religion. m. Grace Winifred Lang, 14 Mar. 1939, 2 sons, 1 daughter. *Education:* University of Melbourne, Theological Hall, Ormond College, Melbourne. *Appointments:* Bacuum Oil Co. -ty. Ltd., 1926-32; Minister of Morwell Presbyterian Church, 1939-41; Chaplain to the Forces Second AIF Ninth Division, 1941-43; Minister of Strathmore Presbyterian Church, 1943-47; Minister of Scots Church, Shepparton, 1947-52; Minister of St John's Presbyterian Church, Warrnambool, 1952-60; Moderator of Presbyterian Church of Victoria, 1958-59; Moderator - General Presbyterian Church of Australia, 1967-70; Delegate to World Assembly of the World Council of Churches, Uppsala, 1968; Minister of Uniting Church, Glen Iris, 1976. *Memberships:* President of Australian Council of Churches, 1968-70. *Hobbies:* Gardening; Golf; Bowls. *Address:* 6 5 Yarrabee Court, Mount Waverley, 3149, Victoria, Australia.

FAIGAN, Julian Goodrich, b. 14 Oct. 1944, Auckland, New Zealand. Museum Director. *Education:* BA, 1966, MA, 1970, University of Auckland; Post-graduate research, University of Melbourne, 1978-. *Appointments:* Assistant Lecturer, Canterbury University, New Zealand, 1969-70; Director, City of Hamilton Art Gallery, Australia, 1975-. *Memberships:* Graduate Union, University of Melbourne; Executive, Australian Gallery Directors' Council Ltd., 1980-81. *Publications:* Master's thesis, Le vocabulaire des armes offensives dans les chansons de geste du XIIe siècle, 1970; Ambrose Bowden Johns, Family and Friends, 1979. Paul Sandby Drawings, 1981; English Decorative Arts at The Hamilton Gallery, in the Australian Antique Collector, Vol. XXIII, 1981. *Honours:* Bourse du governement français, 1970-71. *Hobbies:* Travel; Music; Reading. *Address:* 13 McIntyre Street, Hamilton, Victoria, Australia, 3300.

FAIN, Richard David, b. 9 Oct. 1947, Massachusetts, USA. Financial Executive. m. Colleen J Ferris, 27 July 1969, 1 son, 2 daughters. *Education:* BS. Economics, University of California, Berkeley, USA, 1969; MBA, University of Pennsylvania, Wharton, USA, 1972. *Appointments:* IU International Management Corporation Manager of International Finance, 1972-75; GLSC Senior Vice President, Finance, 1976-. *Memberships:* University Club, New York. *Hobbies:* Photography; Electronics. *Address:* 36 Marryat Road, Wimbledon, London, SW19 5BQ, England.

FAIRCLOUGH, Ellen Louks (Mrs D H G Fairclough) (nee Cook), b. 28 Jan. 1905, Hamilton, Ontario, Canada. Chartered Accountant. m. David Henry Gordon, 1931, 1 son. *Education:* Certified General Accountants; Certified Public Accountants, 1951; Chartered Accountants, Ontario, Fellow, 1965. *Appointments:* Public Practice, 1935-57; City Council, Hamilton, Alderman, 1946-49, Controller, 1950; Mamber of Parliament, Hamilton West, 1950-63; Secretary of State, 1957-60; Minister Citizenship & Immigration, 1960-62; Postmaster General, 1963; Chairman, Hamilton Hydro Electric Commission; Director Canada Permanent Trust Company. *Memberships:* International Treasurer, 1972-76, past Governor, Zonta International; Director and Executive Counil, Canadaian Chamber of Commerce; Patron, Huguenot Society of Canada; Former Dominion Secretary, United Empire Loyalists of Canada; Chancellor, Hamilton Royal College of Music, 1977-80; Zonata Club of Hamilton I; Canadian Club of Hamilton; Albany Club of Toronto; Advertising and Sales Club, Hamilton; Faculty Club, McMaster University. *Publications:* Numerous magazine and newspaper articles and speeches. *Honours:* Princess Six Nations Indian Band Council (Cayuga Tribe), 1962; Chief, Blackfoot Tribe, 1962; Decorations, Coronation, Centennial and Jubilee Medals, 1953, 1967, 1977; Honorary LL.D McMaster University, 1975; Human Relations Award, Canadian Council Christians and Jews. 1979; Province of Ontario, Outstanding Women Award, 1975; Officer of the Order of Canada, 1979; *Hobbies:* Reading; Music; Philately;

Photography. *Address:* 25 Stanley Avenue, Hamilton, Ontario, L8P 2K9, Canada.

FAJAIYEYO, Samuel Mobolaji Oyetunji, b. 23 July 1935, Obuasi Formerly Gold Coast now Ghana. Pharmacist. m. Victoria Titilayo Ige, 1966, 2 sons, 3 daughters. *Education:* Dispensers Course School of Pharmacy, Zaria, 1950-53; Diploma Course in Pharmacy, 1959-62, Diploma in Pharmacy, Nigerian College of Arts Science & Technology. *Appointments:* Pharmaceutical Sales Representative, 1963-66, Superintendent, 1966-68, Glaxo (Nig); Area Sales Manager Northern Nigeria Pfizer Products, 1968-70, Southern Nigeria, 1970-72; National Sales Manager, Merck Shapp & Dohme (Nig) Ltd., 1972-74, Heinrich Mach Nachf (Pfizer Organisation), 1975-78; Pharmaceutical Business Manager, 1978-80, Development Manager, 1980-, Prizer Prodicts. *Memberships:* Pharmaceutical Society of Nigeria; Pharmacy Management International. *Hobbies:* Lawn tennis; Table tennis; Native Indoor Game (Ayo). *Address:* 31 Atiba Osborne Street, Meade Village, Maryland Area, Ikega, Lagos, State of Nigeria.

FAJEMISIN, Joseph Moroti, b. 23 Sept. 1943, Ilesha, Nigeria. Agricultural Research (Plant Pathologist and Breeder). m. Stella Falade, 29 Aug. 1970, 3 sons, 1 daughter. *Education:* BSc, University of Ibadan, Nigeria, 1967; MSc, PhD, University of Illinois, Urbana-Champaign, USA, 1973. *Appointments:* Clerical Officer, Ministry of Works & Transport, Western Region of Nigeria, 1964; Senior Science Teacher St Charles Grammar School, Oshogbo, Nigeria, 1967-68; Research Officer, Chief Research Officer and Leader, Maize Improvement Programme, Federal Fepartment of Agricultural Research Moor Plantation, Ibadan, now National Cereals Research Institute, 1968-81; Visiting Scientist, International Institute of Tropical Agriculture, 1981-. *Memberships:* Association for the Advancement of Agricultural Science in Africa; National Secretary, 1976-78, Genetics Society of Nigeria; Vice-President, 1980, Nigerian Society for Plant Protection; Agricultural Society of Nigeria; Science Association of Nigeria. *Publications:* PhD Thesis, 1973; Contributor to professional journals and conferences. *Honours:* Wheatley Cup, University of Ibadan, Nigeria, 1966; Phi Kappa Phi, University of Illinois, 1973; Gamma Sigma Delta, 1972. *Hobbies:* Gardening; Table tennis; Watching comedy plays. *Address:* No 3 Africa Drive, IITA, PMB, 5320, Ibadan, Nigeria.

FALETAU, Inoke Fotu, b. 1937, Tonga. Diplomat. m. Evelini Maata Hurrell, 3 sons, 3 daughters. *Education:* University of Wales, Manchester University, UK. *Appointments:* Civil Servant Executive, Tonga Civil Service, 1958-65; Assistant Secretary, Prime Ministers Office, 1965-69; Secretary to Government, 1969-71; Resources and External Relations Officer, University of the South Pacific, Fiji, 1971-72; Tonga High Commissioner to UK and Ambassador to France, 1972-, Ambassador to: German Federal Republic, 1976, Netherlands, Belgium, Luxembourg, EEC, 1977, USA., 1979, USSR., 1980, Denmark, Italy, 1981. *Memberships:* Royal Commonwealth Society. *Address:* Tonga High Commission, N Z House, Haymarket, London SW1, England.

FALKINGHAM, Robert Percy, b. 8 May 1915, Busselton, Western Australia. Company Director. m. 4 Mar. 1939, 2 sons, 1 daughter. *Education:* BA,1947, Diploma in Commerce, 1939, University of Western Australia; BC., University of Queensland, Australia, 1948. *Appointments:* Bank of New South Wales, Australia, 1933-57; General Manager,1970-80, John Fairfax Limited, 1957-80(retired); Chairman, Macquarie Broadcasting Holdings Limited, 1980-. *Memberships:* Associate, Australian Society of Accountants; Fellow, Bankers' Institute of Australia; Associate, Australian Institute of Valuers; Sydney Club. *Hobby:* Motoring. *Address:* 7 Byora Crescent, Northbridge, New South Wales 2063, Australia.

FALLOON, George David, b. 12 Nov. 1911, Noapara, North Otago, Dunedin, New Zealand. Minister of Religion. m. Mary Millicent Cock, 8 Mar. 1940, 4 sons. *Education:* BA, University of Otago, New Zealand, 1938. *Appointments:* Chaplain, New Zealand Army, 1942; Moderator of General Assembly, Presbyterian Church of New Zealand. *Memberships:* Foundation Master, Lodge Masterton, No. 356 New Zealand; Foundation President, South Christchurch Rotary; Moderator, Presbyterian Church of New Zealand; Member of Board of Governors of: Solway College, Masterton, Cashmere High School, Christchurch and Geraldine High School, South Canterbury. *Publications:* Produced Stories and Outlines for Several subjects. *Honours:* Awarded Military Cross, 1944; Mentioned in dispatches 35 Battalion; OBE, Queen's Birthday Honours, 1977. *Hobbies:* Walking in Countryside; Photography; Gardening. *Address:* 154 Dyers Pass Road, Christchurch 2, New Zealand.

FALLSHAW, Keith George, b. 17 Nov. 1946, Stepney, London. Exhibition Designer; Artist; Sculptor. *Education:* Studied Typographical Design at London College of Printing under Leonard Cusdens and Don Smith; Pupil of Leonard and Margaret Boden and Edmund Holmes. *Memberships:* Associate member of National Society of Painters, Sculptors and Printmakers, 1978; Institute of Advanced Motorists. *Creative Works:* Exhibited Deben Gallery, Woodbridge, Suffolk, 1976,77; N S and U A Mall Galleries, London, 1978, 79, 80 and 81. *Hobbies:* Music; Photography; Theatrical Production. *Address:* Bay Tree Cottage, No. 1 Crown Terrace, Bishop's Stortford, Hertfordshire, England.

FAMOYE, Jethro Oluyemi, b. 27 June 1936, Igbotako, Ondo State, Nigeria. Personnel Manager. m. Iyabo Williams, 2 Oct. 1959, 4 sons, 1 daughter. *Education:* Grade III Teachers Certificate, 1955-56, Grade II, 1959-60. *Appointments:* Teaching in various schools in Nigeria, 1954-70; Supervisor, Flour Mills of Nigeria Ltd., Shift Supervisor, 1974, Shift Manager, 1976, Personnel Manager, 1979, Nigerian Bag Manufacturing Company Ltd. *Memberships:* Igbotako Youth League. *Publications:* Short stories for Radio, Children's programmes. *Hobby:* Swimming. *Address:* 13 Jadesola Oshodi Street, Aguda, Suru-Lere, Lagos State, Nigeria.

FANCUTT, Walter, b. 22 Feb. 1911, Blackburn, Lancashire, England. Baptist Minister; Author. m. Amy F M Hawkins, 28 Dec. 1933. *Education:* All Nations Bible College and Central School of Art, London, UK. *Appointments:* Minister at Whitchurch, 1934-37, Acton, 1937-42, Leytonstone and Wanstead, 1942-45, Andover, 1945-51, Ryde, 1952-56; Editorial Secretary, 1957-70, Editorial Consultant, 1970-75, The Leprosy Mission; General Secretary, Southern Baptist Association, 1970-76. *Memberships:* Society of Authors; Radio Writers Association; Baptist Historical Society; Vice-President, National Association of Non-Smokers; Honorary Member, the Rotary Clubs of Mill Hill, London and Ventnor, Isle of Wight; Chaplain, Ventnor Retired Business and Professional Mens' Club. *Publications:* Kingsgate Pocket Poets; Prujean Pocket Poets, 1943; Then Came Jesus, Whitchurch Baptist History, 1952; Waterlooville Baptist History, 1954; In This Will I be Confident, 1957; Beyond the Bitter Sea, 1959; Escaped as a Bird, 1964; Daily Remembrance, 1966; Present to Heal, 1966; The Imprisoned Splendour, 1972; With Strange Surprise, 1974; History of the Southern Baptist Association, 1974; History of Andover Baptist Church, 1974; The Luminous Cloud, 1980. *Honours:* Poetry Prize, School of Religious Journalism, 1942. *Hobbies:* Numismatics; Collecting Prints. *Address:* 4b St. Boniface Gardens, Ventnor, Isle of Wight PO38 1NN, UK.

FARGHER, Kenneth Herbert Francis, b. 26 Oct. 1929, Mildura, Australia. Educationalist. m. Dorothy Pearl Spencer, 19 Dec. 1953, 4 sons. *Education:* BSc.,1952, D.Ed., 1953, B.Ed., 1956, Melbourne University Australia; MBA., 1968, PhD., 1972, University of New South Wales, Australia. *Appointments:* Head, Department of Administrative Studies, 1972, Head, Graduate School of Management, 1975, Royal Melbourne Institute of Technology, Australia. *Memberships:* Fellow, Australian Institute of Management; Fellow, Australian Institute of Export. *Publications:* Cases in Australian Business, 1972; Case Studies in International Marketing (with Weinstein), 1972. *Honours:* Efficiency Decoration; J Storey Memorial Prize, University of New South Wales, Australia, 1968. *Address:* 31 Through Road, Burwood, Melbourne, Australia 3125.

FARMER, Keitha (Mrs Jon Brian Slapley Farmer), b. 4 Feb. 1928, Taumarunui, New Zealand. Medicine (Paediatrics). m. Jon Brian Slopley Farmer, 23 June 1962, 1 son. *Education:* MB ChB, Otago, 1951; DCH, 1955; MRCP(E), 1958; MRACP, 1960; PhD (hon) (Lond), 1963; FRCP(E), 1970; FRACP, 1971. *Appointments:*

House Physician, Auckland Hospital; SHO, Selly Oak Group, Birmingham; House Physician, Hospital for Sick Children, London; Tutor Specialist, Princess Mary Hospital, Auckland, 1960; Research Fellow, Hospital for Sick Children, London, 1961-63; Paedtrician, Princess Mary Hospital, 1964-70; Paedtrician, Infectious Diseases, Princess Mary Hospital, Paediatric National Womens Hospital, Auckland, 1970-. *Memberships:* New Zealand Medical Research Council Fellow in Neonatal Infection, 1970; Past Chairman, Paediatric Society of New Zealand; Sub Committee on Nutrition of Paediatric Society of New Zealand. Contributor to numerous Medical Journals including: A follow up study of 15 cases of neonatal meningoencephalitis due to Coxsackie Virus B5 (co-author), 1975; Intramuscular iron dextran and susceptilility of neonates to bacterial infections, (co-author), 1977; A controlled trial of treatment of vaginal carriers of group B streptococci with oral pencillin (co-author), 1980. *Hobbies:* Swimming; Water, Snow Skiing. *Address:* 88 Ngapuie Road, Remuera, Auckland 5, New Zealand.

FARNSWORTH, Robert Housley, b. 21 Nov. 1936, Sydney, NSW Australia. Medical Practicioner. m. Penelope Gay Crookes, 28 July 1963, 2 sons, 2 daughters. *Education:* MBBS, Sydney, 1960; FRACS, Edinburgh, 1964; FRACS, Australia, 1969; FACRM, Australian College of Rehabilitation, 1980. *Appointments:* Resident Medical Officer, Sydney Hospital, 1960-61; Surgical Registrar, The Prince Henry Hospital, 1963, 1965; Tutor in Surgery, University of NSW, 1966-69; Specialist Urological Surgeon, Prince Henry Hospital, 1969-81; Chairman, Department of Urology, Prince Henry Hospital, 1973-81. *Memberships:* Treasurer, Urological Society of Australasia, 1976-78; British Association of Urological Surgeons; Nephrological Society of Australia; Australian Paediatric Society; Australian Surgical Research Society; Royal Sydney Golf Club. *Publications:* Numerous scientific contributions to Urological Journals. *Hobbies:* Squash; Tennis; Golf. *Address:* 6 Macquarie Road, Pymble, NSW 2073, Australia.

FARNWORTH, Arthur James, b. 30 Sept. 1923, Geelong, Victoria, Australia. Chief General Manager. m. Enid Hinda Brown, 2 sons, 1 daughter. *Education:* Diploma of Industrial Chemistry (AG, Inst. Tech.), Gordon Institute of Technology; M Sc, University of Melbourne; PhD, University of Leeds(uK). *Appointments:* Senior Lecturer in Textile Chemistry/Research Chemist, Gordon Institute, 1948-54; Principal Research Officer—CSIRO, Geelong, 1954-61; Technical Director, Australian Wool Board, 1961-70; Deputy NManaging Director, Australian Wool Board, 1970-71; General Manager, Australian Wool Board, 1972; General Manager, General & Product Operations, Australian Wool Corporation, 1973-74; General Manager, Corporate Services & Research Division, Australian Wool Corporation, 1974-79; Chief General Manager, Australian Wool Corporation, 1979-. *Memberships:* Associate Fellow, Australian Institute of Management; Associate, Royal Australian Chemical Committee; CSIRO Victorian State Committee; Fellow of the Institute of Directors in Australia; Life Member, Geelong & District Community Chest Association & Geelong Apex Club; Sciences Club; Royal Automobile Club of Victoria. *Publications:* Contributor to New International Illustrated Encyclopaedia, 1954; Research papers in scientific literature; Monograph on the Permanent Setting of Wool(with J. Delmenico). *Honours:* MBE, 1959. *Hobbies:* Nature Photography; Fishing; Music. *Address:* 47 The Boulevarde, Doncaster, Victoria 3108, Australia.

FAROUK, Abdullah, b. 1 Mar. 1928, Pabna Town, Bangladesh. University Professor. m. Sophia Husneara, 31 July 1949, 2 sons, 2 daughters. *Education:* BA, 1946, MA, 1948, Calcutta University; PhD, Dacca University, 1954. *Appointments:* Assistant Director of Statistics, 1950-55, Member National Planning Commission, 1976-81, Government of Bangladesh; Lecturer & Reader, 1955-69, Professor of Marketing, 1969-, Part-time Director, Bureau of Economic Research, 1955-69, Dacca University. *Memberships:* Bangladesh Economic Association. *Publications:* Author and co-author of numerous surveys and studies for professional publication including: The Vagrants of Dacca City, 1978; Time Use of Women in Bangladesh, 1980; Various research papers in professional journals including: Land Reforms in East Pakistan, 1962; The Consumer Goods Industries of Pakistan, 1965. *Honours:* Prize for the best book of the year in History in Bengali language,

The Economic History of Bangladesh, 1974. *Hobby:* Travelling. *Address:* 37/F Fuller Road, Dacca University Staff Quarters, Nilkhet, Dacca, Bangladesh.

FAROUNBI, Yemi Bamidele, b. 1 Oct. 1944 Ora, Nigeria. Broadcaster. m. Adenike Farounbi, 20 Apr. 1974, 2 daughters. *Education:* West African School Certificate, 1962; Ba, 2nd Class, 1968; Masters in Public Administration, 1975. *Appointments:* Staff Development Manager, WNTV,WNBS, Ibadan, 1968-75; Controller, Corporate Affairs, WNTV,WNBS, Ibadan, 1975-76; Director of Administration, NTV, Ibadan, 1976-77; General Manager, NTV, Ibadan, 1977-80; General Manager, NTV, Akure, 1981-. *Memberships:* Society of Nigerian Broadcasters; National Secretary, Society of Nigerian Broadcasters; Institute of Personnel Management; International Institute of Communications; Overseas Press Media Association. *Publications:* In Defence of Nigerian Broadcasting, 1976; Whither Nigerian Broadcasting, 1977; Broadcasting Management; An Analysis of Principles & Practice, 1978; Mass Media and The Future, 1979; Television and Society, 1980. *Honours:* Peter Odnmosu Prize for Public Administration, 1975. *Hobbies:* Music; Writing. *Address:* PO Box 7479, Ibadan, Nigeria.

FARQUHARSON, Gordon Mackay, b. 1928, Charlottetown, Prince Edward Island. Director. *Education:* BA, Victoria College, University of Toronto; Osgoode Hall Law School; Called to the Bar of Ontario, 1954; QC, 1965. *Appointments:* Partner, Lang Michener, Cranston, Farquharson & Wright, Toronto, Ontario; Director and Secretary: GSW Ltd/Ltée; Director: Showerlux Canada Ltd.; Canadian Appliance Mfg. Co. Ltd.; Mony Life Insurance Co. of Canada; Valleydene Corp. Ltd.; Shaw Industries Ltd. *Memberships:* President, Eglinton Provincial Liberal Association and of Eglinton Federzl Liberal Association, 1962-67; Don Valley Federal, 1966-68; Convention Chairman, Mitchell Sharp, 1968, Liberal Leadership Convention. *Hobbies:* Skiing; Canoeing; Sailing. *Address:*245 Borden Street Toronto, Ontario, Canada.

FARRER, William Oliver, b. 23 June 1926, Broadstairs, Kent. Socicitor. m. Margery Hope Yates, 16 Apr. 1955 (dec. 1976), (2) Hazel Mary Clark Andrew, 12 May 1979, 2 sons, 1 daughter. *Education:* Eton College, 1939-44; Balliol College, Oxford, 1948-49. *Appointments:* Lieutenant, Coldstream Guards, 1945-47; Solicitor—Admitted 1953; Partner Messrs Farrer & Co., 1956, Senior Partner, 1976. *Memberships:* Brooks's Club; Marylebone Cricket Club; Royal & Ancient Golf Club of St. Andrews; Honourable Company of Edinburgh Golfers; Chairman, Haslemere NMusical Society, 1973-80. *Hobbies:* Golf; Music. *Address:* Popmoor, Fernhurst, Haslemere, Surrey, England.

FARROW, Brian James, b. 8 Aug. 1927, Maidstone, Kent, England. Chartered Secretary; Training Advisor. m. Rosemary Muriel Gardiner, 31 Mar. 1955, 1 son. *Education:* BSc, Bristol University, 1948-51; BA, Oxford University, 1952-55; Institute Secretaries Administrators, 1959; Institute Personnel Management, 1963; Institute Training and Development, 1973; British Institute of Management, 1978. *Appointments:* Army, 1945-52; Statistition/Assistant Company Secretary, 1955-63, General Manager, 1963-73, Motor Trade Distributors; Senior Training Officer, Industrial Training Board, 1973-78; Training Advisor, Polypropylene Woven Sack Manufacturers, Nigeria, 1978-. *Memberships:* Treasurer, Institute of Training and Development (Nigeria Branch); Nigerian Employers Consultative Association, Member Training/Education Committee. *Honours:* MC, 1945; MBE, 1953. *Hobbies:* Music; Theatre; Walking; Photography. *Address:* 21 North Avenue, Apapa, Nigeria.

FARROW, Colin Pyewell, b. 16 June 1919, Wagin, Western Australia. Chartered Engineer. m. (1) Kathleen Murphy, 4 Nov. 1944 (dec. 1977), 3 sons, 1 daughter, (2) Patricia Mary Gluyas, 7 Sept. 1979. *Education:* Bachelor of Engineering, University of Weatern Australia, 1937-41; St. George's College, Crawley, Western Australia, 1937-41. *Appointments:* Engineer, Department of the Interior, Perth, WA, 1941; Draughtsman, De Havilland Aircraft Company, Sydney, 1942; Engineer, The Shell Company of Australia, 1944-46, Construction Manager, 1950, Ocean Terminal Manager, 1956, Operations Manager, The Shell Company, Philippines, 1957, Assistant Branch Manag-

er, 1960, Asphalts Contracting Manager, 1964; Retired, 1979; Consulting Engineer, 1980-. *Memberships:* Institution of Engineers, Australia; Royal Automobile Club of Victoria; Kew Golf Club; Australian Road Federation, President, 1978-. *Honours:* Western Australian Exhibition, 1937. *Hobbies:* Gardening; Golf. *Address:* 8 Millicent Avenue, North Balwin, Victoria 3104, Australia.

FARRUGIA SACCO, Carmelo,b. 22 Aug. 1949, Hamrun, Malta. Lawyer; Magistrate. m. Susan Laivera, 28 Aug. 1976, 1 son. *Education:* BA, in Economics, Italian and English, 1969; Diploma of Notary Public, 1972; Doctor of Laws, 1973. *Appointments:* Magistrate of the Courts of Malta. *Memberships:* Malta Sports Club; Vice-President, Malta Lawn Tennis Association; President, Hamrun Tennis Club; Member Malta Football Association; Cafino 1852; Union Club. *Publications:* Capacity to make a Will. *Hobbies:* Tennis; Football; Wine Making. *Address:* Villa Carinya, Princess Elizabeth Street, Ta'Xbiex, Malta.

FASANYA, Jacob Oluwafemi, b. 18 Feb. 1938, Ola—Ejigbo, Nigeria. Librarianship. m. 28 June 1966, 1 son, 4 daughters. *Education:* BA, Hons. English, University of Ibadan, 1966; Post Graduate Diploma in Librarianship, University of Ibadan, 1967; Masters in Library Science, University of Pittsburgh, USA, 1972; PhD, University of Pittsburgh, USA, 1975. *Appointments:* Assistant Librarian, University of Ibadan, 1967-771; Senior Librarian, University of Ibadan, 1975-76;. Lecturer, 1977; Chief Librarian & Ag. Head of Technical & Library Services Division, Centre for Management Development, Lagos, 1977-. *Memberships:* Nigerian Library Association, 1967-; Ag. Secretary, Nigerian Library Association, 1970-71; American Library Association, 1972-77; Business Manager, Nigerian Library Association, 1976-; National Advisory Committee on Education for Citizenship, 1978-79. *Publications:* Library Antamation—Problems and Prospects, Nigerian Libraries, Vol. 13, 1977; International Library Review, Vol. 9, 1977. *Honours:* Beta Phi Mu; International Library Honor Society, Life Membership, 1972; Hillman Fellow, 1975; Evolved an indexing procedure for the Pittsburgh Courier, a weekly Afro-American journal. *Hobbies:* Photography; Music; Lithography. *Address:* Ile Onsa, Ola—Ejigbo, Oyo State, Nigeria.

FASHEUN, Adebayo, b. 28 Oct. 1951, Ilesha, Oyo State, Nigeria. Research Agricultural-Meteorology. m. Olubusola Fadahunsi, 29 Sept. 1979, 1 son. *Education:* BSc., Hons., 1972-76, MSc., 1979-80, Reading University, Reading, UK; Certificate, Weather Forecasting, British Meteorological Office College, UK, 1972, 75. *Appointments:* Nigerian Meteorological Services, 1971-72; Nigerian Civil Aviation School, Zaria, Nigeria, 1976-77; National Horticultural Research Institute, Ibadan, Nigeria, 1977-. *Memberships:* Fellow, Royal Meteorological Society; Associate, Institute of Physics; Horticultural Society of Nigeria. *Publications:* Contributed two poems to: The Spring Poets, 1974. *Creative Works:* Organized 1st Conference of Horticultural Society of Nigeria; Member of Nigerian Committee planning the West African Monsoon Experiment, sponsored by the World Meteorological Organisation. *Hobbies:* Writing; Reading; Driving. *Address:* AS 14 Itishin Street, Ilesha, Oyo State, Nigeria.

FATAYI-WILLIAMS, Atanda, b. 22 Oct. 1918, Lagos, Nigeria. Jurist, Chief Justice of Nigeria. m. Irene Violet Lofts, June, 1948, 3 children. *Education:* BA, 1946, LLB, 1947, MA, 1949, University of Cambridge; Middle Temple, London, 1947-48. *Appointments:* Private Practice, Lagos, 1948-50; Crown Counsel, Lagos, 1950-55; Deputy Commissioner for Law Revision, W. Nigeria, 1955-58; Chief Registrar, High Court of W. Nigeria, 1958-60; High Court Judge, 1960-67; Justice of Appeal, W. State, 1967-69; Justice, Supreme Court of Nigeria, 1969-79; Chairman, Ports Arbitration Board, 1971; All Nigeria Law Reports Committee, 1972-75; Chairman, Board of Trustees, Van Leer Nigerian Education Trust, 1973-; Member, Nigerian Institute of International Affairs, 1972-; Life Member, Body of Benchers, 1979-80; Chairman, Legal Practitioners' Privileges Committee, 1979-; Chairman, Federal Judicial Service Commission; Chairman, Judiciary Consultative Committee; Chairman, National Archives Committee, 1979-; Chairman, Elder Dempster Trust, 1979-; Trustee, Nigerian Youth Trust, 1979; Chief Justice of Nigeria, 1979-. *Memberships:* Life

Fellow, Royal Society of Arts, London; National Museum Society, Lagos; Chairman, Crescent Bearers, Lagos; Honorary President for Africa, World Peace Through Law Centre, 1981-. *Publications:* Revised Laws of the Western Region of Nigeria, (with Sir John Verity), 1959; Sentencing Processes, Practices and Attitudes, as seen by an Appeal Court Judge, 1970; Editor, Western Nigeria Law Reports, 1955-58. *Hobbies:* Reading; Walking; Swimming; Travelling; Speedboats. *Address:* 15 Ikoyi Crescent, Ikoyi, Lagos.

FATOBERU, Isaac Joy Ayobamidele, b. 1 Feb. 1952, Ibadan, Nigeria. Purchasing and Supplies Management. *Education:* Final Diploma in Purchasing and Supply, 1976 77. *Appointments:* Water Corporation, Ibadan, 1970-77; National Horticultural Research Institute, Ibadan, 1977-. *Hobby:* Table Tennis. *Address:* Quarters NH11, Eleiyele, Ibadan, Nigeria.

FAULDS, Andrew Matthew William, b. 1 Mar. 1923, Esoko, Tanzania. Member of Parliament. m. Bunty Whitfield, 22 Oct. 1945, 1 daughter. *Education:* Glasgow University. *Appointments:* Actor, approximately 35 films, numerous television performances and broadcasts; Council Member British Actors' Equity, 1966-69; Member of Parliament for Smethwick, 1966-74; Parliamentary Private Secretary to Minister of Aviation, 1967-68 and Postmaster General, 1968-69; Opposition Spokesman for the Arts, 1970-73, 1979-; Member of Parliament for Warley East, 1974-. *Memberships:* Chairman, British Branch Parliamentary Association for Euro-Arab Co-operation; Executive Committee Member Great Britain-China Centre; Executive Committee Member Franco-British Council; Chairman, All-Party Parliamentary Heritage Group; Member, UK Commission for Unesco Culture Advisory Committee. *Address:* 14 Albemarle Street, London W1, England.

FAULKNER, Arthur James, b. 20 Nov. 1921, Auckland, New Zealand. Member of Parliament. m. 3 Mar. 1945, 2 sons, 3 daughters. *Appointments:* Sales Clerk; War Service; Secretary-Organiser, Auckland Province, Labour Party, 1952-57; Minister of Defence; Minister of Labour and State Services; President, New Zealand Labour Party, 1976-79; Opposition Spokesman on Industrial Relations and Employment, 1975-79; Opposition Spokesman for Foreign Affairs and Defence, 1979-. *Memberships:* Numerous Parliamentary Select Committees including: Defence, Foreign Affairs; Member of the Labour Select Committee and the Committee of Inquiry into Electoral Law; Caucus Committee on Marketing and Production; Kirk Memorial Trust. *Hobby:* Boating. *Address:* 1 Invermay Avenue, Mt. Roskill, Auckland, New Zealand.

FAULKNER, (Sir) Eric, b. 21 Apr. 1914, St Albans, England. Banker. m. Joan Mary Webster, 7 Sept. 1939, 1 son, 1 daughter. *Education:* Corpus Christi College, Cambridge. *Appointments:* Joined Glyn Mills and Co. (Bankers), 1936, Managing Director, 1950, Chairman, 1963-68; Chairman, 1969-77, Director, 1968-, Lloyds Bank; President, British Bankers Association, 1972-73, 1980-; Chairman, Industrial Society, 1973-76; Chairman, City Communications Organisation, 1976-79. *Memberships:* Trustee, Winston Churchill Memorial Trust; Warden, Bradfield College. *Honours:* Knight Bachelor, 1974; Honorary Fellow, Corpus Christi College, Cambridge, 1975. *Hobbies:* Cricket; Association Football; Fishing; Walking. *Address:* Chart Cottage, Seal Chart, Sevenoaks, Kent, England.

FAUNCE, Marcus de Laune, b. 5 Dec. 1922, Sydney, New South Wales, Australia. Consultant Physician. m. Marjorie Morison, 10 Dec. 1951, 2 sons, 1 daughter. *Education:* MBBS, University of Adelaide, 1946; Fellow of Royal Australasian College of Physicians, 1965; Fellow of Royal College of Physicians of London, 1968. *Appointments:* RMO, Royal Adelaide Hospital, 1946-47; Captain, Australian Army Medical Corps, 1947-49; Senior Registrar, Sydney Hospital, 1950-53; House Physician and Research Assistant, Brompton Hospital, London, 1954-55; Consultant Physician, Royal Canberra Hospital, 1957-; Member of Board of Management, Canberra Hospital, 1967-73; Member, Medical Board of ACT, 1963-74; Group Captain, Senior Consultant Physician, RAAF, 1976-. *Memberships:* Fellow of Royal Society of Medicine; Member of Thoracic Society of Australia; Commonwealth Club Canberra. *Publications:* The Cotton Aerodynamic Anti-G Suit, 1978.

Honours: OBE, 1969; AM (Mil), 1981. *Hobby:* Water colour painting. *Address:* University House, Australian National University, Canberra City, Australia.

FAVARO, Eric William, b. 29 Aug. 1950, Glace Bay, Nova Scotia, Canada. Music Educator. m. Sheila Catherine Gillis, 14 Aug. 1976, 1 son. *Education:* BA., Major in Music, St. Francis Xavier University, 1971; Special Studies in Music Education, University of Toronto, 1972; B.Ed., General Elementary Education, St. Francis Xavier University, 1973; M.Mus., University of Oregon, 1978. *Appointments:* Music Demonstration Teacher, Fine Arts Center, Calgary Separate School Board, Alberta, 1973-75; Grade 3/4 Teacher, Calgary Separate School Board, 1975-76; Music Education Instructor, College of Cape Breton, Sydney, Nova Scotia, 1976-77; Music Specialist, Calgary Separate School Board, 1978-81; Music Ed. Instructor, University of Lethbridge, 1974; Music Ed. Instructor, College of Cape Breton, 1975-79; Music Specialist, Cape Breton Municipal School Board. *Memberships:* Board of Directors, Alberta, Canadian Music Educators Association; Executive Representative, Alberta ATA Fine Arts Council; Past President, Calgary Music Educators Society; Carl Orff Canada, Music for Children, Calgary Chapter. *Publications:* Article on Aleatoric Music for Children, 1975; Music Curriculum Integrating Music and Art Concepts in the Elementary School. M.Mus. Thesis, Integrating Line, Form, Colour, Texture in Art and Music. *Hobbies:* Piano & Organ Playing; Skiing; Skating; Swimming; Cooking. *Address:* Site 4 Box 48, R.R. #1 Glace Bay, Nova Scotia, B1A 1G0.

FAWIBE, Oladiran, b. 20 July 1943, Ilesha, Nigeria. Economist. m. Olu V A Fawibe, 2 daughters. *Education:* BSc, 1969, MSc, 1971, University of Ibadan, Nigeria. *Appointments:* Research Assistant, Nigerian Institute of Social and Economic Research, University of Ibadan, 1969-71; Senior Research Supervisor, Central Bank of Nigeria, 1971-72; Petroleum Economist, Nigerian National Oil Corporation, Lagos, 1972-75; Head of Marketing Department, NNPC, 1975-81; Chief Economist, NNPC, Petroleum Inspectorate, Lagos, 1981-; Member of Nigerian Delegation to OPEC Economic Commission Board, Working Parties and Conferences, 1973-. *Memberships:* Fellow, Institute of Petroleum, London; Institute of Marketing, London; Oxford Energy Policy Club; Nigerian Economic Society. *Publications:* Competition in the Marketing of Petroleum Products in Nigeria; Flow of Foreign Investments to Nigeria: Evidence from Cross-Section Data; The Nigerian Industrial Relations System and the Dynamics of Economic Development; Transfer of Technology to Developing Countries, Ibadan Lafia Canning Factory Case. *Hobbies:* Squash Rackets; Law Tennis; Reading; Trasvelling. *Address:* Block B, Suite 2B, Eko Court Kofo, Abayomi Street, Victoria Island Lagos, Nigeria.

FAZACKERLEY, Brian Bate, b. 25 July 1927, Wigan, Lancashire, England. Medical Practitioner (Radiologist). m. Zélie Elizabeth Josephine Gillespie, 31 Aug. 1955, 3 sons, 1 daughter. *Education:* University of Dublin, BA., 1948, M.B., B.Ch., 1949; D.M.R.D. 1956; M.R.C.R.A., 1962. *Appointments:* Radiologist, Christchurch Hospital, New Zealand, 1958-62; Radiologist, Royal Hobart Hospital, Tasmania, 1962-78; Radiologist, Hamilton Base Hospital, Portland & District Hospital, Victoria Australia, 1979-. *Memberships:* Royal College of Radiologists of Australasia; Royal Automobile Club of Victoria; Hamilton Club, Victoria; Victoria Racing Club; Tasmanian Racing Club. *Honours:* State Exhibition Northern Ireland Schools Senior Leaving Certificate, (Mathematics & Science Group), 1943. *Hobbies:* Golf; Horse Racing. *Address:* 255 King Street, Hamilton, Victoria, Australia.

FEARON, Blair, b. 26 Jan. 1919, Farnham, Prov. Quebec, Canada. Physician & Surgeon (Otolaryngologist). m. Joyce D Ball 1 June 1946, 1 son, 2 daughters. *Education:* BA., Mt. Allison University, 1940; MD., University Toronto, 1944; F.R.C.S., 1950; F.A.C.S., 1968; F.A.A.P., 1977. *Appointments:* Teaching Staff (Assistant Professor), Department Otolaryngology, University Toronto, 1950-; Attending staff (Senior surgeon) Hospital for Sick Children, Toronto, 1950-; Consultant Otolaryngology & Bronchoesophagology, Women's College Hospital and Oakville-Trafalgar Memorial Hospital, 1953-; Chief Otolaryngology, North York General Hospital, 1968-76, Senior Consultant. *Memberships:* Royal College Physician & Surgeons,

Canada; Fellow, American College Surgeons; American Broncho-esophagological Association, President 1966-67; American Laryngological Association, Vice-President 1976-77; American Triological Society; American Academy of Otolaryngology and Head & Neck Surgery; International Broncho-esophagological Society; Canadian Otolaryngological Society; Naval & Military Club, London; Granite Club & Rosedale Golf Club, Toronto. *Publications:* Over 60 publications in international medical journals and chapters in several medical texts. *Honours:* Chevalier Jackson Award, 1976; Chevalier Jackson Award, 1980; Award American Academy Otolaryngology Head and Neck Surgery, 1981. *Hobby:* Photography. *Address:* 13 Douglas Crescent, Toronto, Ontario, Canada, M4W 2E6.

FEEHAN, Harold Victor, b. 27 Nov. 1930, Melbourne, Australia. Administrator. m. Marie Rita Ryan, 4 July 1953, 2 sons, 3 daughters. *Education:* Degree of Bachelor of Commerce with Honours, University of Melbourne, 1962. *Appointments:* Cadet Journalist, Wangaratta Chronicle Despatch, 1950; Commonwealth Department, Customs & Excise, 1951-62; Commonwealth Department, Shipping & Transport, 1962-66; Deputy Chief, Commonwealth Bureau of Roads, 1967-69; Tutor, Statistical Method, University of Melbourne, 1962-69; Registrar, Pharmacy Board of Victoria, 1969-81; Secretary-Registrar, Pharmaceutical Society, Victoria, 1969-73; Executive Director, Victorian College of Pharmacy & Pharmaceutical Society of Victoria, 1973-81; Secretary Hospitals Division, Health Commission of Victoria, 1981-. *Memberships:* Associate fellow Australian Institute of Management and the Institute of Business Administration; Royal Institute of Public Administration, Victoria Branch; Royal Society of Health; Historical Society of Victoria; Genealogical Society of Victoria. *Publications:* Alexander Cameron, Founder of Penola, A Biographical Sketch, 1980; Birth of the Victorian College of Pharmacy, 1981; Scattered Poems, 1980; Bond and Link, Pharmacy Organisations and Education in Victoria, 1857-1977, 1978. *Honours:* Commonwealth Scholarship, 1950; Commonwealth Public Service Tertiary Education Scholarship, 1958. *Hobbies:* Lapidary work and Gemstone Prospecting; Genealogy and History; Writing. *Address:* 17 Winston Drive, Doncaster, 3108, Victoria, Australia.

FELL, Howard Barraclough (Barry), b. 6 June 1917, Lewes, Sussex. Oceanographer & Epigrapher. m. Renee Clarkson, 10 Oct. 1942, 2 sons, 1 daughter. *Education:* University of New Zealand, Wellington, BS.c., 1938, M.Sc., 1939; PhD., University of Edinburgh, Scotland, 1941; D.Sc., University of Edinburgh, 1955; Honorary A.M. Harvard University, USA., 1965. *Appointments:* Associate Professor of Zoology, Victoria University, NZ., 1945-64; Curator of Marine Invertebrates, Museum of Comparative Zoology, Cambridge, USA., 1964-77; Professor of Marine Invertebrates, Harvard University, 1965-77; Professor Emeritus, Harvard University, 1977-; Visiting Professor, University of Tripoli, Libya 1978. *Memberships:* President Epigraphic Society, 1974; Fellow, American Academy, 1964-79, Fellow Emeritus, 1979; Fellow, Royal Society of New Zealand, 1960; Early Sites Research Society, Massachusetts, 1974; Membre Honoris Causa Societe d'etude des anciens peuples, Carcasonne. *Publications:* Deep-Sea Photography, 1967; Treatise on Invertebrate Paleontology, 1966-67; Life, Space & Time, 1974; Introduction to Marine Biology, 1975 America B.C. 1976-77 (Six printings); America B.C. 1977-80 (Pocket Books); Saga America, 1980, also British, Arabic, Spanish and Japanese editions. *Honours:* University of Triploi Prize for Arab History, 1980; America B.C. selected by US Booksellers Association as one of Best Books published, 1966; Hector Medal, 1959, and Hutton Medal, 1962 Royal Society of New Zealand, for scientific research. *Hobbies:* Sculpture; Exploring. *Address:* Epigraphic Society, 6625 Bamburgh Drive, San Diego, CA 92117, USA.-

FELTHAM, Herbert George (Barney), b. 28 Mar. 1924, Raetihi, New Zealand. Radiologist. m. Keren Pratt, 18 Dec. 1947, 2 sons, 2 daughters. *Education:* M.B., Ch.B., University Otago, 1947; D.M.R.D., London, 1953; M.R.A.C.R., 1956; F.R.A.C.R., 1978. *Appointments:* Radiologist Princess Mary Hospital for Children, Auckland, 1954-56; Private Radiological Consulting Practice, Auckland, 1956-; Part-time Visiting Consultant Auckland & Princess Mary Hospitals, 1956-; Visiting Consultant Radiologist, Thames Hospi-

tal, N.Z., 1958-; Chairman Advisory Committee on Radiological Services to Auckland Hospital Board; Member Radiological Services Advisory Committeee N.Z. Department of Health. *Memberships:* Past President, Present Secretary, Auckland Radiological Society; Royal N.Z. Yacht Squadron; Rotary Club of Newmarket, Auckland. *Hobbies:* Sailing; Building & Home improvement. *Address:* 3 Elmstone Avenue, Remuera, Auckland 5, New Zealand.

FENECH, Joseph, b. 2 Apr. 1931, Malta. Advocate; Member of Parliament. m. Marlene Ellal, 1 May 1957, 2 sons, 1 daughter. *Education:* BA, 1952, LLD, 1955; Royal University of Malta. *Appointments:* Practised, Commercial and Civil Law, Malta, 1955-; Elected to Parliament, 1976-; Secretary to Opposition Parliamentary Group and Spokesman for the Opposition on the Department of Treasury and Audit. *Hobbies:* Sports; Reading. *Address:* Villa San Anton, B'Kara Road, Attard, Malta.

FENNELL, Trevor Garth, b. 16 July 1940, Port Augusta, South Australia. Grammarian (Baltic, Romance & General). m. Etiennette Dupuy, 24 Apr. 1963, 1 son, 1 daughter. *Education:* B.A. 1st Class Honours, Adelaide, 1962; Docteur de l'Université, Paris, 1965. *Appointments:* Lecturer, 1966; Senior Lecturer, 1970, Reader in French, 1975; Vice-Chairman, 1968-70, Acting Chairman, 1971, Chairman, 1974-79, School of Humanities, Flinders University of South Australia. *Memberships:* Linguistic Society of Australia; Association for the Advancement of Baltic Studies; Member of the zBaltic Scientific Institute (Stockholm), 1981. *Publications:* La Morphologie du futur en moyen francais, 1975; A Grammar of Modern Latvian, (with H. Gelsen), 1980; Numerous articles on grammatical questions, particularly Latvian. *Honours:* Fellow, Academy of the Humanities of Australia, 1978; Honorary Member of the Latvian-American Association of Professors and Scientists, 1981. *Hobbies:* Gastronomy; Cricket; Music. *Address:* School of Humanities, Flinders University, Bedford Park, South Australia 5042.

FENNER, Frank John, b. 21 Dec. 1914, Ballarat, Victoria, Australia. Medical Research. m. Ellen Margaret Roberts, 2 Nov. 1944, 1 daughter. *Education:* M.D., University of Adelaide, 1941; D.T.M., University of Sydney, 1940; Honorary MD., Monash University, 1964. *Appointments:* Medical Officer, Australian Imperial Forces, 1940-46; Francis Haley Fellow, Walter & Eliza Hall Institute for Medical Research, 1946-48; Professor of Microbiology, John Curtin School of Medical Research, Australian National University, 1949-67; Director, John Curtin School of Medical Research, 1967-73; Director, Center for Resource & Environmental Studies, Australian National University, 1973-79; University Fellow, Australian National University, 1980-. *Memberships:* Foreign Associate, Australian National Academy of Science, 1977; Fellow, Royal Society of London, 1958; Fellow, Australian Academy of Science, 1954, Secretary 1958-60. *Publications:* The Production of Antibodies, (with F.M. Burnet), 1949; Myxamatosis, (with F N Ratcliffe), 1965; The Biology of Animal Viruses, 1968, 1nd edition, 1974; Medical Virology (with D O White), 1970, 2nd edition, 1976; The Classification & Nomenclature of Viruses, 1976; The Australian Academy of Science-8The First 25 Years, (Editor with ALG Reese), 1980. *Honours:* MBE., 1943; CMG., 1976; Mueller Medal, 1964; Britannia Award for Medicine, 1967; Mathew Flinders Lecture, 1967; ANZAAS Medal, 1980; ANZAC Peace Prize, 1980. *Hobbies:* Gardening; Tennis; Fishing. *Address:* 8 Monaro Crescent, Red Hill, Canberra, ACT 2603, Australia.

FENNESSY, Leo Michael, b. 7 June 1907, Warrnambool, Victoria, Australia. Retired Member of Parliament, Victorian State Assembly. m. Celestine Vosti, 17 Feb. 1940, 1 daughter. *Education:* St. Thomas' Christian Brothers College, Melbourne. *Appointments:* Manufacturing Industry, 1923-29; Wheat Farming & Gold Mining Industry, 1929-39; Army Engineers, Middle East, 1939-44; Commonwealth Public Service & Trade Union Official, 1944-55; Victorian State Member of Parliament, 1955-70. *Memberships:* Frankston (Returned Services) Club; 39ers Services Club; Melbourne Legacy Club; Yamala Park Bowling Club. *Honours:* O.B.E., 1974; Commissioner of the Peace, 1954. *Hobbies:* Lawn Bowls; Gardening. *Address:* 2/32 Dunstan Street, Olivers Hill, Frankston, Victoria, Australia.

FENN, Elaine Dorothy, b. 20 Mar. 1937, Cohuna, Victoria, Australia. Concert Pianist. *Education:* BM, Melbourne University Conservatorium, 1955-58; Premier Prix, 1971, Higher Diploma of Virtuosity, 1973, Royal Conservatoire, Brussels, Belgium; Private Piano Studies. *Appointments:* Soloist, Australian Broadcasting Commission, 1956-; Soloist, Victorian Symphony Orchestra, 1958-61; Soloist, Brussels Royal Conservatoire Orchestra, 1972; Soloist, Belgian National Orchestra, 1973; Soloist, British Broadcasting Corporation, 1975-; Wigmore Hall London Debut, 1974; Appeared in Concerts in Australia, Belgium, Holland, Switzerland, England, USA. *Memberships:* Pianists' Foundation of America. *Honours:* Commonwealth Scholarship, 1956; City of Canberra Open Piano Championship, 1962; Belgian Government Scholarship, 1967-73; Premier Prix Brussels Royal Conservatoire, Great Distinction, 1971; Higher Diploma of Virtuosity, 1973. *Hobbies:* Reading; Walking; Theatre. *Address:* 6 Kendal Court, Shoot-up Hill, London, England.

FENWICK, Denton Rowland, b. 31 July 1916, Co. Durham, England. Chartered Electrical Engineer. m. Joan Marguerite Jeffrey, 7 Nov. 1939, 2 sons, 1 daughter. *Education:* Manchester College of Technology, 1937-39; Higher National Certificate, Electrical Engineering, 1939. Design Engineer, Metropolitan-Vickers Electrical Co. Ltd., 1946-56; Engineering Section Leader, MVE Co/AEI Ltd., 1956-60; Departmental Assistant Chief Engineer, AEI Ltd., 1961-62; Departmental Chief Engineer, AEI/GEC Ltd., 1962-69; Chief Instrumentation Engineer, NEI-Parsons, Ltd., 1970-80; Consultant to NEI-Parsons, Ltd., 1981-. *Memberships:* Fellow, Institution of Electrical Engineers. *Publications:* Measurement of Shaft Movements—Paper, 1977; Trends in Excitation Systems, 1976; Auto-Turbine Run-Up System, 1962. *Hobbies:* Radio & Electronics. *Address:* 2 The Glebe, Stannington, Morpeth, Northumberland, NE61 6HW, England.

FERGUSON, Angus MacLeod, b. 1 Jan. 1924, Kettins, Angus, Scotland. Solicitor. m. (1) Frances Minto Waugh 8 Dec. 1951 (dec.), (2) Shirley Marguerite de Beaux Sloan, 6 Apr. 1974, 2 sons, 1 daughter. *Education:* Perth Academy 1941; Army 1942-47; Bachelor of Law, Edinburgh University 1950. *Appointments:* Professional Practice, Edinburgh, 1951; Irving and Bonnar, Lagos, Nigeria, 1951-; Senior Partner, 1960-; Director, of 24 Companies; Chairman of 5. *Memberships:* Caledonian Club, London; Metropolitan Club, Lagos; Nigeria-Britain Association; Lagos Caledonian Society. *Honours:* CBE 1967. *Hobbies:* Work; Cricket; Reading; Listening to Music. *Address:* 5 Louis Solomon Close, Victoria Island, Lagos.

FERGUSON, Malcolm Alastair Percy, b. 19 Dec. 1913, Blackwater, Hants., England. Artist & Teacher. m. 24 Aug. 1942, 1 son, 1 daughter. *Education:* Royal Military College, Sandhurst, 1932 (Invalided soon after); Portsmouth School of Art, 1934-36; Croydon School of Art, 1936-38; Slade School University of London, 1939, 1948-50; Diploma in Fine Art, University of London, 1950; Group II Five Year Trained (Burnham Report) and A.T.D., equivalent, 1950. *Appointments:* In charge of Art at Boston Boy's Grammar, Merchant Taylors' School, Northwood, Brymore Technical School Somerset and Kings College, Taunton, 1942-78; Part-time Assistant Somerset College of Art; At present part-time teaching; Over last ten years carrying out his designs for Fresco in half dome and apse of St. Joseph's Chapel, St. Cuthberts, Transkei, during summer vacation to complete in 1981. *Memberships:* Elected A.R.W.A., 1964 and R.W.A., 1973 and member of various provincial Societies; Formed Minehead Painter's Group, 1960's. *Creative Works:* Work purchased by various public collections, including Plymouth City Art Gallery, Talbot Bequest Britol, Royal West of England Permanent Collection, Somerset Museum Service and public and private collections in England, America, Canada, South Africa, Australia; One-man exhibitions, 1970, White Chapel Public Library Gallery, Port Elizabeth, 1971; Brewhouse Taunton, 1977; Oxford, 1980; Mountbatten Gallery, Portsmouth, 1980. *Address:* 7 Mill Street, North Petherton, Bridgwater, Somerset TA6 6LX, England.

FERLEY, Lorne William, b. 22 Nov. 1934, Teulon, Manitoba, Canada. Education (School Principal). m. Irene Theresa Johnson, 16 July 1960, 2 sons, 1 daughter. *Education:* Graduated, Teulon Collegiate, 1952; Teaching Certificate, Prov. Normal School 1953; BSc, University of Manitoba 1960, BEd, University of Manitoba, 1963. *Appointments:* Teacher, Union Prairie School, Inwood, Manitoba, 1953-55; Teacher, Norris Lake School, Teulon, Manitoba, 1955-57; Science Teacher, Nelson McIntyre Collegiate, Norwood School Division Winnipeg, 1960-71; Principal, Archwood School, Norwood School Division, 1971-. *Memberships:* National Science Teachers Association; Manitoba Association of Principals; Manitoba Schools Science Symposium; Science Teachers Association of Manitoba; Manitoba Teachers Society; Norwood Teachers Association; The Alumni Association, University of Manitoba. *Honours:* Awarded, Recognition and Gratitude for Service Medal by NSTA, 1977; Distinguished Service Citation, STAM 1977. *Hobbies:* Photography; Reading; Music; Collecting Plants; Canoeing. *Address:* 19 Carolyn Bay, Winnipeg, Manitoba, Canada, R2J 2Z3.

FERNANDES, Victor Anthony, b. 8 Mar. 1948, Barbados. Broadcaster. m. Lorna Fernandes, 20 Feb. 1967 (div.), 1 son, 1 daughter. *Education:* Professional Studies, BBC 1974; Operations Management, Barbados Institute of Management and Productivity 1977. *Appointments:* Announcer, Caribbean Broadcasting Corp. 1965-72; Senior Announcer, CBC, 1972-77; Director of Radio, CBC, 1977-80; Manager, CBC Radio, 1980-. *Memberships:* President, Presentation College Old Scholars Association; Chairman, Radio Committee, Caribbean Broadcasting Union. *Honours:* Cropouer Award, 1980. *Hobbies:* Table Tennis; Squash; Music. *Address:* Atlantic Shores, Christ Church, Barbados.

FERNANDO, Anura Christopher Manilka, b. 13 Aug. 1953, Colombo, Sri Lanka. Chartered Accountant. *Education:* Associate Member, The Institute of Chartered Accounts of Sri Lanka, 1979. *Appointments:* Lecturer, The Polytechnic Colombo, Sri Lanka; Accountant, Delmege Forsyth & Co.; Chief Accountant, Holiday Inn, Abu Dhabi, U.A.E. *Memberships:* President, Chartered Accountant Student Society of Sri Lanka; Member, National Prices Commission of Sri Lanka. *Honours:* IBM Certificate for Computer Programming, 1978. *Hobbies:* Sports. *Address:* 12/6 Spathodea Avenue, Colombo, 5, Sri Lanka.

FERNANDO, Henry Marcus, b. 17 Oct. 1920, Colombo, Sri Lanka. Accountant. m. Christabel May Faustina, 3 May 1948, 3 sons, 2 daughters. *Education:* Fellow, Institute of Cost and Management Accountants, London; Associate, Institute of Chartered Secretaries and Administrators, London; Associate member, British Institute of Management, London. *Appointments:* Secretary/Accountant, Sri Lanka Leather Products Corporation, 1945-50; Group Chief Accountant/Company Secretary and Finance Director, CFT Group of Companies, Sri Lanka, 1950-76; Chief Accountant/Finance Manager, National Grains Production Company Limited, Kaduna, Nigeria, 1976-. *Memberships:* President, CFT Sports Club; President, CFT Death Benefit Society. *Hobbies:* Reading; Gardening. *Address:* 7B Maikano Road, Kaduna, Nigeria.

FERNANDO, Thusew Samuel, b. 5 Aug. 1906, Ambalangoda, Sri Lanka. Law. m. Malini Wickramasuriya, 7 July 1943, 1 son. *Education:* Royal College Colombo; University College, Colombo and London, 1927-31; Inns of Court, (Lincoln's Inn), 1928-31; Barister-at-Law, 1931; LLB (London) 1932; Advocate, Ceylon Bar, 1932. *Appointments:* Crown Counsel, Ceylon, 1936-46; Senior Crown Counsel, 1946-52; Solicitor-General, 1952-54; Acting Attorney-General, 1954-56; Judge of the Supreme Court, 1956-68; President, Court of Appeal, 1971-73; High Commissioner of Sri Lanka, Australia and New Zealand, 1974-77. *Memberships:* International Commission of Jurists, Geneva; International Committee, Institute on Man and Science, 1966. *Honours:* CBE; Queen's Counsel for Ceylon, 1953. *Hobbies:* Social Service; Walking. *Address:* 3 Cosmas Avenue, Barnes Place, Colombo 7, Sri Lanka.

FERRERS (Earl) Robert Washington, b. 8 June 1929, London. Peer of the Realm. m. 21 July 1951, 1 son, 3 daughters. *Education:* Winchester College; MA., Agriculture, Magdalene College, Cambridge. *Appointments:* Coldstream Guards, Malaya, 1948-50; Lord-in-Waiting to H.M. Queen, 1962-64; Opposition Whip,

House of Lords, 1964-67; Lord-in-Waiting, 1971-74; Parliamentary Secretary, Ministry of Agriculture, Fisheries & Food, 1974; Member of Armitage Committee on Political Activity & Civil Servants, 1976; Joint Deputy Leader of the Opposition, House of Lords, 1976-79; Deputy Leader, House of Lords, 1979-; Minister of State, Ministry of Agriculture Fisheries & Food, 1979-. Director, Norwich Union Insurance Group, 1975-79; Chairman, Trustee Savings Bank of Eastern England, 1977-79; Director, Central Trustee Savings Bank Ltd., 1978-79; Director Trustee Savings Bank Trustcard Ltd., 1978-79; High Steward, Norwich Cathedral, 1979-. *Memberships:* President, East of England Agricultural Society, 1979; President, Eastern Counties Region of Mencap, 1979; Beefsteak Club. *Hobbies:* Shooting; Music; Travel. *Address:* Hedenham Hall, Bungay, Suffolk, England.

FERRIER, Alexander Ian, b. 5 Sept. 1928, Port Washington, Long Island, New York, USA. Architect. m. Mercia Philomena Forde, 22 Sept. 1951, 2 sons, 4 daughters. *Education:* St Patrick's College, Ottawa, Ontario, Canada, 1940-45; Bachelor of Architecture McGill University, Montreal, 1946-52. *Appointments:* Consultant Royal Canadian Air Force, 1952-53; Stephenson and Turner Architects, Sydney NSW, Australia 1953-55; Donoghue, Cusick and Edwards, Architects, Brisbane Queensland Australia 1955-57; Practice, A Ian Ferrier and Associates, 1958; Established A Ian Ferrier, Campbell and Associates Pty. Limited 1970-. *Memberships:* President, 1980-81, Royal Australian Institute of Architects; Industrial Design Institute of Australia; Institute of Arbitrators Australia and Councillor of Queensland Chapter; Knight Sovereign Order of St. John of Jerusalem Knights Hospitaller; Councillor, Brisbane Kindergarten Teachers College; Building Committee, Board of Advanced Education; Faculty of Architecture Board, Queensland University. *Honours:* Justice of the Peace Life Fellow Royal Australian Institute of Architects 1981; Honorary Fellow, American Institute of Architects, 1981; Honorary Fellow Royal Architectural Institute of Canada 1981; Building of the Year Award, Queensland Chapter, RAIA 1964; Citations for Meritorious Architecture, Queensland Chapter RAIA, 1958, 1971; Anzac Medal Design Competition 1978. *Hobbies:* Sketching; Golf; Fishing. *Address:* 392 Swann Road, St Lucia, Brisbane, Queensland 4067, Australia.

FEUSER, Willfried Franziskus, b. 23 July 1928, St. Tönis, West Germai. . Educationist. m. 19 Mar. 1962, 1 son, 2 daughters. *Education:* Universities of Würzburg, 1950-51; Dayton, 1951-52; Freiburg, 1952-58; PhD., University Freiburg, 1960. *Appointments:* Lecturer, German, University Glasgow, 1958-60, University Ibadan, Nigeria, 1960-62; Lecturer, French, University Ibadan, 1962-67, Senior Lecturer, 1967-68; Professor, Modern Languages, University Ife Nigeria, 1968-77; Dean, Faculty of Arts, University Ife, 1969-71; Professor French & Comparative Literature, University Port Harcourt, Nigeria, 1977-. *Memberships:* Nigerian Association of French Teachers, President, 1970-71; Modern Languages Association of Nigeria, President, 1974-77; Sociedade Protectora dos Desvalidos, Bahia. *Publications:* Author, Aspectos da Literatura do Mundo Negro, 1969; Africa in Prose, Editor (with O.R. Dathorne), 1969; Afrikanische Religion und Weltanschauung, (Translation), 1974; Editor, Twenty Years of German Studies in Nigeria, 1980 and Jazz and Palm-Wine, 1981. *Hobbies:* Swimming; Gardening. *Address:* Permanent Site, University of Port Harcourt, Nigeria.

FIDDIAN-GREEN, Charles William, b. 17 Apr. 1934, Matatiele, South Africa. Chairman & Chief Executive of Rennies Consolidated Holdings. m. Margild Irmgard Barty-King, 5 Apr. 1978 (second marriage), 2 daughters. *Education:* Michaelhouse, Balgowan, South Africa; University of Cape Town, Cape Town, South Africa; MA., Brasenose College, Oxford, UK; P.M.D., Harvard University, USA; *Appointments:* Assistant Manager, Goldfields of South Africa prior to joinging Rennies as Financial Director, 1967- Appointed Managing Director, 1969, Deputy Chairman, 1972 and Chief Executive Chairman, 1976. *Memberships:* Trustee South Africa Foundation; National Advisory Board of the Graduate School of Business, Cape Town; Oriental Club, London; St Moritz Tobogganing Club; Johannesburg Country Club, South Africa; River Club, Johannesburg; Inanda Club Johannesburg; S. African Cresta Club; Bryanston Country Club, Johannesburg. *Honours:* Captained his

college at Oxford at cricket and squash; Represented Combined South African Universities at Squash, 1954. *Hobbies:* Golf; Fishing; Shooting; Tobogganing; Tennis. *Address:* 29 Rosebank Road Dunkeld, Johannesburg 2196, South Africa.

FIEFIA, Sione Naa, b. 1 Feb. 1931, Haateiho, Tongatapu, Tonga. Educational Administration. m. Iunisi Lui, 17 May 1955, 1 son (adopted), 1 Daughter. *Education:* N.Z. Trained Teachers' Certificate, Ardmore Teachers' College, 1952-53; B.Ed., Degree, University of Hawaii, 1963-65; Diploma Ed. Admin., Reading University, UK., 1968-69. *Appointments:* Assistant Teacher, 1954; Assistant Lecturer, 1955; Senior Lecturer 1960; Census Officer, 1966; Education Officer, 1968; Senior Education Officer, 1970; Director of Education, 1972-. *Memberships:* University Council; Vice-Chairman, South Pacific Board of Educational Assessment; The Tonga International Year for the Child Committee. *Publications:* Census Report of Tonga, 1966. *Honours:* First Tongan to be trained overseas as a Teacher, 1952; Played Rugby for Tonga against an Australian XV, 1954; First Tongan to be Director of Education, 1972; Member of Council of University of South Pacific, representing Tonga Government, 1977; Represented Tonga in many international and Commonwealth meetings. *Hobbies:* Rugby; Reading; Gardening; Travelling; Photography. *Address:* Taufa'ahau Road, Ha-'ateiho, Tongatapu, Tonga.

FIELD, Christopher Rodney, b. 6 Apr. 1940, Woodford, England. Research Scientist. *Education:* BA., (Cantab), Honours, 1962; MA., (Cantab), 1964; PhD., (Cantab), 1968. *Appointments:* Scientific Investigator, Nuffield Unit of Tropical Animal Ecology, Uganda, 1962-69; Research Scientist, Caesar Kleberg Research Programme in Wildlife Ecology, Texas A.M. University, attached to Kenya Wildlife Management Project, Nairobi, Kenya, 1970-75; Senior Ecologist UNESCO, Integrated Project in Arid Lands, Mt. Kulal, Northern Kenya, 1976-. *Memberships:* Society for Range Management; East African Wildlife Society; Fauna Preservation Society. *Publications:* 21 publications as senior author in the fields of wildlife ecology, nutritional ecology, livestock ecology, and arid lands ecology; Co-author of seven publications in similar fields. *Honours:* Leverhulme Research Award, 1962; Honorary Consultant to World Wildlife Fund, Zebra Group, 1977. *Hobbies:* Hiking; Wildlife ecology; Ornithology. *Address:* Stella, Castle Street, Usk., Gwent, NP5 1BU. Wales.

FIELD, Clyde Julian, b. 1 June 1934, Barbados West Indies. Company Director. m. Janice Chandler 5 June 1954, 3 daughters. *Education:* Combermers School, 1940-44; Harrison College 1944-50. *Appointments:* Articled Clerk, Carrington and Sealy, Solicitors; Wireless Operator, Internation Aeradio Limited; Station Officer, B.W.I.A; Insurance Salesman, British American Life; Hardware Salesman, T Geddes Grant Bds Limited; Managing Director, Clyde J Field Enterprises Limited. *Memberships:* Carlton Cricket and Football Club; Barbados Turf Club; Lions Clubs International; Small Business Association. *Hobbies:* Cricket and Football; Horse Racing; Social Work, Blind and Deaf; Reading. *Address:* "Cluffs" Villa Val Halla, St Lucy, Barbados.

FIELD, Jeremy Winston, b. 29 May 1930, Salisbury, Zimbabwe. Farmer & Director. m. Heather Joan Mountain, Oct. 1954, 3 daughters. *Education:* Ruzawi School Marandellas, Zimbabwe, 1937-43; Michaelhouse, Balgowan, Natal, South Africa, 1943-47. *Appointments:* Director of Numerous Companies and Corporations including: Booth Cubitt Engineering Ltd.; Oldham z9 Son Ltd.; Martech (Private) Ltd.; Colcom Central Co-operative Ltd.; Filca (Private) Ltd.; Pig Producers Copopperative Ltd.; Enterprise Construction (Private) Ltd. *Memberships:* Fellow, Institute of Directors. *Hobbies:* Fishing; Boating. *Address:* Karimba, P.O. Box 51, Marandellas, Zimbabwe.

FIFE, Wallace Clyde, b. 2 Oct. 1929, Wagga Wagga, New South Wales. Member of Parliament. m. Marcia Hargreaves Stanley, 31 May 1952, 2 sons, 2 daughters. *Education:* Canberra Grammar School; Gurwood Street Public School, Wagga Wagga. *Appointments:* Field Representative, Liberal Party of Australia, NSW Division, 1948; Elected member for Wagga Wagga, NSW Legislative Assembly, 1957; Assistant Minister for Education 1965-67; Minister for Mines, 1967-75;

Minister for Conservation, 1971-72; Minister for Power, 1972-75; Assistant Treasurer, 1972-75; Minister for Transport and Minister for Highways, 1975; Elected member for Farrer, Commonwealth Parliament, 1975; Minister for Business and Consumer Affairs, 1977-79; Minister Assisting the Prime Minister in Federal Affairs, 1978-; Minister for Education, 1979-. *Memberships:* Union Club, Sydney; Commonwealth Club, Canberra. *Hobbies:* Reading; Swimming. *Address:* "Dullatur", R.M.B. 636, Tarcutta Road, Wagga Wagga, 2650, Australia.

FILION, Louis Jacques, b. 9 Aug. 1945, Trois-Rivières, Québec, Canada. Teacher. m. Maria Gagnon 27 May 1972, 1 son. *Education:* BA., University Montreal, 1966; MA., University Ottawa, 1974; MBA., HEC., University of Montreal, 1976. *Appointments:* Reynolds Metals Co., Baie Comeau, Quebec, 1968-72; Government of Quebec, 1972-73; Woods, Gordon, Montreal, Quebec, 1974; Quinze Publisher, Domino Publisher, Sogides, Montreal, Quebec, 1977-80; University Quebec Trois-Rivieres and HEC, University Montreal; Teacher, Management Science and Business Policy, 1981. *Memberships:* Adm. A., ASAC, Acfas, AMBAQ; MENSA. *Hobbies:* Tennis; Racquet Ball; Ski; Sailing. *Address:* C.P. 172, Brossard, Quebec, Canada, J4Z3J2.

FILSON, Albert Henstock Kofi, b. 8 Jan. 1926, Half-Assinie, Western Region, Ghana. Teaching. m. Sarah Maria Mensah, 30 Dec. 1956, 2 sons, 1 daughter. *Education:* Cambridge School Certificate, St Augustine's College, Cape Coast, 1938-44; Teachers Certificate A, Wesley College, Kumasi, 1948-49; BA(Hons) University of Ghana, Legon, 1960-63. *Appointments:* Pupil Teacher, Catholic Education Unit, Kumasi 1945-47; Certificated Teacher, Methodist Unit, Kumasi 1950-54; Non-Graduate Teacher, Opoku Ware Secondary School Kumasi 1955-60, Graduate Teacher, 1963-65; Headmaster, Amaniampong Secondary School 1966-71; Headmaster, Kaneshire Secondary Technical School, 1972-80; Assistant Director, Ghana Education Service Regional Office, Accra 1980-. *Memberships:* Historical Society of Ghana; Greater Accra Voluntary Work Camps Association; St Theresa's Catholic Church Parish Advisory Council. Hobby: Gardening. *Address:* PO Box M 148, Accra, Ghana.

FINDLAY, Earl Charles, b. 30 Dec. 1915, Toronto, Canada. Mechanical Engineer (ret). m. Norma Willene Lorenson, 17 June 1939, 3 daughters. *Education:* B Sc., M Sc., PhD. *Appointments:* Order Department, Supervisor, Link-Belt Company, Toronto, Montreal and Quebec; Sales Engineer, Sales Manager, United Steel Corp., Montreal and Quebec; Manager of Sales Engineering & Sewage & Sanitation Division, Consolidated Engines and Machinery Company, Montreal; Managing Director, Zurn Industries Canada Ltd., Toronto, later Vice President, General Sales Manager, Zurn Industries, Inc. New England, USA. *Memberships:* American Society of Mechanical Engineers; American Chemical Engineering Society; Association of Naval Architects & Marine Engineers; Power Institute of Canada; Association of Iron & Steel Engineers; Water Pollution Control Federation. *Honours:* Two honorary degrees, 1957, 1959. *Hobbies:* Tree Farming; Swimming; Snow Shoeing; Skiing; Dancing; Organist & Former concert violinist. *Address:* Long Hill Road, Raymond, New Hampshire, 03077, USA.

FINDLAY, Joseph William Oladepoh (Jr.), b. 9 Aug. 1935, Freetown, Sierra Leone. Director General; Head of Mass Media Services. m. 30 Apr. 1960, 2 sons, 3 daughters. *Education:* DIPLOM (Publizistik) Bonn, West Germany, 1961; BA, Iowa, USA, 1969; Post Graduate Certificate in Journalism Education, Iowa, USA, 1970; MA, Iowa, USA, 1971. *Appointments:* Junior Announcer, 1958; Programme Planner, 1960; Programme Manager, 1964; Head of Programmes, 1964; Assistant Director (Progs. & Admin.), 1966; Director, Sound Broadcasting, 1971; Director of Broadcasting, 1971; Director General, 1978; Director General & Head of Mass Media Services, 1979-. *Memberships:* Board of Trustees International Institute of Communications (ITC); Chairman, Broadcasting Organisations of Non-Aligned Countries (BONAC). *Publications:* SLBS Record Vol. 1, 1972; 40 Years of Broadcasting, 1974. *Honours:* Outstanding Foreign Student Award, University of Iowa, USA, 1970-71. *Hobbies:* Reading; Tennis; Cricket. *Address:* PO Box 933, Freetown, Sierra Leone, West Africa.

FINGLAND, (Sir) Stanley James Gunn, b. 19 Dec. 1919, Edinburgh, Scotland. Diplomat (Retired). m. Nell Lister, 10 Oct. 1946, 1 son, 1 daughter. *Appointments:* Major, Royal Signals, 1939-47; Commonwealth Relations Office, 1948; Service, Cwlth Service/FCO in New Delhi, Bombay, Canberra; Adviser on Commonwealth and External Affairs to Governor General of Nigeria, 1958-60; British High Commission, Lagos, 1960-61; Adviser on Cwlth and External Affairs to Governor General of the West Indies, 1961, Trindad, Tobago, 1962; Deputy High Commissioner: Port of Spain, 1962, Salisbury, Rhodesia, 1964-66; British High Commissioner, Freetown, Sierra Leone, 1966-69; Assistant Under Secretary of State, FCO , 1969-72; Ambassador, Havana, Cuba, 1972-75; British High Commissioner, Nairobi, Kenya, 1975-79; British Representative to UN Environmental Programme and HABITAT, Nairobi; Led British Delegation to UN Desertification Conference, Nairobi, 1978; Attended Zimbabwe/Rhodesian Elections as Observer Appointed by HMG, 1980. *Memberships:* Royal Overseas League. *Honours:* Commander of the Order of St Michael and St George, 1966; Knight Commander of the Order of St Michael and St George, 1979. *Hobbies:* Golf; Fishing. *Address:* 34 Ashdown, Eaton Road, Hove, Sussex, England.

FINLAY, John Robert, b. 22 Aug. 1939, Toronto, Canada. Solicitor. m. Janet Louise Little, 17 Aug. 1967, 3 daughters. *Education:* BA, 1961, LLB, 1965, University of Western Ontario, Canada, Chartered Financial Anlayst, 1979. *Appointments:* Solicitor, Holden Murdoch & Finlay, Toronto, 1967-80; Vice-President and Financial Officer, Universal Group of Mutal Funds, 1975-80; Vice-President, Argus Corporation Limited, 1980-; Director of: Commercial Oil and Gas Limited, Hollinger Argus Limited, Industrial Group of Mutual Funds, Labrador Mining and Exploration Company Limited, Mackenzie Financial Coproration, Norcen Energy Resources Limited, Universal Group of Mutal Funds; Vice-President and Director: Argus Corporation Limited, The Ravelston Corporation Limited, USE Fund Management Limited; Appointed Queens Counsel, 1981. *Honours:* QC, 1981. *Hobbies:* Boating; Golf; Tennis. *Address:* 6 St Margaret's Drive, Toronto, Ontario, Canada.

FINLAY, John Ronald, b. 11 Apr. 1915, Western Australia. Mining Engineer. m. Raie Bermingham, 14 Jan. 1942. *Education:* Associate of Sydney Technical College. *Appointments:* Mining Engineering, North Broken Hill Limited, 1935-58; Operations Manager, 1959-69; Manager, 1970-77; Executive Director, 1977-80; Director, North Broken Hill Holdings Limited, 1980-; Chairman Directors, Beach Petroleum NL, 1976-. *Memberships:* Australian Institute Mining; Fellow, Australian Institute of Management; British Institute of Management; Australian Club; Broken Hill Club; Masonic Club. *Address:* 6 Garden Court, Wheelers Hill, Victoria 3150, Australia.

FINLAYSON, William, b. 9 Oct. 1927, Kinross-shire, Scotland. Forestry. m. (1) June Lovett Mercer, 3 Oct. 1953, (2) Theresia Suyati, 9 Apr. 1978, 5 sons, 1 daughter. *Education:* Broughton Secondary School, Edinburgh 1941-44; BSc(For.), University of Edinburgh 1944-47; Colonial Forest Service Course, Commonwealth Forestry Institute, Oxford 1950-51. *Appointments:* Assistant Conservator of Forests, Tanganyika; Lecturer in Forestry, University of Edinburgh; Director, Uganda Forestry School; Director, Papua New Guinea Forestry School; Principal, Cyprus Forestry College; Adviser on Training and Education, FAO, Cameroon, Somalia, Indonesia; Director, Commonwealth Forestry Bureau. *Memberships:* Commonwealth Forestry Association; Institute of Foresters of Great Britain. *Publications:* Numerous papers on forestry education, mensuration and information. *Address:* 1 Tilbury Lane, Oxford, OX2 9NB, England.

FINSBERG, Geoffrey, b. 13 June 1926, London, England. Parliamentary Under Secretary of State. m. Pamela Benbow Hill, 10 Apr. 1969. *Appointments:* Chief Industrial Relations Adviser, Great Universal Stores Limited, 1960-79; Member of Parliament, Hampstead, 1970. *Memberships:* St Stephens Constitutional Club; Fellow, Institute of Personnel Management; Hampstead Borough Council, 1949-65; Camden Borough Council, 1964-74; CBI Council, 1968-79. *Honours:* MBE, 1959, JP, 1962. *Address:* House of Commons, London, SW1, England.

FIRMAN, Ivor David, b. 29 July 1934, London, England. Plant Pathologist. m. Anne Bowles, 27 July 1957, 1 son, 2 daughters. *Education:* BSc, Nottingham University, 1954-57; Dip.Agric.Sci, Cambridge University, 1957-58; DTA, Imperial College of Tropical Agriculture, Trindad, 1958-59; Fellow, Institute of Biology. *Appointments:* Plant Pathologist, Coffee Research Station, Kenya; Lecturer in Plant Pathology, University of Bath, UK; Plant Pathologist, Department of Agriculture, Fiji; Plant Pathologist, Food and Agriculture Organisation of the United Nations, Brazil; Plant Protection Officer, South Pacific Commission, Fiji, 1974-. *Memberships:* Association of Applied Biologists; British Mycological Society; Fiji Institute of Agricultural Science. *Publications:* Numerous publications on plant pathology in scientific press. *Address:* South Pacific Commission, PO Box 2119, Suva, Fiji.

FISHER, Alfred Charles, b. 26 June 1905, Lurgan, County Armagh, Northern Ireland (deceased Aug. 1981). Surgeon (Retired), Company Director. m. Margaret Monica Hanford, 19 Jan. 1941, 3 sons, 1 daughter. *Education:* MBCHB, 1929, FRCS, 1930, MD, 1934, Bristol University. *Appointments:* Chief Medical Officer, Roan Antelope Copper Mines; Visiting Surgeon, Nchanga Consolidated Copper Mines; Director, Rhodesian Selecton Trust; Director, SKF Zambia; Director, Grindlays Bank, Int., Zambia, Limited. *Memberships:* British Medical Association; Fellow, Royal Society of Medicine; Fellow, Royal Commonwealth Society. *Publications:* A Study of Schistosomiasis in Belgian Congo, 1934; Primary Tropical Phlehitis, 1947. *Honours:* Gold Medal, Medical School, Bristol, 1929; Order of British Empire. *Hobbies:* Sussex Cattle Pedigree Breeder. *Address:* Greystone Park, PO Box 20928, Kitwe, Zambia.

FISHER, Darrell Lyell, b. 2 July 1940, Burnie, Tasmania, Australia. Teacher. m. Gail Gwendoline McLagan, 28 Dec. 1962, 4 sons, 1 daughter. *Education:* Bachelor of Science; Diploma of Education; Bachelor of Education; Master of Education; Tasmanian Teachers Certificate. *Appointments:* Assistant Science Teacher, Cosgrove High, Hobart, 1962-65; Senior Master, Natural Sciences, Devonport High, 1966-69; Materials Development Officer, Australian Science Education Project, Melbourne, 1970-72; Consultant, Tasmanian Education Department, 1973; RECSAM, Penang, Malaysia, 1979; Senior Lecturer, Division of Teacher Education, Tasmanian College of Advanced Education, 1974-80. *Memberships:* Australian College of Education; South Pacific Association for Teacher Education; Australian Science Education Research Association; Australian Science Teachers Association; Curriculum Interest Group. *Publications:* Investigating Pollution; Growth and Development; Science units written for Australian Science Education; Articles on classroom learning environment in education journals. *Hobbies:* Bush walking; Gardening; Listening to music; Reading. *Address:* Swan Bay, Dilston, Tasmania, Australia.

FISHER, Donald Gilbert Muuready, b. 27 Apr. 1923, London, England. Artist and Exhibition; TV Designer. m. Lylian Guelfand, 20 Dec. 1952, 1 son, 1 daughter. *Education:* St. Martin's School of Art, Master: Ruskin Speak. *Appointments:* Central Office of Information, Exhibition Division, 1947-49; British Council, Aids and Displays, 1950-54; Electrical Development Association, Exhibitions Division, 1959; Freelance. *Memberships:* Society of Industrial Artists and Designers; Free Painters and Sculptors; Chelsea Arts Club; Players Theatre. *Creative Works:* Numerous Exhibitions; Two One Man Shows; Private Collections: UK, Canada, France, Australia, Sweden; Sketches of numerous celebrities. *Hobbies:* Song writing; Music and Lyrics; Poetry; Writing Biographies; Reading Biographies. *Address:* 119 Beaufort Mansions, Beaufort Street, Chelsea SW3, England.

FISHER, Gladstone Lawrence Isaac, b. 5 Nov. 1939, St Andrew, Jamaica WI. Architect, Divorced 1979 2 sons. *Education:* Senior Cambridge School Certificate, Munro College, 1951-58; Pre-Architecture, Acadia University, 1964-66; Bachelor of Architecture, Nova Scotia Tech. 1966-70. *Appointments:* Project Architect, Rutkowski Bradford and Associates Jamaica, 1970-72; Project Architect, Peter Soares and Partners, Jamaica, 1972-73; Senior Partner, Gladstone L I Fisher and Associates, Jamaica, 1973-77; Project Architect, Sunderland Preston Simard, Canada, 1977-78; Project

Architect, Keith L Graham and Associates, Canada, 1978; Site Architect, Drew Sperry and Associates, Canada, 1978-79; Executive Architect, National Development Agency, Jamaica, 1979-81; Senior Partner, Gladstone L I Fisher and Associates, Jamaica, 1981-. *Memberships:* Jamaica Institute of Architects; Royal Jamaica Yacht Club; Liguanea Club. *Honours:* Nova Scotia Association of Architects Award for thesis project: Low Income Hillside Housing in Jamaica, 1970. *Hobbies:* Sailing; Painting; Stamp Collecting. *Address:* 75 Hope Boulevard, Kingston 6, Jamaica.

FISHER, Kelton John, b. 6 May 1947 Sydney Australia. Health and Physical Education. m. Hilary Jane White 25 Sept. 1976. *Education:* Certificate of Education, St. Luke's 1973; BED, Exeter, UK 1974; MSc Oregon, USA 1975. *Appointments:* Spencer Park School London, UK 1970-74; Beaufoy School, London, 1975-76; Kwinana Senior High School, West Australia 1976; Wanneroo High School 1977-78; Curriculum Branch, W.A. Education Department 1979-80. *Memberships:* Australian Council of Health, Physical Education and Recreation; Health Education co-ordinator West Australia, 1980. *Publications:* A History of Cricket in Sports, Dance and Related Pastimes, 1977; Health Education at Wanneroo High School, 1979; Health Education at Wanneroo, W.A; Health Education for Secondary Schools, 1980. *Honours:* County Cricket Representative, Devon County Cricket Club, UK 1974; Foreign Student Scholarship University of Oregon Eugine 1974-75. *Hobbies:* Sport; Outdoor Pursuits; Cooking; Music. *Address:* 54 Rathay Street, Victoria Park, Perth 6100, Western Australia.

FISHER, Nigel Thomas Loveridge, b. 14 July 1913, Cosham, Hampshire, England. Member of Parliament. m. (1) Lady Gloria Vaughan, 1935, (2) Patricia Ford, 1956, 1 son, 1 daughter. *Education:* MA(Honours), Law, Eton and Trinity College, Cambridge. *Appointments:* MP, Hitchin Division of Hertfordshire 1950-55; MP, Surbiton 1955-74; Kingston on Thames, Surbiton, 1974-; Parliamentry Secretary to Minister of Food 1950-55, Home Secretary 1955-57; Under Secretary of State for the Colonies 1962-63 and Commonwealth Relations, 1963-64; Opposition Spokesman, Commonwealth Colonies Affairs 1964-66; Treasurer Commonwealth Parliament Association 1966-69 and UK branch of CPA, 1977-79, Vice Chairman 1975-76; Deputy Chairman, CPA, 1979-. *Memberships:* MCC: Society of Authors. *Publications:* Official Biography of Iain MacLeod 1973; The Tory Leader 1977. *Honours:* BA 1934; MA 1939; MC 1944; Knighted 1974. *Hobbies:* Tennis; Riding; Walking; Reading; Writing. *Address:* 16 North Court, Great Peter Street, Westminster, London SW1, England.

FISHER, Rosamund Anne, b. 22 May 1924 Hobart Tasmania Australia. Zoo Director and Author. (1) Geofrey Forrester Fairbairn June 1945 2 sons, 1 daughter, (2) John Lord Fisher, 7 May 1970. *Education:* Educated in Australia and England. *Publications:* My Jungle Babies; Marcus Who am I. *Hobbies:* Tapestry; Interior Decorating; Collecting Antiques; Gardening. *Address:* Kilverstone, Thetford, Norfolk, England.

FISHER, William Norman, b. 11 May 1946 Canberra, A.C.T. Australian Diplomatic Service. m. Kerry Jean Gulson, 17 Jan. 1969. *Education:* Bachelor of Economics (Honours) Australian National University. *Appointments:* Australian Mission to UN Geneva; Australian Embassy, Laos; Diplomatic Staffing Officer, Department of Foreign Affairs, Canberra; Australian Consul to New Caledonia and French Polynesia; Australian Consul in the New Hebrides; Head of South Pacific Section, Department of Foreign Affairs; Charge D'Affaires Australian Embassy, Iran. *Memberships:* Australian National University Staff Club. *Address:* c/o Department of Foreign Affairs, Canberra, Australia.

FLAHERTY, Gerald Ambrose, b. 26 Mar. 1934, Alton, Ontario, Canada. Barrister and Solicitor. m. Helen Tarcza, 30 June 1962, 3 sons. *Education:* BA (Political Scienoo and Economics), St Michaels College University of Toronto, 1958; LLB, Faculty of Law, 1961; Certificate in Comparative Law, University of Ottawa 1966. *Appointments:* Articled Law Student Blackwell, Hilton, Treadgold and Spratt, Bay St. Toronto, 1961-62; Legal Counsel, Canadian Broadcasting Corporation 1963-64; Assistant General Counsel, Canadian Broadcasting Corporation, 1964-. *Memberships:* Canadian Bar Association: Federal Lawyers Club; World Association of Lawyers; World Peace Through Law Center. *Publications:* Report on Freedom of the Press in Canada, 1975; Seminar materials on Law affecting Journalists in Canada; Prepared for presentation at seminers for Canadian Daily Newspapers Association, Canadian Conference of Managing Editors, Radio $television News Directors Association; Papers, on Freedom of Information, World Law Conference Manilla 1977; Prior Legal restraints on Media, World Law Conference Madrid 1979 and World Law Conference Sao Paulo 1981. *Honours:* Admitted to Bar of Ontario 1963; Bar of Northwest Territories 1973; Queen's Counsel, Canada, 1979; Honorary President for The Americas, World Peace Through Law Centre 1981. *Hobbies:* Skiing; Cycling; Reading. *Address:* 2252 Quinton Street, Ottawa, Ontario K1H 6V3, Canada.

FLANAGAN, John Richard, b. 20 Sept. 1912, Adelaide, South Australia. m. Olive Mary Casserly, 21 Nov. 1936, 2 sons, 5 daughters. *Education:* St Dominic's College, Dongara; St Patrick's Christian Bros. College, Geraldton. *Appointments:* Assistant Secaretary, Industrial Officer and Secretary, Australian Meat Industry Employees Union, W.A 1952-63; Commissioner, The Western Australian Industrial Commission 1964-74. *Memberships:* Royal Association of Justices of Western Australia; The Celtic Club; East Perth Football Club; Industrial Relations Society of Western Australia. *Honours:* Justice of the Peace 1963. *Hobbies:* Leathercraft; Gardening; Boating. *Address:* 275 Grand Promenade, Doubleview, Western Australia 6018.

FLEMING, Charles Alexander, b. 9 Sept. 1916 Auckland, New Zealand. Palaeontologist (Retired). m. Margaret Alison Chambers 12 Apr. 1941 3 Daughters. *Education:* Kings College, Auckland 1931-34; Auckland University College, University of New Zealand; BA 1938; BSc 1940; MSc 1941; DSc 1952; DSc (Hon.) Victoria University of Wellington 1967; DSc(Hon) University of Auckland 1974. *Appointments:* Assistant Geologist, NZ Geological Survey 1940; Assistant Palaeontologist, Palaeontologist, Senior and Chief Palaeontologist 1952-77; Hon. Lecturer in Geology, Victoria University of Wellington 1977-; Mamber, New Zealand National Parks Authority 1970-80. *Memberships:* Foreign member, American Philosophical Society; FRS; FRSNZ; FGS; FZS; FANZAAS; Corresp. Fellow, American Ornithologists Union; Hon. Fellow Royal Australian Ornithol. Union; Hon. Member Geological Society Australia; Entomological Society NZ; Fellow, Art Galleries and Museums Association of NZ. *Publications:* The Geological History of New Zealand and its Life, 1979; Marwick's Illustrations of NZ Shells 1959; Hochstetter's Geology of NZ 1959; Checklist of NZ Birds 1951; Many periodical articles on NZ Molluscs, Birds, Fossils, Geology, Oceanography, Biogeography and Cicadidae. *Honours:* OBE; KBE; Galathea Medal; Hutton and Hector; Memorial Medals; Hamilton Memorial Prize; Walter Burfitt Medal; ANZAAS Medal; Cheeseman Memorial Prize; NZ Research Medal; Service to Science Medal; McKay Hammer Award; McLea Memorial Lecture. *Hobbies:* Gramophone (classical); Whitebait Fishing. *Address:* 42 Wadestown Road, Wellington, 1, New Zealand.

FLEMING, Robert Ingersoll, b. 25 Dec. 1918 Seattle, Washington, USA. Business Executive. m. Margaret Brocket Slayton 17 Nov. 1942, 3 sons, 1 daughter. *Education:* BA (Economics and History) Yale University 1949; Diploma in Economics, Oxford Univarsity 1950; LSE, London University 1951. *Appointments:* American Foreign Service Officer, Accra, Gold Coast, 1951-54; Assistant, to General Manager, Mobil Oil, West Africa, 1954-58; Director, West Africa Programme, Rockefeller Brothers Fund 1958-63; Prepared Economic Programme for Zambia and N. Rhodesia 1963; Promoted Investment for Western Nigeria in New York 1963-65; Organized Investment promotion center for Tunisia (Ford Foundation) 1966; Committee Chairman, US Department of State Committee on Investment on Investment Pro. Econ. Adviser to ECA, Addis Ababa 1966; Vice President, Mid-America International Development Association Inc. 1966-71; Managing Director, Life Flour Mill Limited, Nigeria, Alt. Director, West African Shrimps Limited 1971-81. *Memberships:* Metropolitan Club of Lagos; Rotary Club of Lagos; Nigerian-American Chamber of Commerce, Lagos; Island Club of Lagos; Lions Club of Sapele, Nigeria; International Club of Accra; Rodger Club of Accra. *Publications:* Have Americans a Place in Africa; Critical Choices for Ameri-

ca. *Honours:* Fulbright Scholar for two years in England. *Address:* 12201 S.W. 82nd Avenue, Miami, Florida 33156, USA.

FLEMING, Robert John, b. 5 Apr. 1925 London, England. Government Administrator. m. Patricia Carruthers Beeman 16 Dec. 1950 1 son. *Education:* Appleby College, Oakville, Ontario 1934-36; Lakefield College, Lakefield, Ontario 1936-41. *Appointments:* Founder and Editor-in-Chief, Pace Programs, Inc. Los Angeles, California 1964-69; Robert J Fleming and Associates International Communicators 1969-71; Executive Director, Royal Commission on Book Publishing 1971-72; Executive Director Ontario Commission on the Legislature 1972-74; Principal Secretary, to Hon. Robert L Stanfield, Official Leader of the Opposition, Ottawa 1974; Director of Administration, Ontario Legislature, Toronto 1974-. *Memberships:* Institute of Public Administration of Canada; Canadian Study of Parliament Group. *Publications:* Various papers relating to the administration of government. *Honours:* Penney/Missouri award for magazine publishing awarded by the University of Missouri School of Journalism 1969. *Hobbies:* Sailing; Hiking. *Address:* 51 Boswell Avenue, Toronto, Ontario, M5R 1M5, Canada.

FLETCHER, C Trevor, b. 24 Nov. 1928 England. Institute of Public Finance Accountant. m. Dorothy Maud (Mollie) Inman, 20 Oct. 1951 1 son, 2 daughters. *Education:* Open Exhibitioner and State Scholar in Classics, Christ Church Oxford 1946-50; BA(Hons) Literae Humaniores 1950; MA 1954; Member of Chartered Institute of Public Finance and Accountancy 1955. *Appointments:* Accountancy Trainee, Hertfordshire County Council 1950-55; Senior Accountant, Luton Borough 1955, Worthing Borough 1955-58; Assistant City Treasurer, Coventry 1958-60; Deputy Borough Treasurer, Brighton 1969-63; Deputy Director of Finance Gas Council 1964-70; Director of Finance, Wales Gas Board 1970-72; Deputy County Treasurer, Cheshire 1972-74; County Treasurer, Cheshire, 1974-81; Bursar, Keble College, Oxford, 1981. *Memberships:* Chartered Institute of Public Finance and Accountancy; Society of County Treasurers; Lions Clubs International. *Hobbies:* Fell Walking; Music Appreciation; Bridge; Gardening; Community Service. *Address:* Keble College, Parks Road, Oxford OX1 3PG, England.

FLETCHER, Edmund Francis, b. 27 Dec. 1916 Sydney, NSW Australia. Medical Practitioner. *Education:* MB, BS University of Sydney. *Appointments:* Resident Medical Officer, Sydney Hospital 1940; Senior Medical Officer, St George Hospital 1941; Captain AAMC; Resident Psychiatrist, Hollywood Hospital 1947; Resident Psychiatrist, Heathcote Hospital 1948-50; Senior Consultant Psychiatrist Fremantle Hospital 1950-; Senior Psychiatrist, King Edward Hospital 1950-. *Memberships:* National Association Medical Specialists; National Society for Medical Education; Fremantle Sailing Club; Sustralian Medical Association. *Publications:* The Use of Muscle Relaxants in Electroconvulsive Therapy; Australian Medical Journal, 1954. *Honours:* Psychiatrist Member Inebriates Advisory Board 1963-73; Commonwealth Medical Referee etc. *Hobbies:* Horse Breeding and Racing; Farming. *Address:* Lot 50, North Beach Road, Gwelup, WA 6021, Australia.

FLETCHER, Jack Donald, b. 30 Dec. 1931, Springhill Nova Scotia Canada. Vice President, Finance. m. Margaret Alder Tant, 18 May 1957, 4 daughters. *Education:* Bachelor of Commerce, Sir George Williams University, Montreal, Canada, 1962; ACIS, 1965. *Appointments:* Accounting Clerk, Douglas Rogers and Amherst, N.S. Canada, 1949-50; Accounting Clerk, Maritime Agencies, Parrsboro NS Canada, 1950-51; Mutual Life of Canada, Halifax and Montreal, 1951-55; Accountant, L M Erricsson, Montreal Canada, 1955-57; Chief Accountant and Corporation Secretary, MSH Industries Limited, Mussens Equipment Limited, Hovermarine Canada Limited, Etc. 1957-74; Vice President Finance, MTM Holdings Limited, Atmas Equipment Limited, Mack Maritime Limited, Train Co. Limited, Thermoking Atlantic Limited, Fredericton, New Brunswick, Canada. *Memberships:* Financial Executives Institute, Maritime Chapter, Canadian Region; Chartered Institute of Secretaries; Capital Winter Club, Fredericton nb canada; Fredericton Golf and Country Club. *Creative Works:* Oil Paintings; Water Colours. *Honours:* Junior Chamber of Commerce, President of the Year Award, Province of Quebec, 1963. *Hobbies:* Painting; Gardening; Golf; Curling; Woodworking. *Address:* 24 Carriage Hill Drive, RR6 Box 17, Fredericton New Brunswick, Canada, E3B 4X7.

FLETCHER, Kenneth Edward, b. 10 Nov. 1940, Melbourne, Australia. Geologist. m. Diana Roberta Meldrum, 8 Nov. 1965, 2 sons, 1 daughter. *Education:* Royal Melbourne Institute of Technology 1955-60; Fellowship Diploma Geology, (FRMIT). *Appointments:* Exploration Manager, Metals Exploration Limited, 1967-70; Managing Director, Queensland Nickel Pty/Ltd, 1971-75; Director, Metals Exploration Limited, 1976; Managing Director, 1979-. *Memberships:* Australian Institute of Mining and Metalluray Geological Society of Australia. *Publications:* Technical Papers. Hobby: Cattle and Sheep Breeding and Grazing. *Address:* 1076 Malvern Road, Armadale, Victoria, Australia.

FLETCHER, Leopold Raymond, b. 3 Dec. 1921 Nottingham, United Kingdom. Politician; Journalist; Playwright and Scriptwriter. m. (1) Johanna Klara Elisabeth Ising 8 July 1948, (2) Catherine Mildred Elliott, 1 stepdaughter. *Education:* Hoghschule Zum Grauen Kloster, Berlin; Humboldt Universitat, Berlin; Doctorate in History and German Literature. *Appointments:* Special Duties, Hamburg District, Rhine Army 1949; Freelance Journalist and Literary Critic, Adult Education Lecturer and Broadcaster 1949-53; Full-time Journalist, 1953-64. Member of Parliament 1964-. *Memberships:* International Institute of Strategic Studies; Anglo-German Society; Various Inter-Parliamentary Union and Commonwealth Parliamentary Association groups in House of Commons, Defence and Foreign Affairs Committee of Parliamentary Labour Party; Co-opted member of Europe sub committee of LP. *Publications:* The Prussion Officer, (play); Fenner; co-author, Oh, what a lovely war; Sixty Pounds a Second on Defence; 8 pamphlets on foreign and defence affairs; Contributor to symposia as follows: Inflation; Wege ins Zukunft; The Coming Confrontation. *Hobbies:* Writing for theatre; Study of the cinema; Collecting rare books; Music; Swimming. *Address:* Brooklands, 23 Ilkeston Road Heanor, Derbyshire, England.

FLORANCE, Brian, b. 11 June 1928 Sydney, NSW Australia. Dermatologist. m. Christine MacLeod 5 Mar. 1960, 1 son, 3 daughters. *Education:* LC 1945; University of Sydney 1946-53; MB, BS 1953; DDM 1960; Foundation Fellow Australian College of Dermatologists 1967; Fellow Royal Society of Medicine 1980. *Appointments:* R.M.O. Royal North Shore Hospital 1954; Fellow in Dermatology Royal Prince Alfred Hospital 1955-56; Clinical Assistant in Dermatology: Sydney Hospital 1956-60, Royal North Shore Hospital 1956-61, Royal Infirmary Hospital Edinburgh 1959-60; Specialist Dermatologist Royal Australian Navy 1956-; Hon. Dermatologist: Royal North Shore Hospital 1961-72, Hornsby and Kuring-gai Hospital 1958-; Consultant in Dermatology to Director General, Naval Health Services Royal Australian Navy 1956-; Surgeon Commander, RANR. *Memberships:* Australasian College of Dermatology; Dermatological Association of Australia; British Association of Dermatology NSW Branch; Fellow St Johns Hospital Dermatological Society; St. Ives Rotary Club; United Services Institute; Naval Historical Society; Aviation Medicine Society of Australia. *Publications:* Sundry Medical papers. *Honours:* Reserve Decoration 1969. *Hobbies:* Model Railroading; Philately; Sailing. *Address:* 10 derby Street, St. Ives, NSW 2075, Australia.

FLOURENTZOS, Nicos, b. 20 Nov. 1923, Ayios Elias, Famagusta, Cyprus. Commercial Representative. m. Tassoula Psyllas, 3 Nov. 1946, 1 son, 1 daughter. *Education:* Famagusta Greek Gymnasium. *Appointments:* Company Secretary, Cyprus Potatoes Growers Corporation Limited, 1951-52; Textiles Merchant, self-employed, Famagusta, 1952-74; Managing Director, The Florentzos and Company Limited, 1981-. *Memberships:* Member, Municipal Council, Famagusta, 1963; President, New Salamis Athletic Club, Famagusta, 1953-73; President, Refugees Association of Limassol District, 1974-76; Member of the Board of Directors, Famagusta Chamber of Commerce and Industry; Member, Pancyprian Committee of Refugees. *Hobbies:* Fishing; Swimming; Gardening. *Address:* 11, Agapinoros Street, Limassol, Cyprus.

FLOWERS, Edward, b. 13 Aug. 1926, County Durham, England. University Librarian. m. Patricia J. Stephenson, 27 Dec. 1954, 1 son, 2 daughters. *Education:* M.A., A.L.A.A. *Appointments:* Deputy City Librarian, Newcastle Public Library, 1952-57; Shire Librarian, Lake Macquarie Shire, 1957-61. *Memberships:* Chairman, Board of Education, Library Association of Australia, 1980-. *Hobbies:* Golf; Gardening. *Address:* 78 Kerr Street, Mayfield, New South Wales, Australia, 2304.

FOLEY, Leslie Bernard, b. 27 Apr. 1924, Sydney Australia. Solicitor. m. Patricia Mary Lynch, 19 May 1948, 2 sons. *Education:* Leaving Certificate, Sydney Boys High School; Bachelor of Laws, University of Sydney. *Appointments:* Solicitor, Commonwealth Crown Solicitors Office, Sydney, 1946-73; Principal Registrar, High Court of Australia, 1973-79; Deputy President, Repatriation Review Tribunal, 1979-. *Memberships:* Law Society of New South Wales; Royal Sydney Golf Club; The Lakes Golf Club; Tattersall's Club; Australian Jockey Club. *Honours:* OBE. *Address:* 41 Mons Avenue, Maroubra, 2035, Sydney, Australia.

FONG, Kin-Wai, Stephen, b. 6 July 1942, Hong Kong. Executive Director and Administrative Manager. m. Emily Poon Suk-yin, 14 July 1974, 2 daughters. *Education:* Teacher's Certificate, Northcote College of Education, 1964-66; Bachelor of Social Sciences, University of Hong Kong, 1969-72. *Appointments:* Certificated Master, Education Department, 1966-69; Management/technology trainer, The Hong Kong Productivity Centre, 1972-75; Executive Director, Cedar Garment, Singapore, 1975-77; Executive Director and Administrative Manager, Wing Tat Electric Company Limited, 1977-. *Memberships:* Member, British Institute of Management; Member, Association of Business Executive; Member, Institute of Supervisory Management. *Honours:* B.Soc.Sc. Honours, 1972; Certificate of Small Industries Consultants Advanced Training, 1974. *Hobbies:* Hiking; Football; Swimming. *Address:* 44, Kung Lok Road, Flat 4B, Kung Lok Building, Kwun Tong, Hong Kong.

FOOKES, Janet Evelyn, b. 21 Feb. 1936, London, United Kingdom. Teacher; Member of Parliament. *Appointments:* Teacher in Independent Schools, 1958-70; Member of Parliament, Merton and Morden 1970-74; mp, Plymouth Drake, 1974-. *Memberships:* Vice Chairman, RSPCA; Council of National Canine Defence League; Councils of SSAFA and the Stonham Housing Association; The Speaker's Panel of Chairmen; Secretary, All Party Mental Health Group; Councillor, County Borough of Hastings, 1960-61 and 1963-70. *Hobbies:* Travel; Gardening. *Address:* 51 Tavistock Road, Plymouth, Devon.

FOOKES, Peter George, b. 31 May 1933, Essex, England. Consultant Engineering Geologist. m. Gwyneth Margaret Jones, 4 Dec. 1962, 2 sons, 3 daughters. *Education:* Queen Mary College, London University, 1957-60; BSc., 1960; F.G.S., 1960; PLD., 1967; F.I.M.M., 1977; DSc.(Eng), 1979. *Appointments:* Engineering Geologist, Binnie and Partners, London, 1960-65; Lecturer, Imperial College, London University, 1966-71; Consulting Engineering Geologist, 1971-. *Memberships:* Member, Geologists Association, 1956-; Fellow, Geological Society, 1960-; Companion, Institution of Civil Engineers, 1966-; Chairman, Engineering Group, 1980-. *Publications:* Contributed to over 80 papers and other publications. *Honours:* Visiting Professor, Queen Mary College, London University, 1979-. *Hobbies:* Industrial Archaeology. *Address:* Winters Wood, 47 Crescent Road, Caterham, Surrey, CR3 6LH, England.

FOOKS, Ernest Leslie, b. 6 Oct. 1906, Bratislava, C.S.R. Architect, Townplanner, Artist, Lecturer. m. (1) 1936, (2) Noemy Matusevics, 8 Feb. 1939. *Education:* Bachelor Degree of Architecture, University of Vienna, 1924-29; Psychology, University of Vienna, 1926-28; Master Degree of Architecture, Doctor Degree of Technical Sciences, University of Vienna, 1930-31. *Appointments:* Private Practice, Vienna, 1932-38; Chief Assistant Housing Commission, Victoria, 1939-48; Lecturer, Royal Melbourne Insitute of Technology, 1944-54; Private Practice, Architect and Town Planner, 1948-. *Memberships:* Fellow, Royal Australian Institute of Architects; Fellow, Town Planning Institute of Australia; Associate, Royal British Institute of Architects; Associate, Royal British Institute of Town Planning; Council Member, National Art Gallery of Victoria; President, Jewish Society of Arts, Victoria, 1964-66; President, B'nai B'rith 'Unity', Melbourne, 1972-76; Member, Rotary Club, 1973-. *Publications:* Towards Physical Planning, 1944; X-Ray The City, 1946. *Creative Works:* Cities Of Yesterday, National Art Gallery of Victoria, 1944; The Two Faced Metropolis, 1952; Tribal Villages; Tribal Architecture, 1980. *Honours:* Third Prize, Competition, The Growing House, Vienna, 1932; Third Prize, Competition, Norrmalm, Stockholm, 1933; Bronze Medal, Architecture, Olympic Games, Melbourne, 1956; House of the Year Award, 1966; Award for own Residence, 1967. *Hobbies:* Photography; Slide lectures. *Address:* 32 Howitt Road, Caulfield 3161, Melbourne, Victoria, Australia.

FOORD, John Murray, b. 9 Feb. 1931, Woolahra, New South Wales. Law. m. 30 Mar. 1959, 1 son, 3 daughters. *Education:* Wavesley College; LLB, Sydney University, 1954. *Appointments:* Admitted NSW Bar 1955; Queen's Counsel 1976; Judge District Court of NSW 1978; Member Education Committee, College of Law, 1980. *Memberships:* Wavesley District Cricket Club; Tattersalls Club, Sydney; Rivestine Club, Wagga Wagga; Wavesley Bowling Club. *Hobbies:* Bowls; Cricket. *Address:* 26 Queens Park Road, Bondi Junction, NSW 2022, Australia.

FOOTS, (Sir) James Williams, b. 12 July 1916, Jamieson, Victoria, Australia. Australian Mining Engineer. m. Thora Hope Thomas, 2 Dec. 1939, 1 son, 2 daughters. *Education:* University High School, Victoria, 1932-33; Melbourne University, 1934-37. *Appointments:* Chairman M.I.M. Holdings Limited, 1970-81. *Memberships:* Director of Bank, New South Wales; Director of the X11 Commonwealth Games, 1982; President of Australian Mining Industry Council, 1974-76; President of Australasian Institute of Mining and Metallurgy, 1974. *Honours:* Institute Medal, Australasian Institute of Mining and Metallurgy, 1972; Kernot Medal, Distinguished engineering achievements, 1975; John Storey Medal, Australian Institute of Management, 1979; Knight Bachelor, 1975. *Address:* G.P.O. Box 2236, Brisbane Q. 4001, Australia.

FORAY, Cyril Patrick, b. 16 March, 1934, Sierra Leonean. University Lecturer. m. Arabella Williams, 19 April 1958, 2 sons 2 daughters. *Education:* B.A., Fourah Bay College, University of Durham, 1952-54; Honours in Modern History, St. Cuthbert's Society, Durham University, England, 1957; Post Graduate, St. Cuthbert's Society, Durham University, England, 1958. *Appointments:* Assistant Master, St. Edward's Secondary School, Freetown, 1958-60; Senior Lecturer and Substantive Head, Department of History, Fourah Bay College, 1977-; Moderator in History, Milton Margai Teachers College, Freetown, 1975-; Sierra Leone's Minister of Foreign Affairs, 1969-71; Dean Faculty of Arts, Fourah Bay College, University of Sierra Leone, since 1978. *Memberships:* Member, Civilian Rule Committee, 1968; Member, Scholarships Advisory Committee, Sierra Leone Government, 1978-. *Publications:* Historical Dictionary of Sierra Leone, 1977; An Outline of Fourah Bay College History, 1979; Contributed to a number of articles on Sierra Leone, 1979. *Address:* K25, Fourah Bay College, USL, Freetown, Sierra Leone.

FORBES, John Allan, b. 16 May 1920, Lismore Victoria Australia. Medical Practitioner. m. Peggy Cail Nicholson, 22 Jan. 1943. *Education:* The Geelong College 1933-38; Melbourne University 1939; War Service 2nd AIF 1940-44; MB, BS 1948. *Appointments:* RMO, Royal Melbourne Hospital 1949; Lecturer in Pathology Melbourne University 1950-52; Senior Medical Officer and Deputy Medical Deputy Medical superintendent, Fairfield Hospital for Communincable Diseases 1953-60 and Medical Superintendent and Dean of Clinical School, 1960-78; Consultant, WHO, Western Pacific Region, 1979-80. *Memberships:* Royal Australasian College of Physicians; Royal Australian College of Medical Administrators; Australian College of Paediatrics; Australian Society for Infectious Diseases. *Publications:* Publications in Infectious Diseases including: Group and its Management, 1961; Rubella: Historical Aspects, 1969; Human Valley Encephalitis, 1974; The Epidemic Variance 1914; Predisposing Rainfall Patterns, 1978. *Honours:* AM 1976. *Hobbies:* Farming;

Fishing. *Address:* 69 Stevenson Street, Kew, Victoria 3101, Australia.

FORBES, John Frederick, b. 6 Mar. 1944, Bendigo, Victoria, Australia. Surgeon. m. Jennifer Joan Daniels, 23 Mar. 1968, 2 daughters. *Education:* Trinity College, University of Melbourne, Australia, 1962-68; MB., BS., 1968; B.Med.Sci., 1973; MS., 1977; FRACS., 1974; FRCS., 1976. *Appointments:* Resident Medical Officer, 1969-70, Surgical Registrar, 1972-75, Royal Melbourne Hospital, Australia; Postgraduate Research Officer, University Department of Surgery and the Cancer Institute, Melbourne, Australia, 1970-71; Fellow in Surgery, Department of Surgery, Welsh National Medical School, Cardiff, UK, 1975-77; Consultant Surgeon, Mid Glamorgan, UK, 1976-77; Senior Lecturer, Department of Surgery, University of Melbourne Royal Melbourne Hospital, Australia, 1977-. *Memberships:* Vice Chairman, Breast Group, Clinical Oncology Society of Australia; Executive Secretary, Management Committee, ANZ Breast Cancer Trials Group; Editorial Board of: Australian and New Zealand Journal of Surgery, Breast Disease, Research and Treatment- Project Grants Committee, National Health and Medical Research Council; Clinical Oncology Society of Australia; Am. Soc. Clin. Oncology; Br. Ass. Surg. Oncol.; Surg. Res. Soc. Aust.; Aust. Soc. Med. Res.; Aust. Statist. Soc.; Cell Biology Society, Victoria; Victoria Society Expt. Pathol. Aust. Soc. Immunol.; International Society of Surgeons; Royal Society of Medicine; Society for Clinical Trials; Life member, Graduate Society, University of Melbourne. *Honours:* Dux Prize, Bendigo High School, 1961; 1st class Hons., Matriculation, Commonwealth Government Award, 1961; Medical Exhibition, 1968; Robert Gartley Healy Prize, Medicine, Keith Levi Memorial Prize, 1968; Denis Glisson Memorial Prize, Royal Australasian College of Surgeons, 1971; Robert Fowler Fellowship, Anti Cancer Council of Victoria, 1975; Nuffield Foundation, Commonwealth Fellowship in Medicine, Australia, 1975-76; John Mitchell Crouch Fellowship, Royal Australian College of Surgeons, 1980. *Hobbies:* History of Surgery; Polio Society; Haklyut Society; Jogging; Gardening. *Address:* 10 Harwood Street, Brighton, Victoria 3184, Australia.

FORBES, Morris Zion, b. 17 Nov. 1919, Sydney, New South Wales. Solicitor. *Education:* B.A., B.L., Sydney University. *Appointments:* Solicitor of Supreme Court of New South Wales; Assistant Crown Solicitor, New South Wales; Associate, Miles Barelay and Company Solicitors, Sydney. *Memberships:* President, Australian Jewish Historical Society; President, New South Wales Public Service Association; Member, New South Wales Cricketers Club. *Publications:* Contributed to several Historical Journals; Law Journals; Australian Dictionary of Biography. Contributor and former Editor of Great Synagogue Journal, Sydney. *Hobbies:* Historical and Cricket Archive collections; Cricket; Religous writing. *Address:* 48 Plowman Street, North Boude, New South Wales, Australia.

FORD, David Wycliffe, b. 20 Oct. 1938, Sydney, Australia. Chief of Protocol, Goverment of Victoria. m. Geraldine Marie Dodds, 27 April 1963, 1 son, 1 daughter. *Education:* Royal Military College, Duntroon, 1956-59. *Appointments:* Military Cadet, R.M.C. Duntroon, 1956-59; Regular Army Officer, Australian Army, 1960-76; Chief of Protocol, Goverment of Victoria, 1977-. *Memberships:* Member, Chartered Institute of Transport, 1971; Naval and Military Club, Melbourne. *Honours:* G.M., 1957; MVO, 1981. *Hobby:* Rugby Union Football. *Address:* 33 Barak Street, Bulleen, Victoria, Australia 3105.

FORD, John Archibald, b. 19 Feb. 1922, Newcastle-under; Lyme, England. HM Diplomatic Service. m. Emaline Burnette, 30 June 1956, 2 daughters. *Education:* BA., 1942, MA., Oriel College, Oxford, UK. *Appointments:* Major, 1947, Royal Artillery, 1941-47; HM Diplomatic Service, 1947; Head of Establishment Department, 1964; Counsellor, commercial, British Embassy, Rome, Italy, 1966; Assistant Under-Secretary, Foreign and Commonwealth Office, 1970; HBM Consul General, New York, Director-General, British Trade Development in USA, 1971; British Ambassador, Jakarta, 1975; High Commissioner, Ottawa, Canada, 1978. *Memberships:* Farmers' Club, London; Yvonne Arnaud Theatre Club, Guildford, UK. *Honours:* Military Cross, 1945; CMG., 1967; KCMG., 1977. *Hobbies:* Walking; Sailing. *Address:* Earnscliffe, Ottawa, Ontario, Canada, K1N 5A2.

FORDE, Henry de Boulay, b. 20 Mar. 1933, Barbados, West Indies. Minister of Government. m. Patricia Yvonne Williams, 25 June 1960, 2 daughters. *Education:* BA., Hons., 1956; LL.B., 2nd class, 1957, MA., 1961, University of Cambridge, UK. *Appointments:* Private practice as Barrister and Attorney-at-Law, 1959-76; Lecturer, Extra-mural Programme, 1961-68, Part-time Lecturer, Caribbean Studies, 1964-68, University of the West Indies; Attorney General and Minister of External Affairs, 1976-. *Memberships:* Alternate Director, Caribbean Press Council; Finance and General Purposes Committee, Cave Hill Campus, University of the West Indies; President, 1968-72, Barbados National Theatre Workshop; Governing Body, St. Gabriel School, 1971; Deputy District Governor, 1970-71, Lions District 60; Joint Chairman, National Insurance Appeal Tribunal, 1970; Deputy Chairman, Public Service Commission, 1969-70; Secretary, Organisation of Commonwealth Bar Associations; Advisory Committee, Anglican Church Property Committee, 1969-; Governing Body, Community High School; Chairman of Board, Contact Limited; Patron, Dorcas League; Secretary, Barbados Bar Association. *Honours:* Senior Counsel, 1976. *Hobbies:* Reading; Walking; Gardening. *Address:* 'Fan Ling', Pine Hill, St. Michael, Barbados, West Indies.

FOREMAN, Eric George, b. 19 Oct. 1915, Perth, Western Australia. State Public Servant (retired). m. Norma Lyle Regan, 31 Oct. 1945, 1 son, 2 daughters. *Education:* Diploma, Public Administration, Diploma, Accounting, Perth Technical College, Australia, 1966-75. *Appointments:* Harbour and Lights Department, 1931-34; Mines Department, Perth and Goldfields, 1934-41; RAAF Aircrew, 1941-46; Clerk of Courts, various centres, Crown Law Department, 1946-59; 1st Registrar of Trade Associations, Secretary, Land Agents' Supervisory Committee, 1960-70; Secretary, Town Planning Department, Secretary, Metropolitan Region Planning Authority, 1970-73; Assistant Chief Electoral Officer, 1973-77, State Chief Electoral Officer and Electoral Commissioner for Western Australia, 1977-80. *Memberships:* Justice of the Peace for Western Australia; Councillor and Immediate Past President, Royal Association of Justices of Western Australia; Associate Fellow, Australian Institute of Management. *Publications:* Development and administration of legislation and instructions regarding Land Agents, Trade Practices and Electoral matters. *Hobbies:* Golf; Bowling; Fishing; Gardening. *Address:* 3 Glenties Road, Floreat Park, Western Australia 6014.

FORINTON, Michael Seymour, b. 4 Feb. 1926, Boston, Lincolnshire, England. Chartered Civil Engineer. m. Roma Luise Ulrike Prüssing, 17 Sept. 1966, 3 sons. *Education:* MA., King's College, Cambridge, UK, 1943-45. *Appointments:* Consulting Engineer, Sir Wm. Halcrow and Partners, UK; Engineer, Glenfield and Kennedy Limited, Hydraulic Engineers, UK; Engineer, Marples Ridgway and Partners; W.C. French Limited; Civil Engineering Contractors; Chief Surveyor, Schweizerische Aluminium AG., Zürich, Switzerland; Self employed Consulting Engineer. *Memberships:* Fellow, Institution of Civil Engineers, London, UK. *Publications:* Civil Engineering Contracts and Claims, 1972. *Hobbies:* Skiing; Shooting; Sailing. *Address:* Knockmourne Glebe, Conna, Co. Cork, Republic of Ireland.

FORRESTER, Peter Garnett, b. 7 June 1917, Cheadle Hulme, Cheshire, England. Professor of Management. m. 2 May 1942, 2 daughters. *Education:* BSc., (Hons.), 1935-38, MSc., 1938-39, Manchester University, UK; C.Eng. *Appointments:* Metallurgist, Thomas Bolton & Sons Limited, 1938-40; Research Officer, Tin Research Institute, 1940-48; Chief Metallurgist, Glacier Metal Co. Limited, 1948-63; Consultant, John Tyzack & Partners, 1963-66; Professor of Industrial Management, 1966-, Director, School of Management, 1967-, Pro-Vice-Chancellor, 1976-, Cranfield Institute of Technology, UK. *Memberships:* Board of Trustees, European Foundation for Management Development; Companion of British Institute of Management; Fellow, Institute of Metallurgists; Fellow, Royal Society of Arts. *Publications:* Many Scientific and Technical papers and articles on metallurgy, tribology, engineering and management. *Honours:* CBE., 1981. *Hobbies:* Sailing; Walking. *Address:* 5 West Road, Wharley End, Cranfield, Bedford, UK.

FORSELL, Peter, b. 2 July 1927, Leicester, England. Medicine. m. Barbara Isabel Bromwich, 28 Dec. 1950, 1 son, 2 daughters. *Education:* Medicine, University College, London, UK, 1945-48; MB., BS., Melbourne University, Australia, 1949-52; Membership, 1968, Fellowship, 1974, Royal Australian College of General Practitioners; Fellowship, Australian College of Allergy, 1980. *Appointments:* Adviser on Antibiotics, Commonwealth Serum Laboratories, Melbourne, Australia, 1970-72; Medical Director, Glaxo Australia Pty. Limited, Melbourne, Australia, 1972-; Clinical Assistant, Prince Henry's Hospital, Melbourne, Australia, 1970-. *Memberships:* Medical and Scientific Committee, Anti-Cancer Council of Victoria; Vice Chairman, Publications Board, Royal Australian College of General Practitioners; President, 1979-80, Association of Medical Directors to Australian Pharmaceutical Industry; Medical Liaison Committee, Australian Pharmaceutical Manufacturers Association; Melbourne Cricket Club, 1979-. *Publications:* A Survey of the Incidence of Resistance of Staphylococcus Aureus to Antibiotics in General Practice, 1971; Diphtheria Immunity in Victoria, 1972; Antibiotic Prescribing in General Practice, 1972; Antibiotics, 1976; Labetalol in the Treatment of Hypertension in General Practice, 1979. *Hobby:* Gardening. *Address:* 2 Trudi Court, Donvale, Victoria 3111, Australia.

FORSYTHE, Victor Leonard Consort, (Dr.) b. 26 Feb. 1925, L'Otoire, West Bank, Demerara, Guyana. University Lecturer; Communication Consultant. m. Ona Thelma Alleyne, 22 Nov. 1969, 2 sons. *Education:* BSc., Hons., 1963, MSc., First Class, 1972, Boston University, USA; PhD., Moscow State University, USSR, 1980. *Appointments:* Broadcaster, BBC, London, UK, 1950's; Senior Broadcasting Officer, 1954-58; CBC., Quebec and English Speaking Caribbean Broadcasting Organizations, 1960's; Guest Radio Reporter for W.I., on the Inauguration of President John Kennedy, 1961; Assistant Programme Director in Ed. TV WGBH-TV & WBUR-TV, Boston, USA, 1962-63; General Elections Broadcaster, Deutsche Welle, West Germany, 1969; Principal Information Officer, 1963-67, Chief Information Officer, 1967-80, Guyana; Director, Guyana Broadcasting Corporation, 1973-; Communication Advisor, Ministry of Information, Georgetown, Guyana, 1981-; Associate Lecturer, 1975-79, Communication Studies Co-ordinator and Lecturer, 1979-, University of Guyana. *Memberships:* International Institute of Communications, London; International Association for Mass Communication Research, London; Chairman, Communication Project Advisory Committee, Caribbean Family Planning Affiliation; UNESCO Standing Working Party for Communication Research in the Caribbean. *Publications:* Publications include: Information and the Public Mind on Coastal Guyana; Trends Towards a National Communication Policy in Guyana; Towards Integration of Communication Training in the Caribbean; Guidelines for the Introduction of TV in a Developing Country; An Evaluation of the Medex/Guyana Two-way Radio Pilot Project; The Development of Broadcasting in Guyana; Four prizewinning plays. *Honours:* Senior Fulbright Fellow, Communication Research, School of Public Communication, 1971-72, Alumni Prizeman for Scholarship and Leadership in Communications field, 1963, Boston University, USA. *Hobbies:* Swimming; Driving; Table tennis; Lawn tennis; Drama; Collecting folk music. *Address:* 23 First Street, Alberttown, Georgetown, Guyana.

FORT, Alec Frank, b. 27 Sept. 1930, Freiwaldau. Professor of Phsyics. m. Jitka Vacek, 14 Sept. 1955, 1 daughter. *Education:* MSc.(Physics) 1953, MA. (Education) 1955, PhD (Nuclear Physics) 1956, DrPh.(Solid State Physics) 1967, Charles' University, Prague, Czechoslovakia. *Appointments:* Assistant Lecturer, Lecturer, Senior Lecturer, Charles University, Prague, Czechoslovakia, 1953-66; Reader, Khartoum University, The Sudan, 1966-71; Advisor, Divisional General Manager, Technical Co-ordinator World Wide, The Plessey Co. Limited, Memories, UK, 1971-74; Director, Martingrade Limited, 1972-74; Consultant, Headlands Chemicals Limited, 1972-74; Visiting Research Scientist, NRC, Canada, 1974-76; Consultant Technical Research International, Chicago, USA, 1974-76; Mineral Processes International, Arizona, USA, 1974-76; Professor and Head of Physics Department, University of Xambia, 1976-. *Memberships:* Fellow, Institute of Physics; Member Institute of Electrical and Electronic Engineers; International Solar Energy Society. *Publica-*

tions: About 35 papers, books, minor works and articles. *Hobbies:* Music; Literature; Tennis. *Address:* 34 Galley Field, Abingdon, Oxfordshire OX14 3RT, England.

FORTIER, Claude, b. 11 June 1921, Montreal, Canada. Medical Scientist. m. Elise Gouin, 8 Sept. 1953, 4 daughters. *Education:* BA., MA., 1941, MD., 1948, Licensed Medical Council of Canada, 1948-; PhD., 1952, University of Montreal, Canada; FRCP(C), 1965. *Appointments:* Research Assistant, Institute Experimental Medicine and Surgery, 1948-51, Lecturer, Neurophysiology, 1947-51, University of Montreal, Canada; Research Consultant, Clinical Medicine, University of Lausanne, Switzerland, 1952-53; Research Associate, Department Neuroendocrinology, University of London, UK, 1953-55; Assistant Professor, Experimental Medicine and Surgery, ibid, 1950-52; Associate Professor Physiology and Director Neuroendocrinology Laboratory, Baylor University, Houston, Texas, USA, 1960-61; Director, Endocrinol Laboratory, 1960, Professor, Experimental Physiology, 1961, Chairman, Department of Physiology, 1964-, Laval University; Consulting Physician, CHUL, 1969-; Vice-Chairman, 1975-78, Chairman, 1978-, Science Council of Canada; SCC Task Force on Research in Canada, 1975-78; Vice President, Parliamentary and Scientific Committee, 1979-; President, Royal Society of Canada, 1974-75; Chairman, Board CFBS, 1973-74; Chairman, National Committee IUPS, 1970-73; Chairman, Advisory Committee, Medical Research Government of Québec, Canada, 1968-70; Vice Chairman, MRC of Canada, 1965-67. *Memberships:* President, 1966-67, Canadian Physiology Society; American Physiology Society; Endrocrine Society; American Thyroid Society; Society for Experimental Biology and Medicine; NY Academy Science; American Association Advanced Science; Association American Physicians; Peripatetic Club; Biomedical Engineering Society; Canadian Society Endocrinology and Metabolism; Canadian Society Clinical Investigation; Council, International Society Neuroendocrinology; Canadian Association; Club de Rome. *Publications:* Over 200 publications on Neuroendocrinology, Physiology, Biomathematics and Science Policy. *Honours:* FRSC., Royal Society of Canada, 1964; CC. Companion of the Order of Canada, 1970; Archambault Research Award of ACFAS, 1972; Science Award of Government of Quebec, 1972; LL.D.(Hon) Dalhousie University, 1978; Wightman Award of Gairdner Foundation, 1979; Marie Victorin Science Award of Government of Quebec, 1980; DU-(Hon), University of Montreal, 1981; DU(Hon), University of Ottawa, 1981. *Hobbies:* Skiing; Sailing. *Address:* 1014 de Grenoble, Ste Foy, PQ, Canada, G1V 2Z9.

FORTIN, Gabriel, b. 27 Feb. 1939, Matane, Quebec, Canada. Attorney. m. Thérèse De Celles, 25 June 1965, 1 son. *Education:* BA., cum laude, Laval University, Canada, 1959; LL.L., cum laude, 1962, DES., 1965, University of Montreal, Canada; LL.M., 1970, Certificate, 1970, J. F. Kennedy School of Government, Harvard Law School, USA. *Appointments:* Attorney, St. Lawrence Region, Canadian National Railway Co., 1963-68; Assistant Professor, Law School and School of Planning, University of Montreal, Canada, 1968-75; Executive Exchange Program, Ministry of Urban Affairs, Ottawa, Canada, 1973-75; President, Consulplan Inc., Montreal, Canada, 1975-77; Vice-President law and Secretary, VIA Rail Canada Inc., Montreal, Canada, 1977-. *Memberships:* Bar of Province of Quebec; National Council, Canadian Bar Association; Chamber of Commerce. *Publications:* Law Review articles; Technical papers. *Honours:* Queen's Counsel, Canadian Government, 1980; Samuel Morse Lane Research Fellowship, Harvard Law School, USA, 1969-70; Central Mortgage and Housing Corporation's Fellowship, 1969-71; Department of Education's honorary Scholarship, Quebec Government, 1969-71. *Hobbies:* Reading; Swimming; Ski; Hiking. *Address:* 522 McEachran Outremont, Quebec, Canada, H2V 3C4.

FORTUNE, Denys Woodeson, b. 10 May 1931, Swansea, South Wales. Pathologist. m. Nora Mary Trump, 23 July 1955, 2 sons, 2 daughters. *Education:* MB.ChB, 1954; MRCPE, 1962; MRC.Path., 1964; FRCPA., 1965; FIAC., FRC.Path., 1976; FRCPE, 1980. *Appointments:* HS, 1954, HP, 1955, Southmead Hospital, Bristol, UK; MO, Royal Army Medical Corps., 1955-57; SHO, 1957-59, Registrar, 1959-61, Southmead Hospital, Bristol, UK; Senior Registrar, Pathology, Royal Devon and Exeter Hospital, UK, 1961-64; Cytopathologist, 1964-66, Director of Pathology, 1966-, Royal Womens Hospital, Melbourne, Australia. *Memberships:* State Councillor for Victoria, Australia, 1977; Royal College of Pathologists of Australasia. *Publications:* Approximately 40 publications in Medical Literature in Obstetric Gynaecological and Perinatal Pathology. *Hobbies:* Music; Sport; Reading. *Address:* 15 Rochester Road, Canterbury, Victoria 3126, Australia.

FOSTER, Hiram Lloyd, b. 9 Mar. 1939, Sav-La-Mar, Jamaica, West Indies. Dental Surgeon; Specialist Pedodontist. m. (1) Linda Lee, 27 Nov. 1967 (deceased), (2) Rose Balck, 26 Aug. 1976, 3 sons, 1 daughter. *Education:* BSc., 1966, DD.S., 1971, Diploma in Pedodontics, 1973, Howard University. *Appointments:* Instructor in Pedodontics, Howard University, 1973-74; Pedodontist, Government of Jamaica, West Indies, 1974-. *Memberships:* Librarian, Jamaica Dental Association; Constant Spring Golf Club. *Publications:* Retention of Sealants on Primary Molars, paper presented at Convention of International Dental Research, Atlanta, Georgia, USA, 1974. *Hobbies:* Lawn tennis; Photography; Gardening. *Address:* 9 Presimmon Avenue, Box 201, Kingston 6, Jamaica, West Indies.

FOULKES, George, b. 21 Jan. 1942, Oswestry, England. Member of Parliament. m. Elizabeth Anna Hope, 4 July 1970, 2 sons, 1 daughter. *Education:* BSc., Edinburgh University, UK, 1964. *Appointments:* President, Scottish Union of Students; Manager, Fund for International Student Coop; Scottish Organiser, European Movement; Director, European League for Economic Co-operation; Director, Enterprise Youth; Director, Age Concern, Scotland; Councillor, Edinburgh Corporation-,UK, 1970-75; Councillor, 1974-79, Chairman, Lothian Region Education Committee; Chairman, Education Committee, Convention of Scottish Local Authorities, 1974-78. *Memberships:* Fabian Society; Co-operative Party; Labour Party; Traverse Theatre Club. *Publications:* Editor: Eighty Years on, History of Edinburgh University S R C. *Honours:* Justice of the Peace. *Hobby:* Boating. *Address:* 31 Monument Road, Ayr, Scotland, UK.

FOUNTAIN, Sally, b. 22 Sept. 1944, Leicestershire, England. Local Government Officer. m. Alan Fountain, 22 Sept. 1973. *Education:* MA., (Cantab.), Historical Tripos, 1967. *Appointments:* Local Government, 1967-, Head of Director-General's and Programme Office, Greater London Council. *Memberships:* Justice of the Peace, Highgate Petty Sessional Division, UK, 1977; Member of Juvenile Panel, 1979; Hon. Sec., Middlesex Magistrates'Association. *Honours:* Queen's Silver Jubilee Medal, 1977. *Hobbies:* Music; Gardening; Painting. *Address:* 25 Finchley Park, London, N12 9JS, England.

FOWLE, Le Clerc, b. Haslar, Hampshire, England. Artist. *Education:* Slade School of Fine Art, University of London, UK. *Appointments:* Many commissions and works in England, America, Switzerland and Australia; Two One-man exhibitions in Bond Street, London. *Memberships:* ROI; Hanging Committee, ARWA; Fellow, Royal Society of Arts, 1972. *Honours:* Gold and Silver Medal Salon Artistes Francais, 1965, 1960; First Prize, Laing Competition, 1979; Exhibited many times at Royal Academy; Royal Institute of Oil Painters; Royal West of England Academy; New English Art Club; Royal Society of Portrait Painters; Pastel Society; Royal Society of British Artists. *Address:* 65 Cheyne Court, Royal Hospital Road, London SW3 5TT, England.

FOWLE, William Randall, b. 27 Jan. 1946, Melfort, Saskatchewan, Canada. Barrister; Solicitor. m. 24 Aug. 1968, 2 sons, 2 daughters. *Education:* LL.B., 1969; BA., 1968. *Appointments:* Barrister and Solicitor, 1970-. *Memberships:* Jaycees International; President and Senator, Board of Governors, Lakeland College; President, University of Alberta Liberals; Vice-President, Young Liberals; Trustee, Lakeland School Division; Chairman, Lions Club of Bonnyville; Chairman, Senior Chamber of Commerce. *Honours:* Senator, Jaycees. *Hobbies:* Boating; Politics. *Address:* Box 1410, Bonnyville, Alberta, Canada, TOA OLO.

FOWLER, Robert William Doughty, (Sir), b. 6 Mar. 1914, Sutton-in-Ashfield, Nottingham, England. Diplomat (retired). m. Margaret MacFarquhar MacLeod, 14 June 1939, 1 son, 1 daughter. *Education:* Emmanuel

College, Cambridge, UK. *Appointments:* Indian Civil Service, Burma, 1937-48; Diplomatic Service, 1948-70; United Kingdom Delgation to the United Nations, 1950-52; Deputy High Commissioner to: Pakistan, 1956-58, Canada, 1960-62, Nigeria, 1963-64; High Commissioner to Tanzania, 1964-65; AMbassador to Republic of the Sudan, 1966-70; Gibraltar Referendum Administrator, Aug-Sept. 1967; HM Forces, 1944-46; Additional Secretary, Governor of Burma, 1947-48. *Memberships:* Royal Commonwealth Society. *Honours:* CMG., 1962; KCMG., 1966. *Hobbies:* Painting; Photography. *Address:* 7 Leicester Close, Henley-on-Thames, Oxon., England.

FOWOWE, Samuel Oluwole, b. 1 Dec. 1944, Ere-ljesha, Via llesha, Nigeria. Librarian. m. Patience Adetoun Lufadeju, 26 May 1973, 1 son, 3 daughters. *Education:* B.A. Hons, 1971, Postgraduate Diploma, 1972, University of Ibadan. *Appointments:* Librarian II, National Library, Lagos, 1972-75; Sub-Librarian II, The Polytechnic Library, Ibadan, 1975-76; Librarian I, 1976-79, Senior Librarian, 1979-81, Principal Librarian, 1981-, University of Ilorin. *Memberships:* The Nigerian Library Association, 1972-; Secretary, The University of Ilorin, Senior Staff Club, 1980-; Vice-President, Egbe Omo Obokun, Ilorin, 1980-. *Publications:* Primary Social Studies, Books 1 and 2, (Macmillan Social Studies series) co-authqr, Dr. H.O. Adesina and Mr. Olu Owolabi, 3rd book in Press. *Hobby:* Farming. *Address:* 248 Abdul Aziz Atta Road, llorin, Nigeria.

FOX, Beryl, b. 10 Dec. 1931, Winnipeg, Manitoba, Canada. Film Producer. m. Douglas Leiterman. *Education:* B.A. University of Toronto, 1958. *Appointments:* Producer, Director of numerous films and coumentary series, 1963-80. *Publications:* include: 'Balance of Terror', 1963; 'The Single Woman and the Double Standard', 1965; 'Summer in Mississippi', 1965; 'The Mills of the Gods; Viet Nam', 1966; 'The Honorable René Levesque', 1966; 'Youth: in Search of Morality', 1966; 'Saigon', 1967; 'The Visible Woman'; 'Here Come the 70's, documentary series 1970-71; 'Surfacing', feature film, 1979; 'By Design', feature film, 1980; 'I'm Getting My Act Together and Taking it on the Road', stage, 1980. *Honours:* include: Winner Wilderness Award, 'One More River', 1963; Winner Vancouver Film Festival, 'The Chief', 1964; Canadian Film Award, Ohio Film Award Commenwealth Film Festival, Vancouver Film Festival, Oberhausen Film Award (Germany), Montreal Festival, Special Mention, 1965; George Polk Mem. Award, U.S., 1966; Winner Atlanta Film Festival Gold Medal for Peace Category, 1969; Silver Medal for Ecol., Atlanta Film Festival. *Hobby:* Arabian Horses. *Address:* 43 Britain Street, Toronto, M5A 1R7, Canada.

FOX, Brian Douglas, b. 20 June 1943, London, England. Rabbi. m. Dr. Dale Stephanie Myers, 31 Jan. 1971, 1 son, 2 daughters. *Education:* BA, Auckland University, New Zealand, 1966; Bachelor of Hebrew Letters, 1972, MA, 1972, Received Ordination as Rabbi, 1972, Hebrew Union College, Cincinnati, O, USA. *Appointments:* Rabbi, Leo Baeck Centre, Victorian Union of Progressive Judaism, Melbourne, Australia, 1972-79; Chief Minister, Temple Emanuel, Woollahra, Sydney, New South Wales, Australia, 1979-. *Memberships:* Zionist Federation of Australia, 1980; Chairman of Immigration and Welfare Sub-Committee, Executive Council of Australian Jewry, 1981. *Hobbies:* Collecting Judaica. *Address:* 10 Vivian Street, Bellevue Hill, Sydney, Australia.

FOX, Eudo Carlile, b. 14 Apr. 1914, Sydney, Australia. Chartered Engineer. m. 4 June 1949, 1 son, 2 daughters. *Education:* BSc., Mechanical and Electrical Engineering BE., Sydney University, Australia, 1932-36. *Appointments:* Post Graduate Training, The British Thomson Houston Co. Limited; The City of London Electric Lighting Co. Limited, London, UK, 1937-39; Australian Military Forces/Australian Imperial Forces, 1940-44; Manager for Victoria, 1950-55, General Manager for India, 1956-59, Deputy Chairman and Managing Director of Australia, 1960-69, The English Electric Co. Limited; Professional Engineering Consultant and Board Director of number of Companies, 1969-. *Memberships:* Fellow of Institution of Electrical Engineers, London; Fellow of Institution of Mechanical Engineers, London; Fellow of Institution of Engineers, Australia; Athaeneum Club, Melbourne; Union Club,

Sydney; Avondale Golf Club, Sydney. *Hobbies:* Golf; Skiing; Sailing; Photography. *Address:* 15 Graham Avenue, Pymble, New South Wales 2073, Australia.

FOXLEE, Thomas Vernon, b. 9 Sept. 1921, Charters Towers. Journalist. m. Maureen Woulfe, 12 March, 1945, 1 son, 1 daughter. *Education:* Charters Towers High; All Soul's College. *Appointments:* Journalist, Courier Mail, 1940-48; Proprietor, Western Star, Roma, 1948-55; Foundation Managing Director, Western Publishers Pty Limited, 1955-59; General Manager, Star Newspapers, 1959-70; Publications Manager, Toowoomba Newspapers Pty Limited, 1970-73. *Memberships:* Twin Towers Club. *Hobbies:* Golf; Gardening. *Address:* 46 Rumrunner Street, Mermaid Waters, Q.4217, Australia.

FOZARD, John William, b. 16 Jan. 1928, Liversedge, Yorkshire, England. Engineer. m. Mary Ward, 1951, 2 sons. *Education:* BSc.,(1st Class Hons.), Aeronautical Engineering, University of London, UK; DCAe., Distinction in Aircraft Design, 1950; Chartered Engineer of the UK. *Appointments:* Project Design Engineer, 1950, Head of Project Office (Advanced Design Group), 1961, Hawker Aircraft Limited, Kingston upon Thames, UK; Chief Designer P1154 (Project cancelled, Feb. 65), 1963, Chief Designer, Harrier, 1965, Deputy Chief Engineer of Kingston Design Team, 1968; Executive Director of Hawker Siddeley Aviation (Hawker Aircraft Limited absorbed into HSA in 1962), 1972; Divisional Marketing Director, Kingston Brough Division, British Aerospace (took over the assets of HSA on Nationalisation of HSA & BAC in 1977), 1978-. *Memberships:* Fellowship, 1963, Elected to Council, 1977, Elected Vice President, 1980, Royal Aeronautical Society; Fellowship of Institution of Mechanical Engineers 1971; Elected to Fellowship of American Institute for Aeronautics and Astronautics 1981. *Publications:* Numerous technical papers contributed to Learned journals and specialist press; Numerous lectures on aeronautics and engineering to audiences around the world—UK, USA, India, Australia, China. *Creative Works:* Chief Designer, Harrier, 1963-78. *Honours:* OBE 1981; British Silver Medal for Aeronautics, 1977; Simms Gold Medal of London Society of Engineers, 1971; Several RAeS prizes for published papers, 1971, 1977. *Hobbies:* Music; History of Engineering. *Address:* Wychbury Cottage, Warreners Lane, St. Georges Hill, Weybridge, Surrey, KT13 OLH, England.

FRAMPTON, Phineas Edward, b. 13 Nov. 1922, London, England. Solicitor. m. Molly Leibowitz, 17 March 1952, 3 daughters. *Education:* University College School, London, 1938; LL.B., Sydney University, 1948; LL.M. London University, London School of Economics, 1951. *Appointments:* J.W. Maund & Kelynack, Solicitors, Sydney, 1940-41, 1945-47; Army, 1941-45; Slaughter & May, Solicitors, London, 1948-52; Stephen Jaques & Stephen, Solicitors, Sydney, 1953; Frampton & Company., Solicitors, 1954-. *Memberships:* Securities Institute of Australia; London House Association of Australia. *Address:* 121 Darling Point Road, Darling Point, Sydney. N.S.W. 2027, Australia.

FRANÇOIS, Hunter Joseph, b. 19 Feb. 1924, Choiseul, St. Lucia. Barrister-at-Law. m. 13 Dec. 1951, 5 sons, 5 daughters. *Education:* Articled Clerk, 1944-48; Admitted to St. Lucia Bar, 1949. *Appointments:* Member, Castries City Council, 1961-64; Elected to St. Lucia House of Assembly, 1964-74; Deputy Premier and Minister of Education and Health, 1966-72; Resigned from Ministry, 1972; Executive Chairman, St. Lucia Broadcasting Corporation, 1979-. *Memberships:* Member of Council, University of the West Indies, 1964-73. *Publications:* First and Last Poems, 1949; Morning, 1978. *Hobbies:* Music; Literature; Billiards. *Address:* Bois d'Orange, St. Lucia, West Indies.

FRANK, (Sir) (Frederick) Charles, b. 6 Mar. 1911 Durban, South Africa. Professor of Physics (retired). m. Maia Maita Asché 28 Apr. 1940. *Education:* BA, BSc 1933; DPhil 1937, Lincoln College, Oxford. *Appointments:* Research: Dyson Perrins Laboratory and Engineering Science Laboratory, Oxford, 1933-37; Kaiser Wilhelm Institut für Physik, Berlin, 1936-38; Colloid Science Laboratory, Cambridge, 1939-40; Scientific Civil Service (temp.) 1940-46; Chemical Defence Research Establishment, Porton 1940; Air Ministry (A.D.I.(Science)) 1940-46; University of Bristol, H H Wills Physics Laboratory 1946-76; Research Fellow in theoretical Physics 1948, Reader 1951, Professor 1954, Henry Overton Wills Professor and Director of the Laboratory 1969; Emeritus Professor, 1976. *Memberships:* Fellow Royal Society; Fellow Institue of Physics; US National Academy of Engineering; Faraday Society; International Organisation for Crystal Growth; British Polymer Physics Group. Athenaeum Club. *Publications:* Publications in Learned Journals, on Dielectrics, Physics of Solids, Crystal Dislocations, Crystal Growth, Liquid Crystals, Geophysics, etc. *Honours:* OBE 1946; Knight Bachelor 1977; Bakerian Lecturer, Royal Society 1973; Royal Medal 1979; Hon. Fellow Lincoln College, Oxford, 1968; Hon. Fellow Institute of Physics 1978; Crystal Growth Award of American Association for Crystal Growth 1978; Gregory Aminoff Gold Medal of the Royal Swedish Academy of Asiences 1978. *Address:* Orchard Cottage, Grove Road, Coombe Dingle, Bristol BS9 2RL, England.

FRANKLYN, Edward Morrissey, b. 1 Aug. 1928, Perth, Western Australia. Barrister. m. Margaret Louise Nash, 20 Sept. 1952, 3 sons, 3 daughters. *Education:* LL.B., Aquines College, University of Western Australia; Admitted to practice as Barrister and Solicitor of Supreme Court of Western Australia, 1950. *Appointments:* Self-employed Solicitor, 1952-68; Commenced practice at Independent Bar as Barrister 1968-. *Memberships:* Former President, Australian Bar Association, 1978; Former member, Council of Law Society of Western Australia; Former President, Western Australia Bar Association, 1975-78; Weld Club. *Honours:* Appointed Queens Counsel, 1975. *Hobbies:* Golf; Tennis; Sailing. *Address:* 6 Irvina Street, Peppermint Grove, Western Australia.

FRAPPIER, Gilles, b. 13 Feb. 1931, Papineauville, Quebec, Canada. Professional Librarian, Director, Secretary Treasurer, Ottawa Public Library. m. Gertrude Mainville, 13 Oct. 1956, 2 sons, 1 daughter. *Education:* B.A., B.Ph., 1945-54, Faculty of Philosophy, B.L.S. Lib. Sc., Library, 1954-55, University of Ottawa; Graduate Studies, Graduate School of Library Science, McGill University, Montreal, 1957-60. *Appointments:* Librarian, Baie Comeau Community Association, Baie Comeau, Quebec, Canada, 1955-57; Branch Librarian, Pulp and Paper Research Institute of Canada, Pointe-Claire, Canada, 1957-59; Librarian, United Aircraft of Canada, Longueuil, Quebec, Canada, 1959-63; Supervisor, Engineering Libraries, Canadair Limited, Montreal, 1963-69; Director, Scientific Libraries, University of Montreal, 1969-70; Associate Parliamentary Librarian, Library of Parliament, Ottawa, Canada, 1970-79. *Memberships:* Library Association of Ottawa; Secretary, Association of Parliamentary Librarians in Canada, 1979; Special Libraries Association; Canadian Association for Information Sciences; Vice-President, CALUPL; CELPLO; L'Alliance Francaise; Societe Des Ecrivains Ottawa-Hull; Canadian Writers Foundation. *Honours:* Kentucky Colonel, Honorable Order of Kentucky Colonels, 1974. *Hobbies:* Golf; Camping; Fishing. *Address:* 423 Carillon Street, Gatineau, Quebec J8P 3P9, Canada.

FRASER, Colin Lovat, b. 23 Feb. 1922, Auckland, New Zealand. Company Director. m. Mary Virginia Hambrook, 18 June, 1947, 1 son, 2 daughters. *Education:* Scotch College, Melbourne; St. Peter's College, Adelaide; Melbourne University. *Appointments:* Reporter, Special writer, Sun News Pictorial, Melbourne, 1938-50; Chief reporter, special writer, Deuputy Chief-of-Staff; Assistant to General Manager, Melbourne Herald, 1950-56; Program Manager, Acting Manager, Herald-Sun Television Pty. Limited, 1956-60; Managing Director, Victorian Country Telecasters Pty. Limited, 1960-64; T.V. Manager, Creative Director, Managing Director, Vice-Chairman, George Patterson Pty, Limited, Melbourne, Australia, 1964-. *Memberships:* Television Society; Athenaeum Club; Naval & Military Club; Royal Automobile Club of Victoria. *Publications:* 'How TV Advertising Works', 1956; Writer of numerous Australian and international award-winning television commercials for Australia's largest Advertising Agency. *Hobbies:* Painting; Building and bricklaying; Fishing; Horse-racing. *Address:* George Patterson Pty. Limited, 394 La Trobe Street, Melbourne. 3000 Australia.

FRASER, Conon, b. 8. March 1930, Cambridge, England. Film Director, Writer. m. Jacqueline Stearns, 17

March 1955, 5 sons. *Education:* Marlborough College, England, 1943-46; Royal Military Academy Sandhurst, 1948-50. *Appointments:* Subaltern Royal Artillery, 1950-53; New Zealand Broadcasting Corporation, 1964-68; TV Producer, Film Director, New Zealand National Film Unit, 1969-. *Memberships:* P.E.N., New Zealand. *Publications:* 8 Boys Adventure Books including: 'The Underground Explorers', 'Oystercatcher Bay'; Numerous other works including: 'Looking At New Zealand', co-author, 'Gardens of New Zealand'; Contributor to New Zealand's Heritage, New Zealand's Landfall, Argosy (United Kingdom) New Zealand Listener; Documentary Films include: 'Children of the Mist', 1974, The Kauri, 1978, Coal Valley, 1979. *Honours:* Several Certificates of Participation in International Film Festivals; Mitra Award of Honour for 'Coal Valley', 26th Asian Film Festival, 1980; Silver Screen Award, U.S. Industrial Film Festival, Chicago, 1980; Silver Medal Festival of the Americas, 1979. *Hobbies:* Walking; Tramping; Gardening; Travel. *Address:* 25 Boundary Road, Kelburn, Wellington 5, New Zealand.

FRASER, Rt. Hon. Sir Hugh Charles Patrick Joseph, b. 23 Jan. 1918. Member of Parliament. m. Lady Antonia Pakenham 1956 (div.) 3 sons, 3 daughters. *Education:* Ampleforth College; Balliol College Oxford; The Sorbonne, Paris. *Appointments:* Ex-Pres. Oxford Union; War Service with Lovat Scouts, Phantom and Special Air Service; PPS to Sec. of State for the Colonies 1951-54; Parly Under-Sec. of State and Financial Sec., War Office 1958-60; Parly Under-Sec. of State for the Colonies 1960-62; Sec. of State for Air, 1962-64. Pres., West Midlands Conservatie and Unionist Association 1967; Director, Sun Alliance, Deputy Chairman Scottish and Universal Investments Limited. *Honours:* Order of Orange Nassau; Order of Leopold with palm; Belgian Croix de guerre. *Address:* House of Commons, London SW1, England.

FRASER, John Denis, b. 30 June 1934, London, England. Solicitor. m. Ann Hathaway, 31 July 1960, 2 sons, 1 daughter. *Education:* Law Society School of Law. *Appointments:* Bank of Australasia, 1950-52; Royal Army Educational Corps, 1952-54; Articled Clerk, 1955-60; Solicitor, 1960-. *Honours:* John Mackrell Prize, Law Society Final Examination, 1960. *Hobby:* Athletics. *Address:* House of Commons, London, SW1A OAA, England.

FRASER, John Malcolm, b. 21 May 1930 Melbourne Australia. Grazier. m. Tamara Margaret Sandford Beggs 9 Dec. 1956, 2 sons, 2 daughters. *Education:* Master of Arts in Philosophy, Politics and Economics, Magdalen College, Oxford University 1949-52. *Appointments:* Member Federal Parliament (Liberal), Wannon, Victoria 1955-; Joint Party Committee, Foreign Affairs 1962-66; Council Australian National University 1964-66; Chairman Government Members Defence Committee 1963-65; Minister for Army 1966-68; Minister for Education and Science 1968-69 and 1971-72; Minister for Defence 1969-71; Leader, Federal Parliamentary Liberal Party and Leader, Opposition, Australia 1975; Prime Minister of Australia 1975-. *Memberships:* President, Melbourne Scots; Melbourne Club; Commonwealth Club. *Honours:* Member of Her Majesty's Most Honourable Privy Council 1976; Companion of Honour 1977; President's Gold Medal for Humanitarian Services; B'nai B'rith International 1980. *Hobbies:* Motorcycles; Fishing; Photography; Vintage Cars. *Address:* Nareen, Victoria, Australia.

FREDERICK, Dolliver H, b. 2 Apr. 1944 Edmonton, Alberta, Canada. Investment Executive. m. Joan Beverly Dickau 28 Aug. 1965 1 son, 1 daughter. *Education:* Alberta College; University of Alberta; Northern Alberta Institute of Technology; Business Administration Graduate. *Appointments:* Marketing Management, Imperial Oil Limited, 1966-73; President and Chief Operating Officer, General Supply Company of Canada and Equipement Federal Quebec Limited and Corporate Vice President Bovis Corporation Limited 1973-79; President, Chief Executive Officer and Director, Can West Investment Corporation 1979-; Director and Chairman of Executive Committee of Board, Na Churs Plant Food Company Marion, Ohio; Director and Chairman of Executive Committee of Board, MacLeod Stedman Inc. Toronto and Winnipeg, Canada. *Memberships:* National Club, Cambridge Club; Toronto Cricket skating and Curling Club; Toronto Board of Trade; Golf Club. *Hobbies:* Golf; Skiing. *Address:* 35 Steeplechase, Aurora, Ontario, Canada, L4G 3G8.

FREEMAN, James Darcy, b. 19 Nov. 1907 Sydney Australia. Catholic Archbishop of Sydney. *Education:* St. Canice's Primary School, Elizabeth Bay; St. Mary's Cathedral High School; St. Columba's College, Springwood; St. Patrick's College, Manly. *Appointments:* Ordained 1930; Assistant Priest in various Parishes 1930-41; Appointed Archbishop's Private Secretary 1941-46; Director Catholic Information Bureau 1946; Priest in Charge, Haymarket, 1949; Parish Priest, Stanmore 1954; Auxiliary Bishop Sydney 1957; Knight of the Holy Sepulchure, Jerusalem 1965; Bishop of Armidale 1968; Archbishop of Sydney 1971; Cardinal 1973. *Honours:* Knight of the Holy Sepulchure, Jerusalem 1965; Knight of the British Empire 1977. *Hobbies:* History; Biography; Sport. *Address:* St. Mary's Cathedral, Sydney, NSW 2000, Australia.

FREEMAN, Capt. Spencer, CBE, b. 1892 Swansea, S. Wales. British Consulting business engineer. m. Hilda Kathleen Toler 1924, 1 son. *Education:* Johannesburg College (Scholarship) and Technical Institute York, Pa USA. *Appointments:* Automotive Industry, USA; Pullman Motor Company York, Pa. and Chalmers Motor Corp., Detroit 1910-14; British Army, 1914-19; Principal Director, Regional and Emergency Services Organization, Ministry of Aircraft Production, 1940-45; Business member Industrial and Export Council 1944-45; Member Radio Board, (British War Cabinet); Member Radio Planning and Production Committee, Radio Production Executive; seconded to Board of Trade to assist reconversion of industry to peacetime production 1945-46; Co-founder and Executive Director, Hospitals Trust Limited Dublin, 1930-81. *Memberships:* Naval and Military London; Kildare St. and University, Dublin. *Publications:* Production Under Fire; Take Your Measure; You Can Get to The Top. *Honours:* Commander, Order of the British Empire 1942; Mons Star; Mentioned in Dispatches WWI; Member Society of Automotive Engineers, USA; Liveryman, Company of Newspaper Makers and Stationers, London England; Sportsman of the Year Irish Republic, 1973. *Address:* Knocklyon House, Templeogue, Dublin 16 Republic of Ireland.

FREUDEN, George, b. 30 Aug. 1932 Budapest, Hungary. Licensed Customs Agent; Company Director. m. Hilary Lacey 15 May 1960, 2 sons, 1 daughter. *Education:* Primary School, Budapest 1942; High School Budapest 1949. *Appointments:* Electrician; Refrigeration Mechanic; Draftsman (Industrial); Toolmaker; Commercial Rep; Taxi-Driver; Shipping Manager; Customs Agent. *Memberships:* International Ski Patrol Federation; Safety Committee, International Ski Federation; Australian Ski Patrol Association; Thredbo Ski Patrol Association; International Society for Skiing Safety; NSW Volunteer Rescue Association; Hakoah Club, Sydney; Vaulluse Yacht Club, Sydney; NSW Bridge Association; Sporting Shooters Association of Australia. *Honours:* Her Majesty the Queen's Silver Jubilee Medal, 1977. *Hobbies:* Skiing; Sailing; Tennis; Bridge; Rifle Shooting. *Address:* 65 Clyde Street, North Bondi, NSW 2026, Australia.

FREUDENSTEIN, George Francis, b. 26 Dec. 1921 Grenfell, NSW, Australia. Farmer and Grazier. m. Joan Elizabeth Parker 25 Aug. 1960. *Education:* Henry Lawson High School. *Appointments:* Rural Bank: Askin-Cutler Ministry, Minister assisting Premier 1969-71; Minister for Cultural Activities and Assistant Treasurer 1971-72; Minister (Acting) for Agriculture 1972; Minister for Conservation and Minister for Cultural Activities 1972-75; Lewis-Cutler Minister, Minister for Mines and Energy 1975-76; Willis-Punch Minister, Minister for Mines and Minister for Energy 1976-. *Memberships:* Royal Automobile Club; Sydney Cricket Ground. *Hobbies:* Reading; Tennis; Golf. *Address:* "Chippendale" Grenfell Road, Young 2594, NSW Australia.

FREW, Ian Johnstone, b. 8 March 1925, Sydney, New South Wales. Economics. m. Jean Allison Roper, 19 Sept. 1956, 4 daughters. *Education:* B.Ec. Sydney University, 1950; Associate Australian Society of Accountants, 1951; Fellow, Australian Institute of Exports, 1959. *Appointments:* Execuitve Director, Australian Insurance Association. *Memberships:* Freeman, Rostrum Clubs of New South Wales. *Hobbies:* Public Speaking; Gardening; Travelling; Lecturing; Bush Walking; Golf; Reading. *Address:* 2 Ormonde Road, Lindfield. 2070, New South Wales, Australia.

FRITH, Harold James, b. 16 Apr. 1921 Kyogle, NSW Australia. Zoologist. m. Dorothy Marion Killen 20 Nov. 1943, 1 son, 2 daughters. *Education:* University of Sydney 1938-41; BSc Agriculture 1941; DSc Agriculture 1961. *Appointments:* Australian Imperial Force 1941-45; CSIRO, Irrigation Research Station 1945-53; CSIRO, Wildlife Survey Section 1953-61, Officer in Charge 1960-61; CSIRO, Division of Wildlife Research Foundation Chief of Division 1961-. *Memberships:* Australian Academy of Science; Australian Academy of Technological Science; Honorary Associate Zoology, University of Sydney; Australian Ecological Society; Australian Mammal Society; Royal Australasian Ornothologists Union; Honorary Fellow of Orinthological Societies of Australia, UK, France USA, Germany; Royal Australasian Ornithologists Union; British Ornithologists Union; Societé Orinthologiqué de France; Deutsche Ornithologen Gesellscheft; American Ornithologists Union. *Publications:* The Mallee Fowl; Waterfowl in Australia; Kangaroos; Wildlife Conservation; Pigeons and Doves in Australia; Author 100 Scientific papers; Editor 6 Books. *Honours:* Whitley Medal for Zoological Books 1980; Officer of Order of Australia 1980. *Hobbies:* Growing Australian Native Plants; Carpentry; Fishing. *Address:* 20 Brown Street, Yarralumla, ACT Australia 2600.

FRITSCH, Adam Edward, b. 11 Jan. 1915, Brisbane, Australia. Business Manager. m. Edna Patience Boustead, 19 Dec. 1942, 2 sons, 2 daughters. *Education:* Commonwealth Institute of Accountants, 1933; Australian Institute of Secretaries, 1934. *Appointments:* Secretary, Innisfail District Canegrowers Executive, 1940-47; Self Employed, Retail and Grain Trades, 1947-60; Secretary, Premier Blinds Pty Limited, 1960-69; Self Employed, Steel Fabrication and Property Development, 1968-. *Memberships:* Fellow, Chartered Institute of Secretaries and Administrators; Fellow, Australian Society of Accountants. *Honours:* Australian Accounting Honours Final Examinations Justice of the Peace. *Hobbies:* Photography; Woodwork; Gardening. *Address:* 10 Donaldson Street, Greenslopes, Brisbane, Australia 4120.

FROST, Alan Charles Hamlyn, b. 8 July 1914, London, England. Chartered Engineer. m. Edith Margery Thomas, 16 April 1938, 3 sons. *Education:* B.Sc (Eng) 1st Hons in Electrical Engineering, 1932-35. *Appointments:* City of London Electric Lighting Company, 1935-36; Merz & MacLellan, Consulting Engineers, London, 1936-42; War Service, Royal Engineers, India, 1943-46; Merz & MacLellan, Newcastle-on-Tyne, 1947-51; Snowy Mountains Authority, 1951-74, Assistant Director, Snowy Mountains Engineering Corporation, 1974-78. *Memberships:* Fellow, Paul Harris; Past-Chairman of various District Committees. *Publications:* Hydro-Electric Engineering Practice, co-author; Paper in Journal of Institution of Electrical Engineers, London, 1950; Several papers on Snowy Scheme, Australia. *Honours:* M.B.E., 1978; Alderman of Cooma, 1962-71; Electrical Engineering Prize. *Hobbies:* Photography; Gardening. *Address:* 72 Orana Avenue, Cooma North, New South Wales 2630, Australia.

FRY, Maurice Alec. b. 11 Dec. 1915 London. Chairman. m. Cozette L.L.E. Cordwell-Green, 20 Dec. 1977 1 son, 2 daughters. *Education:* Bancroft School. *Appointments:* Chairman: Electronic Rentals Group Limited, Group of Companies with six Divisions Television rental in UK, Overseas, Retailing electrical goods with television rental, Camping and Leisure, Property and Miscellaneous. Associated Companies: Telerenta S A Mexico; Camping Leisure Division: Gola Sports Limited England; J Langdon and Sons Limited, Republic of Ireland; Laplaud International S A France; N.R. Components Todmorden Limited England; Polywarm Products Limited England. Elecrent Properties Limited, Englad; Universal Travel Agency Limited, Republic of Ireland; Visionhire Limited England; Colorent Fernsehvermietungs GmbH West Germany; Visionhire Fernsehvermietungs GmbH West Germany; Visionhire Swaziland Limited; Videorent TV Locacao Telvisores Limitada Hong Kong; Colourent)s) Pte Limited, Singapore; Locavision A G Switzerland; Visionhire Pty, Limited, Australia; Visionhire Pty. Limited, South Africa, USA. *Memberships:* Army and Navy, Institute of Directors; St. George's Hill Golf Club. *Hobby:* Golf. *Address:* 4 Belgrave Square, London, SW1, England.

FRYER, Peter Philip, b. 3 Aug. 1929, London, England. Insurance Company Executive. m. Anne Mary Ryan, 4 Apr. 1955, 3 daughters. *Education:* Christ's College, Cambridge, 1950-53; BA, 1953, MA, 1959. *Appointments:* Northern Assurance Company Limited, London, 1953-61; General Reinsurance Corporation, New York, 1961-66; Netherlands Reinsurance Group, Amsterdam, 1966-69; North Atlantic Insurance Company, London, 1969-; British National Life Insurance Society Limited, London, 1980-. *Memberships:* Chartered Insurance Institute; The Catenian Association; Responsibility and Christian Leadership; Woodcote Park Golf Club. *Publications:* Contributions to various technical publications, including, A Practical Approach to the Evaluation of Reinsurance Security. *Hobbies:* Golf; Bridge; Mathematical curiosities. *Address:* 17 Beech Avenue, Sanderstead, Surrey, England.

FUCHS, Vladimir, b. 14 Oct. 1935, Czechoslovakia. Physicist. m. Marie Shanelova, 29 Apr. 1967, 1 son, 1 daughter. *Education:* Promovany Fyzik, 1961, RNDR, 1967, CSC, 1968, Charles University, Prague, Czechoslovakia. *Appointments:* Lecturer, Assistant Professor, Charles University, Prasgue, 1963-68; Research Scientist, IREQ, Quebec, 1968-; Visiting Scientist, MIT, USA, 1979-80. *Memberships:* Canadian Association of Physicists; American Physical Society. *Publications:* A number of scientific papers in the field of Plasma Physics. *Honours:* Ayrton Premium of the Institution of Electrical Engineers, Great Britain, 1974. *Hobbies:* Bridge; Chess. *Address:* 4991 Jean Brillant, Montreal, Quebec, Canada.

FULTON, Edmund Davie, b. 10 Mar. 1916, Kamloops, Canada. m. Patricia Mary Macrae, 7 Sept. 1946, 3 daughters. *Education:* BC, BA, University of British Columbia, 1933-36; BA, Oxford University, 1937-39. *Appointments:* Barrister and Solicitor, 1940; Elected Member of the House of Commons of Canada, Kamloops Constituency, 1945, re-elected 1949, 1953, 1957, 1958, 1962 and 1965; Sworn of the Privy Council of Canada and appointed Minister of Justice and Attorney General of Canada, 1957; Minister of Public Works, 1962, resigned 1963; Partner, Fulton, Morley, Verchere & Rogers, Kamloops, 1945-57, 1963-68; Partner, Fulton, Cumming, Bird, Richards, Vancouver, 1968-73; Judge of the Supreme Court of British Columbia, 1973-81. *Memberships:* Chairman, Canadian delegation in negotiations with USA, Columbia River Treaty, 1962; Elected member, Senate of the University of British Columbia, 1948-57, 1969-72; First Chairman, The Law Reform Commission of British Columbia, 1969-73; Vancouver Club; Shaughnessy Golf and Country Club; Rideau Club; The Royal Canadian Legion. *Honours:* Honourary LLD, Ottawa University, 1960; Honourary LLd, Queen's University, Ontario, 1962. *Hobbies:* Golf; Gardening; Fishing; Shooting. *Address:* 1632 W. 40th Avenue, Vancouver BC, Canada.

FULTON, William Robert, b. 6 Dec. 1916, Salisbury, Zimbabwe. Company Director. m. Grace Alma Fulton,

17 May 1940, 2 sons, 1 daughter. *Appointments:* Founded, Fulton & Evans (PUT) Limited, 1946; Zimbabwe Sports Manufacturers, 1966; Dynamic Sports, 1972. *Memberships:* Royal Salisbury; Ghapman Golf Club, Captain, 1967; President, Mashonaland Junior Golf Association, 1964-69. *Honours:* MBE, 1958; Bronze Medal, Empire Games, 1934, 1938; South African Amateur Boxing Title, 1936-46; Represented Country at Football and Golf. *Hobby:* Gardening. *Address:* Sunihill, 6 Hampstead Road, Highlands, Salisbury, Zimbabwe.

FUNG, King Hey, b. 11 Feb. 1922, Namhoi, China. Company Director. m. Leung Bo Shuen, 1949, 2 sons, 3 daughters. *Appointments:* Chairman & Managing Director, Sun Hung Kai Securities Limited, Hong Kong; Chairman, Sun Hung Kai Finance Company Limited, Hong Kong; Vice Chairman, Sun Hung Kai Properties Limited, Hong Kong; Chairman, Sun King Fung Development Limited, Hong Kong. *Memberships:* Co-Chairman of the Chinese University of Hong Kong Three year MBA Program Advisory Committee; Stanford Research Institute Southeast Asia Advisory Committee; Stanford Research Institute International Committee; Honorary Councillor of Rehabilitation International; Board Member of the Community Chest of Hong Kong; Royal Hong Kong Jockey Club; The Royal Hong Kong Yacht Club; The Hong Kong Country Club; The Royal Hong Kong Golf Club; World Trade Centre Club. *Honours:* Fung King Hey Day, proclaimed by the Borough of Manhattan, New York, 1980. *Hobbies:* Swimming; Boating. *Address:* Admiralty Centre, 3rd Floor, Hong Kong.

FUNG, Tai-Leung, b. 14 July 1940, Canton, China. Manufacturer. m. 1 Feb. 1975, 1 daughter. *Education:* BSc, University of Hong Kong, 1967. *Appointments:* Proprietor, Wacker Industrial Company. *Address:* 27 Berthst, 8th Fl., Kowloon, Hong Kong.

FUREDY, Bela, b. 20 Feb. 1906, Budapest, Hungary. Master Tanner. m. Madge Gardos, Magda, 31 Jan. 1937, 1 son. *Education:* Leaving Certificate, 'gimnazium' High School. *Appointments:* Apprentice, Manager, Managing Director, in Hungary Leather Wholesaler, General Manager, Export Manager, Export Agent, Exporter in Australia. *Memberships:* Former member and Officer; Councillor, International Hide, Skin, Leather Trade Association, London; Councillor, Vice-President, Australian Hide, Skin and Leather Exporters Association; Councillor, Export Development Group of New South Wales; Councillor, Australian Shippers Council. Associate Member, Australian Institute of Export. *Honours:* Export Award Prize, Export Development Group of New South Wales, 1970; Export Award, Federal Government of Australia, 1976. *Hobbies:* Classical Music; Golf; Swimming; Bridge. *Address:* 901/91 Yarranabbe Road, 'Yarranabbe Gds.' Darling Point, New South Wales 2027, Australia.

G

GAGGERO, Charles Germain, b. 28 May 1930, Gibraltar. Economist. m. Jean Lawrance, 18 July 1957, 3 daughters. *Education:* BA, 1952, MA, 1954, Magdalene College, Cambridge. *Appointments:* Director, Charles Gaggero and Company Limited, 1956; Director, Saccone and Speed Limited, Gibraltar, 1968; Director, Saccone and Speed (Malta) Limited, 1970; Director, Saccone and Speed (Iberia) SA, 1971; Director, Amalgamated Builders' Merchants Limited, 1972. *Honours:* Officer, 1967, Commander, 1972, Knight, 1977, Order of St John; Chevalier Order Star of Italian Solidarity, 1969; OBE, 1970; Officer of Merit, Order of Malta, 1978. *Hobbies:* Numismatics; Philstelics. *Address:* 4 College Lane, Gibraltar.

GAGGERO, John George, b. 3 Mar. 1934, Gibraltar. m. 7 July 1961, 2 sons, 2 daughters. *Appointments:* 2nd Lt. XII Royal Lancers, 1953-55; Ailsa Shipbuilding Co. Limited, 1955-58; Director, 1958, Deputy Chairman, 1970, Bland Limited; Director: Gibraltar Airways Limited; Rock Hotel Limited; Stevedoring and Cargo Handling Co. Limited; Cadogan Travel Limited; House of Bellingham Limited; Overland Overseas Tours Inc. *Memberships:* Cavalry and Guards Club; Royal Gibraltar Yacht Club; Royal Institution of Naval Architects; Institution of Engineers and Shipbuilders in Scotland. *Honours:* Knight of the Royal Order of the Bannebrog, First Class, 1981; OBE, 1981. *Hobbies:* Ships; Motor Cruising. *Address:* 15 Brayside Road, Gibraltar.

GAIR, George Frederick, b. 13 Oct. 1926, Dunedin, New Zealand. Politician; Journalist. m. 31 Jan. 1951, 1 son, 2 daughters. *Education:* BA. *Appointments:* New Zealand Herald; BCON Japan; Sun-News Pictorial, Melbourne, Australia; Auckland Star, New Zealand; Auckland Public Relations Officer, Press Officer, Personal Assistant to General Manager, Air New Zealand; Member of Parliament, 1966-; Parliamentary Under-Secretary to Minister of Education, 1970-71; Minister of Customs and Associate Minister Finance, 1972; Minister Housing, Deputy Minister of Finance, 1975-77; Minister of Energy, Minister of National Development and Minister of Regional Development, 1977-78; Minister of Health and Social Welfare, 1978-. *Memberships:* Honorary Member and former President, PRINZ. *Address:* 41 Hauraki Road, Takapuna, Auckland, New Zealand.

GAIRDNER, John Lewis, b. 9 Dec. 1948, Oakville, Ontario, Canada. Investment Banker. m. Jeannette Bernadette, 29 Feb. 1972, 1 son, 1 daughter. *Education:* University of Western Ontario, Canada. *Appointments:* Senior Vice President/Director, Walwyn Stodgell Cochran Murray Limited; Directorships: Mineral Resources International Limited; Yvanex Developments Limited; Cairn Petroleums Limited; Pivot Petroleums Limited; Redcliffe Petroleums Limited; White Eagle Petroleums Limited; Cherokee Energy Limited; Wynall Investments Limited; JSG Holdings Limited. *Memberships:* Oakville Golf Club. *Hobbies:* Tennis; Photography; Fishing. *Address:* 2115 Gatestone Avenue, Oakville, Ontario, Canada.

GALAPPATTI, Anil, b. 8 Jan. 1950, Colombo, Sri Lanka. Management Consultant; Chartered Accountant. m. Ayanthi Gooneratne, 27 Apr. 1981. *Education:* Institute of Cost and Management Accountants, London, 1969-73; Institute of Chartered Accountants of Sri Lanka, 1971-74; MSc.Business Administration, London Graduate School of Business Studies, University of London, 1975-77. *Appointments:* Articled Clerk, Turquand Youngs & Co.Chartered Accountants, Management Consultant, Audit Manager, Management Systems Limited, Colombo, Sri Lanka, 1969-75; Accountant, WEA Records Limited, London, UK, 1975; Systems Accountant, Africa Middle East Management Center, Pfizer International Inc, New York, USA, 1978-80; Joint Managing Director, Partner, GW Consultants Limited, Colombo, Sri Lanka, Partner, GW Associates (Chartered Accountants, 1980-. *Memberships:* President 1973-74, Chartered Accountant Students Society of Ceylon, Colombo; Member of the Council, Royal College Union; London Business School Association. *Honours:* Accountancy Prize, Institute of Chartered Accountants of Sri Lanka, 1972. *Hobbies:* Cine and Still Photography; Philately; Cricket; International Affairs.

Address: 149/10 Suvisuddharama Road, off Havelock Road, Colombo 6, Sri Lanka.

GALBALLY, Bryan Peter, b. 6 Mar. 1926, Melbourne, Australia. Doctor of Medicine. *Education:* MBBS(Hons.), University of Melbourne, Australia, 1944-49; MRACP, 1975; FRACP, 1978. *Appointments:* Resident Medical Officer, 1949-52, Resuscitation Officer, 1952-61, First Director of Intensive Care Unit, 1961-75, First Director of Casualty Medical Services, 1975-, St. Vincents Hospital, Melbourne, Australia. *Memberships:* First President of Australian Society for Parental Nutrition; Chairman of Victorian Association of Casualty Supervisors; Intensive Care Society, UK; Society of Critical Care Medicine, USA; American College of Emergency Physicians. *Publications:* The Planning and Organisation of an Intensive Care Unit, 1966; Procedures in Medicine-Volume Replacement in Shock, 1980. *Honours:* Dux of School, 1943. *Hobbies:* Sailing; Skiing; Tennis; Travel. *Address:* Unit 6, 23 The Loop, Blairgowrie, Victoria 3942, Australia.

GALE, Audrey Mgaere, b. 17 Mar. 1909, New Plymouth, Taranaki, New Zealand. Barrister; Solicitor; Journalist(retired). m. John William Gale, 18 Dec. 1937, 2 sons, 1 daughter. *Education:* LL.B. Canterbury University, New Zealand, 1938; Diploma Journalism, 1935; Admitted to Supreme Court as Barrister and Solicitor, Christchurch, New Zealand, 1939. *Appointments:* Taranaki Daily News, 1936-37; Contributed to New Zealand Freelance, 1937-45; Practised profession of Barrister and Solicitor at Culverden, 1939,40; Elected to Council of Victoria Univrsity of Wellington, New Zealand, 1955-65; Elected to City Council, New Plymouth, 1956; Chairman, City Council's Parks and Recreation Committee, 1966-77; Chairman Executive, Taranaki Museum Board, 1960-78; Appointed by Governor-General, on nomination of Art Galleries and Museums Association of New Zealand to Council of New Zealand Historic Places Trust, 1964-78. *Memberships:* President, New Zealand Library Association, 1966-67; President, New Zealand Institute of Park Administration, 1966-67; Women's Vice-President, New Zealand National Party, 1953; Dominion Councillor, New Zealand National Party, 1951-54; President, 1968,69, Taranaki Branch, New Zealand Federation of University Women; New Plymouth Girls' High School Old Girls' Association; Taranaki Regional Committee, New Zealand Historic Places Trust; Friends of Govett-Brewster Art Gallery Inc; Friends of Taranaki Museum;Associate member, New Zealand Founders Association; Pukeiti Rhododendron Trust Inc; Member and past president, RSPCA, Taranaki Branch; Life member, New Zealand Institute of Park Administration. *Creative Works:* Presidential address delivered to New Zealand Library Association, 1967. *Honours:* OBE, 1979; Queen's Silver Jubilee Medal, 1977;Awards of appreciation from: New Plymouth City Council, 1977, Council of New Zealand Historic Places Trust, 1979. *Hobbies:* Gardening; Reading; Swimming; Theatre. *Address:* 18 Bulteel Street, New Plymouth, New Zealand.

GALLANT, Mavis, b. 11 Aug 1922, Montreal, Quebec, Canada. Author. *Publications:* Green Water, Green Sky, 1959; A Fairly Good Time 1970; The Other Paris (short stories) 1956-57; My Heart is Broken: 8 Stories and a Short Novel (Brit. title An Unmarried Man's Summer) 1964; The Affair of Gabrielle Russier (introductory essay) 1971; The Pegnitz Junction, a Novella and Five Short stories 1973; The End of the World and Other Stories, 1974; (short stories) From the Fifteenth District, 1979; Contributor to New Yorker, 1951. *Honours:* Order of Canada 1981. *Address:* 14 rue Jean Ferrandi, Paris VI, France.

GAME, David Aylward, b. 31 Mar. 1926, Adelaide, Australia. Medical Practioner. m. Patrrica Jean Hamilton, 8 Dec. 1949, 2 sons, 2 daughters. *Education:* Collegiate School of St Peter Adelaide, Australia; MB, BS, University of Adelaide, 1949; Member, Royal Australian College of General Practioners, 1966, Fellow, 1968; Hon. Member College of Family Physicians of Canada, 1976. *Appointments:* Resident Medical Officer, 1950, Registrar, Royal Adelaide hospital 1951; General Medical Practice, Adelaide, 1952-; Senior Visiting Practioner, Primary Care, Royal Adelaide Hospital, 1979-. *Memberships:* Royal Australian College of General Practioners; World Organization of College, Academies and Academic Associations of General

Practitioner/Family Physicians; Royal Society of Medicine; Australian Medical Association; Australian Geriatric Society. *Publications:* Bilateral Ovarian Cysts in a girl aged seven and a half years, 1963; Planning Health Services, 1973; The Health Team Concept, CAn it Work!; Primary Health Care in China—a comparison, 1975; The Role of the Professional Man in the Community, 1975; Training of General Practitioners, 1975; Family Medicine Worldwide—Canada's Contribution, 1975; Visit of Australian Medical Delegation to China, 1975; Editorials for AFP; Various papers printed in Proceedings of World Conference. *Honours:* Rose Hunt Award, Royal Australian College of General Practitioners, 1980. *Hobbies:* Gardening; Painting. *Address:* 50 Lambert Road, Royston Park, South Australia 5070, Australia.

GAMMAGE, Philip, b. 9 Apr. 1936, Oxford, England. University teacher. m. Sarah, 1 daughter. *Education:* Teaching Certificate, Goldsmiths' College, 1956-58, Academic Dip. Ed., Institute of Education, 1961-63, University of London, UK; M.Ed., School of Education, University of Leicester, UK, 1967; PhD (psychology), University of Bristol, UK, 1974. *Appointments:* Schoolteacher, London, UK, 1958-65; Senior Lecturer in Education, Furzedown College, London, UK, 1965-68; Lecturer, Senior Lecturer, University of Bristol School of Education, UK, 1968-; Assistant Professor, Michigan State University, USA, summer 1969; Draper's Visiting Lecturer, University of New England, Australia, 1973; Assistant Professor, University of Manitoba, Canada, summer 1978. *Memberships:* British Psychological Society; Association for Child Psychology and Psychiatry. *Publications:* Teacher and Pupil, 1971; The Child, The School and Society, 1976; Children and Schooling, 1982. *Hobbies:* Mountain and fell-walking; Music; Cycling; Engineering. *Address:* 65 Cairns Road, Bristol 6. England.

GAN, Ee-Kiang, b. 23 June 1944, Penang, Malaysia. Associate Professor. m. Lilian Beng-Guat Yeoh, 27 Nov. 1970, 1 son, 1 daughter. *Education:* BSc, 1969; PhD, 1972. *Appointments:* Part-time Demonstrator, University of Western Australia, 1969-72; Lecturer, 1972-77, Associate Professor, Deputy Dean, 1977-, Associate Professor, Dean, 1980-, School of Pharmaceutical Sciences, Universiti Sains, Malaysia. *Memberships:* Vice-President, Malaysian Society of Pharmacology and Experimental Therapeutics; Associate Member, Malaysian Pharmaceutical Society; Penang Arts Council. *Hobbies:* Reading; Tennis. *Address:* 105 Changkat Minden, Jalan 5, Penang, Malaysia.

GANDAR, (Hon), Leslie Walter, b. 26 Jan. 1919, Wellington, New Zealand. Sheep farmer. m. Monica Justine Smith, 15 Apr. 1944, 4 sons, 1 daughter. *Education:* BSc.(N.Z) DSc. (Massey), FIANZ, F.Inst.P., Victoria University of Wellington, New Zealand. *Appointments:* RNZAF, 1940-44; Sheep farming, 1944-; Member of Parliament, 1966-78; Minister of Education, Science and Technology, 1975-78; High Commissioner for New Zealand in London, 1979-. *Memberships:* Chancellor, Massey University, 1970-75; Chairman, Pohangina County Council, 1956-69. *Honours:* Fellow, New Zealand Institute Agricultural Science; Fellow, Institute of Physics. *Hobbies:* Reading; Music; Wood carving; Cricket. *Address:* c/o New Zealand High Commission, Haymarket, London SW1.

GANDHI, Shrimati Indira, b. 19 Nov. 1917, Allababad, India. Prime Minister of India. m. Shri Feroze Gandhi, 26 Mar, 1942, 2 sons. *Education:* Somerville College, Oxford; Honorary doctoral degrees conferrred by following Universities: Andhra; Agra; Bangalore; Vikram; Punjab; Gurukul; Nagpur; Jamia Milia; Poona; El Salvador of Buenos Aires; Waseda of Tokyo; Moscow State; Oxford; Charles of Prague; Mauritius; Baghdad; USSR Academy of Sciences; Citation of Distinction, Columbia University. *Appointments:* Minister of Information and Broadcasting, Government of India, 1964-66; Prime Minister of India, 1966-77, 1980-; Minister for Atomic Energy, 1967-77; Minister for Space, 1972-77, 1980-; Chairman, Planning Commission, 1966-77; Ministry of External Affairs, 1967-69; Ministry of Finance, 1969-70; Ministry of Home Affairs, 1970-73; Ministry of Information and Broadcasting, 1971-; Ministry of Defence, 1980-. *Memberships:* Associated with numerous organisations and institutions including: President, Board of Trustees of Kamala Nehru

Memorial Hospital; Trustee Gandhi Smarak Nidhi; Trustee, Kasturba Gandhi Memorial Trust; Chairman, Swaraj Bhavan Trust; Founder and Chairman, Bal Sahyog, New Delhi; Chairman, Bal Bhavan Board and Children's National Museum, NewDelhi; Founder and President, Kamala Nehru Vidyalaya, Allahabad; Vice Chairman, Central Social Welfare Board; Life-Patron, Indian Council for Child Welfare; Vice-President, International Council of Child Welfare; Patron-in-Chief, Indian Council for Africa; Patron, Foreign Students Association in India; Chancellor, Visva Bharati University;Indian Delegation to UNESCO, 1960-64; Executive Committee of National Defence Fund, 1962. *Publications:* The Years of Challenge, 1966-69; The Years of Endeavour, 1969-72; India (London), 1975; Inde (Lausanne), 1979; numerous collections of speeches and writings. *Honours:* numerous honours including: Recipient of Bharat Ratna, 1972; Mexican Academy Award for Liberation of Bangladesh, 1972; 2nd Annual Medal, FAO, 1973; Sahitya Vachaspati (Hindi), Nagari Pracharini Sabha, 1976. *Hobbies:* Walking; Reading. *Address:* 1 Safdarjang Road, New Delhi 110 011, India.

GANILAU, Ratu Sir Penaia Kanatabatu, b. 28 July 1918, Fiji. Deputy Prime Minister of Fiji. m. (1) Adi Laisa Delaisomosomo Yavaca 1949, (Dec.) 5 sons, 2 daughters, (2) Adi Lady Davila Ganilau, 1975. *Education:* Provincial School Northern, Queen Victoria Memorial School, Fiji; Devonshire Course for Administration Officers, Wadham College, Oxford University 1947. *Appointments:* FIR 1940-46; Colonial Administration Service 1947; District Officer 1948-53; Member Commonwealth on Fijian Post Primary Education in the Colony 1953; Fiji Military Forces 1953-56; *Memberships:* Hon. Col. 2nd Bn (Territorial), FIR 1973; Fijian Economic Development Officer and Roko Tui Cakaudrove conjoint 1956; Tour Manager and Government Representative, Fiji Rugby Football-tour New Zealand 1957; Dep. Sec. for Fijian Affairs 1961; Minister for Fijian Affairs and Local Government 1965; Leader of Government Business and Minister for Communications, Works and Tourism 1972; Council of Ministers; Official Member Legislative Council; Chairman: Fijian Affairs Board; Fijian Development Fund Board; Native Land Trust Board; Great Council of Chiefs. *Honours:* KBE 1974; OBE 1960; CMG 1968; CVO 1970 DSO 1956; ED 1974. Hobby: Rugby Football. *Address:* Ministry for Fijian Affairs and Rural Development, Suva, Fiji.

GARANIS, Stelios, b. 13 May 1927, Athens, Greece. Industrialist. m. Ekaterini Pieridou, 2 Aug. 1956, 1 son, 1 daughter. *Education:* BSc, Civil Engineering. *Appointments:* Project Engineer, General Construction Co. Limited, Cyprus, 1952-54; Managing Director, Deco Lime and Quarries Limited, Cyprus, 1954-63; Managing Director, Garanis & Petrides Limited, Cigarette Manufacturers, 1963-. *Memberships:* Chairman, Cyprus Athletics Organization; Chairman, Cyprus Federation of Employers and Industrialists; Cyprus Productivity Board; Economic Council of Cyprus Government. *Publications:* Various articles in local press. *Honours:* Scholarship award, University of Oklahoma, USA; Honorary member, Boyscouts of Cyprus. *Hobbies:* Sailing. *Address:* Parthenonos Street, Engomi, Nicosia, Cyprus.

GARDINER, George Arthur, b. 3 Mar. 1935, Witham, Essex, England. Member of Parliament, Political Journalist. m. Helen Hackett, 1980, 2 sons, 1 daughter. *Education:* 1st Class Honours Degree in Philosophy, Politics and Economics, Balliol College, Oxford University. *Appointments:* Journalist, 1958-61; Political correspondent, 1961-74; Member of Parliament, 1974-. *Publications:* Margaret Thatcher: From Childhood to Leadership, 1975. *Address:* House of Commons, London, England.

GARDNER, Brenda, b. 29 Apr. 1907, Palmerston North, New Zealand. Nursing. *Education:* General Nursing Registration, 1936; Maternity Nursing Registration, 1938; Midwifery Nursing Registration, 1943; Diploma, Public Health Nursing, 1946; Plunket Certificate, 1947. *Appointments:* Student Nurse, 1932, Ward Sister, 1937-40, Wllington Hospital; Tutor Sister, Westland Hospital, 1941-42; Staff Sister, Obsteterics, Waikato Hospital, 1943-44; Public Health Nurse, Department of Health, 1945-50; Matron, Country Hospitals, Northland Board, 1951-56; Matron, Whamgarer Base Hospitals, Northland Board, 1957; Supervising Matron, Northland Hospital Board, 1965-67. *Member-

ships: New Zealand Nurses Association, President Whangarei Branch and Honorary Member New Zealand Association; National Council of Women, President for two years, Whangarei branch; Whangarei Council of Social Services, President for two years, Executive 20 years; Northland Hospital Board; Regional Committee Ambulance Transport Advisory Board; Field Staff Organiser, Trust for Intellectually Handicapped People; Birthright Inc, foundation Member, Executive Member, now Honorary member; Life Line, Foundation Member, Executive Member. *Honours:* OBE, 1975. *Hobbies:* Gardening; Landscaping; Reading. *Address:* PO Box 1324, Whangarei, New Zealand.

GAREZE, Charles Joseph, b. 1 Mar. 1925, Gibraltar. Director of Labour and Social Security, Government of Gibraltar. m. Tilly Noguera, 17 Apr. 1952, 1 son, 2 daughters. *Appointments:* Clerk, 1943, Chief Clerk, 1956, Assistant Secretary, 1963, Director of Labour and Social Security, 1968, Gibraltar Government. *Memberships:* Calpe Rowing Club; Gibraltar Garrison Library. *Honours:* OBE, 1978. *Hobbies:* Crossword Puzzles; Walking. *Address:* 31 Scud Hill, Gibraltar.

GARLAND, (Hon) Ransley Victor. b. 5 May 1934. Australian High Commissioner in United Kingdom. m. Lynette May Jamieson, 1960, 2 sons, 1 daughter. *Education:* University of Western Australia; Bachelor Arts, majored in Economics; Fellow, Institute of Chartered Accountants. *Appointments:* Elected Member, House of Representatives, for Curtin, Western Australia, 1969-81 (resigned); Various Government Portfolios, 1971-72, 1977-80, including: Acting Minister for Trade and Resources, 1978-80; Minister to represent the Treasurer at the Ministerial Meeting of the OECD, Paris, 1978; Minister to represent the Government at Ministerial Meeting of the escap, New Delhi, 1978; Chairman, of the Commonwealth Delegations to UNSTAD V, Manila, 1979; Attended Commonwealth Heads of Government Meeting, Lusaka, Zambia, 1979. In practice as Chartered Accountant 1958-70, including university tutoring, director of a number of companies 1960-67. *Memberships:* Councillor Claremont Town Council, 1963-70; Deputy Mayor, 1969; Various offices Liberal Party including some years as Senior Vice-President, Western Australia, and Federal Councillor. *Address:* Richardson Avenue, Claremont, Western Australia.

GARNER, Brian John, b. 26 Feb. 1936, Greenwich, London. Professor of Computing. m. Adelheid L Joseph, 19 June 1961, 2 daughters. *Education:* BSc(Hons), Imperial College, London, 1958; PhD(London), 1961; Diploma of Imperial College (DIC), 1962; Post Doctoral Research Assistant, USA, 1962; NATO Fellow, Wuerzburg University, 1963. *Appointments:* Lecturer, Leeds University, 1964-66; Unilever Research Laboratory, 1966-69; IBM Australia Ltd., 1970-73; BHP, 1974-78; Deakin University (Professor of Computing), 1978-. *Memberships:* Australian Computer Society; Australian Society for Operations Research; President, Australian Computer Association; Mogul Ski Club; Automobile Club of Victoria. *Publications:* Diverse Publications, Scientific Journals, Computer Magazines; Buying Your Computer, Edited for ACUA. *Honours:* Governor's Award (Imperial College), 1958; NATO Fellowship, 1963. *Hobbies:* Skiing; Concert Music; Opera. *Address:* 257 Noble Street, Geelong, Victoria 3220, Australia.

GARNETT, John Lyndon, b. 25 Jan. 1929, Sudney, NSW Australia. Chemist; Educator. m. Wilma Rosalie Young, 3 Nov. 1959, 2 sons. *Education:* ASTC, Sydney Technical College, 1950; BSc(Hons) University of NSW, 1951; MSc University of NSW, 1952; PhD University of Chicago, 1956. *Appointments:* Research Chemist, Taubmans Ltd., Sydney, 1946-50; Demonstrator, University of NSW, 1951-52; Graduate Student, University of Chicago, 1953-56; Associate Professor, School of Chemistry, UNSW, 1957-. *Memberships:* Fellow (Executive Council), Chairman Solid State Division, Royal Australian Chemical Institute, 1977-79; American Chemical Society (Co-Chairman Australia and New Zealand International Committee Polymer (Division); Australian Delegate International Congress on Catalysis Council; UK Chemical Society; Chicago Chapter of Sigma Xi; University of Chicago Alumni Association; Australian and New Zealand Society for the Advancement of Science; University of New South Wales Senior

Common Room Club; University of Sydney Common Room. *Publications:* Author of over 300 publications and 20 patents in Chemistry; Editorial Boards of: Catalysis Reviews; Aspects of Homogeneous and Heterogeneous Catalysis; Metal Catalysis in Organic and Inorganic Chemistry; Journal of Radiation Curing. *Honours:* Fulbright Fellow, 1953-56; HG Smith Medal of the Royal Australian Chemical Institute, 1979. *Hobbies:* Restoring Art Treasures; Restoring Old Houses; Swimming; Reading. *Address:* 56 Arabella Street, Longueville, New South Wales 2066, Australia.

GARNHAM, Frank, b. 17 Dec. 1932, Essex, England. Transparency Technologist; Artist. m. Esther Mould, 15 Feb. 1958, 2 sons. *Education:* South East Essex Technical College, National Certificate of Mechanical Engineering. *Appointments:* Patent Illustrator, 1947-50; Royal Air Force, 1951-53; Technical Illustrator, 1954-65; Pioneer Transparency Technologist/Artist, 1966-. *Memberships:* Old Water Colour Society; Guild of Realist Artists; Wildlife Art Society; Royal Photographic Society, Victorian Artist Society; New Zealand Photographic Society; Australian Photographic Society; MSIA; MTPA; FAIA; FRSA; MIAT; AIAP; AIAM; AIIP. *Creative Works:* Paintings: Innocence of Youth; Eclipse; Golden Touch; Temptation; Autumn Glory. *Honours:* Diploma, London College of Printing, 1965; Gold Medal, Melbourne Art Directors Club, 1974; Presidents Award, Institute of Incorp' Photography, 1979; Diploma, Australian Writers and Art Directors, 1980. *Hobbies:* Chess; Community Service; Photography. *Address:* 335 Beaconsfield Parade, West St. Kilda, Victoria, Australia.

GARRATT, Arthur John, b. 11 Jan. 1916, Aldershot England. Physicist. m. Paloma Gqrratt, 28 July 1948, 2 sons. *Education:* BSc, University College, London. *Appointments:* Scientific Officer, Ministry of Supply; Senior Executive Officer, Festival of Britain; Principal Scientific Officer, National Physical Laboratory; Consultant, Value Management Consultants Limited. *Memberships:* Past Master, Worshipful Company of Scientific Instrument Makers; British Academy of Film and Television Arts; Fellow, Institute of Physics; Fellow, Institute of Directors. *Publications:* Energy from Oil; Editor; Penguin Science Survey, Penguin Technology Survey; Numerous Scientific Papers and Articles. *Honours:* MBE, 1952; Wireless World Prize, Royal Television Society, 1961. *Hobbies:* Travel; Collecting Useless Informastion. *Address:* Le Beuil, Cherval, 24320 Verteillac, France.

GARRETT, Albert Charles, b. 14 May 1915, Kingsclere, Hants. UK. Artist; Writer. m. Jessica Iris, 13 Mar. 1954, 1 daughter. *Education:* Camberwell School of Art, 1947-49; Anglo-French Art Centre, 1949-50; Slade School of Fine Art, 1950-51. *Appointments:* Group Publicity Manager, Newage Group Engineering Companies, London, 1954-61; Public Relations Officer, Pinchin Johnson Association, 1961-62; Lecturer, Art Polytechnic of North London, School of Architecture, 1963, Senior Art Lecturer, 1974-80, Part-time Senior Lecturer, 1980-. *Memberships:* Fellow, Royal Society of Arts; Royal Institute of Oil Painters; President, Society of Wood Engravers; Chairman, Mall Prints Federation of British Artists; Fellow, Free Painters and Sculptors; Colour Group (Great Britain); Life Member Bilan de l'Art Contemporain, Paris; Academie Internationale de Lutece, Paris; Academician Accademia Italia delle Arti e del Lavoro, Salsomaggiore. *Publications:* Wood Engravings and Drawings of Iain Macnab,1973; A History of British Wood Engraving, 1978; British Wood Engraving of the 20th Century, 1980; Works in Public Collections: Derby Art Gallery; Portsmouth Art Gallery; Hull Ferens Art Gallery, Hull; Richter Trust; Polytechnic of North London; Renssellaer Polytechnic Institute, Troy New York; Wiakato Art Gallery, Hamilton, New Zealand. *Honours:* Diplome d'Honneur, 1969; Diplome Mention Speciale, 1976-78; International Arts Guild, Monte-Carlo; Grand Finalist Exhibition of British Artists, Paris and Exposition de Quebec, 1979, 1981; Grand Concours International by Academie Internationale de Lutece, Paris, Silver Medals, 1974, 75, 78; Concours International Academie Internationale de Lutece, Paris, Gold Medals, 1978; Accademia Italia Delle arti e del Lavoro, 1979; Award of Italy by Accademia Italia Arti e del Lavoro, 1980. *Hobby:* Travel. *Address:* 10 Sunningdale Avenue, Eastcote, Ruislip, Middlesex HA4 9SR, England.

GARTON, John Miller, b. 10 Sept. 1928, Sydney Australia. Company Director. m. Valerie Barbara Vaughan, 10 June 1961, 2 sons, 2 daughters. *Education:* BA, Sydney University, 1960. *Appointments:* Chief Executive, United Holdings Limited and Producers and Citizens Life Insurance Company Limited, 1963-69; Chairman of the Board, Luna Park Holdings Limited, 1969-73; Chairman of the Board, Ralph Symonds Limited, 1970-79; Chairman of the Board, Merchant Entrepreneurs Limited, 1972-; Chairman of the Board, Devon Symonds Holdings Limited, 1977-79; Chairman of the Board, Barclay (Insurances) Limited. *Hobbies:* Sailing; Golf. *Address:* 589 New South Head Road, Rose Bay, New South Wales 2029, Australia.

GASS, (Sir) Michael David Irving, b. 24 Apr. 1916, Wareham, Dorset, England. Her Majesty's Overseas Civil Service (ret.). m. Elizabeth Periam Acland-Hood, 21 Aug. 1975. *Education:* King's School, Bruton, 1930-34; Christ Church, Oxford, 1934-38, BA, 1938, MA, 1945; Queens' College, Cambridge, 1938-39, BA, 1938. *Appointments:* Administrative Service, 1939, District Commissioner, 1945. Gold Coast; War Service (East Africa, Burma), 1939-46; Assistant Regional Officer, Ashanti, 1953; Permanent Secretary, Ministry of the Interior, Ghana, 1956; Chief Secretary to the Western Pacific High Commission, 1958; Colonial Secretary, Hong Kong, 1965; High Commissioner for the Western Pacific and British High Commissioner for the New Hebrides, 1969; Retired, 1973; Elected Member of the Somerset County Council, 1977-81. *Memberships:* East India, Devonshire, Sports and Public Schools Club, London; Hong Kong Club; Somerset County Club; Oxford Union Society; Commonwealth Parliamentary Association. *Honours:* CMG, 1960; KCMG,1969. *Hobby:* Ornithology. *Address:* Fairfield, Stogursey, Bridgwater, Somerset, TA5 1PU, England.

GATHERCOLE, Terence Stephen, b. 25 Nov. 1935, Tallimba, New South Wales, Australia. Swim Coach. m. 17 June 1957, 2 sons, 1 daughter. *Education:* Primary & Secondary Schools, West Wyalong, New South Wales, Australia. *Appointments:* Self employed and Owner of Killarney Swim Centre, Killarney Heights, NSW, Australia. *Memberships:* Tattersalls Club, Sydney; Treasurer, Australian Swim Coaches Association; Chairman, Accrediation Committee, Australian Swimming Union. *Honours:* Gold Medalist & Record Holder in Breaststroke and Medley Relay, Commonwealth Games, Cardiff, Wales, 1958; Silver Medalist, Medley Relay, Rome Olympics, 1960; Only man to win seven consecutive Australian Swimming Championships (Breaststroke), 1954-60; World Record Holder in Breaststroke Swimming, 1958-62; Represented Australia, Olympic Games, 1956, 1960, Commonwealth Games, 1958; Australian Womens Swim Coach, Olympic Games, Tokyo, 1964, Commonwealth Games, Jamaica, 1966; Head Coach, Australian Swim Team, Montreal, 1976; Head Coach American Tour, 1980. *Hobby:* Relaxing with Family and Friends. *Address:* 14 Tralee Avenue, Killarney Heights, NSW, Australia.

GAUDRY, Roger, b. 15 Dec. 1913, Quebec, Canada. President of the International Association of Universities. m. 19 June 1941, 2 sons, 3 daughters. *Education:* BA, Université Laval, Quebec, 1933; BSc (Chemistry) Université Laval, 1937; Rhodes Scholar, Oxford; DSc Université Laval, 1940. *Appointments:* Lecturer in organic chemistry, Fac. Medicine, Laval, 1940, Assistant Professor, 1945, Professor, 1950-54; Guest Speaker, La Sorbonne; Assistant Director Research, Ayerst MacKenna & Harrison Ltd, 1954; Director Research, same company and Ayerst Laboritories, New York, 1957-65, Vice-President, 1963-65; Rector University, Montreal, 1965-75; Vice-Chairman Science Council of Canada, 1966-72, Chairman, 1972-75; Chairman Council, The United Nations University, 1974-76,Member Council, 1974-80; President, International Association of Universities, 1975-80. *Memberships:* Corporation of Professional Chemists of Quebec, 1964; Royal College of Physicians and Surgeons, Canada, 1971; Association professionnelle des pharmaciens du Québec, 1972; Royal Society of Canada, 1954; President, Chemical Institute of Canada, 1955-56; President, Canadian Association of Rhodes Scholars, 1960-61; President, Association of Universities and Colleges of Canada, 1969-71; Economic Council of Canada, 1970-73; President, Conference of Rectors and Principals of Quebec Universities, 1970-72; and numerous other memberships. *Honours:* LL D, University of Toronto, 1966; D Sc, Royal Military College of Kingston, 1966; D Sc, University of British Columbia, 1967; LL D McGill University, 1967; Doctorate from Université de Clermont-Ferrand, France, 1967, Numerous other honorary awards including: Province of Quebec Science Award, 1942, 46, 50; Companion of the Order of Canada, 1968; Montreal Medal of the Chemical Institute of Canada, 1974. *Address:* 445 rue Beverley, Montreal, Canada H3P 1L4

GAUR, Ved Prakash Gaur, b. 1 Dec. 1929, Meerut, India. Teacher. m. Mithlesh Gaur, 22 Nov. 1962, 2 sons. *Education:* M.A. (Political Science) University of Allahabad, Inida, 1952; L.L.B. University of Allahabad, India, 1952; PhD., Pilani, Inida, 1971. *Appointments:* Teacher,* Birla Institute of Technology and Science, Pilani, 1964-. *Memberships:* Indian Political Science Association; Indian Society of Gandhian Studies, Allahabad; Ishwari Prasad Institute of History, Allahabad. *Publications:* 'Mahatma Gandhi'; Contributed to several papers on Gandhian Ideology and Current International Affairs. *Hobbies:* Reading; Writing. *Address:* Group Leader, Humanistic Studies, Birla Institute of Technology and Science, Pilani, India.

GAVIN, Angus William Murray, b. 12 July 1944, Amersham, Bucks, England. Architect. *Education:* BA, 1966, DipArch, 1969, MA, 1970, Trinity College, Cambridge; GSD, Harvard University USA, MArch in Urban Design, 1971. *Appointments:* Tripe and Wakeham, Architects, London, 1966-67, 1969-70; Colin St J Wilson and Partners, London, 1971-73, 1975-77; Nayman Gavin Associates, London, Private Practice, 1973-75; Max Lock Group, Nigeria 1977-79; Visiting Associate Professor of Architecture, University of Virginia, USA, 1979-80; Al Sabek, McGaughy Marshall and McMillan Joint Venture, Athens, 1980-81; McKee Associates, Doha, Qatar, 1981-. *Memberships:* Royal Institute of British Architects; Associate, Urban Land Institute, USA; Commonwealth Human Ecology Council; Harvard Alumni Association. *Creative Works:* Projects: Residential Communities, Yanbu New City, Saudi Arabia; British Library, Euston; Joseph Lucas Group Headquarters, Shirley, Birmingham. *Hobbies:* Sailing; Skiing; Climbing. *Address:* 14 Ewald Road, London, England.

GAVIN, Joseph B, b. 30 Aug. 1935, Lansdowne, Ontario, Canada. Historian. *Education:* BA, 1960, PhL, 1961, Gonzaga University; MA, 1966, Columbia University; MA, 1968, STL, 1968, Regis College, Toronto; PhD, McGill University, 1972. *Appointments:* Sessional Lecturer in History, Ignatius College, Guelph, Ontario, 1965-68; Sessional Lecturer, 1971-73, Assistant Professor, 1975-79, Historical Theology, Regis College, Toronto; Visiting Professor of Ecclesiastical History, Università Gregoriana, Rome, 1973-75; President, Campion College, University of Regina. *Memberships:* Canadian Historical Association; Canadian Society of Church History; International Commission of Comparative Ecclesiastical History; International Federation of Catholic Universities; Association of Universities and Colleges of Canada; Council of University Presidents; Board of Governors, Regina Symphony, Executive Member. *Publications:* Numerous Articles in Scholarly Journals on Historical and Theological Topics. *Honours:* Canada Council Fellowship; British Council Grant. *Hobbies:* Singing; Water Skiing; Organist; Ice Skating; Travelling. *Address:* 3769 Winnipeg Street, Regina, Canada.

GAVIN, Peter Murray, b. 27 Feb. 1949, Melbourne, Australia. Member Legislative Assembly of Victoria. m. Barbara Christy, 1 Feb. 1975. *Education:* Completed 8 units of a 10 unit Ba. *Appointments:* Commonwealth Public Servant, 1971-79; Parliamentary Questions Officer, 1975-79; Secretary, Joint Consultative Council of Department of Employment and Industrial Relations, 1976-78; Labour Member for Coburg, Victorian Legislative Assembly, 1979-. *Memberships:* Labour Transport Campaign; Victorian Fabian Society; National Trust; West Coburg Progress Association; Coburg Historical Society. *Hobbies:* Live Theatre; Gardening; Reading; Films; Running; Tennis. *Address:* 65 Boundary Road, Merlynston 3058, Australia.

GAVU, Eniton Ruth Anku, b. 9 Dec. 1941, Gbadzeme. Pharmacist. m. 20 April 1968, 4 sons. *Education:* B.Pharm., Ghana, 1965; Practicals Certificate in Pharmacy, 1968. *Appointments:* Korle By Teaching

Hospital, Accra, 1965; Prin Pharmacist Cocoa Clinic, 1973; Chief Pharmacist, G.C.M.B., Clinics, 1979-. *Memberships:* Member of Council and Honorary Treasurer, Pharmaceutical Society of Ghana; Assistant General Secretary, Zonta Club of Accra (Branch of Zonta International); Council Member, Institute of Pharmacy Management International; Executive Member, Hospital Pharmacists Association; Member, Old Mawuli Students Union. *Hobbies:* Sewing; Reading; Gardening. *Address:* P.O. Box 10234, Accra-North Ghana.

GAY, Norman Rupert, b. 31 Jan. 1941, Sansalvador, Bahamas. Physician/Politician. m. Alicza Corning Clark, 9 Apr. 1976. *Education:* BA, Union College, Nebraska, 1961; MD, Loma Linda University, California, 1965; MBA, University of Miami, 1981. *Appointments:* Senior Medical Officer, Princess Margaret Hospital, 1966-70; Owner, Proprietor, West Bay Medical Clinic, 1970-81; Member of Parliament, 1973-81. *Memberships:* Beta Gamma Sigma; International Academy of Preventive Medicine; Fellow, International Institute of Integral Human Science; International Council of Sports and Physical fitness. *Publications:* Mr Northern Bahamas, over 35, 1980; Second Place, Mr Florida, over 40, 1981; Mr Bahamas, over 35, 1981; Third Place, Mr Southern States, over 35, 1981. *Hobbies:* Billiards; Wind Surfing; Sailing; Music. *Address:* Box N 3222, Nassau, Bahamas.

GAYLE, Fitz Anthony, b. 3 Oct. 1935, Kingston, Jamaica. Commissioned Land Surveyor. m. Natalie Delrose Brown, 26 Aug. 1961, 2 sons, 3 daughters. *Education:* Survey Training School, 1960-63; Diploma in General Administrative Management, Jamaica School of Management Education, 1971. *Appointments:* Survey Assistant, Government Survey Department, 1962-64; Assistant Surveyor, Water Commisssion, 1964; Surveyor, Jamaica Goverment Railway, 1964-65; Surveyor, Ministry of Housing, 1965-67; Private Practise, 1967-. *Memberships:* Member, Land Surveyors Association of Jamaica; Member, Commonwealth Association of Surveying, Mapping and Land Economy; Member, International Federation of Surveyors. *Hobbies:* Swimming; Fishing; Reading. *Address:* 3, Selvon Avenue, Durhaney Park, Kingston 20, Jamaica, W.I.

GAYRE, Robert b. United Kingdom. m. Nina Terry, 1 son. *Education:* MA, Edinburgh University, 1934, Exeter College, Oxford. *Appointments:* Educational Advisor, Allied Military Court, 1940-44; Director of Education, 1944; Chief of Education and Religious Affairs, 1944; Professor, Head of the Post Graduate Department of Anthropogeography, 1954-56. *Memberships:* Fellow, National Acadamy of Science of India; Fellow, National Society of Naples; Fellow, Peloritana Academy of Messina; Fellow, Pontaniana Academy of Naples; Fellow, Royal Society of Health. *Publications:* Contributed to numerous books on Authropology, Heraldry. *Honours:* D.Sc., Naples; D.Phil., Messina; D.Pol.Sc., Palermo; Hon. Leutenent Colonel, State Militia of Alabama and Georgia; E.R.D.; GCMM; GCCN; KCCI; GCLJ. *Hobbies:* Heraldry; Painting; Sailing. *Address:* Minard Castle, Nr. Inveraray, Argyll, Scotland.

GBEGBAJE, Das, b. 18 March, 1940, Ekpan, Warri. Architect. m. Agatha Tureme Mamoh, 10 June 1975, 1 son, 3 daughters. *Education:* Ahmadu Bello University, Zaria, Nigeria, 1965-70. *Appointments:* Nigtr Consultants Architects Practise, 1970-. *Memberships:* Nigerian Institute of Architects, 1977-79; Ikoyi Club, 1938; Board of Governors, Eko Boys High School, Lagos, 1979-. *Creative Works:* Designor of Radiotherapy Block; Lagos University Teaching Hospital, 1970; O.P.P., University Teaching Hospital, 1972; Psychiatric Hospital, Calabar; 481 dwelling units all over Nigeria, including: Principals House, Yaba College of Technology, Lagos; Directors House, Radio Nigeria; Rubber Research Institute, Beniu. *Hobbies:* Badminton; Psychology. *Address:* Plot 1, 2nd Avenue, Beachland Estate, Tin Can Island.

GEARY, Terence John, b. London, England. Businessman, Journalist. m. Patricia Seet, 31 Aug. 1976. *Appointments:* Feature Writer, HongKong Star; South-East Asia Correspondent, Record World; Sole Propreitor, Media House Advertising; Partner, The Entertainment Company; Director, Communication, Advertising and Marketing Limited. *Publications:* 'Guide to HongKong Nightlife',

Co-Author, 1979; Record Producer, EMI Limited, House Records, HongKong. *Address:* Pheonix Court, 39 Kennedy Road, Block 1 Flat 'C', 3rd Floor, HongKong.

GEE, George, b. 11 Nov. 1921, Palmerston North, New Zealand. Company Director. m. Dorothy Bing, 7 Oct. 1940, 1 son, 1 daughter. *Appointments:* Self-Employed, Fruit and Produce Merchant. *Memberships:* Wellington Regional Council; Wellington Harbour Board; retired Mayor of Petowe Borough; Municipal Co-Op Insurance; N2 Walkway Commission; Managing Director Gees Fruit Market Limited; Chairman, Hott Milk Corporation Limited; N2 Milk Board; Joint Council Local Government Service; Chairman, Hutt Valley Drainage Board; Vice-President, N2 Municipal Association. *Honours:* Justice of Peace. *Hobby:* Bowls. *Address:* 2 Buick Street, Pletone, New Zealand.

GEE, Maurice Gough, b. 22 Aug. 1931, Whakatane, New Zealand. Writer. m. Margaretha Garden, 1970, 1 son, 2 daughters. *Education:* MA, University of Auckland, 1953. *Appointments:* Teacher; Librarian; Writer *Memberships:* PEN (New Zealand Centre) New Zealand Writers Guild. *Publications:* Novels: The Big Season; A Special Flower; In My Father's Den; Games of Choice; Plumb; Under the Mountain; The World Around the Corner; Meg; A Glorious Morning, Comrade (Collection). *Honours:* New Zealand Book Award, 1976, 79; James Tait Black Memorial Prize, 1979; Wattie New Zealand Book of the Year, 1979. *Address:* 125 Cleveland Terrace, Nelson, New Zealand.

GEIDANS, Leonids, b. 23 Feb. 1924, Riga, Latvia. Geologist. m. Lilita Eizenija Kalnins, 22 June 1957, 2 sons, 2 daughters. *Education:* French Lyceum in Riga, Latvia; Science, University of Giessen, Germany, 1948-49; Science, Perth Technical College, West Australia, 1953-57; B.Sc. University of Western Australia, 1953-61. *Appointments:* Interpreter, UNRRA and US Miltary Government, Germany and C.E.S. Australia, 1946-51; Geologist, ALCOA, 1962-64; Geologist, North Broken Hill, 1964-68; Consulting Geologist, Watts, Griffis and MacOuat, 1968-69; Self-Employed Consulting Geologist, 1969-73; Resident Geologist, Project Manager, Pechiney Exploration and Minatome, Australia Pty. Limited, 1973-. *Memberships:* Australasian Institute of Mining and Metallurgy; Australian Geological Society; Royal Society of Western Australia; Fellowship, Gemmological Association of Australia. *Publications:* Several Scientific publications including: 'Bauxitic laterites of the South Western part of Western Australia', 1973; 'Zebra Rock' of Western Australia, 1981. *Hobbies:* Music; Studies of genesis of rocks; Studies of role and relationship of planet Earth in solar system and Universe; Farming. *Address:* 1 Lisle Street, Mount Claremont, 6010, Western Australia.

GENDERS, Anselm, b. 15 Aug. 1919, Brimingham, England. Angelican Priest. *Education:* Brasenose College, Oxford, 1939-48; College of the Resurrection, Mirfield, 1948-52; Professed in religious vows and ordained, 1952. *Appointments:* Tutor, College of the Resurrection, Mirfield, 1952-55; Vice-Principal, Principal, Cordington College, Barbados, 1955-65; Treasurer, St. Augustine's Mission, Penhalonga, Rhodesia, 1966-75; Archdeacon of Manicaland, 1970-75; Assistant Bursar, Community of the Resurrection, Mirfield, 1975-76; Bishop of Bermuda, 1977-. *Publications:* Several Magazine contirbutions. *Honours:* Lieutenan R.N.V.R. War Service, 1939-45. *Address:* Bishop's Lodge, P.O. Box 769, Hamilton 5, Bermuda.

GEORGE, Bruce Thomas, b. 1 June 1942, Mid Glamorgan, Wales. Member of Parliament. *Education:* BA. Politics, University College of Wales, Swansea, 1964; MA., Politics, University of Warwick, 1968. *Appointments:* Assistant Lecturer Social Studies, Glamorgan Polytechnic, 1964-66; Lecturer Politics, Manchester, 1968-70; Senior Lecturer in Politics, Birmingham Polytechnic, 1970-74; Member of Parliament, Walsall South, 1974, 1979-. *Memberships:* Patron, National Association of Widows; Vice-Presidetn, Spina Bifida Association; Fellow, Parliament and Industry Trust; President, Gilbert and Sullivan Club.; Royal Institute of Internation Affairs; Internation Institute for Strategic Studies. *Publications:* Several articles on defence, Private Security Industry, American Indian. *Hobbies:* North American Indian studies; Association Football. *Address:* 42 Wood End Road, Walsall, West Midlands.

GEORGE, Donald Scott, b. 19 Apr. 1919, South Australia. Company Managing/Chairman of Directors. m. Irene Clariss Jackett 26 July 1941, 2 daughters. *Education:* Murray Bridge Agricultural High School. *Appointments:* Savings Bank of South Australia 1937-41; Member of Family Company William Jackett and Son Pty Limited, Flour Millers, Grain Exporters, Port Adelaide, 1944-. *Memberships:* Commerce Club Adelaide; Glenelg Golf Club. *Honours:* Export Award for Outstanding Achievement. *Hobbies:* Tennis; Golf; Reading; Theatre. *Address:* PO Box 101, Port Adelaide, South Australia.

GEORGE, Donald William, b. 22 Nov. 1926 Adelaide, South Australia. Chairman, Vice-Chancellor and Principal. m. Lorna Mildred Davey 21 Jan. 1950, 1 son, 1 daughter. *Education:* BSc 1947; BE 1949; PhD 1966, University of Sydney; *Appointments:* Lecturer, University of Technology NSW 1949-53; Experimental Officer, UK Atomic Energy Agency, Harwell UK 1954-55; Research Officer, Australian Atomic Energy Commission, Harwell and Lucas Heights, qnsw 1956-60; Faculty Member, The University of Sydney 1960-74; Vice-Chancellor and Principal, The University of Newcastle and Chairman, Australian Atomic Energy Commission. *Memberships:* Fellow, Australian Academy of Technological Sciences; Institution of Electrical Engineers; Institute of Mechanical Engineers; Institution of Engineers, Australia; Australian Insitute of Physics. *Publications:* 50 or more Scientific Papers. *Honours:* Order of Australia 1979; Premium, Institute of Electrical Engineers, London; Electrical Engineering Prize, Institution of Engineers, Australia. *Address:* 48 Ridgeway Road, New Lambton Heights, NSW 2305, Australia.

GEORGE, Godwin Ekejekwu, b. 18 June 1933, Awka-Etiti, Nigeria. Businessman. m. Mercy Olikeze, 15 June 1958, 5 sons, 3 daughters. *Education:* St Michael's School Aba, 1939-46; St Joseph's College Awka-Etiti, 1951. *Appointments:* Managing Director, GMO and Company Limited, 1957; Director, United African Drug Company Limited, 1964; Chairman, GMO Group of Companies, 1976; Chairman, GODM Shoes Limited, 1978; Director, Ciana Agencies Limited, 1979. *Memberships:* People's Club of Nigeria; Awka-Etiti Social Club; Ikembe Age Group; British Institute of Management, Awka-Etiti. *Honours:* Ezissi Ezenyimba Title 1978. *Hobbies:* Swimming; Table Tennis. *Address:* 18 Obanikoro Road, Ikorodu Road, Vie Yaber, Nigeria.

GEORGE, Hywel, b. 10 May 1924, Holyhead, United Kingdom. University Administration. m. Edith Pirchl, 25 June 1955, 3 daughters. *Education:* BA(Hons), University College of Wales Aberystwyth, 1941-43 and 1946-47; Pembroke College, Cambridge, 1947-48 and 1954-55; MA(Cantab), 1971. *Appointments:* RAF, 1943-46; HM Overseas Civil Service, N. Borneo, 1949-66; Administrator, St Vincent, 1967-69; Governor, St Vincent, 1969-70; Administrator, British Virgin Islands, 1970-71. *Memberships:* Commonwealth Council, British Commonwealth Ex-Servicemens League; Cambridge University Lawn Tennis Club. *Honours:* OBE 1964; CMG 1967; CStJ 1967; PDK (Malaysia) 1974; JMN (Malaysia) 1966. *Hobbies:* Walking; Tennis. *Address:* 70 Storeys Way, Cambridge, England.

GEORGE, Ian Gordon Combe, b. 12 Aug. 1934, Adelaide, South Australia. Priest (Anglican Church of Australia). m. Barbara Dorothy Peterson, 13 June 1964, 1 son, 1 daughter. *Education:* LLB, University of Adelaide 1956; MDiv., General Theological Seminary, New York, 1964; Enrolled, PhD Candidate, University of Queensland. *Appointments:* Assistant Curate, St Thomas' Church, Diocese of New York, USA, 1964-65; St Davids Church, Burnside, Diocese of Adelaide, 1966; Priest in Charge, Australian Regular Army Chaplain, 1967-69; Sub-Warden and Chaplain, St George's College, University of Western Australia, Diocese of Perth 1969-73; Part-time Lecturer and Tutor in History, University of Western Australia; Dean, St. John's Cathedral, Diocese of Brisbane 1973-81; Senior Army Chaplain, 1st Military District, 1975-81; Honorary Chaplain, RAAF, Association of Queensland, St Barnabas Guild for Nurses, Actors' Church Union Theatre Chaplain for Brisbane, Thomas More Society; Rector, Church of St John the Baptist, Canberra 1981-; Residentiary Canon of St. Saviour's Cathedral, Goulburn, Diocese of Canberra and Goulburn 1981-. *Memberships:* Alcohol and Drug Problems Association, Queensland; The Australi-

an Foundation for Alcohol and Drug Dependence; International Society for Education through the Arts; Governor, Queensland Festival of the Arts; Trustee, Queensland Art Gallery; Communit Arts Board, Australia Council; Counsellor, Griffith University, Queensland; Queensland Committee enquiring into Education through the Arts; Australian Liturgical Commission; Church of England Armed Forces Reserve Board; Church of England General Synod Committee on Divorce and Remarriage. *Publications:* Articles in various journals, especially on relationship between religion and the Arts, Art Critic, The News, Adelaide 1966-68; Writer, Weekly Column, The Courier Mail, Brisbane 1974-81; Paintings, The Stations of the Cross 1978; Various graphic works. *Honours:* Bakewell Law Scholar, University of Adelaide, 1952; Australia Council, Community Arts Board Overseas Travel Grant 1978. *Hobbies:* Gardening; Reading; Music; Creative Arts; History; Cooking. *Address:* St John the Baptist Rectory, Anzac Park and Constitution Avenue, Reid, ACT 2600, Australia.

GEORGE, Karachebone Ninan, b. 21 June 1924 Kerala India. Teaching-Designation; Director. m. Grace George 19 Feb. 1961 1 son 1 daughter. *Education:* BSc (Economics) Madras University; MSW (Social Work) Baroda University; MSc (Social Administration) School of Applied Social Sciences, Western Reserve University Ohio USA. *Appointments:* Lecturer, Madras School of Social Work 1953-55; Associate Director, Madras School of Social Work, 1955-57, Director, 1959-. Director of Numerous Teaching and Research in the field of Social Work, Planning, and Community Service. *Memberships:* Panel on Social Work Education in India; Social Welfare Research Advisory Committee, India; Academic Committee, National Insitute of Public Cooperation and Child Development Faculty of Social Work, Baroda; Union Public Serice Commission, India; Sociology and Social Work; Central Social Welfare; International Association of Schools of Social Work; Indian Council of Social Welfare; National Service Scheme. *Publications:* The Beggar Survey in Madras City 1956; Social Welfare in the Slums of Madras 1965; Working Mothers in White Collar Occupations 1970; Several papers in regional and national seminars and published articles in many journals. *Honours:* Citation in recognition of outstanding achievements and services in the field of social welfare by the School of Applied Social Sciences of the Western Reserve University USA; Citation and Gold Medal, by Guild of Service. *Address:* 33 Casa Major Road, Egmore, Madras 600 008, India.

GEORGE, Martin Richard, b. 25 Jan. 1956, Ramsgate, Kent, England. Student. *Education:* Bachelor of Science, 1978; Bachelor of Science with Honours, 1979. *Appointments:* Continuous Study. *Memberships:* President of Astronomical Society of Tasmania, 1973-74 and 1977-; President of Tasmania University Physics Club, 1977 and 1979-80; Tasmanian Bridge Association. *Hobbies:* Amateur Astronomy; Bridge; Photography. *Address:* 157 Gordons Hill Road, Lindisfarne, Tasmania, Australia, 7015.

GEORGIADES, Christakis Costa, b. 10 April, 1937, Limassol, Cyprus. Company Director. m. 3 daughters. *Education:* Limassol Gymnasium, 1955; Diploma, Business Administration, Regent Str. Politechnic, 1958. *Appointments:* Founder, owner, Managing Director, Sun Island Canning Ltd., Limassol, Cyprus, 1970-. *Memberships:* Board of Directors, Cyprus Tourist Organization; President, Limassol Nautical Club; Honorary Secretary, Limassol Chamber of Commerce and Industry; Director, Cyprus Chamber of Commerce and Industry; Rotary Club of Limassol; Fellow, Institute of Directors. *Hobbies:* Sailing; Swimming; *Address:* 1 Evangelistrias Street, Limassol, Cyprus.

GERHARDT, Walter, b. 1 Apr. 1912, Vienna, Austria. Musician. *Education:* Diplomas, Neues Wiener Konservatorium Staatsakademie Für Musik, Vienna. *Appointments:* Leader, Vienna Radio Symphony; Professor State Conservatoire, Ankara, Turkey; Viola Principal, Zurich Radio Symphony; Concert Master South Australian Symphony, Adelaide; Professor London Guild Hall School of Music; Senior Lecturer and Head of String and Orchestra Department Welsh College of Music, Cardiff; Viola Principal, Menuhin Festival Orchestra; Founder and Leader of Gerhardt String Quartet. *Memberships:* Representative, European String Teachers Association, for Wales. *Publications:* Many

Records for EMI, NIXA, Concert Hall Society, VOX, H.M.V. *Honours:* Fritz-Kreisler Prize, Vienna, 1932. *Hobbies:* Collecting String Instruments; Stamp collecting. *Address:* Coed Bach, 38 Queenwood, Cardiff, CF3 7LE, U.K.

GERMAINE, Max, b. 18 July 1914, Melbourne, Australia. Art Valuer and Recorder. m. 15 June 1940, 1 son, 3 daughters. *Education:* Fellow, Australian Institute of Management. *Appointments:* Vacuum Oil Co. Melbourne and Tasmania, 1931-39; Seagoing officer in R.N. and R.A.N., 1940-46; Chief Executive, Max Germaine Pty. Ltd. Group, Tasmania, 1947-64 and F.R. Strange Pty. Ltd. Group, Sydney, N.S.W., 1964-74. *Memberships:* Australian Club, Sydney; Auctioneers and Valuers Association of NS.W. Past President, Hobart Club, 1958-59; Society of Automotive Engineers, Australia. *Publications:* Artists and Galleries of Australia and New Zealand, 1980. *Hobbies:* Writing; Gardening; Tennis. *Address:* Cherry Trees, P.O. Box 59, Dural, NS.W., 2158,, Australia

GERCGIIWITZ, Denis Culin, b. 10 Nov. 1932, South Australia. Insurance Officer. m. Valma Margaret Pethick, 21 May 1960, 3 sons. *Education:* Immanuel College, Adelaide; Associate Banker's Institute of Australasia Licensed Land Broker; Graduate Advanced Management Program. *Appointments:* Bank of Adelaide 1948-; Supertendent, International Division, 1966-68; Manager, London Branch 1969-71; Manager, Adelaide Branch, 1972-73; Assistant General Manager, 1974-76; Deputy General Manager, 1977-79; General Manager, State Government Insurance Commission, 1979-. *Memberships:* Board Management St Andrews Hospital Adelaide; Trustee, Peter Nelson Leukaemia Appeal; Finace Committee: Anti-Cancer Foundation; Scotch College Adelaide; Adelaide Club; Naval, Military and Air Force; Tattersalls, Adelaide. *Honours:* Lieutenent, Royal Australian Artillery. *Hobbies:* Gardening; Golf. *Address:* 7A Serpentine Road, Belair 5052, Australia.

GERVAIS, Richard G, b. 20 Feb. 1942, Montreal, Quebec. Vice-President. m. Marie-Elizabeth Chevrier, 14 June 1976. *Education:* College Stanislas, Outremont; Loyola College, Montreal; Fordham University, NY., USA.; BA Political Science; MA, Political Science; Institut d'Etudes Politiques de Paris, schooling/Doctorat du 3e Cycle, Political Science. *Appointments:* Special Assistant to the Honourable Jean Marchand, Minister of Manpower & Immigration, Ottawa, 1967; P E Trudeau Committee for the Leadership race of Liberal Party, Federal Government, Ottawa, 1968; Special Assistant to the honourable Mitchell Sharp, Secretary of State for External Affairs, 1968; Executive Assistant to Special Joint Committee of Senate & House of Commons on the Constitution of Canada, 1970; Executive Secretary to Task Force on Parole in Canada, 1972; Executive Secretary to Commission of Inquiry on Security of Penitentiaries, 1973; Special Assistant to the Honourable Jean-Pierre Goyer, Minister of Supply Services, 1974; Director: External Affairs, Quebec, Imperial Oil Limited, 1975; Vice-President - Quebec, Public and Industrial Relations Limited, 1981. *Memberships:* International Board of Directors; Board and Vice-President, Maison des Etudiants Canadiens, Paris, France; Chambre de Commerce Francaise au Canada; Chambre de Commerce de Montreal; Canadian Institute of International Affairs, Quebec; Institute of Donations and Public Affairs Research; Associated with several other Societies and Foundations. *Publications:* Commander of the Military and Hospitaller Order of Saint Lazarus of Jerusalem, 1980. *Hobbies:* Wine tasting; Travelling; Reading (Politics and History). *Address:*465 Mount Pleasant Avenue, Westmount, Quebec, Canada.

GHAFUR, Muhammad Abdul, b. 1 July 1931, Rashidabad, Patiya District, Chittagong. Professor. m. 23 Mar. 1953, 2 daughters. *Education:* BA., Honours, Arabic, Dacca University, 1950; MA., Arabic, Dacca University, 1951; PhD., Hamburg University, W. Germany, 1960. *Appointments:* Epigraphical Assistant, Department of Archaeology, Government of Pakistan, 1952-61; Assistant Superintendent of Archaeology, Class I Government of Pakistan, 1962-65; Superintendent of Archaeology, Senior Class, 1965-72; Director of Archaeology, Government of Bangladesh, 1973-74; Professor of Arabic, University of Chittagong. *Memberships:* Asiatic Society of Bangladesh, Dacca; Pakistan Iran Cultural

Society, Karachi; Museums Association, Karachi. *Publications:* Calligraphers of Thatta, 1968; Co-Author, Muslim Architecture & Art Treasure in Pakistan, 1965, Common Cultural heritage of Iran & Pakistan, 1969; Numerous Research Papers including: 14 Kufic inscriptions of Banbhore, the site of Daibul, Pakistan Archaeology, 1966; Muslim Architecture of Sind, 1966; Archaeological Research in Bangladesh, 1972. *Honours:* Tamgha e Qaid e Azam, 1969. *Address:* Vill. Rashidabad, P.O. Shovandandi, Dist. Chittagong, Bangladesh.

GHAI, Vedkumari, b. 16 Nov. 1932, Jammu Tawi India, Teaching. m. Dr Rampratad 15 Dec. 1963, 1 son, 1 daughter. *Education:* MA, Sanskrit; MA, Ancient Indian History, Culture; Diploma, German, Danish; PhD, Sanskrit. *Appointments:* Lecturer, Sanskrit Government College Jammu/Srinyai, J&K State, 1953-63; Lecturer, Department of Sanskrit J&K University, 1963-68; Reader and Head Department, 1968-73; Professor and Head of Department, 1973-. *Memberships:* President, Dogi Research Institute Jammu, Dharatige Vidya Bhawan Jammu; Dogi Sansita Jammus; President, Shri B R V Ghes Dharmmartta Trust Redistered Jammu; Vice President, Home for the Aged and Infirm Jammu. *Publications:* Nilamata Purana Volume I; Nilamata Purana Volume II; Contributions to Dogi Phonetics and Phonology; Sahityika and Sanshritik Nibandhe; Rajendrebarnepurs; Kashmia Darpana; Narendie Darpana. *Hobbies:* Writing; Social Service. *Address:* 173 Raghunathpura, Jammu Tawi, India.

GHALANOS, Panos Christou, b. 30 Oct. 1938, Cyprus. Banker, Chartered Accountant. m. Anthoula, 26 Oct. 1969, 1 son, 1 daughter. *Education:* B.Sc., Economics Honours, London School of Economics, 1959-62; Article Clerk, Qualified as Chartered Accountant, 1965. *Appointments:* Professional Practice in Cyprus, 1966-70; Group Financial Director, Hellenic Mining Co. Ltd., 1970-75; Director, General Manager, Hellenic Bank Ltd., 1976-. *Memberships:* Rotary Club of Nicosia; Vice-Chairman, Electricity Authority of Cyprus; Director, Central Bank of Cyprus, 1970-74. *Hobbies:* Swimming; Tennis. *Address:* 14 Eleftheroupoleos Str. Acropolis, Nicosia, Cyprus.

GHOSH, Debrata, b. 3 Feb. 1929, Calcutta, India. Banking Officer. m. Manjushree, 12 May, 1954, 4 daughters. *Education:* B.Sc., Calcutta University, 1947. *Appointments:* Banking Services since, 1947. *Memberships:* First Bengali Member of American Mathematical Society, 1951-53; Indian Methematical Society; Indian Institute of Bankers. *Publications:* Challenged relativity theory in 1946, and published Paper-back In The Background of the Michelson-Morley Experiment, 1978; Solved Bordered Magic Squares, Even Type; Various other papers on Number Theory. *Hobbies:* Chess; Problem solving in number theory; General correspondence. *Address:* Flat B-50, 16/5, Dover Lane, Calcutta, 700029, India.

GHOSH, Madhab Chandra, b. 1 Sept. 1935, Narisha, District-Dacca, Bangladesh. Medical. m. Renuka, 10 May 1959, 1 son, 1 daughter. *Education:* M.B.B.S., Calcutta University, 1957; M.R.C.P., Glasgow, 1962; M.R.C.P., Edinburgh, 1962; F.C.C.P., USA., 1977; F.R.C.P., Glasgow, 1978; F.R.C.P., Edinburgh, 1979. *Appointments:* Previous- Junior Hospital Medical Officer, Hawkhead Hospital, Glasgow U.K; Visiting Physician, Hospital for Crippled Children, Calcutta; Pool Officer, C.S.I.R., Hospital for Crippled Children; Visiting Physician, Kumar P.N. Roy Group of Hospitals & Rehabilitation Centre, Calcutta; Visiting Physician, Asharam Bhiwaniwalla Hospital, Calcutta; Present- Honorary Visiting Physician, Department of General Medicine, The Calcutta Medical Research Institute, Calcutta; Honorary Consultant in Medicine, S.E. Railway Head Quarters' Hospital, Garden Reach, Calcutta. *Memberships:* Indian Medical Association; Association of Physicians of India; Cardiological Society of India; The National College of Chest Physicians, India; Executive Committee, East India Chapter of American College of Chest Physicians. *Publications:* Contributions in Medical Journals on various topics including: Tongue—its clinical significance; Clinical application of Pulmonary Function Tests; Acromegaly with malignant Lymphoma; Lateral Medullary Syndrome; Critical analysis of 80 cases presenting with upper gastrointestinal haemorrhage; Study on the Etiology of Haemoptysis. *Honours:*

Government Prize in Clinical Medicine; Sir Pardey Luke's Memorial Scholarship in Medicine, Medical College, Calcutta. *Hobbies:* Reading; Writing; Travelling. *Address:* P86/G New C.I.T. Road, Calcutta, 700014, India.

GHOSH, Prasanta Kumar, b. 2 Nov. 1903, Calcutta, India. Professor of Medicine, (Retired). m. Sarala, 7 Oct. 1939. *Education:* M.B., University of Calcutta, 1928; Diploma, Tropical Medicine, Calcutta, 1931; Diploma, Tuberculosis Diseas, University of Wales, 1934; Membership of Royal College of Physicians, Edinburgh, 1935, London, 1935; Fellow of Royal College of Physicians, Edinburgh, 1950; Fellow of the College of Chest Physicians, USA., 1948; Fellow of Public Health Association, India, 1960. *Appointments:* Professor of Medicine (Chest), R.G.Kar Medical College, Calcutta; Medical Consultant to Chloride (Batteries), India; Guest Lecturer to All India Institute of Hygiene and Workers Education Center; Examiner in Medicine, Under-Graduate and Post-Graduate in various Universities; Inspector of various Medical Colleges. *Memberships:* Indian Medical Association; Indian Red Cross Society and Tuberculosis Association of India; Calcutta Medical Club; Leprosy Association of India; Indian Association of Occupational Health; Brahmo Samaj; Indian Association of Chest Diseases; Governor East India Chapter, American College of Chest Physicians, 1953-79. *Publications:* Published approximately 36 Original Papers in Indian and Foreign Journals; Contributed Chapters in text books of Medicine in India; Participated and contributed in various International Conferences in Chest Diseases and Occupational Medicine in Europe, North and South America and India; Introduced Domiciliary Treatment of Tuberculosis in Calcutta, 1948. *Honours:* Obtained various prizes, as a general scholar in medical college; Sir Ardeshir Dalal Memorial Oration, 1963; Warner Oration in Chest Diseases, 1977. *Hobbies:* Travelling; Social and Educational works. *Address:* 8 Tala Park Avenue, Calcutta, 700002, India.

GIBBONS, (John) David, b. 1927. Bermudian politician and businessman. m. Lully Lorentzen, 1958, 3 sons, 1 daughter. *Education:* BA, FBIM, Harvard University. *Appointments:* Social Welfare Board, 1948-58; Board of Civil Aviation, 1958-60; Board of Education, 1956-59; Trade Development Board, 1960-74; Governing Body & subsequently Chairman, Bermuda Technical Institute, 1956-73; Chairman, Board of Governors, Bermuda College, 1973-74; Chairman, Board of Education, 1973-74; Minister of Health & Welfare, 1974-75; Minister of Finance, 1975-; Premier, 1977-. *Memberships:* Harvard Club of New York. *Honours:* Justice of the Peace. *Address:* Leeward, Point Shares, Pembroke, Bermuda.

GIBBS, David Charles Leslie, b. 15 Aug. 1927, Melbourne, Australia. Company Director. m. 20 Mar. 1965, 2 sons, 2 daughters. *Education:* Eton College, Windsor, England, 1941-45; Honours Degree, Politics, Philosophy and Economics, (MA OXON), Chrst Church, Oxford University, England, 1945-48. *Appointments:* Director, Antony Gibbs Holdings Ltd., London, 1958-; Chairman, Gibbs Bright Co. Pty. Ltd., Australia, 1968-; Chairman, Charles Parker, Australia Pty. Ltd., 1974-; Chairman, Baillieu Bowring Pty. Ltd., Australia, 1977-; Chairman, Baillieu Bowring Marsh & MacLennan Pty. Ltd., Australia, 1981-; Director, Australia & New Zealand Banking Group Ltd., 1979-; Director, Perpetual Executors and Trustees Association of Augstalia Ltd., 1981-. *Memberships:* National Museum of Victoria; Trustee, World Wildlife Fund, Australia; Governor, London House for Overseas Graduates. *Hobbies:* Music; Fishing; Ornithology; Collecting Old Master Drawings. *Address:* 21 William Street, South Yarra, Victoria, 3141, Australia.

GIBBS, Humphrey Vicary, b. 22 Nov. 1902, London. Farmer; Director. m. Dame Molly Peel, 17 Jan. 1934, 5 sons. *Education:* Eton and Trinty Cambridge. *Memberships:* Athenaeum; Salisbury; Bulawayo. *Honours:* OBE 1959; KCMG 1960; KCVO 1965; GCVO 1969; PC 1969; Hon. LLD Birmingham 1969; Hon. DCL East Anglia 1969. *Address:* Private Bag 5583 W, Bulawayo, Zimbabwe,

GIBBS, Shirley Ann Morse, b. 18 Jan. 1935, Brisbane, Queensland, Australia. Occupational Therapist. m. Grahame Albert John Gibbs 24 June 1961, 4 sons. *Education:* Leaving Certificate, North Sydney Girls'

High School, 1952; Diploma AAOT, 1955. *Appointments:* Repatriation General Hospital NSW; Far West Children's Health Scheme NSW; Royal National Orthopaedic Hospital UK; North Ryde Psychiatric Centre, NSW; Whitehall Private Hospital NSW; Neringah Rehabilitation Centre NSW; Private Practice, Neurological Dysfunction, Consultant Occupational Therapist, Geriatric Services. *Memberships:* NSW Association Occupational Therapists; SPELD, NSW; Straight Talk Club; Stroke Club Resource Member; NSW Occupational Therapists Private Practice Group. *Publications:* People not Pigeonholes; Life. Be in it. Till Death or Hospital?; A Justifiable Polemic Paradigm?, 1979; Occupational Therapy Private Practice—A necessary development in the 1980s, 1980. *Honours:* Municipal Letter under Seal and mounted Ku-ring-gai Heraldic Crest presented for Voluntary Community Services in connection with IYDP, 1981. *Hobbies:* Family; Music; Literature; Gardening; Homemaking; Politics. *Address:* "Cherrycroft", 25 Melaleuca Drive, St Ives, NSW 2075, Australia.

GIBSON, Alan Hartley, b. 30 Dec. 1933, Sydney, Australia. Biologist. m. Ann Gregory, 9 Sept. 1957, 1 son, 2 daughters. *Education:* B.Sc. Agriculture Honours, University of Sydney, 1956; Ph.D., University of London, 1959. *Appointments:* Commenced as Research Officer, now Senior Principal Research Scientist, CSIRO Division of Plant Industry, Canberra, 1956-; Chairman, Microbiology Section. *Memberships:* Society for General Microbiology; Australian Society of Plant Physiology; Australian Institute of Agricultural Science; A.C.T. Rugby Referees Association, 1960-74, Honorary Secretary 1960-65; Inaugural Honorary Secretary, Australian Society Rugby Referees, 1962-68; Canberra North Rotary Club, 1980. *Publications:* A Treatise on Dinitrogen Fixation, Agronomy and Ecology, (with R.W.F. Hardy); Current Perspectives in Nitrogen Fixation (with W.E. Newton); Author of 60 publications in scientific journals and chapters in books, reviews, etc. *Honours:* First Class Honours and University Medal, University of Sydney, 1956. *Hobbies:* Reading; Rugby; Squash; Rotary; Travel. *Address:* 5 Jukes Place, Hackett, A.C.T., 2602, Australia.

GIBSON, (Sir) Alexander (Drummond), b. 11 Feb. 1926. Principal Conductor and Musical Director, Scottish National Orchestra 1959-. m. Anne Veronica Waggett, 1959, 3 sons. 1 daughter. *Education:* Glasgow University; Royal College of Music; Mozarteum, Salzburg, Austria; Accademia Chigiano, Siena, Italy; LRAM; ARCM ARCO. *Appointments:* Royal Signals 1944-48; Repetiteur and Assistant Conductor, Sadler's Wells Opera 1951-52; Assistant Conductor, BBC Scottish Orchestra, Glasgow 1952-54; Staff Conductor, Sadler's Wells Opera 1954-57; Musical Director, Sadler's Wells Opera 1957-59. *Honours:* Honorary RAM 1969; Honorary FRCM 1973; Honorary FRSAM 1973; Honorary RSA 1975; Order St. John 1975; FRSE 1978; FRSA 1980; Honorary LLD Aberdeen 1968; Honorary DMus. Glasgow 1972; D. University Stirling 1972; Hon. Doctor, Open University 1978; Freeman of the Burgh of Motherwell and Wishaw 1964; St. Mungo Prize 1970; Arnold Bax Memorial Medal for Conducting 1959; ISM Musician of the Year Award 1976; Sibelius Medal 1978; British Music Year Book—Musician of the Year 1980CBE 1967; Knight Bachelor 1977. *Address:* 15 Cleveden Gardens, Glasgow G12, Scotland.

GIBSON, David Sturart, b. 23 May 1925, Hobart, Tasmania. Surgeon. m. Margaret Jeanne Bryce, 14 May 1955, 3 sons, 1 daughter. *Education:* First Year Medicine, University Tasmania, 1947; M.B.,B.S., Ormond College, University of Melbourne, 1948-52; Primary F.R.C.S., Course, Royal College of Surgeons, 1958; F.R.C.S., London, 1959; F.R.A.C.S., Thoracic Surgery, 1960. *Appointments:* R.M.O. Royal Hobart Hospital, 1953-54; R.M.O., Repatriation General Hospital, Heidelberg, Victoria, 1955-56; Registrar, West Suffolk General Hospital, 1958-59; R.S.O., Brompton Hospital, London, 1959; Thoracic Surgeon, Royal Hobart Hospital, Tasmania, 1960-79, Senior Cardio-Thoracic Surgeon, 1979-; Visiting Thoracic Surgeon, Repatriation General Hospital, Hobart, 1960-. *Memberships:* Cardiac Society, Australia & New Zealand; Thoracic Society of Australia; Royal Society of Medicine; State Committee, Royal Australian College of Surgeons, 1965-72, State Chairman, 1971-72; Tasmania Club, President, 1981-82; Australian Medical Association. *Publications:* Cardiac Hydatid Cysts, Thorax, 1964. *Hobbies:* Fishing; Swimming; Boating; Gardening. *Address:* 37 Richards Avenue, Dodges Ferry, Tasmania, 7173.

GIBSON (Sir) Donald Evelyn Edward, b. 11 Oct. 1908, Northenden, Cheshire. Architect, Town Planner, Landscape Architect. m. (1) 19 Oct. 1934 (deceased), (2) 16 Aug. 1978, 3 sons, 1 daughter. *Education:* BA., Honours Architecture, Manchester; MA., F.R.I.B.A., M.R.T.P.I., F.I.L.A. *Appointments:* Scientific Officer, Building Research Station, 1935-37; Deputy County Architect, Isle of Ely, 1937-39; City Architect & Planning Officer, Coventry, 1939-54; County Architect, Nottinghamshire, 1954-56; Director General, War Office, London, 1956-60; Controller General, Ministry of Public Building and Works, London, 1960-70. *Publications:* Papers in Professional Journals. *Honours:* C.B.E., 1952; Knighthood, 1960; President R.I.B.A. Hoffman Wood, Professor of Architecture, Leeds, Coventry award of Merit; Honorary Fellowship of Institute of Landscape Architects. *Hobbies:* Gardening; Fishing; Steam Railways. *Address:* Bryn Castell, Landdona, Isle of Anglesey, Gwynedd, LL58 8TR, Wales.

GIBSON, Jack Andrew, b. 18 Feb. 1951, Winnipeg, Manitoba, Canada. Sports Editor. *Education:* Diploma, MacGregor Collegiate Institute, Manitoba, 1970; BA., Brandon University, (History Major), 1974. *Appointments:* Brandon Sun, Sportswriter, 1973-75; Sportswriter, Winnipeg Tribune, Brandon Sun, 1975-, appointed Sports Editor, 1978. *Honours:* Outstanding Male Athlete, MacGregor Collegiate, 1968,69,70; Varsity Athletic (Basketball) Certificate of Recognition, Brandon University, 1973; Service Appreciation Award, Brandon University, 1975; Citizenship Award, MacGregor Collegiate, 1970; Certificate of Merit, Time Weekly Newsmagazine, 1969. *Hobby:* Reading. *Address:* 1442 Applewood Bay, Brandon, Manitoba, Canada.

GIBSON, Joseph David, b. 26 Jan. 1928. Former High Commissioner. m. Emily Susan Bentley, 3 sons, 2 daughters. *Education:* Teachers Certificate, Auckland Teachers' College; BA, Auckland University, New Zealand. *Appointments:* Assistant Teacher, Suva Boys' Grammar School, 1952-57; Principal, Suva Educational Institute, 1957; Principal, Queen Victoria School, Fiji, 1961-62, (Assistant Teacher, 1958-59; Senior Master, 1959; First Assistant, 1960); Secondary School Inspector, Fiji Education Department, 1964-65; Assistant Director of Education, 1966-69; Deputy Director, 1970; Director of Education and Permanent Secretary for Education, 1971-74; Deputy High Commissioner, London, 1974-76; High Commissioner for Fiji, 1976-; Represented Fiji at: Directors of Education Conferences, Western Samoa and Pago Pago, 1968, Honolulu, 1970; Commonwealth Ministers of Education Meeting, Canberra, 1971; Head of Fiji Delegation, Commonwealth Ministers of Education Meeting, Jamaica, 1974. *Memberships:* University Council, University of South Pacific; Royal Commonwealth Society. *Honours:* CBE, 1979. *Hobbies:* Golf; Fishing; Hockey. *Address:* 97 Platts Lane, London, NW3 7NH, England.

GIBSON, Robert Walter Lockhart, b. 25 May 1937, Brisbane, Australia. Management Consultant. m. Katherine Chalmers, 4 May 1963, 1 son, 2 daughters. *Education:* Bachelor of Engineering, 1956-61, Bachelor of Commerce, 1967, University of Queensland; Business Management, University of Toronto, 1963-66. *Appointments:* Graduate Engineer, Vickers Armstrong Engrs. Ltd., UK, 1962; Industrial Engineer, Corning Glass Works of Canada, 1962-65, Canadian Pacific Subsidiary, 1965-66; Technical Manager, United Packages Ltd., (Brisbane), 1967-70; Production Executive, Besley & Pike Pty. Ltd., 1971-74; Senior Partner, Gibson Associates (Management Consultants), 1974-. *Memberships:* The Institution of Production Engineers; The Institution of Engineers, Australia; Institution of Management Consultants, Australia; Australian Institution of Management; Australian Computer Society. *Publications:* Theses: Pneumatic Gauging in Production, 1961; Capital Expenditure Decision Making, 1970; Study of Envelope Making Industry in Australia. *Hobbies:* Sailing; Antique Furniture; Veteran and Vintage Cars. *Address:* 164 Leybourne Street, Chelmer, 4068, Brisbane, Australia.

GIDIGASU, Mensa Komla Davidson, b. 5 Mar. 1935, Nsuta, Volta Region of Ghana. Civil Engineer. m. Anne Gwendoline West, 8 Aug. 1968, 1 son, 3 daughters. *Education:* M.Sc., Transportation Engineering, 1963; Ph.D., Geotechnical Engineering, Technical University, Warsaw, Poland, 1969. *Appointments:* Highway Engineer, Ghana National Construction Corporation, 1964; Assistant Research Officer, Geotechnical Engineering 1965; Research Officer, CSIR, 1965-72, Senior Research Officer, 1972-75, Principal Research Officer, 1976-; Head, Geotechnical Engineering Division, CSIR, Building & Road Research Institute, 1972-78; Acting Director, Building & Road Research Institute, 1979-. *Memberships:* Executive Committee, Association of African Industrial Technology Organisations; International Society of Soil Mechanics and Foundation Engineering; Institution of Highway Engineers, UK; Ghana Institution of Engineers; Management Board, Ghana Journal of Science; Science Committee of Council for Scientific and Industrial Research, Ghana; Editor, Ghana Engineer, Journal of Ghana Institution of Engineers. *Publications:* Author, Laterite soil engineering, 1976; Editor, Proc. Regional Conference for Africa on Soil Mechanic Foundation Engineering (with A A Hammond & J K Gogo); Ten Research Papers in International Journals; 14 Research Papers in the Proceedings of International Conferences; 16 Research and Technical Papers published by Building & Road Research Institute, Ghana. *Honours:* United Nations Trusteeship Scholarship holder, 1957-64. *Hobbies:* Gardening; Animal husbandry. *Address:* P.O. Box 118, Kadjebi, Volta Region, Ghana.

GIESE, Nancy (Mrs Harry C Giese), b. 31 Jan. 1922, Brisbane, Queensland. Teacher. m. Harry Christian, 4 May 1946, 1 son 1 daughter. *Education:* Teachers Training College, Queensland; Diploma Physical Education, University of Queensland. *Appointments:* Primary Teacher, Queensland Department of Education, 1936-39; Physical Education Specialist Teacher, Queensland Department of Education, 1940-46. *Memberships:* President NT Arts Council, 1972-; Chairman Darwin Community College Council, 1976-; Director, Arts Council of Australia; NT Post-School Advisory Council; Museums & Art Galleries Board of NT; Arts Education Advisory Committee; Alice Springs Community College Council; Brown's Mart. Board of Trustees; Chairman, Darwin Community College Business Committee; Chairman Darwin Community College Advisory Committees on Art, Music, Drama; Past-President National Council of Women of NT; Community Arts Project Committee; Subject Area Committee (Arts) Curriculum, NT., Education Department. Published journal articles, Darwin Community College, 1977, Community Colleges & The Tertiary Education Commission, 1977, The Arts in Remote Areas, 1978. *Honours:* M.B.E., 1971; O.B.E., 1978. *Hobbies:* Music; Reading; Walking. *Address:* 50 Temira Crescent, Larrakeyah, Darwin, N.T., 5790, Australia.

GIFFORD, Alfred Silva Harril, b. 2 Mar. 1897, East Melbourne, Australia. Solicitor & Company Director. m. Gwen Leaven, 2 Mar. 1922, (Deceased), 1 son. *Education:* SA, LL.B, University of Adelaide. *Appointments:* Articled Law Clerk, 1913; Solicitor, South Australia, 1919, Victoria, 1920; Company Director, Andrews Bros. Proprietary Limited, 1921; Company Chairman & Director, 1943. *Memberships:* Chairman of Directors, Union Assurance Society of Australia; President, Federated Taxpayers' Association of Australia. *Honours:* OBE, 1972; Knight of St John, 1947; DCM, 1917. *Hobbies:* Gardening; Playing Piano & Pipe Organs; Reading. *Address:* 3 Audrey Crescent, Burwood, Victoria, 3125, Australia.

GIFFORD, Edwin Chester, b. 16 July 1901, Albert Park, Victoria, Australia. Banking. m. Dulcie Edna Conkey, 20 Feb. 1934, 1 son, 4 daughters. *Education:* Prince Alfred College, Adelaide; Fellow Australian Society of Accountants; Fellow Australian Institute of Management. *Appointments:* Commonwealth Bank of Australia, 1918-64; Retired as Chief Manager for Tasmania, 1959-64. *Memberships:* Chairman of St. John Ambulance Council for Tasmania, 1964-78, Board Freemasons Homes, 1969-, Trustees Grand Lodge of Tasmania, Temples Fund Lodge of Tasmania, Board of Lillian Martin Homes for the Aged, 1969-, Trustees of Ex-Service Womens Homes Association, 1968-, Trustees of Friends of Music, 1974-; President St. John Ambulance Council for Tasmania, 1978-; State President Australian Kidney Foundation, 1969 81; President Australian Institute of Management, 1965-73; Vice-President of Royal Society of Tasmania, 1970-

71, Red Cross, 1964-70; National Vice President Kidney Foundation, 1978-; State Councillor National Heart Foundation, 1960-; Councillor & Past President Save the Children Fund, Tasmania, 1965-. *Honours:* Knight of Grace, Order of St. John of Jerusalem, 1971; Member, Order of Australia, 1976. *Hobbies:* Bowls; Gardening. *Address:* 194 Churchill Avenue, Sandy Bay, 7005, Tasmania.

GILBERT, John Trounsell, b. 19 Apr. 1927, Bermuda. Civil Servant. m. Edythe Margaret Jamieson, 8 Aug. 1970. *Education:* BA., University of Toronto, Canada, 1944-48; Colonial Administrative Service Course, Pembroke College, Cambridge, 1948-49. *Appointments:* British Colonial Administrative Service, Ghana and Bermuda, 1950-60; School Master, England and Bermuda, 1960-74; Civil Servant, 1974-; Assistant Secretary, Bermuda Cabinet, 1974-76; Clerk to the Parliament of Bermuda, 1976-. *Memberships:* Honorary Secretary, Treasurer, Bermuda Branch, Commonwealth Parliamentary Association; Council of the Bermuda Branch of the Royal Commonwealth Society, Chairman, 1978-80; United Oxford and Cambridge University Club, London. *Publications:* Articles published in the Annual Bermuda Heritage Month Magazine. *Honours:* Cup for winning the Round Bermuda Outboard Motorboat Race, 1956. *Hobbies:* Tennis; Outboard Motor Boating; Sailing; Stamp collecting. *Address:* Dunelm, Strawberry Hill, Paget 6-19, Bermuda.

GILCHRIST, Hugh, b. 8 Aug. 1916, Sydney, Australia. Diplomat (Retired). m. Elizabeth Dalton Richardson, 11 Apr. 1950, 1 son, 2 daughters. *Education:* University of Sydney, BA., Honours, 1936, LL.B., 1941. *Appointments:* Admitted to practice as Solicitor in New South Wales, 1940; Australian Army, 1941-45; Department of External Affairs, 1945, Service in Canberra, London, Berlin, Paris, Greece, Jakarta, Pretoria/Cape Town; Australian High Commissioner in Tanzania, 1962-66; Head, Information and Cultural Relations Branch, Department of Foreign Affairs, Canberra, 1966-68; Ambassador to Greece, 1968-72; Head, Legal & Treaties Division, 1974-76; Ambassador to Spain, 1976-79; Retired 1979. *Memberships:* Literature Board of the Australia Council, 1980-; Commonwealth Club, Canberra. *Publications:* Australia's First Greeks (monograph), 1977. *Hobbies:* Historical research into Greek-Australian relations. *Address:* 5 Grey Street, Deakin, A.C.T., 2600, Australia.

GILES, Thomas Harle, b. 9 June 1935, Wellington, New Zealand. Director/General Manager. m. Gwen Isabel Wilson, 9 Nov. 1962, 1 son. *Education:* Master of Business Administration, University of Sydney, 1974-76; Fellow, Australian Society of Accountants, Bankers Institute of Australasia, Australian Institute of Management; Associate, Building Societies Institute Incorporated. *Appointments:* Godfrey Phillips Australia Pty Ltd., 1954-56; Australia & New Zealand Banking Group Ltd., 1959-69; Australian Mercantile Loan & Finance Company Ltd., 1969-71; Australian International Finance Corporation Ltd., 1971-76; United Permanent Building Society Ltd., 1976-; Director of: United Permanent Building Society Ltd., (NSW); United Permanent Building Society Ltd., (Northern Territory); Joint Services Pty Ltd.; United Credit Union Ltd.; Excelsior Insurance Ltd.; Building Societies Indemnity Fund Ltd.; Permanent Building Societies Association of New South Wales. *Memberships:* Permanent Building Societies Advisory Committee, 1980-; Building & Construction Industry Consultative Committee, 1979-; Housing Finance Development Committee; International Union of Building Societies and Savings Associations. *Hobbies:* Philately; Reading. *Address:* 21 Kanowar Avenue, East Killara, NSW, 2071, Australia.

GILHOTRA, Jagmohan Singh, b. 15 Apr. 1946, India. Psychiatrist. m. Gurmeet, 4 Apr. 1971, 1 son. *Education:* MB.,BS, 1969; DPM, (London), 1977; MRC.Psych., (UK), 1978. *Appointments:* Medical Officer in India (Government Service), 1969-73; Senior House Officer, Psychiatry, Oakwood Hospital, Maidstone, UK, 1974-75; Registrar Psych., Belmont Hospital, Sutton, UK, 1975-77; Registrar & Senior Registrar, North Middlesex and St Mary's Hospitals, London, 1977-79; Medical Superintendent, Bloomfield Hospital, Orange, NSW, Australia, 1979-80; Deputy Medical Superintendent, Newcastle Psychiatric Centre, Newcastle, NSW, Australia, 1980-. *Memberships:* Medical Defence Union of

the UK; PMOA of NSW, Australia. *Hobbies:* Music; Travelling; Tennis; Photography. *Address:* 41 Curzon Road, New Lambton, NSW, 2305, Australia.

GILL, Frank, (The Honourable), b. 30 Jan. 1917, Wellington, New Zealand. Airman. m. Barbara Benson, 11 Apr. 1942, 3 daughters. *Education:* St. Patricks College, Wellington; R.A.F., Staff College (P.S.A); U.K., Joint Services Staff College (I.S.S.C.); Imperial Defence College, (I.D.C.). *Appointments:* Royal New Zealand Air Force, 1937-69, including four years in R.A.F., 1939-43; Member of Parliament, 1969-80; Minister of Health and Immigration, 1975-78; Minister of Defence and Police, 1978-80; New Zealand Ambassador in USA., 1980. *Memberships:* Royal New Zealand Yacht Squadron. *Honours:* D.S.O., 1941; C.B.E., 1962. *Hobbies:* Sailing; Farming. *Address:* New Zealand Embassy, 37 Observatory Circle, Washington D.C. 20008, USA.

GILL, K S, b. 25 June 1934, District Lyallpur, Pakistan. Dental Surgeon. m. Bhupinder Kaur, 30 Sept. 1962, 1 son, 2 daughters. *Education:* B.D.S., 1956; M.D.S., 1965; P.D.E.S., (1), Punjab State Dental Education Service, Class I. *Appointments:* Junior & Senior House Surgeon, Government Dental College & Hospital Amritsar, India, 1956-57, Demonstrator, 1957-60, Assistant Professor, 1960-65, Professor & Head of Operative Dentistry Department & Dental Radiology, 1965-79; Head of Dental Wing, Government Medical College, Patiala, India, 1979-. *Memberships:* Dental Council of India; Indian Dental Association, Punjab State Branch (Treasurer for some years); Ex-President of Amritsar Branch of Indian Dental Association; Various academic bodies of Guru Nanak Dev University Amritsar & Punjabi University Patiala. *Publications:* Five publications in the journal of Indian Dental Association, extracts also appear in American Journals; Thesis for M.D.S. *Honours:* Awarded College First Prize in General Knowledge at Khalsa College, Amritsar, 1951. *Hobbies:* Reading books connected with History; Gardening. *Address:* 362 Basant Avenue, Amritsar, India.

GILL, Khem Singh, b. 1 Sept. 1930, V.Kaleke, District Faridkot, Punjab, India. Professor, Dean. m. Surjit Kaur, 1948, 2 sons, 1 daughter. *Education:* B.Sc., Agriculture, Crop Botany, Punjab University, 1949; M.Sc., Agriculture, Genetics & Plant Breeding, Punjab University, 1951; Ph.D., Genetics, California, USA., 1966. *Appointments:* Research Assistant, Department of Agriculture, Punjab, 1951-55, Assistant Oilseed Breeder, 1955-63; Professor, Associate Professor of Genetics, Punjab Agricultural University, 1966-68; Zonal Coordinator, (Wheat), I.C.A.R., 1972-; Professor of Plant Breeding, (Wheat), Punjab Agricultural University, 1968-, Professor & Head of Department, Plant Breeding, 1968-79, Dean, College of Agriculture cum Professor of Plant Breeding, 1979-. *Memberships:* The Crop Improvement Society of India; First President, The Crop Inprovement Society of India, 1974-79; Plant Breeding Association, PAU, Ludhiana, First President, 1971-73; Indian Society of Genetics and Plant Breeding, Vice-President, 1975-76; Indian Society of Genetics and Plant Breeding, 1971-72; The Genetic Association of India, Vice-President, 1976; Fellow, The Indian Society of Genetics and Plant Breeding, The Genetic Association of India; The Society for the Advancement of Breeding Research in Asia and Oceania; Sigma Xi Society of USA. Numerous Office and Committee assignments in professional Societies; Fellow of the Indian National Science Academy. *Publications:* Significant research contributions in the improvement of crop plants, providing guidance as a major advisor to 32 PhD., and M.Sc., students; Developed numerous improved varieties of crops including: Wheat, WG 357, WG 377, WL 711, HD 2009, KSML 3, WL 1562, DWL 5023 & TL 419; Hybrid PHB 47, 1979; Synthetic Hybrid PSB 8, 1979; Linseed, LC 185, 1970, LC 45, 1973, LC 54, 1979. *Honours:* Rafi Ahmed Kidwai Memorial Prize, 1976; Cash Prize by the Punjab Agricultural University. *Hobbies:* Social and religious work. *Address:* 6/7 PAU Campus, Ludhiana, Punjab, India.

GILL, Stephen M, b. 25 June 1932, Sialkot, Punjab, India. Writer/Book Publisher. m. Sarala, 17 Feb. 1970, 1 son, 2 daughters. *Education:* BA., Punjab University, 1956; MA., Agra University, 1963; Doctoral candidate (English Literature), Ottowa University, 1967-70; Oxford University, summer school, (English Literature), 1971. *Appointments:* President, Vesta Publications Ltd. *Memberships:* National Vice President and National Director, World Federalists of Canada; Former editor, Canadian World Federalist newspaper; Emergency World Council; National Officer, in Canada, for the Movement for Political World Union; Founder and former President, Canadian Authors Association, Cornwall Branch. *Publications:* Political Convictions of Shaw; Scientific Romances of H G Wells; Six Symbolist Plays of Yeats; Reflections & Wounds (poems); Life's Vagaries (stories); Discovery of Bangladesh (history); Why (a novel); English Grammar for Beginners; Immigrant (a novel); The Loyalist City (a novel); Sketches of India (essays); Moans & Waves (poems); Editor, Green Snow—an anthology of Canadian poets of Asian origin; Co-editor, Poets of the Capital—an anthology of Ottawa poets; Co-editor, Seaway Valley poets,—an anthology; Editor, Tales from Canada for children everywhere—an anthology; Simon and The Snowman (childrens story book). *Hobbies:* Writing; Dancing; Giving Talks; Meeting people and making friends. *Address:* PO Box 1641, Cornwall, Ontario, K6H 5V6, Canada.

GILLARD, Eugene William, b. 26 Sept. 1939, Melbourne, Australia. Barrister. m. Judith-Ann Gahan, 7 Apr. 1964, 4 sons. *Education:* LL.B, Melbourne University, 1962. *Appointments:* Solicitor, Messrs Evans Masters & Gilbert, Melbourne, 1963-64; Messrs Freshfield, London, 1964-65; Barrister-at-Law, 1965-; Queen's Counsel, 1979. *Memberships:* Victorian Bar Council, 1974-80; Victorian Law Reform Advisory Council, 1981-. *Hobbies:* Cricket; Running; Swimming; Travel. *Address:* 97 South Road, Brighton Beach, Victoria, 3186, Australia.

GILLARD, Reginald, b. 13 Mar. 1920, Lithgow. Former Member of Parliament. m. Irene Audrey Wallace, 3 Apr. 1948, 2 sons, 2 daughters. *Education:* Leaving Certificate, Lithgow High School. *Appointments:* Junior Clerk to Accountant, Lithgow City Council, 1936-56; Managing Prtner, Hassans Walls Motors,Lithgow and Lithgow Soft Drink Company, 1956-75; Member of Parliament, 1975-. *Memberships:* President Lithgow Rotary, 1957-80; Lithgow Legacy 1953-, Secretary for ten years, President, 1961, 1974,75. *Hobbies:* Sport, particularly Bowls; Reading.*Address:* 48 Hayley Street, Lithgow 2790, NSW, Australia.

GILLESPIE, Lyall Leslie, b. 23 July 1919, Queanbeyan, New South Wales. Public Servant. m. Norma Joan Bogg, 6 Sept. 1941, 2 sons, 2 daughters. *Education:* Leaving Certificate Examination, NSW., 1936; Qualified Accountant by correspondence. *Appointments:* Assistant Director, Department of Works, Canberra, 1958-60, Assistant Administrator, Northern Territory, 1960-63; Assistant Secretary, Department of the Interior, Canberra, 1964-72; Commissioner for Housing, Department of the Capital Territory, 1973-78; City Manager, Department of The Capital Territory, Canberra, 1978-. *Memberships:* Australian Society of Accountants; Past-President, Canberra & District Historical Society; Past-President, Horticultural Society of Canberra; Canberra Archaeological Society; Goulburn & District Historical Society; The Heraldry & Genealogy Society of Canberra; Associate Fellow, Australian Institute of Management; Affiliate, Institution of Radio and Electronics Engineers, Australia; Queanbeyan & District Historical Museum Society. *Publications:* Author The Read/Reid Family in Australia 1849-1979, various articles on local history in newspapers and historical journals. *Hobbies:* Archaeology; Historical Research; Gardening; Photography. *Address:* Lynora, 18 Ferdinand Street, Campbell, Canberra City, ACT, 2601, Australia.

GILLIES, William Joseph, b. 13 Mar. 1933, St John's, Newfoundland. Labour disputes mediator, Government of Canada. m. Ruby Earle, 13 Mar. 1961, 2 sons, 2 daughters. *Education:* High School, 1961. *Appointments:* Royal Canadian Air Force; International Representative for International Clerks Union; Secretary Treasurer, Newfoundland Federation of Labour; Labour disputes mediator, Government of Canada. *Memberships:* President, National Karate Association of Canada; Newfoundland & Labrador Amateur Sports Federation; Director, Pan American Karate Union. *Hobbies:* Karate; Dog showing; Writing; Carpentry. *Address:* PO Box 375, Goulds, Newfoundland, Canada A0A 2KO.

GILLIGAN, Bernard Sutcliffe, b. 22 Sept 1934, Warracknabeal, Australia. Neurologist. m. Gwynneth Hamlyn Bignall, 14 Dec. 1957, 2 sons. *Education:* Wesley College, Melbourne, Australia, 1951; M.B.B.S., Melbourne University, 1957; Royal Australian College of Physicians, M.R.A.C.P., 1961, F.R.A.C.P., 1971; F.A.C.R.M., Australian College of Rehabilitation Medicine, 1980. *Appointments:* Senior Neurologist, Alfred Hospital, Melbourne, 1965-; Visiting Neurologist, Fairfield Hospital, Melbourne, 1965-; Consultant Neurologist, Royal Women's Hospital, Melbourne, 1972-; Associate, Monash University Department of Medicine, 1976-. *Memberships:* Australian Association of Neurologists, Council Member, 1977-; Australian Medical Association; Melbourne Club. *Publications:* Numerous articles on various Neurological Disorders. *Honours:* Alfred Hospital Residents Prize in Medicine, 1955; Queens College Scholarship, Melbourne University, 1951, Commonwealth Scholarship, 1951, Grieve Prize in Paediatrics, 1957; Overseas Travelling Scholarship, Royal Australian College of Physicians, 1963. *Hobbies:* Swimming; Walking; Travelling. *Address:* 11 Mulgoa Street, Brighton, 3186, Australia.

GILLING, Ronald Andrew, b. 27 Oct. 1917, Edinburgh, Scotland. Architect. m. Caroline Mary Henty Silvester, 22 June 1944, 2 daughters. *Education:* BA, University of Sydney, 1936-39, 1946-47. *Appointments:* War Service, AIF, 1939-45, Captain, Royal Australian Engineers, Service in Northern Territory of Australia, New Guinea, Borneo; Partner/Director, Joseland Gilling, Architects, since, 1947; Councillor, RAIA NSW Chapter Council, 1958-73; Vice-President, NSW Chapter, 1960-64; President, NSW Chapter, 1964-66; Federal Councillor, 1967-73; Vice-President, RAIA, 1969-70; Federal President, 1970-71; Chairman, National Building and Construction Council, 1970-72; Vice-President, Building Science Forum, 1973-77; Federal Government Nominee, National Capital Planning Committee, 1970-76; NSW Government Nominee, NSW Board of Architects, 1971-; President, Commonwealth Association of Architects, 1973-76; Councillor, International Union of Architects, 1972-78; Vice-President, 1975-78. *Memberships:* World Society of Ekistics; Commonwealth Human Ecology Council, London. *Honours:* OBE, 1977; RAIA Gold Meal, 1977; Life Fellowship RAIA; Honorary Fellowship American Institute of Architects, 1978. *Hobbies:* Skiing; Sailing; Flying. *Address:* 71 Ku-Ring-Gai Avenue, Turramurra, NSW, Australia.

GILLISON, Andrew Napier, b. 24 July 1937, Mackay, Queensland, Australia. Research Scientist, Plant Ecologist & Biogeographer. m. Patricia May Kenway, 7 Dec. 1963, 2 sons, 1 daughter. *Education:* Queensland Diploma in Agriculture, 1956; B.Agr.Sc., University of Queensland, 1963; MSc, 1971, PhD, 1977, Australian National University. *Appointments:* Agricultural Officer, 1957-64, Botanist, 1964-66, Plant Ecologist, Lecturer, 1966-72, Papua New Guinea; Principal Research Scientist, Plant Ecologist, CSIRO, Canberra, ACT, Australia. *Memberships:* Ecological Society of Australia (INC), President, 1981-82; Institute of Australian Geographers; Pacific Science Association. *Publications:* Numerous scientific publications on plant ecology in Australia and south-west Pacific. *Hobbies:* Fishing; Butterfly collecting; Sculpture; Natural History of South-West Pacific. *Address:* 13 Florina Place, Hawker, ACT, 2614, Australia.

GILMORE, Ian George Charles (Brigadier), b. 30 June 1925, Wingham, N.S.W., Australia. Director, Australian Counter Disaster College, Department of Defence. m. Alison Shirley Cayley, 17 Apr. 1954, 2 sons, 1 daughter. *Education:* Royal Military College, Duntroon, 1944-46; Civil Engineering, Sydney University, 1948-50; Royal Military College of Science, Shrivenham, UK., 1954-56; Australian Staff College, Fort Queenscliffe, 1960; US Army Command & General Staff College, Fort Leavenworth, Kansas, 1964-65; Australian Administrative Staff College, Mt. Eliza, 1969. *Appointments:* Australian Regular Army, 1943-78, including service in BCOF in Japan; 1st Commonwealth Division in Korea; 1st Australian Logistic Support Group in Vietnam; Australian Embassy, Washington D.C; ANZUK Force in Singapore & Malaysia; CO 1st Field Engineer Regiment & CRE 1st Aust. Div. 1962-64; Commander 1st Aust. Log. Spt. Gp. Vietnam, 1967-68; Chief Engineer, Northern Command 1969 72; Commander, Puckapunyal Area, 1972-73; Chief of Staff & Dep. Comd., ANZUK Force, 1973-75; Commandant Aust. Staff College, 1975-78;

Director, Australian Counter Disaster College, Mount Macedon, 1978-; Brigadier (Retired). *Memberships:* Legacy; Naval & Military Club, Melbourne; Royal Queensland Golf Club, Brisbane; Barwon Heads Golf Club, Barwon Heads; Fellow, The Australian Institute of Management. *Honours:* MID, Korean War, 1952; OBE, Vietnam War, 1968; ADC to H.M. The Queen, 1977-78. *Hobbies:* Golf; Tennis; Rugby; Gardening. *Address:* The Laurels, Mount Macedon, Victoria, 3441, Australia.

GILMOUR, Clyde, b. 28 Dec. 1923, Brisbane. Public Servant. m. Thelma Ruby Stephan, 13 Dec. 1952, 2 sons, 2 daughters. *Education:* Bachelor of Science Degree; Bachelor of Engineering Degree with Honours; Diploma in Mechanical & Electrical Engineering. *Appointments:* Apprentice with Brisbane City Council Tramways & Power House; RAAF, 1943; Teacher, Central Technical College, Brisbane, 1951; Academic Staff, University of Queensland, Mechanical Engineering Department, 1951; Principal, Central Technical College, 1963; Director, Technical & Further Education, 1964, Deputy Director-General of Education, 1972, Director-General, 1976. *Memberships:* Institution of Engineers (Australia); Fellow, Australian Institute of Management; Society of Mechanical Engineers; Australian College of Education. *Honours:* Florence Taylor Medallion for Australasia, 1972. *Hobbies:* Boating; Fishing; Sailing; Squash. *Address:* 10 Aaron Avenue, Hawthorne, 4171, Brisbane, Queensland, Australia.

GILPIN, Alan, b. 20 Aug. 1924, Whitley Bay, Northumberland, England. Public Servant. m. Sheila Margaret Humphries, 3 Apr. 1954, 2 sons, 1 daughter. *Education:* BSc.(Econ.)Hons.), University of London, UK, 1953; PhD.(Econ.), University of Queensland, Australia, 1974; Chartered Engineer and Fellow of Institute of Energy, UK, 1960. *Appointments:* Chief Environmental Health Officer, Wallasey, England, 1958-61; Planning Engineer, Central Electricity Generating Board, England, 1961-65; Director, Air Pollution Council of Queensland, Australia, 1965-72; Chairman, Environment Protection Authority, Victoria, Australia, 1972-74; Director, Department of Environment, Housing and Community Development, Canberra, Australia, 1975-77; Assistant Director, State Pollution Control Commission, New South Wales, Australia, 1977-80; Assistant Chief Planner, Planning and Environment Commission, New South Wales, Australia, 1980; Commissioner of Inquiry, Ministry of Planning and Environment, New South Wales, Australia, 1980-. *Memberships:* Fellow, Australian Institute of Energy. *Publications:* Control of Air Pollution, 1963; Dictionary of Economic Terms, 1966, 4th ed. 1978; Dictionary of Energy Technology, 1969, 2nd ed. 1981; Air Pollution, 1971, 2nd ed. 1978; Dictionary of Environmental Terms, 1975, Portuguese Ed. 1980; Environment Policy in Australia, 1980; The Australian Environment: Twelve Controversial Issues, 1980. *Honours:* General Editor, Australian Environment Series, University of Queensland Press, 1970-; Visiting Fellow, Australian National University, Centre for Resource and Environment Studies, 1981. *Hobby:* Family Genealogy. *Address:* 14 Jones Place, Weetangera, Canberra, ACT. 2610, Australia.

GINDIN, Jeffrey J, b. 11 Aug. 1946, Linz, Austria. Attorney-at-Law. m. Shellee Mae, 21 July 1975, 1 son. *Education:* BA, 1967, LL.B, 1970, University of Manitoba; Called to Bar of Manitoba, 1971; Called to Bar of Ontario, 1978; Called to Bar of Saskatchewan, 1980. *Appointments:* Walsh, Micay & Co., 1971-78; Gindin, Soronow & Co., 1978-. *Memberships:* Manitoba Trial Lawyers Association; American Trial Lawyers Association; International Commission of Jurists; Canadian Law Teachers Association; Criminal Justice Section of Bar Association. *Publications:* Contributor of articles and Lectures on Law. *Honours:* Dean's Honour List, Law School; Barristers Prize, Law School; Constitutional Law Prize, Law School. *Hobbies:* Tennis; Reading; Writing. *Address:* 116 Queenston Street, Winnipeg, Manitoba, R3N 0W5, Canada.

GIRDWOOD, Ronald Haxton, b. 19 Mar. 1917, Arbroath, Angus, Scotland. Professor; Consultant Physician. m. Mary Elizabeth Williams, 31 July 1945, 1 son, 1 daughter. *Education:* MB., Ch.B.(Hons.), University of Edinburgh, Scotland, 1939; MRCP.Ed., 1941; MRCP.Lond., 1944; FRCP.Ed., 1945; PhD., 1952, MD(Gold Medal),1954, University of Edinburgh; FRCP.Lond., 196; FRC.Path., 1964; FRS.Ed., 1964.

Appointments: Royal Army Medical Corps, Secon World War, 1942-46; Lecturer in Medicine, 1946-50, Senior Lecturer (and later Reader), 1951-58, Professor of Therapeutics and Clinical Pharmacology, 1962-, Dean of the Faculty of Medicine, 1975-79, University of Edinburgh, Scotland; Rockefeller Research Fellow, University of Michigan, USA, 1948-49; Consultant Physician, National Health Service, 1950-; Vice-President, Royal College of Physicians of Edinburgh, Scotland, 1980-. *Memberships:* President, British Society for Haematology, 1963-64; Chairman, Scottish Group of the Nutrition Society, 1961-62; Council of Royal College of Physicians of Edinburgh, 1966-69, 1978-; UK Committee on Safety of Medicines, 1972-; Executive, Medico-Pharmaceutical Forum, 1972-74. *Publications:* Editor (with A N Smith), Malabsorption, 1969; Editor, Blood Disorders Due to Drugs and Other Agents, 1973; Editor (with S Alstead), Textbook of Medical Treatment, 1978; Editor, Clinical Pharmacology, 1979; 200 papers to a wide variety of medical books and journals. *Honours:* Ettles Scholarship; Leslie Gold Medal in Medicine; Royal Victoria Hospital Tuberculosis Trust Gold Medal; Wightman, Keith and Beaney Prizes, University of Edinburgh, 1939; Gold Medal for MD thesis, University of Edinburgh, 1954; Cullen Prize, Royal College of Physicians of Edinburgh, 1970; Lilly Award Lecture, Royal College of Physicians of Edinburgh, 1979; Suniti Panja Gold Medal, Calcutta School of Tropical Medicine, 1980. *Hobbies:* Photography; Painting in oils. *Address:* 2 Hermitage Drive, Edinburgh EH10 6DD, Scotland.

GLADSTONES, John Sylvester, b. 14 Feb. 1932, Perth, Western Australia. Agronomist. m. Helen Patricia Burns,LRAM, 19 Dec. 1962, 1 son, 1 daughter. *Education:* BSc.Agric.(Hons.1st class), 1955, PhD, 1959, University of Western Australia. *Appointments:* Post-doctorate Fellow, Canada National Research Council, Ottawa, Canada, 1958-59; Lecturer and Senior Lecturer in Agronomy, University of Western Australia, 1960-71; Senior and Principal Plant Breeder, Western Australian Department of Agriculture, 1971-. *Memberships:* Australian Institute of Agricultural Science; Royal Society of Western Australia; Swan Valley Vintners Club; Royal Western Australian Historical Society. *Publications:* approximately 60 papers, reviews and monograms on the Agronomy, Botany and Breeding of Agricultural lupins, Subterranean clover and Serradella; on the Trace Element Nutrition of Crop and Pasture plants; and the Ecology of Wine Grape Growing. *Creative Works:* Breeder or co-Breeder to 1981 of seven Commercial varieties of Crop Lupin, Two of Subterranean Clover and one of Serradella. *Honours:* Nuffield Foundation Dominion Travelling Fellowship (Natural Sciences), 1968; Medal of the Australian Institute of Agricultural Science, 1974; William Farrer Memorial Medal, 1975; Foundation Fellow, Australian Academy of Technological Sciences, 1976; Agriculturist of the Decade, named by the Royal Agricultural Society of Western Australia, 1981. *Hobbies:* Music; Wine; Gardening. *Address:* 27 Pandora Drive, City Beach, Western Australia 6015.

GLASER, Walter, b. 28 July 1929, Vienna, Austria. Company Director. m. 10 June 1954, 1 son, 2 daughters. *Education:* Melbourne University. *Appointments:* Managing Director of: Walter Glaser & Associates and Goodwill Products (Consolidated) Pty. Ltd. *Memberships:* Trustee, Committee of Economic Development of Australia; Liberal Party of Australia; National Gallery Society, Japan-Australia Society. *Hobbies:* Japanese Garden Designing; Travel; Economics; Art (Sculpture & Painting); Music. *Address:* 6 Burne Court, Kew, Melbourne, Australia.

GLASGOW, Eric Ferguson, b. 16 Aug. 1931, Cookstown, Northern Ireland. Doctor. *Education:* MB, B.Ch, BAO., 1954, MD, 1972, Queens University of Belfast, Ireland. *Appointments:* House Physician/House Surgeon, Route District Hospital, Northern Ireland, 1954-55; Demonstrator in Anatomy, Queen's University, Belfast, Ireland, 1956-58; Lecturer/Senior Lecturer in Anatomy, University of Western Australia, 1959-65; Senior Lecturer in Anatomy, 1965-67, Associate Professor of Anatomy, 1972-, Monash University, Clayton, Victoria, Australia; Senior Research Fellow in Renal Diseases of Children, Pathology Departments, The Children's Hospital and University of Birmingham, UK, 1967-72; Consultant Renal Pathologist, Prince Henry's Hospital, Melbourne, Australia; Consultant Renal Pathologist, Royal Children's Hospital, Melbourne, Australia. *Memberships:* Anatomical Society of Australia dnd New Zealand; Anatomical Society of Great Britain and Ireland; British Association of Clinical Anatomists; Renal Association (UK); Royal Overseas League(Victoria Branch) Vice President. *Hobbies:* Social cycling; Music; Conversation. *Address:* 15/36 Kensington Road, South Yarra 3141, Australia.

GLASSPOLE, Florizel A, b. 1909. Governor General. m. Ina Josephine Kinlocke, 1934. *Education:* Ruskin College, Oxford. *Appointments:* Member, House of Representatives, 1944; Vice-President, People's National Party; Minister of Labour. 1955-57; Leader of the House, 1955-62; Minister of Education, 1957-62; Member of the House of Representatives Committee which prepared Jamaica's Independence Constitution; Member of Delegation to British Government completing constitution Document, 1962; Governor General of Jamaica, 1974-. *Address:* The Residence of the Governor General, Kingston, Jamaica.

GLEDHILL, John Atkinson, b. 31 Aug. 1927, Salisbury, Zimbabwe. Biologist. m. Agnes MacIver, 15 June 1956, 2 daughters. *Education:* BA.(Cantab.), 1948; MA.(Cantab.), 1968. *Appointments:* Field Assistant, Grassland Improvement Station, Stratford-on-Avon, UK, 1948-49, Beit Scholar, Tsetse Control, Tsetse Research Station, Shinyanga and TPRI, Arusha, Tanganyika, 1950; Tsetse Control Entomologist, Northern Rhodesia, 1951-63; Assistant Director, Tsetse Control, Veterinary and Tsetse Control Services, Research and Specialist, Northern Rhodesia/Zambia, 1963-68; Cotton Research Entomologist, Department Services, Gatooma, 1968-74; Head, Cotton Research Institute, Gatooma, Zimbabwe, 1975-. *Memberships:* Crop Science Society of Zimbabwe; Entomological Society of Southern Africa. *Publications:* 24 publications including: Report on a field trial in the use of dieldrin for the control of G.morsitans, 1962; Notes on tsetse and tsetse control in Zambia, 1967; Notes on the use of one gallon water-based spray volumes in aerial spraying, 1970; Review of some advantages and difficulties in the refinement of pesticide application methods, 1972; Crop losses in cotton caused by Heliothis and Diparopsis bollworms, 1973,1976; The problem of bollworm resistance to insecticides, 1978; Factors determining the setting of cotton planting and destruction dates, 1980. *Hobby:* Ecology. *Address:* Cotton Research Institute, P/Bag 765, Zimbabwe.

GLEESON-WHITE, Michael Anthony, b. 24 Oct. 1925, London. Merchant Banker. m. Judith Lee Street, 21 July 1960, 3 daughters. *Education:* Bachelor of Economics, University of Sydney, 1947-49. *Appointments:* Journalism and economic research, 1950-52; Economist, Ord & Minnett (stockbrokers), 1952-55; Lazard Bros. & Co., Ltd., Merchant Banking, London and New York, 1956-57; Partner, Ord & Minnett, 1958-72, Senior Partner, 1970-72; Chairman & Chief Executive, Schroder, Darling & Co., Ltd., Merchant Bankers, 1973-76; Managing Director, Singapore International Merchant Bankers Ltd., 1977-78; Chairman, Schroder, Darling & Co., Ltd., 1979-81; Commissioner, Trade Practices Commission, 1981; Advisor, Singapore Government Investment Corporation Pte. Ltd. *Memberships:* Chairman of Governors, Winifred West Schools Limited, NSW; The Australian Club; Board of Trustees of the Art Gallery of New South Wales. *Hobbies:* Skiing; Fishing; Music; Art. *Address:* 34 Coolong Road, Vaucluse, New South Wales, Australia.

GLENN (Sir), Joseph Robert Archibald. b. 24 May 1911, Sale, Victoria, Australia. Chartered Engineer; Company Director. m. Elizabeth Mary Margaret Balderstone, 14 Nov. 1939, 1 son, 3 daughters. *Education:* BCE, Melbourne University, Australia, 1930-39; AMP, Harvard University, USA, 1957. *Appointments:* Works Engineer, 1935-37, Design Engineer, 1937-44, ICI Australia Ltd., Special Project Engineer 1944-46, Chief Engineer, 1947-49, General Manager, 1949-52, Managing Director, 1953-63, Chairman and Managing Director, 1963-73, Director, 1970-75, ICI UK Limited; Director, Newmount Holdings Pty Limited, 1973-; Directorships: Bank of New South Wales Australia, 1967-; Alcoa of Australia Limited, 1973-; Hill Samuel Australia Limited, 1973-; Collins Wales Pty. Limited, 1974-; Westralian Sands Limited, 1975-; Chairmanships: Tioxide Australia Pty. Limited, 1973-; I C Insurance Australia Limited, 1973-; Rocky Dam Pty.

Limited, 1971-; Director, Commercial Bank of Australia, 1981-. *Memberships:* Fellow, Institution of Engineers Australia; Fellow, Institution of Chemical Engineers UK; Fellow, Institute of Management. *Honours:* Knight Bachelor, 1967; OBE, 1966; James W Kirby Award for service to Engineering; Doctorate of University, La Trobe U, 1981. *Hobbies:* Rare Books; Cattle farming; Tennis; Golf. *Address:* 3 Heyington Place, Toorak, Victoria 3142, Australia.

GLENNON, Alfred James (Canon), b. 2 Dec. 1920, Sydney, Australia. Anglican Clergyman. *Education:* Licentiate in Theology, Australian College of Theology, 1951; Diploma in Social Studies, University of Sydney, Australia, 1957; *Appointments:* Precentor, 1956-62, Minor Canon, 1968-, St. Andrew's Cathedral, Sydney, Australia; Chaplain, St. George Hospital, Sydney, Australia, 1962-66. *Memberships:* Union Club, Sydney. *Publications:* Your Healing is Within You, 1978. *Hobby:* Heraldry. *Address:* St Andrew's Cathedral, Sydney Square, Sydney, New South Wales 2000, Australia.

GLOVER, Ablade, b. 1 Aug. 1934, Accra, Ghana. Artist. divorced, 2 sons, 2 daughters. *Education:* Art Teachers Certificate, University of Science and Technology, Kumasi, Ghana, 1957-58; NND, Central School Diploma, Central School of Art and Design, London, UK, 1959-62; M.Ed., Kent State University, Kent, Ohio, USA, 1971-72; PhD, Ohio State University, Columbus, Ohio, USA, 1972-74. *Appointments:* Art Teacher, Akodzo Middle School Tema; Art Tutor, Winneba Specialists Training College, Winneba; Exhibition Officer, Ghana Information Services; Lecturer, Senior Lecturer, University of Science and Technology, Kumasi, Ghana. *Memberships:* Royal Society of Arts, London; Italian Academy of Arts; Vice-President, Ghana Association of Artists. *Creative Works:* Oil Paintings: Every Knee Shall Bow, 1979; State Mourning, 1958; Puberty, 1969; Fontomfrom, 1970. *Honours:* Gold Medal, Italian Academy of Arts, 1981. *Hobby:* Billiards. *Address:* 35 Ridge Road, University of Science and Technology, Kumasi, Ghana.

GLOVER, Trevor David, b. 19 Apr. 1940, Ashford, Middlesex, England. Managing Director. m. Carol Mary, 5 Aug. 1967, 1 son, 1 daughter. *Education:* BA (Hons), English, University of Hull. *Appointments:* College Traveller, Sydney Australia, 1964, College Traveller, Sales Manager, General Manager of Professional & Reference Division, Maidenhead, England, 1965-70, McGraw-Hill Publishing Company Limited; UK Sales & Marketing Director, Sales Manager, Penguin Books Limited, Harmondsworth, England, 1970-75; Consultant, Viking Books Inc., New York, USA, 1975-76; Managing Director, Penguin Books Australia Limited, Melbourne, 1976-; Director, Longman Cheshire Publishing Company Limited, Melbourne, Penguin Books Limited, Harmondsworth, England. *Hobbies:* Reading; Photography; Music; Swimming. *Address:* McIntyres Road, Park Orchards, Victoria 3114, Australia.

GLUBB, John Bagot (Sir), b. 16 Apr. 1897, Preston, Lancashire. Military (retired). m. Muriel Rosemary Forbes, 20 Aug. 1938, 2 sons, 2 daughters. *Education:* Cheltenham College, 1911-14; RMA Woolich 1914-15. *Appointments:* Regimental Officer, Royal Engineers, 1915-26; Administrative Inspector, Iraq Government, 1926-30; Commandant Desert Area, Trans-Jordan, 1930-38; Commander, Arab Legion, 1938-56. *Publications:* The Story of the Arab Legion, 1948; A Soldier with the Arabs, 1957; Britain and the Arabs, 1959; War in the Desert, 1960; The Great Arab Conquests, 1963; The Empire of the Arabs, 1963; The Course of Empire, 1965; The Lost Centuries, 1966; A Short History of the Arab Peoples, 1969; The Middle East Crisis, 1967; Syria, Lebanon, Jordan, 1967; The Life and Times of Muhammad, 1970; Peace in the Holy Land, 1971; Soldiers of Fortune, 1973; The Way of Love, 1974; Haroon al Rasheed, 1976; Into Battle: A Soldiers Diary of the Great War, 1977; Arabian Adventures, 1978; A Purpose for Living, 1980. *Honours:* KCB; CMG; DSO; OBE; MC; Knight of St John of Jerusalem; Burton Medal, Royal Geographical Society; Lawrence Medal, Central Asian Society; Livingstone Medal, Royal Scottish Geographical Society. *Address:* West Wood, Mayfield, Sussex TN20 6DS, England.

GLUBE, Constance R., b. 23 Nov. 1931, Ottawa, Ontario, Canada. Justice of the Supreme Court of Nova

Scotia. m. Richard H Glube, 6 July 1952, 3 sons, 1 daughter. *Education:* BA, McGill University, Montreal, 1952; LLB Dalhousie University, Halifax, 1955. *Appointments:* Private Law Practice, 1962-68; Barrister & Solicitor, Legal Department, City of Halifax, 1969-74; City Manager, City of Halifax, 1974-77; Appointed to the Supreme Court of Nova Scotia, 1977-. *Memberships:* Board of Directors: Canadian Council of Christians & Jews, 1975-80; Co-Chairman, Atlantic Region, 1980-; Canadian Institute for the Administration of Justice, 1979-; Canadian Judges Conference, 1979-; Canadian Association Municipal Administrators, 1975-77. Canadian Bar Association. *Honours:* Carswell Book Prize, 1954; Nova Scotia Barrister's Society Scholarship, 1954; Queens Counsel, 1974. *Hobbies:* Sailing; Swimming. *Address:* 404 Francklyn Street, Halifax NS, Canada, B3H 1A8

GLUCKMAN, Ann Jocelyn, b. 13 Aug. 1927, London, England. Secondary School Principal. m. Laurie Kalman Gluckman, 23 Jan, 1947, 4 sons. *Education:* BSc., New Zealand, 1962; MSc.(Hons.), AK, 1964; Diploma Educational Administration, Massey, 1980. *Appointments:* Appointed to Nga Tapuwae College as foundation Principal, 1975. *Memberships:* National Commission for UNESCO, 1977-80; Educational and Social Sciences sub-commission of UNESCO, 1977-80; Executive member, New Zealand Association for Research in Education; Zonta director, Auckland Club, 1981; NZFUW, Pacifica. *Publications:* over 100 papers on Educational administration, Multicultural Education in New Zealand, Geographic topics and travel articles. *Honours:* Department of Education teaching Fellowship in Geography, Auckalnd University, New Zealand, 1971. *Hobbies:* Writing; Collecting antiques. *Address:* 6D 'The Pines', 75 Owens Road, Epsom 3, Auckland, New Zealand.

GLUCKMAN, Laurie Kilman, b. 6 Dec. 1920, Auckland, New Zealand. Psychiatrist. m. Ann Jocelyn Klippel, 23 Jan. 1947, 4 sons. *Education:* MB, ChB, New Zealand, 1944; MD, 1963; MRACP, 1950; FRACP, 1966; FRANZCP, 1970; FRC Psych, 1971. *Appointments:* Psychiatrist, Auckland Public Hospital, 1952-79, National Womens Hospital, 1967-81, Carrington Hospital, 1974-81; Lecturer Psychiatry, Auckland Medical School, 1977-81. *Memberships:* Past Secretary, New Zealand Branch, & Counsellor, Australian & New Zealand College of Psychiatrists; Fellow, Royal Numismatic Society of New Zealand. *Publications:* The Royal Touch in England, a Theory, of origin 1971; Tangiwai a Medical History of 19th Century New Zealand, 1977; Some 130 papers on Psychiatry Medical History. *Hobbies:* Philately; Medical History. *Address:* The Pines, 75 Owens Road, Epsom, Auckland, New Zealand.

GOAMAN, Michael, b. 14 Feb. 1921, East Grinstead, Sussex, England. Stamp and Banknote designer. m. Sylvia Priestley, 19 Sept. 1950, 3 daughters. *Education:* Reading University School of Art, UK, 1938-40; London Central School of Arts and Crafts, UK, 1945-47. *Appointments:* Freelance designer, 1947; General Graphic design, 1948-63; Commenced stamp design for UK, 1952, and for Commonwealth and Foreign countries, 1953; Commenced Banknote design, 1954; Began partnership with wife in stamp design, 1956; Visiting Lecturer, London College of Printing, UK, 1957-61; Member, Ghana Stamp Panel, 1958-62; Consultant designer stamps, Nigeria, 1961-64; Consultant designer for Banknotes to Bradbury Wilkinson & Co. Limited, UK, 1964-. *Memberships:* Fellow, 1957-76, Society of Industrial Artists; Society of Lithographic Artists Designers and Engravers. *Hobbies:* Sailing; Natural History. *Address:* 91 Park Road, Chiswick, London W4 3ER.

GODBEHERE, Walter, b. 8 June 1924, Montreal Canada. Executive. m. Frances Mary Willett, 2 June 1945, 1 son, 1 daughter. *Education:* McGill University, 1943; Certified General Accountant, 1954. *Appointments:* War Service, 1942-45; Senior Management, Northern Telecom, 1940-74; Executive VP, B & K Machinery International Limited, 1974-77; President and Chief Executive Officer, Enheat Incorporated, 1977-81; Retired 1981. *Memberships:* Certified General Accountants Association, Past President; Canadian Manufacturers Association, Member of Executive; Canadian Foundry Association, Director; Canadian Chamber of Commerce, Member International Affairs Comm; Canada-UK Chamber of Commerce. *Hobbies:*

Golf; Fishing; Woodworking. *Address:* 283 Orleans Street, Dieppe NB, Canada.

GODBOLD, Rosemary Elizabeth (Mrs Norman D Godbold), Professional Name Rosemary Margan, b. 12 May 1937, Bendigo, Victoria, Australia. TV Announcer. m. Norman Dosier Godbold, 21 Sept. 1973, 1 daughter. *Education:* St Mary's Convent, Bendigo. *Appointments:* Qualified Ladies Hairdresser; At present working for GTV 9. *Memberships:* Director, Rosemary Margan Fashions Pty, Ltd., Pan Pacific Pictures Pty Ltd., *Honours:* Victorian Water Ski Champion, 1952-62; Won 6 National Water Ski Champion Titles; Australian Water Ski Champion; Australian Jump, Trick & Overall events Champion, 1961-62; Best Female on TV Victoria, 2 awards, 1968-69; Logie Winner, Victoria, 1968-69. *Hobbies:* Water Skiing; Swimming; Reading. *Address:* 23 Studley Avenue, Kew 3101, Australia.

GODDARD, Ronald George, b. 10 Oct. 1921, Gillingham, Kent, England. Mechanical Engineer. m. 19 Sept. 1942, 2 sons, 2 daughters. *Education:* BSc, University of London, 1946-49; Imperial College, London, 1957; Ashridge Management College, 1970. *Appointments:* Design Engineer, W Neill and Sons, St. Helens, 1949-51; Research and Developments Engineer, British Oxygen Company, 1951-53; Senior Project and Development Engineer, British Oxygen Engineering, 1953-56; Deputy Engineering Manager, British Oxygen/Wimpey, 1956-59; Senior Project Engineer/Deputy Project Manager, 1959-63, Proposals Manager, 1963-65, Resident Site Manager, 1965-66, Proposals Manager, 1966-69, Project Manager and Group Project Engineer, 1969-75, Manager Tender Engineering, 1975-79, Administration Manager Operations Department, 1979-81, Procurement Technical Manager, 1981-, Constructors John Brown Limited. *Memberships:* Fellow, Institution of Mechanical Engineer; Fellow, Institution of Nuclear Engineers; British Institute of Management; Royal Air Forces Escaping Society, Authorised Speaker; Honorary Member Union Nationale desÉvadés De Guerre. *Publications:* Various scientific papers. *Honours:* Distinguished Flying Medal, 1943; Citation London Gazette; Royal Air Force Navigation Warrant, 1946; Diplôme D'Honneur De L'Amitie Francaise, 1970. *Hobbies:* Public Speaking; Motoring; Gardening; Woodcraft; Philately. *Address:* 236 Lodge Lane, Grays Thurrock, Essex, England.

GOETZ, Peter Henry, b. 8 Sept. 1917, Slavgorod, Siberia. Artist. m. Helena Warkentin, 9 Aug. 1942, 1 son, 1 daughter. *Education:* Kitchener-Waterloo Collegiate, Waterloo College of Fine Arts; Doon School of Fine Arts. *Appointments:* Taught Adult Education Classes across Western Ontario—Preston, Guelph, Kitchener, Stratford, Ingersoll, Woodstock, Doon School, University of Waterloo. *Memberships:* Ontario Society of Artists; Canadian Society of Painters in Water Colour; Society of Canadian Artists; American Federation of Art; Fellow, International Institute of Arts & Letters; International Platform Association; Centro Studi e Scambi Internazionali. *Creative Works:* Exhibited in all Major Exhibitions and Major Galleries across Canada. *Honours:* Grand Prize, Quebec National Exhibition and Western Ontario Exhibition; Ontario Society of Artists Image 76; Modern Masters Exhibition, Florence. *Address:* 784 Avondale Avenue, Kitchener, Ontario, NZM ZW8, Canada.

GOFF, Robert Lionel Archibald (Sir), b. 12 Nov. 1926, Alyth, Scotland. High Court Judge. m. Sarah Cousins, 12 July 1953, 1 son, 2 daughters. *Education:* Eton College, 1939-44; New College, Oxford, 1948-50; MA, 1953; DCL, 1970. *Appointments:* Lieutenant, Scots Guards, 1945-48; Barrister, Inner Temple, 1951; Fellow of Lincoln College, Oxford, 1951-55; In Practice at the Bar, 1956-75; QC, 1967; High Court Judge, 1975-. *Memberships:* Vice-Chairman, 1971-76, Chairman, 1976-, Council of Legal Education; Chairman, Common Professional Examination Board, 1978-79; Honorary Professor of Legal Ethics, Birmingham University, 1979-81; Judge in charge of the Commercial List, 1979-81. *Address:* Royal Courts of Justice, Strand, London WC2, England.

GOH, Han Teng, b. 31 Dec. 1939, Sumatra. Banker. m. 18 May 1967, 1 son, 1 daughter. *Education:* Perth Technical College, West Australia, 1969; Hemingway Robertson Institute, West Australia, 1971. *Appoint-*

ments: Chairman, Greenery Pte. Limited, Managing Director, Pan Malayan Holdings Limited, Tat Lee Finance Limited, Sin Chuan Development Pte. Limited; Executive Director, Tat Le Bank Limited; Director: Negri Sembilian Oil Palms Bhd; Eng Thye Pln. Bhd; Soctek Sdn. Bhd; Singapore Chinese Chamber of Commerce and Industry. *Memberships:* Honourable Treasurer, Newtown Secondary School Advisory Committee; American Institute of Management; British Institute of Management. *Hobbies:* Lawn Tennis; Table Tennis; Badminton; Squash; Swimming; Golf; Jogging. *Address:* 22 Greenleaf Place, Singapore, 1027.

GOH, Tyau Soon Andrew, b. 29 Aug. 1944, Malacca, Malaysia. Barrister. m. 15 Dec. 1973, 1 son, 1 daughter. *Education:* Diploma in Agriculture, Malaya, 1966; Bachelor of Laws, Hull University, 1969; Barrister-at-Law, Middle Temple, 1969; Master of Laws, London University, 1970. *Appointments:* Private Practice, Advocate & Solicitor, Malacca, Malaysia, 1971-. *Memberships:* President of the College of Agriculture, Malaya Students Union; Chairman of the College of Agriculture, Malaya Sports Council; Various Sports and Social Clubs. *Honours:* Represented Selangor State, 1964-65 and Malacca State, 1971-72, in Rugby. *Hobbies:* Games; Swimming; Reading; Music. *Address:* 293-C Sin Hoe Garden, Bukit Baru, Malacca, Malaysia.

GOLD, Phil, b. 17 Sept. 1936, Montreal, Quebec, Canada. Physician. m. Evelyn Katz, 1960, 2 sons, 1 daughter. *Education:* McGill University, B Sc, 1957, M Sc, 1961, Md., Cm, 1961, Ph D, 1965. *Appointments:* BSc, 1957, MSc, 1961, Md, CM, 1961, PhD, 1965, McGill University, USA. *Appointments:* Junior Assistant Physician, 1967-69 Assistant Physician, 1969-71, Associate Physician, 1972-73, Associate Professor, Medical & Clinical Medicine, 1970-72, Professor, Medical & Clinical Medicine, 1973-, Senior Physician, 1973-, Director, Division Clinical Immunology & Allergy, 1977-, Montreal General Hospital, Canada; Assistant Professor of Physiology, 1968-71, Associate Professor of Physiology, 1972-74, Professor of Physiology, 1974-, McGill, University, USA; Director, McGill Cancer Centre, 1978. *Memberships:* American Academy of Allergy; American Association for Cancer Research; American Association of Immunologists; American Federation for Clinical Research; American Society for Clinical Investigation; Canadian Federation of Biological Sciences; Canadian Medical Association; Canadian Society of Allergy & Clinical Immunology; Canadian Oncology Society (Founding Member); Royal College of Physicians & Surgeons of Canada; Royal Society of Canada, American College of Physicians. *Publications:* 90 Articles; Co-editor of Clinical Immunology with Dr. S O Freedman. *Honours:* E W R Steacie Prize for Science—National Research Council of Canada, 1973; Outstanding Scientist Award, 1976; The Gairdner Foundation Annual Award, 1976; The Gairdner Foundation Award, Canada, 1978. International Research Group for Carcinoembryonic Proteins, 1976; The Gairdner Foundation Award, Canada, 1978; Johann-Georg-Zimmerman Prize for Cancer Research, Germany, 1978. *Address:* 5705 Parkhaven Avenue, Cote St. Luc, H4W 1XC, Montreal, Canada.

GOLDBERG, David Myer, b. 30 Aug. 1933, Glasgow, Scotland. Doctor; Research Scientist; University Professor. m. 9 Mar. 1964, 2 daughters. *Education:* BSc(Hons), 1958, MB ChB, 1959, PhD, 1965, MD, 1974, FRIC, 1972, FRCPath, 1980, University of Glasgow. *Appointments:* Registrar and Senior Registrar, Department Biochemistry, Western Infirmary, Glasgow, 1961-67; Consultant Chemical Pathologist, United Sheffield Hospitals and Honorary Lecturer, University of Sheffield, 1967-75; Biochemist-in-Chief, Hospital for Sick Children, Toronto, 1975-; Professor and Chairman, Department Clinical Biochemistry, University of Toronto, 1977-. *Memberships:* International Society for Clinical Enzymology, Vice-President, 1977-; American Association for Clinical Chemistry; Canadian Association of Clinical Chemists; Canadian Association of Medical Biochemists; Academy of Clinical & Laboratory Physicians; Canadian Society for Clinical Investigation. *Publications:* Editor, Annual Review of Clinical Biochemistry; Co-editor, Enzymes in Health and Disease; Progress in Clinical Enzymology; Author and Co-author of more than 150 scientific papers, book chapters, and reviews. *Hobbies:* Classical Music; Theatre; Cinema; Visual Arts; Squash; Wine. *Address:* 9 Harrison Road, Willowdale, Ontario, Canada, M2L 1V3

GOLDBERG, Mark T, b. 1 Apr. 1952, Toronto, Canada. Medical Researcher; Pharmacologist. m. Susan Buchanan, 1 daughter. *Education:* BSc (Hons.), 1974, University of Ontario; PhD, 1980, Memorial University. *Appointments:* -Ontario Cancer Institute; Ludwig Institute for Cancer Research, Toronto. *Memberships:* Physicians for Social Responsibility; GRAMM (former vice-president); Canadian Pharmacological Society. *Honours:* Grass Fellow, Woods Hole, MA, 1978; Pharmacological Society of Canada's Annual Award for the most outstanding research paper published in the Canadian Journal of Physiology and Pharmacology, 1979; Research Fellow of the National Cancer Institute of Canada, 1980, 1981. *Hobbies:* Music; Croquet. *Address:* 496 Pape Avenue, Toronto, Ontario, Canada, M4K 3P8.

GOLDING, John, b. 9 Mar. 1931. Member of Parliament. *Education:* London School of Economics; BA-(Hons.), University of Keele, Newcastle, Staffordshire. *Appointments:* Assistant Secretary, Post Office Engineers Union, 1960-; MP, Newcastle-Under-Lyme, 1969-; Parliamentary Private Secretary, Ministry of Technology, 1969; Opposition Whip, 1970-74; Lord Commissioner of Treasury, 1974; Parliamentary Secretary, Department of Employment, Chairman, Select Committee on Employment, 1976-79. *Publications:* Trade Unions—ONTO, 1980; Productivity Bargaining, 1980. *Hobbies:* Angling; Horse racing. *Address:* House of Commons, London SW1, England.

GOLDMAN-EISLER, Frieda, (Mrs. Paul Eisler), b. 9 June 1907, Tarnow, Poland. Scientist; Emeritus Professor. m. Dr. Paul Eisler, 29 Feb. 1950. *Education:* Dr. phil., Vienna University, 1928; Postgraduate Studies in Psychology, University College, London, 1938-40. *Appointments:* Science Investigator for Medical Research Council, 1948-56; Lecturer, Reader, Professor in Psycholinguistics, University College, London, 1957-75; Emeritus Professor, 1975-. *Memberships:* include: Fellow British Psychological Society; Fellow, Experimental Psychology Society; Fellow, Royal Society of Medicine. *Publications:* Author, Psycholinguistics—Experiments in Spontaneous Speech, 1968. Contributor of over 50 scientific papers, articles & reports to scientific journals & to Personality on Nature, Society & Culture, 1973. *Hobbies:* Reading; Music; Conversation. *Address:* 57 Exeter Road, London NW2 1YB, England.

GOLDSMITH, James Michael, b. 26 Feb. 1933, Paris, France. Industrialist. m. (1) Maria Isobel Patino (dec. 1954) (2) Ginette Lery, (3) Lady Annabel Vane Tempest Stewart, 3 sons, 3 daughters. *Education:* Eton College, Great Britain. *Appointments:* Chairman: Generale Occidentale S A Paris; Groupe Express (publishers of l'Express); Banque Occidentale pour l'Industrie et le Commerce. Director: Banque Rothschild; Societe des Hotels Reunis; A number of industrial and commercial enterprises. *Memberships:* Buck's London; Brooks's London; Travellers' Paris. *Honours:* Knight Bachelor, 1976; Chevalier de la Legion d'Honneur, 1980. *Address:* 65/68 Leadenhall Street, London, EC3A 2BA, England.

GOLDSTEEN-MALLINSON, Beryl (Mrs) b.25 -july 1916, -waverly, Sydney, Australia. Painter. m. 3 Oct. 1942, 1 son. *Education:* Julian Ashton Art School, Sydney, 1931-36. *Appointments:* Free Lance Commercial Fashion Artist; Painter of Landscapes & Seascapes, in Watercolours & Oils. *Memberships:* Associate Royal Art Society, Sydney; Fellow, IBA (Cambridge); Fellow Academy Art, Italy(With Gold Medal). *Publications:* Women of Parramatta; 100 Years Royal Art Society, Sydney; Howard Hinton's Collection, Armidale College. *Honours:* 1st Prize Sydney Waratah Festival, Water Colours, 1962-63; 1st Prize Water Colours Royal AGR Show, 1965; Fishers Ghost, Cambelltown, 1964, 65, 66; Penrith 1st Prize Water Colours, 1975; 1st Prize Open Air Foundation Week, Parramatta, 1972; 1st Prize Parramatta Historical, 1975. *Hobbies:* Gardening; Growing Orchids; Sculptures (making); Sailing. *Address:* 14 Perry Street, Dundas 2117, New South Wales, Australia.

GOLDSTEIN, Harold Gerald, b. 17 Feb. 1928, Waverley, New South Wales, Australia. Director. m. Nancye Greenberg, 14 Feb. 1951, 2 daughters. *Education:* Sydney Technical College. *Appointments:* Co-Managing Director, J Goldstein and Company Property Limited; Co-Managing Director, Morrisons Outdoor Catering

Property Limited; Director, Harbourside Amusement Park Property Limited. *Memberships:* Most Excellent Order of the British Empire Association, New South Wales. *Honours:* OBE, 1978. *Hobbies:* Tennis; Swimming. *Address:* 11 Echo Street, Roseville, New South Wales 2069, Australia.

GOLDSWORTHY, Eric Roger, b. 17 July 1929, Lameroo, South Australia. Member of Parliament; Deputy Premier of South Australia. m. 12 Apr. 1952, 2 sons, 1 daughter. *Education:* BSc. Dip. T Adelaide University, 1946-49. *Appointments:* Secondary School Teacher (Physics); Member of Parliament. *Memberships:* Royal Commonwealth Society; Australian American Association; Vice-Patron, South Australian Choral Society, Patron numerous Agricultural Societies. *Hobbies:* Classical Music; Managing own Farm. *Address:* Highercombe, Houghton, South Australia 5131.

GOLLEDGE, John Gouldhawke, b. 18 May, 1930, Torquay, Devon, UK. Medicine. m. Patricia Edith Pearcy, 17 Dec. 1954, 4 sons, 1 daughter. *Education:* MB., BS., University of Adelaide, 1949-54; Diploma Soc. Med., University of Edinburgh, 1970-71; Fellow, Royal Australian College of Medical Administrators, 1976; Fellow Royal Australian College of General Practioners, 1968. *Appointments:* R.M.O. Royal Perth Hospital, 1955-56; Private Practice, 1957-64; Chief Casualty Officer, 1964-68, Deputy Medical Superintendent, 1968-72, Royal Perth Hospital; Medical Superintendent, Princess Alexandra Hospital, Brisbane, 1973-. *Memberships:* Chairman, State Health Services, Development Committee; Executive Council of Royal Australian College of Medical Administration; Council of Queensland Institute of Medical Research; Council of Queensland Radium Institute; Medical Faculty Board; Advisory Council on Drugs and Medical Equipment; Advisory Committee on Nurse Education. *Honours:* Wesley College Scholarship, 1942; National Health and Medical Research Council Public Health Travelling Fellowship, 1970-71. *Hobbies:* Golf; Swimming. *Address:* 47 Grounds Street, Yeronga, Brisbane.

GOLLEDGE, Reginald George, b. 6 Dec. 1937, Dungog, NSW, Australia. University Professor. m. Allison L, 15 May 1976, 1 son, 3 daughters. *Education:* BA, 1959, MA, 1961, University of New England, Australia; PhD, University of Iowa, USA, 1965. *Appointments:* Lecturer in Geography, University of Canterbury, Christchurch, New Zealand, 1961-63; Research Assistant, Bureau of Business and Economic Research, University of Iowa, 1964; Assistant Professor, University of British Columbia, Vancouver, 1965-66; Assistant Professor, 1966-67, Associate Professor, 1967-71, Professor of Geography, 1971-77, Ohio State University; Visiting Assistant Professor, 1967, Visiting Associate Professor, 1969, Professor of Geography, 1977-, University of California; Visiting Associate Professor, University of Sydney, 1970; Visiting Professor, University of Texas, 1972, 1973, 1975, University of Auckland, 1976; Chairman, Department of Geography, University of California, Santa Barbara, 1980-. *Memberships:* Association of American Geographers; Institute of Australian Geographers; Regional Science Association; Psychometric Society; North American Classification Society; Environmental Design & Research Association. *Publications:* Traffic in a New Zealnd City, (w. B.W. Johnson, L.J. King & A. Williman), 1965; Behavioural Models in Geography: A Symposium, (w. K.R. Cox), 1969; An Introduction to Scientific Reasoning in Geography (w. D. Amedeo), 1975; Spatial Choice & Spatial Behavior (w. G. Rushton), 1976; Environmental Knowing (w. G. Moore), 1976 (paperback edition, 1978); Cities, Space and Behavior (w. L.J. King), 1978; Work on other books in progress and in press; Contributor of numerous chapters in professional books; Numerous major articles contributed to professional journals including: A Behavioral View of Migration and Mobility Research, 1980; An Experimental Design for Assessing the Spatial Competence of Retarded Populations, 1979; Several Monographs and Government Reports including: Cognitive Maps and Consumer Behavior, taped lecture, 1979; Confirmatory and Exploratory Analysis of Criminal Data (co-author w. L Hubert), 1980; Contributed to numerous Symposia, Discussion Papers, Minor Articles and Reviews. *Honours:* Commonwealth University Scholarship, Australia, 1955; NSW Teachers College Scholarship, 1955-59; University Fellowship, University of Iowa, 1964-65. *Hobbies:*

Fishing; Rugby coaching & refereeing. *Address:* 267 Forest Drive, Goleta, California, 93017, USA.

GOLSON, Jack, b. 13 Sept. 1926, Rochdale, Lancashire, England. University Teacher. m. Clara Lucy, 7 Apr. 1962, 1 son, 1 daughter. *Education:* BA., 1950, MA., 1952, Research Scholar, Faculty of Archaeology & Anthropology, 1951-53, Peterhouse College, University of Cambridge. *Appointments:* Lecturer, 1954-57, Senior Lecturer, 1958-61, Department of Anthropology, University of Auckland, New Zealand; Fellow, 1961-64, Senior Fellow, 1964-69, Department of Anthropology, and Sociology, Foundation Professor, 1969-, Department of Prehistory, Research School of Pacific Studies, Australian National University. *Memberships:* Council Member & Chairman of Standing Committee on Scientific Activities, Pacific Science Association, 1979-; President, Indo-Pacific Prehistory Association, 1980-; Australian Archaeological Association; Secretary, 1955-60, President, 1960-61, New Zealand Archaeological Association; Council Member & Journal Editor, 1958-60, Polynesian Society. Australian Institute of Aboriginal Studies, 1964; Australian Academy of the Humanities, 1975; Explorers Club, New York, USA., 1980. *Publications:* Editor, Polynesian Navigation—A Symposium on Andrew Shapr's Theory of Accidental Voyages, 1962, 3rd edition, 1972; Aboriginal Man and Environment in Australia (Co-Editor with D J Mulvaney), 1971; Sunda and Sahul—Prehistoric Studies in South East Asia, Melanesia and Australia, (Co-Editor with J Allen & R Jones), 1977. *Hobbies:* Reading; Cricket. *Address:* 20 Wongoola Close, O'Connor, ACT 2601, Australia.

GONTHIER, Charles D, b. 1 Aug. 1928, Montréal, Québec, Canada. Justice, Superior Court of Québec. m. Mariette Morin, 17 June 1961, 5 sons. *Education:* College Stanislas, Montréal, Québec; BA., University of Paris, 1947; BCL., McGill University, 1951. *Appointments:* Read Law with Senator John T Hackett, Q.C., called to Bar of Québec, 1952; Q.C., 1971; Practised Law, Hackett, Mulvena & Laverty, Montréal, 1952-57; Hugessen, Macklaier, Chisholm, Smith & Davis, subsequently Laing, Weldon, Courtois, Clarkson, Parsons, Gonthier & Tetrault, 1957-74. *Memberships:* Director, Montréal Legal Aid Bureau, 1959-69; Director, Canadian Judges Conference; Discipline Committee, Québec Bar, 1973-74; President Junior Secretary, 1961-62, Secretary Québec Branch, 1963-64, Canadian Bar Association; Montréal Branch, Canadian Institute International Affairs. *Address:* 221 Outremont Avenue, Outremont, Québec, Canada, H2V 3L9.

GONZALEZ, Anson John, b. 21 Aug. 1936, Trinidad. Educationist. m. 6 Aug. 1961, 2 daughters. *Education:* Teachers Diploma, 1959; BA., 1971. *Appointments:* Teacher, 1953-71; Teachers' College Lecturer, 1971-72; Schools Publications Officer, 1972-81, Acting Supervisor, 1981-. *Memberships:* International Poetry Society; International Biographical Association; International Meditation Society; Public Services Association; TASK International; Writers' Union of Trinidad and Tobago. *Publications:* Score, 1972; National Identity in our Literature, 1972; Trinidad and Tobago Literature, on Air, 1974; The Love-song of Boysie B and other Poems, 1974; Daaga the Warrior, 1975; West Indians in Pan-Africanism, 1976; Photography—an Introduction to a hobby, 1977; Towards Lagos, 1978; Collected Poems, 1979. *Hobbies:* Reading; Writing; Table Tennis; Photography; Lawn Tennis; Martial Arts; Publishing. *Address:* P.O. Box 3254, 1 Sapphire Drive, Diego Martin, Trinidad and Tobago.

GOOCH, John MacLeod, b. 4 Oct. 1917, Korumburra, Victoria, Australia. Medical. m. Margaret Brooke Boothby, 14 Jan. 1950, 2 daughters. *Education:* MB.,BS., University of Melbourne, 1942; Member, Royal College of Physicians, London, 1949; Diploma of Child Health, RCP & S, London, 1950; Member, Royal Australasian College of Physicians, 1975, Fellow, 1978. *Appointments:* Junior Resident Medical Officer, Alfred Hospital, Melbourne, 1942-43; Junior Resident Medical Officer, 1944, Registrar, 1945, Children's Hospital, Melbourne. House Officer, Queen Elizabeth Hospital for Children, London, 1949-50; Pediatrician in charge of Cerebral Palsy Clinic and Associate Physician, Royal Children's Hospital, Melbourne, 1957-79; Part-time Medical Officer, Spastic Society of Victoria, 1980-; Now virtually retired from Medical work. *Memberships:* Australian Medical Association; Australian

College of Paediatrics; Paediatric Society of Victoria. *Publications:* Various scientific papers in Medical Journals. *Honours:* Major Resident Scholar, Trinity College University of Melbourne, 1937; Honorary Consultant Physician to Cerebral Palsy Clinic Royal Children's Hospital, Melbourne, 1980-. *Hobbies:* Farm; Chess. *Address:* Ruffy Road, Longwood, 3665, Victoria, Australia.

GOODALL, Henry Bushman, b. 18 June 1921, Dundee, Scotland, U.K. Medical. m. 15 Dec. 1962, 1 son, 1 daughter. *Education:* MB.,Ch.B., 1944, M.D., 1959, St. Andrews; F.R.C., Pathology, 1970. *Appointments:* House Physician, Hourse Surgeon and Trainee Pathologist, Dundee Royal Infirmary; Graded Pathologist, R.A.M.C; Lecturer and Senior Lecturer in Pathology, University of St. Andrews; Senior Lecture and Honorary Consultant in Haematology, University of Dundee. *Memberships:* Association of Clinical Pathologists; British Society, Haematology; Pathological Society; Scottish Soc. Exp. Med; British Microcire Society; Forfarshire Medical Association. *Publications:* Various publications on Elliptocytosis, Inflammatory Disease of Colon, Anaemia in Pregnancy and Infancy, Disseminated Intravascular Coagulation, in different journals; Chapters in combined textbook of Obstetrics and Gynaecology. *Honours:* Various under-graduate prizes, medals and awards; Gold Medal and Honours for M.D., Thesis. *Hobbies:* Gardening; Golf; Burns Cult. *Address:* 16 Hazel Avenue, Dundee, DD2 1QD, Scotland, UK.

GOODALL, Nigel Roger, b. 29 Mar. 1945, Watford, United Kingdom. Executive Vice-President. m. Lynne Gagnon, 26 July 1979. *Education:* Natural Sciences, Chemistry, St. John's College, Oxford, 1964-68; BA., Oxon, 1968; MA., Oxon, 1971. *Appointments:* Unilever Limited, 1968-80; Marketing/Sales Management, Wall's Meat Company, London, UK., 1968-71; Various Marketing positions up to Vice-President, Hygrade Foods Inc., Canada & N. Bourassa Ltd., Canada, 1971-80; President Canadian Meat Council, 1979; Executive Vice-President, Marketing & Sales, Corby Distilleries Ltd., Canada, 1980-. *Memberships:* Mount Stephen Club. *Honours:* Sir Thomas White Scholarship, 1964; Pfizer Industrial Scholarship, 1964, St. John's College, Oxford. *Hobbies:* Antiques; Skiing. *Address:* 2265 Seneca Road, Town of Mount Royal, Quebec, H3P 2N4, Canada.

GOODALL, Stanley Henry, b. 19 Aug. 1927, Mortlake, Victoria, Australia. Oceanarium Director/Marine Naturalist. *Education:* Technical College. *Appointments:* Commercial Artist, Newspaper Cartoonist; Manager, Tweed Heads Aquarium, Gold Coast, Australia; Managing Director, Pet Porpoise Pool Oceanarium Company, Coffs Harbour, NSW, Australia. *Memberships:* The International Oceanographic Foundation; The Oceans Society of Australia; Marine Mammal Advisory Committee, State Government, NSW, Australia; The Bananacoast Tourist Association, Australia (Secretary); Coffs Harbour Surf Lifesaving Association. *Publications:* Scientific papers, Marine life natural history, Whale conservation; Marine mamal training, The Educational value of Oceanaria; Book illustrating, newspaper cartooning. *Honours:* Sporting trophies. *Hobbies:* Oil painting; Black and white cartooning; Scuba diving; Boating. *Address:* No 2 Fitzgerald Street, Coffs Harbour, NSW, Australia, 2450.

GOODE, Charles Barrington, b. 26 Aug. 1938, Melbourne, Australia. Sharebroker. *Education:* B.Com. *Honours:* M.B.A., Columbia; A.A.S.A; F.S.I.A. *Appointments:* Senior Partner, Potter Partners; Director of: Oliver J Nilsen (Australia) Ltd., Hallmark Cards Australia Ltd; Austin Hospital Foundation Ltd. *Memberships:* Monash University Council; Council of Institute of Public Affairs; L.T.A.V; R.M.G.C. *Hobbies:* Tennis; Golf. *Address:* 1 Millicent Avenue, Toorak. 3142, Australia.

GOODEY, Ronald John, b. 15 Sept. 1938, Melbourne, Victoria, Australia. Otolaryngology. m. Lesley Margaret Allen, 20 Jan. 1962, 1 son, 3 daughters. *Education:* Bachelor of Medical Science, University of New Zealand, 1961; Bachelor of Medicine, Bachelor of Surgery, Otago University, 1963; Fellow, Royal Australasian College of Surgeons, 1969. *Appointments:* Auckland Hospitals, 1964-69; Royal Victoria Eye & Ear Clinic, Belfast, Northern Ireland, 1960-70; Otology Fellow, Wayne State University, Detroit, Michigan, 1970-71; Green Lane Hospital, Auckland, 1972-; University of

Auckland Medical School, 1976-; Private Specialist Practice, 1974-. *Memberships:* Chief Executive Officer, Deafness Research Foundation (N.Z.) Inc., 1973-; President, Auckland Branch, Hearing Association, 1980-81; New Zealand Medical Association; Otolaryngological Society of New Zealand; Politzer Society; Auditory Society (N.Z.); Acoustical Soceity (N.Z.); New Zealand Society for the Deaf. *Publications:* Co-author of: The Reversibility of Anoric swelling of liver slices, 1962; Combined Approach Tymponoplasty in Children, 1972; Antibiotic Treatment of Secretary Otitis Media assessed by impedance Audionating, 1975; The use of intravenous lignocaine in the diagnosis & treatment of tinnetis, 1978; Treatment of Tinnitus with oral anticonvulsants, 1979; Tinnitus in Patient Management, 1980; Drugs in treatment of Tinnitus, 1981. *Hobbies:* Sailing; Swimming; Research & Welfare services for Deafness; Orchardist. *Address:* 13 Ingram Road, Remuera, Auckland, 5, New Zealand.

GOODFELLOW, Ronald, b. 17 Nov. 1937, London. Consultant Chartered Civil Engineer. m. 27 June 1964, 1 son, 1 daughter. *Education:* BSc., Civil Engineering, London University, 1962. *Appointments:* Sandford Fawcett & Partners, 1962-64; Rendel Palmer & Triton, 1965-69; British Petroleum Co., Ltd., 1969-72; Director, Comex-John Brown, 1972-78; Director, Comex Diving, 1974-75; Tokola Underwater Engineer, 1978-80; Gooldfellow Associates, 1980-. *Memberships:* Chairman, British National Committee for E.C.OR; President Engineering Committee for Ocean Resources; Fellow Institution of Civil Engineers; American Society of Civil Engineers; British Institute of Management; Institute of Petroleum; Vice-President, Society for Underwater Technology. *Publications:* Underwater Engineering; Critical Path Analysis; Zakum Sub-Sea Production. *Honours:* Diploma of Public Health; Bronze Medal, Swedish Institute of Technology. *Address:* Tennis; Swimming; Squash; Theatre. *Address:* Northleigh, Westbury Road, Bickley, Bromley BR1 2QB, Kent. England.

GOODING, Grant Leckie, b. 9 May 1928, Toronto, Canada. Professional Engineer; Business Man. m. Carolyn Logan, 31 July 1954, 2 sons, 2 daughters. *Education:* BA Sc Civil Engineering, University of Toronto, 1950; MBA McMaster University, 1971. *Appointments:* Engineer, Toronto Iron Works, 1950-52; Chief Engineer, Central Bridge Company, 1953-59; Vice-President, Corporate Development, Procor Limited, 1960-. The Oakville Club; Engineers Club of Toronto; Board of Trade of Metropolitan Toronto; Canadian Chamber of Commerce; Canadian Association for Corporate Growth; Canadian Manufacturers Association. *Hobbies:* Tennis; Skiing. *Address:* 250 Elton Park Road, Oakville, Ontario, L6V 4C1, Canada.

GOODLAD, Alastair Robertson, b. 4 July 1943, United Kingdom. Member of Parliament. m. Cecilia Barbara Hurst, 7 Dec. 1978, 2 sons. *Education:* King's College, Cambridge, 1962-66; History Exhibitioner, Trevelyan Scholar; MA, Hons; Tripos Part I History, Part II Law; LL.B, International Law. *Appointments:* Contested Crew Division (Conservative), 1970; Elected MP, for Northwich (Conservative), 1974; Joint Honorary Secretary Conservative Parliamentary Trade Committee, 1978-79; Vice-Chairman, 1979; Joint Honorary Secretary Conservative Parliamentary Northern Ireland Committee, 1979; Select Committee on Agriculture, 1979; Joint Honorary Secretary, All Party Group for Population and Development, 1979; Honorary Secretary All Party Heritage Group, 1979; Appointed Government Whip, 1981. *Address:* Common Farm, Tarporley, Cheshire, England.

GOODMAN, Rupert Douglas, b. 25 Nov. 1915, Melbourne, Australia. Educationalist. m. Winnifred Ruthning, 23 Apr. 1946, 1 daughter. *Education:* BA, 1949, Dip. Ed (1st Hons), 1950, BED, 1951, Melbourne, Australia; PhD, Canberra, Australia, 1955. *Appointments:* Teacher Victorian Educational Department, 1934-52; Research Scholar ANU, 1952-55; Headmaster Malvern Grammar School, 1955-59; Lecturer, Senior Lecturer and Reader, Education Department, External Studies, University of Queensland, Australia. *Memberships:* Queensland Commissioner for the Australian Broadcasting VCommission, 1978-; Chairman, Queensland Council for Childrens Films and Television, 1962-; Council Australian College of Education; Queensland Institute Educational Research. *Publica-*

tions: Secondary Education In Queensland, 1860-1960—1970; Toowoomba Grammar School, 1975-1975—A Centenary History. *Honours:* Fellow of Australian College of Education, 1975 (for outstanding service to Australian education). *Hobbies:* Gardening; Reading; Public Speaking. *Address:* 35 Sixth Avenue, St. Lucia, Brisbane, Australia 4067.

GOODSALL, Jon Anthony, b. 10 Aug. 1937, Sydney, NSW, Australia. Civil Engineer. m. Rosemary Salier Bayes, 26 Feb. 1966, 3 daughters. *Education:* Bachelor of Engineering (Civil), University of Melbourne, 1956-59; *Appointments:* Concrete Constructions Group of Companies, 1959-. *Memberships:* Institution of Engineers, Australia; Australian Institute of Building. *Hobbies:* Sailing; Fishing. *Address:* 6 Piccadilly Place, Bulleen, Victoria, Australia.

GOODWIN, Charles Stewart, b. 11 Dec. 1932, London. Physician; Microbiologist; University Lecturer. m. Jean Elizabeth Bruce, 14 Mar. 1959, 2 sons, 2 daughters. *Education:* Clare College, Cambridge, 1951-54; BA, MA, MB, B Chir, MD, St Bartholomews Hospital, London, 1954-57; Dip Bact., Member of Royal College of Pathologists of England, 1965-66; Fellow of the Royal College of Pathologists of Australia. *Appointments:* Hand Research Unit, Christian Medical College, Vellore, India, 1960; Physician & Surgeon, Leprosy Research Sanitorium, Karigiri, India, 1961; Physician & Bacteriologist, Leprosarium, Hong Kong, 1962-64; Senior Bacteriologist, Leprosy Research Hospital, Addis Ababa, Ethiopia, 1967-69; Consultant Microbiologist, Northwick Park Hospital, London, 1971-75; Associate Professor in Clinical Microbiology, University of Western Australia, Head of Department of Microbiology, Royal Perth Hospital, 1976-81. *Publications:* Essentials of leprosy for the clinician, Hong Kong, 1963; Microbial Disease: the use of the laboratory in diagnosis therapy and control, 1979; and numerous publications in medical journals. *Hobbies:* Evangelical Biblical Exegesis & Practice; Anthropology; Archaeology. *Address:* 76 Dalkeith Road, Nedlands, Perth, Western Australia 6009.

GOODWIN, Kenneth Leslie, b. 29 Sept. 1934, Sydney, Australia. University Professor. m. Agnes Elizabeth Shannon, 2 July 1971, 1 son, 2 daughters. *Education:* BA, 1956, DipEd., 1957, MA, 1963, University of Sydney; D.Phil., Oxford University, 1970. *Appointments:* Secondary School Teacher, NSW, Australia, 1957; Lecturer in English, The Teachers' College, Wagga Wagga, NSW, 1958; Lecturer in English, Department of External Studies, 1959-61, Department of English, Lecturer, 1962-67, Senior Lecturer, 1967-69, Reader, 1970-71, Professor, 1971-, University of Queensland; Visiting Professor, Department of English, University of California, Berkeley, USA, 1967; Head, Department of English, University of Queensland, 1974-79. *Memberships:* Chairman, Association for Commonwealth Literature and Laguage Studies, 1977-80; South Pacific Association for Commonwealth Literature and Language Studies, 1975-; Visual & Performing Arts Course Assessment Committee, Board of Advanced Education, Queensland, 1977-; Kelvin Grove College of Advanced Education, Brisbane, 1972-. *Publications:* The Influence of Ezra Pound, 1966; Editor, National Identity, 1970; An Approach to Modern Poetry, 1968; Editor, Commonwealth Literature in the Curriculum—A Teaching Guide, 1980. *Honours:* MacCallum Prize for English Literature and Language, Josiah Symon Scholarship, University of Sydney, 1952; P R Cole Prize, Sydney Teachers' College, 1956; British Council Travel Grant, 1965; Meyerstein Bequest Grant, Oxford University; Balliol College Grant, 1966. *Hobby:* Renaissance music. *Address:* 76 Orchard Terrace, St Lucia, Queensland 4067, Australia.

GOONERATNE, Malini Yasmine, (Mrs Brendon Gooneratne), b. Colombo, Sri Lanka. University Teacher. m. Dr. Brendon Gooneratne, 31 Dec. 1962, 1 son, 1 daughter. *Education:* 1st Class Honours degree in English, Faculty of Arts, University of Ceylon, 1959; PhD English Literature, Cambridge University, 1962; DLitt., Maquarie University, 1981. *Appointments:* Assistant Lecturer, English Literature, University of Ceylon, Peradeniya, 1958-59; Assistant Lecturer, Lecturer, Senior Lecturer, English Literature, 1962-72; Senior Lecturer, Macquarie University, New South Wales, Australia, 1972-75; Associate Professor of English, Macquarie University, Australia, 1976-. *Memberships:* Australasian & Pacific Society for Eigh-

teenth Century Studies; South Pacific Association for Commonwealth Literature & Language Studies; Australian Federation of University Women; South Asian Studies Association. *Publications:* Word, Bird, Motif: Poems, 1971; The Lizard's Cry and Other Poems, 1972; Jane Austen, 1970; Alexander Pope, 1976; English Literature in Ceylon 1815-1878, 1968; Stories from Sri Lanka, 1979; 6000 ft. Death Dive: Poems, 1981; Poems from India, Sri Lanka, Malaysia and Singapore, 1979; Diverse Inheritance, 1980. *Honours:* Exhibition in English, University of Ceylon, 1954; Pettah Library Prize, 1955; Government of Ceylon University Scholarship, Examination in Arts, 1958; Sir Richard Stapley Education Trust Grant, Cambridge, 1960; Girton College Grant, Cambridge, 1960; Bartle Frere Exhibition, Cambridge, 1968; Leon Bequest Special Grant, University of London, 1968; International Research Research Fellowship for English Literature, American Association of University Women, 1968. *Address:* 57 Cheltenham Road, Cheltenham, Sydney, New South Wales, 2119, Australia.

GOONEWARDENA, Neranjanan Gurdip Aswini, b. 2 Apr. 1946, Colombo, Sri-Lanka. *Education:* Institute of Chartered Accountants, Sri-Lanka, 1969-73. *Appointments:* Articled Clerk, M N Sambamurti and Company, Sri-Lanka, 1969-73; Accountant, National Salt Corporation, Sri-Lanka, 1974-76; Accountant, Nihal Ameresekera and Comlpany, Sri-Lanka, 1978; Auditor, Diversified Discount and Acceptance Corporation, Minnesota, USA, 1979-80; Internal Auditor, Cargill, Incorporated Minnesota, USA, 1980-. *Memberships:* Institute of Chartered Accountants of Sri-Lanka; Minnesota Society of Certified Public Accountants, USA. *Address:* 4014 3rd Avenue South, Minneapolis, Minnesota, 55409, USA.

GOPALDAS, Tara, b. 31 Aug. 1932, Professor. m. Pratap Gopaldas, 20 Aug. 1963, 1 son. *Education:* Bachelor of Science, University of Madras, 1951; Master in Biochemistry, Indian Institute of Science, 1954; Doctor in Nutrition, University of Illinois, USA, 1958. *Appointments:* Research Executive, Hindustan Lever Limited, Bombay, 1959-65; Independant Research Consultant and Visiting Faculty Member, Intitute of Catering Technology and Hotel Management, Bombay, 1967-70; Research Consultant and Project Director of POSHAK, 1971-75; Consultant, Programme Evaluation Organization Planning Commission, New Delhi, 1976-77; Professor and Head, Department of Foods and Nutrition, Faculty of Home Science, Maharaja Sayajirao University, Baroda, India. *Memberships:* Nutrition Society of India, Convenor of the Guijarat Chapter; Indian Dietetic Association, President of the Guijarat Chapter; Advisory Board of the Nutrition Foundation of India. *Publications:* Author and co-author of approximately 40 technical papers in national and international journals; Author and co-author of reports and chapters. *Honours:* Recipient of numerous honours and awards for professional services. *Hobbies:* Reading; Indian Classical dance and music; Meeting people of the world; International travel. *Address:* H-9 Alembic Colony, Baroda-3, Gujarat, India.

GOPICHAND, Kalluru, b. 12 Feb. 1934, Kuchipudi, Andhra Pradesh. Professor and Head of Electrical Engineering. m. Akkamma Gopichand, 31 May 1956, 1 son, 2 daughters. *Education:* BSc, 1955; DIISc, 1958; MTech, 1962; PhD, 1964. *Appointments:* Assistant Lecturer, 1958-60, Lecturer, 1960-64, IIT, Kharaghpur; Assistant Professor, 1964-70; Professor and Head of Electrical Engineering, 1970-81, Vice-Principal, 1977-79, Principal, 1978, SV University. *Memberships:* Fellow of Institution of Engineers; Indian Society for Technical Education; Chartered Engineer, India. *Publications:* Electrical Engineering Tables; Contributed articles in field of electrical engineering to professional journals. *Hobbies:* Gardening; Building Construction. *Address:* Q. No. 41, SVU Campus, SV University, Tirupati, India.

GORDON, Charles Addison Somerville Snowden, (Sir), b. 25 July 1918, Liverpool, England. Clerk of the House of Commons. m. Janet Margaret Beattie, 1943, 1 son, 1 daughter. *Education:* Domus Scholar, Balliol College, Oxford, 1936-39; Second Class Degree in History; BA, 1939; MA, 1945. *Appointments:* Royal Navy, 1939-45; Assistant Clerk, 1946, Senior Clerk, 1947, Fourth Clerk at the Table, 1962, Principal Clerk of the Table Officer, 1967, Second Clerk Assistant, 1974,

Clerk Assistant, 1976, Clerk of the House, 1979, House of Commons. *Memberships:* Society of Clerks at the Table in Commonwealth Parliaments; Association of Secretaries; General of Parliament. *Publications:* Joint author, Parliament as an Export, 1966; Contributor to professional journals; Assistant Editor, Erskine May's Parliamentary Practice (19th Edition). *Honours:* CB, 1970; KCB, 1981. *Address:* 279 Lonsdale Road, Barnes, London, SW13 9QB, England.

GORDON, George Edmund, b. 7 Mar. 1910, Sheffield, England. Headmaster (Retired). *Education:* MA, Diploma in Education, Sheffield University, 1927-31. *Education:* Second Master, 1931-48, Headmaster, 1948-75, Dalnada School, Ballymoney. *Memberships:* Founder and Vice-President, Ballymoney Drama Festival; Arts Council, Northern Ireland; Committee, Corrymeela Community; BBC Drama Group. *Publications:* Read own poetry on BBC; Programme of life and poetry on BBC Television; Numerous poems read on BBC Radio. *Hobbies:* Mountaineering; Music. *Address:* 8 Knocklayde Park, Ballymoney, County Antrim, Northern Ireland.

GORDON, John Bowie (Peter), b. 14 July 1921, Stratford, New Zealand. Privy Councillor/Company Director. m. Dorothy Elizabeth Morton, 5 Aug. 1943, 2 sons, 1 daughter. *Education:* St Andrews College, Christchurch; Lincoln College. *Appointments:* Farmer (Sheep and Arable), 1946-; Director of: Insurance, Transport and Shipping Companies; Politician National Party, 1960, retired, 1978; Minister for: Railways, Transport, Civil Aviation, Marine and Fisheries, 1966-72; Labour, State Services, 1975-78; Presently Director of: Meat, Transport, Banking, Insurance etc. *Memberships:* Past President of: West Otago A & P Association; West Otago RSA; West Otago Federated Farmers. *Publications:* Some Aspects of British Farming, 1955. *Honours:* Nuffield Scholar Farming, 1954; USA Leader Grantee, 1964; Privy Council, 1978. *Hobbies:* Golf; Gardening; Cooking. *Address:* Sussex Street, Tapanui, New Zealand.

GORDON, Michael Huntly, b. 19 Oct. 1936, Ottawa, Ontario. Barrister and Solicitor. m. Izetta Anne Elizabeth McAllan, 13 Aug. 1960, 1 son, 1 daughter. *Education:* BA, 1960, MA (History), University of New Brunswick, 1964; LLB, Queen's University, Kingston, Ontario, 1967; Barrister-at-law, Province of Ontario, 1969. *Appointments:* Executive Assistant, Minister of Youth and Welfare, Province of New Brunswick, 1960-64; Freelance broadcaster, 1964-69; Barrister-at-law, Miller, Thompson, Sedgewick, Lewis and Healy, Toronto, 1969-70; Barrister-at-law, Sandler, Gordon and Gleiberman, Toronto, 1970-71; Associate, 1971-73, Partner, Du Vernet, Carruthers, 1973-76; Partner, Du Vernet, Beard, Winter 1976-79; Partner Beard, Winter, Gordon, 1979-. *Memberships:* Law Society of Upper Canada; Canadian Bar Association; Advocates Society; Empire Club; Vice Commodore, Prince Edward Cruising Club; Director, Toronto Institute for Human Relations; Chairman of the Board, Tafelmusik. *Publications:* The Andrew G Blair Administration and the Abolition of Legislative Council of New Brunswick, 1876-1886, MA thesis; Follow-up studies on proceedings under Section 65 of the Labour Relations Act, Ontario issued by Privy Council, Canada; Publications on topical items and reviews of books in the Atlantic Advocate Industrial Canada and Canadian Bar Journal, The Financial Post, 1967-74. *Honours:* Various awards achieved at university. *Hobbies:* Sailing; Building ship's models; Photography. *Address:* 77 Braeside Road, Toronto, Ontario, Canada, M4N 1X9.

GORHAM, Richard Masters, b. 3 Oct. 1917, Paget, Bermuda. Business Executive. m. 21 May, 1948, 3 sons, 1 daughter. *Education:* O Level Matriculation, Ridley College, Ontario, Canada. *Appointments:* President of: A J Gorham Limited, 1948-64, The Supermart Limited, 1954-, Bermuda Paint Company Limited, Bermuda Office Supplies Limited; Political Offices: Parliamentary Secretary for Finance, 1968-76; Government Marketing Board; Board of Public Works; Board of Agriculture; Department of Planning; Armed Forces, 1938-46; Bermuda Volunteer Engineers, 1938; Bermuda Militia Artillery, 1940; Royal Artillery, Pilot Army Air Command, Artillery Spotter, Captain Royal Artillery, 1942; Financial Consultant and Fund Raiser for: The Salvation Army, New Testament Church of God, Matilda Smith Williams Home, The Bermuda

Regiment, Warriors' Chapel and All ex-Servicemen in need; Financial Consultant, Bermuda Diabetic Association; President and Financial Consultant and Organiser of The Home for the Handicapped; General Consultant and Advisor for Financial Affairs of all Bermuda Charities. *Memberships:* President, Bermuda Chamber of Commerce, 1956-58; Chairman, (12 years), Finance Committee, United Bermuda Party; Affiliated to several other Associations and Committees. *Honours:* Distinguished Flying Cross, Italy, 1944; Coronation Medal; CBE, 1976. *Hobbies:* Fund rasing for community service; Education of young people; Rugby (12 years for Bermuda and Regiment in England); Table Tennis (Bermuda Singles Champion); Golf; Tennis; Offshore Yacht Racing (Commodore). *Address:* Westmorland, Pembroke West, Bermuda.

GORTON, (Sir) John Grey, b. 9 Sept. 1911, Melbourne, Australia. Former Politician and Former Prime Minister of Australia. m. Bettina Brown, 16 Feb. 1935, 2 sons, 1 daughter. *Education:* MA, Brasenose College, University of Oxford, 1936. *Appointments:* War Service, 1940-44; Senator, State of Victoria, 1949-68; Minister for the Navy, 1958-63; Minister assisting the Minister for External Affairs, 1960-63; Minister in Charge of CSIRO, 1962-68; Minister for Works and under the Prime Minister in Charge of Commonwealth Activities in Education and Research, 1963-66; Minister for the Interior, 1963-64; Minister for Works, 1966-67; Minister for Education and Science, 1966-68; Government Leader in the Senate, 1967-68; MHR, Higgins, Victoria, 1968-75; Prime Minister of Australia, 1968-71; Minister for Defence and Deputy Leader of the Liberal Party, 1971; Parliamentary Liberal Party Executive and Liberal Party spokesman on Environment, Conservation, Urban and Regional Development, 1973-74; Deputy-Chairman of Parliamentary Joint Committee on Prices, 1973-74; Retired from Parliament, 1975. *Memberships:* Councillor, 1947-52, President, 1949-50, Kerang Shire; Lodden Valley Regional Committee. *Honours:* Privy Councillor, 1968; Companion of Honour, 1971; Kt. Grand Cross of the Order of St. Michael and St. George, 1977. *Hobbies:* Reading; Swimming. *Address:* Suite 3 9th Floor, Qantas House, 197 London Circuit, Canberra City, Australia.

GOSPER, Richard Kevan, b. 19 Dec. 1933, Sydney, Australia. Chairman. m. Jillian Mary, 16 Sept. 1955, 2 sons. *Education:* BA(Hons.) Michigan State University, USA, 1955. *Appointments:* Holding various positions with Shell Australia Limited, 1959-80; Chairman and Chief Executive Officer, 1980-. *Memberships:* International Olympic Committee; Australian Olympic Federation; Australian Institute of Sport; Commonwealth Scientific and Industrial Research Organisation; Melbourne Club; Australian Club; Metropolitan Golf Club. *Honours:* Representation at Commonwealth, Gold Medal and Olympic Silver Medal, Games, 1954-60. *Hobbies:* Amateur Sports Administration; Skiing; Reading; Music. *Address:* 54 Powlett Street, East Melbourne, Victoria 3002, Australia.

GOSS, David Colin, b. 6 Feb. 1933, Sydney, Australia. Diplomat. m. Elizabeth Ann Briant, 31 Mar. 1962, 1 son, 2 daughters. *Education:* Bachelor of Arts (Hons) University of Melbourne 1955. *Appointments:* Minister Australian Embassy, Bangkok, 1973-75; Assistant Secretary, Department of Foreign Affairs, Canberra, 1975-77; Consul General, Chicago, 1977-80; Ambassador to Israel, 1980-. *Hobbies:* Tennis; Philately. *Address:* 78 Rehov Ha'eshel, Herzliya-Pituach, Israel.

GOSTAND, Reba Félice, b. 20 Jan. 1923, Katoomba, NSW, Australia. Lecturer, World Drama; Australian Literature. m. Samuel Gohstand, 28 May 1953, 1 son, 1 daughter. *Education:* BA(1st class Hon.), University of Sydney, 1950; MA, University of Queensland, 1967. *Appointments:* WAAAF, (Cinema Projectionist and part-time Instructor), 1942-44; Editorial Assistant, CSIRO, Sydney, 1951; Lecturer, Department of External Studies, University of Queensland, 1952-53; Part-time marker, Tutor, Public examiner (Senior), 1953-68; Tutor, D.E.S. 1969, Lecturer, Division of External Studies, University of Queensland, 1972-. *Memberships:* ALUMNI, University of Queensland; AULLA; SPACLALS; ASAL; ADSA. *Publications:* Author, The Road to Tocumwal, 1945; At the Initiation, Poems, 1951; The Numberless Sands, 1952; Poems in various periodicals and anthologies; Critical articles in British and Australian publications; Poems set to music. *Honours:* Two,

Henry Lawson Prizes for Poetry, 1947; Thomas Henry Coulson Scholarship, Sydney University, 1948; Wentworth Medal, for critical essay on poet, Furnley Maurice 1949. *Hobbies:* Reading; Music; Theatre; Travel; Food; Dancing. *Address:* 14/36 Jerdanefield Road, St Lucia, Queensland, Australia.

GOSWAMI, DAIBYA Hash, b. 1 May 1938. Educational Administrator. m. Sarita, 24 Nov. 1969, 3 daughters. *Education:* BA, 1957, PhD, 1980, Ganhah University, India; MA, Banaras Hindu University, India, 1960. *Appointments:* Lecturer, St. Edmund's College, 1961-65; Assistant Registrar, 1965-70, Registrar, 1970-, Dibrugarh University, India. *Memberships:* Member, Board of Secondary Education Association; Member, Governing Body, Assam Cricket Association; Senior Vice-President, Bibrugarh University Sports Board. *Publications:* 10 published papers in the fields of University administration, games and sports. *Honours:* Gold Medal in History, 1960; Captain, Banaras Hindu University Cricket team, 1959-60; Represented Assam State in Ranja Trophy. *Hobbies:* Cricket; Tennis; Horticulture. *Address:* Jiban Phukan Nagar, Dibrugarh 786 003, India.

GOTZE, Clas, b. 29 Jan. 1942, Eskholt/Vejle, Denmark. Managing Director. m. Sandra Evans, 15 Dec. 1973. *Education:* 4 year Apprenticeship as a Toolmaker with Laur. Knudsen Electrical Manufacturing Co. Limited, 1962-65; EE Engineer, Copenhagen Engineering College, Denmark, 1965-68. *Appointments:* 2 years in Danish Army, until Apr. 1967; Section Head, Plastic Transfer Test Engineering Group and Electronics Services Manager and Technical Advisor, Fairchild Semiconductor, Mountain View, USA. and Hong Kong respectively, 1969-70; Managing Director, Kulicke & Soffa Limited, Hong Kong, 1970-72; General Technical Consultant, Neckermann Versand, Hong Kong, 1972-73; Managing Director, Kras Asia Limited, Hong Kong, 1973-. *Memberships:* Member, Industrial Affairs Committee, Industrial Development Fund Management Committee, Electronic Committee, Hong Kong General Chamber of Commerce; Management Representative, Hong Kong Productivity Council; Member, Industrial Development Board of Trade, Industry and Customs Department of Hong Kong Government; Hong Kong Country Club; USRC; ABC. *Hobbies:* Sailing; Skiing; Tennis. *Address:* G/F & 1/F, D D 256, Lot %589, Tai Mong Tsai, Sai Kung, Kowloon, Hong Kong.

GOUGH, John Bernard, b. 22 Aug. 1928, Melbourne, Australia. Managing Director. m. Rosemary Olive Upjohn, 15 June 1955, 1 son, 2 daughters. *Education:* Diploma, Tex. Ind., Graduated 1950, Leeds University, UK; Melbourne University Business School; Harvard Business School. *Appointments:* Footwear Division, 1970, Clothing, Fottwear and Textiles Division, 1976, Managing Director, 1980, Dunlop Australia Limited, now Dunlop Olympic Limited. *Memberships:* Chairman, Advisory Board, Graduate School of Business Administration, University of Melbourne, Australia; Fellow of Institute of Management; Chairman, Trade Development Council, Commonwealth Government Department of Trade and Resources; Member Australian Manufacturing Council, Commonwealth Government Department of Industry and Commerce; Member, Premier of Victoria's Economic Adviser's Committee; Member Australia/China Trade Advisory Group; Athenaeum Club, Melbourne; Commonwealth Club, Canberra. *Honours:* OBE, 1980. *Hobbies:* Golf; Tennis; Gardening; The Arts. *Address:* 11 Douglas Street, Toorak, Victoria 3142, Australia.

GOULD, Alan Roy, b. 31 Jan. 1947, Oxford, England. Researcher. m. Stephanie Denise Sibson, 27 Mar. 1975, 1 son. *Education:* BSc.(Biology), University of Sussex, UK, 1971; PhD.(Plant Cell Physiology), University of Leicester, UK. *Appointments:* Research Fellow, Genetics Department, Research School of Biological Sciences, 1975-80, Senior Research Fellow, Department of Developmental Biology, 1981-, Australian National University, Canberra, Australia. *Memberships:* Australian Society of Plant Physiology; International Association for Plant Tissue Culture; American Association for the Advancement of Science; Tissue Culture Association; H E Street Tankard Club No. LXXXVIII. *Publications:* Publications concerning chromosome stability and the control of cell division in plant tissue cultures in several journals. *Hobbies:* Playing jazz. *Address:* Plant Genetics Group, Pfizer Central

Research, Eastern Point Road, Groton, Connecticut 06340, USA.

GOURDAU, Jean-Paul, President and Chief Operating Officer. m. Jeannine Lamarre, 4 children. *Appointments:* Technical Consultant, Department of Health, Province of Québec; Strveyer, Nenniger and Chènevert, Chief Engineer, Municipal Division, 1961-65; Director of Engineering, 1965, Vice President, Operations in 1966; Executive Vice-President, SNC Group, 1972-75; *Memberships:* President, International Federation of Consulting Engineers; Science Council of Canada; Director, l'Ecole de Technologie Supérieure of the University of Québec, Montréal, Ducrois, Meilleur, Roy et Associés Ltée and Didier Refractories Corporation. *Publications:* Author of several articles in the field of Technical background, environmental control, Water Pollution Control. *Honours:* Arthur Sidney Bedell Award, from the Water Pollution Control Federation of Washington, DC. *Address:* St Lambert, Québec, Canada.

GOUTAM, Shri Krishna b. 25 Apr. 1943, Jabalpur, India. Medical Doctor. m. Smt Kusum, 12 Mar. 1967, 1 son, 1 daughter. *Education:* BSc., 1962, MBBS, 1967, MD, 1971, Jabalpur University, India. *Appointments:* Demonstrator in Medicine, Medical College, Jabalpur, India, 1969-71; Medical Officer, 1972-75, Senior Medical Officer, 1975-, P & T D Dispensary, Jabalpur, India. *Memberships:* Secretary, District and State Branch, IMA; Secretary, District Branch, API; American College of Chester Physicians. *Publications:* Izon dextran in Anaemia; Impotence. *Hobbies:* Reading; Gardening. *Address:* Goutam Ganj, Garha, Jabalpur(MP), India.

GOVIL, Narendra Kumar, b. 5 Jan. 1940, Aligarh, India: Teacher; Researcher. m. Urmila Agarwal, 1 Feb. 1964, 2 sons. *Education:* BSc., Agra University, India, 1957; MSc., Aligarh Muslim University, India, 1959; PhD., 1968, Post Doctoral, 1972-73, University of Montreal, Canada. *Appointments:* Research Fellow, Aligarh Muslim University, India, 1962-63; Lecturer, College of Engineering and Technology, Aligarh, India, 1963-64; Lecturer, 1967-68, Assistant Professor, 1968-70, Concordia University, Montreal, Canada; Assistant Professor, 1970-78, Associate Professor, 1978-79, Professor, 1979, Indian Institute of Technology, Delhi, India; Visiting Scientist, Dalhousie University, Halifax, Canada, 1980; Visiting Professor, University of Alberta, Edmonton, Canada, 1981-82. *Memberships:* Indian Mathematical Society; Indian Science Congress; Mathematical Association of India; Member, Executive Council, Society of Mathematical Sciences, Delhi, India. *Publications:* approximately 25 research papers in International Mathematical Journals. *Honours:* Fellow of the National Academy of Sciences of India. *Hobbies:* Music; Travel; Reading. *Address:* House No. 9, Mini Campus, Indian Institute of Technology, New Delhi 110016, India.

GOW, Neil Milne, b. 24 Aug. 1926, Brisbane, Australia. Company Director. m. Jocelyn Exon, 30 July 1955, 2 sons, 1 daughter. *Education:* BApp.Sc. Queensland; Fellow Royal Australian Chemical Institute; Fellow Australian Institute Food, Science and Technology; Fellow, Australian Institute of Management. *Appointments:* Chemist, 1950-52; Chief Chemist, 1952-58; Production Manager, 1958-61; Factory Manager, 1961-69; General Manager, 1969-72; Chairman, R.M. Gow and Company Limited, 1972-. *Memberships:* The Queensland Club; Queensland Cricketers Club. *Honours:* CMG, 1979. *Address:* 59 O'Brien Road, Pullenvale, Queensland, Australia 4069.

GOYAL, Ravindra Nath, b. 14 Sept. 1941, Budaun (UP), India. Telecom Expert. m. Sudha Gupta, 21 Feb. 1968, 2 sons. *Education:* BSc, (Pure Sciences); 1959; BE,(Electrical Engineering), 1962; ME,(Electrical Engineering), 1963; Certificate in Spanish Language and Literature, 1970; Post Graduate Diploma in French Language and Literature, 1972; Diplom de l'ACTIM (Paris), Computer Communications, 1980. *Appointments:* Assistant Director, Telecom Research, 1963-71, Deputy Director, Telecom Training, 1971-73, Senior Deputy Chief Engineer, Telecom Research, 1973-76, Director, Telecom Planning, 1976-, Indian Posts and Telegraphs. *Memberships:* Fellow, Institution of Engineers (India); Council member, UP State Centre, Institution in Electronics and Telecom Division; Fellow, Institution of Electronics and Telecommunication

Engineers of India; Computer Society of India; Rose Society of India. *Publications:* approximately 53 papers in field of Telecommunications in national and international technical journals; numerous literary essays in Hindi and English in magazines and newspapers. *Honours:* Merit Scholarship, 1959-62; Junior Fellowship of University Grants Commission for one year, 1962-63; National Award of Gandhi Centenary Foundation, 1969; University Gold Medal, 1963; French Government's Medal, 1980; Gold Medal of Institution of Engineers (India), 1979-80. *Hobbies:* Horticulture; Numismatism; Photography; Indian archaeology. *Address:* c/o Dr. K N Govil, Civil Lines, Budaun (UP) 243601, India.

GRACE, Henry, b. 14 Nov. 1911, Bristol, England. Chartered Civil Engineer. m. Ann Warren Handran, 20 Mar. 1948, 2 sons, 2 daughters. *Education:* MSc, Bristol University, UK, 1930-33; SM., Harvard University, USA, 1938-39. *Appointments:* A P I. Cotterell & Son, Westminster, London, UK, 1933-34, 1939-42; West Surrey Water Company, UK, 1934-36; Sandford Fawcett & Partners, UK, 1936-38; Royal Air Force, 1942-46; Partner, 1950-76, Senior Partner, 1972-76, Senior Consultant, 1977-, Scott & Wilson, now Scott Wilson Kirkpatrick & Partners by amalgamation with Sir Cyril Kirkpatrick & Partners. *Memberships:* Fellow: Institution of Civil Engineers; American Society of Civil Engineers; Institution of Highway Engineers; Royal Geographical Society; member of Institution of Water Engineers & Scientists; East India Sports Club; St. Georges Hill Golf Club; Director of International Road Federation. *Publications:* various papers to: Institution of Civil Engineers; International Road Federation; Permanent International Association of Road Congresses. *Honours:* Miller prize, Telford premium, Overseas premium, Palmer prize, awarded by Institution of Civil Engineers. *Hobbies:* Photography; Golf;Mountaineering. *Address:* Garthcliff, South Ridge, St Georges Hill, Weybridge, Surrey, KT13 ONF.

GRACE, Radcliffe, b. 25 Dec. 1916, Melbourne, Australia. Hospital Administrator. m. Kathleen Kennedy, 17 Sept. 1953, 1 daughter. *Education:* Fellow, Australian Society of Accountants; Fellow, Institute of Chartered Secretaries and Administrators; Fellow, Australian College of Health Service Administrators; BA. *Appointments:* Edmond J Ryan & Co., Chartered Accountants, Melbourne, Australia, 1934; Chief Executive Officer, St. Vincent's Hospital, Melbourne, Australia, 1942. *Memberships:* Melbourne Cricket Club; Vice-President, Camberwell Cricket Club; Box Hill Golf Club; Vice-President, Australian Cricket Society. *Publications:* A Century to Camberwell Cricket Club; Warwick Armstrong - a biography; Only One Baggy Green Cap. *Honours:* OBE, 1976. *Hobbies:* Cricket; Reading; Golf; Bookbinding. *Address:* 28 Fairmont Avenue, Camberwell, Victoria 3124, Australia.

GRAHAM, Alison Mary, b. 3 Dec. 1922, London, England.Doctor. m. Alexander Joseph Paul, 17 July 1948, 2 sons, 2 daughters. *Education:* London School of Medicine for Women; University of London, 1941-46; MRCS.LRCP., 1947; MB., BS., London, 1947. *Memberships:* Member, Executive Committee, National Council for Social Service; Member, Liaison Committee for National Women's Organisations; Ex Vice-President, National Council for Women; International Standing Committee of Health of International Council for Women-member for Zimbabwe; Member, Executive and National Committees, Zimbabwe Freedom from Hunger Campaign; Past National President, Catholic Women's League; Member, Executive, St. Giles Medical Rehabilitation Centre. *Publications:* Determination of the Neonatal and Infant Mortality Rate in Mufakose, Salisbury, Rhodesia, 1975. *Hobbies:* Cooking; Genealology. *Address:* Rest and be Thankful, 51 Ridgeway North, Highlands, Salisbury, Zimbabwe.

GRAHAM, Charles Edmund, b. 28 Aug. 1927, Sydney, Australia. Orthopaedic Surgeon. m. 27 May 1961, 2 sons, 1 daughter. *Education:* MBBS., University of Sydney, Australia, 1954; FRCSE., 1959; FRACS., 1977; FACS., 1981. *Appointments:* Orthopaedic Surgeon, St George Hospital, Kogarah, Sydney, Australia, 1964-; Orthopaedic Surgeon, Prince of Wales Hospital, Sydney, Australia, 1969-. Foundation member, International Society for the Study of the Lumbar Spine; Corresponding member, Association of Bone and Joint Surgeons of the USA; Selection Committee

for Overseas membership for Association of Bone and Joint Surgeons of the USA. *Publications:* numerous publications including: Hip Arthrodesis, 1963; A Prophylaxis Against Tetanus, 1965; A New Method of Ankle Arthrodesis, 1972; Backache and Sciatica: The Use of Chymopapain in the Treatment of Lumbar Disc Disease, 1972; Chemonucleolysis, 1975, 76, 81. *Hobbies:* Sailing; Skiing; Squash. *Address:* 61 Kambala Road, Bellevue Hill 2023, Sydney, Australia.

GRAHAM, Daisy Agatha, b. 13 Aug. 1935, Jamaica, West Indies. Associate Professor of Education. *Education:* Teachers Diploma, 1961; BA (com laude), 1970; MA., 1971; Professional Diploma in Education, 1973; Certificate in Fiction Writing, 1973; Doctor of Education, 1975. *Appointments:* School teacher, All Saints Government, Kingston Senior Schools, 1961-68; Lecturer in English, EOC, State University of New York, USA, 1973-75; Head of Graduate Studies, University of Guyana, 1975-78; Associate Professor, Head of Research and Evaluation Institute of Extra Mural Services, National University of Lesotho, Africa. *Memberships:* World Council for Curriculum and Instruction; Lesotho Association of Non Formal Education; African Adult Education Association. *Publications:* Experience: Thoughts That Linger; A Critical Analysis of Trends and Patterns of Secondary Education in Jamaica; Lifelong Education in Developing Countries: in Education in a World Perspective; Twenty Triumphant Years: 1960-1980. *Honours:* American Association of University Women Fellowship, 1973-74; Institute of Study for Older Adults Fellowship, 1972-73. *Hobbies:* Creative Writing; Reading; Singing; Music. *Address:* National University of Lesotho, PO Roma, Lesotho, Africa.

GRAHAM, Douglas, b. 25 Aug. 1939, Melbourne, Australia. Barrister-at-Law. m. Sara Anne Harrington, 16 Jan. 1969, 2 daughters. *Education:* Trinity College, University of Melbourne, 1958-61; LLB(Hons), 1962. *Appointments:* Barrister of Supreme Court of Victoria, 1963; Associate to Rt. Hon. Mr Justice Windeyer 1963; Barrister 1964; Barrister of Supreme Court of A.C.T., 1979; Barrister of Supreme Court of NSW, 1980; Queen's Counsel, Victoria, 1978; Queen's Counsel, ACT, 1979; Queen's Counsel, NSW, 1980. *Memberships:* Medico-Legal Society; Australian Bar Association; Melbourne Club; Royal Melbourne Golf Club; Melbourne Cricket Club; Victoria Racing Club. *Honours:* Queen's Counsel: Victoria, 1978, ACT, 1979, NSW, 1980. *Hobbies:* Golf; Music; Bridge. *Address:* 21 Chesterfield Avenue, Malvern 3144, Victoria, Australia.

GRAHAM, John Alexander Noble (Sir), b. 15 July 1926, Calcutta, India. Baronet; Diplomat. m. Marygold Austin, 7 Jan. 1956, 2 sons, 1 daughter. *Education:* BA, Cambridge University, UK, 1948-50. *Appointments:* Army, 1944-47; Foreign Office, 1950, 1954 57, 1961-66, 1977-78, 1980-; Bahrain/Kuwait, 1951-53; Amman, 1953-54; Belgrade, 1957-60; Benghazi, 1960-61; Kuwait, 1966-69; Private Secretary to Foreign Secretary, 1969-72; Washington, 1972-74; Ambassador to Iraq, 1974-77; Ambassador to Iran, 1979-80. *Honours:* KCMG, 1979. *Address:* Foreign and Commonwealth Office, Downing Street, London SW1, England.

GRAHAM, Ronald Anthony, b. 19 Oct. 1956, Christ Church, Barbados. Pharmacist. *Education:* Pharmacy Certificate, Barbados Community College, Barbados, 1974-78. *Appointments:* Assistant Researcher, Barbados Drug Formulary, Project Design and Implementation Unit, Ministry of Health, July 1979-; Collins Limited, Jan.79-March,79; Queen Elizabeth Hospital, March-July,1979. *Memberships:* Barbados Paharmaceutical Society; Secretary, Clapham Sports Club. *Honours:* Highest Academic Achievement, Student Pharmacist, Barbados Pharmaceutical Society; Best Academic Performance, Student Pharmacist, Barbados Community College. *Hobbies:* Sports; Reading; Photography; Music. *Address:* Rendezvous Road, Upper Clapham, St Michael, Barbados.

GRANT, Alan Proctor, b. 27 July 1918, Dublin, Ireland. Consultant Physician. m. Jane Pugh, 26 Apr. 1944, 2 sons, 1 daughter. *Education:* MB., 1940; MD., 1946; Fellow Royal Colleges of Physicians of Ireland, London, Glasgow, Edinburgh; Fellow, International College of Angiology. *Appointments:* Captain, RAMC., 1941-46; Consultant, Belfast City Hospital, Ireland,

1948-. *Memberships:* President, RCP. Ireland, 1977-80. *Publications:* numerous Medical and Antiquarian publications. *Honours:* Mention Dispatches, 1943, 44; CBE., 1980; Hon. Fellow, American College of Physicians, 1978. *Hobbies:* Irish History; Yachting. *Address:* Killenican, Killinchy, Co. Down, Northern Ireland.

GRANT, Alexander Marshall, b. 22 Feb. 1925, Wellington, New Zealand. Dancer; Artistic Director. *Education:* Wellington College, New Zealand. *Appointments:* Dancer, Sadler's Wells Ballet (now The Royal Ballet), 1946-76; Co-Director, 1970-71. Director, 1971-76, Ballet for All; Artistic Director, The National Ballet of Canada, 1976-; numerous leading roles on stage, also in film 'Tales of Beatrix Potter'. *Honours:* CBE, 1965; Scholarship given in New Zealand by Royal Academy of Dancing (London) to study with Sadler's Wells School, London, 1945. *Address:* c/o The National Ballet of Canada, St Lawrence Hall, 157 King Street East, Toronto, Ontario, M5C 1G9, Canada.

GRANT, Carl Thomas, b. 20 June 1933, Ottawa, Ontario, Canada. Barrister and Solicitor. m. Estelle Jacqueline deWilde 1 June 1957, 1 son, 2 daughters. *Education:* BA, Carleton University, Ottawa, 1955; Graduated Osgoode Hall, Toronto 1959; Called to the Bar of Ontario, 1959. *Appointments:* Goodenough, Higginbottem, Toronto, 1959-64; McDonald, Davies, Ward, 1964-66; Aird and Berlis, 1966-. *Memberships:* Law Society of Upper Canada; Canadian Association of Business Valuators; Canadian Bar Association; Canadian Tax Foundation. *Publications:* Editor, Ovens and Beach-Business and Securities Valuation-Legal, 1972; Various articles on business valuation in Canadian professional journals. *Honours:* Queen's Counsel, 1971. *Hobbies:* Tennis; Sailing; Art Collecting. *Address:* J09 Dawlish Avenue, Toronto, Ontario, Canada M4N 1H4.

GRANT, Cedric Hilburn, b. 23 Apr. 1936, Mahaica, Guyana. Professor and Diplomatist. m. Lorene, 4 daughters. *Education:* Universities of Leicester and Edinburgh; PhD. *Appointments:* Resident Tutor, Institute of Adult Education, University of Ghana, 1963-65; Research Fellow, Institute of Social and Economic Research, University of the West Indies, 1965-67; Ford Foundation Fellow, University of Edinburgh, 1967-69; Assistant Professor, University of Waterloo, Canada, 1969-71, Associate Professor, 1971-78; Consultant to Government of Guyana, 1968-71, 1974; High Commissioner in Zambia, 1975-77, in UK., (also accredited to France, Federal Republic of Germany, the Netherlands, Yugoslavia) 1977-. *Publications:* The Making of Modern Belize: Politics, Society and British Colonialism in Central America, 1976. *Hobby:* Music. *Address:* 3 Palace Court, Bayswater Road, London W2 4LP, England.

GRANT, Clifford (Harry), b. 12 Apr. 1929, England. Chief Justice of Fiji (Retired). m. Karen Ann Ferguson, 14 Feb. 1962. *Education:* Harrison College, Barbados; Liverpool College, England tertiary, 1946; Liverpool University, 1949; LLB(Hons); Solicitor of Supreme Court of Judicature, 1951; Commissioner for Oaths, 1958; Barrister and Solicitor, Supreme Court of Fiji, 1969. *Appointments:* Private Practice, London, 1952-58; HM Overseas Judiciary, 1958; Resident Magistrate Kenya, 1962; Senior Magistrate, Kenya, 1963; Crown Solicitor, Hong Kong, 1965; Principal Magistrate, Hong Kong, 1967; Senior Magistrate, Fiji, 1971; Chief Magistrate, Fiji, 1972; Judge of Supreme Court, Fiji, 1974; Chief Justice of Fiji, President, Fiji Court of Appeal, Chairman, Judicial and Legal Services Commission, 1975; Commissioner, Royal Commission of Crime, 1973-79; Acting Governor-General of Fiji, 1980. *Publications:* Report of Royal Commission of Inquiry into Crime, 1976; Various articles for legal journals. *Honours:* Fiji Independence Medal, 1970; Knight Bachelor, 1977; Knight of Mark Twain, 1980. *Hobbies:* Photography; Evolution; Literature; Music. *Address:* 5 The Views, Swan Street, Western Australia.

GRANT, (John) Anthony, b. 29 May 1925, Surbiton, Surrey, England. Member of Parliament; Company Director; Solicitor. m. Sonia, 1 son, 1 daughter. *Education:* Brasenose College, Oxford, UK; Law Society School of Law. *Appointments:* Army Captain, 1943-48; Practising Solicitor in City of London, UK, 1952-70; Conservative MP, Harrow Central, UK, 1964-; Minister, Department of Trade and Industry, 1970-74; Vice Chairman, Conservative party, 1974-76; Chairman, Economic Committee of Council of Europe, 1980-. *Memberships:* Master 1979-80, Guild of Freemen of City of London; Institute of Directors; Law Society. *Hobbies:* Cricket; Rugby; Golf; Napoleonic history. *Address:* House of Commons, Westminster, London, SW1, England.

GRANT, Michael Paul, b. 14 Sept. 1932, Birmingham, England. Educationalist. m. Diane Margaret, 21 Aug. 1961, 2 daughters. *Education:* LL.B (Hons.), 1956, Diploma of Education, 1957, Wales; Certificate Advanced Physical Education, University College of Wales, Aberystwyth, Wales, 1957. *Appointments:* Master, Brookfield Comprehensive School, Kirkby, Lancashire, UK, 1959-60; Senior Master, Swalcliffe Special School, Banbury, Oxon, UK, 1960-61; Lecturer, Ministry of Defence (Army), UK, 1962-70; Director of Resources, St. Helier Boys School, Jersey, C.I., 1971-73; Deputy Head and Head of Resources, Stantonbury Campus, Milton Keynes, UK, 1973-78; Senior Lecturer, Head of Department, Mt Lawley C A E., Perth, Western Australia, 1978-. *Memberships:* Council member, 1973-78, Association of Curriculum Studies, UK; Secretary 1978-81, Media Association of Western Australia; Council member 1979, 80, 81, Friends of Festival of Perth, Australia. *Publications:* Storage and Retrieval of AV Aids, 1978; All You Wanted to Know about AV Aids, 1981; Contributions to Books: Resources for Mixed Ability Groups, 1976; OCCI Retrieval System at Stantonbury; Case Study: Stantonbury Campus, Microforms in Education, 1978; articles to Times Educational Supplement, 1972,74. *Honours:* First Class Diploma of Education with prize for Top Student of the Year, 1957. *Hobbies:* Writing; Theatre and the Arts; Sport. *Address:* 25 Kooringal Court, Kingsley Village, Western Australia.

GRANT, Paul Ainsworth, b. 13 Sept. 1934, Kaifung, China. Patent Attorney. m. Adrienne Mary Hall, 25 July 1959, 3 sons. *Education:* Fellowship Diploma, Electrical Engineering, 1956, Registered Patent Attorney, Australia, 1960, Royal Melbourne Institute of Technology, Australia. *Appointments:* Clement Hack & Co, Melbourne, Australia, Patent Attorneys; FMC Corporation, San Jose, California, USA; G F Redfern & Co (London), UK, Patent Attorneys; Philips Electrical Industries, Sydney, Australia; Commonwealth Scientific and Industrial Research Organization, Canberra, Australia. *Memberships:* Fellow, Institute of Patent Attorneys, Australia; Institution of Engineers Australia; Foundation President: Licensing Executives Society Australia. *Hobbies:* Sailing; Mountaineering; Model Engineering. *Address:* 83 Kambalda Crescent, Fisher, ACT 2611, Australia.

GRANTMESNIL (Duke de), Kenneth Hugh, b. 6 Nov. 1909, Oldham, Lancashire, England. Editor. m. Rosemary Baker, 1 Aug. 1950, 2 sons, 2 daughters. *Education:* Plymouth College; Kings College School. *Appointments:* Director of the Special Office, 1935-41; Editor, Intelligence Digest, 1938-68; Editor, Special Officer Brief, 1969-. *Publications:* Review of World Affairs. *Honours:* Honoured Citizen, New Orleans. *Address:* Yeomans Longborough, Moreton in Marsh, England.

GRASSBY, Albert Jaime, b. Brisbane, Australia. Journalist; Politician; Commissioner for Community Relations. m. Ellnor J Lovez, Feb. 1962, 1 daughter. *Education:* Studied Arts, University of South West, England; Special Studies Agricultural Extension, University of California, Berkeley. *Appointments:* Member, Commonwealth Press Gallery, Canberra, Australia; Tasmanian Parliamentary Press Gallery; CSIRO, Specialist Officer in Information; NSW Department of Agriculture, Extension Service; Executive Officer, Irrigation Rearch and Extension Organisation; Elected NSW Parliament, 1965; Australian Parliament, 1969 and 1972; Minister for Immigration, 1972; Special Consultant to Australian Government on Community Relations, 1974; Commissioner, 1975. *Publications:* Griffith of 4 Faces; The Morning After, 1979; Contributions to journals and general reference publications on migration, population, language teaching, agriculture, racism. *Honours:* Knight Commander of Order of Solidarity of Italian Republic, 1970; Knight of Military Order of St Agata of Paterno 1969; Grand Cross of Military Order Malta, 1974; Citation of University of Santo Tomas, Republic of Philippines, 1974; Freedom of Municipalities of Sinopoli and Plati Italy, 1973; Freedom of Municipalities of Akrata and Platynus, Greece, 1978; Doctorate of Philosophy (Hon.c.) Munich, 1979. *Address:* Commissioner for Community Relations, Box E280, Canberra, ACT 2600, Australia.

GRAY, John Harold, b. 17 July 1928, Auckland, New Zealandl. General Manager and Town Clerk. *Education:* University of Auckland; New Zealand Administrative Staff College, 1970. *Appointments:* New Zealand Army, Territorial Force, 1949-74; Assistant Clerk, Waiheke Road Board, 1947-49; Assistant Town Clerk, One Tree Hill Borough Council, 1949-57; Assistant Town Clerk, 1957-59, Town Clerk and Treasurer, 1959-68, New Lynn Borough Council; Deputy Town Clerk, Dunedin City Council, 1968-71; Deputy Town Clerk, 1971-73, General Manager and Town Clerk, 1973-, Christchurch City Council. *Memberships:* include: New Zealand Society of Accountants; Fellow, Chartered Institute of Secretaries and Administrators, London; New Zealand Institute of Local Authority Administration; Fellow, New Zealand Institute of Town Clerks' and Municipal Treasurers; Canterbury United Council; General Secretary, Christchurch Community Arts Council; Regional Civil Defence Controller, Canterbury Region; Vice President, New Zealand Institute of Town Clerks' and Municipal Treasurers; Legislation Committee, Municipal Association of New Zealand. *Publications:* An Outline of Local Government in New Zealand, 2nd Edition 1978. *Honours:* British Council Study Award to United Kingdom, 1976; Honorary Citizen, Borough of Christchurch, Dorset; Justice of the Peace for New Zealand; OBE. *Address:* PO Box 237, Christchurch 1, New Zealand.

GRAY, Noel Mackintosh, b. 13 Oct. 1920, Perth, Western Australia. Geologist. m. Shirley Evelyn Brown, 20 Jan. 1948, 1 son, 1 daughter. *Education:* Bachelor of Science, University of Western Australia, 1947. *Appointments:* Geological Survey of Western Australia, 1948-52; Metropolitan Water Sewerage and Drainage Board, Sydney, 1952-81; Engineering Geological Consultant, 1981. *Memberships:* Geological Society of Australia; Engineering Geology Specialist Group, Chairman, 1979-81; Australasian Institute of Mining and Metallurgy; Australian Geomechanics Society; Royal Society of New South Wales; Royal Society of Western Australia. *Publications:* Direction of Stress, Southern Sydney Basin, (in press) 1981; Earthquake and Warragamba Dam Storage, (in press) 1981; Co-author of Articles in professional journals. *Hobbies:* Sailing; Photography. *Address:* 1 Centenary Avenue, Hunters Hill, New South Wales, 2110, Australia.

GRAY, Ronald McKay, b. 19 Mar. 1925, Sydney, Australia. Orthopaedic Surgeon. m. Carolyn Brazier, 21 Apr. 1955, 2 sons, 1 daughter. *Education:* MB, BS, University of Sydney, 1947-53; FRCS, Royal College of Surgeons, Edinburgh, 1960. *Appointments:* War Service, 1943-46; Consultant Orthopaedic Surgeon to the RAAF (Retired); Senior Visiting Orthopaedic Surgeon, Modbury Hospital, Adelaide, South Australia. *Memberships:* Australian Orthopaedic Association; Fellow, Western Pacific Orthopaedic Association. *Address:* 16 Grandview Grove, Toorak Gardens, South Australia.

GREATOREX, David Samuel, b. 18 Feb. 1933, England. Insurance Broker. m. Heather Deane 1960 (div.), 2 daughters. *Education:* BA(Hons) Sydney University, 1954; MComm, Victoria University, 1973. *Appointments:* Sales, Computer, IBM, Australia, 1957-61; Victorian Manager, 1962-65; Training Assignment, New York, IBM Corporation, 1966-67; Director, Planning and Services, IBM, Australia, 1968-70; Chairman and Managing Director, IBM, New Zealand, 1971-74; Chief Executive, Willis Faber Johnson and Higgins, 1975-. *Memberships:* Fellow, Australian Institute of Management; Fellow, New Zealand Institute of Management; Fellow, Confederation of Insurance Brokers of Australia; Committee for Economic Development of Australia; Australian Club; Tattersalls Club. *Publications:* Jointly with Professor Graeme Fogelberg, New Zealand Journal of Educational Studies and New Zealand journal of business, The Australian Accountant. *Hobbies:* Films; Art; Jogging. *Address:* 1 York Road, Centennial Park, NSW 2022, Australia.

GREEN (The Honourable Mr. Justice) Guy Stephen Montague, b. 26 July 1937, Launceston. Tasmania Chief Justice of Tasmania. m. Rosslyn Mary Marshall, 1963, 2 sons, 2 daughters. *Education:* Bachelor of Laws, University of Tasmania, 1960. *Appointments:* Admitted to the Bar, Supreme Court of Tasmania, 1960; Partner, Ritchie and Parker Alfred Green and Company, 1963-71; Magistrate, 1971-73; Chief Justice, 1973-. *Memberships:* Faculty of Law, University of Tasmania; Sir Henry Baker Memorial Fellowship Committee; Director, The Winston Churchill Memorial Trust, 1975; Deputy Chairman, National Fellowship Committee Memorial Trust, 1980-; Patron, Inter Church Trade and Industry Mission, 1981-; Vice Patron, The Art Society of Tasmania, 1974-; Vice Patron, The Royal Agricultural Society of Tasmania, 1974-; Member-at-large of the Appellate Court Judges' Section of the World Association of Judges, 1976-; Chairman, Council of Law Reporting, 1978-. *Honours:* Alfred Houston Intermediate Philosophy Scholarship, 1958. *Hobbies:* Tennis; Cycling; Food; Wine. *Address:* Chief Justice's Chambers, Supreme Court of Tasmania, Salamenca Place, Hobart, Tasmania.

GREENBAUM, Geoffrey Michael, b. 12 Nov. 1933, Melbourne, Australia. Medical Practitioner. 2 sons, 1 daughter. *Education:* MBBS, Melbourne University, 1957; FRACGP, 1972; FAMAS, 1978. *Appointments:* Resident Medical Officer, Alfred Hospital, Melbourne, 1958; Private Practice, 1959-. *Memberships:* Honorary Secretary, Victoria Faculty, Royal Australian College of General Practitioners; Chairman of Board, The Bictorian Academy for General Practice Limited; President, The Australian Medical Acupuncture Society; Chairman, Eastern Subdivision AMA. *Publications:* Contributed to various professional journals. *Honours:* Honorary Fellowship, Acupuncture Foundation of Sri Lanka, 1978; Honorary Fellowship, Acupuncture Foundation of India, 1979; Honorary Fellowship, International College of Acupuncture, 1980. *Hobbies:* Medical Education; Woodwork; Farm Management. *Address:* 219 Gore Street, Fitzroy 3065, Melbourne, Australia.

GREENE, Pamela Adjuah Sybil, b. 30 Sept. 1940, Freetown, Sierra Leone. Nutritionist. m. Fennel Dorin Greene, 30 Apr. 1977, 1 daughter. *Education:* Bachelor of Science, 1961, Postgraduate Diploma in Nutrition, 1964; Master of Science, 1969. *Appointments:* Science Teacher, 1961; Professional Development Experiences and Training in various Countries, 1962-78; Lecturer, 1964, Head, Department of Home Economics, 1971, Senior Reseasrch Fellow, 1977, University of Sierra Leone; Regional Assistant Director, Ahea International Family Planning Project, 1978. *Memberships:* include: Vice-President, International Federation for Home Economics; Co-ordinator, Sierra Leone Home Economics Association; Vice-President, Sierra Leone Nutrition Society; Society for International Development; Ministry of Social Welfare, Technical Planning Committee, 1973; Sierra Leone Association of University Women; Consumer Association for Sierra Leone. *Publications:* 14 handbooks, 2 Textbooks; Numerous other Publications and Scientific papers. *Hobbies:* Reading; Sewing; Music; Dancing; Tennis. *Address:* MT3 Murraytown, Freetown, Sierra Leone.

GREENFIELD, Archibald David Mant, b. 31 May 1917, Wallingford, England. University Professor; Dean of Medcine. m. Margaret Duane, 3 Apr. 1943, 1 son, 1 daughter. *Education:* BSc, 1937, MB, BS, 1940, MSc, 1947, DSc, 1953, University of London, MRCP, 1968, FRCP, 1973. *Appointments:* Dunville Professor of Physiology, Queen's University of Belfast, 1948-64; Professor of Physiology, University of London, 1964-66; Foundation Dean, Medical School, Professor of Physiology, University of Nottingham, 1966-; Honorary Consultant Physiologist, Nottinghamshire Area Health Authority. *Memberships:* Physiological Society, 1943-, Member of Committee, 1949-52, 1970-74, 1975-79; Clinical Research Society; Biochemical Society. *Publications:* Numerous Scientific & Medical Papers, in Journal of Physiology, Journal of Applied Physiology, Clinical Science, Lancet & other Journals. *Honours:* CBE, 1977; Hon. LL D, Nottingham, 1977; Hon. DSc, Queens University, Belfast, 1978; Order of St. John, 1978. *Hobbies:* Travel; Watching Birds; Sketching. *Address:* 25 Sutton Passeys Crescent, Nottingham, NG8 1BX, England.

GREENSALL, Douglas Edward, b. 27 Oct. 1935, Astwood Bank, Worcs. England. Banking. m. Janet Homer, 7 June 1958, 1 daughter. *Education:* Associate of Institute of Bankers, United Kingdom 1961. *Appointments:* Joined Staff, 1952, First Managerial appointment, 1972, Midland Bank Limited, England; Midland Bank Group, Representative in Australia at present. *Memberships:* Institute of Bankers; Australian Golf Club. *Hobbies:* Golf; Gardening; Reading; Music. *Address:* 39 Russell Street, Vaucluse, NSW 2030, Australia.

GREENSLADE, Norman Frank, b. 8 Oct. 1910, Gore, New Zealand. Medical Practitioner, Urologist. m. (1) Kyra Gwendoline Payne, 16 Jan. 1936 (dec.) (2) Elaine Wendy Gordon, 8 Feb. 1968, 4 sons, 3 daughters. *Education:* MB, ChB New Zealand, 1933; FRCS, Edinburgh, 1936; FRACS, 1956. *Appointments:* Private Practice, Urological Surgeon, to Christchurch Hospital. *Memberships:* Head, Department of Urology, Christ Church Hospital, NZ; President, NZ Medical Association; Christchurch City Council, 1972-75; Medical Council of New Zealand, 1967-, Chairman, 1972-81. *Publications:* Various Scientific Papers, Medical. *Honours:* OBE, 1977; Queens Silver Jubilee Medal, 1979. *Hobby:* Gardening. *Address:* 8 Daresbury Lane, Christchurch 1, New Zealand.

GREENWAY, Stella (Mrs), b Southampton, United Kingdom. Director of Companies. m. The Hon. Atheling Greenway, (Deceased, 1970), 1 son. *Education:* RADA (Half Leverhulme Scholarship); Southampton School of Art. *Appointments:* WRNS; Journalist on The Farmer; Editor, Womans Magazine, 1960-74; Editor, Travel Magazine, 1960-80; Television Presenter & Interviewer; Consultant, Appropriate Technology Pottery. *Memberships:* International Travel Writers Club; Potters Club; PEN; Chairman & Co-Founder of Adult Literacy Organisation of Zimbabwe, 1960-; Commander, Vivil Defence, Salisbury, 1978-80. *Publications:* Author of numerous Tourist Books on Africa; Books on Specialist Food Preparation, (Deep Freeze in a Warm Climate); Publisher, Africana, Historical & General Books. *Honours:* Silver Medallist, Oxford Festival of Spoken Verse, 1939; Fellow, Institute of Training & Development, 1980. *Hobbies:* Sailing; Gardening; Philately; Pottery. *Address:* Greenway Farm, Box 374, Salisbury, Zimbabwe.

GREENWOOD, Barrie Leck, b. 5 Oct. 1934, Invercargill, New Zealand. Storeman. m. Susan Nichol, 29 Apr. 1978. *Education:* Christchurch, Technical College, 1951-53; Endorsed School Certificate, 1953. *Appointments:* Chorus, New Zealand Opera Company, 1964, 1965. Chorus, Royal Christchurch Musical Society, 1954; Australian and New Zealand Branch International Association of Music Libraries; Court Star of Canterbury, No 2309, Ancient Order of Foresters, 1959-; Canterbury & Westland Shop Assistants Union, 1965, executive member, 1967-68. *Publications:* Antonio Caldara: A Checklist of his Manuscripts in Europe and USA, Vol. 7; Studies in Music, (Nedlands, Western Australia), 1973; Inventory of Music Library of Royal Christchurch Musical Society; Royal Christchurch Musical Society: List of performances, titles of works performed, meetings, notable events etc., 1860-1903; Soloists from 1860-1960. *Honours:* Two Grants, Penrose Fund, American Philosophical Society, Philadelphia, 1972-73. *Hobbies:* Choral Singing; Musicology; History; Reading; Thinking; Writing Poetry. *Address:* PO Box 7382, Sydenham, Christchurch 2, New Zealand.

GREENWOOD OF ROSSENDALE, Anthony, b. 14 Sept. 1911, Leeds, Yorks. Civil Servant. m. Gillian Crawshay Williams, 1 June 1940, 2 daughters. *Education:* Merchant Taylors School, London, 1925-30; Balliol College, Oxford, 1930-33; BA, MA, Doctor of Laws (Honoris causa), Lancaster University, 1979. *Appointments:* Secretary of State for the Colonies, 1964-65; Minister of Overseas Development, 1965-66; Minister of Housing and Local Government, 1966-70. *Memberships:* President: Association of Metropolitan Authorities; Cremation Society of Great Britian; London Society; Housing Centre; River Stour Trust; Essex Association of Local Councils; Isle of Man Parliamentary Group; Vice-President: Association of District Councils; Commonwealth Parliamentary Association; Deputy-Speaker House of Lords. Previous: Vice-Chairman Parliamentary Labour Party; Chairman, Labour Party; Bureau Socialist International; Socialist Educational Association; Labour Students Association; River Thames Society; Pro-Chancellor, University of Lancaster; Local Government Staff Committee; Local Government Training Board; House of Lords Select Committee

on Europe; Director, Commonwealth Development Corporation; Business: Chairman: Greenwood Development Holdings Limited and Subsidiaries; London Cremation Company Limited; London Arena Limited; Nigel Moor and Associates Limited; Calgrad Local Government Information Services Limited; Municipal Mutual Insurance Limited; Britannia Building Society. *Hobby:* Looking at Churches. *Address:* The Old Ship Cottage, East Mersea, Colchester, England.

GREGORIADIS, Gregory, b. 27 Feb. 1934, Athens, Greece. Biochemist. m. Susan, 15 July 1968, 1 son, 1 daughter. *Education:* BSc, University of Athens, 1958; MSc, 1966, PhD, 1968, McGill University, Canada. *Appointments:* Research Fellow, Albert Einstein College of Medicine, 1968-70, Research Fellow, Royal Free Hospital School of Medicine, 1970-72; Senior Scientist, Head of Laboratory on Liposome Research, Clinical Research Centre, Harrow, 1972-. *Memberships:* Harvey Society; Controlled Release Society; Biochemical Society; Hellenic Biochemical Biophysical Society; Society Inherited Disorders. *Publications:* Numerous articles on Drug Targeting and Liposomes; The carrier potential of liposomes in Biology and Medicine, 1976; Targeting of Drugs, 1977; Editor of, Drug Carriers in Biology and Medicine, 1979; Senior Editor, Liposomes in Biological Systems, 1980; Senior Editor, Targeting of Drugs, (in press), 1982. *Honours:* Founder, Gordon Conference series on Drug Carriers in Biology and Medicine, 1978; Founder, NATO Advanced Study Institute Series on Targeting of Drugs, 1981; National Cancer Institute Research Contract Award, 1978. *Address:* 18 Upper Hitch, Carpenders Park, Watford, Herts, WD1 5AW, England.

GREGORIOS, Paulos Mar, b. 9 Aug. 1922, Tripunithura, Kerala, India. Bishop; Educator. *Education:* BA., Goshen College, Indiana, USA, 1950-52; Master of Divinity, Princeton Theological Seminary, USA, 1952-54; STM., Yale University, USA, 1959-60; Doctoral Research at: Oxford University, UK, 1960-61, Gregory of Nyssa Institute, Muenster, Germany; Doctor of Theology, Serampore University, India. *Appointments:* Journalist, India, 1937-42; Secretary, Public Library, Tripunithura, 1939-42; Indian Posts & Telegraphs, 1942-47; Teacher in Secondary Schools, Ethiopia, 1947-50; General Secretary, Orthodox Student Movement of India, 1955-57; Personal Staff and Advisor, Emperor Haile Sellassie, Ethiopia, 1956-59; Executive Secretary, Government Committee for Relief Aid, Ethiopia, 1956-59; Director, Division of Ecumenical Action and Associate General Secretary, World Council of Churches, Geneva, 1962-67; Leader: WCC delegation to UNESCO, 1966, WCC delegation to Heads of African States, 1968; Hein Memorial Lecturer, USA, 1968; Mary Louise Iliff Distinguished Visiting Lecturer, Denver, USA, 1978; Dudley Lecturer, Harvard University, USA, 1979; Chairman, World Conference on Faith, Science & the Future, MIT, 1979; Visiting Professor, College of Wooster, 1981. *Memberships:* Member of num. organisations including: Comparative Education Society in Europe, London; Indian Philosophical Congress; International Society for Metaphysics; Association of Humanist Psychologists International; Indian Institute of World Culture, Bangalore. *Publications:* The Joy of Freedom, 1967; The Gospel of the Kingdom, 1968; The Freedom of Man, 1972; Be Still and Know, 1974; Freedom and Authority, 1974; The Quest of Certainty, 1975; The Human Presence, 1980; Truth without Tradition? 1978; Science for Sane Societies, 1980; Cosmic Man, 1980; Editor and Contributor to: Koptisches Christentum, 1973; Die Syrischen Kirchen in Indien, 1974; Burning Issues, 1977; Science and our Future, 1978; Contributor to numerous Symposia and periodical articles; Lectured at numerous Universities internationally. *Honours:* Certificate of Merit for Distinguished Service and Inspired Leadership of the World Church, by Dictionary of International Biography, Cambridge, UK; Order of St. Vladimir, USSR; Order of St. Mary Magdalene, Poland; Honorary Doctorates, Leningrad Orthodox Theological Academy, USSR, Lutheran Theological Academy, Budapest, Hungary and Prague, Czechoslovakia. *Address:* Orthodox Seminary, PO Box 98, Kottayam, Kerala 686001, India.

GREGORY, Bruce Edward, b. 25 Feb. 1943, Sydney, Australia. Travel Executive. m. Marjorie Lynn Mathieu, 25 May 1968, 1 son, 1 daughter. *Education:* Church of England Grammar School, Sydney, Australia, 1950-60. *Appointments:* Executive Trainee, Sydney, 1960,

Ticket Sales Manager, New York, 1965, Special Sales Representative, Hong Kong, 1970, Marketing Manager, Melbourne, 1974, General Sales Manager, London, 1977, Qantas Airways Ltd.; Director, Delrich Pty. Ltd., 1974; National Sales Development Manager, 1980, National Sales Manager, 1981, Thomas Cook Pty. Ltd., Sydney. *Memberships:* Institute of Marketing; Associate, Australian Institute of Export; Associate, Australian Institute of Travel & Transport. *Publications:* Various travel related articles for Trade Press. *Hobbies:* Farming; Yachting. *Address:* 47 Gould Avenue, St Ives, New South Wales 2075, Australia.

GREGORY-ROBERTS, Frederick, b. Young, New South Wales, Australia. Eye Surgeon. m. 31 Dec. 1938, 1 son. *Education:* MB., Ch.M. University of Sydney, Australia, 1921-26; DO., Oxford, 1931; DOMS., London, 1931; FRACS., 1932; FRACO., 1971; FICS., 1978. *Appointments:* House Surgeon, South Sydney Women's Hospital, Australia, 1926; House Surgeon, 1927, Life Governor, 1936-, RPAH., Sydney, Australia; House Surgeon, Royal Eye & Ear Hospital, Bradford, Yorks, UK, 1930; Clinical Assistant, Moorfields Eye Hospital, 1929, 1931; Junior and Senior House Surgeon, Central London Eye Hospital, UK, 1931-32; Clinical Assistant in Charge, Orthoptic Department, 1933, Junior House Eye Surgeon, 1934-44, RAH Children, Sydney, Australia; Consulting Eye Surgeon, Prince of Wales, Prince Henry, East Suburbs, St. Lukes and Royal South Sydney Hospitals, 1962-; Vice-President, Dr. Barnardo's Homes in Australia, 1955-; Director, Royal New South Wales Institute for Blind and Deaf Children, 1956-; Life Governor, Sydney Hospital, Australia, 1966-; Honorary Major, World War II; Honorary Ophthalmologist, Tresillian Homes for Babies, 1940. *Memberships:* Honorary member, Australian Medical Association; Fellow, Royal Society of Medicine; Fellow, Royal Australian College of Surgeons; Hon. Fellow, Australian Association, Surgeons; Fellow, Royal Australian College of Opthalmologists; Royal Australian Historical Society. *Publications:* Lid Retraction and Eye Fixation in Cataract, 1944; Premedication & Co-operation in Cataract, 1945; Intracapsular Cataract Extraction: Its Most Serious Complications, 1944, 1949; Operation for Correction of Ptosis Trans., 1970. *Honours:* OBE., 1976; O.St.J., 1978. *Hobbies:* Music; Tennis; Golf; Bowls. *Address:* Rose Bay, New South Wales, Australia, 2029.

GREIG, James Carruthers Gorrie, b. 23 Feb. 1927, Moffat, Dumfriesshire, Scotland, United Kingdom. Minister of Religion; Translator; Theologian; Lecturer. m. Elsa Clark Carlile, 20 Sept. 1958, 1 son, 2 daughters. *Education:* BA.(Hons.) Modern & Medieval Languages, 1948, MA, 1952, Gonville & Caius College, University of Cambridge, UK; BD., 1954 supplemented 1955, University of Glasgow, UK; STM summa cum laude, 1955, Union Theological Seminary, New York, USA. *Appointments:* National Service, RAEC, 1948-50; Minister, Closeburn Church of Scotland, Dumfriesshire, Scotland, 1955-59; Professor of New Testament Language, Literature and Theology, Westminster College, Cambridge, UK, 1959-63; Religious Editor, Oliver and Boyd Limited, 1962-67; Lecturer in Religious Education, Jordanhill College of Education, Scotland, 1963-70; Editor, The Scottish Sunday School Teacher, 1965-75; Minister, St Matthew's Church, Paisley, Scotland, 1979-; Theological and general translator, 1955-. *Memberships:* Studiorum Novi Testamenti Societas; The Glasgow Theological Club; John Buchan Society; Scottish Arts Club; German History Society. *Publications:* The Serpent in the Wilderness, 1961; articles in: Studia Evangelica, 1959,68,73; New Testament Studies, 1955; Union Seminary Quarterly Review, 1971; Religion, 1972; Hastings' One Volume Dictionary of the Bible, 1963; Interpreter's One Volume Commentary on the Bible, 1971; The N T in Historical and Contemporary Perspective, 1965; Translations: Essays, 1955; The Messianic Secret, 1971; The Charismatic Leader and his Followers, 1981; short stories in Scots Magazine, 1958. *Honours:* Open Major Scholarship, Gonville and Caius College, Cambridge, 1945-48; Cleland & Rae Wilson Medals, 1953, 54, Robert James Wyllie Fellow, 1954, University of Glasgow; Scots Fellow, Union Seminary, New York, 1954. *Hobbies:* Photography; Painting; Music; Swimming; Walking. *Address:* St John's Croft, Sorbie, Dumfries and Galloway, Scotland.

GRENIER, Fernand, b. 31 Mar. 1927, East-Broughton, Québec, Canada. Geographer; Administrator. *Education:* BA. 1948, B.Ph., 1948, L. ès L., 1950, DES in

History, 1952, Laval, Canada; DES in Geography, Sorbonne, Paris, France, 1955. *Appointments:* Professor of Geography, 1955-76, Head, Department of Geography, 1963-67, Dean, Faculty of Letters, 1967-73, Laval University, Canada; Director General, Télé-université du Québec, Canada, 1973-80; Senior Associate, Inter-American Organization for Higher Education. *Memberships:* Canadian Association of Geographers; Social Sciences Research Council of Canada; Conseil des Sites et Monuments du Québec; President, Festival d'été de Québec; Commission de Toponymie du Québec; Commission des Biens culturels du Québec; Canadian Association of Latin American Specialists. *Publications:* Le Conflit anglo-francais sur l'Ohio, 1745-1756, 1952; Nouvel Atlas du monde contemporain, 1978; Québec. Studies in Canadian Geography, 1972; Atlas Québec-Canada, 1980. *Honours:* Prix Raymond Casgrain, 1952; Canadian Government Scholar in France, 1953-55; Honorary member of Academie Nacional de Historia de Paraguay, 1967; Life member, Société de Géographie de Québec, 1977; Honorary Doctorate of Athabasca University, 1979; Queen's Jubilee Medal, 1977. *Hobbies:* Music; Stamp collecting; Oenology. *Address:* 5 Parc Samuel Holland, Appt. 1168, Québec, Canada G1S 4S2.

GREWAR, Geoffrey Royden, b. 12 June 1932, Adelaide, South Australia. Member of Parliament. m. Pauline Elva Ninham, 10 May 1958, 2 sons, 1 daughter. *Education:* BSc., Agriculture. *Appointments:* Agricultural Adviser; Agricultural Consultant; Farmer and Grazier. *Hobby:* Farming. *Address:* Twilight Beach Road, Esperance, Western Australia 6450.

GREY, Beryl Elizabeth, b. 11 June 1927, London, England. Prima Ballerina. m. Sven Gustav Svenson, 15 July 1950, 1 son. *Education:* Madeline Sharp School., Sadler's Wells School; (Schol.), de Vos School. *Appointments:* Début Sadler's Wells Co., 1941, with Ballerina rôles in same year in Les Sylphides, The Gods Go A'Begging, La Lac des Cygnes, Act II, Comus; 1st ffull-length ballet, Le Lac des Cygnes on 15th birthday, 1942; Has appeared since in leading rôles of many ballets including: Sleeping Beauty, Giselle, Sylvia, Checkmate, Ballet Imperial, Donald of the Burthens, Homage, Birthday Offering, The Lady and the Fool: Film: The Black Swan, 1952; Became free-lance ballerina, 1957; Regular guest appearances with Royal Ballet at Covent Garden and on Continental, African, American and Far Eastern Tours; Guest Artist, London's Festival Ballet, London and abroad, 1958-64; 1st Western ballerina to appear with Bolshoi Ballet, Moscow, Leningrad, Kiev, Tiflis, 1957-58; 1st Western ballerina to dance with Chinese Ballet Co. in Peking and Shanghai, 1964; Engagements and tours abroad include: Central and South America, Mexico, Rhodesia and South Africa, Canada, NZ., Lebanon, Germany, Norway, Sweden, Denmark, Finland, Belgium, Holland, France, Swizerland, Italy, Portugal, Austria, Czechoslovakia, Poland, Rumania; Television of broadcasts in England and abroad; Director-General, Arts Educational Trust, 1966-68; Governor, Dame Alice Owens Girls' School, London, UK. *Publications:* Red Curtain Up, 1958; Through the Bamboo Curtain, 1965; Biographical studies by: Gordon Anthony, 1952, Pigeon Crowle, 1952; Beryl Grey, Dancers of Today, Hugh Fisher, 1955; Beryl Grey, a biography, David Gillard, 1977. *Honours:* Frances Mary Buss Foundation; Hon. DMus., Leicester, 1970; Hon. DLitt., City University, 1974; CBE., 1973. *Hobbies:* Music; Painting; Reading; Swimming. *Address:* Fernhill, Priory Road, Forest Row, Sussex, England.

GREY, Ian, b. 5 May 1918, Wellington, New Zealand. Author; Editor. m. Winsome Warner, 22 Dec. 1944, 1 son, 2 daughters. *Education:* LL.B., University of Sydney, Australia; Barrister-at-Law. *Appointments:* Royal Australian Navy, 1941-45; Foreign and Commonwealth Office, 1946-51; Royal Institute of International Affairs, 1951-55; Commonwealth Parliamentary Association, 1956-. *Publications:* Peter the Great, 1960; Catherine the Great, 1961; Ivan the Terrible, 1964; The First Fifty Years: Soviet Russie 1917-67, 1967; The Romanovs: Rise and Fall of the Dynasty, 1970; A History of Russia, 1970; Boris Godunov, 1973; Stalin, 1980; Editor of the Parliamentarian. *Hobbies:* Music; Walking; Book collecting; Birdwatching. *Address:* 10 Alwyn Avenue, Chiswick, London W4, England.

GRIEVE, Peter William Harvey, b. 6 May 1920, Sydney, New South Wales, Australia. Medical Practitioner.

m. June Crouch, 29 Oct. 1947, 2 daughters. *Education:* MB., BS., Sydney University, Australia, 1938-43; FRACP., 1966; FRACP, 1973. *Appointments:* General Practitioner, 1947-; Secretary General and Chief Executive Officer, RACGP., 1978-; T/Major, RAAMC, RMO 2/9 Australian Cavalry (Commando) Squadron, retired list, 1975. *Memberships:* Council, University of New South Wales, Australia, 1976-81; Commissioner, New South Wales District, St John Ambulance Brigade, 1974-80; Vice President, St John Ambulance Association, New South Wales Centre; Royal Australian Historical Society. *Honours:* Admitted, 1967, Created Knight, 1980, Order of St. John; Service Medal, 1971, Bar, 1976, St. John's Ambulance Brigade. *Hobbies:* Trout fishing; Golf. *Address:* 31 Towns Road, Vaucluse, New South Wales 2030, Australia.

GRIEVE, William Percival, b. 25 Mar. 1915, London, England. Queen's Counsel; Member of Parliament. m. 21 July 1949, 1 son, 1 daughter. *Education:* BA, 1937, MA, 1940, Trinity Hall, Cambridge, UK. *Appointments:* Barrister, Middle Temple, 1938; Army Service, 1939-46; Queen's Counsel, 1962; Master of the Bench, 1969; Member of the Bar of Hong Kong, 1960; Deputy Chairman of Quarter Sessions, Lincolnshire, UK, 1962; Recorder of Northampton, UK, 1965; Recorder of Crown Court, 1971; Member of Parliament(Conservative) Solihull, 1964; served on Parliamentary Select Committees Race Relations and Immigration, Members' Interests; Delegate to Council of Europe and Western European Union, 1969-; Chairman of Legal Affairs Committee Coouncil of Europe and Procedural Committee, W.E..U; Hon. Vice President, Franco-British Parliamentary Committee, Chairman, 1970-75; Chairman, Anglo-Benelux Parliamentary Committee; Chairman, Luxembourg Society. *Memberships:* Carlton Club; Hurlingham Club. *Honours:* Bronze Star (US(: Officer with Crown Irder Adolphe of Nassau; Chevalier Order Couronne de Chene; Croix de Guerre with Palm, Luxembourg; Chevalier, Legion of Honour, France; Officer of Order of the Crown of Belgium, 1980; Commander of Order of Merit of Luxembourg, 1976. *Hobbies:* Swimming; Travel; The Theatre. *Address:* 32 Gunterstone Road, London, W14 9BU, England.

GRIFFIN (Sir), David, b. 8 July 1915, Australia. Company Director. m. Jean Falconer Whyte, 8 Mar. 1941, 2 sons. *Education:* LL.B., University of Sydney, Australia, 1933-39. *Appointments:* Barrister at Law, 1939-48; Solicitor, Supreme Court of New South Wales, Australia, 1948-64; Executive Chairman, Nabalco Pty. Limited, 1964-80; Alderman of the City of Sydney, Australia, 1962-74; Lord Mayor of Sydney, Australia, 1972-73; Chairman, Barclays Bank Group in Australia; Aetna Life and Casualty Limited; Vanguard Insurance Co. Limited; Robert Bosch (Australia) Pty. Limited; Director; John Fairfax Limited; Oil Search Limited. *Memberships:* Royal Sydney Golf Club; Union Club, Sydney; Elanora County Club, Sydney; Pine Valley Golf Club, Philadelphia, USA. *Publications:* The Happiness Box; The Will of the People; verses; short stories; speeches. *Honours:* CBE, 1972; Kt. 1974. *Hobbies:* Golf; Trout Fishing; Gardening. *Address:* 10 Churchill Road, Rose Bay, New South Wales 2029, Australia.

GRIFFITH, Owen Glyn, b. 19 Jan. 1922, Neath, South Wales. Diplomat. m. Rosemary Elizabeth Cecil Earl, 1 Feb. 1949, 2 sons. *Education:* Trinity Hall, Cambridge, UK, 1940-41. *Appointments:* Colonial Service in Uganda, 1944-63; Principal, Commonwealth Office, 1963-65; 1st Secretary and Head of Chancery, Khartoum, 1965-69; 1st Secretary, Commercial, Stockholm, 1969-73; Deputy High Commissioner, Lilongwe, Malawi, 1973-75; Inspector, Foreign and Commonwealth Office, 1976-78; British High Commissioner in Lesotho, 1978-. *Memberships:* Royal Commonwealth Society. *Honours:* MVO, 1954; OBE, 1969; CBE, 1980. *Hobbies:* Golf; Fishing. *Address:* The Sundial, Marsham Way, Gerrards Cross, Bucks, England.

GRIFFITH, Winston Henry, b. 10 Oct. 1931, New Amsterdam, Guyana. General Manager. m. Unaleen Munroe, 30 July 1960, 1 son, 2 daughters. *Education:* Member Institute of Transport, 1968; Diploma, Public Administration, 1972. *Appointments:* Traffic Manager, 1968, General Manager, 1971, T.&.H.D. *Memberships:* President, T.&.H.D. Sports Club. *Publications:* Rationalisation of Transport in Guyana; A short History of T.&.H.D. *Hobbies:* Football; Music. *Address:* 417 Cane

View Avenue, South Ruimveldt Gardens, Greater Georgetown, Guyana.

GRIFFITHS, Ellis Rhys, b. 10 July 1924, Treorchy, Glamorgan, United Kingdom. Orthopaedic Surgeon. m. Patricia, 10 Apr. 1950, 2 sons, 1 daughter. *Education:* MB., BS., St Barts, London, UK, 1947; FRCS., Edinburgh, UK, 1961; FRACS., 1968. *Appointments:* Head of Spinal Department, Royal Perth Hospital, Australia; Practising Orthopaedic Surgeon; Commissioner, St John Ambulance Brigade, State of Western Australia; Consultant Orthopaedic Surgeon, Wing Commander, retired, Royal Air Force. *Memberships:* Vice President, International Medical Society of Paraplegia; Vice President, Paraplegic-Quadriplegic Association; Fellow: British Orthopaedic Association, Indonesian Orthopaedic Association, President Elect, Western Pacific Orthopaedic Association; Australian Orthopaedic Association; Tutor, Orthopaedic Surgeon, University of Western Australia; Royal Agricutural Society of Western Australia. *Publications:* many publications in field of Spinal Injury and Paraplegia. *Honours:* OBE., Military, 1965; O.ST.J., 1973. *Hobby:* Farming-beef cattle. *Address:* 21 Walter Street, Claremont, Western Australia 6010.

GRIFFITHS, Guy Richmond, b. 1 Mar. 1923, Sydney, New South Wales, Australia. Naval Officer (retired); Business Executive. m. Carla Mengert, 1 Aug. 1959, 1 son, 1 daughter. *Education:* Royal Australian Naval College, 1937-40. *Appointments:* Midshipman, HMS Repulse, Revenge, 1941-42, Sub-Lieutenant, 1942; Lieutenant, HMAS Shropshire, 1943-45; Specialised in Gunnery, 1946; HM Gunnery School, Devonport, UK, 1947-49; Lieutenant Commander, HMAS Anzac, 1952-53; RN Staff College, Greenwich, 1954; HMAS, Melbourne, 1955-56, Commander, 1956, Fleet Operations Officer, 1956-58; Personnel, Navy Office, 1958-61; Captain, HMAS Parramatta, 1961-62, Director, Tactics and Weapons Policy, Captain 1964, Naval Staff, Canberra, Australia, 1963-65; Captain, HMAS Hobart, 1965-67; Naval Adviser to Chief of Naval Staff, Royal Malaysian Navy, 1967-69; Imperial Defence College, 1970, Director, General Naval Operations and Plans, 1971-73, Commodore, 1971; Captain, HMAS Melbourne, 1973-75; Rear Admiral, 1976, Chief of Naval Personnel, 1976-78; Flag Officer, Naval Support Command, 1979; Personnel Director, Wormald International, 1980-. *Memberships:* Commonwealth Club, Canberra, ACT. *Honours:* Distinguished Service Cross, 1945; Distinguished Service Order, 1968; Order of Australia, 1979; Campaign Medals for service in World War II, Korean War, Vietnam War. *Hobbies:* Skiing; Tennis; Golf. *Address:* 105 Neerim Road, Castle Cove, New South Wales 2069, Australia.

GRIFFITHS, Paul Frear, b. 21 Sept. 1928, Rangoon, Burma. Stockbroker. m. Prudence Breen, 28 Feb. 1953, 1 son, 3 daughters. *Education:* BA., Amherst College, Amherst, Massachusetts, USA, 1950; Australian Society of Accountants, 1953; Member, Stock Exchange of Melbourne, 1961. *Appointments:* Partner, 1961, Stanley E Watkin & Son, Sharebrokers, Melbourne, Australia, 1953-74; Consultant, Eric J Morgan & Co., Sharebrokers, Melbourne, Australia, 1974-77; Partner, J M Messara & Co., Sharebrokers, Sydney, Australia, 1977-. *Memberships:* Australian Golf Club; City Tatersalls Club; Retired Lieutenant, Royal Australian Naval Reserve. *Hobbies:* Golf; Tennis; Thoroughbred breeding. *Address:* 13 Norfolk Street, Paddington 2021, New South Wales, Australia.

GRIGG, Graeme Lindsay, b. 16 Sept. 1927, Auckland, New Zealand. Consultant Surgeon. m. Frances Mary Oliver, 29 June 1951, 3 sons. *Education:* MB, BS, Melbourne University, 1950; Fellow, Royal Australasian College of Surgeons, 1956; Fellow, Royal College of Surgeons, England, 1958. *Appointments:* Resident training posts, Melbourne, 1951-56; Surgical Registrar, Brompton Hospital, London, 1956-57; Southampton Chest Hospital, 1958-59; Assistant Thoracic Surgeon, Royal Melbourne, Hospital, Honorary Thoracic Surgeon, Prince Henry's Hospital, Melbourne, 1960-63; Consultant Surgeon, Wangaratta, Victoria, 1963-64; Specialist Thoracic Surgeon, Hong Kong, 1965-68; Senior Consultant Cardiothoracic Surgeon & Lecturer in Cardiothoracic Surgery, Kampala, Uganda, 1968-73; Consultant Cardiothoracic Surgeon, Canberra, 1974-. *Memberships:* Cardiac Society of Australia & New Zealand; Thoracic Society of Australia. *Honours:* English-Speaking Union (Victoria) Travelling Scholar, 1957. *Hobbies:* Cabinet making; Painting; Private Flying. *Address:* 8/3 Cabarita Terrace, O'Malley, ACT, 2606, Australia.

GRIGG, Ian Francis, b. 31 Oct. 1931, Melbourne, Victoria, Australia. Executive Director. m. Nanette Wilson, 19 Feb. 1954, 4 daughters. *Education:* BA., Australian National University. *Appointments:* Senior Research Officer, 1956-61, Inspector, 1962-66, Public Service Board; Senior Advisor, Cabinet and External Relations, 1967, First Assistant Secretary, Parliamentary and Government Division, 1969-71, Prime Minister's Department and Secretary Federal Executive Council; Parliamentary Liaison Officer, House of Representatives, 1966-69; Executive member, Joint Parliamentary Delgation to UK., USA., and Europe, 1968; Principal Private Secretary to Prime Minister, 1971-72; Executive Director, Federal Chamber of Automotive Industries, Australia, 1973-. *Memberships:* Director, National Heart Foundation; Commonwealth Club, Yarralumla, ACT. *Hobbies:* Skiing; Fishing. *Address:* 115 Hawkesbury Crescent, Farrer, ACT 2607, Australia.

GRIMES, Donald James, b. 4 Oct. 1937, Albury, New South Wales. Senator for Tasmania. m. Margaret Lynne Schofield, 5 Mar. 1960, 2 sons, 2 daughters. *Education:* MB, BS, Sydney University, 1962. *Appointments:* Medical Practitioner, 1962-74; Senator, 1974-; Shadow Minister for Social Security, 1976; Deputy Leader of the Opposition in the Senate, 1980. *Memberships:* Australian Labor Party. *Hobbies:* Bushwalking; Gardening; Reading. *Address:* 14 Nobelius Drive, Legana, Tasmania, 7251, Australia.

GROCOTT, Alan James, b. 17 Apr. 1943, Sydney, Australia. Engineer, Company Secretary. m. Claudia Ina-Marie Opitz, 31 May 1969, 1 son, 1 daughter. *Education:* BE, University of N.S.W. *Appointments:* IBM (Aust) Ltd., 1967-68; Kinhill Engineers, 1968-69; Management Consultant, Australia & Philippines, 1969-72; Secretary, Island Development & Industry, Republic of Nauru, 1972-79; Manager Admin. & Research Services, Company Secretary, Australian Railway Research & Development Organisation, 1980-. *Memberships:* Board Member, Nauru Insurance Corporation; Secretary, Bank of Nauru; Republic of Nauru Finance Corporation. *Hobby:* Surfing. *Address:* 14 Montalbo Road, Ringwood, 3134, Victoria, Australia.

GROCOTT, Bruce Joseph, b. 1 Nov. 1940, Watford, Hertfordshire, England. Television Political Journalist. m. Sally Barbara Kay Ridgway, 17 July 1965, 2 sons, *Education:* BA, Politics, Upper Second Class Hons, Leicester University 1962; MA, Politics Manchester University, 1967. *Appointments:* Local Government Official 1963-64; Lecturer in Politics 1964-74; Member of Parliament, Labour, Lichfield and Tamworth, 1974-79; Television Journalist 1979. *Memberships:* House of Commons Select Committee on Overseas Development; Former Chairman All Party Group for Penal Reform; Parliamentary Private Secretary, Minister of Local Government, 1974-76 and Minister of Agriculture, 1976-78. *Hobbies:* Cricket; Snooker; Fiction Writing. *Address:* 1 Brookside House, Birch Cross, Uttoxeter, Staffs., England.

GRODON, Minita Elmira, b. 30 Dec. 1930, Belize City, Belize, Central America. *Education:* Associate of the College of Preceptors, London, England, 1961; Post Graduate Certificate in Education, University of Nottingham, England, 1962; Diploma in The Psychology of Childhood, University of Birmingham, 1963; BEd, 1967, MEd, 1969, University of Calgary, Canada; PhD, University of Toronto, Canada, 1980. *Appointments:* School Teacher, 1946-58; Government Training College, 1954-56; Principal, Anglican School, Belize, 1956-59; Belizean Civil Service, 1959; Lecturer, Government Teacher-Training College, 1959-69; Education Officer, Ministry of Education, Belize, 1969-81; Justice of the Peace, 1974, Governor General, 1981, Belize District. *Memberships:* Branch Officer, Belize Branch, British Red Cross Society; District Commissioner, Belize Girl Guides Association; Board of Governors, St Hilda's College, Belize City; Programme Planning Committee; Radio Belize Advisory Committee; National Library Board; Domestic Wages Council. *Publications:* Theses; Dissertations *Creative Works:* Exhibitions of Leather Craft in Canada. *Honours:* Numerous honours including: CIDA Scholarship Award, Canada,

1966-69; Certificate of honour and life membership and badge, British Red Cross Society, 1975; 1st and 2nd Prizes in All Canadian Leather Carving Exhibition, 1979, 1980. *Hobbies:* Travelling; Photography; Reading; Gardening; Youth Work. *Address:* PO Box 201, Belize City, Belize, Central America.

GROGAN, Valerie Margaret, b. 18 Sept. 1934, Sydney, Australia. m. Peter Rex Grogan, 21 Aug. 1959, 1 daughter. *Education:* BA, University of Sydney 1956. *Appointments:* Secondary School Teacher: Presbyterian Ladies' College, Pymble 1957-59; Sydney Church of England Girls Grammar School, Redlands 1960-61; NSW Supreme Court Associate to the Hon. Mr. Justice Jenkyn, 1965-69. *Memberships:* President, The St John Ambulance Brigade Headquarters Auxiliary, NSW District; The St John Council for New South Wales; The St John Ambulance Brigade Nursing Cadet Divisions, NSW District; Council Pymble Ladies' College; Tibetan Friendship Group, Australian Section; Australian-Tibetan Society; Australian Committee, Vrindaban Research Institute; *Honours:* S.S.St.J. 1970; O.St.J. 1977. *Hobbies:* Golf; Opera; Civic and Charitable activities. *Address:* 39 Pymble Avenue, Pymble, NSW 2073, Australia.

GROSS, Harold, b. 30 July 1916, Toronto, Ontario, Canada. Management. m. Roslyn Abrams, 6 Nov. 1939, 1 son, 1 daughter. *Education:* Harbord Collegiate Institute. *Appointments:* Chairman, Gross Machinery Group; President: Harold Gross Machinery Inc; Harold Gross Realty Inc; Halgros Investments Limited; Orgro Holdings Limited; Grocan Intercontinental Limited; Gross International (Far East) Limited, Tokyo; Grocan Sales Limited; Gross Machinery Inc., Detroit. Director and Secretary-Treasurer, Creative Engineering Consultants Limited, 1980-. *Memberships:* President, Machinery Dealers National Association, 1969-71; Canadian Machine Tool Distributors Association; The American Machine Tool Distributors Association; Association of European Machine Tool Merchants. *Honours:* Fellow, American International Academy, 1960. *Hobbies:* Tennis; Skeet Shooting; Swimming. *Address:* 145 Cumberland Street, Suite 2008, Toronto, Ontario, Canada.

GROTH, Peter Frederick, b. 16 Mar. 1935, Wollongong, New South Wales, Australia. Managing Director; Auctioneer/Valuer. m. Isobel Nina Jackson, 16 Aug. 1962, 2 sons. *Memberships:* Australian-Britain Society; President, New South Wales Branch, Royal Commonwealth Society, 1977-79; Vice-President, National Body of Royal Commonwealth Society, 1977-79. *Hobbies:* Reading; Travelling. *Address:* 1 Dugald Road, Mosman, New South Wales, Australia, 2088.

GROVE, Jack William Donald, b. 11 Apr. 1920, London, England. Professor. m. Barbara Susan Marshall, 16 Sept. 1950, 1 son, 1 daughter. *Education:* Privately and Harrow County Grammar School; BSc, (Econ), 1949, Diploma in Public Administration, 1946, London University. *Appointments:* University of Manchester, England, 1949-65; Queen's University, Kingston, Ontario, Canada, 1966-. *Memberships:* Royal Institute of Public Administration; Institute of Public Administration of Canada; Political Studies Association; Canadian Political Studies Association; Society for Social Studies of Science. *Publications:* Central Administration in Britain (with W J M MacKenzie), 1957; Government and Industry in Britain, 1962; Organised Medicine in Ontario, 1969; Numerous monographs, articles and reviews. *Honours:* Rockefeller Travelling Fellow, USA, 1952-53. *Hobbies:* Listening to classical music and jazz; Astronomy. *Address:* 16 Hill Street, Kingston, Ontario, Canada.

GROVES, David Ian, b. 9 July 1942, Brighton, Sussex, England. University Lecturer. m. Suzanne Marie Hatch, 30 Mar. 1964, 1 son, 1 daughter. *Education:* BSc, Honours (1st Class), University of Tasmania, 1963; PhD, University of Tasmania, 1969. *Appointments:* Economic Geologist Geological Survey of Tasmania, 1964-67, 1969-71; Lecturer, 1971-73, Senior Lecturer, 1974-79, Associate Professor, 1980-81, University of Western Australia. *Memberships:* Geological Society of Australia, Chairman Western Division, 1979-80; Society of Economic Geologists; Australasian Institute of Mining & Metallurgy; Western Australian Mining Club. *Publications:* Author of over 70 Papers in scientific journals and books; Editor or Joint-Editor of 8 Geological books, main publications in Economic Geology and Archaean Geology. *Honours:* Old Hobartian Association Leaving Prize, 1958; Geological Survey Scholarship, 1958-62; Mt Lyell Prize for Economic Geology, 1962; Gledden Travel Award, 1974 & 1978. *Hobbies:* Tennis; Golf; Harness Racing. *Address:* 30 Addison Way, Warwick, Western Australia, 6024, Australia.

GRUEN, Fred Henry George, b. 14 June 1921. Professor of Economics. m. Ann 24 May 1947, 2 sons. *Education:* BA, 1945, B.Comm, 1947, University of Melbourne. MSc, (Ag.Econ.), Wisconsin University, 1950; MA, Chicago University, 1951. *Appointments:* Research Officer, Dept. of Agriculture, NSW, 1947-59; Part-time lecturer in Agric. Economics, University of Sydney, 1957-58; Senior Research Fellow, later Senior Fellow, Dept. of Economics, Research School of Social Sciences, ANU, Canberra, 1959-63; Professor of Agricultural Economics, Monash University, Victoria, 1964-72; Part-time Economic Consultant, Department of the Prime Minister & Cabinet, 1973-76; Professor Economics, Department of Economics, RSSSS, ANU, 1972-; Executive Director, Centre for Economic Policy Research, ANU, 1980-; Advisory Committee on Food Production & Rural Development, Commonwealth Secretariat, 1977-78. *Memberships:* President of: Australian Agricultural Economis Society, 1961, Section 25 (Economics) ANZAAS, 1976; Visiting Fellow, Clare Hall, Cambridge, England, 1977; Fellow, 1971, President, 1975-78, Academy of the Social Sciences in Australia. *Publications:* Australian Economics, 1967-77, (Joseph Fisher Lecture), 1978; Editor of, and contributor to, Surveys of Australian Economics, Vols I and II, 1978 & 1979; Changing Production Patterns for Home Consumption, 1980; The Future of Work: An Economic Perspective, 1981. *Hobbies:* Farming; Chess; Skiing. *Address:* Bedulluck, Via Hall, ACT, 2618. Canberra, Australia.

GRUENTHALER, Rudolf Erich, b. 16 June 1922, Leipzig, Germany. Merchant. m. Renate Schmid, 16 Dec. 1972, 2 sons. *Education:* Apprenticeship in Erich Brangsch GmbH, Engelsdorf, Leipzig, Germany. *Appointments:* Soldier in German Army, 1941-45; Manager, Seiler & Co, Leipzig, Germany, 1945; Proprietor & Managing Director, Erich Gruenthaler, Leipzig, Germany, 1945-53; Chief Buyer for Childrens Wear in Merkur, Horten & Co. GmbH, Nuernberg & Duesseldorf, West Germany, 1953-62; Proprietor & Managing Director, Erich Gruenthaler, Aschheim, near Munich, West Germany, later E Gruenthaler, Ltd., Hong Kong. 1962-. *Memberships:* World Trade Centre Club, Hong Kong; Deutsches Haus, Ltd., Hong Kong. *Hobbies:* Dancing; Swimming; Boating. *Address:* B 32 Po Shan Mansions, 15/Floor, 10, Po Shan Road, Hong Kong

GRYLLS, William Michael John, b. 21 Feb. 1934, Folkestone, England. Member of Parliament. m. 1965, 1 son, 1 daughter. *Memberships:* Chairman, Small Business Bureau; Parliamentary Spokesman for Institute of Directors; Chairman, Conservative Industry Committee. *Hobbies:* Sailing; Gardening. *Address:* House of Commons, London SW1, England.

GUILD, Alexander Eddie, b. 30 Oct. 1909, Aberdeen, Scotland. Civil Engineer. m. Mary Gwendoline Bishton, 14 Aug. 1937, 1 son, 1 daughter. *Education:* Robert Gordon's College, 1922-27; BSc, (Eng), Aberdeen University, 1927-30. *Appointments:* Harry C Ritchie & Partners, Consulting Engineers, Liverpool; South Staffordshire Waterworks Company; Water Engineer & Manager, Newport Corporation, Newport & South Monmouthshire Water Board, Gwent Water Board; Divisional Manager, Gwent, Welsh Water Authority. *Memberships:* Chairman, S. Wales Branch, Institute of Civil Engineers; President, Institution of Water Engineers. *Honours:* OBE, 1973. *Hobbies:* Golf; Gardening; Reading. *Address:* 20 Ridgeway Drive, Newport, Gwent, Wales.

GUILLOTTE, Guy Arthur Rene Joseph, b. 15 Oct. 1936, Cowansville, P. Quebec, Canada. Mathematician, Educator, Author, Writer. *Education:* HLC, 1957; BES, 1959; BA, 1961; CAPES, 1975; Dr. Maths, 1975; AFIMA, 1976; D.Ed, 1976; FCC, 1976; BSc, 1977; FNGS, 1978; Br.Ens, 1982. *Appointments:* Accountant, Bank of Montreal, 1959-63; Math Lecturer, Old Montreal College, 1968-70; English & Math Teacher, 1971-74, Sub-Teacher, 1980-81, Massey Vanier High School; English Teacher, Polyvalente J H LeClerc, Granby, P. Quebec, 1974-76; Math Teacher, Father

MacDonald High School, Montreal, 1976-77; Free Lance Writer, 1977-80. *Memberships:* Associate Fellow of the Math Institute & Its application, England, 1974-80; Montreal Gem Association, 1976-79; International Congress of Math, 1970-82; Canadian Math Association, 1967-82; The Learned Societies of Canada, 1970-81. *Publications:* My First Combat with Fermat's Last Theorem, Mutatis Mutandis, 1637, Volume 13, 1981; Emeralds, 1978; Rubies, 1981; Honorary Editor, Open Questions in Mathematics, Volume I-III, 1980; Published over 50 problems in Math Journals; Several research papers. *Honours:* Won a book for Art, 1955; A Math Prize, 1957; Gold Medal for Math, 1975; Officer of the Imperial Order of Constantine, 1975. *Hobbies:* Bridge; Riding; Tennis; Swimming; Bird Watching. *Address:* c/o Les Apps De La Loire, 120 Daigle Apt. 202, Cowansville, Quebec, Canada, J2K 3E4.

GULDEN, Simon, b. 7 Jan. 1938, Montreal, Quebec, Canada. Corporate Executive, Attorney at Law. m. Ellen Lee Barbour, 12 June 1977. *Education:* BA, (Arts), McGill University, Montreal, 1959; Certificate, Université de Rennes, St. Malo, France, 1961; LL.L, (cum laude), Université de Montréal (Law), 1962. *Appointments:* Partner, Genser, Phillips, Friedman & Gulden, Attorneys, Montreal, 1963-68; Secretary & Legal Counsel, Place Bonaventure Inc., Montreal, 1969-72; Legal Counsel, Real Estate, Steinberg Inc., Montreal, 1972-74; Counsel & Prime Attorney, Bell Canada, Montreal, 1975; Vice President, General Counsel & Secretary, Standard Brands Ltd., Montreal & Toronto, 1975-. *Memberships:* Bar of Quebec; Lord Reading Law Society of Quebec; Canadian Bar Association; International Bar Association; International Association of Lawyers and Jurists; International Fiscal Association; Montreal Board of Trade; Toronto Board of Trade; Association des conseils en francization du Québec; Advertising and Sales Executives Club. *Hobbies:* Sailing; Skiing (snow and Water); Horseback riding; Karate; Physical Fitness; Numismatics & Philately; Music; Literature; Theatre; Travel; Politics; Community Organizations. *Address:* 15 Morning Gloryway, Willowdale, Ontario, Canada, M2H 3M1

GULI, Edmondo Piero Giorgio, b. 17 July 1929, Genoa, Italy. Pathologist. m. Catherine Lindsay Yuncken, 24 May 1969, 2 daughters. *Education:* MD, Genoa 1953; Diploma Oncology, Pavia 1956; Docente in Anatomical Pathology, Italy 1961; MRCPath. 1970; FRCPA 1971. *Appointments:* Lecturer, University of Pavia, Italy 1953-54; Lecturer and Senior Lecturer in Pathology, University of Milan, Italy 1955-62; NATO Scholar in Human Genetics, University of Birmingham, UK 1962-63; Associate Professor, Acting Professor and Chairman of Pathology, University of Siena, Italy 1963-69; Associate Professor of Pathology and Immunology, Monash University, Melbourne, Australia, 1969-75; Director of Laboratory Medicine and Hon. Associate Professor, Queen Victoria Medical Centre, Melbourne, Australia 1976-. *Memberships:* Australian and New Zealand Society for Neuropathology; Human Genetics Society of Australasia; Anti-Cancer Council of Victoria, Medical and Scientific Committee; Australian Association of Neurologists; International Academy of Pathology; Australian Society for Pathology and Experimental Medicine. *Publications:* 52 papers dealing with Pathology of Genetic Disorders, Malformations of the Central Nervous System, Antenatal Pathology, Pathology and Immunology of Tumours. *Honours:* Prize, University of Genoa, 1953; Gold Medal for Sciences, Society of Arts, Sciences, Letters French Republic, 1961; NATO Scholarship in Human Genetics, 1962; Yearly prizes for Scientific Work, Universities of Milan and Siena, 1962-67. *Hobbies:* Mechanics; Symbolic Logic; Propositional Calculus. *Address:* 49 Talbot Road, Mount Waverley, 3149, Victoria, Australia.

GULSHAN, Satnam Singh, b. 10 Nov. 1935, Kaura, West Punjab, Pakistan. Teacher. m. Rani, 5 Dec. 1960, 2 sons. *Education:* M.Com, 1958, LL.B, 1965, Ph.D, 1979, University of Delhi. *Appointments:* Senior Lecturer in Commerce, S.T.T.B., Khalsa College, University of Delhi; Deputed as Director of Research and Studies, Institute of Company Secretaries of India, New Delhi, 1975-76; At present, working as Professor and Head, Department of Business Management, Asmara University Ethiopia, on a duputation for two years. *Memberships:* Indian Law Institute, New Delhi. *Publications:* A number of research papers and articles; A few books on management. *Honours:* Obtained First position in M.Com. Examination, University of Delhi, 1958. *Hobbies:* Reading; Writing. *Address:* 100 National Avenue, P.O. Box 744, Asmara, Ethiopia.

GUMI, Abubakar Mahmoud, b. 5 Nov. 1922. Muslim Jurist. (1) 1942, 6 sons, 13 daughters. *Education:* Kano Law School 1943-47; Kano School for Arabic Studies 1949-51; Institute of Education, Bahtur, Rudda, Sudan, 1953-55; *Appointments:* Court Scribe to Chief Alkali's Court 1947; Teacher, Law School Kano 1947-48; Teacher, Education Training College, Maru, 1948-49; Teacher, School for Arabic Studies Kano 1951-53 and 1955-60; Pilgrim Officer, 1960; Deputy Grand Qadi for Northern States, 1960-62; Grand Qadi, Sharia Court of Appeal, N. Nigeria 1962-75; Chairman, National Pilgrims Board, 1975-78; Chairman National Teacher's Institute, 1978-. *Memberships:* Jama'atu Nasril, Islam; World Muslim League, Mecca; Supreme Council, University of Medina; Advisor, Islamic Bank, Jedda; Ahmadu Bello University Council; Majmaul Figh (Jurisprudence) World Muslim League, Jeddah. *Publications:* Tafsir—Raddul Adhhani Ila Ma'anil Qur'an; Translated Qur'an into Hausa Language; Aqidatus Sahiha; Mnatakim Addini in Hausa; Al-Islam Wa ma Yubtiluhu; Guzuri ga mei; Riba—A paper on interest in Islam. *Honours:* National Award, Commander of the Federal Republic, 1965; Uthmaniyya Medal, 1965; Honorary Degree, Ibadan University, Nigeria and Ahmadu Bello University, 1965; Dr of Laws; Many other foreign Honours and distinctions. *Hobbies:* Lecturing; Public Preaching; Reading. *Address:* No 11 Modibbo, Adama Road, Kaduna, Nigeria.

GUN-MUNRO, Sydney Douglas (Sir), b. 29 Nov. 1916. Governor-General. m. Joan Estelle Benjamin, 1943, 2 sons, 1 daughter. *Education:* MB.,BS., Hons. King's College Hospital, London, 1943; DO, Moorfields Hospital, London, 1952; MRCS; LRCP;1943. *Appointments:* House Surgeon, EMS Hospital, Horton, 1943; MO, Lewisham Hospital, 1943-46; District MO, Grenada, 1946-49; Surgeon, General Hospital, St Vincent, 1949-71; District MO, Bequia, St Vincent, 1972-76; Governor, 1977-79, Governor-General, of St Vincent, West Indies, 1979-. *Honours:* GCMH, 1979; Kt., 1977. *Hobbies:* Tennis; Boating. *Address:* Government House, St Vincent, West Indies.

GUNN, Douglas George, b. 11 Jan. 1943, Tillsonburg, Ontario, Canada. Barrister; Farmer. m. Wendy Louise Mansbridge, 25 Jan. 1969, 2 sons, 1 daughter. *Education:* LL.B., University of Western Ontario, London, Canada, 1965; Bar Admission Course, Osgoode Hall, Toronto, Canada, 1967. *Appointments:* Associated in Practice of Law with Fanjoy, Hennessey & Hempster, St Thomas, Ontario, 1967-69, Partner, 1969-72, Partner in Hennessey, Kempster & Gunn, 1972-76; Senior Partner, Gunn, Upsdell, Deck & Eitel, St Thomas, Ontario, 1976-; Instructor, Bar Admission Course, 1976-79; Chairman, Ontario Crop Insurance Arbitration Board, 1981; Farming, 1965-. *Memberships:* Law Society of Upper Canada; Law Society of Alberta; Advocate's Society; Elgin Law Association; Canadian Hereford Association. *Honours:* OAC Alumni Foundation Scholarship, 1960; Queen's Counsel, 1979; Director, South Western Ontario Hereford Association, 1981. *Hobbies:* Carpentry; Construction. *Address:* RR No. 5 St Thomas, Ontario, Canada, N5P 3S9.

GUNN, Graeme Cecil, b. 6 Aug. 1933, Geelong, Victoria, Australia. Architect. m. Grazia Maria Therese Gunn, 12 July 1966, 1 son, 1 daughter. *Education:* Studied Fellowship Diploma in Architecture, Royal Melbourne Institute of Technology, 1956-60. *Appointments:* Lynton Bailey Architect, 1958-60; Grounds Romberg & Boyd, Architects, 1960-62; Private Practice, Graeme Gunn Pty Ltd., 1962-74; Head, School of Architecture and Building, 1972-77, Dean, Faculty of Architecture and Building, 1977-, Royal Melbourne Institute of Technology. *Memberships:* Vice-President, Victoria Chapter, Royal Australian Institute of Architects; Chairman, Victoria Chapter, Public Services Committee, R.A.I.A; Council Victoria Chapter, R.A.I.A; R.A.I.A., Education Committee. *Publications:* Co-author, A Mansion or No House, (with D B D Yencken & J Patterson); Papers: Man and Landscape in Australia, a UNESCO Conference, Conversion of Warehouse Buildings for Residential Use, ANZAAS Congress; Incorporated with Gunn Hayball p/L, 1975; The works of Gunn Hayball Pty Ltd have been published in Journals and

Books in both Australia and overseas. *Honours:* R.A.I.A., Architecture Awards: Bronze Medals, Richardson House, Essendon, 1966, Town Houses, Kew, 1969, Arts Activity Centre, Ararat, 1980; Citations: Plumbers & Gas Fitters Building, Carlton, 1970, Royal South Yarra Lawn Tennis Club, 1971, Winter Park, Doncaster, 1875, Chelsworth Park Pavilion, Heidelberg, 1976, A.M.W.S.U., Headquarters, East Melbourne, 1976. *Address:* 10/112 Millswyn Street, South Yarra, Victoria 3141, Australia.

GUNN, James Thomson, b. 9 Apr. 1932, Gorebridge. Artist, Designer. m. Mary Lang Linton, 22 Dec. 1956, 1 daughter. *Education:* Certificate, Scholarship Award, Heriot-Watt College, 1952-54; Travelling Scholar, Edinburgh College of Art, 1954-56; Diploma, Rhodec International School of Interior Design. *Appointments:* Artist/Designer, Smith & Ritchie Ltd., 1950-54, 1958-59; R.A.F., 1956-58; Studio Manager, Forth Studios Ltd., 1959-73; Free-Lance Artist, 1973-77; Scotsman Publications Ltd., 1977-. *Memberships:* Fellow, International Institute of Arts and Letters; Associate Institute of Professional Designers; Royal Scottish Society of Painters in Watercolour. *Creative Works:* Exhibitions in: Royal Scottish Academy, Royal Glasgow Institute of Fine Art, Pitlochry Festival Theatre; Royal Scottish Society of Painters in Watercolours, Society of Scottish Artists, works in public and private collections. *Honours:* Letter of Commendation from Her Majesty The Queen (RAF), 1957. *Hobbies:* Painting; Music; Philosophy; Poetry; Literature. *Address:* 3 Park Crescent, Easthouses, Dalkeith, Midlothian, Scotland.

GUNNERSEN, Thorold Harvey, b. 29 Nov. 1940, East Melbourne, Victoria, Australia. Managing Director. m. (1) Susan Margaret Stokes (divorced), 25 Jan. 1962, 1 son, 3 daughters, (2) Cherry Edwina Condon, 16 May 1981, 1 son. *Education:* Bachelor of Commerce, Melbourne University; Master of Science, Southampton University. *Appointments:* Church of England Grammar School, Ballarat, 1962-64; LaTrobe University, Melbourne, 1968-70; Managing Director, Marbut-Gunnersen Pty. Ltd., 1970-; Chairman of Directors, Timber Holdings Ltd., 1978-; Director, Softwood Holdings Ltd., 1978-. *Memberships:* Land Conservation Council, Victoria; Church of England Grammar School Council; Melbourne Club; Royal Brighton Yacht Club; Melbourne Cricket Club; Lawn Tennis Association of Victoria; Melbourne Beefsteak Club. *Publications:* Effective Rate of Protection and the Tariff Board, AIDA, 1970; The Victorian Alps: A Resource Base—Forest Industries Resource Management Group, 1977. *Honours:* Gottstein Fellow, 1977. *Hobbies:* Sailing; Skiing. *Address:* 18 Degraves Street, Parkville, Victoria 3052, Australia.

GUNNING, Kenneth Samuel, b. 6 Apr. 1930, Vancouver, Canada. Chartered Accountant. m. Flora Marie Johnson, 2 July 1954, 1 son, 3 daughters. *Education:* Associate, Royal Conservatory of Music, Toronto (ARCT), 1951; Brandon College, University of Manitoba; BA, University of British Columbia, 1952. *Appointments:* Articled XStudent, 1953, Chartered Accountant, 1957, Partner, 1966, Helliwell MacLachlan & Company, Vancouver; Director of Research & Training, 1970, Administrative Partner, 1972, Executive Partner, 1973, Thorne Gunn & Company, Toronto; Deputy Executive Partner, 1974, Executive Partner, 1977, Thorne Riddell & Company, Toronto; Member of Central Management Committee of Klynveld Main Goerdeler, affiliated international accounting firm. *Memberships:* Institute of Chartered Accountants, British Columbia; Institute of Chartered Accountants, Ontario Toronto Club. *Publications:* Author of several articles in professional accounting journals; Frequent speaker at professional conferences. *Honours:* Winner, Canadian Institute of Chartered Accountants, Walter J MacDonald Award, 1975; Fellow of the Chartered Accountants, Ontario, 1976; Fellow of the Chartered Accountants, British Columbia, 1977. *Hobbies:* Squash; Curling; Tennis; Music. *Address:* 539 Blythwood Road, Toronto, Ontario, Canada M4N 1B4.

GUPTA, Baldev Raj, b. 8 July 1942, Chhamal, Pakistan. Teacher; Research. m. Asha, 2 Mar. 1968, 2 sons, 1 daughter. *Education:* MA, 1963; Intensive Course in Spoken Tamil, 1964; PG Diploma, 1966; PhD, 1975; MA, 1976. *Appointments:* Language Teacher, Higher Secondary and High School, 1962-63; Lecturer, Gout College, Chandigarh, 1963-64; Research Scholar, Centre of Advanced Studies, Annamalai University, 1964-66; Junior Research Fellow, 1966-67, Lecturer, 1967-78, Punjabi University; Reader, University of Jammu, 1978-. *Memberships:* Editorial Board: Pa'kha Sanjam, Linguistic Atlas of the Punjab; Linguistic Society of India; Dravidian Linguists Association; Board of Studies in Punjabi, University of Jammu. *Publications:* Research papers in English, Hindi, Punjabi, Sanskrit, Tamil and Dogri; Three Books published on Linguistics; Two Books in Press to be released, 1980, 81. *Honours:* College Prizes, 1957-61. *Hobbies:* Social & Literary Functions; Radio; Concern for Social Situations. *Address:* 45 Gurah, Bakshi Nagar, Jammu Tawi 180001

GUPTA, Chaman Lal, b. 27 Mar. 1933, Ferozepur, Panjab, India. Teacher; Research. m. Shipra, 28 Feb. 1962. *Education:* BSc, St Stephen's College, Delhi, 1952; MSc, University of Delhi, 1961; PhD, University of Roorkee, India, 1967. *Appointments:* Scientist, Central Building Research Institute, Roorkee, India, 1954-57, 1961-68; CSIRO—Division of Building Research, 1968-70; Professor, Sri Aurobindo International Centre of Education, Pondicherry, India, 1971-; Honorary Director, Tata Energy Institute Field Research Unit, Pondicherry, 1975-. *Memberships:* Solar Energy Society of India; International Solar Energy Society; International Centre for Heat & Mass Transfer; Natural Living Association, London; Third world Foundation, London. *Publications:* 90 Research Papers in the field of: Math. modelling in Heat Transfer in Buildings; Solar Energy application to Industrial, Architectural Planning and Rural systems. *Honours:* Hume-Rocla Award of RMIT, Melbourne, 1970. *Hobbies:* Reading; Mystic Literature; Travel; Walking. *Address:* Sri Aurobindo, Ashram, Pondicherry, 605002, India.

GUPTA, Dharma Prakash, b. 27 July 1928, Thakurdwara, Moradabad, India. Teacher; Professor of Mathematics. m. Shashi Gupta, 3 Dec. 1953, 3 daughters. *Education:* MSc, 1950, DPhil, 1959, DSc, 1972, Allahabad University, India; Diploma in French, Saugar University, India, 1964. *Appointments:* Lecturer, University of Saugar, India, 1952-61; Lecturer, 1961-63, Reader, 1963-71, Professor, 1971-, Motilal Nehru Regional Engg College, Allahabad, India; Professor of Mathematics and Head of the Department of Basic Sciences, Higher Petroleum Institute, Tobruk, Libya, 1977-79, 1980-. *Memberships:* Indian Science Congress; Indian, American, Allahabad (Vice-President), Mathematical Societies; Association of Mathematics Teachers of India. *Publications:* Published more than 40 original research papers in international journals on "Approximation and convergence properties of special orthogonal expansions"; 200 review articles for the "Mathematical Reviews" and "The Zentralblatt fur Mathematik". *Honours:* Was invited in 1972 as "Visiting Scientist" to Canada, visited universities in Calgary, Alberta, Montreal. *Address:* M N R Engg College, Allahabad 211 004, India.

GUPTA, Jagdishwar Chandra, b. 6 July 1928, Ambala Haryana, India. Medicine; Pathology; Teacher; Diagnostics; Research. m. Premlata Gupta, 7 May 1950 2 sons, 1 daughter. *Education:* MBBS, University of Madras, 1951; MD, Agra University, 1957. *Appointments:* Demonstrator, 1952-56, Lecturer, 1956-57, Reader, 1957-64, Professor & Head of Department, 1964-, Vice-Dean, 1980-, in Pathology, Medical Colleges of the Madhya Pradesh State, India. *Memberships:* Indian Association of Pathologists & Microbiologists; Indian Medical Association; Indian Academy of Cytologists. *Publications:* 80 papers have been published on various aspects of Pathology & Microbiology in various journals of India and other countries. *Hobbies:* Photography; Reading. *Address:* P-6 Medical College Campus, Jabalpur (MP) 482003, India.

GUPTA, Motilal, b. 18 Sept. 1910, Bharatpur, India. Teaching. m. P D Gupta 15 May 1928, 1 son, 2 daughters. *Education:* MA, Hindi, Sanskrit, English, 1937, 1954, 1944; PhD, Manuscripts 1955; DLitt. Applied Linguistics 1965; D.PR.Sc. Linguistics and Phonetics 1960. *Appointments:* State Government 1933-47; Matsya Government 1947-49; R.E.S. (Raj), 1944-62; University of Jodhpur 1962-73; U.G.C Fellowship, 1976-79; V.R.I. Honorary Director, 1974-81. *Memberships:* Consultation Committee, I.P.S. Tokyo; I.S.PR.S, UNESCO, USA; Hindi Anusandhar Parishad, Allakehad; National Archive of India. *Publications:* Matsya Pradesh Ki Hindi Ko Den 1962; Prataf Rado 1965;

Seniotiès in India 1980; Seniotiès of Braj 1981; History of Khandelwal Community 1970. *Honours:* State Gold Medal 1930; Sir George Lambert Gold Medal 1933; Chintamani Ghost Medal, 1933; U.G.C. Research Fellowship, 1976; British Commonwealth Fellowship, 1959. *Hobbies:* Reading; Touring; *Address:* Mori Charbagh, Bharatpur 321001, India.

GUPTA, Radha Charan, b. 26 Oct. 1935, Jhansi, India. Teaching. m. Savitri Gupta, 12 Dec. 1953, 1 son, 2 daughters. *Education:* BSc, 1955, MSc, 1957, Lucknow University; Dip Mech Engineering, School of Careers, London, 1965; PhD, Ranchi University, 1971. *Appointments:* Lecturer in Mathematics, Lucknow Christian College, Lucknow, 1957-58; Lecturer in Mathematics, 1958-61, Assistant Professor, 1961-76, Associate Professor, 1976-, Birla Institute of Technology. *Memberships:* International Commission on History of Mathematics; British Society for History of Mathematics; Canadian Society for History and Philosophy of Mathematics; Life Member of Indian Mathematical Society; Indian Science Congress Association; Astronomical Society of India. *Publications:* Author of approximately 150 research papers and articles on various subjects; Founder-Editor of the Ganita Bharati, Bulletin. *Honours:* Physics Medal, 1953, Shankar Sahay Gold Medal, 1956, Devi Sahay Misra Gold Medal, 1957, B.I.C. Jhansi, Lucknow University; Prizes for sport. *Address:* BIT Inner Campus, Mesra, Ranchi, India.

GUPTA, Ram Prakash, b. 1 Jan. 1941, New Delhi, India. Surgeon. m. 10 June 1971, 1 daughter. *Education:* MBBS, New Delhi, 1964; FRCS, 1967; MCh, 1971; FRACS, 1974. *Appointments:* Registrar, Surgery, Irwin Hospital, New Delhi, 1968; Lecturer in Thoracic Surgery, 1969-71, Reader in Thoracic Surgery, 1971-74, CMC Vellore, India; Senior Registrar in Open Heart Surgery, Royal Melbourne Hospital, Australia, 1974-75; Associate Professor of Cardiac Surgery, Institute of Cardiology, Kanpur; Honorary Consultant Cardio Thoracic and General Surgeon: Sir Ganga Ram Hospital and Mool Chand Hospital, New Delhi, India. *Memberships:* Association of Surgeons of India; Association of Cardio Thoracic Surgeons of India; Fellow of American College of Chest Physicians; Fellow of International College of Surgeons; Fellow of American College of Cardiologists; Fellow of Denton A Cooley Cardiovascular Surgical Society. *Publications:* Author of approximately 15 papers in International Journals. *Hobbies:* Reading; Surgery. *Address:* SC 11 Railway Bungalow, Basant Lane, New Delhi, India.

GUPTARA, Prabhu S, b. 1949. Freelance Writer, Lecturer, Broadcaster. m. 1976, 1 son. *Education:* BA, 1968, MA, 1970, St Stephen's College, Delhi University. *Appointments:* Lecturer, Delhi University, 1970-73; Lecturer, Postgraduate Department of English, North-Eastern Hill University, India, 1973-76; Warden, Murray Hall of Residence, University of Stirling, Scotland, 1977-79; Visiting Lecturer, Editorial Study Centre, Thomson Foundation, UK, 1980-; Director, Minorities Arts Advisory Service, UK, 1980-. *Memberships:* Fellow, Royal Commonwealth Society; Life Member of the Indian PEN; Asiatic Society, Calcutta; Arts Centre Group, Chairman of the Scottish branch, 1978-79; Literature Advisory Panel, South East Arts Association, 1980-84. *Publications:* Poems: Beginnings, 1975; Continuation, 1979; Modern Indian Poetry in English: An Anthology and Credo, 3rd edition, 1977; Exiles, 1981; Read poems, papers and lectures by invitation at Universities in several Countries; Greenbelt Festival, 1979 and 1980; Biennial Conference of the European Association for Commonwealth Literature and Language Studies, Malta; Annual conference of the Societe d'Etudes du pays du Commonwealth, France; Editor and contributor to varous periodicals. *Honours:* Writer's Award, South East Arts Association, 1980. *Address:* Vine House, Whelford, Fairford, Gloucestershire, England.

GURAYA, Sardul Singh, b. 12 Oct. 1930, Punjab, India. Teaching and Research. m. Surinderpal Kaur, 10 Mar. 1962, 2 sons, 1 daughter. *Education:* BSc, 1954; MSc, 1956; PhD, 1959; Postdoctoral Research Training, USA, 1962-65; DSc, 1971. *Appointments:* Student Demonstrator, 1954-55, Part-time Demonstrator, 1956, Research Scholar, University Grants Commission, 1956-58, Department of Zoology, Punjab University; Pool Officer, CSIR, 1965-66; Assistant Professor of Zoology, Gorakhpur University, 1960-64; Reader in Zoology, Udaipur University, 1966-71; Professor of Zoology, Head, Department of Zoology, Punjab Agricultural University, Ludhiana, 1971-. *Memberships:* Founder Memeber of the Executive Council of Indian Society for General and Comparative Endocrinology; Founder Member of the Executive Council of Indian Society for Invertebrate Reproduction; International Cell Research Organization; Fellow, Indian National Science Academy; Approximately 216 research papers published in International journals; Chapters in books. *Honours:* Gold Medal, VIthe International Congress, France, 1968; Shanti Swarup Bhatnagar Prize, 1973; Prize, Punjab Agricultural University, 1980. *Hobbies:* To observe plants and animals in their natural environment. *Address:* 443-L Model Town, Ludhiana-141002, Punjab, India.

GURNER, Colin Marshall, b. 26 Dec. 1919, Adelaide, South Australia. Medical Practitioner. m. Cynthia Lillian Miller, 20 Dec. 1943, 2 sons, 2 daughters. *Education:* Prince Alfred College, MBBS, Adelaide, 1942; DABR, 1951; MACR, 1952; FRACR, 1957; FRACMA, 1967; FRACS, 1969; FRACP, 1969; Hon. FRCR, 1973. *Appointments:* Residencies, Royal Adelaide Hospital, 1942, 1946-50; Australian Army Medical Corps. AIF, 1942-46; Private Radiology, 1952-60; Honorary Assistant Radiotherapist R.A.H, 1952-60; Honorary Assistant Radiologist, Adelaide Children's Hospital, 1956-60; Deputy Director General, Royal Australian Army Medical Corps, Regular Army, 1960-67; Director General, 1967-75; Surgeon General, Defence Force, 1975-79; Medical Officer, Department of Health, 1980-; Chairman, ACT Medical Board, 1979-. *Memberships:* Melbourne Club; Commonwealth Club. *Publications:* Professional Articles Military Medicine, Radiology. *Honours:* Efficiency Decoration, 1960; CBE, 1969; Officer Order of St John, 1974; Commander, 1980; A.O. 1978. *Hobby:* Gardening. *Address:* 84 Dominion Circuit, Deakin, ACT 2600, Australia.

GURSAHANI, Ganpat, Thakurdas, b. 9 Apr. 1916, Bhiria (Sind); West Pakistan. Teacher. m. (1) Kalan Valiram Motwani 21 May 1938 (deceased 1945), (2) Chandra Bansiram Chhugani, 6 Mar. 1971, 1 son, 1 daughter. *Education:* BSc, 1938, MSc, 1940, BA, 1941, University of Bombay. *Appointments:* Research Assistant, Research Laboratory, Sind P.W.D, Karachi, Pakistan, 1940-45; Research Assistant & Lecturer in Chemistry, D J Sind College, Karachi, 1945-48; Lecturer in Chemistry, Jai Hind College Bombay, India, 1949-61; Professor of Chemistry, Head of Chemistry Department, K J Somaya College, Vidya Vihar, Bombay, 1961-73; Retired as Vice-Principal. *Memberships:* Royal Society of Chemistry; Member of Board of Studies, 1961-73, Member of Faculty of Science, 1962-73; Chairman, Board of Examiners, 1970-72, University of Bombay. *Publications:* Inorganic Chemistry; A Class Book of Practical Chemistry; An Outline of Physical Chemistry, Organic Chemistry and Inorganic Chemistry; A Peep in to an Ancient Sind; A Directory of Sindhis Residing in UK. *Hobbies:* Collection of Books; Reading; Writing; Guiding Students in Science; Social, Cultural & Educational Activities of Sindhis residing in UK. *Address:* 318 Park West, Edgware Road, London, W2 2QR.

GUST, Ian David, b. 15 Jan. 1941, Melbourne, Australia. Medical Virologist. m. 21 Feb. 1969, 3 sons, 1 daughter. *Education:* BSc, 1961, MB.,BS, 1964, MD, 1974, Melbourne University; Diploma Bacteriology, London University, 1968; FRCPA, 1971; MASM, 1977; FRACP, 1979. *Appointments:* RMO, Alfred Hospital, Melbourne, 1965; Pathology Registrar, Fairfield Hospital, Melbourne, 1966; London School of Hygiene and Tropical Medicine, 1967-68; Registrar Regional Virus Laboratory, Glasgow, 1968-69; Director, Virus Laboratory, Fairfield Hospital, Melbourne, 1970; Director, WHO Collaborating Centre for Virus Reference and Research for Western Pacific Region, 1972-; Director, National Hepatitis Reference Laboratory, 1979-. *Memberships:* Australian and American Societies for Microbiology; Royal Australasian Colleges of Pathology and Physicians; Australian Society for Infectious Diseases; Gastroenterology Society of Australia; Asian-Pacific Society for the Study of the Liver. *Publications:* Author of over 100 papers on aspects of Medical Virology. *Honours:* BMA, 1939 (Annual Meeting) Prize for Medical Research, 1980. *Hobbies:* Reading; Writ-

ing; Golf; Travel. *Address:* 8 The Boulevard, Ivanhoe, Melbourne, Victoria, Australia, 3079.

GUTHRIE, Roy David (Gus), b. 29 Mar. 1934, Leatherhead, Surrey, England. Secretary General, Royal Society of Chemistry. 3 sons. *Education:* BSc, 1955, PhD, 1958, DSc, 1968, University of London. *Appointments:* Shirley Institute, Manchester, 1958-60; Assistant Lecturer, then Lecturer, University of Leicester, 1960-63; Lecturer, then Reader, University of Sussex, 1963-73; Foundation Professor, 1973-81, Pro-Vice-Chancellor, 1980-81, Griffith University Brisbane. *Memberships:* Royal Society of Chemistry; Royal Australian Institute of Chemistry; Royal Society of Arts. *Publications:* Introduction to The Chemistry of Carbohydrates, (Three editions, French & Japanese Translations); Over 120 research papers in organic chemistry. *Hobby:* Theatre, both Administration & Acting. *Address:* Royal Society of Chemistry, Burlington House, Piccadilly, London, W1V 0BN, England.

GUYADEEN, Kester Dennis, b. 11 Oct. 1926, British Guiana (Now Guyana). Agricultural Director. m. Dorothea Elsa Bennett, 30 June 1951, 3 sons, 3 daughters. *Education:* Queens's College, Georgetown, 1935-45; DICTS, 1948, AICTA, 1949, Imperial College of Tropical Agriculture, St. Augustine, Trinidad, 1945-51. *Appointments:* Lecturer in Agriculture, Imperial College of Tropical Agriculture, Tinidad, 1949-51; Agricultural Superintendent, British Guiana, 1951-54, Agricultural Officer, 1954-58, Senior Agricultural Officer, Trinidad, 1958-63, Her Majesty's Overseas Civil Service; Agronomist, Caribbean Region, Esso Standard Oil Co., 1964-65; Director & Co-Manager of a United Nations Project, Eastern Caribbean Institute of Agriculture & Forestry, 1965-74; Co-Director, United Nations Forestry Project on Northern Range, Trinidad, 1975-. *Memberships:* Advisory Council, Faculty of Agriculture, University of the West Indies, 1964-67; Board of Management, Agricultural Society of Trinidad and Tobago; International Biographical Association. *Hobbies:* Reading; Gardening. *Address:* 2 Palm Avenue East, Petit Valley, Diego Martin, Trinidad, T.W.1.

GUY, Geoffrey Colin, b. 4 Nov. 1921, Ramsgate, Kent, England. Overseas Civil Servant. m. Joan Elfreda Smith, 3 Sept. 1946, 1 son. *Education:* BA, 1940-41, BA, 1946-47 now MA, Brasenose College, Oxford. *Appointments:* Pilot RAF, 1941-46; District Commissioner, Sierra Leone, 1951-58; Administrator to the Caius Islands, 1958-65; Administrator, 1965-66, Governor, 1966-67, Dominica, West Indies; Administrator, Ascension Island, 1973-76; Governor, St Helena, 1976-81. *Memberships:* Royal Commonwealth Society; *Honours:* MBE, 1957; OBE, 1961; CMG, 1964; CVO, 1966. *Hobbies:* Reading; Swimming; Farming. *Address:* Tamarisk Cottage, Kirk Hamerton, York, England

GWARZO, Alhaji Tukur, b. 1918, Gwarzo, Kano State. Civil Servant (Now Pensioner). m. Mummunai 16 Apr. 1941, 11 sons, 8 daughters. *Education:* Kaduna College, 1935-38; Veterinary Schol Certificate, 1941-43; Diploma School of Hygiene, 1944-46; Certificate, Anti Malaria Control, Yaba, 1953; Diploma, Prevention & Treatment of Tuberculosis, London, 1954; Study Tour, UK, Certificate in preparation & drying of hides and skins, and Abattoir Management, 1957. *Appointments:* Veterinary Assistant; Health Inspector; AG. Health Superintendent; Senior Livestock Superintendent; Administrative Officer; AG. Permanent Secretary; Chairman, Local Government Service Board. *Memberships:* NAPT, UK; Permanent Member and Hon. Assistant Secretary, National Council of Social Work. *Publications:* Preparation and Drying of Hides and Skins. *Honours:* Officer of the Order of Nigeria, 1966. *Hobbies:* Farming; Crops; Livestock. *Address:* 170 Tudun Wazirci, Kano City, Nigeria.

GWEBE-NYIRENDA, Robert Donald, b. 13 Oct. 1928, Kilosa, Tanganyika. Marketing Executive. m. Josephine Manda, 16 Jan. 1954, 2 sons, 2 daughters. *Education:* Junior Management Course, B.A.T., Chelwood Training Centre, 1964; Marketing Management, 1969; Management Development, 1970; East African Staff College, 1973. *Appointments:* Secretary/Manager, K.R.G. Coop, Union, Karonga, Malawi, 1952-57; District Marketing Rep., East African Tobacco Co. Ltd., 1962-65; Divisional Marketing Manager, 1966-73, Marketing Planning Manager, 1977-79, Marketing

Manager, 1980-, B.A.T., Ltd. *Memberships:* Rotary Club, Arusha, Tanzania, 1966-68. *Hobby:* Hunting. *Address:* PO Box 428, Blantyre, Malawi.

GWYNNE-JONES, Allan, b. 27 Mar. 1892, Richmond, Surrey. Painter & Etcher. m. Rosemary Allan, 22 Mar. 1937, 1 daughter. *Education:* Slade School of Art. *Appointments:* Professor of Painting, Royal College of Painting; Staff of Slade School, 1930. *Memberships:* Trustee of Tate Gallery, 1939-46; Royal Academician, 1966; Club Athenaeum. *Publications:* A way of Looking at Pictures; Portrait Painters; Introduction to Still Life. *Honours:* DSO, 1916; RA, 1966; CBE, 1980; Represented by Pictures in collection of The Queen & Queen Elizabeth, the Queen Mother, The Tate Gallery & public galleries of Birmingham, Newcastle, Leeds, Manchester, Oldham, Carlisle, Sheffield & National Galleries of South Africa, Australia and the National Museum of Wales. *Address:* Eastleach Turville, Nr. Cirencester, Gloucester, England.

GYEBI-ABABIO, Kwaku, b. 28 Apr. 1937, Kokofu-Ashanti, Ghana. Buyer. m. Cecilia 14 Mar. 1960, 3 sons, 2 daughters. *Education:* Diploma in International Trade, Thurrock Technical College, Essex, London, 1968-69; Diploma of the Institute of Purchasing & Supply, London, 1974; Post-Graduate Diploma of Purchasing & Suplly, Polytechnic of North London, 1973-74. *Appointments:* Supply Officer: Ministry of Finance Accra, 1975-77; Ghana Institute of Management & Public Administration, Achimota, 1977-81; Assistant Purchasing Manager, State Hotels Corporation, Accra, 1981-. *Memberships:* Institute of Purchasing & Supply, London & Ghana. *Publications:* Co-publisher of a quaterly bulletin. *Hobbies:* Football; Reading; Fish breeding; Back yard Gardening. *Address:* PO Box 200, Keneshie, Accra, North, Ghana.

GYÖRY, A'Kos Zoltan, b. 29 Sept. 1935, Budapest. Medical Academic. m. Ingelore Elisabeth Rubenow, 2 Dec. 1961, 1 son, 2 daughters. *Education:* MB., BS, 1962; MRACP, 1965; MD, Sydney, 1971; FRACP, 1971. *Appointments:* Resident Medical Officer, RNSH, 1962-65; Renal Research Fellow, Sydney Hospital, 1966-68; C J Martin Fellow, NH & MRC, 1969-72; Senior Renal Research Fellow, Sydney Hospital, 1972-74; Research Fellow, NH & MRC, 1973-74, Senior Lecturer, 1974-77, Associate Professor, 1977-, Sydney University; Senior Vis. Spec. Concord, 1973-75; Honorary Physician, Hon. Cons. Ren. Physician, Hon. Cons. Ren. Physiologist, Sydney Hospital, 1974-. *Memberships:* International Society Nephrology; International Soc. for Study of Hypertension in Pregnancy; Australian Society Medical Research; Australian Nephreology Society; Australian Society Clin & Exp. Physiol & Pharmacol; Australian Physiological & Pharmacol Society. *Publications:* 56 publications on Renal Medicine, Renal Physiology and Hypertension in Pregnancy in medical journals. *Honours:* Honorary Editor, Australian & New Zealand Journal of Medicine, of the Royal College of Physicians, 1975-81. *Hobbies:* Stamp Collecting; Carpentry; Hunting. *Address:* 23 Lowry Crescent, St. Ives, 2075 Australia

GYÖRY, Attila Nicholas, b. 1.9 Mar. 1933, Budapest, Hungary. Specialist Physician. m. Elisabeth Gizella Obrincsak, 29 Mar. 1959, 3 sons. *Education:* BSc, Medical, 1960, MB., BS, 1962, MRCP, (UK), 1971, Sydney University; MS, University of Minnesota/Mayo Graduate Medical School, 1974; U.S. Board of Physical Medicine & Rehabilitation Certificate, 1977; Fellow, Australian College of Rehabilitation Medicine, 1980. *Appointments:* Canterbury Hospital, 1962-64; Private General Practice in Sydney, 1965-67; Registrar, Concord Hospital, 1967-68, Royal Newcastle Hospital, 1969; Director Coronary Care/Intensive Care Rachel Forster/Royal Prince Alfred Hospital, 1970; Senior Research Registrar Rheumatology, Guy's Hospital, 1972-72; Fellow Rehabilitation Medicine, Mayo Clinic, 1972-74; Senior Lecturer Anatomy/Kinesiology, Cumberland College, Sydney, 1975; Director Rehabilitation Medicine, Concord Hospital, 1975-. *Memberships:* Deputy Chief Censor and Chairman Board of Examiners, Australia College Rehabilitation Medicine; Past-President, Australia Association of Physical Medicine & Rehabilitation; Collegiate Member, Royal College of Physicians, London; Fellow, Mayo Akumni Association; American Academy of Physical Med. and Rehabilitation; Australian and British Medical Associations; New York Academy of Sciences. *Publications:* Chylothorax of the Right Side, 1964; Orudis in Rheumatoid Arthritis, 1972; Functional Evaluation of Gait, Archives, Physical Medicine and Rehabilitation, 1976; Electrodiagnosis & EMG Biofeedback, 1976; Rehabilitation of Neurological Patients, 1979; Synopsis of Back Pain Assessment & Physical, 1980; Bulletin, Postgraduate Committee, Medical University of Sydney; Biomechanics of Gait, Clin. Orth. & Rel. Res., 1977; Transcut. Electric Nerve Stim., 1980; Rational Use of Muscle Relaxants, Drugs, 1980; EPC of Painful Amputation Stump, Medical Journal of Australia, 1977. *Honours:* Student American Medical Association Research Excellence, 1974; Travel Grant, Postgraduate Federation, Australia, 1972; Commonwealth Scholarship, Medical Course, 1954-61. *Hobbies:* Photography; Swimming; Tennis; Music;Sociology/History. *Address:* 8 Pitt Street, Hunter's Hill, 2110, N.S.W., Australia.

H

HAAS, Richard Joseph, b. 22 Apr. 1910, Darmstadt, Germany. Doctor of Law. m. Ursula Kreindler, 17 Nov. 1946, 1 son, 1 daughter. *Education:* LL.B.; LL.M.; L.LD. *Appointments:* Practising International Law Consultant. *Memberships:* British Institute of International and Comparative Law; American International Academy Washington, USA; London Institute of World Affairs; American Society of International Law; Association of German· Lawyers-Deutscher Juristentag; Anglo-German Lawyers Association; Nigerian Society of International Law; Council of the University College of Buckingham; Commonwealth Human Ecology Council; United Nation Register as Expert and Scholar in International Law; Reform Club. *Honours:* Awarded Croce di' Commendatore Al Merito Melitense from the Sovereign Order of Malta, 1977; Became Freeman of the City of London, 1979; various war decorations. *Hobbies:* Music; Painting; Rugby; Football; Skiing. *Address:* 17 Wadham Gardens, London, NW3, England.

HAASTRUP (Prince), Adedokun Abiodun, b. 3 Jan. 1921, Ilesha, Nigeria. Consultant Legal Practitioner. m. Christiana Olabisi Sadare, 28 Mar. 1948, 4 sons, 3 daughters. *Education:* University Education, University College, London, UK, 1951-53; LLB (Hons) London Barrister at Law of the Middle Temple; Post Graduate Studies in International Law; Comparative Constitutional Law, Administrative Law and Local Government, Institute of Advanced Legal Studies, London, UK, 1953-54. *Appointments:* A D O and Acting Assistant Local Government Inspector in Ijebu Division, 1954-56; Private Secretary to Premier, Western Nigeria, 1956; Secretary to Western Nigerian Government Economic Mission to: Eurpe, America, Canada, 1956, Scandinavian Countries, 1957; Trade Officer, Western Nigerian Office, London, UK, 1957; Various Diplomatic Positions in Washington DC., New York, USA, 1957-60; Counsellor and Head of various divisions, Ministry of External Affairs, Lagos, 1960-64; Member of Nigerian Delegation to: UN Conference on Diplomatic Relations in Vienna, Austria, 1961, Disarmament Conference in Geneva, 1962, various conferences of OAU, 1963,64 and 1966-68, UN General Assembly, 1965; Participant First Dag Hammerskjold Seminar on International Law, The Hague, 1963; Established Nigerian Embassy, Tokyo, 1964; High Commissioner to India, 1964-66; Ambassador to: Ethopia, 1966-68, Western Germany, 1968-73, Italy, Spain, Greece; High Commissioner to Cyprus, 1973-76; Permanent Representative to FAO, Rome, 1975-76; Member and Vice Chairman, 1970-74, Chairman, 1974-76, UN Committee on Elimination of Racial Discrimination; Directorships: (UMARCO) Nigeria Limited, Dadhak Optical Services Limited, International Breweries Limited. *Memberships:* Island Club, Metropolitan Club; Trustee Club Arcade of Nigeria; Chairman of Lagos Chapter, Nigeria Society. *Publications:* Problems of International Law, Diplomatic Relations and Reciprocity. *Honours:* The World.Peace Through Law Center Certificate of Regular Membership for Outstanding Public Service by Contributions to the Cause of World Peace through the Rule of Law. *Hobbies:* Reading; Gardening; Table tennis. *Address:* 'Oluodo Villas', 6 Ogalade Close, Victoria Island Lagos, Nigeria.

HADDAD, John Michael, b. Melbourne, Victoria, Australia. Managing Director, Federal Hotels Limited. m. Agita Freibergs, 6 Oct. 1962, 1 son, 2 daughters. *Education:* Fellow, Catering Institute of Australia. *Appointments:* Nominee, Menzies Hotel, Melbourne, Australia; General Manager, Managing Director, Federal Hotels Limited; Australian National Hotels Limited. *Memberships:* Board member: Melbourne Tourism Authority, Victorian Government Travel Authority; National President, Australian Hotel Association-Residential. *Hobbies:* Piano; Farming; Tennis. *Address:* 2A Merriwee Crescent, Toorak, Victoria, Australia.

HADDON-CAVE, Charles Philip, b. 6 July 1925, Hobart, Tasmania, Australia. Colonial Administrative Service. m. Elizabeth Alice May Simpson, 22 May 1948, 2 sons, 1 daughter. *Education:* MA, 1947; BA, 1944. *Appointments:* Lecturer in Economics, University of Melbourne, Australia, 1946-47; Research Student, King's College, Cambridge, UK, 1948-51; High Commission: East Africa, 1951, Kenya, 1952-61, Sey-

chelles, 1961, Hong Kong, 1962-. *Honours:* CMG, 1973; KBE, 1980. *Hobby:* Golf. *Address:* 45 Shouson Hill, Hong Kong.

HADDRICK, Ronald Norman, b. 9 Apr. 1929, Adelaide, South Australia. Actor. m. Margaret Lorraine Quigley, 10 Mar. 1956, 1 son, 1 daughter. *Appointments:* Shakespeare Memorial Theatre, Stratford-upon-Avon, England, 1954-58; Stage, Film, Television and Radio in all States of Australia, 1959-; Starred in Productions of Australian Plays, London, UK, 1961, 1974, 1980. *Memberships:* Theatre Board, Australia Council, 1974; Board of NIDA; Primary Club of Australia. *Honours:* MBE., 1974; Silver Jubilee Medal, 1977; Played 1st class Cricket for South Australia, 1952. *Hobbies:* Cricket; Golf; Classical music. *Address:* 17 Kessell Avenue, Strathfield West, New South Wales 2140, Australia.

HADFIELD, Geoffrey John, b. 19 Apr. 1923, Long Ashton, Bristol, England. Consultant Surgeon. m. Beryl Sleigh, 21 May 1960, 3 daughters. *Education:* MRCS. LRCP, 1946; MB. BS. 1947; FRCS(Eng),1948; MS.(Lond),1954; London University, St. Bartholomew's Hospital, London, UK; Fellow in Surgery, Memorial Hospital, New York, USA, 1954-55. *Appointments:* House Officer Appointments, 1946-47; Demonstrator of Anatomy, 1947-48; Registrar and Senior Lecturer in Surgery, St. Bartholomew's Hospital, London, UK, 1950-60; Served in: RAMC Far East, 1948-50, TAVR, 1950-73, Col. L/RAMC RARO Hon. Col. 219 General Hospital TAVR; Examiner in Surgery for the Universities of Bristol, Liverpool and Leeds and Visiting Examiner to Universities in the Middle and Far East, 1974-. *Memberships:* Member of Council and Court of Examiners, Royal College of Surgeons of England; Fellow, Association of Surgeons of Great Britain and Ireland; Associated Fellow and Council member of British Association of Urol Surgeons; British Association of Surgical Oncologists; Member of Council, British Association of Clinical Anatomists; Hon. member, Societe Francais de Phlebologie. *Publications:* Current Surgical Practice, (with M Hobsley Arnolds), 1976, 78, 81; articles in Journals and chapters in books in fields of Breast diseases, Cancer, Trauma, Venous disorders and Medical Education. *Honours:* Arris & Gale Lecturer, 1954; Hunterian Professor, 1959; TD, 1963; Erasmus Wilson Demonstrator, 1969; Arnott Demonstrator, 1972; CBE, 1980. *Hobbies:* Sailing; Travel; Walking; Golf.*Address:* Milvererton House, 3 Spenser Road, Aylesbury, Buckinghamshire, HP21 7LR, England.

HADJIOANNOU, Takis N, b. 2 Oct. 1936, Cyprus. Director-General, House of Representatives. m. Georghia, 28 Feb. 1965, 2 daughters. *Education:* Diploma of the Athens School of Economics and Business Studies, Athens, Greece, 1954-58; Degree of Law Faculty, Athens University, Athens, Greece, 1958-61. *Appointments:* Publication Officer, 1961-66, Director-General, 1966-, House of Representatives. *Memberships:* President, National Student's Union of Cypriot Students in Athens; President, Cyprus Football Association; President, Cyprus Lawn Tennis Federation; Cyprus Sports Organization; Cyprus National Olympic Committee; Board of Appeal, the Union of European Football Association; Sports Consultative Committee; President, the Parents Association of Students of Acropolis 'A' Gymnasium; Council of Federation of Parents Associations of Nicosia District. *Publications:* Mercantile Law for Students of Secondary Schools. *Honours:* First winner in: Decathlon, Panhellenic Games, 1956, 400 metres hurdle race, Panhellenic Games, 1957, 400 metres hurdle race, Balkan Games, 1957. *Hobbies:* Chess; Tennis; Hunting. *Address:* 3 Savvas Rosides Street, Dasoupolis, Nicosia, Cyprus.

HADLAND, Rose Lilian, b. 4 Oct. 1915, Taston, Oxfordshire, England. Artist. m. Christopher Ben, 28 Aug. 1938, 4 sons. *Appointments:* Teacher of Painting, Elizabeth Technical College, 1974-78. *Memberships:* Elizabeth Art Society; Royal Society of Arts, Adelaide; Adelaide Art Society. *Creative Works:* over 300 Paintings sold in England and Australia. *Honours:* Artist of the Year, 1965, Elizabeth Art Society; Design chosen for Perpetual Catalogue Cover, Elizabeth Art Society. *Hobbies:* Sculpture; Painting. *Address:* 5 Sampson Road, Elizbath Grove, South Australia 5112.

HADLEE, Richard John, b. 3 July 1951, Christchurch, New Zealand. Professional Cricketer. m. 24 Aug. 1973. *Appointments:* Trainee Manager, Woolworths (NZ(Limited, 1970-72; Department Trainee Manager, Bing Harris, Sargood Limited, General Importers, 1972-75; Sales Manager, Shawnsports Limited, Importers, 1975-78; Professional Cricketer, Nottinghamshire Cricket Club, UK, 1978-; NZ Cricket Council; Tasmanian Cricket Association, 1979-80. *Memberships:* Christchurch Jaycee Inc; Canterbury Commercial Travellers Association. *Publications:* Co-author of biography - Hadlee. *Honours:* MBE., 1980; NZ Sportsman of Year, 1980. *Hobbies:* Video Recording TV; Music; Watching Sport; Gardening; Public Speaking. *Address:* 18 Hawkswood Place, Avonhead, Christchurch, New Zealand.

HAEFLIGER, Walter E, b. 28 Nov. 1941, Lucerne, Switzerland. Bank Representative. m. Charlotte F Friedmann, 27 Sept. 1968, 2 daughters. *Education:* Translator, Paris C C., 1964; New York Institute of Finance, USA, 1968; Swiss Federal Higher Banking Diploma, 1972. *Appointments:* Swiss Volksbank, Lucerne, Switzerland, 1958-61; Credit Suisse, Zurich, 1961-63, 66, 1969-79; Credit Commercial de France, Paris, France, 1963-64; Midland Bank Limited, London, UK, 1965; Swiss American Corporation, New York, USA, 1967; Brown Brothers, Harriman & Co., New York, USA, 1968; Credit Suisse, Hong Kong, 1979-. *Memberships:* Board member, Chairman of Finance Committee, German Swiss International School Association and Foundation; Board member, Rotary Club of Hong Kong South; Hong Kong Club; Hong Kong Country Club; Aberdeen Boat Club. *Hobbies:* Reading; Modelbuilding; Skiing; Mountain climbing. *Address:* 3C Shouson Hill Road, Hong Kong.

HAHLO, Herman Robert, b. 3 Aug. 1905, New York, United States of America. Professor of Law. m. Hanna Blandowski, 26 Sept. 1931, 1 son, 1 daughter. *Education:* Doctor of Laws, University of Halle, Germany, 1931; LL.B., 1937, LL.D., 1964, LL.D.(Hon.causa), 1973, University of the Witwatersrand, Johannesburg, South Africa. *Appointments:* Lecturer, 1940-46, Professor of Law, Dean of the Faculty of Law, 1946-68, University of the Witwatersrand, Johannesburg, South Africa; Professor of Law, Director of the Institute of comparative Law, 1969-75, Professor in Residence, 1975-77, McGill University, Montreal, Canada; Visiting Professor, Faculty of Law, University of Toronto, Canada, 1977-. *Memberships:*President, International Society on Family Law; Selden Society, London; Stigting tot de Uitgaaf van de Oud-Vaderlandse Bronnen, Leiden; Academy of Comparative Law, Paris; Securities Institute, Cambridge. *Publications:* South African Law of Husband and Wife, 1975; South African Company Law Through the Cases, 1977; A Case Book on Company Law (English), 1977; Law of Succession in South Africa, (co-author), 1980. *Address:* 484 Avenue Road, Appt. 504, Toronto, M4V 2J4, Canada.

HAINES, Sidney Caslake, b. 29 Jan. 1921, Christchurch, New Zealand. Medicine. m. 3 sons, 1 daughter. *Education:* MB, ChB, Otago, 1943; FRACP, 1963; FRCP, London, 1974; MCCM, 1980. *Appointments:* Physician—Superintendent in Chief, South Canterbury Hospital Board. *Memberships:* RNZAF; NZART; Civilian Medical Team, Vietnam, 1970; WHO(expert) for Medical Administration, Tonga, 1974; Abortion Supervisory Committee, New Zealand, 1980. *Publications:* Publications on tetanus, pulmonary tuberculosis, hydatid disease, wounding by Elephant fish. *Hobby:*Amateur Radio. 107 Domain Avenue, Timaru New Zealand.

HAINES, Trevor William, b. 19 Feb. 1933, Bangalow, New South Wales, Australia. Public Servant. *Education:* LL.B., University of Sydney, Australia, 1963. *Appointments:* Housing Commission of New South Wales, Australia, 1953-57; Research Officer, 1963, Senior Administrative Assistant, 1969, Assistant Under Secretary, 1976, Deputy Under Secretary, 1977, Under Secretary, 1978, Department of the Attorney General and of Justice, Australia, 1957-. *Memberships:* Attorney General's Deputy, Board of Governors, Law Foundation of New South Wales and College of Law; Councillor, Australian Academy of Forensic Sciences; Board of Sydney Club; Tattersall's Club, Sydney. *Publications:* Many papers in field of law. *Hobbies:* Theatre; Opera; Concerts; Gardening. *Address:* 130 Ryde Road, Hunters Hill, New South Wales 2111, Australia.

HAINSWORTH, Marguerite Dorothy, b. Liverpool, England. College Lecturer; Authoress. *Education:* BSc., Diploma in Education, MA, 1957, University of Liverpool, UK. *Appointments:* Senior Science/Senior Biology Mistress: Faringdon County Grammar School for Girls, Berkshire, Trinity Hall School, Southport, UK, Leeds Girls' High School, UK; Lecturer/Senior Lecturer in Biology, Borough Road College, Isleworth, Middlesex, UK, 1962-76; Senior Lecturer in Science/in charge Biology, West London Institute of Higher Education, Isleworth, Middlesex, UK, 1976-. *Memberships:* Fellow, Institute of Biology; Fellow, Royal Entomological Society of London; Association for Study of Animal Behaviour; Scientific Fellow, Zoological Society of London; American Association for the Advancement of Science; Society of Authors; Committee member of: Spelthorne Joint Committee for the Disabled, Spelthorne Integration Group. *Publications:* Hygiene, 1967; Experiments in Animal Behaviour, 1967; Motile Protista, 1972; Invertebrate Parasites and their Free-living Relatives, 1972; Coelenterates and their Food, 1974; contributions to books and journals in the field. *Honours:* Fellowship of the Institute of Biology, 1973; Recognised Teacher of the University of London, 1975. *Address:* 39 Kingsmead Avenue, Sunbury-on-Thames, Middlesex, TW16 5HL, England.

HALAS, John, b. 16 Apr. 1912, Budapest, Hungary. Film Director. m. Joy Batchelor, 27 Apr. 1940, 1 son, 1 daughter. *Education:* Diploma, Academie de Beaux Arts, Paris, France, 1930; Muhely, Budapest, Hungary, 1930-32. *Appointments:* Creative Director, 1970-, Founder, Halas & Batchelor Animation Limited, London, UK, 1940; Founder, Educational Film Centre, London, UK, 1960; President, International Animated Film Association, 1975-82; President, British Federation of Film Societies, 1980-. *Memberships:* Fellow, Society of Industrial Artists & Designers; Hon. fellow, British Kinematograph Sound & TV Society; Institute of Directors. *Publications:* How to Cartoon, 1959; The Technique of Film Animation, 1969; Film & TV Graphics, 1968; Computer Animation, 1974; Visual Scripting, 1975; Film Animation - A Simplified Approach, 1978; Timing for Animation, 1981; Graphics in Motion, 1981; numerous articles on subject of film animation and graphics. *Creative Works:* Directed and produced over 2,000 animated films, over 170 of which have won awards throughout the world. *Honours:* OBE., 1972. *Hobbies:* Painting; Reading; Theatre; Cinema. *Address:* 6 Holford Road, Hampstead, London NW3, England.

HALBERT, Hugh, b. 14 Apr. 1920, Glengarnock, Ayrshire, Scotland. Company Director. m. Elizabeth Borthwick Findlay, 22 Apr. 1950, 2 daughters. *Appointments:* W S Friend, York Street, Sydney, Australia; Australian Iron and Steel, Port Kembla, Australia; Garnock Engineering Co., Port Kembla, Australia. *Memberships:* Fellow, Australian Institute of Management; Heavy Engineers Advisory Council; Past President, Metal Trades Employers Association; Australian Ship Repairers Association. *Hobbies:* Numismatist; Bowls; Reading. *Address:* 28 Vermont Road, Warrawong, New South Wales 2502, Australia.

HALDAR, Anupam, b. 26 June 1947, Nabadwip, West Bengal, India. Engineer. m. 2 son. *Education:* Bachelor of Engineering, BE(Mech)1st class, University of Calcutta, India, 1963-68. *Appointments:* Assistant Design Engineer, Metal Engineering and Treatment Co., Calcutta, India, 1968-69; Design Engineer, Andrew Yule & Co. Limited, Calcutta, India, 1969-72; Manager, Fan Engineering Division, Air Conditioning Corporation Limited, Calcutta, India, 1972-77; Manager, Sales Department, Hindusthan Development Corporation, Calcutta, India, 1977-. *Memberships:* Associate Secretary, Indian Association for Air Pollution Control Varanasi; Editor and Council member, India Society of Engineers, Calcutta; Chartered Engineer, Institution of Engineers, Calcutta; American Society of Metals, Ohio; Indian Science Congress Association, Calcutta; Calcutta Management Association; Council member, Institution of Public Health Engineers, India, Calcutta; Alumnus of Indian Institute of Social Welfare and Business Management, Calcutta; Diff. sub Committee, Indian Std. Institution. *Publications:* numerous papers published including: Need for Mechanised Ventilation, 1975; Environmental Control and Related Problems,

1978; Electrical and Electronics Engineering: A Glimpse on Worldwide Discoveries, 1979; Environmental Engineering: The Educational and Theoritical Approaches to the Subject, 1979; Environmental Pollution: Effect on Health and Habitats, 1980; Environmental Pollution Control: Cost Analysis - An Over-View, 1981.*Honours:* Good conduct and All-rounder Prizes, Nabadwip Hindu School, 1961, 62 and 63; 2nd in Architecture, College Entrance Examination. *Hobbies:* Contributing Engineering, Science and Literary articles; Free-hand Drawing and Sketching. *Address:* 24 Jyotish Roy Road, New Alipore, Calcutta 700053, India.

HALIM, Emmanuel Chukwunyem, b. 23 March 1922, Ibusa, Bendel State, Nigeria. Civil Servant (retired). m. Alice Halim, 25 March 1951, 2 sons, 1 daughter. *Education:* Teacher's Higher Elementary Certificate, St. Thomas's College, Ibusa, 1936-46; BA., University College of Leicester, England, 1947-50. *Appointments:* Education Officer, Government College, Ughelli, Nigeria, 1950-56; Provincial Education Officer, Delta Province, Nigeria, 1956-57; Vice-Principal, Principal, Western Nigerial Government Colleges, 1957-60; Inspector of Education, Western Nigeria, 1960-63; Permanent Secretary Midwestern State of Nigeria Civil Service, 1963-76; Electoral Commissioner, Federal Electoral Commission, 1976-79. *Memberships:* President, Benin Club, 1972-74. *Publications:* Modern School Mathematics; Primary Mathematics; Modern Primary Mathematics. *Honours:* Officer of the Order of the Niger, 1965; Knight of St Gregory, 1974. *Hobbies:* Golf; Gardening; Music. *Address:* Umuodafe Quarters, P.O. Box 13, Ibusa, Bendel State, Nigeria.

HALKITIS, John Andrew Michael, b. 10 June 1929, Nssau, Bahamas. Engineering Management, Telecommunications. m. Hazel E Fox, 20 Apr. 1954, 1 son, 3 daughters. *Education:* Diploma, Radio and TV Electronics, 1961, 1970, 1973; Diploma, Teleprinter, 1952; Diploma, Business Management, 1971; Diploma, International Business Management, 1972. *Appointments:* Senior Supervisor, Radio Transmission. *Memberships:* Institute of Electrical and Electronic Engineers, 1967; Founding member, Assistant Secretary, 1974-76, The Bahamas Institution of Professional Engineers, 1974; Treasurer, Order of Ahepa, 1964-67; Master Mason, St. Michael's Lodge, No. 1634; Advisory Committee, Christchurch Cath., 1974-76; Anglican Broadcasting & TV Com., 1977-79. *Honours:* Queen's Silver Jubilee Medal, 1977. *Hobby:* Watching: Football, Cricket, US Football, Baseball. *Address:* PO Box 6011 SS, Commonwealth Avenue, Blair, Nassau, Bahamas.

HALL, Arthur Henderson, b. 25 June 1906, Sedgefield County, Durham, England. Artist. m. Winifred Frances zbruce, 6 June, 1942, 1 son, 1 daughter. *Education:* Accrington School of Art, 1923-25; Coventry School of Art, 1925-27; A.R.C.A., Royal College of Art, 1929; Engraving, British School of Rome, 1931; Fellow, Royal Society of Painter Etchers, 1947; Fellow, Royal Society of Painters in Watercolour, 1951. *Appointments:* Apprentice Joiner, 1918-23; Designer of Glassware (Webb and Corbett), 1932-37; Exhibitor, Paintings, Etchings, Illustrator of Books, 1937-. Part-Time Teacher, London Central School of Art, 1937-40, 1947-52, Kingston Polytechnic, 1952-72. *Memberships:* Royal Society of Painters in Watercolour, Painter Etchers Pengravers; Society of Industrial Artists; Head of School of Graphic Design, Kingston Polytechnic; Chelsea Arts Club. *Honours:* Numerous illustrations for: Schools, Childrens Books, Garden Books, Readers Digest, Penguin Books,; *Creative Works:* Exhibitions of Water Colours, Etchings. *Honours:* Watercolour, 'Mist over a Dorset Quarry', purchased by the H.M. Queen Mother, R.A.G. Exhibition, 1965; Invited to submit work for a commission to pain the Portrait of the Chancellor of Newsham College, Cambridge, 1979. *Hobbies:* Travel; Gardening. *Address:* 15, Church Road, East Molesey, Surrey, England.

HALL, David John, b. 3 Nov. 1947, Bristol, England. Higher Scientific Officer. *Education:* L.R.S.C., 1975; HNC, Chemistry, 1974. *Appointments:* Higher Scientific Officer, Long Ashton Research Station, Long Ashton, Bristol, England. *Memberships:* Royal Society of Chemistry; Royal Microscopical Society. *Publications:* Surface Active Agents, Society of Chemical Industry, 1979; Solution/Air Interfaces II, J. Coll. Interface Sci. 51, 1975; C.P.D. for Sem., A semi Automatic Method, J. Miscroc. 113, 1978. *Hobbies:* Motor Rallying; Assistant

Venture Scout Leader; Model Railways; Amateur Dramatics; Cooking. *Address:* 137 High Street, Oldland Common, Bristol, BSIS 6TD, England.

HALL, Peter Reginald Frederick, b. 22 Nov 1930, Bury St. Edmunds, England. Theatre, Opera and Film Director. m. (2) Jacqueline Taylor, 2 sons, 2 daughters. *Education:* M.A. St. Catharine's College, Cambridge; Hon degrees, York 1966, Reading 1973, Liverpool 1977, Leicester, 1977. *Appointments:* Director of Arts Theatre, London, 1955-56; Director of Royal Shakespeare Theatre, 1960; Managing Director, Stratford-on-Avon and Aldwych Theatre, London, 1960-68; Co-Director, RSC, 1968-73; Associate Professor Drama, Warwick University, 1966; Director of the National Theatre, London. *Memberships:* Arts Council, 1969-73; DUniversity York, 1966; *Publications:* Directed several plays including: first productions of Waiting for Godot, South, Waltz of the Toreadors; Formed own producing Company, Internatonal Playwrights' Theatre, 1957; directed his first Opera, The Moon and the Sixpence, 1957; Numerous plays for Theatre including: Love's Labour's Lost, 1956; Gigi, Cat on a Hot Tin Roof, A Midsummer Night's Dream and Coriolanus; Numerous plays produced and directed for Royal Shakespear Company including: Two Gentlemen of Verona, Twelfth Night, Ondine, Becket, Romeo and Juliet, The Collection, The Wars of the Roses; Plays produced and directed for National Theatre including: The Tempest, 1974, John Gabriel Borkman, 1975, No Mans Land, Happy Days, Hamlet, 1975; Numerous other vroductions from 1975-1079; Presenter of Television Programme Aquarius, 1975-77. *Honours:* Tony Award for Best Director, New York, 1966; Hamburg University Shakespeare Prize, 1967; Chevalier de l'Ordre des Arts et des Lettres, 1965; CBE, Knighted 1977; Fellow, St. Catharine's College. *Hobby:* Music. *Address:* National Theatre, London SE1, England.

HALL, Reginald Dalton McKellar, b. 7 Feb. 1897, Broken Hill, New South Wales, Australia. Orthopaedic Surgeon. m. (1) Linda Winifred Anderson, 23 Oct. 1928, 1 son, 2 daughters, (2) Ella Henrietta Irvine, 14 May 1980. *Education:* St Peters College, Adelaide 1908-15; Ormond College, University of Melbourne, Australia, 1910-22; FRCS., Royal College of Surgeons, Edinburgh, UK, 1925. *Appointments:* Resident Medical Officer, Melbourne Hospital, Melbourne, Australia, 1922-4. *Memberships:* Past Hon. Secretary, Past President, Western Australia branch, British Medical Association; Hon. Fellow, British Orthopaedic Association; Past President, Australian Orthopaedic Association. *Publications:* Clay Shovellers Fracture; articles in Orthopaedic Journals. *Honours:* Emeritus Orthopaedic Surgeon, Royal Perth Hospital; Consulting Hon. Orthopaedic Surgeon, Princess Margaret Hospital for Children, Perth, Western Australia. *Hobby:* Work. *Address:* 5 Bayview Terrace, Mosman Park, Western Australia 6012.

HALL, William Cecil, b. 14 Dec. 1938. Bircotes, Doncaster. College Director,. m. Dorothy Walker, 12 Aug. 1960, 2 daughters. *Education:* B.S.c. Hons, Sheffield, 1960; M.Sc. East Anglia, 1969; Ph.D., London, 1973. *Appointments:* Teacher, King Edward VII School, Sheffield, 1960-64; Teacher, King Henry VIII School, Coventry, 1964-65; Science and Maths Editor, Oliver and Boyd Publishing Company, Edinburgh, 1965-67; Head of Physical Sciences, Castle Vale Comprehensive School, Birmingham, 1967-69; Director, Schools Council Project, University of London, 1969-73; Director, Advisory Centre for University Education, University of Adelaide, 1973-77; Director, Mount Gravatt College, Brisbane, 1977-. *Memberships:* South Australian Board of Advanced Education, 1974-77; Queensland Board of Teacher Education, 1977-. Hon. Secretary, Australia Ed. Research Association, 1976-77. *Publications:* Contributed to numerous books and papers. *Hobbies:* Gardening; Painting; Church work. *Address:* 6 Ramita Street, Holland Park West, Queensland, 4121, Australia.

HALLAM, Jack Rowland, b. 10 Sept. 1942, Griffith, New South Wales, Australia. Member of Parliament. m. Lynette Marjorie Beaumont, 23 July 1966, 2 daughters. *Appointments:* Apprentice Plumber; Woolclasser; Farmer and Grazier; Elected member, 1973, Appointed New South Wales Minister for Decentralisation and Minister Assisting the Premier and Deputy Leader of the Government, 1978, Appointed New South Wlaes Minister for Agriculture, 1980, New South Wales Legislative Council, Australia. *Address:* 19 Carrathool Street, Griffith, New South Wales 2680, Australia.

HALLETT, Ian Charles, b. 10 May 1951, York England. Research Scientist. *Education:* BSc., Hons Botany, Reading University, 1969-72; PhD., Reading University, 1972-76. *Appointments:* Research Fellow, 1976-78, Lecturer, 1978-79, University of Auckland, New Zealand; Scientist, Plant Disease Division, D.S.I.R., Auckland, New Zealand, 1979-. *Memberships:* Fellow, The Royal Microscopical Society; British Mycological Society; American Mycological Society; American Phytopathological Society; New Zealand Microbiological Society; New Zealand Society for Electron Microscopy; Music Federation, Auckland. *Publications:* Several publications in Learned Journals. *Honours:* Research Fellowship Award, Royal Commission for the Exhibition of 1851 (London), 1975-77; Research Fellowship Award, University of Auckland, 1976-78. *Hobbies:* Badminton; Painting; Music; Reading. *Address:* 21 Coyle Street, MT Albert, Auckland, New Zealand.

HALL-JONES, John, b. 14 Sept. 1927, Invercargill, New Zealand. Surgeon. m. Pamela Simpson, 27 Dec. 1958, 1 son, 1 daughter. *Education:* MB, ChB, New Zealand, 1953; DLO., London, 1958; FRACS., 1979. *Appointments:* ENT Registrar, Royal Infirmary, Edinburgh, 1957-58; Senior ENT Surgeon, Southland Hospital, Invercargill, New Zealand, 1959-. *Memberships:* President, Otolaryngological Society of New Zealand, 1981-; Secretary, Southland Historical Committee; Hon Ranger Fiordland National Park. *Publications:* Numerous books including: Early Fiordland, 1968; Mr Surveyor Thomson, 1971; Rotary Club of Invercargill, 1974; Bluff Harbour, 1976; Fiordland Explored, 1976; The Invercargill Club, 1979; Fiordland Place-names, 1979; The South Explored, 1979; An Early Surveyor in Singapore, 1980; New Zealand's Majestic Wilderness, 1981. *Honours:* J M Sherrard Award for historical publications, 1979; Awarded FRACS by election, 1979. *Hobbies:* Writing; Historical Research. *Address:* 74 Park Street, Invercargill, New Zealand.

HALPIN, Patricia, b. 15 June, 1935, Sydney, Australia. Publisher, Author. *Education:* Blackfriars Correspondence School; New South Wales State Conservatorium of Music. A.Mus.A., 1950; L.Mus.A. 1953; D.S.C.M., 1956; D.S.C.M, 1957; A.Mus.A., 1960. *Appointments:* Music Mistress at various schools and colleges including: The King's School; Member of faculty New South Wales State Conservatorium of Music, 1964; Owner, Founder, Orpheus Publications, 1974; Many broadcasts as solo pianist for Australian Broadcasting Commission and Commercial Stations, 1951; TV appearances; Concert appearances, solo pianist, orchestra, accompanist, chamber groups; Conductor of choral and orchestral groups. *Memberships:* Order of Australia Association; Australian College of Education; Musical Association of New South Wales; Zonta; Association of Conservatorium Ex-Students and Friends; Royal Australian Historical Society; Society of Australian Genealogists; 1788-1820 Association. *Publications:* Numerous text books on both the theoretical and practical aspects of music. *Honours:* Numerous prizes in Eisteddfods; Various scholarships awarded by Federated Music Clubs and the New South Wales State Conservatorium; Frank Shirley Prize on graduation from New South Wales State Conservatorium, 1957; Fellow, Internation Biographical Association, 1979; Medal of the Order of Australia, 1980. *Hobbies:* Genealogy; Australian History; Handcrafts; Comparative Religion. *Address:* 4 Lilli Pilli Pt., Rd., Lilli Pilli, New South Wales 2229, Australia.

HALSE, Norman James, b. 11 Dec. 1929, Perth Australia. Agricultural Scientist. m. Patricia Spence, 11 Oct. 1952, 1 son, 2 daughters. *Education:* Wesley Colleg, Perth, 1941-46; B.Sc. Agric., 1947-50, M.Sc. Agric., 1955-56, University of Western Australia. *Appointments:* Department of Agriculture, Western Australia, 1951-. *Memberships:* Fellow, Australian Institute of Agricultural Science; Conservation Council of Western Australia; Civil Service Association of Western Australia. *Honours:* Fellowship of A.I.A.S., 1979. *Hobbies:* Fishing; Farming. *Address:* 156 Lockhart Street, Como, Western Australia.

HALSTEAD, Eric Henry, b. 26 May, 1912, Auckland, New Zealand. Chartered Accountant, Politican and

Diplomat. m. Millicent Joan Stewart, 10 March 1940, 3 sons, 1 daughter. *Education:* M.A., 1934, B.Com., 1939, Auckland University; Dott. Academia Tiberina, Roma, 1979. *Appointments:* Head of Commercial and Accounting Department, Auckland Technical College, 1945-49; Member of Parliament, 1949-57; Partner, Mabee, Halstead and Kiddle, Chartered Accountants, 1958-70; Company Director, Auckland Savings Bank, Air New Zealand Limited; Ambassador for several countries, 1970-80. *Memberships:* Fellow, Society of Accountants; Fellow, Chartered Institute of Secretaries and Administrators; Fellow, Institute of Management; Institute of Directors; Vice-President, Institute of International Affairs; Auckland University Council, 1951-54, 1962-70. *Publications:* Several Commercial Practice and Accounting Text Books; Economics and International Affairs Articles; 'Edpeditionary Force'; 'The New Zealanders in North Africa and the Mediteranean,' 1940-45. *Honours:* M.I.D., 1944; E.D., 1954; C.B.E., 1980. *Hobbies:* Golf; Tennis; Bowls; Swimming; Reading. *Address:* 6A Kabul Street, Wellington, New Zealand.

HALSTEAD, John G H, b. 27 Jan. 1922, Vancouver, Canada. Diplomat. m. Jean McAllister Gemmill, 20 June 1953, 2 sons. *Education:* BA, University of British Columbia, 1943, BSc, London School of Economics, 1950. *Appointments:* Department of External Affairs, Ottawa, 1946; Canadian High Commission, London, 1948-52; Canadian Embassy, Tokyo, 1955-58; Permanent Mission to UN New York, 1958-61; Embassy, Paris, 1961-66; Assistant Under-Secretary, Deputy Under-Secretary, Acting Under-Secretary, Ottawa, 1966-75; Ambassador, Bonn, 1975-80; Ambassador to NATO, Brussels, 1980-. *Memberships:* Canadian Institute of International Affairs; International Institute of Strategic Studies. *Hobbies:* Tennis; Sailing; Philately; Painting. *Address:* Canadian Delegation to NATO, Leopold III Boulevard, B-1110 Brussels, Belgium.

HALSTEAD, Ronald, b. 17 May 1927, Lancaster, England. Company Director. m. Yvonne Cecile de Monchaux, 20 July 1968 (dec.), 2 sons. *Education:* MA, BSc, Queens' College, Cambridge, 1945-48. *Appointments:* Research Chemist, HP Bulmer and Company, Hereford, 1948-53; Manufacturing Manager, Macleans Limited, Brentford, 1954-55; Factory Manager, 1955-60, Vice-President, Marketing, 1962-64, Beecham Products Inc; Assistant Managing Director, Beecham Research Labs, UK, 1960-62; President, Beecham Research Labs. Inc, USA, 1962-64; Chairman, Food and Drink Division, 1964-67, Managing Director (Consumer Products), 1973-, Beecham Group Limited; Chairman, Beecham Products, 1967-; Governor, 1970-, Vice-Chairman, 1977, Ashridge Management College; Chairman of the Board, National College of Food Technology, 1978; Director, The Otis Elevator Company Limited, UK, 1978; Non-Executive Director, British Steel Corporation, 1979. *Memberships:* Council Member, Food Manufacturers' Federation Inc; Council Member, Confederation of British Industry; Chairman, Knitting Sector Working Party, National Economic Development Office; Agricultural Research Council; Council Member, University of Reading; President, Institute of Packaging; Council Member, University College at Buckingham, 1973-; Fellow of the Marketing Society, 1981. *Honours:* CBE, 1976; FBIM, 1970; FRSA, 1973; FRSC, 1974; FInstM, 1975; FIGD, 1979. *Hobbies:* Squash; Skiing. *Address:* 37 Edwardes Square, London W8 6HH, England.

HAM, John Mackenzie, b. 20 May 1933, Manchester, England. Surgeon. m. Jacqueline Huie, 2 sons, 1 daughter. *Education:* MB, BS, 1950-56, MD, 1968, University of Sydney; FRACS, 1961; FACS, 1978. *Appointments:* Resident Medical Officer, 1957-58, Registrar and Senior Surgical Registrar, 1959-62, Royal Prince Alfred Hospital, Sydney; Surgical Registrar and Lecturer, The Middlesex Hospital, London, 1964-66; Fellow in Surgery, The Prince Henry Hospital, Sydney, 1967-68; Senior Lecturer in Surgery, 1969, Associate Professor of Surgery, 1970-, University of New South Wales; Chairman, Department of General Surgery, Prince of Wales and Prince Henry Hospitals, 1970-. *Memberships:* Gastroenterological Society of Australia; President, Surgical Research Society of Australasia; Court of Examiners, Royal Australasian College of Surgeons; Asian Pacific Association for the Study of the Liver; Fan-Pacific Surgical Association; Société Internationale De Chirugie. *Publications:* Numerous publications and book chapters; Associate Editor, Journal; Editorial Board, British Journal of Surgery. *Honours:* Clinical Fellowship, New South Wales State Cancer Council, 1963. *Hobbies:* Sailing; Books. *Address:* 7/6 Gladswood Gardens, Double Bay, Sydney, NSW, Australia.

HAMANN, Wolfgang Christof, b. 18 Mar. 1942, Hamburg, Germany. Professor. m. Angela H Hamann, 1967, 1 son, 1 daughter. *Education:* DrMed, Hamburg, 1969; PhD, Edinburgh, 1974. *Appointments:* British Council Scholarship, 1969, Wilson Scholarship, 1970, Wellcome Veterinarian Research Fellowship, 1971, Department of Vet. Physiology, University of Edinburgh; Lecturer and Senior Lecturer, Department of Physiology, Guy's Hospital Medical School, London, 1973; Foundation Professor of Physiology, The Chinese University of Hong Kong, Shatin, Hong Kong, 1980-. *Memberships:* Physiological Society. *Publications:* Research into Cutaneous sensory physiology. *Address:* Physiology Department, Faculty of Medicine, The Chinese University of Hong Kong, Shatin NT, Hong Kong.

HAMBLY, Francis Sutherland, b. 7 Nov. 1935, Melbourne, Victoria, Australia. University Administration. m. Patricia Maree Wyeth, 21 Dec. 1963, 2 sons, 2 daughters. *Education:* Bachelor of Economics, University of Adelaide, 1957. *Appointments:* Australian Public Service, 1957-59; University Administrator, University of Adelaide, 1959-66; Secretary, Australian Vice-Chancellors' Committee, 1966-. *Memberships:* Australian Institute of Tertiary Education Administrators. *Hobbies:* Philately; Australian Rules Football; Cricket. *Address:* 6 Arkana Street, Yarralumla Act, 2600, Australia.

HAMDAN, Sheikh Tahir, b. 27 Apr. 1921, Penang, Malaysia. Vice-Chancellor. m. 1 Sept. 1956, 1 son, 2 daughters. *Education:* University of Nottingham, 1949-50; University of London, 1951; BA, 1956, LLD, 1976, University of Malaya. *Appointments:* Teacher, 1947; Headmaster, 1952-54; Principal, 1957-60; Education Officer, Secondary Schools in Penin, 1956-57, Principal Assistant Secretary, Scholarship and Training Division, 1961-63, Controller of Examination Syndicate, 1963-66, Ministry of Education; Council Member University Malaya, National University of Malaysia, Agricultural University, Director General of Education, 1966-76; Council Member of Technical College, Royal Military College; Secretary General, Malaysian National Commission for UNESCO, 1966-76; Vice-Chancellor, Universiti Sains Malaysia, 1976-. *Memberships:* Chairman, Executive Committee Malaysian Historical Society, 1966-; Chairman, Board of Control, Dewan Bahasa dan Pustaka, 1976-; President, Royal Life Saving Society, Malaysia, 1976-; Penang Development Corporation; Vice-Chairman Tun Sardon Foundation, Penang, 1978-; Vice-Chairman, UNESCO Nat. Association of Malaysia, 1978-; Secretary-Treasurer, Malaysian National Council of ASAIHL, 1978. *Publications:* Education Today for Tomorrow; Several articles. *Honours:* PSM, National Award, 1964; KMN, National Award, 1965; DMPN, State Award, 1977. *Address:* Vice-Chancellor's Residence, No. 2 Universiti Sains Malaysia, Minden, Penang, Malaysia.

HAMEEN, Sulaiman Akanni, b. 22 Feb. 1938, Ede, Oyo, Nigeria. Company Director. 2 sons, 2 daughters. *Education:* University of Lagos; Nigerian Institute of Management; Administrative Staff College of Nigeria. *Appointments:* Bank Clerk, Barclays Bank of Nigeria; Clerical Assistant, British Rails, Western Region; Clerical Officer, British Post Office Saving Bank; Production Superintendent, Tate and Lyle, Nigeria, Limited; Alraine Nigeria Limited; Chairman, Managing Director, Modearo, Nigeria, Enterprises Limited. *Memberships:* Vice-President, Port Harcourt Chamber of Commerce; Nigerian Institute of Management. *Publications:* Two Thesis: The Rise of Black Power Movement; Short History of Nigeria Economic Development and Problems. *Hobbies:* Reading; Swimming; Watching Soccer; Television; Cooking. *Address:* 69G Trans-Amadi, Industrial Layout, Port Harcourt, Rivers State, Nigeria.

HAMER, David John, b. 5 Sept. 1923, Melbourne, Victoria, Australia. Politician, Senator. m. Barbara McPherson, 2 sons, 1 daughter. *Education:* Royal Australian Naval College, 1937-40; MA, Monash University. *Appointments:* War service, 1940-45; Korea War, 1951-52; Staff Course, 1956; Flet Ops. Officer, 1959-

61; Dir. Naval Intelligence, 1962-63; Capt. (D) 10th Destroyer Sqdn. and CO HMAS Vampire, 1963-65; Hon. ADC, to Governor-General of Australia, 1965-68; MHR, Isaacs, Victoria, 1969-74, 1975-77; Senator, Victoria, 1977-. *Memberships:* Melbourne Club; Commonwealth Club; Naval and Military Club. *Publications:* Problems of Australian Defence, 1969; The Australian Senate: An Appraisal, 1977. *Honours:* DSC, 1945. *Hobbies:* Golf; Sailing. *Address:* 17 Victoria Street, Sandringham, Victoria 3191, Australia.

HAMER, Rupert James, b. 29 July 1916, Melbourne, Victoria, Australia. Law. m. April Felicity Mackintosh, 4 Mar. 1944, 3 sons, 2 daughters. *Education:* BA, LLM, Melbourne University, 1935-38. *Appointments:* Solicitor, Smith and Emmerton, Melbourne,1939; War Service, 1939-45; Solicitor, 1946-58; Member of Parliament, Minister of the Crown, 1958-; Premier of Victoria, 1972-. *Memberships:* Naval and Military Club, Melbourne. *Honours:* Supreme Court Judges Prize, 1939; Efficiency Decoration; Mentioned in Despatches. *Hobbies:* Tennis; Sailing; Gardening; Reading; Watching Football; Music. *Address:* 39 Monomeath Avenue, Canterbury, Victoria, Australia.

HAMILTON, David William, b. 30 June 1946, Hobart, Tasmania, Australia. Lecturer in Sculpture. m. 1 Jan. 1972. *Education:* Tasmanian Teachers Diploma of Art, 1966; Diploma of Fine Arts, 1968; Tasmanian Teachers Certificate, 1969. *Appointments:* Teacher, 1969-70; Lecturer, Launceston Technical College, Tasmania, 1971-72; Lecturer, Tasmanian College of Advanced Education, 1973-81. *Memberships:* Vice President, Craft Council of Tasmania; Australian Delegate to World Craft Council Conference, Istanbul, Turkey, 1973. *Honours:* Visual Arts Board Grant. *Hobbies:* Sculpture; Skin Diving; Bush Walking. *Address:* Underwood, Tasmania, Australia.

HAMILTON, James Stuart, b. 16 Jan. 1936, Sydney, Australia. Writer; Editor/Educationist. m. Eileen Veronica Littlehals, Jan. 1967, 2 sons, 1 daughter. *Education:* MA, 1965, BSc., 1958, B.Ed., 1969, University of Melbourne, Australia; M.Ed.Admin., University of New England, Armidale, New South Wales, Australia, 1972; C.Eng; MRAeS; MACE. *Appointments:* Aircraft Research and Development Unit, 1959-63; Maintenance Squadron, RAAF, East Sale, 1964-67; Brighton Grammar School, 1967-69, 1972-74; Elmaco Pty. Limited, 1970-72; Publications and Information Branch, Education Department of Victoria, Australia, 1974-; Editor: The Educational Magazine, 1974-79, Curriculum and Research Bulletin, 1979-. *Memberships:* Committee, 1959-, Secretary, 1967-77, President, 1977-, Victorian Fellowship of Australian Writers; Committee, 1974-, Victorian Council of Educational Administration; Australian Society of Authors; Australian Journalists Association; International PEN; Society of Editors; Royal Aeronautical Society; Australian College of Education; Victorian Association for Teaching English. *Publications:* Festival and other Stories, (co-editor); Bookmark, (co-editor), 1974; Neon Signs to the Mutes (co-editor); Messages in a Bottle (co-editor); Human Beings and Chestnut Trees (co-editor); The Educational Administrator (editor), 1974; many poems and short stories and articles in literary and educational magazines and other publications. *Hobbies:* Reading; Music; Films and TV; Gardening. *Address:* 1/317 Barkers Road, Kew, Victoria, Australia 3101.

HAMILTON (The Hon.), Harold Murray, b. 17 Mar. 1918, Wonthaggi, Victoria, Australia. Member of Parliament; Public Accountant. m. Judyth Margaret Thomas, 19 Jan. 1968, 1 son, 1 daughter. *Education:* B.Com., Melbourne University, Australia, 1950; Associate, July 1950, Fellow, Jan.1968, Australian Society of Accountants. *Appointments:* AIF, Mid East. New Guinea Tarakan, 1940-46; Wounded Mid East. M.I. Despatches, New Guinea; Colonel (ret'd.), Citizen Military Forces, 1948-63; Chief Accountant, Steel Importing Company, 1954-62; Self-Employed, Public Accountant, 1963-67; Elected Member of Legislative Council of Victoria, Higinbotham Province, Australia, 1967-. *Memberships:* Australian Society of Accountants; Commonwealth Parliamentary Association; Melbourne Club; Naval and Military Club of Victoria; Commonwealth Golf Club; Member, Melbourne Cricket Club. *Honours:* Efficiency Decoration, 1958. *Hobbies:* Photography; Classical Music; Military History; Reading. *Address:* 9 Waverley Street, East Brighton 3187, Victoria, Australia.

HAMMOND, Kenneth John, b. 4 June 1920, Hurstville, New South Wales, Australia. Accountant. m. Bernice Mary Williams, 24 Jan. 1942, 1 son, 3 daughters. *Education:* FASA, 1950; ACIS, 1952; AFAIM, 1977. *Appointments:* Secretary, Stegbar Windowalls (NSW) Pty. Limited, Australia, 1960-66; Secretary, Director, 1973, General Manager, 1977, Managing Director, 1979, Graham Group and Associated Companies, 1966-. *Memberships:* United Grand Lodge of New South Wales of Ancient Free and Accepted Masons; Treasurer, 1966-69, Chairman, 1970-, Frank Whiddon Masonic Homes of New South Wales; Chairman, Establishment Committee, Frank Whiddon Masonic Homes Foundation Limited; Parramatta Masonic Club; Institute of Advanced Motorists; City Tattersalls Club; Merrylands Bowling Club; Company Directors Association of Australia 1973. *Honours:* Justice of the Peace. *Hobbies:* Freemasonry; Care of the Aged. *Address:* 2 Major Road, Merrylands, New South Wales 2160, Australia.

HAN, A K, b. 4 June 1948, Johore, Malaysia. Sales and Marketing. m. Choo Choon Hong, 12 May 1974, 2 daughters. *Education:* Bachelor of Business Administration (hons.), University of Singapore. *Appointments:* Marketing Assistant, Tien Wah Press (S) Pte. Limited; Marketing Executive, Sunlight Timber and Products; Sales Manager, Eastern Agencies (S) Pte. Limited. *Memberships:* Rotary Club of Queenstown, Singapore; Singapore Institute of Management; Singapore Swimming Club; Tanglin Club, Singapore. *Hobbies:* Photography; Philately. *Address:* C509 Lakeview, 97 Upper Thomson Road, Singapore 2057.

HANBIDGE, Robert Walter D, b. 5 Apr. 1925, Peterborough, Ontario. President C.E.O. & Director. m. 25 July 1946, 1 son, 3 daughters (one deceased). *Education:* BSA (Economics), Ontario Agricultural College, 1948. *Appointments:* Advertising Supervisor, Gen. Co. and Merchandising Manager, of Textile Fibres, Canadian Industries, (1954) Ltd., 1954-58; Director of Marketing Services, Leetham Simpson Ltd., 1958-61; Commercial Manager, 1961, General Manager, Marketing, 1963, Vice President, Marketing, 1964, Executive Vice President, 1966, President, 1977, BP Canada. *Memberships:* National Granite (Montreal); Mount Royal National Granite (Toronto), Canadian. *Hobbies:* Photography; Restoration of Canadian antiques. *Address:* 14 Salvi Court, Toronto, Ontario, M4A 1P7.

HANCOCK, John Stephen, b. 21 Dec. 1938, Melbourne, Australia. Geologist. m. Jill Keiran McNamara, 21 Jan. 1965, 2 sons. *Education:* BSc, Melbourne University, 1957-60; Certificate of Engineering Hydrology, University of New South Wales, 1962. *Appointments:* Exploration Geologist, Broken Hill Pty. Co., Ltd., 1960-62; Geologist, Groundwater Section, Victorian Department of Mines, 1962-68; Principal, Stephen Hancok & Associates, 1968-69; Director, 1969-76, Managing Director, 1976-, Australian Ground Water Consultants Pty. Ltd. *Memberships:* Australasian Institute of Mining & Metallurgy; Director, 1970, President, 1980-, National Waterwell Association of Australia; Institution of Water Engineers & Scientists; Australian Water & Waste Water Association; Geological Society of Australia. *Publications:* Manual of Australian Groundwater Hydrology Practice (w. others) 1980; Drillers Training & Reference Manual, first edition, 1976 (now in fourth edition); Over 50 technical papers on groundwater. *Hobbies:* Glassical Music; Skiing; Tennis; Swimming; Reading. *Address:* 90 Claremont Avenue, Melvern, Victoria, 3144, Australia.

HANCOCK, Langley George, b. 10 June 1909, Perth, Western Australia. Manager. m. 4 Aug. 1947, 1 daughter. *Education:* Hale School, Western Australia. *Appointments:* Assistant Manager, 1927, Manager, 1934, Mulga Downs, Sheep Station; Part-time prospector. Discovered signs of blue asbestos in Wittenoom Gorge and began development of asbestos industry in Western Australia, developing new techniques for treating asbestos, 1936; Assistant Manager, Australian Blue Asbestos Ltd., 1943; Sold ABA and acquired lease of white asbestos deposits at Nunyerry Creek, 1948; Acquired Whim Creek copper deposits for extraction of mineral for use in commercial superphosphate, 1950; First major discovery of iron ore in the

Pilbara, 1952; Joined with Rio Tinto to secure leases of Koodaideri Mt. Lockyer iron ore deposits, 1962; In conjunction with Rio Tinto secured Temporary Reserves of iron ore in Pilbara, 1961-62; Discovered Paraburdoo iron ore deposits from the air, 1963; Purchased assets of ABA Ltd., from CSR after disclosure of the asbestos mine, later discovered iron ore at Wittenoom, Campana City, Dales Gorge, Yampire and other areas totalling approximately 300 separate major deposits, 1966-67; Negotiated Hanwright Iron Ore Agreement with State Government, 1967; Negotiated contract with Mt. Isa for joint development of McCamey's Monster, 1970; Concluded the Wittenoom Iron Ore Agreement with the Western Australian State Government, 1971; Concluded a deal with Texasgulf Inc., to develop Hancock and Wright's discoveries of iron in the Wittenoom area including the deposit at Marandoo as a 50-50 joint venture, 1972; Worked at developing the downhill railway route from Wittenoom to Ronsard Island; Established the National Miner, a national mining newspaper, 1974; Construction of causeway towards Ronsard Island; Investigation of tidal range, deepwater port and prospects of harnessing tides for generation of power, 1975; Showed New South Wales' Premier Wran and his party over the Pilbara Mining areas, 1977; Showed Premier Bjelke-Petersen and his Mines Minister R Camm, plus party officials over the Pilbara, 1977; Visited Djakarta to negotiate with leaders of the Indonesian Krakatau Steel Mill, to supply ore from the Pilbara, Visited Middle East countries to discuss reciprocal trade and long term investment in Australia fro Middle East funds; Signed extension to The Wittenoom (Iron Ore) Agreement, 1979. *Memberships:* The Explorer's Club. *Publications:* Wake Up Australia, 1979; Published and ran Register of Australian Mining. *Hobbies:* Tennis; Flying; Cricket. *Address:* The Angelas, 49 Stirling Highway, Nedlands, Western Australia, 6009.

HANCOCK, Leonard Harry, b. 11 Sept. 1921, Liverpool, England. Musician. m. Catherine Wilson, 11 Dept. 1971. *Education:* BA, MUS.B, Cambridge University, 1939-46; Royal College of Music, 1946-47. *Appointments:* Music Staff, Royal Opera House, 1947-53; Music Staff and Assistant Conductor, English Opera Group, 1954 and Carl Rosa Opera, 1958; Music Staff, subsequently Head of Music Staff and Assistant to Musical Director, Sadler's Wells Opera, 1958-68; Head of Music Staff and Assistant to Artistic Director, 1968-80 Currently Music Consultant, Scottish Opera. *Publications:* Translations of Opera: Faust (Gounod); Die Fledermaus (J Strauss); Die Lustigeweibern Von Windsor (Nicolai); The Bartered Bride (Smetana); The Two Widows (Smetana); Un Balco in Maschera (Verdi); L'Elisir D'Amore (Donizetti). *Address:* 18 St Mary's Grove, London, N.1.

HANCOCK, Valston Eldrige, b. 31 May 1907, Perth, Western Australia. Retired RAAF. m. Joan Elizabeth Butler, 26 Mar. 1932, 2 sons, 1 daughter. *Education:* Royal Military College, Duntroon, ACT, 1925-28; Flying Training School, RAAF Point Cook, Victoria, 1929-30. *Appointments:* RAAF; Adjutant No. Three Squadron; Director Works & Buildings; CO No. One Bombing & Director Air Staff Plans & Policy; CO 71 Wing New Guinea; Commandant RAAF Academy; Deputy CAS Air Member for Personnel Australian Defence Rep. London; Air Officer Commanding RAF Malays AOE Operational Command RAAF; CAS RAAF; Graduate RAF Staff College; Graduate Imperial Defence College. *Memberships:* President, Royal Commonwealth Society Western Australia, 1975-80; Chairman Australia Defence Association. *Publications:* Military Correspondent Sunday Independent, Perth. *Honours:* OBE, 1940, DFC, 1945; CBE, 1952; CB, 1959; KBE, 1962. *Hobbies:* Fishing; Skiing; Tennis; Camping. *Address:* 108A Victoria Avenue, Dalkeith, Western Australia, 6009.

HANDMER, Walter Philip John, b. 5 May 1926, Bunbury, Australia. Diplomat. m. Norma Brown, 13 Dec. 1947, 3 sons, 2 daughters. *Education:* BA, University of Western Australia, 1950; Diplomatic Studies, Canberra, 1952; Hong Kong University School of Chinese, 1954-57. *Appointments:* Diplomatic Officer, Hong Kong, Singapore, Bangkok, Taipei, Washington; Ambassador to Burma, 1970-73; High Commissoner, to Kenya and Uganda and Ambassador to Ethiopia, 1974-77, to Seychelles, 1975-77; Ambassador to Israel, 1977-80; Ambassador to Pakistan. *Honours:* Hackett

Scholar Perth, 1950. *Hobbies:* Tennis; Golf; Classical Music. *Address:* Australian Embassy, Islamabad.

HANDOO, Jawaharlal, b. 1 July 1941, Srinagar, Kashmir, India. Professor of Folklore. m. Lalita Koul, 6 June 1963, 1 son, 1 daughter. *Education:* BA, 1961; MA, 1963; PhD, 1968. *Appointments:* Assistant Professor in Folklore, Kurukshetra University, 1968-69; Principal investigator, UGC Project on Folklore, 1969-70; Assistant Professor, Kashmiri Language Culture, 1970-71, Assistant Professor of Folklore, 1971-79, Associate Professor of Folklore, 1979-, CIIL; Visiting Professor Folklore, Mysore University, India, 1974-79; Research Associate Folklore, Indiana University, USA, summer 1979. *Memberships:* Secretary, Folklore Fellows of India 1977; Executive Committee, International Society for Folk-Narrative Research, Helsinki, Finalnd, 1979-83. *Publications:* Current Trends in Folklore, 1978; A Bibliography of Indian Folklore, 1977; Kashmiri and Hindi Folksongs, 1971; Kashmiri Phonetics, 1973; Hindi-Kashmiri Common Vocabulary, 1975; Editor, Journal of Indian Folkloristics, 1978; Editor, News Bulletin, Folklore Fellows of India 1977; numerous papers on folklore, language and literature of India. *Honours:* Publication prize for book on Folksongs, Kashmir Academi of Arts, 1970; Indian National prize for book on Kasmiri Folklore, Ministry of Education, 1972. *Hobbies:* Gardening; Interior decoration; Painting; Driving. *Address:* 163 'Brindavan', 11 Main Road, Saraswatipuram, Mysore 570009, India.

HANDOVER, Gordon Frank James, b. 5 Nov. 1909, Acton, Middlesex. Director of Companies. m. Elsie Ruth Christie, 18 Sept. 1948, 2 sons, 2 daughters. *Education:* Beaumont College, Old Windsor London University. *Appointments:* Chairman Dunlop Group of Companies, Zimbabwe. Past President, Confederation of Zimbabwe Industries, Bulawayo Chamber of Industries; Chairman, Small Industries Advisory Service; Natural Resources Board; Chairman, Resource Education Committee. *Hobby:* Painting. *Address:* 63 Circular Drive, Burnside, Bulawayo.

HANKEY, Robert Maurice Alers (Lord), b. 4 July 1905, Croydon, Surrey. Diplomat (retired), Parliamentarian, Comapny Director. m. (1) Frances Bevyl Stuart-Menteth 27 Sept. 1930 (Deceased 1957), 2 sons, 2 daughters, (2) Joanna Riddall Wright, 2 Oct. 1962. *Education:* BA, New College, Oxford, 1923-26; Travelling Fellow, The Queen's College, Oxford, Bonn University, West Germany, Sorbonne University, Paris, 1926-27. *Appointments:* British Diplomatic Service, 1927; Served, British Embassy, Berlin, 1927-28; Paris, 1928-30; Foreign Office, Warsaw, 1936-39; Bucharest, 1939-41; Cairo, 1941; Teheran, 1942; Foreign Office, 1943-45; Warsaw, 1945-46; Head of Northern Department FO, 1946-49; Madrid, 1949-51; Budapest, 1951-53; Cairo; British Ambassador, Stockholm, 1954-60; UK Delegate OEEC Paris & Official Chairman, 1960-61; UK Delegate OECD & Chairman Economoc Policy Committee, 1960-65; Retired from Diplomatic Service, 1965; Vice-President European Institute of Business Administration, 1963-. Director, Alliance Building Society, 1970-. *Memberships:* Royal Commonwealth Society; International Council United World Colleges, 1966-76; International Baccalaureate Foundation Council, Geneve, 1966-76. *Honours:* KCMG, 1955; KCVO, 1956. *Hobbies:* Reading; Music; Skiing; Tennis; Golf. *Address:* Hethehouse, Cowden, Edenbridge, Kent TN8 7DZ, England.

HANNAN, Peter George Blythe, b. 8 June 1925, Melbourne, Victoria, Australia. State Secretary, Air Force Association. *Education:* Scotch College, Melbounre, Australia. *Appointments:* Superintendent, Dhurringile Training Farm, Tatura, Victoria, Australia, 1954-61; Superintendent, Presbyterian Boys Hostel, Kew, Victoria, Australia, 1962-64; Secretary, Victorian Society Prevention of Cruelty to Children, Australia, 1965-72; State Secretary, Air Force Association, Victoria Division, Australia, 1973-. *Memberships:* Life member, Forest Hill Badminton Club; State Secretary, Air Force Club; Honorary Probation Officer, 1963-. *Hobbies:* Badminton. *Address:* 19 Atunga Court, Bayswater North, Melbourne 3153, Australia.

HANNES, Geoffrey Simon, b. 22 Aug. 1928, Berlin, Germany. Mining Engineer. m. June Elisabeth Shrubb, 3 Jan. 1956, 2 sons, 2 daughters. *Education:* Bachelor of Engineering, University of Sydney, Australia, 1950;

Diploma Scientific Management, ICS., 1955; Postgraduate study, London School of Economics for 3 years. *Appointments:* Mining Engineer, West Rand Cons. Mines, South Africa, 1951-53; Mining Engineer to Mine Superintendent, Chibulome Mines, Zambia, 1956-66; Mining Engineer, Anaconda Australia Inc, Australia, 1966-68; General Manager, Queensland Mines Limited, Australia, 1968-70; Mining and Geological Consultant, Sydney, Australia, 1971-. *Memberships:* Fellow, Institute Mining and Metallurgy,UK; Australian Institute Mining and Metallurgy; Rotary Club of Sydney; Royal Automobile Club. *Hobbies:* Chess; Tennis; Swimming. *Address:* 10 Kimo Street, Roseville, New South Wales 2069, Australia.

HANRAHAN, John Chadwick, b. 6 Nov. 1936, Perth, Western Australia. Plastic Surgeon. m. Elizabeth Hiller, 9 Sept. 1961, 4 daughters. *Education:* MB., BS., 1959, FRCS.(Eng)., 1964, FRACS., 1968, University of Western Australia. *Appointments:* Chairman, Department of Plastic and Reconstructive Surgery, Royal Perth Hospital, Perth, Western Australia; Private Practice in Plastic Surgery, Perth, Western Australia. *Memberships:* Chairman, Board of Plastic and Reconstructive Surgery, Royal Australasian College of Surgeons; Executive Committee, International Plastic and Reconstructive Surgeons; Secretary, Australian Hand Club. *Hobbies:* Photography; Wilderness Exploration; Canoeing; Bushwalking. *Address:* 40 Keane Street, Peppermint Grove, Perth, Western Australia 6011.

HANSCHELL, William Henry Albert, b. 5 Jan. 1917, Barbados. Barrister & Attorney-at-Law. m. Mabel Gloria Conliffe, 14 Apr. 1954, 3 sons, 2 daughters. *Education:* BA, Brasenose College, Oxford, 1936-39; Middle Temple, London; Called to Bar, 1945; MA (Oxon), 1965. *Appointments:* Colonial Administrative Service, Central Province & Secretariat, Ghana, 1940-49; Colonial Legal Service, Crown Counsel & District Magistrate, Ghana, 1949-52; Professional Law Practice, Barbados & Eastern Caribbean, 1953-; Admitted to Inner Bar, Queen's Counsel, 1965. *Memberships:* President, Barbados Bar Association, 1971-73; Judicial Advisory Council, 1971-73; Council of Legal Education, Baribbean Region, 1972-73. *Publications:* Contributor to Commision of Enquiry on Native Tribunals in Gold Coast (Ghana), 1943; Chairman, Committee of Enquiry into National Housing, Barbados, 1977-79, reports published, 1980. *Honours:* Somers Cox Memorial Silver Medallist (English), 1935; QC, Barbados, 1965; Honorary Tutor, Council of Legal Education, Caribbean Region, 1973. *Hobbies:* Cricket; Tennis; Swimming; Reading; Bible Study. *Address:* Cana, Crane, St Philip, Barbados.

HANSOR, Joseph, b. 14 May 1920, Sydney, Australia. Trader/Importer. m. Joan Christine Kennedy, 3 June 1943, 1 son, 1 daughter. *Education:* Accountancy Diploma, Sydney Technical College, Australia, 1951. *Appointments:* Accountant, Jacobson Van Den Berg Limited, Sydney, Australia, 1952-54; Managing Director, A W Hansor Pty. Limited, Mfg. Sydney, Newcastle, Port Kembla, Australia, 1954-70; Managing Director, Hansor Investments Pty. Limited, Sydney, Australia, 1958-; Manager Protector, Safety Products Limited, Sydney, Australia, 1970-73; Managing Director, Consor Merchandising Pty. Limited, 1973-; Director, Tall Enterprises Pty. Limited, Melbourne, Australia, 1978-. *Memberships:* Associate Member, Australian Society of Accountants; Returned Servicemens League, Parramatta. *Honours:* Justice of the Peace. *Hobbies:* Bird watching; Bush walking; Fishing. *Address:* 13 Merilbah Road, Bowral, NSW 2576, Australia.

HAQ, Ashab-Ul, b. 4 Dec. 1921, Chuadanga, Kushtia, Bangladesh. Medical Practitioner. m. (1) Momen Ara 19 Jan. 1953, 2 sons, (2) Farida Ashab 16 Nov. 1958, 1 son, 1 daughter. *Education:* Khidirpore Academy, Calcutta, 1935-37; Campbel Medical School, Calcutta, 1938-47; Licentiate-in-Medical-Faculty, East Bengal, 1948. *Appointments:* Senior House Physician, Medical Ward, 1948-49, Senior House Surgeon, Labour & Gynaecological Ward, 1949-50, Mitford Hospital, Dacca; Private Medical Practitioner, 1951-; Member of Parliament, Bangladesh, 1973. *Memberships:* East Pakistan Legislative Assembly, 1970; Bangladesh Delegation to United Nations, 1971; Founder-Chairman, Bangladesh Red Cross Society, 1971; Constituent Assembly of Bangladesh, 1972; Vice-President, Bangladesh Awami League, 1973; Founder-Chairman,

Commonwealth Human Ecology Council, Bangladesh, 1974; Bangladesh delegate to International Parliamentary Union meeting, Abidjan, Ivory Coast, 1974. *Publications:* Contributor of articles to Bangladesh Press. *Hobby:* Politics. *Address:* Muktipara, PO Chuadanga, Kushtia, Bangladesh.

HAQUE, Izhar-Ul, b. 5 Apr. 1942, Kalyanpur District, Jullundhur, Punjab, India. Consultant Orthopaedic Surgeon. m. Naeema Zaidi, 15 Dec. 1968, 1 son, 1 daughter. *Education:* MB,BS, Sind University, Pakistan, 1966; FRCS, Royal College of Surgeons of Edinburgh, 1975. *Appointments:* SHO, Royal Hospital Wolverhampton, 1969-70 and Bath & Wessex Orthopaedic Hospital, Bath, Somerset, 1970-71; Roatational RSO under Cornwall & Isles of Scilly AHA at Truro, Treliske, Camborne, Penzance & Hayle Hospitals, 1971-75; 1975-76; Registrar, Orthopaedics at Lewisham Hospital, London under South East Metropolitan Area Health Authority (Teaching); Senior Registrar (Orthopaedics), 1976-77, Consultant Orthopaedic Surgeon & Honorary Lecturer, 1977-, University Teaching Hospital, Lusaka, Zambia. *Memberships:* Association of Surgeons of East Africa; Rotary International Lusaka Central Club, Community Services Committee; Zambia Blood Donor Services Association, Lusaka; Medical Association of Zambia. *Publications:* Contributor to professional Medical Journals. *Honours:* Kwacha 300, Prize from The Royal Antediluvian Organisation of Buffaolies, 1979; Merit Scholarships 1952-66. *Hobbies:* Reading; Music; Squash. *Address:* PO Box 50083, Lusaka, Zambia.

HAQUE, Muhammed Fzlul, b. 15 Aug. 1937, Dacca, Bangladesh. Economist; Planner; Administrator. m. Nazma Yeasmeen Manju, 6 June, 1960, 3 daughters. *Education:* BA.(Hons.),Economics, 1959; MA, Economics, 1960; Diploma, Agricultural Economics, 1965; PhD. Agricultural Economics, 1970. *Appointments:* General Manager, Sabah Holdings Corporation; Regional Planner, ADB.; Chief of Planning, KPD, Sabah; Visiting Professor, UPLB, Philippines; Visiting Lecturer, University Putanian, Malaysia; Senior Consultant, Easams, UK; Post Doctoral Fellow, London University, UK; Associate Professor, Bangladesh Agricultural University. *Memberships:* American Agricultural Economics Association; Philippine Agricultural Economics Association; Malay Economics Association; Indian Agricultural Economics Society; Bangladesh Economics Association. *Publications:* Fisheries Economic Planning; Land Tenure; Economics of Irrigation. *Hobbies:* Travel; Meditation; Helping others; Writing poems; Discussions on religion and politics. *Address:* 6 Telok Likas, V K, Sabah, Malaysia.

HARBRON, John Davison, b. 15 Sept. 1924, Toronto, Ontario, Canada. Journalist. m. Sheila Elizabeth Lester, 20 Sept. 1950, 2 sons, 1 daughter. *Education:* BA., History, 1946, MA., History, 1948, University of Toronto, Canada; Post-graduate studies, University of Havana, Cuba, 1947-48. *Appointments:* Academic staff of former Canadian Naval College, Royal Canadian Navy until 1953, presently Commander RCN(R) retired; Canadian Editor, Business Week, New York, USA, 1956-60; Editor, Executive Magazine, Toronto, Canada, 1960-66; Associate Editor, The Toronto Telegram, 1966 71; Member, Canadian Department of National Defence Task Force investigate management operations of that Department; Foreign Affairs Analyst, Thomson Newspapers, Toronto, Canada, 1972-. *Memberships:* Royal Canadian Military Institute, Toronto, Canada; Barrie Yacht Club, Barrie, Ontario, Canada; Governor, Board of Governors, St. George's College, Toronto, Canada. *Publications:* Communist Ships and Shipping, 1963; This is Trudeau, 1968; Canada Without Québec, 1977; Canada and the Organization of American States, 1963. *Honours:* Fellow, Royal Society of Arts, London, UK, 1958; Commander, Orden de Isabel la Católica, Spain, 1969; Silver Jubilee Medal, 1977. *Hobbies:* Sailing; Philately. *Address:* 4 Elstree Road, Islington, Ontario, M9A 3Z1, Canada.

HARDING, Gerald Silas Frank, b. 19 Nov. 1925, Kuala Lumpur, Malaysia. Ambassador. m. Mary Helen Telford Crowe, 24 Feb. 1951, 3 sons, 1 daughter. *Education:* BA, Melbourne University, 1946-49; *Appointments:* RAAF, 1944-46; Department of Defence, 1951, then Department of Supply; Department of Foreign Affairs, 1960, Service in Jakarta, Tokyo, Copenhagen, Wellington and Santiage De Chile; Charge De Affairs in Copenhagen, 1971-74; Deputy High Commissioner in Wellington, 1976-79; Ambassador to Chile and Bolivia, 1979-. *Memberships:* Commonwealth Club, Canberra; Press Club Canberra. *Honours:* Melbourne University Blue for Rifle Shooting, 1948. *Hobbies:* Photography; Music; Golf. *Address:* Australian Embassy, Casilla 33, Correo 10, Las Condes, Santiago De Chile.

HARDING, Robert Harold, b. 16 Aug. 1917, South Australia. Accountant. m. Marion Edith Klem, 29 Nov. 1941, 2 sons, 1 daughter. *Education:* AASA., 1937; ACIS., 1938; Diploma of Management, 1953; Australian Administration Staff College, 1969. 03 Harbors Board, South Australian Public Service, 1934-46; Budget Accountant, Broken Hill Assoc. Smelters, Australia, 1946-56; Finance Director, The Rio Tino Mining Co. of Australia, 1956-62; General Manager, Exccutivo Director, 1977-79, Consultant, 1979-, CRA Limited, Australia; Director of: Mary Kathleen Uranium Limited; Consolidated Fertilisers Limited; Legal and General Assurance of Australia Limited; Bougainville Copper Limited; Comalco Limited; Trade Practices Tribunal, Commonwealth of Australia; Councillor, Victorian Solar Energy Council. *Memberships:* Executive Committee, Committee for Economic Development of Australia; Fellow, ex Australian and Victoria Counsellor and Victoria Treasurer, Institute of Directors; executive, Whitley College. *Hobbies:* Photography; Woodwork; Gardening. *Address:* 7 Jacov Gardens Templestowe, Victoria 3106, Australia

HARDY, Godwin Amaewhule, b. 9 Feb. 1945, Mgbuoba Rumuoknute, Nigeria. Craft Technician. m. 20 Jan. 1972, 2 sons, 1 daughter. *Memberships:* Rosicrucian Order. *Honours:* Management Course award of Certificate, 1977; Confirmation in the Church award of Certificate, 1979. *Hobbies:* Football; Tennis; Singing; Music. *Address:* Mgbuoba Rumuoknute, Obio, Port Harcourt, PHLGA Rivers State, Nigeria.

HARDY, Henry Reginald, Jr. b. 19 Aug. 1931, Ottawa, Ontario, Canada. University Professor. m. Margaret Mary Lytle, 5 June 1954, 2 sons. *Education:* BSc., Physics, McGill University, Canada, 1953; MSc., Physics, Ottawa University, Canada, 1962; PhD., Engineering Mechanics, Virginia Polytechnic Institute, USA, 1965. *Appointments:* Scientific Officer and Leader, Rock Mechanics Group, Mining Research Section, 1953-1960, Research Scientist, Physics Section, 1960-66, Fuels and Mining Practice Division, Canadian Department of Energy, Mines and Resources; Associate Professor, 1966-70, Professor, 1970-76, Chairman, Geomechanics Section, 1976-, Department of Mineral Engineering, The Pennsylvania State University, USA. *Memberships:* Past Chairman of Ottawa-Montreal Section, Society for Experimental Stress Analysis; Education Panel, US National Committee for Rock Mechanics; National Academy of Sciences Division of Earth Science; CAP; ISRM; ASTM; AIME; ASMT; AGU. *Publications:* numerous Technical papers including: Emergence of Accoustic Emission/Microseismic Activity as a Tool in Geomechanics, 1977; Application of Microseismic Techniques to the Monitoring of Storage Cavern Stability, 1978; Development of Design Crieria for Salt Cavern Storage of Natural Gas, 1980; Stability Monitoring of an Underground Gas Storage Reservoir, 1980; Monographs and Proceedings include: A Study to Evaluate the Stability of Underground Gas Storage Reservoirs, 1972; First Conference on Acoustic Emission-Microseismic Activity in Geologic Structures and Materials, (co-Editor with F Leighton), 1977. *Honours:* Recipient of the Richard L Templin Award for 1968 presented by the ASTM for an outstanding paper describing new and useful mechanical apparatus and testing techniques; Recipient of the College of Earth and Mineral Sciences Matthew J. and Anne C. Wilson Outstanding Graduate Teaching Award for 1971. *Hobbies:* Sports Cars; Woodworking; Electronics; Travel. *Address:* 1250 Garner Street, State College, Pennsylvania 16801, USA.

HARDY, Peter, b. 17 July 1931, Wath Upon Dearne, England. Member of Parliament. m. Margaret Ann, 28 July 1954, 2 sons. *Education:* Westminster College, London, UK; Sheffield University, UK; College of Preceptors,UK. *Appointments:* Schoolmaster, 1953-70; MP, Rother Valley, South Yorkshire, UK, 1970-. *Memberships:* President, Youth Association of South Yorkshire; Vice-Chairman, All-Party Committee for Nature Conservation; Member of UK Delegation to Council of Europe and Western European Union, since

1976. *Publications:* A Lifetime of Badgers, 1975. *Hobbies:* Watching Wildlife; Dogs. *Address:* 53 Sandygate, Wath Upon Dearne, Rotherham, South Yorkshire, England.

HARDY, Peter John, b. 31 Mar. 1944, Exeter, England. Civil Servant, Tax Commissioner. m. Shirley Delmere Davis, 20 Apr. 1967, 2 sons. *Education:* BA, King's College, Durham University, 1966; MA, School of Graduate Studies, Toronto University, 1967. *Appointments:* Two Teaching Assistantships, Toronto University, 1966-67; Teacher, Berkeley Institute, Bermuda, 1967-70; Bermuda's First Registrar of Companies, 1970-73; Bermuda's First Tax Commissioner, 1973-. *Memberships:* Rotary Club, Hamilton, Bermuda. *Honours:* Ontario Fellowship, 1967. *Hobbies:* Squash; Soccer; Chess; Choral Singing. *Address:* Windward Tide, Daisyfield Estate, Sandys 9-14, Bermuda.

HARE, Robert McKay, b. 22 July 1938, Adelaide, South Australia. Medical Practitioner. m. Geraldine Fay Berg, 7 Apr. 1962, 2 sons, 1 daughter. *Education:* Commonwealth Scholarship, St Peter's College, Adelaide, 1954; MB,BS, 1962; FFARACS, 1967. *Appointments:* First Assistant, Department of Anaesthesia & Resuscitation, Alfred Hospital, Victoria, 1967-68; Chief of Anaesthesia & Resuscitation, The Royal Southern Memorial Hospital, Victoria, 1970-; Visiting Assistant Professor, Department of Anaesthesia, Loma Linda University Hospital, California, 1973. *Memberships:* President, Australian Society of Anaesthetists; Australian Medical Association; South Pacific Underwater Medicine Society. *Honours:* Renton Prize, FFARACS, 1965. *Hobbies:* Yachting; Music; Bridge; Golf; Tennis; Scuba Diving. *Address:* 27 Clive Street, East Brighton, 3187, Victoria, Australia.

HARKER, Don Raymond, b. 25 Dec. 1934, Magrath, Alta., Canada. Logistics Engineer. m. Gail Tenszen, 1 son, 3 daughters. *Education:* Brigham Young University, Provo, Utah, USA, 1954-56; George Washington University, Washington, USA, 1959-60. *Appointments:* Construction manager, Bow Valley Industries, 1970-74; Logistics consultant, Canada Arctic Gas Study Limited, 1974-76; Logistics manager, Thistle A, North Sea oil platform BNOC Development Limited, 1976-78; Logistics manager, North Cormorant Shell/Esso, London, England, Canada, 1979-80; President, Interlog Consultants Limited, Calgary, Canada, 1977-; Logistics consultant, BNOC, 1980-; President, Chief Executive officer, Atlantic Seacare, St. John's, Newfoundland, Canada, 1980-81; Support Services manager, Dome Petroleum, Calgary, Alberta, Canada; Served as officer, AUS, 1957-59. *Memberships:* Member, Society of Logistics Engineers, 1978-80; English Speaking Union; Maple Leaf (London); Canada UK Chamber of Commerce. *Address:* 420 Superior Avenue, S.W., Calgary, Alberta, Canada.

HARKNESS, Philip Vaughan, b. 22 Nov. 1933, Hamilton, New Zealand. Newspaper publisher. m. Leone Diane Phillips, 31 July 1973, 1 son, 3 daughters. *Education:* Diploma Journalism, University of New Zealand, 1957; BJ., University of Missouri, USA, 1958; MA., Stanford University, USA, 1959. *Appointments:* New Zealand Herald, Auckland, New Zealand, 1952-56; Palo Alta Times, California, USA, 1959; Los Angeles Times, California, USA, 1960-62; Editor and publisher, Waikato Times, New Zealand, 1962-72; Deputy managing director, Independent Newspapers Limited, New Zealand, 1972-74; Founder and publisher, Newspapers of Fiji Limited, 1974-; Managing Director, International Press Limited, New Zealand, 1976-. *Memberships:* Board member, International Press Institute, London; Director, New Zealand Press Association; Committee, New Zealand Newspaper Publishers Association; Commonwealth Press Union, New Zealand section; FIEJ, Paris; Institute of Director, London. *Publications:* Contributor to various magazines including: Flying, Christian Science Monitor; People. *Honours:* Justice of the Peace, 1963. *Hobbies:* Flying; Trout fishing; Golf. *Address:* 2 Central Terrace, Wellington, New Zealand.

HARLEY, Ian Allan, b. 4 Apr. 1932, Ipswich, Queensland, Australia. Photogrammetrist and surveyor; Educator. m. Margaret Wendy Hoskin, 11 Jan. 1957, 3 sons, 1 daughter. *Education:* B.Surv., University of Queensland, Australia, 1950-53; PhD, University of London, UK, 1959-62. *Appointments:* Surveyor,

Queensland State Government, Australia, 1954-59; Surveyor, Mt. Isa Mines Limited, Mt. Isa, Queensland, Australia, 1959; Teaching Staff, 1963-, Head, 1974-, Department of Surveying, University of Queensland, Australia, (including 1969 Research Fellow, University of Stuttgart, and 1976, University College, London). *Memberships:* Fellow, Institution of Surveyors, Australia 1969; Photogrammetric Society, London; American Society of Photogrammetry; Australian Institute of Cartographers; University of Queensland Club; Chair of Photogrammetry and surveying in the University of London. *Publications:* Publications in professional and scientific journals in field. *Honours:* Queensland Public Service Scholarship, University of Queensland, Australia, 1950-53; Hilger and Watts Research Bursary, University College, London, 1960-62; Research Fellow of Alexander von Humboldt Foundation, University of Stuttgart, 1969. *Hobbies:* Music; Literature. *Address:* 70 Blackstone Street, Indooroopilly, Brisbane, Australia.

HARLEY, John Douglas, b. 31 Jan. 1929, Gordon, NSW, Australia. Medicine. m. Margaret Mary Sheather, 1 Feb. 1958, 3 sons. *Education:* MB., BS, 1952, MD, 1964, University of Sydney; Member, 1955, Fellow, 1966, Royal Australasian College of Physicians; Fellow, Royal Australian College of Medical Adminstrators, 1979. *Appointments:* Resident & Registrar appointments, Royal Prince Alfred Hospital & Royal Alexandra Hospital for Children, Sydney, 1952-55; Chief Resident Medical Officer, Royal Alexandra Hospital for Children, 1955-58; Self-employed in consulting paediatric practice, 1958-59; Research Fellow, Children's Hospital Research Foundation, Cincinnati, Ohio, 1959-60; Children's Medical Research Foundation, Research Fellow, 1960-66, Director, 1966-77; Regional Director, Western Metropolitan Health Region, 1977-78, Commissioner, 1978-; Health Commission of New South Wales. *Memberships:* Paediatric Research Society of Australia, 1967-, President, 1971-72; Deputy Chairman, New South Wales State Cancer Council, 1979-; Deputy Chairman, New South Wales Drug & Alcohol Authority, 1979-; Australian College of Paediatrics, 1960-; University and Schools Club, Sydney, 1959-. *Publications:* Numerous medical and scientific publication on paediatric, haematological and ophthalmological subjects. *Honours:* Fulbright Scholarship, 1959; University Exhibition to University of Sydney, 1946-51; Tuition Scholarship, Sydney Church of England Grammar School, 1943-45. *Hobbies:* Reading; Gardening; Walking. *Address:* 22 Livingstone Street, Burwood, New South Wales, 2134, Australia.

HARPER, (Sir) Arthur Grant, b. 16 July 1898, Tomoana, Hastings, New Zealand. Government Official (retired); Company Director. m. Hilda Mary Evans (deceased), 14 Apr. 1925, 2 sons, 1 daughter. *Appointments:* New Zealand Civil Service, 1914 58, Appointments include: Chief Electoral Officer, 1945-50; Clerk of the Writs, 1948-58; Secretary for Internal Affairs, 1948-58; Member of Eight Statutory Boards, 1948-58; Director of Royal Tours of New Zealand: Queen and Prince Philip, 1953-54; Prince Philip, 1956; Queen Mother, 1958; since retiring has been a Director of 12 Commercial Companies, Chairman of 7 of them; Currently Chairman of Wareham Associates(New Zealand)Limited; Deputy Chairman, Williams Development Holdings Limited. *Memberships:* Since retiring from Official life has at various times been Patron, President, Vice President, Chairman, Trustee, Member of 40 national and local voluntary organisations dealing with Art, Culture, Recrational and Sporting activities, Theatre, Social and Youth Activities, Travel, Historical Preservation, Philanthropic, Charitable and Community Welfare. *Honours:* KCVO, 1959; CVO, 1954; CBE, 1954; JP, 1949. *Hobbies:* Cricket; Hockey; Tennis; Basketball; Bowls; Swimming; Athletics; Racing; Trotting; Watching TV. *Address:* 1/50 Deveonshire Road, Miramar, Wellington, New Zealand.

HARPER, David Clement Darold, b. 22 May 1943, Sydney, NSW, Australia. Solicitor. m. Diana May, 18 Apr. 1970, 1 son, 2 daughters. *Education:* BA, 1964, LL.B, 1967, Sydney University. *Appointments:* Abbott Tout Creer & Wilkinson, Solicitors, Articled Clerk, 1964, Solicitor, 1967, Parner, 1971-. *Memberships:* Law Society of the Australian Capital Territory, Vice-President, 1976-78, President, 1978-80. Legal Aid Commission ACT, Commissioner, 1981-; Barristers and Solicitors Admission Board of the ACT, 1981 Consultative Committee of State and Territorial Law Admitting Authorities, 1981; Public Officer, 1976, Councillor, 1981, Australian Institute of Judicial Administration. *Hobbies:* Skiing; Cycling. *Address:* 51 Dominion Circt, Forrest, ACT, Australia.

HARRIES, John Robathan, b. 7 Sept. 1941, United Kingdom. Physicist. m. Roberta Bonnell, 14 Dec. 1963, 1 son, 2 daughters. *Education:* BSc, 1963, PhD, 1969, Adelaide; MSc, Minnesota, 1966. *Appointments:* Queen Elizabeth II Research Fellow, University of Adelaide, 1969-70; Research Scientist, Principal Research Scientist, Australian Atomic Energy Commission, 1970-. *Memberships:* Australian Institute of Physics, Treasurer. *Address:* 20 Cassandra Crescent, Heathcote, NSW, 2233, Australia.

HARRINGTON, Conrad Fetjerstonhaugh, b. 8 Aug. 1912, Montreal, Canada. Executive; Company Director. m. Joan Hastings, 6 Aug. 1940, 1 son, 2 daughters. *Education:* BA, 1933, BCL, 1936, McGill University, Montreal, Canada; Certificate, 1937, University of Besançon, France. *Appointments:* Practised Law, Montreal, Canada, 1937-40; Chairman of Board and Executive Committee, Royal Trust Co., Montreal and Toronto, Canada, 1945-77. *Memberships:* Past Chairman, Mount Royal Club, Montreal; York Club, Toronto; Former Director, Mont Bruno Golf, Montreal; Former Director, Toronto Golf Club; Former Member Council, University Club, Montreal; St. James's Club, Montreal; Past President, McGill Graduates Society. *Honours:* K. St.J.; Centennial Medal, Canada, 1967; Canadian Forces Decoration, (C.D(; 2 Mentions in Despatches, 1945. *Hobbies:* Golf; Reading; Painting; Travel. *Address:* 556 Lansdowne Avenue, Westmount, P.Que, Canada H3Y 2V6.

HARRIS, Charles Lloyd, b. 16 Jan. 1920, Maleny, Queensland, Australia. Accountant. m. Mary Agatha Chapman, 7 Dec. 1941, 2 sons, 2 daughters. *Education:* Gympie High School, 1935; Private Study, Matriculation and Accountancy. *Appointments:* Clerk, Agricultural Bank, 1936; Auditor, Department of the Auditor General, 1936-60; Chief Adminstration Officer, Department of Primary Industries, 1960-74; Chairman, The Sugar Board, 1974-80; Chairman, Metropolitan Public Abattoir Board and Bulk Sugar Terminal Consultative Committee; Deputy Chairman, Agricultural Bank Board and Brisbane Milk Board and Export Sugar Committee; Adviser Australian Cattle and Beef Research Technical Committee; Acted as Consultant to the Government of Laos and Fiji on Meat Industry and Abattoir Design Lay-out. *Memberships:* Rural Reconstruction Board, Fruit Industry, Sugar Concessional Committee, Mackay District Abattoir Board. *Publications:* Official Reports, reports of commissions of inquiry, annual reports, most of which tabled in parliament and published. *Honours:* Justice of the Peace; Queen's Jubilee Medal, 1977; Commander of the Most Excellent Order of the British Empire; Fellow, The Australian Society of Accountants. *Hobbies:* Tennis; Fishing. *Address:* 6 Villeroy Street, Wavell Heights, Brisbane, 4012, Queensland, Australia.

HARRIS (KOPPENHAGEN-KALKER), Denise M, b. 21 May 1925, London, England. Former Artist, Linguist and Social Worker. m. R M Harris, 23 June, 1948, 1 son, 1 daughter. *Education:* Art Scholarship, Teacher's Diploma, 1941-42; several qualifications including Photographic Interpretation, and Diploma Child Psychology, Diploma Social Worker, Ruskin College, Oxford, UK, during service with WAAF (WWII), 1943-46; Certificate, Sorbonne, Paris, France, 1961; Fellow of the Institute Linguists (French), 1961; Diplomas in radio, 1967,69; External Student, London University, UK. *Appointments:* Outdoor Publicity Artist, advertising studio, 1947-48; Voluntary worker, Independent Children's Aid Association, 1957-59; Social Worker, NW London Spastic Society, 1959-74; Illustrator (from microscope slides), for book on 'Cancer Research', 1960s. *Memberships:* Contributor to journal, British Mensa Research Association; Association L'Union Polyglotte, Paris. *Publications:* English translation, Baudelaire's 'Les Fleurs-du-Mal, 1960. *Honours:* Essay and music prizes, 1933-40; Music, art and Medical scholarships, 1941-47; Photographic prize (France), 1956. *Hobbies:* Sculpture; Compiling crosswords; Photography; Rifle and pistol shooting; Sports; Making radios; Genetic research; Handicrafts; Computer Data Programming. *Address:* 76 Aylestone Avenue, Brondesbury, London NW6 7AB, England.

HARRIS, David William, b. 17 June 1949, Bournemouth, Dorset, UK. Broadcasting Engineer. m. Prudence Mary Williams, 4 Aug. 1972, 1 son, 1 daughter. *Education:* BSc, University of Southampton, 1967-70; Chartered Engineer, 1977. *Appointments:* Maintenance Engineer, London, 1971, Assistant Station Engineer, BBC Radio, Manchester, 1971-74, British Broadcasting Corporation; Senior Technical Officer, 1974-76, Chief Engineer, 1976-80, Deputy Director of Department of Information and Broadcasting, (Engineering), Government of Botswana Radio Botswana. *Memberships:* Institute of Electrical Engineers; South African Institute of Measurement & Control; Radio Society of Great Britain. *Publications:* Approximately 80 songs; Three Musican Plays including Crossfire, 1974, The Gift of the Magi, 1979. *Hobbies:* Amateur Radio; Drama; Writing Musical Plays; Computing & Electronics. *Address:* Radio Botswana, Gaborone, Republic of Botswana.

HARRIS, Frank Alan, b. 20 July 1930, Liverpool. University Lecturer. m. Helen Janet Robinson, 18 Dec. 1965, 2 sons. *Education:* St John's College, York, 1950-52; Teachers Certificate University of Leeds; Diploma in Speech & Drama, Central School of Speech & Drama, London, 1955-56; Diploma in Philosophy, University of London Institute of Education, 1965-66; Associate, College of Preceptors, 1954. *Appointments:* Assistant Master, Henshaw's Bluecoat School, Oldham, 1952; Assistant Master, Eastlands Secondary Technical School, Rugby, 1953-58; Head of History Department, Dunsmore Boys' Grammar/Modern School, Rugby, 1958-61; Education Officer, Granada TV Network, 1961-63; Lecturer in Education, Christ Church College of Education, Canterbury, 1963-66; Senior Lecturer in Education, St John's College, York, 1966-73; Lecturer in Educational Technology, University of York, 1973-. *Memberships:* Philosophy of Education Society; Council Member, The College of Preceptors; Public Relations Officer, Parish & People. *Publications:* Rebels with a Cause, 1974; Some Needs & Problems of Teachers & Support Staff, 1975; Hail Nigeria, 1977. *Honours:* Honorary Fellow, College of Preceptors, 1976; Walter Hines Page Scholar, English Speaking Union, USA, 1979. *Hobbies:* Music; Drama; Photography. *Address:* 103 Stockton Lane, York, YO3 OJA, England.

HARRIS, Keith Wallington Hills, b. 15 July 1920, Grenfell, NSW Australia. Medical Practitioner. m. Barbara Rosalind Birt, 29 Dec. 1948, 2 sons, 1 daughter. *Education:* MB, BS Sydney 1949; DPH 1959; FRACMA 1967; FCCP 1962; FRIPA 1964. *Appointments:* RMO Royal Perth Hospital 1950-53; RMO Royal Perth Hospital, 1950-51, SMO, 1952-53, Perth Chest Clinic; Assistant T.B. Physician 1953-58; Deputy Director of Tuberculous Division, Department of Public Health, NSW 1958-60; Director of Tuberculosis for NSW 1960-80; Consultant Physician, Parramatta Hospital, Westmead Centre, 1980-; Senior Physician, Parramatta Centre, 1958-81; Consultant Physician, Prince of Wales, Prince Henry Hospital, 1976-. *Memberships:* National Tuberculosis Advisory Council 1960-80; Director Community Health and Anti-Tuberculosis Association; Hon. Sec. Australian Tuberculosis and Ches Association, 1973-81, and TB School Association; Director and Vice President, Queen Victoria Memorial Hospitals; St Johns Ambulance Association; Branch Commissioner for Extension Scouting. *Honours:* Efficiency Decoration. *Creative Works:* Photography; Music. *Address:* 1 Wandeen Road, Clareville, 2107 NSW, Australia.

HARRIS, Philip James, b. 30 May 1923, Ramsgate, Kent, UK. Publisher. m. 16 Dec. 1978. *Education:* BA, 1947, MA, 1950, St Catharine's College, Cambridge; London School of Economics, 1948. *Appointments:* Infantry Officer, (The Buffs), 1942-44; Nigerian Administrative Service, 1949-56; Senior Lecturer in Local Government, Ibadan, 1957-58; Cambridge University Press, West Africa, 1958-62; Education Secretary Cambridge University Press, 1962-65; Director British Book Development Council, 1965-69; Consultant UNESCO 1970; Managing Director, Pitman Publishing Pty Ltd and Chairman Pitman Publishing New Zealand, 1971-. *Memberships:* Deputy Chairman, Australian National Book Council; Executive Committee, Australian Book Publishers Association and the Australian Library Promotion Council. *Publications:* Local Government in Southern Nigeria, 1957; Your Country and You,

1958. *Address:* 214 Macpherson Street, North Carlton, Victoria, 3054, Australia.

HARRIS, Robert, b. 1 Mar. 1908, Hereford, England. Dentist. m. Mary Elizabeth Beech, 14 May 1934, 1 son, 1 daughter. *Education:* Matriculated, University of Sydney 1929, Caird Scholar 1930; Bachelor Dental Surgery, (class I Honours), 1932; Master Dental Surgery 1938; Doctor Dental Science 1978. *Appointments:* Assistant Superintendent, United Dental Hospital 1938-47; Secretary, Australian Dental Association, NSW Branch, 1948-51; Professor, Conservative Dentistry, University of Otago 1952; Assistant Supt, United Dental Hospital 1952-62; Director, Institute of Dental Research, Sydney 1962-72; Lecturer, Preventive Dentistry, University of Sydney 1953-72; Editor, Australian Dental Journal 1956-. *Memberships:* Fellow Royal Australian College of Dental Surgeons 1965-; Hon. Secretary and Registrar of RACDS 1965-80; Hon. Fellow Royal Australasian College of Dental Surgeons 1979; Hon. Life Member, Australian Dental Association 1978; President, Dental Alumni Society, University of Sydney 1954-57; Pierre Fauchord Academy 1975. *Publications:* Co-author, The Temporomandiutar Hiubt Syndrome No4 Monographs in Oral Science; Re Influence of Mechanical Factors in the Design of Inlay Cavity Preparations; Some Aspects of Oral Biology with Special Reference to the Hand Tissues; Author of some 80 scientific papers and a number of essays; Two official Reports for the WHO Thailand Project. *Honours:* Fairfax Memorial Prize, Dental Alumni Society 1960; MBE, 1971; Fellow Dental Surgery, Royal College of Surgeons, 1978; Hon. Member Australian Society Prosthodontists, 1981; Member of the Order of Australia, A.M. 1980. *Hobbies:* Music; Photography; Lawn Bowls. *Address:* 15 Ormond Street, Ashfield, New South Wales, Australia 2131.

HARRIS, Rodney George, b. 26 May 1945, Adelaide, South Australia. Artist/Lecturer. *Education:* Diploma of Art Teaching, South Australian School of Art & Western Teachers College, 1964-66; Two year part-time course in Photography for Education Department Technical Studies Teachers, 1970-71. *Appointments:* Art Teacher, 1967-72, Senior Master of Art, 1973-75, South Australian Education Department; Lecturer-Instructor and originator of Creative Photography for Art Teachers, at the Summer Inservice Conference and Workshop, 1972-75; Lecturer, part-time of Art and Design for the Apprentice Jewellers, 1973-75; Several Study visits to Europe, Scandinavia, USA and Mexico, 1975-80; Lecturer of Art and Photography, The O'Halloran Hill College of Further Education, South Australia, 1976-. *Memberships:* Contemporary Art Society of Australia; Royal South Australian Society of Art; Australian Centre for Photography Ltd; Australian Society for Education for the Arts; National Trust of South Australia; Australian-American Association. *Creative Works:* Numerous paintings, photographs and serigraphs in exhibitions including: Solander Gallery, Canberra, ACT, 1977, Eric Car Gallery, Freemantle, W.A. Glanville Gallery, Perth, Lidums Art Gallery, South Australia, 1978, Colorado Photographic Arts Centre, Denver, Colorado, USA, 1980. *Address:* 68 Devereux Road, Hazelwood Park, South Australia, 5066.

HARRISON, David Charles, b. 12 May 1927, Bulawayo, Zimbabwe.Director of Companies. m. Barbara Burton Gammon 14 Dec. 1968, 3 sons, 2 step daughters. *Education:* Cambridge Certificate, Milton High School Bulawayo 1942. *Appointments:* Chairman: Harrison Holdings, Limited; Harrison and Hughson, Agencies Limited; Tyre Treads Limited; Marathon Vulcanisers Limited; Metco Rubber Products Limited; Equity Insurances Limited; Atlas Finance Corporation Limited; Hatfield Road Property Limited; Leyland Road Investments Limited; Mafeking Road Limited; Midlands Properties Limited 1975; Tyre House Buildings Limited; Watts Road Property Limited; Director: Edgar Allen Limited; Time Engineering Limited; Majestic Industries Limited; Aquarius Construction Limited; Harrison Brothers Limited; Sylvachem Limited; Majestic Locks Limited; Trojan Tyres Limited; Balmoral Properties. *Memberships:* Associated Chambers of Commerce of Zimbabwe; Bulawayo Chamber of Commerce; Bulawayo Club. *Hobbies:* Golf; Snooker. *Address:* 34 Park Road, Suburbs, Bulawayo, Zimbabwe.

HARRISON, Henry, b. 3 Apr. 1914, Victoria, Australia. Engineer. m. Mary Muluenna, 23 1 daughter.

Education: Royal Melbourne Institute of Technology. *Appointments:* Self-employed Manufacturer of Office Furniture and Allied Metal Products. *Memberships:* President of several National and Commonwealth Greyhound and Throoughbred Associations, 1975-81. *Hobbies:* Racing; Thoroughbred Breeding; Clay Target Shooting. *Address:* 5 Maple Grove, Toorak, Victoria, Australia.

HARRISON, (Sir) John Richard, b. 23 May 1921, Hastings, New Zealand. Speaker, House of Representatives, NZ; Member of Parliament for Hawke's Bay; Sheep, cattle and cropping farmer. m. Margaret Agnes Kelly, 30 Sept. 1948, 3 sons, 1 daughter. *Education:* Bachelor of Arts, Canterbury University College, 1941. *Appointments:* Member of Parliament for Hawke's Bay Electorate, 1963-; Junior Government Whip, 1970-71; Member of Committees on Public Expenditure and Statutes Revision; Chairman of Committees on Defence, Human Rights, Road Safety, Library, Standing Orders; Senior Opposition Whip, 1974-75; Chairman of Committees, 1972 and 1976-77; Vice-President of Commonwealth Parliamentary Association, 1977; Speaker, 1978; President of Commonwealth Parliamentary Association, 1978-79. *Memberships:* President, Takapau Returned Services Association; Vestryman, Churchwarden, Lay-reader, Anglican Church; Executive of National Society on Alcoholism and Drug Dependence; Social Policy Group of International Council on Alcoholism and Addictions. *Publications:* Paper on Community Responsibility in Alcoholism, read to summer school of NSADD held at Massey University, 1968. *Honours:* Knight Bachelor, 1980. *Hobbies:* Tramping; Tennis; Swimming; Gardening; Opera; Classical Music. *Address:* Springfield, Takapau, Hawke's Bay, New Zealand.

HARRISON, Kenneth Cecil, b. 29 Apr. 1915 Hyde, Cheshire, England. Librarian. m. Doris Taylor 26 Aug. 1941, 2 sons. *Education:* Fellow of the Library Association, 1938. *Appointments:* Branch Librarian, Coulsdon and Purley, Surrey, 1936-39; Borough Librarian: Hyde, Cheshire 1939-46; Hove, Sussex, 1947-50; Eastbourne, Sussex, 1950-58; Hendon, London NW4 1958-61; City Librarian of Westminster, 1961-80; Executive Secretary, Commonwealth Library Association 1980-. *Memberships:* The Library Association; Commonwealth Library Association; Association of London Chief Librarians; International Association of Metropolitan City Libraries; Royal Commonwealth Society; Zoological Society of London. *Publications:* First Steps in Librarianship, 1980; Libraries in Scandinavia, 1969; The Library and the Community 1977; Public Relations for Librarians 1973; Facts at your Fingertips, 1966; etc. etc. *Honours:* MBE, Military 1946; OBE 1980; Knight 1st class, Order of the Lion of Finland, 1976; Gold Badge of Merit, Finnish Library Association 1980. *Hobbies:* Travel; Cricket; Reading; Writing; Wine; Crosswords. *Address:* 50 West Hill Way, Totteridge, London N20 8QS.

HARRISON, Laurence Graham, b. 18 Apr. 1909, Sydney, Australia. Company Director. *Education:* Barker College. *Appointments:* A S Harrison & Co Pty Ltd., 1928-; Harrison Manufacturing Co Pty Ltd., 1940-; A S Harrison & Co N.Z. Ltd., 1950-. *Memberships:* Sydney Club; Royal Automobile Club; Masonic Club. *Honours:* Justice of the Peace, 1940; Associate, Plastic Institute of Australia, 1947; Fellow, The Plastics & Rubber Institute of Australia; George Milne Medallist, 1972; Hancock Medal, 1978; OBE, 1979. *Hobbies:* Bushwalking; Horticulture; Chinese Ceramics. *Address:* 24/8 Giles Street, Griffith, ACT, Australia.

HARRISON, Neville, b. 11 Apr. 1927, Manchester, UK. Government Auditor. m. Barbara Joyce Moore, 28 Mar. 1959, 1 son, 1 daughter. *Education:* Mathematics & Chemistry to Degree Standard, University College of the South West of England, Exeter, 1945-46, 1948-50. *Appointments:* 2nd Lieutenant, Royal Artillery, 1946-48; Auditor, Kenya, 1951-56; Senior Auditor, Aden, 1956-60; Principal Auditor, 1960-62, Assistant Director of Audit, 1962-64, Federation of Nigeria; Assistant Director of Audit, Basutoland (later Lesotho), 1964-70; Auditor General, Lesotho, 1970-73; Director of Audit, Gibraltar, 1973-. *Memberships:* United Services Sailing Club, Gibraltar; Royal Yachting Association. *Honours:* OBE, 1973. *Hobbies:* Sailing; Gardening; especially potted home plants. *Address:* 2 Mount Road, Gibraltar.

HARRISON, Roger Stancliffe, b. 9 Nov. 1947, Bingley, Yorkshire, England. Marketing and Business Development Manager. m. Lucienne Odette Coutanceau, 23 Apr. 1973, 2 sons. *Education:* BSc (hons) Mechanical Engineering, University of Manchester; DIA, Aston University; C.DIP.FA, Association of Certified Accountants; C.Eng, M.I.Mech.E, M.B.I.M. *Appointments:* Reynolds Tube Commpany (Tube Investments Ltd), 1969-76; Technical Projects Manager in Africa, Asia, Australasia Division, Massey-Ferguson Ltd., 1976-78; Consultant, Metra Consulting Group Ltd., 1978-81; Rockwell International (Brake and Trailer Axle Division) 1982. *Memberships:* Engineering Institutions Foreign Languages Society; London Young Managers. *Publications:* Author, The Algerian Market for British Building Materials; Author Business Opportunites in North Africa; Paper, Is Tractor Manufacture in the EEC countries a Model for the Arab World, 1980. *Hobbies:* Squash; Tennis; Golf; Foreign Languages. *Address:* Coylum Cottage, 95 Chobham Road, Sunningdale, Ascot, Berkshire, England.

HARRISON, Russell Edward, b. 31 May 1921, Grandview, Manitoba, Canada. Banker. m. Nancy Doreen Bell, 18 Oct. 1944, 1 son, 1 daughter. *Education:* University of Manitoba. *Appointments:* Following miitary service in World War II, joined the Canadian Bank of Commerce, 1945 (now Canadian Imperial Bank of Commerce); Head of Bank operations, provice of Quebec, 1956; Executive Vice-President, Chief General Manager, Head Office, 1969; Elected Director of Bak, 1970; President and Chief Operating Officer, 1973; Chairman and Chief Executive Officer, 1976-. *Memberships:* Business Council on National Issues; Stanford Research Institute; The Conference Board Inc; Business School of University of Western Ontario; American Association for the Advancement of Science; Director of California Canadian Bank; Royal Insurance Company of Canada Ltd; Canadian Eastern Finance Ltd; Falconbridge Nickel Mines Ltd., McMillan-Bladel Ltd. *Address:* Canadian Imperial Bank of Commerce, Commerce Court West, Toronto, Ontario, Canada.

HARRY, Ralph Lindsay, b. 10 Mar. 1917, Geelong, Australia. Diplomat, (Retired). m. Elsie Dorothy Sheppard, 8 Jan. 1944, 1 son, 2 daughters. *Education:* LLB, University of Tasmania 1935-38; BA(Jurisprudence) University of Oxford 1939-40. *Appointments:* Australian Department of External Affairs 1940-78; Permanent Representative, Geneva, 1953-56; Singapore, 1956-57; Ambassador Brussels 1965-68; Saigon, 1968-70; Bonn, 1971-75; New York 1975-78; Visiting, Fellow, University of Tasmania 1979; Director, Australian Institute of International Affairs 1979-. *Memberships:* President, Australian Esperanto Association; Commonwealth Club, Canberra. *Publications:* Chapters in, International Law in Australia; Numerous articles in Language Problems and Language Planning, Scienca Revuo, Internacia Jura Revuo, Esperanto, Heroldo de Esperanto, Australian Esperantist and other legal and language journals. *Honours:* Rhodes Scholar for Tasmania 1938; CBE 1963; AC 1980. *Hobbies:* Esperanto; Golf; Gardening. *Address:* 8 Tennyson Crescent, Forrest, ACT, 2603, Australia.

HARRY, Susan Paula (Mrs John I Harry), b. 8 May 1956, Adelaide, South Australia. Agricultural Scientist. m. 21 Jan. 1978. *Education:* Bachelor of Agricultural Science; Currently preparing Thesis for a Master of Agricultural Science, University of Adelaide. *Appointments:* Graduate Research Assistant, Waite Agricultural Research Institute; Currently Quality Control Officer, South Australian Branch, Australian Wheat Board. *Memberships:* Australian Society of Plant Physiologists; Cereal Chemistry Division of the Royal Australian Chemical Institute. *Publications:* Effect of temperature on Edta-Extractable copper in soils; Communications in Soil Science and Plant Analysis (with A M Alston); Tolerance of Triticale, Wheat and Rye to Copper Deficiency and LOw and High Soil, w. R.D. Graham. 1981. *Hobbies:* Needlecraft; Knitting; Restoration work; Tennis; Squash; Jogging. *Address:* 44 Tidworth Crescent, Col. Light Gardens, Sth Australia, 5041, Australia.

HARTE, Geoffrey William, b. 1 Sept. 1919, Christchurch, New Zealand. Broadcasting. m. Heather Carter, 27 Feb. 1947, 2 daughters. *Education:* Boys High School, Timaru. *Appointments:* Timaru Herald, 1946-57; Associate Editor, Evening Star, Dunedin, 1957-64; Regional Editor, South Island Radio & Television Broad-casting Corporation, 1964-75; Controller News & Current Affairs & Sport, Radio New Zealand, 1975-. *Memberships:* Wellesey Club, Wellington; Hutt Golf Club. *Publications:* Histories: Mount Peel is a Hundred; Blueprint for a Century. *Honours:* Kemsley Scholar for 1953-54. *Hobbies:* Golf; Reading. *Address:* 22B Lucknow Terrace, Khandallah, Wellington, New Zealand.

HARTLAND-SWANN, Julian Dana Nimmo, b. 18 Feb. 1936, London. HM Diplomatic Service. m. Ann Deirdre Green 1960, 1 son, 1 daughter. *Education:* Cheam School and Stowe 1945-55; BA History, Lincoln College, Oxford, 1957-60. *Appointments:* Third Secretary, Foreign Office, 1960; Third, Second Securetary, Bangkok, 1961-65; Second and First Secretary, Foreign and Commonwealth Office, 1965-68, Head of External Department, British Military Government, Berlin, 1968-71; Head of Chancery, Vienna, 1971-74; Assistant Head, Republic of Ireland Department, FCO, 1975-77; HM Ambassador, Ulan Bator Brussels, 1977-79; Counsellor and Head of Chancery, 1979-. *Publications:* Article in journal of the Siam Society 1962; Expedition to the Khon Pa (or Phi Tong Luang?). *Hobbies:* French Food; Sailing. *Address:* 5 Burgh Street, London N1.

HARTLEY, Lilian Rose (Mrs), b. 8 Apr. 1901, Birmingham, England. Accountant; Chairman of Directors. m. Samuel Hartley (Dec.), 8 Dec. 1922, 1 son. *Education:* Fellow New Zealand of Secretaries Incorporate, 1933; Fellow of the Chartered Institute of Secretaries of Joint Stock Companies, 1953-. *Appointments:* Chairman of Directors, R A Hammersley Limited, Engineers, Christchurch, New Zealand. *Honours:* Q S M , May 1976, for Services Rendered to the Community, particularly with regard to Education. *Hobbies:* Outdoor and Indoor Bowling. *Address:* 8 Shirley Road, Christchurch, New Zealand.

HARVEY, Ian James, b. 18 Mar. 1930, Dubbo, NSW Australia. University Research Psychologist. m. Heather Grace Lanyon 2 Jan. 1954, 2 sons, 3 daughters. *Education:* LLB, University of Sydney, Law School, 1948-51; MA(Hons), Macquarie University, North Ryde, School of Behavioural Sciences, 1977-80; PhD, Psychology, 1981-83. *Appointments:* Articled Law Clerk, Parish, Patience and McIntyre, Solicitors, Sydney, 1947-52; Solicitor and Attorney, Pigott, Stinson and Company, Sydney, 1952-53; Solicitor and Attorney, Ballina, NSW and Sydney, 1953-75; Managing Director, West Advertising, Melbourne, 1980; Tutor in Psychology, part-time and Commonwealth Post-Graduate Scholarship for PhD research, 1981; Director, Pilgrim International Limited 1961-81. *Memberships:* Australian Psychological Society; The Academic Senate, Macquarie University. *Publications:* Legal Aspects of Adoption Service, 1967; Co-author: Report of the Committee Appointed at the Request of the Archbishop of Sydney, to Consider the adequancy of the laws in NSW, relating to Abortion, 1969; Abortion Report: Report of the Ethics and Social Questions Committee set up by the Synod of the Church of England in Australia, Diocese of Sydney, 1970; Report on Homosexuality: Report of the Ethics and Social Questions Committee to the Synod of the Church of England Diocese of Sydney, 1973; Health and Welfare in Ryde: A Statistical and Social-Psychological Study, 1977; Research Methods in Adoption: Review, Trends, Implications and Future Needs, 1978; Australian Parents for Vietnamese Children: A Social-Psychological Study of Inter-Country Adoption, 1981; plus three reports unpublished. *Honours:* Masters degree, Commonwealth Post-Graduate Scholarship Award, Macquarie University, 1978-79; Doctoral Research, 1981-83. *Hobbies:* Golfing; Philately; Books. *Address:* 16 Karoo Avenue, East Lindfield, NSW 2070, Australia.

HASHIM, (Dato') Mohammed, b. 21 June 1928, Teluk Anson, Perak, Malaysia. Malaysian Administrative & Diplomatic Services. m. Datin Maimunah Bt. Datuk Abdullah, 22 Mar. 1956, 1 son, 4 daughters. *Education:* Senior Cambridge Examination Grade I, Malay College, Perak, 1948; BA (Hons.), University of Malaya in Singapore, 1954; Chinese Examination, Government Officers Chinese Language School, Kuala Lumpur, 1957; Diplomacy & International Relations, London School of Economics & Political Science, 1957-58. *Appointments:* His Malayan Majesty's Consul, Medan, Indonesia, 1958-61; Secretary & Head of Chancery, Malayan Embassy, Tokyo, 1961, Manila,

1962; Principal Assistant Secretary, Ministry of External Affairs, Kuala Lumpur, 1963-65; Minister & Charge d'Affairs, Malaysian Embassy, Rome, 1965; Minister & Deputy Permanent Representative, Malaysian Permanent Mission to the United Nations, New York, 1968; Deputy Director, 1970, Under-Secretary, Ministry of Finance, Kuala Lumpur; Secretary-General, Ministry of Science, Technology & the Environment, Kuala Lumpur, 1973; Diregor- General, Malaysian National Library, Kuala Lumpu, 1981-. *Memberships:* Royal Asiatic Society, Malaysian Branch, 1956-, Vice-President, 1970-. *Honours:* Commander of Most Distinguished Order of the Defender of the Realm, 1978; Knight Commander of the Most Distinguished Order of the Crown of Perak, 1979; Chairman, Commonwealth Science Council, 1980-82. *Hobbies:* Literature;Paintings; Music. *Address:* Sri Impian, No. 7 Lorong 14/37-D, Petaling Jaya, Malaysia.

HASWELL-SMITH, Hamish Haldane, b. 20 Sept. 1928, Glasgow; Scotland. Chartered Architect. m. Jean Aline Hilton, 15 Oct. 1955, 1 son, 1 daughter. *Education:* Dollar Academy, 1937-40; Lawrence Memorial Royal Military School, South India, 1941-44; Strathclyde University, 1945-46; Edinburgh College of Art & Heriot-Watt College, 1946-51; DA, ARIBA, ARIAS, 1951; FRIAS, 1964. *Appointments:* Assistant, Radford & Partners, Architects, Kampala, Uganda, 1951-53; Emergency Service with Kenya Prison Service, 1954-55; Founded, Haswell-Smith & Partners, Edinburgh, Glasgow & Aberdeen, 1955-. *Memberships:* Royal Institute of British Architects; Fellow, Royal Incorporation of Architects, Scotland; East Africa Institute of Architects, 1956, 58; Edinburgh Architectural Association, 1965,66; Edinburgh Merchant Company; British Interplanetary Society; Society of Genealogists. *Publications:* Architecture: Housing, schools, offices, commercial and industrial buildings and rehabilitation of historic properties; Paintings, sculpture: Participated in a number of exhibitions of painting & sculpture. Compositions: Various articles published on diverse subjects including: solar heating, history of Edinburgh, spaceflight. *Honours:* Premiated placing in five international architectural design competitions; Burgess, City of Edinburgh, 1967. *Hobbies:* Music; Historical & genealogical research; Bricklaying; Woodwork; Reading; Growing Heather; Wine; Sketching; Photography; Experiment & Invention; Sailing. *Address:* 1 Oak Lane, Edinburgh, EH12 6XH.

HATFIELD, Richard Bennett, b. 9 Apr. 1931, Woodstock, New Brunswick. Premier of New Brunswick. Leader of the Progressive Conservative Party. . *Education:* BA, Acadia University, Wolfville, Nova Scotia, 1952; LL B, Dalhousie University, Halifax, Nova Scotia, 1956. *Appointments:* Admitted to the Bar of Nova Scotia and later joined the law firm of Patterson, Smith, Matthews and Grant in Truro, Nova Scotia, 1956; Executive Assistant, Federal Minister of Trade & Commerce, Ottawa, 1957-58; Sales Manager, Hatfield Industries Limited, Hartland, New Brunswick, 1958-65; Elected to the NB Legislative Assembly, Progressive Conservative Member, Carlton County, 1961, 63, 67, 70, 74, 78; Leader, Progressive Conservative Party, 1969; Premier of New Brunswick, 1970, 74, 78. *Memberships:* Director, Canadian Council of Christians and Jews; Executive, New Brunswick Division, Canadian Red Cross Society; Board of Directors, Maritime School of Social Work. *Honours:* Honorary LL D, University of Moncton, 1971, New Brunswick, 1972, St. Thomas University, 1973, Mount Allison University, 1975; Honorary Micmac-Maliseet Chief, 1970; Canada-Israel Friendship Award, 1973. *Address:* 7 Elmcroft Place, Fredricton, New Brunswick, E3B 1Y8.

HATTERSLEY, William Martin, b. 31 Mar. 1928, Aldershot, Hampshire, England. Chartered Surveyor. m. Shena Mary Anderson, 1 Sept. 1951, 3 daughters. *Education:* BSc, University of London, 1954. *Appointments:* Gerald Eve & Company, 1950-, Partner, 1958-; Seconded as Chief Resident Valuation Officer, Municipal Council, Kuala Lumpur, 1959-61. *Memberships:* Royal Institution of Chartered Surveyors, 1963; Institution of Surveyors, Malaysia, 1968; Incorporated Society of Valuers & Auctioneers, 1971; British Chapter FIABCI, 1973. *Publications:* Delivered Lectures over a number of years on following subjects: Valuation of Houses for Rating; Revaluation for Rating of Kuala Lumpur; Valuation Problems and Techniques in Canada & Malaysia; Valuations in Canada; Professional

Standards in Member Countries of FIABCI; Articles in Chartered Surveyor. *Honours:* RICS, FIABCI, Yearbook, Marlborough College Register. *Hobby:* Sailing. *Address:* Gerald Eve & Co., 19 Savile Row, London W1X 2BP, England.

HATTON, Leslie, b. 5 Feb. 1948, Manchester, England. Geophysicist. m. Gillian Lesley Libretto, 24 Mar. 1979, 1 son. *Education:* BA, Kings College, Cambridge, 1970; MSc, 1971, PhD, 1973, Manchester University; ALCM, London College of Music, 1980. *Appointments:* HSO Meteorological Office, 1973-74; Senior Research Geophysicist, Western Geophysical Company of America, 1974-79; Technical Director, Merlin Geophysical Company Ltd., 1979-. *Memberships:* FR MET S: European Association of Exploration Geophysicists; Society of Exploration Geophysicists, America. *Publications:* Papers in various journals of Exploration Seismology, Communication Theory and Meteorology. *Honours:* Best Paper Award, Canadian Society of Exploration Geophysicists, 1976; Best Paper Award, American Offshore Technology Conference, 1978; Best Presentation Award, American Society of Exploration Geophysicists, 1978. *Hobbies:* Classical Guitar; Collecting Malt Whisky; Athletics; Playing Banjoes. *Address:* Merlin Geophysical Co. Ltd., Morris House, Commercial Way, Woking, Surrey, England.

HATTORI, Shirô, b. 29 May 1908, Kameyama City, Mie Prefecture, Japan. Professor Emeritus, University of Tokyo. m. Mahira Agi, 31 Dec. 1935, 1 son, 2 daughters. *Education:* BA, 1931, Doctor of Letters, 1943, Faculty of Letters, Tokyo Imperial University. *Appointments:* Lecturer, 1936, Associate Professor of Linguistics, 1942, Faculty of Letters, Tokyo Imperial University; Professor of Linguistics, 1949, Professor Emeritus, 1969, Faculty of Letters, University of Tokyo; Fellow, 1972, The Japan Academy. *Memberships:* President, 1975-77, Vice-President, 1977-, The Linguistic Society of Japan; Honorary Fellow, The Linguistic Society of India, 1968; Un membre correspondent, La Société Hinno-Ougrienne, 1970; Honorary Member, The Linguistic Society of America, 1970; Corresponding member, Türk Dil Kurumu, 1971; Honorary Fellow, Körösi Csoma Társaság, 1973; Honorary Fellow, The British Academy, 1976; Executive Committee of the Permanent International Committee of Linguists, 1967-77. *Publications:* Mongolia and its Language, 1943; A Study of the Chinese Characters Representing the Mongolian Language in the Secret History of Mongols, 1946; Phonetics, 1951; Phonology and Orthography, 1951; The Genealogy of Japanese, 1959; Methods in Linguistics, 1960; A Study in the Basic Vocabulary of English, 1968; On Proto-Japanese, 1978-79. *Honours:* A Person of Cultural Merits (Ministry of Education), 1971; A Prize of Broadcasting Culture (NHK - The Japan Broadcasting Corporation), 1979. *Address:* 1730-10 Kagetori-cho, Totswka-ku, Yokohama-shi, Japan, 245.

HAWKE, Anthony Ralston, b. 2 Aug. 1938, Toronto, Ontario, Canada. Book Publisher. m. Liedewy Romyn, 25 Aug. 1964. *Education:* BA, Queen's University, Kingston, Ontario, Canada, 1961. *Appointments:* J Walter Thompson Advertising, 1962-63; Hayhurst Advertising, 1963-65; MacClelland & Stewart, Book Publishers, 1965-72; Self employed Book Publisher, 1972-. *Memberships:* Association of Canadian Publishers. *Hobbies:* Photography; Reading; Tennis; Swimming; Travel. *Address:* 124 Parkview Avenue, Willowdale, Ontario, Canada, M2N 3Y5

HAWKE, Robert James Lee, b. 9 Dec. 1929, Bordertown, South Australia. Member of Australian Parliament. m. Hazel Masterson, 3 Mar. 1956, 1 son, 2 daughters. *Education:* BA, LLB, Western Australia Rhodes Scholar, 1953, University of Western Australia; B Litt, Oxford University, England. *Appointments:* Research Officer & Advocate, 1958, President, 1970-80, Australian Council of Trade Unions. *Memberships:* Crusaders Cricket Club. *Publications:* Hawke on Israel; The Resolution of Conflict, 1979. *Honours:* Companion of the Order of Australia, 1979; United Nations Association of Australia Peace Prize, 1980. *Hobbies:* Cricket; Tennis; Reading; Snooker; Racing. *Address:* Parliament House, Canberra, ACT 2600, Australia.

HAWKER, Ellison, Octavious. b. 16 Feb. 1914, Kettering, Tasmania, Australia. Bookseller, Newsagent, Stationer. m. Robin, Vera, Agnes, Freeman, 18 Nov. 1944

5 sons. *Education:* Hobart State High School. *Appointments:* Royal Navy, Royal Australian Navy, 1940-46; Managing Director, Ellison Hawker Pty Limited; Retired, 1980. *Memberships:* Alderman, Hobart City Council, 1976-80; Navy, Army, Air Force Club, Hobart; Athaenum Club, Hobart; President, Hobart Rotary Club, 1979-80. *Hobbies:* Travel; Farming. *Address:* 'Belgrove', Kempton, Tasmania 7409, Australia.

HAWKER, Sir, Frank Cyril, b. 21 July 1900, London. Banker, (Retired). m. Marjorie Ann Pearce, 28 May 1931, 3 daughters. *Education:* City of London School 1913-18; Weber's School of German, Bonn-Am-Rhein. *Appointments:* Executive Director, Bank of England 1954-6?; Chairman, Standard Chartered Bank Limited 1962-74; Chairman, Union Zaiboise De Banques, 1968-74; Deputy Chairman, Midland and International Banks 1969-74; Agricultural Mortgage Corporation 1962-72; National Playing Fields Association; Director Head, Wrightson and Company Limited 1962-77; Davy International 1977-79. *Memberships:* President, MCC, 1970-71; Vice President, President, Amateur Football Alliance, 1971-73; Hon. Vice President, The Football Association; Sheriff of County of London 1963. *Honours:* Knight Bachelor 1958. *Hobbies:* Cricket; Football; Sports. *Address:* Pounsley Lodge, Blackboy, Near Uckfield, Sussex, England, TN22 4EY

HAWKER, Richard George (Sir), b. 11 Apr. 1907, Glenelg, South Australia. Grazier. m. Frances C. Rymill, 30 Aug. 1940, 2 sons, 2 daughters. *Education:* M.A., Trinity Hall, Cambridge. *Appointments:* Managing Director, Bungaree Merino Stud, 1932-; Director, Adelaide Steamship Company Limited, 1949-79; Director, Queensland Insurance Company Limited, Local Board, South Australia, 1955-74; Director, Coal and Allied Industries Limited, 1961-78; Director, Amalgamated Wireless (Australasia) Limited, 1971-78. *Memberships:* President, 1962-64, South Australian Stud Merino Sheep-breeders Association, 1959-; President, 1968-71, Australian Association of Stud Merino Breeders, Council, 1962-71; Nominee of Federal Grazier's Council, Australian Wool Industry Conference, 1963-65; Chairman, Roseworthy Agricultural College Council, 1964-73.. *Honours:* Knight, 1965. *Hobbies:* Shooting; Fishing. *Address:* Bungaree, Clare, South Australia 5453.

HAWKSLEY, Philip Warren, b. 10 Mar. 1943, Oswestry, Shropshire, England. Member of Parliament. m. Cynthia Marie Higgins, 1 Apr. 1967, 2 daughters. *Education:* Denstone College, Uttoxeter. *Appointments:* Lloyds Bank Limited on leaving school until election as Member of Parliament for the Wrekin. *Hobbies:* Fishing; Shooting; Travel; Reading. *Address:* The Old Place, The Racecourse, Oswestry, Shropshire. England.

HAWKSWORTH, David Leslie, b. 5 June 1946, Sheffield, UK. Mycologist, Lichenologist, Administrator. m. M Una Ford, 14 July 1968, 1 son, 1 daughter. *Education:* BSc, (Hons), 1967, Ph.D, 1970, DSc, 1980, University of Leicester. *Appointments:* Mycologist, Commonwealth Mycological Institute, Kew, 1969-81; Scientific Assistant to Executive Director, Commonwealth Agricultural Bureaux, Slough, 1981-. *Memberships:* Treasurer, The Systematics Association, 1972-; Editor, The British Lichen Society, 1970-; Secretary, International Mycological Association, 1977-. *Publications:* Author/Editor of several books including: Dictionary of the Fungi, 1971; Air Pollution and Lichens, 1973; The Changing Flora and Fauna of Britain, 1974; Mycologist's Handbook, 1974; Key Works, 1978; Lichenology in the British Isles, 1977; Author of about 200 papers in various scientific journals. *Honours:* Fellow,Linnean Society of London, 1969; Bicentenary Medal, Linnean Society of London, 1978. *Address:* 24 Norwich Road, Northwood, Middlesex, HA& 1NB, England.

HAWLEY, Christopher, b. 27 Jan. 1948, Bridlington, Yorkshire, England. Teacher. *Education:* BA, 1968; Diploma in Teaching English as a Second Language, 1969; Master of Arts (Hons) English Language and Literature, 1970; Victoria University, Wellington, New Zealand. *Appointments:* Lecturer in English, Khon Kaen University, Thailand, 1970-74; Assistant Director, Industrial Language Training Unit for Migrant Workers, Central London, 1975-77; Course Supervisor, Mangere Immigration Centre, Auckland, New Zeal-

and, 1978-81; Visiting Lecturer, NZ, Teachers Team, Nanking University, Nanking, Peoples' Republic of China, 1979-80; National Co-ordinator, Refugee Education, Department of Education, Wellington, New Zealand. 1981-. *Memberships:* New Zealand Association of Language Teachers; Amnesty International; New Zealand Volunteer Service Abroad; New Zealand Ethnic Relations Study Group. *Publications:* Beginnings—A First Course in English for New Settlers to New Zealand. *Hobbies:* Languages; Music; Travel; Gardening; Asian Food. *Address:*18 Hathaway Avenue, Karori, Wellington, 5, New Zealand.

HAWLEY, Donald Frederick, (Sir), b. 22 May 1921, England. HM Diplomatic Service. m. Ruth Morwenna Graham Howes, 16 June 1964, 1 son, 3 daughters. *Education:* MA, Radley and New College, Oxford; Called to Bar, 1951. *Appointments:* HM Forces, 1941-44; Sudan Political Service, 1944-47; Sudan Judiciary, 1947-55; Foreign Office, 1956-58; HM Political Agent Trucial States, 1958-61; Served in Cairo, 1962-64, Lagos 1965-67; Sabbatical Visiting Fellow, Durham University, 1967-68, Baghdad, 1968-71; HM Ambassador to Sultanate of Oman, Muscat, 1971-75; Assistant Under-Secretary of State, Foreign and Commonwealth Office, 1975-77; British High Commissioner to Malaysia, 1977-81; Consultant, Special Advisor to Hong Kong and Shanghai Banking Corporation; Director, Ewbank and Partners Ltd. *Memberships:* Anglo-Omani Society; Athenaeum Club; Travellers Club. *Publications:* 'Courtesies in the Trucial States', 1965; 'The Trucial States', 1970; 'Oman and its Resaissance', 1977; 'Courtesies in The Gulf Area', 1978. *Honours:* MBE, 1955; KCMG, 1978. *Hobbies:* Tennis; Squash; Sailing; Book-Collecting; Golf. *Address:* Carcosa, Pesiaran Swettenham, Jalan Damansara, Kuala Lumpur, Malaysia.

HAY, David Arthur, b. 6 Aug. 1933, London England. Surgeon. m. Penelope Ann Carpenter, 18 June 1960, 3 sons, 1 daughter. *Education:* MBBS, St. George's Hospital, London, 1959; LRCP., MRCS., 1961; FRCS(E)., FRCS(G)., 1970. *Appointments:* Several appointments, St George's Hospital London, 1959-66; Specialist Surgeon, Williamson Diamonds Hospital, Tanzania, 1966-71; Specialist Surgeon, Wankie Hospital, Rhodesia, 1971-79; Senior Specialist Surgeon, Taumarunui Hospital, New Zealand, 1979-. *Memberships:* Orthopaedic Association, New Zealand; Association of Plastic Surgeons of Southern Africa; East African Association of Surgeons. *Publications:* Numerous publications in the medical field including: Two Cases of Gas-Gangrene, 1959; Strangulated Colon in an acquired Diaphragratic Hernia, 1975; Axial Nailing of Vertebrae Bodies through a Posterior Approach - A new concept, 1979. *Honours:* Hon. Consultant Surgeon, Tanzania Government. *Hobbies:* Mozart; Haydn; Legal History; Squash; Tennis; Hockey; Cricket. *Address:* Taumarunui Hospital, Private Bag, Taumarunui, New Zealand.

HAY, Hamish Grenfell, b. 8 Dec. 1927, Christchurch, New Zealand. Company Director. m. Judith Leicester Gill, 14 May, 1955, 1 son, 4 daughters. *Education:* b.com., F.C.A., University of Canterbury. *Appointments:* Trustee, Canterbury Savings Bank, 1962-; Secretary, Deputy Managing Director, Haywrights Limited, 1962-74; Councillor, City of Christchurch, 1959-74; Mayor, City of Christchurch, 1974-; Chairman, Alternative Television Network Limited, 1980-. *Memberships:* Trustee, Canterbury Savings Bank, 1962-; Chairman, Christchurch Town Hall Board of Management, 1962-; Past Chairman, Christchurch Arts Festival, 1965-74; Council, University of Canterbury, 1974-; Canterbury Museum Trust Board, 1974-; Queen Elizabeth II Arts Council, 1975-78. *Hobby:* Listening to good music. *Address:* 70 Heaton Street, Christchurch 5, New Zealand.

HAYDON, Walter Robert (Sir), b. 29 May 1920, London, England. Company Director. m. Joan Elizabet Tewson, 15 June 1943, 1 son, 2 daughters. *Education:* Dover Grammar School. *Appointments:* Served in Army, France, India, Burma, 1939-46; Entered Foreign Service, 1946, London, Berne, Turin, Sofia, Bangkok, London, Khartoum, United Kingdom Mission to United Nations, New York, Washington; Head of News Department, FCO, 1967-71; High Commissioner, Malawi, 1971-73; Chief Press Secretary, 10 Downing Street, 1973-74; High Commissioner, Malta, 1974-76; Ambassador to Republic of Ireland, 1976-80; Director of

Group Public Affairs, Imperial Group. *Memberships:* Travellers Club. *Honours:* CMG, 1970; KCMG, 1980. *Hobbies:* Swimming; Walking; Tennis. *Address:* Director of Group Public Affairs, Imperial Group Limited, Imperial House, 1 Grosvenor Place, London SW 1X 7HB.

HAYES, Dale Thomas, b. 2 Aug. 1937, East St. Louis, Illinois, U.S.A. Professor of Education and Dean of Faculty. m. Eva M. Lilley, Aug 1961, 2 sons, 2 daughters. *Education:* B.A., History English, Bob Jones University, Greenville, S.C, United States of America, 1959; M.A., 1968, Ed.D., 1977, Arizona State University, United States of America. *Appointments:* Professor of Education and Dean of Faculty, Brandon University, Brandon, Canada; Divisional Chairman, University of New Brunswick, Canada; Director of Upward Bound, University of Southern Main; Graduate Professor, School of Advanced Studies, University of Southern Maine; Project Director, U.S.O.E., South Dakota, United States of America; Administrative Co-ordinator of Interns, Arizona State University; Co-ordinator of Learning Assistance Programs, Mt. Royal College Alberta, Canada. *Memberships:* Canadian Association Deans of Education; Society for Study Higher Education; Association Professors of Education; Western Canada Association of Student Teacher Educators; Association of Teacher Educators; Internation Reading Association; Children with Learning Disabilities Canadian Association. *Publications:* Cinderella was a Fat Old Lady, 1975; Dr. Fossil is More Fun than Earth People, 1980; Willie Peter Suntan, 1981; Hoots of Derision, 1981. Several Publications in Professional Journals. *Honours:* Doctoral Fellow, Educational Leadership Development Program, Arizona State University, 1971-72. *Hobbies:* Poetry; Folk Music; Judo; Karate; Bow Hunting; Old Books. *Address:* 14 Christie Bay, Brandon, Manitoba, Canada R7B 2J8.

HAYES, Ross Abbott, b. 6 May 1921, Sydney, Australia. Medical Practitioner, Specialist Pathologist. m. June Joy Broun, 12 Aug. 1949, 4 sons. *Education:* Scotch College Melbourne, 1934-39; M.B., B.S., Melbourne University, 1940-45; F.R.C.P.A., 1956; M.R.C Path, (Eng.) 1966; F.R.C. Path, (Eng), 1973. *Appointments:* Clinical Pathologist, Alfred Hospital, Melbourne, 1950-60; Specialist Private Practice, Sydney, 1960-; Visiting Pathologist, St. Luke's Hospital, 1961-; Visiting Pathologist Royal South Sydney Hospital, 1961-. *Memberships:* University Club; American National Club. *Publications:* Miscellaneous articles to Medical Journals. *Hobbies:* Swimming; Gardening. *Address:* 15A Kulgoa Road, Bellevue Hill, New South Wales 2023, Australia.

HAYES, William, b. 18 Jan. 1913, Dublin, Ireland. Scientist and University Professor, (retired). m. Honora Lee, 2 July 1941, 1 son. *Education:* St. Columba's College, Dublin, 1927-31; BA Natural Science, Trinity College, University of Dublin, 1936; MB, BCh, 1937; Diploma in Public Health, 1941; ScD, 1949. *Appointments:* Lecturer in Bacteriology, University of Dublin, 1947-50; Senior Lecturer in Bacteriology, University of London, 1950-57; Research Fellow, California Institute of Technology, 1953-54; Director, Medical Research Council, Microbial Genetics Unit, 1957-68; Professor of Molecular Genetics, Honorary Director, University of Edinburgh, 1968-73; Professor of Genetics, 1974-78, Emeritus Professor of Genetics, 1979-, Australian National University; Sherman Fairchild Distinguised Scholar, California Institute of Technology, 1979-80; Visiting Fellowship, Botany Department, Australian National University, 1980-. *Memberships:* The Royal Society of London; The Australian Academy of Science; The Royal Society of Edinburgh; The Royal College of Physicians in Ireland; European Molecular Biology Organization; Genetical Society of Great Britain; Society for General Microbiology; Genetical Society of Australia; Australian Society for Microbiology; Pathological Society of South Africa. *Publications:* Discovery of the first bacterial plasmid and the correct interpretation of its role in determining the male, or genetic donor, state in bacterial sexuality; Several Publications including: The Genetics of Bacteria and their viruses, 1964, 2nd edition 1968; Contributed to numerous Scientific articles. *Honours:* Honorary DSc., University of Leicester, 1968, University of Kent, 1973, National University of Ireland, 1973; Honorary LLD, University of Dublin, 1970; Leeuwenhoek Lecture and gift of the Royal Society of London, 1965; Burnet Lecture and Medal,

Australian Academy of Science, 1977; Guest of Honour, 10th Lunteren Lectures, Netherlands, 1979. *Hobbies:* Reading; Music. *Address:* 17 MacPherson Street, O'Connor, A.C.T., Australia 2601.

HAYES, William Alfred, b. 13 Dec. 1937, Dyfed, Wales. Lecturer, Author, Advisor. m. Margaret Bone, 28 July 1963, 1 son, 1 daughter. *Education:* National Diploma in Dairying, University of Wales, 1955-57; B.S.c, in Agriculture, Hons. in Plant Science, Kings College, University of Durham, 1957-61; Ph.D, in Soil Microbiology, University of Newcastle-upon-Tyne. *Appointments:* Glasshouse Crops Research Institute, Littlehampton, Sussex, 1964-71; Department of Biological Sciences, University of Aston, Birmingham, 1971-. *Memberships:* International Society for Mushroom Science; British Association for advancement of Science; Honorary Member, Mushroom Growers Association. *Publications:* Biology and Cultivation of Edible Mushrooms, 1978; Mushrooms, Microbes and Man, New Scientist, 44, 450-452; Nature of the Microbial stimulus affecting sporophore formation in Agaricus bisporus Ann. appl. Biol., 1969; Over seventy publications on Mushroom Science and Cultivation; *Creative Works:* Film: In Search of a Substrate. *Honours:* MGA, Sinden Award for Outstanding contributions in Mushroom Science, 1979. *Hobbies:* Male Voice Choral Music; Rugby; Soccer. *Address:* The Hawthorns, 436 Station Road, Dorridge, Solihull, West Midlands, England.

HAYR, Kenneth James Maxwell, b. 23 Sept. 1906, Auckland, New Zealand. Principal of Teacher Colleges. m. 7 May 1934, 2 sons, 1 daughter. *Education:* Aucklands Teachers College, 1926-27; Auckland and Victoria University, 1938-43. *Appointments:* Held various teaching appointments, 1928-41 including: Toatoa Primary School, Parakao Primary School, Karori West Primary School; Lecturer, Wellington Teachers College, 1942-45, Auckland Teachers College, 1945-50; Inspector of Schools, 1950-56; Senior Inspector, 1957-61; Principal Ardmore Teachers College, 1961-65; Principal, Royang Teachers College, Malaysia, 1966-67. *Memberships:* New Zealand Psychological Society. *Publications:* Teaching of English in the Primary Schools, 1947. *Creative Works:* Film on Active Learning, 1954. *Honours:* B.A. Dip Education, Auckland University; Life member of Aukland Kindergarten Association; Life Member of New Zealand Kindergarten Association. *Hobbies:* Tennis; Golf; Bowls; Gardening. *Address:* 8A Brookfield Street, St. Heliers, Aukland, New Zealand.

HAYWARD, Edward Waterfield, b. 10 Nov. 1903, St. Peters, Adelaide, South Australia, Company Director, Grazier. m. 30 June 1972. *Education:* Collegiate School of St. Peter, Adelaide, South Australia. *Appointments:* Chairman, Coca-Cola Bottlers, Adelaide Limited; Director, Bennet & Fisher Limited; Owner, Silverton Park Hereford Stud, Delamere South Australia, Hillbilly Poll Hereford Stud; Breeder and Owner Racehorses; Company Director and Grazier. *Memberships:* Melbourne Club; Adelaide Club; Australian Club, Sydney; Naval and Military Club, Adelaide; Royal Sydney Gold Club. *Honours:* Kt. Bachelor, 1961; Kt. of St. John & President of St. John Council, South Australia; Lieut. Colonel 2nd A.I.F. Middle East, New Guinea; M.I.D. 1944, Borneo, M.I.D., 1945; Bronze Star Medal United States of America, 1945; Patron, Rats of Tobruk Association. *Hobbies:* Polo; Golf. *Address:* Carrick Hill, Springfield, South Australia.

HAYWARD, Ron, b. 27 June 1917, Bloxham, Oxfordshire. General Secretary, The Labour Party. m. Phylis, 9 Oct. 1943, 3 daughters. *Education:* Royal Air Force Technical Schools. *Appointments:* RAF, 1940-45; Secretary/Agent, Labour Party, 1947-50; Assistant Organiser, 1950-59, Regional Organiser, 1959-69, National Agent, 1969-72, General Secretary, 1972-, The Labour Party. *Memberships:* National Union of Labour Organisers; Vice-President, National Union of Labour Clubs. *Honours:* CBE. *Hobbies:* Oil Painting; Gardening. *Address:* 309 Maritime House, Old Town, Clapham, London SW9, England.

HAZAREESINGH, Kissoonsingh, b. 24 Oct. 1911. Director, Mahatma Gandhi Institute. m. Thara Singh, 18 June 1950, 2 sons. *Education:* Diploma in Social Studies, University of London, 1943-45; Docteur-es-Lettres, University de Paris, Sorbonne, 1961-62. *Appointments:* Labour Officer, 1938; Assistant National

Service Officer, 1939-53; Poor Law Supervisor, 1946-48; Deputy Public Assistance Commissioner, 1948-53; Social Welfare Commissioner, 1953-59; Director, Central Information Office, 1959-66; Principal Private Secretary to Prime Minister, 1966-71; Fullbright Visiting Professor in Sociology, Western Maryland, USA, 1964-65; Visiting Lecturer, Strasbourg University, 1967; Director, Mahatma Gandhi Institute, 1971-. *Memberships:* Secretary, Indian Cultural Association; Associé de l'Académie des Sciences d'Outre Mer; Member of the Council of the University of Mauritius; Mauritius Academy; Member of Council of the Mauritius Instutute of Education; Mauritius Writers. *Publications:* Histoire des Indiens à l'ile Maurice; Undying Values; L'Influence de Tagore à l'ile Maurice; History of Indian in Mauritius; Anthologie de Robert Edward Hart; Anthologie de Léoville L'Homme; Anthologie Générale; Letters to Rajen; Profil de l'ile Maurice; Selected Speeches of Sir Seewoosagur Ramgoolam; Les Pensées de Gandhi; History of Mauritius (awaiting publication). *Honours:* OBE; Officier de l'Ordre Malgache; Chevalier de l'Ordre des Arts et des Lettres; Le Prix de la Langue Francaise de l'Académie Francaise, 1981. *Hobbies:* Reading; Gardening. *Address:* Nalletamby Road, Phoenix, Mauritius.

HEAD, Ivan Leigh, b. 28 July 1930, Calgary, Alberta, Canada. Executive. m. (1) Barbara Spence Eagle, 23 June 1952, 2 sons, 2 daughters. (2) Ann Marie Price, 1 Dec. 1979. *Education:* B.A. 1951, LL.B. 1952, University of Alberta; LL.M. Harvard University, 1960. *Appointments:* Barrister, Solicitor, Calgery, 1953-59; Foreign Service Officer, Department of External Affairs, Ottawa, Kuala Lumpur, 1960-63; Associate Professor, Professor of Law, University of Alberta, 1963-67; Associate Council to Minister of Justice, Canada, 1967-68; Special Assistant to Prime Minister of Canada, Foreign and Defence Policy, 1968-78; President, International Development Research Center, 1978-. *Memberships:* Law Society of Alberta; Vice-President, International Law Association, Canadian Branch; Canadian Council on International Law; American Society of Internation Law; Canadian Institute of International Affairs. *Publications:* 'This Fire-Proof House', 1966; International Law, National Tribunals and the Rights of Aliens, 1971; Pierre Elliott Trudeau, Conversation with Canadians, 1972; Numerous articles in Scholorly Journals. *Honours:* Chief Justice's Medallist in Law, University of Alberta, 1952; Frank Knox Memorial Fellow, Harvard Law School, 1959; Ford Foundation Fellow, 1974; Queen's Counsel, Canada, 1974. *Hobbies:* Skiing; Sailing; Photography. *Address:* 2095 Chalmers Road, Ottawa, Ontario, Canada KIH 6K4

HEATH, Edward Richard George, b. 9 July 1916, Broadstairs, Kent, England. Politician. *Education:* Balliol College, Oxford. *Appointments:* War Service, 1939-45; Civil Service, 1946-47; Journalism and Merchant Banking, 1947-51; Member of Parliament, held various appointments in the Conservative Governments, 1951-64; Assistant Opposition Whip, Lord Commissioner of the Treasury, 1951; Joint Deputy Chief Whip, 1952; Deputy Chief Whip, 1953; Parliamentary Secretary to the Treasury and Government Chief Whip, Privy Councillor, 1955; Minister of Labour, 1959; Lord Privy Seal, 1960; Secretary of State for Industry, Trade and Development and President of the Board of Trade, 1963; party spokesman, economic affairs, Chairman, Committee Planning Future Policy, 1964; elected Leader, Conservative Party, 1965; Prime Minister, 1970-74; resigned as Leader of Conservative Party, 1975; travelled extensively to China, Far East, United States, Middle East and many European countries. *Memberships:* Chairman, 1963-70, London Symphony Orchestra Trust; Founder member, European Community Youth Orchestra; Member of the Independent Commission on International Development Issues, 1977-79. *Publications:* One Nation: A Tory Approach to Social Problems, 1950; Old World, New Horizons, 1970; Sailing—A Course of My Life, 1975; Music—A Joy for Life, 1976; Travels—People and Places in My Life, 1977; Carols—The Joy of Christmas, 1977. *Creative Works:* Conducted at World Festival of Youth Orchestras in Aberdeen, 1977, 1978, and many other orchestras throughout the world, Several LP records. *Honours:* MBE, military Division, mentioned in despatches; Charlemagne Prize, City of Aachen; European Prize for Statesmanship for outstanding services on entry of Britain to the European Community, 1971; Estes J. Kefauver Prize, 1971; Stressman gold medal, 1971;

Captain British Admiral's Cup Team, 1971 and 1979; British Challenge for Sardinia Cup, 1980. Honorary degress from Oxford, Bradford, Westminster College, Salt Lake City, Paris-Sorbonne. *Address:* House of Commons, London SW1, England.

HEATH Henry Vernon Trafford, b. 3 July 1931, Edinburgh, Scotland. Company Director. m. Mary Elizabeth Holder, 12 Nov. 1959, 1 son, 1 daughter. *Education:* George Watsons College, 1948. *Appointments:* Assistant Commercial Sales Manager, Colonial Gas Holdings; Manager, 1960, General Manager, 1965, Director, 1976, Waldorf Appliances. *Memberships:* Deputy Chairman, Australian Council, Asian Business; Hon. Treasurer, Metal Trades Industry Association, Export Council; Deputy President, Gas Appliance Manufacturers Association of Australia. *Honours:* Queen's Silver Jubilee Medal, 1977. *Hobbies:* Golf; Tennis; Reading; Travel. *Address:* 'Tanglewood', 4 Denis Street, Vermont, Vic 3133, Australia.

HEATH, Wiliam Carrick, b. 23 July 1925, Casterton, Victoria, Australia. Consultant Physician. m. Ann Brenan, 26 Jan. 1955, 3 sons, 3 daughters. *Education:* MBBS, Melbourne University, 1953; MRACP, 1959; FACA, 1964; FRACP, 1970; FACC, 1971. *Appointments:* Medical Officer, 1954-56, Consultant Physician, 1965-, Senior Physician, Hypertension Clinic, 1975-, St Vincent's Hospital; Consultant Physician RAAF, 1970-81; Consultant Practice, Cardiovascular and Internal Medicine; Consultant Life Insurance and Superannuation. *Memberships:* Melbourne Club; Athenaeum Club; Naval and Military Club; VRC; MCC; LTAV; Cardiac Society—National Heart Foundation. *Publications:* Cardiovascular Literature. *Hobbies:* Squash; Travel; Reading. *Address:* 124 Anderson Street, South Yarra, Victoria, Australia.

HEAVENS, Oliver Samuel, b. 5 Nov. 1922, London, England. Professor of Physics. m. Eva Dorothea Cohn, 26 Jan. 1946, 3 sons. *Education:* BSc, Birkbeck College, University of London, 1945; PhD, University of Reading, 1951. *Appointments:* Research Assistant, D Napier and Sons, 1943-45; Research Assistant, British Rubber Producers Association, 1945-47; Lecturer, University of Reading, 1947-57; Reader, Royal Holloway College, University of London, 1957-64; Professor of Physics and Head of Department, University of York, 1964-. *Memberships:* Fellow, Institute of Physics; Fellow, Institution of Electrical Engineers; Fellow, Optical Society of America; European Physical Society. *Publications:* The Optical Properties of Thin Solid Films, 1955; Optical Masers, 1964; Lasers, 1971; Author and co-author of 94 articles in various journals. *Honours:* Honorary Doctorate of Université d'Aix Marseille. *Hobby:* Skiing. *Address:* 153 Hull Road, York YO1 3JX, England.

HEBSGAARD, Jens, b. 17 Feb. 1940, Varde, Denmark, Business Consultant. m. 25 July 1964, 2 sons, 1 daughter. *Education:* Graduate Merconom, (Accounts) 1975. *Appointments:* Bookseller, Denmark, 1956-60; Military Service, 1960-62; Publisher (Adult Literacy Material) Nigeria, 1962-65; Manager Bookshop Chain, Nigeria, 1965-72; Free Lance Denmark Teacher, 1975-78; Business Consultant, Nigeria, 1978-80; Northern Area Manager, University Press Limited, Oxford University Press, Nigeria, 1980-. *Hobby:* West African History and Art. *Address:* Mollevejen 68, DK 5960 Marstal, Denmark.

HEDDLE, (Bentley) John, b. 15 Sept. 1943, Ashford, Kent, England. Member of Parliament; Consultant Surveyor; Co. Director and Underwriting Member of Lloyds. m. 18 Apr. 1964, 2 sons, 2 daughters. *Education:* Bishops Stortford College; Voluntary Service Overseas, 1958-60; College of Estate Management, London University, England, 1960-62. *Appointments:* Consultant Surveyor to: Heddle Butler & Co., 1964-70, John Heddle & Co., 1970-80; Consultant Partner, Elliott Son & Boyton, 1980-; Kent County Council, 1973-80. *Memberships:* Fellow, Institute of Directors; Fellow, Royal Society of Arts; Fellow, Incorporate Society of Valuers; Fellow, Rating & Valuation Association; Fellow, Incorporated Association of Architects and Surveyors. *Publications:* A New Lease of Life - A Solution to Rent Control, 1975; The Great Rate Debate, 1980; contributed articles to National press and journals. *Honours:* Freeman, The City of London. *Hobby:*

Relaxing with family. *Address:* The Manor, Barham, Nr. Canterbury, Kent, England.

HEDGES, Dennis Mitchell, b. 29 Nov. 1917, Westcliff-on-Sea, Essex, England. Company Director. m. Margaret Janet Belcham, 2 Jan. 1951, 2 sons. *Education:* Lausanne University, 1936-37; MA, St Catharine's College, Cambridge, 1937-40. *Appointments:* Colonial Service, 1940-61; Provincial Commissioner, Sierra Leone, 1957; Chief Secretary, British Guiana, 1959. *Memberships:* Royal Commonwealth Society; Anglo-Sierra Leonean Society. *Honours:* CBE, 1962. *Hobbies:* Shooting; Golf; Gardening. *Address:* Forshem, Elvetham Road, Fleet, Hampshire, England.

HEERE, Reinier, b. 18 Nov. 1929, Zaandam, The Netherlands. Director of Companies. 1 son. *Appointments:* Various posts in Management and Marketing, Bruynzeel Factories in the Netherlands and overseas, 1950-68; Co-owner, Westfort International Consultants, Paramaribo, Surinam, 1968-70; Co-Director, Caribbean Real Estate and Holding, Aruba, Neth. Antilles, 1970-72; Co-owner/Managing Director, various companies in St. Maarten, Neth. Antilles, Tortula, British Virgin Islands, St. Lucia, West Indies, 1972-. *Memberships:* Past National President, Junior Chamber International, Netherlands; Past President, Foundation for Vocational and Professional Training, St. Maarten. *Honours:* Senator, Junior Chamber International, 1965. *Address:* Almond Grove Estate, St. Maarten, Neth. Antilles.

HEFFERAN, William Vincent, b. 18 Sept. 1938, Brisbane, Australia. Medicine; Ophthalmologist. m. Jenice Faye Gleeson, 28 May 1966, 3 sons, 2 daughters. *Education:* MB., BS., 1962, DO., 1971, Queensland University, Australia; FRACO., 1972. *Appointments:* Resident, 1963, Registrar, Opthalmology, 1969-71, Princess Alexandra Hospital, Australia; Superintendent, Collinsville Hospital, Australia, 1964-68; Consultant Ophthalmologist, 1974-, Senior Consultant Ophthalmologist, 1977-, Repatriation, General Hospital, Greenslopes, Queensland, Australia. *Memberships:* Chairman, RACO., Queensland, 1979-80; Councillor, RACO, Australia, 1979-81; Examiner in Optics, RACO., 1974-. *Hobbies:* Golf; Cricket; Fishing; Stamps. *Address:* 29 Brodie Street, Holland Park, Brisbane 4121, Australia.

HEIDENREICH, Judith, b. 22 Nov. 1936, Mannum, South Australia. Artist, Christian Worker. m. Glen Aubrey Heidenreich, 5 Aug. 1955, 3 sons, 1 daughter. *Education:* Fine Arts Diploma Course, South Australia School of Art, 1960-63. *Appointments:* Self employed, 1963-75; Church Work, Lutheran Church of Australia; Established Christian Community, Manoah, South Australia, 1977-. *Memberships:* Christian Church; St Peters Lutheran Church, Blackwood South Australia; Royal South Australian Society of Arts; Contemporary Art Society; Lyceum Club, Adelaide. *Creative Works:* Numerous paintings and exhibitions in several countries including, America, New Zealand and Australia. *Honours:* Royal Society of Arts prize, 1961, 1964; Olive Dutton Green Prize, 1962; Painting recommended by South Australian National Gallery, purchased by Naracoorte Art Gallery, 1975. *Hobbies:* Singing and Playing Christian Songs; Tennis; Boating; Fishing. *Address:* Manoah Christian Community, Manoah Drive, Upper Sturt, South Australia.

HEIN, Charles Henri Raymond, b. 26 Sept. 1901, Mauritius. Barrister-at-Law. m. 9 Jan. 1928, 4 sons, 4 daughters. *Education:* Scholar, 1920, Royal College, Mauritius; MA., Oxon., Wadham College, Oxford, UK. *Appointments:* Member, Council of Government, 1936-48; Mayor of Port Louis, 1948; Director, 1937-76, President, 1965-76, Mauritius Commercial Bank; Chairman: Swan Insurance Limited, 1967-; Mauritius Life Assurance, 1972-; Anglo-Mauritius Assurance Society Limited, 1973-; New Mauritius Dock Co. Limited, 1960-70 Director, 1937-70; Director, Reinsurance Co. of Mauritius. *Memberships:* Former President: Mauritius Chamber of Agriculture; Mauritius Sugar Industry Res. Institute; Mauritius Turf Club. President, Alliance Française, 1948-54; Former President, Bar Council. *Publications:* Translated Bernardin de St Pierre's Paul et Virginie, 1977; Le Naufrage du Saint Geran, edn. Fernand Nathan, Paris, 1981. *Honours:* Knighted, 1977; Chevalier de la Légion d'Honneur, 1950; QC., 1956. *Hobbies:* Music; Gardening;

Ancient Greek Literature. *Address:* Royal Road, Moka, Mauritius.

HEINRICH, Bretislav, b. 29 July 1940, Prerov, Czechoslovakia. Physicist. m. Anna Heinrich, 25 June 1960, 1 son. *Education:* Master Degree, Charles University, Prague, 1962; PhD, Czechoslovak Academy of Sciences, 1968. *Appointments:* Physics Institute, Czechoslovak Academy of Sciences, 1962-69; Institute of Physical Problems, Soviet Academy of Sciences, 1967-69; Physics Department, Simon Fraser, University Burnaby, Canada, 1969-. *Memberships:* Canadian Association of Physicists. *Publications:* Approximately 50 publications in varous journals. *Hobbies:* Tennis; Skiing. *Address:* 1914 Goleta Drive, Burnaby, BC, Canada.

HEINRICH, Charles G, b. 31 Mar. 1941, Hungary. Management. m. Louise Elizabeth Richardson, 27 Apr. 1968, 2 daughters. *Education:* BSc, Massachusetts Institute of Technology, 1957-64; MBA, McGill University, 1964-66. *Appointments:* Lecturer, Loyola College, Montreal, 1964-67; Research Assistant, Royal Commission on Bilingualism and Biculturalism, Business Sector, 1966-67; Economic Analyst, 1966-68, Superintendent, Planning, Accounting and Treasury, 1968-71, Aluminum Company of Canada Limited; Manager, Reduction, Research and Development, Arvida Research Centre, 1971-74; Vice President and Director, Alcan Smelters and Chemicals Limited, 1974-76; Vice President and Director Corporate Services, 1976-79, Vice President and General Manager, Wire and Cable Division, 1979-, Alcan Canada Products Limited. *Memberships:* Business Environment Committee, Canadian Manufacturers Association; Toronto Chapter, Planning Executives Institute; 1980 Fifth Commonwealth Conference. *Honours:* Canadian Junior Tennis Champion, 1956; Dean's Honour List, 1964; Scholastic Scholarship, McGill University, 1967. *Hobbies:* Tennis; Golf; Skiing; Music; Education. *Address:* 327 Glencairn Avenue, Toronto, Ontario, Canada.

HELLMUTH, Erhart Otto, b. 27 Nov. 1920, Gaernitz, Leipzig, Germany. Plant Eco-Physiologist. m. Eva Hedwig Kuhwald, 10 Mar. 1945, 2 sons. *Education:* Diploma Biology, Germany, 1951; BSc(hons), 1964, PhD, 1969, University of Western Australia; Technical Teachers' Certificate, 1972. *Appointments:* Teacher, 1946-56; Postgraduate Studies, 1964-69; Postdoctoral Research, 1969-70; Lecturer, Biology, Tech. Ed. Division of Western Australia, 1971-. *Memberships:* Convocation, University of Western Australia; Royal Society of Western Australia. *Publications:* Author of several publications on plants in arid Western Australia and eco-physiological methods. *Hobbies:* Watersports; Dancing. *Address:* 53 Drabble Road, Scarborough, Western Australia.

HELLYER, Paul Theodore, b. 6 Aug. 1923, Waterford, Ontario, Canada. Politician; Journalist. m. 1 June 1945, 2 sons, 1 daughter. *Education:* Diploma, Aeronautical Engineering, Curtiss-Wright Technical Institute of Aeronautics, Glendale, California, USA, 1941; BA., University of Toronto, Canada, 1949. *Appointments:* Elected to House of Commons at G.E., 1949, 1953, 1958, defeated General Election 1957-58, re-elected in by-election 1958, 1962, 1963, 1965, 1968, 1972; Parliamentary Assistant to Minister of National Defence, 1956; Member of Privy Council, and Associate Defence Minister, 1957; Minister of National Defence, 1963-67; Minister of Transport, 1967-68; Parliamentary Press Gallery, 1974; Sydicated columnist, Toronto Sun, 1974-. *Memberships:* Fellow, Royal Society for the advancement of the Arts and Sciences; United Nations Association; Canadian Institute of International Affairs; Life Mmeber: Royal Ontario Museum; Ontario Art Gallery. *Publications:* Cities of the Future - Heaven or Hell?, 1970; Agenda, A Plan for Action, 1971; Exit Inflation, 1981. *Honours:* Coronation Medal, 1953; Centennial Medal, 1967; Jubilee Medal, 1978. *Hobbies:* Philately; Music; Water Skiing; Scuba Diving; Gardening. *Address:* 506 - 65 Harbour Square, Toronto, Ontario, M5J 2L4, Canada.

HELPMANN, Robert (Sir), b. 9 Apr. 1909, Mount Gambier, South Australia. Dancer; Choreographer; Actor; Producer. *Appointments:* Made his first professional stage appearance at the Theatre Royal, Adelaide, Australia, 1923; Danced in Anna Pavlova's Co., in Australia, 1926; Became Principle dancer with The

Royal Ballet, London, 1935; Choreographed and appeared in The Red Shoes, famous ballet film, 1948; Headed the Old Vic Theatre Co., in Australia, 1954; Appeared as Guest Artist with Royal Ballet on its tour of Australasia, 1958-59; Commissioned to create The Display, for the Australian Ballet, 1964; Created a seond work, Yügen, 1965; Has appeared as Guest artist with Australian Ballet, dancing and acting many roles including: Dr. Coppelius, Coppelia, The Don, in Don Quizote, Tango in Facade, An Ugly Sister in Cinderella; Henry V; Tales of Hoffman; 55 Days in Peking; The Mango Tree; Produced a full-length ballet version of The Merry Widow, 1975; Has appeared as Guest artist with American Ballet Theater in many roles; Directed Dracula and Stars of World Ballet, 1978; Guest Artist in Maina Gielgud's production at the Old Vic in Steps, Notes and Squeaks, 1980. *Honours:* OBE., 1965; Knight Bachelor, 1968; Knight of the Northern Star by the King of Sweden, 1957; Knight of the Cedars of Lebanon by President Charmoun, 1956; Voted Australian of the Year, 1967. *Address:* 72 Eaton Square, London, SW1, England.

HELSHAM, Hugh Geoffrey, b. 14 Dec. 1933, Colombo, Sri Lanka. Surveyor. m. Marcia Helen Grant, 6 Oct. 1964, 1 son, 2 daughters. *Education:* Higher Grades for Appointment as Trigonometrical Surveyor, 1963; Various courses at School of Military Survey, 1953-61. *Appointments:* Topographical Surveyor, Royal Australian Survey Corps., 1953-62; Surveyor, New South Wales Department of Lands, Australia, 1962-. *Memberships:* Institution of Surveyors, Australia; Australian Institute of Cartographers: New South Wales Staff Surveyors Association. *Publications:* Papers: Position Fixation by Position Line Observations for Land Surveyors, 1960; Adjustment and Maintenance of Geodetic Syrveying Instruments, 1968; Confidence in the Use of EDM Instruments - A Need for Test Lines, 1981. *Hobbies:* Golf; Gardening; Motor Sport. *Address:* 41 Finch Avenue, East Rude, New South Wales 2113, Australia.

HEMINGWAY, Eric William, b. 27 Oct. 1927 Batley, Yorkshire England. Academic Administrator and Chartered Engineer. m. (1) Yvonne Harvey 5 Feb. 1955, (2) Laurie Wilma Hilton 1 May 1979, 3 sons, 2 stepsons. *Education:* Bachelor of Science (Engineering) 2nd Class Honours, London University 1953; Diploma of Imperial College, Gas Turbine Technology, 1955; Master of Science, (Thermodynamics) Birmingham University 1969; Doctor of Philosophy, (Tribology) 1967. *Appointments:* Development Engineer, Joseph Lucas, Gas Turbine Equipment, Birmingham, 1953-54; Development and Performance Engineer, Rolls Royce, Derby, 1955-57; Lecturer in Mechanical Engineering, University of Sydney, 1957-60; Senior Lecturer in Mechanical Engineering, Universtiy Western Australia, 1960-71; Senior Research Fellow in Tribology, University College, Swansea 1967-68; Dean, School of Applied Science, Caulfield Institute of Technology, 1961-; Visiting Consultant, National Centre of Tribology, Risley UK 1979; Numerous consultative assignments in Tribology and internal combustion engines for industry and government utilities. *Memberships:* Fellow, Institution of Engineers Australia; Royal Aeronautical Society, London; Fellow, Institution of Mechanical Engineers, London; Associate Fellow, Australian Institute of Management. *Publications:* About 30 publications in Learned Society Journals, Conferences; Technical journals in fields of Tribology, Internal Combusion engines and the law; Additional confidential documents relating to clients, employers and government agencies. *Honours:* Paul Henderson Memorial Prize 1968; Luxton Prize 1953. *Hobbies:* Sailing; Boat building; Swimming; Reading; Sailmaking. *Address:* 636 Warrigal Road, Chadstone 3148, Victoria Australia.

HEMPHILL, Woodrow, b. 27 Sept. 1918 Mayfield, NSW Australia. Medical Practitioner. m. Betty Degotardi 8 May 1943, 1 son, 1 daughter. *Education:* MB, BS University Sydney 1942; DCH (RCP's, 1956; FRACP 1977. *Appointments:* Resident Medical Officer, Royal Prince Alfred Hospital, 1942-43; Captain, AIF, (AAMC) 1943-46; General Practitioner, Cardiff, New South Wales, Physician, Wallsend District Hospital, 1946-53; Fellow in Paediatrics, Yedz Grotto Fellow, (Rheumatic Disease), John Hopkins Hospital, Baltimore, 1953-55; House Officer, Locum Registrar, Alder Hey Children's Hospital, Liverpool, England, Paediatrics, Liverpool Maternity Hospital, 1955-57; Diploma of Child Health, London, 1956; Director, Bureau School Hygiene, Division for Handicapped Persons, Baltimore City Health Department, Lecturer in Public Health Administration, Committee on Brain Damaged Children, John Hopkins School of Hygiene, Principal Investigator: Survey of Morbidity Present in 1,000 Baltimore School Children, under auspices Children's Bureau of Health, Education and Welfare, 1957-60; Deputy Director, School Medical Services 1960-65; Assistant Director, Bureau of Maternal and Child Health 1966-73; Assistant Physician, Royal Alexandra Hospital for Children, Camperdown, 1968; Principal Adviser, Maternal and Child Health, Health Commission of New South Wales 1973-78; Director, Division of Maternal and Child Health, Health Commission of New South Wales 1978-. *Memberships:* Australian College of Paediatrics; Standing Committee on Child Psychiatry, NSW; Institute of Psychiatry. *Publications:* Comparison of Benzathine Penicillin and Sulphadiazine in Prophylaxis Against Recurrences of Rheumatic Fever, 1955; Sickness and Impairments; Co-author: Height Weight and Other Physical Characteristics of New South Wales Children aged five years and over; Children under five years of age. *Hobbies:* Photography; Cabinet making; Bird watching. *Address:* 19 Linden Avenue, Pymble, NSW, Australia 2073.

HEMPSALL, William John, b. 5 July 1912 Chelsea, London. Chartered Civil Engineer. m. (1) Eunice Anne Robinson, 1939, 1 son, (2) Agnes Kathleen Wathes 23 June 1948, 2 daughters. *Education:* Chelsea Art School, 1928-30; Matriculation, Chelsea Polytechnic 1931-33. *Appointments:* Assistant Engineer, Epsom and Ewell UDC, Town Planning, Roads, Sewers 1935-37, Middlesex County Engineers Department Roads and Bridges, 1937-40; Admiralty CE in C Department, Dover and Chatham, 1940-42; Air Ministry Works Directorate, 1942-47; Senior Assistant Engineer, St Marylebone BC, 1947-49;, Camberwell BC 1949-51; Senior Executive Engineer, Ministry of Works, Uganda, 1951-69; Sir Fredrick Snow and Partners 1969-71; Crown Agents, Ghana and N. Nigeria 1971-74; Deputy Chief Engineer Chemical Construction Limited 1974-75; Chemical Construction, Syricon Limited 1977-; Sir Fredrick Snow and Partners, Zaire, 1975-77 and Belfast Airport, 1978-80, Retired 1980. *Memberships:* Chartered Civil Engineer; FICE; FIMunE; FIHE. *Honours:* MBE 1969. *Hobbies:* Music; Art; Literature. *Address:* 'Cote House', Burton Street, Marnhull, Sturminster Newton, Dorset, DT10 1PP, England.

HENDERSON, Bobby Ray, b. 13 July 1941 Winterville, North Carolina USA. Education/Media. *Education:* BA, St Augustine's College Raleigh, NC 1959-63; MSLS, 1970-72; PhD 1973-78; Certificate, Supervisory Methods in Municipal Administration, University of Georgia Atlanta, 1972. *Appointments:* Branch Head, 1972-77, Model City Coordinator Atlanta Public Library, 1972; Assistant, Georgia Department of Labour, 1971-72; Assistant, Cornell University Medical University, New York 1969-70; Senior Searcher, US Library of Congress Washington DC 1966-68. *Memberships:* Botswana Society; Notswana Library Association; American Library Association. *Publications:* An Investigation of Film Selection Criteria Used by Large Public Libraries in the Southeast; A Survey of Educational Resources/Teaching Aids in Secondary Schools of Botswana; Educational Resources Handbook, University College Botswana; Microteaching: A Manual for Training Teachers. *Honours:* Ford Foundation Fellow 1970. *Hobbies:* Photography; Jazz Collector. *Address:* University College, Botswana Educational Resource Centre, Private Bag 0022, Gaborone, Botswana.

HENDERSON, James Stewart Barry, b. 29 Apr. 1936, Kirkcaldy, Fife, Scotland. Member of Parliament; Management Consultant. m. Janet Helen Sprot Todd, 12 Aug. 1961, 2 sons. *Appointments:* Computer Industry; Member of Parliament for East Dumbartonshire, 1974; Selct Committee on Scottish Affairs, 1979; Vice Chairman, Scottish Conservative Backbench Committee, 1979-; Member, House of Commons Chairmans Panel, 1981. *Memberships:* British Computer Society. *Publications:* The Scottish Conservatives, (co-author). *Address:* House of Commons, London, SW1A OAA, England.

HENDERSON, John Tasker, b. 9 Dec. 1905. Engineering-Physist. m. 30 May 1951, 2 sons, 1 daughter. *Education:* Bachelor of Science, Master of

Science, McGill University; PhD, London University; Post University Course at Sorbonne and Munich. *Appointments:* NRC 1933-70; National Research, RCAF, 1942-46. *Memberships:* President and Director, and Managing Committee of IRF; Union Radio Scientific Radio; Engineering Institute of Ontario. *Publications:* Cathode Ray Direction Finder in Radar, 1942-46; *Honours:* MBE 1943; Royal Society Canada 1944; Fellow Institute Radio Engineers 1955; McNaughton Medal 1969. *Hobbies:* Music; Photography; Reading. *Address:* RR3, Perth Ontario, K7H 3C5, Canada.

HENDERSON, Kenneth Murray, b. 30 Oct. 1927 Edinburgh, Scotland. Managing Director. m. Catherine Denoon Greig 12 Oct. 1963, 1 son. *Education:* BSc Hons, 1944-48, PhD, Edinburgh University 1948-51; Post-Graduate Research: University of Leiden, Holland, Western Ontario, Canada. *Appointments:* Associate Professor, University Western Ontario, Canada; Technical Service Group Leader, M Nairn and Company Kirkcaldy Scotland; New Products Controller, Sterling Winthrop Group, Surbiton, UK; Development Planning Co-ordinator, Nicholas International S.A. Geneva, Switzerland; European Managing Director, Fulford Williams International Switzerland and UK; Managing Director and Director, Mentholatum Company Limited, UK and Nigeria. *Memberships:* Round Table, Surbiton; 41 Club; Proprietary Association of Great Britain. *Publications:* The Rôle of Self-Medication 1969; Self-Medication—The Pharmaceutical Industry Viewpoint, 1978; Co-author, Guide to the Medicines Act 1968. *Hobbies:* Photography; Electronics; Gold; Travel. *Address:* "August Field", Charvil Lane, Sonning, Berks.

HENDERSON, Margaret Mary, b. 13 Nov. 1915, Melbourne, Australia. Consultant Physician. *Education:* MB., BS., 1938, MD., 1941, Universities of Western Australia and Melbourne; FRACP, FRCP, London, UK. *Appointments:* Honorary Physician, 1945-60, Consultant, 1960-, Queen Victoria Memorial Hospital, Australia; Honorary Physician, 1947-75, Specialist Physician, 1975-80, Royal Melbourne Hospital, Australia; Private practice, 1947-. *Memberships:* Australia Medical Association; Thoracic Society of Australia; Victoria Medical Women's Association; Soroptimist International; Lyceum Club. *Honours:* OBE., 1976. *Hobbies:* Music; Drama; Gardening. *Address:* 28 The Avenue, Parkville, Victoria 3052, Australia.

HENDERSON, Neville Vicars, b. 21 Mar. 1899, Longreach, Goulburn, New South Wales, Australia. Solicitor. m. Jean Hamilton Brownhill, 7 Feb. 1934, 1 son, 2 daughters. *Education:* University of Queensland, Australia, 1917-18; BA., 1919, LL.B., 1921, LL.M., 1922, Trinity College, University of Melbourne, Australia. *Appointments:* Solicitor, Foundation member, Consultant, Henderson & Lahey, 1924-71; Company Director; Major, 1942, D.AAG., War Service, 1940-44; Notary Public, 1945; Grazier, 1950-79; Honorary Consul for Australia, 1957. *Memberships:* Council, Queensland Law Association, 1926-27; Secretary, Queensland Law Association, 1926-28; Secretary, Queensland Law Society Incorporated, 1928-54; Secretary, Law Council of Australia, 1939-40; Hon. Secretary, 1947, President, 1954-56, Society of Notaries of Queensland; Dean, Consular Corps. of Queensland, 1977. *Publications:* Managing Editor: Annotated Reprint of the Queensland Statutes, 1962. *Honours:* Final Honours Scholar in Law, Supreme Court Prizeman, University of Melbourne, Australia, 1922; Distinguished Service Order in Gold of Austrrian Republic Knight Cross First Class, 1964; CBE., 1967; Knight Bachelor, 1975. *Hobbies:* Reading; Writing; Swimming. *Address:* Glencraig, 63 Eldernell Avenue, Hamilton, Brisbane, Queensland 4007, Australia.

HENDERSON, Norman Harold, b. 19 May 1920, Sydney, Australia. Managing Director. m. 17 Dec. 1941, 2 daughters. *Appointments:* War service: Royal Australian Navy, 1936-46; Royal Australian Naval Reserve, 1949-80; at this date was placed on retired list as a Lieutenant Commander, RANR (retired); Business Equipment and Engineering Pty. Limited, 1946-49; Sales Manager, Salmond and Spraggon(Australia)Pty Limited, 1949-65; Sales Director, World Agencies Pty. Limited, 1965-66; Managing Director, Chanel(Australia)Pty.Limited, 1966-. *Memberships:* Associate Fellow, Australian Institute Management; Fellow, Institute Directors, Australia; President, 1969, Sunnyfield Association for Intellectually Handicapped. *Honours:*MBE,

Military; Volunteer Reserve Decoration and Clasp; Justice of the Peace; Honorary ADC to Governor of New South Wales, 1964-70. *Hobbies:* Golf; Swimming; Reading; Walking. *Address:* 227 Alfred Street, Cromer, New South Wales 2099, Australia.

HENDERSON, (Honourable), William James, b. 13 Oct. 1916 Empress, Alberta. Justice, Supreme Court of Ontario (Retired). m. Helen MacDougall, 13 Mar. 1943, 2 daughters. *Education:* BA, Queen's University, Kingston, Ontario 1938; Osgoode Hall Law School, Toronto, Ontario 1942; Read law with J M Hickey, Queen's Counsel, Kingston, Ontario; Called to Bar of Ontario, 1942. *Appointments:* Established Law Firm, Henderson and Woods, 1945; General Practice 1945-65; Member of Parliament for Kingston and the Islands, 1949-58; Appointed Judge, 1965; Established Loyalist Farms Limited. *Memberships:* Canadian Bar Association; University Club of Toronto; Cataraqui Golf and Country Club; Trident Yacht Club; Ontario Liberal Association. *Honours:* MBE; Queen's Counsel 1961. Hobby: Stock Breeding. *Address:* 4567 Bath Road, Kingston, Ontario, K7N 1A8, Canada.

HENDRY, Gordon Finlayson, b. 27 Jan. 1929 Hamilton, Scotaland. Personnel and Industrial Relations. m. Flora Duncan Harley 16 Oct. 1948, 3 sons, 2 daughters. *Education:* Personnel Management Diploma 1956. *Appointments:* Personnel Manager, Corporation of the City of Adelaide, 1969-. *Memberships:* Associate Fellow Institute of Personnel Management; Associate Australian Institute of Management; Australian Institute of Public Administration. *Publications:* Two-Way Information Training in a Transport Company 1967. *Hobbies:* Reading; Human Relations; Poetry. *Address:* 119 Gawler Street, Salisbury, South Australia 5108.

HENEINE, Raymond, b. 19 Mar. 1921 Beirut. Ambassador of Lebanon, Australia and New Zealand. m. Eliane Hindi 4 June 1960, 2 sons, 1 daughter. *Education:* Université Saint Joseph, Beirut; Licentiate in Political and Administrative Sciences; Licentiate in Economics and Finance. *Appointments:* Consul General of Lebanon, Rio de Janeiro 1960-64; Counsellor, Embassy of Lebanon, Madrid 1964-65; Chargé d'Affaires, Embassy of Lebanon, Abidjan 1967-72; Chargé d'Affaires, Embassy of Lebanon, Montevideo, Uruguay, 1972-75; Director of the Department for Lebanese Overseas, Ministry of Foreign Affairs, Beirut, 1975-78; Ambassador of Lebanon to Australia 1978-. *Memberships:* Rotary Club. *Honours:* Officer of the National Order of the Cadar; Lebanese Gold Merit of the 1st Class; Officer of the Southern Cross, Brasil; Officer of the Istaklal (Independence), Iraq; Officer of the Polish Restituta, Poland; Officer of the Shining Star, China; Officer of the Order of Sweden; Officer of the Sovereign and Military Order of Malta; Gold Medal of Military Merit of Tamandare, Brazil; Commander of Phoenix, Greece; Commander of Hamayoun, Iran; Commander of the Star of Jordan; Commander of the Italian Merit; Commander of the Austrian Merit; Commander of the Order of German Merit; Commander of the Order of Merit, Spain; Commander of the Southern Cross, Brazil; Commander of the Ivory Merit; Great Officer of the Order of the Throne, Morocco. *Hobbies:* Classical Music; Tennis; Swimming. *Address:* 63 Mugga Way, Red Hill ACT, 2603 Australia.

HENG, Alan B T, b. 21 July 1941, Jakarta, Indonesia. Medical Practitioner. m. Jolie W P W Svasti, 19 Apr. 1969, 2 sons. *Education:* MA., MB.B.Chir., (Cantab), Gonville and Caius College, Cambridge, UK 1966; MRCS., LRCP., 1966, MRCP., 1971, Royal College of Physicians, London, UK; FCCP., American College of Chest Physicians, USA, 1978. *Appointments:* House Physician, Whittington Hospital, London, N.19, UK, 1967; House Surgeon, Connaught Hospital, London, E.17, UK, 1967; Clinical Assistant to Professor G A Ransome, General Hospital, Singapore, 1968-69; Resident Medical Officer, King Edward VII Hospital for Officers, London, W1, UK, 1969-70; Self employed partner, 1971-76; Medical Registrar, 1976-77, Specialist Physician, 1977-81, Prince of Wales Hospital, Randwick, New South Wales, Australia. *Memberships:* Fellow, Royal Society of Medicine, UK; Thoracic Society of Australia; Board of Directors, Lottie Stewart Hospital, Dundas, Australia; Elder of Wesley Central Mission, Sydney, Australia. *Hobbies:* Theology; Photography; Tennis. *Address:* 5 Milroy Avenue, Kensington, New South Wales 2033, Australia.

HENNESSY, Edmund John, b. 23 Apr. 1924 Sydney, Australia. Specialist Surgeon. m. Catherine Twyman 6 Aug. 1948, 1 son, 4 daughters. *Education:* MB, BS Sydney 1947; FRACS 1959. *Appointments:* R.M.O Royal Newcastle Hospital 1948-49; General Practice, 1950-53; Surgical Registrar, 1954-57; Staff Surgeon, 1958-; Director of General Surgery and Urology, 1967-; Fellow in Surgery, Harvard Medical School, Boston, 1968; Senior Clinical Lecturer in Surgery, University of Sydney, 1972-77; Clinical Associate Professor, University of Newcastle 1978-. *Memberships:* Collegium Internationale Chirurgiae Digestivae; Gastroenterological Society of Australia. *Publications:* Ten publications on surgical aspects of gastroenterology. *Address:* 114 Church Street, Newcastle, 2300.

HENNESSY, James Patrick Ivan, b. 26 Sèpt. 1923. HM Diplomatic Service; Governor and Commanderin-Chief of Belize. m. Patricia Unwin, 1947, 1 son (dec'd) 5 daughters. *Education:* Sidney Sussex College, Cambridge, UK; London School of Economics, UK. *Appointments:* Served RA, 1942-46; Appointed to HM Overseas Service, Basutoland, District Officer, 1948; Judicial Commissioner, 1953, District Commissioner, 1954-56, Joint Secretary, Constitutional Committee, 1957-59, Supervisor of Elections, 1959, Secretary, Executive Council, 1960; seconded to Office of High Commissioner, Cape Town/Pretoria, 1961-63; Permanent Secretary, 1964; MLC., 1965; Secretary, External Affairs, Defence and Internal Security, 1968; retired, later appointed to HM Diplomatic Service, FO, 1968-70, Montevideo, 1970; (Chargé d'Affaires 1971-72); Acting, later High Commissioner, Uganda and Ambassador (non-resident) Rwanda, 1973-76; Consul-General, Cape Town, South Africa, 1977-80. *Memberships:* Royal Commonwealth Society. *Honours:* CMG., 1975; OBE., 1968; MBE., 1959. *Address:* c/o Foreign and Commonwealth Office, London, SW1A 2AL, England.

HENNESSY, William Bertrand, b. 16 Nov. 1925, Gulgong, New South Wales, Australia. Physician. m. Stella Humberstone, 22 Dec. 1956, 1 son, 1 daughter. *Education:* MB., BS., 1950, DTM&H., 1962, University of Sydney, Australia; MRCP., 1954, FRCP., 1977, London, UK; MRACP., 1956; FRACP., 1966. *Appointments:* Junior Resident Medical Officer, 1950, Senior Resident Medical Officer, 1951, Deputy Medical Superintendent, 1952, Honorary Clinical Assistant in Medicine, 1955-60, Honorary Relieving Assistant Physician, 1960-61, Honorary Assistant Physician, 1961-71, St. Vincent's Hospital, Sydney; Locum Medical Registrar, Central Middlesex Hospital, London, UK, 1953-54; Resident Medical Officer, Hospital for Tropical Diseases, London, UK, 1954; House Physician, West Middlesex Hospital, London, UK, 1954-55; Honorary Clinical Assistant Physician, 1956-61, Honorary Assistant Physician, 1961-71, Honorary Physician, 1971-76, Lewisham Hospital, Sydney, Australia; Visiting Physician, Prince Henry Hospital, Sydney, Australia, 1957-60; Visiting Physician, 2 Military Hospital, Ingleburn, New South Wales, Australia, 1966-71; Research Medical Officer, School of Public Health and Tropical Medicine, University of Sydney, Australia, Mar-Aug,1961, Dec.1961-Mar.1962, Aug-Oct,1966; Present Appointment: Visiting Gastroenterologist and Part-time Teacher, St. Vincent's Hospital, Sydney, Australia, 1971-; Part-time Research Medical Officer, Commonwealth Institute of Health, University of Sydney, Australia, 1975-. *Memberships:* Gastroenterological Society of Australia; Royal Society of Tropical Medicine and Hygiene; Australian Medical Society on Alcohol and Drugs-related Problems. *Publications:* numerous publications including: Gastrectomy and the blind loop syndrome, (with V J Kinsella), 1960; Studies on post-gastrectomy malabsorption: The importance of bacterial contamination of the upper small intestine, (with V J Kinsella, E P George), 1961; Goitre prophylaxis in New Guinea with intramuscular injections of iodized oil, 1964; Chloroquine-resistant falciparum malaria from Papua New Guinea and its implications for Australia, (with P M Moodie, R H Black), 1977; Alcohol in Australia, Problems and Programmes, 1978; Lay course in tropical medicine, 1979; Cimetidine and acute upper gastrointestinal bleeding: A double-blind controlled trial, (with C G Meredith, M C Kennedy, D N Wade, M V Sweeten, D J Byrnes, D J Frommer), 1980. *Honours:* Awarded Pharmaceutical Manufacturers' Travelling Fellowship of the Royal Australasian College of Physicians, 1972. *Hobbies:* Gard-

ening; Golf; Travel. *Address:* 60 Killarney Drive, Killarney Heights, New South Wales, Australia, 2087.

HENNINGS,John Dunn, b. 9 June 1922, Ipswich, Suffolk, England. High Commissioner. m. Joanna Anita Thompson Reed, 1953, 2 sons. *Education:* Ipswich School; University College, Oxford. *Appointments:* Foreign Office; Berlin, 1947-1949; Colonial Office, 1949-1953 Secretary British Guiana Constitutional Commission, 1951; West African Inter-Territorial Secretariat, Accra, 1953-1955; Colonial Office, 1955-1960; Attaché for Colonial Affairs, British Embassy, Washington, DC, 1960-1963; Commonwealth Relations Office, 1963; Counsellor, HM Diplomatic Service 1965; Head, British High Commission, Residual Staff, Salisbury, Rhodesia, 1966-1968; Counsellor and Head of Chancery, High Commission, Delhi, 1968-1972; Acting High Commissioner, Uganda, 1972; High Commissioner Jamaica, and Ambassador (non-resident) to Haiti, 1973-1976; Assistant Under Secretary of State, FCO, 1976-1978. *Hobbies:* Reading; Photography. *Address:* c/o Foreign and Commonwealth Office, Downing Street, SW1 England.

HENRY, (Hon), David Howard Woodhouse, b. 30 Oct. 1916, London, England. Judge. m. Elizabeth Elaine, 24 Mar. 1945, 1 daughter. *Education:* BA. (Economics and History), Queen's University, 1939; Osgoode Hall Law School, Toronto, Ontario, Canada. *Appointments:* Read law with Mason, Foulds, Davidson and Kellock, Toronto, Ontario, called to the Bar of Ontario, June 1942; created Queens Counsel (Dom.), 1955; practised law with Mason, Foulds, Davidson and Kellock, 1943, and with Fleming, Smoke and Mulholland, Toronto; Junior Advisory Counsel, Department of Justice, 1945; Solicitor to the Treasury, 1949; Director, Advisory Secretary, 1953; Acting Director, Criminal Law Section, 1958; Director of Investigation and Research, Combines Investigation Act, Ottawa, 1960; served in 2nd World War: Commissioned, 1941 in 2nd Battalion, Royal Regiment of Canada; Overseas, 1943-44 with 1st Battalion (England and Normandy) transferred to Judge Advocate General Branch, Ottawa, with rank of Captain, Nov. 1944; Lecturer in Administrative Law, University of Ottawa, Canada, 1961-73; Visiting Lecturer in Law, McGill University, Canada, 1962-73; Chairman, Comte of Experts on Restrictive Business Practices, OECD, Paris, France, 1966-72; Justice Supreme Court of Ontario, Canada, 1973-. *Memberships:* Past president, Federal Lawyers' Clubs; Rideau Club, Ottawa; University Club of Toronto; Anglican. *Hobbies:* Wood-working; Photography. *Address:* Osgoode Hall, Toronto, Ontario M5H 2N5, Canada.

HENRY, Keith Austen, b. 18 Oct. 1923, Winnipeg, Manitoba, Canada. Civil Engineering Consultant. m. Marguerite Irene Hayes, 2 June 1945, 2 sons, 2 daughters. *Education:* BSc. (Civil Engineering) (Hons.), University of Alberta, Canada, 1948. *Appointments:* Surveyor, PFRA, 1946 and 47; Junior Hydraulic Engineer, 1948-51, Hydraulic Model Engineer, 1951-56, River Control, Engineer-St.Lawrence Power and Seaway Project, 1956-61, Ontario Hydro, Canada; Chief Hydraulic and Mechanical Engineer, 1961-63, Project Manager, Hugh Keenleyside Dam, 1963-69, Executive Vice-President, 1963, President, 1969, CBA Engineering Limited, Canada. *Memberships:* Registered Professional Engineer in British Columbia, Alberta, Ontario, and Oregon; Engineering Institute of Canada; Fellow, American Society of Civil Engineers; Consulting Engineers of British Columbia; Director, Association of Consulting Engineers of Canada; Member of Council, International Water Resources Association; Canadian Water Resources Association; Vancouver Club; Terminal City Club; Hollyburn Country Club; Engineers Club. *Publications:* Numerous papers including: River Control of the St. Lawrence River during Construction and Operation; Winter Operation of the St. Lawrence River; Conception and Design of the Arrow Lakes (Hugh Keenleyside) Dam; Earth Dam Built without Dewatering, 1971; International Cooperation in Managing the Great Lakes; Engineering Aspects of the Hadejia River Land Use and Water Resource Study; Sharing Space along the Canada-US Boundary, 1976. *Hobbies:* Tennis; Badminton; Birdwatching; Music; Woodworking. *Address:* 1110 Millstream Road, West Vancouver, B.C., Canada, V73 2C7.

HEPBURN, John, b. 8 May 1929, Glasgow, Scotland, UK. Architect. m. Ruth Christina Anderson, 4 Apr.

1957, 3 sons. *Education:* Diploma of Architecture, Glasgow School of Architecture, Scotland, 1956; Associate, Royal Institute of British Architects, 1957; Fellow, Royal Incorporation of Architects in Scotland, 1974. *Appointments:* Assistant Architect, 1956-65; Principal in Own Private Practice, June 1965-. *Memberships:* President, Glasgow Institute of Architects, 1980, 81, 82; Vice President, Royal Incorporation of Architects in Scotland, 1980, 81, 82; Chairman, New Glasgow Society, 1975-77; Council member, Glasgow Art Club, 1980, 81; Governor, Glasgow School of Art, 1980; Member of Convocation, Strathclyde University, 1980; Scottish Georgian Society; Council member, Charles Rennie Mackintosh Society, 1980-81; Burgess and Guild Brother, Qua Hammerman, 1979. *Creative Works:* Theatre, Swimming Pool, Hall, Eastwood Recreation centre; Recreation Buildings, Factories, Private Houses, Shops and Environmental Housing Rehabilitation, principally in Glasgow, Scotland. *Honours:* MBE, 1979; Saltire Award for Architecture (Rehabilitation), 1980; Access for Disabled Award for Eastwood Recreation Centre, Glasgow, 1976; Silver Medal for Architecture, Glasgow School of Architecture, 1954. *Hobbies:* Skiing; Windsurfing; Gardening; Music; Drawing; Photography; Travel. *Address:* 36 Ormonde Drive, Glasgow G44, Scotland.

HEPPEL, Richard Purdon, b. 27 Oct. 1913, Southsea, Hampshire, England. Diplomat. m. Ruth Theodora Matthews, 2 Sept. 1949, 2 sons, 1 daughter. *Education:* Scholar, Balliol College, Oxford, UK, 1931-35; 1st classical Moderations, 2nd Litt. Hum., Prox. acc. Gaisford Greek verse Prize and Craven and de Paravicini Scholarships, Laming Travelling Fellow, Queens College, Oxford, 1935-36. *Appointments:* Secretary at British Embassies in Rome, Tehran and Athens; Private Secretary, Minister of State for Foreign Affairs; Head of Chancery, Karachi and Madrid; Counsellor at Saigon; HM Ambassador, Phnom Penh; Minister-Counsellor, Vienna; Head of South East Asia Department Foreign Office; Head of Consular Department; HM Consul-General, Stuttgart. *Memberships:* Liveryman, Skinners Company; Oxford Union Society; Hon. Secretary, 1933-34, Oxford University Dramatic Society. *Honours:* CMG., 1959; idc., 1960. *Hobbies:* Theatricals; Gardening. *Address:* Barns Piece, Nether Winchendon, Aylesbury, Bucks HP18 ODU, England.

HEPPLE, Francis James Barnet, b. 3 May 1930, Brisbane, Australia. Orthopaedic Surgeon. m. Ruby Lillian Stanford, 10 Nov. 1956, 1 son, 3 daughters. *Education:* MB., BS., 1953, FRCS., 1963, University of Queensland, Australia, 1963. *Appointments:* Resident Medical Officer, Mater Hospital, Brisbane, Australia, 1954; Resident Medical Officer, 1955-58, Orthopaedic Surgeon, 1966-81, Toowoomba General Hospital, Queensland, Australia; Lecturer in Anatomy, University of Queensland, Australia, 1959; Surgical Registrar, Chelmsford, Essex, UK, 1960-62; Surgical Registrar, Devon, Exeter, UK, 1963; Senior Surgical Registrar, Middlesborough, Yorkshire, UK, 1964; Orthopaedic Registrar, Lord Mayor Trelour Hospital, Hampshire, UK, 1965. *Memberships:* Royal College of Surgeons of England; Australian Orthopaedic Association; Western Pacific Orthopaedic Association; Downs Club. *Hobbies:* Lawn bowls; Snooker. *Address:* 12 Rowbotham Street, Toowoomba, Australia.

HERMANT, Peter Morris, b. 30 Sept. 1939, Toronto, Ontario, Canada. Executive. m. Kathleen Elizabeth Norman, 7 July 1962, 1 son, 2 daughters. *Education:* University of British Columbia, Canada. *Memberships:* Member of Council, Board of Trade of Metropolitan Toronto; Admissions Committee, United Community Fund, 1974-78; International Service Committee, Rotary Club; Past President, Empire Club of Canada; Past Canadian Chairman, Optical Laboratories Association of North America; Worshipful Company of Spectacle Makers. *Honours:* Freeman of City of London. *Hobbies:* Tennis; Theatre; Record Production. *Address:* 202 Roxborough Drive, Toronto, Ontario, Canada M4W 1X8.

HERNON, Rosalie, b. Sarawak, Malaysia. Managing Director. m. Patrick Kieran Hernon, 2 Sept. 1950, 1 daughter. *Education:* Diplomas in Business Administration, Cosmetic Chemistry, Soins esthetiques, Singapore, Paris, Germany, England. *Appointments:* Chairman, Managing Director, Phoenix House of Beauty Pte. Limited; Principal and Sole-Proprietress, Salon Phoenix, Academy of Beauty Culture. *Memberships:* Hon.

Secretary, Chinese YWCA, 1960; Hon. Secretary, Chinese Ladies Association, 1956; Council member, Chinese Women Association; President 1978-79, Inner Wheel Club of Singapore; Chairman, Women Associations Section, Singapore Council of Social Service. *Publications:* Articles on: Beauty; Home Decoration; Poise, Charm and Social Etiquette, in Her World magazine. *Honours:* Paul Harris Fellows award by Rotary Club International, 1981. *Hobbies:* Social work; Golf; Boating; Gardening; Reading. *Address:* 7L Newton Heights, Singapore 1130.

HERRNDORF, Peter A, b. 27 Oct. 1940, Amsterdam, The Netherlands. Broadcasting Executive. m. Eva Czigler, 7 June 1980. *Education:* BA., University of Manitoba, Canada, 1962; LL.B., Dalhousie University, Canada, 1965; MBA., Harvard University, USA, 1970. *Appointments:* Vice-President, General Manager, English Radio and Television Networks, Canadian Broadcasting Corporation. *Address:* 5 Oaklands Avenue, Toronto, Canada.

HERZBERG, Gerhard, b. 25 Dec. 1904, Hamburg, Germany. Physicist. m. (1) Luise (deceased) 1 son, 1 daughter, (2) Monika Tenthoff, 21 Mar. 1972,1 son, 1 daughter. *Education:* Dr. Ing., Darmstadt Institute of Technology, 1928; Post-doctorate work, Universities of Geottingen and Bristol, 1928-30. *Memberships:* Fellow, President, 1966-67, Royal Society of Canada; Fellow, Royal Society, London; Hon. Foreign member, American Academy of Arts and Sciences; Pontifical Academy of Sciences; Hon. member, Optical Society of America; Hon. Fellow, Royal Society of Chemistry; Foreign Associate, National Academy of Sciences, Washington; Hon. member, Japan Academy and Chemistry Society, Japan. *Publications:* Six books; over 200 scientific papers in fields of Spectroscopy, atomic and molecular structure and astrophysics. *Honours:* Companion, Order of Canada, 1968; Faraday Medal, Chemical Society of London, 1970; Nobel Prize for Chemistry, 1971; Royal Medal, Royal Society of London, 1971. *Hobby:* Music. *Address:* 190 Lakeway Drive, Ottawa, Ontario K1L 5B3, Canada.

HESSING, Perle, b. 12 Dec. 1908, Zaleszczyki, former Austrian province. Artist; Housewife. m. Siegfried Hessing, 1926, 1 son. Migrated to Australia 1950 and Naturalized. *Appointments:* Exhibitions include many solo-shows in Australian Capitals; Portal Gallery, 1974, Hamiltons Gallery, 1980, London, UK; Mix Exhibition Women Writers, Painters, etc. in the Commonwealth, London, 1975; Silver Jubilee: London, Native Painters in 6 Exhibitions at Olympia, Embankment, Kensington Town Hall, University of London, City University, National Theatre; International Natives 1977 at Kasper Gallery Morges, 1979; Eisenmann Gallery, Böblingen, 1978, 79, 80; Work represented in Yad Vashem, Museum for Holocaust Art, Jerusalem; Museum Henri Rousseau, Laval; Museum d'Art Naïf de L'Ile de France, Vicq; State Museum, Prague; Australian National Gallery, Canberra; Inner London Education Authority; Museum d'Art Naïf, Anat. Jakovsky, Nice; Numerous other collections in Australia, USA, Europe. Contributed Leonardo, Paris; Speculum Spinozanum, Routledge, London, UK; mentioned in numerous European, Australian and UK journals and books. *Memberships:* Register of Native Artists, London; Friends Hebrew University, Jerusalem. *Address:* 63 Studdridge Street, London SW6 3SL, England.

HESSING, Siegfried, b. 4 Jan. 1903, Czernowitz, Austria. Jounralist; Writer; Librarian. *Appointments:* Daily paper Czernow, Morgenbl., Ostjüd. Zeitung, etc. w. Czernow, until 1935; Foreign correspondent for Languages; various posts during war and postwar periods; Migrated to Australia and naturalized, 1956; Librarian, Sydney, Australia. *Memberships:* Ver. Spinoza Huis, Hague; Brunner Institute, Hague. *Publications:* Contributor to: World Almanach, Minnesota; Neue Brücke, Paris; Revue Philos, Paris; Judaica Zürich; Giorn. Crit. de Ila Fil. Ital. Rome; Philosophia, Ramat Gan; Spinoza Festschrift (German); Spinoza, 300 Jahre Ewigkeit (German); Mosaic Anthology of Poems (English); Speculum Spinozanum (English). *Honours:* Mentioned: Curley: Spinoza Bibliogr.; Preposiet: Bibliogr. Spinoz. Zeidler Castel: Ost. Lit. Geschichte; A. Rivaud: Hist. de Philos. *Address:* 63 Studdridge Street, London SW6 3SL, England.

HETZEL, Basil Stuart, b. 13 June 1922, London, England. Physician; Scientist. m. Helen M Eyles (deceased), 3 Dec. 1946, 3 sons, 2 daughters. *Education:* MB., BS., 1944, MD, 1949, Adelaide University, Australia; MRACP., 1949; FRACP., 1958; MRCP., 1962; FRCP., 1972; FFCM., 1980. *Appointments:* Resident Medical Officer, Clinical Pathology Registrar, Medical Registrar, Royal Adelaide Hospital, Australia, 1945-49; Clinical Research Officer, Institute of Medical and Veterinary Science, Adelaide, Australia, 1949-51; Research Fellow, Department of Medicine, Cornell-New York Hospital Medical Centre, New York, USA, 1951-54; Research Fellow, Department of Chemical Pathology, St. Thomas's Hospital Medical School, London, UKK, 1954-55; Michell Research Scholar/Reader in Medicine, Michell Professor of Medicine, 1964-68, Adelaide University, Australia; Hon. Physician, Queen Elizabeth Hospital, Adelaide, Australia, 1958-63; Visiting Commonwealth Professor, University of Glasgow, UK, 1972-73; Professor of Social and Preventive Medicine, Monash University, Melbourne, Australia, 1968-75; Chief of Division of Human Nutrition, CSIRO, Adelaide, Australia, 1976-. *Memberships:* Deputy Chairman, Council of the International Epidemiological Association; President, Australian and New Zealand Society for Epidemiology and Research in Community Health, 1973-75; President, Endocrine Society of Australia, 1964-66; President, VIII International Thyroid Congress, Sydney 1980; Fellow, World Academy of Art and Science 1970; International Brain Research Organisation, 1981; Member, National Committee, Menzies Foundation for health, fitness and physical achievement. *Publications:* Life and Health in Australia, 1971; Health and Australian Society, 1974; Better Health for Aborigines?, 1974; The Nutrition of Aborigines, 1978; Basic Health Care for Developing Countries, An epidemiological Perspective, 1978; Endemic Goitre and Endemic Cretinism, 1980; Fetal Brain Disorders, Recent approaches to the problem of mental deficiency, 1981. *Honours:* Susman Prize for Medical Research, 1964. *Hobbies:* Music; History; Golf. *Address:* Flat 8, 12 Barnard Street, North Adelaide, South Australia 5006.

HEW, Choy Sin, b. 8 Nov. 1937, Malaysia. Senior Lecturer. m. 26 Feb. 1971, 2 daughters. *Education:* BSc., Nanyang University, Singapore, 1960; MSc., 1965, PhD., 1967, Queen's University, Canada; Postdoctoral Fellow, Brandeis University, USA, 1968-69; Fellow, Linnean Society, London, UK, 1977. *Appointments:* Graduate Assistant, 1960-62, Lecturer, 1969, Senior Lecturer, 1975, Biology Department, Nanyang University, Singapre; Demonstrator in Bilogy, 1962-63, Demonstrator in Botany, 1963-64, Demonstrator in Plant Physiology, 1964-65, Biology Department, Queen's University, Canada. *Memberships:* Honorary Technical Advisor, Nanyang Orchid Society, Singapore; American Society of Plant Physiologists; American Orchid Society; International Horticultural Society. *Publications:* Many publications in International Journals including: Hormonal control of translocation of photosynthetically assimilated 14 C in young soybean plants (with C D Nelson and G Krotkov), 1967; Determination of the rate of CO2 evolution by green leaves in light (with G Krotkov and D T Canvin), 1969; Photosynthetic carbon metabolism of isolated corn chloroplasts (with d o'Neal, E Latzko and M Gibbs), 1972; Do orchid leaves photorespire? (with S C Wong), 1975; Rhythmic production of CO2 by tropical orchid flowers (with Y C Thio, S Y Wong, T Y Chin), 1978; Photosynthesis of young orchid seedlings (co-author); 1980; Conference papers include: Effect of light on the nature of respiratory substrate in green leaves of higher plants (with J Ludwig, I Poskuta and G Krotkov), 1968; Patterns of CO2 fixation in tropical orchids, 1976; Evaluation of certain characteristics in 15 varieties of winged bean (with Y H Lee), 1979; Observations on growth and performance of different winged bean varieties (with Y H Lee), 1980; Contributions to Local Journals include: Herbicidal effect of simazine and atrazine on several common weeds species in Singapore (with C E Lee and Y H Lee), 1972; Polyphenol oxidase in orchid flowers (with T N Tan), 1973; Photosynthesis in certain tropical plant, 1975; Proceedings of Symposium on our Environment, 1977; Facts and Figures of the Singapore Environment, 1978; Proceedings of 2nd Symposium on our Environment, 1980. *Honours:* Rotary Club Fellowship, 1957-58; Lee Foundation Scholarship, 1958-59; 1st in Graduating Class, Nanyang University, 1960; Queen's University Resident Fellowship, 1962-64, Research Assistantship, 1965-67; Brandeis University Post-doctoral Fellowship, 1968-69; Australian-Asian Universities Co-operative Scheme Fellowship, 1973;

German Academic Exchange Services Fellowship, 1975. *Hobbies:* Badminton, Tennis; Swimming; Orchid growing. *Address:* 57A Nanyang Crescent, Singapore 2263.

HEYER, John Whitefoord, b. 14 Sept. 1916, Devenport, Tasmania, Australia. Managing Director; Film Director. m. Dorothy Agnes Janet Greenhalgh, 18 Nov. 1942, 1 son, 2 daughters. *Education:* Scotch College, Melbourne, Australia. *Appointments:* Sound Engineer, Efftee Productions, Melbourne, Australia, 1934-36; Cameraman, Zane Grey Corporation, Los Angeles, USA, 1936-37; Director, Australian Documentary Films, 1938-39; Producer, Allied Works Council; Film Advisor, Prime Minister's Committee; Member, Film Committee, Services Education Council; Director Ealing Studios, 1940-45; Producer, Australian National Film Board, 1945-48; Shell Film Unit, 1948-56; UNESCO and Shell International Petroleum, London, 1956-57; Film Consultant, Rank Organisation, 1967-69. *Memberships:* President, Federation of Film Societies, Sydney, 1944-56; Vice-President, Scientific Film Association, Sydney, 1950-56; President, Sydney Film Society, 1944-54; NSW Government Film Council, 1947-56. *Creative Works:* Numerous Films including: The Back of Beyond, 1954; The Forerunner, 1957; Tumut Pond, 1962; Dream Sound, 1958; The Duel, 1960; Life New, 1963. *Honours:* First British Film Director to win Venice Grande Prise Assoluto, 1954; OBE, 1970; Produced four of six films when Britain won the Coupe de Venice for first time, 1964. *Hobbies:* Pre-cinema. *Address:* 3 Ulva Road, London, SW15 6AP, England.

HEYMANSON (Sir) Randal, b. 18 Apr. 1903, Melbourne, Australia. Journalist. *Education:* MA., BA., University of Melbourne, Australia; Postgraduate work under Professor A J Toynbee, University of London, UK. *Appointments:* European Correspondent, 1928-40, Editor, New York, 1940-69, Australian Newspapers Service; Editor and Publisher, Vital News; Chairman, Political and Economic Research Committee; Participated in pioneering aviation flights including first experimental flight London to Australia. *Memberships:* Vice President, 1948-65, President, 1965-66, Chairman of Board, 1967-, American Australian Association; President, 1946-47, Australian Society of New York; President, 1943, Foreign Press Association, New York; White House Correspondents Association; National Press Club, Washington. *Publications:* Various historical books and contributor to numerous papers and journals. *Honours:* Wyselaskie Scholarship Economics, University of Melbourne, 1924; Dwight Prizeman History, 1924; OBE., 1953; CBE., 1965; Kt., 1972. *Hobbies:* Travel; Art; Bibliomania. *Address:* 7 Mitchell Place, New Yorks 10017, USA.

HIBBERD, (Sir), Donald James, b. 26 June 1916, Sydney, Australia. Company Director. m. Florence Alice Macandie, 4 Apr. 1942, 1 son, 1 daughter. *Education:* Bachelor of Economics, University of Sydney, Australia. *Appointments:* Commonwealth Department of Trade and Customs, 1939-46; Executive Assistant, Commonwealth Treasury, 1946-53; Director, Commonwealth Oil Refinery Limited, 1949-51; Member, Australian Aluminium Production Commission, 1953-57; First Assistant Secretary, Banking, Trade and Industry Branch, Australian Treasury, 1953-57; Executive Director, Commonwealth Aluminium Corporation Pty. Limited, 1957-61; Managing Director, 1961-69, Chairman, 1969-80, Chief Executive, 1969-78, Comalco Limited; Chairman NZ Aluminium Smelters Ltd., 1969-80; Vice Chairman, Queensland Alumina Ltd., 1964-80; President, Australian Mining Industry Council, 1972-73. Director Conzinc Riotinto of Australia Limited, (previously Consolidated Zinc Pty. Limited), Melbourne, Australia, 1962-71; Member, Board of Reserve Bank of Australia, 1966-; Chairman, Munich Reinsurance Australia Limited, 1970-; Member, Melbourne University Council, 1968-; Committee of Management, Royal Victorian Eye and Ear Hospital, Australia, 1958-. *Memberships:* Athenaeum Club; Commonwealth Club; Royal Melbourne Golf Club; Frankston Golf Club. *Honours:* OBE, 1956; Knight Bachelor, 1977. *Hobbies:* Reading; Golf; Gardening. *Address:* 193 Domain Road, South Yarra, Victoria 3141, Australia.

HICKINBOTHAM, Alan David, b. 9 Dec. 1925, Geelong, Victoria, Australia. Chairman and Managing Director, Hickinbotham Group of Comapnies. m. 19 Dec.

1953, 3 sons, 2 daughters. *Education:* BSc., University of Adelaide, Australia, 1948; Associate Commonwealth Institute of Valuers, 1955. *Appointments:* Teacher, Geelong Grammar School, Australia, 1949-51; Horticulture and Real Estate, Mildura and Adelaide, Australia, 1952-59; Chairman: Adelaide, 1954-, Brisbane, 1980-, Hickinbotham Homes; Viticulture, Horticulture and Wine, Clarendon, Australia, 1970-. *Memberships:* Board member, S A Museum, 1980-; Council,1980-, Chairman, 1980-, Civic Trust of S.A; Board of Management, 1968-70, S A National Football League; President, 1965-, South Adelaide Football Club; Council, 1980-, S A Art Gallery Foundation. *Publications:* Engineered Housing - 1954-1979; various articles on Housing, Planning, Development. *Honours:* Interstate Football, S.A., 1946-48; Geelong VFL, 1949-51; District Cricket Footscray (Victoria) and East Torrens (Adelaide). *Hobbies:* Wine; Food; Art; Football; Golf; Tennis. *Address:* 8 Victoria Avenue, Unley Park, South Australia.

HICKMAN, Vernon Victor, b. 28 Aug. 1894, Hobart, Tasmania, Australia. Retired Professor of Zoology. m. Elvie Frances Eddy, 10 Apr. 1920, 2 sons, 1 daughter. *Education:* University of Tasmania, 1912-14; B.Sc., 1915, B.A., 1927, D.Sc., 1937. *Appointments:* Demonstrator in Biology, 1915; Lecturer in Chemistry, Mineralogy, Zeehan School of Mines and Metallurgy, 1915; Head of Chemistry Department, Launceston Technical College, 1920; Ralston Lecturer in charge of Biology, University of Tasmania, 1932; Ralston Professor of Biology, 1943. *Memberships:* Royal Society of Tasmania, 1915, Elected to the Council, 1932-37, Vice-President, 1944-45; Corresponding Member of the Zoological Society of London, 1934; The Entomological Society of Australia, New South Wales. *Publications:* Author of about 50 Technical Papers in various branches of Invertebrate Zoology. *Honours:* Medal of The Royal Society of Tasmania, 1940; Medal of The Royal Physiographical Society in Lund, Sweden, commemorating A.J. Retzius, 1951; Clive Lord Memorial Medal of The Royal Society of Tasmania, 1960; Appointed Officer of the Most Excellent Order of the British Empire, 1979. *Hobbies:* Chess; Gardening. *Address:* 69 Cross Street, New Town, Tasmania, Australia 7008.

HICKS, (Hon) Henry Davies, b. 5 March, 1915, Bridgetown, Nova Scotia. Politician. m. (1) Paulene Agnes, 28 Dec. 1945, (dec. 1964), 2 sons 2 daughters, (2) Margaret Gene MacGregor, 15 April, 1965. *Education:* Mount Allison University; Dalhousie University; Oxford University; Rhodes Scholar 1937. *Appointments:* Teacher, Annapolis County, 1932-33; Served RCA rank of Captain in Canada, United States of America, United Kingdom, Belgium, Holland, Germany; Regent Mount Allison University, 1948-69; First elected N.S. Legis. g.e., 1945; Re-elected g.e. 1949, 1953, 1956; Minister of Education, 1949-55; Provincial Secretary, 1954-56; Leader Liberal Party of Nova Scotia, 1954-61; Chairman, Nova Scotia Power Commission, 1954-56, Nova Scotia Liquor Commission, 1955; Leader of Opposition, 1956-60; Dean Faculty Arts and Science, Dalhousie University, 1960; Vice President, 1961, President and Vice Chancelor, Dalhousie University, 1963-80; President Canadian Commission to Unesco, 1964-66, Canadian Bible Society, 1965-68; Chairman, Association of Atlantic Universities, 1968-72; Representative Associate of University and College of Canada, University of Guyana, 1970-75; Summoned to Senate, 1972. *Memberships:* Halifax Saraguay and Aesculapius Fishing Association. *Honours:* Invested Companion, Order of Canada, 1970. Leader Canadian Delegate to General Conference of Unesco in Paris, 1964, 1966; Canadian Delegate to the 28th General Assembly of the United Nations, 1973. *Address:* 6446 Coburg Road, Halifax, Nova Scotia B3H 2A7, Canada.

HICKS, Robert, b. 18 Jan 1938, Hurrabridge, Devon, England. Member of Parliament. m. Maria Elizabeth Gwyther, 2 March 1962, 2 daughters. *Education:* B.Sc. (Hons) Geography, University College, London, 1957-60; Post Graduate Certificate in Education, University of Exeter, 1960-61. *Appointments:* Lecturer in Regional Geography, Weston-Super-Technical College, 1970; Member of Parliament for Bodmin, 1970-. *Memberships:* Assistant Government Whip, 1973-74; Vice-Chairman, Cons. Parl. Committee for Agriculture, 1971;73, 1974; Select Committee on European Legislation, 1973, 1975-; Vice-Chairman, Cons. Parl. Committee for European Affairs, 1979-80; Chairman,

Westcountry Cons. M.P's, 1976-78. *Hobbies:* Cricket; Golf; Gardening. *Address:* Little Court, St. Ive, Liskeard, Cornwall.

HIDAYATULLAH, M, b. 17 Dec. 1905, Betul, Madhya Pradesh. Lecturer, Vice-President of India. m. Pushpa Sha, 5 May 1948, 1 son. *Education:* Phillips Scholar, Malak Gold Medal, B,A. Morris College, Nagpur; M.A. Nagpur University; M.A., Trinity College, Cambridge; Barrister-at-Law, Lincoln's Inn. *Appointments:* Lecturer, University College of Law, Nagpur University, 1935-43; Advocate, Nagpur High Court, 1930-46; Government Pleader 1942-43; Advocate General, Central Provinces Berar, 1943-46; Puisne Judge, 1946-54; Chief Justice, Nagpur High Court, 1954-56; Chief Justice, Madhya Pradesh High Court, 1956-58; Puisne Judge, Supreme Court of India, 1958-68; Chief Justice of India, 1968-70; Acting President of India, 1969; Elected Vice-President of India, 1979-. *Memberships:* Dean, Faculty of Law, Nagpur University, 1950-54; Faculty of Law, Sagar, Vikram, Aligarh Universities, 1954-58; Chancellor, Muslim National University, New Delhi, 1970-; Pro-Chancellor, Delhi University 1968-70; Chancellor Universities of Delhi, Panjab, Jamia Millia Islamia, 1979; President, Indian Law Institute, 1968-70; President, International Law Association, Indian Branch, 1968-70; Internation Institute of Space Law, Paris, 1966-; International Council of Former Scouts and Guides; Executive Council of World Assembly of Judges Advisory Council for World Peace through Law. *Publications:* Democracy in India and the Judicial Process 1966; The South-West Africa Case, 1967; Judicial Methods, 1969; A Judge's Miscellany, 1972; My Own Boswell (Memoirs) 1980. *Honours:* Hon. Bencher Lincoln's Inn, 1967; LL.D. (Honoris Cause), University of Philippines, 1970, Ravishankar University, 1980, Rajasthan University, 1976, Banaras Hindu University, 1980; Order of the British Empire 1946; Order of Jugoslav Flag with Sash, 1970; Medallion and Plaque of Merit Philconsa, Manila 1970; Kt. of Mark Twain, 1971. *Hobbies:* Golf; Bridge. *Address:* Vice-President's Residence, 10 -janpath, New Delhi, India.

HIELSCHER, Leo Arthur, b. 1 Oct. 1926, Eumundi, Queensland, Australia. Accountant. m. Mary Ellen, 22 May 1948, 1 son, 1 daughter. *Education:* Bachelor of Commerce, Australian Society of Accountants; Associate Accountancy University of Queensland. *Appointments:* Auditor-General's Department, Queensland Government; Accountant, Department of Education, Queensland Government; Assistant Under Secretary, Treasury Department, Queensland; Deputy under Treasurer, Treasury Department, Queensland; Government Under Treasurer, Treasury Department, Queensland Government. *Memberships:* Royal Institute of Public Administration, Queensland Division. *Honours:* Eisenhower Fellow for Australia, 1973. *Hobbies:* Fishing; Golf; Boating. *Address:* 16 Auckland Street, Wishart, Q1. 4071. Australia.

HIGGINS, Huntly Gordon, b. 8 Jan. 1917, Perth, Western Australia. m. Irena Taube, 8 Jan. 1941, 2 sons, 1 daughter. *Education:* B.S.c., 1935-37, B.S.c., hons., 1939, University of Western Australia; Doctor of Applied Science, University of Melbourne, 1962. *Appointments:* Geologist, New Guinea, Western Australia; 1938-40; Lecturer, Kalgoorlie School of Mines; Meteorological Officer, Royal Australian Air Force, 1941-45; Research Scientist in CSIRO Divisions of Forest Products and Chemical Technology, 1945-78; Chief, Division of Chemical Technology, 1979. *Memberships:* Fellow, Australian Academy of Technological Sciences; Fellow, Institute of Physics and Australian Institute of Physics; Fellow, International Academy of Wood Science; Fellow, Royal Australian Chemical Institute; Past President, Appita, International Association of Scientific Papermakers. *Publications:* 110 publications in Scientific Journals. *Honours:* Hackett Scholarship, 1939; Benjamin Medal, 1977. *Hobbies:* Golf; Bridge; Chess. *Address:* 59 Fellows Street, Kew, Victoria 3101, Australia.

HIGGINS, Irving John, b. 3 July 1944, Birmingham, England. Biotechnologist. m. 31 Dec. 1966, 2 sons, 1 daughter. *Education:* B.Sc. Ph.D., Biochemistry, University of Liverpool, 1965-68. *Appointments:* ICI Postdoctoral Fellow, University of Sheffield, 1968-70; Visiting Investigator, Howard Hughes Medical Institute, Miami, United States of America, 1970-71 Lecturer, Biological Laboratory, University of Kent, 1971-78;

Senior Lecturer, Canterbury, Kent, 1978-81; Leverhulme Professor, Director, Biotechnology Unit, Cranfield Institute of Technology, 1981-. *Memberships:* Biochemical Society, London; General Microbiology Society, London; American Society for Microbiology. *Publications:* The Chemistry and Microbiology of Pollution, 1975; Author of several reviews, book chapters; Over 60 papers. *Honours:* BP Energy Prize Award, 1980. *Hobbies:* Gardening; Sailing. *Address:* White Gate, The Street, Staple, Kent, England.

HIGGINSON, James Henry, b. 2 March 1911, Hull, United Kingdom. Educator. *Education:* Hons. England, 1932; Dip., 1933; MEd., 1945; MA, 1939; PhD, 1956; *Appointments:* Senior Lecturer, Education and Warden of Sadler Hall, University of Leeds, 1948-59; Headmaster, County High School, 1959-64; Head Education Studies, Christ Church College, Canterbury, 1964-76; Retired 1976; Part Time University Lecturing and examining. *Memberships:* Alumnus of the American Seminar of Salzburg. *Publications:* Changing Thought in Primary and Secondary Education, 2nd edition, 1972; Contributed to volume of Poems celebrating Silver Jubilee of HM Queen Elizabeth II, 1977; Canterbury Chapters; A Kentish Heritage for Tomorrow, 1977; Entwicklungslinien der Bidungspolitik in England 1945-80; Political or Educational Advance through Secondary Reorganisation? 1981; Numerous articles on work of Sir Michael Sadler to profl. journals and Societies; Selections from Michael Sadler, Studies in World Citzenship, 1979. *Honours:* Médaille de la Reconnaissance Francaise, French Embassy; British Academy award for anthology of Sir Michael Sadler's writings; Felicia Hemans Prize, University of Liverpool. *Hobbies:* Music; Entertaining Friends; Music. *Address:* 'Oastfield', 12 St. Lawrence Forstal, Canterbury, Kent CTI 3PA, England.

HIGGS, Peter Tyson, b. 9 Dec 1944, Miami, Florida, USA. Attorney-at-Law. m Colette Pamela Fletcher 17 August, 1974, 1 son. *Education:* St. Andrews School, Nassau, Bahamas; Cheltenham College, Glostershire, England; Inns of Court Law School, London, England, Barrister-at-Law, Inner Temple, Nov 1967; Attorney-at-Law, Nassau, March 1969; *Appointments:* Clifford-Turner & Co, Solicitors, London, England, 1968; Higgs & Johnson, Consel and Attorney-at-Law, Nassau, Bahamas, 1969-; Partner 1972-; *Memberships:* Royal Nassau Sailing Club; Bahamas Squash Raquets Association Past President; Caribbean Area Squash Raquets Association, Past president (founding); *Hobbies:* Aquatics; Squash; Running; Flying; Sailing; *Address:* Eastlea, E. Bay Street, Nassau, N.P. Bahamas.

HIGGS, Robin James Edgar Dawes, b. 21 May 1943, Aylesbury, England. Orthopaedic Surgeon. m. Judith Mary Higgs, 25 Feb. 1967, 2 sons, 2 daughters. *Education:* M.B.,B.S., St. Bartholomews Hospital Medical School, London University, 1962-67; F.R.C.S., Edinburgh Royal College of Surgeons, 1973; F.R.A.C.S., Royal Australasian College of Surgeons, 1977. *Appointments:* include: Orthopaedic House Surgeon, St. Bartholomews Hospital, London, 1967-68; Senior House Officer, General Surgery, Military Hospital, Hong Kong, 1971; Officer Parachute Field Surgical Team, 1973-74; Retired Rank of Major, 1974; Specialist in Surgery, Cambridge Military Hospital, Aldershot, United Kingdom, 1973-74; Registrar Orthopaedic Surgery, Repatriation General Hospital, Concord, Sydney Hornsby Hospital, Sydney, Margaret Reid Children's Orthopaedic Hospital, Sydney, Prince of Wales Hospital, Sydney, 1975-77; Specialist in Orthopaedic Surgery, Concord Hospital, Sydney, Margaret Reid Children's Orthopaedic Hospital, Joint Services Medical Centre, Canberra, 1977-. *Memberships:* Australian Orthopaedic Association, 1979; Aviation Medical Society of Australia and New Zealand, 1977; Medico Legal Society of New South Wales, 1977; Aviation Law Association of Australia, 1981; Australian Sports Medicine Federation; Royal Australasian College of Surgeons Road Trauma; Chairman, First Aid Advisory Committee. *Publications:* Numerous Scientific Papers including: Caliper Fixation for Fracture Dislocation of the Pelvis with wide Diastasis at the Symphysis Pubis; The Future of Ceramic Materials for use as Orthopaedic Endprostheses; The Experimental Evaluation into the Potential of Silicon Nitride Ceramic for use as Permanently Implantable Orthopaedic Prostheses; Congenetal Carpal Coalition; The Mallet Finger; Total Hip Replacement Using the Autophor Ceramic Prosthesis

with Cement Free Fixtation; Your Child Dead or Crippled by 1990?- Australian Roadwar Continues over the Continent, 1980. *Honours:* Marshall Webb Prize for Medicine, Royal Army Medical College, London, 1968; Tow Prize for Surgery, University of New South Wales, 1977; Duke of Edinburgh Award, 1960. *Hobbies:* Military History; Painting and cartooning; Cricket; Photography; Jogging; Gardening. *Address:* 10 Olsson Close, Hornsby Heights, New South Wales, Australia 2077.

HIGHET, David Allan, b. 1913, Dunedin, New Zealand. Minister of Internal Affairs, Minister of Local Government, Minister of Recreation and Sport, Minister of Civil Defence, Minister for the Arts. m. Shona MacFarlane. *Education:* University of Otago. *Appointments:* Accountant, Public Accountants, New Plymouth; Private Practice, Wellington; General Manager, L.J. Fisher and Company Limited, Auckland, 1960-62; Senior Partner, Cox, Eliffe, Twomey, Highet and Company, Chartered Accountants, Auckland; Fellow Chartered Accountant of The New Zealand Society of Accountants, 1972; Elected to Parliament as Member for Remuera, 1966, 1969, 1972, 1975, 1978; Chairmanship of The Social Services Committee; Membership of The Local Bills, Public Expenditure, Foreign Affairs, Commerce Select Committees; Minister of Internal Affiars, Local Government and Civil Defence, 1972; Associate Minister of Social Welfare; Appointed Minister of Internal Affairs, Local Government, Recreation and Sport, Civil Defence and Minister for the Arts, 1978-. *Memberships:* Chairman, The Public Relations and Cultural Committee, Wellington City Council, 1954-59; Former Executive Director, Auckland City Development Association; Foundation Member, The Queen Elizabeth II Arts Council, Chairman, Drama Committee; Served on the Councils of Auckland and Wellington Chambers of Commerce; Chairman of the First Festival of Wellington and The Auckland Festival Soceity; Past President of Wellington Jaycees and on the National Executive of Jaycees, 1953. *Address:* 28 Burwood Crescent, Remuera, Auckland, New Zealand.

HIGO, Aigboje, b. 22 June 1932, Otuo, Bendel State, Nigeria. Book Publisher. m. 5 Jan. 1932, 3 sons, 1 daughter. *Education:* University of Ibadan, Ibadan, 1956-59; B.A.Hons, London; M.A.,Dip.E.S., University of Leeds. *Appointments:* Head of English Department, St. Andrews College, Oyo, 1959-63; Principal, Anglican Grammar School, Otuo, Bendel State, 1964; Chief Executive, Heinemann Educational Books, Nigeria Limited, Ibadan, 1965-. *Memberships:* Mbari Artists and Writers Club, Ibadan. *Publications:* Occasional Poems in various Magazines and Anthologies. *Honours:* Professor, Mahood Poetry Prize, University of Ibadan, 1958. *Hobbies:* Farming; Golf; Music. *Address:* Plot 2, Block VII, Oba Ademola II Street, G.R.A., Ibadan, Nigeria.

HII, Mee Chung, b. 7 July 1951. Education Officer. *Education:* b.sc. Mathematics, 1976; Diploma in Education, 1976; Currently doing LLB, external course, London University. *Appointments:* Operations Researcher Officer, 1977; Education Officer, Education Department, Sarawak, Malaysia, 1977-. *Memberships:* Malaysian Mathematical Society; Jaycee Malaysia. *Publications:* Dropout study of the pupils at Primary School level in Sarawak, 1978-80; Dropout study of the pupils at Secondary School level in Sarawak, 1978-80. *Hobbies:* Basketball; Lawn-Tennis; Swimming; Reading of Philosophy. *Address:* 10 Fortuna Garden, Sarikei, Sarawak, Malaysia.

HII, Wi Sing, Peter, b. 2 July 1949, Sibu, Sarawak, Malaysia. Businessman. m. Elizabeth Ting Chuo Kiew, 17 April 1971, 4 sons. *Education:* Bio-Chemistry course, Australia, 1969; B.Com. Degree, 1976; M.C.om Degree, 1980. *Appointments:* Managing Director, Yung Kong Company, Yung Kong Metal Works, Yung Kong Tin Factory, 1975-; General Manager, Hotel Longhouse, Kuching, 1976-; Director, Secretary, Yung Kong Construction, 19787, Asia Wire Steel Mesh Manufacturers, 1977, Yung Kong Credit Corporation, 1978-. *Memberships:* Fellow, The British Institute of Management; Fellow, Society of Incorporated Accountant and Auditors; The Institute of Marketing; The Institution of Industrial Managers; Vice Chairman, The Kuching Building and Engineering Contractors' Association, 1980-82; Deputy Chairman, The Kuchingfoochow Association Youth Section, 1981-. *Hobby:*

Touring. *Address:* 33, Jalan Min Ching, Off Jalan Foochow No. 1, Kuching, Sarawak, Malaysia.

HILEY, Thomas Alfred (Sir) b. 25 Nov. 1905, Brisbane, Queensland, Australia. Chartered Accountant, Minister of Crown. m. Marjory Joyce Jarrott, 10 Oct. 1929, 2 sons. *Education:* University of Queensland; Institute of Chartered Accountants. *Appointments:* State Public Service; Public Accountancy; Private Accountancy Practice; Queensland Parliament. *Memberships:* Institute of Chartered Accountants, State Chairman, National President, Life Member; State Chairman, Duke of Edinburgh Award; Faculty of Commerce, University of Queensland. *Honours:* Knight Commander British Empire, 1966; Deputy Premier of Queensland, 1964; Treasurer of Queensland, 1957; Life Member of Chartered Institute of Accountants, 1975. *Hobbies:* Cricket; Bowls; Fishing; Shooting. *Address:* 'Illawong', 39 The Esplanade, Tewantin, Queensland, Australia 4565.

HILGENDORF, Charles, b. 23 Oct. 1908, Lincoln, New Zealand. Farmer. m. Rosemary Helen MacKenzie, 1935, 1 son, 1 daughter. *Education:* M.A. LLD., Canterbury University. *Appointments:* Farming, 1934-; Domminian Council, Meat and Wool Section, 1946-61; New Zealand Meat Producers Board, 1961-80; Lincoln College Council, 1949-61; New Zealand University Grants Committee, 1961-74. *Honours:* Nufield Farming Sclolar, 1951; J.P., C.M.G, 1971; Kt., 1981. *Address:* Sherwood 2 R.D., Ashburton, New Zealand.

HILL, David H, b. 27 Nov. 1939, Ottawa, Ontario, Canada. Barrister and Solicitor. m. Mary C. Malmberg, 17 Aug. 1963, 1 son. *Education:* B.A. (Hon) 1962, LL.B., 1965, Queen's University, Kingston; Called to the Bar of Ontario, Osgoode Hall, 1967. *Appointments:* Read Law with Messrs. Gowling, MacTavish, Osborne and Henderson, Ottawa, 1965-66; Law Clerk to the Hon. G.A. Gale, Chief Justice of Ontario, Toronto, 1967-68; Associate, Gowling, MacTavish, Osborne and Henderson, Ottawa, 1968-70; Partner, Perley-Robertson, Panet, Hill and MacDougall, Ottawa, 1971-. *Memberships:* Law Society of Upper Canada; Canadian Bar Association, National Council 1976-80; County of Carleton Law Association; Vice-Chairman, 1978-79, Chairman, 1979-81, Board of Trustees, Ottawa Civic Hospital, 1976-; Vice President, Treasurer and Director, Canadian Cancer Society, Ontario Division, 1979-81. *Publications:* 'Adjustments of Rent by Consumer Price Index', 1976. *Hobby:* Sailing. *Address:* Townhouse 8, 701 Richmond Road, Ottawa, Ontario, K2A OG6

HILL, Douglas John, b. 27 Jan. 1927, Queanbeyan, New South Wales. Australian Public Service-Deputy Auditor-General. m. Stella Claire Fitch, 4 Dec. 1948, 5 sons. *Education:* Bachelor of Commerce, 1954. *Appointments:* Department of the Treasury, 1944-49, Auditor-General's Office, 1950-53, Department of Works, 1953-56, Department of the Treasury, 1956-76, Department of Finance, 1976-80, Auditor-General's Office, 1980-, Australian Public Service. *Memberships:* Fellow of the Australian Society of Accountants; National Council of Australian Society of Accountants, 1977-; President ACT Division of the Society, 1975-76; Australian Institute of Public Administration. *Hobbies:* Gardening; Golf. *Address:* 15 Booth Crescent, Cook, A.C.T., 2614, Australia.

HILL Gordon Barratt, b. 6 Dec. 1916, Claremont, Australia. Consulting Engineer. m. 1 Sept. 1956. *Education:* B.E. University of Western Australia, 1936-40; D.Phil, Oxford University, 1946-49. *Appointments:* Major Raeme, 1940-45; University of Western Australia, 1951-54; Consulting, 1955-. *Memberships:* Leander Club; Weld Club, Perth; Naval Military Air Forces, Perth. *Honours:* Rhodes Scholar, Western Australia, 1940; C.M.G, 1979. *Hobbies:* Sailing; Gardening. *Address:* 8 Bindaring Parade, Claremont, Western Australia 6010.

HILL, John Aislabie, b. 15 Jan. 1915. Mining Engineer. m. Anne Ruth Rayner 16 Nov. 1940, 2 sons, 2 daughters. *Education:* Royal School of Mines, 1933-37; BSc, London 1937; ARSM. *Appointments:* Various Mining Engineering Appointments 1937-39; Roan Antelope Copper Mines Limited 1946-56; Military Service, 1939-45; Underground Manager, 1956, Mine Superintendent 1960, Assistant Manager and Manager, 1964-67; General Manager, RST (Chibuluma), 1967-68; Vice President, 1968-73, Director RST Ma-

nagement Services and Roan Cons. Mines 1971-73; Mining Consultant 1973-74; Director Zambia Engineering Services 1979-. *Memberships:* Fellow, Institution of Mining and Metallurgy; Chartered Engineer. *Hobbies:* Golf; Pottering. *Address:* 3 Colybank, Rosemary Lane, Colyton, Devon, EX13 6LR, England.

HILL, Robert, b. 24 June 1937 Leeds England. Physicist. m. Nancy Hey 18 Dec. 1965, 1 son, 1 daughter. *Education:* BSc(Hon), Imperial College, London 1958; MSc 1963, PhD 1965, Research Assistant, London University. *Appointments:* Reactor Technology Group UKAEA Windscale, 1958-60; Post-Doctoral Fellow, University of Delaware US, 1966-68; Senior Demonstrator, University of Newcastle upon Tyne, 1968-71; Lecturer, 1971-74, Senior Lecturer, 1974-80; Reader in Opto-Electronics 1980-. *Memberships:* Fellow of Institute of Physics; Newcastle upon Tyne Polytechnic; International Solar Energy Society, UK Section. *Publications:* About 60 papers on Solid State Physics and Solar Cells; Over 20 Reports on Solar Cells and Solar Energy. *Hobbies:* Squash; Music; Pottery. *Address:* 49 Devonshire Place, Newcastle upon Tyne, NE2 2NB, England.

HILLERY, Peter Maxwell, b. 8 Feb. 1946, Kyogle, New South Wales, Australia. Educator. m. Marilyn Anne Waugh, 5 March 1971, 2 daughters. *Education:* Land and Engineering Survey Drafting Certificate, Sydney Technical College, 1966; Bachelor of Science Degree, (Physics Major), University of New South Wales, 1980; Master of Applied Science. *Appointments:* Cadet Survey Draftsman, Western Lands Commission, 1963-64; Engineering Assistant, Housing Commission of New South Wales, 1964-67; Drafting and Computing Coordinator, Amalgamated Decca Surveys Pty, Limited, 1968-70; Teacher, Technical College, Sydney Technical College, 1971-. *Memberships:* Australian Institute of Cartographers; Uniting Church in Australia, (1966-78, various Youth Leadership roles); Action for World Development; Northern District Concert Band; Australian Institute of Physics. *Hobbies:* Music; Bushwalking; Canoeing; Camping. *Address:* 31 Isis Street, Wahroonga, New South Wales, Australia 2076.

HILLIER-FRY, William Norman, b. 12 Aug. 1923, Eltham, England. HM Diplomatic Service. m. Elizabeth Adèle Misbah, 16 Nov. 1948, 2 sons, 2 daughters. *Education:* Colfe's School, London SE 1933-41; BA, St Edmund Hall, Oxford, 1941-42 and 1946. *Appointments:* HM Foreign Service 1946-; Consul-General, Hamburg 1974-79; Ambassador, Kabul 1979-80; High Commissioner, Kampala 1980. *Hobbies:* Music; Theatre. *Address:* c/o Foreign and Commonwealth Office, London, SW1A 2AH.

HILLS, Graham John, b. 9 Apr. 1926 Leigh-on-Sea Essex England. University Vice Chancellor. m. (1) Brenda Stubbington 1 Apr. 1950, (2) Mary Jane McNaughton 12 Sept. 1980, 1 son, 3 daughters. *Education:* BSc, Special Chemistry, 1946; PhD, Physical Chemistry 1950; DSc, Electrochemistry, London University 1962. *Appointments:* Lecturer in Physical Chemistry, Imperial College, London, 1949-62; Professor of Physical Chemistry, University of Southampton, 1962-80; Visiting Professor, National Science Foundation Fellow, Case Western Reserve University, Ohio, USA 1968-69; Principal and Vice Chancellor, University of Strathclyde, Glasgow, 1980-. *Memberships:* Fellow, Royal Society of Chemistry; Honorary Secretary, Faraday Division, Royal Society of Chemistry; Athenaeum Club, London; Caledonian Club, London and Edinburgh. *Publications:* Scientific publications in Learned Society Journals; Books: Reference Electrodes; Polarography. *Honours:* Post-Graduate Scholar, London University 1947-49; Bruno-Breyer Medallist 1968. *Hobbies:* Sailing; Hill Walking; European Political History. *Address:* Penthouse Flat, Livingstone Tower, 26 Richmond Street, Glasgow, G1 1XH, Scotland.

HILTON, Annie Winifred, b. 26 July 1919, Tansley, Matlock, Derbyshire England. Housewife. m. Colonel Peter Hilton 8 Jan. 1942, 2 sons. *Education:* Trinity College of Music London; The National Society's Training College of Domestic Science, Berridge House, London; Pitman's Secretarial College. *Appointments:* Teacher of English and History, and Drama, Hillam Yorkshire; Womens Royal Air Force 1941-45; Chairman Board of Directors, James Smith Scotland Nurseries Limited, Tansley Derbyshire 1965-81. *Memberships:* Womens Royal Voluntary Service; St John Ambulance; Royal British Legion Womens Section; British Heart Foundation; Chairman, NSPCC Derby and District Branch and Mid-Derbyshire; Vice-President and Division Commissioner, Derbyshire Girl Guides Association. *Honours:* Officer Sister and Serving Sister, St John Ambulance; Womens Royal Voluntary Service Medal; County Award Girl Guides Association; LTCL Teaching Diploma Trinity College. Hobby: Gardening. *Address:* Alton Manor, Idridgehay, Derbyshire, England.

HILTON, Jack Dennis, b. 31 Dec. 1909, Sydney, Australia. Metal Merchant. m. Jeanne Isabel Scott 20 June 1942, 2 daughters. *Appointments:* Director: Norman Hill and Company Pty Limited 1938-48; British Metal Corporation, Australia, Limited 1948-52; Managing Director: Jack Hilton, Metals Pty. Limited 1952-73; Wooling Enterprises Pty. Ltd. 1973-; Director, CMC Australia Pty. Ltd. 1980-. *Memberships:* The Royal Motor Yacht Club, NSW; Royal Automobile Club, Australia; The American National Club. Hobby: Mineralogy. *Address:* 21 New South Head Road, Vaucluse, NSW, Australia.

HIMATSINGKA, Bhagwati Prasad, b. 18 Sept. 1926, Dumka, Bihar, India. Industrialist. m. Sushil Goenka 1 May 1945 2 sons. *Education:* Graduate, Calcutta University 1946; Advance Management Course, All India Management Association. *Appointments:* Chairman and Managing Director of India Carbon Limited 1961-; Chairman: Assam Carbon Products Limited, Meghalaya Phytochemicals Limited, Amines and Plasticizers Limited; Director of Assam Petro Chemical Limited; Member, North Eastern Regional Committee of Industrial Development Bank of India; Life Member,: Indian Science Congress, The Institution of Internal Auditors, Inc. New York. *Memberships:* Various Government and semi-Government Bodies; Indian Association for Productivity, Quality and Reliability; Bengal Table Tennis Association; National Alliance of Young Entrepreneurs; Indian Chemical Manufacturers Association; Plastics and Linoleum Export Promotion Council; Panel on Carbon and Graphite Products; Indian Cancer Society Assam Branch; Bharatiya Yatri Avas Vikas Samiti; Executive Council of Indo-American Chamber of Commerce; 5th Indo-US Joint Business Council; Gauhati University Court; National Productivity Council; Calcutta Cosmopolitan Club. *Publications:* Have submitted papers to Indian Science Congress on many occasions which have been reproduced in various journals. *Honours:* Secretary, Plastics Productivity Team, 1959, to Italy, USA and Japan. *Hobbies:* Reading; Sports; Travelling; Promotion of small scale industry in backward area. *Address:* 19B Mandeville Garden, Calcutta 700 019, West Bengal, India.

HINCHLIFFE, Timothy Alexander. b. 6 May 1946, Geelong; Victoria, Australia. Barrister-at-Law. *Education:* Bachelor of Laws, Melbourne University 1972; Barrister and Solicitor of Supreme Court of Victoria 1972. *Appointments:* Solicitor 1974; Barrister-at-Law, Victorian Bar, 1975. *Memberships:* Melbourne Cricket Club; Royal Automobile Club of Victoria; Celtic Club; Essoign Club; The Victorian Bar Council; Wyvern Society of Queen's College; Old Geelong Collegians Association. *Hobbies:* Skiing; Rowing; Live Theatre; Football; Cricket; Squash; Art; Politics. *Address:* 237 Wattletree Road, Malvern, Victoria 3144, Australia.

HINDER, Henry Francis Critchley, b. 26 June 1906, Summer Hill, New South Wales, Australia, Artist; m. Margel Ina Harris, 17 May, 1930, 1 daughter; *Education:* Royal Art Society, East Sydney Technical College; Art Institute of Chicago, Master Institute of Roerich Museum, New York; studied under Emil Bisttram and Howard Giles, New York; *Appointments:* Interested in theatre design; worked in camouflage World War II; Teacher Art School East Sydney Technical College, 1946-1958; Head of Art Department, Sydney Teachers' College, 1958-1964; Trustee Art Gallery of New South Wales, 1974-1978; *Memberships:* Contemporary Art Society & Water Color Institute; Planning Committee Sydney College of the Arts, 1974-1977, Former Member Arts Syllabus Committee, New South Wales, Department of Education; Foundation Member and Past President Contemporary Art Society, New South Wales; *Publications:* Contributed to several professional journals; *Creative Works:* Several one-man and group exhibitions; represented at Art Galleries of Western Australia, Victoria, New South Wales, Canberra, Newcastle, Broken Hill & War Museum Canberra; Joint retrospective exhibition with Margel Winder, Newcastle City Art Gallery, 1973, Art Gallery of New South Wales, NSW, Australia, 1980. *Honours:* Numerous awards, including Blake Prize for religious art, 1952; Awarded Coronation Medal, 1953; Honorary Diploma in Art, Alexander Mackie C.A.E.; 1975; Awarded A.M., General Division, Order of Australia; *Hobbies:* Work; Theatre; Music; *Address:* 36 Nelson Street, Gordon, New South Wales, 2072, Australia

HINDER, Marge Ina, b. 4 Jan. 1906, Brooklyn, New York, USA. Sculptor. m. Henry Francis Critchley Hinder, 17 May 1930, 1 daughter. *Education:* Studied Dancing 1920-24; Studied, School of Fine Arts, Buffalo Academy, Albrigh Art Gallery, 1925; Museum of Fine Arts, Boston, 1926-29. *Appointments:* Commercial Sculpture, 1934-39; Manager, Grosvenor Galleries; 1938; Camouflage Section, Department of Home Security, 1939-44; Guide lecturer, Art Gallery of New South Wales 1948-50. *Memberships:* New Douth Wales Travelling Art Scholarship; Travelling Art Scholarship Committee. *Creative Works:* 3rd Prize The Unknown Political Prisoner Competition, 1953; Awarded Contemporary Arts Society Prizes for Sculpture, 1955, 1957; Invitation Design for Anzac House, Sydney, 1959; 1st Prize Civic Park Fountain, NSW, 1961; 1st Prize for Free standing Sculpture, Reserve Bank, Sydney, 1961; Comalco Invitation Award, 1969; Joint Exhibition with Husband at Newcastle City Art Gallery, 1973; 50 year Retrospective Exhibition with Husband, Art Gallery of NSW, Sydney, 1980. *Honours:* The Comalco Invitation Award for Sculpture in Aluminium, Bonython Art Gallery, Sydney, 1969; Contemporary Art Society Sydney, 1946, 1947, 1948, 1955, 1957, 1959; Blake Prize for Religious Art 1961. *Address:* 36 Nelson Street, Gordon, NSW, 2072, Australia.

HINTON OF BANKSIDE, Baron, Christopher, b. 12 May 1901, Tisbury, Wiltshire. Engineer. m. Lillian Boyer, 19 Jan. 1931 (dec.), 1 daughter. *Education:* Engineering Apprenticeship GWR Company Swindon 1917-23; Senior Scholarship, 1st Class Hons. Mech. Sciences Tripos, John Wimbolt Prize, Second Yeats Prize, Trinity College, Cambridge 1923-26. *Appointments:* ICI, Alkali, Northwich 1926-40, Chief Engineer 1931-40; Ministry of Supply 1940-46, Dep. Dir. Gen., Royal Filling Factories 1942-46; Controller Atomic Energy (Production), 1946-54; Board for Engineering and Production, Managing Director, Industrial Group, UKAEA 1954-57; Chairman, Central Electricity Generating Board 1957-64; International Executive Committee of World Energy Conference 1962-68; Deputy Chairman, Elec. Supply Research Council 1965-; Special Adviser, International Bank for Reconstruction and Development 1965-70; Chancellor of Bath University 1966-80; President, CEI 1976-. *Memberships:* President, Fellowship of Engineering 1976-81; CEI; FEng; HON.F. of ICE; IMechE; IEE; IGasE; I.Weld; I.Metals; FiChemE; FRSA; Hon. Member ASME; Foreign Association National Academy of Engineering USA; Corres. Mem. Mexican National Academy of Engineering; European Academy of Arts, Sciences and Humanities. *Publications:* Engineers and Engineering 1970; Heavy Current Electricity Industry in the UK 1979. *Honours:* OM◆1976; KBE 1957; Kt 1951; Numerous Honours and Fellowships in the field of Engineering,; Rumford Medal, Royal Society 1971; Axel Johnsen Prize, 1957; Wilhelm-Exner Medal, 1956; Castner Medal of Society of Chem Indus. 1956; Albert Medal 1957; Melchett Medal, 1957; James Watt International Medal 1973; Kelvin Gold Medal, 1977. *Address:* Tiverton Lodge, Dulwich Common, London SE21 7EW, England.

HITCHCOCK, William Elton, b. 14 Apr. 1924, Adelaide, South Australia. Farmer and Grazier. m. Patricia Joan Patching 27 Mar. 1948, 3 sons, 3 daughters. *Education:* Leaving Certificate, Marist Brothers Agriculture College, Mount Gambier. *Appointments:* Station Master S.A Railways, 10 years; Hotel Keeper, Lock, 25 years; Farmer Grazier Lock 5 years. *Memberships:* Lock: Town Planning Committee; Football Club; Racing Club; Golf Club; Mount Gambier West Football Club; Eyre Peninsular Golf Association; Lock Progress Association; Eyre Peninsula: Local Government Association; Racing Association; Golf Association; Tourist Association; Lock: Show Society; School Committee;

Cricket Club; Swimming Centre; Medical Centre; Bowling Club. *Honours:* King Scouts Badge Mount Gambier 1940; Local Government 10 year Service Certificate 1973. *Hobbies:* Golf; Bowls; Fishing; Reading; Stamp and Coin Collecting. *Address:* Box 56, Lock, South Australia, 5633.

HIZA, Philip Robert, b. 19 Feb. 1938, Amani. Surgeon. m. Eileen Elizabeth 5 July 1965, 2 sons, 5 daughters. *Education:* MB, ChB, Makerere University 1957-64; (Ed), Royal College of Surgeons, Edinburgh 1967-68. *Appointments:* Internship. Muhimbili Hospital Dares Salaam 1964-65; Medical Officer, Ministry of Health 1965-66; Overseas Training, 1967-68; Specialist Surgeon and Regional Medical Officer, 1969-70; Lecturer in Surgery 1971-72; Senior Lecturer, 1973-75; Associate Professor 1976-78; Professor of Surgery 1979-. *Memberships:* Tanzania Medical Association; Association of Surgeons of East Africa. *Publications:* Medical Publications. *Hobbies:* Swimming; Gardening. *Address:* PO Box 65044, Dares Salaam, Tanzania.

HNATIUK, Roger James, b. 12 Apr. 1946, Grande Prairie, Alberta, Canada. Botanist-Ecologist-Biogeographer. m. Sarah Helen Francis 21 Apr. 1972, 1 son, 1 daughter. *Education:* BSc(1st Class Honours) 1968, MSc (Plant Ecology) University of Alberta, 1969; PhD, (Biogeography) Australian National Unitersity 1976. *Appointments:* Director, Senior Staff Scientist, Royal Society Aldabra Research Station 1973-74; Botanist, Western Australian Herbarium 1976-81; Assistant Director, Australian Bureau of Flora and Fauna, 1981-. *Memberships:* Australian Systematic Botany Society; Ecological Society of Australia; British Ecological Society; Ecological Society of America; Asian Ecological Society; Western Australian Naturalists Club. *Creative Works:* Woodcarvings: Wooden Chests-gothic style and modern; Painting; Myxomycetes. *Honours:* First Class Standing Prize, University of Alberta, 1966; Commonwealth Scholarship and Fellowship Award, 1969-72. *Hobbies:* Bonsai; Bushwalking; Woodworking; Music. *Address:* Australian Bureau of Flora and Fauna, Department of Home Affairs and Environment, Canberra, ACT 2614, Australia.

HO, Lawrence Chow Yeong, b. 30 Dec. 1940, Penang, Malaysia. Medical Practitioner. m. Yean 31 May 1975, 1 son. *Education:* MBBS 1965; FRCS (Ed) 1970; FRACS 1974. *Appointments:* Visiting Plastic Surgeon, Repatriation General Hospital Concord, Sydney NSW Australia; Visiting Plastic Surgeon, Balmain Hospital, Balmain, Sydney, NSW Australia. *Memberships:* Australian Society of Plastic and Reconstructive Surgeons; British Association of Plastic Surgeons; Australian Society of Aesthetic Plastic Surgery. *Publications:* Hypospadias: Extensive Deep Neck Burns; Reconstruction of the Mandible and Temporo—Mandibular Joint; Pinch Grafts in the Treatment of Leg Ulcers. *Address:* 22 Yarrannabbe Road, Darling Point, New South Wales, Australia.

HO, Minfong, (Mrs J V Dennis Jr.), b. 7 Jan. 1951, Rangoon, Burma. Writer and Teacher. m. John Value Dennis, Jr, 20 Dec. 1976. *Education:* Chinese Literature and History, (special non-degree program), Tunghai University, Taichung, Taiwan, 1967-69; BA, Major, Economics & Asian Studies, 1969-73, MFA, Major English Literature, Minor, Nutritional Science, 1978-80, Cornell University, Ithaca, New York. *Appointments:* Teacher, Balestier Hill Secondary School, Singapore, 1973-74; Financial Journalist, Straits Times Press, Singapore, 1974-75; Lecturer, English Department, Chiengmai University, Thailand, 1976-78; Teaching Assistant, Goldwin Smith Hall, 1979-80, Full-time Lecturer, Intensive English Program, Department of Modern Languages & Linguistics, Morrill Hall, 1981-, Cornell University, Ithaca, New York; Teacher, English as a second language, Boces Area Education Center, 1981-5 Sing to the Dawn, 1975; The Scholarship, 1978; Several articles in journals and Technical reviews, 1975-81. *Honours:* First Prize, annual contest of the Council of Interracial Books for Children, NY, 1974; Grant from the Council of Creative and Performing Arts, 1978; Nominated for the Overseas Press Club Award, 1981. *Hobbies:* Bicycling; Growing cyclamens and muskmelons. *Address:* 7 Leedon Park, Singapore, 1026, Singapore.

HO, Peng Yoke, b. 4 Apr. 1926, Malaysia. University Professor. m. Mei-Yiu Fung, 18 June 1955. *Education:*

BSc, 1950; MSc, 1951; PhD, 1959; DSc, 1969; Fellow of the Institute of Physics; Fellow of the Australian Academy of Humanities. *Appointments:* Assistant Lecturer in Physics, 1951-54, Lecturer in Physics, 1954-60, Professor of Chinese Studies, 1964-73, Dean of Arts, 1967-68, University of Malaya; Reader in History of Science, University of Singapore, 1960-64; Foundation Professor, 1973-, Chairman, 1973-78, School of Modern Asian Studies, Griffith University, Brisbane, Australia; Professor of Chinese, University of Hong Kong, 1981-84. *Memberships:* Australia Japan Society; Chinese Club of Queensland; University of Queensland Club. *Publications:* The Astronomical Chapters of the Chin Shu, 1966; Modern Scholarship on the History of Chinese Astronomy, 1977; Science and Civilisation in China (with Joseph Needham), vol. 5 pt. 3, 1976, pt. 4, 1980, pt. 1 (in press); The Birth of Modern Science in China, 1967; The Dating of Taoist Alchemocal Texts, 1979; Numerous Articles in learned journals. *Honours:* Shell Research Fellow, 1951; Carnegie Corporation of New York Grantee, 1965; Edward Hume Lecturer for 1979; Asian Fellow, 1972; Honorary Professor, University of Hong Kong. *Hobbies:* Table Tennis; Tennis; Chess. *Hobbies:* 8 Holdway Street, Kenmore, Queensland, Australia.

HOARE, Michael Edward, b. 10 Mar. 1941, Isle of Ely, England. Historian and Curator. m. Margaret Brown, 31 Aug. 1963, 1 son, 1 daughter. *Education:* BA, University of Hull, 1963; MA, Monash, Melbourne, 1967; PhD, ANU, Canberra, 1974; Diploma New Zealand Council Recreation and Sport, 1980; DipEd, Massey, New Zealand, 1981. *Appointments:* Secondary Teacher, Kingston-upon-Hull Education Authority, 1963-64; Senior Teaching Fellow in German, Monash University, 1964-66; Research Associate and Fellow, Australian Academy of Science and Australian National University, 1966-74; James Cook Fellow, Royal Society of New Zealand, 1975-78; Head of Manuscripts Section, Alexander Turnbull Library, 1978-. *Memberships:* include: Fellow of Linnean Society; President, Archives and Records Association of New Zealand; Australian Society of Authors; Society for Bibliography of Natural History; President of Boys Brigade, Wellington Battalion, 1978-80. *Publications:* Author of several books including: The Tactless Philosopher: J R Forster, 1976; Boys, Urchins, Men: A History of the Boys Brigade in Australia, Papua New Guinea, 1980; The Resolution Journals of J R Forster, 1972-75, 1982. *Honours:* University Prize, Hull, 1963; Humboldt Fellowship, 1970-71; Fellow of Linnean Society, 1976; Canadian Commonwealth Fellow, 1978; Cook Fellowship, 1975-78. *Hobbies:* Reading; Writing; Youth work. *Address:* 58 Beauchamp St, Linden, Wellington, New Zealand.

HOBDEN, Reginald Herbert, b. 9 Nov. 1919, London. Diplomat (Retired). m. Gwendoline Ilma Vowles 23 Jan. 1945, 2 sons, 1 daughter. *Education:* Sir William Borlase's School, Marlow 1931-36. *Appointments:* Colonial Office, London 1936-64; RAFVR, Squadron Leader 1940-46; Seconded to Department of Technical Cooperation, London 1961-62; UK Commission, Malta 1962-64; HM Diplomatic Service 1964-78; Counsellor, Dar es Salaam 1968-69; Councellor, Islamabad 1970-75; High Commissioner to Lesotho 1976-78; Officer of House of Commons 1978-. *Memberships:* Royal Commonwealth Society. *Honours:* Distinguished Flying Cross 1944; Mentioned in despatches 1942. *Hobbies:* Bridge; Chess. *Address:* 14 Belmont Close, Uxbridge, Middlesex, England.

HOCHSTADT, Peggy Wai-Chee (Mrs), b. 14 Nov. 1935, Singapore. Librarian. m. Herman Ronald Hochstadt, 1 son, 1 daughter. *Education:* BA, BA (Hons, Philosophy), 1959, University of Malaya; MA (Lib. Sc.), University of Chicago, 1966; Dip.Ed., University of Singapore, 1969. *Appointments:* Library Assistant, 960-65; Senior Assistant Librarian, 1968; Deputy Librarian, 1972; Librarian, 1973-80; Chief Librarian, 1980-. Board, 1978, Executive Committee, 1978-, Research Fund Committee, 1980-, National Book Development Council of Singapore; Vice-President, Library Association of Singapore, 1972-74; Standing Committee on Bibliographical and Library Cooperation, 1978-; Ad Hoc Advisory Committee on National Information System (NATIS) for Singapore, 1980-; National Archives and Records Centre National Coordinating Committee, 1980. *Publications:* Editor, University Library Buildings in Southeast Asia, 1976; papers: The Provision of library resources relevant to Commonwealth Studies at the University of Singapore, 1980; Centralised/decentralised university services in Southeast Asia, 1980. *Honours:* Beta Phi Mu (International Library Science Honour Society), 1972. *Address:* 44 Sunset View, Singapore 2159, Republic of Singapore.

HODGE, Nancy Lorraine (Mrs), b. 12 Apr. 1915, North Adelaide. Teacher. m. Henry Leonard Hodge, 1 Mar. 1939, 2 sons. *Education:* Fine, Applied and Graphic Arts, South Australia School of Arts, 1927-38. *Appointments:* Art Teacher, South Australian Education Department, 1958-63; Teaching privately and in Private Schools before and since; Judge—Painting Section—Yankalilla, Rapid Bay, Myponga Agricultural & Horticultural Society, 1977, 1978. *Memberships:* Royal South Australia Society of Arts; Adelaide Arts Society Incorporated; Vice-President, Southern Districts Art Society. *Publications:* Exhibitions of own Works: Swan Hill, Victoria, 1977; Strathalbyn, 1978, 79; Victor Harbor, 1978, 79; Encounter Bay, 1980, Southern Australia. Exhibited in Group Displays: Maitland, Hahndorf, Birdwood, Port Elliot, Encounter Bay, Victor Bay, Barossa Valley, Adelaide, Lobethal Strathalbyn, Southern Australia. Numerous honours: Awards for Applied Art Suede Mats; all Australian Exhibition, 1930; South Australian Chamber of Manufacturers Incorporated; Gold Pass for Clay Modelling Competition; Bronze Medal for Handmade Pottery; Royal Adelaide Exhibition, 1957; 1st Prize Australian Wildflowers, Southern Agricultural Art Competition, 1974; 1st Prize, Art Any Subject, Murray Bridge Agricultural Society, 1975; 1st Prize, Transparent Water Colour, Sunshine Valley Art Award, 1978. *Hobbies:* Painting; Studying Wildflowers; Historical Research. *Address:* 108 Franklin Parade, Encounter Bay, Victor Harbor 5211, South Australia.

HODGES, Anthony Whitehead, b. 6 June 1933, Isleworth, Middlesex. Vice-Principal. m. Mary Gwangwadza (2nd Marriage), 27 Sept. 1968, 7 sons, 4 daughters. *Education:* Diploma, Aeronautical Engineering, 1953, Accountancy, 1955, Personnel Management, 1965; BA, 1960; BA (Education), 1969; MA (History), 1979. *Appointments:* Flight Engineer; Secondary School Teacher Training; Training Officer (Motor Industry); Vice-Principal, Teacher Training Colleges and Evelyn Home College, Lusaka, Gambia. *Memberships:* Chairman, Zambia Technical Education Association; General Secretary, Central Africa Party. *Publications:* Numerous papers on Educational topics specialising in those affecting third world countries. *Honours:* Scholarship Royal Aeronautical Society, 1948. *Hobbies:* Flying; Playing Organ and Piano. *Address:* Farm 34A, Gt. East Road, Chongwe, Lusaka, Zambia.

HODGES, Kenneth P. R, b. 24 June 1920, Regina, Saskatchewan, Canada. Barrister and Solicitor. *Education:* BA, University of Manitoba 1941; LLB, University of Saskatchewan 1949. *Appointments:* Private Practice of Law 1950-71; City Clerk/City Solicitor, Moose Jaw, Saskatchewan, 1971-76; Research Director, Law Reform Commossion of Saskatchewan Saskatoon, Saskatchewan 1976-. *Memberships:* Assiniboia Club, Regina, Saskatchewan; Director, YMCA, Regina Branch; Canadian Club; Regina General Hospital, Board of Governors; Globe Theatre Society. *Publications:* Article entitled Musk Ox, 1945. *Honours:* A. F. Sallow's Prize, First Year Law 1947; Second Year Scholarship in Law 1948; Great Distinction in Law 1949; Thomas Dowrick Brown Scholarship in Law; Wetmore Scholarship in Law; Toronto General Trusts Prize in Equity. *Hobbies:* Films; Music; Genealogy; Reading; Collector: Films; Books; Paintings; Antiques; Stamps; Records. *Address:* 69 Potter Crescent; Saskatoon, Saskatchewan, S7H 3L2, Canada.

HODGKINSON, Anthony Hugh Taylor, b. 27 Feb. 1927, Orange, New South Wales, Australia. Orthopaedic Surgeon. m. Ann Purves Lyttle, 7 Mar. 1953, 3 sons, 1 daughter. *Education:* MB, BS, Sydney University, 1951; DIP. OBST. RCOG, 1956; FRCS (Edin), 1957; FRCS (Eng.), 1958; FRACS (Orthopaedics), 1959; FACS, 1968. *Appointments:* Fellow, (Resident) Orthopaedics, Lahey Clinic Programme, Boston City Hospital, USA, 1955; Honorary Assistant Orthopaedic Surgeon, 1962-72, Honorary Orthopaedic Surgeon, 1972-, Mater Misericordiae Hospital, Sydney; Honorary Orthopaedic Surgeon, 1962-78, Consultant Orthopaedic Surgeon, 1979-, Prince Henry & Prince of Wales Hospitals, University of New South Wales. *Memberships:* AMA, BMA, Australian Orthopaedic Associa-

tion; British Orthopaedic Association; Royal Society of Medicine; SICOT. *Honours:* Post-Graduate Medical Foundation Joint Coal Board Travel Grant in Industrial Medicine, 1969. *Hobbies:* Flying; Skiing; Sailing. *Address:* 2 Davidson Avenue, Warrawee 2074, New South Wales, Australia.

HODGSON, John Clifford, b. 6 May 1925, Highgate. School Master. *Education:* Royal Academy of Music, London, 1942-43, 1947-49; LRAM, 1943; LTCL, 1950. *Appointments:* Director of Music, Michaelhouse, Natal, South Africa, 1950-57, Peterhouse, Marandellas, Zimbabwe, 1957. *Memberships:* Chairman, National Musicamp Association; President, Zimbabwe Society of Music Teachers. *Publications:* Church Music in Anthems, Service Settings and Masses; Piano & Vocal Music. *Honours:* Colman Prize, Trinity College of Music, 1950. *Hobbies:* Bridge; Fishing; Cooking. *Address:* 3 Laggan Road, P Bag 3741, Marandellas, Zimbabwe.

HOFF, Ursula, b. 26 Dec. 1909, London. Art Historian; Art Adviser; Freelance Writer on Art. *Education:* PhD (History of Art), Hamburg University, 1935. *Appointments:* Assistant Keeper, 1943-49, Keeper, 1949-56, Curator, 1956, Assistant Director (ret.), 196873, National Gallery of Victoria, Melbourne, Australia; Senior Associate Fine Arts Department, Melbourne University, 1973-75. *Memberships:* Australian Humanities Research Council, 1960-70; Foundation Fell Australian Academy of the Humanities, 1970; Trustee National Gallery Victoria, 1973-75; London Adviser Felton Bequest, 1975-; Purchases Adviser Arts Council of Great Britain, 1981-. *Publications:* Rembrandt und England, 1935; Charles I Patron of the Arts, 1941; Charles Conder, His Australian Years, 1960; Charles Conder, Lansdowne Press, 1972; European Painting and Sculpture, National Gallery of Victoria, 1973; Editor, Part Author, National Gallery of Victoria, Paintings, Drawings, Sculpture, 1968; National Gallery of Victoria, The World of Art Library, 1973. *Honours:* OBE, 1970; Britannica award, 1966; Hon. d Litt, Monash University Victoria, Australia, 1970. *Hobbies:* Reading; Swimming. *Address:* 4 Bonham House, 107 Ladbroke Road, London W11, England.

HOFFMAN, George Richard, b. 29 Feb. 1920, Tatsfield, Surrey. Consulting Engineer. m. 7 Sept. 1946, 2 daughters. *Education:* B Sc (Eng), City and Guilds Institute of London University, 1940. *Appointments:* Joined Sir M MacDonald & Partners, 1947-; Survey, Design, Construction Supervision Hydro-Electric Schemes, Scotland, 1947-57; Irrigation Design for Iraq, 1957-59; Lower Indus Project, Pakistan, 1959-66; Seconded as Leader CENTO advisory group, Iranian Ministry of Water and Power, Teheran, 1966-69; Partner with particular responsibility for Far East, 1969-75; Senior Partner, 1975-. *Memberships:* FICE; FIWES; ECGI; FRSA; MASCE. *Publications:* Papers: Tidal Calculations for the Great Ouse Flood Protection Scheme, 1952; Programme of Investigations in the Former Sind, 1963; The Organisation and Management for Planning and Operation of an Irrigation Project, (co-author), 1972. *Honours:* Palmer Prize, Institution of Civil Engineers, 1966. *Hobby:* Gardening. *Address:* 25 Newton Road, Cambridge, CB2 2AZ, England.

HOFFMANN, William John, b. 10 Oct. 1931, Melbourne Australia. Company Director. m. Elizabeth Kathleen Widowfield Reid, 12 Feb. 1955, 2 sons. *Education:* Wesley College Melbourne; Fellow Charted Institute of Transport. *Appointments:* Transport Industry; Managing Director, Melbourned Based Transport Company. *Memberships:* Executive Australian Olympic Federation, since 1976; Secretary of the Victorian Olympic Council; Secretary of the Victorian Commonwealth Games Association. *Hobbies:* Horse Riding; Golf; Tennis; Swimming. *Address:* "Hughenden" Red Hill Road, Shoreham, 3916, Victoria, Australia.

HOFLEY, Bernard Charles, b. 16 Dec. 1928, Winnipeg, Manitoba, Canada. Lawyer. m. Micheline Fournier 18 Feb. 1958, 3 sons. *Education:* BA, St Paul's College, Winnipeg 1951; LLB, Manitoba Law School 1955. *Appointments:* Legal Officer, Department of Justice, Ottawa, 1955-58; Private Secretary, Minister of National Defence 1958-60; Fournier, Papillon Ltée, 1960-64; Executive Assistant, General Manager of Canadian Corporation for World Exhibition (Expo'67), 1964-67; General Manager Schweppes-Powell Limited 1967-69; Assistant Deputy Solicitor General, Research and

Systems Development 1969-78; Registrar, Supreme Court of Canada, Ottawa 1978-. *Memberships:* Board of Directors of Ottawa Boys and Girls Club. *Honours:* National Defence Sword as Outstanding UNTD cadet, 1952; Centenial Medal, 1967; Queen's Counsel 1980; Canadian Decoration 1980. *Hobbies:* Skiing; Dancing (Scottish). *Address:* 673 Island Park Drive, Ottawa, Ontario, Canada.

HOFT, Leslie Albert, b. 5 Apr. 1929, Petth Western Australia. Officer of Parliament. m. Winsome Lynette Hamon, 1 son, 2 daughters. *Education:* Junior Certificate Perth Boys School 1944; Associate Australian Society Accountants 1961; Diploma Accounting Perth Technical College 1961. *Appointments:* Public Service 1945-62; Parliamentary Staff, Legislative Council: Clerk of Records and Accounts 1963-73; Second Clerk Assistant 1973-78; Clerk Assistant and Usher of The Black Rod, 1978-. *Memberships:* Lions International; The Rhein Donau Club, Perth. *Hobbies:* Reading; Gardening; Golf; Tennis; Sailing. *Address:* 28A Endeavour Avenue, Bullcreek, Western Australia, 6155.

HOGG, William Kirtley, b. 19 June 1936, Bishop Auckland, County Durham, England. Professor. m. 19 Dec. 1959, 1 son, 1 daughter. *Education:* BSc (Hons. Dunelm), 1961; PhD (Dunelm), Durham University, 1966; CEng; FIEE; FInst.P. *Appointments:* Research Engineer, UKAEA, Harwell, 1961; Research Scientist, IRD, Newcastle-upon-Tyne, 1961; Lecturer/Senior Lecturer, 1965, Reader, 1979, University of Strathclyde; Head of Department of Electrical & Electronic Engineering, Brighton Polytechnic College. *Memberships:* Divisional Board, SET, IEE, 1980-. *Publications:* Over 50 publications in IEE, Inst. Physics, IEEE, International Conferences throughout the world on, Dielectrics and the Electrical Properties of h.v. High power Insulating Systems. *Hobbies:* Target Shooting; Writing; Classical Music. *Address:* Little Milbury, 32A Offington Lane, Worthing, West Sussex, BN14 9RT, England.

HOLCOMBE, Yuonne Margaret, b. Sydney, NSW, Australia. Medical Specialist. *Education:* Commonwealth Scholarship; MB, BS, Faculty of Medicine Sydney 1960; FRCPA 1974. *Appointments:* RMO, St. George Hospital Sydney 1960-61; Resist. Path. Prince Henry, Prince of Wales Hospital Sydney 1962-67; Pathol. Sutherland Hospital Sydney 1967-70; Senior Registrar, Path Prince Henry, Prince of Wales Hospitals 1970-71; Senior Registrar, Haem, St. George Hospital 1971-72; Fellow, Path. Royal Prince Alfred Hospital 1972-74; Senior Registrar, 1974-75; Part-time Teacher, Fellow, Pathol. University NSW 1962-67, 1974-75: Lecturer, Clinical Laboratory Medical University, NSW 1976; Lecturer, Department Medicine, 1981-; Clinical Pathologist and Haematologist, Women's Hospital, Sydney 1975-. *Memberships:* Convenor, Historical Committee Royal College of Pathologist of Australasia; Haematology Society of Australia; Medico-Legal Society of NSW; International Haematology Society, Asian-Pacific Division; Australian Thalassaemia Society; NSW Thalassaemia Society; Australian and New Zealand Paediatric Pathology Group; NSW Medical Women's Society. *Publications:* Haemoglobinopathies, 1981; Thalassaemia, 1978; Measurement and Significance of Ala in Amniotic Fluid Lancet, 1981; Disorders of Haemostasis and Haemoglobinopathies in Pregnancy; History of the Royal College of Pathologists of Australia, Small -bwfinninfa 1883, 1979. *Hobbies:* Flautist; Music Opera and Classical; Sport; Painting; Ancient and Modern History. *Address:* 257 Maroubra Road, Maroubra Junction, Sydney, 2035, Australia.

HOLDAWAY, Richard Arthur, b. 24 Oct. 1935, Melbourne, Australia. Financial Consultant. *Education:* B.Comm. (Melbourne), 1958; AASA, 1959; MBA. (Harvard), 1962. *Appointments:* Wm. Haughton & Co. Limited, Melbourne, Australia, 1953-60; Kuhn Loeb & Co. Inc., New York, USA, summer 1961; Morgan Guaranty Trust Co. of New York, New York, USA, 1962-68; Guest & Bell, Melbourne, Australia, 1969-74; Independent Financial Consultant, 1974-. *Memberships:* Athenaeum Club; Harvard Club of New York; Harvard Club of Australia; Harvard Business School Club of Victoria; Metropolitan Golf Club; XX Club of Victoria; Victorian Artists Society; Old Water Colour Society's Club, Australian Branch; Melbourne Press Club. *Publications:* publications include: Australian Banking, 1972; The Australian Banking Industry, 1975; The Australian Finance Industry, 1975; The Australian

Retailing Industry, 1979. *Creative Works:* Oil and water colour paintings include: Still lifes; Landscapes; Seascapes; Portraits and nudes painted in Australia, USA, England, France, Italy and Greece; Represented in private collections in New York, USA and Australia. *Honours:* Melbourne University swimming and water polo blue, 1956-58; Member of Australian Universities Swimming team and Captain of Australian Universities Water Polo team on New Zealand tour, 1959; Victorian backstroke champion, 1960. *Hobbies:* Painting; Swimming; Golf; Tennis; Bridge; Chess; Opera; Roses and sunflowers. *Address:* 244 Highfield Road, Burwood, Victoria 3125, Australia.

HOLDEN, George James Forster, b. 24 Oct. 1925, Felling, Northumberland. Professor of Surveying. m. (1) Kathleen O'Neill 30 June 1950 (Dec.), 3 daughters, (2) Wendy Clarke 17 Feb. 1973. *Education:* Westminster City School London 1937-43; Caius College, Cambridge 1943-44; Diploma Photogrammetry, University College London 1957-58; PhD, University of New South Wales, 1968-72. *Appointments:* Major, Royal Engineers, 1945-65: Commander, 1961-63; Officer-in-Charge of Cartography, Ministry of Defence UK 1963-65; Senior Lecturer, University of Otago, New Zealand, 1965-67; Associate Professor, University of NSW, 1968-81; Professor and Head, School of Surveying, S.A. Institute of Technology. *Memberships:* Fellow, Royal Institution of Chartered Surveyors; Institution of Surveyors Australia; Australian Institute of Cartographers; Fellow, Royal Geographical Society. *Publications:* Several scientific papers in Photogrammetric Record, Photogrammetric Engineering, Australian Surveyor, South African Survey Journal, and University of New South Wales publications. *Address:* 9A Wootoona Terrace, St. Georges, S.A. Australia, 5064.

HOLDERNESS, (Lord), Richard Frederick, b. 5 Oct. 1920, London, England. Peer of the Realm. m. Diana Kellett, 15 Apr. 1947, 1 son, 1 daughter. *Education:* Eton, New College, Oxford. Hon. Doctor of Laws, Sheffield and Leeds Universities, UK. *Appointments:* Served in Army, 1940-43; Member of Parliament for Bridlington, Yorkshire, 1950-79; Parliamentary Secretary to: Ministry of Pensions and National Insurance, 1955-58, 1963-64; Ministry of Labour, 1958-59; Minister of Power, 1959-63; Minister of Pensions and National Insurance, 1963-64; Minister for Overseas Development, 1970-74; Director, Hargreaves Ltd., Regional Director, Lloyds Bank; Chairman Wilton 65; Deputy Lieutenant, County of Humberside. *Memberships:* Hon. Colonel, 4th Battalion, the Royal Green Jackets. *Honours:* Created Life Peer, 1979. *Hobbies:* Gardening; Travel. *Address:* Bishop Wilton, York, England.

HOLESCH de Joyce May, b. Melbourne, Victoria, Australia. Concert Pianist. m. 23 Mar. 1944, 1 son, 1 daughter. *Education:* Diploma of Music, Melbourne University, 1937. *Appointments:* Soloist at 14 years of age; Concerts in countries world wide. *Publications:* Compositions on Australian folk songs; Plays one of these—Homage To Waltzing Matilda, in Hahn film, The Australian Pianist, which outlines her concert career. *Honours:* Bach Prize London, 1939; Josephine Nathan Musical Initiative Prize London 1939; Frank Homewood Memorial Scholarship to Melbourne University Conservatorium 1934; Numerous Press notices World Wide. *Hobbies:* Reading Philosophy; Gymnastics; Yoga. *Address:* Voulangis, 77580 Crécy-la Chapelle, Seine-et Marne, France.

HOLLAND, Alfred Charles, b. 23 Feb. 1927, London. Anglican Bishop. m. 22 Sept. 1954, 3 sons, 1 daughter. *Education:* Raine's School, London; Ba, Dip. Th., St. Chads. College University of Durham, 1948-52. *Appointments:* Assistant Priest West Hackney, London 1952-54; Rector of Scarborough W.A 1955-70; Assistant Bishop, Diocese of Perth W.A 1970-77; Bishop of Newcastle, NSW, 1978-. *Memberships:* Australian Club; Life member Stirling Rugby Football Club; Newcastle Club; Newcastle R.U.F.C. *Publications:* Luke Through Lent, 1980. *Hobbies:* Reading; Painting. *Address:* Bishopscourt, Cnr. Brown and Church Sts. Newcastle, NSW, Australia.

HOLLAND, Philip Welsby, b. 14 Mar, 1917, Middlewich, Cheshire, England. Conservative Member of Parliament. m. Josephine Alma Hudson, 23 Sept. 1943, 1 son. *Appointments:* Royal Air Force, 1936-46; Industrial Management, 1946-59; MP for Acton, London, UK, 1959-64; Personnel Manager, Ultra Electronics, 1964-66; MP for Carlton, Notts, UK, 1966-. *Publications:* The Quango Explosion (co-author), 1978; Quango, Quango, Quango, 1979; Costing the Quango, 1979; The Quango Death List, 1980; The Governance of Quango, 1981. *Hobbies:* World wide travel. *Address:* 2 Holland Park Mansions, Holland Park Gardens, London, W14, England.

HOLLAND, William Nalder, b. 12 Jan. 1927, Mosman, NSW, Australia. Investigations Officer. m. Lois May Hulme 11 Jan. 1958, 2 sons, 1 daughter. *Education:* BA, 1968, PhD, University of Sydney 1974; Diploma of Environmental Studies Macquarie University 1978; Registered Surveyor, Australia, 1951; Registered Surveyor New Zealand 1954; Mining Surveyor, NSW, 1954. *Appointments:* Survey Pupil, Private Surveyors and Department of Lands, NSW, 1945-50; Surveyor, Metropolitan Water Board, Sydney, 1950-55; Surveyor, Ministry of Works, New Zealand 1955-56; Surveyor, British Columbia Power Commission, Canada, 1956; Surveyor, Metropolitan Water Board, Sydney, 1957-58; Surveyor, Department of Main Roads, Sydney, 1958-66; Commonwealth Post Graduate Studentship, University of Sydney, 1967-73; Investigations Officer, Department of Main Roads, NSW, Australia, 1974-. *Memberships:* Geological Society of Australia; Institute of Australian Geographers; Institution of Surveyors, Australia; Institution of Surveyors New Zealand; Australian Institute of Cartographers; Geographical Society of New South Wales; Remote Sensing Society of Australia; Linnean Society of NSW; Katoomba and District Wildfife and Conservation Society. *Publications:* Seven published papers: Investigations of past water levels on Lake George in relation to road levels on state highway No.3—Department of Main Roads,; Two papers in Preparation. *Honours:* Commonwealth Post Graduate Studentship Award, 1969; MA, University of Sydney, High Distinction 1968. *Hobbies:* Geomorphology; Bushwalking; Music. *Address:* 143 Livingstone Avenue, West Pymble, NSW 2073, Australia.

HOLLIER, Donald Russell, b. 7 May 1934, Sydney, Australia. Musician. m. Sharman Ellen Pretty, 9 July 1977, 2 daughters. *Education:* Performers a d Teachers Diploma, New South Wales State Conservatorium, Australia, 1955; Royal Academy of Music, London, UK, 1957-57; BM., 1961, DM., 1975, University of London, UK. *Appointments:* Director of Music, Newington College, 1962-63; Head of Academic Studies, 1967-75, Co-ordinator, 1975-78, Canberra School of Music, Australia; Head of Theoretical Studies, 1979-; Musical Director, Canberra Opera, Australia, 1978-; Musical Director, Canberra Choral Society, Australia, 1979-. *Memberships:* Composers Guild of Australia; Associate, Australian Performing Rights Association; Fellowship of Australian Composers. *Creative Works:* 5 Concerti; 2 Operas: The Heiress, Knights of the Long Knives; 3 Oratorios; Songs; Chamber Music; Works for solo piano, organ. *Honours:* Vasanta Scholarship, New South Wales Conservatorium, 1957; Frank Shirley award, New South Wales Conservatorium, 1955; Henry W Richars Prize, Royal Academy, 1959; Maggs Award, Composition, University of Melbourne, 1975; Churchill Fellowship, 1975. *Hobbies:* Theatre. *Address:* 65 Euree Street, Reid 2601, Australia.

HOLLYOCK, Vernon, b. 13 May 1916, Melbourne, Australia. Medical. m. Mabel Florence Jarman, 1 June 1849. *Education:* MBBS., 1939, MRCOG., 1947, FRACS., 1948, FRCOG., 1965, F.Aust. COG. 1980, University of Melbourne, Australia. *Appointments:* Resident Medical Officer, Royal Melbourne Hospital, Australia, 1940; Captain, Australian Army Medical Corps., 1941-46; Registrar, Liverpool Maternity and Womens Hospitals, UK, 1949-51; First Assistant Professor, Department Obstetrics and Gynaecology, 1951, EXAMINER, Gynaecology, 1966-76, University of Melbourne, Australia; Senior Obstetrician and Gynaecologist, Western General Hospital, Melbourne, Australia, 1952-62; Hon. Gynaecologist, 1951-76, Senior Gynaecologist In Charge, Dysplasia Clinic, 1966-76, Chairman, Gynaecological Staff, 1970-75, Hon. Consulting Surgeon, 1976-, Royal Women's Hospital, Melbourne, Australia; Supervisor, Surgical Training, Royal Australian College of Surgeons, 1970-76; Colposcopist, Alfred Hospital, Melbourne, Australia, 1976-81. *Memberships:* Naval and Military Club, Melbourne; Victoria Racing Club; Moonee Valley Racing Club, Melbourne. *Publications:* Multiple articles on colposcopy and pre-

invasive carcinoma of the uterine cervix, in American and Australian Medical Journals. *Honours:* OBE, 1978. *Hobbies:* Music; Walking; Fishing. *Address:* Flat 2, 76 Studley Park Road, Kew, Victoria, 3101, Australia.

HOLMER, Paul Cecil Henry, b. 19 Oct. 1923, Cairo. Diplomatic Service. m. Irene Beater, 11 Apr. 1946, 2 sons, 2 daughters. *Education:* Balliol College, Oxford, 1941-42, 1946-47; MA, (Oxon). *Appointments:* Lieutenant, Royal Artillery, 1942-46; Colonial Office, 1947-49; Foreign Office and abroad as member of Foreign (later Diplomatic) Service, 1949; Service in Singapore (twice), Moscow, Berlin, Abidjan, (Ambassador to Ivory Coast and to Upper Volta and Niger), Brussels (Minister and UK Deputy Permanent Representative on North Atlantic Council); British Ambassador to Romania, 1979-. *Memberships:* Travellers' Club, London. *Honours:* CMG, 1973. *Hobbies:* Walking; Reading. *Address:* British Embassy, Bucharest.

HOLTEN, Rendle McNeilage, b. 29 Mar. 1922, Melbourne. Member of Parliament. m. Shirley McNeil De Ravin, 6 Jan. 1949, 3 daughters. *Education:* Scotch College, Melbourne, 1938. *Appointments:* Businessman; Member of Australian Federal Parliament, 1958-77. *Honours:* Companion of the Most Distinguished Order of St Michael & St George, 1980. *Hobby:* Sport. *Address:* Administrator, Christmas Island (Australian Territory), Indian Ocean, 6798.

HOLTHAM, Peter Michael, b. 13 Feb. 1947, Birmingham, England. Physicist. m. Katherine Charlesworth, 24 July 1971, 1 daughter. *Education:* BA. (Natural Sciences), 1968, MA., 1972, University of Cambridge, UK; PhD., 1971, University of Bristol, UK. *Appointments:* University of British Columbia, Canada, 1971-75; National Research Council of Canada, 1975-77; Defence Research Establishment of Canada, 1977-. *Memberships:* Institute of Physics, London; Canadian Association of Physicists; American Geophysical Union. *Publications:* Numerous publications and Technical articles in Scientific journals. *Honours:* Open Scholarship, Magdalene College, Cambridge, 1965-68; Prizes in Natural Sciences, Magdalene College, Cambridge, 1966, 67, 68; Killam Fellowship, 1971-73; National Research Council Fellowship, 1975-77. *Hobbies:* Sailing; Travel; Mountain climbing; Classical Music; Theatre; Ski touring; Swimming. *Address:* 964 Saturna Place, Victoria B C, V8Y 1H4, Canada.

HOLYOAKE (Rt. Hon. Sir), Keith Jacka, b. 11 Feb. 1904, Pahiatua, New Zealand. Governor-General of New Zealand (Retired). m. Normá Janet Ingram, 11 Jan. 1935, 2 sons, 3 daughters. *Education:* LL.D., Victoria University, Wellington, New Zealand, 1966; LL.D.(Agric.), Seoul National University, Korea, 1968. *Appointments:* Member of Parliament, National Party, 1932-38, 1943-77; Deputy Prime Minister and Minister Agriculture, Marketing and Scientific Research, 1949-57; Prime Minister and Minister Maori Affairs, 1957; Leader of Opposition, 1957-60; Prime Minister and Minister, Foreign Affairs, 1960-72; Governor General, Oct. 1977-Oct. 1980. *Memberships:* Nelson Provincial President Farmers Union, 103'-41; Vice President, Dominion Executive, Farmers Union, 1940-50; Patron of various National and Local organisations. *Honours:* Freedom of City of London, Uk, 1969; Privy Councillor, 1954; Companion of Honour, 1963; GCMG, 1970; KG., 1980. *Hobbies:* Tennis; Gardening. *Address:* Government House, Private Bag, Wellington, New Zealand.

HOLZBERGER, Ernst August, b. 16 Jan. 1915, Yokohama, Japan. Merchant. m. Anne J Makley, 20 Oct. 1951, 1 son. *Education:* Blankenese High School and College, Hamburg, Germany, 1927-33. *Appointments:* Blembel Bros., Hamburg, Germany, 1933-35; Export Department, Far East. Schering A G, Berlin, E Germany, 1935-37; Departmental Manager, Hong Kong, 1937-39, Manager, Import Department, Mukden, Manchuria, 1939-40, Manager, Import Department, Tsingtao, 1941-42, Manager, Import Department, Tientsin, China, 1943-44, Melchers & Co., Bremen, Germany; Partner, Universal Mercantile Co., Tientsin, China, 1945-48, left for US, Feb. 1949; Internaional Division, 1949, Far East Representative, Japan to Thai and to Indonesia, E R Squibb & Sons, New York City, USA; Proprietor, E A Holzberger in Singapore, 1956, transferred to Hong Kong, 1957; Managing Director, Martin and Thomas Limited, Hong Kong. *Memberships:* Hongkong Philharmic Society; Hongkong Club; Shek O

Country Club, Hongkong; Ladies Recreation Club, Hongkong. *Hobbies:* Music; Golf; Reading. *Address:* 9 May Road, Hong Kong.

HOME, Alexander Frederick, b. 2 July 1903, London. Politician. m. Elizabeth 1936, 1 son, 3 daughters. *Education:* Eton, Oxford. *Appointments:* Member of Parliament; Foreign Secretary 1960-63, 1970-74; Prime Minister, 1963-64. *Publications:* The Way the Wind Blows, 1976; Border Reflections, 1979. *Address:* The Hirsel, Coldstream, Scotland.

HON, Kam Wing, b. 20 Jan. 1942, Hong Kong. Merchant. m. Yeung Yim Fong, 8 June 1966, 1 son, 4 daughters. *Appointments:* Director, Amana Garment Fazctory Limited; Managing Director, Kin Chung Manufacturing Co. Limited. *Address:* 659 Shanghai Street, 10th Floor Mongkoll, Kowloon, Hong Kong.

HONEYCOMBE, Gordon, b. 27 Sept. 1936, Karachi, British India. Writer; TV Presenter. *Education:* MA. (Hons. English Language and Literature), University College, Oxford, UK, 1957-61. *Appointments:* Radio Announcer, 1956-57; Actor, Royal Shakespeare Company, 1962-63; TV Newscaster, ITN, 1965-77; Writer, Author, Playwright, 1960-. *Publications:* Neither the Sea nor the Sand; Dragon under the Hill; Adam's Tale; Red Watch; The Edge of Heaven; Nagasaki 1945; Royal Wedding. *Creative Works:* TV plays: The Golden Vision; Time and again; Stage and Radio plays: The Redemption; Paradise Lost; Lancelot and Guinevere; God Save the Queen! A King shall have a Kingdom; TV presenter and narrator of many programmes including: Family History, BBC TV; Arthur C Clarke's Mysterious World, YTV. *Hobbies:* Genealogy; Brass rubbing. *Address:* c/o Isobel Davie, 13 Bruton Street, London W1X 8JY, England.

HOODLESS, Ian Mark, b. 25 Apr. 1933, Silloth, Cumbria, England. Chemist. m. Shirley Donkin, 20 July 1957, 1 son, 1 daughter. *Education:* BSc, 1954, PhD, 1957, University of Durham. *Appointments:* Post-Doctoral Fellow, National Research Council of Canada, 1957-59; Esso Research Fellowship, 1959-60, Lecturer in Chemistry, 1960-65, University of Glasgow; Lecturer in Chemistry, 1965-68, Senior Lecturer, 1968-70, University of Kent; Professor of Chemistry, Lakehead University, Ontario, Canada, 1970-. *Memberships:* Chemical Institute of Canada; Canadian Association of Physicists. *Publications:* Various joint publications in fields of Solid-State Diffusion and Heterogeneous Catalysis, 1972-79. *Hobbies:* Sports. *Address:* 113 Hogarth Street, Thunder Bay, Ontario, P7A 7G8, Canada.

HOOKE, John Michael, b. 6 Mar. 1946, Melbourne. Musician, Composer. m. Julie Sheffield, 12 May, 1973. *Education:* B. Mus, 1975, B. Mus (Composition), 1976, M.Mus (Composition), 1981, Adelaide. *Appointments:* Police Department, Library Council etc., 1969-72; State Public Service (Victoria); Library Assistant, 1981-. *Memberships:* Fellowship of Australian Composers. *Creative Works:* Tesellations for Piano, 1973; Numerous compositions including: Interaction II for three percussionists, 1981; Interaction III for one percussionist, 1981; Floridale for Solo Flute and Percussion, 1981; Duet for Flute and Bass Trombone, 1981; Kirienko for Solo Trombone and Strings, 1981. *Honours:* Second Prize for Composition at Hartwell Eisteddford, 1970; First and Third Prizes for Composition, Hartwell Eisteddford, 1971. *Hobbies:* Cultivation of Herbs and exotic plants; Study of Rock formations in landscapes. *Address:* 17 St Clements Street, Blair Athol, SA 5084, Australia.

HOPE, Archibald Philip, b, 27 Mar. 1912, Musselburgh, Scotland. Chartered Accountant. m. Ruth Davis, 20 Apr. 1938, 2 sons. *Education:* Eton 1925-30; BA, Balliol College, Oxford, 1930-34. *Appointments:* Kemp Chatteris, 1935-39; Royal Auxiliary Air Force, 1939-45; Airwork Ltd., 1945-56; English Electric Co. Ltd., 1956-77. *Memberships:* Fellow, Royal Aeronautical Society. *Honours:* DFC, 1940; AE, 1942; OBE, 1945; Baronet 1628. *Hobby:* Aviation. *Address:* Manor House, Somerford Keynes, Cirencester, Glos., GL7 6DL, England.

HOPE, Robert Bruce, b. 3 Feb. 1932, Manly, NSW, Australia. Civil Engineering. m. Maureen Jean Murphy, 9 Mar. 1957, 1 son, 3 daughters. *Education:* Civil Engineering Diploma, Sydney Technical College, 1955; Highways & Transportation Systems, University of California, 1958; Introductory Japanese, 1969, Intermediate Japanese, 1974, Australian National University. *Appointments:* Deputy Shire Engineer, Tweed Shire Council, NSW, 1960-63; Manager, Civil Engineering, United States Navy, Perth, Western Australia, 1963-66; Chief Project Engineer, Sentinel Mining Co., Perth, Western Australia, 1966-69; Manager, Engineering, Bougainville Copper Ltd., 1969-74; Manager, New Projects & Chief Engineer, Consolidated Goldfields, Sydney, Australia, 1975-77; Managing Director, Houston Oil & Minerals of Australia, 1977-; President, Houston International Minerals Corp., Denver, USA, 1979-; Managing Director, Date Tenneco Oil & Minerals of Australia, 1981. *Memberships:* Fellow, Institution of Engineers, Australia; Australian Institute of Mining & Metallurgy; American Institute of Mining Engineers. *Publications:* Contributor of papers to Engineering Institutes including: Critical Path Planning in Construction Projects, 1965; Engineering Management of the Bougainville Projects, 1971; Special Aspects of the Bougainville Operations, 1973. *Honours:* Management Award, Institution of Engineers, Australia, 1971. *Hobbies:* Tennis; Squash; Sailing; Skiing. *Address:* Ebrington, 145 Adelaide St East, Clayfield, Queensland, Australia, 4011.

HOPKINSON, Richard Arthur Eric, b. 16 Nov. 1926, Colombo, Sri Lanka. Director/President. m. Lorraine Lasnier, 25 Apr. 1975, 1 son (by former marriage). *Education:* BA, MA, Merton College, Oxford University, 1948-50; Diploma in International Business Administration, Centre D'Etudes Industrielles, Geneva, Switzerland, 1950-51. *Appointments:* Positions in Personnel, General Manager's Office, Accounting Methods, Treasury and Systems Development, Aluminum Company of Canada Ltd., Montreal and Arvida Industrial Complex, Quebec, Canada, 1951-61; Vice-President, Economic Research Corporation, Montreal, 1961-63; Consultant, Management Controls, Peat, Marwick Mitchell & Co., 1963-65; Economist, Canadian National, 1965-67; Senior Specialist, The Conference Board in Canada, 1967-71; Director, Brakeley/Ryerson Group, 1971-75; President, Institute of Donations and Public Affairs Research, 1975-. *Memberships:* Past Chairman, Montreal Branch, Canadian Institute of International Affairs; The Royal Commonwealth Society; Association of Cultural Executives; Institute of Association Executives; University Club of Montreal. *Publications:* Corporate Organization for Pollution Control; Corporate Giving in Canada, 1971-, Annually. *Honours:* Lord Mayor of London's Cup for All-round Services to the City of London School's Games, 1945. *Hobbies:* Reading; Travel; Swimming. *Address:* 443 Prince Albert Avenue, Westmount, Quebec, H3Y 2P6, Canada.

HOPPER, Maxwell Wallace, b. 28 Dec. 1930, Taree, New South Wales, Australia. Director. m Joyce Keeling, 30 Aug. 1955, 1 son, 2 daughters. *Education:* BSc, 1953, DipEd, 1954, Sydney; BA, New England, 1959. *Appointments:* Teacher, 1954-57; University Administration, 1957-60, Assistant Director, 1960-66, Deputy & Acting Director, 1969, Department of External Studies, University of New England; UNESCO Consultant on External Studies and Director of Correspondence Studies, University of Zambia, 1966-68; Director & Principal, Gippsland Institute of Advanced Education, 1970-. *Memberships:* Australian College of Education; International Council for Correspondence Education. *Publications:* Various papers on Distance Education. *Address:* P.O. Box 58, Yinnar, Victoria, 3869, Australia.

HOPPER, Wilbert Hill, b. 14 Mar. 1933, Ottawa, Ontario, Canada. Chairman & Chief Executive Officer. m. Patricia Marguerite Walker, 12 Aug. 1957, 2 sons. *Education:* Scot's College, Sidney, Australia; Wellington College, New Zealand; BSc, American University; MBA, University of Western Ontario. *Appointments:* Petroleum Geologist, Imperial Oil, 1955-57; Petroleum Economist, Foster Associates, 1959-61; Senior Energy Economist, National Energy Board, Ottawa, 1961-64; Senior Petroleum Consultant, Arthur D Little, Cambridge, Mass, 1964-73; Senior Advisor, Energy Policy, 1973-74, Assistant Deputy Minister Energy Policy, 1974-76, Department of Energy, Mines & Resources in Ottawa; President & Chief Executive Officer, 1976-79, Chairman and Chief Executive Officer, 1979-, Petro-Canada, Calgary. *Memberships:* Canadian and American Economic Associations; Canadian and American Societies of Petroleum Geologists; CIMM; Society of Petroleum Engineers. *Address:* 2083 Chalmers Road, Ottawa, Ontario, Canada.

HORA, Heinrich, b. 1 July 1931, Bodenbach/Elbe. Physicist. m. Rosemarie Weiler, 1 July 1956, 1 son, 5 daughters. *Education:* Physics, 1950-56, Diplom-Physiker, 1956, Martin-Luter-University, Halle; Dr.rer.nat. Friedrich-Schiller University, Jena, 1960; DSc. University New South Wales, Sydney, 1981. *Appointments:* Research Physicist, Zeiss Jena, 1956-60; Zeiss Oberkochen, 1960-61; IBM Lab. Böblingen, 1961-62; Institute Plasmaphysik Garching, 1962-67; Senior Res. Physicist, Westinghouse Research Centre, Pittsburgh, Pa., 1967-68; Principle Res. Phys. Max-Planck-Institute, Plasmaphysik Garching, 1965-75; Ad. Asso. Professor of Physics, Rensselaer Polytechnic Institute, Hartford Graduate Center, 1969-75; Professor and Head of Department of Theoretical Physics, University New South Wales, Sydney, 1975-; Visiting Professor, University Rochester, NY, 1973-74; University Bern, Switzerland, 1978-79; Consultant, Messerschmitt-BB, 1969-75; Nuclear Club Wall Street, 1978; University Illinois, 1981-. *Memberships:* Fellow, Institute Physics, (London); Fellow Australian Institute Physics, 1980-; Board of Directors, Society to Advance Fusion Energy, New York; American Physics Society. *Publications:* Laser Plasmas and Nuclear Energy, 1975; Nonlinear Plasma Dynamics, 1979; Physics of Laser Driven Plasmas, 1981; Co-editor, Laser Interaction and Rel. Plasma, 1971-81; Founder and Editor in Chief, Laser and Particle Beams, 1982; 150 publications and 40 Patents on lasers, plasma, solids. *Honours:* Air Force grantee, (Schwarz-Hora-effect), USA, 1972; Lebedev Institute Medal, 1978. *Hobbies:* Piano; Skiing; Golf. *Address:* 12 Duggan Crescent, Connels Point, 2221, Australia.

HORLOCK, John Harold, b. 19 Apr. 1928. Vice-Chancellor. m. Sheila Joy Stutely, 1 son, 2 daughters. *Education:* St John's College, Cambridge; First Class Hons Mech. Sci. Tripos, Part I, 1948; Rex Moir Prize; Part II, 1949; MA, 1952; PhD, 1955; ScD, 1975. *Appointments:* Design and Development Engineer, Rolls Royce Ltd., Derby, 1949-51; Research Fellow, St John's College, Cambridge, 1954-57; University Demonstrator, 1952-56; University Lecturer, Cambridge University Engineering Laboratory, 1956-58; Harrison Professor of Mechanical Engineering & Head of Department, Liverpool University, 1958-66; Professor of Engineering, 1967-74, Deputy Head of Engineering Department 1969-73, Cambridge University; Professorial Fellow of St John's College, Cambridge, 1967-74; Vice-Chancellor, 1974-80, Professor of Engineering, 1976-80, University of Salford; Visiting Assistant Professor in Mechanical Engineering, Massachusetts Institute of Technology, USA, 1956-57; Visiting Professor of Aero-Space Engineering, Pennsylvania State University, USA, 1966; Director, Bicera Ltd., 1964-65; Chairman, ARC, 1979-80; Director; Cambridge Water Co., 1971-74; British Engine Insurance Ltd., 1979-; BL (Technol,) Ltd., 1979-; Vice-Chancellor, Open University, 1981-. *Memberships:* ARC, 1960-63, 1969-72; SRC, 1974-77; Committee of Inquiry into Engineering Profession, 1977-80. *Publications:* The Fluid Mechanics and Thermodynamics of Axial Flow Compressors, 1958; The Fluid Mechanics and Thermodynamics of Axial Flow Turbines, 1966; Actuator Disc Theory, 1978; Contributions to mechanical and aeronautical engineering journals and to Proc. Royal Society. *Honours:* FRS, FEng, FIMechE, FRAeS; Fellow ASME Honorary DSc, Heriot-Watt, 1980; Thomas Hawksley Gold Medal, IMechE, 1969; Honorary DSc, Salford, 1981. *Hobbies:* Music; Cricket; Golf. *Address:* The Open University, Walton Hall, Milton Keynes, MK7 6AA, England.

HORNABROOK, Judith Sidney, b. 26 Oct. 1928, Wellington, New Zealand. Archivist. *Education:* BA, 1946-48, MA, (Hons), 1951, Victoria University of Wellington; Certificate, Archives Principles & Aministration, Canadian Historial Association, 1971; British Council Course, Management of Archives, 1980. *Appointments:* Research Assistant, War History Branch, Department of Internal Affairs, NZ, 1949-56; Library & Research positions, including Royal Institution of Great Britain, London, 1956-58, 1973-; Archivist, 1958-65; Senior Archivist, 1968-73, Chief Archivist, 1973-, National Archives, Department of Internal Affairs, NZ. *Memberships:* Executive Committee, International

Council on Archives, 1982-86; Training Committee, 1976-, Council, 1976-78, Archives & Records Association of NZ; Australian Society of Archivists; Society of Archivists, UK; NZ, Library Association; NZ Historical Association. *Hobbies:* Music; Reading; Natural History. *Address:* 9B Pitarua Street, Wellington, New Zealand.

HORNSBY-ODOI, Mirian Narnole, (Mrs Enoch Hornsby-Odoi), b. 12 Jan. 1929, Accra, Ghana, West Africa. Director of Nursing Service. m. Enoch Hornsby-Odoi, 14 Sept. 1957, 2 sons, 1 daughter. *Education:* State Registered Nursing Certificate, 1951; Central Midwives Certificate, 1953; Public Health Nursing Certificate, 1955; Community Health Nursing Administration Certificate, 1961; Degree in Community Health Nursing, 1979. *Appointments:* Staff Nurse; Public Health Nurse; District, Regional and Principal Public Health Nurse; Deputy Director Nursing Service; Acting Director Nursing Service. *Memberships:* Publicity Officer, Ghana Registered Nurses Association, 1960-70; Committee of the Health and Social Welfare Sector Plan, 1980-. *Publications:* Kwashiorkor with Special Reference Ghana; Why Our Babies Die; Breast Feeding; Role of the Public Health Nurse in Immunization. *Hobbies:* Reading; Sewing; Gardening. *Address:* co Mr E Hornsly-Odoi, Managing Director, T.DC, PO Box, 46, Tema, Ghana

HORNSTEIN, Reuben Aaron, b. 18 Dec. 1912, London, Ontario, Canada. Meteorologist, Broadcaster & Author. m. Helen Christina, 11 Feb. 1956. *Education:* BA, Physics, 1934, MA, Cum Laude Physics, 1936, University of Western Ontario; MA, Meteorology, University of Toronto, 1938. *Appointments:* Meteorologist, Department of Transport & Environment, Montreal, Halifax 1938-72; Meteorological Broadcaster, CBC, Radio & Television, 1946-81. *Memberships:* Canadian Meteorological & Oceanographic Society; Canadian Association of Physicists; Professional Institute of the Public Service of Canada; Nova Scotia Institute of Science. *Publications:* Weather Facts and Fancies, 1948; It's in the Wind, 1951; Weather and Why, 1954; The Weather Book, 1980; 25 or more technical papers. *Honours:* University Graduation Gold Medallist, 1934; MBE, 1946; Patterson Medal, 1963; Canadian Meteorological Service Centennial Plaque, 1972; Federal Institute of Management Special Merit Award, 1977. *Hobbies:* Golf; Bridge; Needlepoint Tapestries; Recording Talking Books for the Blind. *Address:* 1074 Wellington Street, Apt. 301, Halifax, N.S. Canada, B3H 2Z8.

HOROI, Stphen Rex, b. 8 Sept. 1955, Tawatana, Solomon Islands. Teacher. *Education:* Diploma in Education studies at the University of the South Pacific, Fiji, 1975-77; Now studying for BED degree, University of Papua, New Guinea, 1981-82. *Appointments:* T4acher, English and Social Science, St. Joseph's Secondary School, Tenaru, Soloman Islands, 1978-80. *Memberships:* Scout leader, St. Mary's Primary School, Maravovo, Guadalcanal, Solomons and St. Joseph's Secondary School, Honiara; Secretary, The Solomon Islands Students Association & UPNG. *Publications:* Co-author of Grammar Handbook and Communication and Culture Handbook (Soloman Island PIJIN textbooks); Article on the Deteriorating of quality of Artefacts in the Solomons. *Honours:* Governor's prize for School Captain at King George VI School. *Hobbies:* Kungfu; Cricket; Hockey; Rugby; Jogging; Squash; Volleyball; Water Polo; Bushwalking. *Address:* Tawatana Village, Aros G one, San Cristobal, Makira, Ulawa Province, Solomon Islands.

HOROWITZ, Yigal Shalom, b. 22 Apr. 1940, Winnipeg, Manitoba, Canada. Physicist, Associate Professor. m. 1 July 1971, 1 son, 3 daughters. PhD, 1968, MSc, 1965, BSc, 1961, McGill University. *Appointments:* Nuclear Physics Department, Weizmann Institute of Science, 1971-74; Scientific Consultant to Elscint, 1976; Senior Lecturer, Physics Department, 1971-79, Head, Radiation Physics Laboratory, 1973-, Associate Professor, Radiation Physics, 1980-, Ben Gurion University, Negev. *Memberships:* Canadian Association of Physicists; Israel Physical and Nuclear Societies; Israel Association of Medical Physicists. *Publications:* Approximately 50 publications, invited review articles and chapters in International Journals; Book (in preparation) on Thermoluminescence and Thermoluminescent Dosimetry. *Honours:* J W MacConnell Memorial Graduate Scholar, McGill University, 1965-68. *Hob-

bies: Gardening; Stamps. *Address:* Hashita Street, No. 8, Neve Noi, Beersheva, Israel.

HORSFALL, Cliscent Tennyson, b. 30 May 1931, Beguma City Rivers State, Nigeria. Land Surveyor. m. Mercy Adukwei, 3 Apr. 1959, 3 sons, 4 daughters. *Education:* BSc, University of Ibadan, Nigeria, 1958; School of Military Surveys, Newbury, 1959-60; ITC, Delft, Holland, 1961-62; BSc, PhE, 1962; ARICS; USAID Fellowship US Coast and Geodetic Surveys Photogrammetric Research, 1964-65; Nigerian Surveyors Licence, 1967; Fellow, Royal Institution of Chartered Surveyors, London, 1971. *Appointments:* Pupil Surveyor, 1958-60, Surveyor, 1960-62, Surveyor Grade I, 1962-64, Senior Surveyor, 1964-68, Principal Surveyor, 1968-70, Federal Surveys Lagos, Nigiera; Surveyor, General Rivers State, Nigeria, 1970-80 Director and Licensed Surveyor Geodetic Surveys Ltd, Nigeria, 1980, (Retired). *Memberships:* President of: Nigerian Association of Surveying Engineers, 1971-, Association of Senior Civil Servants, 1971-80, Nigerian Society of Photogrammetry and Remote Sensing, 1975-; Nigerian Institution of Surveyors; Science Association of Nigeria. *Publications:* Aerotriangulation Strip Adjustment using fortran and the IBM 1620 Computer, 1965; Electronic Computer Programs for Analytical Aerial Triangulation, 1965; Lectures on Photogrammetry for Beginners Volume 1, 1966. *Hobbies:* Photography; Building Construction; Gymnastics. *Address:* 5 Okarki Street, Borikiri, Port Harcourt, Nigeria.

HORVÁTH, Gábor, b. 22 Mar. 1944, Budapest, Hungary. Biologist. m. Magdolna Droppa, 15 Nov. 1969, 1 daughter. *Education:* Graduated Teacher, Chemistry & Biology, 1968, PhD, 1971, Eötvös L University. *Appointments:* Research Associate, Department of Genetics, Eötvös L University, Budapest; Research Associate, 1971, Research Feklow, 1975, Institute Plant Physiol.Biol.Res. Center, Hungarian Acad. Sci. Szeged; UNDP Fellow, CSIRO, Division of Plant Industry, Canberra, Australia, 1974. *Memberships:* Australian Society of Plant Physiologists. *Publications:* Contributor of numerous articles in professional and scientific journals. *Address:* School of Biological Science, The Flinders University, Adelaide, Australia.

HOSKING, Roger John, b. 28 Nov. 1940, Port Pirie, South Australia. Professor. m. Jacoba Nora Jean Gunther, 22 Dec. 1962, 3 sons. *Education:* BSc, 1961, BSc, Honours Mathematical Physics, 1962, University of Adelaide, 1958-61; PhD, 1965, University of Western Ontario, 1962-65. *Appointments:* Research Officer, Semiconductor Laboratory, Philips Electrical Industries, South Australia, 1960-61; Experimental Officer, Weapons Research Establishment, Salisbury, South Australia, 1962; Research Fellow, Max-Planck-Institut für Physik und Astrophysik, Munich, 1965-66; Visiting Fellow, Department of Theoretical Physics, Institute of Advanced Studies, Australian National University, 1968-69; Associate, Theory Division, Culham Laboratory, U.K.A.E.A., 1970-71; Lecturer/Senior Lecturer, School of Mathematical Sciences, Flinders University of South Australia, 1966-71; Nuffield Foundation Travelling Fellow, to Culham Laboratory and Department of Applied Mathematics and Theoretical Physics, University of Cambridge, 1975-76; Professor of Applied Mathematucs and Chairman of the Division of Computer Applications, Asian Institute of Technology, Bangkok, Thailand, 1980-81; Professor of Mathematics, University of Waikato, Hamilton, New Zealand, 1971-. *Memberships:* New Zealand, Australian, South East Asian, Mathematical Societies; New Zealand Computer Society; New Zealand Astronomical Society; *Publications:* Author First Steps in Numerical Analysis (with Joyce and Turner); Over 30 papers, particularly on fusion energy, plasma physics, engineering and astronomical topics, published in scientific journals; Various popular articles. *Honours:* Commonwealth Scholar and Bursary Award, 1958-61; Canadian National Research Council Studentship, 1962-65. *Hobbies:* Personal computers; Cricket; Travelling. *Address:* 47 Albert Street, Hamilton, New Zealand.

HOSSAIN, Md Fazlee, b. 1 Feb. 1938, Burma. Mathematician, Educator. m. Rosy, 24 Apr. 1959, 3 sons, 3 daughters. *Education:* DU, ISc, 1953; DU, BSc, 1957; DU, MSc, 1958; MSc, Manchester University UK, 1964. *Appointments:* Lecturer in Mathematics, Government Colleges, Bangladesh, 1959-61; Assistant Professor of Mathematics, Goverment College, Chitta-

gong, 1961-68; Assistant Professor of Mathematics, 1968-71, Associate Professor, 1971-76, Professor, 1976-, Chittagong University, Bangladesh; Provost, Suhrawardy Hall, 1976-81; Dean, Faculty of Science, Chittagong University. *Memberships:* President, Physics, Applied Physics, Mathematics, Statistics and Meteorology Section of Bangladesh Association for the Advancement of Science; Vice-Present, Bangladesh Mathematical Association; Senate, Dacca University Bangladesh; London Mathematical Society; American Association for the Advancement of Science; Executive, Bangladesh Association for the Scientists and Scientific Professions. *Publications:* Various contributions to scientific journals; The Geometry of Numbers, 1974. *Honours:* Brennand Prize, Dacca University, 1957; Text Books Board, Bangladesh for Mathematics, 1970, Social Studies, 1975. *Hobbies:* Gardening; Games. *Address:* Village, Hossainpur, Post Office, Panchgaon, Police Station, Chatkhil, District Noakhali, Bangladesh.

HOSSAIN, Mosharaff, b. 1 Dec. 1930, Dacca, Bangladesh. University Professor. m. Pirkko Inari Marjatta Stahlhammar, 6 July 1956, 2 sons. *Education:* BA, 1948, MA, 1950, Dacca University; MA, Manchester University, 1954; PhD, London School of Economics, 1956. *Appointments:* Lecturer in Economics, Dacca University, 1951-52; Deputy Chief Economist, East Pakistan Planning Board, 1957-58; Economist, Taxation Enquiry Committee, Government of Pakistan, 1958-59; Professor of Economics and Director, Socio-Economic Research Board, 1959-68; Nuffield and Leverhulme Research Fellow, York University, England, 1968-70; Policy Planning Cell, Government of the People's Republic of Bangladesh, 1971; Planning Commission, 1972-73; Visiting Research Fellow, Queen Elizabeth House, Oxford and Christian Michelsen Institute, Bergen, Norway, 1976-79; Professor of Economics, Dacca University, 1974-75, 1979-. *Memberships:* Executive Committees, Pakistan and Bangladesh Economic Associations; Executive Committee, Dacca University Teachers' Association. *Publications:* Federal Finance & Economic Development; Taxation and Economic Development; Socio-Economic study of tobacco-growing areas of Rangpur; Issues in Rural Development; Nature of State Power in Bangladesh. *Honours:* British Council Award, 1955; Leadership Exchange Specialist Grant, US State Department, 1963; Visiting Fellowships, Brookings Institution, Workington, 1963, Nuffield, 1968-69, Leverhulme, 1969-70. *Hobby:* Cooking. *Address:* The Old University Bungallow, 3 Fuller Road, Ramna, Dacca, Bangladesh.

HOUGHTON, Aurthur Leslie Noel Douglas, (Lord of Sowerby), b. 11 Aug. 1898, Long Eaton, Derbyshire, England. Member of House of Lords. m. Vera Travis, 11 Mar. 1939. *Education:* Long Eaton Grammar School. *Appointments:* Civil Servant, 1915-22; Secretary, Inland Revenue, Staff Federations, 1922-60; Member of Parliament, 1949-74; Cabinet Minister, 1964-67; Chairman, Parliamentary Labour Party, 1967-74; Member of the House of Lords, 1974-. *Memberships:* Chairman, Teachers Pay Inquiry, 1974; Committee on State Aid in Political Parties, 1975-76; Committee on Security of Cabinet Documents, 1976. *Honours:* Companion of Honour, 1967; Life Peer, 1974. *Address:* 110 Marsham Court, London S W 1, England.

HOVE, Richard Chemist, b. 23 Sept. 1935, Belingive, Zimbabwe. Minister. m. 18 Sept. 1968, 3 sons, 1 daughter. *Education:* B.Com. Bombay, 1966. *Appointments:* Armed Struggle, 1966-80; Minister, 1980-. *Address:* 24 Argyll Drive, Highlands, Salisbury, Zimbabwe.

HOWE, May (Mavis), (Mrs James Howe), b. 11 Dec. 1911, Torrensville, South Australia. Artist. m. Jemes, 17 Mar 1934, 1 son, 1 daughter. *Education:* Port Adelaide Business College Certificates, 1930; Studied painting, Walter Wotzke Hahndorf Academy, 1959-65, Ruth Tuck, Adelaide, 1962-65. *Appointments:* Tutor in Art, Junior and Adult Classes, Adult Education Department SA Onkaparinga Centre Branch, 1966-75; Tutor in Art to Country Women, Country Womens Association Incorporated, South Australia, 1968-74. Director, Yureilla Art Gallery, Uraidla, South Australia. *Memberships:* Associate, nominated for Fellowship, Royal SA Society of Arts Incorporated 1981; Branch Vice-President, Secretary for Crafts South Australian Country Womens Association Incorporated, 1955-64; Hahndorf

Gallery Committee. *Creative Works:* Landscape Painting to be hung in new District Council Chambers, Strathalbym, South Australia, 1981; Paintings, private collections, in America, New Zealand, South Africa, Northern Territory to the Australian States, Queensland, Victoria & South Australia; Exhibitions in: Melbourne Victoria, 1979; Hahndorf Gallery, 1965; Adelaide Festival of Arts, 1972, 1980; Paintings currently in Hahndorf Academy, McLaren Vale Barn Gallery, Miller Andersons and others. *Honours:* Special Award, Royal Show, Adelaide, 1963; E McArthur Pottery Scholarship, Adelaide Potters Club Incorporated, 1967; First Award for Abstract Painting, Weerama Festival, Murray Bridge, South Australia, 1972. *Address:* 1 Sunter Street, Strathalbyn, South Australia, 5255.

HOWELLS, Gwyn, b. 13 May 1918, Birmingham, England. Doctor. m. Simone Maufe, 14 Feb. 1942, 2 sons, 2 daughters. *Education:* University College School, London; St Bartholomews Hospital, University of London; MRCS, LRCP (England), 1941; MB, BS (London), 1942; MRCP (London), 1950; MD, (London), 1950; MRACP (Australia), 1967; FRCP (London), 1974; FRACP (Australia), 1971. *Appointments:* War Service, 1942-46, Captain RAMC, Major IAMC; House Physician, St James Hospital 1946; Registrar to Neurological Department (United Leeds Hospital), 1947-48; Medical Registrar, Bradford Hospital, 1948-49; General practice, 1950; Senior Medical & Chest Registrar, West Cornwall Clinical Area, England, 1950-53; Chest Physician, Derby Clinical Area, England, 1953-57; Consultant Physician, Thoracic Annexe, Toowoomba, Queensland, Australia; Chest Physician, Toowoomba General Hospital, Queensland, 1957-66; First Assistant Director-General 1966-73, Deputy Director-General, 1973, Director-General, 1973-, Federal Department of Health, Canberra, Australia; Chairman, National Health & Medical Research Council, 1973-; Director, Quarantine for Australia, 1973-. *Memberships:* Commonwealth Club, Canberra, Australia; Imperial Service Club, Sydney, Australia. *Honours:* CB, 1979. *Address:* 23 Beauchamp Street, Deakin, ACT, 2600, Australia.

HOWIE, Ross Nisbet, b. 20 Oct. 1933, Hong Kong. Medical Practitioner. m. Helena Mary Clarkson, 4 Mar. 1961, 2 sons, 1 daughter. *Education:* MB, ChB, University of Otago, 1956. *Appointments:* Research Fellow, National Women's Hospital, 1964-72; Senior Lecturer in Paediatrics, 1972-76, Associate Professor, 1976-, University of Auckland. *Memberships:* Fellow Royal Australasian College of Physicians; Paediatric Society of New Zealand, Secretary, 1970-72; Maternity Servives Committee, 1976-81, Child Health Committee, 1977-81, New Zealand Board of Health. *Publications:* Various contributions on the aspects of health of newborn, especially prevention of respiratory disorders in premature babies (with Prof G C Liggins), and work on provision of special care services for the newborn. *Address:* 114 Wheturangi Road, Auckland, 5, New Zealand.

HOWLAND, William Goldwin Carrington, b. 7 Mar. 1915, Toronto, Canada. Chief Justice. m. Margaret Patricia Greene, 20 Aug. 1966. *Education:* BA, 1932-36, LL.B, 1939, University of Toronto; Osgoode Hall Law School, 1936-39; Called to Bar (Silver Medallist), 1939. *Appointments:* Practised law with McMillan, Binch, 1937-75; Appointed to Court of Appeal on Ontario, 1975; Chief Justice of Ontario, 1977-. *Memberships:* Life Bencher and former Treasurer, Law Society of Upper Canada; Trustee, Wycliffe College; Board of Governors, Upper Canada College. *Honours:* Honorary LL.D, Queen's University, 1972; University of Toronto, 1981. *Hobby:* Travel. *Address:* 2 Bayview Wood, Toronto, M4H 1R7. Canada.

HOWLES, Ralph, b. 5 Feb. 1915, Reddish, Nr. Manchester, England. m. Doris May Abbott, 16 Aug. 1952, 2 sons, 1 daughter. *Education:* BA, 1936, PhD, 1940, MA, 1978, St. John's College Cambridge University, 1933-40. *Appointments:* Royal Navy; Cheshunt Experimental & Research Station, Glasshouse Crops Research Institute, 1947-61; Horticultural Research Officer, Department of Agriculture, South Australia, 1962-77. *Memberships:* Australian Society of Plant Physiologists; Australian Plant Pathology Society; Australian Institute of Agricultural Science. *Publications:* Various papers or technical notes on the inactivation of viruses in seeds. *Address:* Wilshamstead, 21 Gorse Avenue, Hawthorndene, South Australia, 5051.

HOWSAM, Kenneth George, b. 8 March, 1921, Melbourne, Australia. Medical Practitioner; m. Betty Rae Gray, 14 July, 1945, 2 sons, 1 daughter(deceased); *Education:* Scotch College; Melbourne University, MB BS, 1943; Diploma Ophthalmology, 1949; FRACS, 1957; FRACO, 1966, FRACMA, 1968; *Appointments:* Resident Medical Officer Royal Melbourne Hospital; Resident medical Officer, Royal Victorian Eye & Ear Hospital; Medical Officer, Royal Australian Air Force; Medical Director, Royal Victorian Eye & Ear Hospital; *Memberships:* Royal Australian College of Ophthalmologists, President, 1981-1982; Royal Australasian College of Surgeons; Royal Australasian College of Medical Administrators; Lawn Tennis Association of Victoria; *Honours:* Royal Humane Society of Australasia, Bronze Medal, 1939; *Hobby:* Tennis; *Address:* 54 Walpole Street, Kew 3101, Victoria, Australia.

HOWSON, Jack Fingall, b. 22 Nov. 1917, Fremantle, Western Australia. Business Director. m. Elizabeth Wedderburn, 2 daughters. *Appointments:* Captain in British Army, Reserve of Officers in Australian and British Army, Service in India, Burma, Malaysia and Indonesia; Director: The Royal Agricultural Society of Western Australia (Inc); Director and Chairman, State Board, City Mutual Life Assurance Company Limited. *Memberships:* Honorary Secretary Treasurer, 1952-72, President, 1972-, Western Australian Olympic Council; Delegate, 1952, Executive, 1960, Australian Olympic Federation; Chairman Forward Planning Committee Australian Olympic Federation, 1977-; Honorary Secretary/Treasurer Commonwealth Games Association (WA Division), 1954-72, Chairman, 1972, Delegate, 1954-77Honorary Director of Organization, 1962; Honorary Treasurer, 1947-48, Honorary Secretary, 1949-67, President, 1968-71, Imm Past President, 1971-75, Manager, State Team, 1959, Western Australia Amateur Swimming Association; Delegate, 1958-67, Vice-President, 1967-70, President, 1970-73, Imm Past President, 1973-76, Amateur Swimming Union of Australia; President, Australian Rowing Council, 1962 and 1965; President, Amateur Rowing Association of Western Australia, 1956-60, 1961-65. Chairman, Patron, Vice-Patron, President and Vice-President of numerous Associations. *Honours:* OBE, 1962; Helms Award, 1962; Justice of the Peace, 1968; Councillor, Town of Melville, 1965-68; Councillor 1968-73, Mayor, 1973-, City of Melville. *Address:* 18 Cunningham Street, Applecross, Western Australia, 6153.

HSUEH, Shou-Sheng, b. 8 Mar. 1926, Shanghai, China. Rector. m. Grace Tang, 29 June 1957, 1 daughter. *Education:* BA, Yenching University, China, 1949; Lic. ès Sc.Pol., 1951, Doc. ès Sc. Pol., 1953, University of Geneva. *Appointments:* Lecturer, Political Science, University of Hong Kong, 1956-63; Assistant Secretary General of Eastern Regional Organisation for Public Administration & Visiting Professor, University of The Philippines, 1963-66; Reader & Professor in Government and Public Administration, Chinese University of Hong Kong, 1966-72, 1975-80; Vice-Chancellor, Nanyang University, Singapore, 1972-75; Rector, University of East Asia, 1980-. *Publications:* Author of several monographs and numerous articles published in Asia, Europe and the USA. *Honours:* Chevalier de l'Ordre National du Mérite by the French Government, 1975. *Hobbies:* Music; Reading; Sports. *Address:* University of East Asia, Hong Kong Office, Suite 1719, Swire House, Central, Hong Kong.

HU, Hung-lick Henry, b. 15 Jan. 1920, Shaoshing, Chekiang Province, China. Barrister-at-Law. m. Chung Chi-Yung, 12 Nov 1945, 2 sons. *Education:* Bachelor of Law, China, 1942; PhD, 1952, Diploma of High Studies in International Law & Affairs, 1953, Paris University; Barrister-at-Law, Middle Temple, 1954. *Appointments:* Practising Lawyer in Hong Kong, 1955-; President, Shue Yan Post Secondary College, 1971-; Superviser, Shue Yan Secondary School, 1972. *Memberships:* Hong Kong Legislative Council, 1976-; Urban Council, 1965-; Chairman, Board of Review, 1977-; Executive, Hong Kong Housing Authority, 1976-; Vice-Chairman, Hong Kong Reform Club, 1965-; Vice-President, Hong Kong Neighbourhood Advisory Council, 1970-. Le Problème Coréen, 1953; The Post War European Institutions, 1955; Nationality & Human Rights, 1956;

Chinese Law & Custom in Hong Kong, 1956; Suez-Canal Crisis, 1957. *Honours:* OBE, 1976; JP, 1976. *Hobbies:* Reading; Hiking; Travelling. *Address:* Flat 404, No. 114, MacDonnell Road, Hong Kong.

HUANG, Po-Wen, Jr., b. 1 Feb. 1939, Hong Kong. Banker. m. Shuan-Shuan Cheryl Chao, 6 June 1975, 2 sons. *Education:* Bachelor of Arts, Magna cum laude, 1960; Master of Arts, 1961; Doctor of Philosophy, Yale University, USA 1963; Social Science Research Council Post-Doctoral Fellowship, 1967-69. *Appointments:* Loan Officer, International Bank for Reconstruction and Development, World Bank, Washington, DC, USA 1969-71; Asian Representative, Investment Banking Division, Merrill Lynch Pierce Fenner and Smith, and concurrently Executive Director, Trident International Finance Limited, Hong Kong, 1971-78; President, Chief Executive Officer, Financial and Investment Services for Asia, Limited, 1978-. *Memberships:* Rho Psi Society; Kowloon Cricket Club, Hong Kong; Craigengower Cricket Club, Hong Kong; American Club; South China Athletic Association; Yale Club of Hong Kong. *Publications:* Author: The Asian Development Bank: Diplomacy and Development in Asia, 1965. *Hobbies:* Sports; Music. *Address:* Apartment E5, 3 Old Peak Road, Hong Kong.

HUBBARD, Robert Hamilton, b. 17 June 1916, Hamilton, Ontario. Art Historian. *Education:* BA, McMaster University 1937; MA 1940, PhD 1942, University of Wisconsin. *Appointments:* National Gallery 1946; Curator of Canadian Art 1947; Chief Curator 1954-78; Cultural Adviser to the Governor General of Canada, 1978-81; Honorary Historian, Government House Ottawa, 1981. *Memberships:* Royal Society of Canada; (Academy of Humanities and Social Sciences); Canadian Museums Association; International Council of Museums; Canadian Historical Association; Athenaeum, London; Rideau, Ottawa. *Publications:* European Paintings in Canadian Collections, 1954-62; National Gallery of Canada Cat. of Paintings and Sculpture, 1957-60; Ridean Hall, 1977. *Honours:* Officer of the Order of Canada, 1977; Fellow of the Royal Society of Canada, 1962; LLD, Mount Allison University 1965. *Address:* 200 Rideau Terrace, Ottawa, K1M0Z3, Canada.

HUCKSTEP, Ronald Lawrie, b. 22 July 1926, Chefoo, China. Professor of Traumatic & Orthopaedic Surgery. m. Margaret Ann MacBeth, 2 Jan. 1960, 2 sons, 1 daughter. *Education:* Aurora University, Shanghai, 1943; Queens' College, Cambridge University, 1946-48; Middlesex Hospital, London, 1948-52; BA (Hons), 1948; MA, MB, B Chir (Cantab), 1952; MD (Cantab), 1957; FRCS (Edin), 1957; FRCS (Eng), 1958; FRACS, 1973. *Appointments:* Registrar & Chief Assistant, Orthopaedic Department, St. Bartholomew's Hospital and various other surgical appointments; Middlesex & Royal National Orthopaedic Hospitals, London, 1952-60; Professor of Orthopaedic Surgery, and various other appointments, Makerere University, Kampala, 1960-72; Consultant Orthopaedic Surgeon & Honorary Surgeon to various Government & Mission Hospitals in Uganda & Honorary Surgeon Round Table Polio Clinic, Kampala, 1960-72; Professor & Chairman, Department of Traumatic & Orthopaedic Surgery Prince of Wales Hospital, Sydney, and Rotating Chairmen, School of Surgery, University of New South Wales; Consultant Orthopaedic Surgeon, Sutherland & Royal South Sydney Hospital, Australia. *Memberships:* Fellow, Royal Society of Medicine, 1955; Fellow, British Orthopaedic Association, 1967; Founder and Honorary Member World Orthopaedic Concern, 1973; Numerous other Societies, Associations, Councils and Committees concerned with orthopaedic and traumatic surgery and rehabilitation of the physically disabled. *Publications:* Books and Papers: Typhoid Fever and other Salmonella Infections, 1962; Simple Guide to Trauma, 3rd Edition, 1982; Poliomyelitis—A Guide for Developing Countries Including Appliances and Rehabilitation, 1979; Numerous chapters in books, booklets and papers on orthopaedic surgery, injuries, typhoid fever, rehabilitation and other medical subjects. *Honours:* Melsome Memorial Prize, Queens' College, Cambridge, 1948; Raymond Horton Smith Prize, 1957; Hunterian Professor, Royal College of Surgeons of England, 1959-60; Commonwealth Foundation Travelling Lecturer, 1970. 73, 76, 78 and 1980; Irving Geist Award, International Society for Rehabilitation of the Disabled, 1969; CMG, 1971. *Hobbies:* Photogra-

phy; Designing orthopaedic appliances and implants; Swimming; Travel; Organising orthopaedic services for the cripple in developing countries. *Address:* 108 Sugarloaf Crescent, Castlecrag, New South Wales 2068, Sydney, Australia.

HUDSON, Alfred Arthur John, b. 1 Feb. 1922, Dhariwal, Punjab, India. Brigade Secretary (Chief Executive), The Boys' Brigade. m. Betty Clarke, 30 Sept. 1944. *Appointments:* RAF (in ranks), 1939-46; RAF (commissioned service), 1946-74; Wing Commander RAF Regt, retired 1974. *Memberships:* Licensed Reader, Church of England, 1968; British Institute of Management, AMBIM, 1974, MBIM, 1976, FBIM, 1979; British Ornithologists' Union, 1968; RAF Ornithological Society, Founder Chairman, 1966; British Trust for Ornithology, 1968. *Hobbies:* Birdwatching; Gardening; Stamp collecting; Photography; Hill-walking. *Address:* 3 Orion, Roman Hill, Bracknell, Berkshire, England.

HUDSON, Ian George, b. 28 May 1917, Sydney, Australia. Honorary Consul-General & Company Director. m. 26 Feb. 1945, 1 son, 4 daughters. *Education:* The Scots College, Bellevuew Hill, NSW, Australia. *Appointments:* Timber Industry from 1934; Chairman, A Hudson Group of Companies; Consul-General of Thailand, 1971-. *Memberships:* Past District Governor, Rotary International; The Australian Club. *Honours:* A.M; H M Queens Jubilee Honors and Commander of the Most Noble Order of the Throne of Thailand, 1978. *Hobbies:* Ornothology; Gardening; Australaiana. *Address:* High Winds, 661 Old Northern Road, Dural, 2158, NSW, Australia.

HUGH, Thomas Benedict, b. 25 Jan. 1935, Sydney, Australia. Surgeon. m. Marie Judith Cluff, 21 Jan. 1960, 2 sons, 4 daughters. *Education:* MBBS, Sydney University, 1957; FRCS, England, 1961; FRACS, 1966. *Appointments:* Visiting Surgeon, St Vincent's Hospital, Sydney; Visiting Surgeon, Mater Misericordiae Hospital, Sydney. *Memberships:* Tattersalls Club, Sydney. *Publications:* Approximately 30 scientific articles in various Surgical Journals. *Honours:* H J Ritchie Prize in Medicine, University of Sydney, 1957. *Hobbies:* Skiing; Windsurfing; Music. *Address:* 21 Carnarvon Road, Roseville, 2069 NSW, Australia.

HUGHES, Davis (Sir), b. 24 Nov. 1910, Launceston, Tasmania. Company Director. m. Joan Phillipa Johnston, 1 son, 2 daughters. *Education:* Teacher Training Certificate, Department of Education, Hobart, Tasmania, 1929; University of Tasmania, (First, Second and Third Year), Degree not completed. *Appointments:* Teacher, Primary Secondary Schools, Tasmania, 1930-34; Teacher, Friends School, Bibur, 1934-35; Teacher, Caulfield Grammar School, Melbourne, 1936-40; RAAF Squadron leader (Overseas service), 1940-45; Deputy Head Master, The Armidale School, NSW, 1947-50; Member of Parliament, 1950-73; Minister for Public Works, NSW, 1965-73; Agent General for NSW, London, UK Europe, 1973-78; Australian Advisor, Societe General, Australia; Director, Societe General Australia Limited; Chairman, Director, Brambles Crouch Australia Ltd; Chairman Director, Neyri River Coproration Australia. *Memberships:* Councillor, University of New England, NSW, 1950-73. *Honours:* Mayor of City of Armidale, NSW, 1953-56; KB, 1975; Freeman City of London, 1975; Freeman City of Armidale, NSW, 1972. *Hobbies:* Fishing; Golf; Tennis; Cricket; Rowing. *Address:* 91/11 Broadwaters, Sutherland Crescent, Darling Point, Sydney, Australia.

HUGHES, Idwal Wyn, b. 21 Feb. 1932, Bermuda. Entomologist. m. Betsey 11 July 1957, 1 son, 3 daughters. *Education:* BSc, Cornell, 1954; MSA, 1960, PhD, 1967, University of Florida. *Appointments:* Plant Pathologist, Assistant Director, Director, Department of Agriculture & Fisheries, Bermuda. *Memberships:* Vice-President, Bermuda Biological Station for Research; Entomological Society of America; Bermuda Technical Society. *Honours:* MBE. *Hobbies:* Tennis; Gardening. *Address:* Botanical Gardens, PO Box 834, Hamilton, 5, Bermuda.

HUGHES, James Curnow, b. 18 Aug. 1929, Adelaide, South Australia. Major General. m. Janice Mary Wardropper, 3 Aug. 1955, 2 sons, 1 daughter. *Education:* Royal Military College, Duntroon, Graduated, 1950; Australian Staff College, awarded PSC, Graduated, 1964; Royal College of Defence Studies, Awarded,

RCDS, Graduated, 1977. *Appointments:* 3 RAR, Korea, 1951-52; Staff Captain, BCFK Japan, 1952-53; Adjutant Adelaide University Regiment, 1954-57; 3 RAR, Malaya, 1957-59; Instructor, RMA Sandhurst, 1960-62; Australian Staff College, 1963-64; OC 2 SAS, 1964-66 including Borneo, 1966; Director of Army Recruiting, 1966-69; CO 4 RAR, 1969-72, including CO 4 RAR/NZ (Anzac), Vietnam, 1971; Commandant Land Warfare Centre, Canungra, 1972-75; Director General, Training and Education Policy, 1975-76; Royal College of Defence Studies, 1977; Controller of Establishments, Department of Defence, 1978-81; GOC Logistic Command, 1981-. *Memberships:* Naval, Military and Air Force Club of South Australia; Naval and Military, Melbourne. *Publications:* Occasional contributions to professional journals. *Honours:* DSO, 1971; Military Cross, 1951; Foreign Awards (US & South Vietnam). *Hobbies:* Rugby Union; Rowing; Pony Breeding; Farming. *Address:* Nangara, Murrumbateman, NSW, 2582, Australia.

HUGHES, James Cyril, b. 3 Jan. 1931, Llangeitho, Ceredigion, Wales. Director, Chief Executive of Urdd Gobaith Cymru. m. Margaret Lloyd Hughes, 17 Aug. 1957, 2 sons. *Education:* LLB, University College of Wales, 1948-51. *Appointments:* Farming, 1952-56; Personal Assistant to the Director of Urdd Gobaith Cymru, 1956-64; BBC Wales Assistant Information Officer, 1964-68; Deputy Director and Director Designate of Urdd Gobaith Cymru, 1969-; Director of Urdd Gobaith Cymru, 1973-. *Memberships:* Court, Council and various Committees of the University College of Wales; Court of Royal National Eisteddfod of Wales; Executive Committee of Welsh Theatre Society. *Publications:* Short articles in various publications. *Hobbies:* All aspects of Welsh Culture, with particular emphasis on the Welsh Language; Sports; Caravanning; Foreign Travel. *Address:* Sycharth, 54 Maes Hendre, Aberystwyth, Dyfed, Wales.

HUGHES, Richard, b. 5 Mar. 1906, Melbour,e Australia. Foreign Correspondent. m. Anne Lee, 1 Oct. 1973 (two earlier marriages, both deceased), 1 son. *Education:* Christian Brothers College, StKilda, Melbourne, 1912-20; *Appointments:* Boy Shunter, Victorian Railways, 1920; Public Relations Officer, Victorian Railways, 1932; Junior Reporter, The Star, Melbourne, 1934-35; Chief of Staff, Sunday Telegraph, Sydney, 1939; War Correspondent, North Africa, 1942-43; Far East Representative, The Sunday Times (London) Based Tokyo, Hong Kong, 1948-; Respreentative, The Economist (London), Tokyo, Hong Kong, 1948-, The Times (London), Hong Kong 1973, The Herald and The Sun, Melbourne, 1958-. *Memberships:* Foreign Correspondents' Club, Hong Kong. *Publications:* Dr Watson's Case Book—Studies in Australian Crime, 1944 (reprint); The Chinese Communes, 1960 (Reprint); Hong Kong - Borrowed Place, Borrowed Time, 1965 (Reprint), Revised 1975 (Reprint); Foreign Devil, 1972 (Reprint). *Honours:* CBE, 1980. *Address:* Apartment 1, Castle Tower, 1 Castle Road, Hong Kong.

HUGHES, Robert Ernest Weston, b. 6 Mar. 1946, Melbourne, Australia. Community Arts and Development. m. Rita Elizabeth Preiss, 14 Mar. 1979, 1 son. *Education:* Yoga Education Centre, 1974-. *Appointments:* Drover, Steelworker, Administrator, Poet, 1964-74; Cartage Contactor, Poet, 1974-76; Director, Footscray Community Arts Centre, 1976-. *Memberships:* Founding Secretary, Poets Union of Australia; Past Chairperson, Community Arts Network, Victoria; Past Co-Ordinator, Salt Water River Festival; Past Co-Ordinator, Down to Earth Festival; Co-Ordinator, Yarraville Village Festival. *Publications:* Dreamer, Poetry and Poems, 1979. *Hobbies:* Poetry; Drawing; Fishing; Entertaining. *Address:* 5 Tenterden Street, Spotswood 3015, Victoria, Australia.

HUGHES, (Sir) Edward Stuart Reginald, b. 4 July 1919. Professor of Surgery. m. Alison Lelean, 30 Dec. 1944, 2 sons, 2 daughters. *Education:* MD; MS; FRCS. Eng; FRACS; FACS; FRCS (Hon). Canada. *Appointments:* House Surgeon, Wingfield Morris Orthopaedic Hospital, Oxford England, 1946-47; Resident Surg. Off., Connaught Hospital, London, Leverhulme Schol., 1947-48; BCOF, Japan, Lt-Col. and Senior Surgeon, Kure Hospital, Japan, 1950-51; Assistant Surgeon, 1953, Hon. Surg, 1964-74, Consultant Surgeon, 1974-, Royal Melbourne Hospital; Surgeon to Out-Patients, 1954-63; Tutor Surgeon, Queen's College,

Melbourne, 1955-63; Censor-in-Chief, Royal Australian College of Surgeons, 1969-73; Senior Vice-President, 1974, President, 1975-; Professor of Surgery, Alfred Hospital, Monash University, 1973-; Consultant Surgeon to the Army; Chief Medical Consultant Hospital and Charities Commission. *Memberships:* Fellow, Queen's College Melbourne University, 1964-; Member, Board of Examiners (Surg.) VRC, 1959-73; First Director of the Menzies Foundation for Health, Fitness and Physical Achievement, 1979-. *Publications:* All About an Ileostomy, 1971; All About a Colostomy, 1976. *Honours:* Henry Simpson Newland Prize Surgery, 1962; CBE, 1971; Kt. cr. 1977. *Hobby:* Tennis. *Address:* Department of Surgery, Monash Medical School, Alfred Hospital, Prahran, Victoria, Australia.

HUGHES-EVANS, David, b. 20 Apr. 1930, Llangeitho, Dyfed, United Kingdom. Editor, Lecturer. m. Jeanne Leger, 28 Feb. 1981. *Education:* BSc, Wye College, University of London, 1950-53. *Appointments:* Senior Lecturer, Life Sciences, Farnborough College of Technology, 1966-; Joint Editor, International Journal, The Environmentalist, 1980-. *Memberships:* International Union for the Conservation of Nature and Natural; Resources (IUCN), Member of the Commission on Education; Executive Officer, World Environment and Resources Council; Commonwealth Human Ecology Council; Science Policy Foundation; Editorial Boards of Environmental Conservation and The International Journal of Environmental Studies. *Publications:* Author/Editor of numerous papers and books on environment, education and training, including the series, Biology—An environmental approach. *Hobbies:* Art; History of Science; Travel. *Address:* 183 Quadrangle Towers, Cambridge Square, London W2, England.

HUI, Check-Wing, b. 28 Nov. 1927, Kwangchou. Jeweller. *Education:* Gemological Institute of America, California, USA. *Appointments:* Managing Partner of New Universal Jewelry Company, Hongkong and Kowloon; Partner of Chan Kwong Kee Jewellery. *Memberships:* include: Chairman of the HK Diamond Importers Association, 1977, 1976, 1975; Former Chairman of the Supervisory Committee and Vice Chairman of the Executive Committee of the Hong Kong Jewellers and Goldsmiths Association; Former Chairman of the Executive Committee and Supervisory Committee of the HK and Kowloon Jewellers and Goldsmiths Employees Association; Permanent Honorary Director of the Hong Kong Jade and Stone Manufacturers Association; Permanent Honorary President of the Hong Kong and Kowloon Jewellers Association; 2nd Vice Chairman of the Tung Wah Group of Hospitals, 1974-; Honorary Advisor of the Tung Wah Group of Hospitals, 1975-; Hong Kong Management Association; Hong Kong Designers Association; Fellow, Photographic Society of Hong Kong; Fellow, Photographic Salon Exhibitors Association of Hong Kong; Fellow, Asia Society of Arts. *Creative Works:* Photographic Colour Prints; Jewellery Creation. *Honours:* Awards and certificates of commendation in the Diamond Design Competition in 1974, 1978, 1979; Awards for originality of thought in the Governor's Award for New Products in 1975, 1977; Awarded Best Colour Print in London International Salon Exhibition 1968; Listed one of the top ten photographers in colour print section by Photographic Society of America in 1972, 1974, 1975. *Hobbies:* Photography; Chinese Kung-Fu. *Address:* New Universal Diamond Company, Diamond Exchange Bldg. 23/F, 20 Ince House Street, Queen's Road Central, Hong Kong.

HULL, David, b. 14 Oct. 1941, Wellington, New Zealand. Barrister. m. Roche Dora-Anne McPherson, 2 daughters. *Education:* LLB, Victoria University of Wellington, 1964. *Appointments:* Private Employment, New-Zealand, 1964-67; Crown Counsel, Hong Kong, 1967-71; Attorney-General, Western Samoa, 1974-77; Parliamentary Counsel, New Zealand, 1971-79; Attorney-General, Gibraltar, 1979-. *Honours:* Queen's Counsel, Gibraltar, 1980. *Hobby:* Fishing. *Address:* 28 South Barrack Road, Gibraltar.

HULME, Peter Joseph, b. 14 Aug. 1930, England. Government Secretary. m. June Evelyn Allen 16 Sept. 1954, 2 sons. *Education:* Douglas High School for Boys, Isle of Man, 1941-46; *Appointments:* Isle of Man Government Service, 1951-. *Memberships:* RAF Association. *Hobbies:* Hill Walking; DIY. *Address:* Government Office, Douglas, Isle of Man, UK.

HULSTON, John Richards, b. 12 July 1932, Christch-urch, New Zealand. Scientist. m. Patricia Jean Quinn, 9 Dec. 1961, 2 sons, 1 daughter. *Education:* BSc, 1952, MSc, 1954, University of Canterbury, New Zealand; PhD, 1964, McMaster University Hamilton, Ontario, Canada. *Appointments:* Physicist, Dominion Physical Laboratory, Lower Hutt, New Zealand, 1955-58; Mass Spectroscopist, 1958-61, Head of Mass Spectrometry Section, 1964-, Institute of Nuclear Sciences, Private Bag, Lower Hutt, New Zealand; Post-graduate study leave, McMaster University, Hamilton, Ontario, Cana-da, 1962-64; Visiting Lecturer, Geothermal Institute, University of Auckland, New Zealand, 1979-. *Memberships:* Australian and New Zealand Society for Mass Spectrometry, Chairman, 1975-77, New Zealand Branch Chairman, 1974-81; Fellow, Institute of Phy-sics; Fellow, New Zealand Institute of Chemistry; Geo-chemical Society, USA; Anglican Church Vestry. *Publi-cations:* Joint contributor of chapter on geothermal systems in Handbook of enviromental Isotope Geo-chemistry; Approximately 40 scientific papers on (a) stable isotopes in geothermal systems, (b) theretical calculations of isotope effects, (c) mass spectrometer instrumentation. *Honours:* International Atomic Ener-gy Agency Fellowship, 1962-63. *Hobby:* Amateur Ra-dio. *Address:* 7 Earlston Grove, Avalon, Lower Hutt, New Zealand.

HUMPHREYS, Benjamin Charles, b. 17 Aug. 1934, Brisbane, Queensland, Australia. Member of House of Representatives. m. Beryl Joan Dixon, 7 Mar. 1955, 2 sons, 3 daughters. *Education:* Qualified Grade A Motor Mechanic; Qualified Airframe Artisifer (RANR NS). *Memberships:* Patron, Balmoral Valley United Stars Club, South Brisbane Sub-Branch RSL; Trustee, Bulim-ba Child Care & Pre-School Centre; Queensland Con-servation Council; Various Clubs and sporting organi-sations. *Hobbies:* Cricket; Boating. *Address:* 29 Virginia Avenue, Hawthorne, Queensland, 4171, Australia.

HUMPHREYS, David Colin, b. 23 Apr. 1925, Sun-ningdale, England. Civil Servant. m. Jill Allison Cran-mer, 8 Nov. 1952, 2 sons, 1 daughter. *Education:* King's Scholar, Eton College, 1938-43; BA, 1949, MA, 1953, King's College, Cambridge, 1946-49. *Appointments:* Air Ministry, 1949; Private Secretary to Secretary of State for Air, 1959; Counsellor, UK Delegation to NATO, 1960; Air Force Department, 1963; Director, Defence Policy Staff, 1971; Assistant Secretary Gener-al (Defence Planning and Policy) NATO, 1972; Under Secretary (Naval staff) 1976; Deputy Under Secretary (Air), 1979. *Honours:* CMG, 1977. *Address:* Rivendell, North Drive, Virginia Water, Surrey, England.

HUNN, (Sir) Jack Kent, b. 24 Aug. 1906, Masterton, New Zealand. Public Servant, (Retired). m. Dorothy Murray, 24 Dec. 1932, 2 sons. *Education:* LLM 1938. *Appointments:* Public Trust Office, 1924; Public Ser-vice Commissioner, 1954; Acting Secretary for Justice, 1950, and Internal Affairs, 1959; Secretary of Maori Affairs, 1960; Secretary of Defence, 1963; United Nations Salary Review Committee, 1956; Public Ad-ministration Adviser, South Pacific Commn. 1957 and SEATO, 1959; UN Adviser to Guyana, 1966; Chmn. Comms. of Inquiry on Wildlife, 1968 and Fire Safety, 1969; Chmn. Amalgamated Wireless (Aust) NZ Limit-ed, 1968; Chmn. Waikanae County Borough Council, 1971; Chmn. NZ Fire Service Commission, 1974. *Mem-berships:* Chairman, Waikanae War Memorial Hall Trust; Patron, Waikanae Beach Bowling Club. *Publica-tions:* Hunn Report on Maori Affairs, 1960; Articles on Defence. *Honours:* CMG, 1964; Knight Bachelor, 1976; Hon. Fellow, NZ Institute of Public Administration, 1968; Hon. Fellow, Institution of Fire Engineers, UK, 1975; Life Member: NZ Chief Fire Officers' Association, 1977; Auckland University Rowing Club, 1978. *Hob-bies:* Reading; Writing; Gardening. *Address:* 17 Kereru Street, Waikanae, New Zealand.

HUNN, John McLeod, b. 28 Mar. 1928, Hobart, Tas-mania. Surgeon. m. Beverley Edith Evaline Isaac, 22 Mar. 1952, 4 sons. *Education:* MB,BS, University of Melbourne, Trinity College, 1951; Diploma Child Health, Glasgow, 1962; FRCS (Edinburgh), 1965; FRACS, 1975. *Appointments:* Launceston General Hospital; Flying Doctor Service of Australia; Spencer Hospital, Wynyard, Tasmania; Princess Margaret Rose Hospital, Einburgh; Hospital for Sick Children, Great Ormond Street, London; Westminster Children's Hos-pital, London; Visiting Senior Surgeon, Surgeon in charge Burns Unit, Royal Hobart Hospital; Visiting Surgeon, Repatriation General Hospital. *Memberships:* Australian Medal Association, Fellow, Federal Council-lor. *Hobbies:* Sailing; Gardening; Cattle Breeding. *Add-ress:* 24 Sonning Crescent, Sandy Bay, Hobart, Tasma-nia, Australia.

HUNNINGS, Thomas Neville March, b. 12 Aug. 1929, Enfield, Middlesex. Barrister. m. Märta Cecilia Edsman, 13 Oct. 1962, 2 sons, 1 daughter. *Education:* University of London, King's College, 1950-53; LLB, 1953; LLM, 1956; PhD, 1964; Diploma Hague Acade-my of International Law, 1957; Called to the Bar, Middle Temple, 1954. *Appointments:* Practice at the Bar, Middle Temple, 1955-58; Information Officer, Central Office of Information, 1958-62; Senior Rese-arch Officer, British Institute of International and Com-parative Law, 1964-72; General Editor, Common Law Reports Limited, 1972-78; Editorial Director, European Law Centre Limited, 1978-; Visiting Lecturer in European Law, King's College, University of London, 1973-74, Queen Mary College, 1975-. *Memberships:* International Commission on Communications Tech-nology and Law; Union Internationale des Avocats, Commission on Law and Technology; Agricultural Law Association; University Association for Contemporary European Studies; Theatres Advisory Council; Society for Theatre Research. *Publications:* Film Censors and the Law, 1967; Legal Aspects of an Enlarged European Community, 1972; Common Market Law Reports, 1964. *Address:* 11 Russell Hill, Purley, Surrey, CR2 2JB, England.

HUNT, Blair Linn, b. 30 Aug. 1938, Labasa, Fiji. Acad-emic. m. Estelle Jeannette Ross, 2 Mar. 1962, 2 sons, 1 daughter. *Education:* Diploma in Chemical Engineer-ing, International Correspondence Schools, 1964; Ba-chelor of Agricultural Economics, (Honours), University of New England, NSW, 1971; Master of Business Administration, University of Southern California, Los Angeles, USA, 1976; Doctor of Philosophy in Business Administration, 1978. *Appointments:* Chemist, CSR Limited, 1957-72; Lecturer in Business Finance, Uni-versity of New England, 1972-74; Australian Govern-ment Overseas Fellow in Management, University of Southern California, Los Angeles, 1974-77; Head, School of Business and Public Administration, NSW Institute of Technology, 1978-; Dean, Faculty of Business Studies, 1980-. *Memberships:* FAIM, Fellow, Australian Institute of Management; Academy of Ma-nagement, USA; Australian Institute of Public Adminis-tration; Institute of Directors; Life Member, Graduate Management Association. *Honours:* Australian Gov-ernment Overseas Fellowship in Management, 1974 and 1977; Beta Gamma Sigma, 1977. Hobby: Golf. *Address:* 31 Lancaster Avenue, St Ives, NSW 2075, Australia.

HUNT, David Anthony (The Hon. Mr. Justice), b. 15 Feb. 1935, Sydney, Australia. Supreme Court Judge. m. Margaret Jennifer Frazer East, 23 Jan. 1959, 3 sons. *Education:* Bachelor of Arts, 1956, Bachelor of Laws, 1958, University of Queensland. *Appointments:* Called to Queensland Bar, 1958, the New South Wales Bar, 1958; Signed the Roll of Counsel in Victoria, 1962; Appointed Queen's Counsel for New South Wales, 1975, and for Victoria, Queensland and the Australian Capital Territory, 1976; Practised mainly in the com-mon law jurisdiction, specializing in defamation litiga-tion; Senior Counsel assisting the Royal Commission into NSW Prisons, 1976; Appointed a Judge of the Supreme Court of NSW, 1979, assigned to the Com-mon Law (Commercial List) and Criminal Divisions. *Memberships:* Australian Club, Sydney. *Publications:* Contributor to professional law journal. *Hobbies:* Ski-ing; Swimming; Reading. *Address:* 223 Eastern Road, Wahroonga, NSW, 2976, Australia.

HUNT, Geoffrey Brian, b. 11 Mar. 1947, Melbourne Australia. Professional Squash Player. m. Teresa Grace Siciliano, 1969, 1 son, 1 daughter. *Education:* BSc, Monash University, Melbourne. *Appointments:* Indus-trial Chemist, Australian Consolidated Industries Limit-ed. *Memberships:* Vice-Chairman, International Squash Players Association; Alma Club. *Publications:* Geoff Hunt on Squash. *Honours:* mbe, 1972; Numer-ous major squash championship titles including: Vic-toria Junior Champion, Australia, 1962-65; Victoria Amateur Champion, 1963-71; Australian Junior Champion, 1963; Australian Amateur Champion,

1965, 1969, 1970 & 1071; World Amateur Champion, 1967, 1969 & 1971; British Amateur Champion, 1970; British Open Champion, 1969, 1974, 1976, 1977 & 1978; Australian Open Champion, 1971, 1973, 1976 & 1977; Irish Open Champion, 1973, 1974, 1976 & 1977; South African Open Champion, 1974, 1975, 1976, 1977 & 1978; Pakistan Masters Champion, 1976, and World Open Champion, 1976 and 1977; World Open Champion, 1980; British Open Champion, 1981. *Hobbies:* Swimming; Fishing; Wine cellaring. *Address:* 24 Hilton Street, Beaumaris, 3193, Victoria, Australia.

HUNT, Ralph James Dunnet, b. 31 Mar. 1928, Narrabri, NSW, Australia. Member of Parliament, Farmer, Grazier. m. Miriam Anne McMahon, 17 Nov. 1954, 1 son, 2 daughters. *Education:* Matriculation, Scots College, Sydney, Australia. Appointments include: Councillor, Boomi Shire Council, 1956-68; Vice President, 1962-68; House of Representives, Gwydir, NSW, 1969, 1969, 72, 74, 75, 77, 80; Minister for the Interior, 1971-72; Member, Joint Opposition Shadow Ministry, 1974-75; Minister for Health, 1975-79; Minister for Transport, 1979-. *Memberships:* Moree and District Local Government Association; Gwydir River Dam Adv. Comm.; House of Reps. Standing Comm. on Aboriginal Affairs. *Hobbies:* Swimming; Tennis; Gardening; Horse Racing. *Address:* 1 Merindah Avenue, Moree, NSW 2400, Australia.

HUNTER, John Morley Withers, b. 24 June 1924, Ottawa. Director of Communications. m. Marion Alice Buckrell, 18 Sept. 1950, 2 sons, 3 daughters. *Education:* Bachelor of Arts, 1948-52; Diploma, Marketing Management, University of Western Ontario, 1969. *Appointments:* Advertising Manager, Emco Limited, London, Ontario, 1952-59; Vice-President, Manager, London Office, James Lovick Limited, Advertising Agency, 1960-67; Director of Advertising and Public Relations, 1968-80, Director of Communications, 1981-. *Memberships:* Sunningdale Golf and Country Club, London, Ontario; London Chamber of Commerce; Canadian Club; Past Master, Mt. Olivet Lodge No 300 AF & AM, Member, London Lodge of Perfection A & ASR, London Sovereign Chapter Rose Croix A & ASR, Moore Sovereign Consistory SPRS 32-Ancient and Accepted Scottish Rite; Mocha Shrine Temple; President Oriental Band; Director, and President Elect, Ontario Division, Canadian Cancer Society. *Honours:* Past President and Director, American Marketing Association, London Chapter; Founding Director, Stoneybrook Sports Association; Past Director, London Chamber of Commerce. *Hobbies:* Golf; Photography; Swimming; Cross Country Skiing. *Address:* 1631 Kathryn Drive, London, Ontario, Canada, N6G 2R7.

HUNTER OF NEWINGTON, Robert Brockie, b. 14 July 1915, Edinburgh. Retired. m. Kathleen Margaret Douglas, 12 Jan. 1940, 3 sons, 1 daughter. *Education:* George Watson's College, Edinburgh; University of Edinburgh: MB, ChD, 1938; FRCPEd, 1950; FACP, 1963; FRSEd, 1964; FInstBiol, 1968; FFCM, 1975; Hon LLD, Dundee, 1969, Birmingham, 1974; Hon DSc, Aston, Birmingham, 1981. *Appointments:* Lecturer in Therapeutics, University of Edinburgh; 1947; Lecturer in Clinical Medicine, University of St. Andrews, 1948; Professor of Materia Medica, Pharmacology and Therapeutics, 1948-67 and University of Dundee, 1967-68; Dean, Faculty of Medicine, 1958-62; Consultant Physician, Dundee General Hospitals and Director Post-Graduate Medical Education; Vice-Chancellor and Principal, University of Birmingham, 1968-81; Clinical Research Bd. MRC, 1960-64; Ministry of Health Committee, Safety of Drugs, 1963-68; Chairman, Clinical Trials Sub-committee UGC 1964-68, Medical Sub-committee, 1966-68; West Midlands RHA, 1974-80; Chairman, DHSS Working Party on Medical Administrators in Health Service, 1970-72; Chairman, DHSS Independent Scientific Committee on Smoking and Health, 1973-80; Chairman, Medical Advisory Committee of Vice-Chancellors and Principals; Nuffield Committee of Inquiry into Dental Education, 1977-80; Management Committee, King Edward's Hospital Fund, 1980-; House of Lords Select Committee on Science and Technology, 1980-. *Memberships:* Oriental Club. *Publications:* The University Today and Tomorrow, 1976; Smoking and Health, 1976; Strategy of the Independent Scientific Committee on Smoking and Health, 1977; Health Service or Sickness Service, 1978; Community Physicians/Clinical Adminstrators,

1979. *Honours:* Life Peerage, 1978; Knighthood, 1977; MBE, 1945; Deputy Lieutenant of the West Midlands County, 1977; Purdue Frederick Medical Achievement Award, 1958; Malthe Foundation Prize, 1958. *Hobbies:* 3 Oakdene Drive, Fiery Hill Road, Barnt Green, Birmingham B45, England.

HUNTER, Robert William, b. 21 Jan. 1931, Co. Durham. Chemist. m. 22 June 1967. *Appointments:* Scientific Technical Officer, NCB, 1947-63; Sewage Works Manager, Consett UDC, 1963-65; Assistant Chemist, Sunderland and South Shields Water Company, 1965-74; Works Chemist, 1974-81. *Memberships:* The Institution of Water Engineers and Scientists. Hobby: Game Fishing. *Address:* 86 Vindomora Road, Ebchester, Co. Durham, DH8 0PP, England.

HUOT, Jacques, b. 26 June 1942, Quebec, Canada. Pharmacologist. m. Nicole Tremblay, 30 June 1968, 1 son, 1 daughter. *Education:* Université Laval: BA, 1963; BSC(Pharm.), 1967; PhD (Pharmacol.), 1972; Fellowship, Lab. Physiol. Cellulaire, Collège de France, Paris, France, 1974-75. *Appointments:* Faculté de Médecine, Département de Pharmacologie, Université Laval. *Memberships:* American Association for the Advancement of Science; New York Academy of Science; Tissue Culture Association; Pharmacological Society of Canada; Canadian Federation Biological Societies; Association Canadienne Française pour l'Avancement des Sciences; Club de Recherches Cliniques du Québec. *Publications:* 27 publications including: Neurochemistry of epilepsies and neurochemical mechanism of action of anticonvulsants, 1973; L'adénylate cyclase de cellules de neuroblastomes synchronisées, 1976; The interactions between phenothiazine, phenobarbital and theophylline on the striatum and cortex cAMP concentrations in mice brain, 1977; A model system for the study of stimulus-enzyme secretion coupling in rat pancreatic acinar cells, 1979; Abstracts include: Fatigue expérimentale et agents psycho-ergotropes, 1966; Transformations métaboliques de la, 1971; Physiological and experimental variations of calcium and magnesium during the cycle of synchronized Hela cells, 1974; Relationships between the cell cycle related fluctuations of calcium content and cyclic nucleotides levels of synchronized neuroblastoma cells, 1977; Regulation of the metabolism of the neurotransmitter glutamate and of its derivatives, glutamine and GABA, in tissue cultures of glial and of neuronal cells, 1980. *Honours:* Burroughs-Wellcome, 1964; Ministère des Affaires Sociales, 1965-67; Frosst, 1966; Horner, 1967; Ministère de l'Education du Québec, 1967; Gouvernement français, 1967; Foundation Canadienne pour l'avancement des sciences pharmaceutiques, 1967; Conseil des Recherches Médicales, Studentship, 1967-69; Fellowship, Conseil des Recherches Médicales, 1974-75. *Hobbies:* Photography; Swimming; Hockey; Bicycle Riding; Skiing. *Address:* 1880 Auclair Blvd, Quartier Laurentien, Ste-Foy, Quebec, P.Q. G2G 1R7, Canada.

HURCOMB, Merle Elaine, Welfare. *Appointments:* Secretary, Sydney City Mission, 1958; Organising Secretary 1960 and 1972; Associate Executive Director, 1972-. *Memberships:* NSW Health Advisory Council, Minister for Health, 1972-78; Homeless Persons Advisory Council, Federal Minister for Social Security 1967-; Vagrants and Intoxicated Persons Committee, NSW State Government; Inner City Legal Services Board. *Honours:* United States Bi-Centennial Fellowship, Study Alcoholism and Mental Health, 1976; A.M., Member of the Order of Australia, 1980. *Hobbies:* Gardening; Yoga; Farming. *Address:* "holly Lodge", Hordens Road, Bowral NSW, Australia 2576.

HURD, Douglas Richard, b. 8 Mar. 1930, Marlborough, Wiltshire, England. Member of Parliament. m. Tatiana Elizabeth Michelle Eyre, 10 Nov. 1960, 3 sons. *Education:* King's Scholar and Newcastle Scholar, Eton College, 1942-48; First class Honours Degree in History, Trinity College, Cambridge, 1949-52. *Appointments:* HM Diplomatic Service, 1952-66; Conservative Research Department, 1966; Head, Foreign Affairs Section, 1968; Private Secretary to Leader of the Opposition, 1968-70; Political Secretary to the Prime Minister, 1970-74; Member of Parliament for Mid Oxon, 1974; Opposition Spokesman on European Affairs, 1976-79; Minister of State for Foreign and Commonwealth Affairs, 1979. *Memberships:* Chairman, Cambridge University Conservative Association; President,

Cambridge Union; Fellow, Nuffield College, Oxford. *Publications:* The Arrow War, 1967; Send Him Victorious, 1968; The Smile on the Face of the Tiger, 1969; Scotch on the Rocks, 1971; Truth Game, 1972; Vote to Kill, 1975; An End to Promises, 1979. *Honours:* Commander, Order of the British Empire, 1974. Hobby: Writing thrillers. *Address:* 2 Mitford Cottages, Westwell, Burford, Oxfordshire, England.

HURLEY, Sir John Garling, b. 2 Oct. 1906, Bondi, NSW, Australia. Company Director. m. (1) Alice E Saunders, 1929, (dec.), 3 daughters, (2) Desolie M Richardson, 1976. *Education: Education:* Sydney Technical High School. *Appointments:* Chairman, William Adams Limited 1963-74, Deputy Chairman 1974-76; Director, Development Finance Corporation Limited 1967-, Australian Fixed Trusts Limited 1970-; Manufacturers' Mutual Insurance Limited, 1954; Royal North Shore Hospital Sydney, 1969-76. *Memberships:* Mufacturing Industries Advisory Council, 1958-71; Berlei Group of Companies 1922-, including: Berlei UK Limited 1931-36; Managing Director, Berlei Limited 1948-69; President, Associate Chambers of Manufactures of Australia, 1955-56, NSW, Chamber of Manufactures 1955-57; Chairman, Standing Committee on Productivity, Commonwealth Minister of Labour Advisory Council 1957; Technical and Further Education Advisory Council NSW; Patron St. Andrew's Cathedral School Building Fund Appeal; National Heart Foundation of Australia; Institute of Directors in Australia. Royal Agricultural Society. *Honours:* Knighted 1967; CBE 1959; FAIM. *Hobbies:* Swimming; Bowls. *Address:* 12 Locksley Street, Killara, NSW, 2071, Australia.

HURLEY, Thomas Henry, b. 25 July 1925, Melbourne, Victoria. Consultant Physician. m. Yvonne Capon, 1 Dec. 1948, 3 sons, 1 daughter. *Education:* University of Melbourne, 1942-48; MB, BS, 1947; MD, 1951; MRCP, 1951; FRACP, 1962. *Appointments:* Resident and Registrar, The Royal Melbourne Hospital, 1947-52, Physician, 1954; Stewart Scholar, University of Melbourne, 1956-58; Professorial Associate University of Melbourne, 1958-. *Memberships:* Board, The Walter and Eliza Hall Institute; Commissioner, Commonwealth Serum Laboratories, also Deputy Chairman; Victorian Anti-Cancer Council; National Health and Medical Research Council; Medical Research Advisory Committee; Governor Potter Foundation. *Publications:* Publications in Medical Journals. *Honours:* OBE, 1980; Fellow, Australian Medical Association, 1979. *Hobbies:* Tennis; Sailing; Literature; Old Books. *Address:* 19 Deepdene Road, Balwyn, 3103, Melbourne, Australia.

HURN, Peter Henry Charles, b. 29 Dec. 1942. Artist. m. Patrizia Daniela Camponovo, 13 Apr. 1967. *Education:* Perth Technical College, Perth Faculty of Arts, Australia; St. Martins School of Art, UK; English Literature, History and Art, University of London, UK. *Appointments:* Exhibiting Switzerland and UIT; Mixed Shows: London, Liverpool, Allaman, Switzerland, Italy. *Hobbies:* Reading; Walking; Collecting Paintings; Art glass; Art pottery; African Sculpture. *Address:* 189C Haverstock Hill, Belsize Park, London NW3, England.

HURRELL, John Gordon Rowan, b. 13 Oct. 1949, Melbourne Victoria Australia. Immunochemist. m. Ella Boyda 15 Dec. 1973. *Education:* BSc 1970, PhD, University of Melbourne, 1977. *Appointments:* Immunochemist, Commonwealth Serum Laboratories, 1971-78; Research Fellow, Harvard Medical School, 1979; Secientific Consultant, Centocor Inc., Philadelphia, 1980; Head, Immunochemistry R&D, Commonwealth Serum Laboratories, 1980-. *Memberships:* Australian Biochemicl Society; Australian Society for Immunology; American Chemical Society; New York Academy of Science. *Publications:* Scientific publications: 42 Papers and Book Chapters. *Honours:* Dunlop Exhibition in Biochemistry, 1970; Commonwealth Postgraduate Research Award, 1973; Fulbright Fellowship, 1979. *Hobbies:* Snow Skiing; Philately; Tennis. *Address:* 32 Dublin Avenue, Strathmore, Victoria, Australia, 3041.

HURST, Francis John Embleton, b. 27 Dec. 1920, Gildersome, Yorkshire, England. Librarian. m. Teresa Anne O'Doherty, 1 Feb. 1968, 1 son, 1 daughter. *Education:* BA, MA, Oxford University, UK, 1946; MA, University of Dublin, Ireland, 1959. *Appointments:* Royal Armoured Corps, 1941-45; Staff-Tutor, Department of Extramural Studies, Durham University, UK,

1947-50; Staff, Manchester Public Libraries, UK, 1951-58; Deputy Librarian, 1958-65, Librarian, 1965-67, Trinity College, Dublin, Ireland; Librarian, New University of Ulster, Northern Ireland, 1967-. *Memberships:* President, 1972-74, Library Association of Ireland; Associate of Library Association; Kildare Street and University Club, Dublin; Royal Irish Yacht Club; Royal Dublin Society; Royal Zoological Society of Ireland. *Publications:* Treasures of Trinity College, Dublin, 1961; articles in Professional journals. *Hobbies:* Gardening; Ornithology. *Address:* 72 Ballywillan Road, Portrush, Co. Antrim BT56 8JN, Northern Ireland.

HUSAIN, Majid, b. 2 July 1938, Vill Banhera (Tanda), Saharanpur, UP, India. Teacher. m. 10 June 1967, 2 sons, 1 daughter. *Education:* BA, Agra University, India, 1957; MA, 1959, LL.B, 1959, PhD, 1963, Aligarh Muslim University, India. *Appointments:* Lecturer, Department of Geography, Jamia Millia Islamia, New Delhi, India, 1963; Reader and Head, Department of Geography, North Eastern Hill University, Shillong-793014, India, 1978-. *Memberships:* Royal Geographical Society, London; National Association of Indian Geographers; National Association of Indian Cartographers; Indian Science Congress; Geographical Society of India, Calcutta. *Publications:* Agricultural Geography, 1979; Human and Economic Geography, 1978; approximately 40 research papers in the field of Agricultural Geography. *Honours:* University Gold medallist for standing First in MA/MSc. Geography, 1959, Aligarh Muslim University, Aligarh. *Address:* 334-H, Batla House, Jamia Nagar, New Delhi-110025, India.

HUSAIN, Mohammad Azim, b. 5 Oct. 1913, Batala, India. m. Nusrat, 30 Sept. 1945, 1 son, 2 daughters. *Education:* BA, Punjab, 1932; BA 1934, MA, 1958, Cantab; Barrister-at-Law, Lincoln's Inn, London, UK, 1937; French, School of Foreign Languages, 1946. *Appointments:* Indian Civil Service: ICS Probation, University College, Oxford, UK, 1936-37; Assistant Commissioner in the Punjab, 1937-39; Under Secretary, Government of the Punjab, Political Department, 1939; Sub-Divisional Officer, Punjab Government, 1939-41; Director of Panchayats (Rural Department, the Punjab, 1941-42; Under Secretary, Ministry of Defence, 1942-44, Deputy Secretary, Ministry of Information and Broadcasting, 1944-48, Government of India; Indian Diplomatic Service: Deputy Secretary, Ministry of External Affairs, in charge of External Publicity; later South East Asia Affairs and Emigration, 1948-52; Consul-General, with rank of Minister, San Francisco, USA, 1952-54; Joint Secretary, Ministry of External Affairs, in charge of United Nations Affairs, later European Affairs, 1954-57; Deputy High Commission, London, rank of Minister; concurrently accredited to Ireland and Spain, 1957-60; Ambassador to Egypt, concurrently accredited as Minister to Lebanon, 1960-62; Ambassador to Libya, 1960-64; Ambassador to Yemen, 1963-64; Additional Secretary, Ministry of External Affairs, Indian Foreign Service Inspector, 1964-65; Promoted as permanent Grade I Ambassador, Indian Foreign Service; Secretary, Ministry of External Affairs, in charge of: (a) Administration of Indian Foreign Service and Re-organisation of Indian Foreign Service, (b) Middle East and African Affairs, (c) Economic Division, Ministry of External Affairs, including technical and economic assistance, 1965-67; Ambassador of India to Switzerland and to the Holy See, 1967-70; Commonwealth Deputy Secretary General, 1970-78. *Memberships:* Gymkhana Club, Delhi; Travellers Club, London; Institute of Strategic Studies, London; Royal Institute of International Affairs, London; Board of Governors, Commonwealth Institute, London; Royal Commonwealth Society, London. *Publications:* History of Lahore, 1938; History of Panchayats in the Punjab, 1941; Fazl-i-Husain: A Political Biography, 1946; articles on Disarmament. *Hobbies:* Music; Photography. *Address:* 14 Lytton Close, London, N2 ORH, England.

HUSAIN, Shahanara, b. 1 Apr. 1937, Brahmanbaria, Comilla, Bangladesh. Professor of History. m. A B M Husain, 27 Sept. 1958, 2 sons, 1 daughter. *Education:* BA.(Hons.), History, 1957, MA, History, 1958, University of Dacca; MA, History, 1960, PhD. History, 1965, University of London, UK. *Appointments:* Lecturer in History, 1960-69, Reader in History, 1969-74, Provost of the Women's Hall, 1966-69, 1972-75, Chairman, Department of History, 1975-78, University of Rajshahi, Bangladesh. *Memberships:* Asiatic Society of Bangladesh; Advisory Committee, Varendra Research Museum, Governor, Institute of Bangladesh Studies, University of Rajshahi; President, Rajshahi Branch, Business and Professional Women's Club; Vice President, National Federation, Business and Professional Women's Club of Bangladesh, 1978-. *Publications:* Books: Every Day Life in the Pala Empire, 1968; General D D Eisenhower's Crusade in Europe, translated into Bengali (with Dr A B M Husain), 1970; Articles include: Nalanda, 1962; Prathamic Madhya Yuge Bengali Nari, 1962; The Terracotta Plaques from Paharpur, 1963; Glimpses in the Village Life of Early Medieval Bengal, 1970; Some Aspects of the Subhasitaratnakosa, 1972; A Terracotta Head from Mahasthangarh, 1975; Position of Women in the Society of Early Medieval Bengal, 1976; Role of Women in the Religious Life of Early Medieval Bengal, 1977; Poems: Amar Ammake, 1980; Palayanbadi (The Escapist), 1979; Atmacinta (Self Reflections), 1980; Poems translated from English to Bangali: Robert Frost, Tree at my Window, 1980. *Honours:* Honours include: Invited to attend UNESCO Conference on the Kushana Studies, Dushanbe, Tadjakestan, USSR, Sept. 1969; Invited to the Congress of Orientalists, Paris, July, 1973; Invited to International Conference on Climate and History, July 1979, Climatic Research Unit, School of Environmental Science, University of East Anglia, UK; Member, Rajshahi University Syndicate, 1968-69, 1974-75; Awarded International Fellowship to visit UK and India under UNESCO Participation Programme, 1980. *Hobbies:* Reading; Composing poems; Social works. *Address:* W-27 University Campus, Rajshahi, Bangladesh.

HUSSAIN, Datuk Abdul Aziz, b. 29 Mar. 1936, Temerloh District, Pahang, Malaysia. Malaysian Civil and -diplomatic Service. m. Datin Dr. Noor Laily Bte Datuk Haji Abu Bakar, 10 Aug. 1963, 1 son, 2 daughters. *Education:* Malay College, Kuala Kangsar, Perak, 1954-55; University of Malaya, Singapore, 1955-59; London School of Economics and Political Science 1970-71; University of Oslo, Norway, 1971. *Appointments:* Assistant Secretary, Ministry of Education, 1959, Prime Minister's Department, 1960, Ministry of Internal Security 1961; First Private Secretary, Malaysian Deputy Prime Minister, 1961-63; First Secretary, Ministry of Foreign Affairs, Singapore Branch, 1964-65; Principal Assistant Secretary, Ministry of Education, 1968-70; State Secretary, Pahan, 1971-74; Deputy Secretary General, Ministry of Home Affairs, 1974-75; Director-General/Registrar General, Department of Co-operative Development, Ministry of Agriculture, 1975-77; Director-General, Department of National Registration, Ministry of Home Affairs, 1977-. *Memberships:* President, Soorts and Welfare Club, National Registration Department, Malaysia; President, Co-operative, National Registration Department, Malaysia; Treasurer, The Malaysian Branch, Royal Asiatic Society; Malaysian Economic Association; UNESCO, National Association of Malaysia. *Honours:* DIMP, Datukship, Pahang State Government, 1974. *Hobbies:* Gardening; Aviary and Aquarium; Tennis; Golf. *Address:* 11a Jalan Bomoh, Bukit Keramat, Kuala Lumpur, Malaysia.

HUSSEIN BIN ONN, Datuk, b. 12 Feb. 1922, Malaya; Barrister and Politician; *Education:* Cambridge School, Indian Military Academy, Dehra Dun, Lincoln's Inn, England; *Appointments:* Commissioned in Indian Army, 1942, Served in Middle East and India; Military General Head Quarters, New Delhi; with British Liberation Forces, Malaya 1945; Malay Administration Service, Kua Kuala Selangor and Klang 1946-1947; National Youth Leader and Secretary-General United Malays National Organization(UMNO), 1947; Member Federal Legislative Council, Jahore Council of State and State Executive Council 1948-1957; called to the Bar, London 1960; rejoined United Malays National Organization 1968, President 1976-; Member of Parliament 1970-; Minister of Education 1970-1973; Deputy Prime Minister 1973-1976; Minister of Finance and Co-ordinator of Public Corporations, 1974-1976; Prime Minister Jan. 1976-; Minister of Defence 1976-1978, 1980-; of the Federal Territory 1978-1980; Seri Paduka Mahkota Johor; *Address:* 3 Jalan Kenny, Kuala Lumpur, Malaysia.

HUTCHEON, Duncan Elliot, b. 21 June 1922, Kindersley, Saskatchewan, Canada. Physician. m. Jean-Marie Kirkby, 7 June, 1946, 1 son, 3 daughters. *Education:* MD, 1945, B.Sc.(Med.), 1947, University of Toronto, Canada, 1940-47; D.Phil., Oxford University,

UK, 1948-50; American Board of Internal Medicine, 1963; FACP, 1965. *Appointments:* Associate Professor of Pharmacology, University of Saskatchewan, Saskatoon, Saskatchewan, Canada, 1950-53; Senior Pharmacologist, Pfizer Therapeutic Institute, Maywood, New Jersey, USA, 1953-57; Resident in Medicine, Jersey City Medical Center, USA, 1957-60; Assistant Professor of Pharmacology to Associate Professor, Seton Hall College of Medicine, 1960-68; Professor of Pharmacology and Medicine, College of Medicine and Dentistry, New Jersey, USA, 1968-. *Memberships:* President, 1970-75, American College of Clinical Pharmacology; Chairman, 1976-80, American Board of Clinical Pharmacology; American Society for Pharmacology and Experimental Therapeutics; President 1980-, Princeton Institute of Environmental Medicine. *Publications:* Editor, Journal of Clinical Pharmacology, 1977-; Publications in cardiovascular and renal pharmacology and the treatment of heart disease. *Honours:* National Research Council Fellowship, Canada, 1947-50; Distinguished Service Award, American College of Clinical Pharmacology, 1975. *Address:* 250 Harriot Avenue, Harrington Park, New Jersey, 07640, USA.

HUTCHESON, David Robertson, b. 5 June 1906, Dundee, Scotland. Pharmacy. m. Susan M R Henry, 18 May 1932. *Education:* Part-time, Heriot-Watt College Edinburgh, 1922-26, Full-time, 1926-27; Chemist and Druggist Certificate, 1927; Royal Veterinary College Edinburgh 1931-32; Personnel Practices Certificate, Sydney Technical College 1951-53; Attorney-Generals Department, Sydney University, Teachers College, NSW; Probation Officer's Certificate. *Appointments:* Howse and McGeorge Limited, East Africa; Wands Limited, Leicester; Genatosan Limited, Loughborough and Sydney; War Service 1939-45; NSW Attorney-General's Department; Australian Department of Health; Prince Henry Hospital, Little Bay, NSW; Part-time demonstrator in Pharmaceutics, University of Sydney. *Memberships:* Workers' Educational Association of NSW; Pharmaceutical Society of Great Britain; Pharmaceutical Society of NSW; Pharmaceutical Society of Australia; Royal Society of Health; Institute of Personnel Management; NSW Association of Health Professions. *Publications:* Articles in Australian Journal of Pharmacy: Professional Behaviour; History and The Professional Fee; The Woolworth Challenge; Pharmacy Technicians; Quality Control and the Patient; Professional Service and The NHS; Payment for Professional Service. *Honours:* Hon. Captain RASC 1945; Efficiency Medal, Territorial 1951; Pharmaceutical Chemist 1957; Fellow, Pharmaceutical Society of Great Britain, 1971. Hobby: Various aspects of education, Liberal Adult Education, Professional Continuing Education, Public Health Education, Human Relations Education; Vice President, Superannuated Commonwealth Officers Association, Serving fellow superannuants; Car maintenance and woodwork. *Address:* 8/123 Old South Head Road, Bondi Junction, NSW 2022, Australia.

HUTCHINGS, Elsie Winifred, b. Ringwood, Hampshire, England. Pianist; Teacher. *Memberships:* British Federation of Music Festivals; Fellow of IBA. *Publications:* Childrens Pianoforte Pieces; National Melodies Book 1; More National Melodies Book 2. *Honours:* AVCM; LVCM; LRAM; Medallist; Prizes for Highest marks in Examinations. *Hobbies:* Dancing; Walking. *Address:* 154 Wellington Flats, Ebury Bridge Road, London, SW1 W8RX, England.

HUTCHINSON (Dr) David Roger, b. 26 Feb. 1955, Ilkeston, Derbyshire, England. Clinical Research Co-ordinator. *Education:* BSc.(Hons.), Biochemistry-Toxicology, 1976, PhD. Clinical Biochemistry, 1980, MIBiol., 1978, Department of Biochemistry, University of Surrey, UK. *Appointments:* Berk Pharmaceuticals Limited, Shalford, Surrey, UK, 1979-81; Farmitalia Carlo Erba Limited, Barnet, Hertfordshire, UK, 1981-. *Memberships:* Liver Club; Association of Clinical Biochemists; Medical Research Society; ACRPI. *Publications:* Biochemical Parameters of Liver Function, 1980; Prealbumin following paracetamol overdose, 1980; Glycylprolyl-p-nitroanilidase in Hepatobiliary disease, 1981; Prealbumin in human hepatobiliary disease, 1981; Publications in Liver Function Testing and Paracetamol Poisoning. *Hobbies:* Soccer; Soccer Management; Golf. *Address:* St. Johns Court, Brookwood, Surrey, UK.

HUTCHINSON, Richard Michael Strode de la Poer, b. 31 July 1934, Southsea, Hampshire, England. Chiropractor. m. Yvonne Margaret Fleming, 4 Apr. 1959, 1 son, 2 daughters. *Education:* Kelly College, Tavistock; Regular Commission, Royal Naval Colleges, Dartmouth and Greenwich, Royal Navy, 1957; Doctor of Chiropractic and Roentgenology Diploma, Anglo-European College of Chiropractic, Bournemouth, UK, 1978. *Appointments:* Served as regular officer in Royal Navy, Specialised in submarines, 1957 and Torpedo and Anti-Submarine Warfare, 1962; Qualified Shallow Water Diver, 1953 and Ships' Diver Officer, 1962; Worldwide Service including submarine staff appointments command and of front line frigate, rank: Lieutenant Commander, 1950-74; Anglo-European College of Chiropractic, Bournemouth, UK, 1974; Qualified as Doctor of Chiropractic and started own private practice in Winchester, Hampshire, UK, 1978-. *Memberships:* Local media spokesman for Hampshire, British Chiropractors' Association; Life Member, Wardroom Mess's HMS Dolphin and Vernon; The Anglo-European College of Chiropractic Alumni Association; The European Chiropractics Union; Self Help Organisation. *Address:* Flettons, 92 Christchurch Road, Winchester, Hampshire SO23 9TE, England.

HUTCHISON, Michael Clark, b. 26 Feb. 1914, Edinburgh, Scotland. Barrister-at-Law; Member of Parliament. m. Anne Taylor, 19 Mar. 1937, 1 son, 1 daughter. *Education:* Honour degree in Law, 1935, MA.Cantab, 1948, Trinity College, Cambridge, UK. *Appointments:* Called to Bar, Grays Inn, London, UK, 1937; Major, Australian Imperial Force, 1939-46; Service in Middle East, Ceylon and Pacific theatres. Colonial Administrative Service, Palestine and Aden, 1946-54; Conservative Member of Parliament, Edinburgh South, Scotland, 1957-79; Director, Talley General Time Limited, Strathleven, Dumbarton, Scotland. *Memberships:* New Club, Edinburgh, Scotland. *Honours:* Mentioned in Despatches. *Hobbies:* Reading. *Address:* Wellcroft End, Bucklebury, Reading, RG7 6PB, Berks, England.

HUTCHISON, Noel Stewart, b. 10 Apr. 1940, St. Leonard's, Sydney, New South Wales, Australia. Sculptor; Art Critic; Lecturer. m. Kathrine Maria Jakubowska, 11 Apr. 1968, 2 daughters. *Education:* BA-.(Hons.), University of Sydney, Australia, 1969. *Appointments:* Part-time teacher of History, Departments of Interior and Graphic Design, East Sydney Technical College and Randwick Technical College, Australia, 1969-70; Tutor, Fine Arts course, Department of Adult Education, 1969-71; Occasional lecturer in Art History, Power Department of Fine Arts, 1960-74; Teaching Fellow, Power Department fine arts and part-time tutor in sculpture, Faculty of Architecture, 1973, University of Sydney, Australia; Lecturer-in-charge, Department of Art, 1974, Senior Lecturer, Department of Art, 1975-80, TCAE, Newham; Principal Lecturer in Fine Art, Prahran CAE, Victoria, Australia, 1980-. *Memberships:* Australian Art Association; Contemporary Art Society of Australia (NSW); International Association of Art Critics. *Publications:* Articles for newspapers and art magazines include: Australian Sculpture in the 1960's Part 1, 1970; Aspects of Geometrically Non-figurative Sculpture in Australia, 1973; Introductory Essay for John Davis Exhibition at Monash University Exhibition Gallery, Melbourne, 1975; Achille Simonetti (1838-1900), 1976. *Creative Works:* Exhibitions include: Mildura Sculpture Triennial; RAS of NSW, Easter Show, Sydney, 1970; Marland House Commission Exhibition, Argus Gallery, Melbourne, 1971; Group show, Watters Gallery and the Sculpture Garden, Sydney, 1973; Tenth Anniversary Show, Watters Gallery and one-man show, Watters Gallery, Sydney, Australia, 1974; One-man show, Queen Victoria Museum and Art Gallery, Launceston, Tasmania, Australia, 1975; Mildura Sculpture Triennial; 'Map' Show, Ewing and George Paton Galleries, Melbourne, Australia, 1978; Australian Sculpture Triennial, Melbourne, Australia, 1981. *Honours:* Sculpture Prize RAS of NSW,

Easter Show, Sydney, Australia, 1970; Mildura Triennial Purchase, 1970. *Hobbies:* Gardening; Music; Camping; Bushwalking. *Address:* 106 Ludstone Street, Hampton, Victoria, Australia 3181.

HUTSON, Victor Massey Tan Sri Dato, b. 30 Aug. 1919, Dublin, Eire. Artist. *Education:* St. Andrews College, Dublin, Eire, 1927-36; Royal College of Art, Dublin, Eire, 1936-39. *Appointments:* Army Service: Royal Engineers; Commission in Royal Corps Signals, 1941; Served in India and Burma, 1942-45; Substantive Major; O C 'O' L. of C. Signals, Malaya, 1945; Joined Socfin Co. Limited, July 1946; Industrial Relations Manager, 1953; Director, Socfin Group. *Memberships:* member of numerous societies and organisations including: Visiting Justice, Salangor, 1955-61; Committee of Discharged Prisoner's Aid, 1956-58; Chairman, Arts Council, 1961; Hon. Secretary, Wine and Food Society, 1957-60, Treasurer, 1962-65, Hon. Auditor, 1966-75; Rotary Club, Kuala Lumpur; Chairman, Council of Selangor Vocational Guidance Association, 1966-71; Standing Industrial Court, 1962; First Chairman, Council of Malayan Zoological Society, 1961; National Family Planning Board, 1968-; National Advisory Council on Industrial Training, 1972. *Hobbies:* Music; Photography; Conservation of Wild Life. *Address:* No. 1 Jalan 5/35, Petaling Jaya, Selangor.

HUXLEY, Andrew Fielding, b. 22 Nov. 1917, London, England. Scientist. m. Jocelyn Richenda Gammell Pease, 5 July 1947, 1 son, 5 daughters. *Education:* BA., 1938, MA., 1941, Trinity College, Cambridge, UK. *Appointments:* Operational Research, Anti-Aircraft Command and Admiralty, 1940-45; Fellow, 1941-60, Demonstrator, 1946-50, Assistant Director of Research, 1951-59, Reader in Experimental Biophysics, 1959-60, Department of Physiology, Cambridge, UK; Director of Studies, Trinity College, Cambridge, UK, 1952-60; Jodrell Professor and Head of Department of Physiology, 1960-69, Royal Society Research Professor, 1969-, University College, London, in the University of London, UK; President, the Royal Society, 1980-. *Memberships:* Honorary member, The Physiological Society; Chairman, 1974-81, Medical Research Committee, Muscular Dystrophy Group of Great Britain; President, 1976-77, British Association for the Advancement of Science; Honorary member, Royal Institution of Great Britain; Fullerian Professor of Physiology and Comparative Anatomy 1967-73; *Publications:* The Croonian Lecture, Royal Society, 1967; Review Lecture on Muscular Contraction, Physiological Society, 1973; Sherrington Lectures, University of Liverpool, 1977; Presidential Address, British Association, at the University of Aston in Birmingham, 1977; Publications in J. Physiology and Proceedings of the Royal Society; The Pursuit of Nature, 1977; Reflections on Muscle, 1980. *Honours:* Shared Nobel Prize for Physiology or Medicine, 1963; Copley Medal of the Royal Society, 1973; Knight Bachelor, 1974; Honorary Doctorates: Saarland, 1964; Sheffield, 1964; Leicester, 1967; London, 1973; St. Andrews, 1974; Aston, 1977; Cambridge, 1978; Birmingham, 1979; Marseille, 1979; York, 1981; Honorary Fellowships: Trinity College, Cambridge, 1967; Imperial College of Science and Technology, 1980; University College, London, 1980; Darwin College, Cambridge, 1981; Institute of Biology, 1981. *Hobbies:* Walking; Designing scientific instruments; Shooting. *Address:* Manor Field, 1 Vicarage Drive, Grantchester, Cambridge CB3 9NG, England.

HYDE, John Martin, b. 2 Feb. 1936, Perth, Australia. Federal Member of Parliament; Farmer. m. Helen Fisher, 14 Jan. 1960, 1 son, 3 daughters. *Appointments:* Farmer at Dalwallinu; Representative of Electorate of Moore in the Federal Parliament, 1974-. *Memberships:* Centre for Independent Studies; Western Australian Club; Farmers' Union; Pastoralists and Graziers Association. *Hobby:* Reading. *Address:* Damarosehay, PO Box 29, Dalwallinu 6609, Western Australia.

I

IACOBUCCI, Frank, b. 29 June 1937, Vancouver, Canada; Law Professor. m. Nancy Elizabeth Eastham, 31 October 1964, 2 sons, 1 daughter. *Education:* B. Commerce, University of British Columbia, 1959; LL.B. 1962; LL.B. Cambridge University, 1964; Diploma in International Law, 1966; *Appointments:* Associated with Law Firm, Dewey, Ballantine, Bushby, Palmer & Wood, New York City 1964-1967; Associate Professor of Law, University of Toronto, Toronto, Ontario, 1967-1971; Professor of Law, University of Toronto, 1971-; Associate Dean, Faculty of Law University of Toronto, 1973-1975; Vice President, Internal Affairs, University of Toronto, 1975-1978; Dean of the Faculty of Law, University of Toronto, 1979-; *Memberships:* Law Society of Upper Canada, 1970nh; Vice President, Canadian Institute for Advanced Legal Studies, 1981-; Vice President, National Congress of Italian Canadians, 1980-; Director, Ontario Multicultural Historical Society, 1976-; Islington United Church Elder, 1972-; Canadian Association of Law Teachers; Canadian Association of University Teachers. *Publications:* Co-author: Business Associations Casebook, 1979; Canadian Business Corporations, 1977; Co-editor: Materials on Canadian Income Tax, 1973, 1974, 1976, 1979 and supplement, 1977; Author of several book chapters, articles, reports and papers. *Hobbies:* Sports (including coaching); Reading. *Address:* 172 Royalavon Crescent, Islington, Ontario, Canada, M9A 2G6

IBE, Okwudili Anthony, b. 10 Oct. 1947, Orsumoghu, Anambra State. Company Director. m. Esther Urobunachi Ibe, 2 sons, 2 daughters. *Education:* H.N.D., Business Administration with N.I.M., 1971. *Appointments:* Self-Employed. *Memberships:* Recreation Club. *Honours:* Nwachinemere I of Orsumoghu, 1980. *Hobbies:* Photography; Swimming. *Address:* 16B Moore Street, Odoakpu-Onitsha, Anambra State, Nigeria.

IBRAHIM, Neelima, b. 11 Oct. 1921, Khulna, Bangladesh. University Professor. m. 14 Dec. 1945, 5 daughters. *Education:* B.A. Honours in Economics, 1939, B.T., 1942, M.A., Modern Indian Languages, 1943, University of Calcutta; Ph.D., 1958, University of Dacca. *Appointments:* Senior Lecturer, 1956, Associate Professor, 1964, Professor, 1972, University of Dacca; Director General, Bengali Academy, 1973-74; Professor, Dacca University, 1972-77. *Memberships:* Life member, Bangali Academy; History Association; Family Planning Association; Asiatic society of Bangladesh; President, Bangladesh Nahila Samity Association; Board of Directors, International Alliance of women. *Publications:* Sarat Protiva; Banglar Kabi Hadhusndan, (Literary Criticism book in Bengali); Origin and development of Bengali drama; 19th century Bengali drama with its Sociopolitical background; Several fiction and drama books; Travel Book. *Honours:* Bangla Academy literary award, Bangladesh, 1964; 'Jay Bangla' literary award, India, 1973. *Hobbies:* Reading; Writing; Plays. *Address:* 63/1 North Brook Hali Road, Dacca, Bangladesh.

IBRAHIM, Saad, b. 3 Aug. 1946, Malaysia. Head Department of Education. m. Zainab, 3 Dec. 1970, 2 sons, 1 daughter. *Education:* B.A.(Hons.), Malaya, 1969; Diploma in Education, Malaya, 1970; M.A.Ed., Wisconsin, 1975; M.A., Pol. Sc., Wisconsin, 1979; PhD., Wisconsin, 1979. *Appointments:* Instructor, Royal Military College, Malaysia, 1970-73; Lecturer, Teachers Training College, Perak, Malaysia, 1973; Lecturer, Department of Education, 1974-80; Head of Department of Education, National University of Malaysia, 1980-. *Publications:* Competing Identities in Plural Society, Singapore, 1980; Social Engineering in Malaysia, 1980; Education and Politics in Malaysia, 1977. *Address:* Persiaran Burhanuddin Helmi, Taman Tun Dr. Ismail, Kuala Lumpur, Malaysia.

IBRU, Elsie Nelly, b. 1 Dec. 1927, Calabar, Nigeria. Executive Director. m. Chief Dr. M C O Ibru, 31 July 1958, 3 sons, 3 daughters. *Education:* Junior Cambridge, 1945; Diploma, Secretarial Practice, 1955. *Appointments:* Teacher; Secretary Typist; Personal Secretary; Personnel Officer; Chairman, Steiner & Co. Limited; Managing Director, Flowershop Limited. *Memberships:* Vice President, YWCF; Inner Wheel Club; Executive Council of the Blind; State Scout Commissioner. *Honours:* Womens Voluntary Services, 1944. *Hobbies:* Reading; Dancing; Gardening; Sewing; Swimming. *Address:* 47 Marine Road, Apapa, Lagos, Nigeria.

IDE, Frederick Palmer, b. 4 Sept. 1904, Ottawa, Ontario, Canada. University Professor (retired). *Education:* BA., 1928, MA., 1930, PhD., 1934, University of Toronto, Canada. *Appointments:* Instructor, 1930-33, Lecturer, 1933-39, Assistant Professor, 1939-50, Associate Professor, 1950-62, Professor, 1962-70, Professor Emeritus, 1970-, University of Toronto, Canada; Wartime Meteorologist, Department of Transport, Air Services, Canada, 1943-45. *Memberships:* Entomological Society of Ontario, Canada, America; Canadian Society of Zoology; Pres., 1957-58, Ontario Society of Biologists; Pres., 1937-38, Toronto Field Naturalist's Club; American Society of Limnology and Oceanography; Society of Systematic Zoology; Society for the Study of Evolution; North American Benthological Society; American Fisheries Society; Federation of Ontario Naturalists; New York Academy of Science. *Publications:* Papers on Taxonomy and Ecology of Aquatic Insects particularly the Ephemeroptera; Stream environment with effect of pollution. *Honours:* Fellow, American Association for the Advancement of Science, 1939; Fellow, Entomolgical Society of America, 1941; Sesquicentennial Long Service Honour Award, University of Toronto, 1977; Hon. Chairman, Third International Conference on Ephemeroptera, 1979. *Hobbies:* Photography; Boating; Skiing. *Address:* PO Box 10, Washago, Ontario, Canada, LOK 2BO.

IDLER, David Richard, b. 13 March 1923, Winnipeg, Manitoba. Biochemist, Marine Scientist. m. Myrtle Mary Betteride, 15 Dec. 1956, 1 sons, 1 daughter. *Education:* B.A. Degree, University of British Columbia, 1949; M.Sc., Degree, University of British Columbia, 1950; Ph.D. Degree, Biochemistry, University of Wisconsin, 1953. *Appointments:* Associate Chemist, 1953-55, Investigator-in-Charge, 1955-59, Assistant Director, 1959-61, Investigator-in-Charge, Director, Steroid Biochemistry, 1961-69, Atlantic Regional Director of Research, 1969-71, Fisheries Research Board of Canada; Director and Professor of Biochemistry, Marine Sciences Research Laboratory, Memorial University of Newfoundland, 1971-. *Memberships:* Founding member, European Society of Comparative Endocrinology; Canadian Biochemical Society; American Association for the Advancement of Science; American Zoological Society; Canadian Society of Zoology; The Endocrine Society. *Honours:* Distinguished Flying Cross, 1945; Babcock Fellowship, University of Wisconsin, 1952-53; Fellow of the Royal Society of Canada, 1972. *Hobby:* Stamp collecting. *Address:* 44 Slattery Road, St. John's, Newfoundland, Canada.

IDORNIGIE, Igonoh Otsemeuno Okumoya, b. 2 May 1932, Ayogwiri Village, Bendel State. Shipping, Clearing and Forwarding. m. Roseline Ekhaiyeme, 13 Oct. 1962, 3 sons, 2 daughters. *Education:* Managment Skills, 1967-68, Effective Budgeting for Management Control, 1969, Accounting for non-Accountants, 1970, Certified Book-keeping, University of Lagos. *Appointments:* Nigerian Police Force, 1950-58; Book Keeper, J.L. Morrison Son and Jones Limited, 1959-61; Branch Manager, Mandilas Limited, 1962-78; Director, General Manager, Joki Nigeria Limited, 1978. *Memberships:* Nigerian Institute of Management; Patron of Nigerian Society for Prevention of Accidents; Patron of O.F.N. Young Farmers Club; Vice President of Bendel Welfare Association; President of Uzairue Progressive Union; Port Harcourt Club. *Honours:* Awarded certificate for 12 years loyal and meritorious service in Mandilas Limited, 1974; Awarded a Gold Pin for best Sales Manager, Volkswagen of Germany, 1976. *Hobbies:* Reading; Music. *Address:* 32 Bekweri Wosu Street, D/Line, Port Harcourt, Nigeria.

IDRIS, Abdulkadir, b. 24 Feb. 1948, Lapai, Nigeria. Management Consultant. m. Fatima Zara, 15 Mar. 1980, 1 daughter. *Education:* Diploma, Commercial Accounting, 1970; B.Eng., (Mech.), 1973; Certificate, Development Banking and Finance, 1977. *Appointments:* Mechanical Engineer, Water Corporation, Ibadan, Nigeria; Terminal Engineer, Mobil Oil Nigeria Limited, Lagos, Nigeria; Investment Executive, Northern Nigeria Investments Limited, Nigeria; Resident Consultant, Project Management Limited, Nigeria; Managing Consultant, A Idris Consultancy Service, Nigeria. *Memberships:* Kano Club; Le Circle Club, Kano; Lebanon Club. *Hobbies:* Sports; Dancing; Current affairs. *Address:* 20 Audu Bako Way, Nassarawa, Kano, Nigeria.

IDRISCU, Abdullahi, b. 30 Dec. 1940, Nigeria. Professional Forester. m. 27 Sept. 1967, 3 sons, 3 daughters. *Education:* BSc. Hons. Botany, 1967; Post Graduate Diploma, Forestry, University of Ibadan, 1969; Project Analysis and Appraisal, Ife University, 1973; Advance Management Course, Ascon, Lagos, 1978. *Appointments:* Pupil Research Officer, 1967-68; Provincial Forest Officer, 1969-72; Headquarter Assistant, 1972-76; Agricultural Chief of forests, 1976-77; Chief Councillor of forests, 1977-. *Memberships:* Forestry Association of Nigeria; Commonwealth Forestry Association; Natural History Society; Treasurer, Ndaduma Development Association. *Publications:* Co-author of Fed. Gov. publication, Agricultural Perspective Plan, 1975-85. *Honours:* Member, Kainji Lake National Park Management Board, 1980; Member, Administrative Committee of Kainji Lake Research Institute, 1976; Member of Nigeria State Tourism Board. *Hobbies:* Gardening; Reading; Table Tennis; Walking. *Address:* House No. 6, Jos Street, Type 'B' Quarters, Minna, Nigeria.

IDUDU, Oghenakpobo Jonathan Awhinawhi, b. 28. Feb. 1945, Nigeria. Chartered Surveyor. m. Dorothy Isiaka Ozomaro, 7 Nov. 1970, 3 sons, 2 daughters. *Education:* BSc., Estate Management, London University, 1969; Elected Profession Associate, Royal Institution of Chartered Surveyors, 1971; Elected Profession Associate, Nigerian Institution of Estate Surveyors and Valuers, 1972; Elected Fellow of R.I.C.S., 1980; Elected Fellow of N.I.E.S.V., 1980. *Appointments:* Surveyor, Barclays Bank Limited, Property Division, London; Surveyor, Knight Frank and Rutley, Nigeria, 1972-73; Partner, Knight Frank and Rutley, Nigeria, 1974-. *Memberships:* Ikoyi Club, Lagos. *Publications:* Various published articles. *Hobbies:* Golf; Table Tennis; Current World Affairs. *Address:* 1 Sofidiya Close, Surulere, Lagos, Nigeria.

IGE, Atinuke Omobonike, b. 4 April 1932, Nigeria. High Court Judge. m. Bolaige, 17 April 1960, 2 sons, 1 daughter. *Education:* University of Ibadan, 1952-54; Law, Lincoln's Inn London, 1955-59; Post Final Course of the Council of Legal Education, London, 1959. *Appointments:* Teacher, 1951-54; Private Legal Practitioner, 1959-62; Appointed Magistrate, Western State of Nigeria, 1962; Senior Magistrate, 1966, 1969; Chief Magistrate, 1972; Chief Registrar, Western State Court of Appeal, 1975-76; High Court Judge, Oyo State, 1977-. *Memberships:* Magistrates Association of Nigeria, 1971-74; Western State delegate to the 4th conference of the Commonwealth Magistrates Association, Kuala Lumpar, 1975; Chairman, Board of Governers, Queens School, Ibadan. *Publications:* Talks in Women Programmes on the Nigeria Radio, 1960-74; Read papers at Magistrates Conferences, Topics included: The Law on Protection of the Policeman while in the execution of his duty; Case for a Law of Adoption in Nigeria; Attended and participated in the 6th Commonwealth Law Conference held in Lagos, 1980; Chairman of 3 papers delivered on 'Essentials of a Fair Trial'. *Hobbies:* Reading; Gardening; Farming. *Address:* Government House, Agodi, Ibadan Oyo State, Nigeria.

IGHARO, Isaac Dele Thaddeus, b. 13 Sept. 1945, Jos, Nigeria. Architect. m. Margaret Henshaw, 9 July 1977, 1 son, 1 daughter. *Education:* B.Arch. Ahmadu Bellow University, Zaria, Nigeria, 1972. *Appointments:* Ona Fowokan City Scape Group, Ibadan, 1972-74; Allied Architects, Lagos, 1974-77; Principal Partner, Environmental Design Associates, Benin-Calabar, Lagos, 1977-. *Memberships:* Nigerian Institute of Architects. *Hobbies:* Chess; Tennis; Travelling. *Address:* 134 Goldie Street, Calabar, Nigeria.

IGNATIEFF, George, b. 16 Dec. 1913, St. Petersburg, ·Russia. Chancellor, University of Toronto. m. Alison Grant, 17 Nov. 1945, 2 sons. *Education:* B.A. University of Toronto, 1935; Rhodes Scholar, Ontario, 1935; M.A., Oxford University, 1938. *Appointments:* Department of External Affairs, Ottawa, 1940; 3rd Secretary, Canada House, London, 1940-44; 2nd Secretary, Ottawa, 1944-45; Diplomatic Advisor, Canadian Del. U.N. Atomic Energy Committee, 1946; Advisor with a Canadian Del., U.N. Assembly, 1946-47; Canadian Alternate Representative, U.N. Security Council, 1948-49; Head of Defence Liaison Division Department of External Affairs, 1955; Ambassador to Yugoslavia, 1956-58; Deputy High Commissioner to United Kingdom, 1959; Assistant Under Secretary of State for External Affairs, 1960-62; Permanent Representative of Canada to NATO, 1963; Ambassador to U.N. Security Council, 1967-68; Permanent Representative of Canada to European Office of U.N. Geneva, 1971-72; Provost, Trinity College, 1972-78; Governor, Heritage Canada, 1978-80; President, United Nations in Canada 1980-; Chancellor, University of Toronto, 1980-. *Honours:* C.C. (Companion of the Order of Canada) 1973; LL.D., Brock University, 1967, University of Toronto, 1968, University of Guelph, 1969, University of Saskatchewan, 1973, York University, 1975, Mount Allison University, 1978; d.c.l. Bishop's University, 1973; D.Litt.S. University of Victoria College, Toronto, 1977; Honorary Fellow, St. John's College, University of Manitoba, 1973; Centenary Medal, 1967; Jubilee Medal, 1977. *Hobbies:* Swimming; Gardening; Cooking. *Address:* 18 Palmers-.ton Gardens, Toronto, Ontario M6G 1V9, Canada.

IGNATIEFF, Vladimir Pavlovitch, b. 28 Aug. 1905, Kiev, Russia. Soil Scientist. m. Florence Mary Hargreaves, 2 June 1934, 1 son, 1 daughter. *Education:* BSc Agriculture, South Eastern Agriculture, Wye College, Kent, England, 1923-27; MSc, Soils Science, University of Edmonton, Edmonton, Canada, 1930-32; PhD, Biochemistry, University of Toronto, Canada, 1932-35. *Appointments:* Manager, Farm Hastings, Sussex, England, 1927; Heardsman, Richmond Jerseys Richmond, Quebec, Canada, 1928; Recorder, Dominion Experiment Substation Beaverlodge Alto Canadian, 1929-30; Research Assistant, Department of Soil Science, University of Alberta, 1930-32; Senior Fellow, Department of Biochemistry, University of Toronto, 1932-36; Lecturer and Assistant Professor of Soils, 1936-40; Major, Canadian Armed Forces, 1940-45; Food and Agriculture Organisation, The United Nations, 1945-70; Head, Soil Science and Fertilizers, Agricultural Division, 1946-57; Chief Soil Resources, Survey Branch, Land and Water Development Division, 1957-64; Deputy Director of Land and Water Development Division, 1964-70. *Memberships:* Agricultural Institute of Canada; Canadian Soil Science Society; International Society of Soil Sciences; Canada Hunger Foundation; Royal Canadian Legion; Canadian Physiological Society. *Publications:* Efficient use of Fertilizers, 1949 and 1958; Determination and behavior of Ferrous Iron in Soil, 1942; Phosphatase distribution in some higher plants, 1932; Numerous papers in the field of Soil Sciences. *Honours:* Fellow, Agriculture Institute of Canada; Fellow, Canadian Soil Sciences Society; Honorary Life member, International Society of Soil Science; Canadian Hunger Foundation; Royal Canadian Legion; Honorary Doctor of Science in Agriculture and Food, University of Laval, Quebec, Canada. Hobby: Gardening. *Address:* Beechmore, RR3 Richmond, PQ, J0B 2H0, Canada.

IGWE, Johnson Okoye (Chief), b. 10 June 1930, Awka-Etiti, Nigeria. Businessman. m. Christiana Azubike, 15 Dec. 1959, 4 sons, 3 daughters. *Education:* St. George's College, Zaria, Nigeria, 1942-46. *Appointments:* Director, G M O & Co., 1957; Chairman, United African Drug. Co. Limited, 1964; Chairman, Ciana Agencies Limited, 1979; Director, Pharma-Deko Limited, 1979; Director, Dumex Industrial (Nigeria) Limited, 1980; Chairman, Hero Construction Limited, 1981. *Memberships:* Executive member: People's Club of Nigeria, Awka-Etiti Social Club; Ikemba Society, Awka Etiti. *Honours:* Ozo Title Holder - Ezissi Akunwanne, Chieftancy Title, August 1981. *Hobbies:* Photography; Music. *Address:* 6 Akobi Crescent, Sumlere, Lagos, Nigeria.

IGWE, Zephaniah Ikejiaku, b. 12 Feb. 1943, Akpulu, Nigeria. Management. m. Abigail Uzoamaka Uzoma, 8 Dec. 1973, 1 son, 1 daughter. *Education:* ACIS., 1973; FCIS., 1980; MBIM., 1976; AMNIM., 1977; MS., Business Management, 1981. *Appointments:* Company Secretary/Accountant, 1975-76, General Manager-/Company Secretary, 1976-78, C Moore Obioha Sons & Co. Limited, Nigeria; Group General Manager, C Moore Obioha Group of Companies, Nigeria, 1979-. *Memberships:* Peoples Club of Nigeria; Branch Secretary, Golden Club of Nigeria. *Hobbies:* Reading; Table Tennis. *Address:* No. 8 Nworu Street, Umungasi, Aba, Imo State, Nigeria.

IGWILOH, Emmanuel Amechi, b. 20 Sept. 1943, Ihiala, Nigeria. m. Charity Nwakaego Nwankwo, 5 May 1973, 1 son, 2 daughters. *Education:* ACCA Correspondence Course, London, UK, 1965-72; Diploma, Accountancy, Benet College, London, UK. *Appointments:* Accountant, Scoa Motors, Enugu, Nigeria, 1972-75; Chief Accountant, Ugochukwu Chemical Industries Limited, Onitsha, Nigeria, 1975-80; Chief Accountant, Standard Polyplastic Industries Limited, Umuahia, Nigeria, 1980-. *Memberships:* Financial Adviser, Ekwueme Social Club of Nigeria. *Creative Works:* Private artist. *Honours:* Cash prize in Drawing and Painting, 1960-64. *Hobbies:* Lawn tennis; Drafts; Swimming. *Address:* PO Box 311, Ihiala, Nigeria.

IHEMADU, Manassen Timothy, b. 22 Nov. 1940, Owo Ahafor Village, Obioma Ngwa, Imo State, Nigeria. Trading/Banking. m. Grace Chinwe Ihemadu, 12 Dec. 1970, 2 sons, 2 daughters. *Education:* First School Leaving Certificate, 1956; Teachers Grade II Certificate, 1965; GCE A/L Teachers Special Grade, 1976. *Appointments:* Teaching, 1957-76; Bank Director, 1976-81; Trading, 1976-. *Hobbies:* Football; Teaching. *Address:* 99 Agikiwe Road, Aba, Imo State, Nigeria.

IKE, Vincent Chukwuemeka, b. 28 Apr. 1931, Ndikelionwu, Anambra State, Nigeria. Creative Writer and Educationist. m. Adebimpe Olurinsola Abimbolu, 13 Dec. 1959, 1 son. *Education:* University College, Ibadan, 1951-55; BA, London, 1955; Stanford University, Palo Alto, California, US, 1966; MA, 1967. *Appointments:* Secondary School Teacher, 1955-56; Admin. Assistant/Assistant Registrar, University College, Ibadan, 1957-60; Deputy Registrar, University of Nigeria, 1960-63; Registrar, 1963-71; Chairman, Planning and Management Committee, 1970; Registrar and Chief Executive, West African Examinations Council, Accra, Ghana, 1971-79; Part-time, Director, The Daily Times of Nigeria Limited, 1971-; University Press, Limited, 1978-; Chairman, Emekike and Company, 1979-. *Memberships:* Nigerian Institute of Management; International Association for Educational Assessment. *Publications:* Toads for Supper, 1965; The Naked Gods, 1970; The Potter's Wheel, 1973; Sunset at Dawn, 1976; University Development in Africa: the Nigerian Experience, 1976; The Chicken Chasers, 1980; Expo '77, 1980. *Honours:* Honorary Fellow, City and Guilds of London Institute, 1978; UNESCO Youth Travel Grant, 1954; Ford Foundation Study Grant, 1966. *Hobbies:* Photography; Assisting authors. *Address:* Chinwuba House, Ndikelionwu Postal Agency, Via Awka, Anambra State, Nigeria.

IKEDE, Basil Orioghae, b. 19 July 1942, Bethel-Oyede, Isoko L.G.A. Bendel State Nigeria. University Professor. m. Joy Aruoribho Okerri, 30 Dec. 1967, 3 sons, 1 daughter. *Education:* B.Vet-Med, Ibadan, DVM (A.B.U) Nigeria 1962-67; Grad-Dip. Diagn. Pathol. (Guelph) Ontario Vet. College, Canada 1970-71; PhD, Ibadan 1972; Cert. Immunol. Ibadan, 1974. *Appointments:* Rockefeller Foundation Research Fellow, 1967-70; Lecturer, 1970-74; Senior Lecturer, 1974-77; Sub-Dean (Postgraduate), 1976-78; Professor, 1977-; Head of Department of Vet. Pathology, University of Ibadan, 1979-; Senior Visiting Fellow, Brunel University, Uxbridge, Middx. 1975; Visiting Professor, Guelph, O.V.C Canada 1979; Visiting Professor, U.C.D, Davis, California, USA, 1979. *Memberships:* Fellow, Royal Society of Tropical Medicine and Hygiene; Nigerian Veterinary Medical Association; Nigerian Society for Animal Production; Science Association of Nigeria; Nigerian Society for Immunology. *Publications:* A monograph on the pathology of African Trypanosomiasis in animals; Over 50 scientific papers on various animal diseases especially those of importance in the tropics. *Honours:* Ibadan University Scholar, 1963-67; Faculty of Agriculture Prize, 1965; Commonwealth Bureau of Animal Health Prize, 1966; Coomassie Prize for Veterinary Science, 1967; C L Davis Journal Award for Advancement of Vet. Pathology, American College of Vet Pathologists, 1973. *Hobbies:* Lawn Tennis; Swimming; Christian Evangelism. *Address:* No 5 Ebrohimie Road, University of Ibadan, Nigeria.

IKEDIFE, Dozie, b. 24 Aug. 1932, Nnewi, Nigeria. Obstetrician and Gynaecologist. m. Christie Anazodo, 10 Sept. 1967, 4 sons, 2 daughters. *Education:* City College, Norwich, England, 1952-53; MB, ChB, University of Glasgow, 1953-59; BSc, External, University of London, 1950-58; FNMCOG, 1974; FWACS, 1978;

FRCOG, 1979. *Appointments:* House Officer, Senior House Officer, Registrar, Stobhill Hospital, Glasgow, 1960-63; Special Grade Medical Officer, Federal Ministry of Health, 1964-66; Eastern Region of Nigeria, 1966-67; Founder, City Hospital Aba, East Nigeria, 1967; Founder, Ikedife Hospital, (Special Medical Centre) Nnewi, Nigeria and Specialist i/c 1975; Visiting Gynaecologist to several Hospitals. *Memberships:* BMA; Society of Obstetricians and Gynaecologists of Nigeria; Fellow, Royal College of Obstetricians and Gynaecologists; Nigerian Medical Council Fellowships in Obstetricians and Gynaecologists; Editorial Committee, Tropical Journal of Obstetrics and Gynaecology. *Publications:* Various medical publications in British Medical Journal, Nigeria Medical Journal. *Honours:* Patron various youth clubs and social clubs in Nigeria. *Hobbies:* Photography; Growing fruit trees; Growing Iroko trees. *Address:* Otolo, Nnewi, Nigeria.

IKOKWU, Godfrey Chibeze, b. 10 Sept. 1910, Oba, Anambra State of Nigeria. Business and Transportation. m. Margarate Ndinma Obinwa, 26 Dec. 1936, 3 sons, 5 daughters. *Education:* General Education. *Appointments:* First Mayor of Portharcourt City Council in Nigeria 1954-56. *Memberships:* Nigerian American Chamber of Commerce; Rotary Club International. *Honours:* Nigerian Senior Citizen in Business Award, 1979. Hobby: Photography. *Address:* Isu Lodge PO Box 9, Oba, Anambra State of Nigeria.

IKPI, Onun Eten, b. 15 Nov. 1915, Ugep, Cross River State, Nigeria. Civil Servant (retired). m. Ekanem Ekpiken, May, 1943, 4 sons, 5 daughters. *Education:* ma., Natural Science, Trinity College, Cambridge University, UK, 1946-48; BSc., Botany, ARCS., Royal College of Science and Technology, London University, UK, 1949-50. *Appointments:* Science Tutor, Hope Waddell Training Institution, 1939-42; Tutor, Army Clerical Training School, Enugu and Yaba, 1942-43; Science Master, School of Agriculture, Moor Plantation, Ibadan, Nigeria, 1943-45; Agricultural Superintendent, Federal Public Service, 1950-52; Administrative Officer (Assistant Secretary), 1952-54, Secretary to Minister of Natural Resources, 1955-56, Director of Recruitment and Training, 1957-58, Permanent Secretary, Ministry of Health, 1963-65, Permanent Secretary, Ministry of Information and Managing Director of Hotel Presidential Limited, 1966, Chairman of Tenders Board, 1958, Eastern Nigeria; Permanent Secretary, Ministry of Town Planning, Lands and Survey, 1959-62; Permanent Secretary, Ministry of Health in Rebel Enclave, 1967-69; Permanent Secretary, Ministry of Economic Development and Reconstruction, South Eastern State, Nigeria, 1970. *Memberships:* Secretary, Eastern States Interim Assets and Liabilities Agency; Chairman, Governing Council, Calabar College of Technology; Chairman, Cross River Basin Development Authority; Commissioner, Federal Government Boundary Adjustment Commission; Director, Nigerian Petroleum Refining Company. *Honours:* Officer of Order of the Niger, 1978. *Hobbies:* Horticulture; Architecture; Building Construction. *Address:* Lebokom, Ugep, Yakuru Local Government Area, Cross River State, Nigeria.

IKRAM, Hamid, b. 24 Dec. 1936. Cardiologist. m. Rosemary Barbara Lilley, 16 June 1973, 2 sons. *Education:* MB, ChB 1959; MD 1974; MRCPE 1965; MRCP 1967; MRACP 1976; FRCPE 1976; FRACP 1978; FACC 1979; FRCP 1981; FICA 1967. *Appointments:* House Physician and Registrar, The General Infirmary Leeds; Teaching Fellow in Medicine, University of Alberta, Canada; Registrar and Senior Registrar, Charing Cross Hospital, London; Cardiologist and Head of Cardiology, The Princess Margaret Hospital, Christchurch, NZ. *Memberships:* The Royal Society of Medicine; Cardiac Society of Australia and NZ; Cardiac Society of Pakistan; New York Academy of Sciences; Canterbury Officers' Club; Royal Commonwealth Society. *Publications:* 72 publications including: Diagnosis of the Mitral Lesion in patients with Giant Left Atria, 1963; The Cardiac Manifestations of Hypothyroidism, 1967; Coronary Angiography, 1971; An Experimental Model for the In-Vivo Study of Coronary Arterial Thrombosis, 1975; The Prevention of Recurrent Myocardial Infarction New Ethicals, 1978. *Honours:* Prize in Clinical Medicine, Hardwicke Prize, University of Leeds; Distinction in Pharmacology, University of Leeds. *Hobbies:* Cricket; Writing. *Address:* 10A Darley Street, Christchurch 2, New Zealand.

ILO, Moses Okechuku, b. 11 Apr. 1934, Amokwe, Udi, Nigeria. Neuro-Psychiatrist. m. Ayagogo Rose Johnson, 11 Feb. 1971, 2 sons, 1 daughter. *Education:* Edo College, Benin City, 1949-54; University College & University College Hospital, Ibadan, 1954-62; MB., BS, (London; University of London, Institutes of Psychiatry, Neurology & Royal Post-graduate Medical School, 1963-67; DPM, 1966; MRC Psych., 1973; FMCP, 1975; FWACP, 1976. *Appointments:* Pre-Registration Royal South Hants, Southampton, Southampton General Hospitals, 1962-63; Spcialist Neurologist & Psychiatrist to the Biafran Armed Forces & in charge of Neurology Clinic, Biafra, 1967-70; Academic Registrar, University Unit of Clinical Neurology, University of London, NHQS, 1970-71; Consultant Psychiatrist, Tooting Bec Hospital, London, 1971-74; Senior Consultant, Ministry of Health, E.C.S., Nigeria; Senior Lecturer & Head of Psychiatry, University of Nigeria, Enugu, 1974-75; Wing Commander, Senior Consultant, Ministry of Defence, NAF Hospital, Kano, 1975-79; Chief Consultant & Commanding Officer, Executive Director, Udunma Centre, Kano, 1979-. *Memberships:* President, Association of Neurophysiologists of Nigeria, 1978-; Executive, Association of Psychiatrists of Nigeria; Nigerian Society of Neurological Sciences; Pharmacological Society of Nigeria; British Association of Psychopharmacologists; Affiliations to African & World Organisations. *Publications:* Invention of the Ilogustometer, 1965, developed for use 1969, awaiting Patent; The Ilo Personnel Section Test; Dokita—Journal of Students Clinical Society, Ibadan, Nigeria, Founder 1960, Editor, 1960-62. *Honours:* Central Government Scholarship, 1949-54; Federal Government Scholarship, 1954-62; Rockefeller Foundation Fellowship, 1963-67. *Hobbies:* Collecting Antiques; Music (Classical & Jazz); Sports; Identifying pathologies, movements, mannerisms, etc. *Address:* 10 Lafia Road, Nasszrawa, Kano, Nigeria.

ILODUBA, Chukwuemeka, b. 18 Oct. 1936, Igbo-Ukwu, Nigeria. Civil and Structural Engineer. m. Roswitha Schultes, 27 Oct. 1972, 2 sons, 2 daughters. *Education:* Diploma Engineering Construction, Enugu Institute of Technology, 1958-61; Government College, Umuahia, Senior Cambridge School Certificate, 1951-56; Diploma Civil Engineering, Senior Technical Institute, Enugo, 1957-60; States Fachlochschule, Karlsruhe, West Germany, 1965-70; BSc, Civil & Structural Engineering. *Appointments:* Civil Engineer, Gruen & Bilfinger, Mannheim, West Germany, 1970-72; Project Engineer, Department of Defense Washington, 1972-77; Managing Director & President, Cimeco (Nigeria) Ltd. 1977. *Memberships:* German Society of Engineers; German Master Builders; American Society of Civil Engineers; Society of American Military Engineers. *Publications:* Presently working on Nigerian Engineers and Future Technological Advancement in Nigeria. *Hobbies:* Photography; Physics, Philosophy. *Address:* 41 Edinburgh Road, Ogui New Layout, Enugu, Nigeria.

ILOGU, Edmund Christopher Onydum, b. 25 Apr. 1920, Ihiala. Minister of Religion and University Professor. m. Elizabeth, 25 Apr. 1946, 5 sons, 3 daughters. *Education:* Senior Cambridge School Certificate, 1938, D.M.G.S., Onitsha, 1935-38; A.L.C.D., 1953, London College of Divinity London University, 1951-53; U.T.S-,M.A,S.T.M., Columbia University, New York, 1957-59; PhD, 1974, State University of Leiden, The Netherlands, 1973-74. *Appointments:* Tutor, Melville Hall, Theological College, Ibdadan, 1953-55; Lecturer and Warden, Nigerian College of Technology, 1955-57; Head of Christian Religious Broadcasting N.B.C., Ikoyi, Lagos, 1959-61; Warden in charge Independence Hall & Lecturer, University College, Ibadan, 1961-66; Senior Lecturer, University of Nigeria, Nsukka, 1966-72; Professor, Head of Department and Dean of Faculty U.N.N., 1972-75; Chairman Teachers Service & Public Service Commissions, Anambra State, 1976-80; Commissioner, Public Complaints Commission, Anambra State, 1980-. *Memberships:* Rotary International. *Publications:* Social Philosophy for the New Nigerian Nation, 1961, Christianity and Igbo Culture, 1974. *Honours:* Shergold Smith Essay Prizeman, London College of Divinity, University of London, 1952. *Hobbies:* Gardening; Driving; Dancing. *Address:* 1 River Lane Street, G.R.A., Enugu, Anambra State, Nigeria.

IMORU, Saibu Olayinka, b. 12 Sept. 1940, Ikare, Akoko, Ondo State, Nigeria. Accountancy. m. Suliat Devi, 30 Oct. 1970, 3 sons, 1 daughter. *Education:* ACCA., 1969; AMBIM., 1973; FCCA, 1980. *Appointments:* Accountant: W & T Avery, Birmingham, UK, 1969-70, Gibbons Brothers Limited, Brierley Hill, UK, 1970-71; Assistant Chief Accountant, National Housing Authority, Zambia, Central Africa, 1971-74; Financial Controller, Head of Finance and Administration, Henkel Chemicals Nigeria Limited, Lagos, Nigeria, 1975-. *Memberships:* Auditor, Muslim Student Society, Birmingham, UK. *Honours:* Best Student in Management Accounts, Wednesbury College of Commerce, Woodgreen, UK, 1967. *Hobbies:* Sports; Games; Reading; Travelling. *Address:* 37 Jubril Martins Street, Surulere, Lagos, Nigeria.

INAMDAR, Narayan, b. 10 Nov. 1926, Madhe, India. University Professor. m. Sharazk Atre, 1 son, 1 daughter. *Education:* M.A. Ph.D., University of Poonal, 1950-54. *Appointments:* Research Fellow, Department of Politics, University of Poonal, 1951-53; Research Scholar Indian Council of World Affairs, 1953-54; Lecturer, Head, Department of Politics, Bombay College, Bombay, 1954-58; Lecturer, Department of Politics and Public Administration, University of Poona, 1958-65; Head of Department of Politics and Public Administration, 1979-. *Memberships:* Life Member, Indian Institute of Public Administration; Panel Chairman, Life Member, Indian Political Science Association, 1978-; Indian Council of World Affairs; President, Mahasashtre Political Science Association; Life member, Mahesestre Sahitya Parashad, Pune 30. *Publications:* Several Research publications including: Report of the Survey of the Administration of the Community development Block Haveli, 1962; Lokahitawadin Chi Shatapatre, 1961; Government and Co-op sugar Factories, 1965; Functioning of Village Panchayats, 1970; Community Development and Democratic Growth, 1976; Several research papers in eminent journals. *Honours:* Awarded Overseas Fellowship of the Indian Institute of Public Administration; Visiting Professor, University Grants Commission of India in Poland during 1969; Elected Chairman, Panel on Rural Government of the Indian Political Science Association, 1978. *Hobbies:* Indian Classical Music; Photography. *Address:* Opp. Sanskrit Centre, Poona University Campus, Pune 411007, India.

INCHAPE, Lord, b. 27 Dec. 1917, Uckfield, Sussex, England. Executive Chairman. m. (1) 1941 (div), (2) Caroline Cholmeley-Harrison, 1965, 5 sons, 1 daughter. *Education:* MA, Trinity College, Cambridge. *Appointments:* War Service, 1939-45; Military Government, Vienna, 1945-46; Mackinnon Mackenzie and Company Limited, Calcutta, 1946-48; Senior Partner, Gray Dawes and Company, 1948-58; Executive Chairman, Inchape and Company Limited; Director: Peninsular and Oriental Steam Navigation Company, (Executive Chairman), British Petroleum Company Limited, Guardian Royal Exchange Assurance Company Limited, Standard Chartered Bank Limited. *Memberships:* Chairman, Council for Middle East Trade, 1963-65; President of Royal India, Pakistan and Ceylon Society, 1972-75; President, The Commonwealth Society for the Deaf; President of General Council of British Shipping, 1976-77; Prime Warden, Worshipful Company of Shipwrights, 1967-68; Prime Warden, Fishmongers' Company, 1977-78. *Hobbies:* Sports; Farming. *Address:* Addington Manor, Addington, Buckinghamshire, England.

INGHAM, Alan John, b. 19 August 1920, Christchurch, New Zealand. Sculptor. m. Ann Nettlefold, 26 December, 1954, 3 daughters. *Education:* Diploma Fine Arts, East Sydney Technical College, 1949. *Appointments:* Assistant Henry Moore, 1950-1953; Grant from Royal Academy, 1949; Part-time Lecturer, Auckland, New South Wales, University (Independent Arts) & Architecture; East Sydney Technical College. *Memberships:* New South Wales Society of Sculptors, 1956-1978, Executive Member and President, 1960-1963. *Creative Works:* Major commissioned works:- Bankstown Council New South Wales, 1964; Snowy Mountains Commission, 1966; 3.M. Company. Pymble, New South Wales, 1968. *Address:* 147, Wallumatta Road, Newport, New South Wales 2106 Australia

INGRAM, Derek Thynne, b. 20 June 1925, Westcliff-on-Sea, Essex, England. Journalist. *Appointments:* Sub-editor, Daily Sketch, London, 1946-47; Daily Express, Manchester, 1947-49; Chief Sub-editor, Night

Editor, Assistant Editor, Deputy Editor, Daily Mail, London, 1949-66; Editor, Gemini News Service, 1967-; Media Adviser, Commonwealth Observer Group, Zimbabwe, 1980. *Memberships:* Deputy Chairman Royal Commonwealth Society, 1979-; President, Diplomatic and Commonwealth Writers of Britain, 1972-73; Board of Governors, Commonwealth Institute; Fellow, Royal Society of Arts; Member, Committee, Britain-Tanzania Society; Zambia Society. *Publications:* Partners in Adventure, 1960; The Commonwealth Challenge, 1962; The Commonwealth at Work, 1969; Commonwealth for a Colour-Blind World, 1965; The Imperfect Commonwealth, 1977; Articles and commentaries on Commonwealth affairs published in Commonwealth countries. *Honours:* Commonwealth Press Union Astor Award, 1978. *Hobbies:* Theatre; Opera; Walking; Reading. *Address:* 5 Wyndham Mews, London, England.

INGRAM, James Charles, b. 27 Feb. 1928, Warragul, Australia. Diplomat; Administrator. m. Odette Koven, 16 Oct. 1950, 1 son, 2 daughters. *Education:* BA., University of Melbourne, Australia, 1950. *Appointments:* Australian Career Foreign Service Officer, 1946; Australian Ambassador, Manila, Philippines, 1970-73; Australian High Commissioner, Ottawa, Canada, 1973-74; First Assistant Secretary, Australian Development Assistance Agency, 1975; Director, Australian Development Assistance Bureau, 1976-. *Hobby:* Yachting. *Address:* 39 Rawson Street, Deakin, A C T 2600, Australia.

INGRAM Kenneth Ross, b. 19 Dec. 1913, Dundee, Scotland, Principal Parliamentary Reporter, Commonwealth of Australia, (retired). m. Margaret Maude Blair, 10 Aug. 1940, 3 daughters. *Education:* Grove Academy, Broughty Ferry, Scotland; Telopea Park High School, Canberra, Australia. *Appointments:* Journalist, Canberra Times, 1932-36; Parliamentary Reporting Staff, 1936-78. *Memberships:* Australian National Press Club, Canberra. *Honours:* O.B.E., 1979. *Hobby:* Woodwork. *Address:* 61 Dominion Circuit, Forrest, Canberra 2603, Australia.

INNES, Brian, b. 4 May 1928, Thornton Heath, England. Author, Publisher, Designer. m. (1) Felicity Anne McNair Wilson (div.) 1 son, (2) Eunice Mary Smith, 1971, 2 sons. *Education:* BSc Kings College, University of London, 1946-49; Chelsea School of Art, Central School of Art, London College of Printing, 1952-56; Member, Institute of Printing; Member, Society of Industrial Artists and Designers. *Appointments:* Research Biochemist, 1949-53; Assistant Editor, Chemical Age, 1953-55; Associate Editor, The British Printer, 1955-60; Art Director, Hamlyn Group, 1960-62; Director, Temperance Seven Limited, 1961-; Director, Innes Promotions Limited and Animated Graphic and Publicity, 1964-65; Proprietor, Brian Innes Agency, 1964-66; Proprietor, Immediate Books, 1966-70; Proprietor, FOT Library, 1970-; Creative Director, Orbis Publishing Limited, 1970-. *Memberships:* Society of Authors; British Actors Equity; Society for Nautical Research; Cruising Association. *Publications:* Author of numerous books including: Book of Pirates, 1966; Book of Revolutions, 1967; Die Seeraüberei, 1969; Saga of the Railways, 1972; The Tarot, 1977; The Red Baron Lives!, 1981; Contributor to Enc. Britannica and to many journals; Films, TV and Radio broadcasts. *Honours:* Royal Variety Command Performance, 1961. *Hobby:* Music. *Address:* 74 Woodland Rise, London, England.

IOANNOU, Anna, b. 17 Mar. 1952, Nicosia, Cyprus. Civil Engineer—Town Planner. 1 daughter. *Education:* BSc, 1972, MPhil, 1975, University College, London. *Appointments:* Traffic Engineer, Van Niekerk Kleyn and Edwards, South Africa; Transport Planner, CSIR, South Africa; Traffic Engineer, Athens Bus Company; Lecturer, Higher Technical Institute, Nicosia, Cyprus; Town Planner, Department of Town Planning, Nicosia, Cyprus. *Memberships:* Associate member of the Institute of Civil Engineers; Royal Town Planning Institute. *Publications:* Other of papers in field of engineering. *Honours:* Chadwick Gold Medal, 1972; R B Hounsfield Prize, 1972. *Hobbies:* Tennis; Swimming; Jogging; Philosophy. *Address:* 8 Pallachos Street, Flat 2, Nicosia, Cyprus.

IRANEE, Behram Behman, b. 9 July 1934, Hong Kong. Company Executive. *Education:* Senior Cambridge examination, 1952; Pitman's College, London,

1955-57; City of London College, 1956-57; Secretarial and Business Administration Courses. Certificates for various commercial subjects from the Royal Society of Arts, The London Chamber of Commerce and Pitman's College, London. *Appointments:* Managing Partner, 1958-76, Proprietor, 1976-, C M Karanjia & Company, Hong Kong. *Memberships:* Founder Member of Hong Kong Arts Centre; National Geographic Society; International Biographical Association. *Hobbies:* Music; Sports; Philately; Reading. *Address:* 28-A Dina House, Duddell Street, Hong Kong.

IRELAND Graeme Kevin, b. 17 July 1929, Australia. Florist. m. Pamela Helen Guy, 25 May 1980, 1 son, 2 daughters. *Education:* Caulfield and Brighton Grammar Schools, Melbourne, Australia. *Appointments:* Managing Director, Ireland's Pty. Limited, Australian Florist Sundries Pty. Limited, G.K. & A.V. Ireland Pty. Ltd. (Importers), Design Inn Pty. Limited, (Indoor Plant Decorators). *Memberships:* Past Master, Freemasons; Past President, Interflora Australian Unit; Past Chairman, Interflora British Group; Past President, Australian Florist Association. *Hobbies:* Swimming; Yachting; Underwater Diving; Photography; World Travel. *Address:* Unit 31, 225 Beaconsfield Parade, Middle Park, Victoria 3206, Australia.

IRFAN, Muhammad, b. 7 Jan. 1933, Meerut, India. Physicist & University Teacher. m. Razia Yousuf, 27 Dec. 1968, 1 son, 1 daughter. *Education:* Intermediate Science, UP Board, India, 1950; BSc (Hons,), Punjab University, Pakistan, 1952; MSc, (Physics), Dacca University, Bangladesh, 1954; PhD, (Nuclear Physics), Glasgow University, 1962. *Appointments:* Lecturer/Demonstrator, University of Karachi, 1955-58; Attaché de Recherche, Université de Montréal, Quebec, Canada, 1962-64; Assistant Professor, 1964-71, Associate Professor, 1971-, Memorial University of Newfoundland, Canada *Memberships:* Canadian Association of Physicists; Canadian Radiation Protection Association; American Physical Society; American Association of Physics Teachers; The New York Academy of Sciences. *Publications:* Author and Co-Author of several publications in Scientific Research Journals in the fields of Nuclear Reactions, Nuclear Detectors and Environmental Radioactivity. *Honours:* Several prizes and awardsschool education, High School, Intermediate Merit Scholarships, 1946-50; Academic Roll of Honour, Government College, Lahore, 1951-52; UNESCO, Fellow, 1958-59; National Research Council of Canada, Post-Doctoral Fellow, 1962-63. *Hobbies:* Reading; Photography; Current Affairs. *Address:* Physics Dept., Memorial University of Newfoundland, St. John's, Newfoundland, Canada, A1B 3X7.

IROHA, Emmanuel Nwankwo Agu, b. 7 Feb. 1942, Ugwele, Uturu, Okigwe, Nigeria. Purchasing. m. Dec. 1970, 2 sons, 1 daughter. *Education:* Read Privately, Diploma in Journalism; Member of Chartered Institute of Transport. *Appointments:* Secretary-Typist, Usaid, Lagos, 1962-73; Purchasing Officer, Volkswagen of Nigeria, Lagos, 1973-75; Distribution Manager, 3M Nigeria Limited, 1975-. *Hobby:* Sport. *Address:* 8 Oladeinde Close, Surulere, Lagos.

IROKA, Luke Amaechine, b. 14 Oct. 1947, Umuna-Orlu, Nigeria. Librarian. m. Juliana O Iroka, 5 Mar. 1972, 2 sons, 2 daughters. *Education:* Diploma in Librarianship, University of Ibadan, Nigeria, 1972-74; Sandwich Library Course, London, 1976; Working on Master of Library Science Degree, Case Western Reserve University, Cleveland, Ohio, USA. *Appointments:* Library Assistant, 1963-72, Librarian, 1974-77, British Council Library, Kaduna, Nigeria; Higher Library Officer, University of Nigeria, Nsukka, Nigeria, 1977-80. *Memberships:* Nigerian Library Association; British Library Association, 1972-77. *Hobbies:* Football; Tennis; Reading. *Address:* Medical Library, University of Nigeria, Enugu Campus, Enugu, Nigeria.

IRUKWU, Joseph Ogbonnaya, b. 20 July 1934, Imo State, Nigeria. Lawyer; Insurance Administrator; Educationist. m. 1964, 2 sons, 3 daughters. *Education:* Barrister-at-Law, Lincoln's Inn, London, 1962; Solicitor & Advocate, Supreme Court of Nigeria, 1962; Fellow Institute of Arbitrators, 1962; Associate of the Chartered Insurance Institute, London, 1964. *Appointments:* Legal Adviser, West African Provincial Insurance Company Ltd., Lagos, 1962-70; Managing Director, Unity Life & Fire Insurance Company Ltd., Lagos,

1970-; Chairman, Nigerian Students Loans Board, 1972-79; Managing Director, Nigeria Reinsurance Corporation, Lagos, 1977-. *Memberships:* Nigerian Bar Association, 1962-; British Insurance Law Association, 1963-; Fellow, Institute of Arbitrators, England, 1962; Chairman, Education Committee, WAICA, 1974-; Past President, Life Councillor, Insurance Institute of Nigeria, 1976-77; President, Nigerian Insurance Law Association, 1977-; Board of Governors, West African Insurance Institute, Montovia, Liberia, 1978; Associate, Nigerian Institute of Management, 1964-. *Publications:* Insurance Law and Practice in Nigeria, 3rd Edition, 1978; Accident and Motor Insurance in West Africa, 1974; Insurance Management in Africa, 1978; Reinsurance in the Third World, 1980. *Honours:* WAICA Book Award, 1976; Ernest Mayer Book Award, 1976; Elected Member of the Governing Council, World Congress on Insurance Law in Madrid, 1978. *Hobbies:* Lawn Tennis; Photography; Dancing; Writing; Cycling. *Address:* Plot 1432, Victoria Island, Lagos, Nigeria.

IRVINE, B(ryant) Godman, MP, b. 25 July 1909, Toronto, Canada. Member of Parliament; Barrister-at-Law; Farmer. m. Valborg Cecilie, 1945, 2 daughters. *Education:* MA, Magdalen College, Oxford; Secretary Oxford Union Society, 1931; Called to Bar, Inner Temple, 1932. *Appointments:* Lt-Commander RNVR, afloat and on staff of Commander-in-Chief Western Approaches and Commander US Naval Forces in Europe, 1939-45; Prospective Candidate, Bewdley Division, Worcs, 1947-49; contested Wood Green and Lower Tottenham, 1951; Elected MP, East Sussex (Rye), 1955; Private Secretary to Minister of Education and to Parliamentary Secretary, Ministry of Education, 1957-59, to the Financial Secretary to the Treasury, 1959-60; Member Speaker's Panel of Chairmen, House of Commons, 1965-76, Joint Secretary Executive Committee, 1922 Committee, 1965-68, Honorary Treasurer, 1974-76; Vice-Chairman, Conservative Agricultural Committee and spoke on Agriculture from Opposition Front Bench, 1964-70; Member, House of Commons select Committee on Agriculture, 1967-69. *Memberships:* Commonwealth Parliamentary Association: Honorary Treasurer, 1970-73; General Council, 1970-73; Executive Committee, 1964-76; Vice-Chairman, Conservative Commonwealth Affairs Committee, 1967-76; Chairman, Conservative Horticulture Sub-Committee, 1960-62; All Party Tourist and Resort Committee, 1964-66. *Hobbies:* Skiing; Travel by sea; Music. *Address:* Great Ote Hall, Burgess Hill, West Sussex, England.

IRWIN Arthur Bonshaw, b. 6 June 1915, North Vancouver, British Columbia, Canada. Professional Engineer. m. Lily Ann Busby, 20 Nov. 1943, 1 son, 1 daughter. *Education:* B.A.Sc., Mining Engineering, 1937, M.A.Sc, Geological Engineering, 1947, University of British Columbia; Ph.D., Geology, MacGill University, 1950. *Appointments:* Mineral Exploration, Central Africa, 1937-40; Mineral Production, Nkana Mine, Zambia, 1940-41; Mine Engineering and Geology, British Columbia, 1941-49; Geological Survey, Government of Canada, 1950-53; Department of Indian Affairs and Northern Development, 1953-77; Management Consultant, Petroleum and Mining rights, 1978-. *Memberships:* Vice-Chairman, Edmonton Branch, Canadian Institue of Mining and Metallurgy, 1955; Association of Professional Engineers of Ontario; Professional Institute of Public Service of Canada; International Friendship Club of Ottawa, 1964-65. *Publications:* Several short articles in Mineral Industry Journals. *Honours:* Commemorative Coronation Medal, Canada for Queen Elizabeth II, 1976. *Hobbies:* Running; Cycling; Mountain climbing; Camping; Motor cycling. *Address:* 118 Bruce Court, Penticton, British Columbia, Canada V2A 6C4.

IRWIN, James Campbell, b. 23 June 1906, Adelaide, South Australia. Architect. m. Kathleen Agnes Orr, 23 Nov. 1933, 1 son, 1 daughter. *Education:* Queen's School; St Peters College; St. Marks College, University of Adelaide; Staff College, Haifa, 1942; F.R.I.B.A., FRAIA, b.s.c. *Appointments:* Partner, Woods Bagot Laybourne-Smith & Irwin, 1930-74. *Memberships:* Royal Australian Institute of Architects; Royal Institute of British Architects; Fellow, Royal Australian Planning Institute, 1957-74; President, 1964-66, Adelaide Festival of Arts, Board Member, 1964-78; National Capital Planning Committee, Canberra, 1964-70. *Publications:* 'The Irwin Family', 1977. *Honours:* OBE, served in

Royal Australian Artillery, 1940-46, Middle East, New Guinea, Philippines, (Lieutenant Colonel), 1945; ED, 1947; Knight Bachelor, 1971; Honorary Fellow, St. Mark's College, 1973; Life Fellow, Royal Australian Institute Architects, 1970; South Australian Institute of Architects' Prize, 1926; Hon. Life Member Adelaide Festival of Arts, 1978. *Hobby:* Reading. *Address:* 124 Brougham Place, North Adelaide, South Australia 5006.

IRWIN, Robert Philip, b. 31 Oct. 1933, Levin, New Zealand. Educator (Tertiary Sector). m. Valerie Jean Judd, 12 Dec. 1959, 2 sons, 1 daughter. *Education:* Diploma of Physical Education, University of Otago, 1952-54; Diploma in Teaching, Christchurch Teachers College, 1955; Associateship, New Zealand Physical Education Society, 1959-61; Master of Science in Health Education, University of Illinois, 1965-66; Doctor of Philosophy, University of Illinois, 1966-69. *Appointments:* Assistant Master, Hutt Valley High School, New Zealand, 1956-59; Lecturer, Hamilton Teachers College, New Zealand, 1960-65; Teaching & Research Assistant, University of Illinois, USA, 1965-69; Senior Lecturer and Head of Department, Hamilton Teachers College, New Zealand, 1969-71; Senior Research Fellow & Director, Department of Sociology, Australian National University, Canberra, Australia, 1971-75; Senior Lecturer, Convenor, Degree of Bachelor of Applied Science in Health Education, and Director of Adult Teaching, Canberra College of Advanced Education, Belconnen, Australia, 1975-81; Principal Lecturer in Health Studies, Canberra College of Advanced Education, Belconnenk, Australia, 1981. *Memberships:* American School Health Association; Australian & New Zealand Society for Epidemiology & Research in Community Health; Sociological Association of Australia & New Zealand; Australian Association for Research in Education; Australian Council for Health, Physical Education & Recreation; *Publications:* Health Teaching, 1975; Drug Education Programs and the Adolescent in the Drug Phenomena Problem, 1976. *Honours:* Efficiency Award, Royal New Zealand Army Medical Corps, 1957; New Zealand University Blue in Athletics, 1958; Diploma Coach to the New Zealand Amateur Athletics Association, 1961; University Summer Fellow, University of Illinois, 1967; Fellow, American School Health Association, 1977. *Hobbies:* Sports observing; Philately; Wood Working. *Address:* 32 Tanumbirini Street, Hawker, ACT, 2614, Australia.

ISA, Ishaka, b. 10 Jan. 1946, Okengwen, Okene Local Government Area, Kwara State, Nigeria. Architect. m. Musili, 18 Dec. 1972, 2 sons, 3 daughters. *Education:* BSc. (Architecture), 1972; MSc. (Architecture), 1974. *Appointments:* Estate Architect, Ahmadu Bello University, Samau, Zaria, 1974-78; Principal Partner, Bestac International Associates, 1978-. *Memberships:* Nigerian Institute of Architects; Architects Registration Council of Nigeria; Zaria Club. *Hobby:* Driving. *Address:* 170 Habibu Road, Samaru, Zaria, Nigeria.

ISA, John Frederick William, b. 8 Aug. 1942, Masasi, Tanzania. Veterinarian. m. Beatrice, 9 Dec. 1972, 2 sons, 3 daughters. *Education:* BVSc., 1968. *Appointments:* District Veterinary Officer, 1968-69, Veterinary Research Officer and Teaching, 1970-76, Tanzania Government; Veterinary Advisor, Pfizer Limited, Zambia, 1976-. *Memberships:* President, 1973-76, Gymkana Club; Lusaka Golf Club; Choma Sports Club. *Honours:* J F Kennedy Scholarship, 1964-68. *Hobbies:* Darts; Reading. *Address:* PO Box 181, Masasi, Tanzania.

ISAAC, K A, b. 10 July 1925, Kanjiramattom, Kerala, India. Teacher. m. Chechamma, 16 May 1955, 2 sons. *Education:* BSc., Travancore, 1947; Diploma, Library Science, 1952, Masters Degree, Library Science, 1953, Delhi, India. *Appointments:* Librarian, Nirmala College, Delhi, India, 1952-53; Librarian, Forest Research Institute, Dehra Dun, 1953-57; University Librarian, 1959-61, University Librarian and Head of Department of Library Science, 1961-72, Professor and Head of Department of Library Science and ex-officio University Librarian, 1972-80, Professor and Head of Department of Library and Information Science, 1980-, University of Kerala, Trivandrum. *Memberships:* Chairman or member of various professional and academic bodies in India. *Publications:* Author of over 60 papers on various aspects of Library and Information Science published in journals or presented at conferences. *Honours:* I rank in the M.Lib.Sc. examination of Delhi University, 1953. *Address:* 17-20 Jagathy, Trivandrum 695014, Kerala, India.

ISHERWOOD, James Lawrence, b. 7 April 1917, Wigan, Lancashire. Professional Artist. m. 28. June 1944, (div.) *Education:* FRSA., FIAL., Wigan College of Art, 1933-39. *Appointments:* Cartoonist, Manchester Evening News, 1952-54; Professional Artist. *Memberships:* Founder, Wigan Art Society, 1952. *Creative Works:* 203 one-man shows, 13 in London, 28 in Cambridge, 25 in Oxford, Salisbury, Winchester, Torquay, Newport Pagnell, Bolton, Blackpool, Manchester and Chorley; 'I am Isherwood', one ½ hr. TV Documentary, 1974-75; Permanent collection of Original Paintings at the Isherwood Banqueting Suite; Portraits of Sir A.E. Richardson PRA, Sir Gerald Nabarro, Jerry Desmonde, Lord Winstanley, Lady Ellaline Terris-Hicks, Lady Hayter, Lord Thomson, Lord Crawford, Cicely Courtneidge, Vis. Newport, Mayors of Southport, Warrington and Wigan. 37 Portrait Demonstrations and Lectures at Warrington U.S.A. Officers Camp, Warrington, Blackpool, Bolton, Wigan, Chorley, Winchester, London and Preston Art Galleries; Currently writing his Life Story, called Mother Lily- A Tribute To Her-the greatest woman in his Life! *Publications:* 'Mother Lily as Lancashire Madonna'; 'The Vicissitudes of an Artists Life'. *Honours:* Silver Medal, Rome, 1958; Sculpted by Stephen Taylor, for 'Isherwood Suite', Southport, 1979; Awarded Life Membership of the International Society of Arts, Switzerland; Honary member by Fellowship of the Royal Society of Arts. *Hobbies:* Stamp collecting; Rowing. *Address:* The Isherwood Collection, Studio Leywood, 151 Wigan Lane, Bellingham, Wigan, Lancashire.

ISLAM, Nurul. b. 1 Apr. 1928, Bangladesh, Cittagong. Consultant Physician. m. Anwara Begum, 26 Dec. 1962, 1 son, 2 daughters. *Education:* MBBS, Calcutta University, 1950; TDD, University of Wales, UK, 1955; MRCP, 1956, FRCP, 1966, Edinburgh University, Scotland; FCCP, USA, 1962; FCPS, University of Pakistan, 1963; FRCP, University of London, UK, 1977. *Appointments:* Professor of Medicine, Medical Colleges, 1962; Joint Director and Professor of Medicine, 1965; Director and Professor of Medicine, Institute of Postgraduate Medicine and Research and Additional Secretary to the Government of Bangladesh, 1968. *Memberships:* President, Bangladesh Association for Advancement of Medical Sciences, National Council of Science and Technology Nutritional Society of Bangladesh; American Society of Tropical Medicine and Hygiene; President, Postgraduate Patients Welfare Society; Patron, National Tuberculosis Relief and Rehabilitation Society; International Advisory Editorial Board-Tropical Doctor, London; President, Bangladesh Medical Research Council; Governing Body, Institute of Nutritiona and Food Science; President, Bangladesh Society of Nuclear Medicine. *Publications:* Described a new method of diagnosis of Hepatic Amoebiasis, 1960; Described a new disease—Eosinophilie lung abscess, 1962; Described Two new methods of Percyssion, 1977; A Simplified Tuberculosis Control Programme for East Pakistan, 1963; Tropical Eosinophilia, 1964; Essentials of Medical Treatment, 1974; Shyastha Shambande Kichu Katha, 1978; History of Institute of Postgraduate Medicine and Research, 1978; Medical Diagnosis and Treatment, 1980; 70 articles in various International Journals. *Honours:* President's Gold Medal, National TB Association, 1963; Sitar-e-Imtiaz (S.I) 1970; Fellow, Bangladesh Academy of Sciences, 1972; FRCP Lond without examination, 1977; Chittagong Association Gold Medal for Meritorious Services, 1979. *Hobbies:* Reading; Writing. *Address:* 'Gulmeher', 63 Central Road, Dhanmondi R A, Dacca-5, Bangladesh.

ISMAIL, Bin Mohamed Ali, b. 16 Sept. 1918, Port Kelang, Selangor, Malaysia. Company Chairman. m. Maimunah binti Abdul Latiff, 12 Mar. 1949, 2 sons. *Education:* BA.(Econs.), University of Cambridge, UK, 1938-41; Barrister-at-Law, Middle Temple, Inns of Court, London, UK, 1943. *Appointments:* Malayan Civil Service, 1946-68; Assistant State Secretary, Selangor State, 1948-50; Assistant Secretary, Economic Division, Federal Treasury, 1950-53; Economic Officer, Penang, 1954-55; Controller, Trade Division, Ministry of Commerce and Industry, 1955-57; Minister, Federation of Malaya Embassy, Washington, 1957-58; Executive Director, World Bank, International Finance Corporation and International Development Association,

Washington, USA, 1958-60; Deputy Governor, 1960-62, Governor, 1962-80, Central Bank of Malaysia; Chairman, Malaysian Industrial Development Finance Limited, 1969-; Chairman, National Equity Corporation, 1978-; Chairman, Commodities Trading Council, 1980-; Chairman, Malaysian Kuwaiti Investment Company, 1980-. *Memberships:* President, 1966-68, Fellow, Malaysian Institute of Management; Board of Governors, Asian Institute of Management, Manila; President, 1964, Royal Selangor Golf Club, Kuala Lumpur. *Honours:* Order of Panglima Mangku Negara, 1964; Order of Panglima Negara Bintang Sarawak, 1976; Order of Seri Paduka Mahkota Selangor, 1977; Order of Seri Paduka Mahkota Johor, 1979; Order of Seri Setia Mahkota, 1980; Honorary Doctor of Laws, University of Malaya, 1973, Award of Tun Abdul Razak Foundation, 1980. *Hobbies:* Golf; Swimming. *Address:* 23 Jalan Taman U Thant, Kuala Lumpur 04-03, Malaysia.

ISMAIL, Zaleha Datin Paduka, b. 18 May, 1936, Selangor, Malaysia. Executive Councillor, Selangor State Government. m. Abdul Rahman Haji Ali, 25 Oct 1959, 3 sons. *Education:* BA, University of Malaya, Singapore, 1960; BA.(Hons.), University of Malaya, Kuala Lumpur, 1961. *Appointments:* Assistant Malay Programme Organiser 1961, English Programme Organiser, 1965, Radio Malaysia; Encyclopedia Editor, 1968, Deputy Head, Text Book Division, 1971, Language and Literary Agency; Political Secretary, 1974; Member, Legislative Assembly of Selangor State, 1978; Executive Councillor, Selangor State Government, 1978. *Memberships:* Supreme Council, United Malay Nationals Organisation; Executive member, Women's Wing of United Malay Nationals Organisation; Selangor State Liaison Umno; Chairman, Selangor Women's Wing of United Malays Nationals Organisation; Chairman, National Advisory Council on Integration on Women in Development in Malaysia; Deputy President, National Council of Women's Organisation Malaysia; President, Child Welfare Council, Malaysia. *Publications:* Articles in Science Encyclopedia and Children's Encyclopedia. *Honours:* Setia Mahkota Selangor, 1979; Kesatria Mangku Negara, 1980; Datuk Paduka Mahkota Selangor, carrying the title DATIN PADUKA, 1980. *Hobbies:* Cooking; Reading; Public Speaking. *Address:* SL9, Jalan Berlian, Taman Perwire Satu, Batu 6, Gombak, Selangor, Malaysia.

ISOLA, Akinwumi, b. 24 Dec. 1939, Ibadan, Nigeria. University Teacher. m. Adebola Aderinola, 27 Sept. 1969, 1 son, 3 daughters. *Education:* BA.(Hons.), 1967, Diploma in Linguistics, 1969, PhD., 1978, University of Ibadan, Nigeria. *Appointments:* Tutor, Wesley College, Ibadan, Nigeria, 1967-68; Lecturer, University of Lagos, Nigeria, 1968-74; Senior Lecturer, University of Ife, Ile Ife, Nigeria, 1974-. *Memberships:* West African Linguistics Society; Yoruba Studies Association of Nigeria; Secretary, Yoruba Creative Writers Association. *Publications:* Book: O LE KU, 1974; Plays: Efunsetan Aniwure, 1970; Kòseégbé, 1981; Madam Tinubu, (in English), 1981; Aye Ye Wón Tan, forthcoming; Were Lesin, forthcoming; Afaimo, (Collection of poems), 1981. *Honours:* 1st Prize, Creative Writing Competition, organised by Egbe Ijinle, Yoruba, 1966. *Hobbies:* Gardening. *Address:* House L 46, Road 19, University of Ife, Campus, Ile Ife, Nigeria.

ITA, Okokon, b. 7 Mar. 1935, Akpap-Okoyong, Calabar, Nigeria. High Court Judge. m. Ekei Ani, 27 Sept. 1975, 3 sons. *Education:* LL.B., London, UK, 1964; Barrister-at-Law and Called to English Bar, 1965; Enrolled in Nigeria as Legal Practitioner, 1965; Certificate of Successful completion of Special Course for Government Legal Officers in Britain, 1969. *Appointments:* Federal Public Service of Nigeria as State Counsel and deployed on Drafting of Legislation, 1965; Transferred to Cross River State Civil Service, 1970; Promoted Legal Draftsman of the State, 1974; Promoted Solicitor-General of the State and Permanent Secretary, Ministry of Justice, 1977. *Memberships:* African Club, Cross River State, Nigeria. *Hobbies:* Reading. *Address:* Judge's Quarters, G R A, Ikot Ekpene, Cross River State, Nigeria.

ITATA, Elizabeth Aniema, b. 6 Nov. 1946, Lagos, Nigeria. Medical Records. m. 17 Dec. 1966, Mr. I W Itata, 3 sons, 1 daughter. *Appointments:* Assistant Medical Records Officer, 1978; Medical Records Officer, 1980. *Honours:* Certificates: 100 Metres, 1962;

220 Metres, 1963; 440 Metres, 1963. *Hobbies:* Letter writing; Cookery; Dressmaking; Athletics. *Address:* 9 Uwanse Street, Calabar, Cross River State, Nigeria.

IYEKOLO, Ezekiel Bolaji, b. 22 May 1942, Odo-Ere, Oyi Local Government Kwara State, Nigeria. Marketing Director. m. 4 Apr. 1970, 2 sons, 2 daughters. *Education:* BSc., Business Administration, Ahmadu Bello University, Zaria, Nigeria, 1969. *Appointments:* Sales Manager, 1969-71, Regional Manager, 1972-76, CSS Bookshop, Zaria, Nigeria; Area Promotion Manager, Oxford University Press, 1976-77; Marketing Manager, 1977-79, Marketing Director, 1979-81, Thomas Nelson Nigeria Limited, Nigeria; Director, Kwara Furniture Manufacturing Company, 1977-79. *Memberships:* British Institute of Marketing, 1971; Zaria Club; Board of Governors, Okutadudu High School, Odo-Ere-Kwara, Nigeria. *Honours:* College Athletic Captain and Prefect, Igbaja Teachers College, 1963. *Hobbies:* Reading; Social Work. *Address:* 35 Ayantuga Street, Mushin, Lagos, Nigeria.

IYER, S R Sivaraja, b. 1 Feb. 1924, Colombo, Sri Lanka. Research Scientist. m. Indrani Chandramouli, 5 May 1958, 1 son, 1 daughter. *Education:* BSc.(Hons.), Sri Lanka University, 1946; MSc., 1951, PhD., 1954, Madras University, India. *Appointments:* Senior Scientific Officer, 1958, Research Associate, 1963-66, 'Atira', Ahmedabad; Research Associate, LeHigh University, USA, 1960-62; Professor of Physical Chemistry and Head, Chemistry Section, Bombay University Department of Chemical Technology, Bombay, India, 1966-. *Memberships:* FRSC., C.Chem. (UK); National Academy of Sciences, India. *Publications:* Several original research publications in various international journals on the subject of surface and interfacial phenomena in dye-polymer systems. *Hobbies:* Reading; Wild Life Conservation; Philately; Indian classical music and dance; Golf. *Address:* Flat 3, UDCT Birla Hostel, Matunga, Bombay-19, India.

J

JACK, Alieu Sulayman (Sir), b. 14 July 1922, Banjul, The Gambia. Politician. m. Marie Cham, 17 June 1946, 4 sons, 4 daughters. *Education:* St. Augustine's High School. *Appointments:* Navy, Army and Air Institute, 1939-44; Bathurst Temporary Local Authority, 1944-48; Private Businessman, 1948-72; Councillor, Bathurst City Council, 1949-62; Speaker of the House of Representatives, 1962-72; Minister of Works and Communications, 1972-77; Speaker of the House of Representatives, 1977 . *Memberships:* Banjul Club; Honourable Society of Gentlemen of the Middle Temple, London. *Honours:* Commander of the National Order of the Republic of Senegal, 1967; Commander of the Order of Merit of the Islamic Republic of Mauretania, 1967; Knight Bachelor, 1970; Commander of the Order of the Federal Republic of Nigeria, 1970; Knight Grand Band of the Republic of Liberia, 1971; Justice of the Peace, 1971; Chancellor of the National Order of the Republic of the Gambia, 1972; Grand Commander of the National Order of the Republic of The Gambia, 1972. *Hobby:* Golf. *Address:* Serekunda, Kombo St. Mary's Area, The Gambia, P.O. Box 376 Banjul, The Gambia.

JACK, Kenneth William David, b. 5 Oct. 1924, Melbourne, Victoria, Australia. Artist. m. Betty J. Dyer, 14 Jan. 1950, 1 son, 2 daughters. *Education:* Art Teachers Certificate, 1949; Art Teachers Diploma, 1951; Trained Teachers Certificate, (Manual Arts). *Appointments:* Worked in the employ of the State Government's Education Department, 1948-68 including: Upwey High School, Assistant to Art Inspector of Technical Schools, Senior Art Instructor, Caulfield Institute of Technology, Founder of Departments of Painting and Printmaking, Deputy Head of Art Department, Caulfield Institute of Technology; Full time Painter, 1968; Member of Council of Caulfield Institute of Technology, 1969-76; Member of Fine Art Advisory Committee for Degree and Diploma, Caulfield Institute of Technology, 1976-; Foundation Member of Federal Government's Artbank Board, 1980-. *Memberships:* Associate of Royal Watercolour Society, London; Australian Watercolour Institute; Patron (formerly President 1978-80) of Old Watercolour Society's Club, (Australian Branch), London; Life Fellow IBA, 1980; Australian Guild of Realist Artists, (formerly foundation Vice-President 1974-80); National Register of Prominent Americans and International Notables, 1974-; Melbourne High School Old Boys Association. *Publications:* 'The Melbourne Book', 1948; 'The Charm of Hobart', 1949; 'Australian Gold and Ghost Towns', 1962; 'The Future Canberra', 1965; 'Kenneth Jack', 1972. *Creative Works:* Designed Mural for Australian Pavilion Expo 67, Montreal; Designed Tapestry Coat of Arms, Australian Pavilion, Expo 70, Osaka; Folio of 44 paintings of South Australia (10), Western Australia (10), Central Australia and Northern Territory (12), Victoria (12); Designed 5 Silver Plates for Franklin Mint; Several Large reproductions of paintings. *Honours:* Over 40 awards including: Art Gallery of New South Wales Trustees Watercolour Prizes, 1967, 1972; Silver Medal, Royal Adelaide Exhibition, 1957; Certificate of Honour, International Graphic Art Exhibition, Leipzig, 1965; Certificate of Merit, 4th International Exhibition of Contemporary Art, New Delhi, 1961; Maude Vizard-Wholohan Watercolour Prizes, 1961, 1963; Print Prize, 1963; Rural Bank Prizes for Oils, 1968, 1969, 1970; Caltex Award, 1968; Bendigo Gallery, Oil, 1959, Watercolour 1945, 1954; Crouch Prize, Watercolour, 1960. *Hobby:* Classical Music. *Address:* Lot 11, Linton Court, Doreen 3754, Victoria, Australia.

JACKLING, Stanley William Redcliffe, b. 5 Nov. 1908, Albury New South Wales, Australia. Solicitor. m. Evelyn Dorothy Arnold, 4 Apr. 1936, 2 sons, 1 daughter. *Education:* Matriculation, Sydney University 1925; Articles of Clerkship in Law, New South Wales, 1926-31; Barrister and Solicitor, 1938-; Associate of Music, Melbourne Conservatorium of Music, 1935. *Appointments:* Solicitor, New South Wales, 1931; Barrister and Solicitor, Victoria, 1938; Chairman of Directors, Statewide Building Society, 1960-. *Memberships:* National President, Life Governor, Apex Clubs of Australia; Savage Club of Melbourne; Albury Club. *Hob-*

bies: Music; Photography; Philately; Flying. *Address:* 1A Bruce Street, Balwyn 3103, Victoria, Australia.

JACKMAN, Harry Hans, b. 2 May 1921, Extension Economist. m. Norma Jones, 15 May 1954, 1 sons, 1 daughter. *Education:* B.A. School of Econ. and Fin. Studies, Macquarie University, 1974; Diploma, Australian School of Pacific Administration, 1965. *Appointments:* Registrar of Co-operative Societies, 1960-62; Chief of Division, Business Training and Management, 1962-68; Chief of Division, Business Extension, 1968-74; Chairman, Co-operative Education Trust, 1970-72; Assistant Staff Economist, United States Trust Territory of the apacific Islands, 1963; Lecturer in Local Government, Mitchell CAE, 1977-79; Visiting Fellow, 1980; Lecturer in Business Management, Riverina CAE, 1981-. *Memberships:* Fellow, Australian Society of Accountants; Fellow, Institute of Chartered Secretaries and Administrators; Associate Fellow, PNG Institute of Management; Amnesty International; International P.E.N., Sydney; United Service Institution, New South Wales. *Publications:* Numerous articles on Business and Economics in Papua, New Guinea, in academic and popular journals. *Honours:* M.B.E. 1978. *Hobby:* Book reviewing. *Address:* S-293, South Wagga-Wagga, New South Wales, 2650, Australia.

JACKS, Bernard, b. 28 March 1930, Brisbane, Australia. Life Underwriter. m. Kirsten Katrina Lefevre-Hansoen, 6 Oct. 1967, 2 sons, 1 daughter. *Education:* Diploma, Australian Insurance Institute, 1966. *Appointments:* Joined National Mutual Life Association of Australasia Limited, 1958-. *Memberships:* Past National President and Past State President, Life Underwriters Association of Australia; Vice Chairman, Membership Communications Committee and Corresponding Member, Constitution and Byelaws Committee, Million Dollar Round Table; President, Temple Shalom. *Honours:* Life Membership, Life Underwriters Association of Australia, 1974; Life Membership, Judean Sports Club, 1952; National Coaching Accreditation Scheme, Australia, 1981. *Address:* 7 MacCaul Street, Indooroopilly Q 4068, Australia.

JACKSON, Alec Harold, b. 7 March 1916, Winnipeg, Canada. Importer. m. 26 Oct. 1946, 2 sons, 1 daughter. *Education:* St. Johns Technicol College. *Appointments:* Importer, Toys and Gifts. *Memberships:* President, Jewish Community Centre, Vancouver, 1964-66; Grand President, B'Nai B'Rith, District 4, 1967-68; President, Jewish Community Fund and Council, 1970; President, Canadian Zionist Federation, Pacific Region, 1974-78; President, Schara Tzedeck Synagogue, 1977-78; Chairman, Israel's Celebration Anniversary, British Columbia, 1973; Chairman, Brotherhood Week Celebration, British Columbia, 1966-67; Ex Board Member of Canadian Council of Chirstians and Jews, 1970-81; Ex Board Member of Canadian Jewish Congress, 1960-81; Commissioner, International Council of B'Nai B'Rith, 1978-. *Honours:* Numerous awards including: B'Nai B'Rith International, Canadian Zionist Federation, Israel Bonds, State of Israel, Schara Tzedeck Synagogue, Jewish Community Centre, United Jewish Appeal, Pioneer Women, City of Vancouver, City of Sacramento; Recipient Akiba Award, B'Nai B'Rith District 4, 1963; Testimonial Dinner, Jewish Community, Vancouver, 1968; Testimonial Dinner, Israel Bonds of British Columbia, 1965; Testimonial Dinner, Negev Dinner Honoree, Jewish National Fund, British Columbia, 1980. *Hobbies:* Singing; Dancing; Racquet Ball; Walking. *Address:* 6573 Pinehurst Drive, Vancouver, Canada.

JACKSON, Donald Robert, b. 12 Oct. 1915, Sunningdale, Berks, England. Australian Regular Army (Retired). m. Anita Mary Urquhart, 6 Dec. 1949, 2 sons, 1 daughter. *Education:* Royal Military College, Duntroon 1934-37; PSC, Middle East Staff College, Haifa 1941; BA, University of Sydney 1938-48. *Appointments:* Sydney University Regiment, 1938; Darwin Mobile Force, 1939; Adjutant 2/1 Inf Bn AIR, Palestine, Egypt, Libya, 1940-41; L.O GHQ Greece, Crete, Staff Capt. HQ, Australian Corps. Syria, 1941; Bm. 24 Aust. Inf. BDE, Syria, El Alamein, 1942-43; Assistant, DMI, Land Forces, S.W.P.A, Papua, New Guinea, Dutch New Guinea, 1943-44; 2/28 Inf Bn AIR, Moluccas, Brit N. Borneo, 1944-45; Comd 67 INF Bn, B.C.O.F Japan, 1946-47; United Kingdom, Sweden, Germany, 1947-48; Comdt. School of Infantry, 1948; Comdt. School of

Tactics, 1949-52; Director of Infantry, 1953; Chief of Staff N. Comd. 1954-56; Comdt. Officer Cadet School 1957; Director of Supplies and Transport 1958-60; Chief of Staff S Comd. 1961-63; Australian Army Representive in United Kingdom, ADC, HM the Queen, 1963-64; Comd Field Training Area 1965-68; Staff Manager, Hamersley Iron Pty. Ltd. 1968-73. *Memberships:* Fellow, Australian Institute of Management; Queensland Olympic Committee 1955-57; President, Queensland Modern Pentathlon Association. *Honours:* Distinguished Service Order 1942. Hobby: Game fishing. *Address:* Soqulu Plantation, Taveuni Island, Fiji.

JACKSON, George Frederic Clarence, b. 5 July 1907, Peterborough, Canada. Bishop, Anglican Church of Canada. m. Eileen de Montfort Wellborne, 14 Sept. 1939, 2 sons, 2 daughters. *Education:* B.A. Toronto, 1932; L.th., Wycliffe, Toronto, 1935; D.D. Wycliffe, 1961; Emmanuel, St. Chad, 1965; St. Johns, 1976. *Appointments:* Teacher, 1927-29; Deacon, 1934; Priest, 1935; Bishop, 1960; Metropolitan, 1970. *Memberships:* Regina Kiwanas Club, 1958-60; Royal Canadian Legion, 1958-77. *Hobbies:* Gardening; Cross-Country; Skiing. *Address:* Box 519, Fort Qu'Appelle, Saskatchewan, Canada SOG 1S0.

JACKSON, Horace Anthony, b. 22 Feb. 1943, Kingston, Jamaica. Plastic & Reconstructive Surgery. m. Cicely Angela Pollard, 8 Apr. 1972, 2 sons, 1 daughter. *Education:* MB., BS., University of West Indies, Jamaica, 1963-69; Internship & Residency in Surgery, Queen Elizabeth Hospital, Barbados, 1969-72; FRCS (Ed.), University of Edinburgh Post-Graduate Medical School and Royal Infirmary of Edinburgh, 1972-73; Resident in Plastic Surgery, Jackson Memorial Hospital, University of Miami, 1976-79. *Appointments:* Associate Consultant Surgeon in General & Urological & Traumatic Surgery, Kingston Public Hospital, 1973-75; Consultant Plastic & Reconstructive Surgeon at the Kingston Public Hospital and the University Hospital of the West Indies; Associate Lecturer, Department of Surgery, University Hospital of the West Indies; Senior Medical Officer (Medical Administration), 1977-. *Memberships:* Associate, Black Psychiatrists of America; Fellow, Royal College of Surgeons of Edinburgh; Association of Surgeons in Jamaica; Medical Association of Jamaica; Paediatric Association of Jamaica; Ralph Millard Jr. Society, (Miami, Florida, USA). *Creative Works:* A unique barrel-type speaker system taking advantage of the principle that low frequency notes are virtually nondirectional (to be patented). *Honours:* Open Scholar, University of West Indies, 1963; Jamaica Government Scholarship, 1972; Henry Arthur Dalziel Ferns Prize, for best candidate in Fellowship examinations, 1972-73. *Hobbies:* Aero-modelling; Photography; Videography; Swimming; High Board Diving; Hi-Fidelity, Audiophile; Fashion & Cosmetology. *Address:* 27 Tucker Avenue, KGN 6, Jamaica, West Indies.

JACKSON, Peter, b. 16 Dec. 1949, Lichfield, Staffs, England. Architect. m. Jutta Bordach, 4 May 1979, 1 son. *Education:* Bartlett School of Architecture, University College, London, 1968-73; B.Sc. Hons, Architecture Planning and Building, 1971; Diploma in Architecture, Field Experience, 1971-73; Dip. Arch, 1973; Riba part III, 1975; B.Sc Hons, Dip. Arch, London, Riba, Mzia, Miaz. *Appointments:* Yorke Rosenberg Mardall, Architects, London, 1971-72; Zisman Bowyer and Partners, Engineers, Richmond Surrey, 1972; John R. Harris Architects, London, Dubai, Muscat, 1973-76; Dig-Architect/Surveyor, Buseirah Excavations by British School of Archaelogy in Jerusalem, 1973, 1974; Montgomerie Oldfield Kirby Architects and Planners, Lusaka, Zambia, 1976-80; Formed Adams Jackson Partnership with Robert John Adams, Salisbury, Zimbabwe, 1980-. *Memberships:* Royal Institute of British Architects, 1976; Zambia Institute of Architects, 1976; Hon. Secretary and Council Member Zia, 1977-78; Secretary, Board of Education, Zambia Institute of Architects, 1977-80; Vice-President, Zambia Institute of Architects, 1978-80; Prehistory Society of Zimbabwe, 1980; Institute of Architects of Zimbabwe, 1981; Secretary, Education Sub-Committee, Institute of Architects of Zimbabwe, 1981. *Publications:* Art and Archaeological Research Paper, 'A Windtower House in Dubai', 1975; Architectural Review 'Bastakia Windtower Houses', 1975; Editor of 'In Situ' Journal of Zia, 1976-80; Regular features, criticisms, reviews and reports for 'In Situ'; Editor of 'Zed' Journal of Institute of Architects of

Zimbabwe, 1981. *Creative Works:* Major Projects include: House Wightman, Lusaka, 1977-79; Lusaka Intercity Bus Terminus, 1977-80, with Ron Kirby; Student Hostel, Lusaka, 1977-80, with Ron Kirby; Laboratory and Workshops, Aspindale, Salisbury, Factory, Salisbury, 12 Town Houses, Salisbury, with R.J. Adams. *Hobbies:* Historical and Historical Architectural Research; Early Stone Age and Archaeology; Architectural Education; Architectural Writing; Cinema. *Address:* 12 Clarence Drive, Salisbury, Zimbabwe.

JACKSON, Peter MacLeod, b. 29 March 1946, Paisley, Scotland. University Professor, Writer. m. Janette Margaret Ritchie, 18 July 1969, 2 daughters. *Education:* B.A. First Class Honours, University of Strathclyde, 1969; Ph.D., University of Stirling, 1974. *Appointments:* Economist H.M. Treasury, London, 1969-71; University Lecturer, Economics Department, University Stirling, 1971-77; Director Public Sector Economics Research Centre, University of Leicester, 1977-; Head of Economics Department, University of Leicester, 1979-. *Memberships:* Royal Economic Society; Royal Commonwealth Society. *Publications:* Public Sector Economics, with C.V. Brown, 1978; Current Issues in Fiscal Policy, with S.T. Cook, 1979; Politcal Economy of Bureaucracy, 1981; Public Sector Policy Initiatives, 1981. *Hobbies:* Reading; Music. *Address:* 39 Stonehill Drive, Great Glen, Leicestershire, England.

JACKSON, Philip Claudius, b. 10 Sept. 1919, Portland, Jamaica, West Indies. Commissioned Land Surveyor and Land Housing Developer. m. Carman Eileen Ramsay, 7 June 1941, 5 sons, 1 daughter. *Education:* Government Trade Scholarship, Kingston Technical School, 1934-38. *Appointments:* Apprentice Survey Draughtsman and Computer, Government Survey Department, 1938-46; Articled Surveyor's Apprentice, 1947-51; Commissioned Land Surveyor, Private Practise, 1951-; Land and Housing Developer, Manderillo, Jamaica, 1963-. *Memberships:* Land Surveyors' Association of Jamaica; Kiwanis Club, Manderillo. *Hobbies:* Bridge; Swimming; Dancing. *Address:* 4 Widcombe Crescent, Kingston 6, Jamaica, West Indies.

JACKSON, Robert (Gillman Allen) (Commander Sir). Under Secretary General of the United Nations. m. Barbara Ward, 1950 (Baroness Jackson of Lodsworth, deceased, 1981), 1 son. *Appointments:* RAN, 1929-37; Malta and RN, 1937; Chief Staff Officer, Governor and C-in-C Malta, 1940; Planned Malta Command Defence Scheme; Rearmament of the Fortress; Developed Co-ordinated Supply Scheme, 1940; Director General, UNRRA, 1945-47; Director-General ME Supply Centre and Principal Assistant to UK Minister Ops./Mil. operations; Developed Aid to Russia Supply route; Established anti-locust campaign, 1942 (CMG); AFHQ for special duties in Greece, 1944-45; transfer to HM Treasury, 1945; Senior Deputy Director of UNRRA, 1945-47; In Charge of UNRRA's operations in Europe, 1945; Supervised transfer of UNRRA's residual functions to WHO, FAO; Assisted in establishment of IRO and International Children's Emergency, 1947; Assistant Secretary General for co-ordination in UN, 1948; HM Treasury for duties with Lord President of Council, 1949; Permanent Secretary, Ministry of National Development, Australia, 1950-52; Advisor to Government of Pakistan, 1952; Chairman of Prepartory Commission for Volta River multi-purpose project, Gold Coast, 1953-56; Chairman, Development Commission, Ghana, 1956-61; Organized, Royal Tours in Ghana, 1959, 1961; advisory Board, Mekong Project, SE Asia, 1962-76; Adviser, President to President of Liberia, 1962-79; Special Consultant to Administrator, UNDP, 1963-72; Special Adviser, 1978-80; Chairman, UN group reporting on Zambia's security, 1963; Commander in Chief, Survey of UN Development Scheme, 1968-71; Under Secretary General in charge, UN Relief Operations in Bangladesh, 1972-74; Under Secretary General, in charge, UN assistance to Zambia, 1973-78, to Indo-China, 1975-78, to Cape Verde Island, 1975-78, to São Tomé and Prícipe, 1977-78. *Memberships:* Committee Fédération Mondiale des Villes Jumelées Cités Unies, 1972; Dag Hammerskjöld Foundation, 1981-. *Publications:* An International Development Authority, 1955; Report of the Volta River Preparatory Commission, 1956; A study of the United Nations Development System, 1969; Report on Senior Volunteers in UN System, 1978; Report on Reinforcement of UN Industrial Development Organization, 1979. 06 OBE, 1941;

CMG, 1944; Knighted, 1956; KCVO, 1962; Honorary DL, Syracuse; International Jury, Prize of Institut de la Vie, 1972. *Address:* United Nations, New York, NY 10017, USA.

JACKSON, Ronald Gordon, b. 5 May 1924, Brisbane, Australia. Company General Manager. m. Margaret Alison Pratley, 3 April 1948, 1 son, 1 daughter. *Education:* Bachelor of Commerce, University of Queensland, 1949. *Appointments:* Joined CSR Limited in 1942, Head, Sugar Marketing Division, 1958-64, Senior Executive Officer, 1964-72, General Manager and Director, C.S.R., 1972-. *Memberships:* Member of the Board, Reserve Bank of Australia; Commonwealth Government's Economic Consultive Group; Board of Governors, Asian Institute of Management, Manila; Australian National Committee, World Energy Conference; Chairman, Commonwealth Government's Consultive Committee on Relations with Japan; Advisory Board of the University of Melbourne's Institute of Applied Economic and Social Research; Foundation Chairman of the Board of the Australian Graduate School of Management; Councillor, Australian Administrative Staff College; Trustee, Mitsui Educational Foundation; Chairman, German Chamber of Industry and Commerce in Australia; Vice-President, Australia, Japan Business Co-operation Committee; Chairman, Order of Australia Association; Councillor, Enterprise Australia. *Honours:* Companion of the Order of Australia, 1976; Commander's Cross of the Order of Merit, Federal Republic of Germany, 1980; James N. Kirby Memorial Award, 1976; John Storey Medal, 1978. *Hobbies:* Sailing; Fishing. *Address:* 1 O'Connell Street, Sydney, New South Wales, Australia 2000.

JACKSON, William Desmond, b. 11 Feb. 1927, Hobart, Tasmania. General Medical Practice. m. Doris Joan Staff, 31 Dec. 1949, 2 sons, 2 daughters. *Education:* First Year Medicine, University of Tasmania 1946; Two Years Service R.A.N 1947-48; Medical Course, University of Melbourne 1949-53. *Appointments:* RMO, Prince Henry's Hospital, Melbourne, 1954; Country Practice, kPyramid Hill, Victoria 1955-64; Surgical Registrar, General Hospital, Launceston, 1964-65; General Medical Practice, Launceston, 1965-; Medical Director, Kings Meadows Health Centre, Launceston, 1976-. *Memberships:* President, Royal Australian College of General Practitioners, 1979-80; Life Governor, Australian Postgraduate Federation in Medicine; Faculty of Medicine, University of Tasmania; Council Victorian Bush Nursing Association. *Publications:* Medical Articles: External Cardiac Massage, 1963; Obstetrical Audit; Red Back Spider Bites; President's pages, Australian Family Physician 1979-80. *Hobbies:* Farming; Music; Amateur Theatre. *Address:* Kings Lane, St. Leonards; Tasmania, Australia 7250.

JACKSON, William (Godfrey Fothergill), (General Sir), b. 1917. British Governor and Commander-in-Chief, Gibraltar. m. Joan Mary Buesden, 1946, 1 son, 1 daughter. *Education:* Royal Military Academy, Woolwich, 1936-37; King's College, Cambridge, 1937-39. *Appointments:* British Army, Regimental and Staff Appointments, 1937-65; Major General, Chief of Defence Staffs' Exercise Planner, 1965-67, Assistant Chief of General Staff, 1968-70; Lt.-General, Commander-in-Chief, Northern Command, 1971-73; General, Quarter-master General, 1974-77; Governor and Commander-in-Chief, Gibraltar, 1978-. *Memberships:* Royal United Services Institute; Institute of Royal Engineers; Fellow, British Institute of Management; Army and Navy Club. *Publications:* Attack in the West; Seven Roads to Moscow; Battle for Italy; Battle for Rome; Alexander of Tunis; North African Campaigns; Overlord, 1944. *Honours:* Knight Grand Cross, Order of the British Empire, 1975; Knight Commander of the Bath, 1971; Knight of the Order of St John of Jerusalem, 1978; Military Cross, 1940, and Bar, 1943. *Address:* West Stowell Place, Oare, Marlborough, Wiltshire, England.

JACOBS, Wilfred (Ebenezer), (Sir), b. 1919. British Governor General. m. Carmen Sylvia Knight, 1 son, 2 Daughters. *Education:* Gray's Inn, London; Barrister-at-Law. *Appointments:* Registrar, St Vincent, 1946; Magistrate, Dominica, 1947; St Kitts, 1949; Crown Attorney, St Kitts, 1952; AttorneyGeneral: Leeward Islands, 1957-59, and Antigua, 1960; Acting Administrator: Dominica, St Kitts, Antigua, various periods,

1947-60; Legal Draftsman and Acting Solicitor General, Trinidad and Tobago, 1960; Solicitor-General and Acting Attorney-General, Barbados, 1961-63; Privy Council and Legislative Council of Barbados, 1962-63; Director of Public Prosecutions, 1964 and Judge of the Supreme Court of Judicature, Barbados, 1967; Governor, Antigua, 1967-; Governor General, Antigua and Barbados, 1981. *Memberships:* Gray's Inn, London; Imperial Society of Knights Bachelor; Royal Commonwealth Society. *Honours:* KOVO; OBE; QC; K St J, 1968. *Address:* Governor General's Residence, Antigua, West Indies.

JACQUES, Claude b. 15 Sept. 1953, Québec, Canada. Physician, Physicist. m. Dominique Dufour, 7 June 1980. *Education:* BSc, Physics, 1976; MSc, Physics, 1978. *Appointments:* Département de Physique, Université Laval. *Memberships:* Association Canadienne des Physiciens. *Publications:* Thése, Etude du carbone hautement ionisé à l'aide de la technique faisceau-lame, 1978; Line identification and lifetime measurements in singly and doubly-excited CIV and in CV, (with E J Kynstautas, R Drouin & H G Berry), 1980; Spectroscopie et mesures de vies moyennes de niveaux de Ni hautement ionise, (with M. Druetta, HG Berry & EJ Knystautas), 1982. Hobby: Music. *Address:* 3335 rue de la Monnerie, #305 Sainte-Foy, Québec G1X IY9, Canada

JAGADEESAN, Kesavan, b. 2 Mar. 1935, Kerala, Quilon, India. Surgeon. m. Meera, 4 Dec. 1960, 1 son, 2 daughters. *Education:* MB., BS, Kerala University, India, 1959; FRCS, Glasgow University, UK, 1965. *Appointments:* United Kingdom Department of Surgery and Trauma and extensive training in Haemodialysis and Transplant in Germany and USA, 1961-63; Five years, Post-Graduate Teaching Institution, Madras; Founded K J Hospital, India. *Memberships:* British and Indian Medical Associations; International Hospital Federation; European Dialysis & Transplant Association; International Medical Science Academy; Surgeons Association of India. *Publications:* Contributed to various professional and medical journals including: Ano-rectal Tuberculosis, 1979; Radiological Review of the size of the Kidneys in 500 cases; Single layer closure of Abdominal Wounds; Our Experience with Total Body Scanner. *Hobby:* Farming. *Address:* 941 Poonamallee High Road, Madras, 600084, India.

JAGAN, Cheddi, b. 22 Mar. 1918, Port Mourant, Guyana. General Secretary, Peoples Progressive Party. m. Janet Jagan 5 Aug. 1943, 2 sons. *Education:* Queens College, Georgetown, Guyana 1933-36; Howard University, Washington DC, USA, 1936-38; BSc, Central YMCA College, Chicago, Illinois, USA 1939-42; Doctor of Dental Surgery, Northwestern University Dental School, Chicago, 1938-42. *Appointments:* Legislative Council 1942-53; Minister of Agriculture, People's Progressive Party, 1953; Minister of Trade and Industry 1957-61; Premier and Minister of Development and Economic Planning 1961-64; Leader of Opposition 1964-73 and 1976-. *Memberships:* Treasurer, Man Power Citizens Association, 1945; Political Affairs Committee, 1946-50; People's Progressive Party, 1950-; President, Sawmill and Forest Workers Union, 1952-54; President, Rice Producers Association, 1955-57; Honorary President Guyana Agricultural Workers Union; Presidential Committee, World Peace Council; *Publications:* Forbidden Freedom 1954 and 1955; The West on Trial; The Fight for Guyana's Freedom, 1966, 67, 72, 75, 80; Caribbean Revolution, 1979; Booklets: Bitter Sugar; Socialism for Guyana; My Credo; Anatomy of Poverty in British Guiana; US Intervention in Guyana; The Role of the CIA in Guyana; Caribbean Unity & Carifta; The Coalition Exposed; The Truth About Nationalisation; The Caribbean and the Centers of International Power. *Honours:* Medal of Honour, International Organisation of Journalists; Lenin Centenary Medal; Order of Peace and Friendship Among Peoples, USSR. Hobby: Swimming. *Address:* 65 Bel Air, Georgetown, Guyana.

JAGAN, Janet, b. 20 Oct. 1920, Chicago, Illinois, USA. Journalist. m. Cheddi Jagan, 5 Aug. 1943, 2 sons. *Education:* University of Detroit; Wayne University; Michigan State College; Cook County School of Nursing. *Appointments:* Georgetown Town Council 1950-52; Deputy Speaker, House of Assembly 1953; Minister of Labour, Health and Housing 1957-61; Minister of Home Affairs 1963-64; Member, National Assembly,

1976-; General Secretary, People's Progressive Party 1950-70; International Secretary, 1970-; Editor, Thunder, Official organ PPP, 1950-55; Editor, Daily and Sunday Mirror 1973-; President, Women's Progressive Organisation 1980-. *Memberships:* Guyana Union of Journalists; International Organisation of Journalists. *Publications:* Army Intervention in 1973 Elections in Guyana; An Examination of National Service; History of the People's Progressive Party. *Honours:* Lenin Centenary Medal. Hobby: Swimming. *Address:* 65 Bel Air, Georgetown, Guyana.

JAIN, Amolak Chand, b. 27 Dec. 1928, Delhi, India. Teaching & Research. m. Vijaya , 8 July 1953, 2 sons, 2 daughters. *Education:* BSc(Hons.), 1948, MSc, 1950, PhD, 1954, Delhi University; PhD, Cambridge University, England, 1958; DSc, USSR, Moscow, 1967. *Appointments:* Lecturer, 1952-60, Reader, 1960-68, Delhi University; Professor & Head of Chemistry Department, Jammu University, 1969-73; Senior Professor, Head of Chemistry Department, Dean of Science & Dean of Academic Affairs, H.P. University, Simla, 1973-79; Professor, Delhi University, 1979-. *Memberships:* Fellow, Indian National Science Academy; National Academy of Sciences of India; Indian Chemical Society; Indian Society of Biol. Chemists; The Chemical Society, (London). *Publications:* Published 180 research papers in national and international journals. *Honours:* Elected FNA; Awarded National Fellowship, U.G.C. India, 1976; Royal Society London, Bursary, 1978; London Chemical Society Research Grants, 1966, 1978; Bhatnagar Prize, 1969; UNESCO Fellowship to work in Moscow, 1966-67. *Hobbies:* Reading; Writing. *Address:* 13 Vaishali, Pitampura, Delhi 110 034, India.

JAIN, Prem Chand, b. 2 July 1944, Delhi, India. Teaching (Lecturer). m. Suman Jain, 8 July 1976. *Education:* BSc(Hons) Physics 1970; MSc Physics 1972; PhD Physics, Delhi University 1976. *Appointments:* Lecturer in Physics, Hindu College, Delhi University, 1976-78; Lecturer in Physics, University of Zambia, Lusaka, 1978-. *Memberships:* International Solar Energy Society, Australia; Renewable Energy Review Information Centre, Bangkok; Abstracts of Selected Solar Energy Technology, United Nations University Tokyo. *Publications:* Author or co-author of 11 research publications in International Journals; Author of 5 popular articles in science. *Honours:* Junior Research Fellowships and Senior Research Fellowships, University Grants Commission India and Council of Scientific and Industrial Research, 1972-76. *Hobbies:* Table Tennis; Chess. *Address:* Physics Department, University of Zambia, P Box 32379, Lusaka, Zambia.

JAIN, Suresh Chand, b. 2 June 1949, Lucknow. Medical Cardiologist. m. Asha 16 Jan. 1979. *Education:* BSc, Part I, Lucknow University, India, 1966; MB.,BS, 1970, MD, (Gen. Med), 1975, K G Medical College, Lucknow, India; Cardiology, National Institute of Cardiology, 1978; Specialist, Mexico City, Mexico. *Appointments:* Internship, 1971, H.O. (Med), 1972, J.R. (Med), 1973, S.R. (Med), 1974, C.R. (Med), 1975, K G Medical College, Lucknow, India; Clinical Attachment, Sunderland General Hospital, UK, 1976; Pool Officer, All India Institute of Medical Sciences, Department of Cardiology, New Delhi, India, 1978-. *Memberships:* Fellow: American College of Chest Physicians, USA; International College of Angiology, USA, Mexican Society of Cardiology, Mexico; Associate Fellow, American College of Cardiology, USA; The Cardiology Society of India; The All India Heart Foundation; The Indian Association for Chest Diseases; The Association of Physicians of India. *Publications:* Theses, 1974, 1978; Contributed to various professional and medical journals. *Honours:* Awarded degree of Specialist in Cardiovascular Diseases, National Institute of Cardiology, Mexico City, 1978. *Hobbies:* Cricket; Hockey; Lawn Tennis; Table Tennis; Music; Gardening; Photography; Sightseeing. *Address:* B-14 South Extension Part I, New Delhi, 110049, India.

JAIRAJ, Prabhakumari, b. 30 Aug. 1942, Kasaragod, Kerala, India. Obstetrician & Gynaecologist. m. 28 June 1971, 1 daughter. *Education:* MB., BS, 1964, D.G.O., 1968, MD, 1969, Kerala University. *Appointments:* Tutor in Obsts. & Gynae, Trivandrum Medical College, 1969-70; Reader in Obsts. & Gynae. Kasturba Medical College, 1970-71; Lecturer, 1972-75, Reader, 1975-78, Associate Professor, 1978-80, Professor in

Obsts. & Gynae, 1980-, C.M.C.H., Vellore. *Memberships:* Obstetrics & Gynaecological Society of India. *Publications:* Comparison of Foam Test and L/L Ratio of amniotic Fluid in the assessment of foetal maturity, 1978. *Honours:* First in the Pre-University Examination, Kerala University, 1958. *Hobby:* Music. *Address:* B-3, Shanti Illam, C.M.C. Hospital Quarters, Vellore, 632 004, India.

JAIRAJ, Puthenveettil Sankaran Nair, b. 16 July 1937, Ashtamichira, Kerala, India. Cardiothoracic Surgeon. m. Prabha Jairaj, 28 June 1971, 1 daughter. *Education:* MB, BS, Kerala University, 1960; Master of Surgery, 1964; FRACS, Cardio-thoracic Surgery, 1971. *Appointments:* Tutor in Surgery, 1964-68, Assistant Professor in Surgery, Medical College, Calicut, 1968-69; Senior Registrar in Cardiothoracic Surgery, St. Vincent's Hospital, Melbourne, and Royal Prince Alfred Hospital, Sydney, Australia 1969-72; Senior Lecturer in Cardiothoracic Surgery, 1972-73, Reader, 1973-75, Surgeon, Christian Medical College, Vellore, 1975-; Associate Professor, 1978-80; Professor of Cardiothoracic Surgery, 1980-. *Memberships:* Association of Surgeons of India; Association of Thoracic and Cardiovascular Surgeons of India; Fellow, Royal Australasian College of Surgeons; Fellow, American College of Chest Physicians. *Publications:* Results of aortic valve replacement, 1973; A case report of retrograde jejunogastric intussusception, Antiseptic, 1966; Experimental microvascular surgery on coronary arteries of dogs, study conducted with a grant from the National Heart Foundation of Australia. *Honours:* MB, BS, 1960. *Hobbies:* Photography; Gardening. *Address:* C.M.C. Hospital Quarters, Vellore 632 004, India.

JAKANDE, Lateef Kayode, b. 23 July 1929, Lagos, Nigeria. Journalism. m. Alhaja Abimbola Fajolu, 23 Mar. 1968, 4 sons, 4 daughters. *Education:* King's College Lagos; Ilesha Grammar School, Ilesha. *Appointments:* Reporter, Daily Service 1949; Associate Editor, 1953; Managing Editor, Nigerian Tribune 1954; Joint General Manager, Amalgamated Press, 1956, Editor-in-Chief, 1956; Editor-in-Chief/Managing Director, Allied Newspapers 1958-68; Editor-in-Chief-/Managing Director, African Newspapers of Nigeria 1968-79; Chairman/Managing Director, John West Publications. *Memberships:* Nigerian Union of Journalists; Nigerian Guild of Editors; Newspaper Proprietors Association of Nigeria; National Press Club of Nigeria; Commonwealth Press Union; International Communications Institute; International Press Institute; National Association for Prisoners Welfare. *Publications:* The Case for Lagos State; The Role of the Mass Media in a Developing Country; The Trial of Obafemi Awolowo. *Hobbies:* Reading; Playing Draughts; Travelling. *Address:* 2 Bishop Street, Ilupeju, Lagos, Nigeria.

JALALI, Bushan Lal, b. 14 June 1943, Srinagar, Kashmir. Research, Teaching. m. Indu, 26 Nov. 1970. *Education:* BSc, (Ag), 1963, MSc, (Ag), 1965, Banaras Hindu University, India; PhD, Punjab Agricultural University, India, 1968; Diploma in German, Goethe Institute, Freiburg, West Germany, 1973. *Appointments:* Assistant Professor, Punjab Agrl. University, 1968-71; Associate Professor (Extn. Pathology), 1971-75, Legume Pathology, 1975-, Haryana Agrl. University; Post-Doctoral Fellow, Federal Research Station for Agriculture, Braunschweig, West Germany, 1973-74; Visiting Scientist, England, West Germany and USA, 1978. *Memberships:* Fellow, Indian Phytopathological Society; British Mycological Society; Association of Applied Bioligists (UK); Federation of British Plant Pathologists; Association of Microbiologists of India, President, 1978-79; Faculty Club, Haryana Agrl. University, Hissar. *Publications:* Published about 40 research papers in various national and international journals; Numerous water-colour paintings; Won several prizes in photography (black & white and colour). *Honours:* Recipient of the National Narasimhan Academic Award for the best original research work in the field of Plant Pathology and its presentation for the years, 1978. *Hobbies:* Photography; Badminton; Music, (Classical). *Address:* Qr.No.9/20 Old Campus, Haryana Agrl. University, Hissar-125004, Haryana, India.

JALLOH, Mohammed Habid, b. 15 Oct. 1940, Mambolo, Freetown, Sierra Leone, W. Africa. Librarian. m. Assanatu Fadliyatu Iyatudide Sanusi, 17 June 1968, 2 sons, 2 daughters. *Education:* Associateship of the Library Association, Polytechnic of North London

School of Librarianship, 1970-74; Master of Library Science, Loughborough University of Technology, 1978-80. *Appointments:* Geological Survey Division. *Hobbies:* Cricket; Football; Reading; Gardening. *Address:* 57 Kelsey Road, Kissy Dockyard, Freetown, Sierra Leone, West Africa.

JAMES, Christopher Roberts Barnes, b. 26 Nov. 1899, Eganstown, Victoria, Australia. Chartered Accountant and Secretary (now retired). m. Ruby Doris Gowlett, 9 Nov. 1921, 2 sons. *Education:* Fellow, Institute of Chartered Accountants in Australia; Chartered Institute of Secretaries and Administrators; Australian Society of Accountants; Municipal Auditor and Inspector of Accounts; Licensed Auditor for Companies. *Appointments:* Chartered Accountant since, 1924; Chartered Secretary, since, 1933. *Memberships:* President, Australasian Institute of Secretaries, 1946-47; President, Chartered Institute of Secretaries, 1949-51; Past President, Rotary Club of Melbourne. *Publications:* Author of Accounting Text Books. *Hobbies:* Bowls; Golf; Gardening; Community Service; Photography; Travel. *Address:* Cridge Lea, Hillcrest Avenue, Narooma, 2546, New South Wales, Australia.

JAMES, Ernest Thomas, b. 29 Jan. 1939, Townsville Nth. Queensland, Australia. Naval Officer, Physical Training Specialist. m. Joan Frances Alexander, 3 Jan. 1959, 2 sons, 1 daughter. *Education:* Diploma of Teaching (Physical Education) Kuring-gai CAE, Sydney, New South Wales, 1979. *Appointments:* Enlisted Royal Australian Navy, 1956; Marine Survey Duties HMA Ships, Warrego & Paluma, 1956-61; Completed Physical Training Qualifying Course, 1961; Physical Training billets in HMA Ships, Watson, Nirimba, Queenborough and Leeuwin, 1962-69; Officers Promotion Course, United Kingdom, Staff Royal Navy Physical Training School, 1969-70; Billets in HMA Ships, Sydney, Nirimba and Stalwart, 1970-78; Full-time Schooling, 1978-79; Staff of Flag Officer Naval Support command as Command Recreation and Visiting Ships Liaison Officer. 1980-. *Memberships:* NSW Secretary, Australian Council of Health Physical Education and Recreation; British Association of Sport and Medicine; Australian Services Rugby Union Referees Association; American Alliance of Health, Physical Education Recreation and Dance. *Honours:* Australian National Medal for Long Service, 1971; Justice of the Peace, New South Wales, 1975. *Hobbies:* Yachting; Rugby Union Fitness Training. *Address:* 92 Chifley Street, Smithfield, NSW, 2164, Australia.

JAMES, John Evans, b. 1 Mar. 1921, Staines, England. Civil & Public Health Engineer. m. Joan Mary Margaret Chapman, 1 daughter. *Education:* St. George's College, Weybridge, 1930-37; Articled Pupil, Walton & Weybridge UDC, 1937-39; Diploma Course in Civil Engineering, Kingston Technical College, 1946-48; Diploma of Institute of Water Pollution Control, 1961. *Appointments:* Assistant Resident Engineer, Ministry of Works, Cumbria, 1948-49; District Engineer, Lake District and Deputy Conservancy Engineer, Forestry Commission, 1949-53; Senior Engineer, West Kent Main Sewerage Board, 1953-58; Resident and Principal Engineer, London County Council and Greater London Council, 1958-70; Engineering Inspector, Department of the Environment, 1970-73; Regional Manager, Anglian Water Authority, 1973-. *Memberships:* Institution of: Civil Engineers; Water Pollution Control (Chairman Met & Southern Branch, 1973-74); Public Health Engineers, (Council, 1968-74); Water Engineers & Scientists. DOE Working Pary on Disposal of Sludge in Liverpool Bay, Technical Secretary, 1971-73; DOE/NWC Standing Technical Committee Waste Water Treatment, Vice-Chairman, 1976-. *Publications:* Design of Extensions to Becton Sewage Treatment Works, London,(co-author), 1972; Effect of Sewage Sludge on the Marine Environment: Case Study in Liverpool Bay, (co-author), 1973; Rationalisation of Sewage Treatment, 1977; Sewage Sludge Disposal—Which Option? 1979. *Honours:* Fredrick Palmer Prize, Institution of Civil Engineers, 1974. *Hobbies:* Historic Buildings; Gardening; Walking. *Address:* 25 St. Hugh's Road, Buckden, Huntingdon, Cambs. PE18 9UB, England.

JAMES, John Ronald, b. 3 Jan. 1917, Cradock, Cape Province, Republic of South Africa. Horticulturist. m. Marian Fowlds, 22 Oct. 1953, 1 son. *Education:* Matriculation Certificate, 1935; Diploma Certificates, Tech-

nical College, 1940; Certificate of the School of Training Institute of Park Administration Inc. UK, 1953. *Appointments:* Apprentice, City of Port Elizabeth, Department of Parks, 1935-40; Military Service, South Africa Engineer Corps, attached to South Africa Air Force, 1940-45; Superintendent of Parks, City of Salisbury, Zimbabwe, 1945; Assistant, 1952, Manager, 1974-, Amenities Department, City of Salisbury; Retirement pending 1982. *Memberships:* Past President, Institute of Park and Recreation Administration; Vice-President, National Association of Garden Clubs, Zimbabwe Orchid Society (founder member), Salisbury and District Garden Club; Chairman, Botanical Society; Aloe and Cactus Society of Zimbabwe; Tree Society; International Federation of Parks & Recreation Administration, Reading, England. *Publications:* Lawns, Trees and Shrubs in Central Africa, 1961; Wrote weekly radio script, local radio, 1968-78; Contributed to local press for 36 years on horticulture; currently contributes to local press, magazines, journals. *Honours:* Certificate of honour for Long and Meritorious Service to Horticulture, 1973; Awarded Life Member Stature by Salisbury and District Garden Clubs, 1980. *Hobbies:* Growing, hybridising and propagating orchids, mainly hybrids; Gemstone cutting and jewellery making; Study of Xerophytic plants, mainly euphorbiaceae, Asclepiadaceae and Aizoaceae. *Address:* 18 Kent Avenue, Avondale, Salisbury, Zimbabwe.

JAMES, Owen Francis, b. 27 Jan. 1936, Sydney, Australia. Anasthesia and Intensive Care; Medical. m. Carolyn Eva, 13 June 1964, 2 sons, 2 daughters. *Education:* MB, BS (Sydney), 1958; DA, 1966; FFA, RCSI, 1966; FFA, RCS, FFA, RACS, 1968; MS (Sydney), 1981. *Appointments:* Director, Anaesthesia and Intensive Care, Royal Newcastle Hospital, 1968-. *Memberships:* AMA; ASA,; ICS; ANZICS; HAICS. *Publications:* Scientific Publications re: Respiratory Failure, Chest Injuries, Anaesthesia Topics. *Address:* 84 Nesca Pde, Newcastle, New South Wales, 2300, Australia.

JAMES, Robert Michael, b. 2 Oct. 1934, Wokingham. HM Diplomatic Service. m. Sarah Helen Bell, 3 Jan. 1959, 2 sons, 1 daughter. *Education:* BA (Hons. History), Trinity College, Cambridge, 1956-58. *Appointments:* Schoolmaster, Harrow School, 1958-60, Cranleigh School, 1960-62; Commonwealth Relations Office, 1963; 3rd Secretary, Wellington, New Zealand, 1963-65; FCO 1st Secretary, Colombo Sri Lanka, 1966-68; FCO, 1969-71; 1st Secretary & Deputy High Commission, Guyana, 1971-74; 1st Secretary, Ankara, Turkey, 1974-76; FCO Information Policy Department, 1976-79; Counsellor & Deputy High Commissioner, Accra Ghana, 1979-. *Honours:* Cambridge Cricket Blue, 1956-58; Rugby LX Club. *Hobbies:* Competitive Games; Travel; Reading; Drawing. *Address:* Warwicks Mount, Warwicks Bench Road, Guildford, England.

JAMIESON, Hamish Thomas Umphelby, b. 15 Feb. 1932, Glenbrook, New South Wales, Australia. Bishop (Anglican Church of Australia). m. Ellice Anne McPherson, 3 Feb. 1962, 1 son, 2 daughters. *Education:* ThL, St. Michael's House (Society of the Sacred Mission), 1952-56; BA, University of New England, 1974. *Appointments:* Ordained Deacon, 1955, Priest, 1956, Member of Brotherhood of the Good Shepherd, 1956-62; A/Curate, Gilgandra, New South Wales, 1957; Priest in Charge, Katherine, N T, 1957-62; Rector, Darwin, NT, 1962-67; Canon of All Souls Cathedral, Thursday Island, Queensland, 1963; Royal Australian Navy, 1967-74; Consecrated Bishop of Carpentaria, Queensland, 1974. *Hobbies:* History; Gardening; Reading. *Address:* The Bishop's House, Thursday Island, Queensland 4875, Australia.

JANAH, Ashis Kumar, b. 29 Oct. 1926, Krishnagar, West Bengal, India. Industrialist. m. 31 July 1954, 1 son, 2 daughters. *Education:* BSc, University Science College, 1949; Commercial Pilot, Civil Aviation Training Centre, 1951. *Appointments:* Works Manager, Rajaniklal Ceramics (Pvt) Limited, Calcutta, 1958-61; Technical Adviser, Dacca Tiles and Potteries Limited, Bangladesh, 1962; Ceramic Consultant, Regional Design Centre, Govt of India, 1965-66; Proprietor, Vallauris Ceramics, 1956-, and Keramos India, Calcutta, 1978-. *Memberships:* Indian Ceramic Society, General Secretary, 1970, 1971, Vice-Chairman, 1981; Studio Potters Association of India, President, 1981; Indian Institute of Ceramics, Founder; Fine Particle Society,

USA; Pottery Manufacturers Association; Crafts Council of India; Rotary Club of East Calcutta. *Publications:* Published papers on Zircon Opacifiers and Opacification of Glazes, Vitreous Enamelling of Aluminium, Low-Temperature Enamelling, Art Pottery, History of Pottery in India. *Honours:* W Bengal State award in Ceramics, 1960; Indian Institute of Art in Industry award, 1963; Best Exhibits award, Indian Ceramic Society, 1970; Self-made Industrialist award, 1978; Transworld Trade Fair Gold Medal, 1980. *Hobbies:* Antiques, Coins, Manuscript collecting. *Address:* 3-B Camac Street, 10th Floor, Flat no. 7, Calcutta 700 016, India.

JARDINE, Velma, b. 3 June 1931, Trinidad. Teacher of Business Studies. m. Gerard Ian Jardine, 19 Oct. 1952, 3 sons, 3 daughters. *Education:* Teacher's Diploma, 1964; Management Certificate, 1978. *Appointments:* Principal, The Stenotype College, 1965-. *Memberships:* UN Standing Committee, International Federation Business and Professional Women; University Women's Club, London; The World Council for Curriculum and Instruction, Minimum Wages Board, 1976-; Past President, Business and Professional Women's Club of Port of Spain, 1974-76; Faculty of Teachers in Commerce, England; Society of Commercial Teachers, England; Co-ordinator/Adviser, Committee for the Concern of Children. *Publications:* Office Practice (co-author). *Hobbies:* Coin and Stamp collecting; Chess; Hockey. *Address:* 55 Cascade Road, Cascade, Trinidad.

JARJIS, Raik A, b. 16 Jan. 1950, Mosul, Iraq. Nuclear Physicist. *Education:* BSc, Physics, 1970; PhD, Nuclear Physics, 1976. *Appointments:* Research Associate in Physics, The University of Manchester, 1975-80; Research Fellow in Physics, The University of Nottingham, 1980. *Memberships:* The Institute of Physics; The British Nuclear Energy Society. *Publications:* Handbook of Nuclear Cross-section Data for Surface Analysis, 1982; 15 Original Publications in Pure and Applied Nuclear Physics. *Hobbies:* Photography; Sketching; Collection of Antique Artistic Prints. *Address:* Department of Physics, University of Nottingham, University Park, Nottingham, England.

JARMAN, Alan William, b. 22 July 1923, Melbourne, Australia. Member of the House of Representatives, Australia, for Deakin, Victoria. m. Alison M. Lemmon, 1 son, 1 daughter. *Education:* Wesley College, Melbourne University, Bachelor of Commerce, (Melbourne); Associate of the Australian Society of Accountants. *Appointments:* Member of the House of Representatives for Deakin, Victoria, from 1966; Deputy Chairman of Committees for House of Representatives; Member of the Parliamentary Joint Committee of Public Accounts, 1969-74; Member of the House of Representatives Standing Committee of Privileges; Member of the Standing Committee of Aboriginal Affairs, 1973-75; Member of the Environment Committee, 1975; Delegate to the Australasian Area Conference of the Commonwealth Parliamentary Association, Sydney, 1969; Member of the Commonwealth Parliamentary Association Conference, Canberra, 1970, Sri Lanka, 1974; Member of the Parliamentary Mission to East Asia, 1969; Member of the Parliamentary Mission to South America, 1980; Military Service: Australian Imperial Forces, 1942-46; Pilot Officer, RAAF Reserve. *Address:* 5 Linum Street, Blackburn, 3130 Victoria, Australia.

JARVIS, William Hugh, b. 23 Aug. 1939, Mansfield, England. Physicist. m. Ann Rintoul, 12 Apr. 1969. *Education:* MA, Magdalen College, Oxford, 1962. *Appointments:* Asst. Physics Teacher, Gordonstoun School, 1962-65; Asst. Physics Teacher, Royal Masonic School, 1965-69; Head of Physics, Rannoch School, 1969-76; Educational Liaison Officer, Unilab Limited, 1976-. *Memberships:* The Institute of Physics; RAF Club. *Publications:* Basic Principles of Electronics (co-author), 1966, 1971; Reviser, Second Course of Electricity, 1973. *Hobbies:* Amateur Radio; Classical Music. *Address:* Salewheel House, Salesbury Hall Road, Ribchester, Preston, England.

JAWARA, Dawda Kairaba (Sir), b. 16 May 1924, Barajali, M I D., The Gambia. Veterinary Surgeon; President of the Republic of the Gambia. *Education:* Achimota College, Ghana; Glasgow University, Scotland, UK; Royal College of Veterinary Surgeons, 1953; Diploma, Tropical Veterinary Medicine, Edinburgh, Scotland, UK, 1957. *Appointments:* Veterinary Officer, 1954, Principal Veterinary Officer, 1957-60, The Gambia Government; Became Leader, Protectorate People's Party, 1960; Elected member, House of Representatives, 1960; Appointed: Minister of Education, 1960-61, Premier, 1962-63; Became Prime Minister on The Gambia's attainment of Internal Self Government, 1963; Led THE Gambia to Full Independence, February, 1965; Led The People's Progressive Party to victory in the General Elections, May, 1966; Appointed Prime Minister, 1966; Became first President of Republic of The Gambia, 1970, 2nd term, 1972, 3rd term, 1977; Chairman, CILSS Heads of State Conference, 1977-79. *Memberships:* Honorary Procurator, Afro-European Dialogue of the Peutinger-Collegium, Munich, Bavaria, Federal Republic of Germany. *Honours:* Knight Bachelor, 1966; Grand Cross of Order of Cedars of Lebanon, 1966; Grand Cross of National Order of Republic of Senegal, 1967; Grand Officer, Order of National Merit of Islamic Republic of Mauritania, 1967; Grand Cross of Order of Propitious Clouds of China, 1968; Grand Cordon of the Most Venerable Order of Knighthood of Pioneers of Liberia, 1968; Grand Commander of National Order of Federal Republic of Nigeria, 1970; Grand Master of National Order of Republic of The Gambia, 1972; Grand Cross of National Order of Republic of Guinea, 1973; GCMG., 1974; Hon. Degree of Doctor of Laws, University of Ife, Nigeria, 1978; Commander of Golden Ark, 1979; Peutinger Gold Medal, 1979; Agricola Medal, 1980. *Hobbies:* Golf; Gardening; Sailing. *Address:* State House, Baujul, The Gambia.

JAY, Douglas Patrick Thomas, b. 23 Mar. 1907, Woolwich, England. Member of Parliament. m. (1) Margaret Garnet, (2) Mary Lavinia Thomas, 27 May 1972, 2 sons, 2 daughters. *Education:* Degree, New College, Oxford; Fellow, All Souls College, Oxford. *Appointments:* Member of Parliament. *Publications:* Who is to Pay for the Peace and the War, The Socialist Case, 1937; Socialism in the New Society, 1962; After the Common Market, 1968; Change and Fortune, 1980. *Honours:* Privy Councillor, 1951. *Hobbies:* Gardening; Walking; Chess; Tennis. *Address:* 6 Hampstead Grove, London, England.

JAYAPAL V, b. 3 May, 1936, Tanjore. Medical. m. Devika Rani, 2 Sept. 1962, 1 son, 1 daughter. *Education:* MB., BS, 1961, MS, 1970, Madras University; FICS, 1972. *Appointments:* Demonstrator in Pathology, Madras Medical College, 1962-63; Honorary Assistant Surgeon, Mahatma Gandhi Memorial Hospital, 1970-80; Chief Surgeon, Dr G Viswcinathan Nursing Home, 1966-. *Memberships:* Fellow, International College of Surgeons; Secretary, Treasurer, Indian Medical Association; President, various cultural societies. *Hobbies:* Stamp collection; Photography. *Address:* 3 Railway Station Road, Srirangam, Trichy, Tamilnadu, India.

JAYASEKAR, Trevine, b. 6 Jan. 1953, Sri Lanka. Chartered Accountant. m. Shirani, 3 May 1979. *Education:* Chartered Accountant; Cost & Management Accountant. *Appointments:* Accountant, Sitken Spence (Shipping) Ltd. Sri Lanka; Audit Supervisor, Coopers & Lybrand, Lusaka, Sambia. *Hobby:* Photography. *Address:* 82A Ward Place, Colombo 7, Sri Lanka.

JAYAWARDENA, Leonard Stanley, b. 22 Apr. 1927, Anuradhapura, Sri Lanka. Vice Chairman, Lever Brothers (Ceylon) Limited. m. Sujata De Silva, 14 May 1950, 2 sons, 3 daughters. *Education:* BA., (Hons.), University of Ceylon. *Appointments:* Income Tax Assessor, 1949-55; Sales Manager, 1955-57, Product Manager, 1957-61, General Advertising Manager, 1961-66, Marketing Director, 1967-78, Vice Chairman and Personnel Director, 1978-, Lever Brothers (Ceylon) Limited. *Memberships:* Chairman, Ceylon Chamber of Commerce; Vice-President of: Meals for Millions Foundation of Ceylon, Sinhala Institute of Culture; Trustee, Cheshire Homes Foundation of Ceylon; Founder President, Sri Lanka Marketing Institute; Past Chairman, Audit Brueau of Circulations for India and Ceylon; Past Vice President, Ceylon Association of Manufacturers; Past Director, Ceylon Tea Propaganda Board; Past District Governor, Lions International District 306. *Hobby:* Photography. *Address:* 8/2 Coniston Place, Colombo 7, Sri Lanka.

JAYEWARDENE, Junius Richard, b. 17 Sept. 1906. Ceylonese politician. m. Elina B Rupesinghe, 1935, 1 son. *Education:* Royal College, Colombo; Ceylon University and Law Colleges. *Appointments:* Honorary General Secretary, Ceylon National Congress, 1940-47; Honorary Treasurer, United National Party, 1946-48, 1957-58; Vice-President, United National Party, 1954-56, 1958-72, Secretary, 1972-73, & President, 1973-; Leader: Ceylon Delegation to Sterling Talks, London, 1948-52; Ceylon Delegation to Commonwealth Talks in Sydney, to International Monetary Fund and World Bank Meeting in Paris, Commonwealth Talks, London; Ceylon Delegation, Japanese Peace Treaty Conference, San Francisco, 1951; Municipal Council, Colombo, 1940-43; MP (United Nat.), 1947-56; Governor, World Bank and International Monetary Fund, 1947-52, Minister of Agriculture and Food and Leader House of Representatives, 1953-56; Minister of Finance, 1947-52, 1952, 1953, 1960 and Leader of the House 1960; MP for Colombo South, 1960-65; 1965-70; 1970-77 and Chief Opposition Whip, 1960-65; Minister of State, Parliamentary Secretary to the Prime Minister and Minister of Defence and External Affairs and Chief Chief Government Whip in the House of Representatives, 1965-70; Leader of the Opposition, House of Reps., 1970-72, National State Assembly, 1972-77; Prime Minister, Minister of Defence, Planning & Economic Affairs and Plan Implementation, 1977; President of Sri Lanka, 1978-; Advocate, Supreme Court, Ceylon. *Publications:* Co-Author of the Colombo Plan for aid to underdeveloped Asiatic countries, 1950; Buddhist Essays; Some Sermons of the Buddha; In Council; Buddhism and Marxism. *Address:* President's House, Colombo, Sri Lanka.

JEAN-FRANÇOIS, Louis Sydney, b. 9 Nov. 1929, Port-Louis, Mauritius. Librarian. m. Thérèse Daisy Ribet, 14 Dec. 1957, 3 daughters. *Education:* BA., London, UK, 1955; Associateship, Library Association, 1959; Fellowship Certificate, International Training Institute, Administration of Libraries, Sydney, Australia, 1978. *Appointments:* Assistant Librarian, 1952, Librarian, 1959, Head Librarian, 1973, Mauritius Institute. *Memberships:* Mauritius Library Association; British Library Association; Mauritius Senior Civil Servants Association. *Publications:* Report: A National Public Libary Service for Mauritius; Paper: The Mauritius Institute Public Library. *Hobbies:* Reading; Tennis; Volley-ball; Swimming. *Address:* 7A Abbé de la Caille Street, Beau-Bassin, Mauritius.

JEGEDE Oluremi (Mrs Michael I Jegede), b. 27 Dec. 1938, Akure, Nigeria. Law Librarian. m. Michael Iyiola, 24 Oct. 1964, 2 sons, 2 daughters. *Appointments:* Barrister at Law, 1964; Master of Library Science, 1967; Private Legal Practice, 1964-65; University of Lagos Library, 1965-79; Nigerian Institute of Advanced Legal Studies, 1980-. *Memberships:* Nigerian Association of University Women; Nigerian Association of Women Lawyers; President, University of Lagos Women Society, 1979-81. *Memberships:* Contributed to various professional and international journals and reviews, including: Nigerian Legal Bibliography, a classified list of legal Materials related to Nigeria, 1975; A Bibliography of the writings of the Honourable Judge T O Elias, 1979. *Hobbies:* Sewing; Gardening. *Address:* 10 Alvan Ikoku Crescent, University of Lagos Campus, Akoka, Yaba, Nigeria.

JELLINS, Jack, b. 5 Nov. 1938, Vienna, Austria. Research Engineer. *Education:* BSc., 1960, B.Eng., 1961, University of Sydney, Australia. *Appointments:* Royal Australian Naval Experimental Laboratory, 1962-64; Barringer Research (Australia) Pty. Limited, 1964-65; Ultrasonics Institute,Australia, 1966-; Consultant in Ultrasound, Royal Prince Alfred Hospital, Camperdown, Sydney, Australia, 1974-; Consultant in Clinical Ultrasonics, Royal North Hospital, St. Leonards, Sydney, Australia, 1978-. *Memberships:* Secretary, Australian Society for Ultrasound in Medicine; Chairman, Organising Committee, International Congress for Ultrasonic Examination of the Breast; Secretary General, Fourth Meeting of World Federation for Ultrasound in Medicine and Biology. *Publications:* Ultrasonic Visualisation of the Breast (w. others), 1971; Ultrasonic Grey Scale Visualisation of Breast Disease (w. others), 1975. *Hobbies:* Literature; Music; Photography. *Address:* PO Box 479, Double Bay, New South Wales 2028, Australia.

JELLIS, John Edwin, b. 21 July 1940, Hampstead, London, England. Orthopaedic Surgeon. m. Pepita Jane Maria Matthews, 8 Dec. 1962, 2 sons, 2 daughters. *Education:* Faculty of Medicine, Kings College, London, UK, 1958-60; The Westminster Hospital, London, UK, 1960-63; LRCP., MRCS., 1963; MB., BS., AKC., 1963; FRCS., 1970. *Appointments:* House Surgeon and Physician, St. Stephen's Hospital, London, UK, 1963-64; Senior House Officer/Registrar, Westminster Hospital, London, UK, 1965-66; General Medical Officer, St. Francis Hospital, Katete, Zambia, 1966-68; Orthopaedic Registrar, Highlands Hospital, London, UK, 1968-70; Senior Registrar, 1970-74, Consultant Orthopaedic Surgeon, 1974-, University Teaching Hospital, Lusaka, Zambia; Honorary Lecturer, University of Zambia, 1974-. *Memberships:* Chairman, Association of Surgeons of East Africa; Overseas Fellow, British Orthopaedic Association; Honorary Surgeon to: Cheshire Home Society of Lusaka, Gymkhana Club of Lusaka, Zambia Horse Society, Lusaka Show Society. *Publications:* Editor: The Proceedings of the Association of Surgeons of East Africa; Papers: Childhood Sciatic Palsies, 1970; Tuberculous Arthritis and Osteitis in Zambia, 1979; The Place of Total Hip Replacement in Africa, 1979; Compression fixation, 1980. *Hobbies:* Cattle Breeding; Riding; Flying; Medical Publishing. *Address:* PO Box 8159, Woodlands, Lusaka, Zambia.

JENKINS, Maurice, b. 9 July 1925, Blyth, Northumberland, England. Company Director. m. Dorothy Tait, 26 Mar. 1951, 1 son, 2 daughters. *Education:* BSc, Manchester University, 1947-50; Post-Graduate, London, University, 1950-51. *Appointments:* Industrial Training, Dorman Long & Company Ltd., Middlesborough, 1943-47; Administrative Officer, H.M. Overseas Civil Service, Nigeria, 1951-62; Rugby Portland Cement Company Ltd., 1963-, Deputy Chairman, 1976-, Managing Director, 1968-; Chairman and Director of Associate Companies including: Chairman, Cockburn Cement Limited, Western Australia, 1974-; Director, A P Bank Ltd., London. *Memberships:* Vice-President, National Council of Building Producers; National Economic Development Committee for Civil Engineering; Companion, British Institute of Management; Fellow, Institute of Directors. *Hobbies:* Family and Business. *Address:* 5 Bilton Road, Rugby, Warwickshire, CV22 7AA, England.

JENKINS, Thomas Richard, b. 23 Aug. 1930, Kirkcaldy, Scotland, United Kingdom. Journalist; Author. m. Elinor Morrison, 29 Dec. 1956, 3 sons, 1 daughter. *Appointments:* Sunday Post, Scotland, UK, 1947-56; Rifle Brigade and Royal Army Education Corps., UK and Egypt, National Military Service, 1949-50; Sunday Express, London, UK, 1956-65; Western Australian, Perth, Western Australia, 1965-. *Memberships:* Lay member, 1979-81, Awards Jury, Australian Institute of Architecture; Planning Committee, Australian College of Education, Western Australia, seminars on education and the media, 1980, 1981; Australian Journalists' Association; Australian Society of Authors; Australian Institute of Urban Studies, 1975-79. *Publications:* Books: We Came to Australia, 1970; The Wise House,(with J James), 1979; Memories of Childhood (with 14 others), 1979; Articles in Newspapers in UK and Australia; Guest lecturer on media, climate-effective housing, etc., at University of Western Australia, Murdoch University, Western Australian Institute of Technology. *Honours:* Highly Commended, Lovekin Prize for Journalism, Australia, 1971. *Hobbies:* The Arts; Architecture; Education; Energy strategies; Conservation; Town planning. *Address:* 25 Rhonda Avenue, Willetton, Western Australia 6155.

JENNAWAY, Ronald James, b. 13 May 1923, Sydney, Australia. Medical. m. Joan Evelyn England, 3 Feb. 1951, 1 son, 2 daughters. *Education:* MB., BS, 1947; FRCS, 1970. *Appointments:* RMO at RPAH., Sydney, 1947-48; Medical Supt., Auburn DH., Sydney, 1948-49; Lecturer Physiology, Sydney University, 1949-54; GP, & ADH, 1951-69, Surgeon & ADH, 1971-79, Auburn, Sydney; Registrar, Bangour Hospital, Scotland, 1969-70; Medical Supt., Lithgow D Hospital, NSW, 1979-81. *Memberships:* President, Sydney University Medical Society, 1949-50; Past District Governor, Rotary. *Honours:* Barker Scholarship, Horner Exhibition for Mathematics, 1941. *Hobbies:* Golf; Fishing; Carpentery; Farming, Grazier. *Address:* PO Box 189, Chez-Nous Villa, Caves Road, Oberon, 2787, Australia.

JENNINGS, Albert Victor, b. 12 Oct. 1896, Melbourne, Australia. Chartered Builder. m. Ethel S Johnson, 23 Sept. 1922, 2 sons. *Appointments:* Founded, 1932, Chairman until retirement in 1972, A V Jennings Industries(Australia)Limited. *Memberships:* Council member, 1943-, Vice-President Housing, 1970-70, Master Builders Association; Commonwealth Building Research and Advisory Committee, 1948-72; Manufacturing Industries Advisory Council to Australian Government, 1962-72; Decentralisation and Development Advisory Committee to Victoria State Government, 1965; Commonwealth of Australia Metric Conversion Board, 1970-72; Trustee, Committee for Economic Development of Australia; Fellow, Federal President, 1964-66, Australian Institute of Building; Fellow, UK Institute of Building, 1971. *Honours:* Knight Bachelor, 1969; Australian Institute of Building Medal, 1970; Total Community Development Award, 1974; Sir Charles McGrath Award, 1976. *Hobbies:* Golf; Swimming. *Address:* 29 Rosserdale Crescent, Mount Eliza 3930, Victoria, Australia.

JENNINGS, Allen Charles, b. 9 Jan. 1926, Wagga Wagga, New South Wales, Australia. Senior Lecturer. m. Helen Chibnall, 26 Aug. 1949, 3 sons, 2 daughters. *Education:* BSc, University of Sydney, 1943-46; MSc, 1962, PhD, 1967, University of Adelaide. *Appointments:* Research Officer, MacMaster Laboratory, 1947-49; Research Biochemist, Institute of Epidemiology and Preventive Medicine, Prince Henry Hospital, Sydney, 1949-51; Analyst, Commonwealth Department of Trade and Customs, Port Adelaide, South Australia, 1952-56; Lecturer, 1956-61, Senior Lecturer, 1962-, Department of Agricultural Biochemistry, Waite Agricultural Research Institute, University of Adelaide. *Memberships:* The Biochemical Society; Royal Australian Chemical Institute; Australian Biochemical Society; Society of Plant Physiologists; Nutrition Society of Australia; National Geographic Society; Secretary, University of Adelaide Staff Association, 1975-77; University of Adelaide Club; Waite Institute Club, Secretary, 1967-71; The Society of Genealogists; The South Australian Genealogy and Heraldry Society. *Publications:* Author of 32 major research publications, on various topics in the disciplines of plant chemistry and biochemistry, in international scientific journals. Many papers have been presented at scientific meetings and seminars. *Honours:* Exhibition to University of Sydney, 1943-46; Royal Society and Nuffield Foundation Commonwealth Bursary, 1964; Fellow, The Royal Australian Chemical Institute, 1969. *Hobbies:* Photography; Hiking; Boating; Genealogy. *Address:* 47 Cambridge Terrace, Malvern, 5061, South Australia.

JENNIS, Francis, b. 12 Dec. 1924, Sydney, Australia. Medical Practioner. m. Judith Ann Sheridan, 12 June 1954, 2 sons, 1 daughter. *Education:* MB., BS, 1953, DCP, 1959, University of Sydney. *Appointments:* Resident Medical Officer, 1953-54, Fellow in Pathology, 1954-56, Assistant Bacteriologist, 1959-65, Royal Prince Alfred Hospital, Sydney, New South Wales; Pathologist, Base Hospital, Shepparton Victoria, 1956-59; Director of Microbiology, Sydney Hospital, 1965-; Part-time Demonstrator in Bacteriology, University of Sydney, 1961-75; Lecturer and Demonstrator in Bacteriology, Sydney Technical College, 1963-73; Lecturer and Demonstrator in Parasitology, New South Wales Institute of Technology, 1970-72; Lecturer in Bacteriology, University of Sydney, 1979-. *Memberships:* FRCPA, 1960; FRCPath, 1976; Australian Society for Microbiology, 1976; Committee ME3, Sterilizing Equipment, Standards Association of Australia, 1969-. *Publications:* Numerous articles on Microbiology in medical journals, 1963-80. *Hobbies:* Mathematics; Reading. *Address:* 147 Killeaton Street, St Ives, NSW, 2075, Australia.

JENNISON, Raymond Barraclough, b. 4 Aug. 1927, Burra, South Australia. Company Director. m. Lola Clarinda Selmes, 13 Apr. 1957, 2 sons, 1 daughter. *Education:* Prince Alfred College, Adelaide, 1943-44; University of Adelaide, 1945-49; BE; Fellow of SA School of Mines. *Appointments:* Post-Graduate College Apprenticeship, Metropolitan Vickers Ltd., Manchester UK, 1950-52; Sales Engineer, AEI Ltd., Adelaide, 1952-56; Managing Director, Jennisons Tyre Service P/L & Exchange Guarantee Co., P/L, 1956-. *Memberships:* Vice-Chairman, Australian Ford Dealer Council; Past Vice-President, SA Automobile Chamber of Commerce; Chairman, District Council of Burra Burra. *Honours:* Justice of the Peace, S Australia; Queens Silver Jubilee Medal, 1977. *Address:* 12 Queen Street, Burra, South Australia, 5417.

JENSEN, Damien Maxwell, b. 15 Aug. 1944, Victoria, Australia. Neurosurgeon. m. Susan Wrigley, 2 Dec. 1972, 1 son, 3 daughters. *Education:* MB, BS, 1968, FRCS, 1973, University of Melbourne; FRACS, 1976. *Appointments:* St Vincent's Hospital; Leighton Hospital, Crewe, England; Western General Hospital, Edinburgh; Walsgrave Hospital, Coventry, UK; Western General Hospital, Footscray. *Hobbies:* Literature; Permaculture. *Address:* 67 Lloyd Street, Strathmore, Victoria, Australia

JENSEN, Elizabeth Jane, b. 29 May 1950, Southport, Queensland, Australia. Australian Commonwealth Public Servant. m. Philip Ross Clark, 13 Apr. 1974. *Education:* BA., 2A Hons., University of Queensland, Australia, 1968-71; MA., War Studies, Kings College, London University, UK, 1976-77. *Appointments:* Research Officer, 1972-76, Adviser, 1977-78, Strategic and International Policy Division, Department of Defence, Canberra, Australia; Adviser, Officer of Women's Affairs, Department of Home Affairs, Canberra, Australia, 1979-81; Co-ordinator, Commonwealth Games Foundation, to organise XII Commonwealth Games to be held in Brisbane, October, 1982, Brisbane, Australia, 1981-. *Memberships:* Women's Electoral Lobby; Former treasurer, Women's Centre, A C T; Counsellor, Abortion Counselling Service; International Institute of Strategic Studies; Australian Institute of International Affairs. *Publications:* Article: WEL Affiliation with the International Alliance of Women, 1981; Contribution to: Copenhagen and Beyond: An Australian Perspective on the World Conference for the UN Decade for Women, 1980. *Hobbies:* Reading; Cooking; Gardening; Travel. *Address:* 11 Cotter Place, Macgregor, A C T., Australia 2615.

JENSEN, John Hjalmar, b. 16 May 1929, Baltimore, Maryland, USA. University Professor. m. Frances Adele Journey, 25 Aug. 1951, 1 son, 4 daughters. *Education:* BA, Houghton College, New York, 1951; AM, 1956, PhD, 1959, University of Pennsylvania, Philadelphia. *Appointments:* Instructor, Mooers Central High School, 1951-52; Graduate Assistant, University of Pennsylvania, 1954-56; Assistant Professor, Rutgers University, College of South Jersey, Camden, 1958-64; Senior Lecturer, 1964-67, Reader, 1967-70, Massey University; Professor & Head of Department, University of Waikato, 1970-. *Memberships:* Vice-President, Manawatu Branch, Royal Society of New Zealand, 1968-69; Australian-New Zealand Association for the Advancement of Science; New Zealand Historical Association, 1979-. *Publications:* Co-editor, The Maclure Collection of French Revolutionary Materials, 1966; General editor and author of many sections, including all of Volume II, The Balance of Power of The European Experience, in five volumes and seven books, 1970-78; General editor and author of three sections, Perspectives in Modern History, 1975-78; Numerous scholarly articles and reviews. *Hobbies:* Walking; Swimming; Trout Fishing; Reading Trollope; Listening to Music. *Address:* 1 Dawson Street, Hamilton, New Zealand.

JEPHCOTT, Bruce Reginald, b. 19 Mar. 1929, Victoria, Australia. Politician, Grazier, Director. m. Barbara Aileen Harpham, 23 Nov. 1956, 1 son, 2 daughters. *Education:* Kings College, Adelaide, 1940-43; Prince Alfred College, Adelaide, 1944-45; BSc, 1948. *Appointments:* Bacteriologist, EH Faulding, Adelaide, 1949-50; Chief Veterinary Biochemist, Animal Industry, Northern Territory, Australia, 1950-59; Manager, Aionora Coffee Plantation, 1959-61; Owner/Manager, Dumpu P/L, PNG, (Cattle & Grain), 1961-; Minister for Transport, Papua New Guinea Government, 1972-78. *Memberships:* C.Chem; MRIC (Britain); ARACI (Australia); Executive of New Guinea Graziers Association. *Publications:* Numerous contributions in scientific publications. *Honours:* Independence Medal, 1975; Honourable for life by the Queen, 1975; CBE, 1976; Silver Jubilee Medal, 1977. *Hobbies:* Golf; Tennis; Polocrosse. *Address:* Dumpu, Box 1299, Lae, Papua, New Guinea.

JESSUP, Ralph Grant, b. 28 Aug. 1941, Fort Macleod, Alberta, Canada. Specialist in Geophysical Fluid Dynamics. m. Chula Kay Graves, 9 Apr. 1977, 2 daughters. *Education:* BSc (Hons. in Physics), University of Alberta; MSc, University of Waterloo. *Appointments:* Research Physicist, Consolidated, Bathhurst Ltd.; Computer Systems Administrator and Senior Scientific Programming Analyst, Canadian Atmospheric Environment Service. *Memberships:* Canadian Association of Physicists. *Publications:* MASc, Thesis, 'On the Problem of Initializing Models Which Employ the Primitive Forecast Equations'. *Hobbies:* Classical Music; Photography. *Address:* 85 Thorncliffe Park Drive, Apartment 4001, Toronto, Ontario, Canada, M4H 1L6.

JEWISON, Norman Fredrick, b. 21 July 1926, Toronto, Ontario, Canada. Film Director. m. Margaret Dixon, 11 July 1953, 2 sons, 1 daughter. *Education:* Malvern Collegiate Institute, Toronto, Ontario, Canada, 1940-44; BA, Victoria College, University of Toronto, 1950; LLD, University Western Ontario, 1974. *Appointments:* Director Belafonte, Danny Kaye, Jackie Gleason, Andy Williams TV shows, 1960; Producer-Director, Judy Garland Specials, pictures directed include: 40 Pounds of Trouble, The Thrill of It All, Send Me No Flowers, Art of Love, The Cincinnati Kid, In the Heat of the Night, The Russians Are Coming, Thomas Crown Affair, Gaily Gaily, Fiddler on the Roof, Jesus Christ Superstar, Rollerball, F.I.S.T., And Justice for All; Producer, The Landlord, Billy Two Hats; Member, Board of Directors, Festival of Festivals, Toronto, 1981; President, D'Avoriaz Film Festival, France, 1981; Executive Producer, Dogs at War, 1981; Produced, Academy Award Show, 1981. *Honours:* Films nominated for 31 Academy Awards, won nine; Academy Award, Best Picture of the year, 1967, In the Heat of the Night; Named Director of Year, National Association Theatre Owners, 1973. *Hobbies:* Farming; Skiing. *Address:* Knightsbridge Films Limited, 18 Gloucester Street, Toronto, Ontario, Canada M4Y 1L5.

JHA, Sudhansu Sekhar, b. 1 Mar. 1922, Malda, West Bengal, India. Retired Army Officer (Lt. Colonel)-Signals. m. Aparna Sen, 14 June, 1947, 2 sons, 2 daughters. *Education:* BA, (Bengali, English, Economics, Mathematics) 1942; Certificate, Works Study, Defence Work Study Institute, 1966; Diploma, Management, Delhi Productivity Council, 1973; Fellow, Institution of Electronics and Telecommunication Engineers India, 1979. *Appointments:* Signal Officer-in-Charge Army Communication Centres of Formation and Theatre of Ops., 1946-49; Staff Officer, Responsible for Signal equipment of Indian Army, 1949-52; Commanding Officers of various Types of Army Signal Units and Regiments 1954-56, 1960-63, 1965-68; Dy Chief Signal Officers of Army Comn Areas, 1963-65, 1968-71; Army Comn Planning Cell, highest level, 1971-72; Advisor, Land Line Comn of Air Force Command, 1972-75. *Memberships:* Dinapur Officers' Club; Officers' Institute Fort William, Calcutta; Kennel Club of India; Common Cause Society of India; Eastern India Automobile Association. *Hobbies:* Dog Breeding; Gardening; Stamp collecting. *Address:* Mazirpur, Malda District, West Bengal, India.

JHAVERI, Jayant, b. 9 Nov. 1929, Halvad (Gujarat State-India.) Diamond and Precious Stones Merchant. m. Sunanda, 4 Dec. 1960, 1 son, 3 daughters. *Memberships:* Gemmological Association of Great Britain; National Geographic Society, Washington, USA; Founder member, The Gujarat Samaj in Hong Kong, (Social and Cultural Activities.); Photographic Society of Hong Kong. *Creative Works:* Abstract and Portrait, Photography. *Hobbies:* Philosophy; Photography. *Address:* 23 Chatham Road South, 2nd Floor, Kowloon, Hong Kong.

JIFFRY, M S Mohamed, b. 17 May 1941, Godapitiya, Sri Lanka. Chartered Accountant. m. Fathima Zibuthaniya, 3 Feb. 1968, 1 son, 2 daughters. *Education:* Diploma in Accountancy, 1968; Associate of the Institute of Chartered Accountants, Sri Lanka, 1974. *Appointments:* Accountant, National Housing Department, Colombo; Accountant, Department of Registrar of Companies; Proprietor, M.S.M. Jiffry and Company, Chartered Accountants. *Publications:* Written about 50 plays for the Sri Lanka Broadcasting Corporation, 1964-. *Address:* 52 Reservoir Road, Colombo 9, Sri Lanka.

JOANNOU, Michael Xenophon, b. 16 Aug. 1933,. Famagusta, Cyprus. Barrister-at-Law. m. Lenia Dionyssiades, 5 July 1959, 1 son, 1 daughter. *Education:* Barrister-at-Law, Gray's Inn, 1956; Fellow, Corporation of Secretaries, 1962; Fellow, Chartered Institute of Secretaries and Administrators, 1970; Member, British Institute of Management, 1975, Fellow, 1980; Academic and Field Course in Public Administration, International Specialists Institute, USA, 1962-63. *Appoint-*

ments: Practised Law, Famagusta and Nicosia, 1957-61; Secretary and Manager, Electricity Authority of Cyprus, 1961-. *Memberships:* Managing Council, Cyprus Football Association; President, Olympiakos, Sports Club Nicosia; President, Ethos, Theatre Group; Member, Board of the Cyprus State Theatre; Chairman, Board of Directors, Cyprus Tourism Co. Ltd. (Government Owned Company for the Cyprus Hilton). *Publications:* Various articles in newspapers; Books: False Truths, 1971; Rain With Sun On the Goldgreen Land, 1974; Straight and Broken Lines, 1977; March and Retrospect 1979; Sounds and Echoes, 1981. *Honours:* Palamas, 1951; Anorthosis 1951; Ehan-Ehag 1951. *Hobbies:* Music; Poetry; Theatre; Football; Tennis; Swimming. *Address:* 10 Metochiou Street, Nicosia (III), Cyprus.

JODA, Ahmadu Mohammadu, b. 13 Feb. 1930, Girei, Gongola State, Nigeria. Agriculturist; Journalist; Civil Servant; Company Director; Rancher. m. Aishatu Umaru, 27 June 1954, 2 sons, 2 daughters. *Education:* School of Agriculture, Ibadan, Nigeria, 1949-51; Pitman's College, London, UK, 1954-55. *Appointments:* Agricultural Research Assistant, Mar-Dec. 1951, Report, Sub-Editor, 1952-53, Nigerian Citizen, 1953-54; Northern Nigerian Organising Secretary, Department of Extra-Mural Studies, University of Ibadan, Nigeria, 1953-54; Daily Express, London, Glasgow, Manchester, UK, 1955-56; Duty Editor, Nigerian Broadcasting Corporation, 1956-60; British Broadcasting Corporation, July-Dec. 1959; Senior Assistant Secretary, Chief Information Officer, Permanent Secretary, 1960-66; Permanent Secretary, Federal Ministries of Information, Education and Industries, 1966-78; Chairman of 3 Nigerian Companies; Director of number of companies including Nigerian National Petroleum Corporation. *Memberships:* Patrol Leader, member of Council, Boy Scouts of Nigeria; Member of National Council, -1978, Nigerian Red Cross Society. *Publications:* Unpublished Government documents on various educational programmes on the development of the Universal Primary Education, Creation of new Universities and Teacher Education as well as National Policy on Eudcation between 1971 and 1975. *Honours:* Officer of Federal Republic of Nigeria, 1965; Commander of the Order of the Niger, 1979. *Hobbies:* Mixed farming; Travelling; Scrabble playing. *Address:* Toungo Quarters, Yola Town, P M B 2165, Yola, Nigeria.

JOEL, Hon. Sir Asher (Alexander), b. 4 May 1912, Sydney, Australia. Company Director and Consultant. m. (1) 1937 2 sons, (2) Sybil Jacobs, 1949, 1 son, 1 daughter. *Education:* Enore Public School; Cleveland Street High School, Sydney. *Appointments:* War Service 1939-45: AIF, 1942, Transf. RAN; Lieut. RANVR, 1943; RAN PRO staff Gen. MacArthur, 1944-45, New Guinea, Halmaheras, Philippines; Chairman, Carpentaria Newspapers Pty Ltd; Chairman, Mount Isa TV Pty Ltd; Chairman, Sydney Entertainment Centre; Nat. Pres., Anzac Mem. Forect in Israel; Dir, Royal North Shore Hospital of Sydney, 1959-81. *Memberships:* Citizens Committee, Captain Cook Bi-Centenary Celebrations, 1970, Welcoming Committee visit Pope Paul VI to Australia, 1970; Sydney Opera House Official, 1972; Fellow, Advertising Institute of Australia; Public Relations Institute of Australia; Institute Management; FInstD; FRSA; Australian Historical Society; Sydney Opera House Trust; Publication: Without Chains, Free (novel), 1977. *Honours:* OBE, 1956; Kt, 1971; KBE, 1974; US Bronze Star, 1943; Ancient Order of Sikatuna, Philippines, 1975; Kt Comdr, Order of Rizal, Philippines, 1978. *Hobbies:* Fishing; Gardening. *Address:* 2 Ormiston Avenue, Gordon, NSW 2072, Australia.

JOGARAO, Sistla. Venkata, b. 2 Oct. 1928, Parvatipuram, Vizianagaram District (A.P.) India. Teaching. m. Pushya Ragam (alias) Pushpa, 15 June 1945, 1 son, 1 daughter. *Education:* MA, 1st Class, I Rank, Andhra University, 1952-53; PhD, Research Medalist, 1957. *Appointments:* Professor of Telugu, Leningrad State University, USSR, 1965-67, and Andhra University, Waltair, 1967-; Principal, Arts, Commerce and Law Colleges, Andhra University Waltair, 1980-. *Memberships:* President, Writers' Coop. Society, Guntur Dist. 1972-76; A.P. Sahitya Academy, Hyderabad; Rotary Club, Guntur; Andhra University Syndicate, Senate, Academic Council and Board of Research Studies; Chairman, and Member, of various Examination Boards and selection committees. *Publications:* Many papers in Tel. and Eng. on a variety of Lit. topic;

Published 17 books (Lit. research, criticism, poetry, playlets, operettas and short stories): History of Tel. Yakshagana (Doctoral Thesis); Lit. of the United States (Translated into Telugu)—Innovated a Lit. type Uha Prahelika; Edited 10 books. *Honours:* MA, 1952; Research Medal, best thesis on Arts, 1959; Honoured by the A.P. Sangeeta Nataka Akademi, Hyderabad, 1970; Madhura Saraswati; Mahakavi; Sahiti Ratnakara; Recipient of A.P. State Award for Meritorious University Teacher 1980. *Hobbies:* Literary discussions; Research guidance; Reading; Creative writing. *Address:* A.U. Professors' Quarters, 5/40 Siripuram, Waltair (A.P.) 530 003, India.

JOGLEKAR, Prabhakar J, b. 15 Jan. 1935, Jalgaon, Maharashtra State, India. Consultant in Electronics. m. Usha Sugwekar, 21 July 1965, 1 son, 1 daughter. *Education:* BE (Telecommunications) 1st class distinction, Poona University, 1956; PhD, Electrical communication Engineering, Indian Institute of Science, Bangalore, 1965. *Appointments:* Engineer, All India Radio, 1957-60; Senior Research Fellow, Indian Institute of Science Bangalore, 1960-63; Lecturer/Assistant Professor, Indian Institute of Technology, Delhi, 1963-71; BBC Engineering Research Department, Kingswood, Surrey, UK, 1965-66; Professor in Electronics and Communication Engineering, Regional Engineering College, Tiruchirapalli, 1971-74. *Memberships:* Fellow Institution of Electronics and Telecommunication Engineers, India. *Publications:* Published several research papers in India, UK, and USA, on atmospheric radio noise. The main contributions are regarding: influence of local thunderstorms on statistical characteristics; short term predictions; frequency spectrum of noise; dependence of noise intensities on sunspot activity. *Honours:* Paper on Correlation between atmospheric noise levels at different frequencies was specially reviewed in IEEE spectrum July 1970 wherein the work was compared with that of the famous astronomer Tycho Brahe. *Hobbies:* Writing; Social Work. *Address:* 5 Rajashree Building, Ram-maruti Road, Thane 400 602, India.

JOHN, Clifton Mortimer Llewellyn, b. 27 Jan. 1925, Guyana, South America. Barrister. m. Evelyn, 21 July 1956, 1 son, 4 daughters. *Education:* LL.B. London, UK; Attorney-at-Law, Lincoln's Inn, London, UK. *Appointments:* Minister of Agriculture, Guyana, 1964-66; Minister of Home Affairs, Guyana, 1967-68; Minister of Local Government, Guyana, 1969; Member of Parliament, Guyana, 1964-69. *Memberships:* Leader, Peoples Democratic Movement, Guyana; National Chairman, Guyana, World Peace Through Law Center. *Publications:* Local Government under the Marshall Plan. *Hobbies:* Farming; Swimming. *Address:* 137 Eldorado Avenue, South Rumveldt Gardens, Georgetown, Guyana, South America.

JOHN, Planthara Jacob, b. 6 July 1940, Tiruvalla, Kerala State, India. Educationist. m. Romaine Pereira, 28 Dec. 1978, 1 son. *Education:* BSc, University of London, UK, 1964. *Appointments:* Teacher of Physics and Mathematics, Christ King College, Tudella, Sri Lanka, June 1964-Dec.1964; Senior Master of Physics and Mathematics, Nyeri High School, Nyeri, Kenya, 1965-68; Teacher of Science and Mathematics, at Mumbwa and Nchelenge Secondary Schools, Zambia, 1968-72; National Executive Secretary of the Junior Engineers, Technicians and Scientists Organisation of Zambia responsible for the Promotion and Popularisation of Science and Technology amongst the Youth in Zambia, 1972-. *Memberships:* Founder member, Society for International Development; Lusaka Sports Club; Practical Subjects Curriculum Committee, Ministry of Education, Zambia; Mathematics Curriculum Committee, Ministry of Education, Zambia; Editorial Board of Zambia Education Journal; Industrial Sub-Committee on Appropriate Technology; Committee on School Science Projects of the Technology Development Advisory Unit of the University of Zambia; Central Committee of the Zambia Association for Science Education; Ex-Officio member, Central Committee of the Zambia Association for Mathematics Education. *Publications:* JETS of Zambia, 1972-74; Production Technology, Vol.1, 1975; Adjudication Criteria for Jets Fairs, 1975; The Jets Quiz, 1976; The Jets Digest, 1981; Papers read at International Forums: Out of School Technical and Scientific Activities of Youth, 1980; Means and Methods of Stimulating and Disseminating Scientific Knowledge, Scientific Skills and Scientific Attitudes Through Extra-Curricular Activities, 1978; The Contribution of Jets In the Promotion of Science and Technology amongst the Secondary School Youth in Zambia and its Proposals for Future Programmes, 1978; Jets Organisation of Zambia, its Activities, Achievements and Proposals for Extension to the Primary and Teacher Training Sectors, 1974; UNESCO Consultant, Afrca Regional Workshop on Training National Leaders for Out-of-School Science and Technology Education an Popularisation of Science, Senegal, 1980; Team leader to first ever African delegation of Young Scientists from Zambia to the Nobel Award Ceremonies, Sweden, 1980. *Honours:* Received two Letter Commendations from His Excellency the President of the Republic of Zambia, Dr. Kenneth Kaunda. *Hobbies:* Social Functions; Magician. *Address:* PO Box 35508, Lusaka, Zambia.

JOHNPILLAI, Ajit Joseph, b. 10 May 1954, Colombo, Sri Lanka. Chartered/Management Accountant. m. Marianne Antoinette Mutukisna, 14 July 1979. *Education:* Associate member, Institute of Chartered Accountants of Sri Lanka, 1979; Associate member, Institute of Cost and Management Accountants, UK, 1981. *Appointments:* Ernst and Whinney, Chartered Accountants, Colombo, Sri Lanka, 1974-79; The Mikechris Group of Companies, Colombo, Sri Lanka, Feb.1979-Sept.79; Touche, Ross Thorburn & Co., Chartered Accountants, Kingston, Jamaica, 1979-81; Charles Kempe & Company, Chartered Accountants, Hamilton, Bermuda, 1981. *Memberships:* Honorary Treasurer, Ceylonese Rugby and Football Club, Colombo, Sri Lanka, 1977,78. *Honours:* Awarded Prizes, Institute of Chartered Accountants of Sri Lanka Examinations; Intermediate Prizes, Accountancy, June 1976; Prizes, Final Part II, Dec. 1977; Accountancy Prize, Final Part I, Dec. 1978; Represented Jamaica in Rugby Football. *Hobbies:* Reading; Contract Bridge; Sports. *Address:* PO Box 463, Hamilton, Bermuda.

JOHNS, Bernard Winton, b. 26 Jan. 1902, Wanganui, New Zealand. Chartered and Registered Architect. m. Mura Lois Ellison, 7 July 1933, 1 son, 1 daughter. *Education:* Atelier, School of Architecture, London University, UK, 1926-29; Elected Member, Royal Institute of British Architects, London, UK, 1929; Elected member, New Zealand Institute of Architects, 1929. *Appointments:* Henry Thomas Johns, Father, 1919-20, 1924; Wm. M Page, 1920-22; Watson, Gooder, Lee, 1922-23; Clere and Williams, 1925; Easton & Robertson, Bedford Square, London, UK, 1926; Joseph Emberton, Regent St, London, UK, 1927; Slater and Moberly, Berners St, London, UK, 1928-29; Own Practice, Wellington, New Zealand, 1929-79. *Memberships:* Commercial Travellers' Club, Wellington; Architect, Central Club, Wellington; Levin Club, Levin; Royal Port Nicholson Yacht Club; Honorary Life member, Levin Art Society; Honorary Life member, New Zealand Academy of Fine Arts; Part Founder and Chairman, Levin Hospital Bus Association; Foundation member, Byrd Memorial, Wellington. *Publications:* Articles on Design concepts of Motorway, Capital City, Wellington and Great North Road, 1960. *Honours:* First Prize winner, War Memorial Stratford, Taranaki, unveiled by Lord Jellicoe, Gov.. General, 1924; Second Prize Winner, Centennial Memorial, Petone, 1940; Bronze Medal of NZIA House of the Year Award, 1942. *Hobbies:* Sports; Walking; Swimming; Gardening. *Address:* 15 Edinburgh Street, Levin, New Zealand.

JOHNS, Stanley Roy, b. 8 July 1935, Cessnock, New South Wales, Australia. Research Scientist. m. Julie Rose Horvath, 24 Aug. 1957, 3 daughters. *Education:* BSc.(Hons.), University of New England, 1953-56; PhD., University of Sydney, Australia, 1958-60. *Appointments:* Burroughs Wellcome Fellow, Department of Pharmacy, University of Sydney, Australia, 1961-62; Post Doctoral Fellow, National Research Council of Canada, Ottawa, Canada, 1962-64; Research Scientist, Senior Principal Research Scientist, CSIRO, Australia, 1964-; Visiting Associate, California Institute of Technology, Pasadena, California, USA, 1972. *Memberships:* Honorary General Secretary, Royal Australian Chemical Institute. *Publications:* 145 Scientific papers in various scientific Journals. *Honours:* Fellowship, Royal Australian Chemical Institute, 1979; Liversidge Lecturer, Royal Society of New South Wales, Australia, 1980. *Hobbies:* Golf; Theatre; Opera; Ballet. *Address:* 13 Kiah Street, Glen Waverley, Victoria 3150, Australia.

JOHNSON, Arthur Joseph Fynney, b. 15 Feb. 1915, Vancouver, B.C. Canada. Lawyer. m. Catharina Van Der Ploeg, 10 Jan 1946, 2 sons, 1 daughter. *Education:* B.A., 1935, M.A., 1936, University of British Columbia; B.A., 1938, B.C.L, 1939; M.A., 1942, Oxford University. *Appointments:* Assistant Supervisor, Foreign Exchange Control Board, Vancouver, 1939-41; Officer, Canadian Army Overseas, 1941-46; Department of External Affairs, Ottawa, 1946-47; Law Practice, Vancouver, 1947-; Partner, Davis & Company. *Memberships:* Past President, Vancouver, United Services Institute; Canadian and Vancouver Bar Associations; Member of Council, Vancouver Institute; Governor, St. George's School, Vancouver; Chairman, Vancouver School Board, 1968; Vancouver Police Commission, 1970-74; Officer Commanding, The British Columbia Regiment, (D.C.O.) 1951-54; Commanding Officers Committee, The British Columbia Regiment; President, British Columbia Regiment Association. *Honours:* Appointed Rhodes Scholar for British Columbia, 1936; M.B.E. (Mil), 1945; C.D. 1948; Q.C., 1969. *Hobbies:* Gardening; Golf; Fishing. *Address:* 1550 Laurier Ave., Vancouver B.C., V6J 2V3.

JOHNSON, Frank Louis, b. 22 Feb. 1930, Marrickville, Sydney, Australia. Physician. m. Eleanor Mary Logan, 5 Mar. 1956, 4 daughters. *Education:* BSc.(Med.), 1953, MB., BS., 1955, Sydney University, Australia; Diploma, Physical Medicine, Royal College of Physicians, London, and Royal College of Surgeons, UK, 1967; Fellow, Royal Australasian College of Physicians, 1971; Fellow, Royal Australian College of Rehabilitation Medicine, 1980. *Appointments:* Junior Resident Medical Officer, Sydney Hospital, Australia, 1955; Resident Medical Officer, Royal Melbourne Hospital, Australia, 1956-58; Consultant Physician in Group General Practice, Southport, Queensland, Australia, 1959-66; Honorary Clinical Assistant Physician to Medical Outpatients, Honorary Physician to Rheumatology Outpatients, Consultant Physician, Physical Medicine and Rehabilitation, Mater Misericordiae Hospitals, Brisbane, Australia, 1963-; Registrar, Department and Physical Medicine, Middlesborough General Hospital, UK, 1966; Senior Registrar, Departments of Rheumatism Research and Physical Medicine, Manchester Royal Informary and Devonshire Royal Hospital, Buxton, UK, 1967-68; Fellow in Rheumatology, Rancho Los Amigos Hospital California, USA, University of Southern California, 1968-69; Visiting Staff Physician in Rheumatology and Physical Medicine, Chairman of Department, Royal Brisbane Hospital, Australia, 1970-; Senior Rehabilitation Medical Consultant, Commonwealth Industrial Rehabilitation Service, Taringa, 1970-72; Visiting Rheumatologist, Repatriation General Hospital, Greenslopes, Brisbane, Australia, 1978-79; Visiting Rheumatologist, Rosemount Repatriation Hospital, Brisbane, Australia, 1978-81; Consultant Physician in Rheumatology, Brisbane and Southport, Australia, 1970-. *Memberships:* Member of numerous organisations including: Australian Rheumatism Association; Chairman, Scientific Committee, Vice President, Queensland Arthritis & Rheumatism Foundation; Australian Medical Association; Australian Association of Physical Medicine and Rehabilitation; Southport Yacht Club; Huntingdon Country Club, Southport, Australia. *Publications:* Agranulocytosis due to Chlorpromazine and Pacatal-Report of a case, 1957; Plasma Antiheparin Activity and the Heparin Precipitable Fraction of Plasma in Rheumatoid Arthritis, 1968; A Method of Measuring Quadriceps Femoris Muscle Strength, 1969; Multiple Sites of Avascular Necrosis in a Patient with Goodpasture's Syndrome. *Honours:* William Kay Prize for Sydney Hospital Fourth Year Students, 1952; BSc.(Med.), 1st Class Hons., 1953; MB., BS., 2nd Class Hons., 1955. *Hobbies:* Boating; Bird watching; Fishing; Surfing. *Address:* 19 Paterson Place, Paradise Point, Gold Coast, Queensland 4215, Australia.

JOHNSON, John Rodney, b. 6 Sept. 1930, India. HM Diplomatic Service. m. Jean Mary Lewis, 11 Sept. 1956, 3 sons, 1 daughter. *Education:* BA.(Hons.), MA., Keble College, Oxford, UK, 1951-55. *Appointments:* HM Overseas Civil Service, District Commissioner, Kenya, 1955-64; Committee of Vice-Chancellors and Principals of UK Universities, 1964-65; Diplomatic Service in FCO, Algiers, Barbados, Nigeria, 1966-; Head of West African Department, FCO AND Ambassador to Chad, 1978-80; High Commissioner to Zambia, 1980-. *Memberships:* Travellers Club; Climbers

Club; Bridgetown Club. *Honours:* CMG, 1980. *Hobbies:* Mountains; Gardening. *Address:* The Gables, High Street, Old Amersham, Bucks, England.

JOHNSON, Julian Stanley, b. 6 Dec. 1926, Kenilworth, Warwickshire, England. m. 21 Apr. 1951, 1 son, 1 daughter. *Education:* LDS., University of Birmingham, UK, 1949; BSc., 1956, MSc., 1959, PhD., 1972, University of London, UK; D.Orth. RCS.(Eng.), 1961; FDS., RCS., (Edinburgh), 1968. *Appointments:* Senior Dental Officer, 1958, Specialist in Dental Surgery, 1961-63, Adviser in Orthodontics, 1961-66, Senior Specialist in Dental Surgery, 1963-66, Senior Specialist in Periodontology, 1963-66, retired as Wing Commander, 1966, Royal Air Force Dental Branch, 1950-66; Consultant Orthodontist, Booth Hall Children's Hospital, Manchester, UK, 1966-71; Consultant Orthodontist and Head of Department of Orthodontics, University of Manchester, UK, 1971-; Regional Adviser in Postgraduate Dental Studies, 1977-80; Visiting Professor to Universities in Turkey, Indonesia and Egypt, 1976-; External Examiner, Royal College of Surgeons of Edinburgh, UK, 1978-; External Examiner, Edinburgh, University, UK, 1980-. *Memberships:* Life Fellow, International Biographical Association; British Society for the Study of Orthodontics; British Association of Orthodontists; British Dental Association; Association of University Teachers of Orthodontics; Chairman, 1970-76, Manchester and Region Orthodontic Study Group; Consultant Orthodontists Group; International Association of Oral Myology. *Publications:* Numerous papers on Treatment of Craniofacial Deformities; Growth and Development of the Face; Facial Variation Resulting from Ethnic and Individual Variation, Mainly Resulting from a new Statistical Approach to the Analysis of any Irregular Shape. *Hobbies:* Cultivation of Varieties of Heather; Hill walking; Classical Guitar. *Address:* 4 Ladythorn Avenue, Marple, Cheshire, SK6 7DR, England.

JOHNSON, Keith Arthur, b. 26 Nov. 1943, Sydney, Australia. Publisher, Bookseller and Genealogist. *Education:* North Sydney Boys High School, until 1960. *Appointments:* Commonwealth Attorney Generals Department, 1961-72; Secretary, National Rehabilitation and Compensation Inquiry, 1973-74; Executive Officer, Australian Law Reform Commission, 1975-79; Co-Director, Library of Australian History, 1979-. *Memberships:* Councillor, 1975-82, Royal Australian Historical Society, 1962; President, 1978-81, Society of Australian Genealogists, 1964-; Committee member, National Trust of Australia, New South Wales Branch, 1961-. *Publications:* Cadmans Cottage, The Coxswains Barrack, co-author J.S. Provis, 1972; Transcripts of Early Sydney Burial Grounds, co-author M.R. Sainty, 1969-79; Index to Notices Sydney Morning Herald, 1831-56; Census of New South Wales, November 1828, 1980. *Honours:* C.H. Currey Memorial Fellowship, 1974; Fellowship, Society of Australian Genealogists, 1971. *Hobbies:* Writing; Australian Historical Research. *Address:* 17 Mitchell Street, North Sydney, New South Wales 2060, Australia.

JOHNSON, Lawrence Alexander Sidney, b. 26 June 1925, Cheltenham, New South Wales, Australia. Botanist. m. 18 Nov. 1950, 4 sons, 1 daughter. *Education:* BSc.(Hons.), 1948, DSc. (Sydney), 1971, University of Sydney, Australia. *Appointments:* Assistant Botanist, National Herbarium of New South Wales, 1948, Director, Royal Botanic Gardens, Sydney, Australia, 1972-; Australian Botanical Liaison Officer, Royal Botanic Gardens, Kew, UK, 1962-63. *Memberships:* Fellow of the Linnean Society of London, Honoris Causa; Corresponding member, Botanical Society of America; Twice past President, member and Councillor, Linnean Society of New South Wales; International Association of Plant Taxonomists. *Publications:* A Classification of the Eucalypts (with L D Pryor), 1971; some 60 scientific papers. *Honours:* Awarded Clarke Medal of the Royal Society of New South Wales for distinguished work in the natural sciences, 1980. *Hobbies:* Music; Family tennis; History; Linguistics; Mathematics; Conservation. *Address:* 357 Sailor's Bay Road, Northbridge, New South Wales 2063, Australia.

JOHNSON, Mobolaji Olufunso Brigadier (rtd.) b. 9 Feb. 1936, Lagos, Nigeria. Company Director. m. Olufunlayo Aganga Williams, 26 Dec. 1961, 3 sons. *Education:* Royal Military Academy, Sandhurst, Camberley, England. *Appointments:* Platoon Commander, United

Nations HQ, Congo (now Zaire), 1962; Commander Brigade of Guards, Nigerian Army, 1963-64; Deputy Adjuctant Quartermaster-General HQ1 2nd Brigade, Nigerian Army, 1964-66; Military Administrator, Fed. territory of Nigeria, 1965-67; Military Governor, Lagos State, 1967-75; Company Director, 1976-. *Memberships:* Nigerian Society for the Blind; Metropolitan Club, Lagos, Nigeria. *Honours:* United Nations Operations in the Congo Medal, 1962; Nigerian Army Long Service Good Conduct Medal, 1969. *Hobbies:* Athletics; Football; Tennis; Squash; Music; Travelling; International Current Affairs. *Address:* 5 Sagamu Avenue, Ilupeju, Lagos, Nigeria.

JOHNSON, Norman, b. 8 May 1923, Barking, Essex, England. Librarian. m. 17 Feb. 1968. *Education:* Associate, Library Association, London, UK. *Appointments:* Senior Assistant Librarian in Charge, North Chingford Branch, Essex County Library, UK, 1951-55; Deputy Librarian, 1955-56, Librarian and Secretary, 1956-, South Rhodesia National Free Library Service, now National Free Library of Zimbabwe. *Memberships:* Past Chairman, Library Association of Rhodesia and Nyasaland; Rotary Club. *Publications:* Professional articles. *Hobbies:* Miniature Model Railways; Gardening. *Address:* 11 Valley Road, Burnside, Bulawayo, Zimbabwe.

JOHNSON, Richard Norman, b. 15 Dec. 1923, Armadale, Victoria, Australia. Professor. m. Jane Meade-Waldo, 24 Mar. 1944, 3 sons. *Education:* BArch, University of Sydney, 1951. *Appointments:* Partner, McConnel Smith and Johnson, 1955-75; Director, McConnel Smith and Johnson Pty. Limited, 1971-; Professor of Architecture and Head of School of Undergraduate Studies in Architecture, 1967-, Dean, Faculty of Architecture, 1968-, University of Sydney; Councillor, 1967-, Deputy Chancellor, 1981-, New South Wales Institute of Technology. *Memberships:* LFRAIA, RIBA; President, New South Wales Chapter RAIA, 1968-70; Council member, 1979-, Vice President, 1981-, Commonwealth Association of Architects; Chairman, Commonwealth Board of Architectural Education of the Commonwealth Association of Architects, 1973-77; Vice-President, Royal Australian Institute of Architects, 1981. *Creative Works:* Various large scale and small scale buildings, including: Sydney Water Board building; Commonwealth State Law Courts, Sydney; Benjamin Offices, Canberra. *Honours:* Order of Australia, 1980; Wilkinson Award, 1964. *Hobbies:* Music; Films; Trout fishing; Ethnic art. *Address:* 29 Greville Street, Chatswood, New South Wales, Australia.

JOHNSON, Stanley Ross, b. 18 Apr. 1929, Calgary, Alberta, Canada. Life Insurance Executive. m. Muriel Fairley, 15 July 1953, 2 sons, 2 daughters. *Education:* Bachelor of Commerce, University of British Columbia, 1952; Degree, Chartered Life Underwriter (CLU), 1959. *Appointments:* Agent, Assistant Manager, Management Assistant, Agency Manager, Supervisor of Western Offices, Superintendent of Agencies, Resident Vice-President for Canada, New York Life Insurance Company; Executive Vice-President, National Life Assurance Company; Elected, Board of Directors, The Continental Insurance Company of Canada and The Dominion Insurance Corporation, 1981. *Memberships:* Delta Upsilon Fraternity, Past International Vice President; United Church. *Honours:* University of British Columbia Alumnus of the Year, 1974; Elected to Board of Directors, National Life, 1980. *Hobbies:* Fishing; Swimming; Sports; Model Building. *Address:* •1312 Cleaver Drive, Oakville, Ontario, Canada.

JOHNSTON, Archibald Dick, b. 5 Mar. 1940, Lethbridge, Alberta, Canada. Chartered Accountant. m. 16 May 1964, 1 son, 3 daughters. *Education:* BA, University of Calgary; MBA, University of Alberta. *Appointments:* Chartered Accountancy Practice, D Johnston and Associates, 1969-75; Director of several private corporations in Alberta, 1969-75; Member, Alberta Legislative Assembly for Lethbridge East Constituency, 1975, 1979; Minister of Municipal Affairs, 1975; Minister of Federal and Intergovernmental Affairs, 1979. *Memberships:* Institute of Chartered Accountants of Alberta; Victorian Order of Nurses, Former Director; Lethbridge Community College, Former Board Member. *Hobbies:* Skiing; Mountain climbing; Reading. *Address:* 3223-105th Street, Edmonton, Alberta, Canada.

JOHNSTON, John Alan, b. 25 Feb. 1941, Sydney, Australia. Information Processing. m. Helen Patricia Bowen, 9 Mar. 1963, 2 sons. *Education:* Accountancy Certificate, Sydney Technical College, 1961. *Appointments:* Branch Accountant, J I Case (Australia) Ptyl Ltd., 1962; Systems Analyst, Representative, National Industry Marketing Manager, Marketing Manager, IBM Australia Ltd., 1977; Joint Managing Director, Johnston Brown and Associates Pty. Ltd., 1981-; Chairman, Johnston Brown and Associates Incorporated; Director: Fountain Management Services Pty. Ltd., Hotel Systems Incorporated, JBA (HK) Pty. Ltd., JBA (Singapore) Pty. Ltd., *Memberships:* Associate, Australian Society of Accountants; Company Directors Association. *Hobbies:* Golf; Tennis. *Address:* Hunters Hill, Sydney, Australia.

JOHNSTON, Marshall lewis, b. 20 July 1923, Canberra, Australia. Diplomat. m. 30 Aug. 1952, 2 sons. *Education:* B.A., University of Melbourne, 1949. *Appointments:* Australian Department of Foreign Affairs, 1947; Australian Ambassador to Burma, 1965-68, Israel, 1979-72, Khmer Republic, 1972-73, Thailand, 1974-78, Iran, 1978-80, Greece, 1980-; Australian High Commissioner to Cyprus. *Honours:* Officer of the General Division of the Order of Australia, 1980. *Address:* Department of Foreign Affairs, Canberra A.C.T., 2600 Australia.

JOHNSTON, Raymond Leslie, b. 9 Jan. 1944, Sydney, Australia. Linguist. m. 14 May 1966, 3 sons, 1 daughter. *Education:* BA, 1967, MA, 1972, Sydney University; Dip. Rel. Educ., Melbourne Coll. Div, 1973; PhD, ANU, 1978. *Appointments:* Department of Youth and Welfare, NSW, 1961-66; Public Service Board of NSW, 1967-68; Field Linguist, 1970-74, Field Consultant, 1978-, Summer Institute of Linguistics. *Memberships:* Linguistic Society of America; Linguistic Society of Papua New Guinea; Editor, Journal of Linguistic Soc. PNG; Australian Linguistic Society. *Publications:* Expatriate Poems; Lower Than The Angels, Devotional Poems. *Honours:* Commonwealth Scholarship, 1961; Commonwealth Post-graduate Research Award, 1975; ANU Research Scholarship, 1975. *Hobbies:* Fishing; Family recreation; Creative Writing. *Address:* Box 97 PO, Ukarumpa, Via Lae, Papua, New Guinea.

JOHNSTON, Walter Ian Harewood, b. 16 Feb. 1930, Melbourne, Australia. Medical Practitioner. m. Christine De Stoop, 2 Sept. 1971, 2 sons, 3 daughters. *Education:* M.B.B.S., 1954, M.G.O., 1962, University of Melbourne; Post-Graduate, Royal Women's Hospital Melbourne, 1957-59, Department of Obstetrics and Gynaecology; University of Melbourne and Liverpool, England; M.R.C.O.G., 1960; F.R.C.O.G., 1974; F.R.A.C.O.G., 1978, Foundation Fellow. *Appointments:* Assistant Obstetrician and Gynaecologist, 1962-64, Junior Gynaecologist, 1964-71, Senior Gynaecologist, 1971, Chairman, Reproductive Biology Unit, 1969, Chairman, Senior Medical Staff, 1980, Royal Women's Hospital. *Memberships:* The Chicago Gynaecological Society; Australian Obsterians and Gynaecologists Research Society; Committee, National Work Shop on A.I.D. of Australian; International Society for advancement of Humanistic studies in Gynaecology; American Association of Gynaecological Laparoscopists; The Neuro Muscular Society of Australia; The XX Club of Victoria. *Publications:* Collection of Human Oocytes at Laparoscopy, 1974; Dydrogesterone and Endometriosis, 1976; In Vitro Fertilization of Pre-Ovulatory Human Eggs, 1978; The Ultrastructure of the Pre-Ovulatory Human Egg Fertilized in Vitro, Vol. 33 No. 1; In Vitro Fertilization - The Challenga of the Eighties, (in press), 1981; Chapter contributions to: 'The Infertile Couple'; 'Handbook on A.I.D. in Australia'. *Hobbies:* Skiing; Sailing; Tennis; French Wine. *Address:* 73 Robinson Road, Hawthorn 3122, Melbourne, Australia.

JOHNSTONE, Ross Allan, b. 24 Apr. 1936, Weyburn, Saskatchewan, Canada. Architect. m. 5 Apr. 1958, 2 sons, 1 daughter. *Education:* University of Saskatchewan, 1957; Dip. Arch. (with distinction), Regent Street Polytechnic, 1963. *Appointments:* Architect with Building Design Partnership, London, 1963-64; Designer and Project Architect, Izumi Arnott and Sugiyama, 1964-67; Chief Architect for Saskatchewan Department of Public Works, 1968; Associate, Gordon R Arnott and Associates, 1969-74; Partner, Vice-President, Arnott MacPhail Johnstone and Associates Limited, 1974-81; Vice-President, Wiens Johnstone Architects Limited. *Memberships:* Member of Council, Saskatchewan Association of Architects; President, Saskatchewan Association of Architects; Chairman, Regina Chapter of Architects; Council Member, Royal Architectural Institute of Canada; Ongoing Committee work for Saskatchewan Association of Architects; National Research Council's Industry Advisory Committee on Modular Co-ordination; Chairman, Regina Chapter Solar Energy Society of Canada; Associate of the Royal Institute of British Architects. *Publications:* Canadian Architect, 1980. *Creative Works:* Designer and Planner of numerous buildings and programmes including: TC Douglas Building (Offices fo Dept. of Health), Regina; Childrens Library, Regina; Psychiatric Centre, Weyburn; Canadian Wildlife Service Building, Saskatoon; Uranium City Primary School; Uranium City Police Station; Senior Citizens Apartments, Moose Jaw; United Nations Environments Programme and Habitat, Nairobi, Kenya. *Honours:* Saskatchewan Association of Architects, Design Awards Program First Award, 1979. *Hobbies:* Running; Squash; Travel; Philately. *Address:* 2827 McCallum Avenue, Regina, Saskatchewan, Canada.

JOLLY, Mark, b. 9 Sept. 1923, New South Wales, Australia. University Professor. m. Adrienne Pamela Hill, 2 March 1957, 2 daughters. *Education:* B.D.S., 1950, M.D.S., 1953, D.D.Sc., 1965, University of Sydney. *Appointments:* Prctice, 1950-51; Lecturer in Operative Dentistry, 1951-54, Senior Lecturer Operative Dentistry and Oral Surgery, 1954-64, Associate Professor in Oral Surgery, 1964-65, McCaughey Professor of Oral Medicine and Oral Surgery, 1965-, University of Sydney. *Publications:* Author of numerous Scientific papers published in United Kingdom, United States of America and Australia. *Hobbies:* Kitchen Antiques; Photography; Gardening. *Address:* 87 Shirley Road, Roseville, New South Wales 2069, Australia.

JONA, Walter, b. 17 July 1926, Melbourne, Australia. Cabinet Minister. m. Alwynne Burley, 10 Jan. 1972. *Education:* University of Melbourne. *Appointments:* Member for Hawthorn, Victoria, 1964-; Parliamentary Secretary of Cabinet, 1973-76; Assistant Minister of Health, 1976-79; Minister of Immigration and Ethnic Affairs, 1976-79; Minister for Community Welfare Services, 1979-. *Memberships:* National Trust of Australia; Naval and Military Club. *Publications:* Articles in various Journals. *Honours:* Queen Elizabeth Jubilee Medal. *Hobbies:* Cycling; Walking; Watching Cricket and football. *Address:* 11 Kildare Street, Hawthorn East, Victoria, Australia.

JONASSON, Eric Leonard, b. 17 Nov. 1948, Winnipeg, Manitoba, Canada. Genealogist/Publisher. m. Elizabeth Molly Cazakoff, 4 May 1974, 1 daughter. *Education:* University of Minnesota, Minneapolis, USA, 1975-78. *Appointments:* Photogrammetrist/cartographer, Western Photogrammetry Limited, 1968-71; Photogrammetrist/cartographer, Production Manager, 1974-75, Applied Photogrammetric Sciences Limited; Partner, Carto Graphics, 1975-79; Owner, Publisher, Wheatfield Press, 1975-; Partner, Canadian Ancestral Research Institute, 1979-; Instructor, University of Manitoba, 1981-. *Memberships:* Association of Professional Genealogists, Trustee, 1980-; International Genealogy Consumer Organization, Member, Board of Professional Advisors, 1981-; Manitoba Genealogical Society, Founder, 1976, President, 1976-79; Historical and Scientific Society of Manitoba, Member of Governing Council, 1980-; Icelandic-Canadian Magazine, Member, Editorial Board, 1979-. *Publications:* Tracing Your Icelandic Family Tree, 1975; The Canadian Genealogical Handbook, 1976, 2nd edition, 1978; A number of miscellaneous articles on genealogy which have appeared in a number of different publications in Canada and USA. *Hobbies:* Gardening; Woodworking; Historical Research; Playing Guitar, Ukelale. *Address:* 255 Strathmillan Road, Winnipeg, Manitoba, Canada.

JONATHAN, (Joseph) Leabua (Chief), b. 30 Oct. 1914. Lesotho Politician. *Education:* Mission School, Leribe. *Appointments:* Mines in South Africa 1934-37; Court President 1938; Politics 1952; District Council 1954; National Council 1954; Member, Panel of 18, 1956-59; Founded Basutoland National Party 1959; Leader 1959-. *Memberships:* Legis. Council 1960-64; Delegate, Constitutional Conference 1964; Prime Min-

ister of Basutoland 1965-; Minister of Public Service, External Affairs 1965-71; Defence 1965-; Civil Service 1965-68, and 1969-70; International Security 1968-; Development and Planning 1968-74; Citizenship, Training and Statistics 1968-70; Chief of Electoral Affairs 1971-. *Address:* Prime Minister's Office, PO Box 527, Maseru, Lesotho.

JONES, Arfon Rowland, b. 10 Sept. 1937, Penycae, Clwyd, Wales. Head Master. m. Jane Lesley Jones, 29 July 1977. *Education:* BA, (Hons.), 1960; Postgraduate Diploma in Education, 1961; MA, 1966. *Appointments:* Research Assistant, Faculty of Education, Aberystwyth; Education Officer, Department of Technical Cooperative, Uganda; Deputy Representative (Wales) British Council; Lecturer in English, Senior Lecturer in Education, Northern Counties College; Deputy Head, Sydney Stringer School; Head, Community College, Coventry. *Memberships:* Trustee, Coventry & Warwickshire Award Trust; Governor, Coventry Technical College. *Publications:* Prawf Cymraeg C1, 1963; Community Participation and Democratic Control, 1978; Efforts to Combat low achievement, 1979; Sydney School and Community College, 1980. *Hobbies:* Squash; Tennis; Hockey; Poetry. *Address:* 4 Hammonds Terrace, Kenilworth, West Midlands.

JONES, David Lewis, b. 2 Feb. 1926, Adelaide, South Australia. Medical Statistician. m. Ena Louisa Lawrence, 4 Dec. 1954, 3 daughters. *Education:* M.B.B.S., 1950, B.Sc., 1963, University of Adelaide. *Appointments:* Royal Adelaide Hospital, South Australia, 1951; General Medical Practice, South Australia, 1952-53; Royal Perth Hospital, Western Australia, 1953; General Practice, Busselton, Western Australia, 1954-58; South Australian Public Health Department, 1959-60; Lung Cancer Registry, Department of Medicine, University of Sydney, 1963-64; Health Commission of New South Wales, Sydney, 1965-. *Memberships:* Statistical Society of Australia, New South Wales Branch, Council, 1980-; Australian Mathematical Society; Australian Medical Association; Medical Statistics Committee, National Health and Medical Research Council, 1964-67. *Publications:* Height, Weight and other Physical characteristics of New South Wales Children, 1973-74; Edited Data and produced tabulations for 'The National Trachoma and Eye Health Program'; The Size of the Homeless new population of Sydney; A survey of the Incidence of Defective vision and Strabismus in Kindergarten age children. *Hobbies:* Music; History. *Address:* 3 Rosebery Road, Killara, New South Wales 2071, Australia.

JONES, Glynne, b. 7 Nov. 1927 Merthyr Tydfil, Mid-Glam, South Wales. Music. *Education:* University College of Wales, Cardiff; BA(Hons.) Music and Welsh; Diploma in Education. *Appointments:* Head of Music, County Grammar School, Merthyr Tydfil 1955-65; Music Adviser for Monmouthshire 1965-74; Senior Music Adviser for Gwent 1974-; Conductor of the Pendyrus Male Choir, Rhondda 1963-. *Memberships:* Royal College of Organists; Arts' Panel of the South East Wales Arts Association; Guild for the Promotion of Welsh Music; Co-founder, Newport International Piano Competition. *Publications:* Music arranger and writer of music scripts for radio. *Honours:* Guild for the Promotion of Welsh Music, for services to contemporary Welsh music, 1968. *Hobbies:* Music; Broadcasting in Welsh and English; Cooking; Driving fast cars. *Address:* 3 Glendower Street, Dowlais, Merthyr Tydfil, Mid-Glam. CF48 3SG.

JONES, Graham Havard, b. 21 Oct. 1932, Rabaul, Papua New Guinea. Head, NSW Government Authority, Australia. m. Gwendolene M Busuttin, 11 Apr. 1953, 1 son, 1 daughter. *Education:* Associate Degree, Australian Society of Accountants, 1964; Fellow, Australian Society of Accountants, 1980. *Appointments:* Department of District Services and Native Affairs, 1953-57; Senior Examiner of Accounts, The Treasury, 1957-59; Budget Officer, The Treasury, 1959-61; Accountant, Department of Education, 1961-65; Executive Officer, Administration and Finance, Department of Education, 1965-66; Chairman, Promotions Appeal Committees Public Service Commission, Papua, New Guinea, 1962-66; Assistant General Manager and Secretary, 1966-75; General Manager and Chief Executive, NSW Fish Marketing Authority, Australia, 1975-. *Memberships:* Practitioner of the Transcendental Meditation and TM Sidhi's Programme; City Tattersalls Club, Sydney; Mandarin Club, Sydney; Eastern Suburbs Leagues Club, Bondi. *Honours:* Life Governer, Aged Masons Widows and Orphans Institutions, Queensland, Australia 1964. *Hobbies:* Body Surfing; Swimming; Jogging; Chess; Reading. *Address:* 41/17 Raglan Street, Mosman 2088, NSW, Australia.

JONES, Hon. Charles Keith, Politician. m. 1 son, 1 daughter. *Appointments:* Minister for Transport, Canberra 1972-75, M.H.R. (A.L.P.) for Newcastle N.S.W. since 1958, Opposition spokesman for Transport 1966-72, Post & Telecommunications & Tourism, 1977; Member Parliamentary Labor Party Executive 1966-75, 1977; Temporary Chairman of Committees 1964-67, 1980; Member of Australian Delegations 22nd Session of General Assembly of United Nations; Deputy Leader Australian Delegation to Inter Parliamentary Union Lisbon, 1978, Bonn, 1978, Prague, 1979, Caracas, 1979, Oslow, 1947-59, Lord Mayor, 1957; Inaugural Councillor Shortland County Council 1957-59. *Hobby:* Fishing. *Address:* Dangar House, 14 Brown Street, Newcastle, New South Wales, 2300, Australia.

JONES, Jack James Larkin, b. 29 Mar. 1913, Liverpool, United Kingdom. General Secretary, Transport and General Workers Union, (Retired). m. 24 Oct. 1938, 2 sons. *Education:* Elementary School, Liverpool. *Appointments:* Engineering Apprentice and Dock-Worker, 1937-39; Trade Union Official, 1939-, Executive Officer, TGWU, 1963, General Secretary, 1969-78. *Memberships:* General Council, Trade Union Congress; Transport International Committee TUC; National Ports Council; National Economic Development Council. *Publications:* Annual Dimbleby Lecture, 1977. *Honours:* Companion of Honour, 1978; DLitt (Hon) Warwick University; Visiting Fellow, Nuffield College, Oxford, 1970-78; Associate Fellow, London School of Economics, 1978-; Vice-President, International Transport Workers Federation, 1972-80; Founding member, Executive Board, European Trade Union Confederation; Fought in Spanish Civil War, International Brigade, Wounded Ebro Barrio, 1938. *Address:* 74 Ruskin Park House, Champion Hill, London SE5, England.

JONES, Leslie Thomas, b. 17 Mar. 1918, Christchurch, New Zealand. Electrical Engineer. m. Lillian Julie Hampton, 2 Dec. 1950, 2 sons, 1 daughter. *Education:* Electrical Engineering, Technical College and University; Member, Association of Supervising Electrical Engineers, England; Registered Electrician, New Zealdnd Institute of Electricians. *Appointments:* Managing Director and Major Share Holder, T L Jones and Son Limited, Electrical and Lift Engineers, Christchurch, New Zealand; Director, Several Associated Companies, and a Private Company in Christchurch. *Memberships:* New Zealand Crippled Children Society, Christchurch; Rotary; Christchurch Businessmens Club. *Hobbies:* Gardening; Power Boating. *Address:* 13 Clouston Street, St Martins, Christchurch 2, New Zealand.

JONES, Lloyd Hugh Parker, b. 3 Nov. 1922, Ballarat, Victoria, Australia. Research Chemist. m. Angela Alice Milne, 24 May 1962, 1 son, 1 daughter. *Education:* Queens College, University of Melbourne 1940-49; BAgrSc 1944; PhD 1949; CChem, FRSC, FRACI, FIBiol. *Appointments:* Officer in Charge, Mineral Nutrition Investigations Unit, Commonwealth Scientific and Industrial Research Organization, University of Melbourne and Honorary Lecturer in Agricultural Chemistry, 1953-67; Associate Research Soil Scientist, University of California, Berkeley, California, 1957; Research Soil Scientist, US Plant, Soil and Nutrition Laboratory, Ithaca, New Yor and Visiting Professor, Agronomy Department, Cornell University, 1965; Head, Soils and Plant Nutrition Department, (Senior Principal Scientific Officer), Grassland Research Institute, Hurley, Berkshire and member, Academic Staff, University of Reading, Berkshire, 1967-. *Memberships:* Royal Society of Chemistry; Royal Australian Chemical Institute; Institute of Biology; American Association for the Advancement of Science; Royal Society of Arts; Sigma Xi, The Scientific Research Society; American Chemical Society; American Society of Plant Physiologist; American Society of Agronomy; Society of Chemical Industry; Farmers' Club, London; Sciences Club, Melbourne. *Publications:* Contributions to scientific journals in Gt. Britain, USA and Australia; Silica in soils, plants and animals, 1967; Air pollution and plants and farm animals, 1978; The fate of heavy metals, 1981. *Honours:* James Cuming Prize in Agricultural

Chemistry, Melbourne University, 1943; Nuffield Foundation Dominion Travelling Fellowship in Natural Science, 1951-52; Advanced Fulbright Scholar, 1957. Hobby: Conservation of natural environment and man's cultural inheritance. *Address:* The Oaks, Station Road, Shiplake, Oxon RG9 3JR, England.

JONES, Michael Edward Wall, b. 4 Aug. 1944, Portsmouth, England. Physicist. *Education:* HNC Applied Physics, 1969; Graduate Examination Institute of Physics, 1971; Radiological Protection Course, 1972; Certificate for Teaching in Further Education, 1976; MSc in Subsea Systems, 1981. *Appointments:* Technical Assistant, Cynamid Great Britain Pharmaceutical Manufacturing Industry, 1961-64; Scientific Officer, Royal Naval Scientific Service, Admiralty Experiment Works: Hydrodynamics, 1965-72; Scientific Officer, Scientific Science, Institute Naval Medicine: Nuclear Physics, 1972-75; Lecturer-Freelance, 1976-78; Research Physicist, Offshore Technology and Subsea Systems, University of Glasgow, 1978-. *Memberships:* Institute of Physics; Graduate Inst. of Electronic and Radio Engs.; Society of Underwater Technology. *Publications:* Deep Water Oil and Gas Production and Manned Underwater Structures, 1981. *Hobbies:* Sailing; Industrial Archaeology; Alternative Technology; Reading. *Address:* Manuel Stables, Manuel Burn, Linlithgow, West Lothian, Scotland.

JONES, Norman William, b. 5 Nov. 1923, Chorlton-cum-Hardy, England. Banker. m. Evelyn June Hall, 18 Nov. 1950, 2 sons. *Education:* Gravesend Grammar School; Harvard Business School (A.M.P.). *Appointments:* Held various Managerial appointments in Head Office and London branches, 1940-72; Assistant General Manager, 1972; General Manager (Group Co-ordination) 1973; Assistant Chief General Manager, 1975; Deputy Group Chief Executive, 1976; Director, Main Board of Lloyds Bank Limited, 1976; Group Chief Executive, 1978. *Memberships:* Naval and Military Club; Overseas Bankers' Club. *Honours:* Territorial Decoration, 1962; Fellow of the Institute of Bankers, 1972. *Hobbies:* Sailing; Photography; D-I-Y; Gardening. *Address:* 21 College Avenue, Grays, Essex RM17 5UN, England.

JONES, Paul Tobin, b. 29 June 1949, Wolverhampton, England. Hotel General Manager. m. (Divorced), 1 daughter. *Education:* Diploma, Final Membership of the Hotel and Catering Institute. *Appointments:* Assistant Manager, Balalaika Hotel, Johannesburg; Food and Beverage Manager: Edward Hotel Durban, Kimberley Hotel Kimberley, Elanefani Hotel Durban, Landdrost Hotel Johannesburg; General Manager, Saint Geran Hotel, Casino and Golf Club, Mauritius. *Memberships:* Secretary, Mauritius Hotels and Restaurants Association; Gymkhana Club; Saint Geran Golf Club. *Publications:* Author: A Taste of Mauritius, 1980. *Honours:* Southern Sun Hotel Corporation, General Manager of the Year, 1980. *Hobbies:* Golf; Tennis; Jogging; Music; Cooking; Philately. *Address:* Saint Geran Hotel, Poste Restante, Mauritius.

JONES, Philip M, b. 12 Mar. 1928, Bath, England. Musician. m. Ursula Strebi, 1 Aug. 1956. *Education:* Royal College of Music London, ARCM, 1947. *Appointments:* Principal trumpet with all the major London Orchestras; Head of School of Wind and Percussion, Royal Northern School of Music, Manchester, 1975-77; Foundation of Philip Jones Brass Ensemble, 1951; Principally engaged in Ensemble activities, Editor of brass music for Chester Music London, 1977. *Creative Works:* About 40 records with Philip Jones Brass Ensemble; Just Brass, music series, Chester Music, London. *Honours:* OBE 1976; FRNCM 1977; Composers Guild Award 1979; Grand Prix du Disque 1977. *Hobbies:* Mountain Walking; Skiing. *Address:* 14 Hamilton Terrace, London NW8, England.

JONES, Roy Geoffrey, b. 9 July 1921, Charters Towers, Queensland. Chairman. m. Rae Gwen Morgan, 7 Feb. 1953, 4 sons. *Education:* Brisbane State High School, 1934-36; Associate, Australia Federal Institute of Accountants, 1948. *Appointments:* Wilson Meats Pty. Ltd. Brisbane, 1936, Company Secretary, 1948-58, General Manager, 1958-63; AIF, Pacific Area, 1941-44; F J Walker Limited, Sydney, Manager, 1963-68, Executive Director, 1968-77; Chairman, Australian Meat and Live-stock Corporation, 1977-; Association/Committee Membership: Chairman, NSW

Meat Exporters Association, 1966-68; Vice Chairman, Australian Meat Exporters Federal Council, 1967-69; Chairman, 1969-71, Vice Chairman, 1971-73; Member, Australian Meat Board, 1973-77, Research Committee, 1977-80, Chairman, 1980-; Australia-Japan Business Co-operation Committee, 1977; Executive member, Pacific Basin Economic Council, 1968-; Vice president, Australia-Korea Business Co-operation Committee, 1978-80, President, 1980; Australian Club, Sydney; Killara Golf Club; North Sydney Anzac Memorial Club. *Hobbies:* Golf; Swimming; Tennis. *Address:* 4A Bundabah Avenue, St Ives, NSW 2075, Australia.

JONES, William Gordon. b. 13 Jan. 1927, Port Pirie, South Australia. Corporate Relations Officer. m. Heather Doreen Piller, 5 March 1946, 2 daughters. *Education:* Port Pirie High School. *Appointments:* The Broken Hill Associated Smelters Limited, Port Pirie. *Memberships:* Mayor, City of Port Pirie, 1979-; Port Pirie City Council, 1963-; Sydney Journalist Club. *Honours:* Duke of Edinburgh's Commonwealth Study Conference, Canada, 1962; Awarded leader Grant by United States Government, 1964. *Address:* 139 Esmond Road, Port Pirie, South Australia 5540.

JOPLIN, Albert Frederick. b. 22 Feb. 1919, Victoria, Canada. Transportation Exective. m. (1) Margaret Brigid MacMorragh-Kavanaugh (dec) 1 daughter. (2) Dorothy Anne Cook, 29 July 1977. *Education:* Senior Matriculation, King Edward High School, Vancouver, 1938; B.A.p.Sc. Civil Engineering, University of British Columbia, 1948. *Appointments:* Various Engineering Appointments in British Columbia with Canadian Pacific Railway, 1947-62; Development Engineer, Vancouver, 1962-65; Manager, Special Projects, President, Project 200 Limited, General Manager, Marathon Realty, 1965-68; System Manager Planning Canadian Pacific, Montreal, 1968-69; Director, Development Planning, Canadian Pacific, 1969-71; Vice President, Marketing and Sales, 1971-74; Vice President, Operation and Maintenance, 1974-76; President and Chief Executive Officer, Canadian Pacific, Bermuda Limited, 1976-; Director of various Companies including: Shaw Industries Limited, Toronto; Expo Oil Limited, Sydney, Australia; Britannia Steamship Insurance, London; Canadian Pacific International Freight Services Limited; Canadian Pacific Shipmanagement (Hong Kong) Limited. *Memberships:* Association of Professional Engineers of British Columbia; Engineering Institute of Canada; Canadian Society of Civil Engineers; North American Society for Corporate Planning; The Bermuda Maritime Museum Association; The Bermuda Trust; The Bermuda Biological Research. *Honours:* Order of St. John, 1975; Royal Canadian Airforce, 1941-45. *Hobbies:* Golf; Photography. *Address:* Cliff Lodge, Harbour Road, Paget, Bermuda.

JORDAN, Alma Theodora, b. 29 Dec. 1929, Tunapuna, Trinidad, West Indies. Librarian. m. Lennox Jordan, 20 Oct. 1962. *Education:* B.A. Hons, London University, 1951; A.L.A. Eastern Caribbean Regional Library School, 1954; A.R.C.M. Royal College of Music, London, 1957; M.S. 1958, D.L.S. 1966, School of Library Service, Columbia University, New York. *Appointments:* Junior Assistant Librarian, 1949-52, Senior Assistant Librarian, 1952-54, Central Library of Trinidad and Tobago; Librarian-in-Charge, Carnegie Free Library, San Fernando, Trinidad, 1954-56; Librarian, Industrial Development Corporation, Trinidad, 1959-60; Campus Librarian, University of West Indies, Trinidad, 1960-. *Memberships:* Chairman, Standing Committee, Section for Latin America and the Caribbean, Federation of Library Associations, 1978-79; President, Association of Caribbean University Research and Institutional Libraries, 1969-70; President, Seminar on the Acquisition of Latin American Library Materials, 1978-79; Chairman, Library Association of Great Britain; Asociación Interamericana de Bibliotecarios y Documentalistas Agricolas. *Publications:* The development of Library Service in the West Indies through Inter-Library Co-operation (Scarecrow Press) 1970; Research Library Co-operation in the Caribbean; Papers of the first and second conferences of the Association of Caribbean, University and Research Libraries (ACURIL) Editor, (ALA), 1973. *Honours:* Beta Phi Mu, 1958; Grolier Society Fellowship, Columbia University, 1957-59; Acuril dedicatory honour, 1972. *Hobbies:* Music; Gardening. *Address:* 28 Gilwell Road, Valsayn Park, Valsayn, Trinidad and Tobago, West Indies.

JOSEPH (Major) V.I., b. 3 May 1930, Telok Anson, Perak. Institutional Manager. m. Margaret Jospeh, 10 Jan. 1953, 3 sons, 1 daughter. *Education:* St. John's Institution, Kuala Lumpur; Metropolitan College, St. Albans, London; M.I.M.A., London; M.R.S.H. *Appointments:* Superintendent of Hostels, University Technology Malaysia, Jalan Gurney, Kuala Lumpur. *Memberships:* Secretary-General, St. John Ambulance, Malaysia; Officer Commanding, 13 Malaysian Signal Squadron, (Territorial Army); Chairman, Indian Artistes Association, Kuala Lumpur; Patron, Tamil Bell Club. *Honours:* Long Service and Good Conduct Medal, St. John Ambulance, 1964; Pingat Peringat Malaysia (PPM) 1966; St. John (SB.St.J) 1966; Ahli Mangku Negara (AMN) 1970; Pingat Jasa Kebaktian (PJK) 1972; Kesatria Mangku Negara (KMN) 1974; Pingat Kebaktian (PK) 1978. *Hobbies:* Radio and Television; Public and Social Service. *Address:* 24 Jalan Maktab, Off Jalan Gurney, Kuala Lumpur 15-02.

JOY, Thomas Alfred, b. 30 Dec. 1904, Oxford, England. Company Director. m. Edith Ellis. *Education:* Bedford House, Oxford, England. *Appointments:* Librarian, Manager, Book Department, Harrods, London, 1935-45; Deputy Manager, Director, Army and Navy Stores, London, 1945-65; Managing Director, Hatchards Limited, Piccadilly, London, 1965-. *Memberships:* Book Trade Benevolent Society; Booksellers Association of Great Britain, 1957-58; Chairman, Education Board, 1954; Employers' Representative, President, Employers Bookselling and Stationery Trades Wages Council, 1946; Hon. Life Member, Society of Bookmen. *Publications:* The Right Way To Run a Library Business, 1949; Bookselling, 1953; The Truth about Bookselling, 1964; The Bookselling Business, 1974; Mostly Joy (autobiography) 1971. *Honours:* Royal Victoria Order, 1979; Queen's Silver Jubilee Medal, 1977; Fellow, Royal Society of Arts, 1967-. *Hobbies:* Reading; Salmon and trout fishing; Motoring; Travel. *Address:* 13 Cole Park Gardens, Twickenham, TW1 1JB, England.

JOYCE, William Joseph, b. 9 June 1932, Greymouth, New Zealand. Senior Inspector of Secondary Schools. m. Heather Edith Pitcaithly, 5 May 1963, 1 son, 3 daughters. *Education:* B.A., 1953, M.A., 1954, Canterbury University College, University of New Zealand; Diploma of Teaching, 1956. *Appointments:* Master, Palmerston North Boys High School, 1956-58; Master, Paeroa College, 1959-61; Master, Hastings Boys High School, 1962; Senior Assistant, Te Whanau-a-Apanui District High School, 1962-63; Lecturer, Auckland Teachers' College, 1963-64; Head of Department, Paeroa College, 1964-66; Head of Department, Otumoetai College, Tauranga, 1966-70; Inspector of Secondary Schools, Christchurch, 1970-72; Senior Inspector of Secondary Schools, Hamilton, 1972-. *Memberships:* President, Australasian Association of Institutes of Inspectors of Schools; Vice-President, New Zealand Association of Inspectors of Schools; District Governor's Representative, Rotary Club of Fairfield, District 999; New Zealand Geographical Association; Geographical Association; National Geographical Association. *Publications:* Articles in Educational Journals; Official Department of Education Publications. *Hobbies:* Travelling; Writing; Classical Music; Trout Fishing; Cacti Growing; Gardening; Swimming. *Address:* 1 Mayfair Avenue, Chartwell, Hamilton, New Zealand.

JUCHNOWICZ, Stanislaw, b. 10 June 1923, Lida, Poland. Architect; Town Planner; Professor. m. 15 July 1962, 3 daughters. *Education:* Fac. of Arch. BSc, Architecture, Technical University Lwow and Krakow, Poland, 1942-45; MSc Architecture, Technical University Gdansk, Poland, 1946-48; Research Fellow/Ford Foundation Grant, University of Pennsylvania, 1959-60; PhD, Technical Sciences, Krakow Poland 1962; DSc, Habitation in Urban and Regional Planning, Poland 1965. *Appointments:* Government Design Office, Gdansk, Poland, 1948-50; Planning and Design Office, Krakow, Poland, 1950-59; Technical University, Krakow, Poland, 1954-; University of Pennsylvania, Institute of Urban Studies, Philadelphia, USA, 1959-60; Ahmadu Bello University, Zaria, Nigeria 1973-81; United Nations Expert, Ibadan, Nigeria. *Memberships:* Numerous Societies including: International Union of Architects; Regional Science Association; Polish Institute of Architects. *Publications:* Author of numerous scientific papers and research studies on Urban and Regional Planning, Architectural and Environmental Problems. *Honours:* State Prize for creative achievements in Architecture and Town Planning, Poland 1956; Distinction in International Competition, Design of Monument of Warsaw Heroes, 1958. *Hobbies:* Classical Music; Tourism; Photography. *Address:* 6 Armii Ludowej Street, 31-537 Krakow, Poland.

JULIUS, Awdry Francis, b. 13 Nov. 1900, Fremantle, West Australia. Consulting Engineer (retired). m. (1) Agnes Yolande Wood Wansey, 15 June 1926, 1 son, 3 daughters, (2) Edna Mary Drane, 2 July 1972. *Education:* B.Eng., Honours, Sydney University, 1919-22. *Appointments:* General Electric Company, United States of America, 1923-25; Partner, 1943-51, Senior Partner, 195175, Julius, Poole and Gibson, Consulting Engineers, Sydney Australia, 1925-75. *Memberships:* Fellow, Member of Council, Institution of Engineers, Australia; 1st President, Member of Council, Hon. Life Member, Association of Consulting Engineers, Australia; Member of Council, Standards Association of Australia. *Honours:* The Consulting Engineers Advancement Society Medal awarded by the Association of Consulting Engineers for outstanding contribution to Australian Engineering. *Hobbies:* Golf; Lawn Bowls; Stamp collecting. *Address:* 6 Plymouth Close, Wahroonga, New South Wales, Australia 2076.

JUMBE, (Mwinyi) Aboud, b. 1920, Zanizbar. Tanzanian Politician. *Education:* Secondary School Zanzibar; Makerere University College Uganda. *Appointments:* Teacher 1946-50; Leader, Zanzibar National Union 1953; Zanizibar Township Council; Afro-Shirazi Party 1960-77; Organizing Secretary Head 1972-77; Vice Chairman, Chama Cha Mapinduzi 1977-; National Assembly of Zanzibar 1961-; Opposition Whip 1962-64; Minister of Home Affairs, Zanzibar 1964; Minister of State, First Vice-President's Office, Tanzania 1964-72; Ministry of Health and Social Services 1964-67; First Vice-President of Tanzania 1972-77, Vice-President 1977-; Chairman, Zanzibar Revolutionary Council 1972. *Address:* Office, Vice-President, Zanzibar, United Republic of Tanzania.

K

KABDEBO, Thomas, b. 5 Feb. 1934, Budapest, Hungary. Librarian. m. Agnes Lily, 1959, 2 daughters. *Education:* University of Budapest, 1956; BA, University of Wales, UK, 1959; Librarianship Diploma, University of London, UK, 1961; MPhil., 1969; MPhil, Library Association of Great Britain, 1975. *Appointments:* Assistant Librarian, University College, London, UK, 1961-69; Librarian, University of Guyana, South America, 1969-72; Librarian, City of London Polytechnic, UK, 1973-74; Sub-Librarian, University of Manchester, UK, 1974-. *Memberships:* Member of Professional Associations including: Fellowship, Library Association; PEN. *Publications:* Author of several books including: Hundred Hungarian Poems Minden Idök (of all times), 1978. *Honours:* Short story competitions winner, 1952, 1975; Poetry prizes, 1969, 1971. *Hobbies:* Fishing; Sailing. *Address:* 6 Albion Road, Manchester 14, England.

KABIR, Lutful, b. 1 Feb. 1918, Village-Uttarballavpur, Post office-Darogahat, District-Noakhali, Bangladesh. Teacher. m. 15 July 1943, 3 sons, 5 daughters. *Education:* BA, Dacca University, Bangladesh, 1941; LL.B., Calcutta University, India, 1955; PhD. in Law, London University, UK, 1965. *Appointments:* Assistant, Office of Director General Munition and Production, Ministry of Defence, Government of India, 1942-43; Viceroy's Cōmmissioned Officer, His Majesty's Indian Land Forces, Royal Indian Army Service Corps, 1943-46; Senior Lecturer in Law, 1955-67, Associate Professor in Law, 1967-73, Professor of Law, 1973-80, Head of Department of Law, 1972-74, Dean of the Faculty of Law, 1972-77, Provost of Surja Sen Hall, 1972-77, Law Officer, 1976-77, Dacca University Bangladesh; Visiting Professor, University of Dar-es-Salaam, Tanzania, 1980-. *Memberships:* Dacca University Club. *Publications:* Land Laws of Bangladesh; Lectures on Penal Code; Roman Law; The Rights and Liabilities of Raiyats under the Bengal Tenancy Act, 1885 and the State Acquisition and Tenancy Act, 1950; *Honours:* War Medal for meritorious services, 1946; University Gold Medal; Kedarnath Banerjee Gold Medal; J Chaudhury Silver Medal; Sir William Ritchie Prize; University Prize in books; S N Law College Prize in books, 1955; recently recommended for UNESCO Prize. *Hobbies:* Gardening; Horticulture. *Address:* c/o Mrs Dileara Muhit, 1/7E Asad Avenue, Mahammadpur, Dacca-7, Bangladesh.

KABLE, Herbert John, b. 28 June 1953, Hobart, Tasmania, Australia. Legal Practitioner. *Education:* LL.B., University of Tasmania, Australia; Barrister and Solicitor, Supreme Court of Tasmania, Australia, 1977. *Appointments:* Associate to Honourable Chief Justice of Tasmania, Australia, 1975-76; Legal Practitioner, 1977-79; Partner in Legal firm, Zeeman and Kable, 1980-. *Memberships:* Tasmanian Racing and Gaming Commission; Committee member, Tasmanian Bar Association. *Hobbies:* Sport; Theatre. *Address:* 13 Bennet Street, Launceston, Tasmania 7250, Australia.

KADAFUR, Usman Alhaji, b. 1928, Biu, Borno State, Nigeria. m. 2 May 1952, 2 sons, 2 daughters. *Education:* School of Medical Auxiliaries, 1949-50. *Appointments:* Civil Servant, Biu Local Government, Nigeria, 1948-68; Business, 1968-. *Memberships:* President, Lake Tilla Club; Chairman, Jama a tu Nasurul Islam. *Hobby:* Farming. *Address:* J/32 Ali G. Street, Biu, Borno State, Nigeria.

KAEDING, Gregory Fredrick, b. 23 Dec. 1955, Swanborne, Western Australia. Environmental Scientist. m. Rowena Marian Grist, 13 Dec. 1980. *Education:* Bachelor of Applied Science, (Chemistry/Geology), 1980; Certificate of Applied Chemistry, 1972; Diploma of Applied Chemistry, 1974. *Appointments:* Research Assistant (Soil Chemistry), Department of Soil Science and Plant Nutrition, University of Western Australia, 1973-78; Research Assistant (Plant Physiology), 1978-80, Environmental Scientist, 1981-, Alcoa Australia Limited, Pinjarra, Western Australia. *Memberships:* Ecological Society, Australia; Australian Society of Plant Physiologists; Alumni Association of the Western Australian Institute of Technology. *Publications:* Mineralisable Organic Nitrogen in Soil Fractionated According to Particle Size, 1979; Assessment of Topsoil

Handling Techniques for Rehabilitation of Sites Mined for Bauxite Within the Jarrah Forest of Western Australia, 1980; Development and Evaluation of a Rapid Technique for the Physical Breakdown of Lateritic Soil Cores Suited to the Determination of Root Content Environmental Research Note, 1980. *Honours:* Phillips Industries Prize for Laboratory Technique and Laboratory Practices, Mount Lawley Technical College, 1972. *Hobbies:* Canoeing; Caving; Climbing; Hiking; Numismatics; Philately. *Address:* 34 Lofties Street, Forrestdale, Western Australia 6112, Australia.

KAGGWA, Norbert, b. 19 Mar. 1938, Mitala Maria, Mpigi District, Central Buganda Province. Artist; Lecturer; Development Educator. m. Betty Nakityo, 19 Feb. 1966, 3 sons, 2 daughters. *Education:* Diploma, Margaret Trowell School of Art, Diploma, Makerere University, Kampala, Uganda, 1958-62; Diploma, Postgraduate Training, Makerere University, Kampala, Uganda, 1962-64. *Appointments:* Head of Art Department, Trinity College, Nabbingo, Uganda, 1964-66; Art Lecturer, Head of Department, National Teachers College, Kampala, Uganda, 1966-81; Consultant, Contractual Visual Communication, Pan African Afrolit Society, 1980-. *Memberships:* Chairman, African Association for Developmental Communication; Chairman, Uganda National Art Panel; Life member/Consultant, Pan African Afrolit Society; African Adult Education Association; Uganda National Adult Education Association. *Publications:* Articles subscribed for training manual 'Illustrations for Development'. *Hobbies:* Photography; Traditional music and related dances. *Address:* PO Box 4214, Kampala, Uganda.

KAHN, Razia Amin, b. 16 Feb. 1936, Faridpur, Bangladesh. Lecturer. m. A Amin Khan, 3 Mar. 1961, 1 son, 1 daughter. *Education:* BA(Hons) English 1957; MA, English and American Literature, Dacca 1958; MA, English Literature, Birmingham United Kingdom 1961. *Appointments:* Editor, Children's Page Young Pakistan 1955-56; Casual Artist, English, Bengali Announcer, Drama Artist Dacca Radio 1955-59; Part-time Lecturer in English Central Womens' College Dacca 1958-59; Lecturer, Rajshahi Varsity, 1959, Senior Editor, Dacca Observer 1961-62; Senior Lecturer, Associate Professor, Dacca 1962-. *Memberships:* Film Censor Board, Censor Reforms Committee; National Film Awards Committee; Films Society; Bangladesh Federation of Film Societies. *Publications:* PEN Award winning play Aborto 1956; Novel, Anukalpa, Baftala 1958; Bengali Poetry, Mahfil, Indiana University Journal, Chitra Bengali novel 1975; Argus, English Poetry 1956; Camel A Peril 1977; Shonali Bengali Poetry 1978; Kabya novel in Bengali 1980. *Honours:* Pope Gold Medal, English Literature 1957; PEN Student prize for play 1956; Bengali Academy Award, 1974. *Hobbies:* Travelling; Entertaining; Listening to European Classical Music. *Address:* House 30 Road 30, Grulshan, Dacca, Bangladesh.

KAINJA, Gautoni, b. 25 May 1956, Lilongwe, Malawi. Lawyer. *Education:* LL.B.(Hons.), 1980. *Appointments:* Legal practitioner, 1980. *Memberships:* Law Society of Malawi. *Honours:* Awarded the National Bank Best Student Award, 1980. *Hobbies:* Reading; Films. *Address:* Mguwata Village, PO Box 567, Lilongwe, Malawi.

KAJUBI, Nuwa Womeraka, b. 29 Mar. 1928, Makeerere, Kampala, Uganda. Educationist. m. Ada Navuga Lubinga, 6 Nov. 1954, 3 sons, 1 daughter. *Education:* Makeerere University College, Kampala, Uganda, 1949-51; AB. (Sec. Ed,), Eastern Mennonite College, Virginia, USA, 1955-56; Post Graduate Certificate, in Education, University of Exeter, UK, 1956-57; Further Post-Graduate work, University of Glasgow, Scotland, 1963-64; UNESCO Short Fellowship, Bolton College of Education (Technical), Bolton, UK, 1979. *Appointments:* Teacher, Ndejje Junior Secondary School, Bbombo, Uganda, 1952; Teacher, Lubiri Secondary School, Kampala, Uganda, 1957-58; Tutor, Namutamba Teacher Training College, Mityana, Uganda, 1959-63; Lecturer, National Teachers Training College, 1964-65; Teacher, Kako Secondary School, Masaka, Uganda, 1965; Teacher, Kibuli Secondary School, Kampala, Uganda, 1966-69; Headmaster, Iganga Secondary School, Busoga, Uganda, 1969-72; Lecturer, National Teachers College, Kyambogo, Kampala, Uganda, 1972; Tutor, St. John the Baptist's Teacher Training College, Ggaba, Kampala, Uganda, 1972-77; Senior Lecturer and Head of Department, 1977-, Uganda

Technical College, Kyambogo, Kampala, Uganda. *Memberships:* Hon. Adviser, Scripture Union of Uganda; Board member, African Evangelistic Enterprise; Life member, The Bible Society of Uganda; Committee member, The Uganda Keswick Convention. *Publications:* Edit- Technology Perspective, 1981; Edited Institution Magazines at 3 colleges. *Hobbies:* Bible related writing; Light reading; Singing. *Address:* Makeerere Village, PO Box 16044, Kampala, Uganda.

KAKODKAR, Purushottam, b. 18 May 1913, Kakodem, Post Curchorem, Goa, India. Socio-political Worker. m. Kamala, 20 June 1941, 1 son, 1 daughter. *Education:* Portuguese Lyceum Course for 3 years; Shastri Degree, Government College, Benares, India, 1939. *Appointments:* Ten years in political exile in Portugal, 1946-56; Elected and re-elected President of State Committee of Indian National Congress Party, 1962-72 and 1978-79; Elected Member of Parliament, House of the People, 1971-77. *Memberships:* Associated Life member, Indian Parliamentary Group of the Inter-Parliamentary Union; Member-Trustee, The Tristao Braganza Cunha Charity Trust, Panjim, Goa, India. *Address:* Kakodhar Printing Press, Margao Goa, India.

KALE, Balvant Keshav, b. 24 Nov. 1933, Dhulia, India. Professor of Statistics. m. Donde Sushila Malhar, 25 Dec. 1956, 1 son, 1 daughter. *Education:* BA.(Hons.), 1954, MA, 1956, University of Bombay, India; PhD, University of Poona, India, 1963. *Appointments:* Lecturer, University of Bombay, India, 1962-64; Faculty Member, Iowa State University, Ames, USA, 1964-67; Professor and Head of Department of Statistics, University of Manitoba, Winnipeg, Canada, 1967-79; Professor of Statistics, University of Poona, India, 1976-78, 1979-. *Memberships:* American Statistical Association; Indian Statistical Association; Statistical Society of Canada; Founder member, Statistical Association of Manitoba, Canada; Governing Council of Indian Statistical Association. *Publications:* Several research publications including a book in the areas of Statistical Inference with current emphasis on inference problems for data involving possible outliers; Associate Editor of Canadian Journal of Statistics, 1976-79, Utilitas Mathematica, 1971, Journal Indian Statistical Association, 1979; Reviewer for Zentralblatt für Mathematik, 1964-; Referred several papers for Statistical Journals in USA; Canada; India. *Honours:* Fellow of American Statistical Association, 1971; Visiting Lecturer for Statistical Societies of North America, 1972-75, 1976-79; Recipient of research grants from National Science foundation, USA, National Science and Engineering Research Council, Canada, University Grants Commission, India; Presented invited talks-seminars at many Universities in Canada, Japan, India, UK and USA. *Hobbies:* Music; Literature; Cricket; Badminton; Bridge. *Address:* 3 Divyakunj Apts, Gokhale Road, Pune MS, India, 411016.

KALENGA, Bibiana Chibomba, b. 1 May 1946, Monze, Zambia. Librarian. m. George, 14 Apr. 1968, 2 sons, 2 daughters. *Education:* Diploma in Library Studies, University of Zambia, 1974. *Appointments:* Library Assistant, Lusaka Public Library, 1968-71; Assistant Librarian, Department of Technical Education and Vocational Training, 1971-76; Librarian, National Institute of Public Administration, 1977-. *Memberships:* Board of Library studies representing Government Libraries, University of Zambia, School of Education; Zambia Library Association. Hobby: Reading. *Address:* Plot 6125 Mwinilunga Road, Sunningdale, Lusaka, Zambia.

KALKOA, George Ati, b. 1937, Vanuata(formerly New Hebrides); Politician. m. 3 sons *Education:* Teachers Training College, Fiji, 1955-1956; Senior Administration Course, Fiji, 1970; *Appointments:* British National Service Education Department, later transferred to British National Service Administration; seconded to Solomon Islands, 1961; Assistant Secretary for Social Services, British Residency Vila, 1970-1977; Twice elected to Advisory Council, 1964 and 1968-1974; Elected to Representative Assembly 1975; Minister of Public Administration in Government of National Unity 1978; President Elect 1980. *Memberships:* Founder Member Vanuaaku Pati. *Honours:* President Elect 1980, awarded chiefly rank, and now known as SO-KOMANU, His Excellency Ati George. *Address:* Port Vila, Vanuata (formerly New Hebrides).

KALOKERINOS, James, b. 2 June 1926, Glen Innes, NSW, Australia. Medical Practitioner. m. Jocelyn R Marshall, 30 Apr. 1958, 1 son. *Education:* MB, BS, Sydney 1948; DMRD, London 1956; FFR, London 1960; ROHAN 1964; FCRA 1966; FACBS 1968; FRCP, Edinburgh 1981. *Appointments:* RMO Sydney Hospital 1948-50; Receiving Officer, Hillingdon Hospital 1951-53; Registrar, Glasgow Royal Infirmary 1955-56; Director Radiology, Royal North Shore Hospital, Sydney 1956-67; Radiological Practice, Newcastle Australia 1967-. *Memberships:* Celtic Fellowship of Australia; Gaelic Association of Australia. *Hobbies:* Traditional Scottish Gaelic Music; Woodworking. *Address:* 82 Violet Town Road, Belmont North, NSW, Australia 2280.

KALSAKAU, George Kaltoi, b. 14 Aug. 1930, Port Vila, Vanuatu New Hebrides. Policeman. m. 23 June 1955, 6 sons, 4 daughters. *Education:* Iririki District School, Port Vila, 1945-46; High School, All Hallows School, Pawa, BS Protectorate, 1949-51; Certificate, UK, 1959-60; Fiji CID and SB courses, 1966; Certificate Australia, 1975. *Appointments:* Clerk, Presbyterian, Paton Memorial Hospital, Vila, 1947-48; Wireless Operator TSF Condominium Government Vila, 1952-53; Police, British Division of New Hebrides Constabulary, 1953-77; NH Self Government, Chief Minister, 1978; President of the National Assembly 1978-79; Vanuatu Capital City, Port Vila, Mayor, 1981. *Memberships:* President, Kiwanis Club of Port Vila; President, British Supervised Co-operative Federation Vanuatu, New Hebrides. *Honours:* Guard Commander for the Joint Guard of Honour for Prince Philip's visit, 1971; Guard Commander for the Joint Guard of Honour for the Queen's visit, 1974; Member of Constitutional Committee 1979; Colonial Police Forces for long Service and Good Conduct, 1953-71. *Hobbies:* Gardening; Fishing; Cricketing. *Address:* Fila Island, Port Vila, Box 911, New Hebrides.

KALU, Udensi Esowe, b. 31 Oct. 1928, Okon-Aku, Ohafia, Aro/Ohafia LGA, Imo State, Nigeria. Librarian. m. 10 Jan. 1957, 6 sons. *Education:* ALA, 1963, School of Librarianship, Loughborough, Leics, England, 1959-63; MSLS, 1977, MA,(Educ.) 1977, Case Western Reserve University, Cleveland, Ohio, USA, 1976-77. *Appointments:* Librarian, Yaba College of Technology, Lagos, 1963-64; Assistant Librarian, University of Lagos Library, 1964-66; Librarian, 1966, Senior Librarian, 1978-, Nnamdi Azikiwe Library, University of Nigeria, Nsukka. *Memberships:* Chairman, Okon Ohafia Development Union, 1977; British Library Association, 1951-; Nigerian Library Association, 1956-; Alumni Association Case Western Reserve University Cleveland, Ohio, 1977-; Board of Governors, Okamu Secondary Commercial School, 1980-; International Association for the Development of Documentation, Libraries &· Archives in Africa, 1979-. *Publications:* Compiled an annotated list of Periodicals & Annuals of the United Nations System available at Nnamdi Azikiwe Library, University of Nigeria, 1979; Paper, An Overview of the United Nations Publications at Nnamdi Azikiwe Library, 1981. *Hobbies:* Fishing; Swimming; Dancing. *Address:* Nnamdi Azikiwe Library, University of Nigeria, Nsukka, Anambra State, Nigeria.

KAMARA, Karifa Ibrahim Sahid, b. 19 Oct. 1944, Kabala, Sierra Leone. Doctor. m. (1) 21 Jan. 1970, 2 sons, 1 daughter, (2) Margaret Ebun Nancy Davies, 22 Aug. 1981. *Education:* MD, Kuban Medical Institute, Krasnodar, USSR, 1969; RAMC, Milbank London & Aldershot, 1973. *Appointments:* Medical Officer, Ministry of Health Freetown, 1969-70, RSLMF Military Hospital, 1971-; Presently on Specialist Training ib Obstetrics and Gynaecology, on the University Hospital, Utrecht, Holland. *Hobbies:* Reading; Cricket; Football; Table Tennis; Music. Department of Obstetrics and Gynaecology, University Hospital, Catharijnesingel 101, 3500 CG Utrecht, P.B. 16250, Holland.

KAMBA, Angeline Saziso (Mrs Walter Joseph Kamba), b. 15 Oct. 1935, Plumtree, Zimbabwe. Librarian. m. 2 Aug. 1960, 3 sons. *Education:* BA, (S.A.), 1957; PCE, London, 1958; MLS, Columbia Univrrsity, New York, 1964. *Appointments:* Assistant Librarian, US Information Service Library, Salisbury, 1959-62; Assistant Librarian, University of Rhodesia, 1964-67; Senior Assistant Librarian, University of London Library, Senate House, 1967-69; Senior Assistant Librarian, University of Dundee, 1969-80; Director, Zimbabwe National Archives, 1981-. *Memberships:* Zimbabwe Library Association; East & Central African Regional Branch of the International Council on Archives. *Hobbies:* Opera; Theatre; Reading; Yoga. *Address:* University of Zimbabwe, PO Box MP 167, Mount Pleasant, Salisbury, Zimbabwe.

KAMBALAMETORE, James Torrey, b. 30 June 1948, Thyolo, Malawi. Chartered Quantity Surveyor. m. Sylvia Vaneress Kaliwo, 30 June 1973, 3 sons. *Education:* Diploma in Building Economics, 1973; Associate Royal Institution of Chartered Surveyors, 1976. *Appointments:* Messrs Gardiner and Theobald, UK, 1973-76; Malawi Housing Corporation, 1977-79; Fitzsimons Northcrofts Associates, 1979-. *Hobbies:* Soccer; Basketball; Softball; Casual Reading. *Address:* PO Box 12, Namadzi 21, Malawi.

KAMBARAMI, Gaylord Tonderayi, b. 17 July 1937, Mrewa, Zimbabwe. Executive Director. m. Angeline Chikwaira, 18 Jan. 1961, 2 sons, 2 daughters. *Education:* Diploma in National Commercial Course, 1958; BSc, Business Administration and Finance, 1968. *Appointments:* Records Clerk, 1956-58; Assistant Storeman, 1959-64; Financial Analyst, 1968-70; Market Research Executive, 1970-71; Business Manager, 1971-76; Executive Director, 1976-. *Memberships:* Chairman Mabvuku Secondary School PTA; National Treasurer of Christian Care and Zimbabwe Christian Council; District Treasurer, United Methodist Church; Executive of the Bible Societies in Africa; Executive and Council Secretary, United Theological College. *Publications:* Annual Reports including: Good News for Rhodesia, God's Word Released His People, The Word and You, A Decade of Translation, Printing and Distribution; The World Aflame. *Hobbies:* Tennis; Soccer; Debates. *Address:* 3 Malvern Road, Mount Pleasant, Salisbury, Zimbabwe.

KAMESWARI, Sistla, b. 3 June 1929, Srikakulam, Andhra Pradesh. Scientist. m. Sistla Sakshi Sidhanti, 15 Mar. 1968. *Education:* BSc, (Chem), Andhra University, 1951; MSc, (Phys.Chem), Nagpur University, 1953; PhD, (DTA of Solid Catalysts), Indian Institute of Technology, Khargpur, 1957. *Appointments:* Research Fellow, Gas Council, Fulham, London, 1957-58; Senior Research Fellow, Central Building Research Institute, Roorkee, 1959-60; Postdoctoral Fellow, Alfred University, Alfred, NY, USA, 1960-63; Pool Officer, Indian Institute of Technology, Delhi, 1964-65; Visiting Scientist, Chemical Technology, Delft, The Netherlands, 1966-67; Pool Officer, Regional Research Laboratory, Hyderabad, 1967-68; Scientist, Defence Metallurgical Research Laboratory, Hyderabad, 1969-. *Memberships:* Secretary, Overseas Science Students Association, London; American Chemical Society; Sigma Xi Alfred University, NY, USA; Catalysis Society of India; Core Group; Indian Women Scientists Association. *Publications:* Author of several papers and reports on hetregeneous catalysis Surface Chemistry and hot corrosion in gas turbines. *Honours:* Atoms for Peace Certificate, 1956. *Hobbies:* Games; Photography; Welfare activities of women. *Address:* 6-3-609/192, Anand Nagar, Khairatabad, Hyderabad, 500004, India.

KAMSAH, Kamariyah, b. 14 May 1954, Malaysia. Student, Landscape Architecture, Urban Planning. *Education:* Diploma in Architecture, Mara Institute of Technology, 1975; Bachelor of Landscape Architecture, Mississippi State University, 1978; Master of Landscape Architecture, University of Illinois, 1981. *Appointments:* Assistant Lecturer, Mara Institute of Technology, 1975; Draughtsman/Designer, LTA Ltd., Mississippi, 1977-78; Returning to Mara Institute of Technology, Malaysia, as a Lecturer in 1981. *Memberships:* Malaysian Institute of Architects. *Publications:* Undergraduate Thesis; Master's Project; Urban Planning Workshop Group Project. *Honours:* Mara Institute of Technology Young Lecturer Scholarship. *Hobby:* Handcraft. *Address:* 7, SS12/3B Subang Jaya, Selangor, Malaysia.

KAMVAZINA, Samuel Simon, b. 3 Mar. 1945, Chileka, Blantyre District, Malawi, Africa. Veterinary Surgeon. m. Felisters Liabuba, 29 Sept. 1973, 2 sons, 3 daughters. *Education:* DVSc, Nairobi; Diploma in Tropical Veterinary Medicine, University of Edinburgh, Scotland. *Appointments:* District Veterinary Officer, Blantyre, 1971-72; Veterinary Education Officer, Mikolongwe Assistant Training School, 1973-74; Re-

gional Veterinary Officer, Central Region, Malawi, 1974-76; Deputy Chief Veterinary Officer, 1976-79, Chief Veterinary Officer, 1980-, Ministry of Agriculture and Natural Resources. *Memberships:* Centre for Tropical Veterinary Medicine; Chairman, SARCCUS, Standing Committee for Animal Health. *Hobbies:* Football; Lawn Tennis; Music. *Address:* c/o Traditional Authority, Kuntaja, Lemu Village, Chileka, Blantyre, Malawi, Africa.

KAN, Lai-bing, b. Hong Kong. Librarian. *Education:* BSc, University of Hong Kong, 1957; MA, MLS, University of California, Berkeley, 1959; PhD, University of Hong Kong, 1968; Medlars Search Analyst Certificate, National Library of Medicine, USA, 1969; Grade I Certification of American Medical Library Association; ALAA, Australia; MI Inf. Sc. Great Britain. *Appointments:* Held various positions at the University of Hong Kong Libraries, 1959-70; Deputy Librarian, University of Hong Kong Libraries, 1970-72; University Librarian and Director of the University Library System, The Chinese University of Hong Kong, 1972-. *Memberships:* Hong Kong Library Association; Australian Library Association; Institute of Information Scientists. *Publications:* Numerous publications including bibliographical works, books and journal articles on libraries and librarianship. *Hobbies:* Theatres; Concerts and other cultural activities. *Address:* University Library, The Chinese Library of Hong Kong, Shatin, NT., Hong Kong.

KAN, Shiu-Cheong Frederick, b. 10 Jan. 1948, Canton, China. Executive Director; Deputy General Manager. m. Liang Yee-woo Evelyna, 1 Sept. 1973, 1 son. *Education:* BComm, University of British Columbia, Canada, 1974. *Appointments:* Credit Officer, Canadian Imperial Bank of Commerce; Assistant Bank Manager, Federal Business Development Bank; Executive Director & Deputy General Manager, Wing Tat Electric Manufacturing Company Limited. *Hobbies:* Sailing; Swimming; Tennis. *Address:* 38A Kennedy Road, 5/F Hong Kong.

KANNAPPAN, Janauikulan Gangadharan, b. 26 Dec. 1934, Coimbatore, Tamil Nadu, India. Orthodontist. m. J K Vasuki, 14 Sept 1961, 2 sons, 1 daughter. *Education:* Bachelor of Dental Surgery, 1957; Master of Dental Surgery (Orthodontics), 1965; PG Training in Paedodontics, London, 1970; Postgraduate Training Course, Hawaii, 1979. *Appointments:* Assistant Reader, 1958-63, Lecturer, 1960-63; Lecturer, 1966-69, Reader, 1969, 1970, Madras Medical College, Madras; Lecturer, 1960-63, 1965-66, Professor, 1981-, Madurai Medical College, Madurai; Professor, 1970-81, Vice-Principal, 1980; Madras Dental College, Madras; Professor, Madurai Medical College, Madurai, 1981. *Memberships:* Indian Dental Association; Indian Orthodontic Society; Tamil Nadu Dental Council; Dental Council of India; Indian Academy of Paediatics; Vice-President, Association of Independent Medical Practitioner of India. *Publications:* Author of Three books in Dentristry; Compiled the Proceedings of Scientific Sessions; Published many scientific papers and read many scientific papers in International Conferences. *Honours:* Scientific School Prize; Book Award, Tamil nadu Government; Plaque Award by Presidnet, Tamil nadu Dental Council; Roll of Honour for 25 years continuous service to the Society. *Hobby:* Teaching. *Address:* Shenbagan Illam, 109 Dr. Radhakrishnan Salai, Madras-600004, India.

KANTUMOYA, Eustace Estance Nyachabashi, b. 7 May 1949, Mwinilunga, Chie Ikelenge. Administrator; Librarian. m. 1970, 1 son, 1 daughter. *Education:* BA, Majored in Public Asministration, Minored in Library Science, 1975. *Appointments:* Adminstrative Manager, Posts & Telecommunications Corporation; Librarian, Kitwe City Council. *Memberships:* Vice-Chairman, Zambia Library Association. *Hobbies:* Table Tennis; Football; Athletics. *Address:* 810B Lukasu Drive, Parklands, Kitwe, Zambia.

KANU, Dr. Sheka Hassan, b. 12 Apr. 1932, Petifu, Port Loko District, Sierra Leone. University Lecturer; Diplomat. m. Fatmatta Bangurah, 16 9 1965, 2 sons, 5 daughters. *Education:* BA(Hons), Teacher's Advanced Certificate, Fourah Bay College; MA, 1967, PhD, 1971, University of Alberta, Canada. *Appointments:* Collegiate School, Freetown, 1956-61; Service Assistant, 1966-67. Teaching Assistant, 1967-69, Lecturer,

1970-71, University of Alberta, Canada; Lecturer, Njala University College, Sierra Leone, 1971-72; Deputy Commissioner for Sierra Leone, London, 1972-73; Ambassador Extraordinary & Plenepotentiary, Federal Republic of Germany, 1973-78, Belgium, The Netherlands and Luxembourg, 1978-; Ambassador to the Commission of the EEC, Brussels, 1978-. *Publications:* A World of Everlasting Conflict, Joyce Cary's view of man and society, 1974. *Honours:* Member of the Order of the Republic of Sierra Leone, 1976; Grand Cross of the Federal Republic of Germany, 1978. *Address:* 21 Beukenlaan, 1980 Tervuren, Brussels, Belgium.

KANUNGO, Madhu Sudan, b. 1 Apr. 1927, Berhampur, Orissa, India. Professor; Biochemist. m. Sarat Kanungo, 21 Apr. 1954, 3 sons. *Education:* BSc (Hons.), Utkal University, Orissa, 1949; MSc (Zoology), Lucknow University, Lucknow, 1951; PhD (Physiology), University of Illinois, USA, 1959. *Appointments:* Lecturer, 1952-61, Reader, 1961-62, Utkal University, Orissa; Reader, 1962-69, Professor, 1970-, Head, Department of Zoology, 1974-76, 1980-, Banaras Hindu University, Varanasi; Visiting Professor of Biochemistry, West Virginia University, USA, 1978. *Memberships:* Life, Executive, Society Biological Chemists (India), 1970-76; Gerontological Society of America, 1978-79; Editorial Boards of three International Journals; University Grants Commission; Council of Scientific Industrial Research; Department Atomic Energy; Indian Council Medical·Research. *Publications:* Biochemistry of Ageing, Academic Press, London, 1980; Published 98 original papers on Biochemistry of Ageing in international journals. *Honours:* Shanti Swarup Bhatnagar Prize for outstanding contributions to Biology, 1971; National Fellow, University Grants Commission, India, 1975-77; Fellow, Indian National Science Academy, New Delhi, 1975-, Indian Academy of Sciences, Bangalore, 1975-; President, Association of Gerontology (India). *Hobbies:* Tennis; Writing. *Address:* New G/1 Jodhpur Colony, Banaras Hindu University, Varanasi—221005, India.

KANU-OJI, Okoronkwo, b. 13 Nov. 1935, Amasu, Arochukwu. Marketing. m. Chinyere Okike, 30 Dec. 1967, 4 sons, 2 daughters. *Education:* Teacher's Grade III Certificate, 1955; Teacher's Grade II Certificate 1959; BSc,)econs.) London 1964. *Appointments:* Teacher, Provincial T.T. College Agbede 1958-60; Manager and Divisional Manager, British-American Tobacco Company Limited, Nigerian Tobacco Company Limited, 1964-76; Marketing Manager and Head of Marketing Department, Golden Guinea Breweries Limited 1976-80; Executive Chairman, Koon, Nigeria, Limited, 1980-. *Memberships:* Nigerian Institute of Management; British Institute of Management; Fellow, Royal Economic Society; Institute of Marketing, United Kingdom; Institute of Sales Technology and Management, UK; American Marketing Association; Trade Policy Research Entre, UK; Boys Scout Movement-Leader; Old Friend Students Christian Movement. *Publications:* Marketing in Nigeria, A new Analysis; Articles written between 1965-81: Management Training in Nigeria; What I consider as the missing link; Industrial Restrictive practices—The Nigerian outlook; Industrial Relations in Nigeria—the new dimensions; What business expects of the Commercial Education graduate; Review of Mr R I Ropers, Labour problems in West Africa. *Hobbies:* Tennis, Lawn and Table; Gardening; Reading; Writing. *Address:* 58 Eket Street, Umuahia, Nigeria.

KAO, Jih Chung, b. 4 Nov. 1920, China (Foochow). Bishop of Methodist Church in Singapore. m. Lim Ai Lang, 5 Sept. 1949, 1 son, 4 daughters. *Education:* Nanking Theological College, 1948. *Appointments:* Pastor: Bukit Panjang Chinese Methodist Church, Singapore, 1946; Hakka Methodist Church, Singapore, 1961; Chinese Methodist Church, Teluk Anson, Malaysia, 1962; Malacca Chinese Methodist Church, Malaysia, 1963; Toa Payoh Chinese Methodist Church, Singapore, 1974; Bishop, The Methodist Church in Singapore, 1977-. *Memberships:* Chairman, Board of Governors: Anglo-Chinese, Primary & Junior Schools; Anglo-Chinese Junior College; Methodist Chinese School; Chairman, Management Committee: Fairfield Methodist Girls' School; Paya Lebar Methodist Girls' School. *Hobby:* Swimming. *Address:* 50 Barker Road, Singapore 1130.

KAPADIA, Ramanlai Ichharam, b. 3 Apr. 1934. Barrister; Solicitor. m. Kalaben, 24 Nov. 1960, 1 son, 1 daughter. *Education:* BA, University of London; Barrister-at-Law (Middle Temple); Commissioner for Oaths; Notary Public. *Appointments:* Practising Barrister, 1958-; Member of the Upper House of Parliament of Fiji, 1970-. *Memberships:* Leader of Government Business in the Senate, 1979-; Chairman of several select committees of the Senate; Suva City Council, 1964-67; Official Arbitrator to settle several industrial disputes. *Hobbies:* Tennis; Yoga. *Address:* 83 Cakobau Road, Suva, Fiji.

KAPUR, Dr. Ashok Kimar, b. 8 Nov. 1942, Nairobi. Medical Practitioner. m. Jeanette E Lasplace, 9 Jan. 1971, 2 daughters. *Education:* MB, ChB, Makerere University, East Africa, 1965. *Appointments:* Medical Officer, Nairobi City Council, 1966; Army Regimental Medical Officer, Captain, 1967-70. *Memberships:* Officer, Kenya Medical Association; Chairman, Nakuru Round Table, 1977; Chairman, Association of Round Tables, Eastern Africa, covering Kenya, Uganda, Tanzania, Ethiopia, Mauritius, Seychelles. *Honours:* Campaign Medal (Army), 1969; Best Round Tabler's Award, 1977. *Hobbies:* Writing; Swimming; Collecting Antiques; Round Tabling. *Address:* PO Box 1199, Nakuru, Kenya.

KAPUR, Tilak Raj, b. 1 July 1921, Jammu, India. Accountant; Auditor; Teacher. m. (1) Smt. Pushpa Rani, 10 June 1947, 2 daughters, (2) Smt. Santosh Kumari 13 Mar. 1953, 2 sons. *Education:* Matriculation, 1939, Intermediate, 1941, BA, 1943, Punjab University; B Com, Commercial University, Delhi, 1963; First & Final in Accountancy, 1956. *Appointments:* Manager/Accountant, M/S Kashmir Knitting Company, Sabzi Mandi, Jammu, 1944-55, M/S Metro Wood & Eng. Works (P) Ltd., Kalol (N. Gujrat) Camp Manali (Dist. Kangra), 1955-57; Chief Accountant, M/S New Kishan Chand Ganesh Dass & Company, Forest Lessees & Timber Merchants, Jammu, 1957-. *Memberships:* Joint Secretary & Fellow of Society of Incorporated Accountants & Auditors of India, Darya Ganj, Delhi; Fellow, All India Commercial Association, Delhi. *Honours:* 1st Prize in Urdu, 1st Prize in Mathematics and II Prize in Economics in II Year, 1941; II Prize in Mathematics A Course & II Prize in Economics in IV Year, 1943. *Hobbies:* Novel Reading; Story Writing; Philately. *Address:* T R Kapur, Incorporated Accountant & Auditor, 46 Lakhdata Street, Purani Mandi, Jammu, India.

KARANTOKIS, Nicolas Georghio, b. 13 Jan. 1917, Nicosia, Cyprus. Contractor, Developer. m. 27 Apr. 1947, 1 son, 2 daughters. *Education:* Athens University, 1935-39. *Appointments:* Interpreter Recruiting Officer, 1941-42; Contractor, British Army, 1943-60; Chairman: Medcon Construction Ltd., 1956, Medcon Construction Group, 1958, Heavy Machinery Association, 1964-68, Com., Tripiotis Ch. Nicosia, 1966-81; President, Churchill Hotels, 1972-. *Memberships:* International Hotel Association. *Address:* Dositheou No. 1, Nicosia.

KARDONNE, Rick, b. 30 Mar. 1947, New York, NY, USA. Composer, Lyricist, Writer, Musical Arranger, Musical Director, Pianist. m. Eda Golub, 11 June 1967, 1 daughter. *Education:* BA, Hiram College, Hiram, Ohio, USA; Graduate work, McGill University; Private Piano and Music theory instruction. *Appointments:* Music columnist: The Canadian Jewish News, since 1972, The Downtowner, Toronto, 1980-; Composed lyrics, soundtrack orchestration for National Film Board of Canada, Columbia Pictures movie, How Things have Changed, 1971; Composer, feature Canadian movie, Rip Off, 1972; Lyricist, Canadian Broadcasting Corporation, radio network programme Inside from the Outside, 1971; Writer of articles for many magazines; Musical Director, orchestrator for countless Totonto area concerts, music events, festivals etc. *Memberships:* The Dramatist's Guild; American Society of Composers, Author and Publishers; American Guild of Authors and Composers; American Federation of Musicians. *Publications:* Research compiler of a soon-to-be-released biography of the late classical pianist Sheila Henig; Stage musical, Despite All Claims to the Contrary, The World is Flat, 1981; Jazz Suite for Harpsichord and Guitar, 1981; 1999, stage musical, 1978; Wrote several other stage musicals which were produced; Many songs performed and recorded. *Hobbies:* Tennis; Summer water sports. *Address:* 1050 Yonge Street, #33A, Toronto, Ontario, M4W 2L1, Canada.

KARGUPTA, Satadal, b. 4 June 1919, Calcutta. Researcher & Journalist. m. Manju SenGupta, 7 Mar. 1947, 1 son, 2 daughters. *Education:* BA, 1941; MA, 1943; Studied Chinese, Viswabharati University and Calcutta University, 1944; Studied Tibetan, Calcutta University, 1944, Sinhalese, 1945; L.LB, 1948, PhD, 1976, Calcutta University. *Appointments:* Lecturer, City College, Calcutta, 1944-45; Research Fellow & Private Secretary, to the Late Dr B M Baruah on cultural mission to Ceylon and adjoining countries on behalf of Calcutta University, 1944; Editor-in-Chief Traveller's Air Guide, 1948-52; Board of Directors, Bengal Fisheries & Agricultural Co (Pvt) Ltd., 1952-56; Honorary Lecturer & Research Fellow in Pali, Calcutta University, 1959-62; Executive Head, National Scientific Works, 1962-64; Advisory Board, Samadhan Weekly, 1964-68; Independent practice in Astro-Dermatoglyphics, Occultism, Recovery of lost birth dates from palmer flexions, 1969-; Editor of: Bengali monthly Jyotish Siddanta, 1978-, Bengali Quarterly Puspanjali, 1971-, English Monthly Vidya, 1978-. *Memberships:* Fellow, Theosophical Society, 1958; Asiatic Society of GB & Ireland, 1978, Calcutta, 1979; Bangiya Jyotish Parishad, 1956; American Oriental Society, USA, 1979; IBA, Cambridge, 1979. *Publications:* More than 130 Research papers published in different journals and magazines; Works also published as a part of the compilation of Books. *Honours:* Inter-college Boxing Championship, 1937; Football captaincy prize; Jyotish-Samrat, 1970; Sahitya-Bhusana, 1979; Jyotish-Ratna, 1978; Jyotish-Martanda, 1981; Lectures given as visiting scholar Glendale Community College, California, 1980 and Pasadena City College, Los Angeles, 1980; Recipient of Award for 1980 of Critic Circle of India (New Delhi) for Research Contribution. *Hobbies:* Football; Badminton; Cards; Carom Board; Astro-dermatogylphics; Occultism. *Address:* 103 Manicktala Main Road, Calcutta 700 054, India.

KARIUKI, Maina, b. 5 Feb. 1955, Thika, Kenya. Business Administrator. m. Nduta 15 Nov. 1980, 1 son. *Education:* BSc 1977; MBA 1978; MIPR 1979. *Appointments:* World Bank; Noble Printers and Publishers Limited; Kenya Tea Development Authority. *Address:* Mnuosa Road, Westlands, Nairobi, Kenya.

KARSH, Yousuf, b. 23 Dec. 1908, Mardin, Armenia-in-Turkey. Photographer. *Education:* Sherbrooke, Quebec; Studied Photography, under John H Garo of Boston, Massachusetts. *Appointments:* Photographic Studio, Ottawa, Canada, 1932; Numerous one-man exhibitions World Wide. *Publications:* Faces of Destiny, 1946; Portraits of Greatness 1959; This is the Mass 1958; This is Rome 1959; This is the Holy Land 1960; These are the Sacraments 1962; In Search of Greatness, an autobiography 1962; The Warren Court 1965; Karsh Portfolio 1967; Faces of our Time 1971; Karsh Portraits 1976; Karsh Canadians 1978; Karsh Portraits which have been used on postage stamps: Dag Hammarskjold; Chief Justice Harlan Stone; Prime Minister William Lyon Mackenzie King of Canada; Her Majesty Queen Elizabeth II; Queen Elizabeth and Prince Philip; Governor General George P. Vanier of Canada; Prince Rainier and Princess Grace of Monaco; Sir Winston Churchill; Pope Pius XII; Konrad Adenauer; General George C. Marshall; Jawaharlal Nehru. *Honours:* Honorary degrees of Doctor of Laws, Doctor of Humane Letters, Doctor of Civil Law, Bachelor of Professional Arts, Doctor of Fine Arts, Achievement in Life Award of the Encyclopaedia Britannica, plus numerous Medals and Fellowships. *Address:* Chateau Laurier Hotel, Suite 660, Ottawa, Canada -k1N 8S7.

KARSTEIN, Hermann, b. 17 Nov. 1914, Wuppertal, West Germany. Marketing Consultant. m. Ruby Evelyn Mildred Beale, 25 Mar. 1943, 1 son. *Appointments:* Commercial Manager, Havero (Bayer) India, 1938-39; Director: Indo Agencies Ltd., Madras, 1948-50, Indo-German Agencies Ltd., Madras, India, 1948-51, German Remedies Ltd., Bombay, India, 1950-52; Sales Director, Sarabhai Chemicals (Squibb), Bombay, 1953-60, Pfizer (India) Ltd., Bombay, 1960-61; Private practice of marketing consultancy, Bombay, 1961-; Visiting faculty member of the University of Bombay, Teaching marketing management, 1963-69. *Memberships:* Past member of the executive and education committees of the Bombay Management Association, Bombay; Management Consultants Association of India. *Publications:* New Horizons in Marketing Vol. 1, 1968, Vol.2, 1969; Marvels of the Mind, 1973; Contributor of numerous articles on management subjects to professional journals. *Honours:* Charat Ram Award, 1965; Escorts Book Award, 1970. *Hobby:* Carpentry. *Address:* Karlyn, 4th Road, Bombay 400 055, India.

KASHOKI, Mubanga Edmund, b. 4 Dec. 1937, Mulobola Mission, Kasama, Northern Province, Zambia. University Professor. m. Juanita MacGriff, 26 Dec. 1965, 1 son, 2 daughters. *Education:* BA, Colgate University, USA, 1964; MA, Michigan State University, USA, 1967. *Appointments:* Chief Literacy Officer, 1967-70; Deputy Team Leader, The Zambia Survey of Language Use and Language Teaching, University of Zambia, 1970-71; Senior Research Fellow, (Linguistics), 1971-75, Research Professor of African Languages, 1976-, Acting Director, Institute for African Studies, 1973-74, Director, 1975-78, Principal, 1978-, University of Sambia, Ndola. *Memberships:* Language Association of Eastern Africa, 1970-, Chairman, 1972-; International African Institute, 1975-84; Vice Chairman, IAI, 1980-84; National UNESCO Commission for Zambia, 1970-; Chairman, Zambia National Monuments Commission, 1973-; Member, 1969-, Chairman, 1969-75, Zambia Language Group. *Publications:* A Phonemic Analysis of Bemba, 1968; Editor, Bane Naatwangaale, 1973; Co-Editor, Language in Zambia (with Sirarpi Ohannessian), 1978. *Honours:* UNESCO ED, 1977; Nessim Habif Prize, 1977; Fulbright Research Sholar, 1977-78. *Hobbies:* Listening to music; Fishing; Canoeing; Swimming. *Address:* 4625 Lunsemfwa Drive, Riverside, Kitwe, Zambia.

KASOMA, Kabwe, b. 2 Nov. 1933, Kasama. Dean of Students, University of Zambia. m. Fausta Bwalya Chambeshi, 22 June 1960, 2 sons, 6 daughters. *Education:* Primary Teachers Certificate, Kitwe, Zambia 1955; Diploma in Social Work, Mwanza Tanzania, 1966; BA (E.D.) University of Zambia, Lusaka, Zambia 1972; MA, Columbia University, New York, 1977. *Appointments:* Primary School Teacher, Kitwe, Zambia 1955-64; Community Development Officer, Kitwe, Zambia 1966-68; Secondary School Teacher, Kitwe, Zambia 1972-; Dean of Students, University of Zambia Lusaka, Zambia 1973-81; Regional Co-ordinator for Project Support Communications for Social Development, UNICEF, Nairobi, 1981-. *Memberships:* Kitwe Dramma Cultural Society; Theatre Association of Zambia; Zambia National Threatre Arts Association; International Theatre Institute. *Publications:* The Long Arts of the Law—A Play, 1969; Black Mamba II, a Play, 1975; The Fools Marry, 1976. *Honours:* 1st Prize Floating Trophy, Zambia Play Writing Competetion, 1969; The Harry Langworthy Award, Best Historical Research Essay, 1972. *Hobbies:* Wataching Soccer; Playing Volleyball; Dramma; Music; Films. *Address:* UNICEF, PO Box 44145, Nairobi, Kenya.

KASSAPIS, George Andreas, b. 1 Jan. 1933, Asha, Cyprus. Planner, Lawyer, Surveyor. m. Lilia, 1 Oct. 1961, 2 sons, 1 daughter. *Education:* BSc, College of Estate Management, London School of Economics, University of London, 1954-58; UNO Fellowship, Postgraduate Diploma in Town & Country Planning, University of Durham, 1961-63; Barrister, Middle Temple, 1972. *Appointments:* Land Officer, Department of Land and Surveys, 1958-61; Divisional Town Planning Officer, Department of Town Planning & Housing Ministry of the Interior, 1963-65; Town Planning Officer Class I, 1965-70; Chief Planner, Development Control and Implementation Specialist, 1970-. *Memberships:* Royal Institute of Chartered Surveyors; Royal Town Planning Institute; Cyprus Bar; Vice-President, Cyprus Association of Chartered Surveyors; Twice President, The Cyprus Association of Town & Country Planning. *Publications:* Contributor of articles in magazines, newspapers and professional journals. *Hobbies:* Tennis; Gardening. *Address:* 14 Pnytogoras Road, Engomi, Nicosia, Cyprus.

KASSIM, Mohamed, b. 20 Nov. 1931, Guyana, Georgetown. Business Executive. Divorced, 3 sons, 2 daughters. *Education:* Junior School Certificate, Cambridge 1947; Senior School Certificate, Cambridge 1948. *Appointments:* Self-employed 1950-61; Managing Director, Guyana Import-Export Limited 1962-71; Director, Guyana Bauxite Limited 1971-78; G.D.R. Trade Representative. *Memberships:* Georgetown Cricket Club; Georgetown Rowing Club; Guyana Motor Racing Club. *Hobbies:* Swimming; Cricket. *Address:* 158 Waterloo Street, Georgetown, Guyana.

KASTURIRANGAN, K, b. 14 Oct. 1940, Ernakulam, India. Scientist. m. Lakshmi, 1968, 2 sons. *Education:* BSc, 1961, MSc, 1963, Bombay University; PhD, Physical Research Laboratory, Gujarat University, 1971. *Appointments:* Research Scholar, 1963-67, Research Associate, 1967-71, Physical Research Laboratory; Physicist, SSD/ISRO, 1971-73; Head, Physics Group, 1974-78, Project Engineer (Spacecraft, 1975-76, ISAC, ISRO; Project Director, BHASKARA (SEO-I), Spacecraft Project, 1976-80; Project Director: SEO-II Project, 1979-, Indian Remote Sensing Satellite Project, 1980-. Astronomical Society of India; Indian Physics Association; Fellow, Institution of Electronics & Telecommunication Engineers. *Publications:* Numerous and varied contributions in scientific and professional journals. *Honours:* Prize for the book BHASKAR (in Hindi), 1980. *Hobby:* Cricket. *Address:* 196 Mahalakshmi, Layout, Bangalore 560 010, India.

KASWA, Jackson, b. 5 Apr. 1942, Mityana, Uganda. Science Tutor. m. Nalongo, 19 Aug. 1965, 2 sons, 3 daughters. *Education:* Diploma in Education (Science), Makerere University, 1969; Diploma in Book Production, University of London, 1972. *Appointments:* Teacher, Bukomeru Junior Secondary School, 1962-64; Headmaster, Kyarrkowe Junior Secondary School, 1965-66; Science Tutor: Buloba College, 1968-71, Busuubizi TTC, 1972-. *Memberships:* Uganda Teachers' Association; Board of Governors, Busuubizi SSS; Management Committee, Kiyinda Primary School. *Publications:* Several books including: Louis Pasteur; Okyiga; Omunaku Kaama; Omuganda N'Enswa; Teaching Science in Primary Schools; The Human Body; Kkoyi Kkoyi. *Hobbies:* Photography; Writing; Research. *Address:* PO Box 244, Mityana, Uganda, East Africa.

KATANEKWA, Nicholas Mwitelela, b. 21 Jan. 1948, Mongu, Zambia. Director. m. Anne Sepiso Mwanamwale, 1973, 1 son, 1 daughter. *Education:* BA, University of Zambia, 1973; Post-Graduate Diploma in African Studies, 1975; MA, University of Birmingham, 1977. *Appointments:* Keeper, Prehistory Department, Livingstone Museum, Zambia, 1973-80; Director, National Monuments Commission, 1980-. *Memberships:* Historical Association of Zambia; The Southern African Association of Archaeologists. *Publications:* Contributed articles to various professional journals. *Honours:* Bradley Memorial Prize, 1976-77. *Hobbies:* Reading; Music; Site-seeing. *Address:* 72 Kanyanta Road, Livingstone, Zambia.

KATHIRESAN, Annamala, b. 5 Oct. 1926, Kovilpatti, India. Professor. m. Saratha, 2 Feb. 1956, 1 son. *Education:* MB., BS, 1950, TDD, 1957, MD, 1965, Madras University. *Appointments:* Lecturer in Tuberculosis, Madurai Medical College, Madurai, India, 1957-67; Professor of Tuberculosis & Chest Diseases, Kilpauk Medical College & Superintendent, Government TB Hospital, Madras, 1967-. *Memberships:* College of Chest Physicians, USA; The Indian Medical Association; The Tuberculosis Association of India; The Indian Association of Chest Physicians. *Publications:* Several books on medical subjects including: Tuberculosis, Chest Diseases, Biochemistry, Diabetes, Paediatrics, Brain, Anatomy, Physiology & infectious diseases in Tamil. *Honours:* Awarded cash prize and certificate of merit for book on Tuberculosis and its preventive methods, 1973; Awarded Gold medal, a certificate of merit and cash prize for the book, Know your Child, 1974. *Hobbies:* Writing Books in Tamil; Social work on prevention of Tuberculosis; Tennis. *Address:* 24 Temple Street, Alagappa Nagar, Madras, 600010, India.

KAUFMAN, Gerald Bernard, b. 21 June 1930, Leeds, England. Member of Parliament. *Education:* MA, The Queen's College, Oxford, 1949-53. *Appointments:* Assistant General Secretary, Fabian Society, 1954-55; Political Staff, Daily Mirror, 1955-64; Political Correspondent, New Statesman, 1964-65; Parliamentary Press Liaison Officer, Labour Party, 1965-70; Member of Parliament, Ardwick, Manchester, 1970; Under-Secretary of State for the Environment, 1974-75, for Industry, 1975; Minister of State, Department of Industry, 1975-79; Elected Parliamntary (Shadow Cabinet), 1980; Opposition Spokesman on the Environment. *Publications:* Co-author, How to Live under Labour; Editor, The Left; To Build the Promised Land; How to be a Minister. *Honours:* Privy Councillor, 1978. *Hobbies:*

Cinema; Music; Theatre; Travel. *Address:* 87 Charlbert Court, Eamont Street, London, NW8 7DA, England.

KAUL, Autar Krishen, b. 4 Oct. 1933, Srinagar, Kashmir, India. Professor of Dental Surgery, Oral Surgeon. m. Nancy Ganju, 9 Aug. 1957, 2 sons, 1 daughter. *Education:* BDS, 1956; MDS, (Oral Surgery), 1971. *Appointments:* Dental Surgeon, Jammu and Kashmir Government, 1956; Lecturer, Eastman Dental Centre and University of Rochester, School of Medicine and Dentistry, New York, USA, 1958-59; Assistant Professor and Head of Department of Dentistry, Government Medical College, Sribnagar, 1963; Associate Professor & Head of Department, 1967, Professor and Head of Department of Dentistry, 1979, Government Medical College, Jammu; Professor and Head of Department of Dentistry, Government Medical College, Srinagar, Kashmir, 1980-. *Memberships:* Indian Dental Association, Vice-President, 1979; Fellow, International College of Dentists, USA, 1972, International Association of Oral Surgeons, Sweden; Perri Fauchard Academy, USA; British Association of Oral Surgeons; Association of Oral Surgeons of India; Indian Red Cross Society. *Publications:* Contributions to Dental Journals including: Clinical trial of carbamazapine in the management of trigeminal of glasso pharyngeal Neuralgia, 1973; Facial Pain and its management, 1974. *Honours:* Honours, Certificate in Operative Dentistry, 1956; Honours in Oral Surgery, 1956; Prof B G Acharya Memorial Prize, Lucknow University. *Hobbies:* Music appreciation; Gardening; Sculpture. *Address:* 7-B Jawahar Nagar, Srinagar 190008, Kashmir, India.

KAUL, Mohan Kishen, b. 7 Aug. 1934, Lahore. Electronic & Telecommunication Engineer. m. Savitri 25 June 1959, 1 son, 1 daughter. *Education:* Second Class Radiotelegraph Operators' Certificate of Competency, 1952; BA, 1956; Graduateship of the Institution of Electronics & Telecommunication Engineers, India, 1967; Advanced Diploma in French Language, 1974. *Appointments:* Officer-in-Charge, 1959-68, Technical Assistant Grade I, 1965-68, Engineer, 1968-78, Wireless Planning & Co-ordination Wing, Ministry of Communications, Government of India; Assistant Director (Communications), Directorate of Preventive Operations, Customs & Central Excise, (Communications Division), Ministry of Finance, Government of India, 1978-. *Memberships:* Institution of Engineers, India; Amateur Radio Relay League Inc., USA; Fellow of and various posts held within the Institution of Electronics & Telecommunications Engineers, India, 1976-; Member of the Governing Council and Honorary Treasurer and Vice Chairman of Delhi Chapter. *Publications:* Contributed articles on Ham Radio in various Ham Radio magazines. *Hobby:* Radio Ham. *Address:* White House, B-3/13 Safdarjung Enclave, New Delhi, 110029, India

KAUL R N, b. 28 Feb. 1931, Srinagar, Kashmir, India. Teaching & Research. m. Shanta, 11 Oct. 1953, 2 sons. *Education:* MA (Prev), 1950-51, MA, (Final), 1952-53, Lucknow University; PhD, Delhi University, 1960; Post-Doctorate, University of California, Berkeley, USA, 1964-65. *Appointments:* Lecturer in Mathematics, Meerut College, 1954-58, Banaras Hindu University, 1958; Deshbandhu College, University of Delhi, 1958-64, 1966-68, San Fernando Valley State College, USA, 1965-66, University of California, Berkeley, USA, 1966; Reader in Maths, 1968-75, Professor of Maths, 1975-, University of Delhi. *Memberships:* Indian Mathematical Society; Operational Research Society of India; Society of Mathematical Sciences, Delhi, Joint Secretary; Indian Science Congress Association. *Publications:* 53 Papers published in International journals of repute; Reveiwed three books for Mathematical Reviews; Supervised the work of PhD, Thesis awarded to 13 candidates. *Honours:* Fulbright Scholarship, 1964-65; Visiting Fellowship, the Indian Institute for Advanced Study, 1974; Dean, Faculty of Mathematics, 1976-78, Head of Department of Mathematics, 1976-79, University of Delhi. *Hobbies:* Music; Bird-watching. *Address:* 20 Malkaganj, Main Bazar, Delhi, 110007, India.

KAUNDA, Josina Ngwarakone (Mrs Martin M Kaunda), b. 22 Aug. 1923, Mphahlele. m. Martin M 19 Dec. 1949, 1 son 5 daughters. *Education:* BSc, Hygiene, 1947; ACP, London, 1955; Depolima in Education, London, 1962; MS, in Nutritional Sciences, 1974. *Appointments:* Health Assistant, Springfield Health

Centre and Groblersdal Health Centre, South Africa, 1948-50; Assistant Teacher, Chalimbana Teacher Training College and Munali Secondary School, 1950-66; Deputy Head Mistress, Kabulonga Secondary School for Girls, Lusaka, 1966-68; Head of Department of Science & Health, Evelyn Hone College of Further Education, Lusaka, 1968-72; Study leave at Wisconsin University, 1972-74; Head of Department of Nutrition at Natural Resources Development College, Ministry of Agriculture & Water Development, 1974-. *Memberships:* National Cultural Group; Acting Chairman, National Food and Nutrition Council of Zambia; Advisory Boards for Lusaka Hospital and Chainama Mental Hospital and University's Provisional Council; National Nutrition Commission; Board of Directors, Poultry Development Company Ltd; Advisory Committee of Mwachisompola Zone; Advisory Board of Education. *Publications:* Play entitled, Marriage in a closed Society; Two Booklets on I Want to Know and Know your Body; Nutrition Contribution in Africana Encyclopaedia. *Honours:* Certificate in Role of Women in Community Development, 1963; Certificate in Family Planning and Population Dynamics, 1973; Certificate in Food Irradiation, 1976. *Hobbies:* Sewing; Crotchetting; Knitting; Reading; Gardening. *Address:* PO Box 30445, Lusaka, Zambia, S Africa.

KAUNDA, Kenneth David, b. 1924. President of Zambia, (formerly Prime Minister Northern Rhodesia). m. Betty Banda, 1946, 7 sons, 2 daughters. *Education:* Munali Secondary School and Lubwa Training School. *Appointments:* Teacher and Headmaster Lubwa Training School; Offices in African National Congress; District Secretary, 1950-1952; Provincial Organizing Secretary, 1952-1953; Secretary-General, 1953-1958; National President, Zambian African National Congress 1958-1959; and United National Independence Party, 1960; Chairman Pan-African Freedom Movement for East, Central and South Africa 1962; Minister of Local Government and Social Welfare, N. Rhodesia 1962-1963; Prime Minister of Northern Rhodesia Jan. 1964-Oct. 1964; President of Zambia 1964-. *Publications:* Black Government (1961); Zambia Shall Be Free (1962); Humanism in Zambia and a Guide to its Implementation (1967); *Honours:* Honorary LLD Universities of Fordham (U.S.A.), Sussex, Dublin, York, Windsor (Canada) and Chile; Chancellor University of Zambia 1966-. *Address:* State House, PO Box 135, Lusaka, Zambia.

KAUNGAMNO, Ezekiel Enock, b. 25 Nov. 1937, Tanzania. Director, Tanzania Library Services. m. Elizabeth Tosiri, 5 June 1971, 2 daughters. *Education:* BA, (Econ), Oberlin College, USA, 1960-64; MLS, Kent State University, USA, 1964-66. *Appointments:* Tutor-/Librarian, Dar es Salaam College of National Education, 1966-69; Training and Recruitment Officer, 1966-69 Assistant Director, 1969-70, Acting Deputy, Director, 1970-71, Director, 1971-, Tanzania Library Service. *Memberships:* Chairman, Tanzania Library Association, 1974-75, 76; Twice Vice-Chairman, Tanzania Unesco National Commission; Council for Library Training; Institute of Adult Education; National Audio-Visual Institute; Institute of Education; National Museum; Chairman, National Archives and Records Management Advisory Council; Regional Adviser, American Library Association's World Encyclopaedia of Library and Information Services. *Publications:* Library Services in West and East Africa, 1979; Library Services in Tanzania, 1979; Contributions of numerous articles to books and numerous papers and articles to professional journals; Various International Conferences, seminars, workshops, courses and study tours. *Honours:* Best Alumnus of the Year Certificate, Kent State University Library School, USA, 1974. *Hobbies:* Music; Writing; Gardening. *Address:* PO Box 9283, Dar Es Salaam, Tanzania.

KAUSIMAE, David, b. 12 Oct. 1931, Aahua, West Areare, Malaita, Solomon Islands. Politician. m. 21 Feb. 1951, 3 sons, 3 daughters. *Education:* Self. *Appointments:* Director: Are Are Maasina Development Company Limited; Concret Industry Limited; Mendana Hotel Limited; Maasina Enterprises Limited; Maasina Saw Mills Limited; Solomon Islands Investment Limited; Solomon Wholesales Union Limited. *Memberships:* Commonwealth Parliamentry Association; Guadalcanal Club; Honiara Golf Club; Lions Club of Guadalcanal. *Honours:* OBE, 1974. Hobby: Reading. *Address:* Maasina Hill, Via Kiu Postal Agency, West Are Are, Malaita, Solomon Islands.

KAVUMA, Paulo Neil, b. 30 Jan. 1900, Namungo, Uganda. Business Director. m. twice: widower and divorcee, 4 sons, 8 daughters. *Education:* King's College, Budo, 1917; 1st class Certificate, and Government Examination with distinction. *Appointments:* Head Clerk and Interpreter, DC's and Residents Office, 1920-43; African Assistant, Resident Buganda; County Chief: Buruli and Kyaggwe counties; Prime Minister, Buganda Kingdom; Publicity Secretary Lint and Coffee Marketing Boards; Mayor, City of Kampala. *Memberships:* Secretary and Treasurer, Budonians Club; Chairman of several Educational Boards; President Mityana Secondary School, (old Boys); President Uganda Red Cross Society; Managing Director, Kavuma's Motors Limited. *Publications:* Author of Exile of Muteesa II (King of Buganda). *Honours:* Coronation Medal, 1952; OBE, 1954; Independence Medal, 1962. *Hobby:* Reading. *Address:* Lungujja Hill, PO Box 2459, Kampala, Uganda.

KAY, Henry Buckhurst, b. 23 Oct. 1915, Melbourne, Victoria, Australia. Physician. m. Jean Hailes, 21 Nov. 1951, 1 son, 2 daughters. *Education:* MB, BS, 1938, MD, University of Melbourne, 1941; MRACP, 1944; MRCP (London), 1947; FRACP, 1953; FRCP, 1964. *Appointments:* JRMO, 1939, SRMO, Royal Melbourne Hospital 1940; AAMC, AIF, 1940-46; Physician, 1946-80, Consultant Physician Alfred Hospital, Melbourne 1980-; Visiting Physician Repatriation Hospital, 1948-80; Associate Faculty of Medicine, Monash University 1970-81; Honorary Fellow, Baker Institute 1948-. *Memberships:* President, The Australian Postgraduate Federation in Medicine; Chairman, Victorian Medical Postgraduate Foundation; Board of Directors, National Heart Foundation; Cardiac Society of Australia and New Zealand; Fellow, Australian Medical Association; Naval and Military Club; Melbourne Club. *Publications:* Publications in various journals on Diseases of the Heart including: Amoebic Dysentery in Northern Territory, 1943; Atrial Septal Defect with Pulmonary Artery Thrombosis, 1956; Angina pectoris, 1977. *Honours:* Nuffield Foundation Fellowship, National Heart Hospital, London, 1946-47; Pfizer Travelling Scholarship, Royal Australasian College of Physicians, 1959; Member, Order of Australia, A.M, 1979. *Hobby:* Golf. *Address:* 62 Hopetoun Road, Toorak, Victoria, Australia 3142.

KAYE, Clive Mervyn, b. 18 Feb. 1945, London. Research Scientist. m. Delia Sandra Baker, 4 July 1971, 1 son. *Education:* BSc, Chemistry/Human Physiology, 1966; BSc(Hons). Biochemistry, Liverpool University, 1967; PhD, Biochemistry, London University, 1971. *Appointments:* Demonstrator and PhD student, Biochemistry Department, 1967-70, Assistant Lecturer, St Thomas's Hospital Medical School, Waterloo, London, 1970-72; Senior Research Biochemist, Department of Clinical Pharmacology, The Medical College of St Bartholomew's Hospital, St Pauls, London, 1972-76; Section Head, Drug Metabolism Department, 1976-78, Head, Clinical Assay Unit, May and Baker Limited, Dagenham Essex, 1978-. *Memberships:* The Biochemical Society; The Royal Institute of Chemistry; The British Pharmacological Society; The Institute of Biology. *Publications:* The principles of clinical pharmacology applied to heart disease; Indications for measurement of cardiac drugs; Methods of assaying cardiac drugs; Drugs for Heart disease; The gas chromatographic analysis of drugs in biological fluids; Progress in Drug Metabolism. *Honours:* BSc; PhD; CChem.; MRSC; MIBiol. *Hobbies:* Gardening; Chess; Decorating and painting; Science Fiction. *Address:* 28 Clivedon Road, Highams Park, London, E4 9RN, England.

KAYE, John Harold, b. 2 Apr. 1910, London, England. Company Director and Management Consultant. m. 26 Jan. 1937. *Education:* Bachelor of Commerce, Queensland University; Diploma Public Administration, Sydney University. *Appointments:* Head Teacher, School of Management, Sydney Technical College, 1946-51; Executive, Bradford Cotton Mills Limited, 1952-62; Director of Personnel, Standard Telephone and Cables Property Limited, 1963-75; Chairman and Director, Human Resource Systems Property Limited, 1975-. *Memberships:* Foundation Member, Chancellor of the New South Wales Institute of Technology, 1956-70; Foundation Member, Chairman of the New South Wales Council for Technical and Further Education, 1949-81; Foundation Member, State and National President of the Institute of Personnel Management of

Australia, 1943-81; Honorary Fellow, IPMA; Honorary Fellow, Sydney Technical College; Fellow, Australian Institute of Management; Chairman of the Scout Association of New South Wales; Chairman, Productivity Promotion Council of Australia, New South Wales branch and of the National Board, 1970-81. *Honours:* MBE, 1967; Silver Kangaroo, Scout Award; Queens Jubilee Medal. *Hobby:* Golf. *Address:* 71 Florence Avenue, Eastlohe 2018, New South Wales, Australia.

KAYUMBO, Hosea Yona, b. 16 Feb. 1935, Tabora. Entomologist. m. 4 June 1964, 3 sons, 2 daughters. *Education:* BSc, 1961, MSc, 1963, London; PhD, 1975. *Appointments:* Research Assistant, Ministry of Agriculture Research Institute, Ukiriguru, Mwanza, 1961; Research Officer, Entomology, Ministry of Agriculture Research Institute, Ukiriguru and Nachingwea, 1964-68; Lecturer in Agricultural Zoology/Agricultural Entomology, 1969-75, Professor of Agricultural Entomology, 1975-78, Faculty of Agriculture, University of Dar Es Salaam; Director General, Tanzania National Scientific Research Council, 1978-. *Memberships:* Member of the Board of Trustees of the International Foundation for Science; Council Member, President of Convocation, University of Dar Es Salaam. *Publications:* Author of a number of Scientific Papers, Articles and Essays on Entomology, Ecology and General Science and Technology issues related to Africa. *Address:* Tanzania National Scientific Research Council, PO Box 4302, Dar Es Salaam, Tanzania.

KAZI, (The Hon. Khangsarpa of Chakhung) Lhendup Dorji, b. 10 Nov. 1904, Pakyong, Sikkim. Kazi of Sikkim, Head Lama, Rumtek Monastery. m. Elisa-Maria Kazini, 13 July 1957. *Education:* Privately by Maharajah Sidkeong Tulku. *Appointments:* Chief Minister of Sikkim. *Memberships:* Institute of Tibetology, Gangtok, Sikkim. *Publications:* Mainly Political Treatises with reference to Sikkim and its neighbours, geo-political, literary, religious and Sikkimese painting and art. *Hobbies:* Gardening; Studying the Buddhist scriptures; Collecting orchids; Walking; Interest in the welfare of the Sikkimese villagers. *Address:* Chakhung House, Kalimpong, West Bengal, India.

KAZIE, Mmaju Imo, b. 29 Sept. 1932, Item, Imo State, Nigeria. Civil Engineer. m. Nnenna Eke 31 Mar. 1962, 3 sons, 1 daughter. *Education:* University College Ibadan 1954-56; BSc Engineering, Northampton College of Advanced Technology, University of London 1956-60. *Appointments:* Assistant Engineer, Sir William Halcrow and Partners, London 1961-63; Executive Engineer, Federal Ministry of Works Lagos 1963-64; Civil Engineer, Niger Dams Authority, Kainji Dam, 1964-66; Executive Engineer, Ministry of Works, Port Harcourt, 1966-67; Civil Engineer, Shell-BP Development Company of Nigeria, Port Harcourt 1967-70; Senior Civil Engineer, Akin Taylor and Company Limited, Lagos 1970-74; Chief Projects Engineer, Aticon Limited 1974-81. *Memberships:* Chartered Engineer, United Kingdom; Institution of Civil Engineers, London; Nigerian Society of Engineers; Nigerian Institute of Management; Item Union Lagos. *Publications:* The Construction of the Kainji Hydroelectric Dam Scheme, 1967; The Extension and Rehabilitation of the Lagos Airport Runways, Taziways and Parking Apron, 1975; The Development of Indigenous Contracting Industry in Nigeria. *Hobbies:* Reading; Classical Music; Tennis. *Address:* 22 Sere Close, Ilupeju Estate, Lagos, Nigeria.

KEALY, John Kevin, b. 20 June 1921, Dublin, Ireland. Veterinary Surgeon. m. Joan Kealy, 5 Apr. 1961, 3 sons, 3 daughters. *Education:* Member of the Royal College of Veterinary Surgeons, 1950; Bachelor of Veterinary Medicine, 1950, Master of Veterinary Medicine, 1967, National University of Ireland; Kellogg Fellow in Agriculture, University of Pennsylvania, 1957-58. *Appointments:* General Practice, Carrickmacross, County Monaghan, 1950-55; Lecturer in Veterinary Surgery, Veterinary College of Ireland, 1955-60; Senior Lecturer, 1960-73, 1975-77, Professor and Head, 1977-, Department of Veterinary Surgery, Obstetrics and Radiology, University College, Dublin; Head of Radiology, Iowa State *University, Ames, USA, 1973-75. *Memberships:* International Veterinary Radiology Association, President, 1973-76; British Veterinary Radiological Association, Chairman, 1967; Irish Veterinary Association, President, 1967; Life Member, Royal Dublin Society; Irish Veterinary Council. *Publications:* Diagnostic Radiology of the Dog

and Cat, 1979; Editor and Guest Editor of Journals; Author of approximately 30 scientific papers in various professional journals. *Honours:* Kellogg Foundation Fellowship, 1957; OECD, Senior Visiting Fellowship, 1964; Foundation Diploma in Veterinary Radiology, 1967; Phi Zeta, Honorary, 1975. *Hobby:* Golf. *Address:* 15 Frankfort Park, Dundrum, Dublin,' 14, Ireland.

KEANE, Horace James Basil, b. 21 Mar. 1926, Boston Mass. USA. Dentist. m. Eunice R Gardener, 31 Mar. 1965, 1 son, 1 daughter. *Education:* BSc, Howard University College of Liberal Arts, 1945-48; DDS, Howard University College of Dentistry 1948-52. *Appointments:* USNR, Dental Corp, 1952-54; Clinical Instructor, Howard University College of Dentistry 1954-57; Dental Officer, Jamaica Government, 1957-60; Private Practice, Dental Adviser to Minister of Health 1969-80; K.S.A.C. Councillor 1969-74. *Memberships:* Jamaica Dental Association; Omega Psi Phi. *Publications:* Preacher in film, Harder they Come; Preacher, Film, Marujana Affair; Colonel, Film Countryman; Publications in Daily Cloaners, Radio and Television appearances on Current issues. *Honours:* Howard University Dental Alumni Award 1976; Jamaica National Award, Order of Distinction. *Hobbies:* Sports; Art; Gardening; Travelling. *Address:* 2 Riverside Heights, Gordon Town, P O, Jamaica, West Indies.

KEANE, Mervyn Rex, b. 3 June 1920, Invercargill. Journalist. m. Ngaire Joyce Cunningham, 9 Apr. 1949, 1 son, 5 daughters. *Education:* Otago University, 1945-46. *Appointments:* Prain and French, Barristers and Solicitors, 1939-40; War Service, 1940-45; Southland Daily News, 1946-53; Otago Daily Times, 1954; Evening Star, 1954-57, Assistant Editor, 1966-79; Wairarapa Times, Editor, 1957-66. *Memberships:* 23 Battalion Association (Otago Branch) Committee. *Publications:* Daily Columnist for 13 years; Editorials, Feature Articles on wide range of human affairs; 53 Short Stories. *Honours:* Italy Star, 1939-45; Defence Medal; War Service Medal; Illuminated Scroll for services rendered as Editor. *Hobbies:* Foreign Affairs; Writing; Reading; Photography. *Address:* 120 Arthur Street, Dunedin, New Zealand.

KEAR, Allen Richard, b. 4 Mar. 1929, Kingston, Ontario, Canada. Political and Social Scientist, Historian, Bilingual Professor. m. 23 Aug. 1969. *Education:* BA, Royal Military College of Canada; BA, MA, Queen's University, Kingston, Ontario. *Appointments:* Deputy City Clerk, Kingston; Provincial Treasurer's Department, Saskatchewan; Federal-Provincial Relations Division, Canadian Finance Department, Ottawa; Royal Commission on Bilingualism and Biculturalism, Ottawa; Broadcaster, Interviewee, Canadian Broadcasting Corporation; Brandon University, Manitoba; University of Saskatchewan; Unversity of New Brunswick; St. Lawrence College, Québec; University of Manitoba. *Memberships:* Canadian Political Science Association; Societe Quebecoise de Science Politique; Executive Member sice 1975, Vice Chairman, 1978-79, Chairman, 1979-81 of Winnipeg Regional Group of Institute of Public Administration of Canada; Honorary Vice President, 1975-76, Honorary Secretary, 1976-80, Manitoba Historical Society; Institute of Public Administration of Canada. *Publications:* Nine Papers on Canadian Political Science in English or French; 18 Publications on Confederalism, the second known political scientist in the world having published on Confederalism; 14 Publications on Federalism; 32 Publications in French; 23 known Citations of publications in English and French. *Honours:* Two prizes from RMC, Queen's University and the Quebec Provincial Government; Invited Visiting Fellow, Leicester University, Leicester, England. *Hobbies:* Canadian Studies in the Social Sciences and Humanities; Helping Franco-Manitobans achieve their goals collectively and individually through La Société Franco-Manitobaine. *Address:* 615 Churchill Drive, Fort Rouge, Winnipeg, Manitoba, Canada.

KEAR David, b. 29 Oct. 1923, London, England. Geologist. m. Joan Kathleen Bridges, 25 Aug. 1948, 2 sons, 1 daughter. *Education:* BSc (Eng), 1941-44, BSc, 1947-48, PhD, 1963, Imperial College, London University; ARSM, 1944. *Appointments:* Engineer Officer, Royal Navy, 1944-47; Prospecting Officer, Ministry of Fuel and Power, 1947; Geologist, New Zealand Geological Survey, 1948; District Geologist, Ngaruawahia, 1949-58; District Geologist, Auckland, 1958-65; Chief Economic Geologist, 1963-67; Director, 1967-74, Assistant

Director-General, 1974-80, Director-General, 1980-, New Zealand Department Scientific and Industrial Research; United Nations Consultant, Western Samoa, 1969-74. *Memberships:* Royal Society of New Zealand, Vice-President, 1975-79; Geological Society of New Zealand, President, 1959-60; Australian Institute of Mining and Metallurgy; New Zealand Executive Management Club, President, 1978-79. *Publications:* Approximately 100 scientific papers, bulletins and maps on New Zealand geology, volcanology and mineral resources, and Western Samoa geology and water supply, resources. *Honours:* Warrington-Smyth Prize, 1949; Frecheville Prize, 1952; Fellowship, Royal Society of New Zealand, 1973. *Hobbies:* Golf; New Zealand Science; Theatre. *Address:* 14 Christina Grove, Lower Hutt, New Zealand.

KEAR-COLWELL, John James, b. 25 Mar. 1937, London, England. Clinical Psychologist. m. Valerie Hope Hyslop Edgar, 10 Aug. 1962, 1 daughter. *Education:* BSc, University of Durham, 1956-59; DCP, University of Glasgow, 1960-62; MBCS, 1969; FBPsS, 1979. *Appointments:* Lecturer, Department of Mental Health, University of Aberdeen, 1962-66; Senior Clinical Psychologist, Crichton Royal, Dumfries, 1966-71; Principal Clinical Psychologist, Southern General Hospital, Glasgow, 1971-75; Consultant Clinical Psychologist, Cleveland Area Health Authority, 1975-. *Memberships:* British Psychological Society, Fellow; British Computer Society; Royal Commonwealth Society, Fellow; Cleveland and South Durham Council on Alcoholism, Chairman; The Heraldry Society. *Publications:* Contributed to various professional journals. *Hobbies:* Photography; Heraldry; Military History; Fishing. *Address:* Gyleburn, Near Lockerbie, Dumfriesshire, Scotland.

KEAY, Ronald William John, b. 20 May 1920, Richmond, Surrey, England. Scientist. m. Joan Mary Walden, 18 Aug. 1944, 1 son, 2 daughters. *Education:* BSc, MA, DPhil, St John's College, Oxford. *Appointments:* Colonial Forestry Service, Nigeria, 1942-62; Director of Forest Research, Nigeria, 1960-62; Deputy Executive Secretary, 1962-77, Executive Secretary, 1977-, The Royal Society, London. *Memberships:* Linnean Society of London, Vice President, 1965-67, 1971-73, 1974-76; Science Association of Nigeria, President, 1961-62; African Studies Association of United Kingdom, President, 1971-72. *Publications:* Flora of West Tropical Africa, 1954-58; Nigerian Trees, 1960-64; Papers on tropical African plant ecology and taxonomy; science policy. *Honours:* OBE, 1966; CBE, 1977. *Hobbies:* Gardening; Walking; Natural History. *Address:* Flat One, 6 Carlton House Terrace, London, England.

KEECH, Donald Bruce, b. 15 Mar. 1923, Broken Hill, Australia. Scientist. m. Muriel Joan Eckersley, 27 Nov. 1944, 5 sons. *Education:* BS, 1953, BS (Hons), 1954, Doctor of Philosophy, 1958, University of Adelaide. *Appointments:* Lecturer, 1961, Senior Lecturer, 1963, Reader, 1968, Department of Biochemistry, University of Adelaide. *Memberships:* Australian Biochemical Society. *Publications:* 47 Publications in International Scientific Journals. *Honours:* War Medals, 1939-45; Lemberg Lecturer, 1980. *Address:* 130 Edward Street, Clarence Gardens, South Australia.

KEEN, Henry Edward, b. 29 Mar. 1929, Temora, New South Wales, Australia. Public Servant/Journalist. m. Marie-Josephine Ella Greenslade, 14 June 1957, 2 daughters. *Education:* BA, Australian National University, Canberra, Australia, 1971. *Appointments:* Editorial Staff, Australian Consolidated Press, 1947-59, including overseas correspondent, Fleet Street, London, 1955-56; Editorial Television News Staff, Australian Broadcasting Commission, 1959-60; Publicity Branch, Department of Immigration, Canberra, 1960-63; Migration Information Officer, Australian Embassy, The Hague, 1963-66; Assistant Director, Information Branch Department Immigration, Canberra, 1966-71; Assistant Chief Migration Officer, Information, London, 1972-75; Counsellor Information, Australian High Commission, London, 1975-77; Publicity Advisor, Queen's Silver Jubilee Appeal for Young Australians, 1977; Director, News Media Centre, Commonwealth Heads of Government Regional Meeting, Sydney, 1978; Director, Honours Secretariat, Department of Administrative Services, Canberra, 1978-. *Memberships:* Founding Vice-President National Press Luncheon Club, Canberra (Now National Press Club);

Wig and Pen, London. *Hobbies:* Golf; Gardening; Reading; Listening to Music. *Address:* 9 Yarrow Place, O'Connor, Canberra, Act, 2601, Australia.

KEEN, Timothy Frank, b. 9 Nov. 1953, Pinner, Middx. England. Computer Company Executive. *Education:* BSc(Hons) Mining Engineer, 1971-74; PhD, University of Nottingham, 1974-77. *Appointments:* Managing Director, Keen Computers Limited, 1979-; Co-Director, Microsystems UK Limited, 1980-; Vice president, Keen Computers Ltd., San Francisco, 1980; Chairman and Vice Chairman, Computer Retailers Association; Chairman, Apple UK User Association; Institute of Mining Engineers. *Publications:* Several Articles Published in UK Computer journals on impact of Microcomputers in UK, 1979-81. *Honours:* Prizes and Awards limited to motor racing activities, 1971-75; University Colours (Gold Award) for Motor Sport, 1974. *Hobbies:* Music; Motor Sport; Science Fiction; Skiing; Scuba Diving. *Address:* The Mews House, Hope Drive, The Park, Nottingham, England.

KEENAN, Patrick John, b. 7 Jan. 1932, Montreal, Canada. President and Chief Executive; Director. m. Barbara Fraser, 14 Feb. 1959, 1 son, 3 daughters. *Education:* Bachelor of Commerce, McGill University, Montreal, 1954; Chartered Accountant, Chartered Secretary, 1956. *Appointments:* Directorships: Patino Management Services Limited; Patino Mines, Quebec Limited; Lemoine Mines Limited; Patino Mining, N.V.; Patino International; Compagnie Francaise d'Entreprises Mineres; Metal et d'Invest; Patino Mining Investment Limited; Patino Overseas, N.V.; Brascan Limited; Westmin Resources Limited; Great Lakes Power Corp. Limited; Hatleigh Corp.; Foodex Corp.; Mining Association of Canada, London Life Insurance Company; Lonvest Corporation; Assistant-Treasurer, Controller, 1964, Treasurer, 1965-66, Vice President, Finance and Treasurer, Patino Mining Corp. 1967-70; Treasurer, Director, Patino, N.V. The Hague 1971; Vice President, Treasurer and Director, 1972-74, President, Chief Executive and Director, Patino, N.V 1975-; Chief Executive, Director, Consolidated Tin Smelters Limited, London, England 1971-74; Vice Chairman, 1975; Chief Executive, Amalgamated Metal Corp. Ltd., London, England 1971-75. *Memberships:* National Club; Board of Trade. *Honours:* Laddie Millen Memorial Scholarship, McGill University, 1952; Institute of Chartered Secretaries Gold Medal, 1962. *Hobbies:* Skiing; Golf; Sheep farming. *Address:* 16 Whitney Avenue, Toronto, Canada.

KEESING, Nancy Florence, b. 7 Sept. 1923, Sydney, Australia. Writer. m. A M Hertzberg, 2 Feb. 1955, 1 son, 1 daughter. *Education:* Diploma, Social Studies, University of Sydney, Australia, 1947. *Appointments:* Social Worker, Royal Alexandra Hospital for Children, Sydney, Australia, 1947-50; Freelance Writer; Chairman, Literature Board of Australia Council, 1974-77. *Memberships:* Chairman, N S W Committee, National Book Council; Vice-President, English Association, Sydney Branch; Board of Management: Australian Jewish Historical Society, Sturt Craft Workshop, Mittagong. *Publications:* Poetry: Imminent Summer, 1951; Three Men and Sydney, 1955; Showground Sketchbook, 1968, Hails and Farewells, 1977; Represented in numerous anthologies including: Australia Writes, 1953; Australian Signpost, 1956; A Book of Australian Verse, 1956; Australian Poets Speak, 1961; Poetry in Australia II, 1964; Songs for All Seasons, 1967; Australian Verse from 1805, 1976; A Map of Australian Verse, 1975; Literary Criticisms: Elsie Carew: Australian Primitive Poet, 1965; Douglas Stewart, 1969; By Gravel and Gum, 1963; The Golden Dream, 1974; Memoirs: Garden Island People, 1975; Editor with Douglas Stewart of Australian Bush Ballads, 1955; Old Bush Songs, 1957; Pacific Book of Bush Ballads, 1967; Biography: John Lang and The Forger's Wife, 1979; Compiled with Introduction and Notes: Gold Fever, 1967; Compiled with Introduction: Transition, 1970; The Kelly Gang, 1975; The White Chrysanthemum, 1977; Henry Lawson: Favourite Verse, 1978; Shalom, 1978. *Honours:* Order of Australia. *Hobby:* Reading. *Address:* c/o Australian Society of Authors, 22 Alfred Street, Wilsons Point, New South Wales, Australia 2061.

KEEVES, John Philip, b. 20 Sept. 1924, Adelaide, South Australia. Educational Research. *Education:* BSc(Hons) Adelaide, 1947; Dip.Ed (Oxon), 1952; MEd,

Melbourne, 1967; PhD (ANU), 1972; fil.dr. (Stockholm), 1972. *Appointments:* Master, Prince Alfred College, Adelaide, 1947-49, 1953-61; Master, Radley College, Berkshire, 1949-51; Senior Research Officer, ACER, Melbourne, 1962-67; Research Fellow, ANU, 1967-71; Senior Visiting Scholar, Institute for International Education, Stockholm, 1971-72; Associate Director, ACER, 1972-77; Director, ACER, 1977-. *Memberships:* Fellow, Australian College of Education; Fellow, Academy of the Social Sciences in Australia; Australian Association for Research in Education; Australian Science Teachers Association. *Publications:* Some aspects of Performance in Mathematics in Australian Schools, 1969; Educational Environment and Student Achievement, 1972; Science Education in Nineteen Countries, 1973; Literacy and Numeracy in Australian Schools, 1976. *Hobbies:* Walking; Squash. *Address:* 23 Statenborough Street, Leabrook, South Australia, 5068.

KEHINDE, James Adetunji Babatunde, b. 10 Nov. 1943, Oyo, Nigeria. Accountancy. m. R Tunrayo, 20 Aug. 1970, 2 sons, 2 daughters. *Education:* BSc., Maths., University of Ife, Nigeria, 1965-69; ACCA., 1972-74, Diploma, Administration Management, Oct-Dec. 74, South West London College, London, UK. *Appointments:* Audit Clerk, Knox Cropper, London, UK, 1974-75; Financial Accountant, Cocoa Industries, Ikeja, Nigeria, 1975-76; Managing Accountant, Dunlop Nigeria Limited, Ikeja, Nigeria, 1976-77; Chief Accountant, Mag. (Nigeria) Limited, Oregun, Nigeria, 1977-80; Chief Accountant, Nicholas Lab. (Nigeria) Limited, Ilupeju, Nigeria, 1980-. *Memberships:* Association of Certified Accountants; Institute of Chartered Accountants of Nigeria; Institute of Administrative Management; Nigerian Institute of Management. *Publications:* Religious Publication: How I Became a Christian. *Hobbies:* Reading; Dressmaking. *Address:* 17 Lawal Street, Oregun Village, Ikeja, PO Box 4149, Ikeja, Lagos, Nigeria.

KEITA, Jean-Djigui, b. 1938 Barania C/ Kita Mali. Forester. m. Rokiatou NiDiaye, 1 Aug. 1964, 2 daughters. *Education:* Preparation and Courses, Sup. Agro, Dipl. Ing. Agronomic School, Rennes, France, 1956-61; Faculty of Science, Rennes, Mineralogy, Pedology, Ecology, Geobotanique, 1960-61. *Appointments:* Soil Conservation Division, Bamako Mali, 1962; Director General Forestry, Fisheries and Wildlife Department, Mali, 1962-78; Technical Advisor, Minister of Rural Development, 1970-72; Regional Forestry Officer, Bureau for Africa, FAO/UN 1978-. *Memberships:* Association Malienne pour la Promotion de la Pharmacopèe Traditionnelle. *Publications:* Technical unpublished papers on Forestry Policy in Mali; Energy Strategy in Sahel toward 2,000 (Fuelwood). *Honours:* Chevalier de l'ordre National du Mali 1976; Officier du Merite de la Rep Française (Etranger) 1975. *Hobbies:* History; Architecture. *Address:* FAO Regional Office, PO Box 1628, Accra, Ghana.

KEITH, John Dow, b. 23 Feb. 1908, Winnipeg, Canada. Physician, Cardiologist. m. Mary MacLaren Carson, 2 July 1938, 1 son, 2 daughters. *Education:* University of Toronto Medical School, 1926-32; Internee and Assistant Resident, Strang Memorial Hospital, Rochester University, 1932-34; Assistant Resident, 1934-35, Resident Medical Officer, Birmingham Children's Hospital, 1935-36; Athol Moynihan Fellowship, England, Research, Rheumatic Health Disease, 1936-38. *Appointments:* Head Cardiac Department, Sick Childrens Hospital, 1938-73; Surgeon-Lieutenant Commander, Royal Canadian Navy, 1942-46; Professor of Pediatrics, University of Toronto. *Memberships:* Fellow, Royal Society Physicians, Canada; Canadian Heart Association; Canadian Heart Foundation; International Cardiological Society; Canadian Cardiovascular Society; American College of Cardiology; American Heart Association. *Publications:* Author and associate author in 108 scientific medical publications in the field of cardiology; Publication of a text on Heart disease in Infancy and childhood. *Honours:* Award of Merit of Canadian Heart Foundation and Canadian Cardiovascular Society; Gairdner award of merit for contributions in the field of cardiovascular disease in childhood. *Hobbies:* Log cabin building; Sailing. *Address:* RRI Caledon East, Ontario, Canada, LON 1E0.

KEITH-LUCAS, David, b. 25 Mar. 1911, Cambridge, England. Chartered Engineer; University Professor. m. Dorothy de Bauduy Robertson, 25 Apr. 1942, (deceased 1979), 2 sons, 1 daughter. *Education:* BA., Mechanical Sciences Tripos, 2nd Class Hons., 1933, MA., 1956, Gonville and Caius College, Cambridge, UK, 1929-33. *Appointments:* Steam Turbine Design, C A Parsons & Co. Limited, 1935-39; Chief Aerodynamicist, 1940-49, Chief Designer, 1949-57, Technical'Director, 1957-65, Short Brothers Limited; Professor of Aircraft Design, 1965-72, Professor of Aeronautics, 1972-76, Cranfield Institute of Technology, UK; Director, John Brown, UK, 1970-78; Chairman, Airworthiness Requirements Board, UK, 1971-; Proesor Emeritus of Aeronautics at the Cranfield Institute of Technology. *Memberships:* Hon Fellow: Royal Aeronautical Society, American Institute of Aeronautics and Astronautics; Fellow: Fellowship of Engineering, Institution of Mechanical Engineers. *Creative Works:* Designer of Short SCI, Britain's First Jet Lift, Vertical Take-off Aircraft. *Honours:* CBE., 1973; Gold Medal of Royal Aeronautical Society, 1975; Hon. DSc., Belfast, 1968, Cranfield, 1975. *Hobbies:* Small boats; Vintage car. *Address:* Manor Close, Emberton, Olney, Bucks MK46 5BX, England.

KELLEHER, John Arnold, b. 22 Sept. 1925, Wellington, New Zealand. Journalist. m. Ursula Jean Sheehan, 2 June 1953, 3 sons, 2 daughters. *Appointments:* Reporter, sub-editor, columnist, various newspapers, New Zealand and Australia, also sports broadcaster, 1944-62; Chief Reporter, 1962-65, Editor, 1968-79, The Dominion; News and Features Editor, 1965, Editor, 1966-68, New Zeland Sunday Times; Group Relations Editor, Independent Newspapers Limited, 1980-. *Memberships:* Executive New Zealand branch, Commonwealth Press Union. *Publications:* No Remedy for Death (with P P Lynch), 1970. *Honours:* New Zeland newspaper feature writing prizes, 1954-64; Aviation writing prize, 1957; Gold Badge, New Zealand Jounralists Association, 1962; US Foreign Specialist Award, 1960. *Address:* 43 Menin Road, Raumati Beach, New Zealand.

KELLY, Frank Heron Churchward, b. 1 Jan. 1915, Lithgow, NSW, Australia. Technical Consultant, Process Engineering. m. Enid Jessie Cleak, 5 Feb. 1938, 1 son, 2 daughters. *Education:* Bachelor of Science, 1934; Master of Science, University of Melbourne, 1936; Doctor of Science, University of Tasmania, 1958; Diploma of Applied Chemistry, Melbourne Technical College, 1937; Certificates in Metallurgy and Assaying, Melbourne School of Mines, 1932. *Appointments:* Research Officer, Technical, Kalamia Sugar Mill, Ayr, Queensland Australia, 1936-46; Industrial Plant Investigator, Electrolytic Zinc Co. A/sia.Risdon, Tasmania, 1946-52; Senior Lecturer in Applied Chemistry, University of Tasmania, 1952-59; Reader in Applied Chemistry, 1959-68; Professor of Applied Chemistry University of Singapore, 1968-74; Malayan Sugar Manufacturers' Professor of Industrial Chemistry, University Sains, Malaysia, 1977-80; UNIDO Technical Consultant for sugar technology assignments 1973-. *Memberships:* Fellow Royal Australian Chemical Institute; Australian and New Zealand Association for the Advancement of Science; Institution of Engineers Australia; International Society of Sugar Cane Technologists; Australian Society of Sugar Cane Technologists. *Publications:* More than 100 publications in scientific and technical journals; Practical Mathematics for Chemists, 1963; The Sucrose Crystal, 1975; The Calcium Carbonate Crystal in the Sugar Industry, 1981. *Honours:* Alexander Rushall Scholarship, 1933-35; President's Medal, Queensland Society of Sugar Cane Technologists, best conference paper 1942 and 1946. *Hobby:* Travel. *Address:* 11 Bambaroo Close, Nambour, Queensland, Australia, 4560.

KELLY, Gerald William, b. 9 Feb. 1948, Fremantle, Western Australia. Market Researcher. m. Estelle Doust, 17 May 1971, 1 son, 1 daughter. *Education:* BSc., (Hons.), University of Western Australia; Diploma of Business (Marketing), Caulfield Institute of Technology, Australia. *Appointments:* Hamersley Iron Pty. Limited, 1969-70; Dulux Australia Limited, 1970-75; Managing Director, Nexus Research, Australia, 1976-. *Memberships:* Chairman, Victorian Division, Market Research Society of Australia; Royal Australian Chemical Institute; Melbourne Chamber of Commerce. *Publications:* Several articles and lectures, etc., on Market Research theory and practice. *Honours:* Marketing Prizes from: Gillette and Market Research Society,

1974, McPherson's Limited, 1975, Rosella and BP Australia, 1976. *Hobbies:* Tennis; Reading; Wine. *Address:* 10 Sharrow Road, Mitcham, Victoria 3132, Australia.

KELLY, Roslyn Joan, b. 25 Jan. 1948, Sydney, Australia. Member of Parliament, m. 20 Mar. 1970. *Education:* BA., 1965-69; Diploma, Education, 1968. *Appointments:* Secondary School Teacher, 1969-72; Consultant, Peter Cullen Prop. Limited, 1973-80; Member, A C T Legislative Assmebly, 1974-79; Member, A C T Consumer Affairs Council, 1974-79; Chairman, A C T Schools Authority, 1978-79. *Memberships:* National Press Club; Institute of International Affairs; A W U Staff Club. *Hobbies:* Reading; Tennis. *Address:* Parliament House, Canberra, ACT 2600, Australia.

KEMP, David Alistair, b. 14 Oct. 1941, Melbourne, Australia. Political Scientist. m. Patricia Marcard, 27 Jan. 1968, 3 sons. *Education:* LLB, 1964; BA(Hons.), Melbourne University, 1966; MPhil, 1971; PhD, Yale University, 1975. *Appointments:* Tutor, 1967, Lecturer, (temporary), 1968, Lecturer, Department of Political Science, Melbourne University, 1972-75; Graduate Fellow, Yale University, New Haven, USA; Senior Advisor: Office of the Leader of the Opposition, 1975, Private Office of the Prime Minister, 1976; Senior Lecturer, Department of Political Science, Melbourne University, 1977-78; Professor of Politics, Monash University, Victoria, Australia, 1979; Director, Private Office of the Prime Minister, Canberra, ACT Australia, 1981. *Memberships:* Australasian Political Studies Association; Australian Institute of Political Science; Alfred Deakin Lecture Trust; International Political Science Association; Australian Institute of International Affairs; Frankston Golf Club; Liberal Party of Australia. *Publications:* Society and Electoral Behaviour in Australia, 1978. *Hobbies:* Golf; Tennis; Sailing; Swimming; Hiking; Camping; Gardening. *Address:* 10 Dirrawan Gardens, Reid, ACT 2601, Australia.

KEMP, Haddon Reginald, b. 21 Dec. 1906, Sydney, NSW, Australia. Oral Surgeon (Retired). m. Daphne Scott Bennett, 9 Nov. 1935, 2 sons. *Education:* Bachelor of Dental Surgery, 1932; Doctor of Dental Science, University of Sydney, 1939; FRACDS, Australian College, 1965. *Appointments:* Superintendent, United Dental Hospital, Sydney, NSW, 1935-46; Oral Surgery Specialist Practice, Brisbane, 1946-55 and Sydney, NSW, 1956-76; Part-time Lecturer, Sydney University, Oral Surgery, 1956-75; Part-time Oral Surgeon, Royal Brisbane General Hospital, 1946-55. *Memberships:* International Society of Oral Surgeons; Australian and New Zealand Society of Oral Surgeons; Rotary International; Australian Club; Queensland Club. *Publications:* Thesis, Regional Anaesthasia, 1939. *Honours:* BDS, Sydney University Second Class Honours, 1932; Honorary FDSRCS, Edinburgh University, 1954. *Hobbies:* Swimming; Fishing; Hand loom weaving; Collecting Antiques. *Address:* 146 Scenic Road, Killcare Heights, NSW 2256, Australia.

KENILOREA, Rt. Hon. Peter, b. 1943. Solomon Islands Politician. m. Margaret, 1971, 2 sons, 2 daughters. *Education:* Diploma in Education. *Appointments:* School master, 1968-71; Assistant Secretary, Finance, 1971; Admin. Officer, 1972-73; Lands Officer, 1973-74; Deputy Secretary: to the Cabinet and to the Chief Minister, 1974-75; District Commissioner, 1975-76; elected Member of Parliament, 1976; elected Chief Minister, 1976-78; 1st Prime Minister of Solomon Islands, 1978-. *Memberships:* Gideons International. 05 Articles in various South Pacific journals. *Honours:* Queen's Silver Jubilee Medal; Privy Councillor, 1979. *Address:* Prime Minister's Office, Honiara, Solomon Islands.

KENNEALLY, Kevin Francis, b. 27 Nov. 1945, Cottesloe, Western Australia. Botanist. *Education:* Perth and Fremantle Technical Colleges; BSc, University of Western Australia, 1973. *Appointments:* Botany Department, University of Western Australia, 1964-73; National Service, RAAMC, Instructor Medical Pathology, Military Hospital, Yeronga, Queensland; Queensland Institute of Technology and Queensland Institute Medical Research, 1967-68; Botanist, Western Australian Herbarium, Department of Agriculture, 1973. *Memberships:* Western Australian Naturalists' Club; Western Australian Gould League; Spelthorne Natural History Society, United Kingdom; Fellow Linnean Society, Lon-

don. *Publications:* The Natural History of the Wongan Hills, 1977; Mangroves of Western Australia 1978. *Honours:* Anthropological Society Prize in Science, 1973; Churchill Fellowship, 1979. *Hobbies:* Photography; Australiana; Swimming. *Address:* 24/70 Broadway, Nedlands 6009, Western Australia.

KENNEDY, Eamon, b. 13 Dec. 1921, Dublin, Ireland. Ambassador of Ireland. m. 4 Feb. 1960, 1 son, 1 daughter. *Education:* BComm, 1942; BA, 1943; MA, University College, 1946; PhD, National University of Ireland, 1970. *Appointments:* Ambassador to Nigeria, 1961-64; Ambassador to Federal Republic of Germany, 1964-70; Ambassador to France, 1970-74; Ambassador to United Nations, New York, 1974-78; Ambassador to United Kingdom, 1978-. *Memberships:* Garrick, London; Royal Wimbledon, London; Institute of Public Administration, Dublin. *Publications:* Labour Theory of Value in Marxian Economics, (PhD thesis). *Honours:* Grand Cross of Order of Merit, Bonn, 1970; Grand Cross of Order of Merit, Paris, 1974. *Hobbies:* Music; Theatre; Golf. *Address:* 17 Grosvenor Place, London SW1, England.

KENNEDY, (George) Michael (Sinclair), b. 19 Feb. 1926, Manchester, England. Journalist. m. eslyn Durdle, 16 May 1947. *Appointments:* Editorial staff, The Daily Telegraph, Manchester, UK, 1941-; Service in Royal Navy, 1943-46. *Publications:* The Hallé Tradition, 1960; The Works of Ralph Vaughan Williams, 1964, rev. 1979; Portrait of Elgar, 1968, rev. 1982; History of the Royal Manchester College of Music, 1971; Barbirolli, 1971; Portrait of Manchester, 1970; Mahler, 1974; Richard Strauss, 1976; Britten, 1981; Editor: Concise Oxford Dictionary of Music, 1980. *Honours:* OBE., 1981; Hon. MA, Manchester University, UK, 1975; Fellow, RNCM, 1981; Hon. RMCM., 1971; FJI., 1967. *Hobby:* Cricket. *Address:* 3 Moorwood Drive, Sale, Cheshire, England.

KENNEDY, John Timothy, b. 15 July 1940, Yarrawonga, Victoria, Australia. Surgeon. m. Anna Christine Mary Tehan, 1 Feb. 1966, 3 sons, 1 daughter. *Education:* MBBS, University of Melbourne, Australia, 1963; FRACS, 1968; MS, University of Iowa, USA, 1973; Diplomate, 1972, Fellow, 1973, American Board Opthalmology and Otolaryncology; FACS, 1980; Fellow, American Facial and Plastic Reconstructive Surgery, 1975. *Appointments:* Senior ENT & Head Skull Surgeon, 1975-, St. Vincent's Hospital Fitzroy, Victoria, Australia, 1963-69, 1975-. *Memberships:* Fellow, Royal Australian College Surgeons; Fellow, American College of Surgeons; Melbourne Cruising Club; Victoria Racing Club; Executive member, Moone Valley Racing Club; Vicotian Amateur Turf Club; Victoria Golf Club; Souento Golf Club. *Publications:* 12 publications in E.N.T. World Literature. *Honours:* Ryan Prize, Surgery, 1973; Young Investigator Award, Centennial Conference on Laryngal Cancer, Toronto, 1974. *Hobbies:* Thoroughbred Racing and Breeding; Golf; Tennis. *Address:* 24 Edward Street. Kew. Victoria, Australia.

KENNEDY, Pearl Alberta Sinclair, b. 23 Jan. 1915, Tofield, Alberta, Canada. Teacher; School Librarian; Public Librarian. m. Thomas Alexander Kennedy, 28 Feb. 1935, 1 son, 1 daughter. *Education:* BA, 1950, Bachelor of Library Science, 1962, University of British Columbia, Canada; Secondary School Teaching Certificate, Vancouver Normal School, Canada, 1958. *Appointments:* Teacher; Librarian, Vancouver Public Library System, Canada; High School Librarian, Ladner, British Columbia, Canada; Self-employed, Section of Dillee Cottages Limited, Vancouver, Canada. *Memberships:* Vice-Chairman, Library Advisory Council of British Columbia; President, British Columbia Library Trustees' Association; Vancouver Public Library Board; Western Vice-President, Canadian Federation of University Women; President, University Women's Club, Vancouver; Volunteer Board of the City of Vancouver; Arbutus Club; Terminal City Club. *Publications:* Short stories for various Newspapers; Editor of Bulletin for University Women's Club, Vancouver; Editor of Newsletter, The Open Door, for Library Trustees Association. *Honours:* Scholastic award for the highest standing in Government examinations, Garneau High School, Edmonton, Alberta, Canada, 1930. *Hobbies:* Writing; Gardening; Music. *Address:* 1758 West 49th Avenue, Vancouver, British Columbia, Canada, V6M 2S5.

KENNEDY-GOOD, John, b. 8 Aug. 1915, Gouburn, New South Wales, Australia. Dental Surgeon (retired);

Mayor. m. June Clement Mackay, 7 Dec. 1940, 4 sons, 3 daughters. *Education:* BDS., Otago University, New Zealand, 1936-40. *Appointments:* Lecturer, Otago University, New Zealand; Locum, Dunedin, New Zealand; Private practice, Opotiki, New Zealand; Private practice, Lower Hutt, New Zealand, 1942-72. *Memberships:* Councillor, 1962-, Mayor, 1970-, Lower Hutt City Council; Chairman, New Zealand Council of Social Service, 1975-; Deputy Chairman, Wellington Regional Council, 1980-; Chairman, Dowse Art Gallery Board, 1970-; National Art Gallery & Museum Trust Board, 1970-; Wellington Harbour Board, 1970-80; HV.Power Board, 1971-77; Municipal Association Executive, Hutt Balley Drainage Board; President, 1959, Hutt Rotary Club; Wellington Branch, New Zealand Dental Association; Chairman, New Zealand Dental Health Council, 1948-54; Founder member, Hutt Club, 1945-; Academy of Fine Arts; Hutt Golf Club; Wellington Racing Club. *Honours:* QSO, 1976; Queens Jubilee Medal, 1977; Justice of the Peace, 1970; Fellow, Royal Society of Arts and Commerce, 1973; Order Merit, New Zealand Litter Control Council, 1979. *Hobbies:* Golf; Gardening; Reading; Homecrafts. *Address:* 'Greenwood', 64 Kings Crescent, Lower Hutt, New Zealand.

KERALAPURA, Krishnamoorthy, b. 30 July 1923, Keralapura, Hassan District, Karnataka State, India. University Teacher. m. Smt. K Saroja, 22 Apr. 1942, 7 daughters. *Education:* BA.(Hons.), 1942, MA, 1943, Kannada Pandit, 1942, BT, 1944, Mysore University, India; PhD, Bombay University, India, 1947. *Appointments:* Lecturer in Kannada and Sanskrit, Basaveswara College, Bagalkot, India, 1944-49; Lecturer, Sharadavilas College, Mysore, India, 1949-52; Lecturer, Kanara College, Kumta, India, 1952-59; Reader and Head, 1959-68, Professor and Head, 1968-, Department of Sanskrit, Karnataka University, Dharwar, India. *Memberships:* Joint Secretary, All India Oriental Conference; Executive Committee, The PEN All India Centre, Bombay; Nagarjuna Research Foundation, Faizabad. *Publications:* Dhvanyaloka and its Critics, 1968; Essays in Sanskrit Criticism, 1963; Some Thoughts on Indian Aesthetics, 1968; Kaldasa, 1972; Banabhatta, 1976; Critical Editions of Sanskrit works with English translation, Introduction and Notes: Yasodharacarita; Kavikaumudi; Subhasita Sudhanidhi; Dhvanyaloka; Vakroktijivita. *Honours:* Rani Setu Parvati Prize, Kerala University, 1965; Mysore University Golden Jubilee Award, 1970 and 1978; Karnataka State Sahitya Akademi Award for Literary Work in Kannada, 1973; Karnataka Government Literary Prize, 1972; Kannada Sahitya Parishat Diamond Jubilee Award, 1975; President's Certificate of Honour for outstanding contribution to Sanskrit Literature and Scholarship, 1978. *Address:* 'Datta Nivas', Saptapur, Dharwar-1, Karnataka State, India.

KERNALEGUEN, Anne Paule, b 15 Feb. 1926, St. Brieux, Saskatchewan, Canada. Professor. *Education:* Bachelor of Household Science, 1948; B.Ed., 1957; MA., 1963; PhD, 1968; Specialist in Ageing Certificate. *Appointments:* District Home Economist, Ontario, Canada, 1948-51; School of Agrriculture, Alberta, Canada, 1951-54; High School teaching, Red Deer, Alberta, Canada, 1954-60; Canadian Education Representative, McCalls Corporation, 1960-62; Assistant Professor, Michigan State, USA, 1963-64; Assistant Professor, University of Saskatchewan, Canada, 1964-66; Associate Professor and Department Chairman, Utah State University, USA, 1968-70; Professor and Division Chairman, 1970-80, Professor, 1980-, University of Alberta, Canada. *Memberships:* member of numerous societies including: Research Editor, 50th Anniversary Publication Chairman, Canadian Home Economics Association; President, National Association of College Professor of Textiles and Clothing; President, Western Division, Canadian Psychological Association; Advisory Board to Merchandising Technology, Olds College, Olds, Alberta, Canada; Charter member, 1980, Nominated for executive position, secretary, Nominating Committee, Alberta Association on Gerontology. *Publications:* Clothing Designs for the Handicapped, 1978. *Creative Works:* Slides: Clothing Designs for the Handicapped. *Honours:* Phi Kappa Phi; Omicron Nu; Phi Upsilon Omicron; AHEA-Omicron Nu International Scholarship, 1966-67; UTAH State University Research Grant U-500, 1969; University of Alberta Research Grant, 1970; University of Alberta Alumni Research Grant, 1974, 1976; Federal Department of Manpower—Opportunities for Youth, 1974; Medical

Services Research Foundation, 1974; Alberta Department of Culture, Youth and Recreation, 1974; University of Alberta President's National Research Council Fund, 1978; University of Alberta Humanities and Social Sciences Research Fund, 1980. *Hobbies:* Sewing; Crafts. *Address:* 605, 11027-87 Avenue, Edmonton, Alberta, Canada, T6G 2P9.

KERNER, Fred, b. 15 Feb. 1921, Montréal, Québec, Canada. Publisher; Editor; Author; Journalist. m. Sally Stouten, 18 May, 1959, 2 sons, 1 daughter. *Education:* BA, Sir George Williams University, Montréal, Canada, 1942. *Appointments:* Editorial Writer, Saskatoon Star-Phoenix, Saskatoon, Saskatchewan, Canada; Assistant Sports Editor, Drama Critic, Montreal Gazette, Montréal, Québec, Canada; Editorial Executive, Columnist, Foreign Correspondent, The Canadian Press; City Editor, The Associated Press, New York Bureau, USA; Senior Editor, President, Hawthorn Books, New York, USA; Editor-in-Chief, Fawcett World Library, New York, USA; Editorial Director, Reader's Digest, Canada; Vice-President, Publishing, Harlequin Enterprises, Toronto, Canada. *Memberships:* Member of numerous societies including: Awards Committee Chairman, Mystery Writers of America; Chairman, Election Committee, Awards Committee, Library Committee, Book Night Committee, International Affairs Conference; Edward R Murrow Memorial Fund, Overseas Press Club of America; Vice-President, Canadian Authors Association; International Platform Association; Advertising Club, New York; American Academy of Political and Social Sciences. *Publications:* Co-author of: Eat, Think and be Slender; The Magic Power of Your Mind; Ten Days to a Successful Memory; Secrets of Your Supraconscious; What's Best for Your Child and You; Buy High, Sell Higher; Nadia; Author of: Stress and Your Heart; Watch Your Weight Go Down; It's Fun to Fondue; Contributor to many anthologies, magazines, radio and television; Books Compiled: A Treasury of Lincoln Quotations; Love is a Man's Affair. *Honours:* Crusade for Freedom Award, 1954; Air Canada Award, 1978; Queen's Silver Jubilee Medal, 1979. *Hobby:* Music. *Address:* 25 Farmview Crescent, Willowdale, Ontario, Canada.

KERR, Desmond Moore, b. 23 Jan. 1930. HM Diplomatic Service; High Commissioner, Swaziland. m. Evelyn Patricia South, 1956, 1 son, 2 daughters. *Education:* BA., Hons., Queen's University, Belfast, Ireland, UK. *Appointments:* CRO., 1952; British High Commission: Karachi, 1956-59; Lagos, 1959-62; Second Secretary, 1960; First Secretary, 1965, Commonwealth Office, 1962-66; Deputy British Government Representative, West Indies Associated States, 1966-70; FCO, 1970-76; Deputy High Commissioner, Dacca, 1976-79; High Commissioner, Swaziland, 1979-. *Honours:* OBE., 1970. *Address:* 28 The Millbank, Ifield, Crawley, Sussex, England.

KERR, The Right Hon. Sir, John Robert, b. 24 Sept. 1914, Sydney, Australia. Barrister-at-law; Queen's Counsel. m. (1) Alison Worstead, (deceased), 1938, 1 son, 2 daughters; (2) Anne Dorothy Taggart, 1975. *Education:* LL.B., Sydney University, Australia. *Appointments:* Practised at Bar, 1938-42, Returned to Bar, 1948-66; Member of AIF, 1942-46, Colonel, 1945-46; Principal of Australian School of Pacific Administration, 1946-48; Organising Secretary, South Pacific Commission, 1947-48; Federal Judge, 1966-72; Chief Justice of New South Wales, Australia, 1972-74; Lieutenant-Governor of New South Wales, 1973-74; Governor-General of Australia, 1974-77(retired). *Memberships:* President 1964-66, Vice-President 1962-64, Law Council of Australia; President 1964, New South Wales Bar Association; New South Wales Bar Council, 1960-64; President, Law Society for Asia and Western Pacific, 1966-70; President, Industrial Relations Society of Australia, 1964-66; Hon. Life member, Law Society of England & Wales, 1965; Hon. member, American Bar Association, 1967-. *Publications:* Matters for Judgment, 1979; Uniformity in the Law - Trends and Techniques, 1965; Law in Papua and New Guinea, 1968; The Ethics of Public Office, 1974; various papers and articles on judicial administration, industrial relations, New Guinea affairs, organisation of legal profession. *Honours:* AC, 1975; AK, 1976; CMG, 1966, KCMG, 1974, GCMG, 1976; GCVO, 1977; PC, 1977; K.St.J, 1974; World Lawyer 1977 Award of World Peace Through Law Conference in Philippines. *Address:* c/o Australian

High Commission, Australia House, Strand, London, WC2B 4LA.

KERR, Roderick, b. 16 Jan. 1902, Louisbourg, Nova Scotia, Canada. Barrister and Judge. m. Myra Macdougall, 14 Jan. 1946, 2 daughters. *Education:* BA., 1923, LL.B., 1925, Dalhousie University, Halifax, Nova Scotia, Canada. *Appointments:* Barrister, Nova Scotia, Canada, 1926-40; Lieut.-Captain-Major, Canadian Army Overseas, 1940-45; Legal Adviser, Unemployment Ins. Commission, Ottawa, Canada, 1946-49; Assistant Counsel, 1949-52, General Counsel, 1952-58, Chief Commissioner, 1958-67, Board of Transport Commissioners, Ottawa, Canada; Judge of Exchequer, Court of Canada, 1967-71; Judge, 1971-75, Deputy Judge, 1975-, Federal Court of Canada; Judge, Federal Court of Appeal, Canada. *Honours:* Granted title of 'Honourable' for life by HM The Queen, upon retirement from Federal Court. *Address:* 176 Iona Street, Ottawa, Ontario, Canada.

KERRIDGE, Gordon, b. 7 Apr. 1920. Orthopaedic Surgeon. m. Catherine Isabel Morley, 30 Mar. 1946, 5 sons, 1 daughter. *Education:* MBBS., University of Sydney, Australia, 1943; FRCS, University of Edinburgh, Scotland, 1953; FRACS, 1955; FACS, 1960; FACRM, 1979. *Appointments:* President, Royal Prince Alfred Hospital, Australia, 1943; Captain, RAAMC, AIF, 1944-47; Resident Registrar and Specialist Orthopaedic Surgeon, 1948-, Director, Department of Orthopaedics, 1960-, Royal Newcastle Hospital, Australia; Clinical Associate Professor, Medicine School, University of Newcastle, Australia, 1978-. *Memberships:* Editorial Secretary, 1964-65, Federal Training Committee, 1970-, President, 1978-79, Immediate Past-President, 1979-80, Australian Orthopaedics Association; AMA; President, New South Wales Hand Surgical Association, 1967 and 1977; Court of Examination, Royal Australian College of Surgeons, 1968-78. *Publications:* various professional articles including: Prognosis of Osted Sarcoma; New Technique for reduction of Dislocated Shoulder. *Honours:* Member of Order of Australia, 1978. *Hobbies:* Swimming; Golf; Administration, Rugby Union Fottball. *Address:* 34 Wrightson Avenue, Newcastle, New South Wales 2300, Australia.

KESI, Emmanuel Emonena, b. 24 Aug. 1942, Aviara, Nigeria. Company Director; Chartered Accountant. m. Agnes Adawa, 15 May 1974, 2 sons, 2 daughters. *Education:* BSc., Econ; Studied post Management studies, Oxford, UK, 1967. *Appointments:* S E Area Accountant, Royal Air Force; Chief Accountant, Glendale Furniture Group, UK; Group Financial Controller, Strand Management Group, London, UK; Chairman and Chief Executive of: Emos Dynamics Co. Limited, UK, 1977, Hintonstow Limited, UK, 1979, Emos Dynamics Co. Nigeria Limited, Nigeria, 1978, Ada Co. Limited, Cameroons, 1980; As Senior Parter, A-E Resource Allocations Consultants, acts as Consultant to three Governments in Africa, 1979; Director of Associated companies in Germany and USA. *Memberships:* Association of Certified Accountants, UK; Institute of Chartered Accountants Nigeria; Institute of Directors, UK, British Institute of Management; Institute of Bankers. *Address:* Plot8, Block 47, Magodo Residential Area, G R A., Ijeka, Lagos, Nigeria.

KEULEMANS, Tony, b. 5 Jan. 1930, London, England. Academic. m. Prudence Alexander Ryrie, 16 May 1968, 2 sons. *Education:* B.Com. (Hons.) in Economics, 1964, Grad. Diploma in Human Communication, 1971, University of New South Wales, Australia; PhD. in Communication, University of Colorado, USA, 1974. *Appointments:* Royal Air Force, Final rank, Flight Lieutenant, 1948-55; Australian Broadcasting Commission, Final appointment, Talks Producer, 1957-67; Deputy to Head, Division of Postgraduate Extension Studies, University of New South Wales, Australia, 1967-78; Principal Lecturer in Communication Studies, Acting Dean, School of Social and Behavioural Studies, Caulfield Institute of Technology, 1978-. *Memberships:* International Institute of Communications; International Communication Association; Australian Communication Association. *Publications:* Most recent publications: The Case for Satellites, 1976; Communicating with People, 1976; Report: First Australian Symposium on Methodologies for Social and Technological Forecasting, Melbourne, 1979. *Honours:* Coronation Med-

al, 1953. *Hobbies:* Bridge; Tennis; Snow skiing. *Address:* 28 Park Road, Glen Iris, Victoria 3146, Australia.

KEYA, Shellemiah Okoth, b. 22 Sept. 1941, Angino, South Nyanza, Kenya. Soil Scientist. m. 20 Dec. 1970, 3 sons, 1 daughter. *Education:* BSc. Agriculture, (Hons.), Makerere University, USA, 1968; MSc. Soil Science, 1970, PhD. Soil Science, 1974, Cornell University, USA. *Appointments:* Bank Clerk, 1965; High School teacher and Headmaster, 1965; Research Assistant, 1968, Tutorial Fellow, 1970, Makerere University, Nairobi; Lecturer, 1974, Senior Lecturer and Chairman, Department of Soil Science, 1976-, University of Nairobi, Kenya. *Memberships:* Chairman, Kenya Agricultural Teachers Association; Governing Council, Kenya National Academy for the Advancement of Arts and Science; Committee member, Soil Science Society of East Africa; International Soil Science Society; Association for the Advancement of Agricultural Science in Africa; Society for International Development; Agricultural Society of Kenya. *Publications:* Theses: Factors affecting Rhizobium-legume specificity in Rhizobium trifolii, 1970; Effects of parasitic Bdellovibrio and predetory protozoa on survival of cowpea. Rhizobium in culture and laboratory soil, 1974; Scientific Journals and Proceedings include: Factors affecting growth of Bdellovibrio on Rhizobium (with M Alexander), 1975; Protozoa and the decline of Rhizobium populations added to soil (with S K A Danso and M Alexander), 1975; Soil Management with respect to liming, manuring and other soil ammendments in East Africa. Improved use of Plant Nutrients, 1977; Yield performance and selection for resistance in beans (Phaseolus vulgaris L.) to common diseases in Kenya (with D M Mukunya), 1978; The role of biological nitrogen fixation in Agroforestry, International Council for Research in Agroforestry, Soils Research in Agroforestry, Proceedings of an Expert Consultation, 1979; Books: Agriculture for Primary Schools (with R S Musangi, B Chembeni, P Simiyu, B Kendall), 1979; Agriculture for Primary School (with R S Musangi, B Kendall, R Simiyu, B Chembeni, R H Maxwell), 1980. *Honours:* Uganda Company Exhibition Prize, 1967; Muljibhai-Madhvani Prize, 1968; USAID scholarship, 1968-70; Rockefeller Foundation scholarship, 1972-74; Elected member, International Cell Research Organization, 1979; Elected alternate member, UNEP/UNESCO/ICRO Microbiology Panel, 1979; Commonwealth Foundation Fellowship, 1980. *Hobby:* Gardening. *Address:* Angino School, PO Oyugis, Kenya.

KEYS, Alexander George William, President, The Returned Services League of Australia. *Appointments:* 5 years World War II; Service in Australia, New Guinea and Borneo, Finschhafen and Tarakan campaigns; Korea 12 months, 1950-51; Joined the Returned Services League of Australia, 1944-. *Memberships:* National President, Korea and South East Asia Forces Association of Australia, 1967-; National Committee of Royal Australian Regiment Association of Australia, 1967-; President, International Federation of Korean War Veterans' Associations, 1978-; President, A.C.T. Churchill Fellows Association, 1974-; Trustee, Australian War Memorial, 1975-; Chairman, Capital Permanent Building Society, 1977-; Administrative Review Council, 1978-; National Chairman, Australian Forces, Overseas Fund, 1978-; Chairman, A.C.T. Austcare for 4 years; Nuffield Scholar, 1956; Churchill Fellow, 1969. *Publications:* 'The Serviceman and His Post Service Problems', 1969. *Honours:* Military Cross, 1961; Officer of the Order of the British Empire, 1970; Knight Bachelor, 1980; Life -member R.S.L, 1960; Life Member Korea and South East Asia Forces of Australia, 1965; Korean Order of National Security Merit, 1980$ *Hobbies:* Weekend farming; Painting; Writing. *Address:* P.O. Box 303, Canberra City, A.C.T. 2601, Australia.

KGAREBE, Aloysius William, b. 17 Aug. 1923, Mafeking, South Africa. Educationalist. m. 2 sons, 3 daughters. *Education:* University of South Africa; University of Leeds, UK. *Appointments:* Teacher, St. Joseph's College, Orlando, Johannesburg; Mamelodi, Pretoria, South Africa, 1946-61; Vice-Principal, Teachers College, Lobatse, 1962-65, Principal, 1966-68; Senior Education Officer, 1968-70, Chief Education Officer, 1970-75, Ministry of Education; High Commissioner in Zambia, 1976-78, in UK, 1978-. *Hobbies:* Reading; Tennis; Gardening. *Address:* 95 Platts lane, London, NW3, England.

KHALIL, Ibrahim Mohamed, b. 11 Jan. 1913, Omdurman, Sudan. Veterinary Doctor. m. 26 June 1946, 2 sons, 3 daughters. *Education:* BVSc., University of Khartoum, Sudan, 1941; Special training in Animal Production at Universities in: Liverpool, UK; Denmark; Sweden; Netherlands; USA. *Appointments:* Veterinary Officer: Allied Forces, Abyssinian Front, 1940-41; White Nile Province, 1942-44; Northern Province, 1945-51; Study course in UK, 1951-52; Principal Veterinary Officer, Upper Nile Province, 1953-54; Director of Animal Production, 1955-61; director, Ministry of Animal Resources, 8th Sudan, 1962-65; Chief Veterinary Officer, Kano, North Eastern States, Borno State, Nigeria, 1965-. *Memberships:* Sudan Veterinary Association; Sudan Philosophical Society; Nigerian Veterinary Medical Association. *Publications:* Paper on Livestock Production. *Honours:* King Farouk of Egypt prize, for Best Graduate, Faculty of Veterinary Medicine, 1941; Republican Order, 2nd Class, Egypt, 1956; Grand Medal of Honour, Science and Technology, France, 1960. *Hobbies:* Polo; Hunting; Tennis; Chess; Table tennis; Card games. *Address:* c/o PO Box 221, Omdurman, Sudan.

KHAN, Mobarak Hossain, b. 27 Feb. 1938, Brahmanbaria (Comilla), Bangladesh. Director, External Services, Radio Bangladesh, Dacca. m. Fauzia Yasmin, 16 Aug. 1963, 2 sons, 1 daughter. *Education:* BA., 1956; MA., History, 1960. *Appointments:* Programme Producer, Programme Organiser, Assistant Regional Director, Regional Director-in-Charge, Radio Pakistan; Director of Programme Planning as Officer on Special Duty, Director of Commercial Service, Director of Administration, Head of Department of Radio Publications, Director of Music, Regional Director, Chittagong, in charge of Relay Station at Chittagong Hill Tracts, Director, External Services, Radio Bangladesh. *Memberships:* Member of numerous organisations including: Life member, Banglaa Academy-A National Academy for development of Bengali language; Founder General Secretary, Rangpur Sangeet Academy-A musical Institute; Secretary, Comilla District Cultural Association; Music & Fine Arts sub-committee, Comilla Education Board; Chief Advisor, The Sangeet. *Publications:* Numerous publications including: Books: Sur Lahori; Sur Niye Jar Khela; Translations: Shikarir Guha; Hadiser Kahini; Dilker Tin Sultan; A Number of articles on music in research magazines and journals. *Honours:* Award certificate of talent as all rounder in games and music, 1957; Honoured as the 'Proud Son' of Brahmanbaria, 1979. *Hobbies:* Writing; Reading; Music. *Address:* c/o Ostad Ayet Ali Khan, Kandirpar, Comilla, Bangladesh.

KHAN, Mohammad Salar, b. 2 March 1924, Kakinada, Andhra Pradesh, India. Professor, Principal Investigator. m. (1) Razia Begum, 25 May 1951, (deceased 20 Nov. 1968) 3 daughters, (2) Sufia Begum, 12 July 1970. *Education:* B.Sc. Botany, Zoology, Chemistry, 1944; M.Sc., Botany, Aligarh Muslim University, India, 1947; Diploma in Biology, University of Edinburgh, United Kingdom, 1960; Ph.D., Plant Taxonomy, University of Edinburgh, United Kingdom, 1962. *Appointments:* Lecturer in Botany, Gandhi Faizam College, Shahjahanpur, India, 1947-50; Lecturer in Botany, University of Dacca, 1950-63; Associate Professor, 1963-78, Professor, 1978-, University of Dacca, Bangladesh; Flora of Bangladesh, 1971-. *Memberships:* Asiatic Society of Bangladesh; Editor, Journal of the Asiatic Society, Bangladesh (Science) 1976-79; Bangladesh Botanical Society; Editor, Bangladesh Journal of Botany, 1976; Association of Phytegeography and Taxonomy of the Mediterranean Flora, 1976-. *Publications:* 58 scientific papers on Taxonomy of Angiosperms from the Near East (Aristolochia), from Turkey (Euphorbia), and on the floristics of Bangladesh; Editor, Flora of Bangladesh. *Honours:* Awarded a scholarship under the Technical Co-operation Scheme of the Columbo Plan to pursue a doctoral programme in plant taxonomy at the University of Edinburgh, 1959-62; Awarded a Royal Society Commonwealth bursary from the Society's Scientific Exchanges Fund to carry out post-doctoral research in connection with Flora of Bangladesh at Edinburgh and Kew herbaria, 1975-76. *Hobbies:* Photography; Gardening; Philately. *Address:* Department of Botany, University of Dacca, Dacca 2, Bangladesh.

KHAN, Muhammad Abdul Aziz, b. 1 Feb. 1931, Bangladesh. Teaching and Research. m. Nargis Ara Choudhury, 16 Oct. 1977, 1 son, 1 daughter. *Education:* S.S.C., 1946, H.S.C., 1948, B.S.c., 1950, M.Sc., 1952, Bangladesh; Ph.D., University of Cambridge, England, 1964. *Appointments:* Lecturer, 1953-60, Senior Lecturer, 1960-69, Associate Professor, 1969-72, Dacca University; Associate Professor, 1973-74, Professor, 1974-, Chittagong University. *Memberships:* Bangladesh A.A. Society; Bangladesh Botanical Society; Editorial Brkanch, Bangladesh Journal of Botany; Editorial Branch, Chittagong University Studies. *Publications:* 40 Research papers; 3 Text books. *Hobbies:* Gardening; Agriculture. *Address:* Ram Nagar, Banwari Nagar, Pabna, Bangladesh.

KHAN, Rasheeduddin, b. 11 Sept. 1924, Hyderabad City, India. Professor, Member of Parliament. m. Leela Narayana Rao, 29 Aug. 1965, 1 son, 1 daughter. *Education:* B.A., 1946, MA., 1948, Madras University; Ph.D., Indian School of International Studies, New Delhi. *Appointments:* include: Lecturer in History and Political Science, Osmania University, Hyderabad, 1948-62; Professor and Head, Department of Political Science, Osmania University, Hyderabad, 1965-70; Dean, Faculty of Social Sciences, Osmania University, Hyderabad, 1970; Dean, School of Social Sciences, Jawaharlal Nehru University, New Delhi, 1973-75; Director, United Nations University Research Project on 'Composite Culture and National Socio-Political Change, 1980; Parliamentary appointments include: Member of Parliament, Council of States, Rajya Sabha, 1970, renomination 1976; Member, Delegation of India to the United Nations 24th General Assembly Session, 1969; Member UNESCO Expert Committee on Study of Violence, 1975; Leader, Delegation of India to the International Conference of Builders of Peace, Warsaw, 1977. *Memberships:* Indian Council of Social Sciences Research, 1969-76, 1980-; University Grants Commission Committees; Life Member, All India Political Science Association, 1966, 1974-75; Member Executive Council, Central University of Hyderabad, 1975-77; Chairman, Committee on Curriculum in Civics and Politics, National Council of Education, Research and Training, 1976-77; Vice-President, Indo-Soviet Cultural Society, 1975-; Board of the Salar Jung Museum, Hyderabad, 1973-; Editorial Advisory Board, Economic and Political Weekly, Bombay, Secular Democracy, New Delhi, Editorial Board, Islamic Culture, Hyderabad, 1966-71. *Publications:* Contributed to various articles on 'Problems of Political System and Federal Polity in India'; Foreign Policy and International Relations; West Asian Politics; Educational Problems; Position Paper prepared for the United Nations University Project, Socio-Cultural Development Alternatives in a Changing World; Two papers prepared for the UNESCO Human Rights and Peace Division, Paris. *Honours:* Leader, Delegation of India to the International Conference of Builders of Peace, Warsaw, 1977; Leader, Delegation of India to the Second Binational India-Indonesia Seminar on 'Changing World, Challenges and Prospects', Jakarta, 1976; Convenor, Parliamentarians for Peace, 1977-. *Hobbies:* Photography; Music; Reading Poetry; Walking. *Address:* C-1/13 Pandara Park, New Delhi, Pin 110 003, India.

KHAN, Yasmin, b. 18 May 1951, Kericho, Kenya. Graphic Designer, Librarian. m. (1) Walter Plata, 12 May 1973. (2) 23 March 1977. *Education:* B.A. Design, University of Nairobi, 1973; Dip. Lib., College of Librarianship Wales, 1979. *Appointments:* Part-time Teaching, Kenya Arts Society, 1974-77; Librarian, 1979; Graphic Designer and Documentation Assistant, United Nations Environmental Programme, Nairobi 1980-. *Memberships:* Former member of the Kenya Arts Society; The Library Association, London, 1978-; Kenya Library Association, 1979-. *Creative Works:* 'Art and Design by Yasmin Khan', 1973; 'Paintings and Prints by Yasmin Khan', 1973; 'Visual Communication in Kenya', 1974; Exhibition for the Best Designed Books of Britain for the years 1973,74,75, University of Frankfort, 1976; Exhibition of Water Colour Paintings, depicting Wild and Garden Flowers of Kenya, Goethe Institute, Nairobi, 1980. *Honours:* 2nd Prize in the National Symbol design competition for Kenya Catering Levy Trustees; Special Mention for the poster competition on the theme Lecco-Citta Manzoniana chosen for exhibition at the Palazzo Ghislanzoni, Lecco, Italy, 1972; Award of the Ghandi Smarak Prize in the Faculty of Architecture, Design and Development for good achievement, 1972-73. *Hobbies:* Painting; Designing; Chinese Brush Painting. *Address:* P.O. Box 40037, Nairobi, Kenya.

KHAN MANSHA, Manshaur Rehman, b. 1 May 1924, Pimpalgaon Raja, Dist-Buldana-Maharashtra, India. Lecturer. m. Tajun Nisa Khanam, 4 sons, 2 daughters. *Education:* H.S., 1941; B.A., 1949; M.A., 1952; B.T., Education, 1956; M.A., Persian, 1958; Ph.D., Arts, 1971. *Appointments:* Assistant Master, Anjuman High School, Khamgaon, 1945; Teacher, Lecturer, Government High School, Yeotmal, 1952; Lecturer in Urdu, Nagpur Mahavidyalaya, Nagpur, 1956. *Memberships:* High School Board of Urdu and Persian; Chairman, Board of Studies in Urdu, Nagpur University, Nagpur; M.S. Urdu Academi; Advisory Board of All India Radio, Nagpur; President, Halqua Ahbad Literary Organisation, Nagpur; All India University Urdu Teacher's Conference; Working Committee, Rashtra Bhasha, Nagpur. *Publications:* Collection of Poems including: Jeevan Tarang in Nagari Seript; Aahange Hayat; Nawa-e Dil; Zikre Khooban; Aenae Iqbal; Akse-Dauran; Mutala-e-Mamnoon-Research thesis on life and works of Mir Mamnoon Delhvi; Diwane Mamnoon. *Honours:* 4 Government Awards for literary Services; Puraskar (Honour) for Urdu Literature, Rashtra Bhasha Prachar Samati Wardha; Puraskar (Honour) for Urdu Poetry, M.S. Information Centre, Nagpur; Prizes on Education, Debates-Essays and Poetry Compositions. *Hobbies:* Gardening; Books; Reading. *Address:* 11 Starky Town, Nagpur Maharashtra, India.

KHANNA, Kanahiya Charan, b. 17 Sept. 1924, Lucknow. Industrial Manager. m. Pratima, 26 Jan 1947, 2 sons, 2 daughters. *Education:* B.Sc. Metallurgy, Banaras Hindu University, 1948. *Appointments:* Engineer, Foundry Industry, 1948-56; Engineer, 1956-54, Superintendent, 1964-67, Chief Superintendent, 1967-69, Assistant General Superintendent, 1969-71, Durgapur Steel Plant; General Superintendent, General Manager, 1971-74, Managing Director, 1974-76, Bokaro Steel Limited; Chairman, Managing Director, Kudremukh Iron Ore Company Limited, 1976-80; Chairman, Steel Authority of India Limited, 1980-. *Memberships:* Indian Institute of Metals, Calcutta; All India Board of Management Studies, Ministry of Education, Government of India; Fellow, Institute of Directors, London. *Honours:* National Metallurgists Award, 1964. *Address:* No. 5 Vishav Rockey Street, Lucknow (Uttar Pradesh) India.

KHATRI, Chinubhai, b. 4 Aug. 1931, Patan, Gujarat State, India. Teaching and Research. m. Kanakben, 11 Dec. 1948, 5 daughters. *Education:* SSc, Secondary S C Board, Poona, 1949; BSc, Gujarat University, Ahmedahad, 1953; MSc, Bombay University, Bombay, 1955; PhD, M S University of Baroda, Baroda, 1960. *Appointments:* Lecturer in Statistics, M S University of Baroda, 1955-62; Reader in Statistics, Gujarat University, 1962-69; Professor of Statistics, Indian Statistical Institute, 1967-68; Visiting Professor, Purdue University, 1968; Professor of Statistics, Gujarat University, 1969-. *Memberships:* The Institute of Statistical Mathematics; American Statistical Association; International Statistical Institute; Indian Statistical Institute; Indian Statistical Association, Vice-President, 1980; Founder President, Gujarat Statistical Association, 1969-71; President, Gujarat Ganit Mandal, 1975. *Publications:* Mathematics of matrices, 1971; Introduction to Multiveriate Statistics, (w. M S Sivastava), 1978; Approximately 150 research papers in various statistical journals. *Honours:* Fellow, American Statistical Association, 1970; Fellow, The Institute of Statistical Mathematics, 1972; Hargovandas Lax michand Gold Medal, 1953. *Hobbies:* Meditation; Walking. *Address:* 7 Jay Mangal Society, Mirambika Road, Ahmedabad, 380013, India.

KHATTRI, Shree Nath, b. 31 March 1942, Akbarpur India. Physician and Cardiologist. m. Asha Kapoor, 11 Dec. 1969, 1 son, 1 daughter. *Education:* M.B.B.S., 1965, M.D., 1969, Lucknow University; Cardiology Orientation course, IMA College of General Practitioners, Delhi. *Appointments:* Compulsory rotating Internship, Medical College, Kanpur, 1965; Resident House Physician, 1966; Resident Medical Officer, 1967-68; Research Scholar in Cariology section of Department of Medicine, Medical College, Kanpur, 1968-69; Private Medical Consultant, Akbarpur, 1969-77; Medical attendant of Central Government Employees, 1974-77; Chief Physician, Fatima Hospital, Mau, 1977-. *Memberships:* Fellow, American College of Chest Physician, Illinois, United States of America; Royal Society of Health, London, England; Academy of Medical Specialities, New Delhi; Indian Association of Chest Diseases, New Delhi; Indian Medical Association, Akbarpur Branch; Rotary International, Mau Branch. *Publications:* Diagnostic value of Splenic Puncture in cases of splenomegaly, 1970; Coronary Heart Disease, How to predict and prevent-The Antiseptic, 1978; Angina Pectoris-Recent advances in Management, 1979; Acute Chest Pain, A diagnostic problem, 1979; Japanese B Encephalitis in Eastern U.P., 1980; Read papers in various Medical Conferences; Published health educational articles in various news-papers. *Honours:* Best House Physician in Medical College Award, 1966; Best Student in Biology of B.N. Inter college award, 1958; Services highly acclaimed during Encephalitis Epidemic, 1978. *Hobbies:* Badminton; Reading; Movies; Travelling. *Address:* Fatima Hospital, P.O. Maunath Bhanjan, Distt. Azamgarh, India.

KHETARPAL, Surat Parkash, b. 9 June 1925, Myingkan, Burma. Professor of Law. m. Geeta 19 April 1962, 1 son, 1 daughter. *Education:* B.Sc. Punjab University, 1946; b.l. Rangoon University, 1949; LL.M. London University, 1957; Ph.D., London University, 1959; *Appointments:* Advocate, High Court Rangoon; Lecturer in Law, University of Singapore, 1961; Professor of Law, 1965-. Director of Graduate studios, 1972-80, Chairman, Post Graduate, Diploma in Law, 1980-, University of Alberta, Canada. *Memberships:* Secretary, Organising Committee, South East Asia Conference on Legal Education, 1962; General Secretary, Law Schools and Law Teachers Association, South East Asia, 1964-65; International Family Law Association; Canadian Law Teachers Association. *Publications:* Editor, Report on the proceedings of Regional Conference on Legal Education, 1962; Cases and Materials on Equity, Trusts, Family Law; Articles on Family Law in various Journals. *Hobbies:* Music; Movies; Theatre. *Address:* 8408-118 Street, Edmonton, Alberta, Canada.

KHETARPAL, Vijay, b. 4 Oct. 1958, Jodhpur, India. Management Consulting. *Education:* BA, Economics, St Stephens College, Delhi University, India, 1975-78; International Politics, Jawaharlal Nehru University, Delhi, 1979. *Appointments:* Consultant, Maurice Project Centre Limited, Nigeria, 1979-. *Memberships:* Third World Foundation; Institute of Management Consultants of Nigeria; Delhi Management Association. *Publications:* Article - Nigeria's Industrial Take-off. *Honours:* Staff of the Year, 1980; Most Outstanding Squash Player, 1977; Won several Squash Championships in India & Nigeria, National Junior Champion, 1977. *Hobbies:* Photography; Travelling. *Address:* Commander Fasteners Pvt. Ltd., 106 New Okhla Industrial Complex, Phase I, New Delhi, 110020, India.

KHEW, Khing Ling, b. 26 Jan. 1943, Sarawak, Malaysia. University Lecturer. m. Lean Siew Hong, 12 Nov. 1978, 1 son. *Education:* BSc, Nanyang University, Singapore, 1961-64; MSc, University of Guelph, Canada, 1966-67; PhD, University of California, Riverside, USA, 1968-71. *Appointments:* Teacher, Sarawak, 1965; Research Assistant, University of Guelph, 1966-67, University of California, 1968-71; Lecturer, University Sains, Malaysia, Penang, Malaysia, 1972-. *Memberships:* Malaysian Plant Protection Society; International Society of Plant Pathology. *Publications:* A Number of research papers published in Malaysian and International Journals. *Honours:* Searca Fellowship, 1976; Alexander Von Humboldt Stiftung Fellowship, 1977. *Hobbies:* Photography; Table-Tennis; Travel. *Address:* School of Biological Sciences, University Sains Malaysia, Penang, Malaysia.

KHILNANI, Khemchand Rewachand Fatehchand Khilnani, b. 16 Feb. 1913, Karachi. Diplomacy, Law and Writing. m. Smt. Umadevi, 3 Dec. 1941, 1 son, 5 daughters. *Education:* B.A. Hons, Bombay University; B.A. Hons, Cambridge University; Politics and International Law, Society of Lincoln's Inn, London; Fellow, Royal Economic Society; M.A. Hons, Cambridge University; M.A. Supreme Court of India. *Appointments:* Assignments in Government of India at Home and Abroad including: Ministry of External Affairs, 1948-49; Economic Advisor Commissioner General for Europe, Paris; First Secretary, Embassy of India, Prague, Bulgaria, Rumania, Albania, Hungary, Poland, 1949-51; High Commissioner East & Central Africa, Ambassador of India, Romania & Bulgaria, Leader, Indian Delegation ECAFE I.L.O; Ambassador of India in Senegal and concurrently accreditation as Ambassador to Ivory Coast, Upper Volta and Mauritania and High Commissioner to The Gambia, 1967-68; Counsel High Court of the Punjab and of the Supreme Court, 1968. *Memberships:* Delhi Gymkhana Club, New Delhi; Chairman Programmes Committee and Editor Rotary Journal, Rotary Club Midtown; Chairman, Senior Citizens Committee, Chairman, Public Relations Committee, President, Indian Social Reconstruction Society; Governing Committee; Indian Cultural and Knowledge Society; Advisery Board, International Cultural Association. *Publications:* A number of Articles in Newspapers, Journals and Magazines, India and abroad. *Honours:* Government of Sind Scholar and Sind Exhibition and Fair Prizeman for standing first in the University, Matriculation Examination, Province of Sind; Awarded twice Besant Elocution Cup; Hughlings Prizeman for standing first, University of Bombay; Distinctions in Private Civil Law, English Essay, Viva voce, first class Constitutional in International Law, Civil Service Examinations, London, 1935-36;. *Hobbies:* Gardening; Poetry; Bird watching; Hiking. *Address:* 18 Eastern Avenue, Maharani Bagh, New Delhi-14, India.

KHOFI-PHIRI, Gowoka Nobi Kalowamfumbi, b. 26 Sept. 1931, Nkhota Kota, Malawi. Businessman and Politician. m. Eunice Kulanda Nyamanda, 26 Dec. 1956, 9 sons, 5 daughters. *Education:* Diploma, Bookeeping and Accounts, Secretarial Practice, Business Management and Administration, 1954; Diploma in Economics and Political Science, The Johns Hopkins University, USA. *Appointments:* Acting Secretary General, Malawi Congress Party, 1960; General Manager, Nkhota Kota Rice Co-op. Society, 1961-63; 3rd Secretary, Malawi Embassy, Washing, USA, 1965-66; Member of Parliament, Nkhota Kota District, 1966-70; Alternate Governor, African Dev. Bank; Leader, Malawi Delegation: CPA, London; ADBA, Conference to Abidjan, Nairobi, Fort Lany, 1967, 1968, 1970; Parliamentary Secretary to Ministry of Trade and Industry and Ministry of Economic Affairs; Leader, Malawi Delegation to UNCIAD, New Delhi, 1969; Managing Director, Kadona Gewoka and Company Limited, 1969-70; Administrative Manager, Press Transport; Pensions, Old Mutual. *Memberships:* Malawi Congress Party; Life Member, Commonwealth Parliamentary Association, Malawi; Insurance Institute of Malawi. *Honours:* Independance Medal, Malawi. *Hobbies:* Soccer; Dancing; Music; Cinema. *Address:* Chiboko Village, Tia Malengachanzi, PO Nkhota Kota, Malawi.

KHOO, Gordon Soo-Guan, b. 7 Nov. 1921, Penang, West Malaysia. Land Surveyor. m. Lily Ying-Loong Leong, 2 Oct. 1952, 2 sons, 2 daughters. *Education:* Bachelor of Surveying, Queensland University, 1951. *Appointments:* District Surveyor, Selangor, 1951; District Surveyor, 1951, Chief Surveyor, 1954-55, Trenganu; District Surveyor, 1952, Chief Surveyor's Deputy, 1953, Chief Surveyor, 1956-58, Kedah and Perlis; Training and Research Officer, HQ, Kuala Lumpur, 1955-56; Deputy Surveyor General, Federation of Malaya and Singapore, 1958-62; Principal of S G Khoo and Company Land and Engineering Surveyors, offices in Kuala Lumpur, Singapore, Kulim, Kelantan and Kelang, 1962-73. *Memberships:* Fellow, Institution of Surveyors, Malaysia; Fellow, Singapore Institution of Surveyors; Institution of Surveyors, Australia; State Natural Resources Board, Kedah; State Development Board, Kedah; Kulim Town Board. *Publications:* Contributed articles to various periodicals. *Honours:* Kedah Commemoration Medal, 1957; First Asian to join Malayan Survey Service; First President, Institution of Surveyors, Malaya. *Hobbies:* Stocks and Shares; Horse Racing; Dog Racing. *Address:* 7 Turriff Road, Floreat Park, Perth, Western Australia.

KHORANA, Anand Bhushan, b. 22 July 1938, New Delhi, India. Psychiatrist. m. Suman Gunde, 19 Nov. 1968, 1 son. *Education:* ISc, Birla University, 1956; MB, BS, Rajasthan University, India, 1961; DPM, Ranchi University, India, 1965; MD, Bihar University, India, 1967; MRC, London University, 1973. *Appointments:* Resident, Medical College, Bikamar, 1962; Resident, Medical College, Jaipur, 1963; Medical Officer, Central Institute of Psychiatry, Ranchi, 1965-67; Assistant Professor, 1967-73, Professor and Head of Department of Psychiatry, 1973-, Medical College, Baroda. *Memberships:* Royal College of Psychiatrists, London; World Psychiatric Association, London; Indian Psychiatric Society, 1967-, Member of the Committee on

Medical Association; Life Member, Indian Association for the Advancement of Medical Association; Life Member, Indian Association of Clinical Hypnosis. *Publications:* 53 Research and Scientific Publications in various National and International Journals. *Honours:* WHO Fellowship; Elected to Corresponding Fellowship, American Psychiatric Association.' *Hobbies:* Swiming; Painting. *Address:* M-8 Doctors Apartments, Indira Avenue, Baroda 390001, India.

KHURANA, Bhagwan Dass, b. 12 May 1944, Sandon, Multan, India. Service. m. Asha Khurana, 15 May 1972, 1 son. *Education:* BTech, Indian Institute of Technology, New Delhi, 1962-67. *Appointments:* Electronic Engineer, 1968-70, Division Incharge, 1970-74, The Oriental Scientific Services· Appratus Workshop, Ambala Cantt; Project Officer, Punjab State Industrial Development Corporation Limited, Chandigarh, 1974-75; Project Manager, 1975-77, General Manager, 1977-80, Managing Director, 1980-, Punjab Wireless Systems Limited, SAS, Nagar. *Memberships:* Fellow, The Institution of Electronics and Telecommunication Engineers, New Delhi; Magnetic Society of India. *Hobbies:* Photography; Writing Poetry. *Address:* 1152/Sector 8-C, Chandigarh-160008, India.

KHUSHTAR, Siddiqui Oadri Razui Muhammed Ibrahim, b. 8 Mar. 1930, Jamalpur, India. Muslim Missionary. m. Amtul Qadeer, 23 Feb. 1958, 3 sons, 3 daughters. *Education:* Accomplished scholar in Arabic, Persian, Urdu and English Matriculation; Received all the degrees from Bareilly Alahabad (India), Lahore, Faisalabad (Pakistan) Universities in 1952, 1960, and already teached in India and Pakistan, Mauritius, UK, in above mentioned languages. *Appointments:* Head Priest, Colombo (Sri-Lanka) Mauritius and Manchester Jummah Mosques; Head of the Islamic Affairs for the United Kingdom and Mauritius. *Memberships:* Founder and Chief Patron of the Sunni Razvi Society International and Sunni Razvi Academy, England, Holland, South Africa, Zimbabwe, Mauritius, Sri-Lanka and Pakistan. *Publications:* Holiest Earth of Islam; Le Chamin de la Deliverance; La Mort; The Path of Spiritual Attainments. *Honours:* Street named after him by Ccl; Maulana Muhammad Ibrahim Khushtar Street, Port-Louis, Mauritius, 1969. *Hobbies:* Reading; Writing; Teaching and Preaching. *Address:* 325 Cheetham Hill Road, Manchester M8 7SN, England.

KIAPI, Abraham, b. 1 Apr. 1943, Moyo, Madi District, Uganda. Professor of Law. m. Isabella Mesiku, 31 Dec. 1967, 2 sons, 4 daughters. *Education:* GCE (A) Level, University College Nairobi, 1961-63; LL B, University College, Dar es Sallam; LL M, Columbia University, New York. *Appointments:* Assistant Lecturer, 1966, Lecturer, 1967-69, University College, Dar es sallam; Senior State Attorney, Ministry of Justice, Uganda, 1969; Head Administrative Law, Uganda Institute of Public Administration, 1970-71; Lecturer, Senior Lecturer, Professor of Law, Makerere University, 1971; Professor & Dean of Law, Makerere University, 1975-80. *Memberships:* Uganda Law Society; Association of British Law Teachers; Board of directors of various companies. *Publications:* Civil Service Laws in East Africa; Textbook of East African Administrative Law; The Theory and the Law of the Public Corporation in East Africa; Theory of Government and Constitutional Law in East'Africa; Law and Population in Uganda; Various articles published in international journals all over the world. *Hobbies:* Reading; Piano; Teble Tennis. *Address:* Makerere University, PO Box 7062 Kampala, Uganda

KIBAKI, Mwai, b. 1931, Othaya, Kenya. Kenyan Politician. *Education:* BA., BSc., Makerere University, Kenya. *Appointments:* Lecturer, Economics, Makerere University College, Kenya, 1959-60; National Executive Officer, Kenya African National Union, 1960-62; elected by Legislative Council, one of Kenya's nine representatives in Central Legislative Assembly of East African Common Services Organisation, 1962; Member, House of Representatives, Nairobi Doonholm, 1963-; Parliamentary Secretary to Treasury, 1963; Assistant Minster, Economic Planning and Development, 1964-66; Minister for Commerce and Industry, 1966-69; Minister of Finance, 1969-70, 1978-; Minister of Finance and Economic Planning, 1970-78; Minister of Home Affairs, 1978-79; Vice-President of Kenya, 1978-; Vice-President, Kenya African National Union(KANU), 1978-. *Address:* Office of the Vice-President, Nairobi, Kenya.

KIDDA, Mairo Laku Elinor (Mrs), b. 27 Jan. 1949, LKaltungo, Bauchi State, Nigeria. University Lecturer. m. Mallam Samaila Molangune Boryo (dec.), 6 Jan. 1970, 1 son, 1 daughter. *Education:* BA (Hons) English, Ahmadu Bello University, Zaria, Nigeria, 1971-74; MA, Linguistics, Southern Illinois University, USA, 1978-79. *Appointments:* Nigerian National Youth Service Corporations, 1974-75; Assistant Lecturer, North East College of Arts & Science, Maiduguri, Nigeria, 1975-76; Lecturer, University of Maiduguri, Nigeria, 1976-. *Memberships:* Governing Council for the Bauchi State College of Arts & Science, Nigeria; Women's Association of Maiduguri University; Linguistics Students Association, USA; African Students' Association, USA; International Women's Association, Maiduguri, *Publications:* Master's Thesis (Unpublished); Seminar Papers. *Honours:* Prizes, Best academic student, 1960, 61, 63; Gold Medal, intermediate 200 metres race, Northern Women's Amateur Athletics, Kaduna, 1964. *Hobbies:* Gardening; Travel; Reading; Current International Affairs. *Address:* c/o Mallam Hassan Kidda, Adult Education Office, T/Waja Local Government, P A Billiri, via Gombe, Bauchi State, Nigeria.

KIDDELL, Sidney George, b. 18 May 1908, Enfield, Middlesex, England. Accountant, Organist. m. Christine Henderson, 15 Sept. 1934, 1 son (Deceased). *Education:* Enfield and further education. *Appointments:* Organist at London Churches, 1924-64; Accountant own practice 1945-; Licensed Reader (Church of England), Chelmsford Diocese, 1964-73, Canterbury Diocese, 1973-75, Salisbury Diocese, 1975-. *Memberships:* Editor of Journal, The Gregorian Association; Secretary, Plainsong & Mediaeval Music Society; Chaplain, World Order of Cultural Exchange; Royal School of Church Music; Hymn Society of Great Britain; International Biographical Association. *Publications:* J H Arnold's third edition of Plainsong Accompaniment; Angelus Virginem; Hymn Tune, Adnitt. *Honours:* Hood of World Order of Cultural Exchange, 1978; Admitted as Oblate Order of St Benedict (Nashdom Abbey), 1979. *Hobbies:* Study of Liturgy; Hymnody; Hymnology; Comparative Religions. *Address:* The Church Lodge, Wimborne St Giles, Wimborne, Doreset, BH21 5LZ, England.

KIDU, Buri William, b. 8 Aug. 1945, Pari Village, Port Moresby, Papua, New Guinea. Chief Justice. m. Carol Anne Mullwater, 11 Aug. 1969, 3 sons, 2 daughters. *Education:* LL.B, University of Queensland, 1966-70. *Appointments:* Legal Officer, Department of Justice, 1971-73; Deputy Crown Solicitor, 1973-74; Crown Solicitor, 1975-77; State Solicitor, 1975-77; Secretary for Justice, 1977-79; Secretary of the Prime Minister's Department, 1979-80; Appointed Chief Justice of Papua New Guinea, 1980-. *Memberships:* Interim President, Papua New Guinea Law Society, 1977; Chancellor, The University of Papua New Guinea. *Honours:* Knight Bachelor, 1980; Papua New Guinea Independence Medal, 1975; Queens Silver Jubilee Medal. *Hobby:* Reading. *Address:* Armit Street, Port Moresby, Papua New Guinea.

KIGERA, David Rufus, b. 22 Sept. 1942, Nairobi. Librarian. m. 14 Mar. 1964, 3 sons, 2 daughters. *Education:* Cambridge Certificate, St. Bernard College, 1958-61; Diploma, Library Science, Certificate, Documentation, Certificate Library Studies, Makerere University, 1968-73. *Appointments:* Library Assistant, Ministry of Economic Planning, Kenya, 1964-68; Assistant Librarian, Kenya Polytechnic, 1969-70; Librarian, Mines & Geology Department, Kenya, 1970-74; Librarian/Documentalist, ICIPE, 1974-81. *Memberships:* National Academy of Science, Kenya; Kenya Library Association; Association of Agricultural Librarians and Documentalists; Kenya German Association; Veterinary Laboratory Sports Club, Kenya; African Association of Insect Scientists. *Publications:* Bibliography of: Culux Quinquefasciatus; Glossina Morsitans; Spodoptera Exempta; Maruca Testulalis; Maliarpha Separatella. *Hobbies:* Water Sports; Motor Sports; Farming. *Address:* PO Box 56616, Nairobi, Kenya.

KIGOZI, Dorcas Maria (Mrs), b. Mukono, Uganda. Librarian. m. Eric Kigozi, 1 May 1964, 1 son, 4 daughters. *Education:* BA, London, 1964; Diploma in Librarianship, Wales, 1971; ALA. *Appointments:* Assistant Librarian, Uganda Public Libraries Board, 1970-73; Sub-Librarian, Makerere Institute of Social Research, Sub-Library, 1973-79; Librarian—Periodicals, Gifts &

Exchange Section, Makerere University Library Service, 1980-. *Memberships:* Executive Committee, Uganda Library Association, Uganda Association of University Women. *Publications:* Women-Sexism-The Feminist Movement. A roster of material at the Makerere Institute of Social Research, 1977. *Hobbies:* Poultry Farming; Gardening; Music; Reading. *Address:* PO Box 7062, Kampala, Uganda.

KIHIKA, John, b. 24 June 1931, Bisya Village, Buhweju County, Uganda. Civil Servant (Director of Information). m. Angelica Phoebe Kefuruka, 11 Aug. 1962, 3 sons, 3 daughters. *Education:* Diploma Course in Journalism, Polytechnic, London, 1958-59; Certificate in Information Services, 1963. *Appointments:* Information Assistant, 1954; Assistant Information Officer, 1960; Senior Officer, 1969, Chief Officer, 1972; Director of Information, 1973-; Commonwealth Liaison Information Officer for Uganda, 1970-. Uganda Journalists and Writers Association; Treasurer, Catholic Centenary Memorial Choir. *Honours:* Uganda Independence Medal, 1962. *Hobbies:* Singing; Hunting; Gardening; Astrology; Wine Making. *Address:* 52 Lumumba Avenue, Kampala, Uganda.

KILGOUR, Ronald, b. 29 Apr. 1928, Edinburgh, Scotland. Medical Administrator. m. Gunilla Edstrom, 15 Oct. 1960, 2 sons, 1 daughter. *Education:* MB, Ch B, University of Edinburgh, 1958; AHA, Graduate Diploma, Health Administration, University of New South Wales, 1975, FRACMA, 1975. *Appointments:* National Bank of Scotland; Senior District Medical Officer, Wyndham; Medical Superintendent, Sir Charles Gairner Hospital, Perth, Western Australia. *Address:* 19 Verdun Street, Nedlands 6009, Western Australia.

KILLAM, Gordon Douglas, b. 26 Aug. 1930, New Westminster, British Columbia, Canada. University Teacher. m. Helen Shelagh Ann Anderson 22 Aug. 1959, 1 son, 1 daughter. *Education:* BA(Hons) English, University of British Columbia, 1954; PhD, English, University College, University of London, 1964. *Appointments:* Fourah Bay College, 1963-65; University of Alberta, 1965; University of Ibadan, 1966-67; University of Lagos, 1967-68; York University, Toronto, Canada, 1968-73; University of Dar Es Salaam, 1970-71; Acadia University, Wolfville Nova Scotia, 1973-77; University of Guelph, 1977-. *Memberships:* Association of Canadian University Teachers of English; Association of Commonwealth Literature and Language Studies; International Association of University Teachers of English. *Publications:* Africa in English Fiction, 1968; The Novels of Chinua Achebe, 1968; The Writing of Ngugi wa Thiong'o 1980; African Writers on African Writing, 1971; Critical Perspectives on Ngugi. *Hobbies:* Music; Dogs. *Address:* 108 Glasgow Street N, Guelph, Ontario, Canada.

KILLANIN, (The Rt. Hon. Lord), Michael Morris, b. 30 July 1914, London. Author; Film Producer; Director. m. Sheila Mary Dunlop, 1945 3 sons, 1 daughter. *Education:* Eton; Sorbonne, Paris; Magdalene College, Cambridge; MA. *Appointments:* Director of a number of companies, including: Beamish and Crawford Limited; Chairman: Chubb Alarms, Ireland Limited, Chubb Lock and Safe of Ireland Limited, Chubb Fire Security Ireland Limited; Fitzwilton Limited; Irish Shell Limited; Chairman, Life Association Ireland Limited; Chairman, Northern Telecom, Ireland Limited; Ulster Bank Limited; Ulster Investment Bank Limited; Chairman, Lombard and Ulster Banking Limited; Chairman, Gallaher Dublin Limited; Member, 1952-80, President, 1972-80, Honorary Life President,1980-, International Olympic Committee 1952-80. *Memberships:* Cultural Relations Committee and National Monuments Advisory Council; Irish Sailors and Soldiers Land Trust; Irish Red Cross Society. *Publications:* Four Days; Sir Godfrey Kneller; A Shell Guide to Ireland; The Olympic Games; Films: Associated with, The Quiet Man; Produced a number of films including: The Rising of the Moon; The Playboy of the Western World; Gideon's Day; Associated with: Young Cassidy; Alfred the Great; Film script, Connemara and its Pony. *Honours:* Honorary Degrees, LLD, National University of Ireland 1975; DLitt, New University of Ulster 1977; Chapion d'Afrique Gold Medal 1981; Numerous decorations include: Grand Cross of the Order of Civil Merit, Spain 1976; Grand Officer of the Order of Merit of the Republic of Italy 1973; Grand Officer of the Order of the Republic Tunis 1976; Grand Officer of the Order of the Phoenix of

Greece 1976; Knight of Honour and Devotion, Sovereign Order of Malta 1943; Commander's Cross of the Polonia Restituta Order, Poland 1979; Commander of the Order of Olympic Merit, Finland 1951; Commander of the Order of the Grimaldis 1961; Grand Cross of the German Federal Republic 1972 (Commander); Star of the Sacred Treasure (Second Class) Japan 1972; Order of the Madara Rider, Bulgaria; Commander of the Order of Sports Merit, Ivory Coast 1977; Commander of the Legion of Honour, France 1980; OBE, Military Division; MBE; Chevalier Order of Duarte Sanchez y Mella, Dominican Republic 1977; Star of Solidarity 1st Class, Italian 1957; Medal Miroslav Tyrš, Czechoslovakia 1970; Olympic Order of Merit, (gold) 1980. *Address:* 30 Lansdowne Road, Dublin, 4, Republic of Ireland.

KILLEN, Denis James, b. 23 Nov. 1925, Dalby, Queensland. Federal Cabinet Minister; Barrister-at-Law. m. Joyce Claire Buley 6 Aug. 1949, 2 daughters. *Education:* Dip. Sheep, Wool and Veterinary Science; LLB, Queensland University. *Appointments:* Research Officer Rheem, Australia Pty. Ltd; RAAF, World War II; Barrister-at-Law, Queensland 1965-; Federal Parliament, Liberal 1955; Minister for Defence, 1975-; Minister for the Navy 1969-71. *Memberships:* Johnsonian; Tattersall's; Brisbane Cricket; Irish Association. *Hobbies:* Reading; Horse Racing; Golf. *Address:* 22 Cook Street, Yeronga, Brisbane, Queensland, 4104, Australia.

KIM, Soo Myung, b. 24 Oct. 1936, Chaeryung, Korea. Physicist. m. Un Whan 22 Aug. 1970, 2 sons. *Education:* Seoul National University, B.S., 1959; PhD, University of North Carolina, Chapel Hill, 1968. *Appointments:* Research Associate, University of North Carolina, 1968; Fellow, University of Guelph, 1968-70; NRC Fellow, 1070-72; Research Officer, Atomic Energy of Canada Ltd, Chalk River, 1972-. *Memberships:* American Physical Society; Canadian Association of Physicists; Association of the Korean Scientists and Engineers in America. *Publications:* 40 Publications, 20 Papers and 20 Conference Contributions. *Hobbies:* Piano; Cross-country skiing. *Address:* 114 Frontenac Cr. Deep River, Ontario, KOJ 1PO, Canada.

KIMALEL, Shadrack Kiptenai, b. 7 Dec. 1930. High Commissioner for Kenya. m. Jebitok Rop, 1959, 2 sons, 2 daughters. *Education:* University College, Makerere, Uganda; BA., London, UK; DipEd., East Africa. *Appointments:* Teacher, 1957-61; Education Officer, Administration, 1962-63; Provincial Education Officer, 1964-66; Assistant Director, 1966-67, Deputy Director, 1967-70, Education; High Commissioner for Kenya: to India, 1970-77; to Nigeria, 1977-79, to UK, 1979-. *Memberships:* Hon. Charter Fellow, College of Preceptors. *Hobbies:* Reading; Table tennis; Hockey. *Address:* 78 Winnington Road, Hampstead, London, N2 OTU, England.

KIMATI, Valerian Pius, b. 18 Dec. 1936, Moshi, Kilimanjaro, Tanzania. Doctor, Paediatrician. m. Eugenia Eracara 8 Aug. 1965. *Education:* MB,ChB, Makerere University Medical School, Uganda, 1959-64; DCH, Royal College of Physicians, Glasgow, 1969; DCH, Royal College of Physicians, London, 1970; MRCP, Royal College of Physicians, UK, 1972; MRCPI, Royal College of Physicians, Ireland, 1972; FRCP, Royal College of Physicians, Edinburgh, 1980. *Appointments:* Medical Officer, 1965-70, Senior Medical Officer, 1970-71, Government of Tanzania; Registrar in Paediatrics, Seafield Children's Hospital, Ayr, Scotland, 1972; Specialist Paediatrician, Government of Tanzania, 1972-73; Senior Lecturer and Head, Department of Paediatrics, 1974-75, Associate Professor Paediatrics, 1976-78, Professor of Paediatrics, 1979-81, University of Dar es Salaam. *Memberships:* President, Tanzania Students body at Makerere University, 1959-61; President, Medical Association of Tanzania, 1978-80, Paediatric Association of Tanzania, 1978-81; Council of Association of Physicians of East and Central Africa. *Publications:* The Ten Top Childhood Diseases and Child Health Priorities in Tanzania, 1975; Maternal and Child Health Organization in Tanzania; The problems of Protein-energy Malnutrition in Tanzania; Childhood Pem and Measles in Tanzania, 1978; Huduma za Afya na utunzaji wa watoto Tanzania (Health services and child care in Tanzania), forthcoming; Numerous contributions to medical journals seminars and conferences. *Honours:* Prize as best Paediatric Student, 1963; Lehmann's University prize, 1964; Prize for outstanding

research in nutrition, 1977; Dean's letter of commendation for excellent work in the Faculty, 1980. *Hobbies:* Music; singing; Church organist 1951-. *Address:* PO Box 65062, Dar es Salaam, Tanzania.

KIMBLE, David Bryant, b. 12 May 1921, Horam, Sussex, England. Vice-Chancellor. m: Margareta Westin, 18 Oct. 1977, 4 daughters (by previous marriage). *Education:* BA, 1942, Postgraduate Diploma in Education, 1943, Reading University; PhD, London University, 1960. *Appointments:* Oxford University Staff Tutor in Berkshire, 1946-48; Resident Tutor in the Gold Coast, 1948-49; Director of Extra-Mural Studies, University of Ghana, 1949-61; Professor of Political Science, University of Dar es Salaam, and Director of the Institute of Public Administration, Tanzania, 1961-67; Director of Research, Centre africain de formation et de recherche administratives pour le développement, Tangiers, Morocco, 1967-71; Professor of Government and Administration, 1971-75, Emeritus Professor, 1977-, University of Botswana, Lesotho and Swaziland (later the National University of Lesotho, 1975-77); Vice-Chancellor University of Malawi, 1977-. *Publications:* The Outlook for Adult Education, 1949; Public Opinion and Government, 1950; Adult Education in a Changing Africa (w. Helen Kimble), 1955; The Machinery of Self-Government, 1953 & 1956; A Political History of Ghana, Volume One, The Rise of Nationalism in the Gold Coast, 1850-1928, 1963 & 1966; Education and Research in Public Administration, 1974; Founder and general editor of the IPA Study Series, 1964-68; Founder of UBLS Readings, 1973-75; Founder and joint editor with Helen Kible of West African Affairs, 1949-51; Penguin African Series, 1953-61; The Journal of Modern African Studies, 1963-71; Sole editor of a quarterly survey of politics, economics, and related topics in contemporary Africa, 1972-. *Honours:* OBE, 1962. *Hobbies:* Editing; Cricket. *Address:* University of Malawi, PO Box 278, Zomba, Malawi.

KINARE, Suman, b. 23 Nov. 1930. Pune, Maharashtra, India. Medical. *Education:* MB,BS, Bombay University, 1953; MD, Pathology & microbiology, 1956. *Appointments:* Resident in pathology, 1953-54; Demonstrator in pathology, 1954-58; Assistant clinical pathologist, 1958-62; Assistant Professor in pathology, 1962-66; Professor of pathology, 1966-79; Professor & Head of the Department, 1979-. *Memberships:* Fellow, National Academy of Medical Sciences; Fellow, The International Medical Sciences Academy; Fellow, The Maharashtra Academy of Sciences; The Association of Pathologists & Microbiologists; The Cardiological Society of India. *Publications:* 80 research papers in various journals in the field of pathology & particularly relating to cardiovascular diseases in India; Co-author of a monograph on Nonspecific Aorto-arteritis, 1972. *Honours:* Rockefeller foundation award, 1965; Merit scholarships in school & college education. *Hobby:* Music (Classical Indian). *Address:* Assistant Dean's Quarters, King Edward VII Memorial Hospital, SS Rao Road, Bombay, 12, Bombay, 400012, India.

KING, Alexander Stuart, b. 13 Feb. 1923, Sydney, Australia. Engineer. m. 27 June 1947, 3 sons. *Education:* Bachelor of Engineering, Sydney University, 1943. *Appointments:* Lieutenant, Royal Australian Navy, 1943-46; P R King & Sons Pty. Ltd., 1946-81. *Memberships:* Institute of Engineers of Australia; Avalon Sailing Club; Marrickville Businessmens Club. *Publications:* Three Australian Patents. *Honours:* Third Class Honours on Graduation, Sydney University, 1943. *Hobbies:* Building Sailing Boats and Yachts. *Address:* 73 Lucinda Avenue, Wahroonga, NSW, Australia.

KING, Berenice Eveline, b. 24 June 1929, Christchurch, New Zealand. Researcher (Nursing). *Education:* Diploma of Nursing School of Advanced Nursing Studies, Wellington, New Zealand, 1957; BA, 1964, MA, 1969, University of Canterbury; Doctoral programme, The Ohio State University, Columbus, Ohio, 1981. *Appointments:* Student Nurse, 1947-50, Staff nurse, 1950-51, Charge nurse, 1952-53, 1953-54, Christchurch Hospital; Charge Nurse, Kaikoura Maternity Annex, 1955-56; Tutor Sister, Essex Hospital, Christchurch, 1956; Tutor Sister, Burwood and Christchurch Hospitals, 1957-63; Clinical Supervisor part-time, 1963-; Public Health Nurse, 1964-66 Full-time University and Supervisor of In-service education, North Canterbury Hospital, Board, 1967; Nurse Adviser, Division of Nursing, Department of Health, 1968-70, 1976; Research assistant, Mershon Research Center, Columbus, Ohio, 1972-76; Senior Research Officer, The Management Services and Research Unit, Department of Health, 1976-. *Memberships:* New Zealand Nurses Association; Trustee of the Nursing Education and Research Foundation; Selector for Volunteer Services Abroad. *Publications:* Contributor of various papers on nursing including: The Work-Life of Qaulified Nurses in one Metropolitan Hospital, 1980; The Work-Life of Qualified Nurses, A user's Guide to the Methodology and Mechanics, 1980. *Honours:* Eli Hamilton Trust Award, 1962; Florence Nightingale Scholarship, 1963; 3M International Nursing Scholarship, 1970; Sigma Tlieta Tau, 1971; British Commonwealth Nurses War Memorial Scholarship, 1980. *Hobbies:* Gardening; Reading; Swimming. *Address:* 9 Narbada Crescent, Khandallah, Wellington, 4, New Zealand.

KING, John Oliver Letts, b. 21 Dec. 1914, London. University Professor, Veterinary Surgeon. m. Helen Marion Gudgin, 12 Sept. 1942, 1 son, 1 daughter. *Education:* MRCVS, Royal Veterinary College, London, 1937; BSc, University of Reading, 1941; MVSc, 1949, PhD, 1957, University of Liverpool; FRCVS, 1969; FI Biol. 1974. *Appointments:* Assistant in Veterinary Practice, 1937; House Surgeon, Royal Veterinary College, 1938; Lecturer, 1941, Senior Lecturer, 1948, Reader, 1961, Proffessor, 1969, Animal Husbandry, University of Liverpool. *Memberships:* Royal College of Veterinary Surgeons, President, 1980-; North of England Zoological Society, Council Chairman, 1972-; British Council, Veterinary Advisory Panel, Chairman, 1978-; British Veterinary Zoological Society, President, 1971-74; Association of Veterinary Teachers and Research Workers, President, 1961-62; Lancashire Veterinary Association, President, 1967-68. *Publications:* Veterinary Dietetics, 1961; An Introduction to Animal Husbandry, 1978; Over 90 articles in scientific journals on various aspects of animal husbandry. *Honours:* Dalrymple Champneys Cup, 1976; Honorary Associate, Lancashire Veterinary Association, 1980. *Hobby:* Gardening. *Address:* Arnside, Hooton Road, Willaston, South Wirral, L64 1SL, England.

KINGSBURY, Norman William, b. 7 Dec. 1932, Waimate, New Zealand. University administration. m. Barbara Anne Stephens, 1 Apr. 1959, 3 sons, 2 daughters. *Education:* Canterbury University College, 1952-56; MA, University of New Zealand, 1957. *Appointments:* Teacher and Vocational Guidance Officer for New Zealand Department of Education, 1957-58; Associate Secretary, then Secretary-General of International Student Conference, Leiden, Netherlands, 1959-61; Assistant Registrar, Victoria University of Wellington, 1961-64; Registrar, 1964-74, Assistant to the Vice-Chancellor, 1974-, University of Waikato; Registrar, University College of Botswana and Consultant in Educational Administration under auspices of Commonwealth Fund for Technical Cooperation (on leave from Waikato), 1978-80. *Memberships:* Vice-President, Waikato Branch, New Zealand Institute for International Affairs; New Zealand Labour Party; Foundation member, Waiariki Community College Council; Fairfield College Board; Hamilton Arts Council; New Zealand Council for Volunteer Service Abroad; World University Service, Geneva. *Publications:* Articles on university administration, continuing education and international affairs. *Hobbies:* Gardening; Drama. *Address:* 245 Banwood Road, Hamilton, New Zealand.

KING-SIEM, Bruce, b. 25 Aug. 1940, Altona. Commercial Arbitrator. m. 4 Sept. 1964, 1 son, 1 daughter. *Education:* BS, 1961; Sundry short courses in EDP, Management, Law & Operations Research, 1962-81; Sundry Conferences & Workshops in Management & Law Commercial, 1968-80; BA, 1972; Graudate Diploma, Export Management, 1976; Grade II Law Commercial Arbitration, 1978; Graduate Diploma, Business Administration, 1980. *Appointments:* British Phosphate Commissioners, Pacific, 1962-63; Reynolds Electric Corporation, USA, 1963-64; Ford Motor Co., Australia, 1964-66; Geo A Pockett & Associates Pty, Ltd., Australia, 1966-74; Pacific Engineering Consultants, 1972; Pockett Siem & Partners, Australia, 1974; Australasian Analytical Laboratories Pty Ltd. 1975; Oceanic Research Foundation Ltd., Australia, 1980-. *Memberships:* Junior Chamber and Chamber of Commerce, Melbourne; Vice-Chairman, Computer Society, Australia; Fellow, Society of Senior Executives, Aus-

tralia; Vice-President, Institute of Planning Engineers, Australia; Institute of Arbitrators, Australia; Building & Disputes Practioners Society, Australia; Socieity of Operations Research, Australia; Institute of Export, Australia. *Publications:* Several professional papers. *Honours:* Various sporting prizes, debating awards, public speaking recognititions. *Hobbies:* Sailing; Skiing; Fine Arts; Literature; Fencing; Theatre; Opera. *Address:* Coomalie, Johnson Avenue, Blairgowrie, Victoria, Australia, 3941.

KINGSLAND, Richard (Sir), b. 19 Oct. 1916, Moree, New South Wales, Australia. Head of Government Department. m. Kathleen Jewel Adams, 29 Oct. 1943, 1 son, 2 daughters. *Education:* Royal Australian Air Force Cadet College, Point Cook, Victoria 1935-36; Imperial Defence College, London, 1955. *Appointments:* Manager, Sydney Airport, NSW 1948-49; Regional Director of Civil Aviation for S.A and Northern Territory 1949-51; Assistant Secretary, Department of Air 1952-58; First Assistant Secretary, Department of Defence 1958-63; Secretary, Department of Interior 1963-70; Chairman, Repatriation Commission 1970-; Secretary, Department of Repatriation 1970-76; Secretary, Department of Veterans' Affairs 1976-. *Memberships:* Board of Management, Canberra Theatre Trust, 1965-75; Trustee of Australian War Memorial, 1966-76; Director of Arts Council of Australia, 1970-72; Chairman, Council of Canberra School of Music, 1972-75; Chairman, Council of Canberra School of Art, 1976-; National Secretary, National Heart Foundation. *Honours:* Distinguished Flying Cross 1940; Commander of the Order of the British Empire 1967; Knight Bachelor 1978. *Hobbies:* Reading; Swimming; Listening to Music; Looking at Paintings. *Address:* 36 Vasey Crescent, Campbell, ACT, Australia.

KINGSLEY, Benjamin John Kuenssberg, b. 7 Feb. 1952, Northwood, Middlesex, England. Librarian. m. Zodwa Doris Nhlengethwa, 3 Sept. 1977, 1 son. *Education:* BA.Librarianship (CNAA), University of Leeds, UK, 1974. *Appointments:* Senior Assistant Librarian, 1974-76, Director, 1979-, Swaziland National Library Service, Manzini, Swaziland; Lecturer-in-Charge, Library Studies, Swaziland College of Technology, Mbabawe, 1976-78; Associate, The Library Association, 1981. *Address:* PO Box 652, Manzini, Swaziland.

KINGSLEY, Margaret (Mrs William A Newcombe), b. 20 Feb. 1939, Cornwall, England. Opera Singer, Presssor of Singing. m. William A Newcombe, 8 June 1963. *Education:* Royal College of Music. *Appointments:* Sung for all the major opera companies in this Country (Glyndebourne, Royal Opera, English National etc.,) and in Europe and America; Professor of Singing, Royal College of Music, London. *Hobbies:* Gardening; Cooking; Walking in the country. *Address:* 48 Bowerdean Street, London, SW6 3TW, England.

KINGS NORTON, Harold Roxbee Cox, Kt, (Baron cr 1965 of Wootton Underwood, Life Peer), b. 6 June 1902, Birmingham, England. Engineer. m. Marjorie, 12 July 1927, 2 sons. *Education:* BSc, 1922, PhD, 1926, Imperial College of Science & Technology, 1922-24; Honorary DSc, Birmingham, 1954; Fellow, Imperial College, 1960; Honorary DTech, Brunel, 1966; Honorary LLD, CNAA, 1969; Honorary DSc, Cranfield, 1970; F.Eng. *Appointments:* Engineer on construction of Airship R101, 1924-29; Chief Technical Officer, Royal Airship Works, 1931; Investigations in wing flutter & stability of structures, RAE, 1931-35; Lecturer in Aircraft Structures, Imperial College, 1932-38; Principal Scientific Officer, Aerodynamics Department, RAE, 1935-36; Head of Air Defence Department, RAE, 1936-38; Chief Technical Officer, Air Registration Board, 1938-39; Superintendent of Scientific Research, RAE, 1939-40; Deputy Director of Scientific Research, Ministry of Aircraft Production, 1940-43; Director of Special Projects, Ministry of Aircraft Production, 1943-44; Chairman & Managing Director, Power Jets (Research & Development) Ltd., 1944-46; Director, National Gas Turbine Establishment, 1946-48; Chief Scientist, Ministry of Fuel and Power, 1948-54; Chairman, Gas Turbine Collaboration Committee, 1941-44, 1946-48; Aeronautical Research Council, 1944-48, 1958-60; Chairman, Council for Scientific & Industrial Research, 1961-65; Chairman, Council for National Academic Awards, 1964-71; Chairman, Director, 1957-67, Deputy Chairman, 1959-60, Chairman Metal Box Company, 1961-67; Director, Ricardo & Co., (Engineers), 1927 Ltd., 1965-77; Chairman, Air Registration Board,

1966-72; Chairman, Berger, Jenson & Nicholson, 1967-75; Director, Dowty Rotol, 1968-75; Director, British Printing Corporation, 1968-77; Chancellor, Cranfield Institute of Technology, 1969-; Director, Hoecht, UK, 1970-75; Chairman, Applied Photophysics, 1972-, Landspeed Limited, 1975-, Withers Estates Limited, 1976-, Submarine Products Limited, 1978-. *Memberships:* President, Royal Institution, 1969-76; Past President, Royal Aeronautical Society; Fellow, Imperial College of Science & Technology, 1960; FCGI, 1976; Membre Correspondant, Faculte Polytechnique de Mons. *Publications:* Numerous papers on theory of structures, wing flutter, gas turbines, civil aviation and airships. *Honours:* R.38 Memorial Prize, 1928; Busk Memorial Prize, 1934; Wilbur Wright Lecturer, 1940; Wright Brothers Lecturer (USA), 1945; Medal of Freedom with Silver Palm (USA), 1947; Hawksley Lecturer, 1951; James Clayton Prize, 1952; Kt. 1953; Thornton Lecturer, 1954; Parsons.Memorial Lecturer, 1955; Handley Page Memorial Lecturer, 1969. *Hobby:* Collecting aeronautical antiques. *Address:* Westcote House, Chipping Campden, Gloucestershire, England.

KINNEAR, Edward Hore, b. 22 Nov. 1928, Melbourne, Australia. Company Chairman. m. Julia Webb, 25 Mar. 1957, 1 son, 2 daughters. *Appointments:* Kinnears Limited, 1947-. *Memberships:* Melbourne Club; Athenaeum Club; Royal Yacht Club of Victoria; Royal South Yarra Lawn Tennis Club; Melbourne Cricket Club. *Hobbies:* Yachting; Fishing. *Address:* 246 B Domain Road, South Yarra 3141, Victoria, Australia.

KINROSS, John Stirton, b. 6 Oct. 1929, Inverelll, New South Wales, Australia. Dental Surgeon. m. Elisabeth Anne de Tessier Prevost, 26 Oct. 1956, 1 son, 2 daughters. *Education:* BDS, 1952, MDS, 1961, University of Sydney, New South Wales, Australia; FRACDS, Royal Australasian College of Dental Surgeons, Australia, 1965. *Memberships:* Hon. Secretary, New South Wales Committee, Royal Australasian College of Dental Surgeons; Councillor, Australian Dental Association, 1969-73; International Academy of Gnathology; Australian Society of Prosthodontists; Australian Society of Endodontology; Medical Science Club; Australian Club; Elanora Country Club. *Address:* 6 Killara Avenue, Killara, New South Wales 2071, Australia.

KINYANJUI, William Gitumbi, b. 28 Sept. 1947, Embu Kenya. Teacher; Librarian. m. Beth Wanjiru, 30 Aug. 1969, 2 sons, 3 daughters. *Education:* B.Ed., Nairobi University, Kenya, 1975; Postgraduate Diploma in Library Studies, Wales, UK, 1978. *Appointments:* Teacher (Graduate), High School, 1975-76; Assistant Librarian, Kenyatta University College, Kenya, 1976-80; Chief Librarian, Kenya Technical Teachers College, 1980-; Visiting Lecturer, Kenya Polytechnic, 1979-. *Memberships:* Kenya Library Association. *Publications:* Secondary School library facilities in Central Province, Kenya in Maktaba, 1979; Serials literature: Their exploitation and use in libraries, 1978. *Hobbies:* Reading; Current Affairs; Squash; Tennis; Darts; Watching movies; Farming. *Address:* PO Box 96, Embu, Kenya.

KIPKORIR, Benjamin Edgar, b. 21 Aug. 1939, Marakwet, Kenya. University Lecturer. m. 14 June 1969, 2 sons, 2 daughters. *Education:* BA. (London), Makerere University College, Kenya; PhD. (Cantab.), St. John's College, Cambridge, UK, 1970. *Appointments:* Lecturer/Senior Lecturer, History Department, 1969-77, Director, Institute of African Studies, 1977-, University of Nairobi, Kenya. *Memberships:* Cambridge Historical Society; Hon. Secretary 1970-75, Historical Association of Kenya. *Publications:* The Marakwet of Kenya (with F B Welborn), 1973; The People of the Rift Valley, 1979; Essays in Imperialism of Collaboration in Colonial Kenya, 1980. *Honours:* Hancock Memorial Prize, Makerere, 1962. *Hobby:* Squash. *Address:* PO Box 30197, Nairobi, Kenya.

KIRK, Bradley Wesley, b. 25 Sept. 1952, Owen Sound, Ontario, Canada. Physicist. *Education:* BSc. (Physics), University of Waterloo, Waterloo, Ontario, Canada, 1976; MSc. (Physics), Laurentian University, Sudbury, Ontario, Canada, 1980. *Appointments:* Environmental Scientist, CANMET, Energy Mines and Resources, Government of Canada, Canada, 1976-81; Teaching Master, Sault College of Applied Arts and Technology, Elliot Lake, Ontario, 1981. *Memberships:* Canadian

Association of Physicists; Optical Society of America. *Publications:* An Iris Diaphragm Based Interface for Use in Eriometry, MSc. Thesis, 1980. *Honours:* Ontario Scholar, 1971. *Hobbies:* Music; Gourmet cooking; Raising dogs. *Address:* PO Box 831, 10 Leacock Street, Blind River, Ontario, Canada, POR 1BO.

KIRKCONNELL, Charles Leonard, b. 6 Dec. 1922, George Town, Grand Cayman, Cayman Islands. Master Mariner, Business Executive. m. Carole Jean, 6 Jan, 1969 (Second Marriage), 3 sons, 3 daughters. *Education:* Munro College, Jamaica, 1939-41; Practical Marine Training with father and Theory Training in USA, (Master Marine Certificate). *Appointments:* President, Kirkconnell Brothers Ltd.; Director, R B Kirkconneli & Borthers Ltd., (Ship Owners), Kirkconnell Ltd., (Merchants) Cayman Brac, Kirk Express Co., Ltd., Canadian Imperial Bank of Commerce Trust Company, Pirate Cove Estates Ltd., Kirk Estates Ltd. *Memberships:* Free Mason. *Hobbies:* Swimming; Boating; Fishing. *Address:* South Sound Road, Grand Cayman, Cayman Islands, British West Indies.

KIRKE, Gordon Irwin, b. 2 Mar. 1945, Toronto, Ontario, Canada. Lawyer. m. Nancy-Jo Burtch, 11 July 1969, 1 son, 1 daughter. *Education:* Sociology, Victoria College, University of Toronto, Canada, 1964-66; LL.B., 1966-69, LL.M., 1977, Osgoode Hall Law School, Canada; Graduated with Honours, Bar Admission Course, 1971. *Appointments:* Partner, Goodman and Goodman, Toronto, Canada. *Memberships:* Canadian Bar Association; County of York Law Association; Canadian Tax Foundation; International Council of Shopping Centres; Association of Commercial Finance Attorneys. *Publications:* Contributed: Guarantee and Suretyship; Customs and Excise Tax; Limitation of Actions; to Canadian Encyclopedic Digest; Special Lecturer, Sports and Entertainment Law, Master of Law Course, Osgoode Hall Law School, Canada. *Honours:* Norman McLeod Scholarship; Public Speaking award; osgoode Hall Journal Editor, 1963-64; President, Phi Delta Legal Fraternity, 1968-69; Richard Halliburton Greer prize, Criminal Law, 1967; Harry R Rose Criminal Law Prize, 1967; Samuel Factor Memorial Prize, Contracts, 1967; Highest mark in Torts, 1967; Law Society Scholarship, 1968; Kenneth Gibson Morden Memorial Prize, Evidence, 1968; Reading Law Club prize, Commercial Law, 1968; Bronze Medal, 1969; Matthew Wilson Memorial Scholarship, 1969; Insurance Company of North America prize, Insurance Law, 1969; Canada Permanent Trust Company prize, Law of Trusts, 1969; Law Society prize, Bar Admission course, 1971. *Address:* 122 Argonne Crescent, Willowdale, Ontario, Canada M2K 2K1.

KIRKHAM, Lillias Sidey, b. 26 Aug. 1926, Adelaide, South Australia. Registered Nurse. *Education:* General Reg. Nurse Certificate, 1952-55, Midwifery Certificate, 1955-56, Hospital Nursing and Unit Management Diploma, College of Nursing, Australia, Melbourne, 1962. *Appointments:* Stenographer, Office, 1943-44, 1947-51; Stenographer, Army, 1945-46; Kindergarten Teacher, UK, 1957; Registered Nurse, Adelaide Children's Hospital, Australia, 1959-64; Exchange Nurse, USA, 1964-66; Registered Nurse, Canada, 1967; Nursing Supervisor, Adelaide Children's Hospital, Australia, 1968-81. *Memberships:* Fellow of the College of Nursing, Australia; Executive Committee, Australian and New Zealand Burn Association; Finance Committee, Royal Australian Nursing Federation; Executive Committee, Child and Home Safety, National Safety Council of Australia, South Australian Division. *Publications:* Thermal Injuries in South Australian Children, 1974; Articles on Thermal Injuries and Accident Prevention in Nurse's Journals and Women's Magazines. *Honours:* Good Fellowship Prize, Royal Adelaide Hospital, 1955; Certificate of Merit, Child and Home Safety, National Safety Council of Australia, South Australia Branch), 1978. *Hobbies:* Golf; Tennis; Swimming; Gardening; Contract Bridge; Thermal Injury Research; Prevention Childhood Accidents. *Address:* 4 Gordon Place, Beaumont, South Australia, Australia 5066.

KIRKPATRICK, Ernest Ross, b. 22 Feb. 1920, Croydon, New South Wales, Australia. Australian Insurance Commissioner. *Education:* Admitted as: Barrister of the Supreme Court of New South Wales, Australia, 1965; Practitioner of the High Court of Australia, 1966; Barrister and Solicitor of the Supreme Court of the Australian Capital Territory, 1971. *Appointments:* Senior Executive Positions in Local Government, New South Wales, Australia, 1946-66; Senior Legal Officer, Commonwealth Attorney-General's Department, 1966-67; Senior Legal Officer, Department of External Territories, 1967-69; Director, Commonwealth Auditor-General's Office, 1969-73; Assistant Insurance Commissioner, 1973-79, Commissioner, 1979-, The Treasury. *Memberships:* Fellow, Australian Society of Accountants; Associate, Institute of Municipal Administration; Associate, Town Clerk's Society of New South Wales; Associate, Chartered Institute of Secretaries and Administrators; Fellow, Australian Insurance Institute. *Hobbies:* Golf; Reading. *Address:* 42 Finniss Crescent, Narrabundah, ACT 2604, Australia.

KIRKPATRICK CHALMERS, Susann Louise, b. 13 May 1915, Alexandria, Scotland. Teacher; Portrait painter; Sculptress; Marioneteer. m. 1963. *Education:* Commercial Art, 1933-34, Diploma (DP), 1937, Board of Education, 1938, Glasgow School of Art, Scotland; Jordanhill College of Education, 1938; various Universities. *Appointments:* Strathclyde Education, 1938-50, 1951-80; Australian Teacher College exchange, 1950-51. *Memberships:* Royal Society of Miniaturists; Society of Miniaturists; Glasgow Society of Lady Artists; Director, Scotia Marionette Theatre; El 'Life member of E I S. *Creative Works:* Miniatures include: Sir Thomas White; Alexandra; Queen Salotes Lady; Posthumous portraits of children; Water Colours include: Dame Pattie Menzies; Lady Effingham; Australian Lady in the bush; Biblical compositions; Oil Paintings include: Maharajah Duleepsinghi; Jean Tonks as Queen Nefertiti; Portrait sculptures of dogs; Marionettes: Various newspaper articles. *Honours:* awarded 2 Silver Medals, 1933; ARMS, 1952. *Hobbies:* German Shepherd Dogs; Birds; Rowing. *Address:* Tigh-na-Loch-studio, No 3 Straid Bheag, Clynder, Gare Loch, Scotland.

KISYOMBE, Felix Wellie, b. 1 Nov. 1949, Lupembe Village, Karonga District, Malawi. Biometrician. 1 son. *Education:* BSc.(Hons.), University College of Wales, Aberystwyth, Wales, 1975. *Appointments:* Department of Agricultural Research, 1975-80, Senior Agricultural Research Officer, 1980-, Malawi Government. *Hobbies:* Films; Crossword Puzzles; Reading. *Address:* 1231 S W 3rd Avenue, %302, Gainesville, FL 32601, USA.

KITCHIN, Reginald Jack, b. 18 Feb. 1931, Durban, South Africa. Orthopaedic Surgeon. m. Alison Joan Buchanan, 15 Jan. 1955, 1 son, 5 daughters. *Education:* MB,Ch.B, Kearsney College University WW Rand, 1953; FRCS, (England), Royal College of Surgeons. *Appointments:* House Surgeon, Johannesburg General Hospital; House Physician Baragaronath Hospital; Surgical Registrar, Victoria Hospital, Blackpool; Orthopaedic Registrar, Royal Northern & New End Hospitals; Surgical Registrar, King Edward Hospital, Durban; Orthopaedic Registrar, Royal Newcastle Hospital; Orthopaedic Surgeon, Royal Canberra & Woden Valley Hospitals. *Memberships:* Australian Orthopaedic Association; Australian Medical Association. *Hobbies:* Golf; Tennis; Cooking; Farming. *Address:* 40 Wilsmore Crescent, Chifley, ACT, 2606, Australia.

KITINGAN, (Datuk), Joseph Pairin, b. 17 Aug. 1940, Papar Sabah. Lawyer. m. Genevieve Dorothy Lee, 10 Jan. 1969, 2 sons. *Education:* Sabah College, Kota Kinabalu; LLB, Saltash College, University of Adelaide, Adelaide. *Appointments:* Joined State Legal Service as Cadet Legal Officer and DPP, later became State Counsel 1971-73; Private Legal Practitioner, 1974-75; Assistant Minister to the Chief Minister, 1976; Minister for Local Government and Housing 1976-80; Minister of Man Power and Environmental Development, 1980-. *Memberships:* President, Kadazan Cultural Associaton, Sabah, since 1977; Vice-President of Sabah National Youth Association. *Honours:* Panglima Gemilang Darjah Kinabalu, State Illustrious Order of Kinabalu, 1978. *Hobbies:* Reading; Music. *Address:* 11 Taman Kinabalu, Jalan Kolam, Kota Kinabalu, Sabah, Malaysia.

KLAVDIANOS, George, b. 30 Mar. 1943, Athens, Greece. Civil Engineer, Contractor. m. Angelique Papageorgioy, 14 Nov. 1971, 1 son, 1 daughter. *Education:* Diploma in Civil Engineering, National Technical University of Athens, 1967. *Appointments:* Lieutenant, Engineer Corps, Greek Army, 1968-69; Construction

Engineer, 1970-72, Project Manager, 1973-74, Edok-Eter; Technical Director, 1974-77, Joint Managing Director, 1978-, Edok-Eter-Mandilas Ltd. *Memberships:* Greek Technical Chamber; Greek Association of Civil Engineers; Greek Association of Civil Engineering Contractors; Project Management Institute. *Hobby:* Music (Piano). *Address:* 130 Sapele Road, Benin City, Nigeria.

KLEPFISZ, Arthur, b. 8 Mar. 1941, Warsaw, Poland. Phsychiatrist. m. Marianne Glaser, 27 May 1969, 1 son, 1 daughter. *Education:* MB, BS, Melbourne University Medical School, 1966; Psychiatric training, University Rochester, NY State, USA, 1970-73; MRANZCP, 1974; FRANZCP, 1981. *Appointments:* Junior Resident, St Vicents Hospital, Melbourne, 196768; Senior Resident, 1968-69, Assistant Psychiatrist, 1974-78, Prince Henrys Hospital, Melbourne; Three years resident psychiatrist, Stong Memorial Hospital, Rochester, New York State, USA, 1970-73; Consultant Psychiatrist, private practice, 1974-81; Assistant Psychiatrist, Box Hill Hospital, Melbourne, 1974-81. *Memberships:* College private psychiatrists; American Group Psychotherapy Association. *Publications:* LSD and Homicide, 1973. *Hobbies:* Tennis; Swimming; Football; Chess; Reading; Photography; Bridge.

KLIKA, Karel, b. 14 Apr. 1915, Prague, Czechoslovakia. Civil Engineer. m. 13 Jan. 1950, 1 son, 1 daughter. *Education:* Graduate of University of Prague, Faculty of Civil Engineering, Degree of Civil Engineering, 1945. *Appointments:* Project Engineer, Kosice Airport, 1948-50; Super. Civil Engineer, Roads & Airstrips, US Army West Germany, 1950-55; Construction Engineer, Darwin Airport Project, Australia, 1960-63; Road Planning Engineer, Works Department, Papua New Guinea, 1060-63; Resident Engineer, Road Development North Australia, 1964-66; UN Expert in Tanzania, Technical Assistance Programme and part-time lecturer at University of Tanzania, Dar El Salam, 1966-69; Project Engineer, Special Projects, BMI, Sydney, 1969-71; Director International Marketing Construction and Klika Trading Engineering Equipment, 1971-; Special Appointment UN Expert to Yugoslavia by UN Industrial Development Organisation, 1973; Delegate to 7th International Road Federation Congress, Munich, 1973. *Memberships:* Institution of Engineers, Australia; Institution of Highway Engineers, London. *Publications:* Various contributions to technical magazines and Congresses. *Hobbies:* History; Arts; Politics; Golf. *Address:* 2 Glentrees Avenue. Forestville, NSW 2087, Australia.

KLINEBERG, Iven, b. 29 Aug. 1941, Sydney, Australia. Dentistry. m. Sylvia Blaut, 23 Feb. 1966, 2 sons, 2 daughters. *Education:* BDS, 1962, BSc, 1968, MDS, 1966, University of Sydney; FDSRCS, Royal College of Surgeons of London, 1971; PhD, University of London, 1971. *Appointments:* Private General Practice, 1963; Department of Prosthetic Dentistry, University of Sydney, 1964; Research Fellow, Dental Neurology, Royal College of Surgeons of England, 1968-71; Demonstrator in Restorative Dentistry, The Royal Dental School, University of London, 1969-70; Senior Research Fellow NH & MRC, Department of Prosthetic Dentistry, 1971, Professor of Prosthetic Dentistry, 1978-, University of Sydney; Private Referral Practice, Sydney, 1972-77; Visiting Professor, Department of Occlusion, University of Michigan, 1977-78. *Memberships:* Australian Dental Association; International Association for Dental Research; International Academy of Gnathology; American Equilibration Society; Pierre Fauchard Academy; Australian Society of Prosthodontists, President NSW Branch, 1975-76. *Publications:* Scientific publication in field of Dental materials, 1966-68, Articular neurology of the temperomandibular joint, and orofacial pain, 1970. *Honours:* G S Caird Scholarship, 1960; Percy A Ash Prize, 1961; Dr John H Wilson Prize, 1961; Leslie Raymond Carroll Medallion, 1962; K P Mackinnon Prize, 1962; Dental Health Education & Research Foundation Scholarship, 1966-68; Commonwealth (Medical) Scholarship, 1969-71; Arnott Demonstration, Royal College of Surgeons, 1971. *Hobbies:* Tennis; Skiing; Golf; Photography. *Address:* Faculty of Dentistry, 2 Chalmers Street, Sydney, New South Wales, 2010, Australia.

KLOPPENBURG, Henry Ronald, b. 21 June 1945, Humboldt, Saskatchewan, Canada. Barrister. m. 19 May 1973. *Education:* BA, magna cum laude, 1965, LL.B, 1968, St Thomas More College, University of

Saskatchewan; BCL, (Exeter College), Oxford University, 1968-70; *Appointments:* Law Clerk, Supreme Court of Canada, 1971-72; Private practice with Goldenberg, Taylor & Tallis, 1972-77; Private Practice, Kloppenburg and Kloppenburg, 1977-. *Memberships:* Law Societies of Saskatchewan, Alberta and Northwest Territories; Canadian Tax Foundation; International Associate, American Bar Association; Association of Trial Lawyers of America; University of Saskatchewan Faculty Club. *Honours:* Rhodes Scholarship, 1968; University of Saskatchewan Arts Prize; Brown Prize in Law, University of Saskatchewan. *Hobbies:* Art collecting; Swimming; Ice Skating; Computers. *Address:* 814 Saskatchewan Crescent East, Saskatoon, Saskatchewan, S7N OL3, Canada.

KNAAP, Adrian, b. 10 Mar. 1926, Groningen, Nederland. Industrial Designer. m. Lynette Georgina Gell, 5 Feb. 1957, 4 sons. *Education:* Diploma Business Administration, Utrecht, 1946; Diploma Leerdam Design School, Nederland, 1949. *Appointments:* Designer, Cown Crystal Glass Ltd. Sydney, Australia, 1950-51; Consultant Designer, Knaap-Thoen Associates, 1951-56; Chief Industrial Designer EMI Ltd., 1956-60; Design Manager, Ferris Industries Ltd.,1960-67; Consultant Designer, Adrian Knaap & Associates, 1967-; Managing Director, Industrial Design Research Pty. Ltd., 1973-. *Memberships:* Federal Councillor Industrial Design Council of Australia; Fellow, Industrial Design Institute of Australia, Past State President; Member Judging Panel Prince Philip Prize for Design, 1968,69,70,79. *Publications:* Specialities Product Design and environmental design, Sebel Design Exhibitions Australia, 1967,68,69; Australian Pavilion Expo Montreal, 1967; Port Waratah Coal handling plant, Newcastle NSW, 1977. *Honours:* Frist Prize First Industrial Design Competition, 1952; Transfield Sculpture Pavilion Design, 1966; Award for design, American Zinc Institute Inc., 1965; Zinc Alloy Diecasters Association of Australia Award, 1965; Australian Design Awards, 1965-79. *Hobbies:* History; Music; Offshore sailing; Design. *Address:* 9 Cremorne Road, Cremorne Point, NSW, Australia.

KNAUERHASE, Oscar Carl, b. 27 Apr. 1911, Booleroo Centre, South Australia. Secondary School Teacher (Retired). m. Margaret Lucy Kiek, 18 Dec. 1937, 4 daughters. *Education:* BA, 1934, Dip.Ed., 1938, MA, 1943, Adelaide University; B.Ed., Melbourne University, 1951. *Appointments:* Teacher, Immanuel College, North Adelaide, South Australia, 1934-36; Teacher, Assistant, 1937-45, Senior Master (Social Studies), 1946-63, Acting Deputy Headmaster, 1963, Special Senior Master (English),1964-72, Part-time Instructor, 1973-74, Adelaide Technical High School, Adelaide; Evening Classes (Mathematics), South Australia, School of Mines and Industries, 1937-54. *Memberships:* Immanuel College Old Scholars Association; Australian Psychological Society; Adelaide Art Society; Royal South Australia Society of Arts. *Publications:* Booklet, Adelaide Technical High School in Retrospect, 1975. *Honours:* Anna Florence Booth Prize, Adelaide University, 1943. *Hobbies:* Art (Drawing and painting, landscapes, portraits, buildings). *Address:* 29 Narinna Avenue, Cumberland Park, South Australia, 5041.

KNIGHT, Arthur Lyndon, b. 15 Mar. 1926, Sydney, NSW, Australia. Educator. m. Audrey Marguerite Gilchrist, 24 Mar. 1948, 1 son, 1 daughter. *Education:* BA, Sydney, 1948. *Appointments:* Knox Grammar School, NSW, Australia, 1946; Sydney Grammar School, NSW, Australia, 1947; Managing Director, 1957-60; Governing Director, 1960-, National Fund Raising Counsel of Australia Pty., Ltd.; Governing Director, Knight Howard & Associates Pty. Ltd., 1966-. *Memberships:* Fellow, Australian Institute of Management; Fellow, Institute of Directors; Fellow, Australian Institute of Fund Raising (Past President & Director); Australian College of Education; Association of Business & Professional Men Ltd., (Past President & Director). *Hobbies:* Music; Community Service work with hospitals and welfare organisations. *Address:* 4 Delecta Avenue, Clareville Beach, NSW, 2107, Australia.

KNIGHT (Sir), Harold Murray, b. 13 Aug. 1919, Melbourne. Banker. m. Gwenyth Catherine Pennington, 7 Apr. 1951, 4 sons, 1 daughter. *Appointments:* Commonwealth Bank of Australia, 1936-40; Australian Imperial Forces (Lieutenant), 1940-43; Royal Australian Naval Volunteer Reserve (Lieutenant), 1943-45;

Commonwealth Bank of Australia, 1946-55; Statistics Division, Research and Statistics Department, International Monetary Fund,1955-59, Assistant Chief,1957-59; Research Economist, 1960, Assistant Manager, Investment Department, 1962-64. Manager, 1964-68, Deputy Governor and Deputy Chairman of Board, 1968-75, Governor and Chairman of Board, 1975-, Reserve Bank of Australia. *Publications:* Introduccion al Analisis Monetario, (Spanish), 1959. *Honours:* KBE, cr. 1980, DSC., M.Comm. (Melbourne). *Address:* Reserve Bank of Australia, 65 Martin Place, Sydney, NSW, 2000, Australia.

KNIGHT, James Wilfred, b. 15 Dec. 1920, Hull, Yorkshire, UK. Managing Director. m. Joan Machin, 10 Aug. 1947, 2 sons, 1 daughter. *Education:* BSc (London), 1945; PhD, (London), 1950; FRSC, 1947; FRACI, 1958; FAIM, 1978. *Appointments:* Ministry of Supply, UK, 1940-47; Distillers Company, UK, 1947-50; Reckitt & Colman, UK, 1950-57; Fielders Ltd., Australia, 1957-63; CPC International, Europe, 1963-70; Fielder Gillespie Ltd., Australia, 1970-. *Memberships:* Australian Club. *Publications:* Wheat, Starch and Gluten, 1965; The Starch Industry, 1969. *Hobbies:* Music; Tennis; Gardening. *Address:* 79 Killeaton Street, St Ives, NSW 2075, Australia.

KNIGHT, Michael John, b. 25 May 1946, Melbourne, Australia. University Senior Lecturer. m. J L Carne, 8 Jan. 1970, 2 sons, 2 daughters. *Education:* BSc, 1967, PhD, 1971, PhD, 1972, University of Melbourne. *Appointments:* Land Utilization Officer, Department of Agriculture Stock & Fisheries, Papua, New Guinea, 1971-73; Engineering Geologist, Geological Survey of Papua, New Guinea, 1973-74; Lecturer, Engineering Geology, School of Applied Geology, University of New South Wales, 1974-. *Memberships:* Fellow, Geological Scoiety of London; International Association of Engineering Geologists; Geological Society of Australia; Executive, of Engineering Geology Specialist Group; Australian Society of Soil Science and three other Institutes/Societies. *Publications:* 23 written publications including: Soil Fabric Analysis; Waste Disposal (Industrial liquid, Domestic Solid and Radioactive Wastes); Groundwater; Geomorphology; others in the field of Environmental Geology. *Honours:* Dux in Geology, Commonwealth Scholarship; Australian Institute of Mining & Metallurgy Bursary, 1966; Howitt Natural History Scholarship, 1967; Professor Kernot Scholarship in Geology, 1969; Australian Scoiety of Soil Science Medal, 1980. *Hobbies:* Leadership & Community Service; Church Elder; Parents & Citizens School Committee. *Address:* 54 Wattle Road, Jannali, New South Wales 2226, Australia.

KNIGHT-JONES, Elis Wyn, b. 7 Mar. 1916, Hanford, Staffs. Marine Biologist. m. (1) Mary Morgan-Jones, 9 Dec. 1939 (dissolved 1968), (2) Phyllis Kathleen Fisher, 26 July 1969, 2 sons, 2 daughters. *Education:* Epsom College, 1930-33; BSc, University College of North Wales, Bangor, 1933-39; Jesus College, Oxford, 1939-46; D Phil (Oxon), 1949; DSc (Oxon), 1976. *Appointments:* Military War Service, 1939-46; Senior Scientific Officer, Fisheries Laboratory, Burnham-on-Crouch, 1947-49; Zoologist & Deputy Director, Marine Science Laboratories, Menai Bridge, 1949-56; Professor of Zoology, University College of Swansea, 1956-81. *Memberships:* Institute of Biology. *Publications:* Contributor to Scientific Journals. *Honours:* Mentioned in Despatches, 1946. *Hobby:* Scuba Diving. *Address:* Bryngwyn, Llanrhidian, Swansea, SA3 1EN, Wales.

KNOTT, John Laurence, b. 6 July 1910, Romsey, Victoria, Australia. Company Director. m. Jean Rose Milnes, 22 June 1935, 3 sons, 1 daughter. *Education:* Diploma of Commerce, Melbourne, Universityk, 1947; Associate Australian Society of Accountants, 1947; Fellow, Chartered Institute of Secretaries, 1947; Fellow, Australian Institute of Management, 1973; Licensed Company Auditor, 1947; Graudate Internal Defence College, London, 1949. *Appointments:* Private Secretary to Minister for Trade Treaties, 1935-38; Secretary Eastern Group Supply Mission to New Delhi, 1940; Executive Officer, Secondary Industries Commission, 1943-48; Secretary, Department Defence Production, 1957-58; Australian Defence Mission to USA, 1957; Secretary Department of Supply, Australia, 1959-65; Deputy High Commissioner to London, 1966-68; Vice-President ELDO, 1967-68; Director General Post & Telegraphs, 1968-71; Company Director &

berships: President, English Speaking Union, (Victoria); President, Institute of Management (Victorian Division); Melbourne University Council, 1972-76. *Honours:* Companion of the Order of Australia, 1981; Knight Bachelor, 1971; CBE, 1960. *Hobbies:* Gardening; Bowls; Golf. *Address:* 3 Fenwick Street, Kew, Victoria, 3101, Australia.

KNOWLES, Henry Joseph, b. 22 Jan. 1932, London, Ontario, Canada. Chairman. m. Marilyn Anne Radcliffe, 6 Aug. 1960, 2 daughters. *Education:* London South Collegiate Institute, London, Ontario, 1952; BA, University of Western Ontario, School of Business Administration, 1956; Osgoode Hall Law School, 1960; LL.M, Yale University Law School, 1961; MBA, University of Toronto, School of Business, 1962; Called as a Barrister and Solicitor to the Ontario Bar, 1960; Appointed Queen's Counsel, 1978. *Appointments:* Practised law, Borden & Elliot, 1961-64, Smith, Lyons, Torrance, Stevenson & Mayer, 1965-68, Partner, 1969-80; Seminar Instructor, Osgoode Hall for Bar Admission Couse (Corporate Law), 1966-69; Seminar Instructor, (Income Tax Law), 1974, 1976 & 1977; Chairman, Ontario Securities Commission, Ontario, Canada. *Memberships:* The Institute of Law Clerks on Ontario, 1978; Canadian Bar Association; Canadian Tax Foundation; County of York Law Association. *Publications:* Author, Partnership (a statutory annotation), 1978; Joint author, A Review of The National Energy Board Policies and Practises and Recent Hearings IX, 1971. *Honours:* Business School Merit Award, Business School Council, Producer of University Student Annual Revue; Delta Upsilon; Phi Delta Phi. *Hobbies:* Skiing; Jogging. *Address:* 6 Doon Road, Willowdale, Ontario, M2L 1L9, Canada.

KNOWLES, Leonard Joseph (Sir), b. 15 Mar. 1916, Nassau, Bahamas. Attorney-at-Law. m. Harriet Hansen Hughes, 8 July 1939, 2 sons. *Education:* LL B (Hons), King's College, University of London; Certificate of Honour in Bar Final, Gray's Inn, London. *Appointments:* Assistant Attorney General of Bahamas, Registrar General; Private Practice; Chief Justice, 1973-78; Private Practice. *Memberships:* Royal Commonwealth Society, London. *Publications:* Elements of Bahamian Law; Financial Relief in Matrimonial Cases. *Honours:* Certificate of Honour, English Bar Final, 1939; Lord Justice Holker Scholarship, 1939. *Hobby:* Music. *Address:* Shirley Park Avenue, Nassau, Bahamas.

KNOX, David Laidlaw, b. 30 June 1933, Lockerbie, Dumfriesshire, Scotland. Member of Parliament. m. Margaret Eva Maxwell, 2 June 1980. *Education:* Dumfries Academy, 1948-51; London University, 1957-60; BSc,(Econ) Hons. *Appointments:* Printing Management Trainee, 1953-56; Printing Executive, 1956-62; O & M Specialist & Management Consultant, 1962-. *Publications:* Editor, Law, Liberty & Licence, .1964; Author—Pamphlet—Britains Economic Future, 1974. *Hobbies:* Reading; Watching Association Football. *Address:* House of Commons, London SW 1, England.

KOENIG, Joseph Marie Jacques, b. 13 Dec. 1921, Mauritius. General Secretary, Mauritius Chamber of Agriculture. *Education:* Royal College, Mauritius. *Appointments:* Mauritius Civil Service, 1941-48; Assistant, Mauritius Sugar Syndicate, 1948-49; Assistant Secretary, Mauritius Chamber of Agriculture, 1949-54, Assistant to London Representative, 1954-60, General Secretary, 1959-. *Publications:* Contributed articles and conferences to television and radio networks, local newspapers and local business magazine. *Honours:* Commander of the Most Excellent Order of the British Empire (CBE). *Hobbies:* Reading; Gardening. *Address:* Farquhar Avenue, Quatre Bornes, Mauritius.

KOFOWOROLA, Ezekiel Oyegbile, b. 14 Dec. 1946, Jos, Plateau State, Nigeria. Research Fellow. m. Felicia Ibidunni Odedoku, 6 May 1966. *Education:* Grade Three Teachers Certificate, Government College, Bauchi, 1960; Grade Two Teachers Certificate, SUM College, Grindiri via Jos, 1964; BA, Drama, University of Ibadan, 1974; MA, Ahmadu Bello University, Zaria, 1977; PhD, Candidate, (African Theatre), Ahmadu Bello University, 1977-. *Appointments:* Teacher, Baptist School, Gombe, 1956, Baptist School, Minna, 1960-61, LEA Transferred Baptist School, Kafanchan, 1964-71; Research Fellow, Centre for Nigerian Cultural Studies, Ahmadu Bello University, Zaria, 1975-. *Memberships:* President, Debating Society, Bauchi,

1958; President, Association of Theatre Arts Students, 1973; Chairman, Nigerian Union of Teachers, Jema'a Federation, Kafanchan, 1969-71. *Publications:* Satiric play in English (unpublished), Goran Giya; The Demise—A play, 1979; Audu Dan Birni—A play. *Honours:* First prize awards, Bauchi Government College, 1957-59; Prefectship and Sport prize, 1959; Third Prize award Gindiri College, 1963. *Hobbies:* Farming; Photography; Music. *Address:* Centre for Nigerian Cultural Studies, Ahmadu Bello University, Zaria.

KOH, Seng Siew, John, b. 29 June 1946, Malacca, Peninsular Malaysia. Architect/Plante. m. Judith Loh Foong Lin, 14 Sept. 1980. Examination in Architecture, RIBA, Part I, University of Singapore, 1967-71; Bachelor of Architecture (1st Class Hons), University of Liverpool, 1971-73; ARAIA, 1976; RIBA, 1977; MSIA, APAM, MBIM, 1980. *Appointments:* Design Partnership Architects, Singapore, 1969; Archynamics Architects, Singapore, 1970; Architects Team 3, Petaling Jaya, Peninsular Malaysia, 1974; Development Consortium Architects Team 3, Penang, 1975-79; Implementation of Special Projects Department, City Hall, Kuala Lumpur, 1979-81; Own Architectural Practice, Kuala Lumpur and Malacca, 1981-. *Memberships:* Joint Board of Architects Malaysia and PAM Examination Panel for Part 3 Professional Practice and Practical Examination, 1982; Royal Commonwealth Society. *Creative Works:* Various Architectural Projects including: Sports and Swimming Pools Complex for Cheras New Town; Proposed Residential Condominium Plans. *Hobbies:* Painting; Music; Scuba Diving; Cross-country Running; Travel. *Address:* 11 Jalan SS 3/6, Taman Sentosa, Petaling Jaya, Selangor, Peninsular Malaysia.

KOH, Tommy Thong-Bee, b. 12 Nov. 1937, Singapore. Diplomat; Lawyer. m. Dr. Siew-Aing Poh, 5 Aug. 1967, 2 sons. *Education:* LLB (1st Class Hons), University of Singapore, 1961; LLM, Harvard University, USA, 1964; Diploma in Criminology, Cambridge University, 1965. *Appointments:* Professor of Law, University of Singapore, 1962-; Ambassador to the UN and High Commissioner to Canada, 1968-71, 1974-. *Publications:* Articles in Malayan Law Journal and Malaya Law Review. *Honours:* University Entrance Scholarship, 1957; University Book Prize, 1961; Sir Adrian Clark Memorial Medal, 1961; Leow Chia Heng Prize, 1961; Fulbright-Hays Award, 1963-64. *Hobbies:* Jogging; Swimming; Reading; Music. *Address:* 425 East 58th Street, New York, NY 10022, USA.

KOLADE, Christopher Olusola, b. 28 Dec. 1932, Iddo-Ekiti, Nigeria. Broadcaster; Management Executive. m. 14 Dec. 1957, 2 sons. *Education:* BA, 1954, Dip. Educ, 1955, Durham (Fourah Bay College). *Appointments:* Education Officer, 1955; School Broadcasts, Education Officer, 1957; Controller, Nigerian Broadcasting Corporation, 1960; Director of Television, 1963, Director of Programmes, 1968, Director-General, 1972, Nigerian Broadcasting Corporation; Executive Director, Cadbury Nigeria Limited, 1978-. *Memberships:* Fellow, Nigerian Institute of Management, Society of Broadcasters; President, International Institute of Communications, 1973-75; President, World Association for Christian Communication, 1975-. *Publications:* Contribution to Broadcasting in Africa, 1974; Articles on Broadcasting for COMBROAD, EBU Review. *Honours:* Honorary Doctorate of Civil Law, University of Sierra Leone, 1976. *Hobbies:* Music; Lawn Tennis; Reading. *Address:* 24A Oduduwa Crescent, Government Residential Area, Ikeja, Nigeria.

KOLIA, John Alexander, b. 3 Apr. 1931, Sydney, Australia. Author. *Education:* PhD, Oral History, 1976, University of Papua New Guinea. *Appointments:* Medical Assistant, London; Medical Assistant, Papua; Teacher, Tutor, Researcher, Papua, New Guinea; Acted as Director of Institute of PNG Studies, 1978-81. *Publications:* History of the Balawaia, 1976; Balawaia Dictionary, 1976; Lala Dictionary, 1977; Vaimuru Dictionary, 1978; PNG Write Your Own History, 1977; Novels: The Late Mr. Papua, 1978; A Compulsive Exhibition, 1978; Up The River to Victory Junction, 1978; My Reluctant Missionary, 1979; Close to the Village, 1979; Without Mannerisms, 1980; Victims of Independence, 1980; Plays: Traditionally Told, 1980; Historical Plays, 1979; Stories: Akward Moments, 1980; Poetry: In Between, 1980; Numerous other radio and stage plays and articles in Papers, Gazettes. *Address:* PO Box 1432, Boroko, Port Moresby, Papua, New Guinea.

KOLM, Jan Eric, b. 14 Aug. 1918, Munich, Germany. Chemical Engineer. m. Hana Eva Maria Patek, 25 June 1950, 1 son. *Education:* Ing. chem, Prague. *Appointments:* Lecturer, 1949-50; Development Chemist, 1950, Development Manager, 1956, Manager Patents and Agreements, 1958, Associate Research Manager, Research Manager, Director, Research and Technology, 1964-70, ICI Australia; Member of Board of ICI Australia, Fibremakers Property Limited, ICI Engineering Property Limited, Nylex Corporation Limited, CSR-Chemicals Property Limited, 1973-80; Director of Beach Petroleum NL, 1981. *Memberships:* Councillor and and Fellow, Australian Academy of Technological Sciences; Member of National Energy Advisory Committee; Member of CSIRO Advisory Committee, Chairman of Manuf. Ind. Subcom; Chairman of CSIRO State Committee, Victoria; Member of Standing Committee (Technical) of National Research, Development and Demonstration Council; Associate, Royal Australian Chemical Institute; Fellow, Australian Institute of Management. *Publications:* Editor and Co-author of Research to Reality, 1980. *Hobbies:* Skiing; Painting; Opera. *Address:* 11 Vista Avenue, Kew, Victoria, Australia.

KOMAKECH, Nyeko Girawal, b. 25 Dec. 1950, Gulu, Uganda, East Africa. Physiotherapist. m. Alice, 7 Dec. 1979, 1 son, 1 daughter. *Education:* Diploma, Kenyan Registered Physiotherapist, 1976; Diploma, Physiotherapy in Leprosy, 1978. *Appointments:* Physiotherapist in charge, Kumi Leprosy Centre, 1976; Senior Physiotherapist in charge, 1980. *Memberships:* Uganda Society of Physiotherapists; Uganda Leprosy Association; Kenyan Society of Physiotherapists. *Publications:* Some political articles in local press. *Honours:* East Africa Outward Bound Award, 1969. *Hobbies:* Sport; Dancing; Politics. *Address:* c/o Box 133, Gulu, Uganda, East Africa.

KOMBO, Cuthbert Lambert, b. 28 Jan. 1928, Meheza, Tanzania. Veterinary Surgeon. m. Sarah Gladys Victoria Swai, 7 Jan. 1956, 2 sons. *Education:* Diploma in Veterinary Science, 1953; Bachelor of Veterinary Science, Queensland, 1965; Member of the Royal College of Veterinary Surgeons. *Appointments:* Assistant Veterinary Officer in charge veterinary field and investigation work, 1954-60; Senior Veterinary Officer, 1965-69; Director of Agriculture Arusha Region, 1969-71; Senior Lecturer in Animal Health, University of Dar Es Salaam, 1971-72; Regional Development Director, 1971-76; Senior Lecturer and Head Division of Veterinary Science, 1976-79, Associate Professor, 1977-79, University of Dar Es Salaam; Associate Professor and Head Department of Verinary Medicine and Public Health, 1979-. *Memberships:* Chairman, 1979-80, Vice-Chairman, 1980-81, Tanzania Veterinary Association; Chairman, 1980-81, Tanzania Society of Animal Production. *Publications:* Editor Designate, The Tropical Veterinarian, Tanzania Veterinary Bulletin. *Honours:* Muljibaai Madhivani Prize, Univdrsity of East Africa, 1953. *Hobbies:* Gardening; Golf. *Address:* University of Dar Es Salaam, PO Box 643, Morogoro, Tanzania.

KONG, Stephen, Swee Meng, b. 26 Oct. 1942, Tatau, Sarawak, Malaysia. Land Surveyor. m. Josephine Lee-Hua Yi, 16 Jan. 1971, 1 son, 2 daughters. *Education:* BSc, Otago University, New Zealand, 1969. *Appointments:* Cadet Staff Surveyor, Lands & Survey Department, Christchurch, New Zealand, 1969-71; Staff Survey and Senior Superintendent, Land & Survey Department, Sarawak, 1971-79; Principal United Survey Consultants, 1979-. *Memberships:* Institutions of Surveyors, New Zealand and Malaysia; Royal Institution of Chartered Surveyors, UK. *Hobbies:* Swimming; Badminton; Table tennis. *Address:* 36 Tabuan Jaya, Kuching, Sarawak, Malaysia.

KOREY-KRZECZOWSKI, George b. 13 July 1921, Kielce, Poland. Management Consultant. m. Irene Marie Latacz, 15 July 1944, 1 son. *Education:* LL.M, Department of Law and Administration, Jagellonian University, Cracow, Poland, 1945; Post Graduate Studies, Academy of Political and Social Science, Warsaw, Poland; Department of International Law, University of Bucharest, Rumania; LL.D., Institute of International Law and Department of Law and Political Science, University of Fribourg, West Germany, 1949; DSc,

Econ., Department of Economic Science, University of Tuebingen, West Germany, 1950; Graduate, Insitute of Educational Management, Harvard University, 1975. *Appointments:* Director of Department, Ministry of Culture and Arts, Poland, 1945; Press Attaché, Polish Embassy, Bucharest, Rumania; Vice-Consul of Poland; Cultural Counsellor of Embassy, 1946; Director and Professor, Polish Institute, Bucharest and Consul of Poland, Bucharest, Rumania; Economic Advisor of Embassy; Counsellor, Ministry of Foreign Affairs, Warsaw, Poland, 1947; Consul of Poland in Berlin, Germany; Consul of Poland in Baden-Baden, West Germany, 1948-50; Resigned diplomatic career for political reasons, 1951; Assistant Supervisor, Industrial Engineering Department and Contract Estimating Department, Canadair Ltd.; Assistant Managing Director and Controller, Damar Products of Canada Ltd. and Around-the-World Shoppers Club (Canada) Ltd.; Vice-President and Managing Director, Schlemm Associates Ltd.; Management Consultant on own account; President, Pan-American Management Ltd.; Dean of Business and Vice-President, Ryerson Polytechnical Institute, 1971; Executive Vice-President and Dean, External Programmes, 1973-77; President, 1974-75; President, Canadian School of Management, Toronto, Ontario; President, Northland Open University; International Ltd, Toronto; President, University Without Walls International Council; Former Chairman, Ontario Advisory Council on Multiculturalism; Formerly President, Ryerson Polytechnical Institute and Ryerson Applied Research Ltd.; Vice-President and Director, York-Ryerson Computing Centre; Director, Canadian Operations, Canadian Textile Consultants Ltd.; Werner Management Consultants (Canada) Ltd.; Industrial and Economic Development Division, Management Consultants Inc., New York; Managing Director, Werner Associates, Inc. *Memberships:* Institute of Management Consultants, Quebec and Ontario; Academy of Marketing Science USA; New York Academy of Science; President & Fellow, Canadian International Academy of Humanities and Social Sciences; American Management Association; Academy of Management USA; Inter-American Research Institute; Academy of International Business; Director, Canadian Council for International Co-operation; Canadian Institute of Public Affairs; European Foundation for Management Development; International Inventors Association; Polish Institute, UK; Canadian Association of University Business Officers; President, National Council, Canadian Polish Congress, 1966. *Publications:* Author of: Siedemnasta Wiosna, 1938; Goloborze, 1939; Internationale Rechtsverhaeltnisse Polens im Gebiete des Strafrechts, 1949; Plannung in der Polnischen Landwirtschaft, 1950; Liryki Nostalgiczne, 1974; New Role for the Canadian Economy in the Age of World Food Shortage, 1975; Lunch w Sodomie, 1976; Korey's Stubborn Thoughts, 1980; Numerous articles on management, economic planning, international affairs, foreign markets and marketing; Guest Lecturer on radio and TV, Talks and interviews. *Honours:* Fellow, Royal Economic Society; Fellow, Royal Society of Arts; Knight-Commander of Justice, Sovereign Order of St John of Jerusalem; Knight, Military Constantinian Order of St George; Knight-Commander, Sovereign Order of Syprus; Knight Grand Cross, Military Order of St Agatha di Paterno; Cross of Polish Home Army, 1939-45; Polish Military Medal for World War II; Honorary Citizen, City of Winnipeg. *Hobbies:* Swimming; Skiing. *Address:* 55 Tanbark Crescent, Don Mills, Ontario M3B 1N7, Canada.

KORNER, Paul Ivan, b. 18 Nov. 1925, M Ostrava, Czechoslovakia. Medical Practioner. m. Jennifer Woods, 21 Dec. 1950, 2 sons, 1 daughter. *Education:* BSc, 1946, MSc, 1947, MB,BS, 1951, MD, 1956, University of Sydney; MRACP, 1968; FRACP, 1971. *Appointments:* Senior Lecturer, Physiology, 1956, Associate Professor of Physiology, 1958, Scandrett Professor of Cardiology, 1968, University of Sydney; Foundation Professor of Physiology, University of New South Wales, 1960; Director, Baker Medical Research Institute and Professor of Medicine, Monash University, 1975-. *Memberships:* Fellow, The Australian Academy of Science; Physiological Society; Australian Physiological and Pharmacological Society; Australian Society Clinical & Experimental Pharmacologists; Cardiac Society of Australia and New Zealand; International Society of Hypertension. *Publications:* Papers on Cardiovascular Control and Hypertension. *Honours:* Edgeworth David Medal, Royal Society of NSW, 1960;

R T Hall Prize, Cardiac Society, 1974; Volhard Award, International Society of Hypertension, 1982. *Hobby:* Bushwalking. *Address:* Baker Medical Research Institute, Commercial Road, Prahran, 3181, Victoria, Australia.

KOROMA, Sorie Ibrahim, b. 1930. Sierra Leone Politician. m. Mabinti Kamara, 1955, 2 sons, 3 daughters. *Education:* Cooperative College, Ibadan, Nigeria. *Appointments:* Co-operative Department, 1951-58; Private, 1958-62; First Secretary-General, Sierra Leone Motor Transport Union, 1958; MP., 1962-65, 1967-; Councillor, Freetown City Council, 1964; Deputy Mayor, Freetown, 1964; Minister: of Trade and Industry, 1968-69; of Agriculture and Natural Resources, 1969-71; Vice-President, 1971-; Prime Minister, 1971-75; Minister of Interior, 1971-73; Minister for State Enterprises, 1977-. *Memberships:* Vice-Chairman, FAO Conference, Rome, Italy, 1971; Represented Sierra Leone at: OAU Summit Conference, Addis Ababa, 1971, 73, Morocco, 1972. *Honours:* Lebanon, People's Republic of China, Ethiopia and Liberia. *Address:* Hill Station 59, Freetown, Sierra Leone.

KOSE-KASSA, Christopher Ignatius, b. 24 Nov. 1952, Kingston, Jamaica. Architect; Planner. *Education:* New York State University, Agric. & Tech., Farmingdale, USA; Bachelor of Architecture, University of Oregon, Eugene, Oregon, USA; DPU., University of London, UK. *Appointments:* Architect, Housing, 1975-76, Executive Architect, Works, 1981-, Ministry of Construction, Jamaica; Assistant Regional Planner, Architect/Planner, Town Planning Department, Ministry of Finance and Planning, Jamaica, 1976-81. *Memberships:* Jamaican Institute of Architects; Town and Country Planning Association. 05 2 volumes of unpublished poems; several unpublished short stories. *Creative Works:* Town Plan for: Rose Town/Whitfield Town, 1977; Sav-La-Mar Expansion, Westmoreland, 1977; Port Royal Comm. and Civic Facilities Design, 1978; Environmental Design for Blue Lagoon, 1978; Port Maria Urban Design, 1981; many other development plans. *Hobbies:* Art; Reading; Fishing; Aquatic sports; Jogging. *Address:* 23 University Close, Mona, Kingston 7, Jamaica, West Indies.

KOSKIE, Jack Louis, b. 23 July 1914, Hull, Yorkshire, UK. Artist. m. Hanna Herman, 27 Oct. 1948, 1 son. *Education:* Scholarship, Hull College of Art; Diploma of Art, Hobart Technical College. *Appointments:* Art Editor, Commonwealth Office of Education; Senior Artist/Designer, Invincible Press Sydney; Head of Department of Graphic Design & Printing, Hobart Technical College, Tasmania; Art Master, Mount Scopus College, Melbourne, Victoria; Lecturer in Printmaking, Gordon Institute of Technology, Geelong, Victoria; Lecturer, School of Humanities, Deakin University Geelong, Victoria. *Memberships:* Royal Society of Arts, London; Print Council of Australia; Victorian Artists Society; Bezalel Society of Art. *Creative Works:* Story of Ships, Story of Aircraft for NSW Education Department; Paintings in War Memorial Museum, Canberra, Government House Hobart, Tasmanian Museum & Art Gallery, John Drysdale Library Geelong, Auburn State College Victoria and numerous other galleries. *Honours:* War at Sea, section Australia at War exhibition, 1947; Ben Uri Art Prize, 1966; Cato Prize, 1970; Roland Prize, 1971; Corio Rotary Purchase Award, 1973; Applied Chemicals Prize, 1974; Lord Mayor's Melbourne City Award, 1980; Highly commended in many other exhibtions in NSW & Victoria. *Hobby:* Yachting. *Address:* 53 Tibrockney Street, Highett, Victoria, 3190, Australia.

KOSKY, Robert John, b. 31 Oct. 1940, Melbourne, Australia. Child Psychiatrist. m. Michele Mary Reis, 11 Jan. 1970, 2 sons, 1 daughter. *Education:* Melbourne High School; University of Melbourne; Monash University; BSc, 1969; Dip.Ed., 1961; MB.,BS., (Hons), 1969; MRANZCP, 1976; Certificate of Child Psychiatry, 1977. *Appointments:* Head, Child and Adolescent Psychiatric Services, Mental Health Services of West Australia, 1977-; Director of Training in Child Psychiatry for West Australia, 1980-; Visiting Psychiatrist, Princess Margaret Hospital for Children, 1978. *Memberships:* Chairman Section of Child Psychiatry, Western Australia. *Publications:* Contributions to medical journals including: Children and Huntington's Disease; Patterns of Adolescent Illnesses. *Address:* 6 Helston Avenue, City Beach, 6015, Australia

KOSOY, Ted, b. 30 Apr. 1937, Toronto, Canada. Author and Publisher. *Education:* BA Political Science 1962; MA History 1968. *Appointments:* History Teacher 1964-67; Freelance Writer 1968-. *Memberships:* American Travel Writers Society; Canadian Publishers Association. *Publications:* Kosoy's Guide for Canadians Travelling Abroad; Kosoy's Travel Guide to Europe; Kosoy's Travel Guide to Canada; Kosoy's Travel Guide to the Orient and the South Pacific; Kosoy's Travel Guide to Mexico, Central America and South America; Kosoy's Travel Guide to Florida and the South; The guides are being prepared for publication in foreign languages. *Hobbies:* Squash; Scuba Diving. *Address:* 40 Shallmar Blvd, Toronto, Canada M6C 2J9.

KOTEY, Raymond Ayodele, b. 7 July 1943, Lagos Nigeria. Quantity Surveying. m. Kuby Dawodu 8 Jan. 1977, 1 son, 1 daughter. *Education:* Fellow, Royal Institution of Chartered Surveyors, 1968-80; Fellow, Institute of Quantity Surveyor, 1966-79; Fellow, Nigerian Institute of Quantity Surveyors 1967-80. *Appointments:* Tillipan and Partners, Quantity Surveyors 1966-68; Qu-Ess Partnership, Quantity Surveyors 1969-. Hobby: *Address:* 11A Kinkind Close, Kaduna, Nigeria.

KOTHANDARAMAN, Portko, b. 9 June 1941, Irumbulikkurichi. Teaching and Research. m. K Poongothai, 23 Apr. 1976, 1 son. *Education:* Vidwan, 1961; Pulavar, 1961; BOL, 1963; MA, 1965; Diploma in Bengali, 1967; PhD, 1970. *Appointments:* Department of Linguistics, Annamalai University, Annamalainagar, Tamilnadu, India, 1969-70, 1972-73; School of Oriental and African Studies, University of London, UK, 1970-72; International Institute of Tamil Studies, Adaiyaru, Madras, India, 1973-77; Department of Tamil, University of Madras, Madras, India, 1977-. *Memberships:* Royal Asiatic Society, London, 1970-72; Philological Society, London, 1971-73; Linguistic Society of India; Dravidian Linguistic Association; Linguistic Analysis, America, 1973-76; Dravidian Studies; Indian Literature, 1977-80; Moliyiyal, Executive Editor; Folklore Fellows of India, 1980-81; Editor, Pulamai, 1974-. *Publications:* Poems, Valkkaippunka, 1965, Kotai valavan, 1978; Published about 70 papers and 12 books (in English and Tamil), on Linguistics and Literature. *Honours:* Patron, London Tamil Sangam, 1972-; Honorary Editor, Makkal Nokku, 1973-78, London, Murasu, 1970-72; Several prizes during studies in schools, college and University; Kavignar. *Hobbies:* Writing poems; Collecting coins from different countries. *Address:* 38-B, Bimmanna Mudali Gardon Street, Alwarpet, Madras, 600 018, Tamil Nadu, India.

KOTHARI, Hemraj, b. 10 Nov. 1933 Sujangarh, India. Consultant-Editor, Chartered, Incorporated and Professional Engineer, Publisher, etc. *Education:* BSc, DWP(Lon), ACCGI(Lon), MSE(Lon), CEng. (Lon and India), PE (UK), MMGI, LMIIM, MRTS (Ion), MAS-.Mech.E (USA), FIIPE, FAE, FIE, FBIM (Lon), FIV, FI-MechE (Lon), FSEI, FGMS, FISE, FBIS (Lon), FCI (Lon), FIAM, FIMechE, FIBA (UK), FID (Lon), FIMS (UK), FSAM (USA). etc. *Appointments:* Founder-Principal: Kothari Organisation, controlling India-International News Service, India-International Films; Kothari Publications, (Publishers of Who's Who Series in India) and Kothari Consultants; Partner: Kothari and Sons. *Memberships:* Life Fellow, Fellow, Committee Member, Life Member, Member of about 100 Professional Institutes in the field of Engineering, Management and Journalism including: National Academies and Chambers of Commerce. Executive Committee Member of Indian National Committee of International Chamber of Commerce; Former Governing Council Member: Indian Council of Arbitration; Former Vice-President and Hon. Secretary: Association of Engineers, India; Executive Committee Member: Association of Indian Engineering Industry (ER); Federation of Engineering Industries of India, Industry Sub-Committee of FICCI, etc. *Publications:* Editor: Who's Who Series, India; The Director; Professional Engineer; Export-Import News; What's On In Calcutta; Compact; etc. *Honours:* Indian Council of Arbitration and American Arbitration Association; Assessor of Municipal properties-appointed by the Government of West Bengal; Indian Delegate to various International Conferences and Former Member of few International Commissions. *Hobbies:* Films; Conferences; etc. *Address:* 3D Rajhans, 6, Hastings Park Road, Calcutta 700027, India.

KRIEDEMANN, Paul Edward, b. 31 Jan. 1937 Brisbane, Queensland, Australia. Research Scientist, Biology and Agriculture. m. Janice Mary Sutherst 16 Dec. 1960, 1 son, 1 daughter. *Education:* BA Agricultural Science, 1959; BA(Hons) University of Queensland 1960; PhD University of Melbourne 1964; Post Doctoral Fellow, Purdue University, Indiana USA 1964-66. *Appointments:* CSIRO, Division of Horticultural Research 1966; Visiting, Professor, Purdue University, 1970 and Cornell University, USA 1973; CSIRO, Appointed Chief, Division of Irrigation Research, 1978. *Memberships:* Australian Society and Plant Physiologists; Editorial Advisory Board, Aust. J. Plant Physiology; National Oilands Research Committeè; Victorian Irrigation Research and Advisory Services Committee. *Publications:* Plant Growth and Development; Review Chapters on Crop growth and wintry relations; Original papers in scientist journals on plant physiology and agricultural research. *Honours:* Wheat Industry Reserch Council Scholarship 1960-64; NSF Post-doctoral Fellowship 1964-66; Commonwealth Scholarship, undergraduate studies 1956-59; Bronze medallian, life saving 1954. *Hobbies:* Carpentry; Reading; Classical Guitar. *Address:* 53 Myall Avenue, Kensington Gardens, Adelaide S.A, Australia 5068.

KRISHNA, Ramasamy Chetty, b. 20 June 1940 Ammapet, Salem-3, Tamil Nadu. Doctor. m. Mrs. Nirmala 4 June 1969, 2 sons, 1 daughter. *Education:* MB, BS 1964; MD, (General Medicine, Madras 1969. *Appointments:* Civil Assistant Surgeon, T.B Sanatorium, Tambaram, 1968-69; Assistant Professor of Medicine Stanlay Medical College Madras, and Assistant Physician, Government Stanlay Hospital Madras, 1969-71; Civil Assistant Surgeon, Governmemt Head Quarter Hospital Salem, 1971-76; Director, Intensive Coronary Care Unit, Modern Hospital Salem 1976-; Diabites Specialist and Consultant Physician, Salem, 1976-. *Memberships:* President, Tribal Welfare Association, Tamilnadu, India; President, Bharath Journal Club, Salem; Vice President, Manam (Mind) Association Tamilnadu; People's Union of Civil liberties; Honorary Consultant, NK Charitable Trust and Free Dispensary; Association of Physicians of India; Diabetic Association of India; Indian Medical Association; Fellow, American College of Chest Physicians. *Publications:* Idiopathic Pericarditis, 1970; Unusual manifestation of Bronchoganic Carcinoma, 1970; Immunity: Articles on Drug Trials; Lectures addressed to Rotary Club, IMA RFPT Centre and FCGP Refresher courses. *Honours:* Second Prize in Competitive Examinations in Bacteriogy, Stanlay Medical College 1962; Prize for acting in College Drama 1959; Fellow, Chest College of Physician's USA 1979. *Hobbies:* Social Service; International Friendship; Reading. *Address:* 128, 2nd Agraharam, Salem-1, Madras State, India.

KRISHNAJI, b. 13 Jan. 1922, Allahabad India. Research and Teaching; Professor. m. Bimla 7 July 1946, 2 sons, 2 daughters. *Education:* BSc, Allahabad University 1942; MSc Physics, 1944. *Appointments:* Professor of Physics, Allahabad University, 1967-81; U.G.C. National Fellow 1977-80; Pro-Vice Chancellor, 1973-77; Visiting Professor, H C Webster Research Fellow, University of Queensland Australia 1970-71; Professor of Physics, University of Jodhpur India 1966; Senior Scientific Officer, Ministry of Defence, Government of India 1959-60; Lecturer in Physics 1945-59 and 1960-65; Research Assistant CSIR Allahabad University 1944-45. *Memberships:* National Academy of Sciences, India; Vigyan Parishad India; Lions Club Prayag; Institute of Electronics and Telecom Engineers; Allahabad University Teachers Association; National Committee of International Union of Pure and Applied Physics. *Publications:* 62 Research Papers, 2 Review Articles, 10 Popular Articles, 5 Books, 24 Supervised DPhil Thesis, in the field of Molecular Physics, Microwave Spectroscopy, Dielectrics. *Honours:* Hari Om Trust, Sir C V Raman Award, 1976; U.G.C. National Lecturer in Physics 1976; Sectional President, Physical Sciences, National Academy of Sciences Annual Session; Fellow, Vice President, National Academy of Sciences, India. *Hobby:* Photography. *Address:* 14B Bank Road, Allahabad 211002, India.

KRISHNAKUMAR, Thiyagarajah, b. 22 June 1949, Maniday, Sri Lanka. Chartered Accountant. *Education:* BSc, Sri Lanka 1971; Associate Member, Institute of Chartered Accountants of Sri Lanka 1977. *Appointments:* Chief Accountant Cargo Boat Despatch Company Limited, Colombo; Financial Accountant Ceylon Hotels Corporation, Colombo; Accountant John Keells Group, Colombo. Hobby: Travelling. *Address:* 26/s E S Fernando, Mawatha, Colombo 6.

KRISHNA MOORTHI, C S, b. Vellore, Tamilnadu State, India. Indian Administrative Sèrvice. m. Shantha Sivaswami Aiyar 30 Apr. 1944, 2 daughters. *Education:* Bachelor of Arts (Honours), Economics and Political Science, Banking and Currency and Public Finance, University of Madras. *Appointments:* Research Scholar, Wartime Railway Transport in India, University of Madras, 1940-42; Indian Army Ordnance Corps, 1943-46; Indian Administrative Service, 1947; Divisional Officer in Madras State, 1947-52; Joint Secretary, and Secretary, Board of Revenue, Madras State, 1952-53; Deputy Secretary, Planning, Department of Economic Affairs, Ministry of Finance, 1954-55; Private Secretary, to Minister of Finance, India, 1955-56; Deputy Secretary, Ministry of Finance, Overseas Finance, 1957-58; Board of Executive Directors, World Bank, Washington DC, USA, and Counsellor, then Minister, Economic, Embassy of India, 1958-63; Joint Secretary, External Finance, Department of Economic Affairs, Ministry of Finance, New Delhi, 1963-66; Vice-President, Asian Development Bank, Manila, The Philippines, 1966-78. *Publications:* Participation in various research and publication activities by, Asian Development Back Manila; The Asian Agricultural Survey, 1968; Rural Asian Challenge and Opportunities 1978; Regional Transport Survey of South East Asia; South East Asia in the Seventies. *Honours:* University Prizeman, Madras University 1940. *Hobbies:* Religions and Philosophy; Photography; Ancient History. *Address:* "Chandra Sri", 3, Srilabdhi Colony, Mowbrays Road, Alwarpet, Madras 600 018, India.

KRISHNAN, Thiruvenkata, b. 8 Dec. 1933 Madras, India. Scientist. m. Janaki Parthasarathy 17 Jan. 1963, 1 son. *Education:* Bachelor of Science, Physics, Chemistry and Mathematics, 1952; Bachelor of Arts, Physics, Chemistry, Mathematics and Crystallography, 1955; Master of Arts, Physics, 1959; University of Madras and Cambridge University, England. *Appointments:* Research Assistant, Cavendish Laboratory, University of Cambridge, England, 1955-56; CSIR, Senior Research Fellow, National Physical Laboratory of India, New Delhi, 1956-59; Research Officer, Commonwealth Scientific and Industrial Research Organisation, Government of Australia, Division of Radiophysics, Sydney, Australia, 1959-62; Research Associate and Radio Astronomer, Department of Electrical Engineering, Stanford Radio Astronomy Institute and Radiophysics Laboratory, Stanford University California, 1963-68; National Academy of Sciences/National Research Council Senior Post-doctoral Resident Research Associate, Goddard Space Flight Center, NASA Greenbelt, Maryland, 1968-70; Four Reports in the field of Astro Research, in USA 1970-71; Four Reports for Science Education in Schools and Colleges, in Tamil Nadu, 1972; Director and kProfessor, Madras Institute of Technology, 1971-74; Managing Partner and Director of Research, 1976-. *Memberships:* Numerous Committees from 1971-74; International Radio Science Union; FIETE, India; Indian Society for Technical Education; Fellow, Royal Astronomical Society, London; International Astronomical Union; IEEE, New York. *Publications:* 16 publications including: Decimeter Radio Bursts Concurrent with Solar Type IV Radiation, 1961; Observations of the Six Most Intense Radio Sources , 1965; Radio Evidence for the Occurrence of High Polar Coronal Densities, 1970. *Hobbies:* Reading; Music. *Address:* 234 Avvai Shanmugam Road, Madras 600086, India.

KROEGER, Arthur, b. 7 Sept. 1932, Naco, Alberta Canada. Public Servant. m. Garbielle Jane Sellers, 7 May 1966, (deceased 1979), 2 daughters. *Education:* BA, University of Alberta 1951-55; MA, Pembroke College, Oxford 1956-58. *Appointments:* Government of Canada, 1958-; Department of External Affairs, 1958-71; Treasury Board Secretariat, 1971-74; Deputy Minister of Indian and Northern Affairs, 1975-79; Deputy Minister of Transport, 1979-. *Memberships:* Five Lakes Fishing Club. *Honours:* Rhodes Scholar, University of Alberta, 1955. *Address:* 245 Springfield Road, Ottawa, Canada.

KRONBORG, Royce Harry, b. 18 Aug. 1925, Benalla, Victoria, Australia. Hospital Administrator. m. Audree edna Storey, 21 May 1949, 3 sons. *Education:* Diploma of Hospital Administration, 1954; Certificate of Hospital Administration, University of New South Wales, 1959; Hospital Administrators Development Program, Cornell University, USA, 1965. *Appointments:* Manager of several Victorian country hospitals, 1949-59; Manager, Preston and Northcote Community Hospital, Victoria, 1959-70; Federal Council, 1967-78, National President, 1974-76; Australian Hospital Association; Council of Management, 1969-, Honorary Treasurer, 1979-81, President Designate, 1981-, International Hospital Federation; General Manager, Austin Hospital Heidelberg, Victoria, 1970-; Honorary Director, 1971-78, Deputy Chairman, 1976-78, Community Systems Foundation Australasia; Australian Council on Hospital Standards, 1973-75 and 1978-79; Commissioner, 1974-76, Deputy Chairman, 1976-78, Chairman, 1978-80, Health Insurance Commission; Division 1 Council, 1978-, Directory Honorary Board, 1980-, Victorian Hospitals' Association; National Health and Medical Research Council, 1980. *Memberships:* Fellow, Australian Institute of Management; Fellow, Australian College of Health Service Administrators; Royal Victorian Association of Honorary Justices; Naval and Military Club. *Honours:* MBE, 1972. *Hobby:* Animal Husbandry. *Address:* "Elsinore", Arthurs Creek Road, Nutfield, Victoria, 3099, Australia.

KRUPINSKI, Jerzy, b. 20 Feb. 1920, Warsaw, Poland. Director, Mental Health Research Institute of Victoria, Australia. m. Aniela Pauline Gaslaw 16 Jan. 1941, 2 daughters. *Education:* Medical Degree, Medical Academy in Gdansk 1949; MD, University of Warsaw 1951; Docent, Medical Academy of Warsaw 1953; Specialist, Public Health and Medical Administration 1953; Docent, Medical Academy of Warsaw, 1954; Fellow, Royal Australian College of Medical Administrators 1967. *Appointments:* Chair of Medical Administration, Academy of Warsaw, Poland: Associate Professor, 1951-54; Docent, 1954-60; Mental Health Research Institute, Victoria, Australia: Psychiatric Biostatistical Officer, 1961-63; Medical Statistician 1963-67; Epidemiologist 1967-71; Director of Research 1971-81; Director 1981-. *Memberships:* Vice-President, Victorian Family Council; Chairman, Research Committee: National Marriage Guidance Council, Marriage Guidance Council of Victoria; Medical Sociology and Sociology of Mental Health; International Sociological Association. *Publications:* 125 Publications, in the field of Social and preventive medicine, mental health, medical administration, sociology of marriage and family, and sociology of migration; Books include: Family in Australia; The Health of a Metropolis. *Honours:* Several Polish decorations. *Hobbies:* Swimming; Bridge. *Address:* 33 Campbell Street, Bentleigh, Victoria 3024, Australia.

KRYGIER, Henry Richard, b. 9 Sept. 1917, Warsaw, Poland. Publisher. m. 8 Jan. 1939, 1 son, 1 daughter. *Education:* LLB, Warsaw University, 1939. *Appointments:* Polish Press Office & War Correspondent in Australia, 1943-45; Research Office, Political Research Society; Secretary, Australian Association for Cultural Freedom, 1954-; Publisher, Quadrant Magazine, 1956-; Director of Companies distributing magazines & books. *Publications:* Articles in various magazines and journals in Australia and overseas. *Honours:* OBE, 1981. *Hobbies:* Reading; Travel. *Address:* 43 Carlotta Road, Double Bay, NSW, 2028, Australia.

KUFORIJI Dorcas Bolajoko Ayodele (Mrs), b. 28 Sept. 1936, Lagos, Nigeria. Chartered Accountant/Economist. Separated, 2 sons, 1 daughter. *Education:* Grade II Teacher's Certificate, 1955; BSc, Economics, London University, 1963; Associate Certificate of the Institute of Chartered Secretaries, 1964; Associate Certificate of the Institute of Chartered Accountants of England & Wales, 1967. *Appointments:* Group Finance Controller & Company Secretary, 1968-72; Finance Director, 1972-77; Managing Director, 1977-. *Memberships:* Nigerian Institute of Social & Economic Research; Nigerian Institute of Management; Matron to many educational and social organisations; Institute of Chartered Accountants; Chairman, Education & Research Committee of the Society of Women Accountants of Nigeria. *Publications:* Various articles in professional magaznes and newspapers. *Honours:* Member of the Order of the Niger, 1979. *Hobbies:*

Reading; Literary Debates; Cycling; Music; People. *Address:* 21 Marine Road, Apapa, Nigeria.

KUJORE, Obafemi, b. 9 Mar. 1931, Abeokuta, Nigeria. University Teacher; Classical Philologist. m. Modupe Abimbola Fagunke 3 Mar. 1960, 2 sons, 1 daughter. *Education:* Kuniversity College, Ibadan, Nigeria 1955-59; University College, London, England. BA (Hons. Classics) University of London 1959; PhD Classical Philology, University of London 1966. *Appointments:* Teacher, Secondary Schools in Nigeria, 1959-63; Teacher, St Paul's School, Hammersmith, London, 1966; Lecturer in Classics, University College of Cape Coast, Cape Coast, Ghana, 1966-69; Lecturer, Department of Classics, University of Ibadan, 1969-72; Senior Lecturer 1972-75; Professor 1975-; Head of Department 1978-. *Memberships:* Philological Society London; Society for the Promotion of Hellenic Studies, London; The Classical Association, United Kingdom; The Classical Association of Nigeria; Linguistic Society of America; West African Linguistic Society. *Publications:* Articles in learned journals; American Journal of Philology 1970; Classical Philology 1971, 74; Glotta 1970; Platon 1970, etc.; Book Monographs: Greek Polymorphic Presents: A study of their development and functional tendencies, 1973; A Short Revision Course in Elementary Greek Syntax, 1973 and 1976; A Short Revision Course in Greek Grammar, 1976. *Honours:* Commonwealth Study Fellowship, University of London, Institute of Classical Studies 1972. *Hobbies:* Music; Lawn Tennis. *Address:* 5 Sankore Avenue, University of Ibadan, Ibadan, Nigeria.

KUKOYI, Oludotun Adekunle, b. 23 Jan. 1929, Ijebu Ode, Ogun State, Nigeria. Land Surveying. m. Essie Florence Ibijoke Smith 11 Apr. 1955, 2 sons, 3 daughters. *Appointments:* University College Ibadan Nigeria 1948-52; University College, London, United Kingdom 1953-54; BSc(Maths) 1952; Diploma in Surveying 1954; Nigerian Surveyors Licence 1957; FNIS 1967. *Appointments:* Staff Appointments, Civil Service 1954-57; Supt. Surveyor, Civil Service, 1957-59; Consultant Surveyor, Public Corporation 1959-64; Surveyor, Lagos Executive Development Board 1968-69; Principal, Adekunle Kujoyi and Partners, 1959-; Managing Director, Nigerian Mapping Company Limited 1978-. *Memberships:* Nigerian Institution of Surveyors; Commonwealth Association of Surveying and Land Economy; Rotary Club of Ikeja; Nigeria Olympic Committee; Nigeria Hockey Federation. *Hobbies:* Music; Photography; Travelling; Table Tennis; Sports Organising. *Address:* 7 Ajayi Ogedengbe Avenue, off Ikorodu Road, Obanikoro, Lagos State, Nigeria.

KUKU, Aderemi, Oluyomi, b. 20 Mar. 1941, Ijebu-Ode Nigeria. Mathematician. m. Felicia Osifunke 28 Dec. 1968, 4 daughters. *Education:* BSc (specialk) maths, Upper second class hons., University of London 1962-65; MSc (maths) 1968; PhD (maths) 1971; University of Ibadan 1966-71. *Appointments:* Lecturer, Mathematics, University of Ife, 1967-68; Lecturer, University of Ibadan 1968-75, Senior Lecturer, 1975-80, Reader in maths, 1980-; Various visiting positions, Columbia Auniversity New York US 1970-71, University of Illinois, Urban, Champaign USA 1974, 1975, University of Chicago, USA 1974-75, Universitat Belefeld, West Germany 1976, 1980. *Memberships:* Science Association of Nigeria; Nigerian Mathematics Society; American Mathematics Society; Mathematical Association of Nigeria; Nigerian Association for Mathematiclal Sciences. *Publications:* Published Abstract Algebra; various articles on algebraic K-theory in such Journals as Journal of Lond maths society; Mathematise Seichrift; Proceedings of the American Maths Society, Communications in Algebra; Journal of Algebra and Springer-Verlag Lecture notes Series. *Honours:* Sub-Dean, Postgraduate, Faculty of Science, University of Ibadan 1978-80; Associate Editor: Nigerian Journal for Mathematical sciences 1978-; Journal of Nigerian maths society 1979-; Member Editorial Advisory Board, Nigerian Journal of Science, African Scholarship programme of American Universities 1962, USA, ID Scholarship 1962-65; State Department Travel Fellowship USA 1968; Afgrad Fellowship 1970-71; Hungarian Fellowship 1974; Honorary Citizenship, Huntsville Alabama, USA 1968 DAAD West German Academic Exch. award 1981. *Hobbies:* Ball-room Dancing; Chess; Table-tennis; Gardening. *Address:* No 2 Amure Street, off Adebajo Street, Kongi, Ibadan, Nigeria.

KULATUNGA, Liyanage Laksaman, b. 4 Apr. 1942, Sri Lanka. Chartered Accountant, Management Consultant. m. Daya Rohinie Ubeyratna, 13 Sept. 1972, 1 son, 1 daughter. *Education:* BA, University of Sri Lanka, 1966; Master of Business Administration, Indian Institute of Management, Ahmedabad, India, 1976; Final Examination of the Institute of Chartered Accountants of Sri Lanka, 1971; Final Examination of the Institute of Cost and Management Accountants, London, 1975. *Appointments:* Accountant, Sri Lanka Police Department, 1970-71; Accountant, Department of National Housing, Sirk Lanka, 1971-73; Senior Management Services Officer, Ministry of Public Administration, Local Government and Home Affaìrs, Sri Lanka, j1973-76; Consultant, Sri Lanka Institute of Development Administration, 1976-78; Senior Partner, Kulatunga and Company, Chartered Accountants, 1978-. *Memberships:* President, Secretary, Association of Professionally Qualified Accountants in Public Service, 1971-78. *Publications:* Advanced Auditing, 1978; Thesis; Company Auditing, (in press). *Hobbies:* Poetry; Writing Short Stories; Stamp Collecting; Photography. *Address:* Situmina, Meegahakumbura, Bulatsinhala, Sri Lanka.

KULLEEN, Prem Chand, b. 9 Nov. 1938, Uppal Jagir, Panjab, India. Lecturer. m. Manju Bala Bagai, 13 Apr. 1972, 1 son, 1 daughter. *Education:* BA, Ranchi University, 1967; BLib.Sc, 1969, MLib.Sc, 1970, University of Delhi. *Appointments:* Documentation Assistant, Telco Limited, India, 1963-70; Chief Librarian, Hindu College, University of Delhi, India, 1970-72; City Librarian, Ndola City Council, Zambia, 1972-75; City Librarian, Lusaka City Council, Zambia, 1975-80; Lecturer, Information and Documentation Science, United Nations Institute for Namibia, Lusaka, 1980-. *Memberships:* Zambia Library Association; Zambia India Friendship Association; Life Member, Urdu Samaj, Jamshedpur, India, General Secretary, 1962-68. *Publications:* Approximately 25 short stories in Hindi and Urdu; Approximately 20 articles on library science in various journals; Thesis. *Hobbies:* Writing short stories; Gardening; Social Work. *Address:* 6 Mambulima Road, Rhodes Park, Lusaka, Zambia.

KULLY, Rolf Max, b. 20 Sept. 1934, Solothurn (CH). University Professor. m. 15 Aug. 1967, 2 sons, 1 daughter. *Education:* Dr.Phil., University of Basle, (CH) 1964; Habilitation, University of Basle 1970. *Appointments:* Teacher, Himmelried (CH) 1954-58; Assistant Professor, Basle 1964-70; Dozent, Basle 1970-73; Visiting Professor, University of Florida, Gainesville Fla., 1972; Associate Professor, University of Montreal 1974-78; Full Professor, 1978-; Acting Chairman 1981-. *Memberships:* Linguistic Society of America; Verband Schweizerischer Germanisten; Canadian Association of University Teachers of German; President, Basler Hebelstiftung; Federation of Swiss Societies in Eastern Canada; Association culturelle Canada-Suisse à Montréal. *Publications:* Die Ständesatire in den deutschen geistlichen Schauspielen des ausgehenden Mittelalters, 1966; Johann Peter Hebel, 1969; Die Flurnameu der Gemeinde Himmelried im Kanton Solothurn, 1977; Numerous articles in periodicals. Hobby: Music (Flute, Piano). *Address:* 316 Avenue Querbes, Outremont, P.Q, H2V 3W3 Canada.

KULSHRESHTHA, Surendra Nath, b. 3 Mar. 1941, Agra, India. Teaching. m. Roma Kulshreshta, 29 Oct. 1967, 1 son, 2 daughters. *Education:* BSc.Ag, 1954-58, MSc.Ag, 1958-60, Agra University; PhD, University of Manitoba, 1962-65. *Appointments:* Assistant Professor, Agra University, India, 1960-62; Graduate Research Assistant, 1962-65, Post-Doctoral Fellow, 1968-69, University of Manitoba; Economist, Agric. Canada, Ottawa, 1965-66; Research Economist, Hedlin-Menzies, 1966-68; Assistant, Associate and Full Professor, University of Saskatchewan, 1969-81. *Memberships:* Canadian Agric. Econ. Society (co-editor, Can. J. of Ag. Ec.); American Agric. Econ. Association; Western Agric. Econ. Association; International Association of Agric. Economists; Econometrical Society; American Statistical Association. *Publications:* Contributed to various professional journals. *Honours:* Canada Council, Post-Doctral Fellowship, 1969-70; Honorable Mention for Best Article Award of |Canadian |society of Agric. Econ, 1977, 1978. *Hobbies:* Dancing; Photography; Badminton. *Address:* 82 Harvard Crescent, Saskatoon, Canada.

KUMAR, Har Darshan, b. 25 Feb. 1934, Lahore. Teaching and Research. m. Krishna Bhasin, 8 Feb. 1964, 2 daughters. *Education:* BSc(Hons.), Botany, Zoology, Chemistry, 1954; MSc, Botany, Banaras Hindu University, 1956; PhD Botany—Algal Physiology and Genetics, University of London, England, 1963. *Appointments:* Lecturer, Bihar University, Ranchi, 1956-58; Assistant Professor, 195864, Reader and Head of Botany Department, 1964-66, Professor and Head, 1966-71, Senior Professor and Head, University of Udaipur, 1971-72; Senior Professor of Botany and Head, Division of Biosciences, Himachal Pradesh University, Simla 1972-73; Senior Professor of Botany, 1973-, Head of Department, Banaras Hindu University, Varanasi 1978-80. *Memberships:* Society of Microbial Ecologists of the Tropics; Indian ·Society of Ecology; Executive Committee, Phycological Society of India; Honorary Librarian, Indian Botanical Society; International and American Phycological Societies. *Publications:* Published 100 research and review papers in internatiionally-reputed foreign and Indian journals; Five books on algae, plant metabolism, modern ecology, molecular biology, and plant physiology; Edited five books written in Hindi by Botany teachers. *Honours:* University Grants Commission National Lecturer in Botany 1972-73; Fellowship, Indian Academy of Science, Bangalore, 1975; Fellow, Explorers Club, New York, 1980. *Address:* New G/27 Nizam Colony, B. H. U. Campus, Varanasi 221005, India.

KUMAR, Narendra, b. 1 Feb. 1940, Bilaspur, India. Research and Teaching. m. Ann, 1 Mar. 1977, 2 daughters. *Education:* BTech.(Honours), Electrical Engineering 1962; MTech., Microwave Engineering 1963; PhD, Physics 1971. *Appointments:* Senior Scientific Officer, Institute of Armament Technology, Poona, 1963-64; Senior Scientific Officer, National Chemical Laboratory, Poona, 1964-68; Teaching Fellow, University of British Columbia, Canada, 1968-70; Assistant Professor, Indian Institute of Science, Bangalore, India 1970-75 and Professor, 1975-; Visiting Professor, University of Warwick, UK 1978-79 and Chef de Travaux, University of Liégè, Belgium 1975-76. *Memberships:* International Centre for Theoretical Physics, Trieste, Italy, 1971-. *Publications:* Approximately 90 original scientific papers published in International Journals, covering Solid state Physics, Astrophysics, Biophysics, General Relativity; Co-author, Interachons in Magnetically ordered solids, 1980. *Hobbies:* Reading philosophical writings and Fiction; Electronic Toys. *Address:* 390 Upper Palace Orchards, Bangalore 560082, India.

KUMITSONYO, Eric Blackson Zachariah, b. 24 Oct. 1935, Ntcheu, Malawi. Lawyer. m. Mary Kumitsonyo, 30 Nov. 1957, 2 sons, 3 daughters. *Education:* Diploma in Commercial Teaching, 1963; LLB, 1971. *Appointments:* Teacher; Lawyer and Proprietor of Lilley, Wills and Compaяy. *Memberships:* The Society of Malawi (Historical and Scientific), Committee Member; The Malawi Law Society, Secretary, 1972-74, Chairman, 1974-77; Malawi University Council, 1975-78. *Hobbies:* Reading; Golf; Tennis. *Address:* Kittermaster Avenue, BCA Hill, Limbe, Malawi.

KUMOLU, Joseph Babalola Omoyele, b. 14 Oct. 1934, Imesi Ile, Oyo State, Nigeria. Engineer. m. Gladys Olaiya, 3 Sept. 1960, 1 son, 6 daughters. *Education:* BSc Hons. Mechanical Engineering 1959; MSc, Mechinal Engineering, University of Aberdeen, 1962. *Appointments:* Project Enineer 1963-72; Assistant Chief Engineer 1972-74; Chief Engineer 1974-75; Operations Manager 1975-79; Divisional Manager 1979-81; Director Shell Nigeria 1975-81. *Memberships:* Nigeria Society of Engineers. *Publications:* Petroleum and the Nigeria National Development Plans. *Hobbies:* Jogging; Golf. *Address:* Imesi-Ile, Oyo State, Nigeria.

KUNDU, Chuni Lal, b. 1 Oct. 1936, Kralyar, Rainawari, Kashmir. University Teaching. m. Usha Kundu, 6 June 1963, 1 son, 1 daughter. *Education:* MEd, 1957; MA, 1959; PhD, 1965; TDP, USA. *Appointments:* Research Fellow, Central Institfute of Education, Delhi, 1959-60; Lecturer in Education, Jammu and Kashmir Govt., 1960-66; Lecturer in Education, Jammu and Kashmir University, 1966-67; Lecturer, 1968-71, Reader, 1972-75, Professor, Dean and Head, 1977-, Kurukshetra University; Principal, University College of Education, Kurukshetra, 1975-78. *Memberships:* President, Kurukshetra University Teacher's Club; Vice-President, All India Juvenile Literary Conference, Calcutta; Indian Adult Education Association, Delhi. *Publications:* Educational Psychology; Personality Development: A Critique of Indian Studies; Mental Abilities and School Curriculum; Rorschach Psychodiagnostics: An Indian Case Study; 36 Research papers and projects. *Honours:* Silver Medal for Writing. *Hobby:* Swimming. *Address:* E-45, University Campus, Kurukshetra, India.

KUNOS, George, b. 14 May 1942, Budapest, Hungary. Physician, Medical Researcher. m. Ildiko Vermes, 11 June 1967, 2 daughters. *Education:* Medical School, 1960-66; MD, Semmelweis Medical University, Budapest, 1966; PhD, McGill University, Montreal, 1971-73. *Appointments:* Assistant Professor of Medicine, Semmelweis Medical University, 1967-71; Lecturer in Pharmacology, 1973-74, Assistant Professor of Pharmacology, 1974-79, Associate Professor of Pharmacology, 1979-, McGill University. *Memberships:* American Society for Pharmacology and Experimental Therapeutics; Canadian Society for Clinical Investigation; Society for Experimental Biology and Medicine; Canadian Pharmacological Society; Canadian Hypertension Society. *Publications:* 40 research papers including several reviews on various aspects of neuropharmacology and hormone receptors; Editor of a series of Books on, Neurotransmitter Receptors. *Honours:* Gold Ring of the President of Hungary, 1967; Chercheur-Boursier, scholarship, 1975-81; Senior Research Fellowship, Ontario Heart Foundation, 1979. *Hobbies:* Swimming; Linguistics; Playing Chess. *Address:* 4811 Cedar Crescent, Montreal, Quebec, Canada.

KURIAKOSE, Mankidiyil Uthup, b. 23 Sept. 1935, Kerala India. Manager. m. Achamma Kuriakose 15 May 1961, 1 son. *Education:* BSc (Met. Eng.) Banaras Hindu University 1958; MBA, Cochin University, 2nd Rank 1973. *Appointments:* Research and Development Department and Extrusion Production Department, ALCAN, 1958-78; Comcraft Services Limited, UK, Nigeria. *Memberships:* Fellow, Institution of Engineers, India; Fellow, Institute of Sales and Marketing Management, UK. *Publications:* Prepared more than 50 technical papers on Extrusion of metals; Three publications on Management and Industrial Psychology. Hobby: Studying transactional analysis and usderstanding the human problems of interaction and helping to solve the same. *Address:* PO Box 1717, Ikeja, Lagos, Nigeria.

KURODA, Mizuo, b. 16 Aug. 1919, Osaka Prefecture. Diplomatic Service. m. Mitsuko Unno, 1949, 2 sons. *Education:* Higher Civil Service Examination; Graduated, Tokyo University, Faculty of Law, 1943. *Appointments:* Third Secretary, Embassy, United States of America, 1952; Treaty Bureau, Ministry of Foreign Affairs, 1954; First Secretary, Embassy, The United Kingdom, 1958; Private Secretary to the Prime Minister 1962; Director, Northeast Asia Division, Asian Affairs Bureau, Ministry of Foreign Affairs, 1964; Counsellor, Embassy, The United States of America 1966; Counsellor, Embassy, Philippines, Consul-General, Manila , Minister, 1967-69; Minister, Embassy, The United States of America 1969; Deputy Director-General, United Nations Bureau, Ministry of Foreign Affairs, Director-General, Research and Planning Department, 1971-72;, and Director-General, Public Information Bureau, 1973; Ambassador Extraordinary and Plenipotentiary, Yugoslavia 1976; Ambassador Extraordinary and Plenipotentiary, Egypt 1978; Ambassador Extraordinary and Plenipotentiary, Australia 1980. *Memberships:* Commonwealth, Canberra; Royal Canberra Golf Club. *Hobbies:* Golf; Music. *Address:* 114 Empire Circuit, Yarralumla, ACT 2600, Australia.

KUSHKA, Vratislav, b. 20 May 1949, Nymburk, Czechoslovakia. Entrepreneur, Writer, Journalist. *Education:* Business School, Czechoslovakia; Prague School of Economics; Graduate, Queen's University Kingstod, Canada. *Appointments:* Czechoslovak State Radio, Head Office of Radio Drama; Producer, Director, Czechoslovakia; Creative Consultant, Propagfilm, Czechoslovakia; Editor, Marketing Director, Publishing House Mlada Fronta, Czechoslovakia Book Club; President, Academic Book Club, Ontario, Canada. *Memberships:* Czechoslovak Society of Arts and Sciences, USA. *Publications:* How to Start a Successful International Book Order Service; The Library; Queen Victoria is Alive and Well in Kingston; The Desting; I Love NY AND Paris, works in progress; 4 Radio plays; Numerous newspaper and magazine articles, short stores. *Hob-*

bies: Theatre; Literature; Visual Arts; Architecture; Industrial Design; Travel; Music; Chess; Philosophy. *Address:* 117 Westmoreland Road, Kingston, Ontario, Canada.

KUSI, Benjamin Freeman, b. 24 Feb. 1922, Besease-Atwima, Ashanti. Timber Producer. m. Rebecca Hagan, 20 Apr. 1949, 3 sons, 3 daughters. *Education:* Diploma in Elementary Accounts. *Appointments:* Managing Director, B F Kusi Limited. *Memberships:* Head of Ashanti Abusua Clan, Kumasi, Lodge Morality; Red Cross Society. *Honours:* British Parliamentary Association Award, 1953; Enstool-Ment as Chief of Besease/Atwima, 1975. *Hobbies:* Golf; Swimming; Farming; Reading; Political Debates. *Address:* 1st Circular Road, Ridge Residential Area, Plot No. 1, Kumasi, Ghana.

KUTENA, Frantisek Zdenek, b. 10 Aug. 1919, Dolni Haj, Czechoslovakia. Engineer, Environmental Pollution Control and Management. m. Helen Lenore Watson, 18 Aug. 1955, 2 sons, 2 daughters. *Education:* BE, Czechoslovakia, 1939; Dip. Hydrology, 1954, Master Applied Science, 1980, University of New South Wales, Sydney. *Appointments:* Engineer in Design and Construction, Steel, Chemical, Power Generation Industries, Czechoslovakia, 1939-49; Chief Instructor, Auto Mech. Division, VTT School, Grafenaschau, West Germany, 1949-50; Hydrographic Engineer, Water Conservation and Irrigation Commission of New South Wales, 1950-55; Senior Engineer, Hydrology, Commonwealth Department of Works, Darwin, Port Moresby, 1955-59; United Nations: Hydrologist, Technical Adviser in: Pakistan, Brazil, Tanzania, Venezuela, Spain, Botswana, Argentina, Bangladesh, Thailand; Liason Officer, FAO/UNESCO International Hydrologic Decade; Programme Coordinator, Earth Resources Technology Satellite Programme in Bangladesh and Thailand. *Memberships:* Australian Water and Waste Water Association; Founding Member CHEC Bangladesh; Commonwealth Human Ecologic Council, London. *Publications:* Author of numerous papers and reports in connection with agricultural development in various countries within United Nations; Patent. *Honours:* Svaz Politickych Veznu, 1945, Decoration for work in Underground Resistance Movement. *Hobbies:* Environmental Issues; Mountaineering; Skiing. *Address:* 12 Denning Street, Coogee, New South Wales, Australia.

KUYE, Omowale Ajani, b. 18 May 1931, Ibadan, Nigeria. Civil Servant. m. Priscilla Olabori Adekogbe, 18 Dec. 1961, 1 son, 1 daughter. *Education:* BSc. (Economics), Hons, 1965, Barrister-at-Law, 1966, London University, UK; Diploma Industrial Management, London Scool of Economics, London, UK, 1966; MA. (Economics), Syracuse University, USA, 1971. *Appointments:* Civil Servant, various grades, now Director of Budget Programmes, Revenue, 1981. *Memberships:* Honourable Society of Middle Temple, London; Associate member, African Institute of Management; Fellow, Nigerian Economics Society; Ikoyi Club; Life Vice-President, Executive Chairman, Nigerian Professional Golfers Association; Chairman, Board of Governors, Apatere Community Grammar School. *Publications:* Export Promotion-selected Essays, 1967. *Hobbies:* Golf; Reading of Religious literature. *Address:* 3A Imoru Close, Ikoyi, Lagos, Nigeria.

KWAKYE, Benjamin Samuel Kofi, b. Sept. 1928, Mampong, Ashanti, Ghana. Farmer. m. Victoria Mensah, 1 Mar. 1956, 5 sons, 2 daughters. *Education:* Certificate in Law, Non Professional. *Appointments:* Inspector, 1957, Commissioner, 1971, Inspector General and Commissioner for Interior, 1978, Police, Ghana; Farmer, 1978. *Honours:* DSO; OSG. *Hobbies:* Hunting; Reading. *Address:* PO Box 8, Mampong, Ashanti, Ghana.

KWAN, Ting-on Teron, b. 1 Sept. 1944, Hong Kong. Financial Advisor; China trader; Professional Consultant. m. Annie Lam, 24 Sept. 1970, 1 son, 1 daughter. *Education:* BA.(Hons.), 1965-68, Diploma in Management Studies, 1970-72, University of Hong Kong. *Appointments:* Assistant Treasurer, Chase Manhattan Bank NA, USA; Senior Banking Manager, Trident International Finance Limited; General Manager, Detex Limited; Director and General Manager, Kam Kui International (Holdings) Limited; Managing Director, Dragons United Limited; Managing Director, Winford International Limited; Managing Director, Professionals (Avia) Limited. *Memberships:* British Institute of Management; Rotary Club, Hobg Kong; Hong Kong University Alumni Association; Chinese Club, Hong Kong; Kowloon Tong Club. *Hobbies:* Squash; Chess; Sailing; Classical Music. *Address:* 8 Honiton Road 12/F, Flat B, Hong Kong.

KWO, Chin, b. 28 Oct. 1926, Loyang, Honan, China. Physician; Surgeon. m. 8 July 1962, 1 son, 2 daughters. *Education:* MD, National Defence Medical Centre, Taipei, Taiwan, 1952; MSc, McGill University, Canada, 1969. *Appointments:* Internship, NDMC, 1952, Resident, Chief Resident, 1952-57, First General Hospital, Taipei, Taiwan; Resident Assistant in Surgery and Orthopaedic Surgery, Barrie Memorial Hospital, Québec, Canada, 1962-64; Resident Assistant in Surgery, St. John General Hospital, New Brunswick, Canada, 1966; Resident in Orthopaedic Surgery, Hospital Sacre-Coeur, Mtl.P Q Hospital Ste. Justine, Hospital General Du Christ-Roi, Montreal, Québec, Canada, 1967-70. *Memberships:* Corporation Proffessionelle des Médecins du Québec; Medical Council of Canada; General Medical Council, London; Medical Board, State of Vermont, USA. *Publications:* Experimental Arthritis; Pioneer Can Use Acupuncture Analgesia for Surgery and Dental Surgery. *Hobbies:* Photography; Painting. *Address:* 4866 Westmount Avenue, Westmount, Québec, Canada, H3Y 1Y1.

KWOK, Frank William, b. 25 Mar. 1929, Wellington, New Zealand. Medical Practitioner. m. Nanette Wallis, 14 May 1966, 2 sons. *Education:* BSc., 1948, MB., Ch.B., 1954, University of New Zealand, Otago, New Zealand; DLO. RCP. (Lond)., RCS. (Eng.), 1957, FRCS. (England), 1960, Royal College of Surgeons of England. *Appointments:* House Surgeon, 1954-56, EENT Registrar, 1957, Consultant ENT Surgeon, 1961, Head of ENT Department, 1975, Wellington Hospital, New Zealand; House Officer/Registrar Institute of Laryngology and Otology, Royal National ENT Hospital, London, UK, 1958-59; Senior ENT Registrar and Tutor, Metropolitan ENT Hospital, London, UK, 1960; Private ENT Surgical Practice, Wellington, New Zealand, 1961-; Lecturer (ENT) to: Wellington Clinical School of Medicine; Wellington School of Pharmacy; Wellington Hospital and Polytechnic Schools of Nursing. *Memberships:* Rotary International. *Publications:* Contributor to Educational Medical publications including: New Ethicals: Treatment of Ear Problems in General Practice, 1979; Treatment of Nasal Problems in General Practice, 1979; Patient Management: Hearing Disorders in School Children, 1980. *Hobbies:* Cooking; Electronics; Music. *Address:* 4 Rawson Place, Seatoun, Wellington 3, New Zealand.

KWOK, Reginald Yin-Wang, b. 24 Jan. 1937, Hong Kong. Urban Planner Architect. m. Annette Holmes, 29 Aug. 1964, 1 daughter. *Education:* Diploma Architecture, The Polytechnic, London, UK, 1963; Diploma, Tropical Studies, Architectural Association, London, UK, 1967; MS.Architecture, 1969, MS. Urban Planning, 1969, PhD., 1973, Columbia University, New York, USA. *Appointments:* Assistant Architect, Chamberlin Powell and Bon, London, UK, 1960-61; Architect, Denys Lasdun and Partners, London, UK, 1963-64, 1965-66; Architect, Palmer and Turner, Hong Kong, 1965; Researcher, Institute of Urban Environment, New York, USA, 1968-69; Course Coordinator, Centre for Advanced Studies of the Environment, Architectural Association, London, UK, 1970-71; Assistant Professor, 1974-76, Associate Professor and Director, Planning Program for Developing Nations, 1976-80, Division of Urban Planning, Columbia University, New York, USA; Professor of Urban Studies and Urban Planning and Director, Centre of Urban Studies and Urban Planning, University of Hong Kong, Hong Kong, 1980-. *Memberships:* Royal Institute of British Architects; Americal Planning Association; Architectural Association, UK; Association for Asian Studies, US; Regional Science Association, US; Regional Studies Association, UK; The Asia Society, US; Society for International Development, US; Board of Directors 1976-80, Chinatown Planning Council, New York. *Publications:* Planning Reports include: Hong Kong, Hong Kong Background Report and Comprehensive Development, (with A Kwok), 1967; Development Investigation Proposal for North-East New Territories, 1980; Articles inclding: Use and Abuse, 1969; Open Space Action, 1969; Social Services: Urban Infrastructure, Education and Health, 1976; Policy Paper on Economic Development of Chinatown, 1978; L'Architecture D'Aujourd'hui, 1979; A Synoptic Examination of Urban Studies and Urban Planning, 1981; Trends in Urban Planning and Development in China, 1981; Papers Presented to Professional and Academic Meetings include: Spatial Methods for Analysing Chinese Development, 1976; Development Strategies and Planning for Food Distribution: the Case of Hong Kong Fisherman, 1976; Evolution of Rural Development in China, 1976; The Effects of Recent Policy Changes on Urbanization in China, 1978; Does Hong Kong need Urbanists and Urban Planners Now? 1981; Conference Papers including: Effects of Industrialization on Urban Systems in Developing Nations, 1976; The Role of Government, 1976; Technological Self-Reliance for the Third World: Is It Possible?, 1978; Urban Planning and Development in China, 1979; The New Territories and Its Future, 1980. *Honours:* Mature Student Grant, 1966-67; William Kinne Fellow Travelling Fellowship, 1969. *Hobbies:* Modern American prints; Modern glass and pottery; Theatre; Music; Sports. *Address:* 10 Middleton Towers, 140 Pokfulam Road, Hong Kong.

KYDD, Dermott Harrison, b. 15 Apr. 1928, Frodsham, Cheshire, England. Chartered Surveyor. m. Sylvia Mary Rogers, 14 Dec. 1968, 1 daughter. *Education:* FRICS.(Agriculture and Land Agency); RICS Diploma 20374, 1952. *Appointments:* Military Service, 1946-48; Articled Pupil, Robinson & Hall, Chartered Surveyors, Bedford, UK, 1948-52; Assistant County Land Agent, Wiltshire and Warwickshire, UK, 1952-54; Agricultural Valuer, 1955-63, Chief Valuer, 1963-65, Chief Agricultural Valuer, 1965-79, Lands Department, Kenya; Divisional Estate Manager, Northern, Native Land Trust Board, Fiji, 1980-. *Memberships:* Royal Institution of Chartered Surveyors; Institute of Valuation and Estate Management, Fiji; Farmers Club; Nairobi Club; Paddle Steamer Preservation Society; Vintage Sports Car Club. *Honours:* OBE, 1978. *Hobbies:* Fishing; Ballooning; Vintage cars and ships; Maritime and Naval history. *Address:* Ritora Street, Labasa, Fiji.

KYERE-AMPONSAH, Kofi, b. 16 Sept. 1955, Nsoatre, Brong-Ahafo Region, Ghana. Sales Manager. m. 5 Jan. 1980. *Education:* MDPI Certificate, Marketing Introduction, Ghana, 1980. *Appointments:* Assistant Accountant, Wampo Enterprises, 1976-77; Senior Salesman, 1977-79, Assistant Sales Manager, 1979-80, Sales Manager, 1980-, Adwinsa Publications. *Memberships:* General Secretary, 1975-76, Be Kind to Animals Club of Ghana. *Publications:* Love too Soon, under preparation; Kofi's Love Before Marriage, in preparation. *Hobbies:* Writing; Hunting; Reading; Editing; Gardening. *Address:* Adwinsa House, A/Mdn/947, Madina, Accra, Ghana.

KYNASTON, Bruce, b. 27 Apr. 1931, Brisbane, Australia. Specialist Medical Practitioner in Radiotherapy. m. Gwynnêth Anne Harris, 17 Nov. 1956, 1 son, 1 daughter. *Education:* MB., BS.(hons.2nd Class) University of Queensland, Australia, 1949-54; MRACR, 1958; FRACR, 1968; FRCR, 1963. *Appointments:* Resident Medical Officer, Brisbane General Hospital, Australia, 1955; Medical Officer, 1956-58, Radiotherapist, 1958-77, Assistant Director, 1977-, Queensland Radium Institute, Australia; Part-time Lecturer, University of Queensland, Australia, 1965-; Part-time Lecturer, Queensland Institute of Technology, Australia, 1973-. *Memberships:* National Health and Medical Research Council, 1976-; Fellow, Royal College of Radiologists; Federal Councillor 1967-68, 1975-76, Fellow, Royal Australasian College of Radiologists; British Institute of Radiology; State Councillor 1964-70, 1971-75, Hon. Treasurer 1972-75, Australian Medical Association; Chairman 1970, Medical Staff Association, Royal Brisbane Hospital, Australia; President 1975, Wantima Country Club. *Creative Works:* Embroidery: Crest and Arms, of Royal Australasian College of Radiologists. *Hobbies:* Gardening; Creative Embroidery. *Address:* 30 Janie Street, Aspley, Queensland 4034, Australia.

KYOMO, Martin Luther, b b. 3 Mar. 1936, Issoko, Mbeya, Tanzania. Professor of Animal Production. m. 4 July 1970, 1 son, 2 daughters. *Education:* Higher School Certificate, Makerere University College, Kampala Uganda 1957-59; BSc (Agric.) (London) Kampala, Uganda 1959-62; MSc (Anim. Breeding) Colorado State University 1964-66; PhD University of Dar es Salaam 1972-78. *Appointments:* Research Officer, Livestock 1962-68; Chief Research Officer 1969; Lecturer in Animal Production 1969-71; Senior Lecturer,

1971-73; Associate Professor 1974-78; Professor, 1978-; Dean Faculty of Agriculture, Forestry and Veterinary Science 1973-79. *Memberships:* American Society of Animal Science; British Society of Animal Production; Tanzania Society of Animal Production. *Hobbies:* Tennis; Photograph. *Address: Address:* Animal Science Department, University of Dar es Salaam, Faculty of Agriculture, Forestry & Veterinary Science, University Post Office Branch, Morogoro, Tanzania.

KYPRIANOU, Spyros, b. 1932, Limassol, Cyprus. President of the Republic of Cyprus. m. Mimi, 2 sons. *Education:* Studied Economics and commerce, City of London College and Law at Gray's Inn, London, UK; Called to Bar, 1954; Diploma, Comparative Law. *Appointments:* Secretary in London pf Archbishop Makarios, Ethnarch of Cyprus, 1952; Secretary of the Cyprus Ethnarchy, London, UK, 1954; Panhellenic Committee for Self-Determination for Cyprus, Greece, 1956; Represented Cyprus Ethnarchy in New York, USA, 1956-57; Returned to London until the signing of the Zurich and London Agreements and returned to Cyprus with Archbishop Makarios, 1959; Represented the Greek Cypriot side at Athens Conference for drafting of Agreement on application of Tripartite Alliance (Cyprus-Greece-Turkey) provided under the Zurich-London Agreement; Appointed Minister of Justice on declaration of Independence, 16 Aug. 1960 and a few days later he was given the Ministry of Foreign Affairs, and represented Cyprus at various Conferences, negotiations, meetings and talks; Accompanied the President of the Republic during state and other visits to many countries; accompanied the President to the Commonwealth Prime Ministers Conferences and the Nonaligned Summits in Belgrade, Cairo and Lusaka; Resigned from post as Foreign Minister, 1972; Practised Law, 1974-; Announced establishment of Democratic Party in Cyprus, 1976; Elected President of the House, 1976; Elected President of the Republic, 1977. *Honours:* Grand Cross-Order of George 1 of Greece, 1962; Grand Cross of the Federal Republic of Germany, 1962; Grand Starof the Republic of the UAR, 1961; Grand Cross-Order of Boyaca-of Colombia, 1966; Grand Cross-Order of Merit-of Chile, 1966; Grand Silver Cross, of Austria, 1973; Ecclesiastical decoration of the Order of St. Aekaterini of Sinai, 1966; Star of the Socialist Republic of Romania. *Hobbies:* Literature; Music; Sport. *Address:* Presidential Palace, Nicosia, Cyprus.

KYULULE, Peter Leonard, b. 22 Nov. 1934, Mchombe, Kilombero, Tanzania. Teacher. m. Olga Gerard Kibiriti, 27 Sept. 1961, 1 son, 2 daughters. *Education:* MA, McGill University, Montreal, Canada, 1975; BA-.(Hons.), University of Montreal, Canada, 1968; Diploma Ed., University College, Dublin, Ireland, 1964; Certificate in French, Fribourg University, Switzerland, 1964. *Appointments:* Headmaster, Ifakara MiddleSchool, 1960-62; Principal, Songea College of National Education, 1970-72; Curriculum Developer in Political Education, University of Dar-Es-Salaam, 1973-74; Tutor, Civil Service College, Dar-Es-Salaam, 1975-76; Head, Political Education Department, Party (CCM) Headquarters, Dodoma, 1976-. *Memberships:* Chama Cha Mapinduzi; Historical Association of Tanzania; Historical Association of Kenya; Tanzania Writers Association; Tanzania Presidential Commission on Education, 1980. *Publications:* Speak Swahili, 1968; Education and Politics in Kenya, 1895-1939; Guide to Political Education in Tanzania, CCM Ideology, in Press. *Honours:* Pongezi Mkutano Mkuu Wa Taifa (Maalum), 1980. *Hobbies:* Agricultural Activities; Languages; Debating; Jogging; Walking. *Address:* Kyulule P L., PO Box 173, Ifakara, Tanzania.

L

LACEY, Paul, b. 7 Oct. 1934, Hampstead, London, England. Chartered Civil Engineer. m. Jillian Mary, 8 Oct. 1960, 2 sons. *Education:* HNC and Endorsements, Westminster Technical College, London, UK. *Appointments:* Engineer, London Midland Region, UK, 1954-58; Engineer and Project Manager, Sir Bruce White, Wolfe, Barry & Partners, UK, 1958-77; Projects Manager, Coastal and Water Department, Ove Arup & Partners, UK, 1977-. *Memberships:* Fellow: ICE; Istructe; Highways; Faculty of Building; Royal Society of Arts; Member of: Company of Builders; Concrete Society; Maritime Engineering Board of he Institution of Civil Engineers. *Publications:* Paper in Dock and Harbour Authority - The Port of Tripoli. *Hobbies:* Chess; Wood carving; Tennis; Table tennis. *Address:* 14 Lawford Close, Chorleywood, Herts, England.

LACHAPELLE, Gerard, b. 28 June 1949, St.Francois-du-Lac, P. Québec, Canada. Geodesist. m. Hilary Susan Curtis Rees, 23 Sept. 1972. *Education:* BSc. Applied Sciences, University Laval, Canada, 1971; MSc., University of Oxford, England, 1973; LPh., University of Helsinki, Finland, 1974; Dr.techn., Technical University of Giaz, Austria, 1975. *Appointments:* Head, Research and Development Section, Geodetic Survey of Canada, Department of Energy, Mines and Resources, Government of Canada, 1976-80; Head, Geodetic Research and Development, Sheltech Canada, Shell Canada Resources Limited, 1980-. *Memberships:* Councillor at large, The Canadian Institute of Surveying, 1977-80; Chairman , Geodesy and Control Survey Committee, 1977-80; Vice President, Canadian Institute of Surveying, 1981-82; American Geophysical Union, 1977-; Canadian Geophysical Union; Institute of Electrical and Electronics Engineers; Canadian Representative to the International Association of Geodesy, 1980-83; Member of Executive Committee of International Association of Geodesy, 1980-83. *Publications:* Author of over 20 Scientific articles published in various Scientific Journals and Symposium Proceedings. *Honours:* Scholarships from National Research Council, Canada, 1971-74; Scholarships from Department of Lands and Forests, Province of Quebec, 1973-74; Kenting Award of the Canadian Institute of Surveying, 1980. *Hobbies:* Reading; Biking; Mountaineering. *Address:* 2604-126 Ave, S.W. Calgary, Alberta T2W 3V6, Canada.

LADAPO, James Olawale, b. 2 July 1943, Ile-Ife, Oyo State, Nigeria. Mechanical Engineer. m. Juliana Kikiba, 31 July 1974, 4 sons, 2 daughters. *Education:* HND., Mechanical Engineering, UK, 1973; Diploma, Industrial Management, UK, 1974. *Appointments:* Mechanical Engineer; Works Manager. *Memberships:* British Institute of Management; Nigerian Institute of Management; Institution of Industrial Managers, UK. *Hobbies:* Football; Golf; Lawn tennis; Boating. *Address:* 5 Harley Street, G R A, Port-Harcourt, Rivers State, Nigeria.

LADHARAM, M. P. b. 1 Jan 1915, Hyderabad Sind, West Pakistan. Business Executive. m. Parpati, 9 Dec. 1936, 5 sons, 3 daughters. *Education:* University 1st year Arts. *Appointments:* Retail and Wholesales Salesman, Egypt, 1933-36; Assistant Export Manager, Shanghai, Japan, 1937-39; Export Manager, Shanghai, 1939-47; General Manager Imports, Manila, 1947-49; General Manager Imports Singapore and Indonesia, 1949-59; Managing Director Imports Exports and Financing, 1960-. *Memberships:* Honourary Secretary, Indian Merchants Association, Shanghai, 1946-47; Honourary Secretary, Bombay Merchants Association, Manila, 1948-49; President, Bombay Merchants Association, Jakarta, 1957-59; President, Lions International Club, Hongkong, 1973-74; Vice-President, Hindu Association, Hongkong, 1974-75; Chairman, The Indian Chamber of Commerce, Hong Kong, 1974-75; Vice President, India Association, 1981-. *Address:* 69B Blue Pool Road, 5/F1 Block B, Hong Kong.

LADIPO, Oladapo Alabi, b. 23 Sept. 1941, Ogbomosho, Oyo State, Nigeria. Lecturer; Consultant Obstetrician; Gynaecologist. m. 21 Aug. 1971, 1 son, 2 daughters. *Education:* MB., BcH., Welsh National School of Medicine, Cardiff, UK, 1962-67; Dip. RCOG., 1970; MRCOG., London, 1971. *Appointments:* House Officer, Llandough Hospital, Llandough, UK, 1967-68; Senior House Officer, Royal Gwent Hospital, Newport, UK, 1968-70; Registrar, St. Dvid's Hospital, Cardiff, UK, 1970-72; Senior Registrar, University College Hospital, Ibadan, Nigeria, 1972-73; Lectuere/Consultant, 1973-76, Professor of Obstetrics and Gynaecology, 1980-, College of Medicine, University of Ibadan, Nigeria. *Memberships:* British Obstetric & Gynaecological Society; American Association of Laparoscopists; Society of Obstetricians & Gynaecologists of Nigeria; Nigerian Medical Association; West African College of Surgeons; Foundation member, Nigerian Association of Endocrinology. *Publications:* 46 publications including: Management of the Third Stage of Labour with particular reference to reduction of foeto-maternal transfusion, 1972; Test of Tubal Patency: Comparison of Laparoscopy and hysterosalpingography, 1976; Laparoscopy in Gynaecological Practice in Ibadan, (with J A Adeleye, O A Ojo), 1977; Anaesthesia for Laparoscopy (with J A Adeleye), 1978; An Evaluation of 576 Hysterosalpingograms on Infertile Women, 1979; Experience with Clomephene Citrate and Bromocryptine in the treatment of infertility, 1980; Clinical Correlates of Male Infertility and Herpes Simplex Virus Type - 2 Infection in Ibadan (with B Adelusi), 1981. *Honours:* Governor's prize for Biology, Norwood Technical College, UK, 1961; Distinction in Physiology, Welsh National School of Medicine, UK, 1964; USAID Scholarship, 1973; Population Council Fellowship, 1974; FMCOG, Nigerian Medical Council, 1975; FWACS, West African College of Surgeons, 1975. *Hobbies:* Squash; Football. *Address:* 2 Arulogun Street, Bodija, Ibadan, Nigeria.

LAFAI, Pusinelli, b. 5 July 1957, Nanumanga Island. Head of the Broadcasting and Information Department. *Education:* University of the South Pacific, 1976-77. *Appointments:* News Editor, 1978; Broadcasting Information Officer, 1980-. *Memberships:* Honourary Secretary, Tavalu Civil Servants' Association, 1981-82. *Hobbies:* Sports; World Political and Economic Affairs; Playing and listening to folk, jazz music; *Address:* Vaiaku, Funafuti, Tuvalu.

LAHIRI, Somnath, b. 1 Sept. 1908, Santipur, West Bengal, India. Journalist; Author; Political worker; Trade Unionist. m. Bela Chatterji, Sept. 1942, 1 daughter. *Education:* BSc., Calcutta, 1929. *Appointments:* Elected Councillor, Calcutta Municipal Corporation, 1944; Editor, Daily Swadhinata (in Bengali, 1945-48; Elected member, Indian Constituent Assembly (later Indian Parliament), 1946-47; Elected member, West Bengal State Legislative Assembly at each election between 1957 and 1977; Became Cabinet Minister, West Bengal State Government, 1967, 1969-70, Portfolois: Local Self Government; Development and Planning, Housing, Parliamentary Affairs. *Memberships:* All-India Committee, Indian National Congress; General Council, All India Trade Union Congress; National Council, Communist Party of India; President, Calcutta Tramway Workers' Union. *Publications:* Samyavad - 1st Bengali book on Marxian Socialism, 1930; Kaliyugeyr Galpa - collection of short stories in Bengali, 1952; numerous other pamphlets, bruchures, etc. *Hobby:* Writing short stories. *Address:* B/1 C I T Buildings, 30 Madan Chatterji Lane, Calcutta 700007, India.

LAHZ, John Lister Colless, b. 29 Nov. 1926, Murgon, Queensland, Australia. Orthopaedic Surgeon. m. Jean Blinman Brown, 15 Jan, 1956, 2 daughters. *Education:* M.B., B.S.Qld., 1949, F.R.C.S, England, 1954, F.R.A.C.S., 1960. *Appointments:* Resident Medical Officer, Brisbane General Hospital, 1950; Orthopaedic Registrar, Mater Hospital, 1952; Senior House Officer, Royal National Orthopaedic Hospital, London, 1954, Orthopaedic Registrar, St. Thomas's Hospital, 1955-56; Orthopaedic Surgeon, Princess Alexandra Hospital, Brisbane, 1957-; Orthopaedic Surgeon, Mount Olivet Hospital, 1957-; Orthopaedic Surgeon, Commonwealth Department of Veterans' Affairs, 1957-. *Memberships:* Australian Orthopaedic Association; Past member and Chairman of the Queensland State Committee, Royal Australasian College of Surgeons; Queensland Club. *Publications:* Various papers on Surgical subjects to meetings of the Royal Australasian College of Surgeons and the Australian Orthopaedic Association. *Hobby:* Sports. *Address:* 66 The Gardens, Alice Street, Brisbane 4000, Australia.

LAI, Wah On, b. 29 Aug. 1940, Hong Kong. Managing Director. m. Chan Wai Fong, 29 May 1966, 1 son, 1 daughter. *Education:* Higher Certificate, Mechanical

Engineering, Hong Kong Polytechnic, 1963. *Appointments:* Apprentice, 1957-63; Draughtsman, 1963-65; Works Manager, 1965-67; Sales and Service Engineer, 1967-72; Sales Development Officer, 1972-73; Assistant Sales Manager, 1973-75; Manager, 1975-80; Managing Director, 1980-. *Hobbies:* Swimming; Basket Ball. *Address:* 1-E Merlin Court, 42 Broadcast Drive, Kowloon, Hong Kong.

LAING, Bernard Kojo, b. 1 July 1946, Kumasi, Ghana. m. Josephine Connelly, Sept. 1966, 5 sons, 4 daughters. *Education:* MA., Glasgow; Post Graduate Diploma in Public Administration, Certificate in Local Administration, Ghana; Certificate in Rural Development, Birmingham. *Appointments:* Principal, Eton Schools and Colleges, 1968-69; District Administrator Officer, Ogginso, Ghana, 1969-72; District Administration Officer, Obuasi, Ghana, 1972-74; District Chief Executive, Konongo, Ghana, 1974-78; Principal Assistant Secretary, The Castle, 1978-79; Administration Secretary, Institute of African Studies, University of Ghana, 1979-. *Memberships:* Chairman, District Branch of Ghana Writers and Poets Association, Obuasi, 1973-74; Chairman, District Branch of Ghana Writers and Poets Association, Konongo, 1974-77. *Publications:* Scottish Poetry, 1969; Poem broadcast on B.B.C. 1967. *Honours:* Prize winner, B.B.C. University notebook Poetry Competition, 1967; Prize winner Valco Literary Fund Competition, Ghana, 1977. *Hobbies:* Hunting; Local Administration; Music; Athletics; Farming. *Address:* Box 73, Institute of African Studies, Legon, Ghana.

LAING, Hector (Sir), b. 12 May 1923, Edinburgh. Chairman. m. Marian Clare Laurie, 1 April 1950, 3 sons. *Education:* Jesus College, Cambridge. *Appointments:* Joined 1947, Chairman, 1963, McVitie and Price Limited; Director, 1953-64, Managing Director, 1964-72, Chairman, 1972-, United Biscuits (Holdings) Limited; Director, Court of Bank of England, 1973-; Director, Allied Breweries since 1979. *Memberships:* Whites Club. *Honours:* Knighted - New Year Honours, 1978; American Bronze Star, 1944. *Hobbies:* Gardening; Walking; Flying. *Address:* High Meadows, Windsor Road, Gerrards Cross, Bucks, England.

LAJA, Aderohunmu Oladipo, b. 24 Feb. 1925, Nigeria. Pathologist. m. Margaret Mary Edem, 29 Aug. 1959. *Education:* BSc. (Hons) Chemistry and Biology, 1947-50, Post-Graduate, Chemistry, 1950-51, Howard University, United States of America; M.D., College of Medicine, 1951-55; Diploma in Clinical Pathology, University of London, 1960-61; Licentiate of the Medical College of Canada, 1956; M.R.C., Member of the Royal College of Pathology, London, 1964; Fellow of Nigerian Medical Council, 1970; Fellow, Royal College of Pathology, London, 1973; F.W.A.C.P. Fellow West African College of Physicians, 1976. *Appointments:* include: 3rd Class Clerk, Inland Revenue Department, 1943-47; Medical Officer, General Duties, General Hospital, Lagos, 1957-58; Promoted Consultant Pathologist, Pathology Department, Lagos, 1963; Promoted and transferred to Lagos State Government, Senior Consultant Pathologist, Lagos State Laboratory Service, 1968; Retired voluntarily from Lagos State Public Service, 1975; Senior Lecturer in Pathology, Faculty of Health Services, Unife; Consultant Pathologist, Ife University Teaching Hospitals, 1975; Acting Head of the Division of Pathology, Faculty of Health Sciences, University of Ife, 1975-76; Chief Consultant Pathologist, Federal Ministry of Defence, Lagos, 1978-. *Memberships:* Examination Board of Pathology, Nigeria Medical Council; Governing Council; Executive Council; Chairman Membership Committee of the Institute of Medical Laboratory Technology of Nigeria. *Publications:* Laja, Ahinie, Ession; Salmonella Typi in Amoebie Liver Abscess, 1955; Keratosis Circumscripts, A District Dermatological Entity or A Veriant of Psoriasis, 1977; Schistonomiasis of the Penis, Simulating early Carcinoma; Articles published in Local Magazines including: Your Health; The Air we Breathe, 1973; Sickle Cell Anaemia, 1974. *Honours:* Dean's Honours List, 1947-50; Scholarship Carnegie $foundation, 1951-54; Federal Government Bursary, 1952-56. *Hobbies:* Photography; Sport; Books. *Address:* 33 Ibadan Road, Ijebu-Ode, Ogun State, Nigeria.

LAJUBUTU, Richard Oladiran, b. 16 Nov. 1940, Ilesha, Oyo State, Nigeria. Federal Civil Servant. m. Anike Olufunke Akinnawo, 7 April 1968, 2 sons, 1 daughter.

Education: Teachers Grade II Certificate, 1961; National Certificate of Education, 1966; Bachelor of Education, 1972; Master of Education, Management, Ibadan, 1981; *Appointments:* Teacher, George Burton Memorial College, Ilesa; Teacher, Principal, Government Teachers College, Sokoto; Head of Department, Language Arts, Federal Advanced Teachers College, Abeokuta. *Memberships:* Honourary Secretary, Student Christian Movement, Adeyemi College of Education, 1965-66; President, S.C.M. University of Ibadan Branch, 1969-70; Alumni Association University of Ibadan; Experiment in Internation Living, Ibadan Branch; Teacher Ambassador to Baltimore Maryland, United States of America, 1969-70. *Honours:* Certificate of Achievement, 1970; Certificate of Meritorious Recognition, 1969-70. *Hobbies:* Visiting Handicapped Homes; Youth Work; Table Tennis. *Address:* W124 Oke-Ola Street, Ilesha, Oyo State, Nigeria.

LAKING, George Robert, b. 15 Oct. 1912, Auckland, New Zealand. Chief Ombudsman. m. Alice Evelyn Patricia Hogg, 13 Apr. 1940, 1 son, 1 daughter. *Education:* LL.B., 1935; Post-graduate study in Public Administration. *Appointments:* War Cabinet Secretariat, 1941-46; Counsellor, 1948-54, Minister, 1954-56, New Zealand Embassy, Washington, USA; Deputy Secretary, External Affairs, 1956-58; Acting High Commissioner for New Zealand, London, UK, 1958-61; Ambassador to: The EEC., 1960, USA, 1961-67; Secretary of Foreign Affairs and Permanent Head, Prime Minister's Department, 1967-72; Parliamentary Ombudsman, 1975-77, Chief Ombudsman, 1977-, New Zealand. *Memberships:* President, New Zealand Institute of International Affairs; Public and Adminstrative Law Reform Committee; Past member and Chairman, Board of the New Zealand - United States Educational Foundation. *Publications:* Various articles on Foreign Policy and Public Administration. *Honours:* CMG., 1968. *Hobbies:* Music; Golf; Pursuit of Happiness. *Address:* 3 Wesley Road, Wellington 1, New Zealand.

LAL, Bipen Behari, b. 30 Jan. 1917, Allahabad, India. Public Service. m. Saroj Mathur, 24 Jan. 1943, 1 son, 1 daughter. *Education:* BSc., St. Stephen's College, Delhi University, India, 1936; MSc., Physics, Allahabad University, India, 1938; Fellow, Harvard University, USA, 1965-66. *Appointments:* Joint Magistrate, Gorakhpur, City Magistrate, Varanasi, 1942-47; District Magistrate, Hardoi & Dehra Dun., 1947-51; Joint Secretary, Secretary, Commissioner and Secretary, Finance, 1951-59, Chairman, U P State Electricity Board, Commissioner and Secretary, Irrigation and Power, 1959-65, Chief Secretary, 1967-69, U P; Additional Secretary, Finance, 1969-70, Secretary, Personnel, Industrial Development, Commerce, Planning Commission, 1970-74, Government of India; Chief Executive, 1974-75, Governor, 1975-, Sikkim, India. *Honours:* Various prizes awarded throughout school and college. *Hobbies:* Photography; Reading. *Address:* Raj Bhavan, Gangtok - 737 101, India.

LAL, Jagdish, b. 9 Sept. 1922, India. Engineer, Educationist. m. Swaraj Lata, 17 Oct. 1953, 3 sons. *Education:* BME·Jadarpur, Calcutta, India, 1945; Hydraulic Machines, Zulassung Prufung Sur Doktorarbeit, Zurich, 1949; DSc. Tech, Federal Institute of Technology, Zurich, Switzerland, 1952. *Appointments:* Assistant Engineer, Volkart Brothers, Calcutta, India, 1945-47; Design & Research Engineer with Sulzer Bros Ltd., Winterthur, Switzerland, Escher Wyss Ltd., Zurich, Theodor Bell & Co. Ltd., Kriens, Switzerland, Gilbert, Gilkes & Gorden Ltd., Kendel, England, 1948-52; Lecturer, Indian Institute of Technology, Kharagpur India, Punjab Engineering College, Chandigarh, India, 1952-55; Assistant Professor, 1955-57; Associate Professor, 1957-58; Professor & Head of Mechanical Engineering Department, 1958-67, Principal & Dean, Engineering College, Allahabad, India, 1967-74, 1976-79; Director, Indian, Institute of Technology, Kanpur, India, 1974-76; Professor of Mechanical Engineering, Higher Petroleum Institute, Tobruk, Libya. *Memberships:* Institution of Engineers, India; Indian Societies of Technical Education, and Theoretical & Applied Mechanics; Institution of Mechanical Engineers, London; International Water Resources Association, USA; Indian Science Congress; Academic Councils, Faculty & Board of Studies of various Universities of India. *Publications:* Hydraulic Machines, 6th edition, 1975; Hydraulics & Fluid Mechanics, 7th edition 1974; Theory of Mechanisms & Machines, 4th edition, 1978; Centrifugal Pumps &

Blowers, (with Prof A H Church), 1973; Descriptive Geometry, 1977; Characteristics of Impulse Turbine in its driving as well as braking regions and efficiencies in driving region, 1952; Numerous papers contributed. *Honours:* Numerous prizes received in field of Engineering; Chairman, Institution of Engineers, Centre, Allahabad, 1974; President, Society of Theoretical & Applied Mechanics, India, 1975-76. *Hobbies:* Organisation of New courses and their development; Collection of stamps & coins. *Address:* 6/22 Roop Nagar, Delhi 110007, India.

LAL, Moti, b. 15 Aug. 1939, Punjab, India. Scientist. m. Subhash Sondhi, 15 Mar. 1968, 3 daughters. *Education:* MSc, Punjab University, India, 1961; PhD, Royal College of Science and Technology, University of Strathclyde, Glasgow, 1966. *Appointments:* Sir William Ramsay Memorial Research Fellow, University of Oxford, 1966-67; Scientist, Unilever Research, Port Sunlight Laboratory, 1967-. *Memberships:* Fellow, Royal Society of Chemistry, London; Founder Member and Honorary Secretary, Statistical Mechanics and Thermodynamics Group of RSC; Faraday Standing Committee on Conferences. *Publications:* Macromolecules at Interfaces (co-editor), 1981; Various research publications in profess onal Journals. *Honours:* Hamilton Barrett Research Prize and Medal, University of Strathclyde, 1964. *Address:* 4A The Spinney, Spital, Wirral, Merseyside, England.

LAL, Siddheshwar, b. 1 July 1928, Varanasi, India. Professor of Physics. m. Madhuri Lal, 9 Dec. 1955, 5 daughters. *Education:* BSc, 1951; MSc, 1953; PhD, 1962. *Appointments:* Research, Tata Institute of Fundamental Research, India, 1953-72; Research Associate and Visiting Professor, University of Chicago and University of Denver USA, 1966-70; Professor and Head, Department of Physics, University of Indore, India, 1970-. *Memberships:* Indian Physics Association; Indian Astronomical Society; Indian Academy of Sciences. *Publications:* Approximately 50 research papers in the field of Cosmic rays, Astrophysics, Particle Physics, Tunneling in Semi-conductors. *Honours:* Fellow, National Academy of Sciences. *Hobby:* Indoor games. *Address:* Department of Physics, University of Indore, Indore, India.

LALSANGZUALA, John, b. 24 Sept. 1924, Kulikawn, Aizaql, India. Politician. m. Zokhumi Lalsangzuala, 12 Sept. 1962, 1 son, 4 daughters. *Education:* Army Special Certificate of Education. *Appointments:* British Indian Army, 1941-47; Indian Army, 1947-58; Secretary, Soldiers, Sailors and Airmen's Board, Mizoram, 1959-70; Vice President, Mizo Hills Congress Committee, 1970-71; General Secretary, Mizoram Congress Committee, 1971-75; Elected as Member of Mizoram Legislative Assembly, 1972-77; Minister, including Supply and Transport, Law and Judicial, Parliamentary Affairs, Secretariat Administration, Co-operation, 1974-77; General Secretary, Mizoram Congress Committee, 1977-. *Memberships:* President, Venglai Welfare Organization; President, Pradesh Consumers Council; Chairman, Mizoram Apex Marketing Co-operative Society; Chairman, Mizo Ex-Services Multi-Purpose Co-operative Society; Chairman, Committee on Land Tenure System, Mizoram; Secretary, Mizoram Ex-Services League; National Confederation of Agriculture and Agricultural Co-operatives; Managing Committee on Special fund for the Resettlement and Rehabilitation of Ex-Servicemen; Mizoram Apex Handloom and Handicrafts Co-operative Society. *Hobbies:* Shooting; Social Welfare Activities. *Address:* Mission Veng, Aizawl 796001, Mizoram, India.

LALWANI, Saroj (Mrs), b. 20 Sept. 1940, Udaipur, India. Managing Director. m. Shri J k Lalwani, 12 Dec. 1960, 1 son, 1 daughter. *Education:* 1st Division: Senior Cambridge, 1955; Intermediate, 1957; BA, 1959; MA, 1981 1st class 1st DHB Homeopathy First Class. *Appointments:* Managing Director, Lalwani Litho, 1967-; Editor, Gora Badal, 1970-. *Memberships:* Vice-President, 1978-79, Association President, 1979-80, International Inner Wheels Clubs of India and Sri Lanka; President, Bhopal Club, 1969-70, Editor District 306, 1970-71, 1971-72, District Secretary, 1973-74, Vice-Chairman, 1974-75, Chairman, 1975-76; Honorary Joint Secretary M P Red Cross;Bhopal University Executive Council, 1972-74, 1978-80, Bhopal University Court, 1972-74, 74, 7 77-80; Jain Research Centre, 1975; Executive, All India Board of General Know-

ledge & Moral Education; Press Advisory Board, 1979-81; M P Bal Kalyan Parishad, International year of the child, 1979; Vice-Presdient, Sangeet Kala Sangam, 1972-80; President, Bhopal District T T Association, 1979-80; State Commissioner, Girl Guides; Member National Executive Bharat Scouts, Guides and St. Johns Ambulance Brigade. *Publications:* Numerous Important Articles, Speeches and Talks given at conferences and Learned Societies. Gold Medal for the Best All Rounder, Rajasthan College; Certificate of Merit from President of India for Meritorious Services in Red Cross, 1976; Won Silver Medal, Trophies & Prizes in Numerous activities including: Cooking; Interior Decorating; Painting; Sculpture; Dramatics; Debating; Chess; Badminton; Deputy Leader Indian Delegation Scout & Guides, 1978; Sri Lanka, Widely travelled, India, Far East, Thailand, Singapore, Europe, Yugosavia, attended International Red Cross cadre training programme, USA, Canada, Iran. *Hobbies:* Cooking; Interior Decorating; Flower Decoration; Debating; Painting; Dramatics; Badminton; Chess; Table Tennis. *Address:* Ashiana Bungalow No 2, Ahmadabad, Bhopal.

LAM, Kam Hing, b. 12 Feb. 1947, Hong Kong. Surgeon. m. Kathleen Pik Han, 5 Sept. 1971, 1 son, 1 daughter. *Education:* MBBS (HK), 1970; MS (HK), 1981; FRCS (ED), 1974; FACS, 1980. *Appointments:* Medical & Health Officer, 1971-73; Lecturer in Surgery, 1973-80; Senior Lecturer in Surgery, 1980-. *Memberships:* Association of Surgeons of South East Asia; Hong Kong Surgical Society; Hong Kong Medical Association; British Medical Association; Association of Head & Neck Oncologists of Great Britain. *Publications:* Publications on research in cancer of the Head and Neck, and cancer of the oesophagus. *Hobbies:* Piano music; Tennis. *Address:* D13 New Senior Staff Quarters, Queen Mary Hospital, Pokfulam Road, Hong Kong.

LAMBERT, Bruce Philip, b. 12 Feb. 1912, Gosnells, Western Australia. Consultant Surveyor; Cartographer. m. Gwendoline Catherine Carmichael, 25 Feb. 1929, 1 son, 1 daughter. *Education:* Diploma, Civil Engineering, Melbourne Technical College, Australia, 1932; Licence to Practice, Victorian Government Land Surveyors, Australia, 1936. *Appointments:* Land and Engineering Surveyor, Victoria, Australia, 1936-39; Assistant Director, Military Survey HQ., Australian Corps., War Service, Australian Army, 1939-45; Director of National Mapping, 2nd Chairman, National Mapping Council of Australia, 1951-77, Commonwealth of Australia Public Service, 1946-77; Executive Director, General Assembly International Union of Geodesy and Geophysics, Canberra, Australia, 1977-79; Consultant Surveyor/Cartographer,: UN Philippines Mapping Project, 1980, 1981, Geodetic Survey of Saudi Arabia, 1980. *Memberships:* Fellow, Institution Surveyors Australia; Hon. Fellow, Australian Institute of Cartographers, ACT Branch; Fellow, Royal Commonwealth Society. *Publications:* Several articles for Australian Surveyor. *Honours:* OBE., 1970; Hon. DSc., University New South Wales, Australia, 1977. *Hobbies:* Gardening; Lawn bowls. *Address:* 3 Ord Street, Forrest, ACT 2603, Australia.

LAMBERT, Cynthia Ann (Mrs), b. 25 Apr. 1935, Unley, South Australia. Artist. m. (1) Kenneth James Lambert, 2 sons, (2) Leon Turnbull Sykes, 29 Apr. 1978. *Education:* St. Peters Collegiate Girls School, Adelaide; Various courses in: Painting; Woodcarving; Copper & Glass Work. *Memberships:* Royal South Australian Society of Arts, Adelaide Art Society. *Creative Works:* Paintings in Oils (Australian Landscapes) in Private Collections both Local and Overseas. *Hobbies:* Watercolour & Oil Painting; Woodcarving (Furniture); Copper Beating; Ceramics; Working with Glass; Boating; Fishing. *Address:* 382 Kensington Road, Erindale, South Australia 5066.

LAMBERT, Henry Uvedale Antrobus, b. 9 Oct. 1925, London. Banker. m. Diana Elsworth Dumbell, 19 Jan. 1951, 2 sons, 1 daughter. *Education:* Scholar, Winchester College, 1938-43; Exhibitioner New College, Oxford, 1946; BA, 1948; MA, 1957. *Appointments:* Armed Forces, 1939-45, and subsequently in Royal Naval Reserve, Lieutenant-Commander; Barclays Bank Limited, 1948-, Vice-Chairman, 1973-79, Deputy Chairman, 1979-, Vice-Chairman, Barclays Bank S A, 1974, Chairman, Barclays Bank International Limited, 1979. *Memberships:* Fellow, Winchester College, 1979; Honorary Treasurer, Navy Records Society; Honorary Treasurer, British-North American Research Association. *Hobbies:* Fishing; Golf; Gardening; Naval History. *Address:* c/o Barclays Bank International Limited, 54 Lombard Street, London, EC3P 3AH, England.

LAMONT, Archibald Stewart MacCallum, b. 5 Feb. 1926, United Kingdom. Director of Anaesthetics. m. Hanna, 1 daughter. *Education:* MB, ChB, University of Glasgow, 1949; DA (RCS), 1953; FFARCS (Eng), 1960; FFARCAS, 1978. *Appointments:* Residnet, Falkirk Royal Infirmary, 1949-50; RAF (Anaesthetic Specialist), 1950-52; SHOGlasgow Royal Infirmary, 1952-53; Registrar, Hammersmith Hospital Royal Postgraduate Medical School, London. 1953-55; Senior Registrar, Leeds Hospitals, 1955-60; Consultant Anaesthetist Leeds (St. James's) University Hospital 1960-76; Director of Anaesthesia, Royal Hobart Hospital, 1976; Senior Clinical Lecturer in Anaesthesia, Leeds University, 1981-. *Memberships:* British Medical Association; Australian Medical Association; Society of Anaesthetists, Great Britain and Ireland; Australian Society of Anaesthetists; Former President, Yorkshire Society of Anaesthetists. *Hobbies:* Sailing; Literature; Music. *Address:* 861 Sandy Bay Road, Sandy Bay 7005, Tasmania, Australia.

LAMONT, Byron Barnard, b. 2 Jan. 1945, Perth, Western Australia. Botanist. m. Heather Carol Herrmann,12 June 1973, 2 sons. *Education:* Wesley College, 1958-62; University of Western Australia, 1963-66, 69-73; New South Wales Department Sport & Recreation, 1968; BSc Agriculture, MSc (Prelim), PhD, Dip. Recreation, MAIH, FRHS. *Appointments:* Landscape Gardener, 1967-68; Resident Tutor, Kingswood College, 1969-72; Senior Tutor in Botany, University of Western Australia, 1973; Lecturer, Biology, Western Australian Institute of Technology, 1974-82; Visiting Lecturer in Botany, University of Cape Town, 1980. *Memberships:* Royal Society of Western Australia, 1975-78; Ecological Societies of Britain, America and Australia; International Society of Plant Morphologists; Australian Institute of Horticulture. *Publications:* Over 55 papers, reviews and reports on biology of the Australian flora. *Honours:* Dux, Wesley College, 1962; Northern Districts Scholarship in Agriculture, 1963; Western Australian Youth Council Scholarship, 1968; Commonwealth Postgraduate Research Award, 1970; Study Leave Award, 1980. *Hobbies:* Piano; Low-maintenance gardens; Photography. *Address:* 12 Flamingo Way, Willetton 6155, Western Australia.

LAMORDE, Abubakar Gofolo, b. 17 Aug. 1944, Mubi Gongola State, Nigeria. Veterinarian. m. 23 Sept. 1971, 1son, 3 daughters. *Education:* B Sc, Agriculture, 1968, DVM, 1970, University of Missouri, USA; MPVM, 1973, PhD, 1975, University of California, USA; Certificate Advanced Management, 1977, ASCON/RIPA London. *Appointments:* Livestock Assistant, 1964-70; Lecturer, (ABU Zaria) 1970-76; Assistant Director (NVRI, Vom), 1976-79; Director (NVRI, Vom), 1979-. *Memberships:* President, Veterinary Council of Nigeria, 1979-; Publicity Secretary, Nigerian Society for Animal Production, 1974-76; Vice-President, African Student Union; Institute of Medical Laboratory Technology Council, 1979-; Food & Drug Administration of Nigeria, 1980. *Publications:* The effect of synthetic gonadotrophic releasing hormone (GnRH) on quiescent Ovaries in prepuberal gilts and lactating sores. *Honours:* Honorary Fellow of the Nigerian Institute for Science Technology, 1980. *Hobbies:* Films; Music; Fishing. *Address:* PO Box 61, Mubi Gongola State, Nigeria.

LAMPELL, Marc, b. 24 Aug. 1949, New York City. Stockbroker, Associate Manager. *Education:* BA, Political Science, City College, New York 1971. *Appointments:* Stockbroker, Vice President, Bache Halsey Stuart Shields Inc. 1975-; Operation Manager, Hornblower and Wilks 1973-75. *Memberships:* Bronx Historical Society; Development Officer, Who's Who in the World; Marquis Publication Biographee; Seminars International. *Publications:* Articles regarding interest data Futures for Seminars International. *Honours:* Bache "Millionaires Club" Award 1980. *Hobbies:* Model Railroading; Photography. *Address:* 8 Frognal, London NW3, England.

LAMPERT, Richard Gordon, b. 16 Aug. 1936, Johannesburg, South Africa. Rabbi. m. Diane Else Wohlgemuth, 16 Dec. 1962, 2 daughters. *Education:* BA., University Witwatersrand, South Afica, 1963; BA., Hons., University of South Africa, 1973; Ordination, September, 1971. *Appointments:* Temple Emanuel, Johannesburg, South Africa, 1966-77; North Shore Temple Emanuel, Sydney, New South Wales, Australia, 1978-. *Hobbies:* Sport; Communal Activities. *Address:* 98 Koola Avenue, Killara, Sydney, New South Wales 2071, Australia.

LANDELL-JONES, Charles Kenneth, b. 17 May 1916, Sydney, New South Wales, Australia. Company Director. m. May Helen, 3 Oct. 1944, 1 son. *Appointments:* Junior Executive, Atlantic Union Oil Co., 1932-40; Rose from Private to Major, served in Middle East (including Tobruk), World War II, 1940-45; Founded Fortune Group of Companies, network of advertising agencies, Australia, 1945-. *Memberships:* Australian Club; The American National Club; Australian Jockey Club; American Chamber of Commerce in Australia; Australian-American Association; Australia-Indonesia Business Co-operation Committee; Australian Institute of Management; Fellow, FAIM; Sydney Chamber of Commerce. *Hobbies:* Business; Swimming; Horse racing. *Address:* 38B Wentworth Road, Vaucluse, New South Wales 2030, Australia.

LANDER, Cyril George, b. 5 Jan. 1892, Footscray, Victoria, Australia. Artist; Cabinet Maker. m. Alice Muriel Thomas, 1934, 1 son. *Education:* Applied Arts, Gordon Technical College, Geelong, Victoria, Australia, 1906-10; Diplomas in: Woodcarving, Metalwork, Perspective Solid Geometry, Leather embossing, Design for Furniture, Building Construction. *Appointments:* Carpenter and Joiner for Thomas Lander (Father), 1905; Foreman Carpenter and Joiner, Trigg & Slaven, Geelong, Australia, 1910; Designer and Furniture estimator, Buckley and Nunn, Melbourne, Australia, 1913; Served in AIF, Galipolli and France, 1915-18; Various jobs in Building Industry, 1919-20; Founded own furniture shop, Toorak, Victoria, restoring Antique furniture and making reproductions, 1921; Established Furniture making Shop and Painted Pictures, Perth, Australia, 1945-. *Memberships:* Feilow, Royal South Australian Society of Artists; Institute of Water Colour painters, Sydney; Perth Society of Artists; Life member and patron, Busselton Society of Artists. *Creative Works:* Numerous paintings in Oil and Watercolour; Many items of furniture in America and Australia; Worked with Sculptor Paul Montford, building all the machinery for Paul to sculpt the Melbourne War Memorial; Made the chair for Paul Montford's statue of Adam Lindsay Gordon cast in bronze in Melbourne, Australia. *Honours:* Won the Hotchin Prize twice; The Bunbury Prize twice; The Busselton Prize once; Entered eight Shire Council Competitions in Western Australia and won eight; Exhibitions in Perth, Brisbane, London, USA., and New Zealand. *Hobby:* Painting and making furniture. *Address:* 11 Hudman Road, Boya 6056, Western Australia.

LANDON-LANE, Ian, b. 12 Dec. 1927, Auckland, New Zealand. Public Servant. m. Rayma Saunders, 14 Nov. 1953, 2 sons, 1 daughter. *Education:* BA, Victoria University of Wellington, 1953; Dip. Pub. Ad. 1958; New Zealand Administrative Staff College, 1978. *Appointments:* Primary Produce Marketing, 1946-53; Seconded to Apple and Pear Board, 1954; Department of Trade and Industry Overseas Postings at Intervals, Sydney, Montreal, San Francisco, Santiago, 1955-; Charge D'Affaires, New Zealand Embassy, Lima, 1976; Ambassador, New Zealand Embassy, Santiago, Chile. *Address:* New Zealand Embassy, Casilla 112, Correo Las Condes, Santiago, Chile.

LANE, David Neil, b. 16 Apr. 1928. HM Diplomatic Service. m. Sara Nurcombe 1968, 2 daughters. *Education:* Abbotsholme School; Merton College Oxford. *Appointments:* Army 1946-48; Foreign and Commonwealth Office 1951-53, 1955-58, 1963-68, 1972-74; British Embassy, Oslo, 1953-55; Ankara 1959-61, 1975-78; Conakry 1961-63; UK Mission to the United Nations, New York 1968-72, 1979; *Memberships:* President UN Trusteeship Council 1971-72; UK Delegate International Exhibitions Bureau 1973-74; High Commissioner in Trinidad and Tobago, 1980-. *Hobbies:* Music; Walking; Ski-ing. *Address:* British High Commission, Port-of-Spain, Trinidad.

LANE, David William Stennis Stuart, b. 24 Sept. 1922 Edinburgh. Chairman, Commission for Racial Equality.

m. Lesley Anne Mary Clauson 23 July 1955, 2 sons. *Education:* Eton; Trinity College Cambridge; Yale University. *Appointments:* Royal Navy; British Iron and Steel Federation; Shell International Petroleum Company; Called to Bar, Middle Temple; MP (Cambridge); PPS to Secretary of State for Employment; Parly under-Secretary of State Home Office; Commission for Racial Equality. *Memberships:* MCC. *Hobbies:* Walking; Golf; Cricket. *Address:* 40 Chepstow Place, London, W2, England.

LANGDON, Ian Alan, b. 15 Mar. 1944, Melbourne, Victoria, Australia. Accountant. m. 2 Apr. 1966, 3 daughters. *Education:* M.BA; BComm; Dip Ed. *Appointments:* Teacher Ed. Department Victoria; Lecturer Gordon Institute of Technology; Senior Lecturer, Deakin University; Dean School of Business, Darling Down, Institute of Advanced Education. *Hobbies:* Tennis; Swimming. *Address:* 12 Palm Court, Toowoomba, Queensland Australia.

LANGFORD-HOLT, John Anthony, b. 30 June 1916, Dover, England. Member of Parliament. 1 son, 1 daughter. *Education:* Shrewsbury School. *Appointments:* Officer, Royal Navy; Company Director and Business Consultant; Member of Parliament for Shrewsbury 1945-. *Memberships:* Whites Club; Carlton Club; Royal Yacht Squadron, Cowes. Hobby: Sailing. *Address:* House of Commons, London SW1, England.

LANGGULUNG, Hasan, b. 16 Oct. 1934, Makassar, Indonesia. Associate Professor. m. 23 Sept. 1972, 1 son, 1 daughter. *Education:* BA, Cairo University 1962; Dip.Ed, 1964; MA, Ein Shams University, 1967; PhD, University of Georgia, 1971. *Appointments:* Assistant Professor: University of Malaya, 1971-72; National University, 1972-76; Associate Professor, National University, 1976-; Visiting Professor, Riyadh University, 1977-78. *Memberships:* American Psychological Association; Cross-Cultural Research and Researchers. *Publications:* Twelve Books, over 50 articles published in international as well as local journals in English, Malay and Arabic. *Hobbies:* Tennis; Swimming; Travel. *Address:* B28 Jalan Bukit, Taman Bukit Kajang, Kajang, Selangor, Malaysia.

LANGLEY, Gilbert Roche Andrews, b. 14 Sept. 1919, North Adelaide South Australia. Member of Parliament, House of Assembly. m. Jean Constance Tully 10 Oct. 1942, 2 sons, 2 daughters. *Education:* Colonel Light Gardens Primary School 1925-32; Unly Central School 1933-37. *Appointments:* Government and Opposition Whip, House of Assembly South Australia; Chairman of Committees; Speaker, House of Assembly two years. *Memberships:* Australian Cricket Team 1949-56; Player, Cricket and Football Clubs; House of Assembly South Australia. *Hobbies:* Cricket; Football; Green Bowls. *Address:* 10 Cambridge Terrace, Unly 5061, South Australia.

LANGSFORD, Graeme Douglas, b. 11 Feb. 1946, Palmerston North, New Zealand. Consultant Surgeon. m. Lorraine Teresa Ross 10 Aug. 1972, 1 son, 2 daughters. *Education:* BSc(Med) Hons., 1968; MBBS Hons. University of New South Wales, 1971; FRACS 1978. *Appointments:* Consultant Surgeon, Mersey General Hospital, 1979; Consultant Surgeon, Orange Bse Hospital 1981. *Publications:* Peri-anal Pagets' Disease; Liver Abscess. *Hobbies:* Fruit Growing; Hydrophonics. *Address:* 27 Alkira Way, Orange, NSW2800, Australia.

LANSKY, Peter Joseph Soják, b. 9 Oct. 1921, Prague, Czechoslovakia. Linguist (Comparative and Applied Linguistics); Writer. m. Viera Scheibnerová Chybová 4 July 1975. *Education:* Interpreter's Diploma, 5 Languages, College Rosenberg, 1946; Diploma in English and Lit.(Cantab) 1946; State Diploma in German, St. Gall, Switzerland 1946; State Examination in Economics, Prague Institute of Technology 1948; Absolutorium in Political Science, Berne University 1950; Doctorate in Medicine, Homoeopathy, The Anglo-American Therapeutical Institute 1972. *Appointments:* Assistant, Head of Mission, Allied High Commission for Germany, Berne, Switzerland 1948-51. *Memberships:* Branch President, Liberal Party of Australia; President, Valuers', Assessors' and Art Restorers' Body; Governor, The All Nations Club; Director, The Consulting Linguists' Pool; Principal and Director, The Consulting Linguists' College; National Trust of Australia; National Accreditation Authority for Translators and Interpreters; etc.

Publications: The Life of a Seer, in press; Some 300 news articles in a variety of subjects. *Honours:* Medal and Diploma of Merit, A.C.E.N. New York USA; Certificates of Appreciation by Rotarians and Lyons 1969, 1972, 1975, 1976; Hon. President, E.S.P. Research Association of Australia. *Hobbies:* Music; Healing arts and psychosomatic medicine; Survival of bodily death evidence; Correlations of parapsychologic and extra-sensory phenomena with cosmologican considerations; Collecting: Art works; objets d'art, old time pieces; Debating; Investigation of viable alternative sources of energy in our civilisation; Sports. *Address:* 'Frangipani', 6 Plumer Road, Rose Bay, NSW, Australia.

LARKINS, Richard Graeme, b. 17 May 1943, Melbourne, Australia. Medical Practitioner. m. Caroline Elizabeth Embley Cust 7 Dec. 1966, 3 daughters. *Education:* MBBS, Melbourne 1966; MD 1972; PhD London 1974; FRACP 1975. *Appointments:* Resident Medical Officer, 1966-69, Assistant Endocrinologist, Royal Melbourne Hospital 1970-72; Research fellow, Endocrine Unit, Royal Postgraduate Medical School, London, 1972-74; Physician, Endocrine Laboratory, Royal Melbourne Hospital 1974-77; Assistant, University of Melbourne Department of Medicine, Repatriation General Hospital, Heidelberg 1978-; Director of Endocrine and Metabolic Unit, Repatriation General Hospital, Heidelberg. *Memberships:* Fellow, Royal Australasian College of Physicians; Endocrine Society of Australia; European Association for the Study of Diabetes; Australian Diabetes Society; Australian Society for Medical Research. *Publications:* Author or co-author of over 60 original papers on medical research, particularly concerning diabetes and endocrinology. *Honours:* Churchill Fellow, 1972. *Hobbies:* Golf; Tennis; Reading. *Address:* 10 Hawthorn Grove, Hawthorn, Victoria 3122, Australia.

LARMIE, Ayitey, b. 4 July 1935, Accra, Ghana. Librarian. m. Matilda Adoley Houghman 14 Apr. 1962, 2 sons, 1 daughter. *Education:* Course for Circuit Court Registrars, Green Hill, Achimota, Accra, 1970; Library Assistants Certificate, Hammersmith and West London, College, London, 1975. *Appointments:* Circuit Court Registrar, Libraries, 1967; High Court Rigestrar, 1976; Senior High Court Registrar, 1979. *Hobbies:* Reading; Building Construction; Walking; Music. *Address:* No A770/5, off Guggisberg Road Ext. Dansoman, Accra, Ghana.

LARMOUR (Lady) Nancy (Mrs Edward Noel Larmour (Sir)), b. 7 Apr. 1920, Belfast. College Lecturer. m. Sir Edward Noel (Nick), 6 Jan. 1946, 1 son, 2 daughters. *Education:* Belfast Royal Academy; BA, Trinity College Dublin. *Appointments:* Teaching posts in schools and colleges in Burma, Singapore, Lagos (Nigeria), Kingston (Jamaica) and at Montagu Centre, Southgate Technical College; Presently at Tetherdown Adult Education Centre, Haringey, North London. *Memberships:* Haringey Community Relations Council; Governor of Commonwealth Institute. *Hobbies:* TV; Theatre; Community Relations; Commonwealth Literature; Cooking. *Address:* 68 Wood Vale, London, N10 3DN, England.

LARSEN, Edward Reynolds, b. 1 Apr. 1925, Vancouver B.C Canada. Headmaster. m. Patricia Lillian Jelinek, 4 Oct. 1980. *Education:* BA (Honours Maths), University of British Columbia 1948; BA (Honours in Modern History), 1953, MA, University of Oxford 1963. *Appointments:* Headmaster, Shawnigan Lake School, British Columbia 1958-67; Headmaster, Appleby College, Oakville, Ontario 1968-80; Headmaster, Rothesay Collegiate School, N.B 1981-. *Memberships:* President, JCR, Exeter College, Oxford 1952-53; President Honorary Fraternity, University British Columbia 1948; President Big Block Club, 1948. *Publications:* Founder, The Canadian Independent School Journal; The place of the Independent School, 1978; The Appleby Northward Board Programme, 1976; Spiritual Values in our Schools, 1978. *Honours:* Woodward Scholarship to University 1945; George Pringle Bursary, 1947; IODE Scholarship for B.C to Oxford 1952; Oxford Society Prize, 1953; Quarrel Read Prize 1953; Triple Blue at Oxford, Squash, Basketball, Badminton; Represented Canada in field hockey in World Tournament, Lyon, 1963. *Hobbies:* Squash; Tennis; *Address:* Rothesay Collegiate School, Rothesay, New Brunswick, Canada, E0G 2W0.

LASDUN, Denys Louis, b. 8 Sept. 1914, London. Architect. m. Susan Virginia Bendit, 26 Mar. 1954, 2 sons, 1 daughter. *Education:* Architectural Association; Rugby School. *Appointments:* Wells Coates, 1935-37; Partner in Tecton, 1946-48; Partnership with Lindsey Drake, 1949-59; Formed partnership with Alexander Redhouse and Petr Softley, 1960; Hoffman Wood Professor of Architecture, University of Leeds, 1962-63; Sub-Committee, Jerusalem Town Planning, 1970; Assessor, Competitions for Belgrade Opera House, 1971, and New Parliamentary Building, London, 1971-72. *Memberships:* V & A Advisory Committee, 1973; Trustee British Museum, 1975-; Slade Committee, 1976-; Arts Panel, Arts Council of Great Britain, 1980. *Publications:* A Language and a Theme, 1976; contributions to architectural and other papers including An Architects Approach to Architecture. Works include: Housing and schools for Bethnal Green and Paddington; new store for Peter Robinson, London; flats at St James's Place; Royal College of Physicians; Fitzwilliam College, and Christ's College extension, Cambridge; New Universities of East Anglia and work for Universities of London (SOAS, Institute of Education, Law Institute, project for Courtauld Institute), Licester and Liverpool; National Theatre, South Bank and adjacent buiding for IBM Cental london Offices; new EEC HQ for European Investment Bank, Luxembourg; Sotheby & Co; Hurva Synagogue, Jerusalem. *Honours:* RIBA London Architecture Bronze Medallist, 1960 & 1964; CBE, 1965; FRIBA; Hon Fellow, American Institute of Architects, 1966; Hon. DA Manchester, 1966; Civic Trust Awards, Class I, 1967, Group A, 1969; Special Award, Sao Paulo Biennale, Brazil, 1969; Hon D Litt, E Anglia, 197, Sheffield, 1978; Hon. FRCP, 1975; Kt. 1976; RIBA Architectural Award for London Region, 1978. *Address:* 50 Queen Anne Street, London W1M 0DR, England.

LASKIN, Bora, (Rt Hon), b. 5 Oct. 1912, Fort William, Ontario, Canada. Chief Justice. m. Peggy Tenenbaum, 1 son, 1 daughter. *Education:* BA, 1933, MA, 1935, LL.B, 1936, University of Toronto; Osgoode Hall Law School, 1933-36; Called to the Bar, 1937; LL.M, Harvard University Law School, 1937. *Appointments:* Lecturer in Law and Assistant Professor of Law, University of Toronto, 1940-45; Lecturer in Law, Osgoode Hall Law School, 1945-49; Professor of Law, University of Toronto, 1949-65; Appointed to the Supreme Court of Ontario, Court of Appeal, 1965; Appointed to the Supreme Court of Canada, 1970; Appointed Chief Justice of Canada, 1973. *Memberships:* Council of Management of the British Institute of International and Comparative Law, 1972; President, Association of Canadian Law Teachers, 1953-54, Canadian Association of University Teachers, 1964-65; Chairman and Board of Governors, Ontario Institute for Studies in Education, 1965-69; Board of Governors, York University, 1967-70, Carleton University, 1970-73; Chancellor, Lakehead University, 1971; Queen's Counsel, 1956; Associate Editor, Dominion Law Reports and Canadian Criminal Cases, 1943-65; National Academy of Arbitrators; Honorary Bencher, Lincoln's Inn. *Publications:* Numerous articles in legal periodicals, and books dealing with Land Law and Canadian Constitutional Law; Third revised edition of Canadian Constitutional Law, 1969; The British Tradition in Canadian Law—Hamlyn Lecturer, 1969; The Institutional Character of the Judge—Lionel Cohen Lecturer, 1972; English Law in Canadian Courts since the Abolition of Privy Council Appeals—Bentham Lecturer, 1976. *Honours:* Fellow, The Royal Society of Canada; LL.D, at various Universities between 1965-81; DCL, Universities of New Brunswick, 1968, Windsor, 1970, Western Ontario, 1972; D.Phil., Hebrew University of Jerusalem, 1976; L.Hu.D., Hebrew Union College, Cincinnati, Ohio, 1977. *Address:* Supreme Court Building, Willington Street, Ottawa Ontario, Canada, K1A OJ1.

LATHAM, Ronald Edward, b. 6 May 1907, Whitley Bay, Northumberland, England. Retired. m. Lydia McKean 9 Sept. 1939, 2 sons, 1 daughter. *Education:* BA (1st Class Lit. Hon), MA, Balliol College Oxford, 1925-29. *Appointments:* Assistant Lecturer in Latin, Queen's University Belfast 1929-32; Assistant Editor, Review of Applied Entomology 1933-34; Assistant Keeper and Principal Assistant Keeper, Public Record Office, 1934-67; Seconded to Ministry of Fuel and Power, 1941-46. *Memberships:* Philological Society; FSA; Historical Association. *Publications:* In Quest of Civilization; Translations, Lucretius and Marco Polo; Finding out about the Normans; Medieval Latin Wordlist (revised) and Dictionary. *Honours:* OBE 1967.

Hobbies: Walking; Gardening; Botany; Chess. *Address:* 284 Croydon Road, Caterham, Surrey, CR3 6QH, England.

LAU, Se Hian, b. 3 Aug. 1949, Malaysia. Accountant. m. Tan Lin Sing Acis, 13 June 1976, 1 son. *Education:* BSc, 1971, BSc(Hons), 1972, University of Malaya, Kuala Lumpur; ICMA, UK, 1975. *Appointments:* Research Officer, Defence Research Centre, Ministry of Defence, Malaysia, 1972-74; Management Consultant, Goonting & Chew Management Consultants, Kuala Lumpur, 1975-77; Director General Manager, Safuan Group of Companies, Kuala Lumpur, 1978-81. *Memberships:* Malaysian Institute of Accountants; Institute of Cost & Management Accountants, UK; ICMA Malaysian Centre, Kuala Lumpur. *Publications:* Course leader for management development programms with Malaysian Institute of Management, Kuala Lumpur. *Honours:* Honours degree in Chemistry, University of Malaya, 1972. *Hobbies:* Swimming; Reading; Music; Travelling. *Address:* 8 Jln 24, Overseas Union Garden, Klang Road, Kuala Lumpur, Malaysia.

LAU, Siu Wai, b. 14 Aug. 1932, Teo-Ann, Kwangtung, China. Managing Director. m. Milly Goh Siew Choo, 18 Mar. 1976, 4 sons, 2 daughters. *Education:* Passed form 5 in 1952 and some subjects of Cambridge Higher School Certificate in 1956. Most of the education was acquired through self-study by means of correspondence courses. *Appointments:* Temporary salesman; Typist; Accounts clerk; Water-works superintendent; Engine fitter and welder; Teacher; Headmaster of Secondary School; Mechanical Engineering and pipe-line Maintenance supervisor; Housing developer; Private tutor; Stenographer; Engineer Trainee. *Publications:* A short story entitled, Every Cloud has a Silver Lining. *Honours:* Second prize by the Borneo Literature Bureau. *Hobby:* Photography. *Address:* 12 Dupont Avenue, City Beach, W.A. 6015, Western Australia.

LAU, Teik Soon, b. 5 Feb. 1939, Penang. Associate Professor & Head, Department of Political Science, National University of Singapore. Member of Parliament. m. Low Sai Noi, 23 Apr. 1962, 1 son, 2 daughters. *Education:* BA, University of Singapore, 1966; PhD, International Relations, Australian National University, 1972. *Appointments:* School Teacher, 1959-63; Officer, Ministry of Foreign Affairs, 1966-68; Research Fellowship, Institute of Southeast Asian Studies, 1971-72; University Lecturer, 1972-75; Senior Lecturer, 1976-80; Member of Parliament, 1976-80, Re-elected 1980. *Memberships:* President, Singapore Institute of International Affairs, 1979-81, re-elected 1981; Executive Committee, Singapore Parliamentary Association, 1979-81; Executive Committee, Commonwealth Parliamentary Association, London, 1978-81. *Publications:* Editor, New Directions in the International Relations of Southeast Asia—The Great Powers and Southeast Asia, 1973; papers published in various journals. *Honours:* Research Scholarship, Australian National University, 1968-71; Research Fellowship, Institute of Southeast Asian Studies, 1971-72; US Department of State International Visitor Grant, 1976; Swedish Institute Foreign Visitor Grant, 1978. *Hobbies:* Jogging; Badminton; Golf. *Address:* Department of Political Science, National University of Singapore, Kent Ridge, Singapore, 0511.

LAU, Yuk Ching Alexander, b. 24 Feb. 1954, Hong Kong. General Merchandise Investment Consultant. m. Wong Ho Pik Mabel, 15 May 1977, 2 sons. *Appointments:* Hang Seng Bank Ltd, Foreign Exchange Department 1973-76; Community Organiser, City District Office, 1976-77; Business Manager, Good Harvest Trading Co., 1977-. *Hobbies:* Discussing Economic & Political Situations; Making friends. *Address:* 80-82 Bonham Road, Rhine Court, Flat C-1, 19/F Hong Kong.

LAUCKE, Condor Louis (Hon. Sir), b. 9 Nov. 1914, Greenock, South Australia. Assistant President of the Senate and Senator. m. Rose Hambour, 19 June 1942, 1 son, 1 daughter. *Education:* Immanuel College; Adelaide School of Mines. *Appointments:* Director, F Laucke Pty. Ltd, Flour and Feed Mills; South Australian House of Assembly for Barossa 1956; Whip 1962-65; Liberal Party Senator for South Australia 1967-; President of the Senate 1976-. *Honours:* KCMG 1979. *Hobbies:* Farming; Wine Growing; Gardening. *Address:* "Bunawunda", Greenock, South Australia.

LAURIE, David Douglas, b. 26 Mar. 1916, Sydney, NSW Australia. Company Director/Transportation Consultant. m. Betty Ruse Reynolds 31 May 1941, 3 sons. *Education:* Matriculated Canterbury High School Sydney NSW 1933. *Appointments:* Junior to Chief Clerk Thomas Playfair Limited Sydney 1933-39; Flight Crew Qantas Empire Airways Limited 1939-41; RAAF Transport Command Flight crew to Ground Administration 1941-46; Traffic Manager, Sales Manager, Manager UK & Europe, General Manager Cargo Division, Trans Australia Airlines, 1946-76; Director Blue Circle Taxi Trucks Pty. Ltd. and Domino Pacific Corp. Aust. Pty Ltd, Melbourne Australia 1976-; Australian Manager Pacific Aero Products Inc. Burbank California and Alaska International Air Inc. Anchorage Alaska. *Memberships:* Fellow Chartered Institute of Transport; Naval and Military Club Melbourne; Returned Serviceman's League. *Publications: Honours:* FCIT 1965; War area service medals, Pacific Star. *Hobbies:* Work; Golf; Poker; Charity work for aged and disabled children. *Address:* 22 Netherway Street, Burwood, 3125, Victoria, Australia.

LAURIE, Robert Stephen, b. 5 Nov. 1936, Sydney NSW Australia. Diplomat. m. Diana Victoria Mary Doyne 6 June 1969, 1 son, 1 daughter. *Education:* BA(Hons) Sydney University. *Appointments:* Department External Affairs 1958; Postings, Colombo, Moscow, Washington, Hong Kong; Deputy High Commissioner New Delhi, 1970-71; Ambassador Rangoon Burma 1975-77; Ambassador Poland and Czechoslovakia. *Memberships:* Australian Club; Molonglo Cricket Club; I Zingari Australia. *Hobbies:* Gardening; Music; Cricket. *Address:* 31 Arthur Circle Manuka, ACT 2603, Australia.

LAUTI, Toaripa (Rt. Hon), b. 1930. Prime Minister. m. Sualua Lauti, 3 sons, 2 daughters. *Education:* Christchurch Teachers' College, New Zealand. *Appointments:* Secondary School Teacher, Tarawa 1953-61; Labour Relations and Training Officer, Nauru and Ocean Islands Phosphate Commission 1962-74. *Memberships:* Gilbert and Ellice Islands House of Assembly; Chief Minister Tuvalu 1975-. *Honours:* Privy Councillor 1979. *Address:* Prime Minister's Office, Vaiaku, Funafuti, Tuvalu.

LAVERTY, Colin Robert Andrew, b. 26 May 1937, Sydney, NSW, Australia. Pathologist. *Education:* BSc, (Med) 1958, MB., BS, 1962, DCP, 1968, Sydney; FRCPA, 1969; MIAC, 1978. *Appointments:* Resident Medical Officer, 1962-63, Pathology Registrar, 1965-69, Royal Prince Alfred Hospital; Senior Registrar in Pathology, St Mary's Hospital, Manchester, England, 1970-71; Histopathologist, Royal Womens Hospital, Melbourne, Australia, 1972-73, Royal Prince Alfred Hospital, 1973, Senior Histopathologist, 1975; Head, Department of Pathology, King George V Memorial Hospital for Mothers and Babies, Sydney, 1975-79; Private Specialist practice in Gynaecologic Pathology and Cytology, Sydney, 1979-. *Memberships:* Australian Society for Colposcopy and Cervical Pathology, 1976-; Histologic Nomenclature Committee, International Federation for Cervical Pathology and Colposcopy, 1980-; Medical Advisory Board, Family Planning Association of NSW, 1981-. *Publications:* Numerous contributions to medical journals including: The significance of Non-Condylomatous Wart Virus Infection of the Cervical Transformation Zone, 1978; Condylomatous Wart Virus Infection of the Cervix Cytologic Histologic and Electronmicroscopic Features, 1979; Noncondylomatous Cervical Wart Virus Infection, 1980; Australian Colonial Sporting Painters, 1980. *Honours:* Australian Commonwealth Medical Fellowship, 1970-71. *Hobby:* 19th Century Australian Painting. *Address:* 4/31 Dick Street, Henley, NSW, Australia, 2111.

LAW, David Wing Chiu, b. 30 Apr. 1948, Hong Kong. Businessman. m. Villie Lam, 13 Aug. 1970, 1 son. *Education:* BSc, McGill University, 1970; PhD, University of Michigan, 1975. *Appointments:* Vice-President, Tsang Fook Piano Company. *Memberships:* Hong Kong University Alumni Association; AAAS. *Publications:* University Microfilms Inc. (Ann Arbor); Purification and Properties of a Diabetogenic Peptide from Urine of Diabetic Patients. *Hobbies:* Music; Photography. *Address:* 43 Stubbs Road, B2-10, Hong Kong.

LAW, Francis Chung-Pak, b. 12 Oct. 1941, Hong Kong. University Professor. m. Rosemary Dy Lim, 18

May 1980. *Education:* BSc, 1966, MSc, 1969, University of Alberta, Canada; PhD, University of Michigan, USA, 1972. *Appointments:* Pharmacology Branch, National Institute of Environmental Health Sciences, USA, 1972-75; College of Pharmacy, Dalhousie University, Canada, 1975-. *Memberships:* American Society for Pharmacology and Experimental Therapeutics; The Pharmacological Society of Canada; Society of Toxicology of Canada. *Publications:* Many research papers published in the areas of Pharmacology and Toxicology. *Hobbies:* Music; Film; Swimming; Travelling. *Address:* #10 Bluejay Street, Bridgeview, Halifax, Nova Scotia, Canada, B3M 1V1.

LAW, Phillip Garth, b. 21 Apr. 1912, Tallangatta, Victoria, Australia. Scientist; Explorer and Educationist. m. Nel Allan, 20 Dec. 1941. *Education:* Ballarat Teachers' College, Melbourne University; BSc 1939; MSc 1941; Doctor Applied Science, Hon. 1962; DEd-(Hon.) 1978; FAIP; FRMIT, (Hon) FTS 1976; FRMIT(Hon) 1977; FAA 1978. *Appointments:* Secondary Teacher, Victoria Education Department 1929-38; Lecturer in Physics, University of Melbourne 1943-48; Senior Scientific Officer, Australian National Antarctic Research Expeditions 1943-48; Director, Antarctic Disision, Department of External Affairs and Leader of ANARE 194966; Executive Vice-President, Victoria Institute of Colleges, 1966-77; Chairman, Australian National Committee on Antarctic Research 1966-80. *Memberships:* Fellow Royal Geological Society London; Royal Society of Victoria; Victorian Institute of Marine Sciences; Australian and New Zealand Scientific Exploration Society; Geelong Area Scouts Association of Victoria; Melbourne Film Society; Fellow, Graduate House, University of Melbourne; Deputy President, Science Museum of Victoria. *Honours:* AO 1975; CBE 1961; Gold Medal, Royal Geographical Society London 1960; John Lewis Gold Medal, 1961; Clive Lord Memorial Medal 1958; Award of Merit, Commonwealth Profession Offices Association 1957; Vocational Service Award, 1970; Freeman of Victorian College of the Arts 1977; Hon. Life Member, Institute of Australian Geographers 1960; Hon. Life Member Geog. Society of NSW 1959; Hon. Life Member Melbourne University Mountaineering Club; Patron Melbourne University Sports Union 1979-. *Hobbies:* Tennis; Skiing; Skin diving; Music. *Address:* 16 Stanley Grove, Canterbury 3126, Victoria, Australia.

LAWAL, Olufunke Olufemi, b. 1 Oct. 1948, Sagamu, Ogun State, Nigeria. Lectureship. m. R I O Lawal, 28 Aug. 1971, 1 son, 2 daughters. *Education:* Nigerian Certificate in Education, 1970; BA., English, Hons., 1974, Master of Education, 1977, University of Lagos, Nigeria. *Appointments:* Teacher of English, Western State Schools Board, Nigeria, 1970-71; Teaching under National Youth Service Scheme, Federal Military Government of Nigeria, 1974-75; Lecturer in Language Education, University of Lagos, Nigeria, 1978-. *Memberships:* Nigeria English Studies Association; University of Lagos Women's Society; World Council for Curriculum and Instruction. *Honours:* Post-graduate Scholarship award, University of Lagos, Nigeria, 1975. *Hobbies:* Gardening; Sewing. *Address:* 14A Child Avenue, Apapa, Lagos, Nigeria.

LAWANI, Stephen Majebi, b. 26 Apr. 1944, Igarra, Akoko-Edo, Nigeria. Library and Information Science. m. Evelyn Ayoka Fadairo, 5 Sept. 1967, 4 sons. *Education:* BSc, Chemistry, 1962-66, Postgraduate Diploma in Librarianship, 1966-67, University of Ibadan; MS, Columbia University, New York, 1967-68; PhD, Florida State University, 1978-79. *Appointments:* Head of Library and Documentation Services, International Institute of Tropical Agriculture, 1969-. *Memberships:* Grail Movement of Nigeria; International Association of Agricultural Librarians and Documentalists; Editor-in-Chief and Council of Nigerian Library Association. *Publications:* Eight Monographs and over 20 journal articles. *Honours:* Shell-BP Scholar, 1962-66; Rockefeller Scholar, 1966-69; Rockefeller Fellow, 1978-79; Consultant to FAO, UNESCO and United Nations Secretariat on several occasions. *Hobbies:* Flower Gardening; Classical Music; Tennis. *Address:* 14 Tropical Crescent, lita, Ibadan.

LAWOYIN, Victor Latunde, b. 5 Mar. 1932, Ilora, Oyo State, Nigeria. Medical Practitioner. m. Lucy Lola Ogunleye, 17 Jan. 1975, 2 sons, 1 daughter. *Education:* Grade II Teachers Certificate, Iwo Baptist College,

Iwo, Nigeria, 1953; BA., Oberlin College, Oberlin, Ohio, USA, 1960; MD., Albany Medical College, Albany, New York, USA, 1964; Fellowship in Gastroenterology, Henry Ford Hospital, Detroit, Michigan, USA, 1969-71. *Appointments:* Teacher at: Ade Oshadi Baptist Day School, Baptist Boys High School, Abeokuta, Nigeria, 1954; Registrar Doctor in Medicine, Lagos University Teaching Hospital, Nigeria, 1967; Practised Medicine at Ford Motor Assembly Plant, Dearborn, Michigan, USA, 1971-72; Practised Medicine at Baptist Hospital, Ogbomosho, Oyo State, Nigeria, 1973-76; Chairman, Oyo State Health Council, Ibadan, Oyo State, Nigeria, 1976-. *Memberships:* Michigan State Medical Association; Nigerian Medical Association; Fellow, Nigerian College of General Medical Practitioners. *Publications:* Medical Publications including: Non-Parasitic Cysts of the Liver: Analysis of 36 cases, 1972; Incidence and Causes of Splenomegaly in Lagos. *Honours:* Order of the Niger, 1981; Justice of the Peace, 1981. *Hobbies:* Table tennis; Lawn tennis; Hunting games; Novel reading. *Address:* SW8/839 Olu Ayoola Street, Challenge, Ibadan, Oyo State, Nigeria.

LAWRENCE, Warwick Ritchie Crawford, b. 27 Dec. 1915, Carterton, New Zealand. Journalist. m. Mary Elizabeth Chinchen, 11 May 1940, 2 sons, 1 daughter. *Education:* Auckland University College, Auckland, New Zealand. *Education:* Flight Lieutenant (Reserve of Officers), Royal New Zealand Air Force, World War II, 1939-46; The Mirror, Auckland; Sydney Morning Herald, Sydney, Australia; The Courier-Mail, Brisbane, Australia; J Walter Thompson (Advertising) Limited, Melbourne and Sydney, Australia; Catts-Patterson (Advertising), Wellington, New Zealand; British High Commission, Wellington, New Zealand. *Memberships:* Life member and New Zealand Representative, Friends of St. George's and Association of Descendants of Knights of the Garter; Secretary-Treasuer and Councillor, Royal Commonwealth Society, Auckland; Central Auckland Committee of Patriotic Societies; New Zealand Historic Places Trust; New Zealand Heraldry Society; Outward Bound Trust, New Zealand; New Zealand Historical Association. *Publications:* Three Mile Bush (Early Wairarapa); Vulcan Lane and Other Verses; Yours and Mine. *Honours:* Runner up Rothmans Book of the Year, Biographical section, New Zealand, 1969. *Hobbies:* Historical research; Writing; Travel; Reading; Gardening. *Address:* 28A Mahoe Avenue, Remuera, Auckland, New Zealand.

LAWS, Charles Reed, b. 27 Jan. 1894, Auckland, New Zealand. Retired. m. Evelyn Katie Lee, 21 Dec. 1921, 1 son, 2 daughters. *Education:* BSc, 1923; MSc, 1924; DSc, 1935. *Appointments:* Primary School Teacher; Lecturer, Geography, Dunedin Training College; Lecturer, Geography & Nature Study, Auckland Teachers College; Senior Lecturer, Geology, University of Auckland; Retired, 1959. *Memberships:* Royal Society of New Zealand, 1930-, Fellow, 1950. *Publications:* Numerous papers on New Zealand Tertiary mollusca; DSC, work published in eight parts between 1937 and 1940. *Honours:* Awarded the Premium in BSc, geology, 1920; Sir Julius von Haast Prize, for MSc. *Hobbies:* Gardening; Philately. *Address:* 198 Greenlane West, Auckland 5, New Zealand.

LAWS, Richard, b. 6 Oct. 1925, Killarney, Queensland. Managing Director. m. Ferol Lilian Parker, 20 May 1950, 1 son, 2 daughters. *Education:* Bachelor of Engineering, University of Queensland, 1951; Diploma of Town & Country Planning, Queensland Institute of Technology, 1969. *Appointments:* Engineer, Co-Ordinator, Generals Department, 1950-54; Senior Engineer, Cardno & Davies, 1955-65; Partner, 1965-71, Director, 1971-78, Chairman & Managing Director, 1978-, Cardno & Davies Australia Pty. Ltd. *Memberships:* Fellow, Institution of Engineers, Australia Secretary of General Branch, Society of Professional Engineers PNG, Institute of Arbitrators, Australia; American Society of Civil Engineers; Royal Australian Planning Institute. *Honours:* University of Queensland Open Scholarship Awarded, 1943. *Hobbies:* Lawn Bowls; Collecting paintings by Queensland Artists; Church work. *Address:* 10 Coolaroo Crescent, Jindalee Q 4074 Australia.

LAWS, Richard John Sinclair, b. 8 Aug. 1935, Wau, New Guinea. Radio and television broadcaster. m. Caroline Rosalie Margaret Cameron-Waller, 27 Nov. 1975, 4 sons, 5 daughters. *Appointments:* Started in Radio, at 3BO Bendigo Victoria, Australia, 1955; Other country stations until 1957 when joined 2UE, 1959, 2SM, 1962; Macquarie Network, 1962, 2UE, 1964-69, 2UW, 1969-79, 2UE, 1979-; Written newspaper columns for 4 Sydney Papers, currently writing for Sunday Telegraph; Hosted 4 National television shows; Appeared regularly on 2 national shows; Currently hosts 'John Laws' World', for Channel 10 network; Starred in Film - Nickel Queen, 1971; Starred in stage play - Side by Side by Sondheim, 1977. *Creative Works:* 11 Albums; 4 Poetry Books; 3 Calendars. *Honours:* Honorary Metropolitan Citizen of Nashville Davidson County, USA, 1963; OBE., 1974; Billboard International Award for on-air achievement, 1974; Australian Radio Record Award for country music album, 1975; Golden Tree Award for outstanding services to Country Music, USA, 1976; CBE., 1978; Radio Award for Best Talkback Personality in Australia, 1977, 1978, 1979, 1980. *Hobbies:* Motor sports; Motorcycling; Boating; Reading; Farming; Deer breeding; Photography. *Address:* PO Box 228, Woollahra 2025, Australia.

LAWSON, Basil Anthony Anani, b. 27 Nov. 1935, Lagos, Nigeria. Insurance. m. 23 Dec. 1961, 1 son, 4 daughters. *Education:* Associate Diploma, Chartered Insurance Institute, London, UK. *Appointments:* Fire and Accident Manager, Guinea Insurance Co., 1963-66; Claims Manager, T A Braithwaite Insurance Brokers, 1966-67; Insurance Officer, Electricity Corporation of Nigeria, 1967-72; Agency Manager, 1972-77, Deputy General Manager, 1978-, National Insurance Corporation of Nigeria; General Manager, Manilla Insurance Co., 1977-78. *Memberships:* National Institute for Policy and Strategic Studies. *Hobbies:* Football; Table tennis; Boxing; Athletics. *Address:* Box 1100, Lagos, Nigeria.

LAWSON, Charles Olatunde, b. 20 Mar. 1919, Igbobini, Ikitipupa Division, Ondo State, Nigeria. Statistician, Retired Civil Servant, Chairman. m. 2 sons, 1 daughter. *Education:* Teacher Training Institution, Wesley College, Ibadan, Nigeria, 1937-40; Higher Elementary Teachers Certificate, 1940; Barnett House, Oxford and Exeter College, University of Oxford, 1950-51, 1952-53; BSc, 1950; DPA, (Oxon), 1951; MA (Oxon), BA, 1953; Graduate of Imperial Defence College, London, 1959. *Appointments:* Teaching, 1941-47; Professional Statistician, Federal Civil Service, Nigeria, 1947-58; Administrative Service, 1958; Principal Private Secretary, Prime Minister of Nigeria, 1960; Deputy Secretary, Cabinet, Nigerian Government, 1961; Permanent Secretary, Federal Ministry of Health, 1961-65, Federal Ministry of Communications, 1965-70, Federal Ministry of Transport, 1970-72; Secretary to the Federal Military Government & Head of Federal Civil Service, 1972-75; Chairman, The Boots Company (Nigeria) Ltd., Director, Rank Zerox (Nigeria) Ltd., 1978-. *Publications:* Wage Earners in Enugu, Eastern Nigeria, 1954-55; A Sample Survey of the Social & Economic Conditions of Wage Earners (Mimeographed); National Income of Nigeria, (Mimeographed), 1956. *Honours:* Commander of the Order of the Niger (National Honour), 1979. *Hobbies:* Voluntary Youth Work; Music. *Address:* 22 Okotie-Eboh Street, South West Ikoyi, Lagos, Nigeria.

LAWSON, Robert Ian, b. 24 Feb. 1925, China. Geologist. m. Elizabeth Cameron Douglas, 1956. *Education:* BSc, Edinburgh University, 1952. *Appointments:* Flying Officer and Pilot, Royal Air Force, 1943-47; Geological Survey of Great Britain, Institute of Geological Sciences, 1953-. *Memberships:* Fellow of Geological Society; Mineralogical Society; Canadian Mineralogical Association. *Publications:* Scientific papers on geology, geochemistry, mineralogy, x-ray analysis and computer applications. *Hobbies:* Golf; Photography; Philately; Sport. *Address:* 36 Hillview Terrace, Corstorphine, Edinburgh, Scotland.

LAWTON, Frank Ewart, b. 23 Oct. 1915, Crewe, Cheshire, England. Dental Surgeon. m. Muriel Leonora Bacon, 26 Apr. 1943, 1 son, 1 daughter. *Education:* BDS., (1st class Hons.), University of Liverpool, UK, 1932-37; DDS., 1948, FDSRCS. Eng., 1948, Northwestern University, Chicago, USA, 1947-48. *Appointments:* General Dental Practice, 1937-39; Lecturer, Senior Lecturer, 1939-56, Professor, Operative Dental Surgery, 1956-80, Director of Dental Education, 1957-80, University of Liverpool, UK; President, General Dental Council, 1979-. *Memberships:* President, 1973-74, British Dental Association; Editor, International

Dental Journal, International Dental Federation, 1963-81. *Publications:* Editor: Stones Oral and Dental Diseases, 1966; Contributor to Scientific Journals. *Honours:* Knight Bachelor, 1981; Honorary Membership, British Dental Association, 1980; Honorary DDSc., University of Newcastle, UK, 1981. *Hobby:* Music. *Address:* 55 Woolton Hill Road, Liverpool L25 6HU, England.

LEACH, Grahame Anthony, b. 19 Jan. 1954, London, UK. Research Chemist. m. Eleonora Christine Zaba, 29 Aug. 1975. *Education:* BSc, 1975, University of Bristol, 1972-75; PhD, 1978, DIC, 1978, Imperial College, University of London, 1975-79. *Appointments:* Post-Doctoral Research Assistant, Imperial College, 1978-79; Development Chemist, Berol Ltd., London, 1979-80, B.O.C. (Techsep), London, 1980-. *Memberships:* MRSC. *Publications:* Various chemical publications in professional journals. *Hobbies:* Wine; Music; Reading; Snooker. *Address:* 52 Luther Close, Edgware, Middx. HA8 8YY, England.

LEACH, Philip Stephen, b. 20 Apr. 1940, Manchester, England. m. Elizabeth Susan Warrior, 4 Oct. 1969, 2 sons, 1 daughter. *Education:* BSc., Eng., Imperial College, London, UK, 1961; Associate of City and Guilds Institute, 1961; Associateship, National College of Heating, Ventilating, Refrigeration and Fan Engineering, 1962. *Appointments:* Design Engineer, 1961-68, Branch Manager, 1968-76, Yorkshire Area Manager, 1976-78, Hader Young Limited, UK; Managing Director, Haden Engineering Pty. Limited, Australia, 1978-. *Memberships:* Chartered Institution of Building Services; Past Chairman of Yorkshire Branch of Heating and Ventilating Contractors Association. *Hobbies:* Sailing; Manual work. *Address:* 313 Woolooware Road, Cronulla, New South Wales 2230, Australia.

LEAL, Joseph Lewis Michael, b. 4 Apr. 1910, Vacoas, Mauritius. Director, Chairman. m. 2 sons, 1 daughter. *Education:* Assistant Pharmacist & Chemist Diploma, Royal College, Curepipe, Mauritius, 1932. *Appointments:* Founder & Director, Mauritius Union Assurance, 1948; Director, Rose Hill Transport, 1957-; Founder & Managing Director, L'Express Newspaper, 1961-; Chairman, Rose Hill Co-operative Stores, 1956-64, Cercle de Rose Hill, 1956-57; Town Council, Beau Bassin/Rose Hill, 1953-63, Vice-Chairman, 1956 & 1960, Chairman, 1958. Treasurer Mauritius Labour Party, 1960-70; Member of the Legislative Assembly, 1963; Parliamentary Secretary, Ministry of Education and Works, 1965; Minister of State (Budget), 1966, (Development), 1967, (Works), 1968-70, Chairman, Development Works Corporation, 1971-81; Vice-Chairman, Mauritius Union Assurance, 1980. *Memberships:* Cercle de Rose Hill; Cercle de Beau Bassin. *Honours:* Commandant Det. No 7 British Red Cross, 1942; Commander of the Order of St Michael and St George, 1980. *Hobbies:* Hunting; Fishing. *Address:* Couvent de Lorette Street, Curepipe Road, Mauritius.

LEAN, George Beattie, b. 14 Jan. 1913, Bellingen, NSW. Chartered Accountant, Director. m. Olwen Heather Ayling, 30 Dec. 1935, 1 son, 2 daughters. *Education:* Bachelor of Economics, Sydney University, 1934; Chartered Accountant (FCA), 1935. *Appointments:* Ballard Way & Hardie (now Coopers & Lybrand), Chartered Accountants, 1929-36; Chartered Accountant on own account, 1936-58; Executive Director, 1960-74, Chief Executive, 1974-78, Chairman, 1978-, Peko-Wallsend Ltd. *Memberships:* Director of Australian Mining Industry Council, Australian Korea Business Cooperation Committee; Council Bismuth Institute; Australian-Japan Business 'Cooperation Committee; International House, University of Sydney; Council, Trade Development Council. *Hobbies:* Poll-Hereford Cattle Stud; Gardening. *Address:* 14 Dunois Street, Longueville, 2066, Sydney, Australia.

LEATHER, Edwin Hartley Cameron (Sir), b. 22 May 1919, Toronto, Canada. Author. m. Sheila A A Greenlees, 9 Mar. 1940, 2 daughters. *Education:* Royal Military College of Canada. Directorships: N M Rothschild Bermuda and other Companies; Member of Parliament, 1950-64; Governor and C-in-C, Bermuda, 1973-77. *Memberships:* President, Institute of Marketing, 1960-65; Executive Committee and Board of Finance, Conservative Party, 1965-72; Chairman, N U of Conservative Associations, 1969-70. *Publications:* The Vienna Elephant; The Mozart Score; The Duveen Letter. *Hon-*

ours: Knight Bachelor, 1962; KCMG., 1974; KCVO., 1975; Knight of St. John, 1973; Hon. LL.D., Bath University, 1975; Gold Medal, National Institute of Social Services, New York, 1975. *Hobbies:* Reading; Music; Gardening. *Address:* Margrove View, Paget, Bermuda.

LEBLANC, Fernand E, b. Montreal, Quebec, Canada. Senator. m. Claire LeFrancois, 16 June 1945, 2 sons. *Education:* M.Com., C.A., 1945. *Appointments:* Chartered Accountant. *Honours:* Commander-Ligue Universelle du Bien Public, 1977. *Hobby:* Golf. *Address:* 350 Côte Vertu, Apt. 522, Ville St-Laurent, Quebec, H4N 1E2, Canada.

LECCIA, Jean-Baptiste Paul André, b. 29 June 1943, Settat, Morocco. University Professor. m. Sylviane Perdomo, 20 May 1970, 2 sons. *Education:* Diploma in Political Science, 1964; Diploma of Higher Studies in Public Law, 1966; Licentiate in History (BA equiv.), 1968; Masters in Geography, 1976. *Appointments:* Deputy Director, Centre for Administrative Training & Specialisation, Dakar, Senegal, 1967; Deputy Director, School of Art & Architecture, Marseilles, France, 1968; Director of Architecture & Town-Planning for the South West of the Ivory Coast, 1970; Professor School of Architecture, Marseilles, 1974; Lawyer at the Bar, Marseilles, 1976; Professor, Institute of International Co-operation, University of Ottawa, 1980. *Memberships:* UNESCO Club, Aix-en-Provence; Groupe Tiers-Monde, Marseilles; Association for Environmental Development, Corse à Corte; Franco-Canadian Office of Management & Engineering. *Publications:* Les Parcs Nationaux dans le Monde, Le Sud Ouest Ivoirien, Les Villes du Tiers-Monde, all memoirs. *Honours:* Knight, Ivory Coast Order of Merit. *Hobbies:* Sport; History; Cookers. *Address:* 33 Bd Challier de Nere, 1300 8 Marseille, France.

LECHTE, Ruth Elizabeth, b. 8 Aug. 1932, Melbourne, Australia. South Pacific Area Director, World YWCA. *Education:* Teaching Degree, Science, Melbourne, Australia, 1950-52; Post Graduate Diploma, Youth Leadership Training, Birmingham, UK, 1958-59. *Appointments:* Science Subjects, Secondary School, Melbourne, Australia, 1952-57; Volunteer work, (then) British Solomon Islands Protectorate, 1953-54; Science subjects, Lady Margaret School, Fulham, UK, 1958; Youth Work, Kingsley Hall Community Centre, Bromley by Bow, London, UK, 1959-60; Library of Toronto University, Ontario, Canada, 1961; National Executive Director, YWCA of Fiji, Suva, Fiji, 1962-73; South Pacific Area Director, World YWCA, Nadi, Fiji, 1973-81. *Memberships:* Executive, Pacific Conference of Churches; Vice-President, Fiji Amateur Sports Association; Manager, Fiji South Pacific Games Team, 1969; Extension Services Committee, University of South Pacific; Fiji National Youth Council; Fiji National Council of Women; Fiji Council of Social Services; South Pacific Commission. *Publications:* Articles in various journals including: Appropriate Technology Case Study Samoa; Socio-Economic Implications of Aid for Women; The European and Part-European Communities; Women's Role in Development; People Politics in the Pacific; Youth Work and Urbanisation. *Honours:* Fiji Independence Medal, 1970; Jubilee Scholarship, Selly Oak, Birmingham, UK, 1957. *Hobbies:* Environment and ecology; Sport; Reefs (snorkeling); Bird watching; Gardening; Applications of Appropriate technology. *Address:* 94 Kennedy Avenue, Nadi, Fiji.

LE CLAIR, Maurice, b. 19 June 1927, Sayabec, Quebec, Canada. Corporate Vice-President. m. Pauline Heroux, 22 Nov. 1952, 2 sons, 4 daughters. *Education:* BSc, 1947, MD, 1951, McGill University, Montreal; MSc, University Minnesota, 1958; MD, Sherbrooke University, 1970; DSc, McGill University, 1971; LL.D., McMaster University, Hamilton, 1974. *Appointments:* Dean, University Sherbrooke Medical Faculty, 1968-70; Deputy Minister Health, 1970-74, Science & Technology, 1974-76, Treasury Board, 1976-79, Federal Government of Canada; Corporate Vice-President, 1979-, Senior Corporate Vice-President, 1981, Canadian National Railways. *Memberships:* Fellow, Royal College Physicians & Surgeons Canada, American College of Physicians. *Memberships:* 120 publications in the fields of medicine & administration. *Honours:* Officer, Order of Canada, 1980. *Hobby:* Clock & Watch reparis. *Address:* 53 Maplewood, Outremont, Quebec, Canada, H2V 2L9.

LE CREN, Eric David, b. 12 Oct. 1922, Fairlie, New Zealand. Biological research. m. Katherine L D Woolham, 4 Oct. 1951. *Education:* BA, 1943, MA, 1946, Trinity College, Cambridge University, 1940-42; MS, 1947, University of Wisconsin, USA, 1946-47. *Appointments:* Freshwater Biological Association: Research Assistant, 1942-46, Zoologist, 1947-62, Officer in-charge, River Laboratory, 1962-73, Director, 1973-. Research Assistant, University of Wisconsin, 1946-47. *Memberships:* Fellow, Institute of Biology, 1965; British Ecological Society, Honorary Secretary, 1954-64, Vice-President, 1965-67; Zoological Society of London; Fisheries Society of British Isles, President, 1978-; Cumbria Trust for Nature Conservation, Chairman, 1900-. *Publications:* About 35 papers in scientific journals on fish ecology etc.; Joint Editor of Le Cren, E.D. & Holdgate, M W (Eds) 1962; The exploration of natural animal populations; Le Cren, E.D. & Lowe-McConnell (Eds), The functioning of freshwater ecosystems. *Hobbies:* Photography; Romanesque architecture; Wildlife conservation. *Address:* The Coach House of Oakland, Windermere, Cumbria, LA23 IAR, England.

LEE, Alvin A, b. 30 Sept. 1930, Woodville, Ontario. President, Vice-Chancellor of McMaster University and Professor of English. m. Annie Hope Arnott, 21 Dec. 1957, 5 daughters. *Education:* BA, Arts, University of Toronto, 1953; Divinity, Victoria University, 1957; MA, 1958, PhD, 1961, University of Toronto. *Appointments:* Teaching Fellow, English, University of Toronto, 1957-59; Assistant Professor, English, 1960-65, Associate Professor, 1966-70, Assistant Dean, School of Graduate Studies, 1968-71, Professor, English, 1970-, Dean, School of Graduate Studies, 1971-73, Vice-President (Academic), 1974-79, President and Vice-Chancellor, 1980-, McMaster University. *Memberships:* Association of Canadian Teachers of English, 1974, Universities and Colleges of Canada, 1980-; Community Education Coordinating Committee, 1981; Centre of Applied Research and Engineering Design, Inc. and Canadian Institute of Metalworking, 1980; Chedoke-McMaster Hospitals, 1980; Council of Ontario Universities, 1980-; Council of Ontario Universities Holdings Limited, 1981; Hamilton Association for the Advancement of Literature, Science and Art, Honorary President, 1980; McMaster University Alumni Council, 1980; Mediaeval Academy of America, 1974; Modern Languages Association, 1974-80; Operation Lifeline, Honorary Member, 1980; Hamilton-Wentworth Lung Association, 1980; Health Sciences Liaison Committee, 1980; Director, Nuclear Activation Services, 1980; Royal Botanical Gardens, 1980; President, McMaster University English Society, 1981. James Reaney. Twayne's World Author Series, 1968; The Guest-Hall of Eden (Four Essays), 1972. *Honours:* Sanford Gold Medal in Divinity, Victoria University, 1957; Canada Council Senior Fellowship, 1966-67; Member, Royal Commonwealth Society, London; Canada Council Leave Fellowship, 1971-72; Social Sciences and Humanities Research Council Leave Fellowship, 1979-80. *Hobbies:* Gardening; Swimming; Hiking; Canoeing; Running; Windsurfing; Theatre; Music; Reading. *Address:* Stormont, West Flamborough, Ontario, Canada, L0R 2K0.

LEE, Arthur Geoffrey, b. 22 Sept. 1928, Sydney, Australia. Company Director. m. Christine M, 30 Oct. 1953, 1 daughter. *Education:* Sydney Grammar School. *Appointments:* Chairman & Managing Director, Halmac Services Limited. *Memberships:* Fellow, Australian Institute of Management. *Honours:* Scout Association Silver Kangaroo, 1980; International Commissioner of the Scout Association of Australia. *Hobbies:* Ocean Yacht Racing; Scouting. *Address:* 73 Yarranabbe Road, Darling Point, New South Wales, 2027, Australia.

LEE, David John, b. 28 Aug. 1930, Swanley, Kent. Consultant; Chartered Engineer. m. Helga Bass, 14 Dec. 1957, 1 son, 1 daughter. *Education:* Brixton School of Building, 1946-47; BSc, Tech. (Building), Manchester College of Technology, 1947-50; DIC (Concrete Technology), Imperial College, 1953-54. *Appointments:* Royal Engineers, 1950-52; Re-inforced Concrete Steel Company Limited, 1952-53, 54-55; Managing Partner & Managing Director, Maunsell Consultants Limited, 1956-. *Memberships:* Fellowship of Engineering, 1980-; FICE, MConsE, FRSA; Concrete Society, Vice-President, 1977-78; Committee, Department of Transport ; BSI; South Bank Polytechnic;

IABSE; Major, E & RSC RE. *Publications:* Theory & Practice of Bearings and Expansion Joints for Bridges, 1971; Chapters on Bridges in Civil Engineering Reference Books, 1975, and in Developments in Pre-stressed Concrete, 1978. *Honours:* George Stephenson Medal, 1969; Oscar Faber Award, 1970; Medal of the Federation Internationale de la Précontrainte, 1974. *Hobbies:* Art; Music. *Address:* 26 Paget Gardens, Chislehurst, Kent, England.

LEE, David, Nai-Wai, b. 18 Aug. 1919, Shanghai. Managing Director. m. Lucille Wang Hsieh Tsung, 21 Nov. 1943, 2 sons, 1 daughter. *Education:* BSc, Textile Engineering, Nantung University, Shanghai, 1941; Industrial Management Course, Columbia University, USA, 1947. *Appointments:* Chairman & Managing Director: South Pacific Textile Industries Bhd; Soutex Sdn Bhd; Knitex Sdn Bhd; Vincent Industries (M) Sdn Bhd, Malaysia; South East Metal Industries Pte Limited, Singapore; Naiwai (Pte) Limited, Singapore. *Memberships:* Founder Chairman, Singapore Industrial Promotion Board, 1957-58; Chairman, Singapore Manufacturers Association, 1956-60; President, National Chamber of Malaysian Manufacturers, 1963-65; Founder Chairman, Malaysian Textile Manufacturers Association, 1974-75; Textile Institute, Manchester, United Kingdom. *Publications:* Chief Editor, Voice of Ahuttle, a textile magazine, 1940 & 1941. *Hobbies:* Music; Golf. *Address:* 34 Swiss Club Road, Singapore 1128, Republic of Singapore.

LEE, Henry Hau Shik, b. 19 Nov. 1901, Hong Kong. Banker. m. 1929, 4 sons, 1 daughter. *Education:* St Johns College, Cambridge University, Economic and Law, BA, 1924, MA, 1978. *Appointments:* Chief of Passive Defence Forces, Kuala Lumpur, 1941; Colonel, 1942-45; Co-founder, Alliance Party, 1949; Minister of Transport, 1953-56; Minister of Finance, 1956-59; Director and Vice Chairman, Golden Castle Finance Corporation Limited, Singapore; Vice Chairman, Institute Bank, Malaysia, 1977-; Chairman of several companies including: China Press Limited, Kuala Lumpur; Development and Commercial Bank Limited, Kuala Lumpur; D and C Nomura Merchant Bankers; Financial and Investment Services for Asia Limited, Hong Kong; On Tai Development Sdn Berhad, Kuala Lumpur. *Memberships:* Fellow, Royal Economic Society, England; Chinese Tin Mines Rehabilitation Loans Board, 1946-59; Financial Mission to London, 1957; Malayan Union Advisory Council, 1946-47; Past President of: All Malaya Chinese Mining Association; Associated Chinese Chambers of Commerce, Malaya and Singapore; Oxford and Cambridge Society; Royal Commonwealth Society; United Lee's Association. *Honours:* JP, 1938; CBE, 1948; KBE, 1957; SMN, 1959; Chancellor, 1978. *Hobbies:* Riding; Golf; Tennis. *Address:* 22 Jalan Langgak Golf, Kuala Lumpur, Malaya.

LEE, Hun Hoe, b. 27 Sept. 1925, Alor Star, Kedah. Chief Justice, Borneo. m. Freda Wong Siew Geck, September, 1957, 4 daughters. *Education:* BA, University of Southampton, 1955; Barrister at Law, Lincoln's Inn, London, 1956. *Appointments:* Stipendiary Magistrate, 1956; Crown Counsel, 1960; Registrar of High Court, Borneo, 1964; Judicial Commissioner, 1965; Judge of High Court, Borneo, 1965; Chief Justice, Borneo, 1974. *Memberships:* Sarawak Lodge; Advisory Editorial Board of Malayan Law Journal; Judicial and Legal Service Commission. *Publications:* Cases on Native Customary Law in Sabah; Cases on Native Customary Law in Sarawak. *Honours:* Ahli Darja Kinabalu, 1968; Panglima Gemilang Darja Kinabalu, 1972; Panglima Mangku Negara, 1974; Panglima Negara Bintang Sarawak, 1975. *Hobbies:* Gardening; Tai Chi; Reading; Golf. *Address:* Sri Belian, Rodway Road, Kuching, Sarawak.

LEE, Jack Austell, b. 15 June 1921, Wellington, New Zealand. Justice of the Supreme Court. m. Nancy Rosemary Arnott, 8 July 1978. *Education:* BA., 1941, Bachelor of Laws (1st Class Hons.), 1945, Sydney University, Australia. *Appointments:* Solicitor, 1945-46; Barrister, 1946-66; QC., for: State of New South Wales, Australia, 1962, State of Victoria, Australia, 1965; Justice of Supreme Court of New South Wales, Australia, 1966-; Lecturer in Procedure, Sydney University Law School, Australia, 1963-66. *Memberships:* President: Judge Rainbow Memorial Appeal Fund, St. George Area, N S W Scout Association; Deputy Chairman, Institute of Criminology, Sydney

University, Australia; Consultant, Parramatta Recidivist Group, Parramatta Gaol; Executive member, International Law Association; Past President, New South Wales Branch, Australian Crime Prevention Council; Past Director, Sutherland Hospital; Past Councellor, Council of Alexander Mackie College of Advanced Education; Counsel for New South Wales Government in Bulli Mine Enquiry, 1964; Australian Pioneers Club. *Publications:* Lee on Stamp and Estate Duties; Hammond Davidsons Law and Practice relating to Lndlord and Tenant in New South Wales (with E C Lewis). *Honours:* Silver Jubilee Medal, 1977. *Hobbies:* Swimming; Skiing; Jogging; Yachting; Study of German. *Address:* Supreme Court, King Street, Sydney, Australia.

LEE, Kenneth Ernest, b. 7 May 1927, Wanganui, New Zealand. Research Scientist. m. Norma Engrid Brian, 25 Aug. 1951, 2 son, 1 daughter. *Education:* Wairarapa College 1940-44; BSc, NZ 1948; MSc(Hons.) 1949; DSc 1959. *Appointments:* Soil Biologist, New Zealand Soil Bureau, DSIR 1949-62; Head, Soil Biology Section, NZ 1962-65; Head, Soil Zoology Section, CSIRO, Division of Soils, Australia 1965-; Member, Royal Society London, Solomon Islands Expedition 1965; Leader, Royal Society/Percy Sladen Expedition to the New Hebrides 1971. *Memberships:* International Society Soil Science; International Committee of Soil Zoologists; New Zealand Ecological Society; Royal Society of South Australia; Soil Science Society of South Australia; British Ecological Society; New Zealand Society of Soil Science; Australian Entomological Society. *Publications:* The earthworm fauna of New Zealand, 1959; Termites and soils, 1971; Editor, with E J H Corner, Report of the 1971 Royal Society/Percy Sladen Expedition to the New Hebrides, 1975; 45 scientific papers in various journals and conference proceedings. *Honours:* New Zealand Association of Scientists Research Medallist 1959; Nuffield Foundation Travelling Fellow in Natural Sciences 1961-62; Fellow of the Explorers Club, New York 1979. *Hobbies:* Photography; Cabinet making. *Address:* 1 Mariner Street, Linden Park, SA 5065, Australia.

LEE, Lam Thye, b. 30 Dec. 1946, Ipoh, Perak, Malaysia. Member of Parliament. m. Yap Kooi Hong, 7 June 1975, 2 sons. *Appointments:* Politician. *Memberships:* Deputy Chairman, Consumer Association of the Federal Territory. *Hobbies:* Fishing; Motoring. *Address:* 44 Jalan Pria Tiea, Taman Maluri, Kuala Lumpur, Malaysia.

LEE, Rance Pui-leung, b. 1 Aug. 1943, Guangdong, China. University Teacher. m. Kam-sar Pang, 4 Feb. 1972, 1 son, 1 daughter. *Education:* Bachelor of Social Science, The Chinese University of Hong Kong, 1965; Doctor of Philosophy, The University of Pittsburgh, USA, 1968. *Appointments:* Research Fellow, Department of Behavioural Sciences, Harvard University School of Public Health, 1967-68; Lecturer in Sociology, 1968-75, Director of Social Research Centre, 1973-, Senior Lecturer in Sociology, 1975-80, Reader in Sociology and Dean of Social Science, 1980-, The Chinese University of Hong Kong. *Memberships:* Hong Kong Branch of the Society of Community Medicine; Association for Asian Studies; American Sociological Association; International Sociological Association; American Statistical Association; Population Association of America; American Psychological Association; Committee for Comparative Behavioral Studies in Population; Law and Society Association. *Publications:* Six books; 55 professional articles in the areas of health care, mental illness, effects of high-density living, corruption and other social problems. *Hobbies:* Reading; Swimming; Table Tennis. *Address:* 5A Staff Residence No. 1, The Chinese University of Hong Kong, Shatin, NT, Hong Kong.

LEE, Soo Ann, b. 21 Mar. 1939, Singapore. Economist. 1 son, 1 daughter. *Education:* BA, 1959; BA, with Honours, 1960; MA, 1961; PhD, 1969. *Appointments:* Assistant Secretary, 1960, Director of Projects, 1967-68, Ministry of Finance; Assistant Lecturer in Economics, 1961-64, Lecturer in Economics, 1964-70, Senior Lecturer in Economics, 1971-74, Associate Professor in Economics, 1974-80, Professor of Economics, 1981-, University of Singapore; Deputy Director, 1978, Director, School of Accountancy and Business Administration, 1979-80; Dean, Faculty of Accountancy and Business Administration, 1980-, Director School of Management, 1980-, National University of Singapore.

Memberships: Vice-President, Economics Society of Singapore; President, Boys' Brigade, Singapore. *Publications:* Economic Growth and the Public Sector in Malaya and Singapore, 1974; Singapore Goes Transnational, 1977; Economic Manning and Project Evaluation, 1977; Industrialisation in Singapore, 1974. *Honours:* Ford Foundation Fellowship, USA, 1960-61; Fulbright Travel Grant, 1968-69; Harvard Teaching Institute Research Fellow, 1976-77. *Hobbies:* Chess; Theology; Music; Jogging; Swimming. *Address:* KE Hall at Kent Ridge, Lower Kent Ridge Road, Singapore.

LEE, QC, William Charles, b. 1 May 1929, Gayndah, Queensland Australia. Queens Counsel; Senior Master of the Supreme Court of Queensland. m. Iris Joan Cluff 5 May 1952, 3 sons, 1 daughter. *Education:* Schooling in Gayndah, Maryborough and Bowen; Queensland University: Diploma of Commerce 1959; Associate in Accountancy; 1951; Bachelor of Commerce 1961; Bachelor of Laws 1965; Australian Society of Accountants 1956; FASA 1980; Data Processing, Computers, Queensland Institute of Technology 1977. *Appointments:* Audit Clerk, Chief Railway Auditers Office, Brisbane, 1945-49; Accountant and Office Manager, Steel Company, Queensland 1949-52; Accountant Manager and Director, Group of Companies in Darwin 1952-60; Registered Taxation Agent, 1953-63; Law Clerk, Cannan and Peterson, Brisbane 1963; Associate to Chief Justice of Supreme Court, Queensland 1963-66; Private Practice 1965-; Crown Prosecutor 1973; Queens Counsel 1977-; First and Senior Master of the Supreme Court of Queensland 1980-. *Memberships:* Specific Learning Difficulties Association; Law Council of Australia representative, ACRUPTC; Church of England Grammar School, Brisbane Parents and Friends Association; Grazing Clubs; Tattersalls; St Lucias Club. *Publications:* The Role of Masters in Supreme Court Practice, 1981; A Paper delivered at 21st Legal Symposium of Queensland Law Society and Queensland Bar Association, describing in detail the nature of the office of master, its origins, reasons for creation, jurisdiction powers and role. *Honours:* Dux. Bowen State High School 1944; King Scott Award, 1947; John Hughes Wilkinson Memorial Prize in Law 1965; Virgil Power Prize in Law 1965; Queen's Counsel 1977; Fellow Australian Society of Accountants 1980; First Master of Supreme Court of Queensland 1980. *Hobbies:* Agriculture and Grazing; Movie Photography. *Address:* 9 Carmody Road, St Lucia, Brisbane, Queensland, Australia.

LEELAKRISHNAN, P, b. 1 Nov. 1935, Kerala. Lawyer. m. Dr. Kanakam, 23 Apr. 1964, 1 son. *Education:* BA, Kerala, 1955; LLB, Aligarh, 1957; MA, Political Science, 1957; LLM in Adminstrative Law and Constitutional Law, 1968; PhD, London, 1975. *Appointments:* Lawyer, 1962-68; Lecturer, Universities of Kerala and Cochin, 1969-76; Reader in Law, University of Cochin, 1976-79; Professor of Law, University of Cochin, 1980-. *Memberships:* Indian Law Institute; Indian Institute of Public Administration; Kerala History Association. *Publications:* Papers: Best Judgment in Sales Tax Assessment; Reasons for Administrative Orders; Bias and Administrative Power; Property and Social Control; Statutory Control of Environmental Protection; Can Rule Interfere with Discretion?; Book: Legal Aspects of Stage Carriage Licensing in India, 1979. *Honours:* Cullen Law Prize 1968. *Hobbies:* Reading; Chatting; Walking. *Address:* "Skyam", B.M.C. Post, Cochin 682021, India.

LEE MARTIN, Geoffrey, b. 18 Aug. 1927, Christchurch, New Zealand. Journalist, Chairman of Directors, Hutchinson Public Relations Property Limited. m. (1) 5 daughters, (2) Janice Wilson Power, 17 Dec. 1969, 1 daughter. *Education:* Auckland University; Melbourne University. *Appointments:* New Zealand Herald; Melbourne Herald; London Daily Telegraph; Founded Hutchinson Public Relations Property Limited, Sydney, Australia, 1970-. *Memberships:* Executive member, and Past President, Auckland Journalists' Association; Director, International Nippon, Australia, New Zealand Club, Sydney; Journalists' Club, Sydney. *Honours:* Baird Award, 1968. *Hobbies:* Writing; Skiing; Mountain climbing; Motor racing. *Address:* 126 West Street, Crows Nest, Sydney, New South Wales, Australia.

LEES, Leonard H, b. 19 Sept. 1941, Birmingham, England. Engineer. m. 1 son, 1 daughter. *Education:* BSc Elec. Eng. 1965; MSc (Control) 1966; PhD (Control), University of Aston, Birmingham, 1968. *Appointments:* Laboratory Assistant: Dunlop Rubber Company Limited, Birmingham, England, 1958-60; Student Apprentice, Joseph Lucas Limited, Birmingham, England, 1960-65; Research Student, University of Aston, Birmingham, 1965-68; Assistant Professor, University of Windsor, Ontario, Canada, 1968-71; Senior Lecturer/Professor, University of Witwatersrand, Johnnesburg, South Africa, 1972-74; Visiting Professor, University of McMaster, Canada, 1974-75; Head EE Department, Hong Kong Polytechnic, Hong Kong, 1975. *Memberships:* FIEE, CEng; PEng, Ontario; MIEEE; SMAIIE; FHKIE. *Publications:* Over 20 technical publications. *Hobbies:* Chess; Fly Fishing; Music. *Address:* Flat A6, 9 Shouson Hill Road, Hong Kong.

LEE-STEERE (Sir) Ernest Henry, b. 22 Dec. 1912. Company Director. m. Jessica, 7 Jan. 1942. *Education:* Hale School, Perth; St. Peter's College, Adelaide. *Appointments:* Army-Air Liaison Gp. AIR, SWPA, 1944-45; Government Director, Belele Pastoral Company, 1952-; W.A. Soil Conservation Advisory Committee, 1955-72; Member, Princ. A'sian Bd, 1962-; Dir. Elder Smith Goldsbrough Mort, W.A. 1962; Cr. Fed. Advisory Cl. CSIRO, 1962-71; Chairman, WATC, 1963-; Vice-President RFDS, W A; Chairman, State Committee CSIRO, 1962-72; Chairman, W.A. Woollen Mills, 1964-76; President, Pastoralists and Graziers' Assn. of W.A., 1959-72; Lord Mayor of Perth, W.A., 1972-78. *Memberships:* President, National Trust, W.A., 1962-72; Chairman, W.A. Bd. AMP Society; Chairman, Kia Ora Gold Corporation NL and Uranium and Nickel Exploration NL; Chairman, General Corporation of Australia Limited, Group, Hawkstone Investments Limited; Heytesbury Holdings Limited. *Honours:* KBE. Hobby: Polo. *Address:* 26 Odern Crescent, Swanbourne, Western Australia 6010.

LEFAIVRE, Denis, b. 6 May 1949, Québec City, Québec, Canada. Physicist. *Education:* BSc Physics, Sherbrooke University, 1971; MSc Atomic and Molecular Physics, 1973; PhD Atomic and Molecular Physics, Laval University, 1978. *Appointments:* Substitute Professor, 1977-79, Research-Professor, Université du Québec à Rimouski, Québec, 1979-80; NSERC, Postdoctoral Fellowship, Bedford Institute of Oceanography, N.-S., 1980-82. *Memberships:* Laval University Council, 4-76, Executive Council, 1975-76; Union Grad. Insc. Laval: President, 1974-75, Vice-President, 1975-76, President, 1977; CMOS; Secretary, Halifax Center, 1980-81; CAP; ACFAS. *Publications:* Papers in journals on Atomic and Molecular Physics. Hobby: Sailing. *Address:* 65 Primrose Street, Apt. 222, Dartmouth, N.-S., B3A 4E1, Canada.

LEGERE, Martin J, b. 17 Nov. 1916. Director. m. Anita Godin, 5 June 1950, 3 sons, 1 daughter. *Education:* Caraquet High School; St Francis Xavier University, Antigonish, N.S.; Faculty of Social Sciences, Laval University, Quebec. *Appointments:* Fieldman, Co-Operative Movement, St Francis Xavier University of Antigonish, N.S. 1938-40; Auditor, Credit Unions and Co-Operatives, N.B. Province, 1940-46; Municipal Councillor, 1950-55; Treasurer of Children's Aid Society of Gloucester County, 1948-66; President of Catholic Youth Association, 1940-50; Director, The National Society of Acadians, 1955-60; Director, Maritime Provinces Board of Trade, 1954-62; President, Caraquet School Board, 1960-65; Vice-President, "l'Evangeline", 1950-65, and 1980-; Director, Atlantic Provinces Economic Council, 1956-62; Advisory Committee, Community Development Corporation, 1965-66; Director of La Caisse Populaire de Caraquet, 1938-71; President, New Brunswick Industrial Finance Board, 1960-76; Director, Caraquet Hospital, 1963-74; General Manager, La Fédération des Caisses Populairs Acadiennes Limitée, 1946-; General Manager La Sociéte d'Assurance des Caisses Populaires Acadiennes, 1948-. *Memberships:* I'Union Coopérative Acadienne; La Societé des Artisans; Le Conseil Canadien de la Coopération; La Coopérative de Caraquet; La Chambre de Commerce de Caraquet; Co-operative Fire and Casualty Insurance; Co-operative Life Insurance; International Co-Operative Alliance; La Compagnie de Gestion Atlantique Limitée; Les Oeuvres de Presse Acadienne; Le Conseil de Vie Française; La Villa Beauséjour de Caraquet; Member, La Compagnie des Cent Associes, 1980; Association Internationale des Parlementaires Francophones, 1980. *Honours:* Awarded, Bene Merentis, by His Holiness Pope Pius XII,

1950; Honorary Doctor in Social Sciences, Sacred Heart University, Bathurst, 1953; Honorary Doctor in Administrative Sciences, Moncton University, 1971; Hon. Doctor of Laws, St Francis Xavier University, Antigonish, N.S., 1974; Officer of the Order of Canada, 1974; *Hobbies:* Acadian History; Sports. *Address:* 312 Ouest, Boulevard St-Pierre, Caraquet, N.B. E0B 1K0 Canada.

LEGGE, Bruce Jarvis, b. 20 Jan. 1919, Toronto, Canada. Barrister. m. Laura Louise Down, 21 July 1950, 2 sons, 1 daughter. *Education:* Bachelor of Arts, University of Toronto, 1941; Osgoode Hall Law School, Called to the Bar of Ontario 1949. *Appointments:* District Solicitor, Department of Veterans' Affairs, 1950-65; Chairman, Ontario Workmen's Compensation Board, 1965-73; Chairman, Commission of Enquiry into Workmen's Compensation in the Yukon and Northwest Territories 1966, and Compensation Board of Enquiry, 1973; Governor's Commission to Study Workmen's Compensation Laws, State of New Jersey, USA 1973; Partner, Legge & Legge with Laura Legge, QC. *Memberships:* Chairman of the Board, Canada Safety Council, 1974; President, Canada Safety Council, 1972-73; President: Medico-Legal Society of Toronto, 1973; The Good Neighbours' Club for Aged Men, 1971-73; International Association of Industrial Accident Boards and Commissions 1971-72; Royal Canadian Military Institute, 1966-68; Royal Canadian Legion, Fort York Branch; The Empire Club of Canada; The Empire Club Foundation; Toronto Branch of the Royal Commonwealth Society; Ontario Committee, Army Benevolent Fund; Governor, Canadian Corps of Commissionaires; Phi Delta Phi International Legal Fraternity; The Canadian Institute of International Affairs; The Canadian Club; The Board of Trade of Metropolitan Toronto; The Arts and Letters Club; Canadian Institute of Strategic Studies; Confederation of Church and Business People. *Publications:* Reports on Workmen's compensation in the Northwest and Yukon Territories 1966; Draft Ordinance of the Northwest Territory on workmen's compensation, 1967, etc. *Honours:* ED 1956; QC 1960; Centennial Medal 1967; Canadian Forces Decoration 1968; Commander of the Order of St. John of Jerusalem 1981; CIOR 1972; Award of Merit, City of Toronto 1972; IAIABC 1973; Knight, 'Ordre Souverain et Militaire du Temple de Jerusalem', Oslo, Norway 1974; Silver Jubilee Medal 1977; Commander of the Order of Military Merit 1978; Certificate of Achievement, Reserve Officers Association of the USA 1978; Knight of Grace (KLJ), 1979; Honorary Life Member, Reserve Officers Association, USA 1980. *Address:* 301 Lonsdale Road, Toronto, Canada, M4V 1X3.

LEGUM, Colin, b. 3 Jan. 1919, Kestell, South Africa. Journalist; Writer; Editor. m. Margaret Roberts, 25 July 1960, 1 son, 3 daughters. *Education:* Kestell Government School, Orange Free State, South Africa. *Appointments:* Political and Parliament Correspondent, Sunday Express and Daily Express, Johannesburg, South Africa 1935-39; Editor, Forward and The Mineworker, Johannesburg, 1939-43; Illustrated Bulletin, 1943-42; The Observer, London; Associate Editor and Commonwealth Correspondent 1949-; Television and Publishing Consultant. *Memberships:* Tavistock Institute of Human Relations; South African Labour Party; Johannesbury City Councillor; Southern African Labour Congress; Trustee, African Education Trust; Africa Publications Trust; Commonwealth and Diplomatic Writers Association; Royal Institute of International Affairs. *Publications:* Must we lose Africa? 1954; Congo Disaster, 1960; Pan-Africanism: A Political Guide, 1962, 65; South Africa: Crisis for the West, 1964; Southern Africa: The Secret Diplomacy of Detente, 1975; Ethiopia: The Fall of Haile Selassies's Empire, 1975; After Angola: The War over Southern Africa, 1976; Conflict over the Horn of Africa, 1977; Editor: Praeger Library African Affairs, 1965-70; A Free and Balance Flow of International News 1978; The Western Crisis over Southern Africa 1979; The Horn of Africa in Continuing Crisis, 1979; Africa in the 1980s 1979; Communism in Africa 1979. *Hobbies:* African and Primitive Art; Africana Books. *Address:* 15 Denbigh Gardens, Richmond, Surrey, England.

LEIBLE, Ephraim, b. 14 Mar. 1944, Mogelov, Russia. Civil Engineer. m. Zipora 6 Sept. 1966, 1 son, 2 daughters. *Education:* BSc, Civil Engineering, Technion, The Technological Institute of Israel, Haifa. *Appointments:* Chief Engineer, Roichman (Schomron) Bros. Limited,

Hadera Israel, 1973-75; Chief Engineer (Roads) Solel Boneh, Nigeria Limited 1975-76; Managing Director, Solel Boneh, Nigeria Limited, Ibadan, Nigeria 1976-81. *Memberships:* The Association of Engineers and Architects in Israel; The Nigerian Society of Engineers. *Address:* 18 Akenzua Avenue, Ibadan, Nigeria.

LEIBLER, Isi Joseph, b. 10 Oct. 1934, Antwerp, Belgium. Company Director. m. Naomi Porush, 28 Dec. 1959, 3 sons, 1 daughter. *Education:* Bachelor of Arts (First Class Honours), Melbourne University, 1953-57. *Appointments:* Managing Director, A.S. Leibler and Company; Managing Director, Jetset Tours Pty. Ltd. *Memberships:* Australian Zionist Youth Council; Australian Union of Jewish Students; Victorian Jewish Board of Deputies; Executive Council of Australian Jewry; Member, Board of Presidents of Memorial Foundation for Jewish Culture; Director of Conferences, Jewish Material Claims Against Germany; Asia Pacific Jewish Association; Executive member, Chairman, Asia Pacific Branch of International Advisory Committee of World Jewish Congress. *Publications:* Soviet Jewry and Human Rights, 1964; Soviet Jewry and The Australian Left, 1965; The Case for Israel, 1972. *Honours:* Commander British Empire, 1977. *Hobbies:* Writing; Swimming. *Address:* 116 Kooyong Road, Caulfield North, Victoria 3161, Australia.

LEIGH-PEMBERTON, Robin, b. 5 Jan. 1927, Kent, England. Banker. m. Rosemary Davina Forbes 8 July 1953, 5 sons. *Education:* St Peter's Court 1936-40; Scholar, Eton College 1940-44; MA, Trinity College, Oxford 1948-50. *Appointments:* Birmid Qualcast Limited, Redland Limited, University Life Assurance Society until 1978; Medway Ports Authority 1974-76; Director: National Westminster Bank 1970-77; Chairman oif Birmid Qualcast Limited 1975-77; Chairman, National Westminster Bank Limited 1977; The Equitable Life Assurance Society 1979. *Memberships:* Brooks's; Cavalry and Guards; MCC; Leander; Union Club, New York. *Honours:* Vice Lord-Lieutenant of Kent, 1975. Hobby: Country Life. *Address:* Torry Hill, Sittingbourne, Kent, England.

LEIGHTON, Harold, b. 4 Nov. 1932, London. Ladies Hairdresser. m. 30 Apr. 1956, 2 sons. *Education:* Numerous National and International Awards and Diplomas, Hammersmith School of Arts and Craft. *Appointments:* Hairdresser with Vidal Sassoon, 1947-53, Romaires, Edgware Road and Dumas, Albermarle Street; Creative Director, Dorothy Grey, 1965; Creative Director, Speligman and Latz, International, 1968-74 and 79; Harrods Department Store, London, 1979-; Promotional Consultant, Glemby International, 1974-79; Promotional Consultant around the World. *Publications:* Hair Cutting for Everyone, 1977; The Complete Book of Haircare, 1980; *Honours:* Silver Rosebowl, Spring Fashions, Brighton Festival. *Hobbies:* Writing; Inventing; Keeping Fit; Hairdressing. *Address:* 17 St James Mans, West End Lane, London NW6, England.

LEITO, B M, b. 1923. Governor of Netherlands Antilles. m. Christine A M Koot, 1951, 1 son, 1 daughter. *Education:* Economist, University in Netherlands. *Appointments:* Junior Officer, Netherlands Antilles Department Social and Economic Affairs 1951; Officer, General Affairs Division of Island Territory of Curacao 1952; Officer, Finance Division 1953; Technical Training in Netherlands Antilles 1952-54; Board of Scientific Library Foundation 1953-70; Part-time Teacher, Secondary School 1954-58; Curacao Island Council 1955-63; Curacao and Bonaire School Advisory Board 1956-62; Member, Parliament, Netherlands Antilles 1959-62; Head, Finance Division of Island Territory of Curacao 1961-65; Director, Netherlands Antillean Department of Finance 1965-70; President, Supervisory Directors Bank of Netherlands Antilles 1965-70; Acting Governor 1969-70, Governor of Netherlands Antilles 1970-. *Memberships:* Working Committee Advis. N.A. Goverment; Netherlands Antilles delegation to Surinam 1965; Netherlands Antillean representative, Carib./L.A. Conference, Jamaica 1967; Chairman Socio-Economic Council, 1967-70; N.A. Goverment Delegation to Venezuela 1968; Acting Lieutenant-Governor, Island Territory of Curacao 1968-70; Queen Wilhemina Fund Foundation; Trustee, Prince Bernhard Fund (Neth-Antil) Foundation; Neth/Antil Red Cross; Board of Scientifice Library Foundation. *Honours:* Officer in Order of Oranje Nassau 1970; Gran. Cordon de la Orden del Libertador de Venezuela 1971; Gran. Cruz

Placa de Oro de la Orden del Merito de Duarte Sanchez y Mella, Dominican Rep. 1972; Knight in Order of Netherlands Lion 1973. *Address:* Governor's House, Fort Amsterdam No 1, Willemstad, Curacao, Netherlands Antilles.

LEIVERS, Peter Frederick, b. 21 Sept. 1923, Nottingham. Consulting Engineer. m. EA Taylor, 14 May 1949, 2 sons. *Education:* Trent Polytechnic, Nottingham. *Appointments:* Thomas Danks and Company Limited, Mech and Elec. Contractors, Nottingham, 1940-43; Mellor, Bromley and Company Limited, Air Conditioning Eng. Leic., 1948-49; EG Phillips Son and Partners, Consulting Eng. Nottm. 1949-55; NIFES Energy Conservation Engineers, Nottingham, 1955-65; PF Leivers, Consulting Engineers, Mech and Elect. Services, Nottingham, 1965-. *Memberships:* Chartered Engineer; Chartered Fuel Technologist; Regional Chairman, Chartered Institution of Building Services; Institution Council; Institution of Plant Engineers; Fellow, Chartered Institute of Building Services; Fellow, Institute of Energy; Fellow Institute of Plant Engineers; Fellow, Institute of Hospital Engineers. *Publications:* Technical Papers delivered; Oxford Clarendon Laboratory; Lanchester College of Technology, Coventry, and various refresher courses for Works Managers/Engineers in England and Wales. *Hobby:* Caravaning. *Address:* 198 Mansfield Road, Nottingham, NG1 3HX, England.

LEKALAKE, Lawrence Diphetogo, b. 5 Apr. 1933, Kuruman, South Africa. Assistant Group General Manager, Kgalegadi Management Services. m. Tutula, 31 Oct. 1959, 2 sons, 2 daughters. *Education:* BSc(Hons), 1958; UED, 1959. *Appointments:* Analytical Chemist, 1960-66; Permanent Secretary, Mines Commerce and Industry, 1967-71; Permanent Secretary, Ministry of Works Commonwealth, 1971-76; Director of Personnel, 1976-78; Assistant Group General Manager, Kgalegodi Management Services. *Memberships:* National Development Bank; Chairman, University Council; Maruapola Council; Chairman, Botswana Police Council, 1979-. *Honours:* Presidential Meritorious Service Award. *Hobbies:* Tennis; Table Tennis; Gardening; Cattle Ranching. *Address:* 297 Lengan Close, Graborone, Botswana.

LE MAY, Iain, b. 30 Oct. 1936, Helensburgh, Scotland. Engineer. m. Shona Kirk, 29 Aug. 1963, 3 daughters. *Education:* BSc., ARCST, 1957, PhD., 1963, University of Glasgow. *Appointments:* North British Locomotive Company, 1957; University of Glasgow, 1957-63; Technical Advisor, Mechanical and Metallurgical Engineering, Nuclebras, Empresas Brasileiras Nucleares, Rio de Janeiro, 1975-76; Assistant Professor, 1963-66, Associate Professor, 1966-71, Professor of Mechanical Engineering, 1971-, University of Saskatchewan; President, Metallurgical Consulting Services Limited, Saskatoon, 1978-. *Memberships:* Fellow, American Society for Metals; American Society of Mechanical Engineers; American Society for Testing and Materials; International Metallographic Society; National Association of Corrosion Engineers; Associacao Brasileira de Matais; Institution of Mechanical Engineers; Canadian Institute of Mining and Metallurgy; British Nuclear Energy Society. *Publications:* Numerous published papers; Several books including: I. Le May, 'Principles of Mechanical Metallurgy', 1981; 'Copper in Iron and Steel'; 'Advances in Materials Technology in the Americas—1980'; 'Materials Recovery and Utilization'; Vol. 2, 'Materials Processing and Performance', 1980. *Honours:* Montgomery Neilson Gold Medal and Prize, 1957; Professor Mellanby Prize, 1957; Fellow, ASM, 1977; Fellow, International Technology Institute, 1980; Centennial Award and Medal, ASME, 1980; District 4 Proficiency Medal, CIM, 1980. *Hobbies:* Sailing; Reading. *Address:* 826 East Centre, Saskatoon, Saskatchewan, Canada S7J 2Z7.

LENDVAY, Paul Gabriel, b. 26 Aug. 1938, Hungary. Consultant Plastic Reconstructive Surgeon & Microsurgeon. m. Anna Raza, 1964, 3 daughters. *Education:* MB.,BS., Sydney University Medical School, 1962; FRCS, London, 1966; Training in plastic surgery at The Queen Victoria Hospital, East Grinstead, England, 1965-68; FRACS, 1970. *Appointments:* Junior & Senior Residency, Sydney Hospital, Sydney, Australia, 1960-61; Lecturer in Anatomy, University of New South Wales, Sydney, Australia, 1964; Commenced practice in plastic and reconstructive surgery and microsurgery, Sydnay, Australia, 1968; Established a re-plantation service for amputated digits and extremities at the Auburn District Hospital, NSW, and carried out the first digital and hand replantations in Australia, 1968; Honorary Plastic Surgeon, Auburn District Hospital, NSW, Australia, 1968-77; Honorary Plastic & Reconstructive Surgeon, The Prince Henry, The Prince of Wales, and Eastern Suburbs Hospitals, Sydney, Australia, 1968-. *Memberships:* International Society of Reconstructive Microsurgery; The Australian Hand Club; The Australian Society of Plastic Surgeons; International Society of Aesthetic Plastic Surgery; NXW Chapter of Plastic Surgeons of the Royal Australasian College of Surgeons. *Publications:* Contributions to medical journals including: Replacement of Amputated Digits & Extremities; Functional Recovery After Digital Reimplantation; Reconstructive Microsurgery, 1978. *Hobbies:* Skiing; Water skiing; Tennis. *Address:* 117 O'Sullivan Road, Bellevue Hill, NSW, 2023, Australia.

LEONARD, Hugh Terence, b. 20 July 1938, Greymouth, New Zealand. General Manager. m. Pauline May Joan Lobendahn, 27 Feb. 1965, 1 son, 2 daughters. *Education:* Five years at Marist Brothers High School, Greymouth, New Zealand; Awarded endorsed New Zealand School Certificate; No Tertiary Education. *Appointments:* Announcer: New Zealand Broadcasting Service, 1956-60, Fiji Broadcasting Commission, 1960-67; Production Supervisor, 1967-68, Chief Announcer, 1968-72, Assistant to General Manager, 1972-73, General Manager, 1973-, FBC. *Memberships:* Rotary Club, Suva; Union Club, Suva. *Honours:* Fiji Independence Medal, 1970. *Hobbies:* Restoration of classic motorcycles; Reading; Popular scientific pursuits. *Address:* 136 Prince's Road, Tamavua, Suva, Fiji.

LEONG, Jessie, b. 16 June 1945, Suva, Fiji. Film Producer, Director. *Education:* Senior Cambridge Examination, St. Joseph's Secondary School, Suva, Fiji. *Appointments:* Radio Panel Operator, 1962, Sound Recording Department, 1966, Fiji Broadcasting Commission; Senior Film Technician, 1967, Australian Commonwealth Film Unit, 1970, Film Editor, 1973, Director of Film Production, 1975, Fiji Civil Service; Multi-media Programme Producer, Extension Services, University of the South Pacific, 1979-. *Memberships:* British Kinematograph, Sound and Television Society; Society of Motion Picture and Television Engineers; Y.W.C.A., Suva Board; Founder member, Treasurer, Councillor, Soroptimist International Club of Fiji; Treasurer, Video and Television Association; Australian Communication Association; Treasurer, Secretary, Pan Pacific and South East Women's Association; China Club; Crippled Children's Society; President, St. Joseph's Past Pupils Association. *Publications:* Participated in a workshop in recording Fijian oral traditions, 1976; Represented Fiji at UN Visual Habitat Communication Clinic on human settlements in Bangkok, 1979; Producer of over 42 documentary film screen productions and 40 newsreels in various capacities. *Honours:* Professional Associate award, East-West Centre and the University of the South Pacific. *Hobbies:* Lawn Tennis; Jogging. *Address:* 6 Bau Street, Suva, Fiji.

LERCH, Laurence August, b. 29 May 1942, Rosenfeld, Manitoba, Canada. President, Combac Management Corporation. m. (div) 1 son. *Education:* Bachelor of Commerce, Economics, 1969. *Appointments:* Canadian Pacific, 1961-69; IBM, 1969-74; Itel, 1974-79; Combac Management Corporation, 1979-. *Memberships:* Skyloft Ski and Country Club; Big Bay Point Marina and Yacht Club; Adelaide Club. *Hobbies:* Skiing; Boating; Golf; Racquet Ball. *Address:* RR % 1, Richmond Hill, Ontario, L4C 4X7, Canada.

LESKE, Clemens Theodore, b. 24 Sept. 1923, Rainbow, Victoria, Australia. Pianist, Director. m. (1) Dorcas Noske, 20 May 1950, 2 sons, 1 daughter, (2) Beryl Kimber, 6 Jan. 1969, 1 son. *Education:* Melbourne University, 1940-41, 1945-46, Bachelor of Music, 1947; Eastman School, Rochester, New York, 1957; Masters Course with Edwin Fischer, Luzern, 1958; Diplôme d'Etudes, 1949, Paris National Conservatoire, 1948-49. *Appointments:* Melbourne University, 1947; Teacher of Piano, Elder Conservatorium, 1950, Senior Lecturer, 1966, Reader, 1976, Dean of Faculty, 1974, University of Adelaide; Director, Elder Conservatorium, 1977-; Chairman, South Australian Music Examinations Board, 1977-; Concert Tours, UK, USA, Denmark,

German Federal Republic, Switzerland, USSR, Italy, Netherlands, Asia, New Zealand, Australia, 1950-81. *Memberships:* Patron: South Australian Society for Keyboard Music, 1976-, Adelaide Eisteddfod Society, 1978-, National Music Camp Association of Australia, 1981; Chairman, University Music Society, 1977-. *Honours:* International Church Music Award, St Louis, 1967; National Critics Award, Australia, 1977; Australia Council Grant Concert Tour USSR, 1977; Australian Government Cultural Exchange Concert Tour, Europe, USA, 1975-76. *Address:* Elder Conservatorium, University of Adelaide, Adelaide, South Australia, 5001.

LESLIE, Peter Noel, b. 13 Dec. 1932, Timaru, New Zealand. Medical Practitioner. m. Heather Macallan, 15 Apr. 1967, 3 sons, 1 daughter. *Education:* MB., Ch.B, New Zealand, 1956; MRACP, 1960; FRACP, 1970; MRCP (London), 1961; FRCP (London), 1977. *Appointments:* House Surgeon & Medical Registrar, 1957-59, Chairman, Division of Medicine, 1981-, Wellington Hospital Board; Medical Registrar, The General Hospital, Birmingham, 1960-61; Cardiology Registrar, National Heart Hospital, London, 1961-63; Cardiologist, 1963-, Head of Cardiology Department, 1979-, Wellington Hospital. *Memberships:* Colonel New Zealand Army, DMS, HQ, NZ Land Forces, 1977-81; CO Second (GH) Field Hospital, RNZAMC, 1971-77; Chief Medical Adviser, New Zealand Red Cross Society, 1979-; National Heart Foundation of New Zealand, 1968; Chairman, Health Education Sub-Committeee NHF of New Zealand, 1979-; New Zealand Committee, (Hon Secretary/Treasurer, 1966-73), Cardiac Society of Australia and New Zealand, 1966-79. *Honours:* ED, 1975; OBE, 1978. *Hobbies:* Sailing; Gardening; Skiing; Reading. *Address:* 24 Sefton Street, Wellington, 1, New Zealand.

LEUNG, Leung Sun, b. 15 August, 1936, Hong Kong. Professor of Chemical Engineering. m. Fuk Ching Theresa Chu, 16 Dec. 1960, 2 sons, 1 daughter. *Education:* BSc. Chemical Engineering, Imperial College, University of London, 1958; PhD., Trinity College, University of Cambridge, 1961. *Appointments:* Esso Refinery, Milford Haven, 1961-62; Malayan Acid Works, 1963-67; University of Malaya, 1966-67; University of Queensland, 1967-; University of Wisconsin, 1972-73; Consultant to a number of companies in United States of America. *Memberships:* Fellow, Institution of Chemical Engineers; Fellow, Institution of Engineers, Australia; Fellow, Australian Institute of Energy; Fellow, Australian Institute of Petroleum. *Publications:* 70 Technical Papers on various aspects of Fluidization, Pneumatic conveying and flow of gas solids down standpipes; Monograph on 'Flow of Gas-Solid Mixtures through Standpipes and Valves'. *Honours:* Australian-American Distinguished Senior Scholar Award, 1975; Keynote Lecturer, Engineering Foundation International Conference on Fluidization, 1980; Chairman, College of Chemical Engineers, Australia, 1980-; Personal Chair, University of Queensland, 1980. *Hobby:* Badminton. *Hobbies:* 93 Bank Road, Graceville, Queensland 4075, Australia.

LEUNG, Wai Sun, b. 19 June 1932, Hong Kong. Professor. m. 6 Sept. 1960, 1 son, 1 daughter. *Education:* BSc. Engineering, University of London, England; PhD. Electrical Engineering, University of Leeds, England. *Appointments:* Engineer, English Electric Company Limited, England, 1954-57; Engineer, Brown Boveri and Cie, Switzerland, 1960; University of Hong Kong, 1960-; Dean of Engineering and Architecture, 1972-78; Professor of Electrical Engineering, 1977-; Head, Electrical Engineering Department, 1980-. *Memberships:* F.I.E.E., England; F.I.E.R.E., England; f.h.k.i.e., Hong Kong; Sen.M.I.E.E.E., United States of America. *Publications:* Over 40 research and technical publications in Electrical Machines and Process control including 6 British Patents. *Hobbies:* Tennis; Swimming; Bridge. *Address:* 140 Pokfulam Road, Flat 65, Hong Kong.

LÉVESQUE, René Jules Albert, b. 30 Oct. 1926, St-Alexis, Quebec, Canada. Physicist. m. Alice Farnsworth, 1956 (div) 3 sons. *Education:* BSc. Physics, Sir George Williams University, Montreal, 1952; PhD. Northwestern University, Evanston, Illinois, 1957. *Appointments:* Research Associate, University of Maryland, 1957-59; Assistant Professor, 1959-64, Associate Professor, 1964-67, Professor, 1967-, Director, Nuclear Physics Laboratory, 1965-69, Chairman, Department of Physics, 1968-73, Vice-Dean, Faculty of Arts and Science, 1973-75, Dean, Faculty of Arts and Science, 1975-78, Vice-President, Research, 1978-, Université de Montréal. *Memberships:* President, Canadian Association of Physicists, 1976-77; Vice-President, Commission of Higher Studies, Quebec Ministry of Education, 1977-78;. Vice-President, Interciencia Association, 1979-80; President, The Association of the Scientific, Engineering and Technological Community of Canada, 1980; President, Canada-France-Hawaii Telescope Corporation, 1980; Vice-President, Natural Sciences and Engineering Research Council, Canada, 1981. *Publications:* Numerous publications in the field of Nuclear Structure. *Honours:* Queen Elizabeth Jubilee Medal. *Hobbies:* Cycling; Skiing. *Address:* 190 Willowdale, PH 1, Outremont, P.Q., Canada H3T 1G2.

LEVI, John Anthony, b. 5 March 1943, Sydney, Australia. Physician, Medical Oncologist. m. Margaret Louise Moore, 10 June 1967, 2 daughters. *Education:* Bachelor of Medicine, Bachelor of Surgery with Honours, University of Sydney, 1967; Member Royal Australasian College of Physicians, 1970; Fellow, Royal Australasian College of Physicians, 1974. *Appointments:* Resident Medical Officer, 1967-70, Senior Fellow in Haematology, 1970-72, Honorary Oncologist, 1976-, Sydney Hospital; Visiting Scientist, National Cancer Institute, United States of America, 1973-76; Assistant Professor of Medicine, University of Maryland, United States of America, 1974-76; Head, Department of Oncology, Royal North Shore Hospital, Sydney, 1976-; Director of Oncology, Northern Metropolitan Region, Health Commission of New South Wales, 1976-; Honorary Consultant Oncologist, Gosford District, Mater Misericordiae and Greenwich Hospitals, 1977-. *Memberships:* The Australian Society of Medical Oncology; The American Society of Clinical Oncology; The American Association for Cancer Research; The Clinical Oncological Society of Australia; The American Society of Haematology; The Sydney Co-operative Oncology Group. *Publications:* Seventy-five publications and Book Chapters on Leukaemia, Lymphoma and Solid Tumours, 1970-81. *Honours:* The Norman Rose Travelling Fellowship, 1972; Clinical Fellowship of the New South Wales Cancer Council, Australia, 1973. *Hobbies:* Photography; Oenology; Swimming. *Address:* 2 Lawley Crescent, Pymble 2073, New South Wales, Australia.

LEVICK, William Russell, b. 5 Dec. 1931, Sydney, Australia. Medical Research Scientist. m. Patricia J. Lathwell, 14 Aug. 1961, 2 sons, 1 daughter. *Education:* BSc, Hons 1, Sydney, 1953; MSc, Sydney, 1954; MB, BS Hons 1 Sydney, 1957. *Appointments:* Teaching Fellow, Department Physiology, University of Sydney, 1953; Resident Medical Officer, Royal Prince Alfred Hospital, Sydney, 1957-58; Research Fellow, NH, MRC, Sydney, 1959-62; C.J. Martin Travelling Fellow, Cambridge, England, 1963-64; Assistant, Associate Research Physiologist, University of California, Berkeley, 1965-66; Senior Lecturer Physiology, University of Sydney, 1967; Professorial Fellow, Physiology, Australia, 1967-. *Memberships:* Biological Cybernetics; Photobiochemistry and Photobiophysics; Physiological Society, Great Britain; Registered Medical Practitioner, Australian National University, 1957-; Australian Physiological and Pharmacological Society. *Publications:* Over 50 publications in International Scientific Journals on the Neurophysiology of the Visual System. *Honours:* Fellow of the Australian Academy of Science, 1973; Fellow of the Optical Society of America, 1977; Fairchild Distinguished Scholar, California Institute of Technology, 1980. *Hobby:* Electronics. *Address:* 33 Quiros Street, Red Hill, A.C.T. 2603, Australia.

LEVY, Wilfred Robert, b. 6 Oct. 1942, Burwood, Australia. Medical Practitioner. m. (1) div. (2) Helenne Clare Moore, 3 sons, 3 daughters. *Education:* MB, BS, 1966; M.R.A.C.P. 1970; F.R.A.C.P. 1975. *Appointments:* R.M.O. Royal North Shore Hospital, Sydney, 1967; R.M.O. Royal Alexander Hospital for Children, Sydney, 1968; Medical Registrar, Ryde D.S.M. Hospital, Sydney, 1969; R.M.O. Repatriation General Hospital, Sydney, 1969-70; Paediatric Registrar, 1971-72, Associate Paediatrician, 1973-; Prince of Wales Childrens Hospital, Sydney; Staff Specialist Paediatrician and Director, Department of Paediatrics, The Nepean Hospital, Penrith, Australia, 1973-; Consultant Paediatrician, Windsor Hospital, Australia, 1978-;

Assistant Paediatrician Westmead Centre, Australia, 1981-. *Memberships:* Australian Medical Association; Australasian College Paediatrics. *Hobby:* Philately. *Address:* 110 York Road, Penrith, New South Wales, Australia.

LEWANDO, Jan Alfred (Sir), b. 31 May 1909, England. Company Director. m. 27 May 1948, 3 daughters. *Education:* Manchester University, 1926-29. *Appointments:* Director of: Marks and Spencer Ltd., 1954-70, Carrington Tesit (Italy), 1971-75, Bunzl Pulp & Paper Ltd., 1976-, W A Baxter & Sons Ltd., 1975-, Edgars Stores Ltd., (S Africa), 1976-, Johnston Industries Inc., (USA), 1976-, Royal Worcester Spode Ltd., 1978-79, Johnston Industries Ltd., 1980-; President, Carrington Viyella Inc., (USA), 1971-75; Heal & Son Holdings, 1975-, Deputy Chairman, 1977, Director; Chairman of: Carrington Viyella Ltd., 1970-75, Consolidated Textile Mills Ltd., (Canada), 1972-75, Gelvenor Textiles Ltd., (S Africa), 1973-75, Beaufort Engineering Co., Ltd., 1980-. *Memberships:* Export Council for Europe, 1965-69; British National Export Council, 1969-71; British Overseas Trade Board, 1972-77; European Steering Committee of Confederation of British Industries, 1968-71; British Overseas Trade Advisory Council, 1975-77; Grand Council of Confederation of British Industry, 1971-75; European Trade Committee of British Overseas Trade Board, 1973-; Clothing Export Council, Vice-Chairman, 1966-70; President, British Textile Confederation, 1972-73; Vice President, Transport Trust, 1973-. *Honours:* Knight Bachelor, 1974; Cammander of British Empire, 1968; Companion Textile Institute, 1972; Order of The Legion of Merit (USA), 1946. *Address:* Davidge House, Knotty Green, Beaconsfield, Buckinghamshire, England.

LEWIN, Terence (Thornton), (Sir), (Admiral of the Fleet), b. 19 Nov. 1920, Dover, England. H M Forces, Chief of the Defence Staff. m. Jane Branch-Evans, 1944, 2 sons, 1 daughter. *Education:* The Judd School, Tonbridge. *Appointments:* Joined Royal Navy, 1939; War Service in Home and Mediterranean Fleets in HMS Valiant, HMS Ashanti in Malta Convoys, N Russian Convoys, invasion N Africa and Channel (despatches); Commander HMS Corunna, 1955-56; Commander HM Yacht Britannia, 1957-58; Captain (F) Dartmouth Training Squadron and HM Ships Urchin and Tenby, 1961-63; Director, Naval Tactical and Weapons Policy Division, MoD, 1964-65; Commander HMS Hermes, 1966-67; Assistant Chief of Naval Staff (Policy), 1968-69; Flag Officer, Second-in-Command, Far East Fleet, 1969-70; Vice Chief of the Naval Staff, 1971-73; Commander-in-Chief Fleet, 1973-75; Commander-in-Chief Naval Home Command, 1975-77; Chief of Naval Staff and First Sea Lord, 1977-79; Chief of the Defence Staff, 1979-; Flag ADC to the Queen, 1975-77; First and Principal ADC to the Queen, 1977-79. *Memberships:* frsa-. *Honours:* GCB, 1976 (KCB 1973); MVO, 1958; DSC, 1942. *Hobbies:* Life and voyages of Captain Cook; Walking. *Address:* Chief of the Defence Staff, Ministry of Defence, Main Building, Whitehall, London, SW1A 2HB, England.

LEWINGTON, Rodney John, b. 14 April 1935, Hampshire, England. Economist. m. Gloria Rose Toye, 21 Jan. 1961, 1 son, 1 daughter. *Education:* Bachelor of Commerce, Bachelor of Commerce and Administration, 1966-68, University of Wellington, Victoria. *Appointments:* Research Officer, Economist, New Zealand Department of Statistics, 1961; Assistant Government Statistician, 1979. *Memberships:* New Zealand Association of Economists; New Zealand Statistical Association; Life Member, Wellington Botanical Society. *Hobbies:* Botany; Photography; Scottish Country Dancing. *Address:* 9 Pembroke Road, Wellington 5, New Zealand.

LEWIS, Alexander Ashley, b. 22 Jan. 1931, Adelaide, South Australia. Businessman & Member of Parliament. m. (1) Patricia Ann Symons, 21 May 1955, 1 daughter, (2) Patricia Elizabeth Williams, 2 Dec. 1978. *Education:* St Peter's College, Adelaide; St Mark's College, Adelaide, South Australia. *Appointments:* Founder Manager P S Agencies, Boyup Brook Machinery Dealers, Western Australia; Elected Member for Blackwood Legislative Assembly Seat, 1972; Elected Member for Lower Central Province in Legislative Council, 1974, Re-elected 1980; Secretary Liberal Parliamentary Party and Joint Government Parties, 1977; Chairman of National Parks Select Committee,

1979 & 1980. *Hobbies:* Sport; Reading; Politics. *Address:* 59 Phillip Road, Dalkeith, 6009, Western Australia.

LEWIS, Allen Montgomery, b. 26 Oct. 1909, Castries, St. Lucia. Jurist. m. 26 Dec. 1936, 3 sons, 2 daughters. *Education:* LL.B. Hons. (External) London, UK, 1941; LLD.(UWI), 1974. *Appointments:* Admitted to practice at Bar of Royal Court, St. Lucia (later Supreme Court of Windward and Leeward Islands), 1931; called to English Bar, Middle Temple, London, UK, 1946; in private practice, Windward Islands, 1931-59; Acting Magistrate, St. Lucia, 1940-41; Acting Puisne Judge, Windward and Leeward Islands, 1955-56; QC., 1956; Commissioner for reform and revision of Laws of St. Lucia, 1954-58; Judge: of Federal Supreme Court, 1959-62; British Caribbean Court of Appeal, 1962; Court of Appeal, Jamaica, 1962-67; Acting President, Court of Appeal, 1966; Acting Chief Justice of Jamaica, 1966; Chief Justice, West Indies Associated States Supreme Court, 1967-72; Chairman, National Development Corporation, St. Lucia, 1972-74; Chancellor of University of the West Indies, 1975-; Governor, 1974-79, Governor-General, 1979-80, St. Lucia. *Memberships:* MLC. St. Lucia, 1943-51; Chairman 6 times, Castries Town Council, 1942-56; President, West Indies Senate, 1958-59; Served on numerous Government and other public Committees including Education Board of St. Mary's College Advisory Committee; Represented St. Lucia, Windward Islands and West Indies at various conferences, including Montego Bay, 1947, and Chaguaramas Commission, 1958; Director, St. Lucia Branch British Red Cross Society, 1955-59; Guild of Graduates Representative (St. Lucia) on UWI Council; President, Grenada Boy Scouts Association, 1967-72; Served as President and/or Committee Member, cricket, football and athletic associations, St. Lucia, 1936-59; Chief Scout, St. Lucia 1976-80; President, St. John Association, 1975-80. *Publications:* Revised Edition of Laws of St. Lucia. *Honours:* Coronation Medal, 1953; Kt. Bach., 1968; K.St.J., 1975; Queen's Silver Jubilee Medal, 1977; GCMG., 1979. *Hobbies:* Gardening; Swimming. *Address:* Beaver Lodge, The Morne, PO Box 1076, Castries, St. Lucia.

LEWIS, Elizabeth Ann, b. 30 Jan. 1935, Melbourne, Australia. Neurosurgeon. *Education:* MBBS. (Melbourne), 1958; FRCS. (England), 1965; FRCS. (Glasgow), 1965; FRACS, 1978. *Appointments:* Neurosurgeon, Queen Victoria Medical Centre, Australia; Assistant Neurosurgeon, Royal Children's Hospital, Australia. *Memberships:* Society of British Neurological Surgeons; Neurosurgical Society of Australasia; Victorian Medical Womens Society; Royal Melbourne Tennis Club; Victorian Ladies Yacht Club. *Publications:* Late Presentation of Stricture of the Aqueduct of Sylvius, 1972; Gastroduodenal Ulceration of Neurogenic Origin, 1973. *Hobbies:* Music; Food and Wine. *Address:* 82 Elgin Street, Hawthorn 3122, Victoria, Australia.

LEWIS, Eric Leslie Vallance, b Great Britain. Physicist. *Education:* BSc (1st class Hons.) in Physics, 1964, PhD. in Physics, 1967, Birmingham University, UK. *Appointments:* Research Associate, Birmingham University, UK, 1967-68; Research Fellow, Chemistry, Manchester University, UK, 1968-69; Research Fellow, University College, Cardiff, Wales, UK, 1969-72; Research Fellow, Leeds University, UK, 1972. *Memberships:* M.Inst.P; FRAS; Biblical Creation Society; Leeds Literary and Philosophical Society. *Publications:* Papers: Acta Cryst B25, 1969; J.Phys.E., 1973-79; J.Mater, Sci., 1979; J.Macromol.Sci., 1980; various musical compositions, mainly church and choral music. *Honours:* S W J Smith Prize, Physics, Birmingham University, UK, 1964. *Hobbies:* Music; Astronomy; Fine Arts; Religions and philosophies. *Address:* 16 Sunset Road, Meanwood, Leeds LS6 4LH, England.

LEWIS, Giles Penfold, b. 25 Nov. 1948, Singapore. Publisher. m. Kate, 22 July 1973, 1 son, 1 daughter. *Education:* BA(Hons), Modern History, St. Edmund Hall, University of Oxford, UK. *Appointments:* Consumer Goods Marketing, Reckitt and Colman; Co-Edition Publishing, Elsevier International Projects; Oxford University Press, Kano, Nigeria, Kuala Lumpur, Malaysia, Nairobi, Kenya. *Memberships:* United Oxford and Cambridge Club. *Hobby:* Eclectic. *Address:* Spring Valley Road, Nairobi, Kenya.

LEWIS, Lawrence Vernon Harcourt, b. 13 Mar. 1932, Barbados, West Indies. Bank President, m. 1 July 1961,

2 sons. *Education:* Diploma, Public Administration, University of the West Indies, Jamaica, 1964; Certificate in Industrial Relations, Institute of Labour Studies, Geneva, Switzerland, 1969. *Appointments:* Assistant Accountant, 1957; Accountant, Ministry of Communications and Works, 1963; Administration Assistant, Ministry of Finance, 1965; Senior Personnel Officer, 1966; Senior Training Officer, 1967; Senior Assistant Secretary, Ministry of Education, 1969; Director, Data Processing, 1970; Accountant General, 1971; Permanent Secretary, Ministry of Finance, 1973; Permanent Secretary, Financial Institutions, 1977; President, Barbados National Bank, West Indies, 1978. *Memberships:* Memberships include: Past President, National Union of Public Workers; National Insurance Board, 1968-76; Harbour Advisory Board, 1973-76, Natural Gas Corporation, 1973-76; Alternate Governor, Caribbean Development Bank, 1973-; Chairman, Governing Body, Garrison Secondary School, 1974-76; Director, Barbados Hilton, 1974-; Board of Industrial Development Corporation, 1975-; Director, Land Reclaimers Limited, 1977-; Chairman, Barbados Mortgage Finance Co. Limited, 1977-; Chairman, Insurance Corporation of Barbados, 1978-81; Chairman, Barbados National Bank, 1978-. *Honours:* King's Scout, 1950; Queen's Jubilee Medal, 1977; Fellow, International Bankers Association, 1979. *Hobbies:* Gardening; Lawn Tennis. *Address:* 'Alexandre Court', West Ridge, Dalkeith, St. Michael, Barbados, West Indies.

LEWIS, Michael George, b. 8 Nov. 1953, Nsanje, Malawi. Land Surveyor. *Education:* BSc(1st class Hons.), Land Surveying Sciences, North East London Polytechnic, UK, 1973-76; MSc. Geodesy, Wolfson College, Oxford, UK, 1979-80. *Appointments:* Surveys Department, Malawi Government, 1973-. *Memberships:* Surveyors Institute of Malawi; Royal Institution of Chartered Surveyors. *Honours:* Held national record for 400m. hurdles and represented Malawi in international athletics competitions, 1971. *Hobbies:* Sports; African Literature. *Address:* PO Box 30047, Chichiri, Blantyre 3, Malawi.

LEWIS, Peter Roy, b. 22 Nov. 1940, Liverpool, England. Educationalist; Folk Singer; Writer; Broadcaster. *Appointments:* Research Assistant, Pharmaceutics, 1959-60, Research Assistant, Metallurgy, 1960-63, Liverpool University, UK; Electrical Engineer, Communications Industry, 1963-64; Pioneer in the practical use of 20th century folk collections in places of entertainment, education and evangelism/worship, school assemblies, integrated studies and conferences; Traveller, singer, musician. *Memberships:* Royal School of Church Music; Performing Right Society; Twentieth Century Church light music group. *Publications:* Sing Life, Sing Love, 1971; Contributed to many publications: Compositions include those in: Teach me how to look; Sing it in the morning; Blueprint books; Gospel Songs; Jesus Folk; Folk Hymnal; Recordings: Sing Life, Sing Love LP; Give Yourselves to Me, LP; Big Story, EP; The Rock, EP; Sing about Christmas, EP; A Chance to see, EP; Let's go great; Contributed to recordings including: Moving, EP; Hosanna, LP. *Address:* 363 Wavertree Nook Road, Liverpool L15 7LJ, England.

LEYLAND, Hal Everett, b. 23 July 1918, Toronto, Canada. Dentis (Retired). m. Marguerite Herbert McCowan, 16 June 1956. *Education:* LDS & DDS, Faculty of Dentistry, University of Toronto, 1943. *Appointments:* Candaian Dental Corps, 1942-46; Captain, General Practice and Administration; Associate practice 1946-47; Private practice, Toronto, 1947-54; Private practice, Nassau, 1961-; Executive Director, Florida Dental Association, 1957-61. *Memberships:* Canadian Dental Association, 1975-; Ontario Dental Association; Past President, West Toronto Dental Society, 1953; Academy of Dentistry of Toronto; Convention Committee, Ontario Dental Association, 1949-54; Past President and Founder, Kiwanis Service Club movement in Bahamas, 1962, and in Toronto and Tampa, 1947-; Volunteer Police Sergeant, Royal Bahamas Police Force, 1966-; Co-founder, Bahama Islands Dental Association, 1965, President, 1970, Registrar, Secretary, Treasurer, 1972-78; Amderican Dental Association; National Secretary/Treasurer, Federation Dentaire Internationale, 1971-79; American College of Dentists; Royal Society of Medicine (England), 1976; International Academy of Preventive Medicine; Pierre Fauchard Academy; American Association of Dental

Editors. *Publications:* Contributions to various dental journals; Publisher and Associated Editor, Flordia Dental Society Journal, 1958-61; Editor & Publisher, The Mayan, a private dental journal, the first in America to be published in full colour, sponsored by The Woehler Research Group, 1964-67 (Discontinued because the Group could not sustain the ever-increasing expense). *Hobbies:* Painting; Sketching; Swimming; Ship model building & model railroading; Sailing - Ship rhetoric and paraphernalia; Journal critic. *Address:* #23B, Carefree Apartments, Box N 4811, Cable Beach, Nassau, Bahamas.

LEYTON, Geoffrey Bertrand, b. 25 Aug. 1913, Leeds, Yorkshire, England. Medical Practitioner. m. Sheila Robertson Dalgliesh, 19 Apr. 1945, 1 son, 2 daughters. *Education:* BA, 1935; MB. BChir., 1938; MA., 1943; MD., 1946; Caius College, Cambridge, UK; DCP.(London), 1947; FRC.Path., 1963; FRCPA, 1964. *Appointments:* Director of Laboratory Services, Manitoba, Canada, 1950-53; Consultant Pathologist, Hollymoor Hospital, Birmingham, UK, 1954-63; Director of Pathology, 1963-80, Consultant Pathologist, 1980-, Wimmera Base Hospital, Horsham, Victoria, Australia. *Memberships:* Fellow of the Royal Society of Medicine; Association of Clinical Pathologists. *Publications:* Effects of Slow Starvation, 1946; Ox-Cell Haemolysins in Human Serum, 1952; A Simple Routine Method for Mono and Diamine Oxidase Estimations in Human Serum, 1981. *Hobbies:* Electronics; Tennis; Travel. *Address:* RMB 7432, Horsham, Victoria, Australia 3400.

LIEBER, Frank Steve, b. 19 Sept. 1923, Hungary. Barrister & Solicitor. m. Margaret E Tamas, 10 July 1947, 1 son, 2 daughters. *Education:* BA, LL.B, University of Alberta, 1950. *Appointments:* Senior Partner, Lieber & Koch; President, Ilonka Properties Ltd.; Past Vice-President, Five Star Mines & Minerals Ltd.; Past Vie-President, Silver Chief Minerals Ltd. *Memberships:* Alberta Law Society; Honorary Life President, Edmonton Hungarian Cultural Society. *Honours:* Queen's Counsel, 1971. *Hobbies:* Curling; Golf. *Address:* 13801 Summit Drive, Edmonton, Alberta, T5N 3S8, Canada.

LIELMEZS, Janis, b. 1 June 1926, Riga, Republic of Latvia. Educator; Chemical Engineer. m. Alna M Blaus, 28 Nov. 1970. *Education:* BSc, University of Denver, Colorado, USA, 1954; MSc, Northwestern University, Evanston, Illinois, USA, 1956; Graduate work, Princeton University, Princeton, New Jersey, USA, 1957; Graduate work, Stanford University, Stanford, California, USA, 1959; Graduate work, University of Minnesota, Minneapolis, Minnesota, USA, 1960. *Appointments:* Graduate Teaching and Research Assistant, Northwestern University, Evanston, Illinois, USA, 1955-56; Engineer, US. Army, Corps. of Engineers, Snow, Ice and Permafrost Research Establishment, Wilmette, Illinois, USA, 1956; Graduate Research Assistant, Princeton University, Princeton, New Jersey, USA, 1956-57; Engineer, 1957-58, 1959, Consultant, 1958-59, Shell Development Co., Emeryville, California, USA; Graduate Research Assistant, University of Minnesota, Minneapolis, Minnesota, USA, 1959-60; Research Engineer, 1961-63, Assistant Professor of Chemical Engineering, 1962-63, Michigan College of Mining and Technology, Houghton, Michigan, USA; Assistant Professor of Chemical Engineering, 1963-69, Associate Professor of Chemical Engineering, 1969-78, Professor of Chemical Engineering, 1978-, University of British Columbia, Vancouver, Canada. *Memberships:* Swiss Chemical Society; American Chemical Society; American Institute of Chemical Engineers; Bioelectro-Chemical Society; Association for the Advancement of Baltic Studies; American Association of University Professors; Canadian Association of University Teachers; Fellow, Chemical Institute of Canada; Canadian Association of Physicists; Vice-President, 1979, Association of Latvian Engineers; Latvian American Association of University Professors and Instructors; Fellow, New York Academy of Sciences; Professional and Community Service: Professional Engineer, The Association of Professional Engineers of the Province of British Columbia; Chairman, Executive, 5th West Coast Latvian Song Festival; Director, Latvian Youth Heritage Seminars; Advisor, Latvian National Federation of Canada; Chairman, Latvian Studies Conference, Canada, 1979. *Publications:* 109 Published works (with others); Editor of numerous journals and newspapers; 15 articles, notes

and discussions regarding various scientific, cultural and historic subjects; 13 unpublished papers presented at Conferences. *Honours:* Foreign Scholarship, Denver University, USA, 1953-54; Weiss Honor Scholarship and Windt Scholarship in Chemistry and Chemical Engineering, Stanford University, USA, 1958-59; Phi Lambda Upsilon, Chemistry Honorary Fraternity; Fellow, Chemical Institute of Canada; Fellow, The New York Academy of Sciences. *Hobbies:* Chess; History. *Address:* Chemical Engineering Department, The University of British Columbia, Vancouver, British Columbia, Canada.

LILEY, Bruce Sween, b. 7 Sept. 1928, Havelock North, New Zealand. University Professor. m. Margaret Alison Donner, 2 Apr. 1960, 2 sons. *Education:* MSc (Maths Hons. 1951, Physics, 1955), University of New Zealand, 1947-51. 1953-55; PhD., University of Reading, UK, 1963. *Appointments:* Lt. RNZSigs., Regular Army, 1952-53; Research Physicist, AEI Research Laboratories, Aldermaston, UK, 1955-63; Senior Research Fellow, Research School of Physical Sciences, Australian National University, 1963-69; Professor and Head of Department of Physics, University of Waikato, New Zealand, 1969-. *Memberships:* Fellow of Institute of Physics, UK; Fellow of Royal Society of Arts, UK; American Association for Advancement of Science. *Publications:* Plasma State, 1974; Report of Royal Commission on Nuclear Power in New Zealand, 1978; Research: Plasma physics—Toroidal machines, Sceptre, UK, 1957-60; Tokamak, Australia, 1964-76. *Honours:* Visiting Fellow, ANU, 1973; Visiting Scientist, University of Texas, Austin, 1973-74; Research Associate, UKAEA Culham Laboratories, 1978-79; Member of Royal Commission (NZ) on Nuclear Power, 1976-78; Member of IUPAP Plasma Physics Commission, 1978-. *Hobbies:* Reading; Gardening; Sport. *Address:* 185 Silverdale Road, Hamilton, New Zealand.

LILLEY, Geoffrey Michael, b. 16 Nov. 1919, Isleworth, Middlesex, England. Professor of Aeronautics and Astronautics. m. Leslie Marion Wheeler, 18 Dec. 1948, 1 son, 2 daughters. *Education:* BSc.(Eng.), 1st class Hons., 1943, MSc.(Eng.), DIC, 1945, Imperial College, London, UK, 1942-45; Chartered Engineer. C.Eng. *Appointments:* Engineering Training, 1936-40; Drawing Officer, Wind Tunnel Departments, Vickers Armstrongs, Weybridge, Surrey, UK, 1940-46; Lecturer, 1946, Senior Lecturer, 1951, College of Aeronautics, Cranfield, UK; Deputy Head of Department of Aerodynamics, 1956, Professor Experimental Fluid Mechanics, 1961, Professor of Aeronautics and Astronautics, 1963-, University of Southampton, UK. *Memberships:* Fellow, Royal Aeronautical Society; Fellow, Institute of Mathematics and its Applications; Institute of Mechanical Engineers; American Institute of Aeronautics and Astronautics; Fellow, Royal Society of Arts; American Society for Advancement of Science. *Publications:* Scientific papers on Fluid Motion; Aerodynamic Noise; Inventions on improvements to aircraft and noise reduction. *Honours:* OBE, 1981. *Hobbies:* Chess; Opera; Ballet; Walking. *Address:* 'Highbury', Pine Walk, Chilworth, Southampton, SO1 7HQ, England.

LIM, Chong Eu, b. 28 May 1919, Penang, Malaya. Chief Minister. m. Goh Sing Yeng, 2 sons, 2 daughters. *Education:* MB, ChB, Edinburgh University. *Appointments:* Private Medical Practitioner; Medical Officer, Malayan Auxiliary Air Force, 1951-54; Numerous Appointments in Radical Party including: Federal Councillor, Penang, 1955, Deputy Chairman, Gerakan Rakyat Malaysia, 1968, Chairman, State Operations Committee, 1969, President of Parti Gerakan Rakyat Malaysia, 1971, Member for Kota in the Penang State Elections, Chief Minister of Penang, 1969, 1974, 1978-. *Memberships:* Past President of Penang Medical Practitioners' Society; Malayan Medical Council; Chairman, Board of Trustees of the Silver Jubilee Home, Penang and Province Wellesley; JCI Senator; Patron of Penang and Province Wellesley Welfare Council; Royal Malaysian Commonwealth Society; Commonwealth Parliamentary Association. *Honours:* Honorary Doctorate of Law, University of Science, Malaysia. *Hobbies:* Shooting; Tennis; Contract Bridge; Fishing; Golf. *Address:* 1 Jalan Haji Sudin, Hillside, Tanjong Bungah, Penang, Malaysia.

LIM, Kek-han, b. 17 Dec. 1932, Indonesia. Violin Soloist, Conductor and Professor of violin-playing. m. Chu Yu Chu, 1 Oct. 1966 (Divorced), 2 sons. *Education:*

Diploma C2, Amsterdamch Conservatorium, 1951; Three cultural exchanges representing Holland Conservatory, to Germany, Paris, Brussels, 1950; National Conservatorie of Music, Paris, 1954-57; Moscow Conservatory, 1957-58, later studied under Henryck Szerying; Study and research with Professor David Oistrack and Galina Barinowa. *Appointments:* Concert Master and soloist, Holland Colonial Jakada Radio Orchestra, 1952-55; Principal Violinist, Lim Kek-han String Quartet, 1952-55; Appointed official soloist of Central Symphony Orchestra of Peking, Professor of Central Conservatory of Music, Peking, 1951-64; Visited Russia as a representative of China, playing with leading Russian Orchestra and giving recitals, 1951; Appointed Soloist of Shanghai Symphony Orchestra, 1964; Professor of Shanghai Conservatory of Music; Violin Professor of Baptist College, Chine University of Hong Kong and Hong Kong Conservatory of Music, 1971; Soloist and Guest Conductor of Hong Kong Philharmonic Orchestra, 1971; Conductor, Soloist and Music Director of Lim Kek-han Concert Orchestra. *Publications:* Composition, Lake Wave Fantasy, Violin Concerto; Recordings: The Butterfly lovers concerto, Master Chinese and Western Violin works. *Address:* 2 B Po Shan Mansion, Tai Koo Shing, Quarry Bay, Hong Kong.

LIM, Pin, b. 12 Jan. 1936, Penang, Malaysia. Professor of Medicine. m. Shirley Loo Ngai Seong, 21 Mar. 1964, 2 sons, 1 daughter. *Education:* MB, BChir, 1963, MA, 1964, MD, 1970, Cambridge; MRCP, 1965, FRCP, London, 1976, FRACP, 1978, FRCPE, 1981. *Appointments:* House Officer, Port Registration, Addenbrooke's Hospital, Cambridge; Medical Officer, Ministry of Health, Singapore; Lecturer, Senior Lecturer, Associate Professor, Department of Medicine, University of Singapore; Professor, Department of Medicine, Vice-Chancellor, National University of Singapore. *Memberships:* Founder President, Endocrine and Metabolic Society of Singapore; Master, Academy of Medicine, Singapore; Member, Central Committee, International Society of Endocrinology; Member, National Productivity Council, Singapore; Director, Neptune Orient Lines, Singapore; Director, Applied Research Corporation, Singapore. *Honours:* Singapore Government Queen's Scholarship, 1957; Commonwealth Medical Fellow, 1969. *Hobbies:* Reading; Swimming. *Address:* 32 Faber Drive, Singapore 0512.

LIM, Tow Ming, b. 2 Jan. 1938, Malaysia. Pathologist. m. 20 Aug. 1967, 1 son, 1 daughter. *Education:* BAgricSc, Malaya, 1964; MSc, 1967, DIC, 1967, PhD, 1977, London. *Appointments:* Plantation Advisory Officer, 1964-65; Research Plant Pathologist, 1966-71; Senior Research Plant Pathologist, 1972-. *Memberships:* American Phytopathological Society; Malaysian Plant Protection Society; Malaysian Scientific Association; Agricultural Institute of Malaysia; Incorporated Society of Planters. *Publications:* Numerous publications in professional journals. *Hobbies:* Reading; Gardening. *Address:* 9 Jalan Jenjarom, Off 2½ Miles, Jalan Kelang, Kuala Lumpur, Malaysia.

LIM, Tuan-Kay, b. 21 July 1946, Canton, China. Optical Physicist and Engineer. m. Chiew-Hiong Wong, 24 July 1969, 1 son. *Education:* BSc, Nanyang University, Singapore, 1969; PhD, McMaster University, Hamilton, Canada, 1975. *Appointments:* Teaching Assistant, McMaster University, Canada, 1969-74; Postdoctoral Fellow, Laval University, Canada, 1974-77; Industrial Postdoctoral Fellow, Dale Electronics Limited, Canada, 1977-79; Optical Engineer, NCR Canada Limited, Canada, 1979-. *Memberships:* Optical Society of America; Society of Photo-optical Instrumentation Engineers; Institute of Electrical and Electronics Engineers; Canadian Association of Physicists; Society of Photographic Scientists and Engineers; Society of Information Display; Institute of Physics, Singapore. *Publications:* Thesis, 1974; Approximately 20 technical papers in professional journals and conferences. *Honours:* Chancellor's Gold Medal, Nanyang University, 1969; McMaster Graduate Fellowship; Laval Postdoctoral Fellowship; Quebec Ministry of Education, Postdoctoral Fellowship; NRC, Industrial Postdoctoral Fellowship. *Hobbies:* Reading; Writing; Games; Sports; Music; Chinese Calligraphy. *Address:* 505 Parkside Drive, Apt. 206, Waterloo, Ontario, Canada.

LIM, York Quan, b. 12 Feb. 1935, Sun Wei City, China. Journalist. *Education:* Columbia College; Overseas Chinese Educational College, Taiwan, China. *Appoint-*

ments: City Editor, Chinese Times, Canada, 1950; Staff Writer, Chinese Voice, Canada, 1953-; Staff Writer, Chinatown News, Canada, 1953-; Special Correspondent in Canada: Overseas Chinese Daily News, Central Daily News, Taipei, Taiwan, Hong Kong, Overseas News, Taipei, Taiwan. *Memberships:* Advisor, Federation of Overseas Chinese Associations, Taiwan; Publicity Chairman, Chinese Benevolent Association of Canada; Secretary General, Chinese Canadians Citizens Association; Chinese Culture Association, USA; Senior Warden, Chinese Freemasons of the World. *Publications:* I Came from China, 1950; Our Land—Canada, 1956; History of the Chinese in Canada, 1958; Guide to Canadian Immigration and Citizenship, 1958, revised Edition, 1981; Immigration Act of Canada, 1981. *Hobbies:* Stamp Collecting; Writing; Reading. *Address:* 2640 Prince Albert Street, Vancouver, BC, Canada.

LIMAN, Umaru Mohammed, b. 25 Oct. 1945, Kontagora, Nigeria. Banking. m. 21 Sept. 1972, 2 sons, 1 daughter. *Education:* BSc, (Economics), Ahmadu Bello University, Zaria, 1970; MA, Center for Development Economics, Williams College, USA, 1972. *Appointments:* Economic Planning Officer, 1970-73, Senior Planning Officer, 1973-74, North Western State of Nigeria; Principal Investment Executive (Defunct N W State), 1975-76; Secretary to the Niger State of Nigeria Executive Council, 1976; Principal Private Secretary to the Governor, 1976-78; Principal Secretary, Ministry of Trade & Industry, 1978-79, Niger State of Nigeria; Seconded to the Nigerian Groundnut Board, Kano as Board Secretary, 1979-80; Withdrew from the Civil Service in 1980 to take up appointment with the United Bank for Africa on Management Status as Assistant Area Manager and UBA Lisison Officer for the Federal Capital Territory at Abuja. *Memberships:* Secretary, State Manpower Committee, North Western State, 1970; National Manpower Board representing defunct North Western State, 1972-73; National Wages Advisory Council, 1972-73; Director, to represent the Niger State Government on the Board of the Shiroro Hotels Limited, Minna, 1980-. *Publications:* The correlation between Educational Growth and Economic Development in Nigeria—A Dissertation for the award of a Master's Degree in Development Economics at the Center for Development Economics, Williamstown, Massachusetts, 1914-1970. *Hobby:* Hockey playing. *Address:* United Bank for Africa Limited, Industrial Estate Road, P M B 2192, Kaduna, Nigeria.

LIMANN, Hilla, b. 1934. President of Ghana. m. 5 children. *Education:* Government Teacher Training College; BSc. Econ. London School of Economics 1960; Sorbonne University; PhD Political Science and Constitutional Law, Paris University 1965; BA Hons. History, London University 1964. *Appointments:* Member, Constitutional Commission, 1969; Head of Chancery, Official Secretary, Ghana Embassy, Lome Togo 1968-70; Numerous International Meetings and Conferences: OAU and Non Aligned States, International Labour Organisation, World Health Organisation and International Atomic Energy Agency, International Conference, on the Peaceful Uses of Atomic Energy 1971; First International Conference on Cocoa Agreement 1972; First Review Conference on the Treaty for Non-Proliferation of Nuclear Weapons 1975; Government Delegations; President of Ghana 1979-. *Address:* Ghana High Commission, 13 Belgrave Square, London SW1X 8PR, England.

LIMERICK, Patrick Edmund Pery, (Sixth Earl of), b. 12 Apr. 1930, London, England. British Merchant Banker. m. Sylvia Rosalind Lush, 2 sons, 1 daughter. *Education:* Eton and New College, Oxford; MA; Qualified as Chartered Accountant with Peat, Marwick, Mitchell & Company, 1953-58. *Appointments:* Kleinwort Sons & Co., 1958; Director, Kleinwort Benson Ltd., 1966-72, 1974; Council London Chamber of Commerce and Industry, 1968-79; London Director, Commercial Bank of Australia Ltd., 1969-72; Parliamentary Under-Secretary of State for Trade, 1972-74; President, Association of British Chambers of Commerce, 1974-77, Vice-President, 1977-; British Overseas Trade Board, 1975-, Chairman, 1979-; Director numerous companies; Chairman, Committee for Middle East Trade, 1975-79; Mallinson-Denny Ltd., 1979-80. *Memberships:* President, Ski Club of Great Britain, 1974-; Vice-President, Alpine Ski Club, 1974-76. *Publications:* Numerous specialist articles. *Hobbies:*

Mountaineering; Skiing; Boating. *Address:* Chidding-lye, West Hoathly, East Grinstead, Sussex, England.

LINCOLN, John Francis, b. 30 July 1916, Australia. Judge. m. Joan Alison Hamilton Scott, 24 Jan. 1952, 1 son, 1 daughter. *Education:* Balliol College, Oxford, 1939-40; Honorary Society of Lincoln's Inn; Barrister-at-Law. *Appointments:* Deputy Assistant Judge Advocate General (India & Singapore), 1945-47; Associate to Chief Justice of New South Wales, 1949; Barrister New South Wales Bar, 1949-68; Acting Judge, Supreme Court of New South Wales, 1967; Judge, District Court of New South Wales, 1968-; Deputy-Chancellor of Macquarie University, NSW, 1976-. *Memberships:* Council 1963-, Chairman, Standing Committee of Convocation, 1974-, Chairman of Friends, 1964-, Macquarie University, NSW; State Treasurer, NSW Liberal Party, 1966-68, Member, Federal Council, 1966-67; Chancellor, Diocese of Newcastle, 1978-; Administrative Committee Commonwealth & Empire Law Conference, 1965; President, Prisoner's Aid Association of NSW; Chairman, Northern Suburbs Municipal & Shire Conference, 1957; President Australian University Graduate Conference, 1977-80, Vice-President, 1976. *Honours:* Deputy Mayor, 1954-56, Mayor of North Sydney, 1956-58. *Hobby:* Swimming. *Address:* Stone Lodge, 30-34 Stanley Street, St Ives, New South Wales 2075, Australia.

LINDSAY, Hilarie Elizabeth, b. 18 Apr. 1922, Sydney, Australia. Author, Toy Manufacturer. m. Philip Singleton Lindsay, 19 Feb. 1944, 1 son, 2 daughters. *Education:* Williams Business College, 1938. *Appointments:* Company Secretary, 1945, Director, 1958, AL Lindsay and Company Pty Ltd; Director and Editor, Ansay Pty Ltd., 1972. *Memberships:* President, Australian Toy Manufacturers Association of Australia; Past President, Society of Women Writers, Australia; Past Vice-President, International PEN; President, State Council, Fellowship of Australian Writers; Committee of Management, Australian Society of Authors; National Press Club; Zonta International; Patron, Terrey Hills Library; Australia Opera. *Publications:* 101 Toys to Make, 13 editions; You're on your Own—Teenage Survival Kit, 3 editions; Echoes of Henry Lawson; Grenfell Sketchbook; Midget Mouse Finds a House; The Short Story; Learn to Write; The Gravy Train; The Naked Gourmet; The Withered Tree, 2 act drama; One Woman's World, verse; Editor of: Ink No. 2, So You Want to be a Writer, Culinary Capers. *Honours:* Grenfell Henry Lawson Prose Award, 1966, 1967; MBE, 1974; Queen's Silver Jubilee Medal, 1977; Hilarie Lindsay Award inaugurated by the Society of Women Writers, New South Wales, 1981. *Hobbies:* Tennis; Attending Ballet; Opera; Drama; Gardening; Reading; Public Speaking. *Address:* 7 Centenary Avenue, Hunters Hill, New South Wales, Australia.

LINDSAY, Joseph Fraser, b. 29 Aug. 1921, Dublin, Ireland. Chartered Civil Engineer. m. Mary Geraldine Webb Adams, 20 Apr. 1948, 1 son, 1 daughter. *Education:* BA, BAI, University of Dublin, 1940-44. *Appointments:* Assistant Resident Engineer, KCD Group, 1943-45; Assistant Engineer, Sir Cyril Kirkpatrick and Partners, 1945-53; Senior Assistant Civil Engineer, Senior Engineer, Associate, Scott Wilson Kirkpatrick and Partners, UK, 1954-73; Partner, Scott Wilson Kirkpatrick and Partners, Hong Kong, 1960-. *Memberships:* Fellow, Institution of Civil Engineers (Overseas Corresponding Member for Hong Kong); Fellow, Hong Kong Institution of Civil Engineers; Fellow, Institution of Highway Engineers; Past Chairman, Association of Consulting Engineers of Hong Kong; Association of Consulting Engineers, UK; Permanent International Association of Navigation Congresses. *Publications:* Various articles in technical press and papers to Institutions, Societies and Clubs. *Honours:* Alexander Prize, 1943, Clark Prize, 1943, University of Dublin; Overseas Premium, Institution of Civil Engineers, 1977. *Hobbies:* Walking; Photography; Squash; Golf; Ornithology. *Address:* 34 Kadoorie Avenue, Kowloon, Hong Kong.

LINES, Donald Peter, b. 23 Dec. 1931, Bermuda. Banking. m. 3 Dec. 1960 (Wife deceased), 3 sons, 1 daughter. *Education:* Chartered Accountant courses leading to qualification, McGill University, 1955; Extension courses in management, computers and other specialized subjects, The Executive Development Institute and McGill University; Other seminars on interna-

tional tax and banking. *Appointments:* Creek, Cushing & Hodgson, 1949-65, (Partner, 1958); Partner, Price Waterhouse, Canada, 1965-69; Trust Officer, 1969-, Assistant General Manager, International & Trust and a member of the Executive, 1971, General Manager, 1979, Chief General Manager, 1981, Bank of Bermuda Limited. *Memberships:* Chairman, Economic Committee of the Chamber of Commerce; Economic Forum of the Bermuda Government; Chairman, Water Authority. *Hobbies:* Fishing; Boating; Scuba-diving; Water sports; Reading; Tennis; Golf. *Address:* Mill Point, Fairylands, Pembroke, Bermuda.

LING, Tak-Ming Bill, b. 2 Aug. 1949, Hong Kong. Advertising. *Education:* BA, Ohio Wesleyan University, 1972; MIM, American Graduate School of International Management, 1974. *Appointments:* Director and General Manager, CCAA International Limited. *Memberships:* American Marketing Association; Hong Kong Management Association. *Hobbies:* Boating; Photography; Golf. *Address:* 17 Conduit Road, Apt. 8A, Hong Kong.

LINI, Walter, b. 1942. Prime Minister, Vanuatu. m. 2sons, 1 daughter. *Education:* St John's Kohimarama Theological College, Solomons; St John's Theological College, Auckland; Ordained 1970. *Appointments:* District Priest, Longana, East Aoba 1970-74; President, National Party 1974; Petitioned before UN Committee of 24, 1974 and 1976; Representative Assembly 1975; Leader, Vanuaaka Pati, invited to join Government of National Unity 1978; Deputy Chief Minister, Prime Minister of Vanuatu 1980-. *Address:* Office of the Prime Minister, Vanuatu.

LINNANE, Anthony William, b. 17 July 1930, Sydney, Australia. Professor of Biochemistry. m. (1) Judith Neil (div.) (2) Daryl Woods, 3 May 1980, 2 sons, 2 daughters. *Education:* BSc, 1951, MSc, 1953, PhD, 1956, DSc, 1972, University of Sydney. *Appointments:* Post-Doctoral Fellow, Enzyme Institute, University of Wisconsin, 1956-58; Lecturer, Senior Lecturer, University of Sydney, 1958-62; Reader, 1962-65, Professor, 1965-, Monash University. *Memberships:* Australian Biochemical Society; Australian Society for Microbiology; Australian Society for Genetics; American Association for the Advancement of Science. *Publications:* Approximately 160 Scientific publications in learned journals, papers and reviews; Editor-in-Chief of Biochemistry International. *Honours:* Fellow, Australian Academy of Science, 1950; Fellow, Royal Society, London, 1980; Lemberg Lecturer, Australian Biochemical Society, 1972. *Hobbies:* Reading; Squash; Horse Racing; Tennis. *Address:* 20 Studley Avenue, Kew, Victoria, Australia.

LINNING, Christopher Adrian, b. 7 June 1953, Brisbane, Queensland, Australia. Cartographic Design Draftsperson. *Education:* Associate Diploma in Cartography, 1975; Associate Diploma in Civil Engineering (Pending); Diploma in Genealogy, Australia (Pending). *Appointments:* Civil Engineering Fraftsman, Department of Transport, Australia, Water Resources Commission, New South Australia; Mechanical Design Draftsman, Esso (Australia) Ltd. *Memberships:* Australian Institute of Cartographers; Australian Society of Genealogists. *Hobbies:* Mah Jong; Bridge; Tennis; Swimming. *Address:* 245 Johnston Street, Annandale, New South Wales, Australia, 2038.

LISTER, James, b. 1 Mar. 1923, London, England. Surgeon. m. 22 May 1946, 3 daughters. *Education:* University of Edinburgh, 1940-45; MBChB, 1945; FRCS Ed, 1950; FRCS Glas, 1970; FRCS Eng, 1975; MD, 1972. *Appointments:* Surgeon Lieutenant RNVR, 1945-48; Training appointments in Surgery, Edinburgh and Dundee, 1948-58; Halstead Research Fellow, University of Colorado, 1959; Senior Lecturer in Paediatric Surgery, Institute of Child Health, University of London, 1960-63; Consultant Surgeon, Hospital for Sick Children, Great Ormond Street, London, 1960-63; Consultant Surgeon, Sheffield Children's Hospital, 1963-74; Professor of Paediatric Surgery, University of Liverpool, 1974-. *Memberships:* British Association of Paediatric Surgeons, Honorary Secretary, 1965-73, President, 1974-75; British Paediatric Association; Hon. Fellow Surgical Section, American Academy of Pediatrics; Member of Council, Royal College of Surgeons of Edinburgh, 1978-; Secretary, Treasurer, World Federation of Associations of Pediatric Surgeons. *Pu-*

blications: Various contributions to scientific journals on neonatal and paediatric surgery; Joint editor, Neonatal Surgery, 1979. *Hobbies:* Hill walking; Fishing; Family Activities. *Address:* Kailheugh, Hownam, Kelso, Roxburghshire, Scotland.

LISULO, Daniel Muchiwa, b. 6 Dec. 1930, Mongu. Lawyer and Politican. m. Mary Mambo 1968 (Dec. 1976) 3 sons, 2 daughters. *Education:* Loyola College, Madras University; Law Faculty of Delhi University India. *Appointments:* Active in independence struggle 1953-63; Anglo-American Corporation, Central Africa 1963-64; Assistant Solicitor, Ellis & Company, Lusaka 1964-67; Advocate, Lisulo & Company 1968-; Director, Bank of Zambia 1964-77; Prime Minister,1978-81. *Memberships:* Chairman, Local Government Service Commission 1964-72; National Committee, One Party System in Zambia; Director, various companies; Central Committee United National INdependence Party 1972-; Minister of Legal Affairs and Attorney-General 1977-78; Chairman, Social and Cultural Sub-Committee, UNIP 1981-; ZIMCO 1979-; National Assembly; Legal Counsel of UNIP. *Hobbies:* Swimming; Hunting; Boating; Soccer. *Address:* Lisulo and Company, Kulima Tower, PO Box 32259, Lusaka, Zambia.

LITTLE, James Crawford, b. 22 May, 1922, Dumfries, Scotland. Psychiatrist. m. Catherine E Salt, 2 Apr. 1949, 1 son, 1 daughter. *Education:* MB., Ch.B., 1947, MD., 1965, University of Bristol, UK; DPM., University of Durham, UK, 1954; MRCP., 1955, FRCP., 1971, Edinburgh, Scotland; FRC.Psych., 1971. *Appointments:* Senior Registrar, Joint Department of Psychological Medicine, Royal Victoria Infirmary and University of Durham, UK, 1956-58; Consultant Psychiatrist, St. James's Teaching Hospital, Leeds, and Clinical Lecturer, University of Leeds, UK, 1958-66; Consultant Psychiatrist and Director of Clinical Research, Crichton Royal Hospital, Dumfries, Scotland. *Memberships:* Hon. Secretary, 1971-75, Hon. Secretary. SCP Research Fund, 1975-, Society of Clinical Psychiatrists; Mental Health Group Executive Committee, British Medical Association. *Publications:* Psychiatry in a General Hospital, 1974; numerous papers in clinical and epidemiological psychiatry and research methodology in psychiatry. *Honours:* Martyn Memorial Pathology Scholarship, University of Bristol, UK, 1945. *Hobbies:* Art; Gardening. *Address:* 'Fearnhill', Bankend Road, Dumfries, Scotland, DG1 4TP.

LITTLE, John Miles, b. 28 Dec. 1933, Sydney, Australia. Surgeon. m. Penelope Ann Vincent, 29 July 1978, 1 son, 3 daughters. *Education:* MB., BS., (Hons. II), MS., 1969, MD., 1977, University of Sydney, Australia; FRACS., 1963; Research Fellow, Department of Surgery, Glasgow, UK, 1966. *Appointments:* Medical Officer and Registrar, 1959-64, Clinical Superintendent, Surgical, 1964-66, Assistant Surgeon, 1967-74, Royal Prince Alfred Hospital; Senior Lecturer in Surgery, 1967-71, Associate Professor, 1971-78, Professor, 1978, University of Sydney, Australia; Surgeon, 1974-80; Visiting Surgeon, 1978, Chairman, Division of Surgery, 1978, Westmead Centre; Consultant Surgeon, Queen Elizabeth II Rehabilitation Centre, Camperdown, Australia, 1976; Consultant Surgeon, Parramatta Centre, Australia, 1980; Consultant Surgeon, Royal Alexandra Hospital for Children, Australia, 1980. *Memberships:* Court of Examiners, RACS., 1974-; Collegium Internaionale Chirurgiae Digestivae; International Council on the Future of the University; International Cardiovascular Association; Societe Internationale de Chirurgie; Editorial Boards of Surgical Techniques Illustrated, Boston; Australia and New Zealand Journal of Surgery; Sub-Dean, Faculty of Medicine, University of Sydney; Governing Council, Cranbrook School, Sydney; Trustee, Outstreched Hand Organisation, Sydney. *Publications:* The Management of Liver Injuries, 1971; Major Amputations for Vascular Disease, 1975; Round Trip (Poetry), 1978; numerous articles in medical and surgery literature. *Honours:* Nuffield Dominion Travelling Fellowship in Medicine, 1966; Glissan Memorial Prize, Royal Australasian College of Surgeons, 1967. *Hobbies:* Writing; Birdwatching. *Address:* 28 Cranstons Road, Dural, New South Wales 2158, Australia.

LITTLEJOHN, Murray John, b. 26 Mar. 1932, Perth, Western Australia. Zoologist. m. Patricia Gordon Sloane, 9 Dec. 1955, 2 sons. *Education:* BSc., 1954, BSc., (Hons. Zoology), 1955, PhD. (Zoology), 1958,

University of Western Australia; MSc., University of Melbourne, 1971. *Appointments:* Graduate Assistant, Department of Zoology, University of Western Australia, 1955-57; Instructor, part-time, Department of Zoology, University of Texas, Austin, USA, 1958-59; Lecturer, 1959-62, Senior Lecturer, 1963-68, Reader in Ecology, 1968-, Department of Zoology, University of Melbourne, Australia. *Memberships:* President, Australian Society of Herpetologists, 1967-68; Vice-President, Society for the Study of Evolution, 1969; Vice-President, Ecological Society of Australia, 1978-81; International Committee of International Congress of Systematic and Evolutionary Biology, 1980-. *Publications:* 63 papers and nine chapters in books, dealing with acoustic communication, speciation processes, zoogeography, systematics and ecology, mainly on the anuran amphibians of southern Australia and the United States of America. *Honours:* Commonwealth Scholarship, Australian Government, 1951-54; Hackett Studentship, University of Western Australia, 1958-59; Fulbright Travel Grant, Postgraduate student, 1958-59; Fulbright Travel Grant, Senior Research Scholar, 1966; Member of the Society of the Sigma Xi, 1959; Fellow of American Association for Advancement of Science, 1968; Fellow of the Herpetologists' League, 1971; Honorary Foreign Member of American Society of Ichthyologists and Herpetologists, 1977. *Hobbies:* Photography; Electronics; Sailing. *Address:* 11 Marlborough Avenue, Camberwell, Victoria, Australia 3124.

LIU, Ching, b. 21 July 1932, China. Librarian. *Education:* BA, National Taiwan University, 1954; Diploma, Interpreters' Training School, 1955; MA, Taiwan Normal University, 1960; Certificate, Leeds Polytechnic, UK, 1979. *Appointments:* Lecturer, National Cengchi University; University Librarian, National Tsinghua University; Cataloguer, Singapore Nanyang University; Assistant Librarian, College Librarian, Sub-Librarian, United College, The Chinese University of Hong Kong. *Address:* 77 Pokfulam Road, 5th Floor, Hong Kong.

LIVERIS, Marcus, b. 15 May 1931, Perth, Western Australia. Academic (Dean). m. Leonie Beth Wood, 16 May 1965, 2 sons, 1 daughter. *Education:* BSc.(Hons.), Physical/Organic Chemistry, PhD., University of Western Austrlia, 1949-56; Teacher's Certificate; Teacher's Higher Certificate. *Appointments:* Lecturer/Senior Lecturer in Chemistry, Perth Technical College, Australia, 1957-64; Post-Doctoral Fellow, University of Saskatchewan, Canada, 1965-66; Head, Department of Chemistry, 1967-69, Assistant Director (Applied Science) retitled Dean of Applied Science, 1969-73, Dean of Health Sciences, 1973-, Western Australian Institute of Technology. *Memberships:* Fellow, Royal Australian Chemical Institute; Fellow, Chemical Society, UK; Fellow, Australian College of Education; American Chemical Society; Australian and New Zealand Association for Advancement of Science; American Society of Allied Health Professions; Australian and New Zealand Society for Epidemiology and Research in Community Health; Australian Public Health Association. *Publications:* various publications, initially in scientific research, more recently in health sciences education and health policy. *Honours:* Post-doctoral Fellow, National Research Council of Canada, 1965; World Health Organization Fellow, 1978. *Hobbies:* Community activities; Recreational sports; Gardening. *Address:* 28 Kalari Drive, City Beach, Western Australia 6015.

LIVINGSTONE, Robert Reuel North, b. 14 Oct. 1915, Christchurch, New Zealand. Real Estate Consultant. m. Hilaire Rosetta Hyde, 19 Nov. 1948, 2 daughters. *Education:* B.Comm., New Zealand University, 1947; Fellow, Real Estate Institute of New Zealand, Freinz; Fellow, New Zealand Institute of Valuers, FNZIV; Fellow, Chartered Accountant of New Zealand, FCA. *Appointments:* H G Livingstone Limited, Real Estate, 1935-39; New Zealand Army, Lt. Col., 1939-45; UN-RRA, Middle-East, Byelo-Russia and Europe, 1945-47; HG Livingston Limited, Jones Lang Wotton, 1947-. *Memberships:* President, Royal Empire Society/Royal Commonwealth Society, Christchurch; Chairman, Combined Patriotic Societies, Christchurch; New Zealand President, General Auctioneers Association of New Zealand; Patron, New Zealand Divisional Cavalry Regiment Association; Vestry, St. Barnabas, 1968-81; New Zealand National Party. *Honours:* MBE., 1943; Mentioned in Despatches, 1944; OBE., 1945; ED. &

Bar, 1956; Eighth Army Bar to the Africa Star. *Hobbies:* Cricket; Golf; Gardening. *Address:* 11 Holmwood Road, Fendalton, Christchurch, New Zealand.

LJUNGSTRÖM, Arne Ernst, b. 6 Apr. 1930, Stockholm, Sweden. Data Processing Executive. *Education:* High School in Stockholm, Sweden. *Appointments:* Supervisor of Tabulating Production, 1955-62, Manager, Computer Operations Department, 1962-68, Resident Data Processing Officer, London, England, 1968-71, Data Processing Officer, Toronto Data Centre, 1971-78, Director of Data Processing Services, 1978-, Canada Life Assurance Company, Toronto, Canada. *Memberships:* Canadian Information Processing Society; Chairman, Canadian Federation of Film Societies; Vice-President/Treasurer, Toronto Film Society; National Ballet of Canada; Shaw Festival Theatre Foundation; Stratford Shakespearean Festival Foundation of Canada. *Creative Works:* Co-publisher of: CFFS Index of 16MM & 35MM Feature Length Films Available in Canada. *Honours:* Dorothy and Oscar Burritt Memorial Award, CFFS, 1978; Special Certificate of Merit for years of work within the Film Society Movement in Canada, 1979. *Hobbies:* Photography; Film and the performing arts. *Address:* Apartment 2104, 65 Wynford Heights Crescent, Don Mills, Ontario, Canada, M3C 1L7.

LLEWELLYN, Donald Rees, b. 20 Nov. 1919, Dursley, Gloucestershire, England. Vice-Chancellor. m. Ruth Marian Blandford, 1943, 1 son, 1 daughter. *Education:* BSc, 1941, DSc, 1957, University of Birmingham; DPhil, University of Oxford, 1943. *Appointments:* Research Fellow, University of Oxford, 1941-44, University of Cambridge, 1944-46; Lecturer in Chemistry, University College of North Wales, 1946-49, University College of London, 1952-57; ICI Research Fellow, University College of London, 1949-52; Professor of Chemistry and Director of Laboratories, University of Auckland, 1957-64, Assistant Vice-Chancellor, 1962-64. *Memberships:* Council of Association of Commonwealth Universities, 1970-72; Council of: Hamilton Teachers College, Waikato Technical Institute; New Zealand Atomic Energy Committee. *Publications:* Numerous papers on application of stable isotopes in Journal of Chemical Society and elsewhere. *Honours:* Justice of the Peace. *Hobbies:* Squash; Tennis; Showjumpint (FEI Judge); Photography. *Address:* R D 3, Hamilton, New Zealand.

LLEWELLYN, Frederick John, (Sir), b. 29 Apr. 1915. Director-General (Retired). m. Joyce Barrett, 4 Sept. 1939, 1 son. 1 daughter. *Education:* BSc, 1935, PhD, 1938, DSc, 1951, University of Birmingham. *Appointments:* Lecturer in Chemistry, Birkbeck College, 1939-45; Director, Ministry of Supply Research Team, 1941-46; ICI Research Fellow, 1946-47; Professor of Chemistry, Auckland University College, New Zealand, 1947-55; Vice-Chancellor and Rector, University of Canterbury, Christchurch, New Zealand, 1956-61; Chairman, University Grants Committee, New Zealand, 1961-66; Chairman, New Zealand Broadcasting Corporation, 1962-65; Vice-Chancellor, Exeter University, 1966-72; Director-General, The British Council, 1972-80; Retired, 1980. *Memberships:* Fellow of: Royal Institute of Chemistry, 1944; New Zealand Institute of Chemistry, 1948; Royal Society of Arts, 1952; Royal Society of New Zealand, 1964; Chairman of: New Zealand Council of Adult Education, 1961-66; New Zealand Commonwealth Scholarships and Fellowships Committee, 1961-66; Northcott Theatre Board of Management, Exeter, 1966-72; Vice-President of: Institute of Rural Life at Home and Overseas; Llangollen International Musical Eisteddfod, 1973-; Associated with numerous committees and councils including: Committee, British Volunteer Programme, 1974-79; Franco-British Council, 1975-; Council of Governors, London House for Overseas Graduates, 1975-; Grand Council, Royal Academy of Dancing, 1976-; Chairman, Overall Review of Education in Hong Kong, 1981-82. *Publications:* Crystallographic papers in Chemical Journal; Acta Crystallographica. *Honours:* Honorary LLD: Canterbury, New Zealand, 1962; Victoria University of Wellington, New Zealand, 1966; Exeter, 1973; Birmingham, 1975; Honorary DSc, Salford, 1975; Honorary Doctor of the Open University, 1979; KCMG, 1974. *Address:* 30 Lancaster Road, Wimbledon Village, London, England.

LLEWELLYN-SMITH, Michael John, b. 28 Nov. 1942, Monmouth, South Wales, United Kingdom. City Plan-

ner. m. Ida Frances Jonassen, 1 Dec. 1971, 1 son. *Education:* BA.(Cantab), 1965, Dip.Arch.(Hons.),(Cantab.), 1968, MA.(Cantab.), 1968, Pembroke College, Cambridge University, UK, 1962-66, 1967-68; MTCP., Wesley College, Sydney University, Australia, 1970-71. *Appointments:* Assistant Architect, Roy Grounds & Co., Architects, Melbourne, Australia, 1966-67; Job Architect, London Borough of Barnet, UK, 1968-69; Architect-Planner, The City of London, UK, 1970; Planner, McConnel Smith & Johnson, Sydney, Australia, 1971; Deputy City Planner, City of Sydney, Australia, 1972-79; City Planner, City of Adelaide, 1974-; Commissioner, City of Adelaide Planning Commission, Australia, 1977-; President SA, Royal Australian Planning Institute, 1977-79. *Memberships:* Royal Town Planning Institute; Associate, Royal Australian Institute of Architects; Associate, Royal Institute of British Architects; Royal Australian Planning Institute; Australian Institute of Urban Studies, 1974-; Hawks Club, Cambridge; United Oxford and Cambridge Club, London, 1966-74; The University Club, Sydney, 1971-74; The Rotary Club of Adelaide, 1980. *Publications:* Articles published in the Royal Australian Planning Institute Journal, 1970, 71, 72, 78, 79; Papers presented published in proceedings of ANZAAS, 1972; IFHP, 1975; PACOM, 1979; EAROPH, 1980. *Honours:* Rhodes Travel Scholarship to Canada, 1962; Visiting guest lecturer at the: City University of New York, 1973, Tulane University, New Orleans, 1975, Toronto University, 1977. *Hobbies:* Badminton; Cycling; Theatre. *Address:* 29 Prescott Terrace, Rose Park, South Australia 5067.

LLOYD, Bruce, b. 24 Feb. 1937, Brighton, Victoria, Australia. Member of House of Representatives. m. Heather Campbell Laird, 9 Mar. 1963, 2 sons, 1 daughter. *Education:* Geelong College, Australia. *Appointments:* MHR (NCP) for Murray, Victoria, 1971-; State President, Victorian Country Prty, 1969-71. Young Farmers, 1959-60. *Address:* 42 High Street, Shepparton, Victoria, 3630, Australia.

LLOYD, George Peter, b. 23 Sept. 1926, London, England. Government Service. m. Margaret Harvey, 22 Apr. 1957, 2 sons, 1 daughter. *Education:* MA, King's College, Cambridge 1948-51. *Appointments:* District Officer, Kenya 1951-60; Principal, Colonial Office 1960-61; Colonial Secretary, Seychelles 1961-66; Chief Secretary, Fiji 1966-70; Defence Secretary/Secretary for Security, Hong Kong, 1971-81; Governor, Cayman Islands. *Memberships:* Royal Commonwealth Society; Muthaiga Country Club; Hong Kong Club. *Honours:* CMG 1965; Mentioned in Dispatches 1957. *Hobbies:* Travel; Chess; Bridge. *Address:* Montpelier, Devonshire, Bermuda.

LLOYD, Ian Stewart, b. 30 May 1921, Durban, Natal, South Africa. Economist. m. 1 Mar. 1951, 3 sons. *Education:* University of the Witwatersrand, 1939-41; BCom, University of Cambridge, UK, 1945-49; MA, MSc. *Appointments:* Economic Adviser, Central Mining and Investment Corporation, 1950-53; Member, Board of Trade Industries, 1953-55; Director, Acton Society Trust, 1956; Group Economic Adviser, British and Commonwealth Shipping, 1956-; Member of Parliament, 1964-. *Memberships:* Fellow, Royal Statistical Society; Chairman, Select Committee on Energy, 1979; Chairman, Parliamentary Information Technology Committee, 1980; Brook's Club; Royal Yacht Squadron; Royal Cork Yacht Club; House of Commons Yacht Club. *Publications:* Rolls-Royce, The Growth of a Firm; Rolls-Royce, The Years of Endeavour; Rolls-Royce, The Merlin at War. *Honours:* Alexander Aiken Medal, 1941; Chamber of Industries Prize, 1941; Union Government Post-Graduate Scholarship, 1941; President of the Cambridge Union, 1947. *Hobbies:* Sailing; Music. *Address:* House of Commons, London, SW1, England.

LLOYD, Richard Ernest Butler, b. 6 Dec. 1928, Bromley Cross, Bolton, Lancashire, England. Banker. m. Jennifer Susan Margaret Cardiff, 6 June 1955, 3 sons. *Education:* MA.Oxon in Politics, Philosophy & Economics, Hertford College, Oxford, UK. *Appointments:* Joined Glyn, Mills & Co., 1952; Executive Director, 1964-70, Chief Executive, 1970-78, Williams and Glyn's Bank; Director, 1961-75, Deputy Chairman, 1965-71, Australia and New Zealand Bank and Australia and New Zealand Banking Group; Chief Executive and Deputy Chairman, Hill Samuel & Co. Limited, also

Director, Hill Samuel Group Limited, Jan. 1978-. *Memberships:* Council member, Confederation of British Industry; Companion, British Institute of Management; Fellow and ex member of Council, Institute of Bankers; Worshipful Company of Mercers. *Hobbies:* Gardening; Walking; Fishing. *Address:* Sunridge Place;, Sunridge, Sevenoaks, Kent, England.

LO, Kwock Chuen, b. 19 Dec. 1917, Hong Kong. Printer; Publisher. m. 7 Jan. 1940, 3 sons, 2 daughters. *Education:* Chinese Education. *Appointments:* Proprietor of Chung Nam Printing Co. (Est. 1947); Publisher and Chief Editor, Api Siang Pau, (Est. 1954). *Memberships:* President, Sabah Printers Association, 1973-81; President, Rotary Club of Kota Kinabalu, 1980-81; Past President, 1966-74, Sabah Scouts Council; Past President, 1964-77, Kota Kinabalu High School; Past President, 1968-74, Sabah Exserices Association. *Publications:* Api Siang Pau; Kinabalu Magazine; A Quick Look at Singapore and Philippines. *Honours:* 1939-45 Star; The Pacific Star; The 1939-45 Defence Medal and War medal by British Government, 1946; Certificate of Honour by HE The Yang Di-Pertua Ngeri Sabah, Nov. 1963; PPM, 1967; ADK, 1969; Medal of Merit, National Chief Scout of Malaysia, 1971; Semangate Rinba, Second Highest award of Malaysia Scouts, 1973; ASDK, 1973; PGDK, 1975. *Hobbies:* Reading; Driving; Travelling; Chinese Art Collecting. *Address:* 24 Lorong Dewan, Kota Kinabalu, Sabah, Malaysia.

LOBLEY, Neil John, b. 11 Dec. 1929, Yallourn, Victoria, Australia. Consulting Engineer. m. Jean Maree Neeson, 8 Feb. 1958, 2 sons, 1 daughter. *Education:* Diploma Mechanical Engineering, 1954; Diploma Electrical Engineering, 1951. *Appointments:* State Electricity Commission, Victoria, 1950; Australian Paper Manufacturers, 1951; Hydro Electric Commission, 1952; Commonwealth Department of Works, 1953-55; Thomas Anderson and Associates, Consulting Engineers, 1956-57; Lobley, Treidel, Davies and Partners Pty. Ltd., 1958-. *Memberships:* Fellow, Institution of Engineers, Australia; Athenaeum Club, Melbourne; Past President, Melbourne Junior Chamber of Commerce. *Hobbies:* Squash; Yachting. *Address:* 654 Toorak Road, Toorak, Victoria 3142, Australia.

LOCK, (Lily) Grace, b. 14 Feb. 1902, Prahran Victoria. House wife; Amateur Photography. m. Charles George Lock, 25 May 1922, 1 son, 2 daughters. *Education:* St Michael's Lady College, St Kilda. *Memberships:* Royal Photographic Society of Great Britain; Photographic Society of America; Australian Photographic Society; Luce Society Victoria; Melbourne Camera Club. *Creative Works:* Photo Prints accrideted in 28 Countries. *Honours:* ESFIAP 1971; EFIAP 1973; FRPS 1972; BEM 1981; Commonwealth Medal for Photography 1980; etc. Hobby: Photography. *Address:* 'Corleenth, 185 Coltham Road, Kew, Victoria 3101, Australia.

LOCKHART, Justice John Stanley, b. 2 Oct. 1935. Judge of the Federal Court. m. Margaret Windeyer, 9 Apr. 1960, 1 son, 3 daughters. *Education:* BA, Sydney University; LLB, admitted NSW Bar 1960. *Appointments:* New South Wales Bar Cl. 1961-65, 1972-74; Hon. Secretary NSW Bar Association 1964-65, Hon. Treas. 1974; Director, Counsel's Chambers Limited 1965-78; Marian St. Theatre Limited 1969-76, Chairman 1973-76; Legal Member, NSW Public Accountants Registration Board and NSW Companies Auditors Board 1974-77. *Memberships:* Committee of Inquiry into Legal Education in NSW 1974-80; Trustee Sydney Grammar School, 1977-; International Arts Corporation of Australia; Commsnd. CMF 1956, Sydney University Regiment Captain 1959. *Honours:* Queen's Council 1973. *Hobbies:* Music; Tennis. *Address:* 3 Garden Square, Gordon, New South Wales, 2072, Australia.

LOGAN, Rodman Emmason, b. 7 Sept. 1922, Saint John West, New Brunswick, Canada. Barrister-at-Law. m. Evelyn Pearl DeWitt, 19 June 1948, 3 sons, 1 daughter. *Education:* BA, 1949; BCL, University of New Brunswick 1951; DCL(Hon), Saint Thomas University 1974. *Appointments:* Practised Law, Saint John, New Brunswick, 1951-70; Legislative Assembly 1963-, 1970-, 74, 78; Provincial Secretary and Minister of Labour 1970-74; Minister of Labour, Housing, 1974-77; Attorney-General, Minister of Justice 1977-. *Memberships:* Royal Canadian Legion; Carleton's York Regimental; New Brunswick Barristers Society; Cana-

dian Bar Association. *Publications:* The Role of the Ombudsman in New Brunswick; The Cassin Institute, 1975. *Honours:* CD (Canadian Forces Decoration); QC 1972. Hobby: Reading. *Address:* 37 Buena Vista Avenue, Saint John West, New Brunswick, Canada, E2M 2S7.

LOHREY, John Elliott, b. 4 Dec. 1943, Launceston, Tasmania. Senior Lecturer, Drama and Theatre Arts. m. Kathleen Ashworth, 7 Jan. 1967, (Divorced) 2 sons. *Education:* BA.Dip.Ed, University of Tasmania, 1962-65; MA, University of Exeter, UK, 1969-70; Associate of Drama Board, UK, 1981. *Appointments:* Teacher, Launceston High School, 1966; Teacher, Launceston Matriculation College, 1967-71; Senior Master, Burnie High School, 1972; Lecturer, Division of Teacher Education, Tasmanian College of Advanced Education, 1973-77; Senior Lecturer, 1978-82. *Memberships:* Founder and Artistic Director, Tasmanian Children's Theatre; Director, Tasmanian Theatre Company; Senior Vice-President, Launceston Players; Tasmanian Association for Drama in Education; Educational Drama Association, UK; Associate of Drama Board, UK. *Publications:* Arts Columnist, Drama Critic; Freelance Theatre Director; Adjudicator and Examiner. *Hobbies:* Theatre History; Golf; Reading. *Address:* 1 Chifley Street, Kings Meadows, Launceston, Tasmania 7250, Australia.

LOH SOONG CHEW, John, b. 9 Aug. 1948 Penang, West Malaysia. Chartered Valuation Surveyor. m. Lay-lay Loh, 3 Apr. 1975, 1 son, 1 daughter. *Education:* St Xavier's Institution, Penang; Professional Diploma, Royal Institution of Chartered Surveyors, UK. *Appointments:* Manager, CH Williams, Talhar and Wong PJ Office, 1971-; Director, 1977-. *Memberships:* Royal Institution of Chartered Surveyors; Institute of Housing; Rating and Valuation Association; Institute of Arbitrators; Institution of Surveyors, Malaysia; Board of Surveyors, Malaysia. Lions Club of George Town; Lions Clubs International. *Honours:* Lion of the Year, 1973-74 and 1979-80; Lions International President Appreciation Award, 1973-74; 100% President's Award, 1976-77; District Chairman of the Year, 1977-78; Outstanding Zone Chairman, 1978-79; Outstanding District Chairman, 1979-80; Honorary Citizen, Inchon City, South Korea; Awarded Pingat Jasa Kebaktian, 1978. *Hobbies:* Reading; Social Work. *Address:* 45 Minden Heights, Road 5, Gelugor, Penang, West Malaysia.

LOKOLOKO, Rore, b. 21 Sept. 1930, Iokea Gulf Province, Papua New Guinea. Politician. m. Lalahaia Meakoro, 1950, 4 sons, 6 daughters. *Education:* Sogeri High School, 1945-49; Diploma in Co-operative, India. *Appointments:* Co-operative Society Officer, 1950-68; Member, House of Assembly, 1968-76; Member of Parliament, 1976-77; Governor General, 1977-. *Memberships:* Scout Association of P.N.G; Red Cross Society; St John Ambulance; RSPCA; Rotary International; Lions; Royal Papua Yacht Club. *Honours:* GCMG, 1977; OBE, 1975; K.St.J, 1979. *Hobbies:* Golf; Fishing. *Address:* Government House, PO Box 79, Port Moresby, Papua New Guinea.

LONE, Mohamed Salim, b. 3 Mar. 1943, Kenya. Journalist. m. Patricia Foley, 4 Sept. 1965, 2 sons. *Education:* BA (Literature), Cum Laude, Ohio, 1965; MA (Literature), New York, 1968. *Appointments:* New York Times' Special Projects, 1969-71; Managing Editor, Sunday Post, 1972-74; Editor-in-Chief, Viva Magazine, 1974-; Editor, African Perspectives, 1977-78. *Memberships:* Chairman, Panel of Editors, Journalist of the Year Awards in Kenya; Vice Chairman, Newspapers and Periodicals Association, Kenya. *Publications:* Published in New York Times, The New Republic, The Washington Post, as well as newspapers and magazines in Kenya. *Honours:* ASPAU Scholar, 1961-65; Danforth Graduate Fellowship, 1965-68. *Address:* Viva Magazine, PO Box 46319, Nairobi.

LONERAGAN, Owen William, b. 26 Mar. 1924, Maylands, Western Australia. Forestry Research and development of community education. m. Joan Edith Shaw, 19 Feb. 1949, 2 sons, 1 daughter. *Education:* Arts I University of Western Australia, 1946; Diploma of Australian Forestry School, Canberra, 1951; Bachelor of Science in Forestry, 1954, Master of Science, University of Western Australia, 1963. *Appointments:* Junior Clerk, Public Health Department of Western

Australia, 1940; War Service, 1942-45, RAAF Wireless Operator Aircrew Attached RAF; Forests Department of Western Australia, 1951-; Forest Assessor, Jarrahdale, 1951-52; Assistant Divisional Forest Officer, Dwellingup/Pemberton, 1952-58; Divisional Forest Officer, Silviculturist Manjimup Como, 1959-80; Senior Silviculturist, Como, 1980-. *Memberships:* United Nations Association of Australia; Human Rights; UNESCO; Multicultural Education Council of W.A; Esperanto League W.A; Institute of Foresters of Australia; Royal Society W.A; Australia/New Zealand Association for Advancement of Science; University Convocation W.A; Australian Conservation Foundation; Tree Society; Returned Services League Air Force Association; Good Neighbour Council. *Publications:* Jarrah, Eucalyptus marginata and Karri E. diversicolor regeneration in Southwest Western Australia, MSc Thesis, University of W A Nedlands, 1961; Karri phenology in relation to reforestation, 1979; Focus on Northern Jarrah Forest Conservation and Recreation Areas, 1980; Vegetation Complexes, Atlas of Natural Resources of the Darling System, 1980; Ashbed and nutrients in growth of seedlings of Karri, 1964-80. *Honours:* Australian Government Universties Commission Trainee, 1946-50; Hackett Bursary, University W.A 1947; W.A. Forests Department, 1948-49; Nominee for Australian Forestry School, Canberra. *Hobbies:* International Language, Esperanto and Esperanto Literature; Gardening. *Address:* 16 Deverell Way, Bentley, Western Australia, 6102.

LONG, Norman Pratt, b. Warracknabeal, Victoria, Australia. Consultant; Radiologist (Diagnostic). *Education:* MB, BS Melbourne University 1936; DDR; Fellow, American College of Chest Physicians 1972; MRACR. *Appointments:* Internship, Alfred Hospital Melbourne 1937-38; Base Radiologist, AIF 1939-46; Radiologist, Director and Head Melbourne Hospital 1946-62; Reader in Radiol/Mass X-ray Survey's 1946-78; Deagnostic Radiological Consultant, Williamstown Hospital 1962-78; Toorak Radiology and X-ray Clinic, Melton Radiological Centre, Mount Royal Medical Centre 1962-. *Memberships:* Royal Society of Medicine, London; American College of Chest Physicians; Australian Institute of Management; Royal College of Radiologists, London; Royal Australian college of Radiologists; Royal Commonwealth Society; English Speaking Union. *Publications:* The Steriosopic FluoroscopemrBi-ocular 1949; Monographs: Pseudocarcinoma in Hiatius Hernia et al; Fluoride in Town Water Supplies; Forensic Approach to Radiology. *Honours:* Officer, Order of St John of Jerusalem; ED (Army) 1946; *Hobbies:* Swimming; Reading; Rifle-shooting. *Address:* Denbigh Lodge, 627 Malvern Road, Toorak 3142, Victoria, Australia.

LONGE, Oluwumi, b. 20 Mar. 1932, Ikere-Ekiti, Nigeria. Computer Science. m. Remi Solape Olatuyi, 22 Dec. 1960, 1 son, 2 daughters. *Education:* PhD Computer Science, Ohio State University, Columbus, Ohio, USA, 1971-74; MSc Computer Science, University of Sydney, NSW, Australia, 1963-67; Physics, BSc(London), University College, Ibadan, Nigeria, 1954-59. *Appointments:* Teacher, Christ's School, Ado-Ekiti, Nigeria, 1952-53; Principal, Lisabi College, Abeokuta, Nigeria, 1960; Senior Science Master, Lagelu Grammar School, Ibadan, Nigeria, 1961-63; Operations Manager, UAC Computer Centre, Lagos, Nigeria, 1967-68; Direcor, Ibadan University Computing Centre, Ibadan, Nigeria, 1968-78; Professor and Head of Department of Computer Science, University of Ibadan Nigeria, 1978-. *Memberships:* Fellow, Computer Association of Nigeria; Association for Computing Machinery, USA; Science Association of Nigeria. *Publications:* Continuous Data Input for Digital Computers; Computer Program Flowgraphs; Computer Science Education in Nigeria; Computer Applications to Basic Needs of Developing Nations. *Honours:* Western Nigerian Government Scholarship, 1954-59; Commonwealth Scholarship 1963-65; Rockefeller Foundation Fellowship, 1971-74; First Fellow, Computer Association of Nigeria, 1979. *Hobbies:* Gardening; Table Tennis; Music. *Address:* 2 Pepple Road, University of Ibadan, Ibadan, Nigeria.

LONGLAND, David Walter (Sir), b. 1 June 1909, Queensland, Australia. Public Servant (retired). m. Ada Elizabeth Bowness, 1935, (dec.), 1 son, 1 daughter. *Education:* Colleges, 1926-32. *Appointments:* Teaching, Queensland High Schools, 1926; Treasury,

Queensland Government, 1932; Secretary to Premier of Queensland, 1940; Officer in Charge of Immigration, 1946; Under Secretary, Department of Works, 1957; Chairman, Public Service Board, 1968; Parliamentary Commissioner for Administrative Investigations, 1974; Retired, 1979. *Memberships:* Fellow, Australian Society of Accountants; Fellow, Royal Institute Public Administration; Fellow, Australian Institute of Management; Brisbane Rotary Club; Queensland Art Gallery Foundation; President, Queensland Spastic Welfare League, 1962-; President, Australian Cerebral Palsy, 1963-64. *Honours:* C.M.G., 1972; Knighthood, 1977. *Hobbies:* Tennis; Bowls; Reading; Gardening. *Address:* 88 Lloyd Street, Camp Hill, Queensland, Australia 4152.

LOOMES, Allan Henry, b. 25 April 1917, Burrenjuck, New South Wales, Australia. Diplomat, (retired, Barrister-at-Law. m. Nancy Louise Jennings, 25 July 1942, (dec), 2 daughters, 1 deceased. *Education:* B.A., 1938, LL.B. First Class Honours, 1942, Sydney University. *Appointments:* Department of Justice, Public Trustee, New South Wales, 1935-45; RAAF., 1943-45; Department of External (later Foreign) Affairs, 1945; Consul-General (later Chargé d'Affaires), Bangkok, Thailand, 1949-52; Australian Mission to United Nations Counsellor, 1952-55; Department of Foreign Affairs, Canberra, Pacific Division, 1955-57; Australian Ambassador to Burma, 1957-61; Chairman, Joint Intelligence Committee, Canberra, 1961-63; Australian Ambassador to Thailand, 1963-68; Australian Ambassador to Republic of Korea, 1968-72; Department of Foreign Affairs, Canberra, First Assistant Secretary (Legal and Consular Division), 1972-74; Australian Ambassador to Perú, Ecuador, Colombia and Venezuela, 1974-77. *Memberships:* General Assembly of the United Nations, 1947, 1952-54, 1960, 1971 (New York); U.N. Conference on the Law of the Sea, Geneva 1958, Caracas 1974; South Pacific Commission, Noumea 1956; Council Representative, SEATO, 1963-68; Australian Representative, UNCURK, 1968-72. *Honours:* Officer of the Order of the British Empire, 1962. *Hobbies:* Golf; Swimming; Fishing. *Address:* 43 Kavel Street, Torrens, A.C.T, Australia.

L'ORANGE, Helen, b. 20 Aug. 1942, Mullumbimby, New South Wales, Australia. Director, Women's Co-ordination Unit, Premier's Department. m. Noel Arthur L'Orange, 28 Aug. 1965, 2 sons. *Education:* Teachers' Certificate, 1961. *Appointments:* Teacher, New South Wales, Department of Education, 1962-69; Child Care Co-ordinator, Marrickville Municipal Council, 1977; Executive Director, International Year of the Child National Committee of Non-Governmental Organisations, 1978; Director, Women's Co-ordination Unit, New South Wales Premier's Department, 1980. *Memberships:* Alderman, Strathfield Municipal Council, including Chairperson of Health, Building and Planning Committee, 1968-77; Executive of the New South Wales Local Government Association, 1974-77; Executive Member, Council of Social Services of New South Wales, 1976-78; Member of Women's Electoral Lobby, 1972-. *Publications:* Papers on such topics as Women and Local Government, International Year of the Child, Politics of Information, Community Netwoks. *Honours:* Commonwealth Scholarship, 1959; Award for Services to Local Government in New South Wales from the Local Government Association of New South Wales, 1977. *Hobbies:* Reading; Poetry; Films; Theatre; Australian postcards; Cycling. *Address:* 28 Ada Avenue, Strathfield, New South Wales 2135, Australia.

LORD, Maurice Athol Albert, b. 10 Oct. 1914, Adventure Bay, Bruny Island, Tasmania. Valuer. m. Jean Hallett, 2 Dec. 1939, (dec(, 1 son, (2) Lucia Kinghorn, 26 Aug. 1978. *Education:* Diploma of Valuation, Hobart Technical College, 1957. *Appointments:* With Public Secretary and Accountant, 1944-48; Director, Real Estate Company, 1948-60; Proprietor, Maurice Lord Real Estate, 1960-81; Specialising in Professional Valuation practice, 1970-81; Valuation Director, Baillieu Freeman Duff Pty. Limited, 1981-. *Memberships:* Federal President, 1978-79, General Councillor, 1972-, President Tasmanian Division, Australian Institute of Valuers; Valuers Registration Board, 1974-; Appointed Special Arbitrator under Lands Resumption Act in 1977; President, Real Estate Institute of Tasmania, 1961-62; Auctioneers and Estate Agents Council, 1966-72; Associate Fellow, Australian Institute of Management, 1959-. *Hobby:* Lawn Bowls. *Address:* 6

Strathern Street, Mount Stuart, Tasmania 7000, Australia.

LORD, Robert, b. 18 Mar. 1931, Burnley, England. University Professor. m. Jennifer, Mak Yee Fun, Sept. 1975. *Education:* MA, Russian Language and Literature, London University, 1956-60; BA, Modern and Mediaeval Languages, Oxford University, 1952-55. *Appointments:* HM Civil Service, 1955-56; Brunel College, 1957-60; Lecturer in Liberal Studies, Battersea College of Technology, 1960-63; Senior Lecturer and Head of Department, Department of Linguistic ad Regional Studies, Surrey University, 1963-68; Director of Language Centre and Professor of Applied Linguistics, Hong Kong University, 1968-; Visiting Fellow, Department of English Studies, Comparative Literature, 1980. *Memberships:* Committee on Language, HM Government Education Department; Musical Director, Hong Kong Chamber Orchestra; Hong Kong Chamber Music Society. *Publications:* Comparative Linguistics; Russian Literature; Dostoevsky: Essays, Perspectives; Hong Kong Language Papers; Studies in Bilingual Education; Many articles in papers. *Hobbies:* Music; Historical Research; Archaeology; Translation of Poetry; Orientalia. *Address:* 9 Middleton Towers, 140 Pokfulam Road, Hong Kong.

LOSEY, Joseph, b. 14 Jan 1909, La Crosse, Wisconsin, United States of America. Writer; Director. m. (1) 2 sons, (2) Patricia Mohan, 29 Sept. 1970, 2 step-children. *Education:* B.A., Dartmouth College, New Hampshire, 1929. *Appointments:* Freelance Journalist, 1931; Play and Book reviewer, 1930-31; Stage Manager, Actor, Reader New York Stage Plays, Theatre Guild, 1931-32; Guest Professor Dartmouth, 1970, 1975. *Memberships:* President, Cannes Film Festival Jury, 1972. *Creative Works:* Numerous Films, Stage plays and Documentary and Commercial films including: Little Ol' Boy, Jayhawker, 1934; Galileo Galilei, with Charles Laughton, 1947-48; Living Newspapers for Federal Theatre, New York, 1935-36; A Child went Forth; Youth Gets a Break; Pete Roleum and His Cousins, 1939; The Boy with Green Hair, 1948; The Lawless, 1949; The Prowler, 1951; The Big Night, 1951; Time without Pity, 1957; The Gypsy and The Gentleman, 1957; Modesty Blaise, 1966; A Doll's House, 1972; Director of 60 Educational Films; Films shown in festivals including: London, New York, Montreal, San Sebastian, Paris, Trieste, Mexico City, Milan, Turin, Venice, Cannes, Sorrento, Chicago. *Honours:* Chevalier de l'Ordre des Artes et Lettres, 1957; Litterarum Humaniorum Doctorem, Dartmouth College, 1973; A Gun in his Hand, Academy nomination, 1945; The Damned, 1960, Science Fiction Prize Trieste; The Servant, 1963, Best Foreign film; Accident, Jury Prize, Cannes, 1967; Secret Ceremony, Best Foreign picture, French Academy, 1968; M. Klein, In French, Official French Entry, Cannes, Best Director, Best Picture Best Picture, Best Art Direction, French Cesars, 1976; Les Routes du Sud, 1978; Don Giovanni, 1978; Boris Godunor, Paris Opera, 1980. *Address:* Cowan Bellew Associates Limited, 45 Poland Street, London W1V 4AU, England.

LOUGHLIN, George Frederick, b. 7 July 1914, Liverpool, England. Professor Emeritus. m. Anne Cowell, 12 Aug. 1943, 2 sons. *Education:* D.Mus., M.A., F.R.C.O., Royal College of Music, 1933-36. *Appointments:* Director of Music, Sidcot School, Winscombe, Somerset, 1936-42; Director of Music, Cheltenham College, Gloucester, 1943-50; Associate Professor of Music, University of Toronto, Canada, 1950-53; Lecturer in Music, University of Glasgow, 1954-57; Ormond Professor of Music, University of Melbourne, 1958-79. *Memberships:* Victorian State Chairman of the Australian Music Examination Board, 1958-77; Chairman, Grainger Museum Board, 1960-79; Trustee, Sydney Myer Music Bowl, Melbourne, 1959-79; Member of the Council, Victorian College of Arts, 1973-80; Australian Music Examinations Board; Victorian College of the Arts. *Publications:* Piano Pieces and Chamber works, including: A String Trio, A Sonatina for Violin and Piano Diatonic Harmony; A Sonatina for Violin and Piano; Various Papers and articles in Journals. *Honours:* Fellow, Royal College of Music; Fellow, The Royal Society of Arts. *Hobbies:* French Language and Literature; Swimming; Walking. *Address:* 7 Evans Road, Kew, Victoria 3101, Australia.

LOUGHNAN, Frederick Charles, b. 1 6 April 1923, Sydney, Australia. Geologist. m. Margaret Anderson Armour, 1 March 1952, 2 daughters. *Education:* B.Sc., Sydney University, 1950; Ph.D., University of New South Wales, 1958; D.Sc. University of New South Wales, 1974. *Appointments:* Geological Survey of New South Wales, 1950-53; University of New South Wales, 1953-. *Memberships:* Geological Society of Australia; Mineralogical Society of Great Britain; Mineralogical Society of America; Royal Society of New South Wales; Institute of Mining and Metallurgy, Australasia. *Publications:* 'Chemical weathering of the silicate minerals', 1969; Numerous Scientific Publications. *Honours:* Fulbright Award, 1953. *Hobbies:* Gardening; Music. *Address:* 4 Pindari Avenue, Castlecove, Australia 2069.

LOUREY, Christopher John, b. 23 Sept. 1942, Melbourne, Victoria Australia. Consultant Anaesthetist. m. Margaret Anne Johnston, 19 Dec. 1966, 3 sons, 1 daughter. *Education:* MB, BS, Melbourne University, 1966; FFARACS, Faculty of Anaesthetists, Royal Australian College of Surgeons, 1972. *Appointments:* Co-Chairman, International Affairs Committee, Undersea Medical Society, 1981; Consultant Anaesthetist, Frankston Hospital, Victoria, Australia; Director Intensive Care, Frankston Hospital; Surgeon Lt. Cdr. RAN(R). *Memberships:* South Pacific Underwater Medical Society; Australian Society of Anaesthetists; Australian Medical Association; Undersea Medical Society; International Anaesthetic Research Society; Faculty of Anaesthetists, Royal Australian College of Surgeons; Naval and Military Club, Melbourne; Peninsula Golf Club; Davey's Bay Yacht Club. *Publications:* Caudal Anaethesia in Infants and Children, 1972; Cardiac Reflexes Revisited—Man in The Aquatic Environment, 1980. *Hobbies:* Tennis; Golf; Skiing; Diving; Sailing; Bushwalking. *Address:* 43 Canadian Bay Road, Mt Eliza 3930, Victoria, Australia.

LOVEDAY, Harold Maxwell, b. 12 Sept. 1923, Petersham, New South Wales, Australia. Diplomat. m. Cynthia Nelson, 2 June 1962, 1 son, 1 daughter. *Education:* Sydney University; Canberra University College. *Appointments:* New South Wales Public Service, 1939-40; AIF 1942-45; Department of External Affairs, 1945; Served in China, 1946-50; Private Secretary to Minister for External Affairs, 1951-53; Bonn and Berlin, 1953, 1954; Korea 1954-55; Kuala Lumpur 1955-56; Washington 1959-62; Australian Commissioner South Pacific Commission 1962-66; Australian Ambassador to Indonesia 1966-69; Ambassador and Permanent Representative to UN Office, Geneva 1969-72; A/g Director General, Australian Development Agency, 1972-74; Australian High Commissioner to Canada, 1975-77; Australian Ambassador to FRG, 1977-. *Honours:* M.B.E., 1955. *Hobbies:* Tennis; Skiing. *Address:* C/o Department of Foreign Affairs, Canberra, A.C.T. 2600, Australia.

LOVELL, Alfred Charles Bernard (Sir), b. 31 Aug. 1913, Oldland Common, England. Professor of Radio Astronomy. m. Mary Joyce Chesterman, 14 Sept. 1937, 2 sons, 3 daughters. *Education:* BSc., 1934, PhD., 1936, University of Bristol. *Appointments:* Assistant Lecturer in Physics, 1936-39, Lecturer, Senior Lecturer, Reader, in Physics, 1945-49, University of Manchester; Principal Officer, Telecommunications Research Establishment, Malvern, 1939-45; Professor, Past Director (retired 1980) of Jodrell Bank, Macclesfield, Cheshire, 1951-. *Memberships:* Hon. Foreign Member, American Academy of Arts and Sciences, 1955; Hon. Life Member, New York Academy, 1960; Hon. Member, Royal Swedish Academy, 1962; Hon. Fellow, Society of Engineers, 1964; Hon. Fellow, Institution of Electrical Engineers, 1967; Hon. Fellow American Philosophical Society, 1974; Hon. Fellow, Institute of Physics, 1976; Hon. Freeman, City of Manchester, 1977. *Publications:* Numerous books in the Scientific field including: Science and Civilisation, 1939; World Power Resources and Social Development, 1945; Radio Astronomy, 1951; The Individual and the Universe, 1958; Discovering the Universe, 1963; The Story of Jodrell Bank, 1968; Out of the Zenith, 1973; Man's Relation to the Universe, 1975; P.M.S. Blackett, a biographical memoir, 1976; Contributions to Physical and Astronomical Journals. *Honours:* Royal Medal, 1960; LL.D., 1961; D.Sc., 1961; D.Univ., 1974; Duddell Medal, (Physical Society) 1954; Churchill Gold Medal, (Society of Engineers), 1964; Benjamin Franklin Medal, Royal Society of Arts, 1980; OBE., 1946; FRS., 1955; Knight Bachelor, 1961; Commander's Order of Merit,

Poland Peoples Republic, 1975; Gold Medal, Royal Astronomical Society, 1981. *Hobbies:* Music; Cricket; Gardening. *Address:* The Quinta, Swettenham, Cheshire, England.

LOVERIDGE, David Duncan, b. 13 Jan. 1944, Birmingham, England. Psychotherapist; Clinical Psychologist. m. Merlyn Chesterman, 29 Feb. 1980. *Education:* BA-(Hons.) Leeds University, 1966; MSc, Hong Kong University, 1981. *Appointments:* Ten years in therapeutic work in England in a variety of settings, mainly special education and mental health; Private Practice, Hong Kong. *Memberships:* British Psychological Society; Hong Kong Psychological Society; Association of Psychological and Educational Counsellors of Asia; Specific Learning Difficulties Association of Hong Kong. *Hobbies:* Himalayan Cultures; Rare Books; Chinese Philosophy. *Address:* 24D Peak Road, Cheung Chau Island, New Territories, Hong Kong.

LOWE, Douglas Ackley, b. 15 May 1942, Hobart, Tasmania. Parliamentarian. m. Pamela June Grant, 2 March 1962, 2 sons, 2 daughters. *Education:* St. Virgil's College. *Appointments:* Apprentice, Electrolytic Zinc Company, Risdon, Tasmania; State Secretary, Tasmanian Branch of the Australian Labor Party, 1965-69, State President, 1974-75; Elected Member for Franklin, Tasmanian House of Assembly, 1969; Minister for Housing, 1972; Chief Secretary, 1974; Deputy Premier of Tasmania, Chief Secretary, Minister for Planning and Reorganisation, 1975; Minister for Industrial Relations, Planning and the Environment, 1976; Deputy Premier, Minister for Industrial Relations and Health, 1976; Leader of the Parliamentary Labor Party, 1977; Premier, Miniser for Industrial Relations and Manpower Planning, 1977-79; Premier, Minister for Economic Planning and Development and Minister of Energy, 1979-80; Premier, Treasurer and Minister for Energy, 1980-81; Premier and Treasurer, 1981-; Tasmanian delegate to the Australian Constitutional Convention. *Memberships:* Associated with a number of sporting and welfare organisations. *Honours:* Queen's Silver Jubilee Medal, 1977. *Hobbies:* Amateur athletics; Shooting; Fishing; Walking; Tennis; Football. *Address:* 15 Tooma Avenue, Chigwell, 7011, Tasmania.

LOWE, James Brian, b. 23 Sept. 1917, Auckland, New Zealand. Physician. m. 2 Jan. 1956, 2 sons, 2 daughters. *Education:* MB., ChB., University of Edinburgh, UK, 1935-40; FRCPE., 1957; FRACP., 1965; FRCP., 1967; FRACS., 1975. *Appointments:* House Physician and Surgeon, 1940-41, Registrar, 1946-48, Royal Infirmary, Edinburgh, UK; Medical Officer, Royal Air Force, 1941-46; Senior Registrar: British Post Graduate Medical School, London, UK, 1948-49; Brompton Hospital, London, UK, 1949; National Heart Hospital, London, UK, 1949, 1950; First Assistant, Institute of Cardiology, London, UK, 1951-52; Cardiologist, Green Lane Hospital, Auckland, New Zealand, 1953. *Memberships:* Corresponding member, British Cardiac Society; Corresponding member, Association of European Paediatric Cardiologists; Cardiac Society of Australia and New Zealand; Faculty of Medicine and Human, Biology, Reader in Cardiology, School of Medicine, University of Auckland. *Honours:* OBE., 1968. *Hobbies:* Music; Gardening; Fishing; Photography. *Address:* 4 Golf Road, Epsom, Auckland 3, New Zealand.

LOWREY, Ronald Leon, b. 23 May, 1939, Melbourne, Australia. Company Director. m. Heather Monica Anne Davis, 13 Apr. 1964, 2 daughters. *Education:* MSc., Melbourne University, Australia. *Appointments:* Managing Director of: International Sugar Consultancy; Kenall Refrigeration; W H O'Gorman Limited; Melbourne Insulation Supplies & Services; Director/General Manager, Coocrooms Pty. Limited; Hardie Rubber Co. *Memberships:* President Queensland, Board member, Company Directors Association of Australia; Australian Institute of Refrigeration; Taxation Institute of Australia. *Publications:* Various Papers presented on Solar Energy throughout South East Asia and the Middle East. *Hobbies:* Fishing; Swimming; Golf. *Address:* 48 Whytecliffe Parade, Scotts Point, Queensland, Australia.

LOWRY, Robert Lynd Erskine, Baron Lowry of Crossgar, b. 30 Jan. 1919, Dublin. Lord Chief Justice. m. Mary Audrey Martin, 1 Sept. 1945, 3 daughters. *Education:* Royal Belfast Academical Institution; Exhi-

bition in Classics Scholar, 1939, 1st Class Classical Tripos Part 1, 1939, Part 11 1940, BA 1940, MA 1944, Jesus College, Cambridge; Honorary Fellow, 1977. *Appointments:* Called to Bar of Northern Ireland, 1947; Bencher of the Inn of Court, 1955; Q.C. 1956; High Court Judge, 1964; Lord Chief Justice of Northern Ireland, 1971; Chairman, NI Constitutional Convention, 1975-76. *Memberships:* Army and Navy Club; MCC; Royal and Ancient, St. Andrews. *Honours:* Honorary Bencher, Middle Temple, 1973; Honorary Bencher, King's Inns, Dublin, 1973; Privy Counsellor, NI, 1971; United Kingdom, 1974; Knight 1971; LL.D. Queen's University, Belfast; D.Litt, New University of Ulster. *Hobbies:* Golf; Showjumping. *Address:* White Hill, Crossgar, Co. Down, Northern Ireland.

LOXTON, Alan Hamilton, b. 13 Apr. 1920, Enmore, Sydney, New South Wales, Australia. Solicitor. m. Dorothy Joan Short, 2 Feb. 1946, 3 sons, 1 daughter. *Education:* LL.B., (Hons.), University of Sydney, Australia, 1949. *Appointments:* 2nd Australian Imperial Forces, 1940-45; Solicitor, 1949-; Partner, Allen Allen & Hemsley, 1951-; Board of Directors of: Unisearch Limited, 1977-, Chairman, 1981; United Dominions Corporation (Australia) Limited, 1967-; Chairman of Directors, Noble Lowndes Australia Limited, 1981-. *Memberships:* President, Law Society of New South Wales, 1973-75; Chairman, The College of Law, 1975-; The Council of the University of New South Wales, 1977-; The Council of Kuring-gai College of Advanced Education, 1977. *Publications:* Legal Aspects of Coal Mining in New South Wales, 1980; Legal Education in New South Wales, (with others), 1979; Private Ownership of Coal in New South Wales, 1980. *Hobbies:* Sailing; Golf. *Address:* 6 Hillcrest Street, Wahroonga, New South Wales 2076, Australia.

LUCAS, Percy Hylton Craig, b. 9 June 1925, Christchurch, New Zealand. Land Administrator. m. Kura Joyce Pitcher, 20 Nov. 1948, 1 son, 1 daughter. *Education:* Accountants Professional Exam, University of Canterbury, 1943-49. *Appointments:* Department of Lands and Survey, Christchurch , 1942-46; Shell Company of New Zealand, Christchurch, 1947; Department of Lands and Survey, Christchurch, 1948-; Assistant Commissioner of Crown Lands, Wellington, 1966-67; Assistant Director of Administration, 1967-69; Director of National Parks and Reserves, 1969-75; Assistant Deputy Director-General of Lands, 1975-81; Director General of Lands, 1981-. *Memberships:* Commission on National Parks and Protected Areas, 1971-; Chairman, New Zealand Walkways Commission, 1976; Deputy Chairman, National Parks Authority, 1975-80; Environmental Council, Land Settlement Board; Tourism Advisory Council; Tawa Borough Council, 1971-. *Publications:* 'To the Glory of God', 1965; 'The Blue and Gold', 1966; 'Conserving New Zealand's Heritage, 1970; 'Saultalk', 1974. *Honours:* Winston Churchill Fellowship, 1969; Associate, New Zealand Institute of Park and Recreation Administration. *Hobbies:* Photography; Cricket; Football. *Address:* 8 Wilmshurst Place, Tawa, New Zealand.

LUCKHOO, Lionel, b. Guyana. Attorney-at-Law. 2 sons, 2 daughters. *Education:* Member, Hon. Society of Middle Temple, London, UK, 1940. *Appointments:* Private Practice; Acted in the following capacities: State Prosecutor; Magistrate; Judge of the Supreme Court; High Commissioner and Ambassador for two Countries, Guyana and Barbados accredited to St. James's Court, Paris, Bonn and the Hague; Returned to Private practice and head of Luckhoo and Luckhoo, Legal Practitioners. *Memberships:* Chairman, Legal Practitioners Committee; Drafting Committee, Law; President, Guyana Olympic Association; Chairman, Red Cross Society. *Publications:* Fitzluck Theory of Breeding of Race Horses; number of books and booklets on Christianity; Open Letter to Muslim Friends. *Honours:* Named in Guiness Book of World Records as The most successful Advocate gaining 240 successive murder acquittals; CBE., 1961; Knight Bachelor, 1965; Knight Commander of St. Michael and St. George, 1969; Queen's Counsel, 1955, Mayor Georgetown, 1954, 55, 61, 62. *Hobbies:* Cricket; Racing; Magic. *Address:* 2 Bellair Gardens, Georgetown, Guyana.

LUFT, Arthur Christian (His Honour the Deemster), b. 21 July 1915, Castletown, Isle of Man, British Isles. Her Majesty's First Deemster, Clerk of the Rolls and Deputy Governor. m. 20 June 1950, 2 sons. *Appointments:*

Admitted to Manx Bar, Apr. 1940; HM Attorney-General, Isle of Man, 1972-74; Her Majesty's Second Deemster, Dec. 1974; Her Majesty's First Deemster, Clerk of the Rolls, Deputy Governor, Isle of Man, 1980. *Memberships:* Chairman of: Criminal Injuries Compensation Board, 1974-80; Licensing Appeal Court, 1974-80; Isle of Man Income Tax Commissioners, 1980-; Tynwald Ceremony Arrangements Committee; Tynwald Pensions Scheme; President, Manx Deaf Society. *Hobbies:* Theatre; Watching cricket; Gardening. *Address:* Leyton, Victoria Road, Douglas, Isle of Man.

LUI, Felise Vitolio, b. 9 June 1950, Safai Savai'i, Western Samoa. Public Servant. m. Brigid Janola, 13 Feb. 1973, 1 son, 2 daughters. *Education.* BA., Economics and Administration, U S P., Suva, Fiji, 1970-73; Fellow, EDI., Economic Development Institute, 1975. *Appointments:* Foreign Affairs Officer, Foreign Affairs Division, 1973, Secretary, National ACC, 1976, Acting Secretary to Goverment, Foreign and Internal Affairs, Immigration, 1979, Prime Minister's Department, Western Samoa; Head of Economic Affairs and Aid Section of FAD, 1977. *Memberships:* Fellow, UN Asian Development Institute. *Publications:* Short papers on various aspects of Pacific development issues presented to a number of seminars and conferences around the Pacific and Asian region. *Honours:* Awarded the New Zealand Institute of Chartered Secretaries and Administrators award for best performance in Management and Administration towards BA, CISP courses, 1973. *Hobbies:* Sport; Amateur stamp and coin collecting. *Address:* PO Box 1204, Vaivase-uta, Apia, Western Samoa.

LUK, Joe, b. 22 May 1953, Hong Kong. Administration and Finance. m. 24 Dec. 1978. *Education:* Accounting Diploma, Hong Kong Baptist College, 1977. *Appointments:* Adminstration and Finance Manager, Houston Electrical Engineering Limited; Financial Manager, Ying Kwong Electro-Technique Development Company Limited; Director, Viceo-Tronic Industrial Company Limited; Director, All Gland Industrial Company Limited; Assistant Manager, Hoi Fat and Company. *Memberships:* Student of Association of Certificate Accountant; Hong Kong Management Association. *Honours:* London Chamber of Commerce and Industry Higher Accounting Certificate, 1976. *Hobbies:* Tennis; Basketball; Swimming; Music. *Address:* 232-242 Fa Yuen Street, Oscar Court, 14/F1 Flat E, Kowloon, Hong Kong.

LUM, Robert Sing Ghun, b. 19 Aug. 1947, Honolulu, Hawaii, United States of America. Architect, Urban and Regional Planner. m. 11 June, 1973. *Education:* Master of Urban and Regional Planning, 1976, Bachelor of Architecture, 1972, Blacksburg, V.A., United States of America. *Appointments:* Frank C. Montague, Alexandra, United States of America, 1972-74; Austin L. Spriggs, AIA, Wahsington, United States of America, 1975; Kola Bankole and Associates, FNIA, Lagos, Nigeria, 1976-78; Froehlich and Kow, FAIA, Los Angeles, United States of America, 1978-80; Froehlich and Kow, FAIA, Port of Spain, Trinidad, 1980-. *Memberships:* Nigerian Institute of Architects; Royal Institute of British Architects; American Planning Association; Building Officials and Code Administration; Professional Services Business Management Association; Theta Chi Social Fraternity; Positive Thinkers Club, for Christian Living. *Creative Works:* Caroni Horse Racing Complex, Port of Spain, Trinidad; Ikoyi Hotel Annex, Lagos, Nigeria; Head Quarters Building, Chamber of Commerce and Industry, Lagos, Nigeria; World Health Training Centre, Igbo Ora, Nigeria; Dominion National Bank Building, Alexandra, United States of America. *Honours:* 2nd Place University Chess Tournament, 1970; National Student Register, 1969, 1970, 1971. *Hobbies:* Chess; Origame; Swimming; Fishing; Photography; Travelling; Reading. *Address:* Trinidad and Tobago Racing Authority, Pakistan Building, Corner Keate and Frederick Streets, Port of Spain, Trinidad, W.I.

LUO Xiu-Jin b. 3 Feb. 1933, Kiangsi Province, China. Chemist. m. Xu Li-Juan, 21 Jan. 1960, 1 son, 2 daughters. *Education:* B.S. Chemistry, Kirin University, 1957. *Appointments:* Assistant Lecturer, 1957-68, Lecturer, 1968-78, Department of Chemistry, Kirin University, China; Visiting Scientist, Royal Society Chinese Academy of Science Exchange Program; Liverpool University,

Cambridge University, Research Fellow, British Council, Chinese Ministry of Education, Scientific Exchange Programme, Davy Faraday Research Group, Royal Institution of Great Britain, 1979-81. *Memberships:* Fellow, Royal Society of Chemistry. *Publications:* Applications of Laser in Physics and Chemistry, 1974; Kinetics of Heterogeneous Catalysed Reactions, 1975; 'The Fundamentals of Catalysis', 1980; Revision, a part of 'Chemical Applications of Group Theory', 1971; Translation, 'Reduced Density Matrices in Quantum Chemistry', 1977. *Hobbies:* Laser Photochemistry; Catalysis; Kinetic Analysis. *Address:* Department of Chemistry, Kirin University, Changchun, China.

LUPU, Radu, b. 30 Nov. 1945, Galati, Rumania. Concert Pianist. m. Elizabeth Wilson, 1971. *Education:* Moscow Conservatoire, Russia, 1962-69. *Appointments:* Has played with all the leading British orchestras, his concert career has taken him all over the world; First major American appearance with the Cleveland Orchestra and Daniel Barenboim, New York, USA, 1972; Chicago Symphoney under Carlo Maria Giulini, has appeared and been re-engaged in every important American City; Has played with the Los Angeles Philharmonic under Mehta and Foster, the Chicago Symphony under Solti, the New York Philharmonic and the Boston Symphony, USA; Soloist many times with the Berlin Philharmonic with whom he made his debut at the Salzburg Festival with Herbert Von Karajan, Easter 1978, second appearance with the Vienna Philharmonic with Riccardo Muti, August 1979; Performs regurlarly with the Israel Philharmonic, the Concertgebouw Orchestra and the Orchestre de Paris. *Creative Works:* Twenty records including the complete Moxart violin and piano sonatas with Szymon Goldberg; His recording of Beethoven's Third Piano Concerto with Lawrence Foster and the London Symphony Orchestra was voted the outstanding concerto disc of 1972 in the USA and Europe; His recording of the complete Beethoven Piano Concertos with Zubin Mehta and the Israel Philharmonic Orchestra released 1979. *Honours:* 1st Prize, Van Cliburn International Piano Competition, 1966; 1st prize, Enescu Competition, 1967; 1st prize, Leeds International Piano Competition, 1969. *Address:* c/o Harrison /Parrott Limited, 12 Penzance Place, London W11 4PA, England.

LUSHER, Stephen Augustus, b. 18 Oct. 1945, Sydney, Australia. Member of Parliament. m. Cherie Kenneth, 5 June 1971, 3 sons, 1 daughter. *Appointments:* Development Finance Corporation Limited, 1964-65; Sydney Stock Exchange, Australia, 1966-72; Assistant Director, National Secretariat, 1973-74, Member, House of Representatives for Hume, New South Wales, Australia, 1974-, National Country Party. *Publications:* Editor: Australian Minerals Reference, 1966. *Hobby:* Tennis. *Address:* Waratah, Cootamundra, New South Wales 2590, Australia.

LUTALO-BOSA, Albert James, b. 4 Jan. 1936, Kampala, Uganda. Biochemist. m. Justina Lucia Nankya Mubiru, 29 Dec. 1973. 1 son, 1 daughter. *Education:* BSc (Lond) University College, Nairobi 1961-65; MSc, PhD McGill University 1965-70. *Appointments:* Chemist 1965; Lecturer 1970-73; Senior Lecturer 1973-75; Associate Professor 1975-77; Professor 1977-. *Memberships:* Canadian Biochemical Society; Society of Sigma Xi (McGill University Chapter); Katalemwa Staff Club. *Publications:* Eleven Publications. *Honours:* Physics Prize 1969. *Hobbies:* Squash; Gardening. *Address:* No 7 Katalemwa Estate, Kampala, Uganda.

LUTCHMAN, Harold Alexander, b. 7 Oct. 1937, Guyana. Professor of Political Science, University of Guyana. Barrister at Law. m. Hollis Richards, 5 May 1969, 1 son. *Education:* B.Sc. Econ., 1964, M.Sc. 1965, University of the West Indies; Ph.D. Manchester, 1967; Bar Examinations, Council of Legal Education, United Kingdom, 1975; LL.B. External Private Student, University of London, 1979. *Appointments:* Lecturer, 1968-70, Senior Lecturer, 1970-75, Head, Department Political Science, 1972-74, Professor, 1975, Dean, Faculty of Social Sciences, 1975-78, Head, Department of Management Studies, 1978-, University of Guyana. *Memberships:* Chartered Institute of Arbitrators, 1976; British Institute of Management, 1980; Royal Institute of Public Administration, 1979; Guyana Human Rights Association, 1979. *Publications:* From Colonialism to

Co-operative Republic, 1976; A History of the Guyana Public Service Association, 1973; Selected Readings on Guyanese Politics, 1976. *Honours:* First year Social Sciences Faculty Prize Part 1, 1962; Nethersole Prize for student graduating with the highest aggregate marks in Government at BSc. 1964; University of the West Indies and Merrill Trust Fund Post Graduate Scholarships, 1964; First Scholar under scheme of collaboration between Universities of the West Indies and Manchester sponsored and supported by the British Ministry of Overseas Development, to read for PhD (Govt) degree at Manchester University, 1965. *Hobbies:* Music; Cricket; Reading. *Address:* 27 Oleander Gardens, East Coast Demerara, Georgetown, Guyana.

LUXTON, John Finlay, b. 14 Aug. 1923, Waitoa, New Zealand. Member of Parliament. m. Margaret Joyce Ritchie, 18 April 1945, 3 sons, 1 daughter. *Appointments:* Member of Parliament, 1966; Member of Delegation to Commonwealth Parliamentary Conference, Bahamas, 1968; Leader of Delegation to Commonwealth Parliamentary Conference, Canberra, 1970; Member of Parliamentary Fact Finding Team to Pacific Island, 1971; Member of Parliamentary Team, Guest of Japanese and Indonesian Governments, 1974; Opposition Representative South Pacific Commission, Nauru, 1975; Leader, Parliamentary Delegation to Pacific Islands, 1976; Recipient Leadership Study Grant to United States of America, 1978; Presiding Officers' Conference, Adelaide, 1978; Presiding Officers' Conference, Port Moresby, 1979; Opposition Spokesman on Fishing and Island Affairs, 1974-75. *Memberships:* Chairman, Waitoa Branch of Federated Farmers, 1956-64; Served on Dominion Lands Committee, Federated Farmers, on a special committee set up to report and make recommendations on Agricultural Education in New Zealand; Waikato Agricultural Production Council; Waitoa School Committee; Trustee, Waikato Savings Bank; Chairman, Pacific Islands Industrial Development Scheme; Chairman, House Committee; Chairman, Private Bills Committee; Chairman, Committee on Bills; Director, Tatua Dairy Company; Honorary member, Te Aroha Rotary; Patron of various societies. *Address:* 368 Thames Street, Morrinsville, New Zealand.

LYE, Kum-Chew, b. 2 Aug. 1934, Kuala Lumpur, Malaysia. Professor of Architecture. m. 4 Aug. 1964, 2 sons, 1 daughter. *Education:* B.Arch, Miami University, Oxford, Ohio, United States of America, 1960; MFA, Princeton University, Princeton, New Jersey, 1961. *Appointments:* Office of Edward Durell Stone FAIA, New York, United States of America; Office of The Architects Collaborative, Cambridge, United States of America; Hugh Wilson and Lewis Womerseley, London; Architectural Association, London; Faculty of Architecture, University of Manitoba, Canada; School of Architecture, University of Hong Kong. *Memberships:* Fellow Royal Architecture Institute of Canada; Royal Institute of British Architects; Hong Kong Institute of Architects; Fellow, Hong Kong Institute of Architects. *Publications:* Essays: Tao Ho; Sumet Jumsai; Contemporary Architects, Macmillan, 1980. *Honours:* AIA Medal, Princeton University, 1961; Henry Adams Prize, Princeton University, 1961; Self-Help Communities, Manila, 1965; Shinkenchiku, Design Competition, 1979; Elected Fellow, FRAIC, 1979. *Hobbies:* Travel; Reading; Food. *Address:* 63 Middleton Towers, 140 Pokfulam Road, Hong Kong.

LYKEN, Olive Adriana, b. 15 Mar. 1924. Training Officer; Teacher Educator. *Education:* Teachers Certificate, Cyril Potter College of Education 1947; Certificate in Child Development, Research, 1954; MA Institute of Education, University of London 1956; BSc(Hons) Geography (Special) with Anthropology, Birkbeck College, 1966. *Appointments:* Teacher, Primary School, Guyana 1940-56; Education Officer, Nursery and Infant Education, Guyana 1956-59; Lecturer in Geography, Cyril Potter College of Education, Guyana, 1967-71; deputy Principal 1968-74; Assistant Chief Education Officer, Ministry of Education 1973-74; Principal, Cyril Potter College of Education 1974-79; Consultant, Commonwealth Regional Training Course, Administration and Supervision in Education, South Pacific Region, University South Pacific, Fiji 1978. *Memberships:* Caribbean Conference on Mental Health 1968; PAHO, WHO, Conference on Nutrition 1972; Commonwealth Conference on Teacher Education 1973; Commonwealth Workshop on Administra-

tion in Education; Education visits to Ghana and Nigeria; Methodist Conference 1975; Education Representative, Guyana-Cuba joint Commission 1975; Commonwealth Conference on Science Communication 1976; Graduation Address, Teachers' College 1977; Synod, Methodist Church, Guyana; Convocation, University of London; Advisory Board, YWCA school for early leavers. *Publications:* Paper, Present Trends in Teacher Education, 1972; The Jubilee Handbook, 1978. *Hobbies:* Music (vocal); Art; Drama. *Address:* 341 East Street, Cummingsburg, Georgetown, Guyana.

LYNCH, Kevin Joseph, b. 22 Oct. 1921, Sydney, Australia. Dental Surgeon. m. June Kathleen Gallop, 3 March 1946, 5 sons, 2 daughters. *Education:* Bachelor of Dental Surgery, Sydney University, Australia, 1949. *Appointments:* Self Employed Dental Surgeon; Honorary Dental Surgeon at: Lewisham Hospital, Sydney, St. Margaret's Hospital, Darlinghurst, Sydney, Little Sister's of the Poor, Home for the aged, Drummoyne, Sydney, Australia. *Memberships:* Foundation President, Sydney Serra Club. *Honours:* M.B.E. New Year Honours, 1980. *Hobbies:* Swimming; Racing; Cricket; Football. *Address:* 43 Walworth Avenue, Newport, New South Wales 2106.

LYNCH, Phillip Reginald, (Rt. Hon. Sir) b. 27 July 1933, Melbourne, Victoria, Australia. Politician. m. Leah O'Toole, 2 Feb. 1958, 3 sons. *Education:* Bachelor of Arts, Diploma of Education, Melbourne University, Australia. *Appointments:* Former School Teacher; Management Consultant; Company Director; Elected to the House of Representatives, 1966; Minister for the Army, 1968-69; Minister for Immigration, Assisting Treasurer, 1969-71; Minister for Labour and National Service, 1971-72; Deputy Leader of the Opposition, House of Representatives, 1973-75; Deputy Leader of the Federal Parliament Liberal Party, 1973-; Treasurer, 1975-77; Minister for Industry and Commerce, 1977-; Appointed to the Privy Council, 1977-. *Memberships:* Federal Executive and Federal Council of the Liberal Party; State President, Victorian Young Liberal Movement; Former member, Victorian State Executive of the Liberal Party; Former National President of the Australian Jaycees; Australian Naval and Military. *Honours:* Royal Humane Society Certificate of Merit, for rescuing a student from drowning at Point Lonsdale, Victoria, 1953; Awarded Knighthood of the Order of St Michael and St George, 1981. *Hobbies:* Swimming; Sailing; Tennis. *Address:* Mt Eliza, Victoria, Australia.

LYNE, Michael Charles Edward, b. 12 Sept. 1912, Herefordshire, England. Artist, Author. m. Jessie Muriel, 27 May 1940, 1 son, 1 daughter. *Education:* Russall School, 1922-30. *Appointments:* Artist; Author. *Memberships:* Steward, National Couising Club; Chairman, Oxfordshire Couising Club; President, Irish Wolfhound Couising Club; Cotswold Couising Club; Saluki Couising Club. *Publications:* 'Horses, Hounds and Country'; 'From Litter to Later-on'; 'A Parsons Son'; 'The Michael Lyne Sketch-book'; *Creative Works:* Exhibition of Paintings in the United Kingdom and the United States of America; Many other books illustrated; Numerous Artists Proofs and Prints. *Honours:* Diploma Paintings in The World Sporting Exhibition in Budapest, 1971. *Hobbies:* Field Sports; Agriculture. *Address:* Dunfield House, Fairford, Gloucestershire, England.

LYON, James Traill, b. 15 April 1934, Glasgow, Scotland. Solicitor (Scotland, 1963); Barrister, Solicitor (Nova Scotia, 1966, Saskatchewan, 1980). m. Irmtraut Ebert, 17 Jan. 1981. *Education:* M.A., University of Glasgow, 1955; LL.B., University of St. Andrews, 1960; LL.M., McGill University, 1963. *Appointments:* Sub-Lieutenant (P) RNUR, Fleet Air Arm, 1955-57; Law Practice, Scotland, 1961-65; Assistant Solicitor, Air Canada, 1965-66; Solicitor, Canadair Limited, 1966-69; Manager, Overseas Department, Bank of N.T. Butterfield and Son, Bermuda, 1970-71; Department of Justice, Ottawa, 1972-75, 1977-78 (Director, Legal Services, Energy Mines and Resources, General Counsel, Department of Finance and Treasury, Board); Assistant Deputy Minister, Department of Transport, Ottawa, 1975-77; Vice-President, General Counsel, Eldorado Nuclear Limited, 1978-80; Associate, Messrs. Balfour, Moss, Milliken, Laschuk, Kyle, Vancise, Barristers and Solicitors, Regina and Saskatoon,

Saskatchewan, 1980-. *Memberships:* Law Society of Scotland; Society of Writers to H.M. Signet; Nova Scotia Barristers' Society, Law Society of Saskatchewan; Canadian Cancer Society; Rideau Club. *Publications:* Historical Survey of The Law of Flight, Institute of Air and Space Law, (with Sand and Pratt), McGill University, 1961. *Hobbies:* Law; History; Reading. *Address:* 13-455 Pinehouse Drive, Saskatoon, Saskatchewan, Canada S7K 5K2.

LYONS, Bernard, b. 30 Mar. 1913, Leeds, England. Company Director. m. Lucy Hurst, 18 Dec. 1938, 3 sons, 1 daughter. *Appointments:* Chairman, U D S Group Limited. *Memberships:* Leeds City Council, 1951-65. *Publications:* The Thread is Strong, 1981. *Honours:* CBE., 1964; Deputy Lieutenant, Yorkshire West Riding, 1971; Justice of the Peace, 1959; LL.D., Hons., University of Leeds, UK, 1973. *Hobby:* Farming. *Address:* Upton Wood, Fulmer, Bucks., England.

M

MA, Lin, b. 8 Feb. 1925, China. Educator; University Professor. m. Meng-Hua Chen, 24 Jan. 1958, 3 daughters. *Education:* BSc., West China Union University, Chengtu, China, 1947; PhD., University of Leeds, UK, 1955; Post-Doctorate Fellow, University College Hospital Medical School, London, UK, and St. James's Hospital, Leeds, UK, 1955-56. *Appointments:* Assistant Lecturer, 1957-59, Lecturer, 1959-64. Clinical Chemistry, Department of Pathology, University of Hong Kong; Part-time Lecturer in Chemistry, 1964, Senior Lecturer, 1965-72, Reader, 1972-73, Professor, 1973-78, Dean of Faculty of Science, 1973-75, Vice-Chancellor (President), 1978-, The Chinese University of Hong Kong; Visiting Biochemist, Hormone Research Laboratory, University of California, San Francisco, USA, 1969. *Memberships:* Biochemistry Society, London; Royal Society of Chemistry; Association of Clinical Biochemists, London; American Chemical Society; World Trade Centre Club; Royal Hong Kong Jockey Club; Hong Kong Country Club. *Publications:* Various research papers in academic journals. *Honours:* Justice of Peace, 1978. *Hobbies:* Table tennis; Swimming. *Address:* The Vice-Chancellor's Residence, The Chinese University of Hong Kong; Shatin, N T., Hong Kong.

MABIN, Victoria Jane, b. 28 Dec. 1953, Nelson, New Zealand. Operational Researcher. *Education:* BSc.(1st class Hons.), Economics, with Mathematics, University of Canterbury, Christchurch, New Zealand, 1972-75; Reading for PhD., Operational Research, University of Lancaster, Lancaster, UK, 1977-81, PhD, 1981. *Appointments:* Part-time Teaching Assistant, Department of Economics, University of Canterbury, New Zealand, 1975; Part-time Teaching Assistant, Department of Economics, Victoria University of Wellington, New Zealand, 1976-77; Operational Researcher (Scientist), Applied Mathematics Division, Department of Scientific and Industrial Research, Wellington, New Zealand, 1976-; currently on study leave in UK. *Memberships:* Operational Research Society, UK; Operational Research Society of New Zealand, inc; New Zealand Association of Economists; Treasurer, 1979-80, Lancaster University Overseas Students Society; Committee member 1976-77, OR Society of New Zealand, Wellington Branch. *Publications:* Research reports include: Location of Farm Advisory Officers in New Zealand— An Application of Facility Location Analysis,(with J.R. Rodgers, O. McCarthy), 1972, 75; Trends in Public Transport in the Wellington Region 1966-76, (with H Barr, R Taylor), 1977; Variability in Distribution, thesis for PhD, University of Lancaster, 1981. *Honours:* Senior Scholarship, J.B. Condliffe Scholarship in International Trade Economic Society Prize, 1975; Shirtcliffe Fellowship; UGC. Post Graduate Scholarship; Commonwealth Scholarship, Canada, 1976; National Research Advisory Council Post Graduate Research Fellowship, 1977. *Hobbies:* Music; Sports; Theatre; Photography. *Address:* Flat 1, Bowland College, University of Lancaster, Lancaster, LA1 4YT, England.

MABOMBA, Rodrick Samson, b. 25 Sept. 1948, Blantyre, Malawi. Librarian. m. 2 Nov. 1972, 2 sons, 2 daughters. *Education:* School Certificate 1966; Part i and Part II Library Association Professional Exams, 1969 and 1970; Associateship, Library Association, 1972. *Appointments:* Assistant Librarian, University of Malawi Library, 1970-75; Chief Librarian, British Council Libraries, Malawi 1975-78; Director, Malawi National Library Service 1978-. *Memberships:* The Library Association, United Kingdom; Malawi Library Association. *Publications:* The Encyclopedia of Library and Information Science; The role of archives in national information transfer; ECARBICA journal; Library and information services in Malawi; ALA world encyclopedia of library and information services, 1980. *Hobbies:* Music; Table Tennis. *Address:* Njowe Village, T.A. Somba, Blantyre, Malawi.

McCANCE, Keith Robert, b. 28 Nov. 1929, Ascot Vale, Victoria, Australia. Member of Parliament. m. Joy Myra Cullis, 7 Feb. 1953, 1 son, 1 daughter. *Education:* Wesley College, 1944-47. *Appointments:* Share Registrar, Broken Hill South Limited, Australia (retired). *Memberships:* Melbourne Cricket Club; Carlton Football Club; National Trust, Victoria; Past President, Mayfield Park Tennis Club. *Hobbies:* Tennis; Philately;

Cricket; Australian Rules Football. *Address:* 2 Dallas Street, Mount Waverley, Victoria, Australia.

MACAULAY, Marion Evelyn, b. 16 Mar. 1905, Taree, NSW, Australia. Teacher. *Education:* Sydney Teachers' College; BA, Sydney University 1931; MEd 1961; MACE. *Appointments:* Teacher and Deputy, New South Wales Schools; Headmistress, North Broken Hill, Hallongong and North Newtown Demenstration Infants' School, with Sydney Teachers College and other Colleges and Sydney University's School of Education; Lecturer in Education, Teachers' Colleges, NSW University; Part-time Lecturer-Tutor, University of Sydney. *Memberships:* National Council of Women; Converger of Education; National Convener of Education; International Council of Women; Macquarie University, College of Education; Library Committee; Films and Television Committee; Educational Administration; Chancellor's Committee, Sydney University; Hurstville Historical Society; International Federation of University Darwin, NSW; Royal Australian Historical Society. *Publications:* Teaching Literature to Young Children; Children's Interests in Television; Various articles for education and historical journals. *Honours:* The Coronation Medal 1953. *Hobbies:* Music; Swimming; Drama. *Address:* 17 McLeod Street, Hurstville, NSW, Australia 2220.

McCAUSLAN, John Patrick William Buchanan, b. 19 Jan. 1937, Bournemouth, Dorset, England. Professor of Law. m. Dorrette Elaine Wright-Leigh, 30 Mar. 1968, 1 daughter. *Education:* BA., 1960, BCL., 1961, Wadham College, Oxford, UK, 1957-61; Barrister at Law, 1961. *Appointments:* Lecturer, University College, Dar Es Salaam, 1961-66; Lecturer, London School of Economics, London, UK, 1966-68; Senior Lecturer, 1968-71, Reader, 1971-72, Professor, 1972-, University of Warwick Law School, UK; Visiting Professor: University of Wisconsin, Madison, USA, 1969, Osgoode Hall Law School, York University, Ontario, Canada, 1974; UN Planning and Environmental Law Consultant: Tanzania, 1977-81, Kano State, Nigeria, 1979, Uganda, 1980, Zimbabwe, 1981. *Memberships:* Honourable Society of the Middle Temple; Fabian Society; Town and Country Planning Association; Society of Public Teachers of Law. *Publications:* Public Law and Political Change in Kenya, 1970; Land, Law and Planning Law, 1975; Urban Legal Problems in Eastern Africa (Editor), 1978; The Ideologies of Planning, 1980; General Editor: Modern Legal Studies, 1973; Joint Editor: Urban Law and Policy, 1978. *Hobbies:* Music; Science Fiction. *Address:* 2 Lillington Road, Leamington Spa CV32 5YR, England.

McCAFFREY, John Francis, b. 31 Jan. 1933, Melbourne, Victoria, Australia. Professor of Surgery. m. Denise Carmell Maroney, 24 May 1958, 2 sons, 2 daughters. *Education:* BM., BS,(1st Class Hons.), 1956, MS., 1961, University of Queensland, Australia; Fellow of Royal Australasian College of Surgeons, 1962; Fellow of Royal College of Surgeons England 1963; Diploma Diagnostic Ultrasound, 1979. *Appointments:* Resident Medical Officer, Mater Hospital, 1957; Lecturer in Anatomy, 1958, Teaching Registrar in Surgery, 1959-62, Senior Lecturer in Surgery, 1964-70, Reader in Surgery, 1970-80, Professor of Surgery, 1981-, University of Queensland, Australia; Nuffield Dominion Travelling Fellow in Surgery, Western Infirmary, Glasgow, UK, 1962-63. *Memberships:* Fellow, Academy of Colon and Rectal Surgery; International Cardio-Vascular Society; Australian Ultrasound Society in Medicine. *Publications:* Numerous publications in medical literature. *Honours:* University Medal for outstanding merit; K G Wilson Prize; Ian Robertson Prize; Nuffield Dominion Travelling Fellowship. *Hobbies:* Electronics; Cricket. *Address:* 3' Cluden Street, Holland Park 4121, Queensland, Australia.

McCAHEY, John, b. 30 June 1921, Lisburn North Ireland. Chairman of Directors. m. Elsie Cole 27 Mar. 1948, 2 sons. *Education:* Mitcham Primary School, South Australia; School of Mines, Adelaide. *Appointments:* Cadet Engineer, Metter's Limited Adelaide 1937; Assistant Work's Manager, Melbourne 1958; W9orks Manager, Metters, Melbourne 1961; Director, Tecnicast Pty. Ltd. Melbourne 1962; Director, Centrifugal Casting Australia 1975; Chairman of Directors, Tecnicast and Centrifugal Castings, 1979. *Memberships:* Sir Samuel Way Masonic Lodge No. 48; South Australia Constitution; Thomas Town Rotary Club,

Victoria. *Hobbies:* Photography; Reading; Tennis. *Address:* 53 Carlsberg Road, Eaglemont 3084, Victoria, Australia.

McCAIN, G Wallace F, b. 9 Apr. 1930, Florenceville, New Brunswick. President. m. Margaret L A Norrie, 2 sons, 2 daughters. *Education:* Bachelor of Arts, Mount Allison University; Honorary, Doctor of Law, 1973. *Appointments:* President, McCain Foods Limited, Florenceville, New Brunswick; Chairman of the Board, McCain Australia Pty. Limited, McCain Foods Inc. US and Thomas Equipment Limited; President, McCain Fertilizer Limited, Valley Farms Limited, and Carleton Cold Storage Limited; Director, McCain Expana SA; McCain Europa B.V., McCain Foods GB Limited, England, Day & Ross Limited, McCain Produce Company Limited, Bilopage Inc., and The Prudential Assurance Company Limited. *Hobbies:* Skiing; Swimming; Hunting. *Address:* Riverview Drive, Florenceville, New Brunswick, Canada, EOJ 1K0.

McCAIN, Harold Harrison, b. 3 Nov. 1927, Florenceville, New Brunswick, Canada. Businessman. m. Marion McNair, 4 Oct. 1952, 2 sons, 3 daughters. *Education:* BA, Acadia University, Canada. *Appointments:* Chairman of the Board of: McCain Foods Limited, Florenceville, New Brunswick, Canada, McCain Foods (GB) Limited, Scarborough, UK, McCain Europa b.v., Hoofddorp, Holand; President, McCain Alimentaire, S.A.R.L, Harnes, France; Director of: McCain Australia (Pty) Limited, Wendouree, Australia, McCain Foods Inc., Washburn, Maine, USA, Bank of Nova Scotia, Petro Canada, Thomas Equipment Limited, Day & Ross Limited, McCain Fertilizer Limited, McCain Espana, S.A., Madrid, Spain. *Hobby:* Skiing. *Address:* Riverview Drive, Florenceville, New Brunswick, EOJ 1KO, Canada.

McCALLUM, John, b. 13 Oct. 1920, Glasgow, Scotland. Naval Architect and Shipbuilder. m. Christine Peggy Sowden, 19 June 1948, 2 sons. *Education:* BSc., Engineering (1st Class Hons. in Naval Architecture), Glasgow University, UK, 1939-43. *Appointments:* Sandwich Apprentice, 1938-43, Naval Architect, 1961, Technical Director, 1967, John Brown Shipbuilders Limited; Junior Lecturer, Naval Architecture and Marine Engineering, Glasgow University, Scotland, 1943-44; Ship Surveyor, Newcastle, 1944, Glasgow, 1949, London, 1953, Chief Ship Surveyor, 1970-, Lloyd's Register of Shipping; Upper Clyde Shipbuilders, Scotland, 1969; Consultant Naval Architect, 1981. *Memberships:* Fellow, The Fellowship of Engineering; Fellow, Vice-President and Past Chairman of Council, Royal Institution of Naval Architects; Fellow, Institution of Civil Engineers; Smeatonian Society of Civil Engineers; Past member of Council, Institution of Engineers and Shipbuilders in Scotland; Society of Naval Architects and Marine Engineers, New York; Liveryman and member Education Committee, Worshipful Company of Shipwrights, London; Chartered Civil Engineer; Chartered Engineer. *Publications:* Numerous Technical Publications including: Pressure Distribution over a Model Hull, 1948; Bending Moments in Bracketed Beams, 1957; Design of Large Ships, 1965; Ships of the Eighties, Design and Implementation, 1972; Ship Technology—The Practical Limits, 1974; A Case History—The World Concord, 1981. *Honours:* Prizes: Kirk Memorial, 1943, George Harvey, 1943, Reid-Birrell, 1942 & 43, Glasgow University, Scotland; Premium, Institution of Naval Architects, 1957; Medallist, Association Technique Maritime et Aéronautique, Paris, France, 1978. *Hobbies:* Golf; Piano; Art. *Address:* 'Dala', Garvock Drive, Kippington, Sevenoaks, Kent, TN13 2LT, England.

McCARTHY, John Ernest, b. 11 Sept. 1932, Photogrammetrist. *Education:* Leaving Certificate, New South Wales 1950; EIVF Certificate, Sydney Preliminary Theological Certificate 1960. *Appointments:* Trainee Photogrammetrist, Adastra Air Surveys, Sydney, 1951; Senior Photogrammetrist 1968-76; Photogrammetric Consultant 1976; Senior Photogrammetrist, Qasco Pty. Ltd. Sydney 1977-81. *Memberships:* Australian Institute of Cartographers (NSW Secretary); Australian Photogrammetric Society; Royal Commonwealth Society; National Trust. *Publications:* Cartography—An Introduction, 1979; Short History of St Mark's Church, Pendle Hill, Pamphlet, 1978; Several Radio Scripts; Script for Audio-Visual, Introduction to Cartography, 1975. *Hobbies:* Photography; Water Colour

Painting. *Address:* 43 Wyena Road, Pendle Hill, New South Wales, Australia 2145.

McCARTHY, Richard Bruce, b. 21 Apr. 1945, Canowindra, New South Wales, Australia. Forestry. m. Margaret R Missen, 7 Oct. 1972, 1 son, 1 daughter. *Education:* BSc.Forestry, 1963-67, MSc., Forest Management, 1975-76, Australian National University, Canberra, Australia. *Appointments:* National Service, Rank Sergeant, Royal Australian Education Corp; District Forester, Department of Forests, Papua, New Guinea, 1969-75; Department of Forestry, Australian National University, Canberra, Australia, 1976-77; District Forester, Australian Paper Manufacturers, 1977-; Operations Superintendent APM Forrests. *Memberships:* Treasurer of Gippsland branch, Institute of Foresters of Australia; Australia Pulp and Paper Institute and Technical Association; Traralgon Rotary Club, Victoria. *Publications:* Review of Farm Forestry in Australia-Problems and Possibilities; The Establishment of Eregnans plantations in Gippsland, Victoria, 1980. *Hobbies:* Gardening; Reading; Surfing; Carpentry. *Address:* 9 Josephine Court, Traralgon, Victoria 3840, Australia.

McCARTNEY, (James) Paul, b. 18 June 1942, Allerton, Liverpool. Musician; Composer. m. Linda Eastman, 1969, 1 son, 3 daughters. *Education:* Liverpool Institute. *Appointments:* Skiffle group, The Quarrymen, 1948; Played with John Lennon and George Harrison as trio, The Moondogs, 1959; Toured Scotland with them and Stu Sutcliffe as the Silver Beatles; Beatles, Litherland Town Hall, Liverpool, 1960, Sweden, 1963; Royal Variety Performance, London, 1963; Paris, Denmark, Hong Kong, Australia, New Zealand 1964; TV, USA, and coast-to-coast tour, 1964; France, Italy, Spain, USA, 1965; MPL group of Companies 1970; Pop group, Wings, 1971; Toured: GB, Europe, 1972-73; UK, Australia, 1975; Europe, USA, 1976. *Creative Works:* Songs (with John Lennon) include: Love Me Do; Please, Please Me; She Loves You; etc.; Albums with The Beatles include: Please, Please Me, 1963; With The Beatles, 1963; A Hard Day's Night, 1964; Beatles for Sale, 1965; etc.; McCartney, 1970; Ram, 1971; Wildlife, 1971; etc.; Back to the Egg 1979; McCartney II 1980; Films (with Beatles) A Hard Day's Night, 1964; Help!, 1965; Yellow Submarine, 1968; Let It Be, 1970; Film Scores: The Family Way, 1967; James Paul McCartney, 1973; Live and Let Die 1973; TV score: The Zoo Gang (series), 1973. *Honours:* (With other Beatles) Grammy Awards for best performance by vocal group and best new artist of 1964; National Academy of Recording Arts and Sciences, USA 1965; Awards for arrangements and albums; MBE 1965. *Address:* c/o MPL Communications Limited, 1 Soho Square, London W1V 6BQ, England.

MacCLEMENT, William David, b. 8 Nov. 1936, Cambridge, England. Physics Teacher. m. Bera Angharad Elizabeth Timms, 18 June 1968, 2 sons, 1 daughter. *Education:* BSc.(Hons.), Physics, McMaster University, Hamilton, Canada, 1961; MSc. Solid St. Physics, 1966, PhD. Lower Atmosphere Physics, 1980, University of Western Ontario, London, Canada. *Appointments:* Electronic Engineer, i/c Field Testing, airborne radar, Canadian Westinghouse Co. Limited, Hamilton, Ontario, Canada, 1961-64; Teacher, Physics laboratories, McMaster University, Hamilton, Canada, 1964-66; Teacher, Physics and Science, C. Well. District High School, Fergus, Canada, 1966-68; Teacher, Physics, Science and Mathematics, Ghana Secondary School, Koforidua, Ghana, 1968-69; Gave 1st year Physics course for Biologists, University of Ghana, Legon, Ghana, 1969-70; Teacher, Physics Laboratories, University of Western Ontario, London, Canada, 1970-76; Faculty, Physics Department, Carleton University, Ottawa, Canada, 1976-78; Lecturer, Ahmadu Bello University, Zaria, Nigeria, 1979; Teacher, Physics, Medical School, University of Auckland, New Zealand, 1980; Head of Science, Kristin School, Albany, New Zealand, 1981. *Memberships:* Canadian Association of Physicists. *Publications:* Molecular Reorientation in Ferroelectric LiHzSO4, 1967; VHF Direction-finder for Lightning Location, 1973; VHF Direction-finder Studies of Lightning, 1978; VHF Studies of the Preliminary Proc. of Lightning, 1980. *Hobbies:* Gliding; Sailing. *Address:* 23 Rame Road, PO Box 108, Greenhithe, Auckland 10, New Zealand.

McCLINTOCK, Sir Eric Paul, b. 13 Sept. 1918, Gulgon 6, New South Wales, Australia. Investment Banker. m.

Eva Tray Hurn Lawrence, 18 Apr. 1942, 2 sons, 1 daughter. *Education:* DPA, Sydney University, Australia. *Appointments:* Supply Department, Department of the Navy Australia, 1935-47; served successively in Departments of Commerce, Agriculture and Trade, Washington, New York, Melbourne and Canberra, 1947-61 (1st Assistant Secretary on resignation); Investment Banking, 1962-75; Chairman: Bestobell Australia Limited; Australian Overseas Projects Corporation; Upper Hunter newspapers Pty Limited; Williams Bros. Engineering Pty. Limited; Wilson Electric Transformer Co. Pty. Limited; GS Yuill & Co. Pty Limited; Director: William Adams Limited; Development Finance Corporation Limited; Nedlloyd Australia Pty. Limited; Philips Industries Holdings Limited; Nationwide Investment Corporation Pty. Limited; (Alternate), Brambles-Ruys Pty. Limited. *Memberships:* Australian Advisory Board, Trade Indemnity Co; Australian Club, Sydney; Commonwealth Club, Canberra. *Honours:* Kt. 1981. *Hobbies:* Tennis; Golf. *Address:* 16 O'Connell Street, Sydney, New South Wales, Australia.

McCOLL, Ian, b. 6 Jan. 1933, England. Medicine. m. Dr Jean Lennox McNair, 27 Aug. 1960, 1 son, 2 daughters. *Education:* Scholarship in Classics, St Paul's School, London; Guy's Hospital Medical School; MB, BS 1957; FRCS, FRCSE 1962; MS 1965; FACS 1973. *Appointments:* Junior Staff, Guy's and St Bartholomew's Hospitals; Reader and Sub Dean, Surgery St Bartholomew's Hospital; Professor of Surgery, University of London; Director, Surgical Unit, Guy's Hospital; Honorary Surgeon, King's College Hospital, Guy's Hospital, Edenbridge District Memorial Hospital. *Memberships:* British Society of Gastroenterology; Surgical Research Society; Medical Research Society; Athenaeum. *Publications:* Intestinal Absorption in Man; Papers mainly on Gastroenterology. *Honours:* Golding Bird Prize in Bacteriology, 1956; Arris and Gale Lectureships 1964 and 1975; Royal College of Surgeons; Moynihan Fellowship, Association of Surgeons of Great Britain and Ireland, 1967; Erasmus Wilson Lecturer, Royal College of Surgeons, 1970. *Hobby:* Forestry. *Address:* 10 Gilkes Crescent, Dulwich Village, London SE21, England.

McCOMB, Yvonne Muriel Renee, b. 23 Nov. 1920, Sydney, Australia. Executive Director. m. John Franklyn McComb 9 Nov. 1946, 2 sons, 1 daughter. *Education:* Junior Certificate, State Commercial High School, 1936. *Appointments:* RAAF Civilian Clerk, 1942-45; Research Officer, Liberal Party Queensland, 1945-46; Public Relations, Returned Services League, 1964-69; Public Relations, Royal Flying Doctor Service, 1973-; Consultant Executive Director, McComb Public Relations, 1976-. *Memberships:* Trustee, Australian War Memorial; Liberal Party of Australia; Amnesty International, Queensland; International Women's Forest; Home Management Advisory Service; Friends St. John's Cathedral; Industrial Relations Society; Public Relations Institute; Rural Press Club; War Widows Guild; United Service; University of Queensland Club. *Honours:* OBE, 1977. *Hobbies:* Art; Music; People; Travel. *Address:* 9 Galileo Tower, Mullens Street, Hamilton, Brisbane, Australia.

McCOMBS, Terence Henderson, b. 5 Sept. 1905, Christchurch New Zealand. Teacher. m. Christina Mary Tulloch, 3 Jan. 1955, 4 sons, 1 daughter. *Education:* Canterbury University College; Christchurch Teachers College; MSc 1929; Diploma Teaching 1931; MRSC 1929; FNZIC 1970, (Honorary 1973). *Appointments:* Charles Cook Memorial Research Scholar 1928; National Research Scholar, 1929-30; Christchurch Teachers College 1931; Christchurch Technical College 1932-33; Seddon Technical College, Auckland 1934-35; Christchurch Technical College, 1951-55; Principal Cashmere High School 1956-72 New Zealand Parliament 1935-51; Parliamentary Under-Secretary for Finance 1945-47; Minister of Education and Scientific and Industrial Research 1947-49; High Commissioner for New Zealand, United Kingdom and Ambassador, in Ireland 1973-75. *Memberships:* Chairman and Executive in various Committees in Local Government including: New Zealand Secondary Schools; Redistricting Parliamentary Electorates 1972 and 1977; Commonwealth Foundation, Conference and Minor Grants Committee. *Honours:* OBE 1971; Knight Bachelor 1975; The Honourable 1974; Freeman, City of London 1974; Honorary Freeman of the Worshipful

Company of Butchers 1973. *Address:* 7 Freeman Street, Christchurch 8, New Zealand.

McCONCHIE, Edwin Max, b. 24 June 1928, Melbourne, Victoria, Australia. Civil Servant. m. Gloria Langley Kriegel, 10 Mar. 1950, 2 sons, 1 daughter. *Education:* BA(Honours), Trinity College, University of Melbourne 1947-49; Primary Teaching Certificate 1950; 1st Devonshire Course, Colonial Office, University of London, 1951-52. *Appointments:* HM Colonial Service, Assistant District Officer, Assistant Secretary, 1952-62; Nigerian Ministry of Labour, Ministry of Finance, Ministry of Transport; HM Diplomatic Service, HBM V-Consul to Spanish Guinea; Australian Public Service, Assistant Secretary, Department of Education Deputy Director of Technical and Further Education. *Memberships:* ACT Oriental Rug Society. *Hobbies:* Collecting Oriental Rugs; Gardening. *Address:* 14 Hotham Crescent, Deakin, Canberra, Australia 2600.

MacCONCHIE, Ian Haig, b. 4 Mar. 1917, Melbourne, Australia. Thoracic Surgeon. m. Marjory Weston Sutcliffe, 23 May 1942, 3 sons, 2 daughters. *Education:* Queen's College, Melbourne University; MB, BS 1941; MS 1947; FRACS 1948. *Appointments:* Consulting Thoracic Surgeon: Royal Melbourne Hospital; Repatriation General Hospital; Western General Hospital; Royal Women's Hospital, Melbourne. *Memberships:* Fellow, Royal Australasia College of Surgeons; Australian and British Medical Associations; Thoracic and Cardiac Societies of Australia; Asian/Pacific Thorace and Cardovascular Society. *Publications:* Articles relating to Thoracic Surgery in many journals. *Honours:* Fellow, Queens College, Melbourne University, 1970. *Hobbies:* Reading; Photography; Music; Golf. *Address:* 18 Edward Street, Kew, Victoria 3101, Australia.

McCONNELL, Joyce Marion, b. 21 Aug. 1916, Chatswood, New South Wales, Australia. m. Hugh Graham Douglas McConnell, 31 Aug. 1939, 2 sons, 2 daughters. *Education:* B.Ec., University of Sydney, Australia. *Appointments:* Appointed to 1st National Women's Advisory Council,(NB), NWAC., by the Prime Minister and Cabinet to advise Australian Government on matters affecting women, 1978-80. *Memberships:* President, 1973-76, Hon. Life Vice-President, 1979-, National Council of Women of Australia; Vice-President, 1974-77, Australian Pre-School Association; Life member, International Council of Women; National Council of Australian Federation of University Women. *Honours:* OBE., 1976; Queen's Jubilee Medal, 1977. *Hobbies:* Gardening; Golf. *Address:* 95 Stonehaven Crescent, Deakin, A C T 2600, Australia.

McCRACKEN, K Wayne, b. 5 June 1943, Sarnia, Ontario, Canada. Lawyer. m. Ginette Roberge, 3 Nov. 1977, 1 son, 1 daughter. *Education:* BA., Hons., Queens University, Canada, 1963; MA., 1964, BL., University of Toronto, Canada. *Appointments:* Lawyer, 1969-, Partner, 1974-. Campbell, Godfrey & Lewtas, Canada; own competition law practice. *Memberships:* University Club of Toronto; Lawyer's Club; Canadian Bar Association. *Publications:* Conspiracy and the Competition Act: Certain Questions, 1972; Consumer Product Warranty LAW: Ontario and Places West, 1979; Legal Editor of: The Source: The Authoritative Guide to Advertising and the Law, 1981. *Hobbies:* Billiards; Fishing. *Address:* 60 Greenwich Square, Scarborough, Ontario, M1J 3L1, Canada.

MacCRAE, David James, b. 17 June 1918, Nairobi, Kenya. Entomologist. m. Agnes Somerville Russell, 20 Sept. 1939, 2 daughters. *Education:* BSc, Edinburgh, 1949. *Appointments:* Entomologist, Kenya, 1949-64, Belize, 1966-68, Brunei, 1971-81. *Memberships:* Royal Commonwealth Society; International Gamefish Association. *Publications:* Insects of Agricultural Importance in Brunei. *Address:* 7 Barnett Street, Belize City, Belize, Central America.

MacCREA, John Mark, b. 26 Mar. 1953, Ottawa, Ontario, Canada. Barrister-at-Law. m. Margaret Anne, 2 July, 1977. *Education:* B.Comm., 1974, LL.B., 1978, MBA., 1978, Dalhouse University, Halifax, Nova Scotia, Canada. *Appointments:* Barrister-at-Law, Patterson, Smith, Matthews and Grant, Truro, Nova Scotia, Canada. *Memberships:* various subsections, Nova Scotia Barristers' Society; various subsections, Canadian Bar Association; Truro and District Chamber of Commerce. *Publications:* Legal Accounting Case Book, Nova Scotia

Barristers' Society Bar Admission Course, 1980-; An Understandable Will or one that will go all the way to the Supreme Court, 1981. *Honours:* Grant to aid to student athletes, 1972; Hon. Richard B. Hanson prize, Constitutional Law, Law School, Dalhousie Universit. Halifax, Nova Scotia, Canada, 1977. *Hobbies:* Tennis; Volleyball; Trout and salmon fishing. *Address:* 20 Patterson Avenue, Truro, Nova Scotia, Canada B2N 1S7.

McCREDIE, Hugh George, b. 30 June 1921, Sydney, Australia. University Administrator. m. (1) Gwenda Morphett), 1945, (2) Sheila Steel, 1978, 2 daughters. *Education:* LL.B., 2nd class Hons., University of Sydney, Australia, 1946-47; Fellow, Australian Society of Accountants; Fellow, Chartered Institute of Secretaries and Adminstrators; Non-practising Barrister, Supreme Court of New South Wales, Australia. *Appointments:* Assistant Registrar, 1950-60, Deputy Registrar, 1960-67, Registrar, 1967-72, Secretary, 1972-74, Deputy Principal, 1974-, Part time Lecturer, Accounting, 1953-59, University of Sydney, Australia. *Memberships:* President, Australian Universities Sports Association, 1971-; Secretary: Rhodes Scholarship Selection Committee, New South Wales, 1969-; Rothmans University Endowment Fund, 1960-; Trustee, Caltex Woman Graduate of the Year, 1976-; President, Sydney University Sports Union, 1961-63; Commonwealth Committee, Professional Qualifications Generalist Section; Bursary Endowmen Board of New South Wales; Treasurer, Wesley College, University of Sydney, 1973-; Treasurer/Director the Director, Dunmore Lang College, Macquarie University, 1970-; Trustee, St. Andrews College, University of Sydney; Board International House, University of Sydney, 1974-; Board member, Chromosome Research Foundation Limited. *Honours:* Carnegie Travelling Fellow, 1963; British Council Scholar, 1963. *Hobbies:* Tennis; Sports Administration. *Address:* 11 Werona Street, Pennant Hills, New South Wales 2120, Australia.

McCREDIE, John Daniel, b. 13 Aug. 1921, Melbourne, Victoria, Australia. Career Diplomat. m. Alison Hall, 10 Feb. 1950, 2 sons, 3 daughters. *Education:* BA., (Hons.), University of Melbourne, Australia, 1948. *Appointments:* Appointments in Ottawa, Karachi, Manila, The Hague; Minister, Jakarta; Consul General, San Francisco, USA; High Commissioner to Ghana, Ambassador to Senegal and the Ivory Coast, Accra; Ambassador to G D R, Berlin, 1980-, Australian Department of Foreign Affairs, 1949-. *Honours:* D F C., 1945. *Hobbies:* Golf; Tennis; Gardening. *Address:* 47 Tschaikowsky Street, Niederschönhausen, Berlin 1110, Germany.

McCULLOCH, George Alec, b. 14 Mar. 1933, Buenos Aires, Argentina. Engineering Management. m. Joyce Lindsay Ballantyne, 25 Mar. 1964, 1 daughter. *Education:* BSc, & ARCST, University of Strathclyde and Glasgow University, 1954-58; PhD, Glasgow University, 1958-62. *Appointments:* Head of Production Control & Management Services, 1965-69, Senior Planning Adviser, 1970-73, Manager Investment Planning, Tubes Division, 1975-80, British Steel Corporation; BSc Fellow & Member of Faculty, London Business School, 1973-75; Principal Lecturer, Harrow College of Higher Education, Harrow, Middlesex, 1980-. *Memberships:* Fellow, Institution of Mechanical Engineers and Chartered Engineer. *Publications:* Contributions to reports and congresses on the use of Computers and Microcomputers in Planning, Production and Financial Planning. *Honours:* Montgomerie Neilson Prize, 1958; W McCrone and Greenock Research Fellowships, and Dr James McKenzie Prize, 1958-61; British Steel Corporation Fellowship, 1973-75. *Hobbies:* Photography; Travel; Social, Welfare and Church activities. *Address:* Newhouse, Main Street, Fotheringhay, Peterborough, PE8 5HZ, England.

McCUTCHEON, Alan Douglas, b. 7 Sept. 1925, Melbourne, Australia. Consultant Physician. m. Joan Elizabeth Mackay, 27 Aug. 1949, 1 son, 1 daughter. *Education:* MB., BS., 1950, MD., 1959, Melbourne University, Australia; MRACP., 1958; FRACP., 1970. *Appointments:* Resident Medical Officer, 1951-52, Clinical Supervisor, 1956-58, Research Assistant and Hon. Assistant Physician, Clinical Research Unit, 1961-64, Physician to: Outpatients, 1964-72, Inpatients, 1972-, Alfred Hospital, Melbourne, Australia; Research Fellow, Baker Medical Research Institute, 1959-61; Associate, Department of Medicine, Monash University, Australia, 1978-. *Memberships:* Australian Medical

Association; Fellow, Royal Australasian College of Physicians; Haematology Society of Australia. *Publications:* Numerous publications including: Sulphaemoglobinaemia and Glutathione, 1960; Aetiological Factors in Pancreatitis, 1962; Experimental Pancreatitis: A Possible Aetiology of Postoperative Pancreatitis, 1962; Renal Damage and Phenacetin, 1962; Reflux of Duodenal Contents in the Pathogenesis of Pancreatitis, 1964; A Fresh Approach to the Pathogenesis of Pancreatitis, 1968. *Hobbies:* Music; Tennis. *Address:* 28 Maitland Avenue, East Kew 3102, Victoria, Australia.

McDERMOTT, John Charles, b. 21 Mar. 1929, Boulder, West Australia. Mine Manager; Mining Engineer. m. Betty May Connolly, 5 Jan. 1952, 1 son, 1 daughter. *Education:* Diploma, Mining Engineering, 1962, Certificate, Mine Surveying, West Australian School of Mines; 1st class Mine Managers Certificate of Competency; Quarry Managers Certificate of Service; Underground Supervisors Certificate of Competency. *Appointments:* Mine Surveyor; Underground Supervisor; Assistant Underground Manager; Underground Manager; Manger, Planning and Development; Resident Manager. *Memberships:* Corporate member, Australian Institute of Mining and Metallurgy; Life member, Apex Clubs of Australia; Representative, Australian Federal Council, President, Eastern Goldfields Section, Royal Flying Doctor Service of Australia; Executive Councillor, West Australian Chamber of Mines. *Honours:* Citizen of the Year award for Eastern Goldfields area, Western Australia, 1980; Justice of the Peace, 1977. *Hobbies:* Flying; Sports. *Address:* 71 Ward Street, Kalgoorlie, West Australia.

MACDONALD, Duncan Donald, b. 24 Sept. 1922, Dublin, Ireland. Physician. m. Rita Margaret Ball, 20 July 1965, 4 sons, 2 daughters. *Education:* Repton School, Repton, Derbyshire; Trinity College, Dublin University, Dublin, Ireland, MA, 1948; MB,BCh, BAO, 1950; LM, 1963. *Appointments:* Resident Casualty Officer, Sir Patrick Dun's Hospital, Dublin; Senior House Officer, St Leonard's Hospital, London; Medical Advisor with Parke Davis & Company and Liaison Officer to the Wright-Fleming Institute of Microbiology, St Mary's Hospital, London; Second Secretary Medical Officer, HBM Legation, Bucharest, Rumania; Head, Medical Information Division, May & Baker Ltd, Dagenham, Essex, England; General practice medicine, Deer Lake, NF, Canada. *Memberships:* Newfoundland & Canadian Medical Associations; Kildare Street and University Club; Deer Lake Chamber of Commerce; Red Cross Society; Royal Commonwealth Society. *Publications:* Various contributions in medical journals; Line drawings, water colour and pen sketches in exhibitions. *Honours:* Formerly Surgeon Lieutenant, Deer Lake Royal Canadian Sea Cadet Corps; Knight of the Sauna, Helsinki, Finland; Knight, Teutonic Order of the Levant in Canada; Honorary MPS, Egypt; Honorary Life member, Management Committee, The Health Centre, Deer Lake, Newfoundland, 1973. *Hobbies:* History; Heraldry; Horticulture; Golf; Travel. *Address:* Fairview House, Deer Lane, NF, Canada.

McDONALD, Hugh Roderick, b. 31 Mar. 1929, Brockville, Ontario, Canada. Lawyer. m. Joan Dorothy Gourley, 10 June 1962, 1 son. *Education:* B.Comm., St. Patrick's College, University of Ottawa, Canada, 1954; Barrister-at-Law, Osgoode Hall, Canada, 1960. *Appointments:* Lieutenant, Royal Canadian Navy, 1946-51; Barrister and Solicitor: Low, Honeywell, Murchison, Burns, 1960-70, Private Practice, 1970-78, McDonald & Lnadry Partnership, 1978-. *Memberships:* Chairman, 1971, Commissioner, 1968-76, Nepean Township Hydro Commission; Alderman, City of Nepean, 1978-; Secretary, Ottawa Centre Liberal Association, 1962-80. *Honours:* Canadian Forces Decoration. *Address:* 5 Tower Road, Nepean, Ontario K2G 3E2, Canada.

McDONALD, Ian Alexander, b. 1 Apr. 1922, Australia. Obstetrician, Gynaecologist. m. Roberta Whiteside, 11 Nov. 1947, 2 sons, 1 daughter. *Education:* MB, BS, Melbourne, 1946; FRCS, England, 1949; MRCOG, 1952; FRACS, 1953; FRCOG, 1963; FAGO, 1974; FRACOG, 1979. *Appointments:* Military Service, Major, BCOF, Japan, Officer Commanding Surgical Division, 1947-48; Resident Medical Officer, 1946-47, Gynaecology Registrar, 1948, Assistant Gynaecologist, 1952-66, Honorary Gynaecologist and Gynaecologist in Chief, 1955-, Royal Melbourne Hospital; House

Surgeon, Queen Charlotte's Hospital, London, 1949-50, Chelsea Hospital for Women, London, 1950-51; Registrar in Gynaecology, North Middlesex Hospital, London, 1951; Senior Registrar, Samaritan Free Hospital for Women, London, 1952; Honorary Obstetrician & Gynaecologist, Footscray and District Hospital, 1953-66; Tutor in Obstetrics & Gynaecology, Queen's College, University of Melbourne, 1953-67; Member of Council, Royal College of Obstetricians & Gynaecologists, London, 1963,1970, 1972; Honorary Secretary, Victorian State Committee,, 1957-60, 1964-67, Australian Council, 1957-64, 1965-75, Honorary Secretary, Australian Regional Council, 1960-64, 1967-72, Australian President, 1972-75; Examiner in Gynaecology, 1966, Examiner for MGO, 1968, University of Melbourne; Guest Examiner, Monash University, 1968; Overseas Examiner, Royal College of Obstetricians & Gynaec., London, 1970. *Memberships:* Past Australian President, Royal College of Obstetricians and Gynaecologists. *Publications:* Numerous contributions to medical journals including: Suture of the Cervix for Inevitable Miscarriage; Incompetent Cervix as a Cause of Recurrent Abortion; A Method of Obstetrics and Gynaecology; Congential Absence of the Vagina; Incompetence of the Cervix; Certival Cerclage; Super Ardua—the history of the Royal College of Obstetricians & Gynaecologist in Australia. *Honours:* Exhibition in Biochemistry, Melbourne University, 1944; Nualasy Prize in Operative Gynaecology, 1947; Robert Fowler Travelling Scholarship of the Anti-Cancer Council of Victoria, 1963. *Hobbies:* Music; Swimming; Tennis. *Address:* 7 Ruhbank Avenue, Balwyn 3103, Victoria, Australia.

McDONALD, Kevin Alexander, b. 29 Aug. 1924, Melbourne, Australia. General Manager. m. Eunice Irene Harding, 11 Oct. 1950. *Education:* Fellow, Institute of Engineers, 1950. *Appointments:* Supervising Engineer, 1960-70, Senior Assistant Director General, 1971-75, Post Master General's Department; General Manager, Australian Tourist Commission, 1975-. *Memberships:* Fellow, Australian Institute of Management; Fellow, Institute of Directors and Institute Senior Executives. *Hobbies:* Cabinet making; Boating; Fishing; Films. *Address:* 56 Darling Street, South Yarra, Australia, 3141.

McDOUGALL, William Stewart, b. 2 May 1928, London, England. In Business. *Education:* Geelong Grammar School, Australia, 1940-44; Malvern College, England, 1944-46. *Appointments:* Director, The Kiwi International Co. Limited, Australia and subsidiary and Associated Companies. *Memberships:* Australian Athenaeum, VRC.; Oriental Club, England. *Hobbies:* Antiques; Travel. *Address:* 550 Orrong Road, Armadale, Victoria 3143, Australia.

McDOWELL, Charles William Michael, b. 11 Feb. 1928, Peterborough, England. Consulting Civil Public Health & Highway Engineer & Chartered Arbitrator. m. Audrey Diana, 6 Aug. 1955, 1 son, 3 daughters. *Education:* BSc Civil Engineering, University College, London, 1948-51. *Appointments:* Pupil Engineer, Tanganyka, 1951-53; Resident Engineer, 1954-56, Deputy Resident Engineer, LCC, 1956-58; Principal Engineer, 1958-62, Howard Humphreys & Sons; Private Practice, 1963-. *Memberships:* Fellow, Institution of Civil Engineers; Senior Vice President, Institution of Public Health Engineers; Institution of Highway Engineers; Chartered Institute of Arbitrators; Institution of Town Planning Consultants. *Publications:* Balancing Ponds, IPHE, 1977; Philosophies & Economics of Public Health Engineers Schemes in Developing Countries, 1978; Development of the Design of Building Drainage for a Large Airport Terminal, 1980. *Hobbies:* Veteran athletics; Stamp collecting; Reading. *Address:* St Christophers 13 Gilhams Avenue, Banstead, Surrey, England.

MacEACHEN, Allan J, b. 6 July 1921, Inverness, Nova Scotia, Canada. Member of Parliament. *Education:* BA., St. Francis Xavier University, Canada, 1944; MA., University of Toronto, Canada, 1946; Post-graduate studies, University of Chicago, USA, 1948; Economics & Industrial Relations, Massachusetts Institute of Technology, Boston, USA, 1951-53. *Appointments:* Professor of Economics, 1946-48, Head, Department of Economics & Social Sciences, St. Francis Xavier University, Canada; Elected, 1953, re-elected, 1957, 1962, 1963, 1965, 1968, 1972, 1974, 79, 80; Sworn of the Privy Council and Appointed Minister of Labour, 1963;

Minister of National Health and Welfare, 1965-68; Government House Leader, 1967-68; Minister of Manpower and Immigration, 1968-70; President of the Queen's Privy Council for Canada, 1970-74, 1976-; Secretary of State for External Affairs, 1974-76; Appointed Deputy Prime Minister, 1977, 1980; Appointed Deputy Leader of Opposition and Opposition House Leader, 1979; Appointed Minister of Finance, 1980. *Memberships:* Corporation Visiting Committee to Center for International Studies of Massachusetts Institute of Technology. *Honours:* Honorary Degrees from: St. Francis Xavier University, 1966; Acadia University, 1966; Loyola College, Baltimore, Maryland, USA, 1966; St. Mary's University, 1973; Dalhousie University, 1974; Sir Wilfrid Laurier University, 1976. *Address:* House of Commons, Ottawa, Ontario, Canada.

McEWAN, Geraldine, b. Old Windsor. Actress. 1 son, 1 daughter. *Education:* Windsor County Girls School. *Appointments:* Theatre Royal Windsor, 1949; Who Goes There 1951; For Better for Worse 1953; Summertime 1955; Seasons at Stratford on Avon, 1956/58/61; The Member of the Wedding 1957; The Entertainer 1957-58; School for Scandal in USA 1962; The Private Ear and The Public Eye, USA 1963; Loot 1965; National Theatre Company 1965-71; Dear Love 1973; Not Drowning but Waving 1973; Chez Nous 1974; The Little Hut 1974; Oh Coward 1975; On Approval 1975-76; Look After Lulu 1978; The Prime of Miss Jean Brodie, Television series 1980; Browning Version/Harlequinade, National Theatre 1980-81; The Provoked Wife, National Theatre. *Address:* 3 Goodwins Court, St Marins Lane, London WC2, England.

McEWEN, John, b. 29 Mar. 1900, Chiltern, Victoria, Australia. Cabinet Minister (retired). m. (1) Annie Mills McLeod, dec'd., 1921, (2) Mary Eileen Byrne, 1968. *Appointments:* Elected Federal Parliament, 1934; appointed to Cabinet, 1937; Deputy Leader, 1943-58, Leader, 1958-71, Deputy Prime Minister, 1958-71, Prime Minister, 1967-68, Australian Parliamentary Country Party. *Memberships:* Melbourne Club. *Honours:* Member, Privy Council, 1953; Companion of Honour, 1969; Knight Grand Cross of Most Distinguished Order of St. Michael and St. George, 1971; Order of the Rising Sun, 1st Class, Government of Japan, 1973. *Hobby:* Reading. *Address:* 367 Collins street, Melbourne, Victoria 3000, Australia.

MACFARLANE, George Gray, b. 8 Jan. 1916, Airdrie, Scotland. Electrical Engineer. m. Barbara Grant Thomson, 23 July 1941, 1 son, 1 daughter. *Education:* BSc(1st class Hons) Glasgow University 1933-37; Dr-Ing. Technische Hochschule Dresden 1937-39. *Appointments:* Scientific Staff, Air Ministry Research Establishment Dundee and Swanage 1939-41; Telecommunications Research Establishment, Malvern 1941-60, Deputy Chief Scientific Officer, 1954-60; Deputy DirectDirector, National Physical Laboratory 1960-62; Director Royal Radar Establishment 1962-67; Controller Research Ministry of Technology and Aviation 1967-71; Controller, R&D Establishments and Research Ministry of Defence, 1971-76; Board Member, The Post Office, 1978-; Member National Enterprise Board 1980. *Memberships:* Fellowship of Engineering; Fellow, Institution of Electrical Engineers; Fellow, Institute of Mathematics and its' Application. *Publications:* Numerous papers in learned Societies, such as IEE journal, Proc. Phys. Society, Physical Review, Phil Mag. *Honours:* Kt 1971; CB 1965; Hon.LLD Glasgow University 1966; Glazebrook Medal, Physical Society 1978. *Hobbies:* Walking; Reading. *Address:* Red Tiles, Orchard Way, Esher, Surrey, KT10 9DY, England.

McFARLANE, Ian, b. 25 Dec. 1923, Sydney, Australia. Chairman. m. Ann Shaw 10 Nov. 1956, 1 son, 2 daughters. *Education:* Harrow School, England 1937; Bachelor Science Engineering, Sydney University 1941-44 and Bachelor of Engineering, 1946; MSc (Civil Engineering), M.I.T 1948-50. *Appointments:* Associate, Investment Bankers, Morgan Stanley and Company 1949-59; Sydney Stock Exchange 1959-64; Chairman Trans Pacific Consolidated Limited 1964; Partner Ord. Minnett T J Thompson and Partners; Chairman Southern Pacific Petroleum N.L, Central Pacific Minerals N.L; Deputy Chairman, Magellan Petroleum Limited 1964-70; Director: International Pacific Corp. 1967-73; Australian General Insurance Company Limited 1968-74; Mercantile Mutual Insurance

Company Limited 1969-74; Concrete Constructions, 1972-74; International Pacific Australian Investments Limited 1972-73; *Memberships:* Australian Club Sydney; Queensland Club Brisbane; Commonwealth Club Canberra; University Club N.Y. *Hobbies:* Swimming; Tennis. *Address:* 40 Wentworth Road, Vaucluse, NSW 2030, Australia.

McFARLANE, Jean Kennedy (Baroness of Llandaff), b. 1 Apr. 1926, Llandaff South Wales. Professor of Nursing. *Education:* BSc, Soc., Bedford College, University of London 1966; MA, Birbeck College, University of London 1968; MSc(Hon.) Manchester 1979; DSc(Hon) New University of Ulster 1981; SRN St. Bartholomews Hospital 1951, HV Certificate Welsh National School Med 1953; RCN HV Tutors Certificate 1960. *Appointments:* Staff Nurse, St Bartholomews Hospital London 1950-51; Health Visitor Cardiff 1954-59; Tutor RCN London 1960-62; Education Officer RCN 1962-66; Research Organiser RCN 1966-69; Director of Education RCN 1969-71; Senior Lecturer University of Manchester 1971-74; Professor, Head of Department of Nursing University of Manchester 1974-. *Memberships:* Fellow, Royal College of Nursing; Royal Commonwealth Society; Ladies Voluntary Aide Detachment; Sloane Club. *Publications:* The Problems of Developing Criteria of Quality for Nursing Care, 1969; The Proper Study of the Nurse 1970. *Honours:* Life Peeress 1979; Fellow, Royal College of Nursing 1979. *Address:* 5 Dovercourt Avenue, Heaton Mersey, Stockport, Cheshire, England.

McFARLANE, Neville Attlee, b. 14 Nov. 1946, Lucea PO, Hanover, Jamaica. Geologist. m. Kamla Paragg, 26 Aug. 1972, 2 daughters. *Education:* BSc, 1969, MSc, 1974, University of the West Indies. *Appointments:* Geologist, Senior Geologist, Mines & Geology Division, Government of Jamaica, 1969-79; Senior Principal Scientific Officer, Scientific Research Council, Mineral Resources Division, Jamaica, 1979-. *Memberships:* Secretary, 1973-76, President, 1976-79, Geological Society of Jamaica; Jamaican Society of Scientists and Technologists; Association of Geoscientists for International Development. *Publications:* Numerous contributions to professional journals including: Bauxitization and Clay Occurences in Jamaica (with V.G. Hill), 1979; Some Mineral Resources of South Central Coast of Jamaica, 1979; Metallogenic Bauxite Provinces of Latin America, 1980; Several papers in preparation. *Honours:* Commonwealth Foundation Award, 1977; Science & Technology representative of the Jamaican Government to the O A S, Washington DC, 1980. *Hobby:* Theory and practice of Third World Development. *Address:* 23 Spring Crescent, Bridge Port PO, St Catherine, Jamaica

MacFARQUHAR, Alexander (Sir), b. 6 Nov. 1903, Inverness, Scotland. International Civil Servant. m. Berneice Whitburn, 2 Mar. 1929, 1 son. *Education:* MA 1st Class Honours, Aberdeen University, 1921-25; Emmanuel College Cambridge, 1925-26. *Appointments:* Indian Civil Service, 1926-47; Commerce & Education Secretary, Government of Pakistan, 1947-51; United Nations, 1952-67: Regional Representative Far East, Special Fund, 1952-60; Secretary General's Special Adviser, Congo, 1960-62; Under Secretary (Director of Personnel), 1962-67. *Memberships:* United Nations Association of Great Britain (one-time President, London Region); Pakistan Society (Chairman, 1970-81). *Publications:* Settlement Report of Amristsar District Punjab, with associated reports. *Honours:* KBE, 1952; CIE, 1945; LLD, Aberdeen, 1980; HQA, Government of Pakistan, 1981. *Hobbies:* Walking; Investment. *Address:* Ottershaw, Beverley Lane, Kingston, Surrey, KT2 7EE, England.

McGARVIE, Graham Allan, b. 2 Mar. 1931, Colac, Victoria, Australia. District Inspector of Schools, Victorian Education Department. m. Mary Miller, 16 Apr. 1960, 3 sons, 1 daughter. *Education:* Trained Primary Teacher's Certificate, 1952, BA, 1961, Bachelor of Education Degree, 1966, Melbourne Teachers' College and the University of Melbourne. *Appointments:* Primary School Teacher; Secondary/Technical School Teacher; Teachers' College Lecturer; District Inspector of Schools. *Memberships:* Assistant Secretary, 1974-76, Secretary, 1977, Vice-President, 1978, 1979, President, 1980, 1981, Victorian Institute of Inspectors of Schools; Secretary, 1977-79, Australasian Association of Institutes of Inspectors of Schools; Australian Col-

lege of Education; Victorian Institute of Educational Research; Executive, Primary Education Today. *Publications:* Teaching and Accountability, New Education, 1978; The Inspector and the Quality of Education, Aces Review, 1981. *Hobbies:* Reading; Walking; Tennis; Gardening. *Address:* 20 Stawell Street, Beaumaris, Victoria 3193, Australia.

McGEOCH, Arthur Hector, b. 14 Feb. 1919, Sydney. Physician; (Dermatology). m. 20 May 1944, 3 sons, 2 daughters. *Education:* L Certificate YANCO Agric. H S, 1938; MBBS, 1943, DDM, 1953, Sydney University; FACP (Foundation), 1962. *Appointments:* Fellow in Dermatology, RPAH, 1952; Clinical Assistant, Royal Newcastle Hospital, 1953; Mater Misercordia Hospital, 1954, Wallsend Hospital, 1954; Senior Consultant, Royal Newcastle Hospital, 1975, Mater Misercordia, 1975. *Memberships:* Fellow, Royal Society of Medicine, 1961, British Association of Dermatology, 1954; American Academy of Dermatology, 1975; Pacific Dermatology, 1965. *Publications:* Shakespeare the Dermatologist, 1954; Shakespeare the Syphilologist, 1960; Facial focal dysplasis, 1975. *Honours:* Best Non technical Article, Australian Journal Dermatology, 1980; Captain AAMC AIF RofO. *Hobbies:* Tennis; Golf; Rugby; The Medicine Knowledge of Shakespeare; The Medicine of Famous Historical Figures; Agriculture. *Address:* 135 Parkway Avenue, Hamilton South, Newcastle, New South Wales, Australia.

MacGIBBON, Alastair Arthur, b. 8 Apr. 1913, Christchurch, New Zealand. Medical. m. Jean England Kerr, 16 June 1945, 2 daughters. *Education:* Edinburgh University, 1932-37; MB ChB, 1937; DLO,(London), 1945; FRCS, Edinburgh, 1946. *Appointments:* House Surgeon, Western General Hospital, Edinburgh, 1937-38, Hertford County Hospital ENT, 1938; Edinburgh Royal Infirmary, ENT Department, 1938-39; Cumberland Infirmary Carlisle, Ent. Department, 1939-40; Royal Air Force, Medical Branch, 1941-46; Palmerston North Hospital, New Zealand, 1946-; Private Practice, Ear, Nose and Throat Surgeon. *Memberships:* President, Edinburgh University Union, 1935-36, New Zealand Otolaryngological Society, 1954. *Publications:* Papers given, Pan Pacific Surgical Association, Honolulu, ENT Society Meetings, New Zealand. *Honours:* Anatomy Medal & ENT Prize, University of Edinburgh; Tennis Blue Five Years, University of Edinburgh, 1933-37. *Hobbies:* Tennis; Squash; Claybird & Duck Shooting; Golf; Hockey; Cricket; Photography. *Address:* 49 North Street, Palmerston North, New Zealand.

MacGIBBON, David John, b. 13 May 1934, Brisbane, Australia. Senator. m. Pamela Emmeline Beak, 8 Aug. 1958, 2 sons, 2 daughters. *Education:* BD Sc, University of Queensland, 1956; FDS, RCS, England, 1962; FRACDS, 1966. *Appointments:* University of Queensland, 1957, London, 1962-64, Queensland, 1965-78, Michigan, 1971-72. *Memberships:* Vice-President, Australian Dental Association (Queensland Branch). *Publications:* Contributions to Professional Literature. *Honours:* Mary Moffat Memorial Prize, University of Queensland, 1956; Carlyle C Bastian Prize, University of Queensland, 1956. *Hobbies:* Reading; Talking; Flying. *Address:* 28 Marston Avenue, Indooroopilly 4068, Australia.

McGONIGAL, Harold David, b. 5 Apr. 1916, Geelong, Victoria, Australia. Chartered Builder. m. Marie Theresa Ryan, 18 Apr. 1942, 2 daughters. *Education:* Geelong High School and Swinbourne Technical College, 1934-36. *Appointments:* Senior Management Executive, Jennings Industries Limited, 1945-80. *Memberships:* National President, 1978-80, President, Victorian Chapter, 1973-74, President, Tasmanian Chapter, 1963, The Australian Institute of Building; President, The Master Builder's Association of Tasmania, 1958-59; National Vice-President, Knights of the Southern Cross, 1962-63; Federal Council Master Builders Federation of Australia, 1958-60; Tasmanian Employers Federation, 1959-62; Commissioner, Tasmanian Apprenticeship Commission, 1961-64. *Honours:* Life Member, Knights of The Southern Cross, 1981; Honorary Member, The Master Builders' Association of Tasmania, 1963. *Address:* 46 Koolkuna Avenue, Doncaster, Victoria 3108, Australia.

McGOWAN, Edward Emmanuel, b. 26 July 1923, Dudley, Worcestershire. Social Scientist/Educator. m. Jean Cynthia Terry, 4 sons, 1 daughter. *Education:* TC,

Claremont Teachers' College, Western Australia, 1957; BA, 1963, THL, 1964, MA, 1968, University of Western Australia; Member of Australian College of Education, 1969; DA, Carnegie-Mellon University, Pittsburgh, USA, 1979. *Appointments:* Primary Teacher, 1958-61, Secondary, 1962-64, Western Australia; Lecturer/Senior Lecturer, Technical Education, 1965-71; Lecturer, University of Western Australia, 1971-72, Claremont Teachers' College, 1972-74; Head of Department of Social Sciences, Nedlands College of Advanced Education, 1975-. *Memberships:* Australian College of Education; Western Australian History Association; Royal Western Australian History Society; Political Studies Association. Consultant on mining history, social science, moral education; Many articles on mining/social science journals; Contributor/Co-editor, Mining in Western Australia, 1979; Western Australian Atlas of Endeavour, 1979; preparing volume on Gold Mining in Western Australia, Western Australia in the 1890's. *Honours:* Grant, To research & write history of Goldmining in Western Australia, 1971; War Service, Europe & South East Asia, 1939-47, Wounded, 1944. *Hobbies:* Gardening; Swimming; Reading. *Address:* 2 Grenville Avenue, Sorrento 6020, Western Australia.

McGRATH, Gerald Francis, b. 24 Aug. 1927. Teacher. *Education:* Diploma, Australian Association Teachers of the Deaf 1957; Diploma, National College of Teachers of the Deaf, London, 1956. *Appointments:* Teacher, St Gabriel's School for Deaf, 1949, Principal 1965. *Memberships:* Australian Deafness Council; Australian Association Teachers of the Deaf; Australian Council of Education. *Publications:* Submitted papers to national seminars; Presented a paper, New York Conference of Teachers of the Deaf 1967; Paper accepted, Stockholm Conference on the Education of the Deaf 1972; Paper, Hamburg Conference 1980; Paper, Manchester Conference, Religious Education of the Deaf 1980. *Honours:* Order of Australia, 1980. *Hobbies:* Surfing; Golf; Tennis; Swimming. *Address:* St. Gabriel's School for Hearing Impaired Children, Old Northern Road, Castle Hill, 2154 Australia.

McGRATH, Philip James, b. 13 Aug. 1935, Sydney, Australia. Medical Practitioner (Orthopaedic Surgeon). m. Patricia Ann Cooper, 1 June 1965, 2 sons, 1 daughter. *Education:* MB BS, University of Sydney, 1959; FRCS Ed, 1969; FRACS, 1974. *Appointments:* Visiting Orthopaedic Surgeon, Parramatta Hospital, 1973-, Westmead Centre, 1978-, New South Wales. *Memberships:* Overseas Fellow, British Orthopaedic Association; Australian Orthopaedic Association; Australian Medical Association; United Services Institute of New South Wales. *Publications:* Giant Cell Tumour of Bone, Journal Bone & Joint Surgery, 1972. *Honours:* Efficiency Decoration (ED), 1978. *Hobbies:* Surfing; Bushwalking; Sailing. *Address:* 15 Wellesley Road, Pymble, New South Wales 2073, Australia.

McGREGOR, Alexander Sharpe, b. 27 Apr. 1932, Toronto, Canada. Teacher. Divorced, 2 sons. *Education:* Toronto Teachers' College; BA, Queen's University, Kingston, Ontario; BEd, Toronto University; MA, McMaster University, Hamilton, Ontario. *Appointments:* Registrar Dean, Assistant Professor, Thorneloe University, 1978-; Assistant Professor, Waterloo Lutheran University and Bishop's University; School Teacher Ontario. *Memberships:* Ontario Historical Society; Canadian Professors Peace in Middle East. *Publications:* Numerous articles in Journals and Scholarly publications. *Hobbies:* Swimming; Coaching Soccer, Laurentian University. *Address:* Thorneloe College, Laurentian University, Sudbury, Ontario Canada.

MACGREGOR, Thomas Horatio Oluyomi, b. 7 Jan. 1938, Lagos, Nigeria. Chartered Surveyor. m. Rosemary Iyabo Wilkey, 22 July 1966, 2 sons, 1 daughter. *Education:* St Gregory's College 1953-58; North Western Polytechnic, London 1960-62; Holborn School of Law, London 1962-64; Willesden College of Technology, London 1964-67. *Appointments:* Commission for the New Towns, Welwyn Garden City, Herts England 1968-70; Harriman and Company, Lagos 1970-72; MacGregor and Company, Lagos 1972-73; Principal Partner, MacGregor and Ojutalayo 1973-81. *Memberships:* Fellow, Royal Institution of Chartered Surveyors; Board of Governors, St Gregory's College; Catholic Friendly Society; Metropolitan Club, Lagos; Chieftain Club, British Caledonia; Island Club, Lagos; Ikoyi Club;

Lagos Divisional Football Association; St Gregory's College, Lagos. *Hobbies:* Football; Films; Travelling; Reading. *Address:* Plot 4, Block E, Ogba Residential Estate, Lagos, Nigeria.

McGUINNESS, Michael Francis, b. 18 Apr. 1948, Bath, England. Dental Surgeon. m. Judith Lovell, 26 Sept. 1970, 2 daughters. *Education:* City & Guilds, London Institute Dental Technicians Certificate, 1968; Further Education Teacher's Certificate, UK, 1970; Bachelor of Dental Science, University of Western Australia, 1977. *Appointments:* Dental Surgeon, St George's Tce, Perth, Western Australia. *Memberships:* Western Australian Branch, Australian Dental Association, 1980; Western Australian Branch, Australian Society of Endodontics, 1980-; Charter Member, Rotary Club of Freshwater Bay. *Hobbies:* Tennis; Music. *Address:* 14 Bernard Street, Claremont, W.A., 6010, Australia.

McHARDY, Pauline Sydney, b. 30 May 1944, Kingston, Jamaica. Physical Planner. *Education:* BA, Geography, 1968, MA, Urban & Regional Planning, 1972, University of British Columbia, Vancouver, Canada; Fellow, Economic Development Institute, 1976. *Appointments:* Geography Teacher, Queen's High School for Girls, 1968-69; Planning Officer, 1969-70, Assistant Regional Planner, 1972-74, Town Planning Department; Chief Planner, National Planning Agency, 1974-75. *Memberships:* Honorary Secretary, 1975-77, Executive, 1977-79, President, 1979-81, Town & Country Planning Association of Jamaica. *Publications:* Information needs for urban housing, Kingston, Jamaica, 1979. *Honours:* Canadian Commonwealth Scholarship, 1965-68; United Nations Fellowship, 1970-72. *Hobby:* Batik Cooking. *Address:* 7A Barbican Drive, Kingston, 6, Jamaica, West Indies.

McILRAITH, (Hon) George James, b. 19 July 1908, Lanark, Ontario. Senator. m. Margaret Summers, 1 son, 3 daughters. *Appointments:* First elected to House of Commons for Ottawa West, 1940; Re-elected, 1945, 1949, 1953, 1957, 1958, 1962, 1963, 1965 and 1968; Appointed Parliamentary Assistant to: Minister of Reconstruction and Supply, 1945, Minister of Trade and Commerce, 1948, Minister of Defence Production, 1951; Resigned in 1953; Sworn of the Privy Council and appointed Minister of Transport, 1963; President of the Privy Council, 1964; Minister of Public Works, 1965; Government House Leader, 1964-67; Solicitor General of Canada, 1968, resigned, 1970; Summoned to the Senate, 1972. *Memberships:* Canadian Club of Ottawa. *Honours:* Has represented Canada at a number of Commonwealth and International Conferences; Representative to the Colombo Plan Conference in London, 1950, Karachi, 1952; Headed Canadian Delegation to 17th Commonwealth Parliamentary Conference in Blantyre, Malawi, Africa, 1972; Member of Canadian Delegation to XXth Meeting of Canada-US, Inter-Parliamentary Group, Alberta, Yokon and Alaska, 1979. *Address:* 406-20 Driveway, Ottawa, Ontario, K2P 1C8, Canada.

McINDOE, John Alexander, b. 19 Feb. 1930, Leongatha, Victoria, Australia. Registrar. m. Margaret Ruth Parsons, 28 Mar. 1959, 2 sons, 3 daughters. *Education:* Bachelor of Commerce, Bachelor of Education, University of Melbourne. *Appointments:* Secondary School Teacher, Victorian Education Department, 1957-68; Assistant Registrar, 1968-73, Deputy Registrar, 1973-75, Victoria Institute of Colleges; Registrar, Royal Melbourne Institute of Technology, 1975-. *Memberships:* Australian College of Education; Vice-President, Victorian Branch, Australian Institute of Tertiary Educational Administration; The Higher Education and Research Development Society of Australia. *Hobbies:* Farming; Music. *Address:* 6 Stawell Street, Kew, Victoria, 3101, Australia.

McINERNEY, Robert James Furlong, b. 22 Aug. 1918, Sydney. Consultant Obstetrician & Gynaecologist. m. Betty Rose Stormon, 31 May 1952. *Education:* De la Salle College, Ashfield; MB.,BS, Sydney, 1942; FRCS, England, 1950; FRACS, 1961; FACS, 1966; FRCOG, London, 1967; FRACOG, 1979. *Appointments:* Senior Gynaecologist, St Vincent's Hospital, Sydney and Lewisham Hospital, Sydney; Senior Gynaecologist and Obstetrician, St Margaret's Hospital, Sydney and Mater Hospital, Sydney. *Memberships:* Medical Officer Western Suburbs Rugby League Football Club; Australian Jockey Club; Australian Turf Club; Tattersalls Club; Royal Sydney Golf Club. *Honours:* Dux of School, 1936; Clipsham Prize in operative surgery & Craig Prize in surgical anatomy; Coppleson Prize for surgery and Deithelm prize in Medicine; CMG, 1977; Knight of Malta, 1977; Papal Knighthood, 1977. Guest Professor in Gynaecology, Chulalongchorn Hospital, Bangkok, Thailand, 1977. *Address:* 6 Sortie Port, Castlecrag, NSW, 2068, Australia.

McINNES, Ian Edgeworth, b. 14 Jan. 1931, Melbourne, Australia. Surgeon. m. Ann Patricia Hughes, 3 Feb. 1966, 2 sons. *Education:* Scotch College, 1942-49; MB, BS, Melbourne, 1955; FRCS, London, 1961; FRACS, Melbourne, 1964. *Appointments:* Surgeon, Alfred Hospital, Melbourne and Frankston Hospital, Frankston; Dean of Clinical School, Manash University Melbourne; Consulting Surgeon, R.A.N. *Memberships:* AMA; AAS. *Publications:* Various contributions to scientific journals and books. *Hobbies:* Flying; Golf; Music. *Address:* 64 Roborough Avenue, Mt Eliza, 3930, Australia.

McINTYRE, Graeme Noel, b. 31 Mar. 1940, Hobart, Tasmania, Australia. University Lecturer. m. Helen Lucy Warren, 17 Feb. 1968. *Education:* Certificate of Education, Tasmania 1963; Bachelor of Arts, 1965; Bachelor of Arts (Hon) 1968; Master of Arts, Australian National University, 1974. *Appointments:* Demonstrator, Department of Geography, University of Tasmania, 1966-68; Teacher, Elizabeth Matriculation College, Hobart, Tasmania 1969; Senior Research Officer, Department of National Development, Canberra, 1970-73; Lecturer, Department of Geography, University of Newcastle, NSW 1974-. *Memberships:* Institute of Australian Geographers; Fellow, Royal Meteorological Society. *Publications:* Several Maps in the Atlas of Australian Resources 1970-74; Other Academic papers. *Hobbies:* Chess; Swimming; Photography. *Address:* 4 Beverley Crescent, New Lambton Heights, Newcastle, NSW, Australia 2305.

McINTYRE, John McGillivray, b. 11 Jan. 1924, Blenheim, New Zealand. Civil Engineer. m. Valerie Marie Stuart-Boyle 15 Dec. 1953, 2 sons, 3 daughters. *Education:* Bachelor of Engineering 1947; Member, Institute of Civil Engineers, UK 1952; Fellow, Institute of Engineers, Australia 1970. *Appointments:* Chairman and Managing Director of McIntyre and Associates Pty. Ltd, Consulting Civil Engineers 1952-. *Memberships:* President, The Institution of Engineers, Australia; Australian Universities Council; Director, MIM Holdings Limited; Deputy Chairman, Queensland Electricity Generating Board. Hobby: Horse Racing. *Address:* 50 Gilbert Crescent, Yarrawonga, Townsville, Australia 4810.

McIVER, Margo Anne, (Mrs J.B. Hobbs), b. 27 Sept. 1934, Nanango, Queensland, Australia. Medical. m. J.B. Hobbs, 15 Apr. 1967, 2 sons, 1 daughter. *Education:* University of Queensland, 1952-57; MB,BS, 1967; MRACP, 1964; FRACP. *Appointments:* Part-time Demonstrator, School of Physiology, University of Queensland, 1957; Junior Resident Medical Officer, Brisbane General Hospital, Brisbane Children's Hospital and Princess Alexandra Hospital, 1958; Medical Registrar, Brisbane Children's Hospital, 1959, Princess Alexandra Hospital, 1960-61; Tutor in Medicine, University of Queensland, 1960-61; Medical Registrar, 1962, Registrar, Renal Unit, 1962-63; Senior Registrar, Renal Unit, 1963-64, Chief Resident in Medicine, 1963-64, Prince Henry Hospital, Sydney; Senior Tutor in Medicine, University of New South Wales, 1965-66; Honorary Associate Physician, Royal Hospital for Women, Prince Henry Hospital and Prince of Wales Hospital, 1965-66; Fellow in Renal Disease, Prince Henry Hospital, and Honorary Physician, Royal Hospital for Women, 1966-67; Clinical Fellow, Renal Unit, Children's Medical Centre, Boston, USA, 1967; Clinical and Research Fellow in Medicine, Massachusetts General Hospital, Boston, USA, 1967-69; Teaching Fellow in Medicine, Harvard Medical School, Boston, 1969; Consultant Physician and Nephrologist in private practice, Canberra, Australia, 1970-72; Private Consultant Practice, Melbourne, 1972-81; Part-time Lecturer in Paediatrics, Monash University, Melbourne, 1972-; Fellow, Royal Australasian College of Physicians, 1972; Assistant, Renal Clinic, 1972, Assistant Physician, 1973; Physician to Renal Clinic, 1975-76, Paediatric Nephrologist, Honorary Physician, Queen Victoria Hospital,

Melbourne; Consultant Physician and Nephrologist, Dandenong, 1974-; Honorary Consultant Nephrologist, Prince Henry's Hospital, Melbourne, 1979-; Clinical Teacher in Medicine and Paediatrics, Monash University; Director, Silenus Laboratories, Dandenong. *Memberships:* Australian Society of Nepurology; Inst. Soc. of Paed. Nephrology. Various joint contributions to medical journals including: Vasculopathy of Hypertension in Pregnancy—A Correlation of Clinical Course with Skin and Decidual Red Vessel Lesions; Whole Blood Viscosity in Pre-Eclampsia. *Hobbies:* Spinning; Gardening; Cooking; Australian History. *Address:* Grandview, Morrison Road, Pakenham Upper 3810, Victoria, Australia.

McKAY, (Alick "Alex" Benson, Sir), b. 5 Aug. 1909, Adelaide, South Australia. Non executive Director, News International Limited. m. (1) Muriel Searcy 15 June 1953 (dec.) (2) Beverley Hylton, 30 May 1973, 1 son, 2 daughters. *Education:* Thebarton High School, Australia. *Appointments:* News Limited Adelaide 1933; Manager, Melbourne 1939; Manager Sydney 1941; Director and General Manager, Argus & Australasian Limited 1952; Daily Mirror Group London 1957 Director 1958; Director G Newnes Limited 1961; Director International Pub. Co. Ltd, 1963-. *Memberships:* Chairman, London, Victorian Economic Development Corporation; Australian Business and Businessmen in Europe. *Honours:* CBE 1965; KBE 1977. *Address:* Ellingham, St. Clements Road, Westgate-on-Sea, Kent, England.

McKAY, Heather Pamela, (Mrs B.H. McKay), b. 31 July 1941, Queanbeyan, New South Wales, Australia. Squash Instructor. m. B.H. McKay 13 Dec. 1965. *Education:* Queanbeyan High School. *Appointments:* Squash Club Receptionist; Squash Instructor. *Publications:* Heather McKay's Complete Book of Squash (with Jack Batten). *Honours:* MBE, 1969; Member in the General Division of the Order of Australia, 1979; Australian Broadcasting Commission, Sportsman of the Year, 1967. *Hobby:* Reading. *Address:* 48 Nesbitt Drive, Toronto, Ontario, Canada, M4W 2G3.

McKAY, Irene Betty, b. 25 Apr. 1926, Port Augusta, South Australia. Artist. m. Norman Donald McKay, 21 Dec. 1946, 1 son, 1 daughter. *Education:* Studied History and Theology, Parkin Wesley Theological College 1977; Studied Drawing, S.A School of Art 1968; Drawing, under Mervym Smith 1969; General Painting under, William Davey, 1965-67; Portraiture with Ingrid Erns 1967-69 and 1969-70. *Appointments:* Chemists Assistant, Carrig Chemist Limited Port Augusta 1940-42; Buyer, Birks Chemist Limited, Adelaide 1943-46. *Memberships:* W.E.A. Art Club; Citizen Art Club; Royal S.A. Society of Arts; Friend, Art Gallery of South Australia. *Publications:* Contributor to numerous Exhibitions with various Art Clubs; Involved in several Group Shows; Two One Man Exhibitions: Copper Crest Gallery and Newton Gallery; Represented in Many Adelaide City Buildings and Paintings and Drawings in Private Collections. *Honours:* Associate 1974; Fellow, Royal South Australian Society of Arts 1978. *Hobbies:* Dress Designing; Interior Decorating. *Address:* 230A Cross Road, Unley Park, 5061, Adelaide, South Australia.

McKEAND, Lee Henry, b. 14 Jan. 1918, Melbourne, Australia. Managing Director. m. Joan Mary McMahon, 3 Jan. 1946, 2 sons, 1 daughter. *Education:* Technical and Then RAAF, to Commissioned Rank, Pilot. *Appointments:* G W Bruce A.C.A. Melbourne; Accountant Pre 1940; Import, Export, Merchant House, Lee McKeand and Son Pty. Ltd. Group of Companies Melbourne, 1946-. *Memberships:* Rotary Club of Prahran; Victorian Fruit Exporters Committee; Naval and Military Club, Melbourne; Air Force Club, Melbourne; Toorak R.S.L. (Heroes) Club, Melbourne; Victoria and Royal Melbourne Golf Clubs. *Hobbies:* Golf; Fishing; Gardening. *Address:* 25 Kooyong Koot Road, Hawthorn, Victoria 3122, Australia.

McKEE, James Stanley Colton, b. 6 June 1930, Belfast, Northern Ireland. Professor, Director. m. Christine Savage, 16 June 1961, 1 son, 1 daughter. *Education:* Kitchener Scholar, Queen's University, Belfast, 1948-52; BSc, 1952; Research Student, Queen's University, Belfast, 1952-56; University Studentship, 1953; PhD, 1956; Fellow of the Institute of Physics, 1966; DSc, Birmingham University, 1968. *Appointments:* Assistant Lecturer in Physics, Queen's University, Belfast, 1954-56; Lecturer in Physics, 1956-64,

Senior Lecturer, 1964-74, University of Birmingham; Visiting Professor, Lawrence Radiation Laboratory, Berkeley, California, 1966-67; Summer Visitor, Lawrence Berkeley Laboratory, 1972; Professor of Physics, University of Manitoba, 1974-; Acting Director, 1974-75, Director, 1975-, Cyclotron Laboratory. *Memberships:* Fellow, Institute of Physics; Secretary Nuclear Physics Sub-Committee, 1968-74; Canadian Association of Physicists; Editorial Board, Reports on Progress in Physics, 1968-71; Canadian Nuclear Association; Charter Associate, Solar Thermal Test Facilities Users Association. *Publications:* Editor of Two books and 120 scientific publications. *Honours:* Queen's Orator, Queen's University, Belfast, 1953; Invited speaker to five International and four National conferences; Member of Advisory Committee for six International Conferences in the Few Body and Polarization fields. *Hobbies:* Tennis; Writing. *Address:* 1443 Wellington Crescent, Winnipeg, Manitoba, R3N 0B2.

McKELL, William John, b. 26 Sept. 1891, Pambula, New South Wales, Australia. Boilermaker; Barrister-at-Law. m. Minnie May Pye, 7 Jan. 1920, 1 son, 2 daughters. *Appointments:* Boilermaker; Member of Legislative Assembly; Minister of the Crown; Premier of New South Wales; Governor-General; Barrister-at-Law. *Honours:* GCMG; QC; PC; Hon. LL.D. Sydney; Grand Cordon of Order of Cedars, Lebanon. *Address:* 42/14 Leura Road, Double Bay, New South Wales 2028, Australia.

MacKELLAR, Alasdair, b. 28 July 1921, Edinburgh, Scotland. Paediatric Surgeon. m. J Evelyn Anderson, 30 Nov. 1946, 2 sons, 3 daughters. *Education:* MB ChB, 1944, FRCS, 1948, FRACS, 1957, University of Edinburgh. *Appointments:* Senior Paediatric Surgeon, Princess Margaret Hospital for Children, Perth, Western Australia. *Memberships:* Chairman, Paediatric Section, RACS, 1978; Court Examiners, RACS, 1974; President, West Australian Branch, Australian Medical Association, 1980; Editorial Board, Australian & New Zealand Journal Of Surgery. *Publications:* Articles in various Medical Journals. *Hobby:* Golf. *Address:* Unit 1, 10 The Avenue, Nedlands, Western Australia.

MacKELLAR, Michael John Randal, b. 27 Oct. 1938, New South Wales, Australia. Australian Politician. m. Robin Morey Smith, 21 Mar. 1969, 2 sons, 1 daughter. *Education:* BScAgr, Sydney University, 1957-60; MA, Balliol College, Oxford University, 1962-64. *Appointments:* NSW Department of Agriculture, 1961-69; Member for Warringah NSW, House of Reps 1969-; Member, Council of Australian National Universities, 1970-75; Member, House of Reps Select Committee on Foreign Affairs, 1971-72, Joint Parliamentary Committee on Foreign Affairs & Defence, 1972-74, Joint Standing Committee on Public Accounts, 1972-74; Member, first Australian Parliamentary delegation to People's Republic of China, 1973; Parliamentary Secretary to Leader of the Opposition, 1973-74; Shadow Minister for Immigration, 1974-75; Minister for Immigration and Ethnic Affairs, 1975-79; Minister Assisting the Treasury, 1978-79; Minister for Health, 1979-; Minister for Home Affairs & Environment, 1981; Minister Assisting the Prime Minister, 1979-80; Leader of delegation to UN Habitat Conference, 1976; Member, NSW Advisory Committee for Australian Broadcasting Comm, 1973-75; Member, Council, Royal Blind Society, NSW, 1970-. *Memberships:* Australian Institute of Agricultural Science; Australian Club, Sydney. *Hobbies:* Tennis; Cricket; Golf; Reading; Photography. *Address:* 1 Lewis Street, Balgowlah, New South Wales 2093, Australia.

McKELLAR, Neil Black, b. 25 June 1942, Campbelltown, Scotland. Economist. *Education:* BA (Hons), Strathclyde University, 1966; BSc (Econ) Hons, London University, 1967. *Appointments:* Economist/Statistician, 1967-72, Head of Fishery Economics Research Unit, White Fish Authority; Chief Economist, White Fish Authority, Edinburgh, Scotland, 1973-. *Memberships:* Royal Economic Society; Commonwealth Society; Secretary, Fisheries Economics Newsletter. *Publications:* Contributed to The Effective Management of Resources—The International Politics of the North Sea, 1979. *Hobbies:* Squash; Travel. *Address:* 87 Warrender Park Road, Edinburgh, Scotland.

MACKENZIE, Peter Boyd, b. 31 July 1930, Sydney, New South Wales. Consultant. m. Elizabeth Armstrong, 12 Aug. 1965, 3 daughters. *Education:* Royal Military College, Duntroon, ACT, 1951; Australian Staff College, Victoria, 1959; BEc, Queensland University, Brisbane, 1963. *Appointments:* Lieutenant to Major, Australian Staff Corps, 1951-65, including active service Korea, 1952-53, Malaysian Emergency, 1956-58; Diplomatic Service (Trade Commissioner), Middle East, Far East, Mediterranean, Europe, 1965-75; General Manager, Bradken Consol Limited, 1975-78; Peter Mackenzie Associates, Export Marketing Consultants, 1978-. *Memberships:* United Service Club, Brisbane; Brisbane Club Royal Selangor Club, Kuala Lumpur; Australian Institute of Export; Queensland Confederation of Industry; Metal Trades Insustry Association; Brisbane Chamber of Commerce. *Hobbies:* Gardening; Politics; Foreign Affairs; Golf. *Address:* Kintail, 101 Layfield Road, Mogill 4070, Queensland, Australia.

McKENZIE, Precious Patrick, b. 6 June 1936, Durban, South Africa. Physical Instructor. m. 17 Dec. 1960, 1 son, 2 daughters. *Education:* Only 1st Year College. *Appointments:* Shoe Trade, 1956-75; Physical Instructor, 1975-81. *Honours:* Commonwealth Gold Medals, Weightlifting (Bantamweight), Jamaica, 1966, Edinburgh, 1970, Christchurch, 1974, Edmonton, 1978; World Powerlifting Champion, 1971, 72, 73, 79 and 80; Hall of Fame; MBE. *Hobbies:* Music; Singing; Sterio; Gymnastics; Swimming. *Address:* 35 Reelick Avenue, Pakuranga, Auckland, New Zealand.

MACKENZIE, Roderick Alexander (Hon), b. 17 Oct. 1933, Melbourne, Australia. Member Parliament, Legislative Council, Victoria, Australia. m. Betty Jackson, 8 June 1957, 1 son, 2 daughters. *Education:* Gordon Institute of Technology, Australia. *Appointments:* Plumber; Plumbing Inspector, Designer; Antarctic Expedition member; Technical Officer, Comm. Government; Plumbing Consultant; Member of Parliament. *Memberships:* Royal Australasian Ornithologist Union; Australian Conservation Foundation; Australian National Trust; Geelong Environment Council; Geelong Field Naturalists. *Hobbies:* Ornithology; Cricket; Squash; Golf; Gardening; Reading; Bushwalking. *Address:* 'Melness', Bannockburn, Victoria, Australia 3331.

McKERRACHER, Daniel Wallace, b. 2 Jan. 1935, Renfrew, Scotland. University Teacher. m. Agnes Finlay Hamilton Thornbury, 4 Aug. 1959, 3 sons, 1 daughter. *Education:* MA, 1957, MEd, 1961, Glasgow; Teacher's Certificate, Scotland, 1958; PhD, Sheffield, 1968. *Appointments:* Teacher-Librarian, Knightswood Comprehensive, Glasgow; Research Psychologist, Rampton Hospital, England; Associate Professor, Department Educ. Psychol., Calgary University, Canada; Professor, Department Education, University of Otago, Dunedin, New Zealand. *Memberships:* Assoc. Brit. Psy. Society; Alberta Psych. Assoc., Chairman, Professional Affairs; New Zealand Psych. Assoc.; American Education Research Association; New Zealand Royal Society; Otago Institute for Educ. Research, Past President. *Publications:* Approximately 40 scientific articles in international Journals; Two chapters in published texts. *Honours:* Glasgow University, Bursary Competition History Scholarship, 1953; McLaglan Scholarship, 1953. *Hobbies:* Camping; Gardening; Reading; Writing; Poetry. *Address:* Lauriston, 38 Riccarton Road, East Taieri, Mosgiel, New Zealand.

MACKERRAS, (Alan) Charles (MacLaurin) Sir, b. 17 Nov. 1925, Schenectady, USA. Musician. m. Helena Judith Wilkins, 1947, 2 daughters. *Appointments:* Principal Oboist, Sydney Symphony Orchestra, Australia, 1943-46; Staff Conductor, Sadler's Wells Opera, 1949-53; Principal Conductor, BBC Concert Orchestra, UK, 1954-56; freelance conductor with most British orchestras, 1957-66; Conductor, Hamburg State Opera, 1966-69; Musical Director, Sadler's Wells Opera, later ENO, 1970-79; Chief Guest Conductor, BBC SO, 1976-79; Chief Conductor Sydney Symphony Orchestra, 1982; frequent tours of opera and concerts in Scandinavia, Germany, Italy, Czechoslovakia, Hungary, Rumania, USSR, Belgium, Holland, Australia, S Africa, Canada, USA and Australia, and throughout Europe; frequent broadcasts BBC; TV programmes of opera and ballet; commercial recordings; appearances at many international festivals and opera houses. *Publications:* Ballet arrangements of Pineapple Polland of Lady and the Fool; articles in Opera Magazine, Music and Musicians and other musical journals. *Honours:* Evening

Standard Award for Opera, 1977; Janácek Medal, 1978; Gramophone record of the year award, 1978 and 1980. *Hobbies:* Languages; Yachting. *Address:* 10 Hamilton Terrace, London, NW8, England.

MACKERRAS, Neil Richard MacLaurin, b. 20 May 1930, Sydney, Australia. Solicitor. m. Elizabeth Margaret Moultrie Connolly (decd.) 4 sons, 5 daughters. *Education:* BA, 1951, LLb, 1956, Sydney. *Appointments:* Barrister, 1957-73; Solicitor, Aboriginal Legal Service, Moree, New South Wales, 1973-75; Barrister, 1975-76; Solicitor, Armidale, New South Wales, 1976-78, 1979-. *Publications:* Landlord and Tenant Practice and Procedure in New South Wales, (5th 6th and 7th editions co-author). *Hobbies:* Music; Bushwalking; Genealogy. *Address:* RMB545C, Kelly's Plains Road, Armidale, New South Wales, Australia.

MACKEY, John, b. 11 Jan. 1918, Bray, Co. Wicklow, Eire. Priest. *Education:* MA., University of New Zealand, 1951; PhD., University of Notre Dame, Indiana, USA, 1963. *Appointments:* Priest, 1941-75; Bishop of Auckland, New Zealand, 1975-. *Address:* Bishop's House, New Street, Ponsonby Island, New Zealand.

MACKIE, Douglas Robert, b. 11 Oct. 1928, Peak Hill, New South Wales, Australia. Company Director; Commercial Property Investor. m. Jill Moreen McEvoy, 27 Apr. 1951, 3 sons. *Education:* Associate, Bankers Institute of Australia. *Appointments:* Director: Canberra Commercial Property Trust, Australia; Commercial Property Management Limited, Australia; Canberra Permanent Building Society Limited, Australia; Federal President, Building Owners and Managers Association of Australia Limited. *Hobbies:* Golf; Skiing; Fishing. *Address:* 41 National Circuit, Forrest, A C T., Australia.

MacKINLAY, Bruce, b. 4 Oct. 1912, Perth, Western Australia. Company Director. m. Erica Ruth Fleming, 9 Oct. 1943, 2 sons. *Appointments:* War Service, 1940-45; Director, J Gadsden Australia Limited, 1954-77; Director, Whittakers Limited, 1975-; Chairman, Local Bd, Chamber of Manufactures Insurance Limited, 1977-. *Memberships:* President, Western Australia, Chamber of Manufactures, 1958-61; Vice-President, Associated Chambers of Manufactures of Australia, 1960; Commonwealth Manufg. Industries Adv. Council, 1962-70; Leader: Aust. Trade Mission, E Africa, 1968; WA Trade Mission, Italy, 1970; Employers' Rep., International Labour Conference, 1977; Councillor, 1967-, Chairman, 1981-, Keep Australia Beautiful WA; Chairman, WA Inst. of Dirs, 1975-77; WA Finance Committee for the Duke of Edinburgh's Third Commonwealth Study Conf., 1967-68; University of Western Australia, Member Senate, 1970-; Chairman, Master of Business Admin Appeal, 1973; Councillor, Organising Council of Commonwealth and Empire Games, 1962; Councillor, Australian Council on Population and Ethnic Affairs, 1981-. *Honours:* CBE, 1970; Kt, 1978. *Hobbies:* Swimming; Gardening. *Address:* 9B Melville Street, Claremont, WA6010, Australia.

MacKINNA, John Gilbert, b. 11 Dec. 1906, Goodwood, South Australia. Mining Engineer. m. Elizabeth Mary Beach, 18 Dec. 1937, 2 daughters. *Education:* University of Adelaide. *Appointments:* Assistant Manager, Stonyfell Quarries, 1936-39; Army Service with Australian Imperial Forces, 1939-45; Assistant Manager, 1946-49, Manager, 1949-56, Quarry Industries Limited; Deputy Commissioner of Police, 1956-57; Commissioner of Police for South Australia, 1957-72. *Memberships:* Fellow, Australian Institute of Management; Australian Institute of Mining and Metallurgy; Vice President, The St. John Council for South Australia. *Honours:* DSO, 1944; ED, 1947; MVO, 1963; CBE, 1967; K.St.J, 1971; CMG, 1978. *Address:* 12 McKenna Street, Kensington Park, South Australia.

McKINNA, John Gilbert, b. 11 Dec. 1906, Goodwood, South Australia. Engineer. m. Elizabeth Mary Beach, 18 Dec. 1937, 2 daughters. *Education:* Prince Alfred College and Adelaide University, Australia. *Appointments:* Assistant Manager, Stonyfell Quarries, South Australia, 1934-39; War Service, 2nd A I F., 1939-45; Assistant Manager, 1946-49, Manager, 1949-56, Quarry Industries Limited, South Australia; Deputy Commissioner, 1956-57, Commissioner, 1957-72, Police, South Australia. *Honours:* CMG., 1978; CBE., 1967; DSO., 1944; MVO., 1963; ED., 1947; K.St.J., 1972;

FAIM., 1953; AIMM., 1955. *Address:* 12 McKenna Street, Kensington Park 5068, South Australia.

McKINNON, Colin Donald Angus, b. 13 Nov. 1944, Montreal, Quebec, Canada. Barrister; Solicitor. m. Marie-Paule Nicole Lemieux, 14 June 1969, 1 son, 2 daughters. *Education:* BA., St. Patrick's College, Ottawa, Ontario, Canada, 1965; LL.B., University of Ottawa Law School, Canada, 1968; Bar Admission Course, Osgoode Hall, Toronto, Canada, Called to Bar of Ontario, Canada, 1970. *Appointments:* Assistant Crown Attorney, 1970-72, Special Agent for Criminal Prosecutions, 1973-81, for Ottawa-Carleton, Canada; Partner, Beament, Green, York, formerly Green, McKinnon & Hebert, Canada, 1973-; Special Agent for Criminal Prosecutions, Attorney General of Canada, 1972-75; Special Counsel to British Governemnt for Extradition cases, 1973-. *Memberships:* President, 1981-82, Officer and Trustee, 1975-80, County of Carleton Law Association; President, Common Law Students Society, University of Ottawa Law School, 1967-68; President, St. Patrick's College Student Union, 1965; Instructor in Criminal Law, Law Society of Upper Canada, 1977-; Special Lecturer, Family Law and Immigration Law, Law Society of Upper Canada; Occasional Lecturer, Criminal Law and Family law, University of Ottawa Law School; Law Society of Upper Canada; Canadian Bar Association; Advocates Society; Former Director, Housing and Urban Development Association of Canada, 1976-79. *Honours:* Gavel Award, University of Ottawa Law School; Student Merit Award, University of Ottawa. *Hobbies:* Squash; Running; Music; Theatre; Gardening. Reading. *Address:* 2224 Bowman Road, Ottawa K1H 6V5, Canada.

McKINNON, Donald Charles, b. 27 Feb. 1939, Blackheath, England. Member of Parliament. m. Patricia Moore, 28 Mar. 1964, 3 sons, 1 daughter. *Education:* Lincoln College, 1960-61; Manakau Technical Institute, 1976-77. *Appointments:* Farming in USA, Wairarapa, Canterbury, Rangitikei, Auckland; Real Estate, 1972-78; Agent and Farm Consultant; Elected Member of Parliament for Albany, 1978-; Elected Junior Government Whip, 1980. *Memberships:* New Zealand National Party, Various Offices; President, Auckland Debating Association; Prisoners Aid and Rehabilitation. *Hobbies:* Tennis; Squash; Jogging. *Address:* Vaughans Road, RD2, Albany, New Zealand.

MacKINNON, Graham Charles (Hon), b. 1916, Australia. Member of Parliament. m. Mary Theresa Shaw, 1940, 2 sons. *Appointments:* Minister for Health, Fisheries and Fauna, 1965-71; Environmental Protection, 1970-71; Minister for Education, Cultural Affairs and Recreation, 1974-77; Leader of the Government in Legislative Council Western Australia, 1977-78, 1978-80; Minister for Fisheries & Wildlife, Tourism, Conservation and Environment, 1977-78; Minister for Works, Water Supplies, Tourism, 1978-80. *Memberships:* Chairman, 150th Anniversary Celebrations Committee, 1977-80; State President and member of Australian Cl. of Scouts Association, 1974-77. *Address:* 57 Stockley Road, Bunbury, Western Australia 6230.

McKINNON, Walter Sneddon, b. 8 July 1910, Invercargil, New Zealand. Army. m. Anna Bloomfield Plimmer, 6 Oct. 1937, 4 sons, 1 daughter. *Education:* BSc., Otago University, Dunedin, New Zealand, 1932; Long Gunnery Staff Course and Rdar Course, UK, 1938-40; Staff College, Camberley England, 1944; Joint Staff College, UK, 1948. *Appointments:* Communications Engineer, New Zealand Post Office; Lieutenant, Regular Army, 1935; War Service, highest wartime rank Lieutenant Colonel, UK., Pacific, Italy, Army of Occupation, Japan; Colonel, 1951, Brigadier, 1953, Commander South Military District, 1953-54; Head, New Zealand Joint Staff Mission, Washington DC., USA, 1954-57; Commander, Northern Military District, 1947-58; Adjutant General, 1958-63; Quartermaster General, 1963-65; Major General, C G S., 1965-67; Chairman, New Zealand Broadcasting Corporation, 1969-74; Councillor, Taupo Borough Council, 1977-80; Councillor, Tongairo United Council, 1979-80. *Memberships:* Vice President, 1978-, President, 1974-78, Taupo Regional Musuem Art Centre; President, 1970-74, Presbyterian/Mwthodist Halls of Residence Trust, Victoria University, Wellington, New Zealand. *Honours:* Mentioned in Despatches, 1943; OBE., 1947; CBE., 1961; CB., 1966. *Hobbies:* Golf; Angling; Gardening. *Address:* 43 Birch Street, Taupo, New Zealand.

McLACHLAN, Hugh Kenneth Ian, b. 18 Feb. 1924, Auburn, Melbourne, Victoria, Australia. Medical Pathologist. m. Elizabeth Grace Worland, 18 Dec. 1951, 1 son, 1 daughter. *Education:* MB,BS, University of Melbourne, 1951; FRCPA, 1975. *Appointments:* Laboratory Assistant, Department of Physiology, University of Melbourne, 1940-42, Australian Military Force, 115th Australian General Hospital, 1942-44; Resident Medical Officer, Albury District Hospital, NSW, 1951-52, Canberra Community Hospital, ACT, 1952-53, Repatriation General Hospital, Victoria, 1953-55; Clinical Assistant to Outpatient Physician, Royal Melbourne Hospital, 1953-56; General Practice, Frankston, Victoria, 1956-58; Assistant Clinical Pathologist, Haematology Department, Royal Melbourne Hospital, 1958-60; Demonstrator, Department of Pathology, University of Melbourne, 1958-70; Pathologist, Brighton Pathology, 1958-79; Consultant Pathologist, Brighton Community Hospitzl, 1962-78; Pathologist, Sandringham and District Memorial Hospital, 1964-78, Bethlehem Public Hospital, 1965-78; Regional Pathologist, Central Grippsland Hospital, Traralgon, 1979-; Regional Officer, Red Cross Blood Transfusion Service, 1979-. *Memberships:* British and Australian Medical Associations; Foundation Honorary Treasurer, Australian Society of Geographical Pathology, 1966-70; Australian Division, International Academy of Pathology, 1974-; Victorian Branch, Australian Society of Cytology; Society of Pathologists in Private Practice, 1972-78; Breast Group, Clinical Oncology Society of Australia, 1976-; British Association of Surgical Oncology, 1976-; Affiliate of Royal Society of Medicine, 1976-; Australian Dermatopathology Society, 1979-; Victorian Division, Blood Transfusion Service Committee, Australian Red Cross Society, 1981-. *Hobbies:* Breeder of Stud Cattle; Gardening; Fishing. *Address:* Lochaber-Braes, Murray Grey Stud, RSD, 39, Hamilton's Road, Lardner, 3820, Victoria, Australia.

McLARDIE, Archibald James Arthur, b. 19 Mar. 1928, Ilford, Essex, England. Regional Manager. m. Marjorie Elizabeth Sparrow, 21 Mar. 1952, 1 son, 2 daughters. *Education:* The Kings School; Sydney Technical College. *Appointments:* Vacuum Oil Co., 1946-52; Cox Bros., Retailers, 1952-54; McLardie's Men and Ladies Wear, 1954-60; Lions Clubs International, 1960-. *Memberships:* Odyssey (Anti Drug and Rehabilitation); Director of Board, James McGrath Foundation. *Publications:* Established First Lions Clubs in much of Australia, Indonesia and Papua New Guinea. *Honours:* Order of Australia Medal, 1980; Ambassador of Goodwill, Highest Award of Lions Clubs International. *Hobbies:* Charity Work; Painting watercolours. *Address:* Warumbal, 68 Wrights Road, Drummoyne Bay, Sydney, 2047.

McLAREN, Richard Henry, b. 7 Aug. 1945, Toronto, Canada. Barrister; Solicitor; Law Professor. m. Martha Elizabeth Murray, 3 May 1980, 1 son. *Education:* HBA., School of Business Administration, 1968, LL.B., Faculty of Law, 1971, University of Western Ontario, Canada; LL.M., London School of Economics, University of London, UK, 1972; Called to Bar, Law Society of Upper Canada, 1974. *Appointments:* Law Professor, 1973-, Associate Dean, 1979-, Faculty of Law, University of Western Ontario, Canada. *Memberships:* Law Society of Upper Canada; National Academy of Arbitrators, USA; Arbitrator's Institute of Canada Inc.; Fellow, Chartered Institute of Arbitrators, UK. *Publications:* Personal Property Security Law (with Catzman), 1976; Falconbridge on Mortgages, 1977; Policy and Legislative Responses to Electronic Fund Transfers, 1978; Secured Transactions in Personal Property in Canada, 1979; Commercial Arbitration (with Palmer), 1982. *Honours:* Holder of MacKenzie King Scholarship, 1971-72. *Hobbies:* Sailing; Skiing; Squash; Collector of rare Canadian stamps; Collector of Scriptophilia. *Address:* 287 St. James Street, London, Ontario, N6A 1X4, Canada.

McLAUGHLIN, Sybil Ione, (Mrs V.D. McLaughlin), b. 24 Aug. 1928, Mobile, Ala, USA. Clerk of the Legislative Assembly, Cayman Islands (Parliament). m. Vivian Delworth McLaughlin, 25 Mar. 1949, 2 sons. *Education:* Jamaica Commercial Institute, La Salle Extension University, Chicago; Commonwealth Clerks' Certificate, attachment Houses of Commons, London, 1966, Parliament Grenada, W.I., 1971, Parliament, Trinidad & Tobago, 1971. Dale Carnegie Course in Human Relations & Effective Speaking, 1975; Public Adminis-

tration Workshop (UN) in organising of Government, Development Administration, etc., of Regulatory Administration, 1978. *Appointments:* Clerk-Typist, Cayman Islands Government, 1945-58; Secretary to Commissioner (now Governor), 1958-59; Clerk of the Legislative Assembly 1959-; Secretary, Cayman Islands Branch Commonwealth Parliamentary Association, 1964-. *Memberships:* Secretary, Cayman Islands Christian Endeavour Union; Past President, Cayman Islands Business & Professional Women's Club for two years, Immediate Past President. *Publications:* Brief Constitutional history of the Cayman Islands, 1971; The role of the Legislative Assembly, Cayman Islands, 1977. *Honours:* MBE, 1967; Highest Award for Achievement, Dale Carnegie Course, 1975; *Hobbies:* Reading (Historical novels); Classical music; Lawn Tennis; Dancing; Social work. *Address:* p o Box 549, Grand Cayman, Cayman Islands, West Indies.

MACLEAN, (Sir Fitzroy Maclean of Dunconnel), b. 11 Mar. 1911, Cairo. Writer. m. Veronica Nell Fraser, 12 Jan. 1946, 2 sons. *Education:* Eton; MA(1st class Hons.) Kings College, Cambridge 1932. *Appointments:* Diplomatic Service 1933; Third Secretary, British Embassy, Paris, 1934-37; Second Secretary, Moscow 1937-39; Cameron Highlanders: 2nd Lt. 1941; SAS Retiment 1942; Captain 1942; Lt. Col 1943; Brig. 1943; Local Maj-Gen 1947; Commander, British Military Mission to Yugoslav Partisans 1943-45; Head, Special Refugee Commission, Germany, Austria, Italy, 1947; Member of Parliament, Lancaster Division 1941-59; Bute and North Ayrshire 1959-74; Parliamentary Under-Secretary of State and Financial Secretary, War Office, 1954-57; Member United Kingdom delegation, North Atlantic Assembly 1962-71; Council of Europe 1972-74. *Memberships:* Great Britain and USSR Association; British Yugoslav Society. *Publications:* Eastern Approaches 1949; Disputed Barricade 1957; A Person from England 1958; Back to Bokham 1959; Jugoslavia 1969; A Concise History of Scotland 1970; The Battle of the Neretva 1970; To the Back of Beyond 1974; To Caucasus 1976; Take Nine Spies 1978; Holy Russia 1979; Tito 1980. *Honours:* CBE(Military) 1944; Crois de Guerre, France; Order of Kutuzov, USSR; Partisan Star 1st Class, Yugoslavia; Order of Merit, Yugoslavia; Order of the Flag 1st Class, Yugoslavia; Hon. LLD Glasgow University 1969; Hon. LLD Dalhousie University; Hon. DLitt. Acadia University. *Address:* Strachur House, Strachur, Argyll, Scotland, PA 27 8BX.

MACLEHOSE, (Crawford) Murray, b. 16 Oct. 1917. Governor & Commander-in-Chief, HM Diplomatic Service, Hong Kong. m. Margaret Noel Dunlops, 1947, 2 daughters. *Education:* Balliol College, Oxford, England. *Appointments:* War Service, Lieutenant, RNVR, 1939-45; Joined Foreign Service, 1947; Acting Consul, 1947, Acting Consul-General Hankow, 1948; First Secretary (Commercial), and Consul, Prague, 1951, Seconded to Commonwealth Relations Officer, Wellington, 1954, transferred to Paris, 1956; Counsellor, 1959; Seconded to Colonial Officer and transferred to Hong Kong as PA, Counsellor Foreign Office, 1963; Principal Private Secretary to Secretary of State, 1965-67; Ambassador to Vietnam, 1967-69, to Denmark, 1969-71; Governor of Hong Kong 1971-. *Memberships:* Anthenaeum, Travellers. *Honours:* GBE, 1976 (MBE 1946), KCMG, 1971 (CMG 1964), KCVO, 1975, K.St.John, 1972. *Hobbies:* Sailing; Fishing. *Address:* Beoch, Maybole, Ayrshire, United Kingdom.

McLENNAN, Ian Munro (Sir), b. 30 Nov. 1909, Stawell, Victoria, Australia. Engineer. Company Director. m. Dora Haase Robertson, 3 Aug. 1937, 2 sons, 2 daughters. *Education:* BEE, Melbourne University, 1931. *Appointments:* Cadet Engineer, 1933, Assistant General Manager, 1947, General Manager, 1950, Chief General Manager, 1959, Managing Director, 1967, Chairman, 1971, Retired, 1977, The Broken Hill Proprietary Co. Ltd.; Chairman, Australian Mineral Development Laboratories, 1959-67; Chairman, Tubemakers of Australia Ltd., 1973-79; Director, ICI Australia Ltd., 1976-79; Chairman: Australia and New Zealand Banking Group Ltd., 1977-, Defence (Industrial) Committee of The Australian Government, (retired 1977), Board of Governors, Ian Clunies Ross Memorial Foundation; Executive Committee, and President, 1977-, Australia-Japan Business Co-Operation Committee; Chairman, Interscan Australia Pty., Ltd., 1978-. *Memberships:* President, 1951, 1957, 1972, Australasian Institute of Mining & Metallurgy; Fellow:

Institution of Engineers, Australia, Australian Institute of Management, International Academy of Management, 1978-, Australian Academy of Science, 1980-; Former Australian President, Institution of Production Engineers; President, Australian Academy of Technological Sciences, 1976-; Australian Institute of Metals; Institute of Directors; American Instutute of Mining, Metallurgical and Petroleum Engineers, 1972; The Metals Society (Gt Britain); Foreign Associate, National Academy of Engineering)USA), 1978; Director, Australia-Japan Academic and Cultural Centre, 1978-; Advisory Council of Commonwealth Scientific & Industrial Research, 1979-; Australian Advisory Council, General Motors Corporation. *Honours:* KBE, 1963; KCMG, 1979; Honorary Doctorate of Engineering, University of Melbourne, 1968; Honorary Doctorate of Engineering, University of Newcastle, 1968; Honorary Doctorate of Science, University of Wollongong, 1978; Bronze Medal, Australasian Institute of Mining & Metallurgy, 1959; James N Kirby Medal, Institution of Production Engineers, 1964; Peter Nicol Russell Memorial Medal, Institution of Engineers, Australia, 1968; Kernot Medal, Melbourne University, 1970; Charles F Rand Memorial Gold Medal Award, 1978, Distinguished Member Award, 1979, American Institute of Mining Metallurgical and Petroleum Engineers. *Hobbies:* Farming; Gardening. *Address:* Apartment 3, 112 Walsh Street, South Yarra, 3141, Australia.

McLEOD, Norman William, b. 26 Nov. 1904, Elora, Ontario, Canada. Professional Engineer. m. Irene Marguerite Briggs, 10 Feb. 1931, 2 sons, 3 daughters. *Education:* BSc, Chemical Engineering, University of Alberta, 1930; MSc, University of Saskatchewan, 1936; ScD, Civil Engineering, University of Michigan, 1938. *Appointments:* Saskatchewan Department of Highways and Transportation in charge of asphalt pavement construction and maintenance, 1930-38; Asphalt Consultant, Imperial Oil Limited, 1938-69; Consultant to Transport Canada (Air) on pavements for airports, 1945-; Vice-President and Asphalt Consultant, McAsphalt. Engineering Services, 1970-; Adjunct Professor of Civil Engineering, University of Waterloo, 1970-. *Memberships:* Ontario Association of Professional Engineers, Past Chairman of the Technical Council, Roads and Transportation Association of Canada; Canadian Technical Asphalt Association; Royal Society of Canada; American Society for Testing and Materials; Past President, Association of Asphalt Paving Technologists; Highway Transportation Board; Sigma Xi; American Association for the Advancement of Science. *Publications:* Author of more than 100 technical papers and discussions on soil mechanics, asphalt pavement structural design, and design and construction of asphalt surfaces. *Honours:* USA Highway Research Board Award, 1946; ASTM Charles B Dudley Medal, 1952; Association of Asphalt Paving Technologists, Annual Award, 1952; Distinguished Alumnus, University of Michigan, 1953; Stevenson Travel Award, 1967; Canadian Centennial Medal, 1967; Asphalt Institute Roll of Honour, 1971; New Zealand, Canadian Geotechnical Society, R.F. Legget Award, 1972; Fellow, The Royal Society of Canada, Academy of Science, 1977; Prevost Hubbard Award, 1978; APEO, The Engineering Medal, 1979; ASTM Award of Merit and Fellow, 1980, University of Waterloo, Honorary Doctorate of Engineering, 1980; Recognition of Achievement Award, Asphalt Emulsion Manufacturers Association, 1981. *Hobby:* My work. *Address:* 41 Glenrose Avenue, Toronto, Ontario, Canada, M4T 1K3.

MACLURE, Kenneth Cecil, b. 14 Oct. 1914, Montreal, Quebec, Canada. Defence Research Scientist (Retired). m. Alice Margaret Blackmore, 28 May 1949, 2 sons, 2 daughters. *Education:* BSc, First Class Hon. Maths and Physics, McGill 1934; Associate Actuarial Society, New York, 1939; MSc Physics, 1950; PhD (Nuclear Physics), 1952; Banff School of Advanced Management, Alberta 1954. *Appointments:* Sun Life Assurance Company, Actuarial and Mathematics Departments, Montreal, Canada, 1934-39; Royal Canadian Air Force, 1939-67; Group Captain, 1954, Director, Armament Engineering, 1954-58; Air Attache Warsaw, Poland, 1958-61; seconded Defence Research Board, 1961-67; Defence Research Scientist, 1967-79, Chief Defence Research Staff, London, 1971-75. *Memberships:* Fellow, Royal Institute of Navigation, Canadian Aeronautics and Space Institute; Arctic Institute of North America; Institute of Navigation, USA;

Arctic Circle, Ottawa; Canadian Association of Physicists; Society of Sigma Xi. *Publications:* Various classified papers on Air Navigation subjects and magnetic anomaly detection during service and DRB careers; Proposed, to RAF, Greenwich Grid System of Polar Air Navigation, 1941. *Honours:* E.W. Beatty Scholarship in Mathematics, McGill University 1930-34; 2nd and 3rd Year Scholar in Mathematics and Physics, McGill, 1931-32 and 1932-34; Anne Molson Gold Medal in Mathematics and Natural Philosophy, 1934; First, Thurlow Navigation Award, Institute of Navigation, US, 1945; Air Force Cross, Canada, 1945. *Hobbies:* Photography; Repair Household Appliances; Gardening; Running; Swimming; Canoeing; Sailing; Skiing; Skating. *Address:* 16 Birch Avenue, Ottawa, Ontario, Canada K1K 3G6.

McMAHON, Christopher William, b. 10 July 1927, Melbourne, Australia. Deputy Governor. m. Marion Elizabeth Kelso, 1956, 2 sons. *Education:* University of Melbourne; PPE, Magdalen College, Oxford, 1953. *Appointments:* Tutor in English Literature, University of Melbourne, 1950; Economic Assistant, HM Treasury, 1953-57; Economic Adviser, British Embassy, Washington, 1957-60; Fellow & Tutor in Economics, Senior Tutor, 1961-63, Magdalen College, Oxford, 1960-64; Tutor in Economics, Treasury Centre for Administration Studies, 1963-64; Plowden Committee on Aircraft Industry, 1964-65; Adviser, 1964, Adviser to Governors, 1966-70, Executive Director, 1970-80, Deputy Governor, 1980-, Bank of England. *Memberships:* Chairman, Working Party 3, OECD, 1980-; Steering Committee, Group of Thirty, 1978-. *Publications:* Sterling in the Sixties, 1964; Techniques of Economic Forecasting, 1965. *Address:* Bank of England, Threadneedle Street, London, EC2R 8AH, England.

McMILLAN, John William, b. 25 Apr. 1934, Swan Hill, Victoria, Australia. Tertiary Educational Administration. m. Colleen Mary King, 5 Jan. 1957, 2 daughters. *Education:* BSc Dip.Ed, 1952-55, BEd, Melbourne University, 1962; MEng.Sc, University of New South Wales, 1965; MA, Macquarie University, 1972. *Appointments:* Secondary Teacher, Victorian Education Department, 1956-60; Head, Mathematics and Physics Department, Bendigo Institute of Technology, 1960-63; Lecturer/Senior Lecturer, The New South Wales Institute of Technology, 1963-65; Registrar, 1967-. *Memberships:* The Australian Institute of Tertiary Educational Administrators; The Conference of Directors of Central Institutes of Technology. *Hobbies:* Cricket; Tennis; Golf. *Address:* 8 Carissa Avenue, St Ives, New South Wales 2075, Australia.

McMILLAN, (Rt. Revd.) Keith Alfonso, b. 21 Mar. 1931, Kingston, Jamaica, West Indies. Bishop (Anglican). m. Cynthia Veronica Burgess, 20 Feb. 1960, 1 son, 3 daughters. *Education:* St Peter's Theological College, Jamaica, West Indies, 1954-57. *Appointments:* Civil Servant, Jamaica, 1948-54; Ordained Deacon, 1957; Ordained Priest, 1958; Consecrated Bishop, 1980; Secretary: Anglican Council of North America and The Caribbean, 1975-80, Vice-Chairman, 1980-, Chairman, 1981. *Memberships:* Royal Commonwealth Society; National Geographic Society. *Hobbies:* Reading; Sports. *Address:* Bishopthorpe, Southern Foreshore, PO Box 535, Belize City, Belize, Central America.

MACMILLAN, Richard Francis, b. 14 Oct. 1936 Reading, Berkshire, UK. Company Director. m. Frances Burke, 7 Feb. 1962, 4 sons. *Education:* Ampleforth, 1945-54; Theological Studies, 1954-58; Institut Francais De Gestion, 1977-78. *Appointments:* Regular Army Officer, Worldwide Hovercraft Development and Evaluation, 1959-71; General Manager, Exquisite Fabrics, Jersey Channel Islands, 1972-75; Directeur, Tricot Frances A. Colmar. Haut Rhin, 1975-77; Managing Director, International Paints, West Africa Limited, 1978-. *Memberships:* Lagos Yacht Club; Ikeja Saddle Club. *Hobbies:* Sailing; Shooting; Music; Clothes. *Address:* 5 Remi Fani Kayode, GRA Ikeja, Nigeria.

McMILLAN, Robert Peter, b. 10 Aug 1921, Northam, Western Australia. Lecturer, Environmental Science. m. Millicent Pole Phillips, 5 Feb. 1948, 4 sons, 1 daughter. *Education:* Hale School, Western Australia, 1935-37; BSc, University of Western Australia, 1956. *Appointments:* RAAF, Mid East and Italy, 1940-46; Farming, 1946-52; Senior Biology Master and Housemaster, Guildford Grammar School W.A., 1959-73; Science Lecturer, Claremont College of Advanced Education W.A., 1974-; Associate in Education Simon Fraser University, British Columbia, 1971. *Memberships:* Hon. Associate, Entomology, West Australian Museum; Chairman, Landscape and Conservation Committee, National Trust of Australia, W.A.; Executive Committee and Council, National Trust of Australia; Advisory Panel for the Environment, Australian Heritage Commission. *Honours:* Distinguished Flying Cross, Italy, 1945; Order of Australia A.M., 1980; Australian Industries Development Association Medal for Science Teaching, 1966. *Hobbies:* Entomology; Marine Biology; Environmental; Macro and Micro Photography. *Address:* 82 Railway Street, Cottesloe, Western Australia 6011.

McMYN, John Kerr, b. 31 Oct. 1916 Accrington, Lancashire, England. Radiologist. m. 19 Feb. 1949, 1 son, 1 daughter. *Education:* Manchester Grammar School, 1929-35; BSc, 1938, MB, ChB 1942, MRCS, LRCP, Manchester University 1942; Dip. Medical Radiodiagnosis, 1950. *Appointments:* House Surgeon, Clatterbridge County General Hospital, Cheshire, 1943; Registrar, Thoracic Surgical Unit, Manchester, 1944-47; Royal Army Medical Corps, 1947-49; Radiology Registrar, Oldham Royal Infirmary, 1948-52; Radiologist, Wellington Hospital, New Zealand, 1952-55; Radiologist in Charge, Green Lane Hospital, Auckland, NZ, 1955-81. *Memberships:* Royal Australasian College of Radiologists. *Publications:* Pulmonary Hypertension, 1960; Report on Overseas Tour, 1966; Pulmonary Stenosis 1967; Tetralogy of Fallot 1969; Planning of an X-Ray Department, 1974; Spontaneous Intramural Oesophageal Perforation, 1977. *Honours:* Dauntesey Scholarship, Manchester University 1938. *Address:* 56 Evelyn Road, Howick, New Zealand.

McNAMARA, Neville Patrick, (Sir), b. 17 Apr. 1923, Toogoolawah, Queensland, Australia. Chief of The Air Staff. m. Dorothy Joan Miller, 27 May 1950, 2 daughters. *Education:* Graduate of: RAAF Staff College, RAF Flying College, Joint Services Staff College, United Kingdom. *Appointments:* Joined RAAF, 1941; Fighter Pilot during World War II No 75 Squadron, No 77 Squadron; Air Traffic Control Duties HQ N E Area, 1948; Flying Instructor Central Flying School, 1951-53; No 77 Squadron Korean War, 1953-54; Command Pilot Training Officer HQ Training Command, 1954; Staff Officer Fighter Operations Department Air, 1955; Commanding Officer No 25 Squadron, 1957; Commanding Officer No 2 Operational Conversion Unit, 1959; Commanding Officer and Senior Air Staff Officer RAAF Staff London, 1961; Staff Officer Directorate of Personnel, 1963; Director of Personnel, Officers, 1964; Officer Commanding RAAF Contingent and Commanding Officer Base Squadron Ubon Thailand, 1966; Air Staff Officer Headquarters RAAF Richmond, 1967; Director General of Organization Department of Air, 1969; Commander of RAAF Forces, Vietnam, 1971; Air Attache Washington, 1973; Deputy Chief of the Air Staff, 1975; Chief of the Air Staff, 1979. *Honours:* KBE, 1981; AO, 1976; CBE, 1972; AFC, 1961. *Hobbies:* Golf; Fishing. *Address:* 19 Jukes Street, Hackett, 2602, Australian Capital Territory Australia.

McNEE, John William (Sir), b. 17 Dec. 1887. Consultant Physician. m. Geraldine, 1923. *Education:* MB, Glasgow, Freiburg and Johns Hopkins, USA, Universities, 1909; MD, and Bellahouston Gold Medal, 1914; DSc, 1920. *Appointments:* Served European War, Major, RAMC, 1914-19; Served War of 1939-45, Surgeon Rear-Admiral RN, and Consulting Physician to the Navy in Scotland & Western Approaches, 1939-45; Assistant Professor of Medicine and Lecturer in Pathology, Glasgow University; Assistant Professor of Medicine and Associate Physician, Johns Hopkins University USA; Consulting Physician UCH, London and formerly Holme Lecturer in Clinical Medicne, UCH Medical School; Rockefeller Fellow in Medicine, 1923; Lettsomian Lecturer, Medical Society of London, 1931; Croonian Lecturer, RCP, 1932; Anglo-Batavian Lecturer, all Universities of Holland, 1936; Vicary Lecturer, RCS, 1958; Examiner in Medicine, Universities of Cambridge, St Andrews, Sheffield, Glasgow, Aberdeen, Edinbugh, Leeds, National University of Ireland and Conjoint Board; Inspector for GMC of all Universities in Gt Britain and Ireland and of Final Examinations in Medicine, 1954-56; Visiting Professor, Harvard University, USA, (Brigham Hospital', 1949; Professor of Practice of Medicine, Glasgow University, 1936-52; Professor Emeritus, 1953; Physician to the Queen in Scotland, 1952-54 (and to King George VI, 1937-52); Consulting Physician to Royal Navy, 1935-55; Consulting Physician to University College Hospital, London, and to the Western Infirmary, Glasgow. *Memberships:* President: Royal Medico-Chirurgical Society of Glasgow, 1950-51; Gastro-Enterological Society of Great Britain, 1950-51; Association of Physicians, Great Britain and Ireland, 1951-52; BMA, 1954-55. *Publications:* Diseases of the Liver-Gall-Bladder and Bile-Ducts (third editition, 1929 w. Sir H Rolleston); Textbook of Medical Treatment (w. Dunlop and Davidson), First edition, 1939, sixth edition, 1955; Numerous medical papers, especially on diseases of liver and spleen and various war diseases (Trench Fever, Gas Gangrene, War Nephritis, Immersion Foot (RN)); Rescue Ships (RN), New International Medical Code for Ships. *Honours:* KT, 1951; DSO, 1918; Comm. Military Order Avis; FRCP, (London, Edinburgh and Glasgow); FRS(E). *Hobbies:* Country Sports. *Address:* Barton Edge, Worthy Road, Winchester, SO23 7AG, Hampshire, England.

McNEE, (Sir) David Blackstock, b. 23 Mar. 1925, Glasgow. Commissioner of Police. m. Isabella Clayton Hopkins, 25 Mar. 1952, 1 daughter. *Education:* Woodside Senior Secondary School, Glasgow. *Appointments:* Royal Navy, 1943-46; City of Glasgow Police, 1946; Deputy Chief Constable, Dumbartonshire Constabulary, 1968; Chief Constable, City of Glasgow Police, 1971-75; Chief Constable, Strathclyde Police, 1975-77; Commissioner of Police of the Metropolis, London 1977-. *Honours:* Knighted, 1978; Commander, Order of St John, 1977; Queen's Police Medal, 1975; Companion, British Institute of Management, 1980. *Hobbies:* Fishing; Golf; Music. *Address:* New Scotland Yard, London SW1H OBG, England.

McNEILL, James Charles, b. 29 July 1916, Hamilton, New South Wales, Australia. Chairman of Directors. m. Audrey Evelyn Mathieson, 31 Jan. 1942, 1 son. *Education:* Newcastle High School. *Appointments:* Accountant, 1947-54, Assistant Secretary, 1954-56, Assistant General Manager, Commercial, 1956-59, General Manager, Commercial, 1959-67, Executive General Manager, Finance, 1967-71, Managing Director, 1971-77, Chairman & Director of Administration, 1977-, The Broken Hill Proprietary Company Limited. *Memberships:* Executive Committee, Australian Mining Industry Council; Council & Chairman, Finance Committee, Monash University; Australian Government's Economic Consultative Group. *Honours:* CBE, 1972; Kt., 1978. *Hobbies:* Gardening; Music; Farming. *Address:* 104 Mont Albert Road, Canterbury 3126, Victoria, Australia.

McNICOLL, Alan Wedel Ramsay, b. 3 Apr. 1908, Melbourne, Australia. Naval Officer (Retired). m. (1) Ruth Timmins, 17 May 1937, 2 sons, 1 daughter, (2) Frances Chadwick, 18 May 1957. *Education:* Royal Australian Naval College. *Appointments:* Joined Navy, 1922; War Service in various ships, 1939-45; Chairman, Joint Planning Committee, 1959-60; Commanded Australian Fleet, 1962-63; Chief of Naval Staff, 1965-68; Australian Ambassador to Turkey, 1968-73. *Memberships:* Commonwealth Club (Canberra). *Publications:* Sea Voices (verse), 1932; Odes of Horace, 1979. *Honours:* KBE, 1966; CB, 1964; GM, 1941; Commander Order of Orange, Nassau, 1955. *Hobbies:* Reading; Fly-fishing. *Address:* 6 Hutt Street, Yarralumsa, Act 2600, Australia.

McNULTY, Anthony Bernard, b. 25 May, 1911, Warwick, United Kingdom. Barrister; Retired International Civil Servant. *Education:* Winchester College, 1924-29; Magdalen College, Oxford, 1929-32. *Appointments:* Practising Barrister, 1932-39; Lieutenant-Colonel, Active Service, 1939-, Demobilised, 1947; Manager, Commercial Company, 1950-54; Secretary, European Commission of Human Rights, 1954-76; Director, British Institute of Human Rights, 1977-. *Publications:* Various legal articles. *Honours:* MBE (Military), 1944; CBE, 1976. *Hobby:* Fishing. *Address:* 92 Chesterfield House, Chesterfield Gardens, London, W.1.

MACPHEE, Ian Malcolm, b. 13 July 1938, Sydney, Australia. Minister of State. m. Julie Ann Harriott, 3 Sept. 1973, 1 son. *Education:* LL.B, Sydney; MA, Hawaii. *Appointments:* Public Solicitor's Office, Sydney, 1956-64; Barrister, Supreme Court of Papua and New Guinea, 1964-66; Assistant Director, Chamber of Manufacturers of New South Wales, 1968-71; Director, Victorian Chamber of Manufacturers, Melbourne, 1971-74; Member of House of Representatives, 1974-; Minister of State, 1976-. *Hobbies:* Bridge; Literary and Drama appreciation. *Address:* c/o Parliamet House, Canberra, ACT 2600, Australia.

MACPHERSON, Keith Duncan, b. 12 June 1920, Sydney, Australia. Company Director. m. Ena Forester McNair 23 Nov. 1946, 3 sons, 2 daughters. *Education:* Matriculation Standard, Scotch College, Melbourne, Victoria, 1930-37. *Appointments:* The Herald and Weekly Times Limited, 43 Years. *Memberships:* Melbourne Club; Athenaeum; Melbourne Cricket; Victoria Racing; Victoria Amateur Turf; Moonee Valley Racing; American National Club; Royal Automobile Club of Victoria. *Honours:* Knight Bachelor, 1981. *Hobbies:* Gardening; Swimming. *Address:* Gleneagles, 24 Balwyn Road, Canterbury, Victoria, 3126, Australia.

MacQUARRIE, Lachlan Bruce, b. 11 Feb. 1925, Toronto, Canada. Social Work Educator. m. Helen Aileen Roach, 17 May 1945, 1 son, 2 daughters. *Education:* Matriculation, Malvern Collegiate, Toronto, 1942; BA-(Hons), 1948; BSW, School of Social Work, 1949; MSW, University of Toronto, 1953. *Appointments:* Rehabilitation Officer, Ontario Workmens Compensation Board; Director Welfare Services, Canadian Armed Forces, (Retired Lieutenant Colonel); Director, Hong Kong Council of Social Service; Head, Hong Kong Polytechnic, School of Social Work. *Memberships:* Canadian Club of Hong Kong; HK Government: Advisory Committee on Social Work Training, Rehabilitation Development Coordinating Committee; Narcotics Prevention and Public Education Committee; HK Council of Social Service Executive Committee and Drug Abuse Committee; HK Union Church Deacons Court; HK Christian Service Management Committee. *Publications:* Readings in Hong Kong Social Policy and Administration, 1975; The Continuing Fight Against Drugs, 1978; The Community Development Approach in Narcotics Prevention; Cooperation and Conflict, 1980. *Honours:* RCAF Pilots Wings, 1942; Canadian Forces Decoration (CD) 1962. *Hobbies:* Tennis; Choral Singing. *Address:* 16B Headland Road, Repulse Bay, Hong Kong.

MACQUIRE, Kenneth Victor, b. 16 Feb. 1911, Norwich, Norfolk, England. Secretary. m. Cecily Jean Frances Barthorp, 6 July 1956, 2 sons. *Education:* Norwich School 1922-30; BA(Hons), MA, Cambridge University, 1930-33. *Appointments:* HMOCS, Colonial Adminstrative Service, Fiji, Mauritius, Northern Rhodesia, 1933-65; Secretary, Royal Free Hospital School of Medicine, 1965-68; Registrar, University College of Rhodesia and Nyasaland, 1968-71; University of Rhodesia, 1971-79. *Memberships:* Commonwealth Parliamentary Association; Overseas League; Colonial Pensioners Association; National Sports Centre Zimbabwe. *Honours:* Parker Exhibitioner, Corpus Christi College, Cambridge, 1930-33; OBE, 1949. *Hobbies:* Cricket; Gardening; Church Music. PO Box BW 329, Borrowdale, Salisbury, Zimbabwe.

McSHARRY, Basil James, b. 9 July 1920, Mount Morgan, Queensland. Banker. m. Betty Kitson, 7 Apr. 1947, 1 son, 2 daughters. *Education:* BEcon, University of Queensland, 1958; Associate Bankers' Institute of Australasia 1952. *Appointments:* Commonwealth Bank of Australia, 1938-59; Reserve Bank of Australia, 1960; Deputy Chief Representative, London, 1970-73; Deputy Manager, Exchange Control Admin. 1974; Manager, Securities Markets Admin., 1974-77; Deputy Chief Manager, Banking and Finance Admin., 1977-79; Manager for Queensland, 1979-81; Manager for Victoria, 1981-. *Memberships:* Australian Institute of Directors; Queensland Club; Brisbane Club; Indooroopilly Golf Club. *Honours:* RAAF 1940-45 (m.i.d. 1944). *Hobbies:* Music; Reading; Golf. *Address:* c/o Reserve Bank of Australia, Box 1631M GPO, Melbourne, Victoria 3001.

McSWEENEY, Terence, b. 30 Oct. 1920, Youghal Co. Cork, Ireland. Consultant Traumatic and Orthopaedic Surgeon. m. Joan Frances Murray, 25 Nov. 1947, 3 sons, 2 daughters. *Education:* MB, BCh, BAO, National University of Ireland, 1943; MCh(NUI) 1951; MCh(Orth)

Liverpool 1950; FRCS, England 1951; FACS 1980. *Appointments:* House Surgeon, Royal Infirmary, Hull, Yorks; House Surgeon, Radcliffe Infirmary, Oxford; Senior House Surgeon, Royal Orthopaedic Hospital, Birmingham; Royal Air Force, Medical Branch, Squadron Leader; Registrar, Fulham Hospital London W1; Registrar, Royal Infirmary, Liverpool; Registrar, Robert Jones and Agnes Hunt Orthopaedic Hospital Oswestry, Shropshire; Assistant Surgeon, Royal Orthpaedic Hospital, Birmingham; Consultant, Traumatic and Orthopaedic Surgeon, Robert Jones and Agnes Hunt Orthopaedic Hospital, Oswestry and South Cheshire Hospitals; Surgeon i/c Spinal Injury Unit, Oswestry. *Memberships:* Fellow, British Orthopaedic Association; International Medical Society of Paraplegia; British Medical Association. *Publications:* Papers in Paraplegia, British Journal of Surgery; Chapters in Operative Surgery; Disorders of the Cervical Spine; Text Book of Orthopaedics. *Honours:* Knight of the Holy Sepulchre, 1976; Guest Speaker, New England Orthopaedic Society, 1979; Faculty member, Spinal Injuries Symposium, Phoenix Arizona, 1972-73; Guest Speaker, Eastern Meditterannian Orthopaedic Congress, 1970. *Hobbies:* History; Gardening; Travel. *Address:* 127 Crewe Road, Nantwich, Cheshire, SW5 6JW, England.

McTAGGART, Donald Raymond, b. 26 Sept. 1934, Sydney, Australia. Consultant Physician. m. Judith Helen Benbow, 19 Mar. 1960, 2 sons, 2 daughters. *Education:* MBBS, Sydney University, 1958; MRACP 1963; FRACP 1971. *Appointments:* Consultant Physician, NW Coast, 1963-71; Consultant Physician, NW General Hospital, Burnie, 1971-. *Memberships:* Chairman, Tasmania Committee, Royal Australian College of Physicians, 1978-80; Cardiology Society of Australia; Australian, New Zealand Society of Intensive Care; Thoracic Society of Australia. *Publications:* Intensive Care in a Peripheral Hospital, 1968; A Three Year Review of Intensive Care, 1972; Nursing Training in Intensive Care, 1978; Seven other articles in Medical Journal of Australia. *Honours:* Scholarship, National Heart Foundation, Tasmania, 1973. *Hobbies:* Fishing; Music. *Address:* 6 Arthur Street, Ocean Vista, Burnie Tasmania, Australia.

MADALLALI, Saidi Abdallah, b. 1 July 1936, Kahama, Tanzania. Veterinary Surgeon. m. Amina Mageke Mayunga, 27 Dec. 1958, 5 sons, 5 daughters. *Education:* Veterinary Certificate, Veterinary Training Centre, Mpwapwa, 1958; BVSc, University of Madras, India, 1964; BBSc, Faculty of Veterinary Sciences University of East Africa, Nairobi, 1965; Certificate, Senior African Managers Course, Addis Ababa, 1971; Certificate, Animal Production Course, Australia, 1974. *Appointments:* Regional Veterinary Officer, Morogoro, 1964; District Veterinary Officer, Ufipa, 1964; Regional Veterinary Officer, Kilimanjaro, 1966; Zonal Veterinary Officer, Mbeya and Iringa Regions, 1968; Regional Director of Agriculture, Kagera, 1969; General Manager, National Ranching Company Limited, Dar es Salaam, 1970; Managing Director, Tanzania Livestock Development Authority, Dar es Salaam, 1974; Principal Secretary, Ministry of Agriculture, DSM, 1977; Principal Secretary, Ministry of Livestock Development, Dar es Salaam, 1980-. *Memberships:* Tanzania Society of Animal Production; Tanzania Veterinary Board Member; Tanzania Veterinary Association. *Publications:* Presented a paper on Animal Production in Tanzania at 3rd World Conference on Animal Production, Melbourne, Australia, 1973. *Honours:* Academic award 1st class and top student Veterinary Certificate Course, Mpwapwa, 1957; Best Worker Award, Tanzania, 1978. *Hobbies:* Athletics; Football; Cricket; Table Tennis; Darts. *Address:* Mwendakulima Village, PO Box 94, Kahama, Tanzania.

MADARIKAN, Charles, Olusoji, b. 19 Feb. 1922, Lagos. m. 7 June 1951, 3 sons, 2 daughters. *Education:* Inns of Court School of Law, London, 1947-48; Called to the English Bar (Lincoln's Inn, London), 1948. *Appointments:* Crown Counsel, 1949-56; Senior Crown Counsel, 1956; Chief Registrar, Federal Supreme Court, Nigeria, 1958-59; Director of Public Prosecution, 1959-60; High Court Judge, 1960-67; Justice of the Supreme Court, 1967-72, 1975-77; President, Court of Appeal, 1972-75. *Memberships:* World Association of Judges, 1976; The Appellate Court Judges Division of the World Association of Judges, 1976; Pro-Chencellor and Chairman of the Council of the University of Ife, 1975 and Chairman of the Management Board of the University of Ife Teaching Hospital Complex, 1976. *Publications:* Selected Judgements of the Federal Supreme Court of Nigeria, 1957 — 1958; Criminal Law and Procedure of the Six Southern States of Nigeria, 1974. *Honours:* Commander of the Order of the Niger, 1978. *Address:* Plot 876 Sir Samuel Manuwa Street, Victoria Island, Lagos, Nigeria.

MADDISON, Robert Edwin Witton, b. 8 Sept. 1901, London, England. Consulting Chemist. m. Adelaide Romeril Verdier, 8. Aug. 1923, (d) 8 June 1976, 2 sons. *Education:* B.Sc., Ph.D., King's College, University of London, 1918-1924; Associate of the London College of Music. *Appointments:* Telegraph Condenser Company, 1925; Committee Secretary, International Standard Electric Corporation, 1928; Section Head, Engineering Department, Standard Telephones and Cables, 1929; Assistant Master, Wellington College, Berkshire, England, 1941; Chief Chemist and Consultant, Claud Campbell and Company Limited, 1944-61. *Memberships:* Fellow of the Society of Antiquaries; Fellow of the Royal Astronomical Society; Fellow of the Chemical Society; Fellow of the Institute of Petroleum. *Publications:* The Portraiture of Robert Boyle, London, 1959; Life of Robert Boyle, F.R.S. London, 1969; A Dictionary of Astronomy, London, 1980; Contributions to various Scientific Journals. *Honours:* Leverhulme Research Fellow, 1962-64. *Address:* 2 Alderney Avenue, Heston, Middlesex, England.

MADDOX, John Royden, b. 27 Nov. 1925, Swansea, Wales. Journalist. m. (1) Nancy Fanning, 1949 (Deceased 1960), 1 son, 1 daughter, (2) Brenda Power Murphy, 1 son, 1 daughter. *Education:* Christ Church, Oxford; King's College, London. *Appointments:* Assistant Lecturer then Lecturer, Theoretical Physics, University of Manchester, 1949-55; Science Correspondent, Guardian, 1955-64; Affiliate, Rockefeller Institute, New York, 1962-63; Assistant Director, Nuffield Foundation and Coordinator, Nuffield Foundation Science Teaching Project, 1964-66; Editor, Nature, 1966-73; Chairman, Maddox Editorial Ltd., 1972-74; Director, Nuffield Foundation, 1975-80; Editor, Nature, 1980-. *Publications:* (w. Leonard Beaton), The Spread of Nuclear Weapons, 1962; Revolution in Biology, 1964; The Doomsday Syndrome, 1972; Beyond the Energy Crisis, 1975. *Address:* 9 Pitt Street, London, W.8. England.

MADDREN, James Robert, b. 5 April 1920, Christchurch, New Zealand. Company Director. m. Betty Ngaire Bascand, 31 Oct. 1942, 2 sons, 2 daughters. *Education:* St. Andrews College, 1934-37; Canterbury University, 1939-41. *Appointments:* Director of: Dalgety New Zealand Limited, Donaghys Industries Limited, Suckling Industries Limited, J. Ballantyne and Company Limited, The Shipping Company of New Zealand Limited, Container Terminals Limited; Chairman of: Midland Coachlines Limited, Tasman Rental Cars Limited, MFL Mutual Fund Limited, Ebos Dental and Surgical Supplies Limited, Maddrens Queensland Pty Limited; Chairman and Managing Director, Maddren Brothers Limited. *Memberships:* Christchurch Rotary Club; Canterbury Club; Past Chairman, Japan Centre. *Honours:* C.B.E. 1971; Consul of Belgium for the South Island of New Zealand, 1972; Fellow of the New Zealand Institute of Management, 1975. *Hobbies:* Boating; Reading. *Address:* 56a Clyde Road, Christchurch 4, New Zealand.

MADE, Stanislaus Matienga, b. 20 Aug. 1935, Rusape. Librarian. m. 6 June 1972, 1 son, 2 daughters. *Education:* BA, 1967; MA, 1970; ALA, 1971; FLA, 1978. *Appointments:* Assistant Librarian, UBLS, Roma, Lesotho, 1969-70; Librarian, UBLS, Swaziland, 1971-74; Librarian, University of Malawi, 1975-76; College Librarian, Teachers College, 1977-78; Librarian, University of Zimbabwe, 1979-. *Memberships:* Library Association, United Kingdom, 1967; Zimbabwe Library Association, 1964; Chairman, Malawi Library Association, 1975-76; Chairman, Zimbabwe Library Association, 1978. *Publications:* University Libraries in English-Speaking Central Africa, 1969; Development of Library Services in English-Speaking Central Africa, 1969; 100 Years of Chichewn in Writing 1875-1975, 1976; Directory of Malawi Libraries, 1976; Reading and Library Facilities in Botswana, 1978; Aspects of Library Provision in Newly Independent Neighbouring Countries, 1977; Manpower Needs and Library Education in a Developing Country. *Honours:* Commonwealth

Scholar, 1967-69. *Hobbies:* Gardening; Poultry. *Address:* 33 Amby Drive, Greendale, Salisbury.

MADEDOR, Anthony Omunwarure, b. 1 Aug. 1932, Bendel State, Nigeria. Civil Engineer. m. Daisy MacIntosh, 3 April 1961, 3 sons, 2 daughters. *Education:* BSc Hons, University of Manchester, 1957; MSc., University of Brimingham, 1962; PhD., University of Manchester, 1967. *Appointments:* Pupil and Assistant Civil Engineer, Cementation Company Limited, 1957-60; Assistant Design Engineer, Husband and Company, 1960-61; Executive Engineer, 1963, Principal Executive Engineer, 1969, Chief Engineer, 1972, Assistant Director, 1975, Federal Ministry of Works and Housing; Director, Nigerian Building and Road Research Institute, 1978-. *Memberships:* Fellow, Technical Secretary, Nigerian Society of Engineers, 1971-74; Institute of Civil Engineers, London; American Society of Civil Engineers; Nigerian Geotechnical Association, 1979-; Ikoyi Club. *Publications:* Volume change characteristics of unsaturated clay, 1969; Foundation Design: An Introduction, Fed. Min. of Works, 1973; Engineering Materials in National Development, 1979. *Hobbies:* Classical Music; Folk Music; Squash Rackets. *Address:* 27A Adeyemi Lawson Road, Ikoyi, Lagos, Nigeria.

MADUBUKO, Chukwuma Timothy Nwankwo Mcanto, b. 6 Aug. 1940, Nise, Awka. Architect. m. Grace Uchenna Oranu, 12 Aug. 1972, 1 son, 2 daughters. *Education:* B.Arch Ahmadu Bello University, Zaria, 1962-66; Michigan State University, East Lansin, 1966; B.Arch. Hons., University of Nigeria, Enugu Campus, 1966-67. *Appointments:* Eastern Nigeria Housing Corporation, Port Harcourt, 1967-70; East Central State Housing Development Aughority, Enugu, 1970-76; Mcanto Madubuko Associates, Enugu, 1976-. *Memberships:* Assistant Secretary, Secretary, Nigerian Institute of Architects, Lagos; Rotary Club of Ekulu, Enugh. *Creative Works:* Co-operative Bank of Eastern Nigeria, Office Block, Okpara Avenue, Enugu Anambra State, Nigeria; Co-operative Bank of Eastern Nigeria, Office Block, Okigwe Road, Owerri, Imo State, Nigeria; Amuzu Motors, Mile 4, Obosi, Onitsha, Anambra State, Nigeria; Co-operative Bank of Eastern Nigeria, Banks Branch, Ariaria Market, Aba. *Honours:* Minex Programme to M.S.U. East Lansin, Michigan, United States of America, 1966. *Hobbies:* Outdoor Sports; Indoor Games; Church Activities; Community Development. *Address:* 5 Church Street, Housing Estate, Abakpa-Nike, Enugu, Anambra State, Nigeria.

MADUKA, Vincent Ifeanyi, b. 5 Oct. 1935, Lagos, Nigeria. Broadcast Management. m. Joanna Olutunmbi Layinka, 19 Dec. 1967, 2 sons, 2 daughters. *Education:* B.Sc., Hons, Electrical Engineering, University of Leeds, England, 1959; M.Eng. Sc., Applied Acoustics, National University of Ireland, 1969. *Appointments:* Pupil Engineer, Marconi Company, England, 1959-61; Understudy Engineer, Western Nigeria Radiovision Services Limited, Nigeria, 1961-62; Engineer, Studios, Senior Engineer, Western Nigeria Government Broadcasting Corporation, Ibadan, 1963-69; Chief Engineer, 1969-73; General Manager (WNGBC) 1973-77; Director, General Nigerian Television Authority, 1977-. *Memberships:* Nigerian Society of Engineers; Nigeria Society; The Ibadan Club; The Ikoyi Club. *Publications:* Engineering Management and Broadcasting Articles, Papers and Seminars. *Hobbies:* Photography; Squash. *Address:* 6 Bishop Kale Close, Victoria Island, Lagos, Nigeria.

MAFIANA, Emmanuel Okolie, b. 6 April 1954, Ubulu-Okiti, Aniochal, Bendal State. Businessman; Consultant. m. Gladys Onyeuka, 21 April 1977, 1 son, 2 daughters. *Education:* BEC Diploma English, 1977; Certificate in Administrative Management, 1980; Group Commercial Diploma, England, 1980; Certificate and Diploma, London, 1981; Diploma in Administrative Management, 1981. *Appointments:* Clerk-Typist, Kosa Consultant Agency, Lagos, 1974; Secretary, Eselemos Transport Limited, Warri, 1974-76; Secretary, Admin istration Assistant, Geoavr Nigeria Limited, Warri, 1976-77; Private Secretary, Dello Nigeria Limited, Warri, 1977-78; Confidential Secretary, Sareteme Efficient Services, Warri, 1978-79; Executive Director, Emma Company Syndicate, 1980-; President, Director General, Institute of Professional Secretaries and Administrators, Ubulu-Okiti, 1981-. *Memberships:* President, Idumu-Agbonor, Student Association, Ubu-

Iu-Okiti; General Secretary, Federated Union of Bendel Students, Imba Chapter, Uyo; General Secretary, Ubu-Iu-Okiti Progressive Union, Warri Branch; Member of Parliament, Student Union, Imba-Uyo; Nigerian Association of Practising Company Secretaries, Lagos. *Publications:* When Will My Sun Shine; A Life History of Stephen Ukwamedua. *Hobbies:* Reading; Dancing; Football; Sports; Travelling. *Address:* Emma O. Mafiana, c/o Miss Gloria Mafiana, Okiti Secondary Grammar School, Idumu-Agbonor Quarters, Ubalu-Okiti, Via Issele-Uku-Bds, Nigeria.

MAGANGA, Clement, b. 17 July 1938, Shinyanga, Tanzania. Senior Lecturer. m. Veronica Nyamizi, 9 July 1960, 3 sons, 3 daughters. *Education:* Cambridge School Certificate, 1957; Grade 'A' Teachers' Certificate, 1959; B.A. 1968; M.A., 1969. *Appointments:* Grade 'A' Teacher, 1960-64; Education Officer, 1965-70; Lecturer, Senior Lecturer, 1974; Head of Kiswahile Department, University of Dar es Salaam, 1973-79. *Memberships:* Faculty Board, Arts and Social Science, 1973-79; Member of Senate, University of Dar, 1973-79; Founder Chairman, Federation of Catholic Choirs, 1977-79; Chairman, Kiswahili Curriculum Development Panel, Institute of Education, Dar es Saleam, 1973-79. *Publications:* 15 papers read at various Conferences within and outside Taszania; 2 Book Manuscripts, Misingi Ya Fonetike Matamshi; Matumizi Pasaha Ya Kiswahili, co-author J.S.M. Mwangomango. *Hobbies:* Local Tanzanian Traditional music and dance; Classical Music; Choir singing and conducting. *Address:* St. Paul's Catholic Parish, Msewe, Ubungo, P.O. Box 20973, Dar Es Salaam, Tanzania.

MAGAWI, Benjamin Nashon, b. 25 Nov. 1951, Mombasa. Teacher. m. 10 March 1978, 1 daughter. *Education:* Kenya Advanced Level School Certificate, 1974. *Appointments:* Nyanza Christian College, 1975-78; Muslim Secondary School, 1978-. *Memberships:* Kenya Language Association; Nyanza Province Kiswahili Teachers' Association. *Publications:* Proses and Peotries. *Hobby:* Sport. *Address:* P.O. Box 5, Luanda, Kenya.

MAGINN, Dennis William, b. 11 May 1922. Medical Practitioner; Psychiatrist. m. 7 June 1949, 3 sons, 3 daughters. *Education:* M.B. B.S. Melbourne, 1946; M.D., Melbourne, 1952; D.P.M., Melbourne, 1963; B.Sc. 1963; M.R.A.N.Z.C.P. 1964; F.R.A.N.Z.C.P., 1979. *Appointments:* J.R.M.O., St. Vincents Hospital, Melbourne, 1946-47; J.R.M.O.R., Childrens Hospital Melbourne, 1947-48; Registrar, 1948-52; Private General and Paediatric Practice, 1952-60; Assistant O.P. Physician, 1953-59; Medical Practitioner and Psychiatrist, Royal Park, 1960-64; Superintendent, St. Nicholas Hospital, Melbourne, 1964-81; Deputy Director, Mental Retardation Division, Health Commission of Victoria, 1981-. *Memberships:* Australian College of Paediatrics; Australian Group for the Scientific Study of Mental Deficiency. *Publications:* Foundation Editor, Australian Journal of Mental Retardation; 'Diagnostic Centres', 1964; 'Mentally Retarded People in Society', 1967. *Hobbies:* Lawn Bowls; Golf; Cooking; Australian Eucalypts. *Address:* Darraweit Road, Wallan, Victoria 3654.

MAGWOOD, John McLean, b. 26 Aug 1912, Toronto, Canada. Lawyer. m. Doris Rose Johnston, 18 June 1938, 1 son, 1 daughter. *Education:* B.A, 1933, M.A, 1937, LL.B., 1938, Doctor Juris, 1981, University of Toronto, Canada; Graduate, Osgoode Hall, Called to Ontario Bar, 1936. *Appointments:* Senior Partner, Magwood Pocock Rogers O'Callaghan, 1950-80. *Memberships:* Chairman, Canadian Executive Service Overseas; Past President, National Council Y.M.C.A of Canada, Canadian Council for International Co-operation, York County Law Association; Canadian Bar Association; Strollers Club, Toronto; The University Club, Toronto; The Badminton and Racquet Club, Toronto; Rosedale Golf Club, Toronto; Osler Bluff Ski Club, Collingwood. *Publications:* Competition Law of Canada, 1981. *Honours:* Mention in Despatches to British Secretary of War, 1944; Queen Counsel, 1956; Canadian Centennial Medal, 1967; Queen Elizabeth Jubilee Medal, 1977. *Hobbies:* Skiing; Riding; Harness Driving; Sailing; Tennis; Golf. *Address:* 10 Avoca Avenue, Toronto MUT 2BT, Canada.

MAHAJANI Ganesh S, b. 27 Nov. 1898, Satara, India. Education. m. Indira Paranjbye, 21 Mar. 1927, 1 son, 1 daughter. *Education:* BA, Bombay, 1920; BA, 1924, MA, PhD, 1929, Cambridge, UK. *Appointments:* Maths Professor, 1927-47, Principal, 1929-46, Ferfusson College, Poona; Vice-Chancellor: Rajasthan University, Jaipur, 1947-53, Delhi University, 1953-57; Vice-Chancellor: Udaipu University, 1963-71, Poona University, 1972-75. *Memberships:* Member of the Bombay Legislative Council, 1936-51; Union Public Service, New Delhi Commission, 1957-63; Fellow, Cambridge Philosophical Society; Foundation Fellow: National Institute of Science, New Delhi, India, National Academy of Sciences, Bangalore, India. *Publications:* Contribution to the theory of Ferromagnetic Crystals; Lessons in Elementary Analysis; Application of Moving Axes to Geometry of Curves and Surfaces; Introduction to Pure Solid Geometry. *Honours:* Smiths Prizeman, 1926; Philip Baylis Scholarship, Cambridge, 1926; Honorary Fellow, St John's College, Cambrdige, 1974; Duke of Edinburgh Fellow, Bombay, 1920. *Hobbies:* Tennis; Racing; Novels; Walking; University Training Corps, 1927-47. *Address:* Sambhram, 864 Shivagi Nagar, Poona, 4, India.

MAHBUBANI, Narain Valiram, b. 4 Aug. 1948, Madras, India. Business Man. *Education:* B.A.(Hons) *Address:* Savoy Mansion, 10/F1., Flat 'A', 49 Carnarvon Road, Kowloon, Hong Kong.

MAHENDRA, Sabanayagam, b. 12 April 1927, Colombo, Sri Lanka. Aid Administrator. m. Myra Ingrid Fernando, 20 Oct. 1961, 1 son, 2 daughters. *Education:* BSc., Botany and Forestry, University of Wales, 1948-51; Diploma in Forestry, University of Oxford, 1951-52; Barrister-at-Law, Middle Temple, 1954-57. *Appointments:* Officer-in-Charge, Forestry Field Training School, Sri Lanka, 1953; Practised as a Barrister, Sri Lanka, 1957-60; Special Assistant to the Director, Colombo Plan Bureau, 1961-75; Chief Project Officer, Commonwealth Secretariat, 1975-78; Deputy Director, Commonwealth Foundation, 1978-. *Memberships:* Royal College Union, Sri Lanka; Former member, Executive Committee, Institute of World Affairs, Sri Lanka; London Diplomats' Group, Quaker Peace and Service; Royal Commonwealth Society; Royal Overseas League. *Honours:* Awarded Certificate of Meritous Service by the Colombo Plan Council in 1975 for over fourteen years service to the Colombo Plan. *Hobbies:* Reading; Travel; Walking. *Address:* 18 Ashridge Gardens, Pinner, Middlesex HA5 IDU, England.

MAHER, Keith Alan, b. 18 Feb. 1930, Sydney, Australia. Fund Raising Consultant. m. Beryl Margaret Williams, 4 Sept. 1954, 3 sons, 1 daughter. *Education:* Matriculation, Homebush Boy's High School; Accountancy, Sydney Technical College. *Appointments:* Purchasing and Sales, Automatic Fire Sprinklers Pty., Limited; Area Programming Manager, Wells Organizations Pty., Limited; Chairman and Managing Director, Keith Maher Pty., Limited; Chairman and Managing Director, Direct Mailmasters Pty., Limited; Director, National Fund Raising Counsel Group. *Memberships:* Past Federal President, Australian Institute of Fund Raising Consultants; A Founding National Councillor, The Australasian Institute of Fundraising; National Society of Fundraising Executives, United States of America; Academy of Hospital Public Relations, United States of America; Board of Consultors, The Fund Raising School, United States of America. *Honours:* Elected Fellow of the Australasian Institute of Fundraising, 1980. *Hobbies:* Farming; Golf. *Address:* 91 Homebush Road, Strathfield, New South Wales, Australia, 2135.

MAHIGA, Joseph Phillip, b. 11 Jan. 1929, Tosamaganga, Iringa, Tanzania. Education Officer, Director of Audio-Visual Institute. m. Consolata Seager, 6 June 1953, 2 sons, 2 daughters. *Education:* B.A. Education Degree (Hons) 1970-73. *Appointments:* Teacher, Headmaster of Middle School, 1950-65; Primary School Inspector, 1965-67; Education Officer, Ministry of Education, 1968-69; Director, Audio-Visual Institute, 1973-81. *Memberships:* Tanzania Society; African Adult Education Association; Chairman, Educational Technology Panel, Institue of Education, D'Salaam, 1974-77; Executive Committee Member of the Provisional Secretariat of the African Association for Cinema Co-operation, 1977-81. *Publications:* 'Our Technical and Educational Problems and Needs' in 'Film Making in Developing Countries', 1975; 'The Audio-Visual Institute of Dar-es-Salaam: Its Meaning and Purpose', 1975; 'The Role of the Audio-Visual Institute in Development', 1980. *Honours:* Bachelor of Arts Degree with Honours. *Hobbies:* Sporting; Gardening. *Address:* Hill Road, No. 66/7 Osterbay, D.S.M. Tanzania.

MAHONEY, Dennis Leslie, b. 26 Dec. 1924, Sydney, Australia. Judge of The Court of Appeal of Supreme Court of New South Wales. m. Lesley Helen Barnes, 28 June 1952. *Education:* Bachelor of Arts, 1945, Bachelor of Laws, (Hons) 1948, Sydney University. *Appointments:* Barrister-at-Law, Sydney, New South Wales, 1948; Queen's Counsel, 1960-61; Judge of the Supreme Court of New South Wales, 1972; Judge of Court of Appeal, Supreme Court, New South Wales, 1974. *Memberships:* President, Australian Section, International Commission of Jurists, 1973-74; Executive Counsellor, Australian Branch, International Law Association, 1965-; Human Rights Committee, Lawasia, 1979-. *Honours:* Knight Grand Cross, (c.rib.) Sov. Mil. Hospital Order of St. John of Malta. *Hobbies:* Skiing; Golf. *Address:* c/o Supreme Court of New South Wales, Sydney, Australia.

MAHONEY, John Joseph, b. 10 Sept. 1912, Queensland, Australia. Dental Surgeon. m. Margaret Hickey, 10 Feb. 1945, 2 sons, 1 daughter. *Education:* B.A., 1935 B.D.Sc., 1944, University of Queensland. *Appointments:* Teacher, St. Joseph's College, Gregory Terrace, 1936-39; Lecturer, University of Queensland, Dental School, 1944; Australian Army Dental Corps, 1944-47; Private Practice of Dentistry, 1947-. *Memberships:* Councillor, 1947-78, President, 1969, Australian Dental Association; United Service Club; University of Queensland Alumni Association. *Publications:* Several papers on Dental Subjects. *Honours:* Life member Australian Dental Association, 1978; Life Member Queensland Hockey Association, 1963; University Blue, Hockey, 1932, Cricket, 1935. *Hobbies:* Cabinet Making; Reading. *Address:* 31 Miles Street, Clayfield, Brisbane, Queensland, Australia 4011

MAHONEY, Kevin Patrick, b. 13 Jan. 1939, Brisbane, Australia. Medical Practitioner. m. Mary Deirdre Hirschfeld, 13 Dec. 1965, 1 son, 3 daughters. *Education:* M.B., B.S., 1965; D.Obst., R.C.O.G., 1972; F.R.A.C.G.P., 1977. *Appointments:* Junior Resident Medical Officer, 1966, Residkent Medical Officer, 1967, Occupational Health Medical Officer, 1973-, Royal Brisbane Hospital, Australia; Paediatric Registrar, Royal Childrens Hospital, Brisbane, Australia, 1968-69; Registrar in General Practice, Royal Brisbane Hospital, 1969-71; General Practice, 1972; Occupational Health Officer, Royal Brisbane Hospital, 1973-. *Memberships:* Faculty Board and Faculty Executive R.A.C.G.P.; Hon. Secretary, R.A.C.G.P., 1979-81; United States Club; Post Graduate, Medical Education Committee; Medico-Legal Society; A.M.A.; Australia and New Zealand Society Occupational Medicine, 1978-. *Hobbies:* Fishing; Music; Wine Bottling; Theatre. *Address:* 58 Toorak Road, Hamilton, Brisbane, Queensland, 4007, Australia.

MAHONY, Francis Joseph, b. 15 Mar. 1915, Hamilton, New South Wales, Australia. Solicitor. m. Mary Kathleen Sexton, 9 Dec. 1939, 7 sons, 1 daughter. *Education:* Bachelor of Laws, University of Sydney, 1940. *Appointments:* Admitted as Barrister, Supreme Court of NSW, 1940; Appointed to Commonwealth Crown Solicitor's Office, 1941; Citizens Military Forces and Australian Imperial Forces, 1942-44; Admitted Practioner, High Court of Australia, 1950; Admitted Solicitor, Supreme Court of NSW, 1952; Deputy Commonwealth Crown Solicitor, NSW, 1963-70; Deputy Secretary, Attorney-General's Department, Canberra, 1970-79; Chairman, Criminology Research Council, 1972-79; Chairman, Board of Management of Australian Institute of Criminology, 1973-79; Leader, Australian Delegation to Diplomatic Conference on Humanitarian Law Applicable in Armed Conflicts, Geneva four sessions, 1974-77; Director-General, Australian Security Intelligence Service, 1975-76; Australian Institute of Judicial Administration, 1976-; United Nations Committee, Crime Prevention and Control, 1979; President, Repatriation Review Tribunal, 1979-. *Honours:* OBE, 1972; Companion of the Bath, 1980. *Hobby:* Tennis. *Address:* 92 Cliff Avenue, Northbridge, New South Wales, 2063, Australia.

MAILLU, David G, b. 19 Oct. 1939, Kenya. Writer and Publisher. m. Hannelore Nuthmann, 30 Jan. 1971, 1 daughter. *Education:* Self-Taught in Literature, Fine Art, Philosophy, Music. *Appointments:* Free-lance Writer and Publisher. *Memberships:* Kenya Writers' Association. *Publications:* Kadosa; After 4.30; For Mbatha and Rabeka; Equatorial Assignment; Black Market; My Dear Bottle; Hit of Love, etc., over 15 titles in Print. *Hobbies:* Farming; Nature Study; Reading; Character Analysis and Mind Reading; Guitar playing; Singing; Composing; The Occult; Painting; Broadcasting; General Counselling. *Address:* P.O. Box 10, Koola Town, Via Machakos, Kenya.

MAIN, Albert Russell, b. 6 Mar. 1919, Western Australia. Professor of Zoology. m. Barbara Anne York, 12 Apr. 1952, 1 son, 2 daughters. *Education:* BSc, 1950, PhD, 1956, University of Western Australia. *Appointments:* Lecturer, 1952, Professor of Zoology, 1967-, Zoology Department, University of Western Australia. *Memberships:* Australian Academy of Science; American Ecological Society; Australian Ecological Society; American Society of Ichthyologists and Herpetologists; Geological Society of Australia; Australian & New Zealand Association for the Advancement of Science; Western Australian Wildlife Authority; President, Zoological Gardens Board; Western Australia Environmen-Numerous scientific papers and books. *Honours:* Fulbright Scholarship, University of Chicago, 1950-51; Carnegie Travelling Fellowship, 1958; Britannica Australia Award for Science (shared with H Waring), 1970; Honorary Foreign Member, American Society of Ichthyologists & Herpetologists, 1975; CBE, 1981. *Address:* 39 Marita Road, Nedlands, Western Australia, 6009.

MAINA, Stephen John, b. 26 Dec. 1938, Kilimanjaro, Tanzania. Teacher. m. Theresia Paul, 5 Aug. 1965, 4 sons, 3 daughters. *Education:* Cambridge School Certificate, 1959; Diploma in Education, 1968; Bachelor of Arts Degree, 1973; Master of Arts Degree, 1975. *Appointments:* Teacher, Secondary School, 1962-64; Teacher, Primary School, 1965; Teacher Training, 1967-69; Adult Education, 1970; Language Cordinator, 1974-75; Executive Secretary, The National Swahili Council, 1976-. *Memberships:* The Ruling Chama Cha Mapinduzi; The Union of Workers; Union of Writers and Peots. *Publications:* Articles, Papers on The Development of Kiswahili as a national language in Tanzania; Novels, Tabia and Shida, in publication. *Hobbies:* Gardening; Reading. *Address:* Mabibo-Ubungo, Kinondoni District, Kigogo Road, Opposite Cargo Handling, Dar Es Salaam, Tanzania.

MAITLAND, James Reginald, b. 20 Mar. 1927, Ashington, Northumberland, England. Head of Department of Engineering. m. Mary Jeanette Gardiner, 12 May 1951, 2 daughters. *Education:* BSc.(Eng.), 2nd.class Hons., London University, UK, 1963; C.Eng., F I Mech. E., 1973; MA. Education, Durham University, UK, 1978. *Appointments:* Engineering apprentice, Ashington Coal Co.Limited, UK, 1943-48; Group Draughtsman, National Coal Board, Ashington, UK, 1948-52; Assistant Lecturer, Gateshead Technical College, UK, 1952-54; Assistant Lecturer, Rutherford College of Technology, UK, 1954-57; Lecturer, Northumberland Technical College, Ashington, UK, 1957-64; Lecturer, Teesside Polytechnic, UK, 1964-65; Lecturer, Newcastle Polytechnic, UK, 1965-67; Organiser of Technical Education, Lanarkshire, Scotland, 1967-70; Vice-Principal, Galashiels College of Further Education, Scotland, 1970-73; Head of Department of Engineering, Bishop Auckland Technical College, UK, 1973-. *Memberships:* Vice President, Bishop Auckland Orchestral Society. *Publications:* TEC. Higher Certificate Engineering Science (in preparation). *Hobbies:* Sport; Music. *Address:* 38 The Demesne, North Seaton, Ashington, Northumberland, NE63 9TP, England.

MAKOWSKI, Zygmunt Stanislaw, b. 15 Apr. 1922, Warsaw, Poland. Civil Engineer; Educator. m. Cecylia Grzesik, 20 Oct. 1951, 2 sons, 2 daughters. *Education:* Reale Università di Roma, 1946; Diploma. Engineering, Polish University College, London, UK, 1948; DIC., Imperial College of Science and Technology, London, UK, 1951; PhD., University of London, UK, 1951. *Appointments:* Assistant Lecturer, Polish University College, London, UK, 1948-51; Lecturer, 1951-58, Senior Lecturer, 1958-62, Imperial College of Science and Technology, University of London, UK; Head of Department, Battersea College of Technology, London, UK, 1962-66; Head of Department and Professor of Civil Engineering, University of Surrey, UK, 1966-.

Memberships: Fellow, Institution of Civil Engineers; American Society of Civil Engineers. *Publications:* Steel Space Structures, in 5 languages; Editor and Co-author of: Analysis, Design and Construction of Double-Layer Grids; Analysis, Design and Construction of Braced Domes; over 100 papers on Space Structures, in various languages in scientific, engineering and architectural journals. *Honours:* Special prize by the Institution of Structural Engineers for the design of BOAC hangars at London Airport, 1971; Prize from British Steel Corporation and British Constructional Steelwork Association, 1972; Golden Wing Prize awarded by International Club of Plastics for contribution to research in structural applications on plastics, 1974; Queen's Jubilee Medal, 1977; Freedom of City of London, 1980. *Hobbies:* Reading; Walking. *Address:* Hollister Cottage, Coombe Bottom, Shere, Guildford, Surrey, GU5 9TD, England.

MALABA, Griffiths, b. 24 July 1924, Maphaneni, Zimbabwe. m. Josephine Mloyi, 9 Sept. 1954, 3 sons, 2 daughters. *Education:* BA. (South Africa), English, History, 1949; UED. (South Africa), English, History, 1950; Certificate in Advanced Religious Studies, Union Theological Seminary, New York, USA, 1958; Ordained Minister, Methodist Church in Zimbabwe, 1977. *Appointments:* Founder and 1st Headmaster of Tegwani Secondary School, 1951-63; Principal, Tegwani Secondary, Primary and Teacher Training Institution, 1963-66; Inspector of Schools, 1966-68; Deputy Provincial Education Officer, 1972-76, Provincial Education Officer, 1976-78, Midlands, Rhodesia; Headmaster, Luveve Secondary School, 1969-72; Deputy Chief Education Officer, Standards Control, Head Office, amalgamated Ministry of Education, 1978-79; Member of Public Service Commission, 1979-. *Memberships:* Past Chairman, Gwelo Branch, Jairos Jiri Association; Founder member and First Chairman, Midlands Association of Mentally Subnormal African Children; Rotary Club of Gwelo; Secretary, Students' Representative Council, University College of Fort Hare. *Publications:* Sengizaphutsha: Grade 7 Reader, Ndebele; Ulunguza: Ndebele Novel. *Honours:* Student of the Year award, Kilnerton High School, Transvaal, South Africa, 1945; English, History and Latin Prizes, Matriculation Class, Kilnerton High School, Transvaal, South Africa, 1945; World Council of Churches Scholarship to study Religious Education at Union Theological Seminary, 1957-58; Travel Grant awarded by Government of West Germany to tour educational institutions in Germany, 1962; Commonwealth Grant for Inspector Training in New Zealand, 1965. *Hobby:* Reading. *Address:* 38 Arundel School Road, Mount Pleasant, Salisbury, Zimbabwe.

MALAMI, Shehu Othman, b. Nov. 1936, Sokoto City, Sokoto State, Nigeria. Administration. m. Asmau Ahmed, 29 Mar. 1960, 2 sons, 2 daughters. *Education:* North Devon Technical College, Barnstaple, Devon, UK; Southend-on-Sea Municipal College, UK; Middle Temple, London, UK. *Appointments:* Chairman of various companies; Private Secretary, 1960, Special Assistant, 1970-74, Sultan of Sokoto; District Headof Wurno, 1973-; Member, North-Western State Local Government Reform Commission, 1971; Director: Nigerian Industrial Development Bank, 1966-75, Northern States Marketing Board, 1968-75, Nigerian Produce Marketing Company, 1972-75; Member: Sokoto Local Authority Council, Local Authority Tenders Board and Establishment Committee, 1972-74; Director, Kaduna Textiles Limited, 1970-75; Member, Governing Council, University of Nigeria and The Tenders Board, 1974-80; Chairman, Endowment Fund Committee, University of Nigeria, 1976-80; Chairman, Nigerian Television Authority, North-Western Zone, 1975-77; Member, Governing Council of Sokoto State College of Technology, 1976-78; Chairman, Wurno Caretaker Local Government Council, 1976; Sokoto University Advisory Council, 1976-77; Nigeria's Constitution Drafting Committee, 1975-76; Nigeria's Constituent Assembly, 1977-78; Chairman, Assessment Committee, Nigerian National Merit Award, 1980-81; Chairman, Union Bank of Nigeria. *Memberships:* Britain-Nigeria Association; Nasara Club, Kano; Island Club, Lagos; Sokoto Turf Club; Nigeria Polo Association; Nigerian Economic Society; University Literary Club. *Publications:* Traditional Rulers and Nigeria's Development; Nigeria's New Constitution. *Hobbies:* Reading; Travel; Tennis. *Address:* The Palace, Wurno, Sokoto State, Nigeria.

MALCOLM, Clive Vincent, b. 26 Dec. 1933, Perth, Western Australia. Agricultural Science. m. Fay Dawn Kitchin, 7 Apr. 1962, 4 sons, 1 daughter. *Education:* BSc. Agriculture, 1951-54, MSc. Agriculture, 1963, University of Western Australia; Associate Art of Speech, Australia; MSc., Pollution and Environmental Control, Manchester University, UK. *Appointments:* Western Australian Department of Agriculture, 1955-. *Memberships:* Group Leader, 1st Melville Scout Group; Australia Institute of Agricultural Science; Australia Society of Soil Science; Australia New Zealand Association for Advancement of Science; Australian Rangeland Society; Royal Society of Western Australia. *Publications:* 40 Scientific publications specializing in revegetation of salt affected soil by the use of salt tolerant forage plants. *Honours:* Andro Mayer Research Fellowship, Food and Agriculture Organisation of United Nations, 1966-67; Robert Gledden Overseas Fellowship, University of Western Australia, 1974-75. *Hobbies:* Amateur theatre; Fishing; Tennis; Travel; Farming. *Address:* 9 Jason Street, Melville 6156, Western Australia.

MALCOLM, Harvey Donald Robert, b. 12 Nov. 1936, Sydney, New South Wales, Australia. Agricultural Scientist. m. Judith Perryman, 12 Jan. 1961, 1 son, 2 daughters. *Education:* BSc., General Science, 1959, MSc., 1964, University of Sydney, Australia; PhD., MacQuarie University, Australia, 1970. *Appointments:* Horticultural Research Officer, 1959-66, Plant Physiologist, 1970-81, New South Wales Department of Agriculture, Australia; MacQuarie University, Australia, 1966-70. *Memberships:* Councillor, Royal Society of New South Wales; Councillor, Public Service Association of New South Wales. *Publications:* 45 publications in field of Agricultural Research. *Honours:* Reserve Decoration, 1969. *Hobbies:* Flying; Carpentry; Oyster Farming. *Address:* 61 Union Street, North Sydney, New South Wales 2060, Australia.

MALECELA, John William Samweli, b. 20 Apr. 1934, Buigiri, Dodoma, Tanzania. Minister for Agriculture. m. Ezerina Mwaipopo, 6 July 1962, 2 sons, 3 daughters. *Appointments:* District Officer, DO., 1960-61; 3rd Secretary, UN Representative Office, 1962; Staff Officer, 1963; Regional Commissioner, 1963-64; Ambassador, UN/Ethiopia, 1965-68; Minister: Communication, Administration, EAC., 1969-72; Minister for Foreign Affairs, 1972-75; Minister for Agriculture, 1975-. *Memberships:* Selander Bridge Club; MPs' Football Club. *Publications:* Participated in UN Committees of Decolonisation and Human Rights; Spokesman as per-conferred Ministries. *Honours:* Received an Honorary Doctorate of Law (PhD), Hardin-Simons University, Abilene, Texas, USA; Chairman, Tanzania Commonwealth Society. *Hobby:* Football. *Address:* Mvumi, Dodoma Rural, Dodoma, Tanzania.

MALETNLEMA, Tumsifu Ninatubu, b. 15 Feb. 1934, Moshi, Tanzania. Medical-Human Nutrition. m. Rachel Elikana Kaaya, 18 Dec. 1971, 4 daughters. *Education:* MB., BS., Makerere University, 1963; DHN, 1965, PhD., 1973, London University, UK. *Appointments:* Registrar, medical, 1964; District Medical Officer, 1965; Medical Officer, Nutrition, 1966-73; Director, Tanzania Food and Nutrition Centre, 1974-. *Memberships:* Tanzania Medical Association; Royal Society of Tropical Medicine and Hygiene. *Publications:* Rural Mother and Child Care, Kiswahili; Art You Too Fat? Kiswahili and English; Several chapters and articles in books and journals. *Honours:* Prize for book - Rural Mother and Child Care. *Hobbies:* Music; Gardening. *Address:* PO Box 20265, Dar Es Salaam, Tanzania.

MALIETOA, Tanumafili II, H. H, b. 4 Jan. 1913. Western Samoan Politician. *Education:* Wesley College, Auckland, New Zealand. *Appointments:* Adviser, Samoan Government, 1940; Member, New Zealand delegation to UN, 1958; Joint Head of State, Western Samoa, 1962-63; Sole Head of State, 1963-; Fautua of Maliena. *Address:* Government House, Vailima, Apia, Western Samoa.

MALIK, Gunwantsingh Jaswantisingh, b. 29 May 1921, Karachi. Diplomat. m. Gurkirat Kaur Singh, 15 Sept. 1948, 2 sons. *Education:* BSc, Gujrat College, Ahmedabad, Bombay University, 1938; Hamburg University, 1938-39; Zurich University, 1939; BA, MA, Downing College, Cambridge University, 1939-41, 1942-43. *Appointments:* Physicist, British Industrial

Plastics, Oldbury, Worcester, 1941-42; Technical Officer, Royal Air Force Volunteer Reserve, 1943-46; Indian Foreign Service 1947-79 during which period served as Ambassador to: Philippines, 1965-68, Senegal (concurrently Ivory Coast, Upper Volta and Mauritania also High Commissioner to the Gambia), 1968-70; Chile (concurrently Colombia, Ecuador and Peru), 1970-74; Thailand (concurrently Permanent Representative to Economic and Social Commission for Aisia and the Pacific), 1974-77; Spain, 1977-79. *Memberships:* India International Centre, 1979-; Society for International Development, Delhi Chapter 1979-. *Publications:* Speeches in the countries of accrediation, articles in magazines in India, contributions to Commemorative volumes in India. *Hobbies:* Photography; Motoring. *Address:* 21A Nizamuddin West, New Delhi, 110013, India.

MALLET, Philip Louis Victor, b. 3 Feb. 1926, London, England. H M Diplomatic Service. m. Mary Borlase, 28 Nov. 1953, 3 sons. *Education:* BA, Winchester and Balliol, 1949. *Appointments:* Foreign Office, 1949, 1953, 1961, 1967; Baghdad, 1950; Cyprus, 1956; Aden, 1958; Tunis, 1965; Khartoum, 1969; Stockholm, 1973; Foreign and Commonwealth Office, 1976; High Commissioner in Georgetown and non-resident Ambassador to Suriname, 1978-. *Honours:* CMG, 1979. *Address:* c/o FCO (Georgetown), King Charles Street, London, SW1A 2AH, England.

MALLIA, Emmanuel, b. 24 Jan. 1952, Sliema, Malta. Advocate. m. Nevise Mifsud Bonnici, 9 Aug. 1980. *Education:* Graduated as Legal Procurator, 1973, Graduated as Notary Public, 1979, Graduated as Advocate, 1980, University of Malta. *Appointments:* Solicitor, Legal division, Car Importer Company, 1974-76; Practised in Legal Chambers of Guido De Marco & Associates, 1976-79; Own Practice, Malta, 1979-; also acts as a legal advisor to numerous firms in Malta. *Memberships:* Council member, Main Football Association; President, 1979, Council member, Gozo Tourist Association; Council member, Malta Automobile Federation; Yacht Club; President, Minibus Transport Association; Malta Football Youth Committee; Kiwanis Club Malta; Sliema Lions; Honorary member, Melita Band Club; Msida Football Club; Secretary-General, Yacht Traders' Association, 1978; President, 1973-77, Sectional Committee, Nationalist Party, Gzira electoral division. *Publications:* Proper Law of International Contracts, 1979. *Hobbies:* Chess; Squash; Horse racing; Football; Reading; Writing poetry; Sailing. *Address:* Apartment No.1, Manoel Flats, Moroni Street, Sliema, Malta.

MALM, Howard Leigh, b. 15 Apr. 1941, Medicine Hat, Alberta, Canada. Scientist. m. Caroline Edith May Back, 6 July 1970, 2 sons. *Education:* BSc.Hons. Magna Cum Laude, 1963, MSc. Physics, 1965, University of Alberta, Canada; PhD., Physics, Simon Fraser University, Canada, 1971. *Appointments:* Research Officer, Atomic Energy of Canada; Vice-President, Aptec Engineering Limited, Canada. *Memberships:* American Nuclear Society; Institute of Electrical and Electronic Engineers; Health Physics Society; Instrument Society of America; Canadian Association of Physicists; Canadian Radiation Protection Association; Bohmisch Physical Society. *Publications:* Over 40 Scientific papers in Professional Journals. *Honours:* Governor General's Award, GR.9, 1956; Friends of the University of Alberta Bursary, 1959; President's Scholarship, University of Alberta, 1959; Lister Trophy, 1960; National Research Council Bursary, 1963. *Hobbies:* Stained Glass Design and Construction; Wine Making; Rose Gardening. *Address:* 332 Richmond Street, Richmond Hill, Ontario, Canada L4C 3Z4.

MALOMO, Israel Mofolorunso, b. 4 Mar. 1934, Abeokuta, Nigeria. Medical Consultant. m. Folake Adedoyin, 10 Dec. 1975, 2 sons, 2 daughters. *Education:* University of Ibadan, 1958-63; University College Hospital, Ibadan, 1966-68; DCP, 1969, DPath, 1969, St. Stephen's Hospital, London. *Appointments:* House Physician, Lagos University Teaching Hospital, 1963-64; House Surgeon, 1964, Consultant/Senior Consultant, Pathology, 1970-76, Adeoyo State Hospital, Ibadan; Medical Officer, Western Nigeria, 1964-66; SHO/Registrar, Department of Pathology, University College Hospital, Ibadan, 1966-68; Senior Consultant/Chief Consultant, Pathology, State Hospital, Abeokuta, Nigeria, 1976-. *Memberships:* Nigeria Medical

Association; Nigerian Society for Haematology and Blood Transfusion; Nigeria Society for Immunology. *Publications:* Contributor to various professional journals. *Honours:* FMC, 1975; FWACP, 1976. *Hobby:* Lawn Tennis. *Address:* House 21 Road 6, Housing Corporation Estate, Ibara, Abeokuta, Ogun State, Nigeria.

MALOOK, Saif Ul, b. 26 June 1945, Lahore, Pakistan. Chemist. m. Nargis Bano, 28 June 1974, 1 son, 2 daughters. *Education:* BSc, 1965, MSc, 1968, University of Punjab, Lahore, Pakistan; PhD, University of Surrey, England, 1974. *Appointments:* Assistant Chemist, Pakistan Railway, 1965; Postdoctoral Research Fellow, Department of Chemistry, The Queen's University of Belfast, Northern Ireland; Production Director, Norbrook Laboratories Limited, Northern Ireland, 1976-. *Memberships:* Member Royal Society of Chemistry; Chartered Chemist. *Publications:* A Kinetic Study of the Catalysed Degradation of Cellulose Triacetate in Solution, Thesis. *Hobbies:* Reading; Golf; Squash. *Address:* 11 Rathmore Road, Newry, County Down, Northern Ireland.

MAMATTAH, Charles McCarthy Kwasi, b. 30 Jan. 1921, Keta, Ghana. Eve Historian and Educationist. m. 3 sons, 6 daughters. *Education:* Teaching Certificate, Achimota College, 1939; School of Social Welfare, Accra, 1948; Diploma in Social Administration, University of Ghana, 1959. *Appointments:* Mission School Teacher, 1940-48; Community Development Officer, 1948-63; Senior Civil Servant with Gold Coast-Ghana Government; Registrar, Volta Region House of Chiefs, 1971; Research Writer, Historian, 1971-. *Memberships:* First National Organising Secretary and Founding Member, Anlo Annual Hogbetsotso Festival Committee. *Publications:* The Ewes of West Africa; Togo Ewes, in print. *Honours:* English and Scripture Prizes, 1936-39. *Hobbies:* Sports; Reading; Research Writing. *Address:* Research Publications, PO Box 142, Keta, Volta Region, Ghana, West Africa.

MAMBA, George Mbikwakhe, b. 1932. Swazi Diplomat. m. Sophie Sidzandza Sibandze, 1960, 3 sons, 2 daughters. *Education:* Cambridge Institute of Education, UK; University of Nairobi, Kenya. *Appointments:* Head teacher, Makhonza School, 1956-60; Assistant teacher, Kwalusen Central School, 1961-65; Primary Education Course, Cambridge, UK, 1965-66; Headmaster, Enkambeni Central School, 1966-67; Scout Field Commissions, full time, 1967-68; Inspector of Schools, Manzini District, 1969-70; Welfare/Aftercare Officer, Prison Department, 1971-72; Counsellor, Swazi High Commission, Nairobi, Kenya, 1972-77; Swazi High Commissioner, London, UK, 1978-. *Address:* 64 Aylestone Avenue, London, NW6, England.

MAMISO, Edmond Baden, b. 1928, Vulpi, Nigeria. Personnel Management. m. Anna Todi, 1 son, 2 daughters. *Education:* Bauchi Teachers College, 1950-51. *Appointments:* Teacher, 1948-58; Parliamentary Secretary, 1958-62; Provincial Commissioner, 1962-66; Senior Councillor, 1966-67; Civil Commissioner, 1967-75; Personnel Manager, Savannah Sugar Company, 1975-. *Honours:* OFR. *Hobby:* Table Tennis. *Address:* PO Box 19, Numan, Nigeria.

MAMMAN, Samaila, b. 18 July 1945, Kurfi, Kaduna State, Nigeria. General Manager. m. Halima, 21 Dec. 1972, 4 daughters. *Education:* BSc, 1969-72; Diploma in Dev. Econs., 1973; Banking Course, 1976. *Appointments:* Economic Planning Office, 1972-74; Investment Executive, 1974-77; Investments Manager, 1977-80; General Manager, 1980-. *Publications:* The Native Location of small-scale Industries in Zaria City; Small-scale Industries & Employment Opportunities in Kaduna State of Nigeria. *Hobbies:* Swimming; Indoor Games. *Address:* 10A Kinkino Close, Kaduna, Nigeria.

MANAF, Mohammed Zaini, b. 24 Feb. 1941, Muar, Johor, Malaysia. Certified Management Consultant. m. Noor Aini Md Zin, 27 July 1969, 1 son, 2 daughters. *Education:* University of London; Univesity of the State of New York; Kesington University of California; MSc; PhD; FRGS; FRSA; PE; CMfgE; FBIM; FInstM; FMS; FIIM; FBIS; FInstPet; FIE; FABE; FID; MASME; MIEEE; MIRTE; MCIT; MAIAA; AIMechE; MInstAM; MInstTA. *Appointments:* Technical and Administrative Assistant, Borneo Company (London(Limited and Inchcape

Export Limited, London, 1963-67; Bank Officer, The Chase Manhattan Bank, Kuala Lumpur, 1967-68; Sales Manager, Wearne Brothers, Malaysia Sdn Bhd, 1968-75; General Manager, Pernas Jardine Aviation, 1975-77; Chairman and Principal Consultant, Manaf and Company, 1977-. *Memberships:* President, The Institute of Management Consultants Malaysia; Chairman, Malaysia Centre of the Institute of Road Transport Engineers, UK; Chairman, Malaysia Centre of the Association of Business Executives, UK; Honorary Representative, Malaysia, The Institution of Industrial Managers, UK, Institute of Engineers UK, Institute Transport Administration UK, Institute of Industrial Engineers, Aust. *Publications:* Professional Organisations in Malaysia; The Malaysian Universities; Approximately 40 articles in various professional journals. *Honours:* Fellowship of The Institute of Marketing, UK; Fellowship, The British Interplanetary Society. *Hobbies:* Heraldry; Genealogy; Classical Music; Interior Decoration and Aviation. *Address:* Hampstead Lodge, PO Box 1052 J Semangat, Petaling Jaya, Malaysia.

MANDELBROTE, Bertram, b. 22 Oct. 1923, Cape Town, South Africa. Physician. m. Kathleen Joyce Howard, 24 Nov. 1949, 2 sons. *Education:* SACS, 1930-39; University of Cape Town, 1939-45; MB., ChB., University Capetown, 1945; MSc., Oxford University, 1948; MRCP (London), 1948; Post-graduate School, Hammersmith Londo, 1948-49; DPM, Instutute of Psychiatry, London, Maudsley Hopistal, 1949-52, 1952-53; Institute of Psychiatry, McGill University, Montreal, Canada; MA, (Oxon), 1961; FRCP, (London), 1964; FRCPsych., (London), 1971. *Appointments:* Groote S Hospital, Cape Town, 1946; Rhodes Scholar Oxford, 1946-48; Churchill Hospital, Oxford; P G School, Hammersmith, 1948-49; Registrar, 1949-52, Senior Registrar, 1953-54, Maudsley Hospital, London; Dominion Provincial Research Fellow, McGill University, Montreal, Canada, 1952-53; Physician Superintendent, Consultant Psychiatrist, Coney Hill & Horton Road Hospital, Gloucester, 1956-59; Physician Superintendet, Littlemore Hospital, Littlemore, Oxford; Consultant Psychiatrist, United Oxford Hospitals; Clinical Lecturer, University of Oxford. *Memberships:* President, Oxford Rotary Club, 1975; President Oxford BMA, 1975; Vice-President Oxford Medical Society; Psychosomatic Society; Royal Commonweath Society. *Publications:* Psychiatric Aspects of Medical Practice (w. Prof. M G Gelder), 1972; 60 publications in learned journals. *Honours:* Victoria Scholarship, 1938-39; Dominion Provincial Research Fellow, 1953-54; Rhodes Scholarship. *Hobbies:* Chess; Philately. *Address:* Littlemore House, Littlemore, Oxford, England.

MANEA, Ernest Cosmo, b. 23 Dec. 1926, Albany, Western Australia. Medical Practitioner. m. Clandine Beulah Elaine Snook, 16 Jan. 1952, 2 sons. *Education:* Bachelor of Medicine, Bachelor of Surgery, Adelaide University, 1949. *Appointments:* Resident Medical Officer, 1950, Surgical Registrar, 1951, Royal Perth Hospital; General Practioner, Bunbury, Western Australia, 1953-. *Memberships:* Chairman, St John's Hospital Board, Bunbury, Western Australia, 1980-81; South-West Regional Development Committee, 1974-81; President, Western Australian Trotting Association. *Honours:* Councillor, 1974-81, Mayor, 1966-72, City of Bunbury, Western Australia. *Hobbies:* Farming; Horse Breeding. *Address:* 36 Mangles Street, Bunbury, 6230, Western Australia.

MANGAN, Louis Joseph, b. 26 May 1922, Australia. Managing Director. m. Cecile Joan Wykes, 2 Oct. 1964. *Education:* Master of Commerce (Prelim), Bachelor of Commerce, University of Melbourne; Associate, Australian Society of Accountants. *Appointments:* RAAF, 1942-45; Cost Accountant, 1952, Personal Assistant to General Manager, 1959, Deputy General Manager, 1967, General Manager, 1972, Managing Director, 1981, Carton and United Breweries Limited; Director of various Breweries & Hotel Companies; Chairman Australian Associated Brewers, 1973-. *Memberships: Hobbies:* Yachting; Golf; Swimming. *Address:* 24 Hopetoun Road, Toorak, 3142, Australia.

MANING, Richard Wong, b. 11 Sept. 1944, Penampang, Sabah, Malaysia. Banker. m. Judith Fay Yaxley, 20 May 1967, 1 son, 3 daughters. *Education:* BA, University of Tasmania, 1969; Diploma in Economic Development, University of Oxford, 1974. *Appointments:* Assistant Secretary, Principal Assistant Secretary, Under Secretary, 1970-75, Permanent Secretary, 1976-78, Ministry of Finance of State of Sabah, Malaysia; Senior Tutor in Economics, University of Papua New Guinea, 1975-76; Managing Director, Sabah Development Bank, Malaysia, 1978-. *Memberships:* Institute of Bankers, UK; American Institute of Management, USA. *Honours:* Faithful Member of the Order of Kinabalu, 1977. *Hobbies:* Chess; Snooker. *Address:* Tamarind Grove, Jalan Sugud (Off Mile 9½ Papar Rd), Kg. Kondis, Penampang, Kota Kinabalu, Sabah, Malaysia.

MANIRUZZAMAN, Talukder, b. 1 July 1938, Pabna, Bangladesh. University Teaching. m. Razia Akter Banu, 21 May 1967, 1 son, 1 daughter. *Education:* BA, 1959, MA, 1960, University of Dacca; PhD, Queen's University, Canada, 1966. *Appointments:* Senior Lecturer, 1966-68; Associate Professor and Chairman, 1968-74, Professor and Chairman, 1974, Department of Political Science, University of Rajshahi; Professor and Chairman, 1974-78, Professor, 1978-, Department of Political Science, University of Dacca. *Memberships:* Chairman, Centre for Policy Research, University of Dacca, 1980-82; General Secretary, Bangladesh Political Science Association, 1975-78; American Political Science Association; National Adviser, Central Children's Association, Bangladesh. *Publications:* The Politics of Development: The Case of Pakistan (1947-1958); Radical Politics and the Emergence of Bangladesh; The Bangladesh Revolution and its Aftermath; Contributed many articles to Journals. *Honours:* Nuffield Foundation Fellowship, 1978-79; Commonwealth Academic Fellowship in UK, 1974-75; Congressional Fellowship, 1970-71; Commonwealth Scholarship in Canada, 1963-66; Visiting Fellowship, Australian National University, 1981; United Pakistan Delegation to the 25th Session of the General Assembly of the United Nations. *Hobbies:* Music; Walking; Reading. *Address:* 48/I Dacca University, Staff Quarters, Fuller Road Dacca-2, Bangladesh.

MANLEY, Gerald, b. 17 Dec. 1933, London, England. Medicine. m. Rosalind Cousins, 29 Sept. 1959, 1 son, 3 daughters. *Education:* University of Bristol; Oriel College, Oxford; MB, ChB, 1957; MD, 1962; DPhil, 1965; MRCPath, 1969; FRCPath, 1981. *Appointments:* House Surgeon, Bristol Royal Infirmary; House Physician, Royal Devon and Exeter Hospital, 1957-58; Lecturer in Pathology, University of Oxford, 1959-64; Senior Registrar, Chemical Pathology, Radcliffe Infirmary, Oxford, 1964-69; Lecturer in Cell Biology, University of Exeter, 1969-72; Consultant Chemical Pathologist, Torbay Hospital, Devon, England, 1972-; Honorary Research Fellow, University of Exeter, 1972-. *Memberships:* Association of Clinical Pathologists; Biochemical Society; Association of Clinical Biochemists; British Society for Allergy and Clinical Immunology. *Publications:* Approximately 30 publications in professional Journals. *Honours:* Crosby-Lennard Prize, University of Bristol, 1955; Frewin Prize, University of Oxford, 1965. *Hobbies:* Painting; Photography; Growing and Breeding Rhododendrons; Playing Violin. *Address:* Department of Chemical Pathology, Torbay Hospital, Torquay, Devon, England.

MANLEY, Hon. Michael Norman, b. 1924. Jamaican Politician. m. Beverley Anderson, 1972, 1 son, 2 daughters. *Education:* BSc., Hons., London School of Economics, UK. *Appointments:* Pilot Officer, Royal Canadian Air Force, 1943-45; Freelance Journalist, BBC., 1950-51; Associated Editor, Public Opinion, Jamaica, 1952-53; Executive member, People's National Party, 1952-; Sugar Supervisor, National Workers' Union, 1953-54; NWU Island Supervisor and First Vice-President, Caribbean Bauxite and Mineworkers' Union, 1955-72; organised strike in sugar industry, 1959, which led to Goldenberg Commission of Inquiry; Senator, 19667; MP for Central Kingston, Jamaica, 1967-; President, Peoples' National Party, 1969-; Leader of Opposition, House of Representative 1969-72; Prime Minister, 1972-80. *Publications:* The Politics of Change, 1974; A Voice at the Workplace, 1976; The Search for Solutions, 1977. *Honours:* Order of Liberator, Venezuela, 1973; Doctor of Laws, Morehouse College, Atlanta, USA, 1973; Order of Mexican Eagle, 1975; Order pf Jose Marti, Cuba, 1975. *Address:* Jamaica House, Hope Road, Kingston 6, Jamaica, West Indies.

MANN, Ira Keith, b. 6 Oct. 1939, Alix, Alberta, Canada. Band Director. m. 15 Aug. 1964, 1 son, 1 daughter.

Education: B Education (Music), University of Alberta, Edmonton, Alberta, Canada, 1969. *Appointments:* Teacher, classroom and instrumental music, Spruce View School, Alberta, 1961-63, Elnora School, Alberta, 1963-68; Teacher, instrumental music (grades five through 12), Innisfail Schools, Alberta, 1969-78, Commanding Officer, (Major), Royal Canadian Air Cadet School of Music, (evening credit), Red Deer College, Alberta, 1974-78; Coordinator, Red Deer College School of Music, Red Deer, Alberta, 1978-. *Memberships:* President, (Alberta Chapter & National), Canadian Band Director's Association; Canadian Music Educators' Association; National Band Association; North American Band Directors' Coordinating Council; Music Educators' National Conference; National Association of Jazz Educators; College Band Directors Association; Phi Beta Mu Fraternity. *Publications:* Founding Editor, Canadian Band Directors' Association Journal (quarterly publication). *Honours:* Canada Centennial Medal, 1967; Band Director of the Year, 1974; Nominee, Jaycees' Five Outstanding Young Canadians, 1978; Invited as co-director for the 1980 European tour of the International Collegiate Wind Band, 1979. *Hobbies:* Photography; Camping; Music; Cross Country Skiing; Down Hill Skiing; Woodworking. *Address:* PO Box 75, Penhold, Alberta, TOM 1RO, Canada.

MANN, Peter Woodley, b. 25 July 1924, Perth, Australia. Anglican Bishop. m. Anne Norman, 10 Feb. 1955, 3 daughters. *Education:* University of New Zealand; LTh, Anglican Board of Theological Studies; BD, University of London. *Appointments:* Curate, Napier Cathedral, 1953-54; Curate, Rotorua, 1954-56; Vicar of Porangahau, 1956-60; Vicar of Dannevirke, 1961-66; Vicar of Blenheim and Archdeacon of Marlborough, 1966-71; Vicar and Archdeacon of Timaru, 1971-75; Vicar of Lower Hutt, 1975; Bishop of Dunedin, 1975-. *Memberships:* University Club, Dunedin. *Hobbies:* Tennis; Golf; Fishing; Gardening. *Address:* Bishops House, 10 Claremont Street, Dunedin, New Zealand.

MANN, Robert Bruce, b. 11 Dec. 1955, Montreal, Quebec, Canada. Physicist. m. Nancy Elizabeth Wright 6 May 1978. *Education:* PhD, 1982, MSc, University of Toronto, 1979; BSc, McMaster University, Hamilton, Ontario, Canada, 1978. *Memberships:* Canadian Association of Physicists; Bruce Trail Association. *Publications:* Gravitational Synchrotron Radiation in the Metric of a New Theory of Gravitation, 1980; Particle Spectrum in a New Theory of Gravitation, 1980; Linear Approximation of a New Theory of Gravity, 1981; Gauging the Complex Pioncare Group, 1981; Post-Newtonian Expansion of a New Theory of Gravity, 1981; Tensor Analysis in Generalized Spacetimes, 1981. *Honours:* Commonwealth Scholarship to Cambridge University, 1979 (declined); NSERC Science Scholarship, 1978; Burke Memorial Ring, 1978; Governor General's Medal, 1977; 4-year University Entrance Scholarship to McMaster 1974; Canadian International Amateur Film Festival award for best film by a filmmaker under 14 years of age, 1970; End-to-end award for hiking the entire Bruce Trail 1976. *Hobbies:* Hiking; Film-making; Leading a Church Youth Group; Travelling; Panelology. *Address:* 644 Main Street, W. «703, Hamilton, Ontario, Canada, L8S 1A1.

MANNAN, Abdul, b. 1 Jan. 1932. Professor, Scientist, Chairman. m. Monowara Begum 10 Apr. 1952, 4 sons, 2 daughters. *Education:* BSc(Hons) Chemistry, 1954; MSc bio Thesis, Dacca University, 1955; Dip-In-Fish Tech., 1960; MPharm. University of Toronto, Canada, 1971; PhD (bionucleonics), University of Alberta, Canada 1973. *Appointments:* Assistant Technologist, Government of East Pakistan 1955; Research Officer, BCSIR Lab. Dacca, 1960-61; Senior Lecturer, Department of Biochemistry, Dacca University, 1962-68; Graduate Teaching Assistant, Faculty of Pharmacy, University of Toronto, 1968-71; and University of Alberta 1971-73; Associate Professor, Biochemistry, Dacca University, 1974-79; Professor Pharmacy, Department of Pharmacy, 1980; Chairman, Department of Pharmacy, 1980. *Memberships:* Founder member, World Federation of Nuclear Medicine and Biology; Asia-Oceania Federation of Nuclear Medicine and Biology; Chemical Institute of Canada; International Diabetic Federation; Asia Oceania Society of Endocrinology; Bangladesh Biochemical Society; Bangladesh Association for the Advancement of Science; Bangladesh Society of Nuclear Medicine and Biology; Bangladesh Drug Technical Advisory Board; Bangladesh

Pharmacy Council; Islamic Medical Mission of Bangladesh; Bangladesh Journal of Scientific Research; Bangladesh Journal of Biological Science. *Publications:* Field of Research: Hormonal and metabolic arrangement in diabetes, uremia, hypertension and contraception and Radio-Pharmacy; 72 publications, 28 in international journals. *Honours:* Myrth B. Field Estate Awards, University of Toronto, 1971; Colombo Plan Research Fellowships, Canada 1958-60 and 1968-70; Graduate Teaching Assistantship in Radio-pharmacy and Bionucleonics, University of Alberta 1971-74; Commonwealth Travel grants to attend and Chair a scientific session, Sydney, First Asia and Oceania Congress of Nuclear Medicine and Biology; Travel grant from WHO, 1976; Travel grants from the Yugoslavian Society of Endocrinology and Metabolism, 1978; Grants from Philippine Society of Nuclear Medicine and Biology. *Hobbies:* Reading; Sight Seeing. *Address:* Village Sayed Pur, P.S. Monohardi, District Dacca, Bangladesh.

MANNAN, Abdul Qazi, b. 1 Jan. 1930 Bengal. Educator and Writer. m. Suraya Begum 7 June 1972, 1 son, 1 daughter. *Education:* Honours, 1949, MA Dacca University 1951; PhD London University 1964. *Appointments:* Senior Lecturer, 1958-63; Reader, 1964-70; Professor, Rafshahi University, 1971-; Provost 1972-75; Visiting Professor, Chicago University, USA 1974. *Memberships:* Bengali Research Association, Rajshahi University; Jinnah Institute. *Publications:* One Book in English; Four Books in Bengali; Numerous Research Articles in English and Bengali. *Honours:* National Literary Award for Publications, 1962. *Hobbies:* Hobby: Music. *Address:* Ukilpara, Naogaon, Rajshahi, Bangladesh.

MANNERS, Herbert James, b. 10 Jan. 1923, Bristol, England. Professional Engineer & Works Director. m. Mary, 19 Dec. 1942, 1 daughter. *Education:* ONC, HNC, Mechanical Engineering; ONC, HNC, Production Engineering; Bristol College of Technology; Bristol University; Institutes of Civil, Mechanical and Production Engineers. *Appointments:* Assistant Technical Director, Norris Industrial Consultants, 1950-58; Assistant to Chief Engineer, Vickers Armstrong, Swindon, 1958-60; Engineer, Bristol Siddeley Engines, 1960-61; Works Director, M H Hurst (Engineering) Ltd., 1961-; Industrial & Management Consultant, 1961-. *Memberships:* Honorary Secretary, Founder and Fellow, Institute of Management Specialists; Fellow, Institute of Manufacturing; Institute of Training Officers; FRSA; FMS; Fl.Mech.E; Fl.Prod.E; FR.Plant.E; FBIM. *Publications:* Contributor of various articles to professional journals; Editor & Technical Adviser to a series of six booklets, Management Specialists and Terotechnology; Editor & Technical Adviser to a series of Eight Booklets, The Essentials of Effective Manufacture. *Honours:* First prize award for best student, Whitwood Mining & Technical College. *Hobbies:* Gardening; Swimming; Fishing; Music; Dancing. *Address:* 17 Rouncil Lane, Kenilworth, Warwickshire, England.

MANSFIELD, John Willem, b. 14 Oct. 1937, Turkey. Banker. m. Anne Marie, 11 Sept. 1965, 2 sons, 1 daughter. *Education:* MA, Magdalen College, Oxford, 1958-62; MBA, University of Pennsylvania Wharton School of Finance, 1962-64. *Appointments:* Military Service; Dow Chemical Company; McKinsey & Company Inc; Grindlays Bank Limited. *Memberships:* Royal Hong Kong Yacht Club. *Honours:* Thouron Award, 1962. *Hobby:* Sailing. *Address:* 52C Carolina Gardens, 30 Coombe Road, Hong Kong.

MANSFIELD, Michael, b. 21 Mar. 1931, United Kingdom. Diplomat. m. Annemarie Niesje Hootsen, 10 Dec. 1960, 1 son, 1 daughter. *Education:* BA, University of Canterbury, Christchurch, New Zealand, 1953. *Appointments:* Assistant Master, Huntley School, Marton, NZ, 1949-50; Commissioned in British Regular Army and served in Britain, Malta, Cyprus, 1954-57; Joined New Zealand Ministry of Foreign Affairs, 1957; Asia, Pacific & Defence Divisions, MFA, Wellington, 1957-60; Second Secretary, New Zealand Embassy, Bangkok, 1961-62; Assistant Head Economic Division and Head, Careers and special projects section of MFA, 1963-66; Counsellor, New Zealand Embassy, Bonn, 1966-69; Deputy High Commissioner, New Zealand High Commission, Apia, 1970-72; Special assignment on overseas property purchasing, MPA, 1972-73; Minister, New Zealand Mission to the United Nations, New

York, 1973-76; High Commissioner, in Papua New Guinea, 1976-78, in Malaysia, 1979-. *Memberships:* Royal Selangor Golf Club, Kuala Lumpur; Royal Bangkok Sports Club. *Honours:* Queen's Jubilee Medal, 1977; Represented New Zealand on a number of international conferences and several sessions of the United Nations General Assembly in New York. *Hobbies:* Reading; Gardening; Skiing; Golf; Sailing. *Address:* Ministry of Foreign Affairs, Private Bag, Wellington, New Zealand.

MANSFIELD, Terence Arthur, b. 18 Jan. 1937, Ashby De La Zouch, Leicestershire. Professor. m. Margaret Mary James, 31 July 1963, 2 sons. *Education:* BSc, University of Nottingham, 1955-58; PhD, University of Reading, 1958-61. *Appointments:* Research Associate, University of Reading, 1961-65; Lecturer, 1965-71, Reader, 1971-77, Professor, 1977-, University of Lancaster. *Memberships:* Council of Society for Experimental Biology. *Publications:* Co-author of Physiology of Stomata (with H Meidner), 1968; An editor of the monthly journal The New Phytologist. Contributor of about 100 scientific publications. *Honours:* Appointed to Personal Chair, University of Lancaster, 1977. *Hobbies:* Cricket; Philately; Hill walking. *Address:* Wallace Lane, Forton, Lancashire, England.

MANSINI, Norman James, b. 5 Oct. 1924, Brisbane, Australia. Commonwealth Conciliation & Arbitration Commissioner. m. Marcella Law, 23 Oct. 1948, 1 son, 3 daughters. *Education:* Associate Australian Society of Accountants. *Appointments:* Deputy Industrial Registrar (Queensland), Commonwealth Industrial Court and Commission, 1955-70; Conciliator, 1970-72, Commissioner, 1972-, Commonwealth Conciliation & Arbitration Commission. *Memberships:* Former Vice-President and Committee, Industrial Relations Society of Queensland. *Hobbies:* Golf; Horse Racing; Gardening. *Address:* 21 Oxford Street, Wavell Heights, Brisbane, Queensland, 4012, Australia.

MANSOOR, Abdul Majeed Mohamed, b. 23 Nov. 1937, Ratnapura, Sri Lanka. Chartered Accountant. m. Fathima Saniha, 9 Feb. 1966, 2 daughters. *Education:* BA, Degree in Economics, University of Ceylon, 1962; Associate Member of Institute of Chartered Accounts of Sri Lanka, 1970. *Appointments:* Teacher, Sri Sumana University College; Audit Trainee, Burah Hathy and Company; Senior Accountant, Ceylon Plywoods Corporation; Chief Accountant, Co-operative Wholesale Establishment; Senior Accountant, Saudi Research & Development Corporation Ltd. *Hobbies:* Reading; Bridge; Table tennis. *Address:* 14 Dickman's Road, Colombo, 5, Sri Lanka.

MANSOOR, Mallikarjun, b. 31 Dec. 1910, Mansoor Village, Dharwar Taluka, Dharwar District, Karnataka State. Vocal Musician. m. S Gangawa, 25 Mar. 1920, 1 son, 7 daughters. *Education:* Obtained early training in music under the guidance of the Late Neelakantha Buwa of Miraj; Had intensive training under the well-known musicians Nanjikhan and Brujikhan, sons of Music Wizard Ustad Alladiakhan of Jaipur Gharana. *Appointments:* Performances given all over India from AIR Stations including several National Programmes of Music and Radio Sangeet Sammelans; Worked as Sangeet Salahakar for Dharwar, Pune, Bombay, Bangalore AIR Stations for about Ten years from 1960-; Has given unnumerable Music Performances in well-known Music Organisations all over India; At present Honorary Director, Institute of Music and Faculty of fine Arts, Karnatak University, Dharawar. *Honours:* Honoured by The Sangeet Nataka Academy of the Karnataka State twice in 1962 and 1964; Was conferreed Padmashree, 1970 and Padmabhushan, 1975; D.Litt degree honoris causa, in recognition of the yeomen service and contribution to the field of Music, by The Karnataka University, 1975. *Address:* Shri-Mrutumya, AIR Road, Dharwar, Karnataka.

MANTOVANI, Ennio M, b. 29 Aug. 1932, Riva S/G Trento, Italy. Roman Catholic Priest. *Education:* Philosophy, 1952-54; Theology, 1954-58; Missiology, 1958-62; Doctor Degree. *Appointments:* Bush Missionary, Highlands of New Guinea, 1962-77; Director, Melanesian Institute for Pastoral & Socio-Economic Service, 1977-. *Memberships:* Internationales Institut für missionswissenschaft-liche Forshungen, Bonn, West Germany; Institutum Missiologicum Societatis Verbi Divini, St Augustin, Techny (Illinois), Buenos Aires.

Publications: Several articles in Point, Catalyst and Verbum on missiological issues. *Address:* The Melanesian Institute, PO Box 571, Goroka EHP, Papua New Guinea.

MANUELI, Paul Fanifau, b. 30 Jan. 1934, Rotuma, Fiji. Company Director. m. Lydia Marian Pickering, 22 Feb. 1958, 1 son, 1 daughter. *Education:* Royal Military Academy, Sandhurst, UK; New Zealand Army Schools; Australian Army Staff College. *Appointments:* Held various military appointments culminating in promotion to Colonel, 1974, and appointment as Commander, Royal Fiji Military Forces, 1955-74; Seconded to Government Administration as District Officer, Rotuma, 1960; Retired, 1979; Manager, Planning and Marketing, 1979, Manager, Special Projects, 1980, Manager, 1981, Director, 1981, British Petroleum South West Pacific Limited, Fiji. *Memberships:* Fellow, Australian Institute of Management; Fiji St John Council; Salvation Army Advisory Board; Fiji Club; Defence Club; Fiji Golf Club. *Honours:* OBE, Military Division, 1974. *Hobbies:* Gardening; Golf. *Address:* 1 Deovji Street, Tamavua, Suva, Fiji.

MANYONI (née Arend), Angelika Felizitas, b. 8 May 1942, Leipzig, Germany. Teacher. m. J.R. Manyoni (Separated), 1 son. *Education:* English and Russian Language and Literature: Staatsexamen, University of Köln, Federal Republic of Germany, 1962-68; MA: German Language and Literature, Carleton University, Ottawa, Canada, 1974-77; D.Phil., German Literature, Somerville College, Oxford University, UK, 1977-81. *Appointments:* Assistant Mistress, German, Rowan High School, London, UK, 1969-71; Part-time Teacher of Russian, Adult Education Centre, Merton, London, UK, 1970-71; Sessional Lecturer of German, Carleton University, Ottawa, Canada, 1972-77; Senior German Teacher, Prince William School, Oundle, UK, 1977-. *Memberships:* Canadian Association of University Teachers of German. *Publications:* Langzeilentradition in Walthers Lyrik, Germanic Studies in America, 1980. *Honours:* Carleton University Graduate Scholarship, 1975-76; Ontario Graduate Scholarship, 1976-77; Canada Council Doctoral Fellowship, 1977-79; SSHRCC Doctoral Fellowship, 1979-81. *Address:* Somerville College, Oxford OX2 6HD, England.

MARA, Rt. Hon. Ratu Sir Kamisese Kapaiwai Tuimacilai, b. 13 May 1920. Prime Minister of Fiji; Hereditary High Chief of the Lau Islands. m. Adi Lady Lala Roko Tui Dreketi, 1951, 3 sons, 5 daughters. *Education:* Otago University, New Zealand; MA., Wadham College, Oxford, UK, 1971; Diploma, Economics and Social Administration, London School of Economics, UK. *Appointments:* Administrative Officer, Colonial Service, Fiji, 1950; Fijian MLC, 1953-, and MEC, 1959-61; Member for Natural Resources and Leader of Government business; Alliance Party, 1964-66 (Founder of Party); Chief Minister and member of Council of Minister, Fiji, 1967. *Honours:* Hon. Dr. of Laws, University of Guam, 1969; Hon. LL.D.: University of Otago, New Zealand, 1973; New Delhi, 1975; Hon. DPolSc Korea, 1978; Hon. Dr. Tokai University, 1980; Honorary Doctorate, University of the South Pacific, 1980; Grand Cross, Order of Lion, Senegal, 1975; Order of Diplomatic Service Merit, Korea, 1978; PC., 1973; KBE., 1969; OBE., 1961. *Hobbies:* Athletics; Cricket; Rugby; Football; Golf; Fishing. *Address:* 11 Battery Road, Suva, Fiji.

MARAIKKADAN, Manickavasagam, b. 3 Aug. 1935, Madras, India. Bank Executive. m. Vimala, 24 Apr. 1964, 2 daughters. *Education:* MA., 1957, BL., 1966, Madras University, India; Certified Associate of Indian Institute of Bankers, 1963. *Appointments:* Madras State Coop Bank, Madras, India, 1957; Officer, Indian Overseas Bank, Salem, India, 1958-60; Joint Accountant, Indian Overseas Bank, Central Office, India, 1960-63; Sub-Manager, Indian Overseas Bank, Esplanade Branch, India, 1963-64; Industrial Assistant Superintendent, Industrial Cell, Indian Overseas Bank, 1964-71; Joint Manager, 1971-73, Manager, 1973-79, Indian Overseas Bank, Hong Kong branch; Manager, Oman International Finance Limited, Hong Kong (Wholly owned Sub. of Bank of Oman Limited, Dubai), 1979-. *Memberships:* Hong Kong Economic Association; Hong Kong Bankers Club; India Association, Hong Kong; Tamil Association, Hong Kong. *Publications:* Contributor of articles for publication in Tamil and English in journals in India and Hong Kong. *Hobbies:* Tennis; Community and Social Service. *Address:* Flat 4B, 21st

Block, Baguio Villa, Upper Flats, Victoria Road, Pokfulam, Hong Kong.

MARCANTONIO, Stephen Richard George, b. 16 Apr. 1949, Ealing, London, England. Teacher. *Education:* BA.(Hons.), Geography, University of Hull, UK, 1968-71; Post-graduate Certificate of Education, Northern Counties College, Newcastle-upon-Tyne, UK, 1972-73. *Appointments:* Teacher, Moffat Academy, Scotland. *Memberships:* Past Hon. Secretary, Moffat Pipe Band; Moffat Gala Committee; Past member, Moffat Community Council; ROC; Selkirk Plodders and Moffat Plodders. *Publications:* Wendover Arm of the Grand Union Canal, unpublished; Theory and Practice of Humanities Curriculum Project, unpublished. *Hobbies:* Hill walking; Politics; Reading; Curling. *Address:* 1 Beech Grove, Moffat, Dumfriesshire, DG10 9RS, Scotland.

MARCHANT, Neil Michael, b. 2 Nov. 1946, Melbourne, Victoria, Australia. Public Servant; Teacher of Art. m. Yvonne Turton, 7 Feb. 1970. *Appointments:* Engineering and Water Supply Department; Department of Further Education. *Memberships:* President, South Australian Military Preservation Society; President, Northern Districts Society of Arts; South Australia Antique and Historical Arms Association; Associate, Royal South Australian Society of Arts; United Services Institute; Returned Servicemen's League. *Publications:* Essays on South Australian History; Guide to South Australian Regiments and Battalions, Pre 1901; various Humorous short stories; Complete History of South Australian Military Forces upto the Present, (in preparation). *Creative Works:* Various Painting and Sketching Exhibitions. *Honours:* 3 awards of Merit, Royal South Australia Society of Arts, 1975. *Hobbies:* South Australian Military History; Weapon and Uniform Collecting; Aboriginal History; Pre-Historic Excavation; Japanese Sword Repairs and Valuation; Sculpture; Historical Writing. *Address:* 10 Player Drive, Fairview Park, South Australia, 5126.

MARCUS-JONES, Walter Sydney, b. 3 July 1926, Freetown Sierra Leone. Barrister-at-Law; University Lecturer. m. Anne Joan Turner, 12 Jan. 1963, 3 daughters. *Education:* Certificate in Social Science and Administration, London School of Economics, UK, 1956; LL.B., London University, UK, 1959; Barrister-at-Law, Gray's Inn, London, UK, 1959; LL.B.(Hons.), University of Birminghamm, UK, 1960; LL.M., 1962, JSD., 1965, Yale University, USA. *Appointments:* Barrister and Solicitor, Supreme Court of Sierra Leone; Lecturer and Senior Lecturer, Dean, Faculty of Economic and Social Studies, Fourah Bay College, University of Sierra Leone. *Memberships:* African Bar Association; Past President, Sierra Leone Bar Association; President, Sierra Leone Association of Professional Organisations; President, National Association for Drug Abuse Control; Deputy Commissioner and Commissioner for Legal Affairs, Sierra Leone Boy Scouts Association; National Chairman, World Peace Through Law; Holdsworth Club; Rotary Club of Freetown; Freetown Junior Dinner Club; Freetown Aqua Sports Club. *Publications:* Leading Cases in Sierra Leone (with A Milner, FC Tuboku-Metzger; The Legal Order, Contemporary Social Change and the Development of Law, (with Brokensha, Crowder); Constitutions of the World, (with GFA Sawyer); The Fundamental Rights Provisions of the Sierra Leone Independence Constitution, 1961, unpublished; Legal History and Constitutional Change in Sierra Leone 1787 to 1971, unpublished; Articles include: The Common Law in Sierra Leone; Law Reform in Sierra Leone; Distinguished Sierra Leoneans; Medico-Legal problems. *Honours:* Prize for Moots and Debates, University of Birmingham; BBC Prize for Short Story writing; Ford Foundation Fellow, 1964-65; British Council Bursar, 1952; Sierra Leone Government Scholar, 1954-56; African Educator's Grant, African American Institute, 1976; Commonwealth Foundation Grant, 1978. *Hobbies:* Swimming; Aquatic Sports; Photography. *Address:* K29 Fourah Bay College, Freetown, Sierra Leone.

MARGHI, Bukar Petrol, b. 8 Nov. 1932, Matangale, Damboa LGA, Borno State, Nigeria. Business. m. 11 children. *Education:* Institute of Administration, Ahmadu Bello University, Zaria, Nigeria, 1955-56; Leadership Training College, Cameroons, 1956-57; International Press Institute, University of Lagos, Nigeria, 1965-66. *Appointments:* Local Government Inspector, Borno Emirate, 1955-58; Staff Reporter, Daily Times, Lagos, Nigeria, 1959-63; Provincial Editor, Daily Express, Plateau, Jos, 1963-66; Northern Editor, Daily Times, Kaduna/Kano, 1967-69; Commercial Manager, Daily Times, Northern States, 1969-73; Managing Director, 1973-78, Chairman/Managing Director, 1978-, Marghi Enterprises Limited, Kano, Nigeria. *Memberships:* Marghi Cultural Society; Borno State Branch, Nigerian Chamber of Commerce, Maiduguri; International Chamber of Commerce Committee, Paris; Kano Club, Kano; Le Cercla Club, Kano; Founder, Marghi Tribal Union; Head of delegation to the 1958 Minority Commission appointed by British Government ot ally the fears of the minority people in Nigeria. *Hobbies:* Hunting; Reading; Debates. *Address:* 19 Abaaji Damboa Road, Gamboru Ward, Maiduguri, Nigeria.

MARGOLIS, William, b. 12 Dec. 1913, Kovno, Litjuania. Company Director. m. Sarah Rabinowitz, 19 Jan. 1941, 1 son, 1 daughter. *Education:* MA.(Econ.)., B.Com., University of Cape Town, South Africa. *Appointments:* Director of Companies including: Olivine Industries (Pvt.) Limited, Salisbury, H. Margolis & Co. Limited, Schweppes (Central Africa) Limited, Standard Bank Limited, Central Africa Building Society, Bard Discount House Limited; Past Chairman, Grain Marketing Board; Commission of Enquiry into Protection of Secondary Industries in Southern Rhodesia Memorial Tariff Committee; Programming Officer, Department of Supply during War. *Memberships:* Delegation to Commonwealth Forums in London and UN Trade Organisation in Geneva; Delegation which negotiated Customs Union (Interim) Agreement with Union of South Africa; Commission of Inquiry into Transport Services of Greater Sby and Greater Byo; Commission of Inquiry into Urban African Affairs and Commission of Inquiry into Railway Rating Structure; Cotton Working Party; President, Sby. Ch. of Com., 1960-61; Past member, Tobacco Export Promotion Cel. of Rhodesia; Federal delegate to Conference of African Resources in New York, 1962; World Food Congress, Washington, 1963; Rotary Club; Past Chairman, Agricultural Marketing Authority. *Honours:* MBE., 1950; OBE., 1957. *Hobby:* Golf. *Address:* 13 Lezard Avenue, PO Belverdere, Salisbury, Zimbabwe.

MARK, John, b. 6 Nov. 1928, Czechoslovakia. Company Director. m. Margaret Jane Renshaw, 14 Dec. 1977, 1 son, 1 daughter. *Education:* Hotel Academy (at University level); Economics, part time, University of Bratislava, Czechoslovakia; 2 year management course, RMIT, Melbourne, Australia. *Appointments:* Founder and Managing Director, Brick Securities Limited, established 1969 as Manager of Unit Property and Mortgage Trusts, Superannuation funds, friendly societies, portfolio approx. A$40 million; Managing Director, Brick Securities Finance Group Limited, formed recently as holding company with intention to list on Stock Exchange; Managing Director, Homex Group Pty. Limited. *Memberships:* Chairman, Mortgage Bankers Association of Australia; Fellow, Australian Institute of Management; President, Property Owners Association of Victoria; Fellow, Real Estate and Stock Institute of Victoria; Senior member, National Association of Review Appraisers, USA; Royal Automobile Association of Victoria; Eildon Boat Club; Immediate Past President, Australian Alpine Club; Past Chairman, Patscherkofel Ski Lodge. *Publications:* Occasional articles on Mortgage Banking in various daily newspapers; Regular column on investment advice in Australian Pensioner, Senior Citizens Gazette, Vital Retirement and Property Owners Journal. *Hobbies:* Skiing; Boating; Tennis. *Address:* Unit 4, 23 Wallace Avenue, Toorak, Victoria 3124, Australia.

MARKS, John Hedley Douglas, (Sir), b. 8 May 1916, Sydney, Australia. Chartered Accountant. m. Judith Norma Glenwright 8 May 1941, 2 daughters. *Education:* Chartered Accountant (FCA) and Secretary. *Appointments:* Founder, Development Finance Corporation Limited; Chairman of: Development Holdings Limited; Japan Australia Investment Company Limited; Vice Chairman, Australian Consolidated Industries Ltd.; Brambles Industries Limited; Garratt's Limited; Reinsurance Company of Australasia Limited; Director of: Alcan Australia Limited; Borg-Warner (Australia) Limited; Chep International Finance SA; Chep International Investments S A; Delfin Discount Company Limited; West Lakes Limited; Commissioner, Electricity Commission of New South Wales, 1966-81; Australian

Manufacturing Council, 1977-79; Chairman, Committee of Inquiry into State Taxation (New South Wales), 1975-76; Committee of Community Health Services, 1968-69; Chairman, Prince Henry Hospital and Prince of Wales Hospital; Governor, Queenwood School; Trustee: The Shore Foundation and the National Parks and Wildlife Foundation (NSW) 1969-81; Council, Macquarie University, 1963-76. *Memberships:* Fellow of: Institute of Chartered Accountants in Australia; International Banker Association; Australian Society of Accountants; Australian Instutute of Management. Institute of Directors in Australia; Development Corporation of New South Wales, 1966-72. *Publications:* Number of articles on business topics. *Honours:* Knight Bachelor, 1972; CBE, 1966. *Hobbies:* Golf; Fishing; Painting. *Address:* 6b Raglan Street, Mosman, NSW, Australia.

MARKS, Keith David, b. Melbourne, Australia. Deputy President. m. Estelle Clare Coady, 23 Nov. 1949, 3 sons, 1 daughter. *Education:* Bachelor of Commerce, 1941, Bachelor of Arts, 1947, Bachelor of Laws, 1963, Melbourne University. *Appointments:* Barrister at Law, Victorian Bar, 1964; Queens Counsel, 1976; Deputy President, Australian Conciliation & Arbitration Commission, 1980-. *Publications:* Various papers on Australian Industrial Relations. *Hobbies:* Music; Tennis. *Address:* 18 Willoby Avenue, Glen Iris, 3146, Victoria, Australia.

MARKS, Kenneth Henry, b. 10 Sept. 1924, Melbourne, Australia. Judge. m. Sheila Marion Harbison, 14 Jan. 1955, 2 daughters. *Education:* McEGS, 1930-40; LL.B, 1947; BA, 1952. *Appointments:* RAAF, 1943-46; Victoria Bar, 1950-77; Judge, Victorian Supreme Court. *Memberships:* Chairman, Victorian Bar Association, 1976-77. *Hobby:* Equitation. *Address:* 56 Burke Road North, E Ivanhoe, Victoria, Australia.

MARLES, Donald McLeod, b. 12 Dec. 1927, Warwick, Queensland, Australia. Headmaster. m. Fay Surtees Pearce 7 Aug. 1951, 1 son, 3 daughters. *Education:* Bachelor of Science, 1949; Bachelor of Education, University of Queensland, 1951. *Appointments:* Assistant Teacher, Maryborough Boys' High School, Queensland 1950-51; Assistant Master, Brighton Grammar School, Victoria, 1953-54; Assistant Master, Geelong Grammar School, Corio, 1955; Assistant Master, St Edward's School, Oxford, 1956-57; Assistant Master, 1958-62, Housemaster, Perryhouse, Geelong Grammar School, Corio, 1963-71; Assistant Master, Wellington College, Crowthorne, 1972; Deputy Headmaster and Master of Corio, 1973-78; Headmaster, Trinity Grammar School, Kew, 1979-. *Memberships:* The Australian College of Education. *Hobbies:* Reading; Gardening; Sports; Travel. *Address:* 49 Wellington Street, Kew, Victoria 3101, Australia.

MARRE, (Sir), Alan Samuel, b. 25 Feb. 1914, London, England. British Parliamentary Commissioner for Administration (retired). m. Romola Mary Gilling, 24 Dec. 1943, 1 son, 1 daughter. *Education:* BA., Trinity Hall, Cambridge, 1932-35; John Stewart of Rannoch Scholar, 1935. *Appointments:* British Civil Servant, 1936-71; employed mainly in Ministry of Health (later Department of Health and Social Security) but for short periods also in Ministry of Labour (later Department of Employment); Second Permanent Secretary, Department of Health and Social Security, 1968-71; Parliamentary Commissioner for Administration, 1971-76; Health Service Commissioner, 1973-76; Chairman, Age Concern, England, 1976-79; Vice-Chairman, Advisory Committee on Distinction Awards, 1979-. *Memberships:* Athenaeum Club; MCC. *Publications:* Various articles and contributions to publications, mainly about Ombudsmen. *Honours:* KCB, 1970. *Hobbies:* Walking; Reading; Gardening. *Address:* 44 The Vale, London, NW11 8SG, England.

MARRIOTT, John Russell, b. 8 Mar. 1923, Melbourne, Australia. Government Tourist Officer. m. Pamela Margaret Johnson, 1 son, 2 daughters. *Education:* Certified Aircraft Ground Engineer (Electrical), 1947; Diplomas in Marketing, 1952, Advertising, 1954, Business Administration, 1956. *Appointments:* Trans ,Australia Airlines Ground Eningeer, 1946-48; Technician, Commonwealth Lighthouse Service, 1948-57; Marketing Director, Hemingway Robertson Institute, 1957-68; Regional Director, Australian Tourist Commission, 1968-79; Government Tourist Officer, King-

dom of Tonga, 1979-. *Memberships:* Past President (State, 1960-62, Federal, 1962-64), Australian Marketing Institute; Air Force Association (State 1964-66, also Federal Vice-President, 1966-74; Foundation President, Junior Australian American Association, 1958-59; Vice-President, International Marketing Federation, 1966-68; Trustee RAAF Welfare Trust Fund, 1971-77. *Publications:* Author of numerous articles on management, training, staff development marketing and tourism. Published in Australia, New Zealand, USA, Japan, Philippines, India and South Africa. *Honours:* Honorary life member Australian American Association; Honorary Fellow, Australian Marketing Institute; Honorary Member, South African Institute of Marketing; Certificates of Merit, Air Force Association and Market Research Society of Australia. *Hobbies:* Vintage Cars; Collecting Antiques; Gardening. *Address:* 70 Vuna Road, Sopu, Kingdom of Tonga.

MARSDEN, Arthur Charles Newman, b. 1 Nov. 1925, Atherton, Queensland, Australia. Prosthodontist. m. Olive Millicent Hooper, 17 Oct. 1958, 3 sons, 1 daughter. *Education:* Bachelor of Dental Science, University of Queensland, 1947; Registered Specialist, Prosthodontics, Queensland Dental Board, 1960; Fellow, International College of Dentists, 1978. *Appointments:* Brisbane Dental Hospital, Queensland, 1947-57; General Practice, Dentristry, Brisbane, 1957-78; Specialist Practice, Prosthodontics, Brisbane, 1979-; Part-time Staff, University of Queensland Dental School, 1976-; Appointed Dental Consultant HQ 1 Military District, 1976-, Rank Lieutenant Colonel. *Memberships:* President, 1975, Australian Dental Association, Queensland Branch; President, 1974-75, Australian Society of Prosthodontists, Queensland Branch; Federation Dentaire Internationale, Pierre Fouchard Academy. *Publications:* Article in Australian Dental Journal. *Hobbies:* Music; Bushwalking. *Address:* 91 Buena Vista Avenue, Coorparoo, Queensland 4151, Australia.

MARSDEN, Francis William, b. 19 Dec. 1935, Charters Towers, Queensland. Orthopaedic Surgeon. m. Patricia Anne Cary, 21 Dec. 1960, 2 sons, 1 daughter. *Education:* MB, BS, St. Johns College, University of Queensland, 1960; FRCS (Edinburgh), 1968; FRACS, 1970. *Appointments:* Surgical Training Posts at Princess Alexandra Hospital, Brisbane, Royal National Orthopaedic Hospital, London and, Prince of Wales Hospital Sydney; Research Fellow, Instructor in Orthopaedics, University of Washington; Currently Visiting Orthopaedic Surgeon, Royal Prince Alfred Hospital, Prince of Wales Children's Hospital and Repatriation General Hospital, Sydney; Clinical Lecturer in Orthopaedics and Traumatic Surgery, University of Sydney. *Memberships:* Australian Orthopaedic Association; NSW, Board of Studies Australian Medical Association; Medical Advisory Committee, Australian Council in the Rehabilitation of the Disabled. Royal Zoological Society of New South Wales. *Publications:* Various papers and abstracts on Surgery in Medical Journals. *Honours:* Queensland State Fellowship in Medicine, 1958; Post Graduate Foundation Travelling Fellowship, University of Sydney, 1970; Joint Coal Board Travelling Fellowship, 1970. *Hobbies:* Gardening; Photography. *Address:* 15a Bonnefin Road, Hunters Hill 2110, New South Wales, Australia.

MARSH, Iris May, b. 10 July 1914, St. Kitts, West Indies. Educational Administration. *Education:* BA, 1957; Post Graduate Certificate in Education, London, 1959; Diploma in Education, London, 1961; MEd, 1971; MA, 1972; PhD, in Education, 1975. *Appointments:* Acting Principal and Senior Assistant Teacher, 1940-57; Head of English Department, Secondary School, 1959-63; School Principal, 1963-79; Secondment to the Bermuda Ministry of Education with responsibility for Developing a Principals' Hand Book for Educational System, 1979-80. *Memberships:* Fellow, Royal Commonwealth Society; The Berkeley Educational Society; President, Queen's University, Alumni SAssociation, Bermuda Branch; 1st Vice-President, Business & Professional Women's Association of Bermuda. *Publications:* Treatise and papers presented at educational conferences. *Honours:* Self Portrait presented at Banquet by Parent/Teacher Association for Outstanding Service to Education, 1979; Merit Award from the Governor of Bermuda, 1977. *Hobbies:* Reading; Travel; Audio-Visual Activities; Drama; Photography; Music (Vocal & Instrumental); Writing. *Address:*

Marsh View, West Side Road, Somerset 9, PO Box 275, Bermuda.

MARSH, Loise Matilda (Mrs), b. 31 Oct. 1928, Victoria, British Columbia, Canada. Zoologist. m. Brian à Beckett Marsh, 17 Feb 1950 (divorced), 1 son, 1 daughter. *Education:* BA(Hons), 1950, MA, 1956, University of Western Australia. *Appointments:* Graduate Assistant (Zoology), 1950-53, Part-time Demonstrator, 1954-60, 1968-69, University of Western Australia; Part-time biology teacher, Suva Grammar School, Fiji, 1963-67; Part-time, Graduate Assistant, 1970-73, Assistant Curator, Mollusc Department, 1974-77, Curator, 1977-78, Western Australia Museum; Curator, Department of Marine Invertebrate Zoology, WA Museum, 1979-. *Memberships:* Royal Society of Western Australia; Australian Marine Sciences Association; Western Australian Naturalists Club. *Publications:* Numerous contributions to Professional Journals including: Coral Reef Asteroids of Palau, Caroline Islands, 1977; (with BR Wilson), Coral Reef communities at the Houtman Abrolhos, Western Australia, in a zone biogeographic overlap, 1979. *Hobbies:* Photography; Scuba Diving; Bushwalking. *Address:* 6 Conon Road, Applecross, Western Australia 6153.

MARSHALL, David Saul, b. 12 Mar. 1908, Singapore. Ambassador. m. Jean Davie Gray, 2 Apr. 1961, 1 son, 3 daughters. *Education:* LLB University of London; Barrister-at-Law, Middle Temple, London 1937. *Appointments:* Advocate and Solicitor, High Court of Singapore 1937-78; Chief Minister of Singapore 1955-56; Member, Singapore Legislatie Assembly 1961-63; Ambassador Extraordinary and Plenipotentiary of Singapore 1978-. *Memberships:* Cercle de l'Union Interalliee, Paris. *Honours:* Datuk Kurnia Johan Pahlawan, Sultan of Pahang, Malaysia; Chevalier de la Legion d'Honneur, France 1978. Hobby: Chess. *Address:* 79 Rue De Faisanderie, 75116 Paris, France.

MARSHALL, Edmund Ian, b. 31 May 1940, Manchester, England. Member of Parliament. m. Margaret Pamela Antill, 19 Apr. 1969, 1 daughter. *Education:* Magdalen College, Oxford, 1958-61; PhD, Liverpool University, 1961-65; MA, 1965. *Appointments:* University Lecturer, 1962-66; Mathematician in Industry, 1967-71; Member of Parliament (Labour) for Goole Constituency, 1971-; Parliamentary Private Secretary to the Home Secretary, 1976-79. *Memberships:* World Methodist Council, 1971; Reform Club. *Publications:* Europe: What Next? co-author, 1968; Parliament & The Public, 1982. *Hobbies:* Genealogy; Music. *Address:* House of Commons, London, SW1A OAA, England.

MARSHALL, Rt. Hon. Sir John Ross, b. 5 Mar. 1912, Wellington. New Zealand Lawyer; Politician. m. Margaret Livingston, 1944, 2 sons, 2 daughters. *Education:* Victoria University College, University of New Zealand, BA, LLM. *Appointments:* Barrister & Solictor of Supreme Court of New Zealand, 1936; New Zealand Expeditionary Force, Pacific and Italy, 1941-46; Member of Parliament, 1946-75; Lecturer in Law, Victoria University College, 1948-5, Visiting Fellow, 1975-; Minister Assisting the Prime Minister and Minister for State Advances Corporation, Public Trust Office and Census and Statistics, 1949-54; Minister of Health, 1951-54, of Information and Publicity, 1951-57; Minister of Justice and Attorney General, 1954-57; Deputy Prime Minister, 1957; Deputy Leader of Opposition, 1957-60; Deputy Prime and Minister of Overseas Trade, 1960-72; Minister of Customs, 1960-61; Minister of Industries and Commerce, 1960-69; Attorney General, 1969-71; Minister of Labour and Immigration, 1969-72; Prime Minister, 1972; Leader of Oppostion, 1973-74; Attended various Trade, Economic & EEC Negotiations, conferences between the years, 1953-72; Consultant Partner, Buddle, Anderson, Kent and Company; Hon. Bencher Gray's Inn, 1973. *Memberships:* Chairman of numerous industries; Visiting Fellow Victoria University of Wellington; Advisory Council, World Peace through Law. *Publications:* Editor, Reform of Parliament; Law Relating to Water Courses; Children's Stories: Dr. Duffer and the Lost City; Dr. Duffer and the Treasure Hunt. *Honours:* Hon. LLD; Member Nat. Party, Leader, 1972-74; Companion of Honour; Knight Grand Cross of th Order of the British Empire; Privy Councillor. *Hobbies:* Golf; Fishing; Breeding Connemara ponies. *Address:* 22 Fitzroy Street, Wellington I, New Zealand.

MARSHALL, (Oshley) Roy, b. 21 Oct. 1920, Barbados, West Indies. Vice-Chancellor. m. 15 Sept. 1945, 1 son, 3 daughters. *Education:* Harrison College, Barbados, West Indies; Pembroke College, Cambridge; University College, London, Barbados Scholar, 1938; Barrister-at-Law, Inner Temple, 1947; BA, 1945; MA, 1948. *Appointments:* Assistant Lecturer, 1946-48, Lecturer, 1948-56, Sub-Dean Faculty of Law, 1949-56, University College, London; Professor of Law & Head of Department of Law, University of Sheffield, 1956-69; On secondment to University of Ife, Ibadan, Nigeria as Professor of Law & Dean of Faculty of Law, 1963-65; Vice-Chancellor, University of West Indies, 1969-74; Secretary-General Committee of Vice-Chancellors & Principals, 1974-79; Vice-Chancellor the University of Hull, 1979-. *Memberships:* Vice-Chairman of the Governing Body of the Commonwealth Institute; Chairman, Commonwealth Education Liaison Committee; Council of the Asscoiation of Commonwealth Universities. *Publications:* The Assignment of Choses in Action, 1950; A Casebook on Trusts (with JA Nathan), 1967; Theobald on Wills, 1963. *Honours:* Honorary LLD Sheffield, 1972; West Indies, 1976; Honorary Professor, University of Hull, 1980. *Hobbies:* Racing; Cricket. *Address:* 4 Hull Road, Cottingham, N Humberside, HU16 4QB, England.

MARSHALL, Thomas David Colbeck Hayden, b. 23 Feb. 1939, Welland, Ontario, Canada. Medical Practitioner and Lawyer. m. 30 Dec. 1961, 3 sons, 2 daughters. *Education:* MD, University of Toronto 1963; LLB, Osgoode Hall, Toronto 1970; Studies in Law and Professional Privilege, Oxford University, England 1974-75. *Appointments:* Medical Practitioner, Marshall Clinic, Cayuga, Ontario, 1964; Coroner 1965-; Lecturer in Law and Medicine, University of Toronto 1971-72; Special Lecturer and Assistant Professor, McMaster University, Hamilton, Ontario 1977-; Lecturer, University of Windsor Law School, Windsor, Ontario 1980-; Partner, Marshall, Thibideau and Rous, Federal Building, Cayuga, Ontario. *Memberships:* President, Canadian College of Legal Medicine; Major, CFMS; Canadian Institute of Internation Affairs; Empire Club of Canada. *Publications:* Author, The Physician and Canadian Law 1974; Inquest Law in Canada 1980; Patients' Rights 1976; Contributing editor to Canadian Family Physician 1974-75; Austor: several articles on Law and Medicine in professional journals. Hobby: Flying. *Address:* The Hermitage, Cayuga, Ontario, Canada.

MARSHALL, Victor Christopher, b. 1 Aug. 1920, Sunderland, England. Chemical Engineer: Safety Expert. m. Joan Marjorie Dale, 2 Apr. 1947, 2 sons, 1 daughter. *Education:* Derby Technical College, 1947-49; MPhil, Bradford University, 1965. *Appointments:* Shift Chemist, British Celanese, Derby; Works Chemist, Theodore St Just, Manchester; Senior Design Engineer, Simon Carves Limited, Stockport; Senior Lecturer, Bradford University; Director of Safety Services, Bradford University. *Memberships:* Fellow: Institution of Chemical Engineers; Institute of Energy; Safety & Reliability Society; Royal Society of Arts; Associate, Institution of Occupational Safety & Health; Chartered Engineer; Member, Major Hazards Committee of Health & Safety Commission. *Publications:* Author, Disaster at Flixborough, 1979; Author numerous papers and technical reports. *Address:* 5 Ivy Road, Shipley, West Yorkshire, BD18 4JY, England.

MARSHALL, Walter Charles, b. 5 Mar. 1932, Rumney, Wales. Nuclear Physicist. m. Ann Vivienne Sheppard, 12 Apr. 1955, 1 son, 1 daughter. *Education:* BSc, University of Birmingham 1952; PhD 1954. *Appointments:* Deputy Director, Atomic Energy Research Establishment 1966-68; Director 1968-75; Deputy Chairman, UKAEA 1975-81, Chairman, 1981-; *Memberships:* Board of National Research Development Corporation 1969-75; Chief Scientist, Department of Energy 1974-77. *Publications:* The Theory of Neutron Scattering, 1971. *Honours:* CBE 1973; Fellow of Royal Society 1971; Foreign Associate of National Academy of Engineering US, 1979; 1964 Maxwell Medallist, Glazebrook Med of Institute of Physics 1975. *Hobbies:* Origami; Gardening. *Address:* 11 Charles II Street, London SW1Y 4QP, England.

MARTEN, Harry Neil, b. 3 Dec. 1916, London. Politician. m. 14 July 1944, 1 son, 2 daughters. *Education:* Rossall School Law Society, Qualified Solicitor, 1939.

Appointments: Solicitor, 1939-40; HM Forces (Major), 1940-46; Solicitor, 1946-47; HM Foreign Service, 1947-57; Member of Parliament, 1959-; Junior Minister of Aviation, 1962-64; Minister of State, Foreign & Commonwealth Office & Minister for Overseas Development, 1979-. *Memberships:* Carlton Club, London. *Honours:* Croix De Guerre; Norwegian Order of St Olav, 1st Class; Norwegian War Medal. *Hobbies:* Tennis; Painting; Mountaineering. *Address:* Swalcliffe House, Nr. Banbury, Oxfordshire, England.

MARTIN, Arthur Ronald, b. 6 Dec. 1904, Eastbourne, Sussex, England. Creative Designer, Artist and Consultant. m. Hephzibah Relf 14 May 1932, 1 son. *Education:* Scholarship, Eastbourne School of Art, 1921-24; Studied Art and Graphic Design, Posters, Packaging, Book Jackets, Typography, Photography and Reproduction Processes, Lond 1925-34. *Appointments:* London Art Studios and Advertising Agencies, 1925-30; Design Studios, Leading Colour Printers, London Studios, 1939-45; Ministry of Supply, Chislehurst, Kent, Draughtsman and Technical Illustrator, 1946-54; Free lance Practice, 1954-65; Formed Company with MRN. Hayward Hayward and Martin Limited, National and Overseas Clients: Crittall, BMC Limited, Sangamo-Weston, Foxboro Yoxall, etc, *Memberships:* Fellow, Royal Society of Arts; Society of Industrial Artists and Designers; Fellow, The Society of Industrial Artists and Designers; Society of Graphic Artists, London; Candidate, Pastel Society, London. *Publications:* Illustrating with the Airbrush, 1965; Wood Engraving, (proposed title), Its Future, in press, 1981; Works Accepted: The Royal Academy of Arts, London; RBA, London; R.I. of Watercolours, Lond, etc. *Honours:* Awarded Book, Admiralty and Ruston—Hornsby Limited, 1963; The Royal Charter and Seal. Society of Industrial Artists and Designers, 1976 Certificate for Outstanding Achievements in the field of Endeavour, 1980. *Hobbies:* Walking; Exhibiting and Lecturing. *Address:* 16 Valverde House, Eaton Gardens, Hove, Sussex, BN3 3TU, England.

MARTIN, Charles Albert, b. 15 June, 1915, Johannesburg, South Africa. Engineer. m. 22 Feb. 1941, 1 son, 2 daughters. *Education:* BSc, Engineering, Witwatersrand, 1940. *Appointments:* Rand Gold Mines, 1932-39; Pilot, Engineer, South African Air Force, 1939-45; Rand Mining Group, 1945-54; Managing Director for Central & Southern Africa, The SKF Ball Bearing Co., 1955-76; Assistant General Manager, Armaments Corporation, 1976-78; Director of Companies & Honorary Tutor, Faculty of Engineering, University of Zimbabwe, 1979-. *Memberships:* Institutions of Mechanical & Electrical Engineers; President, 1976, SA Institute of Mech & Elect. Engineers; Vice-President, 1981, Zimbabwe Institutution of Engineers. *Publications:* Author of over 30 technical papers covering aeronautical, mechanical mining & electrical disciplines; Research on earth leakage protection resulting in present day code of practice in South Africa. *Honours:* Sturrok Premium, 1940; VFP Premium, 1941; Institute Certificated Engineers' special prize, 1944; Victoria Falls and Power Corporation Award, 1951; South African Airways and Harbours Award, 1952; Stevens Award, 1957; Zambian Institution of Engineers award; Rhodesian Institute of Engineers Winquist Award, 1968; South African Institute Certificated Engineers Council Award, 1971. *Hobbies:* Metal engraving; Technical writing. *Address:* 44 Pendennis Road, Mount Pleasant, Salisbury, Zimbabwe.

MARTIN, Ian Archibald Scott, b. 4 May 1922, Adelaide, South Australia. Grazier, Director & Dairy Farmer. m. Dorothy Elizabeth Warwick, 20 May 1950, 1 son, 2 daughters. *Education:* South Australian Institute of Technology (formerly S Australian School of Mine & Industry), 1937-44; Diploma in Wool Classing, 1944. *Appointments:* Wool Classing; Grazing & Dairy Farming; Director, Dairyvale Metro, Cheese & Milk Powder Makers and Milk Processors. *Memberships:* Chairman, Yankalilla District Council, 1975-; Chairman Yankalilla Willunga Pest Plant Board; Appointed by South Australian Minister of Agriculture to S Australia Artificial Breeding Board, 1973; Director Myponga Dairying Society; Appointed by S Australia Minister of Agriculture to Committee of Enquiry into Dairy Herd recording in South Australia, 1980. *Honours:* Queen's Silver Jubilee Medal, 1977; Justice of the Peace. *Hobbies:* Rock & Gem stone collecting; Sport; Fishing; Gardening. *Address:* Box 44, Myponga, 5202, South Australia.

MARTIN, Joseph (Joe) Edward, b. 13 Jan. 1937, Kelvington, Saskatchewan. Management Consultant. m. Sally Ann Dagg, 16 July 1960, 2 sons, 2 daughters. *Education:* BA(Hon), University of Manitoba, 1959; Certified Management Consultant, Institute of Management Consultants of Ontario, 1972. *Appointments:* Investment Department, The Monarch Life Co., 1959; Executive Assistant, Premier, Province of Manitoba, 1961; Consultant, Winnipeg Office, 1966, Senior Consultant, 1968, Partner, 1972, Partner-in-Charge, 1978-, Touche Ross & Partners. *Memberships:* President, Institute of Management Consultants of Ontario, 1981-82; Canadian (Coushiching) Institute on Public Affairs. *Publications:* Bloodshed at Seven Oak's, 1966; Apects of Icelandic Settlement, Manitoba Historical Society, 1980; Ontario's Role and Place in Canadian Confederation, Ontario Economic Council, 1974. *Honours:* Regents Medal for the highest standing in the Fifth Year Honours Arts, 1959. *Hobbies:* Ice hockey; Squash; Tennis; History; Politics. *Address:* 215 Glencairn Avenue, Toronto, Ontario, M4R 1N3, Canada.

MARTIN, Kathryn Jean, b. 8 Mar. 1942, Brisbane, Australia. Senator. *Education:* BA., University of Queensland, Australia, 1964; ASDA., A M E B., 1966. *Appointments:* Mathematics Mistress, Ipswich Girls Grammar School, 1964-66; Administration, University of Queensland, Australia, 1966-74; Senator for Queensland, Australia, 1974-. *Memberships:* Hon. Vice President, National Council of Women, Queensland; Hon. member: Lioness International; Beta Sigma Phi; International Hon. member, ESA Women International; Patron, Queensland Debating Union; Trustee, Queensland Children's Leukemia Society. *Honours:* Life Membership, Young Liberal Movement, Queensland Division, 1964; Queensland Singles Debating Champion, 1966; Outstanding Young Australian of the Year, 1976. *Hobbies:* Gardening; Music; Theatre; Reading; Backgammon. *Address:* Commonwealth Parliament Centre, 295 Ann Street, Brisbane, Queensland 4000, Australia.

MARTIN, Peter Marcus, b. 29 Nov. 1938, Wollongong, New South Wales, Australia. Agricultural Scientist. m. Judith Harrison, 1 Sept. 1966, 1 son, 2 daughters. *Education:* BSc.Agr. 1960, MSc.Agr. 1961, PhD, 1972, Dip.Ed., 1962, University of Sydney. *Appointments:* Lecturer in Botany, University of Sydney, 1963-73; Deputy Principal, Hawkesbury Agricultural College, Richmond, NSW, 1973-75; Executive Member, Advanced Education Board, NSW, 1975; Executive Member, NSW Higher Education Board, 1976-; Deputy Chairman, National Accreditation Authority for Translators and Interpreters, 1978-; Australian Council on Awards in Advanced Education, 1977-; Advisory Committee, International Training Institute, 1979-; Nurses Education Board of NSW, 1975-78; Agricultural Syllabus Committee, Board of Senior School Studues, NSW, 1969-75; Board of Directors, Australian Turf Grass Research Institute, 1971-; Reserve Officer, Citizen Military Forces, Royal Australian Corps of Signals. *Memberships:* Linnean Society of New South Wales; Australian Institutes of Public Administration and Agricultral Science; Association of Applied Biologists, UK. *Publications:* Author of various scientific articles and conference papers related to fields of interest. *Honours:* Junior Post-Graduate Studentship, 1960, Senior, 1962, Commonwealth Scientific and Industrial Research Organisation; Jones Medal, Sydney Teachers College, 1961; E and S Wood Travelling Fellowship of University of Sydney, 1968; JN Young Memorial Orator, Australasian Institute of Radiography, 1977. *Hobbies:* Music; Gardening; Restoring old houses; Collecting old scientific books. *Address:* 15 Merrivale Road, Pymble, New South Wales, 2073, Australia.

MARTIN, Robert Jordan, b. 31 Mar. 1925, Adelaide, Australia. Farmer; Grazier. m. Barbara Ferguson, 20 Aug. 1949, 3 sons. *Appointments:* Self employed: Stud Poll Dount Sheep, 1960-81; Stud South Devon Cattle, 1974-79; Grazer, X Brand Lamb Producer, 1946-81; Delegate from UF & S. ASS Meat Committee to Australia Meat & Livestock Association Conference, Sydney Australia, 1980. *Memberships:* Vice Chairman, United Farmers & Stockowners Association of South Australia, 1979-81; Stockowners Association of South Australia, 1967-79; Executive, 1973-81, Vice President, 1974-79, Stockowners Association Council; President, Central Practices Committee, Stockowners Association, 1970-73; Chairman, South Australian Lamb Committee, 1969-73; Lamb Committee Delegate, Australian Meat Board, 1967-74; Vice President, Executive & Finance Committee, 1979-81; Executive Wool and Meat Council, 1979-81; Meat sub Committee, Farming Council, 1979-81; Vice Chairman, South Australia Livestock and Meat Advisory Committee, 1979-80; Chairman, South Australia Livestock and Meat Advisory Committee, 1980-81; Chairman, Liberal Party Yankalilla Branch, 1976; Fire Officer, Yankalilla District Council, 1959-62; Deputy Supervisor, Emergency Fire Service Yankalilla Council Area, 1962-81; Le Fleurian Peninsula Consultative Committee National Banks, to Minister of Environment, 1980-81; Sub-Committee, Livestock Marketing Study Group, 1980-81; South Australia Agricultural Bureau. *Hobbies:* Golf; Water skiing; Tennis. *Address:* 'Talamara', Box 62, Yankalilla, South Australia 5203.

MARTIN, Stanley Leonard, b. 28 Sept. 1903, Sydney, Australia. Physicist. m. Moya Hazel Thresher, 1 Jan. 1927, 1 son, 1 daughter. *Education:* Diploma of Education, 1925, University of Syndey, 1920-24; BSc, Sydney, 1924; MSc, Sydney, 1952; B.Ed., Melbourne, 1938. *Appointments:* High School Teacher, Education Department, NSW, Australia, 1924-27; Head, Applied Physics Department, Royal Melbourne Institute of Technology, 1928-68; Exchange Lecturer in Physics, Birmingham Central Technical College, England, 1936; Honorary research worker, University College, London, 1948. *Memberships:* Fellow, Institute of Physics, Britain; Foundation Fellow, Australian Institute of Physics; Honorary Life Fellowship, Australasian Institute of Radiography, 1974; Former committee and past Chairman Victorian division, Institute of Instrumentation and Control, Australia; Chairman, Victorian Overseas Students Co-ordination Committee, 1955-63; Overseas Students Assistance Fund, 1975-. *Publications:* Basic Physics (with AK Connor), vols. I, 2, 3, 1947; Research papers and articles in various journals. *Honours:* An annual Stanley L Martin Oration, established in 1974 by the Victorian Branch of the Australasian Institute of Radiography; Smith prize (shared) for Physics 1, University of Sydney, 1920; H C Russell prize for Astronomy, 1921; Deas-Thomson scholarship (shared) for Physics 3, 1922. *Hobbies:* Lawn bowls; Reading; Gardening. *Address:* 14/601 Elgar Road, Box Hill North, Victoria, 3129, Australia.

MARTINEAU, Paul A, b. 10 Apr. 1921, Bryson, Québec, Canada. Barrister; Solicitor. m. Halina Neclaw, 3 Jan. 1946, 2 daughters. *Education:* BA., Suma cum Laude, University of Ottawa, Ottawa, Ontario, Canada, 1937-41; Licentiate in Law., Magna cum Laude, Faculty of Law, University of Montréal, Québec, Canada, 1946-49; Accountancy; Applied Psychology; German and Spanish Special Courses at Oxford, UK and La Sorbonne, Paris, France, while member of Canadian Armed Forces. *Appointments:* Cost Accounting, Ottawa Car and Aircraft, Ottawa, Canada, 1941-42; Royal Canadian Air Force, serving in Canada, UK, France, Belgium, Holland and Germany, 1942-46; Admitted to Bar, Province of Québec, Canada, Practised with Asselin, Crankshaw, Gingras & Trudel, Montréal, Canada, 1949; Appointed Crown Prosecutor, Judicial District of Pontiac, Canada, 1950; Private Practice of Law, 1950-58; Member, House of Commons of Canada, for riding of Pontiac-Temiscamingue, 1958-65; Parliamentary Secretary to Prime Minister of Canada, 1959-61; Appointed Deputy Speaker of House of Commons, Chairman of the Committees of the Whole, 1962; Appointed Federal Minister of Mines and Technical Surveys, 1962; member of several permanent committees including: US Canadian Parliamentary Group; Standing Committee on Defence and Foreign Affairs; Commonwealth Pariamentary Association; NATO Parliamentary Association; World Association of Parliamentarians; Agent for the Québec Government for Supreme Court of Canada and the Exchequer Court of Canada, 1966; Member, Royal Commission of Inquiry on the administration of Criminal and Penal Justice in Québec, Canada, 1967-70; Practiced law at Hull, Québec and Campbell's Bay, Québec, Canada, 1966-80. *Publications:* Several articles on political, social, economic and legal subjects. *Creative Works:* Representational and abstract paintings in various art exhibitions. *Honours:* Military service medals for 1939-45 war; Queen's Counsel, 1966; Privy Counsel, 1962; Medal of the Order of Canada; Centennial Medal, 1967; Medal for Silver Anniversary of HM the Queen; Knight Comman-

der of the Order of St. Gregory the Great. *Hobbies:* Painting; Travelling. *Address:* Mountain Road, R R 1, Lucerne, Québec, Canada.

MARTINS, Akinola Oladapo Abiola, b. 25 July 1922, Lagos, Nigeria. Trade & Industrial Consultant. m. (1) T Luther, 29 May 1952 (divorced 1967), 3 sons, 3 daughters, (2) VO Byron, 6 Jan. 1970, 1 son. *Education:* CMS Grammar School, Lagos, 1936-41; Senior Cambridge School Examination Certificate, 1941; Journalism Course, London School of Journalism, 1946-48. *Appointments:* Shorthand Typist, 1942-46; Tuition, London School of Journalism, 1946-48; Shorthand Typist, Huilever SA, Leopoldville, Belgian Congo, 1946-50; Free-lance Journalist, 1946-50; Company Secretary & Sales Representative, Ross, Allen & Elliott, Leopoldville, Belgian Congo, 1950-52; Chief Salesman, WF Clarke (Nigeria) Ltd., Lagos, 1952-54; Founding of own Company, Akin Martins (Nigeria) Co., 1955; Incorporation of Akin Martins (Nigeria) Ltd., 1965. *Memberships:* Assistant Organist, St Paul's Church, Breadfruit, Lagos, 1963-70; Organist & Choirmaster, 1970-; Royal School of Church Music, Croydon, England. *Publications:* Some Religious Musical Compositions especially hymn-tunes and chants and one anthem. *Honours:* Many prizes during both primary and secondary schools career. *Hobbies:* Music (Classical, Religious and Jazz); Singing; Reading; Football; Lawn and Table Tennis; Cinema; TV; Wrestling. *Address:* 22 Osoro Street, Papa Ajao, Mushin, Lagos, Nigeria.

MARVAN, Jirí (George Jan), b. 28 Jan. 1936, Prague, Bohemia. Linguist & Educator. m. Elishka M Cunderliková, 12 Aug. 1963, 1 son, 1 daughter. *Education:* MA, equiv., 1959, PhD, 1966, Charles University. *Appointments:* Czech Language Institute (Academy of Sciences) Prague, 1960-63; Uppsala University, 1963-67; Portland State University, 1968-69; University of California, 1969-72, 1975-76; Pennsylvania State University, 1972-73; Monash University, Australia, 1973-. *Memberships:* Linguistic Society of America; Czechoslovak Society of Arts & Sciences; Australian & New Zealand Slavists' Association. *Publications:* Over 50 titles (Slavic and Baltic linguistics) including books Prehistoric Slavic Contraction, 1979; Modern Lithuanian Declension, 1979; Outline of Underlying Russian Inflection, 1981. *Honours:* Czech Literary Foundation Award, 1963; University of California Scholar, 1971; Fellow, Australian Ministry of Education, 1976; Australian Research Grant, 1981. *Hobbies:* Poetry; Sport; Travelling; Interethnic values and understanding. *Address:* 4 Conrad Place, Mulgrave, Victoria, 3170, Australia

MARWAHA, Gurbachan Singh, b. 11 June 1926, Khairwala, West Panjab, Pakistan. Director. *Education:* Associate (First Class First) in Min. Engg, Indian School of Mines, 1947; Porstgraduate work, University of Birmingham, UK, 1947-49; Mine Managers First Class Certificate of Competency, UK, Coal, 1950, India, Coal, 1950, India, Metal, 1962; Course for Senior Executive, Admin Staff College of India, 1968. *Appointments:* Colliery Manager, 1950; Jr. Inspector of Mines, 1950-54; Joint Director of Mines Safety, 1954-67; Director of Mines Safety, 1967-72; Director, Indian School of Mines, 1972-; Director, Board of M/s Pyrites, Phosphate and Chemicals Ltd., 1979-, Board of Central Mine Planning and Design Institute, 1978-, Board of Mineral Exploration Corporation Ltd., 1976-79; Tech Assessor Court of Enquiry into Chasnala Colliery disaster, 1976; President & Chief Executive, Central Mines Rescue Stations Organisation, 1961-62. *Memberships:* All-India Council for Tech Education, 1966; WB Mining Education Advisory Board, 1968-; Bihar State Commission for Science & Technology, 1974-; GOI Coal Advisory Council, 1975-; CSIR Earth Sciences Research Committee, 1975-77; Chairma, Developemtn Committee of Mining Education Advisory Board, Government of Bihar, 1960-61; Institution of Engineers; President, Mining, Geological & Metallurgical Institute of India, 1979-80. *Publications:* Author of over 100 technical papers in India and abroad and of several monographs and reports. *Honours:* Queta Singh Sabha Medal, Khalsa College, 1943; Pickering Medal, Indian School of Mines, 1947; Government of India Overseas Scholar, 1947-49; President, Rajendra Prasad Memorial Gold Medal, 1965; Fellowship, Indian Standards Institution, 1968; DD Thacker Gold Medal, 1971; First Recipient Overseas Medal, 1973; Krakow Academy Golden Jubilee Medal, 1977; Eminent Scientist, Khalsa College, 1978; Distinguished Alumni Award, 1978, Distinguished Service Award, 1978, Indian School of Mines; Commemoration Award, Warsaw Technical University, 1979. *Address:* Indian School of Mines, Dhanbad, 826004, India.

MASHOLOGU, Mothusi Thamsanqa, b. 7 Mar. 1939, Morija Lesotho. Diplomat. m. Lineo Debrah, 1 Mar. 1969, 1 son, 2 daughters. *Education:* BA (Rhodes), University College of Fort Hare, 1958; PGGE (London), University of Rhodesia and Nyasaland, 1959; BA, Queens University, Belfast, 1963. *Appointments:* Teacher, 1963-65; Counsellor, Lesotho Mission to UN, 1966-68; Ambassador to US, 1969-73; Secretary to Cabinet, 1974-75; Vice-Chancellor of National University of Lesotho, 1975-80; High Commissioner to Canada, 1980-. *Hobbies:* Music; Writing; Tennis. *Address:* 2 Crescent Road, Rockcliffe Park, Ottawa, Canada.

MASINBO, Victor Kenneth Onyechi, b. 20 Nov. 1938, Ogidi, Anambra State, Nigeria. Architect, Planner. m. Norah, 15 Sept. 1971, 2 sons, 2 daughters. *Education:* RIBA (Intermediate), Nigerian College of Arts Science and Technology, Zaria, Nigeria, 1961; MSc, Architecture, University of Science & Technology, Kumasi, Chana, 1966. *Appointments:* Assistant Research Fellow, Department of Housing and Planning Research, UST, Kumasi, Chana, Assistant Lecturer Faculty of Architecture, 1966-71; Architect, Ministry of Works and Transport, Lusaka, Zambia, 1971-73; Assistant Resident Architect, University of Zambia, Lusaka, 1973-75; Architect, Kola Bankole & Associates, 1975-76; Private, Practice, Chairman Mass Design & Associates, 1976-. *Memberships:* Royal Institute of Architects; Nigerian Institute of Architects. *Publications:* Sehlter for Mankind—The case for the Urban Poor, a paper presented at the Bi-annual general meeting of the Nigerian Institute of Architects in Lagos, 1979. *Honours:* Atlas award, Nigerian College of Arts Science and Technology, 1961. *Hobbies:* Photography; Lawn Tennis. *Address:* 48 Adeniran Ogunsanya Street, Surulere, Lagos, Nigeria.

MASIRE, Quett Ketumile Joni, b. 23 July 1925, Kanye, Botswana. Politician. m. Olebile Gladys, Nov. 1957, 3 sons, 3 daughters. *Education:* Teacher Training until 1949. *Appointments:* Founded Seepapitso Secondary School, Kanye, Botswana, 1950; Journalist, 1958, subsequently Director, Editor, 1962, African Echo; Member, Legislative Council, 1962-65; Member, Legislative Assembly, 1965-; Secretary General, Botswana Democratic Party, 1962-80; Deputy Prime Minister, 1966; Vice President, Minister of Development Planning, 1966-1980; Minister of Finance, 1966-80; President, Republic of Botswana, 1980-. *Memberships:* President, Botswana Society; Patron, International Committee Against Apartheid, Racism and Colonialism in Southern Africa; Patron, Okavango Wildlife Society; Chief Scout, Botswana Scouts Association. *Honours:* Justice of the Peace; Hon. LL.D., University of St. John, New York, USA, 1967; Presidential Order of Honour, Gaborone, Botswana, 1972; Hon. LL.D., Williams College, Williamstown, Massachusetts, USA, 1980. *Address:* PO Box 70, Gaborone, Botswana.

MASON, Bruce Edward George, b. 28 Sept. 1921, Wellington, New Zealand. Writer. m. Diana Manby Shaw, 17 Dec. 1945, 1 son, 2 daughters. *Education:* BA, 1945, Victoria University College, Wellington, 1939-41. *Appointments:* Research Archivist, War History Branch, Internal Affairs, Wellington, 1946-48; Assistant Curator of Manuscripts, Alexander Turnbull Library, 1948-49; Travelling in Europe, 1949-51; Orchardist, Tauranga, New Zealand, 1952; Public Relations Officer, New Zealand Forest Service, 1952-57; Senior Journalist, Department of Tourism and Publicity, 1957-58, since then, free lance writer and actor. *Memberships:* President of Honour, PEN New Zealand Branch, 1980-81; Life Member, Downstage, Inc., 1979; President, New Zealand Writers' Guild, 1976-80, President Emeritus, 1980. *Publications:* Plays: The Pohutukawa Tree, 1960; The End of the Golden Weather, 1962-70; Awatea, 1970; Zero Inn, 1970; Bruce Mason, Solo (four plays for Solo Actor,) 1981; Critical: New Zealand Drama, 1973; Every Kind of Weather, 1981. *Honours:* British Drama League Playwriting Competition, 1953; National Playwriting Competition of the Auckland Festival Society, 1958; Hon. Doctorate of Literature, Victoria University of Wellington, 1977;

CBE, (Civil Division), 1980. *Hobbies:* Music; Gardening; Languages. *Address:* 14 Henry Street, Wellington, 3, New Zealand.

MASON, Colin, b. 28 Oct. 1926. Senator and author. *Education:* Diploma Journalism, University of New Zealand. *Appointments:* Australian Broadcasting Commission's Representative and Foreign Correspondent to South-East Asia, 1956-59; Television and radio Executive Producer, 1959-65; SEATO civilian adviser to Thai Government, 1965-66; Elected to Australian Senate, 1977. *Memberships:* Councillor, Australian Institute of International Affairs, 1962-68; National Convenor, Australia Party, 1976-77; Deputy National President, Australian Democrats, 1977-78, Senate Standing Committee on Science & the Environment, 1978-80, re-appointed, 1980; Senate Select Committee on Parliament's appropriation and staffing, 1980. *Publications:* Asia, A First View, 1971; Hostage, 1973; The View from Peking, 1977. *Address:* Australian Parliament Offices, Chifley Square, Sydney, NSW, 2000, Australia.

MASON, Frederick Cecil, b. 15 May 1913, London, England. Diplomat (retired); Company Director. m. Karen Rørholm, 5 Dec. 1941, 2 sons, 1 daughter. *Education:* BA., 1st Class Hons., St. Catherine's College, Cambridge, UK, 1932-35. *Appointments:* Consular Service, Antwerp, Paris, Leopoldville and Faroe Islands, 1935-43; Diplomatic Service, Panama, Santiago, London, Bonn, Athens, Tehran, 1943-73; Ambassador to: Chile, 1966-70; UN., Geneva, 1971-73; Director, New Count Natural Resources Limited, UK, 1973-. *Memberships:* Chairman, Anglo-Chilean Society, 1978-; Iran Society; Hon. member, Canning Club. *Honours:* CMG., 1958; KCVO., 1968. *Hobbies:* Tennis; Golf; Walking; Birdwatching;. *Address:* THE Forge, Church Street, Ropley, Hampshire SO24 ODS, England.

MASON, (Sir), John (Charles Moir), b. 13 May 1927. HM Diplomatic Service; High Commissioner in Australia. m. Margaret Newton, 1954, 1 son, 1 daughter. *Education:* BA., 1950, MA., 1955, Peterhouse, Cambridge, England; Lieutenant, XX Lancs Fusiliers, 1946-48. *Appointments:* Captain, Royal Ulster Rifles, Korea, 1950-51; HM Foreign Service, 1952; 3rd Sec., 1952-54, 1st Sec., 1959-61, 1st Sec. and Assistant Head of Department, 1965-68, Foreign Office; 1st Secretary, Commercial, Damascus, 1961-65; Director of Trade Development and Deputy Consul-General, New York, USA, 1968-71; Head of European Integration Department, 1971-72, Assistant Under-Secretary of State, Economic, 1975-76, Foreign and Commonwealth Office; Seconded as Under-Secretary, ECGD., 1972-75; Ambassador to Israel, 1976-80; High Commissioner, Australia, 1980-. *Honours:* KCMG., 1980; CMG., 1976. *Address:* c/o Foreign and Commonwealth Office, London SW1, England.

MASON, John Marsden, b. 20 Nov. 1928, Rose Bay, New South Wales, Australia. Member of Parliament. m. Lorna Meg Boxsell, 27 Mar. 1953, 4 sons, 1 daughter. *Education:* United Theological Faculty, Sydney University. *Appointments:* Ordained Methodist Minister, 1950, (Served in Inland Mission in Katherine, NT., then Lismore, Goulburn, Newcastle, Dubbo.) Entered NSW, Legislative Assembly, 1965; Parliamentary Secretary to Premier of NSW, 1975; Minister for Lands & Forests, 1975; Deputy Leader of the Opposition, 1977; Leader of the Opposition, 1978-81. *Memberships:* The Royal Commonwealth Society; National Parks and Wildlife Foundation. *Hobbies:* Boating; Fishing; Swimming. *Address:* 9/7 Ithaca Road Elizabeth Bay, New South Wales, Australia.

MASON, Malcolm John, b. 19 Dec. 1912, Pahuatua, New Zealand. Chartered Accountant. m. (1) 28 Oct. 1939, (2) 2 Sept. 1971, 2 sons, 1 daughter. *Education:* BA., B.Com., Dip., Soc.Sc. *Appointments:* New Zealand Government, 1930-39; New Zealand Army, 1940-46; Chartered Accountant Principal, 1947-. *Memberships:* President: Chartered Institute of Secretaries, 1960-61; New Zealand Pen Centre, 1966-69. *Publications:* The Way Out, 1946; The Water Flows Uphill, 1964; Why Not Japan, 1965. *Honours:* OBE., 1962; Military Cross, 1944; Justice of the peace, 1952; Royal Humane Society Medal for Bravery, 1951. *Hobbies:* Gardening; Writing. *Address:* 29 Everest Street, Wellington, New Zealand.

MASSON, Simon Francis, b. 1945, Mauritius. Company Director. m. Madeleine Mesochina, 1972, 3 daughters. *Education:* Hons. Degree, Sugar Technology, Mauritius; Degreee, Personnel Management, London, UK. *Appointments:* Assistant Personnel Manager, David Whitehead & Sons, Tongaat, South Africa, 1970-72; Training Officer, Mauritius Sugar Producers Association, 1972-74; Personnel Manager, Mauritius Hotels Group, 1974-76; Managing Director, Descro International, Taxi Trucks Limited, Mauritius, 1976-. *Address:* St. Clement Street, Curepipe, Mauritius.

MASTER, Bachoo, b. 7 May 1934, Nagpur, India. Paediatrician — Paediatric Cardiologist. m. Rohinton Nariman, 18 Jan. 1973. *Education:* MB,BS, 1956; DCH, 1958; MD (Ped.), 1959; MRCP, 1962; Diploma, American Board of Paediatrics, 1966; Diploma, American Board of Paediatric Cardiology, 1966. *Appointments:* House Officer, 1956-57, Registrar in Paediatrics, 1957-60, Assistant Hon. Paediatrician (Assistant Professor), 1960-65, Jerbai Wadia Hospital for Children; SHO Neonatal Unit, Rottentow Hospital, Glasgow, 1960-61; Resident Medical Officer, Children's Hospital Medical Centre, Boston, USA, 1963; Fellow, Paediatric Cardiology Boston Flating Hospital, 1964-65; Teaching Fellow, Paediatric Cardiology, Tufts University, Boston, 1965-66; Fellow, Paediatric Cardiology, Hospital for Sick children, Toronto, Canada, 1966-67; Pool Officer and Unit in charge, Paediatrics Government Medical College, Nagpur, 1968; Reader & Head of Department, Corporation Medical College, Nagpur, 1969-71; Professor of Paediatrics MGM Medical College and Senior Paediatrician, Tata Main Hospital, Jamshedpur, 1971-. *Memberships:* Indian Academy of Paediatrics; Cardiological Society of India; Clinical Society, Tata Main Hospital; Indian Medical Association, Jamshedpur Branch; Past President, International College of Pediatrics. *Honours:* Rai Bahadur Sengupta Gold Medal, 1956; Ontario Heart Foundation Award, 1966-67; Sandoz India Award 1969—1971; Fellowship International College of Paediatrics, 1978. *Hobbies:* Painting; Photography; Cooking; Travelling. *Address:* 6 Beldih Lake, Jamshedpur, 831001, Bihar, India.

MASTERS, Kerith Vernon McRubie, b. 3 Oct. 1952, St Catherine, Jamaica, West Indies. Land Surveyor. *Education:* Diploma in Land Surveying, College of Arts Science & Technology, 1974-77; *Appointments:* Wilson, Fidler & Lee; Alpart (Farms) Jamaica Ltd. *Memberships:* Land Surveyors Association of Jamaica; Advisory Committee on Land Surveying. *Honours:* Derrick Dunn Award, 1977. *Hobbies:* Debating; Reading. *Address:* 34 McKinley Road, Mandeville PO, Jamaica, West Indies.

MASTERS, William Stowe Jr., b. 5 Sept. 1919, Southampton, Bermuda. Meteorologist & Merchant. m. Aimee Elyce Schroeder, 14 June 1941, 1 son, 1 daughter. *Education:* B Aero Engineering, New York University. *Appointments:* Meteorologist then Chief Meteorologist, United Airlines, NYC, 1940-49; Managing Director and President, Stuart's Distributing Co., Ltd., Hamilton, Bermuda, 1949-81; President, Somers Distributing Co., Ltd., Hamilton, Bermuda, 1981; Director, Colour Processing Centre Ltd. *Memberships:* Bermuda Chamber of Commerce, President, 1976-77; Bermuda Bravery Award Association, President, 1976-80; American Meteorology Association. *Hobbies:* Sailing; Golf. *Address:* Alta Vista, Cavendish Road, Pembroke East 5-01, Bermuda

MAT SARI BIN HAMID, P J K, b. 18 Nov. 1943, Malacca, West Malaysia. Civil Engineering, Building Construction, Property Development. m. Rohani Bte Mat Tahir, 1 son, 2 daughters. *Appointments:* Managing Director. *Memberships:* Subang National Gold Club. *Creative Works:* Land Scaping. *Honours:* Pingat Jasa Kebaktian, Selangor, 1978. *Hobbies:* Gardening; Camping; Touring. *Address:* No. 2 Jalan 22/42, Taman Aman, Petaling Jaya, Selangor, West Malaysia.

MATCHETT, Victor Lewin, b. 17 May 1922, Moree, NSW, Australia. Psychiatrist. m. Cecily Stuart Smiles, 22 July 1949, 1 son, 1 daughter. *Education:* Bachelor of Medicine & Bachelor of Surgery, University of Sydney, 1945; Diploma of Psychological Medicine, University of Melbourne, 1953; Member of the Australian & New Zealand College of Psychiatrists, 1964; Fellow of the Royal Australian & New Zealand College of Psychiatrists, 1979. *Appointments:* Senior Medical Officer,

Sunbury Mental Hospital, 1952-53; Visiting Psychiatrist, Royal Brisbane Hospital, 1954-65; Clinical Lecturer in Psychiatry, University of Queensland, 1954-65; Visiting Psychiatrist, Repatriation Commission, 1954-63; Senior Psychiatrist, 1969-77, Deputy Medical Superintendent, 1977-78, Medical Superintendent, 1978-, Wolston Park Hospital. *Memberships:* Australasian Association of Psychiatrists (Hon Sec, Queensland Committee, 1954-56; Federal Councillor, 1957-58; Membership Committee, 1962-68); Fellow, The Royal Astronomical Society; British Astronomical Association; American Association of Variable Star Observers; Association of Lunar & Planetary Observers USA; Astronomical Amateurs Club of Moreton Bay (Foundation Hon Sec & Editor). *Publications:* Various observations contributed to astronomical societies; Predictions of Astronomical Phenomena contributed to Handbook of the British Astronomical Association. *Hobbies:* Astronomical observing and computing; The History of Astronomy. *Address:* 14 Bougainvillea Avenue, Indooroopilly, Queensland, 4068, Australia

MATERU, Mtengie Ephatha Aiyona, b. 19 Sept. 1933, Moshi, Tanzania. Agricultural Entomokogist. m. 6 Feb. 1965, 2 sons. *Education:* BSc, (London), Makerere University College, Kampala, Uganda, 1959; MSc, Michigan State University, East Lansing, Michigan, USA, 1962; PhD, Unitersity of East Africa, Nairobi, Kenya, 1968. *Appointments:* Assistant Entomologist, Coffee Research Station, Lyamungu, Tanzania, 1959-61; Research, Senior Research Officer, 1962-66, Principal Research Officer, Deputy Director, 1966-70, Chief Research Officer, Director, 1970-76, Tropical Pesticides Research Institute, Auusha, Tanzania; Director, International Red Locust Control Organisation for Central and Southern Africa, Mbala, Zambia, 1976-. *Memberships:* International Centre of Insect Physiology and Ecology; Association of African Insect Scientists; Tropical Pesticides Research Institute Council, Tanzania. *Publications:* Published over 20 research papers in journals and over 50 miscellaneous papers. *Honours:* Awarded First Prize in Zoology in BSc Degree. *Hobbies:* Athletics; Volleyball; Reading; Gardening. *Address:* c/o PO Box 1349, Arusha, Tanzania.

MATHERON, Richard Cavins, b. 13 Apr. 1927, Oxnard, California, USA. Diplomat. m. Katherine Brown Ellenberger, 12 Dec. 1970, 2 daughters. *Education:* AB, University of California, 1948. *Appointments:* US Department of State, 1949-; Assignments to Paris, France; Saigon, Vietnam; Rome, Italy; Lagos, Nigeria; Yaounde, Cameroon; Kinshasa, Zaire; Bukavu, Zaire; Ouagadougou, Upper Volta; Antananarivo, Madagascar; Addis Ababa, Ethiopia in addition to Washington, DC; Presently serving as Ambassador Extraordinary and Plenipotentiary of the United States of America to the Kingdom of Swaziland at Mbabane, Swaziland. *Memberships:* American Foreign Service Association. *Honours:* Superior Honor Award, US Department of State, 1965. *Hobby:* Collection of African sculpture. *Address:* US Ambassador's Residence, Golf Course Road, Mbabane, Swaziland.

MATHESON, John Ross (Colonel His Honour), b. 14 Nov. 1917, Arundel, PQ Canada. Judge. m. Edith May Bickley, 4 Aug. 1945, 4 sons, 2 daughters. *Education:* BA, Queen's, 1940; MA, Mount Allison, 1975; Barrister-at-Law, Osgoode Hall, 1948; LL M, Western, 1954. *Appointments:* Artillery Officer Overseas, 1940-44; Called to the Bar of Ontario, 1948; Matheson, Henderson & Hart, Brockville, 1968; Elected Member of Parliament for Leeds, By-Election, 1961, Re-elected, 1962, 63, 65; Chairman Standing Committee of External Affairs, 1963-65; Parliamentary Secretary to Prime Minister, 1965-68; Appointed Judge, 1968, Judicial District Ottawa-Carleton, 1968-78, County of Lanark, 1978; Colonel, 30th Field Regiment, Royal Canadian Artillery, 1977-. *Memberships:* Canadian Economics Association; Canadian Bar Association; Royal Canadian Artillery Association; Most Venerable Order of St John of Jerusalem, Registrar, 1966-69, Genealogist, 1969; National Trust for Scotland; Legal Fraternity, Phi Delta Phi; Royal Canadian Legion. *Publications:* Canada's Flag: A Search for a Country, 1980. *Honours:* Knight of Justice, Order of St John, 1974; Knight Commander of Merit, Order of St Lazarus; Commonwealth Heraldry Board Essay Prize, 1980; Canadian Forces Decoration, 1977; Created QC , 1967, Armigerous by Lyon Court, 1959, Armigerous by College of Arms, 1972; Citizen of the Year, Brockville, 1967;

Fellow: Royal Economic Society, 1962; Society of Antiquaries of Scotland, 1969; Canadian Heraldry Society, 1980; Distinguished Service Award, Queen's University, 1977; Montreal Medal, 1981. *Hobbies:* Heritage & History; Military Affairs. *Address:* Rideau Ferry, Ontario, Canada, KOG1WO.

MATHEWS, Ian Richard, b. 29 Jan. 1933, Mitcham, Surrey, England. Journalist. m. Joyce Pamela Morris, 30 Apr. 1957, 1 son, 1 daughter. *Appointments:* Clerk, Local Govt., 1949; Clerk, Guy's Hospital, London, 1952-54; Writer, Royal Fleet Auxillary, 1954-55; Kent and Sussex Courier Group of Newspapers, 1955-59; Express and Echo, Exeter, UK, 1959-60; News Limited Adelaide, SA (Australia), 1960-63; Chief Sub Editor, News Editor, Assistant Editor, Editor, The Canberra Times. *Memberships:* National Press Club. *Honours:* Queen's Jubilee Medal, 1979. *Hobby:* Watching junior sport. *Address:* 4 Stone Place, Garran, ACT 2605, Canberra, Australia.

MATHEWS, Kay, b. 1 Jan. 1940, Calicut, India. University Professor. m. Rosie John, 22 Feb. 1975, 1 son, 1 daughter. *Education:* BA, Kerala University, India; MA, Delhi University, 1964; PhD, Jawaharlal Nehru University, New Delhi, 1973. *Appointments:* Lecturer, Political Science, University of Delhi, 1964-76; Senior Lecturer, 1976-79, Associate Professor, 1979-, Political Science, University of Dar Es Salaam. *Memberships:* African Association of Political Science; International Political Science Association; Indian Council of World Affairs and its Executive Committee, 1971-77; Indian Political Science Association; Indian Society of International Law. *Publications:* Foreign Policy of Tanzania: A Reader (Ed.), 1981; Approximately 20 articles and many Book-reviews and review articles published in various academic journals; Research papers written and presented at seminars and conferences; Editor-in-Chief, The African Review, Dar es Salaam. *Honours:* Visiting Scholar, United Nations Institute for Research and Training, New York, 1972. *Hobbies:* Law Tennis; Swimming; Photography. *Address:* PO Box 35128, Dar Es Salaam, Tanzania.

MATHEWS, Leonard Frederick, b. 14 Mar. 1917, London, England. Senior Resident Director. m. Marian Frankland, 9 Dec. 1939, 2 sons. *Education:* Birmingham and Leeds Colleges of Technology. *Appointments:* Royal Navy Fleet Air Arm, 1940-45; BBC, 1946-55; Assistant Technical Controller, 1955-59, Head of Special Projects, 1959-63, Deputy Operations Controller, 1963-64, Midlands Controller, 1965-67, Director and General Manager (Midlands), 1967-74, Senior Resident Director, 1974-, ATV Network Limited; Director, Independent Television Publications Limited, 1975-. *Memberships:* Malvern Festival Society Limited, Chairman; Malvern Festival Society Trust Limited, Chairman; Association of Crossroads Care Attendant Scheme Limited, Chairman; Shakespeare Theatre Trust Limited; Birmingham Hippodrome Theatre Trust Limited; Executive Board of the Variety Club of Great Britain and Chairman of the Birmingham Committee, 1970-78; Governor of the Royal Shakespeare Theatre; Chairman of the University of Birmingham Centre Committee; Appeal Director of the Royal Shakespeare Theatre Barbican Scheme. *Publications:* Numerous technical papers and contributions to television journals. *Honours:* Royal Television Society Pye Premium, 1962; Radar and Electronics Association Award, 1965; OBE, 1970. *Address:* 3 The Mulberry Tree, Stratford-upon-Avon, Warwickshire, England.

MATHUR, Bepin Behari Lal, b. 15 July 1924, Bareilly, India. Medical Teacher, Administrator. m. Saroj Mathur, 15 Feb. 1949, 2 sons, 3 daughters. *Education:* MBBS, 1946; MD, 1951. *Appointments:* House Physician, Thomason Hospital, Agra, 1946-47; Tutor in Pathology, 1947-49, Resident Pathologist, 1949-50, Medical College, Agra; Lecturer in Pathology, MGM Medical College, Indore, 1950-53; Assistant Professor, Pathology, B J Medical College, Ahmedabad, 1953-59; Professor and Head of the Department of Pathology, Aurangabad, Ahmedabad, Jamnagar and Baroda, 1959-; Medical Superintendent, S S G Hospital, Baroda, 1980-. *Memberships:* International Academy of Pathology, President of Indian Division; Indian Association of Pathologists, Executive Councillor; Royal College of Pathologists, London; Fellow, Royal College of Pathologists, London. *Publications:* Autor of 19 articles in professional journals. *Hobbies:* Gardening; Swim-

ming. *Address:* M-9 Doctor's Quarters, Yavteshwar Compound, Indira Avenue, Baroda, Gujarat, India.

MATHUR, Bhupendra S, b. 1 July 1941, Shikohabad, India. Scientist. m. 20 Feb. 1969. *Education:* PhD., Harvard University, USA, 1966; MSc., 1959, BSc., 1957, Allahabad University, India. *Appointments:* Post Doctoral work, Columbia University, USA, 1966-68; Faculty of Indian Institute of Technology, Kanpur, India, 1968-73; Scientist-in-Charge, Time and Frequency Section, National Physicial Laboratory, New Delhi, India, 1973-. *Memberships:* Fellow, Institution of Electronics and Telecommunication Engineers; Leader, Indian Delegation, Interim meeting of Study Group VII on Time and Frequency of CCIR, Geneva, 1980; Indian Delegation of Indo-Soviet Bilateral Exchange Programme on Metrology, USSR, 1977; Secretary, National Committee on Time and Frequency; Study Group, Time Dissemination via Indian Satellite Insat. *Creative Works:* Convener, International Symposiu, 1981, Convener, Study Group Meeting, 1978, Convener, National Seminar, 1976, Editor, Proceedings of National Seminar and Study Group Meeting, Time and Frequency; Invited to Attend and Present paper at Time and Frequency Conference, Canberra, Australia, 1980; 50 publications in International and National Journals. *Honours:* Appointed Guest Editor by Journal of Institution of Electronics and Telecommunication Engineers for its Special Issue on Proceedings of International Symposium on Time and Frequency, New Delhi, 1981; National Phsyical Laboratory, New Delhi award for Outstanding Research work, 1980; Merit Promotion by Parent Organisation, Council of Scientific and Industrial Research, 1980. *Address:* R-862 New Rajinder Nagar, New Delhi 110060, India.

MATHURIN, Eldon, b. 30 July 1935, St. Lucia, West Indies. Regional Civil Servant. m. Jean Rita Martin, 24 Aug. 1957, 2 sons, 1 daughter. *Education:* Diploma in Income Tax Law and Practice, 1966. *Appointments:* GPO Engineer, UK, 1956-60; Tax Officer, Indland Revenue Division, 1961-66; Inspector of Taxes, 1966-67, Assistant Controller, 1967-68, Controller, 1968-73, Indland Revenue, St. Lucia; Tax Administration Adviser, 1973-78, Director, General Services and Administration, 1978-, Guyana-Caricom Secretariat. *Memberships:* Executive Secretary, Caribbean Organisation of Tax Administrators, 1973-78; Secretary, St Lucia Civil Service Association, 1968-69. *Hobbies:* Music; Sport. *Address:* 39 Dadanawa St, Section K, Campbell Ville, Georgetown, Guyana SA.

MATIPA, Henry Kosam, b. 25 Dec. 1938, Mwense. Industrial Economist, Politician. m. Christina Matipa, 23 Aug. 1965, 2 sons. *Education:* MSc, 1965; PhD, 1969. *Appointments:* Senior Economist: Development Division, Office of the Vice President; Ministry of Finance and Planning; Ministry of National Development and Planning; Ministry of Mines and Mining Development; Minister of State, Ministries of Local Govt. and Housing, Commerce, Lands and Agriculture; Cabinet Minister for Luapula Province; Member of Central Committee of UNIP and Admin. Secretary. *Publications:* Role of the Mining Industry in the Industrialisation of the Republic of Zambia; Several papers on economic development of Zambia and role of Trade Unions. *Hobbies:* Lawn Tennis; Swimming. *Address:* Plot 2B/25/377A, Roan Road, Kabulonga, Lusaka, Zambia.

MATTERN, Barry Francis, b. 7 Mar. 1941, Winnipeg, Manitoba, Canada. Federal Government Employee. m. Judith Elizabeth Burt, 23 June 1962, 2 sons, 1 daughter. *Appointments:* Canadian Pacific Railway, 1959; Pepsi Cola Canada Limited, 1961; Federal Government of Canada, 1969. *Memberships:* Ringette Canada; Director, World Sport Friendship Exchange. *Hobbies:* Ringette; Reading. *Address:* 66 Madera Crescent, Winnipeg, Manitoba, Canada.

MATTERS, Thomas Francis, b. 11 June 1932, Adelaide, South Australia. Real Estate Agent. m. Eletha Cocks, 3 Feb. 1955, 2 sons, 1 daughter. *Education:* St Peters College, 1939-49; South Australia Institute of Technology, 1960-70. *Appointments:* Director - Auctioneer, Matters & Co., Real Estate Consultants; Mmeber: Property Agents International; Debenham Tewson International. *Memberships:* Fellow, Real Estate Institute; Real Estate Institute Valuer; Life member, Navy League of Australia. *Hobbies:* Fishing; Surfing; Sailing. *Address:* 2 Hambour Place, Old Wattle Park, South Australia 5066.

MATTHEW, Joseph Algernon, b. 15 Apr. 1944, Montserrat, West Indies. Architect. *Education:* Montserrat Secondary School, Plymouth, Montserrat, 1957-64; BA Architecture, Howard University, Washington DC, 1973. *Appointments:* Architect, Keith Consulting and Gabriel Architectural Group, Regina Saskatchewan, 1974-79; Principal Architect and President, Joseph A Matthew, Architect Limited, Prince Albert Saskatchewan, 1979-81; Senior Architect and Partner, Deith Gabriel Partnership, Engineers and Architects, 1981-. *Memberships:* Royal Architectural Institute of Canada; Saskatchewan Association of Architects; Kinsmen Club of Prince Albert, Saskatchewan; Prince Albert Kinsmen Community Workshop; Sing Out Prince Albert Inc. *Creative Works:* Architectural Designs for numerous Schools, Office buildings, Apartment buildings, commercial and Industrial buildings. *Hobbies:* Reading; Drawing; Music; Dancing. *Address:* 406-515 6th St. South, Lethbridge Alberta, Canada, T1J 2E1.

MATTHEWS, David Morling, b. 15 Dec. 1926, High Wycombe, Bucks, England. Professor of Chemical Pathology. m. Patricia Mary Maxwell, 15 Nov. 1960. *Education:* University College and University College Hospital: MB, BS(Lond.) 1949; PhD (Sheff.) 1956; MD (Lond.) 1964; DSc (Lond.), 1979. *Appointments:* House Surgeon, University College Hospital, 1950-51; Assistant Lecturer, Physiology, University Sheffield Medical School, 1951-54; Assistant Pathologist, Selly Oak Hospital, Birmingham, 1954-56; Lecturer Physiology, University Birmingham Medical School, 1956-58; Lecturer Chemistry, Pathology, Royal Free Hospital, 1958-61; Senior Lecturer, Chemistry Pathology, Institute Neurology, London, 1962-65; Reader, Westminster Medical School, London, 1965-70; Professor, Experimental Chemistry, Pathology, 1970-. *Memberships:* Fellow, Royal College Pathologists; Royal College Physicians; Biochem. Society; Zool. Society; Assn. Clin. Pathologists; Assn. Clin. Biochemistry; Physiol. Society; Medical Research Society; British Society Gastroenterology; Nutrition Society; Editorial Board of Clinical Science. *Publications:* Scientific publications in the fields of intestinal absorption of protein digestion products and of vitamin B_{12} metabolism, e.g.: Intestinal absorption of peptides, 1975; Distribution of cobalamins in the animal body. Vitamin B_{12} and Intrinsic Factor, 1979. *Honours:* Fellowes Gold Medal in Medicine, 1947; Annual Memorial Lecturer of American Gastroenterological Society, 1977; Plenary Lecturer, 3rd European Symposium on Vitamin B_{12} anad Intrinsic Factor, 1979. *Hobbies:* Reading; Walking. *Address:* 7 Firs Avenue, London, N10, England.

MATTHEWS, Gordon MacDonald, b. 26 Feb. 1926, Barbados. Minister of Religion; Real Estate and Investment Consultant. m. (2) Eleanor Dailey, 12 Nov. 1977, 2 sons, 3 daughters. *Education:* Certificates in Insurance, Human Realtions, Public Speaking, Moody Bible Institute. *Appointments:* Assistant Manager, British American Life Insurance Company; Manager, First Federation Life Insurance Company; Manager, Encyclopaedia Britannica Limited; Sentor, 1971-76; Managing Director, Big Mac Enterprises; International Evangelist. *Memberships:* Carlton Club. *Publications:* Contributor to Magazines and Newspapers. *Honours:* Doctor of Divinity, 1976; Numerous awards in Sales. *Hobbies:* Cricket; Gardening; Reading. *Address:* 138 Chancery Lane, Christ Church, Barbados.

MATTHEWS, Horatio Keith, b. 4 April 1917, Eastbourne, England. Justice of the Peace. m. Jean Andree Batten, 8 June 1940, 2 daughters. *Education:* Epsom College, 1931-35; B.A., 1939, Gonville and Caius College, Cambridge, 1936-40. *Appointments:* I.C.S., Madras Presidency, 1940-47; Joined Foreign Office, 1948; Served in Lisbon, Bucharest, Middle East Forces, Canberra, Berlin; Minister Moscow, 1966-67; High Commissioner ACCRA, 1968-70; Under Secretary General UN, 1971-72; Senior Directing Staff, Royal College of Defence Studies, 1973-74; Retired 1974; Justice of the Peace, Isle of Wight, 1975-. *Memberships:* Travellers' Club. *Honours:* C.M.G., 1963; M.B.E., 1946. *Address:* Elm House, Bembridge, Isle of Wight, PO35 5UA, England.

MATTINGLEY, Keith Vaux, b. 13 May 1924, Melbourne, Australia. Journalist. m. Janine Glover Woods, 12 April, 1955, 2 sons, 3 daughters. *Education:* Scotch College, Melbourne. *Appointments:* Journalist, The Herald, Melbourne, 1941; Federal Political Roundsman, 1945-51; Press Secretary Prime Minister's Department, London, 1952-54; Gentleman Usher to Queen, Commonwealth Coronation Ball, 1953; Herald Sub-Editor, later Deputy Cief Sub-Editor, 1955-62; Feature Service Manager, 1962-65; Managing Editor South Pacific Post, Port Moresby, 1965-69; Development Manager, The Herald and Weekly Times Limited, 1969-70; Manager, The Sun News-Pictorial, Melbourne, 1970-79; Group Manager Publications, The Herald and Weekly Times Limited, 1980-; Chairman and Director of various companies including: The Argus and Australasian Limited; Standard Newspapers Limited; Publicity and Promotion, World Bowls Ltd, 1980; Commonwealth Press Union Tour of Australia, 1981; Founding Chairman, Council Australian Newspaper Advertising Bureau, 1981; Joint Executive Director, Australian Publishers' Bureau. *Memberships:* Trustee, Committee Member, Audit Bureau of Circulations; Newspaper Publishers' Association, Melbourne, 1971-; Commonwealth Press Union; International Press Institute; Melbourne Press Club; Papua Club, Papua New Guinea; Athenaeum Club, Melbourne. *Honours:* Honorary Justice of Peace; Life Governor Royal Women's Hospital and Sandringham and District Memorial Hospital. *Hobbies:* Sailing; Tennis. *Address:* 111 Dalgetty Road, Beaumaris. 3193, Australia.

MATTOCKS, John Godfrey Michael, b. 31 Oct. 1921, Upton, Norfolk, United Kingdom. m. 15 Nov. 1942, 3 sons. *Education:* Certificate Ed. College of St Mark and St John, Chelsea, 1940-42; BSc, London University, 1956; MSc, 1971, PhD Bath University, 1978. *Appointments:* RAF Bomber Command, Radar Technician, 1942-46; Head of Science, Monks' Dyke Secondary School, Louth, Lincs, 1946-48; Biology Master, Paston School, N. Walsham, Norfolk, 1948-60; Senior Lecturer, Norwich College of Education, Norwich, 1960-65; Head of Science, Redland College, Bristol, 1965-76; Principal Lecturer in Physiology, Bristol Polytechnic, 1976-. *Memberships:* Fellow, Institute of Biology; Society for Applied Bacteriology. *Publications:* Various scientific papers on Cellulose digestion, Avian Caecology, Education. *Hobbies:* Gardening; Painting; Writing; Bricklaying. *Address:* Manningham House, 12 Station Road, Nailsea, Bristol BS19 2PD, England.

MATUNGULU N'KUMAN TAVUN, H E, b. 26 June 1940, Kimpanda, Zaire. Ambassador. m. Bunkini Mwadi, 1972, 3 sons. *Education:* BA, Social Sciences, Geneva University, Switzerland; Master Degree Political Sciences and International Relations, Laval University of Quebec, Canada. *Appointments:* Department of Foreign Affairs and International Cooperation: in charge of UN Bureau and Institutions, specialised in Administration of International Cooperation and Research Bureau; President's Office, 1969; Department of Foreign Affairs, 1971; Adviser, President's Office, Zaire, 1973; Ambassador of the Republic of Zaire in Republic of Kenya, 1974; First Ambassador of Zaire, Portugal, 1976; Ambassador, of Zaire, Switzerland, 1978; Ambassador in Iran, 1979; Ambassador of Zaire, Great Britain, 1979-. *Honours:* Commandeur de l'Ordre National du Léopard. *Address:* Fairhill, 2 The Bishops Avenue, London N2, England.

MAUNDER, Marie Clare, b. 7 Oct. 1921, Boggabri, Australia. Grazier and Housewife. m. Edward Lionel Maunder, 8 Feb. 1944, 2 sons. *Education:* Armidale High School. *Appointments:* Semi retired Grazier. *Memberships:* CWA of NSW; Keep Australia Beautiful Council; Premiers' Advisory Council NSW; Sydney Committee for Overseas Students; Secretary, Wallabadah Anglican Guild; Quirindi Garden Club; Hospital Auxiliary and Red Cross. *Honours:* Member of the British Empire, 1979; Queen Elizabeth Jubilee Medal, 1977; Justice of the Peace, 1973; Lions Citizen of the Year, 1975; Life Member, CWA of NSW, 1975; Life Member Boggabri Pony Club 1980. *Hobbies:* Handicrafts; Spinning; Gardening; Reading; Theatre. *Address:* "Deepiendi" Wallabadah, NSW Australia.

MAVROYANNIS, Constantine, b. 13 Nov. 1927, Athens, Greece. Theoretical Physicist. m. Patricia Logothetis, 30 Aug. 1961, 2 daughters. *Education:* Bachelor, Chemical Engineering, National Technical University, Athens, Greece, 1957; PhD Physical Chemistry, McGill University Montreal, Canada, 1961; DPhil.,

Mathematics, Oxford University, Oxford, England, 1963. *Appointments:* Assistant Research Officer, 1964-65; Associate Research Officer, 1966-73, Senior Research Officer, National Research Council of Canada, 1974-. *Memberships:* American Physical Society; Canadian Association of Physicists; Fellow, Chemical Institute of Canada. *Publications:* Eighty scientific papers published in scientific journals and books; Scientific Topics of Research: Optical Properties and Many-Body Interactions in Solids; Quantum Optics and Quantum Electronics. *Honours:* Graduate Student Fellowship, National Research Council of Canada, 1959-61; NATO Science Overseas Postdoctoral Fellowship, Oxford University, England, 1961-63; National Research Council of Canada Postdoctoral Fellowship, 1963-64; Visiting Professor, University of Campinas, Campinas, Brazil, 1979. *Hobbies:* Reading; Gardening; Swimming; Cycling. *Address:* 2121 Maywood Street, Ottawa, Ontario, Canada, K1G 1E8.

MAXWELL, Judith Pamella, b. 13 June 1949, Barbados. Physiotherapist. *Education:* Diploma in Physical Therapy; Certificates in Basic Health Management, Basic Principles of Administration, Effective Speaking and Human Relations. *Appointments:* Physiotherapist, Queen Elizabeth Hospital, 1975-. *Memberships:* President, Barbados Association of Rehabilitation Therapists; President, Caribbean Association of Rehabilitation Therapists; Public Relations Officer, Queen's College Old Girls Association.; The Barbados Club of Toatmistress International. *Honours:* Outstanding Performance Award, Dale Carhegie Course, 1981. *Hobbies:* Cooking; Baking; Gardening. *Address:* 'Besamfi' Sandford, St. Philip, Barbados, West Indies.

MAY, Frederick, George Bruce, b. 5 Jan. 1904, Malvern, Victoria, Australia. Chartered Secretary. m. 9 Oct. 1937, 1 son, 2 daughters. *Education:* A.A.S.A., F.T.I.A., De La Salle College, Malvern, Melbourne University. *Appointments:* President, Melbourne Junior Chamber of Commerce, 1942; Chairman Melbourne, Chamber of Commerce Taxation Committee, 1955-78; Chambers Commerce Standing Tax Committee, Canberra, 1957-78; President, Melbourne Chamber of Commerce, 1960-61; President, Royal Melbourne Institute of Technology, 1962; President Assoc. Chamber of Commerce of Australia, 1965-67; Director Gas and Fuel Corporation, Victoria, 1966-78. *Memberships:* Lord Mayor's Fund Appeal Committee, 1958-79. *Hobby:* Walking. *Address:* 330 Alma Road, Caulfield North, Victoria 3161. Australia.

MAY, James, b. 9 May 1934, Gulgong, NSW, Australia. Professor of Surgery. m. Judith Ann Cox, 29 Nov. 1958, 1 son, 1 daughter. *Education:* St Paul's College, 1952-57; University of Sydney, 1952-57; MB, BS, 1958; MS, 1979; Fellowship, Royal Australasian College of Surgeons, 1962. *Appointments:* Resident Medical Officer, 1958-59, Surgical Registrar, 1962-63, Clinical Superintendent, Surgical, 1964, Honorary Surgeon, Royal Prince Alfred Hospital, Sydney, 1966-; Demonstrator and Lecturer in Anatomy, University of Sydney 1960; Research Fellow, Department of Surgery, University of California, San Francisco, 1964-65; Assistant Lecturer, Department of Surgery, University of Manchester, 1965; Surgical Registrar, Hope Hospital, Salford, England, 1966; Honorary Consulting Surgeon, Renal Transplant Unit, Sydney Hospital, 1968-; Visiting Surgeon, Repatriation General Hospital Concord 1968-73; Consultant Surgeon, Haemodialysis Unit, Mater Misericordiae Hospital, North Sydney 1971-; Professor of Surgery, University of Sydney, 1979-. *Memberships:* Societe Internationale de Chirurgie; International Cardiovascular Society; Transplantation Society; European Dialyais and Transplant Association; Australian Medical Association; Australasian Society of Nephrology; Vascular Section, Royal Australasian College of Surgeons. *Publications:* Numerous publications in the medical literature on the topics of arterial surgery, access to the circulation and transplantation. *Honours:* Henry Simpson Newland Prize, 1965; AMA/Kellogg Foundation Fellowship, 1981. *Hobby:* Tennis. *Address:* 20 Burrabirra Avenue, Vaucluse, NSW, Australia.

MAYER, Eric Anton, b. 11 Apr. 1930, Vienna, Austria. Manager. m. 1 Apr. 1930, 2 daughters. *Education:* Tiverton Boys Grammar School, 1940-45; Bromley Boys Grammar School, 1946-47. *Appointments:* National Mutual, 1949-: Manager Systems Division,

1968; Manager for Victoria, 1972, Manager for New South Wales, 1975, Assistant General Manager, 1978-. *Memberships:* Schools Board for Information Science, Victoria Institute of Colleges, 1968-73; Chairman, NSW Life Offices Assn., 1977. *Honours:* Fellow, Australian Computer Society, 1967. *Hobbies:* Gourmet Cooking; Writing. *Address:* 32 Broadway, Camberwell, Victoria, 3124, Australia.

MAYMAN, George Edwin (Ted), b. 11 Sept. 1912, Kalgoorlie, Australia. Banker (Retired), Writer. m. Daphne Beechey, 25 Sept. 1943, 1 son. *Education:* B.A., University of Western Australia, 1952. *Appointments:* Branches of the Bank of New South Wales, Australia, New Guinea, London; World War 11 service, Intelligence Officer, Royal Australian Air Force; Narrator, R.A.A.F., War History Section. *Memberships:* Australian Society of Authors; Fellowship of Australian Writers. *Publications:* The Mile That Midas Touched (co-author Gavin Casey) 1964; View from Kalgoorlie, 1969; Australian Aviator (co-author, Sir Norman Brearley) 1971; Short stories and poems in Australian anthologies. *Honours:* Tom Collins Prize in Australian Literature, University of Western Australia, 1951. *Hobby:* West Australian Goldfields History. *Address:* 55 Alderbury Street, Floreat Park, West Australia 6014, Australia.

MBAEYI, Paul Mmegha, b. 29 June 1937, Onitsha, Nigeria. Teacher. m. Philomena Afubera, 2 sons, 1 daughter. *Education:* Government College, Umuahia, E. Nigeria, 1951-56; University College, Ibadan, Nigeria, 1957-62; St. John's College Oxford, UK, 1962-65; BA Hons., London, 1962; DPhil. (Oxon) 1965; Fellow, Royal Historical Society, 1978. *Appointments:* Temporary Lecturer, Post-Doctoral Research Fellow, and Lecturer in History, University of Ibadan, Nigeria, 1966-67 and 1970-75; Senior Lecturer, History, University of Benin, Benin City, Nigeria, 1975; Acting Head, Department of History and Creative Arts, 1975-77; Acting Head, Department of History, 1977-78; Reader and Head, Department of History, Alvan Ikoku College of Education, Owerri, affiliated with University of Nigeria, Nsukka, Nigeria, 1980-. *Memberships:* Fellow, Royal Historical Society; Historical Society of Nigeria. *Publications:* British Military and Naval Forces in West African History, 1807—1874, 1978; A number of published papers and articles in learned journals. *Honours:* College Scholar, University College, Ibadan, Nigeria, 1959; History Prize, Faculty of Arts Prize, Ibadan, 1962; First Nigerian Rhodes Scholar to Oxford, 1961. *Address:* c/o Holy Rosary School, (Okwu Public School), Umuhu, Okabia, P.A, Orlu, Nigeria.

MBAH, Michael Udeh, b. 22 Apr. 1932, Nigeria. Senior Consultant Ophthalmic Surgeon. m. Cyrilene Braithwaite, Sept. 1967, 3 sons, 3 daughters. *Education:* BSc 1959, MB, ChB, St Andrews University, Scotland, 1963; DO England, 1966; FMCS, Nigeria 1977. *Appointments:* Senior House Ophthalmologist, Hull and Nottingham, 1964; Glasgow 1966; Registrar, Mansfield and Sheffield, 1967; 1967; Consultant Assistant Ophthalmologist, Ministry of Health, Nigeria, 1973; Senior Consultant Ophalmologist, 1977-. *Memberships:* Rotary International Onitsha Branch; Sports Club, Onitsha. *Hobbies:* Table Tennis; Lawn Tennis; Hunting. *Address:* 11 New Nkisi Road, GRA, Onitsha, Nigeria.

MBAKWEM, Mercy Nena, b. 9 Aug. 1928, Abiriba, Nigeria. Educationist. m. (1) Dr. Odim, Jan. 1950, (2) Dr.Onyegbula Benjamin, 29 Feb. 1964, 1 son, 1 daughter. *Education:* Teachers Grade II Certificate, 1947, Teachers Grade I Certificate, 1950, Nigeria; Professors Certificate, 1954, Ministry of Education Certificate, 1955, University of London, UK. *Appointments:* Head Mistress, Junior Primary School, Abiriba, Nigeria, 1948-53; Vice Principal, Teachers College, Umuobasi Amaro, 1956-57; Principal, Women's Training College, Ezeoke Nsu, 1958-66; Principal, Women's Training College, Umuahia, 1972-79; Principal, Teachers Training College, Ehine Mbano, Nigeria, 1979-. *Memberships:* President, 1968-76, Women's Cultural Organisation, Abiriba; President, Umuahia Branch, 1974-79, Business and Professional Women's Club; Council of Women's Society; Bible Society; Doctors Wives Club; Society for prevention of cruelty to children and animals. *Hobbies:* Knitting; Sewing; Gardening; Table tennis. *Address:* Principal's House, Teachers'

Training College, Ehime Mbano, Imo State, Nigeria, West Africa.

MBALANJE, Austin Timothy Bendera, b. 27 Dec. 1937, Kanyemba Village, Nkhotakota, Malawi. Lawyer. m. Loney Mwasambo, 27 Mar. 1963, 2 sons, 4 daughters. *Education:* Bachelor of Laws (Hons.), London, UK, 1973; Cambridge Course on Development, 1976; Public Sector Administration, Royal Institute of Public Administation, London, UK, 1981. *Appointments:* Teacher, various schools, 1962-68; Lecturer, Staff Training College and Institute of Public Administration, 1969-72; Registrar, Supreme Court of Appeal, 1972-73; Lands Officer, 1974-77; Principal Lands Officer, 1977-78; Commissioner for Lands, 1978-. *Publications:* Editor of College Magazine, SC1PA; Contributor to other College Magazines. *Hobbies:* Football; Short Story Writing; Cinema; Sightseeing. *Address:* PO Box 30395, Lilongwe 3, Malawi.

MBANEFO, Arthur Christopher Izuegbunam, b. 11 June, 1930, Onitsha, Nigeria. Chartered Accountant. m. Jacqueline Egbuna, 14 Aug. 1965, 1 son. *Education:* Cambridge School Certificate, 1946-51; FCA, Institute of Chartered Accountants in England and Wales, 1962; Wayne State University Centre for Applied Management and Technology, 1965-66. *Appointments:* Chater, Knight & Co., Chartered Accountants, Brighton, UK, 1957-59; Cooper Bros. & Co., Chartered Accountants, London, UK, 1960-61; Partner, 1965-, Akintola Williams & Co., Chartered Accountants, Lagos, Nigeria, 1962-; Lybrand, Ross Bros. & Montgomery, Certified Public Accountants, Detroit, USA, 1965-66; Price Waterhouse Associates, Management Consultants, London, UK, 1970-71; Managing Director, 1973-, AW Consultants Limited, Lagos, Nigeria, 1972-. *Memberships:* Institute of Chartered Accountants of Nigeria, 1971-, President, 1978-79; Founding Member, Honorary Treasurer, Vice-President, Nigerian Association of Management Consultants; Governing Council, Nigerian Institute of Management; Nigerian Institute of Management Consultants; Governing Council, International Federation of Accountants; Association of Accoutnancy Bodies in West Africa; Nigerian Chapter, The African Association of Public Administration and Management; Non-Executive Director, UAC of Nigeria Limited, Umarco Nigeria Limited, Metal Box, Nigeria Limited; St. John's Lodge No. 3780 EC., Onitsha, Nigeria; Metropolitan Club, Lagos, Nigeria; Ikoyi Club, Lagos, Nigeria. *Honours:* Member, Federal Republic, Investiture by President, 1981. *Hobbies:* Reading International Affairs; Collecting Works of Art; Golf; Tennis. *Address:* 11A Kingsway Road, Ikoyi, Lagos, Nigeria.

MBANUGO, Godwin Chinwendu, b. 5 June 1920, Calabar, Nigeria. Medical Practioner, Company Director. m. Justura Odunim, 10 June 1949, 5 sons, 4 daughters. *Education:* L.S.M., School of Medicine, Lagos, 1943-45. *Appointments:* Medical Officer, General Hospital, 1948-49; Medical Officer, General Hospital, Lagos, 1949-50; Private Medical Practice, 1951-54; Founded and appointed Medical Director, St. Thomas High, 1955-. *Memberships:* 1st Vice National President, Nigerian Medical Association; Distinguished Lodge of Nigeria; Officer of Grand Lodge of England. *Honours:* Distinction in Medicine, 1948; National Honour Commander of Fed. Republic of Nigeria, 1965. *Hobbies:* Reading; Dancing; Gardening. *Address:* St. Thomas Lodge, St. Thomas Street, Enugu, Anambra State, Nigeria.

MBEKEANI, Zandiukila Isaac, b. 1 Jan. 1946, Blantyre, Malawi. Land and Geodetic Surveying. m. May 1970, 2 sons, 1 daughter. *Education:* Associate Degree in Applied Science with Majors in Land Surveying, State University of New York, 1973-75; B.Sc., Surveying, Ferris State College, Michigan, 1975-77. *Appointments:* Staff Surveyor, 1977-79; Superintending Land Surveyor, 1979-80; Principal Land Surveyor, 1980-. *Memberships:* American Congress on Surveying and Mapping; Surveyors Institute of Malawi. *Publications:* Manual on Metrication in construction Industry. *Hobby:* Soccer. *Address:* Malawi Housing Corporation, P.O. Box 414, Blantyre, Malawi.

MBU, Matthew Tawo, b. 20 Nov. 1929, Okundi, Nigeria. Lawyer. m. Katherine Anigbo, 22 Oct. 1955, 4 sons, 2 daughters. *Education:* LL.B.(Hons.), 1959, LL.M., 1964, University of London, UK, External; Diploma in International Affairs, University College, London, UK, 1959; Barrister-at-Law, Middle Temple, London, UK, 1960. *Appointments:* Represented Ogoja, Eastern House of Assembly and House of Representatives, 1952-53; Member for Ogoja, House of Representatives, 1954-55; Federal Minister of Labour, 1953-54; Acting Minister of Transport and Minister of Commerce, 1954-55; Member of Parliament for Ogoja, 1960-66; Minister of Defence, Navy, 1961-65; Minister of Aviation, 1966; Nigerian Pioneer Diplomat; First High Commissioner for Nigeria in UK, 1955-59; First Nigerian Chief Representative in Washington DC, USA, 1959-60; First Nigerian Chief Representative in United Nations, 1959-60; Represented Nigeria at many International Conferences; Appointed Head of OAU Commission to investigate President Sylvanus Olympio's assassination, 1963; Appointed Nigerian Chief Delegate to OAU Conference in Addis Ababa, 1963; Nigerian Chief Delegate to OAU Conference on Army Mutiny, Tanganyika, 1964; Chairman of many private companies including: Alraine (Nigeria) Limited; Legal Consultant to business interests in Nigeria; Solicitor and Advocate of Supreme Court of Nigeria; Pro-Chancellor and Chairman of Council, University of Ife, Nigeria. *Memberships:* Fellow, London Institute of International Affairs; Fellow, Royal Society of Arts; Fellow, Royal Economic Society; Fellow, Nigerian Society of International Law; Fellow, Royal Commonwealth Society. *Hobbies:* Lawn tennis; Table tennis; Swimming; Billiards. *Address:* 2A Fosbery Road, Ikoyi, Lagos, Nigeria.

MBUNDA, Daniel, b. 27 Sept. 1927, Ruvuma, Tanzania. Adult Educator. m. Grace Masawe, 12 May 1979, 2 daughters. *Education:* BA., 1962-65, Higher Diploma in Education, 1965-66, National University of Ireland, Dublin, Ireland; Master of Philosophy, 1979-80, Doctoral Student, Southampton University, UK. *Appointments:* Headmaster, Secondary School Teacher, Kigonsera, Likonde, Tanzania, 1958-71; Assistant Director, Adult Education, National Headquarters of Education, Dar-Es-Salaam, 1972-73; Director of Institute of Adult Education, University of Dar Es Salaam, 1973-75; Director of Institute of Adult Education, Dar Es Salaam, 1975-79. *Memberships:* National Advisory Council to Ministry of Education, 1973-79; Chairman of National Media Study Team, 1979; Sub-Committee on Presidential Commission on Education, 1981; History Association; Trustee, Adult Education Association, Tanzania; Vice-Chairman, African Consultative Group. *Publications:* Adult Education in Tanzania, 1972; Adult Education Revolution, 1972; Mass Campaigns, 1976; Cultural Values and Education Process in African Societies, 1982. *Hobbies:* Reading; Music; Man in action. *Address:* Box 60190, Kawe, Dar Es Salaam, Tanzania.

MDA, Zanemvula Kizito Gatyeni, b. 6 Oct. 1948, Eastern Cape, South Africa. Playwright; Poet; Artist. m. Mpho, Dec. 1971, (separated), 2 sons, 1 daughter. *Education:* Cambridge Overseas School Certificate, 1969; Bachelor of Fine Arts, 1976. *Appointments:* Assistant Teacher, Lesotho Ministry of Education, 1970-71; Deputy Headmaster and High School English Literature Teacher, Ministry of Education, 1976-80; Cultural and Academic Exchange Program Officer, American Cultural Center, 1980-. *Memberships:* Royal Society of Literature. *Publications:* Poetry in New South African Writing, 1977; We Shall Sing for the Fatherland and Other Plays, 1981; Poems and plays in various publications in southern Afrika and Nigeria; Theatrical Productions: We Shall Sing for the Fatherland, Dead End, 1978-79; Dark Voices Ring, 1979; The Hill, 1980; Art Exhibitions: Many locally, one in Bristol, UK, 1976; Edmonton, Canada, 1978. *Honours:* Merit award of Amstel Playwright Society for play 'We Shall Sing for the Fatherland', 1978; Amstel Playwright of Year award for play 'The Hill', 1980. *Hobbies:* Playing the flute; Composing music. *Address:* Cathedral Area, PO Box 1116, Maseru 100, Lesotho.

MEAD, William Bernard, b. 17 Jan. 1932, Dalby, Queensland, Australia. Local Government Administrator; Public Accountant. m. Shirley Dawn McLaughlin, 19 May 1956, 5 sons, 1 daughter. *Education:* Associate in Accountancy, University of Queensland, Australia, 1959; Qualified Local Government Clerk and Fellow of IMA, 1960; Local Government Auditor, 1961; Registered Tax Agent, 1961; Fwllow, Incorporated Association of Cost Accountants, 1962. *Appointments:* Commonwealth Bank Officer, Dalby, Queensland, Australia; Private Practice, Real Estate Business, Dalby, Queensland, Australia; Deputy Town and Shire Clerk, Dalby, Longreach, St. George, Queensland, Australia; Shire Clerk, Murilla Shire, Miles and Gatton Australia. *Memberships:* Institute of Affiliated Accountants; Associate Fellow, Australian Institute of Management; Institute of Commercial Studies; Secretary, South Western Local Authorities Development Association; Committee Chairman, Cub Leader, Group Scout Master, Boy Scouts Association; St. Vincent De Paul Society; Foundation President, Miles and District Marist Old Boys Association. *Honours:* Honorary Life Membership, Ashgrove Marist Old Boys Association; Justice of the Peace of State of Queensland. *Hobbies:* Gardening; Lawn bowls. *Address:* 2 Highview Avenue, Gatton 4343, Queensland, Australia.

MEADOWS, Arthur Wilkes, b. 11 June 1911, England. Psychologist; Statistician. m. Mavis Elizabeth McLennan, 23 Dec. 1935, 1 son, 1 daughter. *Education:* Trained Teachers Certificate, Melbourne Teachers College, Australia, 1934; BA.(Hons.), 1945, MA-.(Hons.), 1948, Melbourne University, Australia; PhD., University College, London University, UK, 1951. *Appointments:* Teacher, Education Department, Victoria, Australia, 1929-38; Psychologist, Stipendiary Probation Officer, Crown Law Department, Victoria, Australia, 1939-49; Principal Psychologist, Health Department, Victoria, Honorary Psychologist, Royal Melbourne Hospital, Australia, 1950-55; Consultant Psychologist, RAAF, 1951-61; Honorary Psychologist, Melbourne Institute for Psychoanalysis, 1945-54; Head of Psychology, Reader, Adelaide University, Honorary Psychologist, Royal Adelaide Hospital, Australia, 1955-60; Manager, Market Research, WD Scott & Co., 1960-61; Senior Lecturer, Applied Psychology & Business Administration, University of New South Wales, Australia, 1961-71; Director, Market and Industrial Research, Arthur Meadows & Co. Pty. Limited, 1971; Editor, Australian Journal of Marketing Research, 1969-75. *Memberships:* Federal Chairman, Market Research Society of Australia; Fellow, British Psychological Society; Fellow, Institute of Statisticians, England; Fellow, Royal Statistical Society, England; Fellow, Australian Psychological Society; Statistical Society of Australia; Ergonomics Society of Australia; American National Club, Australia. *Publications:* Publications in field of industrial psychology and statistical applications to market research. *Honours:* Honorary Life member, Australian Market Research Society, 1973. *Hobbies:* Music; Photography; Gardening; Fishing. *Address:* 8 Beauty Point Road, Beauty Point 2088, New South Wales, Australia.

MEADOWS, Brian Stanley, b. 8 Feb. 1939, London, England. Hydrobiologist; Geologist. m. Patricia Elizabeth Ann Ringrose, 12 May, 1962, 1 son. *Education:* BSc.(Hons.), University of London, UK, 1963-69. *Appointments:* Assistant Pollution Control Officer, 1964-66, Area Pollution Control Officer, 1966-70, Lee Conservancy Catchment Board, Cheshunt, UK; Higher Scientific Officer, Salmon and Freshwater Fisheries Laboratory, Ministry of Agriculture and Fisheries, Whitehall Place, London, UK, 1970-72; Head of Water Quality, 1972-, Senior Assistant Secretary, 1975, under Secretary, 1979, Ministry of Water Development, Pollution Control, Kenya. *Memberships:* Institute of Biology; Institute of Water Pollution Control; Institute of Water Engineers and Scientists; Institute of Fisheries Management; British Ornithologists Union; Fellow, Zoological Society of London; British Ecological Society; Life member, Freshwater Biological Association; London Natural History Society; East Africa Natural History Society. *Publications:* Over 30 Scientific papers including: Water Development and Resources Management, (with D Baker), 1978; The Quality of Water of the Lake Victoria Basin and its Protection, 1979; Chapter on Waste Water Treatment in Water Resources Handbook for Kenya, in press; Book: Birds of East Africa, Their Habitat, Status and Distribution, 1980; Responsible for 14 Families Jacanidae-Rynchopidae, Eurlamidae-Pittidae. *Honours:* Head Boy award, Tottenham School of Commerce, 1954; International Development Research Centre Grantee in Waste-Water Reclamation, 1957-80. *Hobby:* Ornithology. *Address:* PO Box 30521, Nairobi, Kenya.

MEAKIN, Ian Louis, b. 8 Oct. 1944, Sydney, New South Wales, Australia. Orthopaedic Surgeon. m. Elspeth Margaret George, 5 May 1971, 1 daughter. *Education:* MBBS., University of New South Wales,

Australia; FRACS. *Appointments:* Visiting Orthopaedic Surgeon, Western Suburbs Hospital, Bonkstown Hospital, Canterbury Hospital, New South Wales, Australia. *Memberships:* President, Koscüisko Alpine Club; University Club; Elandora Country Club; Cruising Yacht Club of Australia. *Hobbies:* Sailing; Skiing; Tennis; Golf. *Address:* 20 Upper Minimbah Road, Northbridge, New South Wales 2063, Australia.

MEANEY Patrick (Sir), b. 6 May 1925, London, England. Company Director. m. Mary June Kearney, 1 son. *Education:* Wimbledon College. *Appointments:* Group Managing Director, Chief Executive, Thomas Tilling Limited; Director, Midland Bank Limited; Director, Imperial Chemical Industries Ltd. Director, Cable and Wireless Limited; Director, Rank Organisation Limited. *Memberships:* Sdvisory Board, European Management Forum; Confederation of British Industry; British North American Committee; British Institute of Management; President of Institute of Marketing; London Chamber of Commerce; *Publications:* Various articles on Business Education, Economics, Management. *Honours:* Knight Bachelor, 1981. *Hobbies:* Sport; Music; Travel; International Business; Social Education. *Address:* Stambourne House, Totteridge Village, London N20 8JP, England.

MEDNIS, Karlis Fredericks Andreis, b. 1 Apr. 1910, Pensa, Russia. Artist. m. Taissa Demidoff, 11 June 1969. *Education:* University of Riga, Latvia; Riga School of Art, Latvia. *Appointments:* bacteriologist, Riga University Seruminstitut, 1939-44; Teacher, Victorian Artists' Society Art School, 1958-72; Self-employed, Art School, Melbourne, 1972-75. *Memberships:* Old Watercolour Society Club of London; Australian Guild of Realist Artists; Victorian Artists' Society. *Creative Works:* Commissioned painting of the Presentation of The Standard, by His Royal Highness The Prince of Wales, 1981. *Honours:* E T Cato Prize, Melbourne, 1950 and 1967; Latvian Art Festival Prize, in Sydney New York, Melbourne Adelaide and Cleveland; Albury Watercolour Prize 1965; Camberwell Rotary Watercolour Prize 1966 and 1980; The Ronald Prize, Morwell 1971; Artist of the Year award 1979; Mednis as Academician with Gold Medal 1980; Kiwanis Club of Keilor Prize 1981; Works represented in the National Collection, Canberra; Australian State and Provincial Galleries in many important private collections, in Australia and overseas, England, America and Europe. *Hobbies:* Collecting: Antiques; Coins; Books; Photography; Classical Music. *Address:* 16 Rookwood Street, North Balwyn, Victoria 3104, Australia.

MEDWAY, David George, b. 26 June 1939, New Plymouth, New Zealand. Barrister and Solicitor. m. Jeanette Carole Lamont, 23 Oct. 1965, 3 daughters. *Education:* LLB, Victoria University, Wellington New Zealand, 1964. *Appointments:* Barrister and Solicitor 1964-. Fellow Linnean Society of London; Society for the Bibliography of Natural History; Hakluyt Society; Ornithological Society of New Zealand; Royal Australasian Ornithologists Union; Associate member, Cornell Laboratory of Ornithology; Royal Forest and Bird Protection Society of New Zealand; National Parks Authority of New Zealand, etc. *Publications:* Various ornithological contributions in Notornis, journal of the Ornithological Society of NZ; Published works on various aspects of a continuing study of the ornithology of Cook's three voyages of circumnavigation. *Honours:* FLS 1978; Notary Public 1979. *Hobbies:* Ornithology; Conservation. *Address:* 25a Norman Street, New Plymouth, New Zealand.

MEE, Jenny, b. 23 Aug. 1935, Wushi, China. Medical Practitioner. *Education:* Acton Technical College, Acton, England, 1957-59; MB, ChB, University of Birmingham Medical School, 1960-65; D.Obst, RCOG, 1967; MRCP(UK) 1973. *Appointments:* House Officer posts in Surgery, Medicine and Obstetrics, in the Birmingham Group of Hospitals, 1965-67; Senior House Officer, Paediatrics in Poole and Dorset Group Hospitals, 1967-68; Temporary Physician, Edinburgh Medical Missionary Hospital, Nazareth, Israel, 1968-69; Registrar in Medicine and Paediatrics, South London Hospital, England, 1969-71; Registrar in Paediatrics, Birmingham Childrens Hospital and Sorrento Maternity Hospital, England, 1971-73; Paediatrician, Wesley Guild Hospital, Ilesha, Nigeria, 1973-75; Lecturer, Senior Lecturer, Department of Paediatrics, Ahmadu Bello University Hospital, Zaria, Nigeria, 1975-78; Consultant Paediatrician, Mersey General Hospital, Tasmania, Australia, 1979-. *Memberships:* Australian College of Paediatrics; Paediatric Society of Tasmania; North West Walking Club of Tasmania. *Publications:* Phototherapy for Neonatal Jaundice in rural Africa, 1977; BCG for Neonates: A comparison of three methods, 1977; Circulating immune complexes and complement levels in relation to the clinical presentation of Nigerian children with acute poststreptococcal glomerurephritis, 1978; Reye's Syndrome: A report of two cases from Northern Nigeria, 1979. *Honours:* School leaving prize, 1952. *Hobbies:* Reading; Music; Walking; Batik Printing; Painting; Pottery. *Address:* 3 Ventnor Place, Latrobe, Tasmania 7307, Australia.

MEHRA, Pran Nath, b. 27 Oct. 1907, Amritsar, Panjab, India. Education. m. 6 Dec. 1937, 6 daughters. *Education:* MSc Hons. First Class, 1930, DSc, Panjab University, 1942. *Appointments:* Lecturer in Botany, 1932; Reader in Botany, 1947; Professor of Botany, 1950; Professor of Botany and Dean Science Faculty and Agricultural Faculty, Panjab University, 1965-; Research Advisor, Government of India, Himachal Agricultural University, Simla, 1978-79. *Memberships:* Fellow, Indian National Science Academy; American Botanical Society; Fellow, National Academy of Sciences, India; Fellow, Indian Botanical Society; Fellow, Indian Palynological Society; Indian Pharmaceutical Association. *Publications:* Three Books published; 280 Original Research Papers in International journals. *Honours:* Gold Medal of National Academy of Sciences, India, 1951; Education Ministers Gold Medal, 1951; Birbal Sahni Gold Medal, 1968; Institutional Alumini Gold Medal, 1968; Padma Shri Award of Government of India, 1972; Medal as Vice President International Botanical Congress, Leningrad, 1975; Gunner Erdtman International Gold Medal, 1975; Hon. Professor, Tribhuvan University, Nepal National Lecturer, University Grants Commission, 1970. *Hobby:* Hiking. *Address:* Bungalow 1055, Sector 27-B, Chandigarh, India.

MEHTA, Fali Sorabji, b. 2 Apr. 1923, Bombay, India. Dental Surgeon. m. Joan H Bielefeld, 6 May 1961, 2 sons. *Education:* LDSc, Nair Hospital Dental College, Bombay, 1947; DMD, Tufts University School of Dental Medicine, USA, 1949. *Appointments:* Professor and Head of Research Department and Superintendent of Clinics, Nair Hospital Dental College, 1952-65; Chief of Dental Services, Bhabha Atomic Research Centre, Bombay, 1964-; Head, Basic Dental Research Unit, Tata Institute of Fundamental Research, Bombay, 1964-; Honorary Consultant, Maharashtra State Police, 1953-; Honorary Dental Surgeon, Governor of Maharashtra, 1963-. *Memberships:* Willingdon Club, Bombay; WIAA, Bombay; Pierre Fauchard Academy, USA; Indian Dental Association; WHO Expert Advisory Panel on Oral Health; American Academy of Periodontology; Dental Council of India; Indian Dental Association. *Publications:* Principal Investigator, Study of oral cancer and precancerous lesions sponsored by, National Cancer Institute of US Government; Published over 90 research papers in Indian and world journals; Coauthor, Oral Cancer and Precancerous conditions in India, 1971; Early Detection of Oral Cancer and Precancerous Lesions, 1974. *Honours:* Fellow, American College of Dentists, USA; Fellow, Royal Society of Health, London; Fellow, International College of Dentists, USA; Fellow, American Association for the Advancement of Science, USA; Recipient of 'Dr. Ernest Borges Memorial Oration' Award. *Hobbies:* Western Music; Vintage car rallies; Badminton. *Address:* "Sea Side", Women Graduate Union Road, Colaba, Bombay 400 005, India.

MEHTA, Mohan Sinha, b. 20 Apr. 1895, Bhilwara, India. Education; Administration; Social Service. m. Shrimati Hulas Kumari, 15 May 1910, 1 son. *Education:* Graduated, Agra College, Agra 1916; Post Graduate, Allahabad University 1918, Bachelor-in Law, 1919; PhD London University 1928; Barrister-at-Law, Middle Temple London. Lecturer, Government College, Ajmer 1919; Commissioner, Headquarters, Scout Association, India 1920; Revenue Officer, State of Mewar 1922-36; Chief Minister, Banswara State 1937-40; Minister of Revenue and Education, Mewar State Government 1940-44; Chief Minister, Finance and Education Minister, 1944-46, 1946-48; Member, Constituent Assembly of India 1946-47; Ambassador of India, Netherlands 1949-51; High Commissioner of India, Pakistan 1951-55; Ambassador of India, Switzerland,

Austria and the Vatician 1955-58; Indian Delegation, UN General Assembly 1959; Vice-Chancellor of Rajasthan University 1960-66. *Memberships:* Vice-President, All India Seva Samitri; President, Indian Adult Education; Vice-President, National People's Committee; President, N.P.C; Vice-President, Amnesty International; Executive Committee of Udaipur University; Indian Council of World Affairs. *Publications:* Author: Lord Hastings and the Indian States 1929; Vidya Bahawan, a progressive co-education Educational Complex. *Honours:* William Trolly Award Syracuse University US 1969; National Government's Award 1969; National Federation of UNESCO Associations Award 1979; Special Award, Vidma Vibhushasm 1969; Asian and South Pacific, Bureau of Adult Education 1972; G D Parikh Memorial Award 1980; Doctor of Literature (Honor's causa) University of Udaipur. *Hobbies:* Gardening; Camping; Mountain Hiking. *Address:* Seva Mandir, Udaipur 313 001, Rajasthan, India.

MEHTA, Ratanmal, b. 18 Nov. 1938, Jodhpur. Industrialist. m. Mehta Kamala, 24 Nov. 1956, 2 sons, 1 daughter. *Education:* BSc, 1960. *Appointments:* Teacher, 1960-66; Business and Industry, 1966-. *Memberships:* The Sivakasi Chamber of Trade Promotion; Sivakasi Calendar Manufactures Association; Sri Navratna Ayurvedic Hospital, Jodhpur; Paper Merchants Association, Sivakasi; South India Wax Manufactures Association, Sivakasi. *Hobby:* Reading. *Address:* 183 P.P. Colony, Sivakasi, South India.

MEIN, Joy, b. Melbourne Australia. Company Director. m. Ian Pulteney Mein, 27 Nov. 1941 (dec.), 1 son, 1 daughter. *Education:* St Margarets Girls School, Melbourne. *Appointments:* Company Director, 26 years. *Memberships:* State President Liberal Party of Australia, Victorian Division 1976-79; Federal Vice-President Liberal Party 1979-; State Executive 1967; Federal Executive 1974-; Consumer Affairs Council 1973-76. *Hobbies:* Golf; Tennis; Garden. *Address:* Wandilla, 2 Stephens Road, Mount Eliza 3930, Victoria, Australia.

MEINCKE, Peter Paul Max, b. 21 Jan. 1936, Winnipeg, Manitoba, Canada. Physicist. m. Donna Mallinson, 28 June 1958, 1 son, 1 daughter. *Education:* Graduated, Engineering Physics, Royal Military College, Kingston, Ontario, 1958; BSc, Queen's University, Kingston, Ontario, 1959; MA, 1960, PhD, University of Toronto, Low Temperature Physics, 1963. *Appointments:* Lecturer, 1962-63, Assistant Professor, Royal Military College, Kingston Ontario 1963-65; Technical Staff, Bell Telephone Laboratories, Murray Hill, NJ, USA 1965-67; Assistant Professor, 1967-69, Associate Professor with tenure, 1969-, Associate Dean, Erindale College, University of Toronto, 1970-72; Vice Provost, 1972-76, Professor, University of Toronto, 1977-78; President, University of Prince Edward Island, Charlottetown, P.E.I, Canada, 1978-. *Memberships:* Chairman, Board, Institute of Man and Resources; Board of Governors, Holland College; Canadian Environmental Advisory Council; Canadian Military Colleges Advisory Board; National Library Advisory Board. *Publications:* Measurements of Elastic Constants and Search for Collective Oscillations of the Vortex Lattice in a Type II Superconductor, 1969; Effect of Size and Surface on the Specific Heat of Small Lead Particles, 1972; Observation of a Profile on a Superfluid Helium Film on a Rotating Substrate, 1975; Knowledge Space: A Conceptual Basis for the Organization of Knowledge, 1976. *Hobbies:* Swimming; Skiing. *Address:* 181 Fitzroy Street, Charlottetown, P.E.I. Canada C1A 1S3.

MEISEL, John, b. 23 Oct. 1923 Vienna, Austria. Commission Chairman; Political Scientist. m. Murie Augusta Kelly 6 Aug. 1949. *Education:* BA 1948; MA University of Toronto, Victoria College 1950; PhD, London School of Political Science and Econ9omics, 1959. *Appointments:* Chairman, Canadian Radio-television and Telecommunications Commission, 1980-; Professor Political Science, Queen's University, Kingston, Ontario, 1949-79; Head of Department Political Science; Hardy Professor of Political Science. *Memberships:* Royal Society of Canada; Royal Commonwealth Society. *Publications:* Books and Monographs: The Canadian General Election of 1957, 1962; Papers on the 1962 Election, 1964; L'évolution des partis politiques canadiens, 1966; Ethnic Relations in Canadian Voluntary Associations, 1972; Working Papers on Canadian Politics, 1972, 73, 75; Cleavages, Parties and

Values in Canada, 1974; 47 Articles including: A Note on Nato, 1952; The Emerging Nations and the West, 1960; Party Images in Canada, 1970; Leisure, Politics and Political Science 1978; The Larger Context: General Developments Preceding the Election, 1979; Videotapes: People and Power: Host Professor of 25 videotaped series of one hour programs on Canadian Politcs. *Honours:* Canada Council Killam Award—5 years. *Hobbies:* Music; Swimming; Literature; Nature; Skiing; Indoor gardening. *Address:* Colimaison, R.R. #1, Tichborne, Ontario, Canada K0H 2V0.

MEISSNER, Stefan Tadeusz, b. 14 Jan. 1926, Buczynek, Poland. Engineer. m. Aleksandra Ursyn Niemcewicz, 18 Nov. 1946, 5 sons. *Education:* Dipl.Ing, (Mast.Eng.) Polish University College, London, England, 1951. *Appointments:* Engineer, Chief Engineer, Compr. Division, MGR Production, Canadian Ingersoll Rand, Sherbrooke P.Q., 1951-77; Director of Manufacturing Operations, Ingersoll Rand Brazil, Sao Paulo Br., 1977-80; Vice President, Operations, Canadian Ingersoll Rand, Cambridge, Ontario, 1980-. *Memberships:* Engineering Institute of Canada; Order of Engineering of Quebec; Association of Polish Engineers in Canada. *Honours:* Cross for Bravery, Polish Underground Army, Warsaw, 1944. *Hobbies:* Skiing; Swimming; Tennis; Chess. *Address:* RR-33, Cambridge, Ontario, N3H 4R8, Canada.

MEKI, Constantine, b. 9 Sept. 1950, Chilubi Island, Zambia. Forester. *Education:* Diploma in Forestry, Zambia Forest College, 1972; BSc (For), Makerere University, Kampala, 1975. *Appointments:* Silviculturist, 1975-77; Chief Forest Research Officer, 1977-. *Memberships:* Country representative, International Council, The International Union of Forest Research Organizations; American Wood Preservers Association; Zambia Forestry Association. *Publications:* Methods of Establishing and Tending Plantations, 1980. *Hobbies:* Nature Study; Tennis; Swimming. *Address:* No 5 Munali Crescent, Parklands, Kitwe, Zambia.

MELDRUM, Ivor William, b. 28 Aug. 1924, Victoria, Australia. Utility Executive Chief Engineer. m. Verna Elsie O'Brien, 10 Jan. 1945 (Dec.) 1 son. *Education:* Dip.EE, Castlemaine, 1942; BEE, Melbourne, 1949, BMechE 1953; MSEE Stanford, 1957; State Electricity Commission of Victoria Scholar, 1956. *Appointments:* State Electricity Commission of Victoria: Laboratory Assistant, 1945; Draftsman, 1946; Engineer-Electrical design, 1949; Technical Studies Engineer, 1962; Projects Planning Engineer, Fuel and power project, 1964-. *Memberships:* Fellow, Institution of Engineers Australia; National Committees on Environmental Engineering, Electric Energy, Task Force on Energy, Victorian Division Committee; Fellow, Australian Institution of Energy; Institution of Electrical and Electronics Engineers; International Practices Sub-committees on Power Generation and Power System Engineering, Committee on Power and Environmental Sciences; Australasian Institute of Mining and Metallurgy; Royal Society of Victoria; Australian and New Zealand Association for the Advancement of Science, Town and Country Planning Association. *Publications:* Technical papers to Professional and industry associations including: World Energy Conference, Power Engineering Society of IEEE, Institute of Engineers Australia In field. *Hobby:* Raising Stud Aberdeen Angus cattle and operation of grazing property. *Address:* High Park, Lancefield Road, Kilmore, Victoria 3601 Australia.

MELDRUM, Richard John, b. 12 July 1928, Melbourne, Australia. Architect. m. 1951, 2 sons, 2 daughters. *Education:* BArch(Hons) Melbourne; Hons. Melbourne Dip.Arch.; RMIT; FRIBA; FRAIA: ARNZIA: AACI; FIAID. *Appointments:* Senior Partner, Meldrum Burrows and Partners, Australia, Foulsham Meldrum Burrows, Middle East, Partner, Meldrum and Noad, 1954-59; Meldrum and Partners, 1959-64; Senior Partner, 1964-69; Senior Partner, Meldrum Burrows and Partners, 1970-; Partner, I-C Foulsham Meldrum Burrows, Middle East; Saudi F.M.B. ME. *Memberships:* Melbourne City Council; Parks Gardens and Recreations Committee; Strategy and City Planning Committee; Building and Land Use Committee; St. Kilda Road Advisory Committee; Commissioner Melbourne and Metropolitan Board of Works. *Hobbies:* Travel; Reading; Golf; Archaeology. *Address:* 92 George Street, East Melbourne 3002, Australia.

MELDRUM, William Dickson, b. 18 Jan. 1924, Hamilton, New Zealand. Medical Practitioner. m. Florence Rae Burley, 12 Aug. 1950, 3 sons, 2 daughters. *Education:* University National Scholarship, 1941; MBChB, Otago University Medical School, New Zealand, 1947; DA, London, UK, 1955-56; FFARCS, 1956; FFARACS, 1961. *Appointments:* House Surgeon and physician, 1948-49, Anaesthetic Registrar, 1950, Wellington Hospital, New Zeland; Anaesthetic Registrar, Christchurch Hospital, New Zealand, 1951; General practitioner and anaesthetist, Timaru, 1952-; Anaesthetist, 1954-, Director of Anaesthetics, 1965-, Timaru Hospital, New Zealand. *Memberships:* Executive Committee, Past President, South Canterbury Division, New Zealand Branch of BMA subsequently NZMA; Chairman of Committee, 1971-72, Fellow of Faculty of Anaesthetists, Royal Australian College of Surgeons; Royal New Zealand Army Medical Corps; CO., 3rd Field Ambulance, 1966-68; CO., New Zealand Combined Services Medical Team, Vietnam, 1968-69; President, 1979-80, Rotary Club of Timaru; Chairman, Staff Committee, Timaru Hospital, 1979-80. *Hobbies:* Skiing; Yachting; Squash; Golf; Carpentry; Gardening. *Address:* 10 Sealy Street, Timaru, New Zealand.

MELLANBY, Kenneth, b. 26 Mar. 1908, Barrhead, Scotland. Editor and Environmental Consultant. m. (1) Helen Neilson-Dow 3 Oct. 1935, (2) Jean Louie Copeland, 15 May 1949, 1 son, 1 daughter. *Education:* Kings College, Cambridge 1926-30; MA, ScD Cambridge; PhD London. *Appointments:* Research Worker, London School of Hygiene and Tropical Medicine 1930-36; Sorby Research Fellow, Royal Society of London 1936-45; Major, RAMC 1943-45; Reader, Medical Entomology, University of London 1945-47; First Principal, University College, Ibadan, Nigeria 1947-54; Head, Entomology Department, Rothamsted Experimental Station 1955-61; First Director, Monks Wood Experimental Station 1961-74. *Memberships:* Fellow, Institute of Biology; Atheneum Club; Committee of Management; Bedfordshire and Huntingdonshire Naturalists Trust. *Publications:* Scabies, Oxford Press; Human Guineapigs; The Birth of Nigeria's University; Pesticides and Polution; The Biology of Pollution; Can Britain Feed Itself; Talpa—the Story of a Mole; Farming and Wildfife; Editor: International journal, Environmental Pollution. *Honours:* Commander British Empire 1954; DSc Ibadan 1968; DSc Bradford 1970; DSc Leicester 1972; Doctor of the University, Essex, 1980; Professor, Universities of Leicester, Cardiff, Polytechnic of Central London. Hobby: Gardening. *Address:* Hill Farm, Wennington, Huntingdon, PE17 2LU, England.

MELLICK, John Stanton Davis, b. 22 Feb. 1920, Londonderry, Northern Ireland. Pharmacist; University Teacher; Army Officer (retired). m. Violet Katts, 8 Dec. 1941, 1 daughter. *Education:* psc Australian Army Staff College, Duntroon, 1942; PhC, Pharmacy Board of Queensland 1949; MPS 1950; BA(Hons) 1967; PhD, University of Queensland 1978. *Appointments:* War Service, 1940-45; Self-employed Pharmacist, 1949-64; English Department, University of Queensland 1968-80; Australian Army Reserve Lieut-Colonel, Chief Signals Officer Northern Command and Commanding Officer, 1959-70. *Memberships:* Pharmaceutical Society of Queensland; Chairman, Christian Education Committee and Social Services Committee, Presbyterian Church Queensland, 1962-76; Board of Governors, St Andrew's Hospital, Brisbane. *Publications:* Founder-editor, Pharmaceutical Society of Queensland Bulletin; Author, Henry Kingsley (1830-76), The Unfortunate Brother; Editor of Kingsley Anthology; Editor, History of the Pharmaceutical Society of Queensland, 1880-1980. *Honours:* Mentioned in Despatches 1945; Australian Army Efficiency Decoration 1969. *Hobbies:* Golf; Fishing; Reading. *Address:* 11 Havane Street, Ashgrove 4060, Brisbane, Australia.

MELLON, James, b. 25 Jan. 1929, Glasgow. Diplomatic Service. m. (1) Frances Murray 2 Apr. 1956 (dec.) (2) Philippa Shuttleworth Hartley, 10 Aug. 1979, 1 son, 3 daughters. *Education:* MA Glasgow. *Appointments:* Department of Agriculture for Scotland 1953-60; Agricultural Attaché Copenhagen and The Hague, 1960-63; Foreign Office 1963-64; Head of Chancery, Dakar, 1964-66; UK Delegation, European Communities, 1967-72; Counsellor 1970; Head, Science and Technology Department FCO, 1973-75; Commercial Counsellor, East Berlin, 1975-76; Head, Trade Relations and Export Department FCO 1976-78; High Commissioner,

Ghana and Ambassador to Togo 1978-. *Honours:* CMG 1979. *Address:* FCO, King Charles Street, London SW1, England.

MELLOR, Alfred Burdett, b. 2 Nov. 1915, Melbourne, Australia. Stockbroker. m. Phyllis Mary Lorraine (div.), 2 Nov. 1939, (2) Maureen Ann Walsh, 4 Oct. 1974, 4 sons. *Appointments:* Member, Stock Exchange of Melbourne, Australia, 1944-; Senior Partner, Alfred B Mellor & Co., 1944-72; Joint Senior Partner, May & Mellor, 1972-; Chairman, Australian Associated Stock Exchanges, 1960-64; Chairman, 1960-66, Committee, 1949-72, Stock Exchange of Melbourne, Australia. *Memberships:* President School Council, 1973-81, Carey Baptist Grammar School; Vice President 1972-74, President, Victorian Division, 1972-74, Securities Institute of Australia; Hon. Secretary, Australian Brain Foundation, 1971-; Australian Club, Melbourne; Melbourne Club; Royal Automobile Club of Victoria. *Honours:* CBE., 1966; Fellow, Securities Institute of Australia, 1968. *Hobbies:* Reading; Walking; Travel. *Address:* 4/11 Rockely Road, South Yarra, Victoria 3141, Australia.

MELLOR, Warren Leonard, b. 12 Apr. 1942, Sydney, Australia. Academic. m. Maureen, 22 Aug. 1964, 1 son, 1 daughter. *Education:* BA., 1961, Diploma of Education, 1962, University of Sydney, Australia; ME., 1973, PhD., 1975, University of Oregon, USA. *Appointments:* Teacher, New South Wales Department of Education, Australia, 1963-72; Research Assistant, Oregon Board of Higher Education, USA, 1972-75; Lecturer in Education, University of New England, Australia, 1975; Senior Lecturer in Education, Monash University, Australia, 1976-80; Consultant, International Institute for Educational Planning, Paris, France, 1980-81. *Memberships:* Executive Committee, 1978-82, Commonwealth Council for Educational Administration; National Secretary, 1977-79, Australian Council for Educational Administration; President, 1978-79, Victorian Council for Educational Administration; Australian College of Education. *Publications:* Articles include: Structure and rationality in information decision systems, 1976; Patterns and models of educational administration, 1977; Organizational development in schools—an annotated bibliography, 1977; Conference papers include: School management information network, 1976; School reviews and the process of self-evaluation in Victorian secondary schools, 1977; Some problems in the administration of education, 1980; Developing leader effectiveness, 1979; Organization development and the process of school review, 1978; Staff management and the initiation of change, 1977; Monographs include: Nongraded Schools, 1973; Computerized data processing, 1973; Planning strategies for implementing education change in Bangladesh, 1980; Books: Australia's development, 1860-1890, 1972; Senior History Workshop, (co-author), 1967; Higher Certificate History, (co-author), 1967; Research Projects include: Melton-Sunbury Community Resources Study, 1977; Ten effective secondary schools, 1979; Planning strategies for the implementation of administrative reforms in Bangladesh, 1980. *Honours:* Visiting Scholar, New York University, USA, 1980; Visiting Fellow, International Institute for Educational Planning, Paris, France, 1980. *Hobbies:* Tennis; Music; Photography. *Address:* 50 Rose Avenue, Glen Waverley, Victoria, Australia.

MELROSE, Donald Blair, b. 13 Sept. 1940, Hobart, Tasmania, Australia. University Professor. m. Sara Christine Knabe, 30 Aug. 1969, 1 son, 1 daughter. *Education:* BSc., Physics and Mathematics, 1961, BSc.(Hons.), Physics, 1962, Tasmania, Australia; D.Phil., Theoretical Physics, Oxon, UK, 1965. *Appointments:* Research Fellow, Physics, University of Sussex, UK, 1965-66; Research Associate, Physics, Belfer Graduate School of Science, Yeshiva University, New York, USA, 1966-68; Research Fellow, Center for Theoretical Physics, Astronomy Program, University of Maryland, USA, 1968-69; Senior Lecturer, 1969-72, Reader, 1972-79, Theoretical Physics, ANU; Visiting Scientist, CSIRO Division of Radiophysics, Jan-Jun.1973; Visiting Professor, Department of Astro-Geophysics, University of Colorado, USA, Jan-Feb, 1975, May-Dec. 1977; Professor of Theoretical Physics, University of Sydney, Australia, 1979-. *Memberships:* American Astronomical Society; American Geophysical Union; Astronomical Society of Australia; International Astronomical Union; Australian

Institute of Physics. *Publications:* Plasma Astrophysics, vol 1 The Emission, Absorption and Transfer of Waves in Plasmas, 1980; Plasma Astrophysics, vol 2, Astrophysical Applications, 1980; over 100 papers in scientific literature. *Honours:* Sir Philip Fysh Prize (half share) in Physics, 1969; Rhodes Scholar for Tasmania, 1962; Pawsey Memorial Medal, Australian Academy of Science, 1974. *Hobbies:* Squash; Bridge; Cricket. *Address:* 10 Balfour Street, Wollstonecraft, New South Wales 2065, Australia.

MELVILLE, Robert Pope, b. 23 May 1913, Wollongong, NSW, Australia. Medical Practitioner. m. 5 Mar. 1952, 2 sons, 1 daughter. *Education:* MB, BS Honours Class II, Sydney University 1938; Fellow, Royal College of Surgeons, England 1947; Fellow, Royal Australasian College of Surgeons 1950; Fellow, American College of Surgeons 1962. *Appointments:* RMO, Royal Prince Alfred Hospital, 1938-39; Junior Fellow in Surgery, Sydney Post Graduate School in Medicine, 1940; Australian Army Medical Corps, AIF, 1940-46; RSO, Southend on Sea General Hospital United Kingdom, 1947-49; Clinical Assistant and Tutor, Clinical Surgery, Royal Prince Alfred Hospital, 1950-57; Honorary Surgeon, St. George Hospital 1950-73; Lecturer in Surgery, Sydney University 1957-61; Surgeon, NSW State Cancer Councils Special Unit, Prince of Wales Hospital, 1957; Consultant Surgeon Sutherland Hospital 1958; Supervisor of Professional Cancer Education, Post Graduate Committee in Medicine, University of Sydney, 1959; Consultant Surgeon Prince Henry, Prince of Wales and Eastern Suburbs Group of Hospitals 1970; Visiting Surgeon Quirindi Hospital 1973. *Memberships:* Clinical Oncological Society of Australia; Council of the Australian Cancer Society; World Health Organisation International Reference Centre for the Evaluation of Diagnosis and Treatment of Breast Cancer; Sydney Square Diagnostic Breast Clinic; NSW State Committee Royal Australian College of Surgeons; Court of Examiners Royal Australian College of Surgeons; NSW Medico Legal Society; University of Sydney Medical Society. *Honours:* Honours Class Ii, Medicine, Sydney University 1938; Nuffield Travelling Fellow in Surgery 1946; Hallet Prize, Royal College of Surgeons, England 1946. *Hobbies:* Fishing; Golf; Tennis. *Address:* 39D Manning Road, Double Bay, NSW 2028, Australia.

MENDELSOHN, Frederick Arthur Oscar, b. 19 June 1942, Melbourne, Australia. Medical Practitioner; Reader in Medicine. m. Jeannette Milgrom, 11 July 1980, 3 sons, 1 daughter. *Education:* MBBS., 1965, PhD., 1972, MD., 1973, Melbourne, Australia; FRACP., 1972; MRACP., 1969. *Appointments:* Resident Medical Officer, Royal Melbourne Hospital, Australia, 1966-68; NH&MRC Postgraduate medical scholar, 1969-71, Second Assistant, 1976-77, First Assistant, 1977-, Reader, 1981, Department Medicine, Melbourne University, Austin Hospital, Australia; Honorary Physician, Austin Hospital, Heidelberg, Victoria, Australia, 1971; Nuffield Foundation Travelling Medical Fellow, Department Physics, Applied to Medicine, Middlesex Hospital Medical School, London, UK, 1972-73; National Heart Foundation Overseas Medical Research Fellow at Middlesex Hospital Medical School and Department Physiology, University Munich, Germany, 1973-75; Hon. Endocrinologist, 1975-77, Senior Physician, 1977-, Austin Hospital, Australia. *Memberships:* Fellow, Royal Australasian College Physicians; Endocrine Society of Australia; American Endocrine Society; Australasian Society Nephrology; Australian Society Medical Research; Fellow, New York Academy Sciences; Australian Physiological and pharmacological Society. *Publications:* more than 50 publications in scientific journals including: Biochemical Journal, 1971; Clinical Science, 1975, 1976,79; Kidney International, 1980; Endocrinology, 1980; Chapters in: Pharmacological and Therapeutic Aspects of Hypertension, 1980. *Honours:* Boots Prize in Pharmacology, 1962; Ryan Prize in Medicine, 1965; Nuffield Foundation Travelling Medical Fellowship, 1972. *Hobbies:* Music; Bush walking. *Address:* 16 Eaglemont Crescent, Eaglemont 3084, Victoria, Australia.

MENDIS, Anthony Percival Leslie, b. 16 Oct. 1942, Sri Lanka. Accountant. m. Christine, 14 Mar. 1977, 1 daughter. *Education:* BSc., University of Sri Lanka, 1965; Chartered Accountants Final Examination, Sri Lanka, 1969; Diploma, Business Studies, Australia, 1975. *Appointments:* Audit Assistant, Chartered Accountant's form, Sri Lanka, 1966-69; Chief Accountant, Public Company, Sri Lanka, 1970-72; Accountant, Public Company, Australia, 1973-76; Company Secretary, International Company, Australia, 1977-. *Memberships:* Fellow, Institute of Chartered Accountants, Sri Lanka; British Institute of Management; Associate member, Australian Society of Accountants. *Honours:* Winner, Best Company Annual Report in Sri Lanka, 1972. *Hobbies:* Fishing; Photography. *Address:* 10 Lindau Drive, Vermont South, Victoria 3133, Australia.

MENDIS, Devaradura Lucius Oswald, b. 21 Dec. 1931, Colombo, Sri Lanka. Engineer. m. Soma Kumarihamy, 1 Dec. 1960, 2 sons, 1 daughter. *Education:* BSc., Engineering, Ceylon, 1955. *Appointments:* Instructor, Civil Engineering, 1955-56; Assistant Irrigation Engineer, 1956-61, Project Engineer, 1961-62, Thos. Bourne & Associates; Project Engineer, Walker Sons & Co. Limited, 1962-64; Project Engineer, Ceylon Development Engineering Co. Limited, 1964-65; R V D B., successively Civil Engineer, Udawalawe Head Works, Designs and Planning Engineer, Wlaawe & A G M Heavy Construction Division, 1965-69; Deputy Director, 1969-74, Advisor, 1974-78, Techniques, Ministry of Planning and Economic Affairs; Engineer, Planning and Control, Nigerian Construction Consortium Limited, 1979; Technical Director, AAICO Group of Companies, Sri Lanka 1979-. *Memberships:* Pugwash Conference on Science and World Affairs, 1980; Fellow, Institution of Engineers, Sri Lanka; Member of Council, 1977-78, 1980-81, Institution of Engineers, Sri Lanka; Mahaweli Development Board; Director, National Engineering Research and Development Centre; Director, Industrial Development Board; Governing Board, CISIR; President, 1975, Section C, Sri Lanka Association for Advancement of Science. *Publications:* Papers in various Journals on Engineering and Planning including: Planning thw Industrial Revolution in Sri Lanka in Transactions of the Insitution of Engineers, Sri Lanka, 1975; Appropriate Technology—Under development and over development in Economic Review May 1975 and Third World Forum; a few published and many unpublished poems. *Honours:* EOE Pereira Prize, Institution of Engineers, Sri Lanka, 1977. *Hobbies:* Driving; Travel; Reading; Writing; Books. *Address:* 16/1 George E De Silva Mawatha, Kandy, Sri Lanka.

MENDOZA, June, b. Melbourne, Australia. Artist. m. Keith Mackrell, 1 son, 3 daughters. *Education:* Art Department, Swinburne Technical College, Melbourne, Australia; St. Martin's School of Art, London, UK. *Appointments:* Book Illustrations; Illustrated Strips (Historical, Ballet, etc); Book and Record Jackets; Various Forms Commercial Art; Portraiture various media; 3 years as Professional Actress, Radio; TV Revue; mainly straight plays. *Memberships:* Royal Society of Portrait Painters; Royal Institute of Oil Painters; Contemporary Portrait Society. *Creative Works:* Paintings in Institutions; Colleges; Universities; Museums; Parliamentary buildings; Private collections: England, USA; Philippines; Australia; Europe; Israel; Portraits include: HM The Queen; HRH Prince Charles; Duke of Edinburgh; Archbishop of Canterbury; AJP Taylor; Lord Clark of Saltwood; Lord Hunt of Llanfair Waterdine; Alistair Cooke; Sir Colin Davis; Dame Joan Sutherland; Prime Minister of Australia and Fiji; Lord Gardiner; Judi Dench; Max Wall; Sir Harry Secombe. *Honours:* RP, ROI. *Hobbies:* Music; Theatre; Reading; Tapestry. *Address:* 34 Inner Park Road, London, SW 19, England.

MENEZES, Sister Mary Noel, b. 14 July 1930, Guyana. *Education:* Teacher's Diploma of Education 1954; BA, 1964; MA(summa cum laude) 1965; PhD 1973. *Appointments:* Teacher of English Literature, St Joseph High School, Guyana, 1950-52; Head, Sacred Heart Girls' School, Guyana, 1955-63; Lecturer, History, College Misericordia, Dallas, Penn. 1966-67; Lecturer in History, University of Guyana, 1967-75; Senior Lecturer, History, 1975-80; Professor of History, University of Guyana 1980-. *Memberships:* Association of Caribbean Historians; National Honour Society in History-Phi Alpha Theta; National Jesuit Honour Society-Gama Pi Epsilon; The Latin American Studies Association; Convocation, University of London; Society for Caribbean Studies; Caribbean Studies Association; The Latin American Conference of History, etc. *Publications:* British Policy towards the Amerindians in British Guiana 1803-1873, 1977; Goodall's Sketches of Amerindian Tribes, 1977; A Guide to Historical Research, 1978; The Amerindians in Guyana 1803-1873: A Doc-

umentary History, 1979; The Amerindians and the Europeans 1981. *Honours:* Ford Foundation Fellowship 1970-73; Isobel Thornley Bequest Grant for Publication 1978; Honorary Research Fellowship, Institute of Latin American Studies, University of London 1980-81. *Hobbies:* Reading; Music. *Address:* St John Bosco Convent, Plaisance, E.C.D, Guyana.

MENON, V T Aravindaksha, b. 17 July 1921, Kodungalloor, Trichur District, Kerala State, India. Professional Actor. m. L. Sarasamma, 23 Feb. 1947, 2 sons. *Appointments:* 30 years' experience in professional drama troupes including: Acted in Malayan film, Sthree, 1948; Kalanilayalam Permanent Stage, dramascope troupe, 1950-60; Took lead role as Kochunni, in the play Kayamkulam Kochunni; now working in Malayalam films. *Memberships:* Indo-Soviet Cultural Society. *Honours:* National award for best actor in Malayalam Drama, Kendra Sangeet Natak Akademi, New Delhi, India, 1965; Silver Sheild, Citizens of Trivandrum, 1966; Best Actor award in Professional Drama, Vikram Sara Bhai Space Centre Recreation Club, Trivandrum, 1975; Silver Cup, Kerala Kalamandalam, Cheruthuruthy, 1966; Best Actor award, Cochin Shipyard Recreation Club, Cochin, 1976. *Hobbies:* Classical music; Carnatic music. *Address:* Jayakumar Nivas, Pisharathu Street, N Parur, Pin 683513, Kerala State, India.

MENON, Vidyadaran, b. 25 Oct. 1942, Malaysia. Veterinarian; Lecturer. m. 2 daughters. *Education:* DVM (Doctor of Veterinary Medicine); MVS (Master of Veterinary Studies. *Appointments:* Lecturer in Veterinary Anatomy, 1974-. *Memberships:* Secretary, Malaysian Association, 1978-79, Malaysian Primate Research Committee, 1977; Director, University Pertanian Primate Research Programme, 1979-81. *Publications:* Published 10 papers. *Honours:* First Class Honours for DVM Course; Australian—Asian University Council Fellowship, 1972-74, 1979; Australia Meat Council Assistmanship, 1979. *Hobbies:* Hockey; Cricket; Gardening. *Address:* 5814/5 Taman Bangi, Jalan Reko, Kajang, Selangor, Malaysia.

MENSAROS, Andrew, b. 25 Nov. 1921, Budapest, Hungary. Member of Legislative Assembly, Western Australia. *Education:* Doctor of Law and Political Sciences, summa cum laude, Eotuos University, Budapest, Hungary; Graduate of Law, University of Vienna; Diploma of Accountancy, Barristers Examination, Budapest, Hungary. *Appointments:* Tutor, University, Budapest, Hungary; Legal Practice, Budapest, Hungary; Accountancy Practice, Perth, Western Australia; Proprietor, Construction Firm, Perth, Western Australia; Minister for Industrial Development, Mines, Fuel and Energy, 1974-80; Minister for Works and Water Resources since 1980. *Memberships:* The Weld Club, Western Australia. *Publications:* Several publications in Law, Particularly Criminal Law in Hungary. *Hobbies:* Swimming; Classical music; Classical(Latin)Literature reading. *Address:* 40 Hamersley Road, Subiaco, Western Australia 6008.

MENUHIN, Yehudi, KBE (Hon), b. 22 Apr. 1916, New York, USA. Violinist. m. (1) Nola Ruby, 1 son, 1 daughter, (2) 1947, Diana Rosamond, 2 sons. *Education:* Private Tutors; Studied music under Sigmund Anker and Louis Persinger, in San Francisco; Georges Enesco, Rumania and Paris, Adolph Busch, Switzerland; Made début with orchestra, San Francisco, aged 7, Paris, aged 10, New York, 11, Berlin, 13; since then has played with most of world's orchestras and conductors; Devoted part of his time to concerts for Allied Armed Forces & Red Cross, 1939-45; Concerts in Moscow, Israel, Japan and India, 1945-52; Initiated own annual music festival in Gstaad, Switzerland, 1957, Bath, 1959-68; Joint Artistic Director Windsor Festival, 1969-72; Founder Chairman, Live Music Now, 1977. *Honours:* President, Trinity College of Music, 1971; Honorary Fellow, St. Catherine's College, Cambridge, 1970; Honorary DMus Oxford, 1962, Cambridge, 1970, Sorbonne, 1976, and 10 other degrees from British Universities; Freedom of the City of Edinburgh, 1965, Bath, 1966; Gold Medal, Royal Philharmonic Society, 1962; Jawaharlal Nehru Award, 1970; Sonning Music Prize, Denmark, 1972; Handel Medal, New York; Numerous City of Jerusalem Medal Decorations. *Creative Works:* Films: Stage Door Canteen; Magic Bow; The Way of Light. The Violin aix lessons by Yehudi Menuhin, 1971; Theme and Variations, 1972; Violin and

Viola, 1976; Sir Edward Elgar my musical grandfather (essay), 1976; Unfinished Journey, 1977. *Address:* c/o Harold Holt, 134 Wigmore Street, London W1, England.

MENZIES, James Gordon, b. 7 Dec. 1909, North Sydney, NSW, Australia. Retired Banker, Barrister, Company Director. m. Jean Mann, 24 Apr. 1937, 1 son, 1 daughter. *Education:* BEc, 1950, LLB, 1977, University of Sydney; FASA; FCIS; ABIA. *Appointments:* Assistant Chief Superintendent, Commonwealth Savings Bank of Australia, 1952-59; Chief Accountant, Reserve Bank of Australia, 1960-62; Deputy Governor, Central Bank of Malaysia, 1962-66; Manager for Victoria Reserve Bank of Australia, 1966-70; Managing Director, Martin Corporation, 1970-71; Director, Thomas Cook Pty, Ltd., 1970-; Chairman, The Scottish Hsopital, 1970-; Trustee, Presbyterian Church in NSW, 1971-, Chairman of Trustees, 1977-. *Memberships:* Honorary Trustee Committee of Economic Development; Royal Commonwealth Society; School Councils of: Scots College, Sydney, PLC, Sydney, PLC, Armidale, Scots School, Bathurst; Australia-Britain Society; Australian-America Association; Australia-Chinese Society. *Publications:* Postal Savings in Asia & Far East, 1954. *Honours:* Johan Mangku Negara, 1966; Order of Australia, 1980. *Hobbies:* Music; Reading. *Address:* 40 Stafford Road, Artarmon, NSW, 2064, Australia.

MENZIES, Pattie Maie, b. 1899, Alexandra, Victoria, Australia. m. Sir Robert Menzies, 28 Sept. 1920, 2 sons, (1 son deceased) 1 daughter. *Memberships:* Alexandra Club; Lyceum Club. *Honours:* GBE., 1954, in recognition of years of incessant and unselfish performance of public duty, in hospital work, in visiting, addressing and encouraging many thouands of women in every State of Australia, including very remote areas, and in her distinguished representation of Australia on a number of occasions overseas. *Address:* 7 Monaro Close, Kooyong, Victoria 3144, Australia.

MERCHANT, Jaysukhlal R, b. 14 June 1922, Bombay, India. Professor of Organic Chemistry. *Education:* MSc., 1946, PhD., 1949, Bombay University, India; DSc., Zurich E T H, Switzerland, 1953; C.Chem., FRIC., FASc., FIC.; CSIR Fellow, National Chemical Laboratory, Poona, India, 1953-54. *Appointments:* Associate Professor of Organic Chemistry, 1954-67, Professor and Head of Organic Chemistry Division, 1967-, Institute of Science, Bombay, India. *Memberships:* Fellow, Chemical Society; President, W I Section, RIC; Fellow, Vice-President, Associate Editor, Indian Chemical Society; Fellow, Indian Academy of Sciences; Fellow, Institution of Chemists; American Chemical Society. *Publications:* About 175 research publications. *Hobbies:* Music; Literature; Sports. *Address:* 62 Charat Mahal, Dongersi Road, Bombay 400006, India.

MERCIER, Ernest, b. 1 Mar. 1914, Rosaire (Montmagny), Quebec, Canada. Agrologist, Generalist. m. Marcelle Normand, 5 Oct. 1945, 4 sons, 2 daughters. *Education:* BA, College La Pocatiere, 1933-39; BSc.A, Faculty of Agriculture, Université Laval, Auébec, 1939-43; MSc.A, 1943-44, PhD, 1944-46, Cornell University, New York State; *Appointments:* Agricultural and Forestry Worker, 1928-33; Livestock Insturctor, Ministry of Agriculture, Québec, 1943-47; Organizer, Director, Québec Artificial Insemination Centre, St-Hyacinthe, Québec, 1947-50; Director, Livestock Department, 1950-52; Director, 1952-60, Federal Agricultural Research Station, Lennoxville, Québec; Professor & Chairman, Animal Sciences Department, MacDonald College, McGill University, Ste-Anne-de-Bellevue, Québec, 1960; Deputy Minister of Agriculture, Québec, 1960-67; Senior consultant, The Québec Department of Intergovernmental Affairs, The Canadian International Development Agency, 1970-73; Agrologist Consultant, 1979-. *Memberships:* Sigma Xi, 1944; Canadian Society of Rural Extension, 1974; Québec Order of Agrologists, 1957-59; AIC Membership Directory, 1979; International Society of Agricultural Economists. *Publications:* 14 scientific articles; 25 technical articles; 150 administrative memoranda to political authorities; 30 working documents; 50 technical notes to administrative authorities; 275 extension articles; More than 200 speeches to farmers groups, Agrologists and service clubs; More than 15 feasibility studies in developing countries; Co-ordinator of the Derro Project in Morocco. *Honours:* Bursary of Order of the Imperial Daughters of the British Empire, 1941; Derwint Scholarship, Cornell University, 1946;

Fellow, The Agricultural Institute of Canada, 1966; Cammander, Order of Agricultural Merit, 1961; Confederation Medal, Canada, 1967; Lazarre Spallanzani Medal, 1972. *Hobbies:* Singing; Writing; Helping others; Gardening; Genealogy. *Address:* 910 Ave des Braves, Québec, G1S 3C6, Canada.

MERRISON, Alexander Walter, b. 20 Mar. 1924, London, England. University Vice-Chancellor. m. (1) Beryl Glencora Le Marquand, 1948, deceased. 1968, (2) Maureen Michele Barry, 1970, 3 sons, 1 daughter. *Education:* BSc., King's College, London, UK, 1944; PhD., Liverpool University, UK, 1957. *Appointments:* Experimental Officer, Signals Research and Development Establishment, Christchurch, UK, 1944-46; Senior Scientific Officer, AERE, Harwell, UK, 1946-51; Leverhulme Fellow and Lecturer, 1951-57, Professor of Experimental Physics, 1960-69, Liverpool University, UK; Physicist, Euopean Organisation for Nuclear Research, CERN, 1957-60; Director, Daresbury Nuclear Physics Laboratory, SRC, UK, 1962-69; Vice-Chancellor, Bristol University, UK, 1969-. *Memberships:* FRS; Member of Council, Institute of Physics and Physical Society, 1964-66; FRSA. *Publications:* Contributions to Scientific journals on nuclear and elementary particle physics. *Honours:* Knight Bachelor, 1976; Deputy Lieutenant Avon, 1974; Charles Vernon Boys Prize, Institute of Physics and Physical Society, 1961. *Address:* Senate House, Tyndall Avenue, Bristol BS8 1TH, England.

MERRYLEES, Andrew, b. 13 Oct. 1933, Newmains, Lanarkshire, Scotland. Architect. m. Maie Crawford, 3 Apr. 1959, 2 sons, 1 daughter. *Education:* Glasgow School of Architecture, University of Strathclyde, 1951-57; B.Arch., Dip.T.P., RIBA; FRIAS; FSIAD; FFB. *Appointments:* Student vacational employment, 1952-57; Associate, 1968-72, Partner, 1972-, Sir Basil Spence, Glover & Ferguson. *Memberships:* Scottish Arts Club. *Creative Works:* Design of many buildings including: University Libraries at Edinburgh, Dublin, Liverpool, Aston, Heriot-Watt. *Honours:* Design Prize, Glasgow School of Architecture, 1956; RIBA Bronze Medal; Civic Trust Award. *Hobbies:* Painting; Design. *Address:* 25 Gloucester Lane, Edinburgh, Scotland.

MESSARA, John Maurice, b. 7 June 1947, Alexandria, Egypt. Stockbroker. m. Kristine Louise, 7 Jan. 1973, 1 son, 1 daughter. *Education:* Bachelor of Commerce, University of New South Wales, 1965-67. *Appointments:* Various positions in Stockbroking firms; Elected to The Sydney Stock Exchange, 1972; Senior Partner, J.M. Messara & Co., Stock & Sharebrokers, Sydney, 1974-. *Memberships:* The Sydney Stock Exchange Ltd; Australian Society of Accountants; Securities Institute of Australia; Australian Institute of Management. *Honours:* Prize for Business Finance, University of NSW, 1967. *Hobbies:* Thoroughbred Horse Racing & Breeding; Tennis. *Address:* 22 Redan Street, Mosman, New South Wales, Australia.

MESSEL, Harry, b. 3 Mar. 1922, Levine Siding, Manitoba, Canada. Scientist. *Education:* Queen's University, Ontario, Canada; St Andrew's University, Scotland; Institute, Advanced Studies, Dublin; BA; BSc; PhD. *Appointments:* Canadian Armed Forces Overseas service, 1942-45; Senior Lecturer in Mathematical Physics, Adelaide University, 1951-52; Professor of Physics and Head of School of Physics, University of Sydney, 1952-; Director , Science Foundation for Physics within the University of Sydney, 1954-; Commissioner, Australian Atomic Energy Commission, 1975-; Vice-Chairman (Aust.) Survival Service Commission, International Union for the Conservation of Nature, 1978-. *Publications:* Contributions to Progress in Cosmic Ray Physics, 1953; Many books on physics; Papers in learned journals, numerous monographs on surveys of tidal river systems in the Northern Territory. *Honours:* Governor Generals Silver Medal RMC, Canada, 1942; CBE, 1979. *Hobbies:* Water skiing; Hunting; Fishing; Photography. *Address:* Hopewood Gardens, 13 Thornton Street, Darling Point, 2027, NSW, Australia.

MESSERLE, Hugo Karl, b. 25 Oct. 1925, Haifa, Palestine. Electrical Engineer, Physicist. m. Renate U Meyer, 6 Aug. 1955, 1 daughters. *Education:* BEE, 1951, MEng.Sc, 1952, DSc, 1968, University of Melbourne; PhD, University of Sydney, 1957. *Appointments:* Senior Demonstrator, Tutor University of Melbourne, 1951-

52; Lecturer, Senior Lecturer, 1951-52, Reader, Electrical Engineering, 1960-66, Professor of Electrical Engineering, 1966-, University of Sydney; Fulbright Scholar, 1958, Visiting Professor, 1964, Cornell University, NY, USA; Head of School, University of Sydney, 1970-; Guest Professor, Institute für Plasmaforschung, University of Stuttgart, Germany, 1973; Member Electrical Research Board; Member TSC5 of NERDDC; Chairman Aust Computer Research Board. *Memberships:* Delegate, IAEA/UNESCO Liaison Group on MHD Generation; Australian National Committee of CIGRE; Task Force on Energy of IE Australia & Chairman of WP7, 1976-78; Fellow, Australian Academy of Technical Sciences; Fellow Institute of Engineers, Australia; Board of College of Electrical Engineers, Chairman, National Committee on Electrical Energy; FIREE; FIEE; FAIP; Sigma Xi. *Publications:* Dynamic Circuit Theory, 1965; Energy Conversion Statics, 1969; Numerous scientific papers. *Honours:* Electrical Engineering Premium, 1953; Electrical Engineering Prize, 1961, 1970. *Hobby:* Music. *Address:* 35 Howson Avenue, Turramurra NSW, 2074, Australia.

METZGER, Andrew Joysor Besordu, b. 17 Dec. 1939, Kissy, Freetown, Sierra Leone, West Africa. Librarian. m. Cornelia Konie Tabitha, 2 Sept. 1967, 3 sons, 1 daughter. *Education:* Final examination pass of the Library Association (Great Britain), North-Western Polytechnic, London, 1965-68; Degree of Master of Library Studies, Lougborough University of Technology, Loughborough, England, 1975-77. *Appointments:* Library Assistant-in-Training, 1964, Library Assistant, 1965, Sierra Leone Library Board; Librarian, Head, The Northern Regional Library, Makeni, 1969-72; Librarian, Head of the Women Teachers College Library, Port Loko, Sierra Leone, 1972-75; Librarian, Head of the Port Loko Teachers College Library, 1978-; Lecturer on Childrens Literature, Port Loko Teachers College, 1978-; Part-time Lecturer on Childrens Literature, Fourah Bay College, the University of Sierra Leone, 1978-. *Memberships:* Associate of the Library Association (Great Britain); Sierra Leone Library Association. *Publications:* The Place of Literature in the Life of the Sierra Leonean Child—A Dissertation, 1977; Curriculum Proposals for the Teaching of Literature in the Primary Schools in Sierra Leone—A Thesis (to be published). *Hobbies:* Reading; Gardening; Tennis. *Address:* 29 Newcastle Street, Kissy, Freetown, Sierra Leone, West Africa.

MEYER, George Rex, b. 15 Mar. 1928, Croydon, NSW, Australia. Educationalist. *Education:* BA, 1954, BSc, 1951, MEd, 1955, Dip.Ed, 1951, University of Sydney; PhD, University of London, 1959. *Appointments:* Teaching Fellow, Lecturer, Senior Lecturer in Zoology (Biology), University of Sydney, 1952-66; Foundation Director, Centre for the Advancement of Teaching, 1967-79, Fellow in Continuing Education, 1979-, Macquarie University, Sydney. *Memberships:* Foundation President, President, 1971-75, Educational Resources Association of New South Wales; Foundation President, President, 1972-74, Association for Environmental Education, New South Wales; Patron, Educational Suppliers Association of NSW, 1979-; Offices held in numerous educational associations and societies 1950-. *Publications:* Quiz Yourself About East African Mammals (with S Frank); Basic Genetics for Schools & Colleges (with S Frank); Look, Hear, Audio Visual Aids and others; More than 100 professional articles on biology and education in magazines and journals. *Honours:* Fellow of the Australian College of Education; Order of Australia 1981. *Hobbies:* Gardening; Record collecting; Travel. *Address:* PO Box 154, Beecroft, NSW, 2119, Australia.

MEYNELL, Peter John, b. 25 Nov. 1947, Folkington, Sussex, England. Biologist. m. Judith Alexandra Marten, 1 son, 1 daughter. *Education:* Eton College, Windsor, 1960-65; BA, Biochemistry, Pembroke College, Oxford, 1966-70; MSc, Chelsea College, London, 1970-71; MSc, Reading University, 1978-79. *Appointments:* Waste Water Consultants, HB Berridge & Partners, 1971-75; Ministry of Overseas Development, TCO, on Fish Processing in Malawi, 1975-78; Independent Consultant Biologist, specialising in water pollution, Fisheries, Sanitation, Energy from Biomass, Methane Generation, 1979-. *Memberships:* Royal Society of Chemistry; Institute of Biology; Commonwealth Human Ecology Council; Secretary, British Anaerobic and Biomas Association. *Publications:* Me-

thane—Planning a Digester, 1976; Various papers in field in learned journals. *Hobbies:* Ornithology; Photography; Painting; Walking; Tennis. *Address:* The White House, Little Bedwyn, Marlborough, Wilts, England.

MEZU, Sebastian Okechukwu, b. 30 Apr. 1941, Emekuku, Owerri, Imo State, Nigeria. m. Rose U Okeke, 6 Sept. 1968, 2 sons, 7 daughters. *Education:* BA, Georgetown University, Washington DC, USA, 1964; MA, 1966; LL.B, 1966; PhD, Johns Hopkins University, Baltimore, Maryland, USA, 1967. *Appointments:* Director Peace Corps Training Programme, Atlanta, Georgia, 1966; Ambassador of Biafra to Ivory Coast, 1968; Professor of French & Director of African Studies, State University of New York at Buffalo, 1969-73; Consultant, Chairman, Managing Director, Mezu International Ltd, Cosmetics Manufacturers, Printer, Publishers, Building, Road & Civil Engineers, 1973-. *Memberships:* Modern Language Association, America; African Studies Association, USA. *Publications:* Author: The Philosophy of Pan Africanism, 1964; Behind the Rising Sun; Leopold Sedar Senghor; Leopold Sedar Senghor et la défense et illustration de la civilisation noire; Modern Black Literature; Black Leaders of the Centuries; Igbo Market Literature; The Tropical Dawn (poems); Umu Ejima (play). *Honours:* Festival of Arts Certificates in Nigeria, 1950's; UNESCO Fellow, Johns Hopkins University & Sorbonne, Paris; AFGRAD Scholarship Fellow; Alpha Sigmanu, Georgetown University. *Hobbies:* Tennis; Writing. *Address:* Mezuville, Emekuku, Owerri, Imo State, Nigeria.

MHINA FUMBWE, John Edward, b. 3 May 1926, Muheza Tanga, Tanzania. School Master. m. Anne Ruth Hiza Mwaza, 31 Dec. 1955, 4 sons, 4 daughters. *Education:* Diploma in Education, Makerere University, 1950; Diploma in English as a Foreign Language, London University, 1961; BA, History, UCLA, USA, 1963. *Appointments:* School Master, 1951-60; Headmaster, Secondary Schools, 1961-66; Director, Primary Education, Tanzania, 1967-69; Director, Nordic Project, Kibaha, 1970-72; Governor, Ruvuma Region, Tanzania, 1972-75; Ambassador to Nordic Countries, 1976-80. *Memberships:* President, Tanzania Historical Association, 1966-72; President, Tanzania Society, 1969-75. *Publications:* Co-author, History of East & Central Africa; Author, Mashijaa wa Tanzania; several articles on History of Africa. *Honours:* Various honours. *Hobbies:* Tennis; Gardening; Building. *Address:* PO Box 436, Dar es Salaam, Tanzania

MHONI, Matchiya Alexander, b. 19 Apr. 1940, Mzimba Malawi. Legal. m. Chrissie, 2 Feb. 1974, 2 daughters. *Education:* Bachelor of Laws, University of Malwai, 1972. *Appointments:* Assistant Registrar General, 1972, Senior Assistant Registrar General, 1974, Registrar General, 1977, Chief State Advocate, 1980-. *Memberships:* Malawi Law Society. *Hobbies:* Football; Indoor Games. *Address:* Luzi Village, PA Luzi, Rumphi, Malawi.

MICHEL, Raymond, b. 18 Apr. 1940, Port-Daniel (Québec), Canada. Physics Teacher. *Education:* School for Teachers, 1959-63; B Péd University of Montreal; BA, University of Ottawa, 1967; LSc (Physics), 1970, BSc, 1972, DENS (Education), 1972, University of Québec (Laval University), 1968-72. *Appointments:* Teacher, Elementary School, Québec, 1958-59; Mathematics Teacher, High School, Québec, 1963-64; Chemistry & Physics Teacher, Québec, 1965-68; Physics Teacher, High School, Québec, 1972-. *Memberships:* Canadian Association of Physicists; Association des professeurs de sciences du Québec. *Hobbies:* Reading; Listening to Music; Learning Languages; Walking; Travelling. *Address:* 309 rue St-Pierre, App. 306, Matane (Québec), Canada G4W 2C2

MICHENER, Roland (Rt Hon), b. 19 Apr. 1900, Lacombe, Alta. m. Norah Evangeline Willis, 1927, 2 daughters. *Education:* BA., (Alta), 1920; Rhodes Scholar for Alta, 1919; BA., 1922, BCL., 1923; MA., 1929, Universities of Alberta Canada and Oxford, UK. *Appointments:* Served with RAF, 1918; Called to Bar, Middle Temple, UK, 1923; Barrister, Ontario, 1924; KC, Canada, 1943; Practising lawyer, Lang, Michener & Cranston, Toronto, Cnada, 1924-57; Member, Ontario Legislature for St. David, Toronto, Canda, 1945-48; Provincial Secretary and Registrar for Ontario, CANADA, & ½-½—: Elected, 1953, re-elected 1957,58, Canadian House of Commons; Elected Speaker, 1957, 58;

Canadian High Commissioner to India, Ambassador to Nepal, 1964-67; General Secretary for Canada, Rhodes Scholarships, 1936-64; Governor General and Commander-in-Chief of Canada, 1967-74;, Barrister associated as Counsel, Lang, Michener, Cranston, Farquharson and Wright, Toronto, Canada, 1974-. *Memberships:* Chancellor, Queen's University, 1974-80; Chairman of Council, Duke of Edinburgh's Fifth Commonwealth Study Conference, Canada, 1980; Hon. Chairman of Board, Metropolitan Trust Co., Toronto; Honorary Chairman of Board, Teck Mining Corporation Limited; Director, Pamour Porcupine Mines Limited; Board of Governors, Toronto Stock Exchange, 1974-76; Hon. Counsel, Chairman of Executive Committee, President, Canadian Institute of International Affairs; Hon. Counsel, Red Cross Ontario Division; Chairman of Executive, Canadian Association for Adult Education. *Honours:* Chancellor and Principal Companion, Order of Canada, 1967-74; Chancellor and Commander, Order of Military Merit, 1972-74; KJStJ, 1967; Hon. Fellow: Hertford College, Oxford, UK, 1961; Academy of Medicine, Toronto, Canada, 1967; Trinity College, Toronto, 1968; Frontier College, Toronto, 1972; Royal Canadian Military Institute, 1975; Heraldry Society of Canada, 1976; Hon. FRCP(C), 1968; Hon. FRAIC, 1968; Hon. FRSC., 1975; Hon. member, Cnadian Medical Association, 1968; Hon. Bencher, Law Society of Upper Canada, 1968; Hon. LLD., Ottawa, 1948; Queen's, 1958; Laval, 1960; Alberta, 1967; St. Mary's Halifax, 1968; Toronto, 1968; RMC, Canada, 1969; Manitoba, 1970; McGill, 1970; York, Toronto, 1970; British Columbia, 1971; Jewish Theol. Seminary of America, 1971; Hon. DCL; Bishop's, 1968; Windsor, 1969; Oxford University, UK, 1970. *Address:* 24 Thornwood Road, Toronto, Ontario M4W 2S1, Canada.

MICKLEBURGH, Walter Edward, b. 10 Sept. 1922, Hagbourne, Nr. Didcot, Berkshire, England. Psychiatrist. m. June Isabel Ross, 11 Apr. 1953, 2 sons, 1 daughter. *Education:* BSc, 1949, MB, ChB, 1953, Aberdeen University; Diploma in Psychological Medicine, Melbourne University. *Appointments:* General Medical Practice, Yeadon, Yorkshire, 1954-59; Medical Officer, Mental Hospitals Department, Public Service of South Australia, 1959-64; Psychiatrist, Public Service of South Australia, 1964-74; Director of Mental Health, Capital Territory Health Commission, Canberra Australian Capital Territory, 1974-. *Memberships:* Royal Australian & New Zealand College of Psychiatrists, 1965; Royal College of Psychiatrists, England, 1972; University House, Australian National University, 1975. *Publications:* Numerous papers published in Psychiatric Field. *Hobby:* Horticulture. *Address:* 9 Beauchamp Street, Deakin, Canberra, Australian Capital Territory, Australia.

MIDDLEBRO, John Harry Elsworth, b. 21 Apr. 1943, Owen Sound, Grey County, Ontario, Canada. Barrister; Solicitor; Notary Public. m. Edith Anne McNeill, 20 Mar. 1970, 3 sons, 1 daughter. *Education:* Diploma, Owen Sound Collegiate and Vocational Institute, Canada, 1962; BA., 1965, LL.B., 1968, University of Western Ontario, Canada; Admitted to Bar of Ontario, Osgoode Hall, Canada, 1970. *Appointments:* Part-time Crown Attorney, Bruce Co.; Partner, Horton, Middlebro & Stevens, Law Firm, Canada. *Memberships:* Law Society of Upper Canada; Ontario Bar Association; Canadian Bar Association; Grey & Simcoe Foresters Officers Mess; Royal Canadian Military Institute. *Honours:* Valedictorian of Graduating Class, OSCUI, 1962; President, Grey County Bar Association, 1974. *Hobbies:* Yachting; Camping; Golf; Family life; Fishing; Travel. *Address:* 712 2nd Avenue W, Owen Sound, Ontario, Canada, N4K 4M4.

MIDDLETON, Donald King, b. 24 Feb. 1922, Birmingham, England. HM Diplomatic Service. m. Marion Elizabeth Ryder, 1 May 1945, 1 daughter. *Education:* Saltley College, Ministry of Health, UK, 1958-61. *Appointments:* Ministry of Health, UK, 1958-61; Joined Commonwealth Relations Office, 1961 and held following posts: British High Commission, Lagos, Nigeria, 1961-65; Head of Chancery, British Embassy, Saigon, 1970-72; British Deputy High Commissioner, Ibadan, Nigeria, 1973-75; HM Chargé d'Affaires, Phnom Penh, 1975; seconded to Northern Ireland Office, Belfast, UK, 1975-77; British High Commissioner, Port Moresby, Papua, New Guinea, 1977-. *Memberships:* Royal Commonwealth Society; Patron, Papua, New Guinea Branch, Victoria League for Commonwealth Friend-

ship. *Honours:* CBE., 1981. *Address:* British High Commission, Port Moresby, Papua, New Guinea.

MIDDLETON, Roland William Donald, b. 21 Feb. 1928, Maitland, New South Wales. Orthopaedic Surgeon. m. Margaret Willman, 21 June 1952, 2 sons, 2 daughters. *Education:* MBBS, University of Sydney, 1951; Fellow, Royal College of Surgeons, 1955; Fellow, Royal Australian College of Surgeons, 1958. *Appointments:* Head of Department of Orthopaedic Surgery, Royal Alexandra Hospital for Children; Chairman, Department of Orthopaedic Surgery, Royal North Shore Hospital of Sydney. *Memberships:* Australian Pioneers Club; Australian Orthopaedic SAssociation. *Hobby:* Forestry. *Address:* 13 Balmoral Avenue, Mosman 2088, Australia.

MIFSUD BONNICI, Ugo Enrico, b. 8 Nov. 1932, Cospicua, Malta. Lawyer; Member of Parliament. m. Gemma Bianco, 3 May 1959, 2 sons, 1 daughter. *Education:* BA, 1952, LL D, 1955, Royal University of Malta. *Memberships:* President of the General Council, Nationalist Party (founded 1880). *Publications:* Editor of Malta Letteraria; Regular contributor to the weekly '' Il-Mument''. *Address:* 18 Cospicua Street, Cospicua, Malta.

MILBURN, Janis Ann, b. 13 Sept. 1938, Sydney, Australia. Headmistress. m. Kelvin Lloyd Grose, 27 Aug. 1970. *Education:* BA., 1958, Dip. Ed., 1959, M.Ed., 1965, Sydney, Australia; PhD., London, 1969. *Appointments:* Teacher: Strathfield Girls High School, 1959; Sefton High School, 1961; Senior English Mistress, 1971-72, MLC Burwood, Australia, 1962-64; 1970-72; Senior Tutor, Macquarie University, Australia, 1969; Headmistress, New England Girls School, Australia, 1973-. *Memberships:* NSW English Syllabus Committee; Secondary Schools Board, 1970-; Australian College of Education; Australian Federation of University Women; Zonta International; University Women's Club, London. *Publications:* M.Ed. thesis: Girls' Secondary Education in New South Wales, 1880-1930; PhD. Thesis: The Secondary School Mistress: a study of her professional views and their significance in English educational development 1895 to 1914. *Hobbies:* Travel; Reading. *Address:* The New England Girls School, Armidale, New South Wales 2350, Australia.

MILES, Ena Emily, b. 14 May 1906. m. Frank Miles, 13 Aug. 1932. *Memberships:* Life member, CWA. of Tasmania; Life member, ACWW; Life member, Victoria Lwague for Commonwealth Friendship in Tasmania; Chairman, United Commonwealth Societies. *Creative Works:* Choral and Drama work; Meals on Wheels; Girls Hostel Handicraft and Home Industries. *Publications:* Editor of Newsletter, CWA Tasmania. *Honours:* Order of Australia, 1980. *Hobbies:* Tapestry; Needlework; Gardening; Beaton Brass, Copper, Pewter; Home Industries. *Address:* 33 Hamilton Street, Latiobe 7307, Tasmania, Australia.

MILES, Norman Thomas Graeme, b. 16 June 1932. Secretary, Local Government & Shires Association of New South Wales. m. June Young, 7 Nov. 1955, 1 son. *Education:* BEc, FIMA, Sydney University. *Appointments:* Staff of Sir Bertram Stevens—Survey of local government finance, 1955; Research Officer, 1958; Secretary, 1965-, Local Government & Shires Associations of New South Wales; Secretary, Australian Council of Local Government Associations, 1970-77. *Memberships:* Councillor, Warringah Shire Council, 1962-66; Executive, Council of Social Service, 1966-73, 1976-, Honorary Secretary, 1977-79; Library Council of New South Wales, 1976-; Advisory Board of Adult Education, 1965-70; Australian Refugee Advicory Council, 1979-. *Honours:* Town Clerks' Society Prize. *Hobbies:* Reading; Music; Swimming. *Address:* 7 Bower Street, Manly, New South Wales 2095, Australia.

MILLAN, Bruce, b. 5 Oct. 1927, Dundee, Scotland. Member of Parliament; Chartered Accountant. m. Gwendoline May Fairey, 9 Aug. 1953, 1 son, 1 daughter. *Education:* Harris Academy, Dundee. *Appointments:* Member of Parliament for Glasgow Craigton, 1959-; Secretary of State for Scotland, 1976-79. *Address:* 10 Beech Avenue, Glasgow G41, Scotland.

MILLAR, Kenneth John, b. 13 Oct. 1926, Wangaratta, Victoria, Australia. Medical Practitioner (Surgeon). m.

Joan Iris (Glen), 9 Feb. 1955, 2 sons. *Education:* MBBS, Melbourne, 1949; FRCS, London, 1957; FRACS, Melbourne, 1959. *Appointments:* RMO, Royal Melbourne Hospital, 1949-50; RMO, Repatriation Hospitals, 1950-53; Medical Practice, 1953-56; RAAF Medical Reserve, 1956-; Surgical Registrar, Suffolk, UK, 1957-58; Specialist & Senior Specialist, Repatriation Department, 1959-79; Senior Specialist in charge, Victorian Branch, Department of Veterans Affairs, 1979-; Honorary Assistant Surgeon & Clinical Assistant, Prince Henrys Hospital, 1960-72. Veterans Admin. Exchange Fellow, USA, 1972. *Memberships:* Fellow, RACS; Surgical Supervisor, Regional Surgical Training Committee; Senior Associate to Professor of Surgery, Repatriation Hospital, Examiner & Member of Faculty, Melbourne University Medical School. Fellow, RCS; Royal Society of Medicine; Clinical Oncological Society of Australia. *Publications:* Surgical papers on Infection & Cytology Report on Exchange Fellowship to Veterans Affairs, USA. *Hobbies:* Gardening; Fishing; Cycling; Tennis. *Address:* 110 Lavender Park Road, Eltham 3095, Victoria, Australia.

MILLEN, Andrew Lloyd, b. 6 July 1913, York, Western Australia. Company Director; Marketing Consultant. m. Ellen Martha Hopkins, 21 Dec. 1935, 1 son, 1 daughter. *Education:* Hale College, Perth; AASA (Associate Australian Society of Accountants); Diplomas for Management, Marketing etc. *Appointments:* Chief Assessor, Probate & Stamp Office, Western Australia, 1946-50; Assistant Accountant, State Treasury, 1951-55, Inspecting Accountant, 1956-59, State Treasury, Western Australia; Director, Western Australian Government Tourist Bureau, 1960-71; Executive Director, Tennis Foundation of Western Australia, 1972-77; Marketing Consultant, 1977-. *Memberships:* Royal Commonwealth Society; Travel League of Western Australia; National Fitness Council, 1958-59; Community Recreation Council of Western Australia, 1972-75; Rotary Club of Perth. *Honours:* President, Parents Association Perth College, 1953-54, Wesley College, Perth, 1957-58; Flt Lt RAAF, 1942-45. *Hobbies:* Tennis; Gardening; Swimming; Travel. *Address:* 33 Moreing Road, Attadale 6156, Western Australia.

MILLER, Allen Horace, b. 11 Nov. 1925, Sydney, New South Wales, Australia. Education Researcher; Consultant. m. Sibylla Elizabeth Schuster, 29 Dec. 1951, 1 son, 2 daughters. *Education:* B Sc (Hons), 1950, Dip Ed, 1951, University of Sydney; BA (Hons) University of New England, 1971. *Appointments:* Part-time Demonstrator in Botany, Sydney University, 1947-49; Junior Lecturer, Sydney Teachers' College, 1951; Science Teacher, Secondary Schools, New South Wales, 1952-56; Part-time Lecturer, Newcastle University College, 1955-56; Lecturer, Armidale Teachers' College, 1957-70; Part-time Lecturer, University of New England, 1957-70; Senior Lecturer, Canberra College of Advanced Education, 1971-74; Faculty Associate, Simon Fraser University, British Columbia, 1973; Director of Office for Research in Academic Methods, Australian National University, 1975-; Visiting Fellow, University of Sussex, 1973. *Memberships:* Executive Committee, 1979-81, Higher Education Research Development Society of Australasia; Australian Association for Research in Education; Society for Research into Higher Education; Australian College of Education. *Publications:* Changing Education:Australian Viewpoints(with W S Simpkins), 1972; Academia Becalmed: Australian Tertiary Education in the Aftermath of Expansion (with G S Harman and others), 1980; Freedom and Control in Higher Education, 1980; plus more than 20 articles in educational journals and books. *Hobby:* Music. *Address:* 12 Ardlethan Street, Fisher, ACT 2611, Australia.

MILLER, Billie Antoinette, b. 8 Jan. 1944, Barbados. Attorney-at-Law. *Education:* Queens College, Barbados; Durham University, England; Council of Legal Education, London. *Appointments:* Attorney-at-Law, Barbados, 1969-76; Minister of Health, Barbados, 1976-81; Minister of Education, Barbados, 1981-. *Memberships:* Gray's Inn-of-Court, London; Barbados Labour Party; Commonwealth Parliamentary Association. *Hobbies:* Reading; Swimming. *Address:* 31 Halcyon Heights, St. James, Barbados, West Indies.

MILLER, Charles Ernest, b. 9 Feb. 1914. Medical Practitioner. m. Yvonne La Frenais, 5 June 1941, 1 son, 3 daughters. *Education:* University of Queensland; School of Medicine, Edinburgh; LRCP&S (Edinburgh),

LRFP&S (Glasgow), 1939; D.Obst. RCOG, London, 1947. *Appointments:* Obstetric Resident, 1940; Surgeon, Lt. Commander, Royal Naval Volunteer Reserve, 1941-46; General Practitioner, Runcorn, England, 1946-63; Honorary Medical Officer, Runcorn Hospital, 1946-63; General Practitioner, Lindfield NSW, 1963-70; Department of Health and Health Commission of NSW, 1970-81. *Memberships:* British Medical Association, 1946-81. *Publications:* Report on Perinatal Deaths in NSW, 1963-71. *Hobbies:* Golf; Fishing; Shooting; Bird watching; Carpentry. *Address:* 36 Mona Vale Road, Pymble, NSW, 2073, Australia

MILLER, Ian Hugh, b. 5 June 1955, Toronto, Ontario, Canada. Engineer. *Education:* BSc, Queen's University, Kingston, 1978. *Appointments:* Engineering Department, Construction Department, Regional Support Staff, Bell Canada, 1978-. *Memberships:* Association of Professional Engineers of Ontario; Canadian Association of Physicists; Society of Management Accountants. *Address:* 75 Havenbrook Blvd, #511, Willowdale, Ontario, M2J 1A8, Canada.

MILLER, Jacques Francis Albert Pierre, b. 2 April 1931, Nice, France. Medical Research. m. Margaret Denise Houen, 17 March 1956. *Education:* B.Sc. Med. First Class Hons in Pathology, 1953, M.B., B.S., Second Class Hons in Medicine, 1955, University of Sydney, Australia; Ph.D., 1960, D.Sc., 1966, University of London, England; Fellow of the Australian Academy of Science, Australia, 1970; Fellow of the Royal Society, London, England, 1970. *Appointments:* Junior Resident Medical Officer, Royal Prince Alfred Hospital, Sydney, 1956; Pathological Research University of Sydney, 1957; Cancer Research, Chester Beatty Research Institute, London, England, Lecturer, 1958-65; Eleanor Roosevelt Fellowship, National Cancer Institute, Bethesda, Maryland, United States of America, 1963; Reader in Exp. Pathol., University of London, England, 1965-66; Head, Exp. Pathol Unit, Walter and Eliza Hall Institute for Medical Research, Melbourne, Australia, 1966-; Visiting Fellow, Basel Institute for Immunology, Basel, Switzerland, 1972; Visiting Fellow, Centre d'Immunologie INSERM-CNRS de Marseille-Luminy, France. *Memberships:* Am. Associate of Immunol, 1968, Hon. member, 1977-; Fellow of the Royal Society, 1970; Fellow of the Australian Academy of Science, 1970-; Sc. Council, International Agency for Research on Cancer, 1976-80; International Union of Immunological Societies, Council for Australia, 1977-; Officer of the Order of Australia, 1981; *Publications:* Over 260 publications in Scientific Journals, mostly dealing with Immunology and Cancer research. *Honours:* Esther Langer-Bertha Teplitz Memorial Award for Cancer research, 1965; Gairdner Foundation International Award for Immunology Toronto, Canada, 1966; Encyclop., Britannia Australia Award for Immunolgy, Canberra, Australia, 1966; Scientific Medal Zool. Soc. London, 1967; FRS., 1970; FAA., 1970; Burnet Medal, Australian Academy Sci., 1971; Paul Ehrlich-Ludwig Darmstaedter Prize Immunology, Frankfurt, Germany, 1974; Sir William Upjohn Medal, University of Melbourne, 1978; Rabbi Shai Shacknai Memorial Prize for Immunology and Cancer research, Hadassah Medical School, Jerusalem, 1978; Appointed to the Order of Australia, for services to Medical research, 1981. *Hobbies:* Music; Photography; Art. *Address:* 32 Burke Road North, East Ivanhoe, Victoria 3079, Australia.

MILLER, John Osman, b. 10 May 1930, Melbourne, Australia. Public Servant, Academic, Chartered Accountant. m. Margot Yvonne Ford, 22 Dec. 1962, 2 sons, 3 daughters. *Education:* B.Com, 1952, BA, 1968, Melbourne University; B.Ed, Latrobe University, 1976; M.Ed.Admin., University of New England, 1979; FASA, 1963; FCA, 1966; MACE, 1980; FAIM, 1981. *Appointments:* Wangaratta Woollen Mills Ltd., 1953-56; PA Management Consultants, UK, 1957-59; Canada, 1961-62, Australia, 1963; Partner, Hungerfords, Chartered Accountants, 1964-74; Foundation Dean, David Syme Business School, Caulfield Institute of Technology, 1974-81; Director, Victorian Ministry of Consumer Affairs, 1981-. *Memberships:* Victorian President, 1975, National Vice President, 1980-81, Australian Society of Accountants; Victorian President, Company Directors Association of Australia, 1975-77. *Publications:* Financial Measurement for Managers, 1977; Papers: Management Accounting for Smaller Businesses, 1979; Education and Training of Accountants in

Government, 1979. *Honours:* Truscott Scholarship, 1946-47; Commonwealth Scholarship, 1949-52; Kellog Foundation Fellowship, 1977-78; A.O. (Officer of the Order of Australia), 1979. *Hobbies:* Reading; Hockey; Cross Country Skiing; Tennis. *Address:* 7 Wellington Street, Brighton, 3186, Victoria, Australia.

MILLER, Olive Hilda, b. 9 Nov. 1921, Rayleigh, Essex, England. Civil Servant. m. N. Ray Miller, 7 Nov. 1953, 1 son, 1 daughter. *Education:* Diploma, Youth Leadership, SW Essex Technical College, UK, 1945. *Appointments:* Youth Organiser, Church of Scotland, Jamaica, West Indies, 1946-48; Sister and Teacher, Presbyterian Church, Grand Cayman, Cayman Islands, 1948-50; YWCA, London, UK, 1950-51; Organiser for England, The Girls' Brigade, 1951-54; Infant teacher, Cayman Islands Preparatory School, 1962-63; Associate Editor, local newspapers, 1964-71; Government Information Officer, Cayman Islands Government, 1971-. *Memberships:* Secretary, National Council of Social Service; Chairman, Public Library Committee; International Vice-President, The Girls' Brigade; Director, Pink Ladies Volunteer Corps. *Honours:* Queens Badge and Certificate of Honour, Cayman Islands, 1967; MBE., 1977. *Hobbies:* Reading; Church and Social Work. *Address:* PO Box 717, Grand Cayman, Cayman Islands.

MILLER, Peter, b. 21 Mar. 1929, Taree, NSW, Australia. Consulting Metallurgist. m. Ruth Florence Dawson, 21 July 1956, 2 sons, 1 daughter. *Education:* ASTC, Credit Diploma in Metallurgy, Sydney Technical College, 1953. *Appointments:* Engineer, Cominco, Trail, B.C., Canada, 1956-57; Technical Assistant, Inco, Copper Cliff, Ontario, Canada, 1957-59; Shift Supervisor, Technical Assistant, Smelter Superintendent, Electrolytic Refining & Smelting Co., Port Kembla, Australia, 1954-62; Research Officer, Assistant Superintendent, Lead Refinery, Zinc Slag Fuming, Electrolytic Zinc, Broken Hill Associated Smelters, Port Pirie, South Australia, 1963-71; Metallurgical Superintendent, 1971-79, Kalgoorlie Nickel Smelter Western Australia; Consulting Metallurgist, Tennant Creek Smelter, Northern Territory, Australia, 1980-81; Consulting Metallurgist, La Caridad Copper Smelter, Mexico, 1981-. *Memberships:* American Institute of Metallurgical Engineers; Canadian Institute of Mining & Metallurgy. *Publications:* Contributed paper on Flash Smelting at Kalgoorlie Nickel Smelter, Second Flash Smelting Congress, Tokyo, Japan, 1974. *Honours:* Royal Australian Chemical Institute Prize, 1953; Australian Institute of Metals Prize, 1953. *Hobbies:* Sailing; Photography; Surfing. *Address:* Mexicana De Cobre, S.A., Av. Insurgentes Sur No 432, Mexico 7, DF.

MILLER, Walter Geoffrey Thomas, b. 25 Oct. 1934, Queenstown, Tasmania. Diplomat. m. Rachel Caroline Webb, 13 Aug. 1960, 3 sons, 1 daughter. *Education:* B.A. (Hons) 1956; B.A. (Hons) (Oxon) 1958; M.A., (Oxon). *Appointments:* Diplomatic postings in Malaysia, Indonesia, UN, New York; Deputy High Commissioner, New Delhi, 1973-75; Australian Ambassador, Seoul, Republic of Korea, 1978-80; First Assistant Secretary, North and South Asia Division, Department of Foreign Affairs, Canberra, Australia. *Memberships:* Australian Institute of International Affairs; Australian Institute of Public Administration. *Honours:* Tasmanian Rhodes Scholar, 1956. *Hobbies:* Tennis; Reading; Golf. *Address:* 2 Wickham Crescent, Red Hill, ACT, 2603, Australia.

MILLETTE, Emru Douglas, b. 20 Mar. 1939, Trinidad, West Indies. Doctor of Philosophy, Engineering Consultant. *Education:* BSc, Queen's University of Belfast, 1964; MSc, 1971, PhD, 1974, Purdue University, Indiana. *Appointments:* Chief Engineer, Operations & Maintenance Water & Sewerage Authority of Trinidad & Tobago, 1964-76; Managing Director, Integrated Management Engineering Consultants Ltd., 1976-77; Chairman, Managing Director, Millette Engineering (International) Ltd., 1977-; Chairman, Managing Director, Geodata Consultants (Trinidad) Ltd., 1979-. *Memberships:* Professional Engineers Association (Trinidad & Tobago); Institution of Civil Engineers; American Waterworks Association; American Society of Agricultural Engineers; American Geophysical Union. *Honours:* Sigma XI. *Address:* 37 Scotland Terrace, Andalusia, Maraval, Trinidad.

MILLINGTON, Alwyn John, b. 14 June 1910, Wilmington, South Australia. Agricultural Scientist. m. 2

Apr. 1942, 1 daughter. *Education:* BSc, 1940; MSc, 1942; DSc, 1956. *Appointments:* Western Australian Department of Agriculture; Roseworthy Agricultural College South Australia; University of Western Australia Institute of Agriculture; CSIRO Officer-in-Charge, Kimberley Research Station, Western Australia; Office of Regional Administration and the North West. *Memberships:* Royal Society of Western Australia; Australian Institute of Agricultural Science. *Publications:* The Wheat Industry in Australia (with Sir A Callaghan); Man Made Lakes (with Prof N Stanley & M Alpers); Agriculture in Western Australia 1829-1979 (with G H Burville); Kalumburu and the War Years (with E Perez & R Pratt). *Honours:* Order of Australia, 1980; Fellow Australian Institute Agricultural Science, 1970; Fellow, West4ern Australian Institute of Agricultural Technology, 1972. *Address:* 66 Chipping Road, City Beach, 6015 West Australia.

MILLNER, John Robin, b. 2 Apr. 1934, Esher, Surrey, England. Company Director. m. Gill Wood, 8 June 1974, 3 sons. *Education:* St Paul's School, 1947-52. *Appointments:* L Hammond & Co., Ltd; Alexander Howden & Co., Ltd; The HongKong and Shanghai Banking Corporation; Director of 29 Companies. *Memberships:* The Royal HongKong Yacht Club; The Aberdeen Boat Club. *Hobby:* Boats. *Address:* 4 Ardshiel, 45 Plantation Road, The Peak, Hong Kong.

MILLS, Benjamin Leopold, b. 15 Feb. 1923, Sydney, Australia. Company Director & Corporate Adviser. m. (2) Elizabeth Ann Carlson, 14 Oct. 1978, 2 sons, 3 daughters. *Education:* Law Course, Sydney University, 1948-53; Admitted Solicitor of Supreme Courst of NSW, 1958; Bachelor of Arts, Sydney University; Bachelor of Arts, University of New England; Past Associate and Graduate Member of the Institution of Radio Engineers. *Appointments:* Liaison Officer, Council for Scientific and Industrial Research, Sydney University, 1940-41; Armed Forces on Active Service, 1942-46; Legal Officer, Commonwealth Attorney Generals Office, Sydney, 1947-52; Royal Australian Air Force Reserve, 1948-71; Legal Profession of NSW, 1952-76; Company Director and Corporate Adviser, 1976-80; Appointed Consul General for Sierra Leone in Australia, 1972-. *Memberships:* Sydney University Union; Wireless Institute of Australia; British Astonomical Association (England); Returned Servicemen's League of Australia; Legal Panel Royal Australian Navy, Sydney, 1972-76. *Honours:* Fellow of The Royal Geographical Society (England). *Hobbies:* Electronics; Boating; Astronomy. *Address:* 384 Woolooware Road, Cronulla, Sydney, Australia

MILLS, Ivor Henry, b. 13 June 1921, London, England. Physician. m. Sydney Elizabeth Puleston Roberts, 1947, 1 son, 1 daughter. *Education:* BSc, 1942, PhD, 1946, Queen Mary College, London; BA, Trinity College, Cambridge, 1948; MB.,B.Chir., 1951, MD, 1956, FRCP, 1964, St Thomas's Hospital, London. *Appointments:* Professor of Medicine, University of Cambridge and Honorary Consultant Physician, Addenbrooke's Hospital, Cambridge, 1963-; Casualty Officer, 1951, House Physician, 1952, Senior Medical Casualty Officer & Resident Pathologist, 1953, Junior Lecturer in Medicine & Pathology, 1953-55, Lecturer in Medicine & Chemical Pathology, 1955-59, Senior Lecturer, 1959-62, Reader in Medicine & Honorary Consultant Physician, 1962-63, St Thomas's Hospital, London. *Memberships:* Royal Society of Medicine; The Physiological Society; Secretary, 1963-71, Society for Endocrinology; Renal Association; Medical Research Society; *Publications:* Author of Clinical Aspects of Adrenal Function, 1964. *Honours:* Senior Scholar, Trinity College, Cambridge, 1948; Two Prizes at St Thomas's Hospital Medical School, 1951; MRC., Eli Lilly Travelling Fellowship, 1956-57; Visiting Scientist, National Institutes of Health, Bethesda, Md., USA, 1957-58; Pro-Censor, 1974-75, Censor, 1975-76, Royal College of Physicians; Honorary Fellow, The American College of Physicians, 1975. *Hobby:* Gardening. *Address:* Department of Medicine, University of Cambridge, Addenbrooke's Hospital, Hills Road, Cambridge CB2 2QQ, England.

MILLS, Kingsley Wallis, b. 26 Nov. 1928, Melbourne, Australia. Orthopaedic Surgeon. m. Christine Helen Noonan Thorp (2), 21 Nov. 1979, 3 sons, 2 daughters. *Education:* MB.,BS, Melbourne University, 1946-51; FRACS, 1956; FRCS, (England), 1957. *Appointments:*

Resident Medical Officer, 1952-54, Orthopaedic Surgeon, 1970-79, Senior Orthopaedic Surgeon, 1979-, Royal Melbourne Hospital; Pathology Department, Melbourne University & R.M.H., 1955-56; Orthopaedic Registrar, London Hospital, UK, 1957-58; Robert Jones & Agnes Hunt, Orthopaedic Hospital, Oswestry, UK, 1959; Orthopaedic Surgeon, Western General Hospital, Melbourne, 1960-70; Consulting Orthopaedic Surgeon, Royal Womens Hospital, 1979-. *Memberships:* Chairman, Victorian Board of Studies, Australian Orthopaedic Association; Australian Medical Association; Australian Association of Surgeons; Melbourne Club; Metropolitan Golf Club. *Publications:* Contributor of articles in professional medical journals. *Hobbies:* Skiing; Flyfishing; Golf; Photography. *Address:* 43 Erin Street, Richmond, Victoria 3121, Australia.

MILNE, James, b. 27 June 1917, Great Orton, Carlisle, England. Chartered Engineering Consultant. m. Lelia Petri, 24 July 1952, 1 son. *Education:* Bachelor of Technical Science, Manchester University, 1938. *Appointments:* Assistant Engineer, Mid-Cumberland Electricity Co., 1938-39; British Army Royal Signals, Private to Major, Africa, Italy, Burma, Germany, 1940-46; Engineer, India, 1947-55, Traction Manager, India, 1958-67, Contracts Manager, Iran, Manager, Consultant, Balvac, 1967-71; BICC Ltd; Balfour Beatty Ltd., 1972-75, 1975-. *Memberships:* FISE, 1974-; FIEE, 1960-; FIHE, 1979-; FINE, 1958-. *Publications:* Wilberforce our Monkey, 1958; Balfour Beatty Vacuum Impregnation Process invented, 1972. *Honours:* MBE, 1945; OBE, 1971. *Hobby:* Cycling. *Address:* 178 Queen Alexandra Mansions, Judd Street, London, WC1H9DJ, England.

MILNER, Christopher John, b. 3 Apr. 1912, Sheffield, England. Physicist. m. Eirene Joyce Thorburn, 3 June 1937, 2 sons, 2 daughters. *Education:* St. John's College, Cambridge University, 1930-36; BA, 1933; MA, PhD, 1937. *Appointments:* Research Laboratory, 1936-52, Manhattan Project, 1944, Head of Physics Section, 1946-52, BTH Co., Ltd., RugbyUK; Professor of Applied Physics, 1952-76, Dean Faculty of Science, 1956-59, Head, School of Physics, 1968-76, Head, School of Applied Physics and Optometry, The University of New South Wales. *Memberships:* Associate, 1939, Fellow, 1949, Institute of Physics, (UK); Founder Fellow, Australian Institute of Physics, 1961. *Publications:* Approximately 60 papers in scientific journals, also British and Australian Patents. *Honours:* Emeritus Professor, University of NSW, 1977. *Hobbies:* Sailing; Computing; Research & Development in applied physics. *Address:* 21 Dalkeith Street, Northbridge, NSW, 2063, Australia

MILTE, Kerry Leon, b. 12 July 1944, Melbourne, Australia. Barrister-at-Law. m. Elizabeth Anne Fraser, 19 Aug. 1971. *Education:* Bachelor of Laws, 1967, Diploma in Criminology, 1968, Master of Arts, 1978, University of Melbourne. *Appointments:* Senior Superintendent of Australian Commonwealth Police, 1967-70; Barrister in Private Practice, 1971-73; Law Enforcement Adviser to the Attorney-General of Australia, 1973-74; Denior Lecturer, Criminology Department University of Melbourne, 1975-81; Barrister, Victoria, Newsouth Wales and Australian Capital Territory, Senior Research Fellow Brain-Behaviour Research Institute, La Trobe University, Melbourne, Victoria, 1981-. *Memberships:* Naval and Military Club, Melbourne. *Publications:* Police in Australia, 1978; Principles of Police Planning, 1979; Numerous articles on Law, Psychology, Terrorism and general criminolgical matters in Journals. *Hobby:* Aviation. *Address:* 58 MacIlwraith Street, North Carlton 3054, Victoria, Australia.

MILTON-SMITH, John, b. 23 Apr. 1942, Sydney, Australia. Academic Dean. m. Carolyn Edith Plotkin, 24 Feb. 1973, 2 daughters. *Education:* BA, University of Sydney, 1966; MA, Monash University, 1969; PhD, University of Cambridge, 1974. *Appointments:* Market Research Executive, George Patterson P/L, 1962-64; Advertising Account Executive, Lintas P/L, 1965-66; Tutor, History Department, Monash University, 1966-67; Lecturer, History Department, University of Melbourne, 1971-73; Dean, School of Business & Social Sciences, Gippsland Institute of Advanced Education, 1973-78; Dean, 1979-, Acting Director, 1980-, School of Business, Prahran College of Advanced Education. *Memberships:* President, 1978-80, Institute of Business Administration; Associate Fellow, Australian Institute of Management; Member, State Executive of the

Victorian Liberal Party, 1977-79. *Publications:* Editor, Business Administration, 1981-; Contributor of numerous articles in professional journals. *Honours:* J Holland Rose Studentship, University of Cambridge, 1968-69. *Hobbies:* Vintage Wine; Music; Reading; Conversation. *Address:* 72 Fitzgibbon Street, Parkville, Victoria, 3052, Australia.

MINCHAM, Jeffery Dean, b. 26 Feb. 1950, Milang, South Australia. Artist, Craftsman. m. Lexie Christine Barber, 17 Jan. 1976. *Education:* Prince Alfred College, 1969; Advanced Diploma in Art Teaching, Western Teachers College, 1970-73; Post-Graduate Studies in Ceramics, Tasmanian College of Advanced Education. *Appointments:* Art Teacher, Education Department of South Australia, 1975; Established private workshop, 1976; Part-time Lecturing positions, 1975, 1977 & 1979; Director, Ceramics Workshop, Jam Factory Workshops, Adelaide, 1979-. *Memberships:* Vice-President, 1978-81, Crafts Council of Australia; Vice-President, 1978, President, 1979 & 1980, Crafts Council of South Australia; Vice-President, 1980-81, Royal South Australia Society of Arts; Vice-President, 1978, Potters Guild of South Australia. *Creative Works:* Ceramic works represented in various Australian Art Galleries. *Honours:* Gold Medal Award, Potters Guild of South Australia, 1980; Mayfair Ceramic Award, 1980; Awards of Merit, Pug Mill Award, 1976 & 1979. *Hobbies:* Yacht Racing, (International Flying Dutchman Class). *Address:* PO Box 78, Cherryville, South Australia.

MINSON, Wilfrid Gerald a'Beckett, b. 31 Oct. 1942, Melbourne, Australia. Civil Engineer. m. Susan Elaine, 3 Dec. 1976, 1 son. *Education:* B.E. (Civil), University of Melbourne, 1966. *Appointments:* Atlas Construction Limited, Montreal, Canada, 1966-70; Prentice Bros Minson Pty. Limited, Melbourne, 1970-. *Memberships:* Melbourne Club. *Publications:* Proc ARRB, 1967. *Hobbies:* Travel; Reading; Tennis. *Address:* 12 Olympic Avenue, Montmorency, Victoria, Australia 3094.

MINTER, Robert Hugh, b. 9 Sept. 1921, Sydney, Australia. Solicitor. m. Shirley Jeanette Pitt, 7 Jan. 1948, 2 sons, 1 daughter. *Education:* The Kings School, Parramatta, 1933-39 and Sydney University, 1940-41, 1946-47; Australian Imperial Forces, 1942-45. *Appointments:* Directorships: Chairman, Carrier Air Conditioning Limited; Tetra Pak Australia Pty Ltd.; Parker Pen Australia Pty Ltd.; The Colonial Mutual Life Assurance Society Ltd.; Fairfax and Roberts Jewellers Ltd.; Hertz Pacific Ltd.; Wardly Australia Holdings Ltd.; Twentieth Century Fox Film Corp. (Aust) Pty Ltd.; Robert Barrow (Aust) Pty Ltd; Law Clerk; Partner Minter, Simpson and Company, 1948-. *Memberships:* Royal Sydney Golf Club; Aunion Club, Sydney; Australian Club, Sydney; Ski Club of Australia; Royal Prince Edward Yacht Club; Royal Historical Society, Australia. *Honours:* Bachelor of Laws 1948. *Hobbies:* Sailing; Skiing; Reading. *Address:* 3B Buckhurst Avenue, Point Piper, Sydney 2027, Australia.

MINTOFF, Hon. Dominic, b. 6 Aug. 1916. Maltese Statesman; Architect; Civil Engineer. m. Moyra Bentinck, 1947, 2 daughters. *Education:* Royal University of Malta; Rhodes Scholar, Oxford University, UK; MA; BSc; BA & A; A & CE. *Appointments:* General Secretary, Malta Labour Party, 1936-37; Civil Engineer, UK, 1941-43; set up in practice as architect, Malta; rejoined Malta Labour Party, 1944; elected to Council of Government and Member of Executive Committee, 1945; elected to Malta legislative Assembly, Labour, and as Deputy Leader of Labour Party was Deputy Prime Minister, also Minister for Works and Reconstruction, 1947; resigned Ministry and elected Leader of Labour Party, 1949; Prime Minister and Minister for Finance, 1955; resigned office, 1958, to lead Maltese Liberation Movement, Leader of Opposition in House of Representatives, 1962-71; Prime Minister, Minister of Commonwealth and Foreign Affairs, 1971- and Minister of Interior, 1976-; Minister of Foreign Affairs, 1978-. *Publications:* Scientific, literary and artistic works. *Address:* 'Olives', Xintill Street, Tarxien, Malta, G.C.

MIRZA, Firoze Dara, b. 28 Dec. 1932, Bombay, India. Dental Surgeon; Sp. Prosthodontist. m. Elinor Christian, 8 Oct. 1961, 3 sons. *Education:* LDSc, Nair Hospital Dental College, Bombay, 1955; MSD, Tufts University Boston, USA, 1957; Honarary, FICD, USA, 1968;

Honorary, FICOI, USA, 1973. *Appointments:* Assistant Professor, North Western University, Chicago, USA; Professor and Head of Prosthetic Department, 1962-; Acting Dean, 1974-75. *Memberships:* International College of Oral Implantology; Indian Prosthodontic Society; Mid-town Rotary Club; Indian Dental Association. *Publications:* Implantology, (Dental), 1959; Successfully implanted metal tooth in a cancer bone first time, paper published in 1979; Over 30 papers in journals. *Honours:* Quintessenz—International, West Germany, 1973; Indian Council of Medical Research, Fellowship, India. *Hobbies:* Horse Racing; Gardening; Dental Ceramics. *Address:* 10 Setalwad Road, Bombay 400 036, India.

MIRZA, Gholam Hafiz, b. 2 Jan. 1920, Dinajpur, Bangladesh. Speaker, Bangladesh Parliament. m. Abeda Hafiz, 15 Feb. 1953, 1 son, 3 daughters. *Education:* BA(Hons.), 1939, MA, Economics, Calcutta University, 1941; Bachelor of Law, Dacca University, 1948; Advocate, Dacca High Court, 1950; Senior Advocate, Supreme Court, Pakistan, 1960. *Appointments:* Advocate High Court, East Pakistan and Bangladesh; Senior Advocate, Supreme Court, Pakistan and Bangladesh; Minister for Land Administration and Land Reforms, 1978-; Speaker,, Bangladesh Parliament, 1979-. *Memberships:* East Pakistan Provincialk Legislative Assembly, 1954-58; President, Dacca Chamber of Commerce and Industries; President, Supreme Court Bar Association, Dacca; Senate for Dacca and Rajshahi Universities; Vice-Chairman, Bar Council and all Pakistan Bar; Council, Statutory Bodies to regulate legal profession. *Publications:* Parliamentary Law, Procedure and Practices, (In print); Role of the Speaker in the Parliament of a developing Country, (In print). Hobby: Gardening. *Address:* 127, New Eskatan Road, Dacca, Bangladesh.

MISHRA, Brahmanand, b. 11 May 1938, Bhagalpur District. Professor. m. Bimala Mishra, 11 Mar. 1960, 2 sons, 1 daughter. *Education:* BSc, Engineering, Electronics and Communication, 1962; MSc, 1968; PhD, Networks and Systems, Delhi University 1974. *Appointments:* Technical Assistant, Bihar State Electricity Board, 1962; Lecturer Electrical Engineer, 1962-64, Assistant Professor, Bhagalpur College of Engineering, 1964-65; Assistant Professor, Electronics and Communication, Engineer, Birla Institute of Technology, Ranchi, 1965-68; Assistant Professor, Electrical Engineer, 1965-71, Professor Electrical Engineer, Delhi College of Engineering, University of Delhi, 1971-; Professor, Electrical Engineer, National Institute of Electricity and Electronics, INELEC, Boumerdes, Algeria, 1979-81. *Memberships:* MIEEE; FIETE; MISTE; IEEE, India; IETE, Delhi Centre. *Publications:* Synthesis of Four-Terminal RC Active Filters', 1972; Realisation of Complex Zeros, 1972; Minimal Realisation of Biquadratic R.C. Transfer Functions', 1972; Synthesis of n-Terminal RC-Networks, 1973; A Realisability Theorem for Two-Pole Admittance Functions', 1973; RC-Operational Amplifier Synthesis of Two-Port Admittance Functions, 1975; Some Aspects of Grounded Two-Port RC Synthesis, 1973; Synthesis of RC Active Filters, 1971; Realisation of nth order indefinite admittance matrces, 1974; Single Operational Amplifier Realisation of I-Port Driving Point Functions, 1974; Synthesis of Multi-Channel Filters, 1974; Realisation of Low Sensitivity High Q Active Filters, 1976; Realisation of Digitl Filters and Problems of Accuracies, 1976; A New Technic of Designing Digital Base Band Filters, 1980. Hobby: Photography. *Address:* 80, Lucknow Road, Banarsidas Estate, Delhi 110007, India.

MISHRA, Jayamanta, b. 15 Oct. 1925, Haripur P.O. Kaluahi District, Madhubani, Bihar. Vice-Chancellor, Kameshwara Singh Darbhanga, Sanskrit University, Darbhanga. m. m. Smt. Sushila Mishra, June 1946, 5 children. *Education:* BA(Hons.) First Class, 1950, MA Sanskrit, First Class, Patna University 1952; PhD, Bihar, 1961; Shahitya Shastri, First Class, 1944; Sahityacharya, First Class, Bihar, 1946; Vyakaranacharya, Second Class, 1948; Vyakarna-Shastri, First Class, Varanasi, 1942. *Appointments:* Lecturer, Assistant Professor, Reader and HeadUniversity Professor and Head, Senior University Professor and Head, Department of Sanskrit B.U; Professor of Sanskrit, Colombo Plan, Indian Co-operation Mission, Nepal, Ministry of External Affairs, Government of India, 1963-69 and 1972-75; Vice-Chancellor, K.S.D. Sanskrit University, Darbhanga. *Memberships:* All India Oriental Confer-

ence and World Sanskrit Conference; Executive Council and General Council, Rashtriya Sanskrit Sansthan, Ministry of Education and Social Welfare, Government of India. *Publications:* Kavyatma Mimansa; Nibandha Kusumanjalih; Alankara Prakasa; Sanskrit Vyakarana Sara; Sanskrit Vyakaranodayah; Maithili Natak par Sanskritak Prabhava; Literary Heritage of Nepal (in cultural Heritage of Nepal); Works edited: Puspa Cintamani; Saiva Sarasva Sara; Saiva Sarvasva Sara Pramanabhuta Purana Sangraha; Abhilekh Geeta Mala; Ready for publication: Kavya Suarupa Mimansa; Mudita Kuvalayasva Nataka (edited); Madhavanala Katha. *Honours:* BA(Hons) Two Gold Medals and a Prize, Patna University 1950; MA, Sanskrit, Two Gold Medals and Prize, 1952; Gold Medal in I.A., Highest mark, Sanskrit in Allahabad Board Examination. *Hobbies:* Reading; Writing. *Address:* K.S.D. Sanskrit University, Darbhanga, Bihar, India.

MISHRA, Raghu Nath, b. 1 Jan. 1948, Amwa Digar, District Deoria, U.P., India. Teaching. m. Abha Tiwari, 30 Jan. 1973, 1 son, 1 daughter. *Education:* BSc, Electrical Engineer, 1969; MTech. 1971; PhD, 1975. *Appointments:* Senior Research Assistant, part-time, Electrical Engineer, Indian Institute of Technology, Kanpur, India, 1973-75; Assistant Professor in Electrical Engineering, G.B. Pant University of Agriculture and Tech., Pant nagar India, 1975-. *Memberships:* Indian Society for Technical Education; Fellow, Institution of Electronics and Telecommunication Engineers; Institution of Engineers, India; Chartered Engineer, India; Faculty Adviser, GB Pant University of Agriculture and Technology students chapter, Electrical Engineering, Institute of Engineers, (India). *Publications:* Assumptions in theory of Ballistic Galvanometer, 1980; Hybrid Algorithm for Constrained Minimization, 1968; Convergence of Nonlinear Algorithms, 1980; Memory Gradient Method via Bridge Balance Convergence, 1979; International System of Units, 1978; Estimation Detection and Identification Methods in Power System Studies, 1975; Serch Techniques for Power Flow Optimization Problems, 1973; Application of memory gradient method to economic load dispatching problem, 1972. *Honours:* Lala Balak Ramji Kohinoor Memorial Gold-Medal of Banaras Hindu University, Varanasi, India, in Engineering; R.B.G. Modi Medal (gold); N.V.R. Nageswar Iyer Prize, in Electrical Engineering. Hobby: Research and Observation. *Address:* At & P.O., Amwa Digar, Deoria, UP-274 302, India.

MISHRA, Vijay Chandra, b. 4 May 1945, Suva, Fiji. University Lecturer. m. Nalini Singh, 29 June 1973, 1 son, 1 daughter. *Education:* BA., Victoria University of Wellington, New Zealand, 1964-66; Dip. Tchng., Christchurch Teachers' College, New Zealand, 1967; BA.(Hons.), Macquarie University, Australia, 1970-71; MA., Sydney University, Australia, 1974-75; PhD., Australia National University, Australia, 1978-80. *Appointments:* School Teacher, Labasa College, Fiji, 1968-69; Senior Education Officer, Fiji, 1972-73; Tutor in English, Sydney University, Australia, 1975; Senior Tutor and Lecturer, Murdoch University, Perth, Australia, 1976-. *Memberships:* Modern Language Association of America; Australian Universities Language and Literature Association; Association of Commonwealth Languages and Literatures; South Asian Studies Association; Australian Association for the Study of Religions; Australian Literature Association. *Publications:* Rama's Banishment: A Centenary Tribute to Fiji Indians 1879-1979; Short Fiction as Theory; The Literary Reputation of Charles Hrpur; Two Truths are Told: Tgore's Kabir; Principles of Narrative Structure in Indian Literature; The Girmit Ideology Re-examined; V S Naipaul's India; various other articles; Co-editor, Journal of Studies in Mysticism; Advisory Editor, Religious Traditions. *Honours:* Commonwealth Scholar, 1970-71; University of Sydney Scholar, 1974-75; Australia National University Scholar, 1978-79; First Class Honours in English, 1971. *Hobbies:* Swimming; Chess; Classical Music. *Address:* 92 Hensman Street, South Perth, Western Australia.

MISKIN, Raymond John, b. 4 July 1928, Ipswich, Suffolk, England. Chartered Engineer. m. Betty Tavener, 14 July 1951, (divorced, 1981) 1 daughter. *Education:* ONC.(Mechanical), HNC.(Mechanical), Endorsements to same, Southall Technical College, London, UK, 1945-51. *Appointments:* Development Engineer, 1945-54, Deputy Chief Inspector, 1956-63, Fairey

Aviation Co. Limited; Assistant Chief Technician, S P E Co. Limited, 1954-56; Quality Control Manager, Graviner Manufacturing Co. Limited, 1963-69; Secretary, Institution of Quality Assurance, 1969-73; Secretary, Institution of Production Engineers, 1973-. *Memberships:* Institution of Production Engineers; Institution of Mechanical Engineers; Fellow, Institution of Quality Assurance; Royal Aeronautical Society. *Publications:* Various articles in Technical Journals. *Honours:* International Industrial Technology Management Award, San Fernando Valley Engineers Council, 1978; Honorary Fellow, Indian Institution of Production Engineers, 1979; Los Angeles Council of Engineers and Scientists International Contributions Award, 1901. *Hobbies:* Golf; Photography. *Address:* c/o 66 Little Ealing Lane, London W5 4XX England.

MISSEN, Alan Joseph, b. 22 July 1925, Kew, Victoria, Australia. Senator. m. Mary Martha Anchen, 4 May 1963. *Education:* LL.B., 1947, LL.M., 1948, Melbourne University. *Appointments:* Read at Victorian Bar, 1948; Barrister and Solicitor, 1948-74; Partner, Senior Partner, Schilling Missen and Impey, Melbourne; Elected to Australian Senate, 1974, re-elected 1975, 1977; Chairman Senate Standing Committee on Constitutional and Legal affairs and on Regulations and Ordinances Committee, 1978-81; Elected Chairman, Commonwealth Delegated Legislation Committee, 1980. *Memberships:* Past President, Constitutional Club, Melbourne; Former Chairman, Vice-Chairman, Australian Parliamentary Group, Amnesty International; Past President, Debaters Association of Victoria; Australian Debating Federation, 1964-68. *Publications:* 'The Australian Debater', joint author. *Honours:* Silver Jubilee Medal, 1977. *Hobbies:* Tennis; Golf; Contract Bridge. *Address:* 46 Fitzgerald Street, Balwyn, Victoria, Australia 3103.

MITCHELL, David Ian, b. 31 July 1921, Grenada, West Indies. Minister of Religion. m. Norma Patricia Lorde Achee, 20 Oct. 1973, 5 sons. *Education:* Inter BD., London, Caenwood Theological College, Jamaica, West Indies, 1943-46; BD., London, Richmond Theological College, Surrey, UK, 1946-47; BA., London, Wolsey Hall Correspondence College, Oxford, UK, 1948-50; M.Rel.Ed., Union Theological Seminary, New York, USA, 1955-56; Teachers' College, Columbia University, New York, USA, 1956-58; Ed.D., 1964. *Appointments:* Minister, Methodist Church in Caribbean: St. Vincent, Trinidad, Guyana, 1947-55, 1958-60; Director, Christian Education, Methodist Church, Red Bank, New Jersey, USA, 1956-58; Editor, Carib. Xtn. Living Curriculum, Secretary, Carib. Committee, Joint Christian Action, 1960-69; Chairman, South Caribbean Synod, Methodist Church, 1964-69; Lecturer, Education and Religion, Naparima Teachers College, Trinidad, 1969-72; Editor, Cedar Press, 1974-79, Regional Co-ordinator, Education for Development, 1979-; Caribbean Conference of Churches, 1973-. *Memberships:* Amnesty International, 1980-; Caribbean Studies Association, Puerto Rico, 1979-. *Publications:* Eyes Wide Open, 1973; New Mission for New People, 1977; Workers with Christ, (with H. Sawyer), 1977. *Honours:* Fellow in programme of Advanced Religious Studies, Union Theological Seminary, New York, USA, 1955-56. *Hobbies:* Photography; Reading; Swimming. *Address:* 'Rockridge', Black Rock, St. Michael, Barbados, West Indies.

MITCHELL, Denis Noel, b. 13 Dec. 1915, Sheffield, Yorkshire, England. Chartered Civil and Structural Engineer. m. Maisie, 23 July 1938. *Education:* Chartered Structural Engineer Examinations passed, 1941-42; Chartered Civil Engineer Examinations passed, 1949. *Appointments:* Apprentice in Building Trades, 1931-35; Building and Engineering Designer Draughtsman, 1936-43; Cadet, 1943, Lieutenant and Captain, 1944-46, Honorary Captain, 1946-, Royal Engineers; Senior Structural Engineer, 1946-52; Chief Design Engineer, John Laing & Son Limited, 1952-65; Self Employed Consulting Engineer; Senior Principal Lecturer, part-time, Hatfield Polytechnic, UK, 1965-80. *Memberships:* Fellow, Institution of Civil Engineers; Retired Fellow, Institution of Structural Engineers; British Standards Society. *Publications:* Many reviews of books on Building and Engineering for the British Council. *Honours:* Defence Medal, 1939/45 Star, Burma Star, 1945. *Hobbies:* Home and Garden Maintenance; Amateur Illusionist. *Address:* Escafeld, 6 Theobald Street, Radlett, Herts, WD7 7LP, England.

MITCHELL, Derek (Sir), b. 5 Mar. 1922, Wimbledon, England. Director. m. 1 April 1944, 1 son, 2 daughters. *Education:* M.A. (Hons), History, Christ Church, Oxford, 1940-42, 1945-47. *Appointments:* British Civil Service, 1947-77; Principal Private Secretary to Prime Minister, 1964 66; Economic Minister, British Embassy, Washington and UK Executive Director IMF and World Bank, 1969-72; Second Permanent Secretary, H.M. Treasury, 1973-77; Senior Adviser, Lehman Brothers, Kuhn Loet, 1979-; Director, Standard Chartered Bank, 1979-; Director, Bowater Corporation, 1979-; Member, Port of London Authority, 1979-; Member, National Theatre Board, 1977-; Director, The Observer Ltd., 1981. *Memberships:* Garrick; Political Economy; Pilgrims. *Honours:* CB, 1967; KCB, 1974; CVO., 1966. *Hobbies:* Music; Theatre; Travel. *Address:* 9 Holmbush Road, Putney SW15 3LE, London, England.

MITCHELL, Hamilton, b. 24 Feb. 1910, Sydney Australia. Barrister, Solicitor. m. (1) Marion Frances Norman, 24 Nov. 1938, 2 sons, 1 daughter. (2) Dorothy Good, 18 Oct. 1980. *Education:* LL.M., Auckland University, 1928-33. *Appointments:* Judges Associate, 1932-34; Law Clerk, 1936-41; Self-employed, 1941-. *Memberships:* include: President, New Zealand Returned Services Association, 1962-74; Vice President, British Commonwealth Ex Services League, 1962-74; Deputy Chairman, Winston Churchill Memorial Trust Fund, 1966-75; Judge, Courts Martial Appeal Court, 1962-; Chairman, War Pensions Appeal Board, 1978-; Executive Member, Wellington Show Association, 1979-. *Honours:* K.B.E., 1969. *Address:* 78 Orangekaupapa Road, Wellington, New Zealand.

MITCHELL, Julian Guy, b. 28 Aug. 1938, Croydon, England. Government Dentist. Div. 1 son, 1 daughter. *Education:* Guys Hospital Dental School, London University, UK; Licentiate, Dental Surgery, Royal College of Surgeons, UK, 1962. *Appointments:* Private practice, Chelmsford, UK, 1962-63; Assistant to Sir Rodney Swiss in private practice, North Harrow, UK, 1963-65; Private practice, Weybridge and Dental Surgeon to HM Prisons-Wandsworth, Wormwood Scrubs, Holloway, Pentonville, 1965-69; Woking, UK, 1969-71; Appointed to found and manage the industrial dental unit for Gillette Industries, Reading, UK, 1971; Regional Dental Officer, Eastern Caribbean, 1974-. *Memberships:* Secretary/Treasurer, Caribbean Atlantic Regional Dental Association; Founder member, Leeward/Windward Islands Dental Association; Federation Dentaire International; British Dental Association; Association Industrial Dental Surgeons; St Kitts Lawn Tennis Club; Golden Rock Golf Club; Royal St Kitts Hotel Golf Club. *Publications:* Survey Report: Dental Health Among School Children in State of St Kitts/Nevis, 1976; Project for Government Dental Health Service, Commonwealth of Dominica. *Hobbies:* Choral music; Woodwork; Scuba Diving; Underwater photography; Boating; Climbing; Swimming. *Address:* c/o Health Centre; PO Box 236, Basseterre, St. Kitts, Barbados.

MITCHELL, Norris Michael, b. 24 May 1932, Georgetown, Guyana. Architect. m. 30 July 1964, 2 daughters. *Education:* Dip.Arch, School of Architecture, Northern Polytechnic, London, 1956-61; Certificate in Urban Design, World Universities Service Bursary, Rome, 1961; ARIBA, 1964. *Appointments:* Junior Architect, Jackson and Edmunds Architects and Town Planners, 1962-64; Divisional Architect, Government of Northern Nigeria, Kaduna, 1964-66; Senior Architect, Ministry of Works, Government of Guyana, 1966-68; Advisor to Government of Guyana on World Bank Secondary Schools construction Project, 1968-70; Established as Principal, Firm of Norris Mitchell Associates, 1970-. *Memberships:* President, Guyana Society of Architects, 1967-71; President, Guyana Society, 1979-81; Barbados Institute of Architects, 1981-; Royal Commonwealth Society, 1978-; Commonwealth Board of Architectural Education, 1980-. *Publications:* Several published articles on Architecture and the Environment, 1967-77. *Honours:* Bronze Plaque, for Excellence in Architecture, Kiwanis International of Georgetown, 1976. *Hobbies:* Reading; The Performing Arts. *Address:* 'Golfview', Rockley New Road, Christ Church, Barbados. West Indies.

MITCHELL, Roy Ernest Moxombo, b. 19 Oct. 1935, Trinidad and Tobago. Public Relations. m. Germaine Fanelese Eriche, 3 Dec. 1966, 3 sons, 3 daughters.

Education: Fatime College, 1952-55. *Appointments:* 2nd Cl. Clerk, Ministry of Agriculture, Lands and Fisheries, 1956-60; Insurance Underwriter, Sun Life Assurance Company, 1960-63; Insurance Underwriter, Maritime Life Assurance Company, 1964-65; Advertising Representative, Trinidad Express Newspapers, 1966-67; Managing Editor, Art and Man Limited, 1967-69; Public Relations Officer, Trinidad and Tobago Electricity Commission, 1970-; Delegate to several International Conferences representing Trinidad and Tobago. *Memberships:* Founder, President, 1975-76, Executive member, 1977, Vice President, 1980, Public Relations Association of Trinidad and Tobago; President, Advertisers Association of Trindad and Tobago, 1975-77; Ag. Secretary, Advertisers Standard Authority, 1972; Chairman, Sectional Committee of Bureau of Standards of Trinidad and Tobago on Labelling of Goods, Advertising and Conditions of Sale; President, Junior League of Trinidad Labour Party, 1950-52; President, Pegasus Club, 1965-69; Chairman, Model United Nations Committee, 1967-74; President, Beacons Literary and Cultural Club, 1954-56; Chairman, Cultural Awards Committee, 1966-67; Chairman, National Arts Centre Committee, 1965-66; Road Safety Association, 1974-81; Hon. Secretary/Treasurer/Public Relations Officer, Road Safety Association of Trinidad and Tobago, 1978-81; Member, 1978, Council Member International Public Relations Association, 1979-81; Co-Chairman of Public Relations Committee of International Public Relations Association Responsible for Carribean Venezuala, Mexico, Netherland Antilles and Colombia. *Publications:* Papers presented at GB Management Systems Limited seminar entitled 'Establishing a Public Relations Programme': What Management thinks and expects of Public Relations; Influencing Management Decision-Making; Organising for Special Events; Community Relations; Public Relations in Crisis and Controversy. *Creative Works:* Lectured on Public Relations at: Management Development Centre of the Government of Trinidad and Tobago on: How to establish a Public Relations Department; John S. Donaldson Technical Institute of Trinidad and Tobago on: An appreciation of Public Relations; W W Mircon Management Systems Limited; Institute of Higher Learning of Trinidad and Tobago; Frank Jefkins School of Public Relations (UK(International Seminar on Public Relations in Trinidad and Tobago, 1981. *Address:* Sierra Leone, Petit Valley, Trinidad, West Indies.

MITRA, Manohar, b. 24 Feb. 1936, Darbhanga, Bihar, India. Personnel Administration. m. Chobi, 11 Dec. 1962, 1 son. *Education:* MA.(Economics); B.Com.;LL.B-.;Post Graduate Diploma in Public Administration. *Appointments:* Secretary, Ujjain Improvement Trust, Ujjain; Secretary, Jagadhari Improvement Trust, Jagadhari, Haryana; Deputy Administrative Manager, Hindustan Aeronautics Limited, Hyderabad, India. *Memberships:* Vice Chairman, AP Chapter, 1979-80, National Institute of Personnel Mnagement. *Publications:* Essays in national dailies. *Honours:* Gold Medalist in Post Graduate Diploma in Public Administration, Osmania University, 1972. *Hobbies:* Gardening; Reading; Writing. *Address:* C-17 HAL Township, HAL-PO., Hyderabad 500042, India.

MITTELHEUSER, Cathryn Jean, b. Bundaberg, Queensland, Australia. Plant Physiologist. *Education:* BSc.(1st Class Hon.) Botany, 1968, PhD., 1971, University of Queensland, Australia. *Appointments:* Research Fellow, Department of Botany, University of Queensland, Australia, 1971-76. *Memberships:* Wine Service Guild; Queensland Art Gallery Society; Australian Federation of University Women. *Publications:* Twelve publications in scientific books and journals in the fields of plant hormones, senescence, ultrastructure and water relations including: Stomatal closure and inhibition of transpiration induced by (RS) - abscisic acid,(with R F M Van Steveninck), 1969; Rapid action of abscisic acid on photosynthesis and stomatal resistance,(with R F M Van Steveninck), 1971; Effects of ABA and kinetin on ultrastructure of senescing wheat leaves,(with R F M Van Steveninck), 1972; The effects of D-glucosamine on leaf senescence and ultrastructure,(with R F M Van Steveninck), 1974; Rapid ultrastructural recovery of water stressed leaf tissue, 1977. *Honours:* University Medal, University of Queensland, 1968; Wheat Industry Research Council Senior Post Graduate Studentship, 1968-70. *Hobbies:* Winemaking; Archeology; Gardening; Chinese history; Travel;

Horse racing. *Address:* 20 Cottesmore Street, Fig Tree Pocket, Queensland 4069, Australia.

MIZERE, Nelson Thompson, b. 5 Jan. 1940, Mwanga, Malawi. Diplomat. m. Monica Janet Sale, 26 Feb. 1969, 3 sons, 1 daughter. *Education:* BA., (Hons.), Delhi University, India; Diploma in Public Administration, University of Malawi. *Appointments:* Laboratory Assistant, Plant Pathology Laboratory, 1959-63; Bank Clerk, Standard Bank Limited, Limbe, Malawi, 1963; Assistant District Commissioner, Blantyre and Mwanza Districts and Nkhata Bay District, 1966; Administrative Officer, Ministry of Agriculture and Natural Resources, 1967; Administrative Officer, Ministry of Finance,1967-71; Second Secretary promoted to First Secretary, Malawi Embassy, Pretoria, South Africa, 1971-73; Under Secretary, Ministry of Local Government attached to Ministry of External Affairs, Lilongwe, Malawi, Jan-Aug.1974; Ambassador to South Africa; High Commissioner for Malawi to Lesotho, resident in Pretoria, South Africa, 1974-77; Senior Deputy Secretary, Ministry of Trade, Industry and Tourism, 1977-78; Ambassador to Belgium and to European Economic Community, Brussels; Ambassador to Netherlands resident in Brussels, 1978-79; Abassador to Federal Republic of Germany, Sweden, Switzerland, Austria, resident in Bonn, West Germany, 1979-80; Appointed High Commissioner for Malawi to the United Kingdom, May, 1980, resident in London, UK. *Memberships:* Delegation to Organisation of African Unity Meeting, Mauritius, 1976; Delegation to General Assembly Meeting, United Nations, New York, USA, 1976. *Hobbies:* Football and rugby; Dancing; Music; Mountaineering. *Address:* Kwacha House, 70 Winnington Road, London, N2, England.

MKAPA, Benjamin, b. 12 Nov. 1938. Minister of Information and Culture. m. Anna Shauri Joseph, 27 Aug. 1966, 1 son. *Education:* B.A. (Hons) (Engl) (Lon), Makerere University College; School of International Affairs, Columbia University, New York. *Appointments:* Administrative Officer; Foreign Service Officer; Newspaper Editor; Press Secretary to the President; Ambassador; Minister of Foreign Affairs; Member of the Central Committee of Chama cha Mapinduzi, Tanzania's ruling Political Party. *Hobby:* Reading. *Address:* 911 Mfaume Road, Dar Es Salaam, Tanzania.

MNANGAGWA, Emmerson Dambudzo, b. 15 Sept. 1942, Shabani. Advocate. m. 22 Sept. 1974, 1 son, 3 daughters. *Education:* LL.B.(Unza), University of Zambia, 1975; Barrister-at-Law, Law Practice Institute, Zambia, 1976. *Appointments:* Career Soldier, Trained in China, 1963-64; Practised in Zambia, 1976-77. *Memberships:* Law Society, Zambia. *Address:* 15 Cannock Road, Mount Pleasant, Salisbury, Zimbabwe.

MOBERLY, John Campbell, b. 27 May 1925, Exmouth, England. Diplomat. m. Patience Proby, 2 sons, 1 daughter. *Education:* Winchester College, 1938-43; Magdalen College, Oxford, 1947-50. *Appointments:* War Service, Royal Navy, 1943-47; HM Foreign (later Diplomatic) Service 1950-, including: Service in London, Bahrain, Qatar, Kuwait, Greece, 1950-; Canadian National Defence College, 1968-69; Counsellor British Embassy, Washington DC, 1969-73; Director, Middle East Centre on Arab Studies, Shemlan, Lebanin, 1973-75; British Ambassador, Amman, 1975-79; Assistant Under Secretary, FCO, London, 1979-. *Memberships:* Travelers Club, London. *Honours:* Mentioned in Dispatches, 1945; CMG, 1975. *Hobbies:* Mountains; Walking; Skiing. *Address:* 55 Cardigan Street, London SE11 5PK, England.

MOFFAT, John Lawrence, b. 4 Dec. 1916, Brookside, Canterbury, New Zealand. Lecturer; Writer; Composer. m. Edmée Liliane Griesser, 19 June 1948, 2 sons. *Education:* MA., Canterbury University College, New Zealand, 1938; Teachers' Certificate, secondary, Christchurch Teachers' College, New Zealand, 1939; PhD., Bristol, UK., 1949. *Appointments:* Language Master, Christchurch B H S , New Zealand, 1939-53; Principal Lecturer, Post-Primary Language Department, Christchurch Teachers' College, New Zealand, 1954-79. *Memberships:* President, Christchurch Classical Association; Treasurer, Canterbury Institute for Educational Research. *Publications:* The Structure of English, 1968; A Guide to Study, 1971; Viola, violin, 'cello, piano sonatas; Trios, songs, psalms. *Honours:* Cowie Scholarship, 1929; Thomas Miller Prize for

English Literature, 1934; Bevan-Brown Memorial Prize for Classics, 1934; John Connel Scholarship for languages, 1936. *Hobbies:* Music; Photography; Painting; Bookbinding; Nudism; Camping; Walking; Sun bathing; History; Yoga; Writing. *Address:* 'Souls Repose', 51 London Street, Christchurch, New Zealand.

MOGBANA, Anthony John Chukwuemeka, b. 18 May 1936, Abagna, Njikoka Local Government Area, Anambra State, Nigeria. Barrister and Solicitor. m. Chinwe Clementina Constance Ume-Ezeoke, 7 Jan. 1977, 1 son, 1 daughter. *Education:* University of Lagos, 1963-65; Ahmadu Bello University, 1965-66; LLB (Hons) Second Class, University of Nigeria, Nsukka, 1966-67; Nigerian Law School, Lagos, 1970-71, Called to Nigerian Bar, 1971; MS (Legal Inst.); University of Wis., Madison, United States of America, 1971-72; SJD, University of Virginia, Charl., Va., United States of America, 1972-74. *Appointments:* Legal Consultant, Ministry of Industries, East Central State, Nigeria, 1974-75; Senior State Counsel, Ministry of Justice, Anambra State, Nigeria, 1976-77; Secretary, Legal Adviser, Central Investment Company Limited, 1977-. *Memberships:* Nigerian Bar Association, Enugu Branch; Member of Committees on Business Organisations, Investment Companies, Energy and Natural Resources of Section on Business Law, International Bar Association; Hon. Secretary, Ekubu Rotary Club, Enugu. *Honours:* State Scholar, University of Lagos, 1963-65; Book Prize, University of Lagos, Mobil Oil (Nigeria) Limited, 1964; Wisconsin Ford Fellowship, 1971-72; University of Virginia Fellowship, 1972-74. *Hobbies:* Gardening; Lawn Tennis; Table Tennis; Charity Services. *Address:* Plot 640 Independence Layout, P.O. Box 114, Enugu, Anambra State, Nigeria.

MOHAMED ISA, Bin Ibrahim Shah, b. 1 Sept. 1931, Ipoh, Perak, Malaysia. Director. m. 1 Jan. 1957, 1 son, 2 daughters. *Education:* Cambridge School Certificate, (Overseas), 1952; Cambridge Higher School Certificate, 1953; Diploma in Agriculture, College of Agriculture, Malaya, 1954; Post-Graduate Diploma in Social Planning in Developing Countries, London School of Economics and Political Science, University of London, 1976-77. *Appointments:* Assistant Rural Development Officer in Training, 1952-54; Cadet Assistant Rural Development Officer, RIDA, (now MARA) 1954-56; Replanting Officer, Assistant Replanting Officer, Deputy State Replanting Officer, State Replanting Officer, Deputy Chief Replanting Officer, Rubber Industry Replanting Board, 1957-73; RISDA, 1973-; Director of Plantations and Development, Director of Special Functions, Director of Replanting Director of Monitoring and Evaluation. *Memberships:* Hon. Secretary, Agricultural Institute of Malaysia; Malaysian Scientifica Association; Editorial Board, Incorporate Society of Planters; Malayan Nature Society; Selangor Gardening Society; Selangor Shooting Association; Malaysian Professional Centre. *Publications:* papers: Crop planting as determined by soil and environment factors; Oil Palm Planting and the Smallholders; Newplanting and Smallholders Development; Development of Rubber Replanting and the Smallholders Sector; Replanting Programme and the Elastomer requirements. *Honours:* Prizes: Highest Marks in Chemistry, Botany and Principles of Agriculture; Associateship in Malaysian Scientific Association. *Hobbies:* Gardening; Shooting; Hunting; Yoga; Reading; Taxidermy. *Address:* No 29, Jalan U Thant, Kuala Lumpur, Malaysia.

MOHAMMED, Aliko Misau, b. 15 Sept. 1934, Misau, Bauchi State, Nigeria. Chartered Accountant. m. Aisa, 28 Feb. 1965, 1 son, 6 daughters. *Education:* Association of Certified Accountants, United Kingdom; Institute of Chartered Accountants of Nigeria. *Appointments:* Chief Accountnat/Secretary, Gaskiya Corporation, Zaria; Financial Controller, New Nigeria Development Company Limited; Investment Manager, Northern Nigeria Investments Limited; Chairman, National Insurance Corporation of Nigeria; Chairman, Daily Times of Nigeria Limited; Chairman, Bank of the North Limited; Vice-President, Nigerian Stock Exchange, Lagos. *Memberships:* Kaduna Turf Club; Nigerian Institute of International Affairs. *Publications:* Presented several papers to Universities and Seminars. *Hobbies:* Football; Hockey; Horse Racing. *Address:* 3 Sultan Close, Kaduna, Nigeria.

MOHAMMED ARIF BIN RAHMAT, (Al-Haj), b. 1 Sept. 1931, Jitra, Kedah, Malaysia. Education Officer.

m. Hajjah Fatimah Sham Binte Abu Bakar, 15 Mar. 1959, 2 sons, 1 daughter. *Education:* Language Institute, Kuala Lumpur, 1961; BA(Hons) University of Malaya, 1969. *Appointments:* Primary School Teacher, 1948-61; Secondary School Teacher, 1962-68; Education Officer, 1969-; Headmaster, Khin Johari Secondary School S. Petam, 1970-75; Headmaster, Jitra and Abu Baker Secondary School, 1975-76; Principal, Penang Science Secondary School, Penang, 1976-. *Memberships:* Royal Kedah Club, Alor Setar, Kedal; Malaysian Association of Education; Guild of Graduate University of Malaya; Red Cross Society, Central Province Wellesley; United Malaya National Organisation; Malaysian Association of Education. *Hobbies:* Reading; Gardening; Social Works. *Address:* 1149, Sekolah Menengah Sains Pulau, Pinang, Bukit Mertajam, Pulau Pinang, Malaysia.

MOHAMMED, Hallel Omar, The Reverend Canon, b. 14 Nov. 1914, Auchan, Kaduna State, Nigeria. Clergyman (Retired Civil Servant). m. 19 Apr. 1938, 1 son, 4 daughters. *Education:* St Andrew's College, Oyo, Nigeria, 1944; 1st Class Catechist Certificate, 1944; St Edmond Hall, Oxford University, England, 1964-65. *Appointments:* Court Clerk, 1945-50; Registrar of Sessions, 1951-56; Registrar High Court, 1957-61; Admistrative Officer, 1961-69; Under Secretary 1970-72; Deputy Permanent Secretary, 1973-74; Chairman, Statutory Cooporations Standing Tenders Board, 1974-75; Member, Health Services re-organisation, 1976-77; Member, State Public Accounts Committee, 1975-79; Chairman, Nigeria Reinsurance Corporation, 1977-80; Chairman, Impeachment Committee, Re-Governor of Kaduna State, 1981. *Memberships:* Registrar, Diocese of Northern Nigeria 1958-61; Lay Reader, Lagos Diocese, 1939-78; Vicar, St Saviour's Church Kaduna 1978; Vicar of Seven Churches 1978-81; Vicar of St Christopher's Church, Kaduna, 1981-. *Honours:* Order of the British Empire, 1959. *Hobbies:* Reading; Mountain Climbing. *Address:* 5, Align Turaki Road, Kaduna, Nigeria.

MOHAN, Prabandam Rangachar, b. Bangalore, India. Medical Practitioner. m. Rama Devi 15 Mar. 1974, 1 son. *Education:* MB, BS, 1963; MS (E.N.T) 1966. *Appointments:* Assistant Professor, ENT Surgery Osmania University, Hyderabad India, 1966-72; Medical Superintendent, W.R.E. Hospital Woomera S.A, 1975-77. *Memberships:* Medical Staff Society, Whyalla S.A. *Publications:* Otomycosis, Dissertation presented for MS Degree. *Hobbies:* Badminton; Gliding. *Address:* PO Box 610, Whyalla, S.A. 5600, Australia.

MOHANAN, Panakkal Karappan, b. 15 Feb. 1937, Kerala, India. Cost and Management Accountant. m. Ambikadevi 14 May 1970, 1 son. *Education:* Diploma, Accountancy, Diploma, Secretarial Practice,. Sydenham College, Bombay, 1961-63; Graduate, Cost Accountancy, Institute of Cost and Works Accountants of India, 1969. *Appointments:* General Manager: Mwanza Bottling Company Limited, 1973-77; Kilima Bottlers Limited, 1973-77; Shinyanga Bottlers Limited, 1973-77; Mwanza Fishnet Manufacturers Limited, Tanzania, 1976-77; Executive Director, Jumbo Investment and Trading Corporation, Zurich, Switzerland, 1977-79; Director: Nihon KJ Kabushiki Kaisha, Tokyo Japan, 1977-79; KJ Export-Import Limited, Hong Kong, 1977-79; Lucky Manufacturers (M) SND BHD. Johor Bhahru, Malaysia, 1977-79; NAFA Inc. Florida, USA, 1977-79; Executive Director, Jitco Overseas Limited, Leicester, UK, 1978-; Director: Sheerlock Limited, Leicester, UK, 1979-80; Barmesh Limited, Leicester, UK, 1979-80; Montrose Manufacturing Company Limited, Leicester, UK, 1980-; Moncotex Limited, Leicester, UK, 1981-. *Memberships:* Associate, Cost and Works Accountants of India; British Institute of Management; Leicester Charnwood Lions Club; Masonic Lodge. *Hobbies:* Photography; Reading. *Address:* 15, Eden Close, Oadby, Leicester, England.

MOHOME, Paulus, Mokete, b. 27 May 1929, Thaba-Nehu, South Africa. Anthropologist, Lecturer. *Education:* BA, University of South Africa, 1960; MA, Michigan State University, USA, 1965; PhD, Syracuse University, USA, 1969. *Appointments:* Higher Primary School Teacher, Excelsior H.P. School, South Africa, 1952-59; Teacher, Strydom Training College, Thaba-Nechu, 1959-63; Teacher, Lereko Secondary School, Bloemfontein, 1969-; Teacher, Sigoga High School, Matatiele, South Africa, 1970-71; Lecturer in Anthropology, National University of Lesotho, 1971-; Head of Departemente of Social Anthropology/Sociology, 1971-79. *Memberships:* Royal African Society; Lesotho Red Cross Society; Lesotho National Commission for UNESCO; Lesotho Youth Hostels Association; Lesotho Work Camp Association; Mejametalana Dairy Farmers' Association. *Publications:* Book: Manya-apelo (Excretes from the Heart), Lesotho poetry; Articles: Negritude: Evaluation and Elaboration, 1968; The African writer and international recognition, 1970; Naming in Lesotho, its sociocultural basis, 1972; Africa's Independence: A Balance Sheet, 1977. *Honours:* Native Teachers' Bursary, 1949-51; Fulbright-Hays Study Grant, 1963-65; Research Grant from African-American Council, Inc. 1973; University of Botswana, Lesotho and Swaziland Research Grant 1972-73; ILO Research Grant, 1977; Who's Who in the World Certificate, 1980-81. *Hobbies:* Gardening and Peasant Farming; Horse-riding; Travelling; Fishing. *Address:* Lekhalong Ha Sekete, Roma, Lesotho, Africa.

MOI, Daniel Arap, b. 1924. President of Kenya. *Appointments:* Head Teacher, Government African School, Kabarnet, 1946-48, 1955-57; Teacher, Tambach Teacher Training School, Kabarnet, 1948-54; African Rep. mem., Legislative Council, 1957-63; Chairman, Kenya African Democratic Union (KADU) 1960-61; Parliamentary Secretary, Ministry of Education, Apr-Dec. 1961; Minister of: Education, 1961-62, Local Government, 1962-64, Home Affairs, 1964-67, 1967-78; Vice-President of Kenya, 1967-68; President of Kenya, 1978-. *Address:* Office of the President, PO Box 30510, Nairobi, Kenya.

MOK, Wooi Beng, b. 1926, Kuala Lumpur, Selangor, Malaysia. Self-made Man. *Appointments:* Managing Director, Samok, Snd. Bhd.; Zanadu Corpn. Sdn. Bhd., Kenlibenze Properties Sdn. Bhd., Kenli-Uda Sdn. Bhd. and M.Y.T.(M) Holdings Sdn. Bhd; Chairman/Managing Director, Mok Wooi Beng Properties Sdn. Bhd., Mok Wooi Beng Properties, (Mining Department) Sdn. Bhd and Beng Yuen Holdings Sdn. Bhd; Proprietor, Mok Wooi Beng Realty Development and Mok Wooi Beng General Construction; Executive Chairman, Kuala Kangsar Holdings Company, Patron, Rukun Tetangga, Taman Tasek Jaya, Ipoh and Patron, Life of the Red Crescent Society, Johore Bahru District; Hon. Chairman, Youth Association, Klang Road, K.L.; Hon. Chairman, Chinese Chamber of Commerce, Klang; Hon. Chairman, Building Association, Selangor; Hon. Chairman, Ipoh Tebing Tinggi Mutual Aid Association; Hon. Chairman, Perak Sim San Loke Hup Physical Culture Association; Hon. Chairman, Yuen Seng Kok, Ipoh; Hon. Chairman, Perak Table Tennis Association and Hon. Chairman, The Choong Wah Clinic Building Donation Fund Committee. *Memberships:* Hon. Chairman, Board of Governors of S.R.J.K.(D) Sam Chai, Ipoh; Sekolah Pui Nam (SUWA), Ipoh; Seremban Chung Hua High School, Old Students Association; S.R.J.K.(C) Wan Hwa (1) Ipoh; Selangor Shooting Association; Royal Perak Golf Club. *Honours:* PAM House Award, Outstanding Construction Work, 1975; DPMJ 1977; SPMJ 1978; JP 1979. *Hobbies:* Golf; Shooting; Reading; Movies; Music. *Address:* 13 Jalan Telok Panglima Garang, 3rd Mile, Jalan Klang, Kuala Lumpur, Malaysia.

MOKWUNYE, Anombem, b. 23 Nov. 1939, Onicha-Uku, Bendel State. Architect. m. Uzoamaka Bernice Mokwunye 2 Mar. 1968, 2 sons, 3 daughters. *Education:* Bachelor of Architecture, Ahmadu Bello University, Zaria, Nigeria. *Appointments:* Federal Ministry of Works, 1966-68; Private Offices, Lagos, 1969-72; Anombem Mokwunye, Twigg, Brown and Partners, Architects and Planning Consultants, Lagos, 1973-. *Memberships:* Associate of the Royal Institute of British Architects; Member, Nigerian Institute of Architects; Idland Club, Lagos; Ikoyi Club; Lagos Lawn Tennis Club. *Publications: Hobbies:* Lawn Tennis; Reading; Sketching. *Address:* 63 Norman Williams Street, South West, Ikoyi, Lagos, Nigeria.

MOLAPO, Mooki Motsarapane, b. 28 Apr. 1928. High Commissioner for Lesotho in United Kingdom. m. Emily Mamanasse Thamae, 1958, 3 sons, 1 daughter. *Appointments:* Government Service, 1950-; High Commissioner for Lesotho, UK, 1979-. *Hobbies:* Football; Walking; Movies; Theatre. *Address:* 70 Downage, Hendon, London, NW4, England.

MOLLAN, Robert Charles, b. 28 Dec. 1942, Clogher, Co. Tyrone, Northern Ireland. Science Officer, Royal Dublin Society, m. Philippa Caithness 13 Sept. 1969, 1 son. *Education:* BA, Chemistry 1st class, 1964; PhD, Trinity College, Dublin, 1967. *Appointments:* National Institutes of Health, (USA), Post Doctoral Fellowship, Massachusetts Institute of Technology, Cambridge, Mass. 1967-69; Research Fellowship, Oxford University, England, 1969-70; Fellowship, National Science Council, University College, Dublin, 1970-72; Scientific Officer, 1974, Senior Scientific Officer, Institute for Industrial Research and Standards, Dublin, 1972-76; Science Officer, Royal Dublin Society, 1976-. *Memberships:* Member of Numerous Societies including: Fellowship, Institute of Chemistry of Ireland; National Committee for the History and Philosophy of Science; Council Care, Campaign for the Care of Deprived Children. *Publications:* Author, Children first—A Source Book for Parents and other Professionals; Editor, Richard Griffith, 1784-1878; Reprinted papers on Bee Husbandry; John Tyndall—Essays on A Natural Philosopher; Families for Children—Questions and Answers on Adoption and Fostering; Children First Newsletter; Radio Presenter; numerous papers and articles in scientific and social work journals, newspapers, etc. *Honours:* Moderatorship Gold Medal, Trinity College Dublin, 1964; Cocker Prize and Meda, (Organic Chemistry), 1964; People of the Year Award, Rehabilitation Institute, Dublin, 1979. *Hobbies:* Children; Reading; Writing. *Address:* 8 Saval Park Crescent, Dalkey, Co Dublin.

MOLOKWU, Louis Dumaka, b. Onitsha, Dumaka. Accountant. m. Margaret Oyediran, 16 Sept. 1962, 4 sons. *Education:* BSc (Hons), Accountancy, 1976; AIB, 1976. *Education:* Bank Examiner, Central Bank of Nigeria; Director, African Continental Bank; Chairman, Assets -9 Company Limited. *Memberships:* ADO Club, Nigeria. *Hobbies:* Tennis; Athletics. *Address:* 5 Alade Close, Suru Lere, Lagos, Nigeria.

MOLPHY, Ruth, b. 9 Feb. 1924, Australia. Medical Practitioner. *Education:* MB BS., University of Queensland, Australia, 1942-47; DA.England, 1952; FFARCS., 1953; FFARACS., 1955. *Appointments:* Resident Medical Officer, 1948-49, Registrar in Anaesthesia, 1950-52. Director of Anaesthesia, 1953-62, Brisbane Hospital, Australia; Director of Anaesthesia, Prince Charles Hospital, Brisbane, Australia, 1963-. *Memberships:* Australian Medical Association; Society of Anaesthetists; Cardiac Society; Medical Womens' Society of Queensland; Russian Blue and Abyssinian Club, Victoria; Northern Feline Fourey, Queensland. *Publications:* A Review of 182 Cases of Tetanus, 1958; Respiratory Paralysis due to Snake Bite, 1959; The Case of the Patient after Tracheostomy, 1965; Organic Phosphorus Poisoning and Therapy, 1964. *Hobby:* Breeding Russian Blue Cats. *Address:* 40 Union Street, Clayfield, Brisbane, Queensland, Australia 4011.

MONAGHAN, John Vincent, b. 15 Apr. 1926, Sydney, Australia. Economist. m. Anne Josephine Daly, 7 Apr. 1951, 3 sons, 1 daughter. *Education:* Bachelor of Economics (Hons), University of Sydney, 1951. *Appointments:* War Service, 1944-46; New South Wales Public Service, 1942-1951; Various Positions, Bureau of Statistics, 1951-69; Assistant Secretary, Various Branches, Department of the Treasury, 1969-76; First Assistant Secretary, Transport and Industry Division, Department of Finance, 1977-78; First Assistant Secretary, General Economic and Financial Policy, Department of The Treasury, 1979; Deputy Secretary, Director, National Energy Office, Department of National Development and Energy, 1980-81; Commissioner, Australian Public Service Board, 1981-. *Memberships:* Economic Society of Australia and New Zealand; Patron and Past President, Australian Capital Territory; Junior Hockey Association. *Hobbies:* Surfing; Hockey; Cricket. *Address:* 7 Merrit Place, O'Conner A.C.T., 2601 Australia.

MONET, Jacques, b. 26 Jan. 1930, St Jean, Quebec, Canada. Historian; Professor; Ordained a Jesuit Priest, 1966. *Education:* BA., Université de Montréal, Canada, 1955; PhL., ThL., Colège de l'Immaculeé Conception, 1956-57; MA., 1961, PhD., 1964, University of Toronto, Canada. *Appointments:* Teacher of History, St.Mary's University High School, Halifax, Nova Scotia, Canada, 1956-58; Sessional Lecturer, Loyola College, Montreal, Canada, 1964-67; Assistant Professor,

1968-69, Associate Professor, 1969-81, Professor, 1981-, Chairman of History Department, 1972-76, University of Ottawa, Canada; Research Officer to Governor General of Canada, 1976-78; Special Advisor on cultural policy to Secretary of State, 1978-79. *Memberships:* Secretary,1969-74, President, 1975-76, Canadian Historical Association; Institut D'Histoire de L'Amerique Française; Secretary, Academy I, 1979-80, Royal Society of Canada; Royal Commonwealth Society. *Publications:* The Last Cannon Shot: A Study of French Canadian Nationalism, 1969; The Canadian Crown, 1979; La Monarchie au Canada, 1979; many articles in scholarly journals and in Dictionary of Canadian Biography. *Honours:* Jubilee Medal, 1977; Governor General's Gold Medal, 1978. *Address:* 2104, 211 Wurtemburg, Ottawa, Ontario, K1N 8R4, Canada.

MONGEON, Roger, b. 18 Oct. 1933, Montreal, Canada. Educator. m. 11 Nov. 1972. *Education:* BA., Universite Montreal, Canada, 1964; BAC. pecialisé Musique, 1972. *Appointments:* CECM., Montreal, Canada, 1953; Schools in the Province of Quebec, Canada, 1954-63; Return to the CECM., 1963. *Memberships:* JMC., Montreal, Canada, 1964-72; Alliance des Professeurs de Montreal, Comite D'Education Syndicale, 1967-70; President, Fameq, 1969-70; 1976-79; Vice-President, FAQUEA, 1978-80; President, CPIQ., 1975-77. *Hobbies:* Racket Ball; Tennis; Skiing; Lecture Musique. *Address:* 308 Frigon Repentigny, Quebec, Canada, J6A 4B1.

MONGUNO, Shettima Ali, b. 1926, Nigeria. Education. m. 1948, 2 sons, 5 daughters. *Education:* Bauchi Teachers' College, 1944-47; Katsina Higher Teachers' College, 1949-51; College of Science and Technology, Zaria, 1954-56; College of Education, Moray House, Edinburgh, UK, 1958-59; Edinburgh University, UK, 1958-59. *Appointments:* Primary School Teacher, 1947-49; Teacher, Secondary School, 1951-54; Education Secretary, Borno, 1956-57; Councillor for Education, 1961-65; Member of Parliament, 1959-66; Minister of Home Affairs, 1965-66; Minister of Industries and Trade, 1967-71; Minister of Mines and Power, Petroleum and Energy, 1971-75; Pro-Chancellor, University of Calabar, 1976-80; Pro-Chancellor, University of Nigeria, 1980-. *Memberships:* President, International Club, Moray House, College of Education, 1958-59; Chairman, Maidugun Football Association, 1951-57; Appeal Officer, Maidugun Red Cross Society, 1951-57; Nigerian Delegation to UN for Regular and Emergency sessions; Leader, Nigerian Delegation to UNCTAD II, New Delhi, India, 1968; President, OPEC, 1973. *Honours:* 1st class awards from Republics of: Sudan, 1970, Egypt, 1970, Cameroons, 1970, and Ethiopian Empire; Keys to the Cities of: New York, USA, 1967, Quito, Equador, 1973, Louisville, Kentucky, USA, 1981. *Hobbies:* Cycling; Reading; Travel. *Address:* 23 Nimèri Road, Maiduguri, Borno State, Nigeria.

MONIRUZZAMAN, Mohammad, b. 6 Apr. 1939, Jessore, Bangladesh. m. Rashida Zaman, 8 May 1960, 1 son, 1 daughter. *Education:* BA.,(Hons.), 1958, MA., 1st Class, 1959, PhD., 1969, Dacca University, Bangladesh; Post Doctoral Research, School of Oriental and African Studies, University of London, UK, 1969-70. *Appointments:* Literary Editor, The Daily Millat, 1957-58; Fellow, Lecturer, Senior Lecturer, Assistant Professor, Department of Bengali, 1959-69, Assistant Professor of Bengali, 1970-72, Associate Professor of Bengali, 1972-75, Professor of Bengali, 1975, Chairman, Department of Bengali, 1978-81, Dacca University, Bangladesh; Teaching Assistant in Bengali, SOAS, 1970; Script Writer and Broadcaster, Bengali Service, BBC., 1970. *Memberships:* Fellow, Royal Asiatic Society, 1969; Fellow, Bangla Academy, Dacca; District Secretary, Rotary International District 329, 1980-81; President, Rotary Club of Dacca North, 1977-78; Life member, Itihash Samity Dacca; Life member, Itihas Parisad Dacca; Founder President, Poetry Bangladesh. *Publications:* Poetry: Mohammad Moniruzzaman Kavyasangraha, 1976; Selected Poems, Honolulu 1979; Prose: Adhunik Bangla Kavye Hindu Musalman Samparka, 1970; Adhunik Bagla Sahitya, 1965,1972; Bangla Kaviter Chanda, 1970, 1979. *Honours:* Bangla Academy Literary Prize, Poetry, 1972. *Hobbies:* Music; Reading. *Address:* 32 G Fuller Road, Dacca-2, Bangladesh.

MONJOK, (CON), Egbo Emmanuel, b. 1 Sept. 1929, Ogoja, Nigeria. Civil Servant. m. 8 Apr. 1956, 5 sons, 1

daughter. *Education:* BSc. (Economics), 1960, DPA., 1963, RCDS, 1973, London, UK; MA., Dublin, UK, 1963; Teachers Certificate, Grade II, 1951. *Appointments:* Roman Catholic Mission Schhols, 1946-58; Chairman, Ogoja County Council, 1956-59; Administrative Officer, Federal public service, 1964-68; Principal Private Secretary to Military Governor of Cross River State, Nigeria, 1967-68; Deputy Secretary, Executive Council, Cross River State, Nigeria, 1968; Permanent Secretary, Works, Agriculture and Education, 1969-75; Secretary to State Government, 1975-79; Head of State Civil Service, 1979-. *Memberships:* Nigerian Economic Society; Agricutural Society of Nigeria; Patron, Nigerian Society of Commerce; Nigeria Society; Calabar Sports Club. *Honours:* Commandor of the Order of the Niger. *Hobbies:* Gardening; Hunting. *Address:* Head of Service Quarters, 1 Leopard Town Road, Calabar, Nigeria.

MONKS, Peter Rolfe, b. 15 May 1941, Malacca, Malaysia. Art Researcher; Artist. *Education:* Tauranga College, New Zealand; Elam School of Art, New Zealand; BA., Annhurst College, Connecticut, USA; MA.(Art history), Northwestern University, Chicago, USA. *Appointments:* Assistant Journalist, Bay of Plenty Times, 1959-61; Legal Assistant, Edge and Beeche, Auckland, New Zealand, 1962; Executive Assistant, Permanent Trustee Co., Sydney, Australia, 1966 69; Art Research at: Chantilly and Paris, Borobudhur and Prambanon, Java, Ayudhya in Thailand, Nara, Japan, Koryu, Korea, Pagan, Upper Burma; Sarnath, India, Persepolis, Iran, Cloisters, New York, USA, Walters Gallery, Baltimore, USA, Art Institute, Chicago, USA, 1971-74. *Memberships:* Life Fellow of: Royal Geographical Society, Royal Asiatic Society, Royal Society of Arts, Kappa Pi International Art Society. *Creative Works:* Paintings represented in: Blake Prize, Sydney, Australia, 1970, Annhurst College, Connecticut, USA, Bulgarian Orthodox Patriarchate, and in private collections in USA, UK, France, New Zealand and Australia; Stage Set Designs for: WEA Theatre Group, South Auckland Choral Society, Theatre Arts Inc., 1956-63, Annhurst Theatre Group, 1975-77. *Publications:* Catalogue of the Exhibition of Paintings and Drawings by P R Monks, 1972; Compositional Elements in Jean Fouquet's Paintings for the Antiquites Judaiques, 1981. *Honours:* Art Prize and Medal, Annhurst College, 1978. *Hobby:* Archaeology. *Address:* 7 Kennedy Street, Townsville, Australia 4810.

MONTEFIORE, David Goldsmid, b. 28 May 1929, London, England. University Medical Teacher. *Education:* BA., 1950, MA., 1953, MB., B.Chir., 1953, MD., 1960, Clare College, Cambridge, UK; Guy's Hospital Medical School, London, UK, 1950-53; Dip.Bact., London, UK, 1960; MRC.Path., 1964; FRC.Path., 1974; FNMC., 1974; FWACP.Path., 1976. *Appointments:* Assistant House Surgeon, Out-Patient Officer, House Physician and Resident Pathologist, Guy's Hospital, London, UK; Senior House Officer, Clinical Pathology, Bristol, Royal Infirmary, UK; Registrar, Clinical Pathology, University College Hospital, Ibadan, Nigeria; Junior Specialist, Pathology, RAMC., MELF; Lecturer, Senior Lecturer, Associate Professor, Department Bacteriology, Professor, Department Medical Microbiology, Dean, Faculty Basic Medical Science and Pharmacy, University of Ibadan, Nigeria. *Memberships:* British Medical Association; Nigerian Medical Association; New York Academy Sciences; Medical Society for Study Venereal Disease. *Publications:* numerous Scientific papers in fields of Bacteriology and Virology. *Honours:* 1st Class Hons: Nat. Sci. Tripos Part 1, Cambridge, 1949; 1st Class Hons: Moral Sci. Tripos Part 2, Cambridge, 1950; Passingham Prize in Experimental Psychology, Cambridge University, 1950; Exhibitioner, Clare College, Cambridge, 1949; Scholar, Clare College, Cambridge, 1950; Distinction, Academic Diploma in Bacteriology, London University, 1960; OBE, 1979. *Hobby:* Photography. *Address:* University of Ibadan, Nigeria.

MONTEITH, Lionel, b. 6 Aug. 1921, Brighton, England. Psychotherapist; Clinic Director; Minister of Religion. m. Joan Mary Huson, 25 Mar. 1953, 1 son, 1 daughter. *Education:* Theology, New College, London, UK; Dip.Th., University of London, UK. *Appointments:* Chartered Surveyor's Pupil, 1939; Air Ministry Surveyor, 1940-46; Editor, Poetry Commonwealth, 1947-53; New Collge and London University, UK, 1954-58; Minister, West Kensington Congregational Church, UK, 1958-64; FC Chaplain, St. Mary Abbots Hospital, 1960-

64; Minister, Christ Church and Upton Chapel, 1964-69; Affiliate Psychotherapist, University College Hospital, London, UK, 1960-64; Clinic Director, Lincoln Clinic, 1967-; Psychotherapy practice, 1959-. *Memberships:* Fellow, International PEN; Lincoln Clinic and Institute for Psychotherapy. *Publications:* Contributor of poems and literary extracts to journals in Canada, Australia, New Zealand, South Africa, India, UK, USA, Argentina. *Hobbies:* Tennis; Badminton; Music; Boating; Reading. *Address:* 134 Grove Lane, Denmark Hill, London, SE5 8BP, England.

MONTGOMERY, Charles John, b. 18 Feb. 1917, Llandudno, Wales. Banker. m. Gwenneth Mary MacKendrick, 10 Sept. 1950, 2 daughters. *Education:* Colwyn Bay Grammar School, 1931-35. *Appointments:* Chief General Manager, 1973-78, Vice-Chairman, 1978-, Lloyds Bank,. *Memberships:* Overseas Bankers; Naval. *Honours:* C.B.E., 1977. *Hobbies:* Photography; Walking. *Address:* High Cedar, 6 Cedar Copse, Bickley, Bromley Br1 2NY, England.

MONTUORI, Mario Angelo Gabriele, b. 7 July 1921, Salerno, Italy. Professor. m. Margharetha Francine Lodeizen, 7 Sept. 1957, 1 son. *Education:* Dr.Litt; Dr.Phil; LD. History of Philosphy; Prof. Moral Philosophy. *Appointments:* Lecturer at the Universities of: Coimbra, Utrecht, Leiden and London,UK; Cultural Affairs appointments in: Brazil, Portugal, Netherlands, Lebanon, Greece and London, UK; Freelance Journalist. *Memberships:* Accademia Pontaniana, Naples; Accademia degli Incamminati, Bologna; Fellow, Royal Society of Arts, London; Aristotelian Society, London; Society for Hellenic Studies, London; Vice-Chairman, International Research Seminar in Classics, Birkbeck College, University of London; Hon. Fellow in Classics, Birkbeck College, University of London; Hon. member, Philologhicos Sillogos, Athens. *Publications:* Critical Edition of Locke's A Letter Concerning Toleration, the Hague; Socrate Dal Mito alla Storia; Socrate tra Nuvole prime e Nuvole seconde; Sul processo di Anassagora; Critical Edition of Manetti's Vita Socratis; Tre Lettere di Locke a Limborch sull'unità di Dio; Socrate Fisiologia di un Mito, Firenze; Su Fedone di Elide; Les Philosophes di Palissot e la Fortuna di Aristofane nella Storiografia Socratica Moderna; Su Aspasia Milesia; contributor to numerous Italian and foreign newspapers, radio and TV. *Honours:* Decorated Cross of War; Gr. Uff. Order of Merit, Italy; Cav. di G.e D. del SMO Costantiniano; also other foreign orders; Awarded Italy's 1978 Cultural Prize. *Address:* 238 Parco Ersilia, Piano di Sorrento, Naples, Italy.

MONTY, Guy, B.A., B.A.Sc., b. 17 March 1920, Montreal, Quebec. President and Chief Executive Officer, Hydro-Quebec International. m. Béatrice Larose, 1 daughter. *Education:* Applied Sciences (mechanical and electrical engineering), Ecole Polytechnique de Montréal, 1946. *Appointments:* First Polytechnique student hired as such by Montreal Light, Heat and Power Consolidated (which became Hydro-Québec three years later), 1944; Joined Hydro-Quebec permanently, 1946, appointments include: Engineer, Substation Service, Montreal; Engineer, Projects Section, Transmission Division, 1948; Construction Engineer, 1950; Assistant Transmission Engineer, 1957; Transmission Engineer, 1962; Assistant Chief Engineer for Overhead and Underground Transmission, 1964; Director of Transmission Line Projects, 1965; General Manager of Construction, 1969; Commissioner of Hydro-Québec, 1976; Member, Board of Directors; President and Chief Executive Officer, 1978-. *Memberships:* Order of Engineers of Quebec; Engineering Institute of Canada; Institute of Electrical and Electronics Engineers; Study Committee 22, International Conference on Large Electric Systems; Russo-Canadian Committee on Technical and Scientific Cooperation; Canadian Standards Association; Board of Director of the Corporation de l'Ecole Polytechnique; Canada-China Trade Council. *Hobbies:* Cross-country skiing; Golf; Reading. *Address:* 156 Willowdale Avenue, Outremont, Quebec H3T 1E9, Canada.

MOODIE, Alexander Forbes, b. 6 Aug. 1923, Kirkcaldy, Scotland. Physicist. m. Violet Kathleen Lilias Bowles, 7 Aug, 1948, 2 sons, 1 daughter. *Education:* BSc., 1st Hons., St. Andrews University, Scotland, 1941-43. 1946-48. *Appointments:* Lt., Royal Navy, 1943-46; CSIRO., 1948-51, 1952-75, 1976-; Pennsylvania State College, USA, 1951-52; University

of Oxford, England, 1975-76. *Memberships:* Fellow, Australian Academy of Sciences, 1973; Fellow, Institute of Physics, 1961; Electron Diffraction Commission of International Union of Crystallography, 1967-73; Chairman, Australian Crystallographic Committee, 1980. *Publications:* Scientific papers. *Honours:* Commonwealth Professor, 1975-76. *Hobby:* Music. *Address:* 406 Barkers Road, Hawthorn, Victoria 3122, Australia.

MOON, (Sir) Peter (James Scott), b. 1 Apr. 1928. HM Diplomatic Service. m. Lucile Worms, 1955, 3 daughters. *Appointments:* Home Office, 1952-54; Principal, 1958-60, CRO., 1954-56, 1958-60; Second Secretary, Cape Town, Pretoria, South Africa, 1956-58; First Secretary, Colombo, 1960-63; Private Secretary to Secretary of State for Commonwealth Relations, 1963-65; First Secretary, UK Mission to UN, New York, USA, 1965-69; Counsellor, FCO., 1969-70; Private Secretary to Prime Minister, 1970-72; NATO Defence College, 1972; seconded to NATO Internat. Staff, Brussels, Belgium, 1972-75; Counsellor, Cairo, 1975-78; Ambassador (non resident) Madagascar, 1978-79; High Commissioner in Tanzania, 1978-. *Address:* c/o Foreign and Commonwealth Office, London, SW1, England.

MOONEY, William Wall Warner, b. 14 July 1938, Melbourne, Australia. Otolaryngologist. m. Jennifer Radich, 18 Dec. 1965, 2 sons, 1 daughter. *Education:* MBBS., 1962, FRACS., 1971, University of Melbourne, Australia; FRCS., Edinburgh, Scotland, 1969; FACS., Chicago, USA, 1976. *Appointments:* Otolaryngologist, Head of ENT Department, Royal Children's Hospital, Melbourne, Australia, 1977-; Otolaryngologist-in-charge, Royal Victorian Eye and Ear Hospital, Melbourne, Australia, 1980-. *Memberships:* Australian Medical Association; Australian Association of Surgeons; Otolaryngological Society of Australia; Pan-Pacific Surgical Association; Affiliate, Royal Society of Medicine. *Hobbies:* Tennis; Skiing. *Address:* 156 Winmalee Road, Balwyn 3103, Melbourne, Australia.

MOORE, Colin John, b. 9 Sept. 1954, Melbourne, Australia. Ecologist. *Education:* BS., 1974; BSc.(Hons.), 1975; PhD., 1980. *Appointments:* Technical Officer, CSIRO, Katherine, Australia; Technical Officer, Ministry of Conservation, Victoria, Australia; Tutor, Monash University, Australia; Curriculum Consultant, Department of Education, Victoria, Australia; Managing Director, Ecobiol Consultants, Victoria, Australia. *Memberships:* Chairperson 1975-79, Monash Co-operative Bookshop Limited; British Bryology Society; Ecology Society of Australia. *Publications:* The ecology of mosses on a sand dune in Victoria, Australia,(with GAMS Scott), 1979; Fine structure and physiology of the desiccation mosses, (with SE Luff and HD Hallam), 1981. *Honours:* Commonwealth Post-graduate Research Award, 1976-79. *Hobbies:* Pilot; Scuba Diving; Skiing; Natural Photography; Athletics. *Address:* 4 Clendon Road, Armadale, Victoria 3143, Australia.

MOORE, David Rainsford, b. 10 Feb. 1918, Wimborne, Dorset, England. Anthropologist. m. Gwendoline May Annesley, 11 Dec. 1954. *Education:* Hons. in Classical Tripos, 1939, MA., 1966, Christ's College, Cambridge, England; Diploma in Anthropology, University of Sydney, Australia, 1962-65. *Appointments:* Commission in the Essex Regiment, 1940; Major, Burma Regiment, 1942-45; Scriptwriter and Assistant Director, Ealing Studios, London and Sydney, 1945-51; Assistant Editor, Australian Encyclopaedia, Angus and Robertson, Sydney, Australia, 1952-58; Research Officer in Bibliography, Australian Institute of Aboriginal Studies, 1961-65; Curator of Anthropology, Australian Museum, Sydney, Australia, 1965-78. *Memberships:* Hon. Sec. 1965-70, President, 1970-73, Anthropological Society of New South Wales; Hon. Sec., 1966-70, Member, Australian Institute of Aboriginal Studies, 1965; Chairman, 1970-77, Advisory Committee on Aboriginal Relics, New South Wales; Vice-Chairman, 1965-69, Foundation for Aboriginal Affairs, Sydney. *Publications:* Melanesian Art in the Australian Museum, 1968; Results of an Archaeological Survey of the Hunter River Valley, New South Wales, Australia, 1970-80; The Dark Australians,(with D Baglin), 1972; Indonesia Today: An Impressionistic Picture, 1973; Islanders and Aborigines at Cape York, 1979. *Honours:* Churchill Fellow, 1969. *Hobbies:* Reading; Music; Film and Theatre; Art; Walking; Photography. *Address:* 13

Chester Street, Woollahra, New South Wales 2025, Australia.

MOORE, Graham John, b. 13 Feb. 1946, Bristol, England. Assistant Professor. m. Diana Monica Nystrom, 30 Dec. 1978, 1 daughter. *Education:* BSc.Hons. Chemistry, 1967, MSc., Chemistry, 1968, University of Exeter, England; PhD., Biochemistry, University of Ottawa, Canada, 1972. *Appointments:* Max Planck Institut für Molekulor Genetik, Berlin, West Germany, 1972-73; Division of Pharmacology and Therapeutics, Faculty of Medicine, University of Calgary, Alberta, Canada, 1973-. *Memberships:* Society for Endocrinology, UK; Canadian Biochemical Society; Pharmacological Society of Canada; Western Pharmacology Society. *Publications:* 30 publications in field of biochemistry and pharmacology in scientific journals; 20 published abstracts from scientific meetings. *Honours:* MRC Canada Fellowship, 1973-75; Canadian Heart Foundation Scholarship, 1976-82. *Hobbies:* Fishing; Hunting; Skiing; Boating; Soccer; Raquet sports. *Address:* 1762 1st Avenue N.W., Calgary, Alberta, Canada T2N OB1.

MOORE, Kenneth James Edward, b. 17 June 1941, Bulawayo, Zimbabwe. Sales Manager; Company Director. m. Melodie Edith Hope Bunce, 28 Oct. 1967, 3 sons. *Education:* Matriculation Exemption -Cambridge, 1959; City of Guilds Part I, Mechanical Engineering, London Institute, 1962. *Appointments:* Dunlop TRhodesia, Limited, 1959-65; British Automatic Company, UK, 1965-66; National Cash Register Company, UK, 1966-67; Dunlop Zambia Limited, 1967-70; Dunlop Rhodesia Limited, 1970-75; Prudential Assurance Company, 1975-76; Company Director, Own Business, 1977-80; Schweppes (C A) Limited, 1980-. *Memberships:* Finance Committee; General Purpose Committee; Vice-Chairman, Engineering Services Committee. *Publications:* Presented paper on 'Cyclist and Pedestrians' to Local Government, 1977. *Honours:* Runner-up Jaycee's 'Two Outstanding Young People of the Year Award'. *Hobbies:* Philately; Photography. *Address:* 1 Emerald Drive, Granite Park, Hillside South, Bulawayo, Zimbabwe.

MOORE, Patrick William Eisdell, b. 17 Mar. 1918, Bristol, England. Surgeon. m. Doris McBeth Beedie, 21 Dec. 1942, 4 sons. *Education:* MB, Ch B, New Zealand, 1942; FRCS, England), 1950; DLO, London, 1950; FRACS, 1963. *Appointments:* Senior ENT Surgeon, Green Lane Hospital, Auckland; Consultant Otologist, Waiapu Hospital Board; Reader in Otolaryngology, Auckland School of Medicine; Consultant Otologist, Bay of Plenty Hospital Board; Advisor in Otology to the New Zealand Government. *Memberships:* President, Deafness Foundation of New Zealand; Vice-President, Hearing Association; Patron, Auckland New Zealand Federation for Deaf Children. *Publications:* Author, A Great TRun, 1972. *Hobbies:* Master, Pakuranga Hunt; Sketching; Gardening; Writing. *Address:* 229 Remuera Road, Auckland 5, New Zealand.

MORAN, Richard John MacMoran (Lord), b. 22 Sept. 1924, London. HM Diplomatic Service. m. Shirley Rowntree Harris, 1948, 2 sons, 1 daughter. *Education:* Eton College; King's College, Cambridge. *Appointments:* War Service, 1939-45, including: Ord. Seaman, HMS Belfast, 1943; Sub-Lt RNVR in Motor Torpedo Boats and HM Destroyer Oribi, 1944-45; Foreign Office, 1945; Third Sec., Ankara, 1948; Tel-Aviv, 1950; Second Secretary, Rio de Janeiro, 1953; First Secretary FO, 1956; Washington, 1959; FO 1961; Counsellor, British Embassy, South Africa, 1965; Head of Western African Department, FCO, 1968-73; Non-resident Ambassador to Chad, 1970-73; Ambassador to Hungary, 1973-76; Ambassador to Portugal, 1976-81; High Commissioner to Canada, 1981. *Publications:* C.B. A Life of Sir Henry Campbell-Bannerman, 1973. *Honours:* CMG, 1973; Whitbread Award for Biography, 1973; KCMG, 1981; Grand Cross of the Order of the Infante (Portugal) 1978. *Hobbies:* Fly fishing; Bird watching. *Address:* British High Commission, Ottawa, Canada.

MOREAU, Gérald Emile, b. 18 Feb. 1929, Somerset, Manitoba, Canada. Professor. m. Henriette Marie Fournier, 4 July 1970, 2 sons. *Education:* BA, University of Manitoba, 1951; MA, Université Laval, Québec, 1955; Certificado de Español, Madrid, 1957; Ph D, Université de Poitiers, 1957; Diplome du CREDIF,

Saint-Cloud, 1971. *Appointments:* Associate Professor, University of Victoria. *Memberships:* President, La Fédération de la Colombie-Britannique, 1964-66; Conseil de la vie française en Amérique (12 years); L'Association Canadienne des Educateurs de larque Française (2 years); Vice-President, Alliance Française de Victoria, 1970; Le Club Canadien-française de Victoria, 1957-; Southern Vancouver Island Hospital Society, 1980-; Royal Jubilee Hospital Society, 1980-; University of Victoria Faculty Association, 1957-; Canadian Association of University Teachers, 1957-. *Publications:* Le Commis (novel); Anthologie du roman Canadien-Francais (anthology); Le Quebec Hier et Aujord'hui (reader) (co-author). *Honours:* Médaille du Centenaire du Canada, 1967 *Address:* 3125 Midland Road, Victoria, British Columbia, Canada.

MORELLO, Joseph Charles, b. 23 Nov. 1930, Gibraltar. Deputy Commissioner of Police. m. Bendicion Fernandez, 4 Dec. 1954, 1 son, 2 daughters. *Education:* Latimer School, London; School of Building Arts and Crafts, London; Dochyed Technical College; Bramhill College. *Memberships:* Vice-President, Police Social Club; Chairman, Police Football Club. *Honours:* Police Long Service Medals; Colonial Police Medal; Queens Police Medal. *Hobbies:* Reading; Football. *Address:* 3 South Panihin, Gibralter.

MOREY, Phyllis Alice (Mrs), b. 30 June 1907, Coventry, Warwickshire, England. Housewife; Poet. m. Walter Edward Alexander Morey, 29 Sept. 1928, 2 sons, 3 daughters. *Education:* John Gulson Girls School, Leicester Causeway, Coventry. *Appointments:* Domestic Service, 1921; Factory Worker, 1922-30; Ran Smallholding & Guest House, 1948-62; Wrote Poetry, 1948-; Retired, 1968; Part-time Local News, 1969-81; P C C, 1969-81. *Memberships:* National Poetry Society; Plymouth Arts Centre; East Cornwall Literary Association-Stella Browning, Cinque Ports Poets. *Publications:* Poems: Moments of Meditation, 1949; Coronation Prayer, 1953; Christmas Verses, 1962-80; Golden Eagle Heirloom, Limited Edition 500, 1973; Book of Golden Verse, Limited Edition 500, 1974; Silver Jubilee, 1977; Cornwall, 1970; Peace and Beauty, 1979 and numerous others. *Honours:* Three letters from Queen Elizabeth II, 1953, 1970, 1977; Chosen Poets of 1969; A Novel Diploma Awarded, 1980; Companion of Western Europe IBC Cambridge. Wrote Poem on request, 'Spirit of St Clether Church' presented it framed, is permanently in the church, also wrote Hymn, 'St Clether Hymn' which was sung at Dedication Service, 1980. *Hobbies:* Writing; Reading; Light Music; Television; Films of High Standard; Watching Tennis & Snooker. *Address:* 1 Valley View, St Clether, Launceston, Cornwall, PL15 8QJ, England.

MORGAN, Alan Grenfell, b. 7 Sept. 1925, Wellington, New Zealand. Consultant. m. June Laybourn, 3 Dec. 1949, 1 son, 3 daughters. *Education:* MB, Ch B, Otago University Medical School, 1949; FRCS (Eng), 1953; FRACS, 1957. *Appointments:* Demonstrator in Anatomy, Otago University Medical School, 1949; House Surgeon & Registrar, Wellington Hospital; Surgical Registrar, London P G Hospital, Hammersmith; Visiting Surgeon, Wellington Hospital, 1960-; Clinical Lecturer, Wellington Clinical School, Otagu University, 1973; Member New Zealand Court of Examiners, Royal Australasian College of Surgeons; Member, New Zealand Committee RACS. *Memberships:* Royal Society of Medicine; Wellington Club. *Publications:* Paper, The Place of Fundoplication in the Treatment of Hiatus Hernia, 1971. *Honours:* William Ledingham Christie Prize, Applied Anatomy, Otago University, 1947. *Hobbies:* Golf; Skiing. *Address:* 3 Hatton Street, Karori, Wellington, New Zealand.

MORGAN, James Meredith, b. 24 Apr. 1944. Research Scientist. *Education:* BSc.Agr. Sydney University 1966; MSc, 1971, PhD, Macquarie University 1977. *Appointments:* NSW, Department of Agriculture, 1966; Seconded, Macquarie University 1971-74; Agricultural Research Centre, Developing methods of selecting drought tolerant wheats based on the physiology of adaptation, Tamworth, 1975-. *Memberships:* Australian Society of Plant Physiologists; Agricultural Christian Fellowship. *Publications:* A number of research publications, including several in the journal Nature, on adaptation to drought stress in wheat. *Hobbies:* Theology; Music (classical guitar); Sailing; Church activities. *Address:* 86 Upper Street, Tamworth 2340, Australia.

MORGAN, Leo Robert, b. 25 Oct. 1945, Matakau Village, Lemanmanu, Buka Island, Papua New Guinea. Media and Management. m. Angela Dyra Morgan, 27 May 1971, 2 sons, 3 daughters. *Education:* University of Papua New Guinea, Port Moresby, 1966-69; Australian National University, Canberra, Australia, 1970; B.A., Degree, History, Political Science and Economics. *Appointments:* Journalist, Sydney and Canberra, 1970-71; Research Officer, Administrator's Executive Council, 1971-72; Assistant Secretary, Office of the Chief Minister, 1972-74; High Commissioner, Papua New Guinea to New Zealand, 1974-76; Associate Commissioner, PNG Public Services Commission, 1976-79; Chairman and Chief Executive, NBC, Papua New Guinea, 1979-. *Memberships:* Public Service Association; The Masonic Club, Sydney, Australia. *Publications:* Co-author of an authoritative publication for the South Pacific Forum on Foreign Aid in the South Pacific Region; Report for the Government of Papua New Guinea on Housing Policy and Management; Report for the Government of Papua New Guinea on the Media and Communication and Information policy and practices. *Address:* P.O. Box 5345, Boroko, Papua New Guinea.

MORGAN, Michael Hugh, b. 18 Apr. 1925. HM Diplomatic Service. m. Julian Bamfield, 1957, 2 sons. *Education:* Downing College, Cambridge, UK; School of Oriental and African Studies, London University, UK. *Appointments:* Army Service, 1943-46; HMOCS, Malaya, 1946-56; Foreign Office, 1956-57; First Secretary: Peking, 1957-60, Belgrade, 1960-64; attached to Industry, 1964; First Secretary, FCO, 1964-68; Counsellor and Head of Chancery, Cape Town/Pretoria, 1968-72; Counsellor, Peking, 1972-75; Inspector, FCO, 1975-77; High Commissioner, Sierra Leone, 1977-. *Honours:* CMG., 1978. *Address:* Strefford House, Strefford, Craven Arms, Salop SY7 8DE, England.

MORLET, Geoffrey Claude, b. 4 Oct. 1932, Perth Western Australia. Ophthalmic Surgeon. m. Elisabeth Anne Elliott, 22 May 1956, 2 sons, 1 daughter. *Education:* Geelong College, Victoria; St Marks University College, Adelaide, 1951-55; MB, BS, Adelaide 1955; DO, Melbourne 1962; FRACS 1969; FRACO 1978. *Appointments:* RMO Royal Fremantle Hospital 1956-57; ROM Royal Victorian Eye and Ear Hospital, 1961-63; Relieving Ophthalmic Surgeon, Darwin N.T. 1965; Ophthalmic Registrar, Huddersfield, England 1966; Hon Ophthalmic Surgeon, Preston and Northcote Community Hospital 1970-73; Senior Assistant Honorary Ophthalmic Surgeon, Royal Victoria Eye and Ear Hospital 1971-75; Ophthalmic Surgeon, Royal Perth Hospital, 1976-; Chairman of Department of Ophthalmology 1977-80; Council of Royal Australian College of Ophthalmologists, W.A Representative, 1981-. *Memberships:* Captain, RAAMC Reserve; Australian Medical Association; The Weld Club; Naval and military Club, Victoria. *Publications:* A New Binocular Ophthalmoscope, 1970. *Hobbies:* Sailing; Clay Target Shooting. *Address:* "The Eyrie", Boundary Road, Mosman Park, Western Australia 6012.

MOROKOFF, Alex Leo, b. 8 Aug. 1929, Shanghai, China. Company Director. m. Anna Elizabeth Franchich, 1 Oct. 1954, 1 son, 1 daughter. *Education:* Diploma in Engineering, New South Wales University of Technology, 1955. *Appointments:* Australian General Electric, Cadet Engineer, 1952; Overseas postgraduate scholarship, UK and USA, 1955-56; AEG & A E I Group of Companies, Cadet Engineer to Commercial Director of A E I, 1951-67; Business Development Manager, Dravo Corporation, Pittsburgh, USA, 1968; Chairman & Managing Director, Dravo Australia, 1969; Assistant Managing Director, Thiess Holdings, 1972; Managing Director, 1973, Chairman, 1977, Thiess Bros. Chairman, Energy Resources of Australia Ltd; Director, BMI Ltd., and Lend Lease Corporation Ltd. *Hobbies:* Tennis; Swimming. *Address:* 12 Aminga Street, Fig Tree Pocket, Queensland, 4069, Australia.

MORRIS, Alfred, b. 23 Mar. 1928, Manchester, England. Member of Parliament. m. Irene Jones, 30 Sept. 1950, 2 sons, 2 daughters. *Education:* Ruskin College, Oxford, 1949-50; St Catherine's College, Oxford, 1950-53; MA, University of Oxford. *Appointments:* Manchester Brewing Firm, 1942-46; H M Forces, 1946-48; Schoolmaster in Manchester, 1954-56; Industrial Relations Officer, Electricity Supply Industry, 1956-64; Member of Parliament for Wythenshawe,

Manchester, 1964-; Minister for the Disabled, 1974-79; Presently an Opposition Front Bencher. *Memberships:* General Advisory Council of the BBC, 1968-74; Chairman, The Anzac Group of MP's and Peers, 1973-; Chairman, Parliamentary Co-operative Group at Westminster, 1971-72. *Publications:* Human Relations in Industry, 1960; The Growth of Parliamentary Scrutiny by Committee, 1970. *Honours:* Field Marshal Lord Harding Award, 1971; Award of the National Federation of the Blind, 1972; Privy Councillor, 1979. *Hobbies:* Tennis; Gardening; Chess. *Address:* 83 Mayow Road, London, S.E.26, England.

MORRIS, Arnold Alec, b. 11 March 1926, Ranby, England. Engineer, Royal Air Force. (Air Marshal). m. Moyna Patricia Boyle, 8 June 1946, 1 son, 1 daughter (twins). *Education:* King's College, University of London, 1943-45; University of Southampton, 1949-51. *Appointments:* Radar Duties No. 90 (Signals) Group, 1945-50; Guided Weapons Department, Royal Aircraft Establishment, 1953-56; Exchange Duty, United States Air Force, 1958-60; Space Research, Ministry of Technology, 1960-63; Tutor, RAF Staff College, 1963-65; OC Engineering Wing, No. 2 Flying Training School, 1966-68; OC RAF Central Servicing Dev. 1970-72; SASO HQ No 90 (Signals) Group, 1972-74; Director of Signals (Air), MoD, 1975-76; Director General, Strategic Electronic Systems, MOD (PE) 1976-79; Air Officer, Engineering, HQ Strike Command, RAF, 1979-81; Chief Engineer, Royal Air Force, 1981-. *Memberships:* Institution of Electrical Engineers; Fellow, Royal Aeronautical Society; Royal Air Force Club. *Honours:* CB, 1979. *Hobbies:* Tennis; Squash; Gardening. *Address:* Tedder House, 14 Birch Crescent, Uxbridge, Middlesex, England.

MORRIS, Brian Patrick, b. 5 Sept. 1934, Melbourne, Australia. Company Director. m. Joan Hannah Gordon, 15 Sept. 1956, 3 sons, 1 daughter. *Education:* LAI. *Appointments:* Advertising Writer, Compton Advertising; Account director, George Patterson Advertising; Managing Director: Southdown Press; Ten-10 Television Station, Sydney, Australia. *Hobbies:* Tennis; Horse racing. *Address:* 54A Collins Road, St. Ives 2075, Sydney, Australia.

MORRIS, John George, b. 1 May 1934, Sydney, New South Wales, Australia. Physician in Nuclear Medicine. m. Nitaya Smitananda, 1 Mar. 1968, 1 son, 1 daughter. *Education:* L C Hurlstone A H S University Exhibition, 1951; MB., BS, Sydney University, 1959; MRACP, 1963; MCRA (Associate), 1966; FRACP, 1971. *Appointments:* RMO Sydney Hospital, 1959-63; Lecturer of Medicine, University of Sydney, 1964-65; Physician in Nuclear Medicine, 1966, Head, Department of Nuclear Medicine, 1971-, Royal Prince Alfred Hospital. *Memberships:* Fellow, Royal Australasian College of Physicians; Past Secretary & President, Australian & New Zealand Association of Physicians in Nuclear Medicine; Australian & New Zealand Society of Nuclear Medicine; Australian Medical Association. *Publications:* Numerous contributions to medical journals including: Radiopharmaceuticals in Nuclear Medicine, 1970; Pulmonary Embolism as a Complication of Ventriculoatrial shunt, 1970. *Hobbies:* Fishing; Thoroughbred and Standard bred horse breeding. *Address:* 53 Louisa Road, Birchgrove, Sydney, NSW, 2041, Australia.

MORRIS, John Rothwell, b. 12 July 1931, Hobart, Tasmania, Australia. Director, The National Trust of Australia. m. Jocelyn Mary Daly Smith, 26 Oct. 1966. *Appointments:* Secretary, 1954-59, Director, 1957-65, O B M Pty Limited, Booksellers, Hobart, Tasmania, Australia; Hon. Secretary, Southern Committee, National Trust of Tasmania, Australia, 1962-65; Assistant Director, 1965-72, Acting Director, 1973, Director, 1974-, National Trust of Australia, New South Wales, Australia. *Memberships:* Heritage Council of New South Wales; Royal Australian Historical Society; Civic Design Society; Friends of Elizabeth Bay House; Friends of Australian Museum; The Balmain Association. *Hobbies:* Restoring historic buildings; Reading; Photography. *Address:* Kenilworth, 13 Simmons Street, Balmain, New South Wales 2041, Australia.

MORRIS, Yaakov, b. 16 May 1920, Belfast, Northern Ireland. Diplomat. Author. m. Sarah Cynthia Cohen 15 Aug. 1939 (Deceased 1978), 1 son, 1 daughter. *Education:* Mercantile College High School, Belfast, Northern

Ireland. *Appointments:* Head of Section for English Speaking Countries of Yough Department of World Zionist Organisation, Jerusalem, 1949-55; Ministry for Foreign Affairs, Jerusalem, with postings to: New York, Bombay, Stockholm Israel, 1955-80; Ambassador of Israel to New Zealand. *Memberships:* National President, English Settlers Association, Israel, 1968; Staff Committee, Chairman, Ministry of Foreign Affairs, Jerusalem, 1966-68; *Publications:* Masters of the Desert; Israel's Struggle for Peace; Israel; On The Soil of Israel; Pioneers from the West. *Hobbies:* Chess; Music; Literature; Theatre; The Arts; Walking. *Address:* Rehov Bustanai 5, Jerusalem, Israel.

MORRISON, Eurtls Ivanhoe Horace, b. 21 Oct. 1916, Trelawny, Jamaica. Commissioned Land Surveyor. m. Corinne Geddes, 29 Apr. 1945, 1 son, 1 daughter. *Education:* Privately tutored reaching Senior Cambridge Level; Articled to Vermont & Edwards, Land Surveyors, Jamaica, 1937; Qualified as a Commissioned Land Surveyor, 1941. *Appointments:* United States Engineer, 1940-41; Vermont & Edwards, 1941-44; Junior Engineer, KSAC, 1944-45, Jamaica Public Service, 1945-47; Private Practice, 1947-. *Hobby:* Farming. *Address:* Eden Bower, Ocho Rios, Jamaica.

MORRISON, James Fyffe Thomson, b. 11 Apr. 1932, Glasgow, Scotland. Artist. m. Dorothy Jean McCormack, 12 Apr. 1955, 1 son, 1 daughter. *Education:* DA, Glasgow School of Art, 1950-54; Jordanhill College of Education, 1954-55; *Appointments:* Senior Lecturer, Duncan of Jordanstone College of Art, Dundee, Scotland. *Memberships:* Associate of Royal Scottish Academy; Royal Society Watercolourists; Society of Scottish Artists; Royal Glasgow Institute of Fine Arts. *Creative Works:* Author of Aff The Squerr; Works in Permanent Collections: Glasgow, Dundee, Aberdeen Art Galleries; Arts Council; Glasgow, Edinburgh, Stirling Universities; Arts Council Education Committees, Argylle, Tayside, Edinburgh; Kingsway Technical College; Vaughan College Leicester; Department of the Environment; HRH The Duke of Edinburgh; One-man exhibitions include: McClure Gallery, Glasgow, 1956-58; Scottish Gallery, Edinburgh, 1959,64,75,78; Reid Gallery, London, 1962; Richard Demarco Gallery, Edinburgh, 1968-69; Compass Gallery, Glasgow, 1970-71; Galleria Vaccarino, Florence, 1971-72; Steiger Gallery, Moers, West Germany, 1973. *Honours:* Torrance Memorial Prize, RGI, 1958; Arts Council Travelling Scholarship to Greece, 1968; Dusseldord Knutstmesse, 1974. *Hobbies:* Travel; Chamber Music; Gardening. *Address:* Craigview House, Usan, Montrose, Tayside, Scotland.

MORSE (Sir) Christopher Jeremy, b. 10 Dec. 1928. Banker. m. Belinda Marianne, 1955, 3 sons, 1 daughter. *Education:* First Class Lit. Hum. Winchester, New College, Oxford, 1953. *Appointments:* Trained in banking at Clyn, Mills & Co., made a director in 1964; Executive Director, Bank of England, 1965-72; Alternate Governor for UK of IMF, 1966-72; Chairman of Deputies of Committee of Twenty, IMF, 1972-74; Deputy Chairman, 1975-77, Chairman, 1977-, Loyds Bank; Deputy Chairman, 1975-79, Chairman, 1980-, Lloyds Bank International; Chairman, Committee of London Clearing Bankers, 1980-; Director, Legal & General Assurance Society Ltd; Alexanders Discount Co. Ltd. *Memberships:* NEDC, 1977-; Fellow, All Souls College, Oxford, 1953-68. *Honours:* KCMG, 1975. *Hobbies:* Poetry; Problems and Puzzles; Coarse gardening; Golf. *Address:* 102a Drayton Gardens, London S W 10, England.

MORTIMER, Robin Hampton, b. 18 June 1940, St Albans, England. Medicine. m. Iris Beryl Adam, 26 Nov. 1966, 1 son, 1 daughter. *Education:* MB., BS., University of Queensland, 1964; Albert Einstein College of Medicine of Yeshiva University, 1973-74. *Appointments:* Rotating Internship, 1965-66, Residency, Departments Pathology & Medicine, 1967-68, Royal Brisbane Hospital, Brisbane, Australia; Teaching Medical Registrar, Department of Medicine, 1969-71, Research Assistant, National Heart Foundation of Australia, 1972, University of Queensland, Australia. Fellow, Division of Endocrinology, Department of Medicine, 1973-75, Att4nding Physician, 1975-77, Albert Einstein College of Medicine, Bronx, New York; Assistant Attending Physician, 1975-76, Associate Attending Physician, 1976-77, Bronx Municipal Hospital Centre, New York; Assistant Professor of Medicine, Albert Einstein College of Medicine, 1975-77; Endocrinolo-

gist, 1977, Chairman, Department of Endocrinology, 1979-, Royal Brisbane Hospital, Australia; Visiting Endocrinologist, Prince Charles Hospital, Brisbane, Australia, 1979-. *Memberships:* Royal Australasian College of Physicians; Endocrine Society of Australia; Australian Diabetes Society; American Federation for Clinical Research; American Diabetes Association; Endocrine Society, USA; American College of Physicians. *Publications:* Various publications in Endocrinology. *Address:* 19 Sefton Road, Clayfield, Brisbane, Queensland, 4011, Australia.

MORTON, Herbert Myles, b. 1 Feb. 1925, Belleville, Ontario, Canada. Publisher. m. Elizabeth Ann Stone, 7 June 1952, 2 sons, 2 daughters. *Education:* Cantab College, Canada, 1942; University of Toronto, Canada, 1945. *Appointments:* Publisher, The Belleville Intelligencer, Canada; President: Quinte Broadcasting Company, Canada; Cablevue (Quinte) Limited, Canada; Mymore Holdings Limited, Canada; Morville Holdings Limited, Canada; Morpalm Investments Incorporated, Florida, USA; Director: Victoria and Grey Trust Company, Canada; Victoria and Grey Trustco. Limited, Canada. *Memberships:* Canadian Daily Newspaper Publisher's Association Canadian Press. *Hobbies:* Yachting; Golf; Tennis; Photography. *Address:* 'Greenfields', R R I Belleville, Ontario K8N 4Z1, Canada.

MOSHOESHOE II, King (Constantine Bereng Seeiso), b. 2 May 1938. King of Lesotho, Basutoland. m. Princess Tabitha 'Masentle, 1962, 2 sons, 1 daughter. *Education:* LL.B; Corpus Christi College, Oxford, UK. *Appointments:* Paramount Chief of Basutoland, 1960; King, since restoration of Lesotho's Independence, 1966-; exiled from Lesotho, Apr-Dec. 1970. *Memberships:* Chancellor, National University of Lesotho, formerly University of Botswana, Lesotho and Swaziland, 1971. *Address:* The Royal Palace, PO Box 524, Maseru, Lesotho, Republic of South Africa.

MOSKWA, Tad, b. 26 Mar. 1920, Warsaw, Poland. Company Director, Mining Engineer. m. Anna, 15 Nov. 1947, 1 son. *Education:* BSc, Diploma, Royal School of Mines, Imperial College, University of London; Chartered Engineer. *Appointments:* Rhokana Corporation Ltd., Kitwe, Zambia; Barvue Mines Ltd., Quebec, Canada; International Nickel Co., Sudbury, Ontario, Canada; Anglo American Corporation, Salisbury, Rhodesia; Nchanga Copper Mines Ltd., Chingola, Zambia; Broken Hill Mines Ltd., Kabwe, Zambia; Chingola Division, Nchanga Consolidated Copper Mines Ltd; Nchanga Consolidated Copper Mines Ltd., Lusaka, Zambia. *Memberships:* Associate, Royal School of Mines, London; Fellow, The Institution of Mining & Metallurgy; Royal Chartered Engineers, London. *Publications:* Sinking North Shaft, Nchanga, through mud and running sand; Use of Raise Borers & Tunnel Borers in mining; Proposed Electrification of overburden removal at Nchanga Consolidated Copper Mines Ltd. *Honours:* Virtuti Military Cross; Flying Corss; Cross of Valour with three bars. *Hobbies:* Chess; Bridge; Golf. *Address:* PO Box 50330, Lusaka, Zambia.

MOSS, Kenneth Edwin Charles, b. 25 May 1922, Bisley, England. General Manager. m. Margaret Stephenson, 31 Oct. 1942, 2 daughters. *Education:* St Paul's, Cheltenham. *Appointments:* Pilot with Royal Air Force Volunteer Reserve, 1941-46; Field Representative, 1947, District Manager, 1949, Manager, Gwelo, 1956, Manager, Bulawayo, 1961, Manager, Salisbury, 1964, Manager for Rhodesia, 1969, Assistant General Manager (Marketing), 1980, Old Mutual in Zimbabwe. *Memberships:* Fellow, British Society of Commerce; Member, British Institute of Management; Zimbabwe Institute of Management; Past-Chairman, Rhodesian Standing Committee Life Offices' Association of Southern Africa; First Chairman and Present Chairman, L.O.A. Zimbabwe; Executive and Vice-President for two years of Salisbury Chamber of Commerce; Commonwealth Panel of Referees (Boxing); Zimbabwe Board of Boxing Control. *Hobby:* Keen sportsman, especially boxing; Licensed judge and referee. *Address:* 103 San Sebastian, North Avenue, Salisbury, Zimbabwe.

MOSS, William, b. 21 Dec. 1942, Castleford, Yorkshire, England. Composer, Pianist, Teacher. *Education:* NDD, Leeds College of Art; GRSM, LRAM, Royal Academy of Music. *Appointments:* Lecturer in Music and Musical Instrument Technology at Neward Technical College. 09 Large scale compositions include: Concert for Eleven Pianists, (one piano), 1966; Grande Etude for solo prepared piano, 1970; A number of works for mixed chamber groups. *Address:* The Old Bakehouse, High Street, Fulbeck, Grantham, Lincs., England.

MOSTAFA, Mohammed Golam, b. 6 Aug. 1938, Noakhali, Bangladesh. Professor of Statistics. m. Syeda Rizia Banu, 25 Aug. 1961, 1 son, 2 daughters. *Education:* BSc, 1959, MSc, 1960, Dacca University; PhD, London University, 1965. *Appointments:* Lecturer, Assistant Professor, Associate Professor, 1960-70, Professor — Chairman of the Department, 1973-76, Dacca University; Associate Professor & Head of Department, Cittagong University, 1970-73; Visiting Professor, Indian Statistical Institute, 1971-72. *Memberships:* Fellow, The Royal Statistical Society; American Statistical Association. *Honours:* Raja Kali Narayan Scholarship, 1959; President's Scholarship, Best student, 1960. *Hobbies:* Travelling; Music; Literature. *Address:* 23 Atash Khana Road, Lalbag, Dacca, Bangladesh.

MOTHESA, Lusiano Mitengo, b. 15 Feb. 1943. Assistant Librarian. m. Felesta B Mulonsoti, 1963, 3 sons, 2 daughters. *Education:* Junior Certificate, Malawi Government Examination; Three months Regional Documentation and Librarianship Course, Makerere University, School of Librarianship, 1969. *Appointments:* Assistant Librarian of Parliament. *Memberships:* Malawi Library Association. *Address:* Reading; Football; Table tennis; Boxing. *Address:* Chaone Village, T/A Chimaliro, Chimvu, Postal Agency, Thyolo.

MOTT, Hamilton Charles, b. 5 Dec. 1936, Albury, New South Wales, Australia. Foreign Service Officer. m. Elspeth Hall Lewis, 27 Apr. 1963, 2 sons, 1 daughter. *Education:* BA., Melbourne, Australia, 1957. *Appointments:* Journalist, Herald Melbourne, Australia, 1957-59; Reuters, London, UK, 1960-61; Daily Telegraph, London, UK, 1961; Department of External Affairs, 1962; Third Secretary, The Hague, 1963-65; Second Secretary, Karachi-Rawalpindi, 1965-67; UN Section Department, Foreign Affairs, 1968-70; First Secretary, then Counsellor, Mission to UN New York, USA, 1970-74; Rapporteur, First Committee, UN Law of the Sea Conference, 1973-75; Assistant Secretary, Information, British Department Foreign Affairs and Senior Departmental Spokesman, 1975-77; Minister, Australian High Commission, London, UK, 1977-79; High Commissioner of Australia to Nigeria, 1979-; Special Representative and Head of Australian Liaison Office, Salisbury, Nigeria, 1980-. *Honours:* Zimbabwe Independence Medal, 1980. *Hobbies:* Tennis; Gardening; Reading. *Address:* 2 Kofoabayomi Street, Victoria Island, Lagos, Nigeria.

MOUAT, Cecil Thomas Arthur Millar, b. 4 Apr. 1942, Easthouse, Sandsound, Shetland, Scotland. Schoolteacher. m. Irene Bryce, 29 Mar. 1969, 1 son, 1 daughter. *Education:* Anderson Educational Institue, Lerwick, 1954-60; MA, University of Edinburgh, 1960-63; Moray House College of Education, Edinburgh, 1963-64; BSc, External Degree, University of London, 1971. *Appointments:* Assistant Teacher, Mathematics & Geography, High School, Hawick, Roxburghshire, 1964-72; Principal Teacher, Geography, Anderson High School, Lerwick, Shetland, 1972-. *Memberships:* Shetland Representative, Central Advisory Committee on Geography, 1980-; Treasurer of Shetland Folk Society, 1980; Member of the Up-Helly-Aa Committee, 1981. *Publications:* Contributions to geographical journals; Assisted in making filmstrip on geography. *Hobbies:* Astronomy & astronautics; Space stamps; Chess; All aspects of cinema; Classical & popular music; Fishing; Gardening; Golf; Photography; Sailing; Travel; All aspects of Shetland's geography; History; Language; Literature; Folklore; Giving illustrated lectures on Shetland's scenery & landscape. *Address:* Bellevue House, 29 Knab Road, Lerwick, Shetland Isles, Scotland.

MOULDS, Maxwell Sydney, b. 27 June 1941, Sydney, Australia. Entomologist. m. Barbara Joyce Thomas, 16 Dec. 1972, 1 son. *Education:* Alexander Mackie College of Advanced Education, 1960-62. *Appointments:* School teacher, NSW, State Government, 1963-68; Established Australian Entomological Supplies, 1969, sold, 1972; Established Australian Entomological Press, Managing Director, 1970-. *Memberships:* Entomological Society of NSW; Australian Entomological Society; Zoological Society of Lon-

don; Royal Zoological Society of NSW; Society for the Bibliography of Natural History (London); Linnean Society of New South Wales. *Publications:* Founder & Editor, Australian Entomological Magazine, 1972-; Contributor to professional journals; 21 research papers, 1963-81. *Honours:* Associate, Australian Museum, 1974-; Leader of several expeditions to remote areas of Australia to study and collect insects (over 20,000 specimens donated to research institutions throughout Australia). *Hobbies:* Growing Australian native plants; Scuba diving. *Address:* 16 Park Avenue, Waitara, NSW, 2077, Australia.

MOULE, Alexander John, b. 7 Jan. 1950, Kota Bharu, Malaysia. Dental Surgeon, University Senior Lecturer. *Education:* Bachelor of Dental Science, 1971, PhD, 1979, University of Queensland. *Appointments:* Assistant dentist/dentist in charge, Mackay Dental Clinic, Mackay Hospitals Board, 1972-73; Full-time Lecturer in Restorative Dentistry, University of Queensland, 1973-80; Full-time Senior Lecturer in Operative Dentistry, University of Sydney, 1980-. *Memberships:* Committee, Queensland Branch, Australian Society of Endodontology, 1976-79; Committee, 1975-80, President, 1976, The Brisbane Dental Discussion Group; Federal Council, Gemmological Association of Australia, 1977-78. *Publications:* Contributions to Dental and Gemmological journals. *Honours:* Various undergraduate prizes, University of Queensland. *Hobbies:* Qualified gemmologist; Various offices and some lecturers in gemmmology to diploma students and members of jewellery trade; Main interest Organic gemstones. *Address:* Department of Operative Dentistry, University of Sydney, 2 Chalmers Street, Surry Hills, 2010, Australia

MOUNTAIN, Denis Mortimer (Sir), b. 2 June 1929, London, England. Insurance Executive. m. Helene Fleur Mary Kirwan-Taylor, 18 Feb. 1958, 2 sons, 1 daughter. *Education:* Eton College, 1942-46. *Appointments:* Director of 52 Companies. *Memberships:* Institute of Directors. *Honours:* Third Baronet (Baronetcy of Mountain of Oare Manor County Somerset and Brendon in the County of Devon, 1977. *Hobbies:* Fishing; Shooting. *Address:* Shawford Park, Shawford, Nr. Winchester, Hampshire, England.

MOUTIA, Raoul Jean Sydney, b. 22 June 1932, Port Louis, Mauritius. Resident Commissioner. m. Suzie L'Aimable, 18 Oct. 1961, 1 son, 3 daughters. *Education:* Royal College, Mauritius; Dip.Agri., City & Guilds Certificate, College of Agriculture, Mauritius; BSc, Wye College University of London; Dip. Agri. Econ., St John's College, University of Oxford; D.Phil., University of Gauhati. *Appointments:* Agricultural Officer, 1959, Agronomist, 1961, Senior Agricultural Officer, 1966, Mauritius; Lecturer, College of Agriculture, Mauritius, 1961; Principal Agricultural Officer, 1970; Secretary-General Organisation Commune Africaine et Mauricienne, 1974; Resident Commissioner, Rodrigues, 1980-. *Memberships:* Societe Royale des Arts et Sciunces; Societe de Technologie Agricole et Sucrerie; Agricola Club; Rotary Club of Curepipe. *Publications:* Theses and Reports. *Honours:* Scholarship College of Agriculture, 1955; Commonwealth Scholar, 1963. *Hobbies:* Golf; Photography; Walking. *Address:* The Residency, Port Mathurin, Rodrigues, Mauritius.

MOYLE, Lindsay Gordon Crossley, b. 30 May 1930, Burnie, Tasmania, Australia. Merchant Banker. m. Judith Ann Hutchison, 24 Aug. 1956, 2 sons, 1 daughter. *Education:* Associate, Australian Society of Accountants, 1965. *Appointments:* Various positions, Commonwealth Banking Corporation, 1947-71; Managing Director, Investment Corporation of Papua, New Guinea, 1971-74; Deputy Chief Manager, International, Commonwealth Trading Bank of Australia, 1974-76; General Manager, Australian European Finance Corporation Limited, 1976-78; Managing Director: United Dominions Corporation Limited, 1978-81; Chase-N B A Group Limited, 1981. *Memberships:* Director, Government Insurance Office of New South Wales; Chairman, New South Wales branch, Financial Executives Institute; Trustee, Committee for Economic Development of Australia; Councillor, Civic Reform Association; Funds Committee member: Australian Opera Company; Enterprise Australia; Australian (Sydney and Melbourne) Pymble Golf Club; Papua Club. *Hobbies:* Cattle grazing; Surfing; Golf. *Address:* 131

Powlett Street, East Melbourne, Victoria 3002, Australia.

MOYO, Cromwell Themba, b. 9 Dec. 1949, Tegwani, Zimbabwe. Lecturer. m. Jean Pangani, 31 July 1976, 2 sons. *Education:* BA, Malawi; Advanced Diploma in Education, English Language, Exeter. *Appointments:* Bank Clerk; Secondary School Teacher; Lecturer. *Memberships:* English Syllabus Committee for Teacher Training Colleges in Malawi. *Publications:* Collected Poems under publication. *Honours:* Won The British Council Award for Technical Development to study Applied Linguistics at the University of Exeter, 1979-80. *Hobby:* Photography. *Address:* P Bag 502, Limbe, Malawi, Central Africa.

MOYO, Tommy, b. 10 Jan. 1951, Que Que, Zimbabwe. Safety Officer. m. Saziso Sibindi, 11 July 1977, 1 son, 1 daughter. *Education:* GCE 'O' Level, 1969; Diploma in Occupational Safety, 1980. *Memberships:* Chairman, Torwood Theatre Club, The Torwood Salvation Army, Building Committee. *Honours:* Co-directed a play in Torwood Hall called "The Gods are not to Blame", 1976; Won the Best Achievement Trophy organised by the National Theatre Organisation of Zimbabwe. *Hobbies:* Visiting Game Reserves; Reading; Church. *Address:* 27 Hutchings Crescent, Redcliff, Zimbabwe.

MOZIE, Osi,b. 9 Feb. 1929, Onitsha, Nigeria. University Teacher. m. Ann Achike, 5 Apr. 1958, 2 sons, 3 daughters. *Education:* B Sc, Botany, Howard University, USA, 1952; M Sc, Botany, McGill University, Canada, 1954. *Appointments:* Science Education Officer, 1957-62; Lecturer in Botany, University of Nigeria, 1962-70; Senior Lecturer, 1971-. *Memberships:* Society of the Sigma Xi, McGill University; Science Association, Nigeria, West Africa. *Publications:* Thesis and papers in Botany Field. *Honours:* Examination Honour in English, Howard University, Washington DC, USA, 1951; External Examiner in Biology, Institute of Management and Technology, Enugu Nigeria, 1978, 1980, 1981. *Hobbies:* Swimming; Tennis; Reading. *Address:* Department of Botany, University of Nigeria, Nsukka, Anambra State, Nigeria.

MPANGALA, Gaudens Philip, b. 24 Apr. 1941, Sougla, Tanzania. m. Anunciatha Z Njori, 28 Feb. 1976, 2 sons, 1 daughter. *Education:* St More College, Ihungo, 1963-64; BA (Hons), 1965-69, MA, History, 1975-77, University of Dar es Salaam. *Appointments:* Secondary School Teacher, 1969-72; Secondary Headmaster, 1972-73; Curriculum Developer, 1973-78; Lecturer-Senior Lecturer, University of Dar-es-Salaam, 1978-. *Memberships:* National Chairman, Historical Association of Tanzania, 1978-; Executive, Tanzania Writers Co-operative Society, 1977-. *Publications:* Co-author, Maji, Maji War in Clugoni; Participant in Secondary School, Primary, teacher education, adult Education, history text books and syllabuses; Various papers presented in conferences and university seminars. *Hobbies:* Writing; Gardening. *Address:* Kimara Mavarunza, Dar-es-Salaam. Tanzania.

M'PASSOU, Denis, b. 9 May 1932, Mulanje, Malawi. Lecturer. m. 30 Sept. 1978. *Education:* Diploma in Communication, 1971; Bachelor of Philosophy, 1974; Doctor of Divinity, 1976. *Appointments:* Director of Literary Project, Daystar Communications, Rhodesia, 1970-72; Managing Editor, Inform, 1969-74; Editor-in-Chief and Managing Director, Maco-Passou Communications, 1974-76; Provincial Secretary, Church of the Province of Central Africa, 1977-80; Head of Conferences and Research Programme, Mindolo Eumenical Foundation, 1980-. *Memberships:* Association of Central African Christian Training Institutions; Zambia Joint Theological Seminary and Evangelism Commission; Former Chairman, Christian Council of Zambia; Christian Council of Malawi. *Publications:* Stop the Wedding, 1971; The Hyena's Tail, 1972; Wash Your Hands Mr. Monkey, 1973; Stories with a Sting; Likoma Cathedral, 1976; From a Dog-boy to a Bishop, 1979. *Honours:* First Prize, PEN, Prose English Translation, 1975; 2nd Prize, Drum Short Story Competition 1973. *Address:* Mindolo Ecumenical Foundation, PO Box 21493, Kitwe, Zambia.

MPOFU, Pamba, b. 10 Sept. 1933, Zimbabwe. Senior Editorial Officer. m. Rose Moyo, 15 Apr. 1963, 4 sons, 5 daughters. *Education:* Primary Teacher's Lower Certifi-

cate, 1952-53; University Junior Certificate, 1954-55; Joint Matriculation Certificate, 1956-57. *Appointments:* School Teacher, 1958-62; Reader Translator, Editorial Officer, Senior Editorial Officer, 1962-81. *Memberships:* Vice-Chairman, Sobukhazi Secondary School Advicory Council, 1980-; Treasurer, Thorngrove Tenants Association, 1980-. Contributor to Two poetry books, "Kusile Mbongi Zohlanga" and "Ugqozi Lwezimbongi"; Co-author, Izaga (first publication of proverbs in Ndebele). *Honours:* Awarded two First Class Diplomas in Recitation Nad Drama respectively, African Eisteddfod, Bulawayo, 1953. Offered Scholarship by UCCSA for conduct and brilliance. *Hobbies:* Football; Gardener; Poultry Keeper. *Address:* 11566 Sweethorn Road, Thorngrove, Bulawayo, Zimbabwe.

MSANGI, Abdulrahman Salim, b. 18 Oct. 1929, Usangi Pare, Tanzania. Professor; Director. m. (1) Mary Elizabeth Hiza, 11 may 1957, dec'd, (2) Munira J Manongi, 11 Apr. 1975, 2 sons, 6 daughters. *Education:* Makerere University College, 1950-53; BSc., London, UK, 1954; CAP of E., 1957-58, DAP of E., 1962-63, London School of Hygiene and Tropical Medicine, UK; PhD., External student, University of London, UK, 1964-68. *Appointments:* Scientific Officer, East African Institute of Malaria and Vector-Borne Diseases, Tanga, Tanganyika, 1954-60; Education Officer, 1960-61, Medical Entomologist, 1962-63, Senior Lecturer, 1964-68, Reader, 1969-70, Professor of Zoology, 1970-, Director, Institute of Marine Sciences, 1979-, Project Co-ordinator, 1980-, Marine Science and Technology Development, Economic Commission for Africa, Addis Ababa, Ethiopia. *Memberships:* Fellow, Royal Entomological Society, London; Tanzania Society; East African Academy; Chairman, Serengeti Research Institute; Trustee: Tanzania National Parks; LSB Leakey Foundation; Association of African Insect Scientists; Society for International Development. *Publications:* Several publications on mosquito vectors of malaria, snail vectors of schistosomiasis and plague in East Africa and in general marine sciences and marine resources development in Africa. *Hobbies:* Table tennis; Darts; Gardening; Discussion groups. *Address:* 056 Norwegian Mission Compound, Kesanges, Addis Ababa, Ethiopia.

MSHELIA, Elijah Dika, b. Shaffa, Nigeria. Professor of Physics. *Education:* BSc., Technical University, Darmstadt, 1967; MSc., 1969, PhD., 1972, University of Frankfurt, Germany. *Appointments:* Graduate Assistant, 1967-69, Assistant Lecturer, 1970-72, Lecturer, 1972-76, University of Frankfurt/M, Germany; Senior Lecturer, 1977-79, Associate Professor, 1979-81, University of Maiduguri, Nigeria; Professor, Federal University of Technology, Bauchi, Nigeria, 1981-. *Memberships:* German Physical Society; European Physical Society; Nigerian Institute of Physics; University of Maiduguri Council and Senate; University of Bauchi Senate and Council. *Publications:* 14 publications including: Physics Rev. Letter (with R F Barrett and W Greiner), 1972; Nuclear Physics (with K Roos and W Greiner), 1973; Il Nuovo Cimento (with W Scheid and W Greiner), 1975; Lettere al Nuovo Cimento (with P Antony-Spies), 1976; Proeedings of the International School on Nuclear Physics, Predeal, Romania (with others), 1976; Verhandl (with W Scheid and D Hahn), 1981; Il Nuova Cimento, 1981. *Hobby:* Music. *Address:* Department of Physics, Federal University of Technology, PMB 0248, Bauchi, Nigeria.

MSHIGENI, Keto Elitabu, b. 14 Jan. 1944, Pare District, Kilimanjaro Region, Tanzania. Professor of Botany. m. 30 Nov. 1969, 2 daughters. *Education:* PhD., University of Hawaii, 1974; BSc., Hons., University of East Africa, 1969. *Appointments:* Tutorial Assistant, 1969-74, Lecturer, 1974-76, Senior Lecturer, 1976-78, Associate Professor, 1978-79, Professor, 1979-, Botany, Director of Postgraduate Studies, 1980-, University of Dar es Salaam, Tanzania. *Memberships:* Publisher of Tanzania notes and records, Tanzania Society; International Phycological Society; Phycological Society of America; British Phycological Society; International Seaweed Association; Western Society of Pacific Naturalists. *Publications:* Author of some 60 scientific papers, with over 50 papers in refereed journals such as: Marine Biology, Botanica Marina, Nova Hedwigia, Experientia; contributed chapters in scientific books. *Honours:* Awarded University of Dar es Salaam prizes for outstanding performance in examinations, 1966-67, 1968-69; Norwegian Agency for

International Development Research grant award, 1969; Rockefeller Foundation Scholarship award, 1970-74; Awarded International Foundation for Science Research grant, 1976; USA Fulbright Scholarship award, 1979-80; UNESCO Travel grant awards, 1977, 80; UNDP Travel grant, 1981. *Hobbies:* Photography; Music; Bird-watching. *Address:* University of Dar es Salaam, PO Box 35091, Dar es Salaam, Tanzania.

MTAMBO, Michael Charles, b. 6 Sept. 1957, Zomba, Malawi. University Lecturer in Law. *Education:* LL B (Hons), Chancellor College, University of Malawi, 1975-80. *Appointments:* Legal Assistant, Sacranie, Gow & Company, Malawi, 1980-81; Admitted to the Bar as Legal Practitioner & Commissioner for Oaths, 1980; Assistant Lecturer in Law, The Polytechnic, A Constituent College of the University of Malawi, 1981-; Course Tutor Second Diploma in Business Studies at Polytechnic, University of Malawi; Representative Faculty of Commerce of the Polytechnic, University of Malawi, Teaching Methods Senate Committee. *Memberships:* French Club, University of Malawi, 1975-76; Students Law Society, University of Malawi, 1976-80; Malawi Law Society, 1980. Various contributions to Law Symposiums and Law Journals. *Honours:* Book Prize presented by French Embassy in Malawi, 1974. *Hobbies:* Football; Films; Research and Publication; Music. *Address:* Kuchiri Village, c/o Gwaza F P School, Chingale, Zomba, Malawi.

MTURI, Amini Aza, b. 3 Aug. 1942, Usangi-Pare, Tanzania. Archaeologist; Director of Antiquities. m. 21 Apr. 1979. *Education:* BA (Hons), History, University of East Africa, 1966; Post-Graduate Academic Diploma in Prehistoric Archaeology, Institute of Archaeology, University of London, 1968. *Appointments:* Assistant Conservator of Antiquities, 1966-69; Conservator of Antiquities, 1970-73; Director of Antiquities and National Archives, 1973-75; Director of Antiquities, 1975-. *Memberships:* Chairman, Tasmania Society; Administrator, Faculty of Building; Organisation of Museums; Vice-President, Sites and Monuments of Africa. *Publications:* Research work in Ngorongoro, West Kilimanjaro and Lake Ndutu, Tanzania; Annual Reports of the Department of Antiquities, 1968-75; New Hominid from Lake Ndutu, Tanzania, 1976. *Honours:* Gordon Childe Prize, University of London, Institute of Archaeology, 1968. *Hobbies:* Reading; Sports. *Address:* PO Box 2280, Dar-es-Salaam, Tanzania.

MUDALIGE, Daya Bandula Obada, b. 10 Dec. 1931, Colombo, Sri Lanka. Chartered Accountant. m. Freda Mary Whitehead, 5 Sept. 1964. *Education:* Royal College, 1955; Aquinas College, GCE A Levels, 1955-56. *Appointments:* Articled Clerk, Pegg, Robertson & Company, Coleman St. London; Audit Senior: James Edwards, Dangerfield & Company, London; Ford, Rhodes, Thornton & Company, Fort Colombo I; Tansley Witt & Company London; Jocelyn Layton-Bennett, London. Visiting Lecturer, University of Peradeniya, Sri Lanka; Partner, Mudalige & Company, Southall, Middlesex. *Memberships:* Honorary Treasurer, Ceylon Cancer Society, 1973, Buddhist Publication Society, 1973, Age-Link, London, 1981. *Hobbies:* Sports; Badminton. *Address:* Melrose, 2 Hogarth Avenue, Ashford, Middlesex, TW15 1Q4, England.

MUELLER, Peter Ernst, b. 13 May 1943, Switzerland. Hotelier. *Education:* Cook Apprenticeship, Restaurant Edoardo, Zurich, Switzerland, 1963; Grill Cook Restaurant Le Plaza, Friburg, 1964; Diploma for Hotel Supervisor, 1965; ACSE Certificate, Anglo-Continental School for English, England, 1966; Diploma of Administration from Hotel Management School, Lausanne, Switzerland; Diploma for Innkeeper (Hotel Management), Holiday Inn University Memphis, USA. *Appointments:* Secretary (for Diploma), Hotel Viktoria, National, Basle, Switzerland; Front Office Manager in various hotels in Europe, Singapore, Thailand, and Hong Kong; General Manager, Holiday Inn Hotel, Kuching. *Memberships:* Sarawak Tourist Association. *Honours:* Honourable Mention Award for Achievement as an Outstanding Innkeeper from Holiday Inn System, 1980. *Hobbies:* Tennis; Water-sports; Skiing; Ice Skating; Philately; Reading. *Address:* c/o Holiday Inn Hotel, Jalan Tunku Abdul Rahman, Kuching, Sarawak, East Malaysia.

MUGABE, Robert Gabriel, b. 1925. Zimbabwean Politician. m. Sarah. *Education:* Fort Hare University of South Africa and London University. *Appointments:* Teacher, 1952-60; Publicity Secretary, National Democratic Party, 1960-61; Publicity Secretary, Zimbabwe African Peoples Union, 1961-62; Secretary General, Zimbabwe African National Union (ZANU), 1963; President, Zimbabwe African National Union, 1977-; Joint Leader, Patriotic Front, 1976-80; Prime Minister, Zimbabwe, 1980-; Minister of Defence, 1980-. *Address:* Office of the Prime Minister, Salisbury, Zimbabwe.

MUGERWA, John Sebastian, b. Uganda. Agriculturalist. m. Anne Bikuka, 2 May 1970, 4 daughters. *Education:* SDP, NDP, West of Scotland Agricultural College, 1962; BSc, 1965, MSc, 1967, University of Rhode Island, Kingston; PhD, Ohio State University, Colombus, 1969. *Appointments:* Poultry Officer, Uganda Government, 1962; Research Fellow, Ohio Agricultural Research & Development Centre, 1968-69; Lecturer, 1969-72, Senior Lecturer & Head Department of Animal Science, 1972-74, Reader (Associate Professor) & Head Department of Animal Science, 1974-76, Professor, Dean, Faculty of Agriculture & Forestry & Head Department of Animal Science, 1976-, Makerere University. *Memberships:* American Dairy Science Association; American Animal Science Association; Uganda Academy of Arts & Sciences; Uganda Agricultural Society; Chairman, Uganda Animal Production Society; Vice-Chairman Uganda Society; Agricultural Committee of National Research Council. *Publications:* Over 30 publications in Animal Science. *Honours:* Best Student Award, 1962; President's List, University of Rhode Island, 1964; Fellow Ohio State University, 1967, Phi Kappa Phi, 1969. *Hobbies:* Tennis; Football; Squash; Gardening; Pleasure Reading. *Address:* Faculty of Agriculture & Forestry, Makerere University, PO Box 7062 Kampala, Uganda.

MUGGLETON, Louis Miles, b. 8 July 1922, South Africa. Electrical Engineer. m. 20 Dec. 1947, 4 sons. *Education:* BSc, 1947, PhD, 1960, Cape Town. *Appointments:* Professional Officer, Ministry of Posts, Rhodesia, 1950-61; Lecturer, Senior Lecturer, Department of Electrical Engineering, University of Edinburgh, 1961-73; Founder, Dean of Engineering and Head of Department of Electronic and Power Engineering, University of Rhodesia, 1973-78; Director of the Wave Propagation Department, Trans World Radio International, 1979-. *Memberships:* Institution of Electrical Engineers, London. *Publications:* About 20 articles, mainly describing research results in ionospheric radio wave propagation. *Hobbies:* Tennis; Cricket. *Address:* 185 Topsham Road, Exeter EX2 6AN, England.

MUHAMMAD, Rabiu Danlami, b. 23 July 1945, Kano, Nigeria. Lawyer. m. Asabe Aishatu, 4 sons, 1 daughter. *Education:* LL.B., 1972; BL, 1973. *Appointments:* Magistrate, Kano State; Legal Officer, Bank of the North Ltd., Kano; Company Secretary, Northern Nigeria Investments Ltd., Kaduna; Director of Public Prosecutions, Kano State; Solicitor-General, Kano State. *Hobbies:* Photography; Reading. *Address:* No. 6 Tamandu Road, Kano, Nigeria.

MUIR, David John (Sir), b. 20 June 1916, Brisbane, Australia. Chairman, Queensland Cultural Centre Trust. m. Joan Howarth, 6 June 1942, 1 son, 1 daughter. *Education:* Associate in Accountancy, University of Queensland, Australia; Fellow of: Australian Institute of Management; Chartered Institute of Secretaries and Administrators; Australian Society of Accountants. *Appointments:* Permanent Head, Premier and Chief Secretary's Department, 1948-51, Director of Industrial Development, 1964-77, Chairman, Public Service Board, 1977-79, Ombudsman, 1979-, Queensland, Australia; Agent-General for Queensland, London, UK, 1951-64. *Honours:* James N Kirby Medal of Institution of Production Engineers, 1969; Knight Bachelor, 1961; CMG, 1959. *Hobbies:* Golf; Gardening. *Address:* 28 Buena Vista Avenue, Coorparoo, Queensland 4151, Australia.

MUIR, Elaine Patricia, b. Manangatang, Victoria, Australia. Administrator. Widow, 1 son, 3 daughters. *Appointments:* Principal, Medical Receptioniste Training, 1965-68; Administrative Officer, 1968-77, General Secretary, 1977-, The Australian Psychological Society. *Memberships:* The Sciences Club, Vice-President, 1980-81, Melbourne; The Royal Society of Victoria; Australian and New Zealand Association for the

Advancement of Science; International Association of Applied Psychology. *Hobbies:* Writing; MG Car Club activities; Gardening; Music. *Address:* 2 Marks Street, Pascoe Vale, Victoria, Australia, 3044.

MUIR, Laurence Macdonald, b. 3 Mar. 1925, Morwell, Victoria, Australia. Sharebroker (retired). m. Ruth Richardson, 28 Feb. 1948, 2 sons, 2 daughters. *Education:* LL.B., University of Melbourne, Australia, 1947-49. *Appointments:* Lieutenant commander, Royal Australian Navy, 1942-46; J B Were & Sons, Sharebrokers, 1949-57; Vinton Smith & Dougall, Sharebrokers, 1958-61; Partner, 1962-80, Senior Partner, 1976-80, Potter Partners, Australia; Director of: Australia and New Zealand Banking Group Limited; Australian Consolidated Industries Limited; Commercial Union Assurance Co, of Australia Limited; Wormald International Limited; Chairman, Melbourne FM Radio Pty. Ltd; Alex Harvey Industries Ltd.; Herald and Weekly Times Ltd. *Memberships:* Chairman, Canberra Development Board; Parliament House Construction Authority; Council member, Australian National University; CSIRO Victoria Advisory Committee; Victoria Law Foundation; Chairman, State Library and National Museum Buildings Committee; Executive committee, Victoria 150th Anniversary Celebrations; Former Vice-President, Royal Flying Doctor Service, Victoria Division; Chairman, Microsurgery Foundation; Former Vice-Chairman, Anti-Cancer Council of Victoria Appeals Committee; Board member, Alfre Hospital; Director, Baker Research Institute; Former Co-chairman, CEDA Executive Committee; General Motors Australia Advisory Council. *Honours:* Barrister and Solicitor, Supreme Court, 1950; VRD., 1954; Stock Exchange of Melbourne Limited, 1960; Fellow of: Securities Institute, 1962; Australian Institute of Management, 1965; Australian Institute of Directors, 1967; Knight Bachelor, 1981. *Hobbies:* Tennis; Gardening; Fishing. *Address:* 9/5 Grandview Grove, Hawthorn, East Melbourne, Victoria 3122, Australia.

MUIR, Robert Ballantine, b. 25 May 1910, Whithorn, Scotland. Management. m. Margaret Beryl Firth, 3 Aug. 1946, 1 son, 1 daughter. *Education:* BSc, Glasgow University, 1928-32; Graduate Staff College, Camberly, 1946; Graduate Armed Forces Staff College, USA, 1950. *Appointments:* Regular Amy Officer, Royal Engineers, 1933-36; Seconded to Madras Sappers & Miners, Indian Army, 1936-46; Chief of Staff, HQ Hamburg District, BAOR, 1947-50; Various War Office and Command & Staff Appointments, 1951-57; Chief Military Planner, Chief Engineer and Commander Army Task Group, Christmas Island, H Bomb Tests, 1958; Deputy Commandant & Senior Military Director of Studies, Royal Military College of Science, 1959-61; Director General and Chairman, Executive Board of Scottish Industrial Estates Corporation, 1961-76. *Memberships:* C.Eng., FRSA; FICE; FIStruct.E; FIProd.E; FBIM; MIEE; MIMech.E. *Publications:* The Nuclear Test Programme; Christmas Island Nuclear Tests; Sappers in the Malayan War; Numerous Industrial Articles in International Press and publications. *Honours:* Mentioned in Despatches, Malayan Campaign, 1941-42; Honorary Submariner, United States Navy, 1950; CBE, 1959; Honorary Colonel 102 Corps Engineer Regiment, 1962-67; Honorary Colonel 71 (Scottish) Engineer Regiment, 1972-78. *Hobbies:* Lecturing; Military Engineers History; Industrial Strategy; Walking. *Address:* The Beeches, Empress Road, RHU, Helensburgh, Strathclyde, Scotland.

MUKAROBGUA, Thomas, b. June 1924, Rusape, Makoni District, Zimbabwe. Head Attendant, National Gallery, Zimbabwe. m. Brandina Bingura, Aug. 1954. *Appointments:* Farm worker; Attendant, National Gallery, Zimbabwe, 1957; Painter; Stone Sculptor. *Creative Works:* Exhibited Commonwealth Institute, Commonwealth Arts Festival, 1965; Museum of Modern Art, Camden Arts Centre, Musée Rodin, Institute of Contemporary Art; work purchased by Museum of Modern Art, New York, USA, and the National Gallery of Zimbabwe. *Address:* 5833 Old Canaan, Highfields, Salisbury, Zimbabwe.

MUKERJEE, Kim, b. 22 Mar. 1940, London, England. Behavioural Psychologist. m. Wanders Van Zyl, 1 son, 2 daughters. *Education:* BSc., London School of Economics, UK, 1961; PhD., Columbia University, Canada, 1980. *Appointments:* P.L., 1978, The Research Department Limited, 1961-65; Benton & Bowles & Co. Limit-

ed, 1966; McCann Ericson & Co. Limited, 1967-68; Foote Cone & Belding & Co. Limited, 1969; Maisey Mukerjee Russel & Co. Limited, 1970-77; P L., Brand Management, 1978. *Memberships:* Market Research Society of Australia; Design and Art Directors Association, UK. *Publications:* A Brief Study of the Phenomenon of the Unemployed Australian Aboriginid in Contemporary Society, 1980; AN Anthropologist in Adland, 1981. *Honours:* New York Art Directors Show, 1973; 2 Silver and 1 Bronze awards, New York International TV & Film Festival, 1974, 75, 76; Design and Art Directors Show, 1969, 71, 72, 74; Premier Award, 1972, Advertising Creative Circle, 1971, 72, 73, 74, 75, 76, 77; Creativity, 1979, 81; Clio Awards, 1978, 79, 81; Communication Arts awards, 1972-74; Cannes Film Festival, 1968; Silver award, Rizzoli, 1972. *Hobbies:* Reading; Writing; Photography. *Address:* 68-70 Ellerina Road, Mount Martha, Victoria, Australia.

MUKHERJI, Ramaranjan, b. 1 Jan. 1928, Suri, Birbhum, West Bengal. m. Sarati, 28 May 1953. *Education:* BA, 1944, MA, 1946, D.Phil., 1953, Calcutta University; D.Lit, Jadavpur University, 1965. *Appointments:* Lecturer in Sanskrit, Shri Vidyasagar College, Dist. Birbhum, 1948-55; West Bengal Educational Service, 1955-56; Reader in Sanskrit, 1956-60, Professor & Head of the Department of Sanskrit, 1960-70, Jadavpur University; Vice-Chancellor, University of Burdwan, 1970-71, 1973-. *Memberships:* President, Association of Indian Universities; Council of Association of Commonwealth Universities; Fellow, Royal Asiatic Society of United Kingdom; Asiatic Society of India; Secretary, All India Oriental Conference, 1969; President, Classical Sanskrit Section 26th Session of All India Oriental Conference; President, Technical Science & Fine Arts Section 17th Session. *Publications:* An analysis of Aesthetic Experience, 1954; Literary Criticism in Ancient India, 1965; Corpus of Bengal Inscription, 1967; Imagery in Poetry—An Indian Approach, 1972. *Honours:* Ishan Scholarship, University of Calcutta, 1944; University Gold Medal, 1944; University Gold Medal, 1946; Invited by several Indian and foreign Universities to deliver endowment and other series of Lecturers. *Hobby:* Social Service. *Address:* 125/1 Santoshpur Avenue, Calcutta 700 075, India.

MUKHOPADHYAY, Arabinda, b. 27 Oct. 1940, Calcutta, India. Teaching & Research. m. Purabi Banerji, 20 May 1965, 1 son. *Education:* BSc, 1959, MSc, 1961, Calcutta University, India; PhD, 1967, Jadavpur University, Calcutta, India. *Appointments:* Lecturer in Mathematics, Bengal Engineering College, Calcutta, 1962-63; Lecturer in Mathematics, Jadavpur University, Calcutta, 1963-67; Assistant Professor in Mathematics, Regional Engineering College, Durgapur, India, 1967-69; Reader in Applied Mathematics, Calcutta University, India, 1969-; Commonwealth Academic Staff Fellow & Senior Visitor, Department of Applied Mathematics & Theo Physics, University of Cambridge, UK, 1976-77. *Memberships:* FRAS (London); FIMA, (England); American Geophysical Union; Seismological Society of America; Associate, Cambridge Philosophical Society; Calcutta Mathematical Society; Indian Society of Earthquake Technology; Jadavpur Mathematical Society; Seismological Society of India. *Publications:* Numerous contributions to scientific journals including: A Mechanism of Stress Accumulation near a Strike-Slip Fault, 1979; On Stress Accumulation near a continuously slipping Fault in a Two-Layer Model of the Lithosphere, 1980; On Stress Accumulation in a Visco-Elastic Lithosphere containing a continuously slipping Fault, 1980. *Honours:* E V Srinivasan Gold Medal & Silver Medals, Madras University, 1957; McCann Medal, Calcutta University, 1959; University Jubilee Medal, Calcutta University, 1961; P R S Scholarship, 1971; Mouat Medal for research, Calcutta University, 1979; Commonwealth Staff Fellowship, University of Cambridge, 1976-77; Ghosh Travelling Fellowship, 1976-77. *Hobbies:* Literature; History; Music. *Address:* CA17 Sector I, Salt Lake, Calcutta 700064, India.

MUKULA, Pambi Mwape, b. 20 Sept. 1931, Nyamfwa Village, Nchelenge. Director National Archives. m. (1) Esther Musonda (Deceased), 2 sons, 6 daughters, (2) Jennifer Mwape, 19 Aug. 1979. *Education:* Primary Teacher's Certificate, 1954; Bachelor of Arts, 1969. *Appointments:* Bemba Translator for SDA Mission, 1954-59; Primary School Teacher, 1959-66; Assistant Archivist, 1969-70; Director National Archives, 1970-. *Memberships:* Vice-Chairman, ECARBICA; Society of

Archivists; Chairman, National Archives Advisory Council; Professional Board of Libraries; UNESCO Commission. *Publications:* Newspaper articles on Humanism, 1970; Calendars of District Notebooks, Zambia. *Hobby:* SDA, Church . *Address:* Plot 24, Barlaston Park Township, Lusaka, Zambia.

MUKUNDAN, Panangatan, b. 28 Jan. 1918, Manjeri, Kerala State, India. Engineer. m. Padma Vasudevan, 12 May 1946, 1 son, 1 daughter. *Education:* Bachelor of Engineering, 1943, Diploma, 1943, Madras University College of Engineering. *Appointments:* Indian Telegraph Engineering Service, 1943; REME/IEME, 1943-46; Indian Posts & Telegraphs, 1946-48; Automatic Telephone & Electric Co., Liverpool (now Plessey), 1948-49; Plant Manager, Works Manager, Indian Telephone Industries Ltd., 1949-57; Director, Long Distance Maintenance, Indian P & T, 1957-60; Technical Director, Indian Teleprinter Factory Project, 1961-65; General Manager, Calcutta Telephone System, 1965; Technical Manager, later Managing Director, Hindustan Cable Ltd., 1966-71; Project Director, Kerala Government Mini Stell Plant Project, 1971-75; Technical Director, Delton Cable Industries Pvt., Ltd., 1976-. *Memberships:* Fellow, Institute of Electronics & Telecommunication Engineers. *Hobby:* Photography, including processing. *Address:* A 29 Kailash Colony, New Delhi 110 048, India.

MULDOON, Rt. Hon. Robert David, b. 1921, New Zealand. Politician. m. Thea Dale Flyger, 1951, 1 son. *Appointments:* President, New Zealand Institute of Cost Accountants, 1956; MP for Tamaki, 1960-; Parliamentary Under-Secretary to Minister of Finance, 1963-66; Minister of: Tourism, 1967, Finance, 1967-72; Deputy Prime Minister, Feb.-Nov. 1972; Deputy Leader, 1972-74, Leader, 1974-, National Party; Deputy Leader, 1972-74, Leader, 1974-75, Opposition; Prime Minister and Minister of Finance, 1975-. *Publications:* The Rise and Fall of a Young Turk, 1974; Muldoon, 1977; NY Way, 1981. *Honours:* Companion of Honour, 1977; PC. *Address:* Vogel House, 75 Woburn Road, Lower Hutt, New Zealand.

MULEMENA, Anderson Mwelwa Ephraim Chikangabwe, b. 4 Apr. 1934, Mumbwa District Central Province, Zambia. Teacher; Civil Servant. m. 3 May 1964, 1 son, 2 daughters. *Education:* Certificate in Education, University College of Rhodesia and Nyasaland, 1963; BA, History and Political Science, University of Zambia, 1969. *Appointments:* Primary School Teacher, 1957-60; Deputy Head Teacher, Five Acre Plots, Kabwe, 1960-61; Secondary School Master and Head of Department, History/Civics Departments, Kalonga Secondary School, Kabwe, 1969; Deputy Headmaster, Chipepo Secondary School, Southern Province, 1970; Headmaster, Grade II Kawambwa Secondary School, Luapula Province, 1971-73, Headmaster Grade I, Kabulonga School for boys, Lusaka, 1974; Regional Inspector of Schools, Secondary, Southern Province, 1975-77; Principal, Evelyn Hone College of Applied Arts and Commerce, 1977-. *Memberships:* Group Scout Master, Boy Scouts Movement; Commonwealth Association of Polytechnics in Africa. *Hobbies:* Reading; Gardening. *Address:* 5 Kasisi Close, Rhodes Park, Lusaka.

MULIRA, Enoch Emmanuel Keirimba, b. 3 Feb. 1911, Kamese, Koki, Buganda, Uganda. m. Kate Sarah Ndagire Kamulegeya, 9 Jan. 1943, 2 sons, 4 daughters. *Education:* Diploma in Education, Makerere University, E. Africa, 1934-36; Diploma, English Studies, Nottingham University 1938-39; Certificate, Adult Literacy, Hartford Seminary Foundation, USA, 1951-52; MSc, Journalism, Syracuse University, 1952-54; Adult Education, University of London, 1958-59. *Appointments:* English Teacher, Bishop's School Mukono, 1937-38; Teacher, Teachers' College, Mukono, Uganda, 1939-47; Adult Literacy Officer, Uganda Government, 1948-52; Community Development Officer, and Instructor, 1954-58; Field Community Development Officer, 1959-60; Minister of Social Development, Democratic Party, 1961-62; Deputy Headmaster, King's College, Budo, 1962-65; UNESCO Expert, Adult Literacy, 1965-68; Warden and Senior Lecturer, Adult Education, 1969-74; Makerere University; General Manager, Uganda Publishing House, 1974-76; Afrolit Society, Nairobi, 1977-78; General Manager, School Equipment Dealers Limited, 1979-81. *Memberships:* National Adult Education; Buyamba Transport Co-operative

Society; African Adult Education Association; Afrolit Society. *Publications:* Obufumbo n'Obulamu Mu Uganda, 1945; Adult Literacy Primer, 1947; Adult Literacy and Development, 1979; Olugero Lwa Kintu, 1978; Principles and Methods of Adult Basic Education; Several Academic papers, news and magazine articles. *Address:* PO Box 5052, Kampala, Uganda.

MULKEARNS, Ronald Austin, b. 11 Nov. 1930, Caulfield, Victoria, Australia. Catholic Bishop of Ballarat. *Education:* Corpus Christi College, Werribee, Australia, 1949-56; Doctor of Canon Law, Pontifical Lateran University, Rome, Italy, 1957-60. *Appointments:* Ordained priest, 1956; Assistant Priest, Parish of Mentone, Australia, 1957; Assistant Priest, Parish of North Melbourne, Australia, 1960-62; Secretary, Metropolitan Tribunal of Melbourne, Australia, 1962-68; Consecrated Bishop, 1968; Coadjutor Bishop of Ballarat, 1968-71; Bishop of Ballarat, 1971-. *Memberships:* Founding Secretary, Canon Law Society of Australia, now Canon Law Society of Australia and New Zealand; Chairman, Catholic Commission for Justice and Peace, 1971-77. *Publications:* Articles in Racism, The Australian Experience; Compass; Australasian Catholic Record. *Address:* 340 Wendouree Parade, Ballarat, Victoria 3350, Australia.

MULLAN, James, b. 5 Aug. 1921, Newcastle, Australia. Presbyterian Minister. m. Nancy Nenufar, 5 July 1948, 2 sons. *Education:* BA., St. Andrews College, 1943, Cert. Theol., St. Andrew's Theological Hall, 1945, University of Sydney, Australia; Dip. R.Ed., Melbourne College of Divinity, Australia, 1970. *Appointments:* Patrol Minister, Western Riverina, Australia, 1945-48; Parish Minister: Kiama, Australia, 1948-52; Liverpool, Australia, 1952-58; St. David's, Strathfield, Australia, 1958-74; Beecroft, Australia, 1974-. *Memberships:* Moderator General, Presbyterian Church of Australia, 1979-; Clerk of New South Wales General Assembly, 1977-; Lecturer in Polity, Presbyterian Theological Hall, 1975-; Convener, New South Wales Presbyterian Home Mission, 1971-74; Councillor, St. Andrew's College, 1978-. *Publications:* A History of the Presbyterian Church in the Kiama District; Articles in Church journals; Editor of Ecclesiastical Proceedings and Ecclesiastical Law. *Address:* 6 Welham Street, Beecroft 2119, Australia.

MULLANEY, Frank Marshall, b. 19 Feb. 1918, Stockport, Cheshire. Headmaster (Retired). m. Bessie Danson, 30 Mar. 1942, 2 sons, 1 daughter. *Education:* Stockport Grammar School, 1929-36; BSc (Hons. Mathematics), 1939, Teachers' Diploma, Manchester University, 1940. *Appointments:* Captain, HM Forces, 1940-46; Assistant, Stretford Grammar School, 1946-54; Head of Applied Maths. North Manchester Grammar School, 1954-58; Head of Mathematics, 1958-63, Deputy Head, 1962-69, Fairham School, Nottingham; Headmaster, Woodway Park School and Community College, Coventry, 1968-80. *Memberships:* Secondary Heads' Association; Mathematical Association. *Honours:* Hallam Scholarship, 1936. *Hobbies:* Association Football; Cricket; Golf. *Address:* 11 Cannon Close, Coventry, England.

MULLER, Charles Alister, b. 16 May 1925, Frome, England. Lloyds Underwriter and Insurance Broker. m. Mary Nelson Exton, 25 Aug. 1950, 1 son, 3 daughters. *Education:* Certificate, Downside Public School, England. *Appointments:* Engaged in insurance broking, 1942-; Chairman, Interbroke Limited, Switzerland; Deputy Chairman, Clarkson Puckle, (International) Limited; Managing Director, ERAS (International) Limited; Director, Corredores de Reaseguro Internat., Mexico. Delegate and Contributor to International Commission on Large Dam Conference; Council, Royal Borough of Kensington and Chelsea, Mayor 1968-69, Alderman 1969-78; Chairman, South Kensington Young Conservatives; City University, London. *Publications:* Contributor to journals, conferences on environmental insurance and underground space projects; Creator, Ecclesiastical Professional indemnity for Religous denominations. *Hobbies:* Study of Arctic and Collector Inuit Works of Art; Collector of Antique Bottles. *Address:* Flat 3, 12 Abercorn Place, London, NW8, England.

MULLER, Gervase Edward, b. 26 Apr. 1936, Dublin, Ireland. Publisher. *Education:* Fellow, Institute of Directors; Fellow, The Institute of Marketing and Sales

Management; British Institute of Management; Member, Institution of Industrial Managers; Member, American Management Associations, International. *Appointments:* Director: Thomas Nelson, Limited, Nigeria, 1972-81; Thomson Books Limited, United Kingdom, 1976-79; Nelson Africa Limited, United Kingdom, 1972-74; Paper and Printing Supplies Limited, Malawi, 1968-71. *Memberships:* Royal Commonwealth Society; National Trust. *Hobbies:* Reading; Travel; Collecting. *Address:* 1c Albert Street, Stevenage Old Town, Herts, SG1 3NX, England.

MULLER, Ralph Louis, b. 30 June 1933, London, England. Zoologist. m. Annie Badilla, 26 July 1979, 1 son, 1 daughter. *Education:* BSc., Hons., 1955, PhD., 1958, London University, UK. *Appointments:* Scientific Officer, Colonial Office, UK, -1961; Lecturer, University of Ibadan, Nigeria, 1961-65; Senior Lecturer, School of Tropical Medicine and Hygiene, London, UK, 1966-79; Direcor, Commonwealth Institute of Parasitology, England. *Memberships:* Fellow, Royal Society Tropical Medicine and Hygiene. *Publications:* Worms and Disease, 1975; Editor, Advances in Parasitology. *Hobbies:* Photography; Tennis; Fottball. *Address:* 2 Rugby Mansions, London W 14, England.

MULLINGS, Peter Coningsby, b. 17 Dec. 1928, Ashton-upon-Mersey, Cheshire. Television Producer and Director. m. Barbara Greenhalgh, 11 Jan. 1965, 1 daughter. *Education:* St. Bede's College, Manchester. *Appointments:* Various Appointments, Professional Theatre, 1946-; Stage Manager, BBC TV, 1952; Associated-Redifusion TV 1955; Senior Floor Manager, Granada Television 1956; Programme Director 1959; Producer/Director, 1964; Director of Filming and Executive Producer, Materials Science Films, Pennsylvania State University and Massachusets Institute of Technology, 1971-72; Senior Programme Director and Producer, 1972-. *Memberships:* Savage Club; Royal Institution of Great Britain; British Academy of Film and Television Arts; Chairman, 1973-, Manchester and District Cinema and Television Benevolent Fund Committee. *Publications:* Chapter on, Stage Lighting, in Handbook for the Amateur Theatre; Articles in Amateur Photographer, Coins, BAFTA Journal. *Honours:* Member, Order of the British Empire, 1981; What the Papers Say, Award, 1977. *Hobbies:* Photography; Numismatics. *Address:* 2 Penrith Avenue, Sale, Cheshire, M33 3FN, England.

MULLINS, Geoffrey Charles, b. 29 Oct. 1943, Melbourne, Australia. Medical Practitioner. m. 8 Jan. 1968, 2 sons, 2 daughters. *Education:* MB., BS., 1967, FFARACS., 1972, Melbourne University, Australia. *Appointments:* Resident Medical Officer, Royal Hobart Hospital, Tasmania, Australia, 1968-69; Medical Registrar, Sir Charles Gairdner Hospital, Western Australia, 1970; Anaesthetic Registrar, St. Vincents Hospital, Melbourne, Australia, 1971; Anaesthetic Registrar, 1972, Medical Officer, 1973-75, Director, 1975-81, Intensive Care Unit, Royal Children's Hospital, Melbourne, Australia. *Memberships:* Australian Society of Anaesthestist; Australian College of Paediatrics; Australian New Zeland Intensive Care Society; Western Pacific Association of Critical care Medicine. *Honours:* Victorian Father of the Year, 1977. *Hobbies:* Jogging; Swimming; Cycling; Literature. *Address:* c/o Intensive Care Unit, Hospital for Sick Children, 555 University Avenue, Toronto, Ontario, Canada M5G 1X8.

MULOKOZI, Mugyabuso Mlinzi, b. 7 June 1950, Bukoba, Tanzania. Research Fellow, Literature. m. Helena Daudi, 1975, 2 sons, 1 daughter. *Education:* Bachelor of Arts, Education, 1975; MA Candidate, Literature, University of Dar es Salaam; Trainee, Publishing and Printing, Liber Grafiska A.B Sweden, 1977. *Appointments:* Editor, Tanzania Publishing House, 1975-79; Assistant Research Fellow, 1979-80, Research Fellow, Institute of Kiswahili Research, University of Dar es Salaam, 1980-. *Memberships:* Tanzania Writers Union. *Publications:* Mashairi ya Kisasa, an anthology of Poetry, 1973; Malenga wa Bara, an anthology of Poetry, 1976; Mukwava wa Uhehe, a play, 1979; Kunga za Ushairi na Diwani Yetu, (Prosody and Our Anthology). *Honours:* Prize for second overall final year best student in the faculty of Arts and Social Sciences, 1975; Prize for Best Final Year Education Student 1975; Ford Foundation Research Award 1978-79. *Hobbies:* Reading; Writing Poetry; Cinema

and Theatre; Gardening. *Address:* PO Box 876, Bukoba, Tanzania.

MUNATAMBA, Parnwell Mwando, b. 10 Feb. 1948, Kabwe, Zambia. Lecturer. m. Liseli, 28 Aug. 1976, 2 sons, 1 daughter. *Education:* BA., University of Zambia, 1970; Diplome D'Etudes Superieures, 1973, Licence es Lettres, 1973, Maitrise es Lettres, 1975, Doctorat es Lettres, 1979, Universite de Grenoble III, France. *Appointments:* Teacher, Secondary School, 1971-72; Lecturer, Head, Literature and Languages, University of Zambia, 1976-81. *Memberships:* Founder Chairman, Tikwiza Theatre Club; Lusaka Theatre Club; Zambia Writers Association. *Publications:* Articles on Theatre; My Battle Cry, Collection of Poems, 1981. *Creativo Works:* Principal roles in: Che Guevara; Trials of Dedan Kimathi; Houseboy. *Hobbies:* Tennis; Drama; Writing. *Address:* Plot 5771, Kabompo Close, Kalundu, Lusaka, Zambia.

MUNGAI, Evelyn Karungari, b. 14 May 1944, Lower Kabete. Company Chairman (President). m. Arthur Wagithuku Mungai 2 Jan. 1965, 1 son, 1 daughter. *Education:* Mary Leakey Girls School; Kianda Finishing Cshool. *Appointments:* Private Secretary, E A Common Services Organisation, 1963, Assistant Recruitment Officer, Personal Assistant, Firestone E A; Managing Director, Speedway Secretarial Bureau, 1970-78; Company Chairman, (President), Speedway Investments Limited 1978-. *Memberships:* National Council of Women of Kenya; Nairobi Business and Professional Women's Club; Board of Governors, Kiambu Institute of Science and Technology. *Publications:* Publisher, a local Woman's Magazine; Journal Publications Committee, Chairman of the National Council of Women of Kenya. *Hobbies:* Swimming; Squash; Reading; Cooking. *Address:* PO Box 10988, Nairobi, Kenya.

MUNGAI, Joseph James, b. 24 Oct. 1943, Iringa Tanzania. Politician. m. Mary Chawe 15 June 1965, 3 sons, 1 daughter. *Education:* Diploma in Economics, University of Colorado USA; Master of Public Administration, Harvard University. *Appointments:* Training and Development Manager, Singer Sewing Machine Company, Tanzania, 1965-69; General Manager, Tanzania Educational Supplies Limited, 1970-72; Minister for Agriculture, Tanzania Government, 1973-75; General Manager, Sugar Development Corporation, 1976-79; Minister for Agriculture, 1980-. *Hobbies:* Plays; Squash; Dancing. *Address:* PO Box 24, Mafinga, Tanzania.

MUNRO, John George Clarke, b. 2 Jan. 1928, Aberdeenshire, Scotland. Medical Practitioner. m. Muriel Joy Webster, 7 Dec. 1955, 3 sons, 1 daughter. *Education:* BSc., 1944-47, MB., Ch.B., 1948-54, University of Aberdeen, UK; FRACGP., 1974. *Appointments:* House Physician, Royal Aberdeen Hospital for Sick Children, UK, House Surgeon, Aberdeen Royal Infirmary, UK, 1954-55; Lecturer, Materda Medica, University of Aberdeen, UK, 1955-56; General Practice: Coventry, UK, 1956-63; Nambour, Queensland, Australia, 1963-75; St. Lucia, Brisbane, Australia, 1975-76; Senior Lecturer, Community Practice, 1976-, Head of Department, Social and Preventive Medicine, 1978-, University of Queensland, Australia. *Memberships:* Australian Sports Medicine Federation; Australian and New Zealand Society for Epidemiology and Research in Community Health; Education Committee of Council, Board of Examiners, Royal College of General Practitioners. *Publications:* number of published papers on a variety of medical and educational topics. *Hobbies:* Music; Sport; Birdwatching. *Address:* 15 Sutton Street, Chelmer, Brisbane, Queensland 4068, Australia.

MUNRO, Robert (Sir), b. 2 Apr. 1907, Remuera, Auckland New Zealand. President of the Fiji Senate. m. Ragnhilde Mee, 1937, 2 sons, 1 daughter. *Education:* Auckland University College, New Zealand. *Appointments:* Private practice, Barrister and Solicitor, Suva, Fiji, 1934; Chairman, Suva Carnegie Library Committee, 1942-47; Fiji Education Board and Education Advisory Council, 1943-70; Fiji Legislative Council, 1945-46; Foundation Chairman: Fiji Town Planning Board, 1946-53; Fiji Broadcasting Commission, 1953-61; Norwegian Consul for Fiji, Gilbert and Ellice Islands Colony, Phoeniz Islands and Tonga, 1948-; Notary Public, 1951; President, Fiji Law Society, 1960-62, 1967-69; President, Family Planning Association of Fiji, 1963-; Governing body of International Planned

Parenthood Federation, and E & S E A & O. Regional vice-president, I P P F., 1973; Fiji Government representative, ECAFE, Bangkok, regional pre-consultation World Population Conference and at World Population Conference, Bucharest, Hungary, 1974; East Asian & Pacific Copyright Seminar, Sydney, Australia, 1976; Fiji National Health Advisory Committee, 1976-; Presiding Officers' and Clerks' Conferences, Suva, 1971, Perth, Western Australia, 1972, Rarotonga, 1976, Apia, 1977; Fifth Conference of Commonwealth Speakers and Presiding Officers, Canberra, Australia, 1978, Ottawa, Canada, 1981; International Conference of Parliamentarians on Population and Development, Colombo, India, 1979; 1st Lieutenant, F M F., 1940-46. *Memberships:* Grand Inspector, Fiji Masonic Lodges, E C., 1950-76. *Honours:* Knight Bachelor, 1977; CBE., 1962; Order of St. Olav, Norway, 1966; Rifle Shooting Blue; Captain, New Zealand Hockey team, 1932. *Hobbies:* Law and literature; Music; Gardening. *Address:* Foulis, 6 Milne Road, Muanikau, Suva, Fiji.

MUNSHI, Aziz Ahmed, b. 10 June 1940, Ahmednagar, Maharashtra, India. Educator (Rural Social Work). m. Hasina, 19 Nov. 1978. *Education:* BA(Hons.) 1961; MA (Social Work), 1966. *Appointments:* Extension Work, 1967, Lecturer, Centre for Studies in Rural Development, 1969; Officer, Special Duty, National Service Scheme, Pune and M'wada University, 1970; Maharashtra State Liaoson Officer for Volunteers to Refugee Camp Mana, India, 1971; Maharashtra State Prog-Co-ordinator for National Service Scheme, M.S. India, 1973; Head, Department of Social Work, Centre for Studies in Rural Development A'Nagar College, A'Nagar, 1975. *Memberships:* Lions Club of Ahmednagar; Ahmednagar Football Association; Ahmednagar Anti T.B. Association. *Publications:* Training Camps on the National Schemes for College Students, 1971; Health Service Projects under the National Service Scheme; Emerging Pattern of the N.S.S., 1974; Recreation as a means of Social Development, 1974; Laman Child—My future, Samaj Seva, Silver Jubilee Special Issue on Child Welfare 1975; Planning Curriculum Through N.S.S. Experience, 1976; Some Guidelines for Starting—Centres of Learning, 1978; Training Social Workers for Rural Development, 1980. *Hobbies:* Sports and Games. *Address:* Bungalow No. 10, Aurangabad Road, Ahmednagar (M.S.) India

MUNYENYEMBE, Stanford Frank Changara, b. 27 Nov. 1948, Kopa-Kopa Village, Nthalire, Chitipa, Malawi, Africa. Lawyer. m. Ainah Mukonda, 3 Mar. 1976, 2 daughters. *Education:* Diploma, Public Administration, 1972, BL., 1977, University of Malawi; Certificate, Legislative Drafting, Nairobi, Kneya, 1979. *Appointments:* Attorney General's Office, Lilongwe, Malawi, 1977-78, 1979-80; Department of Legal Aid, 1978-79; Principal Magistrate, Judiciary, 1980-. *Memberships:* Chairman, 1975-77, Chancellor College Student's Law Society; Malawi Law Society. *Publications:* Articles for Student's Law Society Journal. *Honours:* Awarded Diploma in Public Administration, with credit, 1972. *Hobbies:* Music; Reading; Football. *Address:* Kopa-Kopa Village, PA Nthalire, Chitipa, Malawi, Africa.

MUPAWOSE, Robbie Matongo, b. 30 July 1935, Mrewa, Zimbabwe. Agronomist. m. 21 Dec., 2 sons, 2 daughters. *Education:* BSc., Pius XII College, Lesotho, 1962; MS.(Agronomy), Davis University of California, USA, 1967; Post Graduate Studies in Research Techniques, 1968. *Appointments:* Science Master, Goromonzi and Mpopoma, 1962-65; Lecturer, Crop Production, Chibero College, 1968-70; Senior Research Officer, Lowveld Research Station, 1970-77; Group Agriculturist, General Manager, Tilcor, 1977-. *Memberships:* President, International Club, Davis, California,USA; Vice-Chairman,Christian Care; Vice-President, Crop Science Society of Zimbabwe; Chairman, Baines Avenue, Cheshire Homes, Zimbabwe. *Publications:* Sesame; Yield Improvement in Maize, Rice and Groundnuts grown on Chisumbarye Basalt Soils; The Resource Environment for Rural Development in Zimbabwe. *Hobbies:* Tennis; Gardening. *Address:* 45 Stonechat Lane, Borrowdale, Salisbury, Zimbabwe.

MURPHY, Lionel Keith, b. 31 Aug. 1922, Australia. Justice of the High Court of Australia. m. Ingrid Gee, 19 Nov. 1969, 2 sons, 1 daughter. *Education:* BSc., LL.B., University of Sydney, Australia. *Appointments:* Admit-

ted to NSW Bar, 1947, Victorian Bar, 1958, QC., New South Wales, 1960, Victoria, 1961; Senator in Federal Parliament, 1962-75; Leader, Opposition in Senate, 1967-72; Leader of Government in Senate, 1972-75; Attorney-General of Australia and Minister for Customs and Excise, 1972-75; Justice of the High Court of Australia, 1975-. *Memberships:* Member Australian Labour Party Federal Executive, 1967-75; Australian Labour Party Federal Conference, 1967-75; Delegate to United Nations Conference on Human Rights, Tehran, 1968; Member, Council of the Australian National University, 1969-73;, Australian Parliamentary Delegation o Australian Constitutional Convention, 1973; Initiated legislative reforms i human rights, family law, anti-trust, consumer protection; Represented Australia at International Court of Justice Nuclear Tests Case, 1973-74. *Hobbies:* Water skiing; Gardening; Tennis. *Address:* High Court of Australia, Canberra, ACT 2600, Australia.

MURRAY, Alasdair Macdougall, b. 11 June 1943, Rothesay, Scotland, United Kingdom. Geologist. m. Eileen Inglis Percy, 8 Feb. 1971, 1 son, 1 daughter. *Education:* MA., BSc.(Hons.), Edinburgh University, Scotland, 1960-67. *Appointments:* Field Geologist, Papua, New Guinea, Solomon Islands, Western Australia, 1967-73; Mining Geologist, 1974-80, Mine Production and Planning Supervisor, 1980-, Alcoa of Australia. *Memberships:* Associate member, Australasian Institute of Mining and Metallurgy; Secretary, 1975-80, Director of Variable Star Section, 1978-, Astronomical Society of Western Australia; Geological Society of Australia; Royal Astronomical Society of New Zealand. *Publications:* Dasrling Range Bauxites, 1976; Bauxites in WA; Mining and Processing of Bauxite,(with E A Kirke), 1979. *Honours:* Scout Association BP Award, 1964; Scout Association Medal for Meritorious Conduct, 1965; Astronomical Society of Western Australia Trophy, 1980. *Hobbies:* Amateur Astronomy; Bush walking. *Address:* 18 Reveley Street, Safety Bay, Western Australia.

MURRAY, (Alice) Rosemary, b. 28 July 1913, Havant, England. *Education:* MA., 1936, DPhil., 1937, BSc., 1934, Lady Margaret Hall, Oxford University, UK. *Appointments:* Lecturer in Chemistry: Royal Holloway College, UK, 1938; University of Sheffield, UK, 1941; Experimental Officer, Admiralty Signals Establishment, UK, 1940; WRNS., 1942; Girton College, 1946, New Half, 1954-, Vice Chancellor, 1975-77, University of Cambridge, UK. *Honours:* DBE., 1977; Hon. DSc.: New University of Ulster, UK, 1972; Leeds University, UK, University of Pennsylvania, USA, 1975; Wellesley College, USA, 1976; Hon. DCL., Oxford University, UK, 1976; Hon. DL., University S. California, USA; Hon. LL.D., University of Sheffield, UK, 1977; Justice of the Peace, City of Cambridge, UK, 1953-. *Address:* New Hall, Cambridge University, England.

MURRAY, Angus, b. 9 Mar. 1919, Scotland, United Kingdom. Business Consultant; Director of Companies. m. Dorothy Anne Walker, 3 Jan. 1950, 2 sons. *Education:* BSc.(Hons.), Mech. Eng., Glasgow University, Scotland; C.Eng., F I Mech.E., CBIM., University of Strathclyde, Scotland. *Appointments:* P E Consulting Group; Expert Tool Group Limited; Tap and Die Corporation; Umbrako Limited; H H Robertson Pty(South Africa)Limited; Metal Sales Co.(Pty)Limited; Chairman: Backer Electric Co. Limited, Crane Fruehauf Limited, Newall Machine Tool Co. Limited; Director of: Newman Industries Limited, Doulton & Co. Limited, Hambros Industrial Management Limited, Sandvik Limited; Chairman of Candover Investments Limited, Redman Heenan International Limited, relinquishing his appointment as Chief Executive of this latter company-,Sept.1976; Deputy Chairman (formerly Chairman), Fairey Holdings Limited. *Memberships:* Advisory Panel to Electra Fund Managers Limited; Committee, Management, Institute of Obstetrics and Gynaecology; Vice-President, Institution of Industrial Managers. *Honours:* Military Cross and Bar. *Hobbies:* Golf; Music. *Address:* Atholl House, Church Lane, Stoke Poges, Buckinghamshire SL2 4NZ, England.

MURRAY (Hon.Justice), Kemeri Ann, b. 28 Jan. 1932, Adelaide, South Australia. Judge. m. Eric Murray, 10 Sept. 1955, 1 son, 1 daughter. *Education:* BA., 1953, LL.B., 1954, A.Mus.A., 1954, Adelaide University, Australia. *Appointments:* Admitted to Bar, S A Sup. Court, 1955; Private practice, 1955-73; Judge, Local and District Criminal Court, 1973; S A Family Court, 1973; Judge, Family Court of Australia, 1976. *Memberships:* Council of Flinders University of South Australia; Chairman, S A Community Welfare Committee; Accidental Injury to Children; Chairman, Interim Bread Industry Authority; Family and Child Welfare Committee of Australian Council Social Services; Church of England Social Responsibilities Commission; Board of Management, Flinders Medical Centre; Commonwealth Government Advisory Council, Intergovernment Relations; Church of England Diocesan Social Questions Committee. *Honours:* Queen's Silver Jubilee Medal, 1976. *Hobbies:* Classical Music; Biography. *Address:* c/o Judges' Chambers, Box 9991, GPO, Adelaide, South Australia 5001.

MURRAY, William Edward, b. 16 Feb. 1920, Leichhardt, New South Wales, Australia. Catholic Bishop. *Education:* Education for Priesthood, Saint Columba's Seminary, Springwood, New South Wales, Saint Patrick's Seminary, Manly, New South Wales, Australia; Doctorate in Social Sciences, Gregorian University, Rome, Italy, 1958. *Appointments:* Ordained Priest, Archdiocese, Sydney, Australia, 1945; Assistant priest in parishes of Bondi, Rockdale, Elizabeth Bay, Meadowbank, Dulwich Hill, Australia; Sydney Matrimonial Tribunal, 1950; Studies at Gregorian University, Rome, 1955-58; Director, Catholic Information Bureau, Sydney, Australia, 1958-67; Parish Priest, Broadway, Sydney, Director of Continuing Theological Education of the Clergy, 1967-73; Rector of St. Columba's Seminary, Springwood, New South Wales, Australia, 1973-75; Bishop of Wollongong, New South Wales, Australia, 1975-. *Publications:* Doctoral thesis: An Examination of the Australian Immigration Legislation, Policy and Programme in the Light of the Principles of the United Nations Organization on Migration. *Honours:* The 1958 Silver Medal 'Bene Merenti', from Gregorian University, Rome for thesis. *Hobbies:* Reading; Walking; Tennis; Swimming. *Address:* Bishop's House, PO Box 1254, Wollongong, New South Wales, Australia 2500.

MURRAY, Winston Churchill, b. 29 Nov. 1934, Tobago, West Indies. Member of Parliament. 2 daughters. *Education:* BA., Spanish Howard University, Washington, USA, 1959; MA., Diplomacy, Georgetown University, Washington, USA, 1963; PhD., American University, Washington, USA, 1970. *Appointments:* Consultant to US Peace Corps; Instructor, Howard University, USA; Assistant Professor, Morgan State University, USA; Assistant Professor, US Military Intelligence College; Foreign Service Officer, Trinidad, Tobago; Member of Parliament; President, Tobago Marketing Cooperative Society Limited. *Memberships:* ETA Sigma Phi; Phi Sigma Alpha; American Academy of Political and Social Science; Gulf and Caribbean Fisheries Institute; International Studies Association. *Publications:* Politics of the Disposed, 1976; Gagged: The Suspension of Dr. Winston Murray APT 'Fargo' James, Governor of Tobago. *Hobbies:* Fishing; Gardening. *Address:* Fargo House, Golden Grove Road, Canaan, Tobago, West Indies.

MURRAY-JONES, Paul Johnnie, b. 26 Sept. 1921, Southsea, Hampshire, England. Naval Officer. m. (1) E A Grayburn, 17 July, 1943, (2) P A Anderson, 1 June, 1972, 2 sons, 2 daughters. *Education:* Royal Naval College, Dartmouth, UK, 1935-38. *Appointments:* Submarines, 1941-61, Royal Navy, 1938-62; Chas. Fulton & Co., Foreign Exchange Brokers, 1962-65; Managing Director, P Murray-Jones International Limited, Foreign Exchange Brokers, 1976-76; Managing Director, Guardforce Limited, 1976-. *Memberships:* Army and Navy Club, Pall Mall; Worshipful Co. of Shipwrights; Freeman of City of London; Royal Naval Sailing Association; Royal Malta Yacht Club; Royal Hong Kong Yacht Club. *Honours:* Mentioned in Despatches, 1944. *Hobbies:* Yachting; Golf; Tennis; Photography; Sub Aqua diving. *Address:* 12 Shek O, Hong Kong.

MURTY, Dangety Satyanarayana, b. 28 Dec. 1927, Visakhapatnam, India. Professor of Physics. m. Krishna Kumari, 11 May 1952, 2 sons, 2 daughters. *Education:* BSc., 1948, MSc., 1951, DSc., 1956, Andhra University, India; MA., Madras University, India, 1950. *Appointments:* Lecturer, Applied Physics, Andhra University, India, 1952-60; Associate Professor and Acting Head, Physics Department, Texas Southern University, Houston, Texas, USA, 1960-63; Associate Professor and Chairman, 1963-69, Professor and Chairman, 1969-72, Professor of Physics, 1972-, Saint Mary's University, Halifax, Nova Scotia, Canada. *Memberships:* Fellow, Institution of Electronic and Radio Engineers, London, England; Fellow, Institution of Electrical Engineers, London, England; Chartered Engineer, Council of Engineering Institutions, London, England; Canadian Association of Physicists, Ottawa, Canada. *Publications:* Approximately 30 research publications in Ionosphere Physics, Mossbauer Effect and Low Energy Nuclear Physics. *Honours:* Colombo Plan Scholar, London, England, 1957-58. *Hobbies:* Tennis; Gardening. *Address:* 1123 Belmont on the Arm, Halifax, Nova Scotia, Canada B3H 1J2.

MURUMBI, Joseph Anthony, b. 18 June 1911, Eldama Ravine, Kenya. m. Sheila Ann Kaine. *Education:* St. Joseph College, Bangalore. *Appointments:* Controller of Imports and Exports, British Military Administration, Somalia; Acting Secretary General, Kenya African Union, 1952; Assistant Secretary, Movement for Colonial Freedom, London, UK, 1952-58; Assistant Press Officer, Moroccan Embassy, London, UK, 1958-62; Treasurer and Organizer, Kenya African National Union, 1962-63; Minister of State, 1963; Minister of Foreign Affairs, 1964-65; Vice-President, 1965; Chairman, Rothmans, Kenya, 1966-. *Memberships:* East African Study Aide, London, UK. *Honours:* Decorations, Humane Order African Redemption, Liberia; Order Nationale, Madagascar; Order National Leopard, Zaire; Ethiopian Order. *Hobbies:* Stamp collecting; Photography; Gardening; Art collector; Book collector. *Address:* Intona Ranch, PO Kilgoris, Via Kisii, Kenya.

MUSGRAVE, (Frank) Cyril, b. 21 June 1900, Ealing, Middlesex, England. Retired. m. (1) Elsie Williams, 1924, dec'd; (2) Jean Soulsby, 1945, 3 sons, 1 daughter. *Appointments:* Entered Civil Service, 1919; Inland Revenue, 1920-37; Air Ministry, 1937-40; Ministry of Aircraft Production, 1940-46; Under Secretary, 1946-51, Deputy Secretary, 1951-53, Second Permanent Secretary, 1953-56, Permanent Secretary, 1956-59, Ministry of Supply; Chairman, Iron and Steel Board, 1959-67; Part-time member, British Steel Corporation, 1967-70; Director, various Companies, 1960-76. *Memberships:* Founder member, British Migraine Trust, 1966. *Honours:* CB., 1946; Knight Commander Order of the Bah, 1955. *Hobbies:* Gardening; Music. *Address:* Black Horse Cottage, Towersey, Thame, Oxfordshire OX9 3QR, England.

MUSGROVE, John Panton, b. 27 Jan. 1931, Christchurch, New Zealand. Family Doctor. m. Olwyn Grace Mason, 28 June 1958, 1 son, 1 daughter. *Education:* MB., Ch.B.(New Zealand), 1955, DCH.(RCP & RCS), 1962, MRCGP., 1963, FRCGP., 1973, FRNZCGP., 1974, Otago University Medical School, Dunedin, New Zealand. *Appointments:* General Practice, Christchurch, New Zealand, 1958-81; Clinical Lecturer, Christchurch Clinical School of Medicine, 1973-80; Interim Coordinator, Canterbury Family Medicine Training Programme, 1978-79. *Memberships:* Chairman, New Zealand Council, RCGP., 1973-74; Chairman, Council, RNZCGP., 1974-76; Chairman, Finance Committee, 1976-81; Chairman, Joint Advisory Committee, New Zealand Family Medicine Training Programme, 1978-80; Auditor, Canterbury Division, New Zealand Medical Association, 1970-81. *Publications:* Articles in New Zealand Medical Journal, New Zealand Family Physician. *Honours:* Ardagh Memorial Prize, Christchurch Hospital, 1955; MSD Fellowship in Family Medicine (RNZCGP), 1974. *Hobbies:* Gardening; Golf; Jogging; Pottery. *Address:* Ilam Medical Centre, 106 Memorial Avenue, Christchurch 5, New Zealand.

MUSISI, Jafred Shalimba, b. 7 Jan. 1934, Kakamega. Librarian. m. Peruce Ikambili, 2 May 1959, 4 sons, 5 daughters. *Education:* Diploma in Librarianship, Makerere University, Kenya; Masters in Library Studies, Loughborough University, UK. *Appointments:* Ministry of Agriculture Library, 1956-69; Nation Newspapers Library, 1970-74; McMillan Memorial Library, 1975; Kenya Science Teachers College, USTC., 1976-. *Memberships:* Kenya Library Association; Standing Conference, Eastern Central and Southern Africa; Commonwealth Library Association Executive Committee. *Publications:* Several articles in Professional journals. *Hobbies:* Soccer; Music; Reading; Writing. *Address:* PO Box 48832, Nairobi, Kenya.

MUSLIM, Mohammed, b. 22 July 1939, Malaysia. Air Force Officer. m. Hamsiah, 27 June 1963, 2 daughters. *Education:* HSC., Royal Military College, Port Dickson, Malaysia, 1958; HND., Electrical Engineering, RAF Technical College, Henlow, UK, 1962. *Appointments:* OCE & I Flt., 1963; SO3 Trg.Mindef (Air), 1965; S Eng O FTS Alor Star, 1967; RAF Staff College, Andover, UK, 1969; S Eng O Labuan, 1970; SOI Eng Mindef (Air), 1971; Dir Eng Mindef (Air), 1973; National Defence College, new Delhi, India, 1978; Project Leader, RMAF Support Command, 1979; AOC, RMAF Support Command, 1980. *Memberships:* President, 1973,74, RMC Old Boys Association; Secretary, 1977, Pudu Rotary Club; President, 1979, Academy of Malay Technologists; Board of Engineers Malaysia; Royal Aeronautical Society, London; Institution of Electrical Engineers, London. *Honours:* Kesatria Mangku Negara, 1976; Setia Mahkota Selangor, 1981. *Hobby:* DIY. *Address:* 134 Taman Perwire Dua, Ampang Jaya, Kuala Lumpur 19-03, Malaysia.

MUSS, Martin Peter Maria, b. 25 Oct. 1941, Delmenhorst, Germany. Company Executive. m. 27 Jan. 1968, 2 sons. *Education:* Certificate of German Clerk Academy. *Appointments:* Sales Manager, Weyhausen Atlas Inc., Caldwell, New Jersey, USA, 1964-65; General Manager, Atlas Hydraulic Loaders Limited, Vere Road, Blackwood, Scotland, 1965-71; Chairman, Managing Director of: Hydraulic Breakers (Scotland) Limited, 1971-, Hydraulic Cranes (Scotland) Limited, 1971-, Hyscot Group, Strathclyde, Scotland, 1975-. *Memberships:* Past President, Kopling Club, Delmenhorst, Germany. *Honours:* Freedom of Village, Neu-Philately; Tennis. *Address:* The Whitehouse, Broompark Drive, Lesmahagow, Strathclyde, Scotland.

MUSTAPHA, Akeem Olabode, b. 12 Mar. 1950, Ibadan, Nigeria. Advertising; Public Relations. m. Olufadekemi, 25 Aug. 1979, 1 son, 1 daughter. *Education:* Diploma, Retailing, 1976; Diploma, Financial Management, 1977. *Appointments:* Intermediate Manager, Karstadt Group, Hamburg, West Germany; Department Store Manager, Vic. Nigeria Limited, Ibadan, Nigeria; President, Labod Advertising Limited, Ibadan, Nigeria. *Publications:* Paper on Retailing in Nigeria. *Honours:* National runner-up, Young Managers Competition, 1977. *Hobbies:* Table tennis; Lawn tennis. *Address:* 18 Fagbemi Road, New Reservation, Ibadan, Nigeria.

MUTASA, Didymus Noel Edwin, b. 27 July 1935, Rusape Zimbabwe. Social Scientist. m. (1) Flora Musengezi, 23 Nov. 1959, (2) Gertruge Munonyara, 16 Oct. 1972, 3 sons, 2 daughters. *Education:* Bachelor of Social Science, 1976. *Appointments:* Speaker, National Assembly of Zimbabwe. *Publications:* Black Rhodesians Behind Bars, 1974. *Honours:* Gold Medal award, Birmingham University, UK, 1980. *Hobby:* Farming. *Address:* 3D16, Chishawasha Road, Sby Salisbury, Zimbabwe.

MUTEMBA, Anrew Bwalya, b. 12 Aug. 1929, Kasama, Northern Province, Zambia. Zambian High Commissioner. m. Agnes Bwalya, 6 sons, 5 daughters. *Education:* Diploma, Administrative course, Oxford University, UK, 1961; Diploma, African History and Political Science, American University, USA, 1969-70. *Appointments:* Minister of State in following places and Ministries: Copperbelt Province, Cooperative, Youth and Social Services; Information, Broadcasting and Tourism, Education, 1963-; Zambian Ambassador Extra Ordinary and Plenipotentiary to: Kingdom of Ethiopia, USA; Non Resident Ambassador, Extra Ordinary and Plenipotentiary to: Sudan, Somalia, Chile, Peru Brazil, Guine, Ghana, Sierra Leone, Liberia, Senegal, Niger, Ivory Coast, The Gambia, Cameroons; Chief Administrative Secretary, Ruling Party United National Independence Party; Director of: Zambia Trade Fair, Northern Electricity Corporation; Chairman and Director of Zambia Youth Service; Serving in Zambia Cabinet; Zambia High Commissioner to Federal Republic of Nigeria. *Memberships:* Zambia National Cultural Commission; International University Service, Zambia Branch; Chairman, Southern Province Political Committee; Chairman, Southern Province Development Committee; Central Committee Ruling Party, United National Independence Party, Zambia; Chairman, Youth and Sports Committee, UNIP Central Committee. *Address:* PO Box 6119, Lagos, Nigeria.

MUTHU-BABU, Gangadhara-Konar, b. 7 June 1932, Gooty, India. Livestock Specialist. m. Kanakavalli, 3 Feb. 1956, 3 daughters. *Education:* BVSc., 1953; MVSc., 1973. *Appointments:* Veterinary Surgeon, Assistant Director, Government of Tamil Nadu; Deputy Director, Technical, ARDC., Reserve Bank of India; Animal Husbandry Officer, Republic of Zambia. *Memberships:* Tamil Nadu Veterinary Council, India; Registered Veterinary Surgeon, Republic of Zambia. *Publications:* Heritability Estimates of certain economic traits in Poultry. *Hobbies:* International living; Outdoor life; Cooking; Listening BBC World Service. *Address:* Box 72219, Ndola, Zambia.

MUTHUKUMAR, R, b. 2 July 1953, Salem Town, India. *Education:* Diploma in Rural Services, National Council for Rural Higher Education, New Delhi, India; Master of Commerce, Commercial University, New Delhi, India. *Appointments:* Manager, Cooperative Store; Purchaser-in-charge, Textile Processing Mill; Accountant, Engineering Company. *Memberships:* Fellow member, All India Commercial Association, New Delhi, India. *Hobbies:* Reading; Meeting Friends; Films. *Address:* s/o M. Rajagiopal, 151 Ambalavanasamy Koil Street, Gidgai, Salem 6, Tamil Nadu, South India.

MUYELA, Ezekiel Lafont, b. 18 July 1931, Bunyore, Kenya. m. Josephine Atuo, 24 Dec. 1978, 1 son. *Education:* BSc., Librarianship, 1969. *Appointments:* Chief Personnel Officer, E A Oxygen; Assistant Librarian, Kenya Polytechnic; Secretary to the Mayor; Acting Librarian, MOH Medical Research Library; Librarian, MOH Medical Training Centre, Nairobi; Librarian, MOH Medical Training Centre, Nakuru, Kenya. *Memberships:* Kenya Library Association; AFYA Co-operative Society; NGA Brotherhood Society; Elwasi Welfare Society. *Honours:* History, 1967; Geography, 1968. *Hobbies:* Religious Knowledge; Football. *Address:* Medical Training Centre, PO Box 10042, Nakuru, Kenya.

MUZE, Mishael Shogholo, b. 20 Nov. 1933, Suji, Tanzania. Commissioner for National Education. m. Siphiwe Mashengele, 4 June, 1966, 1 son, 2 daughters. *Education:* BA., Mathematics-major, 1964; MA., Education, 1966. *Appointments:* Head of Mathematics Department, Shinyanga Secondary School, 1966-68; Headmaster, Mwenge Secondary School, 1969-73; Curriculum Developer, Institute of Education, 1973-75; Lecturer, University of Dar es Salaam, 1975-78; Commissioner for National Education, 1978-. *Memberships:* Chairman, 1975, 76, Mathematical Association of Tanzania; National Council of Teachers of Mathematics, USA. *Publications:* Chapters in Secondary Mathematics, Tanzania, books 1-4; number of articles on Mathematics and Education in various journals; Multiple Choice Questions in Secondary Mathematics. *Hobbies:* Photography; Gardening; Squash. *Address:* Box 9121, Dar Es Salaam, Tanzania.

MWACALIMBA, Hudwell, b. 10 Jan. 1948, Ntitima Village, Kabwe, Zambia. Library Educator. m. 3 May 1975, 2 sons, 1 daughter. *Education:* BA., University of Zambia, 1968-72; MSLS., Syracuse University, New York, USA, 1973-74; Certificate, Library Management, 1977-78, DLIS., 1977-81, University of California, Berkeley, USA. *Appointments:* Assistant Librarian, 1974-75, Lecturer, Department of Library Studies, 1975-, University of Zambia; Lecturer and Head, Department of Library Studies, 1981-. *Memberships:* Zambia Library Association; American Library Association. *Publications:* A Design for Library Human Resource Development in Zambia, 1981; On Library Education, 1978. *Honours:* UNESCO Fellowship, 1973-74; Librarianship Doctoral Fellowships, University of California, Berkeley, USA, 1979•81. *Hobbies:* Photography; Music; Gardening. *Address:* University of Zambia, Department of Library Studies, PO Box 32379, Lusaka, Zambia.

MWAIPAYA, Paul Anyosisye, b. 28 Dec. 1945, Central-Southern Africa. Philosopher. m. 26 Aug. 1972, 2 sons. *Education:* Postdoctoral Fellow, Georg-August University, W. Germany 1976-77; Doctor of Philosophy (with distinction), Louvain University 1975; Magisterkonferens Artium, Aarhus University, Denmark, 1972; Bachelor of Arts, University of Pennsylvania, USA 1971. *Appointments:* Special Research Fellow in Human Relations, 1975-76, Founder of Philosophical Studies, University of Zambia, 1977-80; Associate Dean, Faculty of Humanities and Social Sciences, 1978-79; Member, University Senate, Zambia, 1977-

79; Member, Academic Board, Zambia, 1979-80; Senior Lecturer in Philosophy, University of Papua New Guinea, 1980-. *Memberships:* International Philosophical Society; East African Philosophical Society; University of Zambia Philosophical Association; Club Germania. *Publications:* Belief as the Foundation of Hume's Philosophical System, 1979; The Importance of Quality Leadership in National Development, with special reference to Africa, 1980; The Place and significance of belief in Hume's Philosophy, 1981; African Humanism, a critical analysis of the basic theoretical principle of Zambian Humanism, 1981; The Significance of Ethical Studies in Accounting Programmes, 1981; The Zambian Humanism, 1978; Death Hillock, 1968, etc. *Honours:* Phelps-Stoke Fund Scholarship, 1969-71; UN Award to attend a workshop in Human Relations 1969; Danish Government Postgtaduate Scholarship, 1972; Louvain Doctoral Research Grant 1972-75; Belgium Government Supplementary Research Grant, 1973-75; University of Zambia Postdoctoral Fellowship 1976-77; Chairman, Yagl-Ambu Editorial Board, University of Papua New Guinea, 1981-82. *Hobbies:* Politics; Reading; Music; Performing Arts. *Address:* University of Papua New Guinea, PO Box 4820, Department of Philosophy, Papua New Guinea.

MWALWENJE, Hilary Kennard, b. 29 Sept. 1945, Karonga, Malawi. Civil Engineering. m. Dora Victoria, 16 July 1971, 2 sons, 2 daughters. *Education:* BSc., Hatfield Polytechnic, UK, 1971; MSc., Purdue University, Indiana, USA, 1974; World Bank Economic Development Institute Fellowship, Project Management, 1978; Registered as Professional Engineer, 1975. *Appointments:* Design Engineer, 1971-72, Regional Construction and Maintenance Engineer, 1973-77, Development and Planning Engineer, 1977-78, Engineer;in-Chief, 1978-, Ministry of Works and Supplies, Malawi. *Memberships:* Chairman of: Malawi Board of Engineers; Consultants and Contractors Registration Board; Standards Advisory Committee, Board of Malawi Bureau of Standards; Malawi Polytechnic Board of Governors; Malawi Advisory Council on Technical Education; Former Treasurer, Malawi Students Association of UK and Eire, 1969-70. *Publications:* Training of Roads Personnel in Malawi; Application of Appropriate Technology in Road Construction and Maintenance in Malawi. *Honours:* Awarded 1st class prize of wrist watch, being the best student in Cambridge Overseas School Certificate examinations at Chaminade Secondary School, 1965. *Hobbies:* Soccer; Sports. *Address:* Katolola Village, PO Karonga, Malawi.

MWANZA, Jacob Mumbi, b. 2 Feb. 1937, Petanke. Economist. m. Elizabeth Maria, 30 Dec. 1964, 3 daughters. *Education:* MA Economics, University of Münster, West Germany, 1968; PhD Cornell University USA 1973. *Appointments:* Lecturer, Senior Lecturer, 1968-74; Head, Economics Department, University of Zambia, 1973-74; Managing Director, Zambia Energy Corporation, 1974-76; Vice-Chancellor, University of Zambia, 1976-. *Memberships:* UN Committee for Development Planning; Lusaka Flying Club; Economics Club; Council of University of Dar es Salaam. *Publications:* Rural-Urban Migration and Urbun Employment in Zambia, 1979; The Operation of Public Enterprises in Zambia, 1978; Oreinting Economics Teaching to Development needs, 1973. *Hobbies:* Fishing; Tennis. *Address:* Haundsworth Park, Lumubashi Road 1-5, Lusaka, Zambia.

MWAUNGULU, Dunstain Fipamutima, b. 11 June 1956, Iringa, Tanzania. Lowyer; Senior Resident Magistrate. *Education:* Bachelor of Law, University of Malawi 1978. *Appointments:* State Advocate, State Counsel/Attorney, 1978-81; Senior Resident Magistrate, 1981-. *Memberships:* Law Society of Malawi. *Hobbies:* Preaching; Singing; Badminton; Football. *Address:* Matete Village, V.H. Mwaungulu, PO Chiluluba, Malawi.

MWEMBA, Joseph Ben, b. 28 July 1917, Monze Zambia. Teacher; Diplomat and Politician. m. Norah Nompumelelo Solontsi, 31 Dec. 1952, 2 sons, 3 daughters. *Education:* BA, Dip.Ed, Fort Hare University College, 1952; Sp. Dip. in Secondary School Teaching, Ball State Teachers College, 1960; Dip. in Diplomacy, The American University, Washington DC, 1964. *Appointments:* Primary School Teacher, 1939-41 and 1947-

48; Secondary School Teacher 1952-60; Manager of Schools 1961; Education Officer, 1962-63; Permanent Secretary, Ministry of Education, 1965; Ambassador and Permanent Representative, UNO 1966-68; Com. for Tech. Education and Voc. Trg. 1969; Deputy Director, 1969-74; Member of Parliament, 1973-78; Minister of State 1974-78. *Memberships:* Northern Rhodesia Teachers Association; Commercial Farmers Bureau. *Publications:* Mubekwabekwa, 1957; Mukandeke, 1966; Munampande, 1978. Hobby: Photography. *Address:* PO Box 112, Mazabuka, Zambia.

MWIINGA, Bruno, b. 15 Mar. 1937, Chivuna. Teaching. m. Agnes Mainza, 20 June 1960, 3 sons, 5 daughters. *Education:* Certificate, Teacher Education, University of Queensland, Australia, 1970; BA., 1976; MA., 1980-81, University of Zambia. *Appointments:* Primary School Teacher, 1961-66; Lecturer, 1967-71, Vice-Principal, 1976-80, Principal, 1981-, Primary Teachers' College; Senior Primary Schools Inspector, 1972-76. *Memberships:* Zambia National Arts; Patron, College Drama Club. *Publications:* Cibuye Tapi, 1980; Maanu A Sulwe, 1977; Kweema Kwa Nakalindu, 1980. *Honours:* Certificate of Merit, Zambia Arts Festival, 1971. *Hobbies:* Chicken rearing; Book writing; Reading. *Address:* Inkuku Zya Mweenzuma, PO Box 304, Monze, Zambia.

MWIYERIWA, Steve Simon, b. 19 Mar. 1946. *Education:* Associate of the Library Association, 1972; Master of Library Science, 1980; Master of Arts, History, 1980; Fellow of the Library Association 1979. *Appointments:* Readers Advisor, University of Malawi Library, Chancellor College, 1971-73; Archivist, National Archives of Malawi, 1973-75; Government Archivist, National Archives of Malawi, 1976. *Memberships:* ECARBICA; International Council on Archives; Malawi Library Association; Society of American Archivists; The Library Association, London; Phi Alpha Theta. *Publications:* Vernacular Literature of Malawi, 1854-1975; Articles on publishing, Librarianship and Archives Science to: Society of Malawi Journal; ECARBICA Journal; Mala Bulletin; Africa Book Publishing Record. *Honours:* Oliver Wendell Holmes Award, Society of American Archivists, 1979. *Hobbies:* Photography; Swimming; Travel; Chess. *Address:* Nyalugwe Village, Nyalugwe F.P. School, PO Box 2, Namitambo, Limbe, Malawi.

MYERS, Rupert Horace (Sir), b. 21 Feb. 1921, Melbourne, Victoria, Australia. Commission Chairman and Company Director. m. Edwina King, 9 Dec. 1944, 1 son, 3 daughters. *Education:* BSc., 1942, MSc., 1943, PhD., 1947, CEng., University of Melbourne, Australia. *Appointments:* Commonwealth Research Fellow, University of Melbourne, Australia, 1942-47; Principal Research Officer, Harwell Atomic Energy Research Establishment, UK, 1947-52; Foundation Professor of Metallurgy, 1952-81, Dean, Faculty of Applied Science, 1956-61, Pro-Vice-Chancellor, 1961-69, Vice-Chancellor and Principal, 1969-81, University of New South Wales, Australia; Part-time Chairman, New South Wales State Pollution Control Commission, 1969-; Member, Sydney Opera House Trust, 1976-; Chairman, Committee of Inquiry into Technological Change in Australia, 1979-80; National Energy Advisory Committee, 1980-; Program Advisory Committee, Australian Railway Research and Development Organisation, 1980-; Australian Manufacturing Council, 1980-. *Memberships:* Fellow: Institution of Metallurgists; Royal Australian Chemical Institute; Australian Institute of Management; Australasian Institute of Mining and Metallurgy; Past President, Honorary Member, Australasian Institute of Metals; Australian Academy of Forensic Sciences; Australian and New Zealand Association for the Advancement of Science; Director, CSR Ltd.; Director, Energy Resources of Australia Ltd. *Publications:* Numerous publications and patents in extraction metallurgy, atomic energy and education; Report of the Committee of Inquiry into Technological Change in Australia, 1980. *Honours:* CBE., 1976; KBE, 1981; Honorary DLitt., University o New South Wales, Australia, 1981; Hon DEng., University of Newcastle, (NSW) Australia, 1981. Hon. DSc, University of Wollongong, Australia, 1976; Hon. LLD., University of Strathclyde, UK, 1973; Fellow, Australian Academy of Technological Science. *Hobbies:* Tennis; Music; Silvercraft. *Address:* 135 Neerim Road, Castlecove, New South Wales 2069, Australia.

MYLONA, Lia, b. 15 Apr. 1931, Cyprus. Personnel Manager. *Education:* MA, Social Science Certificate, University of Edinburgh, 1951-55. *Appointments:* Welfare Officer, Cyprus Social Services, 1956-60; Senior Industrial Relations Officer, Cyprus Employers' Association, 1962-67; Personnel Manager, Lanitis Brothers Limited, Coca-Cola, 1967-70; Personnel Manager, Cyprus Petroleum Refinery Limited, 1970-. *Memberships:* Cyprian Association, Equal Rights/Equal Responsibilitie; Socio-Psychological Research Group; Industrial Tribunal; Cyprus Employers Federation. *Publications:* Socio-Psychological Problems of the Refugees of Cyprus, 1976; The Cypriot Woman, in press; Publications: studies on a variety of social themes such as Marriage, Divorce, Working Women, Women in Executive Posts, The Singles, etc. *Honours:* University Merit Certificate on a number of subjects including First Place Certificate in Moral Philosophy, 1955. *Hobbies:* Painting; Social Research; Reading. *Address:* "Christina" Apts. Apt. 62, 10, Terra Santa Street, Nicosia 112, Cyprus.

MZENDA, Simon, b. 1923. Zimbabwe politician. *Appointments:* Teacher, Carpentry, nr Durban, South Africa; returned to Rhodesia, 1961; Member, Zimbabwe African People's Union (ZAPU); Founder member, 1963-, Member, Central Committee, 1977-, Zimbabwe African National Union (ZANU); imprisoned for nationalist activities, 1961, 1965-71; Deputy Prime Minister, 1980-, Minister of Foreign Affairs, 1980-81, for Co-ordination, 1981-. *Address:* Ministry for Co-ordination, Salisbury, Zimbabwe.

N

NABWISO-BULIMA, Wilberforce Frank, b. 30 June 1938, Kaliro, Uganda. Educationist. m. Deborah Aida Kirenda 5 Feb. 1972, 2 sons, 2 daughters. *Education:* Teachers Certificate, Kyambogo Teachers Training College 1959; BA, Hons. University of East Africa, 1967; MA, University of Sussex, 1968; PhD, Adult Education, University of Wisconsin, Madison 1976. *Appointments:* Teacher Trainer, 1960; Primary School Teacher, 1961-62; Radio Newscaster 1963; Secondary School Teacher 1965-67; University Extra-Mural Tutor, 1969-80; Head, Correspondence Unit 1971-72; Consultant Literacy Education 1976; Regional Education Officer, International Planned Planned Parenthood Federation Africa Region 1977-. *Memberships:* African Adult Education Association; African Literacy Society; International Council on Correspondence Education. *Publications:* Evolution of the Kyabazingaship of Busoga, 1967; The Role of Public Lectures in continuing Education, 1972; Teaching by Correspondence in Africa, 1981; The Health Team Approach to Planned Parenthood, 1980; Issues in the Management of Family Planning Associations, 1981. *Hobbies:* Reading; Singing. *Address:* PO Box 1210 Jinja, Uganda.

NADARAJA, Ratnasingham, b. 27 June 1929, Jaffna, Sri Lanka. University Teacher; Senior Lecturer. m. Lorna Gwendoline De Silva, 27 Sept. 1958, 1 son, 1 daughter. *Education:* Bachelor of Veterinary Science, University of Sri Lanka, 1957; Master of Science, 1966; Doctor of Philosophy, Bristol University, England 1975. *Appointments:* Field Veterinarian, Department of Agriculture, Sri Lanka, 1957-64; Post Graduate Study, University of Bristol, 1964-66; Veterinary Research Officer, Department of Agriculture, Sri Lanka, 1966-71; Post Graduate Study: Cornell University, New York, 1972-74 and Bristol University, England 1974-75; Head, Animal Productivity Research Unit, Research Council of Zambia, 1975-77; Senior Lecturer, Animal Science, University of Zambia, 1977-. *Memberships:* Society for the Study of Fertility, England; Sri Lanka Association, Advancement of Science; Sri Lanka Veterinary Association; Sri Lanka Veterinary Graduates Association; Zambia Veterinary Association; Public Realations Officer; Zambia Sri Lanka Friendship Association. *Publications:* Studies on characteristics of bull semen in relation to deep freeze storage and fertility; Hormonal inter-relationships during the oestrus cycle of the cow. *Honours:* FFHC/FAO, Postgraduate Scholarship, Bristol University 1964; Population Council Biomedical Fellowship, New York, USA 1971-74; Leverhulme Trust Fellowship, Bristol University 1974-75; Commercial Farmer's Award for Cattle Embryo Transfer Study in UK 1979. *Hobbies:* Stamp Collection; Dance Music thro' the ages. *Address:* No: 3832, Great East Road, Lusaka, Zambia.

NADDA, Narayan Lal, b. 2 July 1926, Vijaipur, India. Teaching. m. Shrimati Krishna Nadda, 16 Apr. 1946, 2 sons, 3 daughters. *Education:* BCom. 1945; MCom. Beuares Hindu University, 1947; PhD, Patna University, 1958. *Appointments:* Lecturer in Commerce, H.D. Jain College, Arrah, 1947-54; Lecturer, Department of Applied Economics and Commerce, Patna University 1954-59; Reader, Patna University 1959-69; Professor and Head, Department of Applied Economics and Commerce, Patna University 1969-; Vice-Chancellor, Ranchi University, 1978-80. *Memberships:* 17 Societies in the field of Technical Education, Industries, Social Science Research, Commerce and International Insurance. *Publications: Publications:* Lekha Parikshan (Auditing) prescribed for Degree Examination in many Indian Universities, Awarded by U.P. Government; Money & Banking; Capital Market in India; Socio-Economic Survey of Jamshedpur. A Research Project under the auspices of the Research Programmes Committee; Numerous Articles in Research Journals and Newspapers. *Honours:* Gopal Krishna Commemoration Medal, Central Hindu School, 1941; Champadevi Senior Gold Medal, 1945; Award for the book, Auditing, 1959. *Hobbies:* Games; Swimming; Photography. *Address:* Vijaipur, PO Auhar, Bilaspur, Himachalpradesh, Pin 174024, India.

NAGARAJAN, KUppuswamy, b. 15 Sept. 1930, Sirupalai Village, Tamilnadu, India. Scientist. m. Padmalochana, 5 July 1963, 1 son, 1 daughter. *Education:* BSc

Honours (Chem.), 1950; PhD (Chemistry), 1954; Diploma in German, 1956; Certificate in French Madras University, 1957. *Appointments:* Postdoctoral Research Assistant, CSIR scheme, Presidency College, Madras 1954-57; Postdoctoral Research Fellow, Wayne State University, Detroit, 1957-59, California Institute of Technology, Pasadena, 1959-60 and Zurich University 1961-62; Manager, Ciba-Geigy Research Centre, Bombay, India 1963-. *Memberships:* Chemical Society, London; Swiss Chemical Society; Indian Chemical Society; Indian Pharmaceutical Association; Association of Magnetic Resonance Spectroscopists, India; American Alumnus Association, Bombay. *Publications:* 150 publications in national and international chemical journals on research results; Several patents on new discoveries; Development of three new drugs— antidepressant, nasal decongestant, antiprotozoic. *Honours:* CSIR, Bhatnagar prize for Chemical Sciences 1974; Fellowship, Indian Academy of Sciences 1974; Fellowship, Indian National Science Academy, 1975. *Hobbies:* Gardening; Classical Carnatic Music; Bharathanatyam Dance; Tennis. *Address:* CIBA-GEIGY Research Centre, Goregaon East, Bombay 400063, India.

NAGENTHIRAN, Ponnambalam, b. 31 May 1936, Trincomalee, Sri Lanka. Accountant/Internal Auditor. m. Nahulambihai Ambalawarner, 22 May 1972, 1 son, 1 daughter. *Appointments:* Final Examination of the Institute of Chartered Accountants, Sri Lanka 1969; Elected Fellow, Institute of Chartered Accountants. *Appointments:* Accountant Projects, National Paper Corporation, Sri Lanka; Management Accountant; Chief Accountant; Chief Accountant, Kabwe Industrial Fabrics Limited; Internal Auditor, Indeco Limited, Zambia. *Memberships:* Ceylon Rugby Football Club. *Address:* 54 School Lane, Colombo 3, Sri Lanka.

NAIR, Vadavattath Bhaskaran, b. 10 May 1947, Colombo, Sri Lanka. Chartered Accountant. m. Sreelatha Nair, 26 June 1975, 2 daughters. *Education:* Final Examination, Institute of Chartered Accountants Sri Lanka 1971; Final Examination, Institute of Cost and Management Accountants, London 1975. *Appointments:* Assistant Accountant, JB Textiles Industries Limited, Colombo Sri Lanka 1972-73; Accountant, Elephant Lite Corporation Limited, Colombo, Sri Lanka 1973-79; Accountant, Metal Fabricators of Zambia Limited, Luanshya Zambia 1979-. *Memberships:* Associate, Institute of Chartered Accountants, Sri Lanka. *Hobby:* Gardening. *Address:* 3 Mumba Close, Luanshya, Zambia.

NAIR, Vallillath Madhathil Madhavan, b. 8 Oct. 1919, Mangalore, India. Ambassador of India, (Retired). m. 9 Nov. 1945, 1 son, 1 daughter. *Education:* BA(Hons) University of Madras; MA(Oxon), University of Oxford; MA(Cantab) University of Cambridge; Barrister-at-Law, Inner Temple, London. *Appointments:* High Commissioner of India to Malaya 1957-58; Ambassador, of India, Cambodia 1958-60; Ambassador of India, Norway 1960-63; Joint Secretary, Ministry of External Affairs, N. Delhi 1964-67; Ambassador of India, Poland 1967-70; Ambassador of India, Morocco and Tunisia 1970-74; Ambassador of India, Spain 1974-77. *Memberships:* Delhi Gymkhana Club. *Honours:* Northwick Prizeman, University of Madras. *Hobbies:* Reading; Photography. *Address:* 68 Third Main Road, Gandhinagar, Madras 20, India.

NAISMITH, Robert James, b. 4 Mar. 1916, Edinburgh. Architect and Planning Consultant. *Education:* Diploma of Art, Edinburgh College of Art; Architecture, DA(Edin) 1941; Diploma in Town Planning, Edinburgh 1942. *Appointments:* Assistant Architect and Town Planner, Sir Frank Mears P/P.R.S.A. LLD, FRSE 1942-50; Partner, 1950-; Former Chairman: Professional Advisers Cost Engineering Limited, Edinburgh, Glasgow, Newcastle and Hamburg, West Germany, 1979-; Professional Services to the Oil Industry; Lecturer, Edinburgh College of Art, Heriot-Watt University 1960-; Director, National Survey of Buildings, Countryside Commission for Scotland 1978-81. *Memberships:* Fellow, Royal Institute of British Architects; Fellow, Royal Town Planning Institute; Fellow, Royal Incorporation of Architects in Scotland; Fellow, Society of Antiquaries, Scotland; Scottish Georgian Society; Scottish Arts Club. *Creative Works:* Water Colours and Architectural Drawings; Exhibited in Royal Academy, Royal Scottish Academy, Royal Hibernian Academy; Articles on Architecture and Planning; etc. *Honours:*

RIBA Archibald Dawnay Scholarship 1939-40; RIAS Rutland Prize 1940; Bronze Medalist Heriot-Watt College 1941; Andrew Grant Travelling Scholarship 1942. *Hobbies:* Watercolours; Writing; Travelling. *Address:* 14 Ramsay Garden, Edinburgh, EH1 2NA, Scotland.

NAKAMAE, Tadashi, b. 24 Dec. 1938, Hiroshima City, Japan. Chief Economist. m. Noriko Takimura, 14 Apr. 1967, 1 daughter. *Education:* BA, Tokyo University 1962. *Appointments:* Economist, Daiwa Investment Trust and Management Company, Tokyo, 1962-69; Senior Economist, Daiwa Securities, Tokyo, 1969-73; Chief Economist, Daiwa Europe, London, 1973-. *Memberships:* Association Business Economists UK; Association Investment Analysts; Institute of International Affairs. *Publications:* Occasional contributor to Euromoney, the Guardian, etc. 1975-; Columnist Nihon Keizai Shimbun, major Japanese financial newspaper, 1975-; Author, On inflation and the Japanese Yen, 1972; The International Politics of Surplus Capacity with Article Prospects for the 1980's: A Japanese View (co-author). *Hobbies:* Reading; Classical Music; Golf; Tennis; Igo (a Japanese game). *Address:* The Bungalow, Courtlands Farm, Park Road, Banstead, Surrey, England.

NAMALIU, Rabbie Langanai, b. 3 Apr. 1947, Raluana Village, Kokopo, East New Britain Province, Papua New Guinea. Teacher. m. Margaret Nakikus, 10 Oct. 1978. *Education:* Bachelor of Arts, English and History, University of Papua New Guinea 1970; Master of Arts, History and Political Science, University of Victoria, B.C Canada. *Appointments:* Senior Tutor in History, Department of History, University of Papua New Guinea, Lecturer in History, 1973-74; Principal Private Secretary, to Chief Minister of Papua New Guinea, 1974-75; Visting Pacific Fellow, Centre for South Pacific Studies, University of California, Santa Cruz, California, USA, 1975; Provincial Commissioner, East New Britain Province, Papua New Guinea, 1976; Chairman, Public Services Commission of Papua New Guinea, 1976-79; Member, Papua New Guinea Delegation to the United Nations, New York, USA, 1979; Principal Research Officer, Office of the Prime Minister, Port Moresby, Papua New Guinea 1980; Executive Officer, to the Leader of the Opposition, 1980-81. *Memberships:* Australian Institute of International Affairs; Papua Club Inc., Port Moresby, PNG. *Publications:* Plays: Marki, Kaunsil; The Good Woman of Konedobu; Kannibal Tours. *Honours:* Administration Scholarship, University of Papua New Guinea 1966; Vacation Scholarship, Department of Economics, School of General Studies, Australian National University, 1967; Canadian Commonwealth Scholarship, University of Victoria, 1970; Independence Medal 1975; Queen's Silver Jubilee Medal 1977; CMG 1979. *Hobbies:* Squash; Reading. *Address:* S 55 Lot. 20, Lokua Avenue, Boroko, Papua New Guinea.

NAMPONYA, Clemence Rozario, b. 9 Aug. 1946, Blantyre, Malawi. Librarianship. m. Anna Kamanga, 10 Oct. 1971, 1 son, 2 daughters. *Education:* ALA., 1972; FLA., 1976. *Appointments:* Assistant Librarian, 1970, Acting College Librarian, 1975, College Librarian, 1978-, Bunda College, University of Malawi. *Memberships:* Library Association, UK; Malawi Library Association; International Association of Agricultural Librarians and Documentalists. *Publications:* History and development of printing and publishing in Malawi; Characteristics of the literature cited by agriculturists at Bunda College, 1979; Agricultural librarianship in East and Central Africa; Agriculture in Malawi: an annotated bibliography 1930-1980. *Hobbies:* Football; Table tennis; Squash. *Address:* Drawes Village, Naulenga Mission, PA Thucila, Mulanje, Malawi.

NANCE, Charles Trengove, b. 27 Mar. 1919, Dartmouth, England. Air Commodore, RAF; Company Director; Wind Propulsion Consultant. m. Phyllis Ellicott, 6 Apr. 1946, 4 daughters. *Education:* MA., 1944, Clare College, Cambridge University, UK; Fellow: Institution of Mechanical Engineers; Royal Aeronautical Society. *Appointments:* Commissioned RAF Engineer Branch, 1941; Served Fighter Squadrons and Egypt, World War II, 1941-45; Air Ministry, 1946; Group Captain, 1960; USA & Singapore; Air Commodore, 1966; Director of Aircraft, Defence Research Staff, Washington, USA, 1966-68; Director of Ground Training (RAF) Ministry of Defence, 1969; Director of Standardization, MOD, 1972; Director, Medina Yacht Co. Limited, 1976; Chair-

man, Mustang Yachts Limited, 1980. *Memberships:* Founder President, RAF (Per Ardua) Archery Association; Amateur Yacht Research Society; The Royal Yacht Squadron; Royal Yachting Association; RAF Change Yacht Club (Past Commodore); Other Yacht Clubs. *Publications:* Many papers on Commercial sail and wind Propulsion for: Advanced Transit System Symposium, Amsterdam, 1976; Department of Industry Symposium, London, UK, 1979; West European Marine Technology Conference, Norway, 1980; Danish Institute of Engineers, 1980; Royal Institute of Naval Architects, 1980; Series of popular articles magazine Sea Breezes, under pseudonym 'The Commodore'; Contributes to Lloyds List, The Times, Marine Week and others. *Honours:* Mentioned in despatches, World War II; OBE., 1956. *Hobby:* Yacht racing. *Address:* Mornington, Cowes, Isle of Wight PO31 8BL, UK.

NAORA, Hiroto, b. 16 Nov. 1927, Tokyo, Japan. Professorial Fellow, Research School of Biological Sciences, Australian National University. m. Hatsuko Terao, 22 Feb. 1956, 1 daughter. *Education:* BSc., Tokyo University of Literature and Science, 1950; DSc., University of Tokyo, Japan, 1956. *Appointments:* Research Associate, 1956-57, Member, 1960-62, The Cancer Institute, Japanese Foundation for Cancer Research, Tokyo, Japan; International Fellow, Rockefeller Foundation, Université libre de Bruxelles, Belgium, 1957-58; Associate, Rockefeller University, New York, USA, 1958-60; Foundation Chief, Division of Biology, National Cancer Center Research Institute, 1962-68; Professorial Fellow, Head of Molecular Biology Unit, Research School of Biological Sciences, The Australian National University, 1968-. *Memberships:* 18th President, Japan Society of Cell Biology; Council and/or Executive member, Japanese Biochemical Society, Biophysics Society, Cancer Association, Japan Society of Cell Biology. *Publications:* Editor of: Cell Biology, 1967; Biochemical Genetics, 1970 and other books; Papers on biochemistry, molecular biology, cell biology, cytology. *Honours:* Asahi Science Promotion Award, 1953, 1954; Tamiya Prize, 1966. *Hobbies:* Mountaineering; Photography. *Address:* 89 Hilder Street, Weston, Canberra, ACT 2611, Australia.

NARAIN, Prem, b. 20 Nov. 1942, Delhi, India. Teaching and Research. m. Shashi Gupta, 15 May 1977, 1 son, 1 daughter. *Education:* BA., (Hons.), 1960, MA., 1962, Delhi University, India; MS., 1971, PhD., 1973, SUNY, LINY, USA. *Appointments:* Teaching and Research at: IIT., Kampur, India; Ramjas College, Delhi University, India; IIT., Delhi, India; University of Missouri, Rolla, USA; SUNY, Stony Brook, LINY., USA; IIT., Bombay Institute, India. *Memberships:* Life member, Indian Mathematical Society. *Hobbies:* Chess; Hockey. *Address:* C-49, IIT., Powai, Bombay 400076, India.

NARAYANAN, Palayil Pathazapurayil, b. 15 Feb. 1923, India. Trade Union Executive. m. Dakshayani Nambudiri, 25 Apr. 1947, 3 sons, 2 daughters. *Education:* K K.M. School of Commerce and Technical College, Kuala Lumpur, Malaya. *Appointments:* Member, Federal Legislative Council and Finance Committee, 1948-53, 55-59; Member, ILO Plantation Committee, 1950; Delegate to ILO Conference, 1957, 65, 72, and Adviser, 1974, 79; Consultant, ILO Advisory Committee, Rural Development, 1973-; First President, Malayan Trade Union Congress (later Malaysian) MTUC, 1950-52, 1954-55, 1974-76, 1976-78, 1978-80, 1980-; General Secretary, National Union of Plantation Workers, 1954-; President, ICFTU Asian Regional Organisation (ICFTU-ARO), 1960-66, 1969-76; Chairman, ICFTU-ARO Education Committee, 1960-75; Chairman, World Economic Committee, ICFTU, 1968-; President, ICFTU, 1975, 1978-. *Memberships:* Court of University of Malaya, 1972-75; Vice-President, International Federation of Plantation, Agricultural and Allied Workers; National Family Planning Board, 1969-75; National Unity Council, 1969-71; National Joint Advisory Council, National Electricity Board; Fellow, Malaysian Institute of Management; Commonwealth Parliamentary Association; Tamil Jounralist Union; Sri Aurobindo Society; President, Sree Sathya Sai Samithi, P.Jaya. *Publications:* Short story collections: the Interview, Light in Darkness; various trade union publs.; poems in Malayalam; articles in various trade union journals on socio-economic subjects. *Honours:* Gold Medal, MTUC, 1951; Ramon Magsaysay Award for Community Service, 1962; Gold Medal of Railway Union of Malaya, 1966; Golden Key and Freedom of City of Osaka, Japan, 1972; Hon. LL.D., University Sains Penang, 1974. *Hobbies:* Trade unionism; Creation of new employment opportunities; Painting; Sketching; Writing short stories and poems. *Address:* National Union of Plantation Workers, 2 Jalan Templer, Petaling Jaya, Selangor, Malaysia.

NARONE, Jogendra Nath, b. 17 Jan. 1935, Deoghar, India. Obstetrician; Gynaecologist. m. Raj K Varma, 8 Feb. 1969, 1 daughter. *Education:* Intermediate Science, Bihar University, India, 1953; MB., BS., 1959, Master of Surgery, 1965, Patna University, India; Fellowship, Advanced Techniques of Management of Fertility, Washington University, USA, 1974. *Appointments:* House Surgeon in Obstetrics and Gynaecology, 1959-60, Medical Officer in Medicine, Surgery, Obstetrics and Gynaecology, 1966-68, Resident Surgical Officer and Registrar, Obstetrics and Gynaecology, 1968-73, Patna Medical College Hospital, India; Army Medical Corps, Armed Forces, India, 1960-66; Assistant Professor, Obstetrics and Gynaecology, Darbhanga and Patna Medical College, 1973-75; Associate Professor, Obstetrics and Gynaecology, Patna Medical College, India, 1975-78; Head, Department of Obstetrics and Gynaecology, Nalanda Medical College, Patna, India, 1978-79; Senior Lecturer and Consultant, Obstetrics and Gynaecology, School of Medicine, University of Zambia, Lusaka, Zambia. *Memberships:* Fellow; Programme for International Education in Obstetrics and Gynaecology; Founder member, Executive Committee, National Association of Voluntary Sterilisation of India; Secretary of Patna Branch, member of Working Commitee, Indian Medical Association; Federation of Obstetric and Gynaecological Societies of India; Indian Association of Fertility and Sterility; Zambia Medical Association. *Publications:* Place of Vaginal Hysterectomy in the management of Genital prolapse, 1966; Therapy of Toxaemia of Pregnancy, 1972; Cervical healing after electric cauterisation; Oral diuetics in Oedema of Pregnancy, 1972; Menstrual Regulation, 1975; Infective Hepatitis in Pregnancy, 1976; An evaluation of different methods of MTP., 1977. *Honours:* Honours in Obstetrics and Gynaecology, MBBS., Exam of Patna University, 1959; Awarded Gold Medal for having stood first in Obstetrics and Gynaecology, 1959; Awarded College Blue for outstanding services, 1965; Awarded Patna University Blue for distinguished achievements by Smt. Indira Gandhi, 1965; Certificate, Drama Inter-University Youth Festival, Delhi, 1955; WHO Integrated Programme, New Delhi, 1973; Certificate, IMA for Rendering services to Bagladesh Refugees by Governor of Bihar, 1972. *Hobbies:* Reading; Drama; Bridge; Tennis; Table tennis; Badminton. *Address:* Bobby Niwas, 6B, Rajendra Nagar, Patna-800 016, Bihar, India.

NARONE, Raj Kumari, b. 15 Aug. 1941, Jamshedpur, India. Obstetrician; Gynaecologist. m. 8 Feb. 1969, 1 daughter. *Education:* Intermediate Science, 1959, MBBS., 1964, Master of Surgery, 1967, Patna University, India; Fellowship, Advanced Techniques of Management of Fertility, Washington University, USA, 1975. *Appointments:* House Surgeon, Obstetrics and Gynaecology, 1964-65, Maternity Supervisor, 1967-68, Resident Surgical Officer, Obstetrics and Gynaecology, 1968-71, Medical Officer, Medicine, 1971-72, Registrar, Obstetrics and Gynaecology, 1972-74, Patna Medical College Hospital, Patna, India; Post Graduate Fellow, 1965-67, Assistant Professor, Obstetrics and Gynaecology, 1974-79, Patna Medical College, India; Associate Professor, Obstetrics and Gynaecology, Nalanda Medical College, India, Feb. 1979; Senior Lecturer and Consultant, Obstetrics and Gynaecology, School of Medicine, University of Zambia, Lusaka, Zambia, 1979-. *Memberships:* Fellow, Programme for International Education in Obstetrics and Gynaecology; National Association of Voluntary Sterilisation of India; Indian Medical Association; Federation of Obstetric and Gynaecological Societies of India; Indian Association of Fertility and Sterility; Zambia Medical Association. *Publications:* Numerous publications including: Megaloblastic Anaemia in Pregnancy, 1969; Urinary tract infection in the practice of Obstetrics and Gynaecology, 1969; A review of bacterial flora in Obstetric and Gynaecological operations, 1969; Congenital malformation of foetus as a cause of obstructed labour, 1973; Serum and tissue iron and Menorrhagia, 1973. *Honours:* Honours in Surgery, MBBS Exam. of Patna University, 1964; PC Tallents prize for the highest marks at 2nd and final MBBS Examinations taken

together, Patna University, 1964; Wheeler Gold Medal for highest aggregate, MBBS Exam., 1964; Stephenson Gold Medal for having stood first in Surgery; Awarded College Bèst in Academic, 1964-65; Awarded President of India's Medal, 1964-65; Awarded 1st prize in Drame by Governor of Bihar, 1959; Certificate of Prizes for Inter-College and University Debate in English, 1959-62; WHO Integrated Programme, New Delhi, 1973; Washington University, USA for training in MTP & Laparoscopy, 1975. *Hobby:* Reading. *Address:* Bobby Niwas, 6B Rajendra Nagar, Patna-800 016, Bihar, India.

NARULA, Naunidh Singh, b. 15 May 1942, Gujranwala, Pakistan. Businessman. m. Rani, 1969, 1 son, 2 daughters. *Education:* BSc., Hons., University of London, UK; External Student of Bournemouth College of Technology, UK, 1965-68. *Appointments:* Executive Director, 1968-77, Managing Director, 1978-79, Benetone(HK(Co. Limited, Hong Kong; Executive Director, National Investment Co., Bangkok, Thailand, 1968-77; Managing Partner, Thep Thavi Real Estates, R & P., Bangkok, Thailand, 1968-77; Managing Director: Imperial Chemical Co., Bangkok, Thailand, 1980-; United Consortium Limited, Hong Kong, 1980-. *Memberships:* Old England Students Association, Bangkok, Thailand, 1969; Rotary Club of Victoria, Hong Kong; Masonic Lodge, Hong Kong. *Honours:* Tower History Prize for article on Rabindranath Tagore in Competitive Examination, 1961. *Hobbies:* Photography; Swimming; Squash. *Address:* Apt. No. 22A, Garfield Mansions, 23-25 Seymour Road, Hong Kong.

NASH, Arthur Harry, b. 5 Aug. 1922, Perth, Western Australia. m. 3 Sept. 1943, 1 son, 2 daughters. *Education:* BSc.Eng., 1942, BSc., Hons., 1944, M.Ed., 1961, University of Western Australia; PhD., University of Michigan, USA, 1963. *Appointments:* Research Engineer, Amalgamated Wireless, Australasia Limited, 1942-45; Research Officer, Radio Research Board, Commonwealth Scientific and Industrial Research Organisation, 1945-46; Lecturer, Senior Lecturer, Engineering Department, Perth Technical College, Australia, 1946-62; Dean, School of Architecture, Art and Engineering, 1964-74, Dean, School of Engineering and Surveying, 1975-80, Dean, Faculty of Engineering and Surveying, 1981-, Western Australian Institute of Technology. *Memberships:* Fellow and Federal Councillor, The Institution of Engineers, Australia; Past Member, Federfal Executive, Federal Board of Examiners and Federal Electrical College Board; Committee Member and Past Chairman, Western Australian Division, The Institution of Engineers; American Society for Engineering Education; Fellow, College of Education, Australia; Association for Engineering Education in South-East Asia; Austraian Natinal Commission for UNESCO. *Publications:* Applied Mathematics on Closed Circuit Television, 1960; The Impact of Television on Secondary School Children, 1961; A Descriptive Study of Educational Television Stations operated by State Universities in the USA, 1963; Technical Education for Development-Chapter 7-The Education of the Technician, 1966; Student Progress Attitude and Performance in Engineering Courses at the Western Australian Institute of Technology, 1969; Report on the Committee of Inquiry into Higher Education in Papua New Guinea (co-author), 1971; Seminar on Energy Resource for Domestic Use, 1975; The Role of Engineering Schools in the Development of Alternative Energy Sources, Especially for Rural Areas, (Editor), 1979; 23 additional articles, publications in learned journals. *Honours:* Achieved highest aggregate score for Western Australia in Public Leaving Certificate examinations, 1939; Awarded entrance scholarship to University of Western Australia; Gledden Travelling Fellow, Engineering, University of Western Australia, 1962-64; Fulbright Travelling Fellowship, 1962-64; Clifford Woody Memorial Student (Graduate Studies in Education), University of Michigan, USA, 1963-64; Invited to become a Fellow, College of Education, Australia, 1973. *Hobbies:* Swimming; Australian football; Cricket; Reading; Household repair work; Travel; Gardening. *Address:* 36 Todd Avenue, Como 6152, Western Australia, Australia.

NASON, Lynn Alfred, b. 23 June 1943, Tracy, New Brunswick, Canada. Barrister and Solicitor. m. Paulette C Garnett, 10 Aug. 1968, 2 daughters. *Education:* Bachelor of Business Administration, 1965, Bachelor of Civil Laws, 1967, University of New Brunswick, Fredericton, New Brunswick, Canada. *Appointments:* Barrister and Solicitor, 1967-. *Memberships:* Canadian Bar Association; Barristers Society of New Brunswick; Saint John Law Society. *Address:* Martinon, Saint John, New Brunswick, Canada.

NATH, Girishwar, b. 17 July 1932, Chausa, Bihar, India. Scientist. *Education:* MSc(Math.) Patna University, Patna India, 1954; PhD (Fluid Dynamics) Hungarian Academy of Sciences, Budapest, Hungary, 1966. *Appointments:* Lecturer, Mathematics Department, Patna University, 1954-68; Assistant Professor, 1968-75; Associate Professor, 1975-79; Professor, 1979-; Chairman, Applied Maths. Department, Indian Institute of Science, Bangalore, 1978-. *Memberships:* Fellow, Indian Academy of Sciences. *Publications:* 115 research publications in the field of boundary layer theory, hypersonic flow theory, M.H.D. and Turbomachines. *Address:* 20/C, Margosa Road, 9th Cross, Malleswaram, Bangalore, 560003, India.

NATH, Ravindra Nath, b. 7 Apr. 1940, New Delhi. Electronics Engineer. m. Mrs. Deepa, 26 Dec. 1966, 1 son, 1 daughter. *Education:* Senior Cambridge, Cambridge University, 1956; Bachelor of Engineering, Roorkee University 1962; Masters Degree in Business Administration, Delhi University, 1978. *Appointments:* Class I Officers Cadre, Indian Railways, 1964. *Memberships:* Fellow, Institution of Electronics and Telecom. Engineers India; The Institution of Engineers, India; Institute of Rail Transport; Institution of Railway Signal and Telecom. Engineers, India. *Address:* A-9/35, Vasant·Vihar, New Delhi 110057, India.

NATH, Shambhu, b. 2 Apr. 1933, Rautakat, Nepal. Specialist General Surgeon and Urologist. m. Paresia Rana, 14 July 1962, 1 son. *Education:* MBBS, Bihar India, 1958; FRCS, Edinburgh, United Kingdom, 1969; FACS, USA, 1980. *Appointments:* Medical Officer, Kathmandu Nepal, 1964-; House Surgeon, Registrar, Locum Consultant, United Kingdom; Consultant Surgeon and Consultant Urologist, Senior Lecturer, University Teaching Hospital, Lusaka, Zambia, 1976-. *Memberships:* Association of Surgeons of East Africa. *Publications:* Medical Scientific papers. *Hobbies:* Photography; Curio Collector. *Address:* PO Box R.W 50045, Lusaka, Zambia.

NATHAN-MARSH, Oladisun, b. 22 Jan. 1919, Lagos, Nigeria. Barrister. 4 sons, 1 daughter. *Education:* C.M.S. Grammar School, Lagos, 1926-31; Igbobi College for Boys, Yaba, Lagos, 1932-35; LLB Hons. University of Leeds, England 1948-51; Called to the Bar, Inner Temple, London, 1956; Barrister at Law. *Appointments:* Assistant Liaison Officer, Colonial Office, London, 1951-56; Company Secretary, Nigerian Produce Marketing Company Limited, London, 1956 61 and Lagos, 1961-72; Acting Managing Director, 1968-72; General Counsel, Elf Nigeria Limited, 1972-79. *Memberships:* The Metropolitan Club, Victoria Island, Lagos; The Royal Commonwealth Society, London. *Honours:* Chieftaincy Title, Kemo of Ake, Abeokuta, 1960. *Hobbies:* Reading; Exercises; Walking. *Address:* Marsh Villa, 23 Oduduwa Way, Gra, Ikeja, Lagos, Nigeria.

NATTRASS, Peter Christopher Roland, b. 15 Oct. 1941, Perth, Australia. Obstetrician and Gynaecologist. m. Margot Anne Whittaker, 3 sons. *Education:* MB, BS, University of West Australia; Royal College Obstetricians and Gynaecologist, London; MRCOG; FACOG. *Appointments:* Consultant Obstetrician and Gynaecologist, King Edward Memorial Hospital for Women. *Memberships:* Councillor of the City of Perth, Australia. *Hobby:* Early Australian Art. *Address:* 8 Mounts Bay Road, Crawley, West Australia.

NAVIN, Francis Patrick Duffy, b. 14 June 1938, Grande Prairie, Alberta, Canada. Professor of Transportation Engineer. m. Marina MacKinnon, 21 Nov. 1964, 2 son, 1 daughter. *Education:* BEng(Civil), McMaster University, Hamilton, Ontario, Canada, 1963; MS (Transport Engineering), University of Missouri, Columbia, Missouri, USA, 1968; PhD (Urban Transport) University of Minnesota, Minneapolis, Minnesota, USA, 1972. *Appointments:* Officer, Corps of Royal Canadian Engineers, Canada, 1959-66; Research Assistant, University of Missouri, Columbia, Mo, USA, 1966-68; Transit Planning Engineer, Alan M Voorhees and Associates, McLean, Virginia, USA

1968-69; Transport Engineer, Bather-Ringrose-Wolsfeld, St Paul, Minnesota, USA, 1969-70; Partner and Vice-President, RH Pratt Association, Washington, DC, USA, 1970-72; Associate Professor of Transport Engineering, Department of Civil Engineering, University of British Columbia, Vancouver BC, Canada, 1972-81. *Memberships:* Registered Professional Engineer, Province of British Columbia, 1972 and Province of Ontario, 1963-; Canadian Society for Civil Engineers; Canadian Transportation Research Form.; Roads and Transportation Association of Canada; Associate Editor of: RTAC Journal, Canada, Journal, Transportation Planning and Technology, UK, Journal of Advanced Transporation, USA. *Publications:* Over 100 published papers in the field of Urban Transportation, most in Public Transit; Also papers dealing with vehicle loads on long span bridges. *Honours:* Military Engineering Scholarship, 1962; Urban Mass Transit Fellowship, University of Minnesota, 1969-70. *Hobbies:* Sailing; Skiing; Watercolours. *Address:* 4550 West 7th Avenue, Vancouver, British Columbia, Canada, V6R 1X3.

NAWAWI, Mohd. Norwina, b. 19 Feb. 1956, Jokor Bahru, Johore, Malaysia. Architect. *Education:* Bachelor of Architecture, University of Technology, Malaysia, 1979; Professional Certificate, P.A.M. Prt I, 1976; Computer Intensive Potran Course Certificate, 1979; Financial Management Course (Intan) Certificate 1980. *Appointments:* Architects Team 3, 1974 and 1977-78; City Hall, 1976; Public Works Department, Medical and Health Design Group, 1979-. *Memberships:* Old Girls Association of Tunku Khursiah, (Girls') College; Women Graduate Society; Pertubuhan Arkitek Malaysia. *Publications:* Mural, University of Icebangsaan, Malaysia's Design Auditorium, 1977; Measured Drawing of Istana Jahar, Kelantan, 1975; Articles to AAM Magazine. *Honours:* Federal Scholarship, 1973-79. *Hobbies:* Stamp Collecting; Photography; Travel; Writing; Reading; Music; Poetry Writing; Sketching; Designing; etc. *Address:* 8 Jalan SS1/33, Kg. Tunku, Petaling, Jaya, Selangor, Malaysia.

NAWAZ, Tanwir, b. 19 July 1944, Jessore, Bangladesh. Architect and Urbanist. m. Rasheda Khan, 25 Oct. 1970, 1 son. *Education:* Bachelor of Architecture, (1st Class, University of Engineering and Technology, Dacca, Bangladesh, 1967; Master of Architecture, Urban Design (Honours), Texas A & M University, USA, 1969. *Appointments:* Architect and Assistant Professor, Department of Architecture, University of Engineering and Technology, Dacca, 1970-72; Deputy Chief, Physical Planning and Housing, Planning Commission, Government of Bangladesh, 1972-73; Architect, Moffat Moffat and Kinoshita, Toronto, Ontario, 1973-75; Architect, Annau Architect, Toronto, Ontario, 1975-77; Architect, Department of Municipal Affairs, Regina, Saskatchewan, Canada, 1977-79; Planning Co-ordinator, City of Toronto Housing Department, Toronto, Ontario 1979; Principal, Tanwir Nawaz Architect, Regina, Saskatchewan, Canada 1980-. *Memberships:* Royal Architectural Institute of Canada; Saskatchewan Association of Architects; Ontario Association of Architects; Institute of Architects Bangladesh. *Publications:* Inner City Housing policy development for the Government of Saskatchewan, Canada, includes three major unpublished reports; Downtown Improvement Plan for the City of Moose Jaw, Saskatchewan; Physical Development Analysis of South Downtown Saskatoon, Saskatchewan ($100 million development plan). *Honours:* John D. Rockefeller 3rd Fund Fellowship, 1968-69; Canadian Architect Award of Excellence for Bedford Glen Terraced Housing, Toronto, 1976. *Hobbies:* Table Tennis; Cricket; Classical Music; Reading. *Address:* 118 Rawlinson Bay, Regina, Saskatchewan, S4S 6M8, Canada.

NAYAR, Prabodhachandran Nayar, V R, b. 4 Aug. 1938, Parur, Kerala, India. University Professor. m. R Radha Devi, 11 Feb. 1967, 1 son, 1 daughter. *Education:* BSc, Botany, Chemistry, English, Malayalam First Class and First Rank for Malayalam, Kerala 1957; MA, Malayalam Language and Literature First Class and First Rank, 1959; PhD, Linguistic Analysis of Malayalam 1967; PhD, Phonetics and Phonology, University of London 1970. *Appointments:* Lecturer in Malayalam, S.T.H. College, Nagercoil, 1959-63; Lecturer, Reader, Professor of Linguistics and Head, Department of Linguistics, University of Kerala, 1963-79-. *Memberships:* Linguistic Society of India; Dravidian Linguistic Association; Lexicographic Society of India. *Publica-*

tions: Eight books and more than eighty research papers. Books include: Malayalam Verbal Forms, 1972; Malayalam—A Linguistic Description, 1974. *Honours:* Dr. K Godavarma Memorial Prize, University of Kerala, 1959; Commonwealth Scholarship for post-Doctoral Research in Linguistics, School of Oriental and African Studies, University of Lond, 1967-70; Guest Lecturer, Centre of Advanced Studies in Linguistics, Annamalai University, 1978. *Hobbies:* Music; Performing arts like Kathakali. *Address:* Prasadam, Planchery Lane, Trivandrum 695 008, India.

NAYLOR, Frank Derek, b. 17 Feb. 1933, Belfast, Northern Ireland. University Lecturer. m. Pamela McMullen, 13 May 1961, 2 daughters. *Education:* Bachelor of Arts, University of Sydney, 1959; Doctor of Philosophy, University of Melbourne, 1972. *Appointments:* Guidance Officer, NSW Department of Technical Education, 1959-61; Student Counsellor, University of New South Wales, 1961-66; Lecturer, University of Melbourne, 1966-73; Senior Lecturer, University of Melbourne, 1973-. *Memberships:* The Australian Psychological Society; Australian Association for Research in Education; The Sciences Club, Melbourne. *Publications:* Personality and Educational Achievement, 1972; Further publications include chapters of books and articles in learned journals. *Honours:* Fellow of the Australian Psychological Society, 1979. *Hobbies:* Reading; Music. *Address:* 11 Stanley Avenue, Hawthorn East, Victoria 3132, Australia.

NAYLOR, Judy Anne, b. 10 Dec. 1956, Kogarah, New South Wales, Australia. Teacher; Librarian. *Education:* Bachelor of Education, Canberra College of Advanced Education, Australia. *Appointments:* Head Teacher, Librarian, Sadadeen High School, Alice Springs, Australia. *Memberships:* Library Association of Australia; School Library Association of the Northern Territory; Australian Fellowship of Evangelical students; New South Wales Teachers Federation; NT Teachers Federation. *Publications:* A Readers guide to music, 1977; A union list of music serials held in the ACT., 1977; Union list of music books held in high school libraries in the ACT., 1977-78; Union list of music books held in Senior College libraries in the ACT., 1978; Secondary College Libraries and music curricula, 1978; A basic collection of music for Secondary College libraries, 1978-79; Music Curricula in the Open plan school, 1980; Library Skills, 1981; Repair and maintenance of audio visuals by students, 1981. *Honours:* First prize for Nature/wildlife Photography, 1980. *Hobbies:* Photography; Geology; Playing guitar, banjo mandelin and mandeline; Teaching sunday school. *Address:* 36 Ocean View Drive, Terrigal 2260, New South Wales, Australia.

NAZRUL-ISLAM, A K M, b. 31 Jan. 1948, Bangladesh. Teaching. m. 6 Apr. 1980. *Education:* BSc., Hons, 1967, MSc., 1968, Dacca University, Bangladesh; PhD., Sheffield University, UK, 1977. *Appointments:* Lecturer in Botany, 1970-77, Assistant Professor, 1977-, Dacca University, Bangladesh. *Memberships:* Bangladesh Botanical Society. *Hobbies:* Football; Stamp collections; Reading. *Address:* Multagacha, Mymensingh, Bangladesh.

NCHETE, (Rev.), Dominic, b. 25 Dec. 1920, Monze, Zambia. Clergyman. *Appointments:* Parish Priest; Vicar General. *Publications:* 4 books in Thitonga: Maambaamba Musaama; Atubale; Bana Bensika; Banyama Besa Mu Zambia; 1 book in press: Mbaabo Banyama. *Hobby:* Reading. *Address:* Catholic Church, PO Box 224, Mazabuka, Zambia.

NDIBE, Christopher Chukwuneke, b. 22 Sept. 1941, Enugu-Agidi, Nigeria. Computer Consultant. m. 5 Nov. 1969, 4 sons. *Education:* BSc., Edinburgh University, UK, 1964-67. *Appointments:* Computer Systems Consultant, ICL., 1968-75; Data Processing Manager: Royal Exchange Assurance (Nigeria) Limited, 1975-77; British-American Insurance Co. (Nigeria) Limited, 1977-. *Memberships:* Assistant Secretary General, Computer Association of Nigeria; Chairman, ICL Computer Users Association. *Publications:* Information Retrieval, unpublished paper, 1969; Role of Computer on Insurance Business, 1981. *Honours:* Shell Scholarship Award, 1964-67. *Hobbies:* Reading; Music; Badminton; Dancing; Tennis; Squash. *Address:* 9 Lawani Street, Yaba, Lagos, Nigeria.

NDILI, Frank Nwachukwu, b. 6 Oct. 1934, Asaba, Nigeria. Vice-Chancellor; Nuclear Scientist. m. Edna O

Chinweokwu, 28 Sept. 1963, 2 sons, 4 daughters. *Education:* BSc., 1st class Hons., University College, Ibadan, Nigeria, 1961; PhD., University of Cambridge, UK, 1964. *Appointments:* University Lecturer, University of Ibadan, Nigeria, 1964-67; Research Fellow, Institute of Nuclear Research, Warsaw, Poland, 1967-68; Principal Scientific Officer, Daresbury Nuclear Research, Warrington, UK, 1968-71; Head, Department of Physics, 1971-72, 1973-76, Dean, Faculty of Physical Sciences, 1976-79, Deputy Vice-Chancellor, 1979, Vice-Chancellor, 1980-, University of Nigeria, Nsukka, Nigeria. *Memberships:* Fellow, British Institute of Physics, 1977. *Publications:* Several publications in international scientific journals: Physical Review, 1965; Nuovo Cimento 62A, 1969; International Journal of Theoretical Physics 13, 1975; Physical Review D15, 1977; Physical Review D17, 1978. *Hobbies:* Dancing; Gardening. *Address:* Vice-Chancellor's Lodge, University of Nigeria, Nsukka, Nigeria.

NDO, Robert George Komla, b. 8 June 1926, Ve-Gbodome, Volta Region, Ghana. Principal Superintendent of Schools (retired). m. Alwine Adzoa Nyagbenu, 24 Apr. 1951, 3 sons, 3 daughters. *Education:* Teacher's Certificate A, Presbyterian Training College, Akropong, Akwapim, 1947-50; Specialist Music Certificate, Kumasi College of Technology, 1953-55; Dip. Mus., University of Ghana, Legon, Ghana, 1963-66. *Appointments:* Teacher: Abutia-Kloe Evangelical Presbyterian Middle School, 1951-52; Ve-Koloenu Evangelical Presbyterian Middle School, 1956; Music Tutor, 1957-63, Senior Music Master, 1968-73, Peki Training College; Music Tutor, Jasikan Training College, 1966-68; Senior Superintendent of Schools (Music Education): Peki Education District, 1973-74, Jasikan Education District, 1974-77; Principal Superintendent of Schools, General Administration, Jasikan District Education Office, 1977-79; Retired, 1979, now a farmer. *Memberships:* Ghana Music Teachers' Association; Assistant Organizer, Evangelical Presbyterian Church Choirs' Union; Arnu Choral Society; Secretary: Ve Indigenous Teachers' Association; Management Committee, Ve Secondary School. *Publications:* 15 Hymns and Marching songs; 10 Arrangements of Popular Tunes; 33 African Art Choral Works; 1 Composition for Voice, Piano and Drum Ensemble; 2 Voice Solos with Piano Accompaniment; 1 Voice Solo with Bamboo Pipe Accompaniment; Voices and Drums in Ewe Traditional Gabada and Gbolo idioms; A Handbook for the Choirmaster. *Hobbies:* Driving; Research into African Traditional Music. *Address:* Evangelical Presbyterian Church, Ve-Gbodome, PO Box 33, Ve-Golokuati, V/R, Ghana.

NDOSI, Moses, b. 14 Aug. 1938, Arusha, Tanzania. Medical Doctor. m. 2 Feb. 1975, 2 sons, 1 daughter. *Education:* Medical Assistant Training, 1958-60; BA., Hartwick College, New York, USA, 1962-66; Bachelor of Medicine, Bachelor of Surgery, Makerere University, Kampala, Uganda, 1966-71. *Appointments:* Internship, Mukimbili Hospital, Dar-es-Salaam, 1971; Kilimanjaro Christian Medical Centre, Northern Tanzania, 1972-76; Private Consulting Clinic, Mombasa, Kenya, 1976-. *Memberships:* Kenya Medical Association. *Hobbies:* Gardening; Swimming. *Address:* PO Box 99577, Mombasa, Kenya.

NDUKWE, Ndukwe Iwo, b. 4 Oct. 1945, Abiriba, Nigeria. Architect. m. Ngozi, 28 Dec. 1979. *Education:* BSc., Hons., 1970-73, MSc., 1973-75, Ahmadu Bello University, Zaria, Nigeria. *Appointments:* Architect with: Ministry of Works and Surveys, Kaduna, Nigeria, 1975-76; Ekwueme Associates, Lagos, Nigeria, 1976-79; Integrated Consultants, Lagos, Nigeria, 1979-80; Partner, Starc Partnership, Aba, Nigeria, 1980-. *Memberships:* Nigerian Institute of Architects. *Publications:* A Centre for Cultures and Tourism, Argungu, 1975; Housing for 2000 People, 1973. *Honours:* Book prize for Best student of Fine Art, Hwti, Calabar, Nigeria, 1965; Onafowokan Prize for Best student in Design, 1971, National Scholarship award for outstanding students, 1971, Ahmadu Bello University, Zaria, Nigeria; Participant, International Union of Architects Seminar, Lome, Togo, Mar. 1974. *Hobbies:* Tennis; Music; Chess. *Address:* 8 Uche Street, Eziama Gra, Aba, Nigeria.

NEAL, Bernard William, b. 18 July 1924, Melbourne, Australia. Medical Practitioner. m. Enid Elizabeth Murphy, 23 Feb. 1956, 2 sons, 2 daughters. *Education:*

MB., BS., 1947, MD., 1954, Melbourne, Australia; MRACP., 1955; FRACP., 1965; Dip. Ed., Monash, 1978. *Appointments:* Lecturer in Child Health, Liverpool University, Consultant Paediatrician, Alder Hey Hospital, Liverpool, UK, 1955-56; Honorary Paediatrician, Box Hill and District Hospital, Melbourne, Australia, 1957-62; Physician to Outpatients, 1960-73, Physician in Charge, Enuresis Clinic, 1966-, Physician/Head of Unit, 1973-, Dean of Postgraduate Studies, 1976-, Royal Children's Hospital, Melbourne, Australia; Member, 1970-79, Chairman, Medicine Advisory Committee, 1974-79, National Health and Medical Research Council of Australia; Visiting Lecturer, Paediatrics, School of Postgraduate Medical Studies, 1971; External Examiner, Master of Medicine (Paediatrics) Examination, 1972, University of Singapore; Member, Deputy President, 1976-80, President, 1980-, Medical Board of Victoria, Consultative Council on Maternal and Child Health, 1975-, Poisons Advisory Committee, 1977-, Victorian Government. *Memberships:* Honorary Secretary, Australian Paediatric Association, 1966-71; Alternate member, Standing Committee, 1978-80, Standing Commitee, 1980-, International Paediatric Association. Advisory Board, Association of Paediatric Societies of the South-East Asian Region, 1974-. *Publications:* numerous publications including: Meningeal Tuberculosis in Children, a review of Forty Patients, 1951; Myeloid Leukaemia following irradiation, 1970; Coeliac Disease in Two Generations, 1963; The Management of Enuresis, 1972; Congenital Sensory Neuropathy, 1974; Alcohol-Induced Hypoglycaemia, 1979. *Hobby:* Golf. *Address:* 7 Orford Avenue, Kew, Victoria 3101, Australia.

NEAL, Eric James, b. 3 June 1924, England. Company Executive. m. Thelma Joan Bowden, 4 Mar. 1950, 2 sons. *Education:* Engineering Course, South Australian School of Mines, 1940-49. *Appointments:* Engineering Design Department, Electricity Trust of South Australia, 1948; Works Engineer, Broken Hill & Suburban Gas Company, Australia, 1950; Manager, Ballarat Gas Company, acquired by Boral Limited, 1963, 1959; Boral Gas operations, 1964, Chief General Manager and Director, 1972, Chief Executive, 1973, Boral Limited, Australia. *Memberships:* Institution of Gas Engineers, London; Fellow: Australian Institute of Energy; Australian Institute of Management; Past board member, Australian Gas Association; Institute of Directors; Science and Industry Forum, Australian Academy of Science. *Hobbies:* Boating; Reading. *Address:* 93 Pentecost Avenue, St. Ives, New South Wales 2075, Australia.

NEAL, Harold John, b. 9 Apr. 1954, Northampton, England. Senior Medical Cytotechnologist. m. Stephanie Purcell, 17 Dec. 1977. *Education:* ONC, Medical Laboratory Sciences, Kettering Technical College, 1971-73; HNC, Bristol Polytechnic, 1973-76; Special Examination of the Institute of Medical Laboratory Sciences, Histopathology/Cytopathology, Bristol Polytechnic, 1976-78. *Appointments:* Medical Laboratory Scientific Officer, Department of Pathology, Northampton General Hospital, 1971-78; Senior Medical Laboratory Scientific Officer, Cytopathology Department, Leicester Royal Infirmary, 1978-80; Senior Medical Cytotechnologist, Head of Department, Cytopathology Department, Dunedin Public Hospital, 1980-. *Memberships:* Fellow, The Institute of Medical Laboratory Sciences; Associate of New Zealand Institute of Medical Laboratory Technology. *Hobbies:* Flying, Private Pilot Light Aircraft; Squash; Philately; Model Railways. *Address:* 17 Musselburgh Rise, Musselburgh, Dunedin, New Zealand.

NEAL, Laurence William, b. 18 July 1947, Wangaratta, Victoria, Australia. Senator. *Education:* BA, 1972, Diploma of Education, 1973, Bachelor of Education, 1975, La Trobe University, Melbourne. *Appointments:* Secondary School Teacher, 1973-78; Tutor in Education, 1979-80, Deputy Head of Glenn College, 1979-82, La Trobe University; Senator for Victoria, 1980-81. *Memberships:* Australian College of Education; Australian Institute of International Affairs; Australian National University Convocation; La Trobe University Convocation; Commonwealth Parliamentary Association; Inter-Parliamentary Union; Former Vice-President, Victoria, Former Editor, Party Journal—National Outlook and Federal Council of National Country Party of Australia. *Hobbies:* Golf; Tennis; Reading; Music; Photography; Gardening. *Address:* Lyndwood-Gapst-

ed, 18 Noonan Street, Wangaratta, 3677, Victoria, Australia.

NEAL, Stephanie (Mrs Harold Neal), b. 18 Jan. 1956, Kettering, Northants, England. Medical Technologist. m. Harold, 17 December, 1977. *Education:* HNC, Medical Laboratory Sciences, Bristol Polytechnic College, 1976. *Appointments:* Kettering General Hospital, England, 1974-78; Leicester Royal Infirmary, England, 1978-80; Dunedin Public Hospital, New Zealand, 1981-. *Memberships:* Associate of Institute of Medical Laboratory Sciences, UK; New Zealand Institute of Technology. *Hobbies:* Badminton; Swimming; Philately; Squash; Knitting. *Address:* 17 Musselburgh Rise, Dunedin, New Zealand.

NEALE, Marie Draga (Mrs), b. Taranaki, New Zealand. Psychologist, Educator. 1 son, 1 daughter. *Education:* Teacher Training Certificate, Auckland Teachers College, Auckland, 1941; Specialist Teachers Certificate (Physical Education), Dunedin Teachers College, Dunedin, Otago, 1942; BA, 1944, MA, 1945, Dip.Ed., 1945, University of New Zealand, Auckland; Dip.Psych., 1952, PhD., 1956, University of Birmingham, UK. *Appointments:* Teacher, New Zealand, 1942-46; Lecturer, 1947-50, Research Fellow, 1953-56, University of Birmingham; Lecturer, County Borough of Smethwick, 1956; Clinical Psychologist, Monyhull Hospital, Birmingham, UK, 1957-59; Psychologist, Department of Health, New South Wales, Child Guidance Clinics, 1960-61; Senior Lecturer, University of Sydney, 1961-69; Consultant Psychologist, Neurology Outpatients Clinic, Royal Alexandra Hospital for Children, Sydney, 1961-69; Visiting Professor, University of California, Berkeley, USA, 1968; Honorary Consultant Psychologist, Queen Victoria Medical Centre, 1973-; Foundation Professor, Chair of Exceptional Children, 1970-, Founding Director, Dinah & Henry Krongold Centre for Exceptional Children, 1976-, Monash University; Professional Consultancies: National Literature Board of Review, 1968-70; National Film Board of Review, 1970-73; Australian Pre-School Committee, 1972-73; Victorian Committee on Mental Retardation, 1975; Ministerial Standing Committee on Special Education, 1975; State Council for Special Education (Victoria), 1976-; Standing Committee on Teacher Education, State Council for Special Education, 1980-; QECD Advisory Committee on Education, 1978-. *Memberships:* Fellow of the British and Australian Psychological Societies; National Education Committee Australian Council for Rehabilitation of Disabled, 1962-80; Rehabilitation International Education Commission; Board of Directors and Convenor of the Scientific Sub-Committee, Apex Foundation for Research into Mental Retardation; Australian Group for the Scientific Study of Mental Deficiency; Association for the Study of Specific Learning Difficulties, Victoria, and New South Wales. *Publications:* Neale Analysis of Reading Ability, 1958 (revised 1967); Neale Scales of Early Childhood Development, 1976; Film of Administration of the Neale Scales of Early Childhood Development, 1974; Various papers on child psychology, handicapped and gifted children; Experimental programs for Gifted Children; Models for training personnel for work with exceptional children. *Honours:* First woman appointed as Professor in Education in Australasia; First Professor in Studies of Exceptional Children in Australasia, 1970; Rosemary F Dybwad International Award in Mental Retardation, 1972; OBE, 1980. *Hobbies:* Reading; Swimming; Dancing; Music; Theatre. *Address:* Dinah and Henry Krongold Centre for Exceptional Children, Faculty of Education, Monash University, Clayton, Victoria, 3168, Australia.

NEAVE, Richard Arthur Headley, b. 17 Dec. 1936, London. Medical Artist. m. 23 Apr. 1960, 1 son, 1 daughter. *Education:* Hastings School of Art, 1953-55; Medical Art Training, Middlesex Hospital, 1957-59; Fellowship of The Medical Artists Association, 1977. *Appointments:* National Service, 1955-57; Medical Artist, 1959-69, Assistant Director, Department of Medical Illustration, 1969-, University of Manchester. *Memberships:* Council and Education Committee of Medical Artists Association of Gt Britain & Northern Ireland; Council & Education Committee of Institute of Medical & Biological Illustration. *Creative Works:* Egyptian Mummu, 1770, (The reconstruction of human heads from skeletal remains). *Hobbies:* Sailing; Model making; Painting; Drawing. *Address:* 89 Stamford

Road, Altringham Bowdon, Cheshire, WA14 2JJ, England.

NEAVERSON, Michael Anthony, b. 4 Oct. 1933, Peterborough, England. Consultant Physician. m. Desley Hughes, 12 Dec. 1959, 3 sons, 1 daughter. *Education:* MB.,BS., University of Queensland, 1953-59; Royal College of Physicians, 1965; Royal Australian College of Physicians, 1967; Fellow, Royal Australian College of Physicians, 1973. *Appointments:* Resident Medical Officer, Rockhampton Base Hospital, 1959-61; Medical Registrar, St Mary's Hospital, Portsmouth, 1961-64, Barnet Hospital, London, 1965; Senior Medical Registrar, Sydney Hospital, 1966-67; Honorary Consultant Physician, Masonic Hospital, Sydney, 1968-, Senior Physician, Western Suburbs Hospital, Sydney, 1967-; Medical Director, Pacific and Far East Area, Abbott Laboratores, 1967-77; Executive Director, Samati International, Sydney, 1977-. *Memberships:* President, University of Queensland, Medical Students, 1959; Chairman, Western Suburbs Hospital, Medical Staff, 1977-. *Publications:* Numerous Medical contributions on Cardiology and Pharmacology (Clinical). *Honours:* Soccer Blue, University of Queensland, 1959. *Hobbies:* Golf; Rotary. *Address:* 23 Vernon Street, Strathfield, Sydney, Australia.

NEELAKANTAN, Sthanusubramania, b. 22 Apr. 1927, Nagercoil, Tamilnadu, India. Professor. m. P Vasantha, 7 May 1950, 1 son, 1 daughter. *Education:* BSc, 1949; MSc, 1950; PhD, 1955; Diploma in French, 1973; Diploma in Russian, 1976. *Appointments:* Demonstrator in Chemistry, Andhra University; Lecturer and Reader in Chemistry, Delhi University; Professor of Chemistry, Madurai Kamaraj University. *Memberships:* Fellow Royal Institute of Chemistry (Honorary Secretary North India Branch); Fellow, Indian Chemical Society (Council). *Publications:* Approximately 100 research publications. *Honours:* S.S. Bhatnagar Prize, Andhra University, 1949. *Hobby:* Music. *Address:* Karthik, Plot 411, AA Nagar, Madurai-625020, India.

NEIL, Eric, b. 15 Feb. 1918, Maryport, Cumbria, UK. University Professor. m. Anne Baron Parker, 16 Apr. 1946, 2 daughters. *Education:* University of Leeds, 1935-42; BSc, Hons. I Physiology, 1939; MB.,Ch.B., 1942; MD (Distinction), 1944; DSc, 1953; FRCP., 1978. *Appointments:* Lecturer in Physiology, Leeds, 1942-49; Visiting Research Fellow, Kungl. Veterinärhogskolan, Stockholm, 1949; Reader in Physiology, University of London, 1950-56; John Astor Professor of Physiology, Chairman and Head of Department, in University of London at the Middlesex Hospital Medical School, 1956-. *Memberships:* Chairman, European Board of Physiological Reviews, 1962-68; Honorary Treasurer, The Physiological Society, 1961-67; Honorary Treasurer, 1968-74, President, 1974-80, International Union of Physiological Sciences. *Publications:* Reflexogenic Areas in the Cardiovascular System (jointly), 1958; Applied Physiology (jointly) 10th edition, 1961, 11th edition, 1965, 12th edition, 1971, 13th edition, 1982; Circulation (jointly), 1971; The Human Circulation, 1980; William Harvey, 1975; Scientific papers in medical and physiological journals. *Honours:* Queen's Silver Jubilee Medal, 1977; Honorary MD University Ghent; Fellow, The Royal Academy of Medicine, Belgium. *Hobbies:* Piano; Photography; Venetian Painting. *Address:* 53 Talbot Road, Highgate, London N6 4QX, England.

NEILSON, William Arthur, b. b. 27 Aug. 1925, Tasmania. Agent General for Tasmania. m. Jill, 25 May, 1948, 1 son, 3 daughters. *Education:* Ogilvie High School, Hobart, Tasmania. *Appointments:* Clerk in PMG's Department; Labor Whip, 1946-55; House of Assembly for Franklin, Tasmania, 1946-; Minister for Forests, Tourism and Immigration, 1956-58; Attorney General, 1958-59; Treasurer, 1959; Minister for Education, 1958-69, 1972-74; Deputy Premier, Attorney-General, Minister for Police and Licencing and Minister for the Environment, 1974-75; Premier and Treasurer of Tasmania, 1975-; Agent General for Tasmania, 1978-. *Memberships:* President, ALP, Tasmanian Section, 1968-69. *Honours:* Companion of the Order of Australia, 1978. *Hobbies:* Reading; Cards; Chess; Australian Rules Football; Writing; Amateur Theatre. *Address:* Tasmania House, 458 Strand, London, WC2R ORJ, England.

NELSON, Alan John Mark, b. 3 Apr. 1917, Victoria, Australia. Radiation Oncologist. m. Mavis Louise Sad-

ler, 3 July 1943, 3 sons, 2 daughters. *Education:* Diploma of Radiology (Therapeutic), Sydney University, 1946; Diploma of Diagnostic Radiology, Melbourne University, 1947; Fellowship of Royal Australasian College of Radiologists, 1959. *Appointments:* Resident Medical Officer, Royal Melbourne Hospital, 1940; Major, Specialist Radiologist, Australian Army Medical Corps, AIF, 1941; Radiotherapy Registrar, Royal Price Alfred Hospital, Sydney, NSW, 1946-47; Consultant Radiotherapist to Royal Perth Hospital, Sir Charles Gairdner Hospital, Fremantle Hospital, Princess Margaret and King Edward Memorial Hospitals, all teaching hospitals in Perth, Western Australia, 1947-82; Head of the Department of Radiotherapy at Royal Perth Hospital, 1950-80; Private practice as Radiation Oncologist, Western Australia, 1947-. *Memberships:* Cancer Council of Western Australia, 1954-80; Australian Medical Association, 1939-; Chairman, Leukaemia and Allied Diseases Committee Western Australia, 1970-80. *Publications:* Numerous contributions in medical journals including: Microwaves an Adjuvant to Lympohoma Therapy; Problem of Clinical Hyperthermia; Four Years of Microwaves in Cancer Therapy. *Honours:* Archibald Spencer Prize (Medical Student), 1935; Life Membership YMCA, 1976. *Hobbies:* Farming; Author; Music; Piano Performance; Methodist Lay Preacher. *Address:* 7 York Street, South Perth, Western Australia, 6151.

NELSON, Aruna Kojo, b. 27 Apr. 1908, Accra, Ghana. Bishop. m. Grace Kwarkai Quartey-Papafio, 6 Feb. 1936, 3 daughters. *Education:* St Augustine's Theological College, Kumasi, Ashanti, Ghana. *Appointments:* Deacon, 1932; Ordained Priest, 1932; Canon of Holy Trinity Cathedral, 1957; Commissioned first ever Ghanaian Anglican Chaplain to the Ghana Armed Forces, 1959-63; Provost of the Holy Trinity Cathedral, Accra, 1963-77; Consecrated Assistant Bishop of Accra, 1966. *Memberships:* Christian Peace Conference. *Honours:* Visits to Great Britain, Russia, Hungary, Czechoslovakia, Ireland, Lebanon, France, Zaire, Togo, Sierra-Leone; Served with the UNO during the crisis in the Congo, as Chaplain to the Forces, 1961-62. *Hobbies:* Lawn Tennis; Gardening; Walking. *Address:* 71 North Kaneshie Estate, PO Box 3824, Accra, Ghana.

NELSON, Kenneth Davies, b. 3 Aug. 1921, Llandebie, South Wales, UK. Civil Engineer. m. Shirley Dallas Roberts, 12 May 1975, 2 daughters (by previous marriage). *Education:* BSc, University of Wales, Cardiff, 1949; FIE.Aust., 1980; FGS, 1980; MICE, 1956. *Appointments:* Executive Engineer with: Victorian Water Commission; Ministry for Conservation. *Memberships:* Naval and Military Club, Melboune. *Publications:* Dictionary of Applied Geology, 1967; Dictionary of Water & Water Engineering, 1973; Water Resources, 1979. *Honours:* ED, 1971. *Hobby:* Genealogy. *Address:* 151 Domain Park, 193 Domain Road, South Yarra, 3141, Victoria, Australia.

NELSON, Richard Anthony, b. 11 June 1948, Hamburg, Germany. Member of Parliament. m. Caroline Victoria Butler, 20 Apr. 1974, 1 son, 1 daughter. *Education:* MA, Economics and Law, Christ's College, Cambridge University, 1966-69. *Appointments:* Merchant Banker, NM Rothschild & Sons Ltd., 1969-75; Member of the Council of the Bow Group, 1971; Contested East Leeds (Conservative), 1974; Elected Conservative MP for Chichester, 1974; Select Committee on Science & Technology, 1975-79; Appointed Parliamentary Private Secretary to the Minister for Housing and Construction, 1979-. *Memberships:* Fellow, Royal Society of Arts; Treasurer, The British Caribbean Parliamentary Group; Secretary, British Jordanian Parliamentary Group; Secretary, UK Manx Parliamentary Group. *Hobbies:* Music; Rugby. *Address:* House of Commons, London, SW1, England.

NEMAIA, Andrew Tewaea, b. 30 Dec. 1953, Manra Island, Republic if Kiribati. Admihistrator. m. Kobua Kabiri, 16 Mar. 1976, 2 sons. *Education:* St John School, Nila, Shortland, Primary Certificate, 1963-69; Marist Brothers High School, Kieta, School Certificate, 1970-73. *Appointments:* Clerk, Labour Department, 1974-75; Personnel Officer, Ministry of Trade, Industry and Labour, 1976-77; Registrar, Honiara Technical Institute, 1978-. *Hobbies:* Reading; Meeting People; Volleyball; Music. *Address:* Komaleai Village, Nila Postal Agency, Shortland Islands, Western Province, Solomon Islands.

NETTLEFOLD, Brian William, b. 11 Sept. 1921, Hobart, Tasmania, Australia. Barrister. m. Mary Isobel Quinn, 17 June 1944, 4 sons. *Education:* Bachelor of Laws, University of Tasmania, 1959. *Appointments:* Barrister at Law, 1960-; Tutor, Melbourne University, State of Victoria, 1960; Appointed Queen's Counsel for State of Victoria, 1977, for State of Tasmania, 1977. *Memberships:* RACV, 1960; VRC, 1964; VFL, Melbourne, 1969. *Honours:* Mercury Scholarship, 1959; University Prizes for each year of course, 1955-59. *Hobbies:* Gardening; Travel; Sport. *Address:* 7 Rothesay Avenue, East Melvern, 3145, Australia.

NETTUR, Pavithran Krishnan, b. 1 Mar. 1936, Johore, Malaysia. Naval Officer, Commodore. m. Mary Loretta Suranganie, 29 Mar. 1961. 1 son, 2 daughters. *Education:* Royal Naval College Dartmouth, United Kingdom, 1958; Royal Naval College, Greenwich, 1965; Joint Services Staff College, Latimer, 1968. *Appointments:* British Royal Naval Ships, 1958-61; Royal Malaysian Naval Ships in Command, 1961-68; Director of Personnel and Training, Navy Department, Ministry of Defence, 1969-70; Directing Staff, Armed Forces Staff College, 1971-72; Commander Naval Forces West Malaysia, 1973-74, 1977-78, East Malaysia, 1975-76, 1979-80; Director, Defence Planning Staff, 1980, Defence Operations Staff, 1981. *Memberships:* British Institute of Management; Nautical Institute; Royal Institute of Navigation. *Honours:* Malaysian Federal and State awards, AMN, 1967, KMN, 1973, SMJ, 1979, JMN, 1980, ASDK, 1980. *Hobbies:* Fishing; Golf; Tennis. *Address:* The Anchorage, No 8 Jalan Kent 6, Off Jalan Maktab, Kuala Lumpur, Malaysia.

NEUMANN, Bernhard Hermann, b. 15 Oct. 1909, Berlin, Germany. Mathematician. m. (1) Hanna von Caemmerer, 22 Dec. 1938 (Deceased 1971), 3 sons, 2 daughters, (2) Dorothea Frieda Auguste Zeim, 24 Dec. 1973. *Education:* University of Freiburg, Germany, 1928-29; University of Berlin, Germany, 1929-31; D.Phil., (Berlin), 1932; University of Cambridge, England, 1933-35; PhD (Cantab), 1935; DSc (Manchester) 1954; Hon. DSc (Newcastle, New South Wales), 1974, (Monash Universiy) 1982. *Appointments:* Temporary Assistant Lecturer in Mathematics, University College of South Wales and Monmouthshire, Cardiff, 1937-40; Army Service, Pioneer Corps, Royal Artillery, Intelligence Corps, 1940-45; Lecturer in Mathematics, University College, Hull, 1946-48; Lecturer, Senior Lecturer, Reader in Mathematics, University of Manchester, 1948-61; Professor, Head of the Department of Mathematics, 1962-74, Honorary Fellow, 1975-, Emeritus Professor, 1975-, Institute of Advanced Studies, Australian National University; Senior Research Fellow, 1975-77, Honorary Research Fellow, 1978-, Commonwealth Scientific and Industrial Research Organization, Division of Mathematics and Statistics; Visiting appointments (usually as Visiting Professor or Visiting Fellow or Visiting Lecturer): Australian universities, 1959; Tata Institute of Fundamental Research, Bombay, 1959; New York University, Courant Institute of Mathematical Sciences, 1961-62; University of Wisconsin, Madison, 1966-67; Vanderbilt University, Nashville, Tennessee, 1969-70; University of Cambridge, England, 1970; Fitzwilliam College, Cambridge, 1970; University of Illinois, Urbana-Champaign, 1975; University of Manitoba, Winnipeg, 1979; Monash University, Clayton, Victoria, 1980. *Memberships:* Council, 1954-61, Vice-President, 1957-59, Honorary Editor, (Proceedings), 1959-61, London Mathematical Society; Council, 1963-79, Vice-President, 1963-64, 1966-68, 1971-73, President, 1964-66, Editor, 1969-79, Honorary Editor, 1979-, Honorary Member, 1981, Australian Mathematical Society; Council, 1968-71, Vice-President, 1969-71, Australian Academy of Science; Chairman, 1966-75, Australian National Committee for Mathematics, 1963-75; President, 1966-68, Vice-President, 1968-69, Honorary Member, 1975, Australian Association of Mathematics Teachers; President, 1963-65, Vice-President, 1965-66, Honorary Member, 1975, Canberra Mathematical Association; Honorary Member, New Zealand Mathematical Society, 1975-; Wiskundig Genootschap te Amsterdam; American Mathematical Society; Mathematical Association; Mathematical Association of America; Canadian Mathematical Society; Oesterreichische Mathematische Gesellschaft; Glasgow Mathematical Association; Southeast Asian Mathematical Society; Australian Computer Society. *Publications:* Appendix to German and Hungarian translations of A G Kuros: Teorija Grupp, 1953, 1955; Topics in the theory of infinite groups, Bombay, 1962; Special topics in algebra, Vol. I Universal Algebra Vol. II; Order techniques in algebra, New York, 1962. More than 100 papers, mainly on theory of groups, in various mathematical journals. *Honours:* Prize, Wiskundig Genootschap te Amsterdam, 1949; Adams Prize, University of Cambridge, 1952-53; Fellow, Royal Society, 1959; Fellow, Australian Academy of Science, 1964; Fellow, The Australian College of Education, 1970. *Hobbies:* Chess; Classical Music (Cello); Cycling. *Address:* 20 Talbot Street, Forrest, ACT 2603, Australia.

NEWALL, Ian Graham, b. 13 Oct. 1930, Corrimal, NSW, Australia. Health Services Administrator. m. Gwendoline Mary, 15 Sept. 1954, 2 sons, 1 daughter. *Education:* Bachelor of Health Administration, University of New South Wales, 1971. *Appointments:* Secretary, Goodooga District Hospital, NSW, 1958-61; Chief Executive Officer, Vegetable Creek Hospital, NSW, 1961-62; Bourke District Hospital, NSW, 1962-64; Nepean District Hospital, NSW, 1964-70; Regional Administrative Officer, Hospitals Commission of NSW, 1970-74; Deputy Regional Director, Health Commission of NSW, 1974-77; Deputy Chief Executive Officer, Westmead Hospital, NSW, 1977-81; Director of Administration, Department of Hospital and Allied Services, Western Australia, 1981-. *Memberships:* Associate, Australian College of Health Service Administrators; Fellow, Australian Institue of Management; Visiting Committee to the School of Health Administration, University of NSW. *Honours:* Justice of the Peace, NSW. *Hobbies:* Sailing; Art; Golf; Fishing. *Address:* 12A Robert Street, Dalkeith, Western Australia, 6009.

NEWBURY, Colin Walter, b. 4 Mar. 1929, New Zealand. University Teacher. m. 1957, 1 daughter. *Education:* MA, University of New Zealand, 1953; PhD, Australian National University, 1956. *Appointments:* Teaching Fellow, University of Otago, 1953; Postgraduate Scholar, Australian National University, 1953-56; University Lectuer, Department of History, University of Ibadan, Nigeria, 1956-58; Department of Social Sciences, Unesco, 1959; Oppenheimer Studentship, Oxford University, 1959-60; Research Officer, Senior Research Officer, Institute of Commonwealth Studies, Oxford; University Lecturer in Commonwealth History, Fellow of Linacre College, 1964. *Publications:* The Western Slave Coast and its Rulers, 1961; The West African Commonwealth, 1964; British Policy towards West Africa, Select Documents, two volumes, 1965, 1970; The History of the Tahitian Mission, 1799-1830, 1961; Tahiti Nui. Change and Survival in French Polynesia, 1767-1945, 1980. *Hobby:* Sailing. *Address:* 12 Carey Close, Oxford, England.

NEWCOMBE, Kenneth James, b. 25 Sept. 1947, Melbourne, Victoria, Australia. Energy Planner. m. Marte Stojkovic, 29 Mar. 1969, 1 son, 1 daughter. *Education:* BSc, 1969, HSc Hons., 1970, University of Tasmania, Hobart, Tasmania; PhD, 1976, John Curtin School of Medical Research, Australian National University. *Appointments:* Research Fellow, Centre for Resource and Environmental Studies, Australian National University, Canberra, 1976-, (Seconded to Papua New Guinea Government, 19780; Energy Planner and Head Energy Planning Unit, Department of Minerals and Energy, Papua New Guinea, 1978-81; General Manager (interim), Papua New Guinea Electricity Commission, 1981-; Consultant for UNESCO/UNEP/UNDO/BSCAP; Energy and Resource Planning. *Memberships:* The Australian Institute of Energy. *Publications:* Co-author of two books; Author/Co-Author of 50 scientific papers and monographs. *Hobbies:* Tennis; Fishing; Gardening. *Address:* 3 Siale Place, Boroko, Papua New Guinea.

NEWELL, Lawrence James, b. 12 Feb. 1920, Reading, Berks., England. Chairman. m. Jean Ellen Farrell, 27 June 1942, 1 son, 2 daughters. *Education:* Staff Course, Victoria Police Officers' College, 1966; Fellowship, Australian Automobile Association 1967; Postgraduate Course, Traffic Planning and Control, School of Traffic Engineering University of New South Wales, Sydney 1968. *Appointments:* Victoria Police, 1940; Inspector 1966; Director of Studies Victoria Police Officers' College 1968-70; Assistant Commissioner, Personnel, 1971-74; Assistant Commissioner, Traffic, 1974-77; Member Victorian Consultative Council on Road Mortality 1944-77; Deputy Commissioner of Police 1977-78; Chairman, Country Fire Authority, Victoria 1978. *Memberships:* Road Safety Traffic Authority; Victorian Consultative Council on Road Mortality; Australian Assembly of Fire Authorities; C.M.F. Service, Lt. 10 Fd. Regt. RAA 1951; Captain 1954; Temporary Major 15th Lt. Regt. RAA 1955; HQ, RAA 3rd Div. 1957; Major 1957; Lt. Col. and CO 2nd Fd. Regt. RAA 1963-67; S. Commd. Staff and Training Group 1967; Colonel RAA 1972, (Retired). *Honours:* O.St.J; QPM; ED; FAIM; Efficiency Decoration, Australian Army Reserve, 1963; First Clasp to Decoration, 1969; Queen's Police Medal for Distinguished Service 1974; Officer of the Order of St John of Jerusalem. *Address:* 56 Fromer Street, Moorabbin, Victoria 3189, Australia.

NEWMAN, Jack, b. 3 July 1902, Nelson, New Zealand. Company Director. m. 27 Sept. 1926, 4 daughters. *Education:* Nelson College, New Zealand, 1917-20. *Appointments:* Passenger and Freight Transport, Tourist Industry, 1920-80. *Memberships:* MCC; New Zealand Cricket Council and Foundation; Wellesley and Nelson Clubs. *Honours:* CBE 1965; KB 1977. *Hobbies:* Cricket; Golf; Lawn Bowls. *Address:* 36 Brougham Street, Nelson, New Zealand.

NEWNHAM, William Arthur, b. 3 Aug. 1918, Perth, Western Australia. Medical Practitioner. m. Mary Constance Phillipps, 14 May 1947, 2 sons, 2 daughters. *Education:* MBBS, University of Adelaide, 1946; Diploma of Venereology, London, 1975. *Appointments:* General Practice Perth, Western Australia, 1948-71; Honorary Clinical Anaesthetist, Fremantle Hospital, Western Australia, 1955-66 Director Venereal Disease Control Programme, Western Australian Public Health Department, 1971-79; Clinical Staff, Royal Perth and Fremantle Hospitals, 1973-79. *Memberships:* Infectious Diseases Society for Australia; International Union against Venereal Disease and Treponematoses; Alcohol and Drug Authority of Western Australia; Venereal Disease Co-ordinating Committee, Western Australia; Pastoralists and Graziers Society; Royal Agricultural Society; Farm Management Foundation. *Publications:* The recognition and management of Syphilis, 1974; Asymptomatic Genital Gonorrhoea of the male, 1976; The Oral Manifestations of Venereal Disease, 1978; Handbook of Sexually Transmitted Diseases as one of a panel written under the auspices of the National Health and Medical Research Council of Australia; (co-author) Isolation of Adeno-Virus Type 19 from male and female genital tracts. *Honours:* Commonwealth Travelling Scholarship, National Health and Medical Research Council, 1975. *Hobbies:* Farming; Yachting. *Address:* 5 Whitney Crescent, Mt. Claremont Western Australia 6010.

NEY, David Marshall, b. 5 Nov. 1936, Sydney, Australia. Company Director. m. Barbara Jean, 5 Apr. 1980, 2 sons, 3 daughters. *Education:* Matriculation 1954; Carnegie Management, 1959; AFAIM, 1967. *Appointments:* Factory Manager: Beutron, Hong Kong, 1958-60, Sydney, 1961-63; Manager: Beutron, South Africa 1963-65, Sydney 1966-68; Manager, YKK Australia, 1968-75, President 1976-. *Memberships:* Australian Clothing Export Council; Australian Slide Fastner Association; Australian Confederation of Apparel Manufactures; Fashion Industries of Australia; Australian Institute of Management. *Hobbies:* Boating; Tennis. *Address:* 36 Awatea Road, St Ives, New South Wales, Australia.

NG, Chung Tai, b. 11 Aug. 1945, Shanghai, China. Publisher. m. Quach Chuc Hoa, 22 Jan. 1970, 1 son, 2 daughters. *Education:* New Method College, Hong Kong, 1959-64; Matriculated, Queen's College, Hong Kong, 1964-66. *Appointments:* Managing Director: Chung Tai Book Store, 1966-; Chung Tai Educational Press, 1978-; Academic Press Limited, 1979-. *Memberships:* Rotary Club, Hong Kong Island East. *Publications:* Electronic Technology; Chinese and English textbooks and reference books for Hong Kong Schools. *Hobbies:* Music; Reading. *Address:* 63 Electric Road, 6th Floor, Flat A-B, Causeway Bay, Hong Kong.

NGAEI, George, b. 2 June 1944, Rarutunga, Cook Islands. Medical Practitioner. (Surgeon). m. Elizabeth (Bobi) Anne Adair, 1 son, 2 daughters. *Education:* University of Otago Medical School, 1962-68; MB, ChB, Otago, 1968; FRACS 1974.. *Appointments:* Consultant General & Vascular Surgeon, Director, Intensive Care Unit, Surgical Tutor, Southland Hospital; Lecturer in Surgery Trainee Intern Supervisor, Otago

Medical School; Supervisor of Surgical Training, Royal Australasian College of Surgeons. *Memberships:* Hon. Surgeon, Southland Rugby Union; Member of Invercargil Club. *Hobbies:* Big Game and Trout Fishing; Jogging; Squash. *Address:* 64 Albert Street, Gladstone, Invercargill, New Zealand.

NG'ANG'A, Stanley Kamanga, b. 19 Dec. 1951. Teacher/Librarian m. Rhoda Wanjiku, 3 May 1980, 1 daughter. *Education:* Bachelor of Education (Hons), Nairobi; Diploma in Librarianship, Wales. *Appointments:* Graduate Teacher, Kaiboi Technical School, 1975-76; Chief Librarian/Head of Library and Archival training Kenya Polytechnic, Nairobi, 1977-. *Memberships:* Kenya Library Association; Library Association, UK; National Association of Technical Teachers of Kenya. *Publications:* User Education-Thesis-College of Librarianships, Wales, 1977; Bibliography on Gifted children (in preparation); Library Education in Kenya (Manuscripts). *Honours:* Three Mobil Oil Merit Awards. *Hobbies:* Reading; Boxing; Football; Rugby. *Address:* PO Box 53458, Nairobi, Kenya.

NGERI-NWAGHA, Georgiana Kiente, b. 8 June 1945, Twon-Brass, Rivers State, Nigeria. Librarian. m. Herbert N Nwagha, 2 sons 2 daughters. *Education:* BA Hons. English, University of Nigeria, 1972; Postgraduate Diploma in Librarianship, University of Ibadan, Nigeria 1973; Master of Library Science, University of Western Ontario, 1976; Doctoral Candidate, 1978. *Appointments:* Assistant Statistician, Economic Development Institute, Univesity Nigeria; Library Officer, Ministry of Information, Port Harcourt, 1972 -73; Circulations Librarian, College of Science and Technology, Port Harcourt, 1973-75; Principal Librarian, 1978-79; Chairperson, Rivers State Textbook, Review Committee, Governor's Office, Port Harcourt, 1980-. *Memberships:* Nigerian Library Association; American Library Association; Port Harcourt Women's Corona Society. *Publications:* Olali, 1972; The Importance of a good school Library, 1974; Barriers to the accessibility of Scientific journals in Nigeria, 1980. *Honours:* John F Kennedy Essay award, 1964; National Council of the Nigerian Library Association, 1974-76; Rivers State Library Board 1980; Rivers State Curriculum Development Committee 1980. *Hobbies:* Swimming; Tennis; Volleyball; Dancing; Travelling; Music; Reading. *Address:* PO Box 1165, Port Harcourt, Nigeria.

NICHOLAS, (Sir) John William, b. 1924. British Diplomat. m. Dorothy Rita 1947, 2 sons. *Education:* BA-(Hons) Birmingham University. *Appointments:* War Office 1949-57; 1st Secretary British High Commission, Kuala Lumpur 1957-61; Deputy High Commissioner, British High Commission, Zomba, Malawi 1964-66; Diplomatic Service Inspector 1967-69; Deputy High Commissioner, Colombo 1970-71; Director of Establishments and Finance, Commonwealth Secretariat 1972-73; Head of Pacific Dependent Territories Department, FCO 1973-74; Deputy High Commissioner, Calcutta 1974-76; British Consul-Gen., Melbourne 1976-79; British High Commissioner Sri Lanka and Ambassador, Republic of Maldives 1979-. *Memberships:* Travellers; Royal Overseas League. *Honours:* KCVO CMG; *Address:* c/o Foreign and Commonwealth Office, London, SW1, England.

NICHOLLS, Claude Edward Courtenay, b. 12 July 1903, Yarmouth, Isle of Wight, England. Chemist/Chemical Engineer. m. Winifred Agnes Flux, 31 Jan. 1931, 1 son, 1 daughter. *Education:* University College Southampton 1925; BSc Hons. Chem. London; ARIC, FRIC 1942. *Appointments:* Chemist, British American Tobacco Company, 1926-29; Demonstrator in Chemistry, University College, Southampton, 1925-26; Chemist, Brit. Ind. Solvents, 1920-42; Manager, Acetone Pty. Ltd. Australia, 1942-45; Operations Manager, CSR Chemicals, 1947-64. *Memberships:* Royal Institute of Chemistry; Royal Australian Institute; President, RACI, 1960-61; Vice President, Benevolent Society of Australia, 1974-78. *Publications:* Various technical papers in Scientific Journals in Australia. *Honours:* Member of Council, University of New South Wales, 1963-69; Chairman, International House, 1964-67. *Hobbies:* Music; Oil Painting; Sketching. *Address:* 25 Junction Road, Wahroonga, NSW Australia, 2076.

NICHOLLS, Peter Borden, b. 27 Jan. 1935, Glasgow, Scotland. Plant Physiologist (Research). m. Margaret Irene Woolley, 17 May. 1958, 4 daughters. *Education:*

Bachelor of Science, Honours First Class, University of Tasmania 1954-58; Waite Agricultural Research Institute, University of Adelaide 1959-62; Doctorate of Philosophy, 1963. *Appointments:* Post Doctoral Fellow, California Institute of Technology, Pasadena 1962-64; Post Doctoral Fellow, MSU-AEC Plant Research Laboratory, Michigan State University 1965-66; Post-Doctoral Fellow, Flinders University, South Australia; Research Fellow, Waite Agricultural Research Institute, University of Adelaide 1967- *Memberships:* Australian Society of Plant Physiologists; American Society of Plant Growth Substances Association; British Plant Growth Regulators Group; Orienteering Association of South Australia. *Publications:* PhD Thesis, On the Growth of the Barley Shoot Apex; 16 Scientific Papers. Hobby: Orienteering. *Address:* 1 Chelmsford Avenue, Mitcham, S.A. 5062, Australia.

NICHOLSON, Ian Edmond, b. 29 Nov. 1932, Hamilton, Victoria, Australia. Diplomat; Public Servant. m. Judith Wyatt, 10 Dec. 1956, 1 son, 3 daughters. *Education:* LLB., University of Melbourne, Australia. *Appointments:* Department of Foreign Affairs, 1955, served South Africa, Egypt, Cambodia, New Caledonia, India; Assistant Secretary, PNG Branch, DFA, 1974-75; Australian High Commissioner to Malta, 1975-76; Ambassador to Chile, 1976-79; Australian Commissioner, Hong Kong, 1979-. *Memberships:* Former President, National Union of Australian University Students. *Hobby:* Tennis. *Address:* c/o Department of Foreign Affairs, Canberra, ACT, Australia.

NICHOLSON, Peter Theodore, b. 10 Feb. 1926, Sydney, Australia. Engineer. m. Patricia May Ohlsson, 21 Sept. 1949, 2 sons, 2 daughters. *Education:* BSc., 1947, BE., 1949, Sydney University, Australia. *Appointments:* Electric Equipment Corporation, London, UK; Email Limited, Standard-Waygood Limited, Westinghouse Electric Australasia Limited, Electrical Equipment Limited, Sydney, Australia. *Memberships:* Fellow, Institution of Engineers, Australia; Institution of Electrical Engineers, London, UK; Institution of Electrical and Electronic Engineers, USA. *Honours:* Fulbright Travelling Scholarship, 1954. *Hobbies:* Home Workshop; Gardening. *Address:* 99 Copeland Road, Beecroft, New South Wales 2119, Australia.

NICHOLSON, Robert David, b. 7 Aug. 1937, Perth, Western Australia. Barrister; Solicitor. m. Lynette Trumble, 27 Dec. 1967, 1 son, 2 daughters. *Education:* LL.B., 1959, BA., 1971, University of Western Australia; MA., Georgetown University, Washington, DC., USA, 1963; LL.M., University of Melbourne, Australia, 1981. *Appointments:* Partner, Muir Williams Nicholson & Co., 1963-; Secretary-General, Law Council of Australia, 1975-80; Secretary, Australian Legal Education Council, 1977-80. *Memberships:* Australasian Representative, Commonwealth Legal Bureau, 1978-80; Faculty Boards in Law, Melbourne and Monash Universities, Australia; General Committee, Australian Council of Professions, 1977-80; Chairman, Planning Committee, National Conference on Legal Education, 1976; Secretary, Planning Committee, Australian Legal Convention, 1973; Chairman, Optometrists Registration Board, 1969-73; Foundation President, Australian Graduates Conference, 1966-69. *Publications:* Various articles in Australian Legal Periodicals. *Honours:* Rotary Foundation Fellow, Fulbright Travel Grantee, 1961-62; Honorary Life Associate, Guild of Undergraduates, University of Western Australia, 1961; Cruickshank/Routley Memorial Prize, 1958; JN Barker Prize in Law, 1957; Blackstone Society Anniversary Prize for Constitutional Law, 1957. *Hobbies:* Tennis; Jogging; Music; History. *Address:* 39 Riley Road, Claremont, Western Australia 6010, Australia.

NICKEL, Ernest Henry, b. 31 Aug. 1925, Louth, Ontario, Canada. Mineralogist. m. (1) Muriel Jones, 24 Dec. 1949, (2) Eileen Woodward, 15 Mar. 1980, 3 daughters. *Education:* BSc., 1950, MSc., 1951, McMaster University; PhD., University of Chicago, USA, 1953. *Appointments:* Research Mineralogist, Head of Mineralogy Section, Mineral Sciences Division, Mines Branch, Ottawa, Canada, 1953-71; Chief Research Scientist, Division of Mineralogy, CSIRO, Perth, Western Australia, 1971-. *Memberships:* President 1969-70, Mineralogical Association, Canada; Fellow, Mineralogical Society of America; Mineralogical Society, London; Geological Society of Australia; Australasian Institute of Mining and Metallurgy; Australia and New

Zealand Association of Advanced Science. *Publications:* 65 papers published in technical journals; 12 new minerals discovered and characterized. *Honours:* Dean's Honour Roll, McMaster University, 1950; Rollin D. Salisbury Fellowship, University of Chicago, USA, 1951; Peacock Memorial Prize Walker Mineralogical Club, 1953; Hawley Award, Mineralogical Association, Canada, 1967, 1970. *Hobbies:* Bridge; Music. *Address:* 10 Dampier Avenue, City Beach, Western Australia 6015, Australia,

NICOLSON, Ian Ferguson, b. 22 Feb. 1921, Portree, Isle of Skye, Scotland. Writer. m. Doreen Florence Tabor, 15 Oct. 1945, 3 sons, 1 daughter. *Education:* BA., Manchester University, UK, 1938-40; Trinity College, Cambridge, England, 1950-51. *Appointments:* War Service, The Black Watch and 2nd Punjab Regiment, 1940-47; Colonial Administrative Service, Nigeria and Malaya, 1947-62; University research and teaching, Manchester University, UK, and University of Queensland, Australia, 1962-81. *Memberships:* Royal Institute of Public Administration. *Publications:* Books and articles on Government, Politics and Administration. *Honours:* Simon Research Fellow, Manchester University, UK, 1962-64; Haldane Essay Prize, Royal Institute of Public Administration, London, UK, 1976; Visiting Scholar, Nuffield College, Oxford, UK, 1979. *Hobby:* The Three R's. *Address:* Corlea High Street, Port St. Mary, Isle of Man, British Isles.

NICOLSON, Malcolm John, b. 27 Aug. 1922, Wellington, New Zealand. Medical practitioner. m. 16 Dec. 1950, 3 sons, 2 daughters. *Education:* BSc.; MB., CHB., New Zealand; D. Aust., Auckland; MRCOG; MRCGP. *Appointments:* House Surgeon, Wellington Hospital Board, 1955-56; Senior Obstetric and Gynaecological Registrar, National Womens Hospital, Auckland, New Zealand, 1962-64; Specialist and Obstetric and Gynaecological Tutor, Wellington Hospital, New Zealand, 1967-68; Medical Practitioner, Island Bay Medical Centre, Wellington, New Zealand. *Memberships:* Chairman, Wellington Hospital Board, 1971-; Vice-President, New Zealand Hospital Boards Association, 1977-; Hospital Advisory Council, 1977-; Chairman, Wellington Clinical School Council, 1980 -; Executive member, Wellington Division Cancer Society, 1975-; Chairman, Works Committee, 1970-71, Wellington Hospital Board, 1968-. *Hobbies:* Travel; Tramping; Bowls. *Address:* 1B Herbert Gardens, 186 The Terrace, Wellington, New Zealand.

NIEBOJ, Hans-Peter Harald, b. 5 Feb. 1930, Breslau, Silesia, Germany. Safety Engineering Specialist. m. Helga L Roglin, 30 July 1958. *Education:* University of Mainz, Germany, 1950-53; Diploma, Physics, University of Saarbrücken, Germany, 1953-58; Chemical Engineering University of New Brunswick, Canada, 1964-66; Structural Engineering University of Kansas, KS, USA, 1974-79. *Appointments:* Wissenschaftlicher Assistant at: University at Saarbrücken, Germany, 1956-58, University at Münster, Germany, 1958-61; Research Officer, Esso Research Limited, UK, 1961-64; Assistant Lecturer, University of New Brunswick, Canada, 1964-66; Academic Instructor, Institute of Technology, Saint John, New Brunswick, Canada, 1966-72; Assistant, University of Kansas, Department of Civil Engineering, 1974-79; Safety Engineering Specialist, Saskatchewan Power Corporation, Regina, Saskatchewan, Canada, 1980-. *Memberships:* Verein Deutscher Ingenieure; Engineer in Training, Engineering Institute of Canada through Association of Professional Engineers of Saskatchewan; American Concrete Institute; Society for Experimental Stress Analysis; Emergency Measures Organization of Canada; Canadian Association of Physicists; Association of Translators and Interpreters of Saskatchewan, German-Canadian Society 'Harmonie'. *Publications:* Diplom-Thesis: Ueber einige bei Aerosolen anwendbare Widerstansgesetze; Ein physikalisches Prinzip zur Analyse von Mischstäuben; Abstracting for the American Concrete Institute from Russian. *Hobbies:* Motor Vehicles; World Affairs; Civil Defence. *Address:* 2908 Queen Street, Regina, Saskatchewan, Canada, S4S 2E4.

NIGAM, Dinesh Kumar, b. 4 Feb. 1941, Faizabad, Uttar pradesh, India. Medical. m. 16 Nov. 1967, 2 sons. *Education:* BSc., 1958; MB., BS., 1963; MD., 1966. *Appointments:* House Physician, Medicine, SN Hospital, Agra, India, 1963-64; Demonstrator in Medicine, 1964-66, Resident Medical Officer, 1966-68 Lecturer in Cardiology, 1968-69, SN Medical College, Agra, Uttar Pradesh, India; Lecturer in Medicine, 1969-73, Reader in Medicine, 1973-, MLN Medical College, Allahabad, Uttar Pradesh, India. *Memberships:* Scientific Secretary, AMA branch, Indian Medical Association; Association of Physicians of India; Governing Council, Society of Gastrointestinal Endoscopy of India; Chairman, Study Group, GI Pathology and Immunology, 1977, 1978 & 1979, Indian Society of Gastroenterology; President, 1979, 80, 81, Chitra Gupta Vanshaj Sabha, Allahabad. *Publications:* 30 publications in medical journals. *Honours:* Awarded Commonwealth Medical Fellowship, British Council, 1973-7 Awarded Fellowship of: American Geriatric Society, 1967; International College of Angiology, 1975; Chairman of various Study groups and seminars; 1st prize, best research paper, Annual Conference of Association of Physicians of India; Awarded various prizes in genera paper reading competitions, 1961; Awarded prizes and medals for securing one of top positions in MB., BS., 1958-63. *Address:* New Pool Housing Block, Unit-3 Flat 1 (Ground Floor), Moti Lal Nehru Medical College Campus, Allahabad, Uttar Pradesh, India.

NILSSON, Raymond, b. 26 May 1920, Sydney, New South Wales, Australia. Operatic and Concert Singer. m. Mildred Hartle Stockslager, 10 Dec. 1949, 1 son, 2 daughters. *Education:* London University, UK, 1938-39; BA, Sydney University, Australia, 1939-41, 1944-47; Performers and Teachers Diploma, Sydney Conservatory, Australia, 1946. *Appointments:* School Teacher, Sydney, Australia, 1945-47; Self employed, Professional Singer, 1947-; Professor of Voice and Opera, San José State University, California, USA. *Creative Works:* Principal Tenor with: Carl Rosa Opera Co., and English Opera Group, 1948-53; Royal Opera House Covent Garden, London, UK, 1953-61; San Francisco Opera Co., USA, 1961-; Several tours, Opera, Australia Two tours, Opera South Africa, 1965, 1966; Subscription Concerts, Australian Broadcasting Commission; Guest Artist, Opera Houses, Germany, Holland and Belgium; BBC Recitals, Concerts,and TV Operas, 1948-64. *Hobbies:* Golf; Reading; Refereeing; Coaching rugby. *Address:* 1285 Middle Avenue, Menlo Park, California, USA 94025.

NINGKAN, Stephen Kalong, b. 20 Aug. 1920, Betong, Sarawa, Malaysia. Businessman; Politician m. Elizabeth, 23 Oct. 1952, 3 sons, 4 daughters. *Appointments:* Rubber Fund Clerk, 1938-39; Sarawak Constabulary, 1940-46; Teacher, St. Augustine's School, Betong, Malaysia, 1947-50; Hospital Assistant, Male Nurse, Shell Hospital, Kuala Belait, Brunei, 1950-51; Founder, Secretary General, 1961-64, President, 1964-75, Sarawak National Party; Founder, Secretary General, Sarawak National Alliance Founder, 1962, Sarawak United Front (later Sarawak Alliance Party); Secretary General, Sarawak Alliance Party until 1966; Deputy Leader, Malaysia Goodwill Mission to Africa, 1964; Elected Chief Minister of Sarawak, 1963-66; Visited Thailand, Cambodia, India, Italy, France, United Kingdom, USA, Jamaica, Nigeria, Northern Rhodesia, Nyasaland, Malagasy Republic, Uganda, Aden, Tanzania, Kenya, Ethiopia, Japan , Hongkong, Taiwan, Ghana, Hawaii, Argentina and Indonesia; Opposition Leader, Sarawak State Assembly, 1966-74. *Memberships:* Honorary secretary, Shell Dayak Club, 1955-56, 1958-60; Founder President, Dayak Association, Brunei, 1958-60. *Honours:* Knight of the most illustrious order of Mount Kinabalu, Sabah (Panglima Darjah Kinabalu) P D K addressed Datuk which is also equivalent to British title Sir, 1964; Knight of the most illustrious order of the star of Sarawak (Panglima Negara Bintang Sarawak) PNBS addressed Datuk which is equivalent to British Title Sir, 1964; Elected Chairman, Ex-Police Services Association of Malaysia, Sarawak, 1977-78, 1979-80, 1981-82. *Address:* 74 Eveigreen Garden, Jalan Nanas Barat, Kuching, Sarawak, Malaysia.

NIRAGIRA, Deo-Gratias b. 1 June, 1950, Gafunzo, Bugenyuzi, Burundi. Librarian-Documentalist. *Education:* Candidate in Philosophy, 1970-71, Candidate in Economic and Social Sciences, Burundi University, 1971-72, Diplocame d'Enseignement des Arts et Techniques Audiovisuels, Ina-Bry-sur-Harne. *Appointments:* Journalist, 1972-1976; Librarian-Documentalist, 1979-1980, Radio Burundi; Librarian-Documentalist, Eacrotanal, 1980-. *Publications:* Professional contributions to be published soon: Catalogue de la Bibliothegaque de l'Eac-

rotanal (Annual); Catalogue des Publications de l'Afrique de l'Est et Oceaan Indien (Annual) *Hobbies:* Reading; Cinema; Music; Languages. *Address:* Eacrotanal, PO Box 600, Zanzibar, Tanzania.

NISBET, Ian Milton b. 3 Oct. 1921, Kew, Victoria, Australia. Chartered Accountant. m. Joy Ida Lillian Drinkmilk, 2 Feb. 1946, 1 son, 1 daughter. *Education:* Institute of Chartered Accountants, Australia, 1951; Fellow, Institute of Chartered Accountants, Australia, 1963. *Appointments:* Employee, William Kirkhope & Co., Chartered Accountants, 1938-41; Australian Imperial Forces, 1941-46, Discharge Rank-Lieutenant; Senior Partner, Ian Nisbet & Co., Chartered Accountants, 1956 *Memberships:* Royal Commonwealth Society; The Australian Institute of International Affairs; Rotary International (Rotary Club of Balwyn). *Honours:* Member Order of Australia (AM) June 1980. *Hobbies:* Fishing; Boating; Golfing. *Address:* 26 Walnut Road, North Balwyn. Victoria 3104, Australia.

NITHTHYANANTHAN, Ratnam b. 17 Dec. 1941, Sri Lanka. Senior Research Fellow. m. Sarojini Devi Niththyananthan, 27 May, 1967, 1 son, 2 daughters. *Education:* B.Sc(Ceylon) Second Class Honours, Upper Division in Chemistry, 1959-1963 Ph.D(Lond) Chemistry, 1966-69; M.Sc(Lond) Biochemistry, 1973-75. *Appointments:* Assistant Lecturer in Chemistry, University of Ceylon, 1963-66; Lecturer in Chemistry, Univ. of Ceylon, 1970-71; Biochemist North London Blood Transfusion Centre, 1971-72; Senior Research Fellow, St. Mary's Hospital Medical School(Univ. of London) 1972-; Part-Time Counsellor/Tutor in Chemistry, Biochemistry in the Open University, 1972-. *Memberships:* The Royal Society of Chemistry. Part-time Staff Representative in the General Assembly of the Open University. *Publications:* Comparison of effects of different combined oral contraceptive formulations on carbohydrate and lipid metabolism, The Lancet, 1979. Screening for diabetes during pregnancy. British Journal of Obstetrics and Gynaecology Vol 87, 1980. *Honours:* C.Chem; M.R.S.C. *Address:* 179, Norval Road,, North Wembley, Middx. HAO 3SX, England.

NIXON, Peter James, b. 22 Mar. 1928, Orbost, Victoria, Australia. Minister for Primary Industry. m. Jacqueline Sally Dahlsen, 2 sons, 1 daughter. *Appointments:* Farmer and Grazier; Elected to House of Representatives for Gippsland, Victoria, Australia, 1961, 1963, 1966, 1969, 1972, 1974, 1975, 1977, 1980; Ministerial Appointments: Minister for Interior, 1967-72; Minister for Shipping and Transport, 1971-72; Postmaster-General, Nov. 1975-Dec. 1975; Minister for Transport, 1975-79; Minister for Primary Industry, 1979-; Committee Service: Joint Statutory - Public Accounts, 1964-67; Joint - Foreign Affairs, May 1967-Nov.1967; Prices, 1973-74; Pecuniary Interests of Members of Parliament, 1974-75; Joint Select - New and Permanent Parliament House, 1967-69; Attended numerous International Conferences and Delegations to many countries; Federal representative, Central Council of National Party, 1972-; State Executive of National Party, 1972-; Acting Deputy Leader, National Party, 1979-80. *Hobbies:* Fishing; Golf; Chess. *Address:* 'Macclesfield', Orbost, PO Box 262, Victoria, Australia.

NJOKU, Celestine Onwu Ibe, b. 29 Jan. 1940, Owerri, Nigeria. Professor of Veterinary Pathology. m. Susan, 13 Dec. 1975, 2 sons, 1 daughter. *Education:* BSc., 1967, DVM, 1969, PhD., 1972, Kansas State University, USA; FRVCS., Royal Veterinary College, Sweden, 1974. *Appointments:* Instructor, Department of Pathology, Kansas State University, USA, 1969-72; Lecturer II, 1972, Lecturer I, 1973, Senior Lecturer, 1975, Reader, 1976, Professor, 1979, Department of Veterinary Pathology, Ahmadu Bello University, Zaria, Nigeria. *Memberships:* Editor in Chief, 1977-79, J. Nigerian Veterinary Medical Association Deputy Editor in Chief, 1973-77, J. Nigerian Society for Animal Production Association for Advancement of Agriculture in Africa; American Veterinary Medical Association; Kansas Veterinary Medical Association, Assistant Dean: Postgraduate Studies Vet., Student Affairs, Vet., Ahmadu Bello University, Nigeria. *Publications:* 41 publications including: Congenital Cutaneous papilloma in a foal, (with WA Burwash), 1972; Listeri Abortion Studies in Sheep. II Placento-uterine changes, (with SM Dennis), 1973; Pathology of Lister Infection in Domestic Animals (with others), 1974; Sheep pox in North Western and North-Central States of Nigeria (with others),

1975; The Effects of common diseases of sheep and goats on livestock production in Nigeria (with others), 1976; Degenerative cardiomyopath in a captive Kangaroo (with others), 1978; The effect of scrotal streptothricosis on spermatogenesis in bulls (with others), 1979. *Honours:* Usaid Scholarship, 1963-69; Finalist in All University Teaching Award Competition, Kansas State University, USA, 1972; Gamma Sigma Delta, 1971; First Nigerian to become Fellow, Royal Veterinary College of Sweden, 1974; Visiting Associate Professor, Royal Veterinary College, Sweden, 1978. *Hobbies:* Football; Writing poetry; Current affairs; Watching movies; Reading; Travelling. *Address:* G.I, Ahmadu Bello University, Zaria, Nigeria.

NJOROGE, Daniel Lazarus, b. 17 Dec. 1932, Kikuyu, Kenya. Librarian. m. Mary Wakonyo, 9 May 1953, 3 sons, 3 daughters. *Education:* Library Studies Certificate, 1964; Certificate in Documentation, 1969. *Appointments:* Library Clerk, 1952-59, Library Assistant, 1960-64, Assistant Librarian, 1965-72, Librarian, 1972-, Kenya Agricultural Research Institute Library, Nairobi, Kenya. *Memberships:* Kenya Library Association. *Publications:* Has written several sectional reports appearing in Research annual reports, 1972-. *Hobbies:* Football; Athletics; Cinema; Photography; Driving. *Address:* PO Box 114, Kikuyu, Kenya.

NJUGUNA, Carrie Kabura, b. 22 Dec. 1952, Muranga, Kenya. Chartered Librarian. m. Peter E Njuguna Chege, 4 Dec. 1976, 2 daughters. *Education:* ALA Diploma, 1979. *Appointments:* Children's Librarian, 1980-. *Memberships:* Kenya Library Association, 1973-; LA, 1977-. *Hobbies:* Reading; Squash; Swimming; Dancing; Touring. *Address:* PO Box 50590, Nairobi, Kenya.

NKANSA-GYANE, Yaw, b. 11 Feb. 1928, Nkwatia, Eastern Region, Ghana. Private Medical Practitioner. m. Cecilia Asenso, 2 Jan. 1962, 3 sons, 3 daughters. *Education:* BSc., London, University College of the Gold Coast, Accra, Ghanana; 1947-51; Deutsches Staats Examen, 1954-59, MD., 1960, University of Heidelberg, West Germany; DTM., MP., Hamburg, Germany; DSM., West Germany. *Appointments:* Private Medical Practice; Hon. Medical Officer of: Central Organisation of Sports, Ghana, 1962; Ghana Amateur Boxing Association, 1962-73; International Amateur Boxing Association, 1962-74. *Memberships:* Vice-President, International Amateur Boxing Association, 1974-; President, Press & Publications Commission, 1978-; Vice-President, Ghana Olympic Committee, 1978-; President, Ghana Association of Sports Medicine, 1972-80; Vice-President, Commonwealth Amateur Boxing Association, 1978-. *Honours:* Elected Life Hon. Member, Medical Commission of International Amateur Boxing Association, 1978; Awarded Grand Medal for contribution to the development of Medicine and Sports in Ghana in particular and Africa in general, 1979. *Hobbies:* Art; Gardening. *Address:* 2 Kotoka Hill, Airport Residential Area, Accra, Ghana.

NKEMDIRIM, Simon Eke, b. 20 Apr. 1933, Umuobiala, Isuikwuato, Okigweiga, Imo State, Nigeria. Veterinary Surgeon. m. 1967, 1 son. *Education:* BVMS., MRCVS., Certificate in Modern Techniques, Management of Technology, IMT, Enugu, Nigeria. *Appointments:* Veterinary Officer, East Central State, Enugu, Nigeria, 1968; Veterinary Council of Nigeria, 1970-75; Deputy Chief Veterinary Officer, Imo State, Owerri, Nigeria, 1976-. *Memberships:* Nigerian Veterinary Medical Association, 1970. *Publications:* Time Factor and Technomanagerial achievement; Rabies. *Honours:* Prize for essay awarded by Institute of Management and Technology, Enugu, Nigeria. *Hobbies:* Table tennis; Lawn tennis; Swimming; Dancing. *Address:* Plot 211B, 5 Ohaozara Road, Aladinma Housing Estate, Owerri, Imo State, Nigeria.

NKOMA, John Sydney, b. 21 June 1949, Tanzania. Physicist. m. Rehema Kayuza, 25 Aug. 1973, 1 son. *Education:* BSc., University of Dar-es-Salaam, Tanzania, 1971; MSc., 1973, PhD., 1976, University of Essex, UK. *Appointments:* Tutorial Assistant, 1971, Assistant Lecturer, 1972, Lecturer, 1975, Senior Lecturer, 1978, Associate Professor, 1980, Head of Physics Department, 1979, University of Dar-es-Salaam, Tanzania. *Memberships:* Associate member, Institute of Physics, UK, 1975-77; Associate of International Centre of Theoretical Physics, Trieste, Italy. *Publications:* Several

Scientific research publications in physics including: De Gennes correlation function method applied to electron gas problems (with D R Tilley), 1973; Theory of Raman scattering by surface polaritons in a thin film, 1975; Theory of two photon absorption by surface polaritons, 1977; Green functions theory for rare earth metals, 1978; Linear photon and two photon absorption by surface polaritons, 1980; Theory of absorption by exciton polaritons in a spatially dispersive media, 1980. *Honours:* UNESCO Fellowship, 1971-72; British Council Fellowship, 1973-76. *Hobby:* Photography. *Address:* University of Dar es-Salaam, PO Box 35063, Dar es Salaam, Tanzania.

NKPANG, Joseph Ekpo, b. 21 Apr. 1930, Calabar. Transport Executive. m. Akpabio, 25 May 1963, 2 sons, 8 daughters. *Education:* Chartered Institute of Transport, London, 1961. *Appointments:* Management Cadet, 1956-61; Traffic Officer, Principle Traffic Officer, 1961-69; Port Manager, 1969-76; Assistant General Manager, 1976-. *Memberships:* Director, International Association of Ports & Harbours; International Cargo Handling Co-ordination Association; Fellow of the Chartered Institute of Transport, 1981; Nigerian Trade Facilitation Committee. *Hobby:* Reading. *Address:* 8 Child Avenue, Apapa, Lagos, Nigeria.

NOBLE, Janette Rosalind, b. 21 July 1933, Singleton, NSW, Australia. Commissioner, Health Commission of NSW. *Education:* Diploma of Nursing Education, NSW College of Nursing, 1965; Bachelor of Arts, Class 1 Honours, University of NSW; 1972. *Appointments:* District Hospital, Kaikoura, South Island, New Zealand; The National Women's Hospital, Auckland, New Zealand; The Hospital for Sick Children, Great Ormond Street, London; The American Hospital of Paris, Paris, France; The Women's Hospital, (Crown Street), Sydney, Australia; Elizabeth Gates Home, Singleton, NSW, Australia; Repatriation General Hospital, Concord, Sydney, Australia, Royal Alexandra Hospital for Children, Camperdown, Sydney, Australia; Director of Nursing, 1971-79; Commissioner, Health Commission of New South Wales, 1979-. *Honours:* Queens Silver Jubilee Medal, 1977. *Hobbies:* Collecting Glass and Paintings. *Address:* PO Box K110, Hamarket, NSW, 2000, Australia.

NOBLE, Rodney, b. 5 Sept. 1921, Sydney, Australia. Retired RAAF Engineer Officer; Private Consultant. m. Betty Lorraine Pedler, 25 Nov. 1948, 2 sons, 1 daughter. *Education:* Bachelor of Aeronautical Engineering, Sydney University, 1943; RAAF Staff College Graduate, 1954; Industrial Mobilization Course, 1963; Management Certificate, Royal Melbourne Institute of Technology, 1964; Imperial Defence College Graduate, 1968. *Appointments:* Joined RAAF, 1943; Commissioned 1944 and Graduated Pilot Flight Test Duties; Demobilized RAAF, 1946; Performance and Planning Engineer, Trans Australia Airlines, 1946-47; Re-appointed, Permanent Commission, RAAF, 1947; Various field and staff appointments, Australia and Overseas; Promoted Air Vice Marshall, 1975 and appointed Controller, Service Laboratories and Trials, Department of Defence; Appointed Chief of Air Force, Technical Services, 1979; Retired, 1981; Engineering Management Consultant. *Memberships:* Fellow: Institute of Engineers, Australia and Royal Aeronautical Society; Chartered Engineer; Associate Fellow, American Institute Astronautics and Aeronautics; Imperial Service Club, Sydney; Commonwealth Club, Canberra. *Publications:* Technical Reports, RAAF, Classified; Sir Lawrence Wackett Memorial Lecture. *Honours:* Officer in the Military Division of the Order of Australia, 1976; Blues, for Cricket and Rugby, Sydney University. *Hobbies:* Golf; Surfing; Carpentry. *Address:* 22 Gellibrand Street, Campbell, Canberra, ACT, 2601, Australia

NOCK, Frank Foley, b. 27 Feb. 1916, Toronto, Ontario. Bishop. m. Elizabeth Hope Adams, 30 May 1942, 1 son, 1 daughter. *Education:* Trinity College, 1934-38; BA, Divinity, 1938-40; General Synod B.D. Course; Ordained to Diaconate, (Toronto Diocese), 1940; Ordination to Priesthood, 1941. *Appointments:* Curate, St Matthew's, Toronto, 1940-42; Incumbent Christ Church, Korah, Sault Ste Marie, 1942-45; Rector, St Thomas', Bracebridge, 1945-48; Rector, Church of the Epiphany, Sudbury, 1948-57; Rector, St Luke's Cathedral, 1957-74; Dean of the Diocese of Algoma, 1957-74; Bishop of Algoma, 1974; Enthroned and Consecrated, 1975. *Memberships:* Board of Directors, Group

Health Centre; Community Concert Association. *Honours:* DD, Trinity College, 1957; STD, Thorneloe University, 1980. *Hobbies:* Golf; Skiing. *Address:* 134 Simpson Street, Sault Ste. Marie, Ontario, P6A 3V4.

NOEL, Clement Jeremiah, b. 16 Nov. 1933, Union Island, St Vincent. Civil Servant. m. Beatrice Browne, 17 Aug. 1955, 2 sons, 3 daughters. *Education:* Extra Mural Classes and In-service Training, Teachers' College, 1949-55; Erdiston College Teachers' Certificate, 1961; BA, University of the West Indies, Barbados, 1970-74. *Appointments:* Primary School Teacher, 1949-74; Secondary School Teacher, 1974-75; Civil Servant, Clerk of the House of Assembly, 1975-. *Honours:* First prize, Student Teachers' Examination, 1953; First prize, Teachers' Examination, Geography, 1953; Local Preacher, 1951-55. *Hobbies:* Reading; Listening to Music; Swimming; Cricket. *Address:* Fountain, Arnos Vale PO, Saint Vincent, West Indies.

NOEL-BAKER, Philip John, b. 1 Nov. 1889, London. Politician. m. Irene, 12 June, 1915, 1 son. *Education:* Haverford College, Pennsylvania, USA, 1906-07; Kings College, Cambridge, 1908-12. *Appointments:* Member of Parliament for 37 years; Minister of the Crown, 1942-51; Member of the House of Lords, 1977-. *Publications:* The League of Nations at work, 1925; The Arms Race, 1926; The Coolidge Conference on Naval Disarmament, 1927; The Juridicial Status of the British Dominions in Inaternational Law, 1928; Private Manufacture of Arms, 1936; The Arms Race, 1958; The First World Disarmament Conference, 1932-33, and why it Failed, 1979. *Honours:* Whewell Prize in International Law, University of Cambridge, 1911; Fellow, Kings College, Cambridge, 1915; Silver Medal, 1500 Metres, Olympic Games, Antwerp, 1920; Captain of British Olympic Team, Antwerp, 1920, Paris, 1924; Cassell Professor of International Relations, University of London, 1924; Dodge Lecturer in International Relations, Yale University, 1934; Commandant British Olympic Team, Helsinki, 1952; Nobel Peace Prize, 1959; Honorary Fellow of Kings College, Cambridge, 1961; Papal Knight of the Order of St Sylvester, 1977; Olympic Diploma of Merit, 1978; Honorary Degrees at: Universities of Nottingham, Manchester, Loughborough, Queens University, Kingston, Ontario; Colombo University, Sri Lanka; Haverford College, USA. *Address:* 16 South Eaton Place, London, S.W.1. England.

NOLAN, Peter Ian, b. 14 June 1934, Brisbane, Queensland, Australia. Secretary, Australian Council of Trade Unions. m. Sophie Chodan, 1 Sept. 1979, 1 son, 2 daughters. *Education:* Ascot State School; Central Technical College. *Appointments:* Hand and Machine Compositor, 1955-65; Secretary, Printing and Kindred Industries Union, 1965-70; Research Officer, 1970-71, Assistant Secretary, 1971-75, Victorian Trades Hall Council; Assistant Secretary, 1975-77, Secretary, 1977, Australian Council of Trade Unions; Commissioner Australian Telecommunications Commission, 1979-; Board Reserve Bank of Australia, 1981-; Director, 3FM Broadcasting; Director ACTU Enterprises; Chairman, APPM-ACTU Superannuation Fund; Executive, Australian Council of Union Training. *Memberships:* Director, Australia-Japan Foundation; Director and Vice-Chairman, Victorian Section, Australian Bicentenary Authority; Past, Vice-President, Australian Labor Party. *Hobbies:* Music; Painting. *Address:* 8/41 Chapel Street, St Kilda, Melbourne, Australia, 3182.

NOORDIN-KELING, Mohamed, b. 15 June 1926, Kuala Pilah, Malaysia. Veterinary Surgeon. m. Ann Salmiah Majeed, 15 Aug. 1959, 1 son, 1 daughter. *Education:* Graduate in Veterinary Science, Bengal Veterinary College, Calcutta, India, 1947-50; Royal Veterinary College, University of London, 1951-56; Diploma in Tropical Veterinary Medicine, Royal (Dick) School of Veterinary Studies, University of Edinburgh, 1960; Diploma in Veterinary Public Health, School of Hygiene, University of Toronto, Canada; MRCVS. *Appointments:* Veterinary Surgeon, Bedford, England, 1956-57; State Veterinary Officer, Kelantan, 1957-63; Veterinary Officer, Headquarters, Kuala Lumpur, 1963-64, Chief Veterinary Officer, 1965-72; Assistant Director-General, 1972-73, Deputy Director- General, 1973-78, Veterinary Services, Malaysia; Director-General, National Livestock Development Authority, Malaysia, 1978-. *Memberships:* Past President of: Association of Veterinary Surgeons, Malaysia, Malay-

sian Society of Parasitology & Tropical Medicine, Malaysian Society of Animal Production; Board of Trustees, Tunku Abdul Rahman Foundation and Malaysian Professional Centre; Council of the University of Agriculture, Malaysia; Standing Committee on Evaluation of Qualifications; Malaysian Veterinary Council. *Publications:* Various contributions to medical journals and symposiums including: Co-author, An outbreak of Rabies in West Malaysia, 1970; Rabies in Malaysia, 1974. *Honours:* Raymond Star for Best Man of the Year at Bengal Veterinary College, 1950; SMK, 1963; KMN, 1971; PPT, 1976; JMN, 1979; DSNS, 1980. *Hobbies:* Photography; Golf; Reading; Classical Music. *Address:* 10 Lorong Taman Pantai Lima, Bukit Pantai, Kuala Lumpur, Malaysia.

NOR, Zakiah Hanum, b. 15 Sept. 1937, Malaysia. Archivist. m. Mohd. Nor Ismail, 2 sons, 1 daughter. *Education:* BA(Hons), University of Malaya, 1961; Diploma in Archives Administration, New Delhi, 1962. *Appointments:* Archivist, National Archives of Malaysia, 1961; Deputy Director General, 1970; Director General, 1977. *Memberships:* Malaysian Branch Royal Asiatic Society; Malaysia Historical Society; President, PERTIWI; Vice President, Malaysian Child Welfare Council; etc.etc. *Publications:* Articles and publications on archival and related subjects. *Honours:* Johan Setia Mahkota, 1976; Setia Mahkota Selangor, 1981. *Hobby:* Welfare work for the benefit of women and children. *Address:* No. 3 Lorong 16/6A, Petaling Jaya, Malaysia.

NORCROSS, Keith, b. 29 May 1929, Oldham, Lancashire, England. Consultant Orthopaedic Surgeon. m. 23 Oct. 1954, 1 daughter. *Education:* University of Oxford, 1947-51; Clinical Medical School, University of Manchester, 1951-54; BA(Hons) Oxon, 1951; MA, BM, BCh (Oxon) 1954; FRCS, England 1959. *Appointments:* House Officer, Neurosurgery and Neurology, Manchester, 1954-55; Medical Officer, Royal Army Medical Corps, 1955-58; Senior House Officer, Registrar, Senior Registrar, Royal Infirmary and Crumpsall Hospitals Manchester, 1958-66; Fellowship, Hospital for Special Orthopoedic Surgery, New York, USA, 1964. *Memberships:* Secretary, Oxford University Socratic Club; Librarian, O.U. Mountaineering Club; Editoral Board Member, British Journal of Sex Medicine; British Orthopoedic Association; Royal Society of Medicine; Naughton Dunn, Orthopoedic Club; British Sub Aqua Club; British Canoe Union; Ramblers' Association Fell & Rock Climbing Club; Marine Biology Association; Society of Recorder Players; Dolmetscu Foundation; National Trust. *Publications:* Essays in British Medical Journal and Lancet, on Sex Morality, Medical Academicism, Cost Factors in Medicine, 1980; Prospects in Medicine, 1980; Contributor, 1977; Visual Dictionary of Sex; Young Man to Doctor, 1954; Repair After Subtutal, Amputation of Arm, 1961; Minor Chest Injuries, 1965; Articles in the issues of, Recorders International, 1973-78. *Honours:* Various prizes and scholarships from 1939-1981. *Hobbies:* Camping; Canoeing; Climbing; Diving; Cycling; Music; Reading; Ethical Controversy. *Address:* 38 Selly Wick Road, Birmingham, England, B29 7JA.

NORMAN, Denis Robert, b. 26 Mar. 1931, Chalgrove, England. Farmer. m. June Bingham Marshall, 12 Aug. 1955, 1 son, 3 daughters. *Education:* Oxford/Cambridge School Certificate, 1947. *Appointments:* Farmer; Member and Chairman, Rhodesia Grain Producers Association 1968-76; Vice President, and President, National Farmers Union 1976-79; President, Commercial Farmers Union, Zimbabwe, 1979-80; Zimbabwe Minister of Agriculture 1980-. *Memberships:* Farmers Club, Whitehall London; Institute of Directors; Salisbury Club, Zimbabwe. *Honours:* Senator, Zimbabwe 1980. *Address:* PO Box 23, Norton, Zimbabwe.

NORRIS, Cecil Frederick, b. 15 Oct. 1903, London. Flight Lieutenant, Royal Air Force, (Retired). m. 21 Apr. 1955. *Education:* Elementry. *Appointments:* Royal Air Force. *Memberships:* Fellow, Royal South Australian Society of Arts. *Creative Works:* Sculptor. *Honours:* Royal South Australian Society of Arts. *Hobby:* Motor Racing. *Address:* 172 Esplanade, Port Noarlunga South, South Australia 5167

NORRIS, Lesley Grace, b. 24 Dec. 1941, Essex, England. Projects Officer; Freedom from Hunger. 3 sons, 1 daughter. *Education:* Self Educated. *Appointments:* Department of Information, Lesotho, 1966-68; Social

Rehab. of Frail Aged, Greenwood Nursing Home, Sydney, Australia, 1974-78; Trades and Labour Council, ACT, Australia, 1979; Research Officer, Australian Institute of Criminology, Canberra, 1980; Projects Officer, Jobless Action, ACT Australia, 1980. *Memberships:* Womens Electoral Lobby-Australia; Crisis Counsellor for Louisa Womens and Children's Refuge. *Publications:* Domestic Violence, A Family Affair; Child Sex Abuse Victims; The Politics of Domestic Violence; Spouse Murder. *Hobbies:* Music; Reading; Gardening; Theatre. *Address:* 4 Eugenia Street, Queanbeyan, NSW 2620, Australia.

NORRIS, Robin MacKenzie, b. 9 Mar. 1931. Medical Practitioner. m. Iris Gwendoline Wheatley, 31 Aug. 1963, 2 sons. *Education:* MB, (NZ) 1955; MD, Birmingham 1965; FRCP 1977; FRACP 1972. *Appointments:* House Surgeon and Registrar, Auckland Hospital 1956-59; Research Fellow, Department of Medicine, University of Birmingham, 1962-65; Medical Tutor Specialist, Green Lane Hospital, Auckland, 1965-68; Physician, Corinary Care Unit, 1969-. *Memberships:* Cardiac Society of Australia and New Zealand. *Publications:* Myocardial infarction, its presentation, pathogensis and treatment, 1981. *Honours:* Honorary Associate Professor, University of Auckland, School of Medicine; Director, research programme, Medical Research Council of New Zealand. *Hobbies:* Music; Gardening; Travelling. *Address:* 5 Chatfield Place, Remuera, Auckland, 5, New Zealand.

NORTH, Maurice, b. 9 June 1920, Southend on Sea, Essex, England. Sociologist. m. Nerina Anna Gondolo, 10 May 1947. *Education:* BSc(Econ), MSc(Econ), London School of Economics, London University, 1947-51; PhD, University of Marburg, 1961-65. *Appointments:* British Army, 1939-46; Lecturer, Army College, 1951; Lecturer in Sociology, South West Essex, Technical College, 1951-60; Dolmetscher Schule, Zürich, 1960-61; Principal, Berlitz Schule, Marburg 1961-65; Preside, English School, Bologna 1965-66; Principal Lecturer in Sociology, Hatfield Polytechnic, 1966-74; Professor of Social Institutions and Dean of Faculty of Social Studies and Humanities, Preston Polytechnic, 1974-. *Memberships:* International Sociological Association; Advisory Council Member, The Social Affairs Unit, London. *Publications:* The Outer Fringe of Sex, 1970; The Secular Priests 1972; The Mind Market, 1975; Knowledge of NATO, 1980; Many articles plus books on German language. *Honours:* NATO Research Fellowship 1979-80; Professor emeritus, 1981. *Address:* Preston Polytechnic, Corporation Street, Preston, PR1 2TQ, England.

NORTH-COOMBES, Bernard Raymond Mervyn, b. 19 July 1943, Mauritius. Company Director, Industrialist. *Education:* BA (Latin with Greek), Further Education, University of Exeter, England, 1964-68. *Appointments:* Sales Trainee, 1968-69, Export Executive, 1969-70, Export Regional Manager, Rowntree MacKintosh Limited, York, England, 1970-73; Marketing Manager, Food and Allied Industries Limited, Mauritius, 1973-74; Marketing Manager, Floreal Knitwear Limited, Mauritius, 1974-77; Managing Director, Island Clothing Limited, Mauritius, 1977-; Chairman, National Transport Corporation, Mauritius, 1977-. *Memberships:* Chairman, Mauritius employer's Federation; Vice-President, Mauritius Tax Payers' Association; Action Civigue, Mauritius; Governor, College du St. Esprit, Mauritius. *Publications:* Author of several articles on Management and Industrial Relations, published in newspapers and reviews in Mauritius, 1973-; Code of Practice for Enterprises in Mauritius, 1980. *Honours:* Queen's Award to Industry for Export Achievement in 1972; Exportation Award, Floreal Knitwear Limited, 1975 and 1976, and Island Clothing Limited, 1978. *Hobbies:* Good food and Wine; Making Friends; Tennis; Reading. *Address:* Montebello Farm, Pailles, Mauritius.

NORTHMORE, Jack, McKeer, b. 15 Sept. 1920, London, England. Consulting Agricultural Chemist. m. Irma Anna Maria Guizzon, 19 July 1960, 2 daughters. *Education:* Queen Mary College, London University, 1946-48; Regent Street Polytechnic, 1960-63; BSc(Hons)Chem; CChem; FRSC. *Appointments:* Chemist, J Thorley Limited, London, 1949-51; Chemist, Department of Agriculture, Kenya, East Africa, 1952-61; Senior Research Officer, Coffee Research Foundation, Ruiru, Kenya, East Africa, 1962-69; Consulting

Agricultural Chemist, Northmore Laboratories, Canterbury, Kent, England, 1970-. *Memberships:* Royal Society of Chemistry; Association Scientifique internationale du Café; National Institute of Agricultural Botany. *Publications:* Eleven published scientific papers on Tropical Agriculture (mainly Coffee). *Honours:* Mentioned in Despatches, (RASC), 1944. *Hobbies:* Gardening; Microcomputers; Feed Microscopy; Cine photography. *Address:* 1, Churchill Road, Canterbury, Kent CT1 3EB, England.

NOSEGBE, Michael Sunday Chukudi, b. 22 Feb. 1933, Agbor, Bendel State, Nigeria. Chartered Accountant. 1 son, 7 daughters. *Education:* London School of Accountancy, 1964-70; Fellow of the Institute of Charted Accountants. *Appointments:* Management Accountant: J Sainsbury Limited, United Kingdom; The Gas Council, United Kingdom; Deputy Financial Controller, Blackwood Hodge, Nigeria Limited Lagos; Chief Accountant, African Continental Bank Limited, 1974-77; Assistant General Manager, Finance, 1977-. *Memberships:* Island Club Lagos Nigeria; Ika Club Agbor Nigeria. *Hobbies:* Football; Athletics; Reading. *Address:* 8 Alhaji Tokan Street, Alaka Estate, Suru Lere, Lagos, Nigeria.

NOSIRI, Godwin Eto Robert, b. 6 Apr. 1936, Egbu-Owerri, Imo State, Nigeria. Accountancy/Management. m. Mary Ann Amadi, 16 Nov. 1966, 1 son, 3 daughters. *Education:* School of Accountancy, London, 1953-58. *Appointments:* Accountant, Sir Lindsay Parkingson, Nigeria, Limited, 1960-66; Accountant/Buyer, Chief Resident Engineers Office, Niger Dams Authority, Kainji, 1966; Accountant, International Drilling Company, 1966-67; Administrative Manager, Branch Manager, Wiedemann and Walters, Nigeria Limited, 1970-. *Memberships:* Warri Club. *Hobbies:* Gardening; Reading; Tennis. *Address:* No 4 Daji Close, Agaga Layout, Warri, Bendel State, Nigeria.

NOVAK, Jaroslav Peter, b. 15 Oct. 1939, C. Budejovice, Czechoslovakia. Research Scientist. Divorced, 1 daughter. *Education:* State Diploma, College, Litomerice, Czechoslovakia, 1954-57; MSc., Faculty of Mathematics and Physics, Charles University, Prague, 1957-62; DSc., Université du Québec, Canada, 1971- 74. *Appointments:* Faculty of Mathematics and Physics, Charles University, Prague, 1960-68; Research Assistant, 1960-62; Military Service, 1962-64; Assistant Professor, 1964-68; Secretary of the Department, 1966-68; Research Scientist, Research Institute of Hydro-Québec, Varennes, Québec, Canada, 1968-. *Memberships:* Canadian Association of Physicists. *Publications:* Contributions in the field of plasma physics and gaseous kinetics in professional scientific journals. *Honours:* Winner of Czechoslovak national mathematics competition, Mathematics Olympiad, 1957; Ayrton Premium, awarded by IEE, Great Britain. *Hobbies:* Wind-surfing; Skiing; Tennis; Judo (Champion of Charles University, 1961, Academic Champion of Prague, 1961); Creative Writing. *Address:* 6644 Fielding Avenue, Apartment 34, Montreal, Québec, Canada, H4V 1N3.

NSEKELA, Amon James, b. 4 Jan. 1930, Lupepo, Rungur District, Tanzania. Diplomat. m. Christina Matilda Kyusa, 13 July 1957, 2 sons. *Education:* Dip. Ed., 1954; MA., 1960. *Appointments:* School master; District Officer; Clerk to the Cabinet; Permanent Secretary/Principal Secretary; Chief Executive: National Bank of Commerce; National Insurance Corporation; Chairman of Council University of Dar es Salaam, Tanzania; Member of Parliament. *Memberships:* President, Economic Association of Tanzania; Chairman and Managing Director, National Bank of Commerce. *Publications:* Minara ya Historia ya Tanganyika; Demokrasi Tanzania; Socialism and Social Accountability in a Developing Nation; A time to Act; Toward Rational Alternatives. *Hobbies:* Writing; Swimming; Table tennis; Squash. *Address:* 3 View Road, Highgate, London N6, England.

NTABA, George Maurice Justice, b. 4 Nov. 1951, Mvera Mission, Dowa District, Malawi. Legal Practitioner. m. Phyllis, 18 Mar. 1978, 1 son, 3 daughters. *Education:* Bachelor of Laws, Chancellor College, Malawi, 1973-76. *Appointments:* Admitted to Malawi Bar, 1976; Legal Practitioner, Lilley Wills & Co., Limbe, Malawi, 1976-79; Director of 8 companies, 1976-79; Legal Adviser to and Legal Practitioner for Commercial Bank of Malawi Limited, Malawi, 1979-; First in-house corporate lawyer in Malawi. *Memberships:* Malawi Law Society; Founder member, Secretary, 1975-76, Students Law Society, Chancellor College, Malawi. *Honours:* 9th Prize, Malawi National Mathematics competition, 1970. *Hobbies:* Reading; Watching movies. *Address:* Glyn Jones Road, Namiwawa, Blantyre, Malawi.

NTAMBI, Christopher, b. 16 Dec. 1930, Kirazi, Mawokota, Uganda. Lecturer. m. 13 Dec. 1958, 3 sons, 5 daughters. *Education:* City and Guilds of London Institute Full Technological Certificate, UK, 1963; Technical Teachers' Certificate, 1963, HND., 1967, Leeds, UK. *Appointments:* Technical Teacher, 1956-71, Lecturer-/Head of Department, Civil Engineering and Building, 1972-76, Vice Principal, 1976-, Uganda Technical College, Uganda. *Memberships:* Fellow, Institute of Professional Engineering Technicians of Uganda; AIBCC. *Honours:* Awarded Independence Medal in field of Teaching. *Hobbies:* Music; Gardening. *Address:* PO Box 26, Ntinda, Uganda.

NTONYA, Frank Wyllie, b. 13 July 1938, Malawi. Diplomat; Civil Servant. m. Violet Phiri, 14 Jan. 1967, 2 sons, 4 daughters. *Education:* BA., Haile Sellassie University, Ethiopia, 1965; Diploma, International Affairs, 1969, Certificate in Diplomacy, 1969, Columbia University, New York, USA; Certificate, Tourism Development, Shannon, Ireland, UK, 1978. *Appointments:* Assistant Secretary, External Affairs, Malawi, 1965-67; Second Secretary, 1967-68, First Secretary, 1968-69, Malawi High Commission, London, UK; First Secretary, Malawi Legation, Pretoria, South Africa, 1969-71; Chief of Protocol, Malawi, 1969-73; Malawi High Commissioner, Kenya, 1973-75; Under Secretary, 1975-76, 1979, Office of the President and Cabinet, Malawi; Director of Tourism, Ministry of Trade and Tourism, Malawi, 1976-79; Retired from Civil Service, 1979; Stores Superintendent, Malawi Railways Limited, Malawi 1979-. *Memberships:* Executive Club, Lilongwe, Malawi; Malawi Railways Senior Staff Club, Limba, Malawi. *Hobbies:* Farming; Gardening; Photography; Driving. *Address:* House No F6, Railways Estate, Limbe, Malawi.

NUNAN, Francis Michael, b. 13 Mar. 1924, Ealing, London, England. Banker (retired). m. Mildred Elsie Godfrey, 29 Nov. 1947, 2 sons. *Appointments:* Company Secretary, 1970-80, Head, Financial Control Division, 1972-80, Coutts & Co., London, UK; Navigator, Flying Officer, Royal Air Force, 1943-47. *Memberships:* Associate member: Institute of Bankers; Society of Company and Commercial Accountants. *Honours:* MVD., 1976; CVO., 1980. *Hobbies:* Sport; Gardening; Philately; Tropical fish; Reading. *Address:* 28 Clifton Avenue, Finchley, London N3 1BN, England.

NUNGWANA, Selemani Daudi, b. 20 Oct. 1943, Lutale Village, Mwanza District, Tanzania. Manager. m. Ruth Simon Doto, 16 Apr. 1972, 4 sons, 2 daughters. *Appointments:* Bus conductor, 1965; Clerk, Petrol Station, Geita, Tanzania, 1966-69; Salesman, 1972-74, Assistant Distribution Manager, 1979-81, Distribution Manager, 1981-, Bookshop of the Africa Inland Church, Tanzania. *Memberships:* Chama Cha Mapinduzi, Ruling Party in Tanzania. *Hobbies:* Football; Choir; Films. *Address:* PO Box 2372, Mwanza, Tanzania.

NUPEN, Marjorie Eleanor, b. 30 Apr. 1923, Pretoria, Republic of South Africa. Teacher. m. Harald Wernerprang Nupen, 4 Feb. 1946, 1 son, 2 daughters. *Education:* BA., Rhodes University, Grahamstown, South Africa, 1940-43. *Appointments:* Teacher: Roedean School, Johannesburg, South Africa, 1945; Chingola Primary School, Zambia, 1955-68; Acting Head, 1980-, Lady Tait School, Gatooma, Zimbabwe, 1969-. *Memberships:* 1st Vice President, 1977-78, 2nd Vice President, 1975-76, National President, 1979-80, National Federation of Business and Professional Women of Zimbabwe; National President, Women's Voluntary Services, Zambia, 1960-68; Founder President, Gatooma BPW Club. *Publications:* Profiles of Rhodesia's Women (with Mrs J Woods), 1975. *Hobbies:* Gardening; Reading. *Address:* PO Box 403, Gatooma, Zimbabwe.

NURGITZ, Nathan, b. 22 June 1934, Winnipeg, Manitoba, Canada. Lawyer. m. Phyllis Liberman, 4 Sept. 1955, 1 son, 1 daughter. *Education:* Arts, 1952-54, LL.B., Law School, 1958, University of Manitoba, Cana-

da. *Appointments:* Lawyer: Pollock, Nurgitz, Winnipeg, Canada, 1958-81; Thompson, Dorfman, Sweatman, Winnipeg, Canada, 1981-; Elected National Vice-President, 1969, Elected National President, 1970, Progressive Conservative Party of Canada; City of West Kildonan Alderman, 1963-69 Summoned to Senate of Canada, 1979; Vice-Chairman, Senate Committee, Northern Pipeline, 1979-80; Sits on following Senate Committees: Agriculture, Northern Pipeline, Legal & Constitutional Affairs; Statutory Regulations; Delegate to United Nations General Assembly, 1980; Delegate to Study tour of European Communities, 1981. *Memberships:* Elected, 1978, Re-elected, 1980, Chairman, Bencher, The Professional Liability Committee, Law Society of Manitoba; Director of several Associations. *Honours:* Appointed Queen's Counsel, 1977. *Address:* 42 Merriwood Drive, Winnipeg, Manitoba, Canada, R2V 2P4.

NURU, Saka, b. 15 Feb. 1936, Ilorin, Nigeria. Veterinary Surgeon. m. Maryam M. Nuru, 1964, 2 sons, 1 daughter. *Education:* Bachelor of Vet. Science, Bristol University, 1964; Master of Preventive Med. California M.P.V.M. 1972; Doctor of Philosophy, A.B.U. Zaria; Member, M.R.S.V.S. 1964. *Appointments:* Provincial Veterinary Clinician, Kano and Maiduguri, 1964-1965; Provincial Veterinary Officer i/c of Bauchi Province, 1965-1966; Principal, Livestock Services Training Centre, Kaduna, 1967-70; Senior Lecturer, Faculty of Veterinary Medicine, A.B.U., Zaria, 1972-1975; Acting Head of Department of Veterinary Public Health, Faculty of Veterinary Medicine, A.B.U., Zaria, 1974-1975; Deputy Director (Livestock Research), Institute for Agricultural Research, A.B.U., Zaria, 1975-1976; Director, National Animal Production Research Institute, A.B.U. Zaria 1976-; Acting Provost for Agriculture and Veterinary Medicine, A.B.U., Zaria, 1976-. *Memberships:* Veterinary Council of Nigeria, Secretary/Treasurer, 1969-1970 President Nig. Vet. Med. Assoc., 1976-1978; British Vet. Assoc., 1964-1969; Comm. Wealth Vet. Assoc., 1976-1980; New York Academy of Sciences. *Publications:* Contributor of articles to various conferences, and documented reports of committees, panels etc. *Honours:* Best Student in Science Subjects, Bath Tech. College, 1960. Member, New York Academy of Science since 1978. *Hobbies:* Stamp Collection; Horse Riding; Special Constabulary as Superintendent of Police. *Address:* P.O. Box 8, Ilorin, Nigeria.

NUTTER, Daniel Gerald, b. 7 June 1928, Sydney, Australia. Diplomat. m. Dawn Hardy 10 Nov. 1956, 1 son, 2 daughters. *Education:* B.A. Hons. Sydney University. *Appointments:* Diplomatic Staff Cadet, 1949-1950; Counsellor Dept. Foreign Affairs, 1964-1965; Australian Government Observer Vietnam Elections, 1967; Asst. Dir. C'wealth Secretariat, London; 1968-70; Third Sec. Bonn & Berlin; Second Sec. Saigon and Vientiane (Charge d'Affaires Vientiane); First Sec. Tokyo; Dep. High Comm Delhi; Counsellor Katmandu; Minister Australian Embassy Saigon, 1970-1972; Asst. Sec. Dept. Foreign Affairs (SE Asia Branch), 1972-1973; Head National Assessment Staff, Dept. Foreign Affairs, 1973-1974; Aust. Ambassador to Philippines, 1975-1978; Commissioner to Papua New Guinea, 1978; *Memberships:* Royal Overseas League (Lond); Commonwealth (Canb). *Hobbies:* Swimming; fishing; tennis. *Address:* Department of Foreign Affairs, Canberra ACT 2600, Australia.

NWAFOR, Bartholomew Udemmadu, b. 2 Dec. 1939, Abba, Nigeria. Librarian. 4 daughters. *Education:* Associate of the Library Association, Ealing College of Higher Education, London, 1963; MLS, University of Pittsburgh, 1972. *Appointments:* Sub-Librarian/Assistant Librarian, Ahmadu Bello University, Zaria, 1963-66; Sub-Librarian, Enugu Campus, 1966-73, Senior Librarian in charge, Calabar Campus, 1973-75, University of Nigeria; Assistant Librarian and Deputy Librarian, Alvan Ikoku College of Education, Owerri, 1975-76; University Librarian, University of Jos, Jos, Nigeria, 1976-. *Memberships:* Secretary, 1965, Northern Nigeria Branch, Nigerian Library Association; Publicity Secretary, East Central Staff Division, 1971; Executive Committee, Plateau State Division, 1980. *Publications:* Several articles contributed to international journals including: The Library and the Educational Process, 1977. *Honours:* Senior Project, College of The Immaculate Conception, Enugu, 1959. *Hobbies:* Reading; Music; Tennis; Scrabble. *Address:* Abba, PO Box 40, Abagana, Nigeria.

NWAKUCHE, Flora (Mrs), b. Oguta, Nigeria. Writer & Publisher. m. 1967, 1 son, 2 daughters. *Education:* BA (London), University College, Ibadan, 1953-57; Dip.Ed. (Edinburgh), University of Edinburgh, 1957-58. *Appointments:* Woman Education Officer, 1958-62; Assistant Registrar, (Public Relations), University of Lagos, 1962-67; Commissioner, and Executive Council of East Central State of Nigeria, 1970-75; First Nigerian Woman Novelist. *Memberships:* Patron, National Council of Women's Societies; Writers & Readers Club of Nigeria. *Publications:* Edfuru; Idu; This is Lagos; Emeka-Driver's Guard; Never Again; Mammywater, The Miracle Kittens, Journey to Space, (All children's books). *Hobbies:* Reading; Swimming. *Address:* 1 Ogbaru Street, Independence Layout, Enugu, Nigeria.

NWAMEFOR, Raphael Chianumba, b. 27 Feb. 1935, Nri, Anambra State of Nigeria. Librarian. m. Victoria Kechinyere Okoro, 30 Dec. 1967, 4 sons, 1 daughter. *Education:* BA, University of Nigeria, Nsukka, 1963; Dip. Lib. University of Ibadan, Ibadan, 1964; MLS, The university of Alberta, Edmonton, 1974; Certificate in Library Planning & Design, The British Council, London, 1979. *Appointments:* Assistant Librarian, 1964-67; Librarian, 1967-75; Senior Librarian, 1975-78; Deputy Director, National Library of Nigeria, Lagos, 1978; College Librarian, Anambra State College of Education, Awka, 1978-. *Memberships:* Chairman, Standing Conference of Chief Librarians of Colleges and Polytechnics in Nigeria, 1980-82; The Council of the Nigeria Library Association; Nsukka Philosophical Society; Canadian Association of College & Research Libraries. *Publications:* Several contributions to Library Reviews and Journals including: Planning Library buildings for Nigeria Universities, 1975. *Honours:* Federal Government of Nigeria, Undergraduate Scholarship, 1961-63; Federal Government of Nigeria, Postgraduate Scholarship, 1963-64; Canadian International Development Agency Fellowship, 1972-73; British Council Award, 1979. *Hobbies:* Lawn Tennis; Swimming; Farming. *Address:* PO Box 44, NRI, Njikoka Local Government Area, Anambra State, Nigeria.

NWANKWO, Daniel Nwambeze De-Nne, b. 15 Mar. 1943, Aba, Imo State, Nigeria. Chartered Architect and Planner. m. Dora Sarkodie-Mensah, 10 Aug. 1974, 3 sons, 1 daughter. *Education:* BSc, Ahmadu Bello University, Zaria, 1963-66; MSc, University of Science & Technology, Kumasi, Ghana, 1966-68. *Appointments:* Research Assistant, Department of Housing and Planning Research, University of Science & Technology, Kumasi, Ghana, 1968-70; Architect, Kenneth Scott Associates, Accra, Ghana, 1970-71; Architect, Godwin & Hopwood, Lagos & Kaduna, Nigeria, 1972; Principal Partner and Founder of Nwankwo Scott Associates, Chartered Architects, Town Planners and Development Consultants, 1972-. *Memberships:* Royal Institute of British Architects; Nigerian Institute of Architects; Ghana Institute of Architects. *Honours:* Mention for Good Design Work, 1977. *Hobbies:* Lawn Tennis; Hunting; Reading; Travelling. *Address:* No 1 Second Avenue Close, Independence Layout, Enugu, Nigeria.

NWANKWO, Green Onyekaba, b. 11 Sept. 1933, Arondizuogu, Nigeria. Professor. m. Elizabeth Umenwa, 29 Feb. 1956, 2 sons, 5 daughters. *Education:* BSc, University of Strathclyde, 1960-63; MSc, London School of Economics, 1963-65; PhD., School of Oriental & African Studies, University of London, 1965-67. *Appointments:* Lecturer in Monetary Economics, 1967-68; Senior Lecturer, 1968-72, City of London Polytechnic, London; Associate Professor, 1972-74; Professor of Finance, 1974-, University of Lagos; Chairman, Group of 24 Deputies, 1980-81. *Memberships:* Fellow of The Institute of Bankers, England and The International Banker Association, America; Nigerian Institute of Management, Nigeria; Society for International Development; Nigerian Economic Society; Member, United Nations Committee for Development Planning. *Publications:* Basic Economics, An Introduction for West African Students; With Jones, The Groundwork of Commerce, 1980; The Nigerian Financial System, 1980; The New International Economic Order & The World Monetary System, 1976; The Grammar of Money, (An Inaugural Lecture), 1978. *Honours:* University of London Convocation Trust Prize, BSc Examination,

1962; Corporation of Glasgow Trust Prize, to the best student of the Year, 1963. *Hobby:* Boxing. *Address:* 6A Queen's Drive, Ikoyi, Lagos, Nigeria.

NWANWENE, Omorogbe, b. 18 Dec. 1934, Igbanke, Near Benin City. Professor. m. Maria Green, 31 Mar. 1967, 3 sons, 1 daughter. *Education:* BSc, London, 1961; MSc, London, 1963; PhD., London, 1966. *Appointments:* Research Fellow, University of Ife, Nigeria, 1967-68; Lecturer/Senior Lecturer, 1968-75; Associate Professor/Professor 1975-; Director, New Nigeria Bank, 1979-. *Memberships:* Fellow, The Nigerian Institute of Personnel Management of Nigeria; Parliamentary Affairs Association of the Commonwealth; Civil Service Commission of Bendel State, 1971-76; Governing Board, Administrative Staff College of Nigeria, 1973-75; Nigerian Council for Management Educational Training, 1972-75. *Publications:* Several articles in learned journals dealing with Administration and Management; Adviser and Consultant to the World Health Organisation. *Hobbies:* Gardening; Reading. *Address:* No 20 Okungbowa Street, Off Okhoro Road, Benin City, Nigeria.

NWIKINA, Gbole Nanu, b. 4 Apr. 1923, Kono Town, Ogoni District, Rivers State of Nigeria. Chartered Librarian, Retired Library Director. m. Winifred Chijioke Ifeoma Ndefo, 17 Apr. 1954, 1 son, 4 daughters. *Education:* School of Librarianship, Loughborough, Leicester, England, 1949; Associate of the Library Association, 1952; School of Librarianship, Manchester, England, 1952; Columbia University, NY, USA, 1957-58; Unesco Fellowship in Library Administration, 1958; Certificate of Advanced Library Administration, College of Library and Information Service, University of Maryland, Maryland, USA, 1975. *Appointments:* Librarian, US Information Service, Lagos, 1952-54; Librarian, Federal Ministry of Information, Lagos, 1954-56; Deputy Director, Library Board of Eastern Nigeria, Enugu, 1957-70; Director, Library Board of the Rivers State of Nigeria, Port Harcourt, 1970-77; Retired 1977; Board of Directors, National Library of Nigeria, Lagos, 1971-74; Governing Council, Rivers State College of Science and Technology, Port Harcourt, 1978-79. *Memberships:* Secretary/Treasurer, West African Library Association, 1959-62; Secretary/Treasurer, Nigeria Library Association, 1962-66; Library Association, London, 1944-. *Publications:* Contributions to Library Bulletins, Conferences and Unesco Seminars. *Hobbies:* Reading; Sports; Squash Racquets; Table and Lawn Tennis; Socio-Cultural Activities. *Address:* 10 Ernest Koli Street, Old GRA, PO Box 1390, Port Harcourt, Rivers State of Nigeria.

NWODO, Igwe John Ugwu, (His Royal Highness), b. 1918, Ukehe, Igbo, Anambra State, Nigeria. Health Officer, Treasury Clerk. m. Josephine, 1938, 4 sons, 4 daughters. *Education:* Diploma in Public Health; Read Law and Economics; Attended courses on Local Government and Economics at Ibadan and Cambridge University. *Appointments:* Treasury Clerk, 1938-40; Health Officer, 1945-52; Eastern House of Assembly, 1952-66; Parliamentary Secretary, Eastern Nigeria Ministry of Health, 1954-57; Minister of Works, 1957-58; Minister of Commerce, 1959-61; Minister of Local Government, 1961-66. *Memberships:* Chairman, Agricultural Development Corporation, Anambra State of Nigeria; Chairman, Anambra Traditional Rulers' Association; Judicial Panel on Review and Codification of Customary Law, Anambra State. *Publications:* Retrospect on Institution of Traditional Government; The Coming of Missionaries to Ukehe. *Honours:* His Royal Highness, Igwe of Ukehe, Okwuluora II, Obodo Echina, Ejimofor. *Hobbies:* Pigery; Poultry; Tennis; Folk Music. *Address:* Ukehe House, Ukehe, Igbo, Etiti Local Government, PO Box 184, Nsukka, Anambra State, Nigeria.

NWOGA, Donatus Ibeakwadalam, b. 30 July 1933, Umoukrika - Ekwerazu, Ahiazu-Mbaise, Imo State, Nigeria. Professor. m. Patricia McDonell, 21 May 1962, 5 sons. *Education:* BA, Queen's University, Belfast, 1956-60; MA, University College, London, 1960-62; PhD., University of London, 1965; *Appointments:* Tutor, St Peter Clavers Seminary, 1951, Holy Ghost College, Umuahia, 1954, Christ the King College, Onitsha, 1955-56; Assistant Lecturer, 1962-64, Lecturer, 1964-70, Senior Lecturer, 1970-73, Reader, 1973-74, Professor, 1974-, Head, Department of English, 1965-71, 1974-75, 1978-79, Dean Faculty of Arts, 1975-77, Director, Division of General Studies,

1980-, University of Nigeria; Visiting Professor, University of Texas, Austin, 1979, University of Pennsylvania, Philadelphia, 1980. *Memberships:* African Studies Association, USA; Folklore Society, USA; Folklore Society of Great Britain; African Studies Association, Great Britain; Nigerian Folklore Society; Literary Society of Nigeria; Association for Commonwealth Languages & Literary Studies. *Publications:* Editor, West African Verse, 1967; Co-Editor, Poetic Heritage, Igbo Traditional Verse, 1972; Co-Author, Ogugu Igbo, I-VI, 1974-77; Editor, Harsh Flutes, Crisis Poetry From Eastern Nigeria, 1980; Several Essays in professional journals. *Honours:* Eastern Nigeria Scholarship, 1956-62; Hugh Graham Mitchell Bursary Award, Queen's University, Belfast, 1960. *Hobbies:* Tennis; Music (Classical, Jazz, African); Dance. *Address:* 301 Margucritte Cart., Avenue, University of Nigeria, Nsukka, Nigeria.

NWOGUGU, Edwin Ifeanyichukwu, b. 1 Apr. 1933, Iyi-Enugu, Ogidi, Nigeria. Professor of Law. m. Grace Nwamalubia Uzodike, 19 Feb. 1966, 2 sons, 3 daughters. *Education:* LL.B., Hull, 1960; PhD., Manchester, 1963. *Appointments:* Lecturer, University of Lagos, 1963-65; Reader, University of Nigeria, 1974; Professor of Law, 1975; Head, Department of International Law & Jurisprudence, 1974-77; Dean, Faculty of Law, 1977-78; Deputy Vice Chancellor, University of Nigeria, Enugu Campus, 1979-. *Memberships:* American Society of International Law; Nigerian Bar Association; British Institute of International and Comparative Law; International Family Law Association. *Publications:* Legal Problems of Foreign Investment in Developing Countries; Family Law in Nigeria. *Honours:* Commonwealth Scholar, 1961-63; Nuffield College Student, 1963. *Hobbies:* Gardening; Tennis. *Address:* 2 Charles Leme Street, University of Nigeria, Enugu Campus, Nigeria.

NWOKO, Demas, Nwanna. b. 20 Dec. 1935, Idumuje-Ugboko. Painter-Sculptor/Designer & Dramatist. m. Eunice Chijioke Okonkwo, 27 Dec. 1963, 2 sons, 2 daughters. *Education:* Nigerian College of Arts Science and Technology, Zaria, Nigeria, Diploma in Fine Arts, 1957-1961; International Theatre Centre, Ecole des Beaux Arts in Paris, studying theatre design technique, and Fresco painting, 1961-1962. *Appointments:* Fellow in Fine Arts, Department of Theatre Arts University of Ibadan, as a Sceno-grapher, 1962-1978; Play and Dance Director; Artistic Director New Culture Studios, Ibadan, 1970-; Managing Director African Designs Development Centre Ltd. for Architectural, Theatre and Industrial Designs, Production at Ibadan and Ugboko, 1972-; Editor-in-Chief of 'New Culture', a review of Contem- porary African Arts, Art Books, Creative Writings and other Technical books, published and printed by New Culture Studios, 1978nh. *Memberships:* Mbari, Artists and Writers Club; Society of Nigerian Artists. *Creative Works:* Mural Paintings in the University of Ibadan, 1961; Revival of Terra-cotta Sculpting, 1965; Design and Construction of Studios, 1966-1970. A Dominican Monastery at Ibadan, 1970-1975. A cultural centre complex at Benin, 1973. 'New Culture' a review of contemporary African Arts. The Children of Paradise, a dance play written and produced for FESTAC 1977, World Black Festival of the Arts, Lagos. Totem Pillars, Lagos International Airport, 1978-1979. *Hobbies:* Designing of Building and Architectural Decorations; Music and Dances of the World; Reading from Science and Technology Research Publications. *Address:* Addec Ltd., Ugboko-Aniocha LGA, Bendel State, Nigeria.

NWOKOLO, Chukuedu b. 19 April, 1921, Oraifite, Anambra State, Nigeria. Medicine. m. Njideka Okonkwo, 4 July, 1953, 3 sons, 4 daughters. *Education:* School of Medicine of Nigeria, Yaba 1942-1947; Postgraduate Medical Federation, London, 1950-1953; University of Edinburgh, Scotland & Edinburgh postgraduate Board for Medicine, 1952-1953; University of Minnesota, U.S.A. 1963-1964; LSM Nigeria, 1947; MRCS Eng; LRCP, London, 1951; MRCP Edinburgh, 1953; FRCP Edinburgh, 1961; FWACP, 1976. *Appointments:* Senior Medical Specialist Ministry of Health, Enugu, 1961-1962; Senior Lecturer in Medicine, University of Ibadan, 1963-1965; Associate Professor in Medicine, University of Ibadan, 1965-1967; Professor of Medicine, University of Nigeria, 1971-1980; Dean, Faculty of Medicine, University of Nigeria, Enugu Campus, 1972-1975; Chairman, Board National Institute for Medical Research, 1977-1980; Director, National

Medical Clinic, 1980-. *Memberships:* President Association of Physicians of Nigeria, 1971-1973; Vice-President, West African College of Physicians, 1978-1981; Nigeria Medical Association. *Publications:* 40 Publications in Medical Journals, including: Hypothesis on 'Pathogenesis of Juvenile Tropical Pancreatitis Syndrome', Lancet, March 1 1980; An introduction to Clinical Medicine in the tropics to be published by Churchill Livingstone, London, 1981-1982. *Honours:* Rockefeller Foundation Research Fellowship in Gastroenterology, University of Minnesota, U.S.A., 1963-1964; Sir Walter Johnson Prizeman in Organic Chemistry and Public Health, School Medicine of Nigeria, 1942-1947. *Hobbies:* Electronics; Popular Science; Reading. *Address:* 1B River Close, Ekulu Gra, Enugu, Nigeria.

NWUGA, Vincent Chukuka Babatunde, b. 22 Apr. 1939, Lagos, Nigeria. Physiotherapist. m. 12 Sept. 1964, 3 sons, 2 daughters. *Education:* School of Medical Rehabilitation, University of Manitoba, Winnipeg, Canada, 1970-71; Department of Physical Medicine and Rehabilitation, University of Minnesota, Minneapolis, Minnesota, USA, 1973-74; Doctoral Candidate, University of Ife, Ile-Ife, Nigeria, 1974-77. *Appointments:* Physiotherapist: Brook General Hospital, London, UK, Lewisham Hospital, London, UK, 1967-69; University College Hospital, Ibadan, Nigeria, 1969-70, 1971-72; Princess Elizabeth Hospital, Winnipeg, Canada, 1971; Sole Charge Physiotherapist, State Hospital, Akure, Nigeria on behalf of University of Ife, Faculty of Health Sciences, 1972-73; Physical Therapist, Fairview Hospital, Minneapolis, USA, 1974; Consultant Physiotherapist, 1976-, Head, Department of Medical Rehabilitation, 1978-, Ife University Teaching Hospitals Complex, Nigeria; Graduate Assistant, 1972-73, Lecturer II, 1974-76, Lecturer I, 1976-78, Senior Lecturer, 1978-, Acting Head, Department of Nursing and Medical Rehabilitation, 1979-, University of Ife, Nigeria. *Memberships:* Chartered Society of Physiotherapy, UK; Canadian Physiotherapy Association; Nigeria Society of Physiotherapy. *Publications:* Manipulation of the Spine, 1976; 3 Thesis; 20 papers in Professional/Scientific journals; 2 published Conference Proceedings; 6 papers in Medical Students' Association and Physiotherapy Students' Association Journals; 5 tapes in Tape Slide Programme. *Address:* University of Ife, Faculty of Health Sciences, Department of Medical Rehabilitation, Ile-Ife, Nigeria.

NYABUNDI, Monica Rispa, b. 30 Nov. 1947, Siaya, Kenya. Librarian. m. JS Nyabundi, 18 May 1966, 3 sons, 1 daughter. *Education:* Certificate, Librarianship, Makerere University, Kenya, 1972; Mature age entrance, University of Nairobi, Kenya, 1973; Bachelor of Education, Kenyatta University College, Kenya, 1977; Postgraduate Diploma, Librarianship, Leeds, UK, 1980. *Appointments:* Banker, Kenya Commercial Bank Limited, 1967-71; Library Assistant, 1971-74, Assistant Librarian, 1977-, Kenya National Library Services. *Memberships:* Kenya Library Association. *Hobbies:* Knitting; Pop music; Cookery; Reading novels. *Address:* Riverside Drive, Nairobi, Kenya.

NYAGUMBO, Tapfumaneyi Maurice, b. 12 Dec. 1924, Rusape, Zimbabwe. Cabinet Minister. m. Victoria Makoni, 24 Aug. 1955, 6 daughters. *Education:* BA, South African University. *Appointments:* Minister of Mines and Energy Resources, Zimbabwe, 1980. *Publications:* With the People, 1980. *Hobby:* Reading. *Address:* 114 Eastern Road, Greendale, Salisbury, Zimbabwe.

NYAME, Comfort Seiwah, b. 13 Jan. 1945, Accra, Ghana. Librarianship. 1 son. *Education:* BA., University of Ghana, Legon, Ghana, 1969; Post-Graduate Diploma, Librarianship, Ealing Technical College, London, UK, 1975. *Appointments:* Ghana Library Board, 1976-80; Ghana Institute of Management and Public Administration, 1980-. *Memberships:* Financial Secretary of Ruling Party; Volta Reformation party, Volta Hall, University of Ghana, Legon, Ghana, 1968. *Hobbies:* Reading; Gardening; Music. *Address:* PO Box 1799, Accra, Ghana, West Africa.

NYIIRA, Zerubabel Mijumbi, b. 29 Feb. 1940, Masindi, Uganda. Entomologist; Acarologist. m. Rebecca K Musoke, 8 Nov. 1969, 1 son, 4 daughters. *Education:* BSc., 1967; MSc., 1970; PhD., 1975; Diplomas: African Agriculture, 1960; A.Inst.Sc. Tech., London, UK, 1964; City and Guilds Final Certificate, 1964; Certificate,

Research Administration and Management, 1980. *Appointments:* Agricultural Research Assistant, 1960-64; Research Technician, 1964-67; Scientific Officer, 1967-70; Research Officer, 1971-77; Principal Research Officer, 1977-; Director of Research, 1975-; Coordinator of Agricultural Research, 1977-; Research Professor and Chief Research Officer, 1980. *Memberships:* Royal Society of Health; Secretary, African Students Association; California State University; Kiwana Club, USA; Entomoloical Society of America; Uganda Society of Agnomeny; African Association of Insect Scientists. *Publications:* 51 Scientific publications in International and Local journals and in proceedings of various conferences, workshops and symposia. *Honours:* Local Government Bursary, 1953-56; Uganda Government Fellowship, 1961-64; United States of America Aid Scholarship, 1966-68; Uganda Government Fellowship, Rockefeller Foundation Grant, 1969-70; International Development Research Centre Fellowship, 1980. *Hobbies:* Dancing; Lawn tennis; Swimming. *Address:* PO Box 1112, Kampala, Uganda.

NYIRENDA, Angus, b. 16 Feb. 1934, Mchenga, Karonga, Malawi. Surveyor. m. Chrissie Chimaliro, 14 Aug. 1961, 3 sons, 4 daughters. *Education:* Certificates: Surveying, 1957; Engineering Surveying, 1961; Middle Management, NELP., 1980; Diploma, Surveying. *Appointments:* Survey Department, 1957-59, Works Supplies, Design Department, 1971-, Malawi; Comp works, Tanzania, 1959-66; Ingra Company, Tanzania, 1966-67; Murray and Roberts, Nacala Railway Conf., Malawi, 1968-70; C I C., Malawi, 1970-71. *Memberships:* Associate member, Society of Surveying Technician. *Hobbies:* Do it yourself; Music; Football. *Address:* Box 386, Lilongwe, Malawi.

NYIRENDA, Greenwell Khoti Chekacheka, b. 8 Apr. 1943, Nkhata Bay, Malawi. Entomologist. m. 31 Dec. 1978, 2 sons. *Education:* BSc., University of Malawi, 1969; MSc., London, D I C., 1971. *Appointments:* Trainee Entomologist, 1969, Entomologist, 1971-74, Cotton Insect Pest Control, Agricultural Research Council, Malawi; Cotton Entomologist, 1975, Senior Agricultural Research Officer, Cotton Insect Pest Control, 1977, Acting Officer, 1977, Principal Agricultural Research Officer, 1978, Assistant Chief Agricultural Research Officer, 1978, Makoka Cotton Productivity Research Station, Malawi Government. *Memberships:* Association for Advancement of Science in Malawi. *Publications:* Ultra Low Volume Application of Water-Based Formulations of Insecticides to Cotton (with MD Mowlam and JP Tunstall), 1975. *Hobbies:* Current affairs; Gardening; Traditional music. *Address:* Musani Chilelawana FP., School, PO Nichata Bay, Malawi.

NYONG, Antigha Ekpe, b. 26 May 1926, Creek Town, Nigeria. Barrister-at-Law; Solicitor of Supreme Court of Nigeria. m. Nella Otudor Eyo, 19 Dec. 1953, 2 sons, 3 daughters. *Education:* Holborn College of Law, London, UK, 1958-59; LL.B., University College, London, UK, 1959-61; LL.M., course, 1961-62; Inns of Court School of Laws, 1957-59; Called to Bar, Gray's Inn, London, UK, 1960. *Appointments:* Crown Counsel, Lagos, Nigeria, 1962-65; Private Legal Practice: Lagos, Nigeria, 1965-68; Calabar, Cross River State, Nigeria, 1975-; Senior Magistrate, South Eastern State of Nigeria, 1968-69; Senior State Counsel, 1969-70, Registrar of Companies, 1970, Parliamentary Counsel, 1971-73, Principal State Counsel, 1973, Federal Ministry of Justice, Lagos, Nigeria; Solicitor-General and Permanent Secretary, Ministry of Justice, Cross River State, Nigeria, 1974-75; Legal Adviser, Agricultural Development Corporation, Cross River State, Nigeria, 1976-; Legal Adviser/ Consultant, Investment Trust Co. Limited, Cross River State, Nigeria, 1976-; Legal Adviser, Cross Lines Limited, 1976-; Director/Legal Adviser, Archiandy (Nigeria) Limited, 1975-. *Memberships:* Cross River State Branch, Nigerian Red Cross Society; Peoples Club of Nigeria; Nigerian Bar Association; Vice-Chairman, Unity Party of Nigeria, Cross River State Branch; Congregational Board, Presbyterian Church, Creek Town, Nigeria. *Publications:* Editor: The All Nigeria Law Report, 1962. *Honours:* Patron, Creek Town Voluntary Brigade, 1978. *Hobbies:* Swimming; Gardening. *Address:* Plot E1, Duke Town Drive, Housing Estate, PO Box 637, Calabar, Cross River State, Nigeria.

NZEWI, Meki Emeka, b. 21 Oct. 1938, NNewi, Nigeria. Dramatist; Composer; Ethnomusicologist. m. 29 Nov. 1968, 3 sons, 2 daughters. *Education:* BA.,(Hons.), University of Nigeria, 1965; PhD., Queens University, Belfast, UK, 1977. *Appointments:* Music producer, Nigerian Broadcasting Corporation, 1965; Lecturer, Music, 1966, Research Fellow, African Studies, 1970, Senior Research Fellow, Music and Drama, 1976, University of Nigeria, Nsukka, Nigeria; Director, Theatre Company, Biafra, 1967. *Memberships:* International Music Society; Society for Ethnomusicology. *Publications:* Texts: Drama Scene in Nigeria; Traditional Music in Nigeria; Plays: The Lost Finger; A Drop of Honey; Two Fists in one Mouth; The Ombudspirit: Your Life Depends on it; Many articles in journals; Compositions: over 25 including Musicals; A Symphonic Poem; other works for instruments and solo voices or orchestras. *Hobbies:* Travel; Dancing. *Address:* 910 Murtala Mohammed Road, University of Nigeria, Nsukka, Nigeria.

O

OAKES, Alan Graham, b. 7 Feb. 1947, Dewsbury, England. Dental Surgeon. m. Marguerite Ann Sunderland, 14 Oct. 1972, 1 son. *Education:* BDS, Manchester University Dental School, 1965-70. *Appointments:* Private Dental Practice under National Health Service, Manchester, 1970-71; Dewsbury, 1971-72; Barnsley, 1973-. *Memberships:* Barnsley Local Dental Committee, 1972-; Barnsley Area Dental Advisory Committee, 1974-, Secretary, 1979-; Barnsley Family Practitioner Committee, 1976-; General Dental Practitioners' Association, 1974-, Secretary, 1976-. *Hobbies:* Running; Reading; Music. *Address:* 15 Cheviot Way, Hopton, Mirfield, West Yorkshire, WF14 8HW, England.

OAKES, Ray Ernst, b. 31 Oct. 1923, Toowoomba, Queensland, Australia. Chief Executive Officer. m. Joy Ramage, 31 Oct. 1959, 2 daughters. *Education:* Teacher's II, Queensland. *Appointments:* Primary School Teacher, Queensland, 1940-51; Commercial Accounting, 1951-58; Hospital Officer, 1958-. *Hobbies:* Rugby Union and Australian Rules Football; Music; Reading. *Address:* 40 Lady Game Drive, Killara, NSW, 2071, Australia.

OAKES, Reginald James Chad, b. 6 Apr. 1936, Brownhills. Chartered Engineer. m. Brenda Norton, 22 Mar. 1958, 2 daughters. *Education:* HNC Mechanical Engineering. *Appointments:* Section Leader, 1964-68, Project Engineer, 1968-72, Principal Engineer, 1972-78, Rubery Owen (Darlaston), Defence Equipment Division; Chief Engineer, Rubery Owen (Wrexham), 1978-80; Engineering Consultant, 1980-81. *Memberships:* Chartered Engineer; Committee Member, West Cheshire and Clwyd Branch BIM; FI Mech. E; MIED; MBIM; FEANI. *Hobby:* Music. *Address:* 1 Plover Close, Farndon, Chester CH36RG, England.

OAKSHOTT, Robert John, b. 27 Oct. 1930, Lismore, NSW, Australia. Rehabilitation Medicine. m. Catherine Mary, 6 Feb. 1960, 2 sons, 3 daughters. *Education:* MB, BS, Sydney, 1956; FRCS, 1964; FRACS, Australasia, 1967; DFRM, Sydney, 1975; FACRM, Australia, 1980. *Appointments:* Head of Department of Rehabilitation Medicine, Royal North Shore Hospital, St Leonards, NSW, Australia, 1977-; Medical Director, Royal Ryde Rehabilitation Hospital, Ryde, NSW, Australia, 1977-; Consultant in Rehabilitation Medicine, Commonwealth Rehabilitation Service, 1977-; Part-time Clinical Lecturer, University of Sydney, Sydney, Australia, 1980-. *Memberships:* Council & Secretary of Board of Censors, Australian College of Rehabilitation Medicine; Chairman, NSW Division, Australian Council for Rehabilitation of Disabled; Medical Committee, National Advisory Council for the Handicapped; Secretary, NSW Group, Australian Association of Physical & Rehabilitation Medicine; Secretary, Section of Rehabilitation Medicine, Australian Medical Association; Expert Committee on Rehabilitation Engineering, National Advisory Council for the Handicapped. *Publications:* Contributor to professional medical journals. *Address:* 85 Alexandria Parade, Wahroonga, NSW, Australia, 2076

OBAFEMI, Olorungbon Timothy, b. 19 Apr. 1925, Ekinrin Adde, Oyi Local Government, Kwara, Nigeria. Former Carrier Soldier. m. (1) 5 Feb. 1957, (2) 19 June 1969, 4 sons, 3 daughters. *Appointments:* Professional Army Officer, Retired as Substative Major; Company Executive Director. *Honours:* Nigeria Ind and four other medals. *Hobby:* Badminton. *Address:* 11 Bode Thomas Street, Surulere, Lagos, Nigeria.

O'BAHOR, Jonathan Ayheverero, b. 10 Oct. 1940, Warri, Bendel State, Federal Republic of Nigeria. Scientist. m. Sylvania Olympio, 10 Sept. 1963. *Education:* Inter. BSc, (Cambridge & London), Government College, Ughelli, Nigeria, 1958-60; BSc., University of Edinburgh, Scotland, 1961-65; MSc., University of Aston, Birmingham, England, 1965-66. *Appointments:* Assistant Executive Officer (Finance), The Federal Government of Nigeria, 1961; Research & Development Engineer, The Marconi Company Limited, England, 1963-64; Research & Development Engineer, The Standard Telephones & Cables Company Limited, London, 1967-68; Systems Analyst, Messrs. W R Grace

Limited, London, 1968-69; Nuclear Physicist, The Central Electricity Generating Board, London, 1970-75; The Chair of Physics, The Institute of Continuing Education, The Bendel State Government, Benin City, Nigeria, 1976-80; Chairman, The Commonwealth Commodity Company, Warri, Nigeria, 1981-. *Memberships:* General Council of the University of Edinburgh, Scotland; Royal Academy of Arts, England; Benefactor of the Queen's Gate Trust of the Imperial Colleges of Science and Technology, University of London, England. *Publications:* Numerous contributions in the scientific field; Several Oil Paintings including a Self-Portrait, 1959; Sculpture: Union Jack, 1980, Girder gate sculpture in steel, Susannah House, Warri, Nigeria. *Honours:* Queen Elizabeth II Coronation Prize, 1952; Federal Scholar Commonwealth Scholarship Scheme, 1961-65. *Hobbies:* World Affairs; Classical Music; Oil Painting; African & Oriental Art; Horticulture. *Address:* Susannah House, 38 Odion Road, PO Box 1700, Warri, Bendel State, Nigeria, West Africa.

OBANU, Zak Ahamefule, b. 23 Dec. 1943, Umuekwule-Umuopara, Umuahia, Nigeria. Food/Meat Science. m. Joy Nkechinyere Ibeabuchi, 8 July 1972, 2 sons, 1 daughter. *Education:* BSc, University of Nigeria, Nsukka, 1967; MSc, University of Reading, UK, 1972; PhD., University of Nottingham, UK, 1976. *Appointments:* Biology/Chemistry/Agricultural Science Tutor, Girls Secondary School, Abiriba, 1967-70; Assistant Lecturer in Animal Science, 1970;73, Lecturer Grade Two, 1973-76, Lecturer, Grade One, 1976-77, Lecturer Grade One in Food Science & Technology, 1977-78, Senior Lecturer, and Head of Department of Food and Home Science, 1978-79, Senior Lecturer in Food Science and Technology, 1978-, University of Nigeria, Nsukka. *Memberships:* Secretary, Nigerian Institute of Food Science & Technology; Treasurer, Nutrition Society of Nigeria; Nigerian Society for Microbiology; Association of Food Scientists & Technologists (India); Society of Fisheries Technologists (India); Indian Fisheries Association; Associate, Institute of Food Science & Technology, UK; Institute of Food Technology, USA; American Meat Science Association. *Publications:* Author of over 50 research papers in professional journals and conference proceedings; Also actively engaged in many advisory roles. *Honours:* Best student BSc, Final-year class, 1967; Federal (Nigerian) Scholar, 1964-67; Commonwealth Academic Scholar, 1972-76, Travel Fellowship, 1980; Expert Referee in Meat Science and Food Science & Technology for some professional journals. *Hobby:* Active Christian. *Address:* Umuekwule-Umuopara, PO Box 112, Umuahia, Nigeria.

OBASABJO, Olusegun, b. 5 Mar. 1937, Abeokuta, Nigeria. Head of State. *Education:* Primary and later Baptist Boy's High School. *Appointments:* Nigerian Army, 1958-75: Mons Officers Cadet School, 1959; Lieutenant, 1960; Commander, Engineers Corps, 1963; Captain, 1963; Major, 1965; Lieutenant Colonel, 1967; Colonel, 1969; Commander 2 Div Rear, Garrison, Ibadan; GOC 3 Marine Commando 1969-70; Commander, Inspector, Engineers Corps, 1970-75. *Memberships:* Federal Commissioner for Works and Housing, 1975; Chief of Staff, Supreme Headquarters 1975-76; Head of State, 1976-; *Publications:* Author: My Command. *Honours:* General, 1978; Distinguished Fellow, University of Ibadan; Grand Commander, Federal Republic of Nigeria, 1980; Honorary Doctor of Laws, University of Maiduguri 1980. *Hobbies:* Table Tennis; Billiards; Snooker; Draughts; Squash. *Address:* PO Box 2286, Abeokuta, Ogun State, Nigeria.

OBENG, Letitia Eva, b. Anum Ghana. Research Scientist; Scientific Administration; International Civil Servant. m. 20 June 1953, 2 sons, 1 daughter. *Education:* BSc Hons. Zoology, 1952; MSc Parasitology, Birmingham University, 1962; PhD, University of Liverpool, 1964. *Appointments:* Lecturer, College of Science and Technology, Kumasi, Ghana, 1952-59; Research Staff, National Research Council, Ghana, 1960-63; Research Staff, Ghana Academy of Sciences, 1963-65; Director, Institute of Aquatic Biology, Ghana, 1965-74; Chairman, Soil and Water Task Force, UNEP, 1974-80; Director and Regional Representative for Africa, 1980-. *Memberships:* Fellow, Ghana Academy of Arts and Sciences; Consulting Expert, Rachel Carlson Memorial Trust; Commonwealth Human Ecology Council. *Publications:* Editor, Manmade lakes; Environmental Management; Numerous Scientific and general papers in many books and journals. *Honours:* Silver Medal, Royal

Society of Arts, United Kingdom. *Hobbies:* Flowers; Poetry; Reading; Writing. *Address:* UNEP, PO Box 47074, Nairobi, Kenya.

OBI, Bernard Ositadinma, b. 20 Nov. 1952, Umudbia Village, Umudji, Nigeria. Accountant/Company Executive. m. Maria Obiageli Akpaka, 29 Dec. 1952. *Education:* S.C.A. Intermediate, 1975. *Appointments:* Junior Accounts Clerk, 1970-73; Senior, 1973-75; Accountant Assistant, 1975-76; Branch Accountant, 1976-80; Chairman: Ositadinma International Limited, Cornbrough Products, Nigeria Limited, 1980-. *Memberships:* National Party of Nigeria Youth Wing; Umouji Social Club of Nigeria; Fegge Sports Complex; Chamber of Commerce, Industries, Agriculture and Mines. *Hobbies:* Tennis (Lawn and Table); Soccer; Squash; Cricket; Photography; Music; Movies. *Address:* 59 Zik Avenue, Fegge, Onitsha, Nigeria.

OBI IZEDIUNOR, Michael Ezenweani, b. 12 Nov. 1906, Ogwashi-Uku. Traditional Ruler. m. 10 Oct. 1927, 38 sons, 47 daughters. *Education:* Junior and Senior Clerical Entrance Exam, Hope Waddel Institute, Calaber, 1929-30. *Appointments:* Pupil Teacher, R.C.M. Asaba, 1924-25; Assistant Native Court Clerk, O'ulae, 1925-26; Second Class Clerk Poul. Adu. Wam', 1931-34; Ascended Throne of O'ulae, 1934-. *Memberships:* Reformed Ogboni Fraternity, 1960; The Alashe of the House; Member of Various Societies in O'ulaa. *Hobbies:* Hunter; Footballer; Guitarist. *Address:* Royal Palace, PO Box 1, Ogwash-Ulae, Bendel State, Nigeria

OBIOHA, George Ndu, b. 14 Apr. 1948, Enugu, Nigeria. Business Executive. m. Daba Manuel, 14 Jan. 1978, 1 son, 1 daughter. *Education:* BSc Finance, Howard University, Washington DC, USA, 1973. *Appointments:* Sales Executive, Mutual or Omaha Insurance Company. *Memberships:* Lagos Country Club, Ikeja, Lagos. *Honours:* Century Club Award, 1971; Honour Club Award, Mutual or Omaha, 1972, 73 and 74. *Hobby:* Lawn Tennis. *Address:* 28 Commonwealth Avenue, Palm Grove Estate, Lagos, Nigeria.

OBISANYA, Babatunde, b. 21 Apr. 1950, Ibadan, Nigeria. Business-Company Executive. m. 17 May 1974, 2 sons, 1 daughter. *Education:* Diploma in Physical and Health Education, University of Ibadan, 1977. *Appointments:* Business Consultants. *Memberships:* Nigeria Table Tennis Association. *Honours:* International Table Tennis Umpire. *Hobbies:* Table Tennis; Football; Boxing. *Address:* SW 8/561, Bamgboye Avenue, Liberty Stadium Road, Oke-Ado, Ibadan, Oyo-State, Nigeria.

OBOTE, Dr (Apollo) Milton, b. 1924. Ugandan Politician. *Appointments:* Labourer, Clerk, Salesman, Kenya, 1950-55; Founder-member, Kenya African Union; Uganda National Congress, 1952-60; Uganda Legis. Council, 1957-71; Uganda People's Congress, 1969-71; Leader of the Opposition, 1961-62; Prime Minister, 1962-66; Minister of Defence and Foreign Affairs, 1963-65; assumed full powers of Government, 1966; President of Uganda, 1966-71; Exile in Tanzania, 1971-80; President, 1980-; Minister of Foreign Affairs, 1980-. *Address:* Office of the President, Kampala, Uganda.

O'BRIEN, Bernard McCarthy, b. 25 Dec. 1924, Australia. Surgeon. m. Joan Williams, 18 Dec. 1958, 2 sons, 3 daughters. *Education:* Bachelor of Science, 1948; Bachelor of Medicine and Surgery, 1950; Master of Surgery, 1955; Doctor of Medicine, University of Melbourne, 1978; Fellow, Royal College of Surgeons England, 1955; Fellow, Royal Australasian College of Surgeons, 1959; Fellow, American College of Surgeons, 1966. *Appointments:* Senior Demonstrator in Anatomy, University of Melbourne, 1953; Clinical Assistant Plastic Surgery Unit, Royal Melbourne Hospital, 1954-55; General Surgeon Associate, St Vincent's Hospital 1954-55; Demonstrator on Clinical Surgery and Histopathology, 1954-55; Nuffield Assistant in Plastic Surgery, University of Oxford, 1965; Plastic Surgery Registrar, South West Metropolitan Region, Odstock Hospital, Salisbury, England 1957-58; Chief Resident, Plastic and Reconstructive Surgery Department, Roosevelt Hospital, New York, 1959; Director, Plastic Surgeon, Microsurgery Research Unit, St Vincent's Hospital, Melbourne; Senior Associate, University of Melbourne; Consultant Plastic Surgeon. *Mem-*

berships: International Federation of Societies for Surgery of the Hand; International Society of Reconstructive Microsurgery; Royal Australasian College of Surgeons; Pacific, Pan-Pacific Surgical Association; Australian Delegate Societe Internationale de Chirurgie. *Publications:* Microvascular Reconstructive Surgery 1977; 150 publications in International Surgical Journals. *Honours:* Leriche Prize, 1979; Colles Medal, 1980. *Hobbies:* Opera; Classical Music; Athletics; Skiing; Football. *Address:* 22 Chaucer Crescent, Canterbury, Victoria, Australia.

O'BRIEN, Cyril Cornelius, b. 22 Mar. 1906, Halifax, Nova Scotia, Canada. Research Scientist, Psychologist, Composer, Conductor. m. (1) Madeleine Agatha Jones, 4 July 1939 (Dec.) (2) Mary Patricia Florence Davison, 27 July 1957, 2 sons, 1 daughter. *Education:* BA, 1926; Academic Diploma, 1929; Post-Graduate, Halifax Conservatory of Music, 1927-28; Post-Graduate, Dalhousie University, 1930-32; LMus. McGill University, 1931; MA, 1932; BPaed, University of Toronto, 1934; DPaed, University of Montreal, 1937; BMus, Laval University 1937; PhD, University of Ottawa, Canada, 1944; MusD, 1950; Honorary Fellow, Psycho-Acoustics, University of Wisconsin, USA, 1950. *Appointments:* Principal of Schools, Teacher, Church Organist, Lecturer, Professor, Consultant, Director of Research, 1927-77; Vice-President, Interpersonal Communicators, Inc. Illinois and California, 1961; President, Adan Research Company Limited, Edmonton, 1969-; Vice-President, Patra Real Estate and Appraisal Company Limited, Edmonton, Alberta, 1975-; Conductor, Royal Park Philharmonic Chorus and Orchestra, Alberta, 1978-; Director, Prince of Peace Research Institute, Mundare, Alberta, Canada, 1980-. *Memberships:* Fellow, American Psychological Association; Royal Statistical Society, London; Royal Society of Arts; international Institute of Arts and Letters; American Association for the Advancement of Science; International Academy of Forensic Psychology; Massachusetts Psychological Association; Nova Scotia Music Teachers Association; Royal Canadian College of Organists; Royal Society of Teachers, London; Wisconsin Academy of Sciences, Arts and Letters; Associate, American Society of Composers, Authors and Publishers. *Publications:* About 130 articles to journals including: Journal of Psychology; Music Compositions: Oratorio-Invoke her name with Praise; Mass in Honour of St Thomas Aquinas; Mass in Honour of St Mary Magdalen; Motets, Songs, Hymns, Piano Soli, etc. *Honours:* Gold Medalist, in Music, 1926; Honorary Associate, American Institute of Management, 1956; Silver Certificate, Acoustical Society of America, 1972; Knight Commander, Order of St Bridget of Sweden, 1968; Association of Pontifical Knights, 1977; Knight Commander of the Equestrian Order of the Holy Sepulchre of Jerusalem, 1979. *Hobbies:* Camping; Writing; Publishing; Maintaining a Private Library. *Address:* PO Box 503, Clandonald, Alberta, Canada, T0B 0X0.

O'BRIEN, Kevin Benjamin, b. 19 Oct. 1925, Wellington, New Zealand. Business Consultant. m. 7 May 1955, 1 son, 6 daughters. *Education:* Victoria University of Wellington 1942-51; Bachelor of Commerce 1947; Master of Commerce (First Class Honours) 1948; Bachelor of Arts 1952; Associate, Chartered Institute of Secretaries. *Appointments:* Commercial and Managerial Positions 1942-61; Consultant and Chartered Secretary 1961-; Member 1962-65; Deputy Chairman 1965-72; Chairman 1972-76; New Zealand Tariff and Development Plansm 1975-77; Chairman, New Zealand Commerce Commission, 1977-. *Memberships:* Chancellor, Pro-Chancellor, Member of Council, 1949-75-; Chamber of Commerce; Various Offices, Church, Business, Educational and Medical Research Organisations. *Address:* 90 Hataitai Road, Wellington 3, New Zealand.

O'BRIEN, (Rt. Hon. Lord), Leslie Kenneth, b. 8 Feb. 1908, London. Bank and Company Director. m. Isabelle Gertrude Pickett, 2 Apr. 1932, 1 son. *Education:* DSc (Hon) City University; DL(Hon) University of Wales. *Appointments:* Bank of England 1927-; Chief Cashier 1955-62; Executive Director 1962-64; Deputy Governor 1964-66; Governor 1966-73; Commonwealth Development Finance Corporation-Director, 1962-64; President-British Bankers Association 1973-80; Director of Bank for International Settlements 1966-; Vice Chairman 1979-. *Memberships:* Director, Prudential Assurance Company 1973-; Director Prudential

Corporation 1979-; Director Saudi International Bank 1975-; International Advisory Council, Morgan Grenfell 1973-. *Publications:* Inaugural Jane Hodge Memorial Lecture 1971; The Independence of Central Banks, 1978; Numerous speeches and lectures. *Honours:* Knight Grand Cross of the Order of the British Empire, 1967; Privy Counsellor, 1970; Baron, 1973; Knight Grand Cross of the Order of Merit of Italy, 1975; Grand Officer of the Order of the Crown of Belgium, 1976; Fellow, Royal College of Music, 1979. *Hobbies:* Music; Opera; Theatre; Reading; Tennis. *Address:* 23 Burghley House, Somerset Road, London SW19 5JB, England.

O'BRIEN, Terence Phillip, b. 12 Jan. 1937, Melbourne, Victoria, Australia. Botanist, Biologist, Author, Publisher. m. (1) Eva Margaret Bye, 9 Jan. 1960 (Div) 1977, 3 sons, 1 daughter. (2) Carolynn Irene Maynard, 19 May 1979. *Education:* BAgr.Sc, 1959; MSc, Melbourne, 1963; PhD Biology, Harvard, 1966; JF Harvard, 1964; DSc Monash, 1978. *Appointments:* Research Office in Plant Physiology, ICIANZ, 1958-62; Graduate Student and Part-time Teaching Fellow, Harvard, 1962-64; Junior Fellow, Society of Fellows, Harvard, 1964-66; Visiting Research Fellow, Queen's University Belfast, 1966-67; Senior Lecturer, 1967-70; Reader in Botany, Monash University, 1970-. *Memberships:* Society of Developmental Biology USA; Royal Society of Victoria; Australian Society of Authors; Australian Society of Plant Physiology; Australian Institute of Agricultural Science; International Association of Wood Anatomists. *Publications:* Plant Structure and Development, 1969; Manual of Plant Histology, 1972; The Study of Plan Structure, 1981; 65 scientific papers in various aspects of the physiological anatomy of plants, with major emphasis on grasses and cereals. *Honours:* Dux of St Kieran's Central School, 1950; Exhibition in Agricultural Botany, 1957; Exhibition and James Cuming Prize in Agricultural Chemistry, 1957; Exhibition in Agricultural Bacteriology, 1958; Fulbright Travel Grant, 1962; Paul Mazur Fellowship, Harvard University, 1962-64; Leverhulme Fellow, University of Tokyo, 1972; Nuffield Fellowship to Canada, 1975. *Hobbies:* Squash; Cricket; Bushwalking; Music; Stained Glass Making; Publishing; Creative Writing. *Address:* Richardson Hall, Monash University, Clayton, Victoria 3168, Australia.

OBU, Hilary Agwu, b. 12 July 1920, Ajalli, Nigeria. Civil Servant (retired); Consultant. m. (1) Mercy Obu, 3 June 1944, (2) Monica Obu, 29 July 1959, 4 sons, 5 daughters. *Education:* Post Office Training Schools, Birmingham and London, UK; Diploma, Postal Administration, 1953; High Diploma, 1959. *Appointments:* Postal Officer and Telegraphist, 1937-52; Assistant Postal Controller, 1953-56; Senior Assistant Postal Controller, 1957-61; Postal Controller, 1962-64; Deputy Controller of Posts, 1965-67; Principal Assistant Secretary, 1967-69; Deputy Director, Postal Services, 1970-75; Commissioner, Local Government Service Commission, Anambra, Nigeria, 1976-80. *Memberships:* Nigerian Institute of Management; National Geographic Society of America; Divisional Secretary, Postal Workers Union, Eastern Region, Nigeria; General Secretary, Ajalli Improvement Union, Nigeria. *Honours:* Membership Certificate, National Geographic Society of America, 1951; Associate member, Nigerian Institute of Management, 1973. *Hobbies:* Reading; Walking; Dancing. *Address:* PO Box 1, Ajalli, Anambra State, Nigeria.

OCHIENG', William Robert, b. 5 Oct. 1943, Kisumu, Kenya. Historian. m. Margaret Rogo, 1 Jan. 1969, 1 son, 2 daughters. *Education:* BA(Hons.), History, 1968; PhD, History, Nairobi University, 1971. *Appointments:* Lecturer, Kenyan History, University of Nairobi, 1971-74; Senior Lecturer, Kenyan History, Kenyatta University College, Nairobi, 1974-. *Memberships:* Secretary of Bondo Union, Nairobi; Kenya Writers' Association; Historical Association of Kenya; Editor, Kenya Historical Review. *Publications:* Six books including: A Pre-Colonial History of the Gusii of Western Kenya, 1974; The First Word: Essays on Kenyan History, 1975; Eastern Kenya and Its Invadors, 1976; The Second Word: More Essays on Kenyan History, 1976. *Honours:* Visiting Scholar, Stanford University, California, USA, 1976; Visiting Lecturer, UCLA, 1978-79; Fulbright Scholar, Syracuse University, 1980. *Hobbies:* Journalism; Writing Local and African papers. *Address:* De-partment of History, Kenyatta University College, PO Box 43844, Nairobi, ·Kenya.

OCLOO,. Esther Afua, b. Apr. 1919, Ozake Peki, Ghana, West Africa. Industrialist. m. Steven Ocloo, 25 July 1959, 2 sons, 1 daughter. *Education:* Diploma, Cookery, Good Housekeeping Institute of Cookery, London, UK, 1949-50; Diploma, Food Preservation, Long Ashton Research Station, Bristol University, UK, 1950-51. *Appointments:* Executive Chairman, National Food and Nutrition Board, Ghana, 1964-66; President, Ghana Manufacturers Association, 1973-75, 1978-80; Director, Opportunities Industrialization Centre, Ghana, 1974-. *Memberships:* Manufacturers Association; Ecumenical Co-op Development Societies; Ghana Business and Professional Association; Council on Women and Development; Women World Banking; Council of State. *Honours:* Grand Medal for Meritorious Services, 1969; Honorary degree, Doctor of Science, University of Science and Technology, Kumasi, Ghana, 1977. *Hobbies:* Reading; Handicrafts; Gardening; Social work. *Address:* PO Box 36, Medina, Accra, Ghana.

O'COLLINS, Ellen Maev, b. 16 June 1929, Melbourne, Australia. University Teacher; Community Worker. *Education:* BA., Melbourne, Australia, 1950; Diploma, Social Studies, Sydney, Australia, 1951; Master of Science, 1969, Doctor of Social Welfare, 1972, Columbia University, New York, USA. *Appointments:* Family and Child Care Worker, 1952-56, Marriage Counsellor/ Principal Adoptions Officer, 1958-67, Catholic Family Welfare Bureau, Melbourne, Australia; Lecturer, Melbourne University, Australia, 1968-71; part time Administrative and Academic Assistant, Columbia University School of Social Work, USA; part time Lecturer, Chestnut Hill College, Philadelphia, Hunter College, New York, USA; Associate Professor, 1978, Professor, 1979, Chairman, 1981, Department of Anthropology and Sociology, University of Papua, New Guinea, 1972-. *Memberships:* International Association of Schools for Social Work; Australian and New Zealand Association for the Advancement of Science; Sociological Association of Australia and New Zealand; University Club, University of Papua, New Guinea. *Publications:* Papers include: Law and Society; Social Work Education; Student Research; Social Policy issues; UN Agency reports and newsletters; International Social work; proceedings of Asian Regional Association for Social Work Education. *Honours:* 2nd year Fellowship, American Association of University Women, 1967-69; Doctoral Studies award, Columbia University School of Social Work, USA, 1968-70. *Hobbies:* Gardening; Social work. *Address:* Department of Anthropology and Sociology, University of Papua New Guinea, PO Box 4820, Papua New Guinea.

O'CONNOR, Raymond James, b. 6 Mar. 1926, Perth, Western Australia. Deputy Premier of Western Australia. m. (1) Beverley Lydiate, 17 Mar. 1950, (2) Vesna Stampalia, 14 Mar. 1973, 4 sons, 3 daughters. *Appointments:* Member, Western Australian Legislative Assembly, 1959-; Minister for Transport, 1965-71; Minister for Transport, Traffic and Police, 1974-77; Minister for Works, Water Supplies and Housing, 1977-78; Minister for Labour and Industry, Fisheries and Wildlife, Consumer Affairs, Immigration and Conservation and the Environment, 1978-; Deputy Premier, 1980-. *Memberships:* President, Western Australian Sportsmens Association, 1969-74. *Honours:* Awarded Prendergast Medal for fairest and best reserves player, Western Australian National Football League, 1950. *Hobbies:* Golf; Tennis; Swimming; Horseriding. *Address:* 14 Dwyer Street, Karrinyup, Western Australia 6018, Australia.

ODAMTTEN, Silvanus Kone, b. 3 Apr. 1925, Labadi, Accra, Ghana. University Professor. m. Comfort Akuoko Nelson, 3 Mar. 1979, 2 sons. *Education:* BA., Hons., London, University of Ghana, 1952-57; MA., University of Birmingham, UK, 1961-63. *Appointments:* Elementary School Teacher: Presbyterian Middle Schools: Christiansborg, Ghana, 1947-49, Koforidua, Ghana, 1950-52; Senior History Master, 1960-66, Senior Housemaster, 1960-61, Mfantsipim Secondary School, Ghana, 1957-66; Part-time Tutor, Department of Extra-Mural Studies, University of Ghana, Legon, Ghana, 1957-61; Lecturer, African Studies Fellowship, Selly Oak Colleges, Birmingham, UK, 1961-63; Part-time Lecturer, Commonwealth Institute, London, UK, 1962-63; Part-time Lecturer, History Methods, 1965-66,

Lecturer, History of Education and History Methods, 1966-, Senior Lecturer, 1975, Head, Department of Educational Foundations, 1977- 78, Associate Professor, 1977, Dean, Faculty of Education, 1978-79, Pro-Vice-Chancellor, 1978-, Acting Vice-Chancellor, 1978-80, University of Cape Coast, Ghana. *Memberships:* Fellow, Council member, Historical Society of Ghana; Ghana Book Development Council. *Publications:* The Missionary Factor in Ghana's Development up to the 1880s, 1978; Education in Ghana—The Role of some Christian Mission Churches (in press); The Changing Role of the school in Ghana (in press); The Delight in Teaching and Learning History (in press); numerous publications in field of Religion; attended many International conferences and seminars. *Hobbies:* Swimming; Walking; Gardening; Music. *Address:* PO Box A60, Labadi, Ghana, West Africa.

O'DEA, Marjory Rachel, b. 31 July 1928, Melbourne, Australia. Public Servant. m. Raymond John O'Dea, 30 Aug. 1954, 2 sons, 2 daughters. *Education:* BA., Hons., Dip. Ed. Hons., University of Melbourne, Australia, 1946-50. *Appointments:* Senior History Mistress, Huyton Church of England Girls' Grammar School, Kew, Victoria, Australia, 1953-54; Biographer, CSIRO, 1970-73; Research Officer, 1973-74, Department of the Senate, Australian Parliament; Principal Science Adviser, 1974-76, Head, International Activities Section, 1977-78, Head, Information Policy Section, 1979, Department of Science and the Environment; Director, Tourism Programs, Tertiary Industry Division, Department of Industry and Commerce, 1980-. *Memberships:* Inaugural Committee, Australian Capital Territory, 1970, Society for Social Responsibility in Science; Australian Society of Authors; Amnesty International. *Creative Works:* Six Days Between a Second, 1969; Of Jade and Amber Caves, 1974. *Honours:* Exhibitions: Modern History, 1945; English Expression; English Literature; General; to Janet Clarke Hall. *Honours:* Poetry Magazine award of Poetry Society of Australia, 1968; Australian Representative, Struga Poetry Festival and Symposium, Yugoslavia, 1972. *Hobbies:* Dressmaking; Walking. *Address:* 58 Barada Crescent, Aranda, ACT 2614, Australia.

ODEY, John Upan, b. 3 Oct. 1918, Bebuabong Village, Obudu Town, Cross River State, Nigeria. Teaching. m. Christiana, 15 Jan. 1956, 6 sons, 6 daughters. *Education:* Diploma, Apologetics, 1952, BA., 1953, University College, Cork, Eire, Ireland; Postgraduate Diploma, Education, Institute of Education, University of London, UK. *Appointments:* Teacher in Primary and Secondary Schools; Principal, Teacher Training College. *Memberships:* Federal member of Parliament; Eastern Region, Library and Scholarship Boards; Chairman: Public Service Commission, Calabar; Caretaker Committee, Local Government Area, Obudu; NP N Political Party, Obudu, Nigeria; Director, NI Cogen Company. *Publications:* Translated and Printed Catholic Catechism in Bette Language. *Honours:* Papal Knighthood of St. Sylvester, 1975. *Hobbies:* Gardening; Chess. *Address:* 16 Hospital Road, Obudu, Cross River State, Nigeria.

ODEYEMI, John Agboola, b. 4 Apr. 1939, Ile-Ife, Nigeria. Chartered Accountant. m. (1) Felicia Olateju, Oct. 1964, (2) Victoria Obiageli, Jan. 1974, 4 sons, 3 daughters. *Education:* Associate, Association of Cost and Management Accountants, 1971; Associate, Association of Chartered Accountants of Nigeria, 1971; Fellow, Association of Certified Accountants, 1980. *Appointments:* Audit Senior, Coopers and Lybrand, Birmingham, UK, 1968; Accountant/Administration Manager, 1969, Finance Controller, 1972, Finance Director, 1974, Deputy Managing Director, 1979, James Kilpatrick (Nigeria) Limited, Nigeria; Chairman: Cutler Hammer Nigeria Limited, Nigeria, 1980; Intercare and Associates, Nigeria, 1980. *Memberships:* Chairman, Building and Civil Engineering Trade Group, Lagos Chamber of Commerce and Industry; Council member, Lagos Chamber of Commerce, Industry, Mines and Agriculture. *Honours:* Chieftaincy Title 'The Obasewa of Ife', 1980; Rubery Owen prize, most distinguished student of year, Wednesbury College of Commerce and Technology, Staffordshire, UK, 1965. *Hobbies:* Table tennis; Reading; Community developmental activities. *Address:* Ife Ooye House, First Avenue, Beachland Estate, near Tincan Island, Kirikiri-Apapa, Nigeria.

ODGERS, James Rowland, b. 9 Aug. 1914, Adelaide, South Australia. Parliamentary Officer (retired). m.

Helen Jean Horner, 2 Jan. 1939, 2 sons, 1 daughter. *Appointments:* Parliamentary Officer, 1937-79, Clerk of the Senate, 1965-79, Commonwealth Parliament, Canberra, Australia. *Publications:* 5 editions of: Australian Senate Practice, 1953, 1959, 1967, 1972, 1976. *Honours:* CBE., 1968; CB., 1980. *Hobby:* Canaries *Address:* 30 Barnett Close, Swinger Hill, Canberra, ACT 2603, Australia.

ODHIAMBO, Thomas Risley, b. 4 Feb. 1931, Mombasa, Kenya, Africa. University Professor. m. Jerusha Nerea Auma, 30 June 1956, 4 sons, 4 daughters. *Education:* BA., 1962, PhD., 1965, MA., 1960, Cambridge University, UK. *Appointments:* Technical Assistant, Tea Research Institute of East Africa, Kericho, Kenya, 1954-55; Assistant Agricultural Officer, Entomology Division, then Curator of Insect Collections, Ministry of Agriculture Serere Experimental Station then Kawanda Research Station, Uganda, 1955-62; Special Lecturer, Zoology, 1965-67, Senior Lecturer, Zoology, 1967-69, Reader, Zoology, 1969, Professor of Entomology, 1970-77, University of East Africa, Nairobi, Kenya; Head, Department of Entomology, 1970-77, Dean, Faculty of Agriculture, 1970-71, Hon. Professor of Entomology, 1977-, University of Nairobi, Kenya; Director, International Centre of Insect Physiology and Ecology, Nairobi, Kenya, 1970-. *Memberships:* Founder Fellow and Chairman, Kenya Academy of Sciences, 1977; Fellow: Pontifical Academy of Sciences, 1981; Italian Academy of Sciences, 1979; Royal Etomological Society of London, 1959; Foreign Fellow, Indian National Science Academy, 1977; Founder member and President, African Association of Insect Scientists, 1978; Permanent Committee, International Congresses of Entomology, 1980; Chairman, East African Society of Parasitologists, 1979; Fellow, Royal Society of Tropical Medicine and Hygiene, 1978. *Publications:* Look at Life; over 80 Scientific publications; Editor-in-Chief for: Insect Science and its Application, journal; Book series: Current Themes in Tropical Science; Monographic series: East African Monographs in Biology; member of Editorial Board, Entomologia Generalis. *Honours:* Special Scholarship, Makerere University, 1952-53; Uganda Government: Special Scholarship, 1959-62; Meritorious Studies Award, 1963-65; Appointed to Honorary Fellowship, Fauna Society, 1961; Appointed to Honorary Professorship, Entomology, University of Nairobi, Kenya, 1977. *Hobbies:* Reading and writing; Farming; Philosophy. *Address:* 'Pacho' 6 Gitanga Grove, PO Box 59900, Nairobi, Kenya.

ODIFE, Dennis Onyemaechi, b. 29 Aug. 1947, Jos, Plateau State, Nigeria. Stockbroker; Financi Analyst. m. Stella Adaku, 10 July 1970, 3 sons, 1 daughter. *Education:* BSc., Hons., University of Lagos, Nigeria, 1972; MBA., Columbia University, New York, USA, 1974. *Appointments:* Lecturer, Finance, University of Lagos, Nigeria, 1973-76; Manager, Corporate Finance, 1979, Director, 1978-79, ICON Stockbroker Limited, Nigeria; Managing Director, Centre-Point Investments Limited, Lagos, Nigeria, 1980. *Memberships:* Nigerian Economic Society; British Institute of Management; Nigerian Junior Chamber of Commerce; Nigeria Society. *Publications:* The 1977 Budget and the Nigerian Enterprised Promotion Act; Dividend Policy in an era of Indigenization: a comment; The Financial Implications of the New Industrial Policy, 1981; Listing for What, 1981; Nigerian Life-table distributions—a study of the distribution of male Nigerian life-times, 1976; Historical Development and Role of Merchant Banks in Nigeria (co-author), 1977. *Honours:* English prizes from: Edo College, Benin City, Nigeria 1963; Kings College, Lagos, Nigeria, 1964; History, Drama, Literary and Debating prizes, Kings College, Lagos, Nigeria; Faculty prize, Faculty of Business, Unilag, 1967; Deans List, Columbia University, Graduate School of Business, New York, USA, 1974. *Hobbies:* Lawn tennis; Reading; Swimming; Movies. *Address:* 14 Community Road, Akoka, Yaba, Lagos, Nigeria.

ODIGIE, Andrew Dele Stephen, b. 6 June, 1940, Benin, Nigeria. Accountancy. m. Sunbo, 6 June, 1964, 1 son, 2 daughters. *Education:* A.C.I.S., Westminster City College London 1965-1966; F.C.C.A., Catford College of Commerce London, 1966-1968; A.M.N.I.M., Nigerian Institute of Management; F.C.A., Institute of Chartered Accountants of Nigeria, 1970. *Appointments:* Accountant, Union International Co. Ltd. London, 1967-1969; Chief Accountant, Nigerian Sugar

Co. Ltd. Bacita, 1969-1974; Chief Accountant/Company Secretary, Goodyear Bendel Rubber Processing Co., 1974-1976; Finance Director, Adecentro Nigeria Ltd. Ibadan, 1976-1979; Executive Director, Adecentro Nigeria Ltd., Ibadan, 1979-; Chairman, B & O Health Farms Ltd. Lagos, 1980-. *Hobbies:* Table Tennis; Reading; Walking. *Address:* 17 Ogundipe Street, S7/1515A Orita Challenge, P.M.B. 5549, Ibadan, Nigeria.

O'DONNELL, Thomas Henry, b. 1 Sept. 1917, Sydney, New South Wales, Australia. Medical Practitioner. m. Alice Patricia Ann Mead, 6 May, 1944, 2 sons (1 deceased), 5 daughters. *Education:* M.B.B.S., Sydney University, 1942; Diploma in Laryngo-otology (D.L.O.), Sydney University.; FRACS, Fellow of Royal Australian College of Surgeons. *Appointments:* Consultant, Ear, Nose & Throat Surgeon, in Private Practice; Senior Honorary E.N.T. Surgeon, Royal North Shore Hospital of Sydney; Consultant E.N.T. Surgeon, Royal Alexandra Hospital for Children. *Memberships:* Otolaryngological Society of Australia; State Chairman 1966-1968, Deputy-Chairman of Federal Executive 1970-1975, President 1981-. *Hobbies:* Golf; Swimming *Address:* 25 Stanhope Road, Killara, New South Wales 2071, Australia.

O'DONOGHUE, Michael, John, b. 30 Nov. 1934, Leicester. Mineral, gemstone & crystal specialist/consultant: Lecturer, City of London Polytechnic. m. Anne Borley, 26 Feb. 1968, 1 son, 2 daughters. *Education:* MA, Cambridge, 1959; Fellowship Diploma, Gemmological Association of Great Britain, 1968. *Appointments:* National Library of Scotland, 1960-1962; British Museum 1962-. seconded to Science Reference Library. *Memberships:* Fellow, Geological Society of London; Council, Gemmological Association of Great Britain; Deutsche Gemmologische Gesellschaft; Mineralogical Society. *Publications:* Encyclopedia of minerals and gemstones, Orbis, 1976; Synthetic Gem materials, 1976; Synthetic gems, the case for caution, 1975; Guide to man-made gem materials(in press) 1981; Beginner's guide to minerals (in press) 1981; Editor, Gems, Gemmological Newsletter: Synthetic Crystals Newsletter; Over 1,500 other publications in the field of minerals, gemstones and crystal growth. *Hobby:* Playing the Organ. *Address:* 7 Hillingdon Avenue. Sevenoaks, Kent TN13 3RB, England.

ODU, Clifford, Temple, Idigi, b. 3 July 1938, Aba, Nigeria, Professor. m. Margaret A.R. Spiff, 11 Jan. 1968, 2 sons, 4 daughters. *Education:* B.Sc. (London), 1962; Ph.D. (Ibadan), 1967. *Appointments:* Agriculture Officer, Ministry of Agriculture, Eastern Nigeria, July-December, 1962; Lecturer Grade II, 1965-1968; Lecturer Grade I, 1968-1973, Senior Lecturer, 1973-1977; Professor 1977-. Head of Department of Agronomy, University of Ibadan, October, 1978-. *Memberships:* Soil Science Society of Nigeria; Microbiology Society of Nigeria; Soil Science Society of America; International Society of Soil Science. *Publications:* Over 40 Scientific publications in Scientific journals. *Honours:* Faculty Prize in Agriculture 1962 degree examinations; Rockefeller Scholarship, 1965; UNESCO/ICRO Fellowship for Microbiology, 1971; Fulbright-Hays Fellowship, 1977. *Hobbies:* Music; Photography. *Address:* 5 Danfodio Road, University of Ibadan, Ibadan, Oyo State, Nigeria.

ODUMUYE, Samuel Ayo-Oluwa, b. 24 Feb. 1934, Ilisan-Remo, Ogun State, Nigeria. Legal Practitioner. m. Mrs. Olupero Gbemisola Odumuye, 22 Sept. 1960, 4 sons, 1 daughter. *Education:* B.A.(Hons) History, (Lond) University College, Ibadan, 1952-1957; LL.B.(Hons) University of London (External) 1963-1968; LL.B.(Hons) University of Ife, 1964-1968. *Appointments:* Administrative Officer, Western Nigeria Civil Service, 1957-1961; Administrative Officer, University of Ibadan, 1962-1972; Deputy Registrar, University of Ibadan, 1972-1975; Managing Director, The Electronics Instrumentations Ltd. 1975-1976. *Memberships:* Nigerian Institute of Management; National President, University of Ife Alumni Association; National Treasurer, University of Ibadan Alumni Association; Nigerian Bar Association; Governing Council, University of Ife, Nigeria 1981-. *Hobbies:* Broadcasting; Current Affairs; Legal Issues-Radio Lawyer; Lawn Tennis; Table Tennis; Badminton; Community Development; Secretary Town Hall Building Committee, Ilisan-Remo. *Address:* 15 University Crescent, Bodija Housing Estate, Ibadan, Nigeria.

ODUNFA, Samuel Olusola, b. 13 July, 1942, Ibadan, Nigeria. Journalist. m. Adetoun Dawodu 2 May, 1970, 4 daughters. *Education:* IPC Newspaper Training School, Plymouth, England, 1970-1971. *Appointments:* Reporter, Daily Express, 1963-1965, Daily Times, 1966-1970; Editor, Lagos Weekend, 1971-1972, Spear Magazine, 1972-1976; Head of Publications Second World Black and African Festival of Arts and Culture, Lagos, 1977; Editor, Sunday Sketch, 1977; The Punch, 1977-1980; Editor-in-Chief, Punch Newspapers, 1980-. *Memberships:* General Secretary, Nigerian Guild of Editors. *Hobbies:* Swimming; Photography, Music. *Address:* No. 4, Oshinkalu Close, Surulere, Lagos, Nigeria.

ODUNLAMI, Godwin, Oladeinde, b. 12 Feb. 1937, Abeokuta, Ogun State, Nigeria. Legal Practitioner. m. Flora Ayodele Thompson, 7 Sept. 1961, 3 sons, 1 daughter. *Education:* LL.B. London University, 1970; BL Nigerian Law School, 1972. *Appointments:* Private Legal Practice, 1972-. *Memberships:* Honorary Secretary, Nigerian Bar Association; Executive Member, Nigerian Bar Association; Executive Member of the World Alliance; Legal Adviser Lagos YMCA; International Bar Association. *Honours:* Notary Public 7 December, 1978. *Hobbies:* Travelling; Philately; Camping; Gardening; Music; Photography. *Address:* 2 Odunlami Street, Ikate, Surulere, Nigeria.

ODUSOGA, Zacchaeus, Oludele, b. 8 April, 1933, Ikorodu Town, Lagos State, Nigeria. Company Secretary. m. Olaniqun Oyeleye Onafowokan, 28 March, 1964, 4 sons, 2 daughters. *Education:* ACIS, Scottish College of Commerce Glasgow, & Manchester College of Commerce, Manchester, 1966. *Appointments:* UAC Audit Department, Audit Assistant; Central Bank of Nigeria, Lagos, Senior Supervisor; Nigerian Hoechst Ltd., Company Secretary. *Memberships:* Liberty Club, Ikorodu, Vice-President; Christ Progressive League, Ikorodu, Officer, Special Duties; Ikeja Club, Ikeja, Champion 'Whot' Game (1979). *Hobbies:* Lawn Tennis; Table Tennis, Whot; Soccer. *Address:* Plot 3, Aina Eleko Lane, Maryland, Onigbongbo, Nigeria.

OFOSU-APPIAH, Lawrence, Henry, b. 18 March, 1920, Adawso, Ghana. Academic. m. Victoria Boohemaa Addo, 15 July, 1954, 3 daughters. *Education:* BA Hertford College, Oxford, England, 1944-1948; Diploma in Anthropology, Jesus College, Cambridge, 1948-1949; MA Hertford College, Oxford, England, 1951. *Appointments:* Lecturer in Classics, University College of the Gold Coast & Ghana, 1949; Associate Professor of Classics, University of Ghana, 1962; Fulbright Scholar and Visiting Professor of Classics, Dartmouth College, Hanover, NH USA, 1964-1965; Professor Edgar B. Stern University; Professor, Dillard University, New Orleans, 1965-1966; Director and Editor-in-Chief Encyclopaedia Africana Project, 1966nh. *Memberships:* Classical Association of England and Wales; Treasurer & President Classical Association of Ghana; Honorary Secretary and Vice-President, Fellow, Ghana Academy. *Publications:* People in Bondage-African Slavery in the Modern Era; Slavery—A Brief Survey; Encyclopaedia Africana; other publications include several biographies and translations from Homer, Socrates, and Sophocles. *Honours:* Ghana Book Development Council; Prize for Scholarly publications, Nigeria, 1979; Honorary D.Lit. University of Lagos to be awarded in 1981. *Hobbies:* Reading; Writing; Walking; Travelling. *Address:* Encyclopaedia Africana Project, P.O. Box 2797, Accra, Ghana.

OGALI, Chris, Egesi, b. 16 Oct. 1947, Calabar, Cross River State, Nigeria. Chartered Accountant. m. Udeaku Igwe, 17 Dec. 1977, 1 daughter. W.A.S.C. Grade I, Kings College Lagos, 1965; OND Accountancy, Yasa College of Technology, 1973; ACCA, 1974; ACA(Nigeria), 1976. *Appointments:* Trainee Accountant, 1973-1975, Chartered Accountants Nigeria; Audit Senior Partner, Chartered Accountants Nigeria, 1975-1979; Financial Controller, British American Insurance Co. (N) Ltd. 1979-. *Memberships:* Society of Institute of Chartered Accountants of Nigeria, at Lagos. *Honours:* Fourth Place Prize ACCA, examinations December, 1972. *Hobby:* Music. *Address:* 6, Dabiri Close, Surulere, Lagos, Nigeria.

O'GARA, Robert Julian, b. 8 July 1922, Kingstown, St Vincent & The Grenadines. Retired Police Commissioner. m. Winifred Omega John, 27 Dec. 1966 (Deceased), 1 son, 2 daughters. Primary and Private Tuition. *Appointments:* Constable, 1942; Sergeant, 1950; Station Sergeant, 1957; Inspector, 1961; Assistant Superintendent, 1966; Ag. Deputy Superintendent, 1967; Deputy Superintendent, 1968; Superintendent, 1969; Commissioner, 1972-77. *Memberships:* St Vincent & The Grenadines Girl Guides Council, 1968-; Scout Council, 1981; National Awards Committee, Duke of Edinburgh's Award Scheme, 1976-. *Publications:* Poems: The Joys of Xmas Tide; The Police, My Vocation I Accept with Pride; Birthday; Hymns: O God Unseen; Jesus Guard Me. *Honours:* First Prize Essay Competition, 1961; Territorial, 1939-45 War Medal; Colonial Police Long Service Medal, 1960; St Vincent Certificate & Badge of Honour, 1967; HM Queen Elizabeth Jubilee Medal, 1977; MBE, 1977. *Hobby:* Rifle Shooting. *Address:* Chapman Street, New Montrose, Kingstown, PO Box 905, St Vincent, West Indies.

OGBALU, Frederick Chidozie, b. 20 July 1927, Abagana, Njikoka, LGA, Anambra State, Nigeria. Teaching. m. Evelyn Amauchechukwu Chidebelu, Dec. 1957, 5 sons, 2 daughters. *Education:* BSc., (London); LL.B., Inter (London); Nigerian Teachers Senior Certificate; FRES, (London). *Appointments:* Vice-Principal, St Augustine's Grammar School, 1953-57, St Johns College, Port Harcourt, 1958, DMGS, Onitsha, 1965-72; Principal, St Paul's Teacher Training College, Awka, 1972-73, Government College, Owerri, 1973-74; Head of Department of Igbo Language and Culture AICE, Owerri, 1975; Head of Department of Igbo Language and Culture and Dean, School of Arts, Anambra State College of Education, Awka, Nigeria, 1978-. *Memberships:* National Chairman, Society for Promoting Igbo Language and Culture, African Authors Association of Nigeria and Nigerian Socialist Club; Nigerian Society for Arts Through Education; Commonwealth Parliamentary Association. *Publications:* Author of several books in Igbo and English Language, including: Obiefuna; Uwaezuvke; Mbedivgn; Tortoise The Fantastic Winner; Ilu Igbo; Igbo Numeration System; Igbo Attitude to Sex; Igbo Institutions and Customs; Editor of Onuora magazine and Igbo weekly newspaper Anyanwu. *Honours:* Ibeziako Prize Winner, 1944. *Hobbies:* Writing; Sports. *Address:* Anambra State College of Education, Awka, Anambra State, Nigeria.

OGBEMI, Franklin Akomi, b. 2 Oct. 1932, Ugbege, Warri, Nigeria. Consulting Engineer. m. 16 Apr. 1960, 1 son, 3 daughters. *Education:* BSc., Intermediate, University of Ibadan, Nigeria, 1952-54; BSc., Queen Mary College, London University, 1954-58. *Appointments:* Post Graduate Training, Central Electricity Generating Board, UK, 1958-60; Various Engineering positions, Electricity Corporation of Nigeria, 1960-75; Assistant General Manager (Operations) National Electric Power Authority, Nigeria, 1975-78; Chairman, Benin River Basin Development Authority, 1976-79; Chief Consulting Engineer, Nukom Engineering Limited, Lagos, Nigeria, 1978-. *Memberships:* Executive Council, Nigeria Society of Engineers, 1969-77; Council of Registered Engineers of Nigeria, 1972-77. *Honours:* Chartered Engineer UK, 1965; Fellow of: Institution of Mechanical Engineers, UK, 1970, Nigerian Society of Engineers, 1979; British Institute of Management, UK, 1979. *Hobbies:* Swimming; Art work collection. *Address:* 105 Bode Thomas Street, Surulere, Lagos, Nigeria.

OGBOBINE, Rufus Agbebichoma Ijemine, b. 3 June 1928, Usele, Via Warri, Bendel State, Nigeria. Legal. m. 9 Aug. 1957. *Education:* Cambridge School Certificate, King's College, Lagos, 1944-46; Diploma in Social Administration, University of Exeter, 1951-53; Council of Legal Education, London, 1954-56. *Appointments:* High Court Judge, Bendel State, Nigeria. *Memberships:* Chairman, Federal Government College, Warri Advisory Council; President, Edo College, Old Boys' Association, Benin City; President, Warri Cultural Society. *Publications:* Political Scramble in Warri Division, 1964; Materials & Cases on Benin Land Law, 1974; The Urhobo People & Their Land Tenure, 1975; The Juvenile Court and Young Offenders, 1976; The Itsekiri People & The Rights of Over Lordship, 1978; You and Your Problem Child, 1980. *Hobbies:* Swimming; Dancing; Reading. *Address:* Judge's Quarter's, GRA, Asaba, Bendel State, Nigeria.

OGBUAGU, Beremako (Bob) Ewuolonu, b. 25 May 1925, Umukabia, Ohuhu Clan, Umuahia, Imo State, Nigeria. Public Servant/Journalist. m. Cecilia Chinyere, 22 Oct. 1950, 3 sons, 3 daughters. *Education:* Senior Cambridge School Certificate Grade I (with exemption from London Matriculation), 1945. *Appointments:* Proprietor and Editor, Northern Advocate, Jos, Plateau State, 1948-55; Press Officer, Eastern Region Development Corporation, Enugu, 1955-58; Publicity Manager, 1958-59; Secretary/Chief Aministrative Officer, Eastern Nigeria Development Corporation, 1961-70; Area Representative of Utilgas Nigeria and Overseas Gas Company Limited in the Eastern States, 1970-75; Managing Director of East Central State Government Agricultural Development Authority, 1975-76; General Manager, Imo State Government Agricultural Development Corporation, 1976-80; Officer on Special Duties, and Adviser to Imo State Governor on Government Companies and Parastatals, 1980-. *Memberships:* Council, Nigerian Association of Chambers of Commerce, Industry, Mines & Agriculture, 1974-80; Council, West African Federation of Chambers of Commerce, 1974-79; National President, Nigerian Institute of Public Relations, 1980-; First Vice President, All-Africa Federation of Public Relations Association, 1978-; British Institute of Public Relations, 1963; Fellow, The Nigerian Institute of Public Relations, 1971. *Honours:* Officer of the Order of the Niger, 1966. *Hobbies:* Lawn Tennis; Broadcasting (TV & Radio); Golf; Photography. *Address:* PO Box 759, Owerri, Imo State, Nigeria.

OGDEN, Robert Lynn, b. 28 Jan. 1947, Stettler, Alberta, Canada. Civil Servant; Archivist; Cultural Administrator; Businessman; Heritage Consultant. m. Arlene Gail Sharp, 2 Sept. 1966, 2 sons. *Education:* Business Administration and Commerce, 1965-67; BA(Hons), 1967-70; MA, 1970-71; Certificate, APA, 1971. *Appointments:* Woodman and Scott, Chartered Accountants, 1966; Internal Auditor, Alberta Government Telephones, 1967-69; Team Leader, Alberta, Canadian Inventory of Historic Buildings, Historic Sites Alberta, Provincial Museum of Alberta and Parks Canada, 1970; Coordinator, National Business Archives Programme, Public Archives of Canada, 1971-73; City Archivist, City of Vancouver, British Columbia, 1973-75; Regional Director, Canadian Conservation Institute, National Museums of Canada, Ottawa, 1975-79; Executive Director, Canadian Museums Association, Ottawa, 1979-81; Assistant Deputy Minister, Department of Cultural Affairs and Historical Resources, Province of Manitoba, Winnipeg, Manitoba 1981-; Tutor in Canadian History, Carleton University, Ottawa, 1970-72; Lecturer, Archives Administration, University of British Columbia, 1973; Adjunct Professor, 1974-75; Lecturer, Vancouver City College, 1973-75. *Memberships:* Phi Alpha Theta International Honours Society in History; International Council of Museums; Canadian Museums Association; Association of Canadian Archivists; International Institute for Conservation of Artistic and Historic Works; International Institute for Conservation, Canadian Group; Canadian Historical Association. *Publications:* Numerous publications. *Hobbies:* Reading; Writing; Book reviews. *Address:* 99 Briarcliff Bay, Winnipeg, Manitoba, R3T 3H8, Canada.

OGHOMIENOR, Isaac Oritseminone, b. 29 June 1932, Jesse-Sapele, Bendel State, Nigeria. Packaging Technologist. m. Margaret Ajua Thompson, 10 Jan. 1954, 5 sons, 3 daughters. *Education:* Teachers' Certificate Grade II, 1956; BA, (Inter), University of London, 1968; Diploma, Institute of Purchasing, 1970; Diploma, Institute of Packaging, 1973. *Appointments:* Teaching in Catholic Schools and Colleges, Benin Diocese, 1951-60; Product Manager, Purchasing Manager, Packaging Technologist, Lever Brothers, Nigeria Limited, Apapa, 1962-76; Chairman/Managing Director, Ethiope Food Industries, Jesse, Sapele, 1977-. *Memberships:* Director General, Institute of Packaging, Nigeria; Vice Chairman, Institute of Purchasing, Nigeria; Chairman, Advertising Student' Union of Nigeria. *Publications:* Poem, Edo. *Hobbies:* Photography; Writing; Film going. *Address:* 72 Yoruba Road Ext., Sapele, Bendel State, Nigeria.

OGIER, Thomas de Mouilped, b. 20 Feb. 1924, Guernsey, Channel Islands. Master Mariner. m. Mona Atualie Ross, 5 Sept. 1952, 2 sons, 2 daughters. *Education:* HMS Worcester, Greenhithe, Kent, 1938-40; Master Mariner, FG, 1950. *Appointments:* Cadet to

Master, Shaw, Savill and Albion Company Limited, London, 1941-48; Master Mariner, 1971-72; Senior Master Mariner,, 1972-; Head of Marine School, Homiara Technical Institute, Homiara, Solomon Islands. *Memberships:* Younger Brother of Trinity House, London. *Hobbies:* Golf; Walking; Reading; Nautical Astronomy; Gardening. *Address:* GPO Box 368, Homiara, Solomon Islands.

OGILVIE, David Alexander, b. 2 Aug. 1927, Edinburgh, Scotland. Chartered Engineer. m. Rosamond Hilary Hopkins, 31 July 1952, 3 sons, 1 daughter. *Education:* Major Scholar in Classics, St John's College, Cambridge University, 1948-51; Second Class Honours, Mechanical Sciences Trippos, 1951. *Appointments:* HM Colonial Service (Administration), Northern Rhodesia, 1952-54; Manager and Director, Baker Perkins (Exports) Limited, Peterborough, 1955-66; Chief Executive, Small Industries Council for Rural Areas of Scotland, Edinburgh, 1966-75; Head of Small Business Division, Scottish Development Agency, 1975-. *Memberships:* Crafts Council, 1976; Company of Merchants, City of Edinburgh, 1974; HRH Duke of Edinburgh's Study Conference, Canada, 1962. *Publications:* Executive Flight, 1963; Small Scale Industries in Rural Scotland, 1973; Subcontracting by Small Firms in Scotland, 1973; Self-help in International Marketing, US Small Business Administration, 1976; Opportunities for Rural-based Industries in Upland Scotland, 1978. *Honours:* MA., (Cantab), 1955; MIMech.E., 1960. *Hobbies:* Travel; Music. *Address:* 33 Grange Road, Edinburgh, 9.

OGILVY, James Gardiner, b. 6 July 1933, Melbourne. Medical Practitioner. m. Cheryl Patricia Hutchinson, 3 Apr. 1964, 1 son, 2 daughters. *Education:* Ormond College University of Melbourne, 1951-57; MB.BS, (Melbourne), 1957; MRCOG (London), 1966; FRCSE, 1968; F(Aust) COG, 1979. *Appointments:* RMO, Footscray Alfred Royal Childrens, Royal Womens Austin Hospitals, Melbourne, 1957-64; Surgical Registrar, Stirling Royal Infirmary Scotland, 1967-70; Honorary Obstetrician and Gynaecologist, Wangaratta and District Base Hospital, 1972-74; Casualty Director, Austin Hospital, Melbourne, 1978-82. *Memberships:* AMA; Australian Society of Emergency Medicine. *Hobby:* Junior Sport. *Address:* 251 Ironbark Road, Diamond Creek, Victoria, 3089, Australia.

OGUAKWA, James Udengene, b. 5 May 1936, Inyi, Oji-River, LGA, Anambra State, Nigeria. University Lecturer. m. Theresa, AC, 30 May 1965, 1 son, 1 daughter. *Education:* University College, Ibadan, Nigeria, 1957-61; BSc., Hons. (London), 1961; Moscow State University, Moscow, 1962-66; PhD., Chemistry, Moscow State, 1966. *Appointments:* Lecturer Grade II, 1970-74, Grade I, 1974-76; Senior Lecturer, 1976-79, Associate Professor, 1980-, University of Nigeria, Nsukka, Nigeria. *Publications:* Contributor to medical journals including: two publications on a new antibiotic and two on Erythrophleum alkaloids; Six publications on Strychnos alkaloids, 1978-80. *Honours:* Eastern Nigeria Scholarship award, 1958; UNESCO Fellowship Award, 1962. *Hobbies:* Writing books on science for children; Reading narrative stories on valour. *Address:* Central School, Inyi, c/o Inyi PA., Oji-River, LGA, Anambra State, Nigeria.

OGUNADE, Samuel Olumuyiwa, b. 3 Sept. 1940, Ijebu-Ode, Nigeria. Lecturer. m. Emily Ajoke Adenaike, 14 Aug. 1964, 5 daughters. *Education:* BSc., 1965; M.Phil., London, 1969; PhD., Victoria, 1973. *Appointments:* Petroleum Engineer, Shell-BP Petroleum Development Corporation of Nigeria, 1965-66; Lecturer, Department of Physics, University of Ife, Ile-Ife, Nigeria, 1973-. *Memberships:* Institute of Physics; Society of Exploration Geophysicists; American Geophysical Union; European Association of Exploration Geophysicists; Canadian Association of Physicists; Nigerian Institute of Physics; Science Association of Nigeria; Nigerian Union of Radio and Planetary Sciences. *Publications:* Contributor of numerous articles to professional journals and conferences including: Electromagnetic Response of an embedded Cylinder for Line Current Excitation, 1981. *Honours:* Federal Government of Nigeria Post-Graduate Scholarship, 1966-68; University of Victoria Scholarship, 1969-70, 1970-71; Canadian International Development Agency/National Research Council Research Fellowship, 1975-77; Alexander von Humboldt Research Fellowship, 1979-

80. *Hobbies:* Gardening; Table Tennis; Music; Travelling. *Address:* 1 Irede Street, Ile-Ife, Nigeria.

OGUNBANJO, Christopher Oladipo (Chief), b. 14 Dec. 1923, Nigeria. Barrister-at-Law & Solicitor of Supreme Court of Nigeria. m. Hilda Adunola Ladipo, 25 June 1953, 3 sons, 4 daughters. *Education:* LLB. London, 1949. Called to Nigerian Bar, 1950. *Memberships:* Honorary Vice-President, Lagos Chamber of Commerce & Industry; President, Nigerian Maritime Law Association; Chairman, Nigerian Council for Management Education and Training, 1972-76. *Publications:* Various contributions to Seminars and Conferences. *Honours:* Senior Citizen Award for contribution to Industry in Nigeria; Bobajiro of Ijebu-Imushin, Ijebu-Ode, Nigeria, 1961. *Hobbies:* Lawn Tennis; Swimming. *Address:* 2 Ilabere Avenue, Ikoyi, Lagos, Nigeria.

OGUNDARE, Samuel Owolanke, b. 27 Mar. 1939, Akure, Ondo State, Nigeria. Company Administrator. m. Morenike, 30 Dec. 1967, 1 son, 3 daughters. *Education:* Teachers Grade II Certificate, 1960; Corporation of Secretaries Final Examination, 1967. *Appointments:* Primary School Teacher, 1960-66; Account Executive, Bentworth Finance, 1967; Bank Executive, National Bank of Nigeria Limited, 1967-72; Company Secretary, 1973-76, General Manager, Managing Director, 1978-, Skyway Press Limited. *Memberships:* Akure National Union. *Hobbies:* Reading; Gardening; Politics. *Address:* 18 Adeojo Street, PO Box 3934, Ikeja, Nigeria.

OGUNDE, Adedoyin Olayide, b. 1 Dec. 1935, Itele, Ogun State, Nigeria. Chartered Accountant. m. 2 June 1962, 3 sons, 3 daughters. *Education:* Nigerian College of Technology, Ibadan, Oyo State, Nigeria, 1957-59; Article of clerkship at Deloitte, Haskins & Sells, Chartered Accountants, London, 1962-66; FCA (England & Wales); FCA (Nigeria); ACIS. *Appointments:* Peat, Marwick, Ani, Ogunde & Co., 1966-70, Partner, 1971-. *Hobbies:* Lawn Tennis; Table Tennis; Swimming; Gardening. *Address:* 6 Moor Road, Ikoyi, Lagos, Nigeria.

OGUNDIPE, Oladipo Olusegun, b. 6 Feb. 1935, Lagos, Nigeria. Librarian. m. Odunayo Akinhanmi, 2 sons, 1 daughter. *Education:* MA, English Department, Michigan State University, East Lansing, USA, 1963-65; English Department, University College, London, 1958-60; Library Association of Great Britain. *Appointments:* Assistant Librarian, Lewisham Public Library, London, 1950-61; Sub-Librarian, University of Nigeria, Nsukka, 1961-67, University of Ife, Ife, 1967-70; Librarian, Njala University College, Sierra Leone, 1970-73; University Librarian, University of Zambia, Lusaka, 1974-76, University of Benin, Benin City, Nigeria, 1975-. *Memberships:* Executive, Sierra Leone Library Association, 1970-73; President, Zambian Library Association, 1974 and Nigerian Library Association, 1978-80; Editor-in-Chief, Nigerian Libraries, 1981-. *Hobbies:* Motoring; Cinema. *Address:* University Librarian, University of Benin Library, PMB, 1191, Benin City, Nigeria.

OGUNMADE, Albert Abimbola, b. 14 May 1945, Ajagba-Okitipupa, Ondo State, Nigeria. Chartered Accountant. m. 27 Nov. 1973, 1 son, 1 daughter. *Education:* Institute of Chartered Accountants of Nigeria; Institute of Cost & Management Accountants. *Appointments:* British Steel Corporation, Imperial Works, Glasgow, MCS, Glasgow; PZ Industries Limited, Kupeji; Finance Controller, Nigeria General Gas Company Limited, Lagos. *Hobbies:* Swimming; Tennis. *Address:* 13 Chief Innamdi Abikiwe Street, Okupe State, Maryland, Lagos, Nigeria.

OGUNMEKAN, Adeboye Oluwole, b. 2 Nov. 1934, Lagos, Nigeria. Medical Practitioner. m. Dorothy Adebunkola Jadesimi, 20 Nov. 1965, 3 sons. *Education:* Durham University Medical School, King's College, Newcastle Upon Tyne, 1957-62; MB.,BS., 1962; DCH (Glasgow), 1968; MRCP (UK), 1972; MD (Newcastle), 1977. *Appointments:* House Officer, Obstetrics & Gynaecology, 1962-63, General Medicine, 1963, General Hospital, South Shields, Northumberland, England; Senior House Officer, Department of Paediatrics, 1963-64, 1964-66, Consultant Physician, 1975, Lagos University Teaching Hospital, Nigeria; Senior House Officer, Paediatrics, Queen Elizabeth Hospital, Gateshead, County Durham, England, 1967; Supernumerary Senior House Officer, Medicine, Royal Victoria Infirmary, Newcastle Upon Tyne, England, 1967-69; Senior

House Officer, General and Geriatric Medicine, Preston Hospital, North Shields, England, 1969-71; Registrar, General Medicine and Rheumatology, Killearn Hospital, Scotland, 1972; Senior Registrar, Paediatrics, Lagos University Teaching Hospital, Lagos, Nigeria, 1971-73; Clinical Fellow (Neurology), The Hospital for Sick Children, Toronto, Canada, 1973-75; Lecturer Grade I, Department of Paediatrics, 1974, Senior Lecturer, 1978, College of Medicine, University of Lagos, 1978. *Publications:* Association of Consultants, Lagos; Medical Advisory Committee; Medical Records Committee; British Medical Association; Nigerian Medical Association; Paediatric Association of Nigeria; International College of Paediatrics; Nigerian Society of Neurological Sciences. *Publications:* Numerous contributions to professional medical journals. *Hobbies:* *Honours:* Prize for article in Durham University Medical Gazette, 1961-62. *Hobbies:* Lawn Tennis; Athletics. *Address:* Flat CM 2, L U TH Compound, PMB 12003, Lagos, Nigeria.

OGUNSANYA, Adeniyi Alhaji, b. 25 Nov. 1940, Lagos, Nigeria. Insurance. m. 15 Sept. 1971, 2 sons, 2 daughters. *Education:* Diploma Chartered Insurance Institute, 1969. *Appointments:* Federated Employers Insurance Association/Refuge Assurance, Manchester, 1967-71; Nigerian General Insurance Company Limited, Lagos, 1971-. *Memberships:* Lagos Country Club, Ikeja, Lagos; Oriwu Club, Ikorodu, Lagos State; Dynamic Club of Lagos; Unique Club, Ikorodu, Lagos. Board of Directors, Lagos State Development and Property Corporation, 1975-79. *Hobbies:* Footballing; Athletics. *Address:* 7 Awe Crescent, Ikorodu Road, Shomolu, Lagos, Nigeria.

OGUOCHA, Victoria Nkemdilim (Mrs), b. 14 Dec. 1943, Obosi, Anambra State, Nigeria. Accountancy. m Davidson Okeke, 22 June 1974. *Education:* BSc., University of Nigeria, Nsukka, 1967; *Appointments:* Accountant, Ministry of Information in the Former Eastern Nigeria, 1967-70; Group Internal Auditor, IBRU Organisation, 1970-72; Branch Account, IBRU Sea Foods Limited, 1972-75; Accountant, WF Clarke (Nigeria) Limited, 1975-77; Senior Accountant, 1977-80; Finance Manager, 1980-. *Memberships:* British Institute of Management; Executive Financial Society, University of Nigeria, Nsukka. *Honours:* Best student in Home Economics and Mathematics at Queens School, Enugu; Queen of Graduating Class at University of Nigeria, 1967. *Hobbies:* Games; Netball; Volleyball; Cookery; Scrabble. *Address:* Block D, Flat 13, Eric Moore Towers, Surulere, Lagos, Nigeria.

OH, Saewoong, b. 26 Mar. 1931, South Korea. Cyclotron Physicist. m. 2 Nov. 1961, 1 son, 2 daughters. *Education:* BSc., College of Arts and Sciences, Seoul National University, 1956; PhD., University of Birmingham, England, 1969. *Appointments:* Lecturer, Korean Air Force Academy, 1956; Research Scientist, Korea Atomic Energy Research Institue, 1959; Research Associate, Senior Research Associate, University of Birmingham, England, 1965-73; Cyclotron Physicist, University of Manitoba, Canada, 1973. *Memberships:* Canadian Association of Physicists. *Publications:* 21 contributions to periodicals and conference proceedings. *Hobby:* Fishing. *Address:* 3 Golden Willow Crescent, Winnipeg, Manitoba, R2M4E1, Canada.

OH, Teik Sam, b. 15 June 1930, Kuala Lumpur, Malaysia. Chartered Quantity Surveyor & Construction Cost Consultant. m. Nelly, 15 May 1955, 2 sons, 3 daughters. *Education:* Diploma in Quantity Surveying, Malaysia, 1956; Diploma of The Royal Institution Chartered Surveyors, 1970. *Appointments:* Quantity Surveyor in the Public Works Department, Malaysia, 1956-69; Executive Director, M/s Song Pang Seng Contruction Company Limited, 1970-72; Executive Director, M/s Wan Sam Construction Company Limited, 1973-78; Chartered Quantity Surveyor & Construction Cost Consultant, 1978-. *Memberships:* Institute of Surveyors, Malaysia; Master Builders Association Malaysia; Private Sector Consultative Committee for Housing, Malaysia; Technical Committee on Building & Construction of Standards & Industrial Research Institute of Malaysia; Fellow, The Royal Institute of Surveyors, London; Chartered Institute of Arbitrators, London; Institute of Surveyors, Singapore. *Hobbies:* Hunting; Reading; Walking. *Address:* 28 Lorong Lee Hin Neo 1, Ukay Heights, Kuala Lumpur 18-02, Malaysia.

OHABUIKE, Alpheus, b. 13 Apr. 1939, Umuhu-Okabia Orlu. Banking. m. Nneoma Chinke 1 July 1972, 4 sons, 1 daughter. *Education:* BSc Accountancy, University of Nigeria, 1966; ACIS, London, 1970; FCIS, 1976; ABIM, 1976; FIB, 1981. *Appointments:* American Overseas Petroleum Oil Company Limited, 1965-66; Inspector, Cooperative Bank of Eastern Nigeria Limited, 1966-68; Accountant, Head Office, 1968-70; Chief Inspector, 1971-72; Chief Accountant, 1972-73; Chief Personnel Officer, 1974-. *Memberships:* Publicity Secretary, Institute of Banker, Enugu Branch; Institute of Personnel Management; Bankers Club, Enugu. *Hobbies:* Novel Reading; Lawn Tennis. *Address:* Plot 922 Independance, Layout, Enugu, Nigeria.

O'HAIR, John Brian, b. 12 Aug. 1928, Melbourne, Australia. Chartered Engineer. m. Daphne Lorraine Sherwin, 5 June 1954, 1 son. *Education:* Diploma Mechanical and Electrical Engineering, Queensland, 1959. *Appointments:* Estimator, Kelly & Lewis Ltd. Melbourne, 1945-49; Assistant Chief Engineer, Harland Engineering Limited, Melbourne, 1949-51; Chief Engineer, Ajax Pumps Pty. Ltd. Melbourne, 1951-53; Founder 1953; Chairman, Managing Director, O'Hair Engineering Pty. Ltd., Queensland, Dir. Pump Distbrs. Pty. Ltd., Consultant on Turbo Machinery, 1953-. *Memberships:* MIE, Aust. Chartered Engineer, ASME IAHR; BHRA; Australian Pump Manufacturers Association; National Water Well Association; American Plastics Institute, Society of Maufacturing Engineers; A. Inst. Metals. *Creative Works:* Patents. *Hobbies:* Sailing; Golf. *Address:* 7 Victoria Terrace, Bowen Hills, Queensland, 4006, Australia.

OHIAERI, Godson Ebonine Chukuemeka, b. 13 May 1932, Abba, Imo State Nigeria. Agriculturist. m. 7 Jan. 1967, 2 sons, 2 daughters. *Education:* Bachelor of Science, Agriculture, University of London, 1959; Master of Science, Soil Science, Oklahoma State University, 1963; Certificate, Corn Production Cimmyt. Mexico 1973. *Appointments:* Soil Conservation Officer, 1959-64; Senior Soil Conservation Officer, 1964-74; Principal Research Officer, 1974-77; Assistant Chief Research Officer, 1977-79; Chief Research Officer (Extensions), 1979-81; Assistant Director, 1981-. *Memberships:* Agricultural Society of Nigeria; Nigeria Audio-Visual Association. *Publications:* MSc, Thesis: Distribution of Soil Phosphorus Compounds in some representative Soils of Oklahoma, 1963. *Hobbies:* Coin Collection; Stamp Collection; Art Works Collection; Lawn Tennis. *Address:* NC 11 A, Moor Plantation, Ibadan, Nigeria.

OHLSSON, Terence Edward, b. 30 Dec. 1938, Sydney, Australia. Film Director. *Education:* TV Studio Techniques Diploma, North Sydney Technical College, 1957; Sydney University. *Appointments:* Maquarie Radio Network; Artransa Studios; HR-McCann Frickson, Sydney; Ajax Films, Sydney; Ford Film Unit, United Kingdom; Masius Wynne-Williams, UK; Rayant Television UK; Managing Director, Kingcroft Productions, Sydney. *Memberships:* Producers and Directors Guild, Australia; Film and TV Producers Association, Australia; Australian Writers Guild; Royal Motor Yacht Club. *Publications:* Director of many films including: Year of the Cortina, 1964; Davids Day, 1965; First Time Round, 1971; She's A Lady, 1973; Scobie Malone, 1974; Green Machine, 1975; Overseas Connection, 1978; Ninth Life, 1980; Never Never Land, 1981. *Hobbies:* Flying; Sailing. *Address:* Kingcroft Productions Pty. Ltd., 29A Rosalind Street, Crows Nest, NSW 2065, Australia.

OJEHOMON, Norma Thelmadge Thomas, b. 5 Nov. 1931, Tuscumbia, Alabama, USA. Managing Director. m. A Ojeamiren Ojehomon, 2 sons, 4 daughters. *Education:* BA Natural Science, Talladega College, USA, 1952; Ohio State Civil Service Certificate and Teachers Certificate; Diploma, American Society of Travel Agents Inc. 1970; Certificate Advanced Passenger Tariff Training course for IATA-Agents, 1976; Lufthansa Certificate, Seeheim, Germany. *Appointments:* Bacteriology Tech. Western Reserve University, 1952; Bacteriology Tech. State University of New York, 1953-54; Research Tech. Wandsworth Hospital Group, London, 1955-56; Research Assistant/Tech. University of Ibadan, Nigeria, 1956-64; Senior Science Tutor, Anglican Girls Grammar School, Benin, 1966-68; Science Tutor, Benin Delta Teacher Training College, Benin, 1968-70; Originator and Co;founder, Airegin Enterprises and Agencies Ltd. and Airegin Travel Agency, Managing Director 1971-. *Memberships:* Nigeria Association of Travel Agents; Chamber of Commerce and Industry; Young Womens Christian Association; The Benin Club; Science Teachers Association of Nigeria. *Publications:* A Study of Proteus Infections in A Male Urological Ward, 1957; Co-author, Studies on the Succinic Dehydrogenase Activity of Staphylococcus Pyogenes, 1958. *Honours:* Oro Verde International Trophy, 1980; British Caledonian Award for Travel Agency Performance, 1979 and 1980. *Hobbies:* Poetry; Piano; Bridge. *Address:* 49 Forestry Road, PO Box 498, Benin City, Bendel State, Nigeria, West Africa.

OJIENDA OKWANYA, Fredrick, b. 15 June 1936, South East Kano. Typographer. m. 1 Nov. 1957, 4 sons, 5 daughters. *Education:* Diploma in Printing, Ariel Printing School Israel; Certificate in Publishing, Staatlich Leherer Institute für Graphic und Werbung, Berlin, West Germany. *Appointments:* Lake Printing Work Mwenza Tanzania, 1954; Kenya Vernacular Press Nairobi, 1957; English Press Nairobi, 1959; Africa Samachar Nairobi, 1960; Kenya Labour Press, 1964; Foundation Books Limited, 1973. *Memberships:* Printing and Kindred Trades Worker's Union; Kenya Press Club; Kenya Publishers Association; Planning Committee, Regional Centre for Bode Promotia in Africa. *Publications:* Published more than eight titles one with Comb Bode's, Seven with Foundation Books. *Hobbies:* Painting; Writing. *Address:* PO Box 73435, Nairobi, Kenya.

OJO, Abiola Olayinka, b. 30 Jan. 1940, Lagos, Nigeria. Professor of Law. m. Adebisi Fagbulu, 29 July 1966, 3 sons, 1 daughter. *Education:* LLB(Hons) London, 1964; LLM 1965; PhD 1967. *Appointments:* Faculty of Law, University of Lagos. *Memberships:* English Speaking Society, UK; International Common Law Exchange Society, California, USA. *Publications:* The Search for a Grundnorm in Nigeria, 1970; Constitutional Structure and Nature of the Nigerian Military Government, 1976; Constitutional Developments in Nigeria since Independence, 1972; Law and Government in Nigeria; Separation of Powers under the 1979 Constitution in Public Law, 1981. *Hobbies:* Table-tennis; Watching Soccer Games. *Address:* 3 Ozolua Road, University of Lagos Campus, Yaba, Lagos.

OJO, Amos Adesunkanmi, b. 21 June 1947. Clerical Officer; Teacher; Principal Librarian. m. Veronica Morenike, 10 Sept. 1977, 2 sons. *Education:* BA(Hons) French, University of Ibadan, Nigeria, 1968-72; Postgraduate Diploma in Librarianship, 1973-74; MA, University of Sheffield, 1978-79. *Appointments:* Clerical Officer, Nigerian Railway Corporation, 1967-68; Senior French Teacher, Ministry of Education, Lagos, 1972-73; Principal Librarian, Centre for Management Development, Lagos 1974-. *Memberships:* Councillor, Nigerian Library Association; The British Library Association. *Publications:* Library Services to the disadvantaged in Nigeria; A Study submitted in Partial Fulfilment of the requirements for the degree of Master of Arts in Librarianship, 1979. *Hobbies:* Reading; Dancing; Meeting People. *Address:* 13 Olorunimbe Street, Ikeja, Lagos, Nigeria.

OJO, Matthew Olapade, b. 3 Apr. 1936, Ondo, Ondo State, Nigeria. Teaching. m. Augustina A Reis 28 Oct. 1936, 2 sons, 2 daughters. *Education:* BVM&S Edinburgh 1965; MRCVS, UK 1965; Diploma Bact. London, 1969; PhD, Ibadan, 1976. *Appointments:* Veterinary Officer, 1965-67; Teaching, Universities, 1966-. *Memberships:* National Universities Commission; International Organization for Mycoplasmology; Nigerian Society for Immunology; Nigerian Society for Microbiology; FAO/WHO; Editorial Board, Veterinary Microbiology. *Publications:* Author of 39 publications in recognised international journals. *Honours:* Dean, Faculty of Veterinary Medicine, 1979-; WHO Travelling Grant, 1978; UKTA Grant, 1971; DANDA Grant, 1973/74; Rockefeller Fellowship, 1969-71. *Hobbies:* Table Tennis; Reading; Gardening. *Address:* Ojoo Village, Oyo Road, Ibadan, Oyo State, Nigeria.

OJO, Olusola Adewole, b. 1 Feb. 1927, Ibadan, Nigeria. Obstetrician and Gynaecologist. m. Olakunle George, 2 July 1952, 2 sons. *Education:* BA 1952; MB, BcH, BAo 1954; MA 1959; MAO 1959; MRCOG 1960; MD 1964; FNMCOG 1967; FRCOG 1973; FWACS 1973. *Appointments:* Internship in Surgery and Obstetrics and Gynaecology, 1954-55; Appointments in Med-

icine and Paediatrics, 1955-56; Resident, Obstetrics and Gynaecology, University College Hospital, Ibadan, Nigeria, Radcliffe Infirmary Oxford, Western Infirmary, Glasgow, Royal Maternity/Royal Victoria Hospitals, Belfast, 1956-60; Specialist Obstetrician and Gynaecologist, Federal Ministry of Health, Lagos, Nigeria, 1961-62; Lecturer, Senior Lecturer and Professor, Department of Obstetrics and Gynaecology, University of Ibadan, Nigeria, 1962-. *Memberships:* Society of Gynaecology and Obstetrics of Nigeria. *Publications:* Joint Authorship: A Textbook for Midwives in the Tropics; Author of about sixty publications in learned medical journals. *Honours:* Begley Studentship, Dublin University, 1951-52; Nuffield Foundation Fellowship, 1963. *Hobbies:* Lawn Tennis; Squash Raquets; Table Tennis; Reading. *Address:* 35A Rotimi Williams Avenue, Bodija, Ibadan, Nigeria.

OJO-IGBINOBA, Matthew Ena, b. 19 June 1942, Benin City, Nigeria. Librarianship. m. Gladys Enore, 16 Jan. 1970, 4 sons, 2 daughters. *Education:* BA., Hons., 1968; Postgraduate Diploma, Librarianship, 1969; MSc., 1978; AMNIM., 1978. *Appointments:* Librarian: Ministry of Education, Benin City, Nigeria, 1970-71; College of Education, Abraka, Nigeria, 1971-. *Memberships:* Nigerian Library Association, 1970-; Nigerian Institute of Management, Nigeria, 1978-; President, Senior Staff Association, College of Education, Abraka, Nigeria, 1979-; Editorial Board, Abraka Journal of Education; Life member, Benin Amateur Athletics Association, Benin City, Nigeria. *Publications:* Editor, Education, official periodical published by Ministry of Education, Benin City, Bendel State, 1970-71; Editor, Abraka Quarterly, a journal of Education, 1974-77. *Hobbies:* Photography; Sports organisation; Amateur dramatist. *Address:* 6A Oreoghene Street, Benin City, Bendel State, Nigeria.

OJO-OSAGIE, Joseph Idahosa, b. 21 Mar. 1934, Benin City, Bendel State, Nigeria. Chartered Surveyor. m. Feb. 1962, 2 sons, 4 daughters. *Education:* Inter BSc., University of Technology, Ghana, 1956-59; BSc., College of Estate Management, London, UK, 1963; ARICS., 1965; FRICS., 1973. *Appointments:* Senior Estate Officer, Ministry of Lagos Affairs, Nigeria, 1965-68; Senior Surveyor, 1968-70, Partner, 1970, Senior Partner, 1979, Knight Frank and Rutley, Lagos, Nigeria. *Memberships:* Lagos Island Club; Metropolitan Club, Lagos. *Address:* 36 Curtis Adeaiyi Jones Close, Surulere, Lagos, Nigeria.

OJWANG, Vincent Paul, b. 14 Apr. 1951, Soni Lakwar, Kirewa, Tororo District, Uganda. Physiotherapist; Psychologist. m. 6 Jan. 1975. *Education:* Diploma, Physiotherapy, Mulago Physiotherapy School, 1973-76; BA., Makerere University, Uganda, 1978-81. *Appointments:* Physiotherapist, Mulago Hospital, Uganda, 1976-78, 1981-. *Memberships:* Uganda Physiotherapy Association; Uganda Red Cross. *Publications:* A series of poems (unpublished). *Honours:* Received Certificate of Merit in Drama, Tororo College, Uganda. *Hobbies:* Creative writing; Mountaineering. *Address:* c/o Physiotherapy Department, Mulago Hospital, Box 7051, Kampala, Uganda.

OKAFOR, Charles Okolo, b. 8 June 1938, Arochukwu, Nigeria. Chemist. m. Josephine Ifeyinwa Igboko, 1967, 2 sons, 4 daughters. *Education:* BSc., Chemistry (London), 1962, University College, Ibadan (a college of the University of London), 1959-62; PhD., Michigan State University, East Lansing, Michigan, 1962-65; Post-Doctoral Fellowship, Harvard University, Cambridge, Massachusetts, 1972. *Appointments:* Lecturer in Chemistry, 1965-70, Senior Lecturer, 1970-74, Reader, 1974-75, Professor of Chemistry, 1975-, Head, Department of Chemistry, 1975-80, Dean, Faculty of Physical Sciences, University of Nigeria, 1980-81; Chairman, Governing Council, College of Technology, Owerri, Nigeria, 1980-; Technical Editor and Member of the Editorial Board of the Journal of Heterocyclic Chemistry; Visiting Professor of Chemistry, University of South Florida, Tampa, Florida, 1981-82. *Memberships:* Chemical Society of Nigeria; Fellow, Royal Society of Chemistry; American Chemical Society; International Society of Heterocyclic Chemistry; Intra-Science Research Foundation, California; Sigma Xi; Society of Harvard Chemists; Society of Michigan State Chemists. *Publications:* Over 30 publications in international journals. *Honours:* US Travel Grant, 1972; IUC, Fellowship, 1977; Research Seminar, McGill University,

Montreal, 1972; External Examiner at several universities and polytechnics. *Hobbies:* Dancing; Tennis. *Address:* 2105 E Navajo Avenue, Tampa, Florida, 33612, USA.

OKAFOR, Clement Abiaziem, b. 23 Nov. 1944, Umuoji via Onitsha, Nigeria. University Senior Lecturer. m. Rosaline, 4 Nov. 1972, 3 sons. *Education:* BA., University of Nigeria, 1965; MA., University of East Africa; PhD., Harvard University, USA, 1975. *Appointments:* Lecturer, University of Zambia; Senior Lecturer: University of Ibadan, Nigeria; University of Nigeria, Nsukka, Nigeria. *Memberships:* International Comparative Literature Association; African Literature Association; International Institute of Folk Narrative Research; Executive member, Nigerian Folklore Society. *Publications:* The Tonga Chante-Fable: Analysis of an African Narrative Tradition; numerous Scholarly articles in various journals in Europe, America and Africa. *Honours:* Rockefeller Foundation Fellowship, 1965-68; Ford Foundation Fellowship, 1971-72; Harvard University Fellowship, 1972-75. *Hobbies:* Lawn tennis; Yoga. *Address:* Postal Agency, Umuoji-Onitsha, Nigeria.

OKAFOR, (Chief) Raphael Ben Kechi, b. 15 Mar. 1927, Nkwessi Town, Ohaoma Local Government Area of Imo State, Nigeria. Politician. m. (1) Mercy, (2) Florence, (3) Agnes, 18 children. *Appointments:* Teacher, Nkwessi and Lagos Central Schools, Nigeria; 1st class clerk, Treasury, Old Nigerian Secretariat, Marina, Lagos, Nigeria; 1st National Deputy President, Nigerian Civil Service; Politician and Journalist, West African Pilot under Zik; Leading early officer, Zikist Movement and Secretary general of NCNC Youth Wing; Political adviser: Middle Belt State Movement; Zikist National Vanguard; Lecturer, NCNC School of political studies; Became member of Federal House of Representatives, 1959; Member, Federal Government Public Accounts Committee, 1960; Appointed Parliamentary Secretary, Federal Attorney General and Minister for Justice; Appointed Federal Minister for Trade, 1966; Founder, Managing Director, New Era Finance and Estate Co., Port-Harcourt, Nigeria; Founder, Chairman, Managing Director, Continental Lines (Africa) Limited, Nigeria; Chairman of Board, Nigerian Cement Co. Limited, Nkalagu, Nigeria; Appointed to Federal Government Commission, Development of sea and river ports, 1977. *Memberships:* Commonwealth Parliamentary Association; Chairman: Oru Community Council, 1971-72; Oguta Divisional Council, 1973-75; NPP National Planning and Organisation Committees; 1st Deputy Chairman, Nigerian/American Chamber of Commerce; World International Institute of Freight Forwarders. *Honours:* Awarded Scholarship by USAID in collaboration with Federal Ministry of Economic Development, 1961-62; Honorary Citizen of New York, Texas, Atlanta and California, USA; Holds 12 Keys of American Cities. *Hobbies:* Swimming; Lawn tennis. *Address:* 24 Wharf Road, PMB 1073, Apapa, Nigeria.

OKATCHA, Frederick Moses, b. 16 Apr. 1938, Nakuru, Kenya. Educational Psychologist. m. Kathleen, 16 Dec. 1972, 1 son, 1 daughter. *Education:* BA., Hons., 1963, MA., 1965, PhD., 1968, Michigan State University, USA. *Appointments:* Lecturer, Educational Psychology, University College, Nairobi, Kenya, 1968-72; Lecturer, Educational Psychology, 1968-72, Senior Lecturer, Associate 1972-75, Associate Professor, 1975-, Chairman, Department of Educational Psychology, 1970-79, Dean, Faculty of Education, 1975-79, University of Nairobi, Kenya; Visiting Lecturer, Educational Psychology and Social Psychology, Makerere University, Kenya, July-Sept. 1969. *Memberships:* American Psychological Association; International Council of Psychologists; International Rehabilitation Special Education Network. *Publications:* Recall and Comprehension as a Function of Mode of Presentation and Transformational Complexity; The Psychological Reality of Grammatical Structure in Prose Learning; Editor: Cognitive Processes: Theory and Research; Modern Psychology and Cultural Adaptation. *Honours:* Distinguished Alumnus Award, Michigan State University, USA, 1977. *Hobbies:* Reading; Writing. *Address:* University of Nairobi, PO Box 30197, Nairobi, Kenya.

OKE, Ebenezer Folorunso, b. 16 Mar. 1937, Abeokuta, Nigeria. Chartered Accountant. m. Ronke Dania, 5 June 1971, 1 son, 3 daughters. *Education:* BSc., University of Southampton, UK, 1963; Associate, Institute of Chartered Accountants in England and Wales, 1966; Fellow, ACA, England and Wales, 1976. *Appointments:* Senior Accountant, London, 1966, Lagos, 1967-72, Partner, 1972-, Partner, Management Consultancy Practice, 1973-, Coopers and Lybrand, Lagos, Nigeria. *Memberships:* Council member: ICAN; IMCON; Treasurer, NAMCON; Nigeria Society. *Publications:* Various articles in the Nigerian Accountant. *Honours:* Winner of the Plender Griffiths and Leo T Little prizes, in final examinations of ACA, 1966. *Hobbies:* Squash; Lawn tennis. *Address:* 65 Raymond Njoku Street, SW Ikoyi, Lagos, Nigeria.

OKE, Olusegun Ladimeji, b. 17 Sept. 1934, Ibadan, Nigeria. Lecturer. m. Aduke Olajumoke Bucknor, 30 Jan. 1960, 1 son, 4 daughters. *Education:* BSc., 1st class hons., London, UK, 1959; PhD., Reading, UK, 1962; Diploma, Nutrition, Cantab., UK, 1975; C.Chem., 1979. *Appointments:* Government Chemist, Ministry of Agriculture and Natural Resources, Ibadan, Nigeria, 1962; Lecturer, 1962, Senior Lecturer, 1965, Professor, 1976, Head, Chemistry Department, 1979-81, Dean, Faculty of Science, 1981-, University of Ife, Nigeria. *Memberships:* Royal Society of Chemistry; Royal Society of Medicine; Royal Society of Health; Nutrition Society. *Publications:* 81 papers in International journals; series of articles on traditional technologies; published a book on dyeing in Nigeria. *Creative Works:* Tie dyeing of materials for shirts and dresses. *Honours:* Best Student prize, University of Ibadan, Nigeria, 1959; Inter-University Council Senior Fellow, 1969-70. *Hobbies:* Travelling; Photography; Dyeing; Tennis; Jogging. *Address:* House A6, Road 14 Close, University of Ife Campus, Ile-Ife, Nigeria.

OKE, Solomon Akintola, b. 14 Feb. 1939, Effuduasi, Ghana. Publisher; Sales Director. m. Felicia Iyabode, 14 June 1964, 2 sons, 4 daughters. *Education:* Member, Institute of Marketing, 1976. *Appointments:* Sales-/Bookshop Supervisor, University of Ibadan Bookshop, Ibadan, Nigeria, 1962-64; Sales Controller/Assistant Manager, Nigeria Baptist Bookstores Limited, Ibadan, Nigeria, 1964-69; Sales Representative, 1969-74, Sales Manager, 1974-79, Director, 1980, Evans Bros. (Nig. Pub.) Limited, Ibadan, Nigeria. *Memberships:* Chairman, Helpers Club of Nigeria; Council, Oyo State, Nigeria. *Honours:* Justice of the Peace, Oyo State of Nigeria, 1981. *Hobbies:* Golf; Table tennis. *Address:* S7/881, Adeniran Oyinlola Avenue, Ring Road, Ibadan, Nigeria.

OKECHUKWU, Theodore Luckson Cyril, b. 4 July 1923, Enugu, Nigeria. Medical. m. Theodora Edozien, 30 Jan. 1954, 3 sons, 2 daughters. *Education:* MB., B.Ch., BAO., NUI., 1949; DOMS., RCSI., 1952; FMCS., Nigeria, 1970. *Appointments:* House Surgeon and Casualty Officer, Battle Hospital, Reading, UK, 1949; Opthalmic House Surgeon, Royal Infirmary, Hull, UK, 1950; Clinical Assistant, Moorfield Eye Hospital, London, UK, 1951; Senior House Officer, Sussex Eye Hospital, Brighton, UK, 1951-52; Special Grade Ophthalmic Medical Officer, 1952; Consultant Ophthalmologist, 1960; Senior Consultant Ophthalmologist, 1964; Chief Consultant Ophthalmologist, 1972; Director, State Mobile Eye Clinic Programme, 1973-80; Nigeria Medical Council, 1970-78; Chief Executive, Park Lane Hospital, Enugu, 1974-80; Nigeria. *Memberships:* Nigerian Representative, World Council for Welfare of the Blind; Oxford Ophthalmological Congress, UK; International Glaucoma Association, UK; Nigeria Medical Association; Nigerian Representative, International Agency for Prevention of Blindness. *Hobbies:* Music; Photography; Studies in Comparative religion. *Address:* Madonna Villa, Umunuko Village, PO Box 6, Ukpor, Nnewi LGA, Nigeria.

OKEDIADI, Eunice Chinedo, b. 19 Nov. 1920, Egbu, Owerri, Imo State, Nigeria. Teacher. m. Samuel Leslie Okediadi, 9 Jan. 1943, 3 sons, 2 daughters. *Education:* Teacher Grade II, Women's Training College, Umuahia, 1937-40; Department of Education, Edinburgh University, UK, 1960-61; Christian Home and Family Life Seminar, Kitwe, Zambia, 1963; Christian Journalism course, Shagamu, Western Region, 1964. *Appointments:* St. Monica's Girls School, 1930-33; Auxiliary teacher, Owerri, Imo State, 1934-36, School mistress, 1941-45, Owerri, Imo State, Nigeria; Teacher training, Umuahia, Nigeria, 1937-40; Primary School Mistress, Owerri, 1941-45; Preliminary Training Centre for teachers, Owerri, Nigeria, 1946-49; Head-Mistress,

Primary School, Onitsha, Anambra, Nigeria, 1950-59; Secretary, Women's Work, Owerri, Nigeria, 1961-63; Attended Ecumenical Conference, Protestant Churches, Ibadan, Enugu, Umuhuia, 1962-70; Principal, Anglican Secondary School, Asaba, Bendel, Nigeria, 1964; Administrative Secretary, National Council of Women's Societies, Lagos, Nigeria, 1965; Principal, Draspring Girls' Ind. & Training Centre, Onitsha, Nigeria, 1976-; Conducted Vocational training for Women under Christian Council, Nigeria. *Memberships:* Patron, National Council of Womens' Societies, 1961-; Nigerian Union of Teachers, 1944-; Patron, Society for the Promotion of Igbo Language and Culture; Old Pauline Cooperative Housing Society, 1962-, Executive member; Secretary, 1970-73, Ogbaru Women Cooperative Society; Director, Coop Bank of Eastern Nigeria Limited; Diocesan Board member, Niger Anglican Diocese, Onitsha, 1972-; Nigerian's Peoples Party, 1978-; Management Committee, Iyienu Hospital, 1965-73; Girl Guide Captain, 1947-71. *Publications:* Friendship between Boys and Girls (co writer), 1964; A Short Biography of the late Bishop Alphonso Chukwuma Onyeabo, OBE, 1956. *Honours:* Awarded B B M., 1969. *Hobbies:* Freelance writing; Reading; Music; Singing; Gardening. *Address:* 10 Arondizuoga Street, Fegge, Onitsha, Anambra State, Nigeria.

OKEDIJI, Oladejo Olatokunbo, b. 30 Aug. 1933, Nigeria. Teacher. Widower, 1 son, 3 daughters. *Education:* BSc., 1962, PhD., 1966, Columbia University, New York City, New York, USA. *Appointments:* Visiting Research Fellow, Institute of Administration, University of Ife, Ibadan, Nigeria, 1964-65; Visiting Lecturer, Anthropology, New York University, New York, USA, 1965-66; Lecturer, Department of Anthropology and Sociology, City College of New York, USA, 1965-66; Lecturer, Anthropology, Columbia University, New York, USA, 1966-67; Lecturer, Senior Lecturer, Associate Professor, Department of Sociology, 1967-75, Professor of Sociology, 1975-, University of Lagos, Nigeria. *Memberships:* Nigerian Anthropological and Sociological Association; Nigerian Economic Society; American Anthropological Association; Vice President and Alternate Delegate to ISSC, International Union of Anthropological and Ethnological Sciences. *Publications:* Co-Editor: The Sociology of the Yarubas, 1970; numerous Scholarly articles, comments and review articles in national and international journals. *Honours:* Federal Nigerian Government Scholar, 1959-67, Foreign Students' Award, 1966, Columbia University, USA; Ford Foundation Award, University of Ife, Ibadan, Nigeria, 1964-65; UNESCO Consultant Institute for Mass Communication Research, Stanford University, USA, 1971. *Hobbies:* Reading; Driving; Gardening; Listening to Music; Indoor games. *Address:* 7 Oritshejolomi Thomas Crescent, University of Lagos Campus, Akoka, Yaba, Lagos, Nigeria.

OKEKE, Benson Chukwuma, b. 20 Apr. 1946, Enugwu-Agidi, Njika L G A., Anambra State, Nigeria. Architect. m. Florence, 25 Nov. 1978, 1 daughter. *Education:* B. Arch., Hons., University of Nigeria, Enugu Campus, Nigeria, 1970-75. *Appointments:* Supervision of Advanced Teachers' College buildings, Pankshin, Plateau State, Nigeria, Federal Ministry of Education, Lagos, Nigeria, 1975-76; Project Architect, 1976-78, Junior Partner, 1978-80, The Environmental Designers, Lagos, Nigeria; Founding Principal Consultant, Design Plus, now merged with Riccan Associates, 1980; Partner, Riccan Associates, Enugu, Nigeria, 1981; Riccan Associates now merged with Burgess Associates of Cardiff, Wales, UK under the name Riccan Burgess Partnership, Lagos, Nigeria. *Memberships:* Nigerian Institute of Architects. *Creative Works:* State Fire Station, Makudri, Benue State, Nigeria, 1978; Office Complex, Anambra State House of Assembly, Enugu, Nigeria, 1980-81; Benue State Business and Secretariat Complex, Makurdi, Enugu, Nigeria, 1980; Proposal for Institute of Management and Technology Master Plan, 1981. *Hobbies:* Football; Travelling; Films; Music. *Address:* 4 Ikwuato Street, behind Leventis Stores, Uwani Central, Enugu, Nigeria.

OKEKE, H A Nnagbo, b. 2 July 1938, Enugu, Nigeria. Physiotherapy. m. Constance A. 20 Oct. 1969, 2 sons, 2 daughters. *Education:* MCSP., West Middlesex Hospital School of Physiotherapy, Isleworth, London, UK, 1966; BPT., MCPA., University of Manitoba, Canada. *Appointments:* Physiotherapist, General Hospital, Uxbridge, UK, 1966; Physiotherapist, 1970-74, Senior

Physiotherapist, 1974-76, Principal Physiotherapist, 1976-77, Chief Physiotherapist, 1977 -, University of Nigeria Teaching Hospital, Enugu, Nigeria. *Memberships:* Editor of Journal, Nigeria Society of Physiotherapy; Chartered Society of Physiotherapy, UK; Canadian Physiotherapy Association; Cancer Society of Nigeria. *Publications:* Tactics of Social Influence (review); Functional Structure of the Lumbar Spine, 1977; Poliomyelitis: the disease, the victim and the developing nations, 1980; Physiotherapy and the Handicapped child in Nigeria, 1981; Rehabilitation and Integration, 1981; Leprosy: Combined Median/ulnan nerves and physiotherapy, 1974; Trade Union as a management facet, 1979; Mechanics of the Lumbar Spine, 1978; The human hand - a functional indox of fitnoss, 1981; Staff evaluations in Physiotherapy Departments, 1980. *Honours:* Speaker - Rehab. International Year of the Disabled Persons. *Hobbies:* Photography; Reading; Motoring; Soccer. *Address:* 38 River Avenue, Ekulu, G R A Enugu, Anambra State, Nigeria.

OKENWA, Pius Dim Chikwereuba, b. 22 Sept. 1934, Ihitenansa Orlu L G A., Imo State, Nigeria. Business Industrialist; Schools Proprietor. m. (4) Edith, Nkechi, Veronica, Ego, 3 sons, 2 daughters. *Appointments:* Founder/Proprietor: Edo Boys High School, now Adolo College, Benin City, Bendel State, Nigeria; Eastern Boys High School, now Boys High School, Ihitenansa, Orlu L G A, Imo State, Nigeria; Founder, Chairman, Managing Director, Markdealers(Nigeria) Limited, Enugu, Nigeria; Founder, Executive Director, Managing Director, Continental Medical Complex Limited, Oji River, Nigeria; Director, UK based company. *Memberships:* Ogboni Fraternity; Orsu County Council, 1965-66; 1st Chairman, Ihitenansa Community Council, 1971; Traditional Ruler, Autonomous Community of Ihitenansa, Orlu, Nigeria, 1978. *Hobbies:* Reading of Novels; Ludo; Drafts; Swimming; Dancing. *Address:* Traditional Ide Palace, PO Box 272, Orlu, Imo State, Nigeria.

OKIGBO, Pius Nwabufo Charles, b. 6 Feb. 1924, Ojuto, Nigeria. Economist. m. Florence Nnakwe. *Education:* BA., Hons., 1946, BSc., 1949, LL.B., 1952, London University, UK; MA., PhD., Northwestern University, USA; LL.D., Hons., University of Nigeria, 1966. *Appointments:* Lecturer, Northwestern University, Evanston, Illinois, USA, 1955-57; Student, Nuffield College, Oxford, UK, 1957; Economic Adviser: Government of Eastern Nigeria, 1960-62; Federal Government of Nigeria, 1962-67; Managing Director, SKOUP & Co. Limited, Nigeria, 1971-. *Memberships:* American Economic Association; Fellow, Royal Economic Society; Nigerian Society for Economic and Social Science; Econometric Society. *Publications:* Nigerian National Accounts 1950-1957, 1962; Africa and the Common Market, 1967; Nigerian Public Finance, 1965; Nigeria's Financial System: Structure and Growth, 1981. *Honours:* Commander of the Order of the Niger, 1975. *Hobbies:* Music; Chess. *Address:* 3 Nike Avenue, PO Box 39, Enugu, Nigeria.

OKO, Emelia Chinagolum (Aseme), b. 23 Nov. 1945, Oguta, Nigeria. Lecturer. m. 29 July 1969, 3 daughters. *Education:* BA., Hons., English U N N., 1971; MA., Essex, UK, 1974. *Appointments:* Lecturer in English and Literature: University of Nigeria, Calabar Campus, Nigeria, 1973-74; University of Calabar, Nigeria, 1976-77; University of Benin, Benin City, Nigeria, 1977-81. *Memberships:* Literary Society of Nigeria; Modern Languages Association of Nigeria; English Association, University of Nigeria, Nsukka; Nigerian Association of University Women. *Publications:* The Historical Novel of Africa - a sociological study of . Achebe's Things Fall Apart and Arrow of God, 1974; Articles: The Language of Comedy in Nigerian Fiction, 1980; Myth and Reality in Soyinka's Social Vision, 1981; The Liberation of the Individual - Armah's Fragments, 1980; Tradition and History in Achebe's Novels, 1980; Conference Papers: Achebe and a Living Tradition, 1979; The Sociology of Literature - an African Perspective, 1974; Literature and Ideology - a study of Cary's Mister Johnson and Achebe's Arrow of God, 1980; The Criticism of the Nigeria Novel - a review, 1980; 4 Faculty of Arts Lecture Series, The Nigerian Novel and Revolution, University of Benin, Nigeria. *Hobbies:* Reading; Lawn tennis; Swimming; Gardening. *Address:* Dept. of English, University of Calabar, CRS, Nigeria.

OKOGIE, Anthony Olubunmi, b. 16 June 1936, Lagos, Nigeria. Catholic Archbishop of Lagos, Nigeria.

Education: SS. Peter and Paul Major Seminary, Ibadan, Nigeria, 1963; BD., STL., DD., Urban University, Rome, Italy, 1967. *Appointments:* Pastor, Catholic Churches, Lagos, Nigeria, 1967-71; Director of Vocations, Archdiocese of Lagos, Nigeria, 1967-71; Master of Ceremonies, Holy Cross Cathedral, Lagos, Nigeria, 1967-71; Broadcaster, Religious Programme, NBC/tv., 1967-71; Auxiliary Bishop: Diocese of Oyo, Nigeria, 1971-72; Apostolic Administrator, Archdiocese of Lagos, Nigeria, 1972; Archbishop of Met. See of Lagos, Nigeria, 1973-. *Address:* Holy Cross Cathedral, PO Box 8, Lagos, Nigeria.

OKOKON, (Chief) Ita, b. 24 Mar. 1935, Calabar, Cross River State, Nigeria. Banking. m. Edith Henrietta Edet, 22 Feb. 1969, 1 son, 2 daughters. *Education:* BSc., Hons., 1965; Diploma, French, 1961; Organization and Methods Administration, Cranfield School of Management, UK, 1969- 70; Several Management courses, 1976-78; International Certificate, Commercial Banking course, Manchester Business School, UK, 1980. *Appointments:* Statistical Officer, Federal Office of Statistics, Lagos, Nigeria; Assistant Chief Internal Auditor, Assistant Chief Bank Examiner, Central Bank of Nigeria; Company Secretary and Chief of Administration, Controller of Operations, Chief Inspector, Mercantile Bank of Nigeria Limited. *Memberships:* Wolf Cub, King's Scout, Boys Scout Movement, 2nd Calabar Group; Charter President, 1980-81, Rotary Club of Calabar, Nigeria. *Publications:* Publications on Management in local magazines; papers presented at Management Seminars; Paper on Revenue Allocation - presented to the Technical Committee on Revenue Allocation in Nigeria. *Honours:* Awarded Book prize, International Commercial Banking course, Manchester Business School, Manchester University, UK. *Hobbies:* Swimming; Dancing; Table tennis. *Address:* D281 Second Avenue, Housing Corporation Estate, Calabar, Nigeria.

OKOLI, George Uwaekwe, b. 7 June 1930, Oko, Aguata Local Government Area, Anambra State, Nigeria. Electrical Engineer. m. Patience Ijennwa Nwosu, 15 Aug. 1959, 1 son, 5 daughters. *Education:* Inter. Cits Guild, Post and Telegraphs Training Centre, Oshodi, Nigeria, 1954-57; Pre-Engineering, Langston University, Langston, Oklahoma, USA, 1959-61; BSc., University of Washington, Seattle, USA, 1961-64. *Appointments:* Sub-Inspector of Lines in Training, 1954-57, Technical Officer, 1957-59, Post and Telegraphs, Nigeria; Assistant Engineer, Pacific North West Bell Telephones, USA, 1962-65; Communications Engineer, 1965-71, Area Operations Engineer, 1973-75, National Electric Power Authority, Nigeria; Managing Director, George Engineering Co. Limited, Nigeria, 1975-. *Memberships:* Institute of Electrical and Electronic Engineers,1964, Nigerian Society of Engineers, 1974. *Hobby:* Photography. *Address:* 3 Amaigbo Lane, Uwani, Enugu, Anambra State, Nigeria.

OKONKWO, John Chukwunweike, b. 10 Oct. 1942, Ufuma, Aguata Local Government Area, Anambra State, Nigeria. Legal Practitioner and Notary Public. m. Amaka Ezeaku, 10 Aug. 1977. *Education:* LL.B., (Hons.), University of Nigeria, Nsukka, 1962-66; BL, Nigerian Law School, Lagos, 1971; Called to Nigerian Bar, 1971. *Appointments:* Clerk, Barclays Bank DCO, Obun Eko Branch, Lagos, 1961; Reporter, West African Pilot Limited, 1961-62. *Memberships:* United Nations Students' Association, 1963-66; Students' Parliament, University of Nigeria, 1964-66, Speaker, 1965-66. *Hobbies:* Football; Table Tennis; Lawn Tennis; Politics; Music. *Address:* 11 Inyi Street, Achara Layout, Uwani, Enugu, PO Box 2109, Nigeria.

OKONKWO, Okwudili James, b. 15 Sept. 1940, Onitsha, Anambra State of Nigeria. Accountant/Manager. m. 24 July 1965, 2 sons, 2 daughters. *Education:* HNC, Business Studies M/cr, 1968; ICMA, Derby, 1973; AC MA, 1976. *Appointments:* Cost Accountant, Rota Print Limited, Queensbury, 1973-74; Management Accountant, Nigeria Wire Industry, Lagos, 1974-75; Accountant, UAC of Nigeria Limited 1975-; Comercial Manager EMS, UACN Limited, Senior Accountant. *Memberships:* Chairman, MBOSI Development Union. *Honours:* 1st Prize, 1st School Leaving Certificate. *Hobbies:* Chess; Football; Squash; Swimmer. *Address:* AT&P A Division of UAC of Nigeria Limited, P.M.B 4001, Sapele, Bendel State, Nigeria.

OKORIE, Kalu Chima, b. 25 Feb. 1923, Umuhu Ezechi, (Achi) Bende L.G.A. Librarianship. m. Emma Onyeakagbule Eluwa, 29 Dec. 1956, 3 sons, 2 daughters. *Education:* Student, Higher College, Yaba Lagos, 1942-44; Schools of Librarianship: Loughborough, England, 1949-50; Associate of L.A. (A.L.A.), 1950; N.W. Polytechnic, London, 1950-51; Fellowship of LA. (F.L.A.), 1953; Institute of Education, University of London, 1951-52. *Appointments:* Librarian, Lagos Municipal Library 1952-55; Librarian, Eastern Nigeria Government, Enugu, 1955-56; Regimal Librarian/ Director of Liby Services, Eastern Nigeria Library Board, 1957-70; Director, Liby Service, Easte Central State Library Board, 1970-76; Director, Liby Service, Imo State Library Board, 1976-78. *Memberships:* West African Liby Association; West African Library Association; Nigerian Library Association; Councillor Nig. Liby Association; Provisional Council Ife University; Franklin Book Program; East Nigeria Festival of Arts Committee; East Central State/Imo State Liby Boards; etc. *Publications:* Contributed several articles in professional journals UNESCO bulletin for libraries; LAR; Liby Trends; Library Journal; Library World; WALA Libraries; Nigerian Libraries; etc. *Honours:* MBE, 1961; OON, 1964; Carnegie Corporation Commonwealth Travel Grant to Canada and USA, 1962; Ford Foundation Travel Grant to Denmark, Sweden Canada and USA 1966. *Hobbies:* Reading; Classical/ Pop records, tapes collection; Gardening; Art Collection; Table Tennis; Personal Library Collection. *Address:* Obu Onyekachi, Umuhu Ezechi, Bende, L.G.A., PO Box 401, Umuahia, Nigeria.

OKORO, Anezionwu Nwankwo, b. 17 May 1929, Arondizuogu, Nigeria. Physician. m. Eseohe Ayodele Olumese, 2 sons, 3 daughters. *Education:* DMGS, Onitsha, 1946-47; University College Ibadan 1948-52; MB, ChB, University of Bristol, United Kingdom, 1953-56; LRCP, MRCS, 1956; Postgraduate Medical Schools, London and Edinburgh, 1961-63; MRCP, Edinburgh, 1963; FMCP(Nig), 1971; FWACP 1976; FRCP, Edinburgh 1977. *Appointments:* House Surgeon, House Physician, U.C.H. Ibadan, 1956-57; Medical Officer, Ministry of Health, Lagos, 1957-64; Consultant Dermatologist, Lagos and Enugu 1965-67; Senior Lecturer in Medicine, University of Nigeria, 1967-74; Reader in Medicine, 1974-75; Professor of Medicine, 1975-. *Memberships:* British Association of Dermatologists; International Society of Tropical Dermatology; Association of Dermatologists of West Africa; Rotary Club of Enugu; Writers and Readers Club of Nigeria, Enugu. *Publications:* Novels: The Village School, 1966; The Village Headmaster, 1967; Febechi in Cave Adventure, 1971; One Week one Trouble, 1974; Febechi Down the Niger, 1975; Dr. Amadi's Posting, 1975; Double Trouble, 1981; Textbook, Pictorial Handbook of Common Skin Diseases, 1981; Albinism in Nigeria and other medical articles. *Hobbies:* Writing; Chess; Gardening. *Address:* 7 Braithewaite Close, University of Nigeria, Enugu Campus, Enugu, Nigeria.

OKORO, Eugene Odindu Ugochukwu, b. 25 Nov. 1938, Owerri, Imo State, Nigeria. Insurance Executive-/Bank Director. m. Patience Onyemaechi Njoku, 20 Apr. 1968, 3 sons, 3 daughters. *Education:* University of Cambridge School Certificate, 1958; General Certificate of Education, 1960; Insurance Institute of London, 1965; Insurance Institute of Nigeria, 1971; Associate, Institute of Management Specialists, 1979; Associate, Nigerian institute of Management 1979; British Institute of Management, 1980; Executive Council Member, American Institute of Management, 1980. *Appointments:* Insurance Clerk, 1960; Management Trainee 1964; Executive Officer 1965; Resident Representive, Royal Exchange, Onitsha 1967; Assistant to East Area Manager, 1970; Motor Superintendent, Royal Exchange Assurance, Lagos, 1971; Assistant to Accident Manager, Royal Exchange Head Office, Lagos, 1972; Branch Manager, Royal Exchange Assurance, Apapa, Lagos, 1973; Ag. Resident Rep. Guardian Royal Exchange, Monrovia, Liberia, 1974; Manager, Organisation and Methods, 1976; Assistant General Manager, Royal Exchange Assurance, Nigeria Limited 1978; Board of Directors, African Continental Bank Limited, 1980. *Memberships:* Rotary Club of Isolo, Lagos; The Royal Over-Seas League, London; Nigerian Tourist and Passengers' Association. *Hobbies:* Swimming; Table Tennis; Gardening; Reading. *Address:* 34 Ilorin Street, Adelabu, Surulere, Lagos, Nigeria.

OKORO, Nwakamma, b. 17 Dec. 1927, Arochukwu, Imo State, Nigeria. Legal Profession, Real Estate Development. m. Eme Ikpeme 31 Mar. 1959, 2 sons, 4 daughters. *Education:* Diploma in Public Administration, University College, Exeter England, 1953-55; LLB Hons., 1955-57; Barrister-at-Law Lincoln's Inn, England, 1958; LLM, Birmingham University, 1957-58; PhD Law (Cantab.), 1961-63. *Appointments:* Legal Practitioner in Nigeria, 1958-61, 1964-; William Senior Scholar in Comparative Law, Clare College, Cambridge University, 1961-63; Nigerian Constituent Assembly for the Production of the Current Federal Constitution of Nigeria, 1977-78; Senior Advocate of Nigeria, 1978; Director, Nigerian National Petroleum Corporation, 1981-. *Memberships:* President, Nigerian Bar Association, 1976-78; First Secretary-General, National Party of Nigeria. *Publications:* The Customary Laws of Succession in Easter Nigeria, 1966; The Ascertainment of Customary Laws of Succession in Southern Nigeria, 1967; Subject Index of Nigeria Supreme Court Judgments 1956 to 1974-1981. *Honours:* Bracton Law Prize, University College of Exeter, 1957; Senior Advocate of Nigeria, 1978. *Hobbies:* Politics; Tennis; Gardening. *Hobbies:* Amuvi, Arochukwu, Imo State, Nigeria.

OKORO, Simon Nduka, b. 23 Mar. 1923. Barrister-at-Law. m. Olive Williams, 28 Jan. 1961, 3 sons, 1 daughter. *Education:* Studied Law at Lincolns Inn, London, 1951-55, passing Bar Final; Called to the English Bar, 1961. *Appointments:* Crown Counsel, Eastern Nigeria Government Service, 1962; Senior State Counsel, 1971-75, Principal State Counsel, East Central Government Service, 1975-76; Deputy Solicitor-General, Imo State Government Service, 1976-78; Chairman, Capital Finance Company Limited, 1978-. *Memberships:* Owerri Bar Association. *Honours:* Ogogbuzuo I of Arondizuoge, for philanthropic services to the community, 1963. *Hobbies:* Lawn Tennis; Swimming; Reading. *Address:* 22 Ohaozara Street, Aladinma, PO Box 800, Owerri, Nigeria.

OKORONKWO, Timothy Alachulam, b. 18 Sept. 1937, Eziama-Obiato, Imo State of Nigeria. Accountancy. m. 3 Oct. 1964, 5 sons, 6 daughters. *Education:* Associate of: The Institute of Book-keepers, The Nigerian National Accountants, The British and Nigerian Institutes of Management. *Appointments:* Accounts Clerk, 1957-61; Assistant Accountant, 1961-77; Accountant, 1967-77; Chief Accountant, 1977-. *Memberships:* Fellow, The Institute of Financial and Management Executives. *Hobbies:* Reading; Christian activities. *Address:* 28B Ijaoye Street, Igbobi, Yaba, Lagos, Nigeria.

OKOYE, Eddy Obi, b. 3 Mar. 1941, Umunnachi. Banking. m. 20 Apr. 1969, 1 son. *Education:* Fellow of: The Institute of Bankers, The Chartered Institute of Secretaries and Administrators and the British Institute of Management. *Appointments:* General Manager and Chief Executive, Cooperative Bank Limited, Enugu, Nigeria. *Hobbies:* Swimming; Music; Tennis. *Address:* Cooperative Bank Limited, PMB 1321, 28 Okpara Avenue, Enugu, Nigeria.

OKOYE, Levi Ifeanyi Obi, b. 10 Dec. 1939, Ojoto, Anambra State of Nigeria. Civil Servant. m. Mary 27 Dec. 1969, 3 sons, 1 daughter. *Education:* Trained on Medical Records Keeping and Health Statistics, Federal Ministry of Health, Lagos, 1959-61; Diploma in Health Statistics, University of Benin, Nigeria, 1980. *Appointments:* Third Class Clerk, 1959, First Class Medical Statistics Assistant, Ministry of Health, Lagos, 1964; Assistant Medical Records Officer, 1971, Medical Records Officer, 1972, Higher Medical Records Officer, 1977, Senior Medical Records Officer, 1979, Principal Medical Records Officer, Ministry of Health, Enugu, 1980. *Memberships:* Associate, Nigerian Health Records Association; University of Benin Alumni Association. *Publications:* Statistics as a Basis For Planning, a Thesis, 1980. *Hobbies:* Gardening; Listening to good music. *Address:* State Health Management Board, No 1 Colliery Avenue GRA, Enugu, Anambra State, Nigeria.

OKOYE, Samuel Ejikeme, b. 26 July 1939, Umuahia, Imo State, Nigeria. University Professor. m. Chinyere Ugheime Obioha, 12 Apr. 1969, 2 sons, 2 daughters. *Education:* BSc., (London) University College, Ibadan, Nigeria, 1958-62; PhD., University of Cambridge, UK., 1962-65. *Appointments:* Lecturer II, University College, Ibadan, 1965-66; Lecturer II, University of Nigeria, 1970-74, Reader, 1974-76, Professor, 1976, Director, Division of General Studies, 1976-78, Head,

Department of Physics, University of Nigeria, Nsukka, 1978-81. *Memberships:* Fellow, Royal Astonomical Society; American Astronomical Society; International Astronomical Union; Nigerian Institute of Physics; Science Association of Nigeria; Nigerian Union for Planetary & Radio Science. *Publications:* Contributor of chapters and numerous scientific articles in learned journals. *Honours:* College Scholar, 1959-62, Department Prize, University College, Ibadan, 1962. *Address:* 10 Eni Njoku Street, University of Nigeria, Nsukka, Nigeria.

OKPALA, Edmund, Udeze, b. 21 Sept. 1934, Nkpologwu, Aguata L.G.A. Anambra State, Nigeria. Reader, Associate Professor, Plant Pathology. m. Victoria Omelebele Esimai, 27 June, 1961, 4 sons, 2 daughters. *Education:* BSc, Hons., London. Botany 2 class (Old Regu.) University College Ibadan; D.I.C. Mycology and Plant Pathology, Imperial College, London, 1964; Plant Pathology PhD(London), Imperial College London, 1966. *Appointments:* Senior Science Master, Urhobo College, Warri, Nigeria, 1959-1961; Vice Principal, Urhobo College, Warri Nigeria, 1961-1962; Acting Principal, Urhobo College, Warri, Nigeria, 1962-1963; Lecturer II University of Nigeria, Nsukka, Nigeria, 1966-1967; Major, Biafran Army, 1967-1970; Field Director, National Rehabilitation for East Central State, 1970-1971; Lecturer I University of Nigeria Nsukka 1971-1975; Senior Lecturer, U.N.N. 1975-1978; Reader (Associate Professor) 1978-; Head, Department of Crop Science, 1980-. *Memberships:* British Mycological Society; International Society for Horticultural Science; Nigerian Society for Plant Protection; Vice President, Nigerian Society for Plant Protection, 1977-1978; President, Nigerian Society for Plant Protection, 1978-1979. *Publications:* Published over 20 researched work in Plant Pathology; Supervised many PhD and M.Sc researches; Completed work on Compendium of Plant diseases from Nigeria. *Honours:* Won 1st Prize, Nigerian Festival of Arts, 1951-1952 (under 16 years); Commonwealth Scholar, 1963-1966; Senior I.U.C. Fellowship, 1977-1978. *Hobbies:* Gardening; Carpentry; Scrabble; Table Tennis; Farming; Studying Mysteries. *Address:* No. 632 Odim Street, University of Nigeria, Nsukka, Nigeria.

OKPARA, Udensi,Onuke, b. 10 May 1948, Alayi, Bende, LGA, Imo State Nigeria. Civil Servant. m. Theresa Enyidia, 28 Aug. 1978, 2 sons. *Education:* Grade III Teachers Certificate, 1962; Grade II Teachers' Certificate, 1966; Associate in Arts (Hesston College, USA), 1973; BSC Business Administration, Oral Roberts University, USA 1975; MBA, Oral Roberts University, USA, 1977; Doctoral Candidate in Marketing University of Nigeria, Nsukka, 1980-. *Appointments:* School Teacher Abakaliki District, 1958-1967; School Teacher and Games Master, 1971; Principal Assistant Secretary, Nigerian Coal Corporation, Enugu, '1981-. *Memberships:* Nimark (Nigerian Marketing Association); Nigerian Institute of Management. *Publications:* Performance and control in a partial MBO Sales Department. *Honours:* Deans Honour Roll, 1973. *Hobbies:* Soccer; Poetry; Table Tennis. *Address:* 11 Colliery Avenue, Gra Enugu, Anambra State, Nigeria.

OKU, Ekei, Essien, b. 22 January, 1924, Calabar, Cross River State, Nigeria. m. 18 August, 1956. 1 son, 2 daughters. *Education:* Associate ot the British Library Association (ALA), 1953. *Appointments:* Librarian in charge Lagos City Council Libraries, 1955-1969; Librarian in charge Cross River State Library Service, 1969-; Promoted Chief Librarian, 1975. *Memberships:* Secretary, South-Eastern State Branch of the Nigerian Girl Guide Association, 1969-1975; St. John's Ambulance; National Council of Women's Societies; President, Calabar Choral Party, Calabar Branch. *Hobbies:* Sewing; Reading; Singing. *Address:* 3 Diamond Lane, Diamond Hill, Calabar, Nigeria.

OKUDZETO, Samuel Awuku, b. 4 Sept. 1935, Adidome, Volta Region. Lawyer. m. Priscilla, 2 Oct. 1971, 2 sons, 4 daughters. *Education:* Corporation of Secretaries Final Certificate, Leeds College of Commerce, Leeds, Yorkshire, England, 1958; Licentiate Membership, Corporation of Secretaries, 20 Mar., 1959; Bachelor of Law (Hon.), Kings College, London University, 1961; Institute of Advance Legal Studies, 1961-1962; Called to the Bar Inner Temple, London, 1963; College of Europe, Bruges, Belgium, 1962-1963; Certificate of Advance European Studies, College of Europe, June

1963; Hague Academy of International Law Summer Session, 1963; Diploma of College of Europe, October, 1973; Associate Membership, Corporation of Secretaries, 1965; Associate Membership, Chartered Institute of Secretaries, 1970; Fellow, Chartered Institute of Secretaries, 1977. *Appointments:* Private Legal Practitioner 1963-; Assistant Secretary, Eastern Region Branch, Ghana Bar Association 1966-1968; Assistant Secretary General, Ghana Bar Association (National) 1968-1969; Acting General Secretary, Ghana Bar Association, 1969-1970; Treasurer, Ghana Bar Association, 1972-1975 Member of the General Legal Council of Ghana 1974-1976; Member of the Legal Aid Committee, 1974-1976; Member of the Disciplinary Committee of the General Legal Council, 1977-1980; Chairman, Ghana Association of the Institute of Chartered Secretaries and Administrators 1972-1980; Member of Parliament, 1969-1972; A Director and Secretary to a number of Private Companies; Parliamentary Delegate to Australia, Papua New Guinea and India, 1970; Chairman of various Committees and Commissions 1972-1978; Commonwealth Countries Observer Team to Zimbabwe, 1980. *Memberships:* Founding and Executive Member of National Alliance of Liberals (Main Opposition Party, (1969-1972); Founding and Executive Member of the United National Convention, 1979. *Honours:* Paul Harris Fellow, Rotary International, 1972. *Hobbies:* Gardening; Swimming; Driving. *Address:* House No. 12, C.F.C. Estate, Tesano, Accra.

OKUK, Lambakey Palma, b. 1943, Pari, Chimbu Province. Papua New Guinean politician. *Education:* National High School, Sogeri. *Appointments:* Papua New Guinea National Parliament, 1972-; Minister for Agriculture, 1972-73, for Education, 1975; Leader of the Opposition, 1978; Deputy Prime Minister, 1980. *Address:* Office of the Leader of the Opposition, PO Box 3534, Port Moresby 211622, Papua New Guinea.

OKWO, Benedict, Chukwuemeka, b. 20 Mar., 1936, Oturkpo. Engineer. m. Marie Nwayiwunwa, 30 Jan., 1965, 2 sons, 4 daughters. *Education:* BSc. Engineering London, Nigerian College of Arts, Science and Technology, Enugu, 1956-1958; Nigerian College of Arts Science and Technology, Zaria, Faculty of Engineering, University of Ibadan, 1959-1962. *Appointments:* Executive Engineer, Federal Ministry of Works and Housing, 1962-1972; Principal Executive Engineer, 1972-1977; Assistant Chief Engineer, 1977-1979; Political Appointments include: Anambra State Government of Nigeria, Commissioner for Works & Housing, 1975-1978; Establishments 1978; and Industries, Trade & Cooperatives, 1978-1979; Director of African Continental Bank. *Memberships:* Nigerian Society of Engineers; Enugu Sports Club. *Hobbies:* Gardening; Table Tennis; Reading. *Address:* No. 1 Isi-Uzo Street, Independence Layout, P.O. Box 2599, Enugu, Nigeria.

OKWUOWULU, Alphonsus, Onwura, b. 29 Sept. 1935, Nnewi, Nigeria. Librarian. m. 9 June, 1969, 3 sons, 5 daughters. *Education:* Diploma in Education (Ibadan) 1961; A.L.A. (Gt. Britain), 1963; M.S. in L. S. (Case Western Reserve), 1976; M.A. (Case Western Reserve), 1976; Certificate in Medical Librarianship (USA.), 1976. *Appointments:* Librarian Assistant, University of Glasgow, 1963-1964; Assistant Librarian, University of Lagos Medical School, 1965-1966; Sub-Librarian, University of Nigeria, Nsukka 1967-1969; Librarian, University of Nigeria Medical Library, Enugu, 1970-1974; Chief Librarian, University of Nigeria Medical Library, Enugu, 1975-. *Memberships:* Councillor Nigerian Library Association, 1976-1979; Medical Library Association (Nigeria) Vice-Chairman, 1977-; Library Association (Gt. Britain), 1962-1975. *Publications:* Contributed to various medical and educational journals. *Honours:* Beta Phi Mu (USA), 1977. *Hobbies:* Reading; Lawn Tennis; Table Tennis; Billiards; Photography; Auto-Mechanics. *Address:* University of Nigeria, Enugu Campus, Enugu, Nigeria.

OLABIMTAN, Afolabi, b. 11 June, 1932, Ilaro, Ogun State, Nigeria. University Teacher. m. Olubunmi Olurinde, 28 Dec., 1961, 4 sons. *Education:* B.A. (London) University College, Ibadan, 1958-1961; Higher Diploma in Education, University of Dublin, Trinity College, 1962-1963; M.A., Ph.D. University of Lagos, Lagos, 1969-1974. *Appointments:* Graduate Teacher, Lagos, 1961-1969; University Lecturer, University of Lagos,

Lagos, 1969-; Ogun State Commissioner for Local Government and Information, 1976-78; Chairman, Local Government Reform Committee (Ogun State), 1979; Chairman, Governing Council, Ogun State College of Education, 1981. *Memberships:* General Secretary, Ilaro Youth Organisation 1967-1976; Assistant General Secretary EgBE Ijinle Yorube; Executive Yoruba Studies Association of Nigeria; Nigerian Folklore Society; West African Linguistic Society. *Publications:* Publications in Yoruba include: Oluwa L'o M'Ejo Da; a play Kekere ekun, novel; AAdota Arofo, poetry; Olaore Afotejoye, a play; Ayanmo, a novel; Ewi Orisirisi, poetry; Baba Rere, a novel. *Hobby:* Reading. *Address:* 51 Adeniran Ogunsanya St., Surulere, Lagos, Nigeria.

OLADOKUM, Solabomi (Mrs) b. 11 March, 1930 Igbajo, Oyo State, Nigeria. Librarianship. m. Emmanuel Gbadebo Oladokun, 19 Sept. 1954, 2 sons, 2 daughters. *Education:* Teachers' Certificate, Baptist Women's College, Aloeokuta, Nigeria, December, 1953; School of Librarianship, Polytechnic of North London Jan. 1967-Dec 1968; Associate of the Library Association July 1970; M.A. Librarianship, August 1973, Graduate School of Librarianship, University of Denver, Colorado, United States. *Appointments:* Teacher Nigeria Jan 1954-Sept 1962; Library Assistant London Kime 1964-Dec 1966 and Feb 1969-May 1970; Chief Librarian, National Technical Teachers' College, Yaba, Lagos, Nigeria, July 1970-. *Memberships:* The Library Association United Kingdom; American Library Association; Nigerian Library Association. *Hobby:* Pleasure Reading. *Address:* 21 Ikorodu Road, Yaba, Lagos, Nigeria.

OLAKUNRI, Olutoyin Olusola, b. 4 Nov. 1937, Lagos, Nigeria. Chartered Accountant. m. Simeon Moronfolu, 1 son, 6 daughters. *Education:* Fellow, Institute of Chartered Accountants of England and Wales. *Appointments:* Peat Marwick Cassleton Elliot & Co., 1963-65; Nigerian Industrial Development Bank, 1965-72. *Memberships:* Chairman, Society of Women Accountants; International Womens Society of Nigeria. *Hobbies:* Reading; Collecting pottery. *Address:* 20 Norman Williams Street, S W Ikoyi, Lagos, Nigeria.

OLAMBIWONNU, Olatunji Nurudeen, b. 12 Aug. 1938, Lagos, Nigeria. Physician. m. 25 Dec. 1965, 1 son, 2 daughters. *Education:* BA, New York University, New York, USA, 1963; MD, Albert Einstein College of Medicine, NY, USA, 1967. *Appointments:* Bronx Municipal Hospital Centre, Bronx, NY, USA, 1967-68, 1969-70; Montefiore Hospital Medical Centre, Bronx, NY, USA, 1968-69; Los Angeles County, USC Medical Centre, California, USA, 1970-73; University College Hospital, University of Ibadan, Ibadan, Nigeria, 1973-80. *Memberships:* Lo ngeles Pediatric Society; Nigerian Medical Association, Secretary Western Branch; Executive, Nigerian Society of Endocrinology & Metabolism; Nigerian Pediatric Society. *Publications:* Several articles in learned journals in USA & Africa. *Honours:* Fellowship in Physiology, 1964; Commissioner for Health, Lagos State of Nigeria, 1975-78; Commissioner for Finance, 1978-79; Director, Nigerian Hoechst Limited, 1979-. *Hobbies:* Table Tennis; Lawn Tennis; Swimming; Gardening. *Address:* 774 East Mariposa, Altadena, California, 91001, USA.

OLAND, (The Hon.) Victor deBedia, b. 9 Aug. 1913, Halifax, Nova Scotia, Canada. Chairman, Lindwood Holdings Limited. m Nancy Jane, 17 Apr. 1939, 2 sons, 2 daughters. *Education:* BA., Dalhouse University, Canada, 1935. *Appointments:* Armed Forces, 1939-45; Vice-President, 1945-60, President, 1960-68, Oland & Son Limited, Canada; Brigadier-General, Fourth Militia Group, 1956-60; President, Canadian Chamber of Commerce, 1963-64; President, Canadian Tourist Association, 1967-68; Lieutenant-Governor, Province of Nova Scotia, Canada, 1968-73; Chairman, Lindwood Holdings Limited, Canada, 1973; Director of: Expo '67; Organizing Committee, 1976 Olympic Games; Texaco Canada Inc., 1963; Bank of Montreal, 1965; VS Services Limited, Canada, 1966; Tartan Seafoods, Canada, 1966-. *Memberships:* Director, World Wildlife Fund, Canada; National Council, Canadian Human Rights Foundation; Governor, Canada Sports Hall of Fame; Trustee, Fraser Institute; Executive Committee, Canadian Corps of Commissionaires; Former Director, CD Howe Institute; Fellow, Royal Society of Arts. *Honours:* Efficiency Decoration, ED., 1943; Knight of Malta, 1954; Knight of St. John, 1968; DCL., 1969; LL.D.,

1969; D.Litt., 1973; Canadian Forces Decoration, 1977; Honorary Colonel, 1st Field Artillery, RCA., 1972-79; Nova Scotia Sports Hall of Fame, 1980; Order of Canada, 1980. *Hobby:* Yachting. *Address:* 788 Young Avenue, Halifax, Nova Scotia, Canada, B3H 2V7.

OLATEJU, Isola Oyenitun (Chief). b. 22 Nov. 1936, Ayetoro Egbado, Nigeria. Electrical Engineer. m. Margaret Modupe, 1970, 3 sons, 2 daughters. *Education:* Federal School of Science, Lagos, Nigeria; Cornell University, Ithaca, New York, USA; Polytechnic Institute of New York, Brooklyn, New York; BSc., (EE); MSc., (EE); MIEE. *Appointments:* Engineer, Ministry of Communications, Lagos, 1966-72; Director, Littleways Electrical Limited, 1972-80; Senior Lecturer, Ogun State Polytechnic, Abedkuta, 1980-. *Memberships:* Council of Registered Engineers of Nigeria. *Publications:* Chief Oga-llu of Eyetoro, 1978; Chief Jagunmolu of Idofoi Ayetoro, 1981; Commendation award by Federal Government for Professional Work, Telephones, 1968; College Letterman, (Soccer), 1965. *Hobbies:* Music; Travelling; Dancing; Football (Soccer). *Address:* 29 Abeokuta Road, Eyetoro Egbado, Isokan Local Government, Ogun State, Nigeria.

OLATERU-OLAGBEGI, Benson Adeyanju. b. 3 Dec. 1941, Owo, Nigeria, Ondo State. Director. m. Ayodele, 25 Sept. 1971, 1 son, 2 daughters. *Education:* BSc., Hons. Economics; MSc., Business Management; Diploma, Development Economics; Fellow, Economic Development Institute, of the World Bank. *Appointments:* Director, Merchant Banking Operations, Nigerian Bank for Commerce. *Address:* Plot 1262, Adeola-Odeku Street, Victoria Island, Lagos, Nigeria.

OLATUNJI, Francis. b. 28 Dec. 1944, Isanlu Makutu, Kwara State, Nigeria. Librarianship. m. Felicia Funsho Bello, 15 Aug. 1970, 2 sons, 1 daughter. *Education:* BA. (Hons.), 1971; Post-Graduate Diploma in Librarianship, 1974. *Appointments:* Librarian II, Kwara State Library Services, 1974-76; Librarian II, 1976-77, Librarian I, 1977-78, Senior Librarian, 1978-80, Principal Librarian, 1980-, Kwara State College of Technology, Ilorin. *Memberships:* Kwara State Division Secretary, Nigerial Library Association, 1977-80, National Secretary, 1980-. *Publications:* Dissertation: Transports and Transportation in Kafamchan Kagoro Districts, 1971; Bibliography: Markets and Marketing in Independent Nigeria, 1961-73, Ibadan Department of Library Studies, University of Ibadan, Ibadan, 1974. *Honours:* Best Student, Igbaja Teachers College, 1959-61. *Hobbies:* Reading; Driving; Photography. *Address:* B5 Senior Staff Quarters, Kwara State College of Technology, Ilorin, Nigeria.

OLATUNJI, Taoheed Adebola. b. 2 June 1936, Ijebu-Ode, Nigeria. Legal Practitioner. m. 3 sons, 1 daughter. *Education:* LL.B., (London), 1964; Called to Nigerian Bar, 1966. *Appointments:* Private Legal Practice, 1966-70; Executive Director of Opportunities Industrialization Centre, Lagos, 1970-73; Legal Adviser to Investment Holdings Limited, 1974-80; Principal Partner of Adebola Olatunji & Company, Private Legal Practice, 1980-. *Memberships:* Ikoyi Club, 1938; Obanta Social Club; Oduduwa Lodge. *Hobbies:* Lawn Tennis; Squash. *Address:* 69A Patey Street, Ebute-Metta, Lagos, Nigeria.

OLAYEMI, Thomas Folorunsho. b. 20 Aug. 1949, Odo-Ere, Kwara State, Nigeria. Medical Records Administration. m. Joyce Bosede Adeola, 19 May 1973, 2 sons. *Education:* Government College, Keffi, Nigeria, 1964-68; Nalgo Correspondence Institute, London, 1972-74; BSc., RRA, College of St Scholastica, Duluth, USA, 1975-79. *Appointments:* Medical Records Clerk, 1969-75; Honorary NYSC, Higher Medical Records Officer, 1980; Senior Medical Records Officer, 1981. *Memberships:* Nigerian Red Cross Society. *Hobby:* Photography. *Address:* Okutadudu Street, P.A. Odo-Ere, Odo-Ere Via Ilorin, Kwara State, Nigeria.

OLD, Greensill Selby. b. 27 May 1905, North Sydney, NSW, Australia. Retired Librarian. *Education:* BA, Hons., 1928, LL.B., University of Sydney, Australia, 1935; Diploma, Library Training, University College of Dublin, Republic of Ireland, 1939. *Appointments:* Librarian, Law Society of New South Wales, Sydney, Australia, 1948-70. *Memberships:* Library Association of Australia; Law Librarians Group; Friends of Sydney University Library; Book Collectors' Society; Society of

Australian Genealogists; Honorary Secretary, Australian Antiochian Orthodox Diocese Trust; East-West Churches Association; North District Sydney Committee; Scout Association of Australia. *Publications:* Reading List of the books on Orthodox churches in the Fisher Library of the University of Sydney, 1980; Contributor to professional journals including: Story of Historic House, Waverton, 1974; The Old family of Waverton, 1980. *Honours:* MIBA, 1977. *Hobby:* Reading. *Address:* 2/74 Milray Avenue, Wollstonecraft, Australia, 2065.

OLIBAMOYO, Oluyemi, b. 18 Jan. 1949, Igbotako. Chemist. m. Adekunbi Balogin 15 Mar. 1975, 2 sons, 1 daughter. *Education:* BSc., (Hons), Chemistry, University of Ibadan, Ibadan, 1972. *Appointments:* Medical Representative, Senior Medical Representative, Wellcome (Nigeria) Limited; Divisional Manager, Jonssen Pharmaceuticals, Johnson & Johnson (Nigeria) Limited; O.T.C. Manager, Embechem Limited, Ikeja, Lagos, Nigeria. *Memberships:* Nigerian Institute of Management; Associate, Institute of Marketing. *Hobbies:* Football; Swimming; Table Tennis; Singing. *Address:* 17 Erelu Danisa Street, Ijesha-Tedd, Lagos, Nigeria.

OLIVE, Charles Gordon Chaloner, b. 3 July 1916, Brisbane, Australia. Director, Farmer, Artist. m. Beryl Gwendoline North, 2 sons, 2 daughters (one deceased). *Education:* University of Queensland; RAAF College, Point Cook, Victoria. Australia. *Appointments:* Civil Engineering Cadet, 1934-35; Fighter Pilot, RAF, 1937-43; Fighter Pilot, RAAF, 1943-46; Executive in Manufacturing Industry, 1947-81; Chairman, Metropolitan Fire Brigage Board, 1979-; Queensland State Fire Service Council, 1979-; Australian Assembly of Fire Authorities, 1979-; Board member of Brisbane Gas Company Limited, Director. *Memberships:* State Commandant, Air Training Corps, RAAF (Queensland), 1950-70; Commandant No 23 City of Brisbane Squadron (Auxillary), 1960-70; United Services Club, Brisbane, 1946-, President, 1970-71; Guild of Air Pilots & Navigators, Australian Region; Chairman, Australian Chapter, Battle of Britain Pilots Association. *Publications:* Series of Oil Paintings of Battle of Britain. *Honours:* Commander of Order of the British Empire, (Civil Division), 1978; MBE, 1961; Distinguished Flying Cross, 1940; Air Efficiency Award, RAAF, 1970; Cadet Forces Medal, 1965; Honorary Aide de Camp to HM Elizabeth II, 1961-63. *Hobbies:* Painting; Music; Pony Breeding. *Address:* Mail Service 21, Kalbar, Queensland, Q4309, Australia.

OLIVIER, Laurence Kerr (Lord), b. 22 May 1907, Dorking, Surrey, England. Actor, Director. m. (1) Jill Esmond, 1930, (marr. diss. 1940), 1 son, (2) Vivien Leigh, 1940, (marr. diss. 1961), (3) Joan Plowright, 1961, 1 son, 2 daughters. *Education:* MA Hon. Tufts, Mass., 1946; Honorary DLitt: Oxon, 1957, Manchester, 1968, Sussex, 1978; Honorary LLD, Edinburgh, 1964; Honorary DLitt, London, 1968. *Appointments:* First appeared, 1922 at Shakespeare Festival, Stratford-on-Avon special boys' performance as Katherine in Taming of the Shrew; Appeared in innumerable contemporary and classical stage and film productions world-wide; Lieut (A) RNVR until released from Fleet Air Army, 1944 to co-direct The Old Vic Theatre Company; Appointed Director of National Theatre, 1963; Directed numerous stage productions; Produced and Directed several Films; Associate Director, National Theatre, 1973-74 *Memberships:* South Bank Theatre Board, 1967-; South Bank Theatre and Opera House Board, 1962-67. *Honours:* Sonning Prize, Denmark, 1966; Gold Medallion, Swedish Academy of Literature, 1968; Special Award for directorship of National Theatre, Evening Standard, 1973; Albert Medal, RSA, 1976; Honorary Oscar, 1979, for lifetime's contributions to films; Commander Order Dannebrog, 1949; Officier Legion d'Honneur, 1953; Grande Officiale dell' Ordino al Merito della Repubblica (Italian), 1953; Order of Yugoslav Flag with Golden Wreath, 1971; Kt., 1947; Order of Merit, 1981. *Hobbies:* Tennis; Swimming; Motoring; Flying; Gardening. *Address:* 33/34 Chancery Lane, London, WC2A 1EW, England.

OLIVER, Michael Francis, b. 3 July 1925, Borth, Wales. Medicine. m. Margaret Yool Abbey, 1947, (Separated 1979), 3 sons, (one deceased), 1 daughter. *Education:* Marlborough College, Wiltshire, 1939-42; MB.,Ch.B, Edinburgh, 1947; MD., (Gold Medal) University of Edinburgh, 1957; FRCP.Ed., 1957; FRCP., 1969; FFCM., 1973. *Appointments:* Consultant Physician,

Royal Infirmary, 1961; Senior Lecturer, 1961, Reader in Medicine, 1973, Personal Professor of Cardiology, 1977, Duke of Edinburgh Professor of Cardiology, University of Edinburgh, 1978-; President, British Cardiac Society, 1981-. *Memberships:* British Cardiac Society; Chairman, British Atherosclerosis Group, 1970-75; Association of Physicians and Medal Research Society; Chairman, Council on Atherosclerosis and Ischaemic Heart Disease of the International Society of Cardiology, 1968-75; Chairman, Science Committee, Fondation Cardiologique Princess Lilian; Convener, Cardiology Committee, Scottish Royal College; British Heart Foundation. *Publications:* Acute myocardial infarction, 1966; Intensive Coronary Care, 1970, second edition, 1974; Effect of acute ischaemia on myocardial infarction, 1972; Modern trends in cardiology, 1975; High density lipoproteins and arherosclerosis, 1978; Coronary heart disease in young women, 1978; More than 200 contributions to scientific and medical journals on causes of coronary heart disease, biochemistry of fats, myocardial metabolism, mechanisms of sudden death, clinical trials of drugs and population studies of vascular diseases. *Honours:* facc., h.c. 1973; MD., h.c. Karolinska, 1980. *Hobbies:* English porcelain; History; Travelling. *Address:* Ladyurd House, Blythebridge, Peeblesshire, EH46 7DH, Scotland.

OLIVER, Nicholas William John, b. 6 Aug. 1933, Auckland, New Zealand. Consultant Physician. m. Elizabeth Ann Barber, 17 Aug. 1957, 1 son, 3 daughters. *Appointments:* London University, St Mary's Hospital, 1950-56; MB.,BS. (London), 1956; D.Obst. R.C.O.G., 1962; MRCP., (London), 1968; MRACP, 1977; FRACP, 1978. *Appointments:* House Surgeon & House Physician, St Mary's Hospital, London, 1956-57; RAF Medical Officer, 1957-60; Casualty Officer, Obst. Officer, Paediatric Officer, Northampton General Hospital, 1960-61; RAF Medical Officer, 1962-70, (Wing Comdr.); SHO., Brompton Hospital, London, 1968; Medical Specialist, RAF Renal Unit, 1968-70; Medical Registrar, Glasgow Western Infirmary, 1970; Senior Registrar, Cardiff Royal Infirmary, 1971; Consultant Physician, East Glamorgan Hospital, 1972-76; Medical Specialist, Repatriation General Hospital, Hobart, 1976; Senior Medical Specialist, 1977-; Renal Physician, Royal Hobart Hospital, 1978-. *Memberships:* Australian Medical Association; Australian Gerontological Society; Australasian Society of Nephrology; Thoracic Society of Australia; International Society of Nephrology and Hypertension; Renal Association. *Publications:* Various publications on aspects of hypertension and renal disease. *Honours:* Surgical Prize, St Mary's Hospital, 1956; Honorary Councillor, Australian Post-graduate Federation in Medicine; Honorary Chairman of: Tasmanian Postgraduate Medical Committee and Tasmanian Committee, Australian Kidney Association; Honorary Secretary, Tasmanian State Committee, RACP. *Hobbies:* Golf; Walking; Reading; Music. *Address:* 25 Bealey Avenue, Lenah Valley, Hobart, Tasmania, Australia, 7008.

OLIVER, Oscar Neil Blackburne, (The Hon.), b. 16 Aug. 1933, Caulfield, Victoria, Australia. Member of Legislative Council, Parliament of Western Australia. m. Margaret Joy Treloar, 22 June 1962, 2 sons, 1 daughter. *Education:* Royal Melbourne Institute of Technology, Victoria. *Appointments:* Military Service, Australian Military Forces; Wool Broker, Australian and New Zealand; Construction Manager and Company Director, national building company, Australia; Member of Legislative Council, Parliament of Western Australia. *Memberships:* Vice-President and National Director, Multiple Sclerosis Society of Western Australia; Vice-President, Army Museum of Western Australia; Board of Churchlands College of Advanced Education, 1974-78; Chairman, Desirable Levels of Housing & Construction Indicative Planning Council of Western Australia, 1973-77; Councillor Confederation of Western Australia Industry, 1974-79; President, Housing Industry Association of Western Australia, 1975-77. *Honours:* Efficiency Decoration and Bar, 1973; Honorary Colonel, Royal Australian Corps of Transport, 1979. *Hobbies:* Sailing; Snow Skiing; Horse riding; Squash. *Address:* Hatuma Lodge, Old Northam Road, Chidlow, Western Australia.

OLIVEY, Freda Darling (Mrs W S Olivey), b. 31 Dec. 1924, Pembroke Parish, Bermuda. Transportation Specialist. m. Wallace Sterling, 14 June 1962. *Education:* Cambridge University, Junior & School Certificate.

Appointments: United States Government: US Army, 1945-48; US Air Force, 1948-54 (Seconded to Army, 1954-70); US NAVY, 1970-. *Memberships:* Imperial Order Daughters of the Empire, Regent, Educational Secretary; Bermuda Society of Arts; Bermuda National Trust; English Speaking Union; Vice President, International Adviser, Bermuda Girl Guides Association; Vice President, Chorus Chairman, Bermuda Musical an Dramatic Society; President, St George's Historical Society; Coral Beach and Tennis Club. *Honours:* OBE, 1981; Queen's Silver Jubilee Medal, 1977; Bronze Beaver, Girl Guides Association; Bermudiana Award, Bermuda Girl Guides Association. *Hobbies:* Music (Piano & Choral Singing); Gardening; Needlepoint; Tennis; Reading. *Address:* Chartwell, Nr 6 Wellington Park, St George's 1-12, Bermuda.

OLOKO, Simeon Olatunde, b. 27 Aug. 1931, Ibadan, Nigeria. Lawyer; Economist. m. Jessie Ibijola Oye, 5 Jan. 1960, 5 sons, 2 daughters. *Education:* BSc Economics, London School of Economics, 1954-57; Barrister at Law, Hon. Society of the Inner Temple 1956-58; Diploma in Industrial Administration, Centre D'Etudes Industrielles, Geneva Switzerland. *Appointments:*3 Solicitor and Advocate, Federal Supreme Court of Nigeria; Chief Executive, Western Nigeria Development Corporation, 1963-69, Housing Corporation, 1969-73; Secretary, Water Corporation; Executive Director and Company Secretary, Philips Nigeria, Limited. *Memberships:* Chairman, Ibadan Recreation Club; LSE Alumni Association; Western Nigeria Football and Amateur Boxing Association. *Honours:* Alcan Aluminium Presidential Award, 1965. *Hobbies:* Lawn Tennis; Billiards; Music; Art Collection. *Address:* Plot 225 Census Close, Surulere, Lagos, Nigeria.

OLORUNDA, Ayodeji Babatunde, b. 24 Mar. 1953, Ikare, Nigeria. Chartered Architect. *Education:* B.Arch. (Hons.), University of Nigeria, Enugu Campus, 1972-77; Professional Practice Examination, 1979. *Appointments:* Allied Architects, Ibadan, Nigeria, 1974-77, 1978-; Kaduna State Housing Authority, 1977-78. *Memberships:* Nigerian Institute of Architects, Assistant Secretary, Western Chapter. *Publications:* Jericho Market (Resettlement Scheme), Ibadan; Iyo State Government Television Broadcasting Complex, Iwo, Nigeria; Pulp and Paper Complex, Ikiti-Pupa (Thesis Project), 1977. *Honours:* Excellent Thesis Presentation, 1977. *Hobbies:* Painting; Music; Games. *Address:* H/14D Okeruwa Street, PO Box 107, Ikare, Ondo State, Nigeria.

OLORUNTOBA, Barnabas Sanyaolu, b. 30 Sept. 1928, Okeri, Swara State, Nigeria. Agriculturist/Agricultural Consultant. m. Elizabeth Dele Ogunjobi, 30 Dec. 1959, 2 sons, 2 daughters. *Education:* BSc Agriculture, University of Durham, United Kingdom, 1956-59. *Appointments:* Agricultural Assistant, Rice and Resettlement Projects, Shendam and Jamaa Areas, 1951-60; Secondment, Federal Office of Statistics, Agricultural Census Methodology, 1959-50; Senior Agricultural Officer, Zaria Province of Northern Nigeria. 1962-63; Principal Agrucultural Officer, Ministry of Agriculture Headquarters, Kaduna, 1964-65; Chief Agricultural Office, Northern Region of Nigeria, 1966-68; Chief Agricultural Officer Kwara State, Nigeria 1969; Director of Agriculture for Nigeria, 1970-74; Permanent Secretary, Federal Ministry of Agriculture 1975-78. *Memberships:* Overseas Cotton Advisory Board, Cotton Research Corporation; Agricultural Adviser, Lake Chad Basin Commission; Agriculture Adviser, FAO biennial and Regional conferences; Board of Trustees, International Livestock Centre, Ethiopia; Vice-Chairman, International Institution of Tropical Agriculture, Ibadan; Consultant, FAO Seed Industry, Valley Foods Limited, ADP and World Bank, 1972-81. *Honours:* Ford Foundation Grant; Officer of the Federal Republic of Nigeria 1978. *Hobbies:* Golf; Tennis; Photography. *Address:* 32 Yahaya Road, (GRA) Ilorin, PO Box 569, Ilorin, Nigeria

OLSON, Horace Andrew (Bud), b. 6 Oct. 1925, Iddesleigh, Alberta, Canada. Senator and Cabinet Minister. m. Lucille McLachlan, 1 son, 3 daughters. *Education:* Iddesleigh and Medicine Hat, Alberta. *Appointments:* Member of Parliament, Medicine Hat, 1957, 62, 63, 65, 68; Minister of Agriculture, Canada 1968-72; Senate 1977; House Leader Official Opposition, Deputy Leader, 1979; Minister of State, Economic Development, 1980-; Minister Northern Pipeline Agency 1980-.

Memberships: Commonwealth Parliamentary delegation Nigeria, 1962; Chairman, Sub-Committee for revising rules of procedure, 1963-64; Canadian Parliamentary delegation to USSR & Czechoslovakia, 1965; UN General Assembly, 1966; Chairman, Alberta Liberal Caucus 1973-74; Economic Council of Canada, 1975-79; Inter-Parliamentary Union delegation to Bulgaria, 1977. *Honours:* Centennial Medal, 1967; Citation for Distinguished Citizenship, Medicine Hat College, 1968; Hon. Col. South Alberta Light Horse Regiment, 1970; Queen's Silver Jubilee Medal, 1977. *Address:* General Delivery, Iddesleigh, Alberta, T0J 1T0, Canada.

OLUFOWOTE, Johnson Oluwole, b. 11 Aug. 1945, Igbile, Ogun State of Nigeria. Research Scientist, m. 14 Aug. 1976, 2 sons. *Education:* BSc Agriculture, 1969; MSc Agromomy, Plant Breeding and Genetics, 1975. *Appointments:* Rice Breeder, National Cereals Research Institute, Moor Plantation, Ibadan, Nigeria, 1969-81; Sub-Regional Co-ordinator, West Africa Rice Development Association, 1981-. *Memberships:* Genetics Socity of Nigeria; Science Association of Nigeria; West Africa Science Association; Institute of Biology. *Publications:* Thesis: Inheritance of resistance to Bacterial blight, Xanthomonas oryzea (Uyeda and Ishiyama) Dowson in Rice, 1975; 12 articles in Learned Journals; 9 articles in Scientific conferences and Workshop; 8 Training courses; 4 articles in Agricultural newsletters; Attended 16 International conferences and Siminars. *Hobbies:* Tourism; Gardening; Current Affairs. *Address:* No 39 Ndebaninge, Sithole Road, North Labone Estate, Accra, Ghana.

OLUJOBI, Tola, b. 25 Apr. 1941, Abeokuta, Nigeria. Advertising. *Education:* Higher Diploma in Secretarial Practice; Various Management Courses and Training in Company Secretaryship, Advertising and Research. *Appointments:* Personal Secretary, 1962-64; Assistant Company Secretary, 1965-70; Personal Assistant/Executive Secretary, 1970-74; Deputy Company Secretary, 1974-76; Research Co-ordinator, 1974-76; Executive Director, 1976-; Account Director, Advertising, 1976-; Company Secretary 1976-. *Memberships:* Market Research Society, London; Institute of Directors, London. *Hobbies:* Athletics; Dancing; Cooking; Reading. *Address:* 58 Amosu Street, Alaka Estate, Surulere, Lagos, Nigeria

OLUMBA, Ann Nosiri, b. 9 Sept. 1949, Mbieri Owerri, Imo State, Nigeria. Businesswoman. m. Rufus I Olumba, 8 Apr. 1971, 1 son, 3 daughters. *Education:* Colleges and Universities in Washington DC, USA, Iowa, Chicago, Florida and California; LLB 1974; MA 1975; PhD 1976. *Appointments:* Secretary, World Bank, Washington DC USA, 1972-73; Secretary, International University of Communication, Washington DC, 1973-74; Director, Pan African Employment Agencies, Washington DC, 1974-76; Managing Director, Baroness Enterprizes, Imo State Nigeria, 1978-. *Memberships:* Lumumba Foundation; Save Humanity Society of Africa; Afro-American Development Centre; Good Samaritan Order; International Association for the Promotion of African Heritage and Identity. *Publications:* The Social and Cultural Impact of Mass Communication Media on the Nigerian Traditional Society. *Hobbies:* Singing; Dancing; Reading; Debating. *Address:* PO Box 6, Mbieri Owerri, Imo State, Nigeria.

OLUMBA, Rufus I, b. 5 Jan. 1937, Umuduru Mbieri, Owerri, Imo State, Nigeria. Educationist; Businessman; Politician. m. Ann Nosiri, 8 Apr. 1971, 1 son, 3 daughters. *Education:* Howard University, Washington DC, USA; George Washington University; La Salle University, Chicago; DeVry Institute of Technology, Chicago; International University of Communication, Washington DC; Waldon University, Florida; California, National Open University, USA; BA 1967; MSc 1973; LLB 1974; MA 1974; PhD 1975; DBA 1976; DIM 1976; DSc 1978. *Memberships:* Lumumba Foundation, Save Humanity Society of Africa; Afro-American Development Centre; International Association for the Promotion of African Heritage and Identity. *Publications:* Many articles in newspapers and magazines; The Problems of Collective Action; The Case of Portuguese Colonialism in Africa, 1975; Methodological Issues and Problems of Administrative Theories: An Analytical Study. *Honours:* Numerous honours and awards for academic and social services and achievements including: DD; DLitt; DPH; LLD. *Hobbies:* Reading; Dancing; Football; Golf;

Debating. *Address:* Umuduru Mbieri, PO Box Mbieri, Owerri, Imo State, Nigeria.

OLUOCH, Apollo Richard, b. 15 June 1936, Siaya, Kenya. Librarian. m. 15 Jan. 1957, 4 sons, 4 daughters. *Education:* BA,. Makerere University, Uganda, Kenya, 1967; Dip., Lib., ALA., College of Librarianship, Wales, UK, 1969. *Appointments:* Director/Chief Librarian, Kenya National Library Service Club, Kenya. *Address:* 60/229/13 Makina Street, Langata, Nairobi, Kenya.

OLUSANYA, Gabriel Olakunle Olusegun, b. 2 July 1936, Abeokuta, Nigeria. University Professor. m. Megan Rose Clayton, 22 June 1963, 1 son, 4 daughters. *Education:* BA., Hons., London, University College, Ibadan, Nigcria, 1957-60; MA., University of British Columbia, Canada, 1961; PhD., University of Toronto, Canada, 1964. *Appointments:* Lecturer, Commonwealth History, Ahmadu Bello University, Zaria, Nigeria, 1964-66; Lecturer, Senior Lecturer, Professor of History, University of Lagos, Nigeria, 1966-; Director of Courses, National Institute for Policy and Strategic Studies, Nigeria, 1979-; on secondment from University of Lagos, Nigeria. *Memberships:* Historical Society of Nigeria; Vice-President, 1976-, African Association for Public Administration; Nigerian Society for International Affairs; Twelve Friends Auxilliary Society, Holy Trinity Church, Lagos, Nigeria; Methodist Boys High School Old Boys Association. *Publications:* The Second World War and Politics in Nigeria, 1973; The Evolution of the Nigerian Civil Service—The Problems of Nigeranization; The Unfinished Task, 1977; Yomba History and Philosophy, (in press); If Wishes were Horses, 1981; A History of the West African Students Union (in press); With Cook of Killimpray (in press); several articles in learned journals. *Honours:* World University Service Fellowship, 1960-61; Canada Council Fellowship, 1961-64; Sir Joseph Flavelle Fellowship, 1964; Sir Alexander Alexander Research Fellowship, 1964; Senior Inter-University Council Visiting Fellow, Centre of West African Studies University of Birmingham, UK, 1974; Honorary Research Fellow, University of Birmingham, UK, 1974; Visiting Professor, Karl-Marx University of Leipsig, GDR., 1979. *Hobbies:* Drama; Music; Walking; Collecting art work; Dancing. *Address:* National Institute for Policy and Strategic Studies, PMB., 24, Bukuru, Plateau State, Nigeria.

OLUSANYA, Olajide, b. 17 Apr. 1941, Lagos, Nigeria. Architecture. m. Josephine Adeola Bamgbose, 28 June 1980, 1 daughter. *Education:* B.Arch., Hons., 1970; Diploma, Royal Institute of British Architects, 1974. *Appointments:* Kola Bankole and Associates, 1969-; Egbor and Associates, 1970-. *Honours:* AA Prize, Outstanding abilities, 1968; Atlas prize, best thesis, final year, 1970; Ministry of Overseas Development Grant through Professor Douglas-Jones, Bristol, UK, into use of mud for cheap housing in Nigeria. *Hobbies:* Travelling; Gardening; Table Tennis; Lawn Tennis. *Address:* House 31, Cappa Estate, Maryland, Ikeja, Lagos, Nigeria.

OLUTOYE, Olufemi, b. 18 May 1931, Ido-Ani, Ondo State, Nigeria. Major General (retired), Business Manufacturing. m. Omotayo Johnson, 4 Apr. 1958, 3 sons, 3 daughters. *Education:* BSc., London, University College, Ibadan, Nigeria, 1950-54; Postgraduate Certificate, Education, Cambridge University, UK, 1955-56; MA., External, London University, UK, 1975. *Appointments:* Senior Biology Master, Olu-Iwa College, Ijebu-Ode, Nigeria, 1954-59; Chief Education Officer, 1964-67, Director of Rehabilitation 1969-75, Nigerian Army, 1959-77; Federal Commissioner (Minister), Social Development, Youth and Sports, Nigeria, 1975-77; Chairman, Ondo State Health Management Board, Nigeria, 1978-79. *Memberships:* Chairman, 1970-72, OAU Defence Commission; President, 1975-77, Nigerian Olympic Committee. *Publications:* Education of Handicapped Children in Nigeria, 1975 (unpublished). *Hobbies:* Squash rackets; International affairs; Lawn tennis. *Address:* 5 Obanlearo Crescent, Ilupeju, Lagos, Nigeria.

OMABOE, Emmanuel Noi, b. 29 Oct. 1930, Amanokrow, Ghana. Economic Consultant. m. Letitia Odofoley Manko, 29 Oct. 1958, 2 sons, 3 daughters. *Education:* Accra Academcy, Ghana, 1946-50; University College of Ghana, 1951-54; BSc., Hons., London School of Economics, UK, 1954-57. *Appointments:* Economics

Research Fellow, University of Ghana, 1957-59; Government Statistician, Ghana, 1960-66; Commissioner, Economic Affairs, Ghana, 1967-69; Managing Director, EN Omaboe Associates Limited, Ghana, 1969-. *Memberships:* Honorary Fellow, Royal Statistical Society; Past President, Economic Society of Ghana; Past Vice-President, International Statistical Institute; International Union for the Scientific Study of Population; American Statistical Association. *Publications:* Education of Handicapped Children in Nigeria, 1975 (MA Thesis); Study of Contemporary Ghana, (joint author). *Honours:* Grand Medal, Republic of Ghana, 1968; Enstooled Chief, Gyasehene of Akuapem under Stool name, Nana Wereko Ampem II, 1975. *Hobbies:* Golf; Soccer. *Address:* 4 Roman Road, Accra, Ghana.

OMARI, Dunstan Alfred, b. 9 Aug. 1922, Newala, Tanzania. Company Director. m. Fidelia Shangali, 23 Apr. 1962, 2 sons, 1 daughter. *Education:* Diploma, Teaching, Makerere College, Uganda, 1943-45; BA., Hons., University College of Wales, Aberystwyth, Wales, UK, 1949-53. *Appointments:* Teacher, 1946-49; Education Officer, 1953-54; Administrative Officer, District Officer, 1955-58; District Commissioner, 1958-61; Tanganyika's first High Commissioner to UK, 1961-62; Permanent Secretary and Secretary to Cabinet, Tanganyika, 1962-63; Secretary General, East African Common Services Organisation and Community, 1964-68; Company Director, 1968-. *Memberships:* Chairman, East African Currency Board, 1964-72; Chairman, African Medical and Research Foundation; Fellow, Institute of Directors, UK. *Creative Works:* Talks on Citizenship, 1954. *Honours:* MBE., 1961. *Hobbies:* Carpentry; Photography; Badminton. *Address:* PO Box 25015, Nairobi, Kenya.

OMBU, Jigekuma Ayebatari, b. 4 May 1938, Okpoma, Rivers State, Nigeria. Librarian. m. Bomo Orungele, 6 Feb. 1969, 2 sons, 3 daughters. *Education:* Dip. Lib., Institute of Librarianship, University of Ibadan, Nigeria, 1963-64; MLS., 1975, School of Library and Information Science, University of Western Ontario, London, Canada, 1973-75. *Appointments:* Assistant Librarian-/Sub-Librarian, University of Ibadan, Nigeria, 1966-70; Sub-Librarian/Senior Sub-Librarian/ Deputy Librarian/Chief Librarian, College of Science and Technology, Port Harcourt, Nigeria, 1971-80; University Librarian, Rivers State University of Science and Technology, Port Harcourt, Nigeria, 1980-. *Memberships:* Chairman, 1976-78, Council, 1980-, Rivers State Division, Nigerian Library Association. *Publications:* Niger Delta Studies, 1627-1967, 1970; The Benin Kingdom from earliest times to 1969, (in press); 3 articles in professional journals. *Honours:* Best Scholar, Aggrey Memorial College, Arochukwu, Nigeria, 1957. *Hobbies:* Listening to instrumental music; Shortwave broadcasts listening; Photography; Book collecting. *Address:* 4 Road B, Rivers State University of Science and Technology Campus, Port Harcourt, Nigeria.

O'MEALLY, His Honour Judge, John Lawrence, b. 18 Nov. 1939, Coogee, New South Wales, Australia. Law (Judge). m. Mary Ethel Hartley, 7 Jan. 1972, 4 sons. *Education:* LL.B., University of Sydney, Australia, 1962. *Appointments:* Associate to the Hon. Mr. Justice Nagle, 1960-61; Admitted New South Wales and Australian Bars, 1964; Admitted Papua-New Guinea Bar, 1965; Admitted Western Pacific Bar, 1970; Acting Judge, National Court of Justice, Papua New Guinea, 1977; Judge, Workers Compensation Commission of New South Wales, 1979; Commissioned Australian Army Legal Corps, 1967; Colonel, Chief Legal Officer (A Reserve) 2nd Military District; Consultant to Director, Army Legal Services, 1979. *Memberships:* Executive Committee and International Issues Committee, Australian Section, International Commission of Jurists; Director, Sydney University Union, 1961-62; Secretary, 1962, Vice President, 1963-64, Sydney University Law Graduates Association. *Hobbies:* Swimming; Music; Reading. *Address:* Judges Chambers, 131 Macquarie Street, Sydney, New South Wales 2000, Australia.

OMIDIORA, Chief Johnson Olabisi, b. 12 Mar. 1933, Ile-Ife, Nigeria. Chartered Accountant. m. Eyinade Aderemi, 18 Jan. 1958, 1 son, 4 daughters. *Education:* BSc., Hons., London School of Economic and Political Science, UK, 1959-62; Diploma, Communication and Family Planning, University of Chicago, USA, 1970;

ACA., 1966; FCA., 1976. *Appointments:* Chief Accountant, 1975-78, Executive Director, General Manager, R & A Services Division, UAC of Nigeria Limited; Director, United Insurance Co. of Nigeria Limited; Chairman, Vono Products Limited, Nigeria. *Memberships:* Council, Institute of Chartered Accountants of Nigeria; Hon. Treasurer, Family Planning of Nigeria; President, Oduduwa College Old Students Association. *Honours:* Conferred with the Chieftancy Title of Obasegbatan of Ife, the Cradle of Yoruba race for Services done to the town. *Hobbies:* Badminton; Tennis; Farming; Reading history. *Address:* 14 Mekunwen Road, Ikoyi, Nigeria.

OMIGIE, Francis Omoruyi b, 25 July 1934, Benin City, Bendel State, Nigeria. Medical Records Officer. m. Olabisi Turner-Shaw, 26 June 1963, 3 sons, 2 daughters. *Education:* Diploma, Medical Records Sci., Bristol Royal Infirmary, UK, 1961-63. *Appointments:* Deputy Medical Records Officer, Lagos University Teaching Hospital, Lagos, Nigeria, 1964-72; Chief Medical Records Officer, University of Benin Teaching Hospital, Bendel State, Nigeria, 1972-. *Memberships:* National Secretary, 1969-72, National President, 1978-80, Nigerian Health Records Association. *Publications:* Medical Records in National Health Development, 1976; Medical Records in Developing Countries, The Nigerian Experience, 1980. *Honours:* Fellowship, Nigerian Health Records Association, 1979; Elected Nigerian Director, International Federation of Health Records Organisation, The Hague in 1980 for four years, 1980-84. *Hobbies:* Reading; Table tennis. *Address:* House B11, UBTH., Staff Quarters, Ugbowo, Benin City, Bendel State, Nigeria.

OMO-BARE, Adams Osagie, b. 1 Sept. 1954, Benin City, Nigeria. Footwear Technologist. 1 daughter. *Education:* Diploma, Advanced Footwear Technology, Wellingborough Technical College, UK, 1976-78; Diploma, Industrial Management, The Centre for Business Studies, London, UK, 1979. *Appointments:* Stores Control Officer, Omo-Bare & Sons (Nigeria) Limited, 1973-76. *Memberships:* Benin Club. *Publications:* Footwear and its Industry. *Honours:* Best Student awards, Wellingborough Technical College, UK, 1978. *Hobbies:* Music; Lawn tennis; Swimming. *Address:* No 1 Omo Bare Street, Box 210, Benin City, Bendel State, Nigeria.

OMOERHA, Thompson, b. 29 Sept. 1943, Fugar, Etsakor Division, Bendel State, Nigeria. Librarianship. m. Apr. 1972, 1 son, 4 daughters. *Education:* BA., Hons., 1964-68, University of Ibadan, Nigeria; Post graduate Librarianship, 1969-70. *Appointments:* Library Assistant, 1963-64, Assistant Librarian, 1968-69, University of Ibadan, Nigeria; Assistant Librarian, University of Ife, Nigeria, July-Sept. 1969; Archivist, National Archives of Nigeria, Ibadan, Nigeria, 1970-79; Sub-Librarian, University of Benin, Nigeria, 1970-75; Librarian, 1975, Chief Librarian, 1979, Petroleum Tr. Institute, Warri, Nigeria. *Memberships:* Nigeria Library Association; Nigerian Institute of Management. *Publications:* Rapid preliminary communications in science and technology, 1973; The Cataloguing of Arabic materials and the Anglo-American Cataloguing Rules, 1973; African Government publications: problems of acquisition and organisation, 1974; Nigerian Arabic manuscripts: State of Documentation, 1973; Cataloguing and Classification at the University of Benin Library, 1973; Marc-orientated Union Data Base for Nigeria, 1974; Nigerian personal authors and the application of the Anglo-American Cataloguing Rules (with others), 1974; Edo Studies: Preliminary bibliography, 1976. *Honours:* Departmental prize, Librarianship, 1969-70; Inter-University Council award, 6 months visiting Fellowship to study British University Library systems and computer applications; Attended 4 months International Graduate Summer School, University of Wales, UK; Attended London and Frankfurt Bookfair. *Hobbies:* Table tennis; Reading; Gardening. *Address:* A3/8 PTI Staff Quarters, PTI Campus, Effurun, Nigeria.

OMOLAOYE, James Akanmu, b. 6 Mar. 1948, Ilemowu-Iwo, Nigeria. Architecture. m. Elizabeth Olusola Ojo, 1 Jan. 1977, 1 son, 1 daughter. *Education:* BSc., Hons., 1973, MSc., 1975, Ahmadu Bello University, Zaria, Nigeria; MNIA., 1977. *Appointments:* Associate, Archlon, Nigeria, 1975-. *Memberships:* Board of Governors, Ilupesu Grammar School, Ilemowu-Ilo; Planning Advisor, Lagos branch, Telemu Elite Club; Adviser, Ilemowu Elite Club, Ilemowu-Ilo, Nigeria.

Creative Works: Has designed many buildings constructed in Lagos, Nigeria including: Gbagada General Hospital, Mushin, Lagos, Nigeria; Ikorodu General Hospital, Lagos, Nigeria. *Hobbies:* Table tennis; Travelling. *Address:* 26 Obayan Street, Akoka, Yaba, Lagos, Nigeria.

OMOLOLU, Adewale, b. 15 Nov. 1927, Lagos, Nigeria. Public Health Nutritionist. m. Olabisi Olufunke Soetan, 25 Jan. 1955, 1 son. *Education:* LRCPI., LRCSI., LM., Royal College of Surgeons in Ireland, UK; Diploma, Public Health, School of Hygiene and Tropical Medicine, University of London, UK, 1961-62; MRCPI., 1964, FRCPI., 1972, Royal College of Physicians in Ireland, UK. *Appointments:* Houseman, Senior House Officer, Registrar, Paediatrics, UCH. Ibadan, Nigeria, 1953-58; Medical Research Fellow, Institute of Child Health, 1959-61, Lecturer, Senior Lecturer and Reader, Human Nutrition, 1963-67, University of Ibadan, Nigeria; WHO Fellow, Public Health and Nutrition, 1961-63; Professor, Human Nutrition and Consultant Nutritionist, 1972-; WHO Consultant, Government of Mauritius, Nutrition and Maternal and Child Health, 1966; Member, WHO Advisory Panel on Nutrition, 1970-; Member and Vice-Chairman, United Nations University's Advisory Committee on World Hunger, 1974-79; Council member, International Union of Nutritional Sciences, 1974-. *Memberships:* Past Secretary and Treasurer, Nutrition Society of Nigeria; Past Chairman, Association of Sports Medicine; Past President, Society of Health of Nigeria; Paediatric Association of Nigeria. *Publications:* Nutrition and the African Child in Biomedical Lectures, 1970-73 series, 1975; Food Famine and Health, 1974; Nutrition in Africa, 1975. *Honours:* University graduate prize in Physics, Chemistry, Biology, Physiology and Anatomy, Royal College of Surgeons in Ireland, UK; Prize, Diploma in Public Health, University of London, UK, 1962. *Hobbies:* Cricket; Table tennis. *Address:* 24 Elliot Close, University of Ibadan, Ibadan, Nigeria.

OMONIRA, (Chief) Olusola, b. 8 Oct. 1934, Ibasa, Lagos, Nigeria. Economist; Chartered Accountant. m. Ronke Egbaiyelo, 6 Oct. 1962, 4 sons, 2 daughters. *Education:* ACIS., South West London College, UK, 1963; MBIM., Kingston Polytechnic, Surrey, UK, 1965; Dip., Ed., University of London, Garnet College, UK, 1966; MSc., University of Aston, Birmingham, UK, 1967; Associate of Certifited and Corporate Accountants, 1968. *Appointments:* Senior Accounts Clerk, Accounting Assistant, Western Region Marketing Board, 1958-61; Cost Assistant Accountant, British Aircraft Corporation, Weybridge, Surrey, UK, 1963-65; Cost Accountant, AEI-Hill Top Foundry, Wednesbury, UK, 1967-68; Lecturer, Managerial Accounting, School of Management, Surrey, UK, 1968-70; Lecturer, Accounting, Ahmadu Bello University, Zaria, Nigeria, 1970-71; Financial Controller, Ag., General Manager, Nifinco, Ibadan, Nigeria, 1971-72; Financial Controller, National Supply Co. Limited, Nigeria, 1972-74; Principal Consultant and Chairman, Omo Group Organisation, Nigeria, 1974-79; National Assembly, Lagos, Nigeria, 1979-. *Memberships:* Associate, Chartered Institute of Secretaries; Fellow, Association of Certified Accountants; Fellow, Institute of Chartered Accountants of Nigeria. *Publications:* Several publications in professional journals and newspapers. *Honours:* Awarded three Chieftancy titles: Oghetolu of Ugbo, Ilaje; Aseto of Mahin, Ilaje; Iyun Oba of Etikn, Ilaje. *Hobbies:* Fishing; Historical reading; Meeting people. *Address:* National Assembly Street E, Flat 105, Victoria Island, Lagos, Nigeria

OMOSINI, Olufemi, b. 29 Dec. 1941, Eluomoba Ekiti, Ondo State, Nigeria. University Lecturer. m. Bosede Dina, 5 Feb. 1972, 2 sons, 3 daughters. *Education:* BA., Hons., London, University of Ibadan, Ibadan, Nigeria, 1960-64; PhD., Cantab., University of Cambridge, UK, 1965-69. *Appointments:* School teacher, Ado Grammar School, Ado-Ekiti, Nigeria, 1961; History tutor, Ibadan Grammar School, Ibadan, Nigeria, 1964; Assistant Registrar, West African Exams Council, Ghana, 1964-65; Lecturer, 1969-, Senior Lecturer, 1974-, University of Ife, Ile-Ife, Nigeria. *Memberships:* Historical Society of Nigeria. *Publications:* Author of many articles in learned journals including: Journal of Historical Society of Nigeria; International Journal of African Historical Studies; Odu: Journal of West African Studies; Sierra Leone Studies; Africa; Author of several book chapters; British Economic Imperialism and West

African Resistance 1880-1914 (in press). *Honours:* State Scholar, 1960-64, College Scholar, 1961-64, University of Ibadan, Nigeria; Commonwealth Academic Staff Fellow, 1976-77; Elected fellow, Institute of Commonwealth Studies, Oxford University, UK, 1976-77; Elected Associate Fellow, Clare Hall, Cambridge University, UK, 1976-77. *Hobbies:* Photography; Swimming. *Address:* 11 Okenaun Street, Iluomoba Ekiti, Ondo State, Nigeria.

OMOTOSO, Bankole Ajibabi, b. 21 Apr. 1943, Akure, Nigeria. University teacher; Writer. m. Marguerita L Rice, 7 Apr. 1973, 2 sons, 1 daughter. *Education:* BA., Hons., University of Ibadan, Nigeria, 1968; PhD., University of Edinburgh, Uk, 1972. *Appointments:* Lecturer, University of Ibadan, NIgerIa, 1972-76; Senior Lecturer, University of Ife, Nigeria, 1976-. *Memberships:* Union of Writers of African Peoples; Association of University Unions. *Publications:* The Edifice, 1971; The Combat, 1972; To Borrow a Wandering Leaf, 1978. *Honours:* College Scholar, 1965-68, Commonwealth Scholar, 1969-72, University of Ibadan, Nigeria; OUP prize for Playwriting, 1968. *Hobby:* Travelling. *Address:* Osukoti Layout, Akure, Nigeria.

ONABANJO, Samuel Olufemi, b. 13 Sept. 1942, Ago-Iwoye, Ijebu, Nigeria. Medical Practitioner; Neursurgeon. m. Grace Ibiyemi Ogunnaike, 27 Sept. 1969, 3 daughters. *Education:* MB., BS., College of Medicine, University of Lagos, Nigeria, 1969; Fellow, Royal College of Surgeons, Edinburgh, UK, 1977. *Appointments:* Pre-Registration Houseman, 1961-70, Senior House Officer, Surgical Registrar, 1970-72, Senior Registrar in Neurosurgery, 1978-80, University College Hospital, Ibadan, Nigeria; Resident doctor, Walton Hospital, Liverpool, UK, 1974-75; Registrar, Surgery, Worcester Royal Infirmary, UK; Consultant Neurosurgeon, Ring Road State Hospital, Ibadan, Nigeria, 1980-. *Memberships:* Nigeria Medical Association; Neurosurgical Society of Nigeria. *Publications:* Extracranal Vascular Malformations in Nigerians; Delayed Post-Traumatic Extradural Haemorrhage. 1981; Melametric Neuroenteneous Syndrome in a Nigerian Infant. *Hobbies:* Swimming; Photography. *Address:* 40 Apate Street, Shomalu, Lagos State, Nigeria.

ONAH, Julius Onuora, b. 10 July 1939, Orba, Isi-Uzo, LGA., Nigeria. Marketing. m. Bridget N Anieke, 14 Aug, 1966, 1 son, 3 daughters. *Education:* BSc., Hons., University of Nigeria, Nsukka, Nigeria, 1961-65; MBA., MA., PhD., Michigan State University, E Lansing, USA, 1966-71; Diploma, Marketing Management, Research Institute for Management Sciences, Delft, Holland, 1976. *Appointments:* Tutor, Igbo-Ekiti Grammar School, Adada, 1960-61; Teaching Assistant, University of Nigeria, Nsukka, NIgeria, 1965-66; Salesman, Meijers Supermarket, Lansing, USA, 1968-69; Instructor, Lansing Commercial College, Lansing, USA, 1969-70. *Memberships:* American Marketing Association; British Institute of Marketing; Associate member, Market Research Society, UK; Nigerian Institute of Public Relations; 1st Vice-President, Chairman, Eastern Chapter, Nigerian Marketing Association. *Publications:* Books: Nigerian Cases in Business Management; Marketing in Nigeria; Management Practice in Developing Countries; Marketing Management for Developing Countries; Articles: Market Segmentation; Urban Poverty in Nigeria; Product deferentiation of Marketing revisited; Role of Marketing in Developing Countries. *Honours:* USAID/MSU., Fellowship, 1966-68; Royal Dutch Fellow, 1976; World Council of Churches Scholarship, 1969; Alpha Kappa Delta. *Hobbies:* Writing; Jogging; Gardening; Reading. *Address:* House 5, off Braithwaite Avenue, University of Nigeria Enugu Campus, Enugu, Nigeria.

ONAKPOYA, William Henslope, b. 15 June 1945, Abraka, Nigeria. Librarianship. m. 6 Aug. 1970, 5 sons, 1 daughter. *Education:* BA., Hons., 1972; PGDL., 1977; M.Ed., 1980. *Appointments:* Teacher, Bendel State of Nigeria Education Board; Librarian, College of Education, Abraka, Nigeria. *Memberships:* Ukoko Emotor President. *Hobby:* Reading *Address:* Library Department, College of Edu, Abraka, Bendel State, Nigeria.

O'NEIL, Desmond Henry, b. 27 Sept. 1920, Perth, Western Australia. Retired. m. Nancy Jean Culver, 18 Mar. 1944, 2 daughters. *Education:* Leaving Certificate, Aquinas College; Teachers Certificate, Claremont Teachers College. *Appointments:* Lieutenant, AIR,

1940, Captain 1941; Education Department, Western Australia; Member of Parliament, Canning Electorate, 1959; East Melville, 1962; Government Whip, 1962-65; Minister of Housing and Labour, 1965-73; Deputy Leader of Opposition, 1972-73; Minister for Works, Water Supply and Housing, 1974; Deputy Premier, 1975. *Memberships:* South of Perth Yacht Club; Mount Pleasant Bowling Club; Commonwealth Parliamentary Association. *Honours:* Title of Honorable, 1971; Knight Bachelor, 1980. *Hobbies:* Boating; Fishing. *Address:* 42 Godwin Avenue, South Como, Western Australia, 6152.

ONI, Felix Adeshokan, b. 5 Jan. 1951, Ibadan, Nigeria. Construction Executive. m. Helen Ibifaka Oni, 12 Feb. 1976, 1 son, 1 daughter. *Education:* BSc Hons. Political Science, 1972. *Appointments:* Assistant Secretary, 1972-76; Personnel Manager, 1976-78; Administrative Director, Harboni Limited, 1978-. *Memberships:* Ibadan Recreation Club; May Klub Ibadan. *Publications:* Joint Venture in Construction Business, Case Study, University of Edinborough, 1975. *Hobbies:* Football; Lawn/Table Tennis. *Address:* Plot 6, Oluyole Estate, 6th Avenue, Ring Road, Ibadan, Nigeria.

ONIONS, Peter Maurice Christopher, b. 17 May 1916, Oxford, England. Accountant. m. Frances, 2 Mar. 1950, 1 son, 1 daughter. *Education:* Oxford and Cambridge School Certificate, 1934; Fellow of Association of International Accountants, London, 1956. *Appointments:* Lloyds Bank Limited, 1934-39; War Service, 1939-47; Shell-Mex and BP Limited, 1948-50; Solictors, Lungley, Tapping and Roby, 1950-55; Company Secretary, Ricemans Limited, Deal, 1957; Divisional Controller and Company Budget Manager, Eatons of Canada, 1957-65; Divisional Controller, Steinbergs Limited Montreal, 1965-68; Controller, Vice President Finance and Director, Consumers Distributing Company Limited, 1969-81. *Memberships:* Light Infantry Club; Board of Trade of Metropolitan, Toronto. *Honours:* FAIA 1956. *Hobby:* Tennis. *Address:* 12 Crestview Road, Toronto, Ontario, M5N 1H4, Canada.

ONI-ORISAN, Babatunde Abayomi, b. 4 June 1932, Lagos, Nigeria. Librarianship. m. Mercy Omotayo Ibitokun, 1 son, 3 daughters. *Education:* BA (London), University College, Ibadan, 1955-59; PGCE (London), 1961-62; Diploma Librarian, University of Ibadan, 1965-66. *Appointments:* Graduate Teacher 1959-64; Assistant Librarian, 1964-67; Sub-Librarian, 1967-72; Senior Sub-Librarian, Ibadan University, 1972; Deputy University Librarian, University of Ife, 1972-76; Librarian, University of Ilorin, 1976-. *Memberships:* Historical Society of Nigeria; Nigerian Library Association; Advisory Committee on inter-library lending. *Publications:* Education, school Libraries and Nigerian's development plants, 1970-74; Present patterns of Library Services, 1973; A biography of Nigerian History. *Honours:* Fellowship, Special Commonwealth African Assistance Plan, 1971. *Hobby:* Table Tennis. *Address:* University of Ilorin, Ilorin, Nigeria.

ONUIGBO, Wilson Ikechuku Beniah, b. 28 Apr. 1928, Oraifite. Medical Practitioner. m. Edith Odukwe, 30 Sept. 1960, 1 son, 6 daughters. *Education:* BSc London University, 1954; MB, ChB, Glasgow University, 1957; DTM&H, Liverpool University, 1959; PhD London, 1961; MD Glasgow, 1979; FRCPath. Royal College of Pathologists, 1975. *Appointments:* Houseman, 1958, Medical Officer, Ministry of Health, Enugu, 1959; Lecturer on Pathology, College of Medicine, Lagos University, 1962-63; Pathologist, 1963-64, Senior Specialist, 1970, Chief Consultant, Ministry of Health, Enugu, 1974; Visiting Professor and Head of Department of Morbid Anatomy, Enugu Medical School, 1977-78; Founder Director, Medical, Foundation and Clinic, Enugu, 1978-. *Memberships:* Royal Society of Medicine; Pathological Society of Great Britain and Ireland; British Medical Association; Nigerian Medical Association; People's Club of Nigeria; Board of Governors, Oraifite Secondary School. *Publications:* PhD Thesis, Analytical studies on the topographical distribution of adrenal matastases in lung cancer; MD Thesis, studies on the geographical pathology of the Igbos of Nigeria; Over 100 research publications, mainly on cancer, in journales in several countries. *Honours:* Mission Scholar, DMGS, Onitsha, 1942-45; Government Scholar, Higher College, Yaba, 1946-47; John Reid Price, 1955; Mary Ure Prize, 1956; First Prize, Medical Students Essay Competition, 1957; University Research Fellow-

ship, Glasgow, 1962; Onowu Title, Oraifite, 1978. *Hobbies:* Music; Motoring; Writing. *Address:* PO Box 2, Oraifite, Anambra State, Nigeria.

ONWE, Chukwuka Okekpa, b. 21 Jan. 1942, Ngbo, Ishielu Local Government Area, Anambra State, Nigeria. Architecture. m. Ifeoma Henrietta, 29 Sept. 1973, 1 son, 2 daughters. *Education:* BArch (Hons), 1972; University of Nigeria, 1964-66, 1970-72; PPENIA 1974; MNIA 1975; ARCON (Full Reg.) 1975. *Appointments:* Architect Gd. II 1972; Executive Architect, 1974; Senior Architect, 1977; Principal Architect, 1979; Deputy Chief Architect, Housing Development Corporation, 1980-. *Memberships:* Christ Apostolic Church, Nigeria, Enugu. *Creative Works:* Major Architectural Works: Imo State Hotels, Owerri, Afiko, Okigwe, Umuahia, 1976; Benedictine Monastry Amorji Nike Enugu, 1976; Maternity Cum Paediatrix Complex Afikpo, 1976; Residential Building for Chief Al Egbunike Onitsha 1977; High Court Complex, Enugu, 1977; Residential Building for Dr Akanu Ibiam, Enugu, 1978; St Patricks Catholic Cathedral Abadaliki, 1978; Commercial Complex, A.S.H.D.C. Layout, Onitsha 1979. *Hobbies:* Lawn Tennis; Music; Fine Art; Photography; Preaching. *Address:* No 1 Amafor Street, Idaw River Layout, PO Box 2421, Enugu, Nigeria.

ONYANGO-OGONY, Philemon Jashon, b. 7 Nov. 1943, Kabale, Uganda. Doctor. m. Lilian Monica Otieno, 30 Aug. 1975, 1 son, 1 daughter. *Education:* MB, ChB, Makerere Medical School, Uganda, 1968-73; Diploma in Ophthalmology, Institute of Ophthalmology, London University, 1975-77; Master of Medicine, University of Nairobi, 1980. *Appointments:* Internship, Provincial General Hospital, Machakos, Kenya, 1973-74; Senior House Officer, Ophthalmology, 1974-75; Senior House Officer in Ophthalmology, Beckett Hospital, South Yorkshire, England, 1976; Senior House Officer, Aberdeen Royal Infirmary, 1976-77, Woodend General Hospital, Aberdeen Scotland; Provincial Eye Specialist, Eastern Province, Kenya. *Memberships:* Kenya Medical Association; Ophthalmological Society of East Africa; Scouting Movement. *Publications:* Purulent Ophthalmia Neonatorum, 1975; Oculosporidiosis, case report; Cyclopia, Synophthalmos, case report. *Honours:* Scholarship, Alliance High School, 1962; Government scholarship, Institute of Ophthalmology in London, 1975. *Hobbies:* Scouting; Athletics; Soccer. *Address:* Kenyatta National Hospital, PO Box 20723, Nairobi, Kenya.

ONYEAGOCHA, Sunday Chiedo, b. 21 Dec. 1922, Owerri, Nigeria. Forester (Retired Chief Conservator of Forests). m. Justina Ekwebelam, 28 Nov. 1948, 2 sons, 3 daughters. *Education:* OND, School of Forestry, Ibadan 1943-44, HND, 1951-52; BA Forestry, Oxford University, 1960-62. *Appointments:* Agricultural Assistant, 1941; Forest Assistant, 1943-57; Assistant Conservator of Forests to Principal Conservator, 1957-75; Chief Conservator of Forests, Imo State, Nigeria, 1976-77. *Memberships:* Masonic Freemason of English and Scottish Constitutions; Rotary Club of Owerri; Church Warden; Chairman, State Land-Use Committee; Federal Forest Research Institute of Nigeria Governing Body; Trustee, Forestry Society of Nigeria. *Publications:* Soil and Water Conservation in the Southern Zone of Nigeria, 1974; The establishment of Vegetation cover on waste lands in the Southern parts of Nigeria, 1974; The Role of Forestry in Erosion Control and Watershed management in Nigeria, 1980. *Honours:* Member of the Order of The Niger, 1979. *Hobbies:* Cricket; Football; Table Tennis; Painting; Photography; Hunting; Walking; Travelling. *Address:* 14 Ekeonunwa Street, PO Box 264, Owerri, Imo State, Nigeria

ONYEAMA, Charles Dadi, b. 5 Aug. 1917, Eke, Enugu, Nigeria. Barrister-at-Law. m. (1) Susannah Ogwudu 25 Mar. 1950, (2) Florence Wilcox, 5 Aug. 1966, 4 sons, 2 daughters. *Education:* King's College, Lagoa, 1931-35; Achimota College, Gold Coast, 1937; LLB (London) University College, 1937-40; Brasenose College, Oxford, 1940-41. *Appointments:* Chief Magistrate, Nigeria, 1952-57; Puisne Judge, Lagos, 1957-64; Justice of the Supreme Court of Nigeria, 1964-67; Judge, International Court of Justice, The Hague, 1967-76. *Memberships:* Royal Automobile Club, London; Royal Commonwealth Society London; Royal Overseas League, London; Metropolitan Club, Lagos, Nigeria. *Honours:* Doctor of Laws (Honoris causa), University of Nigeria, Nsukka. *Address:* Eke, via Enugu, Nigeria.

ONYESOH, Joseph Anaekwe, b. 5 Mar. 1933, Nigeria. Accountant. m. Chinwe Victoria, 27 Nov. 1971, 3 sons. *Education:* General Certificate of Education 1952; Associate member of the Association of Certified Accountants of the United Kingdom, 1965; Fellow, Association of Certified Accountants 1980; Fellow, British Institute of Management, 1980. *Appointments:* Group Accountant, INDECO Industrial Holdings of Zambia, 1968-71; Managing Director, 1971-75; Financial Controller, Cadbury Nigeria Limited, 1976-77; Finance Director, 1977-. *Memberships:* Council of the Institute of Chartered Accountants of Nigeria; Lagos Country Club. *Hobbies:* Lawn Tennis; Swimming; Travelling; Reading. *Address:* 15 Joel Ogunnaike Street, GRA Ikeja, Nigeria.

ONYIUKE, Gabriel Chike Michael, b. 7 June 1922, Nimo, Anambra State, Nigeria. Legal Profession. m. Vera Nneka Koggee, 15 Nov. 1952, 2 sons, 2 daughters. *Education:* LL.B., London, 1946; BL., 1947; *Appointments:* Director of Public Prosecutions, Eastern Region, Nigeria, 1960-64; Federal Attorney General, Federal Republic of Nigeria, 1966; Judge of High Court, Republic of Tanzania, 1970-74; Legal Consultancy, 1975-. *Memberships:* Founder member, World Association of Lawyers of the World Peace through Law Centre, 1976. *Publications:* Civil Procedure in Anglophonic Africa under the Auspices of Max Planck Institute, Hamburg, Germany, 1972. *Honours:* Officer of Order of Federal Republic of Nigeria, 1962; Queen's Counsel, 1960; Senior Advocate of Nigeria, 1979. *Hobby:* Golf. *Address:* 1 Adeyemi Lawson Road, Ikoyi, PO Box 659, Lagos, Nigeria.

OPARAOCHA, Christopher Ozobia, b. 23 Aug. 1941, Owerri, Nigeria. Veterinary Surgeon. m. Charity, 16 May 1967, 6 daughters. *Education:* BVs., University of East Africa, Nairobi, Kenya, 1967; MS., Royal Veterinary College, University of London, UK, 1971. *Appointments:* Veterinary Research Officer: Kahete, Kenya, 1967-68; Mazaluka, Zambia, 1968-74; Senior Lecturer, University of Zambia, 1974-78; Private Practice, Lusaka, Zambia, 1978-80. *Memberships:* President, University Games Union, Nairobi, 1965; Speaker, University Union, Nairobi, 1966-67; Secretary, Veterinary Association of Zambia, 1967-79; Regional Representative, Commonwealth Veterinary Association, 1978-80. *Publications:* Rabies in Zambia, 1969; Buffalo Disease in Zambia, 1973; Aspects of the pathology of the bovine placenta, 1974; A review of the skilled technical and professional manpower situation in regard to beef production with projections of availability of expertise up to 1981, 1975; Non protein Nitrogen Urea as a protein supplement for ruminants consuming poor Zambian Feeds (with EA Gihad), 1976. *Honours:* Victor Ludorum, University Games, 1965. *Address:* Plot Sub 5 of Sub 349, Great East Road, Lusaka, Zambia.

OPIE, Bruce James, b. 9 Jan. 1924, Shepparton, Australia. Chartered Town Planner. m. Helen Stobo Shera, 24 Apr. 1948, 1 son, 1 daughter. *Education:* Authorised Land Surveyor; Post-Graduate Diploma, Town and Regional Planning, University of Melbourne, Australia, 1952. *Appointments:* Chief Town Planner, 1953-68, Director of Statutory Planning, 1968-69, Town and Country Planning Board of Victoria, Australia; Town Planning member of staff, Russell, Kennedy and Cook, Solicitors, Melbourne, Australia, 1969-72; Private Practice and Managing Director, Planned Environment Services Pty. Limited, Australia, 1972-75; President, Australia Perth Mission, 1975-78; Director for Temporal Affairs, Southeast Asia Area, 1979-. *Memberships:* Fellow, Past Federal President, Divisional President and Federal Councillor, Royal Australian Planning Institute; Institution of Surveyors, Australia; Royal Town Planning Institute, UK; Regional Representative, SW Pacific Region, Commonwealth Association of Planners, 1970-75; Hong Kong Institute of Planners. *Hobbies:* Bush walking; Cricket; Reading. *Address:* 7 Castle Road, Central, Hong Kong.

OPIK, Armin Aleksander, b. 24 June 1898, Lontova Province, Viru, Estonia. Geologist; Palaentologist. m. Varvara Potashko, 28 Nov. 1919, 3 sons, 3 daughters. *Education:* Dr.Phil.,Nat., Tartu University, 1922-26. *Appointments:* Reader, 1926, Professor of Geology, Palaentology, Mineralogy, Tartu University; Director of Geology Institute and Museum; Teacher of Geology, Historical Geology, Palaentology, Mineralogy, Petrography; Teacher, Geology, Greifswald, Germany, 1944;

Worked with S von Bubnoft compiling a regional geology of Europe, 1948; Joined Bureau of Mineral Resources, Australia, 1948-80. *Memberships:* Palaentological Society of America, 1928; Geological Society of London, UK, 1938; Australian Academy of Science Fellow, 1965; Finnish Geological Society; American Association for Advancement of Science Fellow; Swedish Geological Society; Australian Geological Society; Australian Palaentological Society. *Publications:* Numerous publications including: Middle Cambrian Agnostios: Systematics and Biostratigraphy, 1979; Trilobites Dolichmetopio, (in press). *Honours:* Estonian Laureate for Science, 1935; Charles Doolittle Walcott Medal, Smithsonian Institute, USA, 1962; Award of Merit medal, PO Australia, 1966; Clarke Memorial Lecturer for 1965; Geologinen Tutkimuslaitos Medal, 1956. *Hobbies:* Writing poetry; Study of Archaeology; Chess; Study of Linguistics. *Address:* 14 Busby Street, O'Connor L601, Canberra, ACT., Australia.

OPIYO, Mary, Beatrice, Anyango, b. 18 Jan 1938, Kenya. Child Educator/Adult Educator. m. Michael Opiyo L.B. 22 Feb 1959, 4 sons, 1 daughter. *Education:* Communications, Facilitation Training, 1971-1974; Training in Evaluation of Functional Literacy Programmes; Diploma in Adult Education, University of Nairobi, 1980. *Appointments:* Teacher/Tutor, Teacher Training College, 1954-1957; Teacher Primary Schools, 1958-1970; Headmistress, Primary Schools, 1971-1976; Adult Educator, National Trainer of Literacy Workers for Protestant Churches in Kenya, 1976-. *Memberships:* Honorary Treasurer Literacy in Africa Society; Honorary Treasurer, Africa Adult Education Association; Treasurer, Kenya Adult Education Association; Executive Committee and Board member, Bible Society of Kenya; Executive Committee member, Literacy and Evangelism(Kenya); Executive Committee member, Kenya Music Festival. *Publications:* Compositions include Research Studies, Reports and case studies in connection with Literacy training, and adult education. Also published short stories. *Hobbies:* Music, classical and modern; revival of traditional foods; Music, Dance and Folklore of the Luo Tribe in Kenya, especially with women groups in both urban and rural areas, belonging to that tribe. *Address:* P.O. Box 40486, Nairobi, Kenya.

OPPERMAN, (Sir) Hubert Ferdinand, b. 29 May, 1904, Rochester, Victoria, Australia. Director. m. Mavys Paterson Craig, 14 Jan 1928, 1 son, 1 daughter. (deceased) *Education:* State School-Benalla, Melton, Ten Mile Armadale (All Victoria). *Appointments:* Federal Member Corio Victoria, 1949; Chief Government Whip, 1955; Minister Shipping and Transport, 1960; Minister for Immigration, 1963; 1st High Commissioner, Malta, 1967-1972. *Memberships:* U.S.I. Masonic Air Force Association; Bailiff Prior Victorian Priory, St. John of Jerusalem (Hospitallers) K.G.C. OSJ, Patron, Sportsmens' Association of Australia. *Publications:* Autobiography, Pedals Politics and People, 1977. *Honours:* Australian Road Cycling Champion 1924, 1926, 1927, 1929. Winner, French Bold'OR 1928: Paris-Brest. Paris (726 miles non-stop, 1931); Captain Australia Tour de France Team 1928-1931; Winner, United Kingdon Bidlake Memborial Prize, 1934. Holder world's unpaced track record 489 miles-motorcycle paced 24 hours, 860 miles, 1000 miles, 28hrs 55 mins. Awarded Tour de France Medal 1965, Medal Council of Paris 1971, Medal City Brest, Verona 1971, French Medal Merité, 1978; OBE 1952; Knight Bachelor, 1968. *Hobbies:* Swimming; Bushwalking; Cycling. *Address:* 6A Edgewatertowers, 12 Marine Parade, St. Kilda Victoria 3182, Australia.

ORAKWUSI, Alexander Oyibo Obunike, b. 27 Feb 1939, Oba, Anambra State, Nigeria. Lawyer. m. Dr. Ijeoma Nduka, 25 Dec 1975, 3 sons, 1 daughter. *Education:* LLB, University of London, 1963; LL.M. University of London, 1966. *Appointments:* Member Governing Council of University of Benin, Nigeria; Solicitor and Advocate of the Supreme Court of Nigeria. *Memberships:* President, Nigeria Union of Great Britain and Ireland 1965-66. *Hobby:* Photography. *Hobbies:* 2 Jalupon Close, Surulere, Lagos, Nigeria.

ORBIH, John Edward Agekame, b. 21 Dec 1944, Ogbona, Etsako Local Government Area, Bendel State, Nigeria. Architect. m. Cecilia Francisca Ikharelu Audu-Momoh 21 Aug 1976, 1 son. *Education:* B.Sc Hons. (Architecture) Ahmadu Bello University, Zaria, Nigeria,

1973; M.Sc (Architecture) Ahmadu Bello University, Zaria, Nigeria, 1975; P.P.E. 1977; M.N.I.A. *Appointments:* Allied Architects, Ibadan, 1975-1976; Bendel Development and Planning Authority, Benin City, 1976-1980; Hibro Edwards Archi-Services, P.O. Box 1218, Benin City, 1980-. *Memberships:* Honorary General Secretary Edo College Old Boy's Association; Chancellor of the Exchequer and Lieutenant Liege: Alpha Club, A.B.U. Zaria. *Hobbies:* General Reading; Current Affairs; Travelling. *Address:* 31 Ugbowo Housing Estate, Opposite U.B.T.H., Ugbowo, Benin City, Nigeria.

ORCHARD, Barbara, Winifred, b. 14 Aug 1932, Mt. Gambier, South Australia. Medical Practitioner. *Education:* MB.BS Adelaide 1959; DEH England, 1963; FRACMA, 1980. *Appointments:* Royal Adelaide Hospital, RMO, 1959; Adelaide Children's Hospital SMO, 1960; Queen Elizabeth Hospital, Adelaide, SMO, 1961; St. Mary's Hospital, London, Paediatric Registrar, 1963; Hospital for Sick Children, Great Ormond Street, London, SMO, 1962-1963; Various hospital appointments in United Kingdom, plus general practice both in UK and South Australia, 1963-1977; Medical Officer, South Australia Health Commission, School Health Branch, 1977-. *Memberships:* Secretary, Australian Federation of Medical Women; S.A. Medical Women's Society, A.M.A. B.M.A. Australian Association for Adolescent Health; Adelaide University Graduates Union; Australian Federation University Women; Australian Sports Medicine Federation; Member, South Australia Goverment Recreation Advisory Council; Community Fitness Review Committee; Graduates Union Representative, Adelaide University Sports Association; Trustee, South Australian Women's Memorial Playing Fields Trust. Former International Cricketer; Former Secretary, Australian Women's Cricket Council. *Honours:* South Australia Health Commission Study Award, 1978; Adelaide University Blue for Cricket, 1954. *Hobbies:* Music; Gardening; Recreation in general and Sport in particular. *Address:* 43 Coolah Terrace, Marion, South Australia, 5043.

ORCHARD, Peter, Francis, b. 25 March, 1927, Bromley, Kent, United Kingdom. Industrialist. m. Helen Sheridan, 14 May 1955, 2 sons, 2 daughters. *Education:* Magdalene College, Cambridge (Scholar), 1948-1950; 1st class honours Classical Tripos 1950; M.A. (Cantab). *Appointments:* Joined Thomas De La Rue & Co. Ltd, 1950; Managing Director, Thomas de la Rue (Brazil), 1959-1961; Managing Director, Thomas De La Rue International, 1962-1970; Director, The De La Rue Co. Ltd, 1963-; Chief Executive, The De La Rue Co Ltd, 1977-. *Memberships:* Travellers' Club, London; M.C.C.; Court of Assistants, The Drapers Company; Service with KRRC, 1944-1948. *Hobbies:* Gardening; Swimming; Cricket. *Address:* 5 Burlington Gardens, London W1A 1DL, England.

ORIJI, John Nwachimereze, b. 3 Mar. 1944, Eziama, Nvosi, Isiala, Ngwal. G. A, Imo State, Nigeria. Research Fellow. m. Rita Oriji, 31 May 1969, 1 daughter. *Education:* BA(Hons) History, Nigeria, 1967; MA, Johns Hopkins, 1974; MA, New Jersey, 1975; PhD, New Jersey, 1977. *Appointments:* Admin. Secretary, Home Publicity Bureau, Ministry of Information, Enugu, 1967-70; Research Fellow, Institute of African Studies, University of Nigeria, Nsukka, 1970-. *Memberships:* American Society for Ethno History; Educators to African Association; Historical Society of Nigeria. *Publications:* I History of Ngwa People, 1981; Articles: A study of the Palm Oil and Slave Trade in Ngwaland, 1981; Development of Oracular Trade in Ngwaland, 1981; Transformations in Traditinal Ngwa Society, 1981; A Review of the Oral History of the Ngwa, 1981. *Honours:* Foundation Scholarship, University of Nigeria, 1963-67; Federal Government of Nigeria Scholarship, 1972-77; Oilman Scholar, Johns Hopkins University, 1972-73; Teaching Fellowship Award, Rutgers University, 1976-77. *Hobbies:* Music; Dancing; Lawn Tennis; Debating. *Address:* No8 Umukanka Street, University of Nigeria, Nsukka, Nigeria.

ORIMOLOYE, Stephen Ademola, b. 14 Jan. 1935, Akure, Ondo State, Nigeria. Librarianship. m. Grace Aderonke Akeredolu, 1 Feb. 1964, 5 sons, 1 daughter. *Education:* BA, 1958-61, Institute of Librarianship, 1961-62, ALA, 1964, University College, Ibadan. *Appointments:* Assistant Librarian, Ibadan University, 1962-63; Lagos University, 1963-64; Sub-Librarian

and Senior Sub-Librarian, 1965-74, Deputy Librarian, 1974-77, Senior Deputy Librarian, Lagos University, 1977-. *Memberships:* Honorary Secretary, Association of Lagos University Teachers, 1967-68; Chairman, Nigerian Library Association, Lagos Division, 1970-71; Lagos University Senate, 1973-75; Business Committee of Senate, 1973-75; Publications Committee, Lagos University, 1973-; Nigerian Library Association. *Publications:* Biographia Nigeriana, a biographical dictionary of eminent Nigerians, 1977; Many professional articles in Librarianship journals etc. *Hobbies:* Music; Films; Videotapes; Cuff Links Collecting. *Address:* 1 Nana Close, Lagos University Campus, Akoka, Yaba, Lagos, Nigeria.

ORME, Stanley, b. 5 Apr. 1923, Sale, Cheshire, England. Member of Parliament. m. Irene Mary Harris, 1951. *Education:* National Council of Labour Colleges and Workers' Education Association Classes. *Appointments:* Shop Steward, Amalgamated Union of Engineering Workers, 1949-64; Councillor, Sale Borough Council, 1957-65; MP for Salford West, 1964-; Minister of State, Northern Ireland Office, 1974-76; Department of Health and Social Security, 1976; Minister for Social Security, 1976-79; Opposition Spokesman for Health and Social Security, 1979-80; Opposition Spokesman for Industry, 1980-; Chairman, Amalgamated Union of Engineering Workers Parliamentary Group of Labour MPs, 1977-. *Honours:* Privy Councillor, 1974. *Address:* 47 Hope Road, Sale, Cheshire, England.

OROGBU, Damian Nwoye Onuegbunam, b. 27 Dec. 1936, Awka, Anambra State, Nigeria. Telecommunications Engineer. m. Mary Ann Ifeyinwa Ezekwe, 10 Apr. 1966. *Education:* 1st School leaving Certificate, 1951; West Africa School Certificate, 1956; Assistant Technical Officer, P and T School, Oschodi, 1958; Royal West African Frontier Force Officer, Ghana, qualifying, 1959; Queens Commission in Mons, England, 1960; Royal Signals Qualifying Certificate, Caterick, England, 1961; Royal Signals Telecommunications Engineer, Caterick, England, 1965. *Appointments:* Instructor, Military School, Zaria, 1961-62; Brigade Signals Officer, United Nations Nigerian Army, Luluaborg, Congo, 1962; Commandant, Nigeria Army Signals School, Apapa and Second-in-Command Nigeria Army Signals, 1965-67; Promoted Lieutenant Colonel and appointed Chief Signals Officer, Biafra Army Signals, and Director, Armed Forces Communications, 1967-70; Retired. *Memberships:* Roman Catholic Church; President Awka Development Union, Lagos Brach, Nigeria, Netherlands Chamber of Commerce; Royal Signal School, Caterick, England; Chairman/Managing Director, Kucena-Damian, Printers of the National Telephone Directory, Nigeria; Managing Director, Ekkudelta (Nig) Ltd., Publishing Consultants to P & T, Nigeria. *Honours:* United Nations Congo Medal, 1961; Nigeria Independence Medal, 1960. *Hobbies:* Table Tennis; Billiards; Reading Novels; Music. *Address:* 89a Enugu Road, PO Box 644, Awka, Anambra State, Nigeria.

ORR, David Alexander (Sir), b. 10 May 1922, Dublin, Republic of Ireland. Company Chairman. m. Phoebe Rosaleen Davis, 21 Apr. 1949, 3 daughters. *Education:* BA, LL.B., Trinity College, Dublin. *Appointments:* Trainee with Unilever Limited, 1948; Production Manager and then Advertising Manager, Lever Brothers Limited, 1950; Marketing Director and then Vice-Chairman, Hindustan Lever Limited, 1955; Overseas Committee, Unilever Limited, London, 1960; Vice-President, 1963, President, Lever Brothers Company, New York, 1965; Director, 1967, Vice-Chairman, 1970, Chairman, Unilever Limited, London, 1974. *Memberships:* Governor of London Business School; Trustee of: Leverhulme Trust, Civic Trust, Centre for Southern African Studies at York University; Council Member of Chatham House; Vice-President, Liverpool School of Tropical Medicine. *Honours:* Received Knighthood in Queen's Silver Jubilee and Birthday Honours List, 1977; Honorary Degree of LLD, Trinity College, Dublin; Her Majesty Queen Juliana of the Netherlands awarded Commandership of the Order of Oranje Nassau, 1979. *Hobbies:* Golf; Reading; Travel. *Address:* Oakhill, Enton Green, Godalming, Surrey, England.

ORR, Raymond Donald, b. 22 Apr. 1925, Mt Barker. Business Manager. m. Valma Marjory Davis, 19 Mar. 1949, 1 son, 1 daughter. *Appointments:* Joined EFS., 1946; Regional Officer, Country Fire Service; Fire

Control Officer & District Supervisor; Controller, State Emergency Service. *Memberships:* Past Chairman, Adelaide Hills Fire, Fighting Association; Deputy Chairman, Country Fire Service Board and all committees deriving; Trustee, Volunteer Fire Fighters Fund; Councillor. District Council of Mt Barker, 1960-; Chairman, District Council of Mt Barker; Past President, Southern and Hills Local Government Association; Hospital Board, Mt Barker & District Soldiers Memorial Hospital. *Creative Works:* Designed the Australian Standard Rescue trailer, SES; Organised the first St John Ambulance mass training class; Participated in the District formation of Senior Citizen, Meals on Wheels, District Nurse and Service Clubs and assisted with the Royal Flying Doctor Service of South Australia. *Honours:* OAM; JP; MLG; Coroner; Awarded Citation for Meritorious Service EFS, 1969. *Address:* Box 48, Mt Barker, 5251, South Australia.

ORSMAN, William John, b. 9 Mar. 1939, Havelock, New Zealand. Economist. Separated, 2 sons. *Education:* Master of Commerce (Hons), Economics, Canterbury University, New Zealand, 1967; Diploma, Agricultural Science, Lincoln College, New Zealand, 1967. *Appointments:* Economist, 1967-76, Chief Agricultural Economist, New Zealand Ministry of Agrulture & Fisheries, 1979-; Economic Adviser to the Kingdom of Tonga, 1976-78. *Memberships:* New Zealand Association of Economists; Australian Agricultural Economics Society. *Publications:* Various published papers. *Hobbies:* Tennis; Skiing; Art. *Address:* 14 Winston Street, Crofton Downs, Wellington, New Zealand.

ORTIZ, Eduardo Leopoldo, b. 28 Mar. 1931, Buenos Aires, Argentina. Mathematician. m. Elba Susana Perez, 1 son. *Education:* Lic. in Mathematics, 1956, Dr. Mathematical Science, 1961, Faculty of Science, University of Buenos Aires. *Appointments:* Science Officer, Commission of Atomic Energy of Argentina, 1956-58; Assistant Professor, University of Beunes Aires, 1958-61; Research Member, Institute for Advanced Studies, Dublin, 1961-63; Lecturer in Mathematics, Imperial College, University of London, 1963-64; Professor of Mathematics, Royal Applied Mathematics Laboratory, University of Buenos Aires, 1965-66; Professor of Mathematics, Head of Mathematics Department, Faculty of Science, National Engineering University, Lima, Peru, 1966-68; Senior Lecturer in Mathematics, Head Numerical Analysis Section, Co-Director of Postgraduate Studies in Numerical Analysis, Imperial College, University of London, 1968-. *Memberships:* International Union on the History and Phil. of Science, Argentine Group; Fellow, Argentine Mathematical Union, former Editor of the Journal; Argentine Computer Society, former Secretary General; Society for Industrial and Applied Maths., USA; British Society for the History of Science; FIBA. *Publications:* Research papers on Mathematics and the History of Science in international journals; Invited contributor to several books on computational mathematics and approximation theory. *Honours:* Interuniversity Regional Council Scholarship; External Scholarship, University of Buenos Aires; Grants from French Government, British Council. *Address:* 115 Studdridge Street, London, SW6 3TD, England.

OSADEBAY, Chukudebe Dennis, b. 29 June 1911, Asaba, Nigeria. Barrister-at-Law. m. 1951, many children. *Education:* Studied Law, London, 1946-49; Called to the Bar at Lincoln's Inn, London, 1948; Graudated LL.B., London, 1949. *Appointments:* Civil Servant, Department of Customs & Excise, Nigeria, 1030-46; Practised Law in Nigeria, 1949-61; Elected to the Western Nigerian House of Assembly, 1951-54; Elected to the Nigerian House of Assembly, 1951-54; Leader of the Opposition in the Western House of Assembly, 1954-56, Deputy Speaker, 1956-58, once again Leader of the Opposition; Elected, President of the Nigerian Senate, the Upper House of the Nigerian Parliament, 1960 and led the Nigerian Parliamentary Delegation to the USA, Canada and UK, 1962; Acted as Governor-General of Nigeria, 1961; Appointed Administrator of Midwestern Nigeria, 1963; Became First Premier of Midwestern Nigeria, 1964-66. *Memberships:* Chancellor of the Anglican Diocese of Asaba, 1977; Pro-Chancellor & Chairman, Governing Council of the University of Lagos, 1980. *Publications:* Book of one hundred poems entitled, Afria Sings, 1952, reprinted, 1970; A second book of Poems entitled The Poems of a Refugee or Goddess of the Niger is ready for publication; Autobi-

ography, Building a Nation, 1978; Contributor of many papers and newspaper articles on Constitutional and Political Issues affecting Nigeria & Africa. *Honours:* Asaba ,Chieftaincy title of Ojiba, 1956; Holds many chieftaincy titles in Bendel State of Nigeria; Honorary Degree of Doctor of Laws, University of Nigeria, Nsukka, 1964; Grand Commander of the Order of the Niger, 1964; Awarded Doctor of Letters, Honoris Causa, University of Benin. *Hobbies:* African Affairs; Tennis; Football. *Address:* Osadenis House, Cable Point, Box 7, Asaba, Nigeria.

OSASONA, Josiah Taiye, b. 16 Jan. 1947, Eruku, Irepodun, LG, Kwara State, Nigeria. Architect. m. Grace Bike Omotinugbob, 22 Dec. 1979. *Education:* BSc., 1972-75, MSc., Ahmadu Bello University, Zazria, 1975-77. *Appointments:* Nigeria Army Engineers, Jos, Makurdi, 1977-78; Gideon Associates, Ibadan & Ilorin, 1978-. *Memberships:* Nigerian Institute of Architects. *Publications:* Editor of Titcombe College Echoes' (the School Official Yearbook), 1969. *Honours:* Titcombe College Prize for the best student in Form 1, 1964, Form II, 1965, Form III, 1966; Best student in English & Yoruba Languages in Form V, 1968, Best student in General paper & Divinity, 1969; Titcombe College Volleyball & Athletic Captain, 1970; Kwara State of Nigeria 800 Metres Champion, 1968, 69, 70. *Hobbies:* Religious Music; Athletics; Volleyball; Photography. *Address:* Sabo Oke Quarters, Ilorin, Kwara State, Nigeria.

OSBORN, Robert Andrew, b. 29 July 1930, Kalgoorlie, Western Australia. Medical Practitioner, Pathologist. m. Joan Mary Hockley, 10 Nov. 1956, 3 sons, 1 daughter. *Education:* University of London, Middlesex Hospital, 1948-54; BSc., 1952; MB.,BS., 1954; MD (London), 1963; MRCP (Edinburgh), 1960; FRCPA, 1965; MRCPath., 1963; FRCPath, 1975; MAACB, 1968; MIAC, 1976. *Appointments:* House Physician, Middlesex Hospital, 1954-55; Senior Registrar, Pathology, United Sheffield Hospitals; Director of Pathology, Royal Hospital for Women, Paddington, 1963-; Clinical Lecturer in Obstetrics, University of Sydney, 1963-65; Senior Lecturer in Pathology, University of New South Wales, 1971-. *Memberships:* Honorary Secretary, Royal College of Pathologists of Australasia, 1974-80; Honorary Secretary, New South Wales State Committee, RCPA, 1969-74; Teratology Society; Australian & New Zealand Paediatric Pathology Group; Australian Society of Cytology; International Academy of Pathology; International Academy of Cytology; Royal Society of Medicine. *Publications:* Numerous contributions to medical journals. *Hobbies:* Angling; Squash; Tennis. *Address:* 4 Haite Close, West Pymble, New South Wales, 2073, Australia.

OSBORNE, Harold James, b. 9 Mar. 1940, Calgary, Alberta, Canada. Public Relations Practitioner. m. Judith Anne Gollinger, 27 Aug. 1966, 3 daughters. *Education:* BA., University of Alberta, 1972; Professional Accreditation (APR), The Canadian Public Relations Society, Incorporated, 1977. *Appointments:* Editor, The Canadian Press, Ottawa & Edmonton; Chairman, Communications Department, Grant MacEwan Community College, Edmonton, Alberta; Director, Public Relations, University of Regina, Regina, Saskatchewan; Director, Public Relations Northern Telecom Canada Limited. *Memberships:* National Treasurer, Canadian Public Relations Society Incorporated, 1980-81; Director, Council for Canadian Unity; Royal Canadian Military Institute, Toronto, Ontario; Director, Regina Chamber of Commerce, 1978, 79, 80; Journalism Advisory Board, University of Regina; Accreditation Board, Canadian Public Relations Society; Canadian Forces, Public Affairs Task Force (Militia); Director, Royal United Services Institute, Regina, 1979, 80. *Publications:* Co-author, The Accuracy of News Reporters, University of Alberta Technical Paper, 1972; Author of Chapter on Public Relations for a textbook on Public Relations, 1979. *Honours:* Queen's Scout, 1956; First Class Standing, University of Alberta, 1972; Award of Merit, United Way of Regina, 1980. *Hobbies:* Gardening; Reading; Woodworking. *Address:* 24 Nantucket Crescent, Brampton, Ontario, L6S 3X5, Canada.

OSEI-BONSU, Moses, b. 20 May 1940, Nsuta, Ashanti. Librarianship. m. Mary Nyarko, 20 May 1967, 1 son, 3 daughters. *Education:* Associateship of the Library Association, 1970; Master of Library Studies, 1977. *Appointments:* Deputy Regional Librarian, 1965;

Senior Library Assistant, UST., 1965; Assistant Librarian, 1967-71; Principal Library Assistant, 1971-73; Assistant Librarian, 1973-75; Acting Librarian, 1977-. *Memberships:* Associate, British Library Association; Classification & Indexing Group of LA; Association of Assistant Librarians; Ghana Library Association. *Publications:* Contributor of articles to Library Bulletins. *Honours:* Ministry of Overseas Development (Gt Britain) Technical Assistance Study Fellowship, 1975-77. *Hobbies:* Reading; Gardening. *Address:* PO Box 113, Achimota, Ghana, West Africa.

O'SHANE, Patricia June, b. 19 June 1941, Mossman, Queensland, Australia. Barrister-at-Law. Divorced, 2 daughters. *Education:* Queensland Teachers' College, 1960; B.Ed (Not completed), University of Queensland, 1966-69; LL.B., University of New South Wales, 1972-75; LL.M. Candidate, Sydney University, 1978-. *Appointments:* School Teacher (Secondary), Cairns State High School, Queensland, 1961-72; Barrister-at-Law, private practice, 1976-77; Tutor, Law School, University of New South Wales, 1977-79; Appointed first female member, Metropolitan Water, Sewerage Drainage Board, 1979; Co-ordinator, Task Force to Select Committee of the Legislative Assembly (NSW) upon Aborigines, 1979-. *Honours:* United Association of Women's Lady Street Memorial Award, Woman of the Year, 1977. *Hobbies:* Jogging; Swimming; Squash; Golf; Political activities; Listening to Classical Music; Reading. *Address:* Goodsell Building, Chifley Square, Sydney, New South Wales, Australia.

O'SHEA, Amanda Mary, b. 19 July 1953, Adelaide, South Australia. Teacher. m. 6 May 1978, (Divorced). *Education:* Diploma of Teaching; Bachelor of Education. *Appointments:* Physical Education Teacher, Enfield High School. *Memberships:* Australian Council of Health, Physical Education and Recreation. *Hobbies:* Squash; Tennis; Netball; Basketball; Water Skiing. *Address:* 42 Fifth Avenue, Saint Peters, 5069, South Australia.

OSHIN, Ladipo Babatunde, b. 3 June 1931, Kano, Nigeria. Medicine, Ophthalmology. m. Mojisola, 25 May 1965, 1 son, 2 daughters. *Education:* LMSSA, London, 1960; Diploma in Ophthalmology, RCPS, Ireland, 1970; FMCS, Ophthalmology, Nigeria, 1980. *Appointments:* Pre-Registration House Jobs at Croydon General Hospital, London, 1960 and Orpington Hospital, Kent, 1961; Medical Officer, Adeoyo Hospital, Ibadan, Nigeria, 1963-67; SHO Ophthalmology, Kent & Sussex Hospital, Tunbridge Wells, Kent, 1968-69; SHO Registrar, The Royal Eye Hospital, St George's Circus, London, 1970; Consultant Ophthalmologist, Adeoyo Hospital, Ibadan, Nigeria, 1971-73; Senior Consultant, 1973-77, Chief Consultant, State Hospital, Abeokuta, Ogun State, Nigeria, 1977-. *Memberships:* Vice-President, Ogun State, Nigeria Medical Association; Ophthalmological Society of Nigeria; British Medical Association; Ophthalmological Society of the United Kingdom; Delegate from Nigeria at Centenary Meeting, Ophthalmological Society of United Kingdom, 1980. *Honours:* Cricket Colours, King's College, Lagos, 1949. *Hobbies:* Lawn Tennis; Table Tennis; Cricket; Swimming; Hunting; Monopoly; Chess; Ayo (Nigerian Game); Whot; Dominoes. *Address:* HC 13, Road Six, Housing Corporation, Ibara, Abeokuta, Ogun State, Nigeria.

OSIBO, Babafunmi Olayemi, b. 18 Jan. 1938, Lagos, Nigeria. Engineering. m. 1965, 1 son, 3 daughters. *Education:* Queens College, University of St Andrews, 1959-63; University of Surrey, 1966-67; BSc., (Applied Science), 1963; MSc., (Applied Dynamics), 1967. *Appointments:* Graduate Apprentice, British Railways; Development Engineer, Napier & Son, Acton; Engineer, Tate & Lyle Refineries; Chief Engineer, Tate & Lyle (Nigeria), Factory Manager, Works Director, 1974-. *Memberships:* Council, Apapa Branch, Manufacturers Association; Chemical Industries Technical Standards Committee of Nigerian Standards Organisation; University of Ilorin Faculty of Engineering Board; Nigerian Society of Engineers (Secretary then Deputy Chairman of Kwara State Branch); Nigerian Institute of Management; Fellow, Nigerian Institute of Food Science and Technology; Fellow, Nigerian Society of Engineers, 1981. *Hobbies:* Reading; Walking. *Address:* Tate & Lyle (Nigeria) Ltd., PO Box 1240, Lagos, Nigeria.

OSINOWO, Olakunle Oladipo, b. 23 Nov. 1948, Nigeria. Economist. m. Olufunmilayo Okubanke Okuban-

jo, 8 Dec. 1979. *Education:* Bachelor of Business Administration, Texas Southern University, Houston, Texas, 1977; Master of Economics, Prairie View A & M University, Prairie View, Texas, 1978. *Appointments:* Stockbroker. *Memberships:* Nigerian-American Chamber of Commerce; Lagos Chamber of Commerce, Mines and Industry. *Creative Works:* Drawing and Painting. *Hobbies:* Soccer; Table Tennis; Badminton. *Address:* 11B Adediran Ajao Crescent, Ajao Estate, Anthony Village, Lagos, Nigeria.

OSINULU, Clara Olanrewaju (Mrs Samuel A Osinulu), b. 30 Nov. 1934, Lagos, Nigeria. Anthropologist. m. Samuel Adeoye, 20 Dec. 1969, 4 sons, 4 daughters. *Education:* Certificate in Secretarial Studies, Birmingham College of Commerce, 1959-60; BA., Hons. Anthropology, Birkbeck College, University of London, 1960-61, University College, London, 1961-64; Postgraduate Diploma in African Studies, University of Birmingham, UK, 1964-65. *Appointments:* Teacher, St Anne's School, Ibadan, Nigeria, 1955-56; Curator of the National Museum, Lagos, 1965-67; Program Officer, African American Institute, 1967-72; Director-/Program Representative, 1972-. *Memberships:* Fellow, Royal Anthropological Institute; Friends of the National Museum Society; Nigerian Association of University Women (National Secretary, 1969-73); National Council of Women's Societies; The Nigerian Institute of International Affairs; Servas International. *Publications:* The Changing Status of African Women, 1965; Femininity in Yoruba Religious Art, 1969; Nigerian Traditional Works of Art, 1974; Religion and Status of Women, 1975; The Nigerian Woman in Traditional Society: The Family, 1975; Nigerian Women & Development in Relation to Changing Family Structure: Religion & Status of Nigerian Women, 1976; The Role of Women in Population Control, 1975; On being a Woman in Africa Today, 1976; The African Child in the Family, 1979; Women in the Mass Media in Nigeria: The Role of Market Women in Development, 1981. *Hobbies:* Photography; Singing; Country tours; Walking; Climbing; Badminton; Lawn Tennis. *Address:* 5 Ola Ayeni Street, Off Medical Road, Ikeja, PO Box 1178, Ikeja, Lagos State, Nigeria.

OSISI, Alphonsus Okamigbo, b. 15 Feb. 1943, Arondizuogu. Consulting Architect. m. Patience Chinenye Offor, 3 Jan. 1975, 3 sons. *Education:* BSc., Design Hons. 2nd Class lower, 1969; Post-Graduate Diploma Architecture, 1971; Diploma Civil Engineering, 1964. *Appointments:* Nixson & Borys, Architects, 1971-72; Egbor & Associates, Architects, 1972-74; Principal Consultant, Enuiro-Arc, Consultant Architects, 1974-. *Memberships:* Nigerian Institute of Architects; Education Board of the Nigerian Institute. *Publications:* Yet unpublished designs. *Honours:* Best student of the year, 1971. *Hobby:* Lawn Tennis. *Address:* 466 Modupe Johnson Crescent, Surulere, Lagos, Nigeria.

OSISIOGU, Isaac Udo, William, b. 3 Nov 1930, Umuahia, Imo State, Nigeria. Pharmacist. m. Peggy Oyiya Green, 25 Aug 1962, 2 sons, 1 daughter. *Education:* Chemist and Druggist Diploma (1953) of the School of Pharmacy, Yaba, Nigeria; B. Pharm. (1959) University of London, School of Pharmacy; Ph.D (1963) University of London, Chelsea College of Science and Technology. *Appointments:* Hospital Pharmacist, Bamenda, Cameroons, 1953; Lecturer, School of Pharmacy, Yaba, 1954-1955; Lecturer, University of Nigeria, Nsukka, 1963; Senior Lecturer, University of Nigeria, Nsukka, 1967; Professor of Pharmacy, University of Nigeria, 1974-1979; Federal Commissioner (Minister) for Water Resources, 1975-1977; Federal Commissioner (Minister) for Civil Aviation, 1977-1978; Federal Commissioner (Minister) for Trade, 1978-1979; Present Position: Executive Director, Ibafon Chemicals, Lagos, Nigeria. *Memberships:* Science Association of Nigeria. *Publications:* Research papers in Chemistry and Pharmacognosy; Hannah's Poems; Co-author of A Concise School Certificate Organic Chemistry. *Honours:* May & Baker Prize for distinction in the Chemist and Druggist Diploma Course, 1953. *Hobbies:* Music; Gardening. *Address:* P.O. Box 60262, Ikoyi, Lagos, Nigeria.

OSOBU ISOLA, Kanmi (Isola), b. 1 Jan 1937, Ilesa Oyo State, Nigeria. Legal Practice Writer. m. Victoria Abimbola (nee Ajasa), 10 April 1966, 2 sons, 3 daughters. *Education:* Batchelor of Laws (LL.B) University of London, June 1963; Nigerian Law School, July 1965. *Appointments:* Barristers at Law, Solicitors and Advocates-Legal Practitioners of the Supreme Court of Nigeria, July 1965-. *Memberships:* Foundation National Convener, Nigerian Association of Patriotic Writers and Artistes (NAPWA); National Publicity Secretary, Nigerian Bar Association, 1974-1976; Vice Chairman, Lagos Branch, Nigerian Bar Association 1978-1979; Chairman, Social and Publicity Committee, N.B.A. (Lagos). *Publications:* Essays and Writings on Nigeria, African and Black Politics, Culture and Civilisation (in print); Major Contributions to National and International Debates On Way Forward for Africa. *Honours:* Won many Secondary School Awards. *Hobbies:* Reading; Writing; Lecture and Public Speaking Engagements; Touring and Visiting Places of History. *Address:* 122 Murtala, Muhammed Way, Ebute Metta, Lagos, Nigeria.

OSOGO, James Charles, Nakhwanga, b. 10 October, 1932, Bukani, Bunyala Location, Busia District, Kenya. ,Teacher. m. Marie Nakhubaliobara, 16 Aug. 1959, 4 sons, 1 daughter. *Education:* Teacher Training at Kagumo College, 1953-1954. *Appointments:* Teacher, 1955-1962; Politician from 1961-. *Memberships:* Patron, Kenya Youth Hostels Association; Lions Club; Nairobi Club; Chairman of Kenya African National Union District Branch. *Publications:* Kenya's World of Commerce and Industry. *Honours:* Elder of the Golden Heart (Kenya); Member of the Order of the Star of Africa (Liberia); Member of the Grand Cordon of the Star of Ethiopia; Member of the Grand Cross of the Yugoslav Flag (1st Class). *Hobbies:* Fishing; Playing Volleyball and Soccer; Reading. *Address:* P.O. Box 1, Port Victoria, Kenya.

OSOKA, Ogala, b. 2 Dec 1949, Portharcourt, Nigeria, Insurance. m. Elizabeth Nsolo, 25 April 1981. *Education:* Associate Chartered Insurance Institute, 1976; Associate Chartered Institute of Arbitrations, 1976; Member, British Institute of Management, 1977. *Appointments:* Unity Life & Fire Insurance Co Ltd, Lagos, 1971-1974; Greig Fester Reinsurance Brokers, London, 1974-1975; Eagle Star Insurance Company Ltd, London, 1975; Greig Fester (Reinsurance Brokers), London, 1975-1977; Nigeria Reinsurance Corporation, Lagos, 1977-. *Memberships:* Ikoyi Club, Lagos. *Publications:* Publications on current insurance and management topics, various newspapers and magazines. *Honours:* Prize Winner, Insurance Institute of Nigeria, 1974. *Hobbies:* Golf; Tennis; Bicycle Riding. *Address:* 29 Idowu Martins Street, Victoria Island, Lagos, Nigeria.

OSOLA, Vaino, Juhani (Victor, John), b. 24 Jan 1926, Hull, England. Chartered Mechanical Engineer. m. Brenda Lilian Davison, 18 Dec 1948, 2 sons, 1 daughter. *Education:* The Technical College (Sunderland) Engineering Diploma, 1943-1945; B.Sc (Applied Science-Mechanical Engineering), Sunderland Technical College, University of Durham, 1948-1950. *Appointments:* Technical Commission, Corps of Royal Engineers, 1945-1948; C.A. Parsons & Co Ltd, Newcastle upon Tyne, Gas Turbine Research Engineer, 1951-1952; Procter & Gamble Ltd, Newcastle upon Tyne Senior Design Engineer, 1952-1957; Lankro Chemicals Ltd, Eccles, Lancs., Company Chief Engineer, 1957-1965; Divisional Director, Pilkington Brothers Ltd., St. Helens, 1965-1979; Group Managing Director, Redman Heenan International Ltd. Worcester, 1979-; Member of Court, Cranfield Institute of Technology, 1979-; Independent Member of the Mechanical Engineering and Machine Tools R & D Requirements Board of the Department of Industry, 1974- 1979, Chairman, 1977-1979. *Memberships:* Fellowship of Engineering, Member of Executive Committee; Fellow of the Institution of Mechanical Engineer, Vice President and Chairman of the Technical Policy Board; American Society of Mechanical Engineers; Institute of Energy; Fellow of the Royal Society of Arts; Associate of St. George's House, Windsor. *Honours:* CBE., 1980; Mac Robert Award, 1978. *Hobbies:* Music; Offshore Sailing. *Address:* Whiddon End, Yarhampton Cross, Nr Stourport on Severn, Worcs., DY13 0UY, England.

OSOMO, (Chief) Michael Ojo, b. 20 May 1933, Ikaramu, Akokodiv, Ondo State, Nigeria. Company Director. m. 3 sons, 4 daughters. *Education:* Intermediate examination, Chartered Institute of Secretaries, 1957. *Appointments:* Junior Accounts Executive, Shell Co. of West Africa Limited, 1955-58; Accountant, Principal Accountant, Electricity Corporation of Nigeria, later National Electricity Power Authority, 1958-76. *Honours:* Installed Odofin of Ikaramu, Akoko Division, Ondo State, Nigeria, 1980. *Hobby:* Squash rackets. *Address:* 9 Soleye Crescent, Surulere, Lagos, Nigeria.

OSUNDE, Iriowen John, b. 28 Sept. 1939, Benin City, Nigeria. Law and Theology. m. Victoria King, 28 Dec. 1975, 2 sons. *Education:* LL.B., Blackstone of Law, 1964-67; DD., Ministry of Christ School of Theology, 1972-75. *Appointments:* Education Officer, Benin City, Nigeria, 1956-57; Civil Service, Nigeria, 1958-61; Seconded by Federal Government of Nigeria to United Nations Peace Mission to the Congo Republic, now Zaire, 1961-62; Ordained Minister, Ministry of Christ Church Inc., 1975; Elected President, Manson Overseas Trade Corporation, 1976. *Memberships:* Chambers Institute of Management, UK; International Fundamental Human Rights Association, Switzerland; President, African Institute of Education; Founder and President General, International Helpless Children Society Inc. *Publications:* Poem: The World is not as Bad, 1975; The Golden Rod, 1976. *Honours:* Nigerian Independence Medal for Good Services, 1960; United Nations Gold Medal for Struggle for World Peace, 1962. *Hobbies:* Football; Golf; Hockey; Writing. *Address:* 62 Lawanson Road, Surulere, Lagos, Nigeria.

OSUNKOYA, Babatunde Olusiji, b. 26 Oct. 1934, Lagos, Nigeria. Medical. m. Beryl Cosiba Afanu, 2 Feb. 1962, 4 sons. *Education:* MB., BS., London, University College of Ibadan, Nigeria, 1954-61; PhD., University of Ibadan, Nigeria, 1964-66. *Appointments:* House Physician and Surgeon, 1962, Consultant Pathologist, 1968-, UCH., Ibadan, Nigeria; Rural Medical Officer, Western Nigeria, 1963; Medical Research Training Fellow, 1964-66, Lecturer, 1967-69, Senior Lecturer, 1969-71, Pathology, Senior Lecturer, Immunology, 1971-72, Professor of Immunology, 1973-, University of Ibadan, Nigeria. *Memberships:* Fellow: Nigerian Academy of Science; Science Association of Nigeria; Past President, Nigerian Society for Immunology; Past Secretary, Nigerian Cancer Society; Royal College of Pathologists; Pathological Society of Great Britain and Ireland; Association of Pathologists of Nigeria; Past Secretary, UCH., Ibadan Medical Society. *Publications:* 78 publications including: Established Lymphoblastoid Cell Lines (with others), 1971; The Thymus in Burkitt's Lymphoma, 1971; Pleural Effusion in Burkitt's Lymphoma (with others), 1977; Multinucleated Giant Cells in PHA-Stimulated Leucocyte Cultures of Children with Measles (with others), 1973; Neoplasms of the Sella Turcica Region in Ibadan, Nigeria (with others), 1973; A Review of Cancer Research in Ibadan, 1972; Immunopathology of Human Malaria, 1978. *Honours:* University College Scholar, Ibadan, 1956-61; Fellowships: NATO, 1966; UICC, 1969; WHO, 1969, 71, 72. *Hobbies:* Music; Chess; Table tennis; Travelling. *Address:* Plot B Osoba Layout, Bodija, Ibadan, Nigeria.

OSUNTOKUN, Benjamin Oluwakayode, b. 6 Jan. 1935, Ilawe, Nigeria. Physician; Neurology; University teacher. m. Olabopo Cameron-Cole, 15 Dec. 1962, 3 sons, 2 daughters. *Education:* MB., BS., Hons., London, 1961; MRCP., London, 1964; PhD., Ibadan, 1969; MD., London, 1971; FRCP., London, 1974; DSc.. London, 1977; Attended University College, Ibadan, Nigeria; Universities of London, UK, Ibadan, Nigeria, Newcastle-on-Tyne, UK, Welsh National School of Medicine, UK. *Appointments:* House Officer, 1961, Consultant Neurological Physician, 1966, University College Hospital, Ibadan, Nigeria; Senior House Officer, Welsh National School of Medicine, UK, 1963; Smith & Nephew Fellow. National Hospital for Nervous Diseases, London and University of Newcastle-on-Tyne, UK, 1964-65; Medical Research Training Fellow, 1965, Lecturer, 1966, Senior Lecturer, 1968, Professor of Medicine, 1970, Dean, Faculty of Medicine, 1974-78, University of Ibadan, Nigeria; Commonwealth Professor of Medicine, RPMS, University of London, UK, 1978-79; Consultant Neuroscientist to USA Government, NINCDS, National Institutes of Health, Bethesda, USA, 1979-80; Consultant, World Health Organisation, 1972-. *Publications:* Over 160 publications in books and learned journals. *Honours:* Several undergraduate prizes, 1954-61; Sir Langley Memorial prize, University of London, UK, 1971; Frederick Murgatroyd prize, Royal College of Physicians, London, UK, 1976; Officer of Federal Republic of Nigeria, 1978. *Hobbies:* Lawn tennis; Table Tennis; Photography; Hunting.

Address: 34 Osuntokun Avenue, Bodija, Ibadan, Nigeria.

OTENG, Absalom Kenneth, b. 11 Nov. 1928, Barr, Erute, Lira District, Uganda. Veterinary Surgeon. m. Semmy Akello- Alyek, 26 Nov. 1955, 4 sons, 2 daughters. *Education:* Diploma in Veterinary Science, Makerere, Uganda, 1958; Bachelor of Veterinary Science, University of Queensland, Australia, 1965; BVSc (Hons. Para.), 1966; Master of Veterinary Science, 1969; Doctor of Philosophy, Makerere University, Kampala, Uganda, 1973. *Appointments:* Assistant Veterinary Officer, Uganda, 1958-65; Veterinary Officer, 1966-67; Chief Veterinary Research Officer, 1968-75; Director of Veterinary Research Services, Uganda, 1976; Senior Lecturer (Temporary), Faculty of Veterinary Medicine, Nairobi, 1977; Senior Principal Professional Officer, National Council for Scientific Research, Zambia, 1978; Head, Pest Research Unit, NCSR, Zambia, 1979; Head/Chief Scientific Officer, 1980; Consultant, UNECA/mulpoc/lusaka, 1980. *Memberships:* National Research Council, Uganda, 1970; Uganda Veterinary Board; East African Academy; Joint Standing and Research Co-ordinating Committees, East African Community; Trustee of the Uganda Museum; World International Congress of Parasitologist; Commonwealth Veterinary Association, Regional representative, East & Central Africa; Australian Society for Parasitologist. *Publications:* Published 30 papers on professional and scientific topics. *Honours:* Bronze Medal, East African Amateur Athletic Sports, 1951; Mulgibhai Madhvani Prize, Final Year Diploma in Vet. Sc., 1958; Commonwealth Scholarship and Fellowship Plan to Australia, 1962; First prize for outstanding under-graduate research project final year, 1965. *Hobbies:* Photography; Bush walking; Gardening. *Address:* PO Box, 16, Lira, Uganda.

OTENYA, Sylvester C, b. 6 June 1947, Kitale, Librarianship. m. Mary Njoki, 4 May 1967, 1 son, 2 daughters. *Education:* Makerere University, Kampala Uganda 1976; BSc, MSc (Library Science), University of Illinois, USA, 1979. *Appointments:* University of Illinois, 1979; Kenya National Archives, 1979; Kenya National Library Services, 1979. *Memberships:* Kenya National Union of Teachers; Kenya Library Association. *Hobbies:* Jazz Music; Dancing; Reading; Photography. *Address:* PO Box 1937, Nakuru, Kenya.

OTHMAN, Abdul Halim Bin, b. 9 Feb. 1938, Malaysia. University Lecturer (Associate Professor). m. Norlis, 25 Dec. 1960, 1 son, 3 daughters. *Education:* Certificate in Education, Birmingham, 1959; BA(Psychology) Hawaii, 1970; MEd (Ed.Psych.), 1971; MSc (Ed.Psych.) Indiana, 1978; EdD (Counselling), 1979. *Appointments:* Teacher, 1960-67; University Lecturer, 1971-. *Memberships:* Association of Counsellors, Malaysia; Malaysian Psychological Association; American Psychological Association; Old Putera Association. *Publications:* Akademika, Majalah Psikologi, Journal Pendidikan; Thesis: Doctoral, Reports of Research and Seminar Papers. *Honours:* East-West Center Grant, 1967-70; Kouk Brothers Award, 1971; Fulbright-Hays Grant, 1974-78. *Hobbies:* Travels; Hiking; Swimming. *Address:* Lot 11586, Taman Mesra, Batu 13, Kajang, Selangor, Malaysia.

OTHMAN, Morni, b. 28 Dec. 1948, Brunei. Head of Agronomy Section. m. Rauyah Haji Abdul Rahman, 28 Dec. 1973. *Education:* Bachelor of Science, Agriculture (Hons) McGill, Canada, 1973; Doctor of Philosophy (Plant Science) Canterbury, New Zealand, 1980. *Appointments:* Head of Agronomy Section, State Agronomist. *Memberships:* Agronomy Society of New Zealand. *Hobbies:* Golf; Fishing; Travelling. *Address:* B3 Kg Sungai Matan, Jalan Kota Batu, Brunei.

O'TOOLE, John Joseph, b. 12 Aug. 1923, Wyong. Senior Executive. m. Hazel Clare Sullivan, 10 Oct. 1942, 2 daughters. *Appointments:* Director, Royal North Shore Hospital Board, 1978-; Chairman, Works and Planning Committee, Australian Imperial Forces, 5 years. *Memberships:* Australian Rugby Football League Board of Control, 1956-; Secretary, Country Rugby Football League of New South Wales; New South Wales Rugby Football League General Committee, 1954; President/Director, NSW Leagues' Club; Sydney Cricket and Sportsground Trust, Chairman of Finance Committee; Manager, Australian Rugby League Team to England and France, 1960. *Honours:*

Member of the British Empire, 1978; First Grade Rugby League Player; Represented Australian on International Rugby League Conferences. *Hobbies:* Football; Racing; Cricket. *Address:* 165 Phillip Street, Sydney, NSW, Australia, 2000.

OTTAH, Meye Moses, b. 24 Mar. 1926, Agbor, Nigeria. Charted Secretary. m. Edith Ngozi Okwuadi, 1 June 1961, 2 sons 1 daughter. *Education:* Government School, Agbor, 1934-40; Baptist Boys High School, Abeokuta, 1943-45; Private Studies, by Correspondence, 1946-47; CIS Final, Leeds College of Commerce, Leeds, 1955-59; Attended Several International Management Courses and Seminars in USA, Europe and Nigeria. *Appointments:* Royal West African Frontier Force, 1941-42; Civil Servant, Postal Clerk and Telegraphist, 1946-48; Senior Accounts Clerk Oduah Service Agency, 1948-49; Bank Executive, African Continental Bank Limited, 1949-53; Assistant/Accountant, UTC Motors, Lagos, 1953-55; Senior Accounts Executive, Shell Company of Nigeria Limited, Lagos, 1959-65; Cost Accountant, 1966-67, Financial Accountant, 1967-68, Company Secretary and Controller, 1968-78, Managing Director, Wayne, West Africa Limited, 1978-. *Memberships:* ACIS; Associate member, Nigerian Institute of Management; Ika Club; General Secretary, Esato Society, Lagoa. *Publications:* Accredited authority in Agbor Language of Nigeria. *Hobbies:* Lawn Tennis; Table Tennis; Swimming. *Address:* 49 Adisa Bashua Street, PO Box 66, Surulere, Lagos, Nigeria.

OUDENDAG, Egbert, b. 20 Apr. 1914, Raalte, Holland. Artist; Painter. m. Maria Grolman, 20 Nov. 1946, 2 sons. *Education:* Autodidact. *Appointments:* Riding Instructor, Dutch Riding Artillery; Self-employed. *Creative Works:* Paintings include: West Coast Scenes; Fine Arts Series: Howe Sound; Atkinson Light; The Lions. *Honours:* Outstanding Gymnast, ran 100 Metres in 11.2 seconds. *Hobbies:* Chess; Music. *Address:* 15691 Marine Drive, White Rock, BC, Canada, V4B 1E3.

OUELLET, Gary, b. 9 Jan. 1945, Quebec City, Canada. Barrister/Solicitor. m. Renée Frenette 5 May 1973, 1 son, 2 daughters. *Education:* BA (cum laude) Loyola, Montreal, 1964; LL.L (cum laude) Université Laval, Quebec City, 1967. *Appointments:* Lawyer, Lazarovitz, Bernatches and Associates 1967-68; Partner: Des Rivières, Choquette and Associates, 1968-70; de Goumois, L'Heureux, Ouellet, 1970-73; Levasseur, Ouellet and Associates, 1973-. *Memberships:* Canadian Bar Association; Bar of the Province of Quebec; Director-/Vice-President, Jeffery Hale's Hospital; Society for the Prevention of Cruelty to animals; Quebec Garrison Club; Canadian Association of Authors, Publishers and Composers; Ordre illustre des chevaliers de Méduse; Conseil souverain de la Nouvelle-France. *Publications:* Author, Manuel pratique de preuve civile, 1978; Contributing Editor, Canadian Lawyer Magazine, Canada Month Magazine; Contributer, Videonics Videotape Lectures. *Hobbies:* Horticulture; Conjuring. *Address:* 1262 Lemoine, Sillery, QC, Canada, G1S 1A2.

OVERALL, Graham Frederic, b. 18 Oct. 1920, Sydney, Australia. Engineer. m. Brenda Payne 15 Jan. 1944, 2 daughters. *Education:* MechE, Sydney Technical College. *Appointments:* Hadfields Steel Works Limited; Eagle and Globe Steel Company Limited. *Memberships:* Association of Australian Forging Industrys; Royal Prince Alfred Yacht Club; Tattersalls Club; Lindfield Bowling Club. *Hobbies:* Fishing; Lawn Bowling. *Address:* 21 Sylvan Avenue, East Lindfield, NSW 2070, Australia.

OVERALL, (Sir) John Wallace, b. 15 July 1913, Sydney, Australia. Architect-Planner. m. Margaret Joan Goodman, 17 Sept. 1943, 4 sons. *Education:* Overseas Travelling Scholarship, NSW Board of Architects, 1939; Post Graduate Training, Town Planning, London, United Kingdom, 1949. *Appointments:* Private Practice, 1935-40; Lieutenant Colonel, AIF, 1940-46; Chief Architect, South Australian Housing Trust, 1946-49; Partner, Overall and Walkley, 1949-51; Chief Architect, Commonwealth Government of Australia, 1951-58; Commissioner, National Capital Development of Commission, 1958-72; Company Director and Private Practice 1973-; Consultant, United Nations, City Planning, 1972-80; Directorships: CSR Limited, 1973-; Lend Lease Corporation Limited, 1973-; General Property Trust, 1975-; Alliance Holdings Limited,

1975-. *Memberships:* Fellow, Royal Australian Institute of Architects; Fellow, Australian Planning institute of Architects. *Publications:* Observations on Redevelopment of Western side of Sydney Cove, 1964; Papers to Professional Journals; Design, Development and Construction of Canberra. *Honours:* Knight Bachelor, 1968; Commander British Empire, 1965; Military Cross and Bar, 1942-43; Australian Medallion, NSW Board of Architects, 1949; Sydney Luker Memorial Medal, 1964; L/fraia; L/fapi. *Hobbies:* Tennis; Golf. *Address:* 10 Wallaroy Road, Double Bay, Sydney 2028, NSW, Australia.

OVERTON, Cyril David, b. 22 Apr. 1919, London, England. Librarian. m. Angela Marguerite Allott, 1 daughter. *Education:* Associate, 1946, Fellow, 1951, Library Association; MA., London University, UK, 1969. *Appointments:* Public Libraries, UK, 1936-; Superintendent BNBC, National Central Library, UK, 1950-; Librarian, Imperial Institute, UK, 1952; Deputy Librarian, Colonial and Commonwealth Offices, UK, 1954; Chief Librarian, Ministry of Public Building and Works, UK, 1967; Head of Library Services, Departments of Trade, Industry, Energy, Prices, 1967; Technical Co-operation Officer, Overseas Development Administration, Nairobi, Kenya, 1979. *Memberships:* Library Committee of: Royal Commonwealth Society; Hispanic and Luso Brazilian Council; Senior Examiner, Library Association; Kenya Library Association; International Federation of Library Associations; Standing Conference on Library Materials on Africa. *Publications:* Gramophone Record Library, Grafton, 1951; Planning the Administrative Library, IFLA, 1981; Chapters in: Government Information and the Research Worker; Handbook of Special Librarianship; ASLIB; Bibliographies on the Commonwealth, NBL; Articles in: Library Association Record; Library Review; ASLIB Proceedings. *Hobbies:* Reading; Natural history; Mountain walking; Music. *Address:* 11 Daleside, Riverdale Road, Sheffield S10 FA2, England.

OWENS, Ernest Stanley, b. 22 Sept. 1916, Armidale, New South Wales, Australia. Chartered Accountant. m. Margaret Clara Brown, 6 Feb. 1943, 1 son, 1 daughter. *Education:* The King's School, Australia, 1929-34; FCA; FASA; FAIM. *Appointments:* Executive Chairman, Hill Samuel Australia Limited, 1970-; Investigation and reports for Commonwealth Government Tolai Cocoa Project, 1966, 70; Chimbu Coffee Co-operative, 1969, 70; Founding Chairman, Investment Corporation, Papua, New Guinea, 1972-75; Director of many companies. *Memberships:* Alderman, City of Sydney, Australia, 1969-74; President: New South Wales Division, Australian Institute of Management, 1971, 72; Civic Reform Association, 1959-62, 1965-67, 1975-78; Board of Directors, Royal Prince Alfred Hospital; Chairman, Enterprise Australia; Governor, Thalidomide Foundation Limited. *Creative Works:* Founder of AIM's Annual Report Award. *Honours:* Awarded: OBE., 1970; CBE., 1979. *Hobbies:* Bowling; Surfing. *Address:* Unit 11, 574 Pacific Highway, Killara, New South Wales 2071, Australia.

OWIREDU, Peter Augustus, b. 22 Aug. 1926, Cape Coast, Ghana. Teacher. m. Phyllis Dodoo, 1954, 6 children. *Education:* BA., London, 1952; Postgraduate Certificate in Education, London, UK, 1953. *Appointments:* Second Headmaster, old site, 1959, First Headmaster, new site, 1960, Apam Secondary School, Ghana; Examiner in Mathematics, West African School Certificate, 1959-64; Retired as Headmaster, Apam Secondary School, 1979; now manages his personal estates, Mpasatia, Ghana. *Memberships:* Honorary member, Hansard Society for Parliamentary Government, UK; Fellow, International Biographical Association, UK. *Publications:* Apass Comes of Age, 1974; Articles in journals; Book reviewer. *Honours:* Presented with Citation and Gold Tie Pin, Foso Branch, People's Educational Association of Ghana, 1958; Elected National President, VOLU, 1978; Installed as Chief, Mbo-fra-Mfa-Adwene re Nana Mbofra-Mfa-Adwene, 1978; House 5, Apam Secondary School named Owiredu House, 1978. *Hobbies:* Reading; Writing; Gardening; Indoor games. *Address:* PO Box 1474, Kumasi, Ashanti, Ghana, West Africa.

OWOREN, Martin Anslem, b. 1 Sept. 1934, Afaha Obong Clan, Abak Division, Cross River State, Nigeria. Management Development and Consultancy. m. 28 Aug. 1965, 1 son, 2 daughters. *Education:* BS., 1960,

MPA., 1961, Cornell University, USA. *Appointments:* Administrative Assistant to General Manager, 1962-64, Assistant Manager, Special Duties, Assistant Manager, Plantations Division, Senior Manager i/c Oil Palm Plantations, 1965-66, Head, Planning and Control Division, Management Committee, 1966-68, Eastern Nigeria Development Corporation; Head, Plantations Department, South Eastern State Ministry of Agriculture and Natural Resources, Nigeria, 1968-69; Senior Lecturer, Consultant, L/c, 1969-74, Director of Institute Services, 1974-76, Deputy Director-General, 1976-, Nigerian Institute of Management. *Memberships:* Fellow, British Institute of Management; Executive member, American Marketing Association; Institute of Marketing, UK; Institute of Management Consultants of Nigeria, Nigerian Institute of Management. *Publications:* Investment in Oil Palm Plantations in Nigeria (co-author), 1965; Articles: Buying Motivation and Consumer Behavior, 1973; Management Consultancy-It's Role in National Development, 1974; The Marketing Function, 1975; Professionals in Public Utilities, 1976; How Companies can get the Best out of the 3rd (Nigeria) Dev. Plan, 1976; How an Executive Should Go About Making a Decision, 1977; Top Management Soul Searching, 1979. *Honours:* Eisenhower Fellow from Nigeria, 1980. *Hobbies:* Gardening; Reading; Writing. *Address:* 27 James Robertson Road, Surulere, Lagos, Nigeria.

OWUSO-NIMOH, Mercy Adoma, b. 6 Feb. 1935, Kade, Eastern Region, Ghana. Librarian. m. Kwabena Owuso-Nimoh, 6 Feb. 1955, 3 sons, 1 daughter. *Education:* Associate, Library Association, UK, 1961; BSc. (Economics), University of Hull, Yorkshire, UK, 1967. *Appointments:* Lending Librarian, Accra Central Library, Ghana, 1961-62; Assistant Librarian, Sydney Webb Training College, London, UK, 1963; Librarian, Sir Henry Cooper High School, Hull, UK, 1967-72; Children's Librarian, Forest Hill Public Library, London, UK, 1972-73; Organiser of School Libraries, and a special library, 1973-75; Librarian, National Investment Bank, Accra, Ghana, 1975-. *Memberships:* Library Association, UK; Ghana Library Association; Council member, Ghana Book Publisher's Association; Executive member, Children's Literature Foundation. *Publications:* Adventures of Coalpot, 1966; Mosquito Town, 1967; Walking Calabash, 1977; Rivers of Ghana, 1977; Kofizee Goes to School, 1978; Stories of Kofizee, 1979. *Honours:* Authorship Development Fund Award, 1976; VALCO Fund Literary Award and Citation, 1979; MONA Award for African Writers-Honorary Mention, 1980; Ghana Book Development Council-Ghana Book Award and Citation, 1980. *Hobbies:* Writing for Children; Gardening; Farming. *Address:* 'Monim House', PO Box 133, Kade, Eastern Region, Ghana.

OWUSU ANSAH, Cecilia Afua Sarpong, b. 13 Jan. 1943, Tetrefuh, Sawuah, Ashanti, Ghana. Librarian. m. 9 Jan. 1967, 2 daughters. *Education:* BA., Library Studies, University of Ghana, Legon, Accra, 1964-67; Certificate, General Management, Accra, Ghana, 1980. *Appointments:* Library Assistant, Ashanti Regional Library, Kumasi, Ghana, 1963-64; Librarian, Ghana Military Academy, Accra, Ghana, 1967; Teacher/Librarian, Government Secondary School, Tamale, Ghana, 1967-70; Librarian: Ghana News Agency, Accra, Ghana, 1970-73, Ministry of Agriculture Reference Library, 1973-77, Management Development and Productivity Institute Library, Ghana, 1977-. *Memberships:* Ghana Library Association; Association of West Africa Agricultural Librarians and Documentatists; Ghana Public Relations Association; Womens Organiser, Kumasi Youngsters Club. *Publications:* Poems: The Woman's Citadel; The Ideal Man; Which is Which; Ideal Woman; Bibliographies on: Oil Palm, 1975; Rice, 1976; ILO publications in MDPI Library, 1941-77, Mar. 1978. *Hobbies:* Dressmaking; Music; Dancing; Reading. *Address:* House No. B. 14/522, Mataheko, Accra, Ghana.

OYEDELE, Yetunde Adeyinka, b. 3 Apr. 1942, Lagos, Nigeria. Pharmacist. m. Akintola (deceased), 16 Aug. 1969, 2 daughters. *Education:* M.Pharm., Chemico Pharmaceutical Institute, Leningrad, Russia, 1970. *Appointments:* Dispensary Controller, Pharmacy Retail Manager, Kingsway Stores, Lagos, Nigeria; Materials Manager, Quality Assurance Manager, Health Care Products formerly Johnson and Johnson Nigeria, Limited. *Memberships:* Melody Thrift and Cooperative Society; National Association of Industrial Pharmacists; Nigerian Pharmaceutical Society. *Hobbies:* Singing; Cooking; Sewing. *Address:* 25 Adelabu Street, PO Box 2959, Surulere, Nigeria.

OYEDIPE, (Chief) Adekunle Ayodele, b. 25 Feb. 1938, Shagamu, Nigeria. Company Director. m. Tola, 14 Dec. 1966, 2 sons, 2 daughters. *Education:* BA., Hons., University of Ibadan, Nigeria, 1962-65; Diploma, Management Science, University of St. Gall, Switzerland, 1967. *Appointments:* Assistant Secretary, Federal Civil Service of Nigeria, 1965-68; Second Secretary, 1969-70, First Secretary, 1970-71, Nigerian High Commission, London, UK, with accreditation to International Coffee Organisation and other commercial deputations; Manager, John Holt (Liverpool) Limited, UK, 1971-73; Management Consultant, Head of Grants and Liaison Department, Centre for Management Development, Lagos, Nigeria, 1974-76; Board member of many companies. *Memberships:* Kuti Hall Students Governing Body, 1963-64; Board of Governors, Remo Secondary School, 1966-69; Governing Council, University of Port-Harcourt, Nigeria, 1978-; Senior Fellow, School of Textiles, Ikeja, Nigeria, 1979-; Trustee, Institute of Textiles, Nigerian Chapter, 1980-; President, Nigeria/India Association, 1978-80; Governing Council, Nigerian Institute of Management, 1980-; Commonwealth Society. *Publications:* Poems published in Ibadan, journal published at University of Ibadan, Nigeria. *Honours:* Awarded Kuti Hall Master's Prize, 1964, Irving & Bonnar Prize for Classics, 1965, University of Ibadan, Nigeria; Dag Hammarskjold Foundation Fellowship, 1967; Honoured with traditional chieftancy title of Jomu of Ilishan-Remo, 1980; Installed as Lowu of Iperu-Remo, 1980. *Hobbies:* Singing; Dancing; Drama; Travelling; Poetry writing. *Address:* 9 Oremeji Street, Ilupeju, Lagos, Nigeria.

OYELEYE, Victor Olusegun, b. 10 June 1943, Ilesha, Oyo State, Nigeria. Ophthalmologist. m. Mopelola Bolaji Omole, 14 Feb. 1972, 1 son, 2 daughters. *Education:* MBBS., University of Ibadan, Nigeria, 1969; DO., Royal College of Physicians and Surgeons, UK, 1973. *Appointments:* Pre-Registration House Officer, 1969-70, Senior Registrar, Eye Clinic, 1975-76, Consultant, Eye Clinic, 1976-79, Senior Consultant, Eye Clinic, 1979-, General Hospital, Lagos, Nigeria; Medical Officer G.11, Marsey Street Children's Hospital, 1971; Senior House Officer, Ophthalmology, 1971-72, Registrar, Ophthalmology, 1973-74, Lagos University Teaching Hospital, Nigeria; Senior House Officer, Ophthalmology, Sussex Eye Hospital, Brighton, UK, 1972-73; Clinical Assistant, Moor Fields Eye Hospital, London, UK, Mar-Sept. 1975. *Memberships:* Hon. Secretary, Ophthalmological Society of Nigeria; International Society of Geographical Ophthalmology. *Creative Works:* Mobile Eye Unit in Nigeria. *Honours:* Fellowship award, West African College of Surgeons. *Hobbies:* Tennis; Music; Motoring. *Address:* 7 Moorhouse Road, Ikoyi, Lagos, Nigeria.

OYENIJI, Anthony Ola, b. 29 Sept. 1945, Abeokuta, Nigeria. Personnel/Contracts Administration. m. Esther Omobayo, 23 Dec. 1970, 1 son, 2 daughters. *Education:* Diploma, Secretaryship, 1973. *Appointments:* Confidential Secretary to Chairman and Chief Executive, 1971-73, Executive Personal Assistant, 1974-75, Administrative Officer, 1975-77, ITT Nigeria Limited; Personnel and Contracts Manager, Radio Communications Nigeria Limited, 1977-. *Memberships:* Associate member, Faculties of Secretaries and Administrations, UK. *Hobbies:* Table tennis; Reading. *Address:* 3 Oyeniji Street, Akowonzo Village, Agege, Lagos, Nigeria.

OYETAN, John Amuwa, b. 20 Nov. 1939, Ondo, Nigeria. Banker. m. 6 Oct. 1964, 4 sons, 2 daughters. *Education:* Diploma, 1965, Fellowship, 1976, Institute of Bankers, London, UK; Certificate, Chartered Corporate Secretaries, 1967. *Appointments:* Executive Officer, Nigerian Stock Exchange, 1967; Banking Executive, Philip Hill (Nigeria) Limited, 1968-69; Assistant Manager, Controller, Nigerian Acceptances Limited, Merchant Bankers, Nigeria, 1969-. *Memberships:* Council member, Chairman, Education Committee, Nigerian Institute of Bankers. *Honours:* College award for Banking Students, London Polytechnic, UK, 1965. *Hobbies:* Tennis; Music. *Address:* 71B Tinobu Road, Palm Grove Estate, Lagos, Nigeria.

OZOLINS, Irina, b. 16 Oct. 1920, Smolensk, Russia. Artist. m. Karlis Ozolins, 24 Apr. 1945, 2 sons, 2 daughters. *Education:* MSc., Riga, Latvia, 1943; Undergraduate, Academy of Arts, Riga, Latvia. *Appointments:* Research Scientist, Physics, University of Dresden, Germany, 1944, 45; Mathematician, Education Department of South Australia, 1954-81. *Memberships:* President, Latvian Press Society in Australia; Royal South Australian Society of Arts; Contemporary Art Society of Australia; Society of Latvian Artists in Australia. *Publications:* Regular literary and travel articles in the newspaper: Australisas Latvietis. *Creative Works:* One-man exhibition at Miller-Anderson Art Gallery, 1975; Exhibitions at: Latvian Hall, 1976, 1977; Contemporary Art Society of Australia, 1979; Miller-Anderson Art Gallery, 1980. *Address:* 20A Pepper Street, Magill 5072, South Australia.

P

PACK, Clive Wesley, b. 22 Jan. 1937, Sydney, Australia. Management Consultant. m. Geraldine Joyce Whiteley, 14 May 1960, 4 sons, 1 daughter. *Education:* Bachelor of Economics, Sydney University, 1958. *Appointments:* The Coca-Cola Export Corporation, 1959-67; Manager, Strategic Services Group and Partner, PA Management Consultant Pty. Limited, 1967-75; Managing Principal, Asian Pacific Region, Vice-President of Louis A Allen Inc. of California, USA, 1975-. *Memberships:* Australian Institute of Management Consultants; Australian Institute of Management. *Hobbies:* Gardening; Camping. *Address:* 118 Arabella Street, Longueville, NSW 2066, Australia.

PAENIU, Isakala, b. 10 Aug. 1939, Mukulaelae, Tuvalu. Journalism; Accountancy; Political Science. m. 2 Mar. 1968, 2 daughters. *Education:* Secondary Education, Correspondence and Attachment Courses, on-the-job Training and Self Study. *Appointments:* Treasury Executive, 1963-66; Public Relations Officer, 1967-69; Member of Parliament, Minister for Natural Resources, 1970-75. *Memberships:* Chairman, Tuvalu Co-operative Societies Limited; Nukulaelae Branch of Co-operative Store; Nukulaelae Agriculture and Fisheries Association. *Publications:* Contributions in Pacific Islands Regional Magazines. *Hobbies:* Sailing; Farming; Fishing; Sports; Reading. *Address:* Punalei, Nukulaelae, Tuvalu.

PAGE, Alexander Warren, b. 1 July 1914, London, England. Director. m. Anne Hickman, 1 June 1940, (Div.), 2 sons, 1 daughter, (2) Andrea Wharton. *Education:* MA (Hons) Mechanical Sciences, Clare College Cambridge. *Appointments:* Chairman, Metal Box Limited 1979 (Retired); Chairman, Electrolux Luton; Director, Shippams, Chichester; Chairman, Gt Pension Services Limited; Chairman, Paine, St Neots. *Honours:* Knighted, 1978; MBE, 1943. *Hobbies:* Golf; Tennis; Do it Yourself; Farming. *Address:* Merton Place, Dunsfold, Nr. Godalming, Surrey GU8 4NP, England.

PAHANG, H H, (Sultan of, Sultan Haji Ahmad Shah ibni Almarhum Sultan Sir Abu Baker Riayatuddin Almuadzam Shah), b. 24 Oct. 1930, Istana Mangga Tunngal, Pekan. Malaysian Ruler. m. Tengku Jajjaj Afzan binti Tengku Muhammad, 1954. *Education:* Malay College, Kuala Kangsar; Worcester College, Oxford; University College, Exeter; Tengku Mahkota (Crown Price), 1944; State Council, 1955; Regent, 1956, 1959, 1965; succeeded as Sultan; Timbalan Yang di Pertuan Agung (Deputy Supreme Head of State of Malaysia), 1975-79, Yang di Pertuan Agung (Supreme Head of State), 1979-(84). *Appointments:* Captain, 4th Battalion, Royal Malay Regiment, 1954; Commander, 12th Infantry Battalion of Territorial Army, 1963-65, Lieutenant-Colonel. *Honours:* DK; SPCM; SPMJ. *Address:* Pekan Lama, Kuantan, Pahang, Malaysia.

PAHLOW, Pauline Mary, b. 10 Mar. 1922, Sydney, NSW, Australia. Public Servant. (Retired). m. Stephen Silady. *Education:* Secretarial Course, Our Lady of Mercy College, Parramatta, Australia. *Appointments:* Commonwealth Public Service; Secretary, Australian Shipbuilding Board, Controller of Ship Repairs; Australian Aluminium Production Commission; P&O Line; Accountancy; Films; Electronics (Amalgamated Wireless Australasia Limited; New South Wales, Public Service, Department of Education 1964-82. *Memberships:* Public Service Association; Australian Boomerang Association; Doll Collectors' Club of NSW. *Publications:* Poems for children on Australian subjects: The Lyrebird; Kookaburra; Blue Wrens; Guild Poems: Doctors; Chemists; Lawyers: Engineers; Printers; Innkeepers; Stories of Cookland; The Saucepan in the Sky; Co-author, The Australian Boomerang. *Honours:* Australian Navy, Army and Air Force crests. *Hobby:* Books. *Address:* 152 Greville Street, Chatswood, NSW 2067, Sydney, Australia.

PAI, Siu Ting, b. 5 Apr. 1931, Wuan, Honan, China. Physicist; Electrical Engineer. m. Pin Y Yang 29 June 1963, 1 son, 1 daughter. *Education:* BSc Physics, Cheng Kung, Taiwan, 1960; MSc Memorial, Canada, 1965; PhD, Windsor, Canada, 1970; Certificate of Electrical Engineer, Ontario, Canada, 1975. *Appointments:* Assistant Professor, University of Pei, Pei, Ca-

nada, 1966-69; Scientist, Welwyn Canada Limited, London, Canada, 1970-76; President, Chisco Mold Manafacturers Limited, London, Canada, 1975-78; Visiting Professor, National Central University, Taiwan, 1978-79; Scientist, Opto Electronics Limited, Oakville, Canada, 1979-. *Memberships:* Association of Professional Engineers of Ontario, Canada; Association of Canadian Physicists, Canada; Institute of Electronics Engineers, USA. *Publications:* X-ray Induced TL Centres in CaF:Ho3, 1981; Electromigration in Metals & Al2 Films, 1977; Composition of Oxides on Ni-P Deposits, 1973; Annealing Effect on Ni-P Films, 1972; Infrared Absorption of Deuterium, 1966. *Honours:* Memorial Graduate Fellowship, 1964 and 65; Ontario Graduate Fellowship, 1969 and 70. *Hobbies:* Classical Music; Badminton. *Address:* 1576 McClure Drive, London, Ontario, Canada N6G 2L2.

PAIN, Michael Cowper Franklyn, b. 9 Apr. 1936, Sydney, Australia. Consultant Physician. m. L Diane McCoy 9 Nov. 1960, 1 son, 2 daughters. *Education:* MB, BS 1959, MD University of Sydney, 1965; Fellowship Royal Australasian College of Physicians, 1971; Postgraduate Training Royal Postgraduate Medical School, London. *Appointments:* Respiratory Specialist, Royal Melbourne Hospital, 1966-79; Director of Thoracic Medicine, Royal Melbourne Hospital, 1980-; Consultant in Respiratory Medicine, Royal Australian Air Force, 1971-; Professorial Associate in Medicine, University of Melbourne, 1980-. *Memberships:* President, Thoracic Society of Australia; Australasian Pioneers Club; Yarra Valley Country Club. *Publications:* Over 40 publications in the field of clinical respiratory physiology and thoracic medicine. *Hobbies:* Reading; Amateur Radio; Medical History. *Address:* 2 Calderwood Street, Bulleen, Victoria 3105, Australia.

PAKENHAM, Aubrey Cecil, b. 8 Dec. 1928, Port Elizabeth Cape Province, South Africa. General Manager. m. Ceta Burt, Mar. 1 son, 1 daughter. *Appointments:* General Manager, Roben Motors (Pvt.) Limited. *Memberships:* National Vice President and Matabeleland Chairman, Wildlife Society of Zimbabwe; Hon. Warden Department National Parks and Wildlife Management; Bulawayo Gun Club; Bulawayo Angling Society; Zimbabwe Clay Pigeon Shooting Association; Zimbabwe Game Association. etc. *Creative Works:* Involved in creation of Tshabalala Wildlife Sanctuary; Interpretive Centre to make animals available for appreciation and study by city dwellers; Shashi Wilderness Trails, an educational centre, for conservation education. *Hobbies:* Bass Fishing; Wildlife Observation and Photography; Subscriber Bulawayo Philharmonic Orchestra. *Address:* 10 Weir Avenue, Hillside, Bulawayo, Zimbabwe.

PALKHIVALA, Nani Ardeshir, b. 16 Jan. 1920, Bombay. Senior Advocate. m. Nargesh H Matbar, 9 Apr. 1945. *Education:* MA Honours in English, 1942; LLB 1st Class First, 1943; LLB 1st Class First, 1944; Advocate (O.S.), 1946. *Appointments:* Professor of Law, Bombay University; Tagore Professor of Law, Calcutta University; Counsel for India, 1964-66; and 1971-72; Ambassador of India to the USA, 1977-79; Chairman: The Associated Cement Companies Limited, Tata Exports Ltd.; Deputy Chairman: The Tata Iron and Steel Company Limited; Vice-Chairman: Tata Engineering and Locomotive Company Limited, Associated Bearing Company Limited; Director of eight other Companies. *Memberships:* Income-tax Appellate Tribunal Bar Association, Bombay; Leslie Sawhny Programme of Training for Democracy; The AD Shroff Memorial Trust; Auroville Committee, Maharashtra State; The Lotus Trust; Forum of Free Enterprise. *Publications:* Joint Author: Law and Practice of Income-tax; Taxation in India; Author: The Highest Taxed Nation; Our Constitution Defaced and Defiled; India's Priceless Heritage; Various articles on Constitutional law, tax laws and economic subjects. *Honours:* Honorary Membership, The Academy of Political Science, New York, 1975; LLD, Princeton University, USA, 1978; LLD, Lawrence University, USA 1979. *Hobbies:* Reading; Motoring. *Address:* Commonwealth, 181 Backbay Reclamation, Bombay 400020, India.

PALLISER, Arthur Michael, b. 9 Apr. 1922, United Kingdom. Permanent Under Secretary of State, Foreign and Commonwealth Office; Head of Diplomatic Service. m. Marie Marguerite Spaak, 15 June 1948, 3 sons. *Education:* Wellington College, 1935-40; MA,

Merton College, Oxford, 1940-41. *Appointments:* Coldstream Guards, 1942-47; HM Diplomatic Service, 1947-. *Honours:* GCMG, 1977; Chevalier, Order of Orange, Nassau, 1944; Chevalier, Légion d'Honneur, 1957. *Address:* Foreign and Commonwealth Office, London, SW1, England.

PALMER, Elizabeth Ann, Musician. *Education:* Foundation Scholar, Royal College of Music; ARCM, Bassoon Performing, Teaching. *Appointments:* 17 years in London; Played in Major Concert halls in Orchestral and Chamber music Concerts; Taught individuals to play orchestral wind instruments; Junior Exhibitions, Royal College of Music; Highgate Boys, Charterhouse and G.P.D.S.T; Festival Adjudicator. *Memberships:* Incorporated Society of Musicians; Music Masters Association; Royal Society of Musicians; Adjudicator, Federation of Music Festivals. *Honours:* Life Member National Trust; International Society for Music in Education. *Hobbies:* Reading; Walking. *Address:* The Oak, Knoll Hill, Bristol, BS9 1QU, England.

PALMER, Norman Kitchener, b. 2 Oct. 1928, Munda, Solomon Islands. Archbishop of Melanesia. m. Elizabeth Lucy Gorringe, 9 Jan. 1960, 3 sons, 1 daughter. *Education:* Te Aute College, New Zealand, 1952-55; Teachers' Certificate, Ardmore College, New Zealand, 1956-57; LTH., St. John's Theological College, New Zealand, 1962-65. *Appointments:* Teacher, King George VI Secondary School, Auki, Solomon Islands, 1958-60; Deacon/Teacher, 1966, Priest/Teacher, 1966, Pawa Secondary School, Anglican,. Solomon Islands; Priest/Headmaster, Alangaula Anglican Primary School, 1967-69, St. Nicholas Anglican Primary School, 1970-72, Solomon Islands; Dean, St. Barnabas Cathedral, Honiara, Solomon Islands, 1973-75. *Memberships:* Public Service Advisory Board, 1971-75. *Honours:* MBE., 1975; CMG., 1981. *Hobby:* Gardening. *Address:* Archbishop's House, PO Box 19, Honiara, Solomon Islands.

PAMBA, Adrian Kasonde, b. 18 May 1948, Luanshya, Zambia. Librarian. m. Catherine Nalungwe Simfukwe, 14 February 1976, 2 sons, 1 daughter. *Education:* A pre-Theology Catholic College, 1967-1969; Diploma in Library Studies (DIP LS), University of Zambia, Lusaka, 1972-1974. *Appointments:* Joined Municipal Council of Luanshya (now Luanshya District Council in April 1970 as Pupil Librarian of Luanshya Public Library; Founder-Librarian of Helen Kaunda Memorial Library in Luanshya 1975; Joined the President's Citizenship College as the first Zambian Librarian-in-charge of this national leadership College; Started a United Nations Depository Library in September 1978 at the same College (PCC). *Memberships:* Secretary of the Zambia Library Association Council, 1980-1981; Chairman of the Standing Conference of Head Librarians of Zambia, 1979-1981; Chairman of the Copperbelt Branch of the Zambia Library Association, 1975-1976; Copperbelt Representative on Zambia Library Association Council, 1975-1977; Zambia Karate Association. *Honours:* Senior-discus championship of the Central Province, 1969; National Certificate of competency in football refereeing, Referee Association of Zambia, 1968. *Hobbies:* Karate; Gymnastics; Athletics; Dancing; Cinema; Music; Football; Reading. *Address:* The President's Citizenship College, P.O. Box 80415, Mulungushi, Kabwe, Zambia.

PANAYIDES, Christou Tasos, b. 9 April 1934, Ktima, Paphos, Cyprus. Ambassador. m. Pandora Constandinides, 27 July, 1969, 2 sons, 1 daughter. *Education:* Paphos Gymnasium; the Cyprus Teacher's Training College; The University of London and the University of Indiana, USA; Diploma in Public Administration and Masters Degree in Political Science. *Appointments:* Teacher in Cyprus, 1954-1959; First Secretary to the President of the Republic Archbishop Makarios, 1960 and later Director of the President's Office; Ambassador of Cyprus to the Federal Republic of Germany, Switzerland and Austria, 1969-1976; Representative of Cyprus to the International Atomic Energy Agency in Vienna, 1976; Secretary and Dean of the Commonwealth Group in Bonn. High Commissioner in U.K. and Ambassador in Denmark, Malta, Sweden, Iceland, Norway, 1979-. *Publications:* Articles in Periodicals. *Honours:* Grand Cross with a Star and Sash of the Federal Republic of Germany; Grand Cross in Gold with Star and Sash of the Republic of Austria. *Hobbies:*

Reading of History Books; Swimming; Other Sports. *Address:* 5 Cheyne Walk, London, S.W.3, England.

PANDEY, Kapil Deo b. 1 Sept. 1936, Ratsar, Ballia, U.P. India. Teacher. m. Smt. Sonmati Devi, 15 June, 1963, 2 sons, 2 daughters. B.A. Gorakhpur University, 1962; Diploma (French) Sampurnanande Sanskrit University Varanasi, 1964; M.A. (Sanskrit) B.H.U., 1965; Ph.D.(Sanskrit) B.H.U., 1967; Diploma (Kannada), Departmental Examinations, Uttar Pradesha, 1979; Shastri (Neo-grammar) Sampurnananda Sanskrit University," Varanasi, 1980; *Appointments:* Lecturer and Head of the Department of Sanskrit in Arya Mahila Degree College, Varanasi, affiliated to B.H.U. 1968-. *Memberships:* Linguistic Society of India, Poona (India), 1970-; Nagari Pracharini Sabha, Varanasi, 1976nh; Sarvabhauma Sanskrit Prachara Karyalaya, Varanasi, Secretary, 1976-; Abhinaya Bharati, Varanasi, Founder-member; Kavibharati, Varanasi, Secretary; Pt. Ramasahaya Samgita, Vidyahaya, Varanasi. *Publications:* Srngaratilaka (Rudrata), a book on rhetorics; Chhandolamkara-Vimarsha, a book on prosody; and Many Articles on Grammar, Linguistics and Indian Philosophy published in different periodicals. *Honours:* Mitra Gold-medal for securing highest position in Sanskrit, 1955; *Hobbies:* Composing Poems in Sanskrit and Hindi; Taking part in Sanskrit Dramas as an actor. *Address:* C27/111 Jagatganj, Varanasi, India.

PANDEYA, Satish Chandra, b. 1 January 1929, Kanpur, U.P. India. University Professor; m. Sheela, 29 January, 1960, 1 son 3 daughters. *Education:* B.Sc. Agra University, India, 1947, Botany, Zoology & Chemistry M.Sc. Saugar University, India, 1949, Botany, Spl. Ecology; Ph.D. Saugar University, India, 1953, Ecology of Grasslands; Perfetta di Ecologia Agraria, Perugia, Italy, Ecology of Croplands, 1955. *Appointments:* Part-time Lecturer in Botany, Saugar University, 1950-1953; Temporary Lecturer in Botany, Saugar University, 1953-1954; Lecturer & Assistant Professor in Botany, M.P. Government Educational Service, 1954-1960; Reader in Botany, Gujarat University Ahmedabad, 1960-1969; Professor & Head, Department of Biosciences, Saurashtra University, Rajkot, 1969-; *Memberships:* Fellow, Indian National Science Academy; Fellow, Linneous Society of London; Fellow, International Society for Tropical Ecology; Fellow, National Academy of Sciences, India; Fellow, National Institute of Ecology; Fellow, Indian Botanical Society. *Publications:* Conducted Research Projects; Held Positions in Conferences and Summer Institutes in India; Delivered Invited Lectures; Consultant to Government of India & Gujarat; Attended many International Meetings and Conferences; Numerous contributions to professional societies, and journals. *Honours:* Fellow, Indian National Science Academy; Chairman International Grassland Congress, Continuing Committee, 1974-1977, Chaired Leipzig Session, 1977; Member, UNESCO Expert Panel on Synthesis of World Knowledge on Tropical Grazing Land Ecosystems, Paris; National Lecturer, Government of India, 1978-1979. *Hobby:* Astrology. *Address:* 59 Shiva-Shakti, Jankalyan Society, Rajkot 360 001, Gujarat, India.

PANGKATANA, Peter, b. 31 August 1941, Dojo, Sentani Barat, West Papua, New Guinea. Medical Practitioner (University Lecturer). m. Loliu Lepilis, 15 February, 1969, 3 sons, 1 daughter. *Education:* Diploma Medicine & Surgery, Papuan Medical College; Diploma in Public Health, Makerere University; Master of Public Health, Amsterdam. *Appointments:* Medical Officer Grade I, 1966-1968; Paediatric Registrar, 1969-1972; Assistant Paediatrician, 1973-1974; Tutor (University of Papua New Guinea), 1973-1974; Lecturer in Community Health, 1974-1978; Senior Lecturer in Community Health, University of Papua, New Guinea, 1978nh; Dean of the Faculty of Medicine, University of Papua New Guinea, 1979-1980. *Memberships:* Australian College of Paediatrics; South East Asian Paediatric Society; Papua New Guinea Paediatric Society; President of Papua New Guinea Paediatric Society, 1978-1979; Papua New Guinea Medical Society; Papua New Guinea Medical Society President, 1980 ; Member of the Council of the University of Papua New Guinea. *Publications:* Published papers on Health of Children in urban areas, and also problems of medical schools in developing countries. *Hobbies:* Reading Detective Stories; Reading and Listening to Cricket Test Matches; Coaching Soccer (Football) to school children.

Address: Section 70 Lot 2, Valkyrie Street, Korobosea, Papua New Guinea.

PANNELL, Christopher John Masterman, b. 1 April 1938, Middlesex, United Kingdom. Mechanical Engineer. m. Philomena Mary Wohlfahrt, 19 April 1965, 4 sons, 5 daughters. *Education:* Higher National Certificate Mechanical Engineering & Marine Engineering, Bath Technical College, 1958-1960. *Appointments:* Design Draughtsman, Stothert & Pitt Ltd., Bath, U.K. 1958-1960; Application Engineer, Pannell Plant Ltd., Plymouth, U.K., 1960-1963; Design Engineer, Coates & Co. Ltd., Melbourne, Australia, 1963-1965; Sales Manager, N.S.W., Coates & Co. Ltd., Sydney, Australia, 1965-1967; State Manager, N.S.W., Coates & Co. Ltd., Sydney, Australia, 1967-1973; Chairman & Managing Director, Pannell Plant Pty. Ltd., Sydney, Australia, 1971-1978; Chairman & Managing Director, Pannell Holdings Pty. Ltd., Sydney, 1975-; Director, Pannell Plant Ltd., Plymouth, U.K., 1978-. *Memberships:* Associate Member Institute of Plant Engineers, London, U.K. Secretary, St. Cecilia's School, Wyong. N.S.W., Australia. *Honours:* Commonwealth of Australia Industrial Research & Development Grants 1977, 1978, 1979, for Design and Development of Innovative Special Purpose Construction Machinery; Australian Design Award, 1981, By Industrial Design Council of Australia. *Hobbies:* Australian Native Flora; Steam Power & Alternate Energy. *Address:* Torr Hill, Beckingham Road, Berkeley Vale. N.S.W. 2259, Australia.

PANT, Narendra Chandra, b. 28 January, 1924, Dehradun, India. Director, Commonwealth Institute of Entomology. m. Madhuri Pant, 5 Feb. 1952, 1 son, 2 daughters. *Education:* M.Sc (Agriculture) Agra University, India, 1946; Ph.D, London University, UK, 1950; D.I.C., Imperial College, London UK, 1950. *Appointments:* Quarantine Entomologist, Government of India, 1950-1952; Lecturer Zoology, Delhi University, India, 1952-1956; Insect Physiologist, Indian Agricultural Res. Institute, Delhi, India, 1956-1968; Professor of Entomology, Indian Agricultural Res. Institute, Delhi, India, 1968-1971; Dean Agriculture, H.P. University, Simla, India, 1971-1972; Professor & Head Department Entomology, Indian Agricultural Res. Inst. Delhi, India, 1972-1977; Director, Commonwealth Institute of Entomology, London, 1977-. *Memberships:* Fellow of Entomological Society of India (President, 1970-1972) Fellow of the Royal Entomological Society of London; Fellow of the Indian National Science Academy, India; Fellow of the Institute of Biology, London. *Publications:* Published more than 50 Research Papers, several Scientific Reviews, edited two books on Applied Entomology and Insect Nutrition and Symbiosis with Micro-organisms. *Hobby:* Comparative Religion. *Address:* 1 A Orchard Close, Wembley, Middlesex, HA0 1TZ, England.

PANTON, Verma Wevlyn b. 17 April 1936, Malvern, St. Elizabeth, Jamaica W.I. Architect. *Education:* Jamaican Government Scholarship in Architecture, 1958; Bachelor Architecture, McGill University, 1964. *Appointments:* Ministry of Education, Kingston, Jamaica, 1964-1968; McMorris Sibley, Robinson, Kingston, Jamaica, 1968-, Associate. *Memberships:* Jamaican Institute of Architects; McGill Graduate Society, Past Vice President; St. Andrew Business & Professional Women's Club; Liguanea Club, Horticultural Society, Orchid Society; Recipient of Qualifying academic certificate from the Royal Architectural Institute of Canada Certification Board; Past Chairman of Public Relations Committee of the Jamaican Society of Architects; Chairman of Organising Committee of the Pan American Federation of Architects Association Conference held in Jamaica, 1973; Representative of the Jamaican Society of Architects to the Pan American Federation of Architects Conferences held in Latin America and the Caribbean 1974-1975 & 1976; Heart Foundation Club of Jamaica; National Advisory Council on Energy Conservation, Jamaica. *Creative Works:* Ceramics & Jewellery Design & Making. *Honours:* Honorable Mention-House Design, Wood Preservation Ltd. 1967; Honourable Mention, Low Income Housing Design, Redimix Concrete Ltd., 1973. *Hobbies:* Reading; Jogging; Squash; Ceramics; Jewellery Craft; Horticulture. *Address:* 4 Avesbury Avenue, Kingston 6, Jamaica, West Indies.

PANTRIDGE, (James) Frank, b. 3 October 1916, Hillsborough, Co. Down, N. Ireland. Physician and Professor of Cardiology. *Education:* Bachelor of Medicine, Queen's University Belfast, 1939; Doctor of Medicine, Queen's University, Belfast, 1947; Research Fellow, University of Michigan, Ann Arbor, 1948-1949; *Appointments:* Physician in Charge, Cardiac Department, Royal Victoria Hospital, 1954nh; Professor of Cardiology, Queen's University, Belfast, 1971-; Director, Regional Medical Cardiology Centre, Royal Victoria Hospital, Belfast, N. Ireland, 1977-. *Memberships:* British Cardiac Society (Chairman 1978); Member Executive Committee Association Physicians Great Britain; Fellow Royal College of Physicians (London); Fellow American College of Cardiology; Athenaeum Club. *Publications:* Author of The Acute Coronary Attack (Pitman Medical), 1975; Multiple articles, British Heart Journal, American Heart Journal, Circulation, British Medical Journal, Lancet, European Journal of Cardiology. *Creative Works:* Developer of first portable defibrillator; Pioneer Pre-hospital Coronary Care. *Honours:* Commander Order of British Empire, 1978; Military Cross, 1942; Honorary Fellow, Royal College of Physicians (Ireland), 1955; Honorary Doctor of Science, New University of Ulster, 1981; Honorary Doctorate, Open University, 1981; Canadian Heart Foundation Orator; St. Cyres Orator, National Heart Hospital, London. *Hobby:* Fishing. *Address:* Hillsborough, Co. Down, Ireland.

PANTRY, Ansley Gareth Vallis, b. 22 Feb. 1931, Bermuda. Bank Officer. m. Mary Jane, 15 Apr. 1950, 3 sons. *Education:* Saltus Grammar School, Pembroke, Bermuda, 1938-46. *Appointments:* General Post Office, Hamilton, Bermuda, 1947-52; The Bank of Bermuda Limited, Hamilton, Bermuda, 1952-. *Honours:* Justice of the Peace, 1972. *Hobbies:* Boats; Sailing; Fishing; Bird Watching. *Address:* PO Box 46, Flatts Post Office, Smith's Parish, 3-20, Bermuda.

PAO, Cohon, b. 1 Aug. 1913, Shanghai, China. Managing Proprietor. m. Dora Lee, 21 Dec. 1958, 1 son. *Education:* BSc., Fuh Tan University, Shanghai, China. *Appointments:* Senior Engineer, War Production Board, Republic of China; Director of: Taiwan Industrial & Mining Enterprises, Associated Office, Avon Cosmetics (Hong Kong) Limited and Cosmos Products Incorporated, Canada; Managing Director, Kaliwood Enterprises Limited, Kong Kong; Managing Proprietor, Cosmos Development Company. *Memberships:* Hong Kong General Chamber of Commerce; Kowloon Chamber of Commerce; The Chinese Manufacturer's Association of Hong Kong. *Creative Works:* Inventor & Owner of: British Patent No. 1,204,654; 1,215,287; 1,341,811; 1,513,499; US Patent No. 3,774,255; 4,137,926. *Honours:* The New Products Award of 1971, Hong Kong New Products Competition. *Hobbies:* Amateur Violinist; Invention of new products. *Address:* 36 Belleview Drive, 16/F Repulse Bay Garden, Repulse Bay, Hong Kong.

PAPADOPOULOS, Achilles Symeon, b. 16 Aug. 1923, Palekhori, Cyprus. HM Diplomatic Service. m. Joyce Martin (Stark), 17 Jan. 1954, 1 son, 2 daughters. *Education:* The English School, Nicosia. *Appointments:* British Administration of Eritrea, 1943-52; HMOCS: Cyprus, 1953; Tanganyika, 1959; Malta, 1961; HM Diplomatic Service: Malta, 1965; Nairobi, 1965; FCO, 1968; Colombo, 1971; Washington, 1974; Havana, 1974; HM Ambassador to El Salvador, 1977; to Mazambique, 1979; British High Commissioner, Nassau, 1981. *Memberships:* Royal Commonwealth Society. *Honours:* CMG, 1980; MVO, 1972; MBE, 1954. *Hobbies:* Bridge; Golf. *Address:* 5 Lansdowne Close, Wimbledon, London, SW20 8AS, England.

PARAMESHWARAN, Nadarajah, b. 19 Sept. 1925, Sri Lanka. Medical Specialist in Clinical Pathology. m. Dharini de Soysa, 27 Nov. 1952, 1 son. *Education:* MB.,BS., Sri Lanka, 1952; DCP London, 1958; MRCP Edinburgh, 1961; Founder Member of Royal College of Pathologists, UK, 1963, Founder Fellow, 1975; Fellow, Royal College of Physicians, Edinburgh, 1979. *Appointments:* Internship and Pathology trainee in Sri Lanka, 1952-57; Locum Registrar in Warley Hospital, Essex, England, 1960 and St Stephen's Hospital, London, 1962; Consultant Clinical Pathologist in Sri Lanka, 1961-76; Regional Pathologist in Muldura Base Hospital, Victoria, Australia, 1976-81. *Memberships:* Social Secretary, Sri Lanka Medical Association, 1974-76; Honorary Co-Editor, Sri Lanka Medical Journal, 1974-76. *Publications:* Contributor to several professional medical journals; Co-author of Hypertriglyceridaemia in Rye's Syndrome, 1979. *Honours:* Post-graduate scholarship, 1957; Post-graduate scholarship, 1967; Prizes for Tennis and Billiards. *Hobbies:* Philately; Music; Gardening. *Address:* 1 Jenner Court, Muldura, Victoria 3500, Australia.

PARASHAR, Narain Chand, b. 2 July 1935, Fenzepur, India. Teaching; Member of Parliament (Lok Sabha). m. Smt. Swarnlata, 1968, 2 sons, 2 daughters. *Education:* MA, Government College, Punjab University, Ludhiana, Punjab, 1959; BA, DAV College, hoshiarpur, Punjab, 1955; MA, (Prev.) Delhi University; Diploma in Japanese, Chinese and Bengali; Certificate Course in German and Tamil; Proficient in Sanskrit, Urdu, Pahari, Hindi, Punjabi & Pali. *Appointments:* Lecturer in English, Government College, Tanda Urmar, 1958- 62, Ludhiana, 1962-65; Senior Lecturer & Head Department of English (Literature), PGDAV College, Delhi University, New Delhi, 1979-; Parliament of India, 1971-77. *Memberships:* Central Advisory Board of Educators; Vice-President, All India Federation of Educational Associations; Mahabodhi Society of India; Linguistic Society of India; Indian Council of World Affairs; Court of Delhi University, 1974; Court of Himachal Pradesh University, 1971; Indian National Congress, 1965-; Executive, Congress Party in Parliament. *Publications:* Play in Pahari, Graeen Kanen Tisra Gran; Edited Himdhara in Pahari, Yugdisha in Hindi; Short stories and articles (Pahari, Hindi & English). *Honours:* Merit Scholarship; Honoured as writer in Pahari language and literature by Himachal Pradesh State Government, 1970; Presided, First National Conference of Voluntary Associations in the field of Modern Indian Languages, Central Institute of Indian Languages, Mysore, 1974; Vice-President, Steering Committee, First National Convention on the Problems & Potentials of Development in Hill Regions of India, 1975; Delegate to 35th UN General Assembly, 1980. *Hobbies:* Hockey; Philately. *Address:* 9 Mahadev Road, New Delhi-1, India.

PARBERY, Douglas George, b. 27 May 1935, Bega, New South Wales, Australia. Agricultural Scientist, Plant Pathologist, Mycologist. m. Betty Margaret Birkin, 19 May 1962, 3 sons, 1 daughter. *Education:* BSc., Sydney University, 1959; M.Agr.Sc., University of Queensland, 1962; PhD., University of Melbourne, 1970. *Appointments:* Demonstrator in Botany, University of Queensland, 1959-61; Lecturer in Plant Pathology, 1962-78, Reader in Agriculture and Forestry, University of Melbourne, 1978-; Dean, Faculty of Agriculture and Forestry, 1981-83. *Memberships:* British Mycological Society; Australian Plant Pathology Society; Australian Institute of Agricultural Science, Victoria Branch Committee. *Publications:* Over 50 scientific publications in professional journals. *Hobbies:* Reading; Railways History; 19th Century Australian History, especially transport and agricultural development. *Address:* 24 Churchill Street, Mont Albert, Victoria, 3127, Australia.

PARBO, Arvi Hillar, b. 10 Feb. 1926, Tallinn, Estonia. Mining Engineer. m. 4 Apr. 1953, 2 sons, 1 daughter. *Education:* Bachelor of Engineering, University of Adelaide, 1956. *Appointments:* Underground Surveyor, Technical Assistant, Great Western Consolidated N.L; Underground Manager, Nevoria Mine; Technical Assistant to Managing Director, Western Mining Corporation Limited; Deputy General Superintendent, General Manager, Chairman & Managing · Director, WMC; Chairman, Alcoa of Australia Limited; Chairman, BH South Limited. *Memberships:* Fellow, Australian Academy of Technical Sciences and Institute of Engineers, Australia. *Honours:* Knight Bachelor, 1978; Commander's Cross of the Order of Merit of the Federal Republic of Germany, 1979. *Hobbies:* Reading; Carpentry. *Address:* Longwood, 737 Highbury Road, Vermont South, Victoria, 3133, Australia.

PARDON, George, b. 4 Mar. 1942, Germany. Teacher. m. Danielle, 9 July 1966, 1 son. *Education:* Teachers College, University of Toronto, 1969-70. *Appointments:* Auto Body Repairman, Germany, 1956-62, Montreal, Canada, 1962-65, Toronto, Canada, 1965-69; Teacher of Auto Repair in a vocational school. *Memberships:* Canadian Junior Development Committee, 1974-78. *Hobbies:* Reading; Sports; Gardening. *Address:* 169 Wintermute Boulevard, Scarborough, Ontario, Canada, M1W 3M9.

PARECATTIL, Joseph, b. 1 Apr. 1912, Kidangoor, India. Archbishop. *Education:* BA, Madras University; Licentiate in Philosophy and Doctorate in Theology, Papal Athaneum, Kandy, Sri Lanka. *Appointments:* Assistant Parish Priest; Parish Priest; Editor; Bishop; Archbishop; Cardinal, 1969. *Memberships:* Pontifical Commission for the Codification of Latin Canon Law, 1969; President of the Pontifical Commission for the Revision of the Oriental Canon Law, 1972; Vice-Chairman, Catholic Bishops' Conference of India, President, 1972; President, Syro-Malabar Bishops' Conference as well as· of the Kerala Catholic Bishops' Conference; Chancellor of the Pontifical Institute of Philosophy and Theology; Re-elected President, of the Catholic Bishops' Conference of India, 1974. *Address:* Cardinal's House, Post Bag 2580, Cochin, 682031, India.

PARENT, Lucien Adrianus, b. 16 Feb. 1932, Holland. Piano-maker. m. Christine Zealia Ekins, 23 Jan. 1964, 2 daughters. *Education:* Self-educated, following High School; Circa 30,000 hours spent in piano research to date; Studied piano research and design in many important piano factories and museums around the world. *Appointments:* Self-employed, 1953-. *Memberships:* Rotary Club of Unley S.A.; Early Music Society of South Australia; Australian Society for Keyboard Music. *Publications:* Technical paper on Piano Design; Small classical piano solo compositions and improvisations; Traditional paintings; UK Patent No. 846286, for improvements in piano-design. *Honours:* Consultations and work carried out for: Australian Society for Music Educators conference, Canberra, 1977; International Sydney Piano Competition, 1977; Adelaide Festival of Arts Piano Competition, 1978; Victorian College of the Arts Melbourne, at the recommendation of Yehudi and the late Hephzibah Menuhin, 1980 and 1981; Mastered the technique to modify and improve the tone-character and quality of any given make of piano or grand, any size, new or old, to any desired tonal quality. *Hobbies:* Private antique piano museum collection; Painting; Playing the piano; Historic coins; Lawn tennis. *Address:* 2a Angove Court, Rosslyn Park, South Australia, 5072.

PARGAONKAR, Damodar Rangrao, b. 18 May 1934, Aurangabad (Maharashtra), India. Veterinarian (Gynaecologist). m. Ashalata Balkrishna Deshpande, 6 June 1966, 2 sons, 1 daughter. *Education:* BVSc., 1958; MVSc., 1969; FRVCS (Sweden), 1971; PhD., 1979. *Appointments:* Veterinary Officer in charge, Veterinary Hospital, 1958, Key Village Centre, 1959-64; Lecturer, Nagpur Veterinary College, 1965-68; Assistant Professor (Gynaecology), 1969-70; Reader in Gynaecology, 1970-78; Associate Professor of Gynaecology, 1979-; Professor of Gynaecology, 1981. *Memberships:* Secretary, Maharashtra Veterinary Association; Indian Association for Fertility & Sterility; Indian Society for Study of Animal Reproduction. *Publications:* 27 publications. *Honours:* National Livestock Committee, New Delhi awarded Silver Medal in appreciation of good work done in 1964. *Hobbies:* Shuttle Badminton; Bridge. *Address:* Shivaji Nagar, Parbhani 431 401, India.

PARIKH, Pravin, b. 10 Jan. 1931, Bombay. Techno-Comm. Management. m. Sulochana Shah, 19 Jan. 1953, 2 sons. *Education:* BSc., University of Bombay, 1950; MSc., Gujarat University, India, 1954; Doctorate in Science, University of Mainz, West Germany, 1961; Post Doctoral Fellowship, Toshiba Central Research Laboratory, Japan, 1964. *Appointments:* Lecturer in Physics, VP College, Gujarat, India; Max Planck Institute, Mainz, West Germany, 1950-62; Reader in Physics, Punjab University, Chandigarh, 1962-63; Senior Scientific Officer, Full-time Research, SSPL, Delhi, India, 1963; Techno-Comml. & Marketing Management (Electronic Components Division), Peico Electronics & Electricals Limited, Bombay, 1970-. *Memberships:* Fellow, Institution of Electronics & Telecommunications Engineers, Chairman, Bombay Centre; Institute of Electricals & Electronics Engineers Incorporated, Executive Council, Bombay; Magnetic Society of India, Executive Council; *Publications:* 31 Research papers published in international journals; Guided research and application work in various laboratories to team of more than ten scientists and engineers, 1963-; Leading a team of marketing of electronic components; Editing and publishing journal, Electronic Applications News, 1971-. *Honours:* Proposed for RL Wadhwa Prize, Institution of Electronics & Telecommunications Engineers, for research work and industrial development in Electronics in India. *Hobbies:* Photography; Outdoor; Geography. *Address:* 51 Radheshyam Apartments, Barfiwala Lane, (Juhu Lane), Andheri (West), Bombay 400 058.

PARKER, Alec Harry, b. 6 Mar. 1924, England. Entomologist. *Education:* BSc. Hons. Birmingham, 1944; MSc., Birmingham, 1946; PhD., Glasgow, 1955. *Appointments:* Assistant Lecturer in Zoology, University of Birmingham, 1945-46, University of Glasgow, 1946-48, University of Nottingham, 1948-50; Research Officer, West African Institute for Trypanosomiasis Research, Nigeria, 1950-54; Entomologist, Colonial Pesticides Research Unit, England, 1954-57; Senior Lecturer in Zoology, University of Khartoum, Sudan, 1957-60, Sir John Cass College, London, 1966-69; Senior Lecturer/Associate Professor in Zoology, University of Ibadan, Nigeria, 1961-66; Assistant Director, Commonwealth Institute of Entomology, London, 1969-. *Memberships:* MIBiol; FRES. *Publications:* Numerous entomological research papers. *Hobbies:* Music; Theatre; Mythology; Historical Natural History. *Address:* 44 Beaumont Avenue, Wembley, Middlesex, HA0 3BY, England.

PARKER, Geoffrey Frank, b. 10 Sept. 1917, Cooma, NSW, Australia. Bishop. m. Barbara, 14 Apr. 1956, 1 son, 1 daughter. *Education:* BA, University of Sydney, 1937; Th.L., Moore Theological College, Sydney, 1939; BA, 1951, MA, 1955, University of Oxford. *Appointments:* Chaplain: Trinity Grammar School, Summer Hill, NSW, 1941, RAAF, 1942-46, Launceston Grammar School, Tasmania, 1951; Rector, Hurlstone Park, Sydney, 1942; Locum Temens Oddington (Dio of Gloucester, England), 1951; Rector, Aberdeen, (Dio. of Newcastle), 1953, Singleton, (Dio. of Newcastle); Vice-Warden of St John's Theological College, Morpeth, 1964; Rector of Muswellbrook, NSW, 1970; Auxiliary Bishop of Diocese of Newcastle, NSW, 1974. *Memberships:* University of Newcastle, Theological College, NSW. *Honours:* Queen Elizabeth II Jubilee Medal, 1980. *Hobbies:* Jogging; Golf; Fibre Spinning. *Address:* Cathedral Close, Church Street, Newcastle, NSW, 2300, Australia.

PARKER, James Roland Walter, b. 1919. British Diplomat. m. Deirdre Mary Ward, 1941. *Education:* Southall Grammar School. *Appointments:* Ministry of Labour, 1938-57; HM Forces, 1940-41; Labour Attache Tel Aviv, 1957-60; Labour Adviser, Accra, 1960-62, to Lagos, 1962-64; Seconded to Foreign Office, 1965-66; First Secretary, Lagos, 1966; Deputy High Commissioner, Enugu, 1966-67; Foreign and Commonwealth Office, 1968-70; Head of Chancery, British High Commission, Suva, 1970-71; British High Commissioner to the Gambia, 1971-75; HM Counsul-General, Durban, 1976; Governor and Commander-in-Chief of the Falkland Islands, 1976-80. *Memberships:* Travellers'; MCC. *Honours:* CMG; OBE. *Address:* 1 St Edmund's Court, St Edmund's Terrace, London, NW8, England.

PARKER, Kevin Horace, b. 6 Feb. 1937, Kalgoorlie, Western Australia. Law. m. Joan Margaret, 2 sons, 3 daughters. *Education:* LI.B., University of Western Australia, 1958. *Appointments:* Admitted as Barrister and Solicitor, Supreme Court of Western Australia and of High Court of Australia, 1960; Appointed Crown Counsel for Western Australia, 1973; Appointed Solicitor General of Western Australia, 1979. *Memberships:* Chairman, Barristers' Board of Western Australia; Chairman, Privacy Law Committee, Law Council of Australia, 1978-79; Diocesan Advocate, Anglican Diocese of Perth, 1968-; Honorary ADC (Air) to Governor of Western Australia, 1965-70. *Honours:* Appointed Queen's Counsel, 1977; Appointed Honorary ADC (Air) to HM The Queen, 1979. *Address:* 20 Campion Crescent, Attadale, 6156, Western Australia.

PARKER, Nick, b. 20 Sept. 1945, USA (naturalised British, 1977). Principal Adviser to the Royal Family of the Yemen; Underwriting member of Lloyd's and Company Chairman. m. Inge Christa Bromann, 17 Feb. 1967 (Divorced 1972). *Education:* International Correspondence Schools Diploma in Industrial Psychology, 1962; London School of Journalism, 1971-72; Middle East Centre for Arabic Studies, Shumlan, Lebanon, 1972 & 1974. *Appointments:* Professional numismatist, 1961-68; Freelance journalist, specialising in Middle East, 1968-72; Intelligence agent for Royal Family

of Yemen, 1972; Administrator-General, Hamid ed-Din Order of the Crown of Yemen, 1973; Principal Adviser to the Royal Family of the Yemen, 1973; Royal Yemeni Special Ambassador, 1974; Seconded to Greek Royalist Underground, 1974; Underwiring member of Lloyd's, 1979-. *Memberships:* Bureau for International Monarchist Relations, Chairman; Vice-Chairman, Royal Society of St George; Representative, Professional Karate Association. *Publications:* Numerous newspaper and magazine articles, lectures, etc. *Honours:* Grand Cordon, Special Distinction Division, Hamid ed-Din Order of Crown of Yemen, 1973; Style of His Excellency, 1974; Grand Cross Order of the Star of Ethiopia, 1978; Grand Commander, Imperial Order of Glory (Tunesia), 1979, styles (Tunisian) of Shaikh and Bey, 1979; Honorary Tunesian diplomatic status (diplomatic passport), 1981; Freedom of the City of London, 1979. *Hobbies:* Karate; Flying; Languages; Gastronomy; Travel; Snooker; Riding. *Address:* 56 Curzon Street, London, W1Y 7PF, England.

PARKER, Peter (Sir), b. 30 Aug. 1924. Chairman. m. Gillian Row-Dutton, 1951, 3 sons, 1 daughter. *Education:* Bedford School; London University; Lincoln College, Oxford. *Appointments:* Major, Intelligence Corps, 1943-47; Commonwealth Fund Fellowship to Cornell and Harvard, 1950-51; Contested (Lab), Bedford, 1951; Philips Electrical, 1951-53; Head of Overseas Department Industrial Soc. 1953-54; Secretary Duke of Edinburgh's Study Conference on Human Problems of Industry, 1954-56; Joined Booker McConnell Limited, 1956; Chairman: Bookers Engineering & Industrial Holdings Limited, 1966-70; Associated Maltsters Limited, 1971-73; Rockware Group Limited, 1971-76 (pt-time Member, 1976-); Curtis Brown Limited, 1971-76; Victoria Deep Water Terminal Limited, 1971-76; Dawnay Day Group, 1971-76; H Clarkson & Company (Holdings) Limited, 1975-76 (pt-time Member 1976-); Director: Booker Bros McConnell & Company Limited, 1960-70; Renold Group Limited; Chairman-designate, National Ports Authority, 1970; Member of British Airways Board, 1971-; Chairman, British Railways Board, 1976-. *Memberships:* BSC, 1967-70; British Transit Authority Board, 1969-75; Court of London University, Deputy Chairman, 1970; Political and Economic Planning Executive, Vice-Chairman, 1969-70, Honorary Treasurer, 1973-78; Council, BIM, Vice-Chairman; Foundation on Automation & Human Development, 1971-; Engineering Industries Council, 1975-76; Council of Foundation for Management Education; Chairman, Westfield College, 1969-76, Honorary Fellow, 1979; Clothing EDC, 1971-78; Advisory Council, Business Graduates Association; *Honours:* Kt., 1978; MVO, 1957. *Hobby:* Rugby. *Address:* Rail House, Euston Square, London NW1 6DZ, England.

PARKER, Richard Eric, b. 6 May 1925, Leicester, United Kingdom. Chartered Chemist. m.' Elizabeth Anne Howgego, 14 Nov. 1969, 1 son. *Education:* University College, Leicester, 1943-46; King's College, London, 1946-47; BSc Hons. Chemistry, 1946; PhD, 1954. *Appointments:* Assistant Lecturer, 1947-50; Lecturer, Organic Chemistry, University of Southampton, 1950-62; Secretary and Registrar, Royal Institute of Chemistry, 1962-80; Registrar and Secretary for Public Affairs, Royal Society of Chemistry, 1980-. *Memberships:* Fellow, Royal Society of Chemistry; Member of Council, RIC; Fellow, Royal Society of Arts; Savage Club. *Publications:* About 30 papers on physical organic chemistry, mainly in journal of the Chemical Society; occasional articles on position of scientists in society. *Hobbies:* Travel; Watching Rugby Football. *Address:* 6 Woodside House, Woodside, Wimbledon, London, SW19 7QN, England.

PARKIN, Arthur Raymond, b. 24 Sept. 1917, Melbourne, Australia. Pathologist. m. Margaret Mary Powell, 31 Dec. 1970. *Education:* Wesley College, Melbourne, Draper Scholarship, Government Senior Scholarship; Bachelor of Medicine, Bachelor of Surgery, University of Melbourne, 1941; Fellow, Royal College of Pathologist of Australia, 1956. *Appointments:* RMO, Royal Women's Hospital 1942; Captain, Australian Army Medical Corps, 1942-45; Medical Officer, Department of Repatriation, 1945-; Senior Specialist Histopathology, Repatriation General Hospital, Heidelberg. *Memberships:* Australian Orchid Foundation; Melbourne Eastern Orchid Society; Fellow, Royal Horticultural Society; Victorian Orchid Club; Repatriation Wine Tasting Club; Toyota Landcruiser

Club. *Publications:* Conduct a monthly meeting of histopathologists for discussion of cases of interest, 1964-. *Hobbies:* Horticulture; Photography; Snow-Skiing; Outback Touring Australia. *Address:* 12/623 Drummond Street, North Carlton, 3054, Victoria, Australia.

PARKINSON, Michael Warren, b. 19 August 1943, Bombay, India. Banker. m. Kristin Harvey, 11 Dec. 1971, 1 son, 1 daughter. *Education:* Winchester College, United Kingdom, 1956-61; BA Hons. Cambridge University, 1962-65; MBA, Stanford University, USA, 1969-71. *Appointments:* Unilever Limited, United Kingdom 1965-69; First National City Bank, Sydney, Australia, 1971-74; Citi National Holdings Limited, Melbourne, Australia, 1974-78; Managing Director, Grindlays Australia Limited, Melbourne, Australia, 1978-. *Memberships:* Australian British Trade Association; Oriental Club, London; Melbourne Club; Australian Club; Hawks Club, Cambridge. *Hobbies:* Royal Tennis; Riding; Cricket; Reading. *Address:* 223 Burke Road, Glen Iris, Victoria, Australia 3146.

PARKINSON, Nicholas Fancourt, (Sir) b. 5 Dec. 1925, England. Australian Diplomat. m. Roslyn Sheena Campbell, 12 Aug. 1952, 2 daughters. *Education:* BA., Hons., University of Sydney, Australia, 1951; University of London (SOAS) and Middle East Centre for Arab Studies, 1952-53. *Appointments:* Joined Australian Diplomatic Service, 1951; Served in Cairo, 1953-56, Hong Kong 1958-61; Moscow, 1963; Wellington, New Zealand, 1963-65; Kuala Lumpur, 1965-67; Canberra; Australian High Commissioner to Singapore, 1970-74; Deputy Secretary, 1974-76, Secretary, Department of Foreign Affairs, Canberra, Australia, 1977-79; Australian Ambassador to USA., 1976-77, 1979-. *Honours:* Knight Bachelor, 1980. *Hobbies:* Tennis; Bridge; Farming. *Address:* 3120 Cleveland Avenue, Washington DC., 20008, USA.

PARR, Joan Oddny, b. 12 Nov. 1929, Winnipeg, Manitoba, Canada. Publisher. m. John Lloyd Davidson Parr, 9 Jan. 1954, 2 daughters. *Education:* BA., 1952, Bachelor of Paedagogy, 1959, University of Manitoba, Canada. *Appointments:* Teacher, Grandview, Manitoba, Canada, 1952-53; Teacher, Cook's Creek, Manitoba; Supply teacher, London County Council, London, UK, 1954-56; Teacher, English, Viscount Alexander School, Fort Garry, Manitoba, Canada; Part-time teacher, Adult Education Centre and Daniel McIntyre Collegiate Institute, Winnipeg, Manitoba, Canada, 1962-64, 1971-72; Part-time lecturer, English, Med. Rehabilitation Centre, Winnipeg, Canada, 1968-73; Publisher, own Publishing Co., Queenston House, Canada, 1973-. *Memberships:* Association of Canadian Publishers; Vice-President, 1979, Association of Manitoba Book Publishers. *Publications:* Editor: Winnipeg Stories, 1974. *Honours:* Carolyn Berbrayer 2nd Prize, English, 1964; Sellers Scholarship, Arts, 1949. *Hobbies:* Sewing; Interior Design; Carpentry; Gourmet cooking. *Address:* 102 Queenston Street, Winnipeg, Manitoba, Canada, R3N 0W5.

PARRIS, C Deighton, b. 11 Oct. 1922, Barbados, West Indies. Television/Electronics Engineer. m. 23 Nov. 1963, (div), 1 son, 1 daughter. *Education:* Chartered Engineer; Institution of Electronic and Radio Engineers, UK; Television Society, UK; Association of Professional Engineers, Trinidad and Tobago. *Appointments:* Chief Engineer, 1965, General Manager, 1980, Trinidad and Tobago Television Co., West Indies. *Publications:* Regular contributor to publications of Commonwealth Broadcasting Association. *Hobbies:* Lawn tennis; Swimming; Physical culture; Electronics. *Address:* 8 Bimitti Road, Valsayn Park, Trinidad, West Indies.

PARROTT, William Egmont, b. 24 Aug. 1910, Wanganui, New Zealand. Journalist (retired). m. Esther Rebecca Goodland, 11 May 1937, 2 sons, 1 daughter. *Education:* Diploma, Journalism, 1932, BA., 1933, Canterbury University, Christchurch, New Zealand, 1929-33. *Appointments:* Reporter: Taranaki Daily News, New Plymouth, New Zealand, 1927-28; Christchurch Sun, New Zealand, 1933-35; Reporter/Foreign Correspondent, New Zealand Herald, Auckland, New Zealand, 1935-47; Chief correspondent, Reuter-Australian Associated Press; Hong Kong, 1947-51; Singapore, 1951-53; London Editor, Australian Associated Press, 1953-65; Overseas Editor, 1965-

70, Caribbean Manager, 1970-73, Reuters. *Memberships:* Former President, Foreign Correspondents Club, Hong Kong; The Press Club, London, UK; Barbados Press Association; Former Councillor, Commonwealth Press Union, London, UK. *Hobbies:* Gardening; Reading. *Address:* 104 Harbour View Road, Omokoroa, Tauranga, RD2, New Zealand.

PARRY, Tom Evelyn, b. 10 June 1916, Llanrug, Gwynned, North Wales. Medicine. Consultant Haematologist. m. Winifred Margaret Bowen, 2 Sept. 1954, 1 son. *Education:* MB., Ch.B., Victoria University, Manchester, UK, 1941; MRCS., (Eng)., LRCP., (London), 1941; MRCP., (London), 1950; FRC. Path., 1963; FRCP., (London), 1974. *Appointments:* House Surgeon and Resident Clinical Pathologist, Manchester Royal Infirmary, UK, 1941-42; Lieutenant to Major, full specialist, Pathology, Service in India, India-Burma border (Imphal), Hong Kong, Royal Army Medical Corps, 1942-46; Ex Service Registrar, Medicine, Ancoats Hospital, Manchester, UK, 1947-50; Senior Registrar, Pathology, Liverpool Royal Infirmary, UK, 1950-52; Consultant Pathologist, United Cardiff Hospitals and Clinical Teacher, Pathology, 1952-72, Consultant Haematologist, South Glamorgan Area Health Authority (Teaching), Clinical teacher, Haematology, 1972-, Welsh National School of Medicine, England; Honorary Consultant Haematologist, South Glamorgan Area Health Authority, 1981-. *Memberships:* British Medical Association; British and International Societies of Haematology; Pathological Society of Great Britain and Ireland; Association of Clinical Pathologists; Committee, 1976-80, Paediatric Pathology Society. *Publications:* Articles on DNA metabolism, Pathology and Haematology in 'Nature' and in Medical journals. *Honours:* Hon. member, Gorsedd of National Eisteddfod of Wales. *Hobbies:* Motoring; Sailing. *Address:* Awelon, Pen-y-Turnpike, Dinas Powis, S. Glamorgan, CF6 4HG, England.

PARSLOW, Thomas, b. 12 Mar. 1920, Melbourne, Victoria, Australia. Barrister-at-Law; Queen's Counsel; Brigadier. m. Margaret Fraser Brown, 7 Dec. 1946, 2 daughters. *Education:* LL.B., University of Queensland, Australia, 1946-50; Barrister-at-law, 1950; Queen's Counsel, 1971. *Appointments:* Petty Sessions, 1935-50; War Service, 1939-45; Crown Prosecutor, 1950-60; Deputy Parliamentary Draftsman, 1960-64; Senior Assistant Crown Solicitor, 1964-68, Crown Solicitor, 1968-71; Solicitor-General for Queensland, Australia, 1971-80. *Honours:* Lilley Medal, 1931; Star, Pacific Star, Australian War Medal, General Service Medal, Efficiency Decoration with two bars, Queens Jubilee Medal, 1939-45; Virgil Power Prize, 1950; many military honours. *Hobbies:* Music; Painting. *Address:* 27 Southerden Street, Sandgate 4017, Queensland, Australia.

PART, Sir Antony (Alexander), b. 28 June 1916, London, England. m. Isabella Bennett, 26 Mar. 1940. *Education:* 1st class hons. degree, Modern Languages, Trinity College, Cambridge, UK, 1934-37. *Appointments:* Joined Board of Education, 1937; Assistant Private Secretary, Ministry of Supply, 1939-40; Rose from Rifleman to Lieutenant Colonel, Army Service, 1940-44; Rose to Deputy Secretary, Ministry of Education, 1944-63; Commonwealth Fund Fellowship, USA, 1950-51; Deputy Secretary, 1963-65, Permanent Secretary, 1966-68, Ministry of Public Building and Works; Permanent Secretary: Board of Trade, 1968-70; Department of Trade and Industry, 1970-74; Department of Industry, 1974-76; Chairman, Orion Insurance Co., UK, 1976-; Director of: Debenhams; EMI; Life Association of Scotland; Lucas Industries; Metal Box; Savoy Hotel Limited, UK. *Memberships:* Governor, Vice Chairman, 1979-, London School of Economics, 1968-; Governor, Administrative Staff College, Henley, UK, 1968-; Oxford and Cambridge University Club. *Publications:* The Maitland Lecture, Institution of Structural Engineers, 1979. *Honours:* MBE., Military, 1943; CB., 1959; KCB., 1966; GCB., 1974; Hon. D.Tech. Brunel, 1966; Hon. DSc., Aston, 1974; Hon. DSc., Cranfield, 1976. *Hobby:* Travel. *Address:* Flat 5, 71 Elm Park Gardens, London SW10 9QE, England.

PARTRIDGE, (Ernest) John, b. 18 July 1908, Bristol, England. Industrialist. m. (1) Madeline Fabian, 30 June 1934, (2) Joan Johnson, 10 May 1949, 2 sons. 2 daughters. *Education:* LL.D. (Hon), University of Bristol, England, 1972; DSc. (Hon), Cranfield Institute of Technology, England, 1974. *Appointments:* Chairman, Imperial Group Limited, England, 1964-75; Director of various companies; President, Confederation of British Industry, 1970-72. *Memberships:* President, National Council for Voluntary Organisations, 1973-80; Chairman, Council of Industry for Management Education, 1967-71; President, Foundation for Management Education, 1972-; Chairman, CBI Education Foundation, 1976-; National Economic Development Council, 1967-75; Chairman, United World College of the Atlantic, 1979. *Honours:* Knight Commander, KBE., 1971. *Hobbies:* Gardening; Walking; Music. *Address:* Wildwood, Haslemere, Surrey, GU27 1DR, England.

PASCO, Richard Edward, b. 18 July 1926, Barnes, London, England. Actor. m. (1) Greta Watson (dlv), 1 son. (2) Barbara Leigh-Hunt, 18 Nov. 1967. *Appointments:* Student Apprentice Stage Manager, 'Q' Theatre, London, England, 1943; Spent 3 years with Sir Barry Jackson's Birmingham Repertory Co., appeared in Hamlet, 1955; Joined George Devine's English Stage Co., at the Royal Court, England, and appeared in Look Back in Anger; The Entertainer; Teresa of Avila; The Lady from the Sea; Ivanov; The New Men; Look Homeward Angel; Joined the Bristol Old Vic, England, 1964 for the Shakespeare Quatercentenary season, appeared in Henry V; LOve's Labour's Lost; lead the Company on long tour of Europe, Scandinavia and Israel; returned to Bristol he played Hamlet; Peer Gynt; Man and Superman; Measure for Measure; Sixty Thousand Nights; Led the Company on a tour of USA, Canada, Europe and Israel playing Hamlet and Angelo, 1967; played Edmund in The Italian Girl, at Bristol, and Wyndham's Theatre, London, England, 1967; Joined the Royal Shakespeare Co., 1969 and appeared in: The Winter's Tale; Twelfth Night; Women Beware Women; Two Gentlemen of Verona; Henry VIII; Major Barbara; Much Ado About Nothing; The Duchess of Malfi; The Lower Depths; Murder in the Cathedral; Richard II; As You LIke It; King John; The Beast; The Marrying of Ann Leete; Man and Superman; The Seagull; appears at festivals in recital and anthology programmes; is a regular broadcaster; films include: Room at the Top, Yesterday's Enemy; Sword of Sherwood Forest; The Gorgon; Rasputin; Hot Enough for June; A Watcher in the Woods; appeared in many television plays; Returned to Royal Shakespeare Co., appeared in Timon of Athens; Richard III, 1980. *Honours:* Gold Medal, Central School of Speech and Drama, 1950; CBE., 1977. *Hobbies:* Music; Gardening; Reading; Walking. *Address:* c/o MLR Ltd., 194, Old Brompton Road, London SW5 OAS, England.

PASRICHA, Bal Rama, b. 18 Apr. 1917, Sialkot City, Pakistan. Educationalist. m. Raj Bhutani, 12 Oct. 1940, 3 sons. *Education:* BSc., 1936, MSc., 1938, Certificates in: German, 1936, French, 1938, Lucknow University; TD., 1948, MA., 1949, London University, UK; M.Ed., Illinois University, USA, 1953; Certificate, Statistics, Poona University, India, 1957. *Appointments:* Senior Lecturer, Head of Department of Mathematics, Isabela Thoburn College, Lucknow, 1938-43; Emergency Commission, Royal Indian Naval Volunteer Reserve, World War II, 1943-46; Overseas Scholar, Indian Government, Institute of Education, London University, UK, 1946-49; Lecturer, National Defence Academy, K'dakvasta, Poona, India, 1949-58; Teaching and research Assistant, School of Education, Illinois University, USA, 1953-54; Principal, Oak Grove School, Mussorie, India, 1958-70; Headmaster, Laurence School, Sanawar, Simla Hills, India, 1970-74; Senior Registrar, DTEVT., G R Z Contract, 1974-77; Training Officer, NRDC., GRZ Contract, 1978-. *Memberships:* Indian Psychological Society; National Institute of Industrial Psychology, UK; Indian Mathematical Society; Zambia Mathematical Association; Zambia Adult Education; Indian Science Association; Indian Public School Heads Conference. *Publications:* 3 Papers: Humbert and Generalised Hypergermetric Functions, 1942-43; Factor Analysis and Analysis of Variance, 1948-49; Rogerian Technique of Client Centred Non-Directive Guidance, 1953-54; *Honours:* Dux Prize, 1932, 1934; University Scholarship, 1936; Central Government of India Overseas Scholarship, 1946-49; Fulbright & Smith Mundt Scholarship, 1953-54; University Research Fellowship, Illinois University, USA, 1954. *Hobbies:* Duplicate bridge; International Relations and Fellowship; Tennis. *Address:* House No. 33, Natural Resources Development College Campus, PO Box CH99, Lusaka, Zambia.

PATAKI-SCHWEIZER, Kerry Josef, b. 1 Nov. 1935, Peekskill, New York, USA. Behavioural Science and Medical Anthropology. m. Lalitha Shirin Harben, Nov. 1973, 1 son. *Education:* SB, University of Chicago 1960; MA 1965; PhD, University of Washington, 1968. *Appointments:* Reed College, Portland, Oregon, 1967-69; University of Colorado, 1970; University of California, San Francisco 1971-73; University of Papua New Guinea, 1974-. *Memberships:* Royal Anthropological Society; Fellow, World Association for Social Psychiatry; Malaysian Society of Parasitology and Tropical Medicine; Papua New Guinea Medical Society; Association of Academic Psychiatry; Society for Medical Anthropology; Fellow, American Anthropological Association. *Publications:* A New Guinea Landscape: Community, Space and Time in the Eastern Highlands, 1980. *Honours:* Woodrow Wilson Fellow 1960-61; French Government Award for Translation, University of Chicago, 1958; National Institute of Mental Health Predoctoral Research Fellow, 1965-66. *Hobbies:* Private Aviation; Photography; Mountaineering; Literature. *Address:* PO Box 5623, Boroko, Papua New Guinea.

PATEL, Ambalal S, b. 22 Sept. 1918, Ajarpura, Kaira District, Gujarat State, India. Teacher; Researcher; Consultant; Social Worker. m. May 1932, 3 sons, 1 daughter. *Education:* BA (Hons) 1940; STC, Bombay Government, 1942; DPEd, 1943; BT, 1945; MA (Sanskrit) Bombay University, 1949; MEd (Educ.) Baroda University, 1951; MSc Psychology, 1956; MS, 1956; PhD, Wisconsin University, USA, 1957. *Appointments:* High School Teacher, 1940-47; University Lecturer, Baroda, India, 1947-54; University Teaching Assistant and Research Fellow, Wisconsin University, USA, 1954-57; Reader, Department of Psychology, M.S. University, Baroda, 1957-64; Professor: Head of Research Centre 1964-69; Head of Psychology Department, 1969-74; Dean of Faculty of Education and Psychology, 1974-78; Visiting Professor, S.P. University Vallabh Vidyanagar, India, 1978-80; Director, Psycho-Clinic and Assessment Services, Baroda, India, 1980-. *Memberships:* President, Indian Psychological Association; Psychology and Educational Science, Indian Science Congress; Indian Academy of Applied Psychology; All-India Education and Voc. Guidance Association; Many Professional Associations of Psychology, National and International. *Publications:* About 110 research papers in field of Psychology and Education; 15 Research Projects; Research Monographs; Psychological Tests. *Honours:* Foreign Visits and Academic Participations. *Hobbies:* Sports; Social Work. *Address:* 35 Nirman Society, Near Alakapuri, Baroda 390005, Gujarat State, India.

PATEL, Harish, b. 3 Nov. 1939, Morogoro, Tanzania. Biochemist. m. 21 Nov. 1964, 1 son, 1 daughter. *Education:* BSc (Hons) 1963; MSc 1970; PhD 1974. *Appointments:* Agriculture Chemical Department, Makerere University, Uganda, 1963-67; Biochemistry Department, Royal Free Hospital, Medical School, London, 1967-76; Biochemistry Department, Charing Cross Hospital, Medical School, London, 1976-. *Memberships:* Biochemical Society, London. *Publications:* Oral Administration of Insulin by Encapsulation within Liposomes FEBS 62, 1976; Potential Application of Liposomes to Therapy, 1978; Systemic and Oral Administration of Liposomes in Liposomes, 1981; etc. Hobby: Professional Interests, research in drug delivery particularly in insulin therapy. *Address:* Charing Cross Hospital Medical School, Fulham Palace Road, London, W6 8RF, England.

PATEL, Hashim Hashim, b. 20 Nov. 1935, Calcutta, India. Managing Director. m. Zarina Fatima Gulmohamed, 24 June 1977, 2 sons, 2 daughters. *Education:* Mount Hermon School, Darjeeling, India, 1942-46; La Martiniere, 1947-48; St James, 1949-51; Senior Cambridge Overseas Examination. *Appointments:* Aircraft Apprenticeship, Jamair Company Limited, Calcutta, India, 1951-54; Fuelling Superintendant, Shell Oil Aviation Department, Calcutta, 1954-58; Motor Mechanic/Foreman, Broadfields Garage, London, England, 1960-65; Managing Director, Van Cleaves Eng. Ltd. Van Matic Ltd. Van Cleaves Holdings Ltd, 1965-. *Memberships:* Institute of Automobile Marketing Management; Automotive Parts Rebuilders Association, USA; Automatic Transmission Rebuilders Association, USA; Federation of Automatic Transmission Engineers, United Kingdom; Overseas Automotive

Club, USA; British Institute of Management, United Kingdom. *Honours:* Certificates of Merit: Jaguar Motor Car Company, 1963; Chrysler Motor Car Company, 1965; Southgate Technical College, 1968; Borgwarner Automatic Transmission Course, 1974; FBIM, British Institute of Management, London, England, 1981. *Hobby:* Music. *Address:* 59 Beechwood Avenue, Finchley, London, N3 3BB, England.

PATEL, Indraprasad Gordhanbhai, b. 11 Nov. 1924, Baroda, India. Governor, Reserve Bank of India, Bombay. m. Alaknanda Patel, 28 Nov. 1958, 1 daughter. *Education:* BA, PhD; Economist; BA(Hons) Bombay University, 1944; BA(Hons) 1946; PhD, University of Cambridge, 1949; Harvard University, 1947-48. *Appointments:* Professor of Economics and Principal, Baroda College, MS University of Baroda, 1949-50; Economist and Assistant Chief, Financial Problems and Policies Division, IMF, 1950-54; Deputy Economic Adviser, Indian Ministry of Finance, 1954-58; Alt. Executive Director, India, IMF, 1958-61; Chief Economic Adviser, Ministry of Finance, India, 1961-63, 1965-67; Economic Adviser, Planning Commission, India, 1961-63; Visiting Professor, Delhi School of Economics, Delhi University, 1964; Special Secretary, Ministry of Finance, 1968-69; Secretary, 1970-72; Deputy Administrator, UN Development Programme, 1972-77; Governor, Reserve Bank of India, 1977-. *Memberships:* Wellingdon Sports Club, Bombay. *Publications:* Articles on inflation and economic development, monetary and credit policy. *Honours:* James Taylor Prize, 1944; Wranburg Scholar, 1946; Adam Smith Prize, 1948; Honorary Doctorate, Sardar Patel University, India, 1979. *Hobbies:* Reading; Music. *Address:* 5 Carmichael Road, Bombay 400 026, India.

PATEL, Praful Raojibhai Chaturbhai, b. 7 Mar. 1939, Jinja, Uganda. British Race Relations Adviser and Company Director. *Education:* Government Secondary School, Jinja, Uganda; London Institute of World Affairs, Extra-Mural Department, University College, London. *Appointments:* Business Consultant; Industrial Investment Adviser; Company Director. *Memberships:* Royal Commonwealth Society. *Publications:* Many articles in newspapers and journals on race relations and immigration, human rights. *Honours:* Various Travel awards, to East and Central Africa, South Africa, and Middle East; Honorary Secretary, Committee on UK Citizenship; Honorary Secretary, Uganda Evacuees resettlement advisory Trust and Indo-British Cultural Exchange. *Hobbies:* Cricket; Campaigning and Lobbying; Current Affairs; Inter-faith co-operation; Arts; Music. *Address:* 60 Bedford Court Mansions, Bedford Avenue, London WC1B 3AD, England.

PATENAUDE, Jean-Claude, b. 4 Mar. 1946, Montréal, Québec, Canada. Director of information and public relations service. *Education:* Master in History, University Montreal; Course in Management and Publicity Administration, School of Higher Commercial Studies; Certificate in Public Relations, McGill University and British Institute, London. *Appointments:* Grand Postal Establishments, Montreal; Ministry of Manpower and Immigration, Quebec Region; Order of Nurses and Hospital Orderlies of Quebec. *Memberships:* Canadian Society Public Relations; Society of Business Press of Quebec. *Hobbies:* Skiing; Tennis; Fencing; Lectures. *Address:* 1550 Docteur Penfield, Suite 1008, Montreal H3G 1C2, Canada.

PATERSON, (Sir) Dennis Craig, b. 14 Oct. 1930, Adelaide, South Australia. Director and Chief Orthopaedic Surgeon. m. Mary Mansell Hardy, 1 son, 3 daughters. *Education:* St Peters College, Adelaide; MBBS, University of Adelaide, 1953; Fellow, Royal College of Surgeons of Edinburgh, 1958; Fellow, Royal Australasian College of Surgeons, 1962. *Appointments:* Director and Chief Orthopaedic Surgeon, Adelaide Children's Hospital, Adelaide, South Australia; Senior Visiting Orthopaedic Surgeon Royal Adelaide Hospital, Adelaide; Senior Visiting Orthopaedic Surgeon, Queen Victoria Hospital, Adelaide; Senior Visiting Orthopaedic Surgeon, Modbury Hospital, Adelaide; Consultant Orthopaedic Surgeon, The Regency Park Centre for Physically Handicapped Children, Adelaide; Captain, RAAMC Reserve. *Memberships:* Crippled Children's Association of South Australia; Board of Orthopaedic Surgery, Royal Australasian College of Surgeons; Court of Examiners, Royal Australasian

College of Surgeons; Australian Orthopaedic Association; President, Crippled Childrens Association. *Publications:* Over 100 publications of orthopaedic surgery and research in major surgical and orthopaedic surgical journals. *Honours:* Knight Bachelor, 1976; The Queen's Silver Jubilee Award, 1977; The First John C Wilson Visiting Professor, Children's Hospital, Los Angeles, 1977; Delivered with 11th RI Harris Memorial Lecture, Canadian Orthopaedic Association, Vancouver, Canada, 1978; Presidential Guest Speaker, American Academy of Orthopaedic Surgeons, Las Vegas, USA, 1981. *Hobbies:* Tennis; Golf; Gardening. *Address:* 31 Myall Avenue, Kensington Gardens, South Australia 5068.

PATERSON, Donald Edward, b. 28 Mar. 1918, Darlington, England. Diagnostic Radiologist. m. Rachel Moore, 30 Aug. 1952, 4 sons. *Education:* MB, ChB Liverpool University, 1941; MRad, 1948; MD, 1955; DMRD, London, 1948; MRACR, Sydney, 1976. *Appointments:* H.S. Liverpool Royal Infirmary, 1941-42; Captain, RAMC, 1942-46; Radiological Registrar, Liverpool, 1946-48; Radiologist, Hankow China, Union Mission Hospital, 1948-51; Professor, Radiodiagnosis, Christian Medical College, Vellore, S. India, 1951-64; Walsall Hospitals, United Kingdom, 1964-74; Radiologist, Masterton, New Zealand, 1974-. *Memberships:* British Institute of Radiology; Royal College of Radiologists; Council for World Mission, London; Christian Medical Association of India. *Publications:* Bone Changes in Leprosy, MD Thesis, 1955; Leprosy, and on Tropical Radiology, 1964; Radiology of Sprue and Malabsorption Syndrare, 1958-64; Radiology of Hiatus Hernia, 1961. *Honours:* Mentioned in Dispatches, Greece, 1944. *Hobbies:* Mountain Walking; Gardening; Golf. *Address:* Atea Bideford Road, R.D.6 Masterton, New Zealand.

PATERSON, Graham Lindsay, b. 20 Aug. 1934, Adelaide, South Australia. Surveyor; Mine Planning Engineer. m. Cynthia Margaret Saunders, 2 sons. *Education:* Articles in Surveying and Photogrammetry, 1951-54; Mine Engineering, British Institute of Mining Technology, 1955-59; Diploma in Civil Engineering, 1969; ASCE; *Appointments:* Photogram Section South Australia Lands Department, 1951-54; Mine Surveyor, Ildorado, Tennant Creek Limited, 1954-55; Surveyor-/Photogrammetrist, Australasian Petroleum, 1955-57; Exploration Surveyor, Geosurveys of Australia Limited, 1957-59; Chief Surveyor, Development Engineer, Rompin Mining Company, Malaya, 1960-63; Technical Manager, Aero Service (NG) Pty. Ltd., 1964-66; Managing Director, QASCO (NG) Pty. Ltd. 1966-69; Consultant, G L Paterson, Indonesia, 1969-72; Chief Surveyor Bougainnlle Copper Limited, 1973-75; Chief Surveyor/Mine Planning Engineer, Newmont Holdings P/L, 1975-81. *Memberships:* Fellow, American Congress on Survey and Mapping; American Society of Civil Engineers; Society of Mining Engineers; Photogrammetric Society, London; American Society of Photogrammetry; Canadian Institute of Surveyors; Australian Institute of Management. *Publications:* Air Photo Index of Indonesia, 1970; Index of Geological Maps of West Iran 1971; Index of Geological Reports of West Iran, 1971; Road Location Feasibility Studies with Photogrammetry, 1968; A National Mapping Policy Plan for Indonesia, 1971; Air Photography Practice in Papua New Guinea, 1969. *Hobbies:* Yachting; Karate; Mountain Climbing; Painting; Chess; Squash. *Address:* 13 Logan Street, Atherton, Queensland 4883, Australia.

PATERSON, Oliver Douglass, b. 9 Nov. 1916, Hampden, New Zealand. Company Director. m. 1945 (Div. 1967), 1 son, 2 daughters. *Education:* BE (MIning), BSc (Geology), AOSM, Senior Scholarship (Geology), University of Otago, 1934-37; MSc (Geology), 1st Class Honours, University of New Zealand, 1938. *Appointments:* Colonial Mines Service, Malaya, 1945-48; Acting Deputy Chief Inspector of Mines, Chief Research and Development Officer, Department Mines, Malaya, 1949-51; Senior Lecturer in Mining, University of Queensland and Professional Consultant in Detrial Deposits, coal and metalliferous minerals, 1951-56; Director of Exploration, Mineral Deposits Limited 1956-68; Managing Director, Mineral DEposits Limited, Director, Doehler Australia Pty. Ltd., Baroid Australia Pty. Ltd. and Executive Director, Queensland Titanium Mines Pty. Ltd. 1968-. *Memberships:* Queensland Chamber of Mines Limited; Mineral Sands Producers'

Association; Board of Faculty of Engineering, University of Queensland; Associate of Otago School of Mines; Fellow, Institution of Mining and Metallurgy; Fellow, Geological Society; Australasian Institute of Mining and Metallurgy; American National Club; Sydney Cricket Ground; Australian Golf Club; NSW Rugby Club; Southport Golf Club. *Publications:* The Geology of the Lower Shag Valley, N.E. Otago 1939; Mineral Sands in Eastern Australiamrthe Search for Deposits of Rutile & Zircon, 1962. *Honours:* Sir Julius Von Haast Prize, 1938; MBE, 1948; Perak Meritorious Service Medal, 1948. *Hobbies:* Golf; Squash. *Address:* 3 Southern Cross Drive, Cronin Island, Surfers Paradise, Queensland, Australia, 4217.

PATERSON, Thomas Ferguson, b. 31 Jan. 1923, Denny, Scotland. Public Servant. m. Mary Demos, 5 May 1951, 3 sons, 4 daughters. *Education:* BAc., 1956, Bachelor of Commerce, 1953, University of Melbourne, Australia. *Appointments:* Department of the Army, 1940-41, 1946; Commonwealth office of Education, 1947-55; Investigator, Department of Works, 1955-57; Assistant Commissioner, 1963-, Public Service Board Representative, London, UK, 1969-72, Commonwealth Public Service Board, 1957-74; First Assistant Secretary, 1974-75, Department of the Special Minister of State; First Assistant Secretary, Department of Administrative Services, 1975-78; First Assistant Secretary, Department of Home Affairs, 1978-80; First Assistant Secretary, Culture, Sport and Recreation, Department of Home Affairs and Environment, 1980-. *Address:* 30 Finniss Crescent, Narrabundah ACT, Australia.

PATHIK, Bhupendra, b. 24 Oct. 1940, Suva, Fiji. Principal, Fiji School of Medicine. m. Mithlesh, 26 Jan. 1966, 2 daughters. *Education:* MB., BS., Bombay University, India, 1965; MRACP., 1969; FRACP., 1974; MHPEd., New South Wales, Australia, 1978. *Appointments:* House Physician, JJ Hospital, Bombay, India, 1966; Medical Registrar, CWM Hospital, Suva, Fiji, 1967; Senior House Physician, Royal Melbourne Hospital, Australia, 1968; Medical Registrar, Queen Victoria Hospital, Melbourne, Australia, 1969; Senior Clinical Tutor, Medicine, 1970-74, Principal, 1974-, Fiji School of Medicine. *Memberships:* Fellow, Royal Society of Medicine, UK; Vice President, Fiji Medical Association; Vice Chairman, St. John's Council of Fiji; Fiji Medical Council; Fiji Dental Council; Chairman: Academic Board, Fiji School of Medicine; DAV. Colleges Board of Governors; Executive Committee, National Heart Foundation of Fiji. *Publications:* Future Directions for Medical Education in the South Pacific. *Honours:* Desai prize awarded by Fiji Medical Association, 1974. *Hobbies:* Tennis; Gardening; Community self help projects. *Address:* Quarters 49, Fiji School of Medicine, Tamavua, Fiji.

PATHMANATHAN, Subrananiam Nagamutty, b. 23 Aug. 1942, Jaffna, Sri Lanka. Chartered Accountant. m. Peyenthimala, 12 July 1971, 1 daughter. *Education:* Fellow, Institute of Chartered Accountants of Sri Lanka; Institute of Internal Auditors, Florida, USA. *Appointments:* Aiyar & Co., 1970-71; Wickrama Singhs & Co., 1971-74; Coopers and Lybrand, Tanzania, 1974-76; National Import & Export Corporation, Lusaka, Zambia, 1976-78; Expert in Financial Accounting and Auditing, United Nations, UNDICD., 1979-80. *Hobbies:* Chess; Bridge. *Address:* 71 37th Lane, Colombo 6, Sri Lanka.

PATON, Robert, b. 25 Feb. 1926, Cottesloe, Western Australia. Surgeon. m. 8 Dec. 1951, 4 daughters. *Education:* MB., BS., Adelaide, South Australia, 1951; FRCS., England, 1956; FRCS., Edinburgh, Scotland, UK, 1956; FRACS., 1958. *Appointments:* Resident Medical Officer, 1952-54, Hon. Surgeon, 1962-76, Senior Vascular Surgeon, Royal Perth Hospital, Australia, 1967-; Junior Assistant, 1957-59, Senior Assistant, 1960-61, University Department of Surgery, Western Australia; Senior Vascular Surgeon, Sir Charles Gairdner Hospital, Australia, 1967-; Chairman, Interhospitals Vascular Surgical Service. *Memberships:* Past member, State Secretary, State Committee, Royal Australasian College of Surgeons; Society of Vascular Surgeons of Great Britain and Ireland; Australian Associations of Surgeons; Member, International Cardiovascular Society. *Publications:* Number of papers on surgical subjects. *Honours:* Travelling Fellowship of Australian National Heart Foundation, 1966. *Hobbies:* Tennis; Yachting; Gardening.

Address: 28 Saunders Street, Mosman Park, 6012, Western Australia.

PATTANI, Kishor Bhagwanji, b. 16 July 1947, Kahama, Tanzania. Medical Practitioner. m. Renuka, 18 Feb. 1973, 1 daughter. *Education:* MBBS., Bombay University, India, 1973. *Appointments:* Private Practitioner. *Memberships:* Chairman, Coast Division, Kenya Medical Association; Divisional Surgeon, St. John Ambulance Brigade, Mombasa, Kenya; Voluntary Medical Advisor to: Likoni Sheltered Workshop of Association of Physically Disabled of Kenya; Likoni School for the Blind of Salvation Army; Founder member and Medical Advisor to Mkomani Harambee Clinic, Mombasa, Kenya; Director, Giants Group of Mombasa; Assistant Secretary, Lohana Community, Mombasa. *Hobbies:* Tennis; Squash; Swimming; Philosophy. *Address:* Mnazi Moja Road, PO Box 86077, Mombasa, Kenya.

PATTERSON, Colin Isaac, b. 14 June 1929, Reefton, New Zealand. Barrister; Solicitor. m. Margaret Claire Morton, 23 Feb. 1957, 3 sons, 1 daughter. *Education:* LL.B., Otago University, New Zealand. *Appointments:* Barrister and Solicitor; Chairman: New Zealand Securities Commission; New Zealand Contracts and Commercial Law Reform Committee. *Hobby:* Golf. *Address:* 92 Warwick Street, Wilton, Wellington 5, New Zealand.

PATTERSON, Flora Elaine, b. 28 Dec. 1930, Moosomin, Saskatchewan, Canada. Manager. *Education:* BA., McMaster University, Hamilton, Ontario, Canada, 1953; BLS., University of Toronto, Toronto, Canada, 1957. *Appointments:* Reference Librarian, 1957-63, Head, Serials Section, 1963-65, Chief, Serials Division, 1965-71, Chief, Reference and Circulation Division, 1971-73, Co-ordinator for Public Services, 1973; Director, Public Services Branch, 1973-, National Library of Canada. *Memberships:* Canadian Library Association; Canadian Nature Federation; Bibliographical Society of Canada; American Birding Association; National Audubon Society; Ottawa Field Naturalists. *Hobbies:* Nature study; Photography; Travel. *Address:* 70 McEwen Avenue, Apt. 602, Ottawa K2B 5M3, Canada.

PATTERSON, John Stanley, b. 20 Mar. 1922, Barbados, West Indies. Company Managing Director. m. Hazell Herbert, 7 May 1949, 1 son, 2 daughters. *Education:* External Graduate, Queens University, Canada. *Appointments:* Staff, Royal Bank of Canada, 1938-51; Royal Navy, 1942-44; Joined Plantations Limited, Barbados, West Indies, 1951-. *Memberships:* Barbados Employers' Confederation; Past President, Barbados Chamber of Commerce. *Hobbies:* Swimming; Tennis. *Address:* 'Harbour View', Lodge Hill, St. Michael, Barbados, West Indies.

PAUL, John Warburton, b. 29 Mar. 1916, Weymouth, Dorset, England. m. Audrey Weeder, 14 Dec. 1946, 3 daughters. *Education:* BA., MA., (Cantab), Selwyn College, Cambridge, UK, 1936-39. *Appointments:* Regular Soldier, Royal Tank Regiment, 1937-46; Administrative Officer, Sierra Leone, Secretary to the Cabinet, 1959-61, Overseas Civil Service, 1946-61; Governor, Governor-General, The Gambia, 1962-66; Governor: Belize, 1966-71; Bahamas, 1972-73; Governor, Governor-General the Lieutenant Governor, Isle of Man, UK, 1974-80; Chairman, St. Christopher MSA Limited, 1980; Director, Overseas Relations, St. John Ambulance, 1981. *Memberships:* Inner Temple, Barrister-at-Law, 1947. *Honours:* MC., 1940; Mentioned in despatches, 1940; OBE., 1959; KCMG., 1962; GCMG., 1965; K.St.John, 1962. *Hobby:* Painting. *Address:* Sherrens Mead, Sherfield-on-Lodoon, Hampshire, England.

PAVIA, Demetri, b. 19 June 1944, Alexandria, Egypt. Hospital Physicist. m. Bridget Mary Campbell, 6 Nov. 1971, 2 sons. *Education:* Grad. Inst.P., 1966; MSc., Surrey University, UK, 1969; M.Inst.P., 1971; PhD., London University, UK, 1974. *Appointments:* Research Assistant, 1968-74, Research Fellow, 1975-76, London School of Hygiene and Tropical Medicine, London University, UK; Senior Scientific Officer, 1976-81, Principal Scientific Officer, 1981-, Department of Thoracic Medicine, Royal Free Hospital, London, UK. *Memberships:* Institute of Physics; Hospital Physicists Association; Medical Research Society; Breathing Club. *Publications:* 60 publications in scientific and medical journals on: Lung Mucociliary Clearance in Humans; Selective Deposition of Therapeutic Aerosols;

Diagnostic Uses of Aerosols; Deposition and clearance of inhaled particles (with others), 1980. *Honours:* HPA-/Wisconsin Travel Award to USA, 1978; Hon. Lecturer, Academic Department of Medicine, Royal Free Hospital School of Medicine, London, UK, 1981. *Hobbies:* Tennis; Building. *Address:* 181 Feltham Road, Ashford, Middlesex, TW15 1BB, England.

PAYNE, Douglas, b. 28 Mar. 1927, Amersham, Buckinghamshire, England. Adult Education. m. Megan Bolton, 1955, 5 daughters. *Education:* A.Mus.LCM., 1949; ARCM., 1950; Diploma, Adult Education, 1963, MEd., 1967, University of Manchester, UK; MA., Ad.Eundum gradum, University of Tasmania, Australia. *Appointments:* Principal: Harewood School of Music, UK; Almondbury Adult Education Centre, UK; Area Principal, East Surrey Institute of Further Education, UK; State Director of Adult Education, Tasmania, Australia; Chief Executive, WEA, Southern District, UK, 1977-. *Memberships:* Vice-Chairman, 1970-71, Chairman, Association for Adult Education, 1971-73; Executive, Australian Association for Adult Education, 1973-76. *Publications:* Many articles, pamphlets, reports etc. *Honours:* Visiting Fellow, University of Southampton, England, 1979-; FRSA, 1981. *Hobbies:* Reading; Travel. *Address:* 1 Fernlea Gardens, Southampton, England.

PAYNE, Margaret, b. 14 Apr. 1937, Southampton, England. Artist, Painter and Printmaker. *Education:* National Diploma, Design, Painting and Etching, Harrow School of Art, 1955-59; Art Teachers Certificate, Goldsmith's College, London University, UK, 1960. *Appointments:* Part-time teacher, Haggerston School, North London, UK, 1960-61; Part-time Drawing teacher, Harrow School of Art, UK, 1961-62; Part-time art teacher, LCC Youth Clubs, UK, 1962-64; Designer, Audio Visual Aid Centre, South Kensington, London, UK, 1964-65; Art teacher, St. Hilda's School, Bushey, Herts, UK, 1965-68; Senior lecturer, Roehampton Institute of Higher Education, London, UK, 1968-. *Memberships:* Associate, 1962-76, Fellow, 1976-, Royal Society of Painter Etchers and Engravers. *Creative Works:* Exhibited at: Royal Academy Summer Exhibition, 1958, 59, 60, 61, 73, 77; Royal Society of Painter Etchers and Engravers, annually from 1962-81; Paris Salon, 1962, 63; Royal Society, 1963, 64; Society of Women Artists, 1962, 63; Young Contempories, 1959, 60; Cardiff, 1979, Oundle, 1980; Graphics International, New York, 1975-76; Harrogate, 1977; Cardiff, 1978; South London Art Gallery, UK, 1975; Hereford, 1974; Oudle, 1974; Surrey University, UK, 1973; Milton Keynes, UK, 1974. *Address:* 11A Wallorton Gardens, East Sheen, London SW14, England.

PAYNE, Titus, b. 16 July 1935, Mengka, Yunnan Province, Red China. Eye Surgeon; Ophthalmologist. m. 18 Aug. 1962, 1 son, 3 daughters. *Education:* MD., Medical College of Georgia, Georgia, USA; Board qualified, Ophthalmology, USA, 1970. *Appointments:* Evangelical Churches of West Africa, Kano Eye Hospital, Kano, Nigeria, 1967-. *Memberships:* Fellow, Royal Society of Tropical Medicine and Hygiene, UK. *Publications:* Iridoschisis: A Case Report, 1966; Intraocular Involvement in Burkitt's Lymphoma, 1971; A Simplified Way to Remove Pterygia, 1974. *Address:* ECWA Eye Hospital, Box 14, Kano, Nigeria.

PAYTON, Sheila Marguerite, b. 15 Sept. 1932, Henley-on-Thames, Oxfordshire, England. Professional Artist. m. Richard Clifford Smith, 25 Jan. 1969. *Education:* Intermediate, Arts and Crafts, University of Reading, UK, 1953; Certificate, Education, Bath Academy of Art and Drama, UK, 1955. *Appointments:* Head of Art Department: Wick Hill County Secondary School, Bracknell, Berks, UK, 1955-62; St. Bernard's Convent, Slough Grammar School, UK, 1962-68; Free lance designer Furnishing Fabrics, dress, 1966-; Professional Artist (Oils) Portraits, Figures, Animals. *Memberships:* Council member and Publicity Committee, United Society of Artists; Friends of Federation of British Artists; World Wildlife Fund; Friends of the Earth; Fauna Preservation Society; Beauty Without Cruelty; Marwell Zoological Society; Royal Horticultural Society. *Publications:* Book of Poetry: Heart Beat. *Creative Works:* One Woman Shows: Salisbury, Oxford, London, UK; Royal Horticultural Society; Marwell Zoological Society; Group Exhibitions: Royal Academy; Womens International Art Club; Royal Society of British Artists; Royal Institute of Oil Painters; Society of Wildlife Artists; New English Art Club; United Society of Artists; Touring Wildlife Exhibitions in London and the Home Counties, UK. *Honours:* World Wildlife Fund Poetry Prize, 1975. *Hobbies:* Conservation; Tigers; Silversmithing; Upholstery; Writing; Reading; Gardening; Teddy Bears; Allergies; Low Frequency Sounds; Designing Houses; Asia; Sewing. *Address:* The Thatch, Appleshaw, Nr. Andover, Hants, SP11 9BN, England.

PEACOCK, (The Hon.), Andrew Sharp, b. 13 Feb. 1939, Melbourne, Victoria, Australia. Minister for Foreign Affairs, Australia. 3 daughters. *Education:* BL., Melbourne University, Australia. *Appointments:* President, Victorian Liberal Party, 1965-66; former Partner, Rigby & Fielding, Solicitors; Chairman, Peacock and Smith Pty. Limited, Australia, 1962-69; Captain, CMF Reserve, 1966; Liberal member of Parliament (Australia), Kooyong, 1966-; Minister for the Army and Minister: Assisting the Prime Minister, 1969-71; Assisting the Treasurer, 1971-72; Minister for External Territories, Feb.-Dec. 1972; Member, Opposition Executive, 1973-75; Opposition Shadow Minister, 1973-75, Minister, 1975-, for Foreign Affairs. *Hobbies:* Horse racing; Surfing. *Address:* 30 Monomeath Avenue, Canterbury, Victoria 3126, Australia.

PEACOCK, Bruce Clifford, b. 16 Oct. 1937, Brisbane, Queensland, Australia. Plant Physiologist. m. Ruth Elizabeth Spiers, 19 Dec. 1959, 1 son, 1 daughter. *Education:* BSc., Queensland University, Brisbane, Australia, 1960; JSSC., Joint Services Staff College, Canberra, Australia, 1976. *Appointments:* Queensland Department of Primary Industries. *Memberships:* Lieutenant Colonel, Australian Army Reserve; Local Controller, City of Redcliffe, State Emergency Service; Australian Institute of Agricultural Science; Australian Society Plant Physiologists; International Society of Horticultural Science. *Publications:* 21 publications including: The Effect of Temperatures on the Preclimacteric Life of Bananas; The Effect of Temperature on the Preclimacteric Life of Pears; Summation of the Effect of Varying Temperatures on the Metabolism of a biological system; The Role of Ethylene in the Initiation of Fruit Ripening; The Effect of Pre-Harvest Gibberellic Acid Sprays on Ellendale Mandarin Fruit; An Effect of Light on the Preclimacteric Life of Bananas; Effect of Colletotrichum Musae Infection on the Preclimacteric Life of Bananas. *Honours:* Efficiency Decoration, Military, 1970. *Hobbies:* Military Service-Army Reserve; Gardening. *Address:* 39A Boyce Street, Margate, Queensland, Australia 4019.

PEACOCK, Joseph Henry, b. 22 Oct. 1918, Brentford, London, England. Medicine; Surgery. m. 24 June 1950, 1 son, 1 daughter. *Education:* MBChB., 1941, MRCS., LRCP., 1941, CH.M., 1957, MD., 1963, University of Birmingham, UK; FRCS., 1949. *Appointments:* Hon. Major, Surgical and Orthopaedic Specialist, RAMC., 1942-47; Demonstrator, Anatomy, University of Birmingham, UK, 1947; Surgical Registrar, 1948, Senior Surgical Registrar, 1950, Consultant Surgeon, 1954-, United Bristol Hospitals, UK; Lecturer, 1950, Reader, 1965, Surgery, Professor of Surgical Science, 1970, University of Bristol, UK; Consultant Surgeon, South West Region, UK, 1960-. *Memberships:* Founder member: Surgical Research Society of Great Britain; Vascular Society of Great Britain and Ireland; Hon. member, Coller Surgical Society of America; Fellow, Association of Surgeons of Great Britain and Ireland; Founder member, European Society for Surgical Research; General Medical Council of Great Britain; Court of Examiners, RCS of England; South West Regional Health Authority; Past Examiner for Primary FRCS., and Universities of Bristol, Wales, London, UK; Ghana. *Publications:* Many medical and scientific publications in the fields of Vascular Surgery and Transplantations. *Honours:* Rockefeller Fellow in Surgery, 1951-52; Research Fellow, University of Michigan, USA, 1951-52; Jacksonian prize, 1953 and 1967, Hunterion Professor, 1956, Arris & Gale Lecturer, 1960, RCS., of England. *Hobbies:* Shortwave radio; Gardening. *Address:* The Old Manor, Ubley, Nr. Bristol, BS18 6RJ, England.

PEAD, Allan Day, b. 12 Mar. 1913, Fremantle, Western Australia. Chartered Engineer; Educator. m. Thelma Pimm, 30 Apr. 1938, 1 daughter. *Education:* Diploma, Mechanical Engineering, Perth Technical College, Australia, 1942; Swinburne Technical College, Melbourne, Australia. *Appointments:* Engineer, Department of Munitions, 1940-44; Head, Production

Engineering Department, Swinburne Technical College, Melbourne, Australia, 1944-59; Inspector, Technical Schools, Victoria, Australia, 1959-70; Deputy Chairman, (Acting President, 1966), Apprenticeship Commission, 1963-69; President, Industrial Training Commission, Victoria, Australia, 1970-76; National Steering Committee, Training for Industry and Commerce, 1972-73; Consultant, Education and Training. *Memberships:* Fellow: Institution of Engineers, Australia, Management Branch Committee, 1956-65, Chairman, 1965; Institution of Production Engineers, London. *Publications:* Member, Victorian Committee on Status of Women-Report, 1976; Submission to Government Committees of Inquiry into Aircraft Industry; Industrial Support for Defence; Post Secondary Education; Many published papers on Education and Training; Apprenticeship in Victoria—The Development of Legislation and Modular Courses, 1981; Training Skilled Workers—Comparisons between Japan and Australia, 1981. *Honours:* Companion, Imperial Service Order, 1977; Jack Finlay National Award, Institution of Production Engineers, 1978. *Hobbies:* Gardening; Motoring; Photography; Mechanical Work. *Address:* 'Greenbushes', 13 Stutt Avenue, Doncaster, Victoria 3108, Australia.

PEAKE, Kathleen Hetty, b. London, England. Pianist; Piano teacher. *Education:* Brockwell Park College; Tobias Matthay Pianoforte School; 2 Exhibitions, Howard Jones & Samons School of Music; LRAM; Studied with Harold Craxton. *Appointments:* Private Teaching in Harrow, Middlesex, UK and Bricketwood, Hertfordshire, UK. *Memberships:* Incorporated Society of Musicians. *Honours:* Many of her pupils hold Challenge Cups and Silver and Gold Medals from various Music Festivals; Has had good success with Associated Board Examinations from Grade I to VIII with merits and distinctions in all grades; many LRAM Diploma successes. *Hobbies:* Gardening; Painting; Breeding collie dogs. *Address:* 163 Headstone Lane,Harrow, Middlesex, England.

PEARCE, John Trevor Archdall, b. 7 May 1916, Naremburn, New South Wales, Australia. British Colonial Service Administration (retired). m. Isabel Bundey Rankine, 18 Oct. 1948. *Education:* MA., Keeble College, Oxford, UK, 1935-39. *Appointments:* District Officer, 1939-50, District Commissioner, 1950-59, Provincial Commissioner, 1959-61, Permanent Secretary, Office of the Vice-Presidentm 1961-63, Tanganyika; Major, RE., War Service, Kenya, Abyssinia, Ceylon, India, Burma, 1940-46; Chairman, Public Service Commission, Basutoland, 1963-65; Chairman, Public Service Commission, Swaziland, 1965-69; Registrar, University of Technology, LAE, New Guinea, 1969-73. *Honours:* CMG., 1965. *Hobbies:* Golf; Music; Military and Imperial history. *Address:* Clippings, Ferguson Avenue, Buderim, Queensland 4556, Australia.

PEARCE, Robert Lyons, b. 20 Apr. 1940, Plastic and Reconstructive Surgeon. m. Penelope Anne Wilson, 17 Feb. 1968, 1 son, 2 daughters. *Education:* MB, BS, University of Queensland, 1965; ECFMG, 1969; JP, 1970; FRCS, Glasgow, 1972; FICS, 1978; FRSA, 1979; FAIM, 1981. *Appointments:* RMO, Princess Alexandra Hospital, Brisbane, 1966-67; Surgical Registrar, Toowoomba General Hospital, 1968; Research Assistant, 1969; Teaching and Surgical Registrar, Royal Children's, Brisbane, 1970; Surgical Registrar, Royal Infirmary Edinburgh and Northampton, 1971; Plastic Surgery Registrar, Churchill, Oxford, 1972; General Hospital; Senior Registrar Plastic Surgeon, Royal Perth, 1973-75; Private Practice, Plastic, Reconstructive and Hand Surgery, Perth, Western Australia, 1975-; Senior Visiting Plastic Surgeon, Hollywood Hospital, Perth, 1975-. *Memberships:* Australian Resuscitation Council, SLSA National Medical Panel; Australian Medical Association; Australian Association of Surgeons; Australian Sports Medical Federation; Fellow, Royal Society Tropical Medicine and Hygiene; Fellow, Royal Society of Medicine; Safety Institute of Australia; American College of Sports Medicine; Australian Sportsmen's Association; Royal Flying Doctor Service; St. John Ambulance District Surgeon, W.A. *Publications:* Author of numerous scientific papers on Renal Physiology, Genetics, Sports Medicine and Plastic Surgery, Medical and Military History; Sculptor (cast metals). *Honours:* Commonwealth Scholarship, 1958; National Heart Foundation Scholarship, 1963; A E Douglas Surgery Prize, 1964; NHF Essay Prize, 1969; Advance

Australia Award, 1981. *Hobbies:* History; Medical Philately; Flying; Golf; Sculpture; Sports Medicine; Collecting Art and Antiques; Breeding Thoroughbred Horses. *Address:* 25 Launceston Avenue, City Beach, Western Australia, 6005.

PEARN, John Hemsley, b. 18 Mar. 1940, Brisbane, Australia. Medicine (Paediatrics). m. Vena Beatrice White, 1 Dec. 1966, 2 sons, 1 daughter. *Education:* Commonwealth Scholarship, The University of Queensland, 1958-64; MB.,BS., 1964; BSc., 1962; Doctor of Medicine, 1969; MRACP (Australasia), 1969; PhD., (London), in Genetics and Neurology, 1974; MRCP (UK), 1974; Diploma of Child Health (London), 1974; The School of Tropical Medicine & Hygiene, London, 1972; Follow of: Royal Australian College of Physicians, 1974 and Royal College of Physicians of London, 1981. *Appointments:* Resident Medical Officer, The Royal Brisbane Hospital, Brisbane, Australia, 1965; Lecturer (Clinical) in Pathology, University of Queensland, 1966-67; Lecturer (Clinical) in Child Health, The Royal Children's Hospital, Brisbane and the University of Queensland, 1968-70; Paediatrician, Goroka Base Hospital, Papua New Guinea, 1969; The Consultant Physician (an Acting Consultant Psychiatrist), The Australian Force, Vietnam Campaign, First Australian Field Hospital, Vietnam, 1970; Senior Lecturer in Child Health, University of Queensland, 1970-71; Senior Research Fellow, MRC Clinical Genetics Unit, Great Ormond Street, London, 1973, Senior Research Fellow, The Muscular Dystrophy Research Laboratory, Regional Neurological Centre, Newcastle-upon-Tyne, UK, 1971-72; Resident in Neurology and Neurosurgery, The Hospital for Sick Children, Great Ormond Street, London, 1974; Reader in Child Health, University of Queensland at the Royal Childrens Hospital, Brisbane, Australia, 1975-81; Senior Research Fellow, The Pasteur Institute, Paris, 1977, for six months. *Memberships:* Paediatric Research Society of Australia; Australian Medical Association; Australian College of Paediatrics; Royal Australasian College of Physicians; Royal College of Physicians; Human Genetics Society of Australasia, National Executive, 1980, 1981, Vice-President, 1981; The Australian Neurological Foundation; The Australian Association of Neurologists. *Publications:* Numerous contributions to medical journals including: Classification of the Spinal Muscular Atrophies, 1980. *Honours:* Order of Australia (General List), 1979; The National Medal, 1980; The Florey Fellowship, The Royal Society, London, 1970; The Service Medal of The Order of St John, 1981. *Hobbies:* Palaeontology; Anthropology (specifically stone tool cultures); History (specifically medical history and medial philately). *Address:* 121 Banks Street, Newmarket, Queensland, 4051, Australia.

PEARSON, Norman, b. 24 Oct. 1928, Stanley, Co. Durham, England. Company President and Consultant Planner. m. Gerda Maria Josefine Riedl, 25 July 1972. *Education:* Bachelor of Arts Honours, University of Durham, 1951; Canadian Institute of Planners, 1956-59; Ontario Land Economist, 1963; Fellow, Royal Town Planning Institute, United Kingdom, 1955, Fellow, 1972; International Society of City and Regional Planners, 1972; American Institute of Planners, 1973, Charter Member, 1978; Real Estate Professional Appraiser, Alpha Appraisal Association, 1976; Doctor of Philosophy, Land Economics, International Institute for Advance Studies, 1979; Master of Business Administration, Pacific Western University, 1980. *Appointments:* Consultant, Stanley Urban District Council, UK, 1946-47; Planning Assistant, Accrington Town Plan and Bedford County Planning Survey, 1947-49; Planning Assistant, Messrs. Allen and Mattocks, Consulting Planners and Landscape Designers and Architects, UK 1949-51; Administrative Assistant, Scottish Division, National Coal Board, 1951-52; Military Service, 1952-53 and 1953-58; Planning Assistant, London County Council, UK, 1953-54; Planner, Central Mortgage and Housing Corporation, Ottawa, 1954-55; Planning Analyst, City of Toronto Planning Board, 1955-56; Director of Planning, Hamilton-Wentworth Planning Area Board, 1956-59; Director of Planning, Burlington and Suburban Area Planning Board, and Commissioner of Planning, Ontario, 1959-62; Consultant Planner, 1962-; President, Tanfield Enterprises Limited, 1976-; Teaching and research work in Planning, Resources Development Environmental Management and Intergovernmental Affairs 1956-64, 1961-63, at International Institutes and Universities. *Memberships:* Numerous Societies in the field of Social Sciences, Economics and Legal Aspects. *Publications:* Co-author of four books; Author 68 articles in referred academic and professional journals or chapters in books; Author of 171 articles in non-refereed journals, reports, conference papers or abstracts; Author of 46 newspaper articles or book reviews. *Honours:* President's Prize (Bronze Medal) of the Royal Town Planning Institute, UK., 1957. *Address:* 223 Commissioners Road, East London, Ontario, N6C 2S9, Canada.

PEARSON, Vicki (Mrs I.S. Pearson), b. 10 June 1949, Adelaide, South Australia. Medical Superintendent. m. Ian Scott, 5 Jan. 1972. *Education:* Adelaide University, South Australia, MB., BS., 1967-72. *Appointments:* RMO Sydney Hospital & Guys Hospital, London, 1973-75; Assistant Medical Superintendent, Sydney Hospital, 1976-78; Director Accident & Emergency Services, Sydney Hospital, 1978-80; Medical Superintendent, 1980-. *Publications:* Medical writer, Australian Womens Day, 1976-78. *Hobbies:* Music; Food; Wine. *Address:* 19 Mackenzie Street, Rozelle, Sydney, Australia.

PEART, Ernest Grafford, b. 11 May 1918. High Commissioner. m. Dorothy, 1947, 3 sons, 1 daughter. *Education:* RAF College; Letchworth Technical High School, UK; Yatesbury No. Nine Radar School, UK. *Appointments:* Member, House of Representatives (PNP), Western Manchester, 1959-; Member, Parliamentary Public Accounts Committee; Minister of Labour, 1972; Minister of Works, 1976; High Commissioner for Jamaica in London, 1978-. *Memberships:* President, New Green JAS Branch; Jamaica Legion; Parish Chairman, (Manchester), 1963; Area Chairman, 1970-78; Chairman, Mandeville Branch, and Member Island Council; Manchester Secondary School Trust, 1956; Manchester School Board; Board of Governors, Manchester Nursing Home; Board of Visitors, Mandeville Hospital; Local Management Committee, Curphey Home; Executive Committee, Manchester Boy Scouts Association; Manchester Parish Council, 1956-59 (Vice-Chairman, 1958, 1959). *Honours:* CD, 1978. *Hobbies:* Cricket; Football; Table Tennis; Reading. *Address:* Jamaican High Commission, 50 St James's Street, London, SW1, England.

PECK, Edward Heywood, b. 5 Oct. 1915, Hove, Sussex, England. Retired Member of British Diplomatic Service. m. Alison Mary MacInnes, 20 Mar. 1948, 1 son, 2 daughters. *Education:* First Class Honours in Modern Languages, The Queen's College, Oxford, 1934-37; MA (Oxon), 1938; Lanning Travelling Fellow, 1937-38. *Appointments:* Vice-Consul: Barcelona, 1939, Sofia, 1940, Ankara, 1940-44; Consul: Adana, 1944, Iskenderun, 1945, Salonika, 1945-47 with UK Delegation to Sp. Commission on Balkans, 1947; Foreign Office, 1947-50; with British High Commission, Delhi, 1950-52; Deputy Commandant, British Sector, Berlin, 1955-58; with British Commissioner General for SE Asia, Singapore, 1959-60; Assistant Under-Secretary of State, Foreign Office, 1961-66; British High Commissioner in Kenya, 1966-68; Deputy Under-Secretary of State, FCO, 1968-70; British Permanent Representative to North Atlantic Council, 1970-75; Retired from Diplomatic Service, 1975; Honorary Visiting Fellow, Aberdeen University, 1976-. *Memberships:* Royal Geographical Society. *Publications:* Bartholomew's Guide to North East Scotland, 1981. *Honours:* CMG, 1958; KEMG, 1966; GCMG, 1974. *Hobbies:* Mountaineering; Skiing. *Address:* Easter Torrans, Tomintoul, Ballindalloch, Banffshire, Scotland.

PEEBLES, Antony Gavin Ian, b. 26 Feb. 1946, Southborough, Kent, England. Concert Pianist. *Education:* Trinity College, Cambridge, (with Musical Exhibition), 1964-68; LRAM, 1964; Mus.B.Cantab., 1968. *Appointments:* Has given concerts in 75 different countries; Plays regularly on BBC, Royal Festival Hall, Royal Albert Hall, Queen Elizabeth Hall, etc. *Creative Works:* Record: Bartok Studies op. 18; Dellapiccola Quaderno Musicale Di Annalibera; Copland Fantasy. *Honours:* First Prize, BBC Piano Competition, 1971; First Prize, Debussy Competition, 1972. *Hobby:* Tennis. *Address:* 2A Forthbridge Road, London, SW11 5NY, England.

PEET, Lindsay James, b. 5 Oct. 1939, Perth, Western Australia. Real Estate Company Director. m. Laurel Aileen Pilkington, 12 Mar. 1965, 2 sons. *Education:* Bachelor of Science, University of Western Australia,

1964; Diploma in Valuation, Perth Technical College, 1973; Diploma in Real Estate Management, 1977. *Appointments:* Continental Oil Company of Australia, 1964; Post-Graduate Course, University of Western Australia, 1965-66; Geological Survey of Western Australia, 1967; Peet & Company Limited (1894), 1968-. *Memberships:* Real Estate Institute of Western Australia; Royal Aero Club of Western Australia; Council National Theatre Company; International Real Estate Federation; Fellow, Geological Society of London; Council of Royal Society of Western Australia; Royal Commonwealth Society. *Hobbies:* Reading; Flying & Gliding; Movie Photography. *Address:* 39 Beatrice Road, Dalkeith, 6009, Western Australia.

PEIRIS, Sunil, b. 5 Dec. 1954, Colombo, Sri Lanka. Chartered Accountant. m. Nivanka Fernando, 17 July 1980. *Education:* Completed up to professional Stage II of the Examination Conducted by the Institute of Cost and Management Accountants; Associate member of the Institute of Chartered Accountants, Sri Lanka. *Appointments:* Assistant Manager, Neptune Hotel, Beruwala, Sri Lanka, 1979; Financial Controller, Holiday Inn, Sharjah, 1979-. *Memberships:* Honorary Sports Secretary, Chartered Accountants Student Society, Sri Lanka, 1977-78. *Honours:* Leonard Arndt Memorial Prize, St Thomas College, Mt. Lavinia, Sri Lanka, 1974. *Hobbies:* Cricket; Rugger; Soccer. *Address:* Holiday Inn, PO Box 5802, Sharjah, United Arab Emirates.

PEKIĆ, Borislav V, b. 4 Feb. 1930, Titograd, Yugoslavia. Author. m. Lilian, 11 May 1958, 1 daughter. *Education:* University of Belgrade, Yugoslavia, 1954-58. *Appointments:* Dramaturge Lovćen Film, Yugoslavia, 1959-64; Freelance writer, Yugoslavia, 1964-71, England, 1971-. *Memberships:* PEN; Association of Yugoslav Writers; Association of Film Artists of Yugoslavia; Editorial Board of Journal Knjizevne Novine, 1968-69. *Publications:* Books: Time of Miracles, 1965; Houses of Belgrade, 1970; The Rise and Fall of Icarus Gubelkiyan, 1975; The Defense and Last Days, 1977; The Golden Fleece, parts one, two, three, four, five, 1977-81; How to Get Rid of a Vampire, 1977; Theatre Plays: The Generals or A Kinship in Arms, 1971; How Can Mr Martin Be Amused, 1970; Eastwards in Eden, 1971; How to Get Rid of a Vampire, 1977; Categorical Demand, 1977; The Masterpiece or The Destiny of an Artist, 1979; The Correspondence, 1979; The Destruction of Speech, 1980; Radio Plays: The Generals, 1969; Goodbye, Comrade, Goodbye, 1970; How can Mr Martin Be Amused? 1971; Theseus, Did you Kill the Minotaur? 1972; Eastwards in Eden, 1973; The Destruction of Speech, 1973; Who Killed Lilly Schwarzkopf? 1973; The Case of One Commercial Traveller, 1974; How to Get Rid of A Vampire, 1974; Who Killed My Immortal Soul? 1974; The Bad Day on the Stock Exchange, 1974; Judah Triptych (includes The Miracle of Jerusalem, The Miracle in Ghadara and The Miracle in Jabnel), 1975; The Magic Suitcase of Madam X, 1980; The Making of a Gentleman, 1981; Television Play, The Generals, 1973; Essays and Filmscripts. *Honours:* First Prize, film competition for two filmscripts, 1958; Prize for best Yugoslavian novel, 1970 & 1977; Prize for best Yugoslav comedy, 1972. *Hobbies:* Classical Music; Gardening. *Address:* 4 Grand Avenue, London, N10 3AY, England.

PELLEREAU, (Major General) Peter John Mitchell, b. 24 Apr. 1921, Quetta, British India. m. Rosemary Garnar, 30 Apr. 1949, 2 sons. *Education:* Wellington College; BA, 1942, MA, 1957, Trinity College, Cambridge; CEng; FIMechE; FBIM. *Appointments:* Commissioned into Royal Engineers, 1942; War Service in NW Europe, 1942-45; OC 26 Armd Engineers Sqdn, RE, 1946; PTSC, PSC, 1950-51; Secretary, Defence Research Policy Committee, 1960; Assistant Military Secretary, WO, 1961; CO 131 Parachute Engineer Regiment RETA, 1963; Military Director of Studies, RMCS, 1965; Assistant Director RE Equipment Development, 1967; Senior Military Officer, Royal Armament R & D Establishment, 1970; Vice-President, 1973-75, President, 1975-76, Ordnance Board; retired, 1976; Secretary, Association of Consulting Engineers, 1977-. *Honours:* Honorary Colonel, Explosive Ordnance Disposal Squadrons, RE (Vol.), TAVR, 1977-. *Hobbies:* Lawn Tennis; Hockey (as umpire; Vice-President, Surrey Hockey Umpires' Association; President, Oxted Hockey Club). *Address:* Woodmans Folly, Crockham Hill, Edenbridge, Kent, England.

PELTON, Foster, b. 10 June 1933, Newcastle Upon Tyne, England. Civil Engineer. m. Sheila Green, 27 Aug. 1960, 2 sons, 1 daughter. *Education:* BA, (Cantab.), 1957; MA (Cantab.), 1961; MSc., (London University), 1969; DIC, 1969. *Appointments:* Sir Alexander Gibb & Partners, 1957-72; Mott, Hay & Anderson, 1972-74; Sir William Halcrow & Partners, 1974-78; Acres American Incorporated, 1979-. *Memberships:* American Society of Civil Engineers; Institution of Civil Engineers; Institution of Water Engineers and Scientists; Institution of Public Health Engineers. *Hobbies:* Squash Rackets; Golf. *Address:* 34 Glen Oak Drive, East Amherst, New York, 14051, USA.

PENNA, Lakshimakanth Rao, b. 21 Oct. 1938, Hanamkonda, Andhra Pradesh, India. Principal, College of Law. m. Vijay Tiwari, 3 Oct. 1977. *Education:* DICHR, International Institute of Human Rights, Strasburg, France, 1973; LL.M., Stanford University, California, USA, 1964; LL.M., Osmania University, India, 1960; LL.B., 1958; B.Com. Osmania University, 1956; Diploma in Leg. Research, Indian Law Institute, New Delhi, 1961; Certificate of Research, Hague Academy of International Law, 1970 & 1973. *Appointments:* Principal, College of Law, Osmania University, 1972-, in continuous service, 1960-, Lecturer, 1970, Reader, Professor, 1974-75; Visiting Professor, Columbus School of Law, Catholic University of America, Washington, DC, USA; Appointed Visiting Professor North Carolina Central University Law School, 1978; Special Assistant to HE Governor of UP, India, 1976; Research Scientist Program of Policy Studies, George Washington University, USA; Intern at United Nations High Commission for Refugees, International Labor Organisation, International Committee of the Red Cross, 1973; Consultant, National Planning Association, USA, 1968; Advocate High Court, of AP and Supreme Court of India; President, All India Law Teachers' Association, 1978. *Memberships:* International Society of Military Law and Law of War, Brussels, Belgium; Federation of International Human Rights, Paris, France; Board of Recommendations, International Center of Legal Science, The Hague, The Netherlands; International Law Association; American Society of International Law; Indian Society of International Law; Amnesty International; President & Secretary, Osmania University Teachers Association, 1974-76 and 1970-71 respectively. *Publications:* Civil Wars—Regulation of Use of Force; Comparative Constitutional Process: Some Problems Common to India and US; Human Rights; Communications Satellites; Persian Gulf: Delimitation of the Continental Shelf; Development of Transportation in Alaska; Jurisdiction in International Law; Dashmir Dispute; Judicial Review in USA; Over 70 Research Papers. *Honours:* Stood First in University for LL.M., 1960; Ford Foundation Grant for study in US, 1963-64; UNESCO sponsored training in teaching of human rights; Cum Laude, first Indian and second in world from International Institute of Human Rights, Strasbourg, France; Research grants by Hague Academy of International Law, 1970 & 1973, Institute Henri Dunant, Geneva, 1973, International Institute Humanitarian Law, Italy, 1973. *Hobbies:* Photography; Billiards; Tennis; Chess. *Address:* R 3 Osmania University, Hyderabad, 500 007, India.

PEPRAH, Enoch Oppong, b. 11 Jan. 1946, Kumasi, Ghana. Economist; Senior Lecturer. m. Ermestina Jamtuah, 28 July 1973, 2 sons, 1 daughter. *Education:* BSc., (Physics), University of Science and Technology (UST), Kumasi, Ghana, 1971; MA, (Dev. Econ.), Williams College, Williamstown, Mass., USA, 1973. *Appointments:* Economist, Ministry of Finance, Ghana, 1971-74; Lecturer, 1974-78, Senior Lecturer, Ghana Institute of Management and Public Administration, 1978-. *Memberships:* American Economic Association, 1973-. *Publications:* Reports published of Management Audit of six public corporations in Ghana, 1975-81; Published report examining the specific aspects of the structure and procedure of the Ghana Civil Service, 1975. *Honours:* Edward S Mason Fellow, Williams College, 1972-73. *Hobbies:* Tennis; Politics; Music. *Address:* No 4 New Drive, GIMPA, Greenhill, Achimota, Ghana.

PERCY, David, b. 15 Jan. 1933, Coldstream, Berwickshire, Scotland. Mechanical Engineer. m. Norma Isabel Lumsden, 26 Oct. 1957, 3 sons. *Education:* Read for Bachelor of Science Degree in Mechanical Engineering, Harvard Business School, 1969 on an Advanced Management Programme Diploma Course. *Appointments:* Apprentice, Design Authority, Manager, Ferranti Limited, Edinburgh, 1955-64; Deputy General Manager, Ranco Motors Limited, Uddingston, 1964-67; Managing Director, PR Motors Limited, Coventry, 1967-71; Group Managing Director, Melbray Engineering, London, 1971-72; Chairman and Managing Director, British Marc, Grantham, 1972-75; Managing Director & Part Owner, Larkhall Machine Tool, Lanarkshire, 1974-79; Chairman & Managing Director, JH Carruthers Limited, East Kilbride, Kilbride, Glasgow, 1979-; Director, Burmah Engineering Limited, Wythenshaw, Manchester, 1979-; Director, Caruther D & D, Johannesburg, South Africa, 1979-. *Memberships:* Fellow: Insitute of Mechanical Engineers, Institute of Production Engineers, British Institute of Management, Institute of Engineers & Shipbuilders of Scotland, Institute of Directors, Heriot Watt University; Council CBI; Executive EEF. *Hobbies:* Gliding; Dramatics; Rugby; Chess; Golf; Caravanning; Singing; DIY; Badminton; Jogging. *Address:* 12 Cluny Avenue, Edinburgh. EH10 4RN, Scotland.

PEREIRA-KAMATH, Olinda Mary, b. 15 Aug. 1925, Mangalore, India. Education. *Education:* BA, (Madras), 1946; B.Ed., (Madras), 1948; MA. (Banaras), 1962; PhD., (Mysore), 1974. *Appointments:* School Assistant, 1948-60; Social Work Education, 1962-; Director, Institute of Social Service & Principal, School of Social Work. *Memberships:* Indian Psychological Association; National Committee on Women; Board of Studies in Social Work in four universities; Founder member, Institute of Social Service School of Social Work, Mangalore; Founder Member, Council of Catholic Women of India. *Publications:* Adjustment and its correlates among pre-adolescents; Bookets: Understanding children; Behaviour problems of children; The Pre-adolescent stage of Development. *Honours:* Mahatma Gandhi Peace Travel Award, 1979; The Sarth Kamara Award for International Women's Year, 1975. *Hobbies:* Reading; Writing; Walking in the countryside; Playing certain games. *Address:* Roshni Nilaya, Mangalore, 575002, India.

PERERA, Terence, b. 10 May 1923, Sri Lanka. WHO Regional Adviser. m. 21 Jan. 1951, 1 son, 2 daughters. *Education:* MB.,BS., (Ceylon) with honours; MRCP (UK); DCH (London); Diploma MCH (Sweden). *Appointments:* Medical Officer of Health, Consultant Paediatrician, Director of Maternal and Child Health, Ministry of Health, Sri Lanka; WHO Regional Adviser in Maternal and Child Health, South East Asia Region. *Memberships:* College of Physicians, Ceylon; Paediatric Association, Sri Lanka; British Medical Association. *Publications:* Several scientific publications in the field of Paediatrics, Maternal and Child Health and Family Planning. *Honours:* Fellow of: Royal College of Physicians, 1971 and American Academy of Paediatrics, 1981. *Hobbies:* Rowing; Gardening. *Address:* W 72 Greater Kailash I, New Delhi, 48, India.

PERKIN, Harold James, b. 11 Nov. 1926, Stoke-on-Trent, UK. Social Historian (Professor). m. 3 July 1948, 1 son, 1 daughter. *Education:* BA, First with distinction, 1948, MA, 1952, Jesus College, Cambridge. *Appointments:* (AL & L), University of Manchester, 1950-65; (SL & Prof.), University of Lancaster, 1965-; Professor, 1967-; Founding Director, Centre for Social History, 1976-. *Memberships:* Social History Society of UK, founding Chairman, 1976-. Association of University Teachers (UK), President, 1970-71, Vice-President, 1969-70 & 1971-73, Executive, 1961-73; Fellow, Royal Historical Society, 1969. *Publications:* The Origins of Modern English Society, 1780-1880, 1969; New Universities in UK, 1969; Key Profession: History of AUT, 1969; Age of the Railway, 1970; History: An Introduction, 1970; Age of the Automobile, 1976; The Structured Crowd: Essays, 1981. *Honours:* Visiting Fellow, Princeton University, 1979-80; Stenton Lecturer, University of Reading, 1980. *Hobbies:* Foreign Travel; Gardening. *Address:* Borwicks, Caton, Lancaster, LA2 9NB, UK.

PERKINS, Harold Jackson, b. 6 July 1930, London, Ontario, Canada. University President; Biochemist. m. Mary Louise Kreutziger, 21 Aug. 1954, 3 sons, 1 daughter. *Education:* BA, 1951, MSc, 1953, University of British Columbia; PhD., Iowa State University, 1957. *Appointments:* National Research Council (Canada), 1957-58; Canada Department of Agriculture, Research

Branch, 1958-63; State University of New York, 1963-77; Brandon University, 1977-. *Memberships:* Wester Director, Canadian Society of Plant Physiologists, 1962-63; Sigma Xi; New York Academy of Sciences, 1963-75; American Association for the Advancement of Science; Aircraft Owners and Pilots Association. *Publications:* Numerous publications in scientific journals, primarily in the field of Plant Biochemistry, some work in Educational Television. *Honours:* Post-Doctoral Fellowship, National Research Council of Canada, 1957-58. *Hobbies:* Flying (Aircraft); Canoeing; Fly Fishing. *Address:* 463-13th Street, Brandon, Manitoba, Canada, R7A 4P9.

PERKINS, Neville George, b. 4 Jan. 1952, Alice Springs, NT, Australia. Executive Manager. 1 daughter. *Education:* University of Sydney, New South Wales, 1970-73, Graduated Bachelor of Arts, 1974, with Majors in Government and Legal Subjects. *Appointments:* Regional Manager, Aboriginal Hostels Limited, Northern Territory, 1974-76; Executive Director, Central Australian Aboriginal Congress, NT., 1976-77; Member for MacDonnell, Legislative Assembly of the Northern Territory, 1977; Deputy Leader of the Opposition (ALP), 1977-81, Northern Territory; Branch Manager, Aboriginal Developemtn Commission, Canberra, 1981-; General Manager, Aboriginal Hostels Limited, Canberra, 1981. *Memberships:* Adviser, Central Australian Aboriginal Congress, Alice Springs, NT; Secretary (Hon.), Aboriginal Publications Foundation, Canberra, ACT; Patron, Historic Vehicles Club of Central Australia. *Publications:* Aboriginal Australians Yesterday and Today: An Aboriginal Overview, 1973, Pamphlet; Black Australian Civilisation and Historical Awareness, 1977, Colloquium Paper, Second World Black and African Festival of Arts and Culture, Nigeria; Aborigines, Land Rights and Politics in the Northern Territory, 1979, Australian National University Conference Paper on NT Politics. *Honours:* Justice of the Peace for the Northern Territory, 1975. *Hobbies:* Country & Pop Guitar; Reading; Writing; Vintage Vehicles; Travelling. *Address:* 9 Samson Place, Kambah, ACT, 2902, Australia.

PERRET, Cyril John, b. 28 Nov. 1919, Woodford Green, Essex, England. Microbial Biochemist; Theoretical Biologist. m. Dorothy Harriet Card, 9 Nov. 1957. *Education:* Royal Signals Officer Cadet Training Unit, Aldershot, England, 1940; St John's College, Cambridge, 1946-50; BA (Cantab), 1950; MA (Cantab.), 1953; University of London, 1950-57; PhD., (London), 1957. *Appointments:* Territorial Army, 1938: Royal Corps Signals, 1939-46 (Commissioned 1940), active service throughout SE Asia; National Institute for Medical Research, London, 1950-53; Lister Institute of Preventive Medicine, London, 1953-58; Department of Microbiology, University of Western Australia, 1958-. *Memberships:* Biochemical Society; Society for General Microbiology; British Ecological Society; Royal Society of Western Australia. *Publications:* Numerous scientific papers in learned journals; Verse, short stories and articles; Various landscape and semi-abstract paintings; Many BBC Broadcasts on Biology and Philosophy. *Honours:* Sir Joseph Larmor Prize, Cambridge, 1950; Wellcome Research Fellow, Royal Society of Medicine, 1954-57. *Hobbies:* Music; Painting; Photography; Exploring; Arguing. *Address:* 132 Rosalie Street, Shenton Park, Western Australia, 6008.

PERRIN, John Robin, b. 6 July 1930, Los Angeles, California. Professor. m. Jennifer Mary Gibbon, 1 son, 1 daughter. *Education:* BSc., (UCLA), 1951; MBA (UCLA), 1954; PhD., (London), 1958. *Appointments:* Assistant Professor, Mount Allison University, Canada, 1959-61; Senior Lecturer, Nottingham University, 1962-68; Wolfson Professor of Financial Control, Lancaster University, 1968-74; Professor and Director, Centre for Industrial Economic and Business Research, Warwick University, 1974-. *Memberships:* Chartered Institute of Public Finance & Accountancy, 1975-81; English Speaking Union; LSE Society; Association of University Teachers of Accounting, and (formerly) Royal Commonwealth Society. *Publications:* Co-author, The Management of Financial Resources in the NHS, 1978 and Health Care: Priorities and Management; Author of articles on management accounting and health-service topics. *Honours:* Founder Editor of the Journal of Business Finance and Accounting and Consulting Editor for the Thos. Nelson Series in Accounting and Finance. *Hobbies:* Rural Pursuits; Travel. *Address:* University of Warwick, Coventry CV4 7AL, England.

PERRINI, Antonio, b. 8 Feb. 1916, Tarquinia, Italy. Journalist. m. 19 Jan. 1946, 1 daughter. *Education:* Diploma Classic Lycee La Spezia; Degree Jurisprudence, Rome University, 1939. *Appointments:* Il Temp, Rome Daily Newspaper, 1944, now London Correspondent. *Memberships:* Academy of the Incamminati, Italy; Foreign Press Association, London. *Publications:* Novels: Aulo Etrusco; Viva I Butteri. *Honours:* Commendatore Corona D'Italia. *Hobby:* Restoring Antique Fufniture. *Address:* 11 Bedford Road, Bedford Park, London, W4 17D, England.

PERRY, Rayden Alfred, b. 2 July 1925, Port Noarlunga, South Australia. Scientist. m. Pamela Adele Porter, 14 Dec. 1957, 2 daughters. *Education:* BSc., 1946, MSc., 1955, University of Adelaide. *Appointments:* Commonwealth Scientific and Industrial Research Organization, Div. Soils, 1947; Div. Plant Industry, 1948; Div. Land Research and Regional Survey, later Land Research, 1954; CSIRO Rangelands Research Unit, 1969; Chief, CSIRO Division of Land Resources Management, 1973-. *Memberships:* Society of Range Management; Australian and New Zealand Association for Advancement of Science; Australian Institute of Agricultural Science; Australian Society for Animal Production; Australian Rangeland Society (Chairman, Editorial Board); Ecological Society of Australia (President, 1965-66); Arid Zone Research Association of India. *Publications:* Arid Lands of Australia; Over 70 Scientific papers. *Honours:* Foundation Fellow, Australian Academy of Technological Sciences, 1974; Australian Arid Zone Research Liaison Officer, 1967-78. *Hobbies:* Sport; Gardening. *Address:* 34 Chipping Road, City Bearch, Western Australia, 6015.

PETCH, Howard Earle, b. 12 May 1925, Agincourt, Ontario, Canada. President and Vice-Chancellor and Professor of Physics. m. (1) Rosalind June Hulet, 13 Aug. 1949 (Deceased), (2) Linda Jean Schlechte, 27 Mar. 1976, 2 sons, 1 daughter. *Education:* BSc., 1949, MSc., 1950, McMaster University; PhD., University of British Columbia, 1952; Cambridge University, 1953-54. *Appointments:* Served with the Royal Canadian Air Force, 1943-45; Mass Spectrometry Laboratory, Polymer Corporation, Sarnia, Ontario, 1948; Chalk River Laboratories, Atomic Energy of Canada, Limited, 1949; Post-doctorate Fellow, McMaster University, 1952-53; Rutherford Memorial Fellow, Cavendish Laboratory, Cambridge, 1953-54; Assistant Professor of Physics, 1954-57, Associate Professor of Physics, 1957-60, McMaster University; Assumed responsibility for developing a metallurgy department, 1957; Chairman, Department of Metallurgy and Metallurgical Engineering, 1958-62, Professor, 1960-67, McMaster University; Chairman, Interdisciplinary Materials Research Unit, 1964-67, Director of Research, 1961-67, Principal of Hamilton College, 1963-67, McMaster University; Vice-President, Academic, University of Waterloo, 1967-69, President (pro tem), 1969-70, Vice-President, Academic, 1970-74, Professor of Physics, 1967-74; Assistant Secretary, Ministry of State for Science and Technology, Government of Canada, (on leave from University of Waterloo), 1972; President and Vice-Chancellor, University of Victoria, Professor of Physics, 1975-. *Memberships:* Numerous National Science Bodies and Committees: Chairman, Council of Western Canadian University Presidents, 1976-80; Long-Range Planning Committee, Universities Council of British Columbia; Board of Director, Association of Universities and Colleges of Canada; Executive Committee, Association of Universities and Colleges of Canada; Board of Directors, WESTAR; Board of Governors, McMaster University, 1961-63, University of Waterloo, 1965-67; Associated with numerous other councils, Professional Societies and Committees. *Publications:* Contributor of numerous articles in professional journals, including: Deuteron Spin Lattice Relaxation from Hindered otations in Molecular Crystals, 1980; Nuclear Magnetic Resonance Study of Ionic Motions in Ammonium Bifluoride, 1979. *Honours:* Alpha Sigma Mu, 1961; Convocation Founder of Simon Fraser University, 1965; Fellowship, Royal Society of Canada, 1966; Centennial Medal, 1967; Honorary Doctor of Science, McMaster University. *Address:* 3775 Haro Road, Victoria, BC, Canada, V8P 5C3.

PETERS, Daphne Molly, b. 15 July, 1942, India. Medical Practioner. m. Robert Edward Peters, 20 Feb.

1966, 2 sons, 1 daughter. *Education:* MBBS, Institute of Medicine, University of Rangoon, Burma, 1966; MBBS, Medical School, University of Western Australia, 1969; FRCPA, 1975. *Appointments:* RMO, Royal Perth Hospital, 1969-70 and State Health Laboratories, Western Australia, 1970; Registrar, State Health Laboratories, Sir Charles Gairdner Hospital, 1970-75; Senior Registrar, 1975-76; Haematologist/Acting, Senior Specialist, Repatriation General Hospital, 1976-. *Memberships:* Haematology Society of Australia; Sessional/part time Lecturer, University of Western Australia; Western Australian Branch Medical Research Advisory Committee, Department of Veteran Affairs; Leukemia and Allied Disorders Western Australia; Medical Advisory Committee of Repatriation General Hospital. *Honours:* Blues, University of Rangoon, Burma, Hockey, 1963-64. *Address:* Department of Pathology, Repatriation General Hospital, Monash Avenue, Nedlands, 6009 Western Australia.

PETERS, William, b. 1923. British Diplomat. m. Catherine Bailey, 1944. *Education:* MA, Balliol College, Oxford; London School of Economics. *Appointments:* War Service, Queen's Royal Rifles, King's Own Scottish Borderers, & 9th Gurkha Rifles, 1942-46; Joined HM Overseas Service, 1950; Assistant District Commissioner, Gold Coast; also served in Cape Coast, Bawku & Tamale, 1950-59; Assistant Principal in Commonwealth Relations Office, 1959; First Secretary, Dacca, 1960-63, Nicosia, 1963-67; Head of Zambia & Malawi Department CRO, 1967-68; Head of Central African Department, FCO,.1968-69; Director, International Affairs Division, Commonwealth Secretariat, 1969-71; Conference Secretary, Commonwealth Heads of Government Meeting, 1971; Counsellor & Head of Chancery, Canberra, 1971-73; Deputy High Commissioner, Bombay, 1974-77; HM Ambassador, Montevideo, 1977-80; High Commissioner, Lilongwe (Malawi), 1980-. *Memberships:* Diplomatic Service Association; Royal Commonwealth Society; United Oxford & Cambridge University. *Publications:* Diplomatic Service: Formation & Operation: & contributions to professional journals. *Honours:* Royal Victorian Order (member Class IV), 1961; OBE, 1959. *Address:* 12 Crown Court, Deal, Kent, England.

PETERSEN, George Maxwell, b. 29 Oct. 1925, Sydney, New South Wales, Australia. Chairman; Managing Director. m. 24 Oct. 1946, 1 son, 2 daughters. *Education:* Leaving Certificate, Canberra High School, Australia, 1941. *Appointments:* Audit Clerk, Hungerford-Spooner and Company, Chartered Accountants, Sydney, 1941-42; Assistant to Manager, George Petersen, Hotel Kosciusko,, 1946-47; Royal Australian Air Force, 1942-45; Manager, Bermagui Wharf, Illawarra and South Coast Steam Navigation Company Limited, 1948-52; Clearance Officer, Deputy Superintendent, Department of Shipping and Transport, 1952-60; Operations Officer, Qantas Airways, 1960-62; Legal and Collection Officer, Protection Acceptance Limited, 1962-63; Collection Manager, Dunn and Bradstreet Pty. Limited, 1963-67; Chairman/Managing Director, Australian Mercantile Bureaux and Agency Pty. Limited, 1967-. *Memberships:* Executives Association of Australia; Management Committee of Institute of Mercantile Agents; American Collectors' Association, Inc. *Honours:* Justice of Peace for New South Wales; Fellow, Institute of Directors, Australia; Associate Fellow, Australian Institute of Management; Associate Fellow, Australian Institute of Credit Management. *Hobbies:* Billiards and snooker; Snow-skiing. *Address:* 21 Marina Crescent, Gymea Bay, NSW 2227, Australia.

PETERSEN, Gordon Marshall, b. 25 Nov. 1921, San Francisco, USA. Professor of Mathematics. *Education:* BA, 1943; MA, Stanford University, 1947; PhD, Toronto University, 1951; DSc University of Wales, 1963. *Appointments:* University of British Columbia, 1947-49; Teaching Fellow, Toronto, 1949-51; University of Manitoba, 1951-52; University of Arizona, 1952-53; University of Oklahoma, 1953-55; Research Fellow, Swansea University College, 1955-57; University of New Mexico, 1957-59; Lecturer, Swansea University College, 1959-64; Reader, Swansea, 1964-65; Professor, Canterbury University, 1965-66; Head, Department of Mathematics Canterbury University, 1967-. *Memberships:* American Mathematical Association; American Mathematical Society; Canadian Mathematical Congress; London Mathematical Society; New Zealand Mathematical Society. *Publications:* Regular Matrix Transformations, 1966; Theory of Groups, 1959. *Honours:* Fellow, Royal Society of New Zealand, 1973. *Hobbies:* Collecting Roman Coins; Chess sets; Enamelled coins; Puzzles; Travelling. *Address:* 2 Bannister Street, Christchurch, New Zealand.

PETERSON, Bruce Henry, b. 21 Sept. 1918, Sydney, NSW, Australia. Consultant Psychiatrist. m. Dorothy Katherine Speirs, 8 July 1942, 3 daughters. *Education:* MB, BS, Sydney University, 1936-41; DPM, 1952; Fellow, Royal Australian and New Zealand College of Psychiatrists, 1963. *Appointments:* RMO, Sydney Hospital, 1941; RMO, 2/7 Australian Inf. Bn. AIF, 1942-46; Private General Practice, Emmaville, NSW, 1946-49; MO, NSW Health Department Division of Mental Hygiene, 1949-54; Private Psychiatric Practice 1954-; Hon. Psychiatrist, Sydney Hospital, 1964-73; Clinical Lecturer in Psychiatry, Sydney University, 1967-73. *Memberships:* Australian and New Zealand College of Psychiatrists; Family Life Movement of Australia. *Publications:* Contributions to Medical Journals; The Voices of Conscience, 1967; Understanding Psychosexual Development, Family Life Movement, 1970; Growing in Love and Sex, in Press; Editor, Australian journal of Sex, Marriage and Family, 1979-. *Honours:* Mentioned in Despatches, 1943; Military Cross, 1943. *Hobbies:* Music; Boating; Travel; Photography. *Address:* 5 Aspinall Place, Woolwich, NSW, Australia, 2110.

PETERSON, David Robert, b. 28 Dec. 1943, Toronto, Ontario, Canada. Lawyer; Business Executive; Member, Provincial Legislature. m. Shelley Christine Matthews, 16 Jan. 1974, 1 son, 1 daughter. *Education:* Bachelor of Arts, Political Science, University of Western Ontario, 1964; Bachelor of Laws, University of Toronto, 1967; University of Caen, France; Osgoode Hall, Read Law with Thomson Rogers, Called to the Bar of Ontario, 1969. *Appointments:* President, Family business, Electronics Company, 1969; Ontario Legislature, Riding of London Centre, 1975 and 1977; The Law Society of Upper Canada; Select Committee on Hydro and Standing Committee of Public Accounts, Ontario Legislature; Opposition Finance Critic, previously Opposition Energy Critic. *Memberships:* Frontier College, Director of Legal Services, Community youth organization, Yorkville, Toronto; London Canadian Club; United Appeal, Association for the Mentally Retarded; London Chamber of Commerce; Young Men's Christian Association; Secretary, Young Presidents' Organization. *Honours:* MPP, BA, LLB; Queen's Counsel, Ontario, 1981. *Hobbies:* Jogging; Tennis; Skiing. *Address:* 283 Regent Street, London, Ontario, Canada N6A 2H3.

PETROPOULOS, Evangelos Anastassios, b. 14 Jan. 1935, Athens, Greece. Professor of Physiology. m. Panayota N. Tzelas, 12 Nov. 1964, 1 son, 1 daughter. *Education:* MD 1959; Doctorate, University of Athens, Greece, 1964; PhD University of California, San Francisco, 1970. *Appointments:* Intern and Resident, Internal Medicine, Evangelismos Medical Center, Athens, Greece, 1961-64, Intern in Endocrinology, 1964-65; Research Assistant, University of California, San Francisco, 1965-66, Teaching Assistant, 1968; Assistant Research Physiologist I and II University of California, Berkeley 1967 and 1970-72; Special Fellow, US National Institute Health, San Francisco, 1968-70; Resident Associate and Lecturer, University of California, 1972-73; Special Consultant in Endocrinology, Evangelismos Medical Center, Athens, Greece, 1973-75; Professor and Chairman Department of Physiology, School of Medicine, University of Zimbabwe, 1975-. *Memberships:* American Physiological Society; The Endocrine Society, USA; The Society for the Study of Reproduction USA; International Society of Psychoneuroendocrinology; International Society for Developmental Neuro-sciences; International Society of Biometeorology; Society of Sigma Xi, USA; American Association for the Advancement of Science; Medical Research Society, Zimbabwe. *Publications:* 42 research publications in various scientific journals; 8 monographs or chapters in various books, Subjects: Reproductive endocrinology, developmental neurobiology, high altitude physiology. *Honours:* Abraham Rosenberg Research Fellow, University of California; Society of Sigma Xi Research Award; Special Fellow, US Nat. Inst. of Health; Guest Lecturer, University of California, Berkeley. *Hobbies:* Mountain Climbing; Underwater

Fishing; Tennis; Horticulture. *Address:* 9, Old Catton Road, Mount Pleasant, Salisbury, Zimbabwe.

PETTIGREW, Allan, b. 8 Sept. 1932, Bundaberg, Queensland, Australia. Engineer. m. Margaret Anne Harris, 24 Nov. 1956, 2 sons, 2 daughters. *Education:* Diploma in Mechanical and Electrical Engineering, Queensland Institute of Technology, Brisbane. *Appointments:* Cadet Engineer and Engineer, Toowoomba Foundry Pty. Ltd. 1951-61; General Manager, Technical, W G Utting Pty. Ltd. 1961-68; Australian Government SEATO Aid Adviser in South Vietnam, 1968-69; Principal, Pettigrew Engineering Pty. Ltd. 1969-76; Principal, Pettigrew Consultants Pty. Ltd. 1976-. *Memberships:* National President, Australian Water and Wastewater Association; Institution of Engineers Australia; Fellow, Australian Institute of Management; Director, Water Pollution Control Federation, USA; Institute of Water Pollution Control, United Kingdom. *Publications:* Published 11 technical papers dealing with water treatment and in particular the treatment of Industrial Waste Effluents, by-product recovery and the re-use of water. *Hobbies:* Pistol Shooting; Reading; Gardening. *Address:* 3647 Beaudesert Road, Park Ridge, 4125 Queensland, Australia.

PHELAN, Charles Jerome, b. 30 June 1941, Winnipeg, Manitoba, Canada. Barrister. m. Sylvia Shewchuk, 11 Mar. 1972 2 sons, 1 daughter. *Education:* BA 1963; LLB, University of Manitoba, 1967. *Appointments:* Crown Attorney, Province of Manitoba, 1967-68; Partner, Monk, Goodwin and Company, 1968-. *Memberships:* President, Manitoba Motor League, 1976-79; Governor, Canadian Automobile Association, 1976-79; Law Society of Manitoba, 1967-. *Honours:* HM, Silver Medal, 1977. *Hobby:* Photography. *Address:* 32 Falconer Bay, Winnipeg, Manitoba, Canada, R2M 4R5.

PHILIP, George Alexander David, b. 26 Sept. 1927, Glasgow, Scotland. Civil Servant. m. Janet Mathieson Cunningham, 17 Aug. 1951, 2 sons, 1 daughter. *Education:* Bellahouston Academy, Glasgow, UK, 1942-45. *Appointments:* Scots Guards, HM Forces, 1945-48; Temporary Clerk, Inland Revenue, Scotland, 1948-49; Executive Officer, Ministry of Pensions and National Insurance, Scotland, 1949-62; Higher Executive Officer, Scottish Home and Health Department, Scotland, 1962-66; Assistant Private Secretary to Secretary of State for Scotland, 1966-71; Senior Executive Officer, 1971-78, Principal, 1978-, Scottish Office. *Hobbies:* Music; Church choir; Pottering about at home. *Address:* 20 Elsworthy, Thames Ditton, Surrey, England.

PHILIP, Hugh Whitelaw Stuart, b. 1 Jan. 1919, Gourock, Scotland. Professor of Education. m. (1) Esme N Lawdrey, 19 Mar. 1943, (2) Margaret Anne Cullen, 11 May 1959, 2 sons, 4 daughters. *Education:* TC., Sydney Teachers' College, Australia, 1936-37; BA., 1941, MA., 1951, Sydney University, Australia; AM., 1954, PhD., 1958, Harvard University, USA. *Appointments:* Teacher, New South Wales Department of Education, Australia, 1938-41; Australian Army, 1941-46; Research Officer, Commonwealth Office of Education, 1946-54; Senior Lecturer, Sydney University, Australia, 1955-59; Director, Institute for Child Study, UNESCO, Bangkok, 1959-64; Head, Division of Educational Studies and Research, UNESCO, Paris, France, 1964-66; Foundation Professor of Education, Macquarie University, Australia, 1966-. *Memberships:* Fellow: British Psychological Society; Australian Psychological Society; Australian College of Education; Royal College of Preceptors; Foundation President, AARE. *Honours:* Smith Mundt Fellow, Harvard University, USA, 1954; Senior Imperial Relations Trust Fellow, London University, UK, 1972; Bernard van Leer Foundation Fellow, The Hague, 1978; Unesco Silver Medal, 1978. *Hobbies:* Golf; Sailing; Reading; Family. *Address:* 7 Little Street, Mosman, New South Wales 2088, Australia.

PHILIPPE, Madeleine Valentine, b. 4 Mar. 1938, Quatre Bornes, Mauritius. Librarian. m. Jocelyn Philippe, 2 May, 1977. *Appointments:* Town Librarian, Carnegie Library, Curepipe, Mauritius. *Address:* Cité Baissac, Lees Street, Curepipe, Mauritius.

PHILIPPE, Marie Clancy Jocelyn, b. 2 July 1946, Port Louis, Mauritius. Civil Engineer. m. Madeleine Paruit, 2 May 1977. *Education:* BSc., Hons., City University, London, UK, 1970. *Appointments:* Highway Engineer,

Essex County Council, UK, 1970-72; Civil Engineer, Ministry of Works, Mauritius, 1972-75; Town Engineer, Municipality of Curepipe, Mauritius, 1975-. *Memberships:* Institution of Highway Engineers, London, UK; Societé des Ingénieurs et Scientifiques de France; Institution of Engineers, Australia. *Hobby:* Radio Controlled MOdel Aeroplanes. *Address:* Cité Baissac, Lees Street, Curepipe, Mauritius.

PHILLIPS, Beatrice Pauline, b. 28 May 1907, Coolgardie, Western Australia. Teacher; Welfare Officer (retired). m. Leslie Albert Phillips, 5 Mar. 1932, 1 son, 3 daughters. *Appointments:* Lipreading Teacher to adults, Welfare Officer, Secretary, Australian Association for Better Hearing. *Memberships:* National President, State President, 20 years, Australian Association for Better Hearing; Vice President, National Council pf Women; Executive member, Council on the Ageing. *Publications:* History of the West Australian branch of Australian Association for Better Hearing from its inception May 1945 to 1966, now in process of carrying on from 1966 to 1981 for publication. *Honours:* MBE., 1975. *Hobbies:* Reading; Philately; Visiting sick and elderly people. *Address:* 61/8 Bradford Street, Mt. Lawley 6050, Australia.

PHILLIPS, (Sir) Fred, b. 14 May 1918, Brighton Village, St. Vincent, West Indies. m. Gloria Derrick, 25 July 1975. *Education:* Barrister-at-Law, Middle Temple, London, UK, 1956; LL.B., London, UK, 1957; MCL., McGill University, USA, 1968. *Appointments:* Assistant Administrator, Grenada, 1957-58; Senior Assistant Secretary, 1958-60, Secretary to Cabinet, Permanent Secretary, 1960-62, West Indies Federation; Senior Lecturer, University of the West Indies, 1962-65; Administrator, St. Kitts, West Indies, 1966-67; Governor, St. Kitts, Nevis, Anguilla, West Indies, 1967-69; Special Representative and Chief Legal Adviser, Cable and Wireless (West Indies) Limited, 1969-. *Memberships:* Imperial Society of Knights Bachelor. *Publications:* Freedom in the Caribbean: A Study in Constitutional Change; The Evolving Legal Profession in the Commonwealth. *Honours:* CVO., 1967; Knight Bachelor, 1967. *Hobbies:* Reading; Swimming. *Address:* PO Box 206, Bridgetown, Barbados, West Indies.

PHILLIPS, John Grant, b. 13 Mar. 1911, Sydney, Australia. Central Banker. m. Mary Willmot Debenham, 9 Mar. 1935, 2 sons, 2 daughters. *Education:* BE., University of Sydney, Australia, 1928-31. *Appointments:* Research Officer, New South Wales Retail Traders Association, Australia, 1932-35; Economic Assistant, Royal Commission on Monetary and Banking System, 1936-37; Economic Department, 1937-51, Investment Adviser, 1954-60, Commonwealth Bank of Australia; Deputy Governor and Deputy Chairman of Board, 1960-68, Governor and Chairman, 1968-75, Reserve Bank of Australia; Member of Council, Macquarie University, 1967-79; Member of Board, Howard Florey Institute of Experimental Physiology and Medicine, 1971-; Member of Board, Lend Lease Corporation Limited, 1976-; Chairman, Australian Statistics Advisory Council, 1976-. *Honours:* CBE., 1968; KBE., 1972. *Hobbies:* Lawn bowls; Contract bridge; Swimming. *Address:* 2/25 Marshall Street, Manly, New South Wales 2095, Australia.

PHILLIPS, Marian Antoinette Therese, b. 15 June 1954, Colombo, Sri Lanka. Chartered Accountant. m. Edward Francis Jeyakumar Phillips, 26 Jan. 1980. *Education:* Associate member, Institute of Chartered Accountants of Sri Lanka; Foundation Stages A & B and Professional Stage I of the Institute of Cost and Management Accountants, London, UK. *Appointments:* Articled Clerk, Aiyar & Co., Chartered Accountants, Sri Lanka; Group Management Accountant, Lyons Brooke Bond Limited/Oxo Zambia (1969) Limited, Zambia. *Honours:* Best Performance award, Sri Lanka Teachers Association, 1967; Silver Medal for Best Performance in Speech, 1967, General Proficiency award, 1969, Trinity College of Music, London, UK; English prize, 1965, 66, 67, 68, 69. *Hobbies:* Sports; Music; Photography. *Address:* 4 Sutton Court, Fitente Avenue, Ndola, Zambia.

PHILLIPS, Robert Howard Daniel, b. 3 Dec. 1921, Regina, Saskatchewan, Canada. Editor; Publisher. m. Tanyss Bell, 27 Oct. 1951, 2 sons. *Education:* BA., Hons., University of Saskatchewan, Saskatoon, Canada, 1948. *Appointments:* Journalist, Canada and UK,

1948-60; Economist and Director, of Research, Saskatchewan Wheat Pool, farmers' cooperative association, Regina, Canada, 1960-73; Editor and Publisher and General Manager, Western Producer Publications, a division of Saskatchewan Wheat Pool, Regina, Canada, 1973-. *Memberships:* Agricultural Institute of Canada; Canadian Agricultural Economics Society; Canadian Plains Research Center; International Association of Agricultural Economists; Director, Livestock Merchandising Institute; Board of Managers, St. Andrew's Presbyterian Church, Saskatoon, Canada; Saskatchewan Institute of Agrologists; Director, Council for Canadian Unity. *Publications:* Out West, 1977; Stories about persons and places on the Canadian prairies; Newspaper columns, 1948-. *Address:* 49 Churchill Court, Saskatoon, Saskatchewan S7K 3W9, Canada.

PHILP, John, b. 26 Dec. 1909, Fife, Scotland. Chief Fire Officer (retired). m. (1) Mary Louisa, 1 July 1931, (2) Doris Eleanor, 15 Nov. 1972, 2 sons, 1 daughter. *Appointments:* Deputy, 1939, Wellington Fire Brigade, 1926; Chief Fire Officer, Invercargill Fire Brigade, New Zealand, 1942-64. *Memberships:* Past President, Institute of Fire Engineers of Great Britain, New Zealand branch; Associate member, Chairman, 9 years, Southland Harbour Board; Executive, 9 years, New Zealand Harbours Association; Executive, South Island Promotions Association; Executive, Merchant Navy Centre, Bluff; Life Hon. member, Museum Trust Board; Borstal Committee; Marriage Guidance; Deputy Magistrate, Children's Court, 15 years. *Honours:* Appointed Justice of Peace, 1948; Queens Fire Service Medal, 1964; OBE., 1972. *Hobbies:* Indoor basketball; Tennis; Bowls. *Address:* Flat 2, 134 Pomona Street, Invercargill, New Zealand.

PHIRI, Masautso, b. 28 Aug. 1945, Chipata, Zambia. Publishing. m. Faith Chembe, 22 Dec. 1979, 3 daughters. *Education:* BA., University of Zambia, 1973; M.Litt., Edinburgh University, Scotland, 1975; currently completing one-year course in Radio, Film & TV., Bristol University, UK. *Appointments:* Accounts Clerk, 1966-67; Library Assistant, 1967-68; Adult Education Teacher, 1969-71; Part-time Tutor, 1974; English Editor, 1975-77, Senior Editor, 1977-79, Chief Editor, 1980-, Meczam; Freelance Journalist and Columnist, Times of Zambia, 1977-80; Actor, Theatre Director, 1969-. *Memberships:* Lusaka Press Club; Founder member, Production Chairman, 1976-79, Tikwiza Theatre; Executive Committee, 1980, Zambia National Writers Association. *Publications:* Plays: Christ Unlimited; Fanon's Notebook; Novels: Soweto Flowers Will Grow, 1979; Corn in the Field (in press). *Honours:* Presidential Group award to Tikwita Theatre, 1976-79; Commonwealth Scholar, 1973-75; British Council Scholar, 1980-81. *Hobbies:* Theatre; Literary writing; Photography; Hill climbing; Badminton; Walking in countryside. *Address:* Box 50086, Lusaka, Zambia.

PHOON, Wai-On, b. Singapore. University Professor. m. Molly Koh Soh Choo. *Education:* Educated, Universities of Malya, London and Edinburgh. *Appointments:* Vice-Dean, Faculty of Medicine, University of Singapore; Professor and Head, Department of Social Medicine and Public Health, University of Singapore. *Memberships:* President, Asian Association of Occupational Health; Vice-President, Association of Schools of Public Health; Vice-President, International Association for Accident and Traffic Medicine; Executive Vice-President for Asia, World Safety Organization; Singapore Medical Association. *Publications:* Author or main author of Five books. *Honours:* Singapore Medical Association Lecturer, 1972; Gold Medal, International Association for Accident and Traffic Medicine, 1980. *Hobbies:* Chess; Badminton; Table-tennis; Reading. *Address:* 11 Bin Tong Park, Singapore 1026, Singapore.

PICHETTE, Joseph Albert Robert, b. 7 Aug. 1936, Edmundston, New Brunswick, Canada. Public Servant. m. P.R. Roberts, 12 Aug. 1967 (Div. 1980), 2 sons. *Education:* Collège de Saint-Laurent, Montréal; Collège Saint-Denis, Montréal; Université Saint-Louis, Edmundston. *Appointments:* Royal Canadian Air Force, 1955-58; Announcer, French network, Canadian Broadcasting Corporation, Moncton, NB, 1960; Announcer, and Public Affairs Producer, CKCH Hull-Ottawa, 1961-63; Administrative Assistant, Premier of New Brunswick, Fredericton, NB, 1963-66; Deputy

Commissioner, Atlantic Provinces Pavilion Expo 67, 1966-67; Executive Assistant, 1968-70; Chief of Regional Operations, Information Canada, Ottawa, 1971-73; Special Assistant, Federal Commissioner of Official Languages, Ottawa 1973-77; Commissioner's Representative, Atlantic Provinces 1977-. *Memberships:* The Heraldry Society of Canada; Council of St John Ambulance; The Canadian Institute of International Affairs; North American Council of State's Arts Agencies; Governor, Dominion Drama Festival; Vice-President, XIII International Congress of Genealogical and Heraldic Sciences, London, 1976. *Publications:* Monographs, articles and papers in the field of Heraldry, in English and French. *Honours:* Coronation Medal, 1953; Centennial of Canada Medal, 1967; Jubilee Medal 1977; Officer, Order of St. John of Jerusalem, 1978; Knight of Honour and Devotion, the Sovereign and Military Order of Malta, 1970; Knight Commander, the Hospitaller Order of St. Lazarus of Jerusalem, 1975; Fellow, Royal Society of Arts, UK, 1978; Fellow, Heraldry Society of Canada, 1979; Gold Medal, Brazilian Society of Heraldry, 1976; Hon. Colonel and ADC to Governor of Louisiana, USA, 1969; Hon. Citizen of Lafayette, Louisiana, USA, 1966; Lewiston, Maine, USA, 1969; Kedgwick, New Brunswick, Canada, 1965. *Hobbies:* Heraldry; Music. *Address:* 52 Maple Grove Village, Moncton, New Brunswick, E1A 4R2, Canada.

PICKERING, (The Hon.), Edward Phillip, b. 1 Nov. 1939, Newcastle, NSW, Australia. Chemical Engineer. m. Elaine Marion Brock, 16 Feb. 1961, 2 sons, 3 daughters. *Education:* BSc, Chemical Engineering, University of New South Wales, Australia, 1964. *Appointments:* B.H.P Newcastle, 1964-65; Fuel Technologist, The Bellandor Coal Company Limited, Bulli, 1965-75; Executive Coal Cliff Collieries Pty. Limited, 1975-80; Member, New South Wales Legislative Council, 1976-. *Memberships:* M.Aus. IMM; FAIE. *Address:* 28 The Drive, Stanwell Park, 2509, Australia.

PICKERING, Errol Neil, b. 5 May 1938, Geelong, Victoria, Australia. Hospital Administrator. *Education:* Diploma of Hospital Administration, University of Toronto, Canada, 1972; Bachelor of Arts (Honours), York University, Canada 1970; Diploma of Medical Laboratory Technology, Royal Melbourne Institute of Technology, Australia, 1963. *Appointments:* Assistant Administrator, St. Michael's Hospital, Toronto, Canada, 1972-74; Executive Director, Australian Council on Hospital Standards, Sydney, Australia, 1974-80; Executive Director, Australian Hospital Association, Sydney, Australia, 1980-. *Memberships:* University Club, Sydney; Amnesty International; College of Health Service Administrators. *Publications:* Numerous Journal articles including: Hospital Administration in Canada, 1972; Old and Sick, 1973; Organisation in Hospitals in the Peoples Republic of China, 1980. *Honours:* Robert Wood Johnson Award in Hospital Administration, Canada, 1972; Hospital Administration in Canada Journal Article Award, 1973. *Hobby:* Classical Music. *Address:* 68 Audley Street, Petersham, Sydney, New South Wales, 2049 Australia.

PIERCE, Alan Edward, b. 18 Apr. 1920. Researcher. m. Margaret Nance, 14 Nov. 1953, 1 son, 1 daughter. *Education:* MSc, Wisconsin; PhD, London; DSc, London; FRCVS; DVSM; FACVSc. *Appointments:* Res. Officer, UK Ministry of Agriculture, 1943-50; Wellcome Fellow, University of Wisconsin, 1948-49; Agricultural Research Cl. Fell. Lister Institute, London, 1950-52; Principal Science Officer, ARC Institute of Animal Physiology Cambridge, 1952; Ian McMaster Fell. CSIRO Sydney, 1954-55; McMaster Laboratory CSIRO, Sydney, 1962-63; Senior Pricipal Science Officer ARC Institute Animal Physiology, Cambridge, 1964-66; Chief CSIRO, Division of Animal Health, 1966-72; Executive CSIRO, 1973-78; Minister (Scientific), Australian High Commission, London, 1979-81; Farmers' Veterinary Research, London. *Publications:* numerous articles in scientific journals and books. *Honours:* CBE, 1980. *Hobbies:* Music; Art; Travel. *Address:* c/o Australian High Commission, Australia House, Strand, London WC2B 3LA, England.

PIESSE, Winifred Margaret, b. 12 June 1923, Narre Warren, Victoria, Australia. Member of Legislative Council, Parliament of Western Australia. m. Mervyn Charles Piesse, 3 Sept. 1947, (Dec. 1966), 2 sons, 1 daughter. *Education:* Narre Warren State School, Victoria; Dandenong High School, Victoria. *Appointments:*

General nursing, Midwifery nursing and Child Health nursing, Victoria and Western Australia, (Triple Certificate Nurse); Tutor Sister in Child Health (Trudy King System). *Memberships:* Western Australian Branch Royal Justices' Association; Commonwealth Parliamentary Association; President, Red Cross Wagin Branch; Vice President and Secretary National Country Party; Country Womens' Association; Corp Nursing Officer, St Johns Ambulance. *Hobbies:* Gardening; Golf; Bridge. *Address:* 32 Forrest Street, Wagin, Western Australia 6315.

PIGGOTT, John Bruce, b. 22 Aug. 1913, Australia. Chairman, Tasmania Law Reform Commission, 1979-. m. (1) Kathleen Mason, 27 Jan. 1935, 2 sons, 4 daughters, (2) Audrey Beresford, 30 Mar. 1972, 2 sons, 1 daughter. *Education:* LLB, University of Tasmania. *Appointments:* Admitted to the Bar 1935; Senior Partner, Piggott, Wood and Baker, Hobart; President, S. Law Society Tasmania, 1960-62; President Arts Council Tasmania, 1945-49; President Council National Theatre and Fine Arts Society Tasmania, 1949-65; President, Law Council of Australia, 1961-64; Tasmania Representative on Executive Committee, 1960-70; Chairman, UN Appeals in Tasmania, 1948-68; Vice-President and Chairman International Bar Association, 1961-64; Australian Council of International Commission of Jurists, 1963-. *Memberships:* Institute of International Affairs; Representative for Australian and Treas. Law Association of Asia and Western Pacific, 1966-70; National Chairman for Australian World Peace Through Law Centre, NY, 1963-; International Law Association; Australian Rep. Union Internationale des Avocats (Brussels); Chairman and Member, Federation Council Institute of Directors, Australia, etc. *Honours:* CBE, 1962. *Hobbies:* Golf; Literature and the Arts. *Address:* 53 Derwentwater Avenue, Sandy Bay, Tasmania, 7005, Australia

PIGOTT, Peter Hugh, b. 29 Aug. 1936. Company Director. m. 20 Jan. 1960, 2 sons, 2 daughters. *Education:* SEGS North Sydney; East Sydney and Ultimo Technical Colleges. *Appointments:* Managing Director H R Pigott and Company Pty. Ltd, 1960; Founder, Surgical Dynamics Pty. Ltd. 1969; Chairman, Australian Howmedica Surgical Dynamics, Quambi Holding Pty. Ltd, 1971-. *Memberships:* Founder, Native Wildlife Reserve, Mt Wilson, NSW, for endangered species, 1971; Trustee of National Parks and Wildlife Foundation, 1971-; Senior Vice President and Chairman of Projects Committee, 1974-; Chairman, Federal Government Committee of Enquiry Museums and National Collections, 1974-75; Advisory Committee, Blue Mountains National Park; Trustee, The Australian Museum; Founder, Uncle Pete's Toy Warehouse, Sydney; Bicentenary Committee, Australian Museum; Deputy Chairman, Museum of Australia Interim Council. *Honours.* AM 1980. *Hobbies:* Flying; Skiing; Tennis; Swimming; Wildlife Conservation. *Address:* 1/10 Carabell Street, Kirribilli, Sydney, Australia.

PILE, Kenneth Cameron, b. 31 Mar. 1926, Barbados. Civil Servant. *Education:* Accounting, USA Governments Federal West Indies, (Trinidad), 1960; Land Reform Training Institute, Taiwan, 1976; University of Southern California, 1979. *Appointments:* Clerk, 1944-56, Supervisor, Inland Revenue, Post Office, 1956; Accountant, Port Authority, 1962-67; Senior Accountant, Ministry of Communications and Works, Queen Elizabeth Hospital, 1967-72; Assistant Accountant General, Treasury, 1972-74; Collector of Taxes, Rates and Taxes Department, 1974-. *Memberships:* District Officer, Lay Lecturer, St John's Ambulance Brigade; National Training Commissioner, Boy Scouts Association; Treasurer, Duke of Edinburgh Award Scheme. *Honours:* Serving Brother, Venerable Order of St John of Jerusalem, 1959; Queen's Jubilee Medal, 1977; Justice of the Peace, 1979. *Hobbies:* Scouting; Reading; Music; Youth Work. *Address:* Tronvilla No 10, 3rd Avenue, Belleville, St Michael, Barbados.

PILLAI, Jaya Kothai, b. 1 July 1926, Tanjore, India. Professor. m. M M Pillai, 4 May 1945, 4 sons. *Education:* BA (Chemistry, Physics) 1945; BEd, English, Maths and Science, 1949; MEd, History of Education, comparative Education, 1957; MA, Ancient Indian Culture, 1968; PhD, Educational Management, 1973. *Appointments:* Teacher, Maths and Science, Garrison schools of Ambala, Poona, Delhi Public School, Delhi, 1949-59; Lecturer, Loreto College, Calcutta, 1959-69;

Principal, Sri Avinashilingam Teachers' College, Coimbatore, 1969-71; Research Scholar, M.S. University of Baroda, 1971-74; Professor, Technical Teachers' Training Institute, 1974-77; Professor of Education, Madurai Kamaraj University, 1977-. *Memberships:* Commonwealth Council for Educational Administration, University of New England, Australia; All India Association for pre school Education; Indian Association for programmed Learning and Educational Innovations; University Women's Association. *Publications:* The Education System of the Ancient Tamils; Indian Education, Historical Foundations; Organizational Climate, Teacher morale and school quality; The Teaching-Learning process an analytical approach, in Press; Three Monographs. *Honours:* Fellowship for Internation Teacher Development Programme, USA, 1966-67. *Hobbies:* Music; Reading; Short story writing. *Address:* A.20 Tirunagar, Madurai 625 006, India.

PIMPARKAR, Bhalchandra, b. 30 June 1923, Vairag, District Sholapur, Maharashtra State, India. Consulting Physician. m. 15 June 1947, 1 son, 3 daughters. *Education:* LMP, LCPS 1948; MBBS 1950; DSc, Medical 1960; FAMS 1977. *Appointments:* House Physician, 1949; General Practice, 1951-54; Resident in Int. Med. Freedman's Hospital, Howard University, 1954-57; Fellow, Graduate School of Medicine, University of Lenna, 1957-60; Assistant Hon. Professor of Medicine, 1964-71; Hon. Professor of Medicine, 1971-; Hon. Physician, Dr B Nanarrati Hospital, 1961; Hon. Physician, Bombay Hospital, 1965-. *Memberships:* Indian Medical Association; Association of Physicians of India; Indian Society of Gastroententology; Society of Nuclear Medicine India; British Medical Association; Bockus International Society of Gastroenterology; National Academy of Medical Sciences, India. *Publications:* More than 75 publications in National and International journals; Contributor to Gastroentirology; AP1 Text Book of Medicine India. *Honours:* Fellowship, National Academy of Medical Sciences, India; President, Indian Society of Gastroenterology. *Hobbies:* Agriculture; History; Gardening; Sanskrit Literature. *Address:* 708 Cumball Crest, 42 Dr. G Deshmukh Marg, Bombay, 400026, India.

PINDLING, Lynden (Rt. Hon), b. 1930. m. Marguerite M. McKenzie, 1956, 2 sons, 2 daughters. *Education:* LL.B., LL.D. (Hon.), University of London; Middle Temple (Barrister-at-Law). *Appointments:* Practised as a lawyer, 1952-67; Joined Progressive Liberal Party, 1953; Elected to Bahamas House of Assembly, 1956, 1962, 1967 and 1968; Parliamentary Leader of Progressive Liberal Party, 1956; Leader of the Opposition, 1964; Delegations to United Nations Special Committee of Twenty-four, 1965 & 1966; Premier and Minister of Tourism and Development, 1967; led Bahamian Delegation to Constitutional Conference, London, 1968, to Independence Conference, London, 1972; Prime Minister and Minister of Economic Affairs of the Commonwealth of the Bahama Islands, 1969-. *Honours:* PC. *Address:* Office of the Prime Minister, Rawson Square, Nassau, Bahamas.

PINTO, Cholmondeley John lloyd, b. 6 May 1950, Chilaw, Sri Lanka. Chartered Accountant. m. R. Chamindra Coorey, 10 July 1974, 1 daughter. *Education:* Associate member, Institute of Chartered Accountants of Sri Lanka, 1972. *Appointments:* Audit Assistant, Hulugatta Samarasinghe & Co., Sri Lanka, 1972; Accountant: Building Materials Corporation, Sri Lanka, 1973; Carson Cumberbatch & Co., Sri Lanka, 1974; Audit Senior, Coopers and Lybrand, Zambia, 1975; Audit Manager, Pim Whiteley and Close, Zambia, 1978. *Hobbies:* Photography; Wildlife preservation. *Address:* 'Sweenitha', Jetty Street, Chilaw, Sri Lanka.

PIPER, Herbert Walter, b. 27 Aug. 1915, Murray Bridge, South Australia. University Teacher. m. Marie Therese Foristal, 28 Mar. 1944, 1 son, 1 daughter. *Education:* BA., University of Adelaide, Australia, 1938; D.Litt., 1961; BA., MA., 1952, Oxford University, UK. *Appointments:* Lecturer, 1948-50, Reader, 1950-54, University of Adelaide, Australia; Professor and Head of Department, University of New England, USA, 1954-65; Head, Wright College, 1958-59; Professor, 1966-80, Head of School, 1966-70, Emeritus Professor, 1981, Macquarie University, Australia. *Memberships:* President, 1957-59, Australasian Universities Language and Literature Association; New South Wales Board of Senior School Studies, 1962-76; Board of

Directors, Independent Theatre, Sydney, Australia, 1969-75; Editorial Board, Southern Review, 1973-. *Publications:* The Active Universe, 1962; The Beginnings of Modern Poetry, 1967. *Honours:* Rhodes Scholarship, 1946; Carnegie Travel Grant, 1960. *Address:* 182 West Street, North Sydney, Australia.

PIPER, John Anthony, b. 8 Nov. 1930, Shanghai, China. Diplomat. m. Ann Caro, 3 Dec. 1955, 1 son, 2 daughters. *Education:* BNC., Oxford, UK, 1950-53; BA., MA., PPE. *Appointments:* British Army, 1949-50; Australian Department of External Affairs, Canberra, serving in: Delhi, 1955-56, Rome, 1957-58, Karachi, 1961-62, Paris, 1966-70, Ottawa, 1971-72, Ambassador, Algiers, 1976-78, also accredited to Tunis, currently Senior Advisor, Economic Division, 1954-. *Address:* 71 Muggaway, Red Hill, ACT., Australia.

PIRBHAI, (Sir) Eboo, b. 25 July 1905, Bombay, India. Company Director; Rep. of HH The Aga Khan. m. Kulsumbai, 1925, 3 sons, 3 daughters. *Appointments:* Nairobi City Council, Kenya, 1938-43; Parliamentary Legislative Council for Kenya, 1952-60; Past President, Muslim Association; President, HH The Aga Khan's Supreme Council for Europe, USA, Canada and Africa. *Memberships:* Royal Commonwealth Society, UK. *Honours:* OBE., 1946; Knighted, 1952; Given Title of Count, 1954; Brilliant Star of Zanzibar, 1956; Order of Crescent Cross of the Comores, 1956. *Hobby:* Social work. *Address:* 12 Naivasha Avenue, Nairobi, Kenya.

PITBLADO, (Sir) David (Bruce), b. 18 Aug. 1912, London, England. Government Official. m. Edith Mary Evans, 14 Apr. 1941, 1 son, 1 daughter. *Education:* BA., MA., 1937; Emmanuel College, Cambridge, England, 1930-34. *Appointments:* Entered Civil Service, 1935; Assistant Private Secretary to Secretary of State, 19338, Dominions Office, UK, 1935-42; War Cabinet Office, 1942; Under Secretary, 1949, Third Secretary, 1960, HM Treasury, 1942-65; San Francisco Conference, 1945; Central Economic Planning Staff, 1949-51; Principal Private Secretary to Mr. Attlee, Mr Churchill and Sir A. Eden, 1951-56; Vice-Chairman, European Payments Union, 1958-60; Economic Minister, British Embassy and UK, Director, IMF., World Bank, 1961-63; Permanent Secretary, Ministry of Power, 1965-69; Comptroller and Auditor General, 1971-76. *Memberships:* Hon. Treasurer, Soldiers, Sailors and Airmens Family Association. *Honours:* Bar prize, 1938; Hon. Fellow, Emmanuel College, UK, 1972. *Hobby:* Travel. *Address:* 23 Cadogan Street, London, SW32 PP, England.

PITCAITHLY, Ngata Prosser, b. 26 Sept. 1906, Waimate, New Zealand. Principal of College (retired). m. Reena Simpson, 28 Dec. 1933, 2 sons, 1 daughter. *Education:* Otago University, New Zealand, 1925-28; Auckland University, New Zealand, 1928; BA., 1928; MA., 1931; Diploma, Education, Victoria College, New Zealand, 1937-38; Associate, New Zealand Institute of Chemistry, 1931. *Appointments:* Science Master, Auckland Grammar School, New Zealand, 1928-32; Head, Rotorua Junior High School, New Zealand, 1932-33; Science Master, Rotorua High School, 1934-36; Head, Science Department, 1936-46, Deputy Head, 1944-46, Dannevirke High School, New Zealand; Foundation Principal: Northland College, New Zealand, 1946-56; Selwyn College, New Zealand, 1956-66; Feature writer, New Zealand Herald, 1967-77; Promotions and Publicity Officer, Auckland Festival Society, New Zealand, 1967-75. *Memberships:* President, Kaikohe Chamber of Commerce. *Publications:* Distribution of Copper in the Coryno carpus Laevigata, 1933; Secondary Education of the Maori, 1955; Marae and College, 1956. *Honours:* Queen Elizabeth Coronation Medal, 1953; Efficiency Decoration and Clasp, 1956. *Hobbies:* Yachting; Gardening. *Address:* 214 St. Heliers Bay Road, Auckland 5, New Zealand.

PITCHUMONI, Capecomorin Sankar, b. 20 Jan. 1938, Madura, India. Physician; Professor of Medicine. m. Prema, 5 Nov. 1964, 1 son, 2 daughters. *Education:* MBBS., 1960, MD., 1965, Medical College, Trivandrum, India; FRCP., Royal College of Physicians of Canada, 1970; American Board in GE., 1971; American Board in Internal Medicine. *Appointments:* Associate Professor of Medicine, 1972-75, 1975-80, Professor of Clinical Medicine, 1980, New York Medical College, USA; Chief of Gastroenterology, Metropolitan Hospital, New York, USA, 1972-80; Chief of Division of Gastro-

enterology, MIsericordia Hospital, New York, USA, 1980. *Memberships:* Association of Physicians of India; Federation for Clinical Research; Fellow: Royal College of Physicians; American College of Physicians; American College of GE; American GE Association; Indian Society of GE; American Institute of Nutrition; NY GE Association; BX Cty Medical Society; NY State Society; American Medical Association; American Association for the Advancement of Science; President, Kerala Samajam of New York, USA, 1977-78. *Publications:* Scientific articles in leading medical journals on disorders of Pancreas and Alcohol Injury to Stomach. *Honours:* Recipient of Hoechst-Om Prakash award, Indian Society of Gastroenterology. *Hobby:* Oil Painting. *Address:* 178 Fairmount Avenue, Glenrock, New Jersey 07452, USA.

PITFIELD, Peter Michael, b. 18 June 1937, Montreal, Canada. Public Servant. m. Nancy Snow, 27 Dec. 1971, 1 son, 2 daughters. *Education:* BASc., St Lawrence University, 1955; BCL, McGill University, BCL, 1958; DESD, University of Ottawa, 1960; Called to Quebec Bar, 1962; Appointed QC., (Federal), 1972. *Appointments:* Read law with Mathewson, Lafleur & Brown, Montreal, 1958-59; Administration Assistant to Minister of Justice and Attorney-General, of Canada, 1959-61; Secretary and Executive Director, Royal Commission on Publication, 1961-62; Attache to Governor-General, 1962-65; Secretary and Research Supervisor of Royal Commission on Taxation, 1963-66; Entered Privy Council Office and Cabinet Secretariat of Government of Canada, 1965; Assistant Secretary to Cabinet, 1966; Deputy Secretary to Cabinet (Plans) and Deputy Clerk of Council, 1969; Deputy Minister, Consumer & Corporate Affairs, 1973-75; Clerk of Privy Council and Secretary to Cabinet, 1975-79; Mackenzie King Visiting Professor, Kennedy School of Government, Harvard, 1979-80; Clerk of Privy Council and Secretary to Cabinet, 1980-. *Memberships:* Canadian, Quebec and Montreal Bar Associations; Canadian Institute of Public Administration; Canadian Political Science Association; American Society Political and Social Sciences; International Commission of Jurists; Beta Theta Pi; University Club of Montreal. *Honours:* Fellow, Harvard University, 1974; Honorary DLitt, St Lawrence University, 1979. *Hobbies:* Squash; Skiing; Reading. *Address:* 305 Thorold Road, Ottawa, Canada K1M OK1.

PITHEY, Jack William, b. 30 Dec. 1903, Potchefstroom, RSA. President of Senate, Parliament of Zimbabwe (retired). m. Mary Wood Lang, 1 Sept. 1931, 2 sons, 1 daughter. *Appointments:* Secretary for Justice, 1957-63; Member of Parliament, Avondale Constituency, 1964-70; President of the Senate, 1971-78. *Memberships:* 1st Chairman, Greendale Town Council; Civil Service Club. *Honours:* Grand Officer of Legion of Merit; CBE. *Hobbies:* Racing; Gardening. *Address:* 3 Cambridge Drive, PO Greendale, Salisbury, Zimbabwe.

PITKE, Madhukar Vishwanath, b. 31 Mar. 1936, Bijapur, Karnataka, India. Scientific research. m. Shakuntala, 14 May 1968, 1 son, 1 daughter. *Education:* BSc., 1956; MSc., 1958; PhD., 1973. *Appointments:* Research Associate, 1959-63, Fellow, 1966-73, Research Scientist, 1973-78, Senior Research Scientist, 1978, Tata Institute of Fundamental Research, Bombay, India; Visiting Scientist: University of Pisa, Italy, 1963-64; MaxPlanck Institut fur Physik, Munich, West Germany, 1964-65; Visiting Professor, University of Mexico, Mexico City, USA, Jan.-Oct. 1965; Professor and Head, Department of Computer Science, University of Bombay, India, 1978. *Memberships:* Institute of Electrical and Electronics Engineers; Fellow: Institute of Electronics and Telecommunication Engineers; Maharashtra Academy of Sciences. *Publications:* Several papers describing results of research in leading national and international journals and presented at scientific conferences. *Honours:* member of several panels/committees appointed by Government of India for problems dealing with the development of electronics, computers and telecommunication in India. *Hobbies:* Photography; Music; Travelling. *Address:* 204 Colaba Housing Colony, Homi Bhabha Road, Bombay 400 005, India.

PITMAN, (Sir) Isaac James, b. 14 Aug. 1901, London, England. Educator. m. The Hon. Margaret Beaufort Lawson Johnston, 28 Apr. 1927, 3 sons, 1 daughter. *Education:* MA., Christ Church, Oxford, UK, 1920-23.

Appointments: Sir Isaac Pitman & Sons Limited, 1923, 1945-66; Acting S.L., RAFVR., 1941; Director of O & M., HM Treasury, 1943; Conservative member of Parliament, Bath, UK; Director, Bank of England. *Memberships:* Chairman, Royal Society of Teachers; Chairman, Council of ITA Foundation; Vice-Chairman, London University Institute of Education. *Creative Works:* Invented Initial Teaching Alphabet, Selected Spellings to represent a dialect of English which give the greatest similarity to the spelling in Traditional Orthography so that extension from the Initial learning medium to Traditional Orthography may be effortless in context. *Honours:* KBE; Hon. D.Litt from: Hofstra, New York, USA; Strathclyde, UK; Bath, England. *Hobby:* Languages, particularly English and French. *Address:* 58 Chelsea Park Gardens, London, SW3 6AE, England.

PITT, Aubrey, b. 11 Feb. 1934, Melbourne, Australia. Medical Practitioner; Cardiologist. m. Sylvia Kiers, 21 Dec. 1954, 1 son, 1 daughter. *Education:* MBBS, 1957; MD, University of Melbourne, 1961; Royal Australasian College of Physicians, 1961; FRACP, 1970; American College of Cardiology, 1971. *Appointments:* House Staff, Royal Melbourne Hospital, 1958-61, Assistant Sub-Dean, 1962; National Heart Hospital, London, 1963; Johns Hopkins Hospital, 1964-66; Director, Cardiology Service and Associate Professor, Alfred Hospital and Monash University. *Memberships:* Australian Medical Association; Royal Australasian College of Physicians; American College of Cardiology; Cardiac Society of Australia and New Zealand; International Society and Federation of Cardiology; Council on Clinical Cardiology. *Publications:* Author and co-author of over 70 papers and abstracts on cardiology. *Hobbies:* Cricket; Music; Theatre. *Address:* 15 Cantala Avenue, North Caulfield 3161, Australia.

PITT, Christopher Wren, b. 18 June 1942, Blackheath, London, England. Electronics Engineer. m. Brenda Christine Webb, 2 Apr. 1966, 1 son, 1 daughter. *Education:* Ord. National Certificate in Electrical Engineering, Thames Polytechnic, London, 1958-60; BSC., (Eng), Hons., 1961-64; MSc., Solid State Physics, 1966-68. *Appointments:* Semiconductor Device Design and Development Engineer, R&D Laboratory, ITT Semiconductors Limited, Sidcup, Kent, 1964-66; Senior Process Engineer, Planar Devices, 1967-70; Research Fellow, Electronic and Electrical Engineering Department, University College, London, 1971-77; Lecturer and Undergraduate Tutor (1979) UCL, 1978-81; Senior Lecturer and Undergraduate Tutor, 1981-. *Memberships:* Institute of Physics, 1973; Institution of Electrical Engineers, 1974; Organising Committee Chairman, IPAT International Conference. *Publications:* Numerous papers on semiconductor devices, optical circuits, particularly integrated optics, thin film materials and technology; Several patents on semiconductor components and optical devices; Consultant to Imperial Chemical Industries Limited, Corporate Laboratory, General Electric Company Limited, Hirst Research Centre, Sira Limited and other companies at various times; Extensive conference presentations in above field. *Honours:* Research contracts from Science Research Council, Ministry of Defense, UK industrial companies, 1970-. *Address:* 7 The Meadows, Halstead, Sevenoaks, Kent, TN14 7HD, England.

PITT, Harry Raymond (Sir), b. 3 June 1914, West Bromwich, England. Former Vice-Chancellor. m. 1 Apr. 1940, 4 sons. *Education:* Mathematics Tripos I, II, III, First Class Honours, BA, Distinction, Peterhouse Cambridge, 1932-39; PhD., Cambridge, 1938; Fellow, Smith's Prize, 1938; Harvard Fellow, 1937-38. *Appointments:* Assistant Lecturer in Mathematics, Aberdeen, 1939-41; Scientific Intelligence, Air Ministry, 1942-45; Professor of Mathematics, Queen's University, Belfast, 1945-50 and Nottingham University, 1950-64; Visiting Professor, Yale University, 1962-63; Vice-Chancellor, University of Reading, 1964-79. *Memberships:* Fellow, Royal Society, 1957; Fellow, Institute of Mathematics and its application, Vice-President, 1979-; Chairman, Universities Central Council for Admission, 1975-79; Chairman, Standing Conference on University Entrance, 1975-79; Vice-Chairman, Committee of Vice-Chancellors and Principals, 1976-77. *Publications:* Tauberian Theorems, 1957; Measure, Integration and Probability, 1963; Mathematical papers in scientific journals. *Honours:* FRS, 1957; Knighthood, 1978; Honorary LL.D., Aberdeen, 1970, Nottingham, 1970; Honorary DSc., Reading, 1978; Belfast,

1981. *Hobbies:* Walking; Travel. *Address:* 46 Shinfield Road, Reading, Berkshire, England.

PLAISTER, Douglas Robert, b. 25 June 1912, Hobart, Tasmania, Australia. Retired School Teacher. m. Violet Beryl Hay, 25 Aug. 1934 (Deceased), 1 son, 1 daughter. *Education:* Trained Teacher's Certificate. *Appointments:* Army Service, AIF, Artillery, LHQ, Physical and Recreational Training School, Officer in charge of Swimming and Life Saving, Australia and New Guinea, 1941-45; Senior Swimming Teacher, Physical Education Branch, 1946-76; Elected Alderman, Hobart City Council, 1970; Elected Deputy Lord Mayor, 1974; Elected Lord Mayor, 1976-78; Re-elected Lord Mayor, 1978-. *Memberships:* Senior Life Governor, Royal Life Saving Society, Australia, 1981, State President, Tasmanian Branch, 1979-, Life Governor, Hong King Branch; Life Governor, Hong Kong Life Guard Club; Judiciary Committee, National Council, Surf Life Saving Association of Australia, 1980-, Vice-President, 1950-75, President, 1977-, Chairman, Organising Committee, Australian Surf Life Saving Championships, 1969 & 1976, Tasmanian State Centre; Associated with numerous other Swimming, Police, Water Safety and Sportsmen's Associations; President, Southern Tasmanian Honorary Justices' Association, 1976-; Executive, 1976-80, President, 1980-81, Municipal Association of Tasmania, Chairman, Southern Regional Committee; Chairman, Australian Capital Cities Secretariat, 1981; State Chairman, Delegate to Australian Body, Commonwealth Youth Support Scheme; State President, Royal Guide Dogs for the Blind Association of Tasmania, 1978-; Board, 1979, State President, 1979, Royal Tasmanian Society for the Blind and Deaf; Chairman, Southern Regional Committee for the Handicapped; Chairman, Retarded Children's Welfare Association, Woman of the Year Quest, 1976-; Chairman, ANZAC Day Celebrations Committee; Director and Board Member, Tasmanian Fiesta; State Committee, Queen Elizabeth Jubilee Trust Fund; State Committee, Sir Robert Menzies Memorial Trust; President, Hobart Benevolent Society; Committee, Royal Over-Seas League (Tasmanian Branch), 1960; Chairman, Tasmanian Committee, The International Year of Disabled Persons, 1980; Honorary Vice-President, Royal Humane Society of Australia, 1980. *Honours:* Officer of the Order of Australia, 1980; MBE., 1955; Queen's Coronation Medal; Queen's Jubilee Medal; Justice of the Peace, 1970; Vice-President, Life Governor, Service Cross and three Bars, Recognition Badge and one Bar, Honorary Associate Certificate and Badge, Royal Life Saving Society, Commonwealth Council, London; Vice-President, Life Governor, Life Member, Meritorious Service Award, Royal Life Saving Society (Australia), Tasmanian Branch; Merit Certificate, World Life Saving; Certificate of Merit, Royal Humane Society; Thanks Badge, Scouts Association of Australia, (Tasmanian Branch) and Girl Guides Association. *Address:* 18 Osborne Street, Sandy Bay, Tasmania, 7005, Australia.

PLATT, Harry (Sir), b. 7 Oct. 1886, Thornham, Lancashire, England. Consulting Orthopaedic Surgeon. m. Gertrude Sarah Turney, 27 Oct. 1916, 4 daughters. *Education:* MB., Ch.B., Victoria University of Manchester, 1909; MB.,BS., (Honours, Distinction: Medicine and Suregery, with Gold Medal), University of London, 1909; MS, University of London, 1911; FRCS., England, 1912; MD, University of Manchester, (Gold Medal for Thesis on Peripheral Nerve Injuries), 1921. *Appointments:* House Surgeon, Manchester Royal Infirmary, 1909-10; Resident Surgical Officer, Royal National Orthopaedic Hospital, London, 1912-13; Clinical Attaché, Massachusetts General Hospital, Boston, USA and Childrens' Hospital, Boston, USA, 1913-14; Demonstrator of Anatomy, 1911-12, Lecturer in Orthopaedic Surgery, 1926-39, Professor of Orthopaedic Surgery, 1939-51, Emeritus Professor, 1951-, University of Manchester; Honorary Orthopaedic Surgeon, Ancoats Hospital, Manchester, 1914-32, Manchester Royal Infirmary, 1932-51; Surgical Director, Ethel Hedley Hospital, Windermere, 1920-63; Surgical Adviser, Robert Jones and Agnes Hunt Orthopaedic Hospital, Oswestry, Shropshire, 1920-; Consulting Orthopaedic Surgeon, Lancashire County Council, (Education, Public Health and Tuberculosis), 1920-48; Captain, Royal Army Medical Corps, Territorial Forces; Appointed Surgeon-in-Charge of Military Orthopaedic Centre in Manchester. *Memberships:* Founder Member and First Honorary Secretary, 1918, Vice-President, 1930-31,

President, 1934-35, British Orthopaedic Association; Founder Member, Association of Surgeons of Great Britain and Ireland, 1919; Council, 1940-58, Vice-President, 19450, President, 1954-57, Royal College of Surgeons of England; President, Royal Society of Medicine, London Section or Orthopaedics, 1931-32; Founder Member, 1929, British Delegate International Committee, 1929-48, President, 1948-53, Membre d'Honneur, 1973, Société Internationale de Chirurgie Orthopédique et de Traumatologie; President, 1958-66, Honorary President, 1970, International Federation of Surgical Colleges; Honorary member of numerous other Medical Societies worldwide. *Publications:* Part-Author of several text books including: Surgery in Chronic Rheumatism, Bone Tumours; Editor, Modern Trends in Orthopaedics, Monograph, The Surgery of the Peripheral Nerve Injuries of Warfare; Author of selected papers; Numerous contributions to medical journals. *Honours:* Knighted, 1948; Baronetcy conferred, 1958; Honorary Degrees: MD, University of Berne, 1954; LL.D., University of Manchester, 1955, University of Liverpool, 1955, University of Belfast, 1955, University of Leeds, 1965; Docteur Honoris Causa, University of Paris, 1966; Honorary Fellow of: American College of Surgeons, 1934, Royal College of Physicians and Surgeons of Canada, 1955, of South Africa, 1957, Royal Australasian College of Surgeons, 1961, Royal College of University Surgeons of Denmark, 1962, Faculty of Dental Surgery, Royal College of Surgeons of England, 1963, Royal Society of Medicine (London), 1966, Royal College of Surgeons in Ireland, 1976; British Council Lecture Tours: Cyprus and Israel, 1953, India, Pakistan, Ceylon, 1958-59, Latin America, 1959. *Hobbies:* Music; Anglo-American Relations; Travel; Political Philosophy. *Address:* 14 Rusholme Gardens, Platt Lane, Manchester M14 5LS, England.

PLAYFORD, Phillip Elliott, b. 27 Dec. 1931, Perth, Western Australia. Geologist. m. Cynthia Hogbin, 30 May 1964, 2 daughters. *Education:* Bachelor of Science, University of Western Australia, 1949-52; First Class Honours in Geology, 1952; PhD., Geology, Stanford University, 1959-61. *Appointments:* Field Geologist, Commonwealth Bureau of Mineral Resources, 1953; Staff Stratigrapher, West Australian Petroleum Pty. Ltd., 1954-59; Supervising Geologist, Geological Survey of Western Australia, 1962-70; General Manager, Abrolhos Oil, N.L., 1970-71; Deputy Director, Geological Survey of Western Australia, 1972-. *Memberships:* Australasian Institute of Mining and Metallurgy; Petroleum Exploration Society of Australia; Geological Society of Australia; American Association of Petroleum Geologists; Society of Economic Paleontologists and Mineralogists; Royal Society of Western Australia (councillor and past president); National Trust of Australia; Royal Western Australian Historical Society. *Publications:* Author of more than 50 publications dealing mainly with Western Australian geology, energy resources and history; Principal publications deal with Devonian reefs, oil exploration, geology of the Perth Basin and stromatolites. *Honours:* General Exhibition, University of Western Australia, 1948-51; Lady James Prize in Natural Science, 1951; Gledden Research Fellowship, 1959-61; Fulbright Scholarship, 1959-61; Distinguished Lecturer, American Association of Petroleum Geologists, 1978-79; Distinguished Lecturer, Petroleum Exploration Society of Australia, 1980. *Hobby:* Photography. *Address:* 102 Thomas Street, Nedlands, 6009, Western Australia.

PLAZZOTTA, Enzo Mario, b. 29 May 1921, Mestre, (Venezia), Italy. Sculptor. m. (1) Patricia Bloomfield, 1949, 1 son, (2) Gillian Antonia Beamish, 1960, 1 son, 1 daughter. *Education:* Academia de Brera, Milan, 1938-46. *Memberships:* Chelsea Arts Club. *Creative Works:* One-man exhibitions GAM., Paris, 1967; Grosvenor Gallery, London, 1968, 1970; Acquavella Gallery, New York, 1969, 1973; David Jones Gallery, Sydney, 1974; Lad Lane Gallery, Dublin, 1975; Wexford International Festival, 1976; Wildenstein Gallery, London, 1978; Wildenstein Gallery, New York City, 1980; Bedford College, London University, 1980. *Honours:* Order of Merit, (Italy). *Hobbies:* Chess; Tennis. *Address:* 10 Shalcomb Street, London SW10, England.

PLIATZKY, Leo, b. 22 Aug. 1919, Salford, Lancashire, England. Former Government Servant; Company Director & Academic. m. Marian Jean Elias, 11 Nov. 1948, (Deceased, 1980), 1 son, 1 daughter. *Education:* Corpus Christi College, Oxford, First Class Classical Honours, 1938; First Class PPE, 1946. *Appointments:* War Service, 1940-45, (Mentioned in Despatches); Ministry of Food, 1947-50; Secretary, Treasury, 1950-77; Permanent Secretary, Department of Trade, 1977-79; Special duties, reporting to the Prime Minister, 1979-80; Visiting Professor, The City University, 1980-; Non-Executive Director; Associated Communications Corporation, Ultramar Company, British Airways. *Memberships:* FRSA; Honorary Fellow, Corpus Christi College, Oxford. *Honours:* KCB, 1977. *Address:* 27 River Court, Upper Ground, London, SE1, England.

PLIMSOLL, James, (Sir), b. 1917. Australian Diplomat. *Education:* University of Sydney. *Appointments:* Economic Department, Bank of New South Wales, 1938-42; Australian Army, 1942-47; Australian Delegation, Far Eastern Commission, 1945-48; Australian Representative, UN Commission for the Unification and Rehabilitation of Korea, 1950-52; Assistant Secretary, Department of External Affairs, Canberra, 1953-59; Australian Permanent Representative at the United Nations, 1959-63; Australian High Commissioner in India, and Ambassador to Nepal, 1963-65; Secretary, Australian Department of External Affairs, 1965-70; Australian Ambassador to the United States, 1970-74; Australian Ambassador to USSR & to Mongolia, 1974-77; to Belgium, Luxembourg and the European Communities, 1977-80; Ambassador to Court of St James, 1980-. *Honours:* AC, 1978; Kt. 1962; CBE, 1956. *Address:* Australian Embassy, Australia House, Strand, London WC2, England.

PLOWDEN, Edwin Noel, (Baron of Plowden), b. 6 Jan. 1907. Chairman. m. Bridget Horatia, 1933, 2 sons, 2 daughters. *Education:* Switzerland; Pembroke College, Cambridge. *Appointments:* Temporary Civil Servant, Ministry of Economic Warfare, 1939-40; Ministry of Aircraft Production, 1940-46; Chief Executive and Member of Aircraft Supply Council, 1945-46; Vice-Chairman, Temporary Council Committee of NATO, 1951-52; Cabinet Office, 1947; Treasury, 1947-53; Adviser on Atomic Energy Organization, 1953-54; Chairman, Atomic Energy Authority, 1954-59; Visiting Fellow, Nuffield College, 1956-64; Chairman, Committee of Enquiry; Treasury control of Public Expenditure, 1959-61; Organisation of Representational Services Overseas, 1963-64; Aircraft Industry, 1964-65; Structure of Electricity Supply Industry, England and Wales, 1974-75; into CBI'S aims and organisation, 1974-75; Deputy Chairman, Committee of Inquiry on Police, 1977-79; Director Commercial Union Assurance Company Ltd., 1946-78; National Westminster Bank Ltd., 1960-77; Chairman, Equity Capital for Industry, 1976-; Chairman, Police Complaints Board, 1976-80; Independent Chairman, Police Negotiating Board, 1979-; President of Tube Investments Ltd., 1976-, Chairman, 1963-76. *Memberships:* Top Salaries Review Body, 1977-; Chairman, Top Salaries Review Body, 1981-; Ford European Advisory Council, 1976-; Chairman, CBI Companies Committee, 1976-80; Vice-Chairman, CBI President's Committee, 1977-80; President, London Graduate School of Business Studies, 1976-; Chairman, 1964-76; Chairman, Standing Advisory Committee on Pay of Higher Civil Service, 1968-70; Civil Service College Advisory Counsel, 1970-76; Engineering Industries Council, 1976. *Honours:* Baron, 1959; KCB, 1951; KBE, 1946; Honorary Fellow, Pembroke College, Cambridge; Honorary DSc., Pennsylvania State University, 1958; University of Aston, 1972; Honorary DLitt, Loughborough. *Address:* Martels Manor, Dunmow, Essex, England.

POAKWA, Daniel Anini, b. 28 Apr. 1936, Konongo. Educationist. m. 28 Apr. 1955, 2 sons, 2 daughters. *Education:* General Diploma in Music, University of Ghana, Lagos, 1965-69. *Appointments:* Teacher, Onwe, Methodist Primary School, 1958-60, Suame, Kumasi, 1963-65; Music Master, Isei Kyeretwie Secondary School, 1969-73; Senior Music Master & House Master, 1973-78; Assistant Headmaster, Akomadan Secondary School, Akomadan, 1978-79; Acting Headmaster, 1979-80; Training & Course Officer, District Education Office, Offinso, Ashanti, 1980-. *Memberships:* Musicians Union of Ghana; Society of African Music Research; Ghana Music Teachers Association. *Creative Works:* Song: Yehye wo Nsam; Som Ghana Sompa; Nfifisisam ne Anigyee; Abotare; Nyame ne Yen Nam; Ma me man Nsore; Adikanfo; Spiritual (Ibi Hard work-renamed) Ibi Him Christ; English songs: How did Moses Cross the Red Sea?; Child on Cocoyam

Leaves. *Hobbies:* Reading; Listening to Music. *Address:* Ibadan City Academy, PMB 5013, Ibadan, Oyo State, Nigeria.

POCIUS, nee SAKALAUSKAITE, leva, b. 14 Sept. 1923, Piniava, Lithuania. Sculptor. m. Martynas Pocius, 26 Apr. 1943, 1 son, 1 daughter. *Education:* Diploma, Fine Art, South Australia School of Art, Adelaide, Australia. *Appointments:* Part-time Lecturer, Sculpture, South Australia School of Art, Adelaide, Australia, 1964-75; Self-employed. *Memberships:* Fellow, Royal South Australia Society of Arts; Contemporary Art Society. *Creative Works:* 8 Individual Exhibitions, 6 Adelaide, 2 Melbourne, 1963-; has taken part in many invitation and competitive shows in Australia; Exhibited regularly in group and invitation shows in Adelaide. *Honours:* Associate Prize, 1963, Prize for Sculpture, 1965, Royal South Australia Society of Arts; Sculpture Prize, Lithuanian Art Exhibition, 1966; Shared prize, Centenary Art Competition, Bundaberg, Queensland, Australia, 1967; Prize of Honour, International Summer Academy of Fine Arts, Salzburg, Austria, 1970; Represented: Art Gallery of South Australia, Reserve Bank of Australia, South Australia School of Art. *Hobbies:* Travel; Community work amongst Lithuanians in South Australia; Painting pictures for relaxation. *Address:* 2A Tallala Terrace, Myrtle Bank, South Australia 5064.

POCKLEY, (Robert) Peter (Campbell), b. 20 May 1935, Sydney, Australia. University Administrator; part-time Science Writer and Commentator. m. Jenifer Anne Johnston, 10 June 1968, 1 daughter. *Education:* BSc., 1956; Dip.Ed., 1957, University of Melbourne, Australia; DPhil., University of Oxford, Balliol College, UK, 1961. *Appointments:* Science Master: Melbourne Grammar School, Australia, 1958; Wellington College, UK, 1961-64; Resident Tutor, Chemistry, St Paul's College, University of Sydney, Australia, 1964-68; First Director of Science Programmes for TV and Radio, Australian Broadcasting Commission, 1964-73; Adviser, Public Affairs, Head, Public Affairs Unit, The University of New South Wales, Australia, 1973-. *Memberships:* Science and Industry Forum, Australian Academy of Science, 1971-; Film, Radio and Television Board, Australia Council, 1974-76; Foundation Convener, Public Broadcasting Association of Australia; Association of British Science Writers; National Association of Science Writers, USA. *Publications:* The Elements of Physical Chemistry (co-author), 1967; This is Australia (co-author), 1975; Numerous popular science publications, Australian Broadcasting Commission; Editor of UNIKEN Newspaper, quarterly magazine, Occasional Papers series of the University of New South Wales, Australia; Australian correspondent for Nature, 1973-79. *Honours:* Shell Commonwealth Postgraduate Scholarship for Australia, 1958-61. *Hobbies:* Photography; Swimming; Restoring old houses. *Address:* 25 Avenue Road, Glebe, Sydney, New South Wales 2037, Australia.

POEHLMAN, William Fredrick, b. 10 Nov. 1945, St. Catharine's, Ontario, Canada. Professional Scientist; Assistant Professor. *Education:* BS., Niagara University, Canada, 1968; BSc., Brock University, Canada, 1969; MSc., 1972, PhD., 1980, McMaster University, Canada. *Appointments:* Research Technician/Instructor, Brock University, Canada, 1972-74; Research Associate, 1979-81, Professional Scientist, Assistant Professor, Engineering Physics, 1981-, McMaster University, Canada. *Memberships:* Executive Board, Hamilton Chapter, Institute of Electrical and Electronics Engineers; Canadian Association of Physicists; American Association of Physics Teachers; McMaster Institute for Energy Studies. *Publications:* Several contributions to scientific journals. *Honours:* Member of the NATO Advanced Study Institute: Ion Beam Analysis, 1978; National Research Council of Canada Scholar, 1969-71. *Hobbies:* Computer Systems Development; Software Analysis of Domestic Problems; Science Fiction. *Address:* Institute for Materials Research, McMaster University, 1200 Main St. West, Hamilton, Ontario, Canada, L8S 4MI.

POKU, Osei, b. 5 Feb. 1932, Kumasi, Ghana. Journalist. m. Feb. 1955, 7 sons, 2 daughters. *Education:* Studied Economics, Political Science, Industrial Management, Trade Union and Labour Administration, Ruskin and Labour College, UK. *Appointments:* Features Writer; Features Editor, The Peoples' Vanguard; Editor, The Brigadier; Managing Editor, The Peoples' Evening News, The Peoples' Sentinel. *Memberships:* Management Committee, Asante Kotoko Football Club. *Hobbies:* Football; Boxing. *Address:* D243 Dansoman Estate, Accra, Ghana.

POLAK, Julia Margaret, b. 29 June 1939, Buenos Aires, Argentina. Senior Lecturer (Consultant) in Histochemistry. m. Daniel Catovsky, 1961, 2 sons, 1 daughter. *Education:* Physician, 1961, MD., 1964, Buenos Aires; MRC Path., UK, 1974; DSc., London University, UK, 1980. *Appointments:* Senior House Officer, Surgery and Medicine, 1962, Registrar and Senior Registrar, Department of Pathology, 1963-67, Buenos Aires, Argentina; Research Assistant, 1968-69, Assistant Lecturer, 1970-73, Lecturer in Histochemistry, 1973-79, Senior Lecturer in Histochemistry, 1979-, Honorary Consultant, 1979-, Department of Histochemistry, Royal Postgraduate Medical School, London, England. *Memberships:* Secretary, Bayliss and Starling Society; Council, Pathology Section, Royal Society of Medicine; Assistant Editor, Regulatory Peptides; Co-editor: with Dr. S. R. Bloom, book on Gut Hormones; with Dr. P. Stoward, book, Histochemistry, the New Horizons; Editorial Board of: Peptides; Investigative and Cell Pathology; Co-organiser and co-editor of Symposia on Basic Sciences in Gastroenterology; Organiser, (with Dr. S. R. Bloom) of Third International Symposium on Gastrointestinal Hormones. *Publications:* 228 Lectures in field of Medicine, 1975-; 240 Medical publications; 253 Abstracts in field of Medicine. *Honours:* Awarded Benito de Udaondo Cardiology Prize, 1967. *Address:* 12 Dell Way, St. Stephens Road, London W13 8JH, England.

PONTIFEX, (Brigadier) David More, b. 16 Sept. 1922, London, England. Regular Soldier (retired). m. Kathleen Betsy Matheson, 6 Aug. 1968, 1 son, 4 daughters. *Education:* Student, 1951, Instructor, 1967-69, Staff College, Camberley, England; Armed Forces Staff College, Norfolk, Virginia, USA, 1958-59. *Appointments:* Commissioned, The Rifle Brigade, 1942; Italy, 1944-45; HQ Parachute Brigade, 1952-54; Kenya, 1954-56; War Office, 1956-58; Brigade Major, 63 Gurkha Brigade, 1961-62; CO., 1st Battalion Federal Regular Army, Aden, 1963-64; GSO1 2nd Division BAOR, 1965-66; Divisional Brigadier, The Light Division, 1969-73; Deputy Director, Staff Duties, MOD., 1973-75; Deputy Commander and Chief of Staff, South East District, 1975-77; Secretary, Combined Cadet Force Association and General Secretary, Army Cadet Force Association, 1977-. *Memberships:* Secretary, Royal Green Jackets Officers Club; Rifle Brigade Club and Association. *Publications:* Editor: The Cadet Journal; Contributions to Service and Cadet Journals. *Honours:* MBE., 1956; OBE., 1965; CBE., 1977; ADC to the Queen, 1975-77. *Address:* 68 Shortheath Road, Farnham, Surrey GU9 8SQ, England.

POOLE, Barry Leslie, b. 2 May 1941, Darlinghurst, Sydney, New South Wales, Australia. Company Director. m. Külliki Riis, 30 Dec. 1966, 1 son, 2 daughters. *Education:* Sydney Technical College, Australia, 1959-68; Diploma, Printing Administration, 1968. *Appointments:* Assistant Production Manager, Bartlett Murphy & Mackenzie Pty. Limited, Sydney, Australia, 1959-60; Production Manager, MAC Merchandising Advertising Pty. Limited, Sydney, Australia, 1960-61; Assistant to Managing Director, Westmead Printing Services Limited, London, UK, 1961-62; Sales Manager, Joint-Governing Director, Hogbin, Poole (Printers) Pty. Limited, Sydney, Australia, 1963-80; Director, Love Typesetting Services Pty. Ltd., Sydney, Australia, 1982; Chairman, Managing Director, Hideway Island Resorts Ltd., Port Vila, Vanuatu, 1982; Self employed in own family company, Bodlian Holdings Pty. Limited, Australia, 1981-. *Memberships:* President, 1972-75, New South Wales Division, Australian Institute of Graphic Arts Management. *Publications:* The Work Value Concept, 1968; Mergers, Takeovers and Company Acquisitions within the Australian Printing Industry, 1975. *Honours:* Associate Fellow, Australian Institute of Graphic Arts Management, 1969. *Hobbies:* Motor boat cruising; Water skiing; Snow skiing; Swimming. *Address:* 89 Ferguson Street, Forestville, New South Wales 2087, Australia.

POOLE, Robert Keith, b. 21 Sept. 1948, Cardiff, Wales, United Kingdom. University Lecturer; Microbiologist. m. Joy Carol Leonard, 31 Dec. 1979. *Education:*

1st class Hons Degree, Microbiology, 1967-70, PhD., 1970-73, University College, Cardiff, Wales, UK. *Appointments:* Postdoctoral Research Fellow, Department of Biochemistry, University of Dundee, Scotland, UK, 1973-74; Lecturer, Microbiology, Queen Elizabeth College, University of London, UK, 1975-. *Memberships:* Committee, Cell Biology Group, Editorial Board of Journal of General Microbiology, Society for General Microbiology, 1974-; Biochemical Society, 1970-. *Publications:* Over 70 Scientific publications including: The Cell Division Cycle, (co-author), 1981. *Honours:* Science Research Council Postdoctoral Research Fellowship, 1967; Science Research Fellowship, Nuffield Foundation, 1980; Research grants from Royal Society and Science Research Council. *Hobbies:* Music; Cycling; Art; Science. *Address:* 16 Wymond Street, Putney, London SW15 1DY, England.

POROOR, Vikraman, b. 10 Sept. 1936, Malaysia. Physician. *Education:* Maharajas College, Ernakulam; Medical College, Trivandrum; MBBS., 1961; MRACP., 1970; FRACP., 1974. *Appointments:* Resident, Medical College Hospital, Trivandrum, 1961-62; General Hospital, Malacca, 1962-65; St. Vincents Hospital, Melbourne, Australia, 1965-70; Repatriation Hospital, Heidelberg, Australia, 1970; Lecturer, University Hospital, Kuala Lumpur, 1971-73; Royal Melbourne Hospital, Australia, 1973-81; Senior Physician, 1981-, Western General Hospital, Melbourne, Australia, 1974-81; Physician, Department of Nephrology RMH Associate, Department of Medicine, University of Melbourne, Australia, 1981-. *Memberships:* Australasian Society of Nephrology; International Society of Nephrology. *Address:* 16 Smith Crescent, Footscray 3011, Melbourne, Victoria, Australia.

PORRITT, (Lord) Arthur Espie, b. 10 Aug. 1900, New Zealand. m. Kathleen Mary Peck, 20 Dec. 1946, 2 sons, 1 daughter. *Education:* Otago University, New Zealand, 1920-23; MA., M.Ch., Oxford University, UK, 1923-26; FRCS., St. Mary's Hospital, London University, UK. *Appointments:* Surgeon, St. Mary's Hospital, London, UK; Surgeon to: Duke of York; Royal Household; King George VI; Sergeant Surgeon to HM Queen Elizabeth II; Consulting Surgeon, Army; Governor-General, New Zealand. *Memberships:* President: Royal College of Surgeons of England; British Medical Association; Royal Society of Medicine; Association of Surgeons of Gt. Britain and Ireland; American Association of Surgeons; Past Master, Society of Apothecaries; Hunterian Society; American Society Clinical Surgery; French Academy of Surgery. *Honours:* Baronet, 1963; GCMG., 1967; Life Peer, 1973; GCVO., 1970; CBE., 1945; Gold Medal, BMA; Hon. Fellow, Magdalen College, Oxford, UK; Hon. DSc., Oxford, UK; Hon. MD., Bristol, UK; numerous Honorary degrees. *Hobbies:* Life Vice-President, Commonwealth CR Games Federation; Hon. member, International Olympic Committee; Bronze medallist, Olympic Games, Paris, France, 1924. *Address:* 57 Hamilton Terrace, London, NW8 9RG, England.

PORTER, James Forrest, b. 2 Oct. 1928, Frodsham, Cheshire, England. Director, Commonwealth Institute. m. Dymphna Powell, 23 Feb. 1952, 2 daughters. *Education:* Teachers Certificate, 1949; BSc, London School of Economics, 1954; MA, University of London Institute of Education, 1956. *Appointments:* Assistant Master, St George in the East, Secondary School, Stepney, 1948-50; Lecturer in Sociol and Education, Worcester College, 1955-60; Head of Education Department, Chorley College, 1960-62; Deputy Principal, Coventry College, 1962-67; Principal, Bulmershe College of Higher Education, Reading, 1967-78. *Memberships:* Chairman, World Education fellowship, 1978; Council of Royal Commonwealth Society; Management Committee of University of London Institute of Education. *Publications:* The Changing Role of the Teacher, 1977; Columnist, contributor to journals, lecturer, 1970; UNESCO reports, 1975. *Honours:* Leverhulme Fellowship, 1953; Fellow of College of Preceptors, 1978; Fellow, Royal Society of Arts, 1978. *Hobbies:* Writing; The Arts. *Address:* House by the Water, Bolney Avenue, Shiplake, Henley-on-Thames, Oxon., England.

PORTER, Robert (Evelyn) (Sir), b. 10 July 1913, Adelaide, South Australia. Sharebroker. m. June Leah Perry, 30 Mar. 1942. *Education:* St Peters College Adelaide; University of Adelaide. *Appointments:* Honorary Consul for Belgium in S.A. & NT., 1947-; F.W.

Porter & Company, member Stock Exchange, Adelaide, (own business); Lord Mayor of Adelaide, 1968-71. *Memberships:* St John Council; RSPCA (President); Anti-Cancer Foundation; World Wildlife Foundation Trustee (Australia). *Honours:* Knight Bachelor, 1978. *Hobbies:* Polo; Golf; Tennis. *Address:* 1 Edwin Terrace, Gilberton, South Australia, 5081.

POSLA, Haynes, b. 23 Jan. 1939, Dovele, Solomon Islands. Medical. m. Junily Liligeto, 3 Dec. 1969, 3 sons. *Education:* Diploma in Medicine, Medical School, Port Moresby, Papua New Guinea, 1962-66; Diploma Obst., Auckland, New Zealand, 1972; DTM&H., Sydney, Australia, 1975. *Appointments:* Medical Officer, Intern, PNG., 1967, 1968; Medical Officer, 1969-72, Medical Director, 1973-, Atoifi Hospital, Solomon Islands. *Memberships:* National Geographic Society. *Hobby:* Fishing. *Address:* Pabarua, Gatokae, Marovo Lagoon, Solomon Islands.

POSNETT, Richard Neil (Sir), b. 19 July 1919, Kotagiri, India. Colonial Administrator; Lawyer; Diplomat; Businessman. m. ·Shirley Margaret Hudson, 25 July 1959, 2 sons, 1 daughter. *Education:* St Johns, Cambridge, 1938-40, 1946-47; BA, Mathematics and Law Tripos, 1942; MA, 1947; Called to the Bar at Gray's Inn, 1950. *Appointments:* Colonial Service, Uganda, District Officer, Magistrate, Crown Counsel, 1941-58; Colonial Office, London, 1958-60; Judicial Adviser, Buganda, 1960-61; Uganda Permanent Secretary, Social Development, 1961-62; Uganda Post-Independence, Permanent Secretary, External Affairs and Trade, 1962-63; Retired from Uganda Service, 1963; Joined British Foreign Service, 1964; UK Mission to UN, New York, Economic Secretary, 1966-70; Briefly HM Commissioner, Anguilla, 1969; Foreign & Commonwealth Office: Head of West Indian Department, 1970-71; Governor and Commander in chief, Belize (formerly British Honduras), 1972-76; FCO Adviser on Dependent Territories, 1977-79; British High Commisioner in Uganda, 1979; UK Commissioner on Board of British Phosphate Commissioners, 1978-; Governor and Commander in Chief, Bermuda, 1981. *Memberships:* Royal Institute of International Affairs; Royal Commonwealth Society; Uganda Olympic Committee, (Chairman, 1958). *Publications:* Contributor of articles in professional journals; Reports on Ocean Island and the Banabans; Dominica: Termination of Association. *Honours:* OBE, 1963; KStJ., 1972; CMG, 1976; KBE, 1980. *Hobbies:* Skiing; Tennis; Golf; Trees. *Address:* Government House, Bermuda.

POTTER, Michael Anthony, b. 23 July 1951, Birmingham, England. Artist; Poet; Writer. *Education:* Passed First - fourth years, (Intermediate Certificate), Mordialloc, Chelsea High School; Art Courses, Balmain School, Oakleigh, Prahan College. *Appointments:* Australia Post, 1968-71; Black Cabs, 1973-78; Part-time work, 1980-. *Memberships:* Associate, Australian Guild of Realist Artists; Poets Union, Melbourne; Amnesty International. *Creative Works:* Paintings: Loch Lomond; Murray River; Sunset Over Caernarvon; Samson The Shire Horse; Autumn in the Midlands; Southern Flinders Ranges; River near Orange; Asling Beach Eden, NSW; McDonnell Ranges Central Australia; Pink Lakes, South Australia; Beaumaris Sunset; Beethoven Tonal; Victorian Beach Scene; Snowy Mountains and Murray River; Mosman Ferry, 1880; Old Mill, Perth; Sunset over Loch Lomond; Upper Yarra River Warrandyte; Yangtze River, China; Mountain and River Scene, Ayers Rock, NT.; Shute Harbor, Queensland; Mist over Ricketts Point; Seagulls; Sailboat and Fog; Mountains of China; Desert Scent, Arizona; Afternoon Fog over Beaumaris; Gazelle, South Africa; Central Australian Scene; Ghost Gums; Poems: Collective works submitted. *Hobbies:* Photography; Music; Stamp & Coin Collecting; Reading; Gold & Relic Hunting; Movies; Tenpin Bowling; Table Tennis; Beach Combing; Bush Walking; Astrology; Travel. *Address:* 20 Ebb Street, Aspendale, Melbourne, Victoria, Australia.

POTTS, Joseph Henry, b. 17 July 1925, Saskatchewan, Canada. Lawyer. m. Dawn Rober, 3 Mar. 1954, 5 sons, 2 daughters. *Education:* University of British Columbia; University College, University of Toronto; BA., 1949; Trinity College, Cambridge University; BA., 1951; LL.B., 1952; MA., 1977. *Appointments:* Called to English Bay, Gray's Inn, 1952; Called to Ontario Bar, 1953; With firm of Slaght, McMurtry and Company, 1953; McTaggart, Potts, Stone, Winters & Herridge,

1956-. *Memberships:* Canadian Bar Association: Past Chairman of National Membership Committee and Public Relations and Membership Committees (Ont. Br.); President, (Ont. Br.); Governor, Canadian Institute for Advanced Legal Studies: York County Law Association; Canadian Tax Foundation; Lawyers Club (Past President); Canadian Institute of International Affairs; Canadian Civil Liberties Association. *Honours:* Banker's, University of Toronto, 1947; University College Alumni, 1947; Beaver Club, 1949-52; Exhibitioner, trinity College, Cambridge, 1950; Queen's Counsel, 1969; Canadian Forces Decoration (CD), 1959. *Hobbies:* Politics; Camping; Swimming. *Address:* 40 Nanton Avenue, Toronto, Ontario, M4W 2Y9, Canada.

POWLES, Guy Richardson (Sir), b. 5 Apr. 1905, Otaki, New Zealand. Chief Ombudsman of New Zealand (Retired). m. Eileen, 1931, 2 sons. *Education:* Wellington College and Victoria University of Wellington, LL.B., 1927. *Appointments:* In practice as a barrister and solicitor in Wellington, 1927-40; Army service, including Brigade Major 2nd Brigade Group (NS), directing staff of the New Zealand Staff College (Military), With 3rd NZ Division in Solomon Islands as Cdr., 144 Ind. Bty., NZ Artillery, Director of Personal Services (Colonel) Army Headquarters, Wellington, 1940-45; Far Eastern Commission, visited Japan, 1945; Counsellor, New Zealand Legation, Washington DC and New Zealand Representative on Far Eastern Commission, 1946-48; High Commissioner of Western Samoa, 1949-60; High Commissioner for New Zealand in India and in Ceylon, and Ambassador for New Zealand in Nepal, 1960-62; Appointed Ombudsman for New Zealand, 1962; Appointed Race Relations Conciliator under Race Relations Act, 1971, 1972-73; Chief Ombudsman for New Zealand, 1975-77; Resident Consultant, International Ombudsman Institute, Edmonton, Alberta, 1978. *Memberships:* Attended international and regional conferences on behalf of New Zealand, including United Nations Trusteeship Council, Far Eastern Commission, South Pacific Commission, Canberra Conference on Japanese Peace Treaty, International Whaling Conference, Economic Commission for Asia and Far East, Commonwealth Education Conference, Colombo Plan Conference. Founding Secretary (1937) and Past President (1945 and 1967- 71), New Zealand Institute of International Affairs; Commissioner, International Commission of Jurists, Geneva, 1965-, Vice-President, New Zealand Section, 1963-; President, 1980; Senior Counsel Coalition for Open Government, 1980. *Publications:* Numerous articles and addresses on the work of the office of Ombudsman, international affairs, particularly New Zealand and the Pacific Islands and on Human Rights. *Honours:* Efficiency Decoration (ED), 1943; Companion of the Order of St Michael and St George, 1954; Knight Commander of the Order of the British Empire, 1961; Award of Knighthood expressed to be for public service to New Zealand, especially in connection with Western Samoa; Doctor of Laws, (LLD.), Honoris Causa, Victoria University of Wellington, 1969. *Hobbies:* Reading; Gardening; Human Rights. *Address:* 34 Wesley Road, Wellington, New Zealand.

POYNTON, John Orde, b. 9 Apr. 1906, London. Pathologist; Bibliographer. (Retired). m. Lola Horry, 31 Aug. 1965. *Education:* Marlborough College, 1919-1923; Gonville and Cauis College, Cambridge, 1923-27; BA 1927; BCh 1930; MD 1940; Charing Cross Hospital, University London, 1927-30; MRCS (Eng.); LRCP (London) 1930. *Appointments:* Senior Medical Officer, Charing Cross Hospital, 1933-35; Research Pathologist, Institute for Medical Research Federated Malay States, 1936-46; Pathologist, Institute of Medical and Veterinary Science, South Australia, 1948-50; Director, 1950-61; Director, Commercial Finance Company, 1960-70; Consulting Bibliographer, Baillieu Library, University of Melbourne, 1962-74. *Memberships:* Fellow, Graduate House, University of Melbourne. *Publications:* Monographs and contributions to periodicals relating to medicine and bibliography. *Honours:* University Scholar in Pathology, Charing Cross Hospital, 1927-30; Horton-Smith Prize, University Cambridge, 1940; CMG, 1961; Hon. LLD, University of Melbourne, 1977. *Hobbies:* Books; Engravings. *Address:* Lowood, 6/8 Seymour Avenue, Mount Eliza, Victoria 3930 Australia.

PRABAHARAN, Sivanathan Kuganathan, b. 16 Jan. 1953, Jaffna, Sri Lanka. Chartered Accountant. m.

Aloma Germaine, 12 Feb. 1979, 1 daughter. *Education:* Final Examination, Institute of Chartered Accountants, Sri Lanka, 1977; ICMA, UK, 1977. *Appointments:* Audit Manager, Lawrie Muthu Krishna and Company, Sri Lanka, 1977-78; Audit Senior, Coopers and Lybrand, Kitwe, Zambia, 1978-80, Audit Supervisor, 1980-81; Group Management Accountant, Fairway Engineering Group of Companies, Kitwe, Zambia, 1981-. *Memberships:* Zambia Tamil Arts and Cultural Association; Inter Act Club of Sri Lanka. *Honours:* Prize, General Proficiency, Grade 7, 1963. *Hobbies:* Playing Cricket; Reading; Stamp Collection. *Address:* PO Box 23397, Kitwe, Zambia.

PRABHU, Nagur Sheshagiri, b. 25 Feb. 1933, Nagur, Karnataka State, India. Linguist and Specialist, English Language Teaching. m. Praphulla, 14 May 1959, 2 daughters. *Education:* MA, English, Madras Christian College, 1956; Diploma in Teaching English, Central Institute of English, India, 1967; MA, Linguistics, 1971; PhD, University of Reading, UK, 1974. *Appointments:* Lecturer, Reader, English, Academy of General Education, Manipal, India, 1956-66; English Studies Officer, The British Council, Madras, India, 1967-. *Memberships:* English Language Teachers' Association, India; Linguistic Society of India; Dravidian Linguistic Association. *Publications:* English Through Reading, 1975; Gul mohar Graded English Course; Anaphoric Pronouns, 1972; Diachronic Process and Synchronic Rule, 1975; Some Linguistic Concepts for Language Teachers, 1968; Konkani Syntax, PhD Thesis, 1974. *Honours:* First rank in Diploma, Teaching English (CIE, India); MA, Linguistics, University of Reading, UK. *Hobby:* Indian classical music. *Address:* 20 Khader Nawaz Khan Road, Madras 600 006, India.

PRAIN, (Sir) Ronald, OBE, b. 3 Sept. 1907, Iquiqui, Chile. Chief Executive; Chairman. m. Esther Pansy Brownrigg, 23 Apr. 1938, 2 sons. *Education:* Cheltenham College. *Appointments:* Controller, Diamond Die and Tool Control, 1940-45; Controller, Quartz Crystal Control, 1943-45; Chief Executive, 1943-68, Chairman, RST Group of Copper Mining Companies, 1950-72; President, British Overseas Mining Association, 1952; President, Institute of Metals, 1960-61; First Chairman: Agricultural Research Council of Rhodesia and Nyasaland, 1959-63; Merchant Bank of Central Africa Limited, 1956-66; Merchant Bank, Zambia Limited, 1966-72; Chairman: Council of Commonwealth Mining and Metallurgical Institutions, 1961-74; Botswana RST Group, 1959-72; Director: International Nickel Company of Canada Limited, 1951-72; Wankie Colliery Company Limited, 1953-63; Metal Market and Exchange Company Limited, 1943-65; San Francisco Mines of Mexico Limited, 1944-68; Barclays Bank International, 1971-77; Selection Trust Limited, 1944-78; Minerals Separation Limited, 1962-78; Australian Selection Pty Limited; Foseco Minsep Limited; Monks Investment Trust Limited; Pan-Holding S.A; etc. *Memberships:* Hon. President, Copper Development Association; Hon. Fellow, Institution of Mining and Metallurgy; Metals Society, BNF Metals Technology Centre; Institute for Archaeo-Metallurgical Studies; President, Cheltenham College Council, 1972-80. *Publications:* Selected Papers, (4 Volumes); Copper . . . the Anatomy of an Industry, 1975; Reflections on an Era, 1981. *Honours:* ANKH Award, Copper Club, New York, 1964; Gold Medal, Institute of Mining and Metallurgy, 1968; The Institute of Metals Platinum Medal, 1969. OBE, 1946; KT, 1956; *Hobbies:* Cricket; Tennis; Travel. *Address:* Waverley, Granville Road, St. George's Hill, Weybridge, Surrey, KT13 0QJ, England.

PRASAD, Ram Chandra, b. 18 July 1929, Gorakhari, Patna Binar, India. Teaching. m. Sumitra Prasad, 7 June 1947, 2 sons 1 daughter. *Education:* Bachelor of Arts, Honours, 1949; MA, English Literature, Patna University, 1951; PhD, Edinburgh University, UK, 1959; DLitt, Hindi Literature, Patna University, 1966. *Appointments:* Lecturer in English, 1951-67; Reader, Patna University, 1967-73; University Professor and Head, English Department, Bhagalpur University, 1974-78; Patna University, 1979-80; Pro Vice-Chancellor, Bhagalpur University, 1980-. *Memberships:* President, Indian Students' Association, Edinburgh University, 1958-59; General Council; Association Internationale de Sociologie; Patna University Senate; Bhagalpur University Senate, 1977-78, and Syndicate, 1980-. *Publications:* Early English Travellers in India, 1980; Rajneesh: The Mystic of Feeling, 1970; Adhunik

Hindi Alochana par Paschatya Prabhava, 1973; Shai-lee, 1973; Literary Criticism in Hindi, 1976; The Mahat-ma, 1978; Dr. Samuel Johnson: Siddhanta aur Samiks-ha, 1978. *Honours:* Scholarship, Higher Studies Abroad, Patna University, 1957; 9th World Congress of Sociology, Uppsala, Sweden, 1978; UGC's award, Par-ticipation in International Seminars, 1975, 78; Interna-tional Frankfurt Book Fair, 1969. *Hobbies:* Zen; Yoga. *Address:* 3 Rajendranagar, Patna, Bihar, India.

PRASAD, Shyam Shiva, b. 2 Aug. 1921, Buxar, Dis-trict Bhojpur, Bihar, India. Chartered Mining Engineer. m. Shanti Prasad, 5 July 1945, 2 sons. *Education:* Degree in Mining Engineering, Indian School of Mines, 1945; Certificate of Competency, Coal Mine Surveyors, 1945; First Class Coal Mine Managers' Certificate, 1947; First Class Metal Mine Managers' Certificate, 1961. *Appointments:* Junior Inspector of Mines, 1948-51; Senior Inspector, 1951-62; Director, Mines Safety, 1962-71; Deputy Director General, Mines Safety, 1971-74; Chief Inspector of Mines in India and Chair-man, National Council of Safety in Mines, 1974-76; Technical Adviser, Government of India, 1976-79. *Memberships:* Mining, Geological and Metallurgical Institute, India. *Publications:* Contributed 17 technical papers on various platforms; Pillar fires in Indian Coal Mines and Measures to combat the same, paper was read and discussed in 16th International Conference, Washington, 1975; India's principal delegate to ILO 10th session of Coal Mines Committee, Geneva, 1976 and Chairman and Reporter of Safety and Health Sub-Committee; Technical paper, Space Technology, 1977; Speaker, World Instrumentation Symposium, India, 1976. *Hobbies:* Photography; Stamp Collection; Golf. *Address:* Shanti Sadan, Nageshwar Colony, Boring Road, Patna, 800001, Bihar, India.

Prasad, T Rama, b. 15 July 1941, Visakhapatnam, India. Medical. m. V.S. Rajyalakshmi, 15 Nov. 1969, 1 son. *Education:* MB, BS 1965; DTCD 1974. *Appoint-ments:* Medical Officer, Andhra Pradesh Medical Ser-vices, 1966-67; Tutor in Anatomy, Andhra Medical College, 1967; Medical Officer, Ramalingam Tubercu-losis Sanatorium, Perundurai Sanatorium P.O., Periyar District, Tamil Nadu, India, 1967-. *Memberships:* Fellow, Scientific Council of the International College of Angiology, USA; American College of Chest Physi-cians and International Academy of Chest Physicians and Surgeons, USA; National College of Chest Physi-cians; Asthma and Bronchitis Foundation of India. *Publications:* Author of several scientific papers in medical journals and numerous writings in general press. *Honours:* Dr. R Viswanathan Prize, 1974; Some prizes in Art and Photography. *Hobbies:* Ornamental Horticulture; Art; Photography. *Address:* Perundurai Sanatorium P.O, Periyar District, Tamil Nadu, India.

PRATAP, Thayamballi Chalkkaran, b. 2 Oct. 1952, Cannanore, Kerala, India. Dental Surgeon. *Education:* Secondary School, 1967; Pre-Degree, 1969; Bachelor of Dental Surgery, 1977. *Appointments:* Private Prac-tice in Dental Surgery, Quilon, Kerala, India, 1979; Dental Officer, District Hospital, Zambezi, Zambia, Afri-ca, 1979-. *Memberships:* Ashtamudi Boat Club; Jaycees International; Indian Dental Association, Triv-andrum Branch, India; All India Students and Gradu-ates Association; Zambia Dental Association. *Hobbies:* Reading; Corresponding with people; Travelling; Car Racing; Playing Chess; Table Tennis; Cards. *Address:* PO Box 89, Zambezi, Zambia, Africa.

PRATHAP, Kesavan, b. 7 May 1939, Penang, Malay-sia. Pathologist. m. 21 Aug. 1966. *Education:* MBBS, Singapore, 1963; MRCPath, United Kingdom, 1972; MD, Malaya, 1973; FRCPA, 1978. *Appointments:* Pro-fessor and Head, Department of Pathology, Faculty of Medicine, University of Malaya; Deputy Dean, Faculty of Medicine, University of Malaya; Senior Consultant in Pathology, University Hospital, Kuala Lumpur. *Mem-berships:* Editor, Malaysian Journal of Pathology; Vice President, Malaysian Society of Pathologists. *Publica-tions:* Over 70 scientific publications in national and international journals. *Address:* 19 Road 7/2, Petaling Jaya, Selangor, Malaysia.

PRATHER, Rollin Wayne, b. 17 July 1925, Eureka, Kansas, USA. Geologist. m. Gwyneth Mary Evans, 14 Feb. 1975, 1 son 2 daughters, 2 stepdaughters. *Educa-tion:* BSc Honours, Geology, Kansas State University, 1950. *Appointments:* Junior Geologist, Pacific Petro-

leums Limited, Edmonton, Alberta, 1950-51; Consult-ing Geologist, Murray Mitchell and Gray Limited, 1951-55; Division Production Geologist, Imperial Oil Limited, 1955-60; Senior Exploration Geologist, 1960-62; Research Geologist, Standard Oil of New Jersey, Tulsa, Oklahoma, 1962-64; Chief Division Geologist, Imperial Oil Enterprises, Regina, Saskatchewan, 1964-66; Ex-ploration and Research Director, King Resources Com-pany, Calgary, Alberta, 1966-70; Executive Vice Presi-dent and General Manager, Pinnacle Petroleum Limited, 1970-71; Vice President, General Manager and Director, Columbia Gas Development of Canada Limited, 1971-80; President and Chief Executive Offi-cer, 1980-. *Memberships:* Sigma Phi Epsilon Fraternity; Calgary Petroleum; Silver Springs and Cal-gary Golf and Country; DeAnza Desert Country; Borre-go Springs, California. *Publications:* Author, Geology of Gas Occurrences in Paleozoic Rocks of Alberta Plains, 1968; Regional Geology and Hydrocarbon Potential of the Arctic Islands, 1971. *Honours:* Service Medal, South Pacific, 1945; All American Track, 1943, 1947, 1948; All Canadian Football, 1951, 1954. *Hobbies:* Golf; Cross country skiing; Hiking; Reading; Rocks and minerals. *Address:* 15 1901 Varsity Estates Drive, N.W. Calgary, Alberta, Canada T3B 4T7.

PREMADASA, Ranasinge, b. 1924. Sri Lankan Politi-cian. m. Hema Wickrematunga, 1964, 1 son, 1 daugh-ter. *Education:* Lorenz College and St Joseph's College, Colombo. *Appointments:* Member of Colombo Munici-pal Council, 1950; Deputy Mayor of Colombo, 1955; Member of Parliament, 1960 and 1965-, (Colombo Central Constituency); Parliamentary Secretary to Min-istry of Local Government, 1965; Chief Whip, Govern-ment Parliamentary Group, 1965; Parliamentary Se-cretary to Ministry of Information and Broadcasting and to Ministry of Local Government, 1966; Minister of Local Government, 1968; Chief Whip, Opposition Parli-amentary Group, 1970; Deputy Leader, United National Party, 1976; Minister of Local Government, Housing and Construction and Leader of the National State Assembly, 1977-; Prime Minister of Sri Lanka, 1978-. *Publications:* Author of ten books. *Address:* Sucharita Mawatha, Colombo, Sri Lanka.

PREMATUNGA, Upula, b. 2 Mar. 1951, Matara, Sri Lanka. Chartered Accountant. m. Swarna Ranjani Sen-anayaice, 25 Mar. 1981. *Education:* Associate mem-bership, Institute of Chartered Accountants, Sri Lanka. *Appointments:* Accountant, Ceylon Electricity Board, Sri Lanka, 1976-78; Divisional Internal Auditor, NCCM Limited, Kabwe, Zambia, 1978-. *Hobbies:* Reading; Listening to Radio. *Address:* 2 Sable Court, Kabwe, Zambia.

PRENTICE, Reginald Ernest, b. 16 July 1923, Thorn-ton Heath, Surrey, England. Member of Parliament. m. Joan Godwin, 6 Aug. 1948, 1 daughter. *Education:* BSc (Econ) London School of Economics and Political Science, 1946-49. *Appointments:* Civil Servant, 1940-42; Royal Artillery, 1941-46; Head Office, Transport and General Workers Union, 1950-57; Member of Parliament, 1957-79; Labour Government, 1964-70 and 1974-76; Conservative MP, 1979; Minister of State for Social Security, 1979-81. *Memberships:* Re-form Club. *Publications:* Part author: Social Welfare and the Citizen, 1957; Right Turn, 1978. *Honours:* Privy Counsellor, 1966. *Hobbies:* Walking; Golf. *Address:* Bridle Cottage, Ballards Farm Road, Croydon, Surrey, England.

PRENTICE, William Thomas, b. 1 June 1919, Sydney. Judge. m. Mary Dignam, 13 Apr. 1946, 3 sons, 1 daughter. *Education:* BA, Sydney University, 1938; LLB, 1947. *Appointments:* Barrister, New South Wales Bar, 1947-70; Judge Supreme Court, Papua New Guin-ea, 1970; Deputy Chief Justice, 1975-78; Chief Jus-tice, 1978-80, (Retired). *Memberships:* Common-wealth of Australia Administration Appeals Tribunal, 1981-; Tattersalls Club Sydney; NSW Leagues Club. *Honours:* MBE, 1945; Knight, 1975. *Hobbies:* Reading; Swimming; Walking. *Address:* 16 Olympia Road, Nar-emburn, Sydney, New South Wales 2065, Australia.

PRESCOTT, Nigel Ian, b. 9 May 1942, Melbourne, Victoria, Australia. Theatre Administrator. m. Valerie Helen Coxon, 8 Feb. 1964, 2 daughters. *Education:* BA, University of Western Australia. *Appointments:* Execu-tive Officer, Theatre Management Committee, Univer-sity of Western Australia, 1964-72; Manager, Perth

Concert Hall, Australia, 1972-79; General Manager, Perth Theatre Trust, Australia, 1979-. *Memberships:* Chairman, Council of Friends of Festival; Western Australia Representative, Confederation of Australian Arts Centres; Director, Artlook Book Publishers. *Hobbies:* Drama; Music; Collecting keyboard instruments. *Address:* 3 Melville Street, Claremont 6010, Western Australia.

PRESTON, Arthur William, b. 14 Oct. 1912, Brisbane, Australia. Clergyman. m. 7 Mar. 1941, 1 son, 3 daughters. *Education:* Licentiate of Theology, Kings College, University of Queensland, Australia. *Appointments:* Minister: The Methodist Church of Australasia, 1939-77; The Uniting Church in Australia, 1977-; Superintendent, Wesley Central Mission, Melbourne, Australia. *Publications:* Plain Talks for the People; Greater Than Ourselves; We Offer Christ; The Many Splendoured Thing. *Honours:* OBE., 1963. *Hobbies:* Tennis; Swimming. *Address:* 3 Lenne Court, Camberwell 3124, Australia.

PRESTON, Christopher Edward Martin, b. 13 Nov. 1918, Addlestone, Surrey, England. Author. m. Joy Celeste Agatha Davidson, 23 Apr. 1949, 4 sons, 1 daughter. *Education:* Royal Naval College, Dartmouth, 1932-36. *Appointments:* Royal Navy, 1936-58; Bristol Aero-Engines, 1958-60; General Sales Manager, Bristol Siddeley Engines, 1960-67; General Marketing Manager, 1967-74, Director of Marketing, 1974-77, Director of Marine Marketing, 1977-80, Rolls Royce, UK. *Memberships:* Institute of Marine Engineers. *Publications:* Various articles on marine and industrial gas turbines in British, German and Japanese technical magazines. *Honours:* DSC., 1940; OBE., 1980. *Hobbies:* Sailing; Gardening. *Address:* Marston House, Priors Marston, Nr. Rugby, Warwickshire, England.

PRICE, Charles Archibald, b. 20 July 1920, Adelaide, South Australia. University Research. m. 27 Jan. 1945, 2 sons, 2 daughters. *Education:* BA., University of Adelaide, Australia, 1938-40, 1943-44; BA., MA., D.Phil., University of Oxford, UK, 1946-51. *Appointments:* Research Fellow, Fellow, Senior Fellow, 1952-64, Professorial Fellow, Department of Demography, 1964-, Australian National University, Australia. *Memberships:* Director of Immigration Research Project, Academy of Social Sciences in Australia, 1967-; International Union for the Scientific Study of Population, 1957-; Chairman and member, Good Neighbour Council, Canberra, Australia, 1954-69; Chairman, Refugee and Migration sub-committee, Australian Council of Churches, 1969-; Consultant and member, various Australian Government migration committees. *Publications:* Books, Chapters and articles on immigration and ethnic group relations including: German Settlers in South Australia, 1945; Southern Europeans in Australia, 1963; Jewish Settlers in Australia, 1964; The Great White Walls are Built, 1974; Australian Immigration: Bibliography and Digest, 1970, 1980. *Hobbies:* Swimming; Music. *Address:* 31 Rawson Street, Deakin, Canberra, ACT, Australia 2600.

PRICE, (Sir) Francis Caradoc Rose, b. 9 Sept. 1950, Calcutta, India. Barrister; Solicitor. m. Marguerite Jean Trussler, 11 July 1975, 2 daughters. *Education:* LL.B., Hons., Trinity College, Melbourne University, Australia, 1970-73; LL.M., University of Alberta, Canada, 1974-75. *Appointments:* Admitted to Bar: Province of Alberta, Canada, 1976; Northwest Territories, Canada, 1978; Partner, Reynolds, Mirth & Côté, Edmonton, Alberta, Canada; Lecturer, Bar Admission Course, Law Society of Alberta, Canada, 1979-. *Memberships:* Law Society of Alberta; Edmonton Bar Association; Law Society of Northwest Territories; Canadian Petroleum Law Foundation. *Publications:* Book: Pipelines in Western Canada, 1975; Articles: Adoption and the Single Parent, 1975; The Cost of Expropriating in Alberta & Manitoba, 1976; Costs in Foreclosure Actions, 1977; Valuation of Security Interests upon Expropriation, 1979; Agreements for Sale to Corporations—the Remedy of Extra-Judicial Determination, 1981; Surface Rights Acquisition and Compensation (co-author), 1981. *Honours:* Wright Prize, 1973, Butterworths Prize in Family Law, 1973, University of Melbourne, Australia; Annual Prize, 1974, Fellowship, 1974-75, Canadian Petroleum Law Foundation. *Hobbies:* Cricket; Skiing; Squash; Running; Theatre; Opera. *Address:* 9677-95 Avenue, Edmonton, Alberta, Canada.

PRICE, George Cadle, b. 15 Jan. 1919. Premier. *Education:* St John's College, Belize City. *Appointments:* Private Secretary to late Robert S Turton; Entered Politics, 1944; City Councillor, 1947-65 (Mayor of Belize City several times); Founding Member, People's United Party, 1950; Party Secretary, 1950-56, Leader, 1956-; Elected to National Assembly, 1954; under 1961 Ministerial System, led People's United Party to 100 victory at polls and became First Minister; under 1964 Self-Government Constitution, title changed to Premier; *Memberships:* Has led delegations to Central American and Caribbean countries; spearheaded internationalization of Belize problem at international forums; addressed UN's Fourth Committee, 1975, paving way for overwhelming victory at UN when majority of nations voted in favour of Belize's right to self determination and territorial integrity. *Address:* Office of the Premier, Belmopan, Belize.

PRICE, Wordsworth Lawrence Victor, b. 10 Aug. 1930, Port-of-Spain, Trinidad, West Indies. Physicist. *Education:* BSc., University College of the West Indies, 1954; MSc., Birkbeck College, London, UK, 1966; PhD., University of London, UK, 1971. *Appointments:* Demonstrator, Physics, University College of the West Indies, 1954-56; Assistant Master, Kingston College, Jamaica, West Indies, 1956-57; Research Assistant, British Electrical and Allied Industries Research Association, 1957-59; Scientific Officer, British Insulated Callenders' Cables Research and Engineering Division, seconded to British Dielectric Research Limited, UK, 1959-64; Assistant Lecturer, Norwood Technical College, UK, 1964-67; Lecturer, 1967-75; Senior Lecturer, 1975-, Polytechnic of the South Bank, London, UK; Tutor The Open University, UK, 1973-75. *Memberships:* Institute of Physics and Fellow of former Physical Society, 1966; Chartered Engineer, Institution of Electrical Engineers, 1969. *Publications:* The Measurement of the Principal Dielectric Constants of Sapphire by a Mechanical Action Method, 1967; Comments on the paper: The Measurement of the Principal Dielectric Constants of Sapphire by a Mechanical Action Method, 1968; Extension of van der Pauw's theorem for measuring specific resistivity in discs of arbitrary shape to anisotropic media, 1972; Electric Potential and Current Distribution in a Rectangular Sample of Anisotropic Material with Application to the Measurement of the Principal Resistivities by an Extension of Van der Pauw's Method, 1973 in the Journal of Solid State Electronics, 1973; A Theorem in Infinite Products, 1974; On the measurement of fluid viscosities using the Rotating Cylinder Viscometer (co-author), 1974. *Honours:* St. Georges Gold Medal and Challenge Vase at Imperial meeting, 1959, (Rifle Shooting). *Hobbies:* Music; Rifle shooting; Photography. *Address:* 3 Crescent Lane, London, SW4 9PT, England.

PRIDEAUX, (Sir) Humphrey Povah Treverbian, b. 13 Dec. 1915, London, England. Company Director. m. Cynthia Violet Birch Reynardson, 30 Aug. 1939, 4 sons. *Education:* MA.,·Trinity College, Oxford, UK, 1933-36. *Appointments:* Chairman, Navy, Army and Air Force Institutes, 1963-73; Deputy Chairman, Liebig's Extract of Meat Co. Limited, 1968-69; Chairman, Oxo Limited, 1968-72; Director, Brooke Bond Oxo Limited, 1969-70; Chairman, Brooke Bond Liebig Limited, 1972-81; Director, 1964-, President, London Life Association, 1973; Director, 1969-, Vice-Chairman, W H Smith & Son (Holdings) Limited, 1977-81; Trustee, 1963-, Chairman, Lord Wandsworth Foundation, 1966; Chairman: St. Aubyns School Trust Limited, 1975; Stern Farms Limited, 1977; Director, Morland & Co. Limited, 1981. *Memberships:* Companion, British Institute of Management; Imperial Society of Knights Bachelor; Commissioner, Royal Hospital, Chelsea, UK. *Honours:* OBE., 1945; Knights Bachelor, 1971. *Hobbies:* Horses; Books. *Address:* Summers Farm, Long Sutton, Basingstoke, Hampshire, RG25 1TQ, England.

PRIDEAUX, (Sir) John Francis, b. 30 Dec. 1911, London, England. Banker. m. Joan Terrell Hargreaves Brown, 22 Nov. 1934, 2 sons, 1 daughter. *Appointments:* Director, 1936, Chairman, 1964-69, Arbuthnot Latham & Co. Limited, UK, 1930; Chairman, 1969-74, Director, Arbuthnot Latham Holdings Limited, UK; London Advisory Board, Bank of New South Wales, 1948-74; Director, 1955-, Chairman, 1971-77, National Westminster Bank Limited, UK; Director, 1955-, International Westminster Bank Limited, UK; Deputy Chairman, Commonwealth Development Corporation,

1960-70; Chairman, Committee of London Clearing Bankers, 1974-76; Vice President, British Bankers' Association, 1972-77; President, Institute of Bankers, UK, 1974-76; Treasurer, Chairman, Board of Governors, St. Thomas' Hospital, UK, 1964-74; Member, Lambeth Southwark and Lewisham Area Health Authority, UK, 1974-. *Memberships:* Prime Warden, 1972, Court of the Goldsmiths' Company; Chairman, Victoria League for Commonwealth Friendship, 1977-. *Honours:* OBE., 1945; Legion of Merit, USA, 1945; Knighthood, 1974; Deputy Lieutenant for County of Surrey, UK. *Hobby:* All country pursuits. *Address:* Elderslie, Ockley, Dorking, Surrey, RH5 5TD, England.

PRIEDKALNS, Janis, b. 28 Mar. 1934, Barbele, Latvia. Professor of Anatomy and Histology. m. Sarma Kaskurs, 1964, 3 sons, 3 daughters. *Education:* BVSc., University of Sydney, Australia, 1959; PhD., University of Minnesota, USA, 1966; MA., University of Cambridge, UK, 1970; MRCVS., UK, 1971. *Appointments:* Veterinary practice, South Australia, 1959-61; Instructor/ Assistant Professor, Histology and Embryology, University of Minnesota, USA, 1961-67; German Government Humboldt Research Fellow, Universities of München and Giessen, Germany, 1967-68; French Government Research Fellow, Collège de France, Paris, École nationale vétérinaire, Lyon, France, 1968-70; Visiting Scientist and University Demonstrator, Anatomy School. Cambridge University, UK, 1970-72; Visiting Professor, Harvard University Medical School, USA, 1972; Elder Professor and Head of Department, Anatomy and Histology, University of Adelaide Medical School, South Australia, Visiting Professor: University of Buenos Aires, Argentina; Witwatersrand Medical School, Johannesburg, South Africa; Karolinska Institute, Stockholm, Sweden; University of Washington, Seattle, USA, 1972-. *Memberships:* Australian, European and American Societies of Anatomists and Endocrinologists; Fellow, Royal Society of South Australia. *Publications:* Research publications in neuroendocrinology; Contributor to: Histology; Comparative Placentation. *Address:* 2 Collyer Court, Linden Park, South Australia 5065, Australia.

PRIME, Derek Arthur, b. 16 July 1932, Cheadle, Staffordshire, England. Engineering Designer. m. Pamela Dix, 9 Nov. 1963, 1 son, 1 daughter. *Education:* Diploma, Engineering, 1950, HNC., Mechanical Engineering, 1953, North Staffs Technical College, UK. *Appointments:* Draughtsman, Thomas Bolton & Sons Limited, Froghall, UK, 1948-53; Project Designer, 1953-59, Assistant Chief Designer, 1959-64, Chief Designer, 1964-70, Technical Director, 1970-73, Managing Director, 1973-, JCB Research, Rocester, Uttoxeter, UK, 1953-. *Memberships:* Fellow, Society of Industrial Artists and Designers; Institute of Engineering Designers. *Creative Works:* over 20 Patents on Construction Machines. *Honours:* Design Council award for Engineering Products, 1973, 75; Queens award for Technical Innovation, 1974; Presidential award for Design Management, Royal Society of Arts, 1979. *Hobbies:* Gardening; Watching his children show-jumping. *Address:* Bladon House, Lodge Hill, Tutbury, Burton-on-Trent, Staffordshire, England.

PRINDIVILLE, Bernard Francis, b. 4 June 1911, Western Australia. Public Accountant; Company Director. m. Mary Agnes O'Mahoney, 18 Apr. 1938, 3 sons, 2 daughters. *Education:* St. Ildephonous College, New Norcia, Western Austrlia. *Appointments:* Public Accountant and Company Director; Justice of the Peace; Chairman Advisory Board of Management, St. John of God Hospital; Past President, Western Australia Society for Crippled Children; Chairman, Advisory Board of Management St Vincents Hospital, Guildford; National Vice President, Western Australian Committee for the Economic Development of Australia; Foundation Chairman Southern Cross Homes for the Aged. *Memberships:* Fellow Australian Society of Accountants; Fellow, Institute of Directors; Fellow, Australian Institute of Management; Fellow and Past President, Australian Marketing Institute; Fund Raising Committee, YMCA; Finance Committee, Police Boys Federation Public Appeal; West Australian Cricket Association; Chairman, Advisory Board of Management, New Norcia Arts and Cultural Centre; Chairman, Board of Management Villa Pelletier (Inc.) Homes for the frail aged; Lord Mayors Disaster Relief Committee; Trustee Karrakatta Cementery Board; Trustee Pinnaroo Valley Memorial Park Board; Director: Pan Australian Holdings Limited;

Leasing Capital Corporation Pty. Ltd.; Houghton Holdins Limited; Swan Television and Radio Broadcasters Limited; Westralian Forest Industries Limited; Town and Country Permanent Building Society. *Honours:* Companion, Most Distinguished Order of St. Michael and St. George (Imperial Honour), 1979; Knight Commander, Order of St. Gregory The Great, 1973. *Hobbies:* Golf; Tennis; Farming. *Address:* Unit 11,219 Mill Point Road, South Perth, Western Australia 6151

PRINGLE (Sir) Charles Norman Seton, b. 6 June 1919, Dublin. Engineer. m. 21 Sept. 1946, 1 son. *Education:* MA, St John's College, Cambridge, 1937-40. *Appointments:* Royal Air Force, 1941-76; Senior Executive, Rolls-Royce Limited, 1976-78; Director and Chief Executive, Society of British Aerospace Companies Limited, 1979-. *Memberships:* Fellowship of Engineering; Fellow, Royal Aeronautical Society; Council of Engineering Institutions; Fellow, Royal Society of Arts; Companion, British Institute of Management; Member of Institute of Directors. *Publications:* Various Aeronautical Papers. *Honours:* Knight Commander of the Order of the British Empire, 1973. *Hobbies:* Ornithology; Fishing. *Address:* 8 Strangways Terrace, London W14 8NE, England.

PRITCHARD, Norman Macdonald, b. 19 Nov. 1945, Glasgow, Scotland. Minister of Religion. m. Elizabeth Joan Clarke, 5 July 1969, 1 son, 1 daughter. *Education:* MA(Hons), BD(Hons), MTh, for thesis, Worship in the New Testament Church; Glasgow University, 1964-71 and part-time, 1971-74. *Appointments:* Assistant Minister, St George's West Church, Edinburgh Scotland, 1971-74; Minister, St Andrew's Church, West Kilbride, Ayrshire, Scotland, 1974-79; Senior Minister, The Scots' Church Melbourne, Victoria, Australia, 1979-. *Hobbies:* Tennis; Squash; Enjoys Work. *Address:* 6 Griffin Close, Surrey Hills, 3127 Victoria, Australia.

PRITCHETT, (Sir) Victor Sawdon, b. 16 Dec. 1900, Ipswich, United Kingdom. Writer. m. 2 Oct. 1936, 1 daughter. *Education:* Alleyns School, London. *Appointments:* Foreign Correspondent, The Christian Science Monitor, Ireland, Spain; Freelance cont. to London Weekly Reviews; Regular Critic and one time Lit. Editor, New Statesman; Contributor, Story criticism to the Listener, New Writing, Horizon, New Yorker, New York Review of Books, Playboy, Atlantic Monthly etc.; Christian Guest Lecturer, Princeton, 1953; Lecturer, Brondeis, Berkeley Smith College, Chumbra Clast. Lectures, Cambridge, United Kingdom. *Memberships:* International Press PEN Club; President, Society of Authors; Fellow Royal Society Literature. *Publications:* Novels; Short Stories; Travel and Criticism. *Honours:* CBE 1968; Knighted 1976; Hon DLit. Leeds University; Hon DLit. Columbia University; Hon DLit, Sussex University. *Hobbies:* Walking; Gardening. *Address:* 12 Regents Park Terrace, London NW1, England.

PROBER, Jay Charles, b. 23 May 1943, Winnipeg, Canada. Lawyer. m. Rosalind Harper, 22 July 1967, 1 son, 2 daughters. *Education:* BA, 1964; LLB, University of Manitoba, 1967; LLM, London School of Economics and Political Science, 1968; Diplôme De Langue et Lettres, Université D'Aik Marseille Franc, 1975. *Appointments:* Law Clerk, Mr Justice Martland Supreme Court, Canada, 1968-69; Lecturer, Law School, University of Manitoba, part-time, 1969-70, 1971-72, 1979-80; Counsel, Royal Commission of Inquiry into Churchill Forest Industries, 1972-74; Senior Partner, Walsh, Prober, Yard and Co. 1978-. *Memberships:* Law Society of Manitoba; Canadian Bar Association; Law Society of Alberta; Director, X-Kalay Foundation; Winnipeg Squash Club and Wildewood Club. *Honours:* Canadian National Debating Champion, 1967. *Hobbies:* Squash; Tennis; Golf; Swimming. *Address:* 506 South Drive, Winnipeg, Canada.

PROBERT, John Ronald, b. 13 Mar. 1921, Widnes, Cheshire, England. Regular Army Officer, Brigadier (Retired); Chartered Engineer, Aeronautical and Mechanical. m. Betty Helena Boddy, 7 May 1951, 1 daughter. *Education:* University of the Witwatersrand, 1946-47; Royal Military College of Science, 1949-51; University of Rhodesia, part-time, 1977-81; BA(Hons); CEng; FIMechE; FRAcS; FBIM; FZwelE; FZIM; MNZIE; MIPM(SA). *Appointments:* Royal Artillery, United Kingdom and Middle East, 1938-43; Pilot, RAF, Rhodesia, Middle East and United Kingdom, 1943-46; RA and REME, Germany, Malaya, United Kingdom, Kenya,

Hong Kong, New Zealand, 1947-74; Manager, Personnel Services, Air New Zealand, 1974; Chief Executive Officer, City of Salisbury, Rhodesia, 1974-77; Chief Executive, Zimbabwe Institute of Management, 1977-; Elected Member of Parliament for Borrowdale, Salisbury, Zimbabwe, 1981. *Memberships:* Organiser, Salisbury Civil Defence, 1974-77; Chairman, Hong Kong Rugby Football Union, 1964-65; Rotorcraft Committee, Royal Aeronautical Society, UK, 1970-72; Chairman, The Legion, Salisbury Branch; Vice-Chairman, Royal Air Force Association; Commissioner of Oaths. *Publications:* Thesis, The Operation and Maintenance of Army Aircraft in the Modern Army; The Design of Army Rotary Aircraft; Many magazine and newspaper articles including RTV The Second World War. *Hobbies:* Flying; Golf; Military History; Rugby; Sailing. *Address:* Moonrakers, 10 Burlington Road, Salisbury, Zimbabwe.

PROCTOR, (Sir) Roderick Consett, b. 14 July 1914, Sydney, NSW, Australia. Chartered Accountant; Company Director. m (1) Kathleen Mary Murphy, 19 Mar. 1943 (Dec.) (2) Janice Marlene Pryor, 15 May 1980, 4 sons. *Education:* Melbourne Grammar School; Institute of Chartered Accountants, 1955; Fellow, 1958. *Appointments:* Audit Clerk, R Goyne Miller, Chartered Accountant, Perth Western Australia, 1931-33; Taxation Officer, Perpetual Trustee Company, 1934-37; Clerk Clarke and Son Chartered Accountants, Brisbane Queensland, 1937-60; Partner, 1950-76; Company Directorships, 1964-. *Memberships:* Queensland Club; Brisbane Club; Royal Queensland Golf Club; United Service Club; Southport Golf Club. *Honours:* Knight Bachelor, 1978; MBE, 1946. *Hobbies:* Yachting; Surfing; Golf. *Address:* Unit 102 The Gardens, 204 Alice Street, Brisbane, Australia.

PROSSER, Victor Albert, b. 25 Aug. 1926, Adelaide, South Australia. Accountancy. m. Minnetta Isabel Sandery, 11 Apr. 1953, 2 sons, 1 daughter. *Education:* MBM., 1971, BEc., 1951, University of Adelaide; Fellow, The Australian Society of Accountants, 1961; Fellow, the Institute of Chartered Secretaries & Administrators, 1962. *Appointments:* RAAF., 1945; South Australian Law Courts, 1942-47; Treasury, 1959-51; Executive Trainee, 1951-52, Organisation Officer, 1953-55, Broken Hill Associated Smelters Pty. Ltd., 1951-55; Accountant, 1957-67, Group Finance Director, 1967-69, G & R Wills Group of Companies, 1955-79; Executive Director, The Institute of Chartered Accountants in Australia, 1979-. *Memberships:* South Australian President, Australian Society of Accountants, 1974-75; General Councillor, 1973-79; Faculty of Economics, University of Adelaide, 1970-79; Council of Governors, Scotch College, Adelaide, 1975-79; Naval, Military and Air Force Club. *Publications:* Weekly columnist in The Financial Australian, 1980-. *Honours:* John Storey Prize for Business Management, University of Adelaide, 1964. *Hobbies:* Tennis and other sports; Theatre; Gardening. *Address:* 5/15 Thornton Street, Darling Point, New South Wales, 2027, Australia.

PROVAN, John Gilmour, b. 1 Feb. 1931, Ayr, Scotland. Medical Practitioner. m. Mary Taylor Campbell, 27 Mar. 1958, 1 son, 2 daughters. *Education:* MB, ChB, Glasgow University, 1948-53; FRCS(Glas); FRACS; *Appointments:* Resident Medical Officer, Victoria Infirmary, Glasgow, 1953-54; Flight Lieutenant, Medical Branch, Royal Air Force, 1954-56; Registrar in Surgery, Southern General Hospital, Glasgow, 1956-64; Surgeon in Charge, Government of Basutoland, Queen Elizabeth II Hospital, Maseru, Basutoland, Lesotho, 1964-66; Locum Consultant Surgeon, Stracathro Hospital, Brechin, Scotland, 1966; Senior Staff Surgeon, Sydney Hospital, New South Wales, 1967-68; Senior Medical Officer and Surgeon, Carnarvon District Hospital and Medical Officer i/c Royal Flying Doctor Service, Carnarvon, Western Australia, 1968-72; Medical Superintendent, Rockhampton Base Hospital, Queensland, 1972-. *Memberships:* Fellow, Royal College of Surgeons, Glasgow; Fellow, The Royal Australasian College of Surgeons; Queensland Department of Health Hospital Drugs and Equipment Advisory Council; Queensland Ad Hoc Committee on Rural Health and the use of Aerial Transport; Glasgow Medical Chirurgical Society. *Publications:* The Anterior' Lobe of the Thyroid, 1967. *Hobbies:* Sailing; Golf; Painting. *Address:* Medical Superintendent's Residence, Rockhampton Base Hospital, Rockhampton, Queensland 4700, Australia.

PRYKE, Graham Ernest, b. 23 Feb. 1920, Largs Bay, South Australia. Commissioner. m. Marjorie Caroline Casey, 28 Aug. 1943, 1 son, 1 daughter. *Education:* Stott's Business College; Muirden Business College; Associate, Australian Society of Accountants; Fellow of: Australian Institute of Management and English Association of Accountants & Auditors. *Appointments:* Industrial Officer, State Committee of Overseas and Interstate shipping companies, 1943-52; Industrial Director, Chief Industrial Advocate, South Australian Employers' Federation Incorporated, 1952-72; Commissioner, Industrial Commission of South Australia, 1972-. *Honours:* OBE., 1981; Justice of the Peace. *Hobbies:* Swimming; Motoring; Photography. *Address:* 17 Lincoln Street, Largs Bay, 5016, South Australia.

PRYOR, Lindsay Dixon, b. 26 Oct. 1915, Moonta, South Australia. Forester and Landscape Consultant. m. (1) Wilma Brahe Percival, (Deceased, 1975), 2 sons, 2 daughters, (2) Nancy Violet Cook. *Education:* BSc., Forestry, Adelaide, 1936; Diploma Forestry, Australian Forestry School, 1936; MSc., (Adelaide), 1939; DSc., (Adelaide), 1958. *Appointments:* Assistant Forester, ACT, 1936-39; Assistant Research Officer, F & TB, Canberra, 1939-40; Acting Forester, ACT, 1940-44; Director, Parks & Gardens, 1944-58; Professor of Botany, Australian National University, 1959-75; Consultant Forester, 1975-. *Memberships:* President, Royal Society of Canberra; Deputy Chairman, Board of School of General Studies, Australian National University; Council, Australian Institute of Landscape Architects; Fellow of: Australian Academy of Technological Sciences and Institute of Foresters of Australia. *Publications:* Biology of Eucalypts; A Classification of the Eucalypts, (w. L.A.S. Johnson); Trees in Canberra. *Honours:* Schlich Medal, 1935; Verco Medal, 1967; Australian Park Administration Medal, 1969; N.W. Jolly Medal, 1972; Mueller Medal, 1976. *Hobby:* Walking. *Address:* 69 Endeavour Street, Redhill 2603, Canberra, ACT, Australia.

PRYOR, Robin John, b. 7 Oct. 1941, Numurkah, Australia. Demographer; Minister of Uniting Church, Australia. m. Bronwyn B Brewster, 17 Dec. 1966, 1 son, 2 daughters. *Education:* BA., 1963, Dip.Ed., 1964, MA., 1968, Melbourne, Australia; PhD., Malaya, 1972; B.Theol., M C D., 1981. *Appointments:* Tutor, Senior Tutor, Melbourne University, Australia, 1964-68; Commonwealth Research Scholar, University of Malaya, 1968-70; Lecturer, James Cook University, Townsville, Queensland, Australia, 1970-73; Research Fellow, Demography, Australian National University, Canberra, Australia, 1973-78; Consultant, Economic Commission for Europe at the United Nations, Geneva, Switzerland, 1977-78; Graduate Studies in Theology and training for Ordination in the Uniting Church in Australia, 1979-81. *Memberships:* International Union for the Scientific Study of Population; Sociological Association of Australia and New Zealand; Commission on Population, International Geographical Union; Australian College of Education. *Publications:* Migration and Development on South East Asia, 1979; Mobility and Community Change in Australia, (co-author), 1980; numerous articles and monographs on internal migration and urbanisation; The Vocational Needs of Ministers, 1982. *Hobbies:* Family; Pottery; Demographic research—South East Asia and Australia; Community development. *Address:* 3 Quinn Street, Numurkah, Victoria 3636, Australia.

PRYOR, William Joseph, b. 16 Feb. 1927, Horsham, Victoria, Australia. Veterinarian. m. Ann Christine Harris, 2 June 1956, 5 sons. *Education:* BVSc., Sydney University, Australia, 1950; MVSc., University of Queensland, Australia, 1962; PhD., Oregon State University, USA, 1966; FACVSc., Australia, 1972. *Appointments:* Veterinary Officer, Victorian Department of Agriculture, Australia, 1951-56; Senior Lecturer, Reader, Animal Husbandry, 1958-71, Dean, Veterinary Faculty, 1970-71, University of Queensland, Australia; Professor and Dean, Faculty of Veterinary Science, Massey University, New Zealand, 1972-76; Assistant Director, Australian Bureau of Animal Health, ACT, Australia, 1977-. *Memberships:* President: Australian Veterinary Association, 1980-81; Australian College of Veterinary Scientists, 1978-79; Vice-President: Australian Society for Animal Production, 1968-70; University of Queensland Staff Association, 1970-71. *Hobbies:* Classical music; Livestock farming. *Address:* 9 Rosenthal Street, Campbell, ACT 2601, Australia.

PUCHALAPALLI, Pushpamma, b. 31 Dec. 1936, Nellore District, Andhra Pradesh, India. Dean and Principal. m. P.R. Reddy, 27 Aug. 1958, 2 sons, 1 daughter. *Education:* BSc., Andhra University, India, 1954-56; MSc., Banaras Hindu University, India, 1956-58; PhD., Kansas State University, USA, 1964-68. *Appointments:* Assistant Lecturer, College of Agriculture, Department of Agriculture, Bapatla, Andhra Pradesh, India, 1959-64; Associate Professor, 1968-74, Professor of Foods and Nutrition and Principal, 1974-78, Dean and Principal, 1977-, College of Home Science, Andhra Pradesh Agricultural University, Hyderabad, India. *Memberships:* Member of numerous organisations in India and Internationally including: Sigma XI of Kansas Chapter, USA; Association of Food Scientists and Technologists of India; Nutrition Consultant of Indo-Dutch Project, A.P.; Mother and Child Care Project; Chairman, Consumer Guidance Society, Andhra Pradesh branch; Task Force on Home Science, ICAR. *Publications:* 14 Research papers including: Improving protein quality of millet, sorghum and maize diets by supplementation, 1972; Evaluation of nutritive value, cooking quality and consumer preference of Grain legumes, 1975; Liver and serum lipids—Effect of dietary oils, 1976; Problems of Home level storage, 1977; Rural creche: a longitudinal case study, 1978; Nutritional quality of sorghum and legume based food miztures for infants and pre-school children, 1979; Effects of Location and varieties on protein, amino acids and mineral contents of chickpea, 1980. *Hobbies:* Reading; Writing; Cooking; Indoor games. *Address:* Principal Quarters, College of Home Science, Saifabad, Hyderabad 500 004, India.

PULLENAYEGUM, Selvanayagam Arjuna Lohan, b. 2 Nov. 1944, Colombo, Sri Lanka. Chartered Accountant. m. Malkanthi Wijesinha, 20 July 1973, 2 sons, 1 daughter. *Education:* Fellow, Institute of Chartered Accountants of Sri Lanka. *Appointments:* Accountant, Ceylon Oils and Fats Corporation, Sri Lanka; Finance Manager, Sri Lanka Sugar Corporation; Partner, Lawrie Muthu Krishna & Co., Chartered Accountants, Sri Lanka; Chief Accountant, Chilanga Cement Limited, Zambia. *Address:* PO Box 99, Chilanga, Zambia.

PURI, Gopal Singh, b. 18 Aug. 1915, Kallar, Dissh, Pakistan. m. Kailash, 29 Aug. 1943, 1 son, 2 daughters. *Education:* BSc., Hons., 1937, MSc., Hons., 1939, Punjab, India; PhD., Lucknow, India, 1944; PhD., London, UK, 1948. *Appointments:* Polynologist, Burma Oil Co., 1939-40, 1942, 1944-45; Malaria Officer, Indian Medical Services, 1940-42; Research Fellow, University of London, UK, 1945-48; Forest Ecologist, Forest Research Institute, Debradum, 1948-54; Regional Director, Botanical Services of India, Poone, 1954-56; Director, Government of India, Botanical Laboratory, Allahebad, 1956-61; Acting Head, Department of Botany, University of Ibadan, Nigeria, 1961-63; Professor and Head of Department, Agricultural Botany, University of Ghana, 1963-67; Human Ecologist, Liverpool Polytechnic, UK, 1967-80. *Memberships:* Fellow: World Academy of Art and Science; Commonwealth Council of Human Ecology; Fellow and Advisor, National Institute of Ecology; Secretary General, International Society of Tropical Ecology; Technical Secretary, Indian Council of Ecological Research; World Federation of Healing. *Publications:* Indian Forest Ecology, 1960; Res. Method in Ecology, 1968; Indian Food Ecology, 1981; Author of 400 research papers in Ecology and Environment. *Honours:* Ruche Rurn sahui Research Prize, India, 1943; Medals awarded by: Grasland Congress, Sao Paulo, Brazil, 1963; Conservation Society of Russie, 1970; numerous honours and awards for research, teaching from several universities throughout the world. *Hobbies:* Rotary movement; Social services. *Address:* 'Bucklands', 36 Merrilocks Road, Blundellsands, Liverpool L3, England.

PURNELL-WEBB, Edward Alfred, b. 4 Apr. 1921, Brisbane, Queensland, Australia. Commonwealth Public Servant. m. 27 Nov. 1948, 3 sons. *Education:* LL.B., University of Queensland, Australia, 1966; Master's (Foreign-going) Certificate, Sydney, Australia, 1949. *Appointments:* Seafaring, 1938-51; Local Representative, Townsville, Brisbane, Sydney, Australian Stevedoring Industry, 1951-70; Director of Shipping Practices, Department of Trade and Resources, Canberra, Australia, 1970-72; Assistant Secretary and First Assistant Secretary, Fisheries Division, Department of Primary Industry, Canberra, Australia, 1972-81. *Memberships:* Royal Commonwealth Society, London. *Hob-*

bies: Cricket; Golf; Reading; Fishing; Gardening. *Address:* 84 Finniss Crescent, Narrabundah, ACT., 2604, Australia.

PURSLOW, Michael Gordon, b. 22 Nov. 1935, Shrewsbury, England. Printing Management. m. Christine Margaret Taylor, 6 Sept. 1958, 1 son, 2 daughters. *Education:* Diploma, Printing Management, London College of Printing, UK, 1963-65. *Appointments:* Production Manager, Baynard Press, London, UK, 1965-69; Works Manager, 1969-71, General Manager, 1974-76, Vyse Printers, Stoke-on-Trent, UK; Printing Advertisier to Government of Singapore, 1971-74; Commercial Director, 1976-79, Managing Director, 1979-, Monterey Printing and Packaging, Zambia. *Memberships:* Fellow, Institute of Directors; British Institute of Management; Associate, Institute of Printers. *Hobbies:* Community work; Squash; Music. *Address:* 41 Dr Damie Street, PO Box 71042, Ndola, Zambia.

PURSSELL, Anthony John Richard, b. 5 July 1926, Simla, India. Manufacturing Company Executive. m. Ann Margaret Batchelor, 1952, 3 children. *Education:* BA., Hons., Oriel College, Oxford, UK. *Appointments:* Production Director, 1963-66, Personnel Director, 1966-68, Managing Director, 1968-73, Arthur Guinness & Co., Park Royal Ltd, UK, 1948-73; Managing Director, Arthur Guinness Son & Co. (Dublin) Limited, Ireland, 1973-75; Managing Director, Arthur Guinness Son & Co. Limited, UK, 1975-; Joint Deputy Chairman, 1981-. *Memberships:* Fellow, British Institute of Management; Vice President, Institute of Brewing; Incorporated Brewers' Guild; Governor, Ashridge Management College. *Address:* 10 Albemarle Street, London W1X 4AJ, England.

PURVES, Daphne Helen, b. 8 Nov. 1908, Dunedin, New Zealand. Teacher; Lecturer. m. Herbert Dudley Purves, 16 Dec. 1939, 1 son, 2 daughters. *Education:* BA., 1929, MA., 1930, University of New Zealand. *Appointments:* Assistant Mistress: Waitaki Girls' High School, New Zealand, Otago Girls' High School, New Zealand; Otago Boys' High School, New Zealand; Lecturer, Senior Lecturer, Dunedin Teachers' College, New Zealand. *Memberships:* Vice-President, 1971-77, President, 1977-80, Convener, Cultural Relations Committee, International Federation of University Women; President, New Zealand Federation of University Women; Alliance Francaise, Dunedin, New Zealand; Vice President, United Nations Association of New Zealand. *Publications:* Contributions to: educational journals, newspapers, World Conference of the United Nations Decade for Women. *Honours:* DBE., 1979. *Hobbies:* Reading; Public Speaking; Travel; Bridge; Spinning; Gardening. *Address:* 11 Falkland Street, Dunedin, New Zealand.

PUTTERILL, Rodney Ray Jensen, b. 25 Jan.'1917, Harrismith, South Africa. Army Officer (retired). m. Isobel Stewart Mackie, 18 Dec. 1945, 1 daughter. *Education:* PSC., Army Staff College, Camberley, UK, 1952. *Appointments:* Enlisted Rhodesia Regiment (TF), 1937; Rhodesian Army, 1940; 6 (SA) Armed Division, Mid East, 1942-43; 2nd Battalion, Queens Own Cameron Highlanders, 4 Indian Division, Italy and Greece, 1944-45 S. Rhodesia Staff Corps., 1946; Co. N. Rhodesia Regiment, 1956-58; Commander, N. Rhodesia Area, 1959; S. Rhodesia District, 1959-62; Appointed DCGS., Federal Army, Rhodesia and Nyasaland, 1963; Appointed CGS., Rhodesian Army, 1964; Major General (retired), 1968. *Memberships:* Centre Party. *Honours:* OBE., 1960; CBE., 1965; ADC, additional, HM The Queen, 1963. *Hobbies:* Trout fishing; Beekeeping; Small scale fruit farmer. *Address:* 'Wyadera', PO Box 2, Juliasdale, Zimbabwe.

PYM, Rt. Hon. Francis Leslie, b. 13 Feb. 1922, Abergavenny, Monmouthshire, Wales, United Kingdom. Member of Parliament. m. 25 June 1949, 2 sons, 2 daughters. *Education:* Magdalene College, Cambridge, England. *Appointments:* Trainee, Lewis's Limited, UK; General Manager, Merseyside Dairies Limited, UK; Managing Director, Holloway & Webb Limited, UK; Parliamentary Secretary to the Treasury and Government Chief Whip, 1970; Secretary of State for Northern Ireland, 1973; Opposition Spokesman on Foreign Affairs, 1978; Secretary of State for Defence, 1979; Leader of the House of Commons, 1981. *Honours:* Military Cross; Deputy Lieutenant for Cambridgeshire. *Address:* House of Commons, London SW1, England.

Q

QIONIBARAVI, Mosese, b. 10 Sept. 1938,.Nasau, Koro, Fiji. Businessman. m. Anaseini Bekanimoli, 19 Feb. 1961, 2 sons, 2 daughters. *Education:* B.Com., 1962, M.Com. 1964, Auckland University. *Appointments:* Fiji Government: Central Planning Office, 1965-70; Permanent Secretary for Finance, 1971-72; Private Sector: Managing Director, Naviti Investments Limited, 1973-80; Speaker, House of Representatives, 1977-. *Memberships:* President, Commonwealth Parliamentary Association, 1981. *Honours:* Fiji Jaycees Award for Outstanding Young Man of the Year, 1973; CMG., 1979. *Hobby:* Golf. *Address:* Navurevure Road, Tamavua, Suva, Fiji.

QOLONI, Isaac, b. 16 Sept. 1940, Nabusasa Village, Choiseul Island, Solomon Islands. Civil Servant. m. Alice Geisae, 12 Nov. 1966, 1 son, 3 daughters. *Education:* New Zealand Teacher Training Certificate and Diploma of Teaching, 1964; First Class Diploma, Public and Social Administration (UK), 1971; First Class Magistrate, Solomon Islands, 1974. *Appointments:* Teacher, Church Senior Primary School, 1965; Joint Government Service as Administrative Candidate, 1966; Administrative Officer, Solomon Islands, 1968; District Commissioner, Western Province, 1973; Permanent Secretary, 1975; Secretary to the Prime Minister and the Cabinet, 1978. *Honours:* Old Boys Prize, Wesley College, New Zealand, 1959; OBE., (UK Honours), 1976; Solomon Islands Independence Medal, 1978. *Hobbies:* Swimming; Gardening; Bush Walking; Reading; Business. *Address:* PO Box 662, Homiara, Guadal Canal Island, Solomon Islands.

QUAYLE, Robert Brisco MacGregor, b. 6 Apr. 1950, Birmingham, England. Clerk of Parliament. m. Deborah Clare Pullinger, 30 Sept. 1972, 1 son, 2 daughters. *Education:* BA., 1971, MA., 1974, Selwyn College, Cambridge; College of Law, Guildford. *Appointments:* Solicitor, 1974-76; Clerk of Tynwald, 1976-; Secretary, House of Keys. *Memberships:* Honorary Secretary, Isle of Man Branch of Commonwealth Parliamentary Association. *Hobbies:* Church and Charitable Activities; Anglican Lay Reader. *Address:* Mullen Beg, Patrick, Isle of Man.

QUÉNET, Vincent, (Sir) b. 14 Dec. 1906, Worcester, CP, South Africa. Advocate. m. Gabrielle Price, 5 Mar. 1938, 3 sons. *Education:* BA., LL.B., University of Cape Town. *Appointments:* Barrister at Law, Middle Temple; Practised at Johannesburg Bar, QC; Judge of High Court of Southern Rhodesia, 1952-61; Judge of Federal Supreme Court, Federation of Rhodesia & Nyasaland, 1961-64; Judge, Appellate Division, High Court, Rhodesia, 1964-70; Retired. *Memberships:* Chairman, Commission of Inquiry into Wankie Colliery Disaster, 1973; Chairman, Commission of Inquiry into Racial Discrimination, 1976. *Honours:* Knight, 1962. *Address:* Tiger Valley, Domboshawa Road, Borrowdale, Salisbury, Zimbabwe.

QUICK, Peter Vaughan, b. 5 Oct. 1940, Porthcaul, Glamorgan. Wales. Managing Director. m. Lynne, 1979, 1 son. *Education:* BSc., University College of Swansea, 1959-62. *Appointments:* Production Manager, Enfield Rolling Mills; Consultant, PA Management Consultants; Senior Consultant, Coventry Management Training Centre; Unit Manager, Cov-Rad Limited; Managing Director: Self-Changing Gears Limited and Leyland Nigeria Limited. *Hobbies:* Sailing; Flying; Reading. *Address:* 111 Rotimi Williams, Bodija, Ibadan, Oyo State, Nigeria.

QUINN, Neville William, b. 25 Apr. 1934, Melbourne. Oral and Facio-Maxillary Surgeon. m..Ann Galbally, 19 May 1970, 1 daughter. *Education:* BDSc., University of Melbourne, 1959, MB.,BS., (Melbourne), 1965; FRCS., (England, Ireland, Edinburgh), in general surgery, 1972; FDSRCS (England) in dental surgery, 1973. *Appointments:* Junior Resident MO, St Vincent's Hospital, Melbourne, 1966; General Medical Practice, Locum Tenens positions, Melbourne, 1967; Prosector, Anatomy Department, Royal College of Surgeons, England, 1968; Senior Registrar, General Surgery, Repatriation General Hospital, Heidelberg, Victoria, 1969; Registrar, St Vincent's Hospital, Melbourne, 1960-71; Dental Surgery, University of London, Eastman Dental Hospital, London, 1972; Senior Registrar, Institute of Dental Surgery, University of London, 1973, Lecturer in Oral Surgery and Oral Medicine postgraduate courses at this Institute; Senior Registrar in Oral Surgery and Oral Medicine, King's College Hospital, University of London, 1974; Lecturer to undergraduate and postgraduate students; Commenced Specialist Practice, Melbourne, Oral Surgery, Oral Medicine, Facio-Maxillary Surgery, 1975. *Publications:* Contributor to professional medical journals. *Hobbies:* Golf; Sailing; Music. *Address:* 31 Brunswick Street, Fitzroy, Victoria, 3965, Australia.

QUIRION, Joseph, b. 31 Oct. 1917, St-Evariste, Canada. Professor. *Education:* BA, Laval, 1938; LPA, 1941; BTh, Ottawa, 1943; BCom, South Africa, 1955; MSc (Econ), London, 1958. *Appointments:* Lecturer, Registral and Bursar, Pius XII University College, Roma, Basutoland, 1945-60; Dean, Faculty of Social Sciences, University of Ottawa, Canada, 1961-65; Dean, Faculty of Arts, 1965-74; Professor of Economics, 1974-78; Director, Institute for International Cooperation, University of Ottawa, Canada, 1978-. *Memberships:* Fellow, Chartered Institute of Secretaries. *Hobbies:* Swimming; Travelling; Reading. *Address:* 305 Nelson Street, Ottawa, Canada, K1N 7S5.

R

RADCLIFFE, Sheila, b. 26 July, 1914, Adelaide, South Australia. Teacher. *Education:* BA, University of Adelaide, 1944; Diploma in Education, 1953. *Appointments:* Teaching Infant Schools, Education Dept. of South Australia, 1936-45; Secondary Schools, 1946-47; Senior Mistress, Whyalla, Pt. Adelaide, Nailsworth, 1948-56; Head Mistress, Port Adelaide Girls Technical School, Croydon Girls Technical High School, 1957-70. *Memberships:* Head Mistresses Association; Australian Federation of University Women; Adelaide University Graduates Union; Royal S.A. Society of Arts; Adelaide Art Society; Ornithological society of South Australia; Lyceum Club; Victoria League for Overseas Friendship; University Music Society. *Creative Works:* Water colour paintings of landscape and birds; One man show 1981 of overseas work done in 1980 while in G.B. and Europe. *Hobbies:* Playing viola in Burnside Symphony Orchestra; Playing recorder. *Address:* 54 Brigalow Avenue, Kensington Gardens, South Australia 5068.

RADFORD, Susan Patricia, b. 22 July, 1952, Nairobi, Kenya. Scientist. m. 21 Dec. 1980. *Education:* BSc, Aberdeen University, 1974; M.Agr.Sc. Queensland University, 1980; PhD, Sydney University, 1979. *Appointments:* Laboratory Assistant, Malaysian Rubber Producers Research Association, 1975; Part Time Teaching, Sydney Technical College, School of Rural Studies, 1981. *Memberships:* Institute of Biology; Australian Society of Plant Physiologists; Social Convenor, Postgraduate Association, QLD; Council, Sydney University Postgraduate Res. Association; Men of the trees, NSW Branch. *Publications:* M.Agr.Sc. Thesis, Comparitive responses to water deficits of three C4 grasses grown in field and controlled environments, *Honours:* Collie Prize, Aberdeen University, 1974; Scholarship, Draper's Livery Co., 1976-79; Scholarship, New South Wales Nurserymen's Association, 1979-82. *Hobbies:* Music and Theatre; Craftwork; Environmental Studies, Agroforestry. *Address:* 3/50 French Str, Maroubra, Sydney, NSW 2035, Australia.

RADHAKRISHNAN, Narayanan, b. 18 Mar. 1930, Kayangulam, Kerala, India. Naval Officer/ Civil Servant. m. Sita, 16 Aug. 1964. 1 son, 1 daughter. *Education:* Master of Business Administration, Delhi University, 1972; Post Graduate Diploma in Business Administration, Delhi University, 1971; Passed Staff Course, Defence Services Staff College, Wellington, 1963; BSc. Kerala University, 1948-60. *Appointments:* Cadet, Royal Indian Navy, 1949-52 with the Royal Navy along with Special Entry Cadets. Commissioned in the Indian Navy 1951; Served in a number of ships and establishments of the Indian Navy and the National Defence Academy, Kharakvasla; Chief Instructor Signal School, Cochin; Command Operations and Signals Officer, Cochin; Command Communications Officer, Bombay; Fleet Communications Officer, Indian Fleet; Deputy Director of Naval Signals, Naval Headquarters, New Delhi; Prematurely retired 1971; Cabinet Secretarial Government of India, New Delhi, 1972. *Memberships:* Fellow of the Institution of Electronics and Telecommunication Engineers, New Delhi; Delhi Gymkhana Club, New Delhi; Defence Services Officers Institute, New Delhi. *Honours:* Gallantry Award of Shaurya Chakra (SC) on Republic Day, 1977. *Hobbies:* Reading Current Affairs; Tennis. *Address:* C2-3 M.S. Flats, Sector XIII, Ramakrishnapuram, New Delhi, 110066, India.

RADIN, Soenarno (Dato Seri), b. 6 June, 1932, K. Lipis, Pahang, Malaysia. Public Administrative Officer. m. Zabidah, 6 Dec. 1962, 3 sons, 1 daughter. *Education:* BS, University of Malaya, 1959; MPIA, University of Pittsburgh, 1972. *Appointments:* District Officer, 1959-62; Assistant Secretary Prime Ministers Office, 1962-65; Senior Research and Planning Officer, Ministry of Agriculture, 1965-69; State Development Officer, Johor, 1969-70; Deputy Secretary General, Ministry of National and Rural Development, 1970-71; Deputy Secretary General, Ministry of Communications, 1972-75; State Secretary, Perak, 1975-79; Secretary General, Ministry of Lands, since 1979. *Memberships:* President, Perak Royal Golf Club, Ipoh, 1975-80; Royal Golf Club, Selangor. *Publications:* Thesis, Malay Nationalism. *Honours:* AMN 1965; PIS,

1970; JMN, 1977; SPMP 1977. *Hobbies:* Golf; Reading. *Address:* 20 RD 12/19, Petaling Jaya, Selangor, Malaysia.

RADION, Stepan, b. 24 July, 1912, Sylne, Volyn, Ukraine. Journalist; Writer; bibligrapher; Critic. m. Eugenia Anhel, 17 July 1942. 1 son, 1 daughter. *Education:* Diploma: Story and Serial Writing; Freelance Journalism; radio Writing; Verse Writing, Australian School of Journalism in Melbourne. *Appointments:* The Free Thought, 1951-81; The Liberation Path, London, 1957-81; Ukrainian Settler, Melbourne, 1960-81; Oura Front, Melbourne, 1968-81; Ukrainian Voice, Winnipeg, 1975-81; New Pathway, Toronto and other Ukrainian weeklies and magazines, 1976-81. Up to the end of 1980 published 228 book reviews, 311 articles and 10 translated into Ukrainian Australian short stories. 04 Federation of Australian Writers, Melbourne; Ukrainian Writers Association, New York; Shevchenko Scientific Society in Australia; Member Correspondent of Ukrainian Mohyla-Mazeppa Academi of Science, Montreal, Canada. *Publications:* The New Crusade, Adelaide, 1954; Nicolaus Bereza, Melbourne, 1956; Bio-bibliography of Literary Works, Bloomington, USA, 1975; A Survey of History of the Shevchenko Scientific Society in Australia, Melbourne, 1976; Bibliography and Collections of Works, Melbourne, 1978; Bibliography of Works in Ukrainian Language, 1980; Dictionary of Ukrainian Surnames in Australia, 1981. *Hobbies:* Writing; Gardening. *Address:* 8 Eve Court, Springvale North, Victoria, Australia.

RADLEY, David Ewart, b. 8 Oct. 1936, Skelmanthorpe, England. Veterinary Surgeon. m. Carole Elizabeth, 28 Mar. 1964. 1 son, 2 daughters. *Education:* BVM & S., MRCVS., Edinburgh University, 1960; DTVM, Edinburgh University, 1966; PhD, Edinburgh University, 1971. *Appointments:* General Practice, Lancaster, 1960-65; Research fellow, Centre for Tropical Veterinay Medicine, University of Edinburgh, 1966-68; Veterinary Research Officer, EAVRO, Muguga, Kenya, seconded by the Ministry of Overseas Development, 1968-70; Veterinary Research Officer, EAVRO, Muguga, Kenya, seconded by Pfizer Inc. 1971-77; FAO Consultant Burundi, 1977-78; FAO Project Manager in Malawi, 1979-. *Publications:* Senior Author of 20 publications on Theileriosis and Junior Author of a further 25 publications. *Hobbies:* Photography; Music. *Address:* C/O UNDP, PO Box 30135, Capital City, Lilongwe 3, Malawi.

RADMANOVICH, Max (Dr), b. 16 Nov. 1935, Broken Hill, NSW, Australia. m. Jelena, 22 Feb. 1959, 1 son, 4 daughters. *Education:* BE, Sydney University, 1958; MES, Sydney University, 1961; Doctor of Philosophy, University of N.S.W. 1971; Management Certificate Sydney Technical College, 1965. *Appointments:* Mining Engineer, North Broken Hill Ltd., 1960-65; Production Engineer, North Broken Hill Ltd., 1965-69; Assistant Underground Manager, North Broken Hill Ltd., 1969-71; Production Superintendent, Utah Development Company, 1971-72; Mine Manager, Utah Development Company, Queensland, 1972-76; General Manager, The Bellambi Coal Company, NSW, 1977-80; General Manager, Ulan Coal Mines Ltd., North Sydney, 1980-. *Memberships:* Australasian Institute of Mining and Metallurgy; Fellow Australian Institute of Management; Melbourne University Business School Association. *Publications:* Contributed various Papers to Publications and Conferences of Aus.I.MM. A.I.M; Editor published Proceedings of two Annual Conferences of The Aus.I.M.M. *Honours:* Intermediate Scholarship, 1950; Commonwealth Scholarship, 1952; Mines and Metals Bursary, 1955-56; Aus.I.M.M. Students Essay Prize, 1955, 1956, 1957; Sydney Technical College Prizes, 1963-64. *Hobbies:* Furniture Making; Model Aircraft/Trains; Gardening; Painting. *Address:* 44 Cassia Street, Dee Why, N.S.W. 2099, Australia.

RADWANOWSKI, Lech Jan, b. 21 Nov. 1927, Poland. Architect. m. Danuta, 31 Dec. 1960. 1 daughter. *Education:* BSc. and Diploma of Engineer Architect, 1949; MSc. 1955; PhD, 1968; DTSc, 1970. *Appointments:* Building Manager, Chief of Supervision, 1949-55; General Designer in Project Office, 1953-70; Reader in Department of Architecture, Technical University, 1956-78; Professor of Architecture and Chief Architect, 1978-80; Professor of Architecture and Head of Department of Architecture, University of Jos, 1979. *Memberships:* Association of Polish Architects; Head

Council of Technics; International Solar Energy Society; Polish Cybernetics Society; Nigerian Association of Architects. *Publications:* Theory of Geo-Magnetohydrodinamics in Building, 1976; Formulation of Principles of Biocenotics-Technical Discipline for Designing, 1968; More than 100 publications; More than 80 Architectural and Urban Designs. *Honours:* Commemoration Medal of 50 years of the Technical University of Warsaw, 1973; Golden Cross of Merit, 1976; Silver Medal of Architectural Initiative, 1977; Golden Medal for Achievement in Building, 1976; Annual awards of Vice-Chancellor, 1974,75,76,77. *Hobbies:* Physics and Cybernetics. *Address:* University Staff Quarter, Jos, Nigeria, PMB 2084.

RAHMAN, A.H.M. Habibur, b. 30 Oct. 1939, Comilla, Bangladesh, Teacher. m. Khajesta, 29 Jan. 1971, 1 daughter. *Education:* BCom(Hons), Dacca University, 1958; MCom, Dacca University, 1959; PG Diploma in Business Management, Brunel College, Middlesex, England, 1965; PhD, Durham University, England, 1969. *Appointments:* Professor of Finance, Dacca University, 1978; Dean of the Faculty of Commerce, and Chairman, Bureau of Business Research, University of Dacca; Associate Professor, University of Dacca. 1970-78; Founder Chairman, Department of Finance, University of Dacca, 1974-77; Founder Director, Bureau of Business Research, University of Dacca, 1972-80. *Memberships:* Treasurer, Dacca University Club; Foundation for Research on Educational Planning and Development; Associated with several professional and cultural organisations. *Publications:* Major Research work and publications are in the field of Industrial Finance, Small Enterprise Development, Entrepreneurship Development, Rural Industrialisation, Financial Management, Labour Market Adjustment Process in Bangladesh. *Honours:* Received Government Scholarship for higher studies leading to PhD in the United Kingdom, 1964-68; Received UNAPDI-ADIPA Fellowship to work as Visiting Professor at the Management Development Institute, New Delhi, 1980. *Hobbies:* Reading; Writing; Travelling; Photography; Sports and games. *Address:* Village-Ulookandi, PO Marichakandi, Dist. Comilla, Bangladesh.

RAHMAN, Md. Shafiur, b. 31 Dec. 1922, Kushtia, Bangladesh. Teacher. m. Jerina Begum, Oct. 1945, 2 sons, 3 daughters. *Education:* GVSC, 1943; BS, Texas A & M University, USA, 1963; MS, Texas A M University, USA, 1964; PHD, Texas A & M University, usa, 1966. *Appointments:* Assistant Animal Husbandry Officer, 1943-50; Animal Nutrition Officer, 1950-58; Assistant Professor, 1959-68; Associate Professor, 1968-73; Professor, 1973-. *Memberships:* Society of Sigma Xi; American Dairy Science Association; Bangladesh Association for Advancement of Science; Bangladesh Animal Science Asssociation. *Publications:* Research Articles, 20; Review Articles, 7; Popular Articles, 6; Text Book, 1. *Hobbies:* Reading; Indoor Games. *Address:* 33/4 Mahtab Uddin Road, Kushtia, Bangladesh.

RAHMAN, Mustafizur, b. 2 Apr. 1930, Akkelpur, Bogra, Bangladesh. Teacher & Researcher. m. 4 June 1953, 3 sons, 2 daughters. *Education:* BSc, Dacca University, Bangladesh, 1950; MSc, Punjab University, Pakistan, 1952; PHD, University of Adelaide, Australia, 1966. *Appointments:* Lecturer in Zoology, Govt. Colleges, 1952-59; Assistant Entomologist, Jute Research Institute, Pakistan, 1959-66; Senior Lecturer, Rajshahi University, 1967-70; Associate Professor, Rajshahi University, 1970-75; Professor of Zoology, Rajshahi University, 1975-. *Memberships:* Australian Entomological Society; American Entomological Society; Vice President, Bangladesh Association for the Advancement of Science; Vice President, Bangladesh Zoological Society; President, Society of Natural Resources, Rajshahi; Pakistan Zoological Society; Pakistan Society for the Advancement of Science. *Publications:* Published 32 original research papers and two books. *Hobbies:* Reading; Bird watching; insect collecting; Fishing; Expedition. *Address:* W/13-A University Campus, University of Rajshahi, Rajshahi, Bangladesh.

RAHMAN, Shah Mohammad, Azizur, b. 22 Nov. 1925, Kushtia. Politician and Lawyer. *Appointments:* General Secretary All-India Muslim Students Federation, All-Bengal Muslim Students League, 1945-47; Chairman, East Pakistan Combined Opposition Party, 1964; Leader, Awami League Parliamentary Party and Deputy Leader of Opposition, National Assembly of

Pakistan, 1965-69; Senior Advocate, Supreme Court of Bangladesh; Member Bangladesh Parliament for Daulatpore Kushtia constituency; Leader of the House; Minister of Labour and Industrial Welfare, 1978-79; Prime Minister and Minister of Education, 1979. *Memberships:* Bangladesh Bar Council. *Address:* Office of the Prime Minister, Dacca, Bangladesh.

RAHMAT, Bin Ismail Alhaj, b. 10 Dec. 1929, Alort Star Kedah Malaysia. Businessman m. 6 Oct. 1955, 2 sons, 3 daughters. *Appointments:* Special Constable; British Armed Forces; Malaysian Armed Forces; Business. *Memberships:* Vice Chairman, Community Relation Council, Kota Kinabalu Town Sabah Malaysia; Ex Services Association of Sabah & Malaysia. *Honours:* Pingat Angkuan Negara (PPN), Federal Honours, 1966; Pingat Bintang Kinabalu (BK), State Honours, 1969. *Hobbies:* Music; Drama. *Address:* No. 8 Lorong 14, Sembula, Kota Kinabalu, Sabah, Malaysia.

RAHMING, Philip, b. 28 Jan. 1933, New Providence, Nassau, Bahamas. Clergy. m. Madge Elaine, 23 July, 1966, 1 daughter. *Education:* Student Southern Baptist Theological Seminary, Louisville, Master of Divinity Degree, 1969-70; Post Graduate Master in Theology Degree, 1970-71. *Appointments:* Wireless Telegraphist at Remote Receiving Station of Government Telecommunications department, 1948-53; Former Senior Accountant in Accounts Section, Telecoms Dept., 1953-61; Chaplain to the Hon; Speaker of the Bahamas Parliament, 1968-69; Associate Pastor, Mt. Carey Union Baptist Church, Fox Hill, 1971. *Memberships:* 1st Vice-President New Providence District Churches Bahamas Baptist Union, 1979; Director, Mass Communications Bahamas National Baptist Missionary and Education Convention, 1973; Past President, Bahamas Christian Council, 1977-80; Executive Member of the Bahamas Christian Council, 1980. *Publications:* Author of A New Beginning, 1973; National Song; God Bless our Sunny Clime. *Honours:* J.P. Commonwealth of the Bahamas, 1969; Doctor of Divinity Degree, Simmons University, Louisville, Kentucky, USA, 1974; Private conversations with His Holiness, Pope John Paul, II. *Hobbies:* Swimming; Table-tennis; Music; Radio work. *Address:* Nassau East, P.O. Box 5354, Nassau, Bahamas.

RAI, Bhanu Kumar, b. 21 Nov. 1926, Bilaspur (MP), India. Serviceman. m. Bina Narain, 29 Nov. 1954, 2 sons. *Education:* BSc, Banaras Hindu University, 1949; DIISC, Indian Institute of Science, Bangalore, India, 1950; OLT(ME), Military College of Telecommunication Engineering, Mhow, India, 1959. *Appointments:* Chief Executive/Managing Director, UP Electronics Corporation Ltd., Lucknow, UP, India; Director, Chief Executive, Ruttonsha Group of Companies, Bombay, India; Plant Development Manager, Continental Device India Ltd., New Delhi, India; Regular Officer, Corps of Signals, Indian Army; Assistant Engineer, National Radio & Engineering Company Ltd., Bombay, India. *Memberships:* Fellow, Institution of Electronics & Telecommunication Engineers, New Delhi, India; Chairman, Institution of Electronics & Telecommunication Engineers, UP Centre; Institution of Electronics & Radio Engineers, UK; Royal Air Force Amateur Radio Society. *Publications:* A number of Technical articles in leading Electronics Journals. *Honours:* Laghu Udyog Maharishi AR Bhat Award, 1978; Small Scale Marketing Award, 1979; Distinguished Alumnus Award from BHU, Institute of Technology, Varanasi, India, 1980. *Hobbies:* Amateur Radio; Painting; Golf. *Address:* 18/2 Madan Hohan, Malviya Marg, Lucknow 226 001, India.

RAINBOW, Andrew James, b. 18 Dec. 1943, Essex, England. Medical Physicist. m. Anna Omeluck, 22 July 1972, 1 son 1 daughter. *Education:* BSc, (Hons), Physics, University of Manchester, UK, 1965; MSc, Radiation Biology & Radiation Physics, University of London, UK, 1967; PhD, Biology, McMaster University, Canada, 1970. *Appointments:* Associate member, Department of Biology, McMaster University, 1973; Associate Professor, Department of Radiology, McMaster University, 1978; Director, Regional Radiological Sciences Program, Chedoke-McMaster Hospital, 1980-. *Memberships:* Radiation Research Society; Canadian Association of Physicists (Medical & Biological Physics Division); American Society of Photobiology; Canadian Radiation Protection Association. *Publications:* About 20 publications concerning the role of radiation damage and DNA repair in cancer; Host-cell Reactivation of virus, patient exposure and equipment calibration Methods in Diagnostic Radiology. *Honours:* Research Fellow of the National Cancer Institute of Canada, 1968-70; Fellow of the Canadian College of Physicists in Medicine 1981. *Hobbies:* Music; Guitar & Cello playing. *Address:* Department of Radiology, McMaster University, Hamilton, Ontario L8S 4J9, Canada.

RAINSFORD, Eric Richard John, b. 23 Feb. 1937, Melbourne, Australia. Managing Director, m. Sylvia, 13 Feb. 1960, 1 son, 1 daughter. *Education:* Diploma Applied Chemistry, 1959; Advanced Management programme, Melbourne University, 1973. *Appointments:* Plant Manager, Nylex Corporation, 1972; Division Manager, Nylex Corporation, 1976; Director of Manufacturing, Black & Decker, 1977; Managing Director, Black & Decker, 1980. *Memberships:* Institute of Directors; Melbourne University Business School Association. *Hobbies:* Jogging; Gardening; Education; Sports. *Address:* 8 Whitefriars Way, Donvale 3111, Victoria, Australia.

RAJA, Dharmavenkataperumal, D.V.P., b. 10 Sept. 1937. Rajapalayam, Ramnad District, Tamil Nadu. Teacher. m. D.V.P. Bama, 8 Sept. 1967, 1 son, 2 daughters. *Education:* MA, Public Administration; DSSA. *Appointments:* Director & Secretary, Madurai Institute of Social Work, A Post Graduate College affiliated to Madurai Kamaraj University, Madurai. Military Experience, Commissioned Officer Army, 1963-68; Sub-Commander, Julander, Ordance Depote; Company Commander, Army Ordance Centre, Secundrabad; Brigade Ordance Officer, Staff Officer, in Brigade Hqs. *Memberships:* Vice President, Indian Society of Psychiatric Social Work, Head Office Bangalore; President, Indian Association of Trained Social Workers, Madurai Branch, Madurai; General Secretary, Principals' Association, Madurai Kamaraj University Area, Madurai; Secretary, Association of Social Service Organisations in Madurai (ASSOM). *Publications:* Published Book, Thozhilai & Mudalali, in Tamil. *Honours:* Outstanding Young Person for the Year, 1976. *Hobbies:* Kitchen Gardening; Writing. *Address:* 9 Raj Bhavan, Ayyanar Nagar, Madurai 625 020, India.

RAJAGOPALAN, Pylore Krishnaier, b. 27 Oct. 1930, Mukteswar, UP, India. Medical Entomologist & Ecologist. m. Leela, 10 Nov. 1957, 2 sons 1 daughter. *Education:* BSc, 1949; MSc, 1951; MPh, 1959; PhD, 1965. *Appointments:* Virus Research Centre, Poona, India, 1953-70; WHO, Project on Genetic Control of Mosquitoes, New Delhi, 1970-75; Vector Control Research Centre, Pondicherry, India, 1975-. *Memberships:* Indian Society of Medical Microbiologist; Indian Entomological Society. *Publications:* Over 110 Publications in Medical Entomology, Ecology, Arbovirus, Epidemiology & Vector Control. *Honours:* Rockefeller Foundation Fellow, 1958-59; Member of Expert panel of advisors on Vector Control to WHO, 1981-85. *Hobby:* Gardening. *Address:* Ushess, Rajaji Nagar, Pondicherry 605008, India.

RAJAMMAL SUBRAMANIAM, Bahai Aunty, b. 29 May 1933, Trichy, India. Lecturer. m. 5 July 1981 2 sons. *Education:* BA, University of Delhi, 1976; Master of Commerce, Commercial University of Delhi, 1977. *Appointments:* Headmistress, Rajarajeswari School, 1968-70; Headmistress, St. Thyajrara School, 1971-72; Headmistress, Annie Besant School, 1973-75; Lecturer & Head of Department of Commerce & Economics in City Ladies Tutorial, 1978-81. *Memberships:* Bala Bhavan Institute; Chairman, Local Spiritual Assembly, Singapore, 1978-81. *Publications:* Some short stories and childras stories in leading magazines. *Honours:* Prizes in Music competitions, Painting & Embroidery, 1952, 1954, 1959. Best children class Teacher, 1976. *Hobbies:* Playing Chess; Painting; Embroidery, Knitting. *Address:* 655a Black 167, Boonlay Drive, Singapore, 2264.

RAJAN, Balachandra, b. 24 Mar 1920, Toungoo, Burma. University Professor. m. Chandra Saima, Aug 1946, 1 daughter. *Education:* BA, Contab, 1941; MA, Cantab, 1944; PhD, Cantab, 1946. *Appointments:* Director of Studies in English, Trinity College, Cambridge, 1945-48; Member Indian Foreign Service, 1948-61; Professor of English, Delhi University, 1961-64; Visiting Professor, University of Wisconsin, 1964-65; Senior Professor, University of Western Ontario, 1966-. *Memberships:* Milton Society, President, 1972; Intl.

Association of University Professors of English; Academy of Literary Studies; Modern Language Association. *Publications:* Paradise Lost and the Seventeenth Century Reader, London, 1947; New York, 1948; W.B. Years, a Critical Introduction, London, 1965; The Lofty Rhyme, a Study of Milton's Major. Poetry, London, 1970; Carol Gables, 1970; The Overwhelming Question, a Study of the Poetry of T.S. Eliot, Toronto, 1976; The Dark Dancer, A Novel New York, 1958; London, 1959; Tou Lous in the West, A Novel, London, 1961, New York, 1962. *Honours:* Fellow of Trinity College, 1944-48; Fellow, Royal Society of Canada, 1975; Honoured Scholar, Milton Society of America, 1979. *Hobbies:* High Fidelity Reproduction; Photography. *Address:* 478, Regent Street, London, Ontario, Canada, N5Y UHU.

RAJAN, B.P. b. 15 Oct. 1932, Arumuganeri, Tirunelveli DT, Tamil Nadu, India. Dentist. m. Shantha, 10 Dec. 1958. *Education:* BSc, 1953; BDS, 1957; MDS, 1962. *Appointments:* Professor, Operative Dentistry, Dental Wing, Madras Medical College, Dental Surgeon, Government General Hospital, Madras, 1967-78; Professor, Operative Dentistry, Head of Dental Wing, Madras Medical College, Madras, 1978-79; Principal and Professor, Operative Dentistry, Madras Dental College, Madras, 1979-. *Memberships:* Fellow, International College of Dentists; Pierre Fauchard Academy. *Publications:* Role of Medical Practitioners in Dental Health, Nadu State Medical Conference, 1978; Care of teeth Wisdom, 1980. *Address:* 116 Dr. Radhakrishnan Salai, Mylapore, Madras 600004, Tamil Nadu, India.

RAJAN, Veluthevar Kanaga, b. 2 Mar. 1939, Johore Bahru, Malaysia. Diplomat. m. Vijayalakshmi, 7 Mar. 1971, 2 daughters. *Education:* BL, LLB, University of London, 1969; BL, Lincolns Inn, 1977. *Appointments:* Government of Republic of Singapore, Served in several Ministries, Private Secretary to the President of the Republic, The Late Dr. B.H. Sheares, First Secretary at the Singapore High Commission in Australia, 1959-. *Memberships:* British Institute of Management, 1974; Hindu Endowments Board, 1978-81. *Publications:* Recipient of Public Administration, Silver, 1971. *Hobbies:* Gardening; Photography. *Address:* 86 Hawker Street, Torrens Act 2607, Australia.

RAJANEESH, Bhagwan Shree, b. 11 Dec. 1931, Kuchwada, Madhya Pradesh, India. Spiritual Master. *Education:* MA, Saugar University, Philosphy, 1957. *Appointments:* Professorship, Jabalpur University, Philosophy, 1960-66. *Publications:* Extracts from Bhagwan's books have been published in newspapers and magazines all over the world, Translations of his books have been made into 21 different languages, Recent titles include, My Way; The Way of the White Clouds; A cup of Tea; The sound of Running water. *Address:* c/o Shree Rajneesh, Ashram, 17 Koregaon Park, Poona, 411 001, India.

RAJARATNAM, Jesuthasan Mylvaganam, b. 23 Dec. 1927, Alvai, Sri Lanka. Business Executive. m. 1 Dec. 1949, 3 sons, 2 daughters. *Education:* BSc, University of Ceylon, 1949; Fellow, Institute of Chartered Accountants of England and Wales, 1956. *Appointments:* Regional Vice President, Far East Region, The Singer Company, 1976-; Vice President, Finance and Accounting, International Division, The Singer Company, 1973-76; Director, Analysis and Controls, International Division, The Singer Company, 1973. *Memberships:* Fellow, Institute of Chartered Accountants of England and Wales; Fellow, Institute of Chartered Accountants of Sri Lanka. *Honours:* Hons and 12th Certificate of Merit, Intermediate exam of the Institute of Chartered Accountants of England and Wales, 1954; Winner, Debating Prize, London Chartered Accountants Students Society, 1953; Winner, Ceylon Government open scholarships for studies in Accountancy, 1950. *Hobbies:* International Politics and Economics; Oriental Classical Music; Dramatics. *Address:* 20/1 Sukhumvit 43, Bangkok, Thailand.

RAJAYYAN, Kunju Krishnan Nadar K., b. 7 Apr. 1929, Nellikkakuzhi. Teaching and Research. m. Mabel Helena, 23 May 1956, 1 son, 1 daughter. *Education:* MA, Kerla University, 1953; MLitt, Madras University, 1959; AM, George Washington University, 1964; PhD, Madras University, 1965. *Appointments:* Lecturer, Mar Ivanios College, Trivandrum, 1954-56; Research Scholar, Madras University, 1956-58; Lecturer, Sacred

Heart College, Tirupattur, NA, 1958-60; Lecturer, S.V. University, Tirupati, 1960-68; Chief Professor, Presidency College, Madras, 1968-70; Professor of History, M.K. University, Madurai, 1970-80; Visiting Professor, Kerala University, Trivandrum. 1980-81. *Memberships:* Fellow, Institute of Historical Studies; Indian History Congress; Indian Council of Historical Research; Tamil Nadu Council of Historical Research; South Indian History Congress. *Publications:* Administration and Society in the Carnatic; A History of British Diplomacy in Tanjore, South Indian Rebellion, History of Madurai 1736-1801, History of Tamil Nadu 1565-1967, Poligars of Tamil Nadu, History in Theory and Method. *Honours:* Recipient of Fulbright Scholarship for Studies in USA, 1963-64. *Hobby:* Gardening. *Address:* University Road, Rajambadi, Madurai 625021, South India.

RAJENDRAM, Rasiah, b. 5 Aug. 1930, Malaysia. Chartered Architect. m. Shantha Ramani Rajendram, 17 May 1969, 1 son, 1 daughter. *Education:* University of Cambridge, Fitzwilliam College, 1953-56; BA, 1956-58, DipArch; MA, 1960; Associate of Royal Institute of Archictects, 1962; Fellow, Royal Institute of Architects, 1970; Nigerian Institute of Architects, 1969; Nigerian Institute of Architects, 1981. *Appointments:* Assistant Architect, London County Council, 1958-60; Ministry of Works, Lagos, Nigeria, 1960-62, Principal, R. Rajendram and Associates, Chartered Architects, 1963-79; Chairman and Managing Director, R. Rajendram and Associates Development and Technical Consutants, Lagos, Nigeria, 1979-81. *Memberships:* Royal Institute of British Architects, 1963, Fellow, 1970; Architects' Registration Council, United Kingdom, 1963; Nigerian Institute of Architects, 1969, Fellow, 1981; Architects' Registration Council, Nigeria, 1969. *Creative Works:* 113 Works completed by the Firm R. Rajendram and Associates Chartered Architects, the most recent being, Extension to Governor' Lodge for Borno, Bauchi and Gongola States at Lagos. *Hobbies:* Painting; Artwork; Writing; Reading; Music; Research into Ancient Indian Architecture. *Address:* Flat F, John Holt Compound, 149/153 Broad Street, Lagos, Nigeria.

RAJ KUMAR, Dyanand, b. 12 Dec. 1942, Trinidad, Trinidad and Tobago, West Indies. Lecturer in Crop Production, m. 24 Sept. 1977. *Education:* BSc, Agriculture, London UCWI, 1964; MSc. Crop Science, University of the West Indies, 1969; PhD, (Plant Physiology) University of Adelaide, 1977. *Appointments:* Research Agronomist and Field Supervisor, West Indian Tobacco Co. Ltd., Trinidad, 1964-68; Manager, West Indian Tobacco Co. Ltd., Trinidad, 1969-72; Agricultural Officer, Ministry of Agriculture, Trinidad and Tobago, 1977; Lecturer in Crop Production, University of the West Indies, Trinidad and Tobago, 1977-. *Memberships:* The Association of Professional Agrologists of Trinidad and Tobago; Australian Society of Plant Physiologists; Agricultural Society of Trinidad and Tobago; Judge at Annual Flower Show, Horticultural Society of Trinidad and Tobago. *Publications:* Chemical Weed Control in Tobacco in Trinidad - J. Seeyare and D. Raj Kumar; Pans, 1969, 15: 370-372; The effect of fertilizers on growth, yield and quality of flue-cured tobacco in Trinidad; MSc Thesis, UWI, 1969; The Control of vegetative shoot growth in Citrus. PhD Thesis, University of Adelaide, 1977. *Honours:* Trinidad Government Exhibition, providing free secondary education, 1952; Scholarship to pursue BSc, West Indian Tobacco Co. Ltd., 1960; Texaco Agriculture Research Prize for best MSc Thesis, 1969; Australian Commonwealth Scholarship, to pursue PhD, 1972; Canadian Commonwealth Scholarship to pursue PhD, 1972. *Hobbies:* Music; Swimming; Fishing; Sailing; Martial Arts; Gardening. *Address:* 8 Brives Road, Maraval, Port of Spain, Trinidad and Tobago.

RAJMANE, Krishna, b. Chinchanti, Ta, Tasgaon District, Sangli. Teaching, Research and Extension. m. Latika, 24 May, 1964, 1 son 1 daughter. *Education:* BSc. Agri., Poona University, India, 1962; MSc, 1966; PhD, Punjab Agricultural University, 1974. *Appointments:* Lecturer, College of Agriculture, Kolhapur, 1966-69; Assistant Professor of Economics, 1969-75; Head, Department of Economics and Statistics, Marathwada Agricultural University, Parbhani, 1975-. *Memberships:* Indian Society of Agricultural Economics; Indian Science Congress; Marathwade Development Corporation Planning Cell; Maharashtra Standing Committee for Crop Loans; Marathwada Economics Society. *Publications:* Contributor of reviews, mono-

graphs, articles to professional journals and conferences, including Demand and supply projections of foodgrains in Maharashtra (1980-81 to 2000-1), Paper presented in Seminar on Food Futurolog, 1979. *Address:* PO Chinchani, Ta. Tasgaon, Dist. Sangli, India.

RAJU, (Datla) Venkata Subba , b. 21 June, 1928, Godavary District, India. Chartered Engineer. m. 15 May, 1945, 1 son, 1 daughter. *Education:* BSc in Science, India, 1949; DMIT Engineering, India, 1953; Radar Engineering, UK, 1955. *Appointments:* Managing Director, Elico Private Ltd., Hyderabad, India, 1960; Research Officer, Government of India, Ministry of Irrigation and Power, 1959; Development Engineer, Furzehill Laboratories Ltd., Watford, U.K. 1956-58. *Memberships:* Fellow, (FIETE) Institute of Electronic and Telecommunication Engineers, India; IEEE, USA; Secunderabad Club, India; Fateh Maidan Club, India; Dinners Club, India; Rotary Club, India. *Publications:* Seminar short paper on Electronics Industries Assistance. *Honours:* Recipient of Best Import substitution award by the Chamber of Commerce, 1978. *Hobbies:* Visiting Historical places. *Address:* 6-3-1186/10, Greenland Road, Begumpet 500 016, India.

RALPH, Bernhard John Frederick, b. 9 March, 1916, Auckland, New Zealand, Biotechnologist. m. Barbara E. Wills, 28 Aug. 1947, 2 sons, 2 daughters. *Education:* BSc, University of Tasmania, 1938; PhD, University of Liverpool, 1949; *Appointments:* Lecturer, Chemistry Dept, University of Tasmania, 1942-45; Research Officer, CSIR, Div. of Forest Products, 1946; ICI Research Fellow, University of Liverpool, 1946-49; University of New South Wales, 1950-80; Senior Lecturer and Assoc. Professor, 1950-58; Foundation Professor of Biochemistry, 1959-80; Head, School of Biological Sciences, 1956-66; Head, Dept. and later School of Biological Technology, 1965-80; Dean, Faculty of Science, 1962-68; Dean, Faculty of Biological Sciences, 1968-80; Emeritus Professor since 1980; Honorary Associate School of Metallurgy, 1980-. *Memberships:* Fellow, Australian Academy of Technological Sciences; Fellow of Royal Australian Chemical Institute, Federal President, 1965. *Publications:* Over 60 papers in the fields of Fungal Biochemistry, Radiation Chemistry, Fermentation Technology, Bacterial Leaching and Mineral Biodegradation. *Honours:* Leighton Memorial Medallist, 1974, Royal Australian Chemical Institute. *Hobbies:* Gardening. *Address:* 21, Bobbin Head Road, Pymble, New South Wales; 2073; Australia.

RAMACHANDRA, Kanakanatath, b. 18 Aug. 1933, Mandya, Karnataka State, India. Research in Mathematics. m. Saraswathi, K. 5 June 1958, 1 daughter. *Education:* BSC, Mysore University, 1955; MSC, Mysore University, 1956; PHD, Bombay University, 1964. *Appointments:* Joined Tata Institute of Fundamental Research, Bombay, India, 1958; Became a full Professor in the Institute, 1975. *Memberships:* The National Academy of Sciences, India, 1973; The Indian Academy of Sciences, 1975; The Biographical Academy of Commonwealth, 1980; President, The Hardy-Ramanajan Society, 1978. *Publications:* Some Remarks on the Mean Value of the Riemann Zeta-Function and other Dirichlet series III; Annales Acad. Science Fenn, AI, 5, 1980; Progress Towards A Conjecture on the Mean-Value of Titchmarsh Series, 1979. *Honours:* Award of the Hari OM Ashram, Award for research in Theoretical Sciences for 1976, Awarded 1980. *Hobbies:* Devotional Music; Vedic Chantings. *Address:* 702 (A7N) B-I Block, Colaba Housing Colony, Homi Bhabaa Road, Bombay 400005, India.

RAMACHANDRAN, Vangipuram, Seshachar, b. 30 Dec. 1929, Bangalore, India. Scientist. m. Vasundhara, 27 Oct. 1957, 1 son, 1 daughter. *Education:* BSc, 1949; MSc, 1951; PhD, 1956; DSc, Ottawa, 1981. *Appointments:* Senior Scientific Officer, Central Building Res. Inst., India, up to 1968; Associate Res. Officer, Div. Build. Res., National Res. Council, Ottowa, Canada, 1968-71; Senior Research officer, div. Build. Res., 1971-79; Head Building Material Section, 1979-. *Appointments:* Fellow, American Ceramic Society; Chairman, Secretary of various committees. *Publications:* Published 4 books; 8 chapters in books and Annual Reviews; 120 research papers in various journals. *Honours:* Plaque from the Italian II Cemento, 1979; Nominee for Mettler Award, International Conf. Thermal Analysis, 1980, 1981. *Hobbies:* Short Story writing; Poems; Popular Science articles; Classical Indian Music. *Address:* 1079, Elmlea Drive, Ottawa, Ontario K1J 6W3, Canada.

RAMA DAS, Vallabhaneni Sita, b. 5 Feb. 1933, Gudlavalleru, India. University Professor, m. Ahalya Devi, 22 June, 1951, 1 son, 1 daughter. *Education:* BSc. Andhra University, India, 1951; MSc, Delhi University, 1953; D.Phil, Oxford University, England, 1957. *Appointments:* Asst. Professor of Botany, University of Allahabad, India, 1957-59; Research Plant Physiologist, University of California, 1959-60; Lecturer in Botany, Sri Venkateswara University, India, 1960-61; Reader in Botany, S.V. University, Tirupati, India, 1961-67; Associate Professor of Biology, Memorial University of Newfoundland, St. Johns Newfoundland, Canada, 1967-69; Reader and Head of Botany, S.V. University, India, 1969-70; Professor and Head of Botany, S.V. University, India, 1970-78; Professor of Plant Sciences, and Director Centre for Photosynthesis, University of Hyderabad, India, 1978-80; Professor of Botany and Head of the dept. S.V. University, India, 1980-; Dean, School of Biological and Earth Sciences, 1981. *Memberships:* Fellow, Indian National Science Academy, New Delhi; Fellow, Indian Academy of Sciences, Bangalore; Member, Indian Society for Plant Physiology, President, 1973; Member, Andhra Pradesh Akademi of Science, President, 1977-78; Member American Society of Plant Physiology, Japanese Society of Plant physiology, Weed Science Society of America; American Society for Photobiology. *Publications:* Published 152 research papers in Plant Physiology. *Honours:* Recipient of the Award from the Federation of Indian Chambers of Commerce and Industry for outstanding achievement in the field of life sciences, 1978; Best Teacher Award, Government of Andhra Pradesh, India, 1981. *Hobbies:* Gardening. *Address:* Sri Venkateswara University, Tirupati, 517 502, India.

RAMAKRISHNA, Basava Sri, b. 17 Oct. 1921, Vizianagaram, India, Vice Chancellor, Professor and Consultant in Acoustics and Noise control. m. V. Rajeswari, 1 May, 1943, 1 son, 1 daughter. *Education:* BSc, Andhra University, Waltair, India, 1941; MSc. Benares Hindu University, India, 1944; PhD Illinois Institute of Tech. Chicago, Ill. USA, 1949. *Appointments:* Lecturer, Asst. Professor and Professor of Acoustics, Indian Institute of Science, 1949; Visiting Professor of Acoustics, University of Minnesota, Minneapolis, 1967: Vice Chancellor, University of Hyderabad, India, 1980-. *Memberships:* Fellow & Former President of Acoustical Society of India; Fellow, Indian Academy of Science; Fellow, Institution of Electronics and Telecommunication Engrs. India; Member American Institute of Physics; International Commission on Accoustics. *Memberships:* Research monograph: Some aspects of Relative Efficiencies of Indian Languages—An Information Theoretical Study. *Publications:* Scholarship for Study in USA by Government of India. *Hobbies:* Photography and Linguistic Studies from information theory point of view. *Address:* Vice-Chancellors Residence, Santoshnagar, Hyderabad, 500028 India.

RAMAKRISHNA, Pillai M.N., b. 6 Dec. 1910, Changanacherry, Kottayam District, Kerala, India. Accountant/student of Mathematics. m. L. Kamalamma, 18 Apr. 1935, 1 son, 1 daughter. *Education:* BA. SB College, Changanacherry, 1926-30; BL. Law College, Trivandrum, 1933; Diploma in Accountancy, 1936; Lower & Higher Departmental Examinations in Accounts and Audit of the State Government. *Appointments:* Auditor, Accounts Office, Trivandrum, 1931-37; Chief Accountant, Government, Ceramic Concerns-Kundara, 1937-42; responsible for the organisation of accounts and finance Department; Superintendent, Account Generals Office, Trivandrum, 1946-50; Superintendent, 1950-58, Accounts Officer, 1958-66, Indian Audit and Accounts Department; First Financial Advisor and Chief Accounts Officer in Hindustan Latex Ltd, 1966-71. *Memberships:* Indian Mathematical Society, 1945; Life Member, Indian Mathematical Society, 1965; President, Accounts Officer's Association, Accountant General Office, Trivandrum, 1968. *Publications:* A dozen papers presented at the Annual Conferences of the Indian Mathematical Society from 1972-80 on Algebra & Analytical Geometry/Published in Mathematics Education in 1972. Articles in certain magazines on Mathematical subjects; Monograph on Triangles and their associated Determinates, a new approach to the study of the analytical geometry of the

triangle based on symmetric points and shift operators, under publication. *Honours:* Prize for Good conduct and Proficiency in Studies in College, 1930. *Hobbies:* Study of religious literature and Mathematics. *Address:* Kovilvilla East, TC 28-1425, Old Sreekanteswaram Road, Puthenchanthai, Trivandrum-695 001, Kerala, India.

RAMAKRISHNAN, Alladi, b. 9 Aug. 1923, Madras, India. Scientist. m. Lalitha, 21 Aug. 1946, 1 son. *Education:* BSc. Madras University, 1943; PhD Manchester, UK, 1951. *Appointments:* Reader, University of Madras, 1952-59; Professor, University of Madras, 1959-62; Director, Institute of Math. Sciences, Madras, 1962-. *Memberships:* Fellow Indian Academy of Sciences; Founder Fellow and Vice President, Tamil Nadu Academy of Sciences, Madras. *Publications:* Over 150 Research publications, 3 books and contributor of reviews, monographs, articles to professional journals and conferences. *Honours:* FICCI Award, Outstanding Contributions to Mathematical Sciences, 1980. *Address:* 62, Luz Church Road, Mylapore, Madras, 600004, India.

RAMANATHAN, K.V., b. 24 Apr. 1924, India. Retired Government Officer, Malaysia. m. Rukumani, 16 Sept. 1951, 1 son, 2 daughters. *Education:* Senior, English, Cambridge. *Appointments:* Chief Clerk, PWD Federal Headquarters & Federal Stores, Kuala Lumpur; Executive Officer, PWD Federal Headquarters, Kuala Lumpur. *Memberships:* Council member, Malaysian Council for Child Welfare; Malaysian Writers Association; Malaysian Tamils Association; Malayan Tamil Teachers Association; Founder Member, Chairman & Secretary of nearly 54 organisations in Malaysia in the field of sports, youth, culture, social & spiritual. *Publications:* Thondar Thilagam, for spiritual and social work given by the Indian Community of Malaysia in 1973. *Honours:* Recipient of numerous honours and awards for professional and public services including: AMN; PPN; PJK; FIBA. *Hobbies:* Painting; Gardening. *Address:* Lot 4777 Lorong Melor Lima, Taman Cuepacs, 7 Mile, Jalan Cheras, Kajang, Selangor, Malaysia.

RAMANATHAN, Mylvaganam, b. 10 Aug. 1937, Kopay, Sri Lanka, Chartered Accountant. m. Nageswari Arunasalam, 13 May, 1968, 1 son, 2 daughters. *Education:* BA, University of Madras, March, 1959; Final examination of the Institute of Chartered Accountants of Sri Lanka, June 1965. *Appointments:* River Valleys Development Board, 1965-73; Chief Accountant, Galoya Project; Assistant General Manager, Finance of Heavy Construction Division; Chief Accountant of Udawalawe Multipurposes Reservoir Project; Accountant/Chief Accountant, Zimco Ltd and Mindeco Ltd, Zambia, 1973-; Chief Accountant, Zimco Ltd, Lusaka, Zambia, Feb. 1980-. *Memberships:* Institute of Chartered Accountants of Sri Lanka, FCA; British Institute of Management, MBIM; National Geographic Society, Washington USA; Life Member of International Society for Krishna Consciousness. *Hobbies:* Astrology and Palmistry. *Address:* 3, Jifumpa Flats, Plot 6003, Sibweni Road, PO Box 30790, Lusaka, Zambia.

RAMAVATRAM, Sathyavathi, b. 8 Oct. 1934, Latur, India. Physicist. m. Kilambi, 18 Feb. 1957, 1 daughter. *Education:* BSc. Physics, Mathematics, Chemistry, 1954; MSc. 1956; PhD., 1961. Research Appointments in several laboratories, 1961-80, including: Research Associate, ORNL, Oak Ridge, USA, 1978-80; Research Associate, Vanderbilt University, 1978-78; Scientific Associate 1, Brookhaven National Laboratory, Upton, NY 11973, USA, 1980-. *Memberships:* American Physical Society; Canadian Association of Physicists; American Women in Science. *Publications:* Over 30 publications in leading European, American and Canadian Journals on Nuclear Structure, Nuclear Reaction; Theories applied to interpret experimental data and obtain a better understanding of the microscopic aspects of nuclei. *Honours:* Commonwealth University Scholarship as a PhD Student, 1958. *Hobbies:* Travelling to places of Historic and Archealogical interest, understanding different cultures through their art, music etc. Learning languages; Gardening. *Address:* 3, George Avenue, Shoreham, New York, 11786, USA.

RAMBERT, Marie DBE (Dame) b. 20 Feb., 1888, Warsaw, Poland. m. Ashley Dukes, 1918, 2 daughters. *Education:* Studies with Jaques Dalcroze and Enrico Cecchetti. *Appointments:* Founder and Director of Ballet Rambert, London, 1926; Reformed as Modern

Dance Company, 1966; Founded Rambert School of Ballet, London, 1920; Ballet Club at the Mercury Theatre, 1930; Director of the Mercury Theatre Trust Limited, controlling Ballet Rambert. *Memberships:* Member, Grand Council of the Imperial Society of Teachers; Fellow, Vice President, Royal Academy of Dancing; Fellow Royal Society Arts; Institute of Directors; Diploma Associateship Manchester College of Art, 1960; Hon. D.Litt. University of Sussex, 1964; Composers Guild of Great Britain Award, 1978; *Publications:* Translation Ulanova, Her Childhood and Schooldays by Sizova; Co-author, Dancers of Mercury, The Story of Ballet Rambert, by Mary Clark; Interview, 50 Years of Ballet Rambert, Edited Anya Sainsbury/Clement Crisp/Peter Williams, 1976; Autobiography, Quicksilver, Polish Edition, 1978, Marie Rambert on Ballet, with Karsavina, Jupiter recording; Television/Radio personality, Lecturer. *Honours:* Commander British Empire, Coronation Honours, 1953; Queen Elizabeth II Coronation Award, Royal Academy of Dancing, 1956; Dame British Empire, 1962; Legion d'Honneur, 1957; Golden Medal of the Order of Merit, Polish People's Republic, 1979. *Address:* Mercury Theatre Trust Limited, 94, Chiswick High Road, London, W4 1SH, England.

RAMBURN, Lutchmeeparsad, b. 11 Jan. 1925, Curepipe, Mauritius. Sworn & Exchange Broker; Managing Director. m. Krishna Kumaree, 6 July, 1952, 2 sons, 3 daughters. *Memberships:* Lions Club of Port Louis; Triveni Cultural Circle; Chairman of Temple; Deputy Chairman of Chamber of Brokers; Executive Member of Chamber of Commerce. *Hobbies:* Hunting: Fishing. *Address:*Route Du Jardin, Curepipe, Mauritius.

RAMDAS, Laxminarayan, b. 5 Sept. 1933, Bombay. Naval Officer. m. Lalita, 19 Oct. 1961, 3 daughters. *Education:* Graduate of National Defence Academy, 1951; Bachelor Degree, Military Service, 1959; Graduate Royal Naval Staff College, Greenwich, 1968; Alumni of National Defence College, New Delhi, 1980. *Appointments:* Cadet, First Course-National Defence Academy, 1949; Cadet, Britannia RN College, Dartmouth, 1951; Lieutenant, Specialist Communications, 1959; Flag Lieutenant to Chief of the Naval Staff, 1960-61; Squadron Communication Officer, 1961-63; LT CDR Chief Instructor, Signal School, 1963-66; LT CDR, Staff Course - RN College, Greenwich, 1968; Commander Officer in Charge,, Naval Academy, 1969-70; Commanding Officer, INS BEAS, 1971-72; Commander, Executive Officer, INS VIKRANT, 1972-73; Commanding Officer, INS VIKRANT, 1973; Captain, Naval Attache, Embassy of India, Bonn, West Germany, 1973-76; Captain, Commanding Officer, INS ARNALA and Captain (P) 32 Patrol Vessel Squadron, 1976-77; Captain, Director of Personnel, 1978-79; Commodore, Alumni National Defence College, 1980; Commodore, director of Naval Signals, 1981. *Memberships:* Associate Member of British Institute of Management; Fellow of the Institute of Electronics and Telecommunication Engineers (India). *Creative Works:* Thesis on the role of the military in India's National Development. *Honours:* Vir Chakra; Vishisht Seva Medal. *Hobbies:* Photography; Music; Sailing; Trekking. *Address:* Flat No. 406, Block No. 6, Service Officers' Enclave SP Marg, New Delhi-110021, India.

RAMGOOLAM, Seewoosagur, Dr. (the Rt. Hon Sir), b. 1900. Prime Minister of Mauritius. m. Sahoduth Ramjoorawon, 1 daughter. *Education:* Royal College, Curepipe; University College and University College Hospital, London, LRCP, MRCS. *Appointments:* Elected Municipal Councillor, 1940-53; re-elected 1956; Deputy Mayor, Port Louis, 1956; Mayor, 1958; Entered Legislative Council, 1940; Elected Member Legislative Council for Pamplemousos-Riviere du Rempart, 1948; re-elected, 1959; re-eleceted for Triolet, 1959; Member of Executive Council, 1948, 1953; Liaison Officer for Education, 1951-56; Ministerial Secretary to Treasury, 1958; Leader of the House since 1960; Chief Minister and Minister of Finance, 1961; Premier, 1965; Prime Minister, Minister of External & Internal Affairs since 1968; Minister of Information & Broadcasting since March, 1969; Minister of Defence & Internal Security since, 1969; Chairman, OAU, 197677. *Honours:* GCMG; Kt; LECP; MRCS; PC; MLA; Knighted, 1965; Grand Croix de l'Ordre National de la Republique Malagasy; Doctor in Law 'Honoris Causa', University of New Delhi; Fellow University College; Grand Croix, Ordre National de Lion de la Republique du Senegal; Citoyen d'Honneur de la Cite de Port Louis; and numer-

ous other awards. *Address:* 87 Desforges Street, Port Louis, Mauritius.

RAMLOO, Ganta, b. 11 Apr. 1927. Hyderabad, India. Medical Surgeon. m· Mrs. G. Kam 31 Jan. 1952, 5 children. *Education:* MB, BS, March 1954, MS, April 1965. *Appointments:* Assistant Surgeon; Assistant Professor in Surgery; Assistant Professor in Cardiothoracic Surgery; Superintendant of Nursing Home; Consultant Surgeon, Bhavani Clinic. *Memberships:* Association of Surgeons, India; Association of Gastroenterology, India; Nizam Club, Hyderabad; FMC Club, Hyderabad. *Publications:* Several Articles. *Honours:* Recipient of MMMS, First Class. *Hobbies:* Social Work. *Address:* 11/5/152/6, Red Hills, Hyderabad, India.

RAMPHAL, Shridath, Surendranath, b. 3 Oct. 1928, New Amsterdam, Guyana. Commonwealth Secretary-General. m. Lois Winifred King, 16 Aug. 1951, 2 sons, 2 daughters. *Education:* Queen's College, Georgetown, Guyana; LLM, King's College, London, 1952; Called to the Bar, Gray's Inn, 1951; Harvard Law School; Fellow, King's College, London, 1975; London School of Economics, 1979. *Appointments:* Crown Counsel, British Guyana, 1953-54; Assistant Attorney-General, 1954-56; Legal Draftsman, 1956-58; Legal Draftsman, West Indies Federation, 1958-59; Solicitor-General, British Guyana, 1959-61; Assistant Attorney-General, West Indies Federation, 1961-62; Attorney-General, Guyana, 1965-73; Member, National Assembly, 1965-75; Minister of State for External Affairs, 1967-72; Minister for Foreign Affairs, 1972-75; Minister of Justice, 1973-75; Commonwealth Secretary-General 1975-. *Memberships:* Honorary Advisory Committee, Centre for International Studies, New York University; International Committee of Jurists; Board of Vienna Institute of Development; International Honorary Committee, Dag Hammarskjold Foundation; Governing Body, Institute of Development Studies, Sussex University; Independent Commission on International Development Issues; Independant Commission on Disarmament and Security Issues; Chairman, Selection Committee, Third World Prize; Vice-Chairman, Centre for Research on the New International Economic Order, Oxford, United Kingdom; Athenaeum Club, Royal Automobile Club; Travellers's Club. *Publications:* Contributions in journals of legal, political and international affairs, including, International and Comparative Law Quarterly, Caribbean Quarterly, Public Law, Guyana Journal, The Round Table, Royal Society of Arts Journal, Foreign Policy, Third World Quarterly; One World to Share, Selected Speeches of the Commonwealth Secretary-General, 1979; Third World Foundation Monograph, Nkrumah and the'Eighties: Kwame Nkrumah memorial lectures, 1980, 1981. *Honours:* Arden and Atkin Prize, Gray's Inn, 1952; John Simon Guggenheim Fellowship, 1962; Queen's Counsel, 1965; Senior Counsel 1966; CMG, 1966; Knight Bachelor, 1969; Order of the Republic, Egypt, 1973; Grand Cross, Order of the Sun, Peru, 1974; Grand Cross, Order of Merit, Ecuador, 1974; Honorary Degrees, LLD, Panjab University, Chandigar, 1975; Southampton University, 1976; St. Francis Xavier University, Nova Scotia, 1978; University of the West Indies, 1978; University of Aberdeen, 1979; University of Surrey, 1979, University of Essex, 1980; University of Cape Coast, Ghana, 1980; University of London, 1981; Honorary Bencher, Gray's Inn, 1981. *Hobbies:* Boating; Shooting; Cooking. *Address:* The Garden House, 40b Hill Street, London W1X 7FR, England.

RAMSAY, James, Halford, b. 12 Feb. 1930, Melbourne, Australia. Minister of Labour, Industry and Economic Development, Government of Victoria. m. Dorothy E. Gaze, 19 Dec. 1953, 3 sons, 1 daughter. *Education:* BA, Hons, University of Melbourne. *Appointments:* Lecturer, Economics and History, Royal Military College, 1952-54; Printer, Publisher and Company Director, 1955-72; Elected, Victorian Parliament, 1973; Parliamentary Secretary to Cabinet, 1976-78; Minister of Labour and Industry, Minister of Consumers Affairs, 1978-. *Memberships:* Senior Vice President, Victorian Employers Federation, 1970-72; Chairman, Develop Victoria Council, 1968-78. *Hobbies:* Tennis; Fishing. *Address:* 133 Mont Albert Road, Canterbury, Victoria, Australia 3126.

RAMSAY, James, Maxwell, b. 27 Aug. 1916, Hobart, Tasmania. Naval Officer. m. Janet Burley, 24 Nov. 1948, 1 son, 3 daughters. *Education:* Hutchins School,

Hobart; RAN College, Jeruis Bay, RN College, Greenwich; US Armed Forces Staff College; Imperial Defence College. *Appointments:* Royal Australian Navy, 1930-72; Lieutenant Governer, Western Australia, 1974-77; Governor, Queensland, 1977-. *Memberships:* Honorary Colonel, Royal Queensland Regiment; Honorary Air Commodore, 23 Squadron, RAAF; Fellow, Royal Historical Society of Queensland. *Honours:* Recipient of KCMG, 1978; Kt, 1976; CBE, 1966; DSC; US Legion of Merit; K.St.J. *Hobbies:* Fishing; Boating; Golf. *Address:* Government House, Brisbane, Queensland, Australia.

RAMZAN, Mohammed, b. 15 Apr. 1924. Minister for Health. m. Yashoda Devi, 21 Dec. 1940, 3 sons, 5 daughters. *Education:* British Council Bursary, 1958; Member, HRH Duke of Edinburgh's Second Commonwealth Study Conference, Canada, 1962; OCE, Leader Course, USA, 1962; International Labour Organization's Internship Course, Geneva, Switzerland, 1964; Attended three months Geneva International Labour Organization Fellowship Course. *Appointments:* General-Secretary, Public Employees' Union, 1951-73; Elected, Parliament, 1972; Appointed Minster for Urban Development, Housing and Social Welfare, 1972-77; Minister, Commerce and Industry, 1977-81; Minister for Health, 1981-. *Memberships:* Rotary Club of Suva, Fiji. *Honours:* MBE, 1969. *Hobbies:* Shooting; Golf. *Address:* 119 Milverton Road, Suva, Fiji.

RAND, Michael John, b. 19 Aug. 1927, Suffolk, England. Pharmacologist. m. Ilze Kupcs, July 1972. *Education:* BSc, University of Melbourne, 1949; MSc, University of Melbourne, 1955; PhD, University of Sydney, 1957. *Appointments:* Part-time Demonstrator, Physiology Department, Melbourne University, 1950-52; Research Fellow, Pharmacology Department, Sydney University, 1953-56; Demonstrator, Pharmacology Department, Oxford University, 1957-58; Visiting Scientist, Pharmacology Department, Vermont University, USA, 1959; Senior Research Fellow, Pharmacology Department, Sydney University, 1959-60; Wellcome Research Fellow an Lecturer, Pharmacology Department, London University, 1960-65; Professor of Pharmacology, Melbourne University, 1965-. *Memberships:* Australasian Society of Clinical and Experimental Pharmacologists; Australian Physiological and Pharmacological Society; British Pharmacological Society; The Physiological Society; Australian Society for Medical Research; High Blood Pressure Research Council of Australia; The Royal Society of Medicine. *Publications:* Textbook of Pharmacology, W.C. Bowman and M.J. Rand, 1st and 2nd Editions, Published by Blackwell Scientific Publishing Company; An Introduction to the Physiology and Pharmacology of the Autonomic Nervous System, M.J. Rand, C. Raper and M.W. McCulloch, A/asian Pharmaceutical Publishing Company; Some 200 Articles in Scientific and Medical Journals. *Hobbies:* Farming; Wine. *Address:* Amarandra, Spring Flat Road, Heathcote, Victoria 3606, Australia.

RANDLE, Peter Thomas, b. 16 Apr. 1951, Nuneaton, Warwickshire, England. Chemist, Teacher. m. Nova Teasdale, 1 son, 3 daughters. *Education:* BSc Hons, QMC, London University, 1970-73; Queen's University, Canada, MSc, 1973-75; Heidelberg University, 1976; PhD, Queen's University, Canada, 1976-78. *Appointments:* Research Assistant, Queen's University, Canada; Research Assistant, Max-Planck Institute, Heidelberg, West Germany; Chemistry Master, Colbayn's High School, Essex; Chemistry Master, Bristol Cathedral School, Avon; Chemistry Master, Wednesfield High School, West Midlands. *Memberships:* Royal Society for Chemistry; Association of Science Education. *Publications:* An analysis of energy differences in atomic multiplets in connection with the inequality formulation of Hund's rules, Molecular Physics, 1975, Volume 29, Number 6, 1861-75. *Honours:* Recipient of Ernest H. Channon prize, 1969. *Hobbies:* Music; Languages; Travel; Cooking; History of Science. *Address:* 7 Shipton Close, The Willows, Stirchley, Telford, Shropshire, England.

RANGANATHAN, Aiyadurai, b. 28 Apr. 1929, Sri Lanka. Chartered Accountant. m. Kanagambigai Ranganathan, 30 Mar. 1955, 1 son, 3 daughters. *Education:* BA, Econ, 1952; ACIS, 1957; FCA, 1959. *Appointments:* Chief Accountant, Secretary, Aitken Spence Group, Sri Lanka; Director, Aitken Spence Group Eustours Limited, Sri Lanka; Director, Financial Consultants and Allied Services Limited; Financial Advisor PNP X, World Bank Project, Indonesia; Financial Analyst, World Bank, Washington D.C. USA. *Address:* 5705 Lenox Road, Kenwood Park, Bethesda, MD 20034, USA.

RANGOLE, Prabhakar Lokesh Paul. b. 13 Sept, 1930, Nagpur in Maharshtra State, India. Scientist and Project Coordinator, CEERI, PILANI, INDIA. m. Sudha P. Chiney, 5 June 1956, 2 sons. *Education:* BSc, Nagpur University, 1952; MSc, Nagpur University, 1954. *Appointments:* General Electronics Engineering Research Institute, Pilani, Scientist, 1964-72; Scientist and Project Leader and Project Coordinator, 72-*Memberships:* International Coordinator, IEE, 1975; Chairman, Bhagwan sri Sathya Sai Seva Samithi, Pilani, 1979; Vice President III, Lions Club, Pilani, 1980; President, Imperial College India Society, London, 1972. *Publications:* Contributor of review, monographs, articles to professional journals and conferences. *Honours:* UNDP, Fellow, 1969-72; Merit Increaments as Scientist, 1977. *Hobbies:* Oriental Astrology; Social Work; Background of the English Theatre. *Address:* D-21, CEERI Colony, Pilani (RAJ) -333 031, India.

RAO, Chandra Rajeswara, b. 6 June 1914, Managalapuram, India. Political Workers, General Secretary, Communist Party of India. m. Savitramma, 1 son. *Education:* Intermediate Science of the Benares Hindu University. *Appointments:* Joined the Communist Party of India, 1934; Secretary, Andhra State Committee of the Communist Party of India, 1943-61; General Secretary of the Communist Party of India, 1964-. *Memberships:* Vice-President, All India Agricultural Workers' Union. *Publications:* Historic Telengana Struggle, Some Useful Lessons; Problems of India's Agrarian Sector; Lenin's Teachings and Our Tactics. *Honours:* Awarded Order of Lenin by the Supreme Soviet of the USSR on the occasion of his 60th birthday, 1974. *Hobby:* Agriculture. *Address:* Ajoy Bhavan, Kotla Marg, New Delhi-110002, India.

RAO, Chinta Koteswara, b. 7 Nov. 1930, Siripuram, Guntur District, India. m. Kantamamba 19 May, 1950, 2 sons, 1 daughter. *Education:* MBBS, Andhra, 1955; Diploma in Public Health, Calcutta, 1959; Master of Science in Hygiene, Harvard, 1969. *Appointments:* District Health Officer in Andrapradesh, India, 1956-64; Assistant Director, National Institute of Communicable Diseases, Delhi, 1955-71; Deputy Director, National Institute of Communicable Diseases, Delhi, 1972-. *Memberships:* Treasurer, Indian Society for Malaria and other Communicable Diseases, Delhi, 1973-79, Secretary, 1980- *Publications:* Author/Co-author of over 100 scientific publications on Parasitic Diseases. *Honours:* Recipient of Scroll for contributions in the Indian Smallpox Eradication Programme from Union Minister of Health and Family Welfare, 1975, 1977. *Hobbies:* Bridge. *Address:* E81 Sector XIII, R.K. Puram, New Delhi, 110066, India.

RAO, Hangarkatta Tharanath. b. 20 Feb 1934, India. Engineer/Company Director. m. Geetha Rao, 25 Dec, 1966. 2 daughters. *Education:* Bachelor of Engineers, Mechanical; University of Madra, India, 1956. *Appointments:* 1964-70, Works Manager, John Fowler, India; 1970-75, Managing Director, John Fowler, India; 1976-, Managing Director, Tower Aluminium, Nigeria. *Hobbies:* Music and Sports. *Address:* 4, Ladipo Oluwole Avenue, Ikeja, Nigeria.

RAO, Keshavamurthy Ramachandra, b. 25 Feb 1926, Mysore, Karnataka State, India. Scientist, Engineer and Admisitrator. m. Nagalakshmi, 29 Apr 1945, 2 daughters. *Education:* BSc, Mysore University, India, 1945; DIISc, India, 1948; PSc, Wellington, India, 1958; MSc, Cranfield Institute of Technology, UK, 1962. *Appointments:* Director & Member, Governing Body National Remote Sensing Agency, India, 1975; Director, Indian Space Research Organisation, 1965-75; Chairman & Project Administrator, Arri satellite communication Project, India, 1968-72; Indian Air Force, 1949-71; Technical Assistant, All India Radio, 1948-49. *Memberships:* Life, President, Indian Society of Photo interpretation & Remote Sensing; Fellow, Association of Exploration Geophysisists, India, Vice President; Fellow Institution of Engineers, India; Fellow American Society of Photogrammetry & Remote Sensing, USA; Founder, Indian National Cartographic Association.

Publications: About 40 papers, Technical & Non-Technical. *Honours:* Padmashri, by President of India, 1973; Ativisishta Seva medal by President of India, 1972; World Telecommunication Day Award, Government of India, 1973; 3 medals & 5 prizes in University of Mysore, 1943-45. *Hobbies:* Photography; Music, Indian Classical. *Address:* 459, 9th Cross Road, I Block, Jayanagar, Bangalore, 560011, India.

RASTOGI, Suresh Chandra, b. 5 Sept 1944, Lucknow, India. Reader, Mathematician. m. Malti Rastogi, 4 July 1972, 1 daughter 1 son. *Education:* BSc, 1963; MSc, 1966; PhD, 1970. *Appointments:* Lecturer GNLD Rastogi Inter College, Lucknow, 1966-67; Lecturer DAV Degree College, Lucknow University, 1967-69; Lecturer MLK Post Graduate College, Gorakhpur University, Balrampur, 1970; Lecturer BSNV Degree College, Lucknow University, 1971-73; Lecturer University of Nigeria, 1973-74; Senior Lecturer, University of Nigeria, 1974-75; Reader, University of Nigeria, 1975-. *Memberships:* Tensor Society of Japan; Science Association of Nigeria; Bharata Ganita Parishad, Lucknow, India. *Publications:* More than 50, research publications in differential Geometry, in various International Journals. *Honours:* Junior Research Fellowship, UGD, India, 1970; Senior Research Fellowship, CSIR, India, 1971. *Hobbies:* Swimming; Rowing; Water skiing; Badminton; Chess. *Address:* 228/103,A, Raja Bazar Lucknow, UP, India.

RATHNASABAPATHY, Ayyavoo, b. 29 Oct 1939, Coimbatore, Tamil Nadu, Assistant Professor, Madras Medical College, Madras. m. Vadanta, 30 June 1966. *Education:* MBBS, 1963, MD, 1966, Internal Medicine, Madras University. *Appointments:* Assistant Professor, Stanley Medical College, 1966-67; Madras; Assistant Professor, Madras Medical College, Madras, 1967; Assistant Physician, Government General Hospital, 1967-. *Memberships:* Fellow, American College of Chest Physician; Fellow, International College of Angiology; Research Society for Study Of Diabetes in India. *Publications:* Contributor to various professional journals. *Honours:* FCCP; FICA. *Hobbies:* Music; Reading. *Address:* 32, McNichols Road, Chetpet, Madras, Tamil, Nadu, India.

RATNAM, Chaluvadi Venkata Subba, b. 9 Oct 1923, Cumbum, Prakasam District, Andhra Pradesh, India. Chemical Engineer and Technologist Official in United Nations Organisation. m. Smt. C. Sarojini, 24 Aug 1942, 2 sons, 1 daughter. *Education:* BSc, Andhra University, India, 1945; Certificate in Chemical Engineering, Indian Institute of Science, Bangalore, India, 1946; MS, Chemical Engineering, Oregon State University, USA, 1948; PhD, University of North Dakota, USA, 1950. *Appointments:* Adviser on Science & Technology Policy, UN ESCAP Regional Centre for Technology Transfer, ESCAP/RCTT, Bangalore, India, 1980; Expert on Technology Transfer, ESCAP/RCTT, 1977-80; Managing Director, National Research Development Corporation of India, New Delhi, 1970-79; Superintendent, Chemicals, Neyveli Lignite Corporation, Neyveli, India, 1967-70; Superintendent, B&C, India, 1963-67. *Memberships:* Institute of Engineers, India; Indian Institute of Chemical Engineers; Society of R&D Managers of India; Bangalore Management Association. *Publications:* Has published more than 125 papers. *Honours:* Railway Board Gold Medal, 1963; Distinguished Alumni Award, 1969, University North Dakota, USA. *Address:* No.10, 12th Main, Malleswaram, Bangalore, 560 055, India.

RATNASINGHAM, Navaneethasingham, b. 10 May 1944, Malaysia. Chartered Surveyor. *Education:* Fellow of the Royal Institution of Chartered Surveyors; Member of the Institution of Surveyors, Malaysia. *Appointments:* Partner, Jones Lang Wootton, Malaysia. *Memberships:* The Selangor Club; The Lake Club; The Royal Selangor Golf Club. *Hobbies:* Football; Badminton; Cricket. *Address:* No.6 Jalan Aman, Kuala Lumpur, Malaysia.

RATNATHICAM, Sanchayan, b. 3 Nov 1947, Colombo, Sri Lanka. Chartered Accountant. m. Anita R. Sinclair-Ratnathicam, 23 July 1977, 1 daughter. *Education:* Institute of Chartered Accountants of Sri Lanka, 1964-68; University of Portland, USA, Masters in Business Administration, MBA, 1972-73. *Appointments:* Shaw Wallace & Hedges Ltd, Colmbo, Sri Lanka, Assistant Accountant; Consolidated Freightways Corpora-

tion of Delaware, Portland, USA, General Accountant; Mwaiseni Stores, National Import & Export Corporation, Lusaka, Zambia, Chief Accountant; Consolidated Freightways Corporation of Delaware, Portland, USA, Director, Financial Accounting. *Memberships:* Institute of Chartered Accountants of Sri Lanka; Accounting Principles Committee, National Accounting & Finance Council, American Trucking Associations, Washington DC, USA; Financial Reporting & Information Committee. *Hobbies:* Tennis. *Address:* 9975 NW Murlea Drive, Portland, Oregon 97229, USA.

RATTERAY, Edward Stanley Davis, b. 11 June 1934, Paget, Bermuda. Dental Surgeon, Politician. m. Patricia J. Noel, 7 Sept 1956. 1 son 2 daughters. BA, 1956; DDS, 1957. *Education:* BA, 1956; DDS, 1957. *Appointments:* Dental Surgeon, 1957-; Parliamentary Secretary for Education, 1968; Minister for Education, 1969-72; Minister for Planning, 1976-78; Minister for Planning 1978-79. *Honours:* CBE, 1980. *Hobbies:* Music. *Address:* Coral Acres, Southampton, Bermuda.

RAU, U. Shankar, b. 11th June, 1942. Udipi. Physician, m. G. Sudha Vasudeva, 18 Jan. 1967, 3 sons, 1 daughter. *Education:* MB, BS, Madras Medical College, 1964; MD, Madras Medical College, 1968. *Appointments:* Honorary Civil Assistant Surgeon, Government General Hospital; Consultant Physician, National Hospital; Consultant Cardiologist, Life Insurance Corporation of India; Medical Officer, Reserve Bank of India; Managing Director, Hospital Property Private Limited. *Memberships:* Secretary, International Academy of Chest Physicians & Surgeons, South India; Indian Medical Association; Indian Association for Chest Diseases; Treasurer, Tamilnadu Youth Welfare Association. *Publications:* Numerous Scientific Papers: Pulmonary Histopathology in Tropical Eosinophilla, 1967; Tuberculin Anergy in Tuberculous Pleural Effusion, 1968; Suppurative Lung Diseases in India, Recent Advances in Medicine; Book Trust of India, 1982; Chapter on Respiratory Diseases, Medi-clinics; Book Trust of India, 1981. *Honours:* Captained Madras State Basketball at 10h National Championship. *Hobbies:* Stamp Collection; Coin Collection; Pisciculturist. *Address:* 19, Ormes Road, Kilpauk, Madras-600 010, South India.

RAUERT, Leslie Norman b. 29 Jan. 1948, Dimboola, Victoria, Australia. Sports Administration. m. Vickie Suzanne Zadow, 22 Dec. 1978. *Education:* Diploma of Physical Education, Melbourne, 1968; Batchelor of Physical Education, Western Australia, 1979. *Appointments:* Department of Education, Victoria, Australia; Commonwealth Teaching Service, Australia; Northern Territory Department of Education. *Memberships:* Secretary, Australian Schools Sports Council; Secretary, Australian Primary Schools Sports Association; Northern Territory Primary Schools Sports Association, Secretary; Secretary, Northern Territory Secondary Schools Sports Association. *Honours:* ACH PER Award, University of WA, 1979. *Hobbies:* Exercise Physiology. *Address:* 31, Halpin Street, Malak, 5793, Darwin, Northern Territory, Australia.

RAULT, Eugene Gabriel, b. 21 Apr. 1929. Durban, South Africa. Banker. m. Lynne Averil Lanning, 4 Feb. 1961, 2 daughters. *Education:* Fellow, Institute of Bankers in Zimbabwe, July, 1980. *Appointments:* Joined Present Employers in Durban, South Africa in March, 1949. Bank then called Netherlands Bank of South Africa Limited. Appointed Chief General Manager and Chief Executive Officer on 1st Nov. 1978. *Memberships:* Bulawayo Club; Salisbury Club; Royal Salisbury Golf Club; Rotary Club of Salisbury City; Catenian Association. *Hobbies:* Gardening; Reading; Swimming. *Address:* 18, Jenkinson Road, Chisipite, Salisbury, Zimbabwe.

RAVI VALLABA RAY, Raja. b. 23rd Aug. 1957. Vadakkangulam, South India. Business. *Education:* SSLC, 1975-76; PUC, 1976-77; BCom, 1980-81. *Appointments:* Managing Partner of Annai Nilayam, Publishing-House, Sivakasi, 1980-. *Memberships:* Junior Chambers International AICA, New Delhi. *Hobbies:* Gardening; Reading. *Address:* 27/a Amman Kovil Patty, North Street, Sivakasi, Tamilnadu, South India.

RAVUTU, Iliesa, b. 5th Nov. 1940. m. Taina Waqa, 24th Dec. 1968, 2 sons, 3 daughters. *Education:* Printing Management, London School of Printing. *Appoint-*

ments: Government Printer. *Memberships:* Justice of the Peace; Former President of Australasian Government Printers' Association, 1978. *Hobby:* Farming. *Address:* 122, Bureta Street, Suava, Fiji Islands.

RAWLINSON, (Sir) Anthony Keith, b. 5th Mar. 1926. Oxford, England. Civil Servant. m. Mary Hill, 4th Apr. 1956, 3 sons. *Education:* Eton College Kings Scholar, 1939-44; Christ Church Oxford, Open Scholar, 1944; 1st-Class Hons. Mod. Classics, 1949; BA, 1951; MA, 1954. *Appointments:* Ministry of Labour & National Science; Assistant Principal, 1951; transferred to Treasury, 1953, Principal, 1955; On loan to UK Atomic Energy Authority, 1958-60; Returned to Treasury, 1960; Assistant secretary, 1963; Under Secretary, 1968; Deputy Secretary, 1972; Economic Minister, UK Embassy, Washington & UK Executive Director, International Monetary Fund and World Bank, 1972-75; Department of Industry, Deputy Secretary, 1975-76; Second Permanent Secretary, 1976-77; Second Permanent Secretary, HM Treasury, 1977-. *Memberships:* Alpine Club, Honorary Secretary, 1963-66; Vice-President, 1972-73; Chairman, Mount Everest Foundation, 1970-71; United Oxford & Cambridge University Club. *Publications:* Articles and memo's in Mountaineering Journals. *Honours:* CB, 1975; KCB, 1978. *Hobbies:* Mountaineering. *Address:* 105, Corringham Road, London, NW11 7DR, England.

RAY, Ajit Kumar, b. 1st Feb. 1925, Calcutta, India. Scientist-Administrator Educator. m. Ratna, 12th Aug. 1956. 1 son, 1 daughter. *Education:* BSc, (Hons.), 1944, MSc. Appl. Math, 1947, Calcutta University, India; DSc, Gottingen University, West Germany, 1955. *Appointments:* Professor, Applied Mathematics, Asutosh College, Calcutta University, India, 1948-56; Reader, Indian Institute of Science, Bangalore, India, 1956-60; Associate Research Officer, National Research Council of Canada, 1961-64; Mathematical Advisor (Research Scientist), Department of Transport, Government of Canada, 1964-65; Assistant Professor of Applied Mathematics, Clarkson College of Technology, Potsdam, NY USA, 1965-66; Associate Professor, Applied Mathematics, University of Ottawa, Ottawa, Ontario, Canada, 1966-75; Professor, Consultant & Advisor, 1975-. *Memberships:* Fellow and Life member of various societies in India etc; *Publications:* Non-linear partial differential equations of Mathematical Physics, Educational & Science Policy; Classical Numerical Mathematics and Discrete Mathematics; above 40 research publications in 14 different countries of world after presentations in the International congresses, Symposia, NATO-ASI, Academy of sciences etc. *Honours:* Holder, President's Gold-medal, Prize in School, 1940; Asutosh Memoral Scholar, College, 1943; Gold Medallist & University Prizeman of Calcutta University, 1947; Alexander von Humboldt Scholar, 1952-54; Holder of Special Foreign Scholarship of Calcutta University, 1954; Certificate of Merit during Centennial celebrations of Mechanical Sciences of USA, 1980. *Hobbies:* Music; Photography; Flying. *Address:* Suite no. 313, A Innes Park, 2767, Innes Road, Ottawa, KIB414, Ontario, Canada.

RAY Mohit Kumar, b. 4th Jan. 1940. Suri, West Bengal, India. Teaching. m. Meera Gupta, 12th May, 1966, 2 daughters. *Education:* BA. 1959; MA, 1961; PhD, 1967; Diploma in French, 1967; Diploma in German, 1971; Diploma in Arabi Arabic, 1980. *Appointments:* Head of Department of English and Other Modern European Languages, Visva-Bharati, 1977-80; In charge, Central Library, Visva-Bharati since Ist Nov. 1980. *Memberships:* Executive Committee. Indian Association for English Studies; American Studies Research Centre, Hyderabad; Academic Council, Visva-Bharati. *Memberships:* Introduction to Social Sciences, 1966; TS Eliot, Search for a Critical Credo, 1978; Large number of research papers published in scholarly journals; some popular articles and poems in English and Bengali. *Hobbies:* Chess; Painting; Painting Stamps; Folklore; Parapsychology. *Address:* 36, Andrews Palli, Santiniketan, Pin: 731 235, India.

RAY, Timothy Derek, b. 13th Oct. 1942. Cheltenham, England. Barrister. m. Helen Hayward, 25th June, 1966. 2 sons, 2 daughters. *Education:* BA, Ottawa University, Ottawa, Ontario, 1965; LLB, Osgoode Hall, Toronto, Ontario, 1970; Barrister at law, 1972. *Appointments:* Clerk of Committees, Justice & Legal Affairs Committee, House of Commons, Ottawa, 1966-

72; Secretary, Commonwealth Conference of Clerks of Parliaments, Ottawa, 1967; Scott & Aylen, Barristers & Solicitors, Ottawa, 1972-77, Admitted partnership, 1975; Executive Assistant to Honourable Eugene Waelan, Minister of Agriculture, CNDN Government, 1974; Counsel, Royal Commission of Enquiry into the Royal Canadian Mounted Police (McDonald Commission) 1978-81. *Memberships:* Canadian Bar Association; International Commission of Justices, Canadian Section; Carleton County Law Association; Mens Canadian Club. *Honours:* Medal for good service, Boy Scouts of Canada, 1981. *Hobbies:* Painting; Amateur Radio, Hiking. *Address:* 117, Aylmere Road, Aylmere, Quebec, Canada, J9H 5TZ.

RAYMENT, Brian Wade, b. 5th Apr. 1945, Sydney. Barrister. m. Colette Eleanor, 3 sons. *Education:* BA, Sydney University, 1964; LLB, Sydney University, 1967. *Appointments:* Member of New South Wales Bar, 1970-. *Memberships:* NSW Bar Council, 1977, 1979, 1980. *Address:* 14, Victoria Road, Bellevue Hill, 2023, Sydney, Australia.

RAZVI, Mohammed, Husain. b. 2 Oct 1929, Augangabad, Deccan, India. Library Science. m. 14 Feb 1956, 1 son, 4 daughters. *Education:* BA, 1950; MA, 1952; DLSc, 1955. *Appointments:* Assistant Librarian, Osmania University, Hyderabad, 1952-55; Lecturer in Library Science, 1956-60, Aligarh Muslim University Deputy Librarian, Jammu and Kashmir University, Srinagar, 1960-68; Deputy Librarian Maulana Azad Library, Aligarh Muslim University, 1968-70; University Librarian and Professor, Head of the Department of Library Science, Aligarh Muslim University, 1970-. *Memberships:* FID; Executive Council, ILA; Vice President, ITALIS; President, IASLIC; Executive Council, INSDOC. *Publications:* Descriptive Catalogue of Manuscripts added to Maulana Azad Library, 1970-80; Descriptive Catalogue of Manuscripts of Persian Poetry; Directory of Urdu Periodicals; Libraries and Indian Languages. *Honours:* Recipient of numerous honours and awards for professional services. *Address:* Professor's Bungalow A-6, M.C. Colony, AMU Campus, Aligarh 202001, India.

REA, Frederick Beatty, b. 31 May 1908, Dublin, Ireland. Methodist Minister and Missionary. m. 9 Aug 1937, 1 son, 1 daughter. *Education:* BA, BD, Dip. Ed., Hon. LLD, University of Zimbabwe, 1979. *Appointments:* Teacher Training, Waddilove Institution, 1937-40; Army Chaplain, 1940-45; Parish Minister, 1947-56, Bulawayo; Principal Epworth Theological College, 1956-64; Parish Minster, 1965- Salisbury. *Publications:* Alcoholism: Its Psychology and Cure, Epworth Press; Southern Rhodesia, the Price of Freedom, 1964; we Would See'Jesus, 1965. *Honours:* MBE, 1945. *Hobbies:* Golf. *Address:* Mabelreign Methodist Church, II Penzance Road, Mabelreign, Salisbury, Zimbabwe.

REA, Lord Rea of Eskdale, (Right Hon.), b. 7 Feb 1900, London. Peer of the Realm. *Education:* 1913-18, Westminster School; 1919-21, Christ Church Oxford, Exhibitioner; 1920, Granoble University, Phonetique. *Appointments:* 1918-19 Grenadier Guards; 1921, Shipping; 1928-39, Hire Purchase Company; 1939-50, Army and Foreign Office; 1955, President Liberal Party, Liberal Leader, House of Lords. *Honours:* Privy Counsellor, 1955; Officer, Order of British Empire, 1945; MA, Christ Church, Oxford, 1956; Deputy Lord Lieutenant Cumbria, 1950; JP, 1950; Chevalier, Legion; Croix de Guerre; Ordre de Merita, France etc. *Hobbies:* Musical Composition; France by car. *Address:* St. John's House, Smith Square, Westminster, SWIP. England.

READ, John (Emms) Sir, b. 29 Mar 1918, Brighton, UK. Chartered Accountant. m. Dorothy M. Berry, 14 Mar 1942, 2 sons. *Education:* Fellow Institute of Chartered Accountants, 1947; Administrative Staff Collge, Henley, 1952. *Appointments:* Royal Navy, 1939-46; Ford Motor Company, 1946-64; EMI Ltd, 1965-; Company Directorships, 1970; Thorn EMI Ltd, 1979; Chairman, Committee of Management, Institute of Neurology, 1980; Trustee Savings Bank Centre Board, Chairman, 1980-. *Memberships:* Brighton Festival Society, Chairman of Trustees, Fellow of the Royal Society of Ang., 1975; Elgen Foundation, 1978; Armed Forces Pay Review Body, 1976; Chairman, CBI Finance Committee, 1978. *Hobbies:* Music; ARts; Sport. *Add-*

ress: Munster House, 12 Munster Green, Haywards Heath, West Sussex, RH16 4AG. England.

READ, Warwick Olver, b. 10 Sept 1925, Sydney, Australia. Dentist. m. Margaret Drummond Love, 30 Dec 1949, 3 sons, 1 daughter. *Education:* BDS, University of Sydney, 1950; Fellowship, Royal Australasian College of Dental Surgeons, 1968; Fellowship, International College of Dentists, 1976. *Appointments:* Private Practice Croydon, NSW, 1950-52; Sydney, 1952-; Part time Teaching Fellow/Senior Tutor, Department of Operative Dentistry, University of Sydney, 1964-78; Member, Advisory Committee and Council, Dental Health Education and Research Foundation, University of Sydney, 1964-68; Member Council, Royal Australasian College of Dental Surgeons, 1970; Censor in Chief, 1972-74; Hon. Treasurer, 1974-76; Vice President, 1976-78; President, 1978-80; Trustee, Australian Dental Research & Education Trust, 1974. *Memberships:* Australian Club, Sydney. *Hobbies:* Music; Photography; Trout Fishing. *Address:* 6 Dorset Drive, St. Ives, 2075, Australia.

READDAWAY, William Brian, b. 8 Jan 1913, Cambridge. Retired University Professor of Economics. m. Barbara A. Bennett, 17 Sept 1938, 3 sons, 1 daughter. *Education:* BA, 1934; MA, 1938, King's College, Cambridge University. *Appointments:* Assistant Bank of England, 1934-35; Research Fellow, University of Melbourne, 1936-37; Fellow of Clare College, Cambridge, 1938; Assistant Lecturer, Cambridge University, 1939-47; Lecturer, 1947-55; Director Department Applied Economics, 1955-69; Professor of Political Economy, 1969-80; Board of Trade, 1940-47; Organisation for European Economic cooperation, 1951-52; Editor, Economic Journal, 1971-76. *Memberships:* Fellow of British Academy, 1967-' Royal Economic Society, 1936-. *Publications:* Writer of 6 books including The Effects of UK Direct Investment Oversea, 1967,68; The Effects of the Selective Employment Tax, 1970,1973; Articles in many learned periodicals. *Honours:* Foundation Scholar, King's College, 1931; Adam Smith Prize Cambridge University, 1934-5; Fellow of British Academy, 1967; CBE, 1971. *Hobbies:* Walking, Swimming, Tennis, Squash. *Address:* 4, Adams Road, Cambridge, CB3 9AD. England.

READE, Peter, Clarence b. 23 Feb 1930, Adelaide, South Australia. University Professor. m. Ene Looke, 15 Dec 1969, 1 son, 2 daughters. *Education:* BDS, 1952; FDSRCS, 1957; MDS, 1961; PhD, 1964; MDSc, 1968; FRCPath, 1980. *Appointments:* 1952-55, Private dental practice, Adelaide; 1956-58, Registrar Eastman Dental Hospital, London; 1958-64, Lecturer, University of Adelaide; 1964-66, Research Fellow, National Health & Medical Research Council of Australia, University of Adelaide 1966-68, Research Associate; Harvard University; 1968-, Professor of Dental Medicine & Surgery and Chairman of Department, University of Melbourne. *Memberships:* Australian Dental Association, 1953; Board of Directors and ther International Association for Dental Research, 1962; Board of Directors, 1977 and Chairman, Graduate Union, University of Adelaide, 1966; Australian and New Zealand Society of Oral Surgeons, 1968; Councillor and Chairman and Vice, Graduate Union, University of Melbourne; Fellow, International Association Oral Surgeons; Fellow, Graduate University, University of Melbourne; Fellow, Royal Microscopical Society, 1979. *Publications:* Many Scientific and Professional Publications. *Honours:* 1974, Leverhulme Visiting Fellow; Tōkyo Medical and Dental University, Japan. *Hobbies:* Motor Cars; Photography; Equestrian Sports. *Hobbies:* Hill View, Benson Road, Couangalt, 3437, Victoria, Australia.

REBBECK, Denis, b. 22 Jan 1914, Belfast, N. Ireland. Shipbuilder & Marine Engineer. m. Rosamond A.K. Jameson, 21 May 1938. 4 sons. *Education:* BA, Tripos, 1935; MA, 1939; MA, 1945; b.Litt, 1946; MSc, 1946; PhD, 1950, Belfast. *Appointments:* Harland & Wolff Ltd. Belfast, Director, 1946-70, Managing Director, 1962-70, Chairman, 1965-66; Royal Bank of Scotland, Director, 1969-; Iron Trades Insurance Group, Director, 1950-; Belfast Harbour Commissioner, 1962-; Lloyds Register of Shipping, General Committe, 1962-; Nationwide Building Society, 1980- *Memberships:* President, Belfast Association of Engineers, 1947-48; President, Worldship Society, 1978-; Prime Warden, Worshipful company of Shipwrights, 1980-; *Publications:* Papers read before British Association;

Institution of Civil Engineers. etc. *Honours:* CBE, 1952; DL, 1960; Akroyd Stuart Award; Institute Marine Engineers, 1943. *Hobbies:* Sailing. *Address:* The White House, Craigavad, Holywood, Co. Down, Northern Ireland, BTl8 OHE.

REDCLIFFE-MAUD, John Primatt (Life peerO b. 3 Feb 1906, Bristol, England. Academic; Home Civil Service; Commonwealth and Diplomatic Services. m. Jean Hamilton, 20 June 1932, 3 daughters. *Education:* Eton College, Kings' Scholar, 1919-24; Now College, Oxford, 1924-28; First Class Honours, Greats; Harvard College, USA, AB, 1929. *Appointments:* Fellow of University College Oxford, 1929-39; Master of Birktech College, London University, 1939-43; Home Civil Servant, 1939-58; Commonwealth Service, High Commissioner to South Africa, 1959-61; Foreign Service, Ambassador to South Africa, 1961-63; Colonial Service, High Commissioner for Bechuanaland and Swaziland, 1969-63; Life peerage, 1967. *Memberships:* President, British Diabetic Association, 1977; President Royal Institute of Public Administration, 1969-78; Chairman of Council Royal College of Music; Chairman, Royal Commission on Local Government in England, 1966-69; Chairman, Committee on Local Government Management, 1964-67; Senior Fellow, Royal College of Art, *Publications:* English Local Goverment, 1932; City Government, the Johannesburg Experiment, 1938: Chapters in other books. *Honours:* Knight Grand Cross of the Bath, 1955; CBE, 1942; Honorary Degrees, Witwaterstand, Natal, Leeds, Nottingham, Birmingham; Honorary Fellowships, University College and New College, Oxford, Johnathan Edwards College, Yale. *Address:* 221, Woodstock Road, Oxford. England.

REDDY, Neelam, Sanjiva, b. 1913, President of India, m. 1 son, 3 daughters. *Education:* Theosophical High School, Adyar, Madras; Arts College, Anantapur. *Appointments:* Secretary Andhra Pradesh Provincial Congress, 1936-46; Member, Madras Legislative Assembly, 1946, Indian Constituent Assembly, 1947; Minister of Prohibition, Housing and Forests, State of Madras, 1949-51; President, Andhra Pradesh Congress Committee, 1951-52; Member, Rajya Sabha, 1952-53; Deputy Chief Minister & Leader of the Congress Legislature Party, Andhra Pradesh, 1953-56; Chief Minister, 1956-59, President, Indian National Congress, 1960-62; Chief Minister, Andhra Pradesh, 1962-64; Minister of Steel & Mines, Union Government, 1964-65 and of Transport, Aviation, Shipping and Tourism, 1966-67; Speaker of Lok Sabha, 1967-69; President of the Republic since 1977. *Address:* Rashtrapati Bhavan, New Delhi, India.

REDMOND, James, (Sir) b. 8 Nov 1918, Muiravonside, Stirlingshire, Scotland. Electrical & Electronics Engineer. m. Joan Morris, 15 Apr 1942 1 son, 1 daughter. *Education:* Caledonian Wireless College, Edinburgh. *Appointments:* BBC, Edinburgh, 1937-38, Junior Sound Engineer; BBC, Alexandra Palace, 1938-39; Junior Television Engineer; Merchant Navy, 1939-45, Radio Officer; BBC Television, Planning Engineer; Director of Engineering BBC, 1968; Retired 1978. *Memberships:* Club Athanaeum; President, Institution of Electrical Engineers, 1978-79; President, Society of Electronic and Radio Technician Engineers; Vice President, European Broadcasting Union, Technical Bureau; Vice President Engineering, Commonwealth Broadcasting Association; Council, Brunel University. *Publications:* Various technical articles on broadcasting. *Honours:* Knighted, 1979. *Hobbies:* Golf. *Address:* 43, Cholmeley Crescent, Highgate, London, N6 5EX. England.

REECE, David Chalmer, b. 14th Feb. 1926. Winnipeg, Canada. Diplomat. m. 25th Jan, 1958, 1 son, 2 daughters. *Education:* BA, Cambridge 1946-49; MA, 1974; Called to Bar, London, 1951; *Appointments:* English Speaking Union, 1951-52; Department, Export Affairs, Ottawa, Canada, 1952; High Commission to Trinidad and Tobago and Barbados, 1972; Commission to West Indies Associated States; High Commissioner to Ghana, and Ambassador to Togo & Dahomey & Liberia, 1974; Ambassador, Canadian Delegation to the Mutual and Balanced Force Reduction Talks, 1978. *Hobbies:* Walking; Theatre; Reading. *Address:* Suttingergasse 18, 1190 Vienna, Austria.

REED, Malcolm Leonard, b. 19 Feb. 1944, Sydney, Australia. University Lecturer. *Education:* BSc, Agr,

University of Sydney, 1965; PhD, University of Sydney, 1970. *Appointments:* Temporary Lecturer in Biology, University of Sydney, 1968-69; Lecturer/Senior Lecturer, University of Malawi, 1969-74; Research Fellow, Institute for Photobiology of Cells and Organelles, Brandeis University, Massachusetts, 1975; Lecturer/Senior Lecturer, Macquarie University, 1976-. *Memberships:* Australian Institute of Agricultural Science; Institute of Biology; Australian Biochemical Society; Australian Society of Plant Physiologists; American Society of Plant Physiology. *Publications:* Malawi Certificate of Education, Biology, Pupils Workbooks, and Teachers Guides, Years 3 and 4, editor; 12 other publications in plant physiology, five in biology education, 14 radio programmes. *Honours:* Association of Colleges of Agriculture in the Philippines, including Plaque of Appreciation, 1979. *Hobbies:* Roses. *Address:* 28, Victoria Street, Epping, New South Wales, Australia 2121.

REED, Peter Alfred, b. 15th June, 1921. Northumberland, England. Psychiatrist. m. Margaret Vera Jones, 22nd Oct. 1949, 1 son, 1 daughter. *Education:* University College and Medical School, London; LRCP, MRCS, England, 1945; MB,BS, London, 1949; DPM, 1957; FRANZCP, 1979. *Appointments:* Senior Physchiatric Registrar, St. Mathews Hospital, Staffs, 1957; Senior Medical Officer, Ballarat Mental Hospital, Victoria Australia, 1958-61; Psychiatrist Superintendent, Swanbourne Hospital, Western Australia, 1972-81. *Publications:* Contributed to paper on Serum Pyridoxal, Folate & Vitamin B12 Levels in institutionalized epileptics, with R.E. Davis and B.K. Smith; Published in Epilepsia, 1975; *Honours:* Bucknill University Scholarhsip, 1939-46. *Hobbies:* Music; Gardening. *Address:* 55, Boulevarde, Floreat Park, West Australia, 6014.

REES, Merlyn, b. 18th Dec. 1920, Cilfynydd, South Wales. Member of Parliament. m. Colleen Faith Cleverly, 26th Dec. 1949, 3 sons. *Education:* Teachers Certificate, London University, 1940; BSc, London University, 1949; MSc, London University, 1954. *Appointments:* Form Teacher, Harrow Weald Grammer School, 1949-59; Parliamentary Secretary to James Callaghan, Chancellor of the Exchequer, 1963; Under Secretary of State Army, 1964-66; Under Secretary of State, RAF, 1966-68; Under Secretary of State, Home Office, 1968-70; Shadow Spokesman, Northern Ireland, 1971-79; Secretary of State, Northern Ireland, 1974-76; Home Secretary, 1976-79; Shadow Home Secretary. 1979-80; Shadow Spokesman on Energy. *Memberships:* Joined Labour Party, 1939; Served RAF 1941-46, Demobilised, Squadron Leader; President, Students Union, Goldsmiths College London, 1940; *Publications:* The Public Sector in the Mixed Economy, 1972. *Hobbies:* Reading; Walking. *Address:* House of Commons, London, SW1. England.

REESE, Willard Francis, b. 7th Sept. 1925, Janesville, Wisconsin, USA. Professor, Author, Actor, Inventor. m. Barbara Jane Reese. *Education:* BSc. US Merchant Marine Academy, 1944; BEd, University of Wisconsin, Whitewater; MA & EdD, University of Northern Colorado. *Appointments:* Lab School, University of Northern Colorado, 1954-59; University of Alberta, 1960-66; University of Dacca, East Pakistan, 1966-68; University of Alberta, 1968-72; Chelsea College of Science and Technology Visiting, 1972-73; University of Alberta, 1974-. *Memberships:* President, Think Metric Association Limited; Past President 7 Parts Club; Executive, Canadian Authors; Many offices held in National and International organisations in the past. *Creative Works:* Money Tree, LeBel Publishers, 1977; Illustrated Science Test, 1969; Over 100 TV & Radio shows for CBC, METTA, CFRN, and ACCESS Radio and T.V. Published in over 30 different journals. *Honours:* Citation Royal Department of Education, Kathmandu Nepal, 1968; Gold Medal Mayor's Award, Prague, Czechoslovakia, 1971; Consultant's Citation, Institute of Education and Research, Dacca, East Pakistan, 1968; Meritorius Teaching Award, Weld Country Colorado, 1952. *Address:* Room 352 Education Building South, Department of Elementary Education, University of Alberta, Alberta T6G 2G5, Canada.

REFSHAUGE Sir William (Dudley) b. 3 Apr. 1913. Victoria, Australia. Medical. m. Helen E. 29 Aug. 1942, 4 sons, 1 daughter. *Education:* MB,BS University of Melbourne, 1938; FRCOG, 1961; FRACS, 1962; FRACP, 1963; FRACMA, 1968. FRACOG, 1978. *Ap-*

pointments: Medical Superintendent, Royal Womens Hospital, Melbourne 1948-51; Deputy Director General, Australian Army Medical, Services, 1951-55; Director General, Army Medical Services, 1955-60; Director General, Australian Department of Health, 1960-73; Secretary General, World Medical Association, 1973-76; Hon. Consultant, Australian Foundation on Alcoholism & Drug Dependence, 1979; Chairman ACT Committe, Sir Robert Menzies Foundation for Health & Fitness & Physical Achievement, 1979; National Committee and National Executive; Chairman, Blood Transfusion Committee, ACT Branch, Australia, Red Cross Society, 1980; Chairman, ACT Branch, Australia, Red Cross Society, 1960-62; and Chairman or President of numerous other organisations. *Memberships:* Censor in Chief (RACMA) Royal Australian College of Medical Administration, 1968-73; Member: Commonwealth Club; Naval & Military Club, Melbourne; Royal Auto Club of Victoria, Melbourne Cricket Club; National Trustee, Returned Services League, 1962-73, 1976-. *Publications:* Various publications in Professional Journals. *Honours:* World War II, 1939-45, OBE, 1944; Mentioned in Despatches Four Times; CBE 1959; ED, 1965; QHP 1955-1964; Honory Fellow Royal Society of Health: Honorary Life Member, Australian Dental Association, 1976; Knight Bachelor, 1966; Campanion of Order of Australia, 1980. *Hobbies:* Rug Making; Gardening; Bowls. *Address:* 26, Birdwood Street, Hughes ACT 2605, Australia.

REGOLI, Dominik, b. 16 May, 1933. Lucca, Italy. University Professor. m. Uta, 21 June, 1968, 2 sons, 2 daughters. *Education:* MD, University of Siena, 1959; Private Docent Pharmacology, University of Lausanne, 1967. *Appointments:* Resident, Medicine, University, Siena, 1959-60; Guest Scientist, Pharmacology, Ciba, Basel, 1961-63; Guest Scientist, Pharmacology, University London, 1964-65; Assistant Professor, Pharmacology, University Lausanne; Career Investigator, MRCC Physiology, Pharmacol, University Sherbrook 1973; *Memberships:* Canadian Society of Pharmacology, 1971; British Pharmacologica Society, 1965; American Society of Pharmacol & Experimental Therapeautics 1972; Canadian Society of Hypertension. *Publications:* 200 Publications. Regoli, D., Rioux, F. and Park, W.K. Pharmacology of angiotensin. Pharmacol. Rev.26 69-123, 1974; Regoli, D. and Barabe J. Pharmacology of Bradykinin and related kinins. Pharmacol. Rev. 32: 1-46, 1980. *Honours:* Lepetit, Prize for best M.D. Thesis. Siena University, 1959; Invited speaker to Actualities Pharmacologiques, 1981, Paris University, February, 1981. *Hobbies:* Writing; Reading. *Address:* R.R. 3, Magog, Que, J1X3W4, Quebec, Canada.

REICHER, Arthur, b. 19th Aug. 1910. Nowy-Sacz, Poland. Dental Surgeon. m. 18th Dec. 1948, Stephanie Palek-Reicher. 1 son. *Education:* Doctor of Medicine and Surgery, Romania, 1946. Bachelor of Dental Science, University of Melbourne, 1954. *Appointments:* Lectured at the Universities in Poland, 1937-38; After the Second World War, lectured at the University in Bucarest Romania, Dental School; Head of Department of Esthetics and Ceramics, the same university. Since graduation at the Melbourne University self employed as a Dental Surgeon. *Memberships:* President, Australian Friends of Techion, Israel Institute of Technology, Melbourne. *Creative Works:* Metal Porcelain dental Crown, Patented in Poland, France, England No 510,893 Aug. 10,1938; is the basic invention for the VMK Crown in dentistry. To that are related the three Reicher Lines Helping the process of modeling of labial or buccal surfaces of the teeth. X Ray film developed in day light, Australian patent granted in 1955; Obstretrics Forceps prevents injury to the child during delivery, 1946; Silent railway line, 1936, 3 D Film, theory; Rotary engine; Cheap method of using solar engergy. *Hobbies:* Music; Photography; Inventions. *Address:* 3, St. Georges Road, Toorak, 3142 Victoria, Australia.

REID Gregor, b. 14 Oct. 1955, Johnstone, Scotland. Microbiologist. *Education:* BSc, 1978; PhD, 1982 (being completed). *Appointments:* Houghton Poultry Research Station, England, Temporary Vacational, Microbiology Department, 1978; Departmental Demonstrator, Massey University, 1978-82; Research Associate in Medical Microbiology, Department of Biology, University of Calgary, Canada. 1982-. *Memberships:* New Zealand Microbiological Society, 1979-82. *Creative Works:* Two Poems published, 1976 Twentieth Century Poets; Photography, prizes, 1977; Poetry Lyrics, short stories, published in papers, 1976-82; Regular university articles at Massey on Soccer, Poetry, Humour and viewpoints. *Honours:* Recipient of numerous honours and awards including: Rotary Foundation Award to New Zealand, 1981; NZMS, Best Student Award, 1980, 1981. *Hobbies:* Football; Rugby; Tennis; Music; Poems; Amateur Photography; Travel; Being a Disc Jockey. *Address:* 4, Stobs Drive, Barrhead, Glasgow, Scotland, G78 1MZ.

REMEDIOS, Manuel Maurice, b. 25th July, 1952. Hong Kong. Company General Manager. m. 16th Feb. 1974, 2 sons. *Education:* BSc, University of Washington DC USA, 1972. *Appointments:* Market Representative, Duty Free Enterprises, 1972-3; Administrator, Edmunsons Electrical Limited, 1974-6; Market Correspondent, Letraset, 1976-9; General Manager, International Art Supplies Limited, 1979-. *Memberships:* Independent Business & Professional Association of Hong Kong. *Hobbies:* Chess, Swimming; Football; Carpentry. *Address:* 266, Prince Edward Road, Hong Kong.

REMPT, Jan Dirk, b. 14 Sept 1907, Purmerend, Netherlands. Journalist and Writer. m. Elizabeth van den Bosch, 6 Sep 1933. 1 son, 1 daughter. *Education:* Diploma, State Diploma Constitutional Law; Candidatus juris, Leyden University. *Appointments:* Sub-Editor, Trade Journals, Amsterdam, Netherlands, 1930-33; Gallery Netherlands Parliment, The Hague, 1934-40; Press liaison Officer Dutch Department of Agriculture, The Hague, 1941-48; Reporter Farmer and Settler, Sydney, 1952-54; Sub-Editor Poultry Newspaper and The New World, Sydney, 1955-61; Sub-Editor, Cumberland Newspapers Ltd, 1961-63; Editor Publications Australian Government Department of Primary Industry, Canberra, 1963-72; Managing Editor, Dutch International Press, 1972-; Australian correspondent AVRO-Hilversum, Dutch radio station, Belgian Radio, Brussels. *Memberships:* Netherlands Association of Journalists, Australian Journalists Association, Farm Writers and Broadcasters' Association; Australian Society of Authors. *Publications:* Televisie: History and Future, co-author; Dutch title, Wordingsgeschiedenis en Toekomst, 1949; All About Australia, 1952. *Honours:* Honorary Life Member of the Farm Writers and Broadcaster's Association. *Hobbies:* Bush walking; Reading; Photographing. *Address:* 55-57, Fowler Road, Illawong via Menai, NSW, Australia, 2234.

RENAULT, Paul Fernand b. 21 Feb 1916, Quebec City, Barrister and Solicitor. m. Louise Morin 26 Apr 1943, 2 sons, 2 daughters. *Education:* BA, 1937, Ste- Anne de la Pocatiere College; LL.L., 1940, Laval University Quebec; McGill University, Montreal, B.Comm, 1942, *Appointments:* Read Law with St. Laurent, Cagne & Taschereau, Quebec, 1940; Called to the Bar of Quebec, 1940; Barrister & Solicitor with Ogilvy, Renault, 1942; specializing in Labour Law, 1950; Created QC, 1959. *Memberships:* Canadian Bar Association; The Bar of Montreal; Conseil du Patronat du Quebec, labour; Montreal Board of Trade, Labour Relations Section; Chambre de Commerce de Montreal; Director, Singer Company of Canada. *Hobbies:* Golf *Address:* 1545, Docteur Penfield Avenue, Appartment PH4, Montreal, Quebec, H3G 1C7.

RENE, France Albert, b. 16 Nov 1935, Mahe, Seychelles. President of the Republic of Seychelles. m. Geva Adam, 31 Aug 1975. *Education:* University of London/Admission Middle Temple, 1954; Council of Legal Education, 1956; Called to bar, 1957; London School of Economics, Political, Science & Economics, 1961. *Appointments:* Lawyer, 1958-75; Member of the legislative Council, 1965; Member for East Mahe in The Governing Council, 1967; Member for East Mahe in the Legislative Assembly, 1970-74; Minister for Works & Land Development in the Coalition Government, 1975; Prime Minister of Seychelles in the Coalition Government on Independence, 1976; President of the Republic of Seychelles on Liberation Day, 1977; First elected president of the Republic of Seychelles, 1979-. *Memberships:* Founder of the political party, Seychelles People's United Party, 1964; President of the Seychelles People's United Party, 1964-78; President of the Seychelles People's Progressive Front 1978-. *Publications:* Torch of Freedom. *Hobbies:* Gardening, Fishing. *Address:* State House, Victoria Mahe, Seychelles.

RENNIE, Inez, Lola, b. 10 Apr, 1903, Foxton, New Zealand. Housewife, Potter. m. Dr. Bruce Rennie,

FRCS, 29 Jul 1929, 1 son, 1 daughter. *Education:* Massey University Extension Classes. *Appointments:* Housewife, Potter. *Memberships:* Foundation member New Zealand; Potters Society, Wellington delegate; Potters AGM: Past President & Life Member, Wellington Arts Council; Potters Society, New Zealand Arts Council; Artist members of New Zealand Acadamy of Fine Arts. *Publications:* Potters in New Zealand and Overseas. *Hobbies:* Pottery; Gardening; Reading. *Address:* Ardowan, Featherston RD1, New Zealand.

RENTON, David Lockhart-Mure, (Rt. Hon. Lord) b. 12 Aug. 1908, Dartford, Kent, Queens Counsel. m. Clare, Ciceley, 17 July, 1947, 3 daughters. *Education:* MA, BCL, University College, Oxford, 1927-31; Barrister at Law, Lincolns Inn, 1933. *Appointments:* In practice at the bar, 1933-39; 1945-55; 1962-74. Queens Counsel, 1954; Recorder of Rochester, 1964-68; Commissioner, 1966-7; Recorder of Guildford, 1968-71; Deputy Chairman, Kent QS, 1954-55; Deputy Chairman, Essex QS, 1964-69; Served in Territorial Army, 1938; War Service 1939-45. *Memberships:* President, Statute Law Society, 1980-; Chairman of Mencap, 1978-; Treasurer of Lincolns Inn, 1979; President, Conservation Society, 1971; President, National Council for Civil Defence, 1980-. *Publications:* Numerous political, legal and literary articles and pamphlets; Royal Commission on the Constitution, 1971-73. *Honours:* Recipient of numerous honours and awards for professional services. *Hobbies:* Riding; Shooting; Lawn Tennis; Gardening. *Address:* House of Lords, London, S.W.1. England.

REY, Joseph Marcel Francis, b. 16 Oct. 1925, Mauritius, Chartered Secretary and Director. m. Marie Aimee, 27 Apr. 1949. 3 sons 1 daughter. *Education:* Institute of Chartered Secretaries and Administrators, 1960. *Appointments:* Secretary, Central Electricity Board, 1952-65; Secretary, Mauritius Sugar Producers Association, 1965-74; Director, Mauritius Employers Federation, 1974-. *Memberships:* Fellow of the Royal Society of Arts. Fellow of the Royal Economic Society; Member of the Mauritius Institute of Management, 1976-. *Hobbies:* Reading; Photography. *Address:* 34 Stanley Avenue, Quatre Bornes, Mauritius.

RHOADES, Rodney, (Commodore), b. 8 Apr. 1909, Sydney, N.S.W. Australia. Naval Officer. m. Valerie Myra Florence, 2 daughters. *Education:* R.A.N. College, Jervis Bay, N.S.W. 1923-27; Royal Naval College, Greenwich, 1929-30. *Appointments:* Junior Officer, served in various ships of the Royal Navy and Royal Australian Navy. Commanded destroyers HMAS Vendetta nd HMAS Quickmatch throughout world war II. Later as Senior Officer Frigate Flotilla in HMAS Shoalhaven, Commander of Nore Destroyer Flotilla in HMS Opportune and Captain D 10th destroyer Flotilla in HMAS Tobruk. Defence representative, New Zealand, Naval Officer in charge Western Australia and finally NO i/c Victoria. Retired 1963 and was employed till 1975 as Director of the Lord Mayors Fund for Hospitals and Charities in Melbourne. *Memberships:* Committee, Melbourne Club, 1970-75. *Honours:* Distinguished Service Cross, 1941; Mentioned in Dispatches, 1941; Danish Royal Order of Dannebrog, 1951. *Hobbies:* Gardening. *Address:* 92 Burns Road, Wahroonga, N.S.W. 2076, Australia.

RHODES, Emma Dora, b. 15 Jan. 1899, Mexborough, Musician. *Education:* Royal Academy of Music, London. *Appointments:* Music Mistress at the late Hillsborough High School, 1935; Sheffield, Hillsborough Congregational Church, 1930; Choir Mistress, Opera Ballad Songs, 1930; Active in Hillsborough Musical Life; Hillsborough Ladies Choir Mistress, Hillsborough Council Evening School, 1935-8; Assistant Adjudicator, Sheffield Musical Festival, 1935-6. *Memberships:* The late Sheffield Musical Union; Conductor of the late Ladies Choral Group; Council of Social Service; Hillsborough Good Samaritans; Passed Mannequin for worthy causes. *Honours:* Mention in Town and Country News, 1935; Honours in singing, Royal Academy of Music, 1936-7; Numerous prizes successes, 1938-9; International Who's Who in Music and Musicians Directory, 1980; The World Who's Who of Women, 1978; International Register of Profiles, 1977. *Hobbies:* Churches; The Hillsborough National Cruelty to Children; Welfare Work. *Address:* 235 Middlewood Road, Sheffield, Yorkshire, S6 4HE. England.

RHODES, James, Robert, b. 10 Apr. 1933, Murree, Pakistan. Member of Parliament and Author. m. Angela, Margaret, 18 Aug. 1956, 4 daughters. *Education:* BA, Worcester College, Oxford University; 1955, MA, 1964. *Appointments:* Assistant Clerk, House of Commons, 1955-9; Senior Clerk, House of Commons, 1959-63; Fellow of All Souls College, Oxford, 1964-8; Director of the Institute for the Study of International Organisation, University of Sussex, 1968-73; Principal Officer, Executive Office of the Secretary General of the United Nations, 1972-76; Member of Parliament (Conservative) for Cambridge, 1976. *Memberships:* Fellow, Royal Society of Literature; Fellow, Royal Historical Society; Travellers Club, London. *Publications:* Lord Randolph Churchill, 1959; An Introduction to the House of Commons, 1961; Rosebery, 1963; Gallipoli, 1965; (Ed) Chips The Diaries of Sir Henry Channon, 1967; (Ed) Memoirs of a Conservative, 1968; Churchill: A Study in Failure, 1900-39, 1970; Ambitions and Realities, 1972; The British Revolution, Vol I, 1976; Vol II, 1977. *Honours:* Llewellyn Rhys Memorial Prize, 1962; Heinemann Award of Royal Society of Literature, 1964. *Hobbies:* Sailing. *Address:* The Stone House, Great Gransden, Nr. Sandy, Bedfordshire. England.

RHODES, Peregrine Alexander, CMG, b. 14 May 1925. HM Diplomatic Service, High Commissioner, Cyprus. m. (1) Jane M. Hassel (marriage dissolved), (2) Margaret R. Page, 2 sons, 1 daughter. *Education:* Winchester College, New College, Oxford. *Appointments:* Coldstream Guards, 1944-47; Joined FO, 1950; 2nd Sec., Rangoon, 1953-56; Private Secretary to Minister of State, 1956-59; 1st Secretary Helsinki, 1962-65; FCO, 1965-68; Councellor, 1967- Study of International Organisation, Sussex University, 1968-69; Counsellor, Rome, 1970-73; E. Berlin, 1973-75; Secondment as Under Secretary Cabinet Office, 1975-78. *Honours:* Recipient of CMG, 1976. *Hobbies:* Photography; Reading. *Address:* c/o Foreign and Commonwealth Office, SW1, England.

RIBET, Marie Evariste Jaeques, b. 29 Aug. 1911, S. Mauritius. m. Marie Simone Bestel, 11 July, 1938, 1 son 5 daughters. *Appointments:* Commonwealth Police Service, 1931-71; Head of C.I.D. and special branch, Mauritius, 1955-64; Deputy Commissioner of Police, 1965-67; Commission of Police, Mauritius, 1968-71; Managing Director, Securicor, Mauritius Ltd. *Memberships:* International Police Association; International Professional Security Association; Industrial and Commercial Security Association of South Africa; Mauritius Institute of Management. *Honours:* Colonial Police Medal New Years Honour, 1949; Queens Police Medal, New Years Honour, 1969; Commander of the Most Excellent order of British Empire, 1972. *Hobbies:* Reading. *Address:* Le Caprice, Tamarin, Mauritius.

RICE, John Cracroft, b. 9 July, 1933, Norwich, England. Medical Practitioner. m. (1) Julia Ruth, 22 Nov. 1958, 1 son, 3 daughters, (2) Jennifer, 7 Feb. 1981. *Education:* MA, 1960; MB B.Chir, 1958; FRCS, 1962; FRACS, 1967. *Appointments:* ENT House Surgeon, St. Bartholomews Hospital, London, 1958; House Surgeon/House Physician, Norfolk and Norwich Hospital, 1959-60; Demonstrator, Dept. of Anatomy, University of Cambridge, 1960-61; Registrar, Royal National Throat Nose and Ear Hospital, London, 1961-62; Registrar, St. Thomas Hospital and Hospital for Sick Children, Gt. Ormond Street, London, 1963-67; ENT Surgeon, Adelaide Childrens Hospital, 1967-; Presently Chairman, Dept. ENT Surgery, Adelaide Childrens Hospital. *Memberships:* British Medical Association; Australian Medical Association; Otolaryngological Society of Australia; International Society of Audiology; Australian Acoustical Society; Australian and New Zealand Society of Occupational Medicine; The Broken Hill Club. *Hobbies:* Sailing; Music. *Address:* 15 Ilfracombe Drive, Wattle Park, South Australia, 5066, Australia.

RICHARD, Allan E, b. 7 Nov. 1931, Moncton, New Brunswick, Canada, Engineer. m. Elizabeth, 24 Sept. 1955, 2 sons, 1 daughter. *Education:* BSc, University of New Brunswick, 1955. 03 Design Engineer, Montreal Eng. Co. Ltd., 1955-61; Project Manager, Montreal Engineering Co. Ltd., Ceylon, 1961-63; Supervising Engineer, Montreal Engineering Co. Ltd., Montreal, 1963-64; Branch Manager, N. Fodor & Association, Moncton, 1964-66; Project Manager, Montreal Engineering Co. Ltd., Brazil, 1966-70; Assistant Chief Engineer, Montreal Engineering Co. Ltd., Montreal,

1970-73; Vice President - Engineering, Societe de'Ingenierie Cartier Limitee, Montreal, 1973-75; General Manager, Societe d'Ingenierie Cartier Limitee, Montreal, 1975-78; President Societe d'Ingenierie Cartier Limitee, 1979-. *Memberships:* Order of Engineers of Quebec; Engineering Institute of Canada; Institute of Electrical and Electronics Engineers. *Hobbies:* Fishing; Golf. *Address:* 20655 Lakeshore Road, Baie d'Urfe, Que, Canada, H9X 1R5.

RICHARDS, Conrad Freeston, b. 28 May, 1944, Antigua, West Indies. Barrister at Law; Solicitor of the West Indies Associated States Supreme Court. m. Claudia Evelyn Francis, 2 sons. *Education:* BSc. Economics (Honours), University of the West Indies, 1968 LLB, Hons. University of the West Indies, 1973; Legal Education Certificate, 1975. *Appointments:* Assistant to Industrialization Officer, Government of Antigua, 1968; Legal Assistant in Attorney General's Chambers, Government of Antigua, 1975; Additional Magistrate for Districts A, B and C in the State of Antigua, 1976; Registrar of the High Court of Justice and Provost Marshall for the State of Antigua and also a deputy registrar of the West Indies Associated States Court of Appeal, 1977; Barrister at Law in private practice. *Memberships:* Secretary, Antigua Bar Association; Law Reform Commission, Antigua; Director, Four Island Air Services Limited; Director, Antigua Sugar Industry Corporation. *Honours:* Mill Reef Scholarship, 1965. *Hobbies:* Swimming; Table Tennis; Cricket. *Address:* Wireless, Clare Hall, St. Johns, Antigua.

RICHARDS, James Maude, b. 13 Aug. 1907, London, Author; Journalist; Historian. m. Kathleen, 31 July, 1954, 1 son deceased, 1 daughter by previous marriage. *Education:* AA Diploma, 1929, ARIBA 1930. 03 Architect, (London, Dublin, Canada and US), 1929-33; Assistant Editor, The Architects Journal, 1933-35; Assistant Editor, The Architectural Review, 1935-37; Editor The Architectural Review, 1937-71; Architectural Correspondent, the Times, 1947-71; Visiting Professor of Architecture, University of Leeds, 1957-58; Editor, Publications Division, Ministry of Information, 1942-43; Director of Publications, Ministry of Information Middle East, Cairo, 1943-46. *Memberships:* Fellow, Society of Antiquaries; Athenaeum Club, London; Royal Society of Arts. *Publications:* High Street, 1938; Introduction to Modern Architecture, 1940; The Castles on the Ground, 1946; The Functional Tradition, 1958; An Architectural Journey in Japan, 1962; The Professions: Architecture, 1974; Eight Hundred Years of Finnish Architecture, 1978; Memoirs of an Unjust Fella, 1980; Goa, 1981; The National Trust Book of English Architecture, 1981; Editor of several books. *Honours:* CBE, 1966; Knighthood, 1972; Chevalier (First Class), Order of the White Rose of Finland, 1959; Gold Medal, Mexican Institute of Architects, 1963; Bicentenary Medal, Royal Society of Arts, 1971. *Hobbies:* Travel. *Address:* 29 Fawcett Street, London, SW1O. England.

RICHARDS, Novelle Hamilton, b. 24 Nov. 1917, Antigua, West Indies, Diplomat. m. Ruby Beryl Viola, 1 Sept. 1958, 4 sons, 1 daughter. *Education:* Diploma in Journalism, London Polytechnic Institute, 1951. *Appointments:* Editor, Workers Voice Newspaper, Antigua; Minister of Communications and Works Federal Government of West Indies; President, Antigua Senate; Diplomatic Commissioner for West Indies Associated States to Canada; Director of Trade and Tourism in Canada for Government of Antigua. *Memberships:* Honorary, Mill Reef Club, Antigua; Royal Society Commonwealth, Montreal; Canadian Club of Montreal. *Publications:* Socialism and the West Indies; The Struggle and the Conquest Parts 1 and 2; The Twilight Hour (Novel); Tropic Gems, Poetry; Vines of Freedom; Author National Anthem of Antigua and Barbuda. *Hobbies:* Writing; Bridge. *Address:* 1 Oriole Road, 310, Toronto, Ontario, Canada, M4V 2E6.

RICHARDS, Peter Netherton, b. 10 Apr. 1922, Ballarat, Victoria, Australia, Metallurgical Engineer. m. Rae, 7 Dec. 1946. 3 sons. *Education:* B Met E. 1943; ME, 1962; D.App. Sc. 1968; *Appointments:* Metallurgist, Commonwealth Department of Supply; Lecturer, Royal Melbourne Institute of Technology; Senior Lecturer, Port Pirie School of Mines; John Lysaght (Australia) Limited: Senior Research Officer; Assistant Superintendent, Research; Manager, Research; General Manager, Research and Technology. *Memberships:* Fellow, Australian Academy of Technological Sciences; Fellow, American Society of Metals; Fellow Institution of Metallurgists; Chartered Engineer; Australian Institute of Metals; American Institute Mining and Metallurgy; American Association, Iron and Steel Engineers. *Publications:* Numerous professional papers. *Honours:* Simon Frazer (the younger) Scholar; Florence Taylor Medallist; Claude A. Stewart Medallist. *Hobbies:* Swimming; Sailing. *Address:* 26 The Terrace, Newcastle, 2300, NSW, Australia.

RICHARDS, Ross James, b. 15 Mar. 1931, Sydney, NSW, Australia, Scientist, Defence Food Science Adviser. m. Patricia, Lois, 7 Apr. 1956, 3 daughters. *Education:* BSc. Agr(Hons), Sydney University, 1955; PhD, Ohio State University, 1960. *Appointments:* New South Wales Department of Agriculture, 1955-74; Armed Forces Food Science Establishment, Department of Defence, 1974. *Memberships:* Australian Institute of Food Science and Technology; Nutrition Society of Australia; Australian Society of Dairy Technology; State Councillor and Chairman, National Association of Testing Authorities. *Publications:* Over 30 publications in Scientific and Technical journals. *Hobbies:* Golf; Gardening. *Address:* 15 Mary Street, Scottsdale, Tasmania, Australia, 7254.

RICHARDS, William Leslie, b. 28 May, 1916, Capel Isaac, Llandeilo, Dyfed, Deputy headmaster. m. Mair Pamela Jones, 15 Dec. 1942, 1 son, 3 daughters. *Education:* BA Honours First Class, 1938; Diploma in Education, 1939; MA, 1947. *Appointments:* Student-Lecturer, UCW Aberystwyth, 1939-40; Senior Welsh Master, Grammar School, Llandeilo, 1947-69; Head of Welsh Department, County Secondary School, Llandeilo, 1969-81; Deputy Headmaster, 1975-81. *Memberships:* Honorary Druid, Bardic Circle, Royal National Eisteddfod of Wales. Honorable Society of Cymmrodorion; Welsh Panel of Welsh Joint Education Committee. *Publications:* Poetry: Telyn Teilo, 1957; Bro A Bryniau, 1963; Dail yr Hydre, 1968; Adledd, 1973; Ffurfiau'r Awen (6th Edition 1979); Novels: Yr Etifeddion (2nd Edition 1976); Llanw A Thrai 1958; Cynffon o Wellt, 1960; Gwaith Dafydd Llwyd, 1964; Cymraeg Heddiw (4 Vols. with others - 1965-70); Numerous articles in Welsh Language journals. *Honours:* T.E. Ellis Memorial Essay Prize UCW, 1939; Sir John Williams Research Studentship, 1946; Sir Ellis Griffith Memorial Prize, 1965; Fellow International Autobiographical Association, 1980. *Hobbies:* Reading. *Address:* 12 Thomas Street, Llandeilo, Dyfed, SA19 6LB. Wales.

RICHARDSON, Gordon Dalyell, b. 23 Nov. 1917, Librarian & Archivist (Retired). m. (1) Yvonne L Spence (deceased), 1 June 1940, 1 son 2 daughters; (2) Ruth H. Robertson, 17 Dec. 1966. *Education:* MA, Sydney, 1951; FLAA, 1963. *Appointments:* Infantry Officer, Australian Imperial Force, 1940-45, Senior Assistant, State Library of New South Wales, 1946; Dixson Librarian, 1954-58; Deputy Principal Librarian, 1954-59; Mitchell Librarian, 1958-73; Principal Librarian & Executive Member, Library Board of New South Wales, 1959-73; Principal Archivist, Archives Office of New South Wales, 1961-73. *Memberships:* General Secretary, Library Association of Australia, 1954-56; Vice President, 1964-66, President, 1967-68; Vice President, Royal Australian Historical Society, 1956-57; 1961-63; Councillor National Trust of Australia, 1960-73; Australian Advisory Council on Bibl. Services, 1956-73; Chairman 1970-73; N.S.W.. Film Council Advisory Board on Adult Education; Geographical Names Board, Variously 1959-73; Chairman, Australian UNESCO Committee for Libraries, 1967-71; Councillor, Inverness Field Club, 1981. *Honours:* OBE, 1970; HON. FRAHS, 1978. *Hobbies:* Gardening; Motoring; Genealogy. *Address:* 16 Eriskay Road, Inverness, IV2 3LX, Scotland

RICHARDSON, Henry, Lorimer, b. 18 June 1902, Feilding, New Zealand. Retired Agricultural Research Chemist. m. Katherine Jane Fisher, 19 May1938. *Education:* BSc, MSc (1st Class Hons) Victoria University College, Wellington, New Zealand, 1919-24; MSc, Empire Exhibition School, 1924; PhD, Imperial College, London, 1926. *Appointments:* Assistant Chemist, Rothamstead Experimental Station, 1926-37; Research Bureau, Ministry of Agriculture, Free China, 1937-43; Research Grant, British Council, 1943-45; ICI Limited, Eventually Manager, Overseas Agricultural Department, 1945-61; Project Manager, The Fertilizer Pro-

gramme, Food and Agricultural Organisation of the UN, 1961-67; Writing a report, 1967-70; Guest Professor, University of Nanking, Chengtu, 1938-43; Part-Time Editor, Empire Journal of Experimental Agriculture, 1950-53. *Memberships:* Life Fellow, Royal Society of Chemistry; Life Fellow, Royal Geographical Society; Society of Chemical Industry; The Fertiliser Society; International Society of Soil Science; New Zealand Society of Soil Science; The Climbers Club, London; The Farmers Club, London; The Heraldry Society, New Zealand. *Publications:* Number of Scientific and Technical papers on Organic Chemistry, Soils and Fertilizers, Agriculture, Geography, Geology, Heraldry; Monograph, Soils and Agriculture of Szechwan, 1942. *Honours:* Diploma of Distinction, IBC, 1980; A personal grant of arms from the College of Arms, London, 1970. *Hobbies:* Hill Walking; Bush Tramping; Cycling; Camping; Motoring; Rock and Alpine Climbing; Gliding; Bird Watching; Heraldry; Swimming; Playing Rugby Football; Cricket; Travelling; Psychology; Reading; Writing. *Address:* Richardson's Stead, Mullet Point Road, Warkworth RD2, New Zealand.

RICHARDSON, Henry, Walter, Egyarko, b. 15 Nov. 1941, Nsawam, Ghana. Architect, Urban Designer-City and Regional Planner. m. Margaret Thandiwe Chinamora Richardson, 22 Mar. 1975. *Education:* Achimota School, Achimota, Ghana, 1955-61; Diploma, Phillips Academy, Andover, Massachusetts, USA, 1962-63; BArch, 1968, MArch, 1970, Cornell University, Ithaca New York, 1963-71. *Appointments:* Teaching Assistant, 1968-69, Instructor, 1969-70, Assistant Professor, 1971-76, Associate Professor with tenure, 1967-, Assistant Dean, 1971-76; Associate Dean, 1976-80, Acting Chairman of the Department of Architecture, 1979-80, Cornell University, Ithaca, New York. Urban Renewal Agency, Puerto Rico, 1968-69; United Nations Center for Housing and Planning, 1970; Anton J Egner and Associates, Architects and Planners, Ithaca, New York, 1971-76; US AID/Cornell University Technical Assistance Mission to Ghana, 1976; Consultant on Solar Energy Research, AIA Research Corporation, Washington DC, 1979-80; Energy Consultant, International Solar Power Company, San Antonio, Texas, 1979-; Intellect Associates, Consultant, Lagos, Nigeria, 1976-. *Memberships:* American Institute of Certified Planners; American Planning Association; International Association of Housing Science; Gargoyle Society; Rotary International, New York. *Publications:* The Urban System of Ghana, 1971; Basic Housing in Ghana, 1975; Rural Housing Delivery Networks in Ghana, 1976; Solar Cities in America, 1980; New Towns in Africa; *Honours:* First Prize, Achimota School, 1955-1961; Ghana's Ambassador, Experiment in International Living, Trip to the USA, 1961; Charles Goodwin Sands Medal for excellence in architectural design, Cornell University, 1963-68; Research Fellowship, Institute for International Order, 1970. *Hobbies:* Soccer; Tennis; Music; Jazz; Photography; Reading; Writing Poetry; Sculpting. *Address:* 325 North Albany Street, Ithaca, New York, 14850 USA.

RICHARDSON, Melvin Orde Wingate, b. 26 Sept. 1944, London. University Lecturer/Materials Consultant. m. J S Richardson, 26 Oct. 1968, 2 sons. *Education:* B Tech (Hons), 1968; PhD, 1972. *Appointments:* Department of Materials Engineering and Design, Loughborough University; Scientific Branch, Greater London Council; Ault and Wiberg Limited; ERDE, Ministry of Defence; GPO, Materials Branch; London Rubber Company Limited. *Memberships:* Chairman, Sub-Committee, Building and Construction Group of the Plastics and Rubber Institute, FPRI; C.Chem, FRSC. *Publications:* Author of over 40 published scientific papers and learned journal articles and patents; Author of the book, Polymer Engineering Composites, Applied Science Publishers, 1977. *Hobbies:* Skiing; Swimming. *Address:* 47 Tynedale Road, Loughborough, Leicestershire, LE11 3TA, England.

RICHARDSON, Sam, Scruton, b. 31 Dec. 1919, Gosport, England. Administrator. m. Sylvia May McNeil, 1 Apr. 1949, 2 sons, 1 daughter. *Education:* BA, Politics, Philosophy, Economics, Trinity College, Oxford, 1940; MA, 1945; Barrister at Law, 1959; LLD, Nigeria, 1966 Courses in Arabic, 1946-55. *Appointments:* District Commissioner, Sudan Political Service, 1946-54; HM Overseas Civil Service, 1954-66; Attorney General's Chambers, North Nigeria; Director, Institution of Administration, Deputy Vice Chancellor,

Ahmedu Bells University, 1961-67; Professor of Public Administration, Vice Chancellor, University of Mauritius, 1967-68; Principal, Canberra College of Education, Australia, 1968-. *Memberships:* Vice President, International Association of Science, Institute of Administrators'; President, Australian Conference of Prinicipals, 1979-80; President, Conference of Directors Central Institutes of Technology, Australia, 1980; President, Rotary Club, Canberra, 1975. 05 Contributed to various journals. *Honours:* State Scholarship, 1937; Senior Scholarship, LCC, 1938; Mention in Despatches for distinguished service, Burma, 1943; OBE, 1960; CBE, 1965; Officer in the Order of Australia, 1980. *Hobbies:* Travel; Book Reviewing; Gardening. *Address:* 3 Fuller Street, Deakin, Canberra ACT2600, Australia.

RICHEMONT, Robert de, b. 20 Feb. 1925, Lille, France. Company Director, Oil Consultant. m. Martha S Willard, 12 Nov. 1949, 1 son, 3 daughters. *Education:* Law Degree, Paris University, 1946; Diploma, Institute of 'Etudes Politiques, Paris, 1947. *Appointments:* Compagnie Francaise des Petroles, Marketing Manager, Morocco, 1953-55, Assistant General Manager, South Africa, 1955-59, Acting General Manager, Australia, 1959, Director, Italy and Austria, 1960-64; Gulf Oil Corporation, Managing Director, Italy, 1964-67, Vice President, Marketing, Eastern Hemisphere, London, 1967-71, Vice President and World Wide Marketing Co-Ordinator, Pittsburgh, 1971; ISAB Spa Genoa, Managing Director, 1971-77; Vice Chairman, Garrone Group, Genoa, 1978-81. *Memberships:* Rand Club, Johannesburg, Circolo Della Caccia, Rome, Hurlingham Club, London. *Honours:* Recipient of Croix de Guerre, World War 2. *Address:* 49 Grosvenor Square, London, W1X 9AA, England.

RIDE, Edwin, John, Lindsay, b. 12 Nov. 1931, Hong Kong. Diplomat. m. Sandra Jean Stokes, 31 Dec. 1976, 2 sons, 2 daughters. *Education:* Joined Australian Department of External Affairs, Canberra, 1956; Third Secretary, New Delhi, 1957-60; Second Secretary, Rangoon 1966-68; First Secretary, later Charge d'Affaires, Lima, 1968-70; First Secretary, Ankara, 1970-72; Head, South Pacific Section, Department of Foreign Affairs, 1973-74; Deputy High Commissioner, Ottawa, 1974-78; Head, USA Section Department of Foreign Affairs, 1978-79; High Commissioner for Australia to Tanzania, Zambia and Mauritius since 1979; Ambassador, Madagascar, 1980, due to present credentials as High Commissioner to Malawi in August or September, 1981. *Publications:* Author of BAAG Hong Kong Resistance 1942-45, due to be published by Oxford University Press, Hong Kong, September 1981. *Honours:* Member, General Division of the Order of Australia, AM, 1980. *Hobbies:* Photography; Tennis; Skin and Scuba Diving; Theatre. *Address:* c/- Department of Foreign Affairs, Canberra, ACT, 2600, Australia.

RIDE, William, David, Lindsay, b. 8 May 1926, London, England. Zoologist. m. Margaret Eileen Stewart, 25 July 1951, 3 sons, 2 daughters. *Education:* Scotch College, Melbourne, Australia; University of Hong Kong, 1949-51; BA, 1954, MA, DPhil, University of Oxford, England, 1957. *Appointments:* Demonstrator, Vertebrate Zoologist, University of Oxford, 1954-57; Hulme Lecturer, Zoology, Brasenose College, Oxford, 1955-57; Director, WA Museum, Perth, Australia, 1957-75; Director, Bureau of Flora and Fauna, ABRS, Department of Science and Environment, Canberra, Australia, 1975-80; College Fellow in Life Sciences, Canberra College of Advanced Education, Canberra, Australia, 1980. *Memberships:* President, Commonwealth Association of Museums, London, 1974; President, International Commission on Zoological Nomenclature, 1973; Executive, International Union of Biological Sciences, 1976; Fellow, Linnean Society of London, 1957; Scientific Fellow, Zoological Society of London, 1956; Fellow, royal Society of Arts, 1974; President, Section D, Zoology, ANZAAS, 1968; University of Western Australia, 1965-75; Honorary Reader in Zoology, University of Western Australia, 1962; Trustee, The Australian War Memorial, 1975; Council, Canberra College of Advanced Education, 1978; The Commonwealth Club, 1980. *Publications:* A Guide to Australian Native Mammals, 1970; Index to the Genera and Species of Fossil Mammalia Described from Australia, with Mahoney, J.A., 1975, and numerous papers in scientific journals. *Honours:* Recipient of Christopher Welch Research Scholar, University of Oxford, 1953. *Hobbies:* Biological Australiana; Choral Music.

Address: 29 Glasgow Street, HUGHES, A.C.T., 2605, Australia.

RIDGEON, John, b. 7 Feb. 1944, Barking, Essex, England. Musician. m. Delia Norma Shambrook, 28 Mar. 1970, 1 daughter. *Education:* LRAM, ARCM, LTCL, Royal Academy of Music. *Appointments:* Senior Music Adviser, Leicestershire; Teaching Consultant to the Guildhall School of Music & Drama, London. *Memberships:* National Association of Brass Teachers in Education, Chairman. *Publications:* Brass for Beginners; How Brass players do it; Scene one for the Brass Player; Scene Two for the Brass Player; Nine Miniatures; Six Lip Flexibilities for Tuba; Six Lip Flexibilities for Trombone; New Horizons for Beginner Brass. *Address:* Spinneys, Wakerley Road, Oakham, Rutland, Leics, England.

RIDLEY, Annette (Reed) b. 14 Oct. 1924, Wellington, New Zealand. Industrial Chemist now Florist. m. 15 Dec. 1949, 4 sons. *Education:* BSC, Otago, New Zealand, 1949; Dip.Ed, Massey, New Zealand, 1975; MNZIC, 1975. *Appointments:* Owner/Operator, Tokoroa Florist Business, 1977; Teaching, Tokoroa High School, Part-time Teaching of Pianoforte, 1973-77; Teacher, Manurewa High School, 1968-71; Lecturer, Loreto Teachers College, Auckland, 1966-67; Teacher & Student, Melbourne Conservatorium of Music, 1962-65; Teacher, Secondary School, Secretary, NZFUW Wellington 1956-57; Assistant Chemist, Chemistry Division DSIR, 1942-49. *Memberships:* Institute Chemistry, New Zealand; Professional Florists Association; Teleflower Inc. *Hobbies:* Landscape Painting; Floristry; Piano Playing; Pipe Organ Playing; Golf; Tennis; Accordion; Sewing; Gardening; Contract Bridge. *Address:* 27 Ben Alder Crescent, Tokoroa, New Zealand

RIDLEY, Joan Metcalf, (Mrs. W. St. John Oliphant). b. 23 March, 1931, Co. Durham, U.K. Psychiatrist. m. 27 August, 1966, 1 son, 1 daughter. *Education:* LRCP, MRCS, 1955; MB BS (London) 1955; DRCOG. Royal Colleges London and England, 1957; DPM, Royal Colleges, 1960; DPM, Durham, 1960; Founder Member, MRC Psych. 1971; MRANZC, Psych, 1978; FRANZC, Psych. 1980. *Appointments:* Resident House Officer, London; Registrar Psychiatry, Durham Univerzity Medical School, Dept., Psychiatry, Newcastle/Tyne; RMO, Guy's Hospital, London; Senior Registrar, Royal Free, London; Research Fellow, Royal Free, London; Consultant Psychiatrist, Northampton, England; Medical Superintendant, Baillie Henderson Hospital, Toowoomba, Queensland, Australia.- *Memberships:* Chairman, Health, Welfare and Rehabilitation Sub-Committee, Toowoomba; Past Vice-Chairman, University Womens Federation, Toowoomba Branch; IYDP Committee, University Womens Federation Soroptomists, Toowoomba; Member Institute of Group Analysts Royal College of Psychiatrists Section for the Psychiatry of Old Age; Royal Australian & New Zealand College of Psychiatrists Inter-Professional Relationship Committee; Darling Downs Rifle Club. *Creative Works:* Painting for own pleasure and relaxation. *Address:* G.P.O. Box 405, Toowoomba, 4350, Queensland, Australia.

RIECK, Walter Edward, b. 3 Jan. 1926, Port Augusta, South Australia. m. Pamela J. Hanton, 12 Dec. 1966, 1 son, 3 daughters. *Education:* Australian Schools. *Appointments:* Postal Clerk; Shearer; Contractor; Pastoralist. *Memberships:* J.P. South of Australia; Order of Buffaloes; Masonic Orders Rose Croix - Chapter - Craft. *Address:* Merty Merty Station, Near Leigh Creek, South Australia, 5731.

RILEY Douglas Herbert b. 22 Sept. 1936, Sydney, Australia. Information Processing.m. Patricia L. Manning, 23 Dec. 1963, 1 son, 1 daughter. *Education:* Physics Diploma, Sydney Technical College, 1963. *Appointments:* Technical Assistant, Commonwealth Scientific & Industrial Research Organisation, 1954; Customer Engineer, Programmer, Senior Programmer, Systems Engineer, IBM Australia Ltd., 1958; Programming and Systems Manager, Manager Systems & Data Services, International Harvester, 1967; Systems Engineer, IBM Australia Ltd., 1975; Director, Johnston Brown & Associates Pty. Ltd., 1977. Other Companies; Director, Fountain Management Services; JBA (HK) Pty. Ltd.; JBA (Singapore) Pty. Ltd.; JBA Inc.; Hotel Information Systems. *Hobbies:* Photography; Music.

Address: 36, Karina Crescent, Belrose, New South Wales 2085, Australia.

RILEY, Francis Patrick, b. 6 Feb. 1929, Young, New South Wales, Australia. Hospital Executive. m. Pamela M. Haggerston, 26 Dec. 1953, 4 sons, 2 daughters. *Education:* Associate Australian Institute of Management, 1974; Associate Fellow Australian Institute of Management, 1978; Fellow Australian Institute of Management, 1980; Department Technical Education Certificate, Hospital Administration, 1978; licentiate Australian College Health Service Administrators, 1978. *Appointments:* Self-employed, hotels and small business, 1954-65; Assistant Secretary, Manickville District Hospital, 1965-68; Deputy Chief Executive of Bathurst District Hospital, 1968-74; Deputy Chief Executive Officer, The Womens Hospital, Crown Street, 1974-75; Chief Executive Officer, The Womens Hospital, Crown Street, 1975-81-. *Memberships:* Assistant Registrar, Australian College of Health Service Administration; Australian Institute of Management. *Hobbies:* Boating; Rugby; Golf; Cricket. *Address:* 79 Perouse Road, Randwick, New South Wales, 2031, Australia.

RILEY, James Arnold, b. 27 Jan. 1932, Liverpool, England, Mechanical Engineer. m. Elizabeth A. Monk, 4 Aug, 1956, 1 son, 1 daughter. *Education:* B.Sc, Bristol University, 1951-55; MSc. Birmingham University, 1958-59; PhD. Glasgow University, 1970-73; Chartered Engineer, 1965; MI Mech.E., 1961. *Appointments:* Engineer II, Atomic Weapons Research Est., Berkshire, 1955-63; Senior Lecturer, Liverpool Polytechnic, 1963-66; Lecturer in Engineering, Strathclyde University, Scotland, 1966-74; Principal Lecturer, Kingston Polytechnic, Kingston Upon Thames, 1974-. *Memberships:* Founder Member and Member of the National Executive of the Association for Sandwich Education and Training. *Publications:* Contributor of reviews, monographs, articles to professional journals and conferences. *Honours:* Whitworth Society Prize Awarded, 1950; Honorary Bootle Major Scholar, 1951-55; Technical State Scholar, 1951-55. *Hobbies:* Rebuilding and driving Classic cars. *Address:* 366, Vale Road, Ash Vale, Near Aldershot, Hants, England.

RILEY, John Gerard, b. 13 Oct. 1927, Tamworth, New South Wales, Australia. m. Margaret Rogers, 19 June, 1963, 1 son, 2 daughters. *Education:* Christian Bros. College, Tamworth, Sydney University, 1946-48. *Appointments:* East-West Airlines, 1949; General Manager, East-West Airlines, 1960; Director, 1974; Managing Director, 1976; Chairman, 1980. *Memberships:* American National Club; Tamworth Club, past President; Australian Club. *Honours:* Order British Empire, 1979. *Address:* 32, Daymar Place, Castlecove, New South Wales, 2069, Australia.

RILEY, William John, b. 7 Feb, 1934, Perth, Western Australia. Clinical Biochemist. m. Lorraine P. Barker, 27 Feb, 1960, 1 son, 2 daughters. *Education:* BSc, (Honours) University of Western Australia, 1955; PhD, University of Western Australia, 1966. *Appointments:* Laboratory Technologist, 1956-59; Senior Laboratory Technologist, 1959-63, Chemist and Research Officer, 1963-65, Assistant Biochemist, 1965-68, Biochemist, deputy Head of Department, 1968, Royal Perth Hospital; Lecturer, Perth Technical College, 1959-65; Visiting Scientist, Middlesex Hospital, 1970. *Memberships:* Fellow, Foundation Fellowship conferred in 1968, Member of Council, 1967-70, 1979-, Registrar, Board of Examiners, 1977-79, Chairman, Board of Examiners, 1979-, Chairman Education Committee, 1971-74, Australian Association of Clinical Biochemists; Australian Biochemical Society, Endocrinol Society of Australia; Australian Diabetes Society; South of Perth Yacht Club, Milligan 150 Club. *Publications:* Contributed to various professional journals. *Hobbies:* Sailing; gardening. *Address:* 27, McLeod Road, Applecross, Western Australia, 6153.

RILEY, William Joseph, b. 16 Sept. 1920, Chigago, USA. Professional Engineer. m. Alice M. Crook, 8 May, 1948, 6 sons, 3 daughters. *Education:* B.Eng. McGill University , 1948. *Appointments:* Project Engineer, International Harvester Co.1948-50; Assistant Works Manager, Can. Gen. Elec. 1950-53; Works Manager, Sperry Gyroscope, 1953-55, Chief Engineer, Sperry Gyroscope, 1955-62; Director, General Precision, 1962-65; Chief Engineer, CAE Industries, 1965-67; Assistant Director, Conductron, 1967-69; V.P. Can-

Pac. Consulting, 1969-77; G.M. Can. Pac. Investments, 1977-78; President & Chief Exective Officer, Halifax Industries Ltd., 1978-81; President, Ubigue Riley Enterprises Limited, 1981-. *Memberships:* President Professional Engineers of Quebec, 1959-60; Vice-President Can. Society for Mechanical Engineering, 1979-82; Councillor, Engineering Institute of Canada, 1959; Member Professional Engineers of Nova Scotia; American Management Association; Associate Member, U.S.Naval Institute; Member, Halifax Club; Ashburn Golf Club. *Publications:* Contributed to various professional journals. *Honours:* Military Cross, 1944; Canadian Forces Decoration, 1955; Fellow, Engineering Institute of Canada, 1981. *Hobbies:* Golf; Cross Country Skiing. *Address:* 6589, South Street, Halifax, Nova Scotia, Canada, B3H 1V1.

RINGADOO, Veerasamy b. 9 Sept. 1920, Port Louis, Mauritius. Barrister-at-law, Minister of Finance. m. Lydie Vadamootoo, 1 son, 1 daughter. *Education:* Law degree, London School of Economics, 1949. *Appointments:* Minister of Labour and Social Security, 1959-64; Minister of Education, 1964-67; Minister of Agriculture, 1967-68; Minister of Finance, 1968-. *Memberships:* 2nd Vice-President of the African Development Bank, 1974-75; Chairman of Board of Governors of the African Development Fund and African Development Bank, 1977-78; Governor of the International Monetary Fund and African Development Bank. *Honours:* Knighted in 1975; received the Award of Officier, Ordre National Malgache, 1969; Doctor in law, Honoris Causa, of the University of Mauritius, 1975; Honorary Fellow of the London School of Economics , 1976; D. Lit, Honoris Causa, Andhra University, India, 1978. *Hobbies:* Reading. *Address:* Farquhar Avenue, Quatre Bornes, Mauritius.

RINGLANS, Frank Lindsay, b. 22 June, 1923, Belfast, Ireland.m. 5 April, 1952, 2 sons, 1 daughter. 02 RAF, 1941-46; Cambridge Matriculation. *Appointments:* Samuel Stevenson & sons, FFRIBA, Belfast; P.W.D. Nigeria, 1953-61; Native Authorities Housing Corp.1961-70; Northern Nigeria Housing Corp. 1970-74; Northern Nigeria Development Corp., 1974-77; Comprehensive Design and Planning Consultants, 1977-. *Memberships:* Associate RIBA; Member Nigerian Institute of Architects; Life Member, Association of Housing COrps. of Nigeria; Life Member Kaduna Rugby Football Club; Royal Ulster Yacht Club. *Honours:* OBE, 1977 for services to the development of Northern Nigeria. *Hobbies:* Golf *Address:* 2A Dawaki Road, Kaduna, Nigeria.

RIORDAN, James William, b. 10 Oct. 1936, Portsmouth, England. University Lecturer. m. Rashida Davletshina, 1 July, 1965, 1 son, 4 daughters. *Education:* B.Soc.Sc. University of Birmingham, 1959; PGCE, University of London, 1960, Dip. Political Science University of Moscow, 1963; PhD, University of Birmingham, 1975. *Appointments:* Barman, brewery cratestacker; RAF Junior Technician; Danceband Musician; Commercial Salesman; Postman; Translator; Lecturer at College; Polytechnic and University; Senior Lecturer in Russian Studies at the University of Bradford, England. *Memberships:* Council Member, Society for Cultural Relations with USSR; Council Member, International Sports History Association. *Publications:* Sport in Soviet Society, 1977; Sport under Communism, 1978; Soviet Sport: Background to the Olympics, 1980. Author of Folk Tales, Central Russian Tales, 1976; Tales from Tartary, 1977; Mistress of the Copper Mountain, 1975. *Honours:* Soviet Peace Prize for contribution to peace and understanding through translations and publication of Soviet children's and folk literature, 1979. *Hobbies:* Writing for children; Collecting folk tales; Sport. *Address:* 15, Bankfield Drive, Shipley, W. Yorkshire, England.

RISKE, Marcus, b. 4 April, 1906, Edinburgh, U.K. Educator, (Retired). m. Dorothy M. Carmalt, 1937, 2 sons, 2 daughters. *Education:* MA (Honours), 1931, Diploma of Education; 1939, Victoria University of Wellington, Teachers A Certificate, Wellington. Teacher's College. *Appointments:* Primary Schools, NZ, 1926-44; Lecturer in Psychology, Victoria University, 1939-45; Wellington Technical College, 1945-61; Head of Day School, 1958-61; Visiting Lecturer in Maths, University of Illinois, USA, 1959-60; UNESCO Expert in Modern Maths, Uganda & Zanzibar, 1962-63; Visiting Professor Psychology, Bowling Green Stat.

University, Ohio, USA, 1965-66; Professor Maths Education Long Island University, 1966-67; Professor Maths, Staten Island Community College, 1969-71; Adult Educ. Tutor in Child Psychology, Stats. 1940's, 1950's. *Memberships:* Chairman, Wellington Branch, (four times) New Zealand Educational Institute; Life Member, National Executive 1936-38 and 1945-54; National Treasurer, 1948-54; Chamber Music Society; Repertory Society; US National Council Teachers of Maths; UK Maths Association. *Publications:* History of Te Aro School, 1952; School Certificate Maths, 1956; numerous articles of Education, Modern Maths in New Zealand and overseas journals. *Honours:* Senior National Scholarship, 1921; Fulbright Scholar, 1959-60. *Hobbies:* Gardening; Reading. *Address:* 27, The Esplanade, Raumati South, New Zealand.

RITCHIE, Douglas Malcolm, b. 5 Nov. 1929, Melbourne, Australia. Orthopaedic Surgeon. m. 1 Feb. 1957, 1 son, 2 daughters. *Education:* Scotch College, Melbourne; MB.BS University of Melbourne, 1954; FRCS, England, 1960; FRCS, Edinburgh, 1960; FRACS, Orthopaedics 1962. *Appointments:* Assistant Orthopaedic Surgeon, Royal Melbourne Hospital, 1963-69; Assistant Orthopaedic Surgeon, Royal Childrens Hospital, 1962-68; Senior Orthopaedic Surgeon, Queen Victoria Medical Centre, 1968-; Lecturer in Orthopaedics, Monash University; Private Practice, 1962-. *Memberships:* Australian Orthopaedic Association, Executive 1975-79; British Orthopaedic Association; Western Pacific Orthopaedic Association; Royal Melbourne Golf Club. *Publications:* Various scientific papers. *Hobbies:* Golf; Antique Collecting; Gardening. *Address:* 43, Evans Court, Toorak, Victoria, 3142, Australia.

RITCHIE, John Anthony, b. 29 Sept. 1921, Wellington, New Zealand. University Professor. m. Anita Proctor, 12 Feb, 1944, 2 sons, 3 daughters. *Education:* Dip. Tchg. Dunedin Teachers College, 1940-41; Mus.B. Otago University, 1940-42; L.Mus.TCL,LTCL, Trinity College of Music, London, 1945. *Appointments:* Lecturer, Senior Lecturer in Music, University of Canterbury, Christchurch, New Zealand, 1946-61; Professor of Music and Head of Department, 1962-; Visiting Professor, Exeter University, 1967-68; Deputy Vice-Chancellor, University of Canterbury, 1978-80; Musical Director, Xth British Commonwealth Games, 1974. *Memberships:* Trustee N.Z. Composers Foundation Ltd.; Member Royal Musical Association; Secretary-General, International Society for Music Education. *Creative Works:* Lord, When the Sense of Thy Sweet Grace, 1957; Concertino for Clarinet, 1963; Kyrie and Gloria, 1967; Four Zhivago Songs, 1977. *Hobbies:* Golf; Reading. *Address:* Villa 2, 12, Mansfield Avenue, Christchurch, 1, New Zealand.

RITCHIE-CALDER, Peter Ritchie, b. 1 July, 1906, Forfar, Scotland. Author. m. 11 Oct.1927, 3 sons, 2 daughters. *Education:* MA Edinburgh University, 1961; D.Univ. Open University, 1975; DSc, York University, Ontario, 1976. *Appointments:* Police Court Reporter, Dundee Courier, 1922, Daily News, 1926-30; Daily Chronicle, 1930; Daily Herald, 1930-41; Director of Plans and Operations, Political Warfare Executive, 1941-45; Special Adviser Supreme Headquarters, 1945; Science Editor, News Chronicle, 1945-57; Editorial Board, New Statesman, 1945-58; Professor of International Relations, 1961-67; Chairman, Metrication Board, 1969-72; Planning Committee and Council, Open University, 1969-81; Senior Fellow Center for Study of Democratic Institutions, 1972-75; House of Lords Select Committee on Science and Technology, 1980-. *Appointments:* Fellow of World Academy of Arts and Science; Fellow of American Association for Advance of Science; Chairman, Association British Science Writers, 1949-55; Chairman, Advisory Committee on Pollution of the Sea. *Publications:* Life Savers, 1961; Living with the Atom, 1962; World of Opportunity, 1963; Two Way Passage, 1964; Evolution of the Machine, 1968; Man and the Cosmos, 1968; Leonard and the Age of the Eye, 1970; The Pollution of the Mediterranean, 1972; How Long Have We Got?, 1972; Energy, 1980. *Honours:* Life Peerage, Baron of Balmashannar, 1966; CBE, 1945; Kalinga International Award for Promotion of the Common Understanding of Science, 1960; Gollancz Award for Services to Humanity, 1969 Jubilee Medal of New York Public Library. *Address:* Philpstoun House, Linlithgow, W. Lothian, EH49 7NB. Scotland.

RIZVI, Rafat Furrukh, (Mrs. F. Rizvi) b. 25 Dec. 1948, Karachi. Business. m. 19 Feb, 1971, 2 daughters. *Education:* BA(Hons) 1970; MA, 1971. *Appointments:* Director F.R. Linkers Ltd., 1976. *Memberships:* Hong Kong Psychological Society; Society of Old Students of the Department of Psychology, University of Karachi. *Hobbies:* Reading. *Address:* Flat R, 6th Floor, Universal Mansion, 52, Hillwood Road, Kowloon, Hong Kong.

RMSAT, Ralph (Rt. Hon. Baron), b. 4 Feb, 1938, Hobart, Tasmania, Australia. Co. Director, Academic Registrar, m. Margay Ruth Vincent, 19 Dec. 1964, 1 son, 1 daughter. *Education:* FRCD, 1978; B.Arch. RCD, 1979; FRAIC, 1979; Dr.Arch.RAIC, 1981. *Appointments:* Director, Delta Mining Co.1968; Director, Golden Gate Mining Co. 1974; Registrar, RAIC, 1981; Registrar, RCD, 1980; Chartered Arch. 1981; Mem. Money Marketeers Aust. 1973. *Memberships:* NAT, 1965; FRNS, 1965; FNSP. 1968; FRCD, 1978; FRAIC, 1979; Royal Scribe, 1978; JP, 1980; Ch. Arch. 1981; M.M.Aust, 1973. *Publications:* Author of selected speeches and papers in the field. *Creative Works:* Designing International Currency. *Honours:* Companion for Preservation of Rural Australia, 1973; Cr. The Rt. Hon. Baron Rmsat, 1980; Knight Grand Cross, Order of Avram, 1980; Knight Grand Cross, Order of Sacred Sword and Lance, 1981. *Hobbies:* Preserving Rural Australia; Recording History. *Address:* PO Box 11, Exeter, Tasmania, Australia, 7251.

ROBB, William Edward, b. 20 Oct. 1927, Sydney, Australia. Member for Miranda, New South Wales Parliament. m. Heather Hinton, 8 July, 1950, 2 sons. *Memberships:* Life Member and Patron of many Sutherland Shire Community Organisations, including Handicapped Children, Junior Sporting, Parents and Citizens, Ex-Service and Scouting groups. *Hobbies:* Bushwalking, Reading. *Address:* 8 Lancashire Place, Gymea, 2227, Australia.

ROBERTS, Barney, b. 31 Jan. 1920, Flowerdale, Tasmania. Writer/Farmer. m. 1 March, 1947, 3 sons, 1 daughter. *Appointments:* Bank Clerk; Army, POW, Germany; Farmer/Writer, 1946-. *Memberships:* Past State Secretary Fellowship of Australian Writers, Tasmanian Branch. *Publications:* Local History, 1964; The Phantom Boy, 1976; Stones in the Cephissus, 1979; The Penalty of Adam, 1980; A Kind of Cattle, to be published. *Honours:* Australian Arts Council; Literature Board 6 Months Fellowship, 1973; Literature Board, 6 months Fellowship, 1974; Won, placed or Commended in Literary Competitions in Six States of Australia. *Hobbies:* Mountain Climbing; Bush Walking; Growing Trees. *Address:* RD 57B, Flowerdale, 7325, Tasmania, Australia.

ROBERTS, Claudius Matthias, b. 15 Jan. 1913, Anguilla, West Indies. Police Officer. (Retired). m. Eunice S. Mondesire 12 June, 1934, 4 sons, 6 daughters. *Education:* Senior Cambridge Certificate. *Appointments:* Leeward Islands Police Force, 1932 and served in Police Forces of Dominica, St. Vincent, Grenada. Appointed Commissioner of Police, Grenada, 1967; Chief of Police, Anguilla, 1972-76, total Police Service, 45 years. *Honours:* Colonial Police Long Service Medal, 1950; War Medal, 1939-45; Colonial Police Medal for Meritorious Service, 1953; Coronation Medal, 1953; Bar for Gallantry to Colonial Police Medal, 1962; MBE, 1967; Granted Honorary Rank of Lieutenant Colonel, 1967. *Address:* Crocus Hill, P.O. Box 9, The Valley, Anguilla, W. Indies.

ROBERTS, David Gethin Edwards, b. 20 Nov, 1918, Cwmdare, Aberdare, Mid Glamorgan, Wales. Dental Surgeon. m. Nesta Gwendolyn Morgan, 4 Feb. 1952, 1 son. *Education:* Guy's Hospital Dental School, 1936-41; BDS, LDS, RCS, English, University of London, 1941. *Appointments:* Assistant Dental Surgeon, General Practice, 1941; House Surgeon, Guy's, 1941; School Dental Officer, 1941-42; General Practice, 1943; Honorary Dental Surgeon, Merthyr & Aberdare H.MC. 1948-52. *Memberships:* President, British Dental Association, 1979-80; Federation Dentaire Internationale; Honourable Society of Cymmrodorion. *Honours:* M.Sc Honoris Causa, University of Wales, 1980. *Hobbies:* Sailing; Gardening; Collecting Paintings; Theatre; Music; Literature; Furniture Restoring. *Address:* 1 Broniestyn Terrace, Gadlys, Aberdare, Mid Glamorgan. Wales.

ROBERTS, Denys (Tudor Emil) (Sir), b. 19 Jan. 1923, London England, Barrister. m. Jan 1949, Marriage Dissolved 1973, 1 son 1 daughter. *Education:* Wadham College Oxford, MA, 1948, BCL 1949. *Appointments:* Practice as Barrister, London, 1950-53; Crown Counsel, Nyasaland, 1953; Attorney General, Gibraltar, 1960; Solicitor General, Hong Kong, 1962-66; Attorney General, 1966-73; Chief Secretary, 1973-79; Chief Justice, 1979; *Publications:* 5 humourous novels, 1953-65. *Honours:* OBE, 1960; CBE, 1970; KBE, 1975. *Hobbies:* Cricket; Walking; Tennis; Music; Reading. *Address:* Chief Justice's House, Gough Hill Road, The Peak, Hong Kong

ROBERTS, George Brooke, b. 25 May 1930, Philadelphia, PA, USA, Diplomat. m. Zara Bentley, 20 June 1952, 2 sons, 1 daughter. *Education:* BA, Yale, 1952; MA, Yale, 1953. *Appointments:* U.S. Navy, Lieutenant (JG), 1953-57; Third Secretary, American Embassy, Bangkok, 1958-60; Second Secretary, American Embassy, Vientiane, 1960-62; International Relations Officer, Department of State, 1962-66; First Secretary, American Embassy, Dar es Salaam, 1967-69; Counselor, American Embassy, Kingston, 1970-73; Special Assistant to Deputy Secretary, Department of State, 1974; Director for Thai & Burmese Affairs, Department of State, 1974-76; Charge D'Affaires, American Embassy, Vientiane, 1977-79; Ambassador, American Embassy, Georgetown, 1979-. *Hobbies:* Carpentry, Antique Automobiles; Model Aircraft. *Address:* American Embassy, P.O. Box 10507, Georgetown, Guyana

ROBERTS, George Woodrow, b. 12 Nov 1918, Grenada, West Indies. University Professor. m. 6 Nov. 1958, 1 son. *Education:* London School of Economics, 1951-53, 1968-69, BSC, DSC. *Appointments:* Vital Statistics Adviser, Development & Welfare Organisation, 1953-58; Vital Statistics Officer, Federal Govt of West Indies, 1958-61; Senior Lectuter, University of West Indies, Jamaica, 1961-66; Professor of Demography, University of West Indies, Jamaica 1966; United Nations Director, Demographic Training & Research Unit, University of Colombo, Sri Lanka, 1979. *Memberships:* Former Vice President, International Union for Scientific Study of Population; International Statistical Institute; Royal Statistical Society. *Publications:* Population of Jamaica,1957, Reprinted 1979; Study of External Migration affecting Jamaica 1953-55 w. D.O. Mills, 1957; Recent Population Movements in Jamaica, 1974; Fertility & Mating in Four West Indian Populations, 1975; Women in Jamaica w. S.A. Sinclair, 1978; Various papers in Professional Journals. *Hobbies:* Photography. *Address:* Demographic Training & Research Unit, University of Colombo, P.O. Box 1490, Colombo 3, Sri Lanka

ROBERTS, Ivor Anthony, b. 24 Sept. 1946, Liverpool, England. H.M. Diplomatic Service. m. Elizabeth Bray Bernard Smith, 4 May 1974, 2 sons. *Education:* Keble College, Oxford, 1964-68, BA, 1968, MA, 1972. *Appointments:* Third Secretary, FCO, 1968-69; Mecas, 1969; FCO, 1970; Third, later Second Secretary, Paris, 1970-73; Second, later First Secretary, FCO, 1973-78; First Secretary, Chancery, Canberra, 1978-80; First Secretary, Economic Commercial & Agricultural Advisor, Canberra, 1980-. *Memberships:* United Oxford & Cambridge University Club; National Press Club, Canberra. *Hobbies:* Opera; Archeology; Reading; Rugby. *Address:* Fairseat Manor, Fairseat, Near Wrotham, Kent TN15 7LU. England.

ROBERTS, Lloyd Guy Pierre, b. 5 Nov. 1923, Guyana. Banker/Company Director. m. Cynthia Mary Hartwright, 21 Dec. 1946, 3 sons. *Education:* St. Stanislaus College, Guyana; Royal Technical College, Glasgow; Institute of Banking Diploma, 1965; Fellow of the Institute of Bankers, 1965. *Appointments:* Barclays Bank, Dominion Colonial & Overseas, 1941, now Barclays Bank International Ltd. to date; Served in Guyana, Grenada, Jamaica, Belize, Nigeria & Barbados, Caribbean Director, 1971; Senior Caribbean Director, 1975; Since 1977 Chairman & Executive Director of Caribbean Board BBIL of Barclays Finance Corporation Barbados Ltd., Barclays Finance Corporation of Leeward & Windward Islands Ltd.; Chairman & Executive Director of Barfincor Cayman Islands Ltd.; Chairman of Aero Services Barbados Ltd. *Memberships:* Institute of Directors. *Honours:* Officer of the Order of the British Empire, Queen's Birthday Honours List, 1981, for services to British Commercial Interests in Barbados.

Hobbies: Golf; Sailing; Amateur Radio. *Address:* Aberdare, Worthing, Christ Church, Barbados

ROBERTS, Richard Frederick Anthony, b. 12 May 1932, Nassau, Bahamas. High Commissioner for the Commonwealth of the Bahamas, London. m. Melvern Hollis Bain, 1960, 1 son 2 daughters. *Education:* St. John's College. *Appointments:* Personnel Officer, Bahamas Airways, 1963-67; Executive Director & Partner, Venn Livingstone Roberts, 1967-68; Personnel Director, New Providence Development Co. Ltd., 1968; Member of Parliament, Centreville Constituency, 1968-77; Parliamentary Secretary, Ministry of Finance, 1969-72; Parliamentary Secretary, Ministry of Agriculture, 1971-72; Minister of Agriculture & Fisheries, 1972-73; Minister of Home Affairs, 1973; Minister of Agriculture, Fisheries & Local Government, 1974-77. *Memberships:* President, Airline Workers Union; Secretary General Amalgamated Building Construction Engineering Trade Union; Assistant General Secretary, Bahamas Federation of Labour; President, Bahamas Trade Union Congress; Assistant General Secretary, Progressive Liberal Party; 1st Vice-Chairman, Progressive Liberal Party; National General Council Progressive Liberal Party; Advisory Committee to Labour Board; Chairman, Maritime Board; Broadcasting & Television Commission; vice Chairman, Bahamas Agricultural Corporation. *Hobbies:* Fishing; Reading; Sports; Religion. *Address:* Carmichael Road, P.O. Box 565, Nassau, Bahamas

ROBERTS, Shirley Dallas (Mrs Kenneth D Nelson), b. 11 Aug. 1927, Bairnsdale, Victoria, Australia. Radiologist, m Kenneth Davies Nelson, 12 May 1975. *Education:* MB, BS, Melbourne University, 1950; DRACR, 1954; FRCR, 1957; FRACR, 1967. *Appointments:* Deputy Director of Radiology, Alfred Hospital, Melbourne, 1958-63; Director of Radiology, Prince Henry's Hospital, Melbourne, 1963-. *Memberships:* Lyceum Club, Melbourne. *Hobbies:* Victorian History. *Address:* 151 Domain Park, 193 Domain Road, South Yarra 3141, Victoria, Australia

ROBERTSON, Angus, b. 10 June 1949, Dundee, Scotland. Insurance. m. Michele Anne Hutton, 21 Aug. 1981. *Education:* BA, ACII, FCII, University of Strathclyde. *Appointments:* Phoenix Assurance Co. Ltd., 1971; Phoenix of Nigeria Assurance Co. Ltd., Assistant General Manager, 1978. *Memberships:* Treasurer, Lagos Caledonian Society; Nigeria Britain Society; Grand Master, Lagos Hash House Harriers. *Hobbies:* Running; Scottish Country Dancing; Golf; Squash. *Address:* 5C Magbon Close, Ikoyi Island, Lagos, Nigeria

ROBERTSON, Carlyle Charles, b. 6 Mar. 1929, Boolaroo, New South Wales, Australia. Company Director. *Education:* Australian Society of Accountants, 1955; Australian Institute of Management, 1953; Institute of Directors, Australia, 1977; Australian Marketing Institute, 1963. *Appointments:* Chairman, Brisbane & Area Water Board; Chairman, Queensland Trotting Board; Director, The Totalisator Administration Board of Queensland; Managing Director, Carl Robertson Ford Pty Ltd., Ford Dealers, Gold Coast, Australia; Alderman/Deputy Mayor of the Gold Coast, 1972-77. *Memberships:* Brisbane Club, Brisbane; Queensland Turf Club. *Honours:* Justice of the Peace, 1978. *Hobbies:* Horse Racing; Surfing; Golf. *Address:* 17/136 Miskin Street, Toowong, 4066, Queensland, Australia

ROBERTSON, Charles, b. 18 Sept. 1928, Arbroath, Scotland. Architect. m. Sheila MacKenzie, 7 July 1962, 1 son, 2 daughters. *Education:* Diploma in Architecture, Dundee Collage of Art, 1952; fellow, Royal Institute of British Architects, 1953; Fellow, Royal Incorporation of Architects in Scotland, 1953; Fellow, Royal Australian Institute of Architects, 1972; Fellow, Chartered Institute of Building, 1979. *Appointments:* Architect, T.H. Thoms, Dundee, 1952-54; Architect, Essex County Council, 1954-55; Senior Architect, W.M. Wilson, Dundee, 1955-56; Senior Architect, Sir Basil Spence, Edinburgh & London, 1956-62; Director of the Architecture Research Unit, Edinburgh University, 1962-72; Consultant to Sir Robert Matthew on planning & housing In Tripoli, 1970-72; Professor of Architecture & Chairman of Department of Architecture & Building, Melbourne University, Australia, 1972-77; Chief Executive of National Building Agency, Scotland, 1977-. *Memberships:* Royal Society of Arts, 1980; Edinburgh University Staff Clud; New Club, Edinburgh; RIBA

Housing Committee, 1964-72; Chairman, Australian Housing Standards Advisory Council, 1974-77; National House Builders Registration Council, Scotland, 1967-72; Building Research Establishment Scottish Advisory Committee, 1977-; Saltire Society Housing Awards Panel, 1978-. *Honours:* Honorary Research Fellow, University of Edinburgh, 1964. *Address:* Crichton House, Pathhead, Midlothian EH37 5UX, Scotland

ROBERTSON, George Islay MacNeill, b. 12 Apr. 1946, Islay, Argyll, Scotland. Member of Parliament. m. Sandra Wallace, 1 June 1970, 2 sons, 1 daughter. *Education:* MA, University of Dundee, 1968. *Appointments:* Research Assistant, Tayside Study Economics Group; Scottish Organiser, General & Municipal Workers Union, 1969-78; Member of Parliament for Hamilton, Lanarkshire, 1978; Parly. Priv. Secretary, to Secretary of State for Social Services, 1979; Opposition Spokesman on Scottish Affairs, 1979-80; on Defence, 1980-81; on Foreign Affairs, 1981; Chairman, Scottish Labour Party, 1977;78; Board Member, Scottish Development Agency, 1975-78. *Memberships:* Chairman, Royal Society for Prevention of Accidents, Seatbelt Survivors Club; Institute of Strategic Studies; Council, National Trust for Scotland. *Hobbies:* Golf; Photography. *Address:* 3 Argyle Park, Dunblane, Central Scotland, FK15 9D2

ROBERTSON, Giles Henry, b. 16 Oct. 1913, Cambridge, England. University Teacher. m. 3 Apr. 1942, 4 sons, 1 daughter. *Education:* BA, 1936, MA, 1947, New College, Oxford. *Appointments:* Lecturer, 1946-60; Senior Lecturer, 1960-69, Reader, 1969-72, University of Edinburgh; Professor of Fine Art, Watson Gordon, 1972-81. *Memberships:* Royal Scottish Academy; Scottish Arts Club. *Publications:* Vincenzo Catena, 1954; Giovanni Bellini, 1968. *Honours:* HRSA, 1972; Member of Insitute for Advanced Study, Princenton, N.J., 1966-67. *Hobbies:* Painting. *Address:* 4 Saxe-Coburg Place, Edinburgh EH3 5BR. Scotland.

ROBERTSON, James Finlay b. 9 Mar. 1924, Blyth, Northumberland, England. Consultant Psychiatrist. m. Margaret Graham Cranmer, 16 Nov. 1960, 1 daughter. *Education:* MB, CHB, University of Glasgow, 1942-48; RCP&S, Ireland, DPM, 1954; DPH, 1956, MRAMZCP, 1966, University of Glasgow; MRC,Psych, 1972. *Appointments:* Senior Specialist Psychiatrist, Bloomfield Hospital, Orange, NSW., 1965; Private Practice, Lismore, NSW, 1966; Hons. Cons. Psychiatrist, Lismore Base Hospital, 1966; Hons. Cons. Psychiatrist, St. Vincent's Hospital, Lismore, 1966; Hons. Cons. Psychiatrist, Bangalow District Hospital, 1966; Specialist Psychiatrist, Dept. of Veterans Affairs, North Cost, NSW, Psychiatrist Cons. Psychogeriatrics, Willsmere Hospical, Kew, Vic. Vic. Cons, Malvern Clinic, Sen. Part time Lecturere, Melbourne University, 1970; Cons in Charge Smith St Clinic Melbourne, 1974; Cons. Psych. Melbourne Clinic. *Memberships:* British Medical Association; Canadian Psychiatric Association; Royal Australia N.Z. Coll. Psychiatrists; College Psychiatrists; Graduate Union, Melbourne; Alliance francaise de Victoria; World Psychiatric Association. *Publications:* Mental Illness or Metal Illness? Bismuth Subgallate; Hemineurin, Safety in Alcohol Withdrawal, 1979. *Hobbies:* Drawing; Water Colour Painting. *Address:* 38 Gresswell Road, Mont Park, Victoria 3085. Australia.

ROBERTSON, John Gray, b. 17 Nov. 1939, Huntly, New Zealand. Research Scientist. m. Glenys Marian Griffiths, 18 Jan. 1964, 2 sons, 1 daughter. *Education:* BSC, Otago University, N.Z., 1962; MSC, Otago University, N.Z., 1964; PHD, Massey University, N.Z., 1968. *Appointments:* Applied Biochemistry Division, DSIR, Palmerston North, New Zealand from 1965 with period of leave at Roswell Park Memorial Institute, Buffalo, N.Y., U.S.A., 1969; UCONN Health Centre, Farmington, Conn., U.S.A., 1970; Charles F. Kettering Research Lab., Yellow Springs, Ohio, U.S.A., 1978-79. *Memberships:* Honorary Lecturer, Massey University; Fergusson Hall, Massey University, Presbyterian Educational Purposes Trust; N.Z. Institute Chemistry, Palmerston North Branch, Chairman, 1974; Secretary, NZ. Biochemical Society, 1975; N.Z. Microbiological Society; N.Z. Plant Physiology Society; N.Z. Society for Electron Microscopy. *Publications:* Ultrastructure & Metabolism of the developing legume root nodule, 1980. *Honours:* University of Otago Award in Science, 1962; University Post Graduate Scholarship, 1964; Damon Runyon Research Fellowship, USA, 1969-70. *Hobbies:* Swim-

ming Coaching; Movie Photography; Squash. *Address:* 51 Collingwood Street, Palmerston North, New Zealand

ROBERTSON, Robert Gordon, b. 19 May 1917, Davidson, Saskatchewan, Canada. President, The Institute for Research on Public Policy. m. Beatrice Muriel Lawson, 14 Aug. 1943, 1 son 1 daughter. *Education:* BA, University of Saskatchewan, 1938; BA, Oxford University, England, 1940; MA, University of Toronto, 1941; LLD, University of Saskatchewan, 1959. *Appointments:* Third Secretary, Department of External Affairs, Ottawa, Ontario, 1941-43; Assistant to Under-Secretary of State for External Affairs, 1943-45; Secretary to the Office of the Prime Minister, Ottawa, 1945-49; Member of the Cabinet secretariat, Privy Council Office, Ottawa, 1949-51; Assistant Secretary to the Cabinet, Privy Council Office, 1951-53; Deputy Minister of Northern Affairs & National Resources & Commissioner of the Northwest Territories, 1953-63; Clerk of the Privy Council & Secretary to the Cabinet, 1963-75; Secretary to the Cabinet for Federal Provincial Relations, 1975-79; President, the Institute for Research on Public Policy since 1980 & Chancellor, Carleton University. *Memberships:* Cercle Universitaire d'Ottawa. *Honours:* Companion of the Order of Canada, 1976; Fellow Royal Society of Canada. *Address:* 20 Westward Way, Rockcliffe Park, Ottawa, Ontario, canada, K1L 5A7

ROBERTSON, Rutherford Ness, (Sir), b. 29 Sept. 1913, Melbourne, Australia. Biologist. m. Mary Helen Bruce Rogerson, 9 Sept. 1937, 1 son. *Education:* BSC, University of Sydney, 1934; PHD, University of Cambridge, 1939; DSC, University of Sydney, 1962. *Appointments:* Assistant Lecturer, Later Lecturer, Botany, University of Sydney, 1939-46; Senior Research Officer, later Chief Research Officer, Commonwealth Scientific & Industrial Research Organisation, Division of Food Preservation, 1946-59; Member of Excutive, Commonwealth Scientific & Industrial Research Organisation, 1959-62; Professor of Botany, University of Adelaide, 1962-69; Master, University House, Australian National University, 1969-72; Director, Research School of Biological Sciences, Australian National University, 1973-78; Honorary Visitor, University of Sydney 1979-; Chairman, Australian Research Grants Committee, 1965-69; Deputy Chairman, Australian Science & Technology Council, 1977-. *Memberships:* President, Australian Academy of Science, 1970-74; Royal Society of London, 1961; US National Academy of Sciences, 1962; President, Australian & New Zealand Association for the Advancement of Science, 1965-; American Philosophical Society; Royal Society of New Zealand, 1971-; President, XIII International Botanical Congress. 1981. *Publications:* Electrolytes in Plant Cells w. G.E. Briggs & A. B. Hope, 1961; Protons, Electrons, Phosphorylation & Active Transport, 1968; and numerous papers in scientific journals. *Honours:* Companion of the Order of Australia, 1980; Knight Bachelor, 1972; CMG, 1968; Hon. SCD, Cambridge, Hon. DSC., Monash, Tasmania & Australian National Universities; Hon. Fellow, St. John's College, Cambridge, 1973; Clarke Memorial Medal, Royal Society of NSW, 1954; Farrer Memorial Medal, 1963; ANZAAS Medal, 1968; Mueller Medal, 1970; Burnet Medal, 1975. *Hobbies:* Riding. *Address:* P.O. Box 9, Binalong, New South Wales, 2584, Australia

ROBINSON, Edwin Campbell, b. 10 May 1933, Regina, Saskatchewan, Canada. Barrister & solicitor. *Education:* Associate in Arts, Luther College, Regina, 1952; BL, University of Saskatchewan, 1956; BA, University of Saskatchewan, 1956; Admission to Law Society of Saskatchewan as practising Barrister & Soclicitor, 1958. *Appointments:* Articled in and employed with Thom, Bastedo, McDougall & Ready, Regina; Associate with Fyffe & Fyffe, Regina; Executive Assistant, Saskatchewan School Trustees Association, Regina; News Commentator & Open Line Host, Radio CJOC, Lethbrdige, Alberta; Practising Solicitor, Own Firm, 1972. *Memberships:* Law Society of Saskatchewan; Canadian Owners & Pilots Association; Regina Flying Club. *Creative Works:* Poetry in past years; Yearly newsletter which includes annual make-fun of names in the Regina, Saskatchewan Telephone Directory, both local & National Distribution; Radio & Mobile Television sports play by plays. *Hobbies:* Model Railroading; Fishing; Boating; Flying Airplane; Public Address for Sports Events; Play by plays of Sports Events, including Telecasting & Videotaping. *Address:* 3116 Park Street, Regina, Saskatchewan, Canada S4N 2J2

ROBINSON, Eric Laidlaw, b. 18 Jan 1929, Brisbane, Australia. Australian Politician & Company Director. m. Narelle Jones, 1965. *Appointments:* Director of varous companies in Marine & sporting goods; Chairman & Managing Director, Robinson Holdings Pty. Ltd., President, Queensland Division of Liberal Party, 1968-73; Member for McPherson, Queensland House of Representatives, 1972-; Minister for the Capital Territory, 1975-76; For Post & Telecommunications 1976-77; For Finance, 1977-. *Memberships:* Queensland Freedom from Hunger Campaign, 1966-68; Brisbane Chamber of Commerce. *Hobbies:* Fishing; Boating; Water Skiing. *Address:* Parliament House, Canberra ACT 2600, Australia

ROBINSON, Lloyd Anthony Jacques, b. 17 Jan. 1919, Kingston, Jamaica. Architect-Medical Facilities Consultant. m. 17 Aug. 1947, 1 daughter. *Education:* Diploma, Hammersmith School of Architecture, 1950-54; Architect Registration, UK, 1953; ARIBA, 1956; FRIBA, 1968. *Appointments:* Ministry of Works, London, England, 1951-56; District Architect, Government of Ghana, 1956-62; Chief Architect, Ministry of Works, Jamaica, 1962-79; PAHO/WHO Consultant Medical Facilities, Dominica and St. Lucia, 1979-81; Deputy Project Director, Ibro, Primary Care Population Project, Jamaica, 1979-81. *Memberships:* Fellow, Royal Institute of British Architects; Past Vice President, Jamaica Institute of Architects; Past Treasurer and Chairman, Jamaica Institute of Architects; Member of Ghanian Society of Architects. *Publications:* Guest Editor, Magazine Design for Health, issued by Jamaica Institute of Architects. *Honours:* 4th Prize Premium, Architectural Competition Cultural Training Centre; 3rd Prize Premium, National Monument Architect Competition. *Hobbies:* Cricket; Badminton; Tennis. *Address:* 12, Mona Road, Kingston, 6, Jamaica.

ROBINSON, Margaret Anne (Scharp), b. 3 July, 1935, Gilgandra. Director of Nursing. m. Eric Louis Scharp, 8 Apr. 1967. *Education:* Fellow of College of Nursing, Australia; Diploma of Nursing Education; Diploma of Nursing Administration; Registered Nurse; Registered Midwife. *Appointments:* General Training, Royal South Sydney Hospital, 1955-59; Midwifery Training, Womens Hospital, Sydney, 1961-62; Overseas experience in England, Germany & Holland; Principal Teacher, Fairfield Hospital, Victoria, 1972-76; Assistant Matron, 1976; Dep. Director of Nursing Fairfield Hospital, 1977-79; Director of Nursing, Prince Henry's Hospital, 1980. *Memberships:* Association of Directors of Nursing, Victoria; American Society of Nursing Service Administrators; College of Nursing Australia Council; Soroptomist, Wine, Griffith Womens NSW. 06 Churchill Fellowship, 1979. *Hobbies:* Gardening, Playing Bagpipes, Travel; Compiling Family Tree. *Address:* 68 Bryson Grove, Lower Templestow, Victoria 3107, Australia

ROBINSON, Maxwell, John, b. 21 Feb. 1929, Richmond, Victoria Commissioner of Police, Tasmania. m. 6 May, 1950, 1 son, 2 daughters. *Education:* Australian National University, 1973. *Memberships:* Tasmanian Spastics Association; Tasmanian State Committee St Johns Ambulance; Chairman, Tasmanian Heads of Government Departments Association; Rotary Club of Hobart; Royal Yacht Club of Tasmania; Fellow of the Australian Institute of Management. *Honours:* Recipient of QPM, for distinquished service. *Hobbies:* Reading; Fishing; Gardening; Music. *Address:* 7 Acushla Court, Sandy Bay, 7005, Tasmania.

ROBINSON, William Robert, b. 23 Apr. 1951, Toronto, Ontario, Canada. Sport Administrator. m. Barbara Jo, 23 Nov. 1949, 1 daughter. *Education:* Senior High School Diploma; Bachelor of Commerce Degree; Honors Business Degree. *Appointments:* Ottawa Roughriders, 1975-78; Executive Director, Canadian Amateur Football Associaton, 1976-. *Memberships:* President, Ontario Interprovincial League Baseball, 1981; National Press Club of Canada; Recreational Centre of Federal Government. *Creative Works:* Policy and Procedure in Sports Administration; Football Athlete Assistance Development Program. *Honours:* All Canadian Quaterback University Football, 1974; Member of National Football Champions: Saint Marys University, 1973; Western Ontario University, 1974; Ottawa Roughrid-

ers, 1976. *Hobbies:* All Sports; Music; Children. *Address:* 410 Byron Avenue, Ottawa, Ontario, K12 623. Canada.

ROBSON, Robert Alick, b. 5 Jan. 1927, Melbourne, Victoria. Company Director. m. Joan Elizabeth, 12 Dec. 1953, 3 sons. *Education:* BCE, Melbourne, 1951; BA, Melbourne, 1960; MSc, 1964; Harvard Advanced Management Program, Hawaii, 1968. *Appointments:* Civil Engineer, Melbourne and Metropolitan Board of Works, 1951-54; Branch Manager, Rocla Pipes Ltd., Albury, NSW, 1955-56; General Manager, Rocla Pipes Africa P/Ltd., Johannesburg, 1957-65; State Manager, Rocla Industries Ltd., 1965-68; Deputy General Manager, Rocla Industries, 1968-70; General Manager and Director, Rocla Industries Ltd., 1970-75; Managing Director, BMI Limited, 1975-. *Memberships:* President, Employers Federation of New South Wales; Deputy President, Institute of Quarrying; Fellow, Australian Institute of Management; Fellow, Institution of Engineers, Australia Royal Sydney Yacht Squadron, Sydney; Australian Club, Sydney. *Honours:* Commander of the British Empire, 1980. *Hobbies:* Sailing; Fishing. *Address:* 2B/27 Sutherland Crescent, Darling Point, NSW 2027. Australia.

ROCCA, Francis, Joseph, b. 20 Apr. 1934, Gibraltar, Deputy Registrar, Supreme Court: Clerk of The Court of First Instance. m. Mary Elizabeth, 11 Nov. 1981. 1 son, 1 daughter. *Hobbies:* Classical Music; Opera; Cricket; Football; Hockey; Basketball. *Address:* 3/80 Red Sands Road, Gibraltar.

ROCCO, Charles, b. 3 June. 1950, New Jersey, United States. Art Administrator. *Education:* BA Fine Arts Education, Dean's List 1971-72, Newark State College, USA, 1972. *Appointments:* Lecturer, School of Fine Arts-Jewellery Silversmithing and Photography, Institiut Teknoloji Mara, Kuala Lumpur, Malaysia, 1972; Co-ordinator, Media Studies Department, Huntingdale Technical School, Victoria, Australia, 1974; Head of Expressive Arts Department, Tusbab Provincial High School, Madang, Papua New Guinea, 1977; Co-ordinator, Creative Arts Country Services, Victorian Council of Adult Education, Melbourne, Australia, 1979; Director, State Regional Art Gallery at Broken Hill, New South Wales, Australia, 1980; Creative Studies Coordinator, Whitefriars College, Melbourne, 1982. *Memberships:* Deputy Chairman, Regional Galleries Association of New South Wales, 1980; Australian Gallery Directors Council, 1980; Art Museums Association of Australia, 1980. *Honours:* Australian Photographic Society Certificate, 1976; Federation Internationale de l'Art Photographique Certificate,1976. *Hobbies:* Short Story writing; Photography. *Address:* 22/40 Woorayl Street, Carnegie, 3163, Victoria, Australia.

ROCKMAN, Irvin Peter, b. 6 Apr. 1938, Melbourne, Australia. Company Director, divorced, 2 sons. *Education:* BC, 1960; AASA, 1960. *Appointments:* Northrock Group of Companies, 1960-. *Memberships:* Melbourne City Council as Councillor; Lord Mayor, City of Melbourne 8/77-8/79; Chairman, Finance Committee, 1975, 76, 80, 81. *Publications:* Author, Underwater Australia Lansdowne Press, 1974. *Honours:* CBE, 1980. *Hobbies:* Private Flying; Sailing; Underwater Photography; Running. *Address:* 8 Ottawa Road, Toorak, Victoria, 3142, Australia.

RODDIE, Robert Kenneth, b. 30 Aug. 1923, Portadown, Northern Ireland. Consultant Surgeon, m. Anne, 5 Oct. 1957, 2 sons, 1 daughter. *Education:* MB, BCh, BAO, 1946; DLO, 1949; FRCS, 1957. *Appointments:* Resident Medical Officer, City Hospital, Belfast; Senior Registrar, ENT Departments, Belfast Hospital Group, 1947-59; Senior Registrar, Royal National Throat, Nose and Ear Hospital and Institute of Laryngology and Otology, London, 1957-59; Consultant ENT Surgeon, Avon Area Health Authority (Teaching),1960; Clinical Teacher in Otolaryngology, University Bristol, 1960-78; Director, Hearing and Speech Centre, Bristol, 1965; Consultant Aurist to Civil Service Commission, 1970; Clinical Lecturer in Otolaryngology, University Bristol, 1978; Head of Department, Oto Rhino Laryngology, University of Bristol, 1978. *Memberships:* British Association of Otolaryngology, 1960; Council British Association of Otolaryngologists, 1977-81; Fellow of Royal Society of Medicine, 1960; Sections of Otology and Laryngology, Royal Society of Medicine, 1960; Council Section of Laryngology, Royal Society of Medicine,

1970-74; South Western Laryngological Association, 1960; General Committee 1st, 2nd, 3rd, 4th, 5th and 6th British Academic Conferences in Otolaryngology; British Medical Association, 1947; Societe Francaise, Dotorhino, Laryng, 1965-75; Clifton Club, Bristol, 1975; Lansdowne Club, London, 1975. *Publications:* Author, Chapters on ENT Bailey and Love's Short Practice of Surgery, 13th Edition, 1965; Retropharyngeal Cyst of Foregut Origin Associated with Vertebral Abnormality, British Journal of Surgery, 1960; Bilateral Melanoma of Tonsils Journal Laryngology and Otology, 1961; Management of Nasopharyngeal Angiofibroma Bristol Med-Chi Journal, 1974; Treatment of Carcinoma of Hypopharynx and Cervical Oesophagus, Proc. Irish Otolaryn Society, 1975. *Honours:* 2nd Class Honours in Medical Jurisprudence, Queens University, Belfast, 1944; President, South Western Laryngological Association, 1980; One Film awarded the British Life Assurance Trust Certificate of Educational Commendation, 1970; Copies of film bought by the British Council for Distribution in Australia and Canada. Also a copy for the Councils London Film Library. *Hobbies:* Oil Painting; Gardening; Golf. *Address:* Briar Lodge, 1 Briercliffe Road, Stoke Bishop, Bristol, BS9 2DB. England.

RODEN, Adrian, (The Honourable), b. 29 Jan. 1926, Sydney, Australia, Supreme Court Judge. m. Eve, 8 Apr. 1950. *Education:* LLB, Sydney University, 1948; Diploma, Crim. Sydney University, 1973. *Appointments:* Admitted Barrister, NSW, 1949; Assistant Custodian Enemy Property, Tanganyika, 1950; Advocate Tanganyika/Tanzania, 1950-65; Appointed Q.C., NSW, 1974; Judge, NSW District Court, 1977-78; Judge, NSW Supreme Court, 1978-. *Memberships:* Tanganyika Legislative Council, 1958; President, Tanganyika Football Association, 1960-63; President Australian Debating Federation, 1975-78; Life Member Australian Debating Federation; President, NSW Debating Union, 1968-75; Captain Combined Australian Universities Debating Team, 1949; Chairman Criminal Law Committee, Sydney University Law Grad's Association, 1976-79. *Honours:* Editor, Honi Soit, 1948; Consulting Editor, Criminal Law in NSW, (Current). *Hobbies:* Sport Bridge; Gardening; Music. *Address:* 35 Shamrock Parade, Killarney Heights, NSW 2087. Australia.

RODER, John Herbert, (His Honour Judge), b. 5 May, 1928, North Sydney, Australia. Judge of the District Court of South Australia (1970). m. Denise Charlotte, 2 Jan. 1954, 2 sons, 1 daughter. *Education:* MA, 1951; BL, 1951; Master of Town Planning, 1973; Fellow of the Taxation Institute of Australia, 1956; Honorary Fellow of the Royal Australian Planning Institute, 1976. *Appointments:* Senior Partner, Roder Dunstan Lee & Taylor, Barristers and Solicitors, 1952-70; Judge of the District Court of South australia since 1970. *Memberships:* Patron, Australian Keyboard Music Society, 1978; Commerce Club, Adelaide; Naval, Military and Air Force Club, Adelaide; University of Adelaide Club; South Lakes Golf Club; Vice President, Burnside Lacrosse Club. *Publications:* Reports and Inquiries on various international land, building and planning legislation and their effect for Commonwealth and south Australian Governments; Various papers on law, urban and regional planning and fifteenth century English literature. *Hobbies:* Reading; Theatre. *Address:* 73 Dashwood Road, Beaumont, S.A. 5066. Australia.

RODGER, William (Glendinning), (Sir), b. 5 June, 1912, Glasgow, Chartered Accountant. m. Dulcie Elizabeth Bray, 1937, 1 son, 1 daughter. *Education:* BCom, FCA(NZ), FCIS, FCAINZ, FNZIM, Victoria University college, University of New Zealand. *Appointments:* Commercial appointments 1927-41, Public Accounting Firm, 1945-54, in consulting practice 1954; Victoria University of Wellington, New Zealand, 1951-66; Professional Board 1951-61; Dean Faculty of Commerce, 1953-54, 1957, 1959-60; New Zealand Government Company Law Revision Committee, 1951-55; Visiting Professor of Business Administration University of California, Los Angeles, 1957-58; Visiting Professor of Commerce, Queens University, Kingston, Ontario, 1962-63; Agricultural Economist, Ministry of Agriculture, London, 1965; Visiting Lecturer in Farm Management, Wye College University of London, 1966; Jamaican Government Sugar Industry Enquiry Commission, 1966-67; Senior Lecturer in Accountancy University of Auckland, 1967-77; Fellow, Centre for

Continuing Education, University of Auckland, 1977; Visiting Fellow Continuing Education Mitchell College of Advanced Education, Bathurst NSW, 1978-79; Founder Member NZ Administrative Staff College, 1950-65, Course Director, 1953-59; Founder Auckland Executive Management Club, 1968, President 1968-71; University of Auckland School of Architecture Lecturer in Management Studies, 1968-81. *Memberships:* Fellow, New Zealand Society of Accountants, 1946; NZ President, Chartered Institute of Secretaries, 1957; President, New Zealand Institute of Cost Accountants, 1958; President, NZ Institute of Management, 1956; Registrar, NZ Institute of Valuers, 1951-55; President, NZ Branch Heraldry Society, 1980-. *Publications:* Bibliography of Accountancy; Reports on the Valuation of Unlisted Company Shares in NZ; Company Accounts in NZ; An Introduction to Cost and Management Accounting; etc., The Arms of the New Zealand Society of Accountants, ('80); An Introduction to Heraldry and Genealogy in New Zealand ('80); Management in the Medical Practice ('81); Contributor to various professional Journals. *Honours:* Knight Bachelor, 1978; OBE, 1957; USEFNZ Fullbright Travel Award, 1957; NZICA Maxwell Award, 1956; JP, 1946. *Hobbies:* Auckland Art Gallery Associates; Auckland Institute and Museum; Auckland - Los Angeles Sister City Committee; NZ Historic Places Trust; The Red Cross Society. *Address:* 6I Speight Road, St. Heliers Bay, Auckland, New Zealand.

RODGERS, John Hubert Macey, b. 9 Oct. 1915, Wallaceville, New Zealand. Honorary Roman Catholic Bishop. *Education:* Hononorary D.D., Mount St. Mary's Seminary, Greenmeadows, 1953. *Appointments:* Member of Society of Mary, 1936; Ordained priest, 1940; Principal, Api Fo, ou College, Tonga, 1941; Titular Bishop and Vicar Apostolic of Tonga, 1953; Bishop of Tonga, 1966; Bishop of Rarotonga, 1972; Auxiliary Bishop of Auckland, New Zealand, 1977. *Creative Works:* Missal in Tongan, Sacramentary in Rarotongan. *Honours:* Bishop Assistant at the Pontifical Throne, 1971; CMG, 1979. *Hobbies:* Pacific Languages and studies. *Address:* Bishops House, New Street, PO Box 47-255, Ponsonby, Auckland, 1, New Zealand.

RODGERS John Sir, (Bart.), b. 6 Oct. 1906, York, England. m Politician, Company Director, Author. m. Betsy Aikin-Sneath, 2 sons. 20 Dec. 1930 *Education:* MA, Keble College Oxford, Scholar. *Appointments:* J. Walter, Thompson Cl. Limited, Director & Deputy Chairman, 1931-71; Chairman, British Market Research Bureau Limited, 1933-54; Cocoa Merchants Limited, 1965-78, Chairman; Member of Parliament for the Sevenoaks Division of Kent, 1950-79; Parliamentary Private Secretary to Viscount Eccles, 1951-57; Parliamentary Secretary, Board of Trade and Minister for Regional Development and Employment, 1958-61; UK Delegate, Conservatives, at the Council of Europe & Vice President, Western European Union, 1969-79; Chairman, Radio Television Luxembourg, London & Chairman of other Companies, 1980-; Chairman, Caribbean Sub-Committee of Foreign & Commonwealth Affairs committee for 20 years. *Memberships:* Council of the National Trust; Vice-Chairman, Heritage of London Trust; Honorary Treasurer, European-Atlantic Group; Hon Treasurer, Royal National Institute for Deaf; Ex-President, Institute of Practitioners in Advertising, Institute of Statisticies and Society for Individual Freedom; Vice-Chairman, Executive Political & Economic Planning, 1962-68; Master, Worshipful Company of Masons, London; President, Centre European de Documentation et Information; 1963-6€, Vice-President, European League for Economic Co-operation; Original Member, later President of the One Nation Group *Publications:* Mary Word Settlement, A history, 1930; The Old Public Schools of England, 1938; English Woodland, 1941; Industry Works of the New Order, 1941; English Rivers, 1948; One Nation, 1950; Many other pamphlets and booklets on political and economic matters. *Honours:* Created a Baronet, 1964; Grand Cross of Liechtenstein, 1970; Knight Grand Cross, Order of Civil Merit, Spain, 1965; Commander Order of Infante Dom Henrique (Portugal), 1972; Grand Officier, Order Leopold II, Belgium 1978; Order of the Brilliant Star, Republic of China, 1979; Knight Commander, First Class, of the Royal Order of the North Star, Sweden, 1980; Commander, 1st Class, Order the Lion of Finland, 1980; Council of Europe Medal of Merit, 1980.

Hobbies: Travel; Theatre; Reading. *Address:* 72 Berkeley House, Hay Hill, London W1, England.

RODKIEWICZ, Czeslaw Mateusz, b. Poland, Professor. *Education:* Dip.Ing, Polish University College, London, England; MSc, University of Illinois, Illinois, USA; PhD. Cleveland Case Institute of Technology, Ohio, USA. *Appointments:* Research Engineer, English Electric Company, Rugby, England; Technical Assistant, Dowty Equipment, Canada, 1954; Ryerson Institute of Technology, Toronto, Ontario, 1955; Full Professor, Department of Mechanical Engineering, University of Alberta, Edmonton, Canada, 1958. *Memberships:* The New York Acadamy of Sciences; American & Canadian Societies of Mechanical Engineers; Sigma Xi Society; Canadian Medical and Biological Engineering Society; Professional Engineers of Ontario; Honorary President of Engineering Students' Society of the University of Alberta in Edmonton, 1962; Three times elected President, Polish Canadian Congress, Alberta; 1976 he received the Congress highest honor, gold decoration for outstanding service to the community, 1969, 1971, 1973. *Publications:* Reviewed scientific papers for various professional periodicals and received numerous lecture and address invitations. *Address:* Department of Mech. Eng University of Alberta, Edmonton, Alberta, Canada.

RODRIGUES, Francis Michael Anthony Celestine, b. 3 Dec. 1930, Belgium City, Karnataka State, India. Medical Research. m. Jeanette Josephine, 28 Feb. 1965, 3 daughters. *Education:* MB,BS, University of Poona, 1954; PhD, University of Poona, India, 1970; MPH University of California, Berkeley, California, USA, 1970. *Appointments:* Shortly after graduation, joined the National Institute of Virology, Poona, which was formerly known as the Virus Research Centre. For the last 25 years, has been in the continuous employment of the National Institute of Virology. Now holds post, Deputy Director, in charge of Division of Epidemiology. *Memberships:* Member of the Indian Association of Pathologists & Microbiologists; Delta Omega, Honours Society for Public Health in USA, elected 1970; Poona Club, Poona. *Publications:* 40 Scientific publications which have been published in medical journals in India and abroad. *Hobbies:* Music; Stamp Collecting. *Address:* 24 Gulati Mansion, Pudamjee Park, Poona 411 002, Maharashtra State, India.

RODRIGUES, Simon Cyril, b. 28 Oct. 1939, Mangalore, India. Chemical Engineer. m. Hilda Lobo, 28 Oct. 1967, 2 sons. *Education:* BSc, 1960; B.Chem.E, 1962. *Appointments:* Firestone Tyre & Rubber Co. of India Limited, Bombay, Management Trainee, then Class A Supervisor, 4 yrs. Chemical & Plastics India, Madras, Technical Foreman & then Technical Sales Officer, 6 years; ALA Chemicals Limited, Bombay, Sales Development Manager, 5 years; Simsons Polymers Ltd, Bombay, Managing Director, Since 1977- Simsons & Martin, India Ltd, Chairman, 1980-; Simon & Ajay Organics Limited, Chairman, Managing Director, Since March 1981. *Memberships:* Plastic & Rubber Institute; Giants International. *Honours:* Number of papers & articles in various technical journals on Polymer Additives and Urethane Chemicals. *Hobbies:* Driving; Boating & Travelling. *Address:* 302 Kumad, Plot 467, 15th Road, Khar, Bombay-400 052, India.

ROE, Raigh, Dame, b. 12 Dec. 1922, Australia. Farmer. m. James Arthur, 6 Nov. 1941, 3 sons. *Memberships:* World President Associated Country Women of the World; National President, Country Womens Association, Australia. *Honours:* Dame Commander, Order British Empire, 1980; Honorary Member, Deutscher Lan Frauenverband Fed.R.West Germany. 1980; Honorary Ambassador, State Louisiana USA, 1979; Honorary Citizen City, Lancaster, Ohio, USA, 1979; Honorary Colonel Executive Department State, Mississippi, USA, 1979; Honorary World Ambassador, Western Australia, Week Council, 1977; Australian of the year, 1977; Commander Order British Empire, 1975; Honorary Life Member, CWA, 1972. *Hobbies:* Communicating. *Address:* 76 Regency Drive, Crestwood, Thornlie 6108, Western Australia.

ROGERS, Benjamin, b. 3 Aug. 1911, Vernon, British Columbia, Canada. Diplomat. m. Frances Morrison, 27 Nov. 1939, 1 son. *Education:* BA, Dalhousie University, Halifax, NS Canada, 1933; MSc(Econ), University of London, 1935. *Appointments:* Research Assistant,

Royal Institute of International Affairs, London, 1935-36; Acting National Secretary, Canadian Institute of International Affairs, 1937-38; Department of External Affairs, Ottawa, 1938-39, 1948-50, 1952-55; Canadian High Commission, Canberra, 1939-43; Canadian Embassy, Washington, 1943-44; Canadian Embassy, Rio de Janeiro, 1944-48; Chargé d'Affaires AI of Canada, Prague, 1950-52; Canadian Ambassador, Lima, 1955-58; Canadian Ambassador, Ankara, 1958-60; Deputy High Commissioner for Canada, London, 1960-64; Canadian Ambassador to Spain & Morocco, 1964-69; Canadian Ambassador to Italy and High Commissioner to Malta, 1970-72; Chief of Protocol, Department of External Affairs, Ottawa, 1972-75; Retired, 1975. *Publications:* Co-Author with R.A. Mackay of Canada Looks Abroad, 1938. *Hobbies:* Writing; Skiing. *Address:* 450, Piccadilly Avenue, Ottawa, Ontario, Canada, KIY OH6.

ROGERS, David William, b. 21st Mar. 1926. Sydney NSW, Australia. Solicitor & Company Director, m. Janette Leslie Christian, 3 sons, 1 daughter. *Education:* LLB, University of Melbourne, Ormand College, 1946-9. *Appointments:* Partner Hedderwick, Fookes & Alston, Melbourne, 1956-; Director, Gatic, Australia Pty Limited, 1962; Chairman, 1974; Director & Chairman, Denso Australia Pty Ltd, 1968; Director, Plumrose, Australia Ltd, 1972; Director, Victorian Board, Australian Mutual Provident Society, 1978; Director ARC Industries, 1978 Chairman, 1979; Director, Woodside Petroleum Ltd, 1979. *Memberships:* Australian Club, Melbourne: Melbourne Club; Metropolitan Golf Club; Royal Melbourne Tennis Club; Royal South Yarra; Lawn Tennis Club. *Publications:* Contributor Medico-Legal Society of Victoria. *Hobbies:* Tennis; Squash; Golf; Fishing. *Address:* 38 Grandview Grove, East Prahran 3181, Victoria, Australia.

ROGERS, Edward Samuel, b. 27 May, 1933, Toronto, Ontario, Canada. Communications Executive. m. Loretta Anne Robinson, 25 Sept. 1963, 1 son, 3 daughters. *Education:* BA, University of Toronto; LLB, Osgoode Hall Law School. *Appointments:* Rogers Telecommunications Limited, 1961-79; Rogers Cablesystems Inc. 1979-. *Memberships:* Toronto Club; Albany Club; Royal Canadian Yacht Club; Rideau Club, Ottawa, Canada, Lyford Cay Club, Nassau, Bahamas. *Hobbies:* Opera; Politics. *Address:* 3 Frybrook Road, Toronto, Ontario, Canada, M4V 1Y7.

ROGERS, Ian James, b. 9 June 1938, Macclesfield, Cheshire. Commercial Manager/QS. m. Joanne M. 27 May 1961. *Education:* Associate of Manchester College of Science & Technology, 1961; Member, British Institute of Management, 1975; Member, Chartered Institute of Building, 1975; Fellow, Chartered Institute of Building, 1980. *Appointments:* 1955-61, Moston Brick & Building Co. Ltd; 1961-62, Allot & Lomax; 1962-64, Tozer & Partners; 1964-67, Rider Hunt & Partners; 1967-72, Regional Director, Mitchell Construction Trinidad, WI; 1972-77, Regional Director, Holst & Co, Scotland; 1977-80, Chief Q.S. John Laing International in Nigeria; 1980-81, Chief Q.S. Feal SPA Milano, Italy; 1981- Widnell & Trollope in Nigeria. *Memberships:* Lodge No.26 St. John, Dunfermline Fife, Treasurer, 1975-77; *Hobbies:* Golf; Squash. *Address:* 16 West Harbour Road, Charlestown, Fife, Scotland.

ROGERS, Kenneth Henry, b. 12 Apr. 1925. Perth, Australia. Diplomatic Service. *Education:* BA, University of Western Australia, 1948. *Appointments:* Joined Department of Foreign Affairs, 1949; Third Secretary, Australian Mission to the United Nations, 1952-56; First Secretary, Australian Embassy, Jakarta, 1958-60; First Secretary, Australian Embassy, Rome, 1961-63; Counsellor, Australian, High Commission, 1965-67; Deputy Permanent Representative, Australian Mission to United Nations, 1967-70; Australian High Commission, Kenya, 1971-74; Australian Ambassador to Mexico, 1977-80; Australian Ambassador to Spain, 1980-. *Hobbies:* Swimming; Scuba diving. *Address:* Australian Embassy, Pareo le la Castellana 143, Madrid 16, Spain.

ROGERS, Robert Louis, b. 23 Nov. 1919, Toronto, Ontario, Canada. Diplomat. m. Elisabeth June Wrong, 17 June, 1949, 3 sons, 1 daughter. *Education:* BA, University of Toronto, 1942. *Appointments:* Canadian Army, 1942-46; Third Secretary, Canadian Embassy, Washington, 1946-49; Second Secretary, Canadian Embassy, Tokyo, 1952-55; Counsellor, Canadian High

Commission, London, 1958-60; Counsellor, Canadian Delegation to NATO, Paris, 1960-63; Head of Far Eastern Division, Ottawa, 1963-65; Ambassador to Israel, 1965-69; Deputy High Commissioner, London, 1969-72; Ambassador to Yugoslavia, 1972-74; Director General Asian & Pacific Affairs, Ottawa, 1974-77; High Commissioner, india, 1977-79; Ambassador at Large for Conference on Security & Co-Operation in Europe, 1979-. *Publications:* History of the Lincoln & Welland Regiment, Canadian Army. *Honours:* Mentioned in Despatches, 1945. *Hobbies:* Reading; Music. *Address:* 1404-71 Somerset St. W., Ottawa, Ontario, K2P 2G2, Canada.

ROHR, James Bruce, b. 9 Aug. 1942. Sydney, New South Wales, Australia. Medical Practitioner, Dermatologist. m. Christine Mary Strong, 22 May, 1967, 5 sons, 3 daughters. *Education:* MB, University of Sydney; BS, 1966; Diploma FACD, 1971. *Appointments:* Chairman, Department of Dermatology, Royal Perth Hospital; Head of Department of Dermatology, Fremantle Hospital; Part-time Clinical Lecturer, University of Western Australia. *Memberships:* W.A. Faculty, Australasian College of Dermatologists, Chairman; Royal Kings Park Tennis Club; WA Turf Club; Lake Karrinyup Golf Club. *Publications:* The Skin of the Newborn, Australian Journal of Dermatology, dec. 1975. *Honours:* Squibb Fellow in Dermatology, 1970. *Hobbies:* Tennis; Gardening. *Address:* 27 Airlie Street, Claremont, Perth 6010, Western Australia.

ROLANDIS, Nicos, b. 10 Dec. 1934, Limassol, Cyprus. Minister of Foreign Affairs. m. Lelia Aivaliotis, 26 Dec. 1959. 1 son, 2 daughters. *Education:* Middle Temple, London, 1956. *Appointments:* Law Practitioner and Businessman, 1956-78; Minister of Foreign Affairs, March 1978-. *Address:* c/o MFA, Nicosia, Cyprus.

ROLLE, Alvan Kenneth, b. 8th Feb. 1945, Exuma, Bahamas, Architect/Educator. m. Bessie May, 5th July, 1975, 1 son, 1 daughter. *Education:* Diploma in Architectural Technology , Miami Dade Community Junior College, 1968; BA, Business Administration Californian Western, 1977; MS, Business Administration Californian Western, 1978; BS, Florida International, 1979. *Appointments:* President, Alvan K Rolle and Associates, 1969-; Provost, Soldier Road Campus, College of the Bahamas, 1977-; Divisional Chairperson, Technical and Vocational Division, 1975-77; Lecturer, CR, Walker Technical College, 1972-75. *Memberships:* Who's Who Among Students in American Universities and Colleges; Faculty of Architects and Surveyors; The Incorporated Association of Architects and Surveyors; The Institute of Bahamian Architects Corporate Member. *Honours:* Honorary Doctorate of Fine Arts; Phi Kappa Phi Honor Society; Sigma Lambda Chi Honor Society. *Hobbies:* Writing; Reading; Movies. *Address:* PO Box N7401, Nassau, Bahamas.

ROLLE, Ian Richard, b. 18th Mar. 1932, Sydney, Australia. Publishing. m. Judith Ann, 12th June, 1957, 2 sons, 1 daughter. *Education:* Sydney Grammar School, 1942-48. *Appointments:* HS Holt, Pty Limited, 1950-56; KV Chapman P/L, 1956-61; Greater Publications, 1961/80; Thomson Publications, Australia Pty Ltd. 1980/81. *Memberships:* Chairman, Australian Association of Business Publications; Executive Member, Circulations Audit Board; Executive Member, Audit Bureau of Circulation; Vice-President, International Advertising Association. Advertising Club. *Hobbies:* Sailing; Golf; Publishing. *Address:* 26A Ku-Ring-Gai-Avenue, Turramurra 2074, Australia.

ROLLISON, Ronald Alexander Andrew, b. 27th Mar. 1926, Adelaide, South Australia. Medical Practitioner. m. Miss Jeannie Curran, 26th Aug. 1965, 1 son, 1 daughter. *Education:* Mb, BS, Sydney University, 1946-52; DA, RCP & S, Royal College of Surgeons & Physicians, 1954; FFA, RCS, Royal College of Surgeons, England, 1961. *Appointments:* Senior Specialist, Prince of Wales Hospital, Sydney, 1961-63; Honorary Anaesthestist, 1963-75; Late Honorary Anaesthetist Fairfield District Hospital; Late Consultant, Anaesthesia, Liverpool District Hospital, Liverpool, New South Wales; Director of Anaesthesia, The Woolongong Hospital, New South Wales, 1970-. *Memberships:* Australian Medical Association, Australian Society of Anaesthetists; Woolongong Club. *Publications:* Suxamethonium in Hot Climates, Anaesthesia, 1958;

Place of Respiratory Unit in General Hospital, 1964; Haemophilia and Hepatitis Causing Airway Obstruction, Australian Medical Journal, 1965. *Honours:* FFA, RACS, by election for services to anaesthesia, 1970, Brisbane, Australia. *Hobbies:* Sailing; Fishing; Golf. *Address:* Townsville General Hospital, Eyre Street, Townsville, Queensland 4810, Australia.

ROMER, John Dudley, b. 9th Sept. 1920, Richmond, Surrey, England. Retired Zoologist. m. Raymonde Mason, 7th Nov. 1945, 3 sons. *Education:* MI Biol, May, 1950; Fl.Biol, March, 1976. *Appointments:* War Service, India, engaged on rodent control, anti-malaria work and prevention of biological deterioration of stores and equipment, 1941-46; Technical Assistant, Rodent Control Research Branch, Infestation Control Division, Ministry of Food, London, 1947; Rodent Control Officer, Hong Kong Government, 1947-51; Experimental Officer, British Ministry of Supply, Tropical Testing Establishment, Port Harcourt, Nigeria, 1951-52; Pest Control Officer, Hong Kong Government, 1952-71; Senior Pest Control Officer, Hong Kong Government, 1971-80. *Memberships:* Foundation and Honorary Member, British Herpetological Society; Scientific Fellow, The Zoological Society of London; American Society of Ichthyologists and Herpetologists; Society for the Study of Amphibians and Reptiles, USA; Co-Founder and Honorary Member, The Hong Kong Natural History Society. *Publications:* Observations on the Habits and Life-history of the Chinese Newt, 1951; Annotated Checklist with Keys to the Adult Amphibians of Hong Kong, 1979. *Honours:* MBE, 1971; ISO, 1980 *Hobbies:* Herpetology. *Address:* 3 Rose Close, Brading, Sandown, Isle of Wight, PO36 0HY, England.

RONALD, Peter Bruce, b. 17th Oct. 1921, Berwick, Victoria, Australia. Grazier. m. Heather Barry Lambert, 27th April, 1949, 2 sons. *Education:* Geelong Grammar School, Corio, Victoria, left 1937. *Appointments:* Hon. Justice of the Peace from 1956-; Member, Town & Country Planning Board, 1971-74; Director, Gas & Fuel Board of Victoria, 1978-. *Memberships:* Royal Agricultural Society of Victoria, President, 1973-77; Berwickshire Council, President, 1956-64; Melbourne Hunt Club, Joint Master, 1958-67; Pakenham Agricultural Society, President, 1941-52; Pakenham Racing Club, President, 1958-67, 1978-. *Honours:* CMG, Companion of the Most Distinguished Order of St. Michael and St. George, 1979. *Hobbies:* Fishing; Watching Football. *Address:* Box 119, Pakenham, Victoria 3810, Australia.

RONNIE, Mary Allan, b. 12th June, 1926. Glasgow, Scotland. National Librarian of New Zealand. *Education:* BA, 1951; MA, 1965; Cert. New Zealand Library Association, 1946; Diploma, New Zealand Library School, 1952; Fellow of the New Zealand Association, 1975. *Appointments:* Dunedin, New Zealand, Public Library, 1944-76; Library Assistant and Reference Librarian 1944-51; Head of Lending, 1952-60; Glasgow Public Libraries, relieving Branch Librarian, 1960-61; Dunedin Public Library, Deputy Librarian, 1961-68; City Librarian, 1968-76; National Librarian of New Zealand, 1976-. *Memberships:* New Zealand Library Association, Member of council, 1968-78; President 1973-74; NZLA Education Committee, 1968; NZLA, Board of Examiners, 1969-76; Visiting Lecturer at Library School, 1968-; Council of University of Otago, 1974-76; Council of Victoria University of Wellington, 1977-; Council of Wellington Teachers College, 1978-. *Publications:* Professional articles in library journals and conference proceedings; Essay on Local Government; Essays to celebrate the Silver Jubilee of Queen Elizabeth. *Honours:* Queens, Silver Jubilee Medal. *Hobbies:* Reading; Scottish Country Dancing; Walking. *Address:* F/2, 1, Wesley Road, Wellington 1, New Zealand.

RONSON, R. Louis, b. 21 Feb. 1915, Toronto, Canada. m. Hildegarde Joann, 13 Aug. 1947, 1 son, 1 daughter. *Education:* BSc, BChE, University of Toronto and Lawrence Institute of Technology, Michigan. *Appointments:* 42 years with Work Wear Corporation of Canada Ltd, Became President and CEO in 1970; Deputy Chairman and CEO, 1981; Chairman of the Board, 1981-82; Director: Bank Hapoalim (Canada); Constitution Insurance Company of Canada; Textile Rental Services Association of America; Mount Sinai Hospital; National Retinitis Pigmentosa Foundation of Canada. *Memberships:* Ontario Chamber of Commerce; Toronto Board of

Trade. *Publications:* National Human Relations Award by the Canadian Council of Christians and Jews, 1979. *Hobbies:* Photography; Golf; Community Service. *Address:* 326 Betty Ann Drive, Willowdale, Ontario, Canada, M2R 1B3.

ROOK, James Michael Ward, b. 16 Sept. 1941, Guildford, Surrey, England. Marketing/Advertising Executive. *Education:* Member, Institute of Marketing Management; Member, Zimbabwe Institute of Management. *Appointments:* Marketing and Advertisement Manager of Modern Farming Publications, The Publicity Arm of the Commercial Farmers' Union, Zimbabwe. *Memberships:* Ex-Vice Chairman and present Committee member of the Quill Club, Zimbabwe's National Press Club. *Publications:* Marketing and Advertisement Manager of the Publication Zimbabwe Agricultural and Economic Review. *Hobbies:* Travel. *Address:* 10 39th Avenue, Haig Park, Salisbury, Zimbabwe.

ROOKE, Denis Eric, b. 2 Apr. 1924, London. Chartered Engineer, Chairman, British Gas Corporation. m. Elizabeth Brenda Evans, 22 Jan. 1949, 1 daughter. *Education:* BSc, University College, London, 1944; Honorary Degrees, Doctor of Science, Salford University, 1978, Leeds University, 1980. *Appointments:* Assistant Mechanical Engineer in coal-tar & by-products works, 1949-54; Deputy Manager of Coal-tar & by-products works, 1954-57; Seconded North Thames Gas Board, 1957-59; Development Engineer, South Eastern Gas Board, 1959; Development Engineer, Gas Council, 1960-66; Member for Production & Supply, Gas Council, 1966-71; Deputy Chairman, Gas Council, 1972-76; Chairman, British Gas Corporation, 1976-. *Memberships:* Athenaeum; English Speaking Union. *Publications:* Numerous papers to Learned Societies and Professional Associations. *Honours:* Knight Bachelor, 1977; CBE, 1970; Fellow, Royal Society, 1978; Elected to Fellowship of Engineering, 1977. *Hobbies:* Photography; Listening to Music. *Address:* British Gas Corporation, Rivermill House, 152 Grosvenor Road, London, SW1V 3JL, England.

ROONEY, Denis Michael Hall, b. 9 Aug. 1919, Liverpool. m. Ruby T. Lamb, 29 Aug. 1942, 3 sons, 3 daughters. *Education:* Stonyhurst College; MA, Downing College, Cambridge. *Appointments:* Deputy Managing Director, Balfour Beatty Limited, 1969-73; Managing Director, Balfour Beatty Limited, 1973-77; Chairman, Balfour Beatty Limited, 1975-80; Chairman, BICC International Ltd, 1978-80; Executive Vice-Chairman, BICC Ltd, 1978-80; Chairman, SE Asia Trade Advisory Group, BOTB, 1975-79; Member, British Overseas Trade Advisory Council, 1976-80; Member, BOTB, 1979-80; Member, Export Group for Construction Industries, 1964-80; Vice Chairman, Export Group for Construction Industries, 1979-80; Chairman, National Nuclear Corporation Limited, 1980-. *Memberships:* Fellow, Institution of Mechanical Engineers, Institution of Electrical Engineers; Companion, British Institute of Managment; Christian Association of Business Executives, Council, 1979-80; Christian Association of Business Executives, Advisory Council, 1980-. *Publications:* Contribution, Brazilian Railway Electrification; IEE Journal. *Honours:* CBE, 1977; FEng, 1979; FRSA, 1980; Liveryman, Worshipful Company of Turners 1974. *Hobbies:* Golf; Sailing. *Address:* Tor House, Station Road, Woldingham, Surrey CR3 7DA, England.

ROPER, Thomas William, b. 6 Mar. 1945, Chatswood, NSW, Australia. Member of Parliament. m. Marily Ann Joyce, 20 July 1968, 2 daughters. *Education:* BA, Sydney, 1966. *Appointments:* Education Vice President, National Union of Australian University Students, 1968-70; Tutor, Senior Tutor, Faculty of Education, La Trobe University, 1970-73. *Publications:* Aboriginal Education, The Teachers Role, 1968; The Myth of Equality, 1970; Under Five In Australia, 1973. *Hobbies:* Politics; Reading; Tennis. *Address:* Parliament House, Spring Sr, Melbourne, 3002, Victoria, Australia.

RORKE, Peter Charles, b. 22 Feb 1928, Pretoria, South Africa. Musician/Film and Television Director. m. Wanda L. G. Dommett, 2 sons, 2 daughters. *Education:* Royal Academy of Music, London; Conservatorium of Music, Holland; Pianoforte, LRAM: LTCL: UTLM; UPLM; Violin, LTCL; Harmony and Counterpoint, UTLM. Film and Television, BBC, Training School. *Appointments:* Private practice as Music teacher; As-

sistant Conductor, London Festival Ballet; Musical Director; ISCOR Symphony Orchestra; Music Producer, BBC Manchester; Film and TV Director, Music and Arts, BBC Television Centre; Supervisor of Music for Victoria, Australian Broadcasting Commission; Executive Producer, TV Music Unit, ABC Melbourne; Head of the Music Programme, Darling Downs Institute of Advanced Education, Toowoomba, Queensland; Associate Dean, School of Arts, DDIAE. *Publications:* Sinfonietta for Chamber Orchestra, 1950; Divertimento for strings, 1952; Burlesque for piano and Strings, 1955; The New Vicar' - One-act comic opera, 1956; The Reluctant Corpse, TV opera, 1959; Variations on Waltzing Matilda, 1972; Overture, Tesso, 1978. *Honours:* University of South Africa Overseas Scholarship, 1847; Lionel Tertis Prize for Composition, Royal Acaderny of Music, London, 1948; University of South Africa Examiner's Scholarship, 1958. *Hobbies:* Carpentry; Electronics; Golf. *Address:* 9 Hilltop Crescent, Toowoomba, Queensland, Australia 4350.

ROSA, Antoine, b. 8 Jan 1924, Larnaca, Cyprus. Director and Secretary, Bata (Cyprus) Ltd. *Appointments:* Bata (Cyprus) Limited, Accountancy, Administration, Personnel Management, Industrial Relations, Corporate Affairs, 1945-. *Memberships:* Industrial Disputes Court; Council member of the Cyprus Employers' Federation; Secretary of the Footwear Industies' Association. *Hobbies:* Art; Architecture; Interior Decoration; Languages (Greek, English, French, Italian). *Address:* 11 Prevezis Str., Nicosia, Cyprus.

ROSCOE, Adrian Alan, b. 5 June, 1939, Ellesmere Port, Wirral, Cheshire, England. Professor of English. m. Janice G. Dean, 22 July, 1961, 1 son, 3 daughters. *Education:* BA, University of Sheffield, 1960; Diploma in Education, 1961; MA, McMaster University, 1965; PhD, Queen's University, Canada, 1968. *Appointments:* Head of English, St. Leo's Training College, Nigeria, 1961-63; Assistant Master, St. Anselm's College, Birkenhead, 1963-64; Teaching Fellow, Department of English, McMaster University, 1964-65; Teaching Fellow, Queen's University, 1965-68; Lecturer, University of Nairobi, Kenya, 1968-70; Visiting Professor of African and British Literature, State University of New York, 1970-72; Senior Lecturer in English, University of Malawi, 1972-76; Dean, School of Arts, University of Malawi, 1976-78; Professor of English, University of Malawi, 1978-. *Memberships:* Board of Governors, Designated Schools Board, Malawi; Founding Editor, Malawian Writers Series; Founding Editor, Busara Magazine, Nairobi; Editorial Panel, Pan-African Journal, 1970-72. *Publications:* Mother is Gold, Cambridge University Press, 1971; Keep My Words, Luo Oral Literature, East African Publishing House, 1974; Tales of Old Malawi, Montfort Press, 1976; Uhuru's Fire, African Literature East to South, Cambridge University Press, 1977; Reviews and Articles in Journals and Periodicals; Radio Broadcasts, BBC, Voice of Kenya; Malawi Broadcasting Corporation. *Hobbies:* Squash (SRA coach); Tennis; Orchestral Playing and Choral Conducting. *Address:* Department of English, University of Malawi, Box 280, Zomba, Malawi.

ROSE, Clyde, b. 7 Aug 1937, Fox Island, Newfoundland, Canada. Publisher. m. 2 May 1970, 1 son, 1 daughter. *Education:* MA, English. *Appointments:* Naval Officer, RCN: Teacher; Professor; Publisher. *Memberships:* President, Breakwater Books Ltd. *Publications:* Editor, Baffles of Wind & Tide; East of Canada; The Blasty Bough. *Honours:* Founded Newfoundlands first Publishing house, Breakwater; National Awards for Children's books; Books of humour. *Hobbies:* Swimming. *Address:* Portugal Cove, Newfoundland, Canada.

ROSE, John Desmond, b. 14 Mar 1920, Rotorua, New Zealand. Financier. m. Sheila M. A. Sinclair, 8 Apr. 1950, 4 sons. *Education:* 1946, University of New Zealand B.Com; Fellow Chartered Accountant, New Zealand; Fellow Institute Chartered Secretaries & Administrators. *Appointments:* 1947-62, Public Practice, Chartered Accountant; 1963-80, Managing Director, Marac Holdings Ltd; 1981, Ex Chairman, Marac Merchant Bank (SE Asia) Ltd. *Memberships:* Officers Club, Northern Club, Auckland, New Zealand; Tanglin Club, Singapore. *Publications:* Professional Papers *Honours:* CBE, 1981; ED, 1955; Eisenhower Fellow, 1965. *Hobbies:* Tramping, Travel. *Address:* 37C4 Nassim Road, Singapore 1025.

ROSE, John Murray, b. 14 Dec 1939, Dunedin. Sheep Farmer. m. Christine M. Fulton, 20 Oct. 1966, 4 daughters. *Education:* University Entrance, 1956. *Appointments:* Farming from 1960; Member of Parliament, 1969-72. *Memberships:* New Zealand, Federated Farmers Dominion Council, 1980; Presbyterian Church Assembly Finance Committee, 1978; Moderator Clutha Presbytery, 1979; Lawrence Lions Club President, 1981; Various Parliamentary Committees; 1970-72. *Honours:* Young Farmers Club Radio Leadership, 1965. *Address:* Rutherglen, Waitahuna, Otago, New Zealand.

ROSE, Raymond James b. 17 Nov 1942, Liverpool, NSW, Australia. Biological Scientist, Plant Physiology. m. Joy. E. Rose, 27 Feb 1965, 1 son, 1 daughter *Education:* 1960-63, Sydney University, BSc, Agr; 1966-69, School of Biological Sciences, Macquarie University, Phd. *Appointments:* 1964-66, Research Officer, NSW Department of Agriculture; 1969-71, Post doctoral Fellow, Department Biological Sciences, Carleton University, Canada; 1971-73, Lecturer, Department Botany and Zoology, Massey University, New Zealand; 1973-75, Research Scientist/Senior Research Scientist, CSIRO, Division of Horticultural Research, Adelaide, Australia; 1975-, Lecturer/Senior Lecturer, 1978, Department Biological Sciences, The University of Newcastle, NSW, Australia. *Memberships:* Australian Society of Plant Physiologists; Australian Institute of Agricultural Science; Australian Biochemical Society; Canadian Society of Plant Physiologists. *Publications:* Publications in a number of scientific journals on the structure and function of plant cells and their organelles, particularly chloroplasts. *Honours:* CSIRO, Postdoctoral Fellowship for Overseas Study, 1969; PL, Goldacre Award from the Australian Society of Plant Physiologists in recognition of research on chloroplast DNA, 1977. *Hobbies:* Tennis. *Address:* 15 Myamblah Crescent, Merewether 2291, NSW, Australia.

ROSENBERG, Louise, b. 19 Feb 1914, Mosman, Sydney, NSW, Australia. Secretary. m. Moshe Rosenberg, 29 Mar 1938, 1 daughter. *Education:* Sydney University Extension Classes, 1938. *Appointments:* Honorary Secretary, Adult Jewish Studies, 1958; Honorary Secretary of Australian Jewish Historical Society, 1966; Honorary Secretary, Great Synagogue Social & Cultural Committee; Member of Great Synagogue Journal Committee; Secretary/Treasurer, Great Synogogue Jewish Museum, 1981-. *Memberships:* Honorary Secretary, Australian Jewish Historical Society, Editorial Committee; Honorary Secretary, Adult Jewish Studies Circle; Committe of Great Synagogue Congregational Journal; Honorary Secretary, Social & Cultural Committee of Great Synagogue. *Publications:* Monographs, Articles, regular contributions to publications, biography entries for various dictionaries, including Australian dictionary of biography. *Hobbies:* Breeding bull-terriers; Gardening; Music; Contributor to Communal and educational publications. *Address:* 5 Deepwater Road, Castlecove, NSW 2069, Australia.

ROSS, Angus, b. 19 July 1911, Otepopo, Otago, New Zealand. University Professor. m. Reda M. Evans McKenzie (dec'd) 26 May 1937; (2) Margaret C. Wood n. Garrett, 11 Nov 1950. 1 son. *Education:* University of Otago, 1930-33; University of Cambridge, Kings' College, 1947-49; The Staff College, Camberley, 1944; MA, New Zealand, 1934; PhD, Cantab, 1949. *Appointments:* University Lecturer and Senior Lecturer, 1936-56; Reader, 1956-64; Professor of History, 1965-76, University of Otago; Military, Platoon commander, Intelligence officer, Brigade Liaison officer, in 23rd New Zealand Bn., 1944; Commanding Officer, 1st Battalion Otago & Southland Regt., 1951-54; Hon. Colonel, 4th Bn., Royal New Zealand Infantry Regiment, 1964-66. *Memberships:* University Grants Committee, 1967-74; Dean, Faculty of Arts, Otago, 1959-61; Council of University of Otago, 1951-56; Foundation Chairman, Otago Regional Committee, New Zealand Historic Places Trust, 1956-61; Management Committee, Otago Museum, 1951-56; Trust Board, Otago Museum, 1956-61; Vice President, New Zealand Institute of International Affairs, 1976; Editorial Advisory Committee, New Zealand Heritage, 1971-72; Dunedin Club Otago Officers Club. *Publications:* 23 Battalion, New Zealand Official War History, 1959; Knox Church, 61960 1960; New Zealand Aspirations in the Pacific Islands in the 19th Century, Oxford UP, 1964; New Zealand's Record in the Pacific Islands in

the 20th Century, Longman-Paul, 1969; They Built in Faith, 1976, Sundry articles and chapters in books. *Honours:* Officer, Order of the British Empire, 1980; Military Cross, 1943; Bar to Military Cross, 1944; Aristion Andrias, Greek Order of Valour, 1944; Efficiency Decoration, EC 1956; Smuts Visiting fellow, Cambridge, 1971-72; Commonwealth Fellow, St. John's College, Cambridge, 1962; JR Orford Scholarship, King's College, Cambridge, 1948-49; Parker Waddington Studentship, 1947-48, King's College, Cambridge. *Hobbies:* Reading; Gardening; Spectator Sports. *Address:* 134 Cannington Road, Maori Hill, Dunedin, New Zealand.

ROSS, James Alexander, b. 10 June 1930, Palmerston North, New Zealand. Government Official; Assistant Director-General of Education. m. Margaret F. Fisher, 15 Jan. 1955, 2 daughters. *Education:* Victoria University, 1949-50; Otago University, 1951; BA, Canterbury University, 1952-53; MA, Christchurch Teachers College, 1954, Dip Tchg. *Appointments:* Assistant Director General of Education, 1980-; Assistant Secretary, Schools and Development, 1979; Assistant Secretary, 1977-78; Director of Technical Education, 1975-76; Superintendent of Curriculum Development, 1972-74; District Senior Inspector of Secondary Schools, Auckland, 1971; Senior Inspector of Secondary Schools Head office and Inspector of Secondary Schools, Wellington Region, 1966-70; Deputy Principal, Upper Hutt College, 1963-65. *Memberships:* Chairman, School Certificate Examination Board; Chairman, National Advisory Committee in Pre-School Education; New Zealand Vocational Training Council; Universities Entrance Board; Various Government Official Committees. *Publications:* Publications include World Geography, 1962; Atlantic World, 1961; Pacific World, 1960; articles in geographical and educational journals. *Honours:* Associate Fellow, New Zealand Institute of Management, 1978. *Hobbies:* Director, Wellington Central Rotary; Licensed Lay Reader; Church of England; Wellesley Club; Recreation includes Swimming; Angling. *Address:* 80 Heke Street, Nigaio, Wellington, New Zealand.

ROSS, James, b. 28 Sept. 1933, Wishaw, Lanarkshire, Scotland. m. 1 Apr. 1961, 1 son, 1 daughter. *Education:* BSc, Glasgow, 1955; Scottish Secondary Teachers Certificate, Jordanhill College of Education, 1956. *Appointments:* Dalziel High School, Motherwell, Assistant Teacher of Geography; Bellshill Academy, Principal teacher of Geography, Head of Lower School; Jordan Hill College of Education, Lecturer in Geography; Hutchesons' Grammar School, Assistant teacher in Geography. *Memberships:* Scottish Association of Geography Teachers; Geographical Association; Royal Geographical Society, Elected to be fellow 1977. *Publications:* Landscapes in Towns, Heineman, 1976; Networks & Communications, 1978; A Study of 3 Indian Punjab Villages, Commonwealth Institute, London, 1975. *Hobbies:* Music, Piano Playing; Gardening; Philately; Golf. *Address:* Bahati, 47 Blackthorn Avenue, Lenzie, Glasgow G66 4DH, Scotland.

ROSS-EDWARDS, Peter, b. 11 July 1922, Corowa, NSW, Australia. Member of Parliament. m. Joy E. Perry, 27 Apr 1953, 4 sons, 1 daughter. *Education:* Melbourne University, 1949-51, Bachelor of Laws Degree. *Appointments:* Employee of P.V. Feltham & Co (Solicitors), 1952-53; Partner of PV Feltham & Co (Solicitors), 1953-76; Consultant of PV Feltham & Co (Solicitors), 1976-; Member of Parliament, 1967-; Leader of the National Party of Victoria, 1970-. *Memberships:* Naval & Military Club, Melbourne; Athenaeum Club, Melbourne. *Hobbies:* Golf; Tennis; Swimming. *Address:* 14 Waters Road, Shepparton, Victoria, Australia.

ROTHWELL, Donald Stuart, b. 25 Apr. 1929, Chicago, Illinois, USA. Transportation Executive. *Education:* BEng, McGill University, 1952; MBA, McGill University, 1967; PhD, McGill University, 1973. *Appointments:* Peacock Brothers Ltd, Branch Manager; De Laval Turbine Canada Ltd, District Manager; Economic Council of Canada, Senior Advisor; Great Lakes Waterway Development Association, President. *Memberships:* Rideau Club; Association of Applied Economics, Director; Canadian Club; Transportation Research Forum; Association of Professional Engineers, Ontario. *Publications:* Many Articles and Speeches on Transportation, Management and Economics. *Honours:* Canada

Council Awards, 1969, 1970, 1971, 1972. *Hobbies:* Antique Automobiles. *Address:* 17 McLeod Street, Ottawa, Ontario, Canada, K2P OZ4.

ROUTLEY, Stuart Waldemar Leslie, b. 5 Apr. 1896, Horsham, Victoria, Australia. Director, Company. m. Steela Syer, 2 Jan 1922, 1 son, 1 daughter. *Appointments:* Royal Victoria Honorary Justices Association, 1950; Chairman, Festival of Empire and Remembrance in Melbourne, 1950-61; Commander and Senior Vice-President, Life Member, of the Victoria Returned Soldiers League, 1950; Central and District Citizens Appeal Committees, Red Cross, 1950-72; Director of the Lord Mayor's Children's Camp Fund, 1956; Honorary Life Governor of Austin Hospital 1945; Royal Children's Hospital, 1947; Life Governor of Prince Henry's Hospital, Melbourne, 1959; Life Member of Seymour Racing Club, Victoria, 1971; Trustee of Young Oakleigh Club for 20 years; Trustee Royal Melbourne Hospital, 1959; Full Member Marylebone Cricket Club. *Honours:* 1917, Military Medal; 1950, JP; 1959 OBE. *Hobbies:* RSL Welfare Work; Youth Clubs; Charities. *Address:* 1512 Dandenoug Road, Oakleigh 3166, Victoria, Australia.

ROWE, Helen Elizabeth, b. 21 Aug. 1952, Essex, England. Archivist. *Education:* BA, London; Diploma in Archives Administration, London. *Appointments:* 1975-, Archivist in Bermuda Archives. *Memberships:* Bermuda Historical Society; St. George's Historical Society; Bermuda National Trust. *Publications:* A Guide to the Records of Bermuda. *Hobbies:* Community Activities. *Address:* Bermuda Archives, Government Administration Building, Parliament Street, Hamilton, Bermuda.

ROWE, Peter Brock, b. 24 April, 1936, Murwillumbah, New South Wales, Australia. m. Joanne E. Hawtin, 31 May, 1961, 2 sons, 3 daughters. *Education:* MB,BS, University of Sydney, 1959; MD, University of Sydney, 1973; FRACP. *Appointments:* House Officer, Registrar, Clinical Super. Royal North Shore Hospital, 1959-64; Instructor in Medicine, Duke University, N. Carolina, 1964-65; Instructor in Medicine, University of Pennsylvania, 1965-67; Asst. Prof. Medicine, Duke University, N. Carolina, 1967-69; Sen. Lecturer Child Health, University of Sydney, 1969-73; Assoc. Prof. Child Health, University of Sydney, 1973-80; Lorimer Dods Professor, Director Childrens Medical Research Foundation, University of Sydney, 1980-. *Memberships:* Fellow of the Royal Australasian College of Physicians; Australian College of Paediatrics; Australian Biochemical Society; Paediatric Research Society of Australia, President, 1974; American Association for the Advancement of Science. *Publications:* Publications in the fields of purine and folic acid metabolism. *Honours:* Kleberg Visiting Professor, Baylor College of Medicine, Houston, Texas, 1978-79; Senior overseas Scholar, Australia American Educational Foundation, 1978-79. *Hobbies:* Reading; Swimming. *Address:* 83, Northwood Road, Northwood, New South Wales, 2066, Australia.

ROWELL, Alfred Gordon, (Brigadier) b. 2 June 1913, Sydney, New South Wales, Australia. Dental Surgeon. m. Yvonne Jeanne Rundle, 9 May 1942, 2 sons, 1 daughter. *Education:* MDS, 1947, BDS, University of Sydney, 1934; DDS, Northwestern University, Chicago, USA, 1936; Fellow in Dental, Surgery, Royal College of Surgeons, 1965; Fellow Royal Australasian College of Dental Surgeons, 1965; Fellow of American College of Dentists, 1956; Fellow International College of Dentists, 1962, Master, 1980, Fellow Academy of Dentisty International, 1980. *Appointments:* General Practice, 1936-39; Lt. Col., War Service with A.I.F., 1939-1947, Twice mentioned in despatches; General Practice and University Teaching since 1947; Colonel Commandant, Royal Australian Army Dental Corps, 1977-81; Dental Consultant, Army Headquarters, 1970-73; Consultant Prosthodontist, RADC, 1960-64; Director, Denta Services Army Headquarters, 1964-70; Chairman, Dental Services Advisory Committee, Department of Defence, 1964-70. *Memberships:* Chairman, Armed Forces Dental Services Commission, Federation Dentaire Internationale, 1970-73; President, International College of Dentist, 1978-79; President, Australasian Section, International College of Dentist, 1971-78; President, Australian Dental Association, 1960-62; President, New South Wales Branch A.D.A., 1953-54; First President & President, Royal Australasian College of Dental Surgeons, 1965-68; Chairman, Australasia for Pierre Fauchard Academy; Chairman, Medical Benefits, Dental Practitioners, Appeals Committee, Federal, 1971-. *Publications:* Contributions to Australian and Overseas Dental Journals and Periodicals. *Honours:* AO; CBE; ED(RL); Recipient of numerous honours and awards for professional services. *Address:* 120 Bellevue Road, Bellevue Hill, New South Wales, Australia 2023.

ROWELL, John Joseph, b. 15 Feb. 1916, Brisbane, Queensland, Australia. Solicitor & Company Director. m. Mary Kathleen de Silva, 27 Aug. 1947, 3 sons, 2 daughters. *Education:* BA, University of Queensland. *Appointments:* President, Queensland Law Society, 1964-66; Hon. Consul, Queensland of Federal Republic of Germany, 1963; Chairman, Lega L/AID Commission of Queensland, 1978; Member, Law reform Commission of Queensland; Director, Boral Ltd. & Boral Resources Ltd.; Chairman, Brisbane Gas Co. Ltd.; Chairman, Concrete Constructions Pty. Ltd.; Chairman, The Boral Group of Companies in Queensland. *Memberships:* Brisbane Club; United Service Club. *Honours:* CBE, 1974; Kt Bachelor, 1980. *Hobbies:* Golf; Fishing. *Address:* 48 Walcott Street, St. Lucia, Brisbane, Queensland, Australia

ROWLAND, Douglas John, b. 2 Jan. 1927, Salisbury, Zimbabwe. Mechanical Engineer. m. Margaret Lucy Barrie, 17 Mar. 1951, 2 daughters. *Education:* S. Africa Advanced Tech. Cert.II, 1955; S.A. National Engineering Diploma, 1957; M.Inst. Mechanical Engineers, 1970; Chartered Engineer, 1971. *Appointments:* National Railways of Zimbabwe: Engineering Mechanical Draugtsman, 1949, Assistant Mechanical Engineer, 1957, Production & Planning Engineer, 1970, Mechanical Engineer, 1972, Assistant Chief Mechanical Engineer, Motive Power, 1980; Director of Local Departmental Store, Vice Chairman, 1977-; Chairman, Board of Management, Railmed Medical Aid Society; Elected Councillor, City of Bulawayo, 1974, Deputy Mayor, 1977, Mayor, 1978-79, Re-elected Deputy Mayor, 1980-81, Elected Mayor, 1981, First Black Majority Bulawayo City Council. *Memberships:* Bulawayo Club; Rotary International; Institution of Zimbabwe Engineers, M.I.Zwe.E; South African Institute Mechanical Engineers, M.S.A.I.Mech.E. *Honours:* Efficiency Decoration, E.D., 1962; Military Forces Commendation, 1970; Defence Medal for Meritorious Service, DMM, 1973; Honorary Colonel 2nd Battalion, 6th BN, 9th BN, Rhodesia Regiment, 1977. *Hobbies:* Cricket; Rugby. *Address:* 5 Munda Drive, Burnside, Bulawayo, Zimbabwe.

ROWLAND, James Anthony, (Sir), b. 1 Nov. 1922, Armidale, New South Wales, Australia. Aeronautical Engineer, Pilot, Service Officer. m. Fay Alison Doughton, 20 Apr. 1955, 1 daughter. *Education:* BE, Aero, University of Sydney, 1940-41, 1946-47; Empire Test Pilots School, Farnborough, England, 1949; RAAF Staff College, Point Cook, 1956; Royal College of Defence Studies, London, 1971; Chartered Engineer, 1970. *Appointments:* Royal Australian Air Force, 1942-45, Pilot; 1948-79, Pilot & Engineer; Test Pilot, Aircraft Research & Development Unit, 1948-54; Staff duties and Maintenance Officer, 1955, 1957, OCR & D, ARDU, 1958-60, Test Pilot & Senior Engineer, RAAF Mission, France, 1961-64, Engineering Staff Officer on Major Projects, 1965-67, S. Eng. SO Operational Command, 1969-70, DG Eng & Air Member for Technical Services, 1972-75, Chief of the Air Staff, RAAF, 1975-79, Engineering Consultant, 1980, Governor of New South Wales, 1981. *Memberships:* Fellow, Royal Aeronautical Society; Fellow, Institute of Engineers, Australia; Freeman, Guild of Air Pilots & Navigators. *Publications:* Contributions to Journals; Classified Reports. *Honours:* KBF, 1977; DFC, 1944; AFC, 1953. *Hobbies:* Carpentry; Surfing; Reading. *Address:* Government House, Sydney, NSW, Australia.

ROWLEY, John William Fellowes, b. 5 Dec. 1943, Linfield, Sussex, England, Barrister. m. Dora Janet Newman, 14 Aug. 1971, 2 sons. *Education:* Carlton University, Ottawa, 1961-65; LL.B, University Gold Medal, University of Ottawa, 1965-68. *Appointments:* Called to Bar of Ontario with Honours, 1970; Called to Bar of Quebec, Special call, 1977; Special Assistant to Director, Combines Branch, Dept. of Consumer & Corporate Affairs, Ottawa, 1967-68; McMillan, Binch, Toronto, Ontario, 1970; Law Clerk to The Hon. Mr. Justice R.A. Ritchie, Supreme Court of Canada, Ottawa, 1971; Rejoined McMillan, Binch, 1972. *Memberships:* The Canadian Bar Association; County of York

Law Association; International Bar Association; The Advocates Society; The Lawyers Club; Rideau Club, Ottawa; University Club, Toronto. *Publications:* Various articles on competition and other economic policy issues; Co-editor with Prof. W.T. Stanbury, Competition Policy in Canada, Butterworths, 1978; Regularly writes for The Financial Post on trade regulations and combines policy; Instructor since 1973, Bar Admission Course of Ontario; Ocassional Lecturer, Law Society of Upper Canada, Fordham Law School, Corporate Law Institute, New York City. *Honours:* University Gold Medal, University of Ottawa, 1968. *Hobbies:* Fishing; Shooting. *Address:* 58 Binscarth Road, Toronto, Ontario, Canada, M4W 1Y4.

ROWLEY, Stuart Duncan, b. 2 Mar 1952, Sale, Cheshire, England. Hospital Administrator. m. Dawn Maree Tipping, 5 May 1973, 2 daughters. *Education:* Certificate of Business Studies, Hospital Procedures, 1976; Bachelor of Health Administration, University of New South Wales, 6th Stage, 1982; Associate Member, Australian Institute of Management; Professional Associate, Aust. College of Health Service Administrators. *Appointments:* Administrative Assistant, Mount Royal Hospital, 1972; Administrative Officer General, Mount Royal Hospital, 1974; Deputy Manager, Echuca District Hospital, 1976; Manager, Echuca District Hospital, 1978. *Memberships:* Registered Critic, Australian Rostrum; President, Rostrum Club No. 44, Echuca; Secretary, Echuca Care of the Aged Program Committee. *Hobbies:* Squash; Golf; Swimming. *Address:* 16 Francis Street, Echuca, 3625, Victoria, Australia.

ROWLISON, Eric Bjorn, b. 13 Nov. 1939, Norwalk, Connecticut, USA. Co-ordinator/ Special Projects, Victorian Ministry for the Arts. *Education:* BA Honours, Lafayette College, Easton, PA, 1961; New York U. Institute of Fine Arts, 1962-63. *Appointments:* Cataloguer, Assoc. Registrar, The Museum of Modern Arts, New York, 1962-70; Registrar of Collections, Art Gallery of New South Wales, Sydney, Australia, 1971-73; Registrar, The Museum of Modern Art, New York, 1973-75; Director, National Gallery of Victoria, Melbourne, Australia, 1975-80; Co-Ordinator/Special Projects, Victorian Ministry for the Arts, Melbourne, 1980-. *Publications:* Rules for Handling Works of Art, 1973, Film with Elizabeth L. Burnham, 1975; A Cataloguers Manual for the Visual Arts, Editor, 1980; Also numerous articles and published lectures. *Honours:* Queen Elizabeth II Silver Jubilee Medal, 1977. *Hobbies:* Study of Oceanic Tribal Art. *Address:* 24 Fitzwilliam Street, Kew, Victoria 3101, Australia.

ROY, Biren, b. 28 Aug. 1909, Calcutta, India. Editor, Writer, Developer of Estates, Parliamentarian. m. Dawn Meghmala Mukherji, 16 July 1939. *Education:* BSc, Physic Hons, Presidency College, 7th in order of Merit, ISC, Calcutta University, 1927; Scholar in Matric, 1925; Doctor of Science, Jadavpur University; Trained in Radio Science, Calcutta University, 1927-28; Licenced Pilot, 1929-69 as an Aviator; *Appointments:* Technical Assistant in RCA, London, 1930; Editor of First Radio Journal of India, 1926-29; Bengal Municipal Gazett, 1935-40; Editor in Chief, The Indian Airman & Spaceman, 1947-82; Writer of Scenario & Story of Films, Agni Yuger Kahini, Musafur, Kamalakanta & Lure of the Unknown; Director, Film Shilpa Sanstha & New Era Printing Works, 1964, & Indropa; Member, Bengal Legislative Council, 1943-52; Member, Bengal Legislative Assembly, 1952-57; Member, Parliament of India, 1957-72; Chairman, S.S. Municipality, 1932-48. *Memberships:* President, Bengal Flying Club; Chairman, Aeroclub of India, 1949-52; President, All Bengal Municipal Assosiation, 1936-50, 1956, 1975; President, Airmail Society of India, 1970; Indian Academy of Arts, Science Congress, Asiatic Society; Indian Parliamentary Group; Presidency College Alumni Assosiation; Mohun Bagan Club. *Publications:* The Mahabharata, in English, German & Begali; Ramayana, English & German; Flying for all, English & Hindi; Practical Set-Making & Science of Radio. *Honours:* Recipient of numerous Honours and awards for professional services. *Hobbies:* Stamp Collecting; Aero-Modelling; Photography; Flying; Motoring. *Address:* Roy Mansions, Behala, Calcutta 34, India.

ROY, Chunilal, b. 31 Oct. 1936, Jagannathpur, Bangladesh. Teaching & Research in Physics. m. Amita Ghosh, 25 Feb. 1969. *Education:* ISC, Silchar G.C. College, Gauhati University, 1954; BSC, 1st Class Hons

in Physics, Vidyasagar College, Calcutta, Cal University, 1956; MSC in Physics, Calcuttal University, 1958; PhD in Physics, Indian Institute of Technology, Kharagput, 1967; Postgraduate Studies in Physics, Copenhagen University, Denmark, 1964; Postgraduate Studies, Uppsala University, Sweden, 1975. *Appointments:* Lecturer in Physics, G.C. College, Silchar, 1958-59; Lecturer in Physics, S.N. College, Calcutta, 1959-60; Lecturer in Physics, I.I.T., Kharagpur, 1961-68; Postdoctoral Research Fellow, Ghent University, Belgium, 1975; Assistant Professor of Physics, I.I.T., Kharagpur, 1968-80; Professor of Physics, I.I.T., Kharagpur, 1980. *Memberships:* The Institute of Physics, London; American Physical Society; The Institution of Electronics & Telecommunication Engineers, India; Indian Science Congress Association; Indian Physics Association. *Publications:* Author of about 60 research papers published in Professional, National and Internation Journals of repute; Author of several Research papers in the proceedings of the Conferences and Symposia; Author of several popular scientific articles. *Honours:* Recipient of numerous honours and awards for professional services. *Hobbies:* Badminton; Table Tennis; Brdige & Chess; Writing; Reading. *Address:* c/o Gopika Ranjan Roy, Station Road, P.O. Silchar 3, Dt. Cachar, Assam, India

ROY, Denis, b. 21 Nov. 1946, Cap-Chat, Quebec, Canada. Physicist, Atomic & Molecular Physics. m. Anne-Marie Masson, 6 July 1968. *Education:* BSc, Physics, Universite Laval, 1970; MSC, Physics, Universite Laval, 1971; DSc, Physics, Universite Laval, 1974. *Appointments:* Associate Professor, Universite Laval, 1974-1980. *Memberships:* Association Canadienne-francaise pour l'Avancement des Sciences; Canadian Association of Physicists, CAP/ACP; American Physical Society; Royal Astronomical Society of Canada; Canadian Nature Federation. *Publications:* About 40 scientific publications, in refereed Conference proceedings or scientific journals, and two book chapters; Fields: Atomic & Molecular Physics, Electron Spectroscopy. *Honours:* Awarding of a Research Associateship of NSERC/CRSNG, at Universite Laval, 1980. *Hobbies:* Outdoor activities; Photography; Reading. *Address:* 1407 rue Petitclerc, Cap Rouge, Quebec, GOA 1KO, Canada

ROY, Tuhin Kumar, b. 1 Aug. 1923, Monghyr, India, Consulting Engineer, m. Silva Mardiste, 1 Jan. 3 sons. *Education:* BSc, Calcutta University; MSc, Calcutta University; MS, Massachusetts Institute of Tech. USA; ScD, Massachusetts Institute of Technology. *Appointments:* Head, Metals Research, Chemical Construction Corp, New York, 1951-54; Professor and Head Chemical Engineering Dept. Jadapur University, Calcutta, 1954-56 & 1958-60; Consultant, Freeport Mineral Co. New Orleans, 1956-58; Managing Director, Industrial Consulting Bureau, New Delhi, 1960-63; Senior Executive, Scientific Design Co. New York, 1963-65; Managing Director, Chemical & Metallurgical Design Co.(P) Ltd., 1966-. *Memberships:* Indian Institute of Chemical Engineers, President, 1970-71; Indian Academy of Sciences, Fellow; Member American Institute of Chemical Engineers; Chairman, Association of Indian Engineering Industry; Member American Chemical Society; Vice-President, National Association of Consulting Engineer. *Publications:* Contributor of reviewa, monographs, articles to professional journals and conferences. *Creative Works:* Invented new processes in Hydrometallurgy and was issued 15 patents. *Honours:* Calcutta University Gold Medal, 1945; Choudhury Memorial Lecturer, Indian Institute of Chemical Engineers; Sigma XI, USA. *Hobbies:* Hiking; Chess. *Address:* C6/3 Safdarjung Development Area, New Delhi, 110016, India.

ROYALL, Bruce Walter, b. 20 June, 1922, m. Elma Barrett, 22 Jan. 1949, 3 sons. *Education:* MB; BS: DTM & H *Appointments:* Chief Medical Officer, Unit of Drug Evaluation and Monitoring, World Health Organisation, Geneva, 1967-76; Medical Consultant, Sandoz Ltd. 1977-78; Medical Officer, Drug Evaluation, Australian Department of Health, 1979-. *Hobbies:* Sailing; Cricket; Golf. *Address:* 90, Darling Street, East Balmain, New South Wales, 2041, Australia.

ROYCE, Robert Dunlop, b. 14 March, 1914, Perth, W. Australia. Botanist. m. Lesley F.L. Brownlie, 3 June, 1944, 4 sons, 1 daughter. *Education:* BSc.(Agric.), University of Western Australia, 1934-37 *Appoint-*

ments: Department of Agriculture, 1937-74; Member of National Parks Board of Western Australia; West Australian Wild Life Authority; Curator, Western Australian Herbarium, 1962-74; Zoological Gardens Board of Western Australia. *Memberships:* Royal Society of Western Australia, Treasurer, Secretary, Assistant Editor, Asst. Librarian; Naturalists Club of Western Australia, President 2 year term. *Publications:* Contributed to various professional journals. *Honours:* Honorary Life Member of Royal Society of Western Australia, 1977; Honorary Zoo Associate from Zoological Gardens Board of Western Australia. *Hobbies:* Gardening; Carpentry; Lapidary. *Address:* P.O. Box 144, Midland, 6056, Western Australia.

ROYLE, John Peterson, b. 12 July, 1934, Victoria, Australia. Vascular Surgeon. m. Pamela A. More, 6 Feb. 1960, 1 son, 3 daughters. *Education:* Matriculation, 1951, Honours-Phys.,Chem, Pure Maths, Applied Maths; University of Melbourne Medical School, 1952-57; Commonwealth Government Scholarship, 1952; Trinity College Resident Exhibition, 1954; Roentgen Prize and Gold Medal in Physics, 1952; Graduated MB, BS, 1957; Diplomas, FRCS (Ed.) 1963; FRCS, 1963; FICA, 1966; FRACS, 1967; FACS, 1970. *Appointments:* Resident Medical Officer, Royal Melbourne Hospital, 1958-59; Surgical Registrar, Alfred Hospital, Melbourne, 1960-62; Assistant Medical Superintendant, Alfred Hospital, 1963; Lecturer in Surgery, St. Bartholomews Hospital, London, 1964-65; Vascular Surgical Registrar, Chelmsford & Essex Hospital, England, 1966; Assistant Surgeon, Alfred Hospital, Melbourne, 1967; Assistant Surgeon, Austin Hospital, Melbourne, 1967; First Assistant, Dept. of Surgery, Austin Hospital, 1968; Acting Professor of Surgery, Austin Hospital, 1971; Honorary Surgeon, Austin Hospital, 1972-77; Senior Vascular Surgeon & Head of Vascular Surgery Unit, Austin Hospital, 1977-; Director of Vascular Surgery Unit, Austin Hospital, 1981. *Memberships:* Vice-President, International College of Angiology; Chairman, Vascular Section, Royal Australasian College of Surgeons; Deputy Chairman, Board of Examiners, Royal Australasian College of Surgeons; Secretary, Victorian State Committee, Royal Australasian College of Surgeons; Member International Cardiovascular Society; Member, Surgical Research Society; Pan Pacific Surgical Association; Australian Medical Association. *Publications:* Multiple Choice Questions in the Basic Medical Sciences; Sciences; Published over 30 papers in the medical literature. *Creative Works:* Films, Profunda Femoris Stenosis (Bronze Award British Medical Association Film), 1971; Thoracic Outlet Syndrome (Commendation British Life Assurance Trust for Health Education for Film), 1976. *Honours:* Roentgen Prize and Gold Medal in Physics, 1952; Outstanding Member of Junior Medical Staff, Chelmsford Group of Hospitals, 1967; Travelling Scholarship, Wellcome Trust, 1967; Travelling Scholarship, Alfred Hospital, 1967; Merrell Award for Film RACS, 1971; Merrell Award for Film RACS, 1976. *Hobbies:* Tennis; Little Athletics, Golf. *Address:* 1, Myambert Avenue, Balwyn, 3103, Victoria, Australia.

ROYSE-SMITH, Terence, b. 4 Nov. 1921, Sydney, Australia. Dental Surgeon. m. Barbara J. Smith, 14 June, 1946, 2 daughters. *Education:* The Armidale School, Matriculated 1938; Sydney University, BDS, 1945. *Appointments:* Private Practice, 1945-. *Memberships:* President, Dental Health Education & Research Foundation, University of Sydney, 1962-75; Honorary Dental Surgeon, East Subs. Hospital, 1947-75; Member, Council Australian Dental Association, 1951-66; Director, 16th Australian Dental Congress 1961; Member, Council of Professions, 1967-80, President, 1971-74; Member, ADA & ICD, Pierre Fauchard Academy; FDI, Sydney Dental Alumni. *Honours:* AM; BDS; FICD; Awarded Fellowship of International College of Dentists, 1962; Fairfax Reading Memorial Prize of University of Sydney, 1978; Member of the Order of Australia, 1980. *Hobbies:* Sailing; Golf; Croquet; Fishing. *Address:* 1, Wallaroy Crescent, Double Bay, New South Wales, Australia.

ROZALLA, Michael Alexander, b. 25 June, 1920, Simla, India. Medical Practitioner. m. 11 April, 1966, 1 son, 1 daughter. *Education:* MB, Calcutta, 1945; DPH, England, 1957; DTM & H, England, 1960; MFCM, United Kingdom, 1974. *Appointments:* Medical Officer, Colonial Medical Service, Sarawak & Brunei, 1949-60; Assistant Director of Medical Services, Sarawak,

1960-64; Deputy Director of Medical Services, Sarawak, 1964-70; Deputy Medical Officer of Health, Department of Health, New South Wales, 1970-74; Deputy Regional Director of Health and Medical Officer of Health, Health Commission of New South Wales, 1974-80, retired; Part-time Community Physician, Health Commission of New South Wales, 1980-. *Memberships:* Australian Medical Association; Sarawak Specialist Society; India Study Circle. *Publications:* Contributor of reviews, monographs, articles to professional journals and conferences. *Honours:* Awarded War Medal, 1945; Appointed an Officer of the Order of the British Empire, 1969; Awarded Sarawak Long Service Medal, 1970; OBE. *Hobbies:* Philately. *Address:* 18 Furness Street, Bathurst, New South Wales, 2795, Australia.

RUBESS, Bruno R, b. 21 Dec. 1926, Riga, Latvia. President, Volkswagen Canada Inc. m. Biruta Broks, 24 May, 1953, 1 son, 2 daughters. *Education:* Advanced Management Programme, Harvard Business School. *Appointments:* Journalist in Germany and Canada, 1950; Life Insurance Underwriter, 1953; Automobile Salesman with Mercedes Benz, becoming Manager of largest retail branch in Canada, 1955; Sales Training Manager, Volkswagen Canada Inc., 1962; Joined Harbridge House Inc. Management Consultants to help establish Harbridge House, Europe in Frankfurt, advancing to Vice-President, 1964-69; Vice-President, Harbridge House Inc. 1970; President and Chief Executive Officer, Volkswagen, Canada, 1972-. *Appointments:* Director, Automobile Importers of Canada, 1981; Member, Ontario Economic Council, 1978-80; Council Member, School of Continuing Studies University of Totonto, 1978-80; Harvard Business School Club of Toronto, President 1977-78, Director, 1978; Director, Ontario Chamber of Commerce, 1978; Chairman Automobile Importers of Canada, 1974-75; Director, Metro Toronto Caravan, 1974-75; Executive Vice President, Latvian Foundation Inc. 1970-76. *Hobbies:* Involvement with young people; Violin; Organ; Chess; Bridge and Reading. *Address:* 162, Munro Boulevard, Willowdale, Ontario, M2P 1C8, Canada.

RUDDER, Geoffrey Malcolm, b. 19 May, 1933, Barbados. Meteorologist. m. Doreen, 17 May, 1958, 2 daughters. *Education:* Advanced Level Certificates, Harrison College, Barbados, 1945-52; BSc. University College of the West Indies, Jamaica, 1952-55; Forecasters Certificate, Meteorological Office Training School, UK, 1957; Scientific Officers Certificate, Met. Office Training School, 1962-63; MS, Florida State University, USA, 1967-69; Post Graduate work, Florida State University, 1969-71. *Appointments:* Teaching Staff, Harrison College, Barbados, 1955-56; Teaching Staff, Presentation College, Trinidad, 1956-57; Assistant Meteorologist, West Indies Meteorological Service, Trinidad, 1957-62; Meteorologist-in-charge, Barbados, 1963-67; Principal, Caribbean Meteorological Institute, Barbados, 1971-79; Chief, Training Projects Branch, World Meteorological Organisation, Geneva, 1979- *Memberships:* American Meteorological Society; Rotary Club, Barbados West, Member, 1979, President, 1977-78. *Hobbies:* Fishing and small boating. *Address:* 17, Chemin des Palettes, 1212, Grand Lancy, Geneva, Switzerland.

RUDD-JONES, Derek, b. 13 April, 1924, Agricultural Research Director. m. Joan Hancock Newhouse, 4 Dec. 1948, 2 sons, 1 daughter. *Education:* Emmanuel College, Cambridge, 1942-48, BA, 1945; MA PhD,1948. *Appointments:* Research Studentship, Agricultural Research Council, University Cambridge Botany School, 1946-48; Plant Pathologist, East African Agriculture and Forestry Research Organization, 1949-52; Post Doctoral Fellow, National Research Council Canada at University Saskatchewan, Saskatoon, 1952-53; Imperial Chemical Industries, Akers Research Lab. The Frythe, Welwyn and Jealotts Hill Research Station, Bracknell, 1953-59; Scientific Adviser, Agricultural Research Council, 1959-71; Director Glasshouse Crops Research Institute, Littlehampton, 1971-. *Memberships:* Fellow, Institute of Biology; Member Association of Applied Biology Council, 1962-67; Founder Chairman, British Crop Protection Council, 1968-72. *Publications:* Scientific papers in Nature, Journal of Experimental Botany, Annals of Applied Biology. *Honours:* CBE, 1981. *Hobbies:* Horse Riding; Fly-fishing; Gardening. *Address:* Bignor Park Cottage, Pulborough, W. Sussex, RH20 1HQ, England.

RUDE, George Frederick Elliot, b. 8 Feb. 1910, Oslo, Norway, University Professor of History. m. Doreen de la Hoyde, 16 March, 1940. *Education:* BA 1931, MA, 1950, Cambridge University; BA Hons, 1948, PhD, 1950, London; D. Letters, 1967, University of Adelaide. *Appointments:* Stowe School, Buckingham, 1931-35; St. Pauls School, London, 1936-49; University of Adelaide, 1960-67; FLinders University, S. Australia, 1968-70; Concordia University, Montreal, 1970-82; Visiting Professor at Tokyo University, 1967, Stirling, Scotland, 1968, College of William & Mary, 1980-81. *Memberships:* Committee Societe des Etudes Robespiernstes; Fellow, Royal Historical Society; Fellow, Australian Academy of Humanities; President, Ancient Order of the Biscuit. *Publications:* The Crowd in the French Revolution, 1959; Wilkes and Liberty, 1962; Revolutionary Europe, 1783-1815, 1964; The Crowd in History, 1965; Captain Swing, 1969. *Honours:* Alexander Prize, Royal Historical Society, 1955; Knight of the Mark Twain Society, 1979. *Hobbies:* Travel; Lecturing. *Address:* The Oast House, Hope Farm, Beckley, E. Sussex, England.

RUGUMYAMHETO, Joseph Asa Muhumuza, b. 26 June, 1946, Ngara, Tanzania. Civil Servant. m. 2 Sept. 1971, 2 sons. *Education:* University of Dar Es Salaam, BA Hons. 1971; Dip. in Econ. Policy & Planning, Iss the Hague, 1978. *Appointments:* Manpower Planning Officer, 1971; Senior Manpower Planning Officer, 1976; Director of Manpower Planning, 1978. *Memberships:* Fellow of the Economic Development Institute, Washington DC, 1974. *Hobbies:* Watching Sports; Reading History; Leisure Talks. *Address:* P.O. Box, 2483, Dar Es Salaam, Tanzania.

RUNDLE, Marjorie Constance Sarah (Mrs.), b 17 Apr. 1913, Pietermaritzburg, Natal, South Africa. Administrator/Journalist. m. Harold Leslie Osborne Rundle, 12 Feb. 1944, 1 son, 3 daughters. *Education:* Pitmans Shorthand Certificate, English, 150 wpm, Afrikaans, 100 wpm, 1933; Typing, Advanced Certificate. *Appointments:* Shorthand-Typist, Government of South Africa; Senior Shorthand-Typist, Dairy Produce Board, Pretoria; Confidential Secretary, Copperbelt Cold Storage Co., Kitwe, N.R.; Journalist, Kitwe & Lusaka; General Secretary, N.R. Civil Servants' Association, Lusaka; Administrative Manager, Agricultural & Commercial Society of Zambia, Position currently held. *Memberships:* Business & Professional Women's Organisation; Vic-President, 2nd World; Chairman, World Membership; President, P.R.O.; Secretary, BPW Association, Zambia; District Commissioner, Girl Guides, N.R. & Zambia. *Honours:* Order of Distinguished Service, Zambian Honour, 1978. *Hobby:* Gardening. *Address:* Plot 2374, Great East Road, Lusaka, Zambia.

RUSSELL, David Gray, b. 3 Feb. 1937, Timaru, New Zealand. Professor of Physical Education. m. Ruth Lesley Voice, 26 Mar. 1959, 1 son, 1 daughter. *Education:* BPE, 1970; MPE, 1971; MA, 1972; PHD, 1974; MAPSS, 1974; MACE, 1974. *Appointments:* Area Organiser, South Auckland, New Zealand; Assistant Area Organiser, Physical Education, Palmerston North, New Zealand; Adviser on Physical Education, Southland, New Zealand; Lecturer, School of Education, UNW, British Columbia, Canada; Research Assistant Professor, Children's Research Center, University of Illinois, USA; Senior Lecturer, Human Movement Studies, University of Queensland, Australia; Professor & Director, School of Physical Education, University of Otago, New Zealand. *Memberships:* Australian Psychological Society; Australian College of Education; American Psychological Assocation; Australia & New Zealand Association for the Advancement of Science; New Zealand Association for Health Physical Education & Recreation; New Zealand Sports Medicine Federation. *Honours:* Cahper Medal, University of British Columbia, 1970; Foundation Travel Fellow, Australia-Japan Foundation, 1977. *Hobbies:* Tennis, Jogging, Scuba; Reading. *Address:* Box 6010, Dunedin North, New Zealand.

RUSSELL, Hilary Maude, (Mrs.) b. 6 Feb. 1922, Stanthorpe, Queensland, Australia. Company Director. m. Charles Wilfred Russell, 27 July 1944, 4 sons 1 daughters. *Appointments:* Tresillian Mothercraft Nurse, 1942-44; Member, School Council, New England Girls School, Amidale, New South Wales; Company Director, School Council of New England, Amidale, New South Wales. *Memberships:* Patroness, Dalby Show Society;

Dalby Women's Forum Club; Royal Overseas League; British Empire Association; National Trust. *Honours:* Officer of the Most Excellent Order of the British Empire, Queen's Birthday Honours, 1979. *Hobbies:* Gardening; Q.C.W.A. work; Forum Club Activities. *Address:* Jimbour House, Jimbour, 4352 Queensland, Australia.

RUSSELL, Thomas, b. 27 May 1920, Melrose, Roxburghshire, Scotland. Her Majesty's Overseas Civil Service. m. Andree Desfosses, 2 Jan. 1951, 1 son. *Education:* MA, St. Andrews University, 1938-40; Dip. Anthrop., Cambridge University, 1946-47. *Appointments:* War Service, 1940-46; Service in Cameronians, Scottish Rifles, & Parachute Regiment; Captain, P.O.W., 1944-45; Appointed to Colonial Service, 1948; Served in Solomon Islands & Fiji, as District Commissioner, Establishment Secretary, Financial Secretary & Chief Secretary until 1974; Governor, Cayman Islands & Presiding Officer of Legislative Assembly, 1974-82. *Memberships:* Royal Anthropological Institute; Royal Commonwealth Society; President, Cayman Islands Branch of Commonwealth Parliamentary Association. *Honours:* CMG, 1980; CBE, 1970; OBE, 1963; Doctor of Humanities, Hon., 1980. *Hobbies:* Anthropology; Archaeology. *Address:* 49 Trafalgar Court, Firgrove Hill, Farnham, Surrey, England.

RUSSELL, Thomas Hendry, b. 23 Oct. 1925, Geelong, Victoria, Australia. Civil Engineer, Chairman Country Roads, Board, Victoria. m. Patricia Myrle Elliott, 15 May 1953, 1 son 1 daughter. *Education:* M.Eng.Sc., Hons, Melbourne University, 1950; B.CE, Melbourne University, 1949; Dip.CE, Gordon Inst. of Technology, Geelong, 1943; F.I.E.Aust; F.C.I.T. *Appointments:* Assistant Divisional Engineer, 1950-59, Assistant Engineer, Plans & Surveys, 1959, Assistant Bridge Engineer, 1959-68, Chief Bridge Engineer, 1968-70, Deputy Chief Engineer, 1970, Chief Engineer, 1970-71, Board Member, 1971-75, Deputy Chairman, 1975-78, Chairman of Country Roads Board, 1978-. *Memberships:* Past President & District Governor, Association of Apex Clubs; Hawthorn Rotary Club, Past President. *Hobbies:* Golf; Jogging. *Address:* 6 View Point Road, North Balywn, Victoria, Australia 3104.

RUTAHAKANA, Lawrence Leonard, b. 10 Aug. 1918, Mugana, Bukoba, Tanzania. M.A. Economist & B.A. Business Adminstration. m. Theresia K. Christian, 28 May 1949, 8 daughters, 2 sons. *Education:* B.A., 1960; MA, 1961. *Appointments:* Bukoba Native Coffee Board, 1947-57; Bukoba Native Co-operative Union Ltd., 1957-58 (General Clerk to Administrative Officer); Tanganyika Coffee Board, 1962-77; Executive Officer, General Manager, Coffee Authority of Tanzania, 1977-79; Chairman, International Coffee Council, International Coffee Organization, 1977-78; Inter African Coffee Organization, Director, 1962-1978. *Memberships:* President for two Terms, Lions Club of Kilimanuari; Chairman, Income Tax Committee, Northern Zone, Tanzania; Executive Committee Member, Chamber of Commerce, Moshi, Tanzania; Councilor, Moshi Town Council. *Publications:* Coffee Improvement Programme in Tanzania; Coffee Expansion in Tanzania; The Coffee Flower is Worth His Salt; Church Liturgy; The Christian Way of Life. *Hobbies:* Reading; Writing; Golf. *Address:* P.O. Box 1016, Moshi, Tanzania.

RUTHERFORD, Stuart James, b. 9 Mar. 1921. Caarshalton, Surrey, England. Executive/ Chartered Accountant. m. Margaret J. Park, 12 Oct. 1946, 3 sons. *Education:* Chartered Accountants Degree, 1950. *Appointments:* Riddell, Stead, Graham, Hutchison, C.A., 1939-42; Canadian Army, 1942-46; Riddell, Stead, Graham & Hutchison, C.A., 1946-53; J.A. Johnston Co. Ltd., 1953-64; Subsidiary Genesco of Canada Co. Ltd., 1964-; Parent Company Genesco Group Inc, 1964-. *Address:* 311 Shakespeare Place, Waterloo, Ontario, Canada.

RUXTON, Bruce Carlyle, b. 6 Feb. 1926, Melbourne, Victoria, Australia. Company Director. m. Ruth Proud, 5 June 1952, 1 son. *Education:* Diploma in Foreign Trade Procedures, Royal Melbourne Institute of Technology. *Appointments:* Family Business, General Stationers Pty Ltd; War Service, 2nd AIF 2/25th Battalion, 1943-49; State President of the Victorian Branch of the Returned Services League of Australia, 1979-; Honorary Secretary, 2/25th and 2/31st Battalions Association, 1952-; Honorary Secretary, Victorian

Association of the Most Excellent Order of the British Empire; Trustee, Shrine of Remembrance, Melbourne; Trustee, War Veterans' Homes Trust of Victoria; Trustee, Victorian Branch of RSL; Member, Discharged Servicemen's Employment Board of Victoria; Chairman, Anzac Day Commemoration Council of Victoria; Governor of the Corps of Commissionaires; Governor of the Victorian Overseas Foundation. *Memberships:* Beaumaris RSL Club; MCC; RACV. *Honours:* M.B.E. 1975; O.B.E., 1981; Life Member with Gold Badge Returned Services League of Australia; Honorary Life Member with Gold Badge, 7th Australian Division, AIF Association. *Hobbies:* Boating; Fishing; Stamp & Medal Collecting. *Address:* 24 Glenwood Avenue, Beaumaris, Victoria, Australia 3193.

RWECHUNGURA, Cleophas Claver, b. 10 Apr. 1940, Bukoba, Tanzania. Agriculturist & Journalist. m. 19 Feb. 1966, 3 sons. *Education:* Certificate in Agriculture, Tanzania, 1962; Diploma in Journalism, Indiana University, USA, 1965. *Appointments:* Field Officer (Agriculture) 1962-72; Editor (Agricultural Magazine) 1972-. *Memberships:* Tanzania Journalist Association. *Publications:* Author of three books on agriculture (in Kiswalili) Kilimo da Mboga: Cassava Growing; Maize Growing; Vegetable Growing. *Hobby:* Table Tennis; Home Gardening. *Address:* Chang'ombe Qrts. No 165 Basra Road, Dar es Salaam, Tanzania.

RWEGELLERA, George, Gregory, Celestine, b. 2 Sept. 1936, Bukoba, Tanzania. Psychiatrist. m. Mary Agnes Mzinga, 6 Feb. 1965, 2 sons, 3 daughters. *Education:* LMS, EA, 1963; MB, ChB, University of East Africa, 1967; DPM, RCP, London, RCS, England, 1969; MPhil, London, 1970, with a commendation for the Thesis; MRC, Psych, United Kingdom, 1973; MD, Makerere, 1974; Membership Certificate of the American Psychiatric Association, 1976. *Appointments:* Senior House Officer, Psychiatry, Maudsley Hospital, London, 1968-69; Registrar in Psychiatry, The Maudsley Hospital, London, 1969-70; Senior Registrar, Honorary Lecturer, Bethlem Royal and Maudsley Hospital, London, 1971-74; Senior Lecturer, Honorary Consultant Physician in Psychiatry and Clinical Neurophysiology, University of Zambia, Lusaka, 1974-78; World Health Organisation, Medical Officer/Tutor in Psychiatry, Honorary Senior Lecturer and Consultant Physician in Psychiatry and Clinical Neurophysiology, Ahmadu Bello University Teaching hospital, Kaduna. *Memberships:* Royal College of Psychiatrists, United Kingdom; Fellow, Royal Society of Medicine, London; American Psychiatric Association; International Association for the Study of Pain USA; Member, Mental Health Association, Zambia, 1974-78; Association of Psychiatrists, Nigeria. *Publications:* Suicide Rates in Zambia, Preliminary Observations; Psychological Medicine, 8, 423-432, 1978; Differential use of Psychiatric services by West African, West Indian and English patients in London; British Journal of Psychiatry, 137, 428-432, 1980; The Present State of Psychiatry in Zambia and Suggestions for Future Development; Psychopathologie Africaine Volume XV1, Number 1 21-38, 1980. *Honours:* Recipient of numerous honours including, Misereor Fellowship, to study Psychiatry, 1966-70; Ciba Foundation Associateship of the Royal Society of Medicine, 1968-73; May and Baker Research Grant, 1971; Roche Products, United Kingdom, Research Grant, 1971-72. *Hobbies:* Photography; Gardening; Music; Home-brewing; Wine-making; Walking; Golf; Tennis; Reading; Languages. *Address:* 7A Kwato Road, Government Reserved Area, GRA, Kaduna, Nigeria.

RWIZA, Raphael, b. 26 Feb. 1953, Bukoba, Tanzania. Industrial Sociologist, (Personnel Officer). *Education:* BA, Hons, 1977; MA, University of DSM. *Appointments:* Manpower Management Officer, Ministry of Manpower Development and Administration, Dar-Es-Salaam; Assistant Lecturer, University of Dar-Es-Salaam, 1978-80; Personnel Officer, Tanzania Audit Corporation, Dar-Es-Salaam. 1980-. *Publications:* Decision making and Rural Development Planning in Tanzania, 1977; The Intergration of the Matengo into the Capitalist System and the Rise of Labour Migration in Mbinga District. MA Thesis, 1979. *Honours:* DAAD (German Technical Assistance) in-Country Scholarship for MA Studies. *Hobbies:* Film; Reading; Music. *Address:* PO Box 25207, Dar-Es-Salaam, Tanzania.

RYAN, John Anthony, b. 7 Sept. 1922, Portland, NSW, Australia. University Lecturer. m. Patricia, 15

Jan. 1955, 2 sons, 2 daughters. *Education:* Diploma, Armidale Teachers College, NSW; BA, Hon. University of Sydney, NSW; MA, Hon. University of Sydney. *Appointments:* Teacher, NSW Education Department; Senior Lecturer, Macquaire University. *Memberships:* Fellowship Committee, Royal Australian Historical Society; NSW Committee, Australian Dictionary of Biography; President, Macquarie University Australian Historical Society. *Publications:* Contributor, Sport, Money, Morality and the Media, 1981; Articles on Social, Political History, published in Australian Library Studies, Australian Journal Econ History Drylight, The Bulletin. *Honours:* Fulbright Scholarship to Western Reserve Academy, Ohio, USA, 1955-56. *Hobbies:* The Australian Bush; Australian Horse Racing; History. *Address:* 10 Grayling Road, West Pymble, NSW 2073, Australia.

RYAN, John Sprott, b. 2 Apr. 1929, Dunedin, New Zealand. University Teacher and Writer. m. Alison Rosalie Norbury, 27 Mar. 1976, (marriage dissolved), 2 step sons. *Education:* BA, NZ, 1951; MA, NZ, 1952; Dip of Hons. NZ, 1953; BA, 1957, MA, 1960, Oxon, PhD, Cantab, 1967; Dip.Cont.Educ. NE, 1980. *Appointments:* University of Nottingham, 1957-58; University of New England, 1959; Lecturer 1959; Senior Lecturer, 1964; Associate Professor, 1969, Tutoring, Peterhouse, etc. Cambridge, 1964-66, 1974-75; Visiting Lecturer, Wollongong University, 1969; Research Fellow, University Otago, 1972; Hocken Lecturer, University Otago, 1979; Visiting Lecturer, Marburg, 1965; Bucharest, 1967, etc; Fellow, Wright College, UNE, 1958; Senior Fellow, 1968-72; Actng. Master, 1972-74; Hon. Fellow, 1976. *Memberships:* Phildogical Society, 1958; English Place Name Society, 1958; Ling. Society of Great Britain, 1966; Australian Ling. Society, 1965; NZ Ling. Society, 1976; Dickens Fellowship, 1964; Mod. Langs. Assn. 1964; *Hobbies:* Walking; Talking; Sailing; Book Collecting; Matters Scandinavian; Archaeology; Learning. *Address:* 30 White Avenue, Armidale, NSW 2350, Australia.

RYAN, Keith William, b. 19 June, 1922, Armidale, NSW, Australia. Company Director. m. Patricia Louise, 6 Feb. 1945, 2 sons, 1 daughter. *Appointments:* Flight Lieutenant, RAAF; Chairman and Managing Director: E.T. Miller Pty Ltd.,; E.T. Miller (Vic) Pty Ltd.,; H.S.G. Wolfe Pty Ltd.,; Sumner Industrial Supplies Ltd., *Memberships:* Past President, Bondi Diggers Club Ltd., Sydney; Registered Clubs Association, NSW; Tattersalls Club Ltd.; Bonnie Doon Golf Club; Waverley Bowling Club. *Honours:* Star, 1939-45; Pacific Star War Medal, 1939-45; Australia Service Medal, 1939-45; USA Presidents Citation Award. *Hobbies:* Swimming; Golf; Bowls. *Address:* 2 Kenilworth Street, Bondi Junction, Sydney, NSW 2022, Australia.

RYAN, Neil Joseph James, b. 20 Mar. 1930, Manchester, England. Publisher. m. Josephine, 1 Feb. 1969, 2 sons. *Education:* BA Hons. University of Bristol, 1949-52; Diploma Ed, University of London, 1952-53. *Appointments:* HM Overseas Civil Service, 1953-65; Malayan Education Service 1953-65; Headmaster, Malay College, Kuala Kangsar, Malaysia, 1959-65; Longman Group 1966-; Publishing Manager, Hong Kong, 1966-71; Managing Director, Longman Malaysia, 1971-77; Deputy Divisional Managing Director, Asia Pacific, Melbourne, Australia, 1977-81; Managing Director, Longman, Australasia and the Pacific, 1981. *Memberships:* Hong Kong Club; Hong Kong Football Club; Lake Club, Kuala Lumpur; Selangor Club, Kuala Lumpur; President, St. Patricks Society, Malaysia, 1975; Vice President, Malaysian Rugby Union, 1962-4, 1973-74. *Publications:* Malaya Through Four Centuries, Oxford UP, 1959; The Making of Modern Malaya, Oxford UP, 1962; History of Malaysia and Singapore, Oxford UP, 1976; Cultural Heritage of Malaya, Longman, 1971; India: Nationalism and Independence, Longman, 1977. *Honours:* PMP, 1965; OBE, 1966. *Hobbies:* Rugby Refereeing; Squash; Music. *Address:* 19 Belle Vue Road, North Balwyn, Melbourne, 3104, Australia.

RYAN, Susan Maree, b. 10 Oct. 1942, Sydney, Australia. Senator, Australian Federal Parliament. 1 son, 1 daughter. 02 BA, Sydney University, 1963; MA Australian National University, 1973. *Appointments:* School teacher; Tutor; National Executive Officer, Australian Council of State School Organisations, 1973-75; Education Officer, Secretariat for International

Women's Year, 1975; Member, ACT Legislative Assembly, 1974-75; Senator, 1975-; Shadow Minister for Media, the Arts and Womens Affairs, 1977-80; Shadow Minister for Aboriginal Affairs, Womens Affairs and the Arts, 1980-. *Publications:* Numerous articles on the arts, sexism in education, community involvement in education, women and politics etc; MA thesis, Women in Eighteenth Century Verse Satire. *Hobbies:* Swimming; Theatre; Music; Reading. *Address:* Parliament House, Canberra, ACT, 2600, Australia.

RYDGE, Alan Graham, b. 24 June, 1952, Sydney, Australia. Company Director. *Education:* The Scots College, Sydney. *Appointments:* Present occupation, Assistant to the Managing Director, The Greater Union Organisation Pty, Limited; Chairman, Enbeear Pty. Limited; Chairman Amalgamated Holdings Limited; Chairman, amalgamated Pictures Proprietary Limited; Chairman, The Greater J. D. Williams Amusement Co. Pty. Limited; Chairman, Wests Pty. Limited; Chairman, Carlton Investments Limited; Chairman, Carlton Hotel Limited; Chairman, Eneber Investment Co. Limited, Chairman, The Manly Hotels Pty. Limited; Director, The Greater Union Organisation Pty. Limited; Director, Guo Film Distributors Pty. Limited; Director, Guo Theatre Supplies Pty. Limited; Director, Rank Xerox (Australia) Pty. Limited; Director Rank Xerox (Finance) Pty. Limited; Director, Canberra Theatres Limited. *Memberships:* American National Club, Sydney; Tattersalls Club, Sydney; Royal Motor Yacht Club of New South Wales; Young Achievement Australia. *Hobbies:* Boating; Water Sports; Gardening; Photography. *Address:* 53 Wunulla Road, Point Piper, 2027, Australia.

RYMAN, Brenda, Edith, (Mrs. H. B. Barkley), b. 6 Dec. 1922, Bristol, England. Professor of Biochemistry, Charing Cross Hospital Medical School and Mistress of Girton College, Cambridge. m. Harry Barkley (died 1978), 11 June, 1949, 1 son, 1 daughter. *Education:* MA, Cambridge, 1945; PhD, Birmingham, 1947; FRIC, 1976; FRCPath, 1979. *Appointments:* Research Chemist, Glaxo Laboratories, 1943-45; Research Student, Birmingham University, 1945-58; Lecturer, Senior Lecturer, Reader in Department of Biochemistry, Royal Free Hospital School of Medicine (University of London), 1948-72; Professor of Biochemistry, Charing Cross Hospital Medical School (University of London), 1972; Mistress of Girton College, Cambridge, 1976. *Memberships:* Trustee of the Smith, Kline and French Foundation; Council of Queen Elizabeth College (University of London); Biochemical Society (Council Member, 1976-80). *Publications:* Articles in Essays in Biochemistry, Nature, Biochemical Journal, Biochimica et Biophysica Acta, European Journal of Biochemistry, European Journal of Cancer, British Medical Journal, etc. *Address:* 54 Primrose Gardens, Hampstead, London, NW3 4TP, England.

S

SAAD, Ronald Shaloub, b. 16 Jan. 1924, Sydney, Australia. Ophthalmologist. m. Margarida Dorotea Saad (née Boude), 27 July 1956, 2 sons . *Education:* MB, BS, Sydney University, 1951; DO, London University, 1962; FRACO, Royal Australian College of Ophthalmologists, 1978. *Appointments:* Repatriation n General Hospital, 1952-54; Australian Department of Immigration (Europe) 1954-60; Institute of Ophthalmology (London) 1961; Department of Veterans' Affairs, New South Wales, 1962-81. *Publications:* Diphyllobothriasis in Finland, 1960; Assessment of Visual Impairment, 1976; Pterygium, Pinguecula and Visual Autivity, 1977; Pterygium: Intensity and Frequency of Autivity, 1978. *Address:* 7 Bapaume Road, Mosman, New South Wales 2088, Australia.

SACHITHANANDAN, Vaithinathaswami, b. 7 Mar. 1928, Terizhandur. Teacher. m. Sivabagyam, 7 June 1957, 1 son, 2 daughters. *Education:* MA, 1949; MLitt, 1960; PhD, 1968; Diploma in Sanskrit, 1969. *Appointments:* Lecturer in English, 1949-69; Reader in English, 1969-72; Professor of English, 1972-. *Memberships:* Indian Association for English Studies; American Studies Research Centre. *Publications:* The Impact of Western Thought on Bharati; Whitman and Bharati: A Comparative Study; A Dictionary of Western Literary Terms (Tamil); An Introduction to Comparative Literature (Tamil) and 23 research papers. *Honours:* Sir George Stanley Prizeman of Annamalai University, 1949; Fulbright/Smith-Mundt scholar, Indiana University, USA, 1963-64. *Address:* 34 Viswasapuri II Street, Madurai - 625 016, India.

SACRANIE, Abdul Hamid, b. 14 Jan. 1939, Limbe, Malawi. Company Director. m. Margriet Johanna Simons, 9 Mar. 1968, 1 son, 1 daughter. *Education:*Senior School Certificate, 1956. *Appointments:*Buyer, Lever Brothers Ltd., 1957; Started the Central Bookshop, 1960; Sustained spinal injuries in car accident 1963, returned to business May, 1966. *Hobbies:*Reading; Music; Current Affairs. *Address:*BCA Hill, Limbe, Malawi, South Africa.

SADA, Pius Oghenerukowho, b. 15 Dec. 1934, Ivori, Bendel State, Nigeria. University Professoor of Geography. m. Rebecca O. Sada, 17 Jan. 1960, 2 sons, 1 daughter. *Education:* BSc, (Hons) Geography, University of Nigeria, 1964; MA (Geograpy) Indiana University, Bloomington, Indiania, USA, 1965; PhD (Geography), 1968. *Appointments:* Lecturer, University of Nigeria, Nsukka, 1966; Lecturer, University of Lagos, Lagos; Senior Associate Research Fellow, Human Resources Unit, 1971-75; Visiting Assistant Professor, Department of Geography, University of Iowa, 1972; Profes University of Benin, 1976-; Fulbright Scholar, Research Triangle Institute, North Carolina, USA. *Memberships:* President, Nigerian Geographical Association; Member (of the following): Nigerian Economic Society; International Geographical Union; The International Federation for Housing and Planning; African Studies Association, USA; Commonwealth Geographical Association. *Publications:* Urbanisation Processes and Problems in Nigeria, Heinemann Publishing Co., Ltd.; Settlements Systems in Nigeria, Published by the Geography Dept., University of Benin. *Honours:* Federal Scholar; Fulbright Scholar Award, USA; Foreign Students A through the United States' Assistance for International Development. *Hobby:* Gardening. *Address:* No. 1 Awadi Layout, Ivori-Irri, Isoko Local Govt. Area, Bendel State, Nigeria.

SADIQ, Ali, b. 4 Apr. 1910, Udaipur. Governor of Tamil Nadu, India. m. Sept. 1951. *Education:* Graduated from the Allahabad University, Uttar Pradesh, 1929. *Appointments:* Permanent Secretary, All India Congress Committee, 1938-47; General Secretary, Indian National Congress 1958-69 (with brief interruptions); President, Congress (O) 1971-73; Chairman, Gandhi National Museum and Library, Delhi; Member, Lok Sabha, 1951-52; Member, Rajya Sabha, 1958-70; Governor of Maharashtra, 1977-80; Governor of Tamil Nadu, 1980-. *Publications:* The Congress Ideology and Programme; Know Your Country; The Culture of India; The General Elections 1957—A Survey; also Chief Editor of AICC Economic Review, 1960-69. *Address:* Raj Bhavan, Madras - 600 022, India.

SADOH, James Omondiogbe, b. 18 May 1936, Ukhun, Nigeria. Legal Practitioner. m. Maria, 17 Nov. 1936, 1 son, 4 daughters. *Education:* LLB, 1964; Barrister at Law, 1964. *Appointments:* Engaged in Private Practice, 1965-. *Memberships:* Rotary Club, Benin; President, Elite Society, Benin; St. Vincent dePaul, Catholic. *Hobbies:* Golf. *Address:* 1 Sadah Drive, GRA, Benin City, Nigeria.

SAGE, Ivon Myer, b. 1 Oct. 1908, Melbourne, Australia. Regalia Manufacturer. m. Grace Kessler, 5 Sept. 1932, 2 daughters. *Education:* Matriculation, Melbourne C of E Grammar School, 1914-24. *Memberships:* Tattersalls Club, Sydney; President, City of Hawthorn Bowling Club, 1979-81. *Hobbies:* Bowling; Swimming; Freemasonry. *Address:* 581 Glenferrie Road, Hawthorn, Victoria 3122, Australia.

SAGEL, J. Frederick, b. 7 Sept. 1948, Hannover, West Germany. Barrister. m. Tammy Dunn Sagel, 15 June 1974, 1 son, 1 daughter. *Education:* BA, (Honours, History & Government) McGill University, Montreal, 1970; LLB, Dalhousie Law School, Halifax, Nova Scotia, 1973; BAC, Osgoode Hall, Toronto, 1975; Torts Specialty, Harvard Law School, Cambridge, 1981. *Appointments:* Partner, Thomson, Rogers, Barristers & Solicitors, Toronto. *Memberships:* Vice-President, Multiple Sclerosis Society of Canada; Member of International Federation of Multiple Sclerosis Societies; International Commission of Jurists; Trial Lawyers of America; Canadian Bar Association; Advocates Society; York County Law Association. *Honours:* Gold Key, Dalhousie Law School, 1973; President, Law Students Society, Dalhousie Law School. *Hobbies:* Swimming; Jogging; Squash; Hiking; Camping. *Address:* 2360 Mississauga Road N, Mississauga, Ontario, Canada.

SAHEED, Mohamed Mohideen, b. 1 July, 1952, Matara, Sri Lanka. Accountant. m. Kshama Hussain Barrie, 23 Sept. 1977, 2 daughters. *Education:* Associate Member of the Institute of Chartered Accountants of Sri Lanka, 1976; Finalist, The Institute of Cost & Management Accountant, London. *Appointments:* Audit Manager, Burah Hathy & Co., Sri Lanka, 1976; Assistant Accountant, Hayleys Ltd., Sri Lanka, 1976; Senior Accountant, Finance Division, Saudi Research & Development Corporation, Jeddah, Saudi Arabia, 1976-79; Financial Controller, Al Sabah Maritime Services Co. Ltd.,; Chief Accountant, Crest Group of Companies, Sri Lanka, 19 *Memberships:* Assistant Treasurer, The Muslim Orphanage, Ratmalana, Sri Lanka; Member, The Moors Sports Club. *Hobbies:* Collecting Antiques and Gems. *Address:* 32 Charles Place, Colombo 3, Sri Lanka.

SAIDI, Sylvester William, b. 8 May 1937, St. David's Mission, Marandellas, Zimbabwe. Journalist. m. Beauty Masenga, 1975, 1 son, 2 daughters. *Education:* University Junior Certificate; One-year private course in English Bible Study; Apprenticeship as journalist. *Appointments:* Reporter, deputy sports editor, editor African Parade magazine, columnist, African Newspapers Ltd., Salisbury, 1957-61; Production editor, news editor, columnist, leader writer, Central African Mail, Lusaka, Zambia, 1963-68; News editor, leader writer, columnist, assistant editor, deputy editor, deputy-editor-in-chief, Times Newspapers Ltd., Lusaka and Ndola, 1969-80; Assistant Editor, The Herald, Salisbury, 1980; Stringe for BBC Africa Service, The Times of London, UPI and Associated Press. *Memberships:* Chairman, Lusaka Press Club, 1972-73; Foundermember, New Writers' Group of Zambia, 1964; Chairman, Zambian Section, Commonwea Press Union, 1979-80. *Publications:* Short stories published in USA, Soviet Union, Nigeria, South Africa, Zimbabwe (S. Rhodesia), Zambia; Novels, The Hanging, publish in TEMCO, Zambia; Short story, Nightmare, published in Anthology of Afro-Asian Short Stories, published in Cairo. *Honours:* Joint First Prize winner of nationwide Short Story Contest in Zambia, 1966. *Hobbies:* Writing; Reading; Football (as spectator); Draughts. *Address:* 225 Arcturus Road, Greendale, Salisbury, Zimbabwe.

SAIDU, Patrick Kakpindi, b. 22 Nov. 1945, Kayiehun, Njama Kowa, Sierra Leone. Librarian. m. Rosaline Amie (née Koroma), 17 May I964, 2 sons, 3 daughters. *Education:* BA, (Durham), Fourah Bay College, Freetown, 1969; ALA (Professional Exams) Birmingham Polytechnic, England, 1973; ALA Chartered Librarian, 1975; MA, Library Studies and Education, Loughborough University, England; 1978; *Appointments:* Teacher (French and English Language), Taiama Secondary School, 1969-70; Trainee Librarian, Njala University College, 1970-71; Assistant Librarian, Njala University College, 1973; *Memberships:* Associate of the Library Association (London). *Hobby:* Gardening. *Address:* Kayiehun, Njama Kowa, Via Mano, Sierra Leone.

SAILAPATHY, Aiyah Iver, b. 15 Dec. 1926, Madurai, Tamil Nadu, South India. m. Kamakshi, 8 Feb. 1952, 2 sons, 1 daughter. *Education:* BSc Chemistry, 1946, MB & BS, 1952, MD General Medicine, 1962, All at Madras University, South India. FCCP, USA, 1972. *Appointments:* Civil Assistant Surgeon, Madras Medical Service, 1955-62; Assistant Professor of Medicine & Assistant Physician, 1962-68; Professor of Medicine & Physician, 1968-. *Memberships:* Member, Indian Medical Association, Past President of Tirunelveli Branch. Member, Association of Physicians of India. *Publications:* 60 publications in Indian Medical Journals. *Honours:* Second prize for essay by Indian Medical Association at Salem, South India, 1980. *Hobbies:* Vocal Carnatic Music. *Address:* 20 Perumalpuram, Tirunelveli-627007, South India.

SAINSBURY, Maurice Joseph, b. 18 Nov. 1927, Sydney, Australia. Psychiatrist. m. Erna June (nee Hoadley), 22 Aug. 1953, 1 son, 2 daughters. *Education:* MB, BS, University of Sydney, 1952; DPM (RCP & S), 1960, FRANZOP 1971, 1963; FRC Psych. 1975, 1971; MHP, New South Wales University. *Appointments:* General Practice, HMO Wollongong District Hospital, 1953-57; Psychiatric Postings, St. Clements Hospital, Claybury Hospital, North Middlesex Hospital, St. Bartholomew's Hospital, England. 1957-1962; Psychiatrist, Macquarie Hospital, 1962-65; Deputy Medical Superintendent, 1965-1968; Director, New South Wales Institute of Psychiatry since 1968; Honorary Psychiatrist, Hornsby and Ku-ring-gai Hospital, 1967-69; Sydney Hospital, 1971-77 *Memberships:* Member and Councillor, Australian Academy of Forensic Sciences, 1974; Member, WHO Expert Advisory Panel on Mental Health, 1980; Royal Australian and New Zealand College of Psychiatrists, NSW Branch Secretary, 1966-68, Honorary Federal Treasurer, 1970-74, President, 1976; Consultant Psychiatrist (Colonel) Defence Departmen Army Office, 1976; Member, Australasian Pioneers Club, Imperial Service Club, North Ryde Golf Club. *Publications:* Key to Psychiatry 1973. *Honours:* Recipient of Robin May Memorial Prize, University of Sydney, 1952. Boxing Blue, Sydney University, 1948. *Hobbies:* Gardening, Golf, Electric Welding, Tennis. *Address:* 3 Bimbil Place, West Killara, NSW 2071, Australia.

SAINT ANTOINE, de L. Jacques, b. 29 Nov. 1923, Mauritius, Chemical Engineer. m. Marise Sauzier, 16 Jan 1950, 2 sons, 1 daughter. *Education:* Honours Diploma, Mauritius College of Agriculture, 1942-45; BSc. Chemical Engineering, Louisiana State University, 1947-49. *Appointments:* Head Lecturer, Sugar Technology & Engineering, Mauritius College of Agriculture, 1950-53; Assistant, then Ag. Registrar, Central arbitration & Control Board, Department of Agriculture, 1954; Sugar Technologist, Mauritius Sugar Industry Research Institute, 1956; Assistant Director, MSIRI, 1969-80; Director, MSIRI, 1980-. *Memberships:* Regional Chairman, International Commission for Uniform Methods of Sugar Analysis (ICUMSA); Regional Vice Chairman, International Society of Sugar Cane Technologists (ISSCT); President, Societe de Technologie Agricole & Sucriere de Maurice, 1970'71'79'80; President, Comite de Collaboration Agricole, Maurice-Reunion-Madagasc Comores; Member, Sugar Industry Technologists Inc., Professional Engineers' Association, Mauritius, Royal Society of Arts & Sciences, Mauritius. *Publications:* Attended various missions abroad, 1956-1980; Contributor of numerous scientific and technical reports concerning the Mauritius Sugar Industry. *Hobbies:* Reading, Shooting, Fishing. *Address:* Sugar Industry Research Institute, Reduit, Mauritius.

ST JOHN, Rosemary Innes (Mrs Robert Clarke) b. 26 May 1926, Lee-on-Solent, Hampshire, England. Harpist. m. Georexander, 20 June 1943, 2 daughters. *Education:* Matriculation, Brighton and Hove High School, 1942; ARCM, (Performers), Royal College of Music, 1945. *Appointments:* 1st harp, Sadlers Wells Ballet, 1946; 1st harp, Scottish National Orchestra, 1946-47;

2nd harp, Covent Garden Opera, 1947-48; 1st harp, Halle Orchestra, 1948-50; 2nd harp, Covent Garden, 1954-55; 1st harp, Covent Garden, 1955-60; BBC Concert Orchestra, 1960-67; New Zealand S.O. 1967; BBC Concert Orchestra, 1968-69; Adelaide SO, 1970; Teachers of Harp at University of Adelaide, 1970. *Memberships:* United Kingdom Harpists Association; American Harp Society; President, Harp Society of South Australia; Life Member, National Trust. *Hobbies:* Travel to remote areas. *Address:* 11 Lomond Avenue, Kensington Park, Adelaide, S. Australia, 5068.

SAINT-LOUIS, Jean, b. 13 Aug. 1948, Cap-de-la-Madeleine, Quebec, Canada. Pharmacologist. m. Cecile Bosse, 22 Aug. 1970, 1 son, 2 daughters. *Education:* BSc. Biology, Universite de Sherbrooke, 1970, MSc. Pharmacology, Universite de Sherbrooke, 1972, PhD Pharmacology, Universite de Sherbrooke. *Appointments:* Fellow of the Counseil de la Recherche en Santé du Québec, Dép. de Pharmacologie, Faculté de Médecine, Université de Sherbrooke, 1975-76, Fellow of the Medical Research Council of Canada and Visiting Scientist, The Welcome Res. Labs., Beckenham, Kent, England. 1976-77, Research Associate, Centre de Recherche en Reproduction animale, Faculté de Médecine Vétérinaire, Université de Montreal, 1977-81. *Memberships:* British Pharmacological Society, Pharmacological Society of Canada, Association Canadienne pour l'Avancement des Sciences, Club de Recherches Cliniques de Québec, National Geographic Society. *Publications:* Contributed to various professional journals. *Hobbies:* History, Woodcraft, Country Skiing. *Address:* 16280, Des Sorbiers, Saint-Hyacinthe, Québec, Canada. J2T 4M1.

ST-PIERRE, Jacques, b. 30 Aug. 1920, Trois-Riviéres, Québec, Canada. University Administrator and Professor. m. Marguerite Lachaine, 15 July, 1947, 5 sons, 1 daughter. *Education:* LSc (Phys), University of Montreal, 1945; LSc (Maths), University of Montreal, 1948; MSc (Maths), University of Montreal, 1951; PhD, (Math Stat), University of North Carolina, Chapel Hill. *Appointments:* Assistant Professor, University of Montreal, 1947; Associate professor, University of Montreal, 1956, Full Professor, University of Montreal, 1960-; Director, Computing Centre, University of Montreal, 1964-71; Director, Computer Science Department, 1966-69; Director, Applied Math Research Centre, 1969-71, Vice President Planning, 1971-. *Memberships:* President, Canadian Association of University Teachers, 1964-65; Institute of Mathematical Statistics, American Statistical Association Biometrics Society, Canadian Operational Research Society, Canadian Mathematical Congress. *Publications:* Thirty five Scientific publications in Learned journals in Mathematical Statistics, Applied Statistics, Biometry. *Honours:* Recipient of Lieutenant Governer General's Medal, 1945, Canada's Centennial Medal. *Hobbies:* Reading, Music. *Address:* 1795 Croissant Daviault, Duvernay-Laval, P. Quebec, Canada, H7G 4E2.

SAKYIAMA, Kofi Pari, b. 1 Nov. 1907, Kumasi, Ashanti, Ghana. Clerk in Holy Orders, Archdeacon Emeritus. m. (1) Christiana Augustina Odoom, 5 July, 1941 (dec.); (2) Lucy Hayford, 6 May, 1967, 3 sons, 2 daughters. *Education:* Elementary Education at Kumasi, 1910-1918; Cape Coast, 1919-22; St. Nicholas Grammar School, now Adisadel College, Cape Coast, 1923; Cambridge School Certificate, with exemption from Cambridge previous 1927; St. Augustins Theological College, Kumasi, Ashanti, 1928-31. *Appointments:* Assistant Priest, Sekondi, 1931-37; Parish Priest, Obo, 1937-41; Whole-time Chaplain, Order of the Holy Paraclete, Mampong, Ashanti, 1941-47; Parish Priest, Mampong, Ashanti, 1941-47; Parish Priest, Bekwai, Ashanti, 1947-50; Parish Priest, Sekondi, 1950-61; Hon. Canon and Chapter Clerk, Holy Trinity Cathedral, Accra, 1955-77; Archdeacon of Sekondi, 1960-61; Parish Priest and Archdeacon of Kumasi, (In charge of Ashanti, Brong-Ahafo, Northern Ghana and Upper Ghana), 1961-65; Vicar-General (of all Ghana), 1968-73; Vicar-General (Exclusive of the Diocese of Kumasi), 1968-77; Parish Priest and Archdeacon of Koforidua, 1965-69; Parish Priest and Archdeacon of Cape Coast, 1969-77; Parish Priest, Saltpond, 1978-79; Archdeacon Emeritus, 1978. *Memberships:* International Order of Oddfellows; Ancient Order of Foresters; *Hobbies:* Poetry, Journalism and Photo-albuming; *Address:* 5 Seventh Sakumolink, Lartebiokorshie, Accra, Ghana.

SALI, Avni, b. 19 Oct. 1940, Australia. Surgeon. m. Hana Mrazek, 1 son, 1 daughter. *Education:* MBBS, Monash University, 1966; Fellow of Royal Australasian College of Surgeons, 1972; PhD, Monash University, 1977. *Appointments:* Resident Medical Officer, Alfred Hospital, Melbourne, 1967; Senior Resident Medical Officer, Alfred Hospital, 1968; National Health and Medical Research Council Research Fellow, Monash Universi Department of Surgery, 1969-71; Surgical Registrar, Prince Henry's Hospital, Melbourne, 1972-73; Lecturer, Monash University Dept. of Surgery, Prince Henry's Hospital, 1974-75; Research Fellow, University of Glasgow, Dept. of Surgery, 1976-77; Specialist Surgeon, Veterans' Administration 1977, Melbourne; Honorary Surgeon, Austin Hospital, Melbourne, 1978-. Professional First Assistant, Melbourne University Dept. Surgery, Repatriation General Hospital, Melbourne. *Memberships:* Royal Society of Medicine; International Society of Surgery; Collegium Internationale Chirurgiae Digestivae; International Biliary Association; Australian Gastroenterological Society; Surgical Research Society of Australia; Clinical Oncological Society of Australia; Nutrition Society of Australia; Australian Sports medicine Federation; Australian Medical Association; *Publications:* Co-author of the following books, The Practice of Biliary Surgery, Biliary Disease 1980; Proceedings First Australian Pancreas Congress; Natural High Fibre Cookery; Articles in Medical Journals. *Hobbies:* Walking; Cars; Tennis; Thoughts on environment and disease. *Address:* 61 Mary Street, Hawthorn, Melbourne, Australia, 3122.

SALMAN, Aliyu Alarape Olanrewaju, b. 2 Oct. 1942, Ilorin, Icwara State. Barrister & Solicitor. m. 2 Oct. 1970, 1 son, 3 daughters. *Education:* LLB Hons degree, June, 1967; BL, June,1968. *Appointments:* From Pupil State Counsel, North Western State, (defunct) to Deputy State Counsel; Attorney General, Kwara State; Private Legal Practice; Member Judicial Service Commission, Kwara, 1980-. *Memberships:* Life Member (banned), National Union of Nigerian Students; Vice President, National Affairs Muslim Students Society of Nigeria; Legal Advisor, Jamatu Nasr-ul-Islam Society of Nigeria; Legal Advisor, Ansarzil-Islam Society of Nigeria; *Hobbies:* Watching Drama (life); Reading especially criminal fictions; *Address:* Plot 53 Adeleye Road, G.R.A. Ilorin, Kwara State.

SALMON, John Robert, b. 10 Aug. 1926, Geelong, Victoria, Australia. Regular Army Officer. m. Jennifer Anne Davidson, 16 Dec. 1956, 1 son, 2 daughters *Education:* Geelong College, 1939-43; Royal Military College, Duntroon, 1944-46; Long Gunnery Staff Course, AA, Wales, 1954-55; Australian Army Staff College, Queenscliff, Victoria, 1967; Joint Services Staff College, Latimer, England, 1966; Royal College of Defence Studies, Belgrave Square, London, 1974. *Appointments:* A Distinguished career of regimental, instructional, artillery command and staff appointments including: British Commonwealth Occupation Force, Japan, 1947-49; Troop Commander 16 Field Regiment, Royal New Zealand Artillery, Korea (wounded in action); British Army of the Rhine, Germany, 1955; Instructor Staff Duties and Tactics, Royal Military College, Duntroon, 1958-60; Officer Commanding, 103 Field Battery Royal Australian Artillery, Malaysia, 1961-63; Staff Officer Grade 1 (Training Doctrine), Directorate of Military Training, Army Headquarters, Canberra, 1963-65; Commanding Officer and Chief Instructor, School of Artillery, North Head, Manly, NSW, 1967-68; Deputy Director of Staff Duties, Army Headquarters, Canberra, 1969-70; Chief of Staff, Australian Army Force, Vietnam, 1971; Director of Personnel Administration, Army Headquarters, Canberra, 1972; Brigadier Army Reorganization, Army Headquarters, Canberra, 1972-73; Director General Coordination and Organization, Army, 1975-77; Commandant Australian Joint Services Staff College, 1978-80; Adviser to Malaysia on the setting up of their Armed Forces Defence College, Head Review of Resources Management within the Army, 1981; Short Brothers (Australia) Pty Ltd, 1981. *Memberships:* Commonwealth Club, Canberra; Naval and Military Club, Melbourne; National Press Club (ACT); Fellow Australian Institute of Management; United Services Institution of the ACT; Joint Services Staff College Association; Royal Australian Artillery Association (ACT & NSW); Society of the Order of the British Empire (ACT). *Honours:* Recipient of CBE, 1972. *Hobbies:* Tennis; Cricket;

Fishing; Horseriding; Rural pursuits. *Address:* 95 Wybelena Grove Cook, ACT, 2614, Australia.

SALMON, John Tenison, CBE, b. 28 June 1910, Wellington, New Zealand. University Professor (Retired). m. Pamela Naomi Wilton, 7 Dec. 1948, 4 sons. *Education:* DSc (New Zealand) 1945; FRS (New Zealand), 1949; FRES, 1937; FRPS, 1966; Hon. Member, American Entomological Society. *Appointments:* Entomologist and Photographer, Dominion Muspane, 1934-48; Senior Lecturer, Biology, 1948-58, Associate Professor, Zoology, 1959-64, Professor of Zoology and Head of Department, Victoria University of Wellington, 1965-75; Nuffield Travelling Reasearch Fellow in Natural Sciences, 1950-51; Carnegie Travelling Fellow, 1958; Professor Emeritus, Victoria University of Wellington, 1976-; Councillor, Waikanae Community Council, 1978-. *Memberships:* Council Member, Royal Society of New Zealand, 1948-65, Editor, 1953-65; Secretary, New Zealand Association of Scientists, 1940-45, VP, 1948-49, President, 1949-50; Foundation Member, New Zealand Natu Conservation Council, 1963-; Chairman, National Conservation Week Campaign Committee, 1975-; President, Entomological Society of New Zealand, 1957; and many others. *Publications:* An Index to the Collombola, 1964; Heritage Destroyed, 1960; New Zealand Flowers and Plants in Colour, 1963; Butterflies of New Zealand, 1968; Field Guide to the Alpine Plants of New Zealand, 1968 The Native Trees of New Zealand, 1980. Also Research and General Pap and numerous articles in magazines. *Hobbies:* Photography; Gardening. *Address:* 65 Seddon Street, Waikanae, New Zealand.

SALTER, Adrian Arthur, b. 1 Dec. 1943, Sydney, Australia. Horticulturist. m. Lynne Beatrice Leith Picking, 8 July, 1972, 2 sons. *Education:* `Horticulture Certificate, Sydney Technical College, 1963; BSc, University of New South Wales, 1978. *Appointments:* Worked in wholesale and retail plant nurseries and Sydney's Royal Botanical Gardens; Own business in Landscape Design and Construction 3 years; Medical student, 1969; Technical Officer, School of Botany, 1972-76, while doing part-time Science degree; Manager, Kasteels Nursery, 1976-; Lecturer, Ryde School of Horticulture. *Memberships:* The Spiritual Assembly of the Bahá'is of Randwick Ltd., 1971, Secretary, 1973-75; The Spiritual Assembly of the Bahá'is of Warringah Ltd., 1976-, Secretary, 1979-; Australian Institute of Horticulture, Inc., 1971-, International Plant Propagators Society; The Rhodesian Ridgeback Club (Australia), Secretary, 1979-; Australian Society of Plant Physiologists; American Society for Horticultural Science. *Creative Works:* Landscape Designer, Bahá' Temple Gardens, Sydney, Australia. *Hobbies:* Personal Computers; Chess; Fishing; Rhodesian Ridgeback dogs, New Technology. *Address:* 124A Booralie Road, Duffy's Forest 2084, Australia.

SALTUPS, Andris, b. 15 June 1934, Riga, Latvia. Cardiologist. m. Vita Bog 31 Dec. 1976. *Education:* Matriculation, Melbourne University High School, 1953; MB, BS, Melbourne, with Honours in Medicine, 1960; MRACP, 1964; FRACP, 1971; FACC, 1977. *Appointments:* RMO, Royal Melbourne & Royal Children's Hospitals, Melbourne, 1961-63; Registrar, Prince Henry's Hospital, Melbourne, 1964-65; Lecturer, Monash University Department of Medicine, 1966-67; Research Assistant, Cardiology, Mayo Clinic, Rochester, Minnesota, USA, 1968-69; Instructor, Department of Medicine (Cardiology), University of Chicago Director, Coronary Care Unit, Billings Hospital, Chicago, Illinois, USA, 1969-70; Staff Cardiologist, Prince Henry's Hospital, Melbourne, 1970-72; Senior Lecturer (part-time) Monash University Department of Medicine, 1970-; Director, Cardiology Service, Princ Henry's Hospital, 1973-. *Memberships:* Cardiac Society of Australia & New Zealand, Victorian Branch; Member, State Committee & Education Committee; Mayo Cardiovascular Society. *Publications:* on Angina Pectoris, Complications of Myocardial Infarction, Cardiac Catheterization, Coronary Arteriography, Results of Aorto-Coronary Bypass Surgery. *Honours:* Overseas Clinical Scholarship, Royal Australasian College of Physicians; Fulbright Travelling Scholarship. *Address:* 4 Christowel Street, Camberwell, Victoria 3124, Australia.

SAMARAKOON, Neville Dunbar Mirahawatte, b. 22 Oct. 1919, Badulla, Sri Lanka. Chief Justice of the Democratic Socialist Republic of Sri Lanka. m. Mary

Patricia Mulholland, 22 July 1949, 1 son, 2 daughters. *Education:* Enrolled as Advocate, 1st May, 1945. *Appointments:* Crown Counsel, Attorney-General's Department, 1948-51; Reverted to Private Bar, 1951; Member of the Bar Council and the Disciplinary Board for Lawyers; Appointed one of Her Majesty's Counsel 1968; Appointed Chief Justice, 1977; Chairman, Judicial Service Commission, Council of Legal Education. *Address:* 129 Wijerama Mawatha, Colombo 7, Sri Lanka.

SAMARATUNGA, Yahampath Atchchige Don Sugathadasa, b. 24 Sept. 1926, Colombo, Sri Lanka. Chartered Accountant, Cost Management Accountant, United Nations Consultant. m. Daisy Sardha peiris, 5 Jan. 1965, 1 son. *Education:* BCom, London, 1949; BSc, Economics, London, 1950; ATII, 1954; FCMA, 1954; FCA, England & Wales, 1955; FCIS, 1955; JDip-MA, 1976. *Appointments:* Lecturer, Sri Lanka Technical College, Colombo, 1951-65, Principal, 1965-66; Director of Education, Government of Sri Lanka, 1966-69; Professor of Commerce, University of Sri Lanka, 1969-71; Commonwealth Fund (CTFC) Specialist Adviser in Management Accounting Institute of Administration, University of Ife, Nigeria, 1973-75; United Nations Expert in Government Accounting & Auditing, Professor of Accountancy, University of Ife, Nigeria, 1975-78; UN Consultant in Accountancy Training, Government of the Sudan, 1978; UNESCO Specialist in Accounting Education, Auchi Polytechnic, Nigeria, 1978-80; UN Expert in Financial Management, African Training and Research Centre in Administration for Development, Morocco, 1980-. *Memberships:* Fellow, Institute of Chartered Accountants of Sri Lanka, Member Council, 1959-66, Vice President, 1972; Fellow, Institute of Charter Accountants in England and Wales; Fellow, Institute of Cost and Management Accountants, Fellow; Chartered Institute of Secretaries and Administrators; Associate, Institute of Taxation; Fellow, British Institute of Management; Member, Royal Overseas League. *Publications:* Accountancy, Society and Economic Development, 1976; Adapting Government Accounting Systems to PPBS Needs, 1976; also contributor of numerous articles to professional journals. *Honours:* Sri Lanka Government Scholarship in Accountancy, UK, 1952-55; Justice of the Peace, 1961-65; served on numerous boards, councils, and committees. *Hobbies:* Collector: stamps, coins, picture postcards, etc. *Address:* 25 Rawlins Close, Crossways, Addlington, South Croyden CR2 8JS, England.

SAMAROO, Daniel Joseph, b. 27 Aug. 1927, Trinidad, West Indies. Director, Business Execut Agriculturist and Teacher. m. 7 Jan. 1968, 1 son, 1 daughter. *Education:* Modern Academy High School; Malvern High School; Pamphyillian High School. *Appointments:* Teacher, Malvern High School, Pamphyillian High School; Assistant Manager, Scott Furnishing Company; Assistant Druggist, Beharry & Scott Limited; Sales Director, Kirpalani's Limited; Merchandise Director, Stephens & Johnsons Limited. *Memberships:* President, West India Club, Venereal Disease Association, Trinid & Tobago Red Cross Society, Princess Elizabeth Home for Handicapped Children; Member, Trinidad & Tobago Orchid Society; Director, Young Men's Christian Association; Secretary, Father of the Year Council; Mason, Several English & Scottish Lodges in Trinidad & Tobago. *Publications:* Short story writer (Trinidad Vernacular); Classic short story Taxi Mister accepted by BBC and international journals and included in the Anthology of Short Stories: From the Green Antilles; Winner of National Cultural award for short story The Milking of Betsy; and short story, Big Brains, included in Caribbean Rhythms, the emerging literature of the West Indies. *Honours:* Justice of the Peace, Trinidad & Tobago; Recipient of the Humming Bird Medal for Community Service, 1976; Winner of an award by the National Cultural Council. *Hobbies:* Cricket; Gardening. *Address:* 84B Saddle Road, Maraval, Trinidad, West Indies.

SAMBASIVAN, Sundaralingam, b. 12 Aug. 1951, Colombo, Sri Lanka. Chartered Accountant. m. Sundhari, 10 Sept. 1980. *Education:* GCE, Ordinary Level, 1966; GCE, Advanced Level, 1969; Intermediat Exam, Chartered Accountancy, 1972; Final Exam, Chartered Accountancy, 1975. *Appointments:* Articled Clerk, 1971-74; Audit Senior, 1975; Qualified Assistant, 1975-77; Accountant, 1977-. *Memberships:* Member, Local Association of Sri Lanka Tamil Arts and Cultural Association in Zambia, Association for Creative Intelligence in Zambia. *Honours:* Merit Certificates, 1963, 1969; Best Articled Clerk Award, 1973; General Proficiency Prize, Mahajana College, 1961-67. *Hobbies:* Photography; Touring; Game Viewing. *Address:* PO Box 21430, Flat 8, Windsor Court, Kabengele Avenue, Kitwe, Zambia.

SAMBONDU, Nyasununu, Charles, b. 2 Aug. 1953, Mwinilunga, Zambia. Librarian. m. Alice, 26 Nov. 1977, 1 son. *Education:* Certificate in Librarianship, 1972-73; Diploma in Librarianship, 1976-79. *Appointments:* Librarian, Helen Kaunda Memorial Library, 1970-. *Memberships:* Chairman, Zambia Library Association, Copperbelt Branch, 1979-80; Member, Professional Board of Library Studies, University of Zambia, 1981-83. *Hobbies:* Soccer; Table Tennis. Member of most charitable organisations in Luanshya District. *Address:* 1 Masasa Street, Luanshya, Zambia.

SAMIOS, James Miltiadis, b. 10 Sept. 1933, Brisbane, Queensland, Australia. Solicitor. m. Rosemary Joan Napier Nicolson, 24 June 1968, 1 son. *Education:* BA, LLB (Queensland), CEGS Brisbane, University of Queensland. *Memberships:* Imperial Service Club; Member, The Special Broadcasting Service (Board Member) 1981; Committee of Review on Migrant Assessment (CROMA) 1981, Interim Cte to establish the independent & multicultural broadcasting corporation, 1980-81; Chairman, Migrant Settlement Counc of New South Wales, 1979, Community Refuge Settlement Committee, 1979, Ethnic Communities' Council of New South Wales, 1979; Treasurer, Association for Classical Archaeology, Sydney University, 1980; Member, NSW Consultative Council on Ethnic Affairs, 1975-79; Chairman, St Basils Homes, 1969-72, 1980-81, Director, 1969; Member, Mixed Council of Clergy & Laity of the Greek Orthodox Archdiocese, 1965; Director, Greek Orthodox Archdiocese of Australia Property Trust, 1965; Member of Executive of the Good Neighbour Council, New South Wales, 1978-80. *Honours:* MBE; Archon of the Oecumenical Patriarchate, Greek Orthodox Church. *Hobbies:* Tennis; Theatre; Classical Music. *Address:* 3 Rosemont, 410 Edgecliff Road, Woollahra, NSW 2025, Australia.

SAMKI, John Kinyala, b. 16 Oct. 1941, Kanji Kirua Vunjo Moshi, Tanzania. m. 8 Apr. 1971, 2 sons, 2 daughters. *Education:* Primary Education, 1950-57; Secondary Education, 1958-62; University Education (University of Canterbury, Christchurch, New Zealand) 1963-66. *Appointments:* Research Officer in Soils, 1967-71; Senior Research Officer, Director of Agricultural Research Institute, 1972-; and co-ordinator of soil research in Tanzania. *Memberships:* Member, East Africa Soil Science Society, Eastern African Soil Correlation committee. *Publications:* A number of articles in the World Soil Resources Reports, published by FAO, Rome. *Hobbies:* Chess. *Address:* ARI Niligano, Ngonemi, Tange, Tanzania.

SAMMAKO, Iliya. b. 5 May 1952, Malumfash, Kaduna State, Nigeria. Medical Records. m. Yalwa Bahago, 7 Dec 1974, 2 sons and 2 daughters *Education:* Primary seven, 1965-68; West African School Certificate, 1969-73; Preliminary Certificate in Medical Records; Nigerian Health Records Associations Certificate, 1977-78; Student (Diploma) in Medical Records, 1981-82 *Memberships:* Dormitory Prefect, Member of Saint de Vincent De Paul Society, Member of Young Farmers Club, Member Nigerian Health Records Association, Young Christian Student, Nigerian Red Cross Society. *Creative Works:* Muffler Making. *Hobbies:* Football, Athletics, Music, Travelling, Letter writing. *Address:* 4G Marafa Estate, Kaduna, Nigeria.

SAMMAN, Peter Derrick, b. 20 Mar. 1914, Darjeeling, India. Physician (Dermatologist). m. Judith Mary Kelly, 24 Oct. 1953, 3 daughters. *Education:* King Williams College (Isle of Man), 1925-33; Emmanuel College, Cambridge, 1933-36; Kings College Hospital, London, 1936-39; BA (Cantab), 1936; MB.BChir, 1939; MA MD, 1948; MRCP (London), 1946; FRCP (London), 1963. *Appointments:* House Physician, Kings College Hospital, 1940; RAFVR, 1940-46; Senior Registrar, United Bristol Hospitals, 1947-48; St. John's Hospital for Diseases of the Skin, 1949-50; Physician, Dermatological Department, Westminster Hospital, London, 1951-79; Physician, St. John's Hospital for Diseases of the Skin, 1959-79; Dean, Institute of Dermatology,

1965-70. *Memberships:* British Medical Association; British Association of Dermatologists; St. John's Hospital Dermatological Society. *Publications:* The Nails in Disease, 3rd Edition, 1978; Tutorials in Postgraduat Medicine, Vol 6; Chapters in Books, Contributions in Professional Journals. *Honours:* Jelf Medal, 1939; Parkes Weber Lecturer and Medalist, 1975. *Hobbies:* Gardening. *Address:* 18 Sutherland Avenue, Orpington, Kent BR5 1QZ, England.

SAMPLES, Reginald, McCartney, b. 11 Aug. 1918, Liverpool, England. Retired British Diplomat; Assistant Director, Royal Ontario Museum, Torono, Canada. m. Elsie Roberts Hide, 2 sons, 1 step-daughter. *Education:* Rhyl County School, 1929-35; B.Com, Liverpool University. 1935-40. *Appointments:* Lieutenant, Fleet Air Arm, 1940-46; DSO, 1942; Central Office of Information, London, 1946-48; Commonwealth Relations Office, Economic Information Office, Bombay, India, 1948-52; Editor-in-Chief, British Information Services, New Delhi, 1948; Information Counsellor and Director, B.I.S, India, 1952-56; Information Counsellor and Director, B.I.S, Pakistan, 1956-59; Assistant Under Secretary, Commonwealth Office, London, 1968; Senior British Consul-General, Toronto, Canada, 1969-78; Retired British Diplomatic Service; appointed Director of Development & Assistant Director, Royal Ontario Museum, Toronto, Canada, 1978. *Memberships:* York Club, Queen's Club, Arts & Letters Club, Toronto; Naval Club, London; President, Board of Directors, National Ballet Company of Canada, Director Canadian Aldeburgh Foundation; Director, Canadian-Scottish Philharmonic Foundation; Life Member, St. George's Society, Toronto; Member, Royal Commonwealth Society. *Honours:* DSO, 1942; OBE, 1962; CMG, 1970. *Hobbies:* Tennis; Listening to Music; Watching Ballet. *Address:* 44 Jackes Avenue, Apt. 1105, Toronto, M4T 1ES, Canada.

SAMUEL, Godfrey Everard, b. 30 July 1956, St. Vincent. Teacher. *Education:* Diploma in Social Work, 1980. *Appointments:* Teacher. *Memberships:* Vice President, National Youth Council; Present post General Secretary. *Hobbies:* Teaching; Travelling; Working with young people. *Address:* Belmont P.O., East St. George, St. Vincent, West Indies.

SAM-WOODE, Kwesi, b. 28 Nov. 1938, Enyan Abaasa, Ghana. Publishing Managing Director. m. Mary Adoko, 2nd Dec. 1962, 1 son 2 daughters. *Education:* Secondary School, Adisadel College, Cape Coast. University, B.A. (Hons) Study of Religions, University of Ghana, Legon. *Appointments:* Teacher, Adisadel College, Cape Coast, l965-67; Travelling Secretary, World Student Christian Federation, 1967-69; Publisher's Representative, Evans Brothers Ltd., London; Publisher and Managing Director, Afram Publications (Ghana) Ltd; Chairman, XYGL (Africa) Ltd; Ghana Publishing Corporation, Member of the Board of Directors. *Memberships:* Ghana Book Publishers Association, Council Member; Full member, Ghana Institute of Management; Member, Achimota Golf Club; Council Member, Ghana National Book Development Council. *Publications:* Publisher of Students World Educational Magazine. *Hobbies:* Carpentry; Vocational Counselling. *Address:* No. 5 3rd Norla Street, North Labone, Accra.

SANDBERG, Michael Graham Ruddock, b. 31 May 1927, London, England. Banker. m. Carmel Sandberg, 11 Feb. 1954, 2 sons, 2 daughters. *Education:* St. Edward's School, Oxford. *Appointments:* General Manager, Executive Director, Deputy Chairman, Chairman, 1949-77; Chairman of the British Bank of the Middle East and Mercantile Bank Limited; Chairman, Hong Kong and Shanghai Banking Corporation, 1977-. *Memberships:* Unofficial Member of the Executive Council of Hong Kong; Treasurer of the University of Hong Kong; Vice-chairman of the Hong Kong Arts Festival Society Limited; President of the Society for the relief of Disabled Children; Steward of the Royal Hong Kong Jockey Club; Chairman of th Board of Stewards of the Royal Hong Kong Jockey Club, 1981. *Honours:* Recipient of OBE, (1977), FIB, (1977). *Address:* Sky-high, 10, Pollock's Path, The Peak, Hong Kong.

SANDERS, Donald Neil, b. 21 June 1927, Sydney, Australia. Banking. m. Betty Elaine Constance, 19 Apr. 1952, 4 sons, 1 daughter. *Education:* Wollongong High School; University of Sydney; BEc, Sydney. *Appointments:* Commonwealth Bank of Australia, 1943-60;

Department of the Treasury, 1956; Bank of England, 1960; Reserve Bank of Australia, 1960; Superintendent, Credit Policy Division, Banking Department, 1964-66; Deputy Manager, Banking Department, 1966-67; Deputy Manager, Research Department, 1967-70; Australian Embassy, Washington D.C., 1968; Chief Manager, Securities Markets Department, 1970-72; Chief Manager, Banking and Finance Department, 1972-74; Adviser and Chief Manager, Banking and Finance Department, 1974-75; Deputy Governor and Deputy Chairman of Board, 1975-. *Address:* Reserve Bank of Australia, 65 Martin Place, Sydney, N.S.W. 2000, Australia.

SANDERSON, Kelvin Thomas, b. 11 June 1941, Lincoln, New Zealand. Agricultural Economist/Development Planner. m. Lesley Margaret Haydon, 7 May 1966, 2 sons, 2 daughters. *Education:* BAgSc, Lincoln College, University of Canterbury, NZ, 1960-64; MAgSc (Hons in Agricultural Economics). *Appointments:* UN Secretary General's Emergency Mission to Lesotho and Botswana, 1977; Project Manager, NZ State Planning Project, Trengganu, Malaysia, 1978-80; Project Manager, UNDP/OPE Public Investment Project, Belize, C.A., 1981-83. *Memberships:* Member, NZ Institute Agricultural Science; Member, Economic Society of Australia and New Zealand. *Publications:* Numerous consultant and development studies including A Fiscal Review of Western Samoa, CFTC, 1971; A Prefeasibility of Narathiwat Port, South Thailand, ENEX, 1973; Policy papers on Livestock Development in Tanzania, 1975-78; Settlement Structure Planning for Economic Development, Trenggover, 1980. *Honours:* Entrance Bursary, Christ College, 1954; ANZ Bank Scholar in Agricultural Economics, 1964. *Hobbies:* Yachting; Tramping. *Address:* 38A Rona Street, Eastbourne, Wellington, New Zealand.

SANDERSON, Raymond Frederick, b. 20 Jun. 1922, Napier, New Zealand. Marine Surveyor & Consultant. m. Margaret Patricia Hazledon, 28 May 1954, 2 sons, 2 daughters. *Education:* Matriculation, Wellington, NZ; Correspondence Course, Social Physchology, Baliol College, Oxford. *Appointments:* R.F. Sanderson & Assocs, Sanderson Public Relations & Assocs, Royal NZ Naval Voluntary Reserve, Commanding Officer, Canterbury Division, Rank: Commander, 1964-71. *Memberships:* NZ Jaycees, Wellington Council; NZ Institute of Management, Wellington Council; Outward Bound Trust of NZ, Chairman, Canterbury Birthright NZ Inc., (Canterbury Branch Exec)., Navy League of NZ Inc., National Vice President; National President, Institute of Loss Adjusters, NZ Inc; Member, Public Relations Institute of NZ Inc. *Publications:* Public Relations House Journals and writings. *Honours:* Recipient of OBE, New Year Honours List, 1971, for service to the Royal NZ Navy; Volunteer Reserve Decoration, VRD and Clasp to above. *Hobbies:* Work; Writing; Naval History *Address:* 69 Armagh Street, Christchurch, New Zealand.

SANI, Stephen Nyam, b. 5 July 1938, Kwoi, Jema'a Fed. LGA, Kaduna State, Nigeria. Veterinarian. m. Amina Gaga, 24 Feb. 1973, 2 sons, 1 daughter. *Education:* VOM Diploma, Veterinary School, 1961-63; Polish Language School, Lodz, 1963-64; MSc. Vet, Veterinary College, Warsaw, 1964-1970. *Appointments:* Veterinary Assistant, Northern Nigeria Government, 1961-1963; Veterinary Officer, Kaduna St. Government, 1970-77; Ag. Chief Vet Officer, 1977-79; Chief Vet. Officer, 1979-. *Memberships:* Nigerian Vet. Medical Association, President of Kaduna State Branch. *Hobby:* Reading. *Address:* 11 Etsu Road, Kaduna, Nigeria.

SANJEEVI, Natesan, b. 2 May 1927, Tiruchirappalli. Teacher and Researcher. m. Krishna, 14 July 1953, 1 daughter. *Education:* MA, 1950; M.Litt, 1963; PhD, 1969; Diploma in Anthropology; Diploma in Politics and Public Administration. *Appointments:* Head, Department of Tamil, Pachaiyappa's College, Kanchipuram, 1950-60; Lecturer, Department of Tamil, University of Madras, Madras, 1960-66; Reader, Department of Tamil, University of Madras, Madras, 1966-71; Professor of Tamil, University of Madras, Madras, 1971-. *Memberships:* President, Tamil Writers Association, Madras, 1969; President, Academy of Tamil Culture, Madras, 1970-72; Secretary, Tamilakap Pulavarkulu (Academy of Tamil Scholars), Tiruchi, 1971-4; Life Member, Saiva Siddhantha Maha Samajam, Madras, 1960-; life Member, Dravidian Linguistics Association,

Trivandrum, 1970-. *Publications:* Published 17 books and more than 100 papers in English and Tamil; Edited 10 books in English and Tamil; Published a few poems. *Honours:* Recipient of Rev. Lazarus Gold Metal for First Rank in Tamil Honours; Centhamil Ilakkiyac Cemmal by Dharmapura Adhinam, Mayuram; Nulari Pulavar by Kunrakkudi Adhinam, Kundrakkudi. *Hobbies:* Travel; Writing; Poems and collection of rare books and manuscripts. *Address:* Natesa Narayana Nilayam, 4 Thalaiyari Street, Mylapore, Madras-600 004, Tamil Nadu, India.

SANKAR, Ramaiyer, b. 13 Feb. 1934, Srivaikuntam, Tirunelvely, India. Teacher and Researcher. m. Padmavathy, 6 July 1960, 2 sons. *Education:* BA Honours, Mathematics, Delhi, 1952; MA, Mathematics, Delhi, 1954; DPhil, Computing, Oxford, 1967. *Appointments:* Lecturer, St. Stephens College, Delhi, 1954-57; Lecturer, Indian Institute of Science, Bangalore, 1957-61; Scientist, National Aeronautical Laboratory, Bangalore, 1961-75; Professor of Computer Science, Indian Institute of Technology, Kanpur, 1975; Head, Computer Centre, IIT Kanpur, 1979. *Memberships:* Fellow of the Institute of Mathematics and its applications, England; Member, Computer Society of India; Member, Executive Council; Life Member, Indian Mathematical Society. *Publications:* 30 Scientific Research Publications in Mathematics and Computing. *Hobbies:* Household Repairs and Gardening. *Address:* 659 IIT Campus, Indian Institute of Technology, Kanpur, Pin-208016, India.

SANTAMARIA, Joseph, Natalino, b. 21 Dec. 1923, Brunswick, Victoria, Australia. Medical Profession. m. Dorothy Cook, 23 Feb. 1952, 2 sons, 3 daughters. *Education:* MB, BS, Melbourne University, 1948; MRACP 1956; FRACP 1968. *Appointments:* Medical Officer, St. Vincent's Hospital, Melbourne, 1949-50; Research Officer, St Vincent's Hospital, Melbourne, 1953-54; Private Practice, 1955-70; Director, Dept, Community Medicine, St. Vincent's Hospital, Melbourne, 1970-; Honorary Clinical Haemat, (Sessional) - R.C.H. 1968-75. *Memberships:* Member, Melbourne Cricket Club; Member, Graduate Union, University of Melbourne; President, Natural Family Planning Council of Victoria. *Publications:* Author, Co-author and contributor of some 45 publications to learned journals, symposia and proceedings in Australia and New Zealand. *Hobbies:* Farming; Tennis. *Address:* 7 Powlett Street, Heidelberg 3084, Victoria, Australia.

SANTIAGO, Sam Mathew, b. 23 Sept 1950, Coonoor. Tea Taster, Buyer & Blender. m. Hilda Christabel, 1 Mar. 1981. *Education:* BCom (FICA), 1979. *Appointments:* With M/S Matheson Bosanquet & Company Limited as a tea-man, 1969-79; With Standard Tea Exports, as a tea-man, 1979-81. *Memberships:* Vice-President, Wellington Y's Men's Club and also secretary to the District Governor of West India Region of Y's Men International Board Member. *Publications:* Tea Experiments. *Hobbies:* Football; Reading; Writing; Travelling; Interior Decorating. *Address:* Post Box 41, Standard Tea Exports, Coonoor 643101, India.

SARAF, Babulal Saraf, b. 2 Dec. 1923, Badnawar. Teacher and Researcher. m. Vimla, 21 May 1947, 3 sons, 1 daughter. *Education:* BSc, University Merit Rank, College Gold and Silver Medals, 1947; MSc, University Rank Second, 1949; PhD, Thesis on 'Inner Bremstrahlung Spectra in Electron Capture Decay', 1958; *Appointments:* Lecturer in Physics, Agra College, Agra, India. 1950-52; Research Fellow, Bartol Research Foundation, Swarthmore, Pa, USA, 1952-55; Scientist, Atomic Energy Establishment, Bombay, India, 1955 Professor of Physics, University of Rajasthan, Jaipur, 1965-; Visiting Professor, Indiana University, Bloomington, Indiana, USA, 1980. *Memberships:* American Physical Society, USA; Indian Physics Association, India. *Publications:* Published several research papers in national and international journals; Physics Through Experiment, Vol 1, EMF Constant and Varying, (co-author); Physics Through Experiment, Vol 2, Mechanical Systems, (co-author). *Honours:* Recipient of First Prize at the Eleventh Biennial Apparatus Competition, New York, 1979. *Hobbies:* Travel; Technology. *Address:* C-8, University Campus, Jaipur, 302 004 India.

SARDAR, Ziauddin, b. 31 Oct. 1951, Northern Pakistan. Author, Science Journalist, Information Scientist. m. 9 Aug. 1978, 1 daughter. *Education:* BSc. (Hons) Physics, The City University, 1974; MSc, Information Science, The City University, 1975; PhD. Information Science, The City University, 1980. *Appointments:* Information Consultant, King Abdul Aziz University, Jeddah, 1975-79; Muslim World Correspondant, Nature, 1978-80; Middle East Science Consultant, New Scientist, 1980-; Third World Science Consultant, ATV Science in Society Unit, Crucible, 1980. *Publications:* Science, Technology and Development in the Muslin World; Hajj Studies, Vol. I; Islam: Outline of a Classification Scheme; The Future of Muslim Civilization; Science and Technology in the Middle East, Turkey and Pakistan. *Hobbies:* Science policy and development in the Middle East; Long range planning in the Muslim World. *Address:* 1 Orchard Gate, London, NW9, England.

SARKAR, Makbular, Rahman, (Dr.), b. 1 Jan. 1928, Rangpur, Bangladesh. Teaching and Research in Applied Physics & Electronics. m. K. A. Fashima, 16 July, 1959, 1 son, 1 daughter. *Education:* PhD in Solid State Physics & Electronics, University of Liverpool, England, 1956; MSc in Physics, Dacca University, Dacca, 1950; BSc. Honours in Physics, Dacca University, Dacca, 1948. *Appointments:* Professor of Applied Physics & Electronics, The University of Rajshahi, 1976-. and has held positions from Lecturer to Professor since 1951. *Memberships:* Member, Council for Scientific Affairs of Information for Third World Movement (I.T.M.) Paris; Member, Rajshahi University Senate; Member, Academic Council, Rajshahi University and holds numerous memberships of scientific societies. *Publications:* Author, co-author and contributor of some 15 important publications to scientific journals in India. *Honours:* Recipient of UNESCO Travel Grant, 1977. *Hobbies:* Photography; Tennis; Gardening. *Address:* Residential Quarter No. W-28, Rajshahi University Campus, Rajshahi University, Bangladesh.

SARKAR, Sakti Prasad, b. 1 Mar. 1923, Calcutta, Service. (Secretary, Post Graduate Councils of Science, Technology, Agriculture & Engineering, Calcutta University). m. Ira, 25 Feb. 1950, 2 daughters. *Education:* BSc, Calcutta University, 1944; MSc. Calcutta University, 1946; DSc, Leiden State University, Netherlands, 1960. *Appointments:* Lecturer in Zoology, City College, Calcutta, 1947-60; Professor and Head, Dept. of Zoology, Anauda Mohan College, Calcutta 1960-67; Professor of Zoology, University of Libya, Tripoli, 1963-65; Secretary, P.G. Council of Science, Technology, Agriculture and Engineering, Calcutta University, 1967-. *Memberships:* Life Member and Ex General Secretary, The Zoological Society, Calcutta; Council Member of the Indian Science News Association; Member The Indian Science Congress Association; Member, The Science Club; Executive Committee Member, The Physiological Society of India *Publications:* Contributor of distinguished articles to medical publications. *Honours:* Recipient of Fellowships from Zoological Society, Calcutta, 1962; and Netherlands Bureau of Technical Assistance, 1959-60. *Hobbies:* Travelling; Music (Indian Classical). *Address:* 16 Central Park, Calcutta - 32, India.

SARKIS, Samir, b. 15 May 1936, Avisdik, El-Kouna, North Lebanon. Civil Engineer/Director. m. Marie Saifi, 15 Sept. 1968, 2 sons, 2 daughter *Education:* High School Diploma with Honours, Bichmizzeen High School, El-Kouna, Lebanon, 1952; Sophomae Engineering Diploma, Aleppo College, Aleppo, Syria, 1954; BS, Civil Engineering, American University of Beirut, 1961. *Appointments:* School teacher in Kafarhota, El-Kouna, 1954-55; Chief Clerk/Interpreter with Qotor Petroleum Development Co. Ltd., 1955-57; Civil Engineer, Project Manager, Agent, and Director with the Contracting and Trading Co. Ltd., 1961-. *Memberships:* Member, Lebanese Order of Engineers, American Society of Civil Engineers, Nigerian Society of Engineers. *Creative Works:* Succeeded and managed in bringing up a company to a very flourishing state through hardwork and perseverance from limited resources and under difficult conditions and unfavourable circumstances; Mechanical and Pipeline Projects in different areas; Bridge Design and Construction; Drainage Works; Roadworks; Design and Construction of Pipeline, Terminals, Office and Residential Buildings, Pumping Stations and Dam Construction. *Hobbies:* Hunting; Running. *Address:* 35 Odibo Estate, Warri, Nigeria.

SASTRY, Mukkavalli Lingappa, b. 21 May 1910, Vishakapatnam, India. Engineer. m. Ramalakshmi, 30 Mar. 1930, 2 sons, 2 daughters. *Education:* BA, English and Mathematics, 1st class, Andhra University; BSc, Electrical and Mechanical Engineering, 1st class; Graduate, Institute of Electrical Engineers, England; City and Guilds, Radio Engineering, London Institute. *Appointments:* All India Radio: Junior Engineer, Station Engineer, Engineer in Charge High Power Transmitters, Research Engineer, Deputy Chief Engineer & Chief Engineer; U.N. Expert, Chief Technical Advisor TV & Broadcasting Saudi Arabia. *Memberships:* Fellow of the Institution of Electronic and Telecommunication Engineers, India; Council Member, 1963-66. *Publications:* Conceived, compiled and presented India Plan for frequency assignment of World Broadcasting stations at Mexico City in 1949. *Honours:* BA, Brabazon Merit Scholarship, 1929; BA, English and Mathematics, 1930; Couselant Physical Culture Cup, 1932; Prince of Wales, Gold Medal, For Electrical and Mechanical Engineering, 1934; Represented India at High Frequency Broadcasting, Technical Planning Committees, Administrative Radio and Plenipotentiary Conferences in Atlantic City, 1947, Geneva, 1948, Mexico City, 1949, Paris, 1949, Florence and Rapallo, 1950, Buenos Aires, 1951; Represented India at Commonwealth Broadcasting Conference, Montreal, 1963; Asian Broadcasting Conferences, Tokyo, 1958, Kuala Lumpur, 1962, Seoul, 1963, Sydney, 1964; Invitation from Government of Burma, advising on Radio Frequeny Management. *Hobbies:* Literature; Philosophy; Contract Bridge and Chess. *Address:* 28 Sea Bird, 114 B.J. Road, Bandra, Bombay 400 050, India.

SATOW, Michael Graham, b. 15 May 1916, Bushey, Hertfordshire, England. Engineer. m. Margaret Anne Barrowcliff, 14 Sept. 1945, 2 sons, 1 daughter. *Education:* Diploma of Loughborough College, Mechanical Engineering, 1936-39. *Appointments:* Fraser & Chalmers Engineering Works, Special Apprentice, Erith, 1934-36; Mather & Platt Limited, 1939-40; I.C.I., India, PVT Limited, 1957-71; Locomotion Enterprises, 1975-80. *Memberships:* Fellow, Institution of Mechanical Engineers; Honorary Life Member, Bengal Club, Calcutta, President, 1970-71; Member, Oriental Club, London, 1962-; Member, Advisory Committee, National Railway Museum, York. *Publications:* Railways of the Raj, Joint with R. Desmond, London, 1980; The Last Parade, joint with others, London, 1977; Honorary Adviser, Government of India, Ministry of Railways, for rail Transport Museum, New Delhi, 1969-. *Honours:* Recipient of OBE, 1971. *Hobbies:* Industrial Archaeology; Indian History; Engineering; Social Work. *Address:* 50 Church Lane, Ormesby, Middlesbrough, Cleveland TS7 9AU. England.

SATTAR, Abdus, b. 1 Feb. 1931, Golora, Tangail, Bangladesh. Servoce. m. Fatima Begum, 6 June 1951, 3 sons, 2 daughters. *Education:* Matriculation, Calcutta University, 1947; Intermediate, Dacca Board, 1949; BA, Dacca University, 1951. *Appointments:* Upper Division Assistant, 1952; Superintendent, Revenue Department, 1958; Sub-Editor, Assistant Editor, Editor, Department of Films & Publications, 1962-1972-. *Memberships:* Fellow, Bangla Academy, Dacca; Joint Secretary, Bangladesh Folklore Parishad; Adviser, Tribal Cultural Academy; Founder Member, Bangladesh Ethnological Society. *Publications:* Some 65 publications on poetry, books of research, translation works and books for children. Most recent are Aamar Banabas, 1981; Moulana Rumi, 1980; Aarbi Galpa, 1975; Mian Taansen, 1980. *Honours:* Recipient of Dawood Prize for Literature, 1966; Bangla Academy Prize for Literature, 1975; Abul Mansur Sahitya Purushkar, 1980; Gold Medal for Literature, 1968, by Aurani Sahitya Sangstha of Tangail. *Hobbies:* Chess Playing. *Address:* 59/4 Circular Road, Dhanmondi, Dacca-5, Bangladesh.

SATTAR, Abdus, b. 1 Mar. 1906, Birbhum, India. Justice. m. Sayema Khatoon. *Education:* Graduated from Presidency College, Calcutta, 1926; Master's Degree, Calcutta University, 1928; Bachelor in Law, Calcutta, University, 1929. *Appointments:* Judge, Dacca High Court, 1957; Judge, Supreme Court of Pakistan, 1968; President, Bangladesh Institute of Law and International Affairs, 1973-; Convenor, Bangladesh National Group for Nomination of Members to the International Court of Justice, 1975-. *Memberships:* Honorary Member, Dacca Rotary Club; Honorary Mem-

ber, Dacca Lions Club. *Hobbies:* Reading; Gardening. *Address:* House No.4, Road No. 4, Dhanmondi Residential Area, Dacca-5, Bangladesh.

SATTERTHWAITE, John Richard, b. 17 Nov. 1925, Whicham, Cumbria, England. Bishop. *Education:* Millom Grammar School, 1936-42; BA, History, Leeds University, 1943-46; GOE, Theology, College of the Resurrection, Mirfield, 1948-50. *Appointments:* History Master, St. Luke's School, Haifa, 1946-48; Curate, St. Barnabas, Carlisle, 1950-53; Assistant Priest, St. Aidan, Carlisle, 1953-54; Assistant General Secretary, C of E Council on Foreign Relations, Lambeth Palace, 1955-59; General Secretary, 1969-70; Priest in Charge, St. Michael Paternoster, Royal, EC4, 1954-59; Vicar of St. Dunstan in the West, 1958-70; Bishop of Fulham and Gibraltar, 1970-80; Bishop of Gibraltar in Europe, 1980-. *Memberships:* Athenaeum Club. *Honours:* Recipient of Honorary Canon of Canterbury, 1963-70; Honorary Canon of Old Catholic Cathedral of Utrecht from Chaplain and Prelate Chaplain of the Sovereign Order of St. John, 1968; Prelate Brother of the Sovereign Military Order of the St. John of Jerusalem Knights, Malta, 1981. *Hobbies:* Music; Fell Walking; Archaeology. *Address:* Flat 1, 19 Brunswick Gardens, London W8 4A8, England.

SAUL, David John, b. 27 Nov. 1939, Warwick, Bermuda. Senior Civil Servant. m. Christine Hall 31 Aug. 1963, 1 son, 1 daughter. *Education:* Certificate of Education, Nottingham, 1961; Diploma, Loughborough, 1962; BA, Queen's, Canada, 1968; MEd, 1969; PhD, Toronto, 1971. *Appointments:* School Master, Bermuda, 1962-67; Graduate Assistant, University of Toronto, 1969-70; Visiting Professor, 1970; Permanent Secretary for Education, Bermuda Government, 1972-76; Finnancial Secretary, 1976-. *Memberships:* Bermuda National Trust; Bermuda Cycle Association; Bermuda Squash Association; Mid Atlantic Athletic Club. *Hobbies:* Painting; Stamp Collecting; Lepidoptery; Gardening; Long Distance Running. *Address:* "Rocky Ledge", Devonshire Bay, Bermuda.

SAUNDERS, Adrian Dudley, b. 4 Jan. 1954, Kingstown, St. Vincent, Caribbean. Attorney-at-Law. m. Marilyn Angela Joslyn, 3 Oct. 1980. *Education:* St. Vincent Grammar School, 1965-72; LLB, Honours, University of the West Indies; Legal Education Certificate, Hugh Wooding Law School, Trinidad & Tobago, 1975-77. *Appointments:* Practising Attorney-at-Law, St. Vincent, 1977-. *Memberships:* Treasurer, Local Development Fund, CADEC: Member, Executive Committee, St. Vincent Table Tennis Association. *Hobbies:* Reading; Table Tennis. *Address:* Cane Garden, Kingstown, St. Vincent, Caribbean.

SAUNDERS, Colin Robert, b. 23 Aug. 1934, Selukwe, Zimbabwe. Medical Practitioner. m. 1 July, 1961, 1 son, 3 daughters. *Education:* MB, ChB, University of Cape Town, 1958; Diploma in Tropical Medicine & Hygiene, University of Liverpool, 1980. *Appointments:* Government Medical Officer, 1959-63; Medical Officer, Triangle Sugar Estates, 1963-70; Chief Medical Officer, Triangle Limited, 1970-. *Memberships:* Chairman, Parks and Wildlife Board of Zimbabwe, 1975-; Founder Member, Conservation Trust of Zimbabwe; Founder Chairman, Lowveld Round Table; Founder Chairman, Lowvels Natural Museum Commit 1965-. *Publications:* Recipient of Memorial Cup for Service to Sport, University of Cape Town, 2955-56; Blacklock Medal for International Community Health, University of Liverpool, 1980. *Hobbies:* Conservation; Natural History. *Address:* Lowveld Lodge, PO Box 17, Triangle, Zimbabwe.

SAUNDERS, Jamie William Sutherland, b. 17 Oct. 1949, Yorkton, Saskatchewan, Canada. Barrister. m. Gayle Jean Tope, 14 July 1973, 1 son, 2 daughters. *Education:* BA (Hons) English and Political Science, Bishop's University, Lennoxville, Quebec, 1966-70; LLB, Dalhousie University, Halifax, N.S., 1970-73; Called to the Bar of Nova Scotia, 1974. *Appointments:* Parole Officer, National Parole Board, 1971-72; Associate, Patterson, Smith, Matthews and Grant, 1974-79; Partner, Patterson, Smith, Matthews and Grant, 1980-. *Memberships:* Civil Litigation, Canadian Bar Association; Colchester Co. Barristers' Society; Dalhousie Law School; Officer, Fellowship Lodge, AF and AM; Boys and Girls Clubs of Canada; Planning Committee, Continuing Legal Education Society, Nova Scotia.

Publications: Update on Damages in Civil Litigation, 1981; Corporal Punishment and Child Abuse, 1981; Lecturer, Insurance and Damages, Bar Admission Course, Nova Scotia Barrister's Society; Lecturer, Nova Scotia Commission on Drug Dependency High School Lecturer on Family and Criminal Law. *Honours:* Golden Mitre Award, Bishop's University, 1970; Smith Shield award, Dalhousie Law School 1973. *Hobbies:* Travel; Literature; Movies; Football; Squash. *Address:* 10 Church Street, Box 1068, Truro, Nova Scotia, Canada.

SAUNDERS, Percy Oswald, b. 11 Dec. 1933. Parliamentary Clerk. *Education:* Bahamas Public Schools. *Appointments:* Principal School Teacher, 1952-57; Customs Officer Grade 1, 1957-69; Parliamentary Clerk, 1969-. *Hobbies:* Flying; Skeet Shooting; Bowling; Water Sports. *Address:* Amerelleys Avenue, Garden Hill Estates, PO Box N-3003, Nassau, Bahamas, British West Indies.

SAUNDERS-NORTH, Diane G (Mrs Winston V Saunders), b. 10 Mar. 1944, Nassau, Bahamas, West Indies. m. 15 Apr. 1968. *Education:* BA, University of Newcastle upon Tyne, UK; MPhil, University of the West Indies. *Appointments:* Teacher, Government High School, 1967-68; Public Records Officer Bahamas Government, 1970-71; Archivist, Ministry of Education and Bahamas Government, 1971-80; Chief Archivist, Ministry of Education and Bahamas Government, 1980-. *Memberships:* Chairman, Broadcasting Committee, Mental Health Association, 1972-73; Secretary, Bahama Drama Circle, 1969-71; Chairman, Red Cross Ball Committee, 1978-80; President of the Caribbean Archive Association, 1975-79; First Vice President, Bahamas Historical Society Chairman, Committee on Preservation of Historic Buildings. *Publications:* Guide to Records of the Bahamas, 1973, (co-author); Historic Nassau, 1979, (co-author). *Honours:* Recipient of Boss of the Year, Nassau, Bahamas, 1979. *Hobbies:* Painting; Tennis; Drama. *Address:* PO Box N-3937, Nassau, Bahamas, West Indies.

SAUVE, Jeanne (Mrs Maurice Sauve) b. 26 Apr. 1922, Prud'homme, Saskatchewan, Canada. Speaker of the House of Commons. m. 24 Sept. 1948, 1 son. *Appointments:* French Teacher, London County Council, 1948-50; Assistant to Director, Youth Section UNESCO, Paris, 1951; Journalist Broadcaster, Canadian Broadcasting Corporation and la Societe Radio-Canada, 1952-72; Director, Bushnell Communications Ltd and Radio Station CKAC, Montreal; Freelance editor, Montreal Star, 1970-72; Founding Member, Institute of Political Research, 1972. *Memberships:* National President, Jeuness Catholique Movement, 1942-47; Founder, Federation des mouvements de jeuness du Quebec, 1947; Vice President, Union des Artistes, Montreal, 1968-70. *Honours:* Honorary Doctorate of Science, University of New Brunswick, 1974 Ordre de la Pleiade, 1980. *Hobbies:* Literature; Music; Tennis; Swimming. *Address:* 281 McDougall Avenue, Montreal, QUE, H2V 3P3, Canada.

SAVAGE, Michael Albert Henry, b. 2 Oct. 1942, Sale, Cheshire, England. Quantity Surveyor. m. B. D. Lemon, 13 Feb. 1976, 1 daughter. *Education:* Associate of the Royal Institution of Chartered Surveyors, 1975; Associate of the Nigerian Institute of Quantity Surveyors, 1978. *Appointments:* Venning, Hope & Partners; F. H. Wood & Partners, Fletcher, Millet & Partners; Mercer & Miller; Widnell & Trollope; Widnell & Trollope, Nigeria. *Address:* 27A Lugard Avenue, Ikoyi, Lagos, Nigeria.

SAVARIMUTHU, John Gurubatham, (Rt. Rev. Tan Sri) b. 29 Nov. 1925, Kulasekharapatnam, S. India. Bishop (Anglican Church). m. Catherine, 9 Apr. 1947, 2 sons, 1 daughter. *Education:* FA, Madras University, 1943-45; BD, Serampore University, 1948-52; DipTh, St. Augustine's College, Canterbury, England, 1962-63. *Appointments:* Assistant Priest, St. Mark's Church, Seremban, Malaysia, 1952-55; Vicar of Negeri Sembilan, St. Mark's Church, Seremban, 1956-62; Vicar of South Johore, St. Christopher's, Johore Bahru and Bishop's Examining Chaplain, 1964-70; Vicar, St. James' Church, Kuala Lumpur, 1971-72; Archdeacon and Director of Theological Training, 1970-72; Bishop of West Malaysia, 1973. *Memberships:* National Secretary, Church Union Negotiating Committee, 1970-73, and National President, 1973; National Vice President, Council of Churches of Malaysia, 1973-75; National

President, Council of Church of Malaysia, 1979; President, Seminari Theoloji, Malaysia, 1979. *Honours:* Recipient of Rottler Prize for Competitive Thesis on Comparative Religion in Theological College, 1951; Royal Award of Panglima Setia Mahota (PSM) with the title Tan Sri for himself and Puan Sri for his wife. *Hobbies:* Reading. *Address:* Rumah Bishop, 14 Pesiaran Stonor, Kuala Lumpur 04-08, West Malaysia.

SAVJANI, Krishna, . b. 2 Mar. 1947, Jamnagar, India. Barrister-at-Law. m. Rita Choksi, 11 July 1977, 2 sons. *Education:* Barrister-at-Law, Gray's Inn, London, 1969. *Appointments:* Savjani & Co., Legal Practitioners, proprietor of firm, Limbe, Malawi. *Memberships:* Chairman, Asian Liaison Circle, 1971-; Chairman, Indian Sports Club, Malawi, 1972-; Educational Governor, Board of Governors of Southern School, Blantyre, Malawi, 1975-. 08 Photography; Reading; Fishing and Travelling. *Address:* PO Box 5234, Limbe, Malawi.

SAW, Evan Staples, b. 20 Sept. 1900, Fremantle, Western Australia. Chartered Accountant and Chartered Secretary. m. Eileen Milford Tindale, 1928, 2 sons. *Education:* FCIA, Australia; FCIS, Great Britain; FASA, Australia. *Appointments:* Chartered Accountant, numerous Australian Companies, 1919-1981. *Memberships:* West Australian Turf Club; Weld Club, Perth; The United Club of Perth; Past President, Life Member, Royal Perth Golf Club; Life Member, Australian Bank Officials' Association; Rotary Club of Perth, 1930-80, 1982. *Hobbies:* Gardening; Swimming; Golf. *Address:* 19 Angelo Street, South Perth, 6151, Western Australia.

SAW, Huat Lye, b. 13 Feb. 1935, Selangor, Malaysia. General Manager, Malaysian Airline System. m. Wong Yuit Leng, 7 Sept. 1959, 2 daughters. *Education:* BA, Economics, University of Malaya, Singapore, 1958. *Appointments:* Assistant District Officer, Kinta South; Assistant State Secretary, Perak; Chairman, Town Council, Taiping; Assistant Commissioner of Lands; Deputy Secretary General, Ministry of Transport; Retired from Government service and appointed by the Government as General Manager of Malaysian Airline System, 1971. *Memberships:* Fellow, Chartered Institute of Transport, 1975; Member of the Board, Institute of Air Transport, 1978; Member, Board of Management, Tourist Development Corporation of Malaysia; Director, PTM Sdn. Berhad. *Honours:* Honoured by His Majesty the King with the award, Kesatria Mangku Negara, KMN, 1969; and with the award, Johan Mangku Negara, JMN, 1976. *Hobbies:* Golf; Hunting. *Address:* No. 6, Jalan Damansara, Permai, Kuala Lumpur.

SAWERS, Ronald John, b. 26 Oct. 1919, Adelaide, South Australia. Medical Practitioner. m. Mary Elizabeth Harman, 20 Sept. 1950, 2 sons. *Education:* MB, BS, University of Adelaide, 1942; MRACP, 1950; FRACP, 1963; FRCPath, 1972; FRCPA, 1965. *Appointments:* Resident Medical Officer, Royal Adelaide Hospital, 1943; Australian Army Medical Corp, 1944-47; Registrar, Prof. Department medicine, University of Queensland, 1947-50; Honorary Assistant Haematologist, Alfred Hospital, Melbourne, 1954-64; Clinical Pathologist, Alfred Hospital, Melbourne, 1960-64; Director, Department of Haematology, Alfred Hospital, Melbourne, 1964-. *Memberships:* Member: Australian Medical Association; International Society of Haematology; International Society on Thrombosis & Haemastasis. *Hobbies:* Sailing. *Address:* 105 Elizabeth Street, Kooyong, Victoria 3144, Australia.

SAXENA, Surrendra Kumar, b. 3 Apr. 1926, Aligarh, India. Director. m. Ingalill Gunnel Amanda Friberg, 18 Sept. 1961, 2 sons, 2 daughters. *Appointments:* Regional Director, ICA, 1959-68; New Delhi South East Asian Office, 1968-; Director, International Cooperative Alliance, London. *Memberships:* Member, Independent Disarmament Commission, Vienna, Austria; Chairman, Executive Committee, India Development Group, London; Life Member, Indian Institute of Public Administration, New Delhi. *Publications:* Many articles dealing with various aspects of cooperative movements in different countries of the world. *Honours:* Recipient of Severin Jorgensen Prize, Copenhagen, 1978; Meda, Indian Cooperative Movement Congress, 1979. *Hobbies:* Golf; Gardening; Indian and Western operatic music; Extensive reading especially in social sciences, biographies etc. *Address:* 6 Hoe Meadow, Beaconsfield, Bucks, HP9 1TD, England.

SAXTON, Beryl, b. 11 Dec. 1934, Sutton in Ashfield, Notts. Teacher of Music. *Education:* ALCM, 1961; LLCM, 1961; FLCM 1962; LTCL. 1969; FTCL, 1972; ATCL, (TD), 1976. *Appointments:* Private Practice. *Memberships:* Incorporated Society of Musicians; Trinity College of Music Guild Diploma Holders Association, London College of Music. *Hobbies:* Gardening; Photography; Woodwork; Do it yourself activities. *Address:* Overstones, 41 Dales Avenue, Sutton in Ashfield, Notts, England.

SAXTON, Roy Gerald, b. 3 Feb. 1945, Kenilworth, Warwickshire, England. Schoolmaster. m. Patricia Eileen Broadbent, 15 Sept. 1973, 1 son, 2 daughters. *Education:* BSc, Bristol, 1969; PhD, Bristol, 1973. *Appointments:* Head, Department of Chemistry, Repton School, 1976-. *Memberships:* Member, Royal Society of Chemistry. *Publications:* The Chemistry of Cyclooctatetraene and its Derivatives (co-author); Concise O-Level Chemistry (co-author) 1979; Fundamental Organic Reactions, 1980. *Hobbies:* Publishing (educational books). *Address:* 22 Brook End, Repton, Derby, DE6 6FW, England.

SAYERS, Edward George, b. 10 Sept. 1902, Christchurch, New Zealand. Consultant Physician. m. (1) Jean M. Grove, 1928; (2) Patricia D. Coleman, 1971. *Education:* MD, NZ; Hon DSc, Otago; FRCP, FRACP; Hon. FACP; Hon. FRCP, Edin.; FAAA, FRS, NZ; DT&H, London. *Appointments:* House Physician, Wellington Hospital, London Hospital for Tropical Diseases; Medical Missionary, British Solomon Islands; Physician, Auckland Hospital; Dean, Faculty of Medicine, University of Otago; Consultant Physician, Dunedin; War Service: Specialist in Tropical Diseases, New Zealand Forces, Middle East; Consultant Physician, New Zealand Forces in Pacific, rank of Colonel. *Memberships:* President, Royal Australasian College of Physicians; Chairman, Medical Council of New Zealand; President, New Zealand branch of British Medical Association; Chairman, Scientific Committee, Nationa Heart Foundation of New Zealand; Colonel Commandant, Royal New Zealand Medical Corps. *Publications:* Various articles in Medical Journals. *Honours:* Recipient of KB, 1965; CMG, 1956; Legion of Merit, USA, 1944; Knight of the Order of St. John of Jerusalem. *Hobbies:* Fishing; Gardening. *Address:* 27A Henry Street, Maori Hill, Dunedin, New Zealand.

SCANLAN, Brian John, b. 27 Aug. 1927, Brisbane, Australia. Medicine. m. Mary Ellen Murdoch, 8 Dec. 1952, 3 sons, 1 daughter. *Education:* MBBS, 1951; FRACMA, 1973; FHA, 1980. *Appointments:* Bundaberg Hospital, 1951; Goondiwindi Hospital, 1952-53; Private Practice, 1953-69; Department of Veterans' Affairs, 1969-; Chief Executive Officer, Repatriation General Hospital, Greenslopes, 1977-. *Memberships:* United Service Club; State President, Royal Australian College of Medical Administrator; Senior Vice President, State Branch, Australian College of Health Service Administrators. *Honours:* Recipient of Open University Scholarship, 1946; AMA Kellogg Foundation Fellowship, 1981. *Hobbies:* Horse Racing; Fishing. *Address:* 29 Kanofski Street, Chermside West, Brisbane, Queensland 4032, Australia.

SCERRI, Arthur J, b. 31 Jan. 1921 (deceased 1981). High Commissioner for Malta. m. Ruby Howell, 1951, 1 daughter. *Education:* St Albert's College; St Mary's College; HM Dockyard Technical College; Diplomas in Statistics, Work Study, English. *Appointments:* Electrical Engineer, HM Dockyard, Malta, 1937-50; Instrument Draughtsman, United Kingdom, 1950-71; Malta Representative, Malta Labour Party London, and London Correspondent, Voice of Malta, 1954-71; High Commissioner for Malta, London, 1971-; Cyprus, 1972-; Ambassador, USSR and Iran, 1972-. *Memberships:* Integration Round Table Conference, 1956; Independence Conference, 1963. *Publications:* Various articles. *Hobbies:* Politics; Reading; Maltese stamps. *Address:* 15 Upper Belgrave Street, London SW1, England.

SCHAFFER, John Wilson, b. 3 Mar. 1925, Woollahra, New South Wales, Australia. Managing Director. 2 sons, 2 daughters. *Education:* Haileybury College, Melbourne, 1935, 1937; Xavier College, Melbourne, 1938, 1942. *Memberships:* Victoria Golf Club, Victorian Amateur Turf Club; Sandringham Club; Royal Automobile Club of Victoria. *Honours:* Recipient of Honours in

Mathematics and Physics, 1942. *Hobbies:* Golf; Horse Racing. *Address:* 33 Haldane Street, Beaumaris, Victoria 3193, Australia.

SCHEIBNEROVA, Viera, b. 27 Mar. 1935, Bratislava, Czechoslovakia. Micropalaeontologist. 2 daughters. *Education:* DipGeol, 1958; DrNatSci, 1969. *Appointments:* Lecturer, 1958-61, Senior Lecturer, 1961-67; Associate Professor, 1967-68, J. A. Cornelius University, Bratislava, Czechoslavakia; Research Scientist, Micropalaentology, 1969-78; Senior Research Scientist, 1969-72; Principal Research Scientist, 1977-; Geology Survey, New South Wales, Sydney, Australia. *Memberships:* The Royal Society, New South Wales; Geology Society, Australia. *Publications:* About 80 scientific papers in various professional journals. *Hobbies:* Education; Painting; Interior Decorating; Cloth Designing; Sewing. *Address:* 6 Plumer Road, Rose Bay 2029, New South Wales, Australia.

SCHENCK, Michael U. R. von, b. 21 Apr. 1931, Basel, Switzerland. Swiss Diplomatist. *Education:* Humanistisches Gymnasium and University, Basel; and in Lausanne. *Appointments:* Secretary-General, International Society for Volunteer Service, 1967-71; Harvard University, 1972-73; Representative to IAEA and UNIDO, Swiss Embassy, Vienna, 1973-77; Head, Economics Department, Swiss Embassy, Bonn, 1977-80; Ambassador to Ghana (also accredited to Liberia, Sierra Leone and Togo) 1980. *Publications:* An International Peace Corps, 1968; Youth Today, 1968; Youth's Role in Development, 1968; International Volunteer Service, 1969. *Hobbies:* Skiing; Hiking. *Address:* Embassy of Switzerland, POB 359, Accra, Ghana.

SCHENKEL, Barbara Caroline (Mrs Leon T Schenkel), b. 11 Nov. 1919, Warsaw, Poland. Teacher and Writer. *Education:* Teacher of Drama, Victorian Education Department, 1958-80, now retired. *Appointments:* Correspondent, Polish Weekly newspaper; Radio Broadcaster, Special Broadcasting Service, Polish language, Melbourne. *Memberships:* Polish Theatre, Polish Radio Committee, Polish Cultural and Artistic Circle and Polish Art Foundation; Fellowship of Australian Writers, Poet's Union, Victorian Broadcasters Association. *Publications:* Poems, articles and short stories published in magazines and newspapers and books in Polish and English. *Honours:* Recipient of Silver Cross of Merit, 1977. *Hobbies:* Childrens Theatre and Youth Counselling. *Address:* 3/1 Munro Street, Armadale 3143, Victoria, Australia.

SCHIFF, Emile Louis Constant, b. 2 Mar. 1918, The Hague, The Netherlands. Diplomatist. m. Jeannette van Rees, 25 Oct. 1944, 1 son, 1 daughter. *Education:* Law Degree, University of Leiden, The Netherlands. *Appointments:* Netherlands Embassy, Washington, 1945-49; Netherlands Legation, Madrid, 1949-52; Private Secretary, Minister for Foreign Affairs, 1952-54; Deputy Chief of Mission, Netherlands Mission to the United Nations, New York, 1955-59; Minister, Netherlands Embassy, Washington, 1959-64; Ambassador to Indonesia, 1965-68; Secretary-General, Netherlands Ministry of Foreign Affairs, 1968-77; Ambassador to Australia, 1977-. *Memberships:* Royal Canberra Golf Club; Commonwealth Club, Canberra; The Hague Golf and Country Club; The Hague De Witte. *Honours:* Recipient of Netherlands and foreign awards. *Hobby:* Golf. *Address:* 16 Mugga Way, Red Hill, ACT 2603, Australia.

SCHMON, Robert MacCormick, b. 2 Dec. 1923, Glen Ridge, New Jersey, USA. Paper Company Executive. m. Galena Netchi, 2 July 1966, 2 sons. *Education:* BA, Princeton University, 1948. *Appointments:* Quebec North Shore Paper Co., Baie Comeau, Quebec, 1948; Assistant Sales Manager, The Ontario Paper Co. Ltd., 1952; Assistant to the Executive Vice President, 1959; Assistant Executive Vice President, Vice President, Development and Planning, 1960; President, 1964; Chairman of the Board, 1979. *Memberships:* Canadian Pulp and Paper Association; Director, Great Lakes Waterways Development Association; Board of Governors, Ridley College, St. Catharines; Trustee, Quetico Foundation; Director, Quebec-Labrador Foundation (Canada) Inc.; Executive Committee, Princeton Alumni Association of Canada Clubs; Mount Royal Club, Montreal; Niagara Falls, NY, Country Club; Tribune Company (Chicago). *Hobbies:* Golf; Fishing. *Address:* 115

Front Street, Niagara-on-the-Lake, Ontario, LOS 1JO, Canada.

SCHREYER, Edward Richard (Rt. Hon.), CC, CMM, CD, b. 21 Dec. 1935, Beausejour, Manitoba, Canada. Governor General of Canada. m. Lily Schulz, 30 June 1960, 2 sons, 2 daughters. *Education:* BA, United College, Winnipeg; BE,St. John's College; MA, University of Manitoba. *Appointments:* Legislative Assembly, 1958; Professor of Political Science & International Relations, St. Paul's College, University of Manitoba; Member of Parliament, Springfield, 1965; Selkirk, 1968; Leader, NDP, 1969; Member, Legislative Assembly Rossmere and became Premier of Manitoba; Commenced second term as Premier, 1973; Leader of Opposition Manitoba Legislature, 1977; Held portfolio, Minister of Dominion Provincial Relations; Minister of Finance, 1972-1976. *Honours:* Recipient of Vanier Award, 1975. *Address:* Rideau Hall, Ottawa, KIA OAI, Canada.

SCHUBERT, Sydney, b. 22 March, 1928, Brisbane, Queensland, Australia. Civil Engineer. m. Maureen Kistle, 29 Jan. 1961, 2 daughters. *Education:* BE, 1950; BA, 1975; Dip. Highway & Traffic Engineering, 1958; Dip.Bus. Admin, 1970. 03 Main Roads Department, Queensland: Deputy Chief Engineer, Research and Planning, 1965-68; Assistant Commissioner, South Queensland, 1968-69; Co-ordinator General's Department: Chief Engineer, 1969-72; Deputy Co-ordinator General, 1972-77; Co-ordinator General, 1977-. *Memberships:* Fellow, Institution of Engineers, Australia; American Society of Civil Engineers; Australian Institute of Management; Queensland Club; Royal Queensland Golf Club. *Honours:* International Road Federation Scholarship, 1958; Eisenhower Exchange Fellowship, 1972. *Hobbies:* Golf; Tennis; Reading. *Address:* 15 Apex Street, Clayfield, Queensland 4011, Brisbane, Australia.

SCHULTZ, Charles Davis, b. 26 Oct. 1904, Vancouver, BC, Canada. Consulting Forest Engineer and Company President. m. 18 June 1947, 1 son, 2 daughters. *Education:* BASc, Forest Engineering, University of British Columbia, 1931. *Appointments:* Forest Engineer, Department of Lands & Forests, BC Government, 1931-35; BC Timber Commissioner to British West Indies, 1936-39; Resident Engineer, Bloedel Stewart & Welch Ltd., Bloedel, BC, 1940-44; President, C. D. Schultz & Co. Ltd., Vancouver, BC, 1944-79. *Memberships:* Director & Chairman, Natural Resources Committee, Association of Consulting Engineers of Canada, 1962-65; Canadian Forestry Association, 1950-; and numerous related societies and clubs. *Publications:* Your Forest Estate, (issued by Nat. Lib.). *Honours:* Engineering Book Prize, University of British Columbia, 1930; War Medal, 1939-45. *Hobbies:* Golf; Boating; Fishing. *Address:* 3050 O'Hara Lane, Crescent Beach, Surrey, BC, V4A 3E6, Canada.

SCHWARTZ, Gerald Wilfred, b. 24 Nov. 1941, Winnipeg, Canada. Industrialist. 2 daughters. *Education:* BComm, University of Manitoba, Canada, 1962; LLB, 1966; MBA, Harvard University, 1970. *Appointments:* Associate, Corporate Finance, Eastbrook & Co. Inc., NY, 1970; Vice President, Corporate Finance, 1971; Senior Associate, Bear, Stearns & Co., 1973; Vice President, Corporate Finance, Bear, Stearns, & Co., 1974; President and Director, Member of Executive Committee, CanWest Capital Corporation, 1977-. *Address:* 155 Carlton Street, Winnipeg, R3C 3HG, Canada.

SCHWEIZER, Karl Wolfgang, b. 30 June 1946, Mannheim, Germany. Professor m. Elizabeth Wild, 31 May 1969, 1 son. *Education:* BA, 1969, MA, 1970, Waterloo; MA, PhD, Peterhouse College, Cambridge, England. *Appointments:* Professor of British History, Bishop's University, Lennoxville, P.Q., 1976-; Research Associate, Russian and East European Centre, University of Illinois, USA, 1978, 1979; Visiting Professor, University of Guelph, 1973-1974. *Memberships:* Cambridge Historical Society; Conference on British Studies; Canadian Association of Scottish Studies; Inter-University Centre of European Studies, Montreal. *Publications:* Editor, Political Diary of William Cavendish, 4th Duke of Devonshire, 1982; Francois de Callieres: Diplomatic Theory in the Ancien Regime, 1982; Contributor to various professional journals and encyclopaedias. *Honours:* Canada Council Post Doctoral Fellowship, 1977-1978; Elected Associate, Royal His-

torical Society, 1981. *Hobbies:* Fishing; Swimming; Reading. *Address:* 4, Harrold Drive, Lennoxville, P.Q. Canada.

SCOON, Sir Paul, b. 4 July 1935. Governor General of Grenada, 1978-. m. Esmai Monica Lumsden, 1970, 2 step-sons, 1 step-daughter. *Education:* St John's Anglican School Grenada; Grenada Boys' Secondary School; Institute of Education, Leeds; BA, MEd, Toronto University. *Appointments:* Teacher, Grenada Boys' Secondary School, 1953-67; Chief Education Officer 1967-68; Permanent Secretary, 1969; Secretary to the Cabinet, Grenada, 1970-72; Deputy Director, Commonwealth Foundation, 1973-78. *Memberships:* Governor, Centre for International Briefing, Farnham Castle, 1973-78, Vice-President, Civil Service Association, Grenada, 1968; Co-founder, Association of Masters and Mistresses. *Memberships:* GCMG, 1979; OBE, 1970. *Hobbies:* Reading; Tennis. *Address:* Governor General's House, St George's, Grenada.

SCOPPA, Joseph, b. 4 July 1946, Italy. Surgeon m. Billie-Jean, 7 Aug. 1973, 2 sons. *Education:* MB, BS, Sydney University, 1969; FRACS, 1975. *Appointments:* E.N.T. Registrar, St. Vincent's Hospital, Sydney, 1972-75; Visiting E.N.T. Surgeon, Balmain Hospital, Sydney; Liverpool Hospital, Sydney, 1976-. *Memberships:* Otolaryngological Society of Australia; Fellow Royal Australasian College of Surgeons; Australian Medical Association. *Hobbies:* Bridge; Squash; Reading; Painting. *Address:* 24 Viret Street, Hunters Hill, Sydney, Australia.

SCORDO, Thomas James. b. 16 Feb. 1948, Ramacca, Sicily, Italy. Company Secretary m. Josephine Mary Bisignano, 8 May 1976, 2 daughters. *Education:* Dip. Bus. Studies, 1974; ACIS, 1979; AASA, 1976; AAIM, 1975; AIBA, 1979. *Appointments:* Trainee Accountant, W. Pridham, Victoria, Australia. 1969-1972; Accountant Auditor, Priestley & Morris, Melbourne, 1974-1975; Tax Consultant, Cerantonio & Baguley, Victoria, 1975-1976; Accountant, C.J. Coles & Company Ltd., Melbourne, 1976-79; Manager Corporate Legal, C.J. Coles, 1979-80; Company Secretary, C.J. Coles, Feb. 1980-. *Memberships:* Italo-Australian Co-operative Social Club; Past Secretary, Ramacca Social Club. *Hobbies:* Reading; Table Tennis; Gardening; Driving-sightseeing; Special interest in Western Philosophy & Traditions. *Address:* 47, William Street, Keilor Park, Victoria 3033, Australia.

SCOTT, Alfred Geoffrey, b. 11 Sept. 1908, Wellington, New Zealand. Film Production. m. joyce Rebecca Thomas, 7 June, 1939, 1 daughter. *Appointments:* Played piano silent movies & theatre orchestras, 1926; Installed and operated first talking picture machines, 1929; Technical supervision, theatre management & film distribution, 1932-41; Foundation Member, N.Z. National Film Unit, 1941; Technical Director N.Z.F.U., 1945-50; Manager & I/C Production N.Z.F.U. 1950-73. *Memberships:* President, Senior Trustee, 33 Club (INC); Rotary Club of Wellington South; Kilbirnie Bowling Club. *Creative Works:* Executive Producer, 700 short films of N.Z.; Devised & produced 3 screen Expo Film, This is N.Z.; Co-inventor Photofinish Camera System, 1943; Devised many Cinematograph techniques. *Honours:* MBE, 1968; OBE, 1972; Newmans 'Man of the Year' award, 1973; N.Z. National Film Unit won over 120 awards in International Competition, 1950-73. *Hobbies:* Bowling; Piano. *Address:* 99, Overtoun Terrace, Hataitai, Wellington, New Zealand.

SCOTT, Arthur Finley, b. 30 Nov. 1907, Kroonstad, Orange Free State, S. Africa. Teacher, Lecturer, Author. m. (1) Margaret Strawson, 1936, 2 children; (2) Margaret C. Smith, 1954. *Education:* BA, 1930; MA, 1934, Cambridge University, England. *Appointments:* Senior Lecturer, Borough Road College of Education, Greater London, U.K. 1951-1973; University Teacher, London University, 1968-73; Examiner in English, London University; Reader for Macmillan, Cambridge University Press, Harrap, Heinemann; Director of Scott & Finlay Ltd. *Memberships:* Life Fellow of the Intercontinental Biographical Association. *Publications:* Author of over 130 books, over 11 million sold, including 'Meaning & Style' 14th edition; 'Poetry & Appreciation' 14th edition; Ten books for schools in India. *Hobbies:* Gardening; Oil Painting. *Address:* 59 Syon Park Gardens, Osterley, Isleworth, Middlesex, TW7 5NE, England.

SCOTT, Avernell Zenil Foster, b. 24 Feb. 1915, West End, Cayman Brac, British West Indies, Business Manager. m. Clyde E. Scott, 7 Jan. 1933, 7 sons, 2 daughters. *Education:* Business Operator and Manager. *Hobbies:* Swimming; Sewing and Crochet. *Address:* West End, Cayman Brac, Cayman Islands, British West Indies.

SCOTT, David, Sir, b. 3 Aug. 1919, London, England. H.M. Diplomatic Service (retired).m. Vera K. Ibbitson, 21 Jan. 1941, 2 sons, 1 daughter. *Education:* Charterhouse School, 1933-38; Birmingham University, 1938-39. *Appointments:* Commonwealth Relations Office, 1948-50; served Union of South Africa, 1951-53; Joint Services Staff College, 1953-54; Cabinet Office, 1954-56; Singapore, 1956-58; Assistant Secretary, Monckton Commission on Central Africa, 1960; Deputy British High Commissioner to Federation of Rhodesia & Nyasaland, 1961-63; Imperial Defence College, 1964; Deputy High Commissioner to India, 1965-67; British High Commissioner to Uganda, 1967-70; Asst. Under-Secretary of State responsible for Dependant Territories, 1970-73; High Commissioner to New Zealand and Governor, Pitcairn Is. 1973-75; H.M. Ambassador to Republic of S. Africa, 1976-79; Chairman, Ellerman Lines Ltd., 1982; also Director of Barclays Bank International Ltd., Mitchell Cotts. Group Ltd., Delta Metal Overseas Ltd. *Memberships:* Vice-Chairman Royal Overseas League, 1981; Royal African Society, 1972-. *Publications:* Africa in Black and White, 1981. 06 CMG, 1966; KCMG, 1974; GCMG, 1979. *Hobbies:* Birdwatching; Music. *Address:* Wayside, Moushill Lane, Milford, Surrey, GU8 5BQ, England.

SCOTT, Douglas Michael, b. Stirling, U.K. Registered Teacher of Music, Lecturer and Choral Conductor. *Education:* LTCL, CMT Methods; ARCM Piano Teaching; LRAM in Singing; LGSM in Singing Teaching; ACP in Educ. Psychology & Methods. *Appointments:* Visiting Teacher of Music, Dunblane & Rural Schools; Assistant Music Master Dollar Academy, Scotland; Principal Teacher of Music, Bannockburn High School; Principal Teacher of Music, Auchterarder High School; Organist and Choir Master, Barony Church, 1971-75; Extra Mural Lecturer, Universities of Glasgow and Stirling; Private Teacher of piano, organ, singing and theory. *Memberships:* Society of Friends of Dunblane Cathedral; Scottish School Music Association. *Honours:* Life Fellow of I.B.A. Cambridge, England; Chairman & Speaker various IBC congresses in the world; Choir Director of IBC choir, Amsterdam and Beverly Hills. *Hobbies:* Travel; Reading; Photography. *Address:* 19, Charles Street, Dunblane, FK 15 9 BY, Scotland.

SCOTT, Edward John Rankin, b. 3 Jan. 1939, London, U.K., Merchant. 02 Eton College, 1952-57; McGill University, 1957-60 B.A.(Hons) *Appointments:* Chairman John Swire & Sons, Australia, 1960-63; Hong Kong 1963-65; Japan 1965-66; Australia 1967-81. *Memberships:* Union Club Sydney; Melbourne Club; M.C.C.; Fishmongers Company; Australian Jockey Club. *Honours:* Recipient of Lt. Governor's Gold Medal in History, McGill University, 1960. *Hobbies:* Sport; Opera. *Address:* 275 Edgecliff Road, Woollahra, Sydney, N.S.W., Australia.

SCOTT, Eric Cameron, b. 24 May, 1926, Picton, Ontario, Canada, Banker. m. Jane E. Goodchild, 3 sons, 1 daughter. *Education:* B.A.Sc., University of Toronto, 1949. *Appointments:* Design Engineer, Canadian International Paper Co., 1949-51; Plant Supervisor, Canadian Industries Ltd., 1951-58; Senior Manager, Executive Vice President, Federal Business Development Bank, 1958-. *Memberships:* Engineering Institute of Canada; International Council for Small Business. *Publications:* Various articles and booklets on small business management and papers to international conferences on this subject. *Hobbies:* Boating; Music; Photography; Tennis. *Address:* 98 Fifteenth Street, Roxboro, Quebec, Canada.

SCOTT, Gerald William, b. 12 Jan. 1931, London, England. Surgeon. m. Beryl Elizabeth Hubbard, 14 May 1955, 3 sons, 2 daughters. *Education:* MB, 1955; FRCS, 1964; MS, 1964; Dip. Am. Bd. Surg, 1965; *Appointments:* Surgeon, Calgary General Hospital, Holy Cross Hospital, Calgary, 1965-68, Foothills Hospital, Calgary, 1967-73; Consulting (Surgeon) W.W. Cross Cancer Institute, 1973-; Chief of Surgery, Charles Camsell Hospital, 1973-78, Surgeon, 1978-;

Professor of Surgery and Director, Surgical-Medical Research Institute, 1978-. *Memberships:* Canadian Association of Clinical Surgeons; European Society for Surgical Research; Canadian Asssociation of Gastroenterology; Canadian Medical Association; Alberta Medical Association. *Publications:* Contributed to various professional journals. *Honours:* Fulbright Scholarship, 1960-64; E. Starr Judd Award, 1965. *Hobbies:* Landscape painting. *Address:* 14707 59 Avenue, Edmonton, Alberta, T6H 4T5, Canada.

SCOTT, Marianne Florence, b. 4 Dec. 1928, Toronto, Ontario, Canada. Librarian. *Education:* BA, McGill University, Montreal, Quebec, Canada, 1949-. BLS McGill University, Montreal, Quebec, Canada, 1952. *Appointments:* Assistant Librarian, Bank of Montreal, 1952-55; Law Librarian, McGill University, 1955-73; Law Area Librarian, McGill University, 1973-75; Director of Libraries, McGill University, 1975-. *Memberships:* Member, International (Director, 1974-77); American, Canadian (President, 1963-69; Executive Board, 1973-75; Archivist) Associations of Law Libraries, Quebec Library Association, President, 1961-62; Corporation of Professional Librarians of Quebec (VP, 1975-76); Canadian Association of Research Libraries, President, 1978-79; Past President, 1979-80; Executive, 1980-81; The Centre for Research Libraries Board of Directors, 1980-81; Canadian Library Assistant President Elect, 1981; *Publications:* Canadian Association of Law Libraries, First Honoured Member, 1979-80; Canadian Silver Jubilee Medal recipient, 1978; *Address:* 3848 Melrose Avenue, Montreal, Quebec, H4A 2S2, Canada.

SCOTT, Sir Michael, b. 19 May 1923. HM Diplomatic Service. m. (1) Vivienne Sylvia Vincent-Barwood, 1944, 3 sons, (Div) (2) Jennifer Cameron Smith Slawikowski, 1971. *Education:* Dame Allan's School; Durham University. *Appointments:* Durham Light Infantry, 1941; 1st Gurkha Rifles, 1943-47; Colonial Office, 1949; CRO, 1957; First Secretary, Karachi, 1958-59; Deputy High Commissioner, Peshawar, 1959-62; Counsellor and Director, British Information Services in India, New Delhi, 1963-65; Head, East and Central Africa Department, FCO 1965-68; Counsellor, British High Commissioner, Nicosia, 1968-72; RCDS 1973; Ambassador to Nepal, 1974-77; High Commission in Malawi, 1977-79; High Commission in Bangladesh, 1980-81. *Honours:* MVO 1961; CMG, 1977; KCVO, 1979. *Address:* 87a Cornwall Gardens, London SW7 4AY, England.

SCOTT, Nicholas Paul, b. 5 Aug. 1933, London, England, Company Director, m. Cecilia Anne Hawke, 18 Apr. 1979, 1 son, 2 daughters. *Appointments:* Member of Parliament, Paddington South, 1966-74; Chelsea 1974-; Parliament Under Secretary, Department of Employment, 1974; Shadow Cabinet (Housing), 1974-75. *Memberships:* MCC; Bucks; Turf; Pratts. *Publications:* Contributor of Various Pamphlets. *Honours:* Recipient of MBE, 1964. *Hobbies:* Cricket, Golf, Tennis, Flying. *Address:* 12 Anhalt Road, London, SW11 England.

SCOTT, Philip John. b. 26 June 1931, Auckland, New Zealand. Academic Physician. m. Elizabeth Jane MacMillan, 10 Mar. 1956, 1 son, 3 daughters. *Education:* BMedSc 1952, MBChB 1955, University of Auckland & University of Otago; MD, University of Birmingham, 1962. *Appointments:* Isaacs Memorial Medical Research Fellow, Department of Medicine, Auckland Hospital; Senior Lecturer, University of Otago, Auckland, 1969; Associate Professor of Medicine, 1973; Personal Chair in Medicine, 1975; *Memberships:* Royal College of Physicians, London, 1959; Fellow, Royal College of Physicians, ondon, 1975; Fellow, Royal Australasian College of Physicians 1959; Royal Australasian College Physicians, 1966; Medical Research Society (United Kingdom), Nutrition Society of New Zealand; Australasian Atherosclerosis Discussion Group; Australian & NZ Society of Epidemiology and Research in Community Health; Australasian Society for Medical Education; Former Chairman (for NZ) Scientific Committee, RACP; Former Secretary NZ Board of Censors, RACP. *Publications:* Sundry scientific articles, chapters & books; Contributor to 1973 & 1978 reports of Coronary Disease, Heart Foundation of New Zealand. *Hobbies:* Pottery; Gardening; Medical History; English Literature; Medico-Legal Aspects of Cancer Therapy & Fringe Medicine. *Address:* 64 Temple Street, Meadowbank, Auckland 5, New Zealand.

SCOTT, Robert Harden. b. 23 Feb. 1916, Sydney, Australia, Economist. m. Joan M. Hall, 4 Jan. 1943, Joan T. Parsons, 17 Apr. 1974, 1 Daughter. *Education:* BEc. University of Sydney, Australia, 1941. *Appointments:* Economist, Commonwealth Bank of Australia, 1948-1960; Economist, Reserve Bank of Australia, 1960-1979; Visiting Fellow, Dept. of Economic History, Research, School of Social Sciences, Australian National University, Canberra, 1979-1980. *Memberships:* Central Council, Economic Society of Australia & New Zealand, 1974-; Australian & New Zealand Association for the Advancement of Science. *Publications:* Sundry Technical papers in Professional Economic Journals in Australia. *Hobbies:* Gardening. *Address:* 5 Sidaway Street, Chapman A.C.T. 2611, Australia.

SCOTT, Timothy. b. 31 Mar. 1952, London, England, Physicist. *Education:* BSc (Mathematics) 1973; PhD 1976. *Appointments:* 1976-1978, NATO Postdoctoral Research Fellow Department of Chemistry, University of Southern California, Los Angeles, USA; 1979-1981, Senior Research Assistant, Department of Physics, University of Durham, England; 1981-; Senior Scientific Officer (UKAEA), Atomic Energy Establishment, Winfrith, Dorchester, England. *Memberships:* Member of the Institute of Physics. *Publications:* Various papers on Electron-Atom Collisions published in Journal of Physics B: Atomic and Molecular Physics and also in Journal of Computational Physics. *Hobbies:* Hiking; Travel; Photography, Chess. *Address:* 23 Lower Hillside Road, Wool, Wareham, Dorset, England.

SCOTT, William John, (Hon.) b. 9 Sept. 1916, Te Awamutu, New Zealand. Company Director. m. Mary Royal Jackson, 21 Aug. 1945. *Appointments:* Minister of Broadcasting, 1963-66; Senior Government Whip, 1961-63; Deputy Chairman, Commonwealth Parliamentary Association, 1963-64; Postmaster-General, Minister of Marine, Minister in Charge of Government Printing Office, 1964-69; Director, Seatrans Consolidated (NZ) Ltd., 1970-74; Chmn. Lakewood Trading Co. Ltd., Chmn. N.Z. Historic Places Trust, 1970-73; Director, North Shore Ferries; Waiheke Shipping Co. Ltd; Kawan Island Ferries Ltd.; Overon Surfdale Transport Ltd.; Tanaki Ferries Ltd. *Memberships:* Auckland Club; Royal New Zealand Yacht Squadron; Coast Guard Member. *Honours:* Member of Executive Council, 1963-69; Hon. Kentucky Colonel; Freeman at City Louisville, (USA). *Hobbies:* Gardening; Fishing. *Address:* 31A Stanley Point Road, Auckland 9, New Zealand

SCOTT-MORGAN, John. b. 27 Feb. 1954 Stanford Brook, London, England, Historical Writer of Transport Subjects. *Appointments:* Freelance Writer and Researcher, 1971-1981 of Industrial Historical Publications for Davids Charles Ltd. Gemini Pub Co. and The North Western Museum of Science & Industry (Manchester). *Memberships:* Railway Club; Greater London Industrial Archeology Soc.; Chairman, British Overseas Railway Historical Soc.; Society of Authors; Transport Trust. *Publications:* The Corris Railway Company, 1977; The Colonel Stephens Railways, 1978; British Independant Light Railways, 1980; The Lobito Route, A. History of the Benguela Railway/North Western Museum of Science & Industry, 1981. *Hobbies:* Collecting Water Colour Paintings of Industrial/Historical Subjects. *Address:* 27 Tasmania Close, Basingstoke, Hants, England.

SCRIVENER, Barrie, Pedder, b. 3 Aug. 1927, Sydney, Australia. Medical Practitioner (Otologist). m. 17 Sept. 1955, 2 daughters. *Education:* MB, BS, 1951, DLO, University of Sydney, Australia, 1956; FRCS (Eng and Ed), 1958; FRACS, 1959. *Appointments:* RMO, RPA Hospital, Sydney, 1951-55; Registrar, Royal National Throat Nose and Ear Hospital, London, England. 1957-58; Foreign Attache to Professor Michel Portmann, Bordeaux, France, 1976; Hon. ENT Surgeon, R.P.A. Hospital, Sydney, 1956; Lecturer in Otology, University of Sydney, 1977. *Memberships:* Chairman, NSW Section, Otolaryngological Society of Australia, 1979-81; NSW State Committee, Royal Australasian College of Surgeons, 1972-79. *Publications:* Recipient of Major Scholarship, Scots College, Sydney, 1941. *Hobbies:* Athletics; French Language. *Address:* 2 North Parade, Hunters Hill, NSW, 2110, Australia.

SEABORN, James Blair, b. 18 March 1924,Toronto, Ontario, Canada. Public Servant. m. Carol Allen Trow, 9 Sept. 1950, 1 son, 1 daughter. *Education:* BA, 1947, MA 1948, Trinity College, University of Toronto, Canada. *Appointments:* Head, Eastern European Division, Dept. of External Affairs, 1966-67, Head, Far Eastern Division, 1967-70; Assistant Deputy Minister (Consumer Affairs), Dept of Consumer and Corporate Affairs 1970-74; Deputy Minister, Dept. of the Environment, 1974-. *Memberships:* Rockcliffe Lawn Tennis Club; Five Lakes Club (Past-President); Le Cercle Universitaire d'Ottawa. *Hobbies:* Cross-country Skiing; Tennis; Squash; Canoeing; Fishing. *Address:* 79 MacKay Street, Ottawa, Ontario, K1M 2E4 Canada.

SEAMAN, Keith Douglas, b. 11 June,1920, Tatachilla, Near McLaren Vale, South Australia. Governor of South Australia. m. Joan Isabell, 17 Aug 1946, 1 son. 1 daughter. *Education:* B.A, 1951, LLB, 1955, University of Adelaide. *Appointments:* Governor of South Australia since 1977; South Australian Public Service, 1937-54; Entered Methodist Ministry, 1954, Renmark, 1954-58, Adelaide Central Methodist Mission from 1958-1977; Secretary, Christian Television Association of South Australia, 1959-73; Member, Executive World Association of Christian Broadcasting, 1963-70; RAAF Overseas Headquarters, London, 1941-45. Flight Lieutenant; Member, Austrailian Government Social Welfare Commission, 1973-76; Superintendent Adelaide Central Mission and Chairman 5KA, 5AU, and 5RM Broadcasting Companies, 1971-77; Director, 5KA-5AU-5RM from 1960. *Memberships:* Adelaide Club. *Honours:* OBE 1976; K.St.J. 1978. *Hobbies:* Reading; Gardening. *Address:* Government House, Adelaide, South Australia, 5000.

SEARELL, Pamela Renee (Mrs. D. Ross McQueen), b. 2 Aug. 1926, Putaruru, New Zealand. Artist; Sculptor; Writer. m. D. Ross, 19 Dec. 1949. *Appointments:* Art & Crafts Intinerant Teacher, 1948-53; Scientific draughtsman to Reader of Mineralogy, Oxford University, England, 1955-56; Scientific Illustrator, Montpellier University Centre, Emberger, 1966; Art reviews, feature talks, news commentaries for Radio, New Zealand, 1966-78. *Publications:* Academy of Fine Arts, New Zealand; Association of New Zealand Art Societies; New Zealand Archaeological Association; New Zealand Film Society. *Creative Works:* Paintings, Sculptures, Lithographs, Commissioned Murals, Biographical Writing for New Zealand Heritage, 1971; Nature Heritage 1974-76; Paul Hamlyn Publisher. *Honours:* Work selected for Hocken collection of New Zealand art; Special Award, National Bank mural competition, 1969-70; Prize for Radio Feature Programme, Radio New Zealand, 1971. *Hobbies:* Music; Films; Theatre; Hill-walking. *Address:* 11 View Road, Titahi Bay, New Zealand.

SEED, Richard Gibson Francis Lloyd, b. 24 Aug. 1935, London. Medical Practitioner/Consultant Anaesthetist. m. Josephine Mary, 3 Nov. 1962, 1 son, 1 daughter. *Education:* MBBS 1960; FFARCS, 1967; FFARACS, 1979. *Appointments:* Six senior Medical Posts held in London hospitals, 1960-74; Director, Department of Anaesthesia, Guys Hospital, London, 1974-78; Director, Department of Anaesthesia, Royal Perth Hospital, Perth, Western Australia, 1978-; Clinical Lecturer in Anaesthesia, University of Western Australia, 1980-. *Memberships:* Fellow of Royal Society of Medicine, London; Association of Anaesthetists of Great Britain and Northern Ireland; Anaesthetic Research Society (past member of Committee); South East Thames Society of Anaesthetists (Past President); Australian Society of Anaesthetists. *Publications:* Over 40 papers and articles on anaesthesia, intensive care and related topics published in anaesthetic, pharmacological, cardiovascular and other journals. *Honours:* Distinction award (NHS). *Hobbies:* Swimming; Photography; Boating; Model Making; Reading. *Address:* 97 Stanley Street, Nedlands, Western Australia, 6009.

SEETHARAM, H. R. Bapu, b. 3 May, 1926, Mysore City, India. Communication Engineer/ Manager. m. M. S. Shamala, 26 Apr. 1951. *Education:* BSc, Mysore University, India, 1945; DIISc, Indian Institute of Science, Bangalore 1949. *Appointments:* Research Assistant, Indian Institute of Science, Bangalore, 1949-51; Technical Officer, Civil Aviation Department, Government of India, 1951-61; Bharat Electronics Ltd., Bangalore, 1961-81. *Memberships:* Secretary, IAQR, 1972-81, Chairman, Bangalore Branch, 1972-79; Publisher, Editorial Board Member, QR Journal 1974-81;

Vice President, Instrument Society of India, 1972-74; President, IISAA, 1981; FIETE, 1980-82. *Publications:* Contributor to various journals. *Honours:* Recipient of numerous honours and awards for professional services. *Hobbies:* Occasionally Photography. *Address:* Jyothi, 695, 10A Main, 34th Cross, IVth Block, Jayanager, Bangalore-560 011, India.

SEFTON, Allan Roy, b. 4 May, 1921, Hobart, Tasmania, Australia. Naturalist, Ecologist, Conservationist, Author. m. Dorothy, 4 sons, 1 daughter. *Appointments:* Lifetime involvement with natural history and preservation of environment has been in an amateur or non professional status. *Memberships:* South Coast (NSW) Conservation Society; Illawarra Bird Observers Club; Chairman, Convenor, Five Islands Nature Reserve, 1960-80; President, Illawarra Natural History Society, 1962-68; and Member or Life Member of 8 related societies. *Publications:* Some 150 Papers and articles etc. on Natural History and Preservation of the environment. *Honours:* British Empire Medal (BEM), 1975; Australian Natural History Medallion, 1978; Justice of the Peace, 1953. *Hobbies:* Communing with nature and watching Cricket; *Address:* 15 Station Street, Thirroul, New South Wales, Australia 2515.

SEGAN, Berek, Robert, b. 22 June, 1919, Lida, Poland. Company Director. m. Maria Segan, 2 sons. *Appointments:* Chairman and Managing Director, Emerald Trading Pty Ltd., Emerald Wines, Harcourt Forest Industries, Hartwell Investments, The Pine Centre. *Memberships:* Australian Broadcasting Commission subscribers Committee; Appointed to A.B.C. Concerts in Australia; President Soirees Musicales Chamber Music Society of Australia; State Committee Kidney Foundation of Australia; Wine and Press Club of Victoria. *Creative Works:* Several compositions for Violin and Piano. *Honours:* OBE June, 1980; Grand Companion de Bordeaux, Mousquetaire de Armagnac, Jurade de St. Emilion, Commandeur de Medocet Graves. *Hobbies:* Swimming; Snow skiing; Water skiing; Violin playing and mandolin performances with orchestra; Tennis; Miniature bottle collector and ancient bottles in Cognac and Armagnac. *Address:* 52 Burke Road North, East Ivanhoe. 3079, Australia.

SEGBAWU, Courage Kwami, b. 8 July, 1939, Dabala, Volta Region, Ghana. Publisher. m. Florence Gifty, 5 sons. *Education:* University of Ghana, Legon, 1962-66; BA Hons, 1965; MA (African Studies) 1968. *Appointments:* Deputy Superintendent of Police, Ghana Police Service, 1966-69; Publishing Executive, Longman Group Ltd ., Accra, Ghana, 1969-71; Manager, Longman Group Ltd., Accra, Ghana, 1971-74; Operational Director, Ghana Area (i.e. English Speaking West Africa outside Nigeria). 1975; Publisher/Managing Director, Sedco Publishing Ltd., Accra, Ghana, 1976. *Memberships:* President, Ghana Book Publishers Association, 1978-80. *Publications:* Makers of African History Series; Osei Bonsu-Warrior King of Asante. *Honours:* Recipient of Junior Academy Award for History from Ghana Academy of Sediences, 1965. *Hobbies:* Small-Scale livestock farming; Swimming, Reading. *Address:* McCarthy Hill, Accra, Ghana.

SEGNIT, Edgar, Ralph, b. 5 Sept. 1923, Adelaide, South Australia. Research Mineralogist. m. 21 Oct. 1950, 1 son, 1 daughter. *Education:* BSc, Hons, Adelaide, 1944; MSc. Adelaide, 1945; Ph.D, Cambridge, 1950. *Appointments:* Research Officer, CSIRO Australia, 1945-53; Senior Lecturer in Geology, University of Adelaide, 1953-57; Research Associate, University of California, Los Angeles, 1957-58; Research Associate, Princeton University, 1958-59; Senior Principal Research Scientist, CSIRO Australia, 1960. *Memberships:* Mineralogical Society of America; Mineralogical Society, London; Australian Ceramic Society (President, 1976-80); President, Mineralogical Society of Victoria, 1981; Indian Ceramic Society; Australian and New Zealand Association for the Advancement of Science; Royal Society of Victoria. *Publications:* Some 120 scientific publications in the fields of mineralogy, applied mineralogy, silicate chemistry and ceramic science. *Honours:* Tate Medal University of Adelaide, 1945; CSIRO Overseas Studentship, 1947; Fulbright Travel Award, 1957. *Hobbies:* Horticulture; Philately; Tennis. *Address:* 24 Grant Street, East Malvern, Victoria 3145, Australia.

SEGUIN, Robert-Lionel, b. 7 Mar. 1920, Rigaud, Comte Vaudreuil, Quebec. Ethnologist. m. Huguette

Servant, 27 Oct. 1957, 1 son. *Education:* Dr. Letters and Human Scis., Sorbonne (University Paris), 1972; Dr. Letters and Ethonology, University Strasbourg, France, 1981; Dr. Letters and History (University Laval, Quebec), 1964; Dip. in History, University Laval, Quebec, 1957; Lic. Soc. Scis., University Montreal, Quebec, 1951. *Memberships:* Member, Royal Soc. Can.,; Societe Des Dix, Quebec; Societe d'Ethnologie francaise, Paris. *Honours:* Gov. Gen of Can. prize, 1967; Broquette-Gonin prize Acad. francaise, 1967; France-Quebec prize, Paris, 1973; Duvernay prize (Soc. St. Jean Baptiste, Montreal, 1975. *Publications:* Twenty books and about 175 articles on folk civilization of Quebec. *Address:* 440 Grande-Ligne, Rigaud, comte Vaudreuil, Quebec, Canada.

SEIGNORET, Eustace Edward, b. 16 Feb. 1925. High Commissioner for Trinidad and Tobago, London 1977-. m. 2 sons, 1 daughter. *Education:* Howard University, Washington; BSc, University of Wales, Bangor. *Appointments:* Agricultural Officer, Department of Agriculture, Trinidad and Tobago, 1953-58; West Indies Fedn Public Service, 1958-62; Assistant Secretary, Trinidad and Tobago Public Service, 1962; First Secretary 1962-65; Counsellor, 1965-68; Trinidad and Tobago Perm. Mission to UN; Deputy High Commissioner in London, 1969-71; Perm. Rep. to UN, 1971-75. *Address:* Trinidad and Tobago High Commission, 42 Belgrave Square, London SW1X 8NT, England.

SELKIRK, George Nigel (Earl), b. 4 Jan. 1906, Dorset. Advocate. m. 6 Aug. 1949. *Education:* MA, Balliol, Oxford, 1924-28; LLB, Edinburgh University, 1931-35; *Memberships:* Member of Edinburgh Town Council, 1933-40; Commissioner of General Board of Control (Scotland), 1936-39; Commissioner for Special Areas in Scotland, 1937-39; Served War of 1939-45 (OBE Despatches twice). A Lord in Waiting to the Queen, 1952-53 (to King George VI, 1951-52); Paymaster General, 1953-55; Chancellor of the Duchy of Lancaster, 1955-57; First Lord of the Admiralty, 1957-59; UK Commissioner for Singapore and Commissioner General for SE Asia, 1959-63; UK Council Representative to SEATO, 1960-63; Chairman, Conservative Commonwealth Council, 1965-72; Freeman of Hamilton. President, National Ski Federation of Great Britain, 1964-68; Anglo-Swiss Society, 1965-74; Building Societies Association, 1965; Royal Society for Asian Affairs, 1966-76; Association of Independent Unionist Peers, 1967-79; Chairman, Victoria League, 1971-77; Hon. Chief, Saulteaux Indians, 1967. *Address:* 60 Eaton Place, London, SW1, England.

SELVARATNAM, Viswanthan, b. 4 Dec. 1934, Ipoh, Malaysia. m. 19 June, 1962, 1 son 2 daughters. *Education:* BA (Hons), University of Malaya, Singapore, 1960, 1961; MA Delhi, School of Economics, University of Delhi, India. 1965; MA, PhD, University of Manchester, England, 1966-77. *Appointments:* Teacher, Malay College, Kuala Kangsar, Malaysia, 1961; Auditor, Federal Audit Department, Malaysia. 1961-1963; Research Fellow, Didsbury College of Education, Manchester, England, 1967-68; Lecturer, Faculty of Economics and Administration University of Malaya, Malaysia. 1968-76; Chairman, Division of Rural Development, Visiting Fellow, IDS at the University of Malaya, Malaysia. 1970-73; Visiting Fellow, University of Sussex, Brighton, England, 1973-75; Associate Professor, University of Malaysia, Malaysia, 1976; Director, Regional Institute of Higher Education and Development, Singapore. 1979; Member of Commission on Futurology of International Union of Anthropological and Ethnological Sciences, 1978-82. *Publications:* Prolific writer and contributor of reports, studies and articles. *Memberships:* Malaysian Economics Association; Indian Sociological Association; Malaysian Sociological Association; British Sociological Association; International Sociological Association; World Future Studies Federation Rural Sociological Association. *Publications:* Prolific writer and contributor of reports, studies and articles. *Hobbies:* Collecting Antiques. *Address:* No. 5IA, Duchess Avenue, Singapore 1026.

SELWYN, Andrew Peter, b. 18 Apr. 1945, Sussex, United Kingdom. Doctor of Medicine. m. 24 Apr. 1974, 1 son, 1 daughter. *Appointments:* MB, CHB, (Distinction), University of Cape Town, South Africa, 1969; MRCP (UK) Royal College of Physicians, UK, 1974; MD, University of Cape Town, South Africa, 1980; FACC Amencau College of Cardiology, 1980. *Appointments:*

Groote Schuuer Teaching Hospital, Cape Town, South Africa; St. Stephens Hospital, London; Brompton Hospital, London; Hammersmith Hospital and Royal Post graduate Medical School, London. *Memberships:* Medical Research Society, England; British Cardiac Society, England; Royal College of Physicians, England; Amencau College of Cardiology, England. *Publications:* More than 100 publications of original scientific research into coronary disease. *Honours:* Esther Barman Medal in Medicine, 1969; Gold Medal in Surgery, 1969. *Hobbies:* Boating; Historic Architecture; Family. *Address:* 1 Fan Court, Longcross, Surrey, England.

SEMEGA-JANNEH, Bocar Ousman. b. 1910. Gambian Diplomat. *Education:* Mohammedan Primary School and Methodist Boys' High School. *Appointments:* High Commissioner of Gambia, London; Ambassador to West Germany, Belgium, Sweden, Switzerland, France and Austria, 1971-80; Accredited, Ambassador to Federal German Republic, France, Austria, Switzerland, The Vatican. *Memberships:* Delegate to UN General Assembly and to OAU, 1968. *Honours:* Grand Officer, Order of Merit. *Address:* Gambia High Commission, 60 Ennismore Gardens, London SW7, England.

SEMMENS, Edgar Henry, b. 11 Apr. 1925, Devonport, British Council Representative, Nigeria. m. Barbara Jean, 18 Aug. 1948, 3 sons, 1 daughter. *Education:* BA (Hons), London, 1949; PGCE, Exeter, 1950. *Appointments:* Senior French Master, Harwich Grammar School, 1950-3; Malayan Education Service, 1954-62; British Council 1962-81. *Memberships:* Soccer Captain, Exeter University College, 1949-50; Table Tennis Captain, Exeter University College, 1948-49; rear Commodore, Ndirante Sailing Club; Member, Churston Golf Club. *Honours:* Recipient of OBE, 1979. *Hobbies:* Golf; Sailing; Choral Singing; Silversmithing. *Address:* 22 Broadsands Road, Paignton, Devon, TQ4 6HQ, England.

SEMPEBWA-SERUGO, Charles Michael, b. 12 Jan. 1938, Masaka, Uganda. Veterinary Surgeon. m. H. K, 4 Feb. 1958, 2 sons, 2 daughters. *Education:* BVSc, AH, University of Bombay, 1964-67. *Appointments:* Uganda Government Veterinary Department, 1967-68; Research Officer, East African Community, 1969-72; Provincial Veterinary Officer, Zambian Government, 1972-78; Principal Zambian Institute of Animal Health, Zambian Government, 1978-. *Memberships:* Member of Livestock Development; Secretary, Uganda Student Association, 1963-67; Sports Captain, 1964-67; Member, Dairy Club, Masalla District, Uganda, 1967-69. *Publications:* Clinical Observations of East Coast fever disease; Wild Life; Cattle developments in Zambia; East Coast fever in Zambia; Variety of Departmental reports. *Honours:* Degree of BVSc and AH, 1967; Variety of prizes in sports, Natural Science subjects etc. 1965-67; Trophies in sports, football, and Debating, 1965-67. *Hobbies:* Writing; Photography; Wild Life; Football. *Address:* P.O. Box 237, Mazabuka, Zambia.

SEN, Jyoti Prakash, b.25 Dec. 1934, Nagpur. Professor of English. *Education:* BA, Nagpur University, 1952; LLB, Nagpur University, 1954; MA, Nagpur University, 1955; PhD, Jabalpur University, 1965. *Appointments:* Professor of English, National College, Nagpur, 1955-56; Professor of English, City College, Nagpur, 1955-56; Professor of English, Govt. Science College, Nagpur, 1955-56; Professor of English, Robertson College (Government Post-graduate Arts College, Jabalpur, 1956-69; Head, Dept. of English, Department of Post-graduate Studies and Research in English, University of Jabalpur, 1969-. *Memberships:* Executive member of All India English Teacher's Conference. *Publications:* The Progress of T.S. Eliot as Poet and Critic, 1971; The Progress of T.S. Eliot, International Edition, 1979; Working on another book on T.S. Eliot on an invitation from the Rockefeller Foundation and the British Council. *Honours:* UGC Fellowship, 1975. *Hobbies:* Reading and Writing. *Address:* 74 Napier Town, Jabalpur-482 001, India.

SEN, Tapas, b. 11 Sept. 1924, Dhubri, Assam, India. Lighting Designer and Theatre Consultant. m. Gita, 11 Dec. 1953, 1 son, 1 daughter. *Appointments:* Designed Pavilions of the International Trade Fairs, New Delhi, 1959-72; Participated in Sound and Light experiments with USIS (American Centre) and various other concerns; Lighting Consultant of Royal Nepal Academy, Kathmandu. *Memberships:* President of Little Theatre

Group, Calcutta; Technical Adviser, Calcutta Puppet Theatre. *Publications:* Contributed articles for various National and International journals, Seminars, etc. *Honours:* Received the Sangeet Natak Academy of India Award, 1974 *Hobbies:* Astro Physics; Biology, Newology; Optics. *Address:* 26H Naktala Lane, Calcutta-700047, India.

SENGUPTA, Devabrata, b. 25 Nov. 1936, m. Jayoti Sengupta, 15 Nov. 1936, 2 sons. *Education:* Hons BSc, Physics, 1959. *Appointments:* Civil Servant, Under Secretary, Ministry of Education Government of India; Section Officer, Ministry of Education and Social Welfare, Government of India, New Delhi; Deputy Director, Central Institute of Hindi, Agra, India 282005; Under Secretary, Ministry of Education and Social Welfare, Government of India, New Delhi. *Memberships:* Indian Anthropological Association, New Delhi; Indian Anthropological Society, Calcutta; Indian Sociological Society Bombay; Linguistic Society of India; International Dravidian Linguistic Association. *Publications:* A large number of articles on Sociology, Linguistics, education etc. *Honours:* Recipient of General Knowledge Prize, St. Stephens College, University of Delhi and a large number of other prizes. *Address:* 22 South Patelnager, New Delhi, India, 110008.

SENGUPTA, Nirmal Kumar, b. 1 Nov. 1912, Dacca, Bangladesh. Electrical/Mechanical/ Telecommunication Engineer. m. Vani Mazumdar, 13 July 1940. 1 son. *Education:* Matriculation, 1928; Intermediate Science, 1930; BSc Engineering, 1935. *Appointments:* Member, Telecommunication Development, P & T Board, Indian P & T Department; Managing Director, M/S Hindustan Cables Ltd.; Managing Director, Mining and Allied Machinery Corporation; Duke of Edinburgh's Commonwealth Conference, Canada, 1962. *Memberships:* Fellow, Institute of Engineers India; Founder Member and Fellow, Indian Institute of Telecommunication Engineers; Fellow, Indian Statistical Institute. *Hobbies:* Photography. *Address:* I-1710 Chittaranjan Park, New Delhi - 110 019, India.

SEN GUPTA, Ranjit Kumar, b 5 Jan. 1924, Lucknow, India, Government Servant (Telecom Engineer), m. Usha Ghose, 1 daughter. *Education:* MSc Lucknow University 1946. 03 Assistant Technical Maintenance Officer, Government of India 1954-1961; Assistant Radio Officer, Government of Uttar Pradish, 1961-1965; Additional Radio Officer, Government of UP 1965-1971; State Radio Officer, Government of UP, 1971-1974; Deputy Inspector General Police Telecom., Government of UP, 1974-. *Memberships:* Fellow of the Institution of Electronics & Telecommunication Engineers, India. *Creative Works:* Light Vocal Music, Broadcasting from all India Radio, Lucknow. *Honours:* Police Medal for Meritorious Service 1973; President's Police Medal for Distinguished Service 1981. *Hobbies:* Light Vocal Music. *Address:* Quarter No. G-1, Police Radio Colony, Mahanagar, Lucknow 226006, India.

SENKOYA, Samuel Babajide, b. 3 June 1948, Ibadan Oyo State of Nigeria, Businessman, m. 11 Apr. 1978, 1 son 1 daughter. *Appointments:* Salesman, 1965-70; Company Director, 1970-81. *Memberships:* Member of Made in Europe. *Hobbies:* Travelling, Sports (Football). *Address:* SW8/500 Oke-Ado, 2nd Market Street, Off NTC Road, Ibadan, Oyo State of Nigeria.

SEOW, Pin Kwong, b. 11 Jan. 1941, Penang, Malasia, Research Chemist, m. Wan Chen Goh, 30 June, 1968, 4 sons. *Education:* B.Sc. University of Malaya, Kuala Lumpur, 1967; Docteur es Sciences, University of Louis Pasteur, Strasbourg, 1974. *Appointments:* Polymer Chemistry Lecturer, Mara Institute of Technology, Malaysia, 1974-75; Research Officer, Rubber Research Institue of Malaysia, 1975-. *Memberships:* Malaysian Institute of Chemistry; Malaysian Scientific Association; Association of Graduates of French Universities; Science Society, University of Malaya; Senior Officers Association. *Publications:* Contributor of reviews, monographs, articles to professional journals and conferences. *Hobbies:* Music; Chess; Travelling. *Address:* 8 Church Road, Benges, Hertford, SG4 3DP, England.

SERIES, Joseph Michel Emile (Sir) b. 29 Sept 1918, Curepipe, Mauritius. Chairman & Managing Director, Weal Group. m. Rose-Aimee Jullienne, 15th June 1942, 2 sons, 2 daughters. *Education:* Royal College,

Curepipe, London University, R.R.C.Dbn, ICL's Tech. Centre Cookham, England, Metropolitan College, England. *Appointments:* Accounts Dept., General Electric Supply Co. of Mauritius Ltd (1936-1952) (final position, Chief Acct.); Chief Acct. & Ecc. Adviser, Flacq United Estates Ltd. (1952-61); Estate Manager, Flacq United Estates Ltd, 1961-1968; Chairman & Managing Director, FUEL and WEAL Group 1968; Member of the Board of Trustees of the Mahatma Gandhi Institute. *Memberships:* Dodo, Mtius Turf, Grand'Baie Yacht. *Honours:* Kt., 1978; CBE, 1974; Chevalier de l'Ordre National due Merite (France) M.Com., FCIS., FAIA., FSCA. FBIM., FRSA., FREcon.S., Mem.AMA.& NAA., N.Y. *Hobbies:* Photography, Shooting, Horse-Racing, Sailing, Classical Music; *Address:* c/o F.U.E.L., Union Flacq, Mauritius.

SERPELL, Ronald Alexander, b. 24 Aug. 1922, Charlton, Victoria, Australia, Real Estate Agent, Valuer, Auctioneer. m. Rose Ena Whitford, 5 Apr. 1947, 1 son 2 daughters. *Appointments:* Commonwealth Public Service, 1955; Baillieu Allard Pty. Ltd., 1956; Associate Director, 1964; Director, 1968; Managing Director, 1974; Chief Executive, 1976; Deputy Chairman, Baillieu Real Estate Australia Pty Ltd., 1981. *Memberships:* Commonwealth Institute of Valuers; Australian Institute of Valuers (FAIV); Australian Institute of Valuers (Victorian Division); President of Australian Institute of Valuers (Victorian Division). *Hobbies:* Trout Fishing, Reading and Community Affairs. *Address:* 39 Bentley Street, Surrey Hills 3127, Victoria, Australia.

SETHI, Rajinder Singh, b. 1 Feb. 1938, Nowshera, Pakistan. Research & Development in Electronics m. Harbans Kaur Ahuja, 12 Jan. 1969, 2 daughters. *Education:* BSc 1960; MSc 1962; PhD 1966; C.Chem, MRSC 1972. *Appointments:* 1966-70 Postdoctoral Research Assistant, Department of Metallurgy, Imperial College of Science & Technology, London; Senior Principal Scientist, Allen Clark Research Centre, Northants, 1970-. *Memberships:* Royal Society of Chemistry; Electrochemical Society (USA); Society for Electrochemistry (Faraday Division); Molten Salt Discussion Group; Electroanalytical Chemistry Society (Analytical Division); Macro Group. *Publications:* Publications in International Scientific Technical Journals. *Hobbies:* Table Tennis, Photography, Jazz Music and Gardening. *Address:* 38 Norman Road, Northampton, NN3 2SG, England.

SETHI, Subash Chandra, b. 8 Feb. 1956, Komanda, Puri Orissa, India. Commerce. *Education:* B.Com. (FICA), D.C. University, New Delhi. *Appointments:* Agent, Indian Oil, Balugaon, Puri Orissa, India. *Memberships:* Fellow, Indian Commercial Association, New Delhi. *Publications:* Written books on Drama & Songs. *Honours:* Awarded Certificate in Astrology, Orissa, 1972. *Hobby.* Music. *Address.* Komanda, Odgaon, Orissa, India.

SETHI, Satya Pal, b. 12 March, 1930, Bhera, Army Officer, m. Shail Sawhney, 1 Oct. 1957, 1 son, 1 daughter. *Education:* B.A. East Punjab University. *Appointments:* National Security Management Course, Industrial College of Armed Forces, Washington, DC, USA. *Memberships:* Fellow of Institution of Electronics and Telecommunication Engineers, New Delhi; Member Gymkhana Club, New Delhi; Defence Service Institute, New Delhi; Narmada Club, Jabalpur. *Publications:* Contributed articles on professional subjects in Service Magazine. *Hobbies:* Gardening. *Address:* No. 7111/6/PR (Pub), Directorate of Public Relations, Ministry of Defence, DHQ PO New Delhi, India - 110011.

SETTY, Channagiri Subba Gapala Krishna, b. 6 May, 1928, Shimoga Town, Karnataka State, India. Professor of Physics. m. Shanta K. Setty. *Education:* BSc. Mysore University, India, 1950; MSc. Mysore University, 1951; PhD. Cambridge University, 1956. *Appointments:* Employed at Universities of Delhi, Mysore, Cambridge, New England, 1951-. *Memberships:* Inst. of Physics and Physical Society; Inst. of Electronics and Telecomm. Engrs. India. *Publications:* Over 100 publications in Scientific journals. *Honours:* Inst. of Telecommunications Award, 1962; Poorna Krishna Rao Medal. *Address:* F14/3 Model Town, Delhi-110009, India.

SETTY, M.G. Anantha Padmanabha, b 19th Sept. 1926, Hulivar, Karnataka State, India Research Scientist in Geological Oceanography. m. Vimala 8th June 1956, 1 son 1 daughter. *Education:* B.Sc. University of Mysore, India, 1949; MSc University of Utah, USA, 1950; PhD University of Utah, USA, 1963; *Appointments:* Lecturer in Geology, University of Mysore, 1953-59; Teaching and Research Asst., University of Utah, USA, 1959-63 International Indian Ocean Expedition, (UNESCO) Indian Program, 1964-66; National Insitute of Oceanography, 1966 to date. *Memberships:* Sigma Xi; American Association for Advancement of Science; Society of Economic Paleontologists & Mineralogists; Society of Economic Paleontologists & Mineralogists; Geological Society of India; Indian Society of Earth Scientists; Rotary International, Director & Chairman. *Publications:* Over 50 Publications in Marine Micropaleontolgy, Geological Oceanography, Tertiary Sediments. *Hobbies:* Billiards; Cricket, Reading. *Address:* Block 2, Type V, N10 Qrs., Dona Paula, 403 004 Goa, India.

SHADBOLT, Gillian Eve Muriel (Mrs) b. 21 April 1929, Sydney, Australia. Journalist; Tutor/Housewife, 3 sons, 1 daughter. *Appointments:* Journalist, Evening Post; Editor, Pen Gazette; Public Relations Officer, NZ Post Office; Tutor, Wellington Polytechnic. *Hobbies:* Renovating old Houses, Gardening, Listening to people and mod. music, Photography. *Address:* 31, Winchester Street, Kaiwaharawhara, Wellington, New Zealand.

SHAGARI, Shehu Aliyu, b. 1925. President of Nigeria. *Education:* Sokoto Middle School; Kaduna College; Teacher Training at Zaria. *Appointments:* Teacher, Sokoto Middle School, 1945-51; Headmaster, Senior Primary School, Argunga, 1951-53; British Council Sponsorship to UK, Education Course, 1953-54; Senior Visiting Teacher Sokoto Province, 1954-59; Formed Sokoto branch of Northern People's Congress (NPC) 1949; Member for Sokoto-West in Federal House of Representatives, 1954-58; Parliamentary Secretary, Prime Minister, 1958; Acting Federal Minister of Trade and Industry, 1959; Minister of Economic Development 1959-60; Federal Minister of Establishments and Service Matters, 1961-62; Federal Minister of Internal Affairs, 1962-65; Federal Minister of Works 1965-66; Secretary, Sokoto Province Educational Development Fund, 1967-68; Director, Northern States Marketing Board, Kaduna, 1968; Commissioner for Education, NW State, 1969-70; Federal Commissioner for Econ-omic Development and Reconstruction, 1970-71; Federal Commissioner for Finance, 1971-75. *Memberships:* IMF's Committee of Twenty; Chairman, Peugeot Auto-mobile Nigeria Limited, 1976-79; Chairman, Sokoto Urban Development Authority, 1976-79; President and Commander in Chief of Armed Forces, 1979. *Honours:* Turakin of Sokoto, 1963; Hon. LLD Ahmadu Bello University, 1976. *Address:* State House, Marina, Lagos, Nigeria.

SHAH, Kapurchand, b. 16 Sept. 1938, Sagna, Kenya, East Africa. Technical Adviser. m. Bhanu 1962, 1 son, 1 daughter. *Appointments:* Production Manager, Steel Africa Ltd, Mombasa Kenya, 1962-65; Uganda Steel Ltd, Tororo, Uganda, 1966-72; Director, Kalamu Ltd; Managing Director, Mifuko Ltd, 1973-. *Memberships:* Associate Member of Automobile Associate of India; Galvenizer of Japan; Lion Club of Tororo; Rotary Club of Dar Es Salaam. *Hobbies:* Sports, Swimming, Music, Travel. *Address:* 1089 Msasani, Dar Es Salaam, Tanzania.

SHAH, Natoobhai, b. 3 Aug. 1926, Godhra (Gujarat) India. Consultant Cardiologist & Physician. m. Sundri n. Malkani, 1 son, 1 daughter. *Education:* MD, Bombay University, 1954; MRCP, 1958; Fellow of American College of Cardiology, 1970; Fellow of Royal College of Physician & Surgeons, 1972. *Appointments:* Honorary Associate Physician, G.T. HOspital, Honorary Professor of Medicine, Grant Medical College, Bombay, 1959-74; Honorary Physician & Cardiologist, Bombay Hospital, Bombay, 1960-. *Memberships:* Founder President of National Council of Hypertension; Association of Physicians of India; Cardiological Society of India. *Publications:* Author of A Handbook of Endocrinology, 1959. *Hobbies:* Golf; Badminton; Table Tennis. *Address:* 4/D, Ananta, Rajaballi Patel Road, Opp. Breach Candy Hospital, Bombay, 400 026, India.

SHAH, Shantilal Harjivan, b. 30 July 1897, Broach, Gujarat, Solicitor. m. Hiralaxmi, Jan. 1913, 1 son 2 daughters. *Education:* BA, LLB. *Appointments:* Minister Government of Bombay, 1952-60; Minister, Government of Maharashtra, 1960-66; Elected to Parliament, 1967; Trustee, Navajivan Trust founded by Mahatma Gandhi. *Address:* 10th Road, Khar, Bombay, India.

SHAH, Sharad Chaturlal, b. 31 July, 1937, Miraj, Maharashtra, Doctor. m. Aruna B. Shah, 16 June, 1965, 1 son, 2 daughters. *Education:* MBBS, 1962; MD, 1965; MRCP (G), 1966; MRCP (ED), 1967; FACG (USA), 1979. *Appointments:* Honorary Assistant Physician, Sir, J.J. Hospital, Assistant Professor of Medicine, Grant Medical College, 1968-; Assistant Honorary Physician, Air Harkisonda Nurrotamda Hospital, 1973-. *Memberships:* Indian Medical Association; Indian Society of Gastroenterology; Society for Gastrointestinal Endoscopy of India. *Publications:* Contributor of reviews, monographs, articles to professional journals and conferences. *Honours:* Henry Peer Dimmock Medalist; Pandit Ramabai Ranade University Scholarship; Bhagwandin Dube Scholarship. *Hobbies:* Reading, Sightseeing. *Address:* Goolestan, Block No.2, 34, Bhulabhai Esai Road, Bombay - 400 026, India.

SHAHABUDDIN, M. b. 1 Jan. 1917, Mymenshingh, Bangladesh. Librarianship. m. Jamila Akhtar Khatun, 8 May 1945, 2 sons, 2 daughters. *Education:* ISc, 1935; BSc, 1937; MSc, 1940; MA (Lib.Sc.) 1962. *Appointments:* Teacher in Physics, Eng. College, Dacca, 1948; Asst. Librarian, 1962; Librarian, 1965, University of Eng. & Technology; Teacher Lib.Sc., Dacca University & Institute of Library Education. *Memberships:* President, Library Assoc. Bangladesh, 1971-1979. *Publications:* Author of 'Practical Physics for Degree Students', Number of articles published in Journals. *Hobbies:* Readings and Writing and Playing indoor games. *Address:* 7/B Engg. University, Staff Quarters, Dacca, Bangladesh.

SHAHABUDDIN, Syed, b. 4 Nov. 1935, Ranchi, India. Lawyer and Politician. m. Shaher Bano Majid, 30 Jan. 1958, 1 son, 5 daughters. *Education:* BSc, Patna Univ., India, 1954; BL part I Patna Univ. First class, 1955; MSc. Patna Univ., First class First, 1956, BL II, Patna Univ. 1969. *Appointments:* Lecturer, Physics, Univ. Dept. Physics, Patna, 1956-58; Indian Foreign Service, 1958-78; Member of Parliament, 1979-; General Secretary, Janata Party, 1980. *Memberships:* Delhi Gymkhana Club; Indian Council of World Affairs; Institute of Defence Studies & Analysis; Institute of Constitutional & Park Studies. *Publications:* Large number of articles in newspapers and journals. *Hobbies:* Reading and travel. *Address:* 8, Feroz Shah Road, New Delhi, 110001, India.

SHAHANE, Vasant Anant, b.18 Dec. 1923, Parbhani. Professor of English. m. Ratnaprabha, 7 June 1946, 1 son, 1 daughter. *Education:* BA English, 1944; LLB, 1946; MA English, 1947; PhD, Leeds, 1957. *Appointments:* Instructor, English, July 1947-Nov 1957; Ass. Prof. English, 1957-65; University Prof. English, 1965-; Dean, Faculty of Arts, 1965-1978; Principal, University College, 1973-1974. *Memberships:* Member of Modern Language Assoc. of America; PEN Club. *Publications:* A prolific author of books and research papers in his field, the most recent of which is E.M. Forster: A study in Double Vision. *Honours:* Best Teacher Award by the Government of Andhra Pradesh for University Teachers. *Hobbies:* Watching Cricket and Playing Table Tennis. *Address:* 3-4-1013/22, Barkatpura, Hyderabad 500 027, India.

SHAHJAHAN, Muhammad, b. 2 Jan. 1939, m. Mahmuda, J. 20 Sept 1967, 1 son, 1 daughter. *Education:* BSc, Bangladesh, 1960; MS, USA, 1963; PhD, UK, 1970. *Memberships:* Institute of Engineers (Bangladesh). *Publications:* A text book on Engineering, numerous publications, reports. *Hobbies:* Tennis, Cricket, Hunting. *Address:* Flat 23/A, Engineering Staff Quarters, Dacca, Bangladesh, India.

SHAHRIMAN, (Tunku Dato), b. Tunku Sulaiman, b. 4 Feb. 1932, Negri Sembilan, Malaysia. Group Chairman, Perbadanan Nasional Berhad. m. 1 Oct. 1959, Datin Siti Hamidah bte Hassan, 1 son 5 daughters. *Education:* BA, Hons, University of Malaya, Singapore, 1958. *Appointments:* Malayan Civil Service, Assistant State Secretary, Perak; Assistant District Officer, Pahang Districts, Temerloh and Rompin, 1961; Cabinet Secretariat, Prime Minister's Department, 1961; District Officer, Kuala Kangsar, Perak, 1961; State Secretary, Pahang, 1968; Director General of Implementation, Co-Ordination and Development, Administration Unit, Prime Minister's Department, 1968; Group Chairman, Perbadanan Nasional Berhad, 1974. *Memberships:* Board of University Kebangsaan, Malaysia; Fellow, Institute of Bankers', Malaysia; Institute of Bankers', Malaysia; Yagasan Sains and Teknoloji Malaysia; Council Member, Malay Chambers of Commerce and Industry. *Honours:* Recipient of Pingat Jasa Kebaktian, Perak; Darjah Indera Mahkota Pahang, Pahang; Ahli Setia Daarjah Kenabalu, Sabah. *Hobbies:* Golf; Reading. *Address:* 49 Persiaran Duta, Kuala Lumpur, Malaysia.

SHAIKH, Hefazuddin. b. 1 Sept. 1926, Nadia, India. University Teaching & Research. m. 21 July, 1959, 1 son, 1 daughter. *Education:* DVMS, Dacca University, 1948; Master of Science Degree, Texas A & M University, USA, 1963; PhD, 1965. *Appointments:* Veterinary Assistant Surgeon (Meherpur-Kushtia, Bangladesh), 1948; Assistant Superintendent Veterinary Research Institute, Dacca, 1954; Lecturer, Parasitology, College of Veterinary Science & Animal Husbandry, Mymensingh, Bangladesh, 1958; Associate Prof, & Head, Dept. of Pathology & Parasitology, Bangladesh Agricultural University, Mymensingh, 1966; Presently Dean, Faculty of Veterinary Science for two years (on rotation basis). *Memberships:* Indian Society for Parasitology; Bangladesh Assoc. for Advancement of Science; Bangladesh Veterinary Association; Editorial Board, Bangladesh Veterinary Journal. *Publications:* Scientific Publications (31) *Hobbies:* Photography and Scouting. *Address:* Professor and Head, Department of Parasitology. Bangladesh Agricultural University, Mymensingh, Bangladesh.

SHAIKH, Mohamed Usman, b. 21 Oct. 1942, Malshiras, Maharashtra, India. m. Azmat-jehan, 26 Apr. 1972, 3 daughters. *Education:* MBBS, 1965, MS, 1970, BJ Medical College, University of Poona. *Memberships:* Associatian of Surgeons of India; Indian Society of Gastroenterology; Indian Medical Association; Collegium Internationale Chirure Digestive, Rome, Italy. *Publications:* Many important papers read at Conferences. *Hobbies:* Swimming; Tennis; Badminton; Trekking. *Address:* Dr. Hamid Memorial Hospital, Dewas Road, Ujjain, India.

SHAKO, Levi Madoka, b. 1918, Shigaro, Taito District, Kenya. Teacher. m. Patience Keziah, 4 sons, 6 daughters. *Appointments:* District Officer, North Nyanza, 1959-60; District Commissioner, Kitui, 1962; First Kenyan Ambassador to France & Federal Republic of Germany, 1964-66; Minister for Tourism and Wildlife, 1970-74; Chairman, Leyland Kenya Limited, Thika, 1975-. *Memberships:* Rotary Club, Mombassa. *Honours:* Recipient of First Prize for English Language, Alliance High School, 1936. *Hobbies:* Church Music; Gardening. *Address:* PO Box 1054, Wundanyi, Kenya.

SHAMS-UD DOHA, Aminur Rahman, b. 1929. High Commissioner for Bangladesh, United Kingdom, 1977-. m. Wijiha Moukaddem, 1981. *Education:* BSc(Hons), BA, Calcutta and Dacca Universities. *Appointments:* Commnd 2nd Lieutenant, Pakistan Artillery, 1952; School of Artillery and Guided Missiles Ft Sill. Okla. USA, 1957-58; General Staff College, Quetta, 1962; Inf. Bde HQ 1963; RMC, Shrivenham, 1964-65; Sen. Instr. Gunnery, 1965; GS GHQ, 1965-66 (Retired); Editor and Publisher, Interwing, Rawalpindi, 1968-71; Member, Central Executive, Bangladesh Nationalist Party, 1978-; Chairman, Commonwealth Fund for Tech Coop, 1978-79; Delegate to CHOGM Lusaka, 1979, Melbourne, 1981; Chairman, Board of Trustees, Islamic Centre, London; Delegate Non-Aligned Summits, Algiers, 1973, Colombo, 1976, Havana, 1979; Ambassador to: Yugoslavia and Roumania, 1972-74; Iran and Turkey, 1974-77. *Memberships:* Associate Member, Institute of Strategic Studies London. *Publications:* Arab-Israeli War, 1967; Aryans on the Indus (MS). *Honours:* C-in-C's Commendation, 1964; several military awards and decorations; Order of the Lance and Flag, Cl. 1 (Yugoslavia); Participated All India Trials for World Olympics, London, 1948. *Address:* 7 Spaniard's Close, London NW11, England.

SHANKAR PILLAI, Keshav, b. 31 July 1902, Kayamgulam Kerala, India. Political Cartoonist, Writer. m. Thankam, 18 May 1931, 2 sons, 3 daughters. *Educa-*

tion: BA, University College, Trivandrum Kerala, 1927. *Appointments:* Staff Cartoonist, The Hindustan Times, New Delhi, 1932-46; Own cartoon journal, Shankar's Weekly, 1948; Began Shankar's International Children's Competition, 1949; Organised first On-the-Spot Painting Competition, Delhi, 1953; Founded Children's Book Trust, 1957; Founded Shankar's International Dolls Museum, 1965; Founded Dolls Designing Centre & Workshop, 1967; Closed Shankar's Weekly, 1975; Started Writers' Workshop, 1977. *Creative Works:* Active political cartooning, 1929-75; writer of 40 books. for children, illustrating four himself; prolific editor; most popular books, Life with Grandfather, Tales from Indian Classic, Panchatantra. *Honours:* Recipient of many national and international awards 1955-80. *Hobbies:* Bridge; Reading; Writing for Children. *Address:* 9 Purana Qila Road, New Delhi, 110001, India.

SHAPIRO (formerly Pizzey), Erin Patricia Margaret, b. 19 Feb. 1939, Tsingtao, China. Therapist, Founder Advisor for Refuges for Women and Children. m. (1) John Leo Pizzey, 10 Feb. 1961; 2 daughters; (2) Jeffrey Scott Shapiro, 17 Dec. 1980. *Appointments:* Founder, Chiswick Women's Aid, 1971; Appointed Therapeutic Consultant, Chiswick Family Rescue, 1978. *Publications:* Scream Quickly or the Neighbours Will Hear, 1974; Infernal Child, 1979; Sexually Abused Children, 1980; Violence among Families, 1981; regular contributor to Cosmopolitan, 1981; Futura, Slut's Cookbook. *Hobbies:* Cooking; Travelling; Reading; Gardening; Lying in bed. *Address:* 397 Goldhawk Road, London W6, England.

SHARALAYA, William Louis, b. 3 May, 1920, Mercara, Coorg District, Karnataka State, India. m. Rajamma Daniel Mathi, 15 May 1944, 1 son, 1 daughter. *Education:* BCom, Commercial University, Delhi, India, 1955; FISC, London, 1955; FBIM, London, 1963; FSAA, 1954. *Appointments:* Secretary, India Financial Association, 1962-66; Business Manager, Spicer Memorial College, 1967-72; Treasurer, Services Association of Seventh Day Adventists, 1973-76; Manager, 1977-81. *Memberships:* Institute of Secretaries, Bombay, 1949. *Publications:* Has written series of articles to Business and Religious Magazines; Editor of Adventist Business Graduates' Association Review for two years. *Hobbies:* Stamp and Coin Collecting. *Address:* Salisbury Park, Box 15, Pune, 411001, India.

SHARFUDDIN, Shaik Mohammad, b. 17 Nov. 1929, Kushtia, Bangladesh. Service, Teacher, Research and administration. m. Roquiya Begum, 6 Nov. 1955, 2 sons. *Education:* PhD, London University, UK, 1964; Master Degree, Calcutta University, India, 1951, Bachelor Degree, (hons. in Mathematics), Calcutta University, 1948. *Appointments:* Assistant Professor of Mathematics, Bangladesh Engineering University, 1953; Professor of Mathematics, Chittagong Government College, 1959-62; Professor Mathematics, Bangladesh Senior Education Service, 1965; Professor & Chairman, Department of Mathematics, Jahangirnagar University, Dacca, 1971; Professor & Director, Institute for Advancement of Science & Technology Teaching, Dacca, 1972-; Visiting Professor to different Universities abroad. *Memberships:* Institute of Mathematics & Its Applications, UK; London Mathematical Society; Deutsche Academy Der Wissenchaften, Bangladesh Mathematical Society, vice president, 1972-74; President, Society International for Islam and Modern Age. *Publications:* Over 150 publications in Mathematics, Mathematical Sciences and Mathematics Education in different International Journals. Adviser to many UNESCO publications on Mathematics Education. Referee to various International Journals. *Hobbies:* Reading books and journals. *Address:* 58 Lake Circus, Kalabagan, Dacca-5, Bangladesh.

SHARMA, Bhu Dev, b. 21 June 1938, Bijnor, U.P. India. Professor of Mathematics. m. Kusum Sharma, 9 July, 1959, 2 sons, 2 daughters. BSc, 1955, MSc, 1957, Agra University, India; PhD, Delhi University, India, 1970. *Appointments:* Lecturer, Mathematics, NAS College, Meerut, 1957-63; Head, Department of Mathematics, Municipal Degree College, Mussoourie, 1963-64; Vaish College, Shamli, 1964-66; Lecturer, Mathematics, 1966-72; Reader, 1972-79, University of Delhi; Professor of Mathematics, University of West Indies, St. Augustine, Trinidad, 1979-. *Memberships:* General Secretary, Forum for Inter-disciplinary Mathematics; Chief Editor, Journal of Combinatories, Infor-

mation & System Sciences; Regional Editor & Associate Editor, Jrnl. of Information & Optimization Sciences; Bulletin Calcutta Math Society; Aligarh Journal of Statistics, Caribbean Jrnl. of Mathematics; Jrnl. of Physical & Natural Sciences. *Publications:* About 100 Research Papers in the areas of Information Theory, Functional Equations, Combinatorial Mathematics; 18 books on different topics in Mathematics. *Hobbies:* Photography; Philosophical Readings; Tourism. *Address:* 24 Warner Street, St. Augustine, Trinidad, West Indies.

SHARMA, Bhupenira Narain, b. 30 Aug. 1929. Officer in the Indian Army. m. Indu Sharma, 1 Jan. 1957, 1 son, 1 daughter. *Education:* BSc, Allahabad University, India, 1948; MSc, Delhi University, 1950. *Appointments:* Officer, Communication Engineering Duties, Corps of Signals; Instructor, Military College of Telecommunication Engineering; Instructor, Infantry School and College of Combat; Instructor, Defence Services Staff College; Command of Communication Units; General Staff Officer, Civil Affairs; Commander Communication Electronics Combat Group; Chief Signal Officer, Corps. *Memberships:* Fellow, Institution of Electronics & Telecommunication Engineers, India; Defence Services Officers' Institute, New Delhi. *Publications:* Established writer on Military Tactics, Strategy, Military History, etc. *Honours:* Honorarium on articles of original work published in military Digest. *Hobbies:* Study of Literature, Philosophy, History; Music; Drama. *Address:* 512/12 Services, Officers' Enclave, SP Marg, New Delhi-110021, India.

SHARMA, Jagdish Saran, b. 29 Apr. 1924, Gazzalpur, Delhi, India. Librarian-cum-Professor of Library Science. m. Prem Lata, 2 sons, 1 daughter. PhD, 1954, MA, 1949, University of Michigan, USA; Post-Graduate Diploma in Library Science, University of Delhi, 1948; MA, St. Stephens College, University of Delhi. *Appointments:* Research Officer and Librarian, AICC, New Delhi, 1954-56; University Librarian & Head, Library Science Department, Banaras Hindu University, Varanasi, 1956-59; University Librarian-cum-Professor, Library Science, 1959-. *Memberships:* Indian Library Association; Association of Special Libraries and Information Centre. *Publications:* Prolific writer of pamphlets, reviews, etc., author and co-author of 32 books. *Honours:* Recipient of Meritorious Library Service Award, 1966. *Hobbies:* Reading; Writing; Walking. *Address:* F-15, Sector 14, Chandigarh 160014, India.

SHARMA, Krishna Dayal, b. 6 Sept. 1931, Pratapgarh, India. Indian Foreign Service. 2 sons. *Education:* BA, MA. *Appointments:* Ministry of External Affairs, New Delhi, India, 1956-58; Third Secretary, Embassy of India, Belgrade, 1958-60; Under Secretary, Ministry of EA, New Delhi, 1960-63; First Secretary, Embassy of India, Tehran 1963-66, Washington, 1966-69; Director, Ministry of External Affairs, New Delhi, 1969-71; High Commissioner for India, Port Louis, 1971-74, Dar-es-Salaam, 1974-78; Joint Secretary, Ministry of External Affairs, New Delhi, 1978-80; High Commissioner for India, Canberra, 1980-. *Memberships:* Delhi Golf Club; Delhi Gymkhana Club; Royal Canberra Golf Club. *Hobbies:* Golf; Reading; Photography. *Address:* 34 Mugga Way, Red Hill, Canberra, Australia.

SHARMA, Ramesh Kumar, b. 23 Dec. 1926, Tehri, India. Teacher. m. Bimlakumari munshi, 1 daughter. *Education:* BA, 1947; MA, 1949; LLB, 1952; PhD, 1958; DLit, 1978. *Appointments:* Lecturer in Hindi, Agra University, 1949; Became Dean Faculty of Arts, Kashmir University, India, 1979. *Memberships:* Director, Kashmir Hindi Sansthan; Dean Faculty of Arts and syndicate member, Kashmir 'University; President Drama Club and Secretary Argan Club, Agra; Member, Central Council of J.K. Academy of Arts, Culture and Languages. *Publications:* Author of five books, and contributor of 45 research papers. *Honours:* Certificate and Tamrapatra (Copper Plate); Certificate in Theatre Arts, 1961. *Hobbies:* Photography; Hunting; Journalism; Trekking. *Address:* J-34, Government Quarter, Jawahar Nagar, Srinagar, Kashmir, India.

SHARMA, S. S. b. 1 Jan. 1919, Gopalpur, Gaya. Service. m. Girja Deri, Mar. 1944, 1 son, 3 daughters. MA, Patna University, India, 1946; PhD, Durham University, United Kingdom, 1956. *Appointments:* University Professor of Philosophy, Senior Professor of Philosophy, Behar University, Muzaffarpur, 1971, 1975;

Pro-Vice Chancellor, Behar University, Muzaffarpur, 1980. *Memberships:* Indian Philosophical Congress; President, Indian Philosophical Congress. *Hobbies:* Reading; Writing. *Address:* Gopalpur, Makhar, Akbarpur, Behar, India.

SHARMA, Surendra Mohan Sharma, b. 2 Aug. 1959, New Delhi. Accountant. Hons BCom, 1978, FSIAA, India, 1981. *Memberships:* Society of Incorporated Accountants of Auditors of India; Rotary International. *Publications:* A few articles on Accountancy and Taxation published in several Professional Journals. *Hobbies:* Reading; Writing; Cricket. *Address:* 19/2 West Patel Nagar, New Delhi-110008, India.

SHARP, David, Henry, b. 24 Feb. 1917, Cleethorpes, England. Chemist/Chemical Engineer. m. Enid Catherine Williams, 18 July 1942, 2 sons, 1 daughter. *Education:* BSc, Hons Chemistry, London, 1939; PhD, london, 1946, Fellow Royal Society of Chemistry, 1954; Fellow Institution of Chemical Engineers, 1972. *Appointments:* Technical Director, FBI/CBI, 1961-68; General Secretary, Industrial Chemical Engineering, 1969-1975; General Secretary, Society of Chemical Industry, 1975-. *Memberships:* Society of Chemical Industry; Chairman, Industrial Water and Effluent Group, 1967-69. *Publications:* Published number of papers in technical press. *Honours:* Recipient of Commander's Cross of Order of Merit of Federal Republic of Germany, 1981. *Hobbies:* Model Railways; Swimming; Colour Photography. *Address:* Green Hill House, Shoreham Road, Otford, Sevenoaks, Kent, England.

SHARP, Lindsay, Gerard. b. 22 Aug. 1947, Bromley, Kent, England. Museum Director. *Education:* MA, 1972; DPhil, Oxon, 1976. *Appointments:* Oxford University Press, Toronto, Canada, 1969-1970; Queen's College, Oxford, 1972-1975; Assistant Keeper, Pictorial Collection, Science Museum, London, 1976-1978; Museum of Applied Arts and Science, 1978-1981. *Memberships:* Museum Association, Australia; American Association of Museums; Wine Society, England. *Honours:* Scholarship to Wadham College, Oxford, 1966; Clifford Norton Research Fellowship, History of Science, Queen's College, Oxford, 1976. *Hobbies:* Swimming; Reading; Writing short stories; Collecting wine. *Address:* 6 Scouller Street, Marrickville, Sydney 2204, Sydney, New South Wales, Australia.

SHARP, Richard, William, b. 9 Mar. 1908, Westport, New Zealand. New Zealand Diplomatic Service, Retired. *Education:* Mt Albert Grammar School, 1922-25; BA, Victoria University of Wellington, 1929; LlM, Victoria University of Wellington, 1932. *Appointments:* Legal Offices, Wellington, 1929-34; Barrister and Solicitor, 1933; Government Service, 1934-46; Ministry of Foreign Affairs, 1951-73; New Zealand Consul, New York and First Secretary, New Zealand Mission to United Nations, 1960-63; Deputy High Commissioner and Minister, Ottawa, Canada, 1968-70; Consul General for North Western States, USA, 1970-73. *Memberships:* New Zealand, Law Society; Chairman, New Zealand Inter-Church Council on Public Affairs; English Speaking Union. *Honours:* Created Companion of the Queen's Service order, Consular Services, 1977. *Address:* 9 Crawford Road, Kilbirnie, Wellington, New Zealand.

SHARPE, John, (Sir), (Hon), KT, CBE, JP,MP. b8 November 1921, Bermuda, Merchant. m. Eileen Margaret Morrow, 3 Sept. 1948, 1 son, 1 daughter. *Education:* Warwick Academy, Bermuda; Mount Allison Commercial College, Canada. *Appointments:* Member of Parliament, 1963-; Served in Armed Forces: Bermuda Volunteer Rifle Corp. 1939-42; Royal Canadian Air Force 1942-45; qualified as Navigator in Canada, posted UK, served with RAF Bomber Command in operations over Europe; Business Directorships, Purvis Limited, 1950-; Bank of Bermuda Limited, 1978-. *Memberships:* Former Secretary & President, Bermuda Athletic Association; Bermuda War Veterans Association; Former President, BVRC Overseas Association; Hon. Vice-Patron, Royal Air Force Association; Coral Beach & Tennis Club; Royal Hamilton Amateur Club; Honorary Vice-President, Bermuda Football Association; Chairman, Bermuda National Olympic Council; National Trust; Royal Bermuda Yacht Club; Warwick Arbor Society, former President. *Honours:* CBE, 1972; Knight Bachelor, 1977. *Hobbies:* Reading; Bridge;

Gardening; Tennis. *Address:* Uplands, Harbour Road, Warwick West, Bermuda.

SHAW, Basil, John, b. 14 Mar. 1933, Brisbane, Queensland, Australia. Teacher. m. Lesley Elizabeth Kronk, 13 Aug. 1955, 4 sons. *Education:* BA, University of Queensland, 1963; Bachelor of Education, 1969; MA, University of London, 1972, MA, University of Queensland, 1975. *Appointments:* Teacher, Principal, Head, Queensland Schools, 1952-74; Head, Languages & Literature Department, Kelvin Grove College of Advanced Education, 1975-77; Head, Humanities Division, KGCAE, 1978-80; Acting Deputy Director, 1981. *Memberships:* Australian College of Education; Australian Association of Teachers of English; Canadian Council, Teachers of English. *Publications:* Times & Seasons: an Introduction to Bruce Dawe, 1974; Teaching: First Out, 1976. *Honours:* Fulbright Award, Washington, USA., August 1965-66; Visiting Professor, Calgary, Alberta, Canada, December 1979-80. *Hobbies:* Tennis; Philately. *Address:* 42 Highview Terrace, St. Lucia, Queensland, 4067, Australia.

SHAW, Hugh, Michael, b. 18 Jan. 1919, London, England. Orthopaedic Surgeon. m. Joan Fraser Craigie, 17 Jan. 1945, 1 son, 1 daughter. *Education:* MB,BS, Melbourne, 1943; FRCS, London, 1952; FRACS, 1954. *Appointments:* Resident Medical Officer, Royal Melbourne Hospital, 1943-45; Captain, Royal Australian Army Corps, 1945-47; Associate Surgeon, Royal Melbourne Hospital, 1949-52; Senior Registrar, Essex County Hospital, 1953; Consultant Orthopaedic Surgeon, Melbourne, 1954-; Orthopaedic Surgeon, Prince Henry Hospital, Melbourne, 1954-79; Consultant Orthopaedic Surgeon, Australian Repatriation Department, 1954-81. *Memberships:* Australian Orthopaedic Association; Royal Melbourne Golf Club. *Hobbies:* Photography; Carpentry. *Address:* 5 Devorgilla Avenue, Toorak, Melbourne, Australia 3142.

SHAW, John, b. 22 Dec. 1940, Sydney, Australia. m. Robin, 7 Mar. 1964, 1 son, 3 daughters. *Education:* MB BS, 1965; MRACP, 1968; FRACP, 1974; PhD, 1974. *Appointments:* Medical Officer and Registrar Royal Prince Alfred Hospital, 1965-68; Research Fellow, National Heart Foundation of Australia, 1968-71; Overseas Research Fellow, National Heart Foundation of Australia, 1972-74; Fellow, Cardiovascular Division, Johns Hopkins Hospital, Baltimore, USA, 1972-73; Research Fellow, Medical Unit, St. Mary's Hospital, London, 1973-74; First Assistant, Clinical Pharmacology, University of Melbourne, 1974-79; Director of Clinical Pharmacology, The Royal Melbourne Hospital, 1977-79; Professor of Clinical Pharmacology, University of Sydney, 1979. *Memberships:* Fellow of numerous Societies throughout Australia and New Zealand. *Publications:* Various publications in Medical Journals on Cardiovascular Physiology and Pharmacology; Contributor to chapters in specialized monographs. *Hobbies:* Tennis; Sailing. *Address:* 171 Deepwater Road, Castle Cove, NSW, 2069, Australia.

SHAW, Mansergh, b. 8 Jan 1910, Liverpool, England. Engineer (retired). *Education:* BE, ME, Sheffield University, 1932-35; M.Mech.E, University of Melbourne, 1939; M.Eng, University of Queensland, 1945. *Appointments:* Draughtsman, Davy Bros, Sheffield, 1929-32; Whitworth Scholar, Sheffield University, 1932-35; Assistant Lecturer, Sheffield University, 1935-37; Senior Lecturer, University of Melbourne, Australia, 1937-47; Research Fellow, University of Birmingham, England, 1948; Professor of Mechanical Engineering, University of Queensland, 1948-75; Emeritus Professor, 1975. *Memberships:* F.I. Mech. E. Chairman of Queensland Branch, 1970; F.I.E. Aust, Chairman of Queensland Division; F.I. Prod. E, Chairman of Brisbane Section, 1976; M.Qld. Society of Sugar Cane Technologists, 1951; M. International Society of Sugar Cane Technologists & Chairman of Manufacturing Section of Durban Conference. *Publications:* Papers in Proc. Q.S.S.C.T, international proceedings of I.S.S.C.T., Paper in Proc. I Mech. E. *Honours:* Whitworth Scholar, 1932; O.B.E. 1976; Emeritus Professor, 1975; Hon. M. Aust. Inst. Man., 1978; James N Kirby Memorial Award, Medal, Institute of Production Engineers, 1974. *Hobbies:* Woodcarving, travel. *Address:* 31, Ironside Street, St. Lucia, Brisbane, Queensland, Australia, 4067.

SHAW, Margaret Eleanor, b. 19 Aug 1921, Melbourne, Australia. Hospital Administrator. *Education:*

Matriculation, 1937. *Appointments:* Accountant, Audit Clerk, 1938-49; Assistant Manager/Chief Accountant, Queen Victoria Memorial Hospital, Melbourne, 1949-57, Assistant Manager/Chief Accountant, Royal Dental Hospital, Melbourne, 1957-66 Manager, After Care Hospital, Melbourne, 1967. *Memberships:* Australian Society of Accountants; Australian Institute of Management; Australian Institute of Chartered Secretaries & Administrators; Australian College of Health Service Admistrators; Girl Guides Association, Assistant State Commissioner, Zonta International Melbourne Club. *Honours:* Red Kangaroo Award, National Award for service, Girl Guides Association, Australia. *Hobbies:* Reading, History, Scottish Country Dancing, Philately, Travel. *Address:* 2/90 Yarrbat Av, Balwyn, Victoria, Australia, 3103.

SHAW, Maxwell, Kenneth, b. 22 May 1938, Newcastle, NSW, Australia, m. Elva C. Dean, 1 son, 5 daughters, *Education:* BSc, 1960, University of Queensland, Australia; MSc, 1964, University of Queensland; PhD, 1966, University of California, Davis, USA. *Appointments:* Research Assistant, National Health & Medical Research Council Australia, 1959-60; Research Scientist, CSIRO, 1960-70; Group Manager, R & D Mauri Bros. & Thompson Ltd, 1970-77; Present Technical Consultant, Shaw Consulting Services, 1977-. *Memberships:* Hon. Gen. Sec. & Executive Secretary, Australian Institute of Food Science & Technology (A/FST); Secretary, Australian Industrial Research Group (AIR6), Australian Society for Microbiology; Chairman, Biological Registration Advisory Committee of National Association of Testing Authorities. *Publications:* 15 Scientifc articles in international journals. *Honours:* CSIRO Overseas Postgraduate Traineeship, University of California, Davis, 1963-66. *Hobbies:* Care & counselling of needy and disturbed people. *Address:* 14, Brisbane Road, Castle Hill, NSW, Australia, 2154.

SHAW, Michael Emerson Andez, b. 17 Dec. 1932, St. Mary, Jamaica, Agronomist. m. Gloria Scot Jacobs, 27 Dec. 1958, 2 sons, 1 daughter. *Education:* BSc McGill Univ. (Macdonald College), Quebec, Canada, 1954-58. *Appointments:* Agronomist, Sugar Manfts. Assoc. Jamaica, Research Dept. 1958; Deputy Director, 1970; Director, Sugar Industry Research Inst. Mandeville, Jamaica, 1975-; Chairman, Sugar Houst Ltd. Director, National Commercial Bank Jamaica Ltd; Chairman, Black River Morass Development Co., Jamaica. *Memberships:* Director, Rotary Club Mandeville, Jamaica; Freemason (Pastmaster). Ewing 3258EC & Adair 8146EC Lodges; Member, Exec Committee, Jamaican Assoc. Sugar Technologists; Councillor, International Society of Sugurcane Technologists. *Publications:* 17 Technical papers on Scientific and Agricultural subjects; Several papers of 'Popular' nature both locally and international. *Hobby:* Gardening. *Address:* Broadlands, Kendal Road, Mandeville, Jamaica.

SHEA, Brian Joseph, b. 18 Nov 1928, Sydney, New South Wales, Australia. Psychiatrist. m. Cecile Pearce Delbridge, 9 Feb 1958. 2 sons, 2 daughters. *Education:* MB, BS, University of Adelaide, 1945-51; DPM, Melbourne University, 1958-61; FRACMA, 1967, FRANZCP, 1967, FRC Psych, 1973; FAIM, 1973; FHA, 1973. *Appointments:* R.M.O., Royal Adelaide Hospital, 1951-52; R.M.O., Glenside Hospital, S.A., 1952-54; M.O. Claremont Hospital, W.A., 1954-55; Deputy Supt. Glenside Hospital, S.A., 1955-62; Supt. Callan Park Hospital, NSW, 1962-64; Ag. Director, State Psychiatric Services, NSW, 1964-65; Director-General of Medical Services, SA, 1967-77; Chairman, S.A. Health Commission, 1977-79; Director, Community Psychiatry, SA, 1979-. *Memberships:* President Elect, Royal Australian & New Zealand College of Psychiatrists. Medical Board of S.A; Medical Research Advisory Committee of NH & MRC, 1978; Naval Military & Air Force Club, Adelaide. *Publications:* Psychiatry & The Community, 1969, Sydney University Press; Numerous publications on medical administration of psychiatry. *Honours:* O.St. J, 1977; O.B.E., 1981. *Hobbies:* Reading, Golf. *Address:* 13, Cross Road, Kingswood, South Australia 5062.

SHEARER, Ian John, b. 10 Dec. 1941, Whakatane, New Zealand. Minister for the Environment Minister of Science and Technology, Minister of Broadcasting. m. Sandra May Griffiths, 1 son, 1 daughter. *Education:* Master of Agricultural Science (Massey University); PhD. (Nottingham University, UK); Certificate in Radi-

oisotope Techniques (Loughborough University of Technology UK). *Appointments:* Research Scientists at Ruakura Agricultural Research Centre, Hamilton, New Zealand. *Memberships:* NZ Institute of Agricultural Science; NZ Association of Scientists; NZ Society of Endocrinology; Amnesty International (NZ); Friends of the Earth (NZ); Native Forests Action Council; NZ Club of Rome; Project Jonah; Royal Forest and Bird Protection Society; Vice President NZ Crippled Children Society; Vice President NZ Society for the Intellectually Handicapped (South Auckland Branch) Vice President, Prisoners Aid & Rehabilitation Society; Patron, Solo Parents (Waikato); Hamilton Branch Youth Hostel Association. *Publications:* Published 32 Scientific and General papers in Nutrition & Physiology. *Honours:* Associate Member of World Wide Academy of Scholars, 1975; Cultural Doctorate in Humanities from World University Roundtable, 1976; Waikato-Thames Valley-King Country area Finalists, 1974; Wills Oustanding Young Man of the Year Award. *Hobbies:* Active Interest in all Sports. *Address:* Parliament Buildings, Wellington, New Zealand.

SHEARER, John, b. 2 Feb, 1897, Perth, Western Australia. Physicist (retired). m. Muriel Jane Aitken, 22 May 1931. 1 son, 1 daughter. *Education:* BA, 1918; BSc, 1920; BSc 1st class hons., 1921; MSc, University of Melbourne, 1926. *Appointments:* 1921-23, Observer, Geophysical Observatory, WA: 1926-28, Lecturer, Nat. Phil. University Melbourne; Queen's College University, Melbourne Resident Tutor Nat. Phil., 1924-28, Acting Vice-Master; 1929, Appointed Lecturer in Physics University WA: 1962, Retired Reader in Physics, University WA. *Memberships:* Fellow of the British Institute of Physics; Foundation Fellow of the Australian Institute of Physics; Perth Club. *Publications:* Contributor to scientific journals from 1927; Author Music & Drama—A Commentary on Wagner and Shakespeare. *Honours:* 1928, CSIRO Research Grant; 1948, Gledden Research Fellow. *Hobbies:* Music, Literature. *Address:* 89, Thomas St, Nedlands, Western Australia, 6009.

SHEARER, Peter Henry, b. 16 April 1913, Berlin. Industrial Consultant. m. Barbara, 12 Apr. 1948. *Appointments:* Efficiency Engineer, F.W. Hughes P/L Sydney, 1938; Director Manufacturing, Hilton Corporation, 1954; Chief Execut. Pelaco Lt., 1970-78; Chairman & Chief Exec. 1978-79; Chairman & Consultant, 1979. *Memberships:* Melbourne Hunt Club; Findon Harriers Hunt Club, Victoria Golf Club; Angus Society of Australia. *Hobbies:* Hunting; Riding; Golf; Sailing. *Address:* 80, Leopold Street, South Yarra (VIC), Australia.

SHEARMAN, Donald, Norman, b. 6 Feb 1926. Sydney, Australia. Bishop. m. Stuart Fay, Nov 1952, 3 sons, 3 daughters. *Education:* ThL, St. John's Theological College, Morpeth, NSW, 1950. *Appointments:* Deacon, 1950, Priest, 1951; Diocese of Bathurst; Assist. priest Dubbo, 1951-52; Assistant Priest Forbes, 1953-56; Rector, Coonabarabran, 1957-58; Director, Religious Education & Promotion, 1959-62; Canon All Saints Cathedral, Bathurst, 1962; Archdeacon of Mildura Victoria, 1962-63; Bishop of Rockhampton Qld, 1964-71; Chairman, Australian Board of Missions, 1971-73; Bishop of Grafton, NSW, 1973. *Honours:* O.B.E., 1978. *Hobbies:* Philately, Fishing. *Address:* Bishopsholme, 35, Victoria Street, Grafton, NSW, 2460, Australia.

SHECHAMBO, Fanuel C.M. b. 22 May 1950, Lushoto, Tanzania, Librarian. m. D. Msagati, 2 Apr. 1975, 1 son, 2 daughters. *Education:* Dip. Lib (Makerere), 1974; *Appointments:* Librarian, Kiuukoni College, Dar-es-Salaam, 1974-1976; Librarian, National Central Library, Dar-es-Salaam, 1976-1979; Student at the University of Dar-es-Salaam, 1979. *Memberships:* Tanzania Library Association; Economics Association of the University of DSM; University of Dar-es-Salaam, Students Organisation (MUWATA)-Secretary, 1979-81. *Publications:* The soils of East Africa. *Honours:* Best Student at the East African School of Librianship, 1974. *Hobbies:* Organist, Trombone Player. *Address:* University of Dar-es-Salaam, P.O. Box 35081, Dare-es-Salaam, Tanzania.

SHEH, Violet Mae, b. 3 June 1919, Prince Rupert, British Colombia, Canada. Journalist. m. Kenneth Sheh, 19 Feb. 1948, 2 sons, 1 daughter. *Appointments:* Journalist, Chinatown News, Vancouver, British Colombia, 1957-58; Social and consumer columnist, Richmond Review, Richmond, British Colombia, Canada,

1967-72. *Memberships:* Life Fellow, International Biographical Association. *Hobbies:* Piano; Swimming; Gardening; Needlepoint; Collecting spoons from around the world; World Travel and Ceramics. *Address:* 10251 Aintree Crescent, Richmond, British Colombia, Canada V7A 3T9.

SHELTON, Harold Herbert, b. 1 July, 1913, Lancashire. Artist/Designer. m. Joanna, 2 Nov. 1941, 1 son. *Education:* Royal College of Art, South Kensington, London; School of Social Studies, University of Edinburgh, 1941-42. *Appointments:* Textile Producer/Designer, Calico Printers Association, Manchester, 1946-47; Principal, Carlisle College of Art, 1947-57; Principal, Hornsey College of Art, 1957-73; Assistant Director, Middlesex Polytechnic, 1973-77. *Memberships:* President, National Society for Art Education, 1963; Awarded Fellowship of the National Society for Art Education, 1963; Associate, Society of Industrial Artists & Designers, 1964; Member, Burnham Further Education Committee, 1964-77; Member, Council Society of Industrial Artists and Designers, 1965-68; Governing Body, Suffolk College of Higher Education, 1977-. *Creative Works:* Paintings, drawings and etchings in wide range of exhibitions. *Honours:* OBE, 1978; Leverhulme Scholarship, 1961. *Hobbies:* Gardening; Golf; Cricket; Tennis. *Address:* Stambourne Hall, Stambourne, Halstead, Essex, England.

SHENOLIKAR, Balwant, b. 22 Nov. 1923, Kolhapur, India. Surgeon/Civil Servant. m. Audrey (dec.), 1 son, 1 daughter. *Education:* MBBS, Calcutta, 1947; FRCS, Edinburgh, 1955; FRCS, England, 1957. *Appointments:* Lecturer in Anatomy, University of Nagpur, 1947-52; House Surgeon, Hammersmith Hospital, London, 1953-54; Resident Surgical Officer, Royal Infirmary, Halifax, 1955-56; Surgical Registrar, Manchester Regional Board, 1957-58; Consultant Surgeon, Mercy Hospital, Georgetown, 1958-62; Senior Surgeon, Government Hospital, Georgetown, 1963-67; Senior Medical Officer, 1967-. *Memberships:* Corresponding Fellow, Association of Surgeons of Venezuela; Past President, Guyana Table Tennis Association. *Publications:* Publications in various medical journals. *Honours:* First class honour in Medicine and Surgery Gold Medal in Pathology and Bacteriology. *Hobbies:* Golf; Music. *Address:* 164 Lower Morden Lane, Morden, Surrey, SM4 4SS.

SHEPHERD, Bruce Dalway, b. 26 Oct. 1932, Tamworth, N.S.W. Australia. Orthopaedic Surgeon. m. Annette, 8 Apr. 1961, 1 son, 1 daughter. *Education:* BDS Sydney, 1953; MB, BS, Sydney, 1958; FRCS, Edinburgh, 1961; FRCS, England, 1961; FRACS, 1964. *Appointments:* Resident Medical Officer, Royal Prince Alfred Hospital, Sydney, 1958-59; Lecture Demonstrator in Anatomy, Sydney University, 1960; Surgical Registrar, Royal Prince Alfred Hospital, 1961; Orthopaedic Registrar, St. Thomas' Hospital, London, 1962-63; Honorary Orthopaedic Surgeon, Mater Misericordiae Hospital; Honorary Orthopaedic Surgeon, Mona Vale District Hospital; Honorary Orthopaedic Surgeon, Auburn District Hospital; Lecturer in Orthopaedics, Sydney University. *Memberships:* Member of executive and Chairman of the Continuing Education Committee, Australian Orthopaedic Association; Pan-Pacific Surgical Association; Western Pacific Orthopaedic Association. *Creative Works:* Founder of Shepherd Centre for Deaf Children and Their Parents, Sydney University. *Hobbies:* Photography; Skiing; Tennis. *Address:* 28 Julian Street, Mosman, 2088, Australia.

SHEPHERD, Stuart John Hunt, b. 13 Apr. 1925, Maryborough, Victoria, Australia. Medical Practitioner. m. Shirley, 3 sons, 1 daughter. *Education:* MB, BS, University of Melbourne, 1953; Diploma, Hospital Administration, University of N.S.W. 1968; FRACMA 1969; DGM, 1978. *Appointments:* Medical Superintendent, Mount Royal Hospital, 1961; Hon. Geriatrician, Royal Melbourne Hospital, 1966; Hon. Visiting Geriatrician, St. Vincents Hospital, 1970-78; Director, Victorian Postgraduate Geriatric Medical Training Programme. *Memberships:* President, Royal Australian College of Medical Administrators, 1975-77; Secretary, Royal Australian College of Medical Administrators, 1966-72; Vice President, Australian Association of Gerontology, 1969; President, Victoria Medical Superintendents Association, 1970; *Publications:* Papers on Accidents to the elderly, Preparation for retirement, Ethics in the aged, Postgraduate Geriatric Medical

Training. *Creative Works:* Farming; Gardening; Sailing. *Address:* 81 Buchanan Avenue, North Balwyn, 3103, Victoria, Australia.

SHEPPARD, Peter Floyd, b. 31 Dec. 1929, Christchurch, New Zealand. Medical Practitioner; Physician. m. Robin Marianne, 2 May, 1964, 1 son, 2 daughters. *Education:* MB. ChB, Otago University; DCH 1958; MRCP, London, 1961; MRACP, 1962; FRACP, 1970; FRCP, London, 1981. *Appointments:* Resident Christchurch Hospital, 1955-56; House Physician, Southend General Hospital, 1957; Medical Registrar, Orsett Hospital, Essex, England, 1958-60; RMO, London Chest Hospital, 1961; RMO, Christchurch Hospital, New Zealand, 1961-64; Visiting Physician & Gastroenterologist, Christchurch Hospital, New Zealand, 1964-. *Memberships:* Chairman, Canterbury Post Graduate Medical Society, 1972-74; Secretary Canterbury Division, New Zealand Medical Association, 1964; Committee Member, New Zealand Society of Gastroenterology, 1968-70; Executive Member, St. George's Hospital, since 1972; Christchurch Club, Christchurch Golf Club. *Publications:* Medical papers only. *Hobbies:* Golf; Skiing; Yachting; Tennis; Music. *Address:* 42 Memorial Avenue, Christchurch, New Zealand.

SHEPPERSON, George Albert, b. 7 Jan. 1922, Peterborough, England. University Professor. m. 31 Dec. 1952, 1 daughter. *Education:* 1st class Hons, English Tripos Part 1, St. John's College, Cambridge, 1942; 1st class Hons, Historical Tripos, Part 2, St. John's College, Cambridge, 1948; 1st class Certificate of Education, Cambridge University, 1948. *Appointments:* Edinburgh University: Lecturer, 1948; Senior Lecturer, 1960; Reader, 1961; Professor of Commonwealth and American History, 1963; Dean of the Faculty of Arts, 1974-77; Founder member, Centre of African Studies and Convenor, 1964-66, and 1973-74; Founder member, Centre of Canadian Studies, 1974; Convenor, 1979. Overseas Universities: Visiting Professor, Roosevelt and Chicago Universities, 1959; Makerere College, Uganda, 1962; Dalhousie University, 1968-69. *Memberships:* Chairman, British Association for American Studies, 1971-74; Vice President, British Association of Canadian Studies, 1980-81; Chairman, Commonwealth Institute, Scotland, 1973; Member, Edinburgh Branch, Royal Commonwealth Society; African Studies Association of the UK. *Hobbies:* Collecting African and Afro-American documents; Theatre. *Address:* 23 Ormidale Terrace, Edinburgh, EH12 6DY, Scotland.

SHER, Jeffrey, Leslie, b. 26 May, 1936, Sydney, N.S.W. Barrister. m. Diana Vicki, 14 Apr. 1959, 2 sons, 2 daughters. *Education:* LLB, Melbourne University, 1957; Matriculated, Haileybury College, 1972. *Appointments:* Deputy Crown Solicitors, 1957-58; John Don, Solicitor, 1959-60; Victorian Bar, 1961; QC, Victoria, 1975; Tasmanian Bar, 1977; Q.C. Tasmania, 1977; N.S.W. Bar, 1980; Q.C. N.S.W. (1981). *Memberships:* Chairman, Board Victoria State Opera, 1979-81; Member, Cranbourne Golf Club, 1974. *Hobbies:* Opera; Tennis; Reading; Classical Music; Gardening. *Address:* 17 Yuille Street, Brighton 3186, Victoria, Australia.

SHERIDAN, John Patrick, b. 2 May, 1933, Toronto, Ontario. Mining Engineer. m. Marjorie, Ann, 11 Oct. 1958, 3 sons, 1 daughter. *Education:* BASc, University of Toronto. *Appointments:* Chief Geophysicist, C.C. Huston and Associates, Toronto, 1956; Founded Sheridan Geophysics Ltd., 1956; Member: Canadian Exploration Geophysical Society; Canadian Institute of Mining; Association of Professional Engineers; President, Sheild Development Co.; Past President, Kidd Copper Mines; White Star Copper Mines; Belleterre Quebec Mines. *Memberships:* Engineers' (Toronto); Albany; Aspen Alps, Aspen, Colorado; Craig Leith Ski; Mach Busters; Explorer's Club, New Yorks; Cambridge Club; Toronto Cricket, Skating and Curling Club, Toronto. *Hobbies:* Skiing; Fishing; Squash; Sports. *Address:* 14 Park Lane Circle, Toronto, Ontario, Canada.

SHIELDS, Francis Edward, b. 22 Mar. 1940, Buxton, Derbyshire, England. m. Brigitte Pamela Phillips, 30 March, 1968. 3 sons. *Appointments:* Farmer, 1964; Assistant Organiser, Devon Young Farmers, 1964-69; Secretary to National Proficiency Tests Council, 1969; General Secretary/Treasurer of the National Federation of Young Farmers Clubs, 1969-. *Memberships:* Director, United Kingdom Sponsoring Authority; Vice-Chairman, National Council for Voluntary Youth Services; Executive Representative on Local Councils Committee, National Council for Voluntary Youth Organisations; Treasurer, National Hedgelaying Society. *Creative Works:* The Young Farmers Club Movement of England and Wales, 1981; Essentially for Clubs, Series of general training material for Young Farmers Clubs; Various training material for the Young Farmers Movement. *Honours:* MBE, 1981. *Hobbies:* Road Running; Voluntary work. *Address:* 26 Woodcote Avenue, Kenilworth, Warwickshire, Warwickshire.

SHIJA, Joseph, Kayoba, b. 13 Sept. 1939, Tabora, Tanzania. Consultant Paediatric Surgeon, Professor of Surgery. m. (1) Lucia Hiyobo, 21 Dec. 1968; (Deceased, 1975), 2 sons; (2) Margaret Makule, 4 March, 1978. *Education:* MBCHB(EA) Makerere University; Kampala, Uganda 1961-67; FRCSEd, Fellow of the Royal College of Surgeons of Edinburgh, 1970-72; Bowater-Ralli Fellow in Paediatric Surgery, Institute of Child Health, London, 1974. *Appointments:* Internship, Muhimbili Hospital, Dar Es Salaam, Tanzania, 1967-68; Surgical Registrar, Muhimbili Hospital, Dar Es Salaam, Tanzania, 1969-70; General Surgeon, Lecturer in Surgery, University Teaching Hospital, Dar Es Salaam, Tanzania, 1972-73; Paediatric SUrgeon, Senior Lecturer in Surgery, University Teaching Hospital, Dar Es Salaam, Tanzania, 1974-76; Associate Professor/Head of Surgery, Muhimbili Medical Centre, Dar Es Salaam, Tanzania, 1976-79; Professor & Head of Surgery, Muhimbili Medical Centre, Dar Es Salaam, Tanzania, 1979-. *Memberships:* Fellow, Royal College of Surgeons of Edinburgh, 1972; President, Medical Association of Tanzania, 1976-78; Member British Association of Paesiatric Surgeons, 1977; Fellow, Royal Society of Tropical Medicine & Hygiene, 1977; President (Chairman) Association of Surgeons of East Africa, 1979-80; Vice-President, Commonwealth Medical Association, 1976-80; Chairman, Tanzania Professional Centre, 1979-. *Publications:* Prolific author of books, papers, scientific publications in his field. *Honours:* Recipient of numerous honours and awards for professional services. *Hobbies:* Reading; Current Affairs; Professional Activities; Gardening. *Address:* P.O. Box 827, Dar Es Salaam, Tanzania.

SHILLINGFORD, Romeo Arden Coleridge, b. 11 Feb. 1936. High Commissioner for the Commonwealth of Dominica, London 1978-. m. (1) Evelyn Blanche Hart, 1 son, 1 daughter. (2) Maudline Joan Green, 3 sons. *Education:* Wesley High School; Roseau Boys School, Dominica; Grammar School; School of Law; Hon. Society Inner Temple. *Appointments:* Dominican Civil Service, 1957; Solicitor's Clerk, Junior Clerk various Government Departments, Dominica, 1957-59; Clerk of Court, Chief Clerk, Magistrates' Office, 1960-61; Eastern Caribbean Commn. London, 1965; Migrants' Welfare Officer, Students' Officer, Assistant Trade Secretary and PA to Comr. 1968-71; Administration Assistant, Consular and Protocol Affairs, 1973-78. *Memberships:* Numerous committees and ad hoc bodies for West Indian Immigrant Welfare and Education; Deputy Chairman, Board of Governors, West Indian Students' Centre, 1970-75; Chairman, 1976-79; West India Committee; Liaison Officer, Victoria League for Commonwealth Friendship; Founder-member and Vice-Chairman, Jaycees. *Honours:* MBE, 1977. *Hobbies:* Cricket; Collecting authentic folk music; Swimming. *Address:* Dominica High Commission, 10 Kensington Court, London W8 5DL, England.

SHIN, Yong-Moo, b. 14 June, 1931, Seoul, Korea. Physicist, Professor. m. Myoung Ja Shin, 16 sept. 1967, 1 son, 1 daughter. *Education:* BSc. Yonsei University, Seoul, 1957; MSc, University of Pennsylvania, Philadelphia, 1960; PhD, University of Pennsylvania, Philadelphia, 1963. *Appointments:* Assistant Professor, University of Texas, 1963-65; Assistant Professor, University of Saskatchewan, 1965-69; Associate Professor, University of Saskatchewan, 1969-75; Professor, University of Saskatchewan, 1975; Director, Accelerator Lab; University of Saskatchewan; 1975. *Memberships:* Canadian Association of Physicists, Vice Chairman, Div. of Nuclear Physics; American Physical Society; Korean Physical Society. *Publications:* 49 Research Papers. *Hobbies:* Painting; Music; Carpentry. *Address:* 506, Quance Avenue, Saskatoon, Sask, Canada.

SHINKFIELD, Anthony James, b. 7 Aug. 1934, St. Peters, S. Australia. Headmaster. m. 12 May, 1956, 2

sons, 1 daughter. *Education:* BA Dip.Ed, Dip.T, University of Adelaide, 1952-55; B Ed. Hons. University of Queensland, 1971-73; MA Ed.D, Western Michigan University, 1976-78. *Appointments:* High School Teacher, Headmaster, South Australian Schools, 1956-72; Inspector of High Schools, S. Australia, 1973-75; Graduate Assistant, W. Michigan University, 1976-78; Headmaster, Church of England Collegiate School of St. Peter (S. Australia), 1978-. *Appointments:* Australian College of Education, 1966; American Education Research Association, 1977; Association for Supervision & Curriculum Development, 1978; S. Australian Institute for Educational Research, 1972; S. Australian Institute for Educational Administration, 1973. *Publications:* 15 publications in learned journals during the last decade. *Hobbies:* Music; Gardening; Cricket; Squash; Reading. *Address:* Headmaster's House, St. Peter's College, St. Peters, S. Australia. 5069

SHINYI, Mathias Asor, b. 26 Sept. 1954, Mkar-Gboko, Benue State, Librarian. *Education:* WASC, Bristow Sec. School, Gboko, 1968-72; HSC, Government Sec. School, Katsina-ala, 1973-74; BLS, Ahmadu Bello University, Zaria, 1975-78. *Appointments:* Army Library Service, Lagos, Nigeria, 1978-79; Librarian Ministry of Information, Makurdi, Nigeria, 1979-79; Serials Librarian, Mucast Library, Makurdi, Nigeria, 1979-. *Memberships:* Member of The Nigerian Library Association. *Hobbies:* Lawn Tennis; Table Tennis; Music. *Address:* NKST Adikpo, P.O. Gboko, Benue State, Nigeria.

SHIRLEY, Douglas, Marshall, b. 2 May, 1920, Dunedin, New Zealand. Chartered Accountant. m. Ella Theadora Silva, 17 Sept. 1948, 1 son, 2 stepsons. *Education:* Otago BHS, OU; ACA; AIAO. *Appointments:* Dunedin City Corporation, 1937-80 *Memberships:* Member, Otago Officers Club; New Zealand Returned Services Association; Otago Peninsula Trust; Outward Bound; Royal Commonwealth Society; Heritage. *Publications:* Prepared and presented papers on various subjects to Professional Institutes in New Zealand and Australia. *Honours:* Mentioned in despatches (World War II); William Brown Memorial Prize in Auditing, University of Otago, 1954; OBE, New Year's Honours, 1980. *Address:* 81, Cannington Road, Maori Hill, Dunedin, New Zealand.

SHIVANATH, Sivasamboo, b. 15 June, 1949, Badulla, Sri Lanka, Financial Management cum Management Accountancy. *Education:* Nalayini Savithiri Selvarajah, 6 Dec. 1976, 1 daughter. *Appointments:* Associate Member, Institute of Cost and Management Accountants, London, passed final 1975, admitted as Member in 1978; Associate Member Institute of Chartered Accountants of Ceylon (Sri Lanka), passed final in 1974, admitted as Member in 1975. *Appointments:* M.N. Sambamurti & Co., Chartered Accountants 1975-75; Sri Lanka Sugar Corporation, 1975-76; Zambia Electricity Supply Corporation Ltd., 1977-79; Endless Investment Holdings Ltd., 1980-. *Hobbies:* Reading; *Address:* Flat No.22, Zecco Flats, Independance Avenue, Kitwe, Zambia.

SHODEINDE, Biliaminu Adegboyega, b. 20 June, 1942, Ibadan, Nigeria. Architect. m. Bukunola Omeyemi, 2 Dec. 1969, 2 sons, 1 daughter. *Education:* Graduate Studies, Comprehensive University, Frankfurt/Main, W. Germany, Grad-Ingenieur; Post Graduate, Technical University, Berlin, W. Germany, Dip.Ingenieur, MSc.Arch. *Appointments:* Architect, Hochtief A.G. Frankfurt/Main, W. Germany, 1968-69; Architect II, Ministry of Works & Transport, Ibadan, 1969-74; Senior Architect/Principal Architect, Western Nigerian Housing Corporation, Ibadan, 1974-76 First Chief Architect, Ministry of Works & Transport, Akure, 1976-80; Chief Architect, Ministry of Works & Transport, Ibadan, 1980-. *Memberships:* Corporate Member, Royal Institute of British Architects; Member, Association German Architects & Engineers, BDB; Member, Nigerian Institute of Architects. *Publications:* Rural Development in Perspective, Ekiti Division of Ondo State as a case study. *Honours:* Merit Award State Government's Programme, September, 1980. *Hobbies:* Football; Table Tennis; Squash. *Address:* Plot 3, Block V, Ikolaba, Bodija, Ibadan, Nigeria.

SHODUNKE, Michael Oluwole, b. 23 Dec. 1940, Modakeke, Oyo State, Nigeria, Accountant. m. Olayide A. Adeleke, 19 Oct. 1963. *Education:* Diploma in Co-operative Studies, Co-operative College, Ibadan, 1959-60; ACCA Final 1, North Western Polytechnic, London, 1963-65. *Appointments:* Accountant, Federal Ministry of Finance, Lagos, 1968-68; Accounts Manager in Training, Lever Brothers Ltd, Nigeria, 1968-68; Senior Accountant, West African Exam. Council, 1968-71; Chief Finance Officer, West African Exam. Council, 1971-73; Chief Accountant, Nigerian Bank for Commerce & Industry, Lagos, 1973-78; Director, Nigerian Bank for Commerce and Industry, Lagos, 1978-. *Memberships:* Ikoyi Club. *Hobbies:* Tennis; Swimming; Gardening; Reading. *Address:* 4, Bishop Oluwole Street, Victoria Island, Lagos, Nigeria.

SHOLL, John Reginald, b. 16 Nov. 1931, Melbourne, Australia, Public Relations Consultant. m. Lynette Ann, 1 son, 1 daughter. *Education:* Melbourne University, 1949-51. *Appointments:* Newspaper Reporter, Sun News Pictorial & Melbourne Argus, including 2 years in London, 1949-57; Public Relations Officer, H.C. Sleigh Ltd., 1957-58; Consultant with various Firms, 1958-68; Established own P.R. Consultancy, 1968-. *Memberships:* Public Relations Institute of Australia: International Public Relations Association. *Hobbies:* Farming. *Address:* SRS Public Relations Pty. Ltd., 505, St. Kilda Road, Melbourne, Australia.

SHONEKAN, Ernest Adegunle, Oladeinde, b. 9 May, 1936, Lagos, Nigeria, Barrister. m. 4 Dec. 1965, 2 sons, 2 daughters. *Education:* LLB Hons. London, 1962; BL, Middle Temple, 1962. *Appointments:* Legal Assistant, UAC of Nigeria Ltd., 1964-67; Assistant Legal Adviser, UAC of Nigeria Ltd., 1967-75; Deputy Legal Adviser, UAC of Nigeria Ltd., 1975-76; Legal Adviser, UAC OF Nigeria Ltd., 1976-78; Genreal Manager, Bordpak Premier Packaging, 1978-80; Chairman/Managing Director, UAC of Nigeria Ltd., 1980-. *Memberships:* Metropolitan Club; Deputy Chairman, Nigerian Youth Trust Council; Council Member, St. John's Ambulance. *Hobbies:* Swimming; Squash. *Address:* 2 Cameron Road, Ikoyi, Lagos, Nigeria.

SHONGA, Prince Casten, b. 11 Jan. 1951, Mrewha Mission, Zimbabwe. Journalist. m. Catherine Nelly Mbizi, 29 Dec. 1977, 1 son 1 daughter. *Education:* Diploma in Journalism, 1979, Africa Literature Centre. *Appointments:* Printer; Journalist. *Memberships:* Chairman, The Editorial Advisory Board, Moni Popular publications. *Publications:* Fiction; News & Features Writer; Photo-Journalist. *Hobbies:* Reading, Writing. *Address:* Ezondweni Village, P.A. Mtwalo, P.O. Ewendeni, Mzimba District, Malawi.

SHOOBRIDGE, Michael Philip Kendal, b. 24 Oct. 1921, Hobart, Tasmania. Medical Practitioner (Pathologist). m. Audrey T. Jacobson, 11 Nov. 1950, 2 sons, 2 daughters. *Education:* MB, BS University of Melbourne (& Trinity College) 1940-45; University of London, Internal course for Diploma of Clinical Pathology at Hammersmith Hospital. DCP 1952-1953. *Appointments:* Resident Medical Officer at Launceston General Hospital, Tasmania 1945; Senior RMO & Acting Pathologist at LGH Tasmania, 1946; Assigned Royal Melbourne Hospital (Victoria Pathology), 1946-47; Pathologist, LGH. Tasmania, 1947-56; Pathologist Box Hill & District Hospital, Victoria, 1956-. Tutor Medical Students, Pathology University of Melbourne, 1956-. *Memberships:* Fellow & Chairman of various posts in Australia. *Hobbies:* Carpentry, Sculpture, Genealogy. *Address:* 23 Naughton Grove, Blackburn, 3130, Victoria, Australia.

SHORE, Mary Catherine, b. 9 Mar. 1943, Edmonton, Alberta, Canada. Music Educator, Organist/Choirmaster. m. Kenneth William Thomas Carleton, 16 Apr. 1977. *Education:* ARCM, 1964, LRAM, 1965, Royal College of Music, London; FTCL, 1974, University of London; BM, 1975, University of London; MA, 1980. *Appointments:* Head, Music Department, St. Joseph's Acadamy, Blackheath, 1970-; Assistant Examiner, University of London, 1977-; Schools Council Steering Committee N & F Level Music, 1975-77; Music Panel, LREB, 1979-; Music 16 plus Working Party 1980-; Visiting Examiner AEB, 1976; Organist/Choirmaster, St. Margarets Parish Church, Lee, 1979. *Memberships:* CNAA Music Board; Southwark Diocesan Exec. Comm., Royal Schl. Ch. Music; Incorporated Soc. Musicians; Royal College of Organists; University of London Subject Advisory Panel, 1980. *Honours:* Winner, Vancouver Int. Festival in Organ Perf. 1964. *Hobbies:* Coach-

ing Swimming, Tennis. *Address:* 74 Micheldever Road, Lee, London SE12 8LU, England.

SHOUCRI, Magdi Mounir, b 1 Oct. 1940, Alexandria, Egypt. Physicist. m. Fayza Melek, 6 Oct. 1946, 2 daughters. *Education:* BSc, Faculty of Engineering , Alexandria, Egypt, 1965; MSc, Stanford University, California, USA, 1970; MSc, University of Iowa, USA, 1972; PhD, University of Iowa, USA, 1974. *Appointments:* Atomic Energy Establishment, Egypt, 1965-68; Dept. of Electrical Engineering, Laval University, Quebec, Canada, 1974-77; Institute de Recherche Hydro, Quebec (IREQ), Canada, 1977-. *Memberships:* IEEE; APS (American Physical Society); Smithsonian Association. *Hobbies:* Classic Music, History. *Address:* 30 Frontenac O, St. Bruno J3V1B7, Canada.

SHOYOMBO, L. Ayinde, (Chief) b. 22 June 1930, Abeokuta, Nigeria. Business Administrator. m. 10 Jan. 1952, 5 sons, 6 daughters. *Education:* FID London, 1974; AMIM, Nigeria, 1975. *Appointments:* Stores Building Materials Manager, 1954-64; Managing Director, 1964-73; Chairman, 1974-81. *Honours:* FIFA Grade in Refereeing of Football; Fellow, Institute of Directors, London; Associate Member, Nigerian Institute of Management. *Hobbies:* Sports, Writing, Reading, Swimming. *Address:* 81 Olateju Street, Challenge, Mushiu, Lagos, Nigeria.

SHRIVASTAVA, Benode Krisbna, b. 7 July 1928, Darbhanga, Bihar, India. Doctor. m. Prem Manishrivastava, 19 June 1947, 2 sons. *Education:* MBBS 1952; MD, 1958; PhD, 1964; All Patna University, India. *Appointments:* Demonstrator in Physiology 1953-58; Lecturer in Physiology, 1958-64; Professor of Physiology, 1964-77; Principal Head of the Department of Physiology & Dean Faculty of Medicine, 1977-80. *Memberships:* Secretary Indian Medical Association; Convenor PreMedical & Dental Research; Editor & Secretary, Patna Medical College, Magazine. *Publications:* Contributor of reviews, monographs, articles to professional journals and conferences. *Honours:* Physiology, 1949; Colombo Plan Fellow, University of Western Australia. *Hobbies:* Fishing, Vocal Music. *Address:* Principal's Quarter, Bhagalfour Medical College, Bhafalfour, Bihar, India.

SHUKLA, Mahendra Pratap, b. 18 June 1932, Kanpur, India. Engineer. m. S. Shukla, 19 Jan. 1956, 3 sons. *Education:* Degree Electrical Engineering, 1951-55. *Appointments:* Project Manager/Divisional Manager, 1972-76; General Manager, Indian Telephone Industries, Naini, Allahabad; Chairman/Managing Director, Telecommunications Consultants India Ltd., 1978-. *Memberships:* Fellow, Institute Electronics & Telecommunication Engineers (India). *Publications:* Author, number articles published in Newspapers & Magazines on Management of Indian Telephone Industries. *Hobbies:* Tennis, Bird Watching. *Address:* E-21, Panchsheel Park, New Delhi 17, India.

SHURING, Catriona Gail, b. 25 Apr. 1945, Chelmsford, Essex, England. Librarian. m. Peter Richard Graham Moule, 28 Nov. 1970. *Education:* BSc, University Liverpool, 1966; MSc, University Birmingham, 1972; Dip. Librarianship University, New South Wales, Australia, 1974. *Appointments:* National Vegetable Research Station, Wellesbourne, Warwickshire, Assistant Experimental Officer, Plant Pathology Section, 1966-72; Marrickville Municipal Library, Sydney, NSW, 1972-74; Hellyer Regional Library, Burnie, Tasmania, 1975-. *Memberships:* Secretary, NARG, 1975-76; Burnie Field Naturalists Secretary, 1977-. *Publications:* Technical Articles in plant pathology field. *Hobbies:* Natural History, Sociology, Bushwalking, Local Historical Research. *Address:* 33 McPhee Street, Havenview, Burnie, Tasmania 7320, Australia.

SHUTE, John Lawson, b. 31. Jan. 1901, Mudgee, NSW, Australia. Primary Production Involving Allied Organisations. m. Constance Winifred Mary Douglas, 16 Jan. 1936, 2 sons. *Appointments:* Secretary, Director, Chairman etc. of many Government & Commercial Companies. *Memberships:* Chairman, Australian Meat Board, 1946-70; Chairman, Australian Committee of Animal Production, 1947-70; Chairman, Australian Cattle Beef & Meat Research Committee, 1960-70; NSW Rural Reconstruction Board, 1942-71; Australia/Britain Society Eastwood District Rugby Football Commercial Travellers Club; Royal Agricultural Society of NSW. *Honours:* OBE 1959; CMG 1970; Freedom of City London, 1951; Life Member, Rural Youth Movement, NSW, 1961; Hon. Life Member, Australian Veterinary Association 1969; Life Member, Eastwood District Rugby Union Football Club, 1951. *Hobbies:* Football/Rugby Union International, Cricket, Swimming. *Address:* The Wold, 2 Woonona Avenue, Wahroonga, NSW, Australia 2076

SICHULA, Maxwell Duncan, b. 7 Dec. 1938, Chingola, Zambia. Business Executive. m. Tina Mwimba, 7 Aug. 1969, 2 sons, 2 daughters. *Education:* BA, University Manitoba, Canada, 1966; BL, University of Zambia, 1980. *Appointments:* Assistant Personnel Superintendent, Roan Consolidated Mines, 1970-71; Group Personnel Manager, Indeco Breweries, 1972; general Manager, Timber Merchant, Zambia, 1973; Manager, Roan Consolidated Mines, 1973-1976; Personnel Director, Roan Consolidated, 1976-. *Memberships:* Chairman of Zambia Federation of Employers; Vice Chairman of Zambia Institute Personnel Management. *Honours:* Awarded Fellowship of the Institute of Personnel Management of Zambia, 1977; Won Sports Administrator Award, 1978. *Hobbies:* Sports playing & Organisation. *Address:* Plot 5488, Msanzara Road, Kalundu, Lusaka.

SIDAMBARAM, OBE., Mootoosamy, b. 3 Nov. 1926, Port Louis, Mauritius. Bank Manager. m. Logersoondery Atmarow, 25 Mar. 1959, 1 daughter. *Appointments:* General Manager, Mauritius Co-Operative Central Bank Ltd.; Chairman, State Insurance Corporation of Mauritius; Director, Development Bank of Mauritius; Consultant, Food and Agricultural Organisation of the U.N. on Agricultural; Credit, Co-operative Banking and Rural Development; President, Co-operative Development Council, Mauritius; Chairman, National Co-operative Planning Commission. *Memberships:* Tamil League; Mauritius Gymkanah Club; Saint Geran Golf Club; Trou Aux Biches Golf Club. *Publications:* Role and functions of Co-operative Bank. *Honours:* OBE 1974. *Hobbies:* Golf; Tennis: Swimming. *Address:* 18 Bis Frere Felix de Valois, Port Louis, Mauritius.

SIDERIS, Andreas, b. 3 Sept. 1932, Patras, Greece. Mechanical/Electrical Engineer. m. Despina Irene, 30 Jan. 1958, 1 sons. *Education:* MSc Mechanical/Electrical Engineering, Technical University of Athens. *Appointments:* 3rd Engineer, Merchant Navy, 1956-57; Served Military Service, 1958-60; National Organisation of Tourism, Greece, 1960-61; Self employed, Construction of 400V and 11KV O/H Lines for national power authority, Greece. Chief Engineer, Paterson, Zochonis Industries Ltd., 1964-. Technical Director, 1974-. *Memberships:* Technical Institute of Greece. *Hobbies:* Chess; Reading. *Address:* 51 Sobo Arobiodu, Gra, Ikeya, Nigeria.

SIDHU, Sher Singh, b. 10 Oct. 1933, Gabbe Majra, India. Dentist (Orthodontist). m. Swarn, 18 Oct. 1959, 2 sons. *Education:* BDS, Punjab University, 1956; MDS, Bombay University, 1966; DFR diploma, Oslo University, 1972. *Appointments:* Demonstrator, Dental Wing, Madras Medical College, Madras, 1956-57; Demonstrator, Dental College and Hospital, Amritsar, 1957-58; Chief Dental Surgeon, B.R. Singh Hospital, Calcutta, 1958-60; Head, Department of Dental Surgery, All India Institute of Medical Sciences, New Delhi, 1960-. *Memberships:* Chairman, 15th Indian Orthodontic Conference, 1980; President, Delhi Dental Association, 1979-80; Scientific Editor, Journal of International College of Dentists, India Section since 1974; Chairman, Council on Dental Health, 1967-69; Member, Dental Council of India, 1978-81. *Publications:* 93 Publications; Editor Recommendations of W.H.O. Workshop on Dental Disease and Oro-facial Anomalies in Children, 1979. Your Teeth in Hindi is in press. *Honours:* Recipient of numerous honours and awards for professional services. *Hobbies:* Gardening. *Address:* Department of Dental Surgery, All India Institute of Medical Sciences, New Delhi-110029, India.

SIGAMANY, Gladys, (Mrs. A. G. Sigamany), b. 17 Mar. 1926, Coimbatore, Tamilnadu, India. Nursing. m. Alexander Gnanam, 27 Dec. 1954, 1 son, 2 daughters. *Education:* BSc, Nursing, Madras University, India, 1952; MSc, Nursing University of Wasington, USA. *Appointments:* Sister-Tutor, Bai Jerbai Wadia Hospital for Children, Bombay, 1956-57; Sister-Tutor, St. Margarets Hospital, Poona, 1959-63; Senior Lecturer, L.T.

College of Nursing, S.N.D.T. Women's University, Bombay, 1966-70; Principal, L.T. College of Nursing S.N.D.T. Women's University, Bombay. 1970-; Dean, Faculty of Nursing, 1978-. *Memberships:* Member and Chairman of various boards in Bombay. *Publications:* Masters Thesis, Changes in the Status of Women and their implications for the Growth and Development of nursing; Role of nurses in Family Planning, Published in the Journal of Family Planning Association of India. *Honours:* Recipient of numerous honours and awards for professional services. *Hobbies:* Stamp collecting; Monogram spoons from various countries. *Address:* 3rd Floor, S.N.D.T. Women's University, Bombay, 400 020, India.

SIGOLA, Simon Madewe, b. 1907 Esiphezini, Essexvale. Farmer/Chief (Tribal). m. 1934, 18 children. *Appointments:* Member: The Natural Resources Board; The Mpilo Hospital Committee; The Whaley Commission; The Moncton Commission; Chairman of Esiphezini Council; Member of the Chief's Council; The Senate; The Dumbutshena; Commission of Enquiry. *Honours:* MBE, ICD. *Hobbies:* Hunting. *Address:* Box 2113, Bulawayo, Zimbabwe.

SIJUWADE, Okunade Adele, (His Majesty), b. 1 Jan. 1930, Ile Ife, Oyo State, Nigeria. Traditional Ruler. m. Nee Oyetunde Oyebode, 20 Oct. 1959, 1 son, 4 daughters. *Education:* Diploma in Business Administration, 1955. *Appointments:* Trainee Manager, 1957; Manager, 1959; Assistant to group Chairman, 1962; Director of many companies, 1968; Chairman and Shareholder of many companies, 1970. *Memberships:* Member, Island Club; Patron, Yoruba Tennis Club; Patron, Ife Country Club; Patron, Ife Action Committee. *Honours:* JP, 1981. *Hobbies:* Swimming; Squash; Horse Riding. *Address:* The Palace,, Ile Ife, Oyo State, Nigeria.

SILADY, Stephen, b. 18 Dec. 1922, Kotoriba, Yugoslavia. Company Director (3) Engineering. m. Pauline, 1 July 1967. *Appointments:* Stromberg Carlson Aust. Pty Ltd., Derwent Thermostats Pty Ltd., Derwent Controls; Derwent Plastics; Derwent Book Company; World trip with the Boomerang; Television appearances in Canada, United States and London. *Memberships:* Australian Boomerang Association. *Publications:* The Australian Boomerang, Co-author with wife Pauline Pahlow. *Honours:* Australian distance boomerang champion, 1964. *Hobbies:* Making and throwing returning boomerangs; Gardening. *Address:* 152 Greville Street, Chatswood, 2067, Sydney, Australia.

SILLITOE, Alan, b. 4 Mar. 1928, Nottingham. Author. m. 20 Oct. 1959. *Education:* Hon. Degree, Manchester Polytechnic, 1975. *Appointments:* Labourer, 1942; Capstan Lathe Operator, 1944; Air Traffic Control Assistant with Ministry of Aircraft Production, 1945-6. *Memberships:* Royal United Services Institute; Royal Geographical Society; Savage Club. *Publications:* Prolific writer of novels, stories, poems and plays, 1958-80, including: Her Victory, 1982; The Second Chance, 1980; Snow on the North Side of Lucifer, 1979; Three Plays, 1979. *Honours:* Hawthornden prize for literature, 1960. *Hobbies:* Cartography; Wireless communication; Navigation; Travel. *Address:* 21 The Street, Wittersham, Kent, England.

SILUNGWE, Annel Musenga, b. 10 Jan. 1936, Mbala, Zambia. Lawyer, Barrister at Law, LLM. m. Abigail, 2 sons, 4 daughters. *Appointments:* Resident Magistrate; Senior Resident Magistrate, Puisne Judge; Minister of Legal Affairs and Attorney-General; Chief Justice. *Memberships:* Past President, Rotary Club of Lusaka Central; District Governor Elect, Rotary International, 1982-83; Chairman, Physical Handicap Society; Vice President, Zambia Students Association, UK; Member of the Executive, Christian Council of Zambia; Board Member, Bible Society of Zambia; Member of the Synod Executive, United Church of Zambia. *Honours:* State Counsel, 1975. *Hobbies:* Golf, Lawn and Table Tennis; Photography; Music. *Address:* 15 Kafue Road, Roma Township, Lusaka, Zambia.

SIMBOTWE, Philip Malumo, b. 25 June, 1950, Mazabuka, Southern Zambia. Research Biologist. m. 7 May 1976, Mirriam, 1 son, 1 daughter. *Education:* BSc. 1975; MS, Systematics and Ecology, 1979, Universities of Zambia and Kansas, USA respectively. *Appointments:* National Museums Board of Zambia, 1975; Keeper of Herpetology and Head of the Research Division, Department of Natural History, 1975-81. *Memberships:* Member of various societies including: The New York Academy of Sciences; The Herpetologists League; The Ecological Society of Australia; The Wildlife Conservation Society of Zambia. *Publications:* Reproductive Biology of Zambian Reptiles, 1980; Feeding Habits of Zambian Reptiles, 1979; Parasites of Zambian Reptiles, 1979; Research Activities at the Livingstone Museum; (Department of Natural History) Herpetology, 1979; A Survey of Snakebite in Zambia, 1981. *Honours:* Recipient of numerous honours and awards for professional services. *Hobbies:* Playing Soccer; Listening to Music (Classics); Reading Fiction; Going to Movies. *Address:* Kabompo 64, Livingstone, Zambia.

SIMINIALAYI, Alpheus Biedimado Siminialayi, b. 19 Feb. 1930, Opoba-Town, Rivers State Nigeria. Industrial Chemist. m. Aster Arinye Pepple, 16 Jan. 1949, 1 son 3 daughters. *Education:* BSc, Maukato State College, Minnesoto, USA. 1953-57. *Appointments:* Principal, Academy Secondary Grammar School, Sapele; Chemist, Nigerian Glass Coy. Ltd., Port Harcourt; Deputy Works Managers, Calabar Cement Co. Ltd. Calabar. *Memberships:*Chairman, Ugele Nkpa Society of Nigeria; Nigerian Chemical Society. *Hobbies:* Swimming, Lawn Tennis. *Address:* Sodienye Villa, Opobo Town, Rivers State, Nigeria.

SIMMONDS, Edward Harold Stuart, b. 7 Aug. 1919, Little Hampton, Sussex, England. University Professor. m. Patricia Gilder, 28 July 1953. *Education:* BA 1948; MA 1952; University of Oxford. *Appointments:* Lecturer in Linguistics SOAS, University London 1948-51; Lecturer in Tai, University of London 1951-66; Reader in Tai Language & Literature, 1966-70; Professor of Language & Literature South East Asia University London, 1970-; Pro-director, SOAS, 1981-. *Memberships:* Asiatic Society President, 1973-76; Director, 1965-68; Philological Society, Siam Society, Royal Institute of International Affairs etc. *Publications:* The Royal Asiatic Society, Its History & Treasures, 1979; Numerous Articles in learned Journals on Literature, Linguistics & politics of Thailand and Laos. *Address:* 18 J. Lennox Gardens, London SW1, England.

SIMON, Barry Douglas, b. 1 Apr. 1936, Dandenong, Victoria, Australia. Ministerial Secretary. m. Ruth Gottlieb, 7 Mar. 1961, 3 sons. *Education:* LLB, Melbourne, 1962. *Appointments:* Barrister & Solicitor, Melbourne, 1962-72; MP, House of Representatives, Parliament of Commonwealth Australia, 1975-80; Principal Private Secretary to Hon. Andrew Peacock MP, Minister for Industrial Relations, Australian Parliament. *Address:* Bathe Road, Pakenham, Victoria, Australia.

SIMON, Pierre, b. 12 Dec. 1929, Mulhouse, France, Management Consultant. *Education:* MA, 1971, PhD, 1975, University of Montreal, Canada. *Appointments:* Freelance Management Consultant, 1972-78; Analytical Research Consultants (ARC), Montreal, Quebec, President, Chief Executive Officer, 1970. *Publications:* Author of nine books, some 30 articles in various journals and some 20 research documents. *Hobbies:* Ski, Tennis, Scuba Diving, Bridge, Poker, Chess, Baggomon, Fine Arts, Music. *Address:* 5703 Durocher, Outremont, Montreal, H2V 3Y3, Quebec, Canada.

SIMOS, Theodore, b. 26 Apr. 1934, Katoomba, NSW, Australia. Barrister. m. Helen Mary Donnelly, 10 Jan. 1962, 2 sons, 1 daughter. *Education:* BA, University Sydney, 1953; LLB, 1956 BLitt, University Oxford, 1958; MLitt, 1980; LLM, Harvard University, 1959. *Appointments:* Admitted New South Wales Bar, 1956; Queen's Counsel, 1974; Lecturer (part-time) in Equity, University of Sydney Law School, 1966-74; Part-time Member, Australian Reform Commission, 1982. *Memberships:*Australian Bar Association, Honorary Secretary, 1968-69; NSW, Bar Association, Member, Council, 1965-67, 1976-79; Commercial Law Association of Australia Ltd.; Member Council, 1975-82; Sydney University Law Graduates Association, Vice President; Harvard Club of Australia, President, 1974-76. *Publications:* Editor, Australian Bar Gazette, 1966-70; Student Editor in Chief Sydney Law Review, 1955. *Honours:* University of Sydney Medal for LLB Degree, 1956; University of Sydney Post Graduate Research Travelling Scholarship, 1956-58. *Hobbies:* Tennis, Fishing. *Address:* Wentworth Chambers, 180 Phillip Street, Sydney, NSW 2000, Australia.

SIMPSON, Bruce Butler, b. 16 Aug. 1936, Townsville, Queensland, Australia. Chartered Accountant. m. Janette Reynallt Hopkins 1 Sept. 1960, 3 sons, 1 daughter. *Education:* FCA, Institute of Chartered Acountants, Australia, 1958; ACIS, Institute of Chartered Secretaries & Administrators 1959. *Appointments:* Deloitte, Haskins & Sells, Chartered Accountants, 1954, Partner, 1970-. *Memberships:* Insitute of Chartered Accountants, Australia; Institute of Chartered Secretaries & Administrators (ACIS). *Hobbies:* Golf, Photography, Travel. *Address:* 2 Culworth Avenue, Killara, NSW, Australia 2071.

SIMPSON, Elizabeth Robson (Mrs. Alfred Moxon Simpson), b. 16 Oct. 1910 Sydney, NSW, Australia. m. 3 Aug. 1938, 1 son. *Education:* BSc, 1931, First Class Honours, 1933, MSc, 1935, University of Adelaide. *Appointments:* Demonstrator in Charge Zoology, University of Adelaide, 1932-38; Lecturer in Biology, Member of Education Committee, Member of College Council, Chairman of Kindergarten Union of S. Aust. 1945-74; Vice President, Acting President of Kingston College of Advanced Education, 1974-78; Appointed to Board of the South Australian Museum 1952-. *Memberships:* Fellow of Royal Society of S. Aust; Contemporary Arts Society of S. Aust.; Fellow of Royal Society of Arts of S. Australia. *Publications:* Contributed to various professional journals. *Honours:* 1929 John Bagor Scholarship & Medal, University of Adelaide. *Hobbies:* Painting, Travel in Outback Central Australian Deserts, Skiing, Gardening, Tapestry, Study of child development. *Address:* 31 Heatherbank Terrace, Stonyfell, South Australia 5066.

SIMPSON, Newton Lloyd, b. 11 Sept. 1930, Wudinna, South Australia. m. Doreen May Heier, 2 sons, 2 daughters. *Education:* 1952 College of the Bible, Glen Iris, Melbourne, Studies for Leaving Certificate. *Appointments:* Board member of Apex; Chairman, Wudinna Area School Council; Chairman, District Council of Le Hunti. *Creative Works:* Country Fire Service, 1956-. *Hobbies:* Table Tennis. *Address:* Box 79, Wudinna, South Australia 5652.

SIMPSON, Robert Gordon, b. 27 Dec. 1920, Warkworth, New Zealand. Master Mariner; Company Director. m. Helen Irene Whale, 27 Feb. 1944, 2 sons. *Education:* Master Mariner, Foreign Going Vessels, London, 1946. *Appointments:* General Manager/Director, Brisbane Wharves and Wool Dumping Pty. Ltd; Chairman/Directors, Newstead Wharves Pty. Ltd; Director, Brisbane Carrying Company Pty. Ltd. *Memberships:* Fellow, Australian Institute of Management; Fellow, The Chartered Institute of Transport; Company of Master Mariners of Australia; Fellow, Society of Senior Executives; The Institute of Materials Handling; The Mission to Seamen, Brisbane. *Honours:* Justice of the Peace, Queensland. *Hobbies:* Fruit Growing; Wine Making; Fishing. *Address:* 365 Swann Road, St Lucia, Brisbane, Queensland 4067, Australia.

SIMPSON, William, b. 5 Mar. 1917, Wick. Company Director/Consultant. m. Maisie Helen Fraser, 15 Sept. 1942, 1 son 1 daughter. *Education:* MA, 1937, Dip. Ed. 1938, Edinburgh University. *Appointments:* British Army, 1939-46, Major; HMCS, Nigeria, Permanent Secretary Minister of Health, Ministry of Internal Affairs, Secretary, Public Service Commission, 1946-61; Director, Communications Consultants (Nigeria) Ltd.; Cutler Hammer (Nigeria) Ltd. *Memberships:* Chairman, Anglo-Cameroon Society, London. *Hobbies:* Sailing. *Address:* 5 Northcliffe Gardens, Broadstairs, Kent, England.

SIN, Ka Fung Paul, b. 6 Nov. 1948. Guangzhou, China. Building Services Engineer. m. 14 Mar, 1975, 2 daughters. *Education:* Certificate in air conditioning engineering, 1973, University of Hong Kong; Endorsement certificate in refrigeration, 1972, Hong Kong Polytechnic; Higher certificate in mechanical engineering, 1971. *Appointments:* Engineering assistant, public works department, Hong Kong Government, 1968-72; Engineer in J. Roger Preston & Partners, 1972-75; Senior B.S. Engineer in Bylander Meinhardt partnership, 1975-76; Project engineer in Hutchison Boag Engineering Ltd., 1976-78; Senior partner of K.C.T.C. & Associates Mechanical. & Electrical Consultant Engineers, 1978- *Memberships:* Hon. Secretary of A.E.E. (Hong Kong Chapter); T. ENG. (CEI): ACIBS: M Inst. R; MASHRAE; MAIRAH; MIEEE; MBIM; MPSHK;

MAEE; AMHKIE. *Publications:* Paper presented in a seminar by the Physical Society of Hong Kong. *Hobbies:* Music; Football; Boating; Reading; Planting. *Address:* Flat 1, Block E, 8th Floor, Shun Tai House, Shun Chi Court, Clearwater Bay Road, Kowloon, Hong Kong.

SINCLAIR, Barry, Whitley. b. 23 Oct. 1936, Wellington, New Zealand. General Manager. m. Helen Mavis Reynolds, 4 Jan. 1967, 2 sons. *Appointments:* Shell Oil, NZ Ltd., 1955-61; Goodyear Tyre & Rubber Co. NZ Ltd., 1961-70; Ponsford, Newmay & Benson 1948 Ltd., 1970-78; L.D. Nathan (Wholesale) Ltd., 1979-; Beverage Services Ltd., 1981. *Memberships:* Kilbirnie Cricket Club, Wellington; North Shore Cricket Club, Auckland; New Zealand Cricket Representative, 1960-70; Captain, 1966-68; Ngataringa Tennis Club, Auckland. *Address:* 23b Stanley Point Road, Stanley Bay, Auckland, 9, New Zealand.

SINCLAIR, Ernest Keith, b. 13 Nov. 1914, Hawthorn, Victoria, Australia. Journalist, Consultant, Department of Prime Minister & Cabinet, 1967-80; Company Director. m. Jill Eddison, 23 June, 1949, 1 son. *Education:* Bendigo, Hampton & Melbourne High Schools, 1920-32; matriculation (Hons.) 1932. *Appointments:* Journalist, Consultant, Company Director, 1932-81, including Editorial Staff, 'The Age', Melbourne, 1932-38; War Service, Royal Air Force, 1940-45; Editorial Staff 'Sydney Morning Herald', London, 1945-46; Editor, 'The Age', Director, Gen. Telev. Corp. Channel 9, Director Australian Associated Press, 1958-66, Chairman, 1965-66; Commissioner, Australian Tourist Commission, 1967-75; Director, Australian Paper Manufacturers Ltd., 1966-; Associate Commissioner, Industries Assistance Commission for specific enquiries, 1974-80; Commissioner, Australian Heritage Commission, 1976-81. *Memberships:* Library Council of Victoria, 1966-79; Board of Studies, Journalism, Melbourne University, 1958-63; Humanities Board, Victoria Institute of Colleges, 1967-71. *Publications:* Literary articles on Historical and Current Affairs in Daily press. *Honours:* DFC, 1943; Mentioned in Despatches, 1944; OBE (Mil), 1945; CMG, 1966; Awarded USA Smith Mundt Leader Grant, 1963. *Hobbies:* Gardening; Reading. *Address:* 21-23 Spindrift Avenue, Flinders, Victoria, Australia, 3929.

SINCLAIR, Geoffrey William Gladstone, b. 10 Nov. 1929, Melbourne, General Surgeon. m. Marjorie Diane Woodfull, 1 Feb. 1955, 5 sons, 1 daughter. *Education:* Scotch College, Melbourne, 1939-47; Bachelor of Medicine; Bachelor of Surgery University, Melbourne, 1953; Master of Surgery, University of Melbourne, 1959; FRACS, 1958; FRCS, England, 1959. *Appointments:* Asst. Surgeon, Royal Melbourne Hospital, 1960-65; Honorary Jnr.Surgeon, Queen Victoria Hospital, Melbourne, 1960-64; Honorary Surgeon, Footscray & District Hospital, 1962-64; Honorary Surgeon, Box Hill & District Hospital, 1964-75; Senior Surgeon, Box Hill Hospital, 1975; Visiting Surgeon, St. George's Hospital, Kew. *Memberships:* Chairman, State Committee Australian Association of Surgeons, 1978-79; President, Federal Council, 1979-80. *Hobbies:* Golf. *Address:* Wimba, 235, Cotham Road, Kew, 3101, Victoria, Australia.

SINCLAIR, Ian MaCahon, (The Rt. Hon) b. 10 June 1929, Sydney. Grazier, Member of Parliament. m. (1) Margaret Tarrant (Deceased), 1 son, 2 daughters; (2) Rosemary Fenton, 1956, 1 son. *Education:* Grazier, Glenclair, Bendemeer, New South Wales, 1953; Country Party Member, Legislative Council, New South Wales, 1961-1963; Elected Federal Member, New England House of Representatives, 1963; Ministerial Portfolios include: Minister for Social Services, 1965-1968; Minister for Shipping and Transport 1968-71; Minister for Primary Industry, 1971-1972, 1975-1979; Minister for Communications, 1980-. *Address:* Glenclair, Bendemeer, New South Wales, Australia.

SINCLAIR, John, b. 13 July, 1939, Maryborough, Queensland. Public Servant; Educationist. m. Helen Grace, 19 May, 1962, 3 sons. *Education:* Queensland Diploma in Agriculture, 1959; Bachelor of Economics, University of Queensland, 1974; Diploma in Continuing Education, University of New England, 1980 *Appointments:* Organiser of Rural Youth Clubs, Queensland Dept. of Education, 1960-67; Organiser of Adult Education Programmes, Queensland Dept. of Educa-

tion, 1967-. *Memberships:* Vice President, Australian Conservation Foundation; President, Fraser Island Defenders Organisation Ltd., President, Wildlife Preservation Society of Queensland; Environmental Planning Commission of International Union for Conservation of Nature (IUCN). *Publications:* Author of Discovering Fraser Island & Discovering Cooloola. *Honours:* Recipient of Australian of the Year, 1976. *Hobbies:* Conservation; Natural History; Researching Australianna. *Address:* 27 Quarry Street, Ipswich, Queensland, 4305, Australia.

SINCLAIR, Peter Malcolm, b. 6 Oct. 1935, Auburn, NSW, Australia, Business Consultant. m. 6 April 1956, 1 son, 1 daughter. *Education:* Fellow, Australian Institute of Export, 1971; Fellow, Institute of Directors, 1980. *Appointments:* Bakers Milk (TAS) Pty Ltd, 1954; General Manager & Director, Bakers Milk (TAS) Pty Ltd, 1971-75; Director-General, Planning & Development, Tasmania, 1977-1980; Business Consultant, 1980-. *Memberships:* Australian President, Market Milk Fed., 1969-1971; President, Lions Club of Hobart, 1971-1972; Director, Australian Bicentennial Authority, 1980; Chairman, Private Forestry Council, 1978; Athenaeum (Hobart); MCC (London); Kingston Beach Golf Club; Royal Hobart Bowls Club. *Hobbies:* Bowls; Golf; Sailing; Reading. *Address:* 3, Binney Court, Sandy Bay 7005, Tasmania, Australia.

SINGBAL, Sadananda Yeshwant, b. 22 Feb. 1942, Betruz, Ponda, Goa, India. Scientist. m. 23 Dec. 1977. *Education:* MSc. University of Bombay; Diploma Marine Pollution, University of Liverpool. *Appointments:* Junior Scientific Asst., 1970-71; Senior Scientific Asst., 1971-74; Scientist B, 1974-79 Scientist C, 1979-. *Memberships:* Member of Indian Association for Water Pollution Control; Member of Fisheries Tech. of India. *Publications:* Approx. 30 papers relating to Chemical Oceanography & marine Pollution. *Hobbies:* Readings; Chess Play. *Address:* Near the Church, Napusa 403507, Goa, India.

SINGH, Ajit, b. 4th Nov. 1924, India, Professor, Physiologist. m. Shil A. 8th Dec. 1951, 2 Daughters. *Education:* BVSc, Punjab University, 1946; MCSc, Punjab University, 1956; MS Ohio State University, USA, 1958; PhD, Michigan State University, USA, 1966. *Appointments:* Lect. Dept. Physiology. Vet. College Hissar, 1947-55; Asst. Prof. Physiology, Vet. College Hissar, 1956-58; Prof. Physiology, Vet. Collect/Punjab Agricul. Univ. Hissar, 1959-61; Prof. & Head of Dept of Physiology & Pharmacology, Punjab Agricul. Univ. Hissar, 1967-69; Dean, College of Vet. Med. PAU Ludhiana, 1970-73, Prof. Dept. Human Physiology, Admadu Bello Univ. Zaria, Nigeria, 1973-. *Memberships:* Memberships of Several Professional and Academic Societies. *Publications:* Contributed 67 articles to Professional Journals. *Honours:* Won Government merit scholarship, 1945; Awarded medal, 1945; Awarded Fellowship, ICA, 1957-58; Awarded Fellowship, Rockefeller Foundation, 1964-66; FIBA, 1980. *Hobbies:* Educational; Social Work. *Address:* Professor, Human Physiology Dept, Ahmadu Bellow Univ., Zaria, Nigeria.

SINGH, Bhagwant, b. 7 July 1926, Simla, India. Professor of Economics. *Education:* PhD, University of Maryland, 1962; MS, Cornell University, 1957; MA. Forman Christian College, Punjab Univ., 1948; Certificate Economics, Ohio State University; Co-sponsored by Economic and Cultural Council, New York, 1958; *Appointments:* Teaching, Consulting, Administrative & Research Experience in Universities & Academic Institutions of Higher Learning in North America, South America, Europe, Africa and Asia, particularly in Commonwealth Countries. Most recent appointments. Visiting Professor, Faculty of Arts & Sciences, Harvard Univ. USA, 1977-78; Professeur invite, Universite de Montreal (Dept de Sciences Economiques), 1977; Colombo Plan Visiting Prof of Economics at University Sains Malaysia, Penang, Malaysia, 1972-73. *Honours:* Certificate of Merit for distinguished service in International Economic Development from the Dictionary of International Biography; Certificate for distinguished achievements from The International Who's Who of Intellectuals and International Register of Profiles; Certificate of Proclamation and Fellow Membership of Preferential standing of the Publication Board of the American Biographical Institute; Community Leaders and Noteworthy Americans Award; and Notable Americans of Bicentennial Era Award. *Publications:* Contributor of reviews, monographs, articles to professional journals and conferences. *Address:* 17, Limerick Place, St. John's Newfoundland, Canada, A1B 2H2.

SINGH, Garnish Benedict, b. 2 Dec. 1927, Lusignan, ECD, Guyana. Roman Catholic Bishop in Guyana. *Education:* MA, 1951; STD, 1957. *Appointments:* Parish Priest, 1959; Chancellor of the Diocese of Georgetown, 1969; Auxiliary Bishop of Georgetown, 1971; Bishop of Georgetown, 1972. *Memberships:* Sacred Congregation for the Evangelisation of Peoples (Rome); Antilles Episcopal Conference; Guyana Council of Churches. *Hobbies:* Conjuring. *Address:* 27, Brickdam, Georgetown, Guyana, (South America).

SINGH, Joseph Sukhendra, b. 28 Oct. 1938, Suva, Fiji Islands. Land Economist. m. Caroline, 8 Aug. 1957, 5 sons, 2 daughters. *Appointments:* Trainee, Local Construction Company, 1954; Technical Assistant, Survey-/Civil Engineering, New Zealand Ministry of Works; Held many senior posts, Fiji Government Department of Lands, 1959-75; Land Economist/Property Manager, Carpenters Fiji Ltd., 1977. *Memberships:* President of the Institute of Valuation and Estate management of Fiji; Committee of Review Agricultural Landlord and Tenant Act. *Creative Works:* Radio Broadcaster direct commentaries and Commentator of soccer matches for Radio Fiji since 1975. *Hobbies:* Meeting people; Service to School and Church organisations; Reading; Travelling. *Address:* 54 Votua Road, Samabula North, Suva, Fiji.

SINGH, Kirpal, b. 10 Mar. 1949, Singapore. Lecturer. m. Sandie, 21 Jan. 1979. *Education:* BA, Singapore, 1972; MA, Singapore, 1978; PhD, Adelaide, 1980. *Appointments:* Lecturer, University of Singapore, 1980. *Memberships:* Vice Chairman, Association of Commonwealth Language and Literature Studies, Singapore, 1979-80; Editor of SINGA Journal of the Ministry of Culture, Singapore, 1980; Member, Industrial Society for Education, Art; *Publications:* Singapore Pot-Pourri, 1970; Articulating, 1972; Twenty Poems, 1978; Wonder and Awe, 1980. *Honours:* Awarded the Singapore National Book Development Council Research Award, 1979. *Hobbies:* Stamps; Coins; Travelling. *Address:* 3 Preston Road, Singapore, 0314.

SINGH, Surjeet, b. 11 June 1942, Delhi, India. Teaching & Research. m. Nispal Kaur, 12 May 1968, 2 sons, 2 daughters. *Education:* BSc, Hons, Delhi University, 1961; MSc, Delhi University, 1963; PhD, Delhi University, 1969. *Appointments:* Research Fellow, CSIR, Delhi, 1963-64; Assistant Lecturer, Delhi University & K.M. College, 1964-65; Lecturer, Kirori Mal College, 1965-69; Reader, Aligarh Muslim University, Aligarh, 1969-75; Professor, Guru Nanah Dev University, Amritsar, 1975-. *Memberships:* Member, Indian Academy of Science, Allahabad; American Mathematical Society; Indian Mathematical Society. *Publications:* A number of Research Papers published. *Honours:* Visiting Scientist, various Universities: Ohio University, USA, Kuwait University, McMaster University, Canada, 1973-81. *Address:* Department of Mathematics, Kuwait University, P.O. Box 5969, Kuwait.

SINGH, Vishwanath Prasad, b. 2 Feb. 1931, Rharhapur, India, Management Consultant. m. 8 July 1945. *Education:* BCom; MCom; MSIIR; MAB; PhDCom. *Appointments:* Management Consultant. *Memberships:* International and Industrial Relations Association; Society of Professional in dispute relations; President, Sri Sathya Sai Baba Spiritual Council, Canada. *Hobbies:* Social Work. *Address:* 3582 Huntington Avenue, Windsor, Ontario, Canada, N9E 3M8.

SINGHAL, Damodar Prasad, b. 24 Sept. 1925, India. University Teacher. m. Dr. Devahutti, 18 May 1950. *Education:* MA, East Punjab, 1949; PhD, London, 1955; DLitt, Queensland, 1974. *Appointments:* Lecturer, History, University of Malaya, Singapore, 1956-61; Senior Lecturer, History, University of Queensland, Brisbane, 1961-63; Reader, History, University of Queensland, Brisbane, 1964-69; Professor, History, University of Queensland, Brisbane, 1969-. *Memberships:* Fellow, Royal Historical Society, London; Fellow, Royal Asiatic Society, London. *Publications:* The Annexation of Upper Burma; British Diplomacy and the Annexation of Upper Burma; India and Afghanistan: A Study in Diplomatic Relations 1876-1907; Nationalism in India and Other Historical Essays; India and World Civilization. British Diplomacy in Burma. *Hobbies:* Theatre; Travel; Reading. *Address:* 193 Carmody Road, St. Lucia, 4067, Brisbane, Queensland, Australia.

SINGHI, Shanti Tekchandra, b. 3 Feb. 1935, Bombay, Maharashtra, India. Gastroenterologic Medicine. m. Sushila Mohabatmal Modi, 1 son, 1 daughter. *Education:* MB, BS, University of Bombay, 1960; MD, Medicine and Therapeutics, University of Bombay, 1966. *Appointments:* Fellow, Gastroenterology, Northwestern University, Chicago, USA, 1969-70; Fellow, Gastroenterology, Mount Sinai Medical Center, Milwaukee, USA, 1970-71; Pool Officer, CSIR, Lokamanya Tilak Municipal General Hospital and Medical College, Bombay, 1971-73. *Memberships:* Life Member, Honorary Secretary, Society of Gastrointestinal Endoscopy, India, 1979-82; Life Member, Honorary Treasurer, Indian Society of Gastroenterology, 1981-84; Life Member, Association of Physicians, India; Member, Indian Medical Association; Fellow, American College of Gastroenterology; Active Member, The Bockus Alumni International Society of Gastroenterology. *Publications:* Contributed to various professional journals. *Honours:* Recipient of First Prize at Spring Clinic Day Conference at Mount Sinai Medical Centre, 1971; Recipient of First Prize for Carrom Tournament, Malad Medical Association, 1976-77. *Hobbies:* Photography; Carrom; Sight seeing; Reading. *Address:* Shanti-kunj, 56 Anand Road, Malad West, Bombay, Maharashtra, India 400 064.

SINGLETON, William Brian, b. 23 Feb. 1923, Darlington, County Durham, England. Veterinary Surgeon. m. Hilda Stott, 1 Jan. 1947, 2 sons, 2 daughters. *Education:* Queen Elizabeth Grammar School, Darlington; Royal Dick Veterinary College, Edinburgh. *Appointments:* Large Animal Practice, Barnard Castle, County Durham, 1945-47; Small Animal Practice, Bromley, 1947-48; Equine Practice, Epsom, 1948-49; Fisheries and Food Officer, Ministry of Agriculture, 1949-50; Research, Animal Health Trust, 1950-54; Small Animal Practice, Knightsbridge, London, 1954-77; Director, Animal Health Trust, 1977-. *Memberships:* Council, Royal College of Veterinary Surgeons, 1961-; British Small Animal Veterinary Association; World Small Animal Veterinary Association; Royal Veterinary College, London; Veterinary Consultant to Independent Broadcasting Association. *Publications:* 32 Professional Publications. *Honours:* Fellow, Royal College of Veterinary Surgeons, 1976; Hon. Diplomat, American College of Veterinary Surgeons, 1973; Commander of the British Empire, 1974. *Hobbies:* Photography; Sailing; Ornithoogy, Gardening. *Address:* Flat 4, Lanwades Hall, Kennett, Near Newmarket, Suffolk, CB8 7PN, England.

SINHA, Amarendra Kumar, b. 29 Oct. 1948, Bhagalpur, Bihar, India. Medical Doctor, Cardiologist. m. Mrs. Prativa Sinha, 27 June 1971, 2 sons. *Education:* MB, BS, 1971; MD, New Jersey, USA, 1975; DTMH, England, 1975; MAMS, Austria, 1978; MCCP, USA, 1975. *Appointments:* Internship and Housemanship at AMCH, India; Residency in Medicine and Cardiology, New Jersey, USA: Private Practice, Cardiology and Medicene; In charge of Cardio-Pulmonary division, K.K. Nursing Home and Research Centre, Bhagarpur, Bihar, India. *Memberships:* School of Tropical Medicine, Liverpool, England; American College of Chest Physicians, USA; National College of Chest Physicians, India. *Honours:* Recipient of Hons. MBBS, Anatomy, 1967; Gold Medal, Pathology, 1968; Iniversity Merit Scholarship, 1967-69. *Hobbies:* Photography; Teaching. *Address:* Kamla House, U.N. Bagchi Road, Bhagalpur, Bihar, India.

SINHA, Jnanendra Prasad, b. 1 Sept. 1923, Chandpara, Birbhum, West Bengal, India. Industrial Promoter and Publisher. m. Prakriti, 16 Aug. 1959, 1 daughter. *Education:* BCom, 1946; MA Com, 1949; MA Econ, 1953. *Appointments:* Partner, Scientific Book Agency; Director, Prasun Engineering Works Private Limited; Director, S.P. Sinha and Company, Private Limited. *Memberships:* Indo-German Chamber of Commerce; International Society for Krishna Consciousness. *Hobbies:* Swimming; Photography. *Address:* 49/13 Hindusthan Park, Calcutta 700029, India.

SINHA, Prajeskumar, b. 6 Jan. 1940, Calcutta, India. Surgeon. m. Dr. Andali, 1 Oct. 1965. 1 son, 1 daughter.

Education: MBBS, Calcutta, 1965; FRCS, Edinburgh, 1974. *Appointments:* Junior and Senior House Surgeon, Department of Surgery in NRS Medical College, 1965-68; Senior House Officer, Thoracic Surgery, Walsgrave Hospital, Coventry, 1969; Senior House Officer, Surgery, 1970-72, Residential Surgical Officer, 1972-75, Burton-on-Trent General Hospital; Senior Registrar, Lusaka, 1975-77; Consultant Surgeon, Lusaka, 1977-78; Senior Lecturer, Surgery, University of Zambia, 1978-. *Memberships:* Association of Surgeon, East Africa; Medical Association, East Africa. *Publications:* Contributed to various professional journals. *Hobbies:* Travel; Photography; Music. *Address:* Postal Box 50501, 3877 Manda Hill Road, Lusaka, Zambia.

SINHA, Ratneshwar Prasad, b. 1 Mar 1918. Chapra. Doctor. m. Urmila, 19 May 1943. 2 sons, 3 daughters. *Education:* MBBS, Patna University; MD, 1955, Patna University; DTM, 1946, Calcutta; FRCP, Glasgow, 1973; DCH, 1959; FCCP, USA, 1962; FICA, USA, 1967; FACC, USA, 1970. *Appointments:* Tutor in medicine, 1951-57; Lecturer in medicine, 1957-67; Professor of medicine, 1967-76, Patna Medical College, India; Professor and Head of the Department of Medicine, India; Consultant Physician, Jayaprabha Hospital, India. *Memberships:* Patna Medical Journal; Journal of Indian Medical Association; Association of Physicians of India; British Medical Journal, BMA. *Address:* Raw Krishna Avenue, Patna, 800004, India.

SINKER, Charles Adrian. b. 29 Apr 1931. Cambridge, England. m. Margaret Dibb, 28 Sept 1957. 1 son, 1 daughter. *Education:* BA, MA University of Cambridge, 1952. *Appointments:* Assistant Warden, Malham Tarn Field Centre, 1952-56; Warden Preston Montford Field Centre, 1956-73; Director, Field Studies Council, 1973. *Memberships:* Fellow of the Institute of Biology; Council for Environmental Education; British Ecological Society; Shropshire Conservation Trust; Botanical Society of the British Isles. *Honours:* OBE, 1979. *Hobbies:* Reading; Writing; Botany. *Address:* North Mytton House, Montford Bridge, Shrewsbury, SY4 1EU, England.

SIONE, Tomu M, b. 17 Nov 1941. Niutau, Tuvalu, Politician. m. 4 sons, 1 daughter. *Appointments:* Member of Parliament, 1970-81. *Hobbies:* All outdoor games. *Address:* Ministry of Commerce & Natural Resources, Funafuti, Tuvalu.

SISYA, Harold Elias Dukuma, b. 15 June 1940. Blantyre, Malawi. Lawyer. m. Rosemary, 22 June 1962. 1 son, 3 daughters. *Education:* LLB London, 1965. *Appointments:* Resident Magistrate, 1965-74; Judge of the High Court of Tanzania, 1974-. *Hobbies:* Gardening, Music. *Address:* House No. 8, New Nguvumali, Tanga, Tanzania.

SITSKY, Larry, b. 10 Sept 1934. Tientsin, China. Composer, Pianist, Musicologist, Teacher. m. Magda, Wlczek, 8 Feb 1961. 1 son, 1 daughter. *Education:* Diploma NSW State Conservatorium of Music; Post Graduate studies with Egon Petri, San Francisco Conservatory of Music. *Appointments:* Chief study piano teacher, Queensland Conservatorium of Music; Lecturer, University of Queensland; Lecturer, Extension studies, Australian National University; Head, Keyboard studies, Canberra School of Music; Head, Department of Composition & Electronic Music Studies, Canberra School of Music; Head, Department of Composition and Musicology, Canberra School of Music. *Memberships:* Chairman, Composers Guild of Australia; Director, Australia Contemporary Music Ensemble; ACT, representative; Fellowship of Composers; Australian Society for Music Education. *Creative Works:* 4 Operas; 4 Orchestral pieces; 2 Concerti; Many pieces of Keyboard, etc. *Honours:* Recipient of numerous honours and awards, including International competition for music for wind instruments; Australia's most commissioned composer. *Hobbies:* Psychic Research, Gardening, Translating from Russian. *Address:* 29 Threlfall Street, Chifley ACT, Australia, 2606.

SIU, Hemann Chan-kin b. 28 Dec 1973. Hong Kong. Merchant. m. Margaret K. Sy Lam, 23 Dec 1973. 1 son, 1 daughter. *Education:* BSc, 1963, Chu Hai College, Hong Kong; Dipl. Mgt., 1980, Chinese University, Hong Kong Certificate Export Promotion, 1980, The Carl Duisberg Society, Bremen & Cologne, Germany. *Ap-*

pointments: Assistant Engineer, 1958, Shanghai Metal Manufactory; Engineer, 1958-63, Tai-Cheung Steel Manufactory, China; teacher, 1967-71, Hong Kong; Chinese Manufactory Association of Hong Kong, 1971-77; Proprietor, Tallways' Crafts Manufactory, 1977; Managing Director, China Trade, Alloted Chinese Distributors Limited, 1980-. *Memberships:* Hong Kong Management Association. *Hobbies:* Paintings, Water Colour, Chinese Painting, Classical Music, Fishing. *Address:* 76D Fa Yuen Street, 11th Floor, Kowloon, Hong Kong.

SIVALINGAM, Sangarapillai, b. 1 May 1922, Jaffna, Sri Lanka. Specialist Pathologist. m. Chandrothayam Maruthappu, 26 Apr 1952. 1 son, 3 daughters. *Education:* MBBS, Ceylon, 1947; DCP, London, 1959; PhD, London, 1962; MRCPath, UK, 1963; FRCPath, UK, 1972. *Appointments:* Medical Officer, Government Department of Health, 1947-51; Medical Officer, Medical Research Institute, Colombo, 1951-61; Consultant Pathologist, Head of Department of Pathology, MRI, 1962-73; Senior Specialist, Institute of Medical and Veterinary Science, Whyalla, South Australia, 1973; Director, 1974, Senior Director, 1976. *Memberships:* International Academy of Pathology; Ceylon Association for the Advancement of Science; International Association for Tamil Research; Ceylon Medical Association. *Publications:* Various publications in International Medical and Scientific journals. *Honours:* Ceylon Government scholarship, 1958. *Hobbies:* Chess, Bridge, Golf, Ballroom Dancing, Fishing and Gardening. *Address:* 2, Eyre Boulevard, Pasadena, SA 5042, Australia.

SIVALINGAM, Visvanather Sivasegaram, b. 7 July 1932, Sri Lanka, Chartered Accountant. m. Jeevaranee Senathirajah, 5 Feb 1961. 2 daughters. *Education:* BA, Economics. *Appointments:* Chief Accountant, Mercantile Credit Co. Ltd; Group Accountant, E.B. Creasy & Co; Chief Accountant, Industrial Credit Co. Ltd. Zambia. *Memberships:* Fellow of the Institute of Chartered Accountant of Sri Lanka. *Honours:* Scholarship to do Accountancy, 1957, by Accountancy Board in Ceylon. *Hobbies:* Astronomy, Reading, Chess, Lawn Tennis. *Address:* 59, Vanniah Street, Trin Comalee, Sri Lanka.

SIVASITHAMPARAM, Murugesu, b. 20 July 1923, Jaffna, Sri Lanka. Attorney-at-Law. m. Sarathadevi, 5 Sept 1949. 1 son, 1 daughter. *Education:* Law degree at the Ceylon Law College. *Appointments:* Attorney-at-Law, 1950-; Member of Parliament, 1961-69; Member of Parliament, 1969-; Deputy Speaker of Ceylon Parliament, 1967-69. *Publications:* Pamphlets and Articles on Current Political Subjects. *Address:* 100 Norris Canal Road, Colombo 10, Sri Lanka.

SIVASUBRAMANIAM, Amirthalingam, b. 7 Feb 1943, Sri Lanka. Chartered Accountant. m. Gowry, 24 Aug 1971. 2 daughters. *Education:* BSc, 1965; ACA, 1969; FCA, 1981. *Appointments:* Chief Accountant/Secretary, Cargo Boat Despatch Co. Ltd, Sri Lanka, l969-73; Audit Supervisor, Cooper & Lybrand, Tanzania, 1974-77; Group Accountant, Tantrust Limited, Tanzania, 1978-81. *Address:* Niruvadhambai, Urickadu, Valvettiturai, Sri Lanka.

SIVIOUR, Trevor Raymond, b. 17 April 1949, Temora, NSW, Australia. Agricultural Scientist (Turf). m. Kim Coker, 11 March, 1978, 1 daughter. *Education:* BSc (2nd Class Honours) Sydney University, Australia. *Appointments:* Australian Turf Grass Research Institute; Australian Plant Pathologist, 1972-1979; Australian Research Director, 1979-. *Memberships:* International Turfgrass Society; American Society of Agronomy; Australian Plant Pathology Society; Royal Australian Institute of Parks and Recreation, State Secretary. *Publications:* Contributor of reviews, monographs, articles to professional journals and conferences, including, Redescription of Ibipora Iolii (Siviour 1978) comb. n Nematoda; (Belonolaimidae) with Observations on its Host Range and Pathogenicity. Nematologica, in Press. *Hobbies:* Squash; Furniture; Restoration; Football (Rugby). *Address:* 15, Simla Road, Denistone, Sydney, New South Wales 2114, Australia.

SJOQUIST, Kirsten Marie, b. 28 March 1911, Denmark. m. Sigurd P. 2 January 1940, 2 sons. *Appointments:* Diploma Acadamy of Design & Drawing, Copenhagen Denmark. *Publications:* The Print Council of Australia, The Print Circle; Nine Printmakers, NSW.

Honours: Works in Oil, Etchings, Screenprints and Sculpture. Exhibited in Australia, Canada, Denmark and Germany. *Hobbies:* Interior Decorating, Floral Art and Horticulture. *Address:* 12/26 Etham Avenue, Darling Point, NSW, Australia 2027.

SKINNER, James John, b. 23 July, 1923, Dublin, Ireland. Chief Justice. m. Brigitte Reisse, 21 October 1950, 3 sons, 2 daughters. *Education:* King's Inn, Dublin, Barrister at Law; Gray's Inn, Barrister at Law. *Appointments:* Leinster Circuit, 1946-51; Bar of Zambia, 1951-69; Minister of Justice, Zambia, 1964-65; Attorney General of Zambia, 1965-69; Minister of Legal Affairs, 1967-68; MP (UNIP) Lusaka, 1964-68; Chief Justice of Zambia, March to September, 1969; Irish Bar, 1969-70; Chief Justice of Malawi, 1970. *Honours:* QC (Northern Rhodesia), 1964; Grand Commander of the Order of Menelik II of Ethiopia, 1965. *Hobbies:* Reading. *Address:* Chief Justice's House, Kabula Hill, P.O. Box 30244, Blantyre, South Malawi.

SKINNER John McPhail, b. 2 December, 1921, Glasgow. Analytical Chemist. m. Elizabeth Haig Crawford, 26 March 1956, 2 sons. *Education:* BSc, Glasgow University, 1944; PhD. Glasgow University, 1950. *Appointments:* Anglo Iranian Oil Co. Ltd, 1944-45; Ragosine Oil Co Ltd, 1945-47; Babcock and Wilcox Ltd, 1950-55; ICI Agricultural Division 1955. *Memberships:* Fellow, Royal Society of Chemistry; Institution of Industrial Managers. *Publications:* Papers on analysis in various journals. *Hobbies:* Golf, History of Motion Pictures. *Address:* 18, Highfield Drive, Eaglescliffe, Stockton-on-Tees, Cleveland, TS16 ODN, England.

SLADE, Dennis Bertram, b. 12 May 1928. North Curry, Somerset. Medical Laboratory Scientist. m. Guinivere Mary Garbutt, 3 sons. *Appointments:* Area Laboratory, Musgrove Park Hospital, Taunton, 1948-1974; Principal Medical Laboratory Scientific Officer, Area Central Laboratory, Royal United Hospital, Bath, 1975-. *Memberships:* President, Institute of Medical Laboratory Sciences; Treasurer, International Association Medical Laboratory Technology. *Publications:* Aids to Medical Laboratory Management (in preparation). *Honours:* FIMLS, 1955; Justice of the Peace, 1970-1974. *Hobbies:* Golf, Music. *Address:* 14, Penn Lea Road, Bath, BAI 3RA, England.

SLADE, John George (Edouard), b. 26 Feb. 1932 Alderney, Channel Islands. Academic Lecturer. *Education:* Diploma of the University of Rennes, BA (London), Postgraduate Certificate (Newcastle upon Tyne); LTCL, LGSM, LLCM, FIL, FCI, FFT Com., ACP, ALAM. *Appointments:* Director of Relief Programme for displaced persons, Interpreter for US Army in Germany, Civil Servant in Jersey, C.I., Industrial Interpreter in Switzerland and Germany, Academic Lecturer in English and Business Studies at German Universities. *Memberships:* FRSA, FRGS, FRHS, FBSC, FIMS, MPS, MJI, M.Inst.CM., AIHE, AMIISE., Affil.R.S.H; Historical Association, Military Historical Society, Royal Institution, Royal Society of Literature, Royal Photographic Society, Royal Society of St George; Associate of: Royal Aeronautical Society. *Publications:* The Pioneer Days of Aviation in Jersey; Behind the Siegfried Line (military history study); numerous newspaper articles on Channel Isles' history; numerous translations of technical and tourism literature. *Honours:* Bronze, Silver and Gold (Honours) Medals LAM (Public Speaking). *Hobbies:* Genealogy, Vintage records. *Address:* Gerberstrasse 41, Postfach 3235, D-5810 Witten 3, Germany.

SLATER, Gordon James Augustus, b. 1922. British Diplomat. m. (1) Beryl Ruth Oliver, 1952 (Div.) (2) Gina Michelle Lambert, 1976, 1 son, 1 daughter. *Education:* Sydney, Australia. *Appointments:* Commonwealth Relations Office and Foreign and Commonwealth Office, 1958-78; British High Commissioner, Solomon Islands, 1978-. *Address:* 17 Astor Close, Kingston, Surrey, England.

SLATER John Philip, b. 19 May 1931, Bradford, United Kingdom, Director. m. Patricia Murgatroyd, 22 Aug., 1958, 3 sons. *Education:* BSc Honours *Appointments:* Unilever Ltd, U.K., 1955-59; Avon Cosmetics Ltd. U.K., 1959-1970; Avon Products Pty Ltd, 1970-1978; Hanimax Pty Ltd, 1978-80; Thorn EMI Pty Ltd, 1980-. *Memberships:* Royal Institute of Chemistry; Institute of Directors; Chamber of Manufacturing NSW; Royal

Prince Alfred Yacht Club; American Club. *Honours:* Recipient of Queens Jubilee Medal. *Hobbies:* Yachting. *Address:* 19, Walker Avenue, St. Ives. NSW 2075 Australia.

SLATYER, Ralph Owen, b. 16 Apr., 1929. Melbourne, Australia. Diplomat. m. June Helen Wade, 16 May 1953, 1 son, 2 daughters. *Education:* BSc University of Western Australia, 1951; MSc. University of Western Australia, 1954; DSc, University of Western Australia, 1959. *Appointments:* CSIRO, Canberra Research Scientist, Chief Research Scientist, 1951-1967; Professor of Environmental Biology, Institute of Advanced Studies, Australian National University, Canberra, since 1967; Visiting Professor of Botany, Duke University, North Carolina, USA, 1963-64; Visiting Professor of Biological Science Ford Foundation Fellow, University of California, Santa Barbara, California, 1973-74; Australian Ambassador to UNESCO, 1978-81. *Memberships:* Fellow of Royal Society of London; Foreign Member, US National Academy of Science, Fellow, Australian Academy of Science; Australian National Commission of UNESCO, Chairman, 1976-78; Ecological Society of Australian, President, 1969-71; Foreign Member, American Academy of Arts and Sciences; Chairman, Australian Biological Resources Study Advisory Committee. *Publications:* Numerous publications in scientific journals, also author and editor of several books. *Honours:* Edgeworth David Memoral Prize, 1960; Medal of Australian Institution of Agricultural Science, 1967; Andrew Stewart Lecturer, University of Western Australia, 1969; Mortlock Lecturer, University of Adelaide, 1977; *Hobbies:* Bushwalking, Skiing. *Address:* 10 Tennyson Crescent, Forrest ACT 2603, Australia.

SLEE David Julian, b. 19 Dec. 1936. Bangalore, India. Actuary. m. Renate Carola, 15 Aug 1963, 2 sons 1 daughter. *Education:* Fellow of the Institute of Actuaries. *Appointments:* Managing Director, Underwriting & Insurance Ltd. *Memberships:* Tasar Association of Victoria, Hon. Secretary; Rotary Club of Prahran. *Publications:* Paper to Internatioal Congress of Actuaries, Zurich, 1980; Valuation of the Shares of an Australian Life Insurance Company. *Address:* 228 Kooyong Road, Toorak, Victoria, Australia.

SLEEMAN, Frank Northey, b. 4 Mar 1915, Sydney, Australia. The Right Honorable Lord Mayor of Brisbane. m. Norma, 2 sons. *Education:* Canterbury Boys High School, Sydney, NSW. *Appointments:* World War II, First Commando Company; established New agency business, Brisbane after war; Alderman Nudgee Ward (renamed Banyo ward 1973), since 1961; Life member of ALP, Treasurer, Local Government Assn. Queensland, 1961-73; Executive member; Vice President, Cities and Towns Local Government Association, 1967-70; President, 1971; Executive Member, 1972-1975, Commonwealth Games Management Advisory Committee, Chairman, Australian Day Council, Queensland (V-Pres) Warana Spring Festival Committee, Vice-President. *Memberships:* Tattersalls, Rotary, Banyo Australian Football, Mayne Sporting, Norths Netball Association, Windsor-Zillmere Australian Football; Banyo Bowls; Queensland Ex-POW Assn.; Australian Conversation Foundation; Association for the Welfare of Children in Hospital, Help Industries. *Hobbies:* All sport, particularly hockey and soccer. *Address:* 344, Zillmere Road, Zillmere, Queensland 4034, Australia.

SMALES, Oliver Richard Clayton, b. 21 Apr. 1944, Yealmpton, Devon, England. Medicine. m. Elizabeth Ann Miller, 1 Apr. 1967, 1 son, 2 daughters. *Education:* Marlborough College, Wiltshire, 1958-62; Medical College, St. Bartholomew's Hospital, London, 1963-69; MRCS, 1969, LRCP, 1969; MBBS, 1969; DCH, 1971; MRCP, 1972; MD, 1979. *Appointments:* House Physician and Surgeon, St. Bartholomew's Hospital, London, 1969-70; House Physician, Hospital for Sick Children, Great Ormond Street, London, 1973; Lecturer, Department of Child Health, University of Nottingham, 1973-77; Fellow, Royal Children's Hospital, Melbourne, Australia, 1976-77; Consultant Paediatrician, Hawker Bay Hospital Board, New Zealand, 1979. *Publications:* Author of 12 contributions to medical journals, the most recent being, Renin and Anglotensin Levels in Children, with F. Broughton-Pipkin and M. J. O'Callaghan. *Hobbies:* Sailing; Opera; Gardening; Shooting; Tramping. *Address:* 700 Charles Street, Hastings, New Zealand.

SMALLWOOD, Denis Graham, b. 13 Aug. 1918, Warwickshire, England. Military Aviator and Adviser. m. 14 Oct. 1940, 1 son, 1 daughter. *Education:* King Edward VI School, Birmingham. *Appointments:* Joined Royal Air Force, 1938; Fighter Command, 1939-45; Group Captain, 1957; Commanded RAF Guided Missiles Station, Lincolnshire, 1959-61; Air Officer Commanding and Commandant, Royal College of Air Warfare, Manby, 1961-62; Assistant Chief of the Air Staff, Operations, 1962-65; Air Officer Commanding Number 3 Group, RAF Bomber Command, 1965-67; Senior Air Staff Officer, Bomber Command, 1967-68; Deputy Commander in Chief, Strike Command, 1968-69; Air Officer Commanding, Near East Air Force, Commander, British Forces Near East, and Administrator, Sovereign Base Area, Cyprus, 1969-70; Vice Chief of the Air Staff, 1970-74; Commander in Chief, RAF, Strike Command, 1974-76; Commander in Chief, United Kingdom Air Forces, NATO, 1975-76; Retired from the Royal Air Force, 1976; Aide-de-Camp to the Queen, 1959-64; Military Adviser, British Aerospace, 1977. *Memberships:* Royal Society of Arts; Royal Aeronautical Society; President of the Air League. *Publications:* RAF Biggin Hill. *Honours:* Recipient of DFC, 1942; DSO, 1944; MBE, 1949; CBE, 1959; CB, 1965; KCB, 1970; GBE, 1976. *Hobbies:* Shooting; Horsemanship; Dog Training; Swimming; Gardening. *Address:* The Flint House, Owlswick, Aylsbury, Buckinghamshire, England.

SMART, Patricia Betty, University Lecturer. *Education:* Teaching Certificate, Bishop Otter College, Sussex, 1951; BA, Philosophy, Exeter University, 1961; MPhil, Philosophy, Birkbeck College, London, 1968; MSc, Philosophy of Science, University College of London, 1970. *Appointments:* Primary School Teacher; Lecturer in College of Education, Hockerill College, Bishop Stortford; Lecturer, Senior Lecturer, Department of Philosophy, University of Surrey. *Memberships:* Association of University Teachers. *Publications:* Thinking and Reasoning, 1972; The Concept of Indoctrination in New Essays in the Philosophy of Education, 1973. *Hobby:* Gardening. *Address:* 63 Bray Road, Guildford, England.

SMEETON, Patricia, May, b. 14 Dec. 1921, Mount Lawley, West Australia. Farmer. m. Ernest Fisher Smeeton, 3 Feb. 1951, 1 son, 1 daughter. *Education:* Perth College, Mount Lawley, West Australia, 1928-35. *Appointments:* Account's Clerk, Raphael's Limited, 1936-41; Staff Sergeant, Australian Army, 1941-46; Account's Clerk, Page Carrying Company, 1946-50; Working Partner of Family Farming Property. *Memberships:* President, Chairman, Treasurer and Ministers' Nominee of various Australian Associations and Committees. *Honours:* Recipient of OBE, 1981; JP, 1980. *Hobbies:* Reading; Tapestry; Gardening. *Address:* Box 92, P.O., Wongan Hills 6603, Western Australia.

SMITH, Arnold Cantwell, b. 18 Jan. 1915, Toronto, Ontario, Canada. Diplomat, Statesman Educator. m. Evelyn Hardwick Stewart, 8 Sept. 1938, 2 sons. *Education:* Upper Canada College, Toronto, 1924-27, 1928-32; Lycee Champoleon, Grenoble, 1927-28; 1932-35, University of Toronto, BA, Political Science and Economics and Rhodes Scholarship, 1935; Christ Church, Oxford, 1935-38; MA Jurisprudence; BCL 1938; Gray's Inn, London. *Appointments:* Editor, The Baltic Times, Assistant Professor of Pol. Economy, Tartu University, Estonia, 1939-40; Attaché Br. Embassy, Cairo, 1940-41; Head, Propaganda Division Office of UK, Ministry of State for ME, 1941-43; Associate Director, National Defence College of Canada, 1947-49; Alternate Rep. of Canada to UN Security Council and Atomic Energy Comm., 1949; Counsellor, Embassy, Brussels, 1950-53; Special Assistant to Secretary of State for External Affairs, Ottawa, 1953-55; Commissioner, International Truce Commission, Cambodia, 1955-56; Canadian Minister, London, 1956-58; Ambassador to UAR, 1958-61; and to USSR 1961-63; Assistant Under Secretary of State for External Affairs, Ottawa, 1963-65; Elected First Secretary-Genera of the Commonwealth, 1965-75; Lester B. Pearson Professor of International Affairs, Carleton University, Ottawa since 1975; 04 Chairman of the Board, North-South Institute, Ottawa; Chairman of the Board, International Peace Academy, U.N. Plaza, New York; Chairman of the Board, Hudson

Institute of Canada, Montreal; Honorary President, Canadian Bureau for International Education, Ottawa; Trustee, Hudson Institute, New Yorks; Life Vice-President, Royal Commonwealth Society, London; Honorary Fellow, Lady Eaton College, Trent University; Honorary President, Canadian Mediterannean Institute; Advisory Committee, Shastri Indo-Canadian Institute; Chairman, Membership Committee and Member of Executive Committee and Council of HRH the Duke of Edinburgh's Fifth Commonwealth Study Conference, Canada, 1980. *Publications:* Stitches in Time—The Commonwealth in World Politics, 1981; Many articles in learned journals; Innumerable Official Reports when CSG. *Honours:* Invested Companion of Honour by HM Queen Elizabeth II, 1975; Zimbabwe Independence Medal, 1980; Honorary DCL, 1966, 1977; Honorary LLD, 1964, 1966, 1968, 1969, 1975, and 1979; Awarded R.B. Bennett Commonwealth Prize, Royal Society for the Arts, 1975. *Hobbies:* Fishing; Reading; Travelling; Farming in France; Photography. *Address:* Town house Five, 300 Queen Elizabeth Driveway, Ottawa, K1S 3M6, Canada.

SMITH, Barbara Francis, b. 16 Feb. 1923, Timaru, New Zealand. Veterinarian. *Education:* BSc, University of New Zealand, 1944; BVSc, Sydney, (2nd class Hons.), 1948. *Appointments:* Assistant in small animal practice, Sydney, 1949-50; Veterinary Officer, Ministry of Agriculture, Fisheries & Food (UK), 1951-52; Research Veterinarian & Head of Quality Control of Research Veterinarian with Virus Research & Development, Tasman Vaccine Laboratory, Upper Hutt, 1954-75; ICI Tasman Limited, Currently Technical Advisor to Export Department, 1975-. *Memberships:* Councillor, 1970-71, Vice President, 1971-72, President, 1972-73, Senior Vice President, 1973-74, New Zealand Veterinary Association; Foundation Member and Councillor, Australian College of Veterinary Scientists, 1971-80; Convenor, New Zealand Sub-Council, 1977-80; NZVA Representative on World Vet Association, 1979-, elected Vice President, 1979; Elected Fellow of Australian College of Veterinary Scientists, 1979. *Hobbies:* Gardening; Music; Theatre; Art; Entertaining. *Address:* 1067 Fergusson Drive, Upper Hutt, New Zealand.

SMITH, David Iser, b. 9 Aug. 1933, Melbourne, Australia. Official Secretary to the Governor-General of Australia. m. June Francis, 4 Apr. 1955, 3 sons. *Education:* BA, Australian National University, Canberra, 1967. *Appointments:* Department of Customs and Excise, Melbourne, 1954-57; Training Officer, Department of Interior, Canberra, 1957-58; Private Secretary to Minister for Interior and Minister for Works, 1958-63; Executive Assistant to Secretary, Department of Interior, 1963-66, Executive Officer (Government), Department of Interior, 1966-69; Senior Adviser, Government Branch, Prime Minister's Department, 1969-71; Secretary, Federal Executive Council, 1971-73; Assistant Secretary, Government Branch Department of Prime Minister and Cabinet, 1972-73; Official Secretary to the Governor-General of Australia since 1973; Secretary of the Order of Australia since, 1975. *Memberships:* District Commissioner, Capital Hill District, Scout Association of Australia, 1971-74. *Honours:* CVO, 1977; C.St.J, 1974. *Hobbies:* Music; Reading. *Address:* Government House, Canberra ACT 2600, Australia.

SMITH, Edgar Anthony Tweedie, b. 20 Feb. 1922, South Africa. Law: Judge. m. June, 1 son, 3 daughters. *Education:* BA, 1947, LLB, 1950, University of the Witwatersrand. *Appointments:* Law Officer, The Office of The Attorney General, Southern Rhodesia, 1951; The Bar, 1953; Solicitor-General of Rhodesia, 1964-68; Member of the Bar Council of Rhodesia, 1962-65; Attorney-General of Rhodesia, 1968-75; Judge of The High Court of Rhodesia since 1975. *Honours:* GLM, 1975; ID,1970; IM, 1980; QC, 1965. *Hobbies:* Gardening; Fishing. *Address:* 29 Argyll Drive, Highlands, Salisbury, Zimbabwe.

SMITH, Edward Durham, b. 27 May, 1922, Sunderland, England, Paediatric Surgeon. m. Dorothy Lois, 29 Dec. 1948. 4 sons. *Education:* MBBS, University of Melbourne, 1948; MD, University of Melbourne, 1967; MS, University of Melbourne, 1972; FRACS, Fellow, Royal Australasian College, 1963; FACS Fellow, American College of Surgeons, 1963. *Appointments:* Post Graduate training in Registrar Posts at Alfred Hospital, Melbourne and Royal Childrens Hospital, Melbourne,

1949-58; Overseas Training: London, UK; Boston, USA; Paediatric Surgeon, Alfred Hospital, Melbourne, 1956-65; Assistant Surgeon, Royal Childrens Hospital, Melbourne, 1956-65; Senior Research Fellow, Royal Childrens Hospital, Melbourne, 1947-75; Surgeon, Senior Staff, Royal Childrens Hospital, Melbourne, 1965-; Hon. Paediatric Surgeon, Mercy Maternity Hospital, Melbourne, 1970-. *Memberships:* Councillor (Elected 1978) on Council of Royal Australasian College of Surgeons; Australian Association of Paediatric Surgeons; British Association of Paediatric Surgeons; Pacific Association of Paediatric Surgeons; Urological Society of Australasia; Australian Medical Association; Naval and Military Club, Melbourne. *Publications:* Spina Bifida and Total Care of Myelomenincocele, 1963; Ano-Rectal Anomalies, 1971; Chapters in 6 other Medical Text Books; 51 Papers in Medical and Surgical Journals. *Honours:* Simpson Smith Essay Prize on Spina Bifida of the Institute of Child Health, University of London, 1959. *Hobbies:* Music; Sport; Various Workshop Activities; Travel; Navy. *Address:* 12 Hardy Terrace, Ivanhoe, Victoria, 3079, Australia.

SMITH, Eric Norman, b. 28 Jan. 1922. HM Diplomatic Service. m. Mary Gillian Horrocks. *Education:* Colfe's School, London. *Appointments:* Royal Corps of Signals, 1941-46; Foreign Office 1947-53; HM Embassy, Cairo, 1953-55; UK Delegation to UN, New York, 1955-57; Foreign Office 1957-60; HM Embassy, Tehran, 1960-64; Foreign Office, 1964-68; British Information Services, New York, 1968-71; FCO, 1971-75; Singapore, 1975-79; British High Commissioner in The Gambia, 1979-. *Honours:* CMG, 1976. *Hobbies:* Music; Photography. *Address:* c/o Foreign and Commonwealth Office, King Charles Street, London SW1A 2AH, England.

SMITH, Ewart, b. 26 Apr. 1920, Manly, NSW, Australia. Law, Barrister and Solicitor. m. Janet, 27 Feb. 1943. 3 daughters. *Education:* LLB, Sydney University, 1942. *Appointments:* Tutor, Australian School of Pacific Administration; Assistant Officer in Charge, Law Revision Section, Dept. of External Territory, 1946-50; Parliamentary Drafting Division, Commonwealth Attorney Generals Department, rising to Assistant Parliamentary draftsman, 1952-62; Advising Division, Attorney Generals Dept. rising to Head of the division, 1962-70; Deputy Secretary, Attorney Generals Department, 1970-80; Senior Non Presidential Member of the Commonwealth Administrative Appeals Tribunal, 1980-. *Memberships:* Canberra Club, Canberra. *Publications:* Assistant Editor of Annotated Laws of the Territory of Papua, 1888-1945; The Annotated Laws of the Territory of New Guinea, 1920-45; Contributor of Poetry to 1981 International Voices. *Honours:* OBE, 1976. *Hobby:* Cricket. *Address:* 10 Chowne Street, Campbell, Canberra, ACT 2601, Australia.

SMITH, Francis Godfrey, b. 15 Feb 1920, London, England. Scientist and Author. m. Joan I Bardwell, 25 Mar 1945. 3 sons, 1 daughter. *Education:* BSc, (Forestry), University of Aberdeen, 1946-49; Doctor of Science, 1956; National Diploma in Beekeeping, 1959. *Appointments:* Royal Artillery (Field), 1939-46; Beeswax Officer, Department of Agriculture and Forests, Tanganyika, 1949-62; Commandant, Special Constabulary Tabora; Officer in Charge, Apicultural Branch, Department of Agriculture, Western Australia, 1962-74; Director of National Parks, Western Australia, 1974-80. *Memberships:* International Bee Research Association; Royal Society of Western Australia; Commonwealth Forestry Association; Institute of Foresters of Australia. *Publications:* Beekeeping in the Tropics, Longmans, 1960; Beekeeping, Oxford University Press, 1962; Bee Botany in Tanganyika, DSc, Thesis Aberdeen, 1956; Editor, Apiculture in Western Australia, 1963-70; Vegetation Maps, Pemberton & Irwin Inlet, 1972; etc. *Hobbies:* Sailing; Photography. *Address:* 36 Vincent Street, Nedlands, 6009, Western Australia.

SMITH, Frederick E. b. 4 Apr 1922, Hull, Yorkshire, England. Author and Playwright m. Shelagh McGrath, 7 July 1945. 2 sons. *Appointments:* Local Government Officer in Hull Corporation, 1938-39, and 1946; RAF, 1939-46; Accountant, Premier Steel Corporation, Cape Town, South Africa, 1950-52; Professional Author and Playwright, 1952-. *Memberships:* The Pathfinders, London; Crime Writers Association. *Publications:* Writer of 30 novels from 1954, the most recent of which are, 633 Squadron: The Tormented, 1974; Operation Cobra, 1981; The War God, 1980; A Play, The Glass

Prison. *Honours:* Mark Twain Literary Award, American, A Killing For The Hawks, 1967. *Hobbies:* Travel; The Countryside; Sport; Conversation. *Address:* 3 Hathaway Road, Southbourne, Bournemouth, Dorset BH6 3HH, England.

SMITH, Ian Winton, b. 25 Nov 1939, Terang, Victoria. Farmer/Politician. m. Jennifer L. Bartlam, 9 Feb 1967, 2 sons, 3 stepsons. *Education:* Honours Agricultural Science. *Appointments:* Elected to Victorian Parliament, 1967; Minister for Water Supply, 1970; Minister for Social Welfare, 1971-73; Minister for Youth, Sport and Recreation, 1973; Minister of Agriculture, 1973. *Memberships:* Glenormiston Foundation; Royal Society for Prevention of Cruelty to Animals; Victorian Farmers & Graziers Association, Employers. *Honours:* P & O Scholarship to study Farming in Britain, 1959. *Address:* Jingella, Terang, 3264, Australia.

SMITH, Joan Ross, b. 6 Mar 1948, New Zealand. Agricultural/Rural Economist. m. Robert McAllan Davison, 25 Oct 1975. *Education:* BSc, 1969; Diploma in Agricultural Science, Lincoln College, 1971; Certificate in Systems Analysis, Wellington Polytechnic, 1974. *Appointments:* Farm Advisory Officer, Department of Agriculture, 1969-70; Lincoln College, 1970; Farm Advisory Officer, Ministry of Agriculture, 1970-71; Land Management Economist, Department of Lands Survey, Wellington, 1971-76; Senior Research Officer, Rural Banking & Finance Corporation of New Zealand, 1976-77; Chief Economist, N.Z. Forest Services, Wellington, 1979-. *Memberships:* National Treasurer, N.Z. Institute of Public Administration; National Councillor, N.Z. Institute of Agricultural Science; N.Z. Society of Farm Management; N.Z. Association of Economists. *Publications:* Guest Editor, N.Z. Journal of Agricultural Science, Vol. 9, No.4. *Hobbies:* House Renovations; Knitting; Cats; Swimming; Home Cooking; Entertaining; Pot Plants. *Address:* 38, Ponsonby Road, Karori, Wellington, New Zealand.

SMITH, John, (Rt. Hon.), b. 13 Sept, 1938, Dalmally, Argyll. Member of Parliament. m. 5 July 1967. 3 daughters. *Education:* MA, 1960, LLB, 1963, University of Glasgow. *Appointments:* Advocate (Scottish Bar), 1967; MP, North Lanarkshire, 1970; Parliamentary Under Secretary Of State for Energy, 1974-75; Minister of State for Energy, 1975-76; Minister of State, Privy Council Office, 1976-78; Secretary of State for Trade, 1978-79; Member of Shadow Cabinet, 1979; Prinicipal Oppositon Spokesman on Trade. *Honours:* Made a Privy Counsellor, 1978. *Hobbies:* Tennis; Hill Walking. *Address:* 21, Cluny Drive, Edinburgh, Scotland.

SMITH, John Herbert, b. 21 Nov 1909, Fredericton, New Brunswick, Canada. Consultant Engineer, Retired chairman, De Havilland Aircraft of Canada Ltd., 1974-78; Retired Chairman and Chief Executive Office Canadian General Electric Co. Ltd, 1957-72. m. Eldred M. Schaidle, 19 July 1937. *Education:* BSc, 1932, University of New Brunswick; MSc, 1936, DSc, 1958; Assumption University DSc, 1961. *Appointments:* Test Course, Canadian General Electric Company Limited, Petersborough, 1932; Sales Engineer, Hamilton, 1936; Manager, Supply Sales, Toronto, 1945; Manager, Apparatus Division, Toronto, 1948; General Manager, Wholesale Department, Toronto, 1952; Vice-President, Toronto, 1953; General Manager, Appliance Department, Montreal, 1955; Apparatus Department, Peterborough Ontario, 1955; President and Chief Executive Officer, Toronto, 1957; Chairman and Chief Executive Officer, Toronto, 1970-72; Chairman, DeHavilland Aircraft of Canada Ltd., 1974-78. *Memberships:* President, Association of Professional Engineers of Ontario, 1953; Engineering Institute of Canada; Fellow, Institute of Electrical and Electronics Engineers. *Honours:* Awarded Canada Centennial Medal, 1967. *Address:* Apt 4811, 44 Charles St. W., Toronto, M4Y 1R8, Canada.

SMITH, Lancelot Bales, b. 17 Jan 1910, Felixstowe, Suffolk, England. Retired Farmer. m. Jessica L. Hughes, 10 Jan 1941, 1 son, 1 daughter. *Education:* Fellow, British Optical Association, 1931. *Appointments:* Optician, 1931-34, Ipswich; British South Africa Police, 1939-45; Pindi Park Farm, 1946; Rhodesian Front MP. Lomagundi, 1962-70; Hatfield, 1970-74; Deputy Speaker, 1964-65; Minister, Agriculture, 1965-68; Minister, Internal Affairs, 1968-74; Chairman, Natural Resources Board, Rhodesia, 1976-80; Zimbabwe, 1980-. *Memberships:* Zimbabwe Historical Society; Scientific Society. *Honours:* 1939-45, War Service, Independence Decoration; Rhodesia Grand Officer Legion of Merit, 1975; Zimbabwe Independence Decoration, 1981. *Hobbies:* Sailing; Fishing; Game viewing. *Address:* Pindi Park, Box 4, Banket, Zimbabwe.

SMITH, Lesleigh George Windmell, b. 20 July 1906. Brisbane. Builder. m. Amy Violet n. Cooper. 22 Apr 1933. 1 son, 2 daughters. *Memberships:* Wondaishire Council, 1945; Chairman, Wondaishire Council, 1948; Australian Institute of Building FAIB: Old Master Builders Association; J.P. President, Wide-Bay Bernett Local Government; Regional President, South Burnett Local Government Association; *Honours:* CBE, Commander of British Empire, 1976; OBE, Officer of British Empire, 1970. *Hobby:* Building. *Address:* 70 Bramston Street, Wondai, Queensland, Australia, 4606.

SMITH, Neil Andrew, b. 5 July 1920. Melbourne, Australia. Accountant. m. Patricia M. Butcher, 15 Feb 1951. 2 sons, 1 daughter. *Education:* AASA, 1947; ACIS, 1947; RCA, 1948; Companion I. Gas E., 1978; FAIE, 1978. *Appointments:* Chairman and Managing Director, Gas and Fuel Corporation of Victoria, 1970-, General Manager, Gas and Fuel Coporation of Victoria, 1968; Executive Director, Ansett Transport Industries Limited, 1958. *Honours:* CMG, 1981; DEd, Honoris Causa, 1980; JP, 1963. *Address:* 8, Montana St., Burwood, Victoria, 3125, Australia.

SMITH, Philip John, b. 23 July 1926, Newcastle, Australia. Clinical Psychologist. m. Fredericka Fenton, 30 Jan 1971. 3 sons 2 daughters. *Education:* Bachelor of Education, University Western Australia, 1955; Master of Arts, University of New York, USA, 1973; Doctor of Education, Columbia University, New York, USA, 1975. *Appointments:* Royal Australian Air Force, 1944-46; Royal Australian Army Psychology Corps., 1951-52; Master, Hale & John Curtin Schools, Western Australia, 1952-61; Lecturer, Teachers College, West Australia, 1962-69; Foundation Head of Department Psychology & Education, Lawley College of Advanced Education, Western Australia, 1970-75: Visiting Faculty, Brooklyn College, City University, New York, USA, 1974; Clinical Psychology, Sydney, Australia, 1976. *Memberships:* American Association on Mental Deficiency; Australian Society for Clinical & Experimental Hypnosis, Chairman, 1979-80; International Society for Hypnosis. *Publications:* Contributor of reviews, articles to professional journals and conferences, including Verbal and Non-verbal Tasks of Predict Behaviour in Down's Syndrome, Other Retarded and Non-retarded Populations, Doctoral Dissertation Columbia Universtiy, 1975; Medical Journal of Australia, 1976. *Honours:* 1974, Foreign Student Scholarship, Columbia University, New York, USA; Citation, American Association on Mental Deficiency. *Hobbies:* Farming; Antiquities. *Address:* 14 Carr Road, Bringelly, NSW, Australia, 2165.

SMITH Richard Max, b. 22 February 1930, Gladeville NSW Australia. Mining Engineer & Member of Parliament. m. Helen May Glover, 3rd October 1953, 1 son 2 daughters. *Education:* BE Mining Sydney University, 1951 *Appointments:* Australian Iron & Steel Limited, 1951-1962; Rio Tinto Colleries P/L, Superintendent of Colleries, 1962-1965; Kembla Coal and Coke P/L Superintendent of Colleries 1965-1966; Ran own business, Mining Systems Consultants, 1966-1973; Coalex PTy Limited Tech & Operations Director, 1973-1978; M.P. Pitwater NSW Parliament 1978- *Memberships:* Lions International; Surf Life Saving Association; B.P. Guild (Scouts) Secretary Parliament Board; Royal Volunteer Coastal Patrol; Krait Committee; Royal Price Alfred Yacht Club; Palm Beach RSL Club. *Publications:* Chairman of Technical Committee that designed Botonay Bay Coal Loader, Developed the Lithgow Coalfield Exploration Feasibility and Development of Clarence Colliery. *Honours:* Attended First Duke of Edinburgh's Conference 1956 at Oxford. *Hobbies:* Sailing; Car Repairs; Painting; Play Music; Bushwalking. *Address:* 16, Pacific Road, Palm Beach, NSW, Australia.

SMITH Robert Cherer, b. 10 October, 1919. Bothaville, South Africa. Chartered Secretary. m. Elizabeth Lucienne, Croudace, 25th July, 1945, 1 son, 2 daughters. *Education:* Vierfontein High School . *Appoint-*

ments: Buyer Post & Telegraph, Department S. Rhodesia; Stores Manager P & T Department S. Rhodesia; Controller Stores and Transport, Federal Ministry of Posts; Assistant Chief Accountant, Federal Ministry of Post; Chief Accountant, Rhodesian Ministry of Posts; Assistant Postmaster General, Rhodesian Ministry of Posts; Deputy Postmaster General, Rhodesian Ministry of Posts; Executive Secretary Agricultural Research Council. *Memberships:* History Society of Zimbabwe - National Chairman; Aloe & Cactus Society of Zimbabwe - Committee member; National Trust of Zimbabwee - National Council; Crop Science Society of Zimbabwe; Grassland group of S/African Grassland Society; Christian College of S.Africa - Chairman. *Publications:* Rhodesia, A Postal History, Stamps Posts and Telegraphs; plus two supplements; The House of Cherer; The Maize Story; Avondale to Zimbabwe. *Honours:* Harvey Pirie Memorial Prize 1975. *Hobbies:* Gardening; Photography; Woodwork; History; Writing. *Address:* 6, Rayl Road, P.O. Borrowdale, Zimbabwe.

SMITH Roy Gordon b. 4 March 1924. Brighton, Sussex, England. Chartered Surveyor and Company Director. m. Wendy Margaret Norrington, 3rd June 1950, 1 son, 2 daughters. *Education:* St. Andrews University, Scotland, 1941-42 (thereinto RAF); Qualified as an Associate of the Royal Institution of Chartered Surveyors; elected a fellow of the Royal Institution of Chartered Surveyors; Elected a Fellow of the Commonwealth Institute of Valuers in 1965. *Appointments:* Articled Pupil, 1947-50; Inland Revenue - Valuation Office, 1950-1962; Chairman and Managing Director of Richard Stanton & Sons Pty Limited, 1962-79; Chairman of the Benchmark Group - Australia Wide; Chairman of Richard Stanton & Sons Pty Ltd, Managing Director, Taylor Woodrow Property Group in Australia, 1979. *Memberships:* Australian Club - Sydney; Institute of Directors. *Hobbies:* Opera; Swimming; Gardening. *Address:* 17A, Macquarie Road, Pymble, NSW 2073, Australia.

SMITH Samuel Olatunde, b. 22 August, 1941, Lagos Nigeria. Chartered Accountant. m. Dorcas Adejoke Smith, 24 December, 1969, 1 son. *Education:* Final Examinations Institute of Chartered Accountants 1971. *Appointments:* Deloitte Haskins & Sells (Audit Senior), 1971-1974; Nigerian Dredging and Marine Limited, Lagos, Nigeria Financial Controller, Administrate Director, 1974-. *Publications:* Contributor - Nigerian Accountant Journal; Official Journal of the Institute of Chartered Accountants of Nigeria. *Hobbies:* Reading; Table Tennis; *Address:* PMB 1029, Apapa, Lagos, Nigeria.

SMITH William George, b. 19 July, 1933. Pembroke Dock S. Wales. Teacher. m. Anne Lovett, 21 June 1958, 1 son, 1 daughter. *Education:* University College of Wales Bangor, 1951-1955; BA with joint honours and diploma in education 1955; ACP, 1974; *Appointments:* Jervis High School, Hull. Teacher, 1957-58; Greatfield High School, Hull, Head of English, 1958-61; Head of Liberal Studies Hull College of Technology, 1961-66; Head of Business and General Studies at Derby College of Further Education, 1966-71; Principal of Crosskeys College, Gwent, 1971. *Memberships:* Royal Society of Arts Secretary for S. Wales Region; College of Preceptors, Chairman South Wales and on Central Council; Member of Wales Committee of the English Speaking Board; Governor of Williams' Charity, Caerleon; Vice Chairman of Gwent District Manpower Committee; South Gwent Community Health Council; Magistrate; Chairman of Gwent for Professional Associaton of Teachers; Director, Gwent Theatre in Education. *Publications:* Poems in Country Quest; Voice etc. *Honours:* FRSA, 1963; FRGS, 1964; MRSH, 1965; MBIM 1965; MIIM, 1978. *Hobbies:* Music and Drama. *Address:* Ty Newydd, Lodge Hill, Caerleon, Gwent, Wales.

SMITHERS, Sir Reginald Alfree, b. 3 February 1903, Echuca, Victoria, Australia. Law m. 17 December 1932, 2 sons, 1 daughter. *Education:* LLB., Melbourne University, 1921-24. *Appointments:* Victorian State Public Service, 1920-22; Employment with Law Company, 1922-29; Engaged as Barrister at Victorian Bar, 1929-1942; War Service with RAAF, 1942-45; resumed practice as barrister, taking silk in 1951, 1945-61; Judge of Supreme Court of Papua-New Guinea, 1962-64; Judge of Supreme Court of Australian Capital Territory and additional Judge of Supreme Court of

Northern Territory of Australia, 1964; Judge of Australian Industrial Court, 1965-73; Judge of Federal Court of Australia; 1973- Deputy President of Administrative Appeals Tribunal, 1975-78. Chancellor of La Trobe University, 1972-80. *Memberships:* Medico Legal Society, President, 1953; Melbourne Club; Savage Club; Commonwealth Club - Canberra; Royal Australian Auto-Mobile Club of Victoria. *Honours:* Knighthood, January 1980. *Hobby:* Working on farm. *Address:* 11 Florence Avenue, KEW. Victoria 3101, Australia.

smithfield, Edward Matthew, b. 6 June 1944, Manchester, England. Company Manager. *Education:* BA-(Hons), Cambridge University 1966. *Appointments:* Freelance Advertising Consultant 1966 76; Manager, Interfridge Products 1975-. *Hobbies:* Golf; Reading. *Address:* 13 Canterbury Avenue, Ely, Cambs CB6 3DW, UK.

SMITHURST, Barry Anthony, b. 2 Sept. 1928, Sydney, Australia. Physician - University Reader. m. Maureen P. Menkens, 2 March, 1968, 1 son, 2 daughters. *Education:* MBBS (Hons) Sydney University, 1945-50; MRACP, Australasian College of Physicians, 1957; FRACP, Australasian College of Physicians, 1971; MFCM, Faculty of Community Medicine (RCP of UK), 1972. *Appointments:* Resident Medical Officer, St. Vincents Hospital, Sydney, 1951; RMO, Royal Hobart Hospital, 1952; Registrar, Alfred Hospital, Melbourne, 1953-54; Asst. Medical Superintendant, St. Vincents Hospital, Melbourne, 1955-60; Fellow in Internal medicine, Johns Hopkins Hospital, Baltimore, 1960-61; Snr. Lectur in Social & Preventive Medicine, University of Queensland, 1957-7 Reader (Clinical) in Social & Preventive Medicine, University of Queensland, 1971; Physician in Geriatric Medicine, The Prince Charles and Royal Brisbane Hospital, 1977-. *Memberships:* Fellow, Royal Society of Medicine; BMA and AMA; District Surgeon; St. John's Ambulance Brigade, Queensland; United Services Club of Queensland. *Publications:* Author of 'Fundementals of Social and Preventive Medicine'; Contributor of over 35 papers and articles on scientific topics in learned Journals. *Honours:* USPHS Fellowship, 1960-61; ED, 1964; SB St. John, 1977; Knight of Malta,1978. *Hobbies:* History; Squash; Walking. *Address:* 29, Ryan Road, St. Lucia, Brisbane, Queensland, 4067, Australia.

SMITH-WHITE, Spencer, b. 14 April, 1909, Sydney, Australia. Emeritus Professor, Retired 1974; Hon. Associate, 1974-81. m. 15 Dec. 1939, 2 sons, 1 daughter. *Education:* HDA, Hawkesbury Agricultural college, 1927; BSc.(AGR), University of Sydney, 1932; DSc.(AGR), University of Sydney, 1957. *Appointments:* Teacher, Scotch College, Mitcham, S.A. 1933-34; Plant Breeder N.S.W. Dept. of Agriculture, 1935-37; Economic Botanist, Technological Museum, Sydney, 1937-47; Lecturer, Snr. Lecturer, Reader, Botany Dept. University Sydney, 1948-63; Professor of Biology (Genetics) University of Sydney, 1963-74. *Memberships:* Linnean Society of NSW. 1942-64; President, 1959; Genetics Society of Australia, President, 1968, Hon. Life Member, 1980; Australian Academy of Science, FAA, 1962. *Publications:* Numerous Scientific publications dealing with essential oils of Australian plants and Cytology and Evolution of Australian Flora. *Honours:* Nuffield Award, 1956; Clarke Medial, Royal Society of NSW, 1968. *Hobbies:* Boating; Fishing; Gardening. *Address:* 25 Robin Avenue, Turramurra, New South Wales, 2074, Australia.

SMOCOVITIS, Dimitrios, b. 6 Sept. 1929, Grammeni, Lamia, Greece, Medical Physicist. m. Alexandra, 15 Aug. 1954, 1 daughter. *Education:* Dip. of Physics, National & Kapodistrian University of Athens Greece; 1947-52; Master of Science, University of British Columbia, Vancouver, B.C. Canada, 1964-66. *Appointments:* Teacher of Physics, High school, Neapolis, Laconia, Greece, 1954-55; Teacher of Physics, Greek High School, Mansurah, Egypt, 1955-62; Medical Physicist, Ontario Cancer Foundation Windsor Clinic, Windsor, Ontario, Canada, 1966-. *Memberships:* Div. of Medical and biological Physics of the Canadian Association of Physics, Secretary-Treasurer, 1978-81, Editorial Board of Physics in Medicine and Biology; Canadian Radiation Protection Assoc.; Greek Community of Windsor, Ontario, Canada, Treasurer, 1971-75, President, 1976-77. *Publications:* Apparent absorption of the gamma rays of radium in water, (with others), 1967. *Honours:* Recipient of The National Cancer Institute of Canada, Fellowship, 1965-66. *Hobbies:* Photography; Gardening. *Address:* 1140, Grand Marais W, Windsor, Ontario, N9E 1C7, Canada.

SMOLICZ, Jerzy, Jaroslaw (George), b. 2 Feb. 1935, Warsaw, Poland, University Reader, m. Ewa M. Kraszewska, 19 March, 1960, 1 son, 1 daughter. *Education:* BSc. and PhD, Edinburgh University, 1960. *Appointments:* Asst. Lecturer in Chemistry, Edinburgh University, 1959-61; Carnegie Research Fellow, Lincoln College & Dyson Perrins Labs. Oxford University, 1961-63; Lecturer in Chemistry, Leicester University, 1963-65; Lecturer,1965,Snr. Lecturer,1967, & Reader, 1972 in Education, Adelaide University; Chairman of Dept. of Education, Adelaide University, 1971 & 1975-80; Visiting Fellow, Clare Hall, Cambridge University, 1972; Visiting Fellow, research School of Social Sciences, Australian National Universit 1970. *Memberships:* Fellow, Academy of Social Sciences in Australia, 1976; Royal Society of Arts, 1975; Australian College of Education, 1974; Royal Institute of Chemistry, 1970. *Publications:* Books, monographs, papers and articles are published in Australia, United Kingdom, France, Poland, Belgium, Singapore, Hong Kong and the Phillipines on sociology of science, sociology of culture and sociology of education, inlcuding Culture and Education in a Plural Society, 1979. *Honours:* Hope Prize in Chemistry, Edinburgh University, 1958; Theodore Fink Memorial Lecturer, Melbourne University, 1975. *Hobbies:* Reading; Writing; Talking; Travelling; Theatre; Gardening; the Wines. *Address:* 30 Avenue Street, Millswood, S.Australia, 5034.

SNEDDEN, Billy Mackie, b. 31 Dec 1926, Perth, Western Australia. Australian Barrister & Politician. m. Joy, 10 Mar, 1950. 2 sons, 2 daughters. *Education:* LLB University of Western Australia; Admitted to the Bar of Supreme Court, Western Australia 1951; Admitted to the Bar of Supreme Court, Victoria, 1955; Appointed Queen's Counsel, 1964. *Appointments:* Migration Officer Italy, England, 1952-54; Member of the Hous of Representatives for Bruce, Victoria Commonwealth Attorney General 1963-66; Leader of the House of Representatives, 196671; Minister for Immigration, 1966-69; Minister for Labour & National Service, 1969-71; Treasurer, 1971-71; Deputy Leader of Liberal Party, 1971-72; Leader of the Opposition, 1972-75; Speaker of the House of Representatives, 1976. *Memberships:* Melbourne Club; Naval & Military Club, Melbourne; Councillor, Melbourne Scots. *Publications:* Various articles for Parliamentary and Academic journals. *Honours:* Appointed as Member of the Privy Council, 1972, KCMG, 1978. *Hobbies:* Sport; Tennis. *Address:* 22, Pine Crescent, Ringwood, Victoria, 3134, Australia.

SNELL, Geoffrey Stuart, b. 25 Oct. 1920, Exeter, England. Rt. Revd. m. Margaret Lonsdale Geary, 2 sons, 1 daughter. *Education:* MA, Oxford University, 1949; Bar, Inner Temple, London, 1957; Ridley Hall Theological College, Cambridge, 1961; London College of Divinity, 1961-62. *Appointments:* Overseas Administrative Civil Service 1949-54; Gabbitas-Thing Educational Trust (Founder & Managing Governor) 1954-61; Theological College, 1961-62; Priest, Emmanuel Church, Northwood (Diocese London) 1962-63; Fellow Central College of the Anglican Communion, St. Augustine's, Canterbury 1964-75; Founder & Director, CORAT, 1968-75; CORAT, (Africa) 1975-77; Bishop, Croydon & HM Forces 1977-. *Memberships:* United Kenya Club, Nairobi; Honorary President, Croydon Philharmonic Society; Honorary President, Croydon Symphony Orchestra. *Publications:* Nandi Customary Law. 1955. *Hobbies:* Music, Travel. *Address:* 52 Selhurst Road, London SE25 5QD.

SOARES, Victor Adebowale, b. 8 Apr. 1944, Lagos, Nigeria. Sales/Marketing. m. Moronke Adedayo Alase, 5 Oct. 1974, 2 sons, 1 daughter. *Education:* BSc, Economics, 1968, MBA, 1979, University of Ibadan, Nigeria. *Appointments:* Divisional Manager, Vono Products Ltd, Nigeria; General Sales Manager Vono Products Ltd., Nigeria; Sales Developments Manager, Lever Brothers Nigeria Ltd. *Memberships:* Nigerian Economics Society; University of Ibadan Alumni Association; Nigerian Institute of Management; Nigerian Institute of Marketing. *Publications:* Contributor of reviews, monographs, articles to professional journals and conferences. *Honours:* Best English literature Student, High School, 1961; Best Economics Student,

Higher School Certificate Class 1963; Best All Round performance, Citizenship & Youth, Fellowship Company, Nigerian Sea School, APAPA 1971. *Hobbies:* Lawn Tennis, Table Tennis, Squash Racket, Reading & Writing, Biographies. *Address:* 1 Oladapo Street, Oregun, Ikeja, Lagos, Nigeria

SOBANDE, Adesiyen Bola Amoke (Mrs.) b. 18 Feb. 1942, Abeokuta, Ogun State, Nigeria. Architect Chartered. m. Victor Olufemi Sobande (Des.) 25 Apr. 1963, 3 sons, 1 daughter. *Education:* B.Arch, Ahmadu Bello University, Zaria, 1970. *Appointments:* Qualified Architect, Messrs. Kola-Bankole Association, 1970-, Became Partner 1977. *Memberships:* Nigerian Institute of Architects; First Board of Governors, Queen's School, Ibadan, 1977-79; Board Member, Zonta Club International, Ibadan; Executive Committee of the Nigerian Red Cross Society 1980. *Publications:* Queen's School, 1956, Represented Nigeria in The Children of the Commonwealth Arts Exhibition. *Honours:* At University, won a Bond-free Scholarship, for Most progressive student, in the faculty of Architecture for that year. *Hobbies:* Art, Needlework Dressmaking, Flower Arrangement, Home Decorating & Cooking, Tennis, Squash. *Address:* Plot 24, Phase IV, Dejo Oyelese Road, Oyo State Development, Corporation Housing Estate, Bodija, Ibadau, Nigeria

SOBANTU, Millicent Thembeka, b. 20 Apr. 1948, Bulawayo, Zimbabwe. Pharmacist. *Education:* BSc London, 1970; BPh University of Wales, 1975. *Appointments:* Science Teacher, Amaveni Secondary School & David Livingstone Secondary School, Zimbabwe, 1971-72; Pharmacist, Impilo Central Hospital, Bulawayo, 1975-76; Pharmacist, Pfizer Private Ltd., 1977; Pharmacist, Karoi Pharmacy & Regal Pharmarcy, 1978; Pharmacist, Havari Central Hospital, Salisbury, Zimbabwe 1979-. *Memberships:* Pharmaceutical Society of Zimbabwe. *Honours:* Upper Second Class Honours, B. Pharm., UWIST, Cardiff, Wales, 1975; Commonwealth Scholarship, for B.Pharm degree, 1972-75. *Hobbies:* Dancing, Music, Dressmaking, Cooking. *Address:* 25 Nevitt Road, Cranborne Park, Salisbury, Zimbabwe.

SOBHUZA II, H.R.H. King, b. 22 July 1899. King (Ngwenyama) and Head of State of Swaziland. *Education:* Zombodze, Swaziland, Lovedale Institute (Cape). *Appointments:* Constitutional Ruler, 1921; led deputation to London to petition against land lost under the Partitions Proclamation of 1907, 1922; Petitioned King George VI of England, 1941; Officially recognized by Britain as King and Head of State, 1967; Assumed all executive powers in Swaziland, 1973; Chancellor University of Botswana and Swaziland, 1975-76; University College of Swaziland, 1976-79. *Address:* Official Residence of the Ngwenyama, Lozithehlezi, Kwaluseni, Swaziland.

SOBTI, Prem, b. 28 June 1921, Simla, India. Medical. m. Vinod Mehra, 16 Jan. 1955, 1 son, 1 daughter. *Education:* BSc 1943, Punjab Undivided, India; MBBS, 1948, Punjab Indi MRCP, 1953, Edinburgh, England; FRCP, 1970, Edinburgh, England, FCCP, FICA, 1971, USA. *Appointments:* House Physician in Delhi, India, 1949; Registrar in Medicine, Wigan Infirmary, England, 1951-52; Senior Honorary Physician, Irwin Hospital, New Delhi, 1954-69; Honorary Teacher in Medicine, Delhi University, 1960-69; Regional South East Asia staff Physician to WHO, Delhi, 1969-; Consultant in Medicine to Northern Railways, 1970-; Honorary Adviser in Cardiology to Armed Forces, India 1970-; Practising Consultant Physician, Delhi, 1954-. *Memberships:* British Medical Association; Indian Medical Association; Indian Association of Chest Diseases of India; Cardiological Society of India; Association of Physicians of India; Director & Vice President of Asthma & Bronchitis Foundation of India; Director of Heart Foundation of India. *Publications:* Published many papers in India & Abroad on the subject of Medicine. *Honours:* Signed Role of Honours in Athletics (Rowing) at Govt. College Lahore; BSc, Hons, Zoology, Punjab University. *Hobbies:* Music, Trekking. *Address:* S-281, Panchshila Park, New Delhi-110017, India.

SODING, William Michael, b. 28 Apr. 1927, Canterbury, Victoria, Australia. Company Sectretary. m. Margaret Teresa Smyth, 9 Feb. 1955, 2 sons, 1 daughter. *Education:* Accounting, 1948, Australian Society of Accountant; Cost Accounting, 1950, Australian Institute of Cost Accountants; Diploma Industrial Accounting & Management, 1953, Royal Melbourne Institute of Technology; Fellow of Australian Society of Accountants, FASA, 1965. *Appointments:* Watkins Products Inc., Melbourne Australia, 1944-60, Accountant & Cost Accountant; Rocca Industries Ltd., Melbourne, Australia, 1960-, 1960, Assistant Chief Accountant, 1963. Chief Accountant, 1972, Assistant Company Secretary, 1976-, Company Secretary. *Memberships:* Chairman, Southern Division, Association of Superannuation Funds of Australia, 1976-78; Federal President, Federal Council, 1979-80. *Hobbies:* Squash; Music; Travel. *Address:* 147 Weatherall Road, Cheltenham, Victoria 3192, Australia.

SODIPO, Gbemi, b. 18 Apr. 1945, Abeokuta, Ogun State, Nigeria. Publishing. m. Funmilayo Ajayi 17 Dec. 1977, 1 son 1 daughter. *Education:* BA, University of Ife, Nigeria, 1971; Diploma Course in Publishing, Oxford Polytechnic, Oxford, England, 1976. *Appointments:* Secondary School Teacher, 1971-74; Assistant Editor, 1974-75; Editor, 1975-77; Senior Editor/Head of Unit 1977-80; Managing Director 1980-. *Memberships:* Mayor, Alpha Club, University of Ife, 1971; Social Scribe, 1970. *Creative Works:* Has taken part in several stage and Television Productions. *Hobbies:* Drama; Music. *Address:* 15 Okejigbo Street, Iporo Ake, Abeokuta, Ogun State, Nigeria.

SOFOLUWE, George, Oluwole, b. 24 Apr 1931, Ilugun-Abeokuta, Nigeria. Physician. University Professor. m. 1 son, 2 daughters. *Education:* MB, ChB, St. Andrews University, Scotland, 1957; Diploma in Public Health, DPH, 1961; Diploma in Industrial Health, DIH, 1965. *Appointments:* Assistant Medical Officer of Health, Lagos City Council, 1959-61; Senior Assistant & Deputy Medical Officer of Health, 1961-63; Lecturer, Ibarapa Rural Community Health Project, University of Ibadan, Ibadan, Nigeria, 1964; Lecturer/Senior Lecturer Comm. Health, University of Lagos, 196470; Regional Adviser, WHO/Regional Officer for Africa, 1970-72; WHO Professor of Comm. Health, Univesity of Zambia, 1972-73; Specialist Comm. Medicine, Environment, Birmingham, 1974-75; Professor of Community Health, University of Benin, 1975-. *Memberships:* President, African Regional Association of Occupational Health; President, Nigerian Society of Occupational Medicine; Society of Occupational Medicine of the UK; Permanent Commission and International Association of Occupational Health; Society of Community Medicine, UK; Royal Society of Health, London: Founder First Secretary and Director of the Nigerian Society of Health. *Publications:* Some original publications in the fields of Public Health, Community Health, Social Medicine and Occupational Health. *Honours:* Honorary Diploma of Sports Medicine, Mexico, 1967: Honorary Citizen of Sioux City, Iowa, USA, 1969. *Hobbies:* Sports Administration; Golf; Swimming. *Address:* Senior Staff Quarters, Permanent Campus, University of Benin, Benin City, Nigeria.

SOKOINE, Edward Moringe, b. 1938, Masai District. Tanzanian Politician (Retired). *Education:* Umbwe Secondary School; Mzumbe Local Government School. *Appointments:* Executive Officer, Masai District Council, 1956; National Assembly for Masai, Chama Cha Mapinduzi, formerly Tanganyika African Nation Union, 1965-; Parliamentary Secretary, Ministry of Communications, Transport and Labour 1967; Minister of State in Second Vice-Presidents Office, 1970; Minister of Defence and National Service 1972-77; Prime Minister, 1977-80. *Memberships:* Chairman, Masai Range Development Committee, 1965-67; Transport Licensing Authority, 1967-70. *Address:* c/o Office of the Prime Minister, Dar es Salaam, Tanzania.

SOLADOYE, Elijah Ebun, b. 21 Nov. 1930, Igosun, Kwara State, Nigeria. Educationist, Public Administrator. m. Abosede, 4 sons, 3 daughters. *Education:* BA, Ibadan University College, 1955-58; PGCE, London Universi Institute of Education, 1958; MEd, PhD, Harvard University, 19641974-5. *Appointments:* School Master, 1949-53; 1959-62; Principal, Secondary School, Advanced Teachers College, 1962-68; Chief Inspector of Education, 1970-73; Permanent Secretary, Ministry of Economics Development, 1973-75; Permanent Secretary Ministry of Works, 1976; Secretary to State Government and Head of Service, 1976-79; Directing Staff, National Institute for Policy and

Strategic Studies, Kuru, 1980-. *Memberships:* Nigerian Historical Society. *Publications:* Prize, Short Story in the Northern Festival of Arts, 1955. *Honours:* Proficiency Prize 1947; Chapel Reading Prize, 1955; Northern Festival of Art, 1955; Phi Delta Kappa, Harvard University, 1965; UNESCO Fellowship, 1964-5; Carnegie Corporation Fellowship, 1970, 74, 75. *Hobbies:* Music; Table Tennis. *Address:* 15B Abdul Razaq Road, LDA, PO Box 310, Ilorin, Kwara State, Nigeria.

SOLEBO, Monsuru Oyetunde, b. 22 Aug. 1940, Lagos, Nigeria. Supply Manager. m. Elizabeth Olabisi, 16 July 1966, 5 sons, 1 daughter. *Education:* Diploma in Management Studies; Diploma, Institute of Purchasing and Supply; Ansar-Ud-Deen School, Alakore, Lagos, 1949-56, Isolo, 1957-61; North Western Polytechnic, London, 1969; Kingston Polytechnic, Kingston on Thames, 1970. *Appointments:* Assistant Supervisor, Federal Census Board, Ikoyi; Audit Clerk, John R Kern and Company, Certified Accountants London; Senior Audit Clerk, Hackett Radley and Johnson, Chartered Accountants, London; Purchasing Manager, Vincent Shaw Entertainment, London; Administrative Manager, Pride Clarke Limited, Moter Dealer, London; Purchasing Manager, Panalpina World Transport (Nig.) Limited; Apapa, Shipping Company; Assistant Manager of Administration, West African Portland Cement Company Limited, Ewekoro Works; Supply Manager, Drake and Scull (Nig.) Limited, Lagos. *Memberships:* Institute of Purchasing and Supply; British Institute of Management; Nigerian Institute of Management. *Address:* 10 Awofeso Street, Shomolu/Palmgrove, Lagos, Nigeria.

SOLOMON, Deva Dassan, b. 14 Aug. 1941, Malaysia. Investment Consultant. m. 23 Aug. 1975, 1 son, 1 daughter. *Education:* BA, University of Malya, 1966; MA, University of British Columbia Canada, 1968; PhD, University of Hawaii, USA, 1977. *Appointments:* Secondary School Teacher, 1962-63; Lecturer, University of Malaya, 1968-78; Group Economist, Sime Darby Holdings, 1978-79; Investment Analyst and Consultant, 1980-. *Memberships:* Economic Association of Malaysia; Management Institute of Malaysia; Selangor Club. *Publications:* Stock of the Month Column in Malaysian Business, 1972-77; Population and Employment Strategy for West Malaysia; Role of Social Sciences in National Development; Exchange Rate Fluctuation in South East Asia. *Honours:* Federal Scholarship, 1959-61; Graduate Assistantship, University of British Columbia, 1967/68; Graduate Research Fellowship, University of Hawaii, 1971-72; United Nations Fellowsh 1975-77; Urbanization and Employment in Kuala Lumpur, 1975. *Hobbies:* Lecture Tours, Travel and Spending time with the family. *Address:* 17 Jalan 22/42, Petaling Jaya, Malaysia.

SOLOMON, Isidor, b. 28 Mar. 1928, Melbourne, Australia. m. Genia, 18 Aug. 1968, 2 sons. *Appointments:* Company Director and Accountant. *Memberships:* Australian Jewish Historical Societies; Victoria Branch Commit since 1955; Victoria Racing Clubs; Melbourne Cricket Club; Royal Automobile Clubs of Victoria. *Publications:* Over 80 published articles on Australian History, particularly relating to early Jewish Settlement; Contributor, Encyclopaedia Judaica, Jerusalem, 1972. *Hobbies:* World Travel; Australian History. *Address:* 35 St. Georges Road, Toorak 3142, Australia.

SOMARE, Michael Thomas, b. 9 Apr. 1936, Rabaul, Papua, New Guinea. Member of Parliamen m. Veronica Bura, Dec. 1964, 3 Sons, 2 daughters. *Education:* Matriculation Diploma of Teaching. *Appointments:* Teacher, Education Dept, Papua, New Guinea; Broadcaster and Journalist, Government Information Services, 1965-67. *Memberships:* Public Service Association Secretary, 1965-67; Lions Club, 1972-80; Rotary Club, Paul Harris Fellow, 1980. *Publications:* Sena, Autobiography Michael Somare. *Honours:* Privy Councillor, Queens Birthday Honours 1977; Companion Honours, Queens Birthday Honours, 1979. Queens Silver Jubilee Medal, 1977; Independence Medal, 1975. *Hobbies:* Football; League Fishing Golf; Reading; Photography. *Address:* Wewak, PO Box 102, Wewak, Papua-New Guinea.

SOMERSET, Henry Beaufort, b. 21 May, 1906, Mount Morgan, Queensland. Industrial Chemist. m. Patricia Agnes, 4 Nov. 1930, 2 daughters. *Education:* MSc, Trinity College, University of Melbourne, 1924-

27; *Appointments:* ICI, Billingham, U.K. 1929-34; ICIANZ, Melbourne, 1934-36; Managing Director, Associated Pulp and Paper Mills Ltd., 1937-69; Deputy Chairman, Associated Pulp and Paper Mills Ltd., 1969-. *Memberships:* FTS; FRACI; M Aus IMM; 1958 and 1966; President APPITA, 1948 Council of CSIRO 1965-73; Council of National Museum of Victoria, 1968.77; Chairman, Council of Australian Mineral Foundation, 1970; Australian Academy of Science Forum to 1975. *Honours:* CBE, 1961; KT, 1966; Chancellor, University of Tasmania, 1964 Hon. DSc, Tasmania, 1973; Leighton Memorial Medal, RACI, 1977. *Hobbies:* Natural History. *Address:* Flat 10/1, 193 Domain Road, South Yarra, Victoria 3141, Australia.

SONI, Balbir Krishna, b. 8 Apr. 1928, Pilibhit, India. Veterinary. m. Leela Soni, 12 June, 1955, 3 sons, 1 daughter. *Education:* PhD, Washington State University, Pullman, USA, 1954; MSc, Washington University, Pullman, USA, 1952; BVSc, Punjab University India, 1950. *Appointments:* Regional Animal Production and Health Officer, FAO of the United Nations, Bangkok, Thailand, 1979-; Deputy Director Genera (Animal Sciences) ICAR Government of India, New Delhi, 1971-79; Dean College of Vet. Medicine and Animal Husbandry, G.P, Pant. Agricultural University, Pantnagar, India, 1961-71; Professor and Head of the Department of Physiology, Veterinary College, Bikaner, 1955-61. *Memberships:* Fellow National Academy of Sciences of India; President, Indian Association of Animal Production, 1975-79; Secretary, Animal Production and Health Commission for Asia and Pacific; Past President Rotary International Club, Bikaner, India; Sigma XI; Council Member, The World Association for Animal Production. *Publications:* More than 75 publications of international standing in the areas of livestock production and health. *Honours:* Fellowship of National Academy of Sciences of India. *Hobbies:* Coin Collection. *Address:* Dreamland Court, Apt. 302, Prom Si 2, Off Soi 39, Sukhumvit Road, Bangkok, Thailand.

SOOPRAYEN, Paul Henry, b. 21 Apr. 1941, Port-Louis, Mauritius. Director. *Education:* BA, London University, 1966; CA, French National Archives, Paris, 1970; DdU, Aix-en-Provence University, 1974. *Appointments:* Teacher, 1961; Clerical Officer, Registrar General's Department, 1961-64; Senior Archives Assistant, 1964-73; Deputy Chief Archivist, 1973-77; Chief Archivist, 1977-. *Memberships:* Association des Instituts de recherches et de development dans l'Ocean Indien, the International Council on Archives and the Indian Historical Records Commission, 1977; Indian Ocean International Historical Association; Government Servants Association, 1970-73; Mauritius Library Association, 1973-75; Senior Civil Servants Association 1973-. *Publications:* Le Militaire de l'Ile de France, 1721-1810. *Hobbies:* Reading; Theatre going. *Address:* 7 Wellington Street, Port Louis, Mauritius.

SOUICH, du, Bertrand Patrick, b. 2 April, 1944, Paris. Professor. m. Annie, 23 Apr. 1968, 1 son, 1 daughter. *Education:* MD, University of Barcelona, Spain, 1968; ECFMG, 1970; Spanish Board of Internal Medicine, 1972; Doctoral Thesis in Pharmacology, 1976; Certificate of Approved Training in Clinical Pharmacology, San Antonio, Texas, USA, 1977; License of the Medical Council of Canada, 1979. *Appointments:* Hospital Clinico, Universidad of Barcelona, Spain, 1968-72; Hospital de la Sante Cruz y de la San Pablo, Universidad Autonoma de Barcelona, Spain, 1972-1976; University of Texas HSC at San Antonio, USA, 1976-1977; State University of New York at Buffalo, USA, 1977-78; Universite de Montreal, Canada, 1978-; Hospital Hotel-Dieu de Montreal, Canada, 1978. *Memberships:* American Society of Experimental Pharmacology and Therapeutics American Society for Clinical Pharmacology and Therapeutics; The Pharmacological Society of Canada; American Federation for Clinical Research. *Publications:* Research interests are oriented towards drug metabolism and the influence of disease on drug disposition. Selected publications: J. Pharmacol. Exp. Ther. 207; Ibid 207: 208, 1978 Clin. Pharmacol. Ther. 25: 161, 1979; Ibid 26: 757, 1979; Ibid 29: 242, 1981; J. Reticuloendothelial Soc.: In press Drug Metab. Disp.: In press. *Honours:* Magna Cum Laude, Doctoral Thesis in Pharmacology, 1976; Merck Sharp and Dohme International Fellowship in Clinical Pharmacology, 1976-78; Research Scholar of the Conseil de la Recherche en Sante du Quebec, 1979. *Address:* 8490 Sorbone, Brossard, Quebec, Canada, J4X 1N3.

SOUTH, Graham Robin, b. 27 Oct. 1940, Norwich, England. University Professor. m. Barbar Ann, 4 June, 1966, 2 daughters. *Education:* BSc. University of Liverpool, 1963; PhD, University of Liverpool, 1966. *Appointments:* Assistant Professor and Curator of Phycological Herbarium, Memorial University, Newfoundland. 1967-71; Associate Professor, Memorial University, Newfoundland. 1971-76; Professor and Head of Biology Department, Memorial University, Newfoundland, 1976-; Visiting Professor, University Helsinki, Finland, 1971; Research Fellow, University Canterbury, New Zealand, 1973-74; Editor, Phycologia, Journal of the International Phycological Society, 1977-. *Memberships:* Executive Board, Biological Council of Canada; President, Canadian Committee of University Biology Chairmen; International Phycological Society; Marine Biological Association, U.K.; Phycological Society of America; British Phycological Society; International Association of Plant Taxonomists; Canadian Botanical Association; Linnean Society of London; Royal Society of New Zealand; Pacific Science Association; Western Society of Naturalists; Norfolk Naturalists Trust; Honory Foreign Member, Societas Pro Fauna Et Flora Fennica. *Publications:* Contributor of reviews, monographs, articles to professional journals and conferences. *Honours:* Elected Foreign Member, Societas pro Fauna et Flora Fennica, 1981; Elected Fellow of the Linnean Society of London, 1975; NATO Post Doctoral Fellowship, awarded 1966-67. *Hobbies:* Writing Fiction, Poetry; Art (oils); Music (violincello); Photography. *Address:* PO Box 215, R.R. 1, Portugal Cove, Newfoundland, Canada, AOA 3KO.

SOUTHAN, David Eric, b. 6 Mar. 1936, Sydney. DentalSurgeon. m. Judith Ann, 7 Jan. 1965, 2 sons, 2 daughters. *Education:* BDS, University of Sydney, 1957; MDS University of Sydney, 1959 FDSRCS, England, 1962; FRACDS, 1965; PhD, University of Sydney, 1968. *Appointments:* Teaching Fellow, Department Operative Dentistry, University of Sydney, 1957-59; Lecturer in Operative Dentistry, University of Sydney, 1963-67; Senior Lecturer in Operative Dentistry, University of Sydney, 1967-73; Guest Research Associate, Royal Dental College, Copenhagen, 1970-71; Private Dental Practice, Crown and Bridge Work, Sydney, 1973. *Memberships:* Councillor NSW Branch, Australian Dental Association, 1974-76; Australian Society of Prosthodontists; Secretary, Royal College of Surgeons Dental Society of Australia and New Zealand, 1964-67; President N.S.W. Branch, 1968-74; Federal President, 1974-80; Pierre Fauchard Academy. *Honours:* 17 Publications - mainly on dental ceramics. *Hobbies:* Boating; Fishing. 07 19 Sherwin Street, Henley, N.S.W. 2111, Australia.

SOUTHEY, Robert John (Sir), b. 20 Mar. 1922, Melbourne, Australia. Company Director. m. Valerie Janet, 20 Aug. 1946, 5 sons. *Education:* MA Magdalen College, Oxford. *Appointments:* William Haughton and Co. Ltd., 1949-80, Chairman 1968-80; Director of the British Petroleum Company of Australia Ltd.,; Kinnears Ltd.,; International Computers, Australia Pty Ltd.,; General Accident Assurance Group (Advisory Council). *Memberships:* Federal President, Liberal Party of Australia, 1970-75; Federal Executive Liberal Party, 1966; Chairman, Australian Ballet Foundation, 1979; Melbourne Club, Australian Club, Melbourne Union Club, Sydney; Cavalry and Guards Club, London; Marylebone Cricket Club; Royal Melbourne Golf Club. *Publications:* Co-author (with C. J. Puplick) of Liberal Thinking, 1980. *Honours:* CMG, 1970, Knight Bachelor, 1976. *Hobbies:* Golf; Fishing. *Address:* 3 Denistone Avenue, Mt Eliza, Victoria, Australia 3930.

SOWDEN, John Percival, b. 6 Jan. 1917, m. Joyce Diana Mary Timson, 11 July 1969. *Education:* BSC(Eng.), ACGI, FCGI, FI.Struct.E., City & Guilds College, Imperial College of Science. *Appointments:* Joined Richard Costain Ltd., 1948, Site Project Manager on various construction projects, including Festival of Britain, Apapa Wharf, Nigeria, & Bridgetown Harbour, Barbados, 1948-60; Joint Managing Director, Richard Costain (Associates) Ltd., 1961-62; Costain-Blankevoort International Dredging Co. Ltd., 1963-65; Richard Costain Ltd., Manager, International Area 1969-70; Chief Executive 1970-73; Chairman and Group Chief Executive 1973-75; Chairman 1975-80; Director, 1980-; Central London Regional Board, and Lloyds Bank, 1980-. *Memberships:* Governing Body of Imperial College of Science & Technology 1971, Fellow

1980. *Hobbies:* Reading, Joinery. *Address:* 22 Wildcroft Manor, Putney Heath, London SW15 3TS, England.

SPANN, Richard Neville, b. 5 Mar. 1916, Manchester, England. University Professor. *Education:* Balliol College, Oxford, 1934-38; MA, Oxford. *Appointments:* Lecturer in Government, University of Manchester, 1940-53; Lieautenant RNVR in Wartime; Rockefeller Fellow, United States, 1950-51; Professor of Government, University of Sydney, 1954-. *Memberships:* President, Australasian Political Studies Association, 1955-56 Australian Research Grants Committee. *Publications:* Government Administration In Australia, 1979 Other books & Articles in learned journals. *Honours:* OBE, 1977; Fellow, Academy of Social Sciences in Australia. *Address:* St. Andrew's College, Newtown, NSW, Australia.

SPARE, Peter Dennitts, b. 27 Oct 1926, Northampton, England. Clinical Chemist. m. 3 Sept. 1955, 1 son 1 daughter. *Education:* Laboratory Sciences, Sir John Cass College, 1953; Fellowship, Sir John Cass College, 1955; MS, Biology, Lakehead University, 1979; Doctor of Philosophy, Walden University, 1980. *Appointments:* Clinical Chemist, Sudbury Memorial Hospital, Sudbury, Ont., Lecturer in Clinical Chemistry Memorial School of Med. Sci., 1955-65; Clinical Chemist, McKellar General Hospital, Thunder Bay, Ontario, Lecturer in Clinical Chemistry, Thunder Bay School Medical Science, 1965-; Program- Co-Ordinator, Division of Medical Laboratory Sciences, Lakehead University, Thunder Bay, Ontario, 1974-. *Memberships:* Fellow, Institute of Medical Laboratory Sciences; Fellow Royal Society of Health; American Association for Clinical Chemistry; American Association for the Advancement of Science; Chemical Institute of Canada; International Platform Association; New York Academy of Science; Canadian Society of Clinical Chemists. *Publications:* Articles published in the Lancet, Canadian Medical Journal; American Journal of Clinical Pathology & Clinical Chemistry. *Address:* 101 Whalen Street, Thunder Bay, Ontario, Canada.

SPEIGHT, James Holmes, b. 7 Feb. 1918, Leicestershire, England. University Administrator. m. 2 Apr. 1945, 1 son, 1 daughter. *Education:* BA, Corpus Christi College, Cambridge 1940; MA, Corpus Christi College, Cambridge, 1944. *Appointments:* Research Chemist, ICI Mond Division, 1940-63; Section Manager, Research Department, ICI, 1963-73; Administrative Officer, School of Biological Sciences, University of Leicester, 1974-. *Hobbies:* Theology, Music, Caravanning. *Address:* Treyarnon, 231 Markfield Lane, Markfield, Leicester, England.

SPENCE, David Ralph, b. 10 Mar. 1942, Hamilton, Ontario, Canada. Clergyman. m. Carol Anne Beatty, 1 son, 2 daughters. *Education:* BA, MacMaster Univeristy, 1963; L.TH, Wycliffe College, University of Toronto, 1968; King's College, Cambridge, 1975. *Appointments:* Curate, St. Georges, Guelph, Ontario, 1968; Rector, St. Bartholomew, Hamilton, Ontario, 1970; Rector, St. John's, Thorold, Ontario, 1974; Regional Dean of Niagara, 1979; Canon, Christ Church Cathedral, Hamilton, 1980. *Memberships:* Director, Heralory Society of Canada; Past President, North American, Vexillological Association. *Publications:* Published in Heraldry & Flag Journals. *Honours:* Order of St. John Knight, Yugoslavia. *Hobbies:* Collects Flags. *Address:* The Rectory, 38 Claremount Street, Thorold, Ontario, Canada.

SPENCE, John Deane, b. 7 Dec. 1920, Northern Ireland. Member of Parliament. m. A. E. Hester Nicholson, 20 Nov. 1944, 1 son 1 daughter. Queens University, Belfast. *Appointments:* British Industrialist; Member of Parliament. *Memberships:* IPU, 1979-; CPA, 1979-; NFU, Country Landowners Association; Yorkshire Derwent Trust; Anglo-Israel Friendship Society. *Hobbies:* Golf; Walking; Travel. *Address:* Greystones, Maltongate, Thornton Dale, Nr. Pickering, North Yorkshire, England.

SPENCER-BOWER, Catherine Olivia Orme, b. 13 Apr. 1905, St. Neots, Huntingdonshire, England. Painter. *Memberships:* President, Canterbury Society of Arts; Native Forest Action Council; Zonta. *Creative Works:* Noted in fluent water colours style paintings in most galleries of New Zealand & in private collections.

Honours: A water colour of Queenstown was presented to Princess Anne by the New Zealand Government. *Hobbies:* Gardening; Travel; Seeing New Zealand. *Address:* 15A Leinster Road, Christchurch, New Zealand.

SPENDER, John Michael, b. 2 Dec. 1935, Sydney, Australia. Member of The House of Representatives. m. Carla Zampatti 19 Sept. 1975, 2 daughters. *Education:* Majored in Political Science, Yale University, USA, 1953-57; Studied Law, Gray's Inn, Londond, 1957-59. *Appointments:* Admitted to practise as a barrister in England & New South Wales, 1960. Since admitted to practise in the Australian Capital Territory, Victoria, Tasmania & Hong Kong; Practising Barrister, 1961-80; Appointed Queen's Counsel, 1974; Elected to the House of Representatives, 1980. *Memberships:* Royal Sydney Golf Club. *Hobbies:* Reading; Travel. *Address:* Suite 601, 6th Floor, 83 Mount Street, North Sydney, NSW 2060, Australia.

SPICER, William John, (Dr.), b. 3 Nov 1935, Melbourne, Australia, Infectious Disease Physician, Microbiologist. m. Heather May Watson 14 Jan 1961, 2 sons, 2 daughters. *Education:* MBBS University of Melbourne, 1959; MRACP, Royal Australasian College of Physicians 1972; DTM & H University of Sydney, 1973; Dip. Bact, University of London, 1974; FRACP, 1975; MASM, Australian Society of Microbiology, 1976; FRCPA, Royal College of Pathologists of Australasia, 1977. *Appointments:* Resident & Registrar, Alfred Hospital, Melbourne, 1960-64; Resident Queen Victoria Hospital, Melbourne, 1965; Medical Superintendent, Joyramkura Christian Hospital, Bangladesh, 1966-70; Clinical Supervisor, Alfred Hospital, 1971-72; Commonwealth Medical Fellow, Post Graduate Study. 1973-74; Physician in Bacteriology, Alfred Hospital, 1975-78; Director of Bacteriology, Alfred Hospital, Senior Lecturer, Monash University, 1979-. *Memberships:* Fellow, Royal Australasian College of Physicians; Royal College of Pathologists of Australasia; Australasian Society of Infectious Diseases; Pathological Society of Great Britain and Ireland. *Publications:* Numerous publications in Antibiotic Therapy and in control of Hospital Infection. *Honours:* Commonwealth Scholarship 1953; Alfred Hospital Travelling Scholarship 1973; Commonwealth Medical Fellowship 1974; Bayer Art Prize, 1976. *Hobbies:* Oil Painting; Model making; Gardening; Carpentry; Music making; Teaching Medicine & Microbiology. *Address:* 10 Rochester Road, Canterbury, Melbourne, Australia 3126

SPIRO, Eran, b. 28 Dec. 1941, Ramat-Gan, Israel. Architect Urban Planning & Design Consultant. m. Tina Matkovic, 14 Aug. 1970, 1 son, 1 daughter. *Education:* MSC,MUP, Hunter College & Columbia University, New York, USA, 1968; BSC, BA, Columbia University, New York, 1966; Agricultural Academic Diploma, Israel. *Appointments:* Development Planning & Design Consultant, Adama Intenational Investment Corporation, Cayman Islands, 1979-; Eran Spiro & Associates, Kingston, Jamaica, 1970-; Office of Design, City Planning Commission, New York, USA, 1966-70; Architect, Urban Planning & Design Consultant & Research Assistant, Columbia University, New York, USA. *Memberships:* American Society of Consulting Planners; American Planning Association; Jamaican Institute of Architects; Association of Engineers & Architects, Israel. *Publications:* Slum Conditions and Growth in Kingstown Jamaica, 1975; Columnist, Jamaica Daily News, 1972-75; Contributed Articles to various Newspapers & Periodicals. *Honours:* Award of Merit, Coconut Grove Shopping Complex, 1975. *Hobbies:* Gardening, Horticulture, Reading, Fishing, Photography. *Address:* Hummingbird Hill, Bamboo, St. Anne, Jamaica W.1.

SPITERI, Chevalier Joseph Francis, b. 22 Feb, 1912, Sliema, Malta, Engineer, Businessman, Banker. m blanche, 11 May, 1944, 4 sons, 3 daughters. *Education:* Stella Maris College, 1920-26; Dockyard Technical School, 1926-29, Marine Engineering course under Prof. Nixon, 1929-31; Scientific Taxidermy, Omaha, Nebraska, U.S.A. 1933. *Appointments:* Engineering apprentice, H.M. Dockyard, 1926-32; Writer, H.M. Dockyard, 1935-39; Machinery Surveyor, Manager Engineer's Dept., H.M. Dockyard, 1944-47, Leading Machinery Surveyor, Manager Engineer's Dept. H.M. Dockyard, 1948; Managing Director, Joseph F. Spiteri & Co. 1948-77; Board of Prison Visitors, 1972-79; Wine Advisory Board, 1977-78; Director, Bank of Valet-

ta Ltd., 1974-79; Vice-Chairman, Marsa Flour Mills Ltd., 1976-79; Chairman, Portelli Int. Ltd., 1974-79; Chairman, Monninghoff Metals, (Malta) Ltd., 1977-79; Chairman, Mqqabba Marbles ltd., 1977-79; Created Knight of Grace, Sovereign Order of St. John of Jerusalem, 1977; Elected Prior of Malta, 1981. *Memberships:* Marsa Sports Club, Malta; Society for the Study & Preservatio of Nature, Malta; Agrarian Society, Malta; Royal Horticultural Society, London; Royal Commonwealth Society, London. *Honours:* Recipient of numerous honours and awards for professional services. *Hobbies:* Gardening; Fruit farming; Shooting; Taxidermy. *Address:* Gilda Court, St. Andrew's Rd., St. Andrew, Malta.

SPOONER, Frank Bakeo, b. 11 Nov. 1936, Ndui Ndui, Ambae, Vanuatu, (New Hebrides), Medical Officer, Director of Health Services. m. Fulori Golesobu, 3 daughters. *Education:* DSM, Fiji School of Medicine, 1962; D.Obst., University of Auckland, 1972. *Appointments:* Medical Officer, British National Service, New Hebrides, 1962-74; Superintendant, Vila Base Hospital, 1975-77; Chief Medical Officer and Director of Health, 1978-79; Director of Health, Vanuata Government, 1980-. *Memberships:* Vice-Chairman British Red Cross Society, New Hebrides, 1975-8 British Ex-Servicemens Club, 1981. *Honours:* MBE 1975 New Year Honours. *Hobbies:* Rugger; Table Tennis; Gardening. *Address:* Picardie Street, Port Vila, Vanuatu, New Hebrides.

SPRAGG, Griffith Silas, b. 24 Jan. 1922, Maitland, N.S.W, Medical practitioner. m. Patricia M. Lamberth, 18 April, 1955, 1 son, 1 daughter. *Education:* MB. BS Sydney University, 1953; DPM, Sydney University, 1967; MRANZCP, 1968; FRANZCP, 1978. *Appointments:* Resident Medical Officer, Royal South Sydney Hospital, 1953-55; N.S.W. Dept, of Health, 1963-72; Dept. Veterans' Affairs, Sydney, 1972-74; Senior Specialist in Charge, Psychiatry, NSW, 1974; Consultant Psychiatry, Australian Dept. Veterans Affairs, 1975-. *Memberships:* Australian Medical Association; Fellow, Royal Australian & New Zealand College of Psychiatrists. *Publications:* Psychiatry in the Australian Military Forces. *Hobbies:* Golf. *Address:* 51, Horace Street, St. Ives, N.S.W. Australia.

SPRINGER, Hugh, Worrell (Sir), b. 22 June, 1913, Barbados, Barrister at Law; Consultant on Education & Development. m. Dorothy D. Gittens, 1 Aug.1942, 3 sons, 1 daughter. *Education:* BA 1936, MA 1944, Hartford College, Oxford; Barrister at Law, The Inner Temple, London, 1938; Fellow, Harvard University Centre for International Affairs, 1961-62; Snr. Visiting Fellow, All Souls College, Oxford,1962-63. *Appointments:* Organiser and First General Sec, Barbados Workers union, 1940-47; General Secretary, Barbados Labour Party, 1940-47; Practice at the Bar, Barbados, 1938-47; Registrar, University of the West Indies, 1947-63; Director, U.W.I. Institute of Education, 1963-66; Commonwealth Assistant Secretary General, 1966-70; Secretary General Association of Commonwealth Universities 1970-80. *Memberships:* Chairman, Member, Fellow, of various bodies and institutions within the West Indies and the Commonwealth. *Publications:* Reflections on the Failure of the First West Indian Federation, Harvard, 1962; numerous articles and publications on Education and Development in journals and periodicals. *Honours:* OBE, 1954; CBE, 1961; KCMG, 1971 and numerous honours and awards for professional services. *Hobbies:* Reading; Talking; Writing. *Address:* Gibbes, St. Peter, Barbados, West Indies.

SPRY, John, Farley, b. 11 March, 1910, Cambridge, England, Solicitor.m. Stella M. Fichat, 4 Oct. 1953, 1 son, 1 daughter. *Education:* Perse School, Cambridge, 1919-29; Peterhouse, Cambridge, 1929-32; Exhibitioner, 1929; MA, 1933. *Appointments:* Colonial Legal Service: Assistant Registrar of Titles & Conveyancer, Uganda, 1936-44; Chief Inspector of Land Registration, Palestine, 1944; Assistant director of Land Registration, Palestine, 1944-48; Registrar-General, Tanganyika, 1948-50; Registrar-General, Kenya, 1950-52; Registrar-General, Tanganyika, 1952-56; Legal Draftsmam. Tanganyika, 1956-60; Principal Secretary, Public Service Commission, Tanganyika, 1960-61; Puisne Judge, High Court, Tanganyika, 1961-64; Justice of Appeal, Court of Appeal for Eastern Africa, 1964-70; Vice-President, Court of Appeal for East Africa,

1970-75; Legal Chairman, Pensions Appeal Tribunals, 1975-76; Chief Justice, Gibraltar, 1976-80; Justice of Appeal, Gibraltar Court of Appeal, 1980-. *Publications:* Sea Shells of Dar Es Salaam, 1961-64; Civil Procedure in East Africa, 1969; Civil Law of Defamation in East Africa, 1976. *Honours:* Knight Bachelor, 1975. *Hobbies:* Conchology; Bird-watching. *Address:* 15, De Vere Gardens, London, W8 5AN, England.

SPURLING, Arthur Dudley (Sir), b. 9 Nov. 1913, Bermuda. Barrister & Attorney. m. 19 June, 1941 3 sons, 1 daughter. *Education:* MA,Law, Trinity College, Oxford, England, London, 1933-36. *Appointments:* Senior Partner, Appleby, Spurling & Kempe, 1948-81; Member Lincoln's Inn, London; Called to English Bar, 1937. *Memberships:* Bermuda Historical Society; The English Speaking Union, 1965; Institute of Directors, London; Oxford and Cambridge University Club, London. *Honours:* Justice of the Peace, 1957; CBE, 1963; Knighthood, 1975. *Hobbies:* Golf; Boating; Swimming; Horticulture; Carpentry. *Address:* 'Three Chimneys', Wellington, St. Georges, Bermuda.

SQUIRE, John Michael, b. 27 June, 1945, Grappenhall, Cheshire, England. University Lecturer, m. Melanie Rae, 12 Aug. 1969, 4 daughters. *Education:* BSc (Physics) 1966; AKC, 1966; PhD, 1969; M.Inst.P, 1979. *Appointments:* Biophysics Institute, Aarhus University, Denmark; Zoology Department, Oxford; Department Metallurgy and Materials, Science, Biopolymer Group, Imperial College, London. *Memberships:* British Biophysical Society; Biophysical Society of America, Royal Microscopical Society, Institute of Physics. *Publications:* General model for the structure of all myosin-containing filaments, 1971; The role of tropomyosin in muscle regulation: analysis of the X-ray diffraction patterns from relaxed and contracting muscles, (with D.A.D. Parry), 1973; General model of myosin filament structure III: molecular packing arrangements in myosin filaments, 1973; Cryo-ultramicrotomy and myofibrillar fine structure, (with M. Sjostrom), 1977; Organisation of myosin in the thick filaments of muscle, 1979; The structural basis of muscular contraction, 1981. *Hobbies:* Music; Photography; D.I.Y.; Drawing. *Address:* 8, Chestnut Drive, Englefield Green, Surrey, TW20 OBJ, England.

SREEDHARAN, Thekkeyil, b. 25 Oct. 1927, Calicut, S. India. Doctor. m. Dr. Sudha, 2 sons, 1 daughter. *Education:* BSc. University of Madras, 1948; MBBS, University of Karnatak, 1960; DTM & H, University of Liverpool, 1967; DTCD, University of Wales, 1969; MRSH, Royal Society of London, 1969; FCCP, 1974. *Appointments:* Rotating Internee, Demonstrator/Lecturer and Tutor in Indian hospitals and Colleges, 1959-72; Registrar & SHO, Llangwyfan Hospital, Wales, U.K, 1966-70; Consultant Physician, Central Chest Clinic, Calicut, India, 1972-. *Memberships:* Member of I.M.A., 1960- *Publications:* Contributed to various journals. *Honours:* Distinguished Alumni Award from Kasturba Medical College, 1979. *Hobbies:* Classical Karnatic Music; Advanced study in Applied Medicine. *Address:* Aravinda Ghosh Road, Near 3rd. Ry Gate, Central Chest Clinic, Calicut.1. Kerala State, South India.

SREENIVASAN, Kasi, b. 10 July, 1899, Hebbur Village, Tumkur Taluk, Karnataka State, India. Electronics and Radio Engineering. *Education:* BSc. University of Mysore, India, 1920; Diploma and Associateship in Electrical Technology, Indian Institute of Bangalore, 1926; *Appointments:* Assistant Professor of Electrical Communication Engineering, Indian Institute of Science, Bangalore, 1932-45; Professor of Telecommunication Engineering, College of Engineering, Madras, 1945-48; Professor and Head of Department of Electrical Communication Engineering, Indian Institute of Science, Bangalore, 1948-59; Acting Director, Indian Institute of Science, Bangalore, 1955-57; Director, Madras Institute of Technology, Madras, 1960-71. *Memberships:* Fellow of the Indian Academy of Sciences, and of the Institution of Electrical Engineers, London; Distinguished Fellow of the Institution of Electronics and Telecommunication Engineers, and Senior Member of the Institute of Electrical and Electronics Engineers, New York. *Publications:* About a dozen papers published in Indian, European, & American radio journals, relating mostly to radio wave propagation. About 10 articles on nationwide broadcast development in India in Indian journals. *Hobbies:* Reading; Gardening. *Address:* Krishna Kripa, 275/31- 17th

Cross Road, Upper Palace Orhcard, Bangalore-560080, India.

SRIVASTAVA, Chandrika Prasad, b. 8 July, 1920, Unnao, India. Secretary-General, inter-Governmental Maritime Consultative Organization, (United Nations), m. Nirmala Salve, 7 April, 1947, 2 daughters 02 1st.cl.BA, 1940; 1st cl. BA Hons, 1941; 1st cl. MA, 1942; 1st cl. LLB, 1944 , gold medals for proficiency in English Literature and Political Science. *Appointments:* Under-Secretary to the Government of India, Ministry of Commerce, 1948-49; City Magistrate, Lucknow, India, 1950; Additional District Magistrate, Meernut, India, 1951-52; Officer on Special Duty, Directorate-General of Shipping, 1953; Deputy Director-General of Shipping, 1954-57; Deputy Secretary, Ministry of Transport and Private Secretary to the Ministry of Transport and Communications/Minister of Commerce and Industry, 1958; Senior Deputy Director-General of Shipping, 1959Managing Director, Shipping corporation of India Ltd., Bombay, 1961-64; Joint Secretary to the Prime Minister of India, 1964-66; Chairman of the Board of Directors and Managing Director, Shipping corporation of India Ltd., 1966-73; Chairman of the Board of Directors, Mogul Line Ltd., 1967-73; Director, Central Board, Reserve Bank of India, 1972-73; Secretary-General, Inter-Governmental Maritime Consultative Organization, 1974-. Also, President, Chairman, Vice-President and Member of various other organizations. *Memberships:* Willingdon Sports CLub, Bombay; Curzon House Club, London; Delhi Symphony Society. *Publications:* Articles on shipping in newspapers and journals. *Honours:* Padma Bhushan, 1972 *Hobbies:* Music,; Tennis; Reading. *Address:* 56, Ashley Gardens, Ambrosden Avenue, London, S.W.1, England.

SRIVASTAVA, Sushil Kumar, b. 26 Feb. 1920, Rewa M.P. India. Teaching and Social Service. m. Smt. Kusum, 23 May, 1949, 2 sons, 3 daughters. *Education:* BSc. (Hons) University of Allehabad; MSc, Allahabad University, 1944 PhD, Sagar University, 1974; *Appointments:* Demonstrator in Physics, Degree College, Rewa, 1940; Lecturer, Allahabad University, 1947; Lecturer, Darbar Degree College, Rewa, 1947; Administrative Officer, Ministry of Defence, 1959-62; Professor and Head, P.G. College, Satna, 1974; APS University, Rewa. *Memberships:* Indian Mathematical Society; National Academy of Sciences, India; Chairman Board of Studies in Mathematics, APS University, Rewa; In college service till 1978; *Publications:* Published papers in Mathematics in Scientific Journals; Composed verses in English and Hindi; Wrote papers entitled Food for Thought, 1, 2, etc. on Political Ills. *Honours:* Recipient of numerous honours and awards for professional services. *Hobbies:* Writing articles (English and Hindi); Composing verses and poetry (English and Hindi); Teaching undergraduates and living in solitude. *Address:* Uprahti, Rewa (MP), India.

SSENNYONJO, Leonard, b. 30 Aug. 1936, Mpigi, Uganda. Librarian. m. Maurice Nabakoza, 9 May 1970, 1 son, 4 daughters. *Education:* STB, Fribourg, Switzerland, 1961-63; DipLib, University of East Africa, 1965-67; BA, University of East Africa, 1969-72; DipLib of InformSc, London,1972-73. *Appointments:* Special Assistant, Makerere University, 1964-72; Assistant Librarian, Makeure University, 1972-77; Medical Librarian, Makeure University, 1978-. *Memberships:* Uganda Library Association; Kyengera Savings Association. *Publications:* Contributed to various professional journals. *Hobbies:* Gardening; Swimming. *Address:* Albert Cook Library, Makerere Medical School, P.O. Box 7072, Kampala, Uganda.

STAAS, Sydney, b. 17 Mar. 1921, Newcastle, Natal, South Africa. Company director. m. Daphne Alma, 8 July 1944, 3 sons. *Education:* FCIS, Chartered Institute of Secretaries; FASA, Australian Society of Accountants. *Appointments:* Lieutenant, AIF, 1940-45; Technical School Teacher, 1945-47; Managing Director, Own Business, 1947-. *Memberships:* N.S.W. Golf Club; St. George's Leagues Club; St. George's Motor Boat Club; Matraville R.S.L. Club; Australian Jockey Club. *Hobbies:* Horseracing; Gardening. *Address:* 18 Castle Street, Blakehurst, N.S.W. 2221, Australia.

STACE, Clifford, Jack, b. 27 Dec. 1910, Wellington, New Zealand. Retired Lawyer. m. 25 July 1942. *Education:* LLB, Victoria University of Wellington, 1928-32;

Admitted as Barrister and Solicitor, Supreme Court, 1933. *Appointments:* Chief Administration Officer, Department of Maori Affairs, 1952-58; Commissioner of Maori Land Court, Judicial and Administration, 1958-62; Chief Judge, High Court, Cook Islands, 1960-61; Judge, Native Land Court, Niue and Cook Islands, 1960-62; President, Land Appellate Court, Cook Islands, 1960; Solicitor, Island Territories Department, New Zealand, 1961-65; Acting Solicitor, Office of the Ombudsman, 1964; Chairman, New Zealand Public Service Appeal Board, 1965-74. *Memberships:* New Zealand Federation of Tuberculosis Associations, 1954-58; Honorary Legal Advisor, New Zealand National Maori Council, 1965-68; Founding Committee, Friends at Court, Wellington, 1977. *Publications:* Contributed to various journals. *Honours:* Prox Accessit for initial Chief Justices' Prize, VUW, 1930; Senior National Scholarship, 1926. *Hobbies:* Rugby; Cricket; Tennis; Golf; Swimming; Bush-walking; Relaxing; Punting. *Address:* 1 Waerenga Road, Days Bay, Eastbourne, New Zealand.

STACK, Ellen, Mary, b. Sydney, Australia. Medical Practioner. m. Thomas Robert Lawler. 3 sons. *Education:* Australian music Associateship; Bachelor of Medicine; Bachelor of Surgery, University of Sydney; Fellow, Royal Australian College of General Practioners. *Appointments:* RMO, Eastern Suburbs Hospital, Sydney; General Practice, Merr Sydney; RMO/CMO, Department of Health, Darwin N.T., General Practice, Darwin N.T., Medical Officer Sessional, Department of Health, Darwin N.T. *Memberships:* Lord Mayor, Darwin, 1979-80; Mayor, Darwin, 1975-79; Alderman, Darwin City Council, 1969-75; Councillor, St. John's Ambulance Council, Councillor inaugural Council, Darwin Community College; N.T. Medical Registration Board; N.T. Consultative Committee, Social Welfare; World Wildlife Fund. *Publications:* Contributed to various journals. *Honours:* Recipient of CBE, 1979; SSSt J, 1978. *Hobbies:* Music; Reading; Golf. *Address:* Box 167, P.O. Darwin N.T., 5794, Australia.

STADEN, Wolfgang Oskar, Von, b. 14 Oct. 1928, Niedersachswerfen, Germany. Veterinary Surgeon. m. 7 Sept. 1957, 1 son, 1 daughter. *Education:* Graduated, Doctor of Veterinary Medicine, Ontario Veterinary College, 1962. *Appointments:* General Practitioner. *Memberships:* SVMA; CVMA; MVMA. *Hobbies:* Collecting paintings; Coins. *Address:* Box 280, Redvers, Saskatchewan, Canada, SOC2HO.

STALEY, Anthony Allan, b. 15 May 1939, Horsham, Victortia, Australia. m. Elsa Mary Harper, 11 Sept. 1962, 3 sons, 1 daughter. *Education:* First Class Hons, Law and Political Science, University of Melbourne. *Appointments:* Senior Lecturer in Government, University of Melbourne; Member for Chisolm, Federal Parliament, 1970-80; Parliamentary Secretary to Sir W. Sneddon and Right Honorable M.Fraser, Minister for Capital Territory; Minister Assisting Prime Minister in the arts in the phase of Government; Minister for Post and Telecommunication in the second Fraser Government; Director, Reed Stenhouse Limited, Ausonics PTY Limited, Mitsubishi Motors, Australia, PTY Limited, Ogilivy and Mather PTY Limited *Memberships:* Confederation of Australian Professional Performing Arts; National Multiple Sclerosis Society of Australia; Impaired Hearing for Children; Yarra Valley Church of England School; Old Scoth Collegians Assocation. *Hobbies:* Poetry; Music; Sport; Drama. *Address:* Yarraview, St. Huberts Road, Coldstream, Victoria, Australia.

STANBROOK, Ivor, Robert, b. 13 Jan. 1924, London, England. Member of Parliament and Barrister. m. Joan Clement, 17 Apr. 1946, 2 sons. *Education:* BSc, Econ, University College, London, 1946-48; Pembroke College, Oxford, 1948-9, 1956-7; Called to the Bar, 1960. *Appointments:* Colonial Administrative Service, Nigeria, 1950-60 ; Practising Barrister, Inner Temple, 1960-; Member of Parliament, Orpington, 1970 *Memberships:* Founder, Britain-Nigeria Association, 1961; Chairman, British-Nigerian Parliamentary Group, 1980-*Publications:* Extradition, The Law Practice, 1979. *Hobbies:* Film-making. *Address:* 6 Sevenoaks Road, Orpington, Kent, England.

STANLEY, Papalii, Alexander, Edward, b. 2 Oct. 1924, Apia Western Samoa, Vaiusu. Customs Officer. m. Helene Christina Oldehaver, 16 Aug. 1954, 3 sons, 4 daughters. *Education:* Technical College, Wellington,

New Zealand, 1948. *Appointments:* Port Administrator, Marine Department, 1972-75; Collector of Customs, Customs Department, 1976-77; Comptroller of Customs, Customs Department, 1977- *Memberships:* Masonic Lodge, Calliope; Boomerang Social Club; Public Service Association; Lions Club; Church Activities. *Hobbies:* Shooting; Fishing; Stamp Collecting. *Address:* P.O. Box 510, Apia, Western Samoa.

STARK, Andrew Alexander Steel, b. 30 Dec. 1916, Fauldhouse, West Lothian, Scotland. H.M. Diplomatic Service, Retired, Company Director. m. Rosemary Helen Oxley Parker, 24 Aug. 1944, 3 sons. *Education:* Bathgate Academy, 1927-33; University of Edinburgh, 1933-38; MA Hons, English Literature, 1938. *Appointments:* Major, H.M. Forces, The Green Howards, 1945; British Diplomatic Service, 1948; First Secretary British Embassy, Vienna, 1951-53; Assistant Private Secretary, Foreign Secretary, 1953-56; First Secretary, British Embassy, Belgrade, 1956-58; First Secretary, British Embassy, Rome, 1958-60; Counsellor, Foreign Office, 1960-64; Counsellor, British Embassy, Bonn, 1964-68, Ambassador, UK Mission to UN, New York, 1968; Under secretary General, United Nations, 1968-71; British Ambassador, Denmark, 1971-76; Deputy Under Secretary of State, Foreign and Commonwealth Office, 1976-77; Chairman, Maersk Company Limited; Director, Scandinavian Bank Limited; Director, Carlsberg Brewery Limited, 1978- *Memberships:* Chairman, Traveller's Club, 1978-81; MCC, Anglo-Danish Society. *Publications:* Articles for United Nations Journal. *Honours:* Recipient of KCMG, 1975; CVO, 1965; Grosses Verdienst Kreuz, German Federal Republic, 1965;Grand Cross, Order of the Dannebrog Denmark, 1974. *Hobbies:* Reading; Music; Shooting; Tennis; Golf. *Address:* Fambridge Hall, White Notley, Witham, Essex, England.

STARK, Denis John, b. 15 Nov. 1937, Crow's Nest, Queensland, Australia. Ophthalmologist. m. Mary Jane Perkins, 21 May 1962, 6 sons, 2 daughters. *Education:* MB, BS, 1962; FRCS, 1970; FRACO, 1970. *Appointments:* Resident Medical Officer, Townsville General Hospital, 1963-65; Surgical Registrar, Mater Hospital, Brisbane, 1966; Ophthalmic Registrar, Brisbane Mater Hospital, 1967-68; Ophthalmic Registrar, Tennant Institutee of Ophthalmology, University of Glasgow, 1969-70; Ophthalmologist, Mater Hospital, Brisbane, 1970-78; Consultant Ophthalmologist, Mater Childrens Hospital, Brisbane, 1970-; Director, St. Andrews Neurosensory Unit, Brisbane, 1978-. *Memberships:* Chairman Queensland Branch, Royal Australian College of Ophthalmologist, 1978-79; Council, 1978-80; Executive, 1979-80; International Socieity of Clinical Electrophysiology, 1978-; AMA, 1962. *Hobbies:* Fishing; Rugby. *Address:* 25 Lloyd Street, Camp Hill, Brisbane, Queensland, Australia.

STEEL, David Martin Scott, b. 31 Mar 1938. Kirkcaldy, Scotland. Member of the Liberal Party since 1976. Member of Parliament. m. Judith MacGregor, 26 Oct 1962. 3 sons, 1 daughter. *Education:* MA, LLB, Edinburgh University. *Appointments:* Assistant Secretary, Scottish Liberal Party, 1962-64; Television Reporter, BBC Scotland, 1964; MP, 1965-. *Publications:* No Entry, 1968; A house divided, 1980. *Honours:* Privy Counsellor, 1979. *Hobbies:* Walking; Fishing; Riding; Motoring. *Address:* House of Commons, London, England.

STEELE, Colin Robert, b. 2 Mar 1944, Hartlepool, Co. Durham, England. Librarian. m. Anna Elizabeth, 22 July 1967. 2 sons. *Education:* BA, Liverpool University, 1965; Diploma in Librarianship University College, London, 1967; MA, Liverpool University, 1971. *Appointments:* Standing Conference of National University Libraries (SCONUL) trainee, Liverpool University Library, UK, 1965-66; Assistant Librarian, Bodleian Library, UK, 1967-76; Deputy Librarian, Australian National University, 1976-80; University Librarian, Australian National University, 1980- *Memberships:* Commonwealth Club, Canberra; University House, Canberra; Canberra Oxford Association, Secretary; Bibliographical Society of Australia & New Zealand; Magellan Society, Co Secretary; Hakluyt Society; Library Associations of UK & Australia. *Publications:* Contributor of reviews, monographs, articles to professional journals and conferences. *Honours:* Hartlepool Grammar School, Chairman of Governor's Prize, 1959; British Academy, American Visiting Fellowship, 1974.

Hobbies: Sport; Science Fiction. *Address:* 11 Elsey Street, Hawker, ACT 2614, Australia.

STEELE, Ian William, b. 2 Jan 1931, Sydney, Australia. Consulting Engineer. m. Pauline Gaillard, 17 Aug 1957. 3 sons, 1 daughter. *Education:* Bachelor of Engineering, 1962, University of New South Wales, Australia. *Appointments:* 1947-54 Engineering Trainee with Australian Iron and Steel Limited; 1954-57, Joined McLellan and Partners, UK: 1957-64, Joined the joint Australian office of Merz and McLellan and McLellan and Partners; 1964-67, Manager of the joint Melbourne office of Merz and McLellan and McLellan and Partners; 1967-71, Manager of the joint Perth Office of Merz and McLellan and McLellan and Partners; 1971-77, Joined the partnership of Merz & McLellan and Partners on its formation in Jan 1971; 1978, Managing Partner for Australia of Merz & McLellan & Partners; 1979, Senior Partner of Merz & McLellan & Partners. *Memberships:* Chairman of National Committee on Electric Energy; Western Australian Division Committee of the Institution of Engineers; WA Electrical Branch Committee of the Institute of Engineers; Electrical College Board of the Institute of engineers; Council of the Institute of Engineers; WA Chapter Committee of ACEA; WA Secretariat of the Institution of Electrcal Engineers; Overseas Representative for WA of the IEE; Councillor of the Perth Chamber of Commerce; The Institute of Arbitrators; Energy Advisory Council Work Party on Energy Research. *Hobbies:* Yachting. *Address:* 12, Malton Place, City Beach, 6015, Western Australia.

STEIDL, Peter Emil, b. 13 Nov 1949, Vienna. Senior Lecturer in Commerce, Vice Consul of Austria for South Australia and Northern Territory. m. Diana S.d.R.B. Lewis, 4 Nov 1978. 2 sons, 1 daughter. *Education:* MBA, 1971; PhD, 1973. *Appointments:* Wissenschaftliche Hilfskraft, Wirtschaftsunivesitaet Wien; Universitaetsassisten Wirtschaftsunivesitaet Wien; Teaching Fellow, University of Adelaide; Senior Teaching Fellow, University of Adelaide; Lecturer, University of Adelaide; Senior Lecturer, University of Adelaide *Memberships:* Director, Institute for Community Resource Development; Child and Home Safety Centre, Chairman Research Subcommittee; Australian Market Research Society, SA Division, President, 1980; American Marketing Association; Australian Society of Accountants; Australian Marketing Institute. *Publications:* Author of a book on Experimental Market Research; Co-editor of Australian Marketing Reading; Author of more than 15 articles and contributions to books. *Hobbies:* Skiing; Problem solving. *Address:* 18, Baliol Street, College Park, 5069, Australia.

STEINER, Michael David, b. 27 May 1946, Prague. Ophthalmic Surgeon.m. Imogen E. Osborne, 1 June 1971. 2 sons. *Education:* MB, BS, 1970; DO, (Syd), 1974; FRACO, 1974, Cranbrook School Sydney University. *Appointments:* JRMO, SRMO, 1970-71, Sydney Hospital; Ophthalmic Registrar St George Hospital Sydney, 1972; Registrar, Sydney Eye Hospital, 1973-74; Part-time Lecturer, Sydney University, Department of Ophthalmology, 1975; Honorary Ophthalmic Surgeon, The Bankstown Hospital, 1975; Lewisham Hospital, 1975; Private Practice, Ophthalmic Surgery, 1975- *Memberships:* Honorary Secretary Royal Australian College of Ophthalmologists Australian Association of Surgeons, NSW committee; Australian Medical Association; The Oxford Ophthalmological Congress. *Address:* 15 Point Road, Northwood, 2066, Sydney, Australia.

STENDERUP, Vibeke, b. 3 Mar. 1921, Copenhagen, Denmark. Research Librarian. m. Aksel Stenderup, 20 Dec. 1947, 2 sons, 1 daughter. *Education:* Cand.mag., Århus and Copenhagen, Universities, English Language and Literature, Physical Culture, 1952; Diploma Royal School of Librarianship, 1968. *Appointments:* Free-lance scriptwriter, Danish Broadcasting Company, 1943-45; Assistant Librarian State and University Library, Århus, 1953-55; Instructor in Ergonomics, Post-graduate Nurses College, 1957-63; Research Librarian, 1964-67; Chief Cataloguer, 1968-72; Readers Service Librarian, University South Pacific Library, Fiji, 1972-73; Senior Research Librarian, State and University Library, Århus, 1973-; Subject specialist in Modern English Literature, Commonwealth Literature and Oceanic Cultures. *Memberships:* Danish Masters of Arts and Science, Library Section; President, Women's Debating Club, Århus, 1970-72; International Federation of University Women; Association of Commonwealth Language and Literature Studies, European and South Pacific Branches; Danish Research Librarians Association; Nordic Association of Research Librarians. *Publications:* Radio scripts; Articles; Lectures, etc. on libraries and librarianship in Scandinavia and the South Pacific; Bibliographical work on writers from the Commonwealth; Co-ed.: Documentation on Developing Countries in Nordic Research Libraries, 1980; Ed. Guide to Documentation on Developing Countries in Nordic Research Libraries, 1981. *Honours:* International Federation of University Women, Winifred Cullis Grant 1980. *Address:* Saralystvej 15, DK-8270 Hojbjerg, Denmark.

STENING, Samuel Edward Lees, b. 14 May 1910, Sydney Australia. Medical Pratitioner (Paediatrics). m. 19 Aug 1941. 1 daughter. *Education:* MB, BS 1933, Sydney University; DCH, Royal Colleges of Physician & Royal College of Surgeons, 1937; MRACP, 1938; fracp, 1950. *Appointments:* General Practice, Sydney, 1937; Honorary Relieving Assistant, Physician, Royal Alexandra Hospital for Children, 1938-46; MRACP, 1938; Surgeon Lieutenant, 1939; Surgeon Lieutenant Commander, R.A.N.R, 1945; Specialist Paediatrician, 1945-Honorary Assistant Physician, Royal Alexandra Hospital for Children, 1946-50; Senior Honorary Paediatrician, The Women's Hospital, Sydney, 1947-Honorary Consulting Paedia trician, St. Luke's Hospital, Sydney, 1951- Honorary Physician, Royal Alexandra Hospital for Children, 1950-56; SEnior Honorary Physician, Royal Alexandra Hospital for Children, 1956-68; FRACP, 1951. *Memberships:* Australian Club, Royal Sydney Golf Club; Australian Jockey Club; President Australian Paediatric Association, 1968-69. *Honours:* DSC, 1945. *Hobbies:* Fishing; Philately. *Address:* 53, Fairfax Road, Bellevue Hill, 2023, Sydney, Australia.

STEPHEN, William Francis, b. 23 July 1921, Fremantle, Western Australia. Political Advisor and Seedsman, Proprietor. m. May T. Waters, 15 Feb 1947; 2 sons, 2 daughters. *Education:* COMM/OFF, RAAF, Aircrew 5 years, 1942-46. Sqd. Gunnery Wireless & radar Leader RAF 95 Sqdn. *Appointments:* Farmer 1948/73; Member Victorian Legislative Assembly as MP for Ballarat South, 1964-79; Voluntarily Retired, Acting Speaker, 1973-79; Chairman all Party State Development committee, 1974-79; Political Advisor, 1979- Seed Merchant, 1956, Still operationg own business. *Memberships:* Chairman of Directors 15 Co-op Housing Societies; President Victorian Seed Merchants Association, 1973; Patron Spastic Society; Airforce Association. *Honours:* Queen's Silver Jubilee Medal, 1977; Special Life Member Sovereign Hill (Ballarat Historical Park Association; Honorary Life Member for Services Rendered, Elderly Citizens and Disabled. *Hobbies:* Lawn bowling; Tennis; Racing; Billiard. *Address:* 4, St Aidans Drive, Ballarat 3350, Victoria, Australia.

STEPHENS, Benedit, b. 3 July, 1926, Kudat. Director. m. 25 Aug 1951. 4 sons, 4 daughters. *Education:* Diploma In Political Science and Public Administration, Carlon University, Ottawa, Canada, 1959-60. *Appointments:* Hospital Assistant, Queen Elizabeth Hospital, 1945; Town Board Inspector, Jesselton Town Board, 1958; District Officer, Keningau, 1962; District Officer, Sandakan, 1963-64; Assistant Secretary, (Defence), Chief Minister's Department, 1964-65; Permanent Secretary, Ministry of Agriculture and Fisheries, 1966; resident, Tawau, 1966; Resident West Coast, Kota Kinabalu, 1969-71; Resident, Sandakan, 1971; Director of Establishment, Chief Minister's Department, 1976; Director and Board Member, Sabah Foundation, since 1976. *Publications:* British Empire Medal, UK, 1957; Panglima Gemiland Darjah Kinabalu, Sabah, 1972; Seri Panglima Darjah Kinabalu, Sabah, 1980. *Hobbies:* Golf; Cricket; Gardening. *Address:* Yayasan House, Mile 3/half, Tuaran Road, Kota Kinabalu, Sabah, Malaysia.

STEPHENS, Ian, b. 19 May 1940, Great Linford, Bucks, England. Artist. m. Valerie Aldridge, 7 March 1964, 2 sons. *Education:* Northampton School of Art, National Diploma in Design, 1961; Leicester Polytechnic, Diploma in Educational Studies, Art Education, 1975. *Appointments:* Art Teacher, Olney Secondary Modern School, 1961-62; Graphic Designer, Gayton Advertising, Leicester, 1962-64; Art Teacher Northampton, 1964-78; Freelance Artist Printmaker &

Typographic Designer, 1978- *Memberships:* Associate of the Royal Society of Painter-etchers & Engravers; Northampton Town & County Art Society; Kettering & District Art Society. *Publications:* Relief Prints, mainly wood engravings; landscape and man's works upon it. *Honours:* Elected ARE, 1981. *Hobbies:* Walking; Cricket; Orienteering; Local History; Natural History Architecture; Heraldry; Roads; Tracks; Railways. *Address:* 25 Knight's Lane, Kingsthorpe, Northampton, NN2 6QN, England.

STEPHENS, Rupert St. John, b. 24 June 1917, Oswestry, Shropshire, England. Teacher. m. 8 Dec 1941. *Education:* MA, St. John's College Oxford, 1936-39. Oxon, 1945. *Appointments:* Hurstpierpoint College, 1949-56; Kingston Grammar School, 1956-81. *Memberships:* Kingston & Malden Conservative Association; Executive. Committee Councillor, 1974; Hon. Treasurer, Norbiton Ward, Kingston, Director, Lansdowne Club. KAC. *Honours:* Appointed JP, 1976 *Hobbies:* Cinema; Squash; Hockey. *Address:* 9, Vicarage House, Cambridge, Kingston Upon Thames, Surrey, KT1 3NE, England.

STEPHENS-NEWSHAM, Lloyd George, b. 30 April 1921, Saskatoon, Saskatchewan, Canada. University Professor. m. Lois R. Brown, 28 June 1950, 2 daughters. *Education:* BA, University of Saskatchewan, 1943; PhD, McGill University, 1948. *Appointments:* 1944-45, Lecturer in Physics, University of Manitoba; 1948-51, Assistant Professor Of Physics, Dalhousie University; 1952-66, Assoc. Professor of Physics and of Raiology, McGill University and Radiation Physicst, Royal Victoria Hospital Montreal, Consultant Physicst to Hotel Dieu de Montreal, Montreal Childrens Hospital, Jewish General Hospital, Montreal; 1966- Professor, University of Alberta. *Memberships:* Canadian College of Physicist in Medicine, Fellow; Canadian Association of Physicists, President of Medical Physics Division, 1956-57; Society of Sigma Xi; Biophysical Society. *Publications:* More than 20 publications in Medical Physics and Physiology. *Honours:* National Research Council of Canada Fellowship, 1947; Nuffield Foundation Travel Grant, 1973. *Hobbies:* Study of Celtic Laguages, Photography. *Address:* 13003 63rd Avenue, Edmonton, Alberta, T6H 1R9, Canada.

STEPHENSON, John Brian Ensor, b. 5 Oct 1933, Canberra, Australia. Orthopaedic Surgeon. m. Margaret Christine Meere, 4 Apr 1964. 4 sons. *Education:* Bachelor of Commerce, University of Melbourne, 1956; MB, BS, University of Sydney, 1961; Fellow Royal College Surgeons Edinburgh, 1966; Fellow Royal College Surgeons, England, 1967; fellow Royal Australasian College Surgeons, 1969. *Appointments:* Visiting Orthopaedic Surgeon, Port Kembla District Hospital: Campbelltown Hospital, NSW: Visiting orthpaedic Surgeon, Military Hospital, Ingleburn, NSW. *Memberships:* Australian Medical Association; British Medical Association; british Orthopaedic Association; Australian Orthopaedic Association NSW, Branch Committee ADA, 1980-81; NSW, Hand Surgery Association Angora Breed Society, Australia; Pan-Pacific Surgical Association South West Pacific Orthopaedic Association. *Hobbies:* Angora Goat Breeding. *Address:* Carroll's Road, Douglas Park, NSW 2569, Australia.

STEPHENSON, Neville Charles, b. 4 Nov 1928, Sydney, Australia. Scientist, Educator. m. Joan, 3 Oct 1952, 3 sons. *Education:* BSc, 1951, Sydney; MSc, 1952, Sydney; PhD, 1961, NSW; DSc, 1971, NSW. *Appointments:* Lecturer, Associate Professor, University NSW, 1954-74; head of School, Chemical & Earth Sciences, NSWIT, 1974; Dean of Faculty of Science, NSWIT, 1975; Visiting Professor, University, NSW, 1981; Post-Doctoral Fellow, Canadian National Research Council, 1952-54; Visiting Research Professor, University Pittsburgh, 1962; Visiting Scientist, National Bureau of Standard, 1969. *Memberships:* Fellow Royal Australian Chemical Institute; President Society of Crystallographers in Australia, 1978-80; National Committee Committee for Crystallography, 1978-80; NSW Board of Senior School Studies Examination Committee; Australian Selection Committee for Postgraduate Awards at College of Advanced Education; President, Rotary Club of Sutherland, 1974; Director of number of Sydney based companies dealing in Technology Transfer. *Publications:* Author of over 88 Scientific publications in International journals and books. *Honours:* Canadian National Research Council Scholarship, 1952-54; Australian Research Grant Committee Award, 1966-75; Australian organiser of Department of Science sponsored scientific team participating US/Australia/Japan workshop in Hawaii 1979. *Hobbies:* Fishing; Golf; Music. *Address:* Dean's Office, Faculty of Science, New South Wales Institute of Technology, PO Box 123, Broadway, New South Wales 2007, Australia.

STEPHENSON, Russell Arthur, b. 2 Oct 1944, Brisbane, Australia. Agricultural Scientist. m. Merrilyn K. Taylor, 21 Dec 1974, 2 daughters. *Education:* 1963 Queensland Diploma of Horticulture; 1964, QHD (Hons); 1969, B.Agr Sc., Queensland; 1974, PhD. *Appointments:* 1974, Post-Doctoral Research Fellowship, University of Georgia, USA; 1975, Lecturer, Agricultural Faculty, University of Papua New Guinea; 1977-78 Dean, Agriculture Faculty; 1979, Senior Lecturer; 1980, Horticulturist, Queensland Department of Primary Industries. *Memberships:* Australian Institute of Agricultural Science; Australian Society of Plant Physiologist; Papua New Guinea Society for the Promotion of Agriculture, newsletter editor, 1977-80. *Publications:* Editor of The Winged Bean Flyer, an international newsletter/abstracting journal for researchers and others involved with the development of the winged bean, a high protein, under utilized crop. *Address:* 1 Berringar Court, Nambour, Queensland, 4560, Australia.

STERN, Lionel, b. 4 Sept 1911, Jerusalem, Israel. Engineering Consultant. *Education:* Diploma in Aeronautical Engineering, 1937. *Appointments:* Design Draftsman Commonwealth Aircraft Corporation, Melbourne, 1938; Chief Draftsman, 1939; Development Engineer, 1941; Development Engineer and Quality Engineer, 1943-47; Chief Design Engineer Overseas Corporation. 1947; Chief Engineer Research & Development Repco Ltd., 1951; General Manager Repco Research Pty. Ltd., 1965; Consultant Manufacturing Services Repco Ltd, 1973-retirement end Dec 1980; Engineering Consultant, 1981. *Memberships:* Fellow Austalian Academy of Technological Sciences, FTS; Councillor, 1975-77; Fellow Institution of Engineers, Australia; FIE.Aust; Member Society of Automotive Engineers, USA, MSAE; Society of Automotive Engineers, Australasia, MSAE-A; President 1968-70; Councillor since 1963; Executive since 1965; Australian Industrial Research Group 1966-73; *Publications:* Over 30 patents, many of which are world patents. *Honours:* Hartnett Medal SAE-A, 1963; Prince Philip Prize, 1972; Britannica Australia Award in Science, 1972; A.G.M. Michell Medallist of I.E.Aust., 1981. *Hobbies:* Music; Reading. *Address:* 3/47 Studley Park Road, Kew, Victoria, 3101, Australia.

STEVENS, Iris Eliza, b. 3 Aug 1928, Murray Bridge, South Australia. Judge. m. Dr. John A. Fortingston Stevens, 3 sons, 1 daughter. *Education:* LLB, University of Adelaide 1960. *Appointments:* 1961-66 Private Legal Practice; 1966 Crown Law Department; 1970, Assistant Crown Solicitor, 1973, Commissioner, Public Service Board, 1977; Judge, Local & District, Criminal Courts. *Memberships:* Land Agents' Board; Land & Business Agent's Board; Land Brokers Licensing Board; Council Institute of Technology; Council University of Adelaide, Chairman Teachers' Appeal Board. *Address:* 6 George Street, Walkerville, SA 5081, Australia.

STEVENS, Neal Francis, b. 16 Feb 1919, Sydney Australia. Chartered Accountant. m. 29 Jan 1949, 2 sons, 2 daughters. *Education:* BEc, Sydney University, 1935-38. *Appointments:* Audit Clerk, 1934-39, Partner of ES Wolfender; War Service, 1939-46; Chartered Accountants, 1950-79; Audit Clerk, 1946; Company Security, 1947-50; Company Director, 1977. *Memberships:* Institute of Chartered Accountants in Australia, 1940; *Honours:* OBE, 1972 *Hobbies:* Sailing. *Address:* 31, Kyhi Avenue, Killara, NSW 2071, Australia.

STEVENS, Siaka Probyn, b. 1905. First Executive President of the Republic of Sierra Leone. m. Rebecca Stevens 1940, 7 sons, 5 daughters. *Education:* UBC School, Moyamba; Albert Academy, Freetown; Ruskin College, Oxford, 1947. *Appointments:* Sierra Leone Police 1923-30; Iron Ore Mining Company DELCO, 1930; Station Master, Stenographer at the Mines; Co-Founder, United Mine Workers Union, General Secretary, 1931-46; Protectorate Assembly in Bo, 1945;

Perm. mem. Standing Committee Protectorate Assembly, 1948; Legislative Council 1951 and First Minister of Lands & Mines; Founder mem. Sierra Leone Organising Society; Deputy Leader, People's National Party, 1958-60; Leader of the Opposition, APC, 1962; Mayor of Freetown, 1964; First Prime Minister, Republic of Sierra Leone, 1971; Executive President, 1971-. *Memberships:* Secretary General, APC 1979. *Honours:* Hon. DCL, University of Sierra Leone, 1969; Chancellor, University of Sierra Leone, 1973; Grand Commander of the Republic of Sierra Leone, 1974. *Address:* State House, Freetown, Sierra Leone.

STEVENS, Sinclair McKnight, b. 11 Feb 1927, Equesing Township, Halton Co., Ontario, Canada. Barrister and Solicitor, Member of Parliament. m. Noreen M. Charlebois, 17 May 1958. *Education:* BA, University of Western Ontario, 1950; Osgoode Hall Law School, Barrister-at-Law, 1955. *Appointments:* Lawyer, Fraser and Beatty, 1955-57; Lawyer, Stevens and Stevens, 1957-72; President, York Centre Corporation, 1960-67; 1970-79; Chairman, Comtech Group International Ltd., 1969-79; Chairman, York Centre Corporation, 1981; Director, Eagle Star Insurance Co, Of Canada, 1969-78; Member of Parliament, York-Simcoe, Elected 1972; Re-elected 1974; Member of Parliament, York-Peel, Elected, 1979; Re-elected, 1980; President of the Treasury Board of Canada, 1979-80. *Memberships:* Albany Club, Toronto, Ontario; Canadian Club of New York; Metropolitan Club of New York; The Institute of Directors in Canada; The Royal Commonwealth Society. *Honours:* Queen's Counsel, 1971; Privy Councillor, 1979. *Hobbies:* Farming. *Address:* Room 449-D, Centre Block, House of Commons, Ottawa, Canada K1A OA6.

STEVENSON, Richard Newell, b. 1 May 1918. Whakatane, New Zealand. Accountancy and teaching. m Bertha J. Fitness, 29 June 1942, 2 sons, 1 daughter. *Education:* BA, B-Com, Dip. Ed, Dip. Teaching, FCA, ACIS; Trained Teachers Certificate, 1941 Auckland Training College; Bachelor of Commerce, University of New Zealand, 1948; Associate Chartered Accountant, NZ Society of Accountants, 1948; Diploma in Education University of Auckland, 1954; Bachelor of Arts, University of Auckland, 1967; Fellow Chartered Accountant, NZ Society of Accountants, 1969; Diploma in Teaching, Department of Education, 1980. *Appointments:* 1946, Commercial Teacher, Seddon Memorial Technical College Auckland; 1952, Head of Commercial Department, Northcote College, Auckland; 1956-81, Managing Secretary, Auckland Division Cancer Society of New Zealand Inc. (Retired, 81). *Memberships:* Hospice Foundation of Auckland, Chairman; Auckland Hospital Board, 1958-71; 1972-74 Deputy Chairman; Northcote College Board of Governors, Deputy Chairman; Crippled Children's Society, Auckland Branch. *Honours:* Member Civil Division of the most excellent order of the British Empire, MBE 1979; Justice of the Peace, New Zealand, 1972. *Hobbies:* Music, *Address:* 73, Sylvan Avenue, Northcote, Auckland, 9, New Zealand.

STEWART, Alexander William, b. 11 January, 1911. Melbourne, Australia. Agricultural Scientist & Company Director. m. Margaret Morgan, 31 December 1976. 2 daughters. *Education:* Bachelor of Agricultural Science (BAgr.Sc), Melbourne University, 1930-1936; Post Graduate Studies, Cambridge University 1937-38. *Appointments:* Technical Service-Commonwealth Fertilisers Limited, 1939; Personal Assistant to Managing Director ACF & Shirleys Fertilisers - Queensland, 1945-46; War Service, Armed Services and Explosives Department, 1940-45; Co-principle, Alex StStewart Co, 1954-57; Directorships as follows: Austral Standard Cables Pty. Limited, 1951-79, Associated Pulp and Paper Mills Ltd, 1953; Broken Hill South Limited, 1955; Metal Manufactu Ltd (Representing Broken Hill South), 1956-80; Commonwealth Aircraft Corporation Limited, 1971-; Queensland Phosphate, 1973-. *Memberships:* Melbourne Club; Australian Club (Melbourne); Royal Melbourne Golf Club; Royal Sydney Golf Club; Australian Red Cross Society (Council & Financial Committee, Chairman Victorian Division 1959-61 & 1975-80); Victoria Racing Club; Victoria Amateur Turf Club; Australian Institute of Agricultural Science, Associate member; Royal Australian Chemical Institute; Fellow Institute of Directors. *Hobbies:* Fishing; Golf. *Address:* 6, Kenley Court, Toorak, Victoria 3142, Australia.

STEWART Cameron Alexander, b. 30 Dec. 1929, Sandgate. Medical Practitioner (Haematologist). m.

Daphne Wright, 22 Feb. 1958, 3 sons 1 daughter. *Education:* MB BS. University of Queensland 1957; FRCPA. Royal College of Pathologists, 1969; FRACP. Royal College of Physicians, 1976. *Appointments:* Royal Brisbane & Alexandra Hospitals, 1958-59; Chinchilla - General Practice, 1959-64; Repatriation General Hospital, Greenslopes, 1964-71; University College Hospital, London, 1971-72; Repatriation General Hospital, Greenslopes, 1972-1980; Medizinische Universitats Klinik Hamatologie Onkologie Abteilung, April-August, 1980; Clinical Haematology Private Practice, 1981. *Memberships:* Queensland State Committee Royal College Pathologists of Australia, 1974-80; Queensland Red Cross Blood Transfusion Service Committee Member, 1975-81; Advisory Committee in Medical Technicology (Queensland Institute of Technology), 1979 Australian and International Societies of Heamatology and Australian Medical Association. *Publications:* Medical Journal, Australia, Chronic Di Guglielmo Disease, 1971; Medical Journal Australia, The Laboratory Control of Heparin Therapy, 1971; Control of Heparin Anticoagulation, 1975; Pathology, Leucocyte Alkaline Phosphatase in Myeloid Maturation, 1974-76; The occurrence of foetal haemoglobin in a patient with Hepatoma, 1971; Medical Journal Australia, Spleno Hepatic Tuberculosis due to Myobate ri Kansasii, 1976; Pathology, Systemic Form of Weber-Christian Disease, 1978; Pathology, Carcinoid Tumour of the Thymus with a Cushing's Syndrome, 1980. *Honours:* Commonwealth Scholarship, 1971-72; DB Duncan Training Fellowship, Queensland Cancer Fund, 1980. *Hobbies:* Bushwalking; Reading. *Address:* 7, Lois Street, Kenmore 4069, Australia.

STEWART, John Charles, b. 24 Sept. 1930. Kirkcaldy, Scotland. Medical Practitioner. m. Isabel Lean Pirrie, 20 July, 1955. 2 sons, 1 daughter. *Education:* MB, ChB Edinburgh, 1954. FRACGP 1970. *Appointments:* RMO appointments Kirkcaldy and Inverness 1954-55; RAMC, 1955-57; Trainee in general practice, Brora, 1958-59; District Medical Officer, King Island, Tasmania, 1960-61; Medical Superintendent, Mersey General Hospital, Latrobe, Tasmania, 1962-65; Private Medical Practice, Launceston, Tasmania 1966; Part time appointment, Thyroid Clinic, Launceston General Hospital, 1967; Commonwealth Medical Officer, Launceston 1970. *Memberships:* Endocrine Society of Australia; Censor Tasmanian Faculty, Royal Australian College of General Practitioners. *Publications:* Scientific papers concerning iodine nutrition and thyrotoxicosis. *Hobbies:* Horses; Farming; *Address:* Wester Brownfield, Riverside, Tasmania, 7250, Australia.

STEWART, Philip John, b. 8 Jan., 1939. London. Human Ecologist. m. Lucile Monjauze. 26 July 1969 3 sons, 1 daughter. *Education:* BA, MA, Oriental College, Oxford, 1958-65; First class Honours in Oriental Studies, 1961, and in Forestry, 1965. *Appointments:* Food & Agriculture Organisation, 1965-66; Algerian Government (Forestry Research Officer), 1967-69; War on Want (Forestry Projec Director, Algeria) 1970-71; Algerian Government (Forestry Lecturer 1971-74; Institute of Development Studies, University of Sussex, (visiting Fellow) 1974-75; University of Oxford (Lecturer, Forest Economy) 1975; Fellow of St. Cross College. *Memberships:* Commonwealth Forestry Association; Commonwealth Human Ecology Council. *Publications:* Translation from Arabic of Children of Gebelawi; 1981. *Honours:* Commonwealth Forestry Institute Jubilee Prize, 1965. *Hobbies:* Local History; Mathematical games. *Address:* Brahim, Berkeley Road, Boars Hill, Oxford, London OX1 5ET, England.

STOCKDALE, Judith Ellen, b. 23 July, 1941. Melbourne, Australia. Company Director m. Charles William, 27 Oct. 1962. 1 son, 1 daughter. *Education:* Diploma of Business studies, Methodist Ladies College, 1958. *Appointments:* Cranemakers P/L - Director; Conveyor Engineering P/L, Director. *Memberships:* Sandringham Yacht Club (Committee Member) *Hobbies:* Yachting; Cordon Bleu Cooking; Golf. *Address:* 13, Mariemont Avenue, Beaumaris, Victoria 3193, Australia.

STOCKWELL, Barry, b. 16 May, 1945. Chingford Essex, United Kingdon. Estate Manager & Valuer. m. Denise Prevost, 10 Feb. 1978, 1 son. *Education:* UE, 1962; AAIV, 1969; FIV, 1980. *Appointments:* Government of Papua, New Guinea, 1963-73; Government of hong Kong, 1974-76; Jones Lang Woo Hon (South

Australia), 1977-79; Native Land Trust Board, Fiji. 1980-81. *Memberships:* President, Institute of Valuation and Estate Management, Fiji. *Hobbies:* Chess; Tennis; Basketball. *Address:* 26 Derwent Avenue, Magill, South Australia 5072.

STODART, James Sinclair, b. 15 Oct. 1921. Longreach, Queensland, Australia. Merchant - Hon. Counsul for Sweden in Queensland. m. Katharine Anne, 4 July, 1949. 3 sons, 3 daughters. *Education:* Church of England Grammar School, East Brisbane. *Appointments:* RAAF Aircrew, 5 years, South East Asia/India RAF F/Lt. *Memberships:* Queensland Club - United Service Club; Queensland Rugby Club; RACQ; President of the State Council of the Queensland Ambulance Transport Brigade; Director of Ceremonies of the Priory of the Order of St. John of Australia; A past President of the Royal Automobile Club of Queensland. *Honours:* K. St. J. Royal Vasa Order (First Class) (Swedish). *Address:* 374, Jesmond Road, Fig Tree Pocket, Brisbane, Australia.

STOIK, John Lentis, b. 5 Mar. 1920, North Battleford, Saskatchewan, Canada. President & Chief Executive Officer, Gulf Canada Limited, Toronto. m. Margaret Mary Marshall, 23 Aug. 1943, 2 sons. *Education:* Chemical Engineering Degree, University of Saskatchewan, 1947; *Appointments:* Assistant Chemist, Moose Jaw, Refinery, 1947; Assistant Manager, Moose Jaw Refinery, 1957; Assistant Manager, Clarkson (Ontario) Refinery, 1961; Manager, Moose Jaw Refinery, General Manager, Refining, Gulf Canada Limited, 1965; Vice President, Refining, Gulf Canada Limited, Toronto, 1968; Executive Vice President & Chief Executive Officer, Korea Oil Corp, Seoul, Korea, 1970; Senior Vice President, Gulf Canada Limited, Toronto, 1974; President & Chief Operating Officer, Gulf Canada Limited, Toronto, 1976; President & Chief Executive Officer, Gulf Canada Limited, Toronto, 1979. *Memberships:* Engineering Insitute of Canada; American Petroleum Institute Business & Industry Advisory Committee (BIAC) for Energy and Raw Materials to the Organisation for Economic Co-operation and Development (OECD); Granite Club, Toronto; St. George's Golf & Country Club, Toronto; Canadian Club, Toronto; Masonic Lodge; Engineer's Club, Toronto; Rideau Club, Ottawa. *Honours:* Honourary Doctor of Laws Degree, St. Francis Xavier University, Antigonish, Nova Scotia, Sept. 1980. *Hobbies:* Curling; Golf. *Address:* 79, Rebecca Court, R.R. 2, Maple, Ontario, LOJ 1EO, Canada.

STOKES, John Gerard, b. 16 Oct. 1923, Perth West Australia. Company Director. m. Ingrid Christine Elizabeth Straberger of Nels, Austria, 21 May, 1962. 2 sons, 2 daughters. *Education:* Bachelor of Science in Engineering University of West Australia, 1943; Various Post Graduate Courses. *Appointments:* Served as Lieutenant in Australian Army, 1943-45 (RAE); Then various positions to Chief Engineer and Assistants: Milling Superintendent, State Saw Mills, Australia 1946-56; General Manager, Katangadoo Timber, Australia, 1956-60; Development Manager, Kauri Timber, Melbourne 1960-63; Managing Director ABC (Aust) Pty Limited, 1963-73; Director Asian & Pacific Areas ABC Inc of Miami USA; MD for Europe & U.K.; Vice President, International ABC INC USA, known as Gang Nail Systems Inc. Miami USA. *Memberships:* World President, World Council of Young Men's Service Clubs (Round Table etc) 1963-64; Vice Chairman, United Nations Industry Co-operative programme, 1973-74; The Club of Rome; President, Royal Guide Dogs for the Blind, 1975-76; Board of Governers, Foundation for International Training, Toronto, Canada: President Underwater Explorer's Club, 1954-56; Member the Naval & Military Club, Melbourne; Weld Club Perth; Royal Freshwater Bay Yacht Club, Perth. *Publications:* Various Articles and Papers Published on Wood, Resources Etc., *Honours:* Honoury Vice Patron, Royal Guide Dogs for the Blind. Honoury Member, Active International USA; Freedom of City Sacramento USA; Honory Life Member Apex Club of Claremont WA. *Hobbies:* Skiing; Underwater Exploration; Wood Turning; Carving & Cabinet Making; Yachting; Surfing; Game Fishing. *Address:* 3, Riley Road, Claremont, West Australia 6010.

STONEHAM, Roy, b. 10 May, 1916, Catford, London, England. Chartered Secretary. m. Joan Pauline Dyett, 26 June, 1940. 1 son, 1 daughter. *Education:* Polytechnic Regent Street, London; Associate member Chartered Institute of Secretaries. *Appointments:* Milk Marketing Board, Thames Ditton Surrey; Tasman Pulp and Paper Co. Limited, Kawarau, New Zealand. 04 Mayor Borough of Kaweray, 1965; President Bay of Plenty Local Authorities Association; Vice-Chairman, Bay of Plenty Catchment Commission; Manager, New Zealand, Team Commonwealth Paraplegic Games, 1974. *Honours:* Certificate of Gallantry, 1945; Justice of Peace; Order of British Empire; Queen Elizabeth Silver Jubilee Medal. *Hobbies:* Building a Town. *Address:* 179, River Road, Kawerau, Bay of Plenty, New Zealand.

STOREN, Robert Thomas, b 30 Jan. 1943, Adelaide, South Australia. Dental Surgeon. m. 3 May, 1968, 2 sons, 1 daughter. *Education:* Education at Christian Brothers College, 1950-60; BDS Adelaide University, 1966. *Appointments:* Partnership Dental Practice, Port Lincoln S.A. 1967-71; Partnership Dental Practice, Adelaide South Africa, 1971; Partnership Dental Practice, Burra, South Australia, Clare, S. Australia, Riverton, S. Australia, Hamley Bridge, South Australia, 1978. *Memberships:* Australian Dental Association; Australian Society of Prosthodontists; Federation Dentair International; South Australian Jockey Club; Gleneg Golf Club. *Honours:* Queens Scout, 1959. *Address:* 15, Andrews Street, Walkerville, South Australia, 5081.

STOREY, Gerald Francis, b. 14 May, 1927. Edinburgh. Civil Engineer. m. Marjorie Purves, 28 June, 1954, 1 son, 1 daughter. *Education:* BSc. Edinburgh University, 1944-48. *Appointments:* Argyll County Council; Air Ministry Works Directorate; Macartney Limited, Civil Engineering Contractors; Department of Agriculture & Fisheries for Scotland; Department of Transport seconded to Scottish Development Department, 1962-; From 1974 Assistant Chief Engineer. *Memberships:* Institution of Civil Engineers; Road Engineering Board & Committee Member of Endinburgh & East of Scotland Association of Institution; Institution of Highway Engineers, Formerly Committee Member & Chairman of Central & Southern Scotland Branch. *Publications:* Papers on Scotland's Arterial Roads, Roads to the Oil; M90 Motorway, etc. *Hobbies:* Golf; Motoring. *Address:* 21, Hawkhead Crescent, Edinburgh, EH16 6LR, Scotland.

STOREY, Hon Haddon QC, MLC. b. 15 May, 1930. Melbourne. Attorney, General of Victoria. m. Cecile, 6 Sept. 1958. 3 sons. *Education:* LLB Melbourne University, 1951; LLM (Hons), 1952 *Appointments:* Admitted to Bar, Practising Barrister since 1955, 1954; Lecturer in Council of Legal Education's Law Course, 1963-76; Appointed Queen's Council, 1971; *Memberships:* Bar of Council. 1971-75; Royal Dental Hospital Council, 1973-79. *Publications:* Real Estate Agency in Victoria (2nd edition. 1975); Articles on: Consumer Credit, Privacy & Community Consultation in law reform published in professional and academic journals *Hobbies:* Reading; Cinema. *Address:* 58, Broadway, Camberwell, Victoria, 3141, Australia.

STOUT, John David, b 13th June, 1925. Wellington, New Zealand. Scientist. *Education:* MA (Hons), 1948; PhD. 1952. *Appointments:* Chief Microbiologist: Soil Bureau, New Zealand, Department of Scientific and Industrial Reasearch. *Memberships:* Royal Society of New Zealand (Wellinton Branch); Society of Protozoology; New Zealand and International Societies of Soil Science; New Zealand Microbiological Society; New Zealand Association of Scientists. *Publications:* About 100 Scientific Papers. *Honours:* Visiting Fellow Cornell University, 1977. *Hobbies:* Music; Swimming. *Address:* 11, Kotare Street, Waikanae, New Zealand.

STRAHAN, Edward George, b. 2 March, 1915. Hawthorn, Victoria, Australia. Medical Practitioner. m. (1) Patricia Evans, 9 Apr. 1941 3 sons; (2) Maxine Lesley Clark, 3 March 1967, 2.daughters. *Education:* Bachelor of Medicine, Bachelor of Surgery, 1939. *Appointments:* Royal Perth Hospital, 1939-40; Orthopaedic Section, Royal Childrens Hospital, 1940. Royal Australian Air Force 1940-45; General Medical Practice, 1945-49; Specialist Consultant, 1949-. *Memberships:* Australian College of Allergy; American Academy of Allergy; Fellow of the American College of Allergy; Fellow of American Association for Clinical Immunology & Allergy; Aerospace Medical Associate; International Association of Asthmology. *Publications:* Several Publications on Allergy in the Medical Journal of Australia. *Honours:* Emeritus Consultant Allergist, Royal Perth Hospital; Consultant Allergist, Fremantle Hospital; Consultant Allergist, Royal Australian Air Force, (Wing Commander RAAF Reserve Retired). *Hobbies:* Music; Music Research & Recordings. *Address:* 44a View Street, Peppermint Grove, Western Australia 6011.

STRANG, William John, b. 29 June, 1921. Torquay, Devon. Aircraft Designer. m. Margaret Nicholas Howells, 21 March, 1946. 3 sons, 1 daughter. *Education:* BSc. Class Hons, Kings College, London, 1946-48; Phd. 1950. *Appointments:* Deputy Head Guided Weapons Department, Bristol Areoplane Co Limited, 1951; Head of Aerodynamics & Flight Research, Bristol Areoplane Co. Limited, 1952; Chief Designer, Bristol Aeroplane Co Limited, 1955; Director & Chief Engineer (Aircraft) British Aircraft Corporation, 1960-67; Deputy Engineering Director, Anglo French Concorde Organisation, 1961; Technical Director, Anglo French Concorde Organisation, 1967; Technical Director, British Aircraft Corporation, Filton Division, 1967-71; Technical Director, BAC Civil Aircraft Division, 1971-78; Deputy Technical Director, British Aerospace, Aircraft Group, Headquarters. *Memberships:* Founder Member of CAA Airworthiness Requirements Board, 1972; Graduate of Royal Aeronautical Society, 1942; Associate Fellow of Royal Aeronautical Society, 1946; Fellow of Royal Aeronautical Society, 1956; Fellowship of Engineering, 1977; Fellow of the Royal Society, 1977. *Publications:* Papers in Proc. Rov. Soc. A and ARL Series. *Honours:* Baden Powel Memorial Prize, 1941; The British Silver Medal for Aeronautics, 1971; CBE, 1973; Royal Aeronautical Society Gold Medal, 1976. *Hobbies:* Sailing and Gardening. *Address:* 11, Broom Park, Teddington, Middlesex, England.

STRANGER, Donald McKinnon, b. 12 May, 1929. Hobart. State Public Servant. m. Janet anne Barnett, 7 Sept. 1972. 1 son, 1 daughter. *Education:* Hobart High School; The Hutchins Scool; BA University of Tasmania, 1966; Dip Pub. Admin., 1966. *Appointments:* Secretary to Attorney-General and Assistant to Leader of Government in Legislative Council 1956-1963; Clerk of the Peace, 1956-1976; Secretary, Publications Board of Review 1954-1975; Registrar, Restricted Publications Board, 1975-1980; Assistant Secretary (Administration) Attorney-General's Department since 1971; Chairman, Childhood Injury Investigation Committee, 1972-75. *Memberships:* Lt. 6 Fd. Regt. RAA (CMF) 1952-56; Hobart (Royal) Tennis Club; Kingston Beach Golf Club, Justice of the Peace since 1965. *Publications:* Reflections on Australian Censorship 1966, Unpublished. *Hobbies:* Royal Tennis; Golf; Fishing; Gardening. *Address:* 17, Chessington Court, Lower Sandy Bay, Tasmania 7005, Australia.

STRATTON, Nigen Ian Bruce, b. 24 Apr. 1940. Leeds, Yorkshire, England. Orthopaedic Surgeon. m. Dr. Shirley Chen, 27 Oct. 1974. 2 sons, 1 daughter. *Education:.* MB, BS Sydney University & St. Paul's College, 1964; FRCS Edinburgh, 1970; FRACS (Orthop), Sydney, 1974. *Appointments:* Resident Medical Officer, Royal Prince Alfred Hospital, Sydney, Australia, 1965-66; Registrr posts in Orthopaedics various NHS Hospitals, in U.K. including Registrar & Research Assistant to Sir John Charnley FRS FRCS at Wrightington Hospital, 1967-72; Consultant Orthopeadic Surgeon, Blacktown & Bowral District Hospitals, N.S.W., 1973-78; Consultant Surgeon to Ministry of Health Nuku' Alofa, Kingdom of Tonga, (Australian Aid Position), 1978-80; Consultant Orthopaedic Surgeon, Dubbo Base Hospital, Dubbo, NSW, 1982. *Memberships:* Australian Medical Association, Australian Orthopaedic Association; Australian Association of Surgeons; Western Pacific Orthopaedic Association; The Low Friction Society; World Orthopaedic Concern. *Publications:* Surgical Management of 104 Club Feet in Tongan Children, a two year on-going study. Presented paper at the Fifth Combined Meeting of the Australian & New Zealand Orthopaedic Associations 23/3/81 in press. *Hobbies:* Sailing; Skiing & Bushwalking. *Address:* 48 Carrington Avenue, Dubbo, New South Wales, 2830, Australia.

STRATTON, Richard James, b. 1924. British Diplomat. *Education:* Merton College, Oxford, BA, MA. *Appointments:* Foreign Office, 1947; First Secretary British Embassy, Bonn, 1958-60 and Abidjan, 1960-62; Private Secretary to Lord Carrington, Minister without Portfolio, FCO, 1963-64 and to Minister of State for Foreign Affairs, FCO, 1964-66; Counsellor and Head of Chancery, British High Commission, Rowalpindi, 1966-69; Imperial Defence College, 1970-71; Head, UN (Political) Department, FCO, 1971-72; Political Adviser to Government of Hong Kong, 1972-74; HM Ambassador, Zaire, 1974-77; Assistant Under-Secretary of State FCO, 1977-80; High Commissioner to New Zealand, 1980-. and concurrently to Western Samoa. *Honours:* CMG; Companion of the Order of St. Michael and St. George, 1974. *Address:* 18 Clareville Court, Clareville Grove, London, SW7 5AT, England.

STRAYER, Barry Lee, b. 13 Aug. 1932, Moose Jaw, Sakatchewan, Canada. Lawyer; Civil Servant. m. Eleanor Staton, 2 July 1955, 2 sons. 1 daughter. *Education:* BA., 1953, LL.B., 1955, University of Saskatchewan; BCL., Oxford University, 1957; SJD, Harvard University, 1966. *Appointments:* Instructor in Law, 1957-58, Professor of Law, 1962-68, University of Saskatchewan; Crown Solicitor, 1959-62, Government of Saskatchewan; Director, Constitutional Review, 1968-74, Assistant Deputy Minister of Justice, 1974-, Government of Canada. *Memberships:* Law Society of Saskatchewan; Canadian Bar Association; International Commission of Jurists. *Publications:* Judicial Review of Legislation in Canada, 1968; Periodical articles and essays on public law subjects. *Honours:* Queen's Counsel, Canada, 1974. *Hobbies:* Cabinet Making; Golf; Cross-country Skiing. *Address:* 504 Queen Elizabeth Driveway, Ottawa, Ontario K1S 3N4, Canada.

STREET, Anthony Austin, The Honourable. b. 8 Feb. 1926. Melbourne, Australia. Member of Australian Parliament, Primary Producer. m. V.E. Rickard 6 July, 1951. 3 sons. *Education:* Melbourne Church of England Grammer School - Matriculation. *Appointments:* Primary Producer to 1966; Member of Australian Parliament 1966-; Minister for Employment and Industrial Relations 1975-78; Minister for Industrial Relations, 1978-. *Memberships:* Marlybone Cricket Club; Melbourne Cricket Club (Australia): Melbourne Club (Victoria Australia); Royal Melbourne Golf Club. *Hobbies:* Flying; Golf and Cricket. *Address:* Eildon, Lismore, Victoria, Australia.

STREET, Philip Whistler, b. 7 Feb, 1926. Sydney, NSW, Australia. Grazier. m. Janice Anstruther Tod, 4 Nov. 1950, 1 son. 2 daughters. *Education:* Hawkesbury Agricultural College (NSW), 1947-49. *Appointments:* Northern Territory Manager, Bennett & Fisher Limited, 1950-52; South Australian Manager, London Woolbrokers Pty Limited, 1953-58; Director, Bedford Wool Dumping Co. Pty Limited, 1953-58; Director, Port Lincoln Wool Dumping Co Limited, 1953-58; Chairman American Field Service International Scholarships, (Armidae Committee 1971-72); Deputy Chairman, Walcha District Hospital Board, 1969-81. *Memberships:* Councillor, Royal Agricultural Society of New South Wales since, 1978; President, Agricultural Societies, Council of NSW - since 1980; President WALC-HA Show Society, 1970-71; President Walcha Pony Club, 1964-67; Northern Zone: President, Pony club Association of NSW, 1965; New England, District Councillor, Graziers Association of NSW, 1965. *Honours:* Appointed Justice of the Peace (JP) in New South Wales, 1960 *Hobbies:* Wood work and Gardening; Sports: Cricket; Tennis Golf. *Address:* Blaxland, Walcha, New South Wales 2354, Australia.

STRETTON, Alan, Bishop, b. 30 Sept. 1922, Melbourne, Australia. Army Officer. m. Valda Blanche Scattergood, 18 Dec. 1943, 1 son, 2 daughters. *Education:* Scotch College, Melbourne; Royal Military College of Australia, 1943; Psc, Australian Staff College, 1948; LLB, University of Queensland, 1966; RCDS, Royal College of Defence Studies, 1972. *Appointments:* Commanding Officer, Australian Battalion, Malaya, 1961-63; Director, Administrative Planning, Australian Army, 1966-69; Chief of Staff, Australian Force, Vietnam, 1969-70; Australian National Intelligence Committee, 1972-74; Director General, Australian Natural Disasters Organisations, 1974-78; Barrister, High Court, Australia, 1969; Supreme Commander of the Australian Relief Force After City of Darwin destroyed by Cyclone Tracey. *Memberships:* Naval and Military Club, Melbourne; Melbourne Cricket Club; Canberra Club; Law Society of the Australian Capital Territory; Royal Canberra Golf Club; Patron, Batemans Bay Retirement Village Trust. *Publications:* The Furious Days -

The Darwin Disaster, 1976; Soldier in a Storm, 1978. *Honours:* Recipient of MBE, 1954; OBE, 1964; CBE, 1970; US Bronze Star, 1970; DSO, 1970; AO, Officer of the Order of Australia, 1974; Australian of the year Award, 1975. *Hobbies:* Golf; Chess. *Address:* 129 Carnegie Crescent, Red Hill, Australian Capital Territory, 2603, Australia.

STRICKLAND, Benjamin Vincent Michael, b. 20 Sept. 1939, Southampton, England. Merchant Banker. m. Tessa Mary Edwina Grant, 6 Feb. 1965, 1 son, 1 daughter. *Education:* MA, Philosophy, Politics and Economics, University College, Oxford, 1963; FCA, 1967; Advanced Management Programme, Howard Business School, 1978. *Appointments:* Lieutenant, 17th/21st Lancers, 1959-60; Junior Manager, Price Waterhouse and Company, London, 1963-68; Director, J. Henry Schroder Wagg and Company Limited, London, Chairman, G.D. Peters and Company Limited, Peters Packaging Limited, 1974-76; Chairman, Chief Executive, Schroder Darling and Company Limited, 1978-; Schroder Darling Property Fund. *Memberships:* President, Junior Common Room, University College, Oxford, 1962-63; President, Blue Ribbon Club, Oxford, 1963; Canning Club, Oxford, 1963. *Publications:* Collaborated with Laurence Reed, formerly MP for Bolton East, on production of Bow Group Booklet on the outlook for resources from the sea, 1967. *Hobbies:* Reading; Travel; Collection of Victorian Campaign Medals; Shooting. *Address:* 1/124 Wolesley Road, Point Piper, Sydney, New South Wales, Australia.

STRONG, John Clifford, b. 1922. British Diplomat. m. Janet Doris Browning, 1942, 3 daughters. *Education:* LL.B., London University, 1940-42. *Appointments:* HM Overseas Civil Service, Tanzania, 1946-63; HM Diplomatic Service, Kenya, 1964-68, London, 1968-73, Tanzania, 1973-78; Governor, Turks & Caicos Islands, 1978-. *Memberships:* Royal Overseas League (London). *Honours:* CBE., 1980. *Address:* c/o Foreign & Commonwealth Office (Grand Turk), King Charles Street, London, SW1A 2AH, England.

STRONG, Roy Colin, b. 23 Aug. 1935, London, England. Museum Director. m. Julia Trevelyan Oman, 10 Sept. 1971. BA, Queen Mary College, University of London, 1956; PhD, Warburg Institute, London, 1959. *Appointments:* Assistant Keeper, National Portrait Gallery, 1959-67; Director and Secretary, National Portrait Gallery, 1967-74; Director and Secretary, Victoria and Albert Museum, 1974-. *Memberships:* Fellow, Society Antiquaries; Royal Archaeological Institute; The Arundel Castle Trustees; The Chevening Trustees; Westminster Abbey Architectural Panel; The Council of the Royal College of Art; The Fine Arts Advisory Committee of the British Council; Dilittante Society; Clubs, Garrick, Grillions, Beefsteak. *Publications:* Prolific writer of Historical Books, including the following titles, And When Did You Last See Your Father?, The Victorian Painter and the British Past, 1978; The Renaissance Garden in England, 1979; Britannia Triumphans: Inigo Jones, Rubens and Whitehall Palace, 1980; He is also a regular contributor to learned journals and a reviewer for newspapers. *Honours:* Recipient of Shakespeare prize from FVS Foundation, Hamburg, 1980. *Address:* Director's Office, Victoria and Albert Museum, London, S.W.7, England.

STUDDY, John Bradridge, b. 19 July 1929, Sydney, New South Wales, Australia. Chartered Accountant. m. Gillian Colvin Clark, 10 Dec. 1971, 2 sons, 1 daughter. *Education:* Sydney University, BEc; FCA; FAIM. *Appointments:* Partner, Coopers & Lybrand, 1958-72; Manager Director, Abbey Capital Property Group, 1972-77; Director, A.M.P. Morgan Grenfell Limited; Acrow Australia Limited; Beneficial Finance Corporation Limited; Cluff Oil, Australia, N.L; Fielder Gillespie Limited; Chairman, Mortgage Guaranty Insurance Corporation of Australia Limited; McEwan's Limited; Pillar Pacific Limited; Wood Hall Limited; Chairman, Black and Decker, Asia, Limited; Chairman, Capital and Counties, Australia, Limited; Rank Industries Australia Limited; Wilh. Wilhelmsen Agency Limited. *Memberships:* President, National Multiple Sclerosis Society of Australia, 1979; Alderman, Municipality of North Sydney, 1980; The Institute of Directors, Australia; Fellow, The Australian Institute of Management; Trustee, Committee for Economic Development of Australia; Australian Club, Sydney. *Publications:* Author of international paper, The Audit Report, Tenth International

Congress of Accountants, Sydney, 1972. *Hobbies:* Sailing; Gardening. *Address:* 11 Walker Street, Lavender Bay, New South Wales, Australia 2060.

STURMAN, Paul, b. 14 Oct. 1943, Hitchin, Hertfordshire, England. Professor/ Author. m. Carol Willis, 29 Dec. 1979. *Education:* Royal Academy of Music, 1962-65; Wycliffe Hall, Oxford, 1965-66; Royal Antwerp Conservatoire, Belgium, 1966-67; GRSM, London, 1965; LRAM, 1963; ARCM, 1964 *Appointments:* Examiner, East Anglican Examinations Board, 1967-; Professor of Harmony and Composition, London College of Music, 1974-; Organist/Choirmaster, Woodford Parish Church, 1967-76; Examiner/Adjudicator, 1967-; Lecturer in Music, All Saints College of Education, 1977 80. *Memberships:* Royal Academy of Music Club. *Publications:* Publications, Creating Music 1980; Harmony Melody and Composition; Compositions, Educational Songs; Published, Christ's Complaint, My Song is in Sighing; Psalm 93 for Choirs and Orchestra; Organ Variations; Season's, Song Cycle; Piano Pieces. *Hobbies:* Theatre; Travel; Reading; Biographies; Gardening. *Address:* 15 Hillside Road, Thorpe Saint Andrew, Norwich, England.

STURROCK, Robert Ralph, b. 1 July, 1943, Dundee. Anatomist. m. Fiona Lesley, 23.Sept. 71. 1 daughter. *Education:* MB, ChB, St. Andrews University, 1961-67; DSc. University of Dundee, 1980. *Appointments:* House Surgeon, Perth Royal Infirmary, 1967-68; House Physician, Stirling Royal Infirmary, 1968; Demonstrator, Anatomy Dept., University of Dundee, 1968-69; Lecturer, University of Dundee, 1969-77; Visiting Associate Professor of Neuroanatomy, Iowa University, 1976; Senior Lecturer, University of Dundee, 1981; Reader in Neuranatomy, University of Dundee, 1977; *Memberships:* Anatomical Society of Great Britain and Ireland; Fellow of the British Association of Clinical Anatomists; Internation' Society for Developmental Neuroscience; British Neuropathological Society. *Publications:* Papers on the development of neuroglia and the reponse to environmental and pathological stress including ageing. *Honours:* Symington Memorial Prize in Anatomy, 1979. *Hobbies:* Reading; Swimming; Serving as RMO to Tayforth Universities, OTC. *Address:* 6 Albany Terrace, Dundee, Scotland.

STUYVENBERG, Daniel Willem, b. 14 Apr. 1909, Utrecht, Netherlands. Priest, Now Archbishop of Honiara, Catholic Church. *Education:* Two years Philosophy and one year Theology, three years Theology in Belgium, Arlon. *Appointments:* Priest, Visale, two years; Priest, nineteen years, Buma, Malaita; Archbishop, Honiara, twenty-three years. *Memberships:* Society of Mary or Marist Fathers, General House of the Marists is in Rome. *Publications:* Creative work has been in the pastoral field in the diocese of Honiara in the Solomon Islands. The work of a priest. *Publications:* Recipient of CBE. *Hobbies:* Sport. *Address:* Holy Cross Cathedral, P.O. Box 237, Honiara, Solomon Islands, Oceania.

STYLES, Ronald Arthur, b. 8 Nov. 1917, Heanor, Derbyshire. Schoolmaster. m. Celia, 3 Apr. 1954, 1 daughter. *Education:* MA, Downing College, Cambridge, 1935-40. *Appointments:* Chemist, Irvine Royal Ordanance Factory, 1940-45; Teacher, Felsted School, 1945-47; Teacher, Christs Hospital, 1948-51; Chemist, Rolls Royce Ltd., 1952-56; Teacher, Hymers College, 1956. *Memberships:* Fellow of Royal College of Organists; Fellow of Trinity College of Music; British Academy of Forensic Sciences. *Publications:* Various articles to Medicine Science and the Law and Health. *Honours:* D.Mus, Central School of Religion, 1980. *Hobbies:* Music; Motoring; Relaxation Therapy. *Address:* The Organists House, 50 Bondgate, Helmsley, York, YO6 5EZ, England.

SUBASINGHE, Tikiri Banda, b. 26 Aug. 1925, Kadahapola, Sri Lanka. Public Servant. m. Chandravalee Wijeratne, 8 Aug. 1955, 1 son, 2 daughters. 02 BA, University of Ceylon, 1953; MS, Columbia University, New York, 1966; Certificate in Plan Implementation and Project Evaluation, Bangkok, 1969; Diploma in Economic Planning, ISS The Hague, 1971. *Appointments:* Assistant Teacher, Dharmaraja College, Kandy, 1953-55; Inspector of Labour, Labour Department, 1955-57; Medical Records Officer/Statistician, Health Department, 1957-68; Market Intelligence Officer, Marketing Department, 1968-71; Economist, Ministry of Agriculture and Food, 1968-71; Deputy Director of

Agricultural Development, Ministry of Agriculture and Lands, 1971-75; Chairman, Ceylon Fertilizer Corporation, 1975-77 Director, Agrarian Research and Training Institute, 1977. *Memberships:* Nutrition Society of Sri Lanka - President, 1981; Sri Lanka Association for the Advancement of Science. *Publications:* Report on Rural Employment in Sri Lanka prepared for the ILO. *Hobbies:* Reading. *Address:* 114 Wijerama Mawatha, Colombo 7, Sri Lanka.

SUBERU, Alhaji (Chief) Arasi Ade, b. 10 Apr. 1925, Ibadan, Chairman and Managing Director. m. Alhaja Sikiratu, 11 Nov. 1963, 2 sons, 5 daughters. *Education:* Diploma, School of Agriculture, Ibadan. *Appointments:* Agricultural Assistant; Agricultural Superintendent in training; Business Directors. *Memberships:* Scout Movement of Nigeria first class. *Honours:* Chief Abese Parakoyi of Ibadan, 1979. *Hobbies:* Football. *Address:* SW9/919 Adebayo Avenue, Ibadan, Niveria.

SUBLOO, Gordon, Neil, b. 14 Apr. 1953, Innistail, Queensland, Australia. Crushed Metals Company Executive, Managing Director. m. Noelleen, J. Sander, 9 Feb 1974. 2 sons, 2 daughters. *Appointments:* Mechanic, See Poys Motors Innistail, 1967-69; Truck Driver, Machinery Operator, H. Subloo & Co, 1969-71; Manager, Hudson Crushed Metals Pty Ltd, Innistail, 1971; Managing Director, Hudson Crushed Metals Pty Ltd, 1971-. *Memberships:* Aircraft owners and Pilots Association of Australia; Club Innistail, AERO. *Publications:* Designed Pipe Making Machine. *Honours:* Diploma of Ground Training School, Hinchinbrook Air Services. *Hobbies:* Flying; Fishing; Reading. *Address:* 43, Maple Street, Innistail, North Queensland, Australia, 4860.

SUBRAMANIAM, Chidambaram, b. 30 Jan 1910, Coimbatore-Tamil Nadu, India. Law and Politics. m. Sakuntala. 1 son, 2 daughters. *Education:* BA, 1930; Bachelor of Law, 1932. *Appointments:* Practised Law, 1935-52; Member, Constituent Assembly of India, 1946-52; Minister of Finance, Education and Law-Government of Madra, 1952-62; Minister of Steel, Heavy Industries Mines & Minerals, Government of India, 1962-64; Minister of Food and Agriculture, 1964-67; Chairman, Committee on Aeronautical Industry, 1968-69; Chairman, Indian Agricultural Commission, 1969-70; Minister of Planning Science and Technology, 1971-72; Minister of Industrial Development, Science and Technology, 1972-74; Minister for Finance-Government of India, 1974-77; Minister for Defence, Government of India, 1979-80. *Memberships:* Cosmopolitan Club, Madras; Cosmopolitan Club, Coimbatore. *Publications:* India of My Dreams; War On Poverty; The New Strategy in Indian Agriculture; Travelogues and other books in Tamil. *Honours:* Hon. Doctorate, Andhra University, Andhra Pradesh; Hon. Doctorate, Venkateswara University, Andhra Pradesh; Hon. Doctorate, Madurai University, Tamil Nadu. *Hobbies:* Practice of Yoga. *Address:* River View, Madras-85, India.

SUFFIAN, Tun Mohamed, b. 12 Nov. 1917, Kota Lama Kiri, Malaysia. Lord President, Malaysia; Pro-Chancellor, University of Malaya. *Education:* Honorary LLD, Singapore, 1972; Honorary D.Litt, Malaya, 1972; MA, Cantab, 1965; LLB, Cantab, 1940; BA, Cantab, 1939; Barrister at Law, 1941. *Appointments:* Malay broadcaster, All India Radio, New Delhi; Head, Malay Unit, All India Radio, New Delhi, 1941. Head, BBC Malay Section, 1945-46; Malayan Civil Service, 1946; Legal Service, 1949; Federal Counsel, Kuala Lumpur, 1954; Legal Adviser, Pahang, 1954; State Secretary, Pahang, 1954; Senior Federal Counsel, 1957; Sole Malayan delegate, UN Conference Geneva on the Law of the Sea, 1958; Leader, Malayan Delegation, Second U.N. Conference, Geneva, 1960; Judge, High Court, Kuala Lumpur, 1961; High Court in Alor Star, 1962; Judge of the Federal Court of Malaysia, 1968; Chief Justice, High Court, Malaya, 1973; Lord President, Malaysia, 1974. *Memberships:* Chairman, Eisenhower Exchange Fellowship Malaysian Nomination Committee, 1966-80; Vice President Oxford and Cambridge Society, Kuala Lumpur, 1967-9, President, 70-71; President, MalaysianAmerican Society, Kuala Lumpur, 1971-2, 1978-80; Council member of Lawasia, 1978-; Vice President representing Malaysia, Asean Law Association and Chairman of the Malaysian National Committee; Vice-President, 1976, President, 1979-, Commonwealth Magistrates Association; Honorary

member, Indian Society of International Law, 1980; Honorary fellow, Malaysian Institute of Management, 1980; Honorary fellow, Malaysian Scientific Association, 1980; President, Malaysian Branch, Royal Asiatic Society, 1978-. *Publications:* First official translation of Malayan Constitution, 1963; An Introduction to the Constitution of Malaysia (2nd edition in 1976), 1972; The Constitution of Malaysia—Its Development 1957-77 with F.A. Trindade and H.P. Lee published by Oxford University Press, 1978. *Honours:* Setia Mahkota Brunei by H.R.H. the Sultan of Brunei, 1959; Johan Mangku Negara by H.M. the Yang Dipertuan Agong, 1961; Pingat Jasa Kebaktian by H.R.H. The Sultan of Pahang, 1963; Panglima Setia Mahkota by H.M. The Yang Dipertuan Agong, 1967; Darjah Indera Mahkota Pahang by H.R.H. The Sultan of Pahang, 1969; Seri Setia Mahkota by H.M. The Yang Dipertuan Agong, 1975; *Hobbies:* Gardening; Reading; Ceramics; Antiques. *Address:* 6 Jalan Taming Sari, Kuala Lumpar, Malaysia.

SUHAIMI, Ariffin, b. 19 Jan 1937, Perak, Malaysia. Educator/Academician. m. Marhamah Bt Haji Mohamed, 31 Jan 1966. 1 son, 2 daughters. *Education:* BSc, Malaya, 1959; Dip. Ed., Malaya, 1961; MSc, Singapore, 1966; PhD, Reading, 1973. *Appointments:* Prinicipal, Sekolah Alam Shah, Kuala Lumpur, 1966-69; Head of Science, Royal Military College, Kuala Lumpur, 1969-70; Lecturer, National University of Malaysia, 1970; Head of Sains Asasi, University Pertanian Malaysia, 1973-75; Dean of Science and Environmental Studies, University Pertanian Malaysia, 1975-. *Memberships:* Malayan Nature Society, Life; Environmental Protection Society of Malaysia; Selangor Consumers Association, life; Fellow of Malaysian Scientific Association; Council member of SIRIM; Council member of Environmental Quality of Malaysia; National Committee for International Hydrological Programme; Advisory Committee of PUSPATI. *Publications:* Environmental Effects of Development of Food Production; Water Quality Management in Malaysia; Environmental Control by Legislation; Policy Considerations in the Evolution of Environmenta Impact Assessment in Malaysia; WHO/UNEP. *Honours:* PK, Awarded by Ministry of Defence, 1974; AMN, Paramount Ruler of Malaysia, 1969; Fellow of the Institute of Environmental Sciences, Miami University, USA. *Hobbies:* Soldiering; Reading. *Address:* C16 Universiti Pertanian, Malaysia Campus, Serdang, Selangor, Malaysia.

SUJAK, bin Rahiman, Dato b. 21 Mar 1922, Johor Bahru, Malaysia. Director of Companies. m. Rosina H.A. Karim, 24 Dec 1953, 3 sons, 3 daughters. *Education:* BSc, (Econ) QUB, 1953. *Appointments:* 1940-55, Johor State Civil Service, 1955-76, Malaysian Civil Service. *Memberships:* Founder, Royal Commonwealth Society; Vice-President, Management Committee of Malaysian Zoological Society; Malaysian Historical Society; President, Malaysian Chapter of Federation of Real Estate; Royal Asiatic Society; Malaysian, American Society; Treasurer of Housing Developer's Association, Malaysia. *Honours:* AMN, JMN, DPMJ. *Hobbies:* Reading. *Address:* No. 16 Jalan 16/5, Petaling Jaya, Selangor, Malaysia.

SUKHADIA, Mohan Lal, b. 31 July 1916, Jhalawar in Rajasthan State of India. Farmer. m. S. Indu Bala, 1939. 2 sons, 5 daughters. *Education:* Licentiate of Electrical Engineering from Victoria Jubli Technical Institute, Bombay. *Appointments:* 1946, Minister for Civil Supplies, PWD Dept. Relief & Rehabilitation, Mewar State, 1948; Minister for Development, Group of Rajasthan, 1951-52; Minister of Civil Supplies, Agriculture & Irrigation, Government, 1952-54; Minister of Land Reforms and Purchayat Raj in Government of Rajasthan, 1954-71; Chief Minister of Government of Rajasthan; Governor, Karnatoka State, 1972-75; Andhra Pradesh, 1976; Tamil Nadu, 1976-77; Member, Lok Sabha, House of People of India, elected, 1980. *Publications:* Our Administrative Problems; Articles on Political, Economic and Social Subjects. *Hobbies:* Farming. *Address:* Durga Nursery, Udaipur, Rajasthan, India.

SUKUMAR, Israel Purushotham, b. 18 July 1935, Vellore, India. Doctor of Medicine-Paediatric Cardiologist. m. Ann Rajan, 10 May 1963; 1 son, 1 daughter. *Education:* MB, BS, University of Madras, 1957; MRCP, Edinburgh, 1961; DM, University of Madras, 1967; FRCP, Edinburgh, 1972; FACC, USA, 1975; FISE, India, 1980; FIMSA, 1981. *Appointments:* Medical Registrar, Cambridge UK, 1959-60; Senior Registrar, West London Medical School, 1960-61; Lecturer in Cardiology, CMC Hospital, Vellore, India, 1961-69. *Memberships:* Association of Physicians of India, Governing body, Scientific subcommittee, Editorial Board; Cariological Society of India, President-elect; Chairman, Scientifc subcommittee and Editorial Board; Fellow, American College of Cardiology; Scientific subcommittee of Paediatric cardiology of the International Society & Federation of Cardiology; Hon. European Association of Paediatric Cardiology, Honorary, Cardiac Society of Australia, New Zealand & Founder, Asean Society of Paediatric Cardiology; President of Cardiological Society of India. *Publications:* Over 100 scientific publications in Indian and Overseas journals Contributor to; API Textbook of Medicine; Progress in Cardiology No.9; Paediatric Cardiology; Guest Editor, Teaching number on Congenital heart disease of the Indian Heart Journal; Progress in cardiology. *Honours:* B.C. Roy Oration, Calcutta; AFMRC Annual Oration Poona; 1st Annual Oration, Nepal Medical Association, Kathmandu; Amalananda Das Gold Medal Oration; Dr. G. Shetty Annual Oration, Bangalore. *Address:* 37, Jubilee Ground, CMC Hospital Campus, Vellore, 632 004, India.

SULEIMAN, Ahmad, b. 5 Mar 1948, Muar, Johore, Malaysia. Chartered Valuation Surveyor. m. Faridah I. Suleiman, 4 Nov 1971. 2 sons, 2 daughters. *Education:* BSc, UK; Professional Member of the Royal Institution of Chartered Surveyors, UK; Member of the Institution of Surveyors, Malaysia; Registered Surveyor under Board of Surveyor's, Malaysia; *Appointments:* Valuation Officer, Malaysian Treasury, Valuation Division, 1971-75; Properties and Valuation Officer, Bank Bumiputra, Malaysia; Berhad, Kuala Lumpur, Malaysia, 1975-76; Manager Properties and Valuation Department, 1976-80, Bank Bumiputra, Malaysia, Berhad; Principal, Suleiman & Co., Chartered Surveyors, Valuers' Estate Agents & Property Manager, 1980-. *Hobbies:* Swimming; Reading; Outdoor Activities. *Address:* 35, Jalan Taman, Seputeh Dua, Kuala Lumpur, Malaysia.

SULLIVAN, James Horace, b. 13 Sept. 1924, Melbourne, Australia. Zoo Director. m. Joan Mary Hilliard, 6 June 1950, 1 son, 1 daughter. *Education:* Accountancy, Hemingway Robertson Institute, 1941-42. *Appointments:* Senior Administrative Officer, Melbourne City Council, Parks Department, 1946-63; Executive Officer, Royal Melbourne Zoological Gardens, 1963-64; Director, Royal Melbourne Zoological Gardens, 1964-; Director, Zoological Parks and Gardens, Victoria, 1976-. *Memberships:* President, Royal Australian Institute of Parks & Recreation, 1976; President, Association of Zoo Directors of Australia & New Zealand, 1976-79, President Elect. 1982-83. *Publications:* Annual Report, Melbourne Zoological Gardens, 1964-76; Various articles in miscellaneous journals. *Honours:* Fellow, Royal Australian Institute of Parks & Recreation, 1967. *Hobbies:* Photography. *Address:* Director's Residence, Royal Melbourne Zoological Gardens, P.O. Box 74, Parkville, Victoria, 3052, Australia.

SUMMER, Christopher John, b. 17 Apr. 1943. Melbourne, Australia. Barrister, Solicitor & Member of Parliament. m. Suzanne Raymonde Pony, 1 son, 1 daughter. *Education:* LLB, University of Adelaide, 1966; BA, University of Adelaide, 1967. *Appointments:* Attorney General, Minister of Consumer Affairs; Minister Assisting the Premier in Ethnic Affairs; Leader of the Government in the Legislative Council 1979, Since September 1979; Leader of the Opposition in the Legislative Council, Shadow Attorney General; Shadow Minister of Consumer Affairs & Shadow Minister of Ethnic Affairs. *Address:* 45, Clifton Street, Prospect, South Africa.

SUMMERS, Anthony Bruce, b. 21 Dec. 1942, Bournemouth, England. Author & Journalist. m. Susan Kent, 26 Jan. 1967. Divorced. *Education:* BA, New College, Oxford University. *Appointments:* Researcher, World in Action, Granada TV, London, 1963; Scriptwriter, Swiss Broadcasting Corporation, Berne, 1964; Writer, BBC TV News, 1965; Assistant Producer, Senior Film Producer, BBC TV, Current Affairs Group, 1965-74; Author & Freelance documentary film producer, 1974-. *Memberships:* P.E.N., London; National Union of Jourralist; Assistant Cinematograph, TV & Allied Technicians. *Publications:* The File On the Tsar, 1976; Conspiracy, 1980; Documentaries for BBC TV include films cn both the above. *Honours:* Golden Dagger

Award for best non-fiction work on crime of 1980. *Hobbies:* Travel; Swimming. *Address:* Deborah Rogers Literary Agency, 5-11 Mortimer Street, London, S1N 7 RH, England.

SUMMERS, Anthony Gilbert, b. 14 April, 1943, Australia. Company Director. m. Christine H. Paterson, 3 sons, 1 daughter. *Education:* RDA, 1963; AAIV, 1968; MATAA, 1972. *Appointments:* Co-Founder, Shareholder, Managing Director of Intensive Industries Pty. Ltd., 1972; Director, Australian Bacon Limited., 1974; Managing Director, Australian Bacon Ltd., 1976; Member of Young Presidents Organisation of New York, 1978; Warden, St. Peters Cathedral, Adelaide, 1978; Council, St. Peters Cathedral, Adelaide, 1978; Chairman of Directors, Australian Bacon Ltd., 1979; Member of Council of Institute of Directors, 1980; Member of Board of Governors of the Adelaide Festival of Arts Incorporated, 1980; Member of the Australian Trade Development Council, 1981; Australian Trade Development Council Committee for Funding of Trade Promotional Activity, 1981; Australian Trade Development Council Committee for Export Franchise Limitations, 1981-. *Memberships:* Adelaide Club; Adelaide Commerce; Victoria Racing Club, (VRC); South Australian Jockey Club, (SAJC). *Hobbies:* Skiing; Theatre. *Address:* 58 Strangways Terrace, North Adelaide, 5006, S. Australia.

SUMMERTON, Oswald, b. 19th Aug. 1926. Adelaide, S.A. Australia. Physhotherapist, (Transactional Analyst). *Education:* BSc (India); PGCE (London); MS (Operations Research); CWRU Cleveland)Lic Phil (Melbourne); Lic Theol (Kurseong). *Appointments:* Teacher at St. Xavier's School, Hazarilbagh, 1953-57; Principal, Teachers Training Institute, Sitagarha, 1962-68; National Secretary, Jesuit Educational Association of India, Delhi, 1968-79; Co. Director, Transactional, Analytic Centre for Education & Training, 1980. *Memberships:* AINACS, All India Association of Catholic Schools (Vice President); AIFEA, All India Federation of Educational Associations, Member, Board of Trustees; JEAI, Jesuit Educational Association of India (Secretary; ITAA, International Transactional Analysis Association (Member Training Standards Committee); TASI, Transactional Analysis Society of India (President). *Publications:* An Operation Research Approach to Transactional Analysis; University Microfilms, Michigan, 1976; Transactional Analysis—Basic Concepts, Manohar, Delhi, 1979; Games Since Eric Berne, Manohar, Delhi, 1979. *Honours:* Misereor International Scholarship, 1973-75; Visiting Professor, University of San Francisco, 1978-82. *Hobbies:* Walking, Writing; Backgammon; Singing. *Address:* C5/4O, Safdarjang Development Area, New Delhi, 1100 16, India.

SUMMY, Ralph Victor, b. 18th June, 1929. Allentown, Pennsylvania, USA. Academic & Journalist. m. Gay Reid McCarthy, 14th July, 1967, 1 son, 1 daughter. *Education:* AB. Harvard University, 1950; Dip.Tr. Admin., Northwestern University, 1959; Dip. Ed., University of New England, 1965; MA., University of Sydney, 1969. *Appointments:* Director, Greater Boston Committee for Sane Nuclear Policy; Teacher, Department of Education, New South Wales, Australia; Tutor, Department of Government, University of Queensland, Australia; Lecturer, Division of External Studies, University of Queensland, Australia; Editor, Social Alternatives. *Memberships:* Peace Institute of Australia, Vice President; Gandhi Marg, International Consultant; Noviolence, Contributing Editor; Australian, New Zealand, American Studies, Association, Executive member; Australian Political Science Association, Harvard Club, Australia. *Publications:* Numerous articles and reviews in Social Alternatives and other journals and newspapers. With Malcolm J Saunders, The Australian Peace Movement: From Sudan to Vietnam and Beyond (forthcoming 1982). *Honours:* Media Peace Prize, 1980; George Essay Prize, 1981. *Hobbies:* Tennis. *Address:* 14, Millwood Street, Rainworth, Queensland 4065, Australia.

SUN, Kuo-Tung, b. 11 Oct. 1922. Canton, China. Educator. m. Ho Bing-Ge, 31 Aug. 1947, 2 sons, 2 daughters. *Education:* BA, National Ching-che University, 1947; New Asia Institute of Advanced Chinese Studies (MA), 1957; PhD., Hong Kong University, 1974. *Appointments:* Chief Columnist, Chun-Nan Daily News, Hong Kong, 1955; Head of History Department, New Asia College, Hong Kong, 1963-73; Dean of Faculty of Arts, New Asia College, Hong Kong, 1973-77; Supervisor, New Asia Middle School, Hong Kong, 1973; Director, New Asia Institute of Advanced Chinese Studies, 1973; Head of History Department, The Chinese University of Hong Kong, 1977. *Memberships:* Board of Trustees, New Asia College; Board of Trustees, New Asia Educational and Cultural Association; Council Member, The Chinese University of Hong Kong. *Publications:* Life and Thoughts, 1954; A Strong Life, 1955; General Chinese History, 6 volumes, 1962; A Study of the Channels of Promotion of Important Civil Officials in T'ang Central Government, 1979; Essays on Historical Studies of the T'ang and Sung China, 1980. *Address:* University Residence No. 7., Flat 8B, The Chinese University of Hong Kong, Shatin, N.T. Hong Kong.

SUN, Stephen Wing Fai, b. 22 Jan, 1948. Hong Kong. Business Executive. University, Sacramento, USA; 1972 MBA, 1974. *Appointments:* Fing Ping Fan Group of Companies: Assistant to Joint Managing .Director, 1974-79; General Manager, 1979-; A. Gransfield & Co Limited (A Mamber of FPF Group), Manager, 1975-77; General manager, 1977-79; Director & General Manager, 1979-. *Memberships:* Royal Hong Kong Jockey Club; Nautilus Club; Royal Hong Kong Club (Yacht) Island Squash Rackets Club; Aberdeen Boat Club; Squash Rackets Association; National Geographic Society; The Cousteau Society; Sea Dragon Skindiving Club; National Association of Underwater Instructors. *Honours:* AMF Hatteras Yachets - Million Dollar Sales Club, 1980 *Hobbies:* Riding; Squash; Scuba Diving; Underwater Photography; Flying; Classical Music. *Address:* 6, Marconi Road, Faber Gardens C2 4/F, Kowloon Tong, Hong Kong.

SUNDAR RAO, Pamidipani Samuel Simon, b. 24 Sept. 1934. Madras, Tamilnadu, India. Professor of Biostatistics. m. Kasturi, 23 Jan. 1961, 3 sons. *Education:* BSc. (Hons) Madras University, 1955; MA., Madras Universiy, 1956 MPH. University of California, Berkeley, Calif, 1964; Dr. Ph. Columbia University, New York, 1976. *Appointments:* Lecturer in Biostatistics, Christian Medical College and hospital, Vellore, India, 1955-62; Senior Lecturer, 1964-68; Reader, 1968-71; Associate Professor, 1971-73; Head of Department of Biostatistics, 1964; Professor, 1973. *Memberships:* American Statistical Association; Biometric Society; Christian Medical Association of India; The India Association for the Advancement of Medical Education; The Royal Statistical Society; Nutrition Society of India; Research Panel of India Council of Medical Research; Life Member, India Society of Human Genetics and Member Governing Body. *Publications:* Co-Author for more than 90 publications, National and International Journals; An Introduction to Biostatistics, a manual for students in health sciences. *Honours:* Delta Omega USA, 1963. *Hobbies:* Reading; Coin collecting. *Address:* CMC College Campus, Vellore, 632002, Tamilnadu, India.

SUPPIAH, Nagan, b. 24 Feb. 1942. Gampola, Sri Lanka. Chartered Accountant. m. Mangayarkarasi, 19 Oct. 1975, 1 son. *Education:* BSc. University of Ceylon, 1965; AVA, Institute of Chartered Accountants of Sri Lanka, 1971; Affiliate of the Institute of Cost & Management Accountants, London. Qualified Assistant, Lawrie Muthu Krishna & Co Colomboll, 1966-74; Finance Manager, St. Anthony's Industries Group, Colomboll, 1974-75; Principal Manager, Cephas & Associates, Kampala, Uganda, 1975-79; Supervisor, Coopers & Lybrand, Lusaka, Zambia, 1979-. *Memberships:* Hony Secretary of Good Hope, Education Fund, 1974-75: *Hobbies:* Photography; Stamp Collection. *Address:* Flat No. 3 Arlberg Court, Adis Ababa Drive, Lusaka, Zambia.

SUR, Mriganka Mohan, b. 3 Mar. 1899. Calcutta, India. Sheet Iron Vitreous Enamel Expert. m. Kamala Prova Biswas, 10 Aug. 1921. 1 daughter, 3 sons. *Education:* Science Graduate of the Calcutta University. Had in-plant training in various Enamel Industries in the U.K., Austria, France, U.S.A. and Japan to acquire manufacturing know-how on vitreous enamelling. Was the First enamellist in India. *Appointments:* Was the pioneer to set up the First vitreous enamel factory in the Indian sub-continent—styled as Sur Enamel & Stamping Works Private Limited. Was the pioneer to set up the First Refrigerator manufacturing plant in India— styled as Sur Industries Private Limited. *Memberships:*

Emeritus Member, American Ceramics Society; Fellow, Institute of Ceramics UK; Honorary Fellow, Indian Institute of Ceramics; Past President, Indian Ceramic Society. *Honours:* Member of the Senate of an Indian University and Paper Setter & Examiner on Enamelling for a decade in the Forties. Member of Indian Parliament (Upper House) for 18 years from 1954. Past President, Bengal National Chamber of Commerce and Industry. Received Plaques and Scrolls from the Indian Ceramic Society in recognition of his contribution to the development of enamelling industry in India. *Hobbies:* Agriculture; Gardening; reading Technical and Religious Books and Journals. *Address:* 163, Acharyya Jagadish Bose Road, Calcutta 700 014, India,

SURJEET, Harkishansingh, b. 23 Mar. 1916, Jullenden, India. Social Worker, Member of Parliament. m. Pritam Kam, June, 1935, 2 sons, 2 daughters. *Education:* Matriculation from Punjab University, 1932. *Appointments:* Member of the Congress party before 1940; Editor of Urdu Monthly Magazine, 1938-39; Editor of Punjab Weekly, 1959-62; Editor of Punjab Daily, 1969-80; Editor of Hindi Weekly, 1979-80. *Appointments:* Fellow and Member of various political societies in India *Memberships:* Author of mamy pamphlets on Agrarian Questions and current politics. *Hobbies:* Politics; Culture. *Address:* 8 Teen Murti Lane, New Delhi-110001, India.

SURVEYOR, Ivor, b. 9 June 1933, London. Physician. m. Mary Elizabeth Ashworth, 6 Oct. 1961, 2 sons, 1 daughter. *Education:* MB, ChB, Bristol, 1958; MD, Bristol, 1967; FRACP, 1975; FRCP, 1981. *Appointments:* Medical Registrar, Queen Alexander Hospital, Portsmouth, England, 1960; Registrar in Nuclear Medicine, Leeds General Infirmary, England, 1962; Senior Medical Registrar, University Hospital of Wales, 1965; Assistant Physician, Nuclear Medicine, Royal Perth Hospital, 1972. *Memberships:* Royal Society of Medicine; Society of Nuclear Medicine; Chairman, W.A-.Branch, ANZANM; Australian Medical Association; British Medical Association; Royal Freshwater Bay Yacht Club. *Publications:* Discrepancies Between Whole-body Potassium Content & Exchangeable Potassium, (with D. Hughes) 1968; The Radioisotope Spleen Scan in the Assessment of Patients with Suspected Spleen Trauma, 1979; Prostaglandins and Excretion of 99 mTc HIDA in the Rat. 1980. *Hobbies:* Yacht Racing. *Address:* 28 Dempster Road, Karrinyup, Western Australia, 6018.

SUTER, Keith Douglas, b. 25 July 1948, Harrow, England. Church Official. *Education:* BA (Hons), University of Sussex; PhD, University of Sydney. *Appointments:* Ministry of Defence, London, 1964-69; Human Rights Secretary, United Nations Association, London, 1972; Director of Adminstration, Wesley Central Mission, Sydney, 1976-81; General Secretary, Commission for Social Responsibility Uniting Church in Australia, 1982; Dean of Students, Wesley College, University of Sydney, 1979-. *Memberships:* President, United Nations Association of Australia, 1979; Chairman, World Federalists of Australia, 1978; Council International Law Association of Australia, 1978; Institute of Directors in Australia, 1980. *Publications:* Protecting Human Rights, 1978; Antarctica & World Law, 1979; Alternative to War, 1981. *Honours:* Gladstone Essay Prize, University of Sussex, 1970; Norman Angell Travelling Scholarship, 1972; Earle Page Prize, 1973. *Hobbies:* Work, Travelling Overseas. *Address:* Wesley College, P.O. Box 84, Camperdown 2050, Australia.

SUTHERLAND, Hugh Brown, b. 22 Jan. 1920, Glasgow, Scotland. Chartered Civil Engineer (Professor). m. Sheila Doris Oliphant, 16 June 1953, 1 son, 1 daughter. *Education:* SM, Harvard University, USA, 1946-47. *Appointments:* Assistant Civil Engineer, Oscar Faber & Partners, 1940-42; Lecturer, University Glasgow, 1942-46; Research Associate, Harvard University, 1947-48; Lecturer, Senior Lecturer, Reader University, Glasgow, 1948-64; Professor, Cormack Chair of Civil Engineering, University of Glasgow, 1964-; Consultant to UNESCO. *Memberships:* Fellow of Institution of Civil Engineers; Fellow of Institution of Structural Engineers; University Athletic Club. *Publications:* Author & Co-Author of over 40 research publications in journals of Professional Societies; Served on various Government Advisory Committees including Tip Safety Committee (Aberfan Tribunal Decision). *Honours:* Fellow of Royal Society of Edinburgh FRSE, 1955; Fellowship of Engineering, F. Eng., 1980. *Hobbies:* Athletics Administration; Rugby; Golf; Gardening. *Address:* 22 Pendicle Road, Bearsden, Glasgow G61 1DY, Scotland.

SWARUP, Gopal, b. 30 May 1928. Azamgarh (UP), India. Scientist. m. Madhuri, 6 June 1957, 1 son, 1 daughter. *Education:* MSC. Ag, 1948; Assoc., IARI, 1950; MS, Kansas, USA, 1954; PhD, Kansas, USA, 1955. *Appointments:* Assistant Mycologist/Assistant Plant Pathologist, 1956-63; Plant Pathologist, (Nematodes), 1963-74; Deputy Secretary, 1974-78; Head of the Division of Nematology, 1978-. *Memberships:* President, Nematological Society of India; Chief Editor, Indian Journal of Nematology; General Secretary, Nematological Society of India; Indian Phytopathological Society; Nematological Society of India; European Society of Nematologists; Society of Nematologists, USA; Association of Seed Pathologists, India. *Publications:* About 100 publications on diseases of crop plants caused by fungi and plant parasitic nematodes, specially host parasite relationships. *Hobbies:* Stamp collection; Music. *Address:* 155C DDA Flats (MIG), Rajouri Garden, New Delhi-110027, India.

SWARUP, Sanjiv, b. 19 Nov. 1958, Madras, India. Professional Accountant & Manager. *Education:* EC, Senior Cambridge, 1979; MC, Calcutta University, 1980; Institute of Chartered Accountants of India. *Appointments:* Director, Emery India Pvt. Ltd. *Memberships:* Chairman, Udayan Club; Sumair Sports Club, Life Member. *Publications:* Publications in various House Journals. *Honours:* Numerous prizes won in various sports. *Hobbies:* Sports; Reading; Socialising. *Address:* Emery, Bedeshwar, Jamnagar, India, 361002.

SWEDE, George, b. 20 Nov. 1940, Riga, Latvia. Teacher/Writer. m. 23 July 1975, 2 sons. *Education:* BA, University of British Columbia, 1964; MA, Dalhousie University, 1965. *Appointments:* Instructor, Vancouver City College, 1966-67; School Psychologist, Scarborough Board of Education, 1967-68; Instructor, Ryerson Polytechnical Institute, 1968-71; Director, Developmental Psychology, Open College/Ryerson, 1972-76; Professor, Ryerson Polytechnical Institute, 1971-. *Memberships:* The Writer's Union of Canada; Canadian Society of Children's Authors, Illustrators & Performers; League of Canadian Poets; Haiku Society of Canada; Canadian Psychological Association. *Publications:* 10 Collections of Poetry; 6 Children's Books; 1 collection of essays on the Haiku form Poems & articles in numerous periodicals; Editor of 1 anthology of Haiku. *Honours:* Various Awards for Haiku, 1977-. *Hobbies:* Tennis; Reading. *Address:* 70 London Street, Toronto, Ontario, Canada, M6G 1N3.

SWEENEY, Charles Augustine, b. Melbourne, Victoria, Australia. Barrister. m. Geraldine Vandeleur, 2 sons, 2 daughters. *Education:* LLB, LLM, formerly part-time lecturer in Commercial Law, Trade Practices & Taxation, University of Melbourne & Leo Cussen Institute. *Appointments:* Member of the Bars of New South Wales, Victoria, Tasmania & Northern Territory. *Memberships:* Royal Melbourne Golf Club, VRC, VATC, MCC, LTAV. *Publications:* Revenue Law in Australia; Duties of Liquidators; Assistant Editor, Australian Law Journal, 1977-; Australian Correspondent, Lloyds Maritime & Commercial Law Quarterly, London, 1974-; Editor Federal Law Reports. *Hobbies:* Sailing; Tennis. *Address:* Wentworth Chambers, 180 Phillip Street, Sydney 2000, Australia.

SWEENEY, John Patrick, b. 14 Aug. 1929, Sharebroker. m. Doreen Kathleen Minter, 11 Oct. 1961, 1 son 1 daughter. *Education:* Fellow, Securities Institute of Australia. *Appointments:* Member of Sydney Stock Exchange, Elected 1959; Chairman of Directors, The Union-Fidelity Trustee Company of Australia Ltd., 1978; Director, G.J. Trewin Industries Ltd., 1980. *Memberships:* Committee Member, Sydney Stock Exchange, 1975-78. *Hobbies:* Golf; Surfing. *Address:* 21 Village Lower Road, Vaucluse, New South Wales, 2030, Australia.

SWEENEY, M. Eamonn, b. 26 July 1934, Sligo, Ireland. Engineer. m. Eileen Henley, 8 Aug. 1960, 1 son, 4 daughters. *Education:* BE, Mechanical/Electrical Engineering; FIMECHE, CENG. *Appointments:* Texaco Trinidad Incorporated; Foster Wheeler Ltd.; Bechtel;

Responsible for Design of Major Oil Refineries in Europe; BP Sweden; Texaco Belgium; Chevron Belgium; Manager of Engineering, Bechtel, Great Britain; Assistant to Division Manager. *Memberships:* Fellow of Institute of Mechanical Engineers: Bechtel Director-/Advisory Group; Trustee Bechtel Pension Fund. *Honours:* Responsible for Design of Fastest ever built 100.000 Barrels per day refinery in 18 months; Currently responsible for design of largest ever built refinery of ARAMCO. *Hobbies:* Golf; Fishing; Bowling; Rugby. *Address:* 552 Allegheny Drive, Walnut Creek, California, CA 94598, USA

SYME, James Robert, b. 29 Aug. 1928, Brisbane, Australia. Radiologist. m. Helen Catherine Fitzgerald, 20 Apr. 1957, 2 sons. *Education.* MB, BS, University of Queensland, 1951; MD, University of Melbourne, 1959; Diploma of Diagnostic Radiology, University of Melbourne, 1961; Fellow, Royal College of Radiologists, London, 1964; Fellow, Royal Australasian College of Radiologists, 1969; Fellow, Royal Australasian College of Physicians, 1971. *Appointments:* Registrar, Professorial Medical Unit, Royal Melbourne Hospital, 1959; Radiology Registrar, Royal Melbourne Hospital, 1960-3; Assistant Radiologist, Royal Melbourne Hospital, 1964; Deputy Director of Radiology, Royal Melbourne Hospital, Since 1965. *Memberships:* Royal Australasian College of Radiologists, Federal Council 1968; Chairman, Victoria Branch, 1972-76; Secretary, Salaried Medical Specialists, Royal Melbourne Hospital, 1968; Australian Society for Ultrasound in Medicine, 1976. *Publications:* Various Scientific papers on Radiological Topics. *Honours:* Thomas Baker Memorial Fellow, Royal Australasian College of Radiologists, 1964-65; Rohan Williams Travelling Professor, Royal Australasian College of Radiologists and Royal College of Radiologists, London, 1979; Honorary Member, Australian Institute of Radiography, 1981. *Hobbies:* Photography; Philately, Gardening. *Address:* 2 Allison Avenue, Glen Iris, Victoria 3146, Australia.

SYME, James Robert, b. 28 Sept. 1938, Sydney, Agricultural Science. m. Janice R. Wood, 31 Dec. 1960, 2 sons, 2 daughters. *Education:* BSc Agriculture, (Hons) Sydney, 1960; PhD, Nottingham, 1963; Diploma Ceramic Studies, 1978. *Appointments:* N.S.W. Department of Agriculture, Plant Breeder, 1960-69; Senior Research Fellow, University of Queensland, 1970-74; Supervising Plant Breeder, Queensland Department Primary Industries, 1975-81. *Memberships:* Australian Institute of Agricultural Science; Wheat Breeding Society of Australia, Vice President; Darling Downs Potters Club (past President). *Publications:* Breeder or Co-Breeder of the Wheat Varieties, Condor Egret, Jabiru, Oxley, Cook and Banks; also contributor of 30 scientific publications on Cereal Breeding, Physiology and Genetics. *Honours:* Pawlett Travelling Scholarship, University of Sydney, 1961; Wheat Industry Council Award for Overseas Study, (Mexico), 1975; Royal Society and Nuffield Foundation Commonwealth Bursary, PBI, Cambridge, 1980. *Hobbies:* Squash; Pottery; Music. *Address:* 30, Rome Street, Toowoomba, Queensland, 4350, Australia.

SYMMONDS, Algernon Washington, b. 19 Nov. 1926, Barbados. Solicitor, Attorney-at-Law. m. Gladwyn Ward, 1 son, 1 daughter. *Education:* Combermere School, Barbados; Harrison College, Barbados; Codrington College, Barbados. *Appointments:* Solicitor, Barbados, 1953; Solicitor, U.K. 1958; Deputy Registrar, 1955-59; Crown Solicitor, 1959-66; Permanent Secretary, Ministry of Home Affairs, 1966-72; Permanent Secretary, Ministry of Education, Youth Affairs, Community Development and Sports, 1972-76, Barbados; Permanent Secretary, Ministry of External Affairs, 1976-79, Barbados, Appointed to rank of Ambassador, 1977; High commissioner to the United Kingdom, 1979-. *Memberships:* Summerhayes Tennis Club, (Past President), Barbados; Empire Cricket Club, (Past Vice-President), Barbados; Life Member, Barbados Cricket Association. *Honours:* Gold Crown of Merit, Barbados National Honours, 1980. *Hobbies:* Lawn Tennis, Cricket; Football; *Address:* Iverta, Burtenshaw Road, Boyle Farm, Thames Ditton, Surrey, England.

SYMONS, Gerald Gordon, b. 7 Sept, 1922, Lachine, Quebec, Canada, Insurance Executive. m Norma H. McElligot, 1 March, 1946, 4 sons, 2 daughters. *Education:* Sir George Williams University, Montreal, Quebec; RCAF Pilot, Coastal Command, England, 1942-75.

Appointments: Ontario Manager, Stewart Smith (Canada) Ltd., 1947-51; Director, Morgan Insurance Services Ltd., 1956, Vice-President Morgan Insurance Services Ltd., 1958; Formed G. Gordon Symons Co. Ltd., 1964-. Chairman & President: Symons General Insurance Company, Canada; Rushmore Insurance Company Ltd., Bermuda; Chairman & Chief Executive Officer, Symonsure Group Ltd; IMG Insurance Management Group Ltd, Canada; IMG Insurance Management, Florida, USA; Symons Financial Holings Ltd, Canada; Canadian Marketing Management Ltd, Canada; Am-Can International Ltd, Bermuda; Chief Agent in Canada; Fire Insurance Company of Canada; Centennial Insurance Company, USA; Director: Insurdata Ltd., Canada; Bott & Associates Ltd., Bermuda. *Memberships:* Life-Governor, Montreal General Hospital; Society for Emotional Development in Children; Director, Society Member, Canadian Schizophrenic Foundation; Member Lakeshore General Hospital *Creative Works:* Prosport professional sport insurance programme. *Hobbies:* Golf; Squash; Flying. *Address:* Belle Cove, Tucker's Town, Bermuda.

SZENT-IVANY, Joseph Julius Hubert, b. 3 Nov. 1910, Budapest, Hungary. Zoologist, Entomologist, Zoogeographer, Conservationist. m. Marie Louise Lakatos, 1 daughter. *Education:* Diploma Econ. & Pol, 1930; PhD, Major in Systematic Zoology, 1936; Dr Habil. in Zoogeography, 1943. Entomologist, Dept. of Agriculture, Stock and Fisheries, Papua, 1954; Snr. Entomologist, 1959; Class IV Prin. Entomologist, 1966; Res. Assoc. Hon. Assoc. in Entomology, B.P. Bishop Mus., Honolulu, 1966-81; Hon. Assoc. in Entomology, S. Australian Museum, Adelaide, S. Australia, 1966-. *Memberships:* Standing Comm. Pacific Entomology, Pacific Sci. Association, Member, 1955-57, 1961-66; Chairman, 1957-61; Papua New Guinea Sci. Soc. President, 1965-66; Royal Soc. of S. Australia, Vice-President, 1976-77, President, 1977-78. *Publications:* 157 Professional publications. *Honours:* Recipient of numerous honours and awards, including, National Defence Cross, Hungarian Government, 1943; Kt. Starcross of Society and Order of St. Ladislaus, 1976; Kt., International Constantinian Order, 1977; Cdr. of Australian Commandery, International Constantinian Order, 1980. *Hobbies:* Table Tennis; Zoological and Botanical Philately. *Address:* Boroko, 39, Addison Avenue, Athelstone, S. Australia, 5076

SZOKOLAY, Steven Vajk. b. 22 Nov. 1927, Budapest. Architect, Educator. m. Katalin Edelenyi, 2 sons by previous marriage. *Education:* Dip. Arch. University of New South Wales, 1961; M. Arch. University of Liverpool, 1968; PhD, University of Queensland, 1978. *Appointments:* Lecturer, University of Liverpool, 1965-68; Seconded to University of East Africa, Nairobi, 1965-67; Senior Lecturer in Environmental Science, Polytechnic of Central London, 1968-74; Senior Lecturer, Dir. of Architectural Science Unit, University of Queensland, 1974-; Reader 1980-. *Memberships:* Chairman, ANZ Section, Intern. Social Energy Society, 1978-80; President, ANZ Architectural Science Association, 1980; Fellow, 1972, Associate, 1962, Royal Australian Institute of Architects; Royal Institute of British Architects, 1964. *Publications:* World Solar Architecture, 1980; Design of first Solar heating system in U.K.- Milton Keynes, 1974; Designer of Solar air conditioned house, Brisbane, 1978; Editor of Solar Progress quarterly, 1980-: also contributor of over 100 articles and papers presented at various conferences. *Hobbies:* Reading: Theatre; Opera; Records. *Address:* 50, Halimah Street, Chapel Hill, Brisbane, 4069, Australia.

SZOMANSKI, Eugeniusz b. 29 Aug. 1918, Pawlograd, Ukraine. Engineer-Educator, retired. m. Johanna Maria, 9 May, 1981, 2 daughters by previous marriage. *Education:* Polish Degree of M.Sc.(Eng), 1st CLass Hon. 1944; Bachelor of Economics, University of Tasmania, 1956; Post Graduate Studies in Electrical Engineering, University of Syracuse, New York, USA, 1960. *Appointments:* War Service, RAF, UK, 1939-46; Project Designer, Rolls Royce Ltd., Derby, UK 1946-51; Senior Lecturer in Fluid Dynamics, University of Tasmania, 1951-56; Senior Research Engineer, Stratos Fairchild Co., N.Y. 1956-59; Staff Eng. Advanced Technology Dept., IBM, NY, 1959-60; Senior Lecturer Fluid Mech. & Thermodyn, Mechanical Engineer, University of NSW, Sydney, 1961-62; Principal Research Scientist, Dept. Chief Eng. Research Div., Australian Atomic Energy Commission, 1962-68; Principal Gordon Institute of Technology, Geelong, Vic. 1968-77; Asst. Vice-Chancellor, Deakin University, 1975-77; Asst. to Vice-President, Victoria Institute of Colleges, Armidale, 1977-78; Retired 1978; Visiting Fellow, University of New England, NSW, 1981. *Memberships:* Fellow, Royal Aeronautical Society; Fellow Institution of Mechanical Engineers, Chairman Australian branch Council Member, 1976-78; Fellow, Institution of Engineers, Australia; Chartered Engineer UK and Australia; Member, America Society of Mechanical Engineers; Australian College of Education; Life Fellow, International Biographical Association. *Publications:* Published many research papers and has delivered many public lectures. *Hobbies:* Painting; Contract Bridge. *Address:* 7, Pleasant Street, Newtown, Victoria, 3220, Australia.

T

TABAL, Ieremia Tienang, CMG, b. 1949. m. Meleangi Kalofia, 1974, 1 daughter, 1 son. *Education:* Senior Assistant Accountant, 1973; Member, House of Assembly, Gilbert Island, 1974; Leader of the Opposition, 1975-77; Chief Minister, 1978-79; President of the Republic of Kiribati since Independence, July 12th, 1979. *Honours:* Companion, Order of St. Michael and St. George, 1979. *Address:* Temoto, Nonouti Island, Kiribati.

TADGELL, Robert Clive, b. 15 Mar. 1934, Brisbane, Queensland. Judge of The Supreme Court of Victoria since 1980. m. Christina, 4 Jan. 1967, 2 sons. *Education:* LLB, Trinity College, University of Melbourne, 1957. *Appointments:* Associate to Mr. Justice Sholl, Supreme Court of Victoria, 1958; Victorian Bar, 1960; (QC, 1974); New South Wales Bar, 1963; (QC, 1979). *Memberships:* Melbourne Club; Australian Club, Melbourne; Metropolitan Golf Club, Melbourne; Melbourne Cricket Club. *Hobbies:* Woodworking; Gardening. *Address:* 19 Henderson Avenue, Malvern, 3144, Victoria, Australia.

TAFT, Rodney David, b. 8th Nov. 1940. Melbourne, Australia. Medical Practitioner, Diagnostic Radiology. m. Aviva Devora Kanatopsky, 20th Dec. 1967. 3 daughters. *Education:* MB,BS, Melbourne University, 1964; MRACR, 1969; FFR, 1971; FRCR, 1975. *Appointments:* Resident Medical Officer, Alfred Hospital, Melbourne, 1965; Radiology Registrar, Prince Henrys Hospital, Melbourne, 1966-70; Research Assistant in Radiology, Bristol United Hospitals, Bristol, 1970; Senior Radiology Registrar, St. Thomas Hospital, London, 1971; Radiology Registrar, National Hospital for Nervous Diseases, London, 1972; Sessional Radiologist, Prince Henrys Hospital, Melbourne, 1972-; Private Practice in Partnership with Drs. Taft, Shnier & Liu. *Memberships:* Royal Australasian College of Radiologists, Treasurer of Victorian Branch Committee; Royal College of Radiologists, FRCR; Australian Society for Ultrasound in Medicine; Graduate union, University of Melbourne, Life Member. *Publications:* Budd-Chairman Syndrome, Australasian Radiology, Feb 1969. *Hobbies:* Photography; Tennis; Swimming. *Address:* 11, Chatfield Avenue, Balwyn, Victoria 3103, Australia.

TAGGART, Joan Margaret, b. 2 Apr, 1917, Sydney, Australia. m. William Taggart, 30 Mar. 1940, 1 son, 1 daughter. *Education:* St. Scholastica's College, Glebe Point, Sydney, Australia. *Appointments:* Personal Assistant, Tooheys Limited, 1954-64; Administrative Assistant, Australian National University, 1964-74; Executive Assistant, The Pipeline Authority, 1974-. *Memberships:* Junior Vice President, Australian Labour Party, 1979-; National Executive, Australian Labour Party, 1973-; Secretary, Australian Federation of Business Professional Women, 1972-76; First Vice President Australian Federation ABPW, 1976-78; President, ACT Branch of Australian Labour Party, 1976-77; President, Canberra Labour Club, 1979-81; Secretary of Zonta International, Canberra Branch, 1979-82. *Honours:* Recipient of Queens Jubilee Medal. *Hobbies:* Music; Theatre, Reading. *Address:* 17, Robe Street, Deakin ACT, Australia 2600.

TAGGART, Peter Irwin, b. 13 Nov. 1932, London. Doctor of Medicine. *Education:* Senior Physician, the Cavendish Medical Centre, London; Hon. Senior Lecturer to the Department of Medicine (Cardiology), The Middlesex Hospital Medical School, London, 1975-; Formerly Medical Registrar, Kings College Hospital, London; British Heart Foundation Research Fellow and Hon. Senior Registrar The Middlesex Hospital, London; Lecturer in Cardiology and Hon. Senior Registrar, The Radcliffe Infirmary, Oxford. *Memberships:* British Cardiac Society; Medical Research Society; Harveian Society of London; British Academy of Forensic Sciences. *Publications:* Scientific papers on (1) the influence of emotional and physical stress on the heart and cardiovascular system, and (2) cardiac electrophysiology. *Honours:* Leverhulme Research Scholarship, 1966; British Heart Foundation Research Award, 1968. *Hobbies:* Tennis. *Address:* Flat 3, Sussex House, 162/164 Kensington Church Street, London, W.8. England.

TAHIR, Ahmad, b. 10 Feb. 1940, Girei, Gongola State, Nigeria. m. (1) Khadijah, 24 Apr. 1964 (Deceased), Rabi, 27th July, 1975, 3 sons, 2 daughters. *Education:* BA, Ahmadu Bello University, Nigeria, 1967; MLib, University of Washington, USA, 1970: MA, McGill University, Canada, 1977; PhD, Still in progress, McGill University, Canada. *Appointments:* Graduate Trainee, Kashim Ibrahim, 1967; Head of Technical Services of Library, ABC library, Kano, 1970; Head Cataloguing Section, KIL, 2971; Head, President Kennedy Library, 1973; Sponsored, Inter-University Council, 6 months course, Library Administration, England, 1975; Deputy University Librarian. *Memberships:* Nigeria Library Association, 1970; Secretary/Treasurer, NLA, 1970-72; Editorial Board, Northern Division, 1972-73; Council member of the NLA, 1971-74; Treasurer, NLA, Standing Committee on Cataloguing, 1974; Standing Committee, School Libraries. *Publications:* Thesis, Change in Egypt as Reflected in Najib Mahfuz's Novels, 1945-50. *Hobbies:* Library Administration, Cataloguing; Arabic Literature; African History. *Address:* President Kennedy Library, Institute of Administration, Zaria, Nigeria.

TAIWO, Cornelius Olaleye, b. 27 Oct. 1915, Oru, Ijebu, Nigeria. Educationist, Administrator, Legal Practitioner. m. Susanna Olufowoke, 25 Dec. 1941, three sons, three daughters. *Education:* MA, Trinity College, Cambridge; MSc, MA, PhD, University of London Institute of Education; Barrister at Law, Middle Temple London; D.Lit. University of London; LLD(Hon), University of Cape Coast, Ghana. *Appointments:* Principal, Edo College, Nigeria; Permanent Secretary, Western Region of Nigeria; Professor of Education & Provost, University of Lagos College of Education; Executive Chairman of Thomas Nelson (Nigeria) Ltd. *Memberships:* Nigerian Association for Educational Administration & Planning; Nigerian Bar Association; Many Local voluntary organisations and societies. *Publications:* Henry Carr, African Contribution to Education; Nigerian Education System; Mathematics Teaching in Schools; Several articles, reports and papers. *Honours:* OBE, 1962; OON, 1964; Title, The Agbon of Oru, December, 1958. *Hobbies:* Scouting; Music; Voluntary & Church Organisations. *Address:* 12, Oduduwa Street, Ikeja, Nigeria.

TAKOMANA, Macray Moses, b. 24 Feb. 1950, Lawyer. m. Ruth Faith Nkanaunena, 30 June, 1979, 2 daughters. *Education:* Diploma Education, University of Malawi, 1972; Bachelor of Laws Degree, University of Malawi, 1978. *Appointments:* Secondary School Teacher, 1972-75; Employer Ministry of Education, 1978-; Lawyer, Assistant Registrar General, Ministry of Justice. *Memberships:* Malawi Law Society. *Hobbies:* Reading; Radio Listening; Taking Family Out. *Address:* Nkutu Mula Village, Banda Postal Agency, TA Kwataine, Ntcheu, Malawi, Central Africa.

TALBOYS, Brian Edward, Rt. Hon., PC, BA, b. 1921, New Zealand, Politician. m. Patricia F. Adamson, 1950, 2, sons. *Education:* University of Manitoba; BA, Victoria University. *Appointments:* Parliamentary Under Secretary to the Minister of Industries & Commerce, 1961-62; Minister of Agriculture, 1962-69; Minister of Science, 1963-72; Minister of Education, 1969-72; Minister of Industries & Commerce, Minster of Overseas Trade, 1972; Deputy Prime Minister since 1974; Minister of Foreign Affairs and Minister of Overseas Trade since 1975; Deputy Leader, New Zealand National Party since 1974. *Address:* 1 Hamilton Avenue, Winton, Southland, New Zealand.

TALLIS, Christopher Geoffrey, b. 12th April, 1944, Heswall, Cheshire. Hotelier. m. Susan Carol Greaves, 6th Sept. 1969, 1 son, 1 daughter. *Education:* Birkenhead School, Cheshire, 1955-62. *Appointments:* British Transport Hotels Limited, Training in various hotels within the UK, France, Germany & Spain, 1962-68; Trusthouse Forte Hotels Limited, Various Assistant Management & Management posts within UK, 1969-74; General Manager, Grosvenor House Hotel, Sheffield, 1975-80; Vice President & General Manager, Jamaica Pegasus Hotel, Kingston, Jamaica, 1980-. *Memberships:* Member, Hotel Catering and Institutional Management Association. *Hobbies:* Jogging; Collecting stamps and antiques. *Address:* Jamaica Pegasus Hotel, P.O. Box 333, 81, Knutsford Boulevard, Kingston 5, Jamaica.

TALUKDAR, Banajit Kumar, b. 27th June, 1929, Barpeta, Assam, India. Chartered Engineer. m. Runi Talukdar, 8th May, 1963, 1 son, 1 daughter. *Education:* BSc, Cotton College, Gauhati, Assam, India, 1950; MSc, University College of Science & Technology Calcutta, 1952; MSc, Tech, Manchester College of Technology. *Appointments:* Electrical Engineer with BICC UK, 1955-56; Graduate Trainee, Phillips Croydon Works Limited UK, 1956-58; Development Engineer, Bush Radio Limited, UK, 1958-59; Assistant Professor in Assam Engineering College, Assam, 1959-61; Chief Engineer of Bush India Limited, Bombay, 1961-. *Memberships:* Institution of Electrical Engineers, UK; Institution of Electronics and Telecommunication Engineers, India; Associate Manchester College of Technology. *Publications:* Article on Television in the Journal of Assam Science Society, 1960. *Hobbies:* Gardening; Photography; Carpentry. *Address:* Anand Bhuyan, 20, ML Dahanukar Marg, Bombay 400 026, India.

TAM, Chi-Sing Laurence, b. 12th Dec. 1933. Canton, China. Curator. m. Tsui Yee-May Margaret, 3rd Aug. 1963, 2 sons. *Education:* Museology, University of Toronto, 1975; MA, University of Hong Kong, 1970; BA, London University, 1965; Diploma for Teaching of English, Moray House College of Education, 1961; Teachers Certificate, Northcote College of Education, 1956. *Appointments:* Teacher of Wah Yan College, Kowloon, 1956-71; Assistant Curator, Hong Kong Museum of Art, 1971-75; Present Curator, Hong Kong Museum of Art, 1976-. *Memberships:* Ontario Museum Association; Canadian Museum Association; Oriental Ceramic Society of Hong Kong; Hong Kong Diocesan Liturgical Commission; Min Chiu Society; Member of Honour of Japan International Artists Society; Adviser of the One Art Group. *Publications:* Over 20 publications on various branches of Chinese Art and Art Education, including Kwangtung Painting, An Anthology of Chinese Ceramics, Six Masters of Early Qing, A Study of Wu Li. *Hobbies:* Painting, Photography; Pottery Making; Reading and Creative Writing. *Address:* 83 Waterloo Road, Excelsior Court, Flat 2D, Kowloon, Hong Kong.

TAM, Wah Ching, b. 17th Aug. 1926. China. Managing Director. m. Madam Tong Lan Fong, May 1955, 1 son. *Memberships:* Lions Club of Hong Kong. *Honours:* Honours and Awards from Lions International Club, Po Leung Kuk, Scouts Association. *Address:* 12, Essex Crescent, Kowloon Tong, Kowloon, Hong Kong.

TAMBIMUTTU, Jeyasekeran Erman, b. Sri Lanka. Chartered Accountant. m. Barbara Lumini Jean Joseph, 29th Dec. 1979. *Education:* Passed Final Examination in Chartered Accountancy, 1978. *Appointments:* Qualified Assistant, M/s Hulugalle Canaga Sooryam & Monsoor & Co, Chartered Accountants; Chief Accountant, Liberia Sugar Corporation Incorporated, 1978; Senior Accountant, Firestone Planatations Co. 1981-. *Hobbies:* Writing; Reading; Golf; Swimming. *Address:* Firestone Plantations, Harbel, Liberia, W. Africa.

TAMER, Shiv Kumar Tamer, Dr. b. 15th April, 1951, Mungeli District, Bilaspur MP, India. Medical, Paediatrician. m. Ujwal Akojwar, 25th Jan, 1977, 1 daughter. *Education:* BSc, CMD College, Bilaspur,'1969; MB, BS, Government Medical College, Jabalpur, 1974; MD, Medical College, Jabalpur, 1978. *Appointments:* Rotating House Officer, Medical College, Jabalpur, 1974-75; Senior House Officer, Paediatrics, Medical College, 1975-76; Clinical Demonstrator in Paediatrics, 1976-78; Consulting Paediatrician in Hackman Memorial Hospital, Bilaspur, 1978-79; Medical Officer, Paediatric Care, MPEB, Hospital, Korba, 1979; Junior Medical Officer in Department, Paediatrics Main Hospital, Bhilai, April, 1979-. *Memberships:* Indian Academy of Paediatrics; Board for Library, Main Hospital Library, Bhilai. *Publications:* Research in field of Social Paediatrics, paper presented National Conferences of Indian Academy of Paediatrics, Feb, 1981; Research, Children of permanently sterilised parents; Paper presented, National Conference, Benglor, 1980 & Inter Steel Medical Officers' Conference at Durgapur. *Honours:* Awarded James Flett Endowment National Gold Medal, best research work in field of Community Paediatrics for 1980 at Benglore, Feb 1980. *Hobbies:* Research in field of social paediatrics. *Address:* Russion Blocks, Qr.

No. 1-B Avenue E, Sector VI Bhilai District, Durg, MP India.

TAN, Koon Swan, b. 24th Sept, 1940. Kuala Lumpur, Company Director & Member of Parliament. m. Katherine Chong Yoke Mei, 1963, 1 son, 1 daughter. *Education:* Advanced Management, Harvard University, 1976. *Appointments:* Inland Revenue Officer, Inland Revenue Department, 1962-68; Tax Adviser, Esso Malaysia Bhd, 1968-70; General Manager of Genting Highlands Hotel, Bhd, 1970-77; Managing Director, Operations, Multi Purpose Management, Sdn. Bhd., 1977-. *Memberships:* Vice President, Harvard Business School, Alumnae Club of Malaysia; Director, Federation of Malaysian Manufacturers; Director, Selangor Tung Shing Hospital; Standing Committee Chinese Assembly Hall; Board of Governors of chiao Nam School; Honorary Treasurer, Federation of Keng Chew Associations; Secretary General, Selangor Keng Chew Association; President, Malaysian Martial arts Association; President, KL & Selangor Chinese Martial Arts Association. *Honours:* Justice of Peace, Sultan of Pahang, 1973; Ahli Mahkota Pahang, Sultan of Pahang, 1977. *Hobbies:* Listening to Music; Playing Badminton. *Address:* 90 Jalan Bukit Pantai, Kuala Lumpur, Malaysia.

TAN, Soo-Hai, b. 5th Jan, 1934, Penang, Malaysia. Consultant Planner/Landscape Architect. m. Tan Ding-Eing, 20th July, 1957, 3 sons. *Education:* BA-(Hons), University of Malaya, 1955; MCD, University of Liverpool, UK, 1958; DipLD, University of Durham, UK, 1959. *Appointments:* Assistant Commissioner, Town & Country Planning, Federal Government, Malaysia, 1959-62; State Director, Town & Country Planning, States of Selangor, Negri Sembilan, & Malacca, 1962-66, Kelantan & Trengganu, 1966-67; Planning Development Consultant, Housing Specialist, 1967-. *Memberships:* Tin Mine Club; Royal Commonwealth Society; Malaysian American Society; American Management Association; Malaysian Scientific Association; Town & Country Planning Association; Malaysian Economic Association; Fellow, Royal Town Planning Institute, London, 1965; Fellow, Royal Geographical Society, 1969; International Association of Assessing Officers; Fellow, 1972, Vice President, 1972-74, President, 1975-76, Malaysian Institute of Planners; President, Technological Association of Malaysia, 1965-67; Chairman of Planning Commission, EAROPH Malaysian Chapter, 1975-76; Central Committee Member, HDA, 1978-80 Senior Vice President, Technological Association of Malaysia, 1978-79; Honorary Consultant, General Manager of National Housing Authority, Philippines. *Publications:* Contributor of reviews, monographs, articles to professional journals and conferences. *Honours:* Meritorious Service Medal, Selangor, 1964. *Hobbies:* Reading; Writing Articles; Golf; Jogging. *Address:* 9, Jalan 16/1, Petaling Jaya, Selangor, Malaysia.

TAN, Teng Huat, b. 22 June, 1940, Singapore. Civil-/Public Health Engineer. m. Khoo Gim Loon, 1 May, 1968, 1 son, 1 daughter. *Education:* DIC, Imperial College, London, 1968; Professional Diploma in Civil Engineering, Singapore Polytechnic, 1962. *Appointments:* Pupil Engineer, Sewerage Branch, PWD, Singapore, 1963; Engineer, Sewerage Branch, PWD Singapore, 1966; Executive Engineer, Sewerage Branch, PWD Singapore, 1970; Higher Executive Engineer, Sewerage Department, Ministry of Environment, Singapore, 1972; Senior Executive Engineer, Sewerage Department, Ministry of Environment, Singapore, 1974; Chief Engineer, Sewerage Department, Ministry of the Environment, Singapore, 1976; Assistant Director, Environment Engineering Division, Ministry of Environment, 1981. *Memberships:* Member, Institution of Engineers, Singapore; American Society of Civil Engineers; Institute of Water Pollution Control, U.K. Professional Engineer, Singapore. *Publications:* Papers in Field of Interest, Sewerage and Sewage Treatment. *Honours:* Public Administration Medal, Singapore, 1976. *Hobbies:* Philately; Numismatics; Gardening; Sports. *Address:* 11, Faber Avenue, Singapore 0512, Republic of Singapore.

TAN, Yaw Kwang, b. 28th Feb. 1932, Kuching, Malaysia. Doctor. m. Hew Yin Sim, 2 sons, 1 daughter. *Education:* MBBS, Singapore, 1954-60; MPH, TM, Tulane, USA, 1969-70. *Appointments:* Medical Officer 1967; Senior Medical Officer, 1970; Assistant Director,

Medical Services, Sarawak, 1971; Deputy Director, Medical Services, Sarawak, 1971; Director of Medical Services, Sarawak, 1975-. *Memberships:* National Executive Council, Red Crescent Society, Malaysia; President, Sarawak Medical Club Council, 1975; Committee Member, National Sports Council, Ministry of Health, Malaysia, 1975; Deputy Chairman, Government Services Welfare & Recreational Council, Sarawak, 1976; Vice Chairman, State Applied Food & Nutritional Committee, 1975; Committee Member, Pemadam, 1976; Kuching Water Board, 1975. *Honours:* Pingat Perkhidmatan Cemerland, State Honour, 1978; Johan Setia Mahkota, Federal Honour, 1979. *Hobbies:* Playing Tennis; Reading; Swimming; Listening to music. *Address.* 27C, Jalan Lowlands, Kuching, Sarawak, Malaysia.

TANDAU, Alfred Cyril, b. 6th Jan, 1936, Mbinga District, Tanzania. Trade Unionist. m. 28th May, 1963, 4 sons, 2 daughters. *Education:* Financial Secretary, Transport & General Workers Union, 1959-62; Deputy Secretary, General TFL, 1962-64; Deputy Secretary General, NUTA, 1964-68; General Manager, URAFIKI, 1968-69; General Secretary, NUTA, 1969-78; General Secretary, JUWATA, 1978-; Minister in Union Government, 1972-. *Honours:* Recipient of TFL na Kuzaliwa Kwa NUTA. *Hobbies:* Reading; Gardening; Indoor Games. *Address:* PO Box 1827, and 1851 D'Salaam, Tanzania.

TANG, Hans, b. 24 Sept, 1915, Hong Kong. Physician Investor. m. Nancy Chan, 10 Aug. 1943, 1 son, 2 daughters. *Education:* MD, 1936; DMR, 1937; MD, 1939; MRCP, London, 1948; MRCP, Edinburgh, 1948; LRCP, London, 1951; MRCS, London, 1951; FICS, 1957; FACCP, 1958; FACC, 1972; FRCP, Edinburgh, 1980. *Appointments:* Resident, Louvain Hospital, Belgium, 1937-39; Professor, Shanghai Medical College; President, Radium Institute; President, Red Cross Hospital, 1945-48; Consultant, Hong Kong Hospitals, 1951-; President, Sherman Investment Corporation; Director, Victoria Finance & Investment Co; Fulton Corporation; Far East Consortium; Pearl City Investment Co; American Investment Co. etc. *Memberships:* Society of Physicians of Hong Kong, President, 1957; President, Hong Kong Chinese Medical Association, 1978; British Medical Association; Hong Kong Medical Association; British Institute of Radiology; Alliance Francaise de Hong Kong, President, 1979; World Trade Centre Club; Hong Kong Royal Golf Club; Hong Kong Royal Jockey Club. *Publications:* Les Bases experimentales de Radiotherapie totale et subtotale; Effects of Peroxides in Tumours; Biology of Radiations; Neoplastic diseases in China; Comparative studies of cardiovascular diseases in China & Western countries. *Honours:* Chevalier de l'Ordre de Leopold, 1967. *Hobbies:* Kinetics; Calligraphy; Arts Collection. *Address:* 44, Plantation Road, The Peak, Hong Kong.

TANIERA, Matita, b. 31st Jan. 1925, Maiana Island, Kiribati. School Teacher Primary. m. Anna Matia, 1950, 2 sons, 4 daughters. *Education:* Teachers Course, Christchurch Teachers College, New Zealand, 1944-55; Commonwealth Teachers Course, Cambridge Institute of Education, UK, 1967-68. *Appointments:* School Teacher, Primary, 1947-78; Clerk to Kiribati House, of Assembly, 1978-. *Memberships:* Chairman, Protestant Church Committee at Bairiki; Secretary, Bairiki Cooperative Society Committee; Honorary Secretary, Kiribati Branch of Commonwealth Parliamentary Association. *Publications:* Special Study on Teaching of Mathamatics for the first two years in the Infant Classes of the Gilbert Islands, written at the requirement of the Cambridge Institute of Education, 1968. *Honours:* Kiribati Certificate and badge of honour, 1978. *Hobbies:* Reading; Gardening; Fishing. *Address:* Bairiki, Tarawa, Republic of Kiribati.

TANNER, Edgar Miles Ponsonby, b. 19 Mar. 1947, Melbourne, Victoria, Australia. Member of the Legislative Assembly of Victoria. m. Mary Elizabeth Adams, 19 Aug. 1972, 1 son, 1 daughter. *Education:* Educated at Melbourne, Church of England Grammar School. *Appointments:* Private Secretary, Minister of Health, Victoria, 1971-73; Personal Assistant, Chief Secretary, Victoria, 1973-76; Victoria Tourist Industry Representative for Europe, 1976-79; Member of Parliament, Caulfield, 1979-. *Memberships:* Council of the Victorian Amateur Boxing Association; Fellow, Australian Society of Senior Executives; Australian Institute of Public Administration; Commonwealth Parliamentary Association; Lawn Tennis Association of Victoria. *Hobbies:* History; Reading; Tennis; Running. *Address:* 10 Cambridge Street, East Brighton, Victoria, 3187, Australia.

TASCHEREAU, Pierre, *Appointments:* Appointed Acting Chairman of the Board and Chief Executive Officer of Air Canada, 1975; Relinquished responsibilities of Chief Executive Officer, 1976, upon appointment of Claude I Taylor as President, but remained Acting Chairman, 1976; Confirmed Chairman of the Board, 1977; Retired, 1979, Appointed to Board as Director, 1979; Appointed, Chairman of the Board, Director, on a part-time basis pending the appointment of a permanent part-time Chairman. *Address:* 1 Place Ville Marie, Montreal, P.Q., H3B 3P7., Canada.

TASMAN-JONES, Clifford, b. 21 Dec. 1928, Darfield, New Zealand. Medical Practitoner. m. Beverley Anne North, 8 Dec. 1956, 4 sons. *Education:* Canterbury College, University of New Zealand, 1948-50; Otago University, 1951-56; London University, 1960; BSc, 1950; MB, ChB, 1956; MRCP, 1961; MRACP, 1963; FRACP, 1970; FRCP, 1977. *Appointments:* Research Fellow, General Hospital, University of Birmingham, 1961-62; Medical Specialist, Tutor, Greenlane Hospital, Auckland, 1962-64; Visiting Specialist, Physician Gastroenterologist, Auckland Hospital Board, 1965-71; Senior Lecturer, Medicine, University of Auckland, 1971-73; Associate Professor, Medicine, University of Auckland, 1973-. *Memberships:* Nutrition Society of New Zealand, Asian-Pacific Association of Gastroenterology; Coeliac Society, New Zealand Branch; Asia-Pacific Association for Study of The Liver; Gastroenterology Society of New Zealand; Nutrition Foundation of New Zealand; National Committee on Nutritional Science; International Society of Endoscopy; Organising Committee, Asian Pacific Congress of Gastroenterology; Asian Pacific Gastroenterology Research Committee; American Foundation for Clinical Research; Australian and New Zealand Association for the Advancement of Science; Cancer Society of New Zealand, Auckland Division, Medical Advisory Committee; Medico-Legal Society; Rotary International Auckland East Club; Tibetan Children's Relief Society. *Publications:* Contributed to various professional journals. *Hobbies:* New Zealand History; Deep Sea Fishing; Cultivation of New Zealand Plants; Gardening. *Address:* 34 Fern Glen Road, St Heliers, Auckland 5, New Zealand.

TAUFA'AHAU TUPOU IV, His Majesty King, b. 4 July 1918, The Royal Palace, Nuku'alofa, Tonga. The King of Tonga. m. Halaevalu Mata'aho 'Ahome'e, 10 June 1947, 2 daughters. *Education:* Tupou College, Tonga; Newington College, Sydney, New South Wales; BA, 1939, LLB, 1942, Sydney University, First Tongan to receive a degree. *Appointments:* Minister of Education upon return from University, 1943; Prime Minister, 1949-65; Crowned the King of Tonga, 1967. *Publications:* Late forties he initiated the reformation of the Tongan orthography resulting of the publication by the Oxford University Press of a Grammar and two Dictionaries of the Tongan Language. *Honours:* Recipient of CBE; KBE; KCMG; GCVO; GCMG; DLitt, 1972, USP; LLD, 1975, New Delhi; Dr. Humanities, 1976, Brigham Young. *Hobbies:* Accomplished Musician; Fishing; Experiments with Animal Breeding specifically with domestic fowls, ducks and geese. *Address:* The Royal Palace, Nuku'alofa, Tonga.

TAY, Keng, Quee, b. 11 July. 1949, Malaysia. Director of Consulting Quantity Surveying Firm. m. Madam Loo Goek Wee, 30 Dec. 1974, 2 sons. *Education:* Diploma in Quantity Surveying, Technical College, Kuala Lumpur; Associate Diploma in Quantity Surveying, Royal Melbourne Institute of Technology. *Appointments:* Rider Hunt and Partners, Melbourne; Pakatan International Kuala Lumpur. *Memberships:* Institution of Surveyors, Malaysia; Singapore Institute of Surveyors; Australian Institute of Quantity Surveyors; General Institution of Surveyors, Malaysia. *Hobbies:* Reading; Billiard Game. *Address:* 162 Pesiaran Zaaba, Taman Tun Dr. Ismail, Kuala Lumpur, Malaysia.

TAY, Tian, Hock, b. 23 Jun. 1943, Malaysia. Research Officer. m. Low Siew Eng, 19 Jan. 1970, 1 son. *Education:* BAgric, Sci, Malaya, 1967; MSc, Singapore, 1975; PhD, Cantab, 1980. *Appointments:* Research Officer, Malayan Pineapple Industry Board, 1967-74; Senior

Research Officer, Malaysian Agricultural Research and Development Institute. *Memberships:* International Peat Society; Malaysian Soil Science Society. *Publications:* Technical publications only. *Hobbies:* General Reading. *Address:* 19 Jalan Durian 4, Yulek Heights, Kuala Lumpur, Malaysia.

TAYLOR, Alexander, b. 1933. m. 1956, 4 children. *Education:* BSc, Hons, Engineering, University of London, 1955. *Appointments:* President, Chief Executive Officer, Canatom Limited, 1970-73; President, Chief Executive Officer, SNC/GECO, 1973-77; Chairman, Canatom, 1977-79; Group Vice-President, SNC Group, North America, 1978-80; Executive Vice-President, SNC Group, 1980; Director, Canadian Nuclear Association, Canatom Incorporated; The Benham Blair SNC Group, Hensley-Schmidt Incorporated; The SNC Corporation, SNC/FW Limited; Singmaster and Breyer. *Memberships:* Ordre des Ingenieurs du Quebec; Institute of Mechanical Engineers; Canadian Nuclear Association; Canadian Electrical Association; Engineering Institute of Canada; Canadian Society of Mechanical Engineers; Beaconsfield Golf Club; Montreal Athletic Club. *Hobbies:* Golf; Squash. *Address:* 9 Garrison Lane, Beaconsfield, Quebec H9W 5 C3, Canada.

TAYLOR, Alexander, Francis, b. 10 June 1917, Rushworth, Victoria, Australia. Medical Practitioner. m. Glenys V Coldwell, 4 Mar. 1944, 2 sons, 2 daughters. *Education:* MB, BS, Melbourne, 1941; DGO, Melbourne, 1945. *Appointments:* Resident Medical Officer, St. Vincent's Hospital, Melbourne, 1941-42; Resident Medical Officer, Women's Hospital, Melbourne, 1942-43; Captain, Australian Army Medical Corps, 107AGH, 1943-44; Clinical Assistant, Royal Women's Hospital, 1944-47; Honorary Obstetrician and Gynacologist, 1947-65; Consultant Obstetrician and Gynacologist, Goulburn Valley Base Hospital, Shepparton, Victoria. *Memberships:* Australian Medical Association. *Hobbies:* Golf; Fishing; Amateur Radio; Callsign VK3AT. *Address:* 108 Maude Street, Shepparton 3630, Victoria, Australia.

TAYLOR, Claude Ivan, b. 20 May 1925, Salisbury, New Brunswick, Canada. President and Chief Executive Officer of Air Canada. m. Frances Bernice Watters, 1 son, 1 daughter. *Education:* Robinson Business College, 1942; RIA, McGill University Extension, 1950-53. *Appointments:* General Manager, Commercial Planning, 1962-64; General Manager, Marketing Services, 1964-67; Vice-President, Strategic Development, 1970-71; Vice-President, Government and Industry Affairs, 1971-73; Vice-President, Public Affairs, 1973-76; President, Chief Executive Officer, 1976. *Memberships:* President, International Air Transport Association, IATA, 1979-80; Chairman, Air Transport Association of Canada, 1975-76; Past President, Travel Industry Association of Canada; Executive Council of the Canadian Chamber of Commerce; The Professional Corporation of Industrial Accountants of Quebec, RIA; Director of Guinness Peat Aviation; Mount Stephen Club, Montreal; Mount Royal Club, Montreal; Forest and Stream, Montreal; Rideau Club, Ottawa. *Honours:* Recipient of numerous honours and awards. *Address:* Air Canada, 1 Place Ville Marie, Montreal, Quebec H3B 3P7, Canada.

TAYLOR, Donald Bevin, b. 5 Apr. 1934, Warrnambool, Australia. Art Gallery Director. *Education:* Diploma, 1975, Art, Warrnambool Institute of Advanced Education. *Appointments:* Self-employed Painter, Potter; Director, Rockhampton Art Gallery, Queensland, Australia, 1975-. *Memberships:* Australian Gallery Directors Council; Art Museums Association of Australia; National Trust, Rockhampton; Arts Council, Rockhampton. *Publications:* Rockhampton Art Gallery Catalogues. *Hobbies:* Pottery; Collecting Books; Stamps and coins. *Address:* Rockhampton Art Gallery, Victoria Parade, Rockhampton, Queensland 4700, Australia.

TAYLOR, Edwin Llewellyn, b. 3 May 1924, St. Michael, Barbados. Methodist Minister of Religion. m. Marguerite Elaine Rogers, 29 Apr. 1953, 2 daughters. City of the Bahamas, 1974. *Education:* Harrison College, Barbados, 1936-41; Caenwood Theological College, Jamaica, 1946-50; BD, Richmond College, University of London, 1957-58; Ecumenical Institute, Bossey, Geneva, Switzerland, 1958, 1964; MScEd, University of Miami, 1979. *Appointments:* First Secretary, Methodist Church, Caribbean and Americas, 1967-70; Chairman, Bahamas District of the Methodist Church, 1970-77; Superintendent Minister, Nassau Circuit of Methodist Church, 1970-76; Superintendent, Grand Bahama Circuit of Methodist Church, 1977-; President of Conference Methodist Church in the Caribbean and the Americas, 1982. *Memberships:* President, Bahamas Christian Council, 1974-77; President, Bahamas Mental Health Association, 1975-77; President, Grand Bahama Christian Council, 1981-; President, Grand Bahama Mental Health Association, 1981-; Central Committee, World Council of Churches, 1968-75; World Methodist Council, 1966-76; Convocation University of London, 1958-; Commission on World Mission and Evangelism of World Council of Churches, 1968-75. *Publications:* Editor, Methodist Quarterly, Bahamas Methodist Church; Area Editor, Caribbean, Encyclopaedia of World Methodism, 1974; Author, The Role and Influence of the Methodist Church in Education in the Bahamas, 1979; Joint Editor, with Mr John Hicks, LLM, of the Constitution and Discipline of the Methodist Church in the Caribbean and the Americas. *Honours:* Elected, Bahamas Secretary's Association, Boss of the Year, 1974; Appointed Justice of the Peace, Bahamas, 1981. *Hobbies:* Historical Research; Jogging; Swimming. *Address:* Superintendent, Grand Bahama Circuit, P.O. Box F. 21, Freeport, Grand Bahama, Bahamas.

TAYLOR, Frederick Leslie Charles, b. 8 Nov 1919, Sydney, Australia. Engineer. m. Marie A. Wilsher, 22 July 1950, 1 son 1 step daughter. *Education:* BSc, 1942, Melbourne University. *Appointments:* Director Posts & Telegraphs, NSW, 1974-75; State Manager, Telecom Australia, NSW, 1975; General Manager, Engineering Department, Telecom Australia Headquarters, 1975-80; Director NEC, Printing Ltd, 1980-. *Honours:* Member, Order of Australia, AM, 1980. *Hobbies:* Boating, Music. *Address:* 14 Edith Court, Doncaster, Victoria, 3108, Australia.

TAYLOR, John Anthony, b. 2 Mar 1936, London, England. Food Technologist, Chief Chemist. m. Patricia C. 31 Mar 1956, 1 son, 1 daughter. *Education:* Post Graduate Diploma of Microbiology, 1961; BSc, 1959; Diploma Meat Technology, 1967. U3 Unilever, 1957-65, T. Wall & Son Ltd; 1965, Vienna Sausauge Manufacturing Co. Chicago, USA; 1968, Prima Meat Co. Johannesburg, S. Africa; 1972, Chief Chemist, J.C Hutton (NZ), Hamilton, New Zealand. *Memberships:* American Institute of Food Technology, 1964; American Society of Microbiology, 1968; New Zealand Institute of Food Technology/Science, 1975; President, Waikato Chapter; New Zealand Institute of Chemistry, 1978. *Publications:* Spore Forming Organisms in Vaccum Packed Ham, 1962; Microbiology of the British Fresh Sausage, 1961. *Honours:* MNZIC, Dip. Bact; MIFST: Microbiological Laboratory Awarded National Registration, 117 under New Zealand Testing Laboratory Registration Act, 1972; Registration Personalised to self, 1979. *Hobbies:* Photography. *Address:* 1 Ridge Road, Waiake, Auckland, New Zealand.

TAYLOR, John Benjamin, b. 19 Mar. 1944, London, England. Teacher/Writer. *Education:* Certificate of Education to teach, 1972; Diploma in Education, 1975. *Appointments:* Teacher, West Bromwich Education Authority; Teacher, Merton Education Authority; Teacher, West Sussex Education Authority. *Memberships:* Workshop Writers, Twickenham, Inaugurator and Director. *Publications:* Liberty Contribution to periodicals, New Poetry, Radio, TV; There Were No Lovely Birds, Workshop Press; Spring, No Time To Stand and Stare?, Poplar Press. *Honours:* Claudine Curney Memento Poetry Award, 1975. *Hobbies:* Music; Swimming; Photography; Sketching; Graphic Design. *Address:* 1 Muchison Road, Flat 12, Leyton, E10 6NA, England.

TAYLOR, Julien Charles, b. 27 June 1921, London, England. Neurological Surgeon. m. Joan Forbes Stewart, 21 Jan 1959, 1 son, 1 daughter. *Education:* Universtiy of London, King's College and Westminster Hospital Medical School, MB; BS, London, 1944; FRCS, 1950. *Appointments:* Resident Surgical Officer, St. Helier Hospital, Carshalton, Surrey; F/Lieutenant RAFVR, Surgical Registrar Westminster Hospital; Surgical Registrar Dept. Neurosurgery, St. George's Hospital, London; Senior Resident in Neurosurgery, Chicago Children's Memorial Hospital; Senior Registrar in Neurosurgery, St. George's Hospital, London; National Hospital, Queen Square London, and Hospital for Sick Children, Gt. Ormond Street; Regional Neurosurgeon, Trent Regional Health Authority; Consultant Neurosurgeon Derbyshire Royal Infirmary; Consultant Neurosurgeon Nottingham University, General and City Hospitals; Clinical Teacher, University of Nottingham Medicial School. *Memberships:* Society of British Neurological Surgeons; Fellow British Association of Clinical Anatomists; Hospital Consultants and Specialists Association. *Publications:* Papers on neurosurgical subjects. *Honours:* MB, BS, Lond. with Honours, 1944. *Hobbies:* Music; Art collecting; Art History; Gardening. *Address:* The Willows, Ambaston, Derbyshire, DE7 3ES, England.

TAYLOR, Lionel Roy, b. 14 Dec. 1924, Manchester, England. Research Biologist, Agriculture. m. Jean M. Bathgate, 11 June 1949, 1 son, 1 daughter. *Education:* London External BSc, Part-time; DSc, London. *Appointments:* Rothamsted Experimental Station, 1948-64; 1965-81; Visiting Professor, Kansas State University, 1964-65; Visiting Professor, Queen Elizabeth College, London, 1978-81. *Memberships:* Fellow of Institute of Biology, Council, Committees; Chairman of Editorial Board of Biologist; British Ecological Society, Council, Editor Journal of Animal Ecology, 1973-81; Fellow of Royal Entomological Society, Committees; Association of Applied Biologists, editorial Board; Association for the Study of Animal Behaviour. *Publications:* Joint author, Introduction to Experimental Ecology, 1967; Editor, The Optimum Population for Britain, 1970; Joint Editor, Population Dynamics, 1979; Contributor to books on ecology, Agriculture; Over 100 Research publications on similar subjects *Honours:* Senior Foreign Fellowship, US National Academy Science, 1964-65; Research Medal of the Royal Agricultural Society of England, 1977. *Hobbies:* Book Collecting; Travel; Music; Natural History; Archaeology; Architecture; Gardening. *Address:* 12 Carisbrooke Road, Harpenden, Hertfordshire, England.

TAYLOR, Peter Alfred, b. 26 Apr 1924, London. Research Scientist, Chartered Engineer. m. Jean M. Billington, 16 June 1946, 1 son 2 daughters. *Education:* University of Birmingham, BSc, 1946-50. *Appointments:* 1950-52, Fuel Research Station, Department of Scientific and Industrial Research; 1952-58, National Institute of Agricultural Engineering; 1958-, CSIRO Division of Mechanical Engineering. *Memberships:* MI.Mech.E; MIE.Aust; MI.Agr.E; Royal Victorian Aero Club. *Publications:* Various scientific publications. *Honours:* I.Mech.E Engineering in Agriculture prize, 1967. *Hobbies:* Flying. *Address:* 14 Woolston Drive, Frankston, Victoria, Australia.

TAYLOR, Robert Edward, b. 12 Apr. 1944, Balham, London. Radio Announcer/Presenter. m. Margaret Cameron Divers, n. Brown, 30 Sept. 1967, 1 son, 1 daughter. *Education:* Technical Education to Trades Certificate Building; Drama School; Announcer Training School, Maori, French, German. *Appointments:* Carpenter, Auckland, Dunedin, London Exhibition Halls, 1961; Salesman, Selfridges, Drama TV, 1965; Radio Announcer, Commercial NZBC, 1967; Radio Announcer, Bunbury Western Australia, 1969; Television, News & Weather, Australian Broadcasting Commission, 1970; Radio Announcer, All Night Programme, 1973; Radio Announcer, Presenter, 1974; Radio New Zealand Breakfast Session, 1981; Undiscovered Country, a 6 part Documentary, Script and Narration. *Memberships:* National Conservation Campaign Committee; Royal Forest and Bird Protection Society; Confederate Historical Association. *Publications:* Radio Scripts, Theatre/Documentaries; Children of Tane, Long Playing Record, Forest Birds, Script & Narration; Friends of Maui, Long Playing Record, Sea Birds; Birds of New Zealand, LP of Bird Calls, Script and Narration. *Honours:* Non Commercial Announcer of year, 1979 & 1980. *Hobbies:* Wildlife Studies; Bird Watching; Hunting; Hiking; Historical Studies of Warfare; Black Powder Shooting. *Address:* 12 Watohu Road, York Bay, Eastbourne, New Zealand.

TAYLOR, Walter Harold, b. 2 Dec 1905, Melbourne, Australia. Civil, Concrete, Research and Educational Engineer. m. Ainslie, E.J. 1 Feb 1957. *Education:* Bachelor and Master of Civil Engineering, BCE, MCE, 1931, 1937; Diplomas in Civil and Municipal Engineering, Business and Municipal Administration; Post-ter-

tiary Research and Development. *Appointments:* Governmental and Professional Engineering Enterprises, 1925-45; Commonwealth Scientific and Industrial Research Organization, Building Research Division, 1945-70; John Connell Group of Consulting Engineers, 1971-76; Royal Melbourne Institute of Technology, National and International Faculties on Concrete Technology and Practice, 1945-. *Memberships:* Fellowships and Branch Chairmanships, Institution of Civil Engineers, Britain, Institute of Engineers, Australia; Honorary Life Membership of the Concrete Institute of Australia; Council of Engineering Institutions, Britain; Australian Institute of Management; Standards Association; Cement & Concrete Association; English-speaking Union and Loyal Societies; Masonic Grand Lodge, Century Club and United Service Institutions. *Publications:* Author, Concrete Technology and Practice, 1965; 4th edition in SI metric units, 1977; Literary contributor to over 20 professional publications. *Honours:* Election to Honorary Life Membership of the Concrete Institute of Australia for outstanding services over many years in advancing Concrete Technology, 1979; Building Science Forum of Australia Book Award, 1968; Argus and Simon Fraser Engineering Awards of the University of Melbourne, 1928-31. *Hobbies:* Philanthropic serviceability and Building Trusts; continuing Education Research; Seminar and Publication Programmes; masonic ceremonials, pennant bowling activities. *Address:* 19, Lawson Street, Hawthorn East, Victoria. 3123, Australia.

TEAL, Albert Joseph, CBE, JP, b. 19 Feb 1919, Sydney, NSW, Australia. Company Director. m. Halcyone A. 24 Jan 1942, 1 daughter. *Education:* Sydney Technical College; University of Sydney. *Appointments:* 1947-51, Industrial Advocate, Metal Trades Employers Association; 1951-81, Personnel Manager, General Motors Holdens Ltd, Australia; Director Public Relations; Director Government Relations; Administrator, Australian Advisory Council, General Motors Corporation, Detroit, USA. *Memberships:* Royal Victorian Association St.p. Justices; Past President Federal Chamber of Automotive Industies; Pastmember Auto Advisory Council to Australian Government; Faculty of Economics, University of Melbourne, Victoria; Vice-President, Committee for Economic Development of Australia. *Honours:* 1979, Commander, most excellent order of the British Empire; 1977, Queens Silver Jubilee Medal. *Hobbies:* Painting; Sculpture. *Address:* The Quadrant, 9/2, Munro Street, McMahons Point 2060, NSW, Australia.

TEBBIT, Donald Claude, Sir, b. 4 May 1920, Cambridge. HM Diplomatic Service, Retired. m. Barbara M. Olson Matheson, 10 Apr 1947, 1 son, 3 daughters. *Education:* Perse School Cambridge, 1931-39; Trinity Hall, Cambridge University, 1940, MA. *Appointments:* British Embassy Washington, 1948-51; British Embassy, Bonn, 1954-58; Private Secretary to Minister of State, 1958-61; Secretary of Committee on Representational Services Overseas, 1961-64; Counsellor and Head of Chancery, British Embassy, Copenhagen, 1964-67; 1967, Commonwealth Office; Assistant Under-Secretary of State FCO, 1968-70; Minister, British Embbassy, Washington, 1970-72; Chief Clerk FCO, 1972-76; British High Commissioner, Canberra, 1976-80; Director General, British Property Federation; Director, Rio Tinto Zinc Corporation Ltd.; Member of Appeals Board, Council of Europe, President Old Persean; Society Governor, Nuffield Nursery Homes Trust. *Memberships:* President (UK) Australian/British Trade Association; Chairman Diplomatic Service Appeals Board; Council Australia Britain Society; Council Fairbridge Society. *Honours:* CMG, 1965; KCMG, 1975; GCMG, 1980. *Hobbies:* Golf; Gardening; Old Maps. *Address:* Priory Cottage, Toft, Cambridge, CB3 7RE, England.

TEELOCK, Leckraz, Sir, b. 1909. Mauritian Diplomat, m. Vinaya Kumari Prasa, 1 son, 1 daughter. *Education:* Royal College Curepipe; Edinburgh University; Liverpool University and Dublin. *Appointments:* Medical Practitioner, 1939-64; Member of the Legislative Assembly, 1959-63; Chairman, Mauritus Family Planning Association, 1959-62; Director, Mauritius Free Press Service Ltd, 1940-63; Commissioner for Mauritius in UK, 1964-68; High Commissioner since 1968; concurrently Ambassador Extraordinary and Plenipotentiary to the Holy See, Luxembourg, Netherlands, Denmark, Norway, Sweden and Finland; Ambassador Extraordinary and Plenipotentiary to Belgium and the EEC, 1971-75. *Honours:* CBE, 1968; MB, ChB, DTM, LM. *Address:* Flat 1, Chelsea House, 26 Lowndes Street, London, SW1, England.

TEH, (Datuk), Hong Piow, b. 14th Mar. 1930, Singapore. Chairman, Banker, Industrialist, Managing Director. m. Datin Tay Sock Noy, 8th Feb. 1956, 1 son, 3 daughters. *Education:* Educated in Anglo-Chinese School, Singapore; FIBA, Australia, Diploma; FCI, UK, Diploma. *Appointments:* Overseas-Chinese Banking Corporation Ltd, Singapore, 1950-59; Sub-Manager, Malayan Banking Berhad, Malaysia, 1960, Manager, 1962; Area Manager, State of Selangor, Apr.-Aug. 1964; General Manager, 1964-66; Member of Senior Credit Seminar, Chase Manhattan Bank, National Association, New York, USA, 1962; Director and Chief Executive, Public Bank Berhad and Public Finance Berhad, 1966.- Appointed Chairman, Public Bank Berhad and Public Finance Berhad, 1978-. *Memberships:* Honorary President, Singapore Branch, Institute of Administrative Management, UK; Fellow, Institute of Administrative Accounting & Data Processing, UK Malaysia District Society; Fellow, Institute of Directors, UK; Fellow, Institution of Industrial Managers, UK; Fellow, British Institute of Management, UK, Fellow, Association of Business Executives, UK; Associate, Malaysian Economic Association, Malaysia; Associate, Institute of Credit Management, UK; Institute of Administrative Management, UK; Malaysian Institute of Management, Malaysia; Life Member of Selangor Teo Chew Pooi Ip Association, Selangor; Honorary Administrator, Teo Yeonh Huai Kuan, Singapore. *Honours:* Dato Kurnia Sentosa from the Sultan of Pahang, 1966. This carries the title of Datuk; Justice of the Peace from the Sultan of Pahang, 1967; Dato Paduka Mahkota Johore from the Sultan of Johore, 1973. This carries the title of Dato; Dato Sri Paduka Mahkota Johore, The Most Honourable Order of the Crown of Johore from the Sultan of Johore, 1974. This carries the title of Dato Sri; Darjah Sultan Ahmad Pahang from the Sultan of Pahang, 1978. This carries the title of Datuk; Dato Sri Setia Sultan Ismail Johore from the Sultan of Johore, 1978. This carries the title of Dato Sri. *Hobbies:* Photography; Reading. *Address:* c/o Public Bank Berhad, 5th Floor, Bangunan Public Bank, Jalan Sulaiman, Kuala Lumpur 01-33, Malaysia.

TEKAMP, Bernard Ben William, b. 13 May 1945, Netherlands. Manager, Manutronics Division, AEL Microtel Ltd. m. 27 June 1969, 2 sons. *Education:* 1970, Industrial Management, St. Lawrence College; 1972, Certified Engineering Technologist, CET. *Appointments:* Manager, Mauntronics Division, AEL Microtel Ltd. *Memberships:* Ontario Association Certified Engineering Technicians and Technologists; Officers Mess, Brockville Rifles, RCIC; Brockville Rowing Club; Past President; President Canadian Amateur Rowing Association; Past Treasurer, Ontario Rowing Association; Director, Canadian Olympic Association; Director, Sports Federation of Canada; International licensed Referee FISA; National Referee Class I license, CARA; 1976, Olymic Canadia Team Managers. *Honours:* 1976, Special Achievement Award, Ontario, Canada; 1976, Presidents Award, CARA; CD, Decoration Canadian Armed Forces Services Award. *Hobbies:* Rowing; Sport Administration; Hockey; Baseball; Football. *Address:* 1309 Brockmount Place, Brockville, Ontario, Canada, K6V 5Z6.

TEKULU, Belshazzar Gina, b. 20 Oct. 1946, Ranongga Island, Western Province, Solomon Islands. Principal. m. Eileen Mason Robinson, 21 Oct 1972. 1 son, 1 daughter. *Education:* Teaching Diploma, Ardmore, New Zealand, 1971; Certificate in Secondary School Administration & Management, Durham, UK 1975-76; Certificate in Education Administration & Management, TJI, Sydney, Australia, 1977; Bachelor in Education, Papua New Guinea, 1980. *Appointments:* Maths Teacher, 1972-76; Deputy Principal, 1976-78; Principal, 1978-. *Memberships:* Church and Society; Tri-Edcation Association, 1st President, Current President. *Hobbies:* Drama Production; Stamp Collecting; Photography; Fishing; Travelling. *Address:* P.O. Box 53, Gizo, Western Province, Solomon Islands.

TELFORD, Robert, Sir, CBE, b. 1 Oct 1915, Liverpool, England. Chartered Electrical Engineer. m. (2) Elizabeth M. 20 Feb 1958, 3 daughters, 1 son. *Education:* Christ's College, Cambridge, MA. *Appointments:* 1940-46, Manager, Hackbridge Works, The Marconi Company Ltd; 1946-50, Managing Director, Companhia Marconi Brasileira; 1950-53, Assistant to General Manager, The Marconi Company Ltd, 1953-61, General Works Manager, The Marconi Company Ltd, 1961-65, General Manager, The Marconi Company Ltd; 1965-81, Managing Director, The Marconi Company Ltd; 1981-, Chairman, The Marconi Company Ltd; 1968-; Managing Director of GEC-Marconi Electronics Ltd. *Memberships:* Royal Air Force Club; F.Eng; FIEE; FI-ProdE, Vice President; CBIM; FRSA. *Honours:* 1978, Knight Bachelor; 1967, CBE. *Hobbies:* Gardening; Silviculture; Reading. *Address:* Rettendon House, Rettendon, Chelmsford, Essex, CM3 5DW, England.

TEN RAA, William Frederick Eric Rykeld, b. 14 Jan 1924, Castricum, Netherlands. Associate Professor of Anthropology, University of Western Australia. m. Lee Bickford (2), 4 daughters. *Education:* University of Oxford, St. Catherine's College, Dip.Anthrop, 1964; D.Phil, 1967. *Appointments:* Pilot, RAF and RNAS, 1944-48; Banking, South America, 1950-51; Manager, Commercial firm in Kenya and Tanganyika, 1952-57; Civil Service, Tanganyika, 1958-63; Academic, Lecturer, Senior Lecturer, Associate Professor, University of Western Australia, 1967-. *Memberships:* Fellow, Royal Anthropological Institute of Gt. Britain and Ireland; Foreign Fellow, American Anthropological Association; Associate, Current Anthropology; Life Member, Tanzania Society, British East Africa Institute; Founder member, African Studies Association of Australia and the Pacific; International African Institute, Association of Social Anthropologists of the Commonwealth; African Studies Association of the UK, Australia-China Society; Royal Society of WA, Oxford Society; President WA Anthropological Society, 1972; Honorary Secretary, Australian Association of Social Anthropologists 1969-72. *Publications:* Author of numerous articles relating to East African Ethnography; Linguistics ; History; Mythology; Dictionary of the Western Desert Language of Australia; reviews, Researches into the structure of Myth. *Honours:* Nuffield scholar, 1964-66; Visiting Fellow, St. Catherine's College, Oxford, 1974; AIAS, ARGC Grants, 1970s. *Hobbies:* African Art; English Caricatures; Model Trains; Ships; Carpentry; Bricklaying; Tennis; Photography; Painting; Philately; Australian Wines; Duck-keeping; Primitive Cookery. *Address:* Anthropology Dept., University of Western Australia, Nedlands, WA 6009, Australia.

TENG, Pin Hui, b. 15 Jan. 1911, Fukien, China. Medical Officers. *Education:* MB, BS, Hong Kong; DPh, London. *Appointments:* Hong Kong Government Medical Officer, 1939-63; Director of Medical and Health Services, Hong Kong Government, 1963-70; Professor of Preventive Medicine, Part Time, 1959-70; Full Time Professor of Preventive Medicine, Hong Kong University, 1970-74. *Memberships:* FRSH: FFCM RCP, UK; FRCS, Hon. Edinburgh; British Medical Association; Faculty of Community Medicine; Royal Society of Health. *Honours:* CMG, 1967; OBE, 1962; LLD, Honours, Hong Kong, 1970; Justice of the Peace, 1947-; Professor Emeritus, Hong Kong University, 1974. *Address:* B2 4th Floor, Villa Monte Rosa, 41a Stubbs Road, Hong Kong.

TEO, Sir (Fiatau) Penitala, b. 23 July, 1911. m. (1) Muniara A. Vaitupu, 1931, 1 daughter 1 son (deceased); (2) Uimai T. Nanumaga, 1949, 8 sons, 3 daughters, (1 deceased). *Education:* Elisefou, Vaitupu, Tuvalu. *Appointments:* Resident Commisioners Officer, Ocean Islands, 1937-42; Special Clerk, 1944; Assistant Administration Officer and Member, Gilbert and Ellice Island Defence Force, 1944; Assistant and Acting District Officer for Ellice Islands, 1944-50; Information Office, Tarawa, 1953; Deputy Commissioner for Western Pacific, 1960; District Commissioner, Ocean Islands, 1963; Ellice Islands, 1967-69; Assistant and Acting Superintendant of Labour British Phosphate Commissioners, Ocean Islands, 1971-78; ADC, to High Commissioner of Western Pacific, 1954-57; District Officer for visit of Prince Philip to Vaitupu Islands, Ellice Islands, 1959. *Honours:* GCMG, 1979; ISO, 1970; MBE,1956; Coronation Medal, 1953. *Hobbies:* Fishing; Cricket; Football; Rugby; Local Games. *Address:* Alapi, Funafuti, Tuvalu.

TERRILL, Neil Warren, b. 22 May 1930, Bairnsdale, Victoria, Australia. Science Education. m. Lois, 23 Jan 1956, 3 daughters. *Education:* Melbourne Technical

College, Dip.App.Chem., 1954; Foundation Student, Technical Teachers College of Victoria, MSc, University of Bristol, 1972. *Appointments:* Works Chemist, Monsanto Avs. 1949-51; Technical Teacher, Foundation Staff, Mildura Technical School, 1956-65; Head Chemistry Department, Yallourn Technical College, 1966; Foundation Senior Lecturer, Gippsland Institute of Advanced Education, 1969; Principal Lecturer, Applied Science 1975; Member, Board of Studies, Victoria Institute of Colleges, 1972-80; 1978 appointed to Victorian Brown Coal Research Advisory Committee; Present Positions, Dean, Applied Science & Engineering, Gippsland Institute of Advance Education, 1978-. *Memberships:* Fellow Australian Institute of Energy; Foundation Chairman, Gippsland Group Associate, Royal Australian Chemical Institute; Former Chairman Gippsland Section; Royal Society of Chemistry, UK; APEX Club of Mildura, 1958-65; President, 1961-62, District Governor, 1965. *Honours:* Victoria Institute of Colleges Overseas Study Award, 1971. *Hobbies:* Gardening, Bushwalking. *Address:* Curragundi, Lindners Road, Jerralang Junction, Victoria 3840, P.O. Box 25, Churchill, Australia.

THAKARE, Vinayak Keshaorao, b. 25 May 1929, Pawani, Sakraji, Dist. Amrarah, Maharstra, India. Professor of Zoology. m. Misa Kusum, 23 June, 1966. 1 son,. 1 daughter. *Education:* MSc, Zoology, Nagbur University, India; PhD, (Entomology) Nagpur University, India. *Appointments:* Lecturer in Zoology, Government Science College Nagpur, 1958; Lecturer in Zoology, National College Nagpur, 1962-63; Lecturer in Zoology, University Department of Zoology, Nagpur, 1968-73; Reader in Zoology, Nagpur University; Professor in Zoology, Nagpur University, 1973-. *Memberships:* Fellow, The National Academy of Science, India; Fellow, Academy of Science; Founder President, Zoological Society, Nagpur University; Founder Member and Past President, Vidarbta Club; Indian Science Congress Association. *Publications:* Published 150 papers on Marbiology, Physiology, Endocrinology and Reproductive Biology of Insects. *Hobbies:* Religious Discourses; Study of Animal Behaviour. *Address:* Opp. Commerce College, Gorepeth, Nagpur 440010, India.

THAKUR, Upendra, b. 2 Jan. 1929, Darbhanga, Bihar, India. Teacher. m. Rama, Thakur Mar. 1952, 1 son, 2 daughters. *Education:* BA, Honours; MA; DPhil. *Appointments:* Lecturer, Patna University, Patna, Bihar, 1956; Lecturer, Gorakhpur University, Gorakhpur, U.P., 1957; Reader, Magarth University, 1964; Professor and Head, Department of Asian Studies, Magarth University, 1970. *Memberships:* Indian History Congress; International Association of Historians of Asia; Explorers Club, New York; Numismatic Society of India; Bihar Research Society, Patna; Editor, Proc. International Buddhist Conference, Tokyo-Bodhgaya; Editor, JBRS. *Publications:* History of Mithila; Studies in Jainism of Buddhism in Mithila; History of Suicide in India; The Hunas in India; Mints and Minting in India; Some Aspects of Ancient Indian History & Culture; Homicide in India; Corruption in Ancient India; On Karthikeya; India an Laos; and other titles; 90 research papers in Indian and foreign journals. *Honours:* Akbar Silver Medal for outstanding contributions to numismatic studies. *Hobbies:* Reading; Writing. *Address:* Department of Asian Studies, Magadh University, Bodhgaya, Bihar, India.

THAM, Seong-Chee, b. 18 Oct 1932, Kuala Lumpur, Malaysia. University Professor. m. Siew Oi Lan, 29 Mar 1958, 3 sons. *Education:* MTTC, University of Liverpool, 1955; MTTC, Psychology, University of Liverpool, 1960; BA, University of Malaya, 1965; PhD, Univeristy of Singapore, 1971. *Appointments:* Teacher, Methodist Boys' School, Kuala Lumpur, 1956-62; Education Officer, Ministry of Education, Malaysia, 1965; Lecturer, Teachers' Training College, Kuala Lumpur, 1966-67; Lecturer, University of Singapore, 1971-74; Senior Lecturer, University of Singapore, 1975-78; Associate Professor, National University of Singapore, 1979-81. *Memberships:* President, United Nations Association of Singapore; Council Member, Singapore Association for the Advancement of Science; President, Academic Staff Association, University of Singapore; International Sociological Association. *Publications:* Malays and Modernization, 1977; Language and Cognition, 1977; Social Science Research in Malaysia, Institute of Developing Economies, 1980/81. Literature and Society in Southeast Asia, University of Singapore Press, 1981.

Honours: Commonwealth Academic Fellow, University of London, 1974-75. *Hobbies:* Gardening; Swimming. *Address:* 34 Maryland Drive, Singapore, 1027.

THANGARAJAH, Palaniyandi, b. 1 Nov. 1955, Sri Lanka. Student. *Education:* M. Com., FICA. *Honours:* Gold Medal, First Mark in Pre-university examination held in 1974, Madras University; Conducted by Chamber of Commerce, Tamilnadu. *Hobbies:* Stamp Collection; Story Book Reading. *Address:* C-98,10-B,W.E, Thillainagar, Trichy 620 008, India.

THAPAR, Bal Krishen, b. 24th Oct, 1921, Ludhiana, India. Archaeologist. m. Susheela, 2nd March, 1952, 1 son. *Education:* BA, Government College, Ludhiana, 1941; MA, Forman Christian College, Lahore, 1943; Orientalisches Seminar Heidelberg, University of Heidelberg, 1959-60. *Appointments:* Deputy Superintendant Archaeologist, Archaeological Survey of India, 1953-55; Superintendant Archaeologist, 1955-66; Director, Explorations & Expeditions abroad, 1966-73; Joint Director General, 1973-77; Additional Director General, 1977-78; Director General, 1978-81; Jawaharlal Nehru Fellow, 1981; Fellow, Alexander von Humboldt Stifting, Bonn, 1959-60; Fellow, Churchill College, University of Cambridge, UK, 1971. *Memberships:* Royal Asiatic Society of Great Britain & Ireland; Permanent Council, Congress Internationale des Sciences Prehistorique et Protohistorique; Vice-President, Executive Committee of International Council of Monuments and Sites; Associate, Current Anthropology; Indian Archaeological Society; Central Advisory Board of Archaeology; History Panel, University Grants Commission; International Editorial Committee of UNESCO for the preparation of History of Civilisations of Central Asia; Regional Editor, Asian Perspective. *Publications:* Author of over 75 research papers, contributed to various journals both in India and abroad, dealing with researches in Indian archaeology and excavation reports; Directed many major excavations in India, including Kaliliangau, a Metropolis of Indian Civilisation. *Address:* P-8-3, Multi storeyed Flats, RK Puram, Sector XIII, New Delhi, 110022, India.

THARMARATNAM, Dhayalan Samuel Richards, b. 14th June, 1945, Colombo, Sri Lanka. Management Consultant. m. Marina Anneliese Fernando, 17th Aug. 1973, 1 daughter. *Education:* Associate Member, Institute of Chartered Accountants, Sri Lanka. 1970; Associate Member, Institute of Cost and Management Accountants, UK, 1978; Master in Business Administration, IMEDE/University of Lausanne, Switzerland, 1978. *Appointments:* Assistant to Chairman, Ceylon Oils and Fats Corporation, 1970; Cost Accountant, Richard Pieris & Company Limited, 1971; Finance Manager, Sterling Drug Inc, Sri Lanka, India, Pakistan, 1972-74; Audit Senior, Pannell Kerr Forster & Co, British Virgin Islands, West Indies, 1974-77; Director, Consulting, Industrial & Commercial Consultants, Limited. 1979-80. *Memberships:* Chairman Archives Committee, Rotary Club of Colombo; Public Interest Committee; International IMEDE Alumni Association, Sri Lanka Representative; The Gymkhana Club; Ceylon Sea Anglers Club; The Capri Club; The Rifle Club of Colombo. *Publications:* Attitudes of Multinational Corporations to Investment in Sri Lanka, IMEDE, 1978; Concept of Management Educations, Journal of the Institute of Chartered Accountants, Sri Lanka; Case Studies in Management, Journal of the Institute of Chartered Accountants, Sri Lanka. *Honours:* First in order of Merit and awarded Sword of Honour, No. 1 Volunteer Officers Course, Royal Ceylon Air Force. *Hobbies:* Stamps and Coin Collecting; Collecting Old books on Ceylon; Playing Squash & Tennis; Big Bore Rifle Shooting. *Address:* 30/2 Park Road, Colombo 5, Sri Lanka.

THATCHER, Rt. Hon. Margaret, b. 1925, Grantham, Lincolnshire, England. Prime Minister and First Lord of the Treasury. m. Dennis Thatcher, 1951, 1 son, 1 daughter. *Education:* BSc., Somerville College, Oxford, England; MA., Oxford University, England. *Appointments:* Research Chemist; Elected to House of Commons representing Finchley, London, 1959; Parliamentary Secretary to Ministry of Pensions and National Insurance, 1961-64; Front-Bench Spokesman in Opposition, 1964-70; Member of Shadow Cabinet, 1967-70; Secretary of State for Education and Science, Privy Counsellor, 1970-74; Shadow Cabinet, Opposition Front-Bench spokesman on Environment and later on

Treasury matters, 1974; Elected Leader of Conservative Party and thus Leader of the Opposition, Feb. 1975; As Leader of the Opposition made several major tours including: USA; Canada; Australia; New Zealand; India; Pakistan; China; Japan; Hong Kong; Has visited many European and Middle Eastern countries; Appointed Prime Minister and First Lord of Treasury, 1979-; She is Britain's first woman Prime Minister. *Memberships:* Former President, Oxford University Conservative Association. *Address:* 10 Downing Street, London, England.

THAVENDRAN, Arulnandhy, b. 18th Dec. 1932, Point Pedro, Sri Lanka. Chartered Accountant. m. Indrani Rajaratnam, 24th May, 1967, 2 sons, 1 daughter. *Education:* BSc, University of Sri Lanka, 1953; BSc, University of London, 1954; ACA, Sri Lanka, 1958; FCA, Sri Lanka, 1970. *Appointments:* Joined the Colombo Commercial Co. Ltd, Colombo, as Accountant in 1958; Group Finance Director,The Maharaja Organisation Ltd, 1972-75; Financial Consultant & Group Finance Director, Crest Group of Companies, 1976-. Chairman, K. Paul Associates Limited, 1976-. *Memberships:* Council of the Institute of Chartered Accountants of Sri Lanka, 1970-73 and 1978-79; Chairman, Gem Traders Section of Ceylon Chamber of Commerce, 1975-77. *Hobby:* Playing Bridge. *Address:* 14, Palmgrove, Colombo-3, Sri Lanka.

THEAGARAJAH, Manickam Vallipuram, b. 13th Oct. 1931, Jaffna, Sri Lanka. Company Director. m. Lingeswary Thanabalasuriar, 26th Jan. 1967, 3 daughters. *Education:* Fellow of the Institute of Cost and Management Accountants, UK, Elected Associate, 1961; Elected Fellow, 1972. *Appointments:* Assistant Accountant, Associated Electrical Industries, Cables Division, Gravesend, UK, 1960-61; Cost Accountant, 1962-63; Group Cost Accountant, 1963-65, Group Cost & Financial Accountant, 1965-68, Finance Director, 1969-79, Deputy Chairman & Finance Director, 1979-, Browns Group of Companies, Colombo, Sri Lanka. *Memberships:* Vice-President, Institute of Cost & Management Accountants, Sri Lanka Branch, 1968; President, Rotary Club of Colombo West, 1979; Chairman, Free Trade Zone Manufacturers Association, 1979-80. *Hobbies:* Gardening. *Address:* 23/2 Independence Avenue, Colombo-7, Sri Lanka.

THEALL, Donald Francis, b. 13th Oct. 1928, Mount Vernon, New York, USA. Educator. m. 14th June, 1950, 5 sons, 1 daughter. *Education:* Diploma, AB Davis High School, 1946; BA, Yale University, 1950; MA, University of Toronto, 1951; PhD, University of Toronto, 1954. *Appointments:* Teaching Fellow, University of Toronto, 1950-52; Lecturer to Full Professor, University of Toronto, 1952-65; Chairman, Joint Departments of English, University of Toronto, 1964-65; Professor, Chairman Department, English & Director Communications, York University, Toronto, 1965-66; Professor, Chairman Department English, McGill University, 1966-74; Molson Professor, McGill, 1972-79; Director, Graduate Programme in Communications, 1976-79; President & Vice Chancellor, Trent University, Peterborough, Ontario, 1980-. *Memberships:* First President, Canadian Communications Association, 1979-80; Chairman of English, Philological Society of Great Britain, Canadian Association; Past Director, Ontario Council Teachers; Corresponding Fellow, Academy Medicine, Toronto. 05 Report on the Cultural Effects of Advertising in Quebec, 1978 Co-ed, Studies in Canadian Communications, 1975; Report on the Creation of Visual Arts Information Service for Canada, 1968; The Medium is the Rear View Mirror; Understanding McLuhan. *Honours:* First Cultural Exchange Professor between Canada & People's Republic of China, 1974-75; High School graduation scholarship awards from Yale, Princeton, Columbia and MIT, 1946. *Hobbies:* Swimming; Music; Films. *Address:* 1604, Champlain Drive, Peterbrough, Ontario, Canada K9L 1N6.

THEKA, Downs Stainer, b. 18th Nov. 1940, Chikwawa District, Malawi, South Africa. Land Surveyor. m. Daphne, 30th Nov. 1974. 1 son, 1 daughter. *Education:* Diploma in Land Survey, Khartoum, Sudan, 1962-66; Certificate in Land Survey, Hyderabad, India, 1972-74; *Appointments:* Government Surveyor, Malawi, 1966-72; Surveyor in Malawi/Canada Railway Project in Malawi, 1974-75; Surveyor, Lilongwe Land Development, Malawi, 1975-78; Regional Surveyor, Malawi Government, 1978-81. *Memberships:* Malawi Institute

of Surveyors; Civil Service Football Club, Chairman. *Honours:* Represented Malawi Government at International Congress for Photogrammetry, Hamburg, Germany, 1980. *Hobbies:* Football; Music; Swimming. *Address:* NSOMO Village, TA Ngabu, PO Ngabu, Malawi, South Africa.

THEVAKUNCHARAPATHY, Supiramaniam, b. 12th Oct. 1938, Inuvil, Sri Lanka. Chartered Accountant. m. Sakuntala, 28th Jan. 1974, 2 daughters. *Education:* BS (Economics), University of London, External Student, International Economics, 1964. *Appointments:* Audit Assistant, Ford, Rhodes, Thornton & Co, Chartered Accountants, Colombo, Sri Lanka, 1967-72; Accountant, Walker Sons & Co, Colombo-1, Sri Lanka, 1972-74; Head of Accountancy Training; DAR School of Accountancy, c/o the Treasury, Dar es Salaam, Tanzania, 1974-75; Finance Accountant, Lakes Fisheries of Zambia, Kitwe, Zambia, 1975-77; Chief Accountant, 1977-78; Chief Accountant, Company Secretary, Copperbelt Steel Manufacturing Co, Kitwe, Zambia, 1978-. *Memberships:* Associate, Institute of Chartered Accountants of Sri Lanka; Associate, Institute of Chartered Secretaries & Administrators, London. *Hobbies:* Badminton; Swimming. *Address:* PO Box 22351, Kitwe, Zambia.

THOMAS, Abator Medwin, b. 10th Aug, 1941, Freetown, Sierra Leone, West Africa. Librarian. Divorced, 2 sons, 2 daughters. *Education:* ALA, Northwestern Polytechnic, 1962-66. *Appointments:* Library Assistant, Kensington Public Libraries, 1966-67; Branch Librarian, Gateshead Public Libraries, 1967-68; Childrens Librarian, Sierra Leone Library Board, 1968-69; Librarian, Milton Margai Teachers College, Godench, Sierra Leone, 1969. *Memberships:* Past President, ex Secretary & Ex Editor, Sierra Leone Library Association; Programme Officer, Resource Materials, Centre for Research into the Education of Secondary School Teachers, (CREST). *Hobbies:* Reading; Interior Decorating. *Address:* 70B Wilkinson Road, Freetown, Sierra Leone, West Africa.

THOMAS, Andrew Murray, b. 14 Mar. 1936, Blyth, South Australia. Senator for Western Australia. m. 27 Mar. 1958, 2 sons, 1 daughter. *Education:* Clare High School, South Australia, 1951. *Appointments:* Farm and Stud Manager, 1952-62; Farmer, Pastoralist and Stud Sheep Breeder, 1963-75; Senator for Western Australia, 1975-. *Memberships:* Foundation President, Australian Merino Society Incorporated; Executive Member, West Australia Stud Merino Breeders Association; Director, Western Australian Farmers Co-operative Limited; Chairman, Senate Standing Committee on National Resources. *Publications:* Contributed professional articles and reports. *Honours:* Recipient of Silver Jubilee Medal, 1977. *Hobbies:* Tennis; Golf; Lawn Bowls; Reading. *Address.* 98 Blencowe Road, Geraldton, Western Australia.

THOMAS, Anthony William, b. 15 Nov. 1949, Adelaide, South Australia. Physicist. m. Joan E. Thomas, 22 May 1971, 2 daughters. *Education:* BSc, Flinders University, 1969; BSc, Hons, Flinders University, 1970; PhD, Physics, Flinders University, 1973. *Appointments:* Killam Postdoctoral Fellow, University of British Columbia, 1973-75; Paid Scientific Associate, CERN, 1975-76; Research Scientist, TRIUMF, 1976-. *Memberships:* American Physical Society; Australian Institute of Physics; Canadian Association of Physicists. *Publications:* Editor, Modern Three Hadron Physics, Springer-Verlag, 1977; Proceedings Eight International Conference on High Energy Physics and Nuclear Structure, North Holland, 1980, D.F.Measday and A.W.Thomas; Invited speaker at seven international conferences; Over fifty published scientific papers. *Honours:* Recipient of Advertiser Prize, 1966; BHP Medal, 1967; Flinders University Medal, 1971. *Hobbies:* Reading; Cricket; Squash; Travel; Languages. *Address:* 2758 W39 Avenue, Vancouver, British Colombia, Canada, V6N 2Z4.

THOMAS, Claudius Cornelius, b. 1 Oct. 1928, Saint Lucia, West Indies. Diplomat. *Education:* LLB, University of London, 1952-56; Called to the Bar, Gray's Inn, 1957; LLD, University of Strasbourg, 1958-60; Hague Academy of International Law, 1960. *Appointments:* Cadet Office, Legal, West Indies Commission, 1961-62; Translator, Common Market, Brussels, 1962-63; Attache, International Institute of Administrative

Science, Brussels, 1963-63; Assistant to Professor of Inter, Foreign and Comparative Law, 1963-72; Assistant Professor of Law, Free University, West Berlin, 1972-75; Commissioner for East Caribbean Governments, London, 1975-; High Commissioner for Saint Lucia, 1979; Saint Vincent and the Grenadines, 1979; High Commissioner for Antigua an Barbuda, 1981. *Memberships:* British Institute of International and Comparative Law; Fellow, Royal Commonwealth Society; Vice-President, West Indies Committee. *Publications:* A number of professional publications, including Constitutional Theory and Practice in West Indies. *Honours:* Recipient of CMG, 1979. *Hobbies:* Table Tennis; Sailing; Listening to Music. *Address:* Paddock Cottage, Hampton Court Road, Hampton Court, London, England.

THOMAS, Derwyn Lewis, b. 15 Mar. 1927, Aberystwyth, Wales. Registered Pharmaceutical Chemist, Civil Servant. m. Margaret Grace Mitchell, 12 Sept. 1959, 2 sons, 1 daughter. *Education:* PhC, University of Nottingham; Chelsea, UCL, BSc, Allied Science, University of London, 1957; MPS, 1954; MRSH, DBA, 1958. *Appointments:* The Pharmaceutical Adviser to Secretary of State for Wales, Welsh Office and Welsh Health Technical Services Organisation, 1974; Area Pharmacist, Derbys Hospital Pharmaceutical Services, 1973-74; Group Pharmacist Derbys Royal Infirmary, 1965-73; Deputy Chief Pharmacist, Royal Berkshire Hospital, 1960-65, following London experience at St. George's Hospital; UCH; Parke-Davis Limited; Charing Cross Hospital; Allen and Hanburys Limited; Westminster Hospital. *Memberships:* Welsh Office Observer at meetings of United Kingdom Medicines Commission and Department of Health and Social Security, Regional Pharmaceutical Officers' Committee; Standing Pharmaceutical Advisory Committee, England and Wales; Welsh Medical and Pharmaceutical Committees; Welsh Committee for Postgraduate Pharmaceutical Education; All Wales Drugs and Dressings, Contracts, Committees; Chairman, meetings of Chief Administrative Pharmaceutical Officers with Officers of the Welsh Office; Past Chairman, Secretary, Pharmaceutical Bodies. *Publications:* Contributed to various professional journals. *Honours:* Recipient of FPS, 1975. *Hobbies:* Gardening; Countryside; Buildings, Ancient and Modern; Browsing through books; Music. *Address:* Swyn-y-Cor, 1 Greenwood Lane, St Fagans, Cardiff, CF5 6EL, Wales.

THOMAS, John, Warren, Nevill, b. 7 Feb. 1938, Toronto, Ontario, Canada. Business Executive. m. Susanne E Thomas, 12 Sept. 1964, 3 sons, 1 daughter. *Education:* BComm, Trinity College, University of Toronto; MA, Econ, Queens University; MBA, York University; CFA, University of Virginia. 03 Investment Banking, Corporate Finance Director of Research Midland Doherty Limited, 1967-; Chairman of Board, Plumbing Mart Corporation, Autocrown Corporation. *Memberships:* Royal Canadian Yacht Club; University Club of Toronto; Metropolitan Club of New York; Canadian Club of New York. *Hobbies:* Sailing; Travelling. *Address:* Devonshire Hall, 110 Sandringham Drive, Toronto, Ontario, Canada.

THOMAS, Keith Henry Westcott, b. 20 May 1923, Portsmouth, Hants England. Civil Servant. m. Brenda Jeanette Crofton, 31 Aug. 1946, 2 sons. *Education:* Royal Naval Engineering College, Keyham, 1943-44; Royal Naval College, Greenwich, 1944-47. *Appointments:* Director General, Naval Design, Department of Navy, Canberra, Australia, 1970-73; Planning Manager, H.M. Dockyard, Rosyth, 1973-75; General Manager, H.M. Dockyard, Rosyth, 1975-7; General Manager, H.M. Dockyard, Devonport, 1977-79; Chief Executive, Royal Dockyards, Head of Royal Corps of Naval Constructors, 1979. *Memberships:* Royal Corps of Naval Constructors, 1979; Fellowships of engineers; Fellow, Royal Institution of Naval Architects; Fellow, British Institute of Management; Fellow, Institution of Industrial Managers; Institution of Royal Commonwealth Club. Recipient of OBE, 1962. *Hobbies:* Fencing; Music; Lapidary. *Address:* 11 Englishcombe Way, Bath, Avon, BA2 2EU, England.

THOMAS, Norman Randall, b. 22nd Dec. 1932, Caerphilly, Wales, UK. Dentistry. m. EAJ Thomas, 5th Dec. 1953, 4 sons, 1 daughter. *Education:* BDS, University of Bristol, 1957; BSc, University of Bristol, 1960; Royal College of Surgeons, Oral Pathology, 1960-62; PhD,

University of Bristol, 1962-65; Certificate, Oral Pathology, 1976-77. *Appointments:* Dental Officer, Gloucester County Council, UK, 1957; Nuffield Fellow, University of Bristol, 1958-60; Medical Research Council Scientific Assistant, Royal College of Surgeons, England, 1960-61; Lecturer Dental Medicine, Oral Biology, University of Bristol, 1962-68; Assoc. Professor and Professor of Dentistry, 1968-; Chairman, Physiology Division, FAC Dent, University of Alberta, 1981. *Memberships:* Counsellor, IADR, Canadian Division; Chairman, Research Council, CDA; Lodge Master, AF & AM, Alberta Jurisdiction; Cymrodurion, UK; Chairman, Research Committee, ACFD; American Academy of Oral Pathology, Alberta, Biofeedbag Association, Vice-President. *Publications:* Publications in Oral Physiology Tooth Eruption; Neurophysiology of Oral Mechanisms; Oral Pathologymr Dental Carles; Osteogenosis; Imperfecta Carcinogenesis, Oral. *Honours:* Gold Medalist, University of Bristol, 1957. *Hobby:* Music. *Address:* 5412, 142 St., Edmonton, Alta, Canada T6G 4B8.

THOMAS, Patrick Alan, b. 1 June, 1932, Brisbane. Conductor, Music. m. 31 May, 1958, 1 son, 1 daughter. *Education:* A.Mus.A, Piano; A.Mus.A, Organ; AASA, Brisbane State High School. *Appointments:* Resident Conductor, Australian Elizabethan Theatre Trust opera, 1964; Australian Ballet, 1964; Assistant Conductor, Adelaide Symphony, Musical Director, ABC Adelaide Singers, 1965-72; Chief Conductor, Queensland Symphony, 1973-77; ABC, Conductor, in residence, 1978-. *Memberships:* AASA: Council, Queensland Conservatorium, 1973-77; Course Consultant Committee, Northern Rivers, CAE. *Publications:* Recordings, EMI, Polygram, WRC, Festival, ABC, etc. *Honours:* Churchill Fellowship, 1972; MBE, 1978. *Hobbies:* Gardening; Photography; Family Life. *Address:* 14 Boronia Avenue, Turramurra, NWS 2074, Australia.

THOMAS, Ralph Percy, b. 26th Mar. 1908, Perth, Western Australia. Research Metallurgist. m. Florence Irene Miles, 26th June, 1943, 2 daughters. *Education:* Diploma in Metallurgy, Kalgoorlie, Western Australia, 1957. *Appointments:* Officer in charge of BHP's Manganese deposit at Peak Hill, West Australia, 1949; Head Assayer, Analyst, precious metals, BHP, Kalgoorlie, 1950; Commonwealth Scientific Institute & Research Organisation, Kalgoolie, 1953; Part time lecturer, WASM, 1959; Accepted to become full time lecturer in Metallurgy and Chemistry Department at WASM, Kalgoolie, until retirement 1961-70. *Memberships:* Associate of the Royal Society of Western Australia; Associate of Graduates Association of Western Australian School of Mines, 1958; Associate of Australian Institute of Mining and Metallurgy; Mandural Bowling Club; Prospectors & Leaseholders Association of Western Australia. *Publications:* The Yarri Octahedrite Iron Meteorite, Journal of the Royal Society of Western Australia, 1969. *Honours:* Associateship with Royal Society of Western Australia. *Hobbies:* Stamp Collecting; Photography; Prospecting, meteorites, telktites, gold and base metals. *Address:* Unit 9, 8 Creery Street, Mandurah, Western Australia, 6210.

THOMAS, Rt. Hon. (Thomas) George, *Education:* University College, Southampton. *Appointments:* Parliamentary Private Secretary, Ministry of Civil Aviation, 1951; Chairman, Welsh Parly Labour Party, 1950-51; Member, Chairman's Panel, House of Commons, 1951-64; President, National Brotherhood Movement, 1955; Schoolmaster; VicePresident, the Methodist Conference, 1960-61; MP, Labour, Cardiff Central, 1945-50; Cardiff West, 1950-76; First Chairman of the Welsh Parliamentary Grand Committee; Joint Parly Under-Secretary of State, Home Office, 1964-66; Minister of State, Welsh Office, 1966-67; Commonwealth Office, 1967-68; Secretary of State for Wales, 1968-70; Deputy Speaker and Chairman of Ways and Means House of Commons, 1974-76; *Memberships:* Honorary Fellow, UC Cardiff, 1972; Honorary LLD, Asbury College, Kentucky, 1976; University of Southampton, 1977; University of Wales, 1977; Birmingham, 1978; Freeman, Borough of Rhondda, 1970; City of Cardiff, 1975; Dato Setia Negara Brunei, 1971; Athenaeum Club, London; County Club, Cardiff. *Honours:* Freeman, Worshipful Company of Blacksmiths, 1980; Freeman, City of London, 1980; Honorary Member, Cambridge Union Society, 1982. *Publications:* The Christian Heritage in Politics. *Address:* Tilbury, 173 King George V Drive East, Cardiff, Wales.

THOMAS, Vadakethu Abraham, b. 15 Aug. 1914, India. Malaysian Citizen. m. Ruth de Alwis, 2 Nov. 1942, (deceased 1979), 5 sons. *Education:* College Diploma, Kuala Lumpur, Telecommunication Engineering and allied subjects, Johore, Malaysia, 1940; Chartered Electrical Engineer, UK; Graduate membership of the Institution of Electrical Engineers, London; Telecommunication Department, Cambridge. *Appointments:* Assistant Controller of Telecommunications, Regional Controller, 1961, Johore, Penang; Director of Telecommunications, 1967; retired, 1969; Founder, Director and Principal of Institute of Technology, Jaya, Kuala Lumpur. *Memberships:* Fellow, Institution of Electrical Engineers, London; Fellow, Institution of Engineers, Malaysia; Society of Engineers, London. *Hobbies:* Reading; Hiking; Golf. *Address:* No 22 Jalan 8/1A, Section 8, Petaling Jaya, Kuala Lumpur, Malaysia.

THOMAS, Vijayamma, b. Kerala, India. Associate Professor. m. Mr. Keluthara Thomas, 13 Apr. 1950, 2 sons, 1 daughter. *Education:* BSc, Travancore, 1951; MSc, Madras, 1955; PhD, Malaya, 1964. *Appointments:* Lecturer, College of Agriculture, Serdang, Malaysia, 1957-66, Demonstrator, 1967-68, Lecturer, 1967-75, Department of Parasitology, Faculty of Medicine, University of Malaya; Principal, 4th Residencial College, University of Malaya, 1971-73; Short-term WHO Consultant in Delhi, India, 1973; Associate Professor, Department Parasitology, Faculty of Medicine, University of Malaya, 1976; Member, WHO Expert Advisory Panel on Vector Biology & Control, 1975-80; Advisor to SWG Group on Malaria, Panama City, WHO, 1979; Member, WHO Expert Advisory Panel on Parasitic Diseases, General Parasitology, 1980. *Memberships:* Life Member, Malaysian Society Parasitology Tropical Medicine, Acting President, 1976, Vice-President, 1976, Honorary Treasurer, 1968, Council Member, 1964; Life Fellow, Royal Society Tropical Medicine Hygiene, London; Life Fellow, Indian Society, Malaria and Other Communicable Diseases; Life, Malaysian Scientific association; Nigerian Society of Parasitology; Associate Member, Malaysian Medical Association. *Publications:* Over 80 scientific papers in National/International Scientific journals in the field of Medical Parasitology/Entomology. 2 books, co-author, Malariology; Pararsitology Perubatan. *Honours:* Government of India Scholarship, 1953-55; WHO Fellowship, 1964; China Medical Board of New York Fellowship, 1973-74; Senior Inter-University Council Fellowship, 1977; WHO Fellowship, 1978; WHO Visiting Scientist Grant, 1979. *Hobby:* Reading. *Address:* 6 Jalan 12/2 Petaling Jaya, Selangor, Kuala Lumpur, Malaysia.

THOMPSON, Gabriel Amorighoye, b. 10 Dec. 1944, Benin. Librarian. m. Matilda A. June. 1972, 3 sons, 3 daughters. *Education:* WASC, 1961-65; BSc, University of IFE, 1968-71; Diploma in Librarianship, University of Ibadan, 1974-75; MLS, 1979-81. *Appointments:* Principal Librarian and Head, Library and Information Department, NITR. *Memberships:* Health Sciences Library and Information Group; Kaduma inter-library scheme, Treasurer; Nigerian Association of Agricultural Librarians and Documentalists; Member of the Insitute of Information Scientists, London. *Publications:* Library Service through Network patern, paper, Nigeria, 1977; Thompson GA Book Selection Principles and Book Collection Development, 1979; Bibliometric Analysis of African Trypanosominosis Literature. Literature of Science and Technology; The role and contribution of selected Research Institute in Nigeria, paper, 1979. *Hobbies:* Table Tennis; Lawn Tennis; Badminton. *Address:* Block BI, NITR Quarters, Surame Road, Kaduna, Nigeria.

THOMPSON, Godfrey, b. 28 June. 1921, Coventry, England. Librarian, Art Gallery Director. m. Doreen Cattel, 27 May. 1946, 1 son. *Education:* King Henry VIII, School Coventry, 1932-38; Loughborough University. *Appointments:* Librarian, Coventry, 1937; Deputy Borough Librarian, Chatham, 1948; Deputy City Librarian, Kingston Upon Hull, 1952; Deputy City Librarian, Manchester, 1958; City Librarian, Leeds, 1963; Guildhall Librarian and Director of Art Galleries, City of London, 1966; Library Planning Consultant in 7 countries, 1978. *Memberships:* President, the Library Association, 1978; Fellow, Society of Antiquaries; Fellow, Royal Society of Arts; Governor, the St. Bridge Foundation. *Publications:* Planning and Design of Library Buildings, 1977, Architectural Press; Encyclopedia of

London, DENT; London Statues, DENT; London for Everyman, DENT. etc. *Address:* 24 Morden Road, Blackheath, London, SE3, England.

THOMPSON, Joe Slater, b. 25 July, 1921, Manly, New South Wales, Australia. MP and Trade Union Secretary. m. Norma Joyce Taylor, 21 July, 1943, 3 sons, 1 daughter. *Education:* Intermediate Certificate, New South Wales Education Department, 1938; Senior Course Administration Staff College, 1962; Industrial Relations, Harvard University, 1968. *Appointments:* Trade Union Official, 1960-74; Trade Union Secretary, 1974-; Member of Parliament, 1974-. *Memberships:* Commonwealth Parliamentary Association, New South Wales Division, Executive Member; Enfield Returned Service Club. *Publications:* A Report on Industrial Relations, Harvard University; An Australian looks at the United Auto Workers Union of America; Future of the World Auto Industry. *Honours:* Churchill Fellowship, 1967; Awarded Order of Australia, 1981. *Hobbies:* Swimming; Boating. *Address:* 8 Allan Avenue, Belmore, 2192, Australia.

THOMPSON, Mark, Lindsay, b. 13 Dec. 1949, Sculptor/Arts Administrator. *Education:* Diploma of Fine Art, Painting, South Australian School of Art, 1972; Diploma of Design, Ceramics, Torrens College of Advanced Education, 1975. *Appointments:* Prepared and introduced ceramics course, Darwin Adult Centre, 1966-67; Art Master, Preparatory School, Prince Alfred College, 1972-78; Lecturer in Industrial Ceramics, Torrens College of Advanced Education, 1977; Director, Jam Factory Workshops Gallery, Design and training, 1978. *Memberships:* Fellow Royal S.A. Society of Arts; Member, Art Museums Association of Australia; Contemporary Art Society of South Australia; Craft Council of South Australia. *Creative Works:* Numerous exhibitions and awards, group exhibitions, one-man exhibitions etc. *Address:* 10 Margaret Street, Walkerville, South Australia.

THOMPSON, Neil George Hugh, b. 7 March, 1940, Sydney, Australia. Orthopaedic Surgeon. m. 4 July, 1970, 1 son, 2 daughters. *Education:* MB, BS, University of Sydney, 1958-64, Fellow, Royal College Surgeons, Edinburgh, 1970; Fellow, Royal College Surgeons, London, 1971, Fellow, Royal Australasian College of Surgeons, 1974. *Appointments:* Resident Medical Officer, Parramatta Hospital, 1965-67; Surgical Registrar, Liverpool Regional Hospitals Board, 1969-70; Orthopaedic Registrar, Addenbrooke's Hospital, Cambridge, 1970-71; Orthopaedic Registrar, Prince of Wales Hospital, Sydney, 1973; Orthopaedic Registrar, Lewisham Hospital, Sydney, 1974; Relieving/Orthopaedic Surgeon, Parramatta Hospital, 1975-76; Relieving Visiting Orthopaedic Surgeon, Repatriation General Hospital, Concord, 1975-76; Visiting Orthopaedic Surgeon, Lismore Base Hospital, 1976-. *Memberships:* Australian Orthopaedic Association, 1975; The Lismore Club, 1977. *Honours:* Commendation for Brave Conduct, 1978; Silver Medal of Royal Humane Society of Australia, 1978. *Hobbies:* Golf; Surfing; Furniture Restoring; Classical Music. *Address:* Skyline Road, Goonellabah, New South Wales, 2480, Australia.

THOMPSON, Norman Sinclair, b. 7 July, 1920, Redcar, Yorkshire, England. Chairman, Mass Transit Railway Corporation, Hong Kong. m. Peggy Sivil, 2 sons. *Education:* FCA Chartered Accountant, 1947; ACMA. *Appointments:* Merchant Seaman, War, 1940-45; Assistant Secretary, Paton's and Baldwin's Ltd., 1947; Commercial Manager, Cowans Sheldon and Co. Ltd, 1955; Group Secretary, Richardson's Westgarth & Co Ltd. 1957; Financial Director, David Brown & Sons (Huddersfield) Ltd, 1961; General Manager, Malta Drydocks, Swan Hunter Group Ltd., 1963; Appointed Swan Hunter Board, 1964; Overseas Director, 1967; Deputy Managing Director, 1969; The Cunard Steam-Ship Co Ltd., Managing Director, Cargo Shipping, 1970; Managing Director, 1971-74. *Memberships:* Oriental Club; Royal Hong Kong Jockey Club; Royal Hong Kong Yacht Club; Hong Kong Club; Royal Automobile Club. *Honours:* CBE, 1980 *Hobbies:* Sailing; Music; Philately. *Address:* Apartment 1, 5 Headland Road, Repulse Bay, Hong Kong.

THOMPSON, Terence James, b. 19 Jan. 1928, Staffordshire, England. Teacher/Musician. *Education:* ABSM, Performer and Teacher of Clarinet, 1950; ABSM, (TTD), 1950. *Appointments:* Music Master,

Technical High School, West Bromwich, 1950-59; Clarinet Teacher, School of St. Mary and St. Anne, Abbots Bromley, 1957-; Head of Music, March End School, 1960-66; Lecturer, West Midlands College of Higher Education, 1965-; Senior Teacher, Wolverhampton Music School, 1968-. *Memberships:* Wolverhampton Teachers Association; Walsall Education Society; Composers Guild of Great Britain; The Black Country Society; Clarinet and Saxophone Society of Great Britain; Schools Music Association; Performing Right Society. *Publications:* 35 various compositions and arranged works, published or in the library of the British Music Information Centre. *Hobbies:* Philately; The Canal Scene. *Address:* 58, Willenhall Road, Bilston, West Midlands, WV14 6NW, England.

THOMPSON, William Edward, b. 17 Dec. 1933, Eleuthera, Bahamas. Clerk in Holy Orders. m. Rosemarie Bailey, 26 April, 1968. *Education:* Educated at Public and Private Schools in Bahamas until 1950; BA(Hons), University of Durham, 1956; MA, University of Durham, 1967. *Appointments.* Ordained Deacon in Anglican Church, 1956, Priest, 1957; Priest-Missioner, 1957-59; Priest-in-charge St. Andrews Parish, Bahamas, 1959-61; Master at St. Johns College, 1961-65; Priest at Long Island, Bahamas, 1965-67; Rector of St. Agnew, Nassau, Bahamas, 1967-; Examining Chaplain to Bishop of Nassau, 1957-. *Memberships:* Bahamas Public Service Appeal Board; Bahamas Public Disclosure Commission; Vice-President, Bahamas Christian Council; Board of Governors, Codrington College, Barbados; Former Member, Amglican Consultative Council as representative of Church in te Caribbean; Former member, Provincial Synod of Anglican Church in the Caribbean. *Publications:* Contributor to newspaper; one of contributors to, Moving into Freedom, a book on trends in Caribbean Theology. *Hobbies:* Reading; Arm Chair Sports. *Address:* The Rectory, Market Street, Nassau, N.P. Bahamas.

THOMSON, David Scott, b. 21 Nov. 1924, Sale, Victoria, Australia. Federal Member of Parliament, Minister for Science and Technology. m. Judith Anne Rogers, 22 Sept, 1955, 3 sons. *Education:* Scotch College, Melbourne; Royal Military College, Duntroon; Staff College, Quetta, Pakistan. *Appointments:* Australian Army, 1942-73; 2/16 Battalion South West Pacific, 1945; British Commonwealth Occupation Force, Japan, 1946-48; 1 Royal Australian Regiment, Military Cross, Korean War, 1954; Staff College, Quetta, 1956; Instructor Royal Military College, Duntroon, 1957-59; Instructor, British Army Staff College, Camberley, 1961-62; Commanding Officer, 4th Battalion, Royal Australian Regiment, 1964-66; Malaysia and Sarawak, 1965-66; Director of Infantry and Regimental Colonel, Royal Australian Regiment, Canberra, 1967-70; Commander, 3 Task Force & 11 Task Force and North Queensland Area, 1970-72; Brigadier, Army Reserve, 1972; Owner of Tourist Resort, North Queensland, 1973-75; Federal Member for Leichhardt in Australian Parliament, 1975; Minister for Science and the Environment, 1979-80; Minister for Science and Technology, 1980. *Honours:* Military Cross. *Hobbies:* Scuba Diving; Swimming; Riding; Reading. *Address:* Parliament House, Canberra, ACT 2600, Australia.

THOMSON, Ian (John) Sutherland, b. 8 Jan. 1920, Glasgow, Scotland, Independent Chairman, Fiji Sugar Industry, .and Chairman, Fiji Economic Development Board. m. Nancy Marguerite, 1 Sept. 1945, 7 sons, 1 daughter. *Education:* MA, (Hons), Glasgow University, 1936-40. *Appointments:* Colonial Administrative Service, Fiji, 1940; Army service during World War II in Black Watch, Royal Highland Regiment, 1940; Fiji Military Forces, 1941-45; Civil Service, Fiji, 1946-53; Secretarial and District Administration. Seconded to Colonial Office, London, 1953-56; Deputy Commissioner, Native Lands and Fisheries Commission, Fiji, 1957; Chairman, Native Lands and Fisheries Commission, 1958-63 and Commissioner Native Land Reserves; Divisional Commissioner, Western Fiji, 1963-1966; Acting Colonial Secretary and Governor's Deputy, 1966; Administrator, British Virgin Islands, 1967-71; Independent Chairman, Fiji Sugar Industry, 1971-; Chairman, Coconut Board and Advisory Council, 1973-; Chairman, Economic Development board, 1980-; Acting Governor General of Fiji, 1980 and 1981. *Memberships:* Deputy Chairman, YMCA, Fiji, 1973-. *Honours:* MBE, (Mil), 1945; CMG, 1968. *Hobbies:*

Gardening; Playing Golf. *Address:* GPO Box 644, Suva, Fiji.

THOMSON, John Adam (Sir), b. 27 April, 1927, H.M. Diplomatic Service. m. Elizabeth A. McClure, 1953, 3 sons, 1 daughter. *Education:* Phillip's Exeter Academy, USA; University of Aberdeen; Trinity College, Cambridge. *Appointments:* Foreign Office, 1950; Third Secretary, Jedda, 1951; Damascus, 1954; Foreign Office, 1955; Private Secretary to Permanent Under-Secretary, 1958-60; First Secretary, Washington, 1960-64; Foreign Office, 1964; Acting Head of Planning Staff, 1966; Counsellor, 1967; Head of Planning Staff; Foreign Office, 1967; seconded to Cabinet Office as Chief of Assessments Staff, 1968-71; Minister and Deputy Permanent Representative to North Atlantic Council, 1972-73; Head of UK Delegation to MBFR Exploratory Talks, Vienna, 1973; assistant Under-Secretary of State, FCO, 1973-76. *Publications:* Crusader Castles with R. Fedden, 1956. *Hobbies:* Carpets; Castles; Walking. *Address:* Lochpatrick Mill, Kirkpatrick, Durham, Castle Douglas, Kirkcudbrightshire, Scotland.

THOMSON, Neal Latta, b. 4th Oct. 1935, Sydney, Australia. Medical Practitioner, Orthopeadic Surgeon, m. Janette Margot Perier, 7th Dec. 1960 1 son. *Education:* MBBS, University of Sydney, 1962; Fellow, Royal College Surgeons of Edinburgh, 1968; Fellow, Royal Australian College Surgeons, Orthopaedics, 1970. *Appointments:* St. George's Hospital, Sydney, Australia, 1962-64; Department Anatomy, University of New South Wales, 1965; Repatriation General Hospital Concord, Sydney, Australia, 1966-67; St. Vincent's Hospital, Sydney, Australia, 1969; Prince of Wales Hospital, Sydney, Australia, 1970; Royal Alexandra Hospital for Children, Sydney, Australia, 1970; Honorary Medical Officer, Balmain Hospital, 1971-81; Honorary Medical Officer, Rachael Forster Hospital, 1971-74; Visting Medical Officer, Concord Repatriation Hospital, 1972-74; Honorary Medical Officer, Lewisham Hospital, 1972-81; Honorary Medical Officer, Auburn District Hospital, 1972-81 Consultant, Institute of Sports Medicine, Lewisham, 1972-81. *Memberships:* Australian Orthopaedic Association; Australian Medical Association; Australian Association of Surgeons; Royal Sydney Yacht Squadron, Kirribilli, Australia. *Honours:* Wolfe Solomon Brown Prize in Anatomy, 1968. *Hobbies:* Snow Skiing; Boating. *Address:* 9, Coonah Parade, Riverview, New South Wales, 1066, Australia.

THOMSON, Norman John Perry, b. 8th May, 1931, Toowoomba, Queensland, Australia. Agricultural Scientist. m. 13th June, 1959, 2 sons, 1 daughter. *Education:* B.Agri.Sci, University of Queensland, 1956; MSci, University of Western Australia, 1964; PhD, University of New England, 1971. *Appointments:* Instructor in Plant Breeding, Queensland Agricultural College, Lawes, Queensland, 1956-58; Agronomist, Kimberley Research Station, Western Australia, 1958-72; OIC CSIRO Cotton Research Unit, Narrabri Research Station, 1972-. *Publications:* Over 30 publications on various aspects of cotton agronomy and plant breeding. *Hobbies:* Gardening; Hobby Farming. *Address:* Cashell, PO Box 344, Narrabri, New South Wales 2390, Australia.

THOMSON, The Rt. Hon. Lord, b. 1 Sept. 1923, Toronto, Newspaper Proprietor. m. Nora Marilyn, 2 sons, 1 daughter. *Education:* Upper Canada College; BA, MA, University of Cambridge, England, 1947. *Appointments:* President and Director, Dominion-Consolidated Holdings Limited; Fleet Street Publishers Limited; Kenthom Holdings Limited; The Standard St. Lawrence Company Limited; Thomfleet Holdings Limited; Thomson International Corporation Limited; Thomson Mississauga Properties Limited; Thomson Works of Art Limited; Vice President and Director: Cablevue (Quinte) Limited; Veribest products Limited: Director: Abitibi-Price Inc.; The Advocate Company Limited; Caribbean Trust Limited; Central Canada Insurance Service Limited; Dominion-Consolidated Truck Lines Limited; Hudson's Bay Company; International Thomson Holdings Inc.; Load & Go Transport Inc.; McCallum Transport Inc.; Nipa lodge Co. Ltd.; Orchid Lodge Co. Ltd.; Scottish & York Holdings Limited; Simpsons, Limited; Thomson Scottish Associates Limited; Thomson Television Limited; The Toronto-Dominion Bank: Began in editorial department of Timmins Daily Press, Timmins, 1947; Advertising Department Cambridge

(Galt) Reporter, Cambridge, 1948-50; General Manager, 1950-53. Returned to the Toronto Head Office of Thomson Newspapers to take over direction of Companys Canadian and American operations. Served in 2nd World War with R.C.A.F. *Memberships:* York Downs; National; Toronto; York; Granite; Toronto Hunt. *Hobbies:* Collecting antiques and Old Master Paintings; Baptist Church. *Address:* 8 Kensington Palace Gardens, London, W.8. England.

THORP, Richard Graham, b. 8 June, 1944, Sydney, Australia. Architect. m. Judith, 20 Nov. 1970. *Education:* BA, University of Melbourne, 1967. *Appointments:* Daryl Jackson, Evan Walker Architects, Melbourne, 1966-8; Andrews, Downie and Kelly Architects, London, 1969-70; Mitchell/Giurgola Architects, Philadelphia, 1971-2; Frank Schlesinger and Associates, Architects, Washington DC, 1973; APR Associates, Washington DC, 1974-6; Brown and Daltas Architects, Rome, 1977; Mitchell/Giurgola Architects, New York, 1978-80; Mitchell/Giurgola and Thorp Architects, Canberra, 1981. *Memberships:* Royal Institute of British Architects, 1969; American Institute of Architects, 1979; New York Society of Architects, 1979; Royal Australian Institute of Architects, 1980. *Honours:* Partner in firm (Mitchell/Giurgola and Thorp Architects); Winner of Parliament House Design Competition, Australia, Canberra, 1980; Nominated as Project Architect, Parliament House, Australia. *Hobbies:* Skiing; Squash; Photography. *Address:* 29 Drevermann Street, Farrer ACT 2607, Australia.

THORPE, Brian Arthur, b. 12th May, 1940, Lower Swanwick, Hants, England. Financial Adviser, British Development Division, Barbados. m. Valerie Green, 18th Sept, 1965, 3 daughters. *Education:* Many schools throughout the world. *Appointments:* Commonwealth Relations Office, 1957-65; Ministry of Overseas Development, 1965-72; Second Secretary, British Embassy, Bangkok, 1972-75; Ministry of Overseas Development, 1975-77; Financial Adviser, BDD Barbados, 1977-. *Memberships:* Bridgetown Club; Society of Conutes, Founder. *Hobbies:* Philately; Bird Watching; Travel. *Address:* Las Brisas, Windy Ridge, Christ Church, Barbados.

THROSSELL, Ric Prichard, b. 10 May, 1922, Western Australia. Public Servant and Playwright. m. Eileen Dorothy Jordan, 3 Oct. 1947, 1 son, 2 daughters. *Education:* University of Western Australia; University of Sydney. *Appointments:* Department of Foreign Affairs, Canberra, 1943-80; Australian Legation, Moscow, 1945-46; Australian Legation, Brazil, 1949-52; Australian Development Assistance Agency, Director of International Training and Education, 1961-76; Assistant Secretary, International Cultural Relations, 1976-80; Director Commonwealth Foundation, 1980. *Memberships:* Australian Society of Authors; Australian Writers Guild; Canberra Repertory Society. *Publications:* The Day Before Tomorrow; For Valour, The Sweet Sad Story of Elmo and Me; Wild Weeds and Wind Flowers etc. *Hobbies:* Theatre; Walking; Photography. *Address:* 45B Redington Road, Hampstead, London, England.

THROWER, Lyle Boyce, b. 21 Mar. 1923, Melbourne, Australia. University Professor (Biology). m. Stella Lavinia, 10 Jan. 1960. *Education:* BS, University of Melbourne, 1950; MS, University of Melbourne, 1952; Doctor of Philosophy, University of Melbourne, 1963; Doctor of Agricultural Science, University of Melbourne, 1981. *Appointments:* Plant Pathologist, Department of Agriculture, Stock & Fisheries, Papua New Guinea, 1954-57; Lecturer in Botany, University of Melbourne, Australia, 1958-61; Senior Lecturer in Botany, University of Melbourne, 1961-65; Professor of Botany, University of Hong Kong, 1965-73; Dean, Faculty of Science, 1966-68; Pro-Vice-Chancellor, 1968-71; Professor of Biology, The Chinese University of Hong Kong, 1973; Dean, Faculty of Science, 1979. *Memberships:* Fellow, Linnean Society of London; British Mycological Society; British Ecological Society; International Phytopathological Society; Royal Asiatic Society, Hong Kong Branch; Royal Commonwealth Society. *Publications:* Approx. 60 papers published in scientific journals. *Honours:* Justice of the Peace, Hong Kong, 1970; Officer, Order of the British Empire, 1977. *Hobbies:* Bird-watching; Walking; Fishing; Music. *Address:* Flat 6B, Residence 6, The Chinese University of Hong Kong, Shatin, N.T., Hong Kong.

THUMBOO, Edwin Nadason, b. 22 Nov. 1933, Singapore. 1 son, 1 daughter. *Education:* BA (Hons), University of Singapore, 1957; PhD, University of Singapore, 1970. *Appointments:* Professor of English, University of Singapore, 1979-80; Professor of English, National University of Singapore, 1980; Dean, Faculty of Arts and Social Sciences, National University of Singapore, 1980. *Memberships:* International Shakespeare Association; Association for Commonwealth Language and Literature Studies; Research Associate of the Centre for Research in the New Literature in English; Editor, Tenggara; Editor, CRNLE Review; Associate Editor, World Literature Written in English. *Publications:* Rib of Earth, 1956; Seven Poets, 1973; Editor, Second Tongue, An Anthology of Poetry from Malaysia and Singapore, 1976; Gods Can Die, 1977; Ulysses by the Merlion, 1979; Several articles in scholarly journals. *Honours:* Recipient of numerous honours and awards for professional services. *Address:* 23 Phoenix Walk, Singapore 2366, Republic of Singapore.

TILL, Christopher Martin, b. 29 Nov. 1951, Johannesburg, South Africa. Gallery Director. m. Edwyn Probart Bassingthwaighte, 6 Dec. 1974, 1 son 2 daughters. *Education:* Bachelor of Fine Art, Rhodes, 1975; Master of Fine Art, Rhodes, 1976. *Appointments:* Keeper, National Gallery of Zimbabwe, 1977; Assistant Director, National Gallery of Zimbabwe, 1977; Director, National Gallery of Zimbabwe, 1980. *Memberships:* Fine Arts Committee; International Council of Museums; Executive Committee; National Arts Council of Zimbabwe. *Creative Works:* Paintings and Sculpture, Various group exhibitions with the Grahamstown Group, 1972-76, Work purchased for private and public collections in Southern Africa. *Hobbies:* Squash. *Address:* 2 Meath Road, Avondale, Salisbury, Zimbabwe.

TILLER, Mavis Ada (Mrs.), b. Wellington, New Zealand. m. Leslie Walter Tiller, 11 Sept. 1937, 2 sons (1 deceased), 1 daughter. *Education:* BSc(Hons), C.Chem, MRSC, London, Bedford College. *Appointments:* Teacher, Roedean School, Johannesburg, S. Africa, 1924-26; Chemist, Broken Hill Dev. Corp. Ltd.. N. Rhodesia, 1928-29; Personal Assistant, Supt. Metallurgy Department, National Physical Laboratory, Teddington, Middlesex, England, 1931-37; Commissioner on The Royal Commission on Social Security in New Zealand, Report 1972; Served on Commission for Expo '70. *Memberships:* Convenor, International Council of Women Standing Committee on International Relations & Peace, 1976-; Parliamentary Watch Committee of National Council of Women of New Zealand; National President, National Council of Women of New Zealand, 1966-70; Vice Convenor, I.C.W. Standing Committee on International Relations & Peace, 1973-76; President, Wellington Branch N.C.W., New Zealand, 1961-66; President for 17 years, Mothers Helpers Association, Wellington; Past President, Women's Auxiliary Primary & Secondary Schools; Board of Governors, Queen Margaret College; Rongotai College. *Honours:* OBE, 1971; Centro Culturale Italiano Premio Adelaide Ristori 1976 Award. *Hobbies:* Travel; Interest in Public Affairs. *Address:* 54 Khandallah Road, Wellington 4, New Zealand

TILLEY, Raymond Francis, b. 21 Feb. 1923, Launceston, Tasmania. Retailing. m. 12 Jan. 1952, 4 sons. *Education:* Fellow, Retail Management Institute of Australia; Fellow, Australian Institute of Management; Licensed Pilot & Radio operator; Trade Activities: President, Tasmanian Booksellers Association; Former Vice President, Australian Booksellers Association; Past President, Retail Traders Association of Tasmania. *Appointments:* Managing Director, A.W. Birchall & Sons Pty. Ltd. & Associated Companies: Booksellers, Stationers, Publishers, Launceston & Hobart; Owners of Birchalls Launceston Australia's Oldest Bookshop 1844; Government Appointments: Justice of the Peace; Member of the Consumer Affairs Council of Tasmania, 1970; Alderman, Launceston City Council, 1973-76; National Parks Advisory Committee; Employer Representative, Tasmanian Wages Board, 1960, 1973; Committee, Tasmanian Orchestral Advisory A.B.C., 1973-76. *Memberships:* Chairman, Council of Honorary Justices Associations, Tasmania; Past President, Honorary Justices Association, Tasmania; Past President, Tasmanian Aero Club; Royal Flying Doctor Service; Past President. Northern Tasmanian Alpine Club; Rotary International F.A.I.M. *Creative Works:* Designing, Building & Inventing, Patents Pending;

Projects Completed. Built & Flew Tasmania's first amateur built aircraft; Rebuilt three vintage aircrafts; Built three boats, one hydrofoil; Constructed Tasmania's first Geodesic Dome. *Honours:* Member, Australian International Ski Team, 1949; New Zealand Cross Country Ski Champion, 1949; Member, Tasmanian Ski Teams, 1940, 1949. *Hobbies:* Music; Woodworking; Metalworking; Outdoor Activities. *Address:* 56 Bald Hill Road, Launceston, 7250, Tasmania, Australia.

TILLEY-GYADO, Jacob, b. 15 Dec. 1944, Ihugh, Benue State, Nigeria. Scientist, Businessman & Industrialist. m. (1) Joyce, 26 Dec 1970. (2) Margaret, 22 Apr. 1977, (3) Biola, 18 Mar. 1978, 5 sons, 2 daughters. *Education:* BSc(Hons), Ahmadu Bello University, Zaria, 1966-69; Diploma in International Management, University of Rome, 1974. *Appointments:* Various Managerial positions with the Nigerian Tobacco Co. Ltd., 1969-72; General Manager, Tilley Gyado Group, 1972-74; Group Managing Director, Tilley Gyado Group of Companies, 1974. *Memberships:* British Institute of Management; Nigerian Institute of Management. *Honours:* Life Fellow, Botanical Society, 1979; Grand Patron, Medical Students Union, Jos, 1981. *Hobbies:* Travelling; Gardening; Music. *Address:* 25 Naraguta Avenue, Jos, Nigeria.

TIMBS, Maurice Carmel, b. 14 July 1917, Glen Innes, New South Wales, Australia. Company Director. m. Heather Joan Woodhead, 24 Apr. 1943, 1 son. *Education:* B.EC, University of Sydney, 1942; A.ASA, 1947. *Appointments:* Public Service, 1936-40; Service, Australian Imperial Forces, RAA-AIF, 1940-45; Public Service, 1945-76; Prime Ministers Department, First Assistant Secretary, 1950-60; Executive Commissioner, Australian Atomic Energy Commission, 1960-72; Permanent Head, Department of Administration Services, 1973-76; Commissioner for Australia, British Phosphate Commission, BPC, 1976-; Christmas Island; Deputy Chairman, Bridge Oil Ltd., 1976; Company Director, National Properties Ltd; Cass International Pty. Ltd, (CIPC), 1976-. *Memberships:* Australian Institute of Directors; Royal Institute Public Administration; Executive Australian/French Association of Professional & Technical Specialists; Australian Institute of Energy; Deputy Chairman, Board Australian Opera, 1970-80. *Honours:* Life Governor, Royal New South Wales Institute for Deaf and Blind Children, 1971; Member of Board of Trustees, World Wildlife Foundation, 1980; Officer of the Order of Australia, A.O., 1981; Vice President, Sovereign Military Order of Hospitaliers St. John of Jerusalem, Rhodes & Malta, Member, 1979, V.P., 1981. *Hobbies:* Bowls; Swimming; Golf. *Address:* 5 Chatsworth, 59 Woolseley Road, Point Piper, New South Wales, 2027, Australia.

TING, Hok-Shou Dennis, b. 13 Sept. 1933, Shanghai, China. Merchant. m. Emily Tsang Wing Hin, 18 Mar. 1961, 2 sons, 2 daughters. *Education:* BA, Colby College, Waterville, Maine, USA, 1960. *Appointments:* Managing Director, Kader Industrial Co. Ltd.; Managing Director, Qualidux Industrial Co. Ltd.; Director, Tindux Metal & Electronics Ltd.; Director, Vita Electronics Corp. Ltd.; Director, Kondux International Ltd. *Memberships:* Chairman, Hong Kong Shippers' Council, 1964-; Chairman, Federation of HK Ind. Plastic L2, Sub-Committee, 1968-; President, Hong Kong Plastic Manufacturers' Association, 1972-; Chairman, IA, Hong Kong General Chamber of Commerce, 1974-; Hong Kong Toy & Gift Fair Organizing Committee, 1974-; Founder President, President, Rotary Club of Hong Kong South, East. *Honours:* Justice of the Peace, 1977. *Hobbies:* Swimming; Hiking. *Address:* Fontana Gardens, No.22, 20/Floor, Causeway Bay, Hong Kong.

TING, Ing Chiew, b. 23 July 1938, Sibu, Sarawak. Architect/Developer. m. Teresa Law, 19 June 1965, 1 son, 2 daughters. *Education:* Bachelor of Architecture, Melbourne, 1964. *Appointments:* Worked with Leighton Irwin Architects, Melbourne, Australia, 1965-66; Worked with Public Works Department, Sibu, Sarawak, 1966-68; Started own firm, Ting & Associates, 1968-. *Memberships:* The Royal Australian Institute of Architects, 1966; The Royal Institute of British Architects, 1967; The Corporate Member of Pertubuhan Akitek, Malaysia, 1970; The Royal Australian Institute of Architects, 1974; Board of Architects, Malaysia, 1976; Chairman, Malaysian Institute of Architects, Sarawak Branch. *Hobbies:* Swimming; Golf; Volleyball; Badmin-

ton. *Address:* 18 Ong Hap Leong Road, Kuching, Sarawak, Borneo.

TINGLEY, Richard James, b. 13 Mar. 1941, St John, New Brunswick, Canada. Barrister/ Solicitor. m. Ann Marie Hovey, 12 Aug. 1967, 3 daughters. *Education:* BA, St. Dunstan's University, Charlottetown, P.E.I., 1960-64; BCL, University of New Brunswick, Frederiktown, New Brunswick, 1964-67. *Appointments:* Tingley, Senechal & Tingley, 1967-68; Sole Practioner, Richard J. Tingley, 1968-76; Senior Partner, Tingley & Humphrey, 1976-80; Senior Partner, Tingley, Humphrey's & Blanchard, 1981-. *Memberships:* Mayor, City of Campbellton, New Brunswick, Canada, 1980-; President, Inter-Provincial Municipal Association, New Brunswick; President, Campbellton Legion War Memorial Company, 1977-80; President, Campbellton Branch of New Brunswick Cancer Society; President, Campbellton Liberal Association, 1970-73; Canadian Bar Association; New Brunswick Barrister's Society; City Council, 1975-80. *Honours:* Maritime Intercollegiate Scoring Champion, 1963; Captain St. Dunstan's University, Varsity Hockey, 1964. *Hobbies:* Oldtimer Hockey; Tennis. *Address:* 5 Athol Street, Campellton, New Brunswick, Canada, ESN1Y2.

TIRUMALACHAR, Mandyam Annadhurai, b. 6 June 1943, Mysore City, India. Physician. m. Rama Mandayam Osuri, 29 June 1967, 1 son, 1 daughter. *Education:* MBBS, Bangalore University, 1966; MRCP, London, England, 1974. *Appointments:* Victoria Hospital, Bangalore, India, 1966-67; General Hospital, Sunderland, England, 1967-68; House Physician, St. Bartholomews Hospital. Rochester, England, 1969-70; Medical Registrar, St. Bartholomews, Rochester & Gravesend, North Kent Hospital, 1971-75; Lecturer in Medicine, St. Johns Medical College, Bangalore, India, & Physician, St. Martha's Hospital, Bangalore, India, 1976-77; Consultant Physician, Medway Group of Hospitals, Kent, England, 1978; Specialist Physician, New Guinea Islands Region, Rabaul, Papua New Guinea 1979-. *Memberships:* Royal College of Physicians, London, England; Indian Medical Association, Bangalore, India; Mandyam Association, Bangelore, India. *Honours:* Certificate of Merit, Bangalore Science Forum, for speaking on Peptic Ulcer, 1964. *Hobbies:* Travel; Photography; Listening to Western & Indian Classical Music. *Address:* SMO Physician, Nongabase Hospital. FMB, Rabaul, ENBP, Papua New Guinea.

TIRVENGADUM, Deva Duttun, b. 6 Sept. 1936, Rose Hill, Mauritius. Director, Mauritius Institute. m. Claudine Gillet, 16 Dec. 1978. *Education:* BSC, Biology, University of Madras, India, 1965; Commonwealth Teacher Training Bursary Scheme Certificate, University of Hull, England, 1969; Certificate d'Entomologie Systematique, Museum National d'Histoire Naturell, Paris, France, 1971; Pre-doctoral certificate in systematic biology, Smithsonian Institution, Washington DC, USA, 1975. *Appointments:* Biology Teacher, St. Mary's College, Mauritius, 1965; Researcher, Laboratoire de Phanerogamie, Paris, 1970; Scientific Assistant, Laboratoire de Phanerogamie, Paris, 1976; Director, Mauritius Institute, Port-Louis, 1978. *Memberships:* Board of Ancient Monuments and Nature Reserves, Chairman; Pamplemousses Gardens Advisory Committee; Man and Biosphere Committee; National Committee for UNESCO. *Publications:* Revision of Connaraceae of Ceylon, A Revised Handbook to the Flora of Ceylon, Vol 1, 1980; Revision of Pittosporaceae of Ceylon, A Revised Handbook to the Flora of Ceylon, Vol.II, 1980; Revision of Rosaceae of Ceylon, A Revised Handbook to the Flora of Ceylon, Vol.III, 1981. *Address:* N5 River Walk, Vacoas, Mauritius.

TISCH, Johannes Hermann, b. 11 Dec. 1929, Graz, Austria. University Professor and Head of Department; Educator; Ethnic Affairs Worker. m. Regula B.C. Wackernagel, 2 sons, 2 daughters. *Education:* St. Fidelis College, Stans Nidwalden, Switzerland; Federal Matriculation, 1949; University of Basle, Switzerland, 1949-53; University of Oxford, England, J.F. Cooper Research Scholar, Basle, 1953-54; University of Goettingen, Federal Republic of Germany, 1954-55; Dr. Phil. Basle, 1961, insigni cum laude; *Appointments:* Lecturer in German, University of Oxford, 1957-60; Lecturer in German, Australian National University, 1961-63; Senior Lecturer in German, University of Sydney, 1964-65; Visiting Professor, Germanic Studies Department, University of Pittsburgh, USA, 1970; Visiting Professor,

Comparative Literature School, La Nouvelle Sorbonne, Paris, France, 1973-74; Foundation Professor of German and Joint Head, Modern Languages Department, University of Tasmania, 1966. *Memberships:* President, Australian and New Zealand Association for Medieval and Renaissance Studies, 1972-74; Vice President Australia, Australasian Neo-Latin Association, 1974-77; President, Tasmanian Branch, Australian Goethe Society, 1968-73 and 1975-76; President and Vice President, Modern Language Teachers Association of Tasmania, various terms; Executive member, Tasmanian Branch, Australian Goethe Society, 1980; Vice President, German Australian Student Exchange Society, Tasmania, 1975 and Member of many national and international scholarly bodies and associations. *Publications:* Numerous publications in scholarly journals, congress proceedings and encyclopedias and in book form, including Der Ruhmesbegriff bei Milton, 1961; J C Gottsched, 1966; The German Speaking Countries, with R.B. Farrell et al. 1966; Andreas Gryphius: Leo armenius, 1968, second edition, 1980; 15th Century German Courts and Renaissance Literature, 1971; Renaissance and Rococo, 1973, second edition, 1978; Major publications in preparation including The Christian Homer: Milton in 18th century Switzerland. *Honours:* Recipient of many honours, awards and civic responsibilities. *Hobbies:* Operatic Singing; Swimming; Bush-walking. *Address:* 1 Cedar Court, Sandy Bay Hobart, Tasmania 7005, Australia.

TIZARD, Robert James, b. 7 June, 1924, Auckland, New Zealand. Member of Parliament. m. Catherine Anne, 12 May, 1951, 1 son, 3 daughters. *Education:* Master of Arts, Honours in History, Auckland University, 1946-9. *Appointments:* War Service RNZAF, 1943-6; Lecturer in History, Auckland University, 1949-53; Assistant Master, Mt. Albert Grammar, 1955-57; Member of Parliament, 1957-60; Assistant Master, Tamaki College, 1961-62; Member of Parliament, 1963; Minister of Health, 1972-74; Deputy Prime Minister and Minister of Finance, 1974-75; Deputy Leader of Opposition, 1976-79. *Memberships:* Captain and now Patron, Remuera Golf Club, 1939-; Remuera Squash Club, 1962-78. *Hobbies:* Golf; Squash; Stamp Collecting. *Address:* 69 Alfred Street, Onehunga, Auckland, 6, New Zealand.

TOBIN, Michael Emanuel, b. 17 Apr. 1956, Sydney, Australia. Chartered Accountant, Company Director. *Education:* ACA, 1977-80; BEc, University of Sydney, 1973-76. *Appointments:* Company Director, Rest-Ezi Furniture P/L; Consultant, Coopers and Lybrand; Consultant, Arthur Andersen & Co. *Memberships:* Association Internationale Des Etudiants En Sciences Economiques Et Commerciales, 1973-79; National President (Australia), 1978-79; National Exchange Controller (Australia), 1975-76. *Creative Works:* Active role in developing AIESEC in Australia, so that as many Australian business students as possible can gain the benefit of AIESEC training schemes within Australia and overseas, and reciprocally foreign business students in Australia; Active role in ensuring the Australian AIESEC plays an active part with the other 56 AIESEC member countries. *Hobbies:* Wine; Sailing; Investment Markets. *Address:* 10 Hesperus Street, Pymble, NSW 2073, Australia.

TODD, John Francis James, b. 20 May, 1937, Leeds, England. University Senior Lecturer and College Master. m. Mavis Georgina, 15 June, 1963, 3 sons. *Education:* BSc Class 1 Hons, Leeds University, 1955-59; PhD, Leeds University, 1959-62; Associate of Royal Institute of Chemistry, 1961; Fellow of Royal Institute of Chemistry, 1974; Chartered Chemist, 1975. *Appointments:* Research Fellow, Leeds University, 1962-63; Research Fellow, Yale University, USA, 1963-65; Assistant Lecturer in Chemistry, 1965-66, Lecturer in Chemistry, 1966-73, College Tutor, 1966-74, Senior Lecturer in Chemistry, 1973-, Master of Rutherford College, 1975-, re-elected, 1980, Kent University; Chairmn, Canterbury an Thanet Health Authority, 1982. *Memberships:* International Union of Pure and Applied Chemistry (Titular member) and Chairman of Mass Spectroscopy Sub-Committee, 1979-83; Chairman, British Mass Spectrometry Society, 1980-82; Fellow, Royal Society of Chemistry; Institute of Measurement and Control and Chartered Measurement and Control Technologist, 1978; Institution of Environmental Science. *Publications:* Dynamic Mass Spectrometry, Vol. 4 published 1976; Vol 5 published 1978; Vol 6

published 1981 jointly edited with D. Price, London. *Honours:* Lowson Chemistry Prize, Leeds Grammar School, 1953; J.B. Cohen Prize in Chemistry, Leeds University, 1963; Fulbright Research Scholar, USA, 1963-65. *Hobbies:* Travel; Music. *Address:* West Bank, 122 Whitstable Road, Canterbury, Kent, CT2 8EG, England.

TOFT, Luke Alexander, b. 21 Nov. 1923, Wandsworth, London, England. Chartered Engineer, Fellow, Institute of Mechanical Engineers. m. Florence Sarah Brown, 3 Dec. 1949, 2 daughters. *Education:* ONC, HNC, Wimbledon Technical College, 1938-43; HNC & ONC endorsements, Portsmouth Municipal College, 1943-44. *Appointments:* Cabinet Shop Labourer, Vickers Sewing Machines Ltd., 1938; Machinist, Watliff Ltd., Morden, Surrey, 1938-39; Toolroom Apprentice, Bryce Ltd., Hackbridge, Surrey, 1939-43; Draughtsman, Ministry of Aircraft Production, Aircraft Torpedo Development Unit, Gosport, Hants. 1943-46; Engineering Assistant, Ministry of Works, London. 1946-56; Inco Europe Ltd., originally The Mond Nickel Co., Ltd., Clydach, Swansea, W. Glamorgan, Development Engineer, 1956-68, Head of Engineering Design and Development Section, 1968-. *Memberships:* Institution of Mechanical Engineers, South Wales Branch Committee; The Gower Society, Committee member, 1973-; The National Trust; Royal Institution of S. Wales. Rotary Kiln Nickel Carbonyl Plant. *Publications:* Patents on Rotary Kiln Seals and Scoops; Booklets, Parish and Church of St. Mary, Pennard, Gower, and Noteworthy Gower Churches, 1981; Historical papers in Gower Society Journals Nos. 23, 26 and 31 also in Welsh Churchman, 1972. *Hobbies:* History—Local and Industrial; Photography; Natural History. *Address:* 42 Sunningdale Avenue, Mayals, Swansea, West Glamorgan, Wales.

TOH, Chin Chye, b. 10 Dec. 1921, Perak, Malaysia. Physiologist. *Education:* Graduated in Science from Raffles College, S'pore and the University of London, 1947; Post graduate studies for a PhD in physiology at National Institute for Medical Research, London, 1952. *Appointments:* Physiology Lecturer, University of Singapore, 1953-58; Reader, (Physiology), University of Singapore, 1958-64; Deputy Prime Minister, 1959-68; Research Associate, University of Singapore, 1964; Vice-Chancellor, University of Singapore, 1968-75 and Minister for Science and Technology; Minister for Health, 1975-. *Memberships:* Singapore Association for the Advancement of Science. *Publications:* Effects of Intracerebroventricularly Injected Nerveside on Free Behaviour and EEG Activity of Rats, A Pilot Study (with R. Scherschlicht, E.P. Bonetti) Arch. Int. Pharmacodyn Therap. 239, 221-229, 1979; A Regional Institute of Higher Education and Development in South East Asia in the World Year Book of Education 1972-3; Universities Facing the Future; Science and Technology for Two Million, 1975. *Honours:* Hon.D.Litt, University of Singapore, 1976. *Address:* 23 Greenview Crescent, Singapore, 1128.

TOM, Jean Marion, (Mrs. W. E. Tom), b. 8 Aug. 1922, Romsey, Victoria, Australia. Grazier. m. William Ernest, 6 July, 1946, 1 son, 4 daughters. *Education:* BS, 1943; MS(Hons), 1946. *Appointments:* School of Physiology, University of Melbourne, 1944-46. *Memberships:* State President, Country Womens Association of Victoria, 1979-81; National C.W.A. Conferences in Hobart, 1973, Brisbane 1975, Melbourne, 1977; Leader of Delegation, Adelaide, 1979; Attended Sydney, 1981; Leader delegation Nairobi, Kenya, 1977; Fiji, 1979; Hamburg, W. Germany, 1980; Planning Committee Member, Regional Conference, Victoria, 1982; Status of Women Committee, Victoria, 1977-79; Fairlea Womens Prison Council, 1979-81; Freedom from Hunger Committee, Victoria, 1979-81; Victoria and its People Committee, 1979-84; Planning for 150th Anniversary of White Settlement in Victoria in 1984-85. *Honours:* Exhibition in Physiology and Biochemistry, 1943. *Hobbies:* Reading; Craft; Gardening. *Address:* Chintin Grange, Wallan, 3654, Victoria, Australia.

TOMES, David, b. 1 Apr. 1932, Shepshed, Leicestershire, England. Schoolmaster. *Education:* MA, St. Catherines, Oxford, 1951-54; Certificate of Education, St. Catherines, Cambridge, 1955-56; Fellow, Institute of Physics, 1971. *Appointments:* Bristol Grammar School, 1955-60; Clifton College, Bristol, 1960-67; Wellington College, 1967-78; Head of Science, Eton College, 1978-. *Memberships:* Fellow, Institute of

Physics; Oxford Cambridge Club. *Publications:* Editor, Physics Monographs (Macmillan's); Joint Author, Physics Questions (Heinemann Educational); Originator of Physics and Maths—a new A level. *Hobbies:* Travel; Music; Theatre. *Address:* Baldwin's End Cottage, Eton College, Windsor, SL4 6DB, England.

TOM-GEORGE, Sotonye, b. 15 Sept. 1949, Buguma, Nigeria. Legal Practitioner. m. 3 Jan, 1976, 2 daughters. *Education:* LLB Hons., B.L. *Appointments:* Manager, Dewe Export and Importing; Manager, Denton West Enterprises; Part-time Managerial Supervision of Companies in England; Retains and still holds Legal Retainer to a number of Companies and Banks; Retains and still holds Board Appointment of Private and Government Companies. *Memberships:* Rosicrucian Order, Legal Adviser; Federation of International Women; Lawyers Association; Nigerian Bael Association. *Hobbies:* Travelling; Dancing; Reading; Singing; Swimming; Golfing. *Address:* 11 Ogoloma Street, P.O. Box 2349, Port Harcourt, Nigeria.

TOMKINSON, John Stanley, b. 8 Mar. 1916, Stafford, England. Gynaecologist and Obstetrician. m. Barbara Marie, 31 Mar. 1954, 2 sons, 1 daughter. *Education:* MB, ChB, Birmingham University, 1941; MRCS, LRCP, Conjoint Board, England, 1941; FRCS, England, 1949; MRCOG, 1952; FRCOG, 1967. *Appointments:* Consultant Gynaecologist and Obstetrician, Guys Hospital, Queen Charlottes Maternity Hospital, Chelsea Hospital for Women, London, England, 1953-79; Consultant Adviser in Gynaecology and Obstetrics to the Department of Health and Social Security, England and Wales, 1966; Secretary, General International Federation of Gynaecology and Obstetrics, 1976-. *Memberships:* Continental Society Gynecology and Obstetrics of USA; Gynaecological Society of Great Britain; South African Society of Gynaecology and Obstetrics; Italian Society of Gynaecology and Obstetrics; Spanish Society of Gynaecology and Obstetrics; Romanian Society of Gynaecology and Obstetrics; Nigerian Society of Gynaecology and Obstetrics. *Publications:* Publications in General Surgery, Gynaecology, Obstetrics and Midwifery; Confidential Enquiries in Maternal Mortality in England and Wales, published HMSO 1967-69; 1970-72; 1973-75; 1976-78. *Honours:* Surgical Prize, University of Birmingham, 1939; Priestley Smith Prize Ophthalmology, University of Birmingham, 1941; Commander of the Most Excellent Order of the British Empire, 1981. *Hobbies:* Fly Fishing; Fly Tying; The Arts. *Address:* 140 Priory Lane, Roe Hampton, London, SW15 5JP, England.

TOMLINSON, Alfred Richard, b. 28th June, 1915, Perth, Western Australia. Public Servant. m. Thelma Pitschel, 17th Oct. 1942. *Education:* Associate of the Australian Society of Accountants, 1939. *Appointments:* O/C Vermin Control Branch, Department of Agriculture, Western Australia, 1949; Chairman & Chief Executive Officer, newly created Agriculture Protection Board, Western Australia, 1951; Deputy Chairman & Chief Executive Office, 1954; Retired, 28th June, 1980. *Appointments:* The Royal Society of Western Australia, Resigned 1980. Until retired, was a member of the West Australian Wildlife Authority since its establishment in 1952 and previously a member of the predecessor body; Was the inaugural Chairman of the Vertebrate Pest Committee of the Australian Standing Committee on Agriculture. Established & developed organised control of vertebrate pests in Western Australia and led the successful campaign to control rabbits in the 1950's. *Honours:* Companion of the Imperial Service Order, ISO, 1st Jan. 1981. *Hobbies:* Gardening; Walking; Swimming. *Address:* 6, Kildare Road, Floreat Park, Western Australia, 6014.

TOMLINSON, Robert Peter, b. 4 April, 1943, Bristol, England. Managing Director, Beacon Radio. m. Mary Wild, 19 Aug. 1967, 2 daughters. *Education:* BA, English Literature, Worcester College, Oxford, 1962-66. *Appointments:* Management Trainee, De La Rue, 1966-68; Presenter, HTV, 1968-71; Presenter, Granada TV, 1971-72; Presenter/Announcer, ATV, 1972-79 and Freelance Communications Consultant; Managing Director, Beacon Radio, 1979-. *Memberships:* Lord's Taverners; Institute of Directors; BRSCC; Wolverhampton Chamber of Commerce, Vice-President; AIRC, Council Member. *Hobbies:* Cricket; Game Shooting; Motor Racing. *Address:* White Gates, Blakeshall, Wolverley, Near Kidderminster, Worcs. DY11 5XR, England.

TOMPOROWSKI, Garry Joseph, b. 7 Feb. 1949, Prince Albert, Saskatchewan, Canada. *Education:* Bachelor of Environmental Studies, 1970; Master of Architecture, 1973. *Appointments:* Number 10 Architectural Group, 1972-73; Jack M. Ross, Architect, 1973-75; Design 4 Architects, 1975-76; Dept., Northern Saskatchewan, 1976-77; Tomporowski Architect Limited, 1977-. *Memberships:* Royal Architectural Institute of Canada; Councillor, Saskatchewan Association of Architects; Manitoba Association of Architects. *Creative Works:* Numerous designs for Office, Retail, Hotel, Educational and Recreational Projects in Western Canada; Vice-President of Twin Grand Developments Limited, a Real Estate Development Company. *Honours:* Manitoba Association of Architects Prize for Excellence in Design, 1972. *Hobbies:* Photography; Hunting; Fishing; Firearm Collecting. *Address:* 366 20th St W, Prince Albert, Saskatchewan, Canada.

TOMS, Kenneth Norman, b. 18 March, 1927, Brisbane, Queensland, Australia. Surveyor. M. Susan B. Pinn, 30 July, 1955, 1 son, 1 daughter. *Education:* Bachelor of Surveying, University of Queensland, 1951; BEcon. University of Queensland, 1968; Master of Urban Studies, University of Queensland, 1972. *Appointments:* Surveyor, Joint Court of the New Hebrides, S.W. Pacific, 1952-54; Surveyor with British Petroleum Company in UK and Kuwait, 1954-55; Lecturer in Surveying, College of Estate Management, London, 1956-57; Senior Surveyor-District Surveyor, Her Majesty's Overseas Civil Service in Northern Nigeria and North Borneo, 1957-65; Consultant Surveyor, South East Queensland, 1965-67; Senior Lecturer, School of Engineering, Queensland Institute of Technology, 1967-71; Head of Department of Surveying, Tasmanian College of Advanced Education, 1971-75; Lecturer in Surveying, University of Queensland, 1975-77; Head, Department of Surveying, Queensland Institute of Technology, Brisbane, 1977-. *Memberships:* Professional Associate, Royal Institution of Chartered Surveyors; Fellow, Institution of Surveyors, Australia; Member Australian Institute of Cartographers; The Photogrammetric Society, London. *Publications:* Monograph: Urban Government, Politics and Planning: A Study of The Brisbane Town Plan, 1974; Published eleven journal articles. *Honours:* Member, Order of the British Empire, 1965; Recipient of Institution of Surveyors, Australia R.D. Steele Prize for 1974 and again for 1976. *Hobby:* Boating. *Address:* 27, Chancellor Street, Sherwood, Queensland, Australia, 4075.

TONG, James Stuart, b. 4 Feb. 1913, Owensboro, Kentucky, USA. Administrator. *Education:* MA, Loyola University of Chicago, 1939; Licentiate in Theology, St. Mary's College, Kurseong, India, 1946; Diploma in Hospital Administration, St. Louis University, Missouri, USA, 1961. *Appointments:* Religious Lecturer, 1947-56; Executive Director, Catholic Hospital Association of India, 1957-73; National Director, Catholic Nurses Guild of India, 1958-68; Executive Director, Voluontary Health Association of India, 1974-80. *Memberships:* Society of Jesus; International Hospital Federation; Natural Family Planning Association of India; Catholic News Service of India Society; Catholic Hospital Association of India; Amnesty International; Indian Hospital Association; Transactional Analysis Society of India; Communication for Development Society. *Publications:* Editor of Medical Service; The Lotus and the Lamp; Hospital Administration; Health for the Millions. Stimulated founding of St. Xavier's High School, Delhi, 1959. *Honours:* Ordained Catholic Priest, 1945; became an Indian Citizen, 1958; Honorary Doctorate of Humane Letters, Loyola University, Chicago, 1969; Commissioned a Kentucky Colonel by Governor Wendell H. Ford, 1973. *Hobbies:* Friendships and Letter Writing. *Address:* The Voluntary Health Association of India, C14 Community Centre, Safdarjang Development Area, New Delhi, 110016, India.

TONKIN, Arthur Raymond, b. 21 Jan, 1930, Kelmscott, W. Australia. Member of Legislative Assembly. m. (1) Judith, 10 May, 1958, 2 sons, 1 daughter; (2) Ina, 25 Oct. 1975. *Education:* BA, University of W. Australia, 1958; Diploma of Education, University of W. Australia, 1960. *Appointments:* Teacher of History and Economics; Member of Parliament. *Publications:* The

Example. *Hobbies:* Writing; Reading; Talking. *Address:* 31, Ireland Way, Bassendean, 6054, Western Australia.

TONKS, Robert Stanley, b. 13 Aug. 1928, Aberystwyth, Wales. Pharmacologist and University Dean. m. Diana M. Cownie, 29 July, 1953, 1 son, 3 daughters. *Education:* University College, Cardiff, 1948-49; Welsh College of Pharmacy and Welsh National School of Medicine, 1949-51; Bachelor of Pharmacy, University of Wales; Welsh National School of Medicine, Cardiff, 1951-54; Doctor of Philosophy in Pharmacology, University of Wales; Pharmaceutical Chemist, 1952; Fellow of Pharmaceutical Society of Great Britain, 1954; Fellow of Institute of Biology, 1973. *Appointments:* Organon Post Doctoral Fellow, Medical School, Cardiff, 1954-55; Post Doctoral Fellow, National Health Service, Medical School, Cardiff and Nevill Hall Hospital, Abergavenny, 1955-58; Clinical Lecturer in Pharmacology, University of Wales, 1958-72; Visiting Research Fellow, Faculte de Medicine, Paris, France, 1959; Senior Lecturer in Materia Medica, Pharmacology and Therapeutics, Medical School, Cardiff, 1972-73; Professor, Dalhousie University, 1973-; Director, College of Pharmacy, Dalhousie University, 1973-77; Dean, Faculty of Health Professions, Dalhousie University, Halifax, Canada, 1977-. *Memberships:* Co-Chairman, Northeast Canadian/American Health Council; Member, Canadian Society for Clinical Investigation; International Society on Thrombosis and Haemostasis; Physiological Society, London; British Pharmacology Society; Biochemical Society, London; Fellow, Institute of Biology, London; Fellow, Pharmaceutical Society of Great Britain. *Publications:* Contributed to various professional journals. *Honours:* Honorary Member, Canadian Society for Hospital Pharmacy, 1974; Honorary Member, New Brunswick Pharmaceutical Society, 1977; Certificate of Merit, Nova Scotia Pharmaceutical Society, 1977. *Hobbies:* Skiing; Skating; Hiking; Tenting; Horse-riding; Furniture-making; Painting; Music; Meeting and talking to interesting people. *Address:* 6061, Fraser Street, Halifax, Nova Scotia, Canada, B3H 1R8.

TONSON, Albert Ernest, b. 18 June, 1917, Auckland, New Zealand. Governing Director. m. Josephine M. Stacey, 16 Feb. 1955, (deceased 1981), 3 daughters. *Education:* Druleigh College; University of Auckland. *Appointments:* Company Director, Paramount Enterprises Ltd. Inc. Tonson Publishing House, 1946-. *Memberships:* President, Commonwealth Heraldry Board; Executive Vice-President, Heraldry Society, N.Z. Branch, Inc; Fellow, Heraldry Society New Zealand; Fellow, Heraldry Society Australia; Fellow, Royal Geographical Society; Fellow, Royal Society Arts; Auckland Historical Society; Member, Royal Society Literature; Member Companion, Military and Hospitaller Order of St. Lazarus of Jerusalem. *Publications:* Co-author and editor, Papatoetoe History; Author of Manukau History and about 100 articles on Heraldry; Editor, Commonwealth Heraldry Bulletin and New Zealand Armorist. *Hobbies:* Writing (History & Heraldry); Literature; Music; Fine Arts; Photography; Genealogy and all things Antiquarian. *Address:* 19 Pah Road, Papatoetoe, Auckland, New Zealand.

TOSHNIWAL, Gaurishankar S, b. 2 Apr. 1920, Ajmer. Business. m. Pushpa, 3 July, 1941, 2 sons. 02 BCom, University of Allahabad, 1940; Dr. of Naturopathy. *Appointments:* Founder & Managing Director, Toshniwal Bros. P. Ltd, Bombay, Madras, Calcutta, Cochin, Bangalore, Delhi, Hyderabad, Indore, Ajmer; Founder, Chairman & Managing Director, Toshniwal Bros (SR) P. Ltd, Madras; Chairman, BT Solders P Ltd, Bombay, Mysore; Chairman, Toshniwal Process Instuments P. Ltd, Bombay; Chairman, Toshniwal Instruments Manufacturing P Ltd, Bombay, Ajmer; Toshniwal Charity Trust, Ajmer; Director, Multimetals Ltd, Kota; Director, Toshniwal Industries P. Ltd, Bombay, Ajmer. *Memberships:* President, Arya Putri Higher Secondary School, Ajmer; President, Rajasthan Pranthiya Prakrutick Chikitsa Parishad, Jaipur; Board of Management, Shramik Vidyapeeth, Government of Rajasthan, Ajmer; Working Committee, All India Prakrutik Chikitsa Parishad, New Delhi; Rt. Past President & Senior Active, Rotary Club, Ajmer; Rotary Paul Harris Fellow. *Publications:* Editor, Monthly Magazine, Seva, 1937-40; Articles on various topics in Weekly & Monthly Journals and Magazines. *Hobbies:* Gardening; Photography; Reading & Writing;

Naturopathy. *Address:* Pushp Vatika, Gokhale Marg, Ajmer 305 001.

TOTTENHAM-SMITH, Ralph Norman, b. 4 March, 1923, Constanza, Rumania. Petroleum Executive. m. (1) 1 Jan, 1949, 2 sons, 1 daughter; (2) 18 April, 1981. *Education:* BA(Hons), Cantab, Modern Languages and Geography, Emmanuel College, Cambridge, 1948. *Appointments:* British Petroleum Co. Ltd., 1949-; Area Manager, France and North Africa, 1955-59; BP Shareholders Representative in Paris, 1959-61; Executive Vice-President and then President of BP Canada Ltd, 1961-66; Senior Planner, London, 1967-69; Regional Co-ordinator for Africa, 1969-76; Managing Director, BP Africa Medwest Ltd., Also Director affiliated companies, 1976-. *Memberships:* West African Committee; Royal Commonwealth Society. *Hobbies:* Tennis; Squash. *Address:* 'Georgeville', Hurtmore Road, Godalming, Surrey, England.

TOUCHIN, Colin Michael, b. 3 Apr. 1953, Liverpool, England. Composer, Freelance Musician, Conductor, Clarinet & Recorder. *Education:* BA, Music, Keble College, Oxford, 1971-74; MA, Music, Manchester University, Department of Education, 1974-75; Licentiate of the Trinity College of Music, London, Performer's Diploma on Recorder, 1969. *Appointments:* Peripatetic Clarinet Teacher, Cheshire Education Authority, 1974-78; Clarinet Teacher, William Hulme's G.S, Manchester G.S, Lore to G.S, Altrincham, 1975-80; Staff coach and conductor. Stockport Youth Orchestra, 1975-78; Stockport Recorder College, 1974-; Trafford Youth Orchestras, 1979-; Founder, Bowdon Sinfonietta, 1972, Bowdon Sinfonietta Wind Band, 1977, and Conductor; Musical Director local amateur wind bands and orchestras. *Memberships:* Musicians' Union; Incorporated Society of Musicians, Manchester Branch Committee, 1979-; Performing Rights' Society; Society of Recorder Players, Executive Committee, 1977-79; Clarinet & Saxophone Society of Great Britain; North West Arts Association; Youth Hostelling Association; Friends of Trafford Youth Orchestras. *Publications:* Chamber Symphony, Op. 18, 1974; Divertimento, Op. 22, wind quintent, 1974; Stars in the Dark Clouds, a cantata for spring, 1980; Pale Cast of Thought, 1980; Sinfonietta No.2, 1981; Havelock, a dance-drama, 1981; Over 40 Scores for theatre; Film score, Rebirth, 1979; Concertante, Op.27 bassoon and piano, premiered Wigmore Hall, 1979; LP, Songs from around the World, 1978. *Honours:* 1974, Oxford Festival, Lennox Berkely Composition Trophy for Divertimento; Concerto Medal for Mozart's Clarinet Concerto, 1980; Hale Barns Festival, commission for cantata Stars in the Dark Clouds; 1980, North West Arts Commission, Pale Cast of Thought; 9 performances on NWA Circuit, 1981; Lincolnshire and Humberside Arts Commission for Havelock. *Hobbies:* Cycling; Reading; Theatre; Hostelling; Letter-writing. *Address:* 180 Framingham Road, Brooklands, Sale, M33 3RG, England.

TOUGH, Alan Ronald, b. 25 May 1939, Perth, Australia. Engineer. m. Ingrid Magdalena Huisken, 1963, 3 daughters. *Education:* University of Western Australia, Bachelor of Engineering, (Hons), 1957-62, Master of Business Administration, 1972-76. *Appointments:* W.E. Bassett & Partners, Consulting Engineers, 1963; Geo. Wimpey & Co. London, Construction Company, 1963-66; Manager, Design and Engineering, Austin Anderson, Melbourne, 1967-70; General Manager, J. & E. Ledger Pty. Ltd., Perth, 1970-72; Ministerial Consultant, Department of Industrial Development, Western Australian Government, 1972-73; Director, Merchant Bank, Westralian International Ltd., 1973-76; Managing Director, Seconded from Westralian International Ltd., To Allied Eneabba Ltd., 1976-. *Memberships:* Associate Fellow, Australian Institute of Management; Royal Perth Yacht Club. *Address:* 112 Circe Circle, Dalkeith, Perth, Western Ausralia 6009.

TOWEETT, Taaitta, b. 5 May 1925, Kericho District, Kenya. Politician, Writer, Educator. m. 1952, 1960, 15 sons, 11 daughters. *Education:* BA, University of South Africa, 1956; Diploma in Public & Social Administration, Torquay, 1956; BA(Hons), Unisa, 1959; MA, Linguistics, Nairobi, 1975; PhD, Linguistics, Nairobi, 1977. *Appointments:* Community Development Officer, 1950-58; Member of Parliament, Kenya, 1958-64; Chairman of Federation of Co-operatives, 1964-68; Member of Parliament, 1969-79; President of 19th Unesco General Conference; Was Minister of Government for 12 years while in Parliament in different Ministries; Director of Studies of U.K. Examinations, Secretarial College, 1979-. *Memberships:* The Writers Association of Kenya; Red Cross; Lions Club; The Royal Commonwealth Society; The Historical Society of Kenya. *Publications:* A Study of Kalenjin Linguistics; English, Swahili, Kalenjin Nouns Pocket Dictionary; Oral Traditional History of the Kipsigis; Tears over a Dead Cow & other stories; Epitaph on Colonialism & Shorter Poems; 100 Daily Essays; An African's Year in England; Dr. Toweett's English, Swahili, Kalenjin Verbs Dictionary. *Hobbies:* Inquiring into the meanings of Personal Names. *Address:* P.O. Box 1075, Kisumu, Kenya.

TOWNLEY, Michael, b. 4 Nov. 1934, Hobart, Tasmania, Australia. Senator for Tasmania in Federal Parliament. *Education:* Engineering Degree, University of Tasmania, 1959; Pharmacy Diploma, Hobart Technical College, 1963. *Appointments:* Telecomunications, University of Toronto, Canada; Then Self Employed, Parmacy, 1963-. *Memberships:* Senator for Tasmania, 1971-. *Hobbies:* Squash; Flying; Running. *Address:* 6 Broadwater Parade, Sandy Bay, Tasmania, Australia, 7005.

TOWNROW, Jocelyn Elizabeth Suzanne, (nee Davies), b. 9 Feb. 1932, Masterton, New Zealand. Part-time University Lecturer in Agricultural Botany. m. 7 July 1955 (Divorced), 1 son, 2 daughters. *Education:* BSc Hons., Agricultural Botany, Reading University, England, 1955; Geology I, University of Tasmania, Australia, 1966; Ph.D., Agricultural Science, University of Tasmania, Australia, 1978. *Appointments:* Demonstrator in Biology, Ibadan University College, Nigeria, 1955-56; Research Fellow, Department Agricultural Science, University of Tasmania, 1966; Lecturer, Department Agricultural Science in charge of Plant Taxonomy, University of Tasmania, 1966-; Honorary Research Associate, Department Agricultural Science, University of Tasmania, 1979-. *Memberships:* Board of Trustees, Royal Tasmanian Botanical Gardens, 1978; Royal Society of Tasmania, Councillor, 1979; British Lichen Society, 1968. *Publications:* Some Grasses of South Western, Nigeria; Studies in the Genus Shipa (Graminlae) in Tasmania. *Honours:* Isle of Wight Major Award, 1952-55; Royal Life Saving Society Diploma, 1950; Freda Bage Bursary, 1973; Science & Industry Endowment Fund Grant, 1973. *Hobbies:* Pottery; Sailing; Choral singing; Classical music. *Address:* 10 Senator Street, Newtown, Tasmania 7008, Australia.

TOWNSEND, Sydney Lance, b. 17 Dec. 1912, Geelong, Victoria, Australia. Professor Emeritus. m. 31 Mar. 1943, 1 son, 3 daughters. *Education:* M.B., B.S., University of Melbourne, 1935; M.D., University of Melbourne, 1959. *Appointments:* Appointed Senior Lecturer, Department of Obstectics & Gynaecology, University of Melbourne, 1948; First Professor, Obstetrics & Gynaecology, Australia, 1951-77; In-Patient Gynaecologist, Royal Women's Hospital, In-patient Obstetrician, Royal Women's Hospital, 1951-77; Gynaecologist, Peter MacCallum Clinic, 1960-77. *Memberships:* Dean, Faculty of Medicine, University of Medicine; College of Obstetricians & Gynaecologists, South Africa; American College of Obstetricians & Gynaecologists; American College of Surgeons; Australian College of Medical Administrators; Royal Australasian College of Physicians; Australian College of Obstetrcians & Gynaecologists. *Publications:* Contributor of reviews, monographs, articles to professional journals and conferences. *Honours:* Knight Bachelor, New Year Honours, 1971; MD, BS, MGO, Melbourne; Hon. LLD, Monash; DTM & H, London; FRCS, Edinburgh; FACS, FRACS, FRCOG, FRACP, FRACMA, FRACOG, Hon FRCS, Canada; Hon. FACOG, Hon. FCOG, South Africa. *Hobbies:* Philately; Sailing; Golf. *Address:* 28 Ryeburne Avenue, Hawthorn East, Vicoria 3123, Australia.

TOWNSHEND, Walter John, b. 18 Oct. 1913, Managing Director. m. Dorrian Ida Powell, 31 Dec. 1938, 2 sons. *Appointments:* Salesman & Later Manager, The Sports House, Pretoria, 1930-39; Director, Alick Stuart Ltd, Bulawayo, 1954; Managing Director, Townshend & Butcher, (1957), PVT, Ltd., 1955-; Managing Director, Tower Holdings, PVT, Ltd., 1957-78; Managing Director, Aliwal Investments, PVT. Ltd., 1957-78; Managing Director, Tab Industries, 1961-75; Managing Director, Dorrian Sports PVT Ltd., 1978-; Managing Director, Favex, PVT, Ltd. 1980. *Memberships:* Chair-

man, Rhodesia Education Advisory Board to Minister of Education, 1978-80; Bulawayo Chamber of Commerce, 1972-81; Standards Association of Central Africa, 1977. *Honours:* Awarded Air Force Cross, 1945; Member Legion Merit, 1978. *Address:* P.O. Box 82, 82 Abercorn Street, Bulawayo, South Africa.

TRACEY, Christopher Geoffrey, b. 31 Dec. 1923, Gutu, Zimbabwe. Businessman. m. 10 Aug. 1946, 3 daughters. *Education:* Ruzawi, Zimbabwe; Blundells, England. *Appointments:* Chairman of 45 Companies. *Memberships:* Salisbury Club, Salisbury; The Farmers Club, London. *Honours:* Recipient of Independence Commemorative Decoration, 1970; Officer of the Legion of Merit, 1979; Rhodesian Farming Oscar, 1972; Rhodesian Businessman of the Year Award, 1977. *Address:* Willand, 83 Orange Grove Drive, Highlands, Salisbury, Zimbabwe.

TRAINER, John Patrick, b. 24 Mar. 1943, Norwood, Adelaide, South Australia. Member of State Parliament. m. Rosemary Martha Rutter, 26 Nov. 1964, 1 son, 2 daughters. *Education:* Rostrevor College, 1956-60; Diploma of Teaching, Adelaide Teachers College, 1961-66; AUA, 1967, BA, 1972, Adelaide University, 1961-72. *Appointments:* Secondary School Teacher, 1965-74; Senior Advisory Teacher, Educational Technology Centre, South Australia Education Department, 1975-79; Member, State Parliament for Ascot Park, 1979-. *Memberships:* Australian Labour Party State Executive, 1975-80; Flinders University Council, 1979-; Justice of the Peace, 1980-. *Publications:* Regular column in Sunday Mail Newspaper; Represented South Australian Parliamentarians in televised debate with Oxford University Union Team. *Hobbies:* Reading; Photography. *Address:* 559 Marion Road, South Plympton 5038, South Australia.

TRAPP, George, b. 30 Dec. 1906, Falkirk, Stirlingshire, Scotland, United Kingdom. Biologist. m. Alice Mary Thomson, 26 Dec. 1945, 1 son, 2 daughters. *Education:* MA, University of Glasgow, 1929; BSc, Hons, 1930; PhD, 1934; DIPED, University of Edinburgh, 1933; BCOM, 1940; LLB, 1969; Diplome de la Langue Francaise, Universite de Besancon, 1938; Diplome D'Etudes Francaises, Universite de Nancy, 1939. *Appointments:* Demonstrator, University of Glasgow, 1929-33; Science Master, High School of Falkirk, 1934-36; Head of Biology Department, George Watsons College, Edinburgh; Assistant Director of Education, County of Aberdeen, 1943-48; Rector, The Gordon Schools, Huntly, 1948-60. *Memberships:* Fellow, Royal Society of Edinburgh, 1941; Fellow, The Linnean Society of London, 1944; International Commission of Jurists, 1960; The College Club, Glasgow University, 1976. *Publications:* Contributed to various professional journals. *Honours:* Recipient of Dobbie-Smith Gold Medal for Scientific research, University of Glasgow, 1932; Exhibitioner to the British Association for the Advancement of Science, York meeting, 1932; Alexander Darling Scholarship in Business and Administrative Subjects, University of Edinburgh, 1940. *Hobbies:* Gardening; Travel. *Address:* 11 Moston Terrace, Edinburgh EH9 2DE, Scotland.

TREDREA, Norman Frederick Trevithick, b. 17 Apr. 1927, Perth, Western Australia. Educational Administration and Education. m. Audrey Jean Rutherford, 6 May 1950, 1 son, 3 daughters. *Education:* BE, University of Western Australia, 1957; BA, University of Western Australia, 1961; Graduate Diploma in Educational Administration, Western Australian Institute of Technology. *Appointments:* Superintendent of Education, Kimberley and North West Schools and North East Metropolitan Schools in Western Australia, 1968-71; Superintendent of Education, Country South West Region, 1972-74; Vice Principal of Western Australia Secondary Teachers' College, 1974-76; Assistant Director of Staffing, Primary Schools, Education Department, Western Australia, 1976-81. *Memberships:* Australian College of Education; Institute of Educational Research; President, Western Australian Institute of Superintendents of Education; Australasian Association of Institutes of Inspectors of Schools; Executive Committeeman of the Celtic Club, Western Australia; Convocation of the University of Western Australia; Chairman of the Board, Western Australian Secondary Teachers' College; Councillor, Western Australian teachers' Education Authority; Board for the Teachers' Registration Board. *Publications:* Contributed articles to various professional journals. *Hobbies:* Educational Administration; Staff participation in Government; Solar Energy; Photography; Squash; Jogging. *Address:* 202 Herbert Street, Doubleview 6018, Western Australia.

TRENHOLME, Margery Wynne, b. 20th Apr. 1913, Columbia, MO, USA. Librarian. *Education:* BA, McGill, 1935; High-School Teaching Diploma, McGill, 1936; Bachelor of Library Science, McGill, 1946. *Appointments:* Four years elementary School teacher, 1936-39; Private Secretary, 1939-45; Library Cataloguer, Harvard Law School, 1946-47; Librarian, McGill Fraser Institute, later Fraser-Hickson, Montreal, 1950-. *Memberships:* Canadian Federation of University Women, Office of Membership, Secretary; Recording Secretary, Chairman of Fellowships Committee, 1967-80; University Women's Club of Montreal Inc., Office of President and Treasurer, 1963-66; Life member of the Canadian Library Association, Member of the Corp. of Professional Librarians of Quebec; l'Assn. pour l'avancement des sciences et des techniques de la documentation. Governor, The Montreal General Hospital Foundation. *Hobbies:* Travel; Photography. *Address:* 4990 Clanranald 5, Montreal, Quebec, Canada H3X 2S2.

TRESCOWTHICK, Donald Henry KBE, (Sir) b. 4th Dec. 1930, Ballarat, Victoria, Australia. m. Norma Margaret Callaghan, 25th Oct. 1952, 2 sons, 2 daughters. *Appointments:* Chairman of Directors, Charles Davis Ltd. and Subsidiaries; Chairman of Directors, HSD Property Trust; Chairman of Directors, Investment & Merchant Finance Corporation Ltd. and Subsidiaries; Chairman of Directors, Swann Insurance Ltd. and Subsidiaries; Chairman of Directors, Perpetual Insurance & Securities (Aust.) Ltd; Chairman of Directors, The Signet Group Pty. Ltd. *Memberships:* Lloyd's of London; The Australian Society of Accountants. *Honours:* Knight Commander of the Most Excellent Order of the British Empire. *Hobbies:* Tennis; Swimming; Reading. *Address:* 38A Lansell Road, Toorak, Victoria 3142, Australia.

TREVOR-ROPER, Hugh Redwald, (Lord Dacre of Glanton), b. 15 Jan. 1914, Glanton, Northumberland. Teacher. m. Lady Alexandra Haig, 4 Oct. 1954. *Education:* Christ Church, Oxford, 1932-6. *Appointments:* Research Fellow of Merton College, Oxford, 1938; Student, Tutor and Censor, Christ Church, Oxford, 1945-57; Regius Professor, Modern History, Oxford University, 1957-80; Master, Peterhouse, Cambridge, 1980. *Memberships:* Fellow of the British Academy; Corresponding Member, The American Academy. *Publications:* Archbishop Laud, 1940; The Last Days of Hitler, 1947; Historical Essays, 1957; Religion, The Reformation and Social Change, 1967; Hermit of Peking, 1976; Printers and Artists, 1976. *Honours:* Chevalier de la Legion d'Honneur, 1975; Created Baron Dacre of Glanton, 1979. *Address:* Chiefswood, Melrose, Scotland.

TRIANTAFYLLIDES, Solon, b. 5th Feb. 1932, Nicosia, Cyprus. Company Director, Chartered Accountant and Honorary Consul for Norway. m. Clio, 5th Jan. 1956, 2 daughters. *Education:* Chartered Accountant, qualified, London, 1956. *Appointments:* Director, George Giabra Pierides Ltd, 1957-; Director, Bank of Cyprus, 1962; Kermai Co. Ltd., 1968; Bank of Cyprus, (London), Ltd., Vice Chairman, 1975; Chairman Bank of Cyprus, (London) Ltd, 1978-; Deputy Chairman, Bank of Cyprus Holding Ltd., Cyprus, Bank of Cyprus, 1978-. *Memberships:* Chairman, Cyprus Employers Federation, 1968-70. *Honours:* Member first class of the St. Olavs Order. This is a Norwegian decoration, as The Honorary Consul for Norway in Cyprus since 1957. *Hobbies:* Tennis; Swimming; Reading. *Address:* 8, Aphrodite Street, Nicosia, Cyprus.

TRIBE, Derek Edward, b. 23rd Sept. 1926, England. m. Elizabeth Graham, 7th Sept. 1948, 2 sons, 1 daughter. *Education:* BSc, University of Reading, 1946; PhD, University of Aberdeen, 1949; M.Agr.Sc. University of Melbourne, Special Degree without examination, 1960; D.Agr.Sc. University of Melbourne, awarded for published work, 1969. *Appointments:* Scientific Officer, Rowett Research Institute, Aberdeen, 1949-52; Lecturer in Animal Nutrition, School of Veterinary Science, University of Bristol, 1952-56; Reader in the Physiology of Domestic Animals, School of Agriculture,

University of Melbourne, 1956-66; Professor of Agriculture, styled Animal Nutrition, University of Melbourne, 1966-80; Director, Australian Universities International Development Program, 1981-. *Memberships:* Member, Council, Canberra College of Advanced Education; Australian Institute of Agricultural Science; Australian Society of Animal Production; Royal Society of Arts, London; Council Member, Australian Academy of Technological Sciences. *Publications:* Written or edited seven books and published more than 100 articles and papers in scientific journals. *Honours:* Silver Medal of the Australian Institute of Agricultural Science, for contributions to agricultural research, 1969; Foundation Fellow of the Australian Academy of Technological Sciences, 1975; OBE, for services to education, 1977; Fellow, Australian Institute of Agricultural Science, 1977; Fellow, Australian Society of Animal Production, 1979; Emeritus Professor, University of Melbourne, 1980. *Hobbies:* Music; Literature; Gardening. *Address:* 23 Dugdale Street, Canberra, 2614, Australia.

TRIBE, Kenneth Wilberforce, b. 6th Feb. 1914, Sydney, Australia. Lawyer. 2 sons, 2 daughters. *Education:* LLB, Sydney University. *Appointments:* Solicitor in private practice, 1941-. *Memberships:* Commissioner, Australian Broadcasting Commission, 1979-; Australia Council, 1973-77; Chairman, Music Board, Australia Council, 1974-77; Chairman of Council, Sydney College of Arts, 1976-; Chairman, New South Wales State Cultural Advisory Committee, 1979-; President, New South Wales Adult Deaf Society, 1957-; Treasurer, Australian Deafness Council, 1975-; President and Chairman, Musica Vuia, Australia, 1949-; Interim General Manager, The Australian Opera, 1979-81. *Honours:* Membership of the Order of Australia, 1975. *Hobbies:* Music; Reading; Gardening. *Address:* 95, Elizabeth Bay Road, Sydney 2011, Australia.

TRINCA, Gordon Walgrave, b. 7th Jan. 1921, Melbourne, Australia. Medicine, General Surgeon. m. Elizabeth Harvey Robertson, 4th Dec. 1946, 2 sons, 1 daughter. *Education:* MBBS, Tertiary, University of Melbourne, 1945; Postgraduate, Diploma of Fellow, Royal Australasian College of Surgeons, 1958. *Appointments:* Resident Medical Office, Royal Melbourne Hospital, 1946; Senior RMO, Mooroopna & District Hospital, Victoria, 1947; Part-time Demonostrator in Anatomy, University of Melbourne, 1951-54; Tutor in Pathology, University of Melbourne, 1963-76; Honorary Associate Surgeon, Prince Henry's Hospital, Melbourne, 1956-58; Honorary Assistant Surgeon, Prince Henry's Hospital, Melbourne, 1958-61; Honorary Assistant Surgeon, Preston & Northcote Community Hospital, Melbourne, 1962-69; General Surgeon, Preston & Northcote Community Hospital, 1969-74; Senior General Surgeon, Preston & Northcote Community Hospital, Melbourne, 1974-. *Memberships:* National Chairman, Road Trauma Committee; Royal Australasian College of Surgeons; State Committee, Royal Australasian College of Surgeons; President, Board of Management, Ambulance Service, Melbourne; Vice-President, Western Pacific Region, International Association for Accident and Traffic Medicine; International Representative, Board of Directors, American Association of Automotive Medicine; Melbourne Cricket Club. *Publications:* Contributor of reviews, monographs, articles to professional journals and conferences. *Honours:* OBE, 1980; John Waite Medal, Lions International Award for Road Safety, 1978; The Gerin Medal, Traffic Medicine Award by International Association for Acident and Trafic Medicine, 1978; Award of Merit, American Association for Automotive Medicine, 1981; Honorary Fellow, Australian Institute of Ambulance Officers, 1977. *Hobbies:* Youth Work; Ecology & Conservation of Tropical Rainforests in Australia. *Address:* 29 Tintern Avenue, Toorak 3142, Melbourne, Australia.

TRIPATHY, Sriram Prasad, b. 24 Mar. 1934, Chikati, Orissa, India. Doctor of Medicine. m. Rekha, 22 May, 1956, 2 sons. *Education:* MB, BS(Hons), Utkal University, Cuttak, 1956; MD, (Bacteriology and Pathology), Andhra University, Visakhapatnam, 1961. *Appointments:* Demonstrator in Bacteriology, All India Institute of Medical Sciences, New Delhi, 1957-59; Assistant Professor of Bacteriology, Medical College, Buda, Orissa, 1961-62; Head of Laboratory, Tuberculosis Research Centre, Madras, India, 1962-69; Director, Tuberculosis Research Centre, Madras, India, 1969-.

Memberships: International Union Against Tuberculosis, Paris; Bacteriology Committee of the Eastern Region, International Union Against Tuberculosis; Standing Technical Committee, Tuberculosis Association of India; Indian Association of Pathologists and Microbiologists. *Publications:* Published over 50 papers in International and National Scientific journals either as Senior Author or Co-Author. *Honours:* Awarded, National Tuberculosis Association Fellowship in 1967, for training in USA; Wander-TAI Oration Award by the Tuberculosis Association of India, 1980. *Address:* 3 Sterling Avenue, Nungaunbakkam, Madras, 34, India.

TRIVEDI, Ram Krishna, b. 1st Jan. 1921, Myingyan, Burma. Civil Servant. m. Krishna Trivedi, 26th Feb. 1944, 4 sons, 1 daughter. *Education:* BA, Lucknow University, 1951; BA, Lucknow University, 1952; MA, Lucknow University, 1953. *Appointments:* Chairman & Managing Director, British India Corporation Ltd., Kanpur, UP; Advisor to the Government of Madhya Pradesh; Vice-Chancellor, Bundelkhand University, Jhansi, UP; Secretary to the Government of India, Department of Personnel and Administrative Reforms, Cabinet Secretariat, New Delhi; Addl. Secretary, Incharge, Department of Civil Supplies and Co-operation, Government of India; Addl. Secretary, Incharge, Planning Commission, Government of India, New Delhi; Chairman, UP State Electricity Board, Lucknow; Secretary to the Government of Uttar Pradesh, Department of Finance, Home, Power and Medical Health; Commissioner, Allahabad Division; Principal Officers' Training School, Allahabad; Vice-Principal, IAS Training School, New Delhi; Senior Dy. Director, National Academy of Administration, Mussoorie; District Magistrate and Collector, Kanpur Allahabad, Faizabad, and Tehri-Garhwal. *Memberships:* Executive Council, Indian Institute of Public Administration New Delhi; Governing Body, Asian Centre for Development Administration, Kuala Lumpur, AUN Organisation under ESCAP. *Publications:* Research Paper on the Socio-economic Background of Recruits to the Indian Civil Service/Indian Administrative Service; Growth of personnel and civil expenditure in the Government of India. *Hobbies:* Painting; Photography; Reading; Travelling; Tennis; Swimming. *Address:* Chitrakut, 7/53 Parbati Bagla Road, Kanpur 208002, UP, India.

TROTTER, Walter James, b. 20 Apr. 1920, Sydney, New South Wales, Australia. Company Director. m. Helen Joan Egan, 2nd Mar. 1946, 5 sons, 3 daughters. *Education:* Qualified as Chartered Accountant, 1943; Fellow of Institute of Chartered Accountants in Australia, 1950. *Appointments:* Admitted to Partnership, PJ Egan & Joyner, 1947; Senior Partner, 1957-71, Retired, 1971; Deputy Chairman, Howard Smith Limited; Deputy Chairman, Coal & Allied Industries, Ltd; Chairman, RW Miller Holdings Ltd; Chairman Amarda Holdings Ltd; Director, Broadcasting Station, 2SM Pty Ltd-Group; Director, John G Stephenson, Group of Companies. *Memberships:* Institute of Chartered Accountants in Australia; The Australian Club, Sydney; Royal Sydney Yacht Squadron, Sydney; Australian Jockey Club; Avondale Golf Club. *Publications:* Delivered Paper on Coal Resources in Australia for London Financial Times. *Hobbies:* Golf; Fishing. *Address:* 27 Warrangi Street, Turramurra, Sydney 2074, Australia.

TRUDEAU, Pierre, Elliott, b. 1919, Canadian Politician. m. Margaret Sinclair, 1971, 3 sons. *Education:* Jean-de-Brebeuf College, Montreal; University of Montreal; Harvard University; Ecole des Sciences Politiques, Paris; London School of Economics. *Appointments:* Called to Bar, Quebec, 1943; Practised Law, Province of Quebec; Co-founder of Review Cite Libre; Associate Professor of Law, University of Montreal, 1961-65; Member of House of Commons, 1965-; Parliamentary Secretary to Prime Minister, 1966-67; Minister of Justice and Attorney General, 1967-68; Leader of Liberal Party, 1968-; Prime Minister of Canada, 1968-79 and 1980-. *Memberships:* Bars of Provinces of Quebec and Ontario; Founding Member, Montreal Civil Liberties Union. *Publications:* La Greve de l'Amiante, 1956; Deux Innocents en Chine Rouge, with Jacques Hebert, 1961; Le Federalisme et la Societe Canadienne-Francaise, 1968; Reponses, 1968. *Honours:* Honorary Doctor of Laws, University of Alberta, 1968; Dr.h.c. Duke University, 1974; Hon. Fellow, LSE, 1969; Freeman of City of London, 1975. *Address:* House of Commons, Ottowa, Ontario, K1A 70A6, Canada.

TRUDEL, Claude Louis, b. 2nd Mar. 1942. Montreal, Quebec, Canada. Lawyer. m. Florence Ares, 19th Aug. 1967, 1 son, Divorced, 1981. *Education:* BA, College St. Viateur D'outremont, 1964; LLL, University of Montreal, 1967; MSc, London School of Economics and Political Sciences, 1969. *Appointments:* Lawyer, Geoffrion el Prud 'homme, 1968; Administrative Secretary, Premier of Quebec, 1970-73; Chef De Cabinet, Adjoint, Premier, Ministre of Quebec, 1973-75; President Director General Du cec Depuis, 1979. *Memberships:* Barreau du Quebec, Section de Montreal; Association des Diplomes de l'Universite de Montreal; Association des Diplomes du Graduate School, London School of Economics and Political Science, University of London, England; Canadian Association of Friends of the London School of Economics and Political Science; Chamber of Commerce, Province of Quebec; Conseil du Patronate du Quebec. *Hobbies:* Lectures; Music; Tennis. *Address:* 7100 Giraud 310, Anjou, Quebec H1J 2E7, Canada.

TRUSCOTT, Roy George, b. 30 May 1923, Devonport, England. Chartered Engineer. m. Jean Ewing, 29 May 1949, 1 daughter. *Education:* Technical College, Rochester, Kent; Technical Colleges, H.M. Dockyard, Chatham, Rosyth; Heriot-Watt College, Edinburgh; University of Texas Pipeline School; Certificates of Competency in Engine Fitting, Engineer, Draughtsman. *Appointments:* Iraq Petroleum Company Limited, 1951-68; General Manager, Crest Engineering Incorporated, 1968-74; Black, Sivalls and Bryson, 1974-76; Senior Associate Engineer, Mobil, 1976; Senior Engineering Manager, Central Engineer Headquarters, British National Oil Corporation, Glasgow, 1976-. *Memberships:* Fellow, Institution of Mechanical Engineers; Fellow, Institute of Petroleum. *Publications:* Oil in Britain Convention, 1972. *Hobbies:* Fishing; Gardening; Travel; Caravaning; Horse Show Jumping. *Address:* White Cottage, Buchanan Castle, Drymen, Stirlingshire, Scotland G63 OHX.

TSANG, Yip-fat, Richard, b. 11 Sept. 1952, Kowloon, Hong Kong. Music Lecturer/Radio Music Programme Producer. 1 Aug. 1977, 1 son. *Education:* BA, Hons, Music, Chinese University of Hong Kong, 1976; MM, University of Hull, England, 1978. *Appointments:* Music Teacher, Aberdeen Technical School, 1978; Producer, Fine Music Section, Radio Television, Hong Kong, 1979-. *Memberships:* Executive Committee Member, Asian Composers League, Hong Kong District; Associated Member, Composers and Authors Society of Hong Kong; Organising Committee Member, Asian Composers League Conference and Festivals, 1981; Chief Delegate, Asian Composers League Conference and Festivals, 1981. *Publications:* Various Musical Compositions including, Images of Bells, 1979; Ling Kai, 1980; Dou-Sau, 1980; Contra-Flux, 1980. *Honours:* Recipient of First Prize, Song-writing Competition sponsored by the Grove Magazine, Hong Kong, 1973; First Prize, Composition competition sponsored by the Hong Kong Music Institute, Choral Section, 1976; First Prize, Composition competition sponsored by the Urban Council Cultural Section, 1978; University of Hull, England, Postgraduate Award, 1976-78. *Hobbies:* Reading; Films; Swimming; Meditation. *Address:* 1 New Praya, Wah Po Building, 21st Floor, Block A, Kennedy Town, Hong Kong.

TUCKER, Alan Mark, b. 10 Mar. 1937, Barnstaple, Devon, England. Medical Practitioner. m. Anita Dorothy Lane, 25 June 1960, 1 son, 4 daughters. *Education:* Queen's College, Taunton; MB, BS, University of London, Charing Cross Hospital; DO DOBST, Royal College of Gynaecologists, 1964; DPH, Bristol, 1966; DCH, London, 1967; MFCM, RCP, United Kingdom, 1972; MRCP, United Kingdom, 1975; FRACGP, 1976. *Appointments:* Senior Lecturer, Community Health, Clinical Schol, University of Tasmania, 1976; Consultant Physician, St. John's Park Hospital, Hobart, 1976-; Part-time Lecturer, Departments Medicine, Pharmacy, University of Tasmania; Private Medical Practitioner; Principal Medical Lecturer, Clive Hamilton School of Geriatric Nursing; Area Medical Officer, Royal Australian Army. *Memberships:* Faculty, Royal Australian College of General Practitioners; Tasmania Cancer Registry Committee; Australian Medical Association; Fellow, Royal Society of Medicine, 1974; Chairman, Creek Cottage Centre for Physically Handicapped Adults; Executive Council Multiple Sclerosis Society Tasmania; Examiner, Nurses Registration Board, Tasmania;

Manager, Tasmanian Schoolboys Rugby Union, 1980. *Publications:* Various Publications, General Practice, Epidemiology, Hearing Disorders. *Honours:* Recipient of Pharmacology and Therapeutics Prize, Charing Cross Hospital, 1961; Certificate of Merit, Surgery, Charing Cross Hospital, 1961. *Hobbies:* Tennis; Rugby Union; Cricket; Antiquities; Music. *Address:* Carinya, 15 Fisher Avenue, Lower Sandy Bay, Hobart, Tasmania 7005, Australia.

TUCKER, Gilbert Brian, b. 23 Oct. 1930, Cardiff, Wales, United Kingdom. Scientist. m. Marian Angela Parker, 28 Apr. 1956, 2 daughters. *Education:* BSc, University College of Wales, Aberystwyth, 1948-50; Diploma of Imperial College, PhD, Physics, Imperial College of Science and Technology, London, 1950-54. *Appointments:* Pilot Officer, Flying Officer, Royal Air Force, 1954-55; Principal Scientific Officer, Meteorological Office, United Kingdom, 1955-65; Assistant Director, Research and Development, Bureau of Meteorology, Australia, 1965-69; Officer-in-Charge, Commonwealth Meteorology Research Centre, Australia, 1969-73; Chief, CSIRO Division of Atmospheric Physics, 1973-. *Memberships:* Royal Meteorological Society, United Kingdom, 1952; Australian Branch, Royal Meterological Society, 1979; Joint Organising Committee, Global Atmospheric Research Programme, 1971-80, (Vice Chairman, 1978-80); Joint Scientific Committee, World Climate Research Programme, 1980. *Publications:* Various Scientific papers. *Honours:* Recipient of Darton Prize, Royal Meteorlogical Society, 1962; L.F. Richardson Prize, Royal Meteorlogical Society, 1961; Department of Scientific and Industrial Research Award, 1952-54; Senior Research Fellowship, Co-operative Institute for Research into Environmental Science, USA, 1981. *Hobbies:* Music; Bush Walking. *Address:* CSIRO Division of Atmospheric Physics, Station Street, Aspendale, Victoria, Australia.

TUFNELL, Meriel Patricia, b. 12 Dec. 1948, Winchester, England. Jockey/Instructor. *Education:* Private Tutor. *Appointments:* Self-employed, Owner/Manager, Equestrian Centre, Schooling Horses and Instructing Pupils. *Memberships:* Chairman and Founder of the Lady Jockey Association, 1972; Freeman, City of London, 1974; Freeman, Grocers Company, 1974; Patron of Sparks, 1975; Lady Tavener, 1979; British Empire, 1974; Honorary Member, Curzon House and Crockfords; St. Moritz Tabogganing Club; The British Modern Pentathlon. *Honours:* First British Champion Lady Jockey, 1972; Reserve Champion, 1973; First British Girl to become European Champion; Goya Cup, Joe Coral's Cup, Daily Mirror Award, Dillon Award, 1972; Joe Coral Cup, 1973; Zurich Ladies Cup, 1974. *Hobbies:* Skiing; Swimming; Water Skiing; Lampshade Making; Flower Designing. *Address:* Fowlers Farm, Vernham Street, Andover, Hants, England.

TU'IPELEHAKE, HRH Prince Fatafehi, b. 7 Jan. 1922, Nuku'Alofa, Tonga. Prime Minister. m. HRH Princess Melenaite Tupoumoheofo, 10 June 1947, 2 sons, 4 daughters. *Education:* Nafualu College, Tonga; Newington College, Sydney, Australia; Gatton Agricultural College, Queensland, Australia. *Appointments:* Agricultural Officer, 1944-49; Governor of Vava'u, 1949; Governor of Ha'apai, Minister of Lands, 1949; Prime Minister, Minister of Agriculture, Minister of Foreign Affairs, 1965; Minister of Marines, 1972. *Address:* Fatai, Nuku'Alofa, Tonga.

TUITA, Siosaia Aleamotu'a Laufilitonga, b. 29 Aug. 1920, Lapaha, Tongatapu, Tonga. Minister of the Crown. m. Fatafehi Tupou, 15 Oct. 1949, 2 sons, 2 daughters. *Education:* Tupou College; Wesley College, Auckland, New Zealand; Oxford. *Appointments:* Governor of Vava'u; Minister of Lands, Survey and Natural Resources; Deputy Prime Minister; Member of His Majesty's Cabinet; Member of His Majesty's Privy Council; Member of Parliament. *Memberships:* Tonga Club; Helepeku Club; Nuku'alofa Club; Yacht Club. *Honours:* Succeeded to the Noble Title TUITA, 1972; Award of Commander of the Most Excellent Order of the British Empire, 1976; Award of the title of Baron Tuita of Utungake, 1980. *Hobbies:* Cricket; Rugby. *Address:* Mahina-fekite, Nuku'alofa, Tonga.

TUNGA, Sudhansu Sekhar, b. 4 Dec. 1936, Midnapore, West Bengal, India. Teaching. m. Miss Tapati Mahapatra, 28 Oct. 1974. *Education:* BA, Hons, Calcutta University, 1960; MA, Bengali, Calcutta University, 1962; MA, English, Calcutta University, 1965; MA, Comparative Philology, Calcutta University, 1969; DLitt, Calcutta University, 1981. *Appointments:* Teacher, Bhastara J.S. School, Hooghly, West Bengal, India, 1964-66; Lecturer, Lady Keane Girls' College, Shillong, Meghalaya, India, 1966-68; Lecturer, Gauhati University, Assam, India, 1968-; Teaching Bengali Literature and General and Indo-Aryan Linguistics. *Memberships:* Life Member, Linguistic Society of India, Poona; Asiatic Society, Calcutta, India; Bangiva Sahitya Parishad, Calcutta, India. *Publications:* Ami Ek Sadagar, I'm a Merchant, A collection of Verse in Bengali, Disari, Calcutta, 1960; Santir Pakhira Ebong Tumi, Birds of Peace and You, A collection of Verse in Bengali, Disari, Calcutta, 1961. *Hobbies:* Correspondence; Chess. *Address:* 21 University Campus, Gauhati 781014, Assam, India.

TURBOTT, Ian Graham, b. 9 Mar. 1922, Whangarei, New Zealand. Company Director. m. Nancy Lantz, 24 Aug. 1952, 3 daughters. *Education:* Auckland University; Jesus College, Cambridge; London School of Economics; London University. *Appointments:* 1948-56, Colonial Service, Overseas Civil Service, Western Pacific, Gilbert & Ellice Islands; 1956-58, Principal, Colonial Office; 1958-64, Administrator of Antigua, West Indies; 1960-64, Queen's Representative, Antigua; 1964-67, Administrator and Queen's Representative of Grenada; 1967-68, Governor, Associated State of Grenada; 1970, Chairman, Spencer Stuart & Associates Pty. limited, Australia; 1971-78, Director, Chlorides Batteries, Australia Limited; 1973, Partner, Spencer Stuart & Associates, (World Wide); 1974, Director, Suncoast Group of Companies; 1975, Chairman, Spencer Stuart Associates Pty. Limited, (Hong Kong Limited); 1976, Chairman, TNT Group 4 Total Security Pty. Ltd; 1976-79, Director, Hoyts Theatres Limited; 1976, Deputy Chairman, American International Underwriting (Australian Pty. Limited) Advisory Board; 1978, Chairman, Chloride Batteries Australia Limited; 1978, Director, Spencer Stuart & Associates Limited; 1978, Director City Mutual Life Assurance Society Limited; 1979, Chairman, Hoyts Theatres Limited; 1980, Chairman, Penrith Lakes Development Corporation; 1980, Director, Mutual Acceptance Limited; 1973, Chairman, Sydney Dance Company; 1973, Member, New South Wales Drug Education Advisory Council; 1976, Governor, New South Wales Conservatorium of Music; 1977, Chairman The Sydney International Piano Competition; 1977, Governor, Sydney Hospital Foundation for Research; 1978, Chairman, Stereo FM Pty. Limited; 1978, Trustee, World Wild Life Foundation in Australia. *Memberships:* The Australian Club; Commonwealth Parliamentary Association; fellow, Australian Institute of Management; Fellow, Institute of Directors. *Publications:* Various technical & scientific, 1948-51, Journal of Polynesian Society, on Pacific area. *Honours:* CMG, 1962; CSt.J, 1964; CVO, 1966; Knighthood, 1968, Kt.B.; Silver Jubilee Medal, 1977. *Hobbies:* Farming; Fishing; Boating. *Address:* 27 Amiens Road, Clontarf, NSW 2093, Australia.

TURKINGTON, Don James, b. 17 Aug. 1949, Lower Hutt, New Zealand. Government Adviser. m. Denise J. Turkington, 27 Feb. 1971, 1 son, 2 daughters. *Education:* BCA, Victoria University of Wellington, 1967-69; MComm, University of Canterbury, 1970; PhD, Victoria University of Wellington, 1971-75. *Appointments:* Junior Lecturer in Economics, Victoria University of Wellington; 1973-78, Lecturer in the Industrial Relations Centre, Victoria University of Wellington; 1977, Honorary Fellow in Industrial Relations, University of Wisconsin, Madison, USA; 1979-, Senior Lecturer in the Industrial Relations Centre, Victoria University of Wellington. *Memberships:* President, Wellington Branch of the Industrial Relations Society of New Zealand; New Zealand Association of Economists; American Economic Association; Industrial Relations Research Association of America; International Industrial Relations Association. *Publications:* Industrial Conflict, 1976; The Trend of Strikes in New Zealand, 1971-75; Strike Incidence and Economic Activity in New Zealand, 1975; Change and Conflict on the Waterfront; Industrial Action, 1980. *Honours:* Various prizes and scholarships from Victoria University of Wellington in Economics and Accountancy. *Hobbies:* Tennis; Swimming. *Address:* 113, John Sims Drive, Johnsonville, Wellington 4, New Zealand.

TURNER, John Malcolm, b. 19 Jan. 1950, Portsmouth, Britain. Press and Information Officer. m. Anne Whitehouse, 9 Sept. 1978. *Education:* BA, University of Wales, 1970-73; Held Rotary Foundation Fellowship in International Understanding, Harvard University, 1973-74. *Appointments:* Kent County Council, Assistant to Director of Social Service, 1974-78; Commonwealth Institute, London, Press and Information Officer, 1978-. *Memberships:* Diplomatic and Commonwealth Writers Association. *Hobbies:* Theatre; Music; Reading; Walking. *Address:* 70 Larkhall Rise, London SW4, England.

TURNER, Michael Fisher, b. 27 Oct. 1931, Wilmslow, Cheshire, England Teacher. m. Winifred Farrell, 26 July, 1955, 1 daughter. *Education:* BSc, Queens University, Belfast, 1951-55. 03 Lloyds Bank; Wangandi Collegiate School; Audio-Tactual Braille, Instructor Royal New Zealand Foundation for the Blind; St. Peters College Auckland, Head of Commerce Department; St. Cuthberts College, Auckland. *Memberships:* Royal Commonwealth Society; New Zealand Association of Economists; Commercial and Economics Teachers Association; Full Gospel Business Mens Fellowship International; Government appointed, Of The Board of Trustees, Royal New Zealand Foundation for the Blind; Chairman of the Braille Committee, RNZFB; National Councillor, New Zealand Association of the Blind and Partically Blind; Liveryman, Worshipful Company of Weavers, London. *Publications:* Research papers including Teaching Braille to Adults' as part of pioneering work in developing a new method of teaching Braille to adults by correspondence. *Hobbies:* Model Railways; Philately. *Address:* 68 Meadowbank Road, Remuera, Auckland 5, New Zealand.

TURNER, Michael James, b. 11 May, 1937, Beckenham, Kent. Welding Engineer and Director. m. Joan E.K. Simpson, 4 daughters, 2 sons. *Education:* Associate Institution of Metallurgists, Birmingham University, 1956-59; Battersea Polytechnic, 1959-60; Diploma in Accounting & Finance, Newcastle Polytechnic, 1972-73. *Appointments:* G.A. Harvey (London) Ltd, 1957-59; Bristol Aerojet Ltd, 1960-66; Welding Institute, 1967-70; Swan Hunter Ltd, 1970-76; Govan Shipbuilders, 1976-; Promweld Ltd., 1981. *Memberships:* Council Welding Institute; Professional Board Welding Institute. *Publications:* Author of numerous technical papers, contributor to Financial Times. *Honours:* Fellowship Institution of Metallurgists, 1974. *Hobbies:* Sailing; Music. *Address:* 116 Old Greenock Road, Bishopton, Renfrewshire, PA7 5BB, Scotland.

TURNER, Michael Rex, b. 31 July, 1934, England. Educator. *Education:* BSc, University of London, 1956; MSc, University of London, 1962; PhD, University of London, 1966. *Appointments:* National Health Service, Blood Transfusion Service, 1959-60; Medical Research Council, Human Nutrition Research Unit, 1960-66; University of Southampton, Department of Physiology & Biochemistry, 1966-77; Director-General, British Nutrition Foundation, 1978-. *Memberships:* Royal Society of Health, Fellow; Royal Society of Medicine, Fellow; Nutrition Society, formerly Council, Programmes Secretary, Proceedings Editor; British Diabetic Association; British Dietetic Association; Society of Chemical Industry; Royal Institution; Group of European Nutritionists; European Association for the Study of Diabetics; European Food Law Association; Fellow, British Institute of Management; Fellow, Institute of Biology;·Fellow, Institute of Food Science and Technology. *Publications:* Editor, Nutrition and Lifestyles; Preventive Nutrition and Society; Food and Health a perspective; Co-editor, Nutrition and Diabetes; Author of 4 Chapters and numerous scientific papers, Comment extensively quoted in National and Regional press, *Hobbies:* Music; Dance. *Address:* PO Box 49, Barbican, London, EC2 Y8AE, England.

TURNER, R. Edward, b. 8 June, 1926, Hamilton, Ontario, Canada. Psychiatrist, Forensic. m. Gene A. 27 Sept. 1952, 1 daughter,3 sons. *Education:* BA, McMaster University, Hamilton, Canada, 1948; MD, University of Toronto, 1952; University of Bristol, 1953-55; Psych., University of Toronto, 1957. *Appointments:* Professor of Forensic Psychiatry, University of Toronto, Director and Psychiatrist in Charge, Metropolitan, Toronto Forensic Service from 1977; Medical Director, Clarke Institute of Psychiatry, 1969-77; Supervisor, Medical Jurisprudence, University of Toronto. *Mem-

berships: Royal College of Psychiatrists; Canadian and Ontario Medical Associations; Canadian and Ontario Psychiatric Associations; Toronto Medico-Legal Society-Council; Fellow, Royal College of Physicians and Surgeons of Canada; President, Kenneth G. Gray Foundation. *Publications:* Pedophilia and Exhibitionism, University of Toronto Press, 1964; Criminal Justice System and Mental Health Services, Ontario Council of Health, 1979; 40 papers published in psychiatry and law and forensic psychiatry. *Honours:* Fellow, American Psychiatric Association, 1961; President, Ontario Psychiatric Association, 1975-76; Fellow, Royal College of Psychiatrists, 1972; Deputy Warden, Cathedral Church of St. James, Toronto, 1978-79. *Hobbies:* Photography; History; Music; Art; Theology. *Address:* 163 Bayview Heights Drive, Toronto, Canada, M4G 2Y7.

TURNER, Ralph Eric, b. 25 Apr. 1949, Toronto, Ontario, Canada. Chemist. *Education:* BSc (Hons. Chemistry), University of Waterloo, 1972; PhD (Theoretical Chemistry), University of British Columbia, 1978. *Appointments:* Postdoctoral Fellow, University of Minnesota, Department of Chemistry. *Memberships:* American Physical Society; American Chemical Society; Canadian Association of Physicists; Candadian Institute of Chemistry. *Publications:* 5 Publications in Journals of physics, 4 by R.E. Turner, 1 by R.F. Snider and R.E. Turner. from 1976-80. *Hobbies:* Hockey; Squash; Tennis; Hiking. *Address:* Department of Chemistry, University of British Columbia, Vancouver, British Columbia, Canada V6T 1Y6.

TURNER, Rex John, b. 14 Mar. 1926, Sydney, Australia. Company Manager & Director. m. 5 June, 1954, 3 sons, 1 daughter. *Education:* BA, University of Melbourne, 1950; BEc, University of Sydney, 1954; MBA, University of Sydney, 1976. *Appointments:* Secretary & Chief Accountant, Hospitals Contribution Fund of Australia, 1956-61; Director & Chief Executive Hospitals Contribution Fund of Australia, 1961-. *Memberships:* American National Club; Australian Golf Club. *Publications:* The Case Against Compulsion, OHCF, 1969; Guideline for Reconstruction of Australia's Voluntary Health Insurance Scheme, OHCF, 1969; Dollars & Sense, OHCF, 1977. *Address:* Memorial Avenure, St. Ives, NSW 2075, Australia.

TURNER, Rowland William Lyttleton, b. 18 Feb. 1943, Wynyard, Tasmania. Orthopaedic Surgeon. m. Karin Louise O'Hanlon, 5 June, 1971, 1 son, 1 daughter. *Education:* MB, BS, University of Queensland, 1967; FRCS, 1972; FRACS, Orthopaedic, 1975. *Appointments:* Royal Hobart Hospital, 1968; Royal Northern Hospital, London, 1969; Registrar, Poole General Hospital, Dorset, 1971; Selly Oak Hospital, Birmingham, 1972; Registrar, Sailsbury General Infirmary, 1973; Senior Registrar, Fremantle Hospital, Australia, 1974; Princess Margaret Hospital, 1975; Visiting Orthopeadic Surgeon, Royal Hobart Hospital, 1976.-. *Memberships:* Tasmania Club; AMA; RSM. *Hobbies:* Angling; Gardening. *Address:* 10 Ilfracombe Crescent, Sandy Bay, Tasmania 7005, Australia.

TURNER, Wilfred, b. 10th Oct. 1921, Littleborough, Lancashire, England. Diplomatist. m. June Gladys Tite, 26th Mar. 1947, 2 sons, 1 daughter. *Education:* Heywood Grammar School, 1932-38; BSc, London University, 1939-42; *Appointments:* Ministry of Labour, 1938-42; HM Forces, 1942-47; Ministry of Labour, 1947-55; Assistant Labour Adviser, British.High Commission, New Delhi, 1955-59; Ministry of Labour, 1959-60; Ministry of Health, 1960-66; Commonwealth Office, 1966; First Secretary, Kaduna, 1966-69; First Secretary, Kuala Lumpur, 1969-73; Deputy High Commissioner & Commercial/Economic Counsellor Accra, 1973-77; High Commissioner to Botswana, 1977-. *Memberships:* Royal Commonwealth Society. *Honours:* CMG, 1977; CVO, 1979. *Hobbies:* Hill walking. *Address:* 44 Tower Road, Twickenham, London TW1 4PE, England.

TURYAHIKAYO-RUGYEMA, Benoni, b. 11th Feb. 1942, Kabale, Uganda, East Africa. Academic. 2 sons. *Education:* BA(Hons.) (History), Makerere University, 1965-68; MA (History), McMaster University, Canada, 1968-70; MA, PhD (History, Africa), University of Michigan, Ann Arbor, USA. *Appointments:* Lecturer/Senior Lecturer, Department of History, Makerere University, 1974-78; Executive Director, Makerere Institute of Social Research, 1978-. *Memberships:* Uganda Society

- Honorary Editor, Uganda Journal; Kenya Historical Association. *Publications:* A History of the Bakiga 1500-1930; A Philosophy and Religion of the Bakiga; Editor, Liberation struggle in Southern Africa; A Biography of Paulo Ngologoza; Amin and His Times: has published numerous articles *Hobbies:* Dancing; Mountaineering. *Address:* Makerere Institute of Social Research, Kampala, Uganda.

TWEA, Edward Bandawe, b. 9th Apr. 1956, Bandawe, Nkhata Bay, Malawi, Central Africa. Lawyer. m. 21st Feb. 1981, 1 daughter. *Education:* Bachelor of Law, University of Malawi, 1973-78. *Appointments:* State Advocate, Attorney General Chambers, Ministry of Justice; Senior Resident Magistrate. *Memberships:* Malawi, Law Society; Gymkhana Club, Zomba. *Hobbies:* Travelling; Reading; Physical Exercises; Making friends; Music. *Address:* No. 2, Hospital Road, Zomba, Malawi, South Africa.

TWEDDLE, Denis, b. 23rd Mar. 1949, Corbridge, Northumberland, England. Fisheries Biologist. m. Sharon Christine Tuohy, 1 son. *Education:* BSc, University College of North Wales, Bangor, 1967-70: *Appointments:* Gear Technologists, Entebbe Fisheries Training Institute, Uganda, VSO, 1971-72; Fisheries Biologist, Monkey Bay Fisheries Station, Malawi, UNV, 1973-75; Fisheries Research Officer, Malawi Government, 1975-. *Memberships:* Institute of Fisheries Management; Limnological Society of Southern Africa. *Publications:* Age, growth and natural mortality rates of some cichlid fishes of Lake Malawi; The ecology of the catfish Clarias gariepinus and Clarias ngamensis in the Shire Valley, Malawi; The zoogeography of the fish fauna of the Lake Chilwa Basin, studies of change in a tropical ecosystem; An annotated checklist of the fish fauna of the River Shire, South of Kapachira Falls, Malawi; The river fishes of Malawi, with a discussion on the relationships between the various river systems. Paper presented at LSSA Annual Congress, Grahamstown, 1980. *Honours:* John S. Schlesinger Fellow - JLB Smith Institute of Ichthyology, Rhodes University, Grahamstown, South Africa, July, 1980. *Hobbies:* All aspects of Angling; Waterskiing; Photography; Badminton. *Address:* c/o 1 Davis Drive, Amble, Morpeth, Northumberland, England.

TWENTYMAN, George Edward, b. 3rd Aug. 1928, Waipawa, New Zealand. m. Shiela Kathlene Godfrey, 8th Sept. 1951, 2 sons 3 daughters. *Education:* Educated at Takapau Primary School; Dannevirke Secondary School; Commonwealth Police College, Australia; Bramshill Police College, UK. *Appointments:* New Zealand Police, Wellington & Christchurch, in various ranks. Deputy Assistant Commissioner and to command of the Christchurch Police District in 1977, 1947-77.- *Memberships:* Patron, Canterbury Outward Bounders Association; Christchurch Rotary Club. *Publications:* The Wahine Disaster; The Police Role, 1969. *Honours:* OBE, 1980. *Hobbies:* Wood Carving; Restoring Antiques. *Address:* 62 Parkstone Avenue, Avonhead, Christchurch 4, New Zealand.

TWEREFOO, Gustav Oware, b. 4th Apr. 1934, Nkwatia, Kwahu. Senior Lecturer in Music Education/Therapy. m. Nancy Kwmiwaah, 25th Dec. 1974, Second marriage, 4 sons, 4 daughters. *Education:* General Diploma Music, University of Ghana, Legon, 1963-67; Diploma Orff Schubuerk, Orff Institute, Salzburg, 1971-72; MSc, MEd, University of Illinois, Urbana, USA, 1973-75. *Appointments:* Classroom Teacher, Ghana Education Service, Accra, 1951-67; Senior Music Master, University, Primary School, Legon, 1967-73; Research Fellow, Institute of African Studies, University of Ghana, Legon, 1973-80; Senior Lecturer-/Head of Department of Music, College of Education, UYO, CRS, Nigeria, 1980.- *Memberships:* Board of Directors, International Society of Music Education; Research Commission of International Society of Mus-

ic. Education. *Publications:* 14 publications, including, music education with the Mentally Retarded; Music as a life long education in Ghana; Out of School Music Education Programme; The preparation of Instructional Materials in Music, 1975-80; Film, 30 minute programme on music. *Hobbies:* Farming; Piano Teaching; Choir Practice. *Address:* Prebsyterian Church, PO Box 8, Nkwatia, Kwahu, Ghana.

TWUMASI, Yaw, b. 28 June 1936, Juaso, Ashanti, Ghana. University Teacher and Editor. m. Evelyn, 4 Jan. 1964, 3 sons. *Education:* BSc, (Econ), London as an External Student; MSc, (Econ), London School of Economics, London University, 1961-63; Nuffield College, Oxford University, 1963-64, 1969-71; D.Phil (Oxon), 1972; Post doctoral MA, Michigan State University, 1976. *Appointments:* Lecturer, Department of Political Science, University of Ghana, Legon, Acera, 1965; Editor, Legon Observer, 1966-69 and Founder Editor; Editor, 1979-; Visiting Scholar, Afrika Studiecentrum, University of Leiden, Holland. *Memberships:* Acting Director, School of Journalism and Communication, University of Ghana, Legon, 1979; Board of Governors, Ghana Institute of Journalism, 1979-; 3 Universities of Ghana, on the Press Commission of Ghana, 1980-. *Publications:* Contributor of reviews, monographs, articles to professional journals and conferences, including The Newspaper Press and Political Leadership in Developing Nations; The. Case of Ghana 1964-78, Gazette Vol 26, 1980, pp 1-16. *Hobbies:* Reading; Walking; Playing Table Tennis. *Address:* 41 Little Legon, Legon, Accra, Ghana.

TYE, Walter, b. 12 Dec. 1912, Rochdale, England. Visiting Professor. m. Eileen Mary, 1 July, 1939, 1 son, 1 daughter. *Education:* BSc. Eng. Northampton Engineering College, 1930-34. *Appointments:* Fairey Aviation Co., 1939; Royal Aircraft Establishment, 1935-38; Air Registration Board, 1938-39; Royal Aircraft Establishment, 1939-43; Air Registration Board, 1943-72; Chief Technical Officer, 1946-69; Chief Executive, 1969-71; Civil Aviation Authority, 1971-74; Visiting Professor, Cranfield Inst. 1975- *Memberships:* Royal Aeronautical Society. *Publications:* Articles, journals - particularly Royal Aeronautical Society. *Honours:* OBE. 1948; CBE, 1966; Air Safety Gold Medal, 1968; R.Ac.S Gold Medal, 1970; Hon D.Sc. (Cranfield), 1972; Hon. Fellow, R.Ac.S. 1977. *Address:* The Spinney, Fairmile Park Road, Cobham, Surrey, England.

TZORTZIS, Andreas, b. 22 Dec. 1922, Famagusta, Cyprus. Industrialist. m. Antoniou Antonina, 11 June, 1950, 1 son, 2 daughters. *Education:* Civil Engineering Certificate by correspondence; Ship Building Certificate. *Appointments:* Designer of Building Drawings, 1942; Workshop owner and Managing Director, 1940; Slipway owner and Managing Director, 1948; Rice Mill Factory Owner and Managing Director, 1967; Land Dealer, 1967; Ship Repairing Contractor of the British Army and Airforce vessels based in Cyprus, 1950-; Shipyard main Share Holder (Floating Dock facilities and Managing Director, 1978. *Memberships:* Past President, Rotary International Club; Vice President of Famagusta Chamber of Commerce and Industry; Council of the Cyprus Chamber; President of the Famagusta Exhibition; Famagusta Public Library; Water Authority; Famagusta Sewerage Plant; Founder and 1st President of Cyprus Parents School Committee; Representative of Employers in the Famagusta Advisory Post labour Committee; Cyprus Labour Advisory Board; Various other committees for social activities. *Publications:* Industrial and political orientated articles in National Newspaper publications. *Honours:* Recipient of and award from British Forces in Cyprus for long successful services. *Hobbies:* Stamps collector; Hunting; Fishing; Clay Pigeon Shooting; Collecting coins. *Address:* Fairways Property Holdings Ltd., Grammou Street, Flat N.3, Limassol, Cyprus.

U

UBEROI, J.S., b. 20 Jan. 1945, India. Publishing. m. Veena, 30 Apr. 1967, 2 daughters. *Education:* BA., 1966. *Appointments:* Advertising Director, Allied Newspapers Limited, 1972-74; Managing Director, 1975-79, Publisher, Thomson Press Hong Kong Limited; Publisher, Media Transasia Thailand Limited. *Memberships:* Pacific Area Travel Association; American Society of Travel Agents. *Publications:* Publisher of: Asian Architect and Builder; Asian Hotelkeeper and Catering Times; Asia Pacific Contractor; Construction Asia; Humsafar: PIA inflight magazine; Living in Thailand; Namaskaar: Air India inflight magazine; Style; Swagat: Indian Airlines inflight magazine; Hongkong City; South Asia Travel Review; Thailand Travel Trade; Where. *Hobbies:* Music; Reading; Bridge. *Address:* 64-66 Soi Ngom Duplee, Esmeralda Apt. 70, off Rama IV Road, Bangkok, Thailand.

UDEH, Fidelis Nwankwo, b. 15 Jan. 1933, Ndiowu, Nigeria. Consultant Surgeon; Reader in Surgery. m. Constance Azuka N. Onwurah, Jan. 1970, 2 sons, 3 daughters. *Education:* University College, Ibadan, Nigeria, 1951-55; Oxford University Medical School, UK, 1955-58; LRCP., London; MRCS., Eng., 1958; MBBS., London, 1958; Edinburgh University Postgraduate Medical School, Scotland, UK, 1962-63; FRCS., Edinburgh, 1962; FRCS., Eng., 1963; Johns Hopkins University, The Johns Hopkins Hospital, Baltimore, Maryland, USA, 1964-65. *Appointments:* House Physician to Nuffield Professor of Clinical Medicine, Oxford, UK, 1958-59; House Surgeon/Senior House Officer, 1960-61, Senior Registrar, Surgery, 1963-64, University College Hospital, Ibadan, Nigeria; Registrar, Surgery, Harold Wood Hospital, Essex, UK, 1962-63; Fellow, Urology, Johns Hopkins University/Johns Hopkins Hospital, USA, 1964-65; Lecturer, Surgery, Consultant Surgeon, University of Ibadan, Nigeria, 1965-67; Lecturer, Surgery, Consultant Surgeon, Head, Department of Anatomy, 1967-70, Senior Lecturer, 1970-74, Reader in Surgery, 1974-, University of Nigeria, Nsukka, Nigeria. *Memberships:* Nigerian Surgical Research Society; Fellow: West African College of Surgeons; International College of Surgeons. *Publications:* Several publications including: Appendicitis in the West African; Leucine-Aminopeptidase Activity in Malignant and Benign prostatic Tissue; Carcinoma of the Bladder in Western Nigeria; Re-evaluation of the Band Receptor theory of Control of Renin Secretion. *Honours:* Government College, Umualia Prize, 1951; Nigeria Central Government Scholar, Universities of Ibadan and Oxford, UK, 1951-58; Oxford University Medical School Prize, 1957; Commonwealth Scholar, Edinburgh University Postgraduate Medical School, Scotland, UK, 1962-63. *Hobbies:* Community Development; Gardening. *Address:* 22 Savage Crescent, Ekulu, G R A., Enugu, Nigeria.

UDO, Asuquo Okon, b. 10 Oct. 1937, Afaha Atai, Ibesikpo, Uyo, Nigeria. Banking and Research Economist. 3 sons, 1 daughter. *Education:* BSc., Hons., University of Nigeria, Nsukka, Nigeria, 1966; Senior Management Course, Manchester Business School, UK, 1980. *Appointments:* Teacher: Lutheran Mission Schools, Cross River State, Nigeria; Holy Family College, Abak, Cross River State, Nigeria; Eastern Commercial Secondary School, Aba, Imo State, Nigeria; 1959-62; Research Economist, 1967-76, Deputy Director, Head of Commodities division, Agricultural Finance Department, Central Bank of Nigeria, 1980-; Secretary, Technical Committee on Produce Prices, TCPP, 1966-80. *Memberships:* Lutheran Church of Nigeria; Nigerian Economic Society. *Publications:* Mainly Policy papers, related to Central Banking functions and papers related to the Determination of Producer Prices for the Scheduled Crops. *Hobbies:* Football; Dancing; Photography. *Address:* Agricultural Finance Department, Central Bank of Nigeria, Lagos, Nigeria.

UDWADIA, Farokh Erach, b. 7 Apr. 1931, Bombay, India. Consultant Physician. m. Vera Khusrokhan, 6 Dec. 1959, 1 son, 1 daughter. *Education:* MBBS., 1953, MD., 1956, University of Bombay, India; FCPS., College of Physicians and Surgeons, Bombay, India, 1955; MRCP., Edinburgh, UK, 1958; FRCP., 1969; FCCP; FRSM; FICA. *Appointments:* Consultant Physician, JJ Hospital, 1959; Honorary Professor of Medicine, Grant

Medical College, 1959; Consultant Physician: Parsee General Hospital, India; Breach Candy Hospital, India; Atomic Energy Commission of India. *Memberships:* President, Association of Chest Physicians of India, 1981; Editorial Board of: Journal of Association of Physicians of India; Indian Journal of Chest Diseases and Allied Sciences. *Publications:* Main Creative research work on Tropical Eosinophilia; Pulmonary Eosinophilia: Progress in Respiration Research, 1975; Diagnosis and Management of Medical Emergencies, 1972, 75; Diagnosis and Management of Acute Respiratory Failure, 1979; numerous other publications in national and international journals. *Honours:* Numerous honours, prizes and medals during scholastic and professional career. *Hobbies:* Music; Sports; History. *Address:* 11 C Jl Palazzo, Ridge Road, Bombay 6, India.

UFOT, Essien Okon, b. 11 Nov. 1956, Mkpat, Enin, Cross River State, Nigeria. Medical Records. m. Grace Eakin Udom, 19 July 1976, 2 sons. *Education:* Diploma, Medical Records Administration, 1979; Associate, Association of Health Care Information and Medical Records Officer, UK; Associate, Nigeria Health Records Association. *Appointments:* Medical Records Officer, 1979-. *Address:* Mkpat Enin, Mkpat Enin P.A., Ikot Abasi Local Government Area, Cross River State, Nigeria.

UGOCHUKWU, (Chief) Mathias Nwafo, b. 1926, Umunze, Aguata Local Government of Anambra State, Nigeria. Financier; Industrialist; Philanthropist. m. *Appointments:* Chairman of many companies including: Ugochukwu and Sons Limited; Ugochukwu Chemical Industries Limited; John Holt Nigeria Limited; John Holt Insurance Brokers Limited; Biscuit Manufacturing Co. Limited; Westminster Dredging Co. Nigeria Limited; Director of many Companies including: Afrprint Nigeria Limited; Singer Nigeria Limited; Chanraj Nigeria Limited; 3M Nigeria Limited; Smurfit Flexwrap Limited; Niger Cafe & Foods (WA) Limited. *Hobbies:* Reading; Meeting people. *Address:* Palace of the People, Umunze, Aguata Local Government Area, Anambra State, Nigeria.

UGONNA, Frederick Nnabuenyi Okeke, b. 12 Oct. 1936, Amaokpara Ihitenansa, Orlu, Imo State, Nigeria. University teacher and researcher. m. Judith Ann Corran, 11 Sept. 1971, 4 sons. *Education:* BA., Hons., 1965, MA., 1971, PhD., 1976, University of Ibadan, Nigeria; Sponsored by British Council, University of London Summer School, UK, 1966. *Appointments:* Pupil teacher, Ahiaba, Nbawsi, Imo State, Nigeria, 1951-52; Second master, Primary school, Ebenator, Orlu, Nigeria, 1957-58; Headmaster, St. Anthony's School, Orsuihiteukwa, Orlu, Nigeria, 1959; Principal, PTC, Ihitenansa, Orlu, Nigeria, 1960-61; Senior Tutor, Earnest Gems Grammar School, Akokwa, Orlu, Nigeria, 1962; Lecturer, English, Ahmadu Bello University, Zaria, Nigeria, 1971; Lecturer 2, Lecturer 1, Senior Lecturer, Associate Professor, Igbo Studies, Department of African Languages and Literature, University of Lagos, Lagos, Nigeria, 1971-. *Memberships:* Secretary, 1980, Nigerian Folklore Society; Assistant Secretary, Editor of Society's Journal, Igbo, Society for Promoting Igbo Language and Culture; Executive member, Literary Society of Nigeria; West African Linguistic Society; Linguistic Association of Nigeria; Nigerian Association of African and Comparative Literature. *Publications:* Anthology of Igbo traditional poems, 1980; Igbo Satiric Art (in press); An African Dramatic Tradition: Mmonwu of the Central Igbo (in press); many articles in learned journals. *Hobbies:* Public debates; Music. *Address:* Eziala House, Amaokpara Ihitenansa, Orlu, Imo State, Nigeria.

UGOT, (Chief) Uno Bassey, b. 17 Aug. 1918, Okurike, Biase, Cross River State, Nigeria. Teaching and Administration (Civil Servant). m. (1) G.I. Iyam, 18 Apr. 1942, (2) F.A.M. Osiwunmi, 31 Dec. 1961, 5 sons, 4 daughters. *Education:* Science Masters' Diploma, Higher College, Yaba, Nigeria, 1935-39; BA., 1951, MA., 1954, Cambridge University, UK. *Appointments:* Science Master: HWTI, Calabar, Nigeria, 1939-42; King's College, Lagos, Nigeria, 1944-47; Government College, Ibadan, Nigeria, 1951-56; Civilian Instructor, West African Force, 1942-44; Education Officer, Senior Education Officer, Western Nigerian Government, 1956-57; Administrative Officer: Western Nigeria, 1958-64; Federal Government, 1964-68; South Eastern State, Nigeria, retiring as Permanent Secretary,

1969-73; Chairman, Library Board, South Eastern State, Nigeria, 1973-76; Chairman, Public Accounts Committee, Nigeria, 1976-79; Council member: University of Calabar, Nigeria, 1976-80; University of Jos, Nigeria, 1980-. *Memberships:* Former Secretary, Treasurer, Nigeria Society; Science Association of Nigeria; State Vice-Chairman, Akamkpa LGA, National Party of Nigeria. *Publications:* State Aided Education. *Honours:* Government Scholar: Government College, Umualia, Higher College, Yaba, University of Cambridge, UK. *Hobbies:* Sport; Reading. *Address:* PO Box 376, Calabar, Cross River State, Nigeria.

UGURU, Chima Eme, b. 22 Nov. 1947, Abiriba. Business. m. Felicia, 20 Jan. 1968, 1 son, 1 daughter. *Appointments:* Record clerk, 1960-63, Senior clerk, 1964-72, AJH., Abiriba Hospital; Secretary, Pico Limited, Aba, Nigeria, 1973-74; Chairman and Managing Director: Chefeson Resources Limited, Aba, Nigeria; Chico Agro-Industrial Complex Limited, Aba, Nigeria; QU Bros. Limited, Aba, Nigeria. *Memberships:* Secretary, Assemblies of God Church; Aba Importers Union; Owerri Chamber of Commerce, Nigeria; Nigeria-Netherlands Chamber of Commerce. *Honours:* Recipient of award from Church. *Hobbies:* Singing; Football. *Address:* 36 Akalanna Road, Aba, Nigeria.

UGWU, Godwin Chukwuemeka, b. 31 Jan. 1937, Isu, Awgu LOcal Government Area, Nigeria. Media Management (Television). m. Anthonia Ugo, 4 Sept. 1971. *Education:* BSc., University College, Ibadan, Nigeria, 1955-60; Certificate, TV Engineering, Thomson Foundation TV College, Glasgow, Scotland, UK, 1965; Postgraduate Diploma, Electronic Engineering and Research Work, TV Research and Development Laboratories, Marconi College, Chelmsford, Essex, UK, 1965-66; MIEE., 1967-68; CEE. *Appointments:* Trainee Engineer, 1960, Senior Engineer, 1966, Eastern Nigeria broadcasting Corporation; Chief Engineer, 1971, AG. Director General, 1976, Radio and Television, East Central State Broadcasting Service, Nigeria; General Manager, 1977, Managing Director, Nigerian Television Authority Zone 'C' incorporating Nigerian Television, Enugu, Makurdi, Calabar, 1978-. *Memberships:* Publicity Secretary, East Central State Branch, 1974-75, Nigeria Society of Engineers. *Publications:* Presented Papers in meetings of: Nigeria Society of Engineers; Commonwealth Broadcasting Association. *Hobbies:* Cricket; Lawn and Table tennis; Badminton; Music; Gardening. *Address:* 1 Mount Drive, Independence Layout, Enugu, Anambra State, Nigeria.

UHLENBRUCH, Walter Wilhelm Johannes, b. 21 July, 1936. Recklinghausen, Federal Republic of Germany. Managing Director. m. 6 Oct. 1961, 2 sons, 1 daughter. *Education:* Academy for Worldwide Trade, Frankfurt, Germany, 1955-56; Certificate of Accountancy, Germany, 1956; Hon. Doctorate, London Institute for Business Studies, UK, 1974; Pacific Management, University of Hawaii, Manoa, Hawaii, 1978; CDA., 1976. *Appointments:* Cadet, 1955, Assistant to Sales Director, 1956, Export Group Manager, 1957, travelled to Africa, Australia, East Asia, 1958-61, Westfaelische Metall Industrie, Lippstadt, Germany; Inaugural Director, 1961, Managing Director, Hella-Australia, 1969-; Chairman of the Board, Hella-New Zealand Limited; President and Chairman, Hella-Philippines Inc.; Director of: Astra-Phil. Inc.; Associated Trim Industries Pty. Limited. *Memberships:* Fellow: Institute of Directors of Australia; Company directors' Association; Australian Institute of Management; Vice-President, Federation of Automotive Products Manufacturers; Federal President, 1973-75, Committee of Management, Committee for the Economic Development of Australia; President, Australian-German Welfare Society; Society of Automotive Engineers, Australasia; Australian-German Association; Advanced Education Alumni Association. *Publications:* Project Director and Co-Author of CEDA monograph No. 47: The Motor Vehicle and Component Industry - Policy Origins and Options. *Honours:* Cross of Order of Merit, Federal Republic of Germany, 1977; Senator No. 7652 and Life member, Junior Chamber International, 1968. *Hobbies:* Golf; Reading; Languages; Welfare work. *Address:* 43 Lynch Crescent, Brighton, Victoria 3186, Australia.

UKA, Kalu, b. 2 Mar. 1938, Akanu-Ohafia, Aro/Ohafia Local Government Area, Imo State, Nigeria. University teacher, researcher and writer. m. Ikodiya Mba Uduma,

12 Mar. 1969, 3 sons, 2 daughters. *Education:* BA., Hons., (London), University College, Ibadan, Nigeria, 1959-62; MA., magna laude, University of Toronto, Toronto, Ontario, Canada, 1962-64. *Appointments:* Assistant Producer, Talks Department, Nigerian Broadcasting Corporation, Lagos, Nigeria, 1962; Advertising and Pricing Clerk, ESSO, Toronto, Canada, 1963-64; Assistant Lecturer, Leeds University, Yorkshire, England, 1964-65; Lecturer, Associate Professor, University of Nigeria, Nsukka, Nigeria, 1965-. *Memberships:* Smithsonian Institute of America; Fulbright Alumni Association; Conference on National Literature Association; Association of Nigerian Theatre Artists; Literary Society of Nigeria. *Publications:* Plays: A Harvest for Ants, 1980; A Child is Born, 1975; ikhammaa, 1979; Stonewalls, 1977; Novels: Colonel Ben, 1978; A Consummation of Fire, 1978; Poems: Earth to Earth, 1973. *Honours:* Commonwealth Fellowship, IODE, of Canada, 1962; BA., Finals Award, 1962; Fulbright Scholars Fellowship Award, USA, 1979-80. *Hobbies:* Scrabble; Lawn and Table tennis; Gardening and Landscaping. *Address:* 6 Ako Okwoli Street, University of Nigeria, Nsukka, Nigeria.

UKEGBU, Basil Nnanna, b. 1931, Imerienwe, Owerri, Nigeria. Educationalist; Politician. m. Dorothy Nwanyinna Amuneke, 27 Dec. 1953, 3 sons, 1 daughter. *Education:* BA., Hons., 1955, PhD., 1974, University of London, UK. *Appointments:* Tutor, St. John's College, Kaduna, Nigeria, 1953-54; Principal, New Nigeria High School, Lagos, Nigeria, 1955-57; Founder and Principal, Owerri Grammar School, Imerienwe, Nigeria, 1958-79; Chairman, Governing Council, Alvan Ikoku College of Education, Owerri, Nigeria, 1975-77; Member, Nigerian House of Representatives, 1959-66; NCNC Party Chief Whip; Founder, Imo Technical University, Imerienwe, Owerri, Nigeria, 1981. *Memberships:* Founder, Technological and Economic Development Mission; Nigerian Historical Society. *Publications:* Ngor-Okpala Experiment, 1965; Agrarian Revolution without Tears, 1975; Production in the Nigerian Oil Palm Industry 1900-1954, 1974. *Honours:* Honours College Scholar, St. Patrick's College, Calabar, Nigeria, 1946-49; Nominated Gubernatorial Candidate for Great Nigeria Peoples' Party, Imo State, Nigeria, 1979. *Hobbies:* Farming; Tennis. *Address:* TEDEM, Amafor, Imerienwe, Owerri, Nigeria.

UKEJE, Bennett Onyerisara, b. 22 Apr. 1927, Isulo, Orumba, Aquata, Anambra, Nigeria. Educationalist; University Professor. m. Fidelma Ekwutozia, 1 son, 3 daughters. *Education:* BSc., 1952, MSc., 1953, Ohio University, USA; MA., 1955, Ed.D., 1957, Columbia University, USA. *Appointments:* Principal, New Bethel College, Ouitsha, Nigeria, 1957-61; Lecturer, Education, 1961-64, Senior Lecturer and Reader, 1964-70, Professor of Education and Dean, Faculty of Education, 1970-, University of Nigeria, Nsukka, Nigeria; Provost: Alvan Ikoku College of Education, Owerri, Nigeria, 1974-77; Anambra State College of Education, Awka, Anambra State, Nigeria, 1977-. *Memberships:* President, Nigerian Association for Educational Administration and Planning, 1976-; Commonwealth Council for Educational Administration, 1974-; Committee member, International Intervischahin Programme in Educational Administration. *Publications:* Education for Social Reconstruction, 1966; School and Society, 1975; Pedagogical Problems in Nigeria Today; Foundation of Education, 1979. *Honours:* Fellow, Commonwealth Council for Educational Administration, 1979. *Hobbies:* Lawn Tennis; Hunting. *Address:* Anambra State College of Education, PMB 5011, Awka, Anambra State, Nigeria.

ULRICH, Peter Edward Rooney, b. 16 Mar. 1927, Melbourne, Victoria, Australia. Medical Administration. m. 22 Dec. 1962, 2 sons, 1 daughter. *Education:* Qualified Pharmaceutical Chemist, Victoria College of Pharmacy, Australia, 1950; MB.,BS., Melbourne University, Australia, 1962; Diploma, Public Health, Sydney University, Australia, 1973. *Appointments:* Retail Pharmacy, 1950-52; Lieutenant Pharmacist, RAAMC., 1952-56; Resident Medical Officer, Queen Victoria Memorial Hospital, Melbourne, Australia, 1963-64; General Practice, 1964-70; Medical Officer, 1970-77, Director, Queensland Division, 1977-, Commonwealth Department of Health, Australia. *Address:* 26 Foxton Street, Indooroopilly, Queensland 4068, Australia.

UMECHE, Luke Enyinnaya, b. 15 Sept. 1944, Aba, Imo State, Nigeria. Consultant Architect. m. Elizabeth

Chinwe Umeokwuaka, 14 Aug. 1976, 3 daughters. *Education:* B.Arch., Hons., University of Nigeria, Enugu Campus, Nigeria, 1973; Nigerian Institute of Architects, 1975. *Appointments:* Architect: State Ministry of Works & Survey, Kano, Nigeria, 1973; Onafowokan Cityscape Group, Lagos, Nigeria, 1974-75; Architect and Head of Officer, Ekwueme Associates, Sokoto, Nigeria, 1976-77; Principal, own Practice, Le Chez Consultants, Nigeria, 1978-. *Memberships:* Nigerian Institute of Architects; Peoples Club of Nigeria; President, University of Nigeria Alumni Association, Sokoto, 1980. *Creative Works:* Design for Conference Centre, Argungu Fishing Village, Nigeria, 1979. *Hobbies:* Watching Wild Life; Travel. *Address:* 4B Clapperton Road, PU Box 206, Sokoto, Nigeria.

UMEH, John Anenechukwa, b. 3 Oct. 1934, Nnobi, Nigeria. University Professor; Chartered Surveyor; Land Economist; Feasibility/Viability Appraiser and Valuer. m. Rich Enujioke Oti, 25 May 1968, 2 sons, 4 daughters. *Education:* BSc., 1962, College of Estate Management, University of London, England, 1957-62; MA., 1964, Pembroke College, University of Cambridge, England, 1964-65; MSc., London, England, 1970; MRSH., 1962; ARVA., 1963; AAI., 1965; ARICS., 1965; FNIVS., 1969; FRVA., 1974; FRICS., 1975. *Appointments:* Tutor, Prince Secondary Commercial College, Onitsha, Nigeria, 1953-54; Tutor, Assistant Principal, Etukokwu Secondary Commercial College, Onitsha, Nigeria, 1955-57; Technical Assistant, Architects Department, Town Planning Section, London County Council, UK, summer 1962; Assistant Lecturer, 1962-64; lecturer, 1964-70, Senior Lecturer, 1970-73, Ag. Head, 1970-72, Head, 1973-80, Department of Estate Management, Reader, 1973-74, Ag.Dean, 1973, Dean, 1975, Faculty of Environmental Studies, Professor of Estate Management, 1974-, University of Nigeria; Consultant to a number of firms on Valuation, Property Rating and Land Taxation; Served as external examiner and moderator to several Universities and Technical Colleges; Member of 3 man Property Rates Assessment Appeal Tribunal, Enugu Zone, 27th Sept. 1979-; Present Dean, Faculty of Environmental Studies, 1981-82. *Memberships:* Fellow, member and Associate of numerous Associations. *Publications:* Numerous publications including: Compulsory Acquisition of Land and Compensation in Nigeria, 1973; Feasibility and Viability Appraisal, 1977; The Problems of Urbanisation in Africa, 1972; Human Settlements as a Tax Base, 1978; Editor-in-Chief of The Tropical Environment; Okponku Abu, (Igbo poems), 1981; Nkenu (Igbo legends on Nkenu), 1981. *Honours:* Several University Scholarships and awards. *Hobbies:* Writing; Thinking; Travelling; Music; Reading; Collection of African legends, folktales and proverbs; Igbo philosophy and traditional religion. *Address:* 19 Mulberry Close, Cambridge, CB4 2AS, England.

UMEZURUIKE, Israel Nzeako, b. 30 June 1932, Ude Ofeme, Umuahia in Ikwuano/Umuahia L G A., Nigeria. Lawyer. m. Mercy Nwanganga Ndunaga, 27 Mar. 1963, 3 sons, 1 daughter. 02 LL.B., Kings College, University of London, UK, 1962-65; Called to English Bar, Inner Temple, London, UK, 1964; Nigerian Law School, Lagos, Nigeria, Jan.-Apr. 1965; Called to Nigerian Bar, Solicitor and Advocate, Supreme Court of Nigeria, 1965. *Appointments:* Private Legal Practice, 1965-67, 1976-; Secretary, Legal Adviser, Co-operative Bank of Eastern Nigeria Limited, 1971-74. *Memberships:* National Executive Committee, 1980-, Ombudsman Committee, 1981-, Nigerian Bar Association. *Honours:* Won Moots Final, Law Faculty, Kings College, London, UK, 1964. *Hobbies:* Reading; International affairs; Farming. *Address:* 10 Eziama Street, GRA Aba, Imo State, Nigeria.

UMOH, Stephen Edem, b. 8 June 1953, Ikot Ambang, Ibiono Ibom, Cross River State, Nigeria. Medical Recorder. m. Ikwo Esu, 13 July 1975, 1 son, 2 daughters. *Education:* Diploma, Medical Records, School of Health Technology, Calabar, Nigeria, 1978. *Appointments:* TB Records, Ministry of Health, 1978-79, Nov.1979-Oct.1980; Nigerian Navy, 1979. *Memberships:* Divisional Sergeant, Calabar, St. John's Ambulance Brigade; Affiliate member, Nigerian Health Records Association. *Publications:* Contributor to Nigerian Chronicle. *Honours:* Awarded Prize for Painting, Festival of Arts and Culture, Nigeria, 1973; Awarded Prize for Academic Excellence, School of Health Technology, Calabar, Nigeria. *Hobbies:* Reading; Writing; Travel;

Drama. *Address:* No. 14A Oyo Efam Street, Calabar, Nigeria.

UNDERHILL, Hon. Justice Peter Francis, b. 30 Jan. 1928, Brisbane, Australia. Judge. m. Nancy Dudley Hoffman, 23 Jan. 1962, 2 sons. *Education:* BA., 1955, LL.B., 1957, University of Queensland, Australia. *Appointments:* Practised at Queensland Bar, Australia; Queensland Director, Australian Legal Aid Office, Australia, 1975-78; Judge, Family Court of Australia, 1978-. *Memberships:* Vice Chairman, Executive Committee, World Federation of United Nations Associations, Geneva, Switzerland; Vice President, Unicef Committee of Australia; Chairman, Queensland UNICEF Committee; Councillor, The Australiana Fund; Committee, Australians Care for Refugees. *Honours:* OBE., 1977; UN Peace Medal, 1977; Father of the Year, 1979. *Hobbies:* Surfing; Tennis; Reading; Music. *Address:* 36 Hanlon Street, Chelmer, Queensland 4068, Australia.

UNDERWOOD, William Elphinstone, b. 20 Oct. 1903, Birmingham, England. Surgeon. m. Vera Florence Beck, 1 June 1935, 2 sons. *Education:* Science Scholarship, London University, 1924; MA., (Hons. Natural Sciences Tripos) 1923, MB.,B.Chir., 1928, Cambridge University; MRCS., (England), LRCP., (London), 1927; FRCS., (England), 1929. *Appointments:* Emergency Surgeon, St Andrew's Hospital, London; Consultant Surgeon, Harrow Hospital; Assistant Surgeon, St Pauls Hospital for Genito Urinary Diseases, London; Associate Urologist, West End Hospital for Nervous Diseases, London; Assistant Surgeon & Sub-Dean, Medical College, St Bartholomew's Hospital, London; Chief Surgeon, Johannesburg Hospital & Professor of Surgery, University of the Witwatersrand; Group Medical Consultant, MTD., Management Services, Zimbabwe. *Publications:* Several contributions to professional medical journals. *Honours:* Jacksonian Prize, 1936, Hunterian Professor, 1937, Royal College of Surgeons, England; Mentioned in Despatches, 1940-41; OBE., (Military), 1942; Honorary Colonel, RAMC. *Hobbies:* Music; Ham (Amateur) Radio. *Address:* The Clinic House, Alaska Medical Centre, Private Bag 7540, Sinoia, Zimbabwe.

UNGAR, Gerald Henry, b. 21 July 1930, Vienna. Medical Practitioner. m. Elsa Sobel, 6 Mar. 1964, 1 son, 1 daughter. *Education:* MB.,ChB., University of Liverpool, 1949-55. *Appointments:* Medical Officer, (Flt.Lt.,) RAF., 1956-58; Junior Hospital Medical Officer, Spinal Injuries, Stoke Mandeville Hospital, Aylesbury, Buckinghamshire, England, 1959-61; Registrar, Physical Medicine, Radcliffe Infirmary, Oxford, 1961-64 and St Stephen's Hospital, Fulham, London, 1964-65; Junior Specialist, Rehabilitation (Sqn. Ldr.), Royal Air Force, 1965-68; Senior Registrar, Spinal Injuries, 1968-73, Locum Consultant, 1973-74, Stoke Mandeville Hospital; Deputy Medical Director, Spinal Injuries Unit, Austin Hospital, Heidelberg, Victoria, Australia, 1974-. *Memberships:* International Medical Society of Paraplegia; International Rehabilitation Medicine Association; British Association of Rheumatology & Rehabilitation; *Publications:* Various contributions on spinal injuries. *Hobby:* Licensed Amateur Radio Operator. *Address:* 89 Greenridge Avenue, Templestowe, Victoria, 3106, Australia.

UNIYAL, M. P., b. 25 Nov. 1939, Uttarkashi, UP, India. Teaching; Professor and Head. m. 23 Jan. 1967, 2 daughters. *Education:* MA., (Sanskrit), 1961; M.Ed., (Education), 1966; D.Phil., (Education), 1973. *Appointments:* Lecturer in Government, PG College for Women, Punjab, 1961-64; Lecturer in Education, Allahabad University, 1966-76; Reader in Education, Kumaan University, 1976-80; Professor/Head/Dean, Faculty of Education, Gashwal University, Srinagar (UP), India. *Memberships:* India Academy of Social Sciences; Advisory Board, Model Institute of Educational Research & Training; Advisor, Indian Association of Teacher Educators; Director, Institute of Educational Planning & Developement. *Publications:* 15 Emperical Research papers on Academic Motivation; 17 Research Papers on Educational Change; 27 Articles in different journals; 3 Books. *Honours:* All India Teacher Training, Debate First Prize, 1965; Gold Medal for topping in Teacher Training, 1965; Gold Medal for topping in M.Ed., 1966; MMM Award for the Book, 1975. *Hobbies:* Debating; Poetry writing. *Address:* 112 Allengunj, Allahabad, UP, India.

UNYOVE, Joseph Akpofa (Chief), b. 14 Feb. 1934, Orie. Architecture. m. Koinde Eruagbera, 8 Apr. 1965, 1 son, 2 daughters. *Education:* Nigerian College of Arts, Science and Technology, 1958-61; Ahmadu Bello University, Zaria, 1962-64; AA School of Architecture, London, 1967-68; B.Arch.; ABU; ARIBA; MRSH; MNIA. *Appointments:* Station Master, Nigerian Railways, 1952-58; Architect, Mid-West (now Bendel) State, Public Service, 1964-69; Managing Director/Architect in charge of Consultant Architects Group, 1969-. *Memberships:* Chairman, Nigerian Institute of Architects, Bendel State Chapter; Nigerian Institute of Architects; Royal Institute of British Architects; Royal Society of Health (London). *Publications:* Isoko Numerals (Ikelakele Isoko); Armed Robbery in Nigeria, Causes and Prevention; Various Architectural Designs. *Honours:* Chairman, Bendel State Steering Committee (Electoral Commission), Local Government Elections, 1976-77; Chairman, Bendel Hotels Board, 1976-79; Chief of: Otota of Irri, 1973 and Oketa of Okpe, 1975. *Hobbies:* Writing; Broadcasting. *Address:* 22 2nd Freedom Street, Off Stadium Road, Benin City, Nigeria.

UPTON, Gordon Noel, b. 24 Dec. 1920, Sydney, Australia. Foreign Affairs. m. 14 May 1944, 3 daughters. *Education:* BA., (Sydney), 1941. *Appointments:* Australian Department of Trade and Customs, 1937-41; RAAF., 1941-45; Australian Department of External Affairs, 1946-66; High Commissioner to Sri Lanka, 1966-70; Department of Defence, Canberra, 1970-73; Minister, Australian High Commission, London, 1973-74; Minister, Australian Embassy, Washington, 1974-76; Australian High Commissioner to Fiji, amd Tonga, 1976-79; Western Samoa, 1977-79; Tunalu, 1978-79; Australian High Commissioner to India and Ambassador to Nepal, 1980-. *Hobbies:* Golf; Walking; Reading. *Address:* Australian High Commission, New Delhi, India.

UREN, Thomas, b. 28 May 1921, Balmain, New South Wales, Australia. Member of Parliament. m. *Appointments:* Retailer; Royal Australian Artiller, 1939-45; 2nd AIF, 1941; Bombardier, 2/1 Heavy Battery, Timor; Japanese Prisoner of War in Timor, Java, Singapore, burma-Siam Railway and Japan, 1942-45; Parliamentary Service: House of Representatives, Reid, New South Wales, 1958, 1961, 1963, 1966, 1969, 1972, 1975 and 1977; Ministerial Appointments: Minister for Urban and Regional Development, 1971-75; Acting Ministries: Services and Property, 1973; Parliamentary Pary Positions: Member, federal Parliamentary Labor Party Opposition Executive, 1969-72; Spokesman on Housing and Urban Affairs; Deputy Leader, 1976-77; Spokesman on Urban and Regional Development 1976-77, and on Urban and Regional Affairs; Decentralisation, Local Government, Housing and Construction, 1977-; Member, ALP., National Executive, 1976-77. *Publications:* Member of several Commonwealth Conferences and Delegations; Official visits to Europe, United States and Canada for talks on environmental issues, 1974. *Address:* 10J Bridge Street, Granville, New South Wales, 2142, Australia.

URHOBO, Emmanuel, b. 27 Apr. 1931, Benin City, Nigeria. Economist; Lawyer. m. (1) Pamela, 19 Sept. 1957 (Divorced), 1 daughter, (2) Linda, 16 May 1979, 2 daughters (Adopted). *Education:* Barrister-at-Law, (B1), Middle Temple, London, 1959; BSc., Econ. (Hons), London, 1960; MA., ·The American University, 1973, PhD., 1979. *Appointments:* Practicising Barrister, Nigeria, 1960-66; Owner/Managing Director, Becc and Mann, Ltd., Lagos, 1965-; Executive Director for Relief and Rehabilitation, World Council of Churches/Christian Council of Nigeria during Biafran War, 1969-72; Elected member of the Bendel State House of Assembly, 1979. *Memberships:* Royal Economic Society; Nigerian Institute of International Affairs; Nigerian Institute of Management. *Publications:* Relief Operations in the Nigerian Civil War, 1978; Disaster Relief Administration, 1978. *Hobbies:* Fishing; Swimming; Travel. *Address:* Edjeba Village, Warri, PO Box 1394, Bendel State, Nigeria, West Africa.

URWICK, Alan Bedford, b. 2 May 1930, London. HM Diplomatic Service. m. Marta Yolanda Montagne, 9 Dec. 1960, 3 sons. *Education:* Rugby (Scholar), 1943-47; New College Oxford, 1949-52, First Class Honours Degree in Modern History, 1952. *Appointments:* Entered HM Diplomatic Service, 1952; Brussels, 1953-55; Moscow, 1957-59; Baghdad, 1960-61; Head of

Chancery & Consul, Amman, 1965-67; Washington, 1967-70; Cairo, 1971-78; Central Policy Review Staff, Cabinet Office, 1973-75; Head of Near East & North Africa Department, FCO, 1975-76; Minister, Madrid, 1977-78; HM Ambassador, Amman, 1979-. *Honours:* CMG, 1978. *Hobbies:* Gardening; History. *Address:* The Moat House, Slaugham, Nr Hayward's Heath, Sussex, England.

USHEWOKUNZE, Christopher Machingura, b. 27 Apr. 1944, Selukwe, Zimbabwe. Lawyer/Administrator. m. Juliet, 24 Dec. 1971, 4 sons. *Education:* LLB., (Hons) Edinburgh, 1970; LL.M., (London), 1971; Barrister-at-Law, Middle Temple, 1973. *Appointments:* Lecturer in Law, University of Zambia, 1974-76; Senior Lecturer in Law, United Nations Institute for Namibia, 1976-80; Legal Consultant, UNCTAD, Zimbabwe Project, 1979; Secretary for Mines and Energy Resources, Government of Zimbabwe. *Memberships:* Honourable Society of the Middle Temple, London. *Publications:* Contributor to professional journal. *Address:* PO Box 7709, Causeway, Greengrove, Salisbury, Zimbabwe.

USHEWOKUNZE, Herbert Sylvester Masiyiwa, b. 7 June 1938, Marandellas, Zimbabwe. Former Medical Practitioner; Cabinet Minister. Divorced, 5 sons, 3 daughters. *Education:* Bachelor of Medicine, Bachelor of Surgery, University of Natal, 1963. *Appointments:* Internship, King Edward VIII Hospital, Durban; Railways Medical Officer, Rhodesia Railways; Private practice, 1966; Was the first African General Practitioner in Metabeleland; Was the first African to own and run a Nursing Home in Zimbabwe, The Marondera Polyclinic, Bulawayo; Also had practices in Mkoba Township (Gwelo), amaveni Township (Que Que). Opened a charity clinic in the Gokwe area near the Binga border in response to the peasant cry for primary health care in the area; Pan-Africanist Congress of Azania; Zanu Administration, Matebeleland; African National Council; ANC Central Committee, Deputy National Chairman; ZANU Central Committee, External Wing; ZANU National Executive and Secretary for Health; Overall Commander of the ZANLA Medical Corps; Minister of Health in the ZANU (PF) Government. *Memberships:* Zimbabwe Medical Association; *Publications:* Severl papers on Primary Health Care. *Honours:* Gold Medallist (Obstetrics and Gynaecology), 1963; Charles Drew Post-Graduate Medical School, USA., 1981. *Hobbies:* Soccer; Tennis (Lawn and Table); Cricket; Athletics; Rugby; Badminton; Music; Speech and Drama; Politics; Traditional Medicine. *Address:* 686 Glenwood Drive, Glen Lorne, Salisbury, Zimbabwe.

USMAN, Asaad K, b. 27 Sept. 1905, Siasi, Sulu, Philippines. Lawyer or Barrister. m. Haja Fatima, 29 Sept. 1963, 8 sons, 1 daughter. *Education:* AA, Pre Law, University of Manila, 1934; College of Law, University of the Philippines, 1934-38; Passed Bar Examination, 1939-40. *Appointments:* Circuit Court Judge for Siasi, Tapul, Ubian and Tondubas Districts, 1940-53; General practice, 1953-73; Claimant to North Borneo, now called State of Sabah, a component part of the Federated States of Malaysia, 1962-. *Memberships:* President, Strength of the South, 1934; Vice-President, Sulu Bar Association; Vice-President, Muslim Association of the Philippines; Chairman, Preparatory Independence Commission Constitutional Delegate from Sulu, 1943; Adviser and Chairman to the Sultanate of Sulu, Rumah Bechard (Law Making Body). *Publications:* Mat Salleh, The National Hero of Sabah; Mat Salleh Rebellion, 1894-1902. *Honours:* Captain and Member of The Philippine Olympic Swimming Team in three Far Eastern Olympic Championship Games, held in Osaka, Japan (Medal), Manila (Medal), Shanghai, Chine (Medal), 1923, 1925 & 1927. *Hobbies:* Swimming; Horse Riding; Going places and meeting new friends. *Address:* 2093 Jalan Telok, Likas Bay, Kota Kinabalu, Sabah, Malaysia.

UTZ, John Walter, b. 9 July 1928, Sydney, NSW, Australia. Chairman & Chief Executive. m. June Wawn, 7 Feb. 1952, 1 son, 3 daughters. *Education:* Advanced Management Program Course, Harvard University, 1960. *Appointments:* Commenced with Wormald International Ltd., 1952; Newcastle Manager, 1955; NSW State Manager, 1960; General Manager, 1964; Appointed to Principal Board, 1965; Deputy Chairman and Managing Director, 1968; Chairman and Chief Executive, 1977; Chairman, Australian Mutual Provident Soc., Fire & Gen. Ins. Co. Ltd; Director, Byrne Davidson

Ind. Ltd.; Vice-Chairman, Rothmans of Pall Mall (Australia) Ltd.; Standard Telephones & Cables Pty. Ltd.; Director, NSW br.bd. Australia Mut. Provident Society; Director, Woolworths Ltd.; Director, The Australian Bi-Centennial Authority Group; Chairman, Australia-NZ Businessmen's Council Ltd. *Memberships:* Def. Ind. Com. Dept. Def., Devl.Corp. New South Wales; Com. Econ. Devel. of Australia; Fellow, Australian Institute of Management; Australian Ac.Sci., Institute Directors. *Honours:* Officer, Order of Australia, 1979. *Hobbies:* Water Sports; Golf; Reading. *Address:* 22 Edgecliffe Esplanade, Seaforth, Sydney, NSW, 2092, Australia.

UWADIA, Raymond Aivbore, b. 22 Aug, 1945, Benin City, Nigeria. Marketing. m. 7 Mar, 1969, 3 sons, 2 daughters. *Education:* WAEC, 1965; Diploma in Sales, 1971; News Certificate, 1976. *Creative Works:* Painting and Decoration, Imaginary Drawing & Drawing from Life. *Honours:* Hussey Cup, 1964. *Hobbies:* Sports; Travelling. *Address:* No 6 2nd Guobadia Lane, New Benin, Benin City, Bendel State, Nigeria.

UWAOMA, Hyacinth Chukwuneme, b. 24 Dec.1950, Orlu, Imo State, Nigeria. Missionary/Publisher. *Education:* Missionary Training. *Appointments:* Army: Anti-Aircraft Operator, 1967-70; Missionary Teacher & Christian Youth Leader, 1973-81; Daily Times Newspapers, 1975-80. *Memberships:* President, Christian Contact International Club; Co-ordinator, College Unity; PEN Association. *Publications:* Four religious booklets. *Hobbies:* Drama; Preaching; Sports; Travelling, Farming; Hunting. *Address:* 28 Amore Street, Olodi, Apapa, Lagos, Nigeria.

UYA, Okon Edet, b. 3 Oct. 1942, Okuko, Oron, Nigeria. University Professor. m. Margaret, 29 Jan. 1978, 1 son, 3 daughters. *Education:* BA, (Hons), 2nd Upper (History), University of Ibadan, 1966; MA, 1968, PhD, 1969, University of Wisconsin, Madison. *Appointments:* Senior History Teacher, West African People's Institute, Calabar, Nigeria, 1966-67; Reader, History Department, University of Wisconsin, USA, 1967-68; Project Assistant, University of Wisconsin, Visiting Assistant Professor of History, Beloit College, Wisconsin, Telelecturer, Berea College, Kentucky, USA, 1968-69; Special Consultant on Afro-American Studies, University of Wisconsin, 1969, Visiting Assistant Professor, History Department, 1969-70, Consultant, 1970, Associate Professor, Afro-American Studies Department, 1970-71; Visiting Associate Professor, Amherst College, USA, Visiting Lecturer (part-time), University of Maryland, USA, 1971-72; Associate Professor, African Studies and Research Programe, 1971-72, Professor of History, Howard University USA, 1972-74; William Leo Hansberry Visiting Distinguished Professor of African Historiography, Africana Studies and Research Center, Cornell University, USA, 1973-74; Senior Lecturer, Department of History/Archaeology, University of Nigeria, Calabar Campus, 1974-75; Professor of History, University of Calabar, 1976-. *Memberships:* Historical Society of Nigeria; American Historical Association; Organization of American Historians; Oral History As-

sociation of the USA; African Heritage Studies Association (USA); Society for the Study of Negro Life and History (USA). *Publications:* From Slavery to Public Service: Robert Smalls, 1839-1915, 1971; Black Brotherhood: Afro-Americans and Africa, 1971; African History: Some Problems in Methodology and Perspectives, 1974; Several Monographs; Numerous chapters in books, articles in learned journals and research papers. 06 History, Latin and English Prizes, Hope Waddell Training Institute, Calabar, Nigeria, 1962; Under-Graduate and Post-Graduate Scholarships; University of Wisconsin Graduate School Fellowship; The Civil War Round Table Fellowship, 1970; Several Research Grants. *Hobbies:* Tennis; Debates; Reading. *Address:* 32 Atekong Drive Housing Estate, Calabar, CRS, Nigeria.

UZOCHUKWU, Samuel, b. 23 Apr. 1940, Ebenator, Nnewi Local Government Area. Lecturer. m. Grace Ego Okeke, 5 Sept. 1969, 3 sons, 2 daughters. *Education:* BA, Hons English 2nd Class (Upper Division) University of Ife, 1966; Post-Graduate Diploma in Linguistics, University of Ibadan, 1975; PhD, University of Lagos, 1981. *Appointments:* Teacher, Primary Schools, 1954-62, Secondary Schools, 1966-70, Yaba College of Technology, 1970-74, University of Lagos, 1974-. *Memberships:* Treasurer/Financial Secretary, University of Ife Dramatic Society, 1964-66; Treasurer Ebenator Improvement Union, Lagos Branch, 1973-; Society for Promoting Igbo Language and Culture, 1975-; Standardization Committee on Igbo Language, 1975-. *Publications:* Igbo Elegiac Poetry; Metre and Rhythm in Igbo Oral Poetry; Lexical Matching in Igbo Oral Poetry. *Honours:* Certificate for participating in the Seminar on Igbo Arts and Music, 1976 and Igbo Methodology, 1979. *Hobbies:* Reading; Table Tennis; Draughts. *Address:* Department of African Languages and Literatures, University of Lagos, Nigeria.

UZOMAKA, Osondu John Eze, b. 29 Dec. 1939, Nkwerre, Imo State, Nigeria. Civil Engineer. m. Ngozika Mercy Ukegbu, 18 Sept. 1965, 2 sons, 3 daughters. *Education:* BSc, First Class Hons, Applied Science, 1966, PhD., 1969, University of Newcastle-upon-Tyne, England. *Appointments:* Graduate Engineer, AP Mason Pittendrigh & Parners, Newcastle-upon-Tyne, England, 1966 and Ward Ashcroft & Partners, Liverpool, England, 1969-71; Geotechnical Research & Development Engineer, Cementation Research Ltd., Rickmansworth, England, 1971-73; Lecturer to Professor, University of Nigeria, Nsukka, Nigeria, 1973-80; Principal, College of Technology, Owerri, Nigeria, 1980-. *Memberships:* Registered Engineer, Council of Registered Engineers of Nigeria; Institution of Civil Engineers, England; American Society of Civil Engineers; Nigerian Society of Engineers; International Society of Soil Mechanics & Foundation Engineers; British Concrete Society. *Publications:* Over 30 contributions to International Technical Journals. *Honours:* Fellow, Nigerian Academic of Sciences, 1980. *Hobbies:* Photography; Tennis. *Address:* 19 Ohaozara Street, Aladinma Housing Estate, Owerri, Imo State, Nigeria.

V

VAIDYANATHAN, Trikkur Somanathaiyer, b. 8 Nov. 1930, Coimbatore, India. Financial Management. m. Jaya, 10 July 1964, 1 son, 1 daughter. *Education:* Bachelor of Arts, Madras University, 1949; SAS, Professional Accountancy, Government of India, 1955; Master of Commerce, Delhi University, 1960; Chartered, Institute of Cost and Works Accountants, 1967. *Appointments:* Auditor/SAS Accountant, Accounts Officer, Madras, India; Principal Accountant, Ministry of Health, Lusaka, Zambia 1967-70; Chief Cost Accountant, Ministry of Trade and Industry, 1970-73; Price Controller, Office, Price Controller, Ministry of Commerce, 1973-75; Financial Controller, Agricultural Development Project, Sokoto State, Nigeria, 1975-80; Financial Advisor, World Bank, Northern Integrated Agricultural Development Project, Makeni, Sierra Leone, 1981-. *Memberships:* Fellow, Institute of Cost and Works Accountants; British Institute of Management; National Association of Accountants New York; Treasurer, Tuberculosis Association, Zambia; Chairman, Gusau Project Recreation Club. *Publications:* Many articles in the Zambia Daily Mail and Times, on inflation, prices, OPEC and the World economic situation; Several technical papers on financial management topics in the Management Accountant. *Hobbies:* Comparative Theology; Country Walking; Writing articles of general/special interest. *Address:* B-2 Brindavan, MICO Colony, Apollo Avenue, Besant Nagar, Madras 600 090, India.

VAKATORA, Rayalu Tomasi, b. 18 Sept. 1926, Naivilaca, Noco, Rewa, Fiji. Politician. m. Wainiqolo Rarawa 3 Mar. 1951, 2 sons, 3 daughters. *Education:* Suva Methodist Boys' School; Teachers Training College; London University; Ruskin College, Oxford; London School of Economics. *Appointments:* Teacher, 1948-55; Junior Labour Inspector, 1955-69; Secretary and Commissioner of Labour 1969-72; Permanent Secretary for Transport and Tourism, Ministry of Communications, works and Tourism, Fiji, 1972-74; Senator, Fiji, 1976; Member, House of Representatives and Minister of Tourism, Transport and Civil Aviation, 1977-80; Minister for Labour, Industrial Relations and Immigration, 1980-. *Memberships:* Major, Fiji Military Forces; Great Council of Chiefs. *Address:* 16 Volavola Road, Tamavua, Suva, Fiji.

VALDOVINOS, Jorge, b. 3 Sept. 1922, Chile. Diplomatic. m. Marta Fuenzalida 4 Jan. 1947, 2 sons, 1 daughter. *Education:* Instituto Nacional, Universidad de Chile and Universidad Central de Ecuador: Law degree; PhD, Law Jurisprudence. *Appointments:* Chilean Ministry for Foreign Affairs, 1941; Embassies of Chile, Argentina, Ecuador, USA, Brazil, Japan, Norway; Counsellor and minister Counsellor; Ambassador to Dominican Republic, 1976; Ambassador to Australia 1978-. *Creative Works:* Photographic Exhibitions in Australia, Chile and Dominican Republic. *Honours:* Awarded decorations: Ecuador, Japan, Brazil and Dominican Republic. *Hobbies:* Photography; Listening to Music; Reading History, etc. *Address:* 8 Timbarra Crescent, O'Malley ACT 2606, Australia.

VALENTINE, Roger Stuart James, b. 5 July 1932, Hobart Tasmania Australia. Legal Practitioner. m. Barbara Elizabeth Darling, 1 son, 2 daughters. *Education:* The Hutchins School, Hobart, 1938-50; Bachelor of Laws University of Tasmania, 1951-55. *Appointments:* Private Practice, Partner, Hodgman & Valentine, Lovibond Valentine & Roach, Lovibond Valentine Roach & Thiessen, 1956-77; Senior Solicitor, Public Trust Office, 1977; Chairman, Child Protection Assessment Board, 1977; Chairman, Licensing Board of Tasmania (Alcohol), 1980-. *Memberships:* National Vice President, Australian Chamber of Commerce, 1970-71; Inaugral Chairman Federation, Tasmanian Chamber of Commerce 1968-70; President, Hobart Chamber of Commerce, 1967-68 and 1972; Chairman, Tasmanian Tourist Council, 1974-77; Tribune Confederation of Australian Motor Sport; Deputy State Chairman and Chairman, Metropolitan Division of the Heart Fund Appeal, 1969; Pilot Officer RAAF Reserve. *Hobby:* Water Skiing. *Address:* 35 Norfolk Crescent, Sandy Bay, Hobart, Tasmania, Australia.

VAN DER BYL, Pieter Kenyon Fleming Voltelyn, b. 11 Nov. 1923, Cape Town, South Africa. Landowner. m. Her Serene Highness Princess Charlotte of Liechtenstein, 31 Aug. 1979, 1 son. *Education:* Diocesan College, Cape Town, 1933-41; Pretoria University, 1942; BA(Cantab), Law, Pembroke College, Cambridge, 1946-47; Harvard University 1947-48. *Appointments:* Member of Parliament for Hartley, 1964; Junior Government Whip, 1963; Deputy Minister of Information, Immigration & Tourism, 1964; Minister, 1948; Minister of Foreign Affairs and Defence, 1974; Minister of Foreign Affairs and Public Service, 1976; Minister of Foreign Affairs, Information, Immigration and Tourism, 1977; etc. *Memberships:* Commonwealth Parliamentary Association; Shikar Club; Cavalry & Guards Club; Civil Service Club, Cape Town; Salisbury Club. *Honours:* Grand Officer of the Legion of Merit; Independence Decoration; Commandeur de l'Etoile Equatoriale. *Hobbies:* Big Game Hunting; Shooting; Fishing. *Address:* 4 Bath Road, Salisbury, Zimbabwe.

VAN DER MERWE, Frederick John, b. 14 Aug. 1927, Windhoek, Namibia. Publisher. m. 10 July 1957, 1 son, 2 daughters. *Education:* BA, 1950; UED Natal 1951. *Appointments:* Assistant Teacher, Durban Preparatory High School, Durban Natal, 1952; Marketing Department, Lever Brothers, 1953-54; Principal, Central African Correspondence College, 1955-67; Managing Director, The College Press, 1968-81. *Memberships:* Salisbury Club; New Club; Royal Salisbury Golf Club. *Hobbies:* Golf; Photography. *Address:* 5 Stafford Road, Mount Pleasant, Salisbury, Zimbabwe.

VAN DRIEL, Bertus, b. 23 June 1918, The Hague, Holland. Company Director. m. Henriette Jacoba Munting, 14 May 1947, 2 daughters. *Education:* Matriculation Certificate; Ing. (Holland), Civil Engineering; Higher School of Technology, Holland. *Appointments:* Captain (Res.), Corps of Royal Engineers, Dutch Army; Manager, Dutch Construction Company, Holland; Manager, Dutch Construction Company, Australia; Founder, Managing Director, Van Driel Pty. Ltd., Master Builders and Civil Engineers, Melbourne, Australia; Chairman of Directors. *Memberships:* ERASMUS Cultural Society; Royal Brighton Yacht Club; Royal Geelong Yacht Club. *Publications:* Author: Commando Group Biesbosch, 1945. *Honours:* The Bronze Cross, Holland, 1949; The Order for Order and Peace, Indonesia, 1946-47. *Hobbies:* Sailing; Skiing; Music; Reading; Travelling. *Address:* 81 Bambra Road, Caulfield, Victoria 3161, Australia.

VAN DUSEN, Richard Herbert, b. 12 Oct. 1935, Brockville, Ontario, Canada. Chartered Accountant. m. Ellen Gail Campbell, 22 Nov. 1958, 1 son, 2 daughters. *Education:* Chartered Accountant, 1960; Registered Industrial Accountant, 1965; Senior Managers' Program, Harvard Business School, 1977. *Appointments:* Treasurer, Ames Company of Canada, 1960-66; Management Consultant, United Nations Development Program, Syria, Jamaica, 1966-69; Executive Vice President, Miles-Sankyo Company, Tokyo, 1969-73; General Manager, In charge of Miles' Operations in Japan, 1973-78; Area Vice President, Far East, 1978-. *Memberships:* Institute of Chartered Accountants, Ontario Canada; Society of Management Accountants, Canada; Toronto Board of Trade; Canada Businessmen Association Hong Kong; Foreign Correspondents' Club, Tokyo and Hong Kong; Tokyo American Club; Asiatic Society of Japan; American Chamber of Commerce, Hong Kong; Harvard Alumni; Harvard Business School Association, Hong Kong; Hong Kong Association, Pharmaceutical Industry; Hong Kong Art Centre; Hong Kong Productivity Centre; Hong Kong Archaelogical Society, etc. *Publications:* Cost Accounting, Management Development Centre, Damascus, Syria; Thesis on Management Accounting, SICA Library, Hamilton Ontario; Communication Information, 1968; Through Foreign Eyes, 1972. *Honours:* Valediction of Registered Industrial Accounting Graduating Class, 1965. *Hobbies:* Music; Restoring Old Furniture; Oriental Antiques. *Address:* Apt. C-2 Grenville House, 1-3 Magazine Gap Road, Hong Kong.

VANNI, Victor Oje, b. 25 Feb. 1942, Igueben, Bendel State, Nigeria. Business Director. m. Henrietta Vanni, 25 Aug. 1972, 2 sons, 2 daughters. *Education:* BSc Hons, 1968; ACCS, 1964. *Appointments:* Managing Director: Vanni Int. Security Systems Limited, 1971-; Chubb Alarms, (Nig) Limited, 1975-; Intercontinental

Airlines Limited, 1978-; Hobkarn Holidays Limited, 1980-. *Hobbies:* Swimming; Golf; Table Tennis; Squash. *Address:* Oregun Residential Area, Ogungbe Layout, Ikeja, Nigeria.

VARADE, Supada Bhiku, b. 5 Dec. 1936, Narwel, Maharashtra, India. Professor. m. Shakuntala Varade, 24 May 1964. *Education:* BSc (Ag) Nagpur University, 1959; MSc (Ag) IARI, New Delhi, 1961; PhD, Indian Institute of Tech. Kharagpur, 1966. *Appointments:* Assistant Lecturer, Indian Institute of Tech. Kharagpur, 1963-70; Lecturer, 1970; Soil Physicist, 1970-74; Professor and Head, Marathwada Agricultural University, Parbhani, 1974-. *Memberships:* Indian Society of Soil Science; American Society of Agronomy; Soil Science Society of America; Maharashtra Journal of Agricultural Universities. *Publications:* 120 Research papers; Indian Soil Science Literature, 1966-77. *Honours:* Executive Council member of Indian Society of Soil Science; Scholorship, through out College Education; Fellow, Indian Institute of Technology; Post doctoral Fellow, UCR, Riverside, California, USA. *Hobby:* Studying religious books. *Address:* Agriculture Chem. & Soil Science, Marathwada Agricultural University, Parbhani, Maharashtra, India.

VASAGAM, Namasivayam Manicka, b. 2 July 1901, Kokuvil, Jaffna, Sri Lanka. Financial Assistant (retired). m. Ratnamah Kandish, 2 Feb. 1922, 4 sons, 1 daughter. *Appointments:* District Office, Jelebu, 1918; Land Office, Seremban, 1922, Chief Clerk, Land Office, Port Dickson, 1924, Magistrate Court, Seremban, 1932, Chief Clerk, Land Office, Kuala Pillah, 1934, Registration Clerk, Land Office, Parit Buntar, 1938, Chief Clerk, PWD., Kuala Kangsar, 1939-46, Financial Assistant: PWD Headquarters, K.L., 1947, PWD Selangor, 1948, Grade A PWD Selangor, 1950, General Clerical Service, Government of Malaya; Chief de-Mission for Malaya Team to Ceylon Amateur Athletics Championships, 1953; Chief de-Mission for Malaya Athletics Team to 2nd Asian Games, Manila, Philippines, 1954; Secretary General, Malayan contingent to Melbourne 16th Olympiad; Retired, 1956. *Memberships:* Hon. Secretary of: Athletics Association, Negeri Sembilan; AAA of Malaya; FMAU; Olympic Council of Malaya; Royal Commonwealth Society of Malaysia; Zoological Society of Malaysia. *Honours:* PJK, 1952; MBE., 1955; JP., 1973; AMN., 1980. *Hobbies:* Athletics; Football. *Address:* 259 Jalan Damansara, Kuala Lumpur, Malaysia.

VASQUEZ, Alfred Joseph, (The Hon.), b. 2 Mar. 1923, Gibraltar. Barrister-at-Law. m. Carmen Sheppard Capurro, 10 Apr. 1950, 3 sons, 1 daughter. *Education:* Hons., degree, Law, Fitzwilliam College, Cambridge, UK, 1946-49; Bar Finals, Inner Temple, London, UK, 1950; Called to Bar, 1950. *Appointments:* Senior Partner, Vasquez and Vasquez, Barristers-at-Law, Gibraltar; Speaker, Gibraltar House of Assembly, 1970-; Mayor of Gibraltar, 1970-76. *Memberships:* Chairman: Gibraltar Branch, Commonwealth Parliamentary Association; Commonwealth Educational Bursaries and Scholarships; Gibraltar Public Service Commission. *Honours:* CBE., 1975. *Hobbies:* Sailing; Golf; Fishing; Gardening. *Address:* 2 St Bernards Road, Gibraltar.

VASQUEZ, Louis Joseph, b. 21 June 1924, Gibraltar. Barrister-at-Law. m. Yvonne Bellotti, 3 Sept. 1952, 1 son, 4 daughters. *Education:* BA., Hons., Cantab., Trinity College, Cambridge, UK, 1946-49; Member, Inner Temple, London, UK, Called to Bar, 1950; MA., 1954. *Appointments:* Partner, Vasquez and Vasquez, Barristers-at-Law, Gibraltar, 1951-62; Director of: Cements Limited; Charles Suggin (Builders' Merchants) Limited; Ready Mixed (Gibraltar) Limited; Mix Concrete (Gibraltar) Limited; Amalgamated Builders' Merchants Limited. *Memberships:* Steward and Hon. Secretary, Gilmeter Magistrates Association. *Honours:* JP; OStJ; OBE. *Hobby:* Bridge. *Address:* 'Filomena', North Front, Gibraltar.

VASS, Frank, b. 7 Feb. 1909, Hungary. Public Servant (retired). m. 11 Oct. 1936, 1 son, 1 daughter. *Education:* Pilot Licence, 1931, Aerial Survey Course, 1934, Royal Academy of Ludovika, Hungary; Certificate of Efficiency, Ancient History, WAE., Sydney University, Australia, 1965. *Appointments:* Pilot, 1931, Squadron Leader, 1938, Royal Hungarian Aero Office; Photogrammetrist, 1955, Supervisor, 1970, retired, 1974, Central Map Authority, Sydney, Australia. *Memberships:* Centr.

Councillor, NSW Public Service Association; Founder member, NSW Public Service Association Club; Founder Director, Lands Department Credit Union; Associate, Association Classical Archaeology, Sydney; International Society for the History of Cartography; Past President, Hungarian Archaeology Association, Sydney. *Publications:* Cartography: The Map of Nippur, 1973; Books: Additional Disciples in Archaeology, 1972; Importance of the Pazyryk Graves, 1974; Origin of Hung. Holy Crown (in press). *Honours:* Awards at National Folklore Festival, Opera House, Sydney, Australia, 1977, 78, 79, 80; Distinguished Comm. Medal., Hungarian Veteran Association, 1977. *Hobbies:* Travel; Folk Art; Photography. *Address:* 30 Prince of Wales Parade, Alexandra Hills, Queensland 4157, Australia.

VAUGHAN, Geoffrey Norman, b. 9 Apr. 1933, Sydney, Australia. Scientist; College Principal. m. Jennie P Billing, 7 Feb. 1959, 3 sons, 1 daughter. *Education:* BSc., Hons., 1954, MSc., 1956, University of Sydney, Australia; PhD., University of Melbourne, Australia, 1961. *Appointments:* Lecturer, 1961-64, Senior Lecturer, 1964-67, Head of School, 1968-78, Dean of College, 1979-, Victorian College of Pharmacy, Australia. *Memberships:* Fellow: Royal Australian Chemical Institute; Pharmaceutical Society of Victoria; Royal Society of Victoria; Royal Agricultural Society of Victoria; Australian Pharmaceutical Science Association; Australian New Zealand Association for the Advancement of Science. *Publications:* Publications in Medicinal Chemistry of the Pharmaceutical Sciences. *Honours:* Timbrol Fellow, University of Sydney, Australia, 1954; Churchill Fellowship, 1968. *Hobbies:* Sailing; Tennis; Gardening; Cooking. *Address:* 'Inglesby', Beaconsfield Upper, Victoria 3808, Australia.

VAUGHAN, Joseph Ernest Alfred, b. 28 July 1926, Gibraltar. Director of Tourism. m. Theresa L. (dec. 30 Mar. 1981), 19 Apr. 1954, 1 son, 1 daughters. *Appointments:* Clerical Staff, 1947-60; Executive Officer, Tourist Office, 1961-62; Collector of Revenue, 1963-67; Assistant Secretary, Development, 1968-70; Director of Tourism, Gibraltar, 1970-81. *Memberships:* Institute of Public Relations. *Honours:* MBE. *Hobbies:* Reading; Charity work. *Address:* Sunnymede, 4 Red Sands Road, Gibraltar.

VAYID, Mohamad Amade Hajee Dawdjee Mamode, b. 24 Feb. 1935, Port Louis, Mauritius. Tobacco Manufacturer. m. Sajeda Malleck-Amode, 28 July 1965, 2 daughters. *Education:* MA., Hons., University of Edinburgh, Scotland, UK, 1959. *Appointments:* Administrative Officer, Government of Mauritius, 1960-61; Manager, 1961-75, General Manager/Managing Director, 1975-, BAT Co (Mauritius) Limited; Director of: Swan Insurance Co. Limited, Mauritius, 1968-; Development Bank of Mauritius, 1979-. *Memberships:* Chairman: Central Housing Authority, 1967-76, Mauritius Broadcasting Corporation, 1968-70, 1979-, Mauritius Chamber of Commerce and Industry, 1975-76, Mauritius Employers' Federation, 1976-78; Special Constitutional Tribunal, 1970-; Commission on Prerogative of Mercy, 1973-; Permanent Arbitration Tribunal, 1974-77; Joint Economic Committee, Government and Private Sector, 1974-78; Electoral Supervisory Commission, 1975-; Mauritius Marine Authority, 1976-; Central Electricity Board, 1977-. *Publications:* Newspaper articles. *Honours:* CMG., 1976. *Hobbies:* Writing; Reading; Cinema; Swimming. *Address:* 24 John Kennedy Avenue, Floreal, Mauritius.

VEALE, Richard Stanley, b. 5 Sept. 1893, Lefroy Tasmania, Australia. Public Utility Officer; Public Relations Officer; Naval Officer Commander (retired). m. (1) Myrtle Elvina Homewood, dec'd., 2 Dec. 1916, (2) Nancy Isabel Townsend, 7 Sept. 1943, 1 son, 3 daughters. *Education:* Naval instruction during sea service, 1915-16; Psychology and Social Studies, 1920-21. *Appointments:* Naval duties, 1909-13; Naval Officer, 1914-19, 1939-51; Active Naval Reserve Officer, 1920-39; Journalist, 1919-20; Public Relations Officer, Metropolitan Gas Co., Melbourne, Australia, 1927-39; Political Party Agent, Australia, 1952-65. *Memberships:* Member of numerous Associations and Societies including: Senior State Vice-President, Royal Life Saving Society, Victoria Branch; Victoria Division, Liberal Party of Australia; Victorian State Executive, Nationalist Party of Australia; British Brotherhood of Victoria, Australia; Brighton North Vigilance Committee; Melbourne Naval Centre Committee. *Publications:*

Handbook Royal Life Saving Society, Victoria Branch, 1937; contributed many articles to various Australian journals. *Honours:* Several awards including: Post nominal VD, now VRD., 1928, 1st Clasp, 1940, 2nd clasp, 1945; King George V's Jubilee Medal, 1935; King George VI's Coronation Medal, 1937; CMG., for long and outstanding service to the Royal Life Savings Society and interests of returned service personnel, 1979; Meritorious Service Medal, RLSS, 1979. *Hobbies:* Lawn Bowls; Angling; Lecturing; Commemorative Addresses. *Address:* 7 Joyce Street, Elwood, Victoria 3184, Australia.

VEERASINGAM, Yohomani, b. 23 Nov. 1938, Malacca West, Malaysia. Architect. m. Kishna Sivaprakasam, 20 Jan. 1964, 1 son, 2 daughters. *Education:* Diploma, RIBA, Part I, Technical College, Kuala Lumpur, Malaya, 1960-63; Diploma, Part II, 1975-77, Diploma, Part III, 1979, RIBA., North Polytechnic, London, UK: *Appointments:* Temporary teacher, 1958-60; Technical Assistant, 1963-75; Graduate Architect, Private Firm, 1977-79; Architect, Public Works Department, Malacca, Malaysia, 1979-. *Memberships:* Education Secretary, Ceylonese Association; Graduate member, Malaysian Institute of Architects; RIBA. *Honours:* 1 year Scholarship, Society for Architects and Surveyors. 10 Painting. *Address:* 2385 Bukit Palah, Melaka, West Malaysia.

VEITCH, Patrick L, b. 26 Mar. 1944, Beaumont, Texas, USA. Opera Manager. m. Kathleen Norris, 28 Dec. 1979, 1 daughter. *Education:* BA., North Texas State University, USA, 1967; Certificate, Non-Profit Management, Columbia University Graduate School of Business, USA, 1976. *Appointments:* Account Executive, Ketchum MacLeod & Grove, Inc., New York City, USA, 1967-69; Director of Publications, Manhattan College, New York City, USA, 1969-72; Director of Marketing, Metropolitan Opera, New York City, USA, 1973-81; General Manager, The Australian Opera, Sydney, Australia, 1981-. *Memberships:* Board of Directors, Opera Orchestra of New York, USA; Metropolitan Opera Club. *Address:* 6 Etham Avenue, Darling Point, New South Wales 2027, Australia.

VELLA, Roger, b. 28 Oct. 1940, St Venera, Malta. Dental Surgeon. m. Dorothy, 30 May 1964, 2 sons, 1 daughter. *Education:* BChD, Royal University of Malta, 1963. *Appointments:* General Private Practice. *Memberships:* Hon. Secretary, 1977-80, Vice-President, Dental Association, 1981; MFA, 1967-69. *Hobbies:* Fishing; Wine Making. *Address:* 291 High Street, Hamrun, Malta.

VENDARGON, Dominic Aloysius, b. 29 Aug. 1909, Sri Lanka. Titular Roman Catholic Archbishop of Kuala Lumpur. *Education:* St. Paul's Institution, Seremban; St. Francis Institution, Meleka; Seminary of St. Francis Xavier, Singapore; General College Pulau Tikus, Penang. *Appointments:* Vicar for Indians, Visitation Church Seremban; Acting Vicar of Our Lady of Lourdes, Singapore; Vicar, Church of Christ The King, Kedah Perlis, Kroh; Vicar for Indians, Johore Bahru; Vicar of St. Anthony's Church Telok Anson; Vicar of St. Anthony's Church Kuala Lumpur; Bishop of Kuala Lumpur 1955; Archbishop of Kuala Lumpur 1973. *Hobbies:* Swimming; Gardening; Jogging. *Address:* 528 Jalan Bukit Nanas, Kuala Lumpur, 04-01, Malaysia.

VENERYS, John Efstratios, Consultant Orthopaedic Surgeon. m. Margaret Joan Merton Clifton, 1961, 1 son, 1 daughter. *Education:* MB; BS; FRCS 1965; FRACS 1964. *Appointments:* Surgeon, Australian Surgical Team, Long Xuyen, South Vietnam, 1969; Senior Lecturer in Orthopaedic Surgery, University of Western Australia, 1969-71; Consultant Orthopaedic Surgeon, The Sir Charles Gairdner and Repatriation General Hospitals, Perth. (Hollywood Orthopaedic Service); Clinical Lecturer in Orthopaedic Surgery, University of Western Australia. *Memberships:* Chairman, WA State Committee, Royal Australasian College of Surgeons, 1978-80; Secretary, 1972-78; Chairman, WA State Committee, The Sir Robert Menzies Memorial Trust Foundation; Executive Committee, Australian Orthopaedic Association, WA Branch, 1978-80; Australian Medical Association. *Publications:* A number of articles on total hip arthroplasty, avascular necrosis of the femoral head following intertrochanteric fractures of the femur, reaction of tissues to internal implants in particular total hip replacement, Compression neuropathy of the posterior tibial nerve, Fractures to the neck

of femur and Surgery in pes cavus; Contributor to book on Asepsis in the Operating Theatre. *Hobby:* Tennis. *Address:* 5 Marlin Court, Dalkeith, 6009, Australia.

VENKATARAMAN, B. b. 19 Sept. 1925, Pudukottai, Tamil Nadu, India. Government Service. m. Leela, 8 July 1955, 1 son, 1 daughter. *Education:* BSc(Hons.); MA; Doctor of Literature. *Appointments:* IAS, Training School, 1950; Home Department, Cuttack, 1950; Assistant Collector, Cuttack, 1950; Assistant Collector, Ganjam, 1950; Assistant Collector, Sambalpur, 1950; Assistant Collector, Koraput, 1951; SDO, Ghumsar Division, Ganjam, 1951; Under Secretary, Supply Department, 1952; Deputy Secretary, Supply and Deputy Director of Food and Supply, 1953; Collector, Phulbani 1954; Collector, Keonjhar, 1956; Director of Industries, Orissa, 1957; Ex-Officio, Chairman of a number of Government Industrial Units; Government Director, P.R. Department, 1961; Home Secretary, Education Secretary and Secretary Public Relations and Cultural Affairs Department and Director of Cultural Affairs, 1964; Deputy Secretary, Ministry of Home Affairs, 1965; Joint Secretary, 1966. *Memberships:* Visiting Fellow, Indian Institute of Advanced Study, Simla, 1973-74; Commissioner-cum-Secretary, Department of Industry, Government of Orissa and Chairman, Industrial Development Corporation, 1974-77; Chairman, Orissa Mining Corporation, 1977-79; Addl. Chief Secretary, Orissa, 1979-80; Chief Secretary, Government of Orissa, 1980; Secretary, Government of India, Ministry of Tourism and Civil Aviation. *Publications:* Laddigam; Rajarajeswaram; Temple Art under the Chola Queens. *Honours:* A number of medals and prizes in school, college and university. *Address:* 19 Willingdon Crescent, New Delhi 110011, India.

VEPA, Ram K, b. 12 Dec. 1923, Visakhapatnam, India. Industrial Administration, Government. m. Chandar Vepa, 9 Aug. 1950, 1 son, 2 daughters. *Education:* MA (Physics), Madras University, 1943; M.Tech. (Telecommunication) Indian Institute of Science, 1946; PhD, University of California, 1950. *Appointments:* Research Engineer, All India Radio, 1950-57; Sales Development Engineer, Union Carbide, 1957-58; District Administrator, 1960-64; Industrial Administration, 1964-68; Department of Electronics, Government of India, 1968-75; UNIDO, Sri Lanka, 1975-76; Government of India, 1978-. *Memberships:* Indian Institute of Public Administration; Institute of Electronics & Telecommunication Engineers; Indian Council of World Affairs; India International Centre. *Publications:* Productivity in Small Industry, 1969; Small Industry in th Seventies, 1971; New Technology—A Gandhian Concept, 1975; Mao's China—A Nation in Transition, 1979; Joint Ventures, 1980; How to succeed in Small Industry, 1980; A large number of papers on Industrial Development, Small Industry Technology Transfer. *Honours:* All India Manufacturers Organisation Award for Highest Industrial Promotion, 1977. *Hobbies:* Reading; Writing; Walking. *Address:* C-11/13, Motibagh, New Delhi 110 021, India.

VERMA, Daya-Nand, b. 25 June 1933, Banaras, India. Research Mathematician. m. Meena, 18 Apr. 1970. *Education:* BSc, 1952; MSc, Banaras Hindu University, 1954; PhD, Yale University, 1966. *Appointments:* Teaching: Birla College, Pilani, 1956-57; Delhi Polytechnic, 1957-59; Banaras Hindu University, Lecturer, 1959-60; Instructor, Yale University, 1965-66; New Mexico State University Las Cruces, 1966-67; Professor and Head, Department of Mathematics, North-Eastern Hill University Shillong, 1975-76; Research: Institute for advanced Study, Princeton, 1967-68 and 1977-78; Fellow and Reader, Tata Institute of Fundamental Research, 1968-. *Memberships:* Indian Mathematical Society; American Mathematical Society; Mathematical Association of America. *Publications:* Structure of certain induced representations, 1968; Role of affine Weyl groups in representation theory, 1975; Stability result in invariant theory, 1980. *Honours:* Fellow, The Maharashtra Academy of Sciences; Visiting Invitations: University of Wisconsin, Madison, 1976-77; Clark University, Worcester, 1978; Ohio State University Columbus, 1979; State Universities of Leiden and Utrecht, 1979. *Hobbies:* Nature-walks; Music Classical Indian and Western; Visual Arts; Rubik Cube; Photography. *Address:* 304 Bhaskara TIFR Housing Colony, Homi Bhabha Road, Bombay 400 005, India.

VERMA, Gurdeva S, b. 5 Jan. 1927, Sultanpur, India. Teaching. m. Uma Verma, 25 Jan. 1951, 1 son, 3 daughters. *Education:* BSc, 1945; MSc, 1947; DPhil. 1953. *Appointments:* Research Fellow, Allahabad University, 1947-49; Lecturer, Phys. Department, 1949-66; Professor of Physics, Banaras Hindu University, 1968-; Research Associate, Case Western Reserve University, Cleveland, Ohio, 1957-59 and 1963-64; Commonwealth Visiting Professor, Nottingham, United Kingdom, 1977-78. *Memberships:* Sigma Xi America; American Physical Society, America; Fellow, Acoustical Society of India. *Publications:* 200 publications in the reputed journals of the world; Author, An Introduction to Acoustics; 21 students awarded PhD degree under GS Verma; Author, Fundamantal Aspects of Physical Acoustics, in preparation. *Honours:* Certificate of appreciation, Department of Agriculture, Washington, DC, USA; Sole representative of Asia, International Organising Committee, International Conference on Phonon Scattering Solids, Paris, 1972; Principal Investigator of Two US PL 480 Projects, 1963-68; Commonwealth Visiting Professor, Nottingham, UK, 1977-78; Series of Lectures, Basrah University, Basrah, Iraq. *Hobby:* Music. *Address:* New F/8, Jodhpur Colony, BHU, Varanasi 5, India.

VERMA, Shivendra Kishore, b. 29 July 1931, Patna, India. Teacher. m. Asha, 14 June 1955, 2 sons, 1 daughter. *Education:* BA(Hons.), 1949; MA, Patna University, Patna, 1951; PGCE, University of London, 1956; PG Diploma Applied Linguistics, 1962; PhD, University of Edinburgh, 1964. *Appointments:* Lecturer in English, Patna University, 1951-64; Reader, 1964-66; Professor of Linguistics, Central Institute of English and Foreign Languages, 1966-. *Memberships:* Linguistic Society of India; Dravidian Linguistic Association; Expert, Boards of Studies in Linguistics; Committees on Linguistics in India. *Publications:* Published 4 books and 60 papers. *Honours:* Durgagati Memorial Prize, 1949; Gait English Gold Medal, 1949; British Council Fellowship, 1961-62; Ford Foundation Grant, 1962-64. *Hobby:* Visiting Places. *Address:* 02 Professors' Quarters, CIEFL, Hyderabad 500007, India.

VICTORY, Octavio Lionel, b. 1 July 1932, Gibraltar. Education Officer. m. Encarnacion Oliva, 1 Aug. 1958, 3 sons, 1 daughter. *Education:* Teacher's Certificate, London University, 1954; Diploma Educational Administration, Leeds University, 1976; MA(Ed) Research and Innovation, Southampton University 1978. *Appointments:* Assistant Teacher, Gibraltar, 1954-64; Deputy Headmaster South America, 1964-66; Deputy Headmaster, 1967-70, Acting Headmaster, United Kingdom, 1970-71; Education Officer, Gibraltar, 1972-. *Memberships:* Lion's International, Gibraltar; Lion Tamer; Mediterranean Rowing Club, Gibraltar. *Hobbies:* Football; Hockey; Rowing. *Address:* 28/2 Scud Hill, Gibraltar.

VIGGERS, Peter John, b. 13 Mar. 1938, Gosport, Hampshire, England. Solicitor. m. 7 Dec. 1968, 2 sons, 1 daughter. *Education:* MA, Honours in History and Law, Trinity Hall, Cambridge, 1958-61; Qualified Solicitor, College of Law, London. *Appointments:* Company Solicitor, Chrysler United Kingdom Limited, 1968-70; Director, Edward Bates and Sons Limited, Bankers, 1970-75; Member of Parliament, (Conservative) Gosport, 1974-. *Memberships:* Bow Group. *Publications:* What A Waste of Energy, 1974. *Hobbies:* Country Pursuits; Travelling. *Address:* House of Commons, London SW1, England.

VIJAYAN, Vannan Kandi, b. 19 June 1946, Badagara, Kerala State, India. Medical. *Education:* MBBS., Calicut Medical College, India, 1970; DTCD., VP Chest Institute, Delhi, India, 1975; MD., Lady Hardinge Medical College, Willingdon Hospital, New Delhi, India, 1977. *Appointments:* Resident in Medicine, Jipmer, Pondicherry, India; Resident in Surgery and Medicine, Willingdon Hospital, New Delhi, India; Assistant Research Officer, ICMR., Cardiology, GB Pant Hospital, New Delhi, India; Resident, Chest Diseases, VP Chest Institute, Delhi, India; Senior Research Fellow, Resident in Medicine, Lady Hardinge Medical College and Willingdon Hospital, New Delhi, India; Research Officer, Cardiology, All India Heart Foundation, New Delhi, India; Research Officer, Indian Council of Medical Research, Madras, India. *Memberships:* American College of Chest Physicians; Cardiological Society of India; International College of Angiology; National College of Chest Physicians; Association of Physicians of India; Indian College of Allergy and Applied Immunology; Indian Society of Electro-Cardiology; Indian Chest Society; All India Heart Foundation; Indian Immunology Society; Speaker of School Parliament Working Committee, All Kerala Medical Students Association; Scientific Working Group, ICMR. *Publications:* A Comparison of Serum Enzyme Levels with Other Parameters of Myocardial Injury in Acute Myocardial Infarction, 1976; Correlation of ST Segment Elevation in 12 - Lead Electro-Cardiogram with Serum CPK., in Acute Myocardial Infarction, 1979; Comparative Value of CPK in Acute Myocardial Infarction, 1979. *Honours:* State Government Merit Scholarship, 1956-62; National Merit Scholarship, Government of India, 1963-70; Gold Medal, Pathology, 1969; Senior Research Fellowship, Indian Council of Medical Research, 1975-77. *Hobby:* Reading. *Address:* 'Lakshmi Nilayam', PO Tikkoti, Kozhikode District, Kerala State, India.

VIJAYASENAN, Mithra Ebenezer, b. 10 Sept. 1936, India. Medical Practitioner. m. Premila Dennison, 30 Dec. 1964, 2 sons. *Education:* BSc.; MB., BS.; DIH; DPM; MRCPsych; MRANZCP; FRANZCP. *Appointments:* House Officer, Christian Medical College Hospital, Velloce, India; Medical Officer, Simpson Group Factories, India; Senior House Officer, Bexley Hospital, Kent, UK; Registrar, St. James Hospital, Portsmouth, UK; Assistant Psychiatrist, St. Ann's Hospital, Bournemouth, UK; Consultant Psychiatrist, Porirua Hospital, New Zealand. *Memberships:* Indian Society of Industrial Medicine; Executive member, Medical Society of Alcohol and Alcoholism, New Zealand. *Publications:* Thermal Stress in Industrial Workers, 1966; Sodium Valproate in the Treatment of the Alcohol Withdrawal Syndrome, 1980; Alcohol and Sex, 1981. *Hobbies:* Cricket; Tennis; Music. *Address:* 73 Bodmin Terrace, Cambourne, Plimmerton, New Zealand.

VILASH, Ram, b. 19 Feb. 1933, Naitasiri, Fiji. Chartered Accountant. m. Sumira, 17 Apr. 1965, 2 sons, 1 daughter. 02 B.Com., Victoria University of Wellington, New Zealand, 1963; Graduated Diplomas in: Professional Accountancy, 1963, Cost and Management Accounting, 1966. *Appointments:* Cost Accountant, South Pacific Sugar Mills Limited, Labasa Mill, Fiji, 1964-66; Auditor, Co-operatives Department, Government of Fiji Civil Service, 1967-69; Private Practice, 1970; Merged with Peat, Marwick, Mitchell & Co., Chartered Accountants, 1974, Resident Partner, Suva, Fiji, 1975. *Memberships:* Commissioner, Fiji Public Service Commission; Past President, Council member, Fiji Institute of Accountants; Fiji Girmit Centenary Council. *Hobbies:* Golf; Charitable, cultural and sporting organisations. *Address:* 5 Pathik Crescent, Tamavua, Suva, Fiji.

VILLIERS, John Francis Hyde, b. 24 Jan. 1936, London, England. Historian. m. 19 July 1958, 1 son, 3 daughters. *Education:* Major Scholar, King's College, Cambridge, UK, 1954-57; BA., 1957; MA., 1959; PhD., 1962; Parker of Waddington Studentship, 1957-58. *Appointments:* British Council: Bandung, Indonesia, 1960-64; Warsaw, 1964-67; Athens, 1967-70; Cultural Attache, Bucharest, 1970-72; Director, East Europe and North Asia Department, 1972-75; Representative, Indonesia, 1975-77, Director, Far East and Pacific Department, 1977-79, Director, British Institute in South-East Asia, Singapore, 1979-. *Memberships:* The Siam Society; Royal Asiatic Society. *Publications:* South-East Asia before the colonial period, German edition, 1965, Italian edition 1967, Spanish edition 1970; various articles in learned journals on South-East Asian history. *Hobbies:* Painting; Music; Languages; Collecting antiques; Squash; Badminton. *Address:* 38M Kum Hing Court, Tomlinson Road, Singapore 1024.

VINCENT, Geoffrey Alan, b. 11 Feb. 1941, Melbourne, Victoria, Australia. Accountant. m. Lesley Carolyn McKenzie, 28 Jan. 1966, 2 sons, 1 daughter. *Education:* B.Comm., Melbourne University, Australia, 1961; Senior, AASA; ACIS. *Appointments:* Assistant Secretary, Myer Emporium, Australia, 1963-64; Assistant Accountant, Conzinc Riotinto of Australia, 1964-65; Accountant, Australian Mining and Smelting Limited, Rum Jungle, Australia, 1965-67; Manager, Riotinto Brick Pty. Limited, Australia, 1967-69; Chief Accountant, 1970-72, Treasurer, 1973-74, Controller, 1975-76, Bougainville Copper Limited, Australia; Executive

Director, Australian Society of Accountants, 1976-. *Memberships:* Order of Australia. *Honours:* Queens Honour - Member of Order of Australia, 1981. *Hobbies:* Golf; Tennis; Yachting. *Address:* 368 New Street, Brighton, Victoria 3186, Australia.

VINCETT, Paul Stamford, b. 23 Jan. 1944, Southend, Essex, England. Research Physicist. m. Marion Rosemary Barrett, 21 Aug. 1965, 2 sons, 1 daughter. *Education:* BA., 1965, MA., 1968, PhD., 1968, University of Cambridge, UK. *Appointments:* Post-doctoral Fellow, Simon Fraser University, B.C., Canada, 1968-70; Instructor, Capilano College, N. Vancouver, B.C., Canada, 1969-70; Senior Research Scientist, ICI Corporate Laboratory, Runcorn, UK, 1971-74; Tutor, Open University, UK, 1972-74; Research Staff, 1974-79, Manager, Thin Film Science and Memory, 1979-, Xerox Research Centre of Canada, Mississauga, Canada. *Memberships:* Canadian Association of Physicists; US National Micrographics Association; Secretary, University of Cambridge Society for the Application of Research, 1966-68. *Publications:* Approximately 30 papers in learned scientific journals, on thin film science, solid state and colloid physics, photographic science; Chapter in: Langmuir-Blodgett Films, 1980. *Creative Works:* Several issued patents for thin film and photographic devices. *Honours:* Foundation Scholar, Corpus Christi College, Cambridge, UK, 1965-68; Open Exhibition, Corpus Christi College, Cambridge, UK, 1962-65; Xerox-Canada Special Recognition Award, 1981; Member, Editorial Board, Thin Solid Films (the International Journal on Thin Film Science, published by Elsevier), 1980-. *Hobbies:* Politics and community affairs; Travel; Wine, food and country living; Winter sports. *Address:* RR1, Grand Valley, Ontario, Canada, LON 1G0.

VINER, Robert Ian, b. 21 Jan. 1933, Claremont, Western Australia. Federal Member for Stirling, Minister for Employment and Youth Affairs, Minister Assisting the Prime Minister. m. Ngaire Ellen, 17 May 1956, 3 sons, 4 daughters. *Education:* LL.B., University of Western Australia, 1954-58. *Appointments:* Bank Officer, ANZ Bank, Australia, 1948-53; Articled, 1958-60, Partner, 1960-65, Muir & Williams, Solicitors, Australia; Joined Western Australian Bar, practised as Barrister specialising in Commercial and Industrial Law, 1965-72; Won Federal Seat of Stirling in Commonwealth Parliament, 1972; Appointed, 1975, Re-appointed, 1977, Minister for Aboriginal Affairs; Given additional appointment of Minister Assisting the Treasurer, 1976; Appointed Minister Assisting the Prime Minister, 1977; Appointed Minister for Employment and Youth Affairs, 1978; Leader of the House, 1979; Minister for Employment and Youth Affairs, Minister Assisting the Prime Minister, 1980-. *Memberships:* Western Australia Bar Association; Squadron Leader, RAAF Reserve. *Honours:* Honours in Law, 1958. *Hobbies:* Fishing; Gardening; Hockey. *Address:* 53 West Coast Highway, Waterman, Western Australia 6020, Australia.

VINES, William Joshua, b. 27 May 1916, Terang, Victoria, Australia. Company Director; Grazier. m. Thelma Jean Ogden, 25 Nov. 1939, 1 son, 2 daughters. *Education:* Scholarship to Haileybury College, UK, 1928, Graduated, Royal Military Staff College, 1945. *Appointments:* Wool Department, 1932, Station Auditor, 1936-38, Australian Estates Co. Limited; Secretary, Alexander Fergusson Pty. Limited, Australia, 1938-40, 1945-47; Sales Director, Goodlass Wall Limited, Australia, 1945-48; Private to Captain, 2/23 Australian Infantry Battalion, AIF, War Service, Middle East, New Guinea, Borneo, 1940-45; Managing Director, Lewis Berger & Sons Pty. Limited, Australia, 1948-55; Managing Director, Lewis Berger & Sons (Australia) Pty. Limited, 1952-55; Group Managing Director, Lewis Berger & Sons Limited, London, UK, 1955-61; Managing Director, 1961-69, Board member until 1979, International Wool Secretariat, UK; Purchased "Old Southwood Station, Tara, Queensland, Australia, 1965; Chairman of: Dalgety Australia Limited, 1969-80; Thorn Electrical Industries Australia Limited, 1969-74; Wiggins Teape Limited Australia, 1969-72; Director of: Wiggins Teape Limited, 1969-78; Commercial Union Assurance Co. of Australia Limited, 1969-78; P&O Australian Holdings Pty. Limited, 1969-71; Chairman, Carbonless Papers (Wiggins Teape) Pty. Limited, 1970-78; Chairman, Australian Wool Commission, 1970-72; Managing Director, Dalgety Australia Limit-

ed, 1970-76; Director of: Dalgety New Zealand Limited; Dalgety Limited, London, UK; Chairman, Associated Pulp & Paper Mills Limited; Deputy Chairman of: Tubemakers of Australia Limited; Chairman, Australia and New Zealand Banking Group Ltd.; Australia and New Zealand Banking Group Limited; Director of: C R A Limited; Port Phillip Mills Limited. *Memberships:* Part time member of Executive, Commonwealth Scientific and Industrial Research Organization; Chairman, The Sir Robert Menzies Memorial Trust; Economic Consultative Group to the Commonwealth Government; Australia New Zealand Foundation; Chairman of Council, Hawkesbury Agricultural College. *Honours:* Several honours including: Knight, 1977; CMG., 1969. *Address:* 73 Tarranabbe Road, Darling Point, 2027, Australia.

VIRGO, Bruce Barton, b. 18 Mar. 1943, Vancouver, British Columbia, Canada. Professor of Pharmacology/Toxicology. m. N. Sheila, 17 May 1969, 1 son, 1 daughter. *Education:* PhD., 1974, MSc., 1970, BSc., Hon., 1965, University of British Columbia, Canada. *Appointments:* McGill University, Montreal, Quebec, Canada, 1973-74; University of Montreal, Montreal, Quebec, Canada, 1974-75; University of Windsor, Windsor, Ontario, Canada, 1975-. *Memberships:* Pharmacological Society of Canada; Society of Toxicology of Canada. *Publications:* 12 Publications including: Bird damage in Niagara Peninsula vineyards (with AB Stevenson), 1967; Bird damage to sweet cherries in the Niagara Peninsula, 1971; Effects of dietary dieldrin on the liver and drug metabolism in the female Swiss-Vancouver mouse (with GD Bellward), 1975; The estrogenicity of delta-9-tetrahydro-cannabinol (THC): THC neither blocks nor induces ovum implantation, nordoes it effect uterine growth, 1979; Effects of Fasting and Exercise on the Depletion of Liver and Muscle Glycogen in the Mouse, 1980; Unilaterally ovariectomized pregnant mice: dieldrin induction of the hepatic monooxygenases and plasma progesterone levels, 1980. *Honours:* National Research Council Fellowship, 1973-75. *Hobbies:* Canoeing; Skiing; Hiking; Reading. *Address:* 2091 West Grand Blvd., Windsor, Ontario, Canada, N9E 1G7.

VIVEKANANDA, Rajaratnam, b. 17 Nov. 1917, Perak, Malaysia. Education Officer. m. Daisy Maheswary Sinnatamby, 22 Apr. 1950, 2 sons, 1 daughter. *Education:* Diploma, Arts, Raffles College, Singapore, 1947; BA., Hons., University of Malaya, Singapore, 1952. *Appointments:* Graduate Teacher, English, 1949-56; Headmaster: High School, Kajang, 1957-58; King George V School, Serembar, 1958-60; Chief Education Officer: Nagn Sembilon, 1961-62; Penang, 1962-64; Selangor, 1964-70; Director, Teacher Training, 1970-71; Chief Inspector of Schools, 1971-72. *Memberships:* Education Service Commission, 1974-79; Council of University of Malaya, 1975-78. *Honours:* Johan Setia Mahkota, awarded by HM The King, 1968. *Hobbies:* Motoring; Gardening; Reading; Sport. *Address:* 3 Clove Hall Road, Penang, Malaysia.

VOI, Mali, b. 28 Aug. 1946. Teacher. m. Ruth, 30 Aug. 1969, 2 sons, 1 daughter. *Education:* Teachers' Certificate, 1965-66, Diploma, Principles and Practises of Teaching, 1970, Port Moresby Teachers College, Australia; Certificate, Development Education, Macquarie University, Australia, 1971; Certificate, Oceania Teacher Development, East-West Centre, Hawaii, 1973. *Appointments:* Teacher, Goroka Demonstration School, 1967-69; Associate District Superintendent of Schools, Wewak, 1972; Associate Assistant Director, 1974, Assistant Director, 1975-77, Secondary Education, Penang; Director, National Cultural Council, 1978-79; Director, Third South Pacific Festival of Arts, 1979-80; Masters Student, Macquarie University, Australia, 1981. *Memberships:* Papua New Guinea Institute of Inspectors; Australian College of Education. *Honours:* OBE., 1981. *Hobbies:* Reading; Debating; Sailing; Collecting orchids; Underwater diving. *Address:* 6/163 Herring Road, North Ryde, New South Wales 2113, Australia.

VOLPÉ, Robert, b. 6 Mar. 1926, Toronto, Ontario, Canada. Physician; Professor of Medicine. m. Ruth, 5 Sept. 1949, 2 sons, 3 daughters. *Education:* MD., Faculty of Medicine, University of Toronto, Canada, 1950; FRCP., 1956; FACP., 1965. *Appointments:* Senior Research Fellow, 1957-63, Assistant Professor, 1963-66, Associate Professor, 1966-72, Professor,

1972-, Department of Medicine, University of Toronto, Canada; Attending physician, St Josephs Hospital, Canada, 1957-66; Attending physician, 1966-74, Physician-in-Chief, 1974-, Wellesley Hospital, Toronto, Canada. *Memberships:* President, 1980-81, American Thyroid Association; Past-President, First President, Canadian Society of Endocrinology and Metabolism; Governor for Ontario, 1978-82, American College of Physicians; Endocrine Society; Canadian Society for Clinical Investigation; Royal Society of Medicine, London, UK. *Publications:* Systematic Endocrinology; Thyroid Dysfunction; Thyrotoxicosis; Autoimmunity in the Endocrine System; 130 Scientific publications, mostly on immunology of the endocrine system. *Honours:* Goldie award for Medical Research, University of Toronto, 1971; State of the Art Lecturer, Endocrine Society, San Francisco, USA, 1975; Jamieson Lecturer, Canadian Society of Nuclear Medicine, 1980; numerous other visiting professorships and lectureships. *Hobbies:* Skiing; Sailing; Tennis. *Address:* 3 Daleberry Place, Don Mills, Ontario, M3B 2A5, Canada.

VOWELS, Rex Eugene, b. 25 Jan. 1917, Adelaide, South Australia. Education Pro-Vice-Chancellor and Professor of Electrical Engineering. m. Chloris Jessie Richards, 29 Jan. 1938, 4 sons, 1 daughter. *Education:* Bach. of Eng., 1937, Master of Eng., 1939, University of Adelaide, Australia. *Appointments:* Assistant Electrical Engineer, Hydro-Electric Commission, Tasmania, 1937-41; Lecturer in charge, Electrical Engineering, Swinburne Technical College, Victoria, Australia, 1941-46; Electrical Engineer, State Electricity Commission, Queensland, Australia, 1946-47; Reader, Electrical Engineering, University of Adelaide, Australia, 1947-53; Carnegie Grant and US Education Foundation Grant to USA, 1951-52; Professor of Electrical Engineering, 1954-, Chairman of Professorial Board, 1959-68, Acting Dean of Faculty of Engineering, 1967-68, Pro-Vice-Chancellor, 1967-, Acting Vice-Chancellor, 1971-, University of New South Wales, Australia. *Memberships:* Fellow, Councillor, Institution of Engineers, Australia; MIEE; SMIEEE; Interim Council, Royal Military College, Duntroon, 1967-77; Library Council of New South Wales, 1969-; New South Wales Higher Education Board, 1978-; Matrix and Tensor Society; Board of Directors, Benevolent Society of New South Wales, 1967-78. *Publications:* Numerous papers in professional journals; Contributor to: Information, Computers, Machines and Man, 1971; research in field of machines, circuit theory and power systems. *Honours:* Angas Engineering Exhibition, 1933; John L Young Scholarship for Research, 1938; Carnegie Award, 1951-52; AO., 1980. *Hobbies:* Gardening; Walking; Swimming; Carpentry. *Address:* 49 The Esplanade, Balmoral Beach, New South Wales 2088, Australia.

W

WAACK, Henry Albert, b. 28 Feb. 1928, Edmonton, Alberta, Canada. Professor of Music and Pianist. m. Elenor Helen Rasmussen, 3 Nov. 1957, 6 sons. *Education:* Associate of the Royal Conservatory of Music, Toronto, Performance, 1951; Associate, University of Alberta, Performance, 1953; Studied with leading Leading Canadian, American and European Teachers, 1938-58. *Appointments:* Over 4000 Professional Engagements as Soloist, Accompanist, Musical Director, Concerts, Radio, Television; Professor of Piano, Mount Royal College, Calgary, Alberta, 1958-60; Music Critic, Lethbridge Herald, 1965-70; Professor of Piano and Founding Member, Douglas College, New Westminster, British Columbia, 1970-. *Memberships:* Founding Member, Douglas College, New Westminster, British Colombia; Director, National Board of Canada Music Competitions; President, Surrey Arts Society; Former President, Lethbridge Kiwanis Club; Fellow, International Biographical Association; American Federation of Musicians. *Honours:* Recipient of Sir Alexander Galt Scholarship, Alberta Music Festival, 1951; Timothy Eaton Scholarship, 1952-53; Western Board of Music Scholarship, 1954; Heintzman Scholarship, 1955. *Hobbies:* Coaching Baseball; Coquitlam Baseball Association. *Address:* 327 Gloucester Court, Coquitlam, British Columbia, Canada V3K 5S6.

WADDELL, James, Robert, Erskine, b. 7 Feb. 1926, Darjeeling, India. University Lecturer. m. 6 Oct. 1961, Janet Helen Mould, 2 sons. *Education:* Charterhouse, 1939-44; Oriel College, Oxford, 1947-50; BA, 1950; MA, 1953; MSc, School of Oriental and African Studies, 1967; PhD, University of Papua New Guinea, 1976. *Appointments:* Royal Insurance Company, 1951-56; Harrisons and Crosfield Limited, 1956-61; H.G. Poland Limited, 1961-65; Police College, Bramshill, United Kingdom, 1967-68; University of Papua New Guinea, 1968-74; University of New South Wales, 1974-. *Memberships:* President, Appropriate Technology and Community Environment; Chairman, Research Limited, Non-profit appropriate technology organisation. *Publications:* An Introduction to South East Asian Politics, John Wiley, 1972. *Hobbies:* Lawn Tennis; Gardening. *Address:* 321 Alison Road, Coogee, New South Wales, 2034, Australia.

WADDS, Jean Casselman (Mrs), b. 1920. Canadian Politician & Diplomat. m. (1) 1946, Clair Casselman (deceased) 1 son, 1 daughter; (2) 1964, Robert Wadds (divorced 1977). *Education:* BA, University of Toronto, Canada; Weller Business College. *Appointments:* Member, Canadian Parliament, 1956-58; Member, Canadian Delegation to UN, 1961; Parliamentary Secretary to Minister of Health & Welfare, 1962; Member of Agriculture, Broadcasting, Civil Service & External Affairs Parliamentary Committees; National Secretary of Progressive Conservative Party, 1971-75; Member of Ontario Municipal Board, 1975-79; Canadian High Commissioner to the United Kingdom, 1980-; Freedom of City of London, 1981; Honorary Doctor of Civil Laws Degree, Acadia University, Wolfville, Nova Scotia, 1981. *Address:* 1 Grosvenor Square, London W1, England.

WADE, Henry William, Rawson, b. 16 Jan. 1918, London, England. University Professor, Barrister at Law. m. Marie Osland-Hill, 15 Oct. 1943, 2 sons. *Education:* Gonville and Caius College, Cambridge, England; MA, 1946; LLD, 1959; Howard Law School, 1939-40. *Appointments:* H.M. Treasury, 1940-46; University Lecturer, Cambridge, 1947-59; Reader, 1959-61; Professor of English Law, Oxford University, 1961-76; Rouse Ball Professor of English Law, Cambridge University and Master of Gonville and Caius College, Cambridge, 1976-. *Memberships:* Alpine Club. *Publications:* Administrative Law, 4th Edition, 1977; The Law of Real Property, with Sir Robert Megarry, 4th edition, 1975; Towards Administrative Justice, 1963; Legal Control of Government, with Professor B. Schwartz, 1972; Constitutional Fundamentals, Hamlyn Lectures, 1980. *Honours:* Honorary Bencher of Lincoln's Inn, 1964; Queen's Counsel, 1968; Fellow, British Academy, 1969; Honorary Fellow, St. John's College, Oxford, 1976. *Hobbies:* Climbing; Gardening; Music. *Address:* The Master's Lodge, Gonville and Caius College, Cambridge, England.

WAGNER, Odon, b. 1 Oct. 1944, Budapest, Hungary. Art Dealer. m. Elisabeth, 7 Nov. 1975, 2 sons, 1 daughter. *Education:* Graduation Theresianische Akademie, Vienna, 1965; Diploma of the Academy of Applied Art, Academic Art Conservator, Vienna, 1969. *Memberships:* Canadian Association of Professional Art Conservators; Granite Club, Toronto; Theresianisten Vereinigung, Vienna. *Hobbies:* Hunting; Sailing. *Address:* 24 Donwoods Drive, Toronto, Ontario, M4N 2G1, Canada

WAGSTAFF, John Pankhurst, b. 1 Jan 1936, Muswellbrook, New South Wales, Australia. Managing Director. m. Jill Barbara Watts, 17 Dec. 1959, 3 sons, (1 deceased), 1 daughter. *Education:* Matriculation, The Armidale School, Armidale, New South Wales, 1945-52; Australian Institute of Marketing, 1964; Australian Graduate School of Management, 1978. *Appointments:* Director, Wrightcel Ltd., 1971; Director, Courtaulds Hilton Ltd., 1976; Deputy Managing Director, Courtaulds Hilton Ltd., 1979; Managing Director, Courtaulds Hilton Ltd., 1980. *Memberships:* Institute of Directors in Australia; Associate, Australian Marketing Institute; Executive, Textile Council of Australia; Trustee, Committee for Economic Development of Australia. *Hobbies:* Sailing; Tennis; Theatre; Gardening. *Address:* 10 Maple Court, Keilor 3036, Australia.

WAHHAB, Al-Kamal Abdul Wahhab, b. 31 Dec. 1936, Bangladesh. Service (Government). m. 16 May 1961, 2 sons, 1 daughter. *Education:* MA, Dacca University, 1960; Diploma in Printing Technology, Japan, 1976. *Appointments:* Assistant Publications Officer, Bangla Academy, Dacca, Bangladesh, 1961-72; Assistant Director, Publications & Sales Division, Bangladesh, 1972-73; Deputy Director, Publications & Sales Division, Bangladesh Academy, Dacca, Bangladesh, 1973-79; Director, Publications & Sales Division, Bangla Academy, Dacca, Bangladesh, 1979-. *Memberships:* Bangla Academy, Dacca, Bangladesh. *Publications:* Published 18 books, out of which Mask, Novel, 1974; On Way to Deep Forest, Novel, 1979; Tipu Saltan, the great General for Juvenile, Drama, 1980; The Hunter in Deep Forest, Short Story, 1981; Songs of Birds & Flowers, Poem, 1981; Khiled, the Mighty Warrior, Drama. *Honours:* Recipient of Bank Literary Prize of Bangladesh, 1978; Bangla Academy Literary Prize, 1980. *Hobbies:* Writing; Travelling; Friendship. *Address:* 11 Dilu Road, New Eskaton, Dacca, 17, Bangladesh.

WAHLQVIST, Mark Lawrence, b. 5 Feb. 1942, Consultant Physician/Nutritionist. m. Soo Sien Huang, 25 Nov. 1967, 1 son, 1 daughter. *Education:* BMedSc, Hons, Adelaide, 1962; MB,BS, Adelaide, 1966; MD, Adelaide, 1970; MD, Uppsala, 1972; FRACP, 1975. *Appointments:* Resident Medical Officer, Royal Adelaide Hospital, 1966; Various Clinical & Research posts in Melbourne, Stockholm, Uppsala, Canberra; Senior Lecturer in Medicine, Monash University, 1976-77; Foundation Professor of Human Nutrition, Deakin University, 1978-; Consultant Physician, Prince Henry's Hospital, Melbourne, 1976. *Memberships:* Nutrition Committee; Australian Academy of Science; President, International Society for Heart Research, Australian Section, 1979-80; President Nutrition Society of Australia, Melbourne, 1978-80; Secretary, Australian Nutrition Foundation, Melbourne, 1979-. *Publications:* Scientific publications in the fields of Diabetes, Lipid disorders, Atherosclerosis, Food Analysis and Nutrition; Food & Nutrition in Australia, 1981. *Honours:* Recipient of numerous honours and awards for professional services. *Hobbies:* Farming; Tennis; Music. *Address:* 63 Canterbury Road, Middle Park, Melbourne, Victoria, Australia, 3206.

WAI, Kee-Neng, b. 18 Dec. 1936, Hong Kong, Pharmacist. m. Eugenia Chong, 20 Sept. 1970, 1 son. *Education:* BS, Degree in Pharmacy, University of Wisconsin, USA, 1955-59; MS, Degree in Pharmacy, Purdue University, USA, 1959-61; PhD, Degree in Industrial Pharmacy, Purdue University, USA, 1961-63. *Appointments:* Vanderbilt Research Fellow, Purdue University, Lafayette, Indiana, USA, 1963-64; Head of Pharmacy & Analytical Chemistry Department, Biorex Laboratories, London, England; Head of New Drugs Formulation Section, Imperial Chemical Industries, Macclesfield, Cheshire, England, 1966-71; Director of the following Companies in Hong Kong: The London Ice Cream Company Ltd., Tom Todd Ltd., Euken Company Ltd.,

Kids' Own Company Ltd., Hinds International (HK) Ltd., *Memberships:* The Pharmaceutical Society of Hong Kong; The Pharmaceutical Society of Great Britain; American Pharmaceutical Association; American Chemical Society; The American Association for the Advancement of Sciences; The Society of the Sigma Xi, Rho Chi Society and Phi Lambda Upsilon Society. *Publications:* Contributed to various journals. *Honours:* British Patent 1,093,286. Improvement in or relating to Dosage Unit Form for the Administration of Medicaments and Diagnostic Agent; British Patent, Pharmaceutical Compositions for Sustained Action Polypeptide Crystals for Injection. *Hobbies:* Music; Contemporary Art. *Address:* 5A, 20 Kennedy Terrace, Central, Hong Kong.

WAKEHAM, John, b. 22 June 1932, Godalming, Surrey, England. Chartered Accountant. m. Anne Roberta Bailey, 19 Sept. 1965, 2 sons. *Education:* Charterhouse, 1946-49. *Appointments:* Member of Parliament for Maldon, 1974-; Government Whip, 1979-; Lord Commissioner of the Treasury, 1981-; Under Secretary of State for Industry, 1981. *Hobbies:* Sailing. *Address:* c/o House of Commons, London SW1, England.

WAKEM, Beverley Anne, (Miss) b. 27 Jan 1944, Wellington, New Zealand. Controller of Programmes, Radio New Zealand. *Education:* FTCL, Trinity College, London, Speech & Drama; BA, Victoria University of Wellington, 1968; MA, Mass Communications, University of Kentucky, USA, 1973. *Appointments:* Talks Producer, Radio, NZBC, 1963-66; Senior Public Affairs Officer, NZBC, 1966-67; Executive Producer, Current Affairs, NZBC, 1974-75; Controller of Programmes, RNZ, 1975-. *Memberships:* Chairman, Public Relations Committee, Zonta, 1975-76; Women in Communications Inc.; NZ Government Commission for the Future; Wellington Branch, Royal Society of NZ, 1970-72, 1975-77. *Honours:* Graduate Fellowship, Rotary Foundation, for study in the United States, 1972-73; P.E.O. International Scholarship, 1974; Altrusa International, Grant in aid, 1974; Teaching Assistantship University of Kentucky, 1973; New Zealand Government Grant for participation in United Nations Graduate Intern Programme, 1974. *Hobbies:* Photography; Reading; Theatre; Music; Flying. *Address:* 83 Monroe Street, Seatoun, Wellington 3, New Zealand.

WAKHLU, Omkar Nath Wakhlu, b. 14 Nov. 1933, Srinagar, Kashmir, India. Academician/Civil Engineer. m. Khem Lata Wakhlu, 27 Sept. 1952, 2 sons. *Education:* BSc. (Civil Engg.), First class and Rank, 1953; Post-Graduate Degree in Irrigation Engineering, Hydraulics and Dam Design, First in First Class awarded Gold Medal, 1957; M.Engg., 1959; Ph.D. (Civil Engg.), Birmingham, 1963. *Appointments:* Civil Engineer, Irrigation Department, J & K Government, 1953-58; Lecturer, Roorkee University, 1958-59; Assistant Professor/Reader, Banaras H. University and REC Srinagar, 1959-65; Professor, REC Srinagar, 1965-77; Principal/Director, REC Srinagar and Dean, Faculty of Engineering, University of Kashmir, 1977-. *Memberships:* Institution of Civil Engineers, London; American Society of Civil Engineers, New York; International Association of Hydraulic Research, Holland; Fellow, Institution of Engineers, India; Indian Society of Technical Education; Authors Guild of India; All India Council of Technical Education (NRC); BOG Indian Institute of Technology, New Delhi. *Publications:* Civil Engineering Management, also contributor of reviews, monographs, articles to professional journals and conferences. *Honours:* Recipient of numerous honours and awards for professional services. *Hobbies:* Book Reading; Indian Classical Music; Spritual discourses. *Address:* Principal's Lodge Regional Engineering College, Hazratbal, Srinagar, Kashmir - 190006 India.

WALATARA, Douglas, b. 23 Oct. 1920, Colombo, Sri Lanka. University Teacher. m. Hermia Liyanage, 10 Sept. 1952, 4 daughters. *Education:* BA, (Hons), University of London, 1942; PhD. University of Sri Lanka, 1973. *Appointments:* Lecturer in English and English Teaching Methodology, Government Training College for specialist teachers of English, Maharagama, Sri Lanka, 1951-66; Lecturer at the University of Ceylon, 1970-74; Senior Lecturer in Education, Faculty of Education, Colombo Campus; Director, Institute of Workers Education, University of Colombo, 1980-. *Memberships:* Founder and Fellow of various Educa-

tional Organizations in Sri Lanka. *Publications:* The Princess of the Well—Tales from Sri Lanka, 1975; How to Share Five Nice Cakes—Folk Tales of Asia Vol 6, 1977; Teaching English as a Complementary Language in Ceylon, 1965; Reconstruction—An English Technique for an Asian Context, Silva Kandy, 1974; Education and Attention—a Basis for the Humanities, 1980; Socio-economic and other factors affecting the Teaching of English in Sri Lanka, 1979. *Honours:* Exhibitioner in English, 1938-39; Scholar in English, 1939-41. *Hobbies:* Sea Bathing; Religion; Philosophy and problems of the media study and research; Reading Poetry; Eastern and Western serious Music. *Address:* The West Indian Tobacco Co. Ltd., PO Box 177, Port of Spain, Trinidad.

WALDRON, John Colin, b. 5 Aug. 1939, Brisbane. Experimental Officer. m. Helen Gwendolyn Bathgate, 6 Apr. 1963, 2 daughters. *Education:* BS, University Education at Queensland University, 1962; MS, University Education at Queensland University, 1966. *Appointments:* Laboratory Assistant, University of Queensland, 1958-61; Experimental Officer, David North Plant Research Centre, Brisbane, 1963-77; Visiting Scientist, Tate and Lyle Ltd., Reading, England, 1975-76; Experimental Officer, CSIRO Division of Plant Industry, Canberra, 1977-. *Memberships:* President, Weston Creek Cricket Club (ACT), 1981-82; Australian Society of Plant Physiologists. *Publications:* A number of scientific publications relating to Biochemical research on Sugar Cane and the Biochemistry of Photosynthesis, including Regulation of invertase synthesis in sugarcane: Effects of sugars, sugar derivatives and polyhydric alcohols, 1963; Chlorophyll-protein complexes of a marine green alga, Caulerpa cactoides, 1980. *Hobbies:* Cricket; Woodworking. *Address:* 11 Faulkner Place, Chapman, ACT 2611, Australia.

WALKER, Audley Lawson Tudor, b. 21 Apr. 1935, Barbados. Agronomist. m. Lucille Walker (nee Hutchinson), 14 July. 1962, 4 daughters. *Education:* Awarded John R Bovell Scholarship for 3 years at Imperial College of Tropical Agriculture, 1954; DICTA, The Imperial College of Tropical Agriculture, 1954-57. *Appointments:* Employed as Agronomist at the West Indian Tobacco Co. Ltd., Appointed Director, WITCO, 1957; Seconded to Demerara Tobacco Co. Ltd., as General Manager, 1978-80; Appointed Chairman and Managing Director, WITCO, 1980. *Memberships:* Rotary Club of Central Port of Spain; St. Andrews Golf Club; Queens Park Cricket Club; Trinidad Union Club; Tobago Race Club; Agricultural Society of Trinidad and Tobago. *Hobbies:* Golf; Cricket. *Address:* 15 St. Andrews Terrace, Maraval.

WALKER, Charles Michael, Sir, b. 22 Nov. 1916, Simla, India. Retired from H.M. Diplomatic Service. m. Enid Dorothy McAdam, 16 June 1945, 1 son, 1 daughter. *Education:* PPE 2nd Class Honours, New College, Oxford, 1935-38. *Appointments:* Clerk of House of Lords, 1939; Army Service, 1939-46; Dominions Office, 1947; First Secretary, British Embassy, Washington, 1949-51; UK High Commission in Calcutta and New Delhi, 1952-55; Commonwealth Relations Office, 1955-58; Imperial Defence College, 1958; Director of Establishment and Organisation, 1959-62; British High Commissioner in Ceylon, 1962-65, concurrently first British Ambassador to Maldive Islands, 1965; British High Commissioner in Malaysia, 1966-71; Permanent Secretary, Overseas Development Administration, 1971-73; British High Commissioner in India, 1974-76; Retired from H.M. Diplomatic Service, 1976; Chairman, British Scholarship Commission, 1977; Chairman Festival of India Trust, 1980-. *Honours:* CMG, 1960; KCMG, 1963; GCMG, 1976; Honorary DCL The City. *Hobbies:* Fishing; Gardening; Golf. *Address:* Herongate House, Common Hill, West Chiltington, Pulborough, Sussex, RH20 2NL, England.

WALKER, Harold, b. 12 July, 1927, Manchester, England. Member of Parliament. m. 20 Oct. 1956, 1 daughter. *Appointments:* Engineer; Elected Member of Parliament, 1964; Government Whip, 1967-68; Parliamentary under Secretary of State, 1968-70; Re-appointed Parliamentary under Secretary of State, 1974-76; Minister of State, 1976-79. *Honours:* Appointed Privy Councillor, 1979. *Address:* 25 Grange Road, Bessacarr, Doncaster, South Yorkshire, DN4 6SA, England.

WALKER, James Fairweather, b. 6 Sept. 1917, Montrose, Angus, Scotland. Consultant Zymologist. m. Dorothy Evelyn Stewart, 17 May, 1941, 1 son. *Education:* BSc(Hons), St. Andrews University, 1939; Post-Graduate Certificate (Malting and Brewing), Birmingham University, 1947; Microbiology of Agriculture, Soil, Water, Reading University, 1949-50; Analysis of Foods, Drugs, Water and Effluents, Chelsea Polytechnic, 1952-5. *Appointments:* Chief Chemist, H & G Simonds, Brewers, Reading, 1947-56; Laboratory Manager, Briant and Harman, Consulting and Analytical Chemists, 1956-58; Junior Partner, Briant & Harman, 1958-60; Senior Partner, Briant & Harman, 1960-80; Chairman, Briant & Harman Ltd., 1980-. *Memberships:* Official Analyst to English Vineyards Association; Sub-Group on Methods of Analysis for Wine of MAFF's Consultative Committee on EEC Methods of Analysis; C.Chem., FRSC, MIBiol, MInst.WPC, FRSH, Assoc. Incorp. Brewers Guild; FIFST Referee for papers to be published in the Journal; Inst. of Brewing; Soc. Chem. Industry - Member Food Group, Food Analysis Panel. *Publications:* Fungicides for Optical/Electronic Equipment (jointly with H.J. Bunker) Procurement Executive, Ministry of Defence Report No. DX/102/020-01, 1974; Water Usage in the Fermentation industries: Effects of Variations in Composition Chemistry and Industry, 1976. *Honours:* Mastership in Food Control (MFC) awarded, 1980. *Hobbies:* Zymology, Photography. *Address:* Lanterns, Cade Lane, Sevenoaks, Kent, TN13 1QX, England.

WALKER, Reginald Nelson, b. 31 Aug. 1918, Gosford, New South Wales, Australia. General Secretary, Australian Council of National Trusts. m. Delma Melville, 8 Mar. 1941, 2 sons, 1 daughter. *Education:* BA, Sydney; Diploma of Public Administration; Fellow of the Royal Institute of Public Administration. *Appointments:* Assistant Secretary, Local Government and Shires Associations of NSW, 1946-56; Alderman, Ku-ring-gai Municipal Council, 1950-65; Mayor, Ku-ring-gai Municipal Council, 1962; Trustee, Ku-ring-gai Chase National Park, 1957-67; Member, Ku-ring-gai Chase National Park Advisory Committee, 1967-. Member, National Parks and Wildlife Advisory Council, NSW Government, 1967-72; Councillor and Executive Member, Australian Conservation Foundation, 1965-70; Director, The National Trust of Australia, NSW, 1963-74; Member, National Estate Committee of Enquiry, 1973-74; Commissioner, Australian Heritage Commission, 1976-; Honorary Secretary, Australian Council of National Trusts, 1965-74; General Secretary, Australian Council of National Trusts, 1974-. *Honours:* Member of the Order of Australia, 1975. *Hobbies:* Bowls; Gardening. *Address:* 14 Hesperus Street, Pymble NSW 2073, England.

WALKER, Roy Edward Alan, b. 25 Aug. 1936, Welling, Kent, England. Artist (Painter and Printmaker). m. Margaret A Traylor, 26 Mar. 1960, 2 sons, 1 daughter. *Appointments:* Professional Artist; Director, Penwith Printworkshop, St. Ives, Cornwall. *Memberships:* Penwith Society of Arts, St. Ives, Cornwall; Newlyn Society of Artists, Penzance, Cornwall; Associate of Royal Society of Painters, Etchers and Engravers. *Creative Works:* Prints in the collection of V & A Museum, British Council, Royal Society Painters, Etchers and Engravers, Connecticut College, USA; Paintings in private collection in UK, USA, Germany, France, Spain, Australia, S.A, Switzerland, Belgium. *Hobbies:* Music; Dancing. *Address:* Warwick House, Sea View Terrace, St. Ives, Cornwall, England.

WALKER, William George (Emeritus Professor), b. 2 Sept. 1928, Narrabri, New South Wales, Australia. Chief Executive and Principal. m. Sheila M Truman, 24 Aug. 1951, 3 sons, 2 daughters. *Education:* Teachers Certificate, Balmain Teachers College, 1947; BA, (Honours), University of Sydney, 1952; MA, (Honours), University of Sydney, 1956; PhD, University of Illinois, 1958. *Appointments:* Various Lecturing posts, 1948-65; Professor of Education, University of New England, 1967-79; Foundation Dean, Faculty of Education, University of New England, 1969-76; American Council of Learned Societies Fellow, Centre for the Advanced Study of Education Administration, Eugene, Oregon, 1971; Head, Centre for Administrative Studies, University of New England, 1974-78; Professional Associate, Culture Learning Institute, East-West Centre, Hawaii; Visiting Professor of Education, University of Illinois, 1977; Deputy Chairman, Professorial Board, University of New England, 1976-78; Chairman, Professorial Board, University of New England, also Acting Pro Vice Chancellor, Acting Vice Chancellor, 1978-79; Chief Executive and Principal, The Australian Administrative Staff College, 1980. *Memberships:* President, Commonwealth Council for Educational Administration; Vice President, Australian College of Education; President, AASC Association; Phi Delta Kappa; Australian Institute of Management; Institute of Directors in Australia; Society of Senior Executives. *Publications:* Peter Board, 1957; Headmasters for Better Schools, 1963; The Principal at Work, 1967; Educational Administration, International Perspectives, 1968; Theory & Practice in Educational Administration, 1970; School, College and University, 1972; Explorations in Educational Administration, 1973; A Glossary of Educational Terms, 1973. *Honours:* Recipient of numerous honours and awards for professional services; Royal Honour, Order of Australia. *Hobbies:* Philately; Reading. *Address:* The Australian Administrative Staff College, Kunyung Road, Mt. Eliza, Victoria, 3930, Australia.

WALKER, William Stuart, b. 27 March 1926, Georgetown, Guyana, (formerly British Guiana). Barrister-at-Law, Attorney & Company Director. m. Janet C R Moffat, 28 Dec. 1963, 2 sons, 1 daughter. *Education:* BA, Honours, Law, MA, Law, Trinity Hall, Cambridge, England, 1945-48; Diploma in Business Administration, Centre d'Etudes Industrielles, Geneva, Switzerland, 1952; Called to the Bar by the Inner Temple, Barrister-at-Law, 1950. *Appointments:* Chambers in London, 1950-52; Legal Departments of Organisations in Canada, 1953-63; Founder & Senior Partner, W. S. Walker & Company, Barristers, Solicitors & Attorneys-at-Law, Grand Cayman, Cayman Islands, 1964-. *Memberships:* Past President, Cayman Islands Law Society; Immediate Past President, Cayman Islands Chamber of Commerce; Royal Canadian Yacht Club, Toronto, Canada; West India Committee, London. *Publications:* Co-author of The Cayman Islands—A New Base for Foreign Companies & Trusts; The Cayman Islands—An Important New Tax Haven; The Cayman Islands—An Important Base for Foreign Companies. *Honours:* Recipient of The Order of the British Empire, OBE, 1978. *Hobbies:* Sailing; Gardening; Music. *Address:* PO Box 265, Grand Cayman, Cayman Islands.

WALL, Patrick Henry Bligh, b. 14 Oct. 1916, Bidston, Cheshire. Member of Parliament. m. Sheila E. Putnam, 19 Nov. 1953, 1 daughter. *Education:* Downside Royal Naval Staff College; Joint Services Staff College. *Appointments:* Commissioned in Royal Marines, 1935; Served HM Ships, support craft, with USN and RM Commandos, 1939-45; Qualified Naval Gunnery Officer and Parachutist, 1951-56; Elected M.P. 1954; Parliamentary Private Secretary to Minister of Agriculture and Chancellor of the Exchequer, 1955-59; Vice-Chairman Conservative Parliamentary Commonwealth Committee, 1960-68; Vice-Chairman, Conservative Parliamentary Defense Committee; 1965-71; Chairman, 1977-81, Vice President, Military Committee North Atlantic Assembly, 1980-. *Memberships:* Royal Naval Sailing Association; Royal Yacht Squadron; Knight of Sovereign and Military Order of Malta. *Publications:* RM Pocket Book, 1944; Student Power, 1968; Defence Policy Overseas Aid, 1969; The Societ Maritime Threat, 1973; Prelude to Detente, 1975; The Southern Oceans and the Security of the Free World, 1977, Contributor to magazines in UK, USA and S. Africa. *Honours:* MC, 1943; VRD, 1957; Knighted, 1981. *Hobbies:* Model Ships and Aircraft; Books. *Address:* 8 Westminster Gardens, Marsham Street, London, SW1, England.

WALLACE, Walter Wilkinson, b. 23 Sept. 1923, Edinburgh, Scotland. H.M. Overseas Civil Service. m. Susan Blanche Parry, 11 July, 1955, 1 son, 1 daughter. *Education:* George Heriot's, Edinburgh, 1931-40. *Appointments:* Captain, Royal Marines, 1942-46; HMOCS, Sierra Leone, 1948-55; Colonial Office, 1955-57; Sierra Leone, 1957-64; Bahamas, 1964-67; Secretary to Cabinet, Bermuda, 1967-72; H.M. Commissioner, Angvilla, 1973; Governor, British Virgin Islands, 1974-78; Foreign and Commonwealth Office, 1980-. *Memberships:* Army and Navy Club. *Honours:* CVO, 1977; CBE, 1973; OBE, 1964; DSC, 1944. *Hobbies:* Golf. *Address:* Becketts, Itchenor, W. Sussex, England.

WALLER, John Powell, b. 5 Sept. 1933, Warwick, Queensland. Medical Superintendant, m. Marcella

Gordon, 5 Feb. 1959, 2 sons, 2 daughters. *Education:* Nudgee College, Brisbane; MB, BS, University of Queensland; Fellow, Royal Australian College of General Practitioners, 1970; Fellow, Royal Australian College of Medical Administrators, 1976. *Appointments:* RMO, Royal Brisbane Hospital, 1957; Medical Officer, Thursday Island Hospital, 1958; Medical Superintendant, Dalby Hospital, 1960; Medical Officer, Chest Clinic, 1963; Private Practice, Dalby, 1966; Medical Officer, Wolston Park Hospital, 1970; Medical Officer, Maternal & Child Welfare., 1973; Casualty Supervisor, Royal Brisbane Hospital, 1974; Deputy Medical Director, Princess Margaret Hospital for Children, W. Australia, 1976; Medical Superintendant, Mater Adult Hospital, Brisbane, 1979-. *Memberships:* Tattersalls Club, Brisbane; Royal Queensland Golf Club. *Honours:* Efficiency Decoration, 1974. *Hobbies:* Golf; Squash. *Address:* 33, Dauphin Terrace, Highgate Hill, Brisbane, Queensland, Australia.

WALROND, Errol Ricardo, b. 19 Mar. 1936, Barbados, West Indies. Medical Practitioner. m. Beverley Walrond, 29 Dec. 1973, 1 son, 1 daughter. *Education:* BSc, Honours, Anatomy, London University, England, 1958; LRCP, MRCP, Conjoint college of the Royal College of Physicians & Surgeons, 1960; MBBS, London University, 1961; FRCS, Royal College of Surgeons of England, 1964; Elected Fellow, American College of Surgeons, FACP, 1976. *Appointments:* House Physician & Casualty Officer, Guy's Hospital, London, 1960-61; ENT House Surgeon, Guy's Hospital, 1961; House Surgeon, Putney Hospital, London, 1961-62; Casualty Officer, 1962-63; Surgical Registrar, Alton & Lord Mayor Treloans Hospital, Alton, England, 1963-65; Senior Hospital Registrar, Queen Elizabeth Hospital, Barbados, West Indies, 1965-66; Senior Surgical Registrar, University Hospital, Jamaica, 1966-67; Commonwealth Fellow, Thoracic Surgical Department, Guy's Hospital, London, 1967-68; Lecturer, Department of Surgery, University of the West Indies, 1968; Professor, Department of Surgery, University of the West Indies, Barbados, 1976; Vice Dean, University of the West Indies, Faculty of Medicine, Barbados, 1977. *Memberships:* President, Barbados Association of Medical Practitioners; Advisory Committee, Family Health Care in the Caribbean; Representative of Barbados Government to the Task Force for Mount Hope Medical School in Trinidad & Tobago; World Health Organisation Expert Advisory Panel of Health Manpower; President, Barbados Red Cross Society. *Honours:* Wilson Harris Prize, 1957; BSc, Honours, Anatomy, 1958. *Hobbies:* Painting; Gardening. *Address:* 3 Erdiston Drive, Pine, St. Michael Barbados, West Indies.

WALSH, James William, b. 27 Dec. 1923, Omagh, Co. Tyrone, N. Ireland. Agriculturist. m. Audrey S. Cawood, 24 Dec. 1949, 1 son, 1 daughter. *Education:* BAgr. Queens University, Belfast. *Appointments:* Conservation Officer, Departments of Irrigation, Research and Specialist Services, and Conservation and Extension, S. Rhodesia, 1947-51; Lecturer, Basic Sciences of Agriculture, Gwebi College of Agriculture, 1951-56; Senior Lecturer in and Head of Field Husbandry, Gwebi College of Agriculture, 1956-60; Principal, Chibero College of Agriculture, 1960-69; Head, Education and Executive Branch of the Department of Research and Specialist Services, Ministry of Agriculture, Zimbabwe, 1969-. *Memberships:* Crop Science Society of Zimbabwe; South African Society of Dairy Technology, Zimbabwe Division; Mashonaland Turf Club. *Honours:* Member of the Legion of Merit, Zimbabwe, 1977. *Address:* 26, Bryden Road, Mount Pleasant, Salisbury, Zimbabwe.

WALSH, Michael Hayden, b. 5 March, 1938, Corowa, New South Wales. Company Director and Television Compere. *Education:* Xavier College, Melbourne, Australia. Started in Radio 1960 at 3SR Shepparton, joined 2SM, Sydney, 1962. 1965-71: Television Ten-10 Sydney, GTV-9 Melbourne, HSV-7 Melbourne; The Mike Walsh Show, National Nine Network, 1973-; Directorships: Managing Director, Hayden Enterprises Pty. Ltd., Managing Director, Hayden Theatres Pty. Ltd, Joint Managing Director, Hayden-Price Attractions Pty. Ltd, and Cooke Hayden Price Pty. Ltd. *Memberships:* Tattersalls Club; Mornington Racing Club. *Honours:* Recipient of OBE. *Address:* P.O. Box 50, Willoughby, 2068, New South Wales, Australia.

WALSH, Paul Victor, b. 24 May, 1943, Winnipeg, Manitoba, Canada. Barrister and Solicitor. m. Meeka Settler, 6 May, 1970, 1 son, 1 daughter. *Education:* BA, 1964; LLB, 1967. *Appointments:* Grafton, Dowhan, Muldoon, Lafreniere, Roy and Walsh, 1968-69; Nozick, Ackman & Walsh, 1969-74; Walsh, Tadman and Yard, 1974-80; Walsh, Prober, Yard, Gutkin and McManus, 1980-. *Memberships:* Past President, River Heights Liberal Association; Past President, Contemporary Dancers of Winnipeg; Board Member, National Youth Orchestra of Canada; Board Member, Winnipeg Art Gallery; Forum Institute; Chai Folk Ensemble; Past Vice-President, Manitoba Trial Lawyers Association; Unicity Tennis Club. *Publications:* Copyright for the Canadian Visual Artist, 1978. *Honours:* Dingwald Trophy for Debating Championship of University of Manitoba, 1963, 1964, 1965, 1966, 1967; MacDonald Lauriere Cup Debating Championship of Canada, 1967. *Hobbies:* Tennis; Photography. *Address:* 1188 Wellington Crescent, Winnipeg, Manitoba, R3N OA4, Canada.

WALSH, Robert John, b. 17 Jan. 1917, Queensland, Australia. Medical. m. 5 June, 1944, 3 sons, 1 daughter. *Education:* MB, BS, University of Sydney, 1939. *Appointments:* House Surgeon, Sydney Hospital, 1940-41; Australian Army Medical Corps. 1941-46; Director, New South Wales Red Cross blood Transfusion Service, 1946-66; Professor, Human Genetics, University of New South Wales, 1966-; Dean, Faculty of Medicine, University of New South Wales, 1973-. *Publications:* Contributor to various professional journals. *Honours:* Recipient of OBE, 1970, AO, 1976; Fellow, Australian Academy of Science; Serving Brother Order of St. John; Fellow, Royal A'sian College of Physicians; Fellow, Royal College of Pathologists of Australia. *Hobbies:* Woodwork; Reading; Gardening. *Address:* 237 Midson Road, Epping, New South Wales, 2121, Australia.

WALSHAM, Bruce Taylor, b. 28 Feb. 1936, Grimsby, England. Geologist, Mining Executive. m. R. Ann Barry, 30 Aug. 1962, 2 daughters. *Education:* BSc. Hons. University of Birmingham, 1958. *Appointments:* Geologist, Union Corporation Ltd., South Africa, 1958-62; Geologist, Mackay and Schnellmann Ltd., London, 1962-64; Geologist-in-charge, Cornish Land Ventures Ltd, 1964-68; Geologist-in-charge, Union Corp. (UK) Ltd, London, 1968-71; Exploration Manager, Bond Corporation, Perth, Western Australia, 1971; Resident Director, Mackay and Schnellmann, P.L. Brisbane, Queensland, 1971; Vice-President and Exploration Manager, Freeport of Australia, 1971-76; Senior Staff Geologist, Freeport Reno, 1976-77; Vice-President, Exploration Manager, S.W. USA, Freeport Tucson, Arizona; President and General Manager, Freeport of Australia and Associated Companies, Melbourne, 1979-. *Memberships:* FIMM; CEng; MAusIMM; MAIME; Society of Economic Geologists; Association of Exploration Geochemists; Geological Society of South Africa; Geological Society of Australia; Arizona Geological Society. *Publications:* Diamond Drilling for Tin in West Cornwall, 1967; Various technical notes and publications in UK, Australia. *Hobbies:* Photography; Philately; Soccer; Cricket; Tennis. *Address:* 11 Nevis Street, Camberwell, Victoria, 3124, Australia.

WALTER, Harold Edward, b. 27 April, 1922. Barrister-at-Law. Yvette N. Toolsy, 1942. *Education:* Quartier Militaire Primary School, 1927-32; Royal College, Curepipe, 1932-39; Academy of Officers, Officers Cadet, Cadet Training Unit, NJORO, 1943-44; Staff Officer, Gen. HQ. MELF, 1945-48; Hon. Society of Lincoln's Inn, Council of Legal Education, 1948-51. *Appointments:* Village Councillor, 1952; President, YMCA, Mauritius, 1953; Municipal Councillor, 1956; Member Legislative Council, 1959, re-elected 1963, 1967; Member, Legislative Assembly, 1976; Minister of Works and Internal Communications, 1959-65; Minister of Health, 1965-67; Minister of Labour, 1967-71; Minister of Health, 1971-76; Minister of External Affairs, Tourism and Emigration, 1976-. Chairman, Commonwealth Medical Conference, Mauritius, 1971; Sri Lanka, 1972-74; Chairman, Premieres Journees, Medicales de l'Ocean Indian, Mauritius, 1974; President, 29th Works Health Assembly, Geneva, 1976-77; Chairman, OAU Council of Ministers, 1976-77. *Memberships:* Bar Association, Mauritius, 1951-77; Executive Board, WHO, 1974-77; Commonwealth Parliamentary Association, 1959-; Parliamentary Association of French Speaking MPs, 1974-; Union of African Parliaments, 1976-. *Honours:* Knighted by Her Majesty the Queen, 1971; Commandeur des Palmes

Academiques of the French Republic, 1974; Decorated by Russia, USSR, on occasion of 30th anniversary of the victory over Facism and Nazism, 1975; Commandeur de la Legion d'Honneur, France, 1980; Grand Officier du Merite de l'Ordre Diplomatique, Coree, 1980. *Hobbies:* Hunting; Fishing; Swimming; Reading; Gardening. *Address:* La Rocca Mgr Leen Street, Eau Coulee, Mauritius.

WALTERS, Gordon Heathcot, b. 15 Sept. 1922, Walrond Village, Christ Church, Barbados, W.I. Primary School Teacher, 1936-58; Social Worker, 1958-. m. Bersdeen C. Thompson, 25 Apr. 1946, 2 sons, 2 daughters. *Education:* BSc, University of West Indies, 1971. *Appointments:* Primary School Teacher, 1936-58; Welfare Officer, 1958-59; Organiser, Youth Town, Youth Centre, City, Bridgetown, Barbados, 1959-60; Welfare Officer, 1960-68; Senior Welfare Officer, 1968-72; Deputy Chief Welfare Officer, 1972-76; Chief Community Development Officer, 1976-. *Memberships:* National Festivals Committee, 1973-76; Parent Education for Development, PAREDOS, 1974-; Penal Reform, Committee, 1980; Chairman, Bridgetown, Barbados, 1979-; Hackney, London, Twinning Committee, 1979-. *Honours:* JP. *Hobbies:* Reading; Vegetable Gardening; Travel. *Address:* Sion Hill, Christ Church, Barbados, West Indies.

WALTERS, William Allen Willcox, b. 27 May 1933, Adelaide, South Australia. Medicine/ Obstetrician & Gynaecologist. *Education:* MB, BS, Adelaide, 1956; PhD, London, 1964; MRCOG, 1960; FRCOG, 1973; FRACOG, 1980. *Appointments:* Lecturer, Department of Obstetrics/Gynaecology, University of Aberdeen, 1963-65; Senior Lecturer, Department of Obstetrics/Gynaecology, Monash University, Melbourne, 1965-70; Associate professor, Department of Obstetrics/Gynaecology, Monash University, Melbourne, 1970-; Obstetrician, Queen Victoria Medical Centre, Melbourne. *Memberships:* Australian Medical Association; British Medical Association; Medical Research Society, U.K.; North of England Obstetrical & Gynaecological Society; Australian Society for Reproductive Biology. *Publications:* Numerous papers in Medical & Scientific Journals, Walters, W.A.W, Cardiovascular Function in Pregnancy, In Reproductive Physiology. Edited by R.P. Shearman, 1979. *Hobbies:* Archaeology; Comparative Religion; Music. *Address:* 20 Barry Street, Kew, Victoria 3101, Australia

WALTERS-GODFREE, Dorothy May (Mrs. F.J. Cossey Godfree) b. 21 May, Ilkeston, Derbyshire, England. Teacher, Journalist, Writer. m. (1) Gerald Walters, 24 Apr. 1948 (deceased), (2) F.J. Cossey Godfree, 21 June 1975. *Education:* Certificated Teacher, City of Leeds Training College. *Appointments:* Holy Trinity Primary School, 2 years; Kensington Junior School, 2 years; Hallam Fields Nursery & Reception, 4 years; Journalist, Ilkeston Pioneer. *Memberships:* Chairman, Bath Political Centre, Conservative; Former Chairman, Bath University Ladies Society; Derbyshire Conservative Commonwealth Committee; Vice Chairman, Bath & Wiltshire Branch European Union of Woman; Secretary, European Union of Women for West Country & Wales. *Creative Works:* New Play (1955) for Conservative East Midlands area on Commonwealth called The Crown; Various children's pageants on Commonwealth themes performed in Derbyshire in 1950's; Books of poetry, And Will the Robin Sing Again, Because a Rainbow Danced; Poetry in international journals. *Honours:* West Country poetry prize on Human Rights, 1968; Poem set to music & performed at Human Rights service by award winning choir in Bath; Awards from Academie da Leonardo da Vinci International Poetry Diplomas. *Hobbies:* Study of Animal & Bird behaviour; Painting; Music; Drama; Gardening. *Address:* The High Street, Batheaston, Bath, England.

WALTON, Nancy-Bird, (Mrs. John C. F. Walton) b. 16 Oct. 1915, Kew, New South Wales, Australia. Aviatrix. m. John C F Walton, 16 Dec. 1939, 1 son, 1 daughter. *Appointments:* Pioneer Aviatrix; first woman to operate an aeroplane commercially in Australia, Participated in First Ladies' Flying Tour of Australia, 1934; Owner pilot to the Far West Children's Health Scheme, 1935-36; War Service, Commandant, WATC, 1940-45; Founder & President, Australian Womens Pilots Association, 1950; President, Australian Women's Flying Club, 1940-45; President, Women's Section, National Heart Foundation, 1960; Member, New South Wales Ambulance Board; Pilot to Far West Children's Health Scheme; Flew the Baby Clinic Sister on regular trips from Bourke, New South Wales to remote areas; Operated as an Air Ambulance & Charter pilot; Active involvement in establishment & development of the New South Wales Air Ambulance project since 1961; Active involvement in International Women Pilots Association; Subject of ABC TV programme, A Big Country, 1976, TV programme, This is Your Life, 1976. *Memberships:* Honorary Life Member, Royal Aero Club, New South Wales; Honorary Life Member, Narromine Aero Club; International Women Pilots Association; Aviation Medical Society of Australia & New Zealand; Australian Women Pilot Association; German Women Pilots Association; Australian British Society; Airport Club; Mascot; Queen's Club; Pacific Club. *Publications:* Born to Fly, 1961. *Honours:* OBE, 1966; ARAes, 1938; Dame of Merit, Knights of Malta, Most Excellent Order St. John of Jerusalem Hospitallers. *Address:* P.O. Box 136, St. Ives, New South Wales 2075, Australia.

WALWYN, Daniel Reynold, b. 27 Nov. 1892, Nevis, West Indies. Accountant. m. Mabel Irene Wilson (deceased), 4 sons, 2 daughters. *Education:* Teachers Certificate, 1913; Diploma in Higher Accountancey, 1929. *Appointments:* Chief Audit Clerk, Leeward Islands Colony, 1920-37; Colonial Treasurer, British Virgin Islands, 1937; Acting Auditor, Leeward Islands, 1945-46; Postmaster General, St. Kitts, Nevis, Anguilla, 1946-47; Colonial Treasurer, Montserrat, 1947-53; Managing Director, Nevis Co-operative Banking Company Ltd., 1955; Chairman, Bank of Commerce, St. Kitts, 1978. *Memberships:* President, Nevis Club; Past President, Nevis Lions Club; Methodist Church, Charlestown. *Honours:* Coronation Medal, Queen Elizabeth, II, 1953; Officer of the Order of the British Empire, OBE, 1969. *Hobbies:* Walking; Reading; Travelling. *Address:* Bath Village, Nevis, British West Indies.

WAN, Abraham, b. 14 Oct. 1928. Tsingtao, Clinical Biochemist. m. 15 Aug. 1959, 1 son, 1 daughter. *Education:* BS, National Taiwan University, 1955; MS, University of Minnesota, 1960; PhD, University of Nebraska, 1964. *Appointments:* Biochemist IV, Provincial Lab. Department of Public Health, Regina, Saskachewan, Canada, 1963-64; Biochemist V, Sunland Hospital, Orlando, Florida, USA, 1964-67; Associate Director in Clinical Chemistry, Norfolk Medical Centre, Norfolk, VA, USA, 1969-74; Deputy Director, Department of Biochemistry, Alfred Hospital, Prhran, Victoria, Australia, 1975- Educational Affiliation: Assistant Professor, Department of Bio Chemistry, Eastern Virginia Medical School, Norfolk, Va. 1974; Adjunct Professor, Department of Biology, Old Dominion University, Norfolk, Va, 1969-74; Adjunct Research Professor, Division of Science, Norfolk State University, Norfolk, Va, 1972-74; Clinical Teacher, Monash University, Medical School, Clayton, Victoria, Australia, 1975-. *Memberships:* American Association for Clinical Chemists; New York Academy of Science; Australian Association of Clinical Biochemists; International Society of Clinical Enzymology. *Publications:* Contributor of reviews, monographs, articles to professional journals and conferences. *Honours:* Recipient of Sigma Xi, 1958. *Hobbies:* Tennis; Vintage Cars. *Address:* 14 Tyrol Court, Doncaster East, Victoria, Australia 3109.

WANEATONA, Lency Adomea, b. 25 Oct. 1952, Sulagwalu, North Malaita, Solomon Islands. Librarian. m. Leah Repest, 25 Oct. 1975, 2 daughters. *Education:* DipEd, University of the South Pacific, Fiji, 1973-75; Library Studies, National Library of New Zealand, Wellington, 1976-77; Joint Honours Degree in Librarianship and Education, University College of Wales, Aberystwyth, 1978-81. *Appointments:* Librarian Designate, 1976-80; Chief Librarian, National Library Services, Solomon Islands, 1980-. *Publications:* Overseas Student Association, UCW, Aberystwyth, 1978-81; Solomon Islands Writers Association, 1977-. *Hobbies:* Football; Rugby; Table Tennis; Reading; Photography. *Address:* National Library of the Solomon Islands, P.O. Box 165, Honiara, Solomon Islands.

WANG, Mabel, (Mrs David Neng Hwan Wang) b. 22 July 1924. Melbourne, Australia. Importer/Chairman of Company. m. 8 Oct. 1943, 2 sons, 2 daughters. *Education:* Graduate of Royal Melbourne Institute of Technology; School of Art, 1942. *Appointments:* Co-Founder of David Wang & Company, 1948; Specialist in

Oriental Imports. *Memberships:* President, Melbourne Dai Loong Association; Victorian Government China Advisory Committee. *Hobbies:* Painting; Piano; Reading. *Address:* 152 Bourke Street, Melbourne, Victoria, Australia.

WANG, Thomas Yau-Sam b. 13 Sept. 1935, Shanghai, China. Conductor, Violinist. m. Mabel Y H Hung, 14 May 1960, 1 daughter. *Education:* FTCL, Fellow of Trinity College, London, 1970; LTCL, Licentiate of Trinity College, London, 1968. *Appointments:* Lecturer, Shanghai Conservatory, Shanghai, 1960-62; Lecturer, Hong Kong Academy of Music, Hong Kong, 1965-67; Conductor, University Orchestra, The Chinese University of Hong Kong, 1973-75; Conductor, Hong Kong Youth Symphony Orchestra, Hong Kong Government, 1978-; Lecturer, Hong Kong Conservatory of Music, 1979-; Concert tour with Hong Kong Youth Symphony Orchestra, 1979; Deputy Music Director, 3rd Asian Youth Music Camp, 1979; Conductor, Hong Kong Jing Ying Strings, Israel, Cyprus, 1980; Assistant Music Administrator (Professional), Music Office, Hong Kong Government, 1978-. *Hobbies:* Table-Tennis; Bridge. *Address:* 3B Prince Garden, 284 Prince Edward Road, Kowloon, Hong Kong.

WANSBROUGH, David James b 15 Apr. 1948, Auckland, New Zealand, Artist, Poet, Theologian. m. Ms. Linda Wood, 6 Aug. 1973, 3 sons, 2 daughters. *Education:* Selwyn College, 1963-66; Teaching Diploma, Auckland Teachers College, 1968-71; Licentate in Theology, Seminary of St. Basil the Great, Sydney, 1979-80; Justice of the Peace, New South Wales, 1980. *Memberships:* Honorary Resurgent Prisoner, Parramatta Jail, 1977; Committee of New South Wales Anthroposophical Society, 1978-79; Director of the Australian Institute, of Contemporary Studies, Sydney, 1980; Honorary Secretary of the Western Orthodox Church, Australia, 1976-78; Vice President of Christophorus House Retirement Centre, 1978-80; Associate of Royal Society of Arts, South Australia. *Publications:* Published Biographical papers on Gandhi and Godfrey Miller; numerous one-man Art Exhibitions including: Print Room, 1980, Pointon Gallery, 1980; Exhibitions in Paris, Switzerland & San Fransisco, 1981. *Hobbies:* Examining the Noetics of Aesthetic Notation; Attempting to form a modern Platonic conception of nature. *Address:* 18 The Links, Leura, New South Wales, Australia 2781

WANSBROUGH, John, Sidney, b. 14 Apr. 1944, Wanganui, New Zealand. Television Producer. m. 30 Mar. 1968, Patricia Margaret Haworth, 2 sons. *Education:* Wanganui Technical College, 1956-59. *Appointments:* Radio Servicing, Wanganui, 1960-65; Sound Engineer, Peach Wemyss Productions, Auckland, 1965; Tour Lighting Director, New Zealand Theatre, Incorporating Royal Shakespeare Company Tours and New Zealand Ballet, 1966; Floor Manager, New Zealand Broadcasting Corporation, 1966-68; Stage Director, Black and White Minstrels, 1968-69; Floor Manager, New Zealand Broadcasting Corporation, 1969; Producer/Director Television, New Zealand, 1980. *Memberships:* Television Producers and Directors Assoication, New Zealand. *Publications:* Producer/Director, Opportunity Knocks; Director, On the Mat, Worldwide Distributed Professional Wrestling; Director, Trial by Jury, Highly Commended at Montreux; Director, Star over Bethlehem, 1979; Director, A Week of It, New Zealand Award Winning Satirical Programme; Producer/Director, That's Country, International Country Show. *Honours:* Trinity College Examinations, Piano, Vocal, Speech, Drama, 1960-65. *Hobbies:* Music; Theatre. *Address:* 8 St Andrews Square, Christchurch 5, New Zealand.

WANYAMA, Patrick Gladstone, b. 1 June, 1947, Kenya. Library Assistant. m. Violet, 5 May 1973, 1 son, 2 daughters. *Education:* East African Advanced Certificate, 1972; UNESCO Library Assistant Certificate, 1975; BA, Librarianship Student, Polytechnic of North London, England. *Appointments:* Library Assistant Trainee, 1973-75; Library Assistant, 1976-80. *Memberships:* Kenya Library Association; The Library Association, Britain; Maktaba Co-operative Society; Maktaba Staff Club, Chairman. *Publications:* Articles in Maktaba Library Association Journals. *Hobby:* Christianity. *Address:* 12 Woollaston Road, London, N4, England.

WARD, Alan Dudley, b. 11 June, 1935, Gisborne, New Zealand. University Professor and Land Administrator. m. Helen Tremaine-Park, 25 Aug. 1962, 1 son, 4 daughters. *Education:* BA, Victoria University of Wellington, 1956; MA(Hons), Victoria University of Wellington, 1958; Secondary School Teachers Certificate, Auckland Teachers College, 1957; PhD, Australian National University, Canberra, 1965-7. *Appointments:* Secondary School Teacher, History, New Zealand Education Service, 1958-64; University Lecturer, La Trobe University, Melbourne, 1967-; Senior Lecturer, 1970; Reader, 1975; Secondments: Commission of Enquiry into Land Matters, Papua New Guinea, Permanent Consultant, 1973; Director of Rural Lands Department, Government of Vanuatu, 1981-83. *Memberships:* Foundation Chairman and present member of the Research Centre for Southwest Pacific Studies; Polynesian Society. *Publications:* A Show of Justice, book; Various articles in New Zealand Journal of History; Journal of the Polynesian Society. *Honours:* Senior Scholarship in History, Victoria University of Wellington, 1956; EP Wilson Prize for published historical writing, Victoria University of Wellington, 1977. *Hobbies:* Tennis; Sailing; Bushwalking. *Address:* 86 John Street, Eltham, Melbourne, Australia 3095.

WARD, Arthur Hugh, Sir, b. 25 Mar. 1906, Spalding, Lincs, England. Executive. m. Jean Bannatyne Mueller, 6 Jan. 1936, 1 son, 3 daughters. *Education:* Associate Chartered Accountant, 1932. *Appointments:* Cost Accountant, Cochrane and Co. Teeside, 1922-26; Secretary, Auckland Herd Improvement Association, 1928-36; Technical Officer, (Herd Improvement), N.Z. Dairy Board, 1936-43; Director of Herd Improvement, NZ Dairy Board, 1944-54; General Manager, NZ Dairy Board, 1954-70; Member, Monetary and Economic Council of NZ, 1970-78; Member, Massey University Council, 1967-81; Pro-Chancellor, Massey University Council, 1970-75; Chancellor, Massey University Council, 1975-81; Member, Remuneration Authority, 1971-72; Chairman, National Research Advisory Council, 1970-72; Member, D.S.I.R. Council, 1956-61; *Memberships:* Royal Society of New Zealand; NZ Association of Agric. Scientists; NZ Soc. of Animal Production, President and Founding Secretary; The Wellington Club; President, Paraparaumu Beach Golf Club. *Publications:* Numerous articles on dairy cattle breeding and dairy husbandry; Book, A Command of Cooperatives, 1975, (History of Dairy Industry); Numerous articles on New Zealand economy in relation to primary production. *Honours:* OBE, 1960; KBE, 1979; Queen Elizabeth II Silver Jubilee Medal, 1977; Marsden Medal for services to Science, 1975. *Hobbies:* Reading; Writing; Gardening; Golf. *Address:* 17 Tui Crescent, PO Box 56, Waikanae, New Zealand.

WARD, Deighton (Harcourt Lisle), (Sir), b. 16 May 1909. Governor General, Barbados. m. Audrey D Ramsey, 1936, 3 daughters. *Education:* Boys' Foundation School; Harrison College, Barbados. *Appointments:* Called to the Bar, Middle Temple, 1933; practised at Barbados Bar, 1934-63; Member, Legislative Council of Barbados, 1955-58; Member, House of Representatives, Federation of West Indies, 1958-62; High Court of Barbados, 1963-76; President, Barbados Football Association, 1954-75. *Memberships:* Spartan, Barbados; Hon, Summerhays; Hon, Bridgetown; Hon, Barbados Turf. *Honours:* QC, Barbados, 1959; GCMG, 1976; GCVO, 1977; Knight of St. Andrew, 1980. *Hobbies:* Reading; Bridge; Billiards. *Address:* Government House, Barbados.

WARD, John, b. 30 Oct. 1937, Melbourne, Victoria, Australia. Teacher, Librarian. m. Lynette Margaret Phillips, 2 sons, 1 daughter. *Education:* Bachelor of Social Science, Royal Melbourne Institute technology, 1975; Associate, Royal Melbourne Institute of Technology, 1971; Associate, Library Association of Australia, 1971; Trained Teacher Librarian Certificate, 1957; Trained Primary Teachers Certificate, 1956. *Appointments:* Teacher Librarian, Malvern Central School, 1957-64; Director, Youth Leader Training Programme, Congregational Churches of Australia, 1964-67; Teacher Librarian, Brunswick Central School, in-Service Education Officer, Library Branch, Education Department of Victoria, 1969-74; Executive Officer, Technical School Libraries, ED. OfV., 1974-77; Co-ordinator Support Services, Planning Services, Education Department of Victoria, 1977-. *Memberships:* President, Australian School Library Association, 1977; Foundation Secretary, Australian School Library Association, 1969-76; Vice-President, Australian Library Promotion Council, 1972-; President, School Library Association of Victoria, 1975-; Secretary, School Library Association of Victoria, 1967-74; Vice-Chairman, Childrens Book Council of Australia, 1979-80; Acting President, Childrens Book Council of Australia, 1979-80. *Publications:* Collection Building, Melbourne, Slav, 1967; Planning School Libraries, Melbourne, Slav, 1970. *Honours:* Honorary Associate, School Library Association of United Kingdom, 1973; Honorary Associate, International Association of School Librarianship, 1977. *Hobbies:* Philately; Gardening; Tennis; Collecting Australiana. *Address:* Alukea, Cr, Brougham Rd. & Taylors Rd, Mt. Macedon. 3441, Victoria, Australia.

WARD, Julian Peter, b. 1 May, 1936, Tully, Queensland, Australia. Medical Practitioner. m. Helen Gordon, 15 Aug. 1962, 1 daughter. *Education:* MB, BS, University of Queensland, 1960; FRACS, 1966; MRCOG, 1966; FRCOG, 1979; FRACOG, 1980; B.Ed.Stun, University of Newcastle, 1976; DDU, 1980. *Appointments:* RMO, 1960-61; Registrar, Surgery, Princess Alexandra Hospital, 1962-63; Registrar in Obstetrics & Gynaecology, Princess Alexandra Hospital, 1964-65; Senior Registrar, Obstetrics & Gynaecology, Portsmouth, UK, 1966-67; Staff Specialist in Obstetrics & Gynaecology, Royal Newcastle Hospital, 1968-69; Director of Obstetrics & Gynaecology, Royal Newcastle Hospital, 1970-. *Memberships:* Australian Society, Ultrasound in Medicne; Australian Society, Medical Education; American Association of Gynaecological Laparoscopists. *Publications:* Medical Publications. *Honours:* Kenneth Wilson Prize, First Place in Obstetrics & Gynaecology, 1960. *Hobbies:* Tennis; Cricket. *Address:* 9 Lemnos Parade, Newcastle, New South Wales, 2300, Australia.

WARDROP, Frank Ricardo, b. 4 Feb. 1912, Muswell Hill, London, England. Chartered Electrical Engineer. m. Ann Low Guik Imm, 26 Dec. 1960. *Education:* Norfolk House High School, 1917-21; Merchant Taylor's School, 1921-30; BSc, King's College, London University, 1933. *Appointments:* Sales Engineer, Hogan & Wardrop Ltd, London, 1934-37; Engineer, Osborne & Chapel, Federated Malay States & Malaya, 1937-41 & 1946-47; Engineer & Adviser to General Manager, Electricity Department later, National Electricity Board, Malaysia, 1947-68; Partner, Consulting Engineer, Lee Wardrop & Partners, 1969-. *Memberships:* Freeman of the City of London & of the Merchant Taylors Company; Ipoh Club; Penang Club; FIEE; FIEM; Selangor Club. *Honours:* CBE, 1966; JMN, 1968. *Hobbies:* Reading; Snooker. *Address:* 8-I Jalan Bunga Pudak, Tanjong Bungah; Penang; Malaysia.

WARE, Malcolm Henry, b. 22 June, 1930, Mildura, Victoria. General Manager of General Credits Ltd, Financier. m. Sonia Ellen Gain, 26 Nov. 1955, 1 son, 1 daughter. *Education:* Harvard 59th AMP. *Appointments:* The Commercial Bank of Australia Ltd., 1946-61; Seconded to General Credits Ltd., 1961-; Deputy Chief Manager, 1968, General Manager, 1974. *Memberships:* Athenaeum Club. *Address:* 39 Hopetoun Avenue, Canterbury 3126, Victoria, Australia.

WARK, Bruce Goodman, b. 23 Nov. 1931, Adelaide, South Australia. Prosthodontist. m. Filicia Janice Alison, 17 Sept, 1955, Divorced, 1980, 1 son, 1 daughter. *Education:* Bachelor of Dental Surgery, University of Adelaide, 1953; LDS, Royal College of Dental Surgeons, Ontario, 1959; Doctor of Dental Surgery, University of Toronto, 1959; Certificate of Attendance in Crown & Bridge, University of Michigan; Member of the Royal Society of Health, 1961; Elected Fellow of the Royal Society of Health, 1965; Fellow of the Royal Australasian College of Dental Surgeons, 1965; Fellow of the International College of Dentists, 1976. *Appointments:* Private practice, Specialist practice, 1961 onwards. *Memberships:* Australian Dental Association; Member of the Federation Dentair Internationale; Australian President, Australian Society of Prosthodontists, 1973-76; Foundation Member of General Practice Study Group; Francis B. Vedder Society of C & B Prosthodontics, USA; Australian President, International Academy of Gnathology, USA, 1977-81; Honorary Clinical Assistant of Royal Adelaide Hospital, 1958; Past President, Adelaide University Dental Students Society, 1967; Pierre Fauchard Academy; American

Equilibration Society. *Publications:* Professional publications. *Hobbies:* Golf; represented State at Rugby Union; Sturt Cricket Club; Football. *Address:* 195, North Terrace, Adelaide, South Australia, 5000.

WARNECKE, Mary Isabel, (Mrs Thomas H. Benson), b. 10 June, 1933, Berri, South Australia. Pianist. m. Thomas Harrow Benson, 16 Nov. 1966, 2 sons. *Education:* Diploma of Associate of University of Adelaide, 1954. *Appointments:* Class Music Teacher, Hurstville Boys School, Sydney, New South Wales; Class Music, Social Study, French Teacher, St. Mary's Star of the Sea, High School, Sydney, New South Wales; Head of Music Department, Meriden, Church of England, School for Girls, Strathfield, Sydney; Head of Music Department, Canberra Grammar Boy's School, Canberra; Wilderness Girls School, Head of Music Department, Adelaide; Tutor in Pianoforte, Elden Conservatorium of Music, University of Adelaide; Examiner for Australian Music Examinations Board. *Memberships:* Treasurer of Music Student's Association, 1950-54; Commonwealth Department for Interim Society of Music Education in Perth, West Australia, 1974. *Honours:* Recipient of numerous honours and scholarships. *Address:* 4 James Street, Gilberton, South Australia 5081.

WARNER, James A. McNeil, b. 26 July, 1925, Bermuda. Principal. m. Florence Mont, 12 Nov. 1966, 1 daughter. *Education:* BSc, 1951; Certificate in Administration, 1971. *Appointments:* Teacher, 1945-48, 1951-59; Deputy Principal, 1959-70; Principal, 1970; Seconded to Ministry of Education, 1974-76. *Memberships:* President, ABUT, Chairman, Associated School Principals. *Hobbies:* Music; Travel. *Address:* Sousa Estate, Devonshire, Bermuda.

WARREN, Bruce Albert, b. 2 Nov. 1934, Sydney, New South Wales, Australia. Clinical Professor of Pathology. m. Diana Mary King, 14 Aug. 1964, 1 son, 1 daughter. *Education:* BSc, First Class Honours, Medical, Pathology, Sydney University, 1957; MB, BS, Second Class Honours, Sydney University, 1959; DPhil, Oxford University, England, 1964; MA, Oxford University, 1967; Fellow, Royal College of Pathologists of Australia, 1972; Member, Royal College of Pathologists, 1973; Fellow, Royal College of Pathologists, 1980. *Appointments:* Part-time Tutor, Pathology, Oxford Medical School, 1967-68; Visiting Assistant Professor, Anatomy Department, University of Western Ontario, London, Canada, 1968; Assistant Professor, 1968-69; Associate Professor, 1969-74; Professor, Pathology, 1974-80; Consultant Pathologist, 1972-80; Clinical Professor, Pathology, University of New South Wales, 1980; Director, Department of Anatomical Pathology, Prince Henry Hospital, 1980. *Memberships:* Senate of the University of Western Ontario, 1970-74; Life Fellow, Royal Microscopical Society; Royal Society of New South Wales, 1973-82; Life Member, American Association for the Advancement of Science; Fellow, Royal Society of Medicine; The Athenaeum Club. *Publications:* Thesis, Science Node Biopsy, Sarcoid-like lesions in lymph nodes draining malignant neoplasms, both with P. Schiff; BSc Theses, The structure and function of vascular endothelium; DPhil Thesis, Chapter 1, The Vascular morphology of tumors and Chapter 2, Tumor angiogensis in the book Tumor Blood Circulation, edited by H.I. Peterson, CRC Press Incorporated, Florida, 1979; Associate Editor, Integrated Medicine, Van Nostrand Reinhold, New York, 1981; 60 Publications in professional journals. *Honours:* Public Exhibition and Australian Commonwealth Scholarship, 1952-58; Prosector in Anatomy, 1953-54; G.S. Caird Scholarship, 1955; BSc, Medical, Scholarship, 1955-56; British Commonwealth Scholarship, United Kingdom, 1962-64. *Hobbies:* Swimming; Gardening; Reading. *Address:* 8 Arcadia Street, Coogee, New South Wales 2034, Australia.

WASHBURN, V. Glen, b. 12 Dec. 1928, Flint, Genesee County, Michigan, United States of America. Author/Poet/Teacher. m. Mary Margaret Julia Flynn, 2 Oct. 1976, 1 son. *Education:* Bachelor of Fine Arts, 1966, Master of Fine Arts, 1968, Michigan State University. *Appointments:* Flint Institute of Arts; Michigan State University; Eastern Montana College; Head Start, Parsons College Art Department; 13th Annual Aesthetics Workshop, University of New Mexico; Director, Graphic Arts Center, Parsons College; Artist-in-residence, Parsons College; Darling Downs Institute of

Advanced Education. *Memberships:* Delta Phi Delta; Phi Kappa Phi; Sigma Chi; American Association of University Professors; College Art Association; Kappa Pi; Universal Life Church. *Publications:* Both Sides of the Leaf, East Lansing, 1967; Near the End of All My Sorrows, A and R Sydney, 1978; Poetry in Overland; Your Friendly Fascist; Saturday Club Book of Poetry; New Poetry; Murals for Howard Johnson Motels; Turnpike Motel; Editor, Spartan Magazine; Idiom Magazine; Prints and Paintings exhibited at Brooklyn Museum, American Federation of Arts Travelling Shows; Morris Gallery, Kresge Art Gallery, Detroit Art Institute, Grant Wood American Gothic Trail Exhibition. *Hobbies:* Photography; Aikido; Folk Song collections and performance; Rare Book Collection and restoration, Fruit and Nut Tree Culture; Wine Making; Film Making. *Address:* 230 Perth Street, Toowoomba, Queensland 4350, Australia.

WASTI, Syed Farouk, b. 29 Dec. 1943, Lahore, Pakiston. Medical Doctor. m. 1973. *Education:* MBBS, King Edward Medical College, Lahore, Pakistan, 1966; BSc, Punjab University, Lahore, Pakistan, 1967; DCH, Diploma, Child Health, Punjab University, Lahore, Pakistan, 1968; MCPS, College of Physicians and Surgeons, Pakistan, 1969; DHA, New South Wales University, Australia, 1974; MHP, New South Wales University, Australia, 1976; FRACMA, Royal Australian College of Medical Administrators, 1978; MCCM, New Zealand, College of Community Medicine, New Zealand. *Appointments:* House Physician, House Surgeon, Mayo Hospital, Lahore, Pakistan, 1966-67; Registrar, Paediatrics, Rotorua Hospital, New Zealand; Resident Medical Officer, B.M. Hospital, Katoomba, 1971; Medical Superintendent, Blue Mountains Hospital, Katoomba, New South Wales 2780, Australia, 1972-. *Memberships:* British Medical Association; New Zealand Medical Association; Medical Superintendents Association, New South Wales; Public Service Association; Amnesty International; Katoomba Golf Club; Lawson Bowling Club. *Honours:* Recipient of MBBS, Hons. *Hobbies:* Philately; Philosophy. *Address:* 13 Dulhunty Street, Katoomba, New South Wales 2780, Australia.

WATERHOUSE, Walter Kingsley, b. 17 Aug. 1940, Goomalling, West Australia. Superintendent of Agricultural Education. m. 4 Jan. 1966, Elindre Anne Cole, 1 son, 2 daughters. *Education:* BSc, Agriculture, 1962, MS, Agriculture, 1968, Diploma of Education, 1963, University of Western Australia; Certificate in Personnel Management, Technical Education, 1974. *Appointments:* Education Office, Agriculture, 1974, Senior Education Officer, Agriculture, 1978, Superintendent of Education, Agriculture, 1980, Education Office, Western Australia. *Memberships:* Australian Institute of Agricultural Science; The Association of Open Clubs. *Publications:* Contributed to various professional journals. *Hobbies:* Bricklaying. *Address:* 122 Modillion Avenue, Riverton, Perth, West Australia.

WATERHOUSE, William Stanley, b. 22 Jan. 1922, North Sydney, New South Wales, Australia. Company Director. m. Suzanne R. Dart, 11 May, 1953, 2 sons, 1 daughter. *Education:* BA; LLB. *Appointments:* Barrister; Bookmaker; Company Director; Consul-General, Tonga, Australia. *Hobbies:* Theatre; Sports. *Address:* 63 Kirribilli Avenue, Kirribilli 2061, Australia.

WATKINS, Nari, Elspeth, Hamilton, b. 14 Jan. 1926, Rabaul, Papua New Guinea. Author, Planter, Farmer. m. Leslie Herbert Watkins, 19 Oct. 1959, 1 son, 1 daughter. *Education:* St. Margaret's Girl's School, Berwick, Victoria, Australia; Clyde Girl's School, Woodend, Victoria, Australia. *Appointments:* WAAAF attached to The Coastwatchers, Northern East Area Townsville, Queensland; WAS, B, Prome and Rangoon; Planter on own Plantation, Bougainville, Papua New Guinea; Equestrian, New South Wales and Victoria, 1951-59; Author and Publisher, Papua New Guinea; Chairman of Directors, Camwat Pty Limited, Papua New Guinea. *Memberships:* Australian Society of Authors; Australian Women Writers; President, Berrima District Ex-Servicewomen's Association, New South Wales; Jaguar Car Drivers Club, M.G. Car Club, New South Wales; Royal Automobile Club, Sydney; Eastern Suburbs League Club, Bondi Junction; Planter's Association, Kieta, Bourganville, Papua New Guinea; Clyde Old Girl's Association, Melbourne, Victoria. *Publications:* Laua Avanapu, 1973; The Kangaroo Connection, 1980;

Short Stories, The Awakening, Willy Waffiukuff, Keran's Patrol, The Pool of Good Friends. *Hobbies:* Cars; Coins; Shells; Travel; Horse Racing; Gold Fossicking. *Address:* Farnborough, Illawarra Highway, Moss Vale, New South Wales, Australia.

WATSON, Alan Oliver, b. 16 Jan. 1917, Sydney, New South Wales, Australia. Dental Surgeon. m. Nancy Hilda Sharp, 25 Mar. 1942, 1 son, 2 daughters. *Education:* Faculty of Dentistry, 1935-38, BDS, Hons, Class 2, 1938, DDSc, 1955, Sydney University; FRACDS, Inaugural Member, 1965; FICD, 1975. *Appointments:* Private Practice, 1944-; Visiting Professor, University of Illinois, Chicago, USA, 1961; Lecturer, Treatment of Handicapped Patients, Sydney University, 1962-72; Established and administered an Honorary Dental Panel for Treatment at the Spastic Centre of New South Wales, 1946-78. *Memberships:* Member of several professional Associations; Killara Golf Club, 1948-; Australian Club, 1977-; Sydney Cricket and Sports Ground Trust, 1970-; Royal Agricultural Society, New South Wales, 1965-; Returned Servicemans League, 1944-; Sydney Discussion Group, 1950-; Pierre Fauchard Academy, 1979-. *Publications:* A History of Dentistry in NSW, 1788-1945; Contributed to various professional journals. *Honours:* Mentioned in Despatches, 1943; Honorary Life Member, Spastic Centre, New South Wales, 1979; Meritorious Service Award of International Dental Fraternity Delta Sigma Delta. *Hobbies:* Golf; Photography; Music. *Address:* Myola, 16 Coronga Crescent, Killara 2071, Sydney, Australia.

WATSON, Arthur Christopher, b. 2 Jan. 1927. HM Diplomatic Service, High Commissioner in Brunei. m. 1956 Mary C C Earl, 1 son, 1 stepson, 1 step daughter. *Education:* Norwich School; St. Catharine's College, Cambridge, England. *Appointments:* Naval Service, 1945-48, commissioned RNVR, 1946; Colonial Administrative Service, Uganda, 1951; District Commissioner, 1959; Principal Assistant Secretary, 1960; Principal, Commonwealth Relations Office, 1963; HM Diplomatic Service, 1965; Karachi, 1964-67; Lahore, 1967; FCO, 1967-71; HM Commissioner, Anguilla, 1971-74; Governor, Turks & Caicos Islands, 1975-78. *Memberships:* Royal Commonwealth Society. *Honours:* Recipient of CMG, 1977. *Hobbies:* Boats; Birds. *Address:* c/o Foreign and Commonwealth Office, London SW1, England.

WATSON, Donald Ross, b. 11 Mar. 1928, Sydney, Australia. m. 24 Aug. 1950, 4 sons, 1 daughter. *Education:* BSc, DipEd, Sydney; MA, Melbourne; PhD, Melbourne. *Appointments:* Teacher, Lismore High School, New South Wales, 1949-54; Lecturer, RAAF College Point Cook, Victoria, 1955-60; Senior Lecturer, RAAF Academy, Point Cook, 1961-76; Warden, Head of Department of Aeronautical Science, RAAF Academy, Point Cook, Victoria, 1976-. *Memberships:* Australian Mathematical Society; Economic Society of Australia and New Zealand. *Publications:* Contributions to Professional Journals. *Hobbies:* Sailing; Computer Electronics. *Address:* The Quadrant, Geelong Grammar School, Corio, Victoria 3214, Australia.

WATSON, Henry, b. 2 Dec. 1925, Gosforth, Northumberland, England. m. Dorothy Monica Skevington, 27 Aug. 1949, 1 son, 1 daughter. *Education:* Higher National Certificate, Mechanical Engineering, Rutherford College, 1942-47; BSc, First Class Hons, Mechanical Engineering, Kings College, University of Durham, 1947-50. *Appointments:* Manager of Engineering, English Electric, Steam Turbine Division, 1967; Chief Engineer, GEC Industrial & Marine Steam Turbine Division, 1975; Chief Mechanical Engineer, Kennedy and Donkin, Consultants, Thermal Generation Department, 1975-79; Started own Business, Watson Engineering Consultants Limited, Bramhall, Cheshire, England, Chairman, Managing Director, 1979-; Special Expertise, Power Engineering. *Memberships:* Fellow, Institution of Mechanical Engineers; Fellow, Institution of Marine Engineers; Chartered Engineer; Member, American Society of Mechanical Engineers; Past Chairman, Steam Plant Group of The Institution of Mechanical Engineers; Past President, Rugby Engineering Society. *Publications:* Author of several professional papers; Contributions to Efficient Use of Steam, 1980, and Electrical Engineers' Reference Book, 14th edition. *Honours:* ONC, Institution of Marine Engineers; HNC, Institution of Mechanical Engineers;

College Bursary, University of Durham. *Hobbies:* Painting; History; Walking. *Address:* 18 Roche Gardens, Cheadle Hulme, Cheshire SK8 7QT, England.

WATSON, James, Wreford, b. 8 Feb. 1915, San Yuan, Shensi, China. Geographer. m. Jessie Wilson Black, 24 Aug. 1939, 1 son, 1 daughter. *Education:* George Watson's College, Edinburgh, 1927-31; MA, Edinburgh University, 1932-36; PhD, Toronto University, 1943-45; LLD Hons, McMaster University, 1977; LLD Hons, Carleton University, Ottawa, 1979; LLD Hons, Calgary, 1980. *Appointments:* Chief Geographer, Canada, 1949-54; Professor, Head of Department, Edinburgh, 1954-72; Professor Geography, Director, Centre of Canadian Studies, Edinburgh University, Edinburgh, 1972-82. *Memberships:* President, Royal Scottish Geography Society, 1977-82; President, Institute British Geographers, 1982-83; President, British Association Canadian Studies, 1974-77;President, British Association Advancement Science, 1970; Fellow, Royal Society of Canada, 1954-; Fellow, Royal Society of Edinburgh, 1958-; British National Commission for Geography, 1960-. *Publications:* General Geography, Copp Clark, Toronto, 1952; North America, Its Countries and Regions, Longmans, London, 1st and 2nd Editions, 1963, 1968; Canada, Problems and Prospects, Longmans, Toronto, 1968; Social Geography of USA, Longmans, London, 1978; Geography of the USA, Longmans, London, 1982; Co-Author with Mrs J Watson, Canadians, How they Live and Work, David and Charles, Newton Abbot, 1979; Of Time and the Lover, McClelland and Stewart, Toronto, 1952; Countryside Canada, Fiddlehead University New Brunswick, 1980. *Honours:* Award of Merit, American Association Geographers, 1952; Murchison Medal, Royal Geographers Society, 1960; Research Medal Royal Scottish Geography Society, 1964; Award of Merit, Association of Canadian Geographers, 1977; Governor General's Medal for Poetry, Canada, 1954. *Hobbies:* Photography; Travel. *Address:* Manotick, 67 Bonaly Road, Edinburgh EH13 OPB, Scotland.

WATSON, Laurence Roy, b. 8 Oct. 1918, Murray Bridge, South Australia. Director of Tourism. m. Gwenllian E. Robinson, 31 May, 1941. *Education:* AAIA, Diploma. *Appointments:* Publicity Manager, South Australian Government Tourist Bureau, Adelaide, 1951-58; UK/European Manager, Australian National Travel Association, London, 1959-64; Director of Tourism, Department of the Capital Territory, Canberra, 1965-. *Memberships:* Australian Standing Committee on Tourism since, 1966; Australian Capital Territory, ACT; Advisory Board on Tourism since, 1966; ACT, Liquor Licensing Board, since 1975; ACT, Poker Machines Licensing Board, since 1976. *Memberships:* Producer of 31 Documentary films for South Australian Government, 1951-58; Author, Tourism in the ACT, 1979. *Honours:* King's Air Force Commendation, 1945; Silver Jubilee Medal, 1977. *Hobbies:* Carpentry. *Address:* 46 Lynch Street, Hughes, ACT, 2605, Australia.

WATT, Leon Harold, b. 6 Feb. 1937, Kellerberrin, Western Australia. MLA, MBR of Legislative Assembly. m. Kay Cocker, 27 Jan. 1962, 1 son, 1 daughter. *Appointments:* Elected to State Parliament as Liberal member for Albany, 1974. *Memberships:* Albany, South Coast Lions Club; Apex Club of Albany, life; *Hobbies:* Sailing; Squash; Fishing. *Address:* 4 Bohemia Road, Yakamia, Albany, Western Australia.

WEARNE, Neil Stanton, b. 28 Mar. 1933, Adelaide, South Australia. Advertising Agency Director. m. Jean A. Simpson. 4 sons, 1 daughter. *Appointments:* Rigby Limited, Publishers; Ring Stacey Pty. Ltd, Advertising Agents; News Limited, Newspaper Proprietors; Noel Paton Pty. Ltd, Advertising Agents; Hansen-Rubenjoan-McCann-Erickson, Advertising Agents; Patton Wearne Australia Pty. Ltd, Advertsing Agents; Wearne Australia Pty. Ltd. *Memberships:* Advertising Federation of Australia; Advertising Institute of Australia; Market Research Society of Australia. *Publications:* Fine Arts, Exhibition, Habitat Gallery, 1970; The Mind Worm, My Life and Other Tragedies, Yowie, Novels; Numerous articles published. *Hobbies:* Tennis; Writing; Painting; Music; Reading in History. *Address:* 88 Barnard Street, North Adelaide, South Australia, 5006.

WEARNE, William Maxwell, b. 1 Dec. 1926, Wellington, New Zealand. Orthopaedic Surgeon. m. Judith Goodwill Childs, 10 Jan. 1953, 1 son, 2 daughters.

Education: BSc, New Zealand, 1946; MB, ChB, New Zealand, 1951; FRCS, England, 1959; FRACS, 1963. *Appointments:* Orthopaedic Registrar, Charing Cross Hospital, London, 1959-60; Visiting Orthopaedic Surgeon, New Plymouth Hospital, New Zealand, 1961-63; Assistant Orthopaedic Surgeon, Royal Melbourne Hospital, 1964-76; Orthopaedic Surgeon, Sandringham & District Memorial Hospital, Victoria, 1973-. *Memberships:* Australian Orthopaedic Association; Medico-Legal Society of Victoria; Naval and Military Club. *Publications:* Experience with the Melbourne Knee Prosthesis, 1978; Australian and New Zealand Journal of Surgery, Volume 48. *Honours:* Alan Newton Prize, Royal Australian College of Surgeons, 1964. *Hobbies:* Light Aircraft Flying; Skiing. *Address:* 28 Edward Street, Sandringham, Victoria 3191, Australia.

WEAVER, Paul Richard Carey, b. 5 Sept. 1927, Roxburgh, New Zealand. Professor of Classics. m. (1) Gretchen D. Potts, 22 Aug. 1951, (divorced) 1 son, 1 daughter, (2) Rosina Perry, 15 Aug. 1881. *Education:* BA, University of Otago, 1947; MA, Canterbury University College, Christchurch, New Zealand, 1949; BA, 1955, MA, 1958, PhD, 1965, Kings College, Cambridge, England. *Appointments:* Assistant Lecturer, Canterbuy University College, 1951-53; Lecturer, University of Western Australia, 1956-60; Senior Lecturer, University of Western Australia, 1961-65; Reader, University of Western Australia, 1966; Professor of Classics, University of Tasmania, 1967; Dean, Faculty of Arts, 1967-69; Deputy Chairman, Professorial Board, 1976-77. *Memberships:* Australian Academy of the Humanities, 1976-; Council, Australian Academy of the Humanities, 1978-80; Vice-President, Australian Academy of the Humanities, 1979-80; Overseas Fellow, Churchill College, Cambridge, England, 1978. *Publications:* Familia Caesaris, 1972; Various Articles. *Hobbies:* Golf; Recorded Music. *Address:* Department of Classics, University of Tasmania, GPO Box 252C, Hobart, Tasmania 7001, Australia.

WEBB, Eric George, b. 24 June 1925, Sydney, Australia. Printing & Packaging. m. Beryl Stanton, 5 Apr. 1947, 3 sons. *Appointments:* Sales & Marketing Manager, Collins Bros. Stationers Pty. Ltd, to 1974; Managing Director, The George Lewis Group, 1974-; Chairman of Directors in 5 other Companies; Director of 5 other Companies. *Memberships:* Justice of the Peace; Australian Institute of Management; Australian Marketing Institute; Rotary Club of St. Ives - District 968; Tattersalls Club; City Tattersalls Club; Corontation Club; Commercial Travellers Association; Auburn-Lidcombe Business Mens Club. *Hobby:* Rugby Union. *Address:* 15 Oxley Avenue, St. Ives, NSW, Australia 2075.

WEBB, Kenneth Richard, b. 2 Feb. 1915, Portsmouth, Hampshire, England. Honorary, Senior Lecturer in Chemistry, University of Southampton, 1980. *Education:* BSc, London External, 1935; PhD, London External, 1939. *Appointments:* Lecturer in Inorganic Chemistry, University of Southampton, 1939-73; Vice-Warden of Connaught Hall, University of Southampton, 1945-69; Admissions Tutor for Chemistry, University of Southampton, 1957-71; Senior Lecturer in Chemistry, University of Southampton, 1973-80, retired. *Memberships:* C.Chem; FRSC; British Society for the History of Science; Life, Nottingham Mechanics Institution. *Publications:* 60 papers, articles, notes or letters, inorganic or physical chemistry or history of science, especially chemistry. *Hobbies:* History of Science, especially Chemistry; General History; History of ecclesiastical institutions, persons & buildings; Ecclesiastical Architecture; Bus Travel; Music, listening; General Literature. *Address:* 48 Granby Grove, Highfield, Southampton, SO2 3RZ, England.

WEBB, Robert Arthur John, b. 1 Nov. 1922, Worthing, Sussex, England. Psychiatrist. m. Celia Marjorie, 26 Jan. 1952, 2 sons, 2 daughters. *Education:* LRCP, MRCS, 1951, MB, BS, 1952, Guys Hospital, London; MPH, Johns Hopkins Hospital, Baltimore, USA, 1961; DPM, Sydney University, Sydney, Australia, 1965. *Appointments:* Medical Superintendant, St. Vincent Mental Hospital, 1955; Deputy Medical Superintendant, Barbados Mental Hospital, 1959; MOH, Barbados, 1961; Medical Officer, Gladeville Mental Hospital, 1963; Director, Mental Health & Drug Education Programme, NSW, 1970. *Memberships:* MRC, Psychiatry; FRANZCP, Psychiatry; Vice President, Health Education Association, NSW; Trustee, Mental Health Association, NSW; Vice President, Mental Health Association, Barbados; Australian Consumers Association. *Publications:* 30 published papers on epidemiology of mental illness, preventive psychiatry, drug education. *Honours:* Fellowship, World Health Organisation, 1961. *Hobbies:* Curing & Smoking Food; Wine; Making Paper; Setting up a new religion. *Address:* 26 Sherwin Street, Henley, NSW 2111, Australia.

WEBB, Ronald Campbell, b. 5 Mar. 1925, Melbourne, Australia. Commonwealth Director of Health For Victoria. m. Denise V. Clarke, 16 Dec. 1948, 3 sons, 3 daughters. *Education:* MBBS, Melbourne University, 1951; DTM & H, Sydney University, 1957; FRACMA, 1967; FAIM, 1975; FRACP, 1977. *Appointments:* Medical Superintendent, Alice Springs Hospital, Flying Doctor, 1956; Commonwealth Director of Health for N.T, Australia, 1958-61; Chief Medical Officer and Medical Adviser, Austalian High Commission, Australia House, London, UK, 1962-65; Australian Delegate to World Health Organization Assemblies, Geneva, 1962-65; Commonwealth Director of Health & Chief Quarantine Officer, Western Australia, 1966-67; Consultant to Malaysian Government to Review Organization & Administration of Hospital & Health Services, Columbo Plan, 1972; Representative of Federal Government of Peer Review, Overseas visit to USA, Canada & German Federal Republic, 1976; Commonwealth Director of Health for Victoria since 1968. *Memberships:* Australian Medical Association; Victorian Branch Council; College of Medical Administrators; Victorian & Federal Council; President, Royal Australian College of Medical Administrators. *Publications:* Numerous Articles in Medical Journals. *Honours:* Member of the Order of Australia (AM), 1980. *Hobbies:* Chess; Tennis; Oil Painting; Photography. *Address:* Inveraray, 13 Mountain Grove, Kew, Victoria 3101, Australia.

WEBB, Thomas (Langley) (Sir), b. 25 Apr. 1908, Melbourne, Australia. Company Director. m. Jeannette A Lang, 15 Aug. 1942, 1 son, 1 daughter. *Appointments:* Chairman & Managing Director, Huddart Parker Ltd, Commercial Bank of Australia; Director, Email Ltd.; Chairman, Trustees, Executors & Agency Co. Ltd., Moore Business Systems, Alliance Oil Development Ltd., Metals Exploration Ltd., Deputy Chairman, McIlwraith, McEacharn Ltd. *Memberships:* Australian Club, Melbourne; Melbourne Ciub; Royal South Yarra Tennis Club, Melbourne; Royal Melbourne Golf Club. *Honours:* Recipient of Knight Bachelor, 1975. *Hobbies:* Golf; Tennis. *Address:* 6 Yarrodale Road, Toorak, Victoria, Australia 3142.

WEBB, William Frederick, b. 13 Sept. 1937, Penrith, NSW, Australia. Medical Practitioner. m. Helen M. McIntyre, 18 Apr. 1964, 4 daughters. *Education:* Bachelor of Medicine & Bachelor of Surgery, MB, BS, University of Sydney. *Appointments:* Resident Medical Officer, Royal Newcastle Hospital, 1963; Resident Medical Officer, Prince Henry Hospital, 1964; Research Student, University of NSW, 1965-68; Research Fellow, Australian National University, 1968-69; Family Practice, Castle Hill, NSW, since 1970. *Memberships:* Australian Sports Medicine Federation Honorary Secretary, 1978-81; President-Elect, 1981-82; Royal Australian College of General Practitioners; Australian Medical Association; American College of Sports Medicine. *Publications:* Various Review Articles for Sporting Publications and Professional and Sporting Groups. *Hobbies:* Rowing; Coaching; Classical Music; Vintage Wine Collecting; Sailing; Golf. *Address:* 34 Hannah Street, Beecroft, NSW, Australia 2119.

WEBSTER, Anita Charlotte, b. 31 July, 1896, Auckland, New Zealand. Teacher Speech & Drama. *Education:* Ladies College, Remuera, Auckland; JC Williamson's School of Dramatic Art, Sydney, New South Wales, Australia. *Appointments:* Self Employed, Teacher of Speech & Drama, Producer of Plays. *Memberships:* Member of Council, Royal Commonwealth Society; Executive English Speaking Union; Navy League of New Zealand, Auckland Branch; Committee for four years, Tree Society of Auckland; Royal Forestry & Bird Proctection Society. *Publications:* Plays & Sketches, Published, 1960, 1964; *Honours:* ALCM, 1948; MBE, Voluntary Welfare Services, 1977. *Address:* Bowling; Bridge; Travel. *Address:* 289 Tamaki Drive, Kohimarama 5, Auckland, New Zealand.

WEBSTER, James Joseph, (The Hon), b. 14 June, 1925, Flinders Island, Tasmania, Australia. Diplomat. m. Jean Drake, 5 Mar. 1957, 4 sons. *Education:* Caulfield Grammar School; Melbourne Technical College. *Appointments:* Farmer; Timber Merchant; Company Director; Elected to Australian Senate, 1964; Minister for Science, 1975; Minister for Science and the Environment, 1977; Australian High Commissioner in New Zealand, 1980. *Memberships:* Associate, Australian Society for Accountants; West Brighton Club, Australia; Wellington Club, New Zealand; Hutt Golf Club, New Zealand. *Hobbies:* Squash; Sailing; Tennis. *Address:* 15 Butavas Street, Khandallah, Wellington, New Zealand.

WEBSTER, Maurice Holland, b. 6 Sept, 1914, Banff, Scotland. Medical Practitioner, Lecturer in Law. m. Margaret Patricia Brander, Deceased, 11th Nov, 1939, 1 son, 4 daughters, (2) Anne Harvey Stanley, 6 Feb. 1982. *Education:* Banff Academy, 1920-31; MB, ChB, Aberdeen University, 1931-36; DPH, Aberdeen University, 1938; Batchelor at Law, University of Rhodesia, 1972-76. *Appointments:* Resident Medical Officer, Aberdeen Hospitals, 1936-39; Army Service, 1939-45, DADH, Western Desert Force; ADH, Malta; Assistant Professor of Hygiene, RAM College; DDH, Western Command; DMS, North Rhodesia; Secretary for Health, Rhodesia; Lecturer in Law, University of Zimbabwe. *Memberships:* Fellow of Faculty of Community Medicine; Royal Society of Health; Zimbabwe Medical Association; President, RVWA Country Club; President, Salisbury Rotary Club; Salisbury Club; Ski Club of Great Britain. *Publications:* Numerous Medical Publications. Man Made Lakes & Human Health; Rhodesian Law Journal. *Honours:* OBE, 1960. *Hobbies:* Golf; Trout Fishing; Skiing; Fly Tying. *Address:* 5 Oswald Close, Mount Pleasant, Salisbury, Zimbabwe.

WEE, Dennis Kee Teck, b. 5 Oct. 1949, Sibu, Sarawak, Malaysia. Chartered Quantity Surveyor. m. Cecilia Chew, 28 Feb. 1973, 2 sons, 1 daughter. *Education:* Bachelor of Building, University of Melbourne, 1968-72. *Appointments:* Partner of Group Survey 4, Sarawak, Malaysia. *Memberships:* Professional Associates of Royal Institution of Chartered Surveyors; Associate of Australian Institute of Quantity Surveyors; Institute of Surveyors of Malaysia; Associate, Australian Institute of Building; Associate of Chartered Institute of Arbitrator. *Hobbies:* Badminton; Fishing. *Address:* 386 Penrissen Road, Kuching, Sarawak, Malaysia.

WEEDON, Basil Charles Leicester, b. 18th July, 1923, London. Vice Chancellor. m. Barbara Mary Dawe, 21st Mar. 1959, 1 son, 1 daughter. *Education:* Imperial College,London; PhD, DSc, Hon.D.Tech, ARCS, DIC, FRSC, FRS. *Appointments:* Research Chemist, ICI, 1943-47; Lecturer in Organic Chemistry, Imperial College, London, 1947-55; Reader, in Organic Chemistry, Imperial College, London, 1955-60; Professor, Organic Chemistry, Imperial College, London, 1960-76; Vice-Chancellor, University of Nottingham, 1976-. *Memberships:* The Royal Society; Royal Society of Chemistry; Swiss Chemical Society. *Publications:* Scientific Papers, mainly in Journal of Chemical Society. *Honours:* CBE, *Hobbies:* Listening to music; Vintage radios. *Address:* Highfield House, University Park, Nottingham, NG7 2QH, England.

WEINER, Stanley, b. 9th Nov. 1920, Cracow. Pathologist. m. Elaine Pluess, 18th Aug. 1945, 1 son. *Education:* MB, BS, Zurich, 1946; DYPL.LEK, Cracow, 1947; MD, Zurich, 1949; PhD, Melbourne, 1963. *Appointments:* Resident Medical Officer, Arosa, TB Sanat, 1947; Resident Medical Officer, Surgery & Pathology, Aarau, Switzerland, 1948; Research Kantonsspital Winterthur & GP Work in Several Cantons, Switzerland, 1949; Prince Henry's Hospital, Melbourne, 1950; Lecturer & Senior Lecturer in Pathology, University of Melbourne, 1955; Director of Pathology, Mental Health Division, Health Commission of Victoria, Australia, 1967-. *Memberships:* FRCPA, Melbourne; FRC Pathology, London. *Publications:* A number of publications on Practical Inventions & Technological-Medical Improvements; Last publication, Neuropathology, Selected Topics, Health Commission of Victoria, 1979. *Hobbies:* Leadlights & Stained Glass, Professional level; Four Wheel Driving & Exploration, Simpson Desert Crossing, 1977; UHF Radio; Painting; Photography. *Address:* 81 Greythorn Road, N. Balwyn, Victoria 3104, Australia.

WEINMAN, Darrel Felix, b. 20th Nov. 1929, Colombo, Sri Lanka. Medical. m. Dr. Brinda Mattucumaru, 16th June, 1971. 1 son, 1 daughter. *Education:* MB,BS, Ceylon, 1955; FRCS, Edinburgh, 1960; FRCS, England, 1960. *Appointments:* Neurosurgeon, General Hospital, Colombo, 1962-74; Neurosurgeon, Canterbury District Hospital, Sydney, 1975-; Neurosurgeon, Western Suburbs Hospital, Sydney, 1977-; Neurosurgeon, Masonic Hospital, Ashfield, Sydney, 1966-. *Memberships:* Honorary Editor, Ceylon Medical Journal, 1966-68; Honorary Assistant Treasurer, Ceylon Medical Association, 1964; Honorary Assistant Secretary, Ceylon Medical Association, 1967; Australian Medical Association, 1975-; Life member, Ceylon Medical Association. *Publications:* 27 Publications in various medical journals; Angiography in the diagnosis of extradural haematoma, 1966; Hydrocephalus american Journal of Neurosurgery, 1967; Mortality for Extradural Haematoma, Australian Journal of Surgery, 1968; Vertical Extradural Haematoma, Journal of College of Surgeons, Edinburgh, 1974. *Honours:* Peri Scholarship for most outstanding graduate, 1955; Hallit Prize winner, Royal College of Surgeons, England, 1957. *Hobbies:* Music; Dogs; Gardening. *Address:* 2 Allenby Crescent, Strathfield, New South Wales 2135, Australia.

WEISZ, Thomas James, b. 12 July 1946, Moson Hungary. Lawyer. m. Sasha Ann, 5 Aug. 1968, 1 son, 1 daughter. *Education:* BA, Economics & Business, Dean's Honour List, McMaster University; LLB, stood First in Final Year winning Silver Medal, prize in Insurance, prize in Estate Planning, Osgoode Hall Law School, 1970; LLM, Tax & Estate Planning, Harvard University. *Appointments:* McCarthy & McCarthy, Barrister & Solicitors, Toronto, Ontario, 1970-79; Weisz & Associates, Barrister & Solicitors, Hamilton, Ontario, 1979-; President, The Effort Trust Company, 1979-, Effort Properties Limited, Jamestown Construction Limited, Semper Investments Limited. *Memberships:* Canadian Bar Association; Canadian Tax Foundation; Harvard Club of Toronto. *Publications:* Contributor to various periodicals and journals on tax related matters and a contributor to The Income Tax Law of Canada. *Honours:* Instructor in Income Tax & Estate Planning Section of the Bar Admission Course; Instructor in Income Tax programmes of the Law Society of Upper Canada; Instructor for Tax II Course produced by the Canadian Bar Association, Instructor for Appraisal Institute of Canada programmes. *Address:* 2061 Kerns Avenue, Burlington, Ontario L7P 1P7, Canada.

WELLINGTON, Karl Everard, b. 2 Nov. 1936, Hopewell, Hanover, Jamaica. Animal Geneticist. m. Cecily Veronica Roye, 31 Dec. 1960, 3 sons, 2 daughters. *Education:* PhD, University of West Indies, 1968; BSc, University of West Indies, 1965; Diploma Agriculture, JSA, 1957. *Appointments:* Agricultural Assistant, 1957; Agricultural Officer, 1965; Assistant Director of Research, 1978; Deputy Director of Research, 1979; Director of Research, 1981-. *Memberships:* Jamica Associate of Scientists; Directors of Livestock Research of the Caribbean, Chairman, 1980-81; University of West Indies, Guild of Undergraduates; Treasurer, JSA, Old Students Association. *Publications:* Many Scientific Publications. *Honours:* Most Outstanding Student, Faculty of Agriculture, University of West Indies, 1965. *Hobbies:* Swimming; Gardening; Dominoes. *Address:* Daley's Grove, Knock Patrick, Mandeville, Jamaica.

WELLS, Colin Sidney, b. 7 Dec. 1948, Nassau, Bahamas. Soft Drink Business Executive. Divorced, 4 sons. *Education:* Masters Degree in Business Administration, University of Miami, 1979-81. *Appointments:* Vice President, Pepsi-Cola Bottling Company, 1967-70; Vice President & General Manager, Caribbean Bottling Company, 1970-79; Executive Vice President & General Manager, Bahamas Beverages Ltd. 1979-. *Memberships:* Past President, Rotary Club of West Nassau; Chairman, Building Committee, Fund Raising Committee, Member of Executive Committee, Bahamas Red Cross Society; Young Presidents Organisation; Bahamas Chamber of Commerce. *Hobbies:* Tennis; Travelling; Reading. *Address:* Port Del Mer, Winton, Nassau, Bahamas.

WELLS David Charles, b. 19 Nov. 1918, Inverell, New South Wales, Australia. Naval Officer, Retired, Farmer & Grazier. m. Joan Moira Alice Pope, 18 June, 1940, 1 son. *Education:* St. Peter's College, Adelaide; Royal Australian Naval College; Greenwich, London, England; Imperial Defence College, London. *Appointments:* Naval Commander: Ships: Queensborough, Voyager, Melbourne; Shore: Naval Air Station, Nowra, New South Wales; Sydney, Flag Officer in command East Australia; Singapore, Malaysia, Australian, New Zealand and United Kingdom forces, ANZUK; Flag Officer Commanding Australian Fleet. *Honours:* Kings Medallist, 1936; CBE, 1971. *Hobby:* Farming. *Address:* Pine Ridge, Leadville, New South Wales, 2854, Australia.

WELLS, John Christopher, b. 11 Mar. 1939, Bootle, Lancs, England. University Lecturer; Writer, Broadcaster. *Education:* BA, Classics, Trinity College, Cambridge, 1960; MA, Trinity College, Cambridge, 1964; MA, Gen. Linguistics & Phonetics, University College, London, 1962; PhD, University College, London, 1971. *Appointments:* Assistant Lecturer, University College, London, 1962-65; Lecturer in Phonetics, University College, London, 1965-. *Memberships:* Secretary, International Phonetic Association; Chairman, London Esperanto Club. *Publications:* Concise Esperanto and English Dictionary, Teach Yourself Books, 1969; Practical Phonetics, 1971; Jamaican Pronunciation in London, 1973; Lingvistikaj Aspektoj de Esperanto, 1977; Accents of English, 1982. *Hobbies:* Walking; Reading; Travel. *Address:* 5 Poplar Road, Merton Park, London, SW19 3JR, England.

WELLS, Murray Charles, b. 8 Oct. 1936, Christchurch, New Zealand. Professor of Accounting. m. 16 Jan. 1960, 2 sons, 1 daughter. *Education:* B,Com, University of Canterbury, 1962; M.Com, University of Canterbury, 1964; PhD, University of Sydney, 1974. *Appointments:* Lecturer in Accounting, University of Canterbury, 1964-66; Lecturer in Accounting, University of Sydney, 1967-70; Senior Lecturer in Accounting, University of Sydney, 1971-75; Professor of Accounting, University of Sydney, 1975-. *Memberships:* New Zealand Society of Accountants; Australian Society of Accountants, NSW Division Councillor, 1979-; Accounting Association of Australia & New Zealand, Executive, 1980-; American Accounting Association; Academy of Accounting Historians, USA, Trustee, 1974-. *Publications:* Over 40 Articles in Australia, New Zealand, USA, UK; Accounting for Common Costs, 1978; A bibiliography of cost accounting, 1978; Editor, Engineers' Contributions to Cost Accounting, 1978; Current Cost Accounting-Identifying the Issues, 1979. *Honours:* Hourglass Award for Best Book on Accounting History, 1979. *Hobbies:* Cars; Squash. *Address:* 28 Canberra Crescent, Lindfield, NSW 2070, Australia.

WELLS, Peter Bayford, b. 28 Jan. 1922, Kew, Victoria, Australia. Chartered Accountant and Company Director. m. Elspeth Lockett Lendon, 12 May, 1951, 2 sons. *Education:* FCA, Fellow of Institute of Chartered Accountants in Australia. *Appointments:* Partner, Touche Ross the Chartered Accountants, 1956-72; Member, South Australian Housing Trust, 1970; Director, John Martin & Co Ltd, 1966-81; Chairman, 1980-81; Director, Elders Trustee & Executor Co. Ltd, 1972, Chairman, 1981; Director, CHL, Australia Pty Ltd, 1969; Chairman, DaCosta Samaritan Fund Trust, 1962; Member of State & Federal Councils of Institute of Chartered Accountants, 1962-70; South Australian, Chairman, 1968-69; Insititute of Directors in Australia, South Australian, Chairman, 1975-78. *Memberships:* Life Member, Kathleen Lumley College Inc.; Anticancer Foundation of the Universities of South Australia, Deputy Chairman - Chairman Finance; Winston Churchill Memorial Trust, Director; Adelaide Club; War Service, RANVR, 1941-46. *Hobbies:* Music; Golf; Tennis; Bridge. *Address:* 13 Wilsden Street, Walkerville, South Australia 5081.

WEMBAH-RASHID, John Albert Rauf, b. 6 May, 1937, Masasi, Tanzania. Social Anthropologist. m. Tezrah Wembah-Rashid, 2 sons. *Education:* BA, University of East Africa, 1968; MA, University of Dar-es-Salaam, 1980; MA, University of Illinois, USA, 1980; PhD, Advanced Candidate, University of Illinois. *Appointments:* Information Officer, Tanzania Information Service, 1968-69; Ethnographer, National Museums of Tanzania, 1969-72; Acting/Assistant Director, National Museums of Tanzania, 1972-73; Assistant Director & Ethnographer, Museums of Tanzania, 1973-. *Memberships:* ICOM; OMSA; African Studies Association, US; Tanzania Society; International Union of Anthropological and Ethnological Studies. *Publications:*

The Ethno-History of the Peoples of South East & RN Tanzania, Author; Tanzania through the National Museum, Editor; Several Articles in Journals and occasional Papers. *Honours:* Research Fellowship from, Social Sciences Council Ford Foundation, 1980/81; The Wenner-Gren Foundation, 1980-81; Unesco, 1974/75. *Hobbies:* Reading; Studying and Collecting Plastic Art, African. *Address:* P.O. Box 511, Dar-Es-Salaam, Tanzania.

WEN, (Dato) TK, b. 11 Feb. 1924, Chairman of Public Property Company. *Education:* BA, Fukien Christian University, China; MA, Columbia University, USA. *Appointments:* Chairman of Bungsar Hill Development Co. Ltd.; Chong Chook Yew Ltd.; Central Landholders Ltd.; Chong Khoon Lin Ltd.; Kayin Holdings Ltd.; Selangor Properties Ltd.; T. K. Wen Ltd. *Memberships:* Chairman, Malayan Public Library Assosiation; Trustee & Honorary Chairman, Selangor Kayin Assosiation. *Honours:* DPMP, (Datoship), 1966; JP, 1974 *Address:* 6A Jalan Batai, Damansara Heights, PO Box 2267, Kuala Lumpur, Malaysia.

WERBLINSKI, Sylwester Jan, b. 27 Mar 1928, Warszawa, Poland. Architect. m. Janina Werblinska, 11 Nov. 1949. *Education:* MA, MSc, Qualified Architect & Town Planner, Faculty of Architecture, Gdansk Technical University, Poland, 1951; Chartered Architect, Fellow of the Polish Institute of Architects, SARP, 1958; Chartered Architect, Associate of Ghana Institute of Architects, 1971; Member of the Nigerian Institute of Architects, 1979. *Appointments:* Architect, Design Consulting Office for Dwelling Bldg, Gdansk, Poland, 1950-52; Superintending Architect, Department of Sport Projects, Warszawa, Poland, 1952-54; Project Architect, Design Consulting Office for Radio & TV Projects, Warsaw, Poland, 1954-63; Building & Architectural Expert, Office for Coordination of Warsaw Metropolity, Poland, 1961-65; Regional Architect, Staff Architect, Public Works Department, Ghana, 1965-72; Chief Specialist & Chief Consultant, Warsaw Development Consortium, Warszawa, Poland, 1972-75-; Senior Architect, Estate Department, Ahmadu Bello University, Zaria, Nigeria, 1975-77; Architect, Interstate Architects, Zaria, Nigeria, 1977-. *Creative Works:* Over two hundred Portraits and Human Figure, pastel and oil paintings, among others, portraits of distinguished personalities of Ghana and Nigeria. *Honours:* I Grade distinction (Team Work) in Architectural Competition for the design of Polish Radio Central Broadcasting Station in Warsaw, Award by The Polish Institute of Architects; II Prize (Team Work) in Architectural Competition for Opera House in Krakow, Award by the Polish Institute of Architects. *Hobbies:* Stamps Collecting; Astrology. *Address:* A.B.U. Area F 22, Zaria-Samaru, Nigeria, P.O. Box 464, Zaria, Nigeria.

WERE, John Owen, b. 3 Oct 1912, Wellington, New Zealand. Anglican Priest. m. Shirley Elizabeth Rees, 18 Sept. 1943, 1 son 1 daughter. *Education:* St. Peters College, Adelaide; BA, University of Adelaide, St. Mark's College, Adelaide, 1933; Th. Schol., St. John's College, 1969; Th.L, St. John's College, 1936; BA, Christ Church, Oxford, 1939; MA, Christ Church, Oxford, 1943. *Appointments:* Ordained Deacon, 1936; Priest, DIO Riverina, New South Wales, 1937; Curate, Broken Hill, New South Wales, 1937, (on leave) Oxford, 1937-40; Rector Narranders, New South Wales, 1940-44; Chaplain, P.T., RAAF, 1940-44; Chaplain, Royal Australian Navy, 1944-67; Senior Anglican Chaplain, Archdeacon, R.A.N., 1962-67; Retired R.A.N., 1967; Vicar, Gisborne, Victoria, 1967-77; Retired, 1977. *Memberships:* Naval & Military Club, Melbourne, Victoria. *Honours:* Lucas-Tooth Scholarship, Oxford, 1937; OBE, Military, for service in Royal Australian Navy, 1968. *Hobbies:* Philately; Scouting. *Address:* Wenlock Edge, Red Hill South, Victoria, Australia.

WEST, Francis James, b. 26 June 1927, East Yorks., England. University Professor. Katherine White, 21 May 1963, Marriage Dissolved, 1976, 1 daughter. *Education:* BA, 1947, PhD, 1951, University of Leeds, 1944-47; Institute of Historical Research, University of London, 1947-49; PhD, 1956, Trinity College, Cambridge, 1949-52. *Appointments:* Research Fellow, Australian National University, 1952-55; Senior Lecturer in History, Victoria University of Wellington, 1955-59; Senior Fellow, Institute of Advanced Studies, Australian National University, 1959-64; Professor of Comparative Government, University of Adelaide at

Bedford Park, 1964-65; Professorial Fellow, Institute of Advanced Studies, Australian National University, 1965-76; Dean of Arts & Professor of History, Independent University of Buckingham, 1973-75; Dean of Social Sciences & Professor of History and Government, Deakin University, Geelong, 1976-. *Memberships:* Australian Humanities Research Council, 1966; Fellow, Royal Historial Society, 1966; Fellow, Australian Academy of the Humanities, 1969, Secretary, 1971-73; Australia Defence association, Vice Chairman, 1977-80; United Services Institution. *Publications:* Biography as History, 1973; University House, Portrait of an Institution, 1980; Three dozen articles in Learned & Professional Journals. *Honours:* Rouse Ball Research Studentship, Irinity College, Cambridge, 1949; South East Asian Treaty Organisation Fellow, 1958; Carnegie Commonwealth Award, 1964; Ford Foundation Travel & Study Award, 1970; Thank Offering to Britain' Fellowship, Bristish Academy, 1971. *Hobbies:* Bridge; Tennis; Occasional Journalism; Broadcasting. *Address:* 6 Sylvan Court, Newtown Victoria, Australia 3220.

WESTBURY, June Alwyn (Mrs P W A Westbury) b Hamilton, New Zealand. m. 22 Oct. 1949, 3 daughters. *Education:* Brain's College, Auckland; Studied voice under the noted contralto, Mina Caldow. *Appointments:* First Woman Secretary, Liberal Party, Manitoba, 1968-69; Alderman, Ward I, City of Winnipeg, 1969; Vice-Chairman, Centennial Celebrations Committee, 1970; Member at varying times of following Committees of Council, Parks & Recreation, Health & Welfare, Housing & Urban Renewal, Utilities & Personnel, 1970-71; Board, Winnipeg Municipal Hospitals, 1970-79; Chairman, 1971-75; Vice-Chairman, 1977-78; Chairman, Health & Welfare Committee, Re-elected Councillor, Roslyn Ward, newly unified City of Winnipeg, 1971; First Manitoban elected as Vice-President, Liberal Party of Canada, 1970-73; Member at varying times of Environment Committee & Commission, Winnipeg Heritage Corporation, Chairman, Sub-Committee on Group Homes, 1972-79; Liberal Candidate, Osborne Constituency, 1973; Re-elected Councillor, Roslyn Ward, 1974; Re-elected to newly-constituted Corydon Ward, 1977; Chairman, Advisory Committee on Historical Buildings, 1979; Elected Member of Legislative Assembly, Fort Rouge Constituency, 1979. *Memberships:* Manitoba Action Committee on Status of Women; Manitoba Historical Society; Southern Cross International Association; Women in Trades Association; Manitoba Association for Rights & Liberties. *Honours:* Recipient of Woman of the Year in Politics & Governmental Affairs, 1979. *Address:* 227 Montgomery Avenue, Winnipeg, R3I1T1, Canada.

WESTER, Lars Erik, b. 2 Apr. 1939. Stockholm, Sweden. Company Director. m. Catherine Letitia Anderson, 23 Nov. 1968, 2 daughters. *Education:* Bachelor of Commerce, 1963. *Appointments:* Trainee Brand Manager, Group Product Manager, Unilever Group, 1963-69; Consultant, Senior Consultant, PA Management Consultants, 1969-73; Managing Director, Industrial Development Australia Pty Ltd., 1973-; Managing Director, Parbury Henty Holdings ltd., 1977-. *Memberships:* Australian Club. *Hobbies:* Skiing; Golf; Sailing. *Address:* 11 Iona Avenue, Toorak 3142, Australia.

WHALEY, William, Rae, b. 3 Oct. 1914, Claremont, Cape Province, Republic of South Africa. Attorney, Notary and Conveyancer. m. Edna Blanche, 8 May 1948, 2 daughters. *Education:* Norvals Farm School, Poorti Valley, Shamva, Zimbabwe; Prince Edward School Salisbury, Zimbabwe, 1932; RSA. BA, LLB, University of Cape Town, 1937. *Appointments:* Admitted as an Attorney of the High Court of Rhodesia and Conveyancer, 1938, Notary, 1939; Assistant, Attorneys in Salisbury, 1949, Partner, 1950, Presently Senior Partner; Chairman, Director, Legal Adviser, Joint Legal Adviser of various companies. *Memberships:* Board of Governors, Ranche House College of Adult Education; Institute of Directors; Former Chairman, Constitutional Commission of 1967; Former President, Rhodesian Law Society, 1955-57; Old Hararians Association, 1951-52; Old Hararians Association; Salisbury Club; Salisbury Rotary Club; The Dining Club; Royal Salisbury Golf Club. *Honours:* Recipient of BA, LLB, University of Cape Town, 1937; Senate of Zimbabwe Continuously from 1970, Re-elected, 1980; Chairman,

Senate Legal Committee, 1970-79, Re-elected, 1980; Independance Commemorative Decoration. *Hobbies:* Golf; Gardening. *Address:* 18 Carlisle Drive, Alexandra Park, Salisbury, Zimbabwe.

WHEATLEY, Clifford Bruce, b. 16 Oct. 1947, Saskatchewan, Canada. Lawyer, Barrister. m. Patricia Margaret Hughes, 30 Apr. 1971, 1 son, 2 daughters. *Education:* Bachelor of Civil Engineering, University of Manitoba, 1971; LLB, University of Manitoba, 1974. *Appointments:* Civil Engineer, Canadian Pacific Railway Company; Whittaker Acton and Wheatley, Lawyer. *Memberships:* Law Society of Saskatchewan; Canadian Bar Association; Association of American Trial Lawyers. *Hobbies:* Sports; Stamp and Coin collecting. *Address:* 1611 Pascoe Crescent, Moosejaw, Saskatchewan, Canada.

WHEATLEY, David James, b. 10 Sept. 1949, Sydney, Australia. Dental Surgeon. m. Gillian Wendy Bowler, 23 June 1973. *Education:* BDS, 1973; MDS, 1975. *Appointments:* University of Sydney; Private Practice. *Memberships:* The Australian Society of Prosthodontists; The Australian Society of Periodontists; The Dental Alumni Society of the University of Sydney, 1979-80. *Hobbies:* Motor Cars; Ski-ing. *Address:* 1 Torrington Street, Strathfield, New South Wales 2135, Australia.

WHEELDON, John Murray, b. 9 Aug. 1929, Subiaco, Western Australia. Senator, Barrister, Solicitor. m. 14 Sept. 1970, 2 sons, 1 daughter. *Education:* BA, Hons, University of Western Australia, 1953. *Appointments:* Member, Australian Labor Party, 1951; Senator, Western Australia, 1965; Chairman, Australian Parliamentary Committee on Foreign Affairs and Defence, 1973-75; Minister, Repatriation and Compensation, 1974-75; Minister, Social Security, 1975; Chairman, Australian Parliamentary Sub-Committee on Human Rights in the Soviet Union, 1978-79; Member, Australian delegation to the 35th United Nations General Assembly, New York, 1980. *Address:* Commonwealth Parliament Offices, 44 St George's Terrace, Perth, Western Australia 6000, Australia.

WHEELER, John Oliver, b. 19 Dec. 1924, Mussoorie, India. Geologist. m. Nora Jean Hughes, 17 May 1952, 2 daughters. *Education:* BASc, Geological Engineering, University of British Columbia, 1947; PhD, Geology, Columbia University, New York, 1956. *Appointments:* Research Scientist, Vancouver, British Columbia, 1968-70; Director, Regional and Economic Geology Division, 1970-73; Deputy Director General, Ottawa, Ontario, 1973-79; Research Scientist, Vancouver, British Columbia, 1979-. *Memberships:* President, Canadian Geoscience Council, 1981; Geological Association of Canada, 1970-71; President, Geological Society of America, 1971-74; President, Canadian Geological Foundations, 1974-79; Royal Society of Canada; Canadian Institute of Mining and Metallurgy. *Publications:* Author of about 40 scientific papers, monographs and geological maps. *Honours:* Fellow, Royal Society of Canada, 1969, Queen's Jubilee Medal, 1977. *Hobbies:* Mountaineering; Hiking; Ski-ing. *Address:* 3333 Mathers Avenue, West Vancouver, British Columbia, V7V 2K6, Canada.

WHEELER, Victor Augustus b. 29 Sept. 1928, Cumana, Toco, Trinidad, Teacher, Headmaster. m. Lolitta Desla Maharaj, 23 Feb. 1963, 1 son, 3 daughters. *Education:* BA, Hons, English, University of the West Indies, Jamaica, 1963-66; DipEd, Post Graduate, University of the West Indies, Jamaica, 1966-67. *Appointments:* Primary School Teacher, 1947-53; Secondary School Teacher, 1954-; Deputy Headmaster, Bishop's High School, Tobago, 1967; Principal II, Headmaster, Roxborough Govenment Secondary, Tobao, 1967-72; Principal II, Headmaster, Scarborough Government Secondary, Tobago, 1972-77; Principal II, Headmster, Signal Hill Senior Comprehensive, 1977-. *Memberships:* President, Tobago Cricket Association, 2 years; Tobago Secretary, National Anglican Schools Board of Management; 2nd Vic President, Tobago Lions Club; Society for Caribbean Linguistics. *Creative Works:* Recordings for Broadcasts by Government Broadcasting Units, The Tobago Dialect and Teaching English, 1974; Tobago and the 15 year Education Plan, 1974; Democratising Secondary Education in Tobago, 1977. *Honours:* Commonwealth Scholarship to Leicester University Institute of Education, 1961; Trinidad & Tobago National Scholarship to U.W.I. 1963-67; King

George VI Memorial Cadet Officers award at Frinlay Park, England, 1962. *Hobbies:* Cricket; Music, playing the Piano and arranging music for Steel Bands. *Address:* Old Farm Road, Tobago, West Indies.

WHILE, John Walter, b. 2 Nov. 1921, Sydney, Australia. Company Director. m. Beverly C McGregor, 30 Oct. 1970, 2 daughters. *Education:* Sydney Grammar School. *Memberships:* Royal Motor Yacht Club. *Hobbies:* Yachting; Golf. *Address:* 61 Rosedale Road, Gordon, Sydney, New South Wales, Australia.

WHISHAW, David b. 9 Mar. 1923, Launceston, Tasmania. Studstock Breeder. m. 31 Aug. 1949, 4 sons, 1 daughter. *Education:* Diplomas of Agriculture & Woolclassing, Canterbury Agricultural College, New Zealand, 1946-47. *Appointments:* Flight Lt., RAAF Aircrew, 1941-45; RAAF, 455 Sqdn, England, 1943-45; Self Employed. *Memberships:* President, The Tasmanian Division, Bloodstock Breeders Association of Australia. *Honours:* Distinguished Flying Gross, 1944; Canterbury Agricultural College Special Awards in Animal Husbandry, 1947. *Address:* Sunninghill, Carrick, Tasmania 7257, Australia.

WHITAKER, Margaret Joy (Ms.) b. 30 Oct. 1926, Sunderland, England. Pianoforte Tutor & Pianist. *Education:* Royal Academy of Music, London, 1942-45; LRAM PT P, 1943; ARCM PT P, 1944; LRAM PT T, 1961; studied with Cyril Smith. *Appointments:* Bretton Hall Training College, 1949-52; Visiting Piano Teacher, St. Peters School, York, Private Teaching, Numerous Recitals in U.K. including Yorkshire Symphony Orchestra, 1952-60; Piano Teacher, Allerton High School, Leeds, 1952-63; Director of Music, Harrogate College, 1964-65; Assistant Piano Teacher, Queen Margarets School, York, 1965-66; Studied Organ at York Minster, 1964-65; Private Pianoforte Teacher, 1968-. *Memberships:* European Pianoforte Teachers Association; ISM London; Society for Music Therapy. *Honours:* LFIBA, 1979. *Hobbies:* Art; Cardiac Research; Needlework; Gardening; Geology; Botany; Cricket. *Address:* 133 Wetherby Road, Harrogate, North Yorks, H62 7SH, England.

WHITBY, Lionel Gordon b. 18 July 1926, London, England. Professor of Clinical Chemistry, University of Edinburgh. m. Joan Hunter Sanderson, 1 son, 2 daughters. *Education:* Eton College, King's Scholar, 1939-45; King's College, Cambridge, 1945-48; Middlesex Hospital Medical School, 1953-56; BA, 1948; MA PhD, 1951; MB, BChir, MRCS, LRCP, 1956; MD, 1961; FRCP, 1972; FRCPEd, 1968; FRCPath, 1972; FRSEd, 1968. *Appointments:* Fellow of King's College, Cambridge, 1951-55; Junior Medical Appointment, 1956-59; Rockefeller Travelling Fellowship National Institutes of Health, Bethesda, Md, USA, 1959-60; University Biochemist, Addenbrooke's Hospital, Cambridge, 1960-63; Fellow of Peterhouse, Cambridge, 1961-62; Professor of Clinical Chemistry, University of Edinburgh, 1963-. *Publications:* Editor w. W. Lutz & Contributor, Principles & Practice of Medical Computing, 1971; Author w. IW Percy-Robb & AF Smith, Lecture Notes on Clinical Chemistry, 1975, 1980; Articles on computers in clinical chemistry, screening for disease, clinical enzymology and various other subjects, published in the scientific literature. *Honours:* WA Meek Scholar, University of Cambridge, 1951; Broderip Scholarship, Lyell Medal & Hetley Prize, Middlesex Hospital, 1956; Murchison Scholarship, Royal College of Physicians, 1959. *Hobbies:* Gardening; Photography. *Address:* 51 Dick Place, Edinburgh EH9 2JA, Scotland.

WHITE, Cyril Charles William, b. 7 Sept. 1909, Hastings, New Zealand. Piano Craftsman/ Technical Adviser, Talking Books for the use of the blind. m. 14 Jan. 1939. *Education:* Totally blind person. Jubilee Institute for the Blind, Auckland, New Zealand, 1914-23; Jubilee Institute for the Blind, Auckland, New Zealand, Piano Tuning Training Course, 1923-27; New Zealand Piano Tuners Certificate. *Appointments:* Conducted own piano tuning and repair business, 1927-51; Manufacturer and Supplier to New Zealand Foundation for the Blind of Electric Talking Book reproducers for the use of the Blind, 1951-59; Technical Adviser, New Zealand Foundation for the Blind, Supervising recording of Talking Books, maintenance and distribution of machines and cassettes, 1960-65; Manager, Royal New Zealand Foundation for the Blind's National Braille and Talking Book Library, 1966-75. *Memberships:* National President, New Zealand Association of the Blind, 1954-66, National Secretary, 1968-, Elected Patron, 1980; Board of Trustees, Royal New Zealand Foundation for the Blind, 1956-; New Zealand Representative member World Council for Welfare of the Blind, 1959-79; Executive, International Federation of the Blind from inception, 1964-79, Third Vice-President, 1977-79. *Honours:* OBE, Queen's Birthday Honours, 1975. *Hobbies:* Radio & Hi-Fi Music; Chess; Interest in Research & Development of electronics & research into technical aids. *Address:* 3 Lauriston Avenue, Remuera, Auckland 5, New Zealand.

WHITE, Harold St.Clair, b. 17 Nov. 1936, St. Michael, Barbados, West Indies. Senior Consultant, Pathologist. m. Lucia Bernadette Taylor, 16 Aug. 1975, l son, 1 daughter. *Education:* MB, ChB, Glasgow University Medical School, Scotland, 1964; DCP, Royal Postgraduate Medical School, 1968; Fellowship Society of Medical Technologists, 1979. *Appointments:* Internship, Glasgow, 1964-65; Senior House Officer, Pathology, Queen Elizabeth Hospital, Barbados, 1968-69; Registrar, Pathology, Queen Elizabeth Hospital, 1969-71; Honorary Registrar, Pathology, Hammersmith Hospital, London, 1969; Associate Lecturer, Pathology University, West Indies, 1969-; Consultant Pathologists, Queen Elizabeth Hospital, Barbados, 1971; Senior Consultatn Pathologist, Queen Elizabeth Hospital, Barbados, 1973-. *Memberships:* President, Glasgow West Indian Students Union, 1959-61; British Medical Association, 1966-; Royal Society of Medicine; Association of Clinical Pathologists, UK; Life Member, Glasgow Graduates Association; Secretary, Treasurer, Barbados Branch, British Medical Association, 1969-71; President, Barbados Association of Medical Practitioners, 1973-79. *Publications:* Contributor of reviews, monographs, articles to professional journals and conferences. *Honours:* Commonwealth Scholarship, Postgraduate Work, Pathology, London, 1967-69; Rockefeller Grant, Columbia Presbyterian Hospital, New York USA, Cervical Cytology, 1971. *Hobbies:* Cricket; Tennis; Photography; Literature; Breeding Thoroughbred Race Horses; Music; Philately. *Address:* Glen Fruin, Belle, St. Michael, Barbados, West Indies.

WHITE, Norman Arthur, b. 11 Apr. 1922, Hetten-le-Hole, Durham, England. International Energy Specialists, Independent Company Director & Management Educator. m. Joyce M Rogers, 16 Dec. 1944, 1 son, 1 daughter. *Education:* BSc Engineering, University of London, 1949; MSc, University of Philippines, 1955; Advanced Management Programme, Havard Graduate School of Business, 1968; PhD, London School of Economics, 1973, Chartered Engineer, 1947. *Appointments:* Research Engineer, Deputy Manager, Product Development; Director, Marketing Development; Chief Executive., New Enterprises, Royal Dutch/Shell Group of Companies, 1945-72; Managing Partner, Norman White Associates, 1972-; Special Adviser, Hambros Bank Ltd.,1972-76; Corporate Adviser, Placer Development Co., Vancouver, 1973-78; Various Board Positions, Chairman, Vice Chairman and Director in UK, Canada & USA, 1973-, Including Chairman, ERL Energy Resources Ltd., 1978; KBC Process Consultants Ltd., 1979-; American Oil Field Systems Ltd., 1980; Vice Chairman, The Henley Centre for Forecasting, 1974; Strategy International Ltd., 1976; Transat Energy Inc., Washington, 1977; British Canadian Resources Ltd., Calgary, 1980; Director and Chairman, Executive Committee Tanks Oil and Gas Ltd., 1974-; Visiting Professor of Business Administration, University of Manchester, 1971; Visiting Professor of Management Studies, Henley Management College, 1976; Member of Senate, University of London, 1974. *Memberships:* Fellow, British Institute of Management; Fellow, Royal Society of Arts; Royal Institute of Int. Affairs; FIMechE; Fellow, Inst. of Energy; Fellow, IMM; Member, RAeS; Royal Inst; Am. Society of Petroleum Engineers; Can. Inst. of Mining and Metallurgy; Permanent Council and Ex.Bd. and Deputy Chairman, British National Comm., World Petroleum Congresses, 1977-; Conservation Commission, World Energy Conference, 1979; Parliamentary and Scientific Committee, House of Commons, 1977; Member of Council and Vice President, Inst. of Petroleum, 1975-; Member of Council and Chairman, Engineering Management Division, Institution of Mechanical Engineers, 1982. *Publications:* Author of various books, articles and papers for professional journals in UK and Canada, including Financing International Petroleum Industry, 1977; International Energy Financing Implications for Canadian Energy

Developments, 1979. *Hobbies:* Country and Coastal Walking; Wild Life; Int. Affairs; Comparative Religions; Domestic Odd-Jobbing. *Address:* Green Ridges, 6 Downside Road, Guildford, Surrey, GU4 8PH, England.

WHITE, Norman Harold Stephen, b. 6 Nov. 1922, Sydney, NSW, Australia, Consultant. m. 25 Nov. 1948, 2 sons, 1 daughter. *Appointments:* Royal Australian Navy, 1936-64; Captain, 1962; Managing Director, NHS White and Associates. *Memberships:* Antarctic Club, Australia, (President, 1964-66, 1978-1980); Naval and Military Club, Melbourne; Imperial Service Club, Sydney; Royal Sydney Yacht Squadron; Royal Sydney Golf Club. *Honours:* The GUY REX Trophy, 1955. *Hobbies:* Golf; Yachting; Fishing. *Address:* 10 Claude Avenue Cremorne, NSW, Australia, 2090.

WHITE, Richard, b. 1 July, 1950, London, England. Research Associate (Mathematics). *Education:* BSc, Queen Mary College, London, 1968-72; DIC, Imperial College, London, 1972-73; M.Phil., Imperial College, London, 1972-74; PhD, City of London Polytechnic, 1974-78. *Appointments:* Research Assistant, Department of Mathematics and Statistics, City of London Polytechnic, 1974-77; Research Associate in Department of Mathematics, University of London, Kings College, 1979-. *Memberships:* Fellow of the Royal Meteorological Society; The Optical Society of America. *Publications:* Contributed to various professional journals, also a number of minor papers and letters in J. Meteorology UK, Weather, Applied Optics and Essex Countryside. *Hobbies:* English Local History; The History of English Antiquarianism; Celtic Studies. *Address:* 106 Roding Lane North, Woodford Green, Essex, IG8 8LJ, England.

WHITE, William Harold, b. 9 Mar. 1934, Palmerson, Ontario, Canada. Barrister. m. Marion, 25 Jan. 1964, 2 sons. *Education:* BA, University of Western Ontario, Canada, 1957; LLB, Osgoode Hall Law School, Toronto, 1960; Barrister & Solicitor, Ontario, 1962; Queens Counsel, 1974. *Appointments:* McGibbon, Harper & Haney, 1962, Partner, 1967; Managing Partner, Harper, Haney & White, Waterloo, Ontario, Canada, 1981. *Memberships:* Law Society of Upper Canada; Canadian Bar Association; Trustee, Waterloo Law Association; Past Chairman, Kitchener, Waterloo Hospital Commission; Past President, Canadian Arthritis & Rheumatism Society, North Waterloo Chapter; Legal Counsel to various Municipal Agencies & Corporations. *Hobbies:* Golf; Tennis; Stamps. *Address:* 70 Norwood Cr., Waterloo, Ontario N2L 2P4, Canada.

WHITELAW, Frederick Thomas, b. 25 Sept. 1919, Wynnum, Queensland, Australia. Regular Army Officer (Retired). m. (1) Annabella, 6 Nov. 1949 (dec.) 2 sons, (2) Nancy MacDougall, 1 July 1978. *Appointments:* Commission, 1940; AABty. Comd.; AIF NG Borneo, 1942-45; School of Artillery, 1946; GSO 2, BCOF, Japan, 1947; GSO 1, BCOF, Japan, 1949-51; Seconded Department of Defence, 1952-55; Australian Mission, Washington, DC, 1956-57; Assistant Military Secretary, AHQ, 1958-60; Commander Royal Tasmania Regt. 1960-62; Military Attache, Indonesia, 1962-64; Director of Cadets, AHQ, 1964-66; Military Secretary, AHQ, 1966-71; Commander Australian Army Force, Far East Land Forces, 1971; Comd. ANZUK, Support Group, Singapore, 1971-73; Deputy Chief of Personnel, AHQ, 1973-74. *Memberships:* Elanora Country Club, Sydney; Imperial Service Club, Sydney; Canberra Yacht Club. *Honours:* CBE, 1970. *Hobbies:* Golf; Fishing. *Address:* 20 Carrara Road, Carrara, Queensland, 4211, Australia.

WHITLAM, (Edward) Gough, b. 11 July 1916, Melbourne, Victoria, Australia. m. Margaret E Dovey, 22 Apr, 1942, 3 sons, 1 daughter. *Education:* BA, Sydney, 1938; LL.B, Sydney, 1946. *Appointments:* RAAF, 1941-45; Barrister, 1947; QC, 1962; MP, 1952-78; Deputy Leader, 1960-67) and Leader, 1967-77; Australian Labor Party; Prime Minister and Foreign Minister of Australia; Visiting Fellow, 1978; First National Fellow, 1980 Australian National University; Visiting Professor, Harvard, 1979. *Publications:* On Australia's Constitution (articles and lectures, 1957-77); Reform During Recession, 1978; The Truth of the Matter, 1979; The Italian Inspiration in English Literature, ANUP, 1980; A Pacific Community, Harvard UP, 1981; Australian Federalism in Crisis, Oxford UP, 1981; The Whitlam Government, Penguin, 1982. *Honours:* Companion of the Order of Australia, 1978; Silver Plate of Honour, Socialist International, 1976; Hon. LL.D., Philippines, 1974; Hon. D. Litt., Sydney, 1981. *Address:* 100 William Street, Sydney, NSW, 2011, Australia.

WHYMAN, John, b. 20 Apr. 1939, Gillingham, Kent, England. University Teacher. *Education:* BSc. (Econ) 2nd Class Honours, London School of Economics, University of London, 1958-61; AIPM, 1961-62, (Postgraduate Diploma in Personnel Management); PhD. University of Kent, 1980. *Appointments:* Lecturer in Economic and Social History, University of Kent, Canterbury, 1968-. *Memberships:* Kent Archaeological Society; University of London Convocation; LSE Society; Institute of Personnel Management; Economic History Society; Agricultural History Society. *Publications:* A Short Economic and Social History of Twentieth Century Britain, 1967; Introduction to a History of Faversham, (1774); Essays in Kentish History, 1973; Articles in Archaeologia Cantiana, Cantium, Bygone Kent, Southern History, and The East Kent Critic; Aspects of Holidaymaking and Resort Development Within the Isle of Thanet, with Particular Reference to Margate c.1736-c.1840, 2 volumes, 1981. *Hobbies:* Travel; The Cinema; Good food and wine. *Address:* Haytor, 53 Pierremont Avenue, Broadstairs, Kent, England, CT10 1NT, England.

WHYTE, Cosmo Charles, b. 14 Nov. 1951, Westmoreland, Jamaica, WI. Architect. m. Judith M. Johnson, 21 Dec. 1977. *Education:* The Architectural Association School of Architecture/University of Science and Technology, Kumasi, Ghana, 1970-76. *Appointments:* Ministry of Housing, Jamaica, WI, 1976-80; Urban Dev. Corporation, 1980-. *Memberships:* Jamaica Institute of Architects. *Publications:* Papers - Classical Yoruba Sculpture; Shelter in Context, a study of the dynamics of rural and urban housing in Jamaica; Use of Architectural Space in a Changing Environment - A Historical Analysis of the use of Domestic Space in Ghana; *Creative Works:* Done work in the Ministry of Housing on Rural and Urban Squatter Upgrading in Jamaica; Urban Planning and Design, Urban Development Corporation, Resort Development, Planning an Development of Rural Towns and Villages in Jamaica. *Hobbies:* Photography; Sailing; Cricket. *Address:* 39 Mona Commons, Kingston, 7, Jamaica, West Indies.

WICKHAM, Ashley Brian, b. 27 Nov. 1947, Munda, Western Solomon Islands. Journalist. m. Terokoraoi Terauno, 1 July 1978, 2 sons, 3 daughters. *Appointments:* Communicator Radio, S.I. Government, 1967; Information Officer, S.I. Government, 1968; Member, Legislative Assembly, S.I. Government, 1973-75; News Editor SIBC, S.I. Government, 1977-78; Head of Programmes, SIBC 1979; Manager, SIBC, 1980; General Manager, SI Ports Authority, 1976-82. *Memberships:* Public Service Commissioner, 1980; Chairman of the Board, SI Ports Authority, 1977; Chairman of the Board, Honiara Consumers Co-operative Society, 1978-81. *Hobbies:* Music; Reading; Fishing. *Address:* Koloale Street, Honiara, Solomon Islands.

WICKING, John Oswald, b. 19 May, 1918, Melbourne, Victoria, Australia. m. Janet Tompson, 1 Aug. 1945. *Appointments:* The Trustees Executor and Agency Co. Ltd., 1934-39; Lieutenant, A.I.F. 2/7th Infantry Battalion, 1939-45; Primary Producer, 1945-63; Director, The Kiwi Polish Company Pty. Ltd., 1963-75; Managing Director, The Kiwi Polish Co. Pty. Ltd., 1976-; Chairman, The Kiwi Polish Co. Pty. Ltd., 1980-. *Memberships:* Australian Club; Athenaeum Club; Peninsula Golf Club; V.R.C., Moonee Valley Racing Club; Naval and Military Club; Castle Creek Golf Club; Euroa Sheep Dog Association. *Honours:* A Member of the Order of Australia, (AM) 1981. *Hobbies:* Golf; Farming. *Address:* Ponkeen, Tarcombe, Via Euroa, Victoria, 3333, Australia.

WICKS, Peter Charles, b. 30 Aug. 1947, Brisbane, Queensland, Australia. Academic Administrator and Historian. m. Thuy Trinh, 14 Feb. 1976, 1 son, 1 daughter. *Education:* BA, Honours, University of Queensland, 1969, B.Ed, University of Queensland, 1977; MEd, University of Hawaii, 1978. *Appointments:* Tutor in History, University of New South Wales, 1972; Lecturer in History and Politics, Darling Downs Institute of Advanced Education, 1973-79; Associate Dean, Academic, School of Arts, DDIAE, 1979-. *Memberships:* Australian College of Education; Aus-

tralian Institute of Management; Malaysian Branch, Royal Asiatic Society; Malaysian Historical Association; Australian Institute of International Affairs; Asian Studies Association of Australia. *Publications:* Overseas Students in Australia, 1972; Australia Discovers Asia, 1978; Images of Malaya in the Stories of Sir Hugh Clifford, 1979; Education, Colonialism and a Plural Society in West Malaysia, 1980. *Honours:* Charles Robertson Memorial Prize in History, University of Queensland, 1965; ACV Melbourne Prize in History, University of Queensland, 1966; HE Fitzgerald Memorial Prize in Education, University of Queensland, 1973. *Hobbies:* Reading; Writing; Gardening. *Address:* 66 Debra Street, Toowoomba, Queensland 4350, Australia.

WIDESON-EVRIVIADES, Andreas, b. 5 Apr. 1918, Larnaca, Cyprus. Hotel Owner. m. Kalliopi Kyprianou, 1 son, 1 daughter. *Education:* Diploma of the Pancyprian Commercial Lyceum; Government of Cyprus Examination Diploma, Ordinary and Distinction, 1934. *Appointments:* Cable & Wireless Operator, Cable & Wireless Ltd, Cyprus & Palestine, 1939-42; Founder & Manager, Four Lanterns Hotel, 1947-; Part-time journalist, Cyprus Mail & Eleftheria, 1956-74. *Memberships:* Rotary Club; Board of Directors, Cypus Ports Authority, 1973, 1980-81; Board of Directors, Bank of Cyprus Ltd., 1979-; President, Cyprus Hotel Association, 1973-. *Publications:* Several articles in English & Greek newspapers in Cyprus, including Churchill's Visit to Cyprus, 1907; The History of Larnaca's Water Supply, and others. *Hobbies:* Music, violin; Sailing; Stamp Collecting. *Address:* PO Box 150, Larnaca, Cyprus.

WIGGAN, Lloyd Sullivan, b. 24 Oct. 1933, Hampden, Trelawny, Jamaica. Animal Scientist. m. Norma G Sandford, 1 son, 2 daughters. *Education:* BSc, North Carolina Agricultural & Technical University, 1959; MSc, University of Nebraska, 1961; DPhil, University of London, 1967. *Appointments:* Livestock Research Assistant, Bodles Animal Production Research Station, Ministry of Agriculture, Jamaica, 1954-57; Research Fellow, Department of Animal Science, University of Nebraska, 1949-61; Commonwealth Fellowship, UK Award, Research In Reproductive Physiology towards PhD degree, University of London; Deputy-Head, Artificial Insemination Division, 1961-64; Head, Artificial Insemination Division, Ministry of Agriculture, Jamaica, 1967-73; Livestock Specialist, Jamaica Development Bank; Manager, Agricultural Projects Department, Jamaica Development Bank, 1977-79; Managing Director, Midland Enterprises, Jamaica, Limited, 1980-. *Memberships:* International Society of Fertility; Jamaica Association of Professional Agriculturists; American Society of Animal Science. *Publications:* Contributor to various professional journals, including, Artificial Insemination in Farm Animals, Jamaica Livestock Society Farmers Handbook, 1979. *Honours:* Fellowship, University of Nebraska, 1959; Elected to Honour Society in Agriculture, Gamma Sigma Delta, 1960; Commonwealth Scholarship Award, UK University of London, Royal Veterinary College, 1964. *Hobbies:* Cricket; Classical Music; Farming. *Address:* 17 West Great House Circle, PO Box 77, Kingston 8, Jamaica.

WIJASURIYA, Donald Earlian Kingsley, b. 22 Nov. 1934, Kuala Lumpur, Malaysia. Librarian. m. Annette Jayatilaka, 3 sons. *Education:* BA, University of Ceylon, 1959; ALA, Associate of the Library Association, UK, 1962; FLA, Fellow of the Library Association, UK, 1965; PhD, Loughborough University, England, 1980. *Appointments:* Assistant Librarian, 1964-70, Deputy Librarian, 1971-72, University of Malaya; Deputy Director, 1972-75, Deputy Director General, 1976-, Acting Director General, 1977-80, National Library of Malaysia. *Memberships:* Library Association, UK, 1960-; Malaysian Library Association, 1959-; President, Malaysian Library Association, 1972, 1973, 1975; Chairman, Executive Board, Congress of SE Asian Librarians, 1978-81. *Publications:* Index Malaysiana, 1972; Barefoot Librarian, 1975; The Need to Know: developing public library services for the community, 1977; Blueprint for school library development in Malaysia, 1979; various articles in Libri, IFLA Journal, UNESCO Bulletin for Libraries, Journal of Information Science, International Library Review, Encyclopaedia of Library and Information Science, etc. *Honours:* BCK Bintang Chemerlang Kedah, Kedah, Malaysia, Distinguished Service Star, Royal Award, 1979; KMN Kesatria Mangku Negara, Royal Order of Chivalry, 1980. *Hobbies:* Reading; Tennis; Swimming. *Address:* No. 19, Jalan 17/21, Petaling Jaya, Selangor, Malaysia.

WIJEKOON, Dingiri Banda, b. 30 July 1935, Keppitpola. Chartered Accountant. m. Jayanthi Wedamestrige, 1 son, 2 daughters. *Education:* BA, Gen, Business Administration, Vidyodaya University, Sri Lanka, 1964; Special Trained Teacher, Commerce, 1963; Certificate on Production Management, National Institute of Management, Sri Lanka, 1973; Associate Member, Institute of Chartered Accountants, Sri Lanka, 1974. *Appointments:* Lecturer, Ceylon Technical College, Colombo 10, 1965-71; Accountant, Water Supply & Drainage Department, Sri Lanka, 1974-/4; Accountant, Land Commissioner's Department, Sri Lanka, 1974-75; Director Practical Training, Institute of Chartered Accountants, Sri Lanka, 1976; Accountant, Registrar of Companies Department, Sri Lanka, 1977-78; Chief Internal Auditor, People's Bank, Sri Lanka, 1978-79; Chartered Accountant, Assignment under Commonwealth Fund for Technical Co-operation, 1979-. *Publications:* A text book on Nigerial Taxation, in preparation. *Honours:* Nominated to Council of Institute of Chartered Accountants, Sri Lanka, 1977-79. *Hobbies:* Farming; Stamp Collecting. *Address:* 33 Ramya Place, Asiri Uyana, Moratuwa, Sri Lanka.

WIJESUNDERA, Stanley b. 6 Dec. 1923, Kandy, Sri Lanka. m. Helena Anoja Devi Wijewardene, 19 Jan. 1956, 2 sons, 2 daughters. *Education:* BSc, Ceylon, 1946; BSc, London, 1947; BSc, Oxford, 1952; DPhil, Oxford, 1954. *Appointments:* Assistant Lecturer/Lecturer/Associate Professor of Biochemistry, 1948-77; Professor of Biochemistry, 1978-; Vice-Chancellor, University of Colombo, 1979-. *Memberships:* Member of the Council & President, Chemical Society of Ceylon, 1966-70; Fellow & Chairman, Royal Institute of Chemistry, Ceylon, 1969; Council, Sri Lanka Association for the Advancement of Science for several years; General Research Council of the SLAAS, 1975-79. *Publications:* Several Research Publications in the field of Biochemistry. *Hobbies:* Photography; Mushroom Culture; Gardening; Travel. *Address:* 28 Thurstan Road, Colombo 3, Sri Lanka.

WIJEYESINGHE, Gamini Christopher Bernard, b. 19 Feb, 1934, Colombo. Chartered Accountant. m. Eustelle Abeyesundere, 29 Aug. 1959, 3 daughters. *Education:* Fellow of the Institute of Chartered Accountants of Sri Lanka; Fellow of the Association of Authorised Public Accountants (UK). *Appointments:* Partner, Ford, Rhodes, Thornton & Co., Chartered Accountants, Sri Lanka; Member of the External Audit Committee of the International Monetary Fund, 1979-80. *Memberships:* Vice President, Institute of Chartered Accountants of sri Lanka; Past President, Lions Club of Colombo South. *Address:* 8A, Gregory's Road, Colombo 7, Sri Lanka.

WIKIRIWHI, Matarehua, b. 4 Apr. 1918, Whakarewarewa, Rotorua, New Zealand. Public Servant (retired). m. Jean Hineuira, 30 Oct. 1949, 1 son, 2 daughters. *Education:* Ch.Ch., Lincoln College, 1946-48; Registered Rural Valuer, Licensed Maori Interpreter. *Appointments:* Maori Affairs Department, 1948-76; Farm Supervisor, 1948-57; Maori Welfare Officer, 1958-76. *Memberships:* North Shore, Auckland, Maori Committee; Auckland Returned Services Association, Executive; 28 Maori Battalion Association. *Honours:* Mentioned in Despatches, 1942; Distinguished Service Order, 1943; Military Cross, 1944. *Hobbies:* Golf; Gardening. *Address:* 39 College Road, Northcote, Auckland, 9 New Zealand.

WIKRAMANAYAKE, Drayton Sarath Palita, b. 15 Nov. 1954, Colombo, Sri Lanka. Chartered Accountant. m. Romanie Dharmaratne, 28 June, 1980. *Education:* Associate member of the Institute of Chartered Accountants of Sri Lanka, 1978; The Professional Part II, The Institute of Cost & Management Accountants, London, 1977. *Appointments:* Served Articles of Apprenticeship, M/S Ford Rhodes Thornton & Co, Chartered Accountants, Sri Lanka, 1974-78; Accountant, M/S Aitken Spence & Co Ltd, Sri Lanka, 1978-79; Audit Supervisor, M/S Touche Ross Thorbun & Co, Jamaica, 1979-81; Inspection Officer/Accountant, The Bank of N.T. Butterfield & Son Ltd, Bermuda. *Memberships:* Executive Committee, Institute of Chartered Accountants of Sri Lanka Students' Society, 1976. *Honours:* Institute prize for Company Law and

Taxation by the Institute of Cost & Management Accountants, UK, 1977; Auditing Prize, Institute of Chartered Accountants of Sri Lanka, 1978. *Hobbies:* Music; Reading; Photography. *Address:* 25 Hamilton Drive, Trafalgar Park, Kingston 10, Jamaica WI.

WILBY, Charles Bryan, b. 13 July, 1926, Headingley, Leeds, England. University Professor and part-time Consultant and Author. m. Jean M. Broughton, 19 Aug. 1950, 3 sons. *Education:* Frank Parkinson Prize, Civil Electrical & Mechanical Engineering, Leeds University, 1946; BSc, Leeds University, 1947; PhD, Leeds University, 1949. *Appointments:* Designer-Contracting, The Yorkshire Hennebique Contracting Co. Ltd, Leeds, 1949-50; Contracting, The Yorkshire Hennebique Contracting Co. Ltd, Hull, 1950-52; Deputy Chief Engineer, Twisteel Reinforcement Ltd, Manchester, and Ferrocon Engineering Co. Ltd, 1952-55; Deputy Chief Engineer, Stuart's Granolithic Co. Ltd, The Company's Development Engineer, 1955-58; Lecturer & part-time Consultant & Author, University of Sheffield, 1958-63; Professor and Chairman of Schools of Civil and Structural Engineering & part-time consultant and Author, University of Bradford, 1963-. *Memberships:* FICE: FIStructE. *Publications:* Author of 13 books, including Design Graphs for Concrete Shell Roofs, 1980; Advanced Post-tensioned Prestressed Concrete, 1981; Handbook of Structural Concrete, Chapter 32, Shell Roofs, 1981; Author of about 40 published papers on concrete, plain, reinforced, prestressed and shell. *Honours:* Miller Prize, Institute of Civil Engineers, 1951; Frank Parkinson Prize, 1946; Queen's Garden Party at Buckingham Palace, Silver Jubliee, 1977. *Address:* 20 Yew Tree Avenue, Bradford, West Yorkshire, BD8 OAD, England.

WILDE, William Henry, b. 19 Nov. 1923, Tamworth, NSW, Australia. Associate Professor. m. Ena F McKeough, 20 Dec. 1947, 1 son, 1 daughter. *Education:* BA, 1946; MA, 1963; Diploma in Education, 1947. 03 New South Wales Department of Education, 1948-53; Civil Professional Staff, Royal Australian Naval College, 1953-63; Lecturer and Senior Lecturer, Royal Military College, Duntroon, 1964-68; Senior Lecturer, Faculty of Military Studies, University of New South Wales, 1968-76; Associate Professor, Military Studies, University of New South Wales, 1976-. *Memberships:* Australian College of Education; Chairman, (1969-70) American Field Service Scholarships, ACT Division; Rotary. *Publications:* Three Radicals, Oxford University Press, 1969; Adam Lindsay Gordon, Oxford University Press, 1972; Henry Kendall, Twaynes world Authors, 1976; Australian Literature to 1900, Gale Information Guide Library Series, 1980; Letters of Mary Gilmore, Melbourne University Press, 1980; General Editor, Oxford Companion to Australian Literature in preparation for Oxford University Press. *Honours:* Awarded Australian Research Grants Committee Award for the biography of Dame Mary Gilmore, 1979-81. *Hobbies:* Sport; Grandchildren; Gardening. *Address:* 12 Verco Street, Hackett, Canberra, Australia.

WILDER, Kenneth William, b. 7 June 1927, Chelmsford, Essex, England. Book Publisher. m. Jean Wilder (nee Riches), 17 Sept. 1949, 1 son, 1 daughter. *Appointments:* Hamish Hamilton, 1950-61; William Collins, Australia, 1961; Chairman and Managing Director, also Director, William Collins and Sons (Holding) Ltd., Glasgow, Scotland. *Memberships:* Australian Book Publishers Association; Imperial Services Club, Sydney; Royal Prince Alfred Yacht Club, Sydney. *Publications:* Trade Press articles. *Hobbies:* Yachting; Tennis; Painting; Music. *Address:* Ashford Park, Osborne Road, Burradoo, NSW 2576, Australia.

WILDING, Kalev, b. 7 Oct. 1945, Germany. Orthopaedic Surgeon. m. Lana I. Nuchtern, 10 Apr. 1981. *Education:* MB, BS, University of Sydncy, 1969; Fellow of Royal College of Surgeons (England), 1973; Fellow of Royal Australasian College of Surgeons, 1976. *Appointments:* Resident Medical Officer, Royal North Shore Hospital, Sydney, 1969-70; Surgical Registrar, Harold Wood Hospital, Essex, England, 1971-72; Registrar in Orthopaedic Surgery, Australian Orthopaedic Association, Sydney Training Programme, 1973-76; Medical Officer, Duchess of Kent Childrens Orthopaedic Hospital, 1977; Lecturer, Department of Orthopaedic Surgery, University of Hong Kong, 1977; Visiting Orthopaedic Surgeon, Concord Repatriation Hospital, Sydney, 1978; Visiting Orthopaedic Surgeon, Margaret

Reid Crippled Childrens Hospital, Sydney, 1978-; Visiting Orthopaedic Surgeon, Sutherland District Hospital, Sydney, 1980-; Honorary Clinical Lecturer, (Department of Surgery), University of Sydney, 1980-. *Memberships:* Australian Medical Association; Australian Orthopaedic Association. *Publications:* Actinomycosis of Bone, Australian and New Zealand Journal of Surgery Vol 45 No. 1, 1975; The Place of Dwyer Anterior Instrumentation in Scoliosis, 1977; Collapsing Lordosis, Correction by the Dwyer Technique, 1977; Journal of Bone and Joint Surgery, 1981, Surgical Treatment of Scoliosis Following Poliomyelitis. *Hobbies:* Tennis; Skiing; Chess. *Address:* 339 Woolooware Road, Cronulla, NSW 2230, Australia.

WILHELM, Donald, b. 18 June, 1915, Newark, N.J., USA. Developmental Consultant. m. Muriel J Leverett, (4 children by previous marriage). *Education:* AB, Yale University, 1938; PhD in Political Economy and Government, Harvard University, 1955. *Appointments:* With Office of the Chairman, War Production Board, Washington, 1942-44; Economic Advisor, Office of Technical Services, Washington, 1945-47; Member of Faculty of Grinnell College, 1947-51; University of Teheran, 1956-60; Tufts University, 1965-66; University of Ibadan, 1967-68; Kent State University, 1968-72; International Consultant to the Educational Career Service, Princeton, N.J., 1972-. *Memberships:* American Association for the Advancement of Science; American Political Science Association; British Association for the Advancement of Science; Cambridge Arts Theatre; Cambridge Union Society; Marshall Society; Middle East Institute; National Trust; Royal Society of St. George; Society for International Development. *Publications:* Creative Alternatives to Communism: Guidelines for Tomorrow's World (London, 1977; New York, 1981; and other editions); Emerging Indonesia, London, 1980; Contributor of articles to professional journals. *Honours:* School and University Scholarships. *Hobbies:* Walking; Contemplation; Travel in developing countries. *Address:* 16 Bowers Croft, Cambridge CB1 4RP, England.

WILKINSON, Anthony George, b. 7 Feb. 1927, Birmingham, England. Chartered Surveyor. m. Nancy Ko Li Yi, 10 Mar. 1980, 1 son, 3 daughters. *Education:* Oxford and Cambridge School Certificate to Matriculation Exemption Standard; Fellow of the Royal Institution of Chartered Surveyors; Chartered Auctioneer and Estate Agent; Fellow of the Incorporated Society of Surveyors and Valuers; Fellow of the Rating and Valuation Association (By examination); Fellow of the Institute of Arbitrators. *Appointments:* Senior Partner, A.G. Wilkinson and Associates; A. G. Wilkinson and Company, 1971-80; Property Manager to the Chartered Bank, 1970-71; Rating and Valuation Surveyor with the Hong Kong Government, 1966-70; A.G. Wilkinson and Company and amalgamated with Goodeve, Martin and Moroney in 1963, 1962-66; Manager, Arthur Stanbury and Brown, 1958-61; Salaried Partner, Jack Dixon and Company and Sadler, Wilkinson and Partners, 1954-58; Property Executive, Elliott Advertising Ltd., 1953-54; Manager, Wm. Fowler, Bewlay and Company, 1951-53; Assistant Property Manager, G.F. Fisher, F.A.I, 1949-50; Articled Pupil Hedley, Mason and Hedley, 1947-49. *Memberships:* Hong Kong Club; United Services Recreation Club; The Royal Hong Kong Auxilliary Police Officers Mess. *Hobbies:* Literature; Music; Shooting; Parachuting. *Address:* Flat H, Block 2, Pok Fu Lam Road, Hong Kong.

WILKINSON, John Arbuthnot Ducane, b. 23 Sept. 1940, Slough, England. Member of Parliament. m. Paula Adey, 5 July, 1969, 1 daughter. *Education:* Commissioned, Qualified French Interpreter, RAF College, Cranwell, 1959-61; MA Hons, Churchill College, Cambridge. *Appointments:* Flying Instructor, RAF, 1967; Conservative Central Office and Research Department, 1967-69; British Aircraft Corporation, 1969-70; MP, Bradford West, 1970-74; Various Posts in Aviation, 1974-79; MP, Ruislip, Northwood, 1979-. *Hobby:* Flying. *Address:* House of Commons, London, SW1, England.

WILKINSON, William Henry, Clementson-, b. 27 Aug. 1921, Bath Somerset. Artist. m. Lady Margaret Ewer, 14 Aug. 1956, 1 daughter. *Education:* Winchester and Heidelberg, Royal College of Art, Paris and Florence. RE; FRCA; FIAL, PhD. *Appointments:* Professor of Engraving School, City and Guilds of London

Institute, Consultant, Morris Singer Bronze Foundry; Consultant, Royal Mint. *Memberships:* Royal Society of Painter - Etchers and Engravers; Chelsea Arts Club; Swiss Alpine Club. *Creative Works:* Engraver and painter of Sporting Prints in line-engraving. Work sold in British Isles, America, France, Switzerland, Germany, Australia. *Address:* Crane Cottage, Tatsfield, Westerham, Kent, TN16 RJT, England.

WILL, Barry Fegan, b. 14 May, 1945, Brisbane, Australia. Architect-planner/ Lecturer. m. Dr. Hwai-Ping Sheng, 1 son. *Education:* B.Arch, University of Queensland, 1968; Master of Urban Studies, University of Queensland, 1970. *Appointments:* Architect, Commonwealth Department of Works, Australia; Lecturer, Department of Architectures, University of Hong Kong; Senior Lecturer, School of Architecture, University of Hong Kong; Architect-planner, Private Practice HK. *Memberships:* Vice President, Hong Kong Institute of Architects; Royal Australian Institute of Architects; American Planning Association; Commonwealth Human Ecology Council; Authorised Person List I HK Government, Registered Architect Board of Architects, Queensland. *Honours:* Brian Johnston Prize for Design, 1967; Ballieu Research Scholarship, 1969. *Hobbies:* Sailing; Motor Sports. *Address:* 17 Middleton Towers, 9/F, 14 Pokfulam Road, Hong Kong.

WILLANS, Jean Stone, b. 3rd Oct. 1924, Hillsboro, Ohio, USA. Religious Organisation Executive. m. Richard James Willans, 28th Mar. 1966, 1 daughter. *Education:* Student, San Diego Junior College. *Appointments:* Assistant to Vice-President, Family Loan Co. Miami, Fla, 1946-49; Civilian Supervisor USAF, Washington, USA, 1953-55; Editor, Trinity Magazine, Los Angeles, 1961-65; Co-founder, Vice-President, Director Asian Office, Hong Kong Society of Stephen, Altadena, California, 1967-75; Executive Director, Hong Kong, 1975; Founder, Blessed Trinity Society, Lecturer in field, 1960.- *Publications:* Author, The Acts of the Green Apples, 1974; Co-editor, Charisma in Hong Kong, 1970; Spiritual Songs, 1970: The People Who Walked in Darkness, 1977. *Hobbies:* Contract Bridge; Fishing; Cooking. *Address:* 1 Buxey Lodge, 37 Conduit Road, Hong Kong.

WILLETT, Frederick John, b. 26 Feb. 1921, London. Vice-Chancellor, Griffith University, Brisbane, Australia. m. Jane Cunningham Westwater, 3 Sept. 1949, 1 son, 2 daughters. *Education:* MA, University of Cambridge, Graduate in Social Anthropology, 1948; MBA, University of Melbourne, Australia, 1963; Hon LLD, University of Melbourne, Australia. *Appointments:* Research team member, Medical Research Council, Social factors in coalmining productivity, 1948-51; Production Manager, Turners Asbestor Cement Co, Manchester, 1951-57; Assistant Director of Research, Industrial Management, University of Cambridge, 1957-62; Sydney Myer Professor of Commerce & Business Administration, University of Melbourne, Australia, 1962-72; Pro-Vice Chancellor, Vice Chairman & later Chairman, Professorial Board, University of Melbourne, Australia, 1967-71; Visiting Professor, Organisation Behaviour, Graduate School of Business, Standford University & Carnegie Travelling Fellow, 1968.-; Appointed first Vice-Chancellor, Griffith University, Brisbane, Australia, 1971.-. *Memberships:* President, Melbourne University Community Aid Abroad Group, 1966-68; Vice-President, World University Service, 1968-70; National President, World University Service, 1966-68; President, Citizens' Welfare Service of Victoria, 1970-72; President, Twelfth Night Theatre, 1974-76. *Publications:* Many publications in the fields of: Organisation Theory; Organisational Behaviour; Motivation in Organisations; Business Policy; Management Education. *Honours:* Distinguished Service Cross, Service with the Royal Navy Fleet Air Arm, 1945; Mention in Dispatches, 1942. *Address:* 8 Prenzler Street, Mount Gravatt, Queensland 4122, Australia.

WILLETT, Peter Ronald b. 8 Nov. 1945, Melbourne, Australia. Physicist. m. Anne Therese Murray, 26 Jan. 1970, 2 daughters. *Education:* BSc, Physics, Monash University, Victoria, Australia, 1967; MSc, Physics, University of New South Wales, Australia, 1972. *Appointments:* Research Physicist, X-ray Crystallography, Defence Standards Laboratory, 1968; Research Physicist, 1969-70; Physical Research Officer, 1970-77; Senior Tyre Engineer, 1977-79; Product Performance Manager, The Olympic Tyre & Rubber Co. Pty. Ltd.,

1979-81; Assistant Manager Tyre Performance, Dunlop Olympic Tyres, 1981. *Memberships:* Director, The Tyre & Rim Association of Australia, 1979; Chairman, Standards Sub-Committee of The Tyre & Rim Association of Australia, 1980-81; Secretary, The Plastics & Rubber Institute, Australasian Section, Victorian Branch, 1981; Council Member of the Australasian Section, The Plastics & Rubber Institute; Vice Chairman, Organizing Committee for 5th Australasian Rubber Convention, 1980; Member of Australian Institute of Physics. *Publications:* Hysteretic Losses in Tyre, paper presented at Symposium on Mechanics of Pneumatic Tires, held in conjunction with the International Rubber Science Hall of Fame, University of Akron, USA, 1974; The Physics of Tyre Sound Generation, paper presented second National Congress, Australian Institute of Physics, New South Wales, Australia, 1976; Viscoelastic Properties of Elastomers, paper presented at Symposium held by the PRI, Melbourne, Australia, 1980. *Honours:* Recipient Silver Medal, Awarded by The Plastics & Rubber Institute, London, for best paper of the year published in the Institute's Journal, 1975; Invited guest speaker at a Symposium titled Mechanics of Pneumatic Tire, Held in conjunction with the International Rubber Science Hall of Fame, University of Akron, USA, 1974. *Hobbies:* Photography; Philately; Baseball; Squash. *Address:* 28 Floriston Grove, Eltham, Victoria, 3095, Australia.

WILLETTS, Bernard Frederick b. 24 Mar. 1927. England. Engineer. m. Norah Elizabeth Law, 14 June 1952, 2 sons. *Education:* BSc, Birmingham University, 1948; MSc, 1951; PhD, 1954, Durham University. *Appointments:* Vickers Armstrongs, 1954-58; Massey Ferguson, UK, Ltd., 1958-68; Chief Engineer, 1959; Director Engineering, 1961; Director Manufacturing, 1965; Deputy Managing Director, 1968; The Plessey Co. Ltd., 1968-78; Group Managing Director, 1968; Main Board, 1970; Deputy Chief Executive, 1975; Vickers Ltd., 1978-80; Assistant Managing Director, 1978; Managing Director, 1980; Dubai Aluminium Company, 1981-; Deputy Chief Executive/ Non-Executive Director: Liverpool Daily Post & Echo; Massey Ferguson Holdings Ltd.; Telephone Rentals. *Memberships:* C.Eng;FIMechE; FI Prod E; FIBM; Vice President, Institute Production Engineers; Fellow of Roya Society of Arts. *Hobbies:* Squash; Gardening; Collecting. *Address:* Suna Court, Pearson Road, Sonning, Berks, England.

WILLEY, Spencer Frank, b. 6 Aug. 1926. London, England. Company Director. m. Glenys, 6 Oct. 1951, 1 son, 1 daughter. *Appointments:* Army Intelligence Corps, 1945-48; Miscellaneous employments, 1948-52; Branch Manager, Northern India, Lipton Overseas Ltd., 1952-59; Internal Marketing Consultant, Rank Hovis Macdougall, U.K., 1959-62; Managing Director, Johnson & Johnson Malaya Sdn Bhd, 1962-68; Chairman & Managing Director, Malayan Cement Berhad Group of Companies, 1968-79; Regional Director, Blue Circle Industries, London, 1979-. *Memberships:* Former President, Malaysian International Chamber of Commerce & Industry; Former Vice-President, Malaysian Institute of Management; Former Vice-President, Federation of Malaysian Manufacturers; Former Vice-Chairman, Malaysian Employers Federation; Former President, Royal Society of St. George, Selangor Branch. *Creative Works:* Has sung lead roles in several musical shows, notably Brigadoon, Showboat, Oklahoma, 1776; Has taken leading parts in numerous concerts, cabarets etc. at various venues. *Honours:* CBE, 1978; Fellow of the Institute of Marketing, UK; Fellow of the Malaysian Institute of Management. *Hobby:* Singing. *Address:* 6 Coronation Road West, Singapore 1026.

WILLIAMS, Alban, b. 13 June 1937, Durban, South Africa. City Treasurer. m. Alison Anne Palmer, 28 Dec. 1963, 2 sons, 1 daughter. *Education:* Matriculated, St. Henry's Marist Brothers College, 1954; Bachelor of Commerce, Natal University, 1955-58; Institute of Municipal Treasurers & Accountants, S.A., Inc.: Final Examination, First Place, 1960; Associate Membership, 1961; Fellow, 1980. *Appointments:* City Treasurers Department, Durban, South Africa, 1955-61; Town Treasurer's Department, Gwels, Rhodesia, 1961-64; City Treasurer's Department, Bulawayo, 1964-; Various Accounting posts, E.D.P. Manager, 1966-70; Chief Accountant, 1972-78; Deputy City Treasurer, 1978-80; City Treasurer, 1980-. *Memberships:* Honorary Treasurer, Zimbabwe Colours Control Board;

Past President, Catenian Association, Bulawayo; Rotary Club of Bulawayo. *Publications:* Articles in Professional Journal. *Honours:* Maldwyn Edmund Prize, First Place in IMTA, SA, Final Examination, 1960; Made a Fellow of IMTA, SA, 1980; Made a member of the Computer Society of Zimbabwe, 1974. *Hobbies:* Amateur Artist. *Address:* 12 Bluebird Road, Burnside, Bulawayo, Zimbabwe.

WILLIAMS, Arthur Dennis Pitt, b. 15 Oct. 1928, Margate, England. Property Development Company Director. m. Ngaire Garbett, 8 Dec. 1951, 3 sons, 2 daughters. *Appointments:* Williams Construction Co. Ltd., 1953-; Williams Development Holdings Ltd., 1967-, Chairman of the Board of Directors, 1979-; (Williams Development Holdings Ltd. now named Carrian-Williams Holdings Ltd.); Chairman, Carrian-Williams Holdings Ltd.; Director, Carrian Traders Ltd., Carrian Travel Service Ltd., Carrian Shipping Ltd. *Memberships:* The Institute of Directors; Associate of Australian Institute of Building; Associate of Real Estate Institute of New Zealand; Property Management Institute. *Hobbies:* Horse-racing. *Address:* Cranbrook, R.D., Waikanae, New Zealand.

WILLIAMS, Awadagin, b. 29 Nov. 1932, Freetown, Sierra Leone. Professor. m. Gracie Ashwood, 7 Sept. 1968, 1 son, 2 daughters. *Education:* BSc, Queen's University, Belfast, 1951-54; PhD, Queen's University, Belfast, 1958. *Appointments:* Lecturer in Mathematics, Fourah Bay College, 1958-62; Senior Lecturer in Mathematics, University of Sierra Leone, 1962-70; Professor of Mathematics, University of Sierra Leone, 1970-. *Memberships:* American Physical Society; American Association for the Advancement of Science; Sierra Leone Association of Mathematics Teacher; Director, Sierra Leone, National Development Bank. *Honours:* Purser Studentship, Queen's University, Belfast, 1955-57; Sloan Post Doctorate Fellowship, Mass. Inst. of Tech., 1961-62. *Hobbies:* Farming; Photography. *Address:* 17 Ross Road, Freetown, Sierra Leone.

WILLIAMS, Belmont Evelyn Oredayo (Mrs Donal Herbert), b. 15 Nov. 1931, Freetown, Sierra Leone. Medical Practitioner. m. 25 June 1965, 1 daughter. *Education:* MB, Chb, Bristol University, England, 1960; MRCOG, Royal College of Obstetricians & Gynaecologists, 1967; Diploma in Public Health, Makerere University Medical School, 1971; FRCOG, Royal College of Obstetricians & Gynaecologists, 1979. *Appointments:* House Officer & Senior House Officer appointments in various hospitals in England, 1960-62; Medical Officer, Ministry of Health, Sierra Leone, 1962-64; Senior House Officer, Rochford & Southen on Sea Hospitals, 1964-66; Senior Registrar, Ministry of Health, Sierra Leone, 1967-70; Specialist, 1970-75, Senior Specialist, 1975-76, Obstetrician & Gynaecologist; Director, Maternal & Child Health Services, 1974-76; Deputy Chief Medical Officer, 1976-78; Chief Medical Officer, 1978-. *Memberships:* Sierra Leone Medical & Dental Association; Nutrition Society, Sierra Leone; Local Chapters, West African College of Surgeons & West African College of Physicians; Chairman, Faculty of Community Health of the West African College of Physicians. *Publications:* Maternal & Child Health Manual, 1977; Maternal Mortality in Sierra Leone, 1978; The Traditional Birth Attnedant, Training & Utilization, 1979. *Hobbies:* Reading; Needlework; Dressmaking; Cooking; Gardening; Attending Concerts and Plays. *Address:* 14 Ross Road, Freetown, Sierra Leone.

WILLIAMS, Bruce Rodda, b. 10 Jan. 1919. Warragul, Victoria, Australia. Director of the Technical Change Centre. m. Roma Olive Hotten, 27 July 1942, 5 daughters. *Education:* BA, University of Melbourne, 1939; MA, University of Adelaide, 1942. *Appointments:* Professor of Economics, University of North Staffordshire, 1950-59; Robert Otley Professor of Economics, 1959-63; Stanley Jevons Professor of Political Economics, 1963-67; University of Manchester: Secretary & Joint Director of Research, Science & Industry Committee, 1952-59; Member, UK National Board for Prices & Incomes, 1966-67; Economic Adviser to UK Minister of Technology, 1966-67; Member, UK Central Advisory Council on Science & Technology, 1967; Vice Chancellor & Principal, The University of Sydney, 1967-81; Chairman, New South Wales State Cancer Council, 1967-81; Member, Board of Reserve Bank of Australia, 1969-81; Chairman, Australian Vice Chancellor's Committee, 1972-74; Chairman, National Committee of Inquiry into Education & Training, 1976-79; Deputy Chairman, Parramatta Hospitals Board, 1978-81; Director, Technical Change Centre, 1981-. *Memberships:* Australian Academy of Social Sciences, 1968. *Publications:* Industry & Technical Progress, (w. C.F. Carter) 1957; Investment in Innovation, 1958; Science in Industry, 1959; Investment Proposals & Decisions, 1965; Investment, Technology & Growth, 1967; Science Technology in Economic Growth, 1973; Systems of Higher Education: Australia, 1978; Education, Training & Employment, 1979. *Honours:* KBE, 1980; Honorary D.Litt, University of Keele, 1973; Honorary DEc, University of Queensland, 1980; Honorary LLD, University of Melbourne, 1981. *Address:* 114 Cromwell Road, London SW7 4ES, England.

WILLIAMS, Colin, Leonard, b. 9 Apr. 1934, St. Margaret's, Middlesex, England. Australian Government Trade Commissioner. m. 20 Dec. 1956, 2 sons, 1 daughter. *Education:* Associate Australian Society of Accountants. *Appointments:* Australian Government Trade Commissioner, South Africa, Malaysia, Saudi Arabia, currently Spain and Portugal, 1970. *Memberships:* Australian Society of Accountants; National Press Club, Canberra. *Hobbies:* Sailing; Painting. *Address:* Villa Toranza, Camino de la Huerta 37, La Moraze-ja, Madrid, Spain.

WILLIAMS, Douglas John, b. 2 Jan. 1924, Sunderland, County Durham, England. Entomologist. *Education:* BSc, 1949; PhD, 1953; DSc, 1980. *Appointments:* Entomologist, Commonwealth Institute of Entomology, British Museum, Natural History, London, 1952-65; Entomologist, USDA, Washington DC, USA, 1965-66; Entomologist, Commonwealth Institute of Entomology, British Museum, Natural History, London, 1966-. *Memberships:* Fellow, Institute of Biology; Fellow, Royal Entomological Society, London; Fellow, Linnean Society of London. *Publications:* 60 Scientific papers on the Taxonomy and Biology of Scale Insects, Hemiptera Coccoidea, of the World. *Hobbies:* Sailing. *Address:* 12 Woodmoor End, Cookham, Berkshire, England.

WILLIAMS, Eric, PC, CH (Rt. Hon.), b. 1911. Prime Minister of Trinidad & Tobago since 1962. *Education:* Queen's Royal College, Trinidad, St. Catherine's College, Oxford, BA, 1935, Class I History, DPhil, 1939. Assistant Professor, Social & Political Science, 1939, Associate Professor, 1946, Professor, 1947, Howard University, Washington, DC, USA. *Appointments:* With Caribbean Commission, and Research Council, Deputy Chairman of latter, 1948-55. Founder & Political Leader, People's National Movement, 1956; First Chief Minister and Minister of Finance, 1956; First Premier, 1959; Minister of External Affairs, 1959-62; Minister of Finance Planning and Development, 1967-81; Led Trinidad and Tobago Delegations to London: US Bases 1960, West Indian Federation Conference, 1961, Independence Conference, 1961, Commonwealth Prime Ministers' Conference, 1962; and to EEC, Brussels, 1962, Pro Chancellor, University of West Indies & Hon LLD, University of New Brunswick; Hon DCL, Oxford. *Publications:* The Negro in the Caribbean, 1942; The Economic Future of the Caribbean, 1943; Capitalism and Slavery, 1944; Education in the British West Indies, 1951; History of the People of Trinidad and Tobago, 1962; Documents of West Indian History, Vol. I, 1492-1655; inward Hunger, 1969; From Columbus to Castro, 1970. *Address:* c/o Erica Williams Connell, 6527 SW116 Pl. B, Miami, Florida 33173, USA.

WILLIAMS, Esther Wininamaori Laisani, b. Suva, Fiji. University Librarian. m. Keith William Williams, 1969, 2 sons . *Education:* BA, University of Wellington, New Zealand, 1971; Post Graduate Diploma, Librarianship, Canberra College of Advanced Education, Australia, 1973. *Appointments:* University of the South Pacific, 1972; University Librarian, 1981. *Memberships:* Vice President, Fiji Library Association, 1978; Secretary, Fiji Library Association, 1975; Council Member, Fiji Library Association, 1977; Secretary, Fiji Society, 1979-; Associate of the Library Association, Australia, 1974-. *Publications:* South Pacific Literature written in English; A Selected Bibliography Suva, USPL, 1979. *Hobbies:* Sport; Squash; Sewing; Cooking. *Address:* P.O. Box 1162, Suva, Fiji.

WILLIAMS, James Royal, b. 24 Feb. 1929, London, England. Engineering Executive. m. Marjorie Jill Wedge, 26 Mar. 1955, 3 sons. *Education:* St. Maryle-

bone Grammar School, London, 1946; City and Guilds of London, Telecommunications, 1956. *Appointments:* De Havilland Aircraft Company Limited, Christchurch, Hampshire, 1954-57; Canadair Limited, Montreal, Canada, 1957-59; Computing Devices of Canada Limited, Ottawa, Ontario, Canada, 1959-63; Leigh Instruments Limited, Ottawa, Ontario, Canada, 1963-74; Elinca Communications Limited, Ottawa, Ontario, Canada, 1974-81. *Memberships:* Associate Fellow, Canadian Aeronautics Space Institute; Rideau Club, Ottawa; Director, Elinca Communications Limited; Director, Austin Automation Limited. *Publications:* Earl of March, A Canadian Biographical Viewpoint; A Prospective Coat of Arms for Kanata, Ontario; Various technical papers. *Hobbies:* Alpine Skiing; Golf; Swimming; Historical Data related to communities. *Address:* 12 Rutherford Crescent, Kanata, Ontario, Canada K2K IM9.

WILLIAMS, John Egerton, b. 27 Apr. 1916, Sheffield, England. Medical Specialist. m. Anne Gladys Kirkby, 10 July 1946, 2 daughters. *Education:* Matriculation, Hons, Sheffield University, 1933; MRCS, LRCP, Fellow of the Faculty of Anaesthetists, London, 1940; FFAR-ACS, Royal Australasian College of Surgeons, 1956. *Appointments:* Visiting Specialist Eye and Ear Hospital, 1950; Visiting Specialist Repatriation Department, 1949-55; Director of Anaesthetics Repatriation General Hospital, 1955-77; Consultant Anaesthetist, Repatriation Commission, 1964-77. *Memberships:* British Medical Association; Australian Medical Association; Australian Society of Anaesthetists; Fellow, Faculty of Anaesthetists; Royal Melbourne; Naval and Military Club; Melbourne Cricket Club. *Publications:* Various Medical Publications and Films. *Honours:* Matriculation, Hons, 1933. *Hobbies:* Gardening; Wine Growing; Film-making. *Address:* 3 Surrey Court, Ivanhoe, Melbourne 3079, Australia.

WILLIAMS, John Robert, b. 15 Sept. 1922, London, England. British Diplomat. m. Helga Elizabeth Konow Lund, 6 May 1958, 2 sons, 2 daughters. *Education:* Sheen County School; BA, Fitzwilliam House, Cambridge. *Appointments:* Colonial Office, London, 1949-56; British High Commission, New Delhi, 1956-58; Deputy High Commissioner, North Malaya, 1959-63; British High Commission, New Delhi, 1963-66; Commonwealth Office, London, 1966-70; British High Commission, Fiji, 1970-74; Minister, Lagos, 1974-79; Ambassador, Peoples' Republic of Benin, 1975-79; Assistant Under Secretary of State, Foreign and Commonwealth Office, 1979; High Commission, Kenya, 1979-; Permanent British Representative, United Nations Environment Programme, 1979-. *Memberships:* United Oxford and Cambridge Club; Royal Commonwealth Society; Roehampton Club. *Honours:* Recipient of CMG, 1973. *Hobbies:* Tennis; Music. *Address:* 2 Tchui Road, Nairobi, Kenya.

WILLIAMS, Louis Allan, (The Hon., QC) b. 22 May 1922, Glenavon, Saskatchewan, Canada. Lawyer. m. Marjorie Ruth Lake, 25 June 1948, 1 son, 2 daughters. *Education:* BL, University of British Columbia, 1950. *Appointments:* Practised Law, Paine, Edmonds and Company, Vancouver, 1950-75; Minister of Labour, British Columbia, 1975-79; Attorney General, British Columbia, 1979-; Member, British Columbia Legislative Assembly, 1966-. *Honours:* Recipient of Queen's Counsel, 1979. *Address:* 2060 Gisby Street, West Vancouver, British Columbia, Canada.

WILLIAMS, Maurice, b. 18 Apr. 1932, Birmingham, England. Chemist. m. Patricia Audrey Newman, 6 Oct. 1956, 3 sons, 1 daughter. *Education:* BSc, University of Birmingham, 1953; PhD, University of Birmingham, 1956. *Appointments:* Technical Officer, ICI Metals Division, Birmingham, 1956-58; Lecturer, Analytical Chemistry, Birmingham College of Advanced Technology, 1959-65; Managing Editor, Learned Journals, Pergamon Press, Oxford, 1966-68; Executive Secretary, International Union of Pure and Applied Chemistry, 1968-. *Memberships:* Fellow, Royal Society of Chemistry. *Hobbies:* Golf; Swimming. *Address:* 3 Glovers Close, Woodstock, Oxford OX7 1NS, England.

WILLIAMS, Oladipupo Akanni Olumuyiwa, b. 1 Dec. 1946, Lagos, Nigeria. Legal Practitioner. m. Henrietta Maria Asibong Edet, 15 Apr. 1972, 1 son, 3 daughters. *Education:* King's College, Lagos, Nigeria, 1960-64; Sevenoaks School, Kent, England, 1964-66; BL, University College, London, 1968-71; Nigerian Law

School, 1971-72. *Appointments:* A Legal Practitioner in the Chambers of Chief Rotimi Williams, 1972-. *Hobbies:* Travelling; Scrabble; Movies; Music. *Address:* 20 Idowu Martins Street, off Adeola Odeku Street, Victoria Island, Lagos, Nigeria.

WILLIAMS, Owen Tudor, b. 4 Oct. 1916, London, England. Consulting Engineer. m. Rosemary Louisa Mander, 15 Sept. 1943, 4 daughters. *Education:* Shrewsbury School, 1930-34; Cambridge University, 1934-37; BA, 1937; MA, 1941. *Appointments:* Partner, Sir Owen Williams and Partners, Civil and Structural Consulting Engineers, 1946-66; Managing Partner, Sir Owen Williams and Partners, 1966-. *Memberships:* Fellow, Institution of Civil Engineers; Fellow, Institution of Highway Engineers; Institute of Asphalt Technology; Association of Consulting Engineers; Naval and Military Club. *Creative Works:* Responsible for Planning, Design and Supervision of Construction of Major Road and Bridge Projects, Including M1 Luton-Doncaster, M5/M6 Midland Links and M4 Newport and Port Talbot. *Honours:* Recipient of CBE, 1969; Awarded Telford Gold Medal of the Institution of Civil Engineers, 1961. *Address:* 18 Little Gaddesden, Berkhamsted, Hertfordshire, HP4 IPA, England.

WILLIAMS, Ronald Brian, b. 13 June 1929, Canberra, ACT, Australia. Secretary, New South Wales State Cancer Council. m. Ivy, 23 Dec. 1950, 2 sons, 3 daughters. *Education:* Sydney, New South Wales, Australia; DIPEnt, Certificate, Economics, Mathematics, Sydney, 1973. *Appointments:* Royal Australian Navy, Medical Branch, 1946-53; New South Wales Ambulance Transport Service, 1956-59; Health Commission, New South Wales, 1971; Secretary, New South Wales State Cancer Council, 1979-. *Memberships:* President, Royal Australian Navy Association, 1970-78. *Publications:* First Aid at Sea, 1951; First Aid in War at Sea, 1952. *Honours:* Justice of the Peace, New South Wales; Awarded United Nations Service Medal and Korean Star, (Korean War Veteran). *Hobbies:* Jogging, Golf, Fishing; Chess. *Address:* Unit 38/D9, Northcott Place, Belvoir Street, Surrey Hills 2010, New South Wales, Australia.

WILLIAMS, Shirley Vivien Brittain, (Mrs), b. 27 July 1930, London, England. Politician. 1 daughter. *Education:* Eight Schools in United States and United Kingdom; MA, Open Scholar, Somerville College, Oxford; Smith-Mundt Scholar, Columbia University, New York. *Appointments:* Member for Parliament, Hitchin, 1964-74; Member of Parliament, Hertford and Stevenage, 1974-79; Member of Parliament, Crosby, 1981; Parliamentary Secretary, Ministry of Labour, 1966-67; Minister of State, Education and Science, 1967-69; Minister of State, Home Office, 1969-70; Secretary of State, Prices and Consumer Protection, 1974-76; Secretary of State, Education and Science, 1976-79; Professional Fellow, Policy Studies Institute, 1979-; Co-founder, Social Democratic Party, 1981. *Memberships:* National Executive Committee, Labour Party, 1970-81; Chairman, Communications Committee, Social Democratic Party, 1981-. *Publications:* Politics is for People, Penguin, 1981. *Honours:* Godkin Lecturer, Harvard University, Cambridge, Massachuesetts, 1980; Rede Lecturer, Cambridge University, England, 1980; Janeway Lecturer, Princeton, 1981; Honorary Doctor, Sheffield, Leeds, Bath, Heriot-Watt, Leuven, Belgium, Radcliffe, United States of America, Council for National Academic Awards, United Kingdom. *Hobbies:* Music; Rough Walking; Swimming. *Address:* House of Commons, London, SW1A 0AA, England.

WILLIAMS, William Thomas, b. 18 Apr. 1913, Fulham, London, England. Research Consultant. *Education:* Imperial College of Science and Technology, London, 1930-33; ARCS, BSc, First Class Honours, Botany, 1933; PhD, DIC, Plant Physiology, 1940; DSc, London, 1952; Queensland Conservatorium, 1969-72; AMusA, 1971; LMusA, 1972, Pianoforte performing diploma. *Appointments:* War Service: Sgt. R.A., 2/Lt., RAOC, T/Major, REME; Lecturer, Botany, Bedford College, London, 1946-51; Professor, Botany, University of Southampton, 1951-65; Chief Research Scientist, Division of Tropical Pastures, 1968-73; Research Fellow, Townsville, 1973-80; Research Consultant, Australian Institute of Marine Science, 1978-. *Memberships:* Fellow, Australian Academy of Science, 1978; Fellow, Linnean Society; Fellow, Institute of Biology; Agricultural Research Council, United Kingdom; Secretary, Society for Experimental Biology; Sherlock Holmes Society, London; Editor, Journal of Experimental Botany, Clarendon Press; Council Biometric Society. *Publications:* Collection of Broadcast Talks, The Four Prisons of Man; Editor, Part Author, Pattern Analysis in Agricultural Science, CSIRO and Elsevier; About 200 papers in Scientific Journals, mostly on numerical methods and their application to Taxonomy, Ecology and agriculture; Recitals in Townsville of music for two pianos with colleagues. *Honours:* Recipient of OBE, 1980; Hon, DSc, University of Queensland, 1973. *Hobbies:* Music; Drinking beer with mates in local pub. *Address:* 10 Surrey Street, Hyde Park, Townsville, Queensland 4812, Australia.

WILLIAMSON, John Ramsden, b. 31 Oct. 1929, Manchester, England. Teacher, Composer, Pianist. m. (1) 2 sons; (2) Valmai Roberts, 22 Apr. 1976. *Education:* Royal Manchester College of Music, 1949-52; ARMCM, 1952; Licentiate of Royal Academy of Music, 1961; BMus, Dunelm, 1973; Fellow of London College of Music, England, 1977. *Appointments:* School Music Teacher, 5 schools in England & Wales, 1952-76; Piano Tutor, Notre Dame College of Education, 1976-80; Piano Tutor, St. Mary's College, Rhos on Sea, Clwyd; Private Teacher, Pianoforte & Harmony. *Memberships:* Incorporated Society of Musicians; Composer's Guild of Great Britain; Society for the Promotion of New Music. *Creative Works:* Piano Concerto; 8 Piano Sonatas; Flute Sonata; 13 Pianoforte Preludes; 10 Pianoforte Preludes; Cantata for Children, The Pied Piper; Song Cycle, A Shropshire Lad; String Quartet; numerous Pianoforte Miniatures; publication: 10 Pianoforte Pieces, Musical Pictures. *Honours:* Barlow Cup for Composition, Chester Music Festival, 1972, 1978, 1979; First Prize, Phys James Eisteddfod, Lampeter, 1971. *Hobbies:* Gardening; Cycling; DIY activities. *Address:* 11A Calthorpe Drive, Prestatyn, Clwyd, LL19 9RF, Wales.

WILLSON, Alan John, b. 26 Sept. 1932, Coventry England. University Teacher of Mathematics. m. Jillian Simpson Ball, 27 July, 1957, 2 daughters. *Education:* King Henry VIII School, Coventry, England, 1943-50; St. John's College, Cambridge, 1950-57; BA, 1953; MA, 1957; PhD, 1957. *Appointments:* Teacher of Mathematics, Clifton College, Bristol, 1957-59; Head of Mathematics Department, 1959-63; Department of Mathematics, University of Leicester, Lecturer, 1963, Senior Lecturer, 1965, Reader in Mathematics, 1968.-. *Memberships:* Fellow of Cambridge Philosophical Society; British Society of Theology; Fellow, Institute of Mathematics and its applications. *Publications:* Many papers in scientific journals in applied mathematics. *Honours:* Fellow, St. John's College, Cambridge, 1958-61. *Hobbies:* Chess, Local History. *Address:* 2 Landscape Drive, Evington, Leicester, England.

WILSON, Albert John Greene, b. 20 Jan. 1907, Hamilton, Ontario, Canada. Barrister at Law. m. (1) 2 sons, 2 daughters; (2) Helen R Helson, 7 Apr. 1973. *Education:* BA, University of Toronto, Canada, 1930; MA, University of Toronto, Canada, 1933; Barrister at Law, Osgoode Hall Law School, 1933; Called to Bar of Ontario, 1935. *Appointments:* Practice Law, Toronto, Ontario, Canada, 1935-41; Canadian Army, Legal Officer, 1942-46; Partner, MacGregor & Wilson, 1946-71; Counsel, MacGregor, Wilson & MacKerrow, 1972-75. *Memberships:* Past President, Multiple Sclerosis Society of Canada; Royal Canadian Legion, International Legal Fraternity of Phi Delta Phi; Auguston Society & Fellow of the Society of Antiquaries of Scotland. *Honours:* Hospitaller Order of Saint John of Jerusalem; Order of the Crown of Yugoslavia; Order of St. Sava; Order of St. Lazarus. *Hobbies:* History; Travel & Phalerology. *Address:* 57 Lytton Boulevard, Toronto, Canada M4R 1L2.

WILSON, Brian Graham, b. 9 Apr. 1930, Belfast, Northern Ireland. University, Vice-Chancellor. m. (1) Barbara Elizabeth Wilke, (2) Margaret Jeanne Henry, (1) 27 May, 1959; (2) 22 Apr, 1978, 2 sons, 1 daughter. *Education:* BSc, University of Belfast, 1952; PhD, National University Ireland, 1956. *Appointments:* Postdoctoral Fellow, National Research Council, Canada, 1955-57; Officer-in-Charge, Sulphur Mt. Laboratory, 1957-60; Associate Research Officer, 1959-60; Associate Professor, Physics, University Calgary, 1960-65; Professor, 1965-70; Dean, Arts and Science, 1967-70; Professor Astronomy & Academic Vice President, Simon Fraser University, 1970-78; Vice Chancellor, University of Queensland, 1979.- *Memberships:* Canadian Association of Physicists. *Honours:* 50 Research publications, principally on cosmic rays and X-ray astrophysics. *Hobbies:* Fishing; Swimming. *Address:* 55 Walcott Street, St. Lucia, 4067, Queensland, Australia.

WILSON, Charles William Edgar, b. 29 Nov. 1924, Charlton, Victoria, Australia. Medicine, Consultant Physician. m. Margaret R. Diederich, 6th Sept. 1952, 3 sons, 3 daughters. *Education:* MB, BS, Melbourne University, Melbourne, 1948; MRCP, London, 1956; MRACP, 1958; FRACP, 1973. *Appointments:* Assistant Medical Superintendant, Alfred Hospital, Melbourne, 1951; Alfred Hospital, 1952-53; RGH, Heidelberg, 1954-56; Assistant to Dr.Avery Jones & Dr. Richard Doll, Central Middlesex Hospital, London, 1956-58; Physician, Bon Hill Hospital, Melbourne, 1958-; Physician, Department Veterans Affairs, Victoria, 1960-68. *Memberships:* Australian Medical Association; Navel and Military Club; Commonwealth Golf Club; Melbourne Cricket Club; Alfred Hospital. *Publications:* Mortality of Gas Workers with Special Reference to Cancers of Lung, Blader, Chronic Bronchitis & Pneumoconiosios, *Hobbies:* Tennis; Golf; Trekking; Theatre. *Address:* 6 Fairview Grove, Glen Iris 3146, Australia.

WILSON, David MacKenzie, b. 30 Oct. 1931, Dacre Banks, Director of the British Museum. m. Eva Sjogren, 1955, 1 son, 1 daughter. *Education:* LittD, St. John's College Cambridge, Lund University, Sweden. *Appointments:* Research Assistant, Cambridge University; Assistant Keeper, British Museum; Reader in Archaeology of Anglo-Saxon Period, University of London; Professor of Medieval Archaeology, University of London; Joint Head of Scandinavian Studies, University College, London; Director, British Museum. *Memberships:* BA, FSA, MRIA, Royal Swedish Academy of Science; Royal Gustav Adolf's Academy, Sweden; German Archaeological Institute; Royal Academy of Science and Letters, Gothenburg, Sweden; Honorary Member, Vetenskapssocienteten, Lund Sweden; Polish Archaeological & Numismatic Society; *Honours:* Viking Art, 1966; The Anglo-Saxons, 1960; Anglo-Saxon Metalwork 700-100, British Museum, 1964; The Vikings and Their Origins, 1970; The Viking Achievement, 1970; Reflections on the St Ninians Isle Treasure, 1970; The Viking Age in the Isle of Man, 1974; Anglo-Saxon Archaeology, 1976; The Northern World, 1980. *Honours:* Recipient of Dag Stromback Prize, Royal Gustav Adolf's Academy, 1975; Felix Neubergh Prize, 1978. *Address:* The Lifeboat House, Castletown, Isle of Man.

WILSON, Elizabeth Hornabrook, b. 25 Jan. 1907, Adelaide,South Australia. m. Keith Cameron Wilson (Sir), 24 May, 1930, 2 sons, 1 daughter. 02 Educated at Creveen Private School, North Adelaide, 1913-1923. *Memberships:* Executive Member, Victoria League for Commonwealth Friendship, South Australia, 1930-; Chairman, Victoria League National committee, 1955-58, 1967-70; Past Chairman, Joint Commonwealth Societies Council, South Australia; Executive Member, Australian Red Cross Society, South Australian Division, 1947-; Chairman South Australian Division, 1969-71; President, Tusmore Red Cross Branch, 1939-69, 1973-80; Central Committee Mothers & Babies Health Association, 1945-, President, 1975-; Council member, Liberal Party of Australia, South Australian Division, 1969-81; Vice President, Liberal Party of Australia, 1954-55; President, Austcare, South Australia, 1969-76; Patron of Austcare, South Australia, 1976-81; Patron, Civilian Widows Association, South Australia, 1960-; Patron, Cornish Association in South Australia. *Honours:* Member of the Order of the British Empire, 1947; Commander of the Order of the British Empire, 1959. *Address:* 79 Tusmore Avenue, Tusmore, South Australia.

WILSON, Helen Helga, (Mrs Edward L. Wilson), b. 25 Jan, 1902, Zeehan, Tasmania, Australia, Author. m. Edward L Wilson, 20th Dec. 1928, 2 sons, 1 daughter. *Education:* BA, University of Western Australia, 1923; *Appointments:* Free Lance Journalist; Author. *Memberships:* Australian Society of PEN International, Sydney; Society of Women Writers; Fellowship of Australian Writers; Karrakatta Club, Perth, Western Australia. *Publications:* Quiet, Brat; The Golden Age; If Golde Rust; Where the Wind's Feet Shine; Island of Fire, 1972; Bring Back the Hour, 1977; The Mulga Trees, 1980; Short Stories Collections: A Show of Colours;

The Skedule & Other 15 prize winning stories; Published in seven countries and in six other Anthologies; Australiana: Gateways to Gold, Westward, Gold; The Golden Miles; Cyclone Coasts of North West Australia. *Honours:* Order of Australia Medal, 1980; Accredited Observer to UN Conference in New Delhi, 1962, for International Association of University Woman as Historian, 1975. *Hobbies:* Travelling; Reading; Swimming. *Address:* 40 Bower Street, Manly, New South Wales, Australia.

WILSON, Howie Keith Forbes, b. 4th Nov. 1930, Auckland, New Zealand. Surgeon and Reconstructive Surgeon. m. Barbara Joyce Batty, 3 Oct. 1958, 1 son, 2 daughters. *Education:* MB,ChB, New Zealand, 1954; FRCS Ed, 1959; FRACS, 1962; FRCS, 1959. *Appointments:* Resident Surgical Officer, Waikato Hospital Board, 1961-62; Plastic Surgical Registrar, Middlemore Hospital, 1962-63; General and Plastic Surgeon, Waikato Hospital Board, 1963-; Plastic Surgical Specialist, Middlemore Hospital, Auckland, 1971-72; Central Specialists Committee, 1978-. *Memberships:* Royal New Zealand Yacht Squadron; Section of Plastic Surgery Royal Australasian College of Surgeons; New Zealand Association of Plastic and Reconstructive Surgeons; New Zealand Association of Hand Surgeons; The Australasian Society of Aesthetic Plastic Surgery; The National Confederation of Plastic Surgeons; Central Specialists Committee; Royal Akarana Yacht Club; Ruapehu Ski Club. *Publications:* Use of Neuromuscular Stimulator in Nerve Injuries; Use of Parallel Incisions for Block Dissection of the Groin. *Hobbies:* Yachting and Skiing; Master of pleasure yacht (ocean). *Address:* 98 Lake Crescent, Hamilton, New Zealand.

WILSON, Ian Brownlie, b. 20 Sept. 1929, Brisbane, Australia. Dental Periodontist. m. Marion Elizabeth Jackson, 29th Nov. 1956, 2 sons, 3 daughters. *Education:* BDSc, Tertiary, University of Queensland, 1947-51; DDS, University of Toronto, 1954; BSc, University of Toronto, 1956; Fellow of the Royal Australian College of Dental Surgeons, Fellow of the International College of Dentists. *Appointments:* Private Practice, Brisbane, 1951-52; Private Practice, London, 1952-53; Specialist Practice, Hamilton, Ontario, 1956-57; University of Toronto Staff, Part time, 1954-56; University of Queensland, Part time, 1959-64; Specialist Practice, Brisbane, 1958-. *Memberships:* Rotary Club of Brisbane; Delta Sigma Delta Fraternity; United Service Club; Tattersall's Club; Australian Society of Periodontology, Federal President, 1967-70: Queensland President, Australian Dental Association, 1965; Royal Australian College of Dental Surgeons; Dental Circle Study Club, Past President; Board of Faculty of Dentistry, University of Queensland, 1959-71; Dental Board of Queensland, 1970-75; National Health and Medical Research Council of Australia, Dental Health Committee, 1970-76; Consultant Periodontist, WHO, 1969-; Vice President, 19th Australian Dental Congress, 1970; Wing Commander, RAAF Reserve; Consultant, Mater Misercordiae Hospital, 1959-71; Consultant, Montrose Home for Crippled Children, 1959-78; Honorary Life Member, Australian Society of Periodontology, 1980. *Hobbies:* Horse Stud; Breeding Appaloosa Sprint Race Horses. *Address:* 20 Deerhurst Road, Brookfield 4069, Brisbane, Australia.

WILSON, Jeanne Patricia Pauline, b. 31 May, 1920, London, England. Author, Novelist and Playwright. m. Dr. Wilbert Jeffrey-Smith Wilson, 12 July, 1943, 1 son. *Appointments:* Teacher of Speech and Drama, Wolmer's Girls' School, Kingston, Jamaica, West Indies, 1960-67; Full time writer, 1967-. *Memberships:* PEN, Jamaica Centre, President, 1979-81; Society of Authors, England; Authors Guild, USA; Writers Union of Jamaica, on Executive Committee. *Publications:* Weep in the Sun, 1976; Troubled Heritage, 1977; Mulatto, 1978; The Golden Harlot, 1979 and 1980; Holiday With Guns, children's adventure, 1977; Flight from the Islands, 1978; The House that Liked to Travel, 1978; Various West Indian Plays and other novels. *Honours:* Jamaica Independance Festival Award, 1965; Jamaica Independence Festival Award, 1966; Institute of Jamaica Centenary Medal, 1980. *Hobbies:* Reading; Cooking; Swimming; Working. *Address:* 19k Old Waterloo Place, 19 Waterloo Road, Kingston 10, Jamaica, West Indies.

WILSON, John, b. 17 Nov. 1918, Filey, England. Schoolmaster. m. Eileen M. Edwards, 25 Mar. 1937, 2 sons, 3 daughters. *Education:* Cambridge School Certificate, 1934; Colchester High School. *Appointments:* Engineering Industry, 1935-40; Army Service Rhodesia, 1941-45; Engineering Industry, 1946-61; Education, Teaching Technical Subjects, 1962-. *Memberships:* Educational Institute of Design, Craft & Technology; Zimbabwe Teachers Association. *Hobbies:* Lapidary; Motor Sport, building specials. *Address:* Sinoia High School, Sinoia, Zimbabwe.

WILSON, John Foster, (Sir), b. 20 Jan. 1919, Nottingham, England. International Health Administrator. m. Chloe J. Macdermid, 1944, 2 daughters. *Education:* BA, MA, University of Oxford, Honours School of Jurisprudence, 1937-41. *Appointments:* Teaching Appointments, Oxford University, 1941-42; Assistant Secretary of Royal National Institute for the Blind, 1941-49; British Delegation Touring Africa & Middle East, 1946-47; Founded and first Director of Royal Commonwealth Society for the Blind, 1950; Director, Royal Commonwealth Society for the Blind; President, International Agency for the Prevention of Blindness. *Memberships:* Royal Commonwealth Society. *Publications:* Blindness in British African and near East Territories, 1947; Ghana's Handicapped Citizens, 1960; Travelling Blind, 1962; World Blindness and its Prevention, 1980. *Honours:* CBE, 1965; Knighthood, 1975; Helen Keller International Award, 1970; Leslie Dana Gold Medal, 1976; Lions International Humanitarian Award, 1978; World Humanity Award, 1979; Albert Lasker Special Public Service Award, 1979. *Address:* 22 The Cliff, Roedean, Brighton, Sussex, England.

WILSON, Keith, b. 18 Mar. 1933, Rugby, Warwickshire. Engineer. m. Angela V. Walker, 12 Aug. 1967, 1 son, 1 daughter. *Education:* Matric., C.Eng., FI Mech.E, Birmingham University, 1949-54. *Appointments:* Commander, Royal Navy Graduate Entry, 1954-60; Chief Mechanical Engineer, George Robinson Consulting Engineers, 1960-67; Executive Manager, Kaiser Aluminum Technical Services Inc., 1964-74; Managing Director, Associated Design Group Pty. Ltd, Engineering Managers, 1975-. *Publications:* Various technical publications on Mechanical Engineering subjects. *Hobbies:* Flying; Sailing. *Address:* 32 Barnic Road, Heathmont, Victoria 3135, Australia.

WILSON, Leslie Kenneth Sloan, b. 10 Aug. 1920, Bulawayo, Zimbabwe. Retired Attorney-Solicitor, Director of Companies. m. Joan E. Bradshaw, 21 July, 1945, 2 sons, 2 daughters. *Education:* Attorney at Law, Notary Public and Conveyancer, admitted High Court of Southern Rhodesia, 1951; Admitted Supreme Court of South Africa, Cape Provincial Division, 1958. *Appointments:* Former Partner, Law firm of Gill, Godlonton & Gerrans; later Surgey, Pittman & Kerswell; Chairman, UDC Ltd; Field Industries Ltd; Casalee Zimbabwe Tobacco Ltd; Zimbabwe Inter-Africa News Agency (Ziana) Ltd, Director of CAPS Holdings Ltd; Director, Agricair Ltd; Director, Vanguard Ltd and several smaller companies; Former Chairman of Ministerial and members of Parliament Salaries Commission; Raw Sugar Price Commission etc.; Governor of Ruzawi Schools and others. *Memberships:* RAF Club, London; Farmers' Club, London, Salisbury Club, Zimbawe; Founder Chairman, Conservation Trust of Zimbabwe; Trustee of Family Planning Association of Zimbabwe; Trustee Central Bursary Fund for Independent Schools, Zimbabwe. *Publications:* Report on Prime Minister's, Ministerial & Members of Parliament Salaries for Zimbabwe; Report on Raw Sugar Price for Cane Growers from Millers in Zimbabwe. *Hobbies:* Fishing; Gardening; Game Conservation. *Address:* Kingsmead House, PO Borrowdale, Zimbabwe.

WILSON, Lynton Ronald, b. 3 Apr. 1940, Welland, Ontario, Canada. Civil Servant. m. Brenda J. Black, 23 Dec. 1968, 1 son, 2 daughters. *Education:* BA, McMaster University, Hamilton, Ontario, Canada, 1958-62; MA, Cornell University, Ithaca, New York, USA, 1967. *Appointments:* Deputy Minister, Government of Ontario, Ministry of Industry and Tourism, 1978-81; President, Chief Executive Officer, Redpath Industries Ltd., Toronto, Ontario, Canada, 1981; Director and Member of Executive Committee, Niagara Institute; Director, Ontario Place Corporation; Director, Ontario Energy Corporation; Executive Director, Policy and Priorities Division, 1977-78; Strategic Planning and Development, MacMillan Bloedel Ltd, Vancouver, British Columbia, 1973-74; Vice President and Director, Walpose

Wooworkers Inc., Walpole, Massachusetts, 1974-77; President, Atlantic Forest Products, Inc., 1974-77; Vice President and Director, MacMillan Bloedel Enterprises Inc., Boston, Massachusetts, 1974-77; Director, Habitant Shops, Inc. 1976-77; Director, Industrial America Corporation, Jacksonville, Florida, 1975-76; Government of Ontario, 1972-73; Secretary, Joint Committee on Economic Policy; Consultant to Canadian Committee on the Business Environment; Consultant to Hudson Institute, New York; Government of Canada, 1971-72; Department of Finance, Working Group on Foreign Investment, 1971-72; Ministry of State for Science and Technology, Co-ordinator, Industrial R & D Policy, 1972; John Labatt Limited, London, Ontario, 1969-71; Coporate Economist, 1969-70; Director of Economic Research, 1970 71; Teaching Assistant, Cornell University, Department of Economics, 1968-69, Government of Canada, Department of Trade and Commerce, Foreign Service Officer, Trade Commissioner Service, 1962-68; Assistant Commercial Secretary, Canadian Embassy Vienna, Austria, 1963-65; Second Secretary, Commercial, Canadian Embassy, Tokyo, Japan, 1967-68. *Memberships:* Rideau Club, Ottawa; Board of Trade, Toronto. *Honours:* McMaster University Honour Society, 1962; Woodrow Wilson National Fellowship, Cornell University, 1965-66; McVoy Endowment Fellowship, Cornell University, 1966-67; Phi Kappa Phi Honour Society, Cornell University, 1967. *Hobbies:* Golf; Skiing; Tennis; Swimming. *Address:* 769 Cardinal Place, Mississauga, Ontario, Canada, L5J 2R8.

WILSON, Roger Lenox Kirkland, b. 26 Mar. 1946, Dunedin, New Zealand. Medical Practitioner. m. Jill E. Slade, 19 Nov. 1977, 2 sons. *Education:* Lincoln College, University Canterbury, 1966-68; BAg Science, 1969; Master of Economics, University of New England, NSW, Australia 1971; MBChB, University of Otago, Dunedin, New Zealand, 1977. *Appointments:* Research Fellow, University of New England, 1969-70; Market Economist, Australian Wheat Board, 1971-72; House Surgeon, Dunedin hospital, 1978; Acting Registrar, Dunedin Hospital, 1979; Resgistrar Surgery, 1980; Registrar ENT Department, Dunedin Hospital, 1981; ENT Registrar, Auckland Hospital Group, 1982. *Memberships:* President, Otago Medical Students Association, 1974-75; Vice President, Australasian Medical Students Association, 1974-75; President, Otago Branch, New Zealand, Resident Medical Officers Association, 1978-80. *Publications:* Oesophageal Diverticula, Principles of Management and Appraisal of Classification; John Borrie and Roger Wilson, Thorax, 1970, Vol 3 No.10; Autoimmune Senorineural Deafness: Case Report, co-author Ian A Stewart, 1981. *Honours:* Sir Gordon Bell Prize in Surgery, Otago Medical School, 1977; Stanley Batchelor Prize in Surgery, Otago Medical School, 1977. *Hobbies:* Rec. Squash; Gardening; Tennis; Swimming. *Address:* 511 Manukau Road, Epsom, Auckland, New Zealand.

WILSON, Roland, b. 7 Apr. 1904, Ulverstone, Tasmania. Economist, Financial Consultant, formerly Civil Servant. m. (1) Valeska Thompson (dec'd), 15 June, 1930; (2) Joyce C. Chivers, 18 Jan. 1975. *Education:* B.Com, University of Tasmania, 1922-25; Diploma Economics & Political Science, University of Oxford, Oriel College, 1925-28; D.Phil (Oxon), 1929; Rhodes Scholar for Tasmania, 1925-28; Commonwealth Fund Fellow, 1928-30; PhD, University of Chicago, 1928-30. *Appointments:* Lecturer in Economics, University of Tasmania, 1930-32; Assistant, Commonwealth Statistician & Economist, 1932-35; Commonwealth Statistician & Economic Adviser to Treasury, 1936-51; Permanent Head, Department of Labour & National Service, 1941-46; Secretary to the Treasury, 1951-66; Chairman, Commonwealth Banking Corporation, 1966-75; Chairman, Qantas Airways Ltd, 1966-73; Company Directorships, included, Wentworth Hotel, ICI Australia Ltd, MLC Assurance Co. Ltd, Australian-European Finance Corporation, 1966 *Memberships:* Economic Society of Australia & New Zealand; Fellow of Royal Statistical Society; Australia-Mexico Association, Former President; Honorary Fellow, The Academny of Social Sciences in Australia; Former Fellow, Informational Institute of Statistics. *Publications:* Capital Imports and the Terms of Trade, 1931; Public & Private Investment in Australia, 1939; Facts & Fancies of Productivity, 1946 *Honours:* Beit Essay Prize, Oxford, 1929; Chairman, United Nations Economic & Employment Commission, 1948-51; CBE, 1941; Knight Bachelor, 1955; KBE, 1965; Hon.LL.D. University of Tasmania, 1969. *Hobbies:* Cabinet Making; Engineering. *Address:* 64 Empire Circuit, Forrest, Canberra, ACT 2603, Australia.

WILSON, Winifred Dorothy, b. 4 Mar. 1918, Northern Ireland. Community Development Officer. *Education:* Institute of Chartered Surveyors Certificate, 1949. *Appointments:* Housing Manager, Capetown City Council, 1950-56; Welfare Officer, Buawayo City Council, 1960-64; Community Development Officer in charge of Women Section, Government, 1964-. *Memberships:* President, Soroptimist International Council of Zimbabwe, 1978; National Federation of Business & Professional Women of Zimbabwe. *Honours:* Awarded Leadership Grant by US Government, 1962; Member, Legion of Merit, 1977. *Hobbies:* Reading; Writing; Bridge. *Address:* c/o Tarr, 28 Selous Road, Highlands, Salisbury, Zimbabwe.

WIMALASENA, Nanediri, JP, b. 1914, Ceylonese Lawyer. m. Prema Fernando, 1938, 1 son, 2 daughters. *Education:* Ananda College, Colombo; Ceylon University College, Ceylon Law College; Attorney at Law. *Appointments:* Elected Member of the Kandy Municipal Council, 1946, remaining a member for unbroken period of 21 years; Deputy Mayor Kandy, 1946; Mayor, 1963; Elected Member of Parliament for Senkadagala, 1960, 1965, 1970-77; Deputy Minister of Finance, 1965-70; High Commissioner for Sri Lanka to the Court of St. James's, 1977-. *Memberships:* Law Society in Sri Lanka. *Address:* 35 Avenue Road, St. John's Wood, London NW8, England.

WING, Lindsay William, b. 4 Apr. 1939, Sydney, NSW, Australia. Medical. m. Andrea M. Smith, 12 Dec. 1964, 2 sons, 2 daughters. *Education:* MB, BS, Sydney University, 1962; DLO, Sydney University, 1968; FRACS, 1968. *Appointments:* Self employed Ear Nose & Throat Surgeon, 1968-; Visiting Surgeon, Royal Hobart Hospital, 1968-; Consultant Head & Neck Surgeon, Peter McCallum Clinic, 1968-; Lecturer in Ear, Nose and Throat and Anatomy, University of Tasmania, 1968-; Editorial Committee, Australian & New Zealand Journal of Surgery. *Memberships:* Federal Councillor, Royal Australian College of Surgeons; Federal Councillor, Australian Association of Surgeons; Federal Councillor, Otolaryngological Society of Australia; Clinical Oncological Society of Australia; AMA. *Publications:* Medical publications over 14 years. *Hobbies:* Golf; Farming. *Address:* Greystanes, 3 Melrose Court, Sandy Bay 7005, Australia.

WINNER, Michael Robert, b. 30 Oct. 1935, London, England. Film Director & Producer. *Education:* MA, Downing College, Cambridge University. *Appointments:* Film Critic and Fleet Street Journalist and contributor to: The Spectator, Daily Express, London Evening Standard, etc; Panellist, Any Questions, BBC Radio; Entered Motion Pictures, 1956, Screen Writer, Assistant Director, Editor; Films include: Director, Play It Cool, 1962; Director and Writer, The Cool Mikado, 1962; Director, West Eleven, 1963; Producer and Director, The System, 1963; Producer, Director, Writer, You Must Be Joking, 1965; Producer, Director, Writer, The Jokers, 1966; Producer and Director, I'll never Forget What's 'Is Name, 1967; Producer, Director Writer, Hannibal Brooks, 1968; Producer, Director, The Games, 1969; Producer, Writer, Lawman, 1970; Producer, Director, The Nightcomers, 1971; Producer, Director, Chato's Land, 1971; Director, The Mechanic, 1972; Producer and Director, Scorpio, 1972; Producer, Director, The Stone Killer, 1973; Producer, Director, Death Wish, 1974; Producer and Director, Won Ton Ton The Dog That Saved Hollywood, 1975; Producer, Director, Writer, The Sentinel, 1976; Producer, Director, Writer, The Big Sleep, 1977; Producer Director, Firepower, 1978; Producer, Director, Writer, Death Wish II, 1981; Theatre Productions: The Tempest, Wyndhams, 1974; A Day in Hollywood a Night in the Ukraine, Mayfair, 1978. *Hobbies:* Walking around Art Galleries, Museums and Antique Shops. *Address:* 6/8 Sackville Street, London, W1X 1DD, England.

WINNY, Herbert Frank, b. 12 Apr. 1908, Purley, Surrey. Aeronautical Engineer. m. Sarah M.D. Dalley, 20 July, 1946, 1 son, 2 daughters. *Education:* BSc, Queen Mary College, University London, 1927; PhD, Imperial College, 1930. *Appointments:* Fairey Aviation Co. Ltd, Hayes, Middlesex, 1932; Deputy Chief Technician, 1943; Chief Technician, 1947; Head of Design,

1949; Chief Designer, 1961; Head of Advanced Technology, Westland Helicopters Ltd, Yeovil, 1966; Southall Technical College, Part time Lecturer, Aerodynamics, 1939; Part time Lecturer in structures, University Southampton, 1978-81. *Memberships:* Fellow, Royal Aero. Society, 1944; Chairman, Rotorcraft Section, 1972; Fellow, Institute Mechanical Engineers, 1956; Chartered Engineer. *Publications:* Skin friction of Flat Plates to Oseen's Approximation, 1933; The Distribution of Stress in Monocoque Wings, 1937; Use of Carbon Fibre Composites in Helicopters, 1971; Other publications in Journals etc. on similar subjects. *Hobbies:* Carpentry; Bricklaying; Walking; Swimming; Chess. *Address:* Wincroft, Camp Road, Gerrards Cross, Bucks, SL9 7PD, England.

WINSTON, William Arthur, b. 17 Nov. 1945, Roseau, Dominica. Medical Psychologist. m. Veronica I. Winston, 9 Aug. 1969. *Education:* BSc, 1974; MSc, 1976; Diploma in Psychological Medicine; Diploma in Orthomolecular Medicine. *Appointments:* Director of the Psychological Clinic for the Promotion of Psycho-Nutrition. *Memberships:* International Academy of Preventive Medicine; Orthomolecular Medical Society; International Academy of Biological Medicine; Academy of Orthomolecular Psychiatry; Royal Institute of Medical Psychologist; International Academy of Psychopathologist. *Honours:* Articles in local newspapers; Books on Criminology and Psychology; Booklet on Orthomolecular Medicine. *Honours:* An Award in Psychodietetics, 1980; An Award in Psychonutrition, 1981; Orthomolecular Therapy, 1981. *Hobbies:* Lawn Tennis; Coin and Stamp Collecting; Golf. *Address:* Bradfield House, County Road, St. Michael, Barbados.

WINTON, Leslie Faulks, b. 21 June, 1945. Sydney, Australia. Researcher. m. Clelia, 22 Dec. 1972, 1 daughter. *Education:* BA, 1973; Dip.Ed, 1974. *Appointments:* Marketing, 1962-66; National Service, 1966-68; Fulltime University, 1969; Executive Director, ANOP, Marketing Research, 1975-. *Memberships:* Market Research Society; Geographical Society; Statistical Society. *Honours:* Numerous journal articles; Craft Exhibits. *Hobbies:* Photography; Bush Walking; Bird Watching; Coin Collecting; Jewellery Making; Stained Glass craft; Letter writing; Journalisim; Pre-History; Archeology; Anthropology; Sociology. *Address:* 79 Clanville Road, Roseville, New South Wales, Australia 2069.

WISE, Douglass, b. 6 Nov. 1927, Redcar, Yorkshire, England. Architect. m. Yvonne Jeannine Czeiler, 8 Mar. 1958, 1 son, 1 daughter. *Education:* Bachelor of Architecture, School of Architecture, Kings College, Newcastle, University of Durham, 1951; Diploma in Town Planning, School of Town Planning, Kings College, Newcastle, University of Durham, 1952; Fellow of Royal Institute of British Architecture, 1958. *Appointments:* Principal, Douglass Wise & Partners, Architects, 1959-; Lecturer, Newcastle University, School of Architecture, 1959-65; Professor of Architecture, Newcastle University, School of Architecture, 1965-70; Head of Department, Newcastle University, School of Architecture, 1970-75; Professor of Architecture & Director, Institute of Advanced Architectural Studies, University of York, 1975-. *Memberships:* Chairman, RIBA Committee of Moderators, 1965-73; Chairman, RIBA Examinations Committee, 1965-73; Chairman, RIBA, Special Entry Committee, 1965-73; RIBA Council, 1976-79; Vice-Chairman, North Housing Group, 1974-77. *Publications:* Various publications on Architectural Design & Theory. *Honours:* OBE, 1980. *Hobbies:* Painting; Natural History; Gardening. *Address:* 4 The Green, Skelton, York, YO3 6XU, England.

WISKICH, Joseph Tony, b. 21 July, 1935, Tully, Queensland, Australia. University Reader/Plant Biochemist. m. Diane Lesley Millard, 20 Apr. 1968, 3 sons. *Education:* BSc, University of Sydney, Australia, 1955; BSc(Hons), 1956; PhD, 1960. *Appointments:* Teaching Fellow, University of Sydney, Australia, 1957-60; Post Doctoral Fellow, University of Pennsylvania, 1961-62; Post Doctoral Fellow, University of California, Los Angeles, 1962-63; Post Doctoral Fellow, University of Adelaide, 1963-64; Lecturer, University of Adelaide, 1964-68; Senior Lecturer, University of Adelaide, 1969-74; Reader, University of Adelaide, 1975-. *Memberships:* Biochemical Society, London; American Society Plant Physiologists; American Association, Advance Science; Japanese Society Plant Physiologists; Australian Society Plant Physiologists; Australian Biochemical Society; Australian, New Zealand Association, Advance Science. *Publications:* Original Scientific Publications. *Hobbies:* Sport; Photography. *Address:* 59 Park Road, Kensington Part, South Australia 5068, Australia.

WITT, Howell Arthur John, b. 12 July, 1920, Newport, Gwent, UK. Bishop. m. Gertrude Doreen Edwards, 18 June, 1949, 3 sons, 2 daughters. *Education:* BA, Leeds University; College of Resurrection, Mirfield, Yorkshire. *Appointments:* Assistant Curate, Usk, Gwent, 1944-47; Assistant Curate, Camberwell, 1948-49; Chaplain Woomera Rocket Range, South Australia, 1949-54; Rector St. Mary Magdalene's City & Diocese of Adelaide, 1954-57; Priest in Charge, Elizabeth, 1951-65; Missioner, St. Peter's College Mission, 1954-65; Consecrated Bishop, North West Australia, 1965; Bishop of Bathurst, 1981. *Publications:* Bush Bishop, 1979. *Hobbies:* TV Script Writing. *Address:* PO Box 23, Bathurst, New South Wales 2795, Australia.

WOJDAN, Alexandra Helena, (Mrs. Marian Wojdan) b. 19 May, 1936, Lwow, Poland. Pharmacologist. m. 22 Aug. 1959, 1 son, 1 daughter. *Education:* Master of Pharmacy Degree, Wroclaw Academy of Medicine, 1957. *Appointments:* Assistant Chair of Bromatology, Wroclaw Academy of Medicine, 1958-59; Senior Scientist, Department of Pharmacology, Ayerst Research Laboratories, 1960-. *Memberships:* The Pharmacological Society of Canada. *Publications:* Borella, L., Herr, F., Wojdan, A.: Prolongation of certain effects of amphetamine by chlorpromazine, Canad. J. Physiol. Pharmacol, 1969; The effect of stimulants of gastric acid secretion on the development of multiple ulcers in the rat, 1971. *Hobbies:* Philately. *Address:* 2115 Decelles, Montreal, Canada, H4M 1B6.

WOLF, Joseph, Dr., b. 5 Apr. 1914, London, UK. Private Medical Practitioner. m. Loi Hiang Chiew, 18 Oct. 1976, 3 sons 2 daughters. *Education:* Tentative stidues in Philosophy, Psychology & Arts, Bonn University, 1933-35; Initial study of medicine, Wuerzburg & Bonn University, 1935-37; Completed studies, as a Refugee from Nazi Germany, National University of Ireland, MB, BCh, BAO, 1943; Postgraduate Midwifery Diploma of LM, National Maternity Hospital, Dublin, 1943; MD, Bonn University, 1958. *Appointments:* Various Junior Hospital Posts in England, 1943-45; Senior Medical Officer & Surgical Registrar, St. Giles' Hospital, London, 1945-50; Medical Abstractor, British Medical Journal, London, 1948-50; Medical Officer, Psychiatry, Brentwood Mental Hospital & Leybourne Grange Mental Deficiency Colony, UK, 1951-52; Medical Officer, Colonial Medical Service, Malaya & Brunei, 1952-61; Private Medical Practice, Tawau, Sabah, Malaysia, 1962-; Visting Medical Officer, BAL Estates, Commonwealth Development Corporation, Tawau, 1974-. *Memberships:* British Medical Association, London; Sabah Medical Association; Hong Kong Medical Association; Medical Defence Union, London; Life Fellow, International Biographical Association; Cambridge; Royal Overseas League, London; Tawau Sports Club. *Publications:* Numerous publications to professional journals including: Larson-Johansson's Disease of the Patella, 1951; Testosterone Therapy for Fractures & Certain Malignant & Non-Malignant Bone Conditions, 1955; Case of Fallot's Tetralogy with Multiple Congenital Abnormalities, 1955; Chinese Bound Feet, 1958 & 59. *Honours:* Include: Distinction Award, Plus money prize award granted by West-German University of Bonn, 1958. *Hobbies:* Music, especially piano playing; Colour Photography; Cinematography; Reading; Motoring; Air Travel. *Address:* 2218 Salleh Road, PO Box 567, Tawau, Sabah, Malaysia.

WOLFE, James Nathan, b. 16 Sept. 1927, Montreal, Canada. Professor of Economics. m. Monica Anne Hart, 14 Apr. 1954, 1 daughter. *Education:* BA, McGill University, 1948; MA, McGill University, 1949; Glasgow University; BLitt, Queen's and Nuffield Colleges, Oxford, 1952. *Appointments:* Professor of Economics, University of Edinburgh, 1964-; Lecturer in Political Economy, University of Toronto, 1952-60; Professor of Economics, University of California, Berkeley and Santa Barbara, 1960-64; Brookings Research Professor, 1963-64; Economic Consultant to National Economic Development Office, 1963-64; Economic Consultant to Secretary of State, Scotland, 1965-72; Economic Consultant to Department Economic Affairs, 1965-69; In-

ter-Department Committee, Long Term Population Distribution, 1966-69. *Memberships:* Athenaeum; New Club; New Scottish Arts; American Economic Association; Royal Economic Society. *Publications:* Editor, Government and Nationalism in Scotland, 1969; The Economics of Technical Information Systems, 1974; Clinical Practice and Economics, 1977; An Economic Survey of the Church of Scotland, 1980; Articles in Learned Journals. *Hobbies:* Books; Friends; Golden Retriever, Marshall. *Address:* 3 St. Margarets Road, Edinburgh EH9 1AZ, Scotland.

WOLFF, Terrance Alban, b. 4 Nov. 1931, Peterborough, Ontario, Canada. President & Chief Executive Officer, Scotia Leasing Limited. m. Irene LaPoint, 16th Nov, 1957, 2 sons, 1 daughter. *Education:* BA, BCom, Francis Xavier University, 1954. *Appointments:* President, Director and member of Executive Committee, Equipment Lessors Association of Canada, Canadian Association Equipment Distributors. *Memberships:* The Board of Trade of Metropolitan, Toronto; Donalda Club. *Hobbies:* Golf; Skiing; Swimming. *Address:* 44 King Street West, Suite 1600, Toronto, Ontario, Canada.

WOLFSOHN, Hugo A., b. 22 Feb. 1918, Berlin. Foundation Professor of Politics at La Trobe University. m. Ilse M. 11th June, 1945, 1 son, 1 daughter. *Education:* Humanistic Gymnasium with emphasis upon Greek & Latin up to Abitur Final in Berlin, Germany; BA, Melbourne University. *Appointments:* Part time Tutor, Political Science, Melbourne, 1947; Tutor, Political Science, 1948; Lecturer, Senior Lecturer, Melbourne University, 1957; Foundation Professor of Politics, La Trobe University, 1966. *Memberships:* President, Australasian Political Studies Association, 1968; International Academic Advisory Council of the University College of Buckingham, England. *Publications:* Contributions to books, Co-Author of one book, articles to journals, book reviews, etc. *Honours:* Rockefeller Fellow in 1963 in USA. *Hobbies:* Reading; Photography. *Address:* 9/129 Riversdale Road, Hawthorn 3122, Australia.

WONG, Albert Lim, b. 10 Oct. 1935, Canton, China. Commercial Artist. m. Eva Jam, 6 July 1963, 1 son, 1 daughter. *Education:* Dun Muy School, Hong Kong; Greytown School, Wairarapa College; Wellington Technical College Art School, New Zealand. *Appointments:* J Ilott Limited, Advertising Agency, 1955-. *Memberships:* Artist Member, New Zealand Academy of Fine Arts, 1958; Vice President, Wellington Society of Water Colour Artist, 1979; Wellington Art Club; Committee Member, New Zealand Chinese Association, Wellington Branch, 1974-80; New Zealand Chinese cultural Society; New Zealand China Friendship Society. 05 Represented in New Zealand Art Exhibition to USSR, 1958; One Man Show, 1960; Chinese Landscapes, After Leading a Group of All Chinese Party Tour to China, 1976. *Hobbies:* Promoting Chinese Culture; Photography. *Address:* 54 Collier Avenue, Karori, Wellington, New Zealand.

WONG, Charles Chun-Chu, b. 20 Oct. 1916, Shanghai, China. Civil Engineer. m. Sophia Yee Wei-Fung, 26 Apr. 1942, 3 sons, 5 daughters. *Education:* BSc, Civil Engineering, St. John's University, Shanghai, China, 1942. *Appointments:* General Manager, Yates Construction Company, Shanghai, China, 1942-50; Chief Engineer, Manager, Ahong Construction Company Limited, Singapore, 1950-60; Managing Director, Ahong Construction Company Limited, Hong Kong, Limited, Hong Kong, 1960-. *Memberships:* MIEM, MIES, MHKIE, FASCE, Engineering; FAIB, FCIOB, FFB, Building; AMIAA, Arbitration. President, Society of Builders, Hong Kong, 1977-79; Chairman, Chartered Institute of Building, Hong Kong, 1978-79; President, Building Contractors' Association, Hong Kong, Ltd., 1979-81; International Federation of Asian & Western Pacific Contractors' Association, 1977-; Official Representative of IFAWPCA to Confederation of International Contractors' Association, 1976-; Chairman, Editorial Board of Asian Pacific Contractors, 1980-. *Hobbies:* Advancement to the Construction Industry. *Address:* 20 Beacon Hill Road, Kowloon, Hong Kong.

WONG, Chee-wing, b. 27 Dec. 1949, Hong Kong. Clinical Psychologist. m. Florence Chan Siu-yu, 28 June 1977, 1 daughter. *Education:* BA, University of Hong Kong, 1972; MPhil, University of London, 1974.

Appointments: Head, Psychological Unit, Castle Peak Hospital, Hong Kong; Clinical Supervisor, Graduate Programme, Clinical Psychology, University of Hong Kong; Honorary Lecturer, Department of Psychology, University of Hong Kong. *Memberships:* Associate, British Psychological Society; Clinical Division, British Psychological Society; Associate, Hong Kong Psychological Society. *Publications:* Research Interests in, The Relationship Between Pain Perception and Psychological Variables; The Nature of Cognitive Deficit in Schizophrenia; The Behavioural Approaches to Psychiatric Disorders. *Hobbies:* Music; Sailing; Scuba-Diving. *Address:* 6A Seymour Road, Fair Wind Manor, 3rd Floor, Hong Kong.

WONG, Ing Siong, b. 30 Jan. 1953, Sarawak, Malaysia. General Practice Surveyor. m. Lau Lea Wu, 27 Jan. 1978, 1 daughter. *Education:* BSc, Hons, Estate Management, University of Reading, London, England, 1977. *Appointments:* Land and Survey Department, Sarawak, 1977-; C.H. Williams, Talhar, Wong and Yeo Sdn, Sarawak, Malaysia. *Memberships:* Institution of Surveyors, Malaysia; Rating and Valuation Association; and Royal Institution of Chartered Surveyors. *Hobbies:* Travelling; Reading. *Address:* 7B Lane 13, Lucky Road, Tun Hayi Openg Road, Sibu, Sarawak, Malaysia.

WONG, John, b. 12 Jan. 1941, Hong Kong. Surgeon. m. Cheung Poh-Geak, 8 Jan. 1966. *Education:* University of Sydney Medical School, 1959-65; BSc, Med, First Class Honours, 1964; MB,BS, First Class Honours, 1966; PhD, 1971; FRACS, 1973; FRCS, Edinburgh, 1980; FACS, 1980. *Appointments:* Professorial Registrar, Royal Prince Alfred Hospital, Sydney, 1972; Lecturer, Surgery, University of Sydney, 1974; Honorary Surgeon, Royal Prince Alfred Hospital, Sydney, 1974; Lecturer, Surgery, University of Hong Kong; 1975; Senior Lecturer, Surgery University of Hong Kong, 1977; Professor of Surgery, University of Hong Kong, 1979; Consultant Surgeon, Queen Mary Hospital, 1979. *Memberships:* Honorary Secretary, Association of Surgeons of South East Asia; Council Member, Hong Kong Surgical Society; James IV Association of Surgeons; Surgical Research Society, Australia; Asian Pacific Association for the Study of the Liver; Societe International de Chirurgie. *Publications:* Contributed numerous articles to professional journals. *Honours:* Renwick Scholarship, University of Sydney, 1959-65; G.S. Caird Scholarship, University of Sydney; Grafton Elliot Smith Memorial Prize, University of Sydney; Robert H. Todd Memorial Prize, University of Sydney; National Health and Medical Research Council Fellowship, Australia, 1969-71; Li Koon-Chun Fellowship, Hong Kong, 1978. *Hobbies:* Classical Music; Snow Skiing. *Address:* Department of Surgery, University of Hong Kong, Queen Mary Hospital, Hong Kong.

WONG, Kee Kuong, b. 23 June 1943, Sibu, Sarawak, Malaysia. Mining Engineer. *Education:* BE, Mining Engineering, University of New South Wales, Australia, 1965-69; Management courses from various institutions, Chartered Engineer, Professional Engineer. *Appointments:* Mining Engineer, Plant Engineer, Shift Engineer, Anglo-Oriental, Malaya, Sdn Bhd, Southern Malaya Tin Dredging Limited, 1970-74; Deputy Director, Mines Department, Sarawak and Sabah, 1974-. *Memberships:* Sarawak Club, Kuching, Sarawak; British Institute of Management; Institution of Mining and Metallurgy; Institution of Plant Engineers; Institution of Industrial Managers; Graduate, Institution of Mechanical Engineers. *Publications:* The Synthesis of Manna, Pensee 111; Entropy and Utopia; Twilight of Existence; The Justification of Justification; A Critrique of Pure Faith, Fiat Lux and Scope; Beyond Worlds in Collision, Cosmoanalytical Interpretations, MS; The Other Side of Religion, MS; Multibang Theory of the Universe, MS. *Honours:* Shell Scholar; Colombo Plan Scholar. *Hobbies:* Music; Photography; Gin Rummy; Snooker; Tennis; Travelling; Reading; Writing; Girl Watching. *Address:* 26 Everbright Park, Kuching, Sarawak, Malaysia.

WONG, Kim Min Datuk James, b. 6 Aug. 1922, Limbang, Sarawak, Malaysia. Businessman. m. Datin Valerie Wong Kui Inn, 9 Jan. 1949, 3 sons, 5 daughters. *Education:* St. Mary's School, Kuching; St. Thomas's School, Kuching; School of Agriculture, Serdang. *Appointments:* District Councillor, Limbang, 1952; Council, Negri Sarawak, 1956; Malaysian delegate, Colombo Plan Conference, Singapore, 1956; Malaysian dele-

gate, ECAPE Conference, Manila, 1962; First Deputy Chief Minister, Sarawak, 1966; Deputy Leader, Malaysian Goodwill Mission, Africa, 1964; Malaysian delegate, Commonwealth Parliamentary Conference, New Zealand, 1965; Malaysian Solidarity Consultative Committee and Malaysian inter-Government Committee, which bodies made fundamental contributions towards intergration of erstwhile Borneo States within Federation of Malaysia; Deputy President, Sarawak National Party; Chairman, Managing Director, Limbang Trading Group of Companies. *Memberships:* Sarawak Club; Prison Golf Club. *Honours:* Recipient of Panglima Negara Bintang Sarawak, which carries the title, Datuk. *Hobbies:* Golf; Hunting. *Address:* 42 Middle Road, Kuching, Sarawak, Malaysia.

WONG, Michael Se-Lum, b. 2 Apr. 1941, Shanghai, China. General Manager. *Education:* MAPICS, American Production and Inventory Control Society, 1975; MHKPICS, Hong Kong Production and Inventory Control Society, 1977; AAIM, Australian Institute of Management, 1980; AIMEC, American Institute of Management, 1980; MBIM, British Institute of Management, 1981. *Appointments:* ITT Transelectronics Limited, Kowloon, Hong Kong, 1974-77; Production Control Manager, I.R. Manager, Hong Kong Industrial Company Limited, Hong Kong, 1976-77; Assistant Factory Manager, Maxwell Electronics Limited, Kowloon, Hong Kong, 1978-79; General Manager, Swire Magnetics Limited, 1979-. *Publications:* Fellowship, Australian Institute of Management, South Australia, 1980. *Address:* 230 Nathan Road, 10th Floor, Rear Flat, Kowloon, Hong Kong.

WONG, Mung-Po, Alden, b. 23 Aug. 1949. Publisher. m. 13 Dec. 1975. *Appointments:* Partner, Hwa Yan Book Company; established Po Wen Book Company, one of the most prominent Chinese book publishing companies in the world. *Memberships:* Founder, Hong Kong Buddhist Youth Association. *Hobbies:* Reading & researching on Modern Chinese History & Literature. *Address:* 234 Wanchai Road G/F, E1, E2, F & D, Hong Kong.

WONG, Po Yan, b. 5 May 1923, Hwei-An, Fukien, China. Company Director. m. Ng Lai Ying, 22 Jan. 1946, 2 sons, 4 daughters. *Education:* BSc, National University of Amoy, 1945. *Appointments:* Managing Director, United Overseas Enterprises, Ltd., Interocean Fishery Supply Ltd, Kar Mau Trading Co. Ltd., Kar Yuen Godown Co., Ltd. *Memberships:* Chairman, Hong Kong Plastic Material Suppliers Association; Vice-president, Chinese Manufacturers' Association of Hong Kong; Hong Kong Chemical Society. *Honours:* Recipient of OBE, 1977. *Hobbies:* Classical music; Golfing; Reading. *Address:* 41A Stubbs Road, Block C-1, 16th Floor, Hong Kong.

WONG, Weng Hong, b. 1948, Penang, West Malaysia. Chartered Quantity Surveyor. m. Christina M. Do Yo Ling, 26 Feb. 1972, 1 son, 1 daughter. *Education:* Diploma in Quantity Surveying, Technical College, KL, Malaysia, 1969-71; Diploma in Quantity Surveying, Thames Polytechnic, London, UK, 1971-72; Associate of Thames Polytechnic, London, 1972; Associate Member of the Institute of Quantity Surveyors, UK, 1972; Associate Member of the Royal Institution of Chartered Surveyors, UK, 1973; Member of the Institution of Surveyors, Malaysia, 1973; Registered Member of the Board of Surveyors, Malaysia, 1974. *Appointments:* Assistant Quantity Surveyor, F. Biscoe, Taylor & Son, Quantity Surveyors, 1971-73; Senior Quantity Surveyor, Pakatan International, Quantity Surveyors, 1973-74; Sole Proprietor, JEB Juru Ekonomis Bangunan, Quantity Surveyors, 1974-75; Partner, JEB Juru Ekonomis Bangunan, Quantity Surveyors, 1975-81. *Memberships:* The Befrienders, Telephone Counsellor; Malaysian Foundation for the Science of Creative Intelligence; Success Motivation Institute of the Far East. *Honours:* Shell Malaysia Scholarship to Study Quantity Surveying at Technical College, Kuala Lumpur, Malaysia, 1969-71; Prize medal in Quantity Surveying at Technical College, Kuala Lumpur, Malaysia, 1971; The British Council Overseas Students Award to Study at Thames Polytechnic, London, 1971-72; Distinction in thesis on Construction Management. *Hobbies:* Counselling; Group Dynamics and Motivational Seminars; Meta and Para-Physics. *Address:* 32 Jalan Mutiara Timor, Tiga, Taman Mutiara II, Cheras, Kuala Lumpur, West Malaysia.

WONG, Woon-wah Henry, b. 14 June, 1951, Hong Kong. Developer, Merchant. *Education:* BSc, Syracuse University, New York, USA, 1976; Master of Building Engineering, Project Management, Concordia University, Quebec, Canada, 1979. *Appointments:* Managing Director, Grass Field Limited, Development; Managing Director, Trade Enlarge Limited; Director, The Hong Kong Fruit & Vegetable Trading Co. Ltd. *Memberships:* Cheung Chau Tung Koo Association Limited, Vice Chairman; American Society of Civil Engineers' Committee on Estimating & Cost Control; American Society of Civil Engineers, Associate; General Chamber of Commerce & Industry of the Tung Kun District, Committee & Education Department In-Charge. *Publications:* Applicability of IRR and MPV Models on Real Estate, Acquisition project, Centre for Building Studies, Concordia University, PQ, Canada. *Hobbies:* Tennis; Table Tennis; Architectural Design. *Address:* 19th Floor, Flat A3, Elizabeth House, 250 Gloucester Road, Wanchai, Hong Kong.

WONG, Yuk Heong, Shereen, b. 8 July, 1948, Perak, Malaysia. Microbiologist. m. Sing Fah, P. Wong, 9 Nov. 1974, 1 son, 1 daughter. *Education:* BSc, New Zealand, 1973; Diploma, Medical Microbiology, Malaysia, 1979. *Appointments:* Hospital Microbiologist, Head of Department, 1974-. *Memberships:* Malaysian Society for Microbiology; Malaysian Scientific Association; Infection Control Nurses' Association, ICNA, Britain. *Hobbies:* Reading; Cooking. *Address:* 3 Jalan Udang Gantung Satu, Taman CUEPACS, Sri Segambut, Kuala Lumpur, Malaysia.

WONNACOTT, Ronald Johnston, b. 11 Sept. 1930, London, Canada. Professor of Economics. m. Eloise Howlett, 11 Sept. 1954. 2 sons, 1 daughter. *Education:* BA, University of Western Ontario, 1955; AM, Harvard, 1957; PhD, 1959. *Appointments:* Teaching positions; Harvard Law School, 1956-57; Harvard Economics Department, 1958; Assistant Professor, University of Western Ontario, 1958-61; Visiting Associate Professor, University of Minnesota, 1961-62; Associate Professor, University of Western Ontario, 1962-65; Professor, 1965-; Chairman, Department of Economics, University of Western Ontario, 1969-72. *Memberships:* American Economic Association; President, Canadian Economic Association, 1981-. *Publications:* Articles in the American Economic Review, Journal of Political Economy, Canadian Journal of Economics, and numerous others; Books:- Canadian American Dependence, 1961; Free Trade Between US and Canada, 1967; Introductory Statistics, 1969; Econometics, 1970; Canada's Trade Options, 1975; Economics, 1979; Regression, 1981; about 12 other books. *Hobbies:* Skiing; Golf; Tennis. *Address:* 171, Wychwood Park, London, Ontario, Canada.

WOO, Peter, L.K., b. 24 Sept. 1928, China. Metallurgist. *Education:* BSc, 1952; PhD, 1969. *Memberships:* AIME, American Institute of Mining, Metallurgical and Petroleum Engineers; AISE, Association of Iron and Steel Engineers; ASM, American Society for Metals. *Address:* 16, Fa Po Street, Flat A, First Floor, Yau Yat Chuen, Kowloon, Hong Kong.

WOO, Po-Shing, b. 19 Apr. 1929, Hong Kong. Solicitor. m. Helen S. Fun Fong, 25 Sept. 1956, 4 sons, 1 daughter. *Education:* Bachelor of Law Degree, London University; Law Society's Examination, 1959. *Appointments:* Senior Partner of Woo, Kwan, Lee & Lo, Solicitors & Notaries, Hong Kong; Deputy Managing Director, HG Kailey Enterprises Ltd; Director, Kailey Enterprises Ltd; Director, Sun Hung Kai Properties Ltd; Director, Henderson Development Ltd; Director, Tai Shing Development Ltd; Director, Wing Tai Development Ltd. *Memberships:* Law Society of England; Law Society of Hong Kong; The Institute of Arbitrators; The Institute of Directors; The British Institute of Management. *Address:* 26th Floor, Connaught Centre, Hong Kong.

WOO, Raymond Kok Chew, b. 8 July 1939, Singapore. Architect. *Education:* BArch, University of New South Wales, Sydney, Australia, 1965. *Appointments:* Worked with Harold Smith & Jesse, Architects & Planners, Sydney, 1963-65; Joined Malayan Architects Co-partnership, Kuala Lumpur, 1965; Singapore P.W.D., 1965; re-joined Malayan Architects Co-partnership, Singapore, 1966; joined Architects Team 3, 1966; Partnership with Project Architects, 1970; Formed Raymond Woo & Associates, 1971. *Memberships:*

Royal Building Institute of Architecture; Royal Australia Institute of Architecture; Singapore Institute of Architecture; Malaysian Institute of Architecture. *Creative Works:* Singapore Science Centre Building; World's widest single-span hangar for jumbo jet aircraft at Changi International Airport, Singapore. *Honours:* 1st Award for Architectural Competition for Science Centre Building from Science Centre Board, 1971. *Hobbies:* Gold-fish rearing; Orchid planting; Reading. *Address:* 15th Floor (301) Merlin Plaza, Beach Road, Singapore 0719.

WOOD, Aileen Jocelyn (Mrs Rupert J Wood), b. 11 July 1942, Picton, New Zealand. Medical Laboratory Technologist. m. 12 Jan. 1967, 2 daughters. *Education:* New Zealand Certificate of Proficiency in Medical Laboratory Technology, 1965. *Appointments:* Trainee Technologist, Kew Hospital Pathology Department, Invercargill, New Zealand, 1960-66; Technologist, Clinical chemistry, Hospitals of University of Chicago, USA, 1967-68; Supervisor, Linden Playcentre, Tawa, New Zealand, 1975-77. Technologist, Medical Laboratory, Wellington, Radiochemistry Department, 1979-. *Memberships:* New Zealand Society of Genealogists, Wellington Group; New Zealand Society of Genealogists; ANZIMLT; Higginbottom Family Society; Clan Fergus(s)on. *Publications:* The Wood Family Ancestry and Genealogy, 1980; Ancestor Hunt, a genealogical research aid. *Hobbies:* Genealogy; Gardening. *Address:* 50 Davidson Crescent, Tawa, New Zealand.

WOOD, Ernest John, b. 5 Sept. 1914, Sydney, Australia. Retired Public Servant. m. Betty Shaw, 24 Sept. 1945, 4 sons. *Education:* BEcon, Sydney University, Australia, 1940. *Appointments:* Soldier, Lieutenant, 1942, Australian Imperial Force, 1940-45; Research Officer, Rural Research Division, Ministry of Post-war Reconstruction, Canberra, 1945-46; Senior Research Officer, 1946-47; Senior Research Officer, Bureau of Agricultural Economics, Canberra, 1947-48; Supervising Research Officer, 1948-49; Senior Projects Officer, Branch Officer in Charge, Department of External Territories, Canberra, 1949-56; Assistant Secretary, Department of External Territories, Canberra, 1956-73. *Memberships:* Rats of Tobruk Association, Canberra. *Hobbies:* Reading; Writing. *Address:* 14 Meehan Gardens, Griffith, ACT, Australia, 2603.

WOOD, Lilian Mary (Mrs Donald Charles Wood), b. 15 Nov. 1922, Melbourne, Victoria, Australia. Editor. m. 14 Sept. 1943, 2 sons, 2 daughters. *Education:* Royal Melbourne Institute of Technology, 1972-75. *Appointments:* Editor, Greythorn Gazette; Foundation member, First Executive Officer, Print Council of Australia, 1966-74; Awarded Life Patron Membership of Print Council of Australia, 1975; Editor, Directory of Australian Printmakers, 1976, 1975-77; Editor, Directory of Australian Print Galleries, 1978; Editor, The Australian Accountant, 1979-. *Memberships:* Print Council of Australia; Society of Industrial Editors; Public Relations Institute of Australia, Victoria. *Publications:* Directory of Australian Printmakers, 1976, 1977; Directory of Australian Print Galleries, 1978. *Creative Works:* Australian Broadcasting Commission radio programmes: Sri Lanka, 1975; Hong Kong, 1975. *Honours:* Recipient of Honorary Life Patron Membership by Print Council of Australia, 1975. *Hobby:* Collecting Australian Hand-printed Graphics. *Address:* 12-14 Tannock Street, North Balwyn 3104, Victoria, Australia.

WOOD, Trevor James, b. 25 Sept. 1935, Melbourne, Victoria, Australia. Medical Administrator. m. Betty Thora Martin, 10 Dec, 1960, 3 sons. *Education:* Melbourne University, 1954-60; MB, BS, University of New South Wales, 1968-70; MHA; FRACP, 1967; FRACMA, 1970; FAIM, 1972; FHA, 1978. *Appointments:* Deputy Medical Superintendent, Royal Melbourne Hospital, 1966-72; Director of Medical Administration, Prince Henry/Prince of Wales/Eastern Suburbs Hospitals, 1972-76; Chief Executive Officer, Alfred Hospital, 1976.- *Memberships:* Censor-in-Chief, Royal Australian College of Medical Administrators; Chairman, State Branch, Royal Australian College of Medical Administrators; President, State Branch, Australian College of Health Service Administrators; Councillor, Australian Institute of Management; Rotary Club. *Publications:* Several Publications, Health Service Administration. *Honours:* Bernard Nicholson Prize, Royal Australian College of Medical Administrators, 1970. *Hobbies:*

Electronics. *Address:* 363 Punt Road, Prahran, Victoria, 3181, Australia.

WOOD, William Sealy, b. 24 Aug. 1917, Randalstown, Co.Antrim, Northern Ireland. Surgeon. m. Elizabeth Doreen Williams, 30 Dec. 1947, 2 sons, 1 daughter. *Education:* ATCL, Violin, 1933; MB, ChB, New Zealand, 1940; FRCS, England, 1948; FRACS, 1952; Otago University, 1935-40. *Education:* House Surgeon, Auckland Hospital, 1941-42; Army Captain, New Zealand Medical Corps, 1943-46; House Surgeon, Hammersmith Hospital, 1947; Registrar, Hammersmith Hospital, London, 1948; House Surgeon, Southend-on-Sea General Hospital; Senior Surgical Registrar, Green Lane Hospital, Auckland, 1949; Part time Visiting Surgeon, Green Lane Hospital, Auckland, 1950; Police Surgeon, Auckland, Retired; Consultant Surgeon, Justice Department; Reader in Clinical Surgery, School of Medicine, Auckland. *Memberships:* Auckland Returned Services Association; Auckland Hockey Association, Vice President; Past District Senior Grand Warden, Freemason, Remuera Lodge 1710 EC. *Honours:* Officer, 1964; Commander, 1974; Knight of Grace, 1979; Venerable Order of St. John of Jerusalem; Medal of Royal Australasian College of Surgeons, 1979; OBE, 1978. *Hobbies:* Sport; Music. *Address:* 82 Mountain Road, Epsom, Auckland 3, New Zealand.

WOODARD, Charles Garrard, b. 8 July, 1929, Adelaide, South Australia. Diplomat. m. Helen Cameron, 21 May, 1955, 2 sons. *Education:* LLB, Adelaide, 1951. *Appointments:* Barrister and Solicitor, 1951; Department of Foreign Affairs, Canberra, 1952; Ambassador to Burma, 1973-75; Ambassador to Peoples Republic of China, 1976-80; High Commissioner to Malaysia, 1980-. *Memberships:* Canberra Club. *Hobbies:* Reading; Racing. *Address:* Australian High Commission, Kuala Lumpur, Malaysia.

WOODHAM, Anthony Arthur, b. 5 July 1924, Liss, Hampshire, England. Nutritionist. m. Maisie F Ross, 8 Sept. 1952, 2 sons, 1 daughter. *Education:* BSc, 1949, PhD, 1951, University of Edinburgh, Scotland. *Appointments:* Research Chemist, T. & H. Smith Ltd., Edinburgh, 1951-55; Research Biochemist, Rowett Research Institute, Bucksburn, Aberdeen, 1955-79; Director, Commonwealth Bureau of Nutrition, Bucksburn, Aberdeen, 1979-. *Memberships:* Past Chairman, Scottish Group, Nutrition Society; Fellow, Royal Society of Chemistry; Society of Antiquities of Scotland. *Publications:* 80 publications dealing with various aspects of the nutritional value of proteins. *Hobbies:* Archaeology; Museum management; Growing succulent plants. *Address:* Clava, Cuninghill Road, Inverurie, Aberdeenshire, Scotland.

WOODHOUSE, (Arthur) Owen, (Rt Hon Sir, KBE, DSC), b. 18 July 1916, Napier, New Zealand. m. Margaret L Thorp, 24 June 1940, 4 sons, 2 daughters. *Education:* Napier Boys' High School; LLB, Auckland University, New Zealand, 1939. *Appointments:* War Service, 1939-46; Barrister & Solicitor, 1946; Crown Solicitor, 1954; Judge of the Supreme Court of New Zealand, 1961; and of the Court of Appeal, 1974; President, Court of Appeal, 1981; Chairman, Royal Commission on Compensation and Rehabilitation, New Zealand, 1966-67; Chairman of similar inquiry for Australian Government, 1973-74. *Honours:* DSC, 1944; Knight Bachelor, 1974; Privy Councillor, 1974; KBE, 1981; Honorary LLD, University of Wellington, 1978; Honorary LLD, York University, Toronto, Canada, 1981. *Address:* 45 Portland Road, Auckland 5, New Zealand.

WOODHOUSE, Peter William, b. 13 Apr. 1935, Middlesbrough, England. Chartered Chemist. m. Wendy Kerr, 17 Oct. 1959, 2 sons, 1 daughter. *Education:* Imperial College, London, England, 1953-54; Hull University, 1954-57; Teesside Polytechnic, 1957-60; Graduate Membership, Royal Institute of Chemistry. *Appointments:* Chemist, Industrial Engineer, ICI Wilton, UK, 1957-67; Industrial Engineer, Evans & Associates, UK, 1967-68; O & M Officer, Teesside C.B. Council, 1968-69; Work Study Manager, John Foster & Son, Black Dyke Mills, UK, 1969-74; Management Consultant, Cruickshank & Partners, Melbourne, Australia, 1974-76; Executive Secretary, Royal Australian Chemical Institute, 1976-. *Memberships:* Associate, Royal Australian Chemical Institute; Member, Royal Society of Chemistry; Institute of Management Services; Royal Society of Victoria; Society of Chemical Industry, Victoria; Standards Association of Australia Council; Australian & Victorian Councils of Professions; Sciences Club, Melbourne; Chairman, Membership Committee. *Publications:* Various articles in Chemistry in Australia. Co-author of RACI Code for the disposal of laboratory wastes. *Hobbies:* Music; Theatre; Rugby Football. *Address:* 52 Flinders Street, Mentone, Victoria 3194, Australia.

WOODRUFF, Arnold Henry Waller, b. 21 Jan. 1951, London, England. Geophysicist. m. 3 Sept. 1977, 2 daughters. *Education:* BSc, Honours, Physics, University College, Durham, UK, 1970-73; MSc, Atmospheric Physics, University College of Wales, Aberystwyth, 1973-74. *Appointments:* Lecturer in Physics, Department of Physics, University of Zambia, Lusaka, 1974-75; British Antarctic Survey, Cambridge, England, 1975-79 (Contract Glacial Geophysicist, two field seasons spent in the Antarctic); Elf Oil Exploration an Production, UK Ltd., 1979; Geophysicist, working in the exploration for oil and gas. *Memberships:* Member, Institute of Physics; Petroleum Exploration Society of Great Britain; Society of Exploration Geophysicists, Tulsa; International Glaciological Society. *Publications:* Some Aspects of Onchocerciasis in Sudan Savanna & Rain Forest, 1977; Depolarisation of Radio Waves can distinguish between Floating and Grounded Ice Sheets, 1979; Ellipticity Variations in the Polarisation of Radio Echoes (in press). *Honours:* Elected MInstP, 1979. *Hobbies:* Mountaineering; Hill Walking; Cycling; Jogging; Reading interests; Geology; Astronomy. *Address:* De Ferras, 157 Denmark Hill, London, SE5 8EJ, England.

WOODS, William Alfred, b. 26 May 1931, Liverpool, England. Professor of Mechanical Engineering. m. Dorothy E Hughes, 10 Aug. 1957, 1 son, 2 daughters. *Education:* BEng, Honours, 1953, PhD, 1958, DEng, 1972, University of Liverpool, England. *Appointments:* Technical Assistant, Aero Engine Division, Rolls Royce Ltd., Derby; Lecturer, Senior Lecturer, Reader, Department of Mechanical Engineering, University of Liverpool; Academic Sub-Dean, Faculty of Engineering Science; currently Head, Department of Mechanical Engineering, Queen Mary College, University of London; Visiting Professor, Massachusetts, USA, 1976-77. *Memberships:* Institution of Mechanical Engineers, London; Vice Chairman, Thermodynamics & Fluid Mechanics, 1980. *Publications:* Forces from Gases on Autoclave, 1967; Flow Through Poppet Valves, 1965; Train & Tunnel, 1972; Unsteady Flow with Gradual Mass Addition, 1976; Validity of Theories for Calculating Unsteady Flows in Railway Tunnels, 1979. *Honours:* Liverpool University: Watkinson Prize, 1952; Stitt Silver Medal, 1953; Joseph & Lucy Chadwick Studentship, 1954; Munitions Committee Fellowship, 1955. Institution of Mechanical Engineers: James Clayton Fund Prize, 1959; East Midlands Branch Graduates Prize, 1960; North Western Branch Graduates Prize, 1961; Viscount Weir Prize, 1962. *Hobbies:* Sailing; Fishing; Camping.

WORDSWORTH, David John, b. 9 June 1930, Kashmir. Minister for Lands and Forests. m. Marie-Louise Johnston, 1958, 1 son, 2 daughters. *Education:* Geelong Grammar School; University of New Zealand; Stanford University, USA. *Appointments:* Farmed Hagley House, Tasmania, 1953-67; Founded Duke of Orleans Bay Pastoral Co., Esperance, 1964; Member, State Executive Liberal Party, Tasmania, 1956-57, WA, 1969-71; WA Representative, Inter-Parliamentary Delegation, London, 1974; Member, Esperance Shire Council, 1969-71; MLC, Lib., for South Province, 1971-; Minister for Lands and Forests, 1978 ; Minister for Transport, 1977-78; Leader of Australian Delegation to World Forestry Congress, Jakarta, 1979. *Memberships:* Weld Club. *Hobbies:* Sailing; Photography; Fishing. *Address:* The Homestead, 155 Dempster Street, Esperance 6450, Australia.

WORDSWORTH, Owen John, b. 31 May 1938, Gordonvale, Queensland, Australia. Biophysicist. m. Janice W N Jenkins, 12 Aug. 1961, 1 son, 3 daughters. *Education:* BSc, Physics, 1960, DipEd, 1961, BSc, Honours IIA, 1963, MSc, Physics, 1965, University of Queensland, Australia; MSc, Radiobiology, 1965, PhD, Experimental Pathology, University of Birmingham, England. *Appointments:* Teacher of Physics & Mathematics, Central Technical College, Brisbane, Queensland, Australia, 1961-64; Research Scholar, University of Birmingham, England, 1964-67; Head of Physics Department, 1968-73, Head of School of Applied Science, 1973-74, Deputy Director, 1974-81, Director, 1981-, Queensland Institute of Technology, Australia. *Memberships:* Fellow, Australian Institute of Physics; Australian Institute of Management; Member, Australian College of Education; Tattersalls Club, Brisbane; Queensland Rugby Union Club; John Oxley Beefsteak & Burgundy Club. *Publications:* Author and co-author of eight scientific papers. *Honours:* Awarded University of Queensland Research Scholarship, 1964; Jeanne Liquier Milward Prize for postgraduate study, University of Birmingham, England, 1965. *Hobbies:* Fishing; Shooting. *Address:* 18 El Paso Street, Bardon, Brisbane, Queensland, Australia 4065.

WORTHINGTON, Brian Stewart, b. 9 June, 1938, Oldham, England. Professor of Radiology & Consultant Neuroradiologist. m. Margaret A Mayne, 2 Dec. 1961, 2 sons. *Education:* BSc, Honours, Physiology, London, 1960; LRCP, MRCS, 1963; MBBS, London, 1963; DMRD, 1967; FFR, Rohan Williams Medal, 1969; LIMA, 1979. *Appointments:* House Officer, Guy's Hospital, 1963-65; Registrar and Senior Registrar, London Hospital, 1965-70; Consultant Radiologist, Nottingham & Dery Hospital Groups, 1970-75; Reader in Radiology, University of Nottingham, 1975-. *Memberships:* British Institute of Radiology; British & European Association of Neuroradiologists; British Association of Clinical Anatomists; Royal Statistical Society; Institute of Mathematics and its Applications; British Society for the History of Mathematics. *Publications:* Several publications on Cognitive Aspects of Radiology; Nuclear Magnetic Resonance Imaging; Image Analysis and Transformation and Neuroradiology. *Honours:* Needham Memorial Academic Award, 1956; Ken Clifford Open Entrance Scholarship in Medicine, Guy's Hospital, 1956; Michael Harris Prize in Anatomy; Wooldrige Prize in Physiology, Guy's Hospital, 1959; Charles Oldham Prize in Ophthalmology, 1963; Rohan Williams Medal, Faculty of Radiologists, 1969. *Hobbies:* Archaeology; History of Mathematics. *Address:* 119 Russell Drive, Wollaton, Nottingham NG8 2BD, England.

WREDE, C. Lars-Henrik, b. 10 June 1941, Helsinki, Finland. President & Chief Executive Officer. m. Riitta Walden, 27 Nov. 1965, 1 son, 2 daughters. *Education:* BA, Economics, Helsinki Swedish School of Economics, 1965; Program for Management Development, Harvard University Graduate School of Business Administration, 1972. *Appointments:* Office Manager, Oy Metro-Auto, Ab, GM dealership, Helsinki, Finland, 1965-66; various Sales position, Enso-Gutzeit Osakeyhtio, Helsinki, Finland, 1966-69; Sales Manager, Kraft Paper, Eurocan Pulp & Paper Co. Ltd. Vancouver, British Columbia, 1969-73, Director of Sales, 1973-75, Vice President, Sales, 1975-78, Vice President & General Manager, Sales, 1978-79, President & CEO, 1979-. Directorships: Eurocan Pulp & Paper Co. Ltd.; Chairman, Oy Metro-Auto AB; Seaboard Lumber Sales Company Limited; Seaboard Shipping Company Limited; Eurocan-Enso Far East Co., Ltd.; Chairman, Eurocan South East Asia Co., Pte. Ltd.; Babine Forest Products Ltd.; Council of Forest Industies of British Columbia; Pulp & Paper Industrial Relations Bureau; Canadian Pulp & Paper Association. *Memberships:* Vancouver Club; Terminal City Club. *Hobbies:* Fishing; Hunting. *Address:* 4662 Keith Road, West Vancouver, B.C., Canada.

WREFORD, Elaine (Mrs Robert H Wreford), b. 12 Mar. 1913, Nairobi, British East Africa. Artist. m. 8 July, 1936, 1 son. *Education:* Governesses in Nairobi; Woodlands Church of England Girls' Grammar School, Glenelg, South Australia, 1925-30; School of Fine Arts, North Adelaide, South Australia, 1931-35. *Appointments:* First Exhibited, 1960; Joint Show w. Malcolm Carbins, Peel Street Gallery, Adelaide, 1962; One-man shows: Osborne Art Gallery, 1964, Skinner Galleries, Perth, 1965, South Yarra Gallery, Melbourne, 1965, Osborne Art Gallery, Adelaide, 1966, New Stanley Art Gallery, Nairobi, Kenya, 1968, Osborne Art Gallery, Adelaide, 1969, City of Hamilton Art Gallery, Victoria, 1971, Osborne Art Gallery, Adelaide, 1971, 1974, The Barn Gallery, McLaren Vale, South Australia, 1975, Lombard Street Gallery, North Adelaide, 1978, Avenel Bee Gallery, Stirling, South Australia, 1979; Represented in Commonwealth Collection, Canberra; Art Gallery of South Australia; City of Hamilton Art Gallery

& in private collections throughout Australia, New Zealand, England, and United States of America; Masters' Choice Exhibition, Portrait of Walter Crocker, Adelaide Festival of Arts, 1976; Three times selected for final judging in Flotta Lauro S3000 prize; Twice included in Melrose Portrait Exhibition, Art Gallery of South Australia; Six times included in Maude Vizard-Wholohan Exhibition, Royal South Australian Society of Arts; Twice selected for inclusion, Alice Springs Art Prize; Four times hung in Adelaide Festival of Arts Exhibition, Royal South Australian Society of Arts, twice in Festival of Art Exhibitions, Osborne Art Gallery; Included in Exhibition, Art Gallery of Tasmania, 1967; Illustrated private publication by Sir Edward Morgan, Tales of a Province; Represented in Art and Artists of South Australia by Nancy Benko, 1970; Kalori, Journal of Royal South Australian Society of Arts, 1972; Artists and Galleries of Australia by Max Germaine, 1980; Bronze Head by John Dowie, National Gallery, Victoria. *Memberships:* Royal South Australian Society of Arts; Queen Adelaide Club, Adelaide, South Australia. *Creative Works:* Represented in Australian Commonwealth Collection; Art Gallery of South Australia; City of Hamilton Art Gallery, Victoria. *Honours:* Elected Fellow of Royal South Australian Society of Arts, 1963. *Hobbies:* The pursuit of beauty, manmade & natural; Gardens; Travel. *Address:* 15 Brougham Place, North Adelaide, South Australia 5006.

WRIEDT, Kenneth Shaw, b. 11 July 1927, Melbourne, Victoria, Australia. Member of Federal Parliament of Australia. m. Helga A Burger, 26 Dec. 1959, 2 daughters. *Education:* State School, 1933-40; Melbourne University High School, 1941-43. *Appointments:* Merchant Navy Officer, 1944-58; Insurance Inspector, 1958-68; Member of Federal Parliament of Australia, Senate, 1968-. *Hobbies:* Listening to classical music; Collecting historic nautical publications. *Address:* 25 Corinth Street, Howrah, Tasmania 7018, Australia.

WRIGHT, David Malcolm, b. 31 July 1941, Lancaster, England. Medical Practitioner. m. Susan P Airey, 5 May 1969, 2 sons. *Education:* MB, ChB, University of Liverpool, England 1964; FFARCS, England, 1968; MRCP, UK, 1972; FFARACS, 1977. *Appointments:* Registrar, Guy's Hospital, London, England, 1968; Specialist, British Medical Team, Saigon, 1969; Senior Registrar, Intensive Care Unit, Whiston Hospital, Prescot, Merseyside, England, 1970; Lecturer, Clinical Pharmacology, University of Liverpool, 1972; Director of Intensive Care, Princess Alexandra Hospital, Brisbane, Australia, 1975-. *Memberships:* Australian Medical Association; Australia & New Zealand Intensive Care Society. *Publications:* Various contributions to Medical Journals and Textbooks on topics relating to Intensive Care. *Hobbies:* Walking; Reading; Music. *Address:* 23 Smeaton Street, Coorparoo 4151, Brisbane, Australia.

WRIGHT, Ernest Haynes Mofikpara, b. 27 Nov. 1935, Hastings, Sierra Leone. University Professor. m. Virginia A D Gooding, 4 July 1963, 1 son, 2 daughters. *Education:* BSc, Honours, Chemistry, 1958, PhD, Physical Chemistry, 1961, University of Hull, England. *Appointments:* Demonstrator in Physical Chemistry, University of Hull, 1958-61; Lecturer in Chemistry, Fourah Bay College, 1961-65; Research Fellow, University of Bristol, 1963; Senior Lecturer, Fourah Bay College, 1965-69; Associate Professor in Chemistry, University of Sierra Leone, 1969-71; Professor in Chemistry & Head of Department, University of Sierra Leone, 1969-71. *Memberships:* Fellow, Royal Society of Chemistry; International Chemistry Committee of Association of African Universities; Science Council of Africa; Sierra Leone Science Association; Mano River Union Training & Research Board. *Publications:* Adsorption of methyl laurate and related methyl estars from solution by oxides, 1965; Comparison of the adsorption behaviour of solutions of dicarboxylic acids on carbon blacks, 1966; Surface Chemical studies and radiochemically-determined uptake correlation for some Njala soils, 1978; and various papers tabled, presented or read at International Conferences and major public lectures. *Honours:* Royal Society & Nuffield Foundation Fellowship, 1963; Carnegie Corporation Travelling Fellowship, 1967; German Academic exchange Fellowship, 1971; Visiting Professor, University of Benin, 1981-82. *Hobbies:* Poetry Reading; Detective stories; Gardening. *Address:* Cockerill, Freetown, Sierra Leone.

WRIGHT, James Ernest Frederick, b. 18 Aug. 1922, London, England. Film Producer. m. Janet Jessey, 11 Nov. 1967, 2 sons. *Education:* School Certificate, 1939. *Appointments:* Banking; Film Camera Technician; Film Cameraman; Production Manager; Production Administration; Film Producer & Company Director. *Memberships:* British Academy of Film & Television Arts; British Industrial & Scientific Film Association; Executive Committee, Disablement in the City; Vice-President, Electronic Aids for the Blind; Chairman, Spelthorne Talking News; Executive Committee, Spelthorne Volunteer Bureau; Association of Independent Producers; Guinea Pig Club; St. Dunstans; Wig & Pen Club. 09 Various Documentary Films. *Honours:* Distinguished Flying Cross, 1943; Order of the British Empire, 1981; BAFTA, and other Film Awards. *Hobbies:* Gardening; Sports. *Address:* Chelmick, Manygate Lane, Shepperton, Middlesex TW17 9ER, England.

WRIGHT, James Roderick, b. 19 July 1916, Riversdale, Col. Co., Nova Scotia, Canada. m. Jean M Montgomery, 31 Dec. 1942, 1 son, 1 daughter. *Education:* BSc.Agr, Agricultural Chemistry, McGill University, Montreal, Canada, 1940; MS, Soil Chemistry, Michigan State University, East Lansing, 1948, PhD, Soil Chemistry, 1953. *Appointments:* Nova Scotia Department of Agriculture: Assistant Chemist, 1940-41; Assistant Prov. Chemist, 1945-50; Military Service: Pilot, RCAF, 1941-45, retired with rank of Sqdn-Lder; Head, Soil Genesis Section, Soil Research Institute, Ottawa, Canada, 1951-61; Director, Research Station, Kentville, Nova Scotia, 1961-67; Assistant Director General, Eastern, Research Branch, Ottawa, 1967-68; Director, Research Station, Kentville & Experimental Farm, Nappan, Nova Scotia, 1968-78; Independent Consultant, Chester, Nova Scotia, 1979-; Lecturer, Nova Scotia Agricultural College, 1945-50; Honorary Professor, Acadia University, Wolfville, Nova Scotia, 1964-70; Chief Liaison Officer for Agriculture, Canada, in Nova Scotia, 1977-78. *Memberships:* Past President, Eastern Ontario Branch, Agricultural Institute of Canada; American Association of Advanced Science; American Society of Agronomy; Past President, Canadian Society of Soil Science; Chemical Institute of Canada; International Society of Soil Science; Nova Scotia Institute of Agrology; Nova Scotia Institute of Science; Soil Science Society of America; Acadia University Institute. *Publications:* Published results of personal research on the chemical nature of soil organic matter and on soil development in various scientific journals. Produced many research reports and other technical communications. *Honours:* Macdonald College Scholarship, 1938-40; King's Commendation (Military) 1945; Agricultural Institute of Canada Scholarship, 1947; Fellow, Chemical Institute of Canada, 1964; Honorary Associate, Nova Scotia Agricultural College, 1978; Fellow, Agricultural Institute of Canada; Honorary Member, Nova Scotia Fruit Growers Association, 1979; DSc, Honours, Acadia University, 1980. *Hobbies:* Gardening; Beekeeping; Music. *Address:* PO Box 668, Chester, Nova Scotia, Canada, B0J 1J0.

WRIGHT, Keith Webb, b. 9 Jan. 1942, Toowoomba, Australia. Member of Parliament. m. 28 Mar. 1963, 2 daughters. *Education:* Graduate of Kelvin Grove Teachers' College; Certificate in Education, AED, University of Queensland, Australia; BA, University of Queensland. *Appointments:* School Principal; Member of Parliament. *Memberships:* Founder & President, Queensland Consumers' Association; Founder & President, Rockhampton Community Service Club; President, Rockhampton National Fitness Area Committee. *Publications:* A Manual in Mathematics; Community Services Directory. *Hobbies:* Numismatics; Boomerang manufacturing. *Address:* 20 Bishop Street, Rockhampton, Queensland, Australia.

WRIGHT, Kenneth Irving, b. 6 Sept. 1925, Red Cliffs, Victoria, Australia. Member of Parliament. m. Valda E Gallagher, 2 sons, 1 daughter. *Education:* Matriculation, Mildura High School. *Appointments:* RAAF Pilot, 1943-45; Real Estate Agent; Member for North-Western Province, 1973-; Secretary, Parliamentary National Party, 1978-. *Memberships:* Fellow, Australian Institute of Valuers; Councillor, City of Mildura, 1961-73, Mayor, 1966-67, 1968-70; Member, Committee of Management, North West Victoria Ambulance Service, President, 1959-61; State Junior Vice President, Country Party, 1971-72, Senior Vice President, 1973; Inaugural President, Mildura Branch, Justices' Association,

1966; President, Sunraysia Area Scout Association of Australia, Victoria Branch, 1971-; Mildura Workingman's Club; Mildura Settlers Club; Mildura Golf Club; RSI; Mildura Club; RACV, Melbourne. *Hobbies:* Golf; Tennis. *Address:* 10 Poplar Parade, Mildura, Australia.

WRIGHT, Lillian Mavis, b. 6 July 1903, Adelaide, Australia. Secretary. *Education:* The Misses Ives Private School, 1910-15; St. Peter's Collegiate Girls' School, 1916-17; Cabra Convent, 1918-19; Studied piano 1911-1923. *Appointments:* Worked for father, export agent in dairy produce, 1920-22; State Civil Service, Engineering & Water Supply Department, 1923-63. *Memberships:* Royal South Australian Society of Arts; Musica Viva Australia; friends of the Art Gallery of South Australia; Dickens Fellowship of South Australia. *Creative Works:* Various paintings under the supervision of prominent artists. *Honours:* Associate of the Royal South Australian Society of Arts, 1977. *Hobbies:* Travelling; Gardening; Cooking. *Address:* 28 Hampton Street, Hawthorn 5062, South Australia.

WRIGHT, Peter Charles, b. 30 Apr. 1940, London, England. Physicist. *Education:* BSc, Special, Physics, University of London, 1961-65; Postgraduate Study, University of Bristol, England, 1965-66; PhD, University of Bradford, 1966-71. *Appointments:* Physics Teacher, London Borough of Waltham Forest, 1971-. *Memberships:* Member, Institute of Physics. *Publications:* The D.C. Volume Restivitity of Plasticized Polyvinylchloride (co-author), 1978. *Hobbies:* Flying; Motoring; Motorcycling; Gardening; Photography. *Address:* 26 Cockmannings Road, St. Mary Cray, Orpington, Kent.

WRIGHT, Peter Robert, b. 25 Nov. 1926, London, England. Director & Choreographer. m. 22 Aug. 1954, 1 son, 1 daughter. *Education:* Bedales School, 1935-40, 1941-45; Leighton Park School, 1940-41. *Appointments:* Dancer, Ballet Jooss, 1945-47, 1951-52, Metropolitan Ballet, 1947-49; Sadlers Wells Theatre Ballet, 1949-51, 1952-56; Ballet Master, Sadlers Wells Opera and Teacher, Royal Ballet School, 1956-58; Freelance Choreographer & Teacher, 1958-61; Ballet Master & Assistant Director, Stuttgart Ballet, 1961-63; BBC Television Producer, 1963-65; Frelance Choreographer, 1965-69; Associate Director, Royal Ballet, 1964-77; Director, Sadlers Wells Royal Ballet, 1977-81. *Creative Works:* Ballets created: A Blue Rose, 1957; The Great Peacock, 1958; Musical Chairs, 1959; The Mirror Walkers, 1962; Quartet, 1962; Namouna, 1963; Designs for Dancers, 1963; Summer's Night, 1964; Danse Macarbe, 1964; Variations, 1964; Concerto, 1965; Arpege, 1974; El Amor Brujo, 1975; Summertide, 1976; Own Productions of the Classics: Giselle, Stuttgart, 1966, Cologne, 1967, Royal Ballet, 1968, Canadian National Ballet, 1970, Munich 1976, Dutch National Ballet, 1977, Houston, Texas, 1979, Frankfurt, 1980; The Sleeping Beauty, Cologne, 1968, Royal Ballet, 1968, Munich, 1974, Dutch National Ballet, 1981; Coppelia, Royal Ballet, 1976; Swan Lake, Sadlers Wells Royal Ballet, 1981. *Hobbies:* Potter; Gardener. *Address:* New House, Totteridge Greeen, London, N20 8PB, England.

WRIGHT, Rita Mary (Mrs A W Wright), b. 12 Apr. 1926. Teacher. m. (1) S Ayello, 14 Aug. 1948 (dec.), 1 son; (2) A Wright, 20 Aug. 1955, 2 sons. *Education:* BA, Honours, French, University of Birmingham, England, 1945-47; Licence Libre, Université de Rennes, France, 1949-51; *Appointments:* After three periods as Assistante in College, Lamballe, Lycee, St. Brieuc, Ecole Normale, St. Brieuc. Goole Grammar School, 1953-56, 1961-64, 1964-68; Language Tutor, Vermuyden Institute of F.E., 1968-69; Tideway Comprehensive School, 1969-71; Head of Department of Foreign Languages, Mayfield Comprehensive School, Putney, 1971-74; Senior Lecturer, East Sussex College of Higher Education, 1974-77; Head of Department, Tideway Comprehensive School, 1977-81. *Memberships:* Secretary, Joint Council of Language Associations; Chairman, Modern Language Association, Member of Executive, 1973; Member of executive, UKCEE; Previous member, Governing Body, CILT, 1975-77. *Publications:* As a member of the Research & Development Committee, MLA, Tools for the Job; Mixed Ability Teaching, Modern Languages. *Hobbies:* Music; Theatre. *Address:* 34 Surrey Road, Seaford, East Sussex BN25 2NN, England.

WRIGHTSON, Sydney John, b. 7 May 1942, Moss Vale, New South Wales, Australia. Geographer. m. Suzanne N Dale, 6 Aug. 1966, 2 daughters. *Education:* Scholarship to Australian National University, Canberra, Graduated BA, 1964; Graduate of Australian Joint Services Staff College, 1979. *Appointments:* Defence Officer, Australian Department of Defence, 1964-; Civilian Service with ANZUK Force, Singapore, 1972-74. *Memberships:* Institute of Australian Geographers; Australian Institute of International Affairs; Joint Services Staff College Association. *Hobbies:* Travel; Carpentry; Gardening; Walking; Films. *Address:* 14 Harpur Place, Garran, ACT 2605, Australia.

WRONG, Oliver Murray, b. 7 Feb. 1925, Oxford, England. Physician. m. Marilda Musacchio, 8 June 1956, 3 daughters. *Education:* Upper Canada College, Toronto, Canada, 1936-38; Edinburgh Academy, 1938-41; Oxford University Medical School, Magdalen College, 1942-47; BM, 1947; DM, Oxford University, 1964; MRCP, 1951; FRCP, London, 1967; FRCP, Edinburgh, 1970. *Appointments:* Junior Hospital Posts, Radcliffe Infirmary, Oxford, 1947-48; Service in Singapore & Malaya, Royal Army Medical Corps, 1948-50; Senior Interne in Medicine, Toronto General Hospital, 1951-52; Research Fellow, Massachusetts General Hospital, Boston, Massachusetts, USA, 1952-53; Tutor in Medicine, Manchester University, England, 1954-58; Assistant to Medical Unit, University College Hospital Medical School, London, 1959-61; Lecturer & Senior Lecturer in Medicine, Royal Postgraduate Medical School, London, 1961-69; Professor of Medicine, Dundee University, Scotland, 1969-71; Professor of Medicine, University College, London, 1972-. *Memberships:* Past Honorary Secretary, Renal Association; Past Honorary Treasurer, Medical Research Society; Zoological Society; Royal Society of Medicine; Past Chairman, National Kidney Research Fund. *Publications:* Papers in journals and chapters in books on renal function and disease, body fluids and intestinal function. The Large Intestine (co-author w. C.J. Edmonds, V.S. Chadwick), 1981. *Honours:* DEMY, Magdalen College, Oxford, England, 1973-77; George Herbert Hunt Travelling Fellow, Oxford University, 1951. *Hobbies:* Music; Gardening; Country. *Address:* 1 Bacons' Lane, London N6, England.

WRYELL, Max, b. 31 July, 1922, Launceston, Tasmania, Australia. Public Servant. m. (1) Aileen Schulz (deceased) 9 Feb. 1952, 1 daughter; (2) Betty Firth, 23 Sept. 1978. *Education:* BCom, 1947, DipPubAd, 1952, University of Tasmania, Australia. *Appointments:* Deputy Director-General, Department of Social Security, Canberra, 1974-; First Assistant Director-General, 1971-74; Acting First Assistant Director-General, 1968-71; Assistant Director-General 1963-68; Director, Policy, 1961-63; Director, Research, 1958-61. *Memberships:* Canberra Club, Canberra. *Publications:* Various articles for journals. *Honours:* Recipient of OBE, 1979. *Address:* 16 Bragg Street, Hackett, ACT 2602, Australia.

WU, Spencer Yin-Cheung, b. 10 May 1932, Hong Kong. Dental Surgeon. m. (1) Mary Sadler Feb. 1958 (divorced), 1 son, 1 daughter; (2) Eleanor Yu, Apr. 1976, 1 daughter. *Education:* Diploma, LDS, RCS, England, Guy's Hospital Dental School, University of London, 1955-60; Postgraduate studies, Eastman Dental Institute, London, Orthodontics, 1961; Periodontology, 1961; Partial Metal Denture, 1962; Intravenous Seda-tion, University of Dundee, 1963; course in Ceramco Technique, Ceramco Inc. Education Centre, Los Angeles, California, USA, 1975; Advanced Dental Practice Management, University of New South Wales, Australia, 1979; served three months at Childrens' Department, Guys Hospital, London, 1960. *Appointments:* General Practitioner, Surrey, England, 1960-70, Hong Kong, 1970-76, Sydney, Australia, 1976-. *Memberships:* British Dental Association, 1959-70; Society for Advancement of Anaesthesia in Dentistry, Great Britain, 1971-; Member of Committee of Fight Violent Crimes Campaign, Hong Kong, 1972; Founder member, Chairman, Pioneer Dental Study Group, Hong Kong, 1973; Member of Committee of SARDA, Hong Kong, 1975; Australia Dental Association, 1977-; Australian Society for Advancement of Anaesthesia & Sedation in Dentistry, 1977. *Publications:* Publisher & Editor, The Hong Kong Dental News and The Far East Dental Journal. *Honours:* Award for contribution to the 26th Convention of the Federation of Private Practitioners of The Philippines, 1976. *Hobbies:* Swimming; Table Tennis; Photography; Painting. *Address:* 2/47 Kurrabe Road, Neutral Bay, New South Wales 2089, Australia.

WYDER, John Ernest, b. 3 Jan. 1938, Grand Forks, British Columbia, Canada. Business Executive. m. Glenda Evans, 3 Sept. 1960, 1 son, 3 daughters. *Education:* BASc, University of British Columbia, Canada, 1961; MSc, 1964, PhD, 1968, University of Saskatchewan. *Appointments:* Geological Survey of Canada, 1961-71; Kenting Ltd., 1971-78; E & B Explorations Ltd., 1978-. *Memberships:* Professional Engineer, Provinces of Alberta, British Columbia, Saskatchewan and Manitoba; Geological Association of Canada; Canadian Institute of Mining & Metallurgy; European Association of Exploration Geophysicists, Society of Exploration Geophysicists; Calgary 400 Club. *Publications:* More than 20 scientific publication & papers. *Hobbies:* Backgammon; Reading; Coins; Stamps; Fishing; Mineral Collecting. *Address:* 131 Canterbury Drive SW, Calgary, Alberta, Canada T2W 1H3.

WYSE, Akintola Josephus, Gustavus, b. 4 Feb. 1944, Freetown, Sierra Leone. University Teacher. m. 31 Dec. 1970, 1 son, 2 daughters. *Education:* BA, Honours, History, Dunelm, Fourah Bay College, University of Sierra Leone, 1969; PhD, History, Kings College, University of Aberdeen, Scotland, 1972. *Appointments:* Lecturer in History, 1972-79, Senior Lecturer, 1979-, Fourah Bay College, University of Sierra Leone; Phelps-Stokes Foreign Curriculum Consultant, USA, 1980-81. *Memberships:* Secretary, Historical Society of Sierra Leone, 1975-; Executive member, University of Sierra Leone Senior Staff Association, 1974-77; Assistant Editor, Journal of the Sierra Leone Historical Society. *Publications:* Articles in several learned journals; contribution to The Encyclopaedia Africana; The Dictionary of African Biography, Sierra Leone, Zaire, 1979; The Sierra Leone Krios: A Re-appraisal from the Perspective of the African Diaspora; Global Dimensions of the African Diaspora (forthcoming); Searchlight on the Krio of Sierra Leone, 1980. *Honours:* Government National Scholar, 1965-69; DELCO National Scholar, 1969-72; Commonwealth Academic Fellow, 1976-77. *Hobbies:* Leisure Reading; Crossword Puzzles; Music; People; Walking. *Address:* Upper Faculty Flats, No. 3, Fourah Bay College, University of Sierra Leone, Freetown, Sierra Leone.

X

XAVIER, Christie Leo Chelvarajah, b. 3 July 1950, Colombo, Sri Lanka. Chartered Accountant. m. Sivambihai, 27 Nov. 1977, 1 son. *Appointments:* Ford Rhodes Thornton and Company, Colombo; Nchanga Consolidated Copper Mines Limited, Kitwe, Zambia; Price Waterhouse and Company, Blantyre, Malawi. *Hobbies:* Model Train Building; Reading Contemporary Continental Translations; Listening to Music. *Address:* Mandala Maisonettes, Number Five, Mandala, Blantyre, Malawi.

Y

YAM, Lloyd Chung-Pong, b. 17 Aug. 1936, Canton, China. Civil Engineer. m. Margaret Kuk-Wah Tsang, 8 June, 1961, 2 daughters. *Education:* BSc (Eng), Hong Kong University, 1961; DIC, 1962; PhD, Imperial College, London University, 1967. *Appointments:* Chief Editor, Anglo-Chinese Daily, Hong Kong, 1963-64; Research Assistant, Imperial College, 1964-66; Head of Bridge Analysis Section, Transport and Road Research Laboratory, Crowthorne, Berks, 1967-75; Head of Structural Design Division Building Research Establishment, Garston, Herts, 1975-. *Memberships:* Institution of Civil Engineers; Institution of Structural Engineers. *Publications:* Over 30 papers on inelastic behaviour of structures, study of failures of buildings and bridges in Europe, harmonization of international construction standards; Design of Composite Steel-Concrete Structures, 1980. *Address:* "Apotto, Juniper Grove, Watford, Herts, England.

YAMOAH, Charles Kwaw, b. 2 June 1905, Asamankese, Ghana. Education. m. 31 Dec. 1932, 6 sons, 3 daughters. *Education:* Elementary School Certificate, 1922; Teachers Certificate A, 1930; BD, London, 1956. *Appointments:* Pupil Teacher, 1923-26; Certificated Teacher, 1931-37; Circuit Minister, Methodist Church, 1941-44; Tutor, Trinity Theological College, Kumasi, 1945-47; Circuit Minister, Ketu Church, 1948-54; Tutor, Trinity College, Kumasi, 1956-61; Principal, Osei Tutor Training College, 1961-66; Chairman, Methodist Church Sekondi District, 1966-73; President, Methodist Church, Ghana. *Memberships:* Methodist Church Council. *Honours:* New Testament Greek Prize, Richmond College, Surrey, 1956. *Hobbies:* Music (Organ playing); Gardening. *Address:* PO Box 99, Asamankese, Ghana.

YAMOAH, Gabriel Mensah, b. 18 Nov. 1947. Administration. m. Forence Appiah, 15 Oct. 1975, 2 sons, 2 daughters. *Education:* BA, University of Ghana, Legon, 1970-73; PGCE, University of Cape Coast, 1976-77. *Appointments:* Headmaster, Ahmadiyya Secondary School, Pramso (now Jachi Pramso), 1968-70; Head of Department, (English & Liberal Studies), Kumasi Polytechnic, 1973-77; Editor, Ghana Publishing Corporation, 1977-80; Deputy Administrative Secretary, Ghana Academy of Arts and Sciences, 1980-. *Memberships:* Secretary, Ghana Publishing Corporation Senior Staff Association; Secretary for Transport, University of Ghana Students' Representative Council; Secretary to various other committees of the GAAS including SCOPE, Documents, Prizes and Awards, Publications etc. *Publications:* Written many articles for the Ghana Broadcasting Corporation; At present working on a book for use in Ghanaian Secondary Schools on Sanitation and Environmental Health. *Hobbies:* Gardening; Watching football; Playing draughts; Listening to music. *Address:* E Agbami Close, Airport Residential Area, Accra, Ghana.

YANG, Chee Ming, b. 15 Aug. 1920, Guangdong, China. Editor. m. Chen Ming, 25 Dec. 1929, 2 sons, 1 daughter. *Education:* South China Middle School, 1937. *Appointments:* Propagandist in the China Field Services, 1938-45; Teacher, Bilo College of Shanghai, 1946-48; Editor, Childrens Publishing House, Hong Kong, 1949-51; Assistant Editor-in-chief, Haikuang Press, Hong Kong, 1953-63; Editor, Truth-Good-Beauty Press, Hong Kong, 1963-70; Assistant editor-in-chief, Commercial Press, Hong Kong, 1971-73; Manager and Editor-in-chief, Scenery Pictorial, Hong Kong, 1974-79; Editor-in-chief, The China Tourism Pictoria, Kong Kong, 1980-. *Publications:* Lectures on Children Painting, 1951; China Atlas, 1971; China Scenery, 1972; Travel in China, 1978; A Guide-book for Tourists, 1978. *Hobbies:* Children Painting; Writing. *Address:* Room No 1111, 5 Ma Hang Chung Road, Kowloon, Hong Kong.

YANG, Kung-Chi, b. 12 Mar. 1942, Taipei, Taiwan. Professor. m. Janet Yu-Shin Huang, 8 July 1972, 1 son, 1 daughter. *Education:* BScF, Taiwan Chung-Hsing University, 1965; MScF, University of New Brunswick, Canada, 1970; MSc, University of Toronto, Canada, 1973; PhD, University of British Columbia, Canada, (in progress), 1982. *Appointments:* Lecturer, Faculty of Forestry, University of Toronto, 197475; Assistant

Professor, 1975-80, Associate Professor, 1981-, Lakehead University. *Memberships:* President & Chairman of Board of Directors, Thunder Bay Chinese-Canadian Association; Forest Products Research Society; International Association of Wood Anatomists; Society of Wood Science and Technology; Poplar Council of Canada; Regional Representative Solar Energy Society of Canada and USA Section; North American Representative, Chinese Foresters Association. *Publications:* Contributor to professional journals. *Honours:* NRC, Research Assistantship, University of New Brunswick, 1967-70; NRC, Research Assistantship, University of Toronto, 1970-72. *Hobbies:* Tennis; Wood Carving; Cheses (Chinese Chess, Go). *Address:* 244 Fairbank Crescent, Thunder Bay, Ontario, Canada, P7B 5L9.

YAP, Meow Foo, b. 15 Apr. 1918, West Malaysia. Pschiatrist. m. 1 daughter. *Education:* MB.,BS, 1946, MD, 1959, University of Hong Kong; Institute of Psychiatry, London University, 1956-59; DPM, London, 1959. *Appointments:* Medical Officer, Sigapore Government Medical Service 1947-71; Medical Superintendent, Woodbridge Hospital and Senior Consultant Psychiatrist, 1961-71; Private Consultant Psychiatrist, 1971-77; Consultant Psychiatrist, Mental Health Services, Western Australia 1977-78; Private Consultant Psychiatrist, 1978-. *Memberships:* Academy of Medicine, Singapore; Singapore Medical Association; Psychiatrist Association of Singapore; Singapore Society for Clinical Hypnosis. *Publications:* Complications of Insulin shock therapy with Special Reference of the Role of the liver, MD Thesis, 1959; Aspects of Aggression of the Mentally Disordered, Proceedings of the World Federation for Mental Health Regional Conference, Singapore, 1970; Psychotropic Medication in Singapore, Indonesian Psychiatric Journal, 1970. *Honours:* Postgraduate Study Award, United Kingdom, 1956-59. *Hobbies:* Reading; International Politics. *Address:* 201K, Ponggol 17th Avenue, Singapore 1954.

YASEEN, Maajid, b. 3 Mar. 1934, Lahore, Pakistan. Entomologist. m. Azra Noor-Mohammed 14 July 1968, 1 son, 1 daughter. *Education:* FSc, F.C. College, Lahore, Punjab University, 1950; BSc, 1952; MSc, Government College, Lahore, Punjab University, 1954; PhD, Punjab University, 1970. *Appointments:* Lecturer, Lahore College for Women, Lahore, 1954-55; Lecturer, Islamia College, Civil Lines, Lahore, 1955-63; Entomologist, Commonwealth Institute of Biological Control, Pakistan Station, Rawalpindi, 1963-69; Entomologist, Commonwealth Institute of Biological Control, Trinidad, 1969-79; principal Entomologist, Commonwealth Institute of Biological Control, Trinidad, 1980-. *Memberships:* Fellow, Royal Entomology Society, London; International Organization for Biological Control; Caribbean Food Crop Society; Trinidad and Tobago Field Naturalists Club; Fellow, Pakistan Zoological Society. *Publications:* Author of 23 papers published in various scientific journals and approximately 50 technical reports. *Address:* 60 Gordon Street, Curepe, Trinidad, West Indies.

YASOTHARAN, Balakrishnan, b. 2 Nov. 1954, Moolai, Sri Lanka. Chartered Accountant. m. Vallinayaki Ambalavanar, 16 June 1980. *Education:* Chartered Accountant, Institute of Chartered Accountants, Sri Lanka, 1976; Passed, Professional Part I, Institute of Cost and Management Accountants, United Kingdom. *Appointments:* Group Chief Accountant, KG Group of Companies, Sri Lanka, 1977-79; Audit Senior, Price Waterhouse and Company, Lusaka, Zambia, 1980-. *Memberships:* Central Sports Club, Lusaka. *Hobbies:* Swimming; Reading novels; Fishing. *Address:* 7 Park Lane, Plot No. 2055, Nasser Road, Lusaka, Zambia.

YATES, Deane, b. 27 Feb. 1922, Barnston, Cheshire. Headmaster. m. Dorothy Fitzgerald Hartley, 14 Apr. 1952. *Education:* St. Bees School, Cumberland, 1936-40; BA, Oriel College, Oxford, 1946-49; MA, St Stephen's House, Oxford, 1953. *Appointments:* Assistant Master, Department of Classics, Mill Hill School, London, 1950-53; Headmaster, St Johns College, Johannesburg, South Africa, 1954-70; Charma, Conference of Headmasters and Headmistresses of the Private School of Southern Africa, 1963-67; Founder Headmaster, Maru A Pula School, Gaborone, Botswana, 1971-. Director, New Area Schools Trust, 1981. *Memberships:* Fellow, Royal Society of Arts, 1972. *Honours:* Order of the British Empire, 1977. *Hobby:* Fishing.

Address: 28 St Patrick Road, Houghton, Johannesburg, South Africa.

YATES, Tom Owen Richard, b. 16 Apr. 1919, Newhaven, England. Medical Practitioner. m. (1) Eva Kathleen Crain, 1943, (2) Michie Maeno, 1967, 1 daughter. *Education:* Faculty of Medicine, University of Sydney, 1939-45; Bachelor of Medicine; Bachelor of Surgery, Wesley College, University of Sydney. *Appointments:* Medical Superintendent: Ikkade Mission Hospital, Madras, South India, 1948-53; Queen Victoria Maternity Hospital, Adelaide, 1953-55; Darwin Base Hospital, Northern Territory Australia, 1956-57; Canterbury District Hospital, Campsie, Sydney, Australia, 1958-60; Broome District Hospital, Western Australia, 1960-61; Wallsend District Hospital, Newcastle New South Wales, Australia, 1961-69; Ophthelmic Registrar, St Vincents Hospital Sydney, 1957; Medical Officer, Allandale Hospital Cessnock, NSW, Australia. *Memberships:* Australian Medical Association; Darwin Medical Society. *Publications:* These Are More Sick, 1950; The Tamil Maiden, 1950; Susan Carol and The Colonal (Poems), 1950. *Honours:* Bachelor of Medicine and Surgery, Adelaide University, 1954; Clinical Demonstrator and Lecturer in Obstetrics, Faculty of Medicine, Department of Obstetrics, 1953 and Adelaide University, 1954. *Hobbies:* Reading; Music; Swimming; Heraldry; Stamps; Coines; The Arts; Gems; Finance; Cricket; Asian Studies; English History. etc. *Address:* 284 Burwood Road, Burwood 2134, NSW, Australia.

YATES, William, b. 15 Sept. 1921, Appleby, Westmorland, England. Parliamentarian. m. Camilla Tennant, 25 Apr. 1957, 4 sons. *Education:* Uppingham, 1935-40; MA Law, Oxford, 1945-47; BEd, Melbourne, 1975. *Appointments:* Legal Officer, Foreign Office Administration, Libya, 1949; Staff Officer, Suez Canal Zone, Egypt, 1950; Conservative Member of Parliament, The Wrekin, 1955-66; Classics Master, Brighton Grammar School, Victoria Australia, 1968-75; Federal Liberal Member, The House of Representatives for Holt, Victoria Canberra, Australia, 1975-80. *Memberships:* The Commonwealth Club, Canberra. *Address:* 17 Cypress Grove, Dandenong, Victoria 3175, Australia.

YAZDANI, Golam, b. 1917, Barojachi, West Bengal, India. Medical Practitioner. m. Maleka Begum, 9 Mar. 1980. *Education:* MBBS 1941; DTMH 1965; DGO, Calcutta University, 1967. *Appointments:* Senior House Physician and Demonstrator of Anatomy, Medical College, Bengal Medical Service, 1943; Emergency War Service, IMS/IAMC, 1943-47; RMO, Islamic Hospital, Calcutta, 1949-69. *Memberships:* Cardiological Society, India; Legislative Assembly, West Bengal; Member of Parliament. *Publications:* Contributed many articles in Medical, Library and Islamic subjects in periodicals, 1942-. *Hobbies:* Study of Literature and Islamic subjects; Writing articles and books in medical and Islamic subjects. *Address:* 96, North Avenue, New Delhi, India.

YEE, Ching, b. 3 Nov. 1916, Mui Yuen County, China. Director and General Manager. m. Lee Kin, 10 Sept. 1939, 2 sons, 4 daughters. *Education:* Graduated, Chong Kuo College, Chong Kuo, Mui Yuen County China, 1933. *Appointments:* Merchant, Cheng Hwa Company, Mui Yuen County, China, 1934-45; Merchant, Kwok Hwa Trading Company Limited, Hong Kong, 1946-58; Director and General Manager, Yue Hwa Chinese Products Emporium Limited, Hong Kong, 1959-. *Memberships:* Standing Committee, 2nd Guangdong Provincial Federation of Returned Overseas Chinese; 4th Guangdong Provincial Committee of Chinese People's Political Consultations Conference; Vice Chairman, Hong Kong & Kowloon General Merchandise Merchants' Association Limited; Ka Ying Chow Chamber of Commerce Limited. *Address:* 5A Marigold Road, 1st Floor, Yau Yat Chuen, Kowloon, Hong Kong.

YEEND, Geoffrey John, b. 1 May 1927, Melbourne, Victoria, Australia. Secretary. m. Laurel Mahoney 20 Dec. 1952, 1 son, 1 daughter. *Education:* Bachelor of Commerce. *Appointments:* Department of Post War Reconstruction, 1944-49; Prime Minister's Department, 1950-; Private Secretary to Prime Minister, 1952-55; Assistant Secretary, Australian High Commission, London, 1958-60; Various appointments, Prime Minister's Department, 1961-76; Under Secretary, 1976-78, Secretary, 1979-, Department of Prime

Minister and Cabinet and Secretary to Cabinet. *Memberships:* International Hockey Federation; Royal Canberra Golf Club; Commonwealth Club. *Honours:* CBE 1976; Kt Cmr. 1979; Australian Eisenhower Fellow, 1971. *Hobbies:* Golf; Fishing. *Address:* 1 Loftus Street, Yarralumla, ACT 2600, Australia.

YEGBE, Joseph Bidault, b. 26 Dec. 1933, Avenorpeme, Volta Region, Ghana. Member of Parliament. m. 8 June 1957, 4 sons. *Education:* Teacher's Certificate, Grade I, 1954; Associate Certificate in Education, 1960; BA(Hons) History, 1964; MA (African Studies), 1967; Certificate in Public Administration, 1967; Postgraduate Certificate in Education, 1970. *Appointments:* Teacher, 1954-59; Education Officer, 1967-73; AG. Headmaster, Kadjebi Secondary School, 1973; AG. Principal, Akatsi Training College, 1974; Assistant Director of Education, 1974-79. *Memberships:* Pax Romana; Historical Society of Ghana; Catholic Youth Organization of Ghana. *Publications:* The Anlo and Their Neighbours 1850-1890, Unpublished MA Thesis. *Honours:* Catholic Student of the Year, Ghana, 1963. *Hobbies:* Reading; Gardening. *Address:* c/o Postal Agent, Avenorpeme, Volta Region, Ghana.

YEH, Meou-Tsen Geoffrey, b. 17 Apr. 1931, Shanghai, China. Company Director. m. 28 Jan. 1958, 1 son, 1 daughter. *Education:* Park College, Parkville, Missouri, USA, 1950-51; BSc, University of Illinois, Champaign, Illinois, 1951-53; MSc, Harvard University, Cambridge, Mass. USA, 1953-54. *Appointments:* Engineer, Clarkson Engineering Company, USA, 1954-55; Assistant Managing Director, Hsin Chong Construction Company Limited, 1955-71; Managing Director, Hsin Chong Holdings, (HK) Limited, 1972-74; Chairman and Managing Director 1974-; Chairman and Managing Director, Hsin Chong Properties Limited, 1980-. *Memberships:* Member of the Most Excellent Order of the British Empire (MBE); Justice of the Peace; Chairman, Construction Industry Training Authority; President, Society of Builders; Town Planning Board; Hong Kong Training Council; The Building Contractors' Association Limited. *Hobbies:* Chinese Chess; "Go" game; Alpine Skiing. *Address:* 140 Waterloo Road, Flat D, Kowloon, Hong Kong.

YEO, Beng Siong, b. 28 Dec. 1945, Singapore. Businessman. m. Tan Poh Choo, 18 Dec. 1971, 3 daughters. *Education:* Business Administration. *Appointments:* General Clerk to Assistant Manager, Lian Hock Company, Singapore, 1962-67; Department Manager, 3M Singapore Pte Ltd. 1967-73; Managing Director, Tapes and Insulated Products, Pte Ltd. 1974-; Tapes and Insulated Products Sdn Bhd, Malaysia, 1976; Benson Tradelink Pte Ltd. 1980-; Benson Jaya Sdn, Bhd, Malaysia, 1981-. *Memberships:* Singapore Institute of Management; Institute of Commerce London; Marketing Executives Group; Singapore Cancer Society; Automobile Association of Singapore. *Hobby:* Rearing of Tropical Fish. *Address:* Apartment Block 194, 428L Kim Keat Avenue, Singapore 1231.

YEO, John Douglas, b. 29 Mar. 1933, Dubbo, NSW, Australia. Medical Practitioner. m. Joy Louise Simmons, 2 June 1962, 1 son, 3 daughters. *Education:* MB., BS, University of Sydney, 1956; Post-graduate Diploma, Physical and Rehabilitation Medicine, 1971; MS (Thesis) Experimental Spinal Cord Injury, 1978; Fellow, Royal Australasian College of Surgeons, 1978. *Appointments:* Junior Resident Medical Officer, 1956, Senior Resident Medical Officer, Royal North Shore Hospital, Sydney, 1957; Resident Medical Officer, Royal Alexandra Hospital for Children, Sydney, 1958; Surgical Registrar, Orthopaedics, Urology, General Surgery, Southlands Hospital, Sussex, United Kingdom, 1959; General Practice, Saskatchewan, Canada, 1960; General Practice, Pambula, New South Wales, Australia, 1961; Senior Registrar in Paraplegia, 1965-67 and Head, Spinal Unit, Royal North Shore Hospital, Sydney, 1968-. *Memberships:* Senior Specialist and Head of Spinal Unit; Tutor in Surgery, University of Sydney; Consultant in Spinal Injuries, Mount Wilga Commonwealth Rehabilitation Centre; Medical Consultant, Wheelchair and Disabled Association of New South Wales; 25 memberships in College's Medical and International Societies and Associations. *Publications:* 30 Publications and articles including: Pregnancy and Quadriplegia, 1968; Care of Paraplegics, 1974; The place of isotope myelography in the definition of spinal cord swelling following trauma: An experimental

study, 1974; Rehabilitation of the patient with spinal paralysis, 1978. *Honours:* Churchill Fellowship to study recent advances in the treatment of paraplegia and quadriplegia in USA, Canada, Europe, United Kingdom, Israel and India. *Hobbies:* Golf; Tennis. *Address:* 16 Andrew Avenue, West Pymble, NSW 2073, Australia.

YEOH, Ghim Seng, b. 22 June 1918, Ipoh, Perak. Consultant Surgeon. m. Winnie Khong, 23 June 1941, 5 daughters. *Education:* BA Hons (Cantab), 1941; MA (Cantab); MB and BChir, 1944; FRCS (England), 1950; FRACS, 1957; FACS, 1958. *Appointments:* Surgical Specialist, Singapore Government Medical Service, 1951-55; Professor of Surgery, University of Singapore, 1955-62; Consultant Surgeon, British Military Hospital, Singapore, 1955-74; Hon. Consultant Surgeon, Ministry of Health, Singapore, 1963-; Private Surgeon, 1962-. *Memberships:* British Medical Association; Cambridge Society; Rotary Club. *Hobbies:* Photography; Golf. *Address:* Command House, Kheam Hock Road, Singapore 1129.

YEOH, Tiong Lay, b. 18 Dec. 1929, Klang, Selangor, Malaysia. Building & Civil Engineering Contractor. m. 27 Sept. 1953, 5 sons, 2 daughters. *Education:* Graduate of Hin Hua High School, Klang. *Appointments:* Chairman and Managing Director: Yeoh Tiong Lay & Sons Holdings Sdn. Bhs; Syarikat Pembenaan Yeoh Tiong Lay Sdn. Bhd; Yeoh Tiong Lay Brickworks Sdn. Bhd; Batu Tiga Quarry Sdn. Bhd; Lay Seng Oil Palm Plantations Sdn. Bhd. Chairman Yeoh Cheng Liam Construction Sdn. Bhd; Joint Managing Director Buildcon (Readymixed Concrete) Sdn. Bhd; Deputy Chairman N.S. Tranport Bhd; Director Aerofoam Industry (1969); Director Inter Consortium (M)Sdn. Bhd. *Memberships:* President of Master Builders Association, Malaysia; Vice President of the International Federation of Asian & Western Pacific Contractors' Association; Honorary Treasurer of the Institute of Building, Malaysia; National Consultative Council on Housing, Malaysia; Selangor Chinese Chamber of Commerce. *Honours:* Awarded the Pingat Pangkuan Begara by His Majesty, the King of Malaysia; Awarded the Pingat Jasa Kebaktian by His Royal Highness, the Sultan of Selangor; Fellow, Chartered Institute of Building; Fellow, Australian Institute of Building; Fellow, British Institute of Management; Fellow, Faculty of Building. *Hobby:* Swimming; Table Tennis; Coin Collector. *Address:* 3, Lorong 16/78, Petaling Jaya.

YEUNG, James, Kam-tong, b. 2 Dec. 1947, Wai Yeung, China. Lecturer of Psychology. m. Choi-ha Leung, 21 Mar. 1981. *Education:* BA., Chu Hai College, Hong Kong, 1973; MA., Columbia, USA, 1975; Advanced Certificate, Education, Oxford, UK, 1976. *Appointments:* Lecturer, Department of Extra-mural Studies, University of Hong Kong, 1977-78; Lecturer, Hong Kong Baptist College, 1976-. *Memberships:* International Council Psychologists, Inc.; Hong Kong Psychological Society. *Publications:* 10 articles, Psychology, in Various Journals and Newspapers, 1980; Development of Intelligence, 1981. *Hobbies:* Chinese painting; Reading; Travelling; Mountain Walking. *Address:* Flat 5, 5/F, Chau's Building, 4 Siu Wo Street, Tsuen Wan, N.T. Hong Kong.

YIP, Yat-Hoong, b. 15 Dec. 1934, Malaysia. Professor of Economics. m. Esah Sieh, 15 Dec. 1965. *Education:* BA., 1957, BA., Hons., 1958, MA., 1960, Singapore; PhD., Malaya, 1967. *Appointments:* Assistant Lecturer, Singapore, 1958-59, Assistant Lecturer, Kuala Lumpur, 1959-60, Lecturer, 1961-68, Associate Professor, 1968-73, Dean, Faculty of Economics and Administration, 1968-71, Professor of Applied Economics, 1973-, Deputy Vice-Chancellor, 1973-79, University of Malaya; Director, Regional Institute of Higher Education and Development, Singapore, 1971-73; Director, South-East Asian Central Banks Research and Training Centre, 1979-. *Publications:* Articles: Recent changes in the ownership and control of locally incorporated Tin dredging companies in Malaya, 1968; Managing a University in a period of rapid inflation and financial stringency, 1976; Books include: The Development of the Malayan Tin Mining Industry, 1969; Management Education in Southeast Asia (editor), 1972; Roles of Universities in Local and Regional Development in Southeast Asia (editor), 1973; Report of the ESCAP Review Mission (with others), 1974; Research Projects and Publications of the University of Malaya, 1959-76 (with Ungku A Aziz), 1977. *Honours:*

Cultural and Educational Service Medal, 1st Class, Republic of Vietnam, 1973; Malaysia's Eisenhower Fellow, 1975; Johan Mangku Negara, 1978. *Hobby:* Golf. *Address:* 62 Pesiaran Bruas, Damansara Heights, Kuala Lumpur, Malaysia.

YORSTON, James Roderick, b. 6 Sept. 1923, Nairobi, Kenya. High School Teacher of Geography. *Education:* MA., Aberdeen University, Scotland, UK. *Appointments:* Assistant teacher, Sir E Scott Public School, Tarbert, Harris, Scotland, UK; Geography teacher, Kinross High School, Scotland, UK, 1969-. *Memberships:* Educational Institute of Scotland; Scottish Association of Geography Teachers. *Hobbies:* Badminton coaching; Making marquetry pictures from colour pictures; Interior decorating. *Address:* c/o Miss Colliar, 23 Church Street, Milnathort, Kinrossshire, KY13 7XE, Scotland.

YOUNG, Colville Norbert, b. 20 Nov. 1932. m. Norma Trapp. *Education:* BA., University of West Indies, 1961; D.Phil., York University, UK, 1974. *Appointments:* Teacher, 1947-58, Head of English Department, 1961-71, Principal, 1974-77, St. Michael's College; Head of Sixth Form, Belize Technical College, 1977-81; Part-time: Lecturer, Belize College of Arts, Science and Technology, Director, Belize Office of Caribbean Lexicography Project, 1980. *Memberships:* Society for Caribbean Linguistics; Executive Committee: Belize Library Association; Mesopotamia Credit Union; English Panellist, Caribbean Examinations Council. *Publications:* Music: Several secular and sacred compositions; most notable the 'Missa Caribeanna', mass based on folk rhythms of Belize and Caribbean (unpublished); Drama: 4 plays including: Riding Horse; Creole Proverbs of Belize, 1980. *Honours:* 2 Faculty Prizes for History and English, 1959, Student of the Year Award, 1960, University of West Indies. *Hobbies:* Steel Band music; Collecting and arranging Belizean Folk-songs. *Address:* 13 West Collet, Belize City, Belize, British Honduras.

YOUNG, George Samuel Knatchbull, (Sir), b. 16 July 1941, United Kingdom. Member of Parliament. m. 1964, 3 sons, 2 daughters. *Education:* MA., Christchurch, Oxford, UK; M.Phil., Kobler Research Fellow, University of Surrey, UK, 1967-69. *Appointments:* Economist, NEDO., 1966-67; Economic Adviser, PO Corporation, 1969-74; Councillor, London Borough of Lambeth, UK, 1968-71; Member, GLC., London Borough of Ealing, UK, 1970-73; Opposition Whip, 1976-79; Chairman, Acton Housing Association, UK, 1972-79; Parliamentary Under Secretary of State, Department of Health and Social Security, 1979-; Parliamentary Under Secretary of State, Department of the Environment. *Publications:* Accommodation Services in the UK 1979-1980, 1970; Tourism, Blessing or Blight, 1973. *Hobbies:* Cycling; Squash. *Address:* Formosa Place, Mill Lane, Cookham, Berkshire, England.

YOUNG, John Robert Alexander, b. 17 Oct. 1927, Dervock, Co. Antrim, Northern Ireland, United Kingdom. Company Director. m. Jocelyn Lavinia Williams-Freeman, 16 Dec. 1953, 1 son, 2 daughters. *Appointments:* Managing Director: African Leaf Tobacco Co. (Pvt) Limited; ABRY Investments (Pvt) Limited; Director, Beverley Building Society; Chairman, Eastern Highlands Tea Estates (Bt) Limited; Member, Tobacco Marketing Board of Zimbabwe; President, Tobacco Trade Association, 1972-79. *Memberships:* Institute of Directors, Zimbabwe branch. *Hobbies:* Golf; Tennis; Reading; Music. *Address:* 'Blugleigh', Piers Road, Borrowdale, Salisbury, Zimbabwe.

YOUNG, Nelson Horatio, b. 28 Dec. 1933, Canton, China. Education Consultant. m. Julia Po-lan Yuen, 10 June 1969, 1 son. *Education:* BA., 2nd class Hons., University of Hong Kong, 1956; Postgraduate Certificate of Education, University of London, UK, 1959. *Appointments:* Assistant to Registrar, 1956-63, Academic Registrar, 1963-70, Deputy Registrar, 1970, Registrar, 1970-73, Secretary of University, 1973-80, The Chinese University of Hong Kong; Principal, Young and Associates, Hong Kong, 1980-. *Memberships:* University Court, University of Hong Kong. *Honours:* Unofficial JP, Hong Kong. *Hobby:* Photography. *Address:* 34 Braga Circuit, Ground Floor, Kowloon, Hong Kong.

YOUNG, Sheila, b. 11 Dec. 1943, Newcastle-upon-Tyne, England. Authoress. *Education:* Associate, Trini-ty College of Music, London, UK, 1965. *Memberships:* Fellow, International Institute of Community Service; Society of Authors, London, UK. *Publications:* The Queen's Jewellery, London, UK, 1968, USA, 1969. *Hobbies:* Music; Gardening; Collecting and compiling pictures and information on Royal tours and activities and Royal jewellery. *Address:* 23 Towers Avenue, Jesmond, Newcastle-upon-Tyne, NE2 3QE, England.

YOUNG, William Lambert, b. 13 Nov. 1913, Kawakawa. Minister of the Crown. m. Isobel Joan Luke, 27 Apr. 1946, 1 son, 4 daughters. *Appointments:* Murray Roberts Co. Limited, 1930; War Service, 2NZEF, 1940-43; Russell Imports Limited, 1946-56; General Manager, Radio Corporation of New Zealand, 1956-62; Past Director: Howard Rotovator Co. Limited, JJ Niven & Co. Limited, NIMO Insurance Company, Johnsons Wax of New Zealand Limited, 1962-66; Elected Member of Parliament for Miramar, 1966; Minister of Works and Development, 1975-. *Hobby:* Sport. *Address:* 31 Moana Road, Kelburn, Wellington 5, New Zealand.

YU, Chan-Wah, b. 4 Sept. 1925, Hong Kong. Consulting Engineer. m. 30 Nov. 1957, 1 daughter. *Education:* BSc., University of Hong Kong, 1950; PhD., University of London, UK, 1954; DIC., Imperial College of Science and Technology, UK, 1954. *Appointments:* Assistant Engineer, Sir Bruce White, Wolfe Barry & Partners, London, UK, 1952; Engineer, 1955, Senior Engineer, 1959, Ove Arup & Partners, London, UK; Development Engineer, Portland Cement Association, Chicago, USA, 1959; Lecturer/Senior Lecturer, Imperial College, University of London, UK, 1962; Partner, Harris & Sutherland: Hong Kong, 1974, Far East, 1977, London, 1980. *Memberships:* Fellow, Member of Ultimate Load of Concrete Structures Committee, Institution of Civil Engineers, UK; Fellow, Member of Joint Committee 328 Limit Design, American Society of Civil Engineers; Royal Overseas League, London, UK. *Publications:* Limit State Design of Structural Concrete, 1972; other Technical papers in International journals. *Honours:* Luggard Scholar; Hong Kong Government Scholar. *Hobbies:* Photography; Woodwork. *Address:* Lower Farm, Northall, Dunstable, Bedfordshire LU6 2HD, England.

YU, Henry Lok-Man, b. 21 June 1935, Hong Kong. Businessman. m. Susan YM Ho, 26 Dec. 1970, 2 sons. *Education:* BSc., 1958; DMS., 1980. *Appointments:* Sales Department, May and Baker Limited, 1959-65; Taiwan Manager, Wyeth International Limited, 1965-69; Far East General Manager, International Natriment Inc., 1969-72; Director, Import Department, On Hong Ning Group of Dispensaries, Apr.-June 1972; Managing Director, Asia Pharm Marketing Limited, Hong Kong, 1972-. *Memberships:* Fellow, British Institute of Management; Hon. Secretary, Hong Kong Pharmaceutical Manufacturers Association. *Hobbies:* Travel; Football; Dancing. *Address:* 4D Glee Path, 15th Floor, Mei Foo Sun Chuen, Kowloon, Hong Kong.

YU, John Samuel, b. 12 Dec. 1934, Nanking, China. Medical Practitioner. *Education:* MB., BS., University of Sydney, Australia, 1959; DCH (RCP & S), 1964; MRACP., 1967; FRACP., 1974. *Appointments:* Resident, Royal North Shore Hospital, Australia, 1959; Resident Registrar, 1961, Professorial Registrar, 1965, Staff Physician and Head of Department of Medicine, 1972, General Superintendent, 1978, Royal Alexandra Hospital for Children, Australia; Neonatal Registrar, Hammersmith Hospital, London, UK, 1963; Research Fellow, Nuffield Neonatal Research Unit, Institute of Child Health, University of London, UK, 1964; Research Fellow, Department of Medicine, University of Sydney, Australia, 1966; Medical Officer, Institute of Child Health, UK, 1967. *Memberships:* Honorary Treasurer, Australian Paediatric Association, 1974-77; Councillor, Royal Australasian College of Physicians, 1967-69; Executive, Paediatric Research Society of Australia, 1972-76. *Publications:* Care for Your Child (with others), 1979; Articles on Worcester Porcelain and Southeast Asian Ceramics; over 50 publications in Neonatology, Metabolic Diseases and other aspects of paediatrics. *Hobbies:* Reading; Collecting ceramics and textiles. *Address:* 1 Moruben Road, Mosman, New South Wales 2088, Australia.

YU, Kwok Chun, b. 16 Sept. 1951, Indonesia. Director and Deputy Manager. m. Soe Chi Yau, 11 Mar. 1978, 1 daughter. *Education:* BA., Majored in Accounting,

AASA, Macquarie University, New South Wales, Australia, 1971-73. *Appointments:* Deputy Manager, 1974-77, Director and Deputy Manager, 1977-, Yue Hwa Chinese Products Emporium Limited, Kowloon, Hong Kong. *Memberships:* Chinese General Chamber of Commerce, Hong Kong; World Trade Centre, Hong Kong; Ka Ying Chow Chamber of Commerce Limited, Hong Kong; Advisor, Junior Police Call Clubhouse, Yaumati Division, Hong Kong. *Address:* 11 Verbena Road, Yau Yat Chuen, Kowloon, Hong Kong.

YU, Swee Yean, b. 10 Nov. 1949, Kuala Lumpur, Malaysia. Food Technologist. m. Lye Tuck Thye, 12 Dec. 1978, 1 daughter. *Education:* BSc., Hons., 1971, PhD., 1975, Nottingham University, UK. *Appointments:* Lecturer, Food Technology, Food Chemistry and Biochemistry, School of Applied Sciences, MARA Institute of Technology, Shah Alam, Selangor, Malaysia, 1976; Lecturer, Biochemistry, Department of Biochemistry, Faculty of Medicine, University of Malaya, Kuala Lumpur, Malaysia, 1977; Lecturer, Food Science and Technology, Department of Food Science and Technology, University of Agriculture Malaysia, Serdang, Selangor, Malaysia, 1977-. *Memberships:* Member of numerous societies including: Associate member, Institute of Food Science and Technology, UK; Associate Member, Committee, Research and Publications, Institute of Quality Control, Malaysia; Council Member, Malaysian Institute of Food Technology, 1978-79; Committee, Malaysian Society for Biochemistry, 1978-79. *Publications:* 16 Publications including: Status of Malaysian Intermediate Moisture Meat: The Effect of Sorbic Acid and BHT on Keeping Quality (with C L Siaw), 1978; Soya Bean Foods in Malaysia (with G C Ch'ng), 1978; On the Nature of the Helix-Coil Transition in Tropomyosin, 1978; Nutritive Value of Sauropus Albicans, a Malaysian Leafy Vegetable (with C H Cheah), 1979; Studies on Malaysian Fish Crackers: Effect of Sago, Tapioca and Wheat Flours on the Acceptability (with others), 1980; Microbial Quality of fresh, frozen and frozen-thawed Meat (with M I Karim), 1980. *Honours:* Shields Prize, BSc., course, Nottingham University, UK, 1971; Prize for Best Dessertation in Food Science, Institute of Food Science and Technology, UK, 1971; Awarded Nottingham University, UK, Postgraduate Scholarship to do PhD in Food Science with Professor R A Lawrie, 1971. *Hobbies:* Swimming; Reading; Badminton; Music. *Address:* 29 Lorong Anggur, Klang Road, Kuala Lumpur, Malaysia.

YU, Victor Yu-Hei, b. 16 Aug. 1945, Hong Kong. Consultant Paediatrician. m. Winnie Wing-Yee Wong, 28 June, 1969. *Education:* MB., BS., 1968, D., 1981, Hong Kong; DCH., RCP & S, 1972; MRCP., UK, 1973; MSc., Oxon, UK, 1975; MRACP., 1977, FRACP., 1978, Australia. *Appointments:* Lecturer, Department of Paediatrics, Hong Kong University, Queen Mary Hospital, Hong Kong; Registrar and Research Fellow, Department of Paediatrics, Oxford University, John Radcliffe Hospital, UK; Postdoctorate Fellow, Department of Paediatrics, McMaster University Medical Centre, Canada; Director of Neonatal Intensive Care and Senior Lecturer, Department of Paediatrics, Monash University, Queen Victoria Medical Centre, Australia. *Memberships:* Royal College of Physicians, London, UK; Paediatric Research Society, UK; Neonatal Society, UK; Royal Australasian College of Physicians; Paediatric Research Society of Australia; Australian College of Paediatrics. *Publications:* Cardiorespiratory Responses to Feeding in the Newborn Infant, MSc. thesis; Neonatal Intensive Care for the Very Low Birthweight Infant, MD thesis; 74 Scientific publications in medical journals, 1969-80. *Honours:* Commonwealth Medical Scholarship Award, 1972-75. *Hobbies:* Photography; Travel. *Address:* 3 Beacon Court, Lower Templestowe, Melbourne, Victoria 3107, Australia.

YUEN, Natalis Chung Lau, b. 30 Dec. 1937, China. Medical Practitioner. m. Sandra Judith Johnson, 18 May 1968, 1 daughter. *Education:* MB., BS., University of Queensland, Australia, 1965; Diploma, Tropical Medicine and Hygiene, University of Sydney, Australia, 1967. *Appointments:* Resident Medical Officer, Princes Alexandra Hospital, Brisbane, Queensland, Australia; Surgical Registrar, Bundaberg General Hospital, Queensland, Australia; Medical Officer: Our Lady of Maryknoll Hospital, Hong Kong, Hong Kong Buddhist Hospital, Hong Kong; Private Practice, 1974-; Honorary Part-time Lecturer, Hong Kong University, Hong Kong Chinese University, Member, Medical Council of Hong Kong, 1981. *Memberships:* Vice-President: Hong Kong

Medical Association, 1980-, Hong Kong College of General Practitioners, 1980-; Local Secretary, Royal Society of Tropical Medicine and Hygiene, 1980-; Hon. Secretary, HK Chapter, Fellow, International College of Surgeons; Fellow, Royal Society of Tropical Medicine and Hygiene; Australian Medical Association; British Medical Association; Chairman, Preliminary Investigation Committee, Medical Council of Hong Kong. *Publications:* The Role of the General Practitioners; The Training of General Practitioners. *Hobbies:* Martial Arts; Collection of Gemstones. *Address:* 4A Hamburg Villa, Eastbourne Road, Kowloon, Hong Kong

YUSOF, Ariff, b. 10 Mar. 1930, Malaysia. Career Diplomat; Ambassador of Malaysia. m. Barbara, 7 Apr. 1958, 1 son, 2 daughters. *Education:* BA., Hons., University of Sydney, Australia, 1953-57; Postgraduate course, International Relations and Diplomacy, London School of Economics, UK, 1957-58. *Appointments:* Education Officer, Malaysia, 1957; Diplomatic Officer, 1957-, Overseas Assignments in Thailand, Australia, Washington, USA, United Nations, Nigeria; Malaysian High Commissioner to Nigeria, 1955-57; Malaysian Ambassador to Burma, 1957-80; ASEAN Secretary General, 1973-75. *Hobbies:* Reading; Writing; Horse riding; Fishing. *Address:* Malaysian Embassy, Rangoon, Burma.

YUSOF, Mohamad Hitam, b. 1 Jan. 1936, Malaysia. Diplomat. m. Michiyo Noor Azian Bt Mustakim, 4 Aug. 1966, 3 sons. *Education:* BA., University of Malaya, Singapore; BA., Hons., University of Malaya, Kuala Lumpur. *Appointments:* Assistant District Officer: Rompin Kuantan, Pahang, 1961-63; Assistant Secretary, PM's Office, Malaysia Division, 1963; Executive Secretary, Border Operations Committee, Civilian Planning Officer, 1963-67; Consul of Malaysia, Medan Sumatra, 1968; Counsellor, Embassy of Malaysia, Manila, 1969; Minister, Embassy of Malaysia, Jakarta, Indonesia, 1972; Under Secretary, Political Affairs, MFA, Kuala Lumpur, 1974; Ambassador of Malaysia, Hanoi, Vietnam, 1976; High Commissioner to New Zealand, 1978; Director General, Asean - Malaysia, Kuala Lumpur, 1980. *Memberships:* Secretary, Muslim Society, University of Malaya, Singapore; President, Malay Language Society, University of Malaya. *Publications:* Short stories and poetry. *Creative Works:* Oil paintings. *Honours:* Malaysia Medal, 1963; Johan Setia Mahkota, 1976. *Hobby:* Golf. *Address:* 42/12 Taman Grandview, Ampang Jaya, Kuala Lumpur, Malaysia.

YUZYK, Paul, b. 24 June 1913, Pinto, Saskatchewan, Canada. Senator. m. Mary Bahniuk, 12 July 1941, 1 son, 3 daughters. *Education:* BA., 1945, BA., Hons., 1947, MA., 1948, LL.D., 1977, University of Saskatchewan, Canada; PhD., 1958, University of Minnesota, USA. *Appointments:* Teacher, Public and High School, Hafford, Saskatchewan, Canada, 1933-42; Volunteer, Canadian Army, NCO., 1942-43; Nominated to Senate of Canada for life, 1963-; Assistant Professor, Slavic Studies and History, 1951-58, Associate Professor, History and Slavic Studies, 1958-63, University of Manitoba, Canada; Full Professor, Russian and Soviet History and Canadian-Soviet Relations, University of Ottawa, Canada, 1966-78; Member of numerous Parliamentary delegations and Committees. *Memberships:* Member of numerous societies and associations. *Publications:* Many publications including: Books: The Ukranians in Manitoba: A Social History, 1953, 1977; Ukranian Canadians: Their Place and Role in Canadian Life, 1967; The Ukranian Greek Orthodox Church of Canada, 1918-1951, 1981; For a Better Canada, 1973; Concern for Canadian Cultural Rights: A Conference to Study Canada's Multicultural Patterns in the Sixties (editor), 1968; Articles: Many articles including: The First Ukranians in Manitoba, 1953; The 'Third' Nation and Tomorrow's Canada, 1967; The True Canadian Identity - Multiculturalism and the Emerging New Factor in the Emerging New Canada, 1970; The Soviet Union and the United Nations, 1969; Twenty-fourth Annual Session of the North Atlantic Assembly, 1979; also co-author of many books. *Honours:* Canadian Centennial Medal, 1967; Manitoba Centennial Medal, 1970; Shevchenko Gold Medal, 1968; City of Sudbury Gold Medal, 1968; Ukranian Canadian Committee, Toronto, Gold Medal, 1973; Key to the: City of Buffalo, USA, 1966, City of Rochester, USA, 1976; Queen Elizabeth II Silver Jubilee Medal, 1977. *Address:* 1839 Camborne Crescent, Ottawa, Ontario K1H 7B6, Canada.

Z

ZACHARIADES, Leandros Victor, b. 6 Apr. 1920, Kaimakli, Nicosia, Cyprus. Businessman. m. Malvina Pantelides, Feb. 1945, 6 sons. *Education:* Classic Gymnasium, Kyrenia; English School, Nicosia; Business Studies, United kingdom. *Appointments:* Cyprus Civil Service, 1938-55; Business, 1955-. *Memberships:* Cyprus Employers and Industrialists Federation; Motor Car Importers Association; Industrial Disputes Court; British Institute of Directors; British Institute of Management; Nicosia Rotary Club. *Publications:* Several papers and addresses. *Honours:* Commendatore of the order of Merit conferred by, President of the Republic of Italy, 1973. *Hobbies:* Sports; Politics. *Address:* 5 Menandrou Street, Nicosia, Cyprus.

ZACHARIAS, George, b. 28 Apr. 1926, Bulawayo, Southern Rhodesia. Work Study Engineer. m. Valerie. *Education:* Bulawayo Technical School; Work Study and Industrial Engineering Certificate, London; Fellow, Institute of Management Services; South African Institute for Production Engineering; Work Study Association of South Africa. *Appointments:* Work Study Practitioner, 1961; Planning Assistant, 1971; Assistant Planning Officer, 1980. *Memberships:* Town Councillor, Bellevue Town Council, 1958-70; City Councillor, Bulawayo City Council, 1971-81; Major, Defence Forces of Rhodesia, 1944-80; Matabeleland Education Advisory Board, Ministerial Appointment, 1968-80; Executive Member, Nursery School Association of Rhodesia, 1965-; Chairman, Matabeleland Branch, Nursery School Association; Bulawayo and District Publicity Association; Prisoners Aid Association; Executive Member, Bulawayo Philharmonic Orchestra; Chairman and Member of various school committees and advisory boards. *Honours:* Rhodesia Defence Medal, 1945; General Service Medal, 1974; Territorial and Reserve Service Medal, 1974 and Bar, 1978. *Hobbies:* Bisley Shooting; Stamp Collecting. *Address:* 130 Wellington Road, Montrose, Bulawayo, Zimbabwe.

ZACHARIOU, Dion, b. 5 Aug. 1950, Symi, Greece. Artist. *Education:* Self-taught. *Appointments:* Assisted in painting the interior of the Greek Orthodox Cathedral on Rhodes; Toured the major capitals of Europe, exhibiting and selling my paintings; Commissioned with three other Artists, on restoration of badly damaged Peter Paul Rubens; Restored many oil paintings including: Rubens, a major JMW Turner, A Norman Rockwell, Cornelius Kriehoff, Tom Thomson. *Creative Works:* Exhibitions: Island of Rhodes, Athens, Greece, 1964; Athens, Salonika, Piraeus, Greece, 1965; Constantinople, Turkey, Milan, Italy, 1966; Amsterdam, Rotterdam, Holland, Stockholm, Sweden, Paris, France, Hiroshima, Japan, 1967; Moscow, USSR, Hamburg, West Germany, Kuwait, Kuwait, 1968; Bombay, India, London, England, 1969; Montreal, Canada, 1971; Series of exhibitions throughout Ontario and Quebec, Canada, 1972-; New York City, USA, 1979; Toronto, Canada, 1980; Toronto, Canada, San Francisco, USA, 1981; Collections: Dion's works of art (paintings, sculptures, frescoes etc.) are in many important private and corporate collections through the world. *Honours:* Internationally famed throughout the world. *Address:* 3431 Yonge Street, Toronto, Ontario, M4N 2N1, Canada.

ZAFU, Eyessuswork, b. 14 Jan. 1938, Merhabete, Shoa Province, Ethiopia. Reinsurance Broking. m. Yezabnesh Tadesse Zafu, 20 May 1970, 2 sons. *Education:* BA (Distinction), Haille Selaisse First University, Addis Ababa, Ethiopia, 1958-62; Dag Hammerskjold Fellow, GSPIA University of Pittsburgh, USA, 1964-66; Master of Public and International Affairs. *Appointments:* Life Sales Supervisor, 1962-64; Production Superintendent and Management Trainee, Imperial Insurance Company of Ethiopia Limited, Addis Ababa, Ethiopia, 1966-67; Sales and Public Relation Supervisor, Assistant Manager, Deputy General Manager and Secretary to Board of Directors, 1967-75; Acting General Manager, Pan African Insurance Company S.C., 1975; Acting General Manager and Director, Ethiopian Insurance Corp., 1975-76; Deputy Underwriter, African Insurance and Reinsurance Company Sudan Limited, 1976-77; Technical Adviser, 1977-80, General Manager, Glanvill Enthoven Reinsurance Brokers, Lagos, Nigeria. *Memberships:* University Alumni Association, Addis Ababa, Ethiopia; Imperial Ethiopian Racing Club; Chartered Insurance Institute; Young Toast

Masters, St Paul Minnesota; Ikoyi Club, 1938, Lagos, Nigeria. *Honours:* Various School Prizes for Academic Performance; Elocution Competitions; Prince Makonnen Memorial Award 1962. *Hobbies:* Listening to Music; Playing Ethiopian Flute; Swimming; Lawn Tennis. *Address:* 22 AkinAdesola Street, Victoria Island, Lagos, Nigeria.

ZAHARIA, Flora, b. 8 July 1927, Blood Indian Reserve, Cardston, Alberta Canada. Teacher. m. Stanley Zaharia, 21 July 1962, 2 sons. *Education:* Senior Matriculation, 1946; Standard & Teaching Certificate, 1949; Professional Teaching Certificate, 1958; Bachelor of Education Pre-Master, 1978; Master of Education, 1981; Speaks fluent, Blackfoot, English an French. *Appointments:* Teacher, Alberta Schools, Grouard, Alberta, 1949-59; Winnipeg School Division I, 1959-60; Norway House, Manitoba, Principal, 1960-62; Winnipeg School Division I, 1962-78; assistant Professor and Director of Community Counselling Certificate Program, University of Manitoba, 1978-79; Co-ordinator of Native Education, Department of Education, Manitoba, 1979-. *Memberships:* Native Advisory to Winnipeg Schools; Project Necheewan, Winnipeg; Native Women's Transition Winnipeg; Children's Aid Society; Indian Friendship Centre; International Centre; Provincial Council of Women. *Publications:* Co-author of Tawow Kit, Project Canada West, 1969-74. *Honours:* Honours in Practice Teaching, University of Alberta, 1949. *Hobbies:* Beadwork; Reading; Spoon collecting; Hiking; Watching Hockey. *Address:* 59 Sage Crescent, Winnipeg, Manitoba, R2Y 0X8, Canada.

ZAHRA, John William, b. 14 Oct. 1956, Pieta, Malta. Dental Surgeon. *Education:* BChD, Royal University of Malta, 1978. *Appointments:* Dental Surgeon, Private Dental Clinic, Demajo's Dental Clinic, Valletta, Malta. *Hobbies:* Practically anything: Car Mechanics; Electrical Engineering; Gardening; Historical Research. *Address:* 1 Government Housing Estate, Nakkar, Malta.

ZAIDI, Shamshad Haider, b. 19 Oct. 1943, Dehradun, India. Teaching. m. Husna Perween, 10 Oct. 1970, 3 sons, 1 daughter. *Education:* BA, 1969; MA (Linguistics), 1971; Certificate in French, 1965; Certificate in Applied Linguistics, 1977; Studing for PhD. *Appointments:* Laboratory Assistant; Senior Laboratory Assistant; Research Assistant; Lecturer. *Memberships:* Linguistic Society of India, Deccan College, Pune; All India University Urdu Teachers Association. *Publications:* Linguistic Analysis of Urdu Language, Urdu Script through Hindi, Urdu Script through English, Urdu Text books for Central School organization part one and two, Urdu visual Aid, Urdu Grammar, Dictionary of Linguistics in Urdu, History of Urdu language, Urdu compounds, Urdu and Linguistics. *Honours:* Won various prizes during student life. *Hobbies:* Chess; Hockey; Swimming; Painting; etc. *Address:* Shahid Manzil, Nihtour, Distt. Bijnour, (U.P.) India.

ZAIKOFF, Danielle W., b. 26 Mar. 1944, France. Professional Engineer. m. Pierre Zaïkoff, 15 Sept. 1965, 2 daughters. *Education:* BASc, Civil Engineering, 1967; MASc, Civil Engineering, Soils Mechanics, 1972. *Appointments:* Engineer, Directorate of Contracts, 1967-70; Soils Mechanics Engineer, Geology and Geotechnical Service, 1972-76; Head of Geomechanics Division, 1976-8; Head of Division, Behaviour studies of powerhouse installations, Hydro, Québec 1980-. *Memberships:* Order of Engineer of Quebec; Canadian Council of Professional Engineers; Engineering Institute of Canada; Canadian Geotechnical Society; Association des Diplomés de Polytechnique; Corporation du Collège Marie de France. *Publications:* Talks and conferences on Professionalism, professional legislation, professional engineering and society; Convocation Address; Nova Scotia Technical College, 1980. *Honours:* President, Order of Engineers of Québec, 1976; President, Canadian Council of Professional Engineers, 1978; Woman of Achievement, YWCA, 1976; Queen's Jubilee Medal, 1977; Doctorate in Engineering, Honoris Causa, Nova Scotia Technical College, 1980. *Hobbies:* Reading; Painting; Embroidery. *Address:* 610 Dawson Avenue, Town of Mount Royal, Quebec, H3R 1C6, Canada.

ZAIN Azraai, b. 27 July 1936, Telok Anson, Malaysia. Ambassador. m. Dawn Zain, 1967, 2 daughters. *Education:* Schools in Malaysia; Oxford University, England, 1956; Graduated with Honours, Politics, Economics and Philosophy; International Relations, London

School of Economics and Political Science. *Appointments:* Foreign Service, 1958; Malayan High Commission, London, 1962; Malaysia's Permanent Mission, United Nations, New York, 1962-66; Principal Assistant Secretary and Under-Secretary for Political Affairs, Ministry of Foreign Affairs, 1966-71; Principal Private Secretary to Prime Minister of Malaysia, 1971-76; Malaysian Ambassador, United States, and concurrently accredited to Mexico, 1976-. *Memberships:* Executive Director, World Bank, representing Malaysia, Burma, Fiji, Indonesia, Laos, Nepal, Singapore, Thailand and Vietnam, 1978-; Chairman, Board of Trustees, Malaysian National Art Gallery. *Honours:* Honoured, Datuk, by Malaysia's Supreme Head. *Address:* 2401 Massachusetts Ave, N.W. Washington DC, 20008, USA.

ZAKARI, Alhaji Muhammad, b. 1 Jan. 1936, Bukuru, Plateau State, Nigria. Lawyer. m. Zainab, 2 Apr. 1961, 3 sons, 1 daughter. *Education:* Barrister-at-Law. *Appointments:* Magistrate, 1961-65; Principal State Counsel, 1966-70; Secretary and Legal Adviser, Bank of the North Limited, 1971-72; Attorney General of Kano State, 1972-75; Chairman, Legal Aid Council of Nigeria 1976-78. *Memberships:* Honourable Society of the Middle Temple; Kano Club. *Hobbies:* Horse Riding; Music; General Knowledge. *Address:* 28A Hadeja Road, Kano, Nigeria.

ZAVAHIR, Mohamed Farouk, b. 22 Apr. 1939, Colombo, Sri Lanka. Senior Vice-President; Chartered Accountant. m. Sithy Amina Mansoor, 28 Mar. 1964, 1 son, 1 daughter. *Education:* Fellow, Institute of Chartered Accountants, 1974. *Appointments:* Senior Vice-President, Finance, Saudi Research and Development Corporation Limited, Saudi Arabia. *Honours:* Lander Prize, Intermediate examination, Institute of Chartered Accountants, 1959. *Hobbies:* Sports; Photography; Movies. *Address:* c/o Redec, PO Box 1935, Jeddah, Saudi Arabia.

ZEIDLER, David Ronald, b. 18 Mar. 1918, Melbourne, Australia. Company Director. m. 20 Nov. 1943, 4 daughters. *Education:* Graduated in Science, University of Melbourne, Australia; Joined CSIRO, 1941-51, worked for 1 year during that time at the Massachusetts Institute of Technology, USA. *Appointments:* Research Department, 1952, Research Manager, 1953, Development Manager, 1959, Controller of Dyes and Fabric Group, 1962, Director, 1963, Managing Director, 1971, Deputy Chairman, 1972, Chairman and Managing Director, 1973, retired, 1980, ICI Australia; Director of: The Commercial Bank of Australia Limited, The Broken Hill Proprietary Co. Limited, Amatil Limited, The Queen Elizabeth II Silver Jubilee Trust; Chairman, Metal Manufacturers Limited. *Memberships:* Board member, Walter and Eliza Hall Institute of Medal Medical Research; Board member, Science Museum of Victoria; Chairman, Commonwealth Enquiry into Electricity Generation and the Sharing of Power Resources in South-East Australia, 1980; Commonwealth Committee, Overseas Professional Qualifications; Chairman, Defence Industry Committee; Chairman, Victoria Government Inquiry into State Electricity Commission; Sir Robert Menzies Memorial Trust; Council, Australian Academy of Technological Sciences; Bureau of Industry Economics; Fellow, Royal Australian Chemical Institute, Institution of Chemical Engineers; Institute of Directors; Royal Society; Royal Society for the Encouragement of Arts Manufactures and Commerce, London, UK. *Honours:* Knight Bachelor, 1980; CBE., 1971. *Hobbies:* Tennis; Skiing; Sailing; Fishing; Golf. *Address:* 45/238 The Avenue, Parkville, Victoria 3052, Australia.

ZELENIETZ, Martin Charles, b. 23 Mar. 1951, Chicago, Illinois, USA. Social Anthropologist. m. Jill L Grant, 1 Apr. 1979, 1 daughter. *Education:* BA., Northeastern Illinois University, USA, 1972; MA., University of Manitoba, Canada, 1974; PhD., McMaster University, Canada, 1980. *Appointments:* Teaching Assistant, University of Manitoba, Canada, 1972-73; McMaster University, Canada, 1974-76; Lecturer, Mt. St. Vincent University, Canada, 1979-80, University of New Brunswick, Canada, 1980, Dalhousie University, Canada, 1980-81, St. Mary's University, Canada, 1980-81, Nova Scotia College of Art and Design, Canada, 1981; Visiting Lecturer, University of Papua New Guinea, 1981-82. *Memberships:* Fellow, Association for Social Anthropology In Oceania; Pacific Arts Association; Atlantic Association for Sociology and Social Anthropology; Association of Australasian Specialists/Oceania. *Publications:* Sorcery and Social Change (editor with S Lindenbaum), 1981; Numerous articles (with JL Grant) published in scholarly journals and books dealing with Anthropological Research in Ongaia, Kilenge, Papua New Guinea. *Honours:* Yates Trust Travelling Fellowship, 1976, 77, 79, Research Grant, 1977-78, Benefactor Scholarship, 1974-78, McMaster University, Canada; University Fellowship, University of Manitoba, Canada, 1973-74; Tuition Scholarship, Hebrew University, Jerusalem, 1970-71; Speech Activities Scholarship, Northeastern Illinois University, USA, 1968-70. *Hobbies:* Philately; Reading; Photography. *Address:* Department of Anthropology and Sociology, University of Papua New Guinea, PO Box 4820, University PO, Papua New Guinea.

ZENDE, Govind Kashinath, b. 5 Mar. 1922, Karanji, District Nasik, Maharashtra, India. University Professor. m. Usha, 14 Dec. 1945, 2 sons, 2 daughters. *Education:* BSc., Hons., 1945, BSc., 1949, Bombay University, India; M.Ag.Sc., Melbourne University, Australia, 1953; PhD., 1974, Rakuri; Kovid, Hons., RBPS., Wardha, 1950. *Appointments:* Lecturer, Chemistry, 1945-56, Associate Professor, Soil Science, 1965-70, Agricultural Chemist, 1966, 1969-70, College of Agriculture, Pune and Dharwar; Soil Physicist, 1956-63, Sugarcane Specialist, 1970-72, Sugarcane Research Station, Padegaon; Professor of Chemistry, College of Agriculture, Dhule, 1964-65; Head, Department of Agricultural Chemistry and Soil Science, 1972-80, Associate Dean-Post Graduate, 1978-80, Secretary, Research Council, 1973-77, MPKV., Rahuri, India. *Memberships:* President, Indian Society of Agricultural Chemists, Allahabad; International Society of Soil Science; Indian Society of Soil Science; Indian Society of Agronomy; Indian Science Congress Association; Council, Deecan Sugar Technologists Association; Indian Society of Biological Chemists; Panel for Agronomy and Soil Science; Indian Society of Sugarcane Technologists, Lucknow. *Publications:* 4 books 2 on soils and 2 on sugarcane; 140 Research and Technical papers in India, International and Regional journals. *Honours:* Prize from Deccan Sugar Technologists Association of India Limited, 1963, 72, 73, 81. *Hobbies:* Bridge; Volleyball; Indian games; Reading. *Address:* 1098/4 Model Colony, Pune 411016., M.S., India.

ZIAUR, Rahman, b. 1935, Bangladesh. General; President of Bangladesh. *Appointments:* Officer in Bangladesh army, served in war against Pakistan, 1971; Chief of Staff, Bangladesh, 1975; Deputy Chief, 1975, Chief, 1976, Martial Law Administrator; Minister, of Finance and Home Affairs, 1975, of Commerce and Foreign Trade, 1975-77, of Information and Broadcasting, 1975-76; President of Bangladesh, 1977-. *Address:* Office of the President, Dacca, Bangladesh.

ZIFCAK, Michael Gejza, b. 28 Sept. 1918, Dobsina. Managing Director. m. Ludmila Matos, 31 Dec. 1944, 2 sons. *Education:* B.Com., 1944. *Appointments:* Managing Director, Collins Booksellers Pty. Limited, Melbourne, Australia, 1950-. *Honours:* OBE., 1981. *Hobby:* Tennis. *Address:* 109 Grange Road, Toorak 3142, Victoria, Australia.

ZINNEMANN, Fred, b. 29 Apr. 1907, Austria. Film Director. m. Renée Bartlett, 1936, 1 son. *Education:* Law School, Vienna University, Austria. *Appointments:* First film, directed for Mexican Government, The Wave, documentary, 1934; Initiated, with others, School of Neorealism in American Cinema, directing among other films: The Seventh Cross, 1943; The Search, 1948; The Men, 1949; Teresa, 1950; High Noon, 1951; Member of the Wedding, 1952; From Here to Eternity, 1953; Later films include: Oklahoma, 1956; The Nun's Story, 1959; The Sundowners, 1960; Behold a Pale Horse, 1964; A Man for All Seasons, 1966; The Day of the Jackal, 1973; Julia, 1977. *Memberships:* American Film Institute; Academy of Motion Picture Arts; Directors' Guild of America; Hon. Fellow, BAFTA, 1978. *Publications:* Article on directing films, Encyclopaedia Britannica. *Honours:* Awards include: Academy Award, Los Angeles, USA, 1951, 54, 67; Film Critics' Award, New York, USA, 1952, 54, 60, 67; Golden Thistle Award, Edinburgh, UK, 1965; Moscow Film Festival Award, 1967; DW Griffith Award, 1970; Donatello Award, Florence, Italy, 1978; Gold Medal of City of Vienna, Austria, 1967. *Hobbies:* Mountain climbing; Chamber music. *Address:* c/o S Kamen, 151 El Camino, Beverly Hills, California, USA.

ZITZERMAN, Saul Benjamin, b. 16 Feb. 1936, Winnipeg, Canada. Lawyer; Executive. m. Zelma Goldberg, 2 Sept. 1956, 1 son, 1 daughter. *Education:* BA., 1956, LL.B., 1960, University of Manitoba, Canada. *Appointments:* Associate, Matlin, Kushner & Buchwald, Canada, 1960-61; Partner, Matlin, Buchwald, Zitzerman & Co., Canada, 1962-65; Partner, Buchwald, Henteleff & Zitzerman, Canada, 1965-70; Senior Partner, Buchwald, Asper, Henteleff, Zitzerman, Goodwin, Greene & Shead, Canada, 1970-74; President and Chief Executive Officer, The Imperial Group of Companies, Canada, 1974-79; Associate Counsel, Buchwald, Asper & Co., Canada, 1979-; President, Counsel Management Limited, Canada; Chairman, Orphic Productions Inc., Canada. *Memberships:* Member of numerous Associations including: National Vice-President, Jewish National Fund of Canada; Chairman, Board of Trustees, Talmud Torah Foundation; Lecturer, Taxation, Canadian Bar Association, Manitoba section; Manitoba Bar Association; Law Society of Manitoba; International Commission of Jurists. *Honours:* Graduate prize, Law Society of Manitoba, 1956; Honouree, Winnipeg Hebrew School, 1981. *Hobbies:* Golf; Ten pin bowling; Reading; Collecting Art. *Address:* 3 Ramsgate Bay, Tuxedo, Manitoba, Canada.

ZIVANOVIĆ, Srboljub, b. 21 Dec. 1933, Sarajevo, Yugoslavia. Doctor of Medicine, Anatomist and Anthropologist. m. Sofija Davidovic, 25 May, 1961, 1 daughter. *Education:* MD., University of Belgrade, Yugoslavia, 1959; DSc., University of Novi Sad, Yugoslavia, 1964. *Appointments:* Demonstrator in Anatomy, 1954-59, Assistant Lecturer in Anatomy, 1959-62, Faculty of Medicine, University of Belgrade, Yugoslavia; Assistant Lecturer in Anatomy, Faculty of Medicine, University of Novi Sad, Yugoslavia, 1962-65; Lecturer, Senior Lecturer, Anatomy, Makarere University Medical School, Kampala, Uganda, 1965-68; Senior Lecturer in Anatomy, Medical College, St. Bartholomews Hospital, University of London, UK, 1968-. *Memberships:* Fellow of: Serbian Medical Society, Yugoslav Anthropological Society, Yugoslav Anatomical Society; Royal Anthropological Institute of GB and N. Ireland; Association of Clinical Anatomists of GB; Royal Society of Medicine, London, UK; Anatomical Association of GB. *Publications:* Anatomy and Physiology for Medical School, Belgrade, 1964, 65, 66, 67; Osnovi Osteologije i Antropometrije, Belgrade, 1964; Meniskusi kolena i njihove veze, Belgrade, 1967; Anatomy and Physiology, 1980; Kinesilology, 1980; Translated 4 books from English into Cerbo-Croat including: Anderson's Pathology; published over 100 papers. *Honours:* Special Honours Diploma, Yugoslav Anthropological Society, 1979. *Hobbies:* Boy Scouts; Chess; Rowing; Camping; Mountaineering. *Address:* 1 Westmoreland Place, London, W5 1QE, England.

ZIYAMBI, Tarisai, b. 22 Mar. 1936, Shurugwi, Zimbabwe. Lawyer; Economist; Politician. m. 27 Apr. 1974, 2 sons, 1 daughter. *Education:* BSc(Hons.) Economics, London, UK, 1964; Barrister-at-Law, Inner Temple, London, UK, 1972. *Appointments:* Barrister, London, UK, 1972-74; Advocate of High Court, Zimbabwe, 1975; Deputy Minister, Home Affairs, Zimbabwe, 1980. *Memberships:* President, Students Union, Zimbabwe University, 1963-66; Chief Representative, ZANU, London, UK, 1967-70. *Honours:* Awarded prize, Council of Legal Education, London, UK, 1972. *Hobbies:* Boxing; Football; Reading; Writing. *Address:* 3 Duiker Street, Mandara, Salisbury, Zimbabwe.

ZNAIMER, Moses, b. Kulab, Tajikistan. Entrepreneur; Producer; Broadcaster; Actor; Speaker; Interviewer/Host. *Education:* BA., Hons., McGill University, Montreal, Quebec, Canada, 1963; MA., Harvard University, Cambridge, Massachusetts, USA, 1965. *Appointments:* Producer, Public Affairs Radio, Producer/Director/Co-Host, Public Affairs Television, major Network Television programs such as: Revolution Plus Fifty, Take Thirty, The Way It Is, Canadian Broadcasting Corporation, 1965; Vice-President, Helix Investments/T'ang Management, Venture capitalists, 1969; President/Founder of Canada's 1st 21 Track/Dolby recording studo, Thunder Sound, 1970; Co-Founder/President/ Executive Producer, Canada's 1st Commercial UHF Station, Toronto's Channel 79 Limited, 1971. *Creative Works:* Has presented on stage the World Premier English production of: Miss Margarida; Co-produced the Toronto production of Tom Stoppard's Travesties; Creates and supervises as Executive Producer every production made by City TV; Films:

Louis Malle's Atlantic City; John Trent's Misdeal; Love. *Hobbies:* Squash; Running; Flying; Collecting vintage cars; Pool. *Address:* City TV, 99 Queen Street East, Toronto, Ontario, Canada, M5C 2M1.

ZUBAIR, Feroze Rahim, b. 2 Apr. 1948, Rainapura, Sri Lanka. Chartered Accountant. m. Fathima Minza Sufi-Ismail, 29 June 1980. *Education:* Institute of Chartered Accountants, Sri Lanka, 1972. *Appointments:* Senior Audit Assistant, Burah Hathy and Company, Chartered Accounts, Colombo, 1973-; Management Consultant, Colombo, 1974-76; Chief Accountant, The Iranian Diesel Engineering Company Limited, Tabriz, Iran, 1976-79; Financial Consultant, Colombo, Sri Lanka, 1979-. *Memberships:* The Institute of Chartered Accountants, Sri Lanka; The Moors Islamic Cultural Home, Colombo, Sri Lanka. *Hobbies:* Reading; Travel; Collector of Precious and Semi-Precious Stones. *Address:* 112 Manning Place, Colombo 6, Sri Lanka.

ZUEL, Jehan Roger France, b. 28 June 1922, Port Louis, Mauritius. Head of News, Mauritius Broadcasting Corporation. m. Marie Thérèse Rivière, 28 Feb. 1949, 3 sons, 1 daughter. *Education:* Primary Schools, 1927-34; Royal College, Curepipe, 1935-41; Matriculation, London University, 1942. *Appointments:* Secretary to Public Assistance Commissioner, 1946-50; English Reporter, Mauritius Legislative Council, 1951-56; Reporter, Chief Reporter, Advance daily newspaper, 1957-70; Chief Editor, Advance, 1970-72; Head of News, Mauritius Broadcasting Corporation, 1972-. *Memberships:* Fellow, International Institute of Journalism, West Berlin. *Hobbies:* Reading; Philately; Numismatology. *Address:* 68 Gladstone Street, Rose Hill, Mauritius.

ZURENUO, Zurewe Kamong, b. 5 July 1920, Sattelberg, Finschhafen, Morobe Province, Papua New Guinea. Head Bishop. m. Ereju, 28 May 1941, 2 sons, 3 daughters. *Education:* Primary and Secondary Education, Lutheran Mission Schools, 1929-39; Correspondence Course, English, 1950's. *Appointments:* Teacher, Lutheran Schools, 1939; Church Secretary, Sattelberg Circuit, Lutheran Church, 1953; General Secretary, Evangelical Lutheran Church of New Guinea, 1962; Ordained to Sacred Ministry, 1966; Head Bishop, Evangelical Lutheran Church of Papua New Guinea, 1973-. *Memberships:* Chairman, Melanesian Council of Churches, 1970-73; Chairman, Lae City Christian Council, 1972-. *Honours:* OBE, 1971; Knight Bachelor, (Religious), 1981. *Publications:* Shaping the Future, 1974. *Address:* Evangelical Lutheran Church of Papua New Guinea, PO Box 80, Lae, Papua New Guinea.

ZWANZIGER, Arieh, b. 7 Dec. 1925, Haifa, Israel. Civil Engineer. m. Miriam, 16 July 1951, 1 son, 2 daughters. *Education:* Technion, Institute of Technology, Israel, 1946-51; Diploma of Civil Engineer, 1951; BSc. *Appointments:* Design of Water retaining Structures, Tahal Limited, 1951-56; Engineer, Agent, Project Manager and Area Manager, Cyprus Building and Road Construction Corporation Limited, 1956-63; Managing Director of Cyprus Building and Road Construction Corporation Limited, 1963-76; Technical Manager, Reynolds Construction Company, Nigeria, Limited, 1977-78; Managing Director, 1978-81; Managing Director, NIBARCCO (Nigeria) Limited, 1981-. *Memberships:* Israeli Institute of Engineers and Architects. *Hobbies:* Collecting Stamps and Coins. *Address:* 71 Ademola Street, Ikoyi, Lagos, Nigeria.

ZWICK, Harold Harvey, b. 1 Oct. 1938, Parkman, Saskatchewan, Canada. Physicist. m. Mary Virginia Douglas, 4 June 1966, 1 son, 1 daughter. *Education:* BA, 1960; MA, 1962; PhD, University of Saskatchewan, 1970. *Appointments:* Radiation Physicist, Royal Victoria Hospital, Montreal, Quebec, 1962-66; Senior Staff Scientist, Barringer Research Limited, Toronto, Ontario, 1970-76; Research Scientist, Canadian Centre for Remote Sensing, Ottawa, Ontario, 1976-81; Vice-President, R&D, Moniteq Limited, Toronto, Ontario, 1981-. *Memberships:* The Remote Sensing Society; Canadian Association of Physicists. *Publications:* Numerous publications in the field of auroral measurements, sensor design and operation and multi-spectral image analysis. *Honours:* Honors Physics Award, 1960; Industrial Research IR100 Award, 1975. *Hobbies:* Outdoor sports; Photography. *Address:* 2597 Pinkwell Drive, Mississauga, Ontario, L5K 2B5, Canada.